KNIGHT'S CYCLOPÆDIA OF THE INDUSTRY OF ALL NATIONS

KNIGHT'S CYCLOPÆDIA OF THE INDUSTRY OF ALL NATIONS

By

CHARLES KNIGHT

GYAN

Published by

Gyan Publishing House
5, Ansari Road
Daryaganj, New Delhi-110002
Phone: 011-47034999, 9811692060
E-mail: books@gyanbooks.com

Distribution Network
gyanbooks.com
India, USA, Canada, UK, Australia, France

ISBN : 978-81-212-6751-9 (PB)
First Published, 1851

2nd Impression 2022

Printed at: Gyan Press, Delhi.

KNIGHT'S CYCLOPÆDIA OF THE INDUSTRY OF ALL NATIONS
Author: CHARLES KNIGHT

KNIGHT'S CYCLOPÆDIA

OF THE

INDUSTRY

OF

ALL NATIONS.

1851.

ADVERTISEMENT.

THIS CYCLOPÆDIA has been prepared with the express desire to carry out the most important object connected with the Great Exhibition—that of regarding it as an instrument of education. Here, *at a rate of unequalled cheapness*, will be found *a full explanation of every subject that can suggest itself to the enquiring visitor.*

The information thus given is brought up to the *very latest accession of knowledge.* THE SCIENTIFIC DETAILS, avoiding as much as possible all embarrassing technicalities, aim at precision and accuracy. The GEOGRAPHICAL ARTICLES exhibit the characteristics of the Industry of All Nations, not only as to large States, but as regards Cities and Ports; and these particulars are founded upon the best and most recent statistical information. The PROCESSES of MANUFACTURES are described in most cases from actual observation, and are ILLUSTRATED BY A SERIES OF ENGRAVINGS which embrace the *entire range of Factory production.*

It may be affirmed without presumption that the Visitor to the Exhibition, by reference to the "Cyclopædia of the Industry of all Nations," will be able to regard that wondrous collection, not with a vague curiosity, but an intelligent appreciation. With the Shilling Catalogue to accompany his visits, and the Cyclopædia to direct him, he may accomplish much that is proposed to be attained by Courses of Lectures. Take an example :—

A Visitor purposes to devote a morning to the department of *French* Industry. He refers to the Cyclopædia—perhaps as follows :

France. This article contains a brief general view of all the staple industries of that country.

But the catalogue is headed France and Algiers. He turns to *Algiers* in the Cyclopædia, and finds a similar view of its industry.

The first article in the *French Catalogue* is as follows :

> "1. Adolphe, C. Manufactory, *Mulhouse* (Haut Rhin) and at M. Grebin's, 8, Rue de la Bourse, *Paris.*—Pieces of *silk* and *woollen damask*, wrought by *Jacquard looms.*"

The *words* above marked in Italic indicate the nature of the information which will be found in the *Cyclopædia of Industry* under those heads. He will there learn what is the peculiar industry of Mulhouse (*Mulhausen*)—what the character of the trade of Paris—the processes of silk and woollen manufacture generally, as well as of damask weaving, and the peculiarities of the Jacquard loom. In addition, by turning to the ENGRAVINGS, he will see the processes of *Silk Manufacture*, No. 29 ; and of *Woollen*, Nos. 36 and 37.

It may perhaps be necessary to add that the "Cyclopædia of the Industry of all Nations" IS NOT A TEMPORARY WORK, or one of limited utility. It will be found as useful in the Merchant's Counting-house as in the Mechanics' Institute—as interesting in the School-room as in the Crystal Palace.

This Cyclopædia has been *founded* upon materials which are the copyright of the Publisher ; but these materials have been condensed or added to, with reference to the immediate purpose of the work,—and a great number of original articles have been introduced,—by the Editor, Mr. GEORGE DODD, author of "Days at the Factories," "British Manufactures," &c.

KNIGHTS' CYCLOPÆDIA OF THE INDUSTRY OF ALL NATIONS.

No. 1.

INTRODUCTION.

I. INDUSTRIAL EXHIBITIONS,

AT HOME AND ABROAD.

THE great Industrial Exhibition of 1851—great in every sense of the word, if worthily carried out,—will be a kind of summing up of the labours of half a century. It will be a practical test, whereby we may know how much, and of what kind, the first half of the nineteenth century has been able to achieve in the application of skilled labour. Before the present century, efforts were too scattered to be susceptible of easy comparison; and the great moving forces of industry, (so to speak) were yet in their infancy. In applying this designation to the *steam engine* and the *factory system*, we do that for which there is much warranty: each of these is a mighty agent both for *combination* and for *subdivision;* for applying to all work to be done, just so much force as will meet the requirements of the case; for economising space and time, capital and labour, materials and tools; for rendering invention and supervision doubly effective; and for developing an amount of precision and accuracy which never before marked industrial processes.

In the contributions, too, which science has made to manufactures, the present century stands out in bold contrast to those which preceded it. It was early in the century that Davy made those brilliant discoveries concerning metallic oxides, which have had so much influence in chemical manufactures. The labours of Dalton in respect to atomic laws of combination; Wollaston's researches into the nature of platinum; Davy's safety lamp, and the curious law on which its action depends; Liebig's remarkable labours; the wonders of electricity; the researches into the phenomena of waves and tides—these, and countless other instances, have had a more immediate practical bearing on manufactures, than was generally the case in respect to the scientific labours of former centuries.

It is not the object of the present paper to place the two years 1800 and 1850 before us, and to make them bear witness—each for itself, and each for the other—to the industrial progress which has been made in half a century; but we propose to trace the attempts which industry has made from time to time, to display its results by means of *exhibitions.* It was not until near the commencement of the present century, that men ventured to draw attention to manufactures as the materials for a public show. The glittering of tournaments, the panoply of war, the pomps of royalty, the ceremonies of the cathedral, the fictions of the drama, the fairs of the market-place—all were objects of public assemblages; but the time had not yet come when the artisan was to be the main exhibitor.

Such a time, however, did come at last; and it is creditable to our neighbours across the Channel, that they were the first to strike the key-note of this species of industrial concert—a concert which, national at first, may become inter-national ere long.

Mr. Digby Wyatt has afforded us the means for tracing the proceedings of the French, in respect to Industrial Exhibitions. The Society of Arts, which has within a recent period thrown into its proceedings a vigour analogous to that of its early days, deeming the Paris Exposition of 1849 a favourable occasion for collecting information, deputed Mr. Wyatt to visit that capital, with a view of enquiring into the origin, constitution, merits, and effects, of such enterprises. The result of his visit appeared in the form of a valuable Report, addressed to the President and Council of the Society; and this Report, in its convenient printed form, may safely be taken as an authority on the subject.

It was during the stormy period of the first French Revolution, when the bonds of society seemed to be snapped asunder, and when peril surrounded all the institutions of that country—it was at such a time that industry was first made the basis of a popular exhibition. At that period, and for many years previously, three manufactories in France had been under the especial rule and guidance of the government,—viz., the porcelain works of Sèvres, the tapestry works of the Gobelins, and the carpet works of the Savonnerie. In 1797 the French Directory appointed the Marquis d'Avèze, as commissioner for these national establishments. He found, on his appointment, that they were in a wretched condition: the operatives were reduced to great penury; and proofs were abundant that neither government care nor government funds had flowed in this direction, during the fearful tumults which had marked the infancy of the Republic. The Marquis conceived that he might give a new impetus to these three manufactures, by forming a public exhibition of the choicest specimens of their production. He memorialized the Minister of the Interior, and obtained his sanction; he applied for the use of the Chateau of St. Cloud, (which was then desolate and unfurnished), and obtained it. The floors were covered with superb carpets from the Savonnerie, the walls were hung with Gobelin tapestries, and the saloons and halls were adorned with the finest examples of Sèvres porcelain. A system was planned, whereby a fund might be raised by sales and by a kind of lottery, for the benefit of the workmen. But political vicissitudes cut short the project, and frustrated the object which the Marquis so praiseworthily had in view. A decree of the Directory was published, banishing all the nobility of France from Paris and its vicinity, and allowing only four-and-twenty hours in preparation for departure. The Marquis, as one of the nobles, was included in the proscription; and he had barely time, before the scant number of hours had passed, to place the treasures of St. Cloud under the care of other government authorities. Thus was the first French Industrial Exhibition strangled in its birth, after a few privileged persons had seen it, but before it had been thrown open to the Parisian public generally.

But the idea thus made public, was not lost. The spirit of nationality soon found inducements to further exertions. The Marquis returned from his proscription in the early part of 1798, and immediately made preparations for a second industrial collection. On this occasion he located it—not at St. Cloud—but in the Maison d'Orsay, in the Rue de Varennes. The Parisians here found collected, not only products from the three national establishments, but beautiful specimens of furniture, marqueterie, clocks, watches, bookbinding, silks, &c., contributed by the chief manufacturers.

These two preliminary Expositions may be considered the creation of one individual; but they were speedily followed by others which were more formally under government patronage. When Napoleon returned flushed with victory from his first Italian campaign, with visions of Roman triumphs in his mind, he bethought of a Temple of Industry as a worthy pendant to the Temple of Glory; and such a temple was erected in the Champ de Mars in 1798—with much frippery and tinsel —but with many solid advantages to manufacturers and their productions. The exhibition was open only three days, but the Parisians were nearly crazy with delight and self-laudation at the result. The Jury system (which we shall presently explain) was established; and among the nine jurymen we find the well-known names of Molard, Chaptal, Duquesnoy, and Berthard. We find, too, among the exhibitors and prize holders, the names of Breguet, Lenoir, Clouet, and Payen,—men of great celebrity in many departments of manufactures.

Such was the third French Industrial Exhibition, or the first strictly National, in which the charges were borne by the state. It is usually spoken of as the First Exposition. It was speedily succeeded by a second. The government determined to make them annual, and to admit provincial towns to an equality with Paris, in respect to specimens admitted; but this determination was not fully carried out, for the second exposition did not take place till 1801. The First Consul had by that time become the patron of science and of art, as of armies and navies; he visited—accompanied by Berthollet, Monge, and Chaptal—the manufactories of Paris, Rouen, Milan, Lyons, Brussels, Liège, and Aix la Chapelle, and encouraged the workmen by prizes and medals. It was under such auspices that the second National Exposition took place. It was held in the great quadrangle of the Louvre, which was fitted up with galleries for the purpose. As compared with its predecessor, this exposition was marked by the excellence of its woollens, cottons, carpets, fancy leathers, and printing; and it was made memorable by the first appearance, as an inventor, of the ingenious Jacquard. It is pleasant to bear in mind, at a time when English and French industrial products are about to be placed side by side in friendly competition, that Jacquard in part owed his eminence to the exertions of the English Society of Arts. This society, about the period now under consideration, offered a prize for the invention of a loom for weaving fishing-nets; and Jacquard produced a machine, consequent on this advertisement, which was the means of bringing him into favourable notice by Napoleon. The second exposition was open six days; it counted 229 exhibitors, against 110 in its predecessor; it was marked by the distribution of sixty medals; and its Jury contained the distinguished names of Berthollet, Berthoud, Guyton de Morveau, Prony, and Costaz.

The year 1802 witnessed the third National Exposition, held in the same place as the second. The days of exhibition were seven, the number of exhibitors was 540, to whom 254 medals, decorations, rewards, and "recognitions," were given. The period was marked by much extension of productive art—especially by the increased application of mechanical and chemical science to facilitate production, and the consequent reduction in price of all articles of popular demand. This exposition was the immediate cause of the establishment of the *Société d'Encouragement*, a kind of Society of Arts, which has rendered important service to French manufactures.

The fourth Exposition took place in 1806, under the blaze of the Empire, when the First Consul had become a King-maker. It was held in a fine building constructed on the *Esplanade des Invalides*, and lasted twenty-four days; there were 1422 exhibitors, among whom 610 honours were distributed. The great and distinguishing feature of this display were the variety and beauty of the textile goods. Printed cottons, silk and thread lace, blonde, cloth, imitations of Cachemere shawls—all these were conspicuous for their beauty in this exposition. Steel and iron manufactures, also, presented great marked improvements. It is remarked by Mr. Digby Wyatt, that "the isolation, which for so many years separated in so great a degree manufacturing France from the other producing powers of Europe,—while it placed her in many points of view in an unfavourable position,—yet by *forcing* her energies to supply *alone* what other kingdoms derived from mutual co-operation and dependance on each other, laid the foundation for that facility and universality of manufacture which so eminently distinguish her at the present day."

A long interval took place before France presented another exposition of industry. Napoleon was incessantly engaged in wars, and the drain on the national Exchequer for the support of his myriads of soldiers was continuous; and these circumstances probably tended to withdraw public attention from the more peaceful arts of production. And even after the restoration of the Bourbons—those who "forgot nothing and forgave nothing,"—four years elapsed before the industrial displays were resumed. At length, in 1819, the fifth Exposition was held in galleries constructed in the Court of the Louvre. It was open thirty-five days, and contained articles contributed by 1662 exhibitors, among whom were distributed no fewer than 809 medals and rewards of various kinds. Jacquard was again a prize-holder on this occasion; and the metal-workers, in steel, iron, bronze, plated goods, gold, and silver, exhibited a great advance in skill. The dyers and the calico-printers, too, came out in great force.

In 1823, after an interval of four years, the sixth Exposition occurred. Like its predecessor of 1819, it was held in the Louvre; but it had a longer existence, being kept open fifty days; there were 1642 exhibitors, and 1091 rewards given. Civil engineering displayed, at this exposition, more notable features than any preceding one.

The seventh Exposition was held in the Louvre in 1827, and exceeded all its predecessors in magnitude and duration; it lasted sixty-two days, had 1795 exhibitors, and 1254 prizes and honorary recognitions. The steam-engine and its wonders told more significantly in this exposition than in any former one, in the greater regularity of finish given to various manufactured articles, and in the greater cheapness and distribution of the products. Merinos had become an article of extensive manufacture; shawls, tulles, and blonds, were manufactured on a large scale: silks were, by the steam-engine, made to include products of the spun as well as the thrown material; mixed fabrics of silk and wool had come into use; cotton printing had become available for the gown of the peasant as well as for the dress of the peeress; and the making of paper in sheets of endless length had become one of the conquests made by steam-power.

Charles X. was expelled, and Louis Philippe elected to the monarchy, in the interval between the seventh and eighth Expositions; but these exciting events did not affect the general character of the Exposition of 1834. The site selected on this occasion was the *Place de la Concorde*, on the four sides of which were erected four pavilions. The exposition was open to public view during a period of sixty days; there were 2,447 exhibitors; and there were 1,785 rewards and recognitions distributed. M. Charles Dupin presided over the jury of this exposition, and it had the benefit of his long and intimate acquaintance with the resources and manufactures of France. Cylinder-printing of paper-hangings, the revival of the arts of enamel and niello, India-rubber goods, artificial ultramarine—these were among the novelties of the display.

The ninth Exposition, in 1839, far excelled all that preceded it, in magnitude, importance, and general excellence. The building constructed for it was in the great square (Carré de Marigny) of the *Champs Elysées;* and comprised a grand hall for the textile products of Mulhausen, a Gallery, and eight long apartments; it occupied an area of 120,000 square English feet, and cost 14,560*l.* The exposition lasted 60 days; the number of exhibitors was 3,281, and the prizes and honorary distinctions awarded were 2,305. Almost every department of French manufactures was represented on this occasion.

We shall presently speak of the Great French Expositions of 1844 and 1849; but there are a few illustrative details concerning the mode in which our neighbours manage these matters, which it will be interesting to notice here.

In the management of these Expositions, as brought into a regular system within the last few years, the Minister of Agriculture and Commerce, once in five years, commences the arrangements about twelve months before the stated period of exhibition. He communicates with the various chambers of commerce throughout France, to collect opinions and information that may be valuable. He presents a report and estimates to the legislature, by whom a grant is made sufficient to cover the whole expense of the undertaking. He appoints a central jury at Paris; and he empowers the prefects of departments to choose special juries. He controls every proceeding up to the time of the opening of the exposition: and he is responsible for the judicious expenditure of all the funds placed at his disposal. A considerable portion of the grants made for these French expositions is derived from fees paid on the granting of patents.

The office of the local special juries is a remarkable one, indicative of a thorough centralised mode of proceeding. The special jury for each district has to determine how far the goods forwarded to the chief town of the district may be worthy of admission to the exposition, and of transmission to Paris at the cost of the state; and it has to settle any minor local questions submitted to it by the central jury. In this we see one among many examples of the different spirit in which Englishmen and Frenchmen conduct their proceedings: in England our manufacturers would be very much inclined to rebel against a jury chosen—not by themselves—but by a magistrate, to pass judgment on their manufactured goods; while in France, these things are regarded as a mere matter of course. We must bear in mind, however, that in France the state voluntarily lends a fostering hand to art, science, manufactures, and literature; whereas in England all these are left to struggle into excellence as best they may. It seems to be agreed, moreover, that the persons selected to form the special juries are really fixed upon according to their fitness to judge on the matters submitted to them. The juries collect the manufactured goods in the chief town of the district, and make the necessary arrangements for forwarding them to Paris.

The central jury is a very important body, and always comprises names which France delights (and properly so) to honour. The number of jurymen has increased as the scope of the exhibition has become enlarged. In the first exposition the number was 9; and this number increased gradually to 27, 44, 53, and 64—the last being the number of the jury in 1849. Any one who is acquainted with the names of distinguished living Frenchmen, will recognise many such among the central jury of 1849—Arago, Blanqui, Chevallier, Chevreul, Didot, Dumas, Duperrier, Dupin, Durand, Ebelman, Laborde, Mathieú, Moll, Payen, Peligot, Pouillet, Seguier, &c. In the meetings of the jury, many important questions have to be decided. The hearing of appeals from the special juries,—the decision whether or not dealers shall be admitted to exhibit as if they were manufacturers; the consideration of the claim of dyers to a share of the honours accruing in respect to fine specimens of woven goods; the arrangements for setting models and machinery in motion; the exercise of a power of rejection, in respect to proposed exhibitors whose commercial reputation is not satisfactory,—such are among the matters which come before their notice in the preliminary arrangement.

It is a curious circumstance, and one that shows how little has yet been done towards a good classification of productive industry, that the juries have wavered considerably in their opinions as to the best arrangement of the specimens in the exposition and its catalogue. It is the same, in this respect, in France as in England: all is yet in a tentative state; systems are tried, to see whether they will work well, and then abandoned if not satisfactory, and others substituted. Costaz, Payen, Comte, Dupin, in France; Ure, Babbage, Barlow, Fergusson in England—all have proposed modes of classification of manufactures. In the exposition of 1806, M. Costaz adopted a topographical arrangement, according to the departments of France whence the specimens were sent. In 1819 he attempted to classify all arts into a sort of natural system; but the separate headings amounted to thirty-nine, and were found to be confused and inconvenient. In 1827 M. Payen adopted a classification into five great divisions,—arranging the arts according as they are chemical, mechanical, physical, economical, or (that sad interloper in most classifications) miscellaneous, in their nature. In practice this was found defective, for two or even three of these characteristics often belong to the same manufacture. In 1834 M. Dupin proposed and adopted a classification which was found to work better than any which preceded it. He considered which among the many wants of man are supplied by any one particular branch of manufacture: he viewed man as a locomotive animal, a clothed animal, a domiciled animal &c., &c., and he traced this multiform animal through his various daily wants and employments. He thus arrived at a classification, in which all arts are placed under nine headings, according as they contribute to the alimentary, sanitary, vestiary, domiciliary, locomotive, sensitive, intellectual, preparative, or social tendencies of man. In 1839 the same system was adopted. In 1844 and 1849 attempts were made towards an eclectic combination of two or three of the above systems; but it does not appear—so far as the materials are offered for forming a judgment—that these systems presented any marked advantages.

In France the awarding of medals, decorations, and similar encouragements, is carried to a much greater extent than in England, and is looked up to as matter of great importance. *We* have the art of awarding medals twenty or thirty years after they have been earned, and when the veteran recipients are fast dropping into the grave. The medals of the French expositions have in some years exceeded three hundred in number—gold, silver, and bronze. These have indicated three gradations of merit; and two other gradations are indicated by "honourable mention," and "favourable notice." In some cases the jury awards prizes to persons who have rendered service to the industrial arts of a kind not susceptible of being represented by productions exhibited in their name.

Our own country must now claim a little attention.

It is difficult to say when and where our first exhibitions of industry took place; for they have hitherto been, for the most part, combined with exhibitions of fine arts and of curiosities, knick-knacks and trinkets, marvels and oddities. Perhaps the *Museum of the Society of Arts* is best worthy of being placed at the head of the list—that dusty and old-fashioned looking museum, which so many persons have visited for so many years. We speak not so much of its present, as of its past condition; for what with "mediæval exhibitions" at one time, and "modern exhibitions" at another, this old museum has been somewhat thrown into the shade lately. Those, however, who remember it in its old form, know that it contained much which instructively illustrated the progress of manufactures. There were specimens of Leghorn plait, in juxta-position with those improved British specimens which the Society has done so much to encourage. There were specimens of hemp and flax, designed to show how far England could grow these important materials of manufacture. There were samples of Assam tea, and Assam silk, of English silk, of English wool, of goats' hair; all designed to test the capability of Britain and her colonies in such productions. There were bits of machine-lace placed by the side of other specimens of pillow-lace. There were examples of the contributions which art may be said sometimes to make to the cause of humanity—such as fire-escapes, chimney-sweeping apparatus, teaching apparatus for the deaf and the blind, magnetic mouth-pieces for needle-grinders, &c. There were models of the safety-lamp, and of various other useful contrivances; there was, too, a somewhat extensive collection of pigments, oils, varnishes, cements, and other substances used in the arts; for this useful society does not confine its operations to the encouragement of any art or manufacture in particular, but to the advancement of productive industry generally—whether in the raw material to which manufacturing art is afterwards to be applied, or to the implements or processes by which this manufacture is conducted.

We hardly know how to bring in the *East India Company's Museum* into our list; yet there are a few curiosities of manufacture in that most miscellaneous assemblage. On one side are exhibited models of Asiatic ship-building, such as the Chinese junk and the Sumatran proa; on another are Burmese musical instruments; here we have models of Hindoo looms, ploughs, mills, bellows, coaches, windlasses, pestles and mortars; there we see a collection of sabres, daggers, hunting-knives, pipes, and bowls. Specimens of dress from the Eastern Archipelago; painted tiles; beads and glass trinkets; models of Chinese villas, in ivory and mother-of-pearl; Chinese lanterns, of horn and other materials; Chinese writing, drawing, engraving, printing, and counting-machines; palanquins and howdahs—all such are instructive, in respect to the insight they give concerning the arts in the East.

The *Asiatic Society's Museum* is very similar to the one just noticed, in so far as regards the oriental nature of the contents. Here weapons of offence and defence are very numerous—spears, lances, javelins, darts, bows, arrows, swords, daggers, knives, axes, rifles, muskets, pistols, firelocks, shields, and fighting-dresses. Among other varied objects (which we only notice so far as they illustrate manufacturing art) are vases and vessels of oriental workmanship; Hindoo astronomical and musical instruments; a highly curious collection of japanned wicker baskets, with specimens of the japan and varnish employed in their manufacture; models of Hindoo agricultural machines; models of pagodas and temples, and of the car of Juggernaut; and a miscellaneous collection of articles of Chinese furniture and personal decoration.

The *United Service Museum* has its few specimens of manufacturing skill, mostly in connection with the arts of war, and mostly brought by military and naval officers from foreign countries. Models of shipping and naval apparatus; specimens of life-buoys and safety garments; models of gun-carriages; a model of a bridge of boats: a portable Russian camp-kitchen; military dresses and accoutrements; grenades and shells—these illustrate more or less the ingenuities of manufacture.

Of a different nature is the *Museum of Economic Geology*, in so far as it exhibits the *materials* rather than the *results* of manufacture. Everything that can illustrate the mineral riches of our country is here instructively displayed. There are models of mines, and of the machinery employed in working them; there are specimens of ore, and the various stages of its preparation; there are sections of strata, and of wells sunk through them; there are specimens of coal, of clay, of sand, and of the various materials on which skilled labour is afterwards to be employed —in short there are to be found within these walls the beginnings of the industrial alphabet: the first link of the manufacturing chain.

If we view it aright, the *British Museum* is an exhibition of manufactures, as well as of art, science, and literature. Let us take our stand for a time in the "Ethnographical Room," and look around. This is one of the most instructive rooms in the museum: it contains specimens illustrative of the manners, customs, arts, and implements of various nations. The Chinese, the Hindoos, the Japanese, the Africans, the North American Indians, the Peruvians, the Mexicans, the Guianians, the Chilians, the Yacatans, the Esquimaux, the Australasians, the Polynesians,—all are represented; and these representations do not relate merely to those nations, but were *made by them*, so as to be indices of their manufacturing skill. Dresses, ornaments, furniture, weapons, vehicles, buildings, instruments, vessels, toys, books —all are here to be met with, and all are full of instruction to one who brings an observant mind in aid of an observant eye.

All the above six examples (and there are many others in London and the country) are museums belonging to the nation or to public bodies, and are open gratuitously. There is another class of exhibitions, in which the primary object is a pecuniary one—the shilling, which every visitor pays for admission. Of course the fostering of national manufactures cannot be looked for under such circumstances; yet there have been many interesting collections displayed under such auspices. We will briefly advert to a few of them.

Many into whose hands this sheet may fall will perhaps remember an exhibition which was opened some twenty years ago, at or near the spot on which the National Gallery now stands. It was a collection of manufactures, ornaments, machines, and curiosities, of a somewhat attractive nature; and was, we believe, set on foot by the same society which afterwards instituted the *Adelaide Gallery of Practical Science.* This gallery has changed its flag: it has given up science and manufactures, and has succumbed to casinos and sherry-cobler. Yet we remember when it was a really instructive exhibition. Besides the marvels of the steam-gun, and of the combustion of steel, and the broiling of a beef-steak by a convex lens, there were many arrangements of specimens which tended to illustrate the processes of manufacture. Specimens of geological strata were grouped in one place; specimens of woods used in the arts, in another; while there were many groups, each of which contained a series illustrative of the successive stages through which a manufactured article passes—such as a knife, a fork, a file, a flask, a button, a candlestick, a tea-pot, a needle, a pin, hooks and eyes, combs, hats, glass, earthenware, silk goods, cotton goods, woollen goods, caoutchouc goods, &c. In all these cases we had the rough, the partly finished, and the highly finished articles displayed for us, in such a way that we could trace its manufacturing history in an intelligible series. These epochs in the history of a knife were eight or ten, in that of a fork still more, in that of a needle no fewer than nineteen.

Although the institution just named has slipped out of existence, its younger sister, the *Polytechnic Institution*, still survives, and seems to gain strength as it grows older. Its music, its lectures, its dissolving views, its semi-science, we have not here to do with; but its illustrations of manufactures have the same kind of interest as those which have just passed under our notice. In the "Hall of Manufactures," just within the entrance; on the floor and in the galleries of the great saloon; and in some of the rooms at the two ends of the building—are various specimens, which illustrate either the materials of manufactures, the finished articles themselves, machines for aiding in manufactures, or moving powers for setting the machines in motion.

Why should we not class Mr. Catlin's most unique *Indian Collection* among the exhibitions of industry? Did it not illustrate the ingenuity and manufactures of a remarkable people, as well as their features and their habits of life? Though the pictures were the main object of the collection, they were not the only memorials of the Red Man. There were some of the real products of Indian manufacture. Among them was a wigwam or lodge of the Crow Indians, twenty-five feet in height, and capable of sheltering eighty persons: it was brought all the way from the Rocky Mountains. Then there were Indian cradles, lances, calumets, or "pipes of peace," tomahawks, scalping knives, bows, quivers, spears, shields, mens' and womens' dresses, necklaces, mocassins, belts, pouches, war clubs, robes, mantles, wampums, whistles, rattles, drums, &c.—all of which displayed the mechanical art, such as it is, of these children of the prairies.

The *Chinese Collection*—was not this, too, an exposition of manufactures? Did we not here find an admirable series of illustrations of the art, the invention, the ingenuity, the mechanical contrivances of that remarkable people? When this singular ship's cargo was brought to England in 1842, and when a capacious and well-planned building was constructed for its reception, the Londoners and the visitors to London flocked in thousands to witness the display; and we believe the general tendency of the spectacle was to raise the character of the Chinese in the estimation of those who had before known so little of them. How wonderfully exact were the models of all the manufacturing processes! How life-like were many of the scenes, representing mechanics in their accustomed dresses, pursuing their accustomed avocations, with their accustomed tools, on the accustomed material! The ivory carvings, the inlayings, the turned work, the japan-work, the basket-work, the jewellery, the cutlery, the silks, the cottons, the nankeens, the shoes, the hats, the tools, the implements and instruments, the weapons—all were there, and all gave a most interesting insight into the industrial genius of that remarkable people.

There have been many other exhibitions in this country (and we may suppose in other countries likewise), in which manufacturing skill has been one of the points of attraction, for which visitors are expected to be willing to pay. But we must hasten to the remarkable Expositions of the last ten years: these we shall notice in chronological order, including many both at home and abroad.

One of the first attempts to establish a temporary exhibition in the provinces, in which specimens of manufactures were to fill a place in the programme offered to visitors, took place at *Manchester* in 1839. It was held in the Mechanics' Institution, for whose benefit, as a commercial transaction, it was set on foot. The gentry and the manufacturers lent, for the occasion, whatever they thought might be of striking interest—whether in pictures or other works of art, in machinery and manufactures, or in miscellaneous curiosities. The visitors were numerous, the funds raised considerable, the satisfaction general; and a hint furnished which future years and other towns have not failed to use profitably. It is true that manufactures bore anything than a lion's share in the assemblage; still there was enough to serve as a beginning: Mechanical Industry took its place by the side of Fine Art; and the two have year by year been drawn into closer and closer communion—new ties bind them, as each becomes more and more developed.

Leeds, the metropolis of woollens, did not lose sight of the example furnished by the metropolis of cotton. She, too, had a Mechanics' Institution; and this institution was located in a building so poor and so comfortless, that the thought of imitating Manchester arose—the thought of raising funds towards the payment for a new structure, by an exhibition of mingled art and manufactures. Let us not think lightly of such an attempt because money was one of its motives: the money was to be the return for money's worth, intellectually and otherwise, and was to be worthily applied towards an educational and intellectual object. Would that all exhibitions could claim such a character! The committee invited loans of such objects as might be fitting for such an exhibition; and the invitation was liberally responded to. The pictures were very numerous, but the machinery was also varied and interesting, and the result was that a considerable sum was realised for the object primarily held in view.

Liverpool, and other towns in the north, followed the example of Manchester and Leeds ; indeed, wherever a Mechanics' Institution has existed, there has been an incentive to such exhibitions, not met with where no such nucleus of association exists.

The order of events now again takes us across the channel. The tenth great *French Exposition*, in 1844, was, like its predecessors, exclusively French,—it was a display of the industry of that nation ; and no one could glance around at the tasteful and varied products exhibited—at the countless forms which metal and wood, glass and porcelain, fibre and sap, colours and chemicals, were made to assume—without feeling that such a nation must perforce occupy a lofty position among the industrial workers of Europe.

The arrangements for this display were on a grand scale—a scale which the French know how to adopt in most of their public "demonstrations," whether warlike or peaceful. A plot of ground was appropriated to this purpose in the *Champs Elysées*, the Hyde Park of Paris. This ground comprised an area of more than twenty thousand square yards, almost every inch of which was crowded with the fruits of French industry and taste. Each front of the quadrangular building presented a low, long, architectural composition, simple enough in its way—pierced by pedimented windows, and having a hexastyle portico in the centre. Two or three of the competition drawings for the Hyde Park structure, sent in before the Commissioners had determined on the adoption of Mr. Paxton's plan, and exhibited at the rooms of the Institute of Civil Engineers, bore considerable resemblance to the Paris structure of 1844. The grand entrance was on the north, with a "Royal saloon" on the right, and a "Jury's saloon" on the left, of the portico ; at the centre of the south side was a private entrance, with rooms for the Directors of the Exposition ; while at the centre of the east and west sides were gates for departure. A palisade girded the whole building, at a distance of several yards from the walls ; and within this palisade were a guard house, a depôt for the fire-brigade, and clusters of the coarser varieties of agricultural implements.

Such were the external arrangements of the building, which, in May 1844, was thrown open to the gaze of the admiring Parisians. The hours for the general public were between twelve and four o'clock each day ; but private admission was obtainable at an earlier hour by means of tickets ; and it indicated considerable liberality of feeling, that any stranger who presented his passport at the gate was admitted to the private view without further introduction. The contents of the building were displayed in forty galleries or ranges of stalls, the avenues between which had an aggregate length of more than five miles. In the centre of the whole was a colossal statue of St. Louis, which served as a sort of guide in traversing the numerous avenues. With a few exceptions here and there, a pretty general system of classification was followed out—the larger machinery and metal work being in the centre, the textile fabrics mostly on the south side, the household furniture for the most part on the north side, and the almost endless variety of ornamental manufactures on the east and west. By far the greater number of the galleries ran in ranges from east to west, but those at the ends extended north and south. A visitor looking round him from the central statue, saw lengthened avenues of metal goods of all grades and uses,—steam-engines, fire-engines, spinning machinery, throwing machinery, cutting and punching engines, mechanical inventions, stoves and smiths' work, locks and keys, iron bedsteads, printing presses, jacquard machinery, zinc work, &c. In other places the more fanciful and artistic applications of metal met his view—philosophical and mathematical instruments, balances, guns and pistols, swords and bayonets, bronzes, clocks and watches, lamps, cutlery, jewellery, daguerrotype plates. The products in which earths, minerals, or glass bore a chief part, were represented by mirrors, cut glass, porcelain, earthenware, marble and alabaster work, stuccoes, statuary, &c. The textile or woven collection was most diversified—as any one might expect, who knows how much attention is paid in France to fancy articles in this department: here were woollen cloths, carpets, draperies for hangings, mixed fabrics of cotton and wool, calicoes; there were silks, merinos, muslins, velvets; and at other places damasks, shawls, embroidered goods, prints, handkerchiefs, mousseline-de-laines, tapestry, cachmeres, &c. It was a remarkable feature in this section of the exhibition that cotton goods—the plain, every day, serviceable cotton goods—bore but a very humble share in the display: silk and wool greatly predominated over cotton. There is a deeper reason than mere choice in this circumstance: it is typical of the relative importance in France, of different departments of textile manufacture—in England the strength, commercial if not artistic, lies in another direction. There was not wanting, too, for those whose curiosity led them to seek further specimens of dress, food to satisfy the search: there were felted goods and hair-plaited goods, straw bonnets, feathers, artificial flowers, &c. Chemical ingenuity presented its perfumery, its soaps and candles, and its comestibles. The workers in wood supplied their pianos, organs, billiard tables, cabinets, household furniture generally, and specimens of inlaying; while the printers, the bookbinders, the paper-makers, the umbrella-makers, the saddlers, the coachmakers—all put forth their claims to a meed of approbation. The exposition was open sixty days; there were 3281 exhibitors, of whom 2305 received honorary notices of one form or other.

The late King Louis Philippe, whose eventful life has so recently terminated, took a most active part in the planning of this exposition. It will be a graceful feature in the history of the past, when the chequered events of his career become recorded, that—while often engaged in the turmoils of political strife—he yet urged his countrymen to achieve the peaceful victories of industry. And when the exposition was opened, the King spent several hours a day, on many of the days (Mondays) when it was not open to the public, in a minute examination of the contents, with a view of ascertaining, by the evidence of his own eyes, what his subjects could or could not effect by the force of their own manipulative talent. It is recorded, too, that the chief manufacturers were recognized by the monarch as benefactors, as the nobles of industry, and were treated by him accordingly:—

> "The King can mak' a belted knight,
> A marquis, duke, and a' that,
> But ———————"

We need not follow out Burns's thought: a king cannot make a manufacturing people; but he can give them kindly countenance in their efforts to make themselves such. And what is graceful in a King, can hardly be otherwise in a Prince Consort.

It was in May of the next following year, 1845, that the great "*Free Trade Bazaar*" was held in Covent Garden Theatre; a bazaar which had a bustling and exciting existence of about twelve days. Pity it was, perhaps, that such a creditable and honourable display should be indissolubly connected with a great political movement, which drove men into two antagonistic parties, and gave a party-colouring to an industrial developement. But whatever may be said of *national* exhibitions, it can hardly be doubted that those of an *inter-national* character—such as that which is looked forward to by all the world in 1851—are essentially dependent on liberal commercial principles for their due carrying out, nay, for their very origin; and even if this position were disputed, the industrial results of the bazaar may be studied without reference to any disputed commercial doctrines.

What, then, were the aspects which the bazaar of 1845 presented? Manufacturers in various parts of the country, favourable to those commercial views which were entertained by the managers, sent up to this Bazaar the choicest productions of their skill. The theatre was skilfully arranged for this occasion. The stage, orchestra, and pit were all floored over to make one large hall, while the boxes and walls presented a vertical surface for a gorgeous display of the products of industry. The centre of the vast area was so fitted up with ranges of stalls, as to leave convenient avenues between the stalls and the sides of the building; and the stream of visitors was so judiciously directed, that by following a certain route every stall and stand came successively under the notice of the eye. The visitors were admitted by the room which was then known as the Shakspere gallery, but which Mr. Albano has probably since demolished in his transformation of a temple of Shakspere into a temple of Apollo. From thence the body of the house was entered at the back of the pit; and the moving multitude passed round the north, west, and south sides in succession—emerging at the back of the pit, but by a different door from that which furnished admittance. The extreme western end was occupied as a refreshment room; but all the rest of the area was appropriated to specimens of manufacture. The arrangement of these specimens was striking and interesting; for each manufacturing town had its own stall or group of stalls. Every stall had inscribed over or within it, in characters which were made to bear part in the general decorations, the name of the town to whose industrial products it was set apart. Thus each town told its own tale: each made its appeal to the spectators in a mode more forcible than mere words could do. The social history of each body of artisans was written in the display of goods exhibited in the stalls of the towns to which they belonged. A sort of industrial map of Britain was presented by the whole assemblage, in which the skill and labour and capital of each town's population were indicated, much as a geological map exhibits the relative distribution of mineral wealth beneath the soil.

Nor were the great manufacturing towns of the north the only foci of industry, whose names were inscribed on these walls. If Lancashire had representatives from Manchester, Bolton, Rochdale, Bury, Blackburn, Ashton, Staleybridge, Liverpool, Lancaster and Preston; if Yorkshire were represented by Leeds, Halifax, Bradford, Huddersfield, York, Hull, Barnsley, Wakefield, and Sheffield; if Cheshire sent its delegates from Warrington and Stockport; so did other parts of the north send their industrial products from Carlisle, Newcastle, Stockton, &c.; Scotland, from Edinburgh, Glasgow, Dundee, Paisley, and the far distant Shetlands; the Midland Counties, from the Potteries, Northampton, Dunstable, Luton, Dudley, Birmingham, Wolverhampton, Kidderminster, Leicester, Coventry, Derby, Nottingham, Norwich; the west from Swansea, Exeter, Bristol, Coalbrookdale; while a sprinkling of towns in the east and south found a few hives for their working bees. The display of beautiful forms and colours was almost as unquestionable as the excellence of the handy work: we say "almost"—for it is well to leave a loophole for any improvements, in the aesthetic relations of manufacturing art, which our continental neighbours may suggest to us next year. The much disputed point of the inferiority of English taste to French taste, and the amount of difference if difference there be, will never be decided except by a more extended and a more direct comparison than has yet been presented in any one collection. Our manufacturers know the length and breadth of the field in which they have to contend: they know in which departments of industry they have the reputation of taking the lead before all the world, and in which they are supposed to lag somewhat behind; and the time has arrived for them to prepare for the battle, armed with the best of all weapons—perseverance, supported by science, adorned by art, and quickened by invention.

Every one who has a moderate acquaintance with the localization of manufactures in this country, will form a judgment of the kind of products exhibited in each department of the bazaar. How every combination of cotton fibres which ingenuity can devise, were exhibited in the Lanacashire sections; how the West Riding gloried in its broad cloths from Leeds and Halifax, its merinoes from Bradford, its many-coloured fancy cloths from Huddersfield, its linens and damasks from Barnsley, its cutlery from Sheffield; how Nottingham produced its bobbin-net and its cotton hosiery, Leicester its worsted hosiery and its warm lambs' wool garments for winter, Derby its silk hosiery, Coventry its ribbons, and Norwich its shawls and bombazeens; how North Staffordshire was represented by its exquisite porcelain, and South Staffordshire by its countless varieties of useful articles in iron and steel, Birmingham by its products in almost every metal that has yet been brought within the range of manufacturing art—all this needs scarcely be told. Besides the ordinary products of the workshop and the factory, there were specimens highly interesting for the novelty which they presented. There was a roll of tissue paper a mile in length, made from the fibres of worn-out coal-pit ropes; a tapestry copy of one of Landseer's pictures, containing three quarters of a million of stitches; bobbin-net for ladies' dresses, with a printed pattern impressed on it; horsehair covers for chairs, damasked both in pattern and in colour; copies of the "Queen's Apron," made from the wool of an Alpaca belonging to her Majesty; muslin printed in gold by the electro-metallurgic process, &c.

The same year, 1845, calls our attention to another part of Europe—one of the German states. *Bavaria* has been the first country to provide a *permanent* building for the holding of Industrial Exhibitions. It was fitting that a monarch who had adorned Munich with such choice works of art, who had built such structures as the Glyptothek and Pinakothek as depositories for sculptures and pictures, who had fostered the genius of Von Klenze in architecture, Schwanthaler in sculpture, Kaulbach in encaustics, Cornelius and Schnorr in frescoes—it was fitting that such a sovereign should hold out a hand of encouragement to industrial art, which presents so much to, and receives so much from, art in its higher acceptation. Ludwig of Bavaria will be remembered for all this, when his foibles are forgotten. It was in 1845 that the building above alluded to was finished; and the site chosen for it was near the Glyptothek—a neighbourhood of good augury. The sides of the building are relieved from absolute plainness by ranges of pilasters, supported by a rusticated basement, and supporting a cornice; but the spaces between the pilasters are plain wall, without windows. In the centre of the principal front, towards the Konigsplatz or King's Square, is a portico of fine proportions—octastyle, Corinthian, and elevated on a lofty flight of steps. The pediment contains sculptures from models by Schwanthaler. In the centre is an emblematic figure of Bavaria enthroned, and surrounded by figures representing sculpture, architecture, painting, encaustic printing, glass painting, metal casting, coining and medalling. The extremities and summit of the pediment exhibit two sculptured lions and a phœnix. The interior of the building contains a vestibule and seven large apartments, lighted from the top; besides which there are two rooms and two corridors lighted by windows. Below the main suite of rooms are warerooms for unpacking the articles sent for exhibition, and apartments for the officers of the establishment. The area of flooring in the exhibition rooms is somewhat under 2,000 square yards—consequently less than one-tenth of that presented by the Paris structure of 1844; the flooring is of oak, diversified into pattern by parquetry. The walls are tastefully painted, in subdued colours; the ceiling is coffered, and so provided with skylights as to diffuse an equable light over the rooms; and the roof is covered with metal. The building is fitted for the reception either of works of art or of manufactures. The first exhibition was of the former kind: comprising pictures, drawings, lithographs, statues, busts, medals, stained glass, &c.

Manchester presented its "Exposition of Industrial Art" in 1846, under the auspices of the Directors of the School of Design in that town, and within the walls of the Manchester Athenæum. The Free Trade Bazaar, at Covent Garden Theatre, had had one unfavourable feature attached to it: in so far as it was a bazaar, anything and everything was saleable, if purchasers presented themselves. Consequently many of the stalls were emptied of their contents within a day or two after the opening of the assemblage. The manufacturers were not by any means dissatisfied with such a result; while the lady stall-keepers were anxious to present as favourable a cash-balance as possible, in respect to the object for which they had become amateur tradeswomen. It did not follow that this circumstance should necessarily and directly vitiate the advantages likely to result from a grouping together of the industry of all England; because there was a general desire to produce the *best* in each class; but still it had a tendency to induce the depositors to send a large per centage of trinkets and mere ornaments, instead of productions of a more permanent and solid character. The French have always been averse, in their expositions of industry, to anything which may approach the bazaar system; and it is evident that the real influence of example, of honourable rivalry, in the production of excellence, ought at such places to be kept free from any immediate alloy of bartering and commercial transactions. It is to give producers an opportunity of learning from and profiting by each other, and to the rest of the world an opportunity of seeing what industrial art has in store for them, that the exhibitions are valuable—the buying and selling are to be the fruits of after growth.

At Manchester the specimens exhibited bore immediate relation to the manufactures of Lancashire, rather than to the manufacturing counties generally; but still there was a very varied and beautiful collection; and the exhibitors strove earnestly to show that a high order of decorative art is now exhibited by the manufacturers, aided in part by the instructions which pattern-draughtsmen receive from the several Schools of Design. Being under the management of the directors of the Manchester School of Design, this exhibition was made a means of showing the progress of the pupils: many specimens produced by the pupils being placed around the walls of the exhibition rooms. Prizes were given, not only for the best designs, but also for the best fabrics to which new designs had been transferred. Amongst the productions for which prizes were awarded were a six-coloured mousseline-de-laine, calico-prints in a single colour each, furniture prints or chintzes, models of flowers and natural objects, designs for a single-colour printed muslin, &c. The miscellaneous articles comprised carpets of singular beauty; porcelain and pottery of every class—from the costliest table-services to the humble but neatly formed vessel of earthenware; papier-maché furniture and ornaments; wood-carvings, produced both by hand and by machine; furniture and cabinet work; Spitalfields and other silk goods; bronze and iron castings; glass manufactures; Paisley shawls; wool-mosaics; cabinets and other articles in embossed leather; paper-hangings; caoutchouc manufactures, &c. One of the specimens exhibited had that kind of interest which attaches to all attempts to introduce a new manufacture, a new material, or a domestication in England of a culture usually belonging to other countries. The specimen in question was a rich brocade, made from silk reared in England. That silk-worms *can* be fostered and reared in England, is well known to thousands who have derived an innocent and instructive amusement from the pursuit; and that attempts have been made time after time, to introduce the culture as a commercial enterprise, is equally known to that smaller number of persons who have attended to the history of manufactures. The piece of brocade exhibited was a counterpart to another piece presented to and accepted by the Queen: it was presented by Mrs. Whitby, a lady who had reared the delicate creatures which produced the silk. This lady, with a motive and a perseverance which deserve all praise, devoted eight or ten years to a continuous study of the subject; she imported into England above a thousand mulberry trees from North Italy; she planted them in the grounds of her estate near Lymington; she fed and tended the silk-worms upon the Italian plan; she purchased winding-reels, heating apparatus, and other appliances necessary for the work; and she finally produced silk which was pronounced by competent authorities worthy of being woven into costly tissues. This is not the place to discuss the reasons why such enterprises have never yet been commercially successful in England, owing to rate of wages, uncertainty of climate, and other circumstances; but it *is* the place in which to join in an expression of thanks to a lady who so laudably makes experiments on the actual capabilities of the system.

It was understood, at the time of the Manchester Exposition, that many of the manufacturers were deterred from sending specimens of their choicest patterns, by dishonesty on one side and defective law on the other. A sad blot this! The small calico-printers (small in morals as in capital) have been wont, too many of them, to avail themselves of patterns which have been provided and paid for by the owners of larger establishments. And this—not when the pattern has had its day, and remunerated its inventor—but immediately on its publication; and being free from artistic charges, they have been able to undersell the real owners of the pattern. The wholesale dealers, who are the immediate purchasers from the manufacturer, notified in some cases their determination not to purchase goods, the new patterns of which had been publicly exhibited: on the ground that the patterns might be copied by other printers, and sold to other dealers at lower prices. It would not be difficult to show that—even in respect to these minor manufacturers —"Honesty is the best policy." The bearings of legal protection on artistic and mechanical inventions are more fruitful in results than many readers suppose.

Belgium came forward in 1847, with her "*Exposition de l'Industrie Belge.*" Brussels became in July of that year, a centre of attraction to those who wished to witness the progress of manufacturing art in that country; it was the third exhibition of the kind since Belgium became politically severed from Holland; and it received all the *éclat* which the presence of royalty and of official dignitaries could give. None of the ordinary buildings of Brussels being large enough for the occasion, the specimens were exhibited in the *Nouvel Entrepôt* on the quay, a large square edifice connected with commercial matters. The building is placed in close vicinage to the navigation system and the railway system of Belgium, and has thus admirable facilities for the transport and admission of manufactured products. The Entrepôt in its ordinary commercial arrangement, has an open court in the centre; but on that occasion the court was covered in, to form a large middle hall, while the surrounding building was laid out in galleries. Every available yard of space was occupied. Upwards of one thousand persons or manufacturing firms sent specimens for exhibition.

Some of the towns of Belgium have been so long celebrated for the exquisite specimens of workmanship which the lace-makers are able to produce, that a display of such articles was naturally to be expected at the Brussels exhibition. It was stated that on that occasion Brussels lace was exhibited, made of thread so exquisitely fine, that one pound weight of it was worth 3,500 francs—140*l.* sterling. Linen thread worth three times its weight in pure gold! This is indeed a striking exemplification of the manner in which labour imparts value to raw material. The lace, the damasked linens, the diapers, the table-cloths, these were among the choicest productions exhibited. As to the Brussels point-lace veils and robes, they are so enormously costly, that none but the wealthy can purchase them. On the occasion in question, an exquisite handkerchief, covered with the richest design, was exhibited, made of the costly thread just alluded to: a thread so gossamer-like, that a single filament was scarcely visible, even when backed by a blue ground. One specimen was a handkerchief worked for the Queen of Spain, and valued at 5000 francs or 200*l.*! Here pure gold sinks fairly beneath notice, as a standard of comparison; we might almost venture to say that such an application of linen thread is worth its weight in diamonds. Belgium is rich in various kinds of pottery and porcelain; but in artistic taste she scarcely comes up to her neighbour, France, whose designs are rather servilely copied. Liége is skilled in metallic manufactures, many of which adorned the exhibition. Among articles in glass were tables, an inch in thickness, exquisitely veined or streaked in colours; they pointed out one of the many novel applications for which this beautiful material is adapted.

As, in England, the glass duties of past years tended to repress invention and enterprise in that most attractive branch of manufacture; as our window duties interfere both with our freedom of ventilation and with the architecture of our private houses; as our soap duties offer a kind of premium for unwashed faces and unwashed garments; as our Insurance duties are a direct discouragement to prudence and forethought—so in Belgium certain fiscal arrangements play sad havoc with the free encouragement of manufactures. An annual tax is laid on all household furniture, in the form of a per centage on the assessed value. The consequence is, that the Belgian nobleman spends his fortune rather on pictures and other untaxed luxuries, than on furniture. This is all well for the pictures, and for those who paint them: it is all well for those who are employed in the productions which escape the impost; but it presses hard on those whose time, talent, and capital are expended on the production of the ordinary kinds of household furniture. Most of the Belgian houses are thus under-furnished: their domestic accommodations do not correspond with the wealth of the owner: there is baldness, bareness, cheapness, where else there might be a fair exercise for the display of the ever-varied products of industry in these departments of manufacture. Inventors, mechanicians, artists, philosophers—all may combine to aid the progress of manufacturers; but unless governments float with the stream, there will ever be a hindrance of one kind or other.

In the management of the Brussels exhibition, encouragement was sought to be given to ingenuity and talent, by awarding prizes to the most deserving exhibitors. The delicate task of awarding these prizes was entrusted to a jury, formed of a number of scientific persons deputed by the government; they were to examine all the articles displayed, and report on their merits; the government gave the prizes in accordance with the report; and a copy of the report was ordered to be presented to the minister and consul of every foreign power. The exhibition days were thus arranged—on Sundays, Wednesdays and Fridays, free admission was granted between the hours of ten and three; on Mondays, Thursdays and Saturdays, between the same hours, the admission was by tickets, for which half a franc each was charged; on Tuesdays the exhibition was open only for the Commissioners and privileged persons. All the half-francs thus taken were distributed to the hospitals of the Ursulines and St. Gertrude. In those cases where manufacturers had been put to greater expense than usual in preparing specimens for exhibition, the commission contrived a sort of Art Union lottery for their benefit; tickets were sold at ten francs each, to any who chose to embark in the lottery; and with the produce of those tickets, specimens were purchased by a managing committee—such works being selected as were costly, rather for the labour bestowed upon them than for the value of the material.

We turn from *Belgium* to *France*. That France should have been able to produce such an Exposition as that of 1849, after such a year of tumult as 1848, speaks much for her elasticity. Whether for fighting or dancing, for barricading or manufacturing, her children throw a wonderful amount of energy into their proceedings, and untiring ingenuity in finding out means for setting their plans in operation.

The building for the Exposition of 1849 occupied the same site as that for 1844, between the great avenue of the Champs Elysées and the river Sèine; but it was very much larger. It was about 675 feet long, by 328 wide, exclusive of the space for the agricultural department, and covered an area of 240,000 square feet—about one-third the area of the building in Hyde Park. Around the four sides of the building extended a gallery about 90 feet wide, divided into two avenues by a double range of pilasters; the whole width of gallery was so arranged, that there were four passages for visitors, two rows of manufactured goods on stalls, two rows placed against walls, and one row between and around the pilasters. The interior area of the great quadrangle was crossed by two transverse galleries, which thus left three courts; one court contained a beautiful fountain and a horticultural collection; another had an immense reservoir; and the third contained specimens of large metal-work. In addition to the main building was a shed of large dimensions, about 300 feet long by 100 in width, appropriated to the reception of agricultural implements and live stock—for it was one feature of this Exposition, as compared with its predecessors, that the skill of the grazier was represented as well as that of the manufacturer. The entire range of buildings was constructed of wood, and roofed with zinc; the cost was about 16,000*l.*—the materials becoming the property of the contractors after the termination of the Exposition. The number of Exhibitors was 4,494. The display was open to the Parisians for a period of fifty-six days; and the admission was gratuitous on Mondays, Wednesdays, Fridays, and Saturdays, between the hours of eleven and five; on Thursdays the admission was charged one franc, towards a fund for the aid of the poor; and Mondays were appropriated to the Jury who were, at their leisure, to award the prizes for the various articles exhibited. At hours before and after the public exhibition, on all the days, admission was given by tickets, to learned foreigners, distinguished personages, representatives of the public press, &c.

In glancing over the plan of the building, and the arrangement of the manufactures, as given in Mr. Wyatt's Report, the eye fails to catch any very marked system of classification, although two systems have evidently been attempted—the *topographical* and the *material*. Thus, on the west side we see "Parisian" goods; while on various parts of the north and south sides are named the departments and towns of Gard, Rhône, Lyons, Roubaix, Elbœuf, Haut-Rhin, Rouen, Sedan, Troyes, Orne, Nord, Turcoing, and Rheims. But the classification according to the materials of manufacture is somewhat more distinctly marked, though an arrangement according to *uses* is also observable. We have, for instance, in pretty near approximation one to another, the whole range of textile goods—from coarse flannels and thick woollens to gorgeous ribbons and delicate laces; in another department are miscellaneous articles of dress, such as artificial flowers, feathers, stays, wigs, shoes, boots, furriery, hats, hosiery, gloves, &c.; musical instruments have a department to themselves; costly articles of various kinds are collected at the "Parisian" or western end, including clocks, watches, jewellery, bronzes, porcelain, weapons, lamps, painted glass, &c.; along the south side are household furniture and chemicals, in two great divisions; while the east end is chiefly occupied by metal work and machinery.—The difficulties which the arranger of this collection had to overcome, and the wavering balance of his opinions, may be read by a glance at the engraved plan. Our Hyde Park Committee or Managers will find the classification of their treasures not among the least of their weighty difficulties.

The *Birmingham* Exposition of Industry, opened in September, 1849, was one of a peculiarly interesting character; for the town of Birmingham naturally contributed towards it more largely than any other town, and Birmingham carries on a greater variety of manufactures than any other town (perhaps) in the kingdom. This industrial display was planned to take place at the same time as the meeting of the British Association at Birmingham; and there could hardly be a happier mode of establishing the union and mutuality of science and art. It was held at Bingley House, in Broad-street, which was fitted up with a long array of exhibition-rooms. Members of the British Association were admitted free: other visitors paid a charge of one shilling each; but arrangements were made for admitting schools and bodies of workmen at much lower prices.

The *electro-plate* which now constitutes such an important department of Birmingham manufactures formed one of the most attractive portions of the exposition. If regarded as a substitute for solid silver goods, this beautiful new product would have the bad character of being a sham—a mere coating of costly metal on a substratum of cheaper metal; but if we regard it as an improvement on the silver-plating of past times, its true character comes out at once: both are examples of coating copper or some other metal with silver; but the electro process has shown itself to be far the better of the two. The old massive but clumsy tea-service, with its heavy style of ornament, is superseded by a lighter and more graceful production, in which the utmost delicacy of decoration is quite compatible with soundness of workmanship. In an another article, too, viz., *papier mache*, Birmingham has made similar advances within the last few years.

All the most distinguished manufacturers contributed towards the Birmingham collection. The metal-work for church decoration, exhibited by Messrs. Hardman, were strikingly illustrative of a branch of art at present in high favour. The castings in bronze and iron were beautifully executed, showing that Birmingham has risen nearly, if not quite, to a level with the celebrated Berlin iron-founders. Among the specimens exhibited in this department were a pair of richly cast gates for the Fitzwilliam Museum, a chandelier for her Majesty, and a tripod (in imitation of one of those submerged at Pompeii) for the Duke of Sutherland. An elegant combination of brass-work with porcelain and with turquoise-glass formed the material of many specimens exhibited—a material which many of our readers may have seen as applied to fanciful ornamental productions. Stamped brass-work is now becoming extensively employed in house-fittings and furniture; and Birmingham, with great propriety, exhibited the skill which she has attained in this art. An instructive feature in the exhibition was afforded by a series of specimens in porcelain and pottery, designed to illustrate the progress of the plastic arts in this country. First came a group of beer-mugs and drinking-jugs, made in the time of Queen Elizabeth, of coarse clay covered with brown glaze; then came a candlestick and drinking cups, of a somewhat later date; then several specimens of the date of William and Mary, glazed with salt instead of with lead; then a collection of cups, plates, tureens, and other articles, made in the time of George II., with light-coloured ornaments in relief on a dark ground; then the improved ware of the latter half of the last century, when Dorsetshire clay came into extensive use, and when improved modes of glazing were adopted: and lastly, the exquisite productions which resulted from the liberality, the ingenuity, and the enterprise of

Wedgwood. Such a serial collection as the one here alluded to forms the best history of the department of mechanical art to which it relates. The modern productions of the Staffordshire Potteries were of course amply represented at the Birmingham Exposition. Of the miscellaneous iron manufactures, any one who knows Birmingham and its industry may easily conceive how richly they were illustrated on this occasion—stoves and grates, fenders and fire-furniture, cast-iron glass-frames and tables, hat-holders and umbrella-stands, letter-boxes and letter-plates, tea-urns and coal-vases, gas-fittings, files, cutlery, screws, weighing-machines, locks, keys, hinges, tools, springs, latches, wire, steel pens, gun-barrels—all that iron can be supposed fitted to produce (and a great deal that we could hardly dream to be made of such a material) were here displayed. Engineering did not fail to put forth its claims to admiration, in steam-engines, paper-making machines, ticket-marking machines for railways, Baranowski's ready-reckoning machines, tube-rolling machines, and a multitude of others. We cannot pass over the mention of tubes and pipes, which are made in such incalculable quantities, and of such various materials, in Birmingham, without quoting a pleasant scrap from the *Times* relating to the *sanitary* merits of pipes :—"Pipes appear to be the order of the day. Pipes to let pure water in—pipes to carry foul water out—pipes for warming, drainage, ventilation—pipes to bring in gas for burning—pipes to carry off the products of combustion—pipes to the rich man's marble bath-room—pipes to the poor man's brick-paved kitchen—pipes for the fountains of St. James's—and pipes for the stinking cesspools of St. Giles's. For ornament and pleasure—for economy and cleanliness—for health and comfort—for arresting conflagration and extinguishing pestilence—pipes! The whole sanitary question, indeed, may be regarded as little more than a question of pipes."

The Birmingham Exposition was entirely successful. Nearly 100,000 persons visited it. Free tickets were granted to the pupils of the School of Design, to many school children, and to a large number of work-people. It is an instructive proof that most of the visitors were busily-employed persons, who could only snatch an hour or two to make this pleasant visit, that by far the greater number of persons assembled at one time was between six and eight o'clock in the evening.

The *Society of Arts* has, within the last two or three years, done much to foster a spirit of generous emulation in productive industry, by forming collections of manufactures for exhibition. In 1849 there was one such display, notable for the great beauty and variety of the specimens sent by our leading manufacturers. But the year 1850 has been marked by the unique *Mediæval Exhibition,* which we must not pass over without a brief notice.

The Council solicited in all quarters, for the loan of specimens of middle-age art and manufactures, for a limited period ; and this request was responded to most liberally. Never before was there such a collection displayed to the British public generally ; for it contained the gems of numerous private collections. There were the most exquisite specimens of metal work, in casting, chiselling, engraving, chasing, damascening, embossing, and pouncing ; the metals being gold, silver, copper, brass, pewter, zinc, bronze, iron, and steel. There were beautiful carvings in box-wood, ivory, alabaster, marble, sardonyx, jasper, and agate. There were enamels and incrustations of the most elaborate description. There were clocks and watches of middle-age workmanship ; and there were various specimens of armour and weapons, notable for their high finish. The porcelain and pottery arts were represented by Della Robbia ware, Majolica ware, old Flemish stone ware, Palissy ware, Böttcher ware, and other kinds which exhibit artistic or manipulative skill. The specimens of glass ware—Greek, Etruscan, Roman, Venetian, and early German—were highly curious. Tapestry, embroidery, lace, embossed leathers, mosaic—all tended to swell the list of Mediæval specimens in this highly interesting exhibition.

The Exhibition of *Modern* Industry, displayed at the Society of Arts at the same time, does not call for much remark. It consisted of a small number of specimens in silks, damasks, lace, velvet, poplin, shawls, carpets, papier maché, marqueterie, glass, castings, carvings, modellings, &c.

Dublin has claimed its right to consideration as the centre of an Industrial Exposition. During the month of July in the present year, (1850) a very interesting collection of manufactured products was exhibited, under the auspices of the Royal Dublin Society, and in the rooms belonging to that body. The house of the Society is a handsome structure, with a range of eleven Italian windows in width, and having a garden and lawn in the rear. All the principal rooms were appropriated to the reception of the specimens: such as the gallery, the Agricultural Museum, the Board Room, the Corridor, the Hall, the Library, the Grand Staircase, the Schools, the six rooms occupied as a Museum, &c.; besides which there were an iron house and a wooden-shed constructed on the lawn. Every apartment was divided into sections; every section was marked off into stalls or tables; and every specimen was numbered and catalogued.

The catalogue prepared by the Society is an unusually complete and full one: so good, indeed, that we may almost regret that it had only a temporary utility, terminating when the exhibition was brought to a conclusion. It may be hoped that a few copies of this catalogue will be preserved, for the sake of furnishing hints to future catalogue makers in respect to industrial collections. It is an octavo pamphlet of about 170 pages. At the beginning are thirteen lithographed plans, showing the exact arrangement of the several floors of the building. Next comes the catalogued enumeration of all the specimens exhibited, numbered in order from 1 to 2,850. In most cases, all the specimens sent by one contributor are numbered consecutively, grouped into one section, and entered in the same part of the catalogue: where the name, occupation, and address of the contributor are given. Near the the end of the catalogue is an alphabetical list of contributors' or exhibitors' names; with the room, the section, and the table appropriated to each person's contributions, and the number of the specimen which begins the group belonging to that person. Lastly, there is a classified list of the trades represented at the exposition, and an alphabetical list of all the persons who sent specimens illustrative of each trade.

This classified list shows how wide was the range embraced by this industrial display: for it includes the following headings—silks, linens, damasks, muslins, and chintzes; fringe and coach lace; carpets and rugs; woollen drapery; hosiery; hats; fancy work; lace and embroidery; hair work; leather; oil-cloth; matting; cabinet-making; picture frames; carving and turning; lamps and lustres; glass; marble; porcelain and pottery; watches and clocks; precious metals; electrotypes; iron work; machines and engines; fire-arms; musical instruments; philosophical and mathematical instruments; agricultural and horticultural implements; carriages; paper hangings; printing; bookbinding; soap and candles; perfumery; ink and blacking &c. The raw materials of manufactures did not form part of the collection.

Many of the specimens exhibited could only be ranked as trinkets or curiosities; but by far the larger number bore immediately on the present state of the industrial arts, especially in Ireland. Irish poplins and Irish linens were fittingly and worthily represented; and so were the damasks, taberets, and gold-tissued poplins, which are manufactured in small quantity but of high excellence in Dublin. The specimens of Limerick lace were especially interesting; for the art of lace-making was not known in that locality until about twenty years ago, whereas it is now an important adjunct to the industry of the place. In 1829 a few young women were taken over to Limerick, to teach this art to various females in the humbler grades of society; and there are now at least one thousand women and girls who are earning at the trade a living for themselves and their families, Messrs. Lambert and Bury, lace manufacturers at Limerick, employ at the present time about four hundred hands in their own establishment.—If Ireland and its people, its rulers and its agitators, would eschew politics once now and then, and try to find a home for manufactures within that beautiful country, we should not hear so much of starvation and of wrangling as we now do. The Limerick lace-manufacture is a case in point; and another is furnished by the muslin-embroidery which is carried on so extensively in the neighbourhood of Belfast and Coleraine, where there are many thousand females employed at this work by Glasgow firms; immense quantities of embroidered Scotch muslins are woven in Scotland, but embroidered in Ireland.

Many of the articles exhibited were said to be "French materials, made up in Dublin;" but many were undoubtedly Irish, both in materials and in manufacture; among which were ornamental articles made of Irish bog-oak. There were some copies or imitations of Irish antique ornaments, made from iron ore and gems found on the Marquis of Waterford's estate. There were sets of tea-trays, elaborately carved fire-screens, and small statuettes, in Irish bog-yew. Many of the exhibitors drew attention to the fact, that the specimens exhibited by them, belonged to branches of manufacture, which, though long and familiarly known in England, are yet new to Ireland; among such is wire-woven cloth for paper-making. Dr. Bagot, of Dublin, sent a few remarkable contributions, interesting in an indirect manner to manufactures and manufacturers. One was a collection of fuel-balls, used by the peasantry of Tipperary; they are usually made by women, who manufacture them by mixing together culm and yellow clay in proper proportions, and, whilst gradually adding a sufficiency of water, work the ingredients into a mass with their bare feet; the mass is then formed into balls, which, when dry, are ready to use as fuel. Another contribution by Dr. Bagot was a curious one, consisting of seven specimens of "cod-liver oil," procured from different quarters. This oil is now extensively employed on account of its powerful medicinal qualities; and the specimens were exhibited, to shew how great is the difficulty of knowing good from bad qualities, and how much deception has crept into this branch of commerce; they were charged from twenty-four shillings to forty-four shillings per gallon, and some of them, (among which was the most costly specimen), contained no cod-liver oil whatever, while others were adulterated with three-fourths their bulk of other and commoner kinds of oil.

It would carry us into too wide a field were we to enter further into the arrangement and contents of the Dublin Exposition. Suffice it to say that many of the leading English manufacturers exhibited their strength in the excellence of the specimens submitted:—Hunt and Roskell their costly works in the precious metals; Elkingtons their wonderful productions in electro-plate; the Copelands, the Mintons, the Ridgways, the Chamberlains, their exquisite works in porcelain; Houldsworths, their beautiful Manchester silk goods; Webbs, their curious hair-cloth damasks; Swainsons their chintzes from Preston; Chubbs, their labyrinthine patent locks; Whitworths, their planing and screw-cutting machines; the Ransomes and the Croskills their agricultural implements, &c.

The *Devonport* Mechanics Institute has honourably followed in the path marked out by its northern compeers. A new Hall and Subscription Rooms have been recently opened in that town; and it was thought that a graceful and fitting mode of celebrating the event would be by assembling together specimens of art

KNIGHT'S CYCLOPÆDIA

OF THE

INDUSTRY OF ALL NATIONS.

A'BACUS, in architecture, is the level tablet, formed on the enriched capital of a column, to support the horizontal entablature.

A'BACUS, an instrument employed to facilitate arithmetical calculations. One variety consists of a frame, traversed by stiff wires, on which beads or counters are strung so as to move easily; the beads on the first right hand row are units, those on the next tens, and so on. Such instruments are not now much employed.

ABANDONMENT. Before a person who has insured a ship or goods can demand from an insurer or underwriter the stipulated compensation for a total loss of such ship or goods, he must *abandon* or relinquish to the insurer all his interest in any part of the property which may be saved.

ABATTOIR. An abattoir, in France, is a slaughter-house, in a form which was first adopted at Paris in 1810. There are three on the north side of Paris, and two on the south side, not far from the barriers, and about two miles from the centre of the city. The cattle markets for the supply of Paris are several miles distant, and the cattle are driven from them round the exterior boulevards to the abattoirs, and consequently do not enter the city. At one of the abattoirs each butcher has his slaughter-house, a place for keeping the meat, an iron rack for fat, pans for melting it, and a place with convenience for giving cattle hay and water, and where they may be kept before being slaughtered. A fixed sum is charged for this accommodation, and in 1843 the fee was 6 francs for each ox, 4 francs for a cow, 2 francs for a calf, and 10 cents for a sheep. The income of the establishment, arising from these fees, the sale of manure, &c., was above 48,000*l*. in 1842. An inspector is appointed at each abattoir, and means are taken to prevent unwholesome meat being sold. There are slaughter-houses under public regulations in most of the continental cities; and those of New York and Philadelphia, and some other of the cities of the American Union, are, it is said, placed on a similar footing.

The great cattle-market in Smithfield, for the supply of London, has existed above five centuries, but the spot was originally a piece of waste ground beyond the city, instead of being, as at present, surrounded by a dense population. The cattle sold in Smithfield Market amount annually to about 180,000, and the sheep to about 1,500,000, and at least this number are annually slaughtered within the limits of the metropolis. There are slaughtermen who kill for other butchers frequently above a hundred head of cattle, and perhaps five or six hundred sheep, every week; many butchers kill for themselves to a considerable extent, and there are few who have not accommodation for slaughtering and dressing a few sheep, either in the cellar underneath their shop, or in the rear of their premises. The slaughter houses, for sheep, in Newgate market, many of which are in cellars, and in Warwick-lane, are close to Newgate-street, and within a hundred and fifty yards of Ludgate-street, two of the great thoroughfares of London.

During the last few years searching enquiries have been made respecting the practicability of removing Smithfield market, and establishing abattoirs for the metropolis in a less crowded situation. The city authorities, who levy considerable tolls in the market, have resisted all proposals for removing it to any place beyond their jurisdiction; and the contest has been (and still is) whether such a removal, to Islington or elsewhere, shall take place; or whether Smithfield market itself shall be enlarged and improved. An opulent projector, some years ago, expended upwards of 100,000*l*. in the formation of a cattle market in Lower Islington; twenty-two acres of land were appropriated; and the market was efficiently provided with counting-houses, offices, sheds, lairs, pens, wells, and everything requisite for a market suitable for twice as many cattle as are accommodated at Smithfield; while plans were arranged for abattoirs adjoining. The market was opened in 1833; but this vast scheme failed, from various causes, and the well-arranged area has ever since remained wholly useless. To revive this market, is one among many recent projects.

In 1847 a Committee of the House of Commons enquired into the subject of Smithfield market. The evidence was published, but without any report on the part of the Committee. Among the items of evidence it was stated that the largest Smithfield market-day (down to the end of 1846) occurred in 1844: on one day in that year there were 5,633 cattle and 39,920 sheep exposed for sale at Smithfield. In the voluminous evidence, extending to 400 pages, every part of the subject received much elucidation, and many details were given concerning the abattoirs of Paris; but it became afterwards known that the Committee were too much puzzled by conflicting evidence to form any decided opinion on the main question submitted to them.

Early in the session of 1849 Mr. Mackinnon moved for the appointment of a committee to enquire into the state of Smithfield market, with a view either to its removal or its improvement. There was some opposition to the motion; but the committee was eventually appointed, and evidence was taken, bearing on the subject. About the middle of the year the report of the committee was presented; in which it was stated that Smithfield market, from its deficiency in size, and from the inconvenience which was thereby created, ought to be abolished; that the area of a new market, its site and locality, should be determined by the authorities of the city of London, or, if they declined, by the government; that of the 5¼ acres which Smithfield occupies, 4 acres should be converted into a pleasant open square, and the remaining 1¼ acres devoted to a range of handsome buildings, the rents of which would probably go far to make up for the loss of tolls sustained by the corporation. In a long debate, Mr. Mackinnon pressed upon the government the adoption of plans in conformity with the report; but the session passed away without further results.

In the early part of 1850 a commission investigated the whole subject, and reported on the propriety of removing the market from Smithfield; but no legislative steps have yet been taken; and the city authorities are still planning various improvements (to cost 500,000*l.*) in the existing market. Whilst the authorities of the City of London are thus deliberating how they can best preserve a profitable nuisance, the city of Edinburgh is building an abattoir, that may be a model to municipalities who concern themselves for public good.

ABERBROTHWICK, or ARBROATH, is a sea-port town in Forfarshire, Scotland, at the mouth of the small river Brothock. The principal manufactures are, yarn spun from flax and hemp, canvas, brown and bleached linen, leather, cast-iron, and bone-dust. In the town and suburbs there are 16 spinning-mills, which are driven by the river. About 106 vessels belonged to the port in 1849. There is a harbour-basin, faced with stone; and there are railways from Arbroath to Forfar and Aberdeen, and from Arbroath to Dundee and Perth.

ABERDEEN is situated on the river Dee, Scotland, where it is discharged into the German Ocean. *Old* Aberdeen is on the south bank: *New* Aberdeen on the north; and the two together had, in 1849, a population of about 73,000. The harbour is spacious, and is rendered safe by a pier of granite on the north side of the Dee, which extends into the German Ocean.

Aberdeen is a place of large trade, with many manufactures of cotton, linen, and woollen; extensive iron-works, ship-building yards, (some for large steam-vessels,) and manufactures of most of the articles connected with ships and ship-building. The number of sailing vessels registered at Aberdeen, in January, 1850, was 368, with a tonnage of 62,234. There are upwards of 4,000 vessels entered inwards and cleared outwards annually. There are fine fleets of steamers to London, Leith, and Inverness. The foreign commerce is chiefly with North America, the East Indies, West Indies, Mediterranean, and Baltic. Several ships were formerly employed in whale-fishing, but that trade has entirely ceased. The rivers Dee and Don supply a large quantity of salmon, which are exported to London and elsewhere. The value of the Aberdeen granite, shipped to London and other places, has sometimes exceeded 40,000*l.* a year. A granite-polishing work has been lately established.

ABERDEENSHIRE, Scotland, is chiefly remarkable, in an industrial point of view, for the exhaustless supply of granite which it yields. This granite is frequently found disintegrated, at least in so friable a state as to be easily dug into by the pickaxe and spade;

yet large blocks of fine building stone are frequently quarried in the midst of a mass of disintegrated rock. The rivers Dee and Don supply large quantities of excellent salmon. The Aberdeenshire canal runs from Aberdeen to Inverury; the chief traffic is in lime, coal, dung, bones, and bark, carried up; and stone, slate, grain, and meal brought down. The Aberdeen railway only touches the county; the Great North of Scotland Railway (if constructed) will traverse it. About 10,000 acres of the county are covered with wood, such as birch, alder, poplar, and mountain ash. The planted woods are chiefly larch and Scotch firs. The fir timber of the forest of Mar is, for size and quality, the first in the British Islands. The quantity of cultivated land is but small.

The chief animals reared aro cattle, sheep, and horses, considerable numbers of which are despatched to London by steamers, which may often be seen a little way below the Tower. The cultivation of turnips has been greatly extended in consequence of the facilities afforded by steam navigation for conveying fat cattle to the London market, and the consequent increase of stock.

ABIES, is the botanical name for the invaluable genus of *Fir* trees. There are many well-known species. The *Abies Picea*, or Silver Fir, is a native of the mountains of the middle and south of Europe, in stony, dry, exposed situations. Planks of indifferent quality, on account of their softness, are sawn from its trunk, which also yields Burgundy pitch and Strasburg turpentine. *Abies Balsamea*, the Balm of Gilead Fir, is found in the cold parts of North America; it yields a clear transparent greenish-yellow turpentine, which is commonly known under the name of *Canadian Balsam*. *Abies Webbiana* is a lofty tree, whose wood seems to be valuable; in India it is used by plane-makers. *Abies Canadensis*, or Hemlock Spruce Fir, is a noble species, rising to the height of seventy or eighty feet. The wood is of little value, being neither sound nor durable: it is chiefly employed for the manufacture of laths and for coarse in-door work. Tho bark is exceedingly valuable for tanning; mixed with oak bark, it is said to be much better than oak bark alone. A great deal of the Essence of Spruce is extracted from the shoots of this species. *Abies excelsa*, the Norway Spruce Fir, is a native of the mountainous parts of the north of Europe, where it sometimes constitutes, as in Norway, the principal timber. The wood is of a white colour, of a fine even grain, and very durable; in the market it is known under the name of White or Christiana Deal. *Abies alba*, the White Spruce Fir, is found in the colder regions of North America. The timber is of inferior quality. From the fibres of the root, macerated in water, the Canadians prepare the thread with which they sew together the birch bark that forms their canoes. Its resin is also used to render the seams water-tight. The bark is said to be occasionally used for tanning. *Abies nigra*, the Black or Red Spruce Fir, is a native of the most inclement regions of North America. From its young branches is extracted the Essence of Spruce, so well known as a useful antiscorbutic in long voyages. *Abies Douglasii*, the Douglas Fir, is found in immense forests in North-West America. The young branches have their bark filled with receptacles of resin, as in the Balm of Gilead. The timber is heavy, firm, of as deep a colour as yew, with very few knots, and not in the least liable to warp. *Abies Larix*, the common Larch Fir, is a native of the mountains of the middle of Europe, of Russia and Siberia. It grows with great rapidity, is subject to very few accidents, transplants with little risk, and produces timber of great excellenco and value, not only for domestic but for naval purposes. In mountainous districts in Scotland the Dukes of Athol havo planted it in immense quantities; and it appears, from a report of one of those noblemen to the Horticultural Society, that in situations 1,500 to 1,600 feet above the level of the sea, he has felled trees, eighty years old, that have each yielded six loads of the finest timber. From the boiled inner bark, mixed with rye-flour, and afterwards buried for a few hours in tho snow, the hardy Siberian hunters prepare a sort of leaven. The bark is nearly as valuable to the tanner as oak-bark; it also produces the substance called Venice Turpentine, which flows in abundance when the lower part of the trunk of old trees is wounded. A sort of manna, called Briançon Manna, exudes from its leaves in the form of a white flocculent substance, which finally becomes concreted into small lumps. *Abies Cedrus*, the Cedar of Lebanon Fir, grows in Syria and the Taurus. According to Labillardiére, a French traveller in Syria, the largest of those now remaining on Lebanon is, at least, 9 feet in diameter; the trees are held in great veneration. *Abies Deodara*, the Sacred Indian Fir, is a large tree, with a trunk about 4 feet in diameter. The wood is extremely durable, and so resinous that laths made of it are used for candles. Spars of it have been taken out of Indian temples, known to have been erected from 200 to 400 years, uninjured, except in those parts which originally were sap-wood. Mr. Moorcroft procured specimens from the starlings of a bridge in Ladakh, where it had been exposed to the water for nearly 400 years. Mr. Lambert says, that its wood takes an excellent polish, being very close-grained.

The genus of resinous plants called *Abies*, which we have thus described, comprehends many forest trees of great importance. Some of them, such as the Larch, the Norway Spruce, the Silver Fir, and the Balm of Gilead, are raised in nurseries in the open ground, in large quantities, for the supply of our plantations; others, such as the Cedar of Lebanon and the Douglas Fir, are procured in much less abundance, and are treated with more care, being usually kept in pots until they are finally committed to the earth in the situation they may bo subsequently destined to occupy.

ABINGDON, in Berkshire, is situated at the juuction of the Ock and the Thames. The trade consists of malting, hemp-dressing, and sack-cloth and sail-cloth making; besides which there are two large clothing factories. The corn-market is large. Capacious wharfs and warehouses have been erected at the entrance of the Wilts and Berks canal into the Thames. The Oxford branch of the Great Western Railway passes by Abingdon, near which there is a station.

ABORI'GINES, a term by which we denote the primitive inhabitants of a country. Thus, to take one of the most striking instances, when the contiuent and islands of America were discovered, they were found to be inhabited by various races of people, of whose immigration into those regions we have no historical accounts. All the tribes, then, of North America may, for the present, be considered as aborigines. But the word aborigines has of late come into general use to express the natives of various parts of the world in which Europeans have settled; but it seems to be limited or to be nearly limited to such natives as are barbarous, and do not cultivate the ground, and have no settled habitations. The aborigines of Australasia and Van Diemen's Land (if there are any left in Van Diemen's Land) are so called as being savages, though the name may be applied with equal propriety to cultivators of the ground. Some benevolent people suppose that aborigines, who are not cultivators of the ground, may become civilized like Europeans. But it has not yet been proved satisfactorily that this change can be effected in any large numbers; and if it can be effected it is an essential condition that the aborigines must give up their present mode of life and adopt that of the settlers. The New Zealanders, a people of natural industry and acuteness, will perhaps furnish the most striking example of the dominant influence of civilization. But such a change is not easy: even in the United States of North America it has been only partially effected. The wide expanse of country between the Mississipi and the Atlantic is now nearly cleared of the aborigines, and the white man, who covets the possession of land, will follow up his victory till he has occupied every portion of the continent which he finds suitable for cultivation. The red man must become a cultivator, or he must retire to places where the white man does not think it worth his while to follow him. The savage aborigines do not pass from what we call barbarism to what we call civilization without being subjected to the force of external circumstances, that is, the presence among them of settlers or conquerors. There is no more reason for supposing that huntsmen will change their mode of life, such as it is, without being compelled, than that agricultural people will change theirs. As contributors to the Industry of Nations, the aborigines of North America are important auxiliaries to the commercial skill of the European. The fur trade is supported by the hardihood and sagacity of the Indian hunters and trappers. See FUR TRADE.

ABOUSAMBUL, or IPSAMBUL, a place remarkable for containing two of the most perfect specimens of Egyptian rock-cut temples adorned with sculptures. These excavations are in Nubia, on the west side of the Nile. The smaller temple has on each side of the doorway, three standing colossal figures, about 30 feet high, cut out of the rock and deep sunk in niches, to the back part of which they are attached by a portion of the rock that has been allowed to remain. The figures are in a standing position, with one foot advanced, and looking towards the river. On each side of the larger figures stand smaller ones, from four to six feet high. The larger temple has four enormous sitting colossi in front, which are the largest in all Egypt or Nubia. Each of these figures is 25 feet 4 inche across the shoulders, the face 7 feet long, the nose 2 feet 8 inches, the beard 5 feet 6 inches; the whole height as it sits is about 50 feet, besides the cap, which is 14 feet high. Only two of these monsters are in sight; the others are buried in the sand. Over the door there is a figure in relief of Osiris, 20 feet high, with two colossal figures, one on each side looking towards it.

ABRUZZO. There are in the kingdom of Naples three divisions called respectively *Abruzzo Ultra* 1, *Abruzzo Ultra* 2, and *Abruzzo Citra*. They contain together about 800,000 inhabitants. Aquila, the chief town of Abruzzo Ultra 1, has manufactures of paper, stockings, and leather. The lake of Celano is in this province. The Emperor Claudius undertook a great work for the purpose of draining the lake, or at least preventing it from doing damage by overflowing. Claudius made a canal 3 miles long, partly by perforating and partly by cutting down a mountain: it was finished in eleven years, 30,000 men having been constantly employed thereon.

The natives of the highlands of Abruzzo are chiefly employed in rearing and tending sheep, numerous flocks of which, after feeding on the mountain pastures during summer, migrate to the plains of Puglia at the approach of winter. The shepherds are generally accompanied by their wives and children in these yearly migrations to and from the mountains, and by their large white dogs, which are very fierce to strangers. The sheep's milk is used to make cheese, the wool is an important article of trade, and the skins are exported in great quantities to the Levant. The shepherds also are clothed in them, and wear sandals of untanned leather, fastened with small cords, round the leg. The breed of merino sheep has been introduced into the Abruzzi. The lower parts of the Abruzzi have a productive soil, and export a considerable amount of grain, oil, and almonds: they also produce some cotton.

ABUSHIRE, or BUSHIRE, a sea-port and commercial town in the province of Farsistan, Persia, is situated on the north-east coast of the Persian Gulf. Ships of about 300 tons burthen can lie in the inner roads about six miles north from the town, and ships of larger burthen in 25 feet of water, three or four miles west from the town. Abushire is the emporium of a large commerce between the East Indies and Persia, its merchants supplying almost all Persia with Indian commodities as well as with many of those of Europe, and exporting in return the productions of Persia and Turkey to the East Indies and to Europe. Of the imports from India the most important are indigo, sugar, and spices; of the Persian exports, raw silk is the most important.

ABUTMENT, in building and machinery, is that which receives the end of and gives support to any thing having a tendency to spread. The piers or mounds on or against which an arch that is less than a semicircle, or a series of such arches, rests, are abutments; while the piers at the extremities of a bridge, of whatever form its arch or arches may be, are always termed its abutments. In machinery also the word has a similar meaning, as applied to a fixed point from which resistance or reaction is obtained. Springs, whether used, as in a watch, to impel machinery, or, as in the various kinds of spring-balance, to measure or control force, must have their abutments, as also must all machines in which power is transmitted by means of screws. The name is applied in carpentry to a joint in which the end of one piece of timber is joined to the side of another, so that their fibres form an angle with each other.

ABYSSINIA. This African country is an elevated table-land, lying between 8° 30′ and 15° 40′ N. lat. and between 35° and 42° E. long. The north-eastern edge of the table-land is directed towards the Red Sea, and is from 30 to 60 miles from its shores; the other or inland edges slope away to a lower level on every side; so that if the surrounding part of Africa were covered with water to the depth of a few hundred feet, the whole of Abyssinia would form an island. Though Abyssinia is situated between the tropics, its productions rather resemble those of the temperate than of the torrid zone. Few of the grains of India are found here. The other grains are wheat, barley, oats, Indian corn, durrha, and tokussa. There are some small plantations of coffee; and cotton is grown in the lower parts of the country. Excellent grapes grow at the foot of the rocky masses to the east of Lake Zána. The domestic animals consist of horses, cattle, sheep, goats, mules and asses. There is also the black sheep, which seems to be peculiar to this region; the wool is of a black colour, and about eighteen inches in length. The people take great care of these animals, lest they should get too fat, for then the wool falls off; they are placed on frames, cleaned every day with water, and fed with roasted barley and other food. A skin of good quality is sold for a dollar and upwards, which is a very large sum in that country. These skins are worn by the warriors. Wild animals are very numerous.

Gold has occasionally been found in Abyssinia. The mountains of Lasta are rich in iron-ore, which is worked, and appears to be of good quality. The great salt-plain which lies between the Red Sea and the table-land of Tigré belongs partly to the sovereign of Tigré, and immense quantities of rock-salt are annually taken from it and imported to all parts of the country, as it is not only used for culinary purposes, but also as currency. Large quantities of salt, taken from the salt lake Assal, are annually imported into Shoa, as salt is not found on the table land. Sulphur is found at several places.

The Abyssinians have made tolerable progress in manufactures. The best article is tanned skins, which are used for bedding or for tents: an important article, on account of the numerous caravans which traverse the country. Shields made of the hides of elephants or rhinoceroses are also good. Axes and ploughshares, as well as spear heads, are made at several places; but knives, sword-blades, scissors, and razors, are only made at Gondar and at Kiratza. At Gondar guns are made, but only by some Greeks, not by the natives. Large quantities of coarse cotton-cloth are made in several parts of the country by women, and a finer kind, with a red or blue border, for the more wealthy classes of society. The silk manufactures are limited to some embroidery, made by Mohammedans and worn by their women, and to blue strings, which are worn on the neck by all Christians, as a mark of distinction from Mohammedans or heathens. A coarse stuff is made from the wool and hair of the black sheep and goats, which is also employed in making a kind of counterpanes. Coarse black pottery is made in every part of the country. Printing has not yet been introduced into Abyssinia: so that the copying of manuscripts forms a distinct branch of industry.

Abyssinia has no immediate intercourse with seafaring nations, but its products are carried either to Massówa on the Red Sea, or to Tajurrah on the gulf of Aden. Massówa is the harbour of Tigré and Amhára; and Tajurrah the harbour of Shoa. Nearly all the articles imported into Massówa go to Abyssinia. They comprise raw cotton, pepper, blue and red cotton-cloth, the threads of which are unravelled and woven into the borders of the cloths of native manufacture, raw silk dyed blue, white cambrics, a small quantity of glazed silks, and some common velvet, glass pearls, linen shirts, common red-cloth, some articles of glass, common razors, sword-blades, spica celtica, small parcels of red or green morocco leather, zinc, common Turkish carpets, bottles of a peculiar shape, of which large numbers are used in Abyssinia, and a large quantity of Persian tobacco. The bulk of the goods imported into Abyssinia is probably consumed there, but some of them find their way into the interior of Africa to supply other countries. They are exchanged for the produce of these countries at Báso, where a market is held weekly during the season, which lasts about eight months in the year. The merchants bring from the southern countries slaves, ivory, coffee, civet, gold, cloth, iron, and cattle.

ACA'CIA, a very extensive genus of trees or shrubby plants, inhabiting the tropical parts of both the Old and New World. Some of the species produce *catechu* and *gum-arabic;* the bark of others yields a large quantity of *tannin*, which, in the form of an extract, is annually imported from Van Diemen's Land in considerable quantity. The *catechu* acacia is a tree with a tolerably high and stout stem, found in mountainous places in the East Indies, especially in Bengal and Coromandel; its unripe pods and wood yield, by decoction, one of the sorts of catechu, or terra-japonica, of the shops, a powerfully astringent substance, formerly thought to be a kind of earth. The *Acacia Arabica* or gum-arabic tree, is an inhabitant of the East Indies, Arabia, and Abyssinia, where it forms a tree thirteen or fourteen feet high. This is one of the plants that yield the useful substance called gum-arabic, which is procured by wounding the bark; after which the sap runs out, and hardens in transparent lumps, of various figures, very similar to the concretions found upon the bark of the cherry-tree in this country. Gum-arabic is also produced abundantly by some of the species nearly related to this. Gum-senegal is the produce of a distinct species called *Acacia Senegal*, found in Arabia and the interior of Africa. From this tree are said, by some, to be procured the pods called *bablach* in the continental drug-shops.

ACANTHUS, is the sculptured leaf which is the distinguishing characteristic of the capital of the Corinthian column. The same leaf, however, is used occasionally in other foliated capitals, as well as for the enrichment of modillions, of mouldings, and of vases. This ornament, in the Roman models, is fuller and broader than it is in the Greek.

ACAPU'LCO, a city and port in the republic of Mexico, about 183 miles S. S.W. from the capital; the port is capable of containing 500 ships, and is deep enough to allow vessels to lie close to the rocks. The city of Mexico communicates with the Pacific by the town of Acapulco, which once had a considerable trade, particularly with Manilla. Under the Spanish dominion a vessel of the largest size used annually to leave Acapulco for Manilla about February or March, loaded with commodities and specie. The vessel returned to Acapulco in August, carrying back muslins, printed calicoes, coarse cotton shirts, porcelain, Chinese jewellery, &c. Its arrival was the signal for a great concourse of merchants to Acapulco, who swelled the population for the time to about 9000. The commerce of the town has however since declined. The exports are cochineal, indigo, silver, and skins. Acapulco is not far from the Isthmus of Tehuantepec, one of the narrow tracts by which Central America is crossed on the route from the Atlantic to the Pacific. But the great commercial routes to California are now (1850) being formed further southward, viz., a combined steam-boat and land-route viâ Nicaragua, and a railway viâ Panama.

ACCO'RDION, a musical instrument, which was introduced into England from Germany about the year 1828. It is in the form of a small oblong box. The interior exhibits a row of very small elastic metallic springs, fixed at one end in a plate of metal, so that they may vibrate freely. The upper and lower parts of the box are united by a folding apparatus, or bellows, which supplies the air required to put the springs into vibration; and to these the air is admitted by means of valves acted on by keys, in the manner of an organ. There is also a very simple contrivance by which a base note, or drone, may be added, at the discretion of the performer. These instruments vary in size and in capabilities: the compass of the most complete is from G, the fourth space in the base staff, to E, the seventh additional space above the treble, including all the semitones; and two or more notes can be played at once. The Chinese are known to possess a musical instrument very similar to this.

ACCRINGTON, is one of the seats of the cotton manufacture in Lancashire. It has grown up from an insignificant village to a town of great importance, in a very few years. In the middle of 1850 there were ten extensive cotton, bleach, dye, and print works; and two more were in process of establishment. Two of these works belonging to Messrs. Hargreaves, employed at that time no fewer than 1600 workpeople; and the whole ten establishments gave occupation to nearly 3000. Nothing illustrates more strikingly the vastness of the cotton manufacture, than the rapid growth of these Lancashire towns.

ACCUMULATION OF POWER. In the coining press, a vast accumulation of force is obtained by means of the fly wheel: the reciprocating motion of a piston connected with a steam-engine communicates, by means of a crank, a continuous circular movement to the fly, and at the same time a reciprocating rectilinear motion vertically to the cylindrical shaft (the stamper) on which the screw is formed. With half a revolution of the fly-wheel the stamper is lifted up, and with the other half it is forced down on the metal, which thus receives at once all the motion accumulated in the fly during an entire revolution.

There are in machinery many such examples of accumulation of power. When a heavy body, like the rammer of a pile-driving machine, descends by the action of gravity during a certain time, and impinges on an object, a shock is produced immensely greater than would result from the mere pressure of the body.

ACER, the botanical name for the different species of *Maple* trees.

The *Acer oblongum*, or oval-leaved maple, is an evergreen tree, of rapid growth, native of the northern parts of India.

The *Acer lævigatum*, or polished maple, is found in the woods of the higher mountains of Nepaul; its timber is used by the inhabitants of Nepaul for rafters, beams, and similar building purposes.

The *Acer Tartaricum*, or Tartarian maple, is an ornamental tree, or rather large bush. From its keys, deprived of their wings, the Calmucks form, by the aid of boiling water, an astringent beverage, which, mixed with an abundance of milk and butter, forms a favourite article of their diet. The wood is hard and white, mixed with brownish veins.

The *Acer striatum*, or striped-bark maple, is a native of North America. Its wood is very white, and is used by the North Americans for inlaying cabinet-work; its shoots afford food to various animals, especially to the moose-deer, in winter and spring, whence it has acquired the name of *moose-wood*.

The *Acer obtusatum*, the Neapolitan maple, is a fine tree, which grows to a height of about 40 feet.

The *Acer campestre*, the common maple, is spread over the greater part of Europe. In England this is either a bush or a small tree, of inelegant appearance; and its wood is of little value, except for the use of the turner, who makes it into cups, bowls, &c. In the southern region of Caucasus, we are told by Pallas that it becomes a tree of handsome aspect, with a trunk as thick as a man's body, and that its wood is so hard as to be in request for the manufacture of musket-stocks.

The *Acer pseudo-plátanus*, the sycamore-maple, flourishes in middle and southern Europe. Although the wood of this species is not particularly valuable, being chiefly used for coarse work, where lightness and toughness are required, yet there is scarcely any more universally cultivated for the sake of the striking effect it produces, whether as a single tree, or planted in avenues, or in masses.

The *Acer Platanoïdes*, the Norway maple, is a fine tree, of North and Central Europe. Its wood is valued for turners' work; from its ascending sap a kind of coarse sugar has been procured.

The *Acer saccharinum*, or sugar maple, grows

abundantly in North America. In the autumn the woods of those countries are dyed of a crimson hue by the changing leaves of the sugar maple. The wood is hard, and has a satiny lustre, but it is readily attacked by insects, and is not of much value, except when its grain is accidentally waved, and then it is in request for the cabinet-makers. The saccharine matter contained in its ascending sap is the principal cause of this species being in so much request. From this sap, obtained by tapping the trunk in the spring, during the space of six weeks, a very considerable quantity of a fine brown sugar is procured; as much, it is said, as 33lb. per tree. The sugar maple does not generally succeed very well in England, where it is rarely seen, and where, even when in health, it is not more than 15 or 16 feet high.

ACETATE, a salt resulting from a combination of acetic acid with an alkaline, earthy, metallic, or vegeto-alkaline base—four varieties which may be exemplified by the acetates of soda, lime, lead, and morphia. Although the acetates possess some properties in common, yet, from the very different nature of their bases, they are variously affected by heat; some being merely evaporated, and others wholly decomposed, at high temperatures.

The acetates are a very important class of compounds. Some of them are used in the preparation of acetic acid. The acetate of alumina and the acetate of iron are largely employed by calico-printers; and many of the metallic acetates are used also by them, and by dyers and colour-makers.

ACETIC ACID, or *Acetous Acid*, is the sour part of vinegar, and that to which its peculiar and valuable properties are owing. It is procured, first, by the fermentation of saccharine or sugary matter,—secondly, by the action of heat upon wood; the product of the former constituting *vinegar*, and of the latter *pyroligneous acid*.

1. *Vinegar.* When certain vegetable juices which contain much sugar, such as that of the grape, are fermented, the sugar undergoes the vinous fermentation [FERMENTATION], by which alcohol is produced; and if this process be carried beyond a certain stage, a further fermentation called the acetous fermentation ensues, by which vinegar is produced: so that, in effect, sugar becomes alcohol, and then alcohol becomes vinegar. How this is managed in practice is explained under VINEGAR, where also the peculiar arrangements of the great vinegar-factories are described. Vinegar is, in practice, made from four sources,—wine, malt, sugar, and wood.

Vinegar (or rather Acetic Acid) possesses the usual property of acids to redden vegetable blue colours; it combines with the alkalis, earths, and metallic oxides to form the salts which are termed *acetates*. Vinegar is purified from the sulphuric acid and colouring matter which it contains by distillation; but its smell and taste are then less agreeable, and it is weaker than acetic acid otherwise procured. When vinegar is exposed to a low temperature, it is principally the watery part which freezes.

2. *Pyroligneous Acid.* The second method of obtaining acetic acid is by heating wood, as the dried branches of trees, in hollow iron cylinders, with a proper arrangement of coolers, or condensers, and receivers. Birch and beech are the best woods for yielding it. The pyroligneous acid thus procured is of a dark brown colour, has a strong burnt acid smell, is very sour to the taste, and acts strongly on vegetable blue colours. It contains a quantity of tar and oily matter; from these it is purified, in a considerable degree, by redistillation; and a further purification with lime converts it into a pyrolignite of lime. This pyrolignite, by the chemical action of dilute sulphate of soda, produces acetate of soda, which is a crystalline salt. From these crystals pure acetic acid is produced, by exposing them to the action of sulphuric acid, which combines with the soda of the acetate, and leaves the acetic acid free.

Pyroligneous acid is employed to preserve meat, and to impart to it the smoky flavour usually obtained by drying. Pure acetic acid is used in chemical researches, and especially for preparing various acetates. In a less pure state it is employed in the arts, for preparing acetate or sugar of lead, acetate of copper, or verdigris, and acetate of alumina, which is largely used by calico-printers as a mordant.

ACETIMETER is the name of a kind of hydrometer, used by the Excise authorities in determining the strength of vinegar.

ACETONE, or *Pyro-acetic Spirit*, is a colourless limpid liquid; its odour is peculiar, penetrating, and somewhat aromatic; it mixes in all proportions with alcohol, æther, and oil of turpentine. It is very inflammable, and is not affected by exposure to the air.

ACHARD, FRANZ KARL, born at Berlin, in 1754, died in 1821, was the author of various works, written in German, on experimental physics, chemistry, and agriculture. Achard is however chiefly known for his proposal to extract sugar from beet-root. Another Prussian chemist, Margraff, had discovered the existence of a certain portion of sugar in this root as early as 1747, but deemed his discovery of little practical importance. Achard, on the contrary, described beet-root as 'one of the most bountiful gifts which the divine munificence had awarded to man upon the earth.' The institute of Paris, in 1800, honoured him with a vote of thanks, but reported unfavourably of the practicability of his plan. Napoleon however, in 1812, formed an imperial manufactory at Rambouillet, when the plan of Achard was put in practice, and partly succeeded. Since then the manufacture of sugar from beet-root has been carried on very extensively in France. The manufacture however is a forced one, and therefore of very questionable policy. [BEET: SUGAR.]

ACHROMATIC. [LENS.]

ACIDIMETER. By reversing the mode of using the Alkalimeter, an Acidimeter may be produced, which will determine the strength of the acids employed in commerce or manufactures. [ALKALIMETER.]

ACIDS. The acids are a numerous and important class of chemical bodies. They are generally sour; usually, but not universally, they have great affinity for water, and are readily soluble in it; they change most vegetable blue colours to red; and they unite readily with most alkalis, and with earthy and metallic oxides. Some are natural, some artificial, and some both; some are gaseous, some liquid, and some solid, at common temperatures; some are transparent, and others coloured; some inodorous, and others pungent; some volatile, and others fixed; so that they vary greatly, except in the qualities first named.

No simple or elementary substance has the properties of an acid, and consequently all acids are compounds of two or more of them. In almost every case one of these elements is either oxygen or hydrogen, producing the *oxacids* and the *hydracids*, the former of which are by far the most numerous. In some instances oxygen gives rise to different acids by combining with the same element in various proportions.

Acids occur in all the kingdoms of nature; the phosphoric acids which exist in bone are of animal origin; the citric and the oxalic acids are products of vegetation; the chromic and the arsenic acid enter into the composition of certain minerals; and many of the acids are derivable from two or more of these sources, and are made by chemical agency.

All the acids which are of any importance in the manufacturing arts, will be found described under their proper titles.

ACONITI'NA, a vegetable alkali which exists in *aconite*, in combination with *aconitic acid*. It crystallizes in white grains, and is inodorous, but intensely bitter and acrid. It is obtained and derives its name from the *Aconitum*, or *Wolf's Bane*, the poisonous properties of which are due to the Aconitina. All the parts of this plant are extremely acrid, especially the roots, which are scraped and mixed with food to form a bait for wolves and other savage animals. According to the observations of Orfila, the juice of the leaves introduced into the stomach occasions death in a short time; the root is far more energetic. The poison acts upon the nervous system, especially the brain, producing a sort of frenzy. The use of this dangerous plant is now almost entirely restricted to painful affections of the nerves, and to rheumatic complaints. We are not aware that it is employed in manufactures.

ACORNS were in ancient days more extensively used for food than they are at present. Acorn bread was much eaten both by the Greeks and Romans; and our Saxon ancestors reckoned *mast* or acorns as an important part of their food, especially in years of deficient harvest. When we find, in 'Don Quixote,' that acorns are described as being served after the repast of the goatherd; and that Teresa sends a present of the choicest acorns she could collect to the duchess, we may reasonably conclude that Cervantes had in his thoughts a custom well known among his countrymen. In Greece, Asia Minor, and Barbary, acorns are sold in the streets as food, and are eaten both raw and roasted. The late General Jackson, of the United States, once sent his officers an invitation to a breakfast of acorns, at a time when provisions were scanty. Tolerably good bread may be made from acorns, when shelled, and especially if allowed to germinate before being used, so that part of the farina may become converted into sugar; some persons who have tasted such bread are of opinion that it is very little inferior to oat bread. Acorns, however, are chiefly serviceable in this country as food for swine.

ACOUSTICS, a word derived from the Greek, and signifying the science of sound. The only part of this interesting science which will come within the range of our present volume, is that which determines the particular mode of eliciting sound from the principal musical instruments; for these details we refer to the names of the instruments themselves.

Acoustic instruments for the relief of partially deaf persons, have been invented in considerable number. Dr. Scott's *Soniferon* is a sort of bell-shaped instrument attached to a tube. The bell, instead of resting on its large or open end, is placed horizontally on an upright leg, on which it revolves. The mouth of the bell is covered with a perforated metallic plate; and the interior of the bell is grooved with spiral channels. A pipe of caoutchouc or gutta percha is attached to the bell, and is connected at the other end with a small ivory ear-piece. When a person who is hard of hearing wishes to take part in conversation around a table, the bell is brought opposite the mouth of the speaker, and the hearer places the ivory piece to his ear. It does not differ from other acoustic tubes in its principle, but in its applicability to many persons seated at the same table, and at any distance from the one who is to be primarily benefitted by the invention. [EAR TRUMPET].

ACRE, a measure of land, of different value in the different parts of the United Kingdom. When mentioned generally, the statute or English acre is to be understood. A square whose side is 22 yards long is the tenth part of an acre, which therefore contains 22 × 22 × 10, or 4840 square yards. The chain with which land is measured is 22 yards long; so that ten square chains are one acre. This measure is divided into 4 roods, each rood into 40 perches, so that each perch contains 30¼ square yards. Thus:—

Acre.		Rood.		Perch.		Square yards.	Side of equivalent squares in yards.
1	=	4	=	160	=	4840	69.5701
		1	=	40	=	1210	34.7851
				1	=	30¼	5.5

The Irish acre is larger than the English, 121 Irish acres being very nearly equivalent to 196 English acres. The Scottish acre is also larger than the English, 48 Scottish acres being equal to 61 English acres. The English statute acre is used in the United States of North America.

The *Arpent* is the French square measure which most nearly corresponds with the English acre, an arpent containing 4028.9 square yards.

ACTINO'METER is an instrument employed for the purpose of ascertaining the intensity of heat in the direct rays of the sun. It consists of a hollow cylinder of glass, containing a blue solution of sulphate of copper, with apparatus for measuring the expansion of the liquid under the influence of the sun's heat. In the hands of its inventor, Sir J. Herschel, this instrument has proved highly useful in determining the quantity of solar heat which is absorbed in passing through different strata of the atmosphere. It may also be employed to determine the diminution of heat which takes place during eclipses of the sun. It has not yet been employed in the arts; but when we consider the remarkable phenomena of Photography, it will appear very probable that the Actinometer is destined to take part in many delicate chemical operations.

A'DAMANT, a word now seldom employed as a scientific term, but used chiefly as a poetical expression synonymous with diamond, or as descriptive of some other extremely hard substance. In 1849 M. Dufresnoy exhibited before the Paris Academy of Sciences, a few pieces of adamant so extremely hard, as to be able to polish the diamond. They were considered to bear the same relation to diamond, which emery does to corundum. They were met with in the same alluvial formation whence Brazilian diamonds are usually procured. The largest piece obtained weighed about 66 grains. Its edges were rounded by long-continued friction; and it presented a slightly brownish dull black colour. When viewed with a microscope, it appeared riddled with small cavities, which separated very small irregular laminæ, slightly translucent and iridescent. It cut glass readily, and scratched quartz and topaz. Its density was rather more than three times that of water, about the same as that of the diamond. The smaller specimens retained their aspect, hardness, and weight, after long calcination at a bright red heat in a covered crucible. On analysis, it was found that this adamant contains from 96.8 to 99.8 per cent of pure carbon: the small remainder consisting of vegetable ash.

ADAMANTINE SPAR is one of the many varieties of Corundum or Emery, from which it differs much in quality, but little in composition. [CORUNDUM.]

ADELAIDE, is becoming a commercial city of much importance. It is the capital of the Colony of South Australia, and is built on the river Torrens. Port Adelaide, at the mouth of the river, seven miles distant from the town, is a fine and capacious harbour, well situated in respect to the prevailing winds. At the present time (1850) a railway is being formed from Adelaide to Port Adelaide. Nearly 14,000 emigrants landed at Adelaide in the four years 1844-7, and the number has since still more largely increased.

The discovery of no fewer than seventy rich copper mines in South Australia is tending to make Adelaide an important place of shipment; while the wool-trade is also advancing with great rapidity. Adelaide was, in 1845, made a free port to the ships of all nations. The imports in the year ending April 1849, were valued at 471,556*l*., and the exports at 485,951*l*.; 112,338 tons of shipping entered inward and outward; 16,000 tons of copper ore, and 19,000 cwt. of wool, were exported.

ADEN, a town and harbour on the southern

shores of Arabia, in the province of Yemen. Before the British took possession of it, Aden was an ill-supplied miserable place, consisting of a small number of mud huts covered with mats, and containing about 600 inhabitants. At present it is a flourishing place of trade, containing from 20,000 to 25,000 inhabitants, surrounded with gardens and orchards, in which all the necessaries of life may be had at a moderate price. The British took possession of Aden in 1840, when a steam-boat navigation was established between Bombay and Suez, for which Aden serves as a central depôt. There are about a dozen steam-vessels engaged on this mail route; and if the present discussions (1850) concerning the Australian mail should result in the Singapore route being chosen, Aden will become a still more important place. Since the occupation of Aden by the British, its trade with the surrounding countries has increased, and a number of Banians, Parsees, and other merchants have settled there. It is expected that the whole commerce of the Red Sea, and especially that of Yemen and Hadramaut will soon be transferred to Aden. The exports of British manufactures thither in 1849 amounted to 14,564*l.*

ADHESION, is the property by which two solids, a solid and a fluid, two solids and an interposed fluid, or two fluids, remain attached to each other when their surfaces are brought into contact. It is a property of much importance in machinery, since *friction* depends upon it to a considerable extent. M. Guyton de Morveau found by direct experiments, that when the surfaces of plates of different metals were placed in contact with the surface of mercury, the weights required to separate them from the fluid were as stated in the following table (the metals were pure, the plates circular, one inch diameter, and of equal thicknesses):—

	Grains.		Grains.
Gold	446	Zinc	204
Silver	429	Copper	142
Tin	418	Antimony	126
Lead	397	Iron	115
Bismuth	372	Cobalt	8
Platina	282		

Mr. Bevan has given a table of the adhesion, &c. of different kinds of nails when driven into dry Christiana deal; in this table it appears that a sixpenny nail, 73 to the lb., 2½ inches long, forced 1½ inches into the wood, required 327 lbs. weight to extract it; the percussive force required to drive the sixpenny nail to the depth of one inch and a-half into the dry deal, with a cast-iron weight of 6·275 lbs., was four blows or strokes falling freely, the space of 12 inches, and the steady pressure to produce the same effect was 400 lbs. With different kinds of timber the results varied greatly, and Mr. Bevan concludes that a sixpenny nail driven two inches into dry oak, would require a force of more than half a ton to extract it by steady pressure. Mr. Bevan has also determined the force required to draw screws out of different kinds of wood; the screws used were about two inches in length, .22 diameter at the exterior of the threads, .15 diameter at the bottom, the depth of the worm or thread being .035, and the number of threads in one inch 12. These screws were passed *through* pieces of wood, exactly half an inch in thickness, and drawn out from the following dry woods by the annexed weights: beech 460 lbs., another specimen 790 lbs., ash 790 lbs., oak 760 lbs., mahogany 770 lbs., elm 655 lbs., sycamore 830 lbs. The force required to draw similar screws out of deal and the softer woods, was about half the above.

ADIPOCIRE, a substance of a peculiar nature, being intermediate between fat and wax, and bearing a close resemblance to spermaceti. In 1786, Fourcroy had the opportunity of observing an accumulation of adipocire on a scale of prodigious extent, under circumstances of a peculiar nature, which are highly curious. There was in Paris an immense burial-ground, called La Cimetière des Innocens. This place had been the receptacle of the dead for a considerable part of the population of Paris for several centuries. On account of some improvements in the neighbourhood it was determined to remove this cemetery. The number of burials in this place had amounted to some thousands annually. The bodies were deposited in pits or trenches about thirty feet deep; each pit was capable of holding from twelve to fifteen thousand bodies; and as the pits became full they were covered with a few feet of earth. The extent of the whole area was about seven thousand square yards, and this space became at last occupied by a mass which consisted almost entirely of animal matter, rising several feet above the general level of the soil. Scientific men were especially charged by the government to direct the precautions requisite for securing the health of the workmen in removing this immense mass of putrefying animal matter. When the bodies were exposed to the light of day, the linen which had covered them was slightly adherent to the bodies; beneath the linen was found nothing but irregular masses of a soft ductile matter of a gray-white colour, resembling common white cheese, the resemblance being more striking from the prints which the threads of the linen had made upon its surface. The bones, which were surrounded by this matter, had no solidity, but were readily broken by sudden pressure. Tho head was environed with this peculiar matter; the face was no longer distinguishable; the mouth was disorganized; no trace remained of the viscera of the thorax and abdomen, which were all confused together, and converted into this fatty matter; and this was also invariably the case with the brain. None of this matter was found in bodies isolated from each other, but only in those accumulated in the common graves. From various observations it was found that this fatty matter was capable of enduring in these burying-places for thirty or forty years, but that ultimately it became corrupted and was dissipated.

The substance thus presented for examination under such remarkable circumstances, is considered by M. Fourcroy as an ammoniacal soap, formed of a peculiar oil combined with ammonia. It melts at about 130° Fahr.; by a strong heat it is decomposed with the solution of ammonia. There would of course be something repugnant in using such materials in manufactures; but French and German chemists have made attempts to convert the dead bodies of cattle into adipocire, for candle and soap-making. It is, however, found that adipocire proceeds solely from the pre-existing fat of the dead body, and not from the flesh and cartileges; and the attempts to produce adipocire artificially have not been commercially successful.

ADIPOSE SUBSTANCE, or fat, is an animal oil, which resembles, in its essential properties, the vegetable oils. It is wholly inorganic, though contained in an organized tissue. It varies in its consistence, or rather in the temperature at which it becomes solid. In general, it forms a pretty firm solid, constituting suet, which, when divested of the membrane in which it is contained, is called tallow; but there are animals in which, at the ordinary temperature of the atmosphere, it always remains fluid, as in tho cetacea. At the temperaturo of the human body, it is fluid. It consists of two substances which are capable of being separated from each other, and obtained in a distinct form. Of these substances, one, at the ordinary temperaturo of the atmosphere, is solid; the other fluid. *Stearine*, the solid portion of fat, is a substauce colourless, tasteless, nearly inodorous, soluble in alcohol, separable from this solution in the form of small silky needles, and preserving its solidity at a temperature of 99° Fahrenheit. *Elaine*, the oily principle of fat, is fluid at the temperature of 60° Fahrenheit; it is of a yellow colour, without odour, lighter than water, its specific gravity being 0.913, and easily soluble in alcohol. Fat is the chief ingredient in several important manufactures, especially CANDLES and SOAP; to which articles, and to TALLOW, it may suffice here to refer.

ADIT, or DRIFT, is the horizontal passage which gives entrance to some mines. [MINING.]

ADJUTAGE, or AJUTAGE, is a name given to a tube, generally not exceeding a few inches in length, which may bo applied to a vessel or reservoir, in order to facilitate the discharge of a fluid from such vessel.

ADRIANO'PLE, the second city in European Turkey, is in the province of Romania or Rumelia, 135 miles N. W. of Constantinople. An aqueduct supplies the baths, mosques, and fountains with water. The manufactures of Adrianople are silk, woollen, and cotton stuffs; it has also establishments for dyeing, and distilling rose-water and other perfumes.

ADRIATIC SEA, sometimes called the *Gulf of Venice*, is a large bay of the Mediterranean, between Italy and Turkey. The navigation is easy and safe, the numerous islands on the Dalmatian coast affording excellent shelter in the most violent gales. It has recently become one of the great lines of communication between India and Western Europe, by the route through Egypt, steam-vessels passing from Alexandria to Trieste. It is near the mouth of the Adriatic, that the two small Greek islands are situated, which formed a disputed point in the momentous Greek question of 1850.

ADULTERATION, is the use of ingredionts in the production of any article which are cheaper and not so good, or which are not considered so desirable by the consumer, as other or genuine ingredients for which they are substituted. The law does not generally consider adulteration as an offence, but relies apparently on an evil of this nature being corrected by the discrimination and good sense of the public. Any one acquainted with modern shop-keeping, however, especially on the 'cheap' system, has good cause to know and to lament the difficulty of detecting such nefarious practices. The *morals* of trade are sadly neglected by many who would spurn a charge of direct dishonesty. In Paris, malpractices connected with the adulteration of food are investigated by the Conseil de Salubrité, acting under the authority of the prefect of police. In this country, also, whenever the interests of the revenue are concerned, strict regulations have been resorted to in order to prevent adulteration. Tobacco, beer, drugs, tea, coffee, cocoa, pepper, and bread, are all more or less protected against adulteration, so far as legislation can do it; but with very little real effect.

ADVERTISEMENT. In the English, Scotch, and Irish newspapers, and other periodical works, there are annually published above two millions of announcements known by the name Advertisement. The duty on a single advertisement was formerly 3*s* 6*d*. in Great Britain, and 2*s*. 6*d*. in Ireland; but by 3 & 4 Wm. IV., c. 23, it was reduced to 1*s*. 6*d*. in Great Britain, and 1*s*. in Ireland. In the year previous to this reduction the total number of newspaper advertisements published in the United Kingdom was 1021,943; namely, 787,649 in England, 108,914 in Scotland, and 125,380 in Ireland. The duty amounted to 172,570*l*., and had been stationary for several years. In 1841 the number of advertisements had increased to 1,778,957; namely 1,386,625 for England and Wales, 188,189 in Scotland, and 204,143 in Ireland. The total amount of duty was 128,318*l*.; and it has progressively increased from the time when the reduction took place. In 1849, the total number of advertisements was 2,109,179, of which 1,668,156 were for England and Wales; 234,166 for Scotland; and 206,857 for Ireland. In the last session of parliament, a considerable effort was made to induce the government to surrender this tax upon the publicity of all those announcements which arise out of a highly complicated state of society. The continual increase of advertisements, even under the tax, is a proof of the absolute necessity which exists, of supplying the public with information through this medium. No other mode of publishing is so effectual as the Newspaper Advertisements; and thus the size of newspapers has been doubled in many instances, to allow of the insertion of a greater number. Advertisements generally supply the fund out of which newspapers are supported, as the price at which the newspaper is sold is insufficient to pay the cost of the stamp, the paper, the printing, and the editorial management. The lowest price of an advertisement in a London daily newspaper is now 5*s*. (except applications for places by servants, which, in the last page of the 'Times,' are 3*s*. 6*d*.), which includes the duty: such advertisement must not exceed five lines. The usual practice is to charge 6*d*. per line for each line above four; but when the number of lines exceeds about twenty, the rate of charge is increased, the longest advertisements being charged at the highest rate. The duty on short advertisements constitutes a tax of 66 per cent. If the duty were abolished, the minimum price of advertisements would probably be 1*s*. in all but a few papers. The yearly number of advertisements in the United States, where no duty on them exists, is said to exceed 10,000,000.

ÆGI'NA, a small island in the Gulf of Ægina, forming a part of the modern kingdom of Greece. It is famed for the temple of Jupiter Panhellenius, or the Panhellénium, one of the most celebrated among specimens of classical architecture. This temple was of the Greek Doric style. It had a portico of six columns at each end, and ranges of twelve columns along each side. Internally it was divided into what may be termed nave and aisles, by two ranges of columns, the space between which was uncovered. The cell or body of the temple was a regular parallelogram inclosed by four walls: access was given to the interior by doors in the cross-walls, from inner porticoes formed by the longitudinal extension of the flank walls. The columns of the peristyle on the sides stand nearly as far from the walls as they do from each other; and a kind of gallery was formed on the floor of the peristyle around the body of the temple, raised by three deep steps from a nearly level platform called a peribolus, in the midst of which the temple stood. The extreme length of the temple in front, measured on the face of the lowest step of the regular stylobate, is 49 feet 10.2 inches, and in flank 100 feet 7·7 inches; and on the floor of the peristyle, that is, at the edge of the upper step on which the columns rest, the corresponding dimensions are, 45 feet 2·2 inches, and 96 feet. Both the tympana were highly enriched with sculptures.

The architecture of the Panhellenium indicates an earlier date than that of the Athenian temples of the age of Pericles; but it would hardly lead us so far back as the early part of the sixth century before Christ; though it is not at all inconsistent with that period. This beautiful temple is now a complete ruin. All the walls are levelled to the ground, and only some of the columns and entablatures remain. Yet it is noble, even in its ruin.

The sculptures which occupied the tympana of the pediments of the Panhellenium were discovered in May, 1811, by a party of English and German travellers, among whom were Messrs. J. Foster, of Liverpool, and C. R. Cockerell, of London, who were pursuing their studies as architects. They were found buried under the ruins of the building and accumulations of rubbish, nearly as they had fallen from their places, especially those of the western front, the whole of which were recovered; but unfortunately not more than half of those of the eastern front could be determined. Thorwaldsen was engaged to repair and restore all the statues which were not so completely broken as to render reparation impossible. Restorations of the two pediments of the Panhellenium, with casts and imitations of the figures on the tympana, have been added to the Athenian and Phigaleian marbles in the British Museum; they occupy the upper part of the north and south sides of the Phigaleian saloon, adjoining the Elgin saloon.

ÆO'LIAN HARP, a musical instrument, the sounds of which are drawn from it by a current of air acting on the strings. One may be constructed as follows:—Let a box be made of thin deal, of a length exactly answering to the window in which it is intended to be placed, four or five inches in depth, and five or six in width. Glue on it, at the extremities of the top, two pieces of oak, about half an inch high and a quarter of an inch thick, to serve as bridges for the strings; and withinside, at each end, glue two pieces of beech about an inch square, and of length equal to the width of the box which is to hold the pegs. Into one of these bridges fix as many pegs, such as are used in a pianoforte, though not so large, as there are to be strings; and into the other, fasten as many small brass pins, to which attach one end of the strings. Then string the instrument with small catgut, or *first* fiddle-strings, fixing one end of them, and twisting the other round the opposite peg. These strings, which should not be drawn tight, must be tuned in unison. To procure a proper passage for the wind, a thin board, supported by four pegs, is placed over the strings, at about three inches distance from the sounding-board. The instrument must be exposed to the wind at a window partly open; and to increase the force of the current of air, either the door of the room, or an opposite window, should be opened. When the wind blows, the strings begin to sound in unison: but as the force of the current increases, the sound changes into a pleasing admixture of all the notes of the diatonic scale, ascending and descending, and these often unite in the most delightful harmonic combinations.

ÆOLI'NA, a very small musical instrument, consisting of a number of short elastic metallic springs, fixed in a frame, and acted on by the breath of the performer. The best of the kind comprise three octaves of the diatonic sounds, and are also capable of giving the three simple harmonies of the key.

AERATED WATERS. Dr. Venables, in a recent work on aerated waters, describes the operation of Bakewell's patent apparatus, and the composition necessary for the production of different varieties of these liquids. The aeration is not confined to mere cooling drinks such as soda water, but is applicable to all cases where water is to have an effervescing quality given to it, whether for aperient, tonic, diuretic, antacid, lithotriptic, or pectic purposes. The principal feature of the process is the forced combination of a gas with pure water; and in the case of soda-water this gas is the result of chemical action between sulphuric acid and carbonate of soda.

Bakewell's apparatus consists of an upright vessel supported on a stand, and furnished with pipes and valves. In the lower part of the apparatus is a vessel called the generator, divided into two compartments by a horizontal partition. Sulphuric acid is placed in the uppermost of these compartments, and the carbonate of soda in the lower; and while the vessel is at rest, the two substances are kept wholly separate; but when a working motion is given to it by making it oscillate on two pivots whereby it is suspended, the acid drops at regular intervals through a hole in the side of the upper compartment, and falls into the lower one, where it mixes with the carbonate. A chemical interchange immediately takes place; the soda leaves the carbonic acid and combines with the sulphuric; so that instead of sulphuric acid and carbonate of soda we have carbonic acid and sulphate of soda. The carbonic acid assumes the gaseous form, and ascends to an earthenware vessel in the upper part of the apparatus. This vessel contains water; and as the apparatus is kept oscillating, the water is sufficiently agitated to absorb the gas passed up into it. With a small apparatus capable of holding a gallon at a time, a quarter of an hour's oscillation will suffice to impregnate the water with gas to a pressure of five atmospheres. The apparatus must of course be strong to resist this pressure; it is made of iron, and there is a pressure guage at the top, to measure the amount of the pressure. There is a tap for draining off the aerated liquids. Dr. Venables states that for a gallon of water to be impregnated to the extent of five atmospheres, would require about six ounces of carbonate (or rather sesqui-carbonate) of soda and four ounces of sulphuric acid. The apparatus admits of being used in many ways; for the aerator or upper vessel may be either filled with pure water, and modified only by the gas which ascends from the generator; or the water may previously be made acid or alkaline, and receive a further change by the aeration. The resulting beverage will thus depend, not only on the aeration, but also on the state of the water before aeration.

Messrs. Knight patented an air-tight stopper,

in 1844, for flasks intended to contain the aerated water, when required to keep it some time for further operations; or to transfer it to the common glass-bottles. It is an ingenious piece of apparatus, strong enough to resist the expansive force of the gas, yet easily adjusted for the entrance or exit of liquids.

AERIAL BRIDGE. [BRIDGE.]

AERIAL WHEELS. This name has been given to a new form of wheel, in which the tire is made hollow and very light. [WHEEL.]

AERO-DYNAMICS signifies the science which treats of the motion of the air, or of the mechanical effects of air put in motion. There are not many points in which this science bears directly on manufacturing operations or the arts generally; but we may present a few considerations to shew its influence on moving machinery.

As soon as we begin to move we feel, more or less, the resistance of the air. And, since any body in moving through a fluid, as air, not only displaces a greater number of particles of the fluid in equal times, in proportion as it moves faster, but causes each particle to react against the body more powerfully in proportion as the latter, by moving faster, strikes it with greater force; it follows that the resistance of a fluid at rest against a body moving in it, or the resistance of the fluid in motion against a body at rest, varies with the square of the velocity of the body, or of the air; that is, if the velocity be suddenly made ten times as great, the resistance is made ten times ten, or a hundred times as great. And this is sufficiently near the truth for practical purposes when the velocities are eight or nine hundred feet in a second.

The resistance is nearly in the same proportion as the surface exposed, but a little greater than this proportion on the larger surface; that is, if we take two bodies of the same figure and material (two iron spheres for example), the surface of the second being twice that of the first, the resistance to the larger sphere is a little more than twice that to the smaller, the velocities being the same in both.

The round ends and sharp ends of solids suffer less resistance than the flat ends of the same. Thus, the sharp end or vertex of a cone is less resisted than the flat end or base.

Two solids, similarly formed on the end towards the air, are not equally resisted unless the hinder parts are also similar.

If we suppose both the wind and the body to be in motion, the resistance is variously modified according to the direction of the motions of the two. If the wind and the body move in the same direction, with the same velocity, there is no resistance, for no air is displaced by the body. If the wind move 50 feet per second, and the body 100 feet, the pressure on the body is the same as if it were at rest, with a *contrary* wind of 50 feet per second blowing on it. If the wind and the body move in contrary directions, with velocities of 100 feet, the resistance is that of a wind of 200 feet per second; and so on.

The following table shows in pounds avoirdupois, the pressure which different winds will exert upon a square foot of surface exposed directly against them. The first column is a rough representation of the second.

Velocity of Wind. Miles per hour.	Feet per second.	Force on the square foot in pounds avoirdupois.	Character of the wind.
1	1·47	·005	Hardly perceptible.
2	2·93	·020	Just perceptible
3	4·40	·044	
4	5·87	·079	Gentle pleasant wind.
5	7·33	·123	
10	14·67	·492	Pleasant brisk gale.
15	22·00	1·107	
20	29·34	1·968	Very brisk
25	36·67	3·075	
30	44·01	4·429	High wind.
35	51·34	6·027	
40	58·68	7·873	Very high.
45	66·01	9·963	
50	73·35	12·300	Storm or tempest.
60	88·02	17·715	Great storm.
80	117·36	31·490	Hurricane.
100	146·70	49·200	Destructive hurricane.

A few illustrations of the resistance and pressure of the air will be met with under AIR-GUN, BELLOWS, BLOWING MACHINE, SAILS, WINDMILL, &c.

AEROLITES, or AIR-STONES, are masses of mineral substances which fall to the earth from the higher regions. As they do not bear very closely on the subject of the present work, a few details concerning them, under the heading METEORIC STONES, will suffice.

AERONAUTICS, AEROSTATICS, AEROSTATION. The first of these three words is compounded of two Greek words, which signify literally the science or art of *sailing in air;* while the other two signify the *standing of bodies in air.* The BALLOON, to which article we refer, is the most interesting machine to which these studies relate.

Æ'SCULUS, or the *Horse-Chestnut*, is a genus of plants which subserves a few useful purposes. The popular name of *horse*-chestnut has arisen from the custom among the Turks of grinding the nuts, and mixing them with the provender given to horses that are broken-winded. Starch is yielded in very considerable quantity by the nuts; but they are not used in the preparation of the starch of commerce. They contain, moreover, so large a quantity of potash as to be a useful substitute for soap; on the latter account they were formerly employed extensively in the process of bleaching yarn, but are now seldom used. The bark, which contains a great deal of tannin, is not a bad substitute for Peruvian bark in fevers; and, finally, the starch of the nuts, deprived of its bitterness by maceration in weak ley, has been recommended as excellent and nutritious food for horses, goats, oxen, and sheep. The timber is soft and spongy, and of little value.

ÆSTHETICS. *Æsthetik* is the designation given by German writers to a branch of philosophical inquiry, the object of which is a philosophical theory of the beautiful, or, more definitely expressed, a philosophy of poetry and the fine arts, and which has by them been raised to the rank of a separate science. The word *Æsthetik* is derived from the Greek (that which concerns feeling or perception), and was first used as a scientific term by Alexander Baumgarten, a disciple of Christian Wolf, who in his *Æsthetica* (Frankfort, 1750-58), considered beauty as a given property of objects, of which we are *becoming sensible*. Winckelmann, without embodying his views in a regular system, developed them chiefly in reviewing and appreciating the remains of antient sculpture. Kant denied the possibility of a strict science of beauty, inasmuch as beauty, according to him, is not a property of objects, but has its origin in the disposition of our mental faculties. Beauty, according to Schelling, is that manifestation of the principle of art where the infinite appears contained in, or represented by, the finite, or where, in the very object, the difference between the conscious and the unconscious (mind and nature) is annulled.

Most German writers who have published systematic treatises on æsthetics, have, with greater or less independence, followed the principles laid down by Baumgarten, Kant, or Schelling. They commonly divide their systems into a general part, or a discussion of the essence of beauty and art, and a special one, or an inquiry into the peculiar character and predominant principles of the several branches of poetry on the one hand, and the fine arts (chiefly sculpture, architecture, painting, and music) on the other.

In England it is not customary to write formally on Æsthetics as a science; but the principle of beauty in art has been discussed by Alison, Payne Knight, Burke, Price, Lauder, Reynolds, Bell, Dugald Stewart, Jeffrey, Hay, Ruskin, Fergusson, and others — who have, however, failed to arrive at anything conclusive and generally accepted; for there are few subjects on which opinions are more discordant than on this.

ÆTHER (*αἰθήρ*), a Greek word, now used to signify a highly volatile, penetrating, and combustible fluid, several kinds of which may be produced by the action of different acids upon spirit of wine, or alcohol. Sulphuric, phosphoric, arsenic, fluoboric, chloric, muriatic, nitric, silicic, acetic, benzoic, citric, gallic, oxalic, and tartaric acids—all yield æther by particular modes of treatment.

Sulphuric æther, obtained by distillation from a heated mixture of alcohol and sulphuric acid, is the chief kind. It is a colourless transparent liquid, of a pleasant smell and a pungent taste, extremely exhilarating, producing a degree of intoxication when its vapour is inhaled by the nostrils. Its specific gravity is from .700 to .750. It evaporates so rapidly that if we put some into a small glass vessel surrounded with cloth and containing water, and after dipping it two or three times into æther, allow the æther after each immersion to evaporate, the water in the glass freezes by the cold produced. In the open air æther boils at 96°, and in a vacuum at 20° below zero. In the open air it remains unfrozen at 60° below zero. Its vapour is nearly three times as dense as common air. It combines sparingly with water, but with alcohol in all proportions. Both æther, and the vapour which rises from it, are very inflammable. The resins and most of the oils are dissolved by æther; it dissolves a small portion of sulphur and of phosphorus, and the latter solution becomes luminous in a dark room, when poured on the hands or on hot water. The alkalies, potash and soda, are insoluble in æther.

Most of the other æthers possess properties analogous to those of sulphuric æther. Acetic æther is used for flavouring British brandy.

Æthers present the most perfect examples of volatile stimulants, being unequalled for rapidity of action when immediate aid must be imparted to the muscular system, especially the involuntary muscles, by augmenting the nervous power, and by quickening its development. Sulphuric æther is the most powerful of æthereal preparations, and therefore of diffusable stimulants. It ranks as an antispasmodic of the highest kind. The vapour of æther has been lately employed for the purpose of producing insensibility, during which the most painful operations in surgery have been performed without being felt by the patient. Teeth have been extracted in this state, both in this country and America; and several capital operations have been performed without pain to the patient. It would have been extensively employed in this way, had not *chloroform* been discovered to be a still more effective agent. Æther is usefully employed in many chemical and manufacturing processes.

ÆTNA, a celebrated volcanic mountain in Sicily is noticeable in a commercial point of view for its supplies of pumice and snow. The pumice-stone, that light porous substance which is so useful in many processes of grinding and polishing, is the lava of Ætna and Vesuvius and similar volcanos, where it is found in exhaustless quantities. In many parts of Ætna, strata of lava have been formed 300 feet thick.

For more than half the year the upper part of the mountain is covered with snow; and it forms the great store from which Sicily and Malta are supplied in summer with that necessary of life in a hot climate. After the hot summer of 1828 a search was made for an additional supply of snow; and this elicited the curious fact, that a glacier or field of ice had been prevented, perhaps for ages, from melting, by being covered with a stream of lava. Mr. Lyell supposes that this ice was formed from a mass of drift snow, which was afterwards covered by an enormous thickness of lava, the heat of which was kept from the snow by an intervening layer of volcanic sand.

AFFINITY is a term used to express the tendency of different substances to unite chemically. The expressions chemical affinity and chemical attraction are applied indifferently to that power by which bodies combine and form compounds always possessing some properties very different from those of their constituents, and frequently diametrically opposite to them. It differs from the attraction of gravitation in not acting on masses, and only at sensible distances. In this last property it resembles cohesive affinity, but is distinguished from it by occurring only between the particles of dissimilar bodies. Thus, the particles of a mass of sulphur are held together by *cohesive* affinity, and so also are those of a mass of copper; but if a particle of sulphur be brought into contact with a particle of copper (under a particular application of heat), the two particles being different, and possessing *chemical* affinity for each other, unite by this power, and form sulphuret of copper.

In all mere *mixtures*, such as alcohol and water, or salt and water, the two may act together in almost any proportions; but in the chemical *compounds* brought about by affinity, the proportions are always definite. Some liquids, such as mercury, water, and oil, have no tendency to unite in any proportion whatever, unless by indirect means.

The simplest cases of chemical affinity are those in which two bodies unite into a binary compound. This is the result of what is termed *single affinity*, and this power may be exerted between two elementary or two compound bodies; and also, though it occurs more rarely, between an elementary and a compound substance. Sulphur and copper for example, both elementary bodies, readily unite when heated; and sulphuric acid and oxide of copper, both compounds, combine with great readiness.

The effects of chemical combination, thus induced, are very remarkable. For instance, sulphur is yellow and copper is red, but a compound of the two is black. Acids give a red tint to vegetable blues, and alkalies give them a green tint; but a salt compounded of an acid and an alkali seldom affects the colour. There are numerous other cases in which the form, colour, smell, taste, density, and other physical qualities, and the chemical properties of fusibility, volatility, solubility, and tendency to combination, in the compound, bear no resemblance to those of its constituent parts.

The force with which bodies chemically unite arises from mutual and equal affinity: thus, sulphuric acid and potash combine, not merely on account of the affinity of the acid for the alkali, but of the alkali equally for the acid. Each substance, too, has a power of unity with many others; and as this power or tendency is stronger in some instances than in others, there exists what is termed *elective affinity*, or a sort of preference (so to speak) in the combining action. An example will illustrate this;—Nitric acid is capable of combining by *single affinity* with lime or with magnesia; and if some dilute nitric acid, containing 54 parts of real acid, be mixed with 28 parts of lime, the earth will be dissolved in the acid, and a neutral solution of nitrate of lime is obtained. A similar quantity of this acid forms a neutral solution of nitrate of magnesia by combining with 20 parts of that earth. Now, if we mix together 54 parts of nitric acid, 28 of lime, and 20 of magnesia, it might be supposed that the acid—which is of course incapable of dissolving the whole of both of the earths—would dissolve them in the proportions of 14 of lime and 10 of magnesia: it is found, however, that this is not the case, for the whole of the lime is dissolved, and the magnesia entirely left. This arises from the nitric acid having an *elective affinity* for lime rather than for magnesia.

To exhibit the degrees of elective affinity, tables are constructed, in which the substance whose affinities are to be expressed is placed at the head of a column, and is separated from the rest by a horizontal line; beneath this line are arranged the bodies with which it is capable of uniting, in the order of their respective forces of affinity; the substance which it attracts most strongly being placed nearest to it, while that for which it has the least affinity is placed at the bottom of the column. Such a table is useful, but not always accurate.

Another variety is that of *double elective affinity*, in which two compounds mutually decompose each other. Thus, sulphuric acid, carbonic acid, strontia, and potash, are so characterised with respect to mutual affinities, that if sulphate of strontia and carbonate of potash be made to act on each other, both are decomposed, and the components re-unite to form sulphate of potash and carbonate of strontia.

Chemical affinity works much more powerfully when the bodies are in the liquid than the solid state, in most cases; while others, again, require the gaseous state for its full development.

Proportion, *heat*, *electricity*, and *light*, all influence tho strength and nature of affinitive combination. If sulphuric acid and alcohol be combined in the ratio of equality, they produce sulphuric æther; but if the proportion of acid be ten times as much as that of alcohol, olefiant gas is produced. With respect to *heat*, the difference is not less striking. If we mix oxygen and hydrogen gases, they will remain in a state of mixture for an indefinite period without combining; but if flame be applied to them they combine with explosion, and water is formed. Water dissolves certain salts, but to a limited extent only when cold; boil it, and the solvent power is greatly increased. When mercury is moderately heated in atmospheric air it is converted into peroxide, by combining with the oxygen of the air: heat the compound thus formed more strongly than was required for its production, and the affinity is destroyed: oxygen gas is given out, and the mercury returns to its metallic state. And so on of other bodies.

Electricity possesses remarkable power over chemical affinity. Indeed so intimate is the connection between the two, that it is now known that no chemical action takes place without electric action being also manifested. This part of the subject, developed as it has been by professors Faraday and Daniell, is noticed under ELECTRO-CHEMISTRY. In the mean time the following will serve as an example of the reversal of chemical affinity by electricity. Immerse a piece of copper in a solution of nitrate of silver, the copper is dissolved and the silver precipitated; if we reverse the experiment, and put a piece of silver into a solution of nitrate of copper, no change is effected; if, however, the silver while immersed be touched by a piece of iron, the order of affinity is reversed, the copper is precipitated, and the silver is dissolved.

Light is capable of controlling chemical affinity, both with respect to decomposition and combination. If a mixture of hydrogen and chlorine gases be exposed to the sun's rays, they combine with explosion, and form muriatic acid: this effect does not appear to be produced by the heat which accompanies the light, for a considerably higher temperature is not capable of producing the combination. Or if pale nitric acid be subjected to the action of light, it suffers decomposition to a certain extent, oxygen gas being evolved.

Chemical affinity has a most important influence on many branches of manufacture. Bleaching, dyeing, and calico-printing depend wholly on it; as these processes are guided by relative powers of combination in different substances. All metallurgic processes in which mixed metals are concerned, such as steel, brass, pewter, bronze, &c.; and nearly all operations in which heat or solution are employed—are in like manner dependent on the affinities of different substances one for another.

AFGHANISTAN, or the country of the Afghans, comprehends a large district between India and Persia, lying between 28° and 35° N. lat., and between 62° and 73° E. long. The valley of Kabool contains many fertile and beautiful spots, studded with villages. The dried fruits of Kabool constitute the principal article of trade; they go to Hindustan. Grapes of a dozen different kinds are grown, but only two species bear exportation. Red and white melons are raised in abundance. The wild rhubarb root is used to make preserves; and the vegetables are excellent. On the slope of the Suliman mountains at the eastern part of Afghanistan, is the Salt-range, where extensive beds of rock-salt are found interstratified with limestone.

The central table-land of Afghanistan being very arid, the natives adopt an ingenious mode of forming aqueducts for irrigation, by which the water of a hill or rising ground is brought out at its foot in a rivulet, to be disposed of at the pleasure of the farmer. Such aqueducts, called *karezees*, are made in the following manner. A well is made at the spot where it is intended the water shall issue; above it in the acclivity is dug another at the distance of five to twenty yards, according to circumstances. The wells are continued at distances generally equal, until the quantity of water collected in them is deemed sufficient, or until the depth of the wells becomes so great that the expense exceeds the advantage. If the acclivity is not very gentle, the highest wells must be very deep, as their bottom must be only slightly elevated above the level of the water in the lower wells. All these wells are then connected by means of aqueducts made under the surface of the ground, through which the water from all of them flows to the foot of the hill.

Afghanistan has great mineral wealth. Gold, silver, and copper, are found in various parts; some of the iron found near Peshawur is believed to be nearly equal to that of Sweden, and is largely exported to India. Lead, salt, alum, and saltpetre, are also among the natural products of the country.

The grains cultivated are wheat, barley, peas, beans, maize, rice, and some other grains of Hindustan, as jowary, chuna, musoor, bajra, moth, moong, oord, and murbwa. The most common vegetables are carrots, turnips, radishes, lettuce, cauliflowers, onions, garlic, melons, and cucumbers, with a few others from Hindustan. Madder is extensively grown on the central table-land; and turmeric, assafœtida, and many other useful plants, grow extensively. Forests are only found on the Himalaya mountains and the Sufaid-Coh. There are no woods on the table-land, and all the trees found there are planted generally in rows along the water courses and canals, and around the orchards. The mulberry tree is very extensively cultivated; and among the fruits grown are apples, pears, cherries, plums, apricots, peaches, quinces, and pomegranates.

The most important of the domestic animals are the sheep. There are two kinds, both with the broad fat tail, which in some parts of the Eimack mountains is so large that a small cart or frame is put under the tail to support it. These sheep yield two fleeces: the spring or coarser fleece is used for carpets, grain-bags, and other coarse stuffs; the autumn or finer fleece is manufactured into cloth, cloaks, and mummuds or rugs. Goats are nearly as numerous as sheep; and some of them yield a fine and remarkably soft down, which grows at the root of the hair: the hair is long and usually jet black, but the down is of a shade more or less intensive. Horses, mules, and asses are plentiful; camels and cattle less so. The cats of Kabool are distinguished by their long silky hair, and go under the name of Persian cats, though very few of them are found in Persia, and none are exported from that country. These cats are exported in great numbers from Kabool, where the people encourage the growth of the hair by washing it with soap and combing it.

The chief articles manufactured for export are silk, woollen stuffs, sword-blades, and fire-arms, from Herat and Candahar. Elphinstone enumerates the following as the chief industrial occupations for home produce at Candahar:—Jewellers, gold and silver smiths, booksellers, bookbinders, stationers, makers of kullumdauns (a sort of inkstand and pen-case, of which every man who can write has one), seal engravers, sellers of armour, sellers of shields (these shields are of buffalo's or rhinoceros's hide), gunsmiths, sword-cutlers, polishers of steel, sellers of bows and arrows, sellers of glass ornaments for women, three descriptions of shoemakers, bootmakers, button-makers, silk thread sellers, gold wire and gold thread sellers, saddlers, farriers, painters, fruiterers, cooks, soup-sellers, tobacconists, druggists, perfumers, sellers of sherbet and of fullodeh, confectioners, embroiderers, and people whose business is to sew ornaments on clothes of all descriptions, from jewels to spangles.

As Afghanistan has no navigable rivers, the transport of merchandise is expensive, and the expense is increased by the want of roads, which are not met with in all Western Asia, from the Indus to the Straits of Constantinople. The conveyance of merchandise is therefore effected by beasts of burden. Camels are mostly used in the level countries, and mules or asses in the mountainous districts. Nearly all the land commerce existing between India on one side, and Persia, Turkistan, and China on the other side, must be carried through Afghanistan. Of these lines of communication, the most northern goes by way of Loo-dianah, Lahore, Attock, Pesbawur, to Kabool, on the way to Bokhara. A middle line leads from Lahore to the table-land, where it branches to Ghuznee and Candahar. A southern route reaches Candahar from the mouth of the Indus. From Candahar a route passes westward into Persia.

An active commerce is carried on between

Herat and Meshed and other towns in Persia. The exports from Herat consist of shawls and shawl goods, indigo, carpets of Herat, Mooltanee chintz, Indian brocades, muslin and other cotton-cloth, assafœtida, lead (from the mines of the Eimack), cast-iron, saffron, pistachio-nuts, gums, a yellow dye, carraway seeds, and paper. The imports of Herat are chiefly silk, dates, tobacco, lemon-juice, and ivory heel-taps.

Several caravans go annually from Kabool to Bokhara. They export chiefly articles which have been imported from India, especially shawls and shawl-cloth, white cloth of all kinds, India turbans, Mooltanee chintz, indigo, and spices; and they import from Bokhara principally horses, and gold and silver in coins and bars. Some articles brought from Russia are also imported by these caravans, especially cast-iron pots, cutlery and other hardware, needles, looking-glasses, Russia leather, tin, beads, and spectacles. A fine cloth made of camel's wool, some raw cotton, and some lambskins, are also brought from Bokhara and Balkh.

AFIOUM KARA HISSAR, a city and fortress situated almost in the centre of Asia Minor, about 200 miles from Smyrna, is a great trading thoroughfare; as it lies on the route leading from Smyrna to Armenia, Persia, and the countries bordering on the Euphrates, and as being the rendezvous of the caravans from Constantinople and Smyrna, which from this place proceed further into the interior. Hence nearly all European manufactures and colonial produce, which are distributed eastward and southward, pass through Afioum. This circumstance renders it a place of considerable importance and activity; and in no other town in this part of Asia Minor are the houses so well built or the shops so well supplied. Its manufactures of wool, tapestry, fire-arms, sabres, and red leather are of some importance; but its chief article of commerce is opium ('afioum'), of which a very large quantity is prepared annually. From the cultivation of opium here it derives its name, which signifies "The Black Castle of Opium." In the country between this place and Smyrna most of the Turkey carpets are made.

AFRICA. The Mediterranean coast of Africa has been known from very early times —more remote, indeed, than that of Europe; but down to so late a date as the beginning of the 15th century, the only portion of the west coast of Africa with which European navigators were acquainted was that between the Straits of Gibraltar and Cape Nun, or Nam, or Non, in 28° 40′ N. lat., an extent of not much more than six hundred miles. From this latter point commenced that career of discovery, by the Portuguese, by which the entire coast of Africa has been made known to the modern world. Between the time of Prince Henry of Portugal (1415) and Vasco de Gama (1497), the Portuguese tracked the whole western coast of Africa from the Straits of Gibraltar to the Cape of Good Hope, and the whole east coast to within 1,000 miles of the mouth of the Red Sea, a distance, in all, of more than 10,000 miles.

The 16th and 17th centuries were marked by discoveries and settlements on the rivers Senegal, Gambia, and Zaire, on the west coast.

The Dutch, the Danes, the French, and the English, all made attempts to imitate the Portuguese in their African researches; but little was effected until about sixty years ago. It is since the formation of the African Association, in 1788, that the chief efforts have been made in the prosecution of discovery in the interior; and it is important for us to notice such enterprises here, for they were induced almost wholly by commercial and manufacturing considerations—the principle of interchange of commodities. The expeditions sent out by the Association and by government, and those undertaken by individual adventurers, have sought Timbuctoo and the Niger from various points. But no considerable progress was made till the first journey in 1795 and 1796 of Park, who, on that occasion, proceeding from the west coast in the direction of the Gambia, discovered much new country in the neighbourhood of Timbuctoo, and found reason to think that the Niger or Joliba (hitherto confounded with the Senegal by the Portuguese) was a wholly distinct river. On his second expedition, which was undertaken at the public expense, in 1805, this adventurous traveller succeeded in sailing a considerable way down the Niger, passing Timbuctoo and many other cities, near one of which he was murdered.

After a few partial discoveries, by Hornemann and Riley, an expedition was sent out by the government in 1816, under the command of Captain Tuckey, to the Congo, with the idea that it would be found to be the same with the Joliba or Niger; he ascended that river for about 280 miles, and also examined part of the adjacent country. At the same time Major Peddie, and after his death Captain Campbell, conducted another party from the mouth of the Senegal, through the Foulah territory, as far as Kakundy. In 1817 Mr. Bowdich explored a part of the extensive territories of the Ashantees; and soon afterwards very considerable additions were made to the knowledge formerly possessed both of the geography and the people of interior Africa, by the publication of Mr. Jackson's account of the territories of Timbuctoo and Houssa, from the communications of El Hage Abd Salam Shabeeny, a Mussulman merchant, who had visited these states.

Various discoveries were made by Mollien, Ritchie, Lyon, and Laing, who respectively started for the interior from Senegal, Tripoli, and Sierra Leone. But a more important and successful attempt than any which had been hitherto made to explore the interior of Africa was that of Major Denham and Lieutenant Clapperton, in 1822. These travellers, setting out from Tripoli, along with a caravan of Arab merchants, crossed the desert, and reached the great inland sea or lake called the Tchad. The two travellers, sometimes together, and sometimes separated, visited Bornou, the Fellatah country, and Sackatoo; but they could not trace the Niger (called at Sackatoo the Quorra) to its mouth. In a second expedition Clapperton reached Sackatoo from Guinea, and there died. His servant, Richard Lander, afterwards returned a considerable way towards the south, intending to embark on one of the branches of the Niger, and, if possible, to solve the grand problem of its termination by sailing down the stream. But he was stopped by the natives, and compelled to turn back when he had got as far as Dunrora, which he understood to be due west of Funda, and at no great distance from it. Meanwhile, Major Laing had succeeded in making his way across the desert from Tripoli to Timbuctoo, in August, 1826, and had transmitted somo brief notices of that famous city, where he spent some weeks. But he was murdered on his return, in the desert, and none of his papers have yet been recovered. Timbuctoo was also reached from Sierra Leone by Caillé. The journey, however, which solved the problem of the Niger, was that of Richard and John Lander. Leaving Badagry on the 22nd of March, 1830, these two travellers, following nearly the same route which had been taken by Clapperton through the kingdom of Eyeo, reached Boussa on the 17th of June. They afterwards ascended the river as far as Yaouri, from which they returned to Boussa, where they remained for some time, and then embarked on the river, which they hoped would conduct them to the sea. In this expectation they were not disappointed. After various adventures, Richard Lander had at last the happiness, on the evening of the 18th of November, to find himself at the mouth of the greater branch of the river, here called the river Nun, in that gulf or depression known as the Bight of Biafra.

When the news of Lander's success reached England, a commercial company at Liverpool determined to send out an expedition, with a view of opening an intercourse with the centre of Africa. Mr. Lander, Mr. Macgregor Laird, and Captain Allen, were of the party; and two small iron steam vessels were provided, which it was hoped might ascend the Niger in safety. The expedition sailed in 1832; but it turned out most disastrous, being attended with a fearful loss of life. The merchants of Liverpool, however, succeeded in establishing a commerce with the natives by degrees; and in 1840 the government determined to send out an expedition; under an impression that trade and treaties with the African chiefs might lessen the horrors of the slave trade. This was also attended with much loss. Captain Becroft ascended the Niger about the same time, in a vessel sent out by Mr. Jamieson, of Liverpool. Mr. Holroyd, Mr. Oldfield, and Messrs. Moffat aud Smith, all increased our store of information concerning those regions, shortly before the period just named. In 1842 Captain Allen explored new regions in western Africa. In 1841 and 1842 Dr. Beke spent a year in Abyssinia, and many researches were made by other travellers in the upper valley of the Nile. In 1843 Major Harris returned from his mission to Shoa, by which much knowledge was gained of that region. In 1844 and 1845 many travellers were exploring the northern half of Africa, in various directions: aud the Journal of the Geographical Society now yearly contains the results of such expeditions.

The zeal for discovery in Africa, which has been so strongly felt within the last half century, has also sent out a succession of travellers to explore the southern regions of that vast continent. The principal settlement in this quarter, that of the Cape of Good Hope, was founded by the Dutch about 1650, and remained in their hands till it was finally taken from them by the British in 1806. For more than a hundred years after the establishment of this colony it occupied only the extreme angle of the African continent, or a part of the narrow tract between the sea and the nearest mountains; nor does much information seem to have been obtained with regard to any of the native tribes, except the nearest Hottentots lying beyond that boundary. The first traveller who penetrated any considerable way into the interior was Captain Henri Hop, who was sent out on an expedition of discovery by the Dutch governor in 1761, and traversed a considerable part of the country of the Namaquas. He was followed by Sparrman, Vaillant, Barrow, Trutter, Somerville, Cowan, Donovan, Lichtenstein, and Burchell, who, between 1775 and 1812, traversed much of the country north and east of the Cape. In 1820 and 1823 Burchell and Thompson penetrated far to the north. In 1836 and 1837 Sir J. E. Alexander explored much of the country inhabited by the Boschmans and other tribes north of the Cape of Good Hope. Since this date, exploring expeditions have been made by the missionary Krapf, Lieutenant Ruxton, Mr. Ackermann, M. Maizan, and others in various directions.

In short, it may be stated, that approaches are now being made towards the centre of Africa, from almost every side of that great continent. The recent lion-hunting, elephant-killing excursion of Mr. Gordon Cumming, can hardly be termed a geographical exploration.

The mineral treasures of this immense continent are of course very imperfectly known. Salt is perhaps one of the most universally diffused, being found from the salt lakes of the Cape colony to the northern coast. It will probably be found on inquiry that the mineral treasures of Africa are nearly as various as those of other parts of the world, though at present less perfectly known, and in many cases only observed at spots widely removed from one another. The mineral wealth of Egypt alone is considerable; and that of the interior west of the Mozambique coast is also abundant. Gold dust, however, is that which has the most excited the cupidity of Europeans; and this mineral is found in the sands of the upper streams of nearly all the great African rivers. Besides gold and salt, the chief mineral products are silver, copper, iron, tin, lead, chalk, sulphur, and a few indications of coal.

The nature of African vegetation depends greatly on the latitude. The principal objects of cultivation in the Barbary States are a kind of wheat (*Triticum durum*), the stems of which are solid, and the grain horny rather than farinaceous; barley, which the Moors give their horses instead of oats, maize, durra (*Holcus sorghum*), rice, tobacco, olives, oranges, and figs of the most delicious quality; pomegranates, grapes, and jujubes, together with sweet melons and water melons. In the districts watered by the Nile we find all the richness of vegetation of the spring months of Barbary; abundance of rice, barley, and wheat; rich fields of sugar-canes; olives, figs, vines, and plantains that have been introduced; while in the hotter or drier, or more southern districts, the date is the chief object of the scenery. In the richer parts of the country we find the acacias which produce gum arabic, large tamarisk trees, called atlé, great quantities of the senna plant (*Cassia obtusifolia* and other species), intermixed with various herbs belonging to tropical genera, all of which are either unknown or very rare in the more northern parts of Africa. Cotton, coffee, indigo, and tobacco are cultivated with the greatest success. At Thebes first begins to appear a third race of palms different from the date and the palmetto, namely, the forky-branched doom palm (*Crucifera Thebaica*) of Upper Egypt. In the equinoctial parts of Africa all trees of European vegetation, and even the date tree itself, disappear. The landscape is characterized by masses of the unwieldy baobab (*Adansonia*), the fruit of which affords the natives a grateful drink, huge cotton trees (*Bombax pentandrum*), thick groups of oil palms (*Elais Guineensis*), sago palms (*Sagus raphia*), and others of the same majestic tribe. In some places the woods abound in pine-apples; while the plains are often covered with immense quantities of the papyrus plant. Among the plants cultivated for food are the cassava, the yam, the pigeon pea, and the ground-nut; the papaw, the tamarind, and the nitta or doura tree; the Senegal custard apple, the gray plum, the Safu, and the musanga, the seeds of which are as agreeable as hazel-nuts, and many others less common. Near the Cape of Good Hope the plants partake more of a milder climate.

Among domestic quadrupeds, the horse, the ox, the buffalo, the sheep, the goat, and the camel, may be enumerated. It is in the northern and central regions that the camel and buffalo are used. Dogs are numerous, and in Mohammedan towns have no particular owners, but are tolerated for their utility.

Under the headings ABYSSINIA; BARBARY; CAPE OF GOOD HOPE; EGYPT; GAMBIA; NIGER; SAHARA; SENEGAL; TIMBUCTOO, &c., will be found details respecting the productions, manufactures, and commerce of various parts of Africa.

AFRICAN COMPANY, a regulated trading company, established by act of Parliament in 1754. In the course of time it happened that the whole expense of the Company came to be defrayed by the public, and for this reason the charter of its incorporation was recalled by Parliament in 1821. The possessions of the Company on the west coast of Africa were by this act annexed to and made dependencies upon the colony of Sierra Leone.

AFTER-MATH is the grass which grows after the hay has been made; it is also called

KNIGHTS CYCLOPÆDIA OF THE Industry of all Nations.

No. 3.

latter-math, rowen, or rowett, and when left long on the ground it is called fogg in some places. Where the land is rich and hay valuable, the after-math is often mown and made into hay. This hay is inferior in value and nourishment to the first crop, which contains the flower-stalks of the grass. It is not good for horses, especially those which are driven fast and work hard; it is thought injurious to their wind. Cows and sheep are fond of it, and with them it is not liable to the same objection.

AGA'RICUS is the botanical name by which all the species of *mushrooms*, properly so called, are collectively known. This genus consists, according to the latest writers, of not fewer than a thousand species, inhabiting meadows, heaths, rocks, and masses of decaying vegetable matter, in all parts of Europe, and in many other parts of the temperate regions of the earth. Among them a large proportion are poisonous, a few are wholesome, but by far the greater number are altogether unknown in regard to their action upon the human constitution.

Agaricus Campestris, the common mushroom, is the species that is so frequently raised artificially for food. This is readily known in any state by its fragrant odour, by which alone it may be always recognised, and the absence of which is extremely suspicious. When in a very young state, it resembles little snow-white balls, which are called *buttons;* afterwards it acquires a stalk, separates its cap, and becomes shortly conical, with liver-coloured gills, and a white, thick, fleshy cap, marked with a few particles of gray. At a more advanced age, the cap is concave, the colour gray, and the gills black; in this state it is called a *flap*. Mushrooms appear in the fields chiefly after Midsummer, in the months of July, August, and September. They are indigenous, and spring up abundantly in fields where cattle have been pastured. Much care is bestowed, in some districts, in the artificial culture of mushrooms.

Agaricus pratensis, or *oreades*, the fairy-ring mushroom, is so well known by its popular designation as to require no description. It may easily have gained that name; for, in former times, there would doubtless be great difficulty in imagining how such productions could spring up in a few hours in the regular rings they appear in, without the aid of some supernatural agency. The use to which this species is usually applied is that of being powdered and mixed with rich sauces, after having been previously strung upon a line, and dried in the shade.

AGATE, sometimes called *Scotch Pebble*, is an ornamental stone used in jewellery. It is one of the many forms under which silica presents itself, almost in a state of purity: constituting in the agate 98 per cent. of the mineral. It presents a semi-translucent mass with a sort of resinous fracture; and is sometimes tinted by a minute quantity of iron. The variations both of translucency and of tint in the same stone are often so great as to give much richness of appearance; and this combined with the high polish which they are capable of receiving, imparts great value to some specimens of agate.

These stones generally occur in the form of detached rounded nodules, in a variety of the trap rocks called Amygdaloid. The particles often arrange themselves in layers parallel to the surface; and the centre has in some specimens a hollow space containing crystals of other minerals. It is supposed that agates have been formed in a kind of lava produced by igneous or volcanic action.

There are many gems which so closely resemble the agate in chemical constitution as to render it convenient to notice them briefly in this place. *Carnelian* or *cornelian* is coloured with shades of red and yellow: the deep clear red being the rarest and most valuable. It is brought chiefly from the East Indies, and is much used for engraved seals. *Calcedony* presents generally a milky white or pale yellow colour, with very often a wavy internal structure. It is sometimes met with in the British isles, in such large masses as to be formed into cups and other vessels. *Onyx* has the particles arranged in parallel layers: white alternating with blue, gray, or brown. The onyx was much used by the ancients for cameos: the figure or device being cut out of the opaque white, and the dark part forming the ground. A Roman cameo of this kind, in the Royal Library at Paris, measures as much as 11 inches by 9. *Sardonyx* is a variety of the onyx, in which the opaque white alternates with a rich deep orange brown of considerable translucency. *Mocha Stone* is a semi-transparent calcedony, in which varied tints are produced by the presence of iron and other bodies. *Moss Agate* closely resembles Mocha stone. *Blood-Stone* is a green agate, coloured with bright red spots like drops of blood. *Chrysoprase* and *plasma* are two varieties of calcedony having a green tint.

Sir H. T. De la Beche, in his Anniversary Address to the Geological Society in 1848, drew attention to the artificial colouring of agate. The agate workers of Oberstein are in the habit of imparting colour to that substance: an art derived from the Italians. It depends on the difference of porosity in the different layers of the agate. By immersion for some time in honey and water or olive oil, so that the pores of the agate become more or less filled, a subsequent soaking of the stone in sulphuric acid produces a difference in the tints of the agate according to the porosity of the layers, the most porous becoming black, while the least porous remain white or uncoloured. By immersion in a solution of sulphate of iron, and a subsequent heating of the agate, a cornelian red is in like manner obtained in the most porous layers, while the least porous remain unchanged in colour. It is supposed that some of the agates which have come down to us from antiquity have been artificially coloured.

In the Exhibition of works of Mediæval Art, at the rooms of the Society of Arts in 1850, many exquisite specimens of agate were collected.

AGA'VE, in Botany, comprehends those plants which gardeners call American aloes. There are many species of this genus, one only of which requires to be mentioned here, viz, the *Agave Americana*, or American Aloe. This is a plant, which, when full grown, has a short cylindrical woody stem, which is terminated by hard, fleshy, spiny, sharp-pointed, bluish-green leaves, about six feet long, and altogether resembling those of the arborescent aloes. It is commonly supposed that this plant only reaches maturity at the end of one hundred years; but this, like many other popular opinions, is an error, the period at which the agave arrives at maturity varying, according to circumstances, from ten to fifty or even to seventy years. In hot or otherwise favourable climates, it grows rapidly, and soon arrives at the term of its existence; but in colder regions, or under the care of the gardener, where it is frequently impracticable to attend to all the circumstances that accelerate its development, it requires the longest period that has been assigned to it. Having acquired its full growth, it finally produces its gigantic flower-stem, after which it perishes. This stem is sometimes as much as forty feet high, and is surrounded with a multitude of branches arranged in a pyramidal form, with perfect symmetry, and having on their points clusters of greenish yellow flowers, which continue to be produced for two or three months in succession. The native country of the American aloe is the whole of America within the tropics, from the plains nearly on a level with the sea, to stations upon the mountains at an elevation of between 9,000 and 10,000 feet. The sap may be made to flow by incisions in the stem, and furnishes a fermented liquor, called by the Mexicans *Pulque;* from this an agreeable ardent spirit, called *Vino Mercal*, is distilled. The fibres of the leaves form a coarse kind of thread; the flowering stems dried make an almost imperishable thatch; an extract of the leaves is made into balls, which will produce a lather with water; the fresh leaves themselves cut into slices are occasionally given to cattle; and finally the centre of the flowering stem split longitudinally is by no means a bad substitute for a European razor strop, owing to minute particles of silica forming one of its constituents.

AGE OF TREES. The immense consumption of timber in the manufactures of this and many other countries, renders it interesting to note the circumstances which distinguish different kinds of trees, in respect to duration and growth.

Besides annual and biennial plants (whose age is indicated by their names), the remainder of the more perfect part of the vegetable kingdom, whether herbaceous or shrubby or arborescent, consist of plants which may be classed under two principal modes of growth. One of these modes is to increase, when young, in diameter, rather than in length, until a certain magnitude is obtained, and then to shoot up a stem, the diameter of which is never materially altered. The addition of new matter to a trunk of this kind takes place by the insinuation of longitudinal fibres into the *inside* of the wood near the centre; on which account such trees are called *Endogenous*: they also bear the name of *Monocotyledons.* The other mode is, from the beginning, to increase simultaneously in length and diameter, but principally in length. The addition of new matter to a trunk of this kind, takes place by the insinuation of longitudinal fibres into a space beneath the bark, and on the *outside* of the wood near the circumference; on which account such trees are called *Exogenous*; they also bear the name of *Dicotyledons.*

To the first of these classes belong the palm tribe and some other tropical trees. There is scarcely any well-attested evidence of these plants ever acquiring any considerable age. It has indeed been supposed, that certain Brazilian cocoa-nut palms may be from 600 to 700 years old, and that others probably attain to the age of something more than 300 years. But the method of computing the age of palms, which is either by the number of rings externally visible upon their rind between the base and the summit of the stem, or by comparing the oldest specimens, the age of which is unknown, with young trees of a known age, is entirely conjectural, and not founded upon sound physiological considerations; besides which, the date-palm, which is best known to Europeans, does not at all justify the opinion that palms attain a great age; the Arabs do not assign it a greater longevity than from two to three centuries.

But in exogenous trees, it is quite the reverse: to their existence no limited duration can be assigned. Of the many remarkable cases upon record of a great age attained by exogenous trees, the following are among the more interesting.

At Ellerslie, the birth-place of Wallace, three miles to the S. W. of Paisley, stands an oak, in the branches of which tradition relates that celebrated chieftain to have concealed himself with three hundred of his followers. However improbable the latter circumstance may be, it is at least certain that the tree may well have been a remarkable object, even at the period assigned to it by tradition, namely, in the beginning of the fourteenth century, and if so, this individual must be at least 700 years old. Its branches are said to have once covered a Scotch acre of ground; but its historical interest has rendered it a prey to the curiosity of the stranger, and the limbs have gradually disappeared till little remains except the trunk. Many other cases of oaks of extreme old age are recorded, some of which have been estimated at 1500 or 1600 years.

Of ancient yews several authentic instances can be named. At Ankerwyke House, near Staines, is a yew older than the meeting of the English barons at Runnymede, when they compelled King John to grant the Magna Charta. This tree, at 3 feet from the ground, measures 9 feet 3 inches in diameter; and its branches overshadow a circle of 207 feet in circumference. The yews of Fountain's Abbey, in Yorkshire, are probably more than 1200 years old; and to others an age of from 2500 to 3000 years has been assigned.

Even this degree of antiquity is, however, much less than that of the baobab trees of Africa, estimated by Adanson at 5000 years; and the deciduous cypress of Chapultepec in Mexico, which the younger De Candolle considers still older.

The way in which the age of some of these specimens has been computed is twofold: firstly, by comparing them with other old specimens, the rate of growth of which is known; and secondly, by cutting out a portion of their circumference, and counting the number of concentric rings that are visible; for in exogenous trees the woody cylinder of one year is divided from the succeeding one by a denser substance, which marks distinctly the line of separation of the two years. The first of these methods is sufficiently correct to give at least an approximation to the truth, and the latter would be absolutely correct, if one could be quite sure that observers provided against all possible causes of error. But it has been shown by Dr. Lindley, that in consequence of the extreme inequality in thickness of the annual layers of wood on opposite sides of a stem, a person who judged of the whole age of a tree by the examination of the layers of the stunted side only, would commit errors to the amount of sixty per cent. and more. It is by no means impossible that the great age assigned to the deciduous cypress and the baobab may be connected with an error of this nature.

AGENT. In commercial matters, where one person acts for another, he is called an *agent*, and his employer the *principal*. The relations between the two are of great importance, and are guided in some respects by statutes, and in others by the custom of the particular department of commerce to which they belong.

AGIO, a term used sometimes to express the variations from fixed pars or rates of exchange, but more generally to indicate by per centages the differences in the valuations of moneys. The Italian word *aggio* is explained to mean 'an exchange of money for some consideration.' Thus, if a coin is reduced in weight, and the real value is not equal to the nominal value, the difference is the agio.

Where it is in the power of the state to prevent the degradation of the coin below the standard, no calculations of agio, strictly so called, are rendered necessary. In some states, the currency is made up of the deteriorated coins of the neighbouring countries with which the inhabitants have dealings. Under these circumstances, banks were, at different times, established by the governments of Venice, Genoa, Hamburg, Amsterdam, &c., which, under the guarantee of the state, should be at all times bound to receive deposits and to make payments, according to some standard value. The money or obligations of these banks bears a premium equivalent to the deterioration, and this premium is called the agio of the bank.

As the current coins of every country have a kind of medium value at which they are generally taken, the term agio is also applied to express what must be paid over and above this medium value. The kinds of money on which, in the case of exchange, an agio is paid, are not always the more valuable intrinsically, but those which are most in request.

The term agio is also used to signify the rate of premium which is given, when a person having a claim which he can legally demand in only one metal, chooses to be paid in another.

Thus, in France, silver is the only legal standard, and payments can be demanded only in silver coin: a circumstance which is found to be practically so inconvenient, that the receiver will frequently pay a small premium in order to obtain gold coin, which is more easily transportable: this premium is called the agio on gold.

AGRICULTURAL IMPLEMENTS. A large and important department of manufacturing skill is that which is devoted to agricultural implements and machines—to those mechanical aids by which the produce of the soil is developed. Like most other departments of industry, this has made a great advance within the last few years. The researches of Liebig, Boussingault, Thaer, and other foreign experimentalists, and those of our own countrymen, have taught us what are the relations which each kind of soil bears to each species cultivated, and how the mechanical preparation of the soil can most efficiently be carried on. Our Smithfield cattle shows, and the annual exhibitions of the Royal Agricultural Society, demonstrate how much attention is now paid to the form and manufacture of agricultural implements.

The Comte de Gasparin, in his valuable *Cours d'Agriculture*, presents a useful analysis and classification of agricultural implements, according to the nature of the operations which they are destined to perform. First come *perforating* implements, intended simply to make holes in the ground, generally for the reception of roots or seed; these comprise the single and double dibble, a frame with pointed spikes, a roller with pointed spikes, and other contrivances of a similar kind. The second class comprises implements which *cut* the soil in strips, or *loosen* it in rows; these comprise ploughs, harrows, rakes, scarificators, &c. In the third class are implements used to cut the soil into horizontal *slices;* these are illustrated by paring machines, by turf-cutting machines, by many forms of plough-share, and by extirpators. The fourth class comprises implements which *overturn* long strips of soil upon themselves; among these are to be numbered cultivators, and many minor forms; indeed the plough itself in some of its forms belongs to this class, inasmuch as it exposes new portions of soil to the action of the atmosphere. The fifth class comprises the more complete forms of plough, by which three movements are effected—a vertical cut, a horizontal cut, and an overturning of the portion loosened. In the sixth class are instruments which displace the soil in separate pieces, and not in continuous strips; they comprise spades, pickaxes, hoes, pitchforks, and other simple hand-worked tools. The seventh class comprises implements used in crushing, equalising, smoothing, and pressing the clods which have been loosened by any of the before mentioned means; the various kinds of clod-crushers, rammers, and rollers are included in this class. In the eighth class are comprised the numerous varieties of *sowing* machines, from the simplest to the most complicated drills, &c. The ninth class comprises the *harvesting* or *reaping* machines, such as sickles, scythes, &c.

Gasparin goes on to the formation of other classes; such as implements for preparing grain for the market (flails, thrashing machines, winnowing machines, &c.); implements of transport (baskets, wheelbarrows, and vehicles of every description used upon a farm); and machines of any kind used in irrigation.

Under their proper headings in this Cyclopædia, all the principal agricultural implements are described. There may be many readers who are not aware that the manufacture of such implements has assumed a magnitude and systematic character quite analogous to the great factory system. At the works of Messrs. Ransome and May, for example, at Ipswich, the operations are conducted on a gigantic scale, and with all that subdivision of labour which marks an advanced stage in manufactures. Many hundred persons are here constantly employed in the manufacture of agricultural implements and machines. Mr. Allan Ransome, a partner in this firm, has within the last few years published a valuable illustrated treatise on such implements.

AGRICULTURAL INSTITUTIONS. The Board of Agriculture was established chiefly through the exertions of the late Sir John Sinclair, and was incorporated in 1793. One of its first proceedings was to commence a survey of all the English counties on a uniform plan. The 'Surveys' were useful at the time in developing more rapidly the agricultural resources of the country. During the years of scarcity, at the end of the last and beginning of the present century, the Board of Agriculture took upon itself to suggest, and as far as possible provide, remedies for the dearth, by collecting information and making reports to the government on the state of the crops. The statistics which the board collected were also at times made use of by the minister, or at least were believed to be so, in connection with his schemes of taxation. The board encouraged experiments and improvements in agriculture by prizes, and it naturally exercised considerable influence over the provincial agricultural societies.

The Board of Agriculture was dissolved in 1816.

The Smithfield Cattle Club, which has been in existence half a century, and some of the provincial agricultural societies, especially the Bath and West of England Society, which commenced the publication of its 'Transactions' nearly seventy years ago, have been very useful in promoting agricultural improvement.

With the establishment of the 'Royal Agricultural Society of England,' a new æra commenced in the history of institutions for the improvement of English agriculture. The objects of this society, as set forth in the charter of incorporation, are:—1. To embody such information contained in agricultural publications and other scientific works as has been proved by practical experience to be useful to the cultivators of the soil. 2. To correspond with agricultural, horticultural, and other scientific societies, both at home and abroad, and to select from such correspondence all information which, according to the opinion of the society, may be likely to lead to practical benefit in the cultivation of the soil. 3. To pay to any occupier of land or other person, who shall undertake, at the request of the society, to ascertain by any experiment how far such information leads to useful results in practice, a remuneration for any loss which he may incur by so doing. 4. To encourage men of science in their attention to the improvement of agricultural implements, the construction of farm-buildings and cottages, the application of chemistry to the general purposes of agriculture, the destruction of insects injurious to vegetable life, and the eradication of weeds. 5. To promote the discovery of new varieties of grain and other vegetables useful to man, or for the food of domestic animals. 6. To collect information with regard to the management of woods, plantations, and fences, and on every other subject connected with rural improvement. 7. To take measures for the improvement of the education of those who depend upon the cultivation of the soil for their support. 8. To take measures for improving the veterinary art, as applied to cattle, sheep, and pigs. 9. At the meetings of the society in the country, by the distribution of prizes and by other means, to encourage the best mode of farm cultivation and the breed of live stock. 10. To promote the comfort and welfare of labourers, and to encourage the improved management of their cottages and gardens. The country meetings take place annually in July. England and Wales are divided into nine great districts, and a place of meeting in each is fixed upon about a year beforehand.

The success of the Royal Agricultural Society has revived the spirit of existing associations, or led to the formation of new ones. There are now about four hundred agricultural societies in various parts of England. There are also a hundred and fifty farmers' clubs, which are eminently practical; and the local results which they collect and discuss may become applicable to other parts of the country placed under similar circumstances of aspect, soil, and situation.

The agriculture of Scotland has been largely indebted to the societies which have been established at different periods for its improvement. A 'Society of Improvers in the Knowledge of Agriculture in Scotland,' was established in 1723, and some of its transactions were published. The society becoming extinct, was succeeded by another in 1755; and the society which now stands in the same relation to Scotland as the Royal Agricultural Society to England was established in 1784. It is entitled the 'Highland and Agricultural Society of Scotland.' The constitution and proceedings of the society are as nearly as possible similar to the English society.

In 1841 the 'Royal Agricultural Improvement Society of Ireland' was established on the plan of the Royal Agricultural Society of England.

In England there are no institutions of a public nature which combine scientific with practical instruction in agriculture. The advantage of establishing such an institution was suggested by the poet Cowley; and in 1799 Marshall published 'Proposals for a Royal Institute or College of Agriculture and other branches of Rural Economy.' There is the Sibthorpian Professorship of Rural Economy in the University of Oxford; at the University of Edinburgh there are professorships of agriculture and agricultural chemistry; and at the university of Aberdeen there are lectures on agriculture. The botanical, geological, and chemical professorships and lectures in the different universities are, however, to a certain extent auxiliary to the science of agriculture. The Earl of Ducie has established a model example farm on his estate in Gloucestershire; and farms of this description are of considerable local advantage. There is one on a very complete scale at Harpenden, near St. Alban's, replete with all the apparatus for the chemical analysis of soils, fodder, products, &c. In 1839, the late B. F. Duppa, Esq., published a short pamphlet entitled 'Agricultural Colleges, or Schools, for the Sons of Farmers,' which contains many useful suggestions for the establishment of such institutions. In the Agricultural College and Model Farm at Cirencester the pupils receive an education at once practical and scientific, under a person thoroughly acquainted with the management of a farm, associated with a professor of chemistry, mechanics, &c.

In Ireland the government affords direct encouragement to agricultural education through the instrumentality of the Board of National Education. The persons who are trained for the office of teachers in the national schools are required to attend the lectures of a professor of agricultural chemistry. The Agricultural Seminary at Temple-Moyle, six miles from Londonderry, is one of the most successful experiments which has yet been made in the United Kingdom to establish an institution for agricultural education. It was founded by the North West of Ireland Society in 1827, and up to 1840 had been attended by 418 pupils.

Such societies as the Scottish Agricultural Chemistry Association, established at the close of 1843, are very well calculated to advance the progress of scientific agriculture; and they can be established in any district where a sufficient number of subscribers can be obtained to command the services of a competent chemist. Associations of this nature show how much can be done in this country without any assistance from the state. Landed proprietors who subscribe twenty shillings yearly, are entitled to have performed analyses of soils, manures, &c., according to a scale fixed upon; and if more than a certain number are required, a charge of one-half above the scale is made.

In England, soils are analysed at the Museum of Economic Geology, London, at a charge of one guinea. The establishment is under the superintendence of her Majesty's office of Woods and Forests.

In France there are schools assisted by the state, where young persons can obtain instruction in agriculture, both practical and theoretical. The principal institution of this kind is that at Grignon, where one of the old royal palaces and the domain attached to it, consisting of 1,185 acres of arable, pasture, wood, and marsh land, have been given up on certain conditions. The professors are paid by the government, and the pupils are of two grades, one paying 48*l.* a year, and the other 36*l.* For the purpose of imparting theoretical knowledge, courses of lectures are given on the following subjects:—1. The rational principles of husbandry, and the management of a farm. 2. The principles of rural economy applied to the employment of the capital and stock of the farm. 3. The most approved methods of keeping farming accounts. 4. The construction of farm-buildings, roads, and implements used in husbandry. 5. Vegetable physiology and botany. 6. Horticulture. 7. Forest science. 8. The general principles of the veterinary art. 9. The laws relating to property. 10. Geometry applied to the measurement and surveying of land. 11. Geometrical drawing of farming implements. 12. Physics, as applied to agriculture. 13. Chemistry as applied to the analysis of soils, manures, &c. 14. Certain general notions of mineralogy and geology. 15. Domestic medicine, applied to the use of husbandmen.

Institutions designed for the improvement of agriculture, and supported by the state, have been established in most parts of Germany. In Prussia there is a public model farm and agricultural academy in nearly every province. The most important of these institutions is the one at Mogelin, in Brandenburg, about 40 miles from Berlin, which was founded by the late king. The establishment consists of a college and a model farm of 1200 acres. At Hohenheim, in the kingdom of Wirtemberg, two leagues from Stuttgard, an old palace has been appropriated as an agricultural college. The quantity of land attached to the institution is about 1,000 acres. Lectures are delivered by twelve professors on the following subjects:—Mathematics and physics, chemistry and botany, technology, tillage, and other departments of rural economy, forestry, and the veterinary art. In Bavaria the king has given up the domain attached to the royal palace of Schleissheim for the purposes of a model farm.

There are agricultural institutions supported by the state in several other countries of Europe.

AGRICULTURE. Without attempting any formal treatise on agriculture, useful details will be met with under the names of the chief agricultural instruments and the chief vegetable crops. In several countries of Europe there is a department of government organized either for collecting the statistics of agriculture or superintending institutions which have immediate relation to that branch of industry. In France these duties devolve upon a department of the Minister of Commerce and Agriculture. The councils general of agriculture, &c., in each department of France collect the agricultural statistics from each commune; and the quantity of land sown with each description of grain, the produce, and the quantity of live stock for the whole of the kingdom, are accurately known and published. In Belgium these facts are ascertained periodically, but not every year. In the United States of North America, at the decennial census, an attempt was made to ascertain the number of each description of live stock, including poultry; the produce of cereal grains, and of various crops; the quantity of dairy, orchard, and garden produce, &c., in each State. There are twenty nine heads of this branch of inquiry. The only countries in Europe which do not possess statistical accounts of their agriculture founded on official documents are England and the Netherlands. On the same principle that a census of the population of a country is useful, it must be useful to have an account of its productive resources. The absence of official information is supplied by estimates of a conjectural character, founded at best only on local and partial observation. In France it is positively ascertained that the average produce of wheat for the whole kingdom is under fourteen bushels per acre. In England it is known that the maximum produce of wheat per acre is about forty bushels, and that the minimum is about twenty bushels. The usual conjecture is that the average produce of the kingdom in years of fair crops is about twenty-eight bushels, but the total superficies sown with wheat or any other grain, and the total quantity of the produce, are matters simply of conjecture. It would be most desirable to trace what have been the results of the more scientific cultivation of the last few years. The only statement the public or even the government are in possession of in respect to the quantity of land cultivated and uncultivated, and of land incapable of producing grain or hay, in Great Britain, rests upon the authority of private inquiry made by one person, Mr. Couling, a civil engineer and surveyor, who gave the details to the parliamentary committee on emigration in 1827. From his tables it appears that upwards of forty-six millions of acres were cultivated in the United Kingdom; of which about nineteen millions were cultivated as arable and gardens, and about twenty-seven millions were meadows, pastures, and marshes.

AIGLETS is the French name for what in England are called *tags*, viz., the metal sheaths at the end of laces or points. These *points* are now out of date; they were ties or bows, adorned at the ends with aiglets, and were used instead of buttons for fastening dresses. They were, in the 16th and 17th centuries, not used merely for service, as the modern tag, but were profusely employed as ornaments, glittering like spangles.

In some of the silk-mills of Derby, tags for silk boot-laces are made in a curious manner. A little boy sits before a kind of cutting-machine, with which he cuts a strip of sheet-brass into small pieces, each large enough for one tag; the piece is at the same time bent into a kind of semi-cylindrical form. The pieces are then taken up by another boy, and dropped one by one into a recess in another machine; and the end of a silk-lace being laid in the hollow of a tag, a lever is brought down with the left hand, by which the tag is made to embrace the lace firmly, enclosing it all round. These processes are conducted with astonishing rapidity: the fingers of the two boys moving almost as fast as the eye can follow them.

AIR, is the material of our atmosphere, though in the last century the name was applied to gases of most kinds as fast as they were discovered. The air which envelops the globe is a *mixture* (not a chemical compound) of oxygen and nitrogen, with a very small proportion of carbonic acid, and water in the state of vapour. The two last are considered as accidental ingredients, and not constituent parts; as well on account of the smallness of their quantity, as because they occur in different proportions at different times. Estimated by weight, air is found (nearly, but not with strict accuracy) to consist of one atom or equivalent of oxygen to two of nitrogen; or, estimated by volume, the oxygen is to the nitrogen in the ratio of one to four. The carbonic acid and aqueous vapour, taken together, are not more than one-fiftieth of the whole weight. A thousand cubic inches of dry air, the barometer standing at 30 inches, and Fahrenheit's thermometer at 60°, weigh about 310 grains. The same bulk of water, at the same pressure and temperature, weighs 252,525 grains, or more than 800 times that of air.

The air, in common with all other bodies, has weight. This is proved by weighing a bottle which contains air in a very delicate balance, and then by repeating the process after the air has been exhausted from the bottle by the air-pump. From this we are immediately led to conclude that, like all other heavy fluids, air exercises pressure upon all substances which are in contact with it,—a truth that was very little suspected in ancient times. The density of the air depends upon, and is a consequence of, the pressure of the superincumbent atmosphere; or the air is an elastic fluid; that is, its bulk increases, and its density diminishes, whenever the exterior pressure is wholly or partially removed. Let a loose bladder, tied at the mouth, and not so full of air as to be distended, be placed under the receiver of an air-pump, so that the air which presses the outside of the bladder can be exhausted; the interior air will expand so soon as the exhaustion begins, will presently distend the bladder to its fullest dimensions, and in some cases will even burst it. On the re-admission of the air into the space surrounding the bladder, the latter will gradually resume its former dimensions, and its withered or flaccid appearance. As we ascend the atmosphere, the superincumbent column of air becomes of less weight, and the density becomes less; that is, a cubic foot at the height of (say) 1000 feet above the ground is not so heavy, or does not contain so much air, as a cubic foot at the surface of the earth. The pressure and density of the air are regulated by the following law: *at the same temperature*, the elastic forces of two portions of air (or, which is the same thing, the weights of mercury they will balance) are in direct proportion to the densities, or in inverse proportion to the spaces, occupied by these portions. The human body would be crushed by the pressure of the air on it, were there not a counter pressure from within.

The temperature of air influences its elastic force. It is probable that air would become first liquid, and then solid, if it could be made sufficiently cold. Like all other substances, air gives out heat when it is compressed; a property strikingly illustrated by the fact that tinder can be set on fire when the air in which it is contained is suddenly and violently compressed.

Air, like gases and vapours generally, enlarges its bulk with every increase of temperature, or increases its elastic force if enlargement of bulk be prevented. The quantity of this expansion, when the temperature passes from the freezing to the boiling point of water (that is, from 32° to 212° of Fahrenheit's thermometer, from 0° to 80° of Réaumur's, and from 0° to 100° of the Centigrade), is 375 parts out of a thousand of the bulk which it had at the freezing point. And this enlargement is uniform; that is, whatever expansion arises from an increase of 12° of temperature, half as much arises from an increase of 6°, twice as much from one of 24°, and so on. From the different systems on which the Fahrenheit, Réaumur, and Centigrade thermometers are graduated, it follows that the increase of bulk, corresponding to a rise of *one* degree of temperature in the air (the bulk of 32° F. being taken as a standard) is equal to $\frac{1}{480}$, $\frac{3}{640}$, $\frac{3}{800}$ respectively. In some few cases this regularity of expansion is not quite certain, but it is known to be very near the truth.

On the properties of air with regard to other bodies, we may notice that probably there is a slight adhesion of air to many, if not to all surfaces. A small needle may be made to swim on water, and in this state the water evidently retires from around it, leaving it, as it were, suspended over a hollow in the fluid. This is attributed to the adhesion of a coat of air, which, with the iron, makes the whole specifically lighter than the water. Recent experiments on the pendulum have led some to suspect, that, in addition to the resistance of the air, a slight coating of this substance travels with the pendulum, and thereby causes an irregular addition to its weight.

These few details concerning the general properties of air will meet with various illustrations under AIR-GUN; AIR-PUMP; ATMOSPHERE; BALLOON; COMBUSTION; PNEUMATICS; STOVE; VENTILATION, &c.

AIR-BEDS and CUSHIONS. [WATER-PROOF COMPOSITIONS.]

AIR-BLADDER. Cod-sounds, which are brought in great quantities from Newfoundland, are nothing more than the salted air-bladders of these fishes. The Iceland fishermen, as well as those of America, prepare isinglass of a very excellent quality from cod-sounds; though they are not acquainted with the method of clarifying it, which the Russians practise in preparing that article from the sound of the sturgeon. [ISINGLASS.]

AIR ENGINES. Many attempts have been made within the last few years to produce engines which should have the power of steam-engines without the use of steam. The compression or the rarefaction of air, brought about in some one of many different ways, is the agent relied upon for producing a moving force. In 1840 Mr. Stirling patented such a machine, and read a description of it before the Institute of Civil Engineers in 1846. In this engine two strong air-tight vessels are connected with the opposite ends of a cylinder, in which a piston works in the usual manner. About four-fifths of the interior space in these vessels is occupied by two similar air-vessels, or plungers, suspended to the opposite extremities of a beam, and capable of being alternately moved up and down to the extent of the remaining fifth. By the motion of these interior vessels the air to be operated upon is moved from one end of the exterior vessel to the other; and as one end is kept at a high temperature, and the other as cold as possible, when the air is brought to the hot end, it becomes heated, and has its pressure increased, whereas its heat and pressure are diminished when it is forced to the cold end. Now as the interior vessels necessarily move in opposite directions, it follows that the pressure of the enclosed air in the one vessel is increased, while that of the other is diminished; a difference of pressure is thus produced upon the opposite sides of the piston, which is thereby made to move from one end of the cylinder to the other; and by continually reversing the motion of the suspended vessels or plungers, the greater pressure is successively thrown upon a different side, and a reciprocating motion of the piston is kept up. The piston is connected with a fly-wheel, in any of the usual modes, so as to communicate motion to machinery. There is a furnace to heat one end of the air-vessels, and a water-pipe refrigerator to cool the other; and the air traverses numerous small channels in its course from the one end to the other, in such a mode as to economise the heat. An engine on this construction has been used in an iron foundry at Dundee.

One of the most remarkable projects for an air-engine is the *Carbonic Acid Locomotive*, for which Mr. Baggs took out a patent in 1842. Carbonic acid gas assumes a liquid form under a pressure of about 540 lbs. to the inch, at a temperature of 32°; and the project consists in an attempt to make the sudden vaporisation of this liquid a source of power. Carbonate of ammonia is made by one of the usual chemical processes; and this being separated into its proximate elements of carbonic acid gas and ammoniacal gas, these two gases are brought to the liquid state, either by the chemical method of Mr. Faraday or the mechanical method of Sir M. I. Brunel. The locomotive or other engine is charged with the condensed or liquefied gases, which are contained in very strong wrought iron tubes; and on opening certain valves, the liquids suddenly flash into the vaporic form, mix and combine together, and are condensed into carbonate of ammonia in an adjoining condenser. This carbonate of ammonia can be again used as a source whence to obtain the two gases. The sudden force generated when the liquids expand into vapour, becomes a moving power for the machine. Apparatus must be provided at suitable stations, for making the two gases, and condensing them into the liquid form.—Such is the rationale of this singular scheme; but we are not aware that it has proceeded beyond the specification of the patent.

Mr. H. Pratt published a pamphlet, about 1845, with a view of shewing that the ascensive force of a lofty current of air, when aided by heat, may be applied to the moving of machinery. The common smoke-jack, and many other machines long in use, illustrate the force of an ascending column of heated air; but Mr. Pratt's object is to show that there is an ascensive power in a tall current of air more than equal to the result produced by the heating of the air to a temperature beyond that of the external atmosphere. A large bakery has been established on this principle at New York, the machinery being worked by the ascensive force of a current of air heated by the baking ovens. At a certain height within a lofty vertical shaft is a horizontal wheel, with wings or vanes attached at an angle of 10°; the ascending air causes this wheel to revolve horizontally; drums are fixed on the spindle of the wheel, and straps or bands from these drums drive the machinery for grinding the flour and kneading the dough. The dimensions of the various parts are so calculated as to produce about 200 horse-power.

Baron Von Rathen made trial of an air-locomotive on a common road, in 1848. It travelled from Putney College (where it was constructed) to Wandsworth, at the rate of 10 or 12 miles an hour. The air-reservoir (substitute for a steam boiler) had a capacity of 75 cubic feet; it was capable of being charged with air to a pressure of fifty atmospheres, by a 6-horse power engine.

AIR-GUN, an instrument for projecting bullets, in which the moving power is the rush of condensed air allowed to escape, instead of the formation of gases arising from the ignition of gunpowder.

In the stock of the air-gun is a condensing syringe, the piston of which condenses air into a cavity having a valve opening inwards, just behind the bullet. The barrel is open, and the bullet (which should just fit the barrel) is inserted in the usual way. The trigger opens the valve behind the bullet, and permits the rush of the condensed air, which propels the bullet forward. The moment the finger is withdrawn from the trigger, the air closes the valve, and remains, somewhat less condensed than before, for the next discharge.

The same principle has been variously applied. In the magazine air-gun, there is a reservoir of bullets, in a channel under the barrel, one of which is turned in by a cylindrical cock pierced by a tube, which in one position is a continuation of the reservoir of bullets, and in another, of the barrel. Thus by turning the gun upside down, and turning the cock, a bullet falls into it from the reservoir, which, on returning the cock, is of course in the barrel. In some air-guns, the cavity containing the condensed air is a hollow copper ball, which can be screwed on to the gun after condensation. The *Air-Cane* is so called because it is usually in the form of a walking stick. The handle contains the condensed air, and can be unscrewed and filled by a separate condensing syringe.

No power, but only a convenient adaptation of power, is gained in an air-gun; since the condensation of the air itself requires an expenditure of power. The instrument has hitherto been little more than a toy.

In 1849 a singular air-gun was invented, in which the elastic quality of gutta-percha was brought in aid of the elasticity of air, so as to charge the gun without the necessity for a condensing syringe—such, at least, was the theory of the apparatus.

AIR-PUMP, is an instrument for removing the air out of a vessel. It effects the reverse operation to that performed by the *condensing syringe*, by which additional air is forced into a vessel. Both in the exhausting and the condensing syringe there is a tube closed at one end, excepting an orifice to which a valve or lid is attached. A piston, with a rod and handle, enters at the other end, and can be moved up and down the tube. The piston is not entirely closed, but has a valve opening the same way as the other valve. Both are attached to vessels, the air of which is to be rarefied or condensed. In the exhausting syringe, both valves open upwards or let air only *out* of the vessel and the piston: in the condensing syringe, both open downwards, or let air only *into* the vessel and the piston. In the exhausting syringe, every time that the piston is drawn *upwards*, it leaves a sort of vacuum in the barrel; and the air in the receiver forces up the lower valve to fill up this vacuum. At the next movement, the air thus raised is driven out of the instrument altogether; for the valves are so placed that no air can go from above downwards. By repeated movements of this kind, nearly all the air may be drawn out of the receiver. In the condensing syringe, all the operations are exactly reversed; the *downward* motion of the piston being the efficient agent in forcing into the receiver a quantity of air many times greater than that which it originally contained.

The exhausting syringe is, in principle, the common air-pump. In most forms of air-pump there is at the top a metal plate ground to a perfectly plane surface, on which is placed an inverted glass jar or receiver, whence the air is to be extracted. A hole in the plate is connected with a tube, which communicates with two pump barrels. These barrels are exhausting syringes. One or more guages are attached to the instrument to test the degree of exhaustion of the air. The pistons which work in the two pump-barrels are connected by a rack-and-pinion movement with a handle, in such a way that when the handle is worked in semi-circular movements, the pistons are raised alternately. As the lower part of each barrel is connected with the receiver by means of the tube, the movements of the two pistons gradually draw out the air from the receiver, in the manner of the exhausting syringe; and in this way a nearly perfect vacuum may be produced.

In most of the objects for which an air-pump is required in scientific experiments, a glass receiver, provided with stop-cocks or other adjustments, is placed on the plate of the air-pump to have the air extracted; and experiments or observations are made in the vacuum thus produced.

If the receiver of an air-pump be open at both ends, and the upper orifice be stopped by the hand,—on exhaustion, the pressure of the exterior air will be painfully great on the hand. If a piece of bladder be tied tightly over the orifice, as the exhaustion proceeds the bladder will be pressed inwards, and will finally burst with a loud noise. The weight of the air is proved by exhausting a copper ball furnished with a stop-cock, which is shut before the ball is removed from the air-pump: it will then be found to weigh less than before the exhaustion was made. The presence of air in various substances may be detected by means of an air-pump. A glass of liquid placed under the receiver will give out bubbles of air as soon as the exhaustion begins. A shrivelled apple will be restored to apparent freshness by the expansion of the air which it contains; but will resume its original appearance when the air is allowed to return. The elasticity of air may be shown by placing a bladder under the receiver, not distended, and the mouth of which is tied up; on exhausting the receiver, the air contained in the bladder will expand it more and more, as more of the pressure from the exterior is removed; and the bladder will finally burst from the interior pressure. If a hole be made in the smaller end of an egg which is placed under the receiver, the small bubble of air, which is always found in the larger end, will by its expansion force out the contents of the egg.

In machinery employed in manufactures, the air-pump is applied in various ways, especially with some forms of steam-engines. In such cases no glass-receiver is necessary, and the mechanism of the air-pump is larger and stronger.

AIR-SADDLE. The principle of the air vessel has been applied within the last few years to the production of saddles: the leather being made into a hollow case, and inflated with air, as a means of forming an easy seat for the rider. A patent was taken out for the invention; but it may be doubted whether the jolting action to which a saddle is subjected would not be too severe for an air-stuffed case.

AIR-VESSELS, or *Air-Chambers*, are used in various machines, either to regulate and equalise the propulsion of fluids, as in a FIRE-ENGINE; or to regulate and check the velocity of apparatus which might otherwise attain a dangerous degree of speed. An example of the last-mentioned use is afforded by the contrivance employed by Mr. Timothy Bramah, instead of a fly, to regulate the speed of a tread-mill. In this contrivance the turning of the tread-wheel is made to work a series of large bellows, or air-vessels resembling bellows, in which the apertures for the ingress and egress of air are fitted with sliding plates worked by an apparatus resembling the governor of a steam-engine; so that whenever the speed of the machinery exceeds the desired limit, the apertures are reduced, and a greater resistance is thereby occasioned. Similar contrivances, in which a cylinder and piston may be used instead of bellows, and water or oil instead of air, may be advantageously employed in lieu of ordinary breaks for cranes used in lowering heavy goods, and in various other machines.

AIRDRIE has lately sprung up to be the centre of one of the most important mining districts in Scotland. It is situated about a dozen miles east of Glasgow. The whole district beneath and around Airdrie abounds in the richest ironstone and coal; and some of the largest iron-works in Scotland are here located, around which a numerous population of miners and workpeople is accumulating. Airdrie is connected with Glasgow by the Monkland Canal and by the Caledonian Railway, by which routes its mineral treasures reach the great emporium of Scottish commerce.

AIX, a considerable town of France, in the department of the Bouches du Rhone, carries on an important trade in hardwares, fish, and the productions of the neighbouring country. Among the manufactures are silks, velvets, woollen cloth, and printed calicoes.

ALABA'MA, one of the southern United States of North America, is a flourishing seat of commerce and industry. The forest trees in the middle and north of the state, are post oak, white oak, black oak, hickory, poplar, cedar, pine, chestnut, and mulberry; in the south, pine, cypress, and loblolly. Iron ore is found in various parts of the state, and coal is abundant on the Black Warrior river and the Cahawba river. Cotton is the staple production of the state, but Indian corn, rice, wheat, oats, &c., are produced. The Alabama river is navigable for vessels drawing six feet water, 60 miles above its junction with the Tombigbee, to Claiborne, and has four or five feet water for 150 miles farther, to the mouth of the Cahawba. The Tombigbee is navigable for small sailing vessels to St. Stephens, 150 miles, and for steam-boats to Columbus in Mississippi State; its total length is 450 miles, and it is navigable for boats nearly the whole length. Cotton is the great article of export. The city and port of Mobile is, next to New Orleans, the largest cotton-mart of the southern states, 320,000 bales having been exported in a year. 40,000 bales, of about 500lb. each, are annually shipped from Montgomery in this State.

Manufactures are spreading considerably in this state. Tanneries, iron-foundries, cutleries, distilleries, printing-offices, &c., are rapidly increasing. Since the collisions of opinion between the northern and southern states respecting slavery, the latter have begun to erect cotton mills as a means of fostering their own cotton culture; and Alabama, as one of them, is rising in importance. In the middle of 1850 there were in Alabama 12 cotton mills, with 12,580 spindles and 300 looms; and there were then contracts in force for 20,000 more spindles and 550 more looms. The exports from Alabama in 1848 were valued at 11,927,749 dollars. The population of Alabama has risen from 20,845 in 1810, to 624,827 in 1845. The railways in Alabama at the beginning of 1849 were 113 miles in length, viz., from Montgomery to West Point, and from Tuscumbia to Decatur.

ALABASTER, is a delicate white soft kind of marble, used for ornamental purposes. The name is derived from Alabastron, a town of Egypt, where there appears to have been a manufactory of small vessels or pots, made of a stone found in the mountains near the town.

There are two kinds of alabaster: the one is a *carbonate* of lime; the other is gypsum, or *sulphate* of lime. Many of the ancient perfume vessels are made of the compact crystalline mass deposited from water holding carbonate of lime in solution, which is found in many places in almost every country. It is easy to ascertain of which of the two kinds a vessel is composed; for *carbonate* of lime is hard, and effervesces if it be touched by a strong acid; but *sulphate* of lime does not effervesce, and is so soft that it may be scratched with the nail. The term alabaster is now generally applied to the softer stone. This last, when pure, is a beautiful semi-transparent snow-white substance, easily worked into vases, lamps, and various other ornaments; but it is seldom found in masses large enough for statuary; and, indeed, artists would be unwilling to execute any great work in a material so very liable to injury. It is largely found in Italy and in Derbyshire.

There are many ingenious modes of producing slight modifications in alabaster, in respect to colour or some other of its properties. Alabaster may be *bronzed*, by coating it once or twice with size, and touching it with a bronze powder, of which many different varieties are manufactured. By a judicious use of bronzing, very pleasing effects may be produced in an alabaster statuette. Alabaster may be *cleaned*, by washing with soap and warm water, and rinsing. It may be *polished*, by rubbing it with dried shave-grass, then with a paste of lime and water, and lastly with powdered talc. It may be *hardened*, by coating the surface with a mixture of plaster of Paris and gum arabic; or by heating, cooling, steeping in water, drying, and polishing. It may be *stained* by the same materials and in the same way as marble. It may be *cemented* when broken by a mixture of quicklime and white of egg. And lastly, it may be *etched* by covering it with an etching-ground composed of white wax, white lead, and oil of turpentine, and proceeding in the customary method of the etching process.

The alabaster manufacture is one of some importance in Italy. It employs numerous turning-lathes in Florence, Leghorn, Milan, and other towns. At Florence, especially, the beauty and uniformity of the alabaster enable it to be worked into ornaments of considerable size. The larger masses are cut with steel saws into blocks and pieces of various shapes, which are afterwards worked into the desired form by lathes and tools. Rasps, fine files, fine chisels, and graving tools, are the chief aids employed.

ALARUM. It is curious to mark how much ingenuity has been displayed within the last few years in the invention of alarums, and how many patents have been taken out for the inventions. In all such contrivances there is some little bit of mechanism or other which gives a shrill sound whenever attention is required to be directed to any subject with which the alarum is associated.

Without describing any of the older forms, we may glance at a few of the modern suggestions. A Mr. Allen, in 1844, registered an alarum intended to prevent injury to boilers from the water falling below its proper level. The machine consists of a float within the boiler, a steam-whistle on the exterior, and a tube of connection. When the water is at a proper height in the boiler, the float is buoyed up, and the whistle is silent; but when the water, and with it the float, descends too low, a little valve in the tube opens, and a current of steam from the boiler ascends to the whistle, which immediately gives forth a shrill sound, thereby indicating that the water has sunk too low in the boiler.

The alarums suggested within a recent period for use on railways, are exceedingly numerous. One patented by Mr. Doull, is a railway whistle, so constructed as to yield several notes, capable of being combined into a code of signals. A chemical alarum by Mr. Mowbray consists of a copper cylinder, with a whistle at the top. A piece of carbonate of lime and a little muriatic acid are put into the cylinder, by which carbonic acid gas is speedily generated; and this is forced by some kind of mechanism into the whistle, whenever a sound is required to be produced. A contrivance by Mr. Hoare, described before the Society of Arts, consists of a chain of rods extending from end to end of a railway train, and moving freely on joints. At the end of the chain, in the guard's carriage, is a crank which, when the rods rotate on their axes, comes in contact with a hammer, and causes it to strike a bell. The driver, or the passengers in any carriage, can give a slight rotatory motion to the rods, and thus signals be communicated.

But the busiest contriver of alarums, perhaps, is Mr. Rutter, who has called to his aid the marvels of electricity. In a patent for several such contrivances, taken out by him in 1847, one variety is the *Fire Alarum*, a complicated apparatus intended for use in large buildings. A galvanic battery is placed in one room, the alarum in another, thermometers in every room, and copper wires to connect all these pieces of apparatus. If the temperature of any room be greatly raised, as by accidental fire, the rising mercury in the thermometer comes in contact with a metallic wire, which sets the galvanic battery in action, and this again works the alarum-bell in the same way as an electro-telegraphic clock, but with an adjustment intended to show in which room the rise of temperature has occurred. A second variety, the *Trespass Alarum*, depends for its action on the placing, near every door and window, of a tube containing mercury, open at the top; the opening or closing of the door or window brings a small wire into contact with the surface of the mercury, and this completes a galvanic connection with a battery in another room: all the parts of the apparatus may be the same as those in the fire alarum, except by having open tubes of mercury near doors and windows, instead of thermometers in each room. A third variety, the *Railway Alarum*, is intended to establish signals of communication between the guard and the engine-driver of a railway train. There is a copper wire carried through or upon or beneath each carriage, and connected with another in the adjoining carriage by a flexible metallic cord: the wire and cord being coated with gutta percha to secure isolation. There is thus a wire-communication from end to end of the train. The guard has in his box or seat a very small galvanic battery; and the engine-driver has a series of small studs connected with the rail on which his hand is usually resting. When the guard wishes to communicate with the engine-driver, he sends a slight galvanic shock through the wire to the spot on which the hand of the driver rests; and the duplication or variation of the shock may be made to indicate various signals.—It must be evident that great completeness and exactness would be necessary to render any of the above three kinds of alarum efficient for the purpose intended.

A floating alarum was suggested a few years ago by Mr. Hobbs, of Bristol, to be moored to a sunken rock or other dangerous place at sea. The centre of the machine is an air-vessel or buoy. At each end is a box in which a whistle is fixed, whose mouth is protected from the water. As the water of the sea circulates in certain parts of the interior of the machine, it drives the air alternately from one end to the other, and impels it through the whistles; and the more violently the sea rocks the floating machine, the louder will the whistles give forth their sound. The proposal of the inventor is to make the buoy and whistles of such dimensions that the sound may be heard some miles distant.

Many of the above good things remain in the form of mere suggestions, not yet practically carried out; and it must be owned that some of them are rather cumbrous and complicated.

ALBANIA, a country of European Turkey, stretching along the coast of the Adriatic and Mediterranian seas, is very rugged and mountainous, and has but few rivers of any note. Among the natural productions may be mentioned many species of oak; as the *quercus cerris*, which affords timber of good size and quality; and the Valonia oak (*quercus ægilops*), the acorns of which are used in dyeing, and supply an article of export from many parts of Turkey. Other trees are the chestnut, the plane, the cypress, the ash, the cedar, the pine, and the larch. The wild vine and the elder are also frequent on the mountains, and the woods and wastes nourish the Amphilochian peach, the Arta nut, and the quince. The cultivated fruits are the olive, which might be rendered more productive by better care; the vine, the pomegranate, the orange, the lemon, the mulberry, and the fig. The agricultural produce consists of barley, oats, maize, and other grains, tobacco, and cotton; some portion of it is exported. Horses, asses, cattle, sheep, and goats are reared, and are sold to the Ionian Islanders. The milk of the goats is made into cheese, a small quantity of which is exported; and their skins serve to hold wine (to which, however, they impart a strong flavour).

Agriculture is in a lowly condition. The plough is of simple construction, and in time of harvest they reap their corn, though with little skill, and they never mow it. The business of sowing and reaping is left to the women and to the aged. The young men fell timber or dress the vines. There are few arts or manufactures. The Albanians export a considerable number of capotes annually; and they produce some embroidery on velvet, stuff, and cloth, for which the country enjoys a better reputation than any other part of European Turkey; but this is the work of the Greeks of Joánnina, who are an industrious people, rather than of the Albanians.

The trade consists mainly in the exchange of natural productions for the manufactures of nations more refined. Oil, wool, wheat, maize, and tobacco, are sent to the kingdom of Naples, or to the Ionian Isles and Malta; and sheep, goats, cattle, and horses, to the Ionian Islands. Cotton wool and timber are exported from the Gulf of Arta; but the cotton is brought chiefly from Thessaly, and the timber from ancient Acarnania, on the south side of the gulf. The manufactured goods which they export are—capotes; gun and pistol stocks, mounted in chased silver, plain and gilt; and embroidered velvets, stuffs, and cloths. They import coffee and sugar from Trieste; knives, sword-blades, gun-barrels, glass and paper, from Venice; gold and silver thread, for embroidery, from Vienna; French and German cloth, coarse and ill-dyed, from Leipsic; and caps and a few other articles from various parts. The want of ready means of communication is a great impediment to traffic. Goods are conveyed by pack-horses, four or five of which are attached to each other by cords, and guided by one man.

ALBANY, a district situated at the eastern extremity of the colony of the Cape of Good Hope in South Africa. The bays and inlets along the coast of this district, are frequented by abundance of excellent fish fit for curing. A large natural salt pan is situated near the

Zondag River, in which the salt forms in masses four or five inches thick; this furnishes a supply of salt to the district. The most important part of the trade of Albany consists in the traffic carried on by licensed traders with the native tribes, beyond the boundary line of the colony. This trade is carried on through a wide extent of country, in the Kaffer territory. The principal articles procured in this manner are hides, horns, and ivory, together with a considerable number of live cattle. The attention of the settlers has, within the last few years been drawn to the improvement of the growth of wool; and during 1848 and 1849, many manufactories were established in the towns.

ALBATA, is the name given to one of the numerous varieties of *white metal*, now so largely used in many branches of manufacture at Birmingham. Many different mixtures or alloys will produce a white metal. For example, Mr. Parker obtained in 1844 a patent for five such compounds, all having the properties of whiteness and considerable malleability. One consists of zinc, tin, iron, and copper, in certain specified proportions; another of zinc, tin, and antimony; a third of zinc, nickel, iron, and copper; a fourth of copper, nickel, and silver; and a fifth of nickel, iron, and copper. It seems evident from the specification, that many different proportions of the ingredients may be adopted, in each of the above kinds. The mode of making white metal, of zinc 50, tin 48, iron 1, and copper 3, is thus described:—the iron and copper are first melted together in a crucible, and while in a fused state, the tin is added in such quantities at a time, that the iron and copper shall not become solid; the zinc is then added, and the whole well combined by stirring. The flux is composed of one part of lime, one part of Cumberland ore, and three parts of sal-ammonia. The alloy thus produced may be cast in sand or ingots for rolling.

See further in respect to these compound metals under Alloy.

ALBERT DÜRER. [Dürer.]

ALBUM (White), was a tablet on which the Roman prætor's edicts were written; it was put up in a public place. It was probably called album because the tablet was white. The word was also used to signify a list of any body of persons, as of the senators and of the júdices.

A book which is intended to contain the signatures, or short verses, or other contributions of persons of note or supposed note, is now called an album. The name is also given to a book which is merely intended as a repository for drawings, prints, verses, and such matters. Trifling as it may appear, an album, in the hands of a person possessing good taste, may be made a very graceful article of artistic decoration. Some modern specimens are extremely costly.

ALBU'MEN forms a constituent principle of plants and animals; and its essential properties are found to be the same from whichever kingdom of the organised world it is derived. It is found in the green feculæ of plants in general; in the fresh shoots of trees; in the sap of many plants; in the bitter-almond, the sweet-almond, and the emulsive seeds in general; but it exists in the greatest abundance in such vegetables as ferment without yeast, and afford a vinous liquor. But albumen exists much more abundantly in animals than in plants. It forms a constituent both of the animal fluids and solids. Of the animal fluids, it forms an essential part of the serum of the blood; it abounds in the fluid that moistens the surface of the internal cavities of the body and of the organs they contain; and it exists in large quantity in the watery fluid poured out into those cavities in the disease termed dropsy. White of egg is nearly pure albumen: when liquid it soon putrefies; but if carefully dried it may be long preserved. In the animal solids, albumen forms the principal part of the skin, of fibrin, the basis of muscle or flesh, and of the organs called glands. It is an intricate compound of carbon, hydrogen, oxygen, nitrogen, sulphur, and phosphorus.

The most remarkable property of albumen is its power of solidifying under circumstances which would rather tend to liquefy than to solidify most substances. White of egg shows white fibres at a temperature of 134° F., solidifies at 160°, and becomes horny at 212°. When mixed with water, a higher temperature is required for coagulation. Albumen is precipitated in white fibres, by agitating white of egg with alcohol. Galvanic action will also coagulate albumen. Many of the stronger acids and salts will have the same effect; and so delicate a test of the presence of this substance is the bichloride of mercury, or, as it is commonly called, corrosive sublimate, that if a single drop of a saturated solution of corrosive sublimate be let fall into water containing only the two-thousandth part of albumen, it will occasion a milkiness in the water, and produce a curdy precipitate.

Albumen is not, as a distinct substance, largely used in manufactures; but its presence in many natural substances greatly influences the manufacturing processes adopted. It is employed as a glaze, or species of varnish, and as a clarifier for wines and syrups. *Al-*

bumen powder is made by drying white of egg to a horny consistency, and reducing it to powder; it is in this state exported largely to the West India sugar plantations, where it is used to clarify sugar.

ALBURNUM, in plants, is that part of the stem of trees which timber merchants call *sapwood.* It is the newly-formed unchanged wood lying immediately below the bark, and is always of a very light colour. It consists of little besides vegetable tissue; in which respect it differs from *heartwood* or *durâmen*, which is vegetable tissue combined with solid secretions, the nature of which varies with the species.

While many plants have the alburnum and heartwood distinctly separated, there are others, technically called white-wood trees, which consist of nothing but alburnum. This arises from their not forming any solid secretions which can give durability to the central parts; hence all such trees are quickly perishable.

ALCARRAZAS. [COOLER.]

ALCHEMY was originally the pretended art of making gold and silver; but another and subsequent object of alchemy was the preparation of a universal medicine. Those alchemists who were supposed to be skilled in the art were termed *adepts* or *the adepts.*

According to the doctrine of the alchemists all the metals are compounds, the baser of them containing the same constituents as gold, but mixed with various impurities, which being removed, the common metals would assume the properties of gold. The change was to be effected by *lapis philosophorum*, or the philosophers' stone, which is commonly mentioned as a red powder possessing a peculiar smell.

As the philosophers' stone was said to take a great part in the pretended transmutations, Dr. Thomson in his 'History of Chemistry,' has endeavoured to discover its probable character. After quoting a description given by one of the alchemists, he states that this mysterious agent could hardly have been any thing else than an *amalgam of gold;* and 'there is no doubt,' he adds, 'that amalgam of gold, if projected into melted lead or tin, and afterwards cupellated, would leave a portion of gold; all the gold, of course, that existed previously in the amalgam. It might, therefore, have been employed by impostors to persuade the ignorant that it was really the philosophers' stone; but the alchemists, who prepared the amalgam, could not be ignorant that it contained gold.'

It is thought by some that the alchemists did injury to chemistry, by bringing it into disrepute; but Dr. Thomson remarks, that a compensation was given in another way:—'As the alchemists were assiduous workmen—as they mixed all the metals, salts, &c., with which they were acquainted, in various ways with each other, and subjected such mixtures to the action of heat in close vessels, their labours were occasionally repaid by the discovery of new substances, possessed of much greater activity than any with which they were previously acquainted . . . . . Thus the alchemists, by their absurd pursuits, gradually formed a collection of facts, which led ultimately to the establishment of scientific chemistry.'

ALCOHOL, is the chemical name, (probably derived from the Arabic), for *ardent spirit.* Alcohol is the intoxicating principle of beer, wine, and fermented liquors in general; and when they are subjected to distillation, the alcohol and a considerable quantity of water are vaporized and condensed together. The distilled products have different names and properties according to the substances yielding them.

It is explained under FERMENTATION, that when that process is going on, a compound of carbon, hydrogen, and oxygen, previously existing in the form of *sugar*, is decomposed, and out of it are formed two other compounds, —*alcohol* and *carbonic acid.* It is in this way that alcohol is obtained for use. The alcohol of commerce is, however, always mixed with water, on account of the great affinity between them; and it is a difficult chemical process to produce absolute or pure alcohol.

Alcohol, in its absolute or anhydrous state (free from water), is a limpid, colourless liquid, of an agreeable smell, and a hot pungent taste. It is composed of carbon, hydrogen, and oxygen. Its specific gravity is 0·791 at 68° F., or 0·7947 at 59° F. It has never been frozen, although exposed to a temperature 91° below zero, or 123° below the freezing point of water. It is extremely volatile, producing considerable cold during evaporation; the degree of cold is proportional to its purity. Heat expands alcohol in a greater degree than it does water, for 100,000 volumes become 104,168 by being heated from 32° to 100°; whereas an equal bulk of water heated to the same degree is increased only to 100,908. Under the average atmospheric pressure alcohol boils at about 173°, but in the vacuum of the air-pump, ebullition occurs at 60° and even below it. Alcohol, and the vapour arising from it, are extremely inflammable; it burns with a lambent flame, the colour of which depends upon the strength of the alcohol; the blue tint prevails when it is strong, and the yellow when weak. Although the flame of alcohol yields but little light, its heat is intense; it burns without any smoke. There are several substances which communicate colour to the flame of alcohol: boracic acid and salts of copper impart green, barytic salts yellow, and the salts of strontia an intense and beautiful red colour. These properties are made available in pyrotechny or fire-works.

Alcohol combines in definite proportions with chloride of calcium, nitrate of magnesia, and other salts, with which it forms *alcoates.* It dissolves resins, essential oils, camphor, sugar, soap, and numerous acids, with readiness; it also readily dissolves ammoniacal gas. As alcohol remains fluid at the lowest temperatures, it is advantageously employed in filling thermometer tubes, and in experiments on artificial cold; its antiseptic properties are great, and hence its use in preserving anatomical preparations; on account of its ready inflammability, the purity, and the intense heat of its flame, it is conveniently, but not economically employed in chemical lamps, usually termed *spirit lamps.* There are many other useful purposes to which this remarkable liquid is applied; but its chief employment is in the form of beverages.

ALCOHOLIC DRINKS. The number of alcoholic drinks is surprisingly large and varied. The following are the principal:— *Agua Ardiente*, made in Mexico, from the fermented juice of the Agave; *Arack* or *Arrack*, made in India from the juice of the palm and from rice; *Araka*, made in Tartary, from fermented mare's milk; *Araki*, made in Egypt from dates; *Arika*, made in Tartary and in Iceland, from fermented cow's milk; *Brandy*, made in nearly all wine countries from wine and from fruits; *Geneva* or *Holland*, made in Holland from malted barley or rye, rectified on juniper berries; *Gin*, made in England from malted barley, rye, or potatoes, and rectified with turpentine; *Goldwasser*, made at Dantzic from various kinds of corn, and rectified with spices; *Kirschwasser*, made in Switzerland from the Machaleb cherry; *Lau*, made at Siam from rice; *Maraschino*, made in Dalmatia from the Macarska cherry; *Mahwah Arrack*, made in India from the flowers of the Madhuca tree; *Rum*, made in the West Indies and South America from cane sugar, and molasses; *Rakia*, made in Dalmatia from the husks of grapes, mixed with aromatics; *Rossolio*, made at Dantzic from a compound of brandy with certain plants; *Sekis-Kayavodka* made at Scio from fruit and lees of wine; *Slatkaia-trava*, made at Kamschatka from a sweet grass; *Show-choo*, made in China from the lees of rice wine; *Trosta*, made in the Rhemish provinces from the husks of grapes fermented with barley and rye; *Tuba*, made in the Philippine Islands from palm-wine; *Vino Meresel*, made in Mexico by distilling the fermented juice of the Agave; *Whiskey*, made in Scotland and Ireland from raw and malted grain, and in the south of France from sloes.

However different the above alcoholic beverages may be, they all have a common resemblance in these particulars:—they all consist chiefly of dilute spirit or alcohol; they all contain portions of essential oils, or colouring matter, or extractive matter; they all derive their distinctive character from the nature of these added substances; and they may all be made to yield pure alcohol by rĕ-distillation and rectification.

Numerous as they are, these drinks are wholly distinct from the various rich and luscious CORDIALS and LIQUEURS, of which the reader will find a brief account in subsequent articles.

ALCOHOMETER. The rigorous proceedings of the Excise in collecting the duty on English spirits, render the use of several instruments necessary. One of these is the *Alcohometer*, a sort of hydrometer fitted to ascertain the quantity of pure alcohol in any given mixture of spirit and water, for absolutely pure alcohol never comes before the notice of the public generally; it is always combined more or less with water. Various means have been adopted to test the strength of alcohol—finding the temperature of the vapour produced, determining the temperature produced by admixture with water, or ascertaining the degree of volatility; but the mode which has been found best in practice is by determining the specific gravity, which becomes greater and greater as there is more and more water mixed with the spirit: in other words, a pint of spirit and water is *heavier* than a pint of pure spirit. The Excise charge duty, not on the quantity of liquor manufactured by distillation, but on the quantity of pure spirit contained; and this quantity is determined by the alcohometer or hydrometer.

ALDER. [ALNUS.]

ALDERNEY, or AURIGNY, one of the islands in the English Channel, lying in the bay of Avranches, near the coast of Normandy. The soil is sandy, gritty, and gravelly round the coast, but in the valleys it is very fertile, producing excellent corn and potatoes. In the meadows they grow rye-grass and clover, which give excellent milk and butter. The grass lands occupy about one-third of the area of the island. The land is generally elevated, but consists both of high and low tracts; a good supply of excellent water is procured in every part of the island. The Alderney cows maintain their reputation: they are easily distinguished from those of the neighbouring islands by being remarkably small, and straight in the back.

ALE. The distinction between ale and beer, the processes of manufacture, and the arrangements of the great London breweries, are described under BREWERIES AND BREWING.

ALEMBIC, a chemical apparatus used in distillation. It consists of a *body*, *cucurbit*, or *matrass*, to contain the fluid to be distilled; a *head*, or *capital*, fixed above it to receive and condense the vapour which rises on the application of heat to the cucurbit; and a pipe descending from the head to a *receiver*, or vessel prepared to receive the condensed product of distillation, which in its passage from the head to the receiver, is frequently passed through a *worm* or serpentine pipe immersed in cold water as a refrigeratory. Alembics or stills are made of both glass and metal, the several parts being fitted together with ground or luted joints, and of various forms according to the purpose for which they are employed. They are of great use in manufacturing chemistry.

ALEPPO. [HALEB.]

ALEUROMETER. One of the novelties of 1849 was a contrivance called an Aleurometer, invented by M. Boland, a Paris baker, for ascertaining the panifiable or bread-making qualities of wheaten flour. This determination depends upon the expansion of the gluten contained in a given quantity of flour, when freed from its starch. A ball of gluten being placed in a cylinder to which a piston is fitted, the apparatus is exposed to a temperature of 150°; and as the gluten dilates, its degree of dilatation is marked by the piston rod. The greater the dilatation, the better is the flour fitted for making bread.

ALEUTIAN ISLANDS, situated in the North Pacific Ocean, between Cape Alaska in North America, and the peninsula of Kamtchatka in Asia, are one of the centres of the fur-trade. In 1785 a commercial establishment was formed there, for the prosecution of this trade; and in 1799 this company received great aid and protection from the Russian government, which has ever since continued. The fur animals which the islands yield are bears, beavers, ermines, otters, foxes, and seals. Almost the only occupations of the inhabitants are fishing and hunting, and the preparation of implements necessary for the prosecution of those pursuits. In fishing they make use of a species of canoe, which they call a *baidar*, and which consists of a skeleton of wood, over which a covering of seal skins is extended. Thus constructed, these canoes are so extremely light that they may be carried about by one person without difficulty. Domestic occupations, such as making clothes, and even the covering of canoes, are performed by the women, who likewise make mats, baskets, and other useful articles of straw.

The Aleutian Islands have been recommended by Lieut. Maury as a *coaling* station, on the route of the Pacific Steamers from California to China, planned on his proposed *Great Circle* system.

ALEXA'NDRIA, called *Iskanderieh* by the Arabs, the only seaport of Egypt, stands on an artificial neck of land which joins the continent to the ancient island of Pharos. It has two ports. The old port on the west side of the town, is at the extremity of an extensive roadstead; there are three passages into this roadstead, the deepest of which will admit frigates, and probably vessels of the line. The new port, which is on the east side of the town, is more exposed and shallower than the old port. The fort of Pharos, which is also a light-house, is connected with the island of Pharos by an artificial dyke, made in part of antient granite columns laid transversely.

Alexandria is the chief commercial town of Egypt. All the products intended for foreign export are conveyed by the Nile and Mahmoudieh Canal to Alexandria for shipment. The Mahmoudieh Canal, which was restored and completed by Mohammed Ali, in 1819, joins the Nile at Atfeh, 40 miles from Alexandria. Alexandria has become an important station in the line of communication with the East Indies, and its importance in this respect is annually increasing. Steamboats from England, Marseille, Trieste, and Constantinople, sail to and from Alexandria regularly, and goods and passengers, as well as mails, pass by the Mahmoudieh Canal and the Nile to Cairo, thence across the desert to Suez, then by the Red Sea and Arabian Sea to Bombay; and so from Bombay by the same route back again.

It is an instructive example of the changes which mark the history of commerce, that this same city of Alexandria, which is now growing in trading importance every year, was a great centre of commerce more than 2,000 years ago; while in a great part of the intervening period it sank to a position of insignificance. Humboldt, in his *Cosmos*, says:—"Under Ptolemæus Philadelphus, scarcely half a century after the death of Alexander the Great, and even before the first Punic war had shaken the aristocratic republic of the Carthagenians, Alexandria was the greatest commercial port in the world, forming the nearest and most commodious route from the basin of the Mediterranean to the south-eastern parts of Africa, Arabia, and India. The Ptolemies availed themselves with unprecedented success of the advantages held out to them by a route which nature had marked, as it were, for a means of universal intercourse with the rest of the world by the direction of the Arabian Gulf, and whose importance cannot even now be duly appreciated until the savage violence of eastern nations, and the injurious jealousies of western powers shall simultaneously diminish."

ALGÆ is the name given by botanists to the tribe of plants which comprehends the sea-weeds, lavers, and fresh-water submersed species of similar habits. Some of them are only visible to the naked eye when they are collected in heaps; others grow together in the beds of the ocean, and when they rise to the surface form floating banks of such extent as to impede the course of ships. Nearly all the useful species, and those of large dimensions, are to be found among the jointless varieties. All the kinds that are consumed in the important manufacture of kelp [KELP]; the eatable sorts, which, in the state of birds'-nests, are collected in the islands of the Indian Archipelago and sold at a high price to the Chinese; those which we consume as lava; the species that afford vegetable glue; all those from which the elementary substance called iodine is obtained; and finally the principal part of what our farmers use for manure, belong to the great tribe of *jointless Algæ*, of which 55 genera and about 160 species are known as natives of the coasts or ditches of Great Britain. The *jointed Algæ*, or *confervæ*, and the *disjointed Algæ*, are of less importance in medicine and the arts.

ALGAROTTI, FRANCESCO, a popular French writer of the last century, who had the merit of rendering science and literature fashionable amongst the upper classes of his age, is mentioned here as the author of a calculation often repeated which is a forcible illustration of the value conferred upon a raw material by industrial skill. A pound of iron, he says, cost five sous. This pound of iron is converted into steel; and this steel forms the material of the balance-spring of a watch. Each spring weighs the tenth part of a grain. Allowing for waste, the pound of iron may be fabricated into eighty thousand watch springs. Such a spring is worth eighteen francs; and thus, a material originally worth five sous, acquires a value of one million four hundred and forty thousand francs. The calculation may appear exaggerated; but the principle is unquestionable.

ALGAROVILLA is a substance which was first analysed a few years ago by Dr. Ure. It is produced from a tree which grows in Chili and other parts of South America; and consists of pods bruised and agglutinated with the extractive exudation of the seeds and husks. It contains a good deal of tannin, and may be used for tanning leather; it may be employed as the basis for a very good black ink; and it gives a brilliant yellow dye to cloth, prepared in a particular way for its application.

ALGIERS, frequently called, since its occupation by the French, *Algeria*, or *Algérie*, is better known to English readers as one of the Barbary states. It is situated on the African coast of the Mediterranean, between Tunis on the east, and Marocco on the west. It is gradually losing its Moorish character, and becoming Frenchified; though the Arabs on the southern border are as little disposed as ever to assume European customs. In the twenty years during which the French have possessed this territory (1830-1850) they have had many a struggle to maintain their position.

The fertility for which this country was renowned in ancient times still continues; in the valleys, which are watered by streams, vegetation is extremely luxuriant. The mould is of a very dark colour; in some places it is reddish, and impregnated with nitre or salt. The hills are covered with fruit trees of every kind, and the fruit is generally exquisite. A species of the lotus is found here, the fruit of which is eaten. The palm is indigenous, but the date comes from the southern side of the Atlas. Few timber trees are to be seen except a species of oak, the *quercus ballota*, which bears a very nutritive kind of acorn. The mountains near Bujeiah used to supply the dockyard of Algiers with timber. There are many species of the cypress and chestnut trees. There are also very extensive plantations of the *nessri* or white roses; these flowers are much larger than those of Europe, and yield the essence known by the name of attar of roses. The sugar-cane grows in this country; and a species of it called Soleyman rises to a great height, and gives more sugar than any other species known. The *indigofera glauca* thrives also. The grain sown is wheat, barley, Indian corn, millet, doura, and also rice.

The Kabyles, who form half the native population, are an industrious race in regard to agriculture, mining, and manufactures generally. They make guns, ploughs, and many coarse utensils, which they sell to the Arabs and Moors; they know how to temper steel, and also make sabres and knives of a tolerable quality. They manufacture gunpowder for their own use, but they never sell any of it. Common woollen and linen stuffs, olive oil, and soap made from soda and oil, are among their manufactures. The furniture of their huts is very simple; a few sheepskins or mats spread on the ground, or on a wooden platform in a corner, serve them as beds; their *hykes*, which resemble in shape the plaid of the Highlanders, and their *boornooses* or cloaks with hoods, which constitute their dress by day, serve them as blankets at night; a few baskets, earthen dishes, pots, and jars, for their milk and honey; they keep their grain and fruit in large vats made of clay baked in the sun, or bury them in holes under ground. The Arabs, Turks, and Moors, are similar in their industrial pursuits to those tribes in other countries.

In his address to the manufacturers of France, as to the articles desirable to send to the Exhibition of 1851, M. Charles Dupin enumerates several of the products of Algeria: wools; fruits; cheap oils, fit for manufacturing purposes; cork; woods, so richly coloured, and of such varied shades, for cabinet work; a material for weaving obtained from the fibres of bark or of reeds, the productions made from which are fitted for summer apartments.

ALGO'A BAY is one of those spots in Cape Colony which, by receiving emigrants from Europe, have laid the foundation for commercial intercourse between England and the semi-civilized nations of the south.

ALHAMBRA, an ancient castle and palace of the Mohammedan kings of Granada, is one of the storehouses for examples of the *Arabesque* species of ornament from time to time adopted in modern decorative art. In Mr. Owen Jones's splendid work on the Alhambra, we see how intricate are the patterns and how brilliant the colours of the decorations with which the walls are adorned. A brief account of the existing state of the building may not be misplaced.

The Alhambra is situated on a hill, which runs out to the east of the town of Granada It is surrounded by a strong wall, flanked by square towers, and enclosing an area of 2500 feet in length, and 650 in breadth. The walls follow all the windings of the mountain, and are constructed of 'tapia,' an artificial concrete, consisting of pebbles, rubble, and lime, put moist into a wooden frame. When the mortar was set, the frame was removed, and the portions were used successively in building the walls, which grew harder by time. The colour is reddish, and hence the name 'al-hamra,' 'the red.'

The exterior appearance of the Alhambra is simple and severe, and gives no indication of the gorgeous beauty which once distinguished the interior. The Torre de Justicia, so called because justice was dispensed there after the manner of the East, is a square tower, with a double entrance-gate, the horseshoe arch in front rising to half the height of the tower. Having passed through the double entrance gates, a narrow passage conducts to the Plaza do los Algibes, or 'Court of the Cisterns,' which are two, the largest 102 feet long and 56 feet wide, arched over, and enclosed by a wall six feet thick. On the east side of this Plaza is the Alcabaza, which is a palace built for Charles V. in the Cinquecento style, by the architect Alonso Berreguete. On the north is a very simple and unostentatious entrance to the Mesuar, or common bathing-court, 150 feet in length and 56 in width. It is paved with white marble, and the walls covered with arabesques of admirable workmanship. In the midst of this court is a basin bordered with flowers. At the lower end of the Mesuar is an archway leading to the Patio de los Leones, or 'Court of the Lions.' It is open to the sky, measures 100 feet by 60, and is paved with white marble. In the centre of it is a large basin of alabaster, of twelve sides, resting on tho backs of twelve lions, rudely carved. Over this basin a smaller one rises, from which a large body of water spouts into the air, and falling from one basin into the other is sent forth through the mouths of the lions. This court is surrounded by a gallery supported by above 100 slender and elegant columns, 9 feet high, and 8½ inches in diameter. These columns are very irregularly placed; sometimes they are single, and sometimes in groups of two or three. The walls, up to the height of fifteen feet from the ground, are covered with blue and yellow mosaic tilings. The columns and ceiling of the gallery are beautifully ornamented with arabesques and fret-work in the most exquisite taste. Around the upper face of the Fountain of the Lions are some Arabic verses, which describe, in a style of oriental hyperbole, the wonders and the beauty of the fountain. On each end of the court projects a portico, which is also supported by slender marble columns.

On the left side of the Court of the Lions

is the Sala de los Abencerrages, and opposite to the Sala de los Abencerrages, on the other side of the Court of the Lions, is the Sala de las dos Hermanas, or 'Hall of the Two Sisters,' so called from two huge flags of white marble, without a flaw or stain, which are in the pavement. On the upper end of the Mesuar stands the magnificent Tower of Comares. This massive tower rises above the rest of the building, and overhangs a deep ravine.

The Sala de los Ambajadores, which occupies the whole of the interior of the Tower of Comares, still preserves traces of its past splendour. The walls are richly stuccoed and ornamented with arabesques of exquisite workmanship. The ceiling is of cedar-wood, inlaid with ivory, silver, and mother of pearl. The three sides of the hall are full of windows, formed in the immense thickness of the wall, which thus allow a free circulation to the air, and admit a faint light which produces a surprising effect. In the same manner all the halls of the Alhambra are lighted and ventilated. To the east of the Sala de Comares is the Tocador de la Reina, or Queen's Dressing-room, aud near it is the Garden of Lindaraja, with its alabaster fountain, and groves of roses, myrtles, and orange-trees.

When we examine the halls of the Alhambra, we are no less surprised at the elegance of their construction aud the beauty of their ornaments than at the durability of a work of such a delicate nature; the blue, the carmine, and the gold still preserve all their brilliancy and freshness; the slender columns and apparently fragile filagree work have stood the vicissitudes of five centuries.

ALICANTE, a modern province of Spain, formed of the southern portion of the kingdom of Valencia and a small part of Murcia, is noted for its fertility and industry. The inhabitants are very industrious, aod cultivate the land with great care: irrigation is much and successfully employed. Wheat is little cultivated, but rice, oranges, citrons, figs, almonds, and dates, are grown in large quantities; barilla, the sugar-cane, the cotton tree, and all equinoctial plants flourish. The quantity of wine produced is considerable, and of the best quality, especially that grown in the environs of the city of Alicante. Linen, broadcloth, soap, paper, and worsted-yarn are manufactured: there are several brandy distilleries in the province. Great attention is paid to the rearing of silk-worms and bees, and the tunny, anchovy, aud other fisheries on the coast are very productive. Nearly 1000 ships, Spanish and foreign, enter the harbour of Alicante town yearly. The greater part of its foreign trade consists of imports of linen from France and Genoa, tobacco from the United States of America, and cod-fish from Newfoundland; its exports are, barilla and almonds to England and Ireland, and wine to Brazil and the coast of Barbary. A considerable quantity of wine is also shipped to the port of Cette, in Languedoc, whence it is sent to Bordeaux, to be mixed with the inferior Medoc wines. Alicante likewise exports oil, olives, brandy, and soap: the quality of the last-mentioned article is much esteemed. The communications between the town and the contiguous country are for the most part kept up by means of small coasting vessels of from 20 to 70 tons burthen, the roads being so exceedingly bad, that such goods as are sent by land must be conveyed on the backs of mules and asses. All cotton manufactures being prohibited, a great contraband trade is carried on from Gibraltar, Algiers, and Oran, chiefly by Spanish fishing-boats

ALIQUOT PART. The determination of aliquot parts of weights or of sums of money is of so much use in commerce that it may be briefly explained here. One number or fraction is said to be an aliquot part of a second number or fraction when the first is contained an exact number of times in the second. Thus, 6, 3, 4, 2, $1\frac{1}{2}$, $\frac{1}{2}$ $\frac{1}{3}$, &c., are all aliquot parts of 12, being coutained in it respectively 2, 4, 3, 6, 8, 24, 36, &c. times. The word is principally used in the arithmetical rule called *practice*, and the convenience of using it is as follows. If we want to know how much $30\frac{1}{2}$ yards cost at 1*l.* 15*s.* 6*d.* a yard, the direct process of common arithmetic would be to turn $30\frac{1}{2}$ yards into half yards, giving 61, and 1*l.* 15*s.* 6*d.* into sixpences, giving 71. Then multiplying 61 by 71, and dividing the product by 2, we have the number of sixpences which $30\frac{1}{2}$ yards cost, which must then be reduced into pounds, shillings, and pence. But if we observe that 1*l.* 15*s.* 6*d.* is made up of 1*l.*, 10*s.* the half of one pound, 5*s.* the half of 10*s.*, aud 6*d.* the tenth of 5*s.*, we can proceed as follows:

	£	*s.*	*d.*		£	*s.*	*d.*
$30\frac{1}{2}$ yards at	1	0	0	per yard cost	30	10	0
,,	0	10	0	,,	15	5	0
,,	0	5	0	,,	7	12	6
,,	0	0	6	,,	0	15	3
,,	1	15	6	,,	54	2	9

in which each line is derived from the preceding by simple division, on the obvious principle that at 6*d.* a yard we give the tenth part of what we give at 5*s.* a yard, and so on.

ALIZARIN. [MADDER.]

A'LKALI is a word compounded of the Arabic article *al* and *kali*, the name of the plant by burning which a saline mass is obtained containing the alkali in question; and in this term are comprehended various other bodies possessing similar properties. The alkalies are numerous, and they are all compound substances; they do not result, however, from the action of any specific or alkalizing principle, being very variously constituted. All exist in nature, and some may be artificially formed. The alkalies may be divided into three classes:—

1st. *Ammonia*, existing in the animal fluids, and composed of two gaseous bodies, viz., hydrogen and azote. As it readily evaporates it was formerly called the *volatile alkali*.

2nd. *Compounds of certain metals and oxygen*, among which are potash and soda, which, though long known as the *fixed alkalies*, and usually obtained from the ashes of plants, were discovered by Davy to be metallic oxides. This class also comprehends the alkaline oxides or earths, lime, magnesia, &c. No metal yields two alkalies by different degrees of oxidizement; nor does any one become an alkali and an acid.

3rd. The *vegeto-alkalies*, produced in plants during vegetation. They are, as far as has been ascertained, quaternary compounds of oxygen, hydrogen, carbon, and azote. This class includes *quina*, an active medicinal principle of chinchona or bark, and *morphia*, one of the narcotic principles of opium, &c., [ALKALOIDS.]

The chemical and distinguishing properties of the alkalies are, that their aqueous solutions turn vegetable blues green, and vegetable yellows reddish-brown; and hence infusion of red cabbage and infusion of turmeric, or paper stained with them, are used as tests of the presence of an alkali. The alkalies restore the colour of vegetable blues which have been reddened by acids, and, on the other hand, the acids restore vegetable colours which have been altered by the alkalies. The alkalies have great affinity for and readily combine with acids, forming *salts* and the power of both in altering vegetable colours is generally destroyed. The alkalies are separated at the negative pole of the voltaic trough. In odour, taste, molecular form, and uses in the arts, the alkalies differ considerably. The salts formed with alkalies are apt to *effloresce*, and resolve the crystals into the state of powder, or to absorb water from the air, and *deliquesce*, or become liquid. The alkalies possess a power of rendering albumen soluble: unboiled white of egg is an albuminate of soda. The albumen of the blood is rendered more fluid by alkalies; hence in excess they impair the plastic power of that fluid. The chief practical uses of the alkalies are noticed under the names of the principal varieties, AMMONIA, POTASH, SODA, &c.

ALKALIMETER. Like as acids and alcohols call for the use of acidimeters and alcohometers to measure their strength, so do alkalies require the aid of analagous instruments, which may fittingly be called alkalimeters. Chemists are aware of many methods of effecting this; and neat instruments have been devised for the purpose. The German soap boilers adopt a somewhat clumsy mode of determining the strength of the alkali which they employ; they pour a quart of water on a pound of alkali, then put in a piece of Dutch soap, and add water until the soap sinks: the more water required to bring about this result, the stronger is the alkali supposed to be. But in the land of Liebig such a rough method is not likely to continue: it is being superseded by more scientific processes.

ALKALOIDS, substances which modern chemistry has discovered, are termed sometimes *vegetable alkalies* as hitherto found only in vegetables, and sometimes *organic alkalies*, from requiring a vital power to effect their formation; but the name given to them above is the most appropriate. They possess alkaline properties in the lowest degree, and are either tasteless or have a bitter acrid taste, existing generally in a solid, mostly crystalline form; some, however, are amorphous (Aconitinæ), occasionally in a liquid state (Conia and Nicotina), the latter very volatile, and readily undergoing decomposition, with an evolution of ammonia, at a moderate temperature. The point in which they differ most from the common alkalies (except Ammonia) is in having nitrogen in their composition, one of them (Caffeina) being perhaps the most highly nitrogenized compound known. Sometimes one only exists in a plant, sometimes several in the same plant, as in opium. Generally they are combined with an acid; most frequently it is a peculiar acid. Many of them are with difficulty soluble in water, more so in alcohol; they seldom completely neutralize acids, but the salts which they form are more soluble than the bases; hence various of their salts are used in medicine in preference to the primitive article. The alkaloids are less extensively used in the manufacturing arts than in medicine.

ALKERMES is the name of a favourite cordial, made in some of the northern countries of Europe. It is made from bay leaves, mace, nutmegs, cinnamon, cloves, brandy, syrup of kermes, and orange-flower water.

The first six ingredients are distilled, and the last two are employed to give flavour.

ALLANTOIN, ALLANTOIC ACID, exists in the allantoic liquid of cows, and has the form of brilliant colourless crystals derived from the rhomboid, with a vitreous appearance. It has, we believe, not yet acquired value in the arts.

ALLIUM is the botanical name of the genus of plants which includes the onion, chive, garlic, shallot, and leek. The *allium cepa*, or common onion, has many varieties; the most remarkable are the blood red, which is the most pungent; the Strasburg, which is the hardiest; the silver-skinned, which is the smallest, and the most fitted for pickling; and the Portugal and Tripoli, which are the largest and the most delicate. The *allium fistulosum*, the Welsh onion, is a native of Siberia, and is cultivated chiefly for the purpose of being sold in the markets when very young, at which time its flavour is delicate. The *allium ascalonicum*, the shallot, a native of Asia Minor, is in many respects similar to the chive. Garlic and leek are other well-known species of the genus.

MM. Fourcroy and Vauquelin have found that the common onion is composed, 1, of a white, acrid, volatile oil, holding in solution sulphur which renders it fetid; 2, of a vegeto-animal matter analogous to gluten; 3, of a good deal of uncrystallizable sugar; of a great quantity of mucilage, resembling gum arabic; 5, of phosphoric acid, either free or combined with lime, acetic acid, and a little citrate of lime; and 6, of vegetable fibre. It is to the volatile oil that the irritating properties of the onion are supposed to be owing, and they are consequently dissipated by heat.

ALLOA, a Scottish sea-port town, in the county of Clackmannan, is a place of considerable manufacturing and commercial importance. It contains large distilleries, several breweries, where ale is made which has long been in high repute, woollen manufactories (chiefly for the blanket and shawl trade), glass-works, corn and flour mills, gas works, and a great iron-foundry, chiefly for the making of steam-engines. The Devon iron-works, near the town, contribute largely to the trade of the port. Bricks, tiles, and other earthenware, copper goods, (especially distillers' apparatus), leather, tobacco, and snuff, are also extensively manufactured. The salmon fishery is carried on with considerable spirit. Alloa possesses a commodious harbour, with a depth of water of 16 feet at neap-tides, and from 22 feet to 24 feet at spring tides. Its vessels sail to every quarter of the globe; and their number and burthen was registered in 1818 at 108 vessels of 17,100 tons, including three steamers. The coasting trade is also very extensive: the export of coals alone amounting to 60,000 tons annually. The imports consist of corn, wool, wine, tea, timber, hemp, oak bark, &c.; the exports are coals, and the many industrial products of the town and neighbourhood. There is a large dry dock in the harbour; and capacious steamers work at the ferry over the Forth.

ALLOWANCE, in commerce, a deduction from the gross weight of goods, agreed on between merchants, according to the customs of particular countries and ports, the chief of which is known by the name of TARE.

ALLOXAN, ALLOXANIC ACID, and ALLOXANTIN, are three substances which organic analysis has recently placed within the domain of chemistry. The first and third are crystalline, the second is a liquid. None of them are yet, we believe, employed in the arts.

ALLOY, either a natural or artificial compound of two or more metals, except when mercury is one of them, in which case the mixture is called an *amalgam*. Native or natural alloys, considered as such, are not useful bodies, the only exception, if indeed it may be so reckoned, is the alloy of iron and nickel, constituting *meteoric iron*, of which the knives of the Esquimaux appear to be made; but artificial alloys are of the highest importance, since by uniting different metals compounds are formed which possess a combination of qualities not occurring in any one metal. Gold, silver, tin, antimony, and bismuth are generally alloyed; the first three on account of their softness, and the two latter because they are extremely brittle. Gold and silver are hardened by alloying with copper; copper is hardened by zinc, &c.

The formation of alloys appears to depend upon the chemical affinity of the metals for each other; and in some instances it seems to be wanting, for no combination occurs. Various facts may be assigned for supposing the combination to be the result of chemical affinity. M. Boussingault analysed six different native alloys of gold and silver, and found in all cases that the metals were combined in definite proportions. The change of properties which metals undergo by combining, furnishes strong evidence of its arising from chemical affinity and action; thus, with respect to colour, copper, a reddish metal, by union with zinc, which is a white one, gives the well-known yellow alloy, brass. The fusing point of a mixed metal is never the mean of the temperature at which its constituents melt; and it is generally lower than that of the most fusible metal of the alloy.

BUTTON MAKING, STAMPING, PRESSING AND PUNCHING.

THE BULL RING BIRMINGHAM.

KNIGHTS' CYCLOPÆDIA OF THE Industry of all Nations

No. 4.

All alloys formed of brittle metals are brittle; those made with ductile metals are in some cases ductile, in others brittle; when the proportions are nearly equal, there are as many alloys which are brittle as ductile; but when one of the metals is in excess, they are most commonly ductile. In combining ductile and brittle metals, the compounds are brittle, if the brittle metal exceed, or nearly equal, the proportion of the ductile one; but when the ductile metal greatly exceeds the brittle one, the alloys are usually ductile. The density of alloys sometimes exceeds, and in other cases is less than, that which would result from calculation.

Not only are the properties of metals altered by combination, but different proportions of the same metals produce very different alloys. Thus, by combining ninety parts of copper with ten parts of tin, an alloy is obtained of greater density than the mean of the metals, and it is also harder and more fusible than the copper; it is slightly malleable when slowly cooled, but on the contrary, when heated to redness, and plunged into cold water, it is very malleable: this compound is known by the name of *bronze.* If eighty parts of copper be combined with twenty parts of tin, the compound is the extremely sonorous one called *bell-metal;* an alloy consisting of two-thirds copper and one third tin, is susceptible of a very fine polish, and is used as *speculum metal.*

It is curious to observe in these alloys, that in bronze the density and hardness of the denser and harder metal are increased by combining with a lighter and softer one; while, as might be expected, the fusibility of the more refractory metal is increased by uniting with a more fusible one. In bell-metal the copper becomes more sonorous by combination with a metal which is less so: these changes are clear indications of chemical action.

The principal alloys employed in manufactures are the following:—Arsenic and copper make *packfong;* tin and lead make *solder* and *common pewter;* tin, antimony, copper, and bismuth make *best pewter* and *Britannia metal;* tin, lead, and bismuth make *fusible metal;* tin and copper, in various proportions, make *bronze, speculum metal, bell-metal,* and *gun-metal;* copper and zinc, in different proportions, make *brass* and *Dutch gold;* copper, zinc, nickel, and iron make *German silver;* silver and copper make *standard silver;* gold, silver, and copper make *standard gold.* In many of these alloys, such as the last two, the quantity of one of the metals is extremely small, but still it is sufficient to give a distinct property to the alloy.

Dr. Weiger, of Vienna, proposed in 1845 many modes of making fine alloys, chiefly for the use of dentists. Gold, silver, platina, and palladium are the metals employed; and these are taken—two or three together—in such proportions as to form eight different alloys: platinum being in every case one of the metals. In making alloys for such delicate uses as those of the dentist, the purity of the single metals is as important as the combining of the whole; and Dr. Weiger details processes in respect to both these qualities.

ALLU'VIUM, or ALLUVIAL DEPOSITS, a name given to those accumulations of sand, earth, and loose stones or gravel brought down by rivers, which, when spread out to any extent, form what is called *alluvial land.* There are three successive stages in the formation of the alluvium: viz. the crumbling of the mineral crust of the earth, by the action of the tides, currents, streams, and atmospheric agency; the transportation of the loosened fragments; and their deposition in the form of alluvium at the bottom of rivers, lakes, æstuaries, and the ocean. Alluvium is important to the arts of life in this way; that when such a deposit is made, it is fitted to become the basis of a rich vegetable soil, by converting into dry land tracts which were before covered with water, but which now form *deltas,* such as those of the Nile, the Ganges, the Rhine, the Mississippi, &c., Alluvial action also breaks down the rigidity of mineral deposits, and renders their wealth more easily attainable; as is exemplified in the gold sands of California, the diamond-washings of Brazil, the stream-tin of Cornwall, &c.

ALMADEN, a town in the Spanish province of La Mancha, about 130 miles from Madrid, is famed for its mines of quicksilver, which have been known for more than 2,000 years. The hill in which the mines are found is 120 feet high; and the cinnabar (ore of mercury) is met with in different parts of the mass. It does not appear that this district is so unhealthy as the quicksilver mines of Idria; for a miner sleeps with safety upon a vein of cinnabar. The galley-slaves, who work in these mines, are not exposed to the hardships that are commonly believed. They only work three hours a day, and do nothing but take out the earth in wheelbarrows. Some feign convulsions, and others fits, to excite the compassion of those who visit the mines. The inhabitants of Almaden work willingly double the time, and receive only half of what every slave costs the government.

The cinnabar occurs in veins which traverse the hill; and pure mercury is also found in crevices of sandstone and slate. For roasting the ore, ovens and other apparatus are provided; the ovens are twelve in number, and are called by the names of the twelve apostles. Each is capable of containing ten tons' weight of stone. The oven is kept burning for three days, and the same time is required to cool.

The celebrated German merchants, Mark and Christopher Fugger, leased the mines in the seventeenth century; but they were afterwards worked by the Spanish government.

ALMOND. The favourite fruit *Amygdalus communis*, or common almond, is a native of Barbary. In this country it is only grown for the sake of its beautiful vernal flowers; but in the countries that have a long and hot summer, it is the fruit for which it is esteemed. This, which is produced in immense quantities, is partly exported into northern countries, and partly pressed for oil, or consumed for various domestic purposes. There are two varieties of it, sweet and bitter. Of the sweet almonds the parts which are officinal are the seeds or kernels. The commercial varieties are numerous, but the most esteemed are the Jordan almonds. Triturated with water, sweet almonds form a grateful sweetish emulsion, which possesses considerable nutritous as well as demulcent properties. Almonds, as an article for the dessert, are nutritive but rather indigestible. *Oil of Almonds* may be obtained from either variety, but is yielded in great abundance by the bitter almond. Almonds which have become rancid yet yield by expression good oil, if a little calcined magnesia be added to the bruised almonds before being subjected to pressure. Almond oil is often adulterated with poppy oil. Bitter almonds are smaller and flatter than the sweet. Those most esteemed come from Provence, those least esteemed from Barbary. They have a very bitter taste, and scarcely any odour, but if rubbed between the fingers with a little water, they emit a peculiarly agreeable odour.

About 21,000 cwts. of almonds, and 6,000 cwts. of bitter almonds were imported in 1848.

ALNUS is the botanical name for the genus of *alder* trees, which comprises many useful species. The common alder, called the *alnus glutinosa*, is an inhabitant of swamps and meadows in all parts of Europe, the north of Africa and Asia, and North America. Next to the charcoal from black dogwood (*Rhamnus frangula*), that supplied by the common alder is of the best quality. The bark is valuable for tanning, and the young shoots for dyeing various colours; the veiny knots of its wood are cut into veneer by cabinet-makers, and its stems, hollowed out, are among the best materials, next to metal, for water-pipes and underground purposes.

ALOE, a genus of succulent plants, the best species of which is the *Aloe Soccotrina*, a native of the Cape of Good Hope and the Island of Soccotra. Attention to the mode of extracting the juice might render aloes, whencesoever procured, of excellent quality. But from the different plans of collecting and inspissating the juice, results an article which differs considerably in appearance and greatly in value. Aloes is one of the few drugs in which adulteration is not extensively practised further than by substituting the inferior and low-priced kinds for the superior. When carelessly prepared, sand and fragments of leaves and skins are frequently found in the samples. Caballine, or *horse* aloes, has nearly disappeared from commerce, refinement or fashion in veterinary medicine deeming it not fit for horses. Barbadoes aloes comes to this country in the gourds and calabashes into which it is poured when prepared. Each of these weighs from sixty to even eighty pounds.

Few more valuable drugs exist, as is proved by the numerous preparations made either of aloes alone, or with some other articles combined with it. These combinations have various objects in view, some to heighten its powers, others to modify, and some to get rid of certain well-founded objections to its effects. The use of aloes is almost entirely confined to medicine.

ALOPECU'RUS. [GRASS.]

ALPA'CA, or PACO, is the wool of the *llama*, or goat of Peru and Chili. The introduction of alpaca wool in manufactures has attracted considerable attention, and the question of naturalizing the alpaca in this country, in Germany, and in Australia, is also an object of much interest. The wool of the alpaca is superior to English wool in length, softness, and pliability. The fleece averages from 10 to 12 pounds, while that of our sheep is seldom more than 8 pounds; and while the staple of English wool does not often exceed six inches in length, that of the alpaca varies from eight to twelve inches. The lustrous appearance of the alpaca wool renders it applicable to many of the purposes for which silk is usually employed in textile fabrics; and it is found a useful substitute for Angora wool. The manufacture of plain and figured stuffs from the fleece of the alpaca was commenced at Bradford, in Yorkshire, a number of years ago, and there is a large and increasing use of alpaca wool. In 1844 five different articles were manufactured at Bradford for her Majesty, from the wool of an alpaca which had been kept at Windsor, copies of which articles were exhibited at the Free Trade Bazaar in 1845.

Besides the use of the wool in textile fabrics, the flesh of the alpaca is also wholesome and palatable. The carcase weighs on an average about 180 lbs.

The question of naturalising the alpaca has been taken up with great enthusiasm by a few persons; but very little progress has yet been made in demonstrating its practicability. The alpaca inhabits the mountainous and inhospitable regions of Peru, and is remarkable for its abstemiousness. It thrives on coarse food. Those which have been brought to this country have been confined in parks and richly cultivated lands, and have been treated with too much care and tenderness. Mr. Walton asserts that they will live where our hardiest sheep would starve, and that the wildest parts of Great Britain are best suited to their habits. If the alpaca may be pastured on lands which are now waste and unprofitable, and where the hardiest sheep would starve, the naturalization of the animal would undoubtedly prove a great national benefit; but if this is not the case, it is a question whether a constant demand for the wool as an article of import would not be quite as beneficial.

Alpaca is now used to a very large extent in manufactures—umbrellas, paletôts, and various articles and garments are made of it, as it presents a sort of compound of the qualities of silk and woollen.

ALPS. In a commercial point of view, the Alps are interesting to the extent that they afford practicable passes for carriage roads, across or between their summits. These passes and roads are as follow:—In the *Maritime Alps*, which extend from the Gulf of Genoa to Monte Viso, a distance of about 100 miles, the only carriage-road across is by the Col de Tende, at an elevation of 5887 feet, formed by Napoleon; there are three or four smaller roads practicable for mules. In the *Cottian Alps*, which extend from Monte Viso to Mont Cénis, a distance of about 60 miles, the carriage-road of Mont Genèvre, formed by Napoleon, is the chief pass, leading from the valley of the Durance in France to Susa in Piedmont. In the *Graian Alps*, extending from Mont Cénis to the Col de la Seigne, about 60 miles, is Mont Cénis, one of the best known of the Alpine passes. This pass was only a mule-road till 1803, when Napoleon commenced a magnificent carriage-road, which crosses the chain at a height of 6773 feet. The pass of the Little St. Bernard, which is supposed to be that by which Hannibal entered Italy, crosses the Graian Alps to the Val d'Aosta. In the *Pennine Alps*, extending about 60 miles from Mont Blanc to the Simplon, are Mont Blanc, Monte Rosa, and Mont Cervin, the three loftiest peaks in Europe. On each side of Mont Blanc are cols or passes of the mountains, usually traversed by pedestrians in their tours about Mont Blanc. There are three larger passes, however, viz. the *Great St. Bernard*, with a Hospice at the height of 7963 feet above the level of the sea; the *Cervin*, at a height of 11,096 feet; and the *Simplon*, the pass of which, at an altitude of 6578 feet, is one of Napoleon's most magnificent works. In the *Helvetic or Lepontian Alps*, extending from the Simplon to Mont St. Gothard, a distance of about 60 miles, is the pass of St. Gothard, a valuable carriage-road from Switzerland to Italy, which has a summit level 6890 feet high. In the *Rhætian Alps*, which extend about 80 miles east from St. Gothard, are many good passes for travellers. One is the Mont St. Bernardin, at an elevation of 6700 feet; another the Splugen; another the Maloya, 8130 feet; another the Stelvio, 9174 feet; and another the Brenner, 4660 feet—all of which connect Tyrol and the Grisons on the north with Lombardy on the south. In the *Noric*, *Julian*, and *Carnic* Alps, which bend round from the Tyrol towards the head of the Gulf of Venice, are the high roads from Salzburg to Venice, and from Vienna to Trieste. In these, as in most other parts of the Alpine chains, the neighbouring governments are vying with or rather aiding each other to add to the number of carriage-passes.

The central ranges of the Alps are, in a great measure though not altogether, composed of gneiss, mica slate, talcose slate, and others of the like character. Gneiss may be considered as very abundant: it constitutes the mass of Mont Blanc, and of several other lofty mountains. The mica slates occasionally contain many minerals, among which may be enumerated garnet, staurotide, cyanite, hornblende, tourmaline, and titanite. Other portions of the Alps present newer geological formations, many of which will form a storehouse of materials for manufactures, as soon as man shall have located his industrial establishments in those parts.

The number of mines worked in the Alps is not very considerable, when compared with the great extent of the mountains. A few gold and silver mines are worked, as at the Rathausberg; and others of copper, lead, iron, and anthracite. The iron-mines of Styria, Carinthia, and Carniola, are very productive. The Bleiberg in Carinthia yields some of the best lead in Europe. The quicksilver mines of Idria have been long celebrated. Salt is procured in many parts of the Tyrol and the neighbouring districts.

The vegetation of the Alps differs in many respects from that of the plains beneath. At the foot of the Alps, for instance, are rich vineyards, and wine is one of the staple products of the country; the forests consist of most of the common European trees. But at the low elevation of 1950 feet the vine is no longer capable of existing; at 1000 feet higher sweet chestnuts disappear; 1000 feet farther, and the oak is unable to maintain itself; at the elevation of 4080 feet, less than one-third of the height of Mont Blanc, the birch, as well as almost every other deciduous tree, ceases; the spruce fir alone attains the height of 5900 feet, after which the growth of all trees is arrested, not by perpetual snow, which does not occur for more than 3000 feet higher, but by the peculiar state of the soil and air.

ALSACE, is one of the most important manufacturing provinces in France. It used to consist of two districts, Upper and Lower Alsace, one of which is now included in the Department of Haut Rhin, and the other in that of Bas Rhin. Both districts are watered by the Rhine.

Lower Alsace produces corn of all kinds in quantity more than enough for the consumption. Wheat is the chief grain crop; spelt wheat is extensively grown in the north; rye also is an important crop; oats is but little grown except on the highlands. Madder and tobacco are objects of careful cultivation in the valley of the Rhine; about 25,000 acres of the best soils are under tobacco culture. Excellent hemp is grown. From cabbages, which are extensively cultivated and grow to an enormous size, a great quantity of *choucroute* or sauerkraut is made for export to Strasbourg and Germany. Among other productions must be named oleaginous seeds, onions, beans, hops, and gentian. Great quantities of large plums for preserving are grown; and also cherries, from which excellent kirschwasser is made. About 11,000,000 gallons of wine are produced annually, one half of which goes to the home consumption: the rest is exported to the right bank of the Rhine. There is a great breadth of meadow land in the department. Horses and cows are very numerous, and of good breed: both oxen and horses are employed in agriculture. The number of sheep is comparatively small. Swine are reared in great numbers; and also geese, the livers of which are used in making the famous Strasbourg pies. The woodlands are very extensive; considerable part of the timber is formed into small rafts, and floated down the Rhine to Mainz, where they are united, so as to constitute enormous rafts from 250 to 300 yards long, and 25 to 30 yards broad, conducted each by 300 or 400 men.

Iron ore is very abundant: 28 mines are worked. Lead, antimony, manganese, and some traces of silver are found. Coal mines are worked. Building stone, plaster of Paris, potters' clay, slates, and asphalte are quarried. Pebbles, admitting of a fine polish, are found in the Rhine. The department contains several mineral springs.

The industrial products are very important and numerous; they comprise fine woollen cloths, linen, calico, sailcloth, cordage, straw hats, playing cards, room paper, hair brushes, horn combs, mineral acids, oils, soap, ivory black, ironmongery, hardware, saw-blades and tools of all kinds, fire-arms, swords, surgical instruments, gloves, buff leather, dressed skins, paper, &c. There are numerous madder mills, paper mills, potteries, bleach works, breweries, tan-yards, cannon foundries, and 27 iron forges and furnaces. These branches of industry are chiefly carried on in the towns of Strasbourg, Bischwiller, Hagenau, Wasselonne, Saverne, Bouxwiller, Schélestadt, Weissembourg, Lauterbourg, &c.

Upper Alsace is situated somewhat farther to the south, or higher up the Rhine. Like the Lower district, it has numerous canals which are employed for floating timber and transporting merchandize. The products are similar to those of Lower Alsace, and more than suffice for the consumption, though formerly this was not the case. The annual vintage yields about 12,760,000 gallons, of which a considerable surplus above the home supply is exported to Switzerland and Germany. A large quantity of kirschwasser is also made. The domestic animals are similar in kind and in number to those of Bas-Rhin; but goats are much more numerous. Even amid the mountains there are some very productive valleys. Cultivation is carried on with great care. The abundant supply of wood in the Vosges Mountains furnishes fuel for the various manufactures of the department. It is floated down the streams which flow into the Ill or the Doubs.

Silver, copper, and lead are found: a great number of iron mines are worked; also mines of antimony, coal, and asphalte; rock-crystal, marble, porphyry, granite, building stone, gypsum, potter's clay, marl, ochre, &c., are quarried. There are mineral springs in several localities.

The industrial products are of the most varied description: this being one of the most active seats of the cotton manufacture in France. The manufactures generally comprise calicoes and printed cottons of all descriptions, shawls, handkerchiefs, hosiery, fine woollen cloths, flaxen and hempen fabrics, ornamental paper, straw hats, chemical products, soap, leather of all kinds, ironmongery, iron wire, clock and watch movements, pottery, &c. There are also numerous cotton, thread, and woollen yarn factories; dye-houses; sugar-refineries; establishments for distilling spirits from pressed grapes, corn, cherries, gentian, potatoes, and carrots; iron furnaces and forges, paper-mills, breweries, tanyards, potteries, and glass works. Colmar, Guebwiller, Mariakirche, Rouffach, Wintzenheim, MÜHLHAUSEN, Belfort, Cernay, Thaun, and Massevaux are the chief towns in which these varied manufactures are carried on.

The chief articles of commerce are the leading industrial products, together with wine, corn, spirits, kirschwasser, steel, bar-iron, iron castings, watch and clock movements, fruit trees, cattle, &c. We may reasonably expect that Alsace will well maintain the reputation of French manufactures in the approaching display of the world's industry.

ALSTON, or ALDSTONE, in Cumberland, is the centre of a district which, though mountainous and sterile, is rich in mineral wealth. It is one of the principal lead districts in England, the produce at present being about 9000 tons per annum. Many of the lead-mines belong to Greenwich Hospital, to which they were given on the forfeiture of the estates of the unfortunate Earl of Derwentwater, who was engaged in the Rebellion of 1745. A little copper is raised in the neighbourhood, and a small per centage of silver is extracted from the lead ore. A branch of the Newcastle and Carlisle Railway is now (1850) being constructed from Haltwhistle to Alston.

ALTAI MOUNTAINS, forming a line of division between Siberia and Tartary, are rich in gold, silver, copper, and lead. The mines containing these metals were worked at some remote period, but by whom or when is not known. They were re-opened by the Russians in the last century, and have been since then extensively worked. The region contains poplars, willows, medlars, privets, whitethorns, and wild roses, on the low banks of the Irtish; and large forests of larch, birch, and other trees, on the slopes of the mountain. The inhabitants use as a substitute for tea the dried leaves of the *Saxifraga crassifolia*. Agriculture is carried on, but not to a great extent, in the valleys. With the exception of mining, the chief occupation of the inhabitants is that of pasturing cattle. The mode in which commercial intercourse is kept up between this remote region and the various countries of Europe and Asia, is noticed under RUSSIA and SIBERIA.

ALTAR-PIECE. We are accustomed in this country to give the name of Altar-piece only to paintings on sacred subjects placed over the altar at churches; but in earlier times the same name was given to small elaborately worked productions in gold and silver, and other metals, connected with the offices of religion. The recent exhibition of Mediæval Art at the rooms of the Society of Arts (1850) contained many such specimens in which much skill was often shewn both by the artist and the artificer. One was an altar-piece of silver, partly gilt, enriched with scrolls and garlands, and enclosing enamels and gems.

ALTIMETER, is the name which the Rev. E. L. Berthon gives to a measuring instrument patented by him in 1850. It is a somewhat complicated contrivance, intended to measure the altitude of the sun, moon, or a star. There are two glass bulbs, one containing mercury and the other spirit, and placed in connexion with each other by vertical and horizontal tubes. A telescope is attached through which the object is viewed. The vertical tubes are graduated; and the heights at which the two fluids adjust themselves in these tubes, when the telescope is directed obliquely upwards, is made to indicate the altitude or angle of elevation of the object viewed, by a particular arrangement of the several parts.

ALTON, in Hampshire, has become quite celebrated for the ale produced there; the breweries are conducted on an extensive scale. There are also paper manufactures; and in the vicinity are fine and prolific hop-grounds. The Farnham branch of the South Western Railway is to be extended to Alton.

ALTO-RILIEVO (high relief), a term which designates that kind of sculpture which is executed on a flat surface, but projects considerably above the ground or plane. The most legitimate use of alto-rilievo is where it is introduced in alternate or occasional compartments to give relief by the boldness of its projections to the uniformity of a large surface. Such are the Metopes among the Elgin Marbles, which, alternately with the triglyphs, ornamented the frieze of the entablature which surmounted the exterior colonnade of the Parthenon. Fifteen of these original Metopes, with one cast, are in the British Museum; they are of unequal execution, but several of them may be referred to as the finest examples extant of alto-rilievo.

A'LTONA, the largest and most populous town in the duchy of Holstein, has extensive trade with France, England, the Mediterranean, and the West Indies. Ship-building is carried on to a considerable extent, and several vessels belonging to Altona are annually employed in the herring and whale fisheries. It enjoys in respect of trade several privileges, which constitute it a free port, and all sects, Jews included, have civil and religious liberty. A railroad connects the town with Kiel, a port on the Baltic. The principal manufactures consist of silk, woollen and cotton goods, tobacco, soap, and vinegar; there are also glass-houses, distilleries, breweries, and sugar-refineries in the town.

ALUM, is an earthy salt, which occurs in a nativo state only in small quantities; but it has been long artificially made and extensively employed in various chemical manufactures. Its basis is sulphate of alumina, combined usually with sulphate of potash, but sometimes with sulphate of soda or sulphate of ammonia: when the first alkaline salt enters into its composition, the product is *common* or *potash alum*, the second forms *soda alum*, and the third *ammonia alum*.

At La Tolfa, in Italy, alum is prepared from an alum-stone, which contains all the ingredients mixed with silica. At the alum-works near Whitby, in Yorkshire, alum is produced from alum-slate, the stratum of which is nearly thirty miles in length. Near Glasgow alum is manufactured from *clay slate;* which is obtained from coal mines, and contains a double sulphate of iron and alumina. Alum is also produced in chemical works, by the direct union of the component ingredients.

The alum mine at Hurlet is well worthy of a visit; it possesses many of the striking characteristics of most mines, without being so deep or so dirty as the majority of those underground workings. The land belongs to the Earl of Glasgow, and contains beneath the surface beds of alum, iron, coal, and lime; and what is very curious is, that the owner leases these different kinds of mineral riches to different parties, even though they may occur in immediate juxta-position; thus, the Hurlet Alum Company leases the alum deposits, but must not touch the other treasures, even though they occur in the same excavations; and it thus happens that alum miners and other miners may be met with in the same galleries or passages. We descend a square shaft, the mouth of which is visible in the middle of a field; and after a few lengths of narrow ladder have been descended, the mouth of a dark horizontal passage is reached—rendered by degrees dimly visible by the candles carried by the miners. At one place we encounter a party of coal-miners, with bits of lighted candle stuck in their caps, and occupied in the various operations incident to coal-mining. At another a party of lime-workers come into view, quarrying the hard white stone which forms the object of their labours, and baring the upper parts of their bodies to render the heat more endurable. At a third spot we fall in with the alum-miners, who do not meddle with the iron, the coal, or the lime, which are around them. The philosophy of this multiform mining is thus explained. There is a stratum of lime over a stratum of coal; and between the two is a stratum (varying from two to twelve inches in thickness) of ore containing most of the chemical elements of alum. When the coal has been for some years excavated, the alum ore, by being exposed to atmospheric influence, undergoes a slight mechanical and chemical change, which fits it for being used in the manufacture of alum. Sometimes specimens of ore are met with in which a hard slaty substance is interstratified with layers of a greenish white crystalline body; sometimes the ore presents itself as a brownish-black kind of coaly slate; but for the most part the ore clings to the roof of the excavated passages as a crumbling powdery substance. To collect, then, these various forms and stages of alum ore, is the work of the miners; and the pick and the shovel, the basket and the wheelbarrow, are dimly seen by the flickering light of the candles, acting their part in the operations.

Arrived again in open daylight we find a large area of ground occupied by steeping-pits and other arrangements for the manufacture of alum. If the ore is in the efflorescent state, it is steeped in water containing sulphate of iron and alumina, and the water is boiled, evaporated, and crystallized into alum; but if the ore is in the hard stony state, it requires to be roasted or burned in a large heap built up in the open air, before the elements which compose it can be acted on by the liquid solution.

Alum is colourless, inodorous, has an astringent taste, and crystallizes generally in regular octahedrons; but by the addition of alumina, and particular management, it may be made to crystallize in cubes. It is brittle, and easily reduced to powder; its specific gravity is about 1.731; water, at 60° Fahrenheit, dissolves about one-eighteenth of its weight of alum, and boiling water about three-fourths of its weight. The solution reddens vegetable blue colours strongly; when exposed to dry air, alum effloresces slightly on the surface, but it remains long without undergoing any change internally. When moderately heated, alum dissolves in its water of crystallization; if more strongly heated, the water is evaporated, and when exposed to a very high temperature, sulphuric acid is expelled, and there remains a mixture of alumina and sulphate of potash.

The above-named properties relate to *common* or *potash alum. Soda alum* is produced by the action of sulphate of soda on sulphate of alumina. Their properties are very closely allied to those of potash alum.

Alum is decomposed, not only by heat, but by many of the acids, alkalies, and earths. It is employed for a vast number of purposes. It is used in lake colours, dyeing, calico printing, leather dressing; and by candle-makers to harden the tallow and render it white. It is an ingredient in making pyrophorus; and in medicine it is employed as an astringent.

Mr. Cliff obtained a patent in 1845 relating to the alum manufacture, in which a double useful result is sought to be obtained. Many kinds of fire-clay used for making retorts, crucibles, and similar articles, contain an excess of alumina, which injures the quality of the articles made from them when at a high heat. Mr. Cliff proposes to take a very aluminous clay, such as is found at Wortley near Leeds; to grind it, calcine it, mix it with sulphuric or some other acid, dissolve the alumina out of it, evaporate the solution, and obtain alum from the residue by the usual chemical means. The earthy sediment, which results when all or nearly all the alumina has been removed, is then to be mixed up with ground native clay, to make a fire-clay fitted for retorts, &c. Many other patents have been recently taken out, for various improvements in the alum manufacture.

The proprietors of some of the chemical works near Newcastle intend to exhibit, at the great display of 1851, specimens of alum, in large masses, procured by the direct chemical union of the component ingredients.

ALU'MINA, the earthy oxide of aluminum, sometimes called argil, or argillaceous earth, constitutes the larger portion of all clays, and their plastic property is owing to it. In a pure state it is procured from alum, from which it derives its name. Alumina is widely diffused throughout the earth; the adamantine spar or corundum, the ruby, and sapphire, are alumina nearly pure and crystallized; these substances have not, however, any of the more obvious properties of common clay, for instead of being amorphous, soft, and diffusible through water, they are crystallized, are among the hardest substances in nature, and will not mix with water. The diaspore is a crystallized mineral, which consists almost entirely of alumina and water; and in North America another hydrate of alumina has been found, and called gibbsite.

Alumina is white, powdery, and light; it has neither taste nor smell, and it adheres to the tongue. It is insoluble in water. It shrinks considerably by heat, and may be fused at a high temperature. Alumina is not in itself either acid or alkaline; but it combines with numerous acids to form salts, among which the *acetate of alumina* is much employed in calico printing. It also combines with potash, soda, lime, and magnesia, so as to form salts called *aluminates*.

ALUMINUM, the metallic base of alumina, is prepared with too great difficulty to be useful in the arts in its separate state.

AMADO'U, *touch-match*, or *German tinder*, is a brown leathery substance prepared from the *Bolėtus igniarius*, a fungus which grows on the trunks of cherry, ash, and other trees. The fungus is perennial, and increases yearly in size. The soft spongy substance of the fungus, after removing the outer covering, is cut into thin slices, and beaten with a mallet to soften it. In this state it is used for stopping hæmorrhages, and for other surgical purposes; and by subsequent boiling in a strong solution of saltpetre it is prepared for use as tinder, constituting the *German tinder* of the tobacconists. To render it very inflammable it is sometimes imbued with gunpowder, which gives it a darker colour.

On the Continent, before the use of congreve lights, tobacco-smokers were accustomed to carry about with them a box containing a little amadou and a small flint and steel.

AMALGAM, a compound of two or more metals, of which one is always mercury; and this circumstance distinguishes an *amalgam* from a mere *alloy*. Nature presents us with only one amalgam, which is of silver, and is termed by mineralogists *native amalgam*: it is met with either semifluid, massive, or crystallized. Klaproth found it to exist of 64 parts of mercury and 36 of silver, out of 100 parts. Most metals may be amalgamated with mercury, and the combination appears to depend on chemical affinity. When the cohesion of a metal is slight, as in the cases of potassium and sodium, or when its affinity for mercury is considerable, as in the instances of gold and silver, amalgamation takes place readily by mere contact. When, on the other hand, the cohesion of a metal is strong, or its affinity for mercury is weak, heat, or intermediate action, or both, are requisite to effect amalgamation. The density of an amalgam exceeds that of the mean of the metals; this and the tendency exhibited by one or both metals to oxidize, are indications of chemical combination. Antimony offers an example of metals which will not amalgamate without heat; in order to effect combination, it must be melted, and while liquid mixed with hot mercury. It has been stated, that they may be amalgamated by mixing the filings of the metal with powdered alum, and rubbing them together in a mortar with a little water; after trituration the alum may be washed out. By the intervention of tin or zinc, iron may be combined with mercury, and a double amalgam is formed. Platina also unites with mercury by the intervention of the amalgam of potassium, but not by direct action.

Amalgams are either liquid, soft, or hard; their form being dependent, in some cases, upon the quantity of mercury employed, and, in others, upon the nature of the metal amalgamated: thus, an amalgam consisting of eighty parts of mercury and one part of sodium, is solid, whilst a compound of fifteen parts of mercury and one part of tin is liquid. The liquid amalgams resemble mercury in appearance, except that the greater part of them flow less readily: solid amalgams are brittle. In general, amalgams are white; they are all crystallizable, and they form compounds of definite proportions. The amalgams of the more oxidable metals, as of potassium and sodium, are decomposed by exposure to the air and absorbing oxygen, and they decompose water with the evolution of hydrogen gas; the double amalgam of iron and zinc does not rapidly undergo any change, and is not attracted by the magnet. All amalgams are decomposed by a red heat, the mercury being volatilized, and the more fixed metals remaining. The process of amalgamation and decomposition is employed to separate gold and silver from their ores; the mercury obtained by decomposing the amalgams is distilled, and repeatedly used for the same purpose, with comparatively little loss. The amalgams of gold and silver are employed in the processes of gilding and plating. (For the mode of silvering the interiors of hollow glass globes, see MIRROR.) The amalgam of tin is largely used in what is termed silvering mirrors, and various amalgams of tin and zinc are employed for exciting electricity in the machine. Some curious effects result from the action of amalgams upon each other: if mercury be added to the liquid amalgam of potassium and sodium, an instant solidification ensues, and heat enough to inflame the latter metals is evolved. When, on the other hand, a solid amalgam of bismuth is put in contact wtth one of lead, they become fluid, and the thermometer sinks during their action.

Some of the French dentists use an amalgam of copper to fill the cavities of hollow teeth. It is gray, very hard, and adheres firmly in its place. There are many useful applications for it as a stopper to machines and chemical apparatus wherever other materials cannot conveniently be used. It is said to consist of 70 parts of mercury to 30 of copper.

AMALGAMATION is a term often used to indicate the process of separating gold and silver from their ores. It will suffice to refer to CALIFORNIA; GOLD; MERCURY; SILVER.

A'MAZON, or MARAÑON, or ORELLA'NA. This magnificent South American river (the largest on the globe) produces on its banks cacao, sarsaparilla, copaiba, caoutchouc, fine forest trees, and many other plants; and the river itself yields abundance of fish. But the slow progress of European enterprize in that region has yet done little to make its resources available, although steam navigation has begun to develope itself on the Amazon.

AMBER, a carbonaceous mineral which occurs in beds of lignite, in Greenland, Prussia, France, Switzerland, and some other countries. The greater portion of it comes from the southern coasts of the Baltic Sea, where it is thrown up between Königsberg and Memel. It is also obtained by mining at a distance of 200 feet from the sea, and at a depth of about 100 feet, and is found in small cavities. It is occasionally met with in the gravel beds near London, in which case it is merely an alluvial product. Amber occurs generally in small pieces, which are sometimes colourless, frequently light yellow, or deep-brown, and very commonly translucent.

The amber-gathering on the shores of the Baltic in 1844 was more abundant than was ever before known at the same spot. In the village of Kahlberg alone, where the amber-gathering is farmed, 20,000 thalers' worth of amber was picked up in the course of a few weeks. It is supposed, according to a paragraph in the *Elbing Zeitung*, copied into the English journals, that this increased quantity may have resulted from the violent storms which prevailed on the shores of the Baltic in the preceding winter, by which the treasure was driven up from the bottom of the sea.

Amber is rather harder than common resins, which it resembles in several properties: it is susceptible of a good polish, and when rubbed becomes electrical; indeed, the word *electricity* is derived from ἤλεκτρον, the Greek name for amber. Its density varies from 1.065 to 1.070: when bruised it exhales a slight aromatic odour; and when heated to 448° of Fahrenheit it melts, then inflames and burns with a bright flame, and emits a smell which is not disagreeable.

The subject of the origin of amber is one

which has been much discussed. According to Berzelius it was originally a resin dissolved in a volatile oil or natural balsam; the proofs of this opinion are, he conceives, numerous; it has often the impression of the branches and bark upon which it has flowed and solidified; it often contains insects, some of which are so delicately formed that they could not have occurred except in a very fluid mass. Sir David Brewster concludes, from an examination of the optical properties of amber, that it is an indurated vegetable juice. Humboldt says, in his *Cosmos*, "The petrified wood which frequently surrounds amber had early attracted the attention of the ancients. This resin, which was at that time regarded as so precious a product, was ascribed either to the black poplar, or to a tree of the cedar or pine genus. The recent admirable investigations of Professor Göppert, at Breslau, have shewn that the latter conjecture is the more correct." Amber consists of a mixture of several substances, which are, a volatile oil, two resins soluble in alcohol and in ether, succinic acid, and a bituminous body that resists the action of all solvents, and which is the principal part of amber. Water does not act upon this substance; it does not even dissolve any of the succinic acid. Alcohol takes up a soft, yellow, limpid resin. Sulphuric and nitric acid both dissolve it.

Amber is employed for ornamental purposes in the manufacture of necklaces, &c. It is used also for preparing amber varnish, for obtaining a peculiar oil used in medicine, and it yields succinic acid employed in chemical investigations.

Mr. Stelling has recently introduced an improved method of making varnish from amber. The difficulty hitherto has been in melting the varnish: the subsequent incorporation with oil and the other ingredients is comparatively easy. The melting is effected in a copper vessel of peculiar construction, whereby the amber becomes liquid without any residuum, and without evaporation of its constituent elements; there is less danger from fire than in the older methods, and the vessel is not liable to burst, which the earthen vessels formerly used were apt to be.

The largest piece of amber at present known is in the Royal Cabinet at Berlin; it weighs 18 lbs. The sum of 5000 dollars is said to have been lately offered by some Armenian merchants, for a piece of amber weighing 13 lbs. This substance is joined and mended by moistening the surfaces with linseed oil, and strongly pressing them together, gently heating them at the same time. In the working of amber the material is wrought in a lathe, polished with whiting and oil, and rubbed with flannel. It becomes so electrical during the working that the workmen are said to suffer considerable inconvenience. By a careful application of heat the workmen are enabled to harden amber. The beautiful black varnish used by coach-makers is a very carefully prepared compound of amber, asphaltum, linseed oil, and oil of turpentine. Factitious or imitation amber is often prepared from shell-lac or gum copal.

Amber is admitted duty free, but manufactured articles in amber pay an import duty of 15 per cent.

AMBERGRIS, a substance of animal origin, found principally in warm climates, floating on the sea, or thrown on the coasts. The best comes from Madagascar, Surinam, and Java. It has been found in the intestinal canal of the *physeter macrocephalus*, mixed with the remains of several marine animals which have served it for food; on this account it has been supposed to be a morbid product, analogous to biliary calculi.

Ambergris of good quality is solid, opaque, of a bright gray colour, which is darkest externally, and intermixed with yellow or reddish striæ. When it is heated or rubbed it exhales an odour which is agreeable to most persons. It is sufficiently soft to be flattened between the fingers. Its specific gravity varies from 0.908 to 0.920. When ambergris is heated with boiling alcohol of specific gravity 0.833, until it is saturated, a peculiar substance, called *ambrein*, is obtained as the solution cools, grouped in mammillated, small, colourless crystals. Ambrein, thus obtained, is brilliant, white, and insipid; it has an agreeable odour. When heated upon platina foil it fuses, smokes, and is volatilized, leaving scarcely any residue; by dry distillation it becomes brown. It is very soluble in strong alcohol, either hot or cold, in ether, and in oils both fixed and volatile. Nitric acid converts it into a pecular acid, called *ambreic acid*.

Ambergris is used as a perfume; and as the alcoholic solution is the most odorous preparation of it, it is generally employed in that form.

Ambergris is admitted duty free.

AMBOYNA, one of the Molucca or Spice Islands, in the eastern seas, is a mountainous place, abundantly furnished with trees and underwood. Sulphur is produced among the hills, some of which are encrusted with a copious efflorescence of that mineral. The earliest visit made to Amboyna by any Europeans was in 1511, when the Portuguese traded to, and afterwards took possession of it.

They held it till driven out by the Dutch in the sixteenth century; about which time the English East India Company also wished to have a share in the valuable spice trade of this and the other Molucca Islands. From that time to the present, except for a short period during the last war, the island has belonged to the Dutch. The main object of the different European powers, who endeavoured to possess themselves of Amboyna, was to monopolize the trade in cloves, the cultivation of which spice forms the principal object of industry with the natives. With the desire of keeping the cultivation of the clove-tree completely within their power, the Dutch caused it to be extirpated from every island belonging to them except Amboyna, where they provided for a sufficient production of the spice, by obliging every native family to rear a certain number of clove-trees. In the prosecution of their plans the island was divided into 4,000 allotments, each one of which was expected to support 125 trees, and a law was passed in 1720 rendering it compulsory upon the natives to make up the full complement. The number of trees upon the island accordingly amounted to 500,000, the average produce of which exceeded one million of pounds of cloves annually.

AMBULATORY, in architecture, the space enclosed by a colonnade or an arcade. In the peripteral temple of the Greeks, the lateral or flanking porticoes are properly termed ambulatories; the cloister of a monastery is surrounded by an ambulatory or ambulatories. The aisles of the ancient Basilica, and those of the cathedral, or other large church, are sometimes called ambulatories.

AMERICA. This great continent has been made known to Europeans partly by the eagerness which commercial nations shew to extend the sphere of their operations, partly by mere national glory, partly by a love for geographical science, and partly by missionary zeal. So far as the commercial incentive has been concerned, we may take a rapid glance at the progress of its discovery.

The whole career of Columbus was in effect a carrying out of the commercial spirit which in his days marked the courts of Spain and Portugal. The riches of India having become known, a wish was entertained to find a western route thither; and in searching for this western route, Columbus discovered America. In his first expedition, made in 1492, he discovered San Salvador, Cuba, Hayti, and other islands of the West Indies, which he so named in ignorance that the vast Pacific intervened between them and India proper. In the next expedition Columbus discovered Jamaica. In a third, his discoveries included Trinidad, and the coast of South America near the Orinoco. The success of Columbus soon gave encouragement to private adventurers to the new world, one of the first of whom was Alonzo de Ojeda, who, in 1499, followed the course of Columbus to the coast of Paria, and, standing to the west, ranged along a considerable extent of coast beyond that on which Columbus had touched, and thus ascertained that this country was part of the continent.

In 1497, while Columbus was engaged in his researches, the coast of North America had been reached by an English vessel, commanded by Giovanni Gaboto, or Cabot, a Venetian settled in Bristol, who undertook an expedition in company with his son Sebastian, and explored a long line of the North American coast. In 1498, Sebastian Cabot, in another expedition, visited Newfoundland. In 1500, Gaspar Cortereal, a Portuguese, touched at Labrador; and Brazil was accidentally discovered by a Portuguese fleet under Cabral. The coast of the province of Tierra Firma, from Cape de Vela to the Gulf of Darien, was first visited by Bastidas, a Spaniard, in 1501. Yucatan was discovered by Diaz de Solis and Pinzon in 1508, and Florida by Ponce de Leon, in 1512. In the same year, Sebastian Cabot reached the bay since called Hudson's Bay. The Pacific, or Southern Ocean, was first seen from the mountain tops near Panama, by Balboa, in 1513, and, two years after, a landing was effected on the south-east coast of South America, about the mouth of the Rio de la Plata, by De Solis.

The French now began to participate in the zeal for adventure, and in 1524 an expedition was dispatched by Francis I., under Giovanni Verazzano, a Florentine, who surveyed a line of coast of seven hundred leagues, comprising the United States, and part of British America. But in 1508, Aubert, a Frenchman, had already discovered the St. Lawrence River. Jacques Cartier, also a Frenchman, in 1534 nearly circumnavigated Newfoundland, and entered the Gulf of St. Lawrence. The coast of California, on the west side of the northern division of the continent, was discovered by Ximenes, a pilot, who had murdered Mendoza, a captain, dispatched by Cortez on a voyage of discovery; the Gulf of California, or Sea of Cortez, was first entered by Francisco de Ulloa, another captain sent out by Cortez in 1539. The Spaniards subsequently undertook several unsuccessful voyages, but they did not abandon their hopes, and at the close of the 16th century Sebastian Viscaino advanced along the coast of New Albion as far as the Oregon or Columbia River.

Colonization in North America by England commenced in the time of Queen Elizabeth. Sir Humphry Gilbert was the first to attempt it, though he merely took formal possession of Newfoundland, in 1583; his half-brother, the celebrated Sir Walter Raleigh, in 1584, dispatched an expedition which discovered the country then called Virginia, and he made several attempts to colonize it without effect. The colonies of Virginia and New England were respectively planted in 1607 and 1620, under James I., and it is not a little remarkable that one hundred and six years elapsed after North America was first visited by Cabot, before a single Englishman had effectually settled in the country.

Within the last half century many exploring parties have traversed the interior regions of America. The recent discoveries of treasure in California have led to a new series of overland researches, some of them in connection with a proposed railway.

British researches in North America have been chiefly directed to the examination of the western coast, under Cook, Clarke, Meares, Vancouver, &c; and to arctic or north-west expeditions. In 1818 the British government commenced that series of expeditions which, aided by the Hudson's Bay Company, and by private enterprize, and conducted by Parry, John and James Ross, Lyon, Franklin, Richardson, Beechey, Scoresby, Dease, Simpson, Ray, King, Back, and others, have resulted in those discoveries which have become such a source of public interest in this country. Would that we could close the mention of them with any announcement of the safety of Sir John Franklin and his enterprizing companions!

The exploratory researches in South America have not been so numerous as in the north; but some of them have been of great value, both geographically and commercially: especially those of De la Condamine, Godin, Humboldt, Bonpland, Spix, and Martius.

When America was first discovered, a large part of it consisted of one vast forest, extending nearly from the Atlantic to the Mississippi, and from the Canadian lakes to the Gulf of Mexico—2,000 miles in length, with an average breadth of 1,000. Most of this vast forest yet remains; but the tract west of the Mississippi contains extensive plains. These plains are devoid of trees; but the lower parts of the Mississippi valley, with a portion towards the north, are still covered with a dense forest, spread interminably like an ocean. The *prairies* of this valley are found both on the east and west side of the channel of the river; they are extensive, elevated, and generally irregular tracts, without trees, though sometimes capable of producing them, covered in the spring with countless flowers and long grass, and often possessing a deep rich soil.

South America is rich in mineral produce. Gold is found in New Granada, Peru, Chili, La Plata, and Brazil; and diamonds have been for some time a part of the Brazilian exports. The silver mines in Peru are very rich, and in Chili there are mines of silver, lead, and sulphur; those of copper are still more abundant. There are mines of iron, sulphur, antimony, tin, lead, copper, and quicksilver, in Brazil; but the pursuit of the precious metals appears to have diverted attention from other mining speculations. America also sends to Europe pearls and other precious stones.

In North America we find the bison, the musk ox, the reindeer, the wapiti, the Virginian deer, the elk, the long-tailed deer, and the black-tailed deer of the Rocky Mountains; the Californian sheep, and the Rocky Mountain Goat. The most remarkable forms of American deer are the llamas, alpacas, and vicuñas, which tenant the craggy Andes. Long previously to the arrival of Columbus, the llama was domesticated and used as a beast of burden by the natives; its wool was manufactured into cloth, and its flesh supplied a wholesome food. Among the Rodents many are valuable as fur-bearing animals; of these we may notice the beaver, the musquash, the coypu, various species of squirrel, and the chinchilla of Peru and Chili. Many thousand skins of the beaver, of the musquash, and of squirrels, are annually imported into England from the northern regions of America; and an extensive trade in the skins of the coypu, improperly called *nutria* or otter, and also in those of the chinchilla, is carried on at Buenos Ayres. Bears are hunted by the fur traders for the sake of their skins, as are also various foxes, ermines, martins, polecats, wolverines or gluttons, lynxes and others. America now contains horses, horned cattle, sheep and goats; but these have been introduced since the time of Columbus. Horses and cattle exist in many parts of South America in great numbers, and wild herds roam the plains. They abound also in Mexico, and the great prairies of the western portions of North America.

In the United States the forests consist of pines and larches unknown in Europe, many kinds of oaks, locust-trees, black walnuts of enormous size, hickories and ashes. Tobacco, maize, and wheat, are the staple objects of cultivation.

At about the latitude of Virginia the region of cotton and rice begins. In the countries in and around the gulf of Mexico, besides indigo, coffee, sugar-cane and maize, (which here finds its native home,) the cocoa-tree, from whose seeds chocolate is prepared, is a most important species; the exportation of the seeds of this plant, which is found wild in the most burning districts, is valued at near 80,000*l.* sterling annually. Pineapples grow wild in the woods; the American aloe yields, when wounded, an abundance of sweet fluid, which is fermented into an intoxicating drink called *pulque*, and distilled into an ardent spirit known by the name of Vino Mercal. In the low woods of Honduras are found enormous forests of mahogany and logwood trees. It is here also that the tamarind and the lignum vitæ are found, the vanilla, and the jalap convolvulus. As we proceed farther and farther southward, the vegetable growth gradually changes, and all the rich and varied produce of South America meets the view.

Under the names of the chief countries, rivers, and towns of America, will be found sundry details illustrative of the produce, manufactures, and commerce of this great continent.

AMETHYST. The *Occidental* or *Common Amethyst* is a variety of quartz or rock crystal, which is met with in many parts of the world, as India, Siberia, Sweden, Germany, Spain, &c. It occurs in various forms, massive, in rounded pieces, and crystallized. The primary form of the crystal is a slightly obtuse rhomboid; but it is usually found in the secondary form of a six-sided prism, terminated at one or both ends by a six-sided pyramid. The crystals of the amethyst vary from diaphanous to translucent, and they exhibit various degrees of splendour, both externally and internally. The fracture is commonly conchoidal, and the fragments are of indeterminate form. The colour is violet or purple violet. The amethyst is sufficiently hard to give fire with steel, and to scratch glass.

The composition, by means of which the best imitation of the amethyst can be produced in glass, is said to be the following:—1000 parts of trass or colourless transparent glass; 8 parts of oxide of manganese, 5 parts of oxide of cobalt, and 0·2 parts of purple of cassius.

AMIANTHUS. [ASBESTUS.]

AMIENS, in the department of Somme, in France, has considerable trade and manufactures. Velvet, plush, camlet, quilting, serge, drugget, fine kerseymere, hosiery, and other goods, linen, cotton, and woollen, are either entirely manufactured, or, being brought to Amiens from other places in an unfinished state, are prepared for sale in other parts of the country or for exportation. There are also paper-mills and bleaching-grounds. The town serves as a mart for the numerous manufactures of the neighbourhood as far as the confines of the department. The total value of the commercial industry of the district, of which Amiens is the centre, was estimated in 1843 at 40,000,000 francs. The value of raw silk, wool, and cotton used in manufactures is set down at between 5 and 6 millions of francs, while the value of the products is stated to be between 15 and 16 millions of francs. The railroad between Amiens and Abbeville was opened in 1847.

AMLWCH, a town in the island of Anglesey in Wales, was an insignificant village till 1768, about which time the celebrated and highly productive *Parys* copper mines, in the neighbouring mountains, were discovered by the united exertions of Sir Nicholas Bayley and Messrs. Roe. Soon afterwards the *Mona* mine was discovered, in the same mountains; and both have since proved highly profitable to the Marquis of Anglesea and other proprietors, and also to the town of Amlwch. At one time, in the history of these mines, the copper ore was found in large conglomerate masses, which admitted of being quarried in open day; at another, it occurred in regular veins or lodes; and as the excavations advanced, the metal was found more and more mixed with earthy matters, so that, at the present time, the ore (chiefly sulphuret of copper) does not contain more than 4 per cent of metal, and the produce is far less remunerative than formerly. At one time the mines gave employment to 1500 men; the stock of ore on hand often exceeded 40,000 tons, and the works for smelting the ore were of great magnitude. At the present time (1850) about 1000 persons are employed at the mines, of whom 100 are engaged at the smelting works. The 2nd of March, the day on which the vein of ore at Parys mine was discovered, is kept as an anniversary holiday at Amlwch. A capacious harbour has been excavated out of the solid slate rock, for the reception of the vessels connected with the copper trade.

AMMO'NIA, the modern name of the *volatile alkali*, formerly so called to distinguish it from the more fixed alkalies; it is a gaseous body, and was first procured in that state by Priestley, who termed it Alkaline air. He obtained it from sal ammoniac, and hence the present name of the alkali.

Ammonia, like all the other alkalies, is a compound substance; it consists of nitrogen and hydrogen, in the proportion of one atom of the former to three of the latter; but these two cannot be made to combine by direct action. Ammonia is colourless, transparent, and of course invisible; possessing the elasticity and mechanical properties of atmospheric air. The smell is peculiar and extremely pungent, and its taste is highly acrid. An animal put into it is immediately killed, and a taper when immersed in it is extinguished. The density of ammoniacal gas is to that of atmospheric air, nearly as 0·5902 to 1; 100 cubic inches weigh rather more than 18 grains. It acts strongly as an alkali, turning vegetable blues green, and yellows reddish brown, and saturates acids, forming various salts. The aqueous solution is colourless, transparent, and has the pungency and alkaline property of the gas: by exposure to the air the ammonia escapes, and by the application of heat it is expelled from the water.

Ammonia is produced in many different ways, both natural and artificial. Almost every animal substance contains the elements of ammonia; and when such a substance is exposed to decomposition, oxygen and carbon combine to form carbonic acid, while hydrogen and nitrogen form ammonia; and the two together form carbonate of ammonia. If such substances as bones, hoofs, or horns, are heated in iron cylinders, ammonia is separated in combination with many other matters, and, after purifying, a liquid called *spirit of hartshorn* results. Vegetable matter containing gluten, coal-soot, and coal itself, may also be made to yield ammonia. Ammonia is produced in small quantities by many different chemical processes, but those mentioned above are the chief sources. By the heat of a spirit lamp, ammonia forms with sodium or potassium a yellowish crust of those metals, though the surfaces remain brilliant and smooth. When passed over melted iron or copper, ammonia is absorbed; and by voltaic action ammonia may be made to combine with mercury, producing an amalgam which is soft at 70° or 80° Fahrenheit, but a firm crystalline body at 32°. Ammonia combines with many of the metals to form *ammoniurets*. In many of its practical applications ammonia is used in solution in water, called *liquid ammonia*, as being more convenient than in the gaseous form.

Ammonia produces many valuable salts, when combined with acids; and those salts, as well as liquid ammonia itself, play an important part in many chemical manufactures, but still more in medicine. The carbonate of ammonia is much used by the bakers of fancy bread and light pastry. With a few drops of any aromatic essential oil it forms smelling salts. Crude sulphate of ammonia forms excellent manure. Nitrate of ammonia forms a freezing mixture with water. Muriate of ammonia is employed in dyeing; it is also used to impart pungency to snuff.

AMMONIAC, GUM, a concrete juice procured in Persia and other parts of the East, from the *dorema ammoniacum*. The juice exudes from the stalk, and is also obtained from the root. It consists of grains of various sizes, usually called *tears;* their colour is whitish, but they become yellow by the action of the air; they are shining, opaque, irregular in shape, and more or less globular; when cold, ammoniac is rather hard and brittle; it softens by the heat of the hand, but does not entirely liquify at a stronger heat. The smell is peculiar and disagreeable, and the taste is nauseous, at first mucilaginous and bitter, and afterwards acrid. Its specific gravity is 1·207. When distilled with water it loses its volatile oil, and becomes inodorous; the distilled water has the odour of the gum, and small drops of limpid colourless oil float on its surface. According to Bucholz, ammoniac consists (in 100 parts) of 72 parts of resin, 22·4 parts of gum, and slight traces of bassorine, water, &c. It is used both in medicine and in some manufacturing processes.

AMO'MUM. [CARDAMOMS.]

AMOY, a city and port of China, in an island of the same name, near the coast, is the emporium of the commerce of the province of Fokien. The merchants of Amoy are among the most wealthy and enterprising in the Chinese empire; they have formed connections all along the coast, and have established commercial houses in many parts of the eastern Archipelago. During the south-west monsoon, they freight great numbers of their smaller junks at Formosa with sugar and rice, which they sell at various ports to the northward, returning home with cargoes of drugs. Above 300 junks of the largest class—some of them 800 tons burden—belong to Amoy, and trade with Borneo, Manilla, Macassar, Java, the Soo-loo Islands, Singapore; and with Bankok, the capital of Siam.

Europeans were allowed to trade to Amoy from 1675 to 1681; but after the latter date, such trade was almost entirely prohibited, until the recent arrangements with the English government. On the 26th of August, 1841, Amoy was captured by the British; by the treaty of Nanking, dated August 29, 1842, this port, among others, was opened to our trade, and British subjects and a British consul allowed to reside at Amoy. By a supplementary treaty, dated October 8, 1843, a tariff of imports and exports was established, and other foreigners admitted to the same privileges as British subjects.

AMPHIDESMA, is the name of a genus of bivalve shells, the cartilages of some of the larger species of which, as the mother-of-pearl shells, are sold by the jewellers under the name of *peacock-stone* or *black opals.* They are not so much used now as formerly, but they are still much sought after on the continent, especially in Portugal.

AMPHIPROSTYLE, is used to designate structures having the form of an ancient Greek or Roman parallelogramic temple, with a prostyle or portico on each of its ends or fronts, but with no columns on its sides or flanks.

AMPHITHE'ATRE, was a building used by the Romans for the exhibition of gladiatorial combatants, and of fights with wild beasts. The word literally means a double theatre, or one composed of two theatres. In the theatre the spectators sat in a semicircle placed opposite to the straight line of the stage; in the amphitheatre, which was of an elliptic form, the seats were placed all round.

The form of an amphitheatre, then, is generally an ellipse, with a series of arcaded concentric walls, separating corridors which have constructions with staircases and radiating passages between them. It enclosed an open space called the aréna. The innermost concentric wall bounded the arena, and was from 10 to 15 feet above its level: from this wall an inclined plane ran upwards and outwards over the intermediate wall, staircases, and corridors, to a gallery or galleries over the outermost corridors. The inner and upper part of the inclined plane was covered with a graduated series of benches following the general form of the plan; these benches were intercepted at intervals by radial passages leading by a more easy graduation to and from the staircases which passed through the substructions of the benches to the corridors. These corridors, in the principal stories, continued uninterruptedly all round the edifice, and afforded easy access to every part. In cases where the radiating passages through the bank of benches were few, concentric platforms went round to make the communications complete. The external elevation of an amphitheatre was determined by its internal arrangement and construction, and it generally had two or more stories of open arches, which were necessary to give light and air to the corridors and staircases.

Roman amphitheatres were first constructed of timber. Afterwards they were constructed of brick or stone.

The amphitheatre of the Romans was raised, for the most part, within the town or city, on the level ground, of costly magnificence, and generally of enormous extent. Almost every important Roman colony or city bears indications of a constructed or excavated amphitheatre. The Colosseum at Rome would contain above 80,000 persons; and even the little city of Pompeii contains the remains of an amphitheatre. The Roman garrisons appear to have contented themselves with camp-built amphitheatres alone. Of this sort,—the castrensian amphitheatre,—we have indications still existing in England; the principal are at Cirencester and Dorchester; but these were originally little more than mere excavations or turf-built cinctures, made up with what walling was absolutely necessary to form the grand concentric bank of benches.

The largest amphitheatre ever built was the Flavian Amphitheatre at Rome, commonly called the Colosseum, which was begun by Vespasian and finished by his son Titus, A.D. 80. The plan and elevation can be made out almost completely from the existing remains. It covers more than five acres. The dimensions as given by different authorities, vary a little, but the largest external diameter is about 613 feet, and the shorter diameter about 510 feet. The external elevation is composed of three series or stories of attached or engaged columns with their usual accessories, and a pilastraded ordinance, forming a species of attic, which is pierced with windows,—one in every other interspace. The crowning entablature is made bold and effective by deep modillion blocks or consoles occupying the whole depth of the frieze. Next in size to the Colosseum, of existing structures of the kind, is the Amphitheatre of Verona. The outer dimensions of this structure were 500 feet by 404 feet. The amphitheatre of El Jemm (Tisdrus) in Tunis is 429 feet in extreme length.

History will record that in the year 1851 there was raised a building in London, nearly capable of containing three of the greatest amphitheatres,—a building not devoted to the bloody contests of the arena and the gratification of national pride and individual bravery, but for the promotion of goodwill, and the cultivation of the most valuable arts, amongst all the nations of the earth.

AMPHITYPE. At the York meeting of the British Association, in 1844, Sir John Herschel described a variety of the 'photographic' process to which he gave the name of *Amphitype*. The paper is saturated with one among several chemical solutions named by him; and the paper so prepared and dried takes a negative picture, in a time varying from half an hour to five or six hours. The impression produced varies in apparent force, from a faint and hardly perceptible picture, to one of the highest conceivable fulness and richness both of tint and of detail: the colour being a rich soft brown. The pictures in this state are not permanent: they fade in the dark, though with different degrees of rapidity; but the picture is only dormant; it may be restored, with a change of character from negative to positive, and of colour, from brown to black. This is effected by the employment of a solution of per-nitrate of mercury, into which the paper is steeped; a long and careful process of rinsing, drying, heating, and smoothing follows, by which a changed picture is produced, very much resembling the effect of a copper-plate engraving on a slightly yellow paper. It is from the production, by one and the same action of light, of either a positive or negative picture, according to the subsequent manipulation, that the name of *amphitype* has been applied to the process. The solutions in which the paper is originally steeped are any of the following,—ferro-citrate or ferro-nitrate of mercury: the metal being either the protoxide or the peroxide, or being superceded by the protoxide of lead; and the nitric acid being substituted for those above named. Steepings in these solutions are to alternate several times with steepings in solutions of the ammonia-tartrate or ammonia-citrate of iron.

Another curious process, which is an *Amphitype* on a different principle, also described by Sir John Herschel, depends on the steeping of a piece of paper, before the photographic process, in a solution of ferro-tartrate of silver. If the paper, immediately on being removed from the photographic camera, be placed for a few seconds with its *back* exposed to the sunshine, a positive picture, the exact complement of the negative one on the other side, slowly and gradually makes its appearance, and in half an hour or an hour acquires a considerable intensity, though unequal to the original picture on the other side in sharpness of detail. This is one of the most striking results in the whole range of photography. [DAGUERROTYPE; PHOTOGRAPHY, &c.]

A'MPHORA was an earthen vessel, used by the Greeks and Romans to hold liquids. It received its name from its two ears or handles. It is generally two feet or two feet and a half in height; and the body, which is usually about six inches in diameter ending upwards with a short neck, tapers towards the lower part almost to a point. The attic amphora contained three Roman urnæ, or 72 sextaries, equal to about nine gallons English imperial-measure. The Roman, sometimes called the Italic amphora, contained two urnæ or 48 sextaries, about six gallons. There are specimens of earthen amphoræ in the British Museum, which are supposed to have been used as funeral urns.

There was another amphora among the Romans, which was a dry-measure, and contained about three bushels.

AMRITSIR, or UMRITSIR, the holy capital of the Sikhs, is a large city in the state of Lahore. It has a considerable trade in the shawls and saffron of Cashmere, and is a place of great opulence, owing to the resort of merchants and to its being the residence of some bankers of extensive dealings. Its native manufactures are confined to coarse cloths and inferior silk goods. It is one of the most flourishing commercial towns in Northern India. It fell into the hands of the British in 1848.

AMSTERDAM, the chief city of Holland, is one of the most commercial places in Europe. The dock accommodation is fitted for a large number of merchant ships. The docks front the mouth of the river Y (an arm of the Zuider Zee), and are entered and secured by sluices. In the north-eastern quarter is the Nieuw Oostelijk Dok, the National Dockyard, and the island of Kattenburg, in which are the quays and warehouses of the East and West India Companies, the Arsenal, and the Admiralty buildings. West of the Dam Rack lies the Haring Packerye, or Herring Packery Tower, in the neighbourhood of which all the business connected with the export of herrings used to be transacted. Further west is the Nieuw Westelijk Dok.

The harbour is spacious and the water deep; it has recently been much improved by the construction of the Oostelijk and Westelijk Docks, which are capable of containing 1000 large vessels, and are closed by large sluice gates. Owing to a bank (the Pampus) at the point where the Y joins the Zuider Zee, large vessels going and coming by that sea are obliged to load and unload a part of their cargoes in the roads. The navigation of the Zuider Zee also is very difficult and intricate by reason of its numerous shallows. To improve the access to the port, the Helder Canal, capable of admitting the largest class of merchantmen, was cut from the north side of the port of Amsterdam to Newdiep, opposite to the Texel, a distance of 50 miles. By this canal the Pampus is avoided, as well as the difficult navigation of the Zuider Zee, where ships were frequently detained for three weeks; and vessels can get to and from Newdiep without any risk in 18 hours Steam-boats ply from Amsterdam to Campen on the Yssel, from whence other steam-boats ply to the towns on the Yssel and the Rhine.

Amsterdam has some manufactures of wool, cotton, linen, and silk; its diamond-cutting and jewellery retain a good repute; but its sugar refineries, soaperies, distilleries, tanneries, oil works, tobacco manufactories, and ship building, are the most valuable branches of industry. The various handicrafts and ordinary fabrics common to all large towns are also carried on in Amsterdam. It has also some glass works and iron works. The imports principally consist of sugar, coffee, spices, tobacco, cotton, tea, dye-stuffs, wine and spirits, wool, grain, hemp, flax, pitch, metals, cotton and woollen stuffs, hardware, rocksalt, coal, &c. The exports are cheese, butter, seeds, rape and linseed oils, linen, spices, coffee and sugar from Java, tea, tobacco, indigo, cochineal, cotton, and other eastern and colonial products. About 260 large ships belong to Amsterdam, which are employed in the East and West India trade: 15 small vessels are engaged in the herring and whale fisheries. Upwards of 4000 vessels enter the port annually; and about the same number leave it. The imports in some years have exceeded £ 8,000,000 sterling.

By the adoption of the system of free navigation by the Dutch government, following the recent example of England, the commerce of Amsterdam will doubtless be greatly increased. The new Dutch Navigation Acts, which came into operation on the 15th September, 1850, and will apply to her colonial possessions at the beginning of 1851, will afford absolute freedom of navigation at the Dutch ports, at home and abroad.

AMULET, in barbarous Latin, *Amulétum*, or *Amoletum*. An amulet hung round the neck, or carried in any other way about the person, is absurdly believed to have the effect of warding off morbid infections and other dangers, and even of curing diseases by which the body has been already attacked. The belief in the efficacy of amulets has subsisted at some time among almost every people. The anodyne necklace, which consists of beads formed from the roots of white briony, and is sometimes hung around the necks of infants with the view of assisting their teething, is an instance of the still surviving confidence in the medical virtue of amulets. Such also is the belief entertained by seafaring people, that a child's caul on board their ship will preserve them from being lost. In exhibitions of art, ancient and mediæval, amulets are often to be met with of curious construction.

AMYGDALIN, a substance obtained from bitter almonds after the fixed oil has been expressed. Its properties are—that it has the form of small, white, pearly, crystalline plates, which are inodorous and nearly tasteless. It is very soluble in water, both hot and cold; a hot solution deposits brilliant prismatic crystals in cooling, which contain water.

AMYGDALUS, is the botanical name for several plants, of which the almond is the principal. [ALMOND.]

AMYRI'DEÆ, the botanical name for a natural order of plants consisting of tropical trees, the leaves, bark, and fruit of which abound in fragrant resin. The odoriferous substances called *gum elemi*, *bdellium*, and *resin of Coumia* are all produced by different species of amyrideæ.

ANACARDIA'CEÆ, or the Cashew tribe, is a natural order of plants, consisting exclusively of woody plants, abounding in an acrid resin. Their juice is often used as a kind of varnish, for which it is well adapted, in consequence of its turning hard and black when dry. It is, however, often dangerous to use, because of the extreme acridity of the fumes, which are apt to produce severe inflammation in many constitutions. One species, *Anacardium Occidentale*, if wounded in the stem, yields abundantly a milk, which, when inspissated, becomes intensely black and hard, besides which it secretes a gum not inferior to gum arabic. The nut is a kidney-shaped body, containing in abundance, beneath the outer shell, the black caustic oil of the order, which, when volatilized by heat, as happens in the process of roasting, is apt to produce erysipelas, and other disagreeable affections in the face of persons standing over the fumes; the kernel is a well known wholesome article of food. In the West Indies it is used as an ingredient in puddings, is eaten raw, and is roasted for the purpose of mixing with Madeira wine, to which it is thought to communicate a peculiarly agreeable flavour.

ANACARDIUM INK. [INK.]

ANA'LYSIS. Chemical analysis is the separation of compound bodies, either into their simpler or their elementary constituents. When merely the number and nature of these are ascertained, it is termed *qualitative* analysis; but when their proportions also are determined, the analysis is *quantitative.* If the analysis consist only in determining the quantities of the *simpler* constituents of a compound, it is *proximate*, as when carbonate of potash is separated into carbonic acid and potash: but when the operation is extended, and the carbonic acid is resolved into carbon and oxygen, and the potash into potassium and oxygen, the analysis is *ultimate*; for neither carbon, oxygen, nor potassium (in the present state of our knowledge) is divisible into two or more kinds of matter.

ANAMORPHO'SIS is such a representation of an object that, except when viewed from a particular point directly, or in a cylindrical mirror, or through a polyhedral lens, it will appear to be distorted, or disconnected, or to be a view of something very different from the original object. Such representations are only made for the amusement of young persons, and are of no artistic importance.

ANASTATIC PRINTING. Early in the month of November, 1841, the proprietors of the *Athenæum* received from a correspondent at Berlin, a reprint of four pages of the number of that journal which had been published in London only on September 25th. The copy was so perfect a facsimile, that had it not come to hand under peculiar circumstances, it would have been taken for two leaves out of a sheet actually printed in London; the observable difference was, that the impression was somewhat lighter, and the body of ink less than usual. In reply to further inquiries, the correspondent at Berlin could only discover that the secret was said to be in the hands of a person at Erfurt. He had seen a fac-simile of an Arabic MS. of the 13th century; and another fac-simile of a leaf of a book printed in 1483—both such close copies as hardly to be detected from the originals, and both taken without injury to the originals. It was also stated that a prospectus was issued at Berlin, of a pirated edition of the *Athenæum*, to be produced in a similar way, and sold at a low price.

In January 1845, the *Athenæum* was enabled to announce that the inventor or discoverer of the method was a M. Baldermus, who had communicated the discovery to a person in London; and to convince the proprietors of that journal of the reality of the method, a page of *L'Illustration*, French journal, was faithfully copied in a quarter of an hour. The method became known by the name of *Anastatic printing*; and many of the London journals directed attention to the subject. In the *Art Union* for February, 1845, pages 40 and 41 of the number are printed from zinc plates obtained by the Anastatic process. The compositors "set up" in the usual way, sufficient matter to fill up two quarto pages of the work, leaving spaces for three wood-cuts, three drawings, and a few lines of writing in pen and ink, which were properly adjusted to the blanks left for them. All were alike copied or transferred to the zinc plates, and then printed from to the number of several thousands. The impressions are fainter and less distinct than those from the original types, but they are unquestionably remarkable.

Professor Faraday explained the rationale of the Anastatic process in 1845, at the Royal Institution. The process depends on a few known properties of the articles employed. 1st. Water attracts water; oil attracts oil; but each mutually repels the other. 2nd. Metals are much more easily wetted with oil than with water; but they will readily be moistened by a weak solution of gum. 3rd. The power of wetting metals with water is greatly increased by the addition of phosphatic acid. 4th. A part of the ink of any newly printed book can be readily transferred by pressure to any smooth surface beneath; if, for example, a corner of a newspaper be fixed on a white sheet of paper, and then pressed or rubbed with a paper knife, the letters will be distinctly seen in reverse on the paper; and indeed every one knows that if a book be bound too soon after the printing, the pages become disfigured by the *setting off* or transfer of the ink upon the opposite pages. From these data the rules for the process are derived. The printed paper, whether letter-press or engraving, is first moistened with dilute acid, and then pressed with considerable force by a roller on a perfectly clean surface of zinc; by which means every part of the sheet of paper is brought into contact with the plate of zinc. The acid, with which the unprinted part of the paper is saturated, *etches* the metal, while the printed portion *sets off* on it, so that the zinc surface presents a reverse copy of the work. The zinc plate, thus prepared, is washed with a weak solution of gum in weak phosphatic acid; this liquid is attracted by the etched surface, which it freely wets, while it is repelled by the oil of the ink in which the writing or drawing on the plate is traced. A leathern roller, covered with ink, is then passed over the plate, when a converse effect ensues; the repulsion between the oil, ink, and watery surface over which the roller passes, prevents any soiling of the unfigured parts of the zinc plate; while the attraction between oil and oil causes the ink to be distributed over the printed portions. In this condition the anastatic plate is complete, and impressions are pulled from it by the common lithographic process. When it is required to apply the anastatic process to very old originals, which do not set off their ink on pressure, the page or print is first soaked in a solution of potash, and then in a solution of tartaric acid: by which is produced a perfect diffusion of minute crystals of bi-tartrate of potash through the texture of the unprinted part of the paper. As this salt resists oil, the ink roller may now be passed over the surface without transferring any of its contents, except to the printed parts. The tartrate is then washed out of the paper, and the operation is proceeded with as before, commencing with the moistening by nitric acid.

In No. 1135 of the *Mechanic's Magazine*, it is stated that Mr. Jobbins, the lithographic printer, took copies of printed pages by a process analogous to that of anastatic printing, as far back as the year 1840; and in the same number Mr. Cocks of Falmouth states "In the year 1836 I introduced a process for the transferring of copper plate engravings (by the old masters), as well as letter-press printing, &c., to stone, zinc, tin, pewter, type-metal, fusible metal, lead, copper, glass, &c., and had impressions taken from each; but the original subjects were destroyed by the chemical agents used. Since that time I have succeeded in transferring prints and letter press without even soiling the originals, fixing the same on metal, wood, or paper, and printing from the form any number of copies. The process is so faithful in its operation, that the finest line of the etching needle is preserved." It is evident, indeed, that anastatic printing is but an extension of processes known long before in England.

In 1848 Mr. Strickland and Mr. Delamotte instituted experiments with a view to ascertain how far the anastatic process would be available as a substitute for lithography. They succeeded in transferring or printing from drawings made on paper with lithographic chalk; within an hour after the drawing was made, a perfect anastatic *fac-simile* was produced, hardly to be distinguished from it. The chief difficulty here seems to be the production of a kind of paper which shall possess a surface similar to lithographic stone. A mode has been devised of imparting to India paper a clear sharp granular surface, well fitted for the purpose as far as regards surface; but it is almost too tender in substance. Mr. Strickland found that *metallic paper*, used for metallic pencils, had the required surface. For fine subjects copied in this way, it is essential that the lithographic chalk be of a hard quality; and cut to a fine point.

ANATOMICAL MECHANISM. Considerable ingenuity is exercised in providing mechanical aid for those who, by amputation or other causes, have been deprived of limbs. A few descriptive details on this subject will be found under ARTIFICIAL LIMBS.

ANATTO. [ARNOTTO.]

ANCHOR. Under some form or other anchors must have been as ancient as ships; and they are accordingly mentioned by Greek and Latin authors, by whom also the invention, like many others which from clumsy beginnings have passed through different stages of improvement, is ascribed to various persons. The first anchors were probably only large stones or crooked pieces of wood loaded with heavy weights, but among the Greeks, latterly, they were made of iron; of these the earliest had but one fluke, afterwards the other was added, and finally they were furnished with stocks. Each ship had several, of which the principal one was called *ἱερα* or sacred, and was reserved for the last extremity. This corresponds to that which has since been denominated the 'sheet anchor.'

The number of anchors carried by a ship have been finally reduced to four principal ones, all of which are disposed at the bows. These are the best and small bowers (bowyers), the sheet, and the spare anchor, and to them are added the stream and the kedge anchors, which are used for particular purposes, and are generally carried 'in-board.'

Every complete anchor has a *ring* by which it is suspended, a *stock* or cross-piece immediately below the ring, a *shank* or perpendicular bar, two *arms* proceeding in opposite directions from the lower end of the shank, a *palm* or *fluke* at the end of each arm, and a *bill* or *peak* at the end of each fluke.

When the anchor is let go in any manner from the vessel's side the heaviest end, or crown, will tend to become the lowest part, and the whole mass having reached the bottom will most commonly fall upon the crown and on one end of the stock; from this position therefore the anchor is to be canted or turned over before it can hold. Now, it is evident that if the stock were very short, the pull of the cable would tend rather to drag the end of the stock along the bottom than to lift up one of the flukes, as must be done in canting the anchor; whereas, if the stock were longer, the cable would act with increased leverage, whatever might be the length of the shank; hence the longer the stock, within the practical limits of stowage, the more certainly will the anchor turn properly; and, when hooked in the ground, the more powerfully will it resist any effort to overset it.

When the anchor has been turned, the stock then lying horizontally on the ground, and the point of a fluke touching the ground, it is evident that the force exerted by the ship to draw the anchor towards itself, compounded with the weight of the anchor (exclusive of the stock, and diminished by about one-seventh on account of the loss of weight in water), will produce a resultant force by which the fluke is made to enter the ground. An anchor, when 'dragged,' always tends to rise out of the ground, and does not again sink till it rests.

In *lifting* or *weighing* the anchor, the cable acting perpendicularly to the end of the shank, tends to break it, and hence the thickness of the shank should increase with its distance from the ring; also the breadth of the shank should be downwards, and the like holds good of the arms, the chief dimension of which should be in the plane of the cable and shank, thus opposing the greatest strength to the greatest strain.

Besides the strains to which an anchor is exposed by its office, it is liable to accidents; for instance, an anchor let go on a rocky bottom has been found, on heaving it up, to have lost an arm, which was probably caused by its striking against a rock obliquely in its descent; again, the shank has been found broken in the middle, though this does not seem to have been accounted for satisfactorily; and it may here be observed generally, that the anchor descends much more swiftly with a chain-cable than a hemp one, for the stiffness of the hemp opposes a retarding force, while the greater density of the chain adds a continually accelerating force.

The principal dimensions of the anchors in the navy may be stated shortly thus:—calling the shank 10, the arm is about 3, the breadth and depth of the palm about half this, the thickness or depth of the shank varies from ·4 to ·6, and the breadth about four-fifths of these, the edges being rounded. The weight of an anchor of 10 feet in length is about 11·4 cwt., and since, if the forms of all anchors were alike, the weights would be as the cubes of the lengths, the weight of any anchor might be found by multiplying the cube of its length by ·0114. Thus the weight of an anchor of 14 feet in length would be $14^3 \times \cdot 0114 = 31 3$. cwt.; the weight of this anchor is, in practice, 30 cwt., hence as far as 30 or 35 cwt., the rule is near enough, but for larger anchors it gives the result too small, because their thickness is made greater in proportion. The weight of the anchor includes that of the ring. A general rule in the navy is to allow 1 cwt. to a gun; thus, an 80 gun ship would have an anchor weighing 80 cwt. A merchant-ship of 200 tons having an anchor weighing 10 cwt., 5 cwt. are added for every additional 100 tons; thus, a ship of 300 tons would have an anchor of 15 cwt., and so on. Small vessels require heavier anchors in proportion than large vessels; the sea, sudden gusts of wind, and the pull of the cable, affect the larger vessels less, and they thus preserve a steadier strain.

As to the cost of an anchor, the labour per cwt. is about 24*s.* for an anchor of 10 cwt. and under, and for the largest anchors about 3*l.*; the value of an anchor of 95 cwt., including the iron at about 9*s.* 9*d.* per cwt., is about 300*l.*

The stock consists of two beams of oak, bolted and hooped together; the length is that of the shank and half the diameter of the ring; it is square; the side at the middle is an inch to a foot of the shank, and tapers to half of this at the end. Such a stock is nearly one-fourth of the weight of the anchor. Lieutenant Rodgers has proposed a solid stock of African oak, for the greater convenience of stocking or unstocking. Of late years iron stocks, whose weight is from one-fourth to one-fifth of the anchor, have been much used.

Numerous improvements have been brought forward within the last few years in the form and manufacture of anchors. Lieutenant Rodgers has patented a hollow-shanked anchor, intended to combine strength with lightness. Mr. Pering has introduced a method of forming the arms of anchors by splitting or bisecting the bars which form the shank, and turning the ends back in contrary directions. Mr. Meggitt has patented an anchor in which the flukes are very little broader than the arms. It would be needless to enumerate all the improvements introduced or suggested; but among the changes proposed in the construction of anchors, the most remarkable is, perhaps, that which was brought forward by Mr. Porter, for the purpose of avoiding the consequences of 'fouling,' by the cable passing over the exposed fluke of the anchor when the vessel is swinging in a tide-way, and injury to the vessel herself in the event of settling upon her anchor. The peculiarity consists in giving to the arms a freedom of motion round a pivot or bolt at the end of the shank. The arms and flukes are forged independently of the shank, and have a hole drilled transversely through the centre for the reception of the iron bolt which connects them with the shank. The effect of this construction is, that when the anchor, after being dropped, rests upon the ground, it assumes a position in which the lower peak is in contact with the inferior surface of the shank, and the upper peak is as far as possible from it. The slightest movement of the cable then suffices to bring the anchor to a position in which the lower peak is favourably situated for penetrating into the ground: the penetration then takes place, and at length the shank and stock lie flat on the ground, the upper fluke being close upon the top of the shank.

Whether we view the forging of an anchor under the old state of things, or now that Nasmyth's hammer works such wonders, it is a striking exhibition of industrial art. The shaft of a first class anchor, nearly twenty feet long by ten or twelve inches thick, is too ponderous to be worked out of one piece of metal; and it has consequently to be built up of many pieces. Forty or fifty bars are sometimes laid together in a group, to be welded into one mass by powerful blows while at a white heat; but in modern times a smaller number of wider bars are more frequently used. The bundle of bars is brought to a highly heated state, in a kind of oven formed wholly of coals, which completely surround the iron; but as the length of the shank is so great, only so much of it is heated at once as can be forged before it cools down too low. The fire is urged by ten or a dozen men (the same who afterwards apply their lusty arms to the hammers); and when the mass is brought to a white heat, it is drawn out of the fiery furnace, swung round by means of the crane by which it has been suspended, and brought to bear on a large anvil. The men arrange themselves in a circle around the heated mass; and, guided by a foreman, they wield their ponderous hammers of sixteen or twenty pounds weight, and produce a rough music by their equal-timed blows: they are 'harmonious blacksmiths,' though perhaps not belonging to Handel's corps. Mr. Samuel Ferguson, in his noble poem, 'The Forging of the Anchor,' has some lines which vividly present this picture:—

'The roof-ribs swarth, the candent hearth, the ruddy lurid row
Of smiths, that stand, an ardent band, like men before the foe;
As, quivering through his fleece of flame, the sailing monster, slow
Sinks on the anvil—all about the fiery faces glow—
"Hurrah!" they shout, "leap out—leap out;" bang, bang, the sledges go:
Hurrah! the jetted lightnings are hissing high and low,
A hailing fount of fire is struck at every crushing blow;
The leathern mail rebounds the hail; the rattling cinders strow
The ground around; at every bound the sweltering fountains flow;
And thick and loud the swinking crowd at every stroke pant "ho!"'

But this was in the old times. If we now visit the Government Anchor Smitheries, such as that in Devonport Dock Yard, we find that steam has driven away something of the old picturesqueness—replacing it by a grandeur of its own. The anchor-shaft is no longer buried in a mere heap of blazing fuel, but is heated in a properly constructed furnace; the bellows are no longer worked by hand, but by the powerful blast of a steam-engine; the forgers need no longer to confine their operations to one small length at a time, for a much greater length can now be managed before it cools down too low; and the circle of anchor-smiths no longer wield their hammers, and expend their strength in blows which were once called powerful but which are now deemed puny. A steam-giant has come amongst them. Mr. Nasmyth's steam-hammer is a contrivance in which a powerful hammer or weight is allowed to fall by its own gravity, but is drawn up by the operation of steam-power; and this alternation of rising and falling occurs several times in a minute—much faster indeed than a man could wield a sledge-hammer. The white-hot anchor-shaft is placed upon an anvil immediately beneath this steam-hammer; and the blows which follow are so powerful and so quickly repeated, that the heated mass becomes forged in a wonderfully short space of time. Let the anchor-smiths group themselves as thickly as they may, and wield hammers the heaviest that human muscles can command—they cannot approach the amount of work which the steam-hammer effects. Even the *Hercules* which formed an intermediate stage between the sledge-hammer and the steam-hammer, and which consists of a heavy mass of iron worked by ropes, must yield in efficiency to Mr. Nasmyth's remarkable machine.

ANCHO'VY is a genus of fish, abundant in the Mediterranean and along the coasts of Spain, Portugal, and France. It occurs also on various parts of our coast, as Hampshire, Cornwall, Wales, &c. They vary from four to seven inches in length. The anchovy has been celebrated from the earliest times, and a sauce or condiment called garum prepared from it was held in high estimation among the Greeks and Romans. In preparing this fish for use, the head and viscera are removed, otherwise the pickle would be intensely bitter; the anchovy was in fact once supposed to have the gall in its head. A fish called the *sardine*, common in the Mediterranean, and belonging to the same genus, is frequently mixed with real anchovies, or even sold salted and barrelled as the genuine fish. The sardine may be known by its long taper form, its dark brown colour, and pale flabby flesh.

A large trade is carried on in the preparing of what are termed *British Anchovies*, especially for making anchovy paste or sauce. The humble sprat is made to do duty for the anchovy. According to the receipt given by Mr. Cooley, two pounds of salt, three ounces of bay-salt, one pound of saltpetre, two ounces of prunella, and a few grains of cochineal, are pounded in a mortar, and then laid in a stone pan or anchovy barrel, layers of sprats alternating with layers of the composition. The whole are then pressed down hard, and kept covered close for six months; after which they are ready for use, and 'really produce a most excellent flavoured sauce.'

ANCHU'SA, the botanical name for a genus of plants, which besides other species, contains the following two, valuable in the arts and in medicine. The *Anchusa officinalis*, common alkanet or bugloss, is sometimes boiled and eaten. The roots contain a considerable quantity of gum, and when boiled yield a demulcent drink, which was once in repute as a medicine. In China this plant is used as a provocative of the eruption of small-pox. The *Anchusa tinctoria*, Dyers' Bugloss or Alkanet, is cultivated in the south of France for the sake of the root, which yields a fine red colour to oils, wax, and all unctuous substances, as well as to spirits of wine. Its chief use is in colouring lip-salves, ointments, &c. It is however sometimes employed for staining wood and dyeing cotton. It is also used for colouring many of the beverages sold under the name of port wine, likewise the corks used for the bottles in which this fluid is sold.

ANCIENT ART. Our knowledge of the fine arts of the ancients is more considerable than that of their useful or manufacturing arts, chiefly in relation to architecture and sculpture. There will be found, however, scattered under various headings in this Cyclopædia, brief notices of such works of ancient skill as have come down to our knowledge with sufficient notoriety to make them interesting.

ANCO'NA, a seaport town on the Adriatic Sea, is the most commercial place in the Papal States, carries on a considerable trade by sea, and is a free port. Its harbour, which is good, is protected by two moles, the ancient one raised by Trajan, and the modern one with the light-house constructed by Clement XII. Ancona exports wax, silk, wool, and corn. It is the only good harbour on the Italian coast of the Adriatic between Venice and Manfredonia, and is the common point of departure for the Ionian Islands and Greece.

ANDALUCI'A or ANDALUSI'A, the most southern of the provinces of Spain, comprises the former Moorish kingdoms of Seville, Cordoba, Jaen, and Granada. On the northern side of the Sierra Morena the productions indicate a climate like that of the south of France; but southward of that range are found the mastic tree, the kermes oak, myrtles, American aloes, palm-trees, the olive, the banana, the caper, orange and lemon trees, the pomegranate, and other productions of warm climates; and in some spots the sugar cane and cotton grow. The orange and lemon trees, particularly around convents and monasteries, form groves of considerable extent, which in the time of blossoming fill the air with a delicious perfume. Besides all the species of corn and fruit, wine and oil make the bulk of the productions of the soil. Among the wines, the Xerez (or sherry), the Pajarete, Malaga, Montilla, Espera, Bornos, and Tintilla, are the most celebrated.

The rich pastures of the mountains and valleys feed innumerable herds of cattle, among which the bulls have been renowned from the fabulous times of King Geryon. The woods of oak of the Serrania de Ronda, of Cordoba, and Granada, afford nourishment to a multitude of hogs; and the Loma de Ubeda, the Dehesa of Cordoba, and the Cartuja of Xerez, produce the finest breed of horses in the peninsula. The seas and rivers abound in fish, and the mountains in every species of game. The riches of the mineral kingdom are abundant. Sixty-six mines are known, which produce gold, silver, copper, iron, lead, loadstone, coals, vitriol, and sulphur.

ANDERNACH, a small town on the west bank of the Rhine, in Rhenish Prussia, has a considerable trade, chiefly in millstones, which are cut in the neighbouring villages of Ober-Mendig and Nieder-Mendig, in bricks, clay for tobacco-pipes; and in trass, which is sent to Holland. This trass is an indurated volcanic mud, of which a vast quantity is accumulated in the valley of Brohl, five miles north of Andernach. It is extensively quarried, and when pulverized and mixed with lime makes a mortar suitable for constructions under water. Trass is a corruption of the Dutch word *tiras*, which signifies cement. In Andernach numerous pieces of columnar basalt are employed as posts at the corners of streets, &c. The door-posts and side-pieces of almost all the windows are made of the porous lava of which the famous millstones are formed. This material is also used for paving courts and kitchen floors, and has been employed in the construction of some of the oldest buildings in this town as well as in Coblentz.

ANDERSON, JOHN, gratefully remembered in Scotland as the founder of the Andersonian Institution of Glasgow, and one of the earliest promoters of that popular instruction in science which has so greatly elevated the character of British artisans, was born in the parish of Rosneath, Dumbartonshire, in 1726. He was appointed professor of Natural Philosophy at Glasgow in 1760; and not content with the ordinary duty of lecturing, he employed himself indefatigably in studying and exemplifying the applications of science to the useful arts, visiting for this purpose the workshops of intelligent artisans, and exchanging his scientific information for their experimental knowledge. The better to carry out his views of popular education, Anderson commenced, in addition to his ordinary class, one which he styled his *anti-toga* class, for the instruction of artisans and others unable to enter upon a regular academical course, to whom he delivered familiar extempore lectures illustrated by experiments. Mechanics were allowed to attend these lectures in their working-dress. He closed his useful career in 1796. Shortly before his death he devised his whole property to eighty-one trustees, for the establishment in Glasgow of an institution to be denominated Anderson's University, for the continued provision of those facilities for the un-academical classes of his townsmen which he had so long supplied by his own personal exertions. His comprehensive design was for an institution consisting of four colleges, with nine professors each, for arts, medicine, law, and theology; but as the funds proved insufficient for so extensive a scheme, operations were commenced in 1797, on a limited scale, by the appointment of Dr. Thomas Garnett as professor of natural philosophy. His first course of lectures was attended by nearly a thousand persons, of both sexes. In the following year a professor of mathematics and geography was appointed; and, though the institution has never attained the magnitude contemplated by the founder, it has been progressively increased and extended in usefulness, and has been productive of much public benefit. Dr. Garnett was succeeded in 1799 by Dr. Birkbeck, on occasion of his removal to the Royal Institution in London, which was formed on a similar model to that established by Anderson; and Dr. Birkbeck, who introduced a new course of instruction for five hundred operative mechanics, free of all expense, was succeeded in 1804 by Dr. Ure.

ANDES. This immense American mountain chain is one of the richest mineral storehouses on the globe. Pumice-stone is found to a great extent in many of the volcanoes of the Andes; and volcanic-tuff, which is a stone more or less compact, made up of fragments of hard lava, cinders, and ashes, agglutinated together, covers immense tracts on the flanks of the Andes and on the table-lands. Stone of every description is met with—a storehouse of material ready for the time when manufactures and the arts of civilized life shall find a home in these regions. But it is in metals that the Andes are so especially rich. These mountains have been celebrated for their mines of metal since our earliest knowledge of America. Gold, silver, mercury, platina, copper, and tin, are met with. Gold is found in the form of grains and small rounded lumps, scattered through alluvial soils, which have been derived from the disintegration of rocks containing the metal, and most probably in the form of slender veins. The places chosen for digging into that auriferous soil are called *lavaderos*, because the gravel, sand, and earth, undergo repeated *washings* to separate the heavy particles of gold. The most considerable gold mines are at Petorea, Coquimbo, Copiapo, Pataz, Huailas, Curimayo, Zorata, Antioquia, Choco, and Barbacoas.

Silver is more abundant in the Peruvian than in the Chilian Andes. The richest mines are those of Pasco, in 11° S. lat., which have been worked since the year 1630. Here, as well as in other situations in Peru, the greatest part of the silver is obtained from an ore called in the country *pacos*, which is an intimate mixture of minute particles of native silver with brown oxide of iron. The mines of Chota are also very productive. They are situated in the mountain of Gualgayoc, at an elevation of 13,300 feet, where the thermometer in summer descends every night to the freezing point. The ore lies immediately beneath the surface. But the most celebrated are the silver mines of Potosi, in a lofty mountain. This mountain is perforated in all directions, and it is said that there are not less than 5000 excavations in it, some of them within 120 feet of the top, which is 16,000 feet above the sea-level.

Mercury, in the form of cinnabar or sulphuret of the metal, is met with at Azogué and other parts of the Andes; but the most celebrated, those of Guancavelica, were overwhelmed by incautious mining in 1789. Platina is met with in small quantities in Colombia. Copper and tin are found in the Chilian Andes.

In respect to the commerce of the Andes, little has yet been effected. The passes between the lofty peaks are few in number; and the routes by which the gold and other mining produce reach the ports of shipment are most inefficient. The distance to the Atlantic is in most cases too great to admit of the transfer in this direction: the Pacific ports are for the most part selected.

In a recent number of the *Journal of the*

KNIGHT'S CYCLOPÆDIA OF THE Industry of all Nations.

o. 5.

Franklin Institute, a description is given of a small steam-boat just built at New York for the Andes region. It is 55 feet keel, 12 feet beam, and 5 feet depth of hold. It is to be propelled by two high-pressure engines, of 10-horse power each; with iron paddle-wheels 10 feet in diameter. It is built in separate pieces, all carefully marked and fitted; and for the convenience of carriage, no piece exceeds 350 lbs. weight. It is to be taken by ship to Lima, and the pieces transported on the backs of mules to Lake Titicata, one of the highest lakes on the surface of the globe, in the midst of the Andes. The lake is 140 miles long, and the shores are well timbered; and it is expected that much traffic and commerce will ensue from the establishment of steam navigation there. The pieces of the vessel will be fitted together on the shores of the lake; and if the enterprise succeeds, a larger steamer will be sent out in a similar manner. The surface of Lake Titicata is no less than 12,795 feet above the level of the Pacific; and some parts are nearly 1000 feet deep.

ANDREASBERG, a town of 4000 inhabitants, in the mining district of the Upper Hartz, in the kingdom of Hanover, stands at the southern foot of the Brocken, on a hill 1936 feet above the level of the sea. The neighbourhood is rich in mines, yielding silver, copper, iron, cobalt, and arsenic; and these, as well as the spinning of yarn, lace-making, and the rearing of cattle, afford profitable employment to its inhabitants. The shaft of the Sampson silver mine is 2,333 feet deep.

ANEMO'METER, or *wind-measurer*, is an instrument for ascertaining the force of the wind, generally by finding the mechanical effect which it produces on the apparatus. Wolf's anemometer consists of four small sails, like those of a windmill, which turn on a horizontal axis: this axis is connected by wheel-work with another in which is inserted one end of a bar carrying a weight. The wind acting upon the sails causes this bar to turn in a vertical plane; and, when it is in such a position that the weight on it counterbalances the pressure of the wind, the angle which it makes with a vertical line passing through the axis affords a measure of the wind's force.

Lind's anemometer consists of two tubes of glass, each 9 inches long and $\frac{4}{10}$ inch diameter, which are open at their upper extremities, and are connected at bottom by a bent tube only $\frac{1}{10}$ inch diameter. These are partly filled with water, and the wind acting at the open end of one tube depresses the water in that tube and elevates it in the other, until the difference of height becomes a counterpoise to the pressure of the wind. This difference can be ascertained by a graduated scale, and hence may be obtained the dimensions of a column of water whose weight is equivalent to the force of the wind. The velocity may thence be found, observing that the velocities are nearly as the square roots of the resistances, and that on a square foot, the pressure of wind moving with a velocity of 20 feet per second, is 12 ounces.

In Regnier's anemometer, a bar, carrying a wooden plate at right angles to it, protrudes from a box, through a hole, in the front of which it slides. This bar is met by a spring, which resists its further entry, until force is applied against the plate. In the interior of the box, the under side of the bar carries rackwork, which plays on a cog-wheel, the axis of which, passing through a side of the box, carries a hand round a dial-plate. The anterior surface of the wooden plate is presented to the wind, which presses upon it and forces back the bar, carrying the cog-wheel and hand through an angle, greater or less, according to the greater or less impulse of the wind.

Mr. Elliott, an overman at Pensher Colliery, invented an anemometer in 1835, to measure the rate of the currents of air in coal mines, with a view to regulate ventilation. It consists of a case 12 inches high, 12 broad, and 4½ deep. On a dial are two concentric circles; the inner circle being divided into 48 parts, and the outer into 60. The vanes are connected with two indices or pointers, whose axes of motion are in the centres of the circles, like the hands of a watch; the one pointing to the outer circle and the other to the inner. The movement of one index has a certain ratio of velocity to that of the other; and by the aid of a calculated table, the number of rotations of the slower index within a given time is made to determine the velocity with which the air is moving in or past the machine.

Mr. Biram, in 1843, invented an anemometer for a similar purpose. It consists of a wheel one foot in diameter, having ten oblique vanes of thin sheet copper, perforated for lightness, and covered with tissue paper or varnished silk. The vanes are set at such an angle, that the wheel makes one revolution in the time a current of air two feet in length is passing through it. The axle of the wheel carries an endless screw, into which works a wheel having thirty teeth; and an index is fixed on the axle. As each revolution of the wheel is effected by the action of a current or column of air, two feet in length, one revolution of the index will register the passage of 60 feet of air.

Dr. Whewell's anemometer differs somewhat from others in being calculated to measure the *rate* of the wind rather than its force. It gives no absolute measure of velocity in miles per hour; and the rate is relative only to that of any one instrument at different times, not to that of any common or general standard. At the meeting of the British Association in 1846, Dr. Robinson described an alteration which he had effected in this instrument. On a vertical axis are mounted three or four arms, carrying hemispherical cups at their extremities. These cups oppose much less resistance to air acting on the concave sides than on their convexities, and in such ratio that uniform revolution is produced at the rate of one-third of the velocity of the wind. From this measure, which might be made the same for all sizes of the instrument and in all places, the mean velocity of the wind during a given period could always be obtained in miles per hour. It is believed that this principle of uniform adjustment might be usefully applied to many practical purposes, such as the regulation of wind and water-wheels.

Captain Cockburn devised in 1847 a form of anemometer founded on that of Dr. Robinson, but calculated for use on ship-board. It is seven inches high; the diameter of the wings is sixteen inches; there are four cups placed at right angles, attached by arms to a spindle on which is an endless screw, working in the teeth of two multiplying wheels, marked up to 10,000 revolutions. The concave side of each cup is made so as to receive or contain one-third more wind than the convex side.

Osler's anemometer bears some such relation to the older forms, as the aneroid barometer bears to the common barometer: that is, it acts chiefly by the pressure of the air on a spring, rather than by the rise and fall of a liquid in a tube. The spring is not so delicate in its indications, but it is more manageable in yielding *self-registered* observations. In Osler's anemometer, machinery connected with a spring is made to move a pencil over a piece of paper; so as to keep a continuous register of the variations of wind, both in *intensity* and direction. A fine instrument of this kind is placed on the roof of the Royal Exchange, so arranged as to register its indications in a room below. It also acts as a *pluviometer* or rain-guage.

Mr. Goddard's anemometer, somewhat resembling in principle Mr. Osler's, registers no less than twelve classes of phenomena in respect to the wind; viz.: miles of wind blown during a day; miles of wind blown in each direction; miles of wind blown between any two given periods; hour and minute of the strongest wind; hours in which most wind has blown; times and lengths of calms; velocity of wind at any hour; time occupied by the wind going any certain distance at any period of the day; direction of wind at any minute; mean direction; direction of longest continuance; and direction of the greatest passage of wind.

Professor Phillips described to the British Association in 1846 a simple form of anemometer which depends on a well-known principle. When the bulb of a thermometer, covered with cotton wool, is immersed in water and then exposed to the air, a diminution of temperature ensues, consequent on evaporation from the surface; and when the thermometer is moved through the air, or air be blown upon it, the rapidity of evaporation is increased. Professor Phillips took advantage of this principle, to measure the rapidity of cooling by the rapidity of motion in or through the air, or, conversely, to measure the motion by the cooling. He ascertained the amount of diminution of temperature by simple exposure, and then raised the temperature by the heat of the hand to that of the air, and marked by a seconds-watch the rapidity of cooling when the hand was withdrawn. He next repeated the process when the thermometer was in motion, and he was thus enabled to determine the velocity of a railway carriage in swift movement.

ANE'MOSCOPE, is an instrument for determining the direction of the wind; usually constructed by connecting with the spindle of a weathercock the hand of a dial on which the points of the compass are marked.

ANEROID BAROMETER. At the Swansea meeting of the British Association in 1848, Professor Lloyd introduced a notice of the Aneroid Barometer, which had been patented by M. Fontainmoreau in 1844. Instead of acting by the pressure of the atmosphere on liquids, as most forms of barometer do, this instrument depends on the pressure of the air on thin laminæ or diaphragms of some elastic solid substance. The body of the instrument consists of a hollow brass box, with a dial face on the upper surface. Below the dial face is the diaphragm, stretched all across the box. This may consist of a thin sheet of metal, or of glass, or of caoutchouc, or of some other elastic material; but the patentee mentions especially a thin piece of copper sheet, corrugated circularly, so as to yield sensibly to any pressure. The box beneath the diaphragm is so made that the air can be extracted from it; and the diaphragm is then only protected from the crushing pressure of the air by a number of delicate spiral springs, which are fixed to the interior of the bottom of the box, and support the diaphragm. When the weight of the atmosphere increases (equivalent to the rising of the ordinary barometer) the diaphragm suffers an increased pressure, to which the springs allow it to yield to a certain extent; but a lessened pressure allows it to rise again to its normal state. A delicate piece of mechanism, connected with the centre of the diaphragm, becomes moved when the diaphragm either rises or sinks; and this movement is transferred to index hands, which mark on a graduated dial the amount of rise or fall. The graduations are so made as to correspond with the inches and fractions of an inch in the common barometer.

From a communication made to the *Athenæum* (No. 1117), it appears that an Aneroid barometer was carefully compared for several days with the standard barometer at the Liverpool Observatory. The greatest difference was about four-tenths of an inch; the aneroid showing 31·22 inches on an occasion when the standard barometer showed 30·80. The least difference was one-fiftieth of an inch, the quantities being 29·22 (aneroid) and 29·24 (standard). At a high temperature or a high pressure, the aneroid was generally in excess of the standard barometer; at a low temperature or a low pressure they were nearly on an equality.

It is still a question of doubt among scientific men, to what extent the aneroid barometer may be relied on in various seasons and climates. With respect to the originality of the invention, it is known that something nearly analogous was suggested long ago. The more ordinary instruments for this purpose are described under BAROMETER.

ANGEL, a piece of money anciently coined and impressed with an angel. The angel was originally a gold coin of France, where it was first coined in 1340. It appears to have been introduced, with its minor divisions, the half angel and the quarter angel, into England by Edward IV., in 1465. Charles I. was the last English sovereign who coined the angel. The device on the obverse was the figure of St. Michael standing upon a dragon, and piercing him through the mouth with a spear. The reverse had a ship, with a large cross for a mast, with the royal arms in front. The obverse had the king's titles surrounding the device.

ANGELICA, yields a candy, an extract, a tincture, and an infusion, all useful in medicine. The candy is prepared by boiling the fresh stalks in water, then steeping them for a time in boiling hot syrup, and lastly taken out and dried. The extract, the tincture, and the infusion are obtained in the modes usually adopted for those preparations.

ANGELO BUONARROTI, MICHEL. This great painter, sculptor, and architect, was born in 1474, died 1563. It is not within the objects of this work to enter into minute details of his life, or any critical account of his works. We confine our notice to the mention of the two greatest monuments of his talents, in departments more immediately connected with what we are accustomed to term the industrial arts. Pope Julius gave orders to Michel Angelo to paint the vault of the Sistine Chapel. He most earnestly endeavoured to decline the task, and even alleged that he thought Raffaelle better qualified to perform it; but Pope Julius allowed no impediment to stand in the way of his will, and Michel Angelo, finding himself without an alternative, and impressed with a sense of the vastness and grandeur of the task, commenced his cartoons. He invited from Florence several artists distinguished as painters in fresco, a mode of practice in which he was then inexperienced, and the roof of the chapel was commenced by these assistants, under his direction; their execution, however, fell short of his expectations, and entering the chapel one morning he dismissed them all, threw their work from the walls, and determined on executing the whole himself. Having advanced to the third compartment, he had the mortification to find his labour frustrated by the bad quality of his materials, in which fermentation had taken place, and in utter disappointment he renounced the undertaking. The pope, being made acquainted with this misfortune, sent to him his architect, San Gallo, who investigated the cause of the failure, and taught him how to correct it. Thus reassured he proceeded, and the pontiff hearing at length that the ceiling was half completed, could control his impatience no longer, and ordered the chapel to be opened for his inspection. Many other persons found admission, and among the rest Raffaelle d'Urbino, who then first became acquainted with Michel Angelo's powers as a painter. Struck with admiration he immediately changed his own style, and thanked God that he had been born in the same age with so great an artist. The work was now carried forward without interruption, and the whole was completed within one year and eight months from the time of its commencement; an achievement which, whether we consider the magnitude and sublimity of the performance, or the almost incredibly short time in which it was executed, is unparalleled in the history of art. The effect of the whole work is adapted with admirable accuracy to the vast height at which it is seen, and it is impossible to contemplate it without reverence and astonishment.

To a design which Michel Angelo made at the beginning of his career for the monument of Julius II., we are indebted for the magnificent church of St. Peter. The monument was too vast for the old church, and the pope determined it should be rebuilt. The monument was finished upon a smaller scale, and placed in another church. But St. Peter's was created. The career of Michel Angelo is an example of the splendid results produced by great powers in conjunction with great opportunities. On St. Peter's he was occupied for the last twenty years of his life. As he had occasion, among the number of persons employed in the undertaking, to promote some and dismiss others, he was beset by cabals, and harassed by opposition; and machinations were even employed to deprive him of his office: but he was uniformly supported by the pontiffs, especially by Julius III., who regarded him with profound respect and veneration. For this great work he constantly refused any remuneration, declaring that he dedicated that service to the glory of God. Old age came upon him, not unaccompanied with the physical infirmities which belong to it, but he retained the vigour and alacrity of his mental faculties to the close of his long life.

ANGERS, a town in the French department of Maine-et-Loire, has considerable manufactures of sail-cloth, camlet, serge, handkerchiefs, hosiery, &c; and there are establishments for bleaching wax and refining sugar. Besides the articles from their own factories, the inhabitants carry on a trade in the agricultural produce of the surrounding district, corn, wine and brandy, flax, hemp, wax, honey, and dried fruits. The neighbourhood is famous for its nursery gardens, and especially for its extensive slate-quarries.

ANGLE. Without entering into the science of Geometry, which does not come within the scope of the present work, a few practical details concerning angles may be useful.

An *angle* is the opening of two lines; *rectilinear*, of two straight lines; *curvilinear*, of two curves; *mixtilinear*, of a straight line and a curve. But in truth angle always means rectilinear angle; and when a curve enters, its tangent is the straight line which is used in determining the angle.

A *right* angle is half the opening of a straight line and its continuation: an *acute* angle is that which is less than a right angle; an *obtuse* angle is that which lies between one and two right angles. *Complemental* angles are two which together make a right angle; *supplemental* angles are two which together make two right angles. When lines meet and make a pair of angles, the one less than two right angles is called *salient;* the other, greater than two right angles, is called *re-entrant* or *re-entering.* For salient and re-entering (which are borrowed from fortification) *direct* and *retroflected* have sometimes been used.

The angles which two lines make with the same part of a third, on opposite sides of it, are called *alternate.* Two lines which cross one another make two pair of *vertically opposite* angles. The angles made by adjacent sides of a figure are called *internal;* those made by any sides with adjacent sides produced are *external.* When the angular point is the centre or on the circumference of a circle, the *angle* is said to be *at* the centre, or *at* the circumference. Beginners often confound the angle with the angular point.

A *spherical* angle is made by two circles (usually great circles) of a sphere. When the circles meet at the pole of the equator, and one of them is the meridian, the angle is an *horary* or *hour-angle;* and when neither is the meridian, the angle is frequently called *horary.* The *angle of position* of a star is that made by the circles drawn to it from the poles of the equator and ecliptic. The angle of *elevation* is the angle made by a line drawn from the eye to any object with the horizontal line which is in the same vertical plane as the first line; but when the object is below the horizon, the term is angle of *depression.* When lines are drawn from two points to a third, those two points, and also the line joining them, are said to *subtend* the angle which is made at the third point. The angle which two objects subtend at the eye is their angle of *elongation.* The *angle of the vertical* is a name given to the angle which a line drawn to the spectator's zenith makes with the radius of the earth produced: it is taken as nothing when the earth is supposed to be a perfect sphere.

When one line falls upon another, the angle of *incidence* is the acute angle which the incident line makes with the perpendicular to the other. When the incident line is thrown off again on the same side as that from which it came, the acute angle made with the perpendicular is called the angle of *reflexion;* when on the opposite side, the angle of *refraction.* These terms are nearly confined to optics.

A *dihedral* angle is the opening made by two planes: it is measured by a rectilinear angle, namely, that made by two lines drawn in the two planes perpendicular to their common intersection. A *solid* angle is said to exist when three or more straight lines, not in the same plane, meet at a point.

In measuring angles, a circle is considered as the curved boundary of four right angles. This is divided into 360 degrees (°), each of which is divided into 60 *minutes* (′), and each minute into 60 *seconds* (″). Formerly, the second was divided into 60 equal parts called *thirds*, and so on; but it is now customary to use the tenths, hundredths, &c., of seconds. The present table therefore stands thus:

A whole revolution = 360° = 21600′ = 1296000″
A right angle = 90° = 5400′ = 324000″

Degrees.		Minutes.		Seconds.
1	=	60	=	3600
		1	=	60

In the attempt to effect a universal change of weights and measures which followed the French Revolution, the circle was divided into 400 degrees, each degree into 100 minutes, each minute into 100 seconds, and so on. This innovation obtained only a partial introduction, and is now entirely abandoned. When used, it is customary in this country to distinguish the French degrees by the name of *grades*, and to denote one grade by 1gr. The convenience of this method, from its close affinity with the decimal system, is certainly great: for example, grades and decimals of grades, such as 12gr. 1329 are converted into grades, minutes, and seconds, by mere separation of the figures: thus, 12gr. 13′ 29″.

1gr. is 0°·9	or	54′	or	3240″
1′ „ 0 ·009	„	0′·54	„	32″·4
1″ „ 0 ·00009	„	0′·0054	„	0″·324

ANGLESEY, or ANGLESEA, the most northern county in Wales, is rich in minerals. The Mona and Parys copper mines are noticed under AMLWCH. Lead ore, rich in silver, has been found also in Parys Mountain. Limestone ranges traverse the island; marbles, both white and variegated, are procured; mill-stones are quarried at Redwharf and Penmon; and there are coal-mines at Malltraeth, but they do not appear to have been worked with much success.

This island-county is noteworthy in an engineering point of view, as being placed in connexion with the rest of Wales by Telford's beautiful Menai suspension-bridge, and by Stephenson's still more wonderful Britannia Tubular Bridge, just now (1850) completed.

ANIMAL FOOD, PRESERVATION OF. [ANTISEPTICS].

ANIMAL STRENGTH. The subject of animal strength will continue to be of much importance as long as it shall be found necessary to employ men or animals, either in conveying burdens or in giving motion to machinery; since by it the employer is enabled to ascertain what is the greatest quantity of useful work which may be obtained from such agents without subjecting them to a degree of fatigue which might in time prove injurious to their health or bodily powers.

With respect to men, Coulomb found that when a man travels unloaded on level ground he can walk 31 miles daily. Now, assuming the weight of a man to be 160 lbs., we have 160 × 31 or 4960 for the measure of his strength or the quantity of action, which is, consequently, equivalent to that of a machine capable of carrying 4960 lbs. to a distance of 1 mile, or 1 pound to a distance of 4960 miles in one day.

He found also, from a mean of the work done by the porters of Paris, that with a burden equal to 128 lbs. a man can walk 9·72 miles in a day, from which it follows (the weight of a man being 160 lbs.) that the quantity of action is (160 + 128) × 9.72, or 2799. If the weight of the man be not included, the quantity of action is 128 × 9·72, or 1244; and this is to be considered as the useful effect. Subtracting 2799 from 4960, we have 2161 for the measure of the action lost in consequence of the burden; but the useful effect, which in the first case was nothing, is in the second expressed by 1244.

By means of a formula, which was given by Euler, with the data afforded by these experiments, it is found that 272 lbs. constitute the greatest burden which a man of average strength can support, and under which he cannot move. It is found, moreover, that the useful effect is at a maximum when a man is loaded with 121 lbs.: under this burden he can walk 10½ miles, nearly, in a day; and consequently the greatest useful effect is expressed by 1280.

Coulomb further determined, that when a man ascends a convenient flight of steps unloaded, the vertical heights of all the ascents during one day being added together, were equal to 1·82 miles; the quantity of action may therefore be expressed by 160 × 1·82 or 291, as if the action were equivalent to that of a machine which could raise 291 lbs. to the height of 1 mile vertically, or 1 lb. to the height of 291 miles during a day. When loaded with 150 lbs. the vertical height ascended was 0·494 miles: the whole quantity of action is, therefore, in this case (160 + 150) × 0·494, or 153, while the useful effect is 150 × 0·494, or 74; that is, 74 lbs. raised 1 mile vertically.

It is remarkable that, from the result of Coulomb's experiments on the power of men ascending steps, both the greatest weight which a man can carry without moving, and the weight which he should bear to render his useful effect a maximum, are nearly the same in this case as they were found to be from experiments made with burdens carried on level grouud.

Coulomb has also made experiments to determine the quantity of action in the case which most generally occurs when heavy goods are carried in towns, viz., that iu which a porter, having delivered his burden, returns unloaded for another; and his conclusion is, that, in order to produce the most useful effect iu this case, the greatest burden which a man should carry on level ground is 135 lbs., and with this he should walk 7 miles. The quantity of useful action is therefore 135×7, or 945.

It is said that a London porter can carry 200 lbs. on his shoulders at the rate of 3 miles per hour; but this action can only be continued during a short time.

The following statements of the streugth of men are taken from Hachette's 'Traité des Machines,' and from other sources; the numerical values being reduced so as to express the number of pounds carried by a man one mile per day of eight hours:—

	lbs.
Drawing a vessel on a canal	753,459
Conveying a load (110 lbs.) in a wheel-barrow (1·018 miles per hour)	896
Drawing a small waggon on four wheels over rather unequal ground	857
Pulling horizontally, the weight being raised by a rope passing over a pulley	378
Rowing in a boat	374
Thrusting horizontally, as at a capstan	368
Turning a winch and axle	159
Digging with a spade	85·3
A soldier marching (12·43 miles) with his arms, &c. (60 lbs.) daily	745

With respect to the horse, the most useful way of employing his strength is to make him draw loads in a cart or waggon; but, even for such work, the estimates which have been made of the quantity of action performed daily are various.

According to Tredgold a horse can draw 125 lbs. at the rate of $2\frac{1}{2}$ miles per hour, which, for one day, would give $125\times2\frac{1}{2}\times8$ or 2500. But Messrs. Boulton and Watt ascertained from trials, purposely made, that a strong horse can draw 125 lbs. at the rate of 3 miles per hour; and the measure of the power of such a horse is 3000, which expresses a number of pounds drawn 1 mile in a day. If this be multiplied by the number of feet in a mile, and the product be divided by the number of minutes in eight hours, the result (=33000) denotes a weight in pouuds drawn 1 foot per minute during the eight hours; and that result is now universally adopted as a measure of the power of a horse, and is called *one horse-power*.

The useful effect of a horse when walking in a circle, as in some mills, is considered as equivalent to	800
A horse carrying a soldier with arms, &c. (=200 lbs.), can go 25 miles in a day, which gives	5000
An African dromedary carrying only his rider (160lbs.) can go between 7 and 8 miles per hour during nine or ten hours, which gives $160\times7\frac{1}{2}\times9\frac{1}{2}$, or	11400
An Asiatic camel will carry burdens weighing from 500 to 800 lbs. (suppose 600) at the rate of $2\frac{1}{2}$ miles per hour. This, for a day of eight hours, gives $600\times2\frac{1}{2}\times8$, or	12000

The velocity of a horse iu walking is estimated at $5\frac{1}{2}$ feet per second, or $3\frac{3}{4}$ miles per hour; in trotting 12 feet per second, or $8\frac{1}{2}$ miles per hour; and in galloping 18 feet per second, or $12\frac{1}{4}$ miles per hour.

ANIMAL SUBSTANCES. Among the most important materials of manufactures, are those which are derived from the animal kingdom. Few persons are aware, unless they have actually been eugaged in manufacturing operations, how numerous and varied these materials are. The bounty of nature has placed at the disposal of man so large a number of substances, derived from so large a number of animals, that there is scarcely an article in daily use but can exhibit an application of some such substance, either in its formation or its decoration. The exterior and the interior, the solids and the liquids—all parts of some animals, and numerous parts of many animals, admit of being thus industriously applied.

In the classified list of objects which are admissible to the Industrial Exhibition of 1851, as announced by the Commissioners, the principal materials of manufactures and the arts derived from the animal kingdom are enumerated, and an attempt is made to arrange them into some convenient systematic form. Iu the first place the whole series is divided into three sections, viz; 1st. *Animal substances used as food;* 2nd. *Animal substances used for medicinal purposes;* and 3rd. *Animal substances used in manufactures.*

Almost every part of almost every species of animal serves as food to some variety or other of the human race. The flesh, the eggs of birds, and the milk of mammalia, are obviously the chief forms in which animal food is presented; but there are many other forms to which more or less of preparative process has been applied; such as preserved meats for long voyages; portable soups; concentrated nutriments; consolidated milk; dried gelatine, albumen, and isinglass; caviare, and trepang; sharks' fins; nests of the Java swallow; honey, &c.

The animal substances used in the medicinal art are exceedingly numerous. Those which the Commissioners enumerate as being fit subjects for exhibition, comprise cod-liver and other animal oils; unguents of spermaceti, lard, oil, and various combinations of the three; musk, castoreum, civet, and ambergris, considered as antispasmodics; phosphorus and ammonia, from bones and hartshorn; crabs' eyes (the calcareous concretions formed in the craw-fish), and cuttle-bone, considered as antacids; cantharides, and their essence cantharidine; and iodine, obtained from marine zoophytes and sponge.

But the animal substances used in manufacturing processes, though perhaps not equalling in *quantity* those consumed as food, are far more varied in quality and texture. They are so numerous, that the commissioners have found it convenient to separate this section into five divisions, viz; *Animal substances employed,* 1st. *for textile fabrics and clothing;* 2nd. *for domestic or ornamental purposes;* 3rd. *for serving as agents in the manufacture of other articles;* 4th. *for the production of chemical substances;* and 5th. *for pigments and dyes.* Under the first division come wool, hair, hair bands and ropes; bristles and whalebone; silk from the silkworm, the pinna, and other insects; feathers, down, and fur; skins, hides, and leather; elytra or beetle wings, for ornaments of dress; &c. Under the second division are included bone, horn, hoofs, ivory, tortoise-shell, shagreen, parchment, vellum, quills, pearls, seed-pearls, mother o' pearl, buffalo shells, Bombay shells, black shells, white-edge shells, yellow-edge shells, flat shells, green-snail shells, coral; together with a large number of softer substances, such as sponge, catgut, gold-beaters' skin, bladders, spermaceti, wax, lard, tallows, oils, &c. Under the third division come glue, isinglass, gelatine, bone-black, ivory black, animal charcoal, &c. Under the fourth division are included bones and other substances from which phosphorus, ammonia, cyanides, &c. are procured. Under the fifth division are enumerated cochineal and carmine; dyes from the galls of aphides; gall-stone pigment from ox-gall; lac, in its various forms of stick-lac, seed-lac, lump-lac, shell-lac, lac-lake, and lac-dye; sepia, from the cuttle-fish; essence d'orient, obtained from the scales of the bleak, and used in the manufacture of artificial pearls, &c.

All or nearly all of the above-named substances will be found noticed under their proper headings in this Cyclopædia.

ANISE and ANISEED. There is a genus of plants known botanically by the name of *pimpernella,* which is chiefly interesting as comprising the species of *anise,* the fruit of which is extensively employed as a carminative medicine, and for the purpose of flavouring liqueurs.

The compound spirit of aniseed is made from aniseed, angelica seed, cassia bark, carraways, proof spirit, and water; or (according to another receipt) from oil of aniseed, oil of angelica, oil of cassia, oil of carraway, and proof spirit. It is used as a pleasant cordial. Another cordial made in France, and known by the name of *Ainsette de Bordeaux,* is a compound of aniseed, coriander, sweet fennel seeds, carraway, oil of cassia, proof spirit, &c.

ANIM'E is the name of a yellowish-brown transparent brittle gum, which exudes from a South American tree called the *Courbaril.* It occurs in pieces of various sizes, and often contains numerous insects imbedded in its mass. It can be softened by various means, but it requires a careful process for its liquefaction. It is extensively used by varnish makers, who combine it at a high heat with oils and turpentine.

ANNEALING is a process by which the extreme brittleness common to glass and some metals when cooled suddenly after melting, is avoided or removed. Such brittleness appears to be occasioned by some disturbance in the regular arrangement of the constituent particles in rapid cooling, and is remedied by cooling very slowly and regularly. A pretty example of the effects of non-annealing is afforded by *glass-tears,* or *Prince Rupert's Drops.* These are made by letting drops of melted glass fall into cold water, whereby they become suddenly solidified without annealing; their form resembles that of a pear, rounded at one extremity, and tapering to a very slender tail at the other. If a part of the tail be broken off, the whole drop falls to pieces with a loud explosion.

Glass-houses are furnished with large *annealing-ovens,* in which this object may be attained by the gradual removal of the glass articles from a hotter to a cooler part, or by allowing the heat of the oven to subside slowly. Analogous operations are employed in the manufactures of cast-iron and other metals. Some malleable metals which crystallize on cooling are brittle in their crystalline state, but are rendered tough by heating and rolling. Zinc, for example, though incapable of more than very slight extension under the hammer, without cracking, becomes almost as flexible and tough as copper after being rolled at a moderate heat.

Cast iron may be made malleable, without subjecting it to the process of puddling; this is effected by a sort of annealing. The iron is kept for several hours at a temperature a little below its fusing point, and then allowed to cool slowly.

ANNIHILATOR, FIRE. In addition to the machines noticed under FIRE ENGINE and FIRE ESCAPE, a new mode of attacking the devouring element is Mr. Phillips's *Fire Annihilator.* Mr. Phillips took out his patent in 1849. The materials employed consist of sugar and chlorate of potash, mixed and boiled together into a homogeneous mass. This is placed in a perforated cylinder, within a second perforated cylinder, contained in a third but air-tight cylinder; and the whole put into an outer case. Water is placed in the space between the bottoms of the third cylinder and outer casing; a vertical pipe opens from this space to the space between the second and third cylinders; so that as the metal expands from the application of heat, the water will be forced up the pipe, and made to mingle with the gas generated from the chemical materials, which will afterwards escape through an opening at the top of the case. It is this gas which is intended to act so remarkably upon a burning mass as to extinguish flame.

With this apparatus Mr. Phillips has made many experiments which have attracted a good deal of public attention. A display was made at Vauxhall Gas Works, in Oct. 1849; model houses and ships, filled with combustibles, were set on fire with a view of shewing how rapidly the annihilator could extinguish the flames. The machine is placed where it can be influenced by the heat of the conflagration; and the resulting gas has a remarkable effect in extinguishing flame; but it does *not* extinguish red heat unaccompanied by flame. Experiments were made in the early part of 1850 at Trentham Park, at the Paddington Railway Station, and at the West India Docks; but the annihilator on these occasions scarcely merited the good opinion of its admirers. A 'Fire Annihilator Company' was, however, established. Shortly after this, the Board of Ordnance permitted a brick building to be constructed in Woolwich Marsh, and made to represent as nearly as practicable (without incurring too much expense) a three storied house, which was then filled with cheap furniture. There were near at hand annihilators of various sizes and degrees of power—one so large as to require two horses to draw it; and a day was appointed for having a grand experimental conflagration. The building was set on fire, but the extinction did not take place satisfactorily.

The truth seems to be (so far as has yet been shewn), that in close rooms, or confined spaces generally, the liberated gases of the annihilator may be serviceably used to extinguish flame; but that where there is plenty of access for external air, the action of the machine becomes impaired. So far as the mere setting to work is concerned, it is so easy and simple, that we may hope to find the apparatus available, in a limited if not an extensive degree.

ANNONAY, a town in France on the banks of the Rhone, is celebrated for making the best paper in France; it is also a busy locality for manufactories of silks, woollens, cottons, and leather.

ANNOTTO. [ARNOTTO.]

ANNULET, in architecture, is the small ring or band which enriches the lower part of the moulding of the Doric column, just where it expands from the top of the shaft.

ANNULUS, the geometrical name for a ring. It is sometimes useful to know the area or solid content of a ring of any substance; and this may be done as follows:—To find the surface of a ring, measure the interior and exterior diameters, multiply the sum and difference of these diameters, and multiply this product by 2·4674. To find the solid contents, measure the inner and outer diameters, multiply together their sum and the square of their difference, and multiply by 0·3084.

ANODY'NES, are substances used in medicine for alleviating pain. They appear to be productive of benefit in two ways: first, by rendering the nerves of the part less sensible; and, secondly, by diminishing the violence with which the large vessels propel the blood, when the anodynes are given in sufficient quantity to influence the brain, and through it, by a process extremely complex, which we need not explain here, the contractile power of the heart and arteries. As most of the articles termed anodynes have a powerful influence over the brain, they generally produce sleep, if given in a large dose: hence they are also denominated *hypnotics;* and, from causing insensibility, they are also denominated *narcotics.* The *Anodyne necklaces* (which partake a good deal of quackery) are formed of the roots of hyosciamus, Job's-tears, allspice steeped in brandy, jumble heads, or elk's hoof, to suit the fancies of the prescribers; they are worn with the hope of procuring easy dentition in children, and sleep in fevers.

The substances which are used as anodynes are, with one exception, derived from the vegetable kingdom; they comprise Opium, Henbane, Woody Nightshade, Deadly Nightshade, Prussic Acid, and Carbonic Acid Gas.

ANONA'CEÆ, is the botanical name for an order of plants, different species of which yield the Ethiopian pepper, the custard apple, bark fit for cordage, &c. The trees and shrubs of this order abound in a powerful aromatic secretion, which renders the flowers of some highly fragrant, the leaves of others a grateful perfume, and the dried fruits of many so highly aromatic as to vie with the spices of commerce.

ANSER. [GOOSE.]

ANT. If the ant is not especially useful to us in furnishing food, or materials for manufactures, he is an instructive artisan whose movements we may watch with profit. Let us view him as a *miner*, a *mason*, a *carpenter*.

The modes in which ants construct their cities differ considerably. The red ant, for example (*Myrmica rubra*), which is common in gardens, makes burrows and chambers under stones, or in the ground under roots, and the spade often disturbs a peaceful colony.

The dusky turf ant (*Formico céspitum*) selects a tuft of long grass, the stems of which serve as supports to a slight tenement consisting of small grains of earth, clay, and sand, piled up without any other cement than water, or the dew and moisture of the ground, which produces a sufficient degree of adhesion between the particles. The whole forms a little hillock, underneath which are galleries and chambers. The sanguinary ant, common on the continent (*F. sanguinea*), makes a subterranean city, composed of galleries and chambers, excavated in the earth or clay to a considerable depth. Over the covert ways into this labyrinth is placed a thick coping of dry heath twigs and grass stems to defend it from rain and cold.

The yellow ant *(F. flava)* builds mounds, a foot or more in height, and generally in old pastures. They are composed of particles of soil quarried from below, bits of decayed wood, &c., and are generally built during rainy or moist weather, as these ants have no other means than what the atmosphere affords of tempering their materials. These mounds are smooth externally, and contain chambers and galleries.

The nest of the fallow ant, or wood ant, a large species not uncommon in woods and pleasure grounds, presents a rude appearance: externally it looks like a hillock of earth, intermixed with bits of dried twigs, straws, particles of leaves, and as we have seen, even grains of corn, all mixed together, and forming a large coping or protection to numerous chambers arranged in separate stories, some deeply excavated in the earth, others near the centre or even the surface of the hillock; all communicating with each other by means of galleries; various passages open externally, the entrances being closed or left free, according to the state of the weather.

The colonies of the fuliginous or jet ant (*F. fuliginosa*), make their habitations in the trunks of old oaks or willows, in which with their strong mandibles they work out horizontal galleries separated from each other by thin partitions, and all communicating with each other. These excavations often resemble halls supported by multitudes of pillars, rising story above story, and built of ebony, for the wood is invariably stained black, perhaps in consequence of the action of the formic acid, a peculiar secretion found in ants, and which, dissolved in water, serves the purposes of vinegar in Norway, where the ants are collected and steeped in boiling water, and thus is formed diluted formic acid.

With respect to the ants of hotter climates, the wonderful structures which they make have attracted the notice of most travellers. Some rear huge mounds; some construct large edifices in the forks of trees; some glue leaves together so as to form a purse; some excavate the branches of the trees, working out the pith to the extremity of the slenderest twig.

An accurate observer, Dr. J. R. Johnson, remarks, 'I have often been surprised at the ingenuity of these little creatures, in availing themselves of contiguous blades of grass, stalks of corn, &c., when they wish to enlarge the boundaries of their abode. As these are usually met with in the erect position, they are admirably calculated for pillars; they therefore coat them over with a fine paste of earth, giving them, by additional layers, the solidity they judge necessary for the work.'

ANTACIDS, signify medicines used to correct acidity in the stomach. Though hydrochloric acid (formerly called muriatic acid, or spirit of salt) is present in a free state in the stomach during the process of healthy digestion, yet under particular circumstances it is apt to be generated in excess. Other acids are also occasionally evolved in the stomach, probably from the fermentation of the articles, as vegetables and fruits of different kinds, by which the acetic acid is produced, or introduced ready formed, in wines or hard beer, and in certain vegetables, as sorrel, which contains oxalic acid. The most frequent source of acidity is that first mentioned, the secretion of acid by the vessels of the stomach. It is, therefore, dependent upon constitutional causes, or the state of the system generally.

The medicinal means of remedying this state are all alkaline, either the pure alkalies, or some combination of them—such as solution of potash, or carbonates of soda, potash, magnesia, ammonia, or lime. These medicines are called Antacids.

ANTÆ, a term used by architects to designate the pier-formed ends of a wall, as in the terminations of the lateral walls in a Greek temple, where a plain face returns on each side, having some relation in general proportion to the columns with which they compose. The antæ (for the word is used alike in the singular and in the plural) has a moulded and otherwise enriched cap or cornice, and generally a moulded base. The moulded caps and bases of antæ are, in Greek works, generally continued along the flank walls so as to form the cornice and base of the whole wall, and not of the protruded faces of its ends alone. In Roman works, and in modern imitations of both, breaks are often made on the face of a wall with the caps and bases of antæ, but more frequently with those of columns, and these are called pilasters. In classical Greek works, and in the best Roman works, antæ and pilasters are never either diminished or fluted.

ANTALKALIES, are medicines for counteracting the presence of alkalies in the system. Such remedies consist of the various mineral and organic acids.

ANTEFIXÆ, blocks with vertical faces placed along over a cornice in ancient Greek and Roman buildings, to hide the ends of the covering or joint tiles, and their faces are generally ornamented with a flower, leaf, or other enrichment.

A'NTHEMIS. [CHAMOMILE.] The *Anthemis tinctoria* is used in France by the dyers for the sake of a brilliant yellow tint, which is obtained from it.

ANTHOXANTHUM. [GRASS.]

A'NTHRACITE, a black, light, mineral substance, resembling coal. It is also called *blind coal*, and *glance coal*. Its specific gravity is about 1·400; it is slowly combustible, but without flame; and it contains 96 per cent. of pure carbon: it is, in fact, a mineral charcoal. Naphtha may be considered as one extremity of the mineral carbonaceous substances, and anthracite as the other. Tar, petroleum, bitûmen, asphaltum, and the various kinds of coal, form the intermediate members of the series. Anthracite is now much used as a steam-engine fuel. Sir H. De La Beche and Dr. Lyon Playfair, who were commissioned lately by the Admiralty to investigate the qualities of steam-coal for the navy, have pointed out the many useful qualities of Anthracite. [FUEL]. Small quantities of Anthracite are found in the primary strata of most countries, as, for instance, in the old slate of Cornwall, Devon, and Cumberland, where the appearances led to borings and other works in search of coal. In the south of Ireland anthracite occurs in clay-slate and grauwacke, so thick as to be regularly worked for the purpose of burning the lime of the district; the most considerable collieries have yielded 25,000 tons annually; and all the coal of the province of Munster, with the exception of that of the county of Clare, is of the same sort. It is found in many of our coal-mines, but generally in those situations where the coal comes in contact with clay-slate.

Anthracite, as a fuel for locomotives, has met with but little success. In America, where wood is largely used for this purpose, great desire is exhibited to substitute anthracite for wood; but Professor Johnson communicated a paper to the *Franklin Journal* in 1847, shewing many reasons why it had hitherto not been very successful. There is a want of rapid ignition and lively combustion; the intense local heat tends to destroy the grate-bars, to loosen the rivets, and to blister the iron plates; the ashes of the anthracite fuse into an unmanageable sort of clinker; the sharp angular particles of coal, projected by the violent draught of the furnace obliquely into the ends of the copper tubes, tend to cut the metal near the fire end. Professor Johnson points out modes which, in his judgment, will obviate these several sources of inconvenience, and render the use of anthracite in locomotives desirable.

In a series of experiments made by Messrs. Fairbairn of Manchester, on 280 bars made of different kinds of iron, it was found that anthracite iron, or iron smelted with anthracite instead of other kinds of coal, is superior to other kinds of iron in strength, though not quite equal to some of them in elasticity. The results were communicated *in extenso* to the British Association in 1840.

ANTIDOTES, administered to counteract the effect of poisons, are used with one of three objects, viz., 1, to remove the poisonous substance: 2, to prevent or limit its local effects: 3, to obviate its effects on remote organs, supporting their action by appropriate measures, till the injurious impression has subsided. The first of these is accomplished mostly by mechanical means, such as the cupping-glass or the stomach-pump. The second mode depends on a very intimate knowledge of the chemical elements and action of the poison. The third mode depends on a close study of the physiology of the human system.

ANTI-ATTRITION, is a preparation used to lessen friction in machinery, and also to prevent iron from rusting. It is made by grinding black lead with four times its weight of lard or tallow, and adding a little camphor to the mixture.

ANTI-FERMENT. In the cider-districts a substance under this name is sold for the purpose of correcting fermentation. Mustard seed and clover, or mustard seed and sulphite of lime, are usually the ingredients: they tend to allay the fermentation of cider or perry, or even beer.

ANTI-FRICTION WHEELS. The action of friction or anti-friction wheels in machinery is to diminish resistance by converting what would otherwise be a *rubbing* into a *rolling* contact. Friction rollers, which are generally of small diameter, are not necessarily fixed upon axles or shafts, but are interposed bodily between the rubbing or sliding surfaces which press upon them; and they may thus be employed to alleviate friction between surface. In some arrangements of mechanism, friction rollers are provided with small axles which do not bear any important strain, but are used chiefly for the purpose of keeping the rollers in their proper place. The wheels of an ordinary carriage are in principle very little other than anti-friction wheels or rollers.

The various applications of anti-friction rotation are very numerous; but they all depend on this principle—that when the surfaces of two bodies are made to pass over each other with a rubbing or sliding motion, their inequalities necessarily meet and oppose each other, and thereby cause both resistance and wear; but if rollers or wheels be applied between them, instead of the inequalities of the roller being dragged against those of the surface upon which it rolls, they are successively laid upon (so to speak) and lifted up from them.

ANTIGUA, is one of the sugar colonies of the British West Indies. The sugar produce of 1846 was 102,644 cwt.; that of 1847 reached nearly double this amount; but 1848 proved a deficient year. A considerable quantity of cotton was once produced in this island, but the culture has been discontinued. If the experiment now being made in Jamaica should, however, be successful, cotton planting may again be attempted in Antigua. Antigua took British produce and manufactures, in 1849, to the value of 70,194*l*.

ANTILOGARITHM, as used in this country, means the *number to the logarithm*. Thus, in Briggs's system, 100 is the antilogarithm of 2, because 2 is the logarithm of 100. [LOGARITHM.]

ANTIMONY, a metal sometimes called *regulus of antimony*, occurs, though rarely, native, and is generally procured from the sulphuret, which is the only abundant ore of the metal. When this is heated in contact with iron, the sulphur, on account of its greater affinity for that metal, is separated by it from the antimony, which is consequently reduced to a nearly pure metallic state. Its colour is silver white, lustre considerable, and the fracture fine laminated when pure; but the antimony of commerce is broad laminated. Its specific gravity is about 6·7, and atomic weight 64. When slowly cooled after fusion, it crystallizes in the octahedron or its varieties. When it is exposed to the air, this metal tarnishes, and at a red heat it melts. Fulminating antimony is much employed in fire-works.

Oxygen and antimony may be combined in several modes and in different proportions. There are many ways of producing the *sesquioxide of antimony*, the composition of which is —antimony 2, oxygen 3. This oxide is a dingy white powder, insoluble in water, but it is dissolved by dilute nitric acid, and by strong nitric acid is converted into antimonious acid. Muriatic acid also readily takes it up; the same effect is produced by bitartrate of potash, and the solution on cooling deposits octahedral crystals, which have been long known and employed in medicine under the name of *tartar emetic*, or *tartarized antimony*. It is soluble also in potash, soda, and ammonia. A second compound is the *deutoxide*, or *antimonious acid*, containing antimony 1, oxygen 2. This acid is neither fusible nor volatile at a red heat. Its saline compounds are termed *antimonites*, as antimonite of potash, &c. If it be fused with this alkali, the salt formed dissolves in water, from which the acids throw down a white precipitate of antimonious acid combined with water. A third compound of oxygen and antimony is the *peroxide*, or *antimonic acid*. It is a pale yellow powder, consisting of antimony 2, oxygen 5. Its action on the animal economy is but slight. Antimonic acid is tasteless and insoluble in water.

Chlorine and Antimony unite to form two compounds. The *protochloride*, or *sesquichloride* sometimes called *butter of antimony*, is composed of chlorine 3, antimony 2. It is a soft and nearly colourless solid. At a moderate heat it liquefies, and it absorbs moisture from the air. From it is prepared the submuriate of antimony, formerly employed in medicine under the name of *pulvis Algarotti*. The other compound is a *perchloride of antimony*, consisting of chlorine 5, antimony 2. It is a colourless or slightly yellow fluid, has a strong disagreeable smell, and emits white fumes. It attracts moisture from the air, and when mixed with water it is decomposed, and converted into muriatic acid and antimonic acid.

Bromine and Antimony form *bromide of antimony*. At common temperatures it is solid, colourless, crystallizes in needles, attracts moisture from the air, and is decomposed by water. It melts at about 206° Fahrenheit, and boils at 518°. *Iodine* also combines with antimony to form an iodide.

Sulphur and Antimony combine to form several compounds. The chief of these is the *sesquisulphuret*, or *crude antimony*, which is the principal ore of the metal. It is found in many parts of the earth; it is of a lead gray colour, possessing considerable splendour, and is met with compact, in acicular crystals, and in rhombic prisms. It is composed of sulphur 3 atoms, antimony 2 atoms. It is much employed in preparing metallic antimony, glass of antimony, crocus of antimony, James's powder, and some preparations in the London and other pharmacopœias. It is soluble in a hot solution of potash or soda; on cooling, an orange red substance is deposited, called *kermes-mineral;* this was formerly much used in medicine. When an acid is added to the remaining cold solution, a further portion of a similar precipitate is formed: this is sometimes called the *golden sulphuret of antimony*, and in the 'London Pharmacopœia,' *sulphuretum antimonii præcipitatum*.

The only salt of antimony, strictly speaking, of any great importance, is the double tartrate of potash and antimony, usually termed tartar emetic, or tartarized antimony—the *antimonium tartarizatum* of the 'London Pharmacopœia.' Of all the preparations of antimony this is the most valuable. The Pharmacopœias also contain a preparation in imitation of James's powder, called *pulvis antimonialis*.

Antimony is susceptible of combining with all metals. It makes them very brittle. The principal alloys of antimony are that with lead, employed as *type metal*, and the alloy of antimony and tin, used for plates on which music is engraved.

It has been recently suggested, by Mr. Forrest of Liverpool, that antimony would be a good substitute for lead in the manufacture of white paint. He considers that the oxide of antimony is usually cheaper than white lead, that it is not so apt to lose its colour, and that an equal weight of paint will spread over a much larger surface.

Antimony sells at the present time in the London market at 44s. to 60s. per cwt.

ANTI'PAROS, a small island in the Grecian Archipelago, is interesting in an artistic point of view for the exquisite white marble which it yields. Of this material consists the famous grotto, which is 120 yards long, 113 wide, and 60 feet high; it is an immense arch of white marble, from the roof of which depend large stalactites, 10 feet long and as thick as a man's waist, with festoons and leaves of the same substance; the floor is rough and uneven, with various coloured crystals and stalagmites rising up; and in the midst is one 20 feet in diameter, and 24 feet high. When lighted up, the whole presents a most brilliant and magnificent scene, but the smoke from the torches of the numerous visitors has somewhat dimmed its effulgence.

ANTI'PODES, as a term indicating the inhabitants on two exactly opposite points on the globe, is only interesting to us here so far as it concerns *climate*. Two *antipodal* points of the earth have the same number of degrees of latitude, one north and the other south, unless one of the points be on the equator, in which case the antipodal point is the opposite point of the equator. Their longitude differs by 180° or 12 hours, if we reckon longitude all round the globe; but if we use east and west longitude, the two longitudes must together make up 180° or 12 hours, one east and the other west. We here insert, in opposite columns, the names of a few places which are nearly antipodal.

London . .	Antipodes Island, S. E. of New Zealand.
Nankin . . .	Buenos Ayres.
Bermudas . .	Swan River.
Quito	Middle of Sumatra.
Azores . . .	Botany Bay.

Antipodal places have the same climate, so far as that depends merely on latitude; but have all the seasons, days and nights completely reversed. Thus, noon of the longest day at the Bermudas is midnight of the shortest day at the Swan River. The remark as to the seasons of course does not apply to antipodal places on the equator.

ANTIQUES. This term properly refers to works of Grecian art in sculpture, bas-relief, engraving of gems, medals, &c. As these arts flourished in the states of Greece, and also under the Roman Empire (though most probably they were always successfully cultivated chiefly by Greeks), it is not possible to find any precise chronological limits that shall determine whether a work of art belongs to the *antique* or not. Still, as there was under the Roman Empire a great and progressive deterioration in the arts above alluded to, until in more recent times they have been again improved, it is clear that many works of considerable antiquity cannot be classed under the head of *antiques;* for by the term antiques we understand, in general, works that have decided merit, and may serve as models for imitation; or they are at least works of art that serve to illustrate and explain those ancient authors whose writings, by common consent, are allowed to be deserving of study.

ANTIRRHI'NUM. [OILS.]

ANTIS. A portico is said to be *in antis* when columns stand in a line, in front, with the antæ or projecting ends of the side walls of the temple or other building. There is a good example of the portico *in antis* in North Audley Street, London, which forms the entrance to an episcopal chapel.

ANTISCORBUTICS, the remedies, real or reputed, against scurvy. Sea-scurvy formerly prevailed in a very extensive degree. Commodore Anson, in the course of his voyage round the world, lost above four-fifths of his men, and when he arrived at Juan Fernandez, of the 200 men then surviving, eight only were capable of duty. An entire crew has sometimes fallen a victim to it, and the ship been left without a single hand to guide it through the waters. This happened in the case of the Spanish ship Oriflamma, in which the whole crew perished, and in this state she was discovered with the dead bodies on board.

The causes of this disease appear to be exposure to a cold and damp atmosphere, excessive fatigue, badly ventilated sleeping apartments, and intemperance; but none of these causes singly, nor indeed all of them combined, are adequate to produce scurvy, unassisted by some specific cause, which cause is to be found in the *diet*. The diet of seamen during long voyages was formerly merely salted meat and biscuit; fresh animal food or recent vegetables formed no part of it. It was also often deficient in quantity.

Fresh vegetables, vegetable substances, or articles prepared from them, constitute the *antiscorbutics*, or means of preventing and curing sea-scurvy; but they are not all of equal value, some far surpassing others in efficacy. The *lemon* is the most valuable of all. It may be used in various ways; the best is in the form of the fresh fruit, sucked by the patient: but in the absence of this, lemon-juice may be employed, and this is the usual mode in the naval practice. A quantity of it, having a tenth-part of spirit of wine added to preserve it, are supplied to each ship, and in about a fortnight after leaving port its use is begun; each sailor is allowed one ounce of it and one ounce and a half of sugar to mix with the grog, or in many instances with wine, a stated quantity of which is granted in lieu of a certain quantity of spirits, which is withdrawn. This has the effect of almost invariably preventing scurvy affecting any of the crew. The recent admiralty orders (1850) tend to lessen the use of grog and to increase that of lemon-juice.

In addition to the lemon-juice, ships intended to be sent on long voyages are supplied with animal food, so prepared as to be almost as fresh at the end of six years as if it had been killed but a few days and dressed the day previous to its being used. This valuable discovery, which tends so greatly to lessen the inconvenience of a sea-life, as well as to secure the health of those devoted to it, was made by Mr. Appert.

ANTISEPTICS, are the means of preventing those changes in organized matter which are comprehended under the term putrefaction.

All organized substances do not putrefy with equal rapidity, nor under all circumstances. Decomposition goes on fastest in substances which contain nitrogen, and most slowly in substances which contain carbon; hence animal matters putrefy quickly; vegetable, especially of a woody texture, gradually. The conditions necessary for putrefaction to take place are, tho presence of air, of a certain temperature, and moisture. If any one of these be excluded, the process is prevented. The moisture may either be external, or it may be the fluids of the body itself. The bulk of the animal frame is made up of fluids, which must either be dissipated by heat, abstracted by some chemical process, or rendered solid by a very low temperature, if we wish to preserve any animal substance in the state most near that of its natural constitution.

The modes of preserving food are either natural or artificial. The natural modes comprehend those which effect this end by abstracting or excluding one or more of the chief agents,—heat, moisture and air; the artificial comprehend those methods of preparation or mixture which produce some chemical change in the substance.

1st. Abstraction of heat. The presence of heat is essential to the exertion of those chemical affinities which take place during decomposition, or constitute the process; abstracting it therefore checks or suspends them. Most articles of food keep better in cold than in warm weather. When the heat has been so completely abstracted that the juices are frozen, *i.e.* become solid, the preservation of the substance is more effectually accomplished. Indeed they may thus be preserved for many years, perhaps ages.

On this principle the Russians preserve their poultry, which they kill in October, and pack in tubs with layers of snow between. The markets of St. Petersburg are supplied with veal brought from a great distance in this state, as well as with whole hogs, sheep, and fish. The Canadians preserve their provisions in the same way.

A precaution is necessary in thawing them; for this end, they should always be put into cold water first. Indeed, in the case of persons buried in the snow, recovery is much more likely to be brought about by plunging the individual into cold water, than by placing him in a warm bed.

This method of preserving food is not applicable to vegetables, but when these are frozen they should also be first put into cold water.

2nd. The abstraction of moisture by heat is employed in drying fish and other animal substances, as beef, bacon, &c., though in these the rapid tendency to putrefaction makes the employment of a certain quantity of salt, &c., necessary, along with the drying, unless the process be carried on with great rapidity, which may be effected by a high temperature and a free circulation of air. Hence in many places, where turf or wood is burnt, hams are hung within the wide kitchen chimney. Drying is also employed for the preservation of vegetable substances, such as grain, hay, &c. It is by this means that botanists preserve plants to form a hortus siccus, or herbarium, and many plants are thus preserved for medical use, but for this purpose a high temperature should never be applied, as it dissipates their active principles.

3rd. The exclusion of sources of oxygen gas constitutes another means of preventing or checking putrefaction; and as the atmospheric air is the most common source of oxygen, we shall limit our remarks to the means of excluding it. The effect of such exclusion is very great. Réaumur varnished some eggs, and found that at the end of two years they were yet capable of producing chickens; and Bomare mentions an instance where three eggs were inclosed within the walls of a church in the Milanese, and when found at the end of 300 years, they had not lost their flavour. Lime-water is the best medium in which to place eggs for long keeping. But more valuable articles than eggs are preserved by this means; and in a condition nearly equal to their fresh state. We allude to the method of preserving animal food and vegetables, promulgated by M. Appert. This consists in boiling the articles (if meat, the bones must be first taken out) to nearly as great a degree as if intended for immediate consumption; they are then put into jars or tin canisters, which must be completely filled with a broth or jelly prepared from portions of the same meat. The jars are then corked and covered with a luting, and the canisters carefully soldered down. After this, they are placed in a boiler of cold water, to which heat is applied till the water boils, and the boiling of which is continued for an hour; the fire must then be instantly extinguished, and the water soon drawn off, but the boiler must not be uncovered, or the bottles taken out, for one or two hours after. By this method meat has been kept sound and well-flavoured for six years and upwards, and has been sent to all parts of the globe. The process of exhausting the air from the vessel which contains the substance to be preserved, and then effectually excluding the atmosphere is a method now frequently used.

A simpler method of preserving animal food for sea-stores is the following:—the meat is cut into slices of four to eight ounces, steeped for five minutes in a vessel of boiling water, and dried on a network at a temperature of about 120° Fahrenheit. The liquid or soup formed by steeping the meat is next evaporated to the state of a thick varnish, to which a little spice is added. The dry pieces of meat are dipped into this gravy, and dried again; and this dipping and drying are repeated two or three times. The meat will in this dry state remain good for a year or two; and must then be cooked in the usual way by boiling, &c.

The natural methods of preserving organized substances are few and simple: the artificial more numerous, as well as more complex. They consist either in causing such changes in the elementary constitution of a body as shall form a new and less destructible article, or in introducing some additional principle which shall hinder the exercise of the natural tendency of the substance to decomposition.

The first set of means constitute the various kinds of fermentation, with respect to which we may remark, that the products of them are not only little disposed to undergo decomposition, but have also a powerful effect in preventing other substances from undergoing it; the most remarkable of these are acetic acid, or vinegar, and alcohol. The formation of sugar, another product of fermentation, is a powerful means of preserving fruits, in which it is formed spontaneously, or to which it is afterwards added. The addition of sugar is practised in forming syrups, jellies, and preserves.

Those parts of plants which contain much carbon last the longest. In trees cut down and exposed to air and moisture, the bark, which contains most carbon, endures after the rest has perished. The seed also contains much carbon, and when seeds are sent from India to England they are always wrapped in recently prepared charcoal. When stakes or piles of wood are to be driven into the beds of rivers or marshes, they are previously charred; and to preserve water sent to sea, the inner side of the cask is also charred.

There are many substances which when added to animal matter prevent for a longer or shorter time their decomposition, such as saltpetre (nitrate of potass), and common salt (chloride of sodium), which last is supposed to act by abstracting the elements of water; certain it is that meat is rendered by salting much drier, harder, less easily digested, and consequently less nourishing. Many aromatic substances have a similar power of preventing putrefaction for a time. They were extensively employed in embalming in ancient as well as modern times, as the Egyptian mummies prove. Oils and resinous substances long resist putrefaction, and preserve other substances from it; bitumen, naphtha, and empyreumatic oils, are examples of this. Russia leather, which is dressed with the empyreumatic oil of the birch, not only does not become mouldy, but also preserves the books which are bound with it. The process of decomposition is greatly hastened by the agency of fungi, such as those which cause mouldiness, and the more formidable destroyers which occasion the dry-rot. The fungi which cause mouldiness are generally prevented from developing themselves by the presence of some aromatic oil; and the others which occasion the dry-rot in timber, may be prevented from developing themselves by the process invented by the late Mr. Kyan. [DRY-ROT.]

ANTONINE COLUMN, a lofty pillar which stands in the middle of one of the principal squares of the city of Rome. It was raised by the senate in honour of the Emperor Marcus Aurelius Antoninus, and in memory of his victory over the Marcomanni and other German tribes. The shaft of the pillar is 13 feet 1 inch in diameter at the bottom, and one foot less at the top; its height, including the pedestal and capital, is 136 feet, of which 13 are under ground; and the statue on the top and its pedestal are 27½ feet more, making the whole height 163½ feet. The capital is Doric. The shaft is made of twenty-eight blocks of white marble. A spiral staircase of 190 steps is cut through the interior of the marble, and leads to the gallery on the top, which is surrounded by a balustrade. The exterior of the shaft is covered with bassi-rilievi placed in a spiral line around, which represent the victories of Marcus Aurelius over the Marcomanni and other hostile nations. The style and execution of these sculptures are inferior to those of the Trajan pillar, which the artists evidently purposed to imitate.

ANTONINUS, WALL OF. This was an entrenchment raised by the Romans across the north of Britain under the direction of Lollius Urbicus, legate of Antoninus Pius, about A.D. 140, and is supposed to have connected a line of forts erected by Agricola, A.D. 80. Julius Capitolinus, the only ancient writer who mentions this rampart, calls it a turf wall (*murus cespititius*). The work was composed of a ditch, a rampart with its parapet, made of materials taken from the ditch, and a military way running along the whole line of the entrenchment at the distance of a few yards on the south side. It extended from Dunglass Castle on the Clyde to the heights above Caer Ridden Kirk, a little beyond the river Avon on the Frith of Forth, or probably to Blackness Castle two miles farther on, though it cannot now be traced so far. In its course are nineteen forts, the eighteen distances between which amount to 63,980 yards, or 36 English miles, and the mean distance from station to station is 3554 yards, or rather more than two English miles. In the position of the forts, the Romans chose a high and commanding situation from whence the country could be discovered to a considerable distance, contriving, as far as circumstances would permit, that a river, morass, or some difficult ground should form an obstruction to any approach from the front. Forts were also placed upon the passages of those rivers which crossed the general chain of communication. From inscriptions discovered in Scotland, it appears that the entrenchment was made by the second legion, by vexillations of the sixth and the twentieth legion, and the first cohort of the Tungri. A very considerable portion of the entrenchment may still be traced. The modern name is Grimes Dyke.

ANTRIM, is one of the chief flax-spinning and linen-weaving counties of Ireland. It contains the flourishing towns of Belfast (the head-quarters of this department of industry); Antrim town, with its smiling bleach-greens in the vicinity; Ballymena and Lisburn, and several other towns which present a marked exception to the poverty of most other parts of Ireland.

ANTWERP, one of the nine provinces of the kingdom of Belgium, is distinguished in an agricultural point of view for the district called the *polders*, which extends along the Schelde, from the neighbourhood of Antwerp city to Zantvliet; it was originally a marsh which was flooded by every tide, its surface being lower than the level of the river at high water. Dykes having been built to keep off the tide, the surface of the marsh was drained by means of water-wheels turned by windmills, and what was before an unhealthy swamp was changed into the richest pasture and arable land. The city of Antwerp has a large commerce, and fine docks and quays to accommodate it. The new quay and the great basin were begun by Bonaparte, and were part of the plan by which he intended to make this city a great naval station. The area of the great basin is 17 acres, and of the small one 7 acres. On each side of the great basin are two careening docks, made during the empire of Napoleon for repairing the ships of war constructed here.

Antwerp is the principal seat of the silk manufactures of Belgium, and is especially famous for its black silks and velvets. It has large manufactures of cotton, linen, lace, carpets, hats, cutlery, and surgical instruments; there is also a bleaching establishment which is worked by steam, several sugar refineries, and other establishments common in large towns. It contains a great military arsenal, dockyards, and an extensive rope-walk. The imports consist principally of coffee, sugar, and other colonial products, cotton stuffs, and other manufactured goods, corn, raw cotton, leather, timber, tobacco, wool, dyestuffs, salt, wines, fruits, &c. The exports consist chiefly of flax, cotton and linen manufactures, refined sugar, glass, zinc, oak-bark, grain and seeds, lace, &c.

ANVIL. The anvil on which the swarthy smith pursues his labours is usually made of iron and faced with steel. It is made of seven pieces, forged separately, and welded together into form. These pieces are the core or body, four corner pieces which serve to enlarge the base, a projecting end with a square hole, and a beak or horizontal cone. The welding of these pieces together requires good workmanship. The steel facing is welded upon the iron in a similar way.

The size, the shape, and the finish of an anvil depend upon the use to which it is applied. Those used by watchmakers and jewellers are small and delicate. Perhaps the largest anvil in the world is that which is placed beneath the ponderous *Nasmyth's hammer* at Sir John Guest's Dowlais Iron Works, Merthyr Tydvil; it weighs 36 tons, and was cast in one piece! The foundation prepared for it was of vast depth and strength.

ANZIN, a village in the neighbourhood of Valenciennes, in the department of Nord, is the seat of the most extensive collieries in France. The pits amount to forty altogether, some of which are more than 1400 feet deep. The coal burns fiercely, and is in demand for purposes which require an intense flame; to this circumstance perhaps may be ascribed the establishment of glass-works and manufactories at Anzin. The number of persons employed in the mines amounts to 16,000, and the annual produce is about 200,000 tons.

A'PATITE, a mineral substance crystallized in the regular six-sided prism, usually terminated by a truncated six-sided pyramid. It has usually a yellowish green tint, and is translucent. In hardness it ranks above fluor-spar, and below feld spar. It is a compound of phosphate of lime with fluoride of calcium. It principally occurs in the primitive rocks, and is found in the tin mines of St. Michael's Mount, Cornwall; in those of Bohemia and Saxony; and in mineral beds met with in Estremadura in Spain.

APENNINES, the great mountain-system of Italy, are not so rich in mineral produce as many other mountain chains. The chief among them, perhaps, are the celebrated marble quarries of Carrara and the pumice of Vesuvius. There is also the peculiar stone called *travertino*, which is a deposit from water holding carbonate of lime in solution, by means of the carbonic acid which is common in spring waters; by exposure to air the carbonic acid escapes, and the carbonate of lime is deposited; such springs abound in many parts of central Italy within the volcanic region. There are vast deposits of this travertino, which is used for building purposes.

APHIS. The genus of insects called by this name is a great torment to the farmer. These insects sometimes make sad havoc with the CABBAGE, the HOP, and the TURNIP, as the reader will find noticed.

APIARY, a place for keeping bee-hives, is usually shielded from wind, but authorities differ much as to the best direction in which it can be placed. [BEE-HIVE.]

APIIN, the peculiar principle of parsley, obtained from it by solution in water. It is nearly insoluble in cold water and alcohol, but soluble in either when heated; soluble in the alkalies, in lime water, in sulphuric acid, and in muriatic acid. Many of its solutions assume a gelatinous state.

APIUM. [CELERY.]

APLANATIC LENS, is a lens which should be capable of so refracting all the rays which, diverging from or converging to any one point in the axis, are incident upon it, that after being transmitted through it they may converge to or diverge from one other point in the same axis.

A spherical lens cannot, when formed of any known media, be made strictly aplanatic; and it having been found impossible hitherto to execute lenses with surfaces produced by the revolutions of conic sections, mathematicians have investigated expressions for the form under which, with a given refractive index, the aberration of the focus shall be a minimum.

A few details, illustrative of the aplanatic quality in lenses will be met with under MICROSCOPE; TELESCOPE.

APOLLO BELVEDE'RE, a celebrated statue of Apollo, found at Capo d'Anzo, in the ruins of ancient Antium, about 32 miles from Rome, towards the end of the fifteenth century. It was purchased by Pope Julius II., before his elevation to the pontificate; and was placed by him in the Belvedere of the Vatican, whence it derives its present name. It has been said to be the work of Agasius the Ephesian, but no certain indications of the sculptor are to be traced. But it is now pretty well proved that it was made under the emperors, and probably by the order of Nero himself.

APOLLO'NICON, the name given to a chamber organ of vast power, supplied with both keys and barrels, built by Messrs. Flight and Robson, of St. Martin's Lane, London, and first exhibited by them at their manufactory, in 1817. It has 1,900 pipes, the largest 24 feet in length, and 1 foot 11 inches in aperture, sounding the G, two octaves below the first line of the base, the highest giving the A in altissimo, two octaves above the second space in the treble. The number of stops is 45, and these in their combinations afford very good imitations of the various wind instruments used in an orchestra. As a self-playing instrument, the apollonicon is provided with two revolving cylinders, studded like that of a barrel organ. As a keyed instrument, it has five key-boards, of which the largest comprises five octaves. The swell, the compound pedals, and all the accessory arrangements, are on a very complex scale.

APO'PHYGE, a term applied by architects generally to a concave surface lying between or connecting two flat surfaces not in the same plane, and particularly to a slight concavity which is almost invariably found to terminate the shaft of an Ionic or Corinthian column both above and below. The more familiar English term for the same thing is, the *escape;* and in French, the apophyge is termed the *congé.*

APOTHECARIES' WARES. Under this designation the Customs' department give an entry of the quantity and value of the drugs and chemicals exported from England to our Colonies annually. These quantities and values are larger than many persons would suppose. They amounted in 1849 to 22,691 cwt., valued at 116,546*l.* The East Indies and New South Wales were the chief places of destination.

APOTHECARIES' WEIGHTS AND MEASURES. In buying and selling medicines wholesale, avoirdupois weight is employed; but in *dispensing* medicines the pound troy is divided into 12 ounces, the ounce into 8 drams or drachms, the dram into 3 scruples, and the scruple into 20 grains.

The late Dr. Young calculated, that the relations which exist between apothecaries' weight in England and other countries are as follow: — 1000 English grains equal 1125 Austrian, 989 Dutch, 981 French, 978 Hanoverian, 958 German, 956 Bernese, 955 Swedish, 925 Spanish, 909 Roman, 864 Portuguese, 860 Neapolitan, 850 Genoese, 824 Piedmontese, 809 Venetian.

Apothecaries' *fluid* measure is as follows:— 60 minims one dram; 8 drams one ounce; 20 ounces one pint. A minim of water is almost exactly one drop; and a fluid ounce of pure water is almost exactly equal to an ordinary ounce weight; but this is not the case with liquids either heavier or lighter than water.

APPALACHIAN MOUNTAINS. This important North American mountain chain is chiefly valuable in an economical point of view for its beds of coal. In Pennsylvania there is a vast deposit of coal, associated with sandstones and slates. The coal seems to be of that quality which in Britain is generally called *blind coal* or *anthracite.* One of these coal-fields, in the valley of Wyoming, is 60 miles long by 5 broad; a second is in the valley of the Lehigh river; and others on the Schuylkill, the Susquehanna, and the Lackawanna. Besides these beds of anthracite coal, there are beds of bituminous coal high up in the Alleghanies of Ohio.

Natural springs, extremely rich in salt, are found all along the western slope of the Appalachian system; and from Onondago, in New York, to the southern termination of the mountain system, wherever the earth has been penetrated to any considerable depth, salt water has been found; in some places, where the boring was from 300 to 400 feet, the water rushed up with so much force, as to rise like a fountain several feet above the surface of the ground. Among the mineral products are iron, lead, and gold; but not in large quantity. The trees growing on and near the mountains are the oak, the pine, the hickory, the sugar and other maples, the Weymouth pine, the hemlock spruce, the laurel, the magnolia, the liriodendron, and many others.

APPAREL. In the exports of British and Irish manufactures, numberless small articles are grouped together by the Customs' authorities under the heading *Apparel, Slops*, and *Haberdashery*. The value of this *Apparel*, &c., exported in 1848, amounted to the large sum of 1,512,271*l.* Our best customer was the United States (328,705*l.*), then Australia (308,765*l.*), next British North America (211,889*l.*) then the West Indies (143,249*l.*), the East Indies (115,487*l.*), and the Cape of Good Hope (103,422*l.*)

In 1849 the exports of apparel, &c., to our own Colonies alone amounted to 1,186,832*l.*

APPENZELL, one of the twenty-two Swiss cantons, is worthy of our notice in respect to its industrial features.

Dr. Bowring's Report on the manufactures of Switzerland presents the industry of Appenzel in an interesting point of view. He says that the cotton and linen manufactures form almost the entire wealth of the canton, pay for all the imposts, and keep the canton out of debt. Hand-spinning, both of linen and cotton, had been known for many generations; but the first spinning-machine in Appenzel was put up in 1783. For many years during a recent period England exported about a million lbs. of cotton yarn annually to Appenzel; but the Swiss are now setting up efficient spinning machines for themselves. The factory system, however, is not much acted upon; and it seems therefore probable that England will continue to be able to supply yarn cheaper than the manufacturers of Appenzel can spin it for themselves. The persons chiefly employed are *manufacturers*, *weavers*, and *embroiderers*. The manufacturer or master undertakes the entire production of the woven goods—in some cases only so much as he and his family can weave; but in other cases as much as a hundred other persons can assist him in producing; they sell their goods either unbleached to the traders at home, or bleached to foreigners. The weavers are employed at their own houses, receiving yarn from the manufacturers, and returning the finished goods. The embroiderers are women and young lads; the merchants buy woven muslins, cause a pattern to be stamped upon them, and give them out to be embroidered—an employment at which the embroiderers earn about eighteen kreutzers (6½*d.*) per day.

APPLE. This fruit, which, from its hardiness and great abundance, combined with its excellent flavour, is one of the most important productions of cold climates, is, in its wild state, the austere crab-apple of the hedges.

England is celebrated for the excellence of its apples, and consequently of its cider, a beverage which perhaps acquires its highest degree of excellence in Herefordshire and the neighbouring counties. [CIDER.]

For *cooking*, the best kinds of apples are the following:—for summer use, the Keswick Codlin and the Hawthornden; for autumn the Wormsley Pippin and the Alfriston: for winter and spring the Bedfordshire Foundling, Dumelow's Seedling, Dr. Harvey, Brabant Bellefleur, and Gravenstein; and for drying, the Norfolk Beaufin. Of all these, the Gravenstein, Alfriston, and Brabant Bellefleur are the best.

Of *dessert* apples, the varieties are endless; but by far the greater part of the local sorts and of those commonly cultivated, is of only second-rate quality. The finest variety of all is the Cornish Gilliflower; no other equals this in excellence, but it is unfortunately a bad bearer. Of those which combine productiveness and healthiness with the highest quality, the six following must be considered the best:—Golden Harvey, Old Nonpareil, Hubbard's Pearmain, Ribston Pippin, Dutch Mignonne, Court of Wick. Finally, the best selection that could be made for a small garden, so as to obtain a constant succession of fruit from the earliest to the latest season, would be the following, which are enumerated in their order of ripening, the first being fit for use in June, and the last keeping till the end of April:—White Juneating, Early Red Margaret, White Astrachan, Sugar-Loaf Pippin, Borovitsky, Oslin, Summer Golden Pippin, Summer Thorle, Duchess of Oldenburgh, Wormsley Pippin, Kerry Pippin, Yellow Ingestrie, Gravenstein, Autumn Pearmain, Golden Reinette, King of the Pippins, Ribston Pippin, Fearn's Pippin, Court of Wick, Golden Harvey, Golden Pippin, Beachamwell, Adam's Pearmain, Pennington's Seedling, Hughes's Golden Pippin, Cornish Gilliflower, Dutch Mignonne, Reinette du Canada, Syke-House Russet, Braddick's Nonpareil, Old Nonpareil, Court-Pendu Plat, Lamb-Abbey Pearmain, Newtown Pippin.

Many different methods of *preserving* apples

have been recommended, and almost every one has some favourite plan of his own. A very good method is to allow the fruits, after being gathered, to lie till their superfluous moisture has evaporated, which is what is technically called 'sweating;' the apples should then be wiped quite dry, wrapped in tissue paper, and stowed away in jars or chests of pure silver sand which has been previously dried in an oven. They should always be taken out of the sand a few days before they are wanted, and laid in dry fern or some such substance; they then absorb oxygen, and acquire a little sweetness, which is necessary to their perfection.

Apples are kept in good condition for the London market in the following way. A cool spot is selected, and layers are heaped up—first of straw or paper, and then of apples, alternately, to a height of about two feet: or the alternate layers are placed in baskets, and the baskets piled one on another. For domestic purposes, apples may be preserved by wrapping each in a piece of clean dry paper, placing them in small wide-mouthed jars or honey-pots, piling the pots one on another, and cementing the fissure between the pots with a paste of plaster of Paris. The pots are kept in a cool place; but shortly before using, the apples are placed in a warm room for a few days. Apples may also be preserved by immersing them in bran: each apple being separated from the rest by its envelope of bran. The Americans preserve apples for two or three years, by peeling them, cutting them into eighths, taking out the cores, and drying the rest in the sun or in a kiln until quite hard; when about to be used, the apples are exposed for a few minutes to the action of boiling water.

Apples will yield sugar, by expressing the juice, neutralising the acid with chalk, boiling, clarifying, and evaporating. One cwt. of apples will yield 84 lbs. of juice, from which may be obtained 12 lbs. of crude sugar.

Besides our home growths, the trade in foreign apples is now very large. In 1848 we imported no less than 331,069 bushels; those from British Colonies pay 2*d.* per bushel import duty; from foreign countries 6*d.*

APPRENTICE, signifies a person who is bound by indenture to serve a master for a certain term, and receives, in return for his services, instruction in his master's profession, art, or occupation. In addition to this, the master is often bound to provide food and clothing for the apprentice, and sometimes to pay him small wages; but the master often receives a premium.

The system of apprenticeship in modern Europe is said to have grown up with the system of associating and incorporating handicraft trades in the twelfth century. These corporations, it is said, were formed for the purpose of resisting the oppression of the feudal lords, and the union of artisans in various bodies must have enabled them to act with more effect. The restraint of free competition, the maintenance of peculiar privileges, and the limitation of the numbers of such as should participate in them, were the main results to which these institutions tended. To exercise a trade, it was necessary to be free of the company or fraternity of that trade; and as the principal if not the only mode of acquiring this freedom in early times was by serving an apprenticeship to a member of the body, it became easy to limit the numbers admitted to this privilege, either indirectly by the length of apprenticeship required, or more immediately by limiting the number of apprentices to be taken by each master. In agriculture, apprenticeship, though in some comparatively later instances encouraged by positive laws, has never prevailed to any great extent. The tendency to association indeed is not strong among the agricultural population, combination being to the scattered inhabitants of the country inconvenient and often impracticable; whereas the inhabitants of towns are by their very position invited to it.

Since the twelfth century, apprenticeship has prevailed in almost every part of Europe —in France, Germany, Italy, and Spain, and probably in other countries. It is asserted by Adam Smith, that seven years seems once to have been all over Europe the usual term for the duration of apprenticeships in most trades. There seems, however, to have been no settled rule on this subject, for there is abundant evidence that the custom in this respect varied even in different incorporated trades in the same town.

Neither in Ireland nor in Scotland have the laws relating to associated trades or apprentices been very rigorously enforced. In Ireland the same system of guilds and companies certainly existed; but, as it was the policy of the English government to encourage settlers there, little attention was paid to their exclusive privileges; and in 1672 the lord-lieutenant and council, under authority of an act of parliament, issued a set of rules and regulations for all the walled towns in Ireland, by which any foreigner was allowed to become free of the guilds and fraternities of tradesmen on payment of a fine of 20s. There is no country in Europe in which corporation laws have been so little oppressive as in Scotland. Three years are there a common term of apprenticeship, even in the nicer trades; but the custom is different in different communities.

In England the institution of apprenticeship is of very old date, being probably contemporaneous with the formation of the guilds or companies of tradesmen. The apprentice laws were enacted at a time when the impolicy of such legislation was not perceived. But opinion gradually became opposed to these enactments, and the judges interpreted the law favourably to freedom of trade. Accordingly the decisions of the courts tended rather to confine than to extend the effect of the statute of Elizabeth, and thus the operation of it was limited to market towns, and to those crafts, mysteries, and occupations which were in existence at the time it was passed. And although, in consequence of this doctrine, many absurd decisions were made, yet the exclusion of some manufactures, and particularly of the principal ones of Manchester and Birmingham, from the operation of the act, had probably a favourable effect in causing it to be less strictly enforced even against those who were held to be liable to it.

Apprenticeship, though no longer legally necessary (except in a few cases), still continues to be the usual mode of learning a trade or art, and contracts of apprenticeship are very common. By common law, a person under the age of twenty-one years cannot bind himself apprentice so as to entitle his master to an action of covenant for leaving his service or other breaches of the indenture.

The churchwardens of parishes have long possessed power in respect to apprenticing pauper children; and overseers of the poor possess similar powers.

An indenture is determinable by the consent of all the parties to it; it is also determined by the death of the master. But if there is any covenant for maintenance the executor is bound to discharge this as far as he has assets. By the custom of London, if the master of an apprentice die, the service must be continued with the widow, if she continue to carry on the trade. In other cases it is incumbent on the executor to put the apprentice to another master of the same trade.

A master may moderately chastise his apprentice for misbehaviour; but he cannot discharge him. If he has any complaint against him, or the apprentice against his master, a power is given to punish or discharge the apprentice, and in some cases to fine the master. If any apprentice, whose premium does not exceed 10*l.*, run away from his master, he may be compelled to serve beyond his term for the time which he absented himself, or make suitable satisfaction, or be imprisoned for three months. If he enters another person's service, his master is entitled to his earnings, and he may bring an action against any one who has enticed him away.

Except in the case of surgeons and apothecaries, proctors, solicitors, attorneys, and notaries, there is now no apprenticeship required by law in England.

The peculiar transition state, in Germany, between *apprenticeship* and *journeymanship*, is described under ARTIZANS.

APRICOT. This fruit is in this country produced either upon open standard trees, or upon walls with a westerly aspect. The fruit produced upon walls is the finest, but that from standards is by far the best flavoured. Of the kinds that are cultivated upon walls there are only three that are much worth having, namely, the Orange for preserving, and the Moorpark and Turkey for the table; several others are to be met with in nurserymen's catalogues, but they are of little importance.

Apricots may be dried (or, as it is sometimes termed, candied) in the following way. The stones are thrust out with a wooden skewer; the apricots are peeled, rolled in dry pounded sugar, immersed in cold syrup, and heated gradually nearly to the boiling point. They are scalded again the next day, sweetened with sugar, and allowed to drain on a hair sieve. Sometimes they are preserved, with the peel left on; and sometimes they are cut into quarters or eighths before preserving.

A'PTERAL is a term applied to a temple which has prostyles, or porticoes of columns projecting from its fronts or ends, but of which the columns do not extend laterally, and run along the flanks from one end to the other, which would make it *peripteral*. The parallelogrammic temples of the Romans were for the most part simply apteral prostyles, and their arrangement has been much more followed in modern works than that of the Greek temples, which are, with few exceptions, peripteral.

AQUA REGIA, or NITRO-MURIATIC ACID. [CHLORINE.]

AQUAFORTIS. [NITRIC ACID.]

AQUATINTA ENGRAVING, a mode of engraving which is an imitation of water-colour or India-ink drawings. The inventor, a German artist named Le Prince, was born at Metz in 1723. His method was to sift black resin over a clean copper plate; the resin was fixed by a moderate heat sufficient to make the dust adhere without fluxing or becoming an even varnish: he thus formed a granulated surface, on the plate, usually called a *ground*, which suffered very little from the action of the diluted acid, yet allowed it to corrode very freely in the small spaces left between the grains of the resin. Mrs. Catherine Prestel, also a German, improved much upon the meagre works of Le Prince, and executed several large works with so much success, that little more was found wanting than a ground that would adhere better to the plate and yield a greater number of impressions; this was effected by dissolving the resin in alcohol, and then pouring the mixture over the plate, the quantity of resin determining the coarseness or fineness of the grain. The modern aquatinters have another advantage over their predecessors in using a composition for painting the forms of leaves of trees, or other objects, where the trouble of surrounding the forms by a varnish would be too great. This composition is made of treacle, whiting, and gum. When used, it must be thoroughly dry before the varnish is passed over it; the varnish also must be allowed time to dry; after which, cold water poured on the plate will in a few minutes bring off all the composition and the varnish which had passed over it, leaving the forms perfect, and the ground in those places free to receive the acid again. The remainder of the plate is permanently *stopped out* by a resinous varnish; with this also the margin of the plate is to be varnished, leaving a narrow strip of the ground for trials or tests. The design intended to be engraved is then made on the ground; this is done in the following manner:—The design is first copied on very thin transparent paper, called tracing-paper; between this tracing and the prepared ground on the plate a thin sheet of paper is placed, which has been rubbed over with lamp-black or vermillion, and sweet oil; every line of the design is then gone over with an instrument called a blunt point, with a moderate pressure, and is thus transferred to the ground so securely that the acid cannot destroy it.

Before the acid is poured on the plate, a border or wall of wax (formed of burgundy pitch, bees' wax, and sweet oil), about an inch in depth, is placed round the margin of the plate.

The plate being so far made ready, the completion of the design is resumed by stopping out the highest lights on the edges of clouds, water, &c., with a varnish of Canada balsam, oxide of bismuth, and turpentine. Next pour on diluted aquafortis; let it remain, according to its strength, from half a minute to a minute, then pour it off, and wash the plate three or four times with clean water, and dry it with a clean linen cloth or a pair of bellows. If on trying the strip the tint is found not to be sufficient, repeat the acid for another half minute, and then proceed. The colour of the bismuth varnish must be changed for the second stopping out, by adding a little chrome-yellow, vermillion, or lamp-black, or any other colour that is not destroyed by the acid. The colour is to be changed after each application of the acid, that the engraver may remember in what places he has carried forward his work, what tints have been softened at their edges, &c. The acid should be strengthened a very little after each application. When the ground changes to a gray colour it is beginning to fail, and must be taken off by heating the plate till the bordering wax will lift off; after this, sweet oil is applied to the whole surface, and a brisk heat beneath the plate will bring off all the different varnishes with a linen cloth; then an oil rubber, made of fine woollen cloth, rolled up hard and the end cut off, applied with sweet oil, will take out the stains; tints which are too strong may be softened or even rubbed out. The plate is now cleaned with spirits of turpentine and sent to the printer to prove, after which it is to be exceedingly well cleaned with turpentine, &c., and another ground laid; this should be done in such a manner as to make the grains fall exactly on the granulations of the former ground, which is called *re-biting*. It is done by making the ground much stronger than the one used before. The process for the second ground is the same as for the first; retouching with the acid those tints which require more depth, and stopping out those parts that are sufficiently dark. Another proof must be taken, and the plate then finished with the burnisher, which some use with oil, but others prefer to use dry, previously filling the whole plate with powdered white lead, by which it can be seen how much has been burnished down according to the quantity of colour left in the plate.

AQUEDUCT, or AQUÆDUCT, is usually an elevated channel for the conveyance of water. Aqueducts were most extensively used by the Romans, and in the vicinities of many of their more important cities, in Asia and Africa, as well as in Europe, remains of extensive constructions of the kind yet exist. Rome itself was supplied with water from sources varying from 30 to 60 miles in distance, and at one period of its history no less than twenty aqueducts brought as many different streams of water across the wide plain or Campagna in which the city stands. Great portions of the distance were of course in every case occupied by artificial channels winding along the sides of hills and mountains; and long tunnels carried the streams through these natural barriers when occasion required; but nevertheless the arcaded duct led the streams across the deep valleys, and the aqueduct was in every case required to carry it onwards from the hills over the wide plain into reservoirs in Rome. In one of these Roman aqueducts the series of arches is calculated at nearly 7000, their height being in many places more than a hundred feet. There is nothing more interesting or more really beautiful in the existing ruins of ancient Rome than the remains of these splendid works, three of which, having been restored and repaired, supply the modern city abundantly.

Among the most celebrated modern aqueducts are that of Caserta in the kingdom of Naples, of Maintenon near Versailles in France, and that of Bemfica, called *Agoas Livres*, near Lisbon in Portugal.

The finest aqueduct of modern times, perhaps, is the Croton Aqueduct, which supplies New York with water. It extends 42 miles across a hilly country on the east side of the Hudson river, diversified with ravines, water courses, and public roads. At a place called Sing Sing, the river Croton is dammed up for a distance of five miles, so as to attain at one point a height of forty feet above its original level. The pond of water caused by the dam covers four hundred acres of ground. The water enters the aqueduct from this pond through a tunnel one hundred and fifty feet long; and the gradients are so arranged that the water descends along the aqueduct at the rate of two feet per second. The channel for the conveyance of the water involves very costly engineering. There are fifteen tunnels, varying in length from 150 to 900 feet; the tunnels through rock are left in their natural state, but those in an earthy soil are bricked. The aqueduct is carried across ravines by means of embankments, provided with culverts for streams; and over the larger rivers and the turnpike roads it is carried by well-constructed bridges. One of these bridges consists of a single elliptical arch, considered at the time of its erection to be the largest arch in America; it is 88 feet span, 33 feet versed sine, and 80 feet from the foundation to the crown of the arch. On Manhatten Island there are bridges which cross eight or ten of the public streets, over which the aqueduct is carried. The aqueduct terminates at the part of New York called 144th Street, where there is a receiving reservoir which occupies 30 acres of ground. From this reservoir the water is conveyed to the distributing reservoir on Murray Hill, covering an area of 10 acres: the channel of conveyance from one reservoir to the other being iron pipes. The distributing reservoir is 114 feet above high-water level; and from this point the water is conducted through the city in pipes. The aqueduct crosses the Haarlem river, at a height of 120 feet, by a bridge of fifteen arches, eight of 80 feet span, and seven of 50 feet span. The expense of this great work has been about 12,000,000 dollars; and the power of supply is stated at the enormous quantity of 50,000,000 gallons per day, so that any increase of population can be met by additional draw-pipes from the great reservoir. The reservoir being as high as the cupola of the city hall, the water can be supplied to the summits of nearly all the houses in aud near New York.

One of the most remarkable existing aqueducts is the Alleghany wire suspension aqueduct, built at Pittsburg in 1845. It consists of seven spans, of 160 feet each. The trunk or channel of the aqueduct is made of wood, 1140 feet long, 14 feet wide at bottom, 16½ feet at top, and 8½ feet deep; it is formed of double layers of thick plank, united in a very durable manner. The bottom of the trunk rests upon transverse beams arranged in pairs, four feet apart; and between these are the posts which support the sides of the trunk. There are outside posts, which support the side walk and towing path. Each pair of beams is supported on each side of the trunk by a double suspension rod of 1⅛ round iron, bent in the shape of a stirrup, and mounted on a small cast-iron saddle, which rests on the cable. This cable (of which there are two, one on each side of the trunk) is 7 inches in diameter, perfectly solid and compact, and constructed in one piece from shore to shore of the Ohio, 1175 feet long; it is composed of 1900 wires, ⅛ of an inch thick, laid parallel, and subjected to equal tension; each wire was separately coated with a protective varnish, and the whole bundle is encircled by a close, compact, continuous wrapping of annealed wire. The whole cable appears like a solid cylinder; it is stronger and more elastic than an equal weight of iron chain. The cable passes over the tops of short pyramids, built of masonry, and placed in a line between the trunk and the towing path; the pyramids are so small and so simple that they offer no obstruction to the tow-rope passing over them. The extremities of the cables do not extend below ground, but are connected with anchor-chains which are buried beneath

KNIGHTS CYCLOPÆDIA OF THE Industry of all Nations

No. 6.

masses of masonry sunk in the ground. The theory of construction throughout has been to form a wooden trunk strong enough and firm enough to support its own weight, and to combine this with wire cables of sufficient strength to bear the weight of water in the trunk; and a very efficient and economical structure has been thus produced. Each cable weighs 110 tons; the weight of water in the aqueduct is 2100 tons; the deflexion of the cables between the piers is 14½ feet.

AQUILARIACEÆ, is the botanical name for an order of plants, of which there are three species useful in the arts. *A. Malaccensis*, the *Bois d'Aigle*, or Eagle-wood, is a native of Malacca, and produces a whitish yellow wood. This is the *A. ovata* of some botanists. *A. Agallochum* is a native of the East Indies, where it is called *Ugoor* or *Ugooroo*, by the natives, and *Lignum-aloes*, or Aloe-wood, by the Europeans. The wood has a fine scent, and is supposed to be the *Calambac*, or *Agallochum*, of the ancients. *A. secundaria* is another species which also yields a scented wood, and has been known in the Materia Medica, and used in perfumery, under the names of Agallochum, Lignum-aloes, and Aloe-wood. In a healthy state this wood is said to be white and inodorous; but it is subject to the attacks of disease, which causes the secretion of a resinous matter, and the wood then becomes coloured, and gives out a powerful scent. This secretion resembles camphor in many of its properties, and has a bitter flavour: hence the name of the tree.

ARABESQUE. This name is intended to mean simply 'in the Arabian manner,' and is a French form of that expression. The mode of enrichment which it refers to was practised in the decoration of their structures by the Moors, Saracens, or Arabians of Spain. The most celebrated arabesques of modern times are those with which Raphael ornamented the piers and pilasters of the arcaded gallery of the palace of the Vatican which bears his name. The term Arabesque is more applied to painted than to sculptured ornament, though it is not restricted to the former.

ARABIA; *Products and Industry:*—This country is rich in vegetable productions useful in the arts and in domestic economy. It has long been celebrated for the abundance of its odoriferous plants. The frankincense of Saba is alluded to by the prophets Isaiah and Jeremiah. Herodotus mentions frankincense, myrrh, cassia, cinnamon, and laudanum, as productions exclusively peculiar to Arabia; though his information on the products of Arabia is neither extensive nor exact. Among the Romans, also, Arabian odours seem to have been quite proverbial.

The coffee-shrub is cultivated chiefly on the western descent of the chain of hills which, in the province of Yemen, separates the level country from the high-land: that grown at Bulgosa, near Beit-el-Fakih, and exported from Mocha, still maintains its superiority over the coffee produced in the European colonies in all other parts of the globe. The farinaceous deposit called manna, familiar to all readers from the use made of it by the Israelites during their wanderings in the desert, is now, according to Niebuhr, chiefly, if not exclusively, found on the leaves of a species of oak called *ballôt* or *afs*: according to others, it is a pellucid substance exuded by the leaves of different kinds of trees, chiefly the *hedysarum alhagi* of Linnæus. Grapes are cultivated in several parts of Arabia, though in the Koran wine is forbidden to the Mussulmans. In Yemen, where some pains are bestowed upon agriculture, Niebuhr saw excellent wheat, Turkey corn or maize, durra, barley, beans, lentils, tobacco, &c.; senna and the cotton tree are also cultivated here. Much indigo is grown about Zebid. Niebuhr says that he saw no oats in Arabia: the horses are fed on barley, and the asses on beans. The time of the harvest varies. At Muscat, wheat and barley are sown in December, and reaped in March; in the high-land, near San'á, the time of the harvest for barley is about the middle of July.

Arabia is rich in indigenous trees; the *acacia vera*, from which the gum-arabic is obtained, the date-tree, and many varieties of the palm and fig-tree, deserve to be particularly noticed. Forests appear to be rare. In the barren tracts of the country, the Beduins sometimes supply the deficiency of fuel by the dried dung of the camel.

Among the ancients, Arabia was celebrated for its wealth in precious metals; yet, according to the accounts of modern travellers, Arabia possesses at present no mines either of gold or silver. Iron mines are noticed by Niebuhr as existing in the territory of Saade. The lead mines of 'Omán are, according to him, very productive, and large quantities of lead are exported from Muscat.

The pearl-fisheries of the Persian Gulf are universally celebrated. The bank on which pearl-shells are principally found extends from the Bahreín islands to very near the promontory of Julfar. The northern extremity, near the isles Karek and Bahreín, is distinguished as particularly rich in pearls.

The tents of the Beduins are made of a coarse kind of dark-coloured cloth, woven by their own women. There is but little furniture in a Beduin tent: a mat of straw is used as table, chairs, and bedstead; spare clothes are kept in bags. The kitchen apparatus is very simple and portable. The pots are made of copper lined with tin; the dishes of the same metals, or of wood. Their hearth is easily built; they merely place their caldrons on loose stones, or over a pit dug in the ground. They have neither spoons, knives, nor forks. A round piece of leather serves them as table-cloth, in which the remains of the meal are preserved. Their butter, which the heat soon melts down, they keep in leather bottles. Water is kept in goats' skins; a copper cup, carefully tinned over, serves as a drinking vessel. Wind-mills and water-mills are unknown: all grain being ground in a small hand-mill. There are no ovens in the desert: the dough is either kneaded into a flat cake, and baked on a round iron plate, or it is formed into large lumps, which are laid between glowing coals till they are sufficiently baked.

ARABLE LAND, is that part of the land which is chiefly cultivated by means of the plough.

Land in general is divided into *arable land*, *grass land*, *wood land*, *common pasture*, and *waste*.

The German agriculturist Thacr has given a classification of arable soils of known qualities, worthy of notice. It is as follows :—

No.		Clay, p. cent.	Sand, p. cent.	Carb. of Lime, p. cent.	Humus, p. cent.	Value.
1	First class of strong wheat soils . . .	74	10	4½	11½	100
2		81	6	4	8¾	98
3		79	10	4	6½	96
4		40	20	36	4	90
5	Rich light sand in natural grass.	14	49	10	27	?
6	Rich barley land . .	20	67	3	10	78
7	Good wheat land . . .	58	36	2	4	77
8	Wheat land .	56	30	12	2	75
9	Ditto . . .	60	38	Very insignificant quantities.	2	70
10	Ditto . . .	48	50		2	65
11	Ditto . . .	68	30		2	60
12	Good barley land . . .	38	60		2	60
13	Ditto, second quality . .	33	65		2	50
14	Ditto . . .	28	70		2	40
15	Oat land . .	23½	75		1½	30
16	Ditto . . .	18½	80		1½	20

Below this are very poor rye lands.

In all these soils the depth is supposed the same, and the quality uniform to the depth of at least six inches; the subsoil sound, and neither too wet nor too dry. The last column, of comparative value, is the result of several years' careful valuation of the returns, after labour and seed had been deducted.

Under the article SOIL the comparative qualities of different kinds of agricultural land are noticed. We may in this place briefly illustrate the nature and qualities of arable land by tracing the history of a corn crop.

The better the soil, the less cultivation it requires to produce tolerable crops; hence, where the land is very rich, we find in general a slovenly culture; where the ground is less productive, more labour and skill are applied to compensate for the want of natural fertility. The simplest cultivation is that of the spade, the hoe, and the rake—and on a small scale it is the best; but spade husbandry cannot be carried to a great extent without employing more hands than can be spared from other occupations. The plough, drawn by oxen or horses, is the chief instrument of tillage, and has been so in all ages and nations of which we have any records. Its general form, and the mode of using, are explained under PLOUGH. The main object of ploughing is to turn over the whole surface of the ground, as a preparation for bringing it to a finely pulverized state, and to admit the atmosphere to act upon parts before excluded from it. When grass-land or stubble is ploughed, care must be taken to bury the grass and weeds completely, and the slice cut off by the plough must be turned over entirely, which is best done by making the width of the furrow greater than the depth. When the grass and weeds are rotten, and the ground is ploughed to pulverize it, a narrow deep furrow is best; the earth ploughed up is laid against the side of the preceding ridge, which forms a small furrow between the tops of the ridges, well adapted for the seed to lodge in and to be readily covered with the harrows. The Norfolk farmers are very careful not to break the *pan*, as they call it, in their light lands: this *pan* is formed by the pressure of the sole of the plough and the tread of the horses, and opposes a useful bank to the too rapid filtration of the water; it lies from five to eight inches below the surface. If it is broken, the manure is washed down into the light subsoil, and the crop suffers, especially when sheep have been folded, their dung being very soluble. In such soils an artificial pan may be formed by the *land-presser*, or *press-drill*. [PRESS DRILL.]

The mode in which the soil is prepared most perfectly for the reception of the seed is best shown by following the usual operations on fallows. After the harvest, the plough is set to work, and the stubble ploughed in. The winter's frost and snow mellow it, while the stubble and weeds rot below. In spring, as soon as the weather permits, it is ploughed again, the first ridges being turned over as they were before: this completes the decomposition of the roots and weeds. It is then stirred with harrows, or other instruments, which tear up the roots that remained; and some of these, not being easily destroyed, are carefully gathered and burnt, or put in a heap to ferment and rot, a portion of quick lime being added. Another ploughing and stirring follows, at some interval, till the whole ground is mellow, pulverized, and free from weeds; manure is put on, if required, and immediately spread and ploughed in; the land is then prepared for the seed.

Various instruments have been invented to stir the earth and mix it, subsidiary to the ploughing, and also to loosen and separate roots and weeds. These are described under HARROW; they all consist of series of spikes or teeth, which are made to break up the clods of earth. When the soil turned up by the plough is in large hard lumps, a roller, sometimes with spikes in it, is drawn over the land to break the clods, or mallets are used to break them by hand; but this is seldom necessary except where very stiff soils have been ploughed when too wet, and the ridges have dried and been ploughed again in dry weather.

When the land has been duly prepared, the seed is sown. This is done sometimes before the last ploughing, but then the manure should have been ploughed in before; for, except in planting potatoes, which are not a seed but a bulb, the manure should always be deeper, and not in contact with the seed. When the seed is ploughed in, the furrow should not be above two or three inches deep, and eight or nine wide; and it is only in particular soils that this mode is to be recommended. The most common method is to sow the seed on the land after the last ploughing, and draw the harrows over to cover it: when the land has been well ploughed, and especially if the press-drill has followed the plough, the seed will mostly fall in the small furrows made by two adjoining ridges, and rise in regular rows. The various modes of sowing are described under DRILL and SOWING.

The proper season for sowing each kind of grain, the choice of seed, and other particulars, are explained under the name of the different seeds usually sown. As a general rule, it may be observed, that the smaller the seed, the less it must be covered, and clover or grass seed are not usually harrowed in, but only pressed in with the roller.

It has been found by experience, that besides the general exhaustion of *humus* (decaying vegetable matter) produced by vegetation, especially by those plants which bear oily or farinaceous seeds, each kind of crop has a specific effect on the soil, so that no care, or manure, can make the same ground produce equal crops, of the same kind of grain, for any length of time without the intervention of other crops. The various important circumstances which bear on this question are noticed under FALLOW, FARM, and ROTATION OF CROPS.

The quantity of arable land in Great Britain was roughly estimated some years ago as follows:—England, 10,900,000 acres; Scotland, 2,500,000 acres; Wales, 900,000 acres. It was ascertained in 1847 that in Ireland, in that year, about one-fourth of the whole area (= 5,238,575 acres out of 20,808,271) was under crops, one sixth under corn culture, ond one eighteenth under pasture and clover.

A'RACHIS, is the botanical name of a kind of pulse, called the Earth-Nut, which is much cultivated in the warmer parts of the world: it belongs to the pea tribe, to which and the bean it is botanically related. The seeds are considered a valuable article of food in Africa, and the tropical parts of Asia and America. In flavour they are as sweet as an almond; and they yield, when pressed, an oil in no respect inferior to that of olives. The plant will only grow in a light sandy soil, in which its pods can readily be buried, and it requires a climate as hot at least as that of the south of France.

ARACK, or **ARRAC**, a distilled spirit prepared from different substances, more especially from sweet juice (toddy) extracted from the unexpanded flowers of different species of the palm tribe. In Ceylon, where a large quantity of arack is manufactured, it is entirely distilled from cocoa-nut tree toddy. The 'toddy topes,' or cocoa-nut tree orchards, are very extensive in Ceylon, and their produce is collected for the distillation of arack, and the manufacture of sugar and oil.

In Ceylon, when it is intended to draw toddy from a tope, the toddy-drawer selects a tree of easy ascent, and connects the upper branches of other trees to it, so as to pass readily from one to another. He ties the flowering spath in different places, and bruises it with the blow of a small mallet; this is done twice a day for a week; after which a portion of the spath is cut off, and juice slowly exudes from it. Successive portions of each spath, and successive trees in the tope, are treated in the same way. The juice or toddy is collected in gourds, from which it is emptied into vessels.

Arack may be distilled from toddy the same day it is drawn from the tree, but sometimes this operation is delayed until it becomes sour.

The process of distillation is carried on in the maritime provinces in copper stills, but in the interior of the island earthen vessels are chiefly employed. Toddy yields by distillation about one-eighth part of proof-spirit.

On the peninsula of India, arack is distilled from the flowers of two or three different trees. In Java it is made from molasses, palm-wine, and rice. In Turkey it is made from the skins of grapes, flavoured with aniseed; the mountain Tartars distil it from many berries and fruits; aud the Calmucks from milk.

Ceylon exports annually, and for the most part to the presidencies of Bengal, Madras, and Bombay, from 5000 to 6000 leaguers of arack, each containing 150 gallons. The prime cost of arack at Colombo in Ceylon varies from 8*d.* to 10*d.* per gallon. Ceylon arack is superior to Batavian arack, and it commonly brings a higher price of from 10 to 15 per cent. on the peninsula of India than Javanese manufactured spirits.

It is said that factitious arack is sometimes sold, made by dissolving flowers of benzoin in pale Jamaica rum. The name of *Vauxhall Nectar* has been given to this mock arack.

ARÆO'METER, is an instrument employed for the purpose of ascertaining the specific gravities of light substances, fluid or solid. Nicholson's aræometer consists of a hollow copper vessel, from each extremity of which proceeds a stem; that which, when the instrument is in a vertical position, is uppermost, is a wire of hardened steel about $\frac{1}{40}$ inch in diameter, carrying at its top a small cup in which weights may be placed: to the lower stem, which is short, is attached a stirrup carrying a cup in which may be placed a solid body whose specific gravity it may be required to determine. The instrument is so adjusted that if a weight equal to 1000 grains be placed in the upper vessel, the whole will sink in distilled water at a temperature expressed by 60 degrees of Fahrenheit's thermometer, till a mark made on the stem is on a level with the fluid surface. When the specific gravity of a fluid, whether lighter or heavier than water, is to be determined, the instrument is plunged into the fluid, and weights are placed in the upper vessel till the mark on the stem is at the surface.

To obtain the specific gravity of a solid which does not imbibe water; the instrument is placed in distilled water, the body is laid in the upper vessel, and weights are added till the mark on the stem is at the level of the surface; these weights being subtracted from 1000 grains, leave the weight of the body in air: then, placing the body in the lower vessel, let other weights be added in the upper one till the mark on the stem is again at the surface of the water; these additional weights will express the loss which the body sustains by being immersed in water.

If the substance whose specific gravity is required be, like wood, capable of imbibing water during the experiment, it should be left in the lower vessel, while under water, till the instrument is stationary, when the additional weights in the upper vessel will express the weight of the displaced water together with that which is imbibed; then, having dried the surface, let the substance be placed in the upper vessel and weighed in air as at first: the difference between this weight and that which was found before the substance was put in the water is the weight of the water imbibed; and this must of course be subtracted from the observed weight of the substance in water, previously to substituting the values of the terms in the last proportion.

The instrument more usually employed to determine specific gravities is the HYDROMETER.

A'RAGON; *Produce and Industry*:—This province of Spain produces wheat, barley, rye, oats, Indian corn, leguminous vegetables, esparto or Spanish broom, flax, hemp, sumach, barilla madder, saffron, liquorice, fruits, oil, wine, and timber. The productions of the mineral kingdom are gold, silver, copper, iron, lead, quicksilver, cobalt, alum, jet, coals, and copperas; few of these mines are now worked. Peat earth is found in the district of Teruel, and is used for fuel. The mountains abound in game. Before the Peninsular war the number of sheep was 2,050,000 heads. The produce of grain and wine is more than sufficient for the consumption: but there is a deficiency of horned cattle and mules, which are supplied from France. The industry of Aragon is very limited and consists principally in manufactories of common cloth, hemp sandals, sacks, and cordage, hats, leather, paper, earthenware, and some iron foundries.

ARAUCA'RIA, is the name of a singular genus of gigantic firs, of which the *Norfolk Island pine* is the best known. This tree is found not only in the spot after which it has been named, but also in several other places in the South Seas, as in New Caledonia, Botany Island, Isle of Pines, and in some parts of the east coast of New Holland. It is described as a most majestic tree, growing to the height of from 160 to 228 feet, with a circumference sometimes of more than 30 feet. Its trunk rises erect, and is sparingly covered with long, drooping, naked branches. The bark abounds in turpentine; the wood, which is destitute of that substance, is white, tough, and close-grained. It was once expected that this tree would have been valuable for its timber, and that it would have afforded spars for the navy of great size; but it has been found on trial to be too heavy, and so unsound, that Captain Hunter could only find seven trees fit for use out of thirty-four that he caused to be felled. Its wood is, however, useful for carpenters' in-door work. Several specimens of this tree exist in the collections of this country. Unfortunately it will not live in the open air in the winter, and its growth is so rapid as to render it very soon too large for the loftiest greenhouses.

ARBALEST or ARBLAST, a cross-bow, appears to have been derived from the larger *ballistæ*, and was probably introduced into England by the Normans, who used it with great effect at the battle of Hastings. The arrows used for the cross-bow were called *quarrels*, from the French *carreaux*, a term which indicates the square form of their heads.

ARBORETUM. An Arboretum in its botanic sense, is a plantation of trees; in its *social* sense, it has become associated with an improvement which marks the present age—the planning and laying out of parks for the people: pleasure grounds where the artizan can breathe the fresh air at intervals. The Derby Arboretum is an example of the munificence of a distinguished family of manufacturers, the Messrs. Strutt. Mr. Joseph Strutt presented to the corporation of Derby, in 1840, a people's park or arboretum, on which he had expended about 12,000*l*. It was beautifully laid out by the late Mr. Loudon, and so supplied with trees, shrubs, and flowers, ticketed and labelled, as to be a kind of botanic garden as well as a pleasure-ground. It was given to the inhabitants, with the corporation as trustees. We must express a regret, however, that a *charge* is made for admission, to defray the expense of keeping up the ground: this should not be—after so munificent a gift, the least that the town could do would be to appropriate a small annual sum for maintenance.

ARBOR VITÆ is the familiar name given to a tree, the botanical name of which is *Thuja* or *Thuya*. There are many species. The American Arbor Vitæ is a large shrub or small tree, sometimes called *white cedar;* the wood is very durable, but is difficult to obtain except in small pieces; it makes excellent posts and rails, and the branches are used for making brooms. The Chinese and the Weeping Arbor Vitæ are not much employed in the arts. The Callitris Arbor Vitæ is said by Broquiart and other authorities to yield the useful substance Gum Sandarac [SANDARAC]; and the wood of this tree, under the name of *alerce*, is in great repute in the east for building religious edifices; the roof of the celebrated cathedral of Cordova is built of this wood, and exemplifies the fitness of the material for such purposes.

ARC, a bow, signifies any part of a curve line. The straight line which joins the extremities of the arc is called its chord.

The practical method of finding the length of an arc is as follows:—Divide the arc into a number of smaller arcs, making the number large in proportion to the degree of accuracy required, and add together the chords of the smaller arcs. The sum of the chords will differ very little from the arc, even when the number of sub-divisions is not very large. For instance, the arc of the quadrant of a circle, whose diameter is ten million of inches, is 7,853,982 inches, within half an inch. Divide this quadrant into ten equal parts, and the sum of the chords is 7,845,910 inches: divide the quadrant into fifty parts, and the same sum is 7,853,659 inches, which is not wrong by more than one part out of 24,316. For only twenty sub-divisions the sum of the chords is 7,851,963 inches, wrong only by one part out of 3890. Therefore, for every practical purpose, an arc of a circle (and the same may be said of every other curve) is the polygon made by the chords of a moderate number of sub-divisions of the arc.

ARCADE properly signifies a series of arches on insulated piers, forming a screen, and also the space inclosed by such.

In addition to its proper technical meaning, this term has of late acquired a different signification among us as the popular name for what the Parisians more properly designate a 'passage' or 'galerie,' viz. an alley lined on each side with shops, and roofed over so as to be in fact a sort of in-door street, entirely protected from the weather, and of uniform design throughout in its architecture. As to such a place being a very great public convenience there can be but one opinion,—as in dirty or wet weather, when the advantages attending such mode of building make themselves felt very sensibly. The Burlington Arcade was the first place of the kind in London. Among the Parisian arcades the Passage Colbert is one of the most striking, both for its extent and architectural display, towards which last its Rotunda contributes in no small degree.

ARCH is the general name for any solid work, whether of masonry or otherwise, of which the lower part is formed into an arc of a curve supported at the two extremities.

The lower supports are the *piers* of the arch; the arch is said to *spring* from the tops of those piers; the summit of the arch is the *crown*, and on either side of the crown are the *flanks* of the arch. The lower line of the arch stones is called the *intrados* or *soffit*, the upper, the *extrados* or *back;* the arch stones are called *voussoirs*, and the highest voussoir the *key-stone*. The width from pier to pier is the *span;* and the vertical distance from the crown to the level of the top of the piers is the *height*. The voussoirs are cemented together; and if the cement were sufficiently strong, any form might be given to the arch, or at least any form which would stand if cut out of the solid material. If we suppose the stones uncemented, their friction upon one another would tend to prevent the disturbance of equilibrium, and allow considerable variety of form in arches constructed with stones of the same weight. But if we suppose the stones perfectly smooth, so that each of them is kept from slipping only by the pressure of the adjoining two, then each intrados has one particular form of extrados and one only, so long as the manner in which the stones are cut follows one given law.

The applications of the arch, in practice, are noticed under ABUTMENT; BRIDGE; BUTTRESS; IMPOST; PIER, &c.

Sir M. I. Brunel introduced, a few years ago, a singular mode of constructing arches. In the construction of stone arches, some kind of centering is necessary, to support the single stones until by mutual pressure they can support each other; but Brunel devised the following mode in respect to brick arches. The piers of the bridge or arch having been constructed in the usual manner up to the springing, he commenced building a portion of the arch right and left, on both sides, taking care that both arches progressed at an equal rate, so that they might balance each other. In order to increase the cohesion of the structure, he introduced bands of hoop iron longitudinally between the courses; and by these means he was enabled to carry on the two semi-arches, until they met those produced in a similar way from the opposite piers. A narrow arch, say about four feet in width, having been thus completed, Brunel proposed to extend it to the requisite width by building on each side of it, adding from nine to eighteen inches at a time. To shew that—whatever might be the difficulties in practice—the principle is sound, Sir M. I. Brunel constructed two semi-arches, of bricks laid with mortar prepared with blue lias lime. Several bands of hoop iron, and several slender rods of fir, were inserted longitudinally between the courses, extending throughout the whole length of the structure. The radius of curvature of the arch was 177 feet, and although only 4½ feet wide at the top, it was extended to the length of 40 feet on each side of the centre pier. One end was afterwards extended an additional 20 feet; and as the other end could not be extended in the same way, in consequence of want of space, a weight of 28½ tons was suspended from it as a counterpoise. Although the structure fell about three years after its completion, the fall was owing to circumstances independent of the principle on which the arch was constructed.

The origin of the arch in actual constructions is still unknown; it cannot be stated with any degree of certainty, either in what country or at what epoch it was first used. There is reason to think that it was unknown to the Greeks at the time when they produced their most beautiful temples, in the fifth, fourth, and third centuries before the Christian æra. The want of the arch would lead them to contract the intercolumniations, or spaces between the columns, and to the general and frequent adoption of columns as the only mode of supporting a superstructure.

It is maintained that there are brick arches at Thebes in Egypt, which belong to a very remote epoch, and one long prior to the occupation of that country by Alexander the Great. Etruria seems to have been the first European country in which the arch was used. The great sewer of Rome, commonly called the Cloàca Maxima, is an arched construction, which probably belongs to the age of the Tarquins.

The application of the arched structure is one of the most useful mechanical contrivances. By means of it small masses of burnt clay, and conveniently sized pieces of soft and friable sandstone, are made more extensively useful for the economic purposes of building, than the most costly and promising materials were in the hands of the Greeks and Egyptians. By means of it cellars are vaulted; subways, or sewers, are made to pass under heavy structures and along streets with certainty and safety; and secure and permanent roadways for every purpose of communication are formed across wide, deep, and rapid rivers.

The Romans did not deviate much from the semicircular form. Arches of smaller segments were certainly used by them, as well as elliptical arches, but in these cases they were fortified with enormous abutments, which proves that the architects knew very well the weak points of such a construction. The architects of the twelfth, thirteenth, and fourteenth centuries, showed what could be done by varying the form and construction of the arch.

The pointed arch, upon its invention or first introduction into Europe, seems to have exercised the ingenuity of architects in varying its form and application. This we observe in the numerous ecclesiastical structures in this country, in our beautiful pointed styles, and most particularly in some of the greater churches and cathedrals.

The origin of the pointed arch has been almost as much disputed as the discovery of the principle of the arch itself. It became general in most parts of Europe at nearly the same time, and about the period of the return of the warrior-priests and pilgrim-soldiers of the first crusade. This, and other circumstances which might be adduced, added to the fact of the pointed arch being used in Asia before that period, and that an arch of the pointed form cannot be satisfactorily shown to have been used in the northern and western parts of Europe anterior to it, give a reasonable degree of certainty to the supposition that the notion was brought from the east by the crusaders.

The most notable of the departures from the principle of the arch in building are described under BRITANNIA BRIDGE; SUSPENSION BRIDGE.

ARCH, TRIUMPHAL, a structure which the Romans used to erect across their roads or bridges, or at the entrance of their cities, in honour of victorious generals or emperors. They were of two kinds. Temporary arches were made of wood, on the occasion of a triumph. The others were permanent structures, built first of brick, afterwards of hewn stone, and lastly made of, or at least cased with, marble. Their general form is that of a parallelopipedon, which has an opening in the longer side, and sometimes a smaller opening on each side of the large one. These openings are arched over with semicircular arches, and the fronts are decorated with columns and their accessories on lofty pedestals: the whole is surmounted by a heavy attic, on the faces of which inscriptions were generally placed.

Triumphal arches were erected under the republic. Under the emperors these monuments became very numerous, and were overcharged with ornaments. One erected to Augustus at Rimini has the widest opening of the ancient arches, the gateway being 31 feet. Of the triumphal arches remaining at Rome, that of Titus is the oldest. This arch is ornamented with sculptures representing the triumph of Titus, and the ornaments of the temple of Jerusalem which he brought as spoils to Rome. But arches were also raised in honour of emperors for benefits conferred on their country on some particular occasions; such is the fine arch of Trajan on the old mole of Ancona. Another fine arch in memory of Trajan exists at Benevento; it is ornamented with fine rilievi, and is in very good preservation. All these are single arches; but others have two smaller archways, one on each side of the great central one. These are consequently oblong in their shape, and have a heavier appearance than the single arch. Two of these triple arches still exist at Rome, that of Septimius Severus, and that called the arch of Constantine.

There are other arches in various parts of Italy, at Aquino, Aosta, and Pola in Istria, and several in the south of France, of which those of Nismes and Orange are the best preserved. There are several arches in Syria and in Barbary, particularly one at Tripoli, and another at Constantina. In modern times triumphal arches have been raised in imitation of the Roman arches. Those of the gate of St. Denis and the gate of St. Martin, at Paris, were raised in honour of Louis XIV. Bonaparte also had one constructed on the place du Carousel, after the model of the triumphal arch of Septimius Severus at Rome. The much larger arch, the 'Arc de l'Etoile,' at the Barrrière de Neuilly, was commenced in 1806, after the battle of Austerlitz, and has only recently been finished (1847.) Another arch (L'Arco della Pace) which was begun by Bonaparte's order at Milan, on the opening of the famous road across the Simplon, has since been completed by the Austrian government. In London there is a single arch at Hyde Park Corner.

ARCHANGEL, considered as a province, has very little to do with the industry of all nations. Its climate is severe, and its productions few. The bread in use is a compound of meal, moss, scrapings of the bark of the pine, and grated roots; yet this food, coarse as it is, is unknown to more northern palates, which must be content with dried fish. The southern districts grow hemp and flax, and a few kinds of vegetables. The forests produce very fine timber. Salt and bog-iron form the chief mineral wealth.

The manufacturing and mechanical industry of the people is principally confined to shipbuilding, the preparation of pitch and tar, and the weaving of linen, which latter occupation fills up the leisure hours of the peasant's wife in the circles of Kholmogory and Archangel, and constitutes a lucrative branch of their commerce with St. Petersburg, Moscow, and other Russian marts. Pitch, tar, timber, tallow, train-oil, hemp, flax, mats, canvas, skins, and furs, are the chief exported produce.

But the *town* of Archangel (the chief place in the province), is notable in a commercial point of view. It is the most northern emporium of trade, and the oldest port, in the Russian dominions. It is now the chief mart of the Russian northern trade, as it was formerly of all the traffic between Muscovy and foreign parts. The exports consist of linseed, rye, oats, wheat, barley, flax, tow, tallow, train-oil, mats, deals, battens and ends, pitch, and tar. The imports, which are generally confined to the town and neighbourhood, are sugar, coffee, spices, salt, woollens, hardware, &c. In 1846 there were 634 vessels cleared, of which 368 were British, the cargoes being valued at 1,063,700*l.* The port is connected by canals with the Volga and the Neva. The navigation is open generally from May to the end of September, and during this period the river is covered with vessels and boats of all sizes; the quays and shores are peopled with multitudes, variously and actively employed; and the great road from Siberia is covered with travellers and loaded carts and waggons. An association called the 'White Sea Company,' was formed at Archangel in 1803; it despatches a fleet of vessels every year on fishery expeditions to the coast of Nova Zembla, Kalguiew, and Spitzbergen, at the last of which the crews sometimes winter.

ARCHERY. A few notices of the mechanical construction of the implements of archery will be found under their proper headings.

ARCHIL, *orchil, litmus,* or *tournsole,* is a blue dye procured from the *rocella tinctoria* and *ceanora tartarea,* which are lichens growing abundantly in the Canary and Cape Verde Islands. The colouring matter of these plants appears to be a peculiar vegetable principle which has been called *erythrine*: it may be extracted either by means of alcohol or ammonia, but the latter is employed by those who manufacture the colour, which is generally sold in small flat pieces, and known by the name of litmus.

Archil is brought to market in three states —violet-red liquid paste, blue lumps, and powder. It is employed by chemists to ascertain the presence of acids in solution, because it has the property of changing from blue to red by contact with acids; and it also detects alkalies, by restoring the blue which had been changed by acids. Archil is never used alone as a dye, on account of its want of permanence. It is, however, employed for the purpose of deepening and improving the tints of other dyes, and it imparts a bloom which it is difficult to obtain from other substances. Liquid archil is much used for staining wood, and tinting silk stockings.

M. Clenchard, a French chemist, has recently (1850) patented a mode of using archil in the dyeing and printing of woollen and silk goods; in which the archil is combined with alkalies and lime, and applied to the woven material with a more direct action than in the ordinary mode of its use.

Archil communicates a beautiful violet colour to marble.

The island of Teneriffe is said to yield annually about 30,000 lbs. of the lichen from which archil is prepared.

ARCHIMEDEAN SCREW. The great Greek philosopher, Archimedes, is associated with many valuable discoveries in science, among which the principle of specific gravity, and certain geometrical theorems, stand out prominently. But the hydrostatic *screw* is the contrivance which connects his name more particularly with the arts. Whether it is true that he travelled into Egypt, and invented the screw as a means of raising the water of the Nile to points which it could not otherwise reach, is a disputed question; but it is known that he was aware of the action of such a screw.

In what way the Archimedean screw may be made available for raising water, is explained under HYDRAULICS; while its application to steam navigation is noticed under SCREW PROPELLER.

ARCHIPELAGO. The small but luxuriant islands which speckle the Mediterranean, between Greece and Asia Minor, are rich in produce which forms no inconsiderable part of the commerce of Europe and the Levant. Many of these islands are composed almost entirely of a pure white marble, of which the Parian, from Paros, where it was formerly most worked, is often mentioned by ancient writers. The productions of the islands are wine, oil, gum-mastic, raisins, figs, silk, honey, wax, olives, and various fruits, especially the lemon and orange: cotton is grown in small quantities on Milo and other islands, and might be cultivated to a great extent; it is remarkable for its brilliant white hue. Some of the larger islands contain sulphur, alum, iron, and other minerals. An extensive sponge fishery has also long been established among the Sporades, which are noted for their fine sponges.

ARCHITECTURE. A formal treatise on architecture being beyond the limits of the present work, the reader is referred simply to the names of the chief component parts of an architectural structure, and to some of the most famous buildings.

ARCHITRAVE, is the lower part of any structure supported by pillars, or the lower beam which rests upon the columns and joins them together, on which the whole entablature (or ornamental part which comes immediately above the columns) rests. When pillars support an arch, the voussoirs supply the place of an architrave, by which name they are sometimes called. In the same way the flat-beam, or row of stones coming immediately above a door or window, is called the architrave.

ARCHIVOLT, or ARCHIVAULT, is the ornamented band or moulding which runs round the lower part of all the voussoirs of an arch.

ARCH-LUTE, a large lute, or double-stringed theorbo, formerly used by the Italians for the base parts, and for accompanying the voice. This instrument had fourteen notes, the highest whereof was A, the fifth line in the base, the lowest the double G below. It possessed considerable power. It was about five feet in extreme length, and proportionally large in the body. At the commencement of the last century this instrument was much in use. Handel employed it in many of his early operas.

ARCOGRAPH. [CYCLOGRAPH.]

ARCTIC FOX, a small species of fox (*Canis lagopus*), celebrated for the beauty and fineness of its fur, which has long been considered a valuable article of commerce. The colour of the fur, as is the case with all animals which inhabit very high latitudes, varies according to the season, being slaty blue in summer, and pure white in winter. It is in the latter state that the fur is most esteemed, not only on account of its colour, but likewise because it is of a closer and finer quality than at any other time, and therefore fitted for producing more costly articles.

ARDECHE, one of the southern departments of France, has considerable manufacturing industry. There are numerous tanneries for shoe and glove leather, paper-mills, cotton, woollen cloth and silk factories. Great attention is paid to the rearing of silkworms, for the production of raw silk, of which about 700,000 lbs. are brought to market annually. The department contains mines of lead, copper, iron, manganese, antimony, alum, and coal: marble of different colours, gun flints, porcelain clay, and pumice-stone abound. Particles of gold are found in the Rhone, the Ardèche, the Erieux, and also mixed with antimony in the mines of the commune of Malbosc.

The number of manufacturing towns is considerable. Annonay, the largest town in the department, has numerous establishments for dressing kid and lamb skins for glove leather, the annual value of which amounts to 6,000,000 francs; there are also several silk-mills, and paper factories which produce the best paper in France; the value of the paper made here is stated to be 3,000,000 francs a year; the production of white silk for the manufacture of blondes and tulles has rapidly increased of late years.

ARDENNES, a department of France on the Belgian frontier, has manufactures in ironmongery of all kinds, broad cloth, cashmere shawls and other woollen stuffs, shoe and white leather, hosiery, coarse linen, and hats; there are also several glass-works, iron-furnaces, and brass-foundries. Coal, iron, slate, porcelain clay, and sand used in the manufacture of plate-glass, are found. At Charleville the chief manufactures are fire-arms, hard-ware, and nails; there are also soaperies and brass-foundries in the town. Rethel is a busy place, and is largely engaged in the woollen manufactures; it contains also several tanneries, breweries, and iron-foundries. The environs are fertile, yielding good pasturage and timber, and contain stone quarries and iron-mines. Sedan has been long famous for its fine broad cloths, and especially for its fine blacks. The total yearly value of this manufacture is set down at 16,000,000 francs. The environs are studded with factories and workshops, engaged in the woollen trade; there are also several iron-works, tanyards and dyehouses.

ARDROSSAN is worthy of our attention, for the part which it now fills in the system of steam navigation. Placed on the west coast of Scotland, near Ayr, it has railway communication with Glasgow on the north-east, and with Carlisle on the south-east. The port having many natural advantages, a harbour was commenced there in 1806; it has been for many years in a state to receive shipping, and is now considered one of the safest and most accessible on the west coast of Scotland. Steamers ply regularly from Ardrossan to various ports of England, Scotland, and Ireland.

ARDWICK LIMESTONE, is a calcareous bed or series of beds containing shells and fish remains, in the upper part of the coal formations of Manchester and Lebetwood. There is a coal-bed above it at Manchester.

ARE, is the modern French measure of surface, forming part of the decimal system adopted in that country after the revolution. It is obtained as follows:—the metre or measure of length, being the forty-millionth part of the whole meridian, as determined by a trigonometrical survey, is 3·2809167 English feet; and the *are* is a square, the side of which is 10 metres long. The hectare is generally used in describing a quantity of land. It is 2·4711695 English acres, or 404⅔ hectares make 1000 acres.

A'REA, is the *superficies* or *quantity of surface* in a plane figure. The measuring unit of every area is the square described upon the measuring unit of length: thus, we talk of the square inches, square feet, square yards, or square miles, which an area contains.

Any figure which is entirely bounded by straight lines may be divided into triangles; and the area of each triangle separately determined. This determination may be made in either of two ways. 1st. Measure a side of the triangle, and the perpendicular which is let fall upon it from the opposite vertex, both in *units;* half the product of these two lengths is the number of square *units* in the triangle. 2nd. Measure the three sides in *units;* take the half sum of the three, from it subtract each of the sides, multiply the four results together, and extract the square root of the product; this gives the number of square *units* in the triangle.

To find the area of a *parallelogram*, multiply one side by its perpendicular distance from the opposite side; for a *rectangle*, multiply two adjacent sides.

To find the area of a *circle*, multiply the radius by itself and the result by 355; then divide by 113. In all these cases, the result is in the *square* units corresponding to the *linear* units in which the measurements were made.

The above are a few practical rules, useful for every day purposes.

ARECA. [BETEL NUT.]

ARENG. [PALMS; SAGO.]

AREQUIPA, one of the largest and finest cities of Peru, has considerable industry and commerce. Gold and silver cloths, woollens, and cottons, are manufactured at Arequipa, which carries on a great trade with Buenos Ayres, exporting brandies, wine, flour, cotton, and sugar; and importing cattle, dried flesh, tallow, cocoa, &c. The great commercial road from Lima to the southern provinces passes through the city.

ARFE, is the name of two very distinguished Spanish silversmiths, and the designers and constructors of several of the most costly tabernacles which do or did adorn the cathedrals of Spain.

Henrique de Arfe, the elder, and the grandfather of the other, Juan de Arfe, made, between 1506 and 1524, the silver tabernacles of the cathedrals of Leon, Cordova, and Toledo. He also made the tabernacle of the Benedictine monastery of Sahagun, besides a great many crucifixes and other articles used in Roman worship.

Juan de Arfe y Villafane, the grandson, was born at Leon in 1535. He is the artist of three of the finest tabernacles in Spain—those of Avila, Seville, and Osmas. He made also tabernacles for the cathedrals of Burgos and Valladolid, and one for the church of St. Martin at Madrid. Arfe was much employed by Philip II. and Philip III.; the former appointed him assayer of the mint of Segovia. He was both engraver and writer.

ARGAND LAMP, a kind of lamp in which the wick, and consequently the flame also, is in the form of a hollow cylinder, through the interior of which a current of air is made to ascend, in order to afford a free supply of oxygen to the interior as well as to the exterior of the flame; and thereby to ensure more perfect combustion and greater brilliancy of light than could be obtained either by the use of a single large wick, or by a series of small wicks arranged in a straight line. These objects are more perfectly attained by the addition of a glass chimney, which confines the air immediately surrounding the flame, and produces an upward current which causes it to rise high above the wick. This arrangement was invented about 1782, by Aimé Argand, a native of Geneva. It is made in many different forms, one of which, with a chimney of copper instead of glass, is used in chemical operations for the emission of heat. The principle is also extensively applied to gas-burners.

Mr. Hemmenway took out an American patent in 1841, for a means of avoiding the necessity of removing the oil chamber when an argand lamp is to be replenished with oil. The fountain or reservoir is to be supplied with oil through a short pipe at top, which is hermetically closed by a leather valve and screw cap; and between the bottom of this reservoir and the pipe that conducts the oil to the burner, is an air chamber, which is supplied with air by a tube passing up through the oil reservoir. This air is made one of the means of filling the vessel with oil.

Messrs. Bedington and Docker registered an improvement in 1849, whereby an argand lamp is enabled to maintain a clear light for a greater number of hours than under ordinary circumstances. The central air-tube, instead of terminating, as in the usual argand lamps, nearly on a level with the top edge of the perforated air-cone, is carried about half an inch higher, and has apertures made near its upper end. The outer case is also prolonged at top to a similar extent, and is similarly perforated near the top. By this arrangement, currents of air are directed through the apertures into the wick, just below the point of inflammation; and thus the oil is prevented from becoming thickened or carbonized at that spot, which is so likely to occur in the ordinary form of argand.

Many other improvements have from time to time been introduced in the argand lamp; and our manufacturers in London and Birmingham, in the various Exhibitions of Manufactures which have taken place within the last few years, have shown how much external beauty as well as practical convenience may be imparted to these contrivances.

The name of Argand having become associated with the means of producing a bright light by a judicious arrangement of air-holes, it has been applied not only to lamps, but also to candles and furnaces. During more than forty years, attention has from time to time been directed to the possibility of producing Argand Candles—that is, candles constructed on the argand principle. As, in the argand lamp, air is supplied *within* the circle of the flame, so it has been thought that if air could ascend through the wick of a candle, the flame produced would be more brilliant. Many varieties have been tried, and some of them patented; but none of them have yet become permanently and commercially successful.

The designation Argand Furnace has been lately given to an arrangement, in which a stream of air is made to mingle with the inflammable gases in the furnace, but is previously divided into a number of minute streamlets by passing through small apertures. The principle has been known and partially acted on for a considerable time, but it was brought into a practical form a few years ago by Mr. Williams.

ARGIL. [ALUMINA.]

ARGOL is an acidulous concrete salt which is deposited by wine, and forms a crust on the sides of vessels in which that liquid is kept. This crust becomes hard, brilliant, and brittle; it is easily reduced to powder. The argol brought from Germany, and produced from white wine, is the best. This substance is used by dyers as a mordant, and to neutralize various acid agents; a tartrate of tin is also prepared from it. Argol, also called *Tartar*, is a bitartrate of potash. When purified and crystallized it is called *Cream of Tartar*, and is much used medicinally.

More than 1000 tons of argol are annually imported into this kingdom. It comes to us from almost all wine-producing countries. The best comes from Bologna and Leghorn; Rhenish fetches a lower price. Argol is now admitted duty free. Its price at present in the wholesale market is 30*s*. to 50*s*. per cwt.

ARGYLE can put forth very few pretensions to notice in an industrial point of view. It occupies a position on the western coast of Scotland rather out of the ordinary commercial route. Yet it is not without mineral riches. There are lead mines in several parts of the county, copper in Islay, and coal in Mull and Campbeltown. The slate-quarries of Easdale island have been among the most considerable in Britain; and there are quarries at Balaclulish in Lorn. Eight million slates have been procured from the county in one year. The marble and limestone of the county are of fine quality. The granite quarried near Inverary takes as fine a polish as marble; and the *lapis ollaris* (a kind of micaceous slate), with which the Duke of Argyle's castle at that place is built, is one of the handsomest of the building-stones found within the borders. Strontian, cobalt, and coral, occur in or near the county.

The manufactures of this county are unimportant. The woollen manufacture was established at Inverary, and carried on for many years under the patronage of the Duke of Argyle, but it does not seem to have flourished, and has been given up for some time. The cotton manufacture has gained but little ground; whatever is carried on is about Campbeltown. A more important branch of industry is the herring, cod, and ling fishery; the fish are both good and abundant, and the fisheries employ a great number of men. The chief trade of Campbeltown is in whiskey, the parish containing numerous distilleries.

ARIE'GE. The inhabitants of this department of France, besides the usual agricultural pursuits, are engaged in the manufacture of coarse woollens, linen, soap, hats, combs, porcelain, and pottery. There are also many tan-yards, paper-mills, saw-mills, glass-works, and numerous establishments for smelting iron and copper ores. The principal article of export from the department is iron, which is carried on the backs of mules to Auterive in Haute Garonne, whence it is conveyed down the Ariège to the canal of Languedoc and the Garonne. Wool is largely imported from Spain, which receives in return woollen fabrics, linen, cattle, and wax. Other articles of commerce are rosin, pitch, turpentine, cork, marble, medicinal herbs, and various miscellaneous products.

ARITHMETIC, as a science, does not

claim a place in this work; but a few useful rulos and properties of numbers, applicable to the mechanical arts and to the details of every-day life, are given under various headings.

ARITHMETER, is another name for the ABACUS, sometimes employed in teaching children the rudiments of arithmetic.

ARITHMETICAL PROPORTION, is the relation which exists between four numbers, of which the first and second have the same differenco as the third and fourth. Thus:—

$$1 : 2 \text{ and } 81 : 82$$
$$7 : 3 \text{ and } 16 : 12$$
$$2\tfrac{1}{2} : 3\tfrac{1}{4} \text{ and } 1\tfrac{3}{4} : 2\tfrac{1}{2}$$

are severally in arithmetical proportion, and in every such proportion the sum of the extremes is equal to that of the means. Thus—

$$12 + 7 = 3 + 16$$

ARKANSAS. This fine American river, the largest affluent (except the Missouri) of the Mississippi, has at the present time a commercial interest imparted to it by the proposed railway across America from the Atlantic to the Pacific. The Arkansas has its rise in the Rocky Mountains, and flows 2000 miles to the Mississippi; and one of the railway projects, suggested to the enterprising Amoricans by the discoveries in California and by the possession of Oregon, is to form a railway up the valley of this river, cross the range of the Rocky Mountains at the lowest availablo pass, and descend to the plains of Oregon and California. Whether this stupendous project will ever be executed, remains to be seen; in the mean time the Arkansas is a medium for bringing the produce of the West to the Mississippi and New Orleans.

ARKANSAS, one of the territories of the United States which lie westward of the Mississippi, is too young in civilization to present an important figure in manufactures and industry. It is however progressing rapidly. The chief produco is Indian corn, wheat, rye, oats, potatoes, cotton, wool, tobacco, and hay. It has numerous tanneries and manufactories of leather, distilleries, and flour-mills.

ARKEEKO, a sea-port on the western coast of the Red Sea, exhibits to us the mode in which the products of Arabia and Persia reach Abyssinia. The goods are landed at Arkeeko, where the kafilas or caravans assemble. From Arkeeko the kafilas journey in a southward direction, passing over the Taranta mountains, and proceed to Dixan, the first Abyssinian town on that side, and thence to Adowa, the chief mart of trade in the kingdom of Tigré.

ARKWRIGHT, SIR RICHARD, is so intimately associated with the progress of the mighty cotton manufacture in this country, that that history could not be understood without a notice of his inventions and improvements.

Born in 1732 at Preston, of parents too humble to give him anything more than a very slight education, Arkwright had to earn his living, first as a barber, and then as a dealer in hair. But his mind was busy all this time. To use Carlyle's quaint language—'Nevertheless, in stropping of razers, in shaving of dirty beards, and the contradictions and confusions attendant thereon, the man had notions in that rough head of his! Spindles, shuttles, wheels, and contrivances, plying ideally within the same; rather hopeless looking, which, however, he did at last bring to bear. Not without difficulty.'

Conflicting statements render it difficult to trace the history of the machinery by which Arkwright so greatly improved the cotton manufacture. It is, however, certain that in 1767 he employed a clockmaker named Kay, then residing at Warrington, to make a model, which was speedily followed by a working machine. This machine was first set up at Preston; but, fearing to encounter such riotous opposition as had been called forth shortly before by the introduction of Hargreaves' spinning-jenny, Arkwright removed it to Nottingham, where he obtained pecuniary assistance from the Messrs. Wright, bankers, and shortly entered into partnership with Messrs. Need and Strutt, eminent stocking-manufacturers of that town. By this important connection the mechanical skill of Mr. Jedediah Strutt, who invented the contrivance by which Lee's stocking-frame was adapted to the production of ribbed stockings was brought to bear upon certain deficiencies of the machine with great advantage. In 1769 a patent was obtained for the machine, the most important feature of which was tho use of two pairs of rollers, technically called *drawing rollers*, the first pair revolving slowly in contact with each other, and the second pair revolving in like manner, but with greater velocity. The lower roller of each pair was fluted longitudinally, and the upper one covered with leather, and the two were pressed together with a gentle pressure by means of weighted levers, in order that they might tako sufficient hold of the soft cotton passed between them. The fibres of the cotton-wool were first laid smooth and straight, by *carding* or combing, so as to produce a soft loose ribbon or cord called a *sliver*, the end of which was introduced between the first pair of rollers. In passing between them it received no further change than a slight compression, but as from them it was conducted to the second pair of rollers, moving with twice, thrice, or more times the velocity of the first pair, it was extended or drawn out to two, three, or more times its original length, its thickness being reduced in like proportion. As this action is effected by the sliding of the fibres upon one another, the distance between the two pairs of rollers must be so adjusted, in relation to the average length of the fibres, that the two pairs may never have hold of one fibre at the same time. Such is the beautifully simple principle upon which, with the aid of twisting, the thick soft sliver or carding is converted into a fine, hard, and compact yarn or thread.

Arkwright's spinning-machine was, in the first instance, worked by horse power; but in 1771 the partners built a spinning mill for working by water-power at Cromford, in Derbyshire, from which establishment, 'the nursing-place,' as it has been styled, 'of the factory opulence and power of Great Britain,' the machine took the name of the *water-frame*, and the yarn produced by it that of *water-twist*. It was in the arrangement of this establishment, the first of its kind, that Arkwright manifested that extraordinary talent for mechanical contrivance and adjustment, and for the no less difficult task of training human agents to take their places as part and parcel of a vast and complicated automatic apparatus, which earned for him the title of father of the factory system.

Notwithstanding the superior quality of the water-twist over other yarns, a superiority which rendered it available for use as warp, the prejudiced manufacturers formed a combination to oppose its use, and thus compelled Arkwright and his partners to commence the manufacture of it themselves, first into stockings and afterwards into calicoes similar in quality to those now used.

The invention of the machine for spinning by rollers was followed up by various improvements in the mechanism for carding and for other processes in the cotton manufacture, for which Arkwright obtained a second patent in 1775. As, however, the cheapness and beauty of the new cotton fabrics had by this time led to an extensive demand, the hostile manufacturers altered their tactics, and instead of endeavouring to put down Arkwright's inventions, they soon began to dispute his claim to them, and to appropriate them in defiance of his patent rights. The use of his new mechanism was extended in the course of a few years, by licences granted by the patentees, to a very great extent, and this circumstance rendered piracy more easy. In 1782 Arkwright computed that the new manufacture already employed upwards of 5000 persons, and a capital of 200,000*l*. In some cases the new machinery was destroyed by mobs, connived at, if not encouraged, by the higher and middle classes; while in others the unauthorized use of it without payment to the patentees was carried to a great length. He became involved in costly litigation, during which attempts were made to deprive him of the fame resulting from his inventions; the result has been to give merited praise to one or two earlier inventors who had languished in obscurity, but leaving quite enough to justify the high fame which Arkwright had achieved.

Prosperity continued to attend the establishment of Arkwright and his partners, notwithstanding the adverse decisions of the courts. His partnership with Mr. Strutt terminated in 1783, after which time he retained the works at Cromford, which were subsequently carried on by his son, while Mr. Strutt continued the works at Belper, which were founded about 1776. How greatly the cotton manufacture extended under the stimulating effect of his improvements may be conceived from the fact that the imports of cotton-wool, which averaged less than 5,000,000 lbs. per annum in the five years from 1771 to 1775, rose to an average of 25,443,270 lbs. per annum in the five years ending with 1790.

Arkwright was a very early riser; devoted himself most assiduously to business; was a severe economist of time; was exceedingly sanguine in his disposition; and entertained an unbounded confidence in the wealth-producing powers of machinery and manufactures. To his credit it is recorded that when upwards of fifty years of age he made strenuous efforts to retrieve the deficiencies of his early education; redeeming time from the hours usually devoted to sleep in order to apply one hour a day to grammar, and another to writing and orthography. In 1786, on occasion of presenting an address to George III. after the attempt on his life by Margaret Nicholson, he received the honour of knighthood; and in the following year he served as high sheriff of Derbyshire. He died in 1792, leaving property to the extent of half a million sterling; and his son Richard, who died in 1843, is said to have been the richest commoner in England.

ARLES. The situation of Arles on the banks of the Rhône gives it considerable advantages for trade. There is also a navigable canal, which runs from the Rhône to the sea. The corn, wine, fruits, manna, cattle, soda, salt, wool, and oil, of the surrounding country, find sale at Arles; and several manufactures are carried on, as of glass bottles, soap, silk, tobacco, and brandy. Arles has a very active coasting trade: merchant steamboats ply regularly to Marseille, and passenger steamers up the river to Avignon, Lyon, and Seyssel; about 100 vessels, of from 30 to 180 tons, are constantly under weigh for Marseille or Toulouse.

ARMAGH, one of the north-eastern counties of Ireland is one of the seats of the flax and linen manufacture, which is chiefly in the hands of the small farmers. Cotton is also manufactured, but not to any great extent. Spinning machinery has been introduced in a very limited degree.

ARME'NIA. However important Armenia may be in a geographical and historical sense, its industrial and commercial features are soon enumerated.

Armenia produces abundance of excellent iron and copper, which are exported to Mosul. Rich mines of gold and silver exist near Kebban and Argana, in the two branches of the Taurus which inclose the valley of Karpoot (anciently Sophène), through which the Euphrates passes in its way from Armenia to Syria; rock salt abounds in the valley of Kulpia, which slopes towards the Araxes, four miles below the fortress of Koor Ougley. A range of hills, bordering the valley on the east side, is apparently entirely composed of that mineral, and in the sides of these numerous excavations have been made.

The valleys of Armenia are fertile in grain, tobacco, manna, hemp, cotton, and in fruit-trees, particularly a large description of apple, and walnuts. The excellence of the Armenian cotton was noticed by Marco Polo.

ARMILLA, is a bracelet, or large ring, for the wrist or arm. The wearing of the armilla, or bracelet, as an ornament, is of very high antiquity. It occurs in Genesis, chap. xxiv., 22, 23, where Abraham sends his servant to seek a wife for Isaac. The Amalekite who slew Saul (2 Sam i. 10) 'took the crown that was upon his head, and the *bracelet* that was on his arm,' and brought them to David. The armilla is often mentioned by the Roman writers, and it was worn both by males and females. It was also used as a reward for military bravery.

The Hamilton, Townley, and Knight collections of antiquities, in the British Museum, contain armillæ in great quantities, and of almost every variety of form, in gold, in silver, and in bronze.

These armillæ are interesting in an industrial point of view, in so far as they illustrate metallurgy in early times.

ARMOUR, is a general term for any defensive habit worn to protect the wearer from the attack of an enemy. *Harness* is a name formerly applied in this country to armour in the aggregate.

Some of the earliest manufactures in metal were connected with the making of armour. In the Bible we find the shield, helmet and breastplate mentioned at a very early period; and *greaves*, or armour for the legs, are named among the armour of Goliath. Homer mentions them, and his descriptions of the breastplate of Agamemnon, the shield of Achilles, and the golden armour of Glaucus indicate the highly decorated character of much ancient armour.

The complete Roman armour consisted of the helmet, shield, lorica, and greaves. The lorica was originally of leather, but in the time of Servius Tullius the whole of the Roman body armour was of brass. The Roman lorica was frequently enriched with embossed figures. Each Roman legion had its own device marked upon its shields.

The early Britons appear to have used no armour except the shield; but many of the Anglo-Saxons wore loricæ of leather and four-cornered helmets, having probably derived them from the Romans. The Anglo-Saxon soldiers appear in drawings of the eighth century with no armour besides the shield and helmet, and armed with the sword and spear. Towards the close of the ninth century the *corium*, or *corietum*, was the armour generally used. It was formed of hides cut into the resemblance of leaves, and covering one another. The weight of the ringed byrne seems to have been found a great impediment to activity. Edward the Confessor appears on his great seal in a diadem evidently put upon a helmet. The casque worn by the nobility was of metal, and of a pointed conical shape, but ornamented with gold and jewels, and in the later specimens furnished with a *nasal*, or small projecting piece to shield the nose.

The Danes, on their first appearance in England, seem to have had no armour beyond a broad collar or thorax of flat rings and leather greaves or rather shin-pieces; but about the time of Canute they adopted, probably from the Normans, a tunic with a hood and long sleeves, and *chausses*, or pantaloons, which covered the feet, all of these being coated with perforated lozenges of steel, called from their resemblance to the meshes of a net, *macles*, or *mascles*. They were also a rounded conical helmet, or skull-cap, with a round knob, under which were painted the rays of a star on its apex, and a large broad nasal, to which the hood being drawn up over the mouth, was attached, so as to leave nothing but the eyes exposed. The shield remained as before, and the weapons were spears, swords, and battle-axes, or bipennes.

From the period of the Conquest, seals, especially those of our kings, and monumental effigies, furnish abundant evidence as to the changes which took place in the fashion of armour. The Conqueror himself appears on his seal in a hauberk apparently of rings set edgewise; and in the Bayeux tapestry ring-armour forming both breeches and jacket at the same time is represented. The *chapel de fer*, which resembles in shape a Tartar cap, being a cone which projects beyond the head, appears for the first time upon the seal of Rufus; and *tegulated armour*, which consisted of little plates covering each other in the manner of tiles, and sewn upon a hauberk, without sleeves or hood, appears during the reign of Stephen, towards the close of which the nasal of the helmet seems to have been disused. Henry II. is represented on his seal in a flat-ringed hauberk, and a conical helmet without a nasal. *Pourpointerie*, or *pourpointing*, which consisted of padded work elaborately stitched, appears first in the great seals of Henry III., where the hauberk and chausses appear to be of this description. Some changes appear also in the helmet, which, in his second seal, is cylindrical. *Poleyns*, or coverings for the knees, were worn in this reign. Archers are shown in illuminations of this period wearing leathern vests over hauberks of edge-ringed mail. Armour of interlaced rings, which did not require to be sewn to an under garment, and was probably introduced from the east by the crusaders, was introduced in this reign; in which also the *chanfron*, or armour for the horse's head, appears for the first time.

Considerable improvements were made in armour during the reigns of Edward I., II., and III. *Ailettes*, or shoulder-pieces; mixed armour, partly of plate and partly of mail; *armures de fer*, or richly adorned plate-armour; *mamelieres*, or pieces put upon the breast, and from which chains descended, one to the sword-hilt, and the other to the scabbard; the *cointisse*, or surcoat, ornamented with the warrior's arms, over the armour; moveable visors attached to the *bacinets*, or bason-shaped skull-caps,—all appeared during these three reigns. Increased ornament was a characteristic of the armour of the reigns of Richard II. and Henry IV., about which time Italian armourers were much employed by the English nobility. Chain-mail appears to have been entirely disused soon after 1400, complete armour of plate superseding it. Black armour was often used at this period for mourning. Plate-armour attained its highest perfection about the reign of Richard III., and one of the finest suits preserved in the Tower of London, accompanied by a chanfron, manæfaire, and poitral, for arming the horse, belonged to Henry VII. In his reign fluted armour was occasionally used; and in that of his successor armour was frequently stamped or engraved with arms and devices, and sometimes *damasquinée*, or inlaid with gold.

The use of complete armour began to decline in this country after the time of Elizabeth. The late Sir S. Meyrick's collection of armour at Goodrich Court is perhaps the finest private collection in this country. At the Mediæval Exhibition of 1850, many fine specimens of armour belonging to the feudal ages were collected.

ARMS. The few details which may be deemed fitting on this subject, in the present work, will be found under such headings as ARTILLERY, BOW, CANNON, GUN, RIFLE, SWORD, &c.

ARNOTTO, or ARNATTO, the inspissated extract from the fruit of the *Bixa Orellana*, is used by dyers to give a bright orange colour to silk goods, and to give a deeper shade to simple yellow colours. It is further used in many of our dairies to give a reddish colour to cheese, which it does without adding any disagreeable flavour or unwholesome quality. The Arnotto of commerce is brought to us from South America. It is moderately hard, brown on the outside, and of a dull red within. It comes in cakes of about two or three pounds weight each, and is generally enveloped in large flag-leaves previous to being packed in casks. In this state it receives the name of flag arnotto, to distinguish it from a less known variety called roll arnotto. Arnotto dissolved in potass and water forms Nankin dye; and most of its solutions are effected with alkalies. A varnish is made from it with alcohol.

The consumption of arnotto has been much increased in this country of late years. In 1847 about 270,000 lbs. were imported. Arnotto is now admitted duty free. It sells at present from 10*d.* to 1*s.* 10*d.* per lb.

ARNOTT'S STOVE. Dr. Arnott has distinguished himself by many ingenious contrivances, brought forward by him—not for the sake of profit, but as conducive to general health and comfort. The Water-bed, the Stove, the Ventilator—all are familiarly known by the name of the benevolent physician who invented them.

Arnott's Stove is one of the many varieties of *close* stove, in which the cheerfulness of an open English fire is abandoned for the sake of a more efficient mode of burning the fuel. It was in 1838 that Dr. Arnott published his work on *Warming* and *Ventilation*, in which he so beautifully and simply explains the philosophy of the fire-placo. He shows how, in a common open firo we waste a large amount of fuel, heat our rooms very unequally at different distances from the fire-place, cause cold draughts to flow in from the doors and windows, and a stratum of cold air to lie next the floor and near the feet, leave the rooms without good ventilation, occasion much unnecessary smoke and dust, waste much time in attending to the fire, entail danger to person and to property, and necessitate frequent cleaning of chimneys. It was to remove some of these evils, and to lessen others, that he suggested his new form of stove—the guiding principle of which is, to allow the fuel to burn very slowly, through the controlling agency of a valve for admitting the air. The stove usually consists of an exterior iron case, square or cylindrical, lined with fire clay; the fuel is burned in a box or vessel within the case; there is one opening in the outer case to admit fuel, another to remove ashes, and a third at which a flue may be fixed to carry off the products of combustion. All these apertures being closed, air must enter to feed the fire in some other way. This is admitted by a very small aperturo near the level of the burning fuel; and the aperturo is closed by a valve which forms the distinguishing feature of the Arnott stoves. Many varieties of the valve have been adopted; but all of them are *self-acting*. When the fire is too fierce, the valve closes automatically, and refuses to admit any more air until the heat becomes subdued; but under average circumstances the valve remains open, and a small but steady stream of air enters the stove. The most successful contrivance is found to be a tube containing mercury, placed within the outer case, and bending round to the exterior in the form of an inverted siphon; when the mercury becomes heated, it expands, rises in the tube, and thus moves a small piece of apparatus which governs the valve.

The relation which Arnott's stove bears to stoves and heating apparatus generally, is noticed under WARMING AND VENTILATING.

ARNOTT'S VENTILATOR. Dr. Arnott's contrivances in respect to heat and air all depend on these two points—how to bring pure air *into* a room and a fire; and how to expel impure air *from* a room and a fire. The Ventilator, now happily so much used in ordinary rooms, is an exceedingly simple means of effecting the second object. When the cholera was raging in London in 1849, Dr. Arnott suggested that, in every badly ventilated room, a brick should be taken out of the wall near the ceiling, so as to open a direct communication between the room and the chimney; and he wrote a letter to the *Times*, in which the rationale of this contrivance was described with a clearness and simplicity which few but himself can effect by words alone. He said, 'Every chimney in a house is what is called a *sucking* or *drawing air-pump*, of a certain force, and can easily be rendered a valuablo ventilating pump. A chimney is a pump—first, by reason of the suction or approach to a vacuum made at the open end of any tube across which the wind blows directly; and secondly, because the flue is usually occupied, even when there is no fire, by air somewhat warmer than the external air, and has, therefore, even in a calm day, what is called a chimney-draught proportioned to the difference. In England, therefore, of old, when the chimney breast was made higher than tho heads of persons sitting or sleeping in rooms, a room with an open chimney was tolerably well ventilated in the lower part, where the inmates breathe.' But modern fire-places are made low, and the heated air cannot thus escape. 'If, however, an opening be made in a chimney-flue through the wall near the ceiling of the room, then will all tho hot impure air of the room certainly pass away.... For years past I have recommended the adoption of such ventilating chimney openings; and I devised a balanced valve, to prevent, during tho use of the fires, the escapo of smoke to the room.'

Such is the philosophy and the action of the ventilating valves. They are made rectangular or circular, of iron or of brass, plain or ornamental, balanced in front or behind; but all act alike on the same principle.

Dr. Arnott has devised other and more elaborate ventilators. He was applied to by the Board of Health, a year or two ago, to suggest means for the ventilation of ships; and he has described very efficient means of attaining this end. Quite recently (1850) he has planned a system of ventilation for a large building of a highly curious and scientific kind. The building is the York County Hospital, which has a reservoir of water at a height of 60 feet from the ground; and he resolved that this water should work the apparatus for ventilating the whole building. A large circular vessel has been constructed, which is partly filled with water; floating on the water, or rather resting with its edges on the water, is a kind of gasometer, or inverted air-chamber. A pipe of small diameter extends vertically from the water vessel to the reservoir at the top of the house; and the water, flowing down this pipe, exerts a great hydraulic pressure on a piston, which forces the water into the gasometer, and forces the air from the gasometer into air-passages which ventilate the building. The scientific principles of the hydraulic press, of the air-pump, and of the gasometer, are all involved in the arrangement. The gasometer holds 125 feet of air; it is filled and emptied by the action of the apparatus, sixteen times in a minute; so that 2000 cubic feet of air per minute are forced into the ventilating passages of the hospital.

The general subject of ventilation, in its varied forms, is noticed in the article before referred to. [WARMING AND VENTILATING.]

ARO'MA AND AROMATICS. Aroma is the supposed principle of odour in plants, formerly called by Boerhaave *Spiritus Rector*. This quality generally resides in the essential oil; but there are some vegetables that have a strong odour which yield but little or no essential oil, as the jessamine and the violet; or when an oil in small quantity is procured from them, it has not a powerful smell.

Aromatics exercise a peculiar influence over tho digestive powers, and are possessed of more or less odour or fragrance. Of this odour, by which they can at all times be recognised, the most usual vehicle is an essential or volatile oil, as just stated. Indeed, volatile oil exists in all aromatic plants, and in every part except the cotyledons, save in the nutmeg and a very few other seeds; but this aromatic oil does not reside in the same part in every kind of plant.

Aromatics are seldom applied to the organ of smell for the purpose of influencing the system in a remedial manner, but are usually introduced into the stomach. As all aromatics contain volatile oil, their action is generally referred to this principle; but there cannot be a doubt that the more fixed principles which they contain contribute greatly to their effect. Volatile oils, when separated, act chiefly on the nervous system; but aromatics influence the digestive organs, the function of assimilation, and the circulation. The necessity for the employment of aromatics is greater in warm climates and weather than in cold; and we find the plants which furnish them grow in the greatest abundance in hot countries. Throughout the East Indies the natives restore the powers of the stomach by chewing betel, which consists of slices of the areca nut, sprinkled with fresh lime, wrapped up along with some aromatic in a leaf of the *piper betel*. The Indians of South America use the *Erythróxylum Peruvianum* (called *coca*) along with the leaves of the *Chenopódium Quinoa*, mixed with quicklime, to stimulate the impaired powers of the stomach during their long and toilsome journeys over the heights of the Andes. On the same principle, the Europeans who visit tropical countries use curry and other hot dishes. But in every quarter of the globe we find condiments used along with all articles difficult of digestion, especially vegetables, fish, and young meat, such as veal.

ARPENT. The arpent is one of the French measures of land, intended to be abolished by the metrical system, but still given in various books, and therefore useful to be known. There were, however, four varieties of it; the smallest of which contained 4089 English square yards, and the largest 9770. The crown-lands were measured by the arpent of 6107 English square yards—about 1¼ acres.

ARQUEBUS. This variety of fire-arms, now out of use, was a sort of hand-gun, provided with a small apparatus suggested by the trigger of the cross-bow, to convey with certainty and quickness the burning match to the touch-powder.

The arquebuses made in the 15th century were often very ornamental. At the exhibition of Mediæval Art, in 1850, many such specimens were collected. In one example, belonging to the Board of Ordnance, the stock is inlaid with ivory, the bow is engraved with arabesques partly gilt, and the linstock is engraved with figures of seven deities.

ARRACK. [ARACK.]

ARRAGON. [ARAGON.]

ARRAGONITE. These crystals have been found abundantly in a ferruginous clay in Aragon in Spain, where they occur accompanied by sulphate of lime; and they are also met with in numerous other parts of Europe. Arragonite is a carbonate of lime, chemically almost identical with calc-spar; but of different crystallized form, heavier and harder than that substance.

ARRAN, the rugged island lying off the coast of Ayrshire, in Scotland, affords a few of the crude materials of industry. It has its quarries of white sandstone; a small supply of slate; a little coal (too limited however to repay for working at present); while wanderers over its mountains often pick up transparent stones, worked by the jewellers under the names of Arran stones, cairngorms, and Scotch topazes. There is a manufactory of sulphate of barytes, used in making paint.

ARRIS, in French *Areste* and *Arete*, is a term employed in building to express the intersection or line in which the two straight or curved surfaces of a body, forming an exterior angle, meet each other. The term is synonymous with edge; but the term edge only is used in reference to parallelopipedal bodies, on which the length and thickness may be measured.

ARRIS FILLET, a small triangular piece of wood, used to raise the slates of a roof against the shaft of a chimney or a wall, to throw off the rain more effectually; it is used for the same purpose also in forming gutters round skylights, which have the same inclination as the roof, and are slightly raised above it.

ARROBA, is the name both of a weight and a measure, in Spain, Portugal, and the Canaries. The weight-arroba varies from about 25 to 33 lb. avoirdupois; the measure-arroba varies from 2½ to 3½ gallons.

ARROO, a large island near New Guinea, is a trading depôt for the Chinese, who procure from Arroo pearls, tortoise-shell, edible birds'-nests, and an aromatic bark named missoy, which resembles cinnamon. Birds of paradise are very numerous in these islands: they are caught by the natives for their plumage; their flesh, when preserved by fumigation, is bought by the Chinese traders.

ARROW. [Bow.]

ARROW-ROOT is a farinaceous substance prepared from the roots or tubers of various plants; that from America and the West Indies being the produce of *Maranta arundinacea* and *Maranta indica*, and that from the East Indies being from the *M. indica*, and from several species of *Curcuma*. Among other plants which yield a similar substance is the cuckoo-pint, *Arum maculatum*. Arrow-root is prepared by either grating or beating the tubers in a mortar to a pulpy consistence; separating the fibrous matter from the pulp by mixing it with a quantity of water, and passing it through a hair-sieve; and then suffering the pure farina to subside from the remaining milk-like fluid, and if needful, purifying it still further by successive washings and strainings. The moisture is at length evaporated by exposure to sun and air, and when perfectly dry the powder is packed in boxes or casks, in which state it may be kept for many years. West Indian arrow-root is usually of a pure white, and East Indian has a yellowish tinge. Its taste is insipid, and the powder emits a crackling sound when pressed in the hand, and retains the impression of the fingers, which common wheat-starch does not. Being very easy of digestion, arrow-root constitutes a valuable article of food for children and delicate persons. It is used mixed with boiling water or milk, or in the form of puddings, and may be given plain, or with wine or spices. Potato-starch is not so digestible, and, if prepared from potatoes in the spring, is liable to disturb the stomach. The common English name of this preparation is derived from the use to which the South American Indians applied the roots of a plant once confounded with the Maranta, but now called *Alpinia galanga*, as an antidote to the effect of poisoned arrows.

It is said that a very large portion of that which is sold in the shops under the name of arrow-root consists of potato-starch.

The cultivation of arrow-root has lately been introduced with considerable success into the island of St. Vincent. Machinery of skilful construction is employed to prepare the arrow-root from the plant; and the packing for shipment is very carefully conducted.

Arrow-root from British colonies pays 6d. per cwt. import duty; from foreign countries 2s. 6d. In 1847 about 10,580 cwts. were imported; and in 1848 about 8,100 cwts.

ARSENAL, a public establishment where naval and military engines, or warlike equipments, are manufactured or stored. The Royal Arsenal at Woolwich is the chief establishment of this kind in England. In France the chief arsenal is at Paris. Toulon, Marseille, and Brest, are naval arsenals.

ARSENIC is a peculiar metal, frequently met with in nature; sometimes in its pure metallic state, but more commonly combined with other metals, as iron and cobalt, or with sulphur, and frequently united with oxygen. Arsenic has a steel gray colour and considerable brilliancy; its density is about 5½ times that of water. The native metal is granular, and the artificial crystalline; it is extremely brittle, and consequently easily powdered. When arsenic is exposed to the air, it soon loses its lustre, and becomes black on the surface. When kept under water, it undergoes no change; if heated to 356° Fahrenheit, it is volatilized, without previous fusion; the vapour has a strong smell, resembling that of garlic, and this, to a certain extent, is relied upon as proof of its presence; the vapour readily condenses in small brilliant crystals of metallic arsenic.

Arsenic and oxygen combine in two proportions, and both compounds possess acid properties; that which contains the smaller quantity of oxygen is termed *arsenious acid*, the *white arsenic* of the shops. *Arsenic acid*, which contains the larger quantity of oxygen, exists in nature much more commonly than the arsenious acid, in combination with lime, copper, iron, and lead. It is of a milk-white colour, and is very poisonous. *Arsenic and hydrogen* combine to form a gas, which, however, when subjected to intense cold, is condensed into a limpid liquid resembling æther. The gas has an extremely fetid smell. The *chloride of Arsenic* is a colourless volatile liquid, which combines with oil of olives and of turpentine, and partially dissolves sulphur and phosphorus when heated. *Arsenic and sulphur* may be made to combine in four different proportions; of which two yield *realgar* and *orpiment*. Realgar, a red sulphuret, is of a deep-red colour, brittle, easily reduced to powder, inodorous, tasteless, and insoluble in water. Orpiment, a yellow sulphuret, is commonly composed of thin plates, which are of a very fine yellow colour, and flexible to a considerable degree.

Arsenic and metals in general combine with great facility: those which are malleable it renders brittle, and those which are difficult to melt it renders fusible. These alloys do not form an important class of bodies.

The arsenic and arsenious acids combine with many alkalies and metals to produce salts. These, as well as other preparations of arsenic, are largely used in the arts. Arsenite of potash is used in making cobalt blue; the red sulphuret is used in making fire-works; the yellow sulphuret is used as a dye, as a pigment, and in making fire-works; arsenic in its metallic state is employed for a few purposes, generally in an alloyed state. The *medical* applications of arsenial compounds we do not notice here; further than to say that the common arsenic of the shops is arsenious acid, and that it is too frequently adulterated with plaster of paris and other cheap substances.

The late Mr. Marsh devised some extremely delicate means of detecting the presence of arsenic. The liquid suspected to contain the poison is acidulated with sulphuric acid and placed in contact with metallic zinc, both of which must be previously ascertained to be free from arsenic; if any arsenic be present in the liquid, the hydrogen gas generated reduces and dissolves it, forming arsenuretted hydrogen gas. This gas is to be lighted at a jet, and a piece of white porcelain or of glass is to be held over the flame, when, if any arsenic be present, a brilliant black spot of metallic arsenic is deposited on the glass or porcelain. Another method of proceeding is to boil a slip of bright metallic copper in the fluid suspected, previously acidulated with hydrochloric acid. If arsenic be present, the copper is covered with a whitish alloy, and then by heating the metal in a test tube, the arsenic is volatilized, and sublimes in the metallic state in the cold part of the glass. This method is susceptible of detecting very minute portions of arsenic.

Foreigu arsenic may be imported into this country duty free.

ART-UNIONS are societies for the encouragement of the fine arts by the purchase of works of art out of a common fund raised in small shares or subscriptions; such works of art, or the right of selecting them, being distributed by lot among the subscribers or members. The success of similar associations in Germany and Prussia led to the establishment in 1837 of the Art-Union of London, which, though it has given rise to many others, remains at the head of such societies in this country. In it every member subscribes annually the sum of one or more guineas, receiving accordingly one or more shares in the advantages held out. Part of the sum thus raised is expended in the engraving of one or more works of art, of which every subscriber receives a copy; but, though the prints thus distributed are such as would, in the ordinary course of trade, cost the full amount of the subscription, they are, owing to the combination of a very large body of subscribers, and the avoidance of risk, produced at so small a cost as to leave the greater part of the subscribed funds available for the purchase of original pictures or pieces of sculpture. The sum thus appropriated is divided into prizes of from 10*l.* to 300*l.* or 400*l.*, which are distributed by lot among the subscribers; the prize-holders being allowed, under certain restrictions, themselves to select works of art to the specified amount. These works of art, previous to their delivery to the prize-holders, are gratuitously exhibited for three or four weeks to the subscribers and the public.

In the season of 1850 the subscriptions amounted to 11,180*l.*; the sum laid out in the purchase of pictures, statuettes and medals was 5073*l.*, and on engravings and etchings 3250*l.* The works of art selected by the subscribers amounted in number to 1021.

Doubts having been raised as to the legality of art unions, temporary acts were passed in 1844 and 1845 to indemnify their managers from the penalties to which they were supposed to be subject; and in 1846 an act (9 & 10 Vic. c. 48) was passed to legalize such as have been or may be incorporated by royal charter, or may have their rules and deed of partnership approved by a committee of the privy council. The Art-Union of London was incorporated by royal charter on the 1st of December, 1846.

ARTA, a town of Albania, holds a respectable rank in respect to manufactures. In the quarter set apart for trade, each art has its separate street or bazaar, and articles of dress manufactured here are held in high estimation. The floccatas, or shaggy capotes of Arta, are considered the finest; woollens, coarse cottons, and Russia leather, are also manufactured, and this town derives some commercial benefit as the entrepôt between Joanina and the gulf, by which the produce of Albania reaches the sea.

ARTESIAN WELLS are perpendicular perforations or borings, through which water rises from various depths, according to circumstances, above the surface of the soil. Such perforations have been named Artesian wells, from the opinion that they were first used in the district of Artois in France. They are seldom more than a few inches in diameter, and are made by means of the usual boring instruments. Their action is due to the constant endeavour of water to seek its level.

Let us suppose, for example, that there is an undulating tract of country, with a town placed in a hollow or valley. Near the surface is a thick bed of rock or clay, either impervious to water, or through which it percolates with difficulty. Beneath this is a sandy or porous stratum which 'crops out' or appears at the surface, on certain heights beyond the limits of the town. Beneath this stratum, again, is a close or impervious one. Under these supposed conditions the rain-water, falling on the heights, is absorbed by the 'crop out,' and filters down through the sandy stratum entirely beneath the town: unable to leave that sandy film or layer, because the strata above and below are nearly impervious to water. If, under these conditions, a perforation be made near the town, deep enough to reach the sandy stratum, the water which saturates this sand, the water will rise through the hole—not merely to a level with the town, but will often spout up far above that level, according to the height of the ground where the 'out-crop' of the sandy stratum occurs.

This is the principle of the Artesian well, let it be carried out how it may. The geologist has to determine whether a watery stratum probably exists: the well-borer has to deviso the mode of reaching it.

One of the most celebrated Artesian wells is that at Grenelle, near Paris. It was commenced in 1833, and not finished till 1841. Geologists were aware, from the nature of the formation beneath and around Paris, that any watery sandy stratum must necessarily be at a great depth; but the urgent want of water for the supply of the south-western portion of Paris, determined the authorities to brave all difficulties in the attempt. The boring proceeded slowly, interrupted from time to time by disasters which severely taxed the patience of the engineer. At length, in February 1841, the boring rods suddenly penetrated into the watery stratum; and a stream of pure and limpid water rushed up to the light of day, from the subterranean depths where it had been so long buried. The depth to which the boring was carried exceeded 1800 feet.

In 1837 the inhabitants of Southampton, requiring an improved supply of water, caused an experimental boring to be made on an elevated common about two miles north of the town. The result being deemed satisfactory, measures were taken for the sinking of a shaft. It proved an enormous work. The well-diggers penetrated through 78 feet of alluvium, 300 feet of stiff clay, 100 feet of plastic clay, and about 100 feet of chalk: encountering much difficulty in forming a substantial open shaft. Having thus reached a depth of about 580 feet, the boring rods were used, and were driven to a further depth of more than 700 feet; so that the total depth attained exceeds 1300 feet. The labour and expense were ultimately rewarded; for a flow of 50,000 gallons of water per day was obtained. The expense was nearly 20,000*l*.

The Artesian Wells of Grenelle in France, and Southampton in England, may be taken as types of these works on a large scale. Nearly all the others which have been formed are of less magnitude, and have involved less expense.

In a paper read before the Institute of British Architects by Doctor Buckland, in 1849, he drew attention to the fact that a well is not properly artesian unless the water overflows at the surface. Thirty years ago there were several such wells in and about London; but such has been the oxhaustion of the springs within this district, that there is now hardly a single well of such a kind, although there are about 300 which are called artesian, chiefly from the mode in which they are sunk by boring instead of digging. The water now obtained in London wells does not rise to within many feet of the surface, and expensive machinery is often necessary to make it available. In the artesian well which supplies the fountains in Trafalgar Squaro the water does not reach within forty feet of the surface, whence it is pumped up by a steam engine: the supply is good, but the process of obtaining it is costly. The level of the water in the London wells is gradually sinking, as the number of wells increase. Doctor Buckland estimated the present average level in the London wells at 60 feet below the surface, and he thinks that in twenty years it will have sunk to 120 feet. One of the great porter breweries has now to pump up water from a depth of 188 feet, in a well which a few years ago maintained a level 95 feet below the surface.

These observations, coming from a high authority, have had some influence on the recent discussions concerning the supply of London with water. Whatever may be the plan ultimately adopted, it does not seem that the artesian system would be fitting for such an enormous supply as would be necessary.

The mode of digging or boring for Artesian Wells is described elsewhere. [BORING.]

ARTICHOKE. The artichoke and the cardoon are two species of the same genus of plants. The artichoke came originally from the south of Europe, and though it has long been cultivated in the regions of the north, it does not resist the very severe cold of winter. The root of the artichoke is rather bitter, the stem still more so. It was formerly employed as a diuretic, but it has long been cultivated only as a kitchen-garden plant. The cardoon is found in the southern countries of Europe and in the north of Africa. When cooked it is tender, and its flavour greatly resembles that of the artichoke. It is in general a choice dish, and seldom seen except at the tables of persons in easy circumstances.

ARTIFICIAL FLOWERS. Few employments of a mechanical or manipulative nature are more beautiful in their results than the production of artificial or imitative flowers. Nothing can well exceed the faithfulness of these imitations; every petal, every leaf, every calyx, every bud, is imitated with an accuracy which must have required long observation and much ingenuity on the part of those who have practised this art. A lady may for a shilling procure one of these delicate productions, such as would be deemed a fitting ornament for her attire; but a curious enquirer might also find a shilling not ill-spent, merely for the instruction to be derived from a dissection of this flower, with a view to study its mechanical anatomy.

The petals of flowers are imitated by ribbons, feathers, silk-worm cocoons, cambric, taffeta, velvet, or thin laminæ of whalebone shaped and coloured for the purpose. The stems are mostly formed of wires, wrapped round with paper, silk, or some other material of the requisite colour. The leaves and petals are mostly cut and embossed by stamping with dies having sharp cutting edges, and are united together by means of wires and paste or cement. The modes of colouring are exceedingly various. Seeds and similar objects, and small fruits, such as currants, are imitated by wax, glass, and other substances. Very beautiful imitations of some plants are made with wax, rice-paper, and shells.

This manufacture is generally carried on in private houses, where a large number of persons (mostly females) work together, each taking certain departments, according to the principle of the division of labour; and the whole product is then sold to wholsale dealers, who supply the retail shops.

Our French neighbours are especially distinguished in this art; all their delicacy of taste is brought to bear upon it; and we may reasonably expect that the Great Exhibition of 1851 will afford a favourable display of their skill. M. Dupin, in his recent letter to the French manufacturers, says:—'Let us not forget a branch of trade which, assiduously studied, rivals nature itself; this is the production of artificial flowers in every possible variety. Of these, France sells to the extent of a million francs (40,000*l.*) to the foreigner; and England, with the United States, purchases more than half this amount.'

We will take a *rose*, as a specimen of French imitative manufacture. The petals, the leaves, the calyx, the buds, the stamens, the stalk—all require distinct processes. First, for the *petals*. These are made of the finest cambric, which is cut out with punches; there being as many different sized punches as there are different sizes in the petals of a rose. Each petal is held by pincers at the extreme end, dipped into a carmine dye, then dipped into water to soften the tint at the edges, then touched with a brush to deepen the tint near the centre; and any little variegated spots, or even blemishes, are imitated by tinting with a brush. Next for the *leaves*. These are made of Florence sarcenet, which is dyed to the proper colour, stretched while wet that it may dry out perfectly smooth; the glazed surface of the leaf is imitated by coating the sarcenet with thin gum-water; while the velvety texture of the under surface is imitated either by a wash of coloured starch water, or by a layer of *flock* or cloth powder, such as is used in making flock paper-hangings. To imitate the *ribs* which form such a peculiar and beautiful characteristic of the leaves, several leaves, placed one upon another, are pressed between *gaufroirs* or goffering-irons, cut with the required indentations. Then we have the leaflets which form the *calyx*; the sarcenet for these is stiffened with starch water while yet wet from the dyeing; and when dry, the material is cut to the proper size and shape by punches. The *buds* are made of sarcenet or of kid, dyed or painted according to circumstances; they are swelled out to the proper shape by a stuffing of cotton, gummed flax, or crumb of bread, and are tied with silk at the end of thin iron wires. The *stamens* are made of silk, fixed at the ends of brass wires, and so shaped that the wire shall imitate the filament and the silk the anther; the silk anther being dipped into a glutinous liquid, is made to retain some very small seeds which imitate the pollen. Lastly comes the building-up of the delicate structure; the stalk is made of iron wire, coated with cotton and green paper; and around this stalk are grouped and fastened the several parts which together form the imitative rose.

ARTIFICIAL FUEL. Some of the compositions, recently introduced as substitutes for coal, are noticed under FUEL.

ARTIFICIAL GEMS; ARTIFICIAL PEARLS. The principal methods adopted in imitating the costly gems which take such a high rank in respect to personal adornment, are described in a later article. [GEMS, FACTITIOUS.]

ARTIFICIAL LIMBS, &c. Considerable mechanical ingenuity is displayed in supplying substitutes for limbs or organs which accident or any other cause has removed.

The art of the dentist, for instance, calls for no small amount of mechanical skill. First there is the choice of the ivory which, from its colour, texture, and hardness, affords the best imitation of the natural teeth. Then there is the shaping of this ivory to the size and form of the tooth, whether single or double, front or back, upper or under. And lastly there are the remarkable contrivauces —by means of golden palates, or springs, or wires, or cement, by which the tooth or mouthful of teeth are fixed in their places. Experience seems to shew that few kinds of cheapness are so dear as cheap tooth-making: so great are the difficulties in supplying teeth that will really eat their way through the difficulties presented to them. As for the *succedaneums* and metallic and other *cements* for stopping decayed teeth, their merit depends more on the quality of the material than on the mode of using. We see from time to time patents for new contrivances in dental surgery, which involve no small amount of ingenuity. One such has been enrolled in 1850 by Mr. Dinsdale, in which the manufacture of teeth, palates, and gums are described.

An artificial eye is an example of glass manufacture; the shaping of the glass being much less difficult than the accurate imitation of the cornea and iris by means of pigments and dyes.

All those numerous examples of skill, which may more fittingly be called surgical *operations* than anatomical *contrivances*, we have nothing to do with here; but when a mechanician undertakes to supply an arm, a hand, or a leg, which will render tolerable service as a substitute for one of flesh and blood, we have as much right to claim it as a proof of constructive skill as a loom or a lathe, a plough or a clock. And here we mark how quickly a newly discovered substance becomes brought within the scope of the operations. Is it caoutchouc? Then will the artificial legmaker find out where to use it with advantage. Is it gutta percha? Then will he soon see where the combined elasticity and toughness of that remarkable substance are likely to be valuable. Accordingly we find that many different materials are employed, either to give shape to the artificial hand, arm, or leg, or to give smoothness and softness to the surface, or to form the joints for the requisite movements. Wood, leather, caoutchouc, gutta percha, cork, iron levers, steel springs—all are employed; and much ingenuity is displayed in arranging.

Sir George Cayley, who has exhibited much inventive talent in various mechanical contrivances, has recently made many trials to produce an artificial hand which shall be less costly than those ordinarily constructed. He has made the 'Mechanics' Magazine' the medium of communicating his experience in this matter. His first attempt was in 1845. The son of one of his tenants having lost a hand by accident, Sir George contrived a substitute which has in many ways lessened the severity of the privation. The movements of this instrument are derived from the stump; a light frame-work fixes the apparatus to the upper part of the arm; and a lever connects this frame-work with the artificial hand. The arm is placed within padded rings of metal, which are connected by two long steel bars hinged at the elbow. When the wearer moves his arm by the usual action of the elbow joint, he shifts a small metal bar near the wrist of the machine, which works two cog-wheels acting on each other; and these cog-wheels bring two steel springs together so as to enable them to grasp an object something in the manner of a thumb and fore-finger. The wheels and springs may either be left exposed, in the metallic state, or may be padded so as to represent a thumb and finger.

It was found that although this artificial hand could be turned round a little way, it could not be turned so much as a quarter of a circle from its horizontal towards a perpendicular grasp; and there was, at the same time, no movement equivalent to the usual bending of the wrist, which gives so great a variety of positions to the natural hand. He therefore contrived a new arrangement of mechanism at the wrist, so as to superadd these two movements to those before pos-

SODA FURNACE AT THE FELLING

SULPHURIC ACID CHAMBER

PLATINUM STILL. SULP. AC.

NEWCASTLE

KNIGHT'S CYCLOPÆDIA OF THE Industry of all Nations.

No. 7.

sessed by the apparatus; this involved an increase of rather delicate mechanism.

At one of the soirées given by the President of the Royal Society in 1845, the boy for whom Sir George Cayley made the artificial hand was introduced, and Prince Albert "shook" him by his mechanical appendage. The hand had only one finger worked by the mechanism; but there were the proper number of cork fingers united side by side, and fixed to one broad thin steel plate, jointed, and covered with continuous leather, stitched down to mark the distinction of the fingers under it. But where a more expensive apparatus can be afforded, and the appearance of having a real hand is sought for, the thin steel plate can be separated into digits, though united at the base as in a common hand, and jointed at the proper places in due proportion to each finger.

In another form of artificial hand, made by Sir G. Cayley, in 1847, there is a case or sheath, into which the stump of the arm is introduced. A spiral spring is fixed at one end to this sheath, and at the other to a bent lever; while the middle of the lever is connected with the mechanism of rods which move the artificial thumb and fingers. In this arrangement, the wearer uses his sound hand to work his artificial hand. He presses a little button which is connected with the bent lever; by pressing this towards the wrist, the fingers and thumb open to receive any object they may be intended to grasp; and when this pressure from the other hand is taken off, the grasp takes effect, without further effort, till released by a contrary movement. The mechanism is very simple, and is attached wholly to the lower arm, near the stump. But as the sound hand must be taken from anything else it has to perform, at the time the artificial hand is thus put to work; and as it may on other accounts be inconvenient to work the apparatus in this way, Sir George invented a very ingenious means of working the hand by the movement of the upper arm or shoulder-joint.

M. Magendie described to the Paris Academy of Sciences, in 1845, an artificial arm, invented by M. Van Petersen. A sort of stays are fixed round the breast of the person; and from these are brought cords made of catgut, which act upon the articulations, according to tho motion given to the natural stump. The apparatus was found to be very effective. It was tried (among other patients) on an invalid soldier, who had lost both arms in the wars of the empire, retaining only the stumps. With the aid of two of the artificial arms, he was able to perform many of the functions which had hitherto been performed for him. M. Magendie considers this contrivance to be tho best substitute for a natural arm yet introduced.

ARTIFICIAL STONE. [CEMENT.]

ARTILLERY. This term, since the introduction of gunpowder, has been applied chiefly to large ordnance, together with their ammunition and appurtenances.

The earliest military engines were, in all probability, those for casting large stones. Such machines do not appear to have been used in England until the Norman invasion, and were used by the Normans chiefly in sea-fights, for throwing Greek fire, quicklime, and other combustibles, as well as stones and darts. Richard I. employed against the Saracens some such engines, worked by tho force of the wind acting upon sails. Edward I. used engines at the siege of Stirling Castle, in 1303, which threw stones of 300 lbs. weight.

The invention of gunpowder, though it did not for a long time supersede the ancient artillery, gradually brought about great changes in the art of war. The first cannon, which were called *bombards*, were very clumsy, wider at the mouth than the chamber, and formed of bars of iron bound together with hoops. The earliest cannon-balls were of stone. *Hand-cannon* carried by two men, and fired from a rest in the ground, were early used; and *carts of war*, conveying light artillery, are mentioned in a Scotch act of parliament in 1456. Cannon began to be formed by casting about the middle of the fifteenth century. Iron bullets (of which Monstrelet mentions one weighing five cwt.) began also to be used, but not to the exclusion of thoso of stono. A hard mixed metal, called *font-metal*, or *bronze*, was early invented for the casting of cannon; and the casting of this kind of ordnance was commenced in England in 1535. In the sixteenth century the size of cannon was reduced, and they were made of superior form. One of the largest cast cannon now existing is a brass one at Bejapoor, which was cast in commemoration of the capture of that place by the Emperor Alum Geer, in 1685. Its extreme length is 14 feet 1 inch; the diameter of its bore 2 feet 4 inches. An iron shot for this gun of proper size would weigh 1600 pounds.

For *mortars* we are indebted to workmen who were employed by Henry VIII.; those made for him about 1543 being, according to Stowe, 'at the mouth from 11 to 19 inches wide,' and employed to throw hollow shot of cast-iron, filled, like modern bombs, with combustibles, and furnished with a fuse.

Different names were given about that date to different kinds of cannon; such as *falcon*, *culverin*, *demi-culverin*, *minion*, and *sakar*. *Petards*, which are explosive engines employed in sieges, were first used by the Huguenots in 1580. The *howitzer*, an improvement on the mortar, was first used in 1697; and the *carronade*, a kind of long howitzer, about 1779.

The casting of these instruments of destruction is described under CANNON.

ARTIZANS. In this country it is customary when a young artizan has served his apprenticeship, for him to enter at once as a journeyman; to settle down in some town, usually where he has been apprenticed; and there work for any master who will employ him. Among the less respectable workmen, or when trade in general is dull, the *tramp* system is acted on; the artizan goes from town to town, a sort of homeless wanderer, seeking work wherever it may be found, and often forced to associate with disreputable companions.

But in Germany the custom is different. There a kind of tramp-system is not merely looked forward to, but is compulsory. The *wanderschaft* of a German workman is a transition period between the life of an apprentice and that of a master. In many parts both of Germany and Switzerland, an apprentice cannot obtain his freedom and become a master until he has spent a certain number of years in following his calling beyond his native country. He is furnished on setting out with a book called a *wander-buch*, in which his various employers insert certificates of his service and conduct. In his wanderings he is generally assisted and succoured, not only by the trade to which he belongs, but by the donations of travellers. Many English travellers in Germany must have encountered these young workmen, trudging along the roads, with knapsack on back. Mr. Symonds, ('Arts and Artizans, at Home and Abroad') states that, while certain evils arise from this system, it tends on the other hand to give the young men an amount of general information more varied and extensive than is commonly met with among English workmen.

In the Vorarlberg (a part of the Austrian dominions) the male inhabitants are accustomed to leave home early in the spring, go to Switzerland and France, exercise the trades of masons and house-builders during the summer, live with the utmost possible frugality, and return to the Vorarlberg in autumn with the savings of their labour.

The silk-weavers of Lyons have a very strict system of classification. There are small masters, workmen, and apprentices; besides the capitalist-manufacturers who set all to work. The masters, or *chefs d'ateliers*, are owners of a few looms, and have fixed residences. The workmen, or *compagnons*, have neither capital, looms, nor houses; they work the looms belonging to the master, live and board with him, and receive half the money gained by the looms they work—the other half going for house-rent, risk, wear and tear of machinery, &c. The *apprentices* are from 15 to 20 years of age; they are taught by the *chefs d'ateliers*, with whom and for whom they work.

Without entering far on this tangled subject, we shall notice, under CO-OPERATION, one or two of the recent suggestions for modifying the relations between employers and artizans.

ARTOCARPUS. [BREAD-FRUIT TREE.]

ARTS, FINE. The fine arts are generally understood to comprehend those productions of human genius and skill which are more or less addressed to the sentiment of taste. They were first employed in embellishing objects of mere utility, but their highest office is to meet our impressions of beauty or sublimity, however acquired, by imitative or adequate representation.

The great use of the arts is to humanize and refine, to purify enjoyment, and, when duly appreciated, to connect the perception of physical beauty with that of moral excellence; but it will at once be seen that this idea of usefulness is in a great measure distinct from the ordinary meaning of the term as applicable to the productions of human ingenuity. A positive use results indeed indirectly from the cultivation of the formative arts, precisely in proportion as their highest powers are developed. Again, as illustrating science, the fine arts may be directly useful in the stricter sense, but this is not the application which best displays their nature and value. The essence of the fine arts, in short, begins where utility in its narrower acceptation ends. That this principle exists in nature we immediately feel in calling to mind the merely beautiful appearances of the visible world, and particularly the colours of flowers. The fine arts in general may be considered the human reproduction of this principle. The question of their utility therefore resolves itself into the inquiry as to the intention of the beauties of nature.

With regard to the classification of the arts, those are generally considered the most worthy in which the mental labour employed and the mental pleasure produced are greatest, and in which the manual labour, or labour of whatever kind, is least apparent. This test would justly place poetry first. It would be an invidious as well as a very difficult task to assign the precise order in which painting, sculpture, architecture and music, would follow poetry and its sister, eloquence; but it may be remarked, that the union of the arts is a hazardous experiment, and is often destructive of their effect.

ARTS, MANUFACTURING. As the fine arts are destined to the production of objects beautiful rather than useful; so do the manufacturing arts produce results useful rather than beautiful. But in all the better epochs of society, these two divisions have tended to coalesce into one: the useful and the beautiful, the *utile et dulce*, being found reciprocally to lend strength to each other. The union of Science and Arts, too, is becoming more and more apparent. It has been remarked by a writer in the 'Edinburgh Review,' (vol. 78) that 'Art will not sufficiently develope her powers, nor science attain her most commanding position, till the practical knowledge of the one is taken in return for the sound deductions of the other. Many causes have concurred to place art and science at variance; but these causes have been gradually diminishing; and in the present advanced state of mechanical and useful arts they have almost wholly disappeared.'

The establishment of Art-Manufactures, in which sculptors and painters of eminence are employed to design models and patterns for manufacturers; the formation of Schools of Design, where drawing and modelling, with an especial relation to manufactures, are taught; the still more recent establishment of artizan schools, where similar instruction is given under different arrangements—all point to a union between fine art and manufacturing art; while Mechanics' Institutions, Lyceums, popular Treatises on Science—so far as they have realised the anticipations concerning them—point to a union between Science and Manufactures. Again, such discoveries as those relating to Photography, Electrography, &c., point to a union between science and fine art. Thus do all three—Science, Art, and Industry—stand in intimate relation one to another. [DESIGN, SCHOOLS OF; MANUFACTURES.]

ARUNDEL MARBLES, are certain pieces of sculpture, consisting of ancient statues, busts, mutilated figures, altars, inscriptions, &c., the remains of a more extensive collection, formed in the early part of the seventeenth century by Thomas Howard, Earl of Arundel, and presented in 1667 to the University of Oxford, by his grandson. The earl collected these fine specimens during a residence in Italy about 1613.

We learn from catalogues, that the Arundelian collection, when entire, contained 37 statues, 128 busts, and 250 inscribed marbles, exclusive of sarcophagi, altars, fragments, and the inestimable gems.

Arundel House and gardens were converted into streets about the year 1678, when it was determined to dispose of the statues by sale. One portion, consisting principally of busts, was purchased by Lord Pembroke; these are now at Wilton. A second was purchased by Sir William Fermor (the father of the first Earl of Pomfret,) who removed them to his seat at Easton Neston in Northamptonshire. Henrietta Louisa, countess dowager of Pomfret, in 1755, transferred these marbles to the University of Oxford, where they became again united to the inscribed marbles which had descended to Henry, second son of the former and sixth Duke of Norfolk, and had been presented by him to the University, in 1667. A few statues and broken fragments were given to a Mr. Arundel, a relation of the Duke of Norfolk; one or two of these were subsequently given to the Earl of Burlington, and went to Chiswick House. A few elegant remains were carried to Mrs. Temple's seat at Moor Park, near Farnham, in Surrey. The cameos and intaglios finally became the property of the Dukes of Marlborough; and are now known by the name of the Marlborough Gems.

The greater part of the Greek inscriptions in the Arundel collection now at Oxford were obtained at Smyrna. They arrived in England in 1627, soon after which they were carefully examined by the learned Selden, who in 1628 published his 'Marmora Arundelliana,' a thin quarto volume, in which twenty-nine Greek and ten Latin inscriptions of this collection are deciphered and illustrated.

The Arundel and Pomfret marbles are at present preserved at Oxford in two rooms belonging to the public schools, beneath the picture gallery. Of the Arundel portion, that which the University places at the head of its collection is the Greek inscription known by the name of the *Parian Chronicle*. Among the more important marbles of the Pomfret donation are the colossal torso (for that portion only is antique) of a Minerva Galeata, restored as a statue by Guelfi; a Venus Vestita, or Leda; Terpsichore; a young Hercules; an Athleta, which has been called Antinous; a female figure, unrestored, of early Greek work; and three statues of senators, one of which is usually considered as Cicero.

AS. The Roman As was a weight, consisting of twelve *unciæ* or ounces; it was also called *libra*, *libella*, and *pondo*, or the pound.

As, assis, or *Assarius* was likewise the name of a Roman coin of copper, or rather of mixed metal, which varied both in weight and composition at different periods of the commonwealth; but which originally actually weighed a pound, whence it was called *As libralis*, and sometimes also *Æs grave*. The earliest Ases were cast probably in imitation of the Etruscan coins, which the Romans appear to have copied. In the British Museum there are even four Ases united together, as they were taken from the mould or matrix, in which many were cast at once. In most of the Ases preserved in our cabinets, the edge shows evidently where they were severed from each other, and where the piece at the mouth of the mould was cut off. From being cast, it will be judged that they are not very correctly sized. As the As fell in weight, the smaller divisions were not cast, but struck.

The coined divisions of the As were numerous, including halves, thirds, fourths, fifths, sixths, twelfths, &c. There were also larger coins, representing various multiples of the As.

ASAM or ASSAM, is chiefly interesting in a commercial point of view for the attempts there made to cultivate the tea-plant. This wild country lies north-eastward of Hindustan, and is to a certain extent dependent on the East India Company. Reports having reached the Calcutta Government, relating to the value of the tea-plant found in Asam, a scientific deputation was despatched thither about the year 1836, to enquire into the subject. Tea-plantations were subsequently established, under the management of Mr. Bruce, who examined the surface of the country with a view to select spots favourable to the culture. Chinese labourers were engaged; and small portions of Asam tea have since been annually produced. An Asam Tea Company has been formed, and the tea sent to market is found to possess the customary qualities of Chinese tea. The Asam Tea Company established a steamer on the Brahmapootra, from Calcutta to Asam; and they imported Coolies from the interior of India at vast expense, as labourers; but it has been found that a more cautious expenditure of capital is necessary to the success of the infant enterprise. The tea-plantations are placed in some jeopardy by the hostility of the native Asamese to these new industrial arrangements. [TEA.]

ASBESTUS must be considered in mineralogy, rather as a term implying a peculiar form sometimes assumed by several minerals, than as a name denoting a particular species; it is in fact applied to varieties of the amphibolic minerals, such as actinolite, tremolite, &c., which occur in long capillary crystals, placed side by side in parallel position, and thus giving rise to a fibrous mass. Those varieties, the fibres of which are very delicate and regularly arranged, are called *amianthus*, a Greek term signifying unpolluted, unstained. Of the finest kinds, the individual crystals are readily separated from each other, are very flexible and elastic, and have a white or greenish colour with a fine silky lustre. Though a single fibre is readily fused into a white enamel, in mass it is capable of resisting the ordinary flame, so that when woven it produces a fire-proof cloth. Those varieties in which the crystals are coarser, with scarcely any flexibility, are called common asbestus. It is generally of a dull green, and sometimes a pearly lustre, and readily fuses before the blow-pipe flame. It occurs more frequently than the amianthus, or finer kind, and is usually found in veins traversing serpentine.

There are three other varieties known by the names of mountain feather, mountain wood, and mountain cork, which differ from the common asbestus by the fibres interlacing each other.

In 1845 Mr. Penny of Glasgow described a peculiar substance which had nearly all the characters of asbestus. It was found in a blast furnace, imbedded in the mass of matter which had collected at the bottom of the furnace in the course of two years and a half, and which is technically called the *hearth*. It was in a cavity, about eight inches below the level on which the liquid metal rested. This substance is colourless, inodorous, and tasteless; and occurs in small masses, composed of extremely minute filaments, cohering longitudinally together; these fibres are very easily detached, and are flexible, though not so much so as those of common asbestus; they have a silky lustre, and are unattacked by the common acids; they remain unchanged in the flame of a spirit lamp, and are difficult of fusion even with the blow pipe. This substance consists chiefly of silica, protoxide of manganese, and alumina; it differs from common asbestus chiefly in having about ten per cent. more of silica, and in containing manganese instead of magnesia. Mr. Penny thinks that the occurrence of this substance in an iron furnace furnishes a proof of the igneous origin of asbestus.

Many remarkable proofs have been given, of the power of asbestus to resist heat. Chevalier Aldini about twenty years ago had some asbestus woven into cloth, and the cloth made into garments; he clothed himself in these garments, and exhibited sundry astonishing feats before the Royal Society, such as holding red-hot iron in a gloved hand, &c. This material has sometimes been proposed for firemen's dresses, and for garments calculated to resist heat generally.

ASH. The ash is one of the most useful of our British trees, on account of the excellence of its hard tough wood and the rapidity of its growth. In its appearance too it is singularly graceful for a European tree, often resembling in its slender stems and thin airy foliage the acacias of tropical regions. The principal objection to the ash is the injury it does to the plants which grow in its neighbourhood, by rapidly exhausting the soil of all its organizable materials.

The principal varieties of the ash are:—1, the *Weeping Ash*, with all the characters of the common wild tree, except that the branches grow downwards instead of upwards, so that, if grafted upon a lofty stem, the head will soon reach the ground and form a natural arbour. This is said to have originated accidentally in a field at Gamlingay, in Cambridgeshire; 2, the *Entire-Leaved Ash*; 3, the *Curled-Leaved Ash*, with very short stunted branches, and deep green crumpled leaves; 4, the *Warted Ash*. In this the stems are covered over with a great number of little grayish brown tubercles. 5. The *Small-Leaved Ash*. 6. The *Flowering* or *Common Manna Ash*, whence the manna of the shops is procured.

Tho uses of the ash in the arts are very numerous. The wood is both elastic and tough. It is used for the telloes and spokes of wheels, the beams of ploughs, the tops of kitchen tables, milk-pails, oars, blocks and pulleys, handles for spades and other implements, hop-poles, hoops, crates, basket handles, fence-wattles, and numerous other purposes. In the neighbourhood of the Staffordshire potteries the ash is cultivated to a great extent, and cut every five or six years for crate-wood, which is in much demand in the pottery district. The ashes yield good potash; the bark is used for tanning nets and calf-skins; the leaves and shoots are used for food by cattle, and the dishonest use ash-leaves for adulterating tea; the seeds or *keys* are sometimes pickled as a sort of salad, and they are used in Siberia to give a flavour to water for drinking. The sap is used for some medicinal purposes. The *Flowering Ash*, as before stated, yields a juice which solidifies into manna.

The Mountain Ash is wrongly named; it belongs to another genus of plants.

ASHANTEES. How far distant the time may be when this West African nation will be commercially important, will depend chiefly on the energy of English merchants, and on the lessening of the slave-trade.

The principal manufacture of the Ashantees is that of cotton cloth, which they weave on a loom worked by strings held between the toes, in webs of never more than four inches broad. Silk is sometimes interwoven with the cotton. The cloths which they produce are often of great fineness of texture, and their colouring of the highest brilliancy. They paint their patterns with a fowl's feather. Another of the arts in which they have attained considerable excellence, is the manufacture of earthenware. They also tan leather, and work in iron, brass, and gold. Articles formed of gold abound in the houses of all the wealthier inhabitants; and in the king's palace those of most common use are described as being made of this precious material.

Gold is found in this country both in mines and in particles washed down by the rains. According to Dupuis, the richest gold mines known to exist in any part of Africa are those in Gaman. Some of the richest of these mines are said to be esteemed sacred, and on that account are not worked. The wealthier inhabitants load their persons with lumps of native gold; some which Dupuis saw, he thinks, must have weighed fully four pounds. In Akim, and some other parts of the empire bordering on the Volta, from which much gold was formerly obtained, the mines are now either exhausted, or at least are no longer worked. There are many rich mines in the small district of Adoom, westward from Cape Coast and about three days' journey from the sea; and during the rainy season it is said that not fewer than eight or ten thousand slaves are employed in washing for gold dust on the banks of the Bara, in Gaman.

ASH-BALLS. As a cheap substitute for soap, in various processes of washing and cleansing, the ashes of various kinds of plants, especially ferns, are damped and made into lumps, which are known by the name of *ash-balls*.

ASHES, the remains of anything burned, whether of vegetable or animal origin, and to a certain extent of mineral bodies also.

Vegetable ashes. Ashes vary in composition according to the nature of the plant, the soil in which it grows, and the manure used upon it. The substances usually contained in the ashes of land plants are potash, soda, lime, magnesia, silica, the oxides of iron and of manganese, chlorine, carbonic acid, sulphuric acid, and phosphoric acid. Alumina occurs rarely, and sometimes oxide of copper has been met with. Very frequently more than one half of the ashes of vegetables consists of carbonate of lime. The quantity of ashes varies, not only according to the soil, age, and aspect of the plant, but also in different parts of the same plant, from 2 to 6 per cent. of its weight, after drying in the air. The soluble part of wood ashes consists of the alkaline sulphates, carbonates, and chlorides; while the insoluble matter is chiefly composed of carbonate of lime, and probably of magnesia, phosphate of lime, and phosphate of iron.

The incineration of wood is a most important operation; from its ashes are obtained the immense quantities of impure potash, and the carbonate called *pearlash*, imported from America and other countries. The sap of plants contains also other vegetable acids, as the oxalic, citric, tartaric, malic, &c.; and the salts which these form with potash are decomposed by heat, and yield the carbonate. The ashes of land plants yield principally the salts of potash, such as *barilla*—those of marine plants afford a large quantity of soda salts, and especially the carbonate, such as *kelp*.

Coal ashes are extremely various both in their appearance and composition. Thus, much of the coal of the north of England, under common circumstances, burns to a cinder, which is a mixture of the ashes of the coal with some carbonaceous matter requiring rather a high temperature to burn it, on account of its being enveloped by incombustible matter. The coal of Somersetshire burns to red ashes, evidently coloured by peroxide of iron: those of the Staffordshire coal are nearly white. The quantity of ashes yielded by different kinds of coal varies considerably; according to Kirwan, Wigan coal contains 1·57 per cent. of ashes; Whitehaven coal 1·7, and Swansea coal 3·33 per cent.; they consist principally of silica and alumina, with small quantities of lime, sometimes magnesia, and also peroxide of iron; but they do not contain either the chlorides, phosphates, or alkaline salts found in wood-ashes. *Peat ashes* differ chemically from both the other kinds.

Animal ashes resulting from the burning of bones and other animal solids, consist principally of phosphate of lime, with traces of salts of lime, magnesia, and soda.

Mineral ashes, such as those of Vesuvius, as examined by Vauquelin, were grayish in colour; they were tasteless, and found to consist of alumina, oxide of iron, muriate of ammonia, sulphate of lime, potash, copper, manganese, lime, and charcoal. Vauquelin also analyzed the ashes ejected in the same year from Ætna; they were of a gray colour, and in fine powder; they contained sulphur, sulphates of lime, copper, and alumina, and several other mineral ingredients.

The *ashes* of domestic economy, comprising not only the coal-ash from the grate, but a quantity of dust and miscellaneous fragments, are a valuable commercial article. The ash-heap of a dust contractor has a large money-value, for much of the waste serves as material for manufactures.

ASHFORD, Kent, is one of those towns which, originally only a centre for an agricultural district, has been converted by railway enterprise into an important scene of manufacturing and trading industry. Ashford has been made a first class station for the South Eastern Railway, and the place of junction with the branch lines to Hastings and Ramsgate. The railway company owing to its convenient position have erected near the station a new village, comprising a factory for the repair of their locomotive engines, and extensive buildings for making and storing their carriages, together with about 200 dwellings (completed and in course of erection) for their workmen.

ASHLAR, or ASHLER, is a term applied in masonry to rough stones as they are taken from the quarry, and also to the dressed stones used for the facing of walls, which may be either plain, tooled, or rusticated. The word is spelt both ways; but Nicholson, in his 'Architectural Dictionary,' gives *ashlaring* as the term for the operation of bedding such slabs of stone as are employed for facing brick or rubble walls; and *ashlering* as a term in carpentry for the short pieces of upright quartering used in garrets to cut off the acute angle between the floor and the sloping rafters of the roof.

ASHOVER, in Derbyshire, has somewhat fallen away from its former rank in respect to manufactures. Formerly there were in the parish considerable lead-mines, but they have long ceased to be worked. Limestone is quarried to some extent. Medicinal herbs are cultivated in considerable quantities. There is a twisting mill for the Nottingham lace manufacture. Stocking-weaving, once an important branch of industry, is on the decline, and tambour working has ceased.

ASHTON-UNDER-LINE is one of the busiest of the Lancashire cotton-towns. It has a population of about 25,000 in the town, and 50,000 in the parish. The following details respecting the Ashton cotton mills are taken from a parliamentary paper; they refer to the year 1843, first in respect to Ashton alone, and then to Ashton together with the surrounding neighbourhood of Staleybridge, Dukinfield, Hyde, and Mossley.

	Ashton alone.	Ashton with Staleybridge, &c.
Mule spindles	595,276	1,866,062
Throstle spindles	9,000	33,136
Power looms	6,738	22,706
Steam engine horse power	1,667	5,353
Hands employed	10,520	34,165
Weekly wages	£5,775	£18,763
Weekly consumption of cotton	338,390lb.	1,063,515lb.

Staleybridge nearly equals Ashton in these particulars. Bleaching, dyeing, and calico printing are also carried on. Hats, woollens, and silks are manufactured. There are more than 20 collieries in the immediate vicinity, which employ upwards of 1000 hands. Ashton is connected with various districts by the Ashton and Manchester, the Ashton and Huddersfield, and the Peak Forest canals; also by the Sheffield and Manchester, the Lancashire and Yorkshire, and other railways.

The manufacturers of Ashton are preparing for the Exhibition of 1851, in those departments of industry for which it has become noted; and the operatives there, as elsewhere, have commenced those joint-stock arrangements which will enable them to visit the metropolis during that busy year.

ASIA. To trace the steps by which commercial enterprise has successively discovered the various parts of the Asiatic continent, would be little less than to trace the history of the human race; for, from the time when the Phœnician merchants spread their trading ports far and wide, to the day when the ports of China were laid open to British shipping and manufactures, there has been a continued series of discoveries, which have had commerce and manufactures among their moving impulses.

Nor would it be easy to enumerate the natural productions which Asia affords to the manufacturer and the merchant. Extending as it does from the burning sands of Arabia to the icy shores of Siberia, from the level plains of Tartary to the lofty heights of the Himalaya, it presents a countless variety of mineral, vegetable, and animal products. The fur-bearing and wool-bearing animals, and those numerous animals which yield flesh for food, milk for drink, and skins for leather, are found in great variety and number. Timber trees, plants used in various arts, and plants used for food, are also bountifully supplied. We need only proceed to any details in noticing the chief *mineral* products.

Among the mineral products of Asia, precious stones are very abundant. Rock-crystal is found in the greatest variety; amethysts in the Altai, Himalaya, and Ural Mountains; carnelians and agates, in western India and in the Gobi desert; casholongs and onyxes, in Mongolia; yu, or oriental jade, in Turkistan; different kinds of jasper, in the Altai mountains; pearl-stone, marcasit, on the shores of the Gulf of Okhotzk; beryl, in the mountains near the Lake of Baikal; lapis lazuli, in the same mountains, as well as in the Hindu Coosh, and on the banks of the Oxus; topazes, in the Ural Mountains; circony, chrysoberyl, sapphires, on the island of Ceylon; rubies, in Ceylon and in Badakshan; turquoises, in Khorasan; diamonds in Deccan, Borneo, and the Ural Mountains.

Volcanic products are met with on the Sunda Islands, in Japan, and Kamtchatka, in the neighbourhood of Tauris, and many parts of the high-land of Armenia, and in Western Anatolia.

Steatite, earth-flax, asbestus, and kaolin, or the finest porcelain-clay, are found in China and Japan; talc in Siberia; coals in northern China, and different parts of Hindustan; rock-salt in the Ural Mountains, northern China, the Panjab, Ajmeer, Yemen, Anatolia; salt in the salt-seas of the steppes, and sometimes on the surface of the ground; sal-ammoniac in the volcanic steppes of Central Asia, not far from the river Ili; nitre in Hindustan; borax, or tinqual, in Tibet; petroleum, near Baku, on the shores of the Caspian Sea, on the Euphrates at Hit, and other places, and at Kerkook east of the Tigris; asphaltum on the Dead Sea, in Palestine. Hot springs are very abundant in the snow-covered mountains of the Himalaya range, especially along the upper branches of the Ganges, and also in the N. W. of Anatolia.

Of the metals, gold is found in Japan, Tibet, Yun-nan, Cochin China, Tonkin, Siam, Malacca, Borneo, Asam, Ava, and in the Ural Mountains; many rivers bring down gold in their sands; silver in China, Da-uria, Japan, Armenia, Anatolia, and the Ural Mountains; tin in Malacca, Anam, the Sunda Islands, and the empire of the Birmans; mercury in China, Japan, and Tibet; copper in the Ural and Altai mountains, Japan, China, Nepaul, Azerbijan, Armenia, and Mount Taurus; malachite in China and Siberia; iron from the Ural Mountains, through central Asia as far as the Peninsula beyond the Ganges, as well as in Japan and Persia; lead in Da-uria, China, Siam, Japan, Georgia, and Armenia.

Under the names of the principal countries in Asia, the reader will meet with some further information on the industrial resources of the East.

ASIA MINOR. This rich, outlying portion of Asia, often designated *Natolia* or *Anatolia* by geographers, contains many mines; but the mining operations are not conducted with much skill. There are copper mines near Bákir-Kurehsí, not far from the Black Sea; near Chalwár, on the eastern side of the Lazian group; near Tireból, on the Black Sea; near Tókat, and many other places. There are iron mines near Unieh, on the Black Sea; silver with copper, in the mines of Tireból; silver and lead at Denek, in the Begrek-Dágh, east of the Kizil-Irmák. Nitre is got at Kará Búnár, in the south-eastern part of the central table-land. Rock salt abounds in all parts, especially in the north-eastern part of Asia Minor and in the tract round Angora. Hot springs occur in all the provinces; those of Brúsá are celebrated, and are even visited by European patients.

The northern shores of Asia Minor are covered with magnificent forest trees of various kinds. The forests, stretching west from Boli, the great and almost inexhaustible source of supply to the Turkish navy, contain ash, elm, plane, poplar, larch, and beech, and some oaks of large size. It is known to the Turks by the significant name of *Agatch Deynis*, or Sea of Trees. The mountains of Karamania are in general well wooded, and Alexandria is mainly supplied with fuel from them. The timber of this coast, at least that near the shore, is chiefly pine, but not in general of large dimensions. The mountains of Taurus contain a great variety of forest trees and shrubs.

No road, in the European acceptation of the term, has ever existed of their own construction in the empire of the Turks. Asia Minor still presents remains of the Roman lines of communication; and of the Roman bridges many yet are in use. Relays of post-horses are still maintained by the Turks at distant intervals. They are principally stationed at the large towns of the leading routes. The most frequented road is that from Smyrna to Constantinople, and the only one by which there is a regular communication, except by caravans. Important as is the trade between these great cities and the rest of Europe, this correspondence takes place but twice a month, and is managed by the Austrian mission and consulate, which, as well as the Russian, despatch, at stated periods, a post to the European capitals. The Porte keeps in constant employment a corps of Tatar couriers, by means of whom they make all their communications. On a smaller scale every pasha has a similar establishment. The route from Smyrna to Constantinople passes by way of Magnesia, Thyatíra, and Moukalitsch. Another route extends from Constantinople to the southern Pashaliks. It goes by way of Mudanieh, Brusa, the Olympus range, Kutaya, Afium-Kara-Hissar, Konieh, Káráman, and Gulnar. A third route advancing in the same direction from the Bosporus, at Eski-shehr pursues an exact eastern course, and reaches Angóra, whence two routes branch off.

ASPA'RAGIN, a peculiar substance obtained from asparagus, and also from marsh-mallow root; it is also contained in the potato, liquorice-root, and beet-root. It crystallizes in transparent limpid colourless prisms. It is inodorous, has a mawkish disagreeable taste, and is rather hard.

ASPA'RAGUS. The common cultivated asparagus is found in sandy and maritime places in most parts of the middle and south of Europe, the Crimea, and also of Siberia and Japan. Attention being paid to the preparation of the soil, asparagus is one of the easiest of all vegetables to cultivate; but no art or skill will produce precisely the soil which is most favourable for its growth. This exists naturally in some places in the fittest of all possible states, and it is there only that it is to be obtained in its greatest perfection; as in the rich alluvial soil of Battersea, Mortlake, and other places round London: in some of these villages it is produced of such extraordinary size that 110 heads in a state fit for the kitchen have been known to weigh more than 32 lbs.

In this country asparagus is frequently forced, but seldom with much success. In many parts of Europe, however, especially about Riga, a mode of forcing is adopted which causes the asparagus to be much finer than any obtained in this country by artificial means.

ASPERGILLUS is the blue mould or fungus which appears on cheese, lard, bread, &c. Its colour is sometimes imitated by fraudulent dealers by sticking brass pins into the cheese—the verdigris formed from the pins giving the desired colour.

ASPHALTE is a name given to various bituminous compounds, which have been much used of late for street-pavements, for the platforms of railway stations, and for flooring, roofing, and protecting buildings in various ways from damp. One of the most important of these is the Seyssel asphalte, introduced into this country by Mr. Claridge, under a patent obtained in 1837.

The principal ingredient of the asphaltic mastic of Seyssel is a dark brown bituminous limestone, found near the Jura Mountains. This stone is broken to powder and mixed with mineral tar, when intended for fine work, such as the covering of roofs and arches, the lining of tanks, and application as cement; or, when intended for the coarser purposes of pavement and flooring, with mineral tar and sea-grit; and the whole is exposed for several hours to a strong heat, in large caldrons, until the ingredients, which are continually stirred by machinery, are perfectly united. The mastic is then run into moulds so as to form it into large cakes or blocks, which are broken up and re-melted on the spot in portable caldrons, with wood or coke fires, with the addition of a little more mineral tar; the whole being well stirred to prevent burning, and to ensure the perfect mixture of the ingredients. When ready for use the mastic emits jets of light smoke, and drops freely from the stirring instrument. It should then be carried very quickly to the spot where it is to be applied, in iron ladles or heated iron buckets. In all cases, however, it is desirable to have the caldron as close to the work as possible; and in covering brick arches or arched roofs, it may be hoisted to the top of the building, proper precautions being observed to shelter the finished work from injury.

Pavements of asphalte are laid upon a firm and dry foundation of concrete; and in laying the asphalte the surface is divided by slips of wood, which serve as gauges to regulate the thickness, into compartments of about thirty inches wide, in which the hot cement is spread and levelled with wooden instruments; after which, while the surface is yet soft, sand mixed with slate-dust, dead plaster of Paris, or powdered chalk, or, for coarser work, clean sharp grit is sifted over it, and rubbed or beaten in. The thickness of asphalte used for pavements varies from half an inch to about an inch and a quarter; from half an inch to five-eighths is sufficient for roofs and the covering of arches to prevent the filtration of water, and for the lining of tanks and ponds; and about half that thickness is sufficient for covering the ground-line of brickwork, to prevent the rising of damp.

The experience of the last few years has shown that asphalte is neither a pleasant nor a profitable material for the pavements of the London streets.

ASPHALTUM is one of the varieties of bitumen, arising from the decomposition of vegetable matter. [BITUMEN.] It occurs massive, of a dark brown or black colour, with a conchoidal fracture, and a resinous lustre. It is opaque, and exceedingly brittle at a low temperature, but softens and fuses by the application of heat. It is insoluble in alcohol, but soluble in about five times its weight of naptha, with which it forms a good and useful varnish. Its combustion is rapid and brilliant, with the production of the bituminous odour.

It is found in many countries, but most abundantly on the shores, or floating on the surface of the Dead Sea; at Hit, above Babylon, on the Euphrates; and near the Tigris. In Trinidad in the West Indies it fills a basin of three miles in circumference and of unknown depth. The Earl of Dundonald has recently (1849) made some experiments on the availability of the Barbadoes asphaltum for fuel; he mixed it with coal (two parts of asphaltum to one of coals) and found that it made a good fuel for steamers; he also devised a form of furnace for burning it. There is a pitch-spring in Zante, which is known to have been at work for above 2000 years. Asphaltum is the principal colouring matter of the dark indurated marl, or shale, which is found in coal districts.

A liquid asphaltum, useful as a black japan or varnish, is made by melting asphaltum with Scio turpentine and oil of turpentine; or substituting balsam of copaiba for the Scio turpentine.

Counterfeit asphaltum is occasionally substituted for the real; it consists of the dregs of Barbadoes tar, heated until quite hard.

ASS. This ill-used and ill-appreciated animal (in England, at least) takes an important part in oriental travelling and commerce. The fine Arabian asses are used only for the saddle, and are imported in great numbers into Persia, where, according to Chardin, they are frequently sold for 400 livres; they are taught a kind of easy ambling pace, are richly caparisoned, and used only by the rich and luxurious nobles. A fine breed, of Arab lineage, used exclusively for the saddle, exists in Syria;—a small spirited and graceful kind is also found in Syria, upon which the ladies ride from preference; and besides this there is a stout breed fitted for ordinary labour. Another breed, that of Damascus, is characterized by the length of its body and of its ears; it is much employed by the bakers of Damascus in carrying flour and brushwood. The ordinary asses of Persia are strong, but in other respects not to be compared to those of Arabia. As we proceed farther eastward the ass degenerates, and in India it is very small, of inferior qualities, and used only by the people of the lowest caste. The finest asses of Europe are those of Malta and Spain. Italy also possesses a superior breed; and the same remark applies to some parts of France, as Le Poitou and Le Mirebalais.

It is a curious example of the extent to which nature is imitated by man, either for honest or dishonest purposes, that artificial *asses' milk* is manufactured. One recipe comprises new cow's milk, sugar-candy, ground rice, and eringo root; while another comprises water, hartshorn shavings, lump sugar, new mi k, and syrup of tolu.

ASSAFŒTIDA is a gum-resin, obtained from the roots of the *Ferula assafœtida*, a perennial plant growing in Persia, in the province of Lar, and in Khorassan. In its recent and purest state it is white and transparent, but by exposure to the air it becomes of a clear brown colour, sometimes verging to red or violet, and of a waxy appearance. The inferior sort is dark-brown, of a dull fatty appearance, viscid, and greasy; it is called assafœtida in masses. The smell of assafœtida is penetrating, very disagreeable, and lasts some time. The taste is bitter, unpleasantly aromatic, of an alliaceous or garlic-like character.

Assafœtida acts on the human system as a stimulant, and is employed in various ways in medicine.

ASSAYING. The difference between assaying and chemical analysis may be thus stated; that when an analysis is performed, the nature and proportions of all the ingredients of a substance are determined; but in assaying, the quantity of any particular metal only which the ore or mixture under examination may contain is ascertained, without rereference to the substances with which it is mixed or alloyed. Assaying is sometimes conducted in what is called the *dry way*, or by heat; at other times in the *moist way*, or by acids and other re-agents; and in some cases both methods are necessarily resorted to in assaying the same ore or mixture of metals.

The assaying of silver and gold is effected by a process called *cupellation*. Cupels are small flat crucibles made by pressing bone ash, moistened with water, into circular steel moulds, and they are dried by exposure to the air. The principle upon which the operation depends is, that all metals with which gold and silver are usually alloyed, are convertible into oxides by exposure to atmospheric air at a high temperature, whereas the precious metals remain unacted upon.

To assay *silver* by cupellation, the silver is flattened, and wrapped up in an envelope of lead. A muffle or oven is heated in an assay furnace, and the two metals put into it. The metals melt, and the lead becomes converted into an oxide, which, as well as any baser metals before combined with the silver, is absorbed by the substance of the cupel, until at length the silver is left absolutely pure.

The assaying of *gold* is performed, to a certain extent, exactly in the same way as that of silver; and if the gold were alloyed only with copper, the process would be as simple as that of silver assaying. Usually, however, gold contains silver, and this cannot be got rid of by cupellation, the *parting* process is therefore had recourse to; this consists in dissolving the silver by dilute nitric acid, which leaves the gold perfectly pure.

Iron ores are assayed by separating the oxygen from the iron, by the greater affinity of charcoal for that element at high temperatures. The ore, some charcoal, and an alkaline flux, are heated in a crucible; and the result is that all the impurities in the ore are made to leave the iron, so that the latter is presented in a purely metallic form.

Copper ores for the most part contain sulphur; and in order to assay them, a flux is prepared of fluor spar, borax, slaked lime, argol, and nitre. The ore is pounded, calcined in a crucible at a red heat; then cooled; then heated again with some of the flux until it is brought to a liquid state. The liquid metal is poured into a mould, and quenched when solid but yet hot. There is then found a portion of metal underneath a layer of coarse slag. The metal is separated from the slag, reduced to powder, and again heated until the sulphur is driven off from it.

Lead.—The principal ore of lead is the sulphuret, commonly called galena; but the carbonate, or white lead ore, is sometimes found in considerable quantity. The former of these is assayed by being put into a crucible with iron and flux, all in small grains; and after being covered with a layer of salt, they are heated until the lead becomes separated from all impurities. The second kind of ore is assayed in the same way, but with a different flux.

Tin.—The ores of tin are principally of two kinds, the oxide and the sulphuret. The oxide is assayed by simple fusion with a flux, which removes the oxygen. The sulphuret is assayed by being first pounded and calcined, to drive off any sulphur or arsenic; and then melted again with a flux of alkalies, fluor spar, and lime, by which the tin becomes separated from all the other impurities.

Zinc.—The ores of zinc are of two kinds, the carbonate, or calamine, and tho sulphuret or blende. The carbonate is assayed by being broken into small pieces, brought to a red heat, cooled, reduced to a fine powder, mixed with powdered charcoal, and melted in a crucible, under such conditions that the zinc may leave the ore, and combine with a thin layer of granulated copper so as to produce *brass;* and the quantity of the brass so produced tests the richness of the ore in zinc. The sulphuret, or blende, is assayed nearly in the same way.

ASSIGNAT. The commercial history of an assignat bears some such relation to that of a bank note, as a swindler does to an honest trader. During the early stages of the French Revolution, the government siezed the clergy lands, and made them over to the municipalities; the municipalities gave security for the value, which securities the government ordered should be a legal tender. Paper money was issued to represent these securities; and the paper notes were called *assignats*, or tokens that church-land had been *assigned* to the holder. The government once having began this system, were induced to proceed; and issued more and more assignats, though there was nothing to be represented by them. By the end of 1792 the assignats had been issued to the extent of nearly 3000 million francs; and as they were not convertible into cash, one silver franc became after a time worth two paper or assignat-francs, then three, then six. During a flash of national glory, in 1793, the assignats rose for a brief period to par, but speedily fell again. By 1794 the number had increased to 6,500 millions, and in the next year it increased to 19,000 millions, the market value being less than one-hundredth of the nominal value. In 1796 the sum reached 36,000 million francs; but the scraps of paper were almost entirely worthless; and as the government officials at length refused them in payment of salaries, the whole thing fell to the ground.

The misery which this nefarious system inflicted is incalculable. There are at the present time, in France and Belgium, rooms which have been completely papered with assignats —for all of which money or money's value had been given, but which became utterly worthless.

ASSIZE. In early times there were assizes or ordinances regulating the price of bread, ale, fuel, and other common necessaries of life, called in Latin *assisæ venalium*. The earliest express notice of any regulation of this kind in England is in the reign of King John (1203), when a proclamation was made throughout the kingdom enforcing the observance of the legal assize of bread: many statutes were passed regulating the assize of articles of common consumption; the earliest of these is the assize of bread and ale, 'assisa panis et cervisiæ,' commonly called the stat. of 51 Henry III., though its precise date is doubtful. The stat. 8 Anne, c. 19, repealed the 51 Henry III., and imposed a new assize of bread, and made various other regulations respecting it. Several subsequent acts have been passed on the subject; but by the 55 George III., c. 99, the practice was expressly abolished in London and its neighbourhood, and in other places it has fallen into disuse. Trade is now allowed to settle its own prices.

ASSURANCE. [INSURANCE.]

ASSY'RIA. We refer to BABYLON and NINEVEH for a few notices of the extraordinary works of art found in Assyria and Mesopotamia.

A'STACUS. [LOBSTER.]

ASTI. This province of Piedmont is well adapted for the cultivation of the vine. A sparkling fine-flavoured white wine, called *vino d'Asti*, resembling champagne, is made in the neighbourhood of Villanuova. The soil is also fertile in corn and fruit-trees, especially mulberries, the leaves of which serve to feed the silkworms. The chief town, also called Asti, has some trade in silk and woollen fabrics, wines, and other agricultural produce.

ASTRAGAL, a moulding used in architecture, and applied principally to the upper ends of the shafts of columns and to their bases. It is also used in the entablatures of the Roman Doric, the Ionic, Corinthian, and Composite orders. The form of this moulding is semicircular, projecting from a vertical diameter. In Egyptian architecture, bands curved after the manner of astragals seem to bind the reeds of which the shaft of the column often appears to be formed. The most remarkable example of the use of the astragal in Grecian architecture is in the base employed in the Ionic temple of Minerva Polias at Priene.

ASTRA'GALUS. [TRAGACANTH GUM.]

ASTRAKHAN. This Russian province depends a good deal for its commercial prosperity on its fisheries. The Volga is scarcely equalled by any other stream in the world for abundance of fish. This noble river flows through the province. In the spring of the year its fishing-grounds, particularly between the sea and the capital, are so abundantly stocked with fish, as to employ upwards of five thousand vessels, and twice that number of persons, who are brought by the fisheries from remote places. Isinglass and caviar are brought from this region.

Goats are reared, not so much for the sake of their milk or flesh, as of their hides, with which the Russians prepare morocco-leather: there is a fine species of hair too, which either falls from the animal's back, or is combed from it, out of which a stuff of beautiful texture is occasionally woven. But the greatest resource possessed by the rural population and nomadic tribes of the province is their flocks of sheep, which are valuable both for their wool and for their fat.

To the principal branches of industry already enumerated we may add the manufacturing of magnesia, tallow, and soap, in considerable quantities, distilleries of brandy and spirits, and manufactories of leather, cotton, and silk. Astrakhan soap is in much request among the Russians on account of its firm substance and fragrant scent. The Volga, which secures a ready access to the eastern shores of the Caspian Sea, has hitherto rendered the capital of this province the principal seat of the traffic carried on between Asia and the Russian dominions.

The chief city, also called Astrakhan, has a navigable communication with St. Petersburg, from which it is upwards of 1200 miles distant. The establishments for weaving silks and cottons are nearly one hundred in number; it manufactures also considerable quantities of leather, particularly a superior description of morocco and shagreen, as well as tallow and soap. The business of buying and selling, more than one-half of which has been engrossed by the Armenians, is conducted in twenty-eight khans or bazaars, which contain 1500 stores built of stone, and 560 wooden stalls. Raw silk and silk goods, cotton and cotton-yarn, drugs, dye-stuffs, carpets, oil, rice, and other eastern productions form the chief importations: the exportations are principally woollen cloth, linens, cochineal, velvet, iron, salt, fruits, fish, wine, liquorice, soda, hides, skins, and grain.

The fisheries of the Volga centre principally a little below the city. Every weir has its group of huts, with a little church attached to it, in which from two to three score fishermen reside; they are divided into divers, catchers, salting-men, and makers of caviar and isinglass. Each little colony is provided with spacious ice-cellars, which contain compartments for storing away the fish when salted, with intervals between the compartments which are filled with ice.

ASTRINGENTS are agents which contract the fibres of the muscles and blood-vessels, and lessen the flow of fluids. Without dwelling on their medical uses, we may briefly enumerate the chief substances so employed.

Of vegetable astringents the chief are *barks*, as of oak and willow, such as that of the *quercus robur*. The best willow bark is procured from the *salix pentandra*, or sweet bay-leaved willow, though very excellent bark is yielded by the *salix Russeliana*, or Bedford willow. Roots, as of tormentil (*potentilla tormentilla*); bistort (*polygonum bistorta*); common avens (*geum urbanum*), which are British plants; and rhatany (*krameria triandra*); rhubarb (*rheum palmatum*); pomegranate (*punica granatum*), which are exotic plants; leaves of arctostaphylos (*uva ursi*), petals of the *rosa gallica*, fruits of *prunus spinosa*, or sloe-thorn (*punica granatum*), and secreted juices of many plants, as kino, from *pterocarpus Senegalensis*, and several others; and catechu, from *acacia catechu*, and galls, from *quercus infectoria;* in all of which the astringent principle is tannin, with more or less of gallic-acid; and lastly log-wood, (*hæmatoxylon Campechianum*), in which hæmatine as well as tannin possesses an astringent property. Acetic acid must also be classed among the vegetable astringents.

The mineral astringents are—diluted sulphuric acid, and salts of iron, zinc, copper, silver, and the salts of lead. Cold, in whatever way applied, is also a valuable astringent.

ASTROCA'RYUM, is the botanical name for a genus of palms. One species, the *A. murimuri*, yields a delicious fruit. Another species, *A. airi*, has very hard wood, which is much used in tropical America for bows, and similar purposes, where hardness and toughness are required. The fibres of the leaves of *A. tucuma* are much valued for fishing-nets.

ASTROLABE, among the Greeks, was a circular instrument used for observations of the stars; but in the sixteenth and seventeenth centuries it signified a projection of the sphere upon a plane, being used in the same sense as the word *Planisphere.* To this small projection, which had a graduated rim, sights were added, for the purpose of taking altitudes; and in this state it was the constant companion and badge of office of the astrologer. In later times, before the invention of Hadley's quadrant, a graduated circular rim, with sights attached, called an astrolabe, was used for taking altitudes at sea.

Improved astronomical instruments have thrown the astrolabe quite out of use.

ASTRONOMICAL INSTRUMENTS. Without entering into the scientific details of astronomy, the mechanical construction of the principal instruments employed will be found under the names of the instruments themselves.

"We are rivals with Britain," says M. Dupin, speaking of his countrymen, "in mathematical instruments, and in those of philosophy, optics, and astronomy." Let us hope that the scientific instrument makers of both countries will be worthily represented in 1851.

ASTURIAS. This portion of Spain does not hold a high rank in relation to manufactures and their materials. There are found, however, marble, stone used for grind-stones, copper, mineral amber, cinnabar, iron, zinc, lead, antimony, jet, coals and turf. The mountainous parts of the province are covered with forests of oak, beech, chestnut, and other trees.

The only manufactories of Asturias are—a royal manufactory of fire-arms at Trubia, a few others belonging to private individuals for the fabrication of copper, earthenware, and jet trinkets, some tanneries, and looms for common woollen and linen stuffs, principally for home consumption. A considerable quantity of pickled fish is sent from Asturias to Madrid.

ASTY'LAR, in architecture, signifies without columns. Thus, we speak of Astylar Italian in contradistinction from the columnar class of buildings in that style, or such as are decorated with the orders. In this country we had no examples of the *astylar* class of design, until it was introduced by Mr. Barry, in the Travellers' Clubhouse and Reform Clubhouse, London.

ASY'LUM, in its original meaning, was a place of refuge. In the present day it has the same signification as a hospital or almshouse; and some of the handsomest modern structures in this country are thus called asylums, such as the Lunatic Asylum at Hanwell, and the still larger structure at Colney Hatch.

ATACA'MA, is the slip of Bolivia which lies between the Andes and the Pacific. The surrounding mountains contain mines of gold and silver, but they are not worked, and are inhabited by numerous herds of vicuñas, which the Indians hunt, selling their skins and eating their flesh, which is tender and of excellent taste. It has been proposed to bore Artesian wells at Puerto de la Mar (the only port in Bolivia), in order to remedy the want of fresh water, which is a serious bar to the prosperity, and even to the existence of the town. The interior districts contain veins of crystal of various colours, of jasper, talc, copper, blue vitriol, and alum.

ATCHEEN, or ACHEEN, one of the many petty kingdoms in the large island of Sumatra, carries on a considerable trade with Coromandel, to which it furnishes gold-dust, raw-silk, betel-nut, pepper, sulphur, camphor, and benzoin; receiving in return cotton goods and salt. A considerable trade is also carried on between Atcheen and Singapore. Coarse manufactures of cotton, woollen, and silk are carried on by the inhabitants.

ATH, or AATH, is a flourishing manufacturing town in the Belgian province of Hainault. The manufactures are caps, hats, gloves, cotton and linen cloth, bleaching, and asbestus cloth. It carries on also some trade in grain, and in the products of the neighbouring country, among which are tobacco, poppies, and rape. The mulberry is extensively cultivated in the neighbourhood for the growth of silk.

ATHENS. As long as the memory of ancient art remains, the name of Athens will be respected as the greatest of its supporters. No other city has ever contained so many buildings and sculptures of high artistic excellence. On the hill called the Acropolis is the world renowned *Temple of the Parthenon* [PARTHENON]. Near the hill called the Areopagus is the *Temple of Theseus* [THESEIUM]. Eastward of the Theseium are the remains of the *Stoa* or *Portico of Hadrian*. South of the Stoa is the *Tower of the Winds*. In the south-east quarter of the city is the *Arch of Hadrian*; and within this are all that now remain of the magnificent temple of *Jupiter Olympus*. Not far from this temple is the beautiful *Choragic Monument of Lysicrates*, which has served as the model for the steeple of one of our London churches. The great *Dionysiac Theatre* was on the south-east side of the Acropolis; while on the south west of the Acropolis was the *Odeium* or *Musical Theatre*,—and on the west was the *Propylæa* or military approach. On or near the Acropolis, too, were the large structure or structures, the remains of which are now known as the Erechtheium.

The ELGIN and PHIGALEIAN Saloons at the British Museum are richly adorned with priceless works of sculpture brought from Athens. These are briefly noticed in other parts of this volume.

ATHERSTONE, in Warwickshire, contributes its mite towards the industry of the country. The chief manufacture is that of hats. Ribands and shalloons are also made. The Coventry Canal, which passes close by the town on the west, contributes to its trade. Among the anomalous rocks by which the coal-field is bounded on the south-east, is a peculiar quartzose sandstone, of extraordinary hardness, which is extensively quarried, and sent to a great distance for the purpose of road-making. Nearly adjacent to this is a rich bed of manganese, which at Hartshill has yielded a very profitable return, but which is now nearly exhausted. Coal is found at Baddesley Moor, in the vicinity of Atherstone.

ATHLONE, which is connected with Dublin by the newly opened Midland Great Western Railway of Ireland, had formerly a considerable trade in the manufacture of coarse hats, but it has declined. There are extensive distilleries, breweries, and tanneries here, and a brisk trade is carried on by means of the Shannon navigation and Grand and Royal Canals with Limerick and Dublin.

ATLANTES, is a term applied to figures or half figures of men used in the place of columns or pilasters, to sustain an entablature. In the temple of Jupiter Olympus, at

Agrigentum, restored by Mr. Cockerell, and described in Stuart's 'Athens,' vol. 4, Atlantes are represented standing upon a plinth placed on the entablature above the pilasters of the cella of the temple, and supporting with their heads and arms the entablature on which the beams of the roof were to have been placed. The Atlantes of this temple were twenty-five feet high, built in courses of stone, corresponding with the walls of the cella, and partly attached to it.

ATLANTIC OCEAN, as the watery expanse which separates Europe from America, is one of the most notable of commercial highways.

No first-class river flows into the Atlantic from Europe or Africa, the Rhine, the Danube, the Dnieper, and the Nile being of the second class. Of Africa, about one-half the surface is supposed to be drained by rivers which, directly or indirectly, flow into the Atlantic. But, on the American side, the Atlantic rivers are on the grandest scale; including the Amazon, the Plata, the Orinoco, the Mississippi, the St. Lawrence, and their numerous tributaries. It is calculated that the areas of country drained by rivers which flow into the Atlantic and its seas are six millions in America, six millions in Africa, three millions in Europe, and half a million in Asia.

The Gulf Stream greatly affects the navigation of the Atlantic Ocean. Vessels bound from Europe to North America avoid it as much as possible, because it would create a delay of at least a fortnight if they were to stem it. They therefore either sail to the south or to the north of it, commonly the latter, their course being accelerated as soon as they approach the continent of North America by the counter-currents which run between the Gulf Stream and the coast. The Gulf Stream is now avoided even by vessels returning from the West Indies and the Gulf of Mexico, though by following its course they arrive four or five days sooner in Europe than those which avoid it. But it has been found by experience that such vessels suffer a damage in wear and tear which is greater than can be compensated by the gain of a few days.

It is a known fact that the water of the Atlantic Ocean, in different parts, contains different quantities of salt; and that the specific gravity is less near the poles than near the equator. There is a considerable difference between the specific gravity of the water of the Baltic and Mediterranean seas and the ocean. That of the Baltic contains only one-sixth of the salt which is found dissolved in the ocean, its specific gravity being on an average not more than 1·0040. The Mediterranean Sea contains somewhat more salt than the ocean; to the east of the Straits of Gibraltar, the specific gravity of the sea-water is 1·0338; whilst between Cape St. Vincent and Cape Cantin, it was only found to be 1·0294.

The Atlantic is always busily laden with the produce which is passing from the old continent to the new, and *vice versa*. Magnificent steam ships traverse it from Glasgow, from Liverpool, from Southampton, from Bremen, from Havre, to Halifax, Boston, New York, the West Indies, and South America; while sailing ships traverse its whole length on their route to the Pacific, to the great but almost unknown Southern Ocean, to the Cape of Good Hope, to India and China, and to our Australian Colonies. In a very few weeks after this page reaches the hands of the reader, ships laden with foreign treasures—treasures of productive industry—will be ascending and crossing the Atlantic, on their way to the great Gathering of Nations in 1851.

ATLAS is the historical and geographical name of an extensive mountain-system in North Africa, which, though not inhabited by a manufacturing race, produces many substances useful in the Arts. On the low plains at the southern foot of the mountains, and within its lower ranges, the date palms cover extensive tracts; the higher lands abound in gum trees, almonds, olives, and other productions of the hotter countries; the lower table-lands produce apples, pears, cherries, walnuts, apricots, and other fruits, common to the southern countries of Europe; and, proceeding higher up the ranges, the plains are covered with pines of an immense size, with a species of oak, called the *belute*, with ferns, elms, mountain-ash, and several species of juniper. Higher up, large forests of firs form the principal vegetation.

Rich mines of different kinds exist in that lateral range which separates the province of Suse from the countries on the river Draha; it abounds especially in iron, copper, and lead. Ketewa, a district east of Tarudant, contains rich mines of lead and brimstone; and saltpetre of a superior quality abounds in the neighbourhood of Tarudant itself. Other mines of iron, copper, antimony, lead, and a little silver and gold, are met with in various parts. Salt and sulphur are also found.

ATMOMETER, an instrument employed to measure the quantity of exhalation from a humid surface in a given time. The instrument to which the name is usually applied is one invented by Professor Leslie, consisting of a very thin ball of porous earthenware, two or three inches in diameter, to which is cemented a long tube of glass, marked by a diamond with divisions, each of which is capable of containing as much liquid as would, if spread over the outer surface of the ball, cover it with a film equal in thickness to the $\frac{1}{1000}$th part of an inch. The open end of the tube is fitted with a brass cap and a leather collar; and when in use the instrument is filled with distilled or boiled water, and suspended vertically with the ball downwards, the end of the tube being perfectly closed with the cap and collar. The water then percolates through the porous ball precisely in proportion to the evaporation from its outer surface, of which its waste in the tube forms an accurate indication. The vacuous space above the water in the tube becomes, during the operation, gradually filled with air which enters through the porous ball. When the tube becomes empty, the cap is removed to refill it. This instrument is not only useful in meteorological observations, but is also capable of being applied with advantage in chemical operations, and in the application of science to agriculture.

ATMOPYRE is the name given to an ingenious contrivance, very recently introduced by Mr. D. O. Edwards. *Smoke* is only one of the evils occasioned by imperfect combustion; and Mr. Edwards's invention is intended to lessen these evils. A small cylinder or tube of pipe-clay, from two to four inches long, is perforated with holes only one-fiftieth of an inch in diameter. One end of the tube is fixed upon a gas-burner; and when the gas is turned on, it becomes mixed with atmospheric air in the cylinder. The little jets which penetrate through the minute holes are ignited, the clay cylinder becomes red-hot, and has the appearance of a solid red flame. By placing these clay cylinders within others of larger size, an intense heat may be produced; and this heat (it is proposed) may be applied to many manufacturing purposes. The gas is thoroughly consumed on account of the minuteness of the threads into which it is divided; while the perforations, acting on the principle of those in the safety-lamp, prevent the flame from reaching the interior of the cylinder.

Common gas is estimated by the inventor to yield double as much heat by this method as in the ordinary mode of combustion; and this heat, by a due multiplication and combination of clay-cylinders, is proposed to be used in raising steam for warm-baths and other minor purposes, and for heating rooms. If the principle be sound, the practical applications will speedily develope themselves.

ATMOSPHERE, is the whole body of air or other mixture of gases which envelopes a planet. As we do not here treat of the atmosphere in its scientific relations, it will suffice to refer to AIR, ANEMOMETER, BALLOON, &c., where the practical results of the existence of an atmosphere are brought into prominent view.

ATOMIC THEORY, in chemistry, sometimes termed the *doctrine of definite proportions*. This very important theory, founded on well ascertained facts, has bestowed on modern chemistry an almost mathematical degree of precision. The theory, which is to be distinguished from the experimental part of the subject, supposes that chemical compounds result from the combination of the ultimate atoms of their constituent parts. It has been determined by experiment, and the fact serves as the basis of the theory, that a compound body, when pure, always contains the same proportion of its constituents: thus calcareous spar, and the pure part of marble, chalk, and limestone, consist of carbonate of lime, composed of uniform proportions of carbonic acid and lime; the carbonic acid always contains uniform quantities of carbon and oxygen, and the lime uniform proportions of calcium and oxygen. The same law also exists with regard to all similarly-constituted oxides, sulphurets, and salts, and indeed to all chemical compounds whatever, whether presented to us by nature or formed by art.

Wenzel, Bryan Higgins, Richter, Proust, and other chemists, made many discoveries which tended towards a law of definite proportions in chemistry; but Dalton reduced it to a system by his *atomic theory*, promulgated in 1803. According to his view, the *atomic number*, or *atomic weight*, or *atomic equivalent*, of any substance, represents the relative quantity or weight of each which will combine with other substances; and the labours of later chemists have been directed to the exact determination of these numbers. Dalton thought that if hydrogen were reckoned 1, all other substances might be represented by integers, and this is still frequently done; but these integers are not strictly accurate.

The following diagram will illustrate the mode in which the atomic numbers or combining weights retain their character throughout all the compositions or decompositions which may take place. An atom of nitric acid (hydrogen being taken as 1, and oxygen as 8) weighs 54; and one of barytes 76; forming when combined 130 of neutral nitrate of barytes. An atom of neutral sulphate of potash = 88, is composed of an atom of sulphuric acid = 40, and an atom of potash = 48. Now when an atom of nitrate of barytes = 130, dissolved in water, is mixed with an atom of sulphate of potash = 88, in solution, double decomposition ensues, and two new and perfectly neutral salts are formed, viz. 1 atom of nitrate of potash = 102, consisting of an atom of nitric acid = 54, and an atom of potash = 48. This remains in solution; and there is precipitated an atom of neutral sulphate of barytes = 116, composed of 1 atom of sulphuric acid = 40, and 1 atom of barytes = 76.

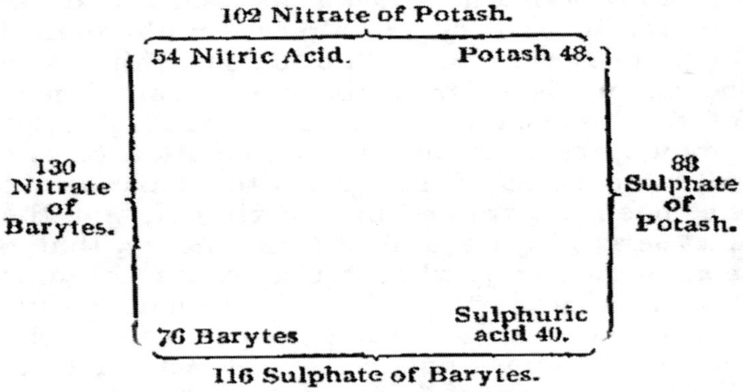

Tables of these combining numbers are now published for the use of chemists.

In 1809 Gay-Lussac published an important memoir on the 'Theory of Volumes,' in which the definite composition of compound gases was placed in a new and instructive light. Suspecting, from the previously ascertained fact that 100 volumes of oxygen gas combine with 200 volumes of hydrogen gas to form water, that other gaseous bodies would be found to unite in simple proportions, he made further experiments, and found that gaseous substances unite in the simple ratio of 1 to 1, 1 to 2, 1 to 3, &c. Thus, for example,—

	By Volume.		By Weight.	
	Nitrog.	Oxygen.	Nitrog.	Oxygen.
Nitrous oxide .	2	1	14	8
Nitric oxide . .	2	2	14	16
Hyponitrous acid	2	3	14	24
Nitrous acid .	2	4	14	32
Nitric acid . .	2	5	14	40

The same rule was found also to apply to the combination of vapours with gases, thus,—

Volumes.		Volumes.	
100 hydrogen gas	with	100	vapour of sulphur.
100 oxygen gas	with	100	„
100 hydrogen gas	with	100	vapour of iodine.

As Chemistry is treated in this work only in respect to some of its practical applications, this brief notice of the atomic theory will suffice.

A'TRIUM, a hall or room of audience in a Roman house. The Cavum Ædium was probably the hollow space in the middle of a Roman house, open to the sky and rain; while the Atrium was the covered part, the hall or room of audience. The Atrium was the most important and usually the most splendid apartment. Here the owner received his crowd of morning visitors, who were not admitted to the inner apartments. Originally the Atrium was the common room of resort for the whole family—the place of their domestic occupations; and such it probably continued in the humbler ranks of life. It consisted of a large apartment roofed over, but with an opening in the centre, called *compluvium*, towards which the roof sloped so as to throw the rain-water into a cistern in the floor called *impluvium*.

In building a marine villa, a Roman Atrium might be introduced with utility and effect; and we can conceive nothing more delightful than the enjoyment of the warm sea-breeze of summer in the cool shade of an Atrium, with a portico open to the sea. In such a design, the Atrium, with its portico, should form the centre feature, and the apartments and offices of the occupants should be arranged round the back and two sides; the Atrium, with the portico, being placed towards the sea, would give a full view of it.

A'TROPA, is the botanical name for the genus of plants which includes *belladonna*, or *deadly nightshade*, and *mandrake;* both of which are very poisonous, except when carefully prepared as medicines.

ATRO'PIA, a vegetable alkali which is found to exist in the juice of the *atropa belladonna*, and in which the poisonous qualities of the plant reside. Atropia forms long transparent colourless crystals which are insoluble in cold water, and very slightly soluble by boiling water and alcohol. It forms with acids peculiar salts, which readily crystallize. During the evaporation of a salt of atropia, the vapour which rises occasions an enlargement of the pupil of the eyes of those exposed to its influence, which continues for several hours.

ATTALE'A is the botanical name for a genus of plants, which includes many species highly valuable to the natives of South America. One species, called by the natives *piaçaba* is found in the native forests of the maritime provinces of Brazil, where it is one of the most valuable gifts which the bountiful hand of nature has conferred on man. The best cordage in America, for naval purposes, is manufactured from the fibres of the leaf-stalks and other parts: such ropes are of great strength, and are extremely durable in salt water. No other cables are employed in a great part of the Brazilian navy. Another species, the *pindora* of the old writers on Brazil, and the *indajà* of the modern Portuguese, forms delightful groves in the interior of the country, growing from twenty to fifty feet clear of its branch-like leaves. The latter are from fifteen to twenty feet long, and about three feet wide. The fruit is the size of a goose's egg, and contains an eatable kernel, of which the negroes are fond. Its leaves form an excellent thatch, and are woven into hats, mats, and baskets. Another species furnishes the nuts which the Brazilians burn for the purpose of smoking the juice of *Siphonia elastica*, or Indian rubber, until it becomes black.

ATTAR (or OTTO) OF ROSES, is an essential oil obtained in India from the petals of the *Rosa centifolia* and *R. sempervivens*, by evaporation from the steeped petals, the attar rising to the top of the water as a kind of yellowish scum. It is a very powerful perfume, and is said by Saussure to be a mixture of two oils, one solid and the other fluid at the common temperature of the air.

Attar of Roses liquefies at about 85° of Fahrenheit, and the solid oil at about 91°; the latter crystallizes by cold into brilliant white transparent laminæ of the consistence of bees' wax.

The Attar is produced in two ways. In one method the rose-leaves are carefully distilled, to produce rose-water of a certain degree of strength; this is poured on a fresh heap of rose-leaves, and distilled to produce stronger rose-water; and this latter (a highly fragrant liquid) is poured into shallow vessels, and left exposed to the fresh air during one night; in the morning the attar or essential oil is found to have collected in a thin film on the top. In the other method, rose-leaves steeped in water are exposed in open vessels to the action of the sun for several days, by which time the attar has collected on the surface of the water.

So intense is the odour of attar of roses, that a morsel on the point of a needle will scent a room during a whole day. One hundred pounds weight of rose-leaves are required to produce only three drachms of attar, even under favourable circumstances; and this will suffice to explain the enormous price of this perfume, when pure.

ATTIC, as a term in building, is applied to the upper room or rooms of a house, with or without a parapet-wall in front. But in architecture the attic comprehends the whole of a plain or decorated parapet wall, which terminates the upper part of the façade of an edifice. There is at Athens a monument, that of Thrasyllus, with an attic over the order of pilasters which form the basement; in the centre was a colossal statue. This example may be taken as the best type of a Greek attic which is at present known. Another example, which bears a closer resemblance to the Roman attic, exists in the upper wall of the nave of the Temple of Jupiter Olympus at Agrigentum, where there is an entire wall with short pilasters at intervals, in the front of which are figures placed above the pilasters of the nave. The attic is a conspicuous feature in the triumphal arches at Rome, and a necessary one: it was not merely intended as a frame-work for the inscription, nor as a support for statues, but is essential to the proportions of the composition.

In all the best examples, and especially in the remains of antiquity at Rome, the attic is decorated with a moulded base and cornice, often with pilasters and figures, as in the arch of Constantine.

The Italian architects who had studied the remains of antiquity in Rome, and those who followed in their school, usually employed an attic in their designs. The attic is in such common use, that there are few public buildings in London without it. Somerset House, in the view towards the street, may be taken as offering a very fine example of this feature of an edifice.

ATTRACTION, in its scientific meaning, denotes that quality by which the bodies of the universe, or the molecules of the same body or of different bodies, approach one another when not prevented from doing so. The tendency by which bodies when unsupported approach the earth is called *Gravitation*; that by which the minute particles of bodies are held together is called *Cohesion*; that by which particles combine together chemically is called *Affinity*; while those actions which exist between the particles of the electrical and magnetic fluids, or between these and the particles of bodies, are called *Electrical* or *Magnetic attractions*.

So far as they have any place in this work, these forms of attraction are briefly noticed under the headings just indicated.

ATTWOOD'S MACHINE. This apparatus was invented by George Attwood, a fellow and tutor of Trinity College, Cambridge, towards the close of the last century. It is intended to demonstrate the law of the velocity of falling bodies.

Suppose weights of six and seven pounds hang over a pulley, the weight and friction of which we neglect for the present; if both weights were six pounds, the machine would not move: therefore, the moving pressure is the one pound by which the one weight exceeds the other. This weight, if it had only its own mass to move, or if it fell freely, would generate $32\frac{1}{6}$ feet of velocity per second; but before this system can move, $6 + 7$, or 13 lbs. must be stirred by 1 lb., and there will only be the 13th part of $32\frac{1}{6}$ feet of velocity produced in one second, that is, about $2\frac{2}{3}$ feet. Therefore, in one second, the heavier weight will fall only $1\frac{1}{5}$ foot; and in five seconds, 25 times as much, or 30 feet. And the velocity acquired may be reduced in any proportion, by making the weights more nearly equal.

Attwood's machine is a pulley, the pivots of which, instead of being placed in a block, are sustained on friction wheels, to diminish the friction. Two weights are hung over this by a string, and the mass moved consists of the two weights, the pulley, and the friction wheels.

The length described in any time is measured by a vertical scale of feet, placed close to the line of motion of one of the weights. To measure the velocity acquired at any point the moving pressure (the excess of one weight above the other) must be taken off, in order that there may be no fresh accession of velocity, or that the system may proceed only with the velocity acquired. This is effected by making the larger weight in two parts, one part equal to the smaller weight, and the other of course to the excess or moving pressure. The latter is so formed that it cannot pass through a certain ring, while the former can. By fixing this ring to any required point of the scale of feet, the moving pressure is taken off when the larger weight passes through it.

Attwood's machine is not wholly satisfactory; but of the four principles—1, the law of uniformly accelerated motion: 2, the constancy of the retardation caused by the having to communicate every acceleration also to the pulley and friction wheels; 3, the constancy of the retardation arising from friction; 4, the smallness of the resistance of the air to small velocities — this machine may be made to prove any one to a spectator who admits the other three.

AUBE. This department of France, formed out of portions of the former provinces of Champagne and Burgundy, possesses a little mineral wealth; iron is found, but no mine is worked; limestone is abundant; building stone, potter's clay, marl, and pipe-clay are found. Turf also is found in some districts, but the fuel of the department is supplied by its forests, the principal of which are those of Clairvaux, Chaource, Montmorency, Orient, and Soulaines.

The principal manufactures are broad cloth, cotton, stuffs, and hosiery. Leather, coarse cloth, cambric, silk, linen, and gloves are also made. Besides these fabrics the department has numerous potteries, tile, porcelain, and glass-works, paper mills, distilleries, vinegar yards, beet-root sugar factories, rope-walks, starch factories, dyeing and bleaching establishments. The trade of the department is in the agricultural and manufacturing products already mentioned, together with cheese, wool, sausages, firewood, and charcoal.

The chief towns in which the manufactures are centred are Troyes, Mery-sur-Seine (the centre of a great honey district containing above 3000 hives), Piney (where there is a large manufacture of ropes and mats from the bark of the lime-tree), Arcis-sur-Aube (where cotton spinning and dyeing are carried on), Ricey (a good wine district), Villenaux, Romilly (where there are several oil and corn-mills), Nogent, Bar sur-Aube, &c.

AUCH, the capital of the department of Gers in France, has a trade in wine, brandy, wool, quills, and fruits; woollen and cotton stuffs, leather, crape, and hats, are manufactured in the town and neighbourhood.

AUCKLAND ISLANDS. These remote islands, lying about 200 miles south of New Zealand, were discovered by Captain Briscoe in 1806. A commercial interest is attached to them at the present time arising out of an attempt to colonize them and make them a depôt for the Southern Whale Fishery.

The Auckland Islands have been granted by government to the Messrs. Enderby on very advantageous terms, in consideration of the services rendered by their father to this country, as also for the more recent discoveries of the southern continent by Captain Briscoe whilst in the employ of the Messrs. Enderby. A company, to which the Messrs. Enderby have ceded their privileges, obtained a charter of incorporation on the 16th of January, 1849, for the purpose of prosecuting the southern whale fishery from the Auckland Islands; and Laurie Harbour has been chosen as the head station of the company, from the superior facilities it affords to whaling vessels. The islands were uninhabited until the Southern Whale Fishery Company, under the conduct of one of the Messrs. Enderby, made a settlement there in 1849. At the first annual meeting of the company, held in February 1850, it was stated that the company had despatched a store-ship, an emigrant ship with settlers, and three whale ships to the island; and that others would soon follow. Quite recently (Nov. 1850) accounts have been received, detailing the successful commencement of the settlement.

AUCTION, a method employed for the sale of property. The Romans gave it the descriptive name of *auctio*, an increase, because the property was publicly sold to him who would offer most for it. In modern times a different method of sale has been sometimes adopted, which is called a Dutch auction, thus indicating the local origin of the practice: it consists in the public offer of property at a price beyond its value, and then gradually lowering or diminishing that price until some one consents to become the purchaser. Fish is often sold in this way on the beach near the fishing-towns. The system adopted at the Cornish mines is a sort of medium between the ordinary and the Dutch auctions; two months' mining is let to a gang or a party of miners who bid the *lowest* sum, that is, who agree to take the smallest per centage of the produce for their reward.

Persons are now sometimes invited to a 'sale by the candle,' or 'by the inch of candle.' The origin of this expression arose from the employment of candles as the means of measuring time, it being declared that no one lot of goods should continue to be offered to the biddings of the persons who were present for a longer time than would suffice for the burning of one inch of candle; as soon as the candle had wasted to that extent, the then highest bidder was declared to be the purchaser.

AUDE, a department of France formed of a portion of the old province of Languedoc, has a fair proportion of produce and manufactures. Mines of coal, plastic clay, and plaster of Paris are profitably worked; limestone, good building stone, and slate are found. The Corbières Mountains contain mines of antimony, manganese, copper, lead, and silver; but none of them are worked. There are several mineral and salt springs. Marble of great beauty is found among the transition limestone and the lower secondary strata in the quarries of Caunes.

The chief manufacture of the department is fine broad cloth, for making which wool is imported from Spain; leather, hats, hosiery, paper, and pottery are made. There are numerous distilleries, flour-mills and saw-mills, furnaces and iron foundries. The exports of the department consist of soda, which is found abundantly on the coast of the Mediterranean; salt, of which about 90,000 tons are annually made in the salt-pans in the neighbourhood of Bages and Sigean; boxwood combs, jet ornaments, and the agricultural, mineral, and industrial products before named.

Besides NARBONNE, the chief manufacturing town is Carcassone, where there is a considerable commerce in mineral products, wine, corn, fruits, &c.; but the town is principally engaged in the manufacture of fine broad cloth, blankets, hosiery, woollen yarn, and linen. There are also several brandy distilleries, soaperies, dye-houses, paper-mills, and naileries in the town. Limoux has important manufactures of broad cloth: there are also woollen-yarn manufactories, tanneries, soaperies, and oil-mills. Limoux has a considerable trade in wine, and is the mart for the iron of the neighbouring furnaces. Castelnaudery has manufactures of coarse cloths, canal boats, pottery, and bricks; there are also brandy distilleries and flour-mills; besides the articles named, the town trades in timber, iron, and hides.

AUGER. The auger is an instrument for boring holes in wood, larger than can be made with an awl or a gimlet. In its simple form, this instrument is too well known to need description. A few years ago a new kind of auger was invented, and introduced into some of our manufacturing establishments; it differs from the common auger in having a spiral like that of a corkscrew, which empties itself of the fragments of wood without having need to be withdrawn from the bore.

AUGITE, a mineral which presents many varieties according to its mode of production. Mineralogists have discussed at much length the connection between augite and hornblende, and their probable formation. Mitscherlich has observed that at many iron-foundries in Sweden and Germany the scoriæ possessed the form, structure, and chemical composition of certain minerals found in nature. From this source he has been led to the opinion, that augite is formed whenever the process of cooling, and consequently of crystallization, is rapid; and horn-blende, when it is conducted more slowly: the chemical ingredients being in both cases nearly the same.

AUGSBURG, the capital of the Bavarian circle of the Upper Danube, is distinguished in commercial matters by its banking and exchange operations, and by its transit of merchandise. It is a staple town also for the deposit and sale of the wines of Italy, Switzerland, and the south of Germany. It has above 200 mercantile establishments, and an annual circulation, varying in value from three to four millions sterling, in bills and merchandise. Augsburg is famous for its plate, jewellery, time-pieces, philosophical and mathematical instruments, books, prints, maps, cotton and woollen manufactures, leather, beet-root sugar, and many other products, which rank it among the chief industrial and commercial cities of Germany.

The manufacturers of Augsburg are making preparations to represent the industry of their town and the surrounding district, in the approaching Industrial Exhibition in Hyde Park.

AUGUSTOVO, one of the districts of Russian Poland, produces considerable quantities of wild hops, which form an article of export to Königsberg. It is likewise rich in forests, those which skirt the Memel being full of linden trees, whence the celebrated 'linden-honey.'

AUK, is a family of oceanic birds, of which some of the species yield products of merchantable value. The razor-bill auk abounds on the shores of Labrador, where thousands are killed for the sake of the breast feathers, and vast numbers of eggs are collected. This species also visits the cliffs of the Isle of Wight, the Isle of Man, and the Scottish isles; where the eggs, which are esteemed a delicacy, are taken in great numbers; but the means by which they are obtained is perilous, and requires no little nerve. A large stake or bar of iron is driven into the top of the cliff (five or six hundred feet in height), and to this is fastened a strong rope, at the end of which a stick is put crosswise, on which rides the adventurer, who is lowered down the front of the precipice. If his object be to secure the eggs only, he shouts to scare the birds away, which rise in countless numbers, uttering discordant cries; but if his object be the feathers, which are valuable, he goes to work in silence, and knocks down all the birds within his reach. The flesh is worthless, but is used by fishermen as a bait for crab-pots, &c. This plan is practised in the Isle of Wight, in the Isle of Man, and the Feroe Islands, as well as along the coast of Norway.

AURANTIA'CEA. A few details respecting the fruits thus named will be found under LEMON; ORANGE.

AU'REUS, or DENA'RIUS AUREUS, was the ordinary Roman coin of gold. It was equivalent to twenty-five silver denarii, or a hundred sestertii.

Gold was first struck at Rome B.C. 207. The earliest coin of gold at this time was named a scruple (scrupulum), and went for twenty sesterces of that age. Pliny says, that it was afterwards usual to coin forty pieces out of the pound of gold (larger of course, bearing the general name of Aurei), and that the Roman emperors by degrees made them forty-five to the pound. The aureus was sometimes called solidus, as opposed to a half and a third. A constitution of Valentinian and Valens declares that the pound of gold must be considered as 72 solidi. An aureus of Julius Cæsar, in the British Museum, weighs 123 grains, which is exactly the weight of an English sovereign, but the Roman coin contains no alloy, or very little. Of the aurei of Constantine in the Museum, one weighs 66 grains, three 67, three 69½, one 73½, and one 81½. The average weight of the aurei of Augustus appears to have been nearly 121 grains; that of Nero's aurei nearly 117.

AURICH, a province (*landrostei*) of Hanover, has a few industrial features to recommend it to our attention. Its inhabitants grow grain, particularly oats and rapeseed; breed great numbers of horses, sheep, and cattle; make much honey; export great quantities of turf; and are actively engaged in foreign commerce and the herring-fishery on the Scotch coast. Besides the town of EMDEN, Aurich contains the busy town of Norden, which has timber and dockyards, tanneries, breweries, distilleries, tobacco aud woollen factories.

AURILLAC, capital of the department of Cantal in France, carries on manufactures in paper, lace, copper, household utensils, and leather; the chief trade is in cattle, cheese, stockings, tapestry, and lace.

AURUNGABAD, like many other cities in India, carries on a considerable traffic in the bazaar, where both European and native goods are exposed for sale; the principal trade is in silk manufactures, mostly of Indian workmanship.

AUSTELL, (ST.) or ST. AUSTLE, is the centre of one of the rich mining districts in Cornwall. It first rose to eminence from its vicinity to the great tin mine of Polgooth and other considerable mines. Polgooth is partly in this parish, and was at one time esteemed the richest mine ever worked in England; it is still productive, the working of it having been recently recommenced. The town still owes its principal importance to the mines, and has formed harbours at Charlestown and Pentewan for the convenience of importing coals from Wales, and of exporting the ores or porcelain clay of the district. A railroad connects the town with the harbour of Pentewan. There is a smelting-house at the west end of the town, and another at Charles town. Copper ore is said to have been smelted at St. Austell before any other place in Cornwall.

AUSTEN, WILLIAM, an English metal-founder of the fifteenth century, is worthy of a brief notice in this place, in so far as he had a great share in the construction of the celebrated tomb at Warwick, in St. Mary's church, of Richard de Beauchamp, earl of Warwick, who died in 1439. In a document given in Dugdale's 'Warwickshire,' William Austen is styled, 'citizen and founder of London,' from which and the details of the agreement, it appears that he was not the designer or modeller of the figures which he cast in brass, for it is expressly stated that he is to work from models made of timber. 'Will. Austen, citizen and founder, of London,' xiv. Martii, 30 H. 6, covenanteth &c. to cast, work, and perfectly to make, of the finest latten (brass) to be gilded, that may be found, xiv. images embossed, of lords and ladies in divers vestures called weepers, to stand in housings made about the tomb, those images to be made in breadth, length, and thickness, &c., to xiv. patterns made of timber. Also he shall make xviii. less images of angells, to stand in other housings, as shall be appointed by patterns, whereof ix. after one side, and ix. after another. Also he must make an hearse to stand on the tombe above and about the principal image that shall lye in the tomb according to a pattern; the stuff and workmanship to the repairing to be at the charge of the said Wil. Austen.

'The said William Austen, xi. Feb. 28 H. 6, doth covenant to cast and make an image of a man armed, of fine latten, garnished with certain ornaments, viz. with sword and dagger; with a garter; with a helm and crest under his head, and at his feet a bear musted (muzzled), and a griffon perfectly made of the finest latten, according to patterns; all of which to be brought to Warwick and laid on the tombe, at the peril (risk) of the said Austen.'

In the opinion of Flaxman, these works of Austen are equal to what was done in Italy at the same time; and though he is mentioned only as the founder, he may possibly be the designer of the figures, as the patterns spoken of in the covenant may have been made in relation to size and costume, and not as exact models to prepare the casts from. The monument, one of the earliest and best in England, is still in a good state of preservation, and is of brass; the meaning therefore of the word latten, which has been disputed, is evidently brass.

AUSTRALIA. The time is not far distant when this island, the largest on the globe, will possess a high degree of commercial importance. All our colonies on its shores—New South Wales, Port Phillip, South Australia, and Western Australia—are gradually advancing in industry and in commerce. The first three are becoming rich in sheep and its produce, while South Australia is also contributing the riches of its mineral produce.

The mineral riches of Australia are being yearly more and more explored. Iron, coal, copper, tin, and lead, are known to exist—some in large quantities. There were in 1847, in South Australia alone, 27 copper mines, 1 lead mine, 2 copper and lead mines, and 1 copper and gold mine. On the estate of the Australian Agricultural Company, near Newcastle, coal was found in 1849; and it was expected that mines would be ready for working on that spot by the beginning of 1850. In 1847 Dr. Van Sommer explored, in a geological survey ordered by the governor, a vast bed of coal in Western Australia, which bids fair to realize the hopes of that hitherto unsuccessful colony; and in 1850 ebony, sandalwood, and guano, have begun to occupy a place among the exports from this colony. Limestones, sandstones, clays, gypsum, roofing slate, are among the abundant materials of manufactures.

From the latest returns from Australia, we find that copper is now offered for sale in considerable quantities. A brig has sailed thence during the present summer to Singapore, with 246 tons of fine tough copper, worth 20,000*l.*; this was collected from four of the South Australian copper works. Tho value of the mineral produce exported from that colony has increased with surprising rapidity—as thus:—

1843	128*l.*
1844	6,437*l.*
1845	19,019*l.*
1846	142,231*l.*
1847	174,017*l.*
1848	320,624*l.*

This Australian copper finds a market in Germany and in France, as well as in England; its quality is said to be very fine. In August 1850, the shares of no fewer than 21 Australian copper mines were in the market, most of them commanding high prices!

The wool trade of Australia, also, is becoming of vast importance. The export of wool from the various colonies of the island in 1847 was about 20 millions of pounds; in 1848 it exceeded 30 million pounds; and in 1849 it rose to the amount of 35 millions.

Efforts are now being made to establish a mail steam-packet route from England to Australia. Four routes are advocated by different interests—1st, across the Isthmus of Panamá and the Pacific; 2nd, by the Cape of Good Hope; 3rd, by Singapore and Western Australia to Sydney; 4th, by Singapore and North Australia to Sydney. The first three routes aro each, in round numbers, about 13,000 miles; the fourth is rather over 12,000. One of the Singapore routes, by placing Australia in connection with India and China, as well as with England, will probably be selected as most advantageous; but an unfortunato difference of view between the government and the East India Company at present exists on this point. It has been recently shown, that tho voyage from Australia to England by the system of what is termed Great Circle sailing, effects a saving in distance of nearly 900 miles, over the old sea route.

Australia will contribute to the Exhibition of 1851.

AUSTRIA. This large empire has been formed by the annexation of so many kingdoms and states, and embraces so great a diversity of soil and productions, that we can only briefly notice its chief industrial features.

Slavonia and the south-eastern and central parts of *Hungary* are richer than most European countries in metals and minerals. Slavonia is traversed from east to west by mountains and hills; and this province, as well as *Croatia*, has alternations of plain and highland which are very fruitful in grain, wine, tobacco, silk, honey, and other products. *Transylvania* being mountainous, the produce is chiefly timber and minerals. *Galizia* is, next to Hungary, a principal granary of the Austrian states, and supplies large quantities of salt, some precious metals, and many other mineral and vegetable productions; but the climate is too cold for the grape. Austrian *Silesia*, next adjoining Galizia, is abundant in pasture and timber, but not in grain. *Moravia*, in its central and southern parts, is a rich land of maize and wine. *Bohemia* has rich and abundant produce. *Upper and Lower Austria* are poor in grain; but fruit, wine, and salt are procured in abundance. The adjoining province of *Styria* is well supplied with pastures, and is besides rich in mineral produce. Next to this is the *Tyrol*, in which the chief products are horses and cattle, grain, wine, fruit, potatoes, timber, salt, iron, copper, silver, lead, and a little gold. *Illyria*, which is composed of *Carinthia*, *Carniola*, and some smaller provinces, includes more varieties of climate and productions than any other part of the Austrian empire. *Dalmatia*, southward of Illyria, supplies much produce, which consists chiefly of marble of excellent quality, wine, oil, figs, almonds, wax, horned cattle, sheep, salt, and more particularly fish. *Austrian Italy* produces grain, maize, rice, millet, peas, beans, potatoes, hemp, flax, vegetables and fruits of all kinds, and, in some parts, saffron; there is no branch of industry more carefully or profitably cultivated than the production and manufacture of silk. The *Alpine* districts yield considerable quantities of iron, copper, coal, marble, and other minerals.

The principal plants cultivated in Austria comprise all the usual kinds of grain, fruit, and vegetables. The chief medicinal plants are—rhubarb, which is raised in Styria, the Lower Ens, Bohemia, and Galizia; liquorice, a favourite article of growth in Moravia, whence 400 tons and upwards are annually exported, and which is also gathered in the wild state in Hungary and Slavonia; manna, derived from the *Fraxinus ornus*, which abounds in the forests of Hungary and Slavonia; and spikenard (*Spica Celtica*), which is collected with much care in the mountains of Carniola, Styria, the Tyrol, and the Upper Ens. An intoxicating spirit is distilled in Carinthia and Styria fram gentian, which is found in most of the elevated regions; and Iceland-moss is collected in considerable quantities on the Carpathian mountains, where it grows in masses of five and six feet in height.

More than one-third of what is deemed the available soil of the Austrian dominions is occupied by woods and forests; and wood is one of the staple productions. Among the products of the Austrian forests we may name potashes, which are chiefly made in Hungary, Galizia, and the Buckowine, Moravia, the Archduchy, and Bohemia. Tar, charcoal, gall-apples, and turpentine should be added to this enumeration of the products of these forests, though they are not of considerable moment.

The quantity of wine annually made in the Austrian territory averages about 8,200,000,000 gallons; of which Hungary produces more than one-half, and of which the inhabitants of the empire are said to consume about seven-eights. Tokay is a Hungarian wine, very choice, but small in quantity.

The rearing of the silkworm, though not wholly neglected in other parts of the south of Austria, is nowhere carried on to such an extent as in the territories of Lombardy and Venice. The whole produce of the empire is estimated at about 6,000,000 lbs., of which about 4,500,000 lbs. are the produce of the Italian provinces. A considerable proportion of this article in the wrought state, chiefly of the sort termed organsine, is exported from the Italian provinces to the English market. Cantharides, or Spanish flies, are a considerable article of export from Hungary and Slavonia; the cochineal insect draws many purchasers into the sandy tracts of Galizia from Turkey and Armenia; and the leech of late years has become an article of considerable trade between Austria and France.

Among the other productions of this monarchy, we may notice that tobacco is a monopoly engrossed by the department of finance in every province but Hungary, Transylvania, and the Tyrol. The annual produce of Hungary alone amounts to 330,000 cwts. There are private manufactories in the three provinces to which this monopoly does not ex-

KNIGHTS CYCLOPÆDIA OF THE Industry of all Nations.

tend. Of seed-oil, though the produce is very considerable in all quarters, enough is not manufactured for the consumption. Large quantities of olive-oil also are obtained from the territories of Lombardy and Venice, particularly the neighbourhood of the Lago di Garda, Illyria, and Dalmatia. The manufactures of paper and of glass are very extensive, and employ a large number of hands.

In *Mineral Productions* Austria surpasses every other country in Europe. With the exception of platinum, it would be difficult to name any metal which it does not possess. The richest of its gold-mines are in Transylvania, which has been called the gold-mine of Europe, and in which no less than forty mines are worked. Silver is largely produced in Hungary; and in smaller quantities in other districts. Schemnitz is the great mining capital for the gold and silver districts. Copper mines and works exist in different parts of the empire: and the annual supply of copper which is raised in the Austrian dominions would appear to amount to about 2500 or 3000 tons. More than double this quantity of lead is produced. Iron is a metal of which almost inexhaustible resources exist, though, on account of the dearness of fuel, the mines have not yet been turned to any very extensive use: the quantity raised throughout the empire is about 80,000 tons per annum. In the Huttenberg, Carinthia possesses one of the oldest and at the same time one of the richest iron mines in Europe, its produce being from 8000 to 9000 tons a year. Tin is raised in no part of Austria but Bohemia, and the whole produce does not exceed 2000 cwt., which is far short of the consumption. The quality, however is good. There is no mine of quicksilver in Europe so rich as the mine at Idria in Carniola. Calamine and zinc are obtained from the Tyrol, the Archduchy, Styria, and Bohemia; cobalt from Hungary, Styria, and Bohemia; arsenic from Hungary, Transylvania, Bohemia, and Salsburg; antimony from Hungary, Transylvania, the Tyrol, and Bohemia; chrome from the Tyrol; and bismuth and manganese from Hungary.

The various species of salt, such as sea-salt, rock, and that made from brine-springs, exist in abundance. The celebrated mine of Wieliczka, which has been worked ever since the year 1253, and lies in the north-western part of Galizia, is but an inconsiderable inroad upon a massive bed extending for a length of nearly 600 miles along the Carpathians, as far as Okna in Wallachia. The whole salt produce of the empire amounts to nearly 300,000 tons yearly. Vitriol, alum, saltpetre, and soda, are among the mineral produc

Wood fuel is much more used than coal or peat; yet there is considerable abundance of these. Every part of the Austrian dominions possesses more or less of native sulphur, but more particularly Galizia, Hungary, Transylvania, and Bohemia. Mineral tar and oil are chiefly obtained in Galizia and the Buckowine; but they are also produced, though but partially turned to account, in the Archduchy, Hungary, Bohemia, Illyria, and Dalmatia.

Among precious stones, the Bohemian carbuncle and Hungarian opal stand in highest repute. The chalcedony, ruby, emerald, jasper, amethyst, topaz, carnelian, chrysolite, and beryl, as well as what is called the 'marble diamond,' in Hungary, must be added to the list of Austrian precious stones. Marble of every description and variety of colour and vein is raised either in Hungary, Transylvania, Bohemia, the Archduchy, Tyrol, Styria, Illyria, Dalmatia, or the Italian possessions of Austria, in which latter the Veronese alone is said to possess 106 distinct varieties. Carinthia and Styria, indeed, supply a quality of white marble no way inferior to the Carrara marble. Alabaster, serpentine, black tourmaline, gypsum, black-lead, slates, and flint, are among the mineral produce.

The principal seats of the linen manufacture, or rather of those productions in which flax and hemp are employed, are Bohemia, Moravia, and Silesia, which furnish the finest articles of this description in Austria, though in diminished quantities as compared with the earlier part of the present century. For variety and goodness of manufacture, the states of Lombardy and Venice deserve to be classed in the next rank to those three provinces. The Tyrol, Hungary, Galizia, and Transylvania produce scarcely any but the middling and coarser species of linen; nor is there much beyond what is termed house-linen made in the Archduchy, Illyria, or the Military-Frontier districts. The raising and preparation of flax alone in Austria are estimated to give employment to 750,000 individuals, and its native manufactures to yield sufficient not only for domestic use, but for partial exportation.

The largest manufactures of woollens, both cloth and other kinds, are established in Moravia and Bohemia. These products in both countries are said to be as much distinguished for their excellence as their variety. In the other parts of the empire, where this branch of industry is proportionably pushed to a much less extent, the principal articles manufactured are of middling and coarse quality, whilst the finer sorts, so far as their domestic consumption requires it, are of Moravian and

Bohemian fabric. Considerable quantities of the latter are exported to foreign parts. The woollen manufacture employs at least 320,000 Austrian hands; and the crown has given no small impulse to it by erecting several establishments, conducted at its own expense, among which is that at Linz, which employs 10,000 spinners and weavers.

The silk manufactures have been rapidly extending in Austria since the introduction of Jacquard's machinery. They are principally carried on in the province of the Lower Ens, and in the Milanese and Venetian territories. The cotton manufacture, though it has been prosecuted with some energy, especially near Vienna, can hardly be said to be prosperous, owing to the difficulty of competing with England and other countries.

The province of the Lower Ens takes the lead in the manufacture of leather, of which the best qualities are made in Vienna. The Upper Ens, Moravia, Styria, Bohemia, and the Tyrol rank next in importance. Hungary abounds in tanneries; and in fact nearly every province in Austria is engaged more or less in this branch.

Iron, the mines of which have been already alluded to, is wrought into marketable form in many parts of the empire. Cast iron is produced in Bohemia, Styria, Hungary, and Illyria; bars and sheets are rolled in the Lower Ens, Styria, Carinthia and Bohemia; iron and steel wire are made in the Archduchy; nails in many of the provinces; and fire-arms and swords in Styria and Hungary. Manufactories of copper, brass, cannon, tin, lead, balls and shot, buttons, gold and silver, are maintained in various parts of the empire.

It was estimated by Lichtenstern, Stein, and Malchus, a few years ago, that the number of manufacturers employed in working up the native produce of Austria, or the raw materials imported from other countries, amounted to 2,365,000, and the yearly value of their productions to 1425 millions of silver currency, representing a sum in British sterling of upwards of 140 millions.

With respect to external trade, no country of equal extent is perhaps more disadvantageously situated; its line of sea-coast is comparatively inconsiderable, and with the solitary exceptions of the Po and the Adige, its finest streams, such, for instance as the Danube and Elbe, lie, even when crossing its frontiers, at a considerable distance from the sea.

Considerable preparations are being made in various parts of the Austrian empire, especially Vienna, to hold a worthy position in the Industrial Exhibition of 1851. The manufacturers hope to produce articles in which combined *cheapness* and excellence will be characteristics. Viennese pianofortes, especially, are expected to illustrate this combination—a feature of much value.

AUTO'MATON, derived from two Greek words, meaning *self-moved*, is a name generally applied to all machines which are so constructed as to imitate any actions of men or animals.

The pigeon of Archytas, the clock of Charlemagne, the automaton made by Albertus Magnus to open his door when any one knocked, the speaking head of Roger Bacon, and the fly of Regiomontanus, are early examples of such machinery, respecting which, however, we have too little information to afford a correct judgment concerning them. In more recent times we read a marvellous account of an automaton group constructed by M. Camus for the amusement of Louis XIV., consisting of a carriage and horses, with a lady who alighted to present a petition; and also, in the 'Memoirs of the Academy of Sciences' for 1729, of a set of actors representing a pantomime in five acts. Less marvellous, though highly ingenious, was the automaton flute-player of Vaucanson, exhibited at Paris in 1738. The same ingenious person subsequently produced a figure which played the flageolet and tambourine; and a duck, which not only imitated the motions and sounds of a real duck, but swallowed food, and digested it by means of chemical substances in the stomach. More recently M. Maelzel exhibited at Vienna an automaton trumpeter; and automata have been made to write, to draw, and to play on the piano-forte. The automaton chess-player is now known to have been worked by a person concealed inside the figure and its table or pedestal, which supposition, however, does not deprive its maker of the credit of great ingenuity in the mechanism by which the hands were set in motion.

The passion for making automata has not yet quite passed away. A recent example was Mr. Faber's *Euphonia*. It consisted of a draped bust and waxen-faced figure, which articulated language with a certain degree of intelligibility. The sounds were produced by striking on sixteen keys. A small pair of bellows was worked with the nozzle in the back part of the head of the figure; and in the head were various arrangements of India rubber and other materials, calculated to yield a particular sound in each part or section. When the exhibitor wished to produce a sentence or word, he first mentally divided it into as many parts as there are actually distinct sounds—not necessarily coinciding with the syllables or the single letters; since the various phonographic systems far more correctly represent distinct sounds. Having determined the first word, the operator pressed his finger on a particular key, which admitted a blast of air to a particular compartment, in which the mechanism was of the kind to produce the sound required. Other keys were similarly pressed, until all the required sounds of the word or sentence were produced. The sounds were near enough to those of the human voice to convey the meaning intended, but they had an unpleasant effect to the ear. By a modification of the action, whispering was imitated.

A remarkable machine was the *Automaton Latin Versifier*, introduced in 1845, by Mr. John Clark of Bridgewater, after a labour of thirteen years. At the first thought such an invention seems inexplicable, owing to the mental character of the process; but a little enquiry shews that it is only a system of permutations, such as a machine can easily be made to produce. The specimens given in the 'Athenæum' and other public journals at the time, are all Latin hexameters, and moreover have all the same grammatical formula and scansion, in respect to dactyls and spondees. The following nine specimens are given, each complete in itself, as an hexametric line, but having no connexion with the others.

1. Horrida sponsa reis promittunt tempora densa.
2. Sontia tela bonis causabunt agmina crebra.
3. Bellica vota modis promulgant crimina fusca.
4. Aspera pila patet depromunt prælia quædam.
5. Effera sponsa fere confirmant vincula nequam.
6. Barbara tela reis præmonstrant nubila dura.
7. Horrida vota bonis progignunt jurgia crebra.
8. Sontia castra modis prositant somnia fusca.
9. Trucida regna quidem conquirunt opera cara.

The exterior of the machine which composes these lines resembles in size and shape a small bureau book-case; in the frontispiece of which through an aperture, the verses appear in succession as they are composed. Mr. Clark, in a communication to the 'Athenæum' (No. 923) makes the following observations on his machine, which he calls the *Eureka*:—"The machine is neither more nor less than a practical illustration of the law of evolution.............. The machine contains *letters* in alphabetical arrangement; out of these, through the medium of numbers, rendered tangible by being expressed by indentures on wheel-work, the instrument selects such as are requisite to form the verse conceived: the *components* of words suited to form hexameters being alone previously calculated, the harmonious combination of which will be found to be practicably interminable.'

Mr. A. J. Cooley, in the same journal, pointed out the existence of a forgotten pamphlet, a century and a half old, in which the author showed how, from a table given, a person might produce millions of hexameter lines. But these were produced by accumulations of words; whereas Mr. Clark's machine, if we rightly understand his description, actually builds up the lines letter by letter.

It is matter of regret that so much ingenuity should be expended in the production of useless results. There are, however, many machines—for calculating, numbering, registering, stamping, paging, &c.—which will be described in various parts of this work, and which illustrate the application of automatic action to useful purposes.

AUTOPHON, is the name given by Mr. Dawson, the organ builder, to an ingenious little contrivance, whereby a barrel organ can be made to play an unlimited number of tunes, instead of the limit usually placed to its action. The tunes or the notes representing them are perforated on sheets of millboard, one to each tune; when one of these is placed within the instrument, the pipes can only sound (on the handle being turned) according to the perforations; so that the tune played depends on those perforations, and not on any particular arrangement of studs in the barrel. There is much of the principle of the Jacquard apparatus in this contrivance. As the perforated tune-cards are sold at a few pence each, a large variety of tunes can be made available. We believe the primary object of the inventor is to make a barrel organ serve for country churches, where it is not convenient to have a player for a keyed instrument. The Autophon was exhibited at the recent Industrial Exhibitions at Dublin and Devonport.

AUTUN, a city in the south of France, is more celebrated for its remains of antiquity than for its industrial features. It has however a respectable amount of trade and manufactures. The trade of the town consists in horses, cattle, wood, and hemp. Serge, cotton-velvet, cloth for regimentals, hosiery, and leather are among its manufactures; and a fabric called *tapisserie de marchau*, fitted for coverlets of beds, horse-cloths, and other purposes, is made. The district round the city contains green porphyry and gray granite; and there are also iron and lead mines near the town.

AUXERRE, a city near the centre of France, stands in a country fruitful in wine. Woollen cloths, serges, druggets, stockings, cotton yarn, bricks, and pottery are made; but the chief trade of the town is in wine, of which about 4,000,000 gallons are sent by water to Paris and into Normandy. Wood and charcoal are also considerable articles of trade at Auxerre.

AUXONNE, a town near the centre of France, has a cannon foundry and powder mills. The trade is chiefly in wine, brandy, grain, melons, and wood; as well as in cloth, and serges, which are sent to Lyon. In return, groceries, silk, and the wines of Mâcon, are received. There are in the neighbourhood quarries of marble and of various kinds of stone. Turquoises and fossil corals are found in these quarries.

AVANTURINE, a variety of quartz, remarkable for the brilliancy with which it reflects light, the effect being in general produced by fine points of mica imbedded within the crystalline mass. From this circumstance it is sometimes employed in jewellery, but it is of little value.

AVANTURINE GLASS. This name has been given to a species of coloured glass, formerly made at Venice, and applied to the manufacture of trinkets and ornaments. The name is given to it on account of its resemblance to the crystal similarly designated. It consists of a yellowish brown kind of glass, enclosing fine thin yellow laminæ or scales, which have a brilliant metallic lustre.

It does not seem to be clearly known in this country how the Avanturine glass is made. Some suppose that the yellow laminæ are produced by melting scales of metal or mica with the glass; but it is deemed more probable that a salt of copper is mixed and melted with the glass, and that a powerful reducing agent decomposes this salt during the melting, and separates the copper in the state of thin metallic scales.

A *tazza* of Avanturine glass was exhibited in the display of Mediæval Art, at the rooms of the Society of Arts in 1850; and many such are preserved as relics of art.

AVEBURY, or ABURY, in Wiltshire, is remarkable as the site of what appears to have been one of the largest Celtic or Druidical temples in Europe. In forming this temple, no less than 650 blocks seem to have been brought together and placed in circles and rows. These stones were of various dimensions, measuring from five to twenty feet in height above the ground, and from three to twelve feet in width and thickness. One hundred were raised on end, and placed in a circular form, within a flat and nearly circular area of about 1400 feet in diameter; and these stones were bounded by a deep ditch and lofty bank, which inclosed the whole work, except at two places, where openings were left for entrances. The bank or mound at present is broken down in four places, but there seem to have been originally only two openings corresponding to the two great avenues which formed the approaches. The inner slope of the bank measured 80 feet, and its whole circumference at the top was 4442 feet: the area within the bank or mound is somewhat more than thirty-five acres. There were two other small circles within the periphery of the great circle. One was a double circle of upright stones, with a single stone raised near the centre, and consisted of forty-three stones. Another circle, of forty-five stones, some of which are still standing and of immense size, was placed a little north of the former, and consisted also of two concentric circles, inclosing a group of three tall stones. These were the component parts and general design and arrangement of the triple temple, as it may be called; but there were two connecting parts which gave a peculiarity to this work distinguishing it from all other Celtic temples. These were avenues of approach, consisting of double rows or lines of upright stones, which branched off from the central work, each to the extent of more than a mile. One of them branched off from the outer circle to the south, turning, near its extremity, to the south-east, where it terminated in two circular or rather elliptical ranges of upright stones. According to Stukeley, this avenue was formed by two hundred stones, being finished at its eastern extremity with fifty-eight stones, which were arranged in a double circle on an eminence called Overton Hill, or the Hakpen Hill, and measured about 146 feet in diameter from outside to outside. The width of the avenue varied from fifty-six to thirty-five feet between the stones, which were on an average eighty-six feet apart from each other in their linear direction. The western avenue extended about one mile and a half, and consisted of 203 stones; its extremity ended in a point or with a single stone. These avenues or grand approaches to the temple were not arranged in straight lines, but in flowing or curved lines.

Only a few stones now remain of this remarkable specimen of Druidical Art.

AVENA. [OATS.]

AVERAGE is a quantity intermediate to a number of other quantities, so that the sum total of its excesses above those which are less is equal to the sum total of its defects from those which are greater. Thus, 7 is the average of 2, 3, 4, 6, 13, and 14. To find the average of any number of quantities, *add them all together, and divide by the number of quantities.*

The average of a set of averages is not the average of the whole, unless there are equal numbers of quantities in each set averaged; for instance, if a harvest were called good because an average bushel of its corn was better than that of another, without taking into account the number of bushels of the two, this might not necessarily be true. The average quantity is a valuable common-sense test of the goodness or badness of any particular lot, but only when there is a perfect similarity of circumstances in the things compared. For instance no one would think of calling a tree well-grown because it gave more timber than the average of all trees; but if any particular tree, say an oak, yielded more timber than the average of all oaks of the same age, it would be called good, because, if every oak gave the same, the quantity of oak timber would be greater than it is. In Marine Insurance, a sum or contribution determined in the following way, is called an Average. If any part of the ship or furniture, or of the goods, is purposely sacrificed for the sake of saving the rest, all parties interested must contribute towards the loss; and this contribution is the Average, or the share of the loss to be borne by each owner.

AVEYRON, a department in France, part of the ancient province of Guienne, produces 6,000,000 gallons of wine yearly. Between the rivers Lot and Aveyron there is a very rich bed of coal. Besides its valuable coal mines, the department contains mines of copper, lead, zinc, sulphur, antimony, iron, and alum. The lead ores are rich, and contain a considerable quantity of silver. Marble, rock-crystal, kaolin, millstone grit, flint, emery, chalk, marl, plaster of Paris, &c., are found. The abundant water power of the department is applied to good purpose in various factories for the manufacture of paper, iron, cotton, leather, woollen stuffs, &c. The trade of the department is in the mineral and industrial products already named, together with corn, plums, chestnuts, almonds, wax, bacon, cattle, hides, wool, hemp, timber, turnery, oak planks, &c. Cheese also, made of ewe's milk mixed with that of goat's, is manufactured in great quantities in the south of the department, especially in the neighbourhood of Roquefort and forms an important article of export.

These departments of industry are carried on in numerous towns of moderate size. In Rodez, serges, coarse woollens, woollen yarn, and leather, are manufactured. At La Guiolle, a large quantity of good cheese, and some woollen stuffs are made. St. Geniez has several woollen and cotton factories, besides numerous tan-yards, dyeing establishments and naileries, the produce of which, together with timber, wool, and turnery, are the chief articles of trade. At Millau, broad cloths, gloves, and leather of different kinds, are made; there are also some silk-throwing establishments. These products, with wool, hides, timber, oak-staves, cheese, wine, and cattle, are the chief articles of trade. The same products are met with at St. Affrique. Near Roquefort there are extensive grottoes, in which about 18,000 cwts. of cheese are annually made. In Villefranche, the manufacturing industry is important: there are several large linen factories, copper and iron foundries, tan-yards, and paper-mills. At Aubin there are rich coal mines, which produce 500,000 to 600,000 tons per annum; there are also mines of sulphur, alum, and iron, and several large iron furnaces in the neighbourhood.

AVIGNON, the capital of the department of Vaucluse, in France, has been rapidly advancing lately in trade and manufactures. Silk stuffs of various kinds are largely manufactured; of taffeta (florence), about 5,000,000 yards are annually made, the value of which is estimated at upwards of 8,000,000 francs; there are also a cannon foundry, a foundry for sheet-iron, copper, and tin, a saltpetre refinery, tanneries, paper-mills, type-foundries, cotton factories, and various other industrial establishments in the town. Avignon has also a large trade in books, corn, wine, brandy, sumac, colonial products, and cattle. A great part of the trade of Avignon is carried on through the port of Marseille, to and from which goods are conveyed on the Rhone by way of Arles. There is constant communication by steamers with Lyon, Arles, and Marseille, and by diligence with Paris and Marseille several times a day. A railroad now in course of construction between Lyon and Marseille passes through Avignon.

AVILA, a district of Old Castile in Spain, produces grain, fruit, oil, wine, and flax. There are at Avila (the chief town in the district) manufactories of woollen stuffs, cotton prints, and hats, besides the royal manufactory of cloth, the machinery of which is moved by water.

AVOIRDUPOIS, or AVERDUPOIS is the

common system of weights in England, now applied to all goods except the precious metals and medicines. Thus, a pound of tea is a pound *averdupois*, and contains 7000 grains; a pound of gold is a pound *troy*, and contains 5760 grains. The ancient pound was heavier than the averdupois, and weighed 7600 grains. The earliest regulations on the subject fix the *troy* weight.

A cubic foot of water, at 62° Fahrenheit and 30 in. barometrical pressure, weighs 997·14 ounces, which, being very nearly 1000 ounces, gives an expeditious rule for deducing the real weight of a cubic foot of any substance from its specific gravity. For example, if the specific gravity of gold be 19·36, the weight of a cubic foot of gold is 19360 ounces averdupois.

AXIS, AXE. This word is used in so many different senses, that it may be defined as follows: any line whatsoever which it is convenient to distinguish by a specific term, with respect to any motion or other phenomenon, is called the axis. Thus we have axes of coordinates, of oscillation, of inertia, of rotation, of polarization, &c. The word, when used by itself, generally means either *Axis of Rotation*, or *Axis of Symmetry*. An axis of rotation, or revolution, is the line about which a body turns; an axis of symmetry is a line on both sides of which the parts of the body are disposed in the same manner, so that to whatever distance it extends in one direction from the axis, it extends as far in the direction exactly opposite. Or if perpendiculars to the axis be drawn from all points and in all directions through the body, the whole of each perpendicular which is within the limits of the body will be bisected by the axis. Such is the middle line of a cone, any diameter of a sphere, the line drawn through the middle of the opposite faces of a cube, &c.

AXLE. Since the extensive use of locomotives, the theory of the action of axles, and the enquiries into the cause of their fracture, have been the result of elaborate enquiry among engineers. Rowan's patent axles are intended to lessen the ordinary amount of friction, by the use of friction rollers applied in a peculiar way. Mr. Bessemer, in a recent paper on the frequent breakage of the axles of railway carriages, attributes it mainly to the oscillations of the carriage. Whether solid or hollow axles, with a given weight of metal, are the stronger, is a disputed point among engineers; Mr. Yorke, in a paper read before the Institute of Civil Engineers in 1843, contends for the superior strength of hollow axles; but this conclusion is disputed by others.

The theory of axles may, indeed, be considered at present in a tentative state; meanwhile patents are frequently obtained for improvements in form and in mechanical action.

Hardy's patent axles have shown the possession of such a remarkable degree of toughness, that the Privy Council in 1849 granted a continuation of the patent; and remarks were made in the House of Lords relating to the lessening of railway accidents by their use. Since that period the patent has been sold for a considerable sum to a company at Birmingham, established for the manufacture of these axles on a large scale.

AXMINSTER. This Devonshire town was formerly celebrated for its manufacture of carpets. In this it rivalled the productions of Turkey and Persia so successfully, that the carpets of Axminster were considered little inferior to those imported. They were woven in one entire piece. But after lasting for 100 years, this manufactory was given up, the demand not being found equal to the expense of producing the article.

AYLESBURY is chiefly an agricultural town. There is one silk factory; but the lace manufacture which once flourished here has greatly declined. The making of straw-plait is more prosperous; and the straw-plait market established some years back is still (1850) held every Saturday. Many of the inhabitants of the neighbourhood add to their income by their skill in breeding ducks, of which they send a considerable number to the metropolis about Christmas.

The straw-plait of the Aylesbury district will occupy a place in the industrial display of 1851.

AYRSHIRE maintains a goodly rank among the commercial counties of Scotland. The mineral riches are considerable. Coal is abundant, especially in the middle and northern parts of the county. The coal is of different varieties, among which is the blende coal, found in the earth charred, or reduced to the state of a cinder; it burns without smoke or much flame, and is used for drying grain and malt. Considerable quantities are exported to Ireland and to the Western Isles. Near Saltcoats eleven different strata or seams of coal of various quality have been discovered. The proprietor constructed the harbour of Saltcoats, and built salt-pans, in order to use profitably the otherwise useless part of the coal.

The county affords abundance of limestone. Freestone is quarried in great quantity; and there is some whinstone and puddingstone. Mill-stones of coarse granite are quarried at Kilbride, near the northern part of the coast, and are in great request for their hardness and durability; they are exported to the West Indies and to America. Near Auchinleck is a quarry of black stone much used for building ovens, on account of its power of resisting the action of fire. The whetstone known by the name of Water-of-Ayr stone is found near the banks of the river Ayr. Marl also is procured in many places.

Ironstone is also abundant, and at a few places extensive iron works are carried on. Lead, plumbago or black-lead, antimony, and copper (of each of which the quantity is small) may be considered as nearly completing the list of minerals of Ayrshire.

The manufactures of Ayrshire are important, for the district possesses considerable advantages. Fuel is abundant; materials for building are at hand; and channels of communication of all kinds are open in every direction. The vicinity of Glasgow and Paisley seems to have given an impulse to improvement. Carpets, cloths, and stockings are manufactured; and the most improved machinery is in use. The woollen manufacture has long been extended to all parts of the county, and is carried on to a considerable extent by the aid of machinery. Dyers and fullers have established themselves in connection with it. The linen manufacture has never been carried to any great extent. The silk manufacture was tried but did not become permanent. The cotton manufacture, established in Glasgow and Paisley, soon extended itself into Ayrshire. Great cotton works were erected at the village of Catrine on the river Ayr; and the weaving of muslins has been established nearly all over the county. Bleaching, as connected with the cotton trade, has also been extensively carried on. Woollen bonnets and serges are largely made.

Leather is another manufactured article of considerable importance. Tanneries have been greatly extended; the leather is employed in making shoes, boots, and saddlery. Of the latter some is exported to foreign parts. Pottery for domestic purposes is made, but not to any great amount, or with much profit. Kelp, soda, and salt have all been made to advantage along the shore.

A'ZIMUTH. The azimuth of a celestial body is the angle contained between the plane of the meridian of any station and that of a vertical circle passing through the body. The instruments by means of which the azimuth of a celestial body may be directly observed are the theodolite and the altitude and azimuth circle. [CIRCLE; THEODOLITE.] An instrument is said to be moved *in azimuth* when it is turned on a vertical axis, so that any line in it drawn through the axis points to the same altitude in the heavens, but not to the same azimuth.

AZOF, or AZOV, called by the Turks Assak, the once-busy town on the shores of the once-important lake of the same name, has fallen to insignificance, chiefly by the shallowing of the water near the shore. Taganrog is the only town on the lake which carries on commerce to any extent.

AZORES. These beautiful islands, which stand so invitingly in the track of ships voyaging down the Atlantic, are very fertile. The lava districts are cultivated with vines, oranges, and lemons; but, where decomposition has afforded richer land, it yields wheat, Indian corn, beans, &c. Both European and tropical fruits arrive at the greatest perfection; and the face of the earth is so diversified as in many places to exhibit within a small extent gardens of aromatic flowers, pastures, vineyards, orangeries, &c. The islands, though still abounding in uncultivated lands, produce much more than sufficient for the supply of their present population, not only of the necessaries but also of the luxuries of life. Vessels touching at any of them are certain of being able to procure an abundant stock of refreshments; and the cattle are equal to any in the world. On the flanks of the mountain called the Peak of Pico are produced the finest wines, which, though inferior to those of Madeira, being much cheaper, find a good market both in Europe and America. The inhabitants of the islands import woollens, hardware, boards, staves, pitch, tar, iron, &c.; in return for which wine and fruit are the chief payments.

AZOTE. English chemists now mostly concur in giving the name of NITROGEN to the gaseous element which used to be called *Azote*.

AZURE BLUE. [COBALT.]

B

BAALBEC, or BALBEC, in Syria, is celebrated for three temples and other relics of ancient works of art. The great temple was peripteral, having ten columns in front and nineteen on the flank; the length of the temple is near 290 feet, and the width 160: in its perfect state, the height from the ground to the top of the pediment was 120 feet. The shafts of the columns consist of three pieces, united so exactly, that the blade of a knife cannot be inserted between the joints. The two smaller temples, like other buildings whose ruins are strewed about this once-important city, are mostly of the Corinthian order.

BABLAH, is a name given to the rind of the fruit of the *mimosa cineraica*, brought from the East Indies and Western Africa. It is used as a substitute for more expensive dye-drugs to impart a drab colour to cotton.

BABYLON. This world-renowned city is still, in its ruin and desolation, a place of interest to the artist and the artificer, on account of the huge fragments which it contains. These ruins consist of mounds of earth formed by the decomposition of buildings, channelled and furrowed by the weather; the surface of them is strewed with pieces of brick, bitumen, and pottery.

In the eastern quarter of the city there is one remarkable group of ruins. It forms a mass which is 1100 yards in length and 800 in its greatest breadth; its figure nearly resembles that of a quadrant; its height is irregular; but the most elevated part may be about 50 or 60 feet above the level of the plain, and it has been dug into for the purpose of procuring bricks. Just below the highest part of it is a small dome, in an oblong enclosure, distinguished by the name of Amram Ibn Ali. On the north is a valley of 550 yards in length, the area of which is covered with tussocks of rank grass, and crossed by a line of ruins of very little elevation. To this succeeds another grand heap of ruins, the shape of which is nearly a square of 700 yards' length and breadth, and its south-west angle is connected with the north-west angle of the mound of Amran by a ridge of considerable height and nearly 100 yards in breadth. About 200 yards from this mound is a ravine, hollowed out by those who dig for bricks, in length 100 yards, and 10 feet wide by 40 or 50 deep. On one side of it a few yards of wall remain standing, the face of which is very clean and perfect, and appears to have been the front of some building. A little to the west of the ravine is the Kasr, or palace, a huge mass of brickwork in a surprising state of preservation. A mile to the north of the Kasr is a ruin called the Mujelibè, meaning the *overturned:* its shape is oblong, and its height, as well as the measurements of its sides, irregular. The sides face the cardinal points; the northern is 200, the southern 219, the eastern 182, and the western 186 yards in length; and the elevation of the south-east, or highest angle, is 141 feet. The western face, which is the least elevated, is the most interesting, on account of the appearance of building it presents. Near the summit of it appears a low wall, with interruptions, built of unburnt bricks mixed up with chopped straw or reeds, and cemented with clay-mortar of great thickness, having between every layer a layer of reeds; and on the north side are also some vestiges of a similar construction. The summit is covered with heaps of rubbish, in digging into some of which layers of broken burnt brick cemented with mortar were discovered, and whole bricks with inscriptions are sometimes found. The whole is covered with innumerable fragments of pottery, brick, bitumen, pebbles, vitrified brick or scoria, and even shells, bits of glass and mother-of-pearl. It appears that the walls were lined with a fine burnt brick to conceal the unburnt bricks, of which the body of the building was principally composed. About 70 yards to the north and west of the Mujelibè are traces of a very low mound of earth, which may have formed an inclosure round the whole.

But the most vast ruins are those of the Tower of Belus, or Birs Nimroud. These form a mound of an oblong form, the total circumference of which is 762 yards. At the eastern side it is cloven by a deep furrow, and is not more than 50 or 60 feet high; but at the western side it rises in a conical figure to the elevation of 198 feet, and on its summit is a solid pile of brick, 37 feet high by 28 in breadth. The fine burnt bricks of which it is built have inscriptions on them; and so excellent is the cement, which appears to be lime-mortar, that it is nearly impossible to extract one whole. The other parts of the summit of this hill are occupied by immense fragments of brickwork of no determinate figure, tumbled together and converted into solid vitrified masses, the layers of brick being perfectly discernible. These ruins stand on a prodigious mound, the whole of which is itself a ruin, channelled by the weather, and strewed with fragments of black stone, sandstone, and marble.

Buttresses and pilastres were component parts of Babylonian buildings, which were sometimes decorated with niches; the edifices generally were of bricks, either dried in the sun or burnt in a kiln or furnace. Tiles were also painted and glazed for the purpose of decorating buildings, and a very fine sort of brick was employed to case thick walls built of common bricks or rubbish. These bricks were impressed with characters. The clay of which they were formed appears to have been mixed up with chopped straw or reeds. When baked or dry they were laid in hot bitumen, sometimes in clay-mortar, and sometimes also in a fine lime-mortar. Thick piers were used for columns. Timber was scarce; and the wood-work of the houses, which were sometimes of three and four stories, was made of the date-tree. Round the posts reeds were twisted, on which a coat of paint was laid. The bitumen used in the building of Babylon is not by any means so tenacious as the mortar. Mr. Rich thinks that lime-cement was most generally employed.

In the British Museum there are many specimens of Babylonian bricks. Stones, elegantly engraved, and seal-rings were in general use among the Babylonians. Heeren is of opinion that these stones and the engraved cylinders served for signatures. These cylinders were made not only of clay, but of the hardest stones, and the Babylonians had brought the art of cutting these stones to a very high state of perfection. Heeren mentions a cylinder of jasper, and Sir R. K. Porter another of white agate.

BACON. Every one knows that bacon is pork prepared by a process in which salt, heat, and smoke are employed. Unless of the best kind, it is either prepared from inferior meat, or prepared in a defective manner. Good bacon has a thin rind; the fat has a firm consistency and a reddish tinge; and the lean adheres strongly to the bone.

As there is no excise duty on bacon, there are no means of ascertaining the quantity made in this country. Imported bacon pays a duty of 14*s.* per cwt. from foreign countries, and 3*s.* 6*d.* from the colonies. Our imports of bacon in 1848 amounted to 211,000 cwt. We export a small quantity every year to the colonies and the East Indies.

In a recent Liverpool commercial list, it is stated that the sale of foreign bacon in this country has not been brisk during the year 1850. 'We attribute this to the very plentiful supply and consequent cheapness of both Irish and English bacon. The cure of the former is estimated to have been nearly as great as during any previous season, while that of the latter has been undoubtedly much larger.' The prosperous condition of the working classes in this country enabling them to neglect almost entirely the ordinary and even middling kinds of bacon, the dealers have lately had difficulty to find a market for any but the best.

BACON. Were it possible to trace the services which were rendered to industry, through the medium of science, by Roger Bacon in the 13th century, and by Francis Bacon in the 16th and 17th, the list would doubtless be an important one; but it would belong to the biography of Science rather than of Art. The *Opus Majus* of Roger Bacon laid the groundwork for better reasoning in later ages; but the great points by which Bacon is known are his reputed knowledge of gunpowder and of the telescope. With regard to the former, it is not at all clear that what we call gunpowder is intended, though some detonating mixture, of which saltpetre is an ingredient, is spoken of as commonly known. In respect to the telescope, it must be admitted that Bacon had *conceived* the instrument, though there is no proof that he carried his conception into practice, or *invented* it. The question has been agitated whether the invention of spectacles is due to Bacon, or whether they had been introduced just before he wrote. He certainly describes them, and explains why a plane convex glass magnifies. But he seems to us to speak of them as already in use.

In respect to the far greater Francis Bacon familiarly known as Lord Bacon, the contributions to Art or Industry were more indirect; for his scientific labours applied chiefly to the logic of science, to the best means by which the human mind may master the difficulties which lie at the threshold of all scientific enquiries. He was in fact removed two stages from the philosophy of manufactures: he taught the man of science how to grasp theoretical principles; and the man of science, thus taught, was in a condition to apply his science to the practical wants of the manufacturer, the mechanist, and the engineer.

BADAKHSHAN, one of the khanats of Turkistan, is rich in gems. The celebrated ruby mines of Badakhshân, often alluded to by Persian poets, are situated at a place called Gharan, near Shughnân, near the Oxus. They are at present worked by the command of the chief of Kundûz, who has conquered this part of the country. The rubies are said to be found like round pieces of pebble or flint, and imbedded in limestone.

BADEN. The grand-duchy of Baden is rich in many kinds of produce. Agriculture is the chief occupation of its inhabitants, and yields a surplus of produce for which Switzerland and France afford a ready market. Only six acres in a thousand are said to be waste land. On an average it is stated to produce abont 1,358,000 quarters of all descriptions of grain, and exports between 75,000 and 93,000. It yields also hay and other fodder for horses and cattle in superabundance. The upper and lower districts produce rapeseed, hemp, flax, and opium; and the lower districts in particular, which include the former Palatinate of the Rhine, where the best husbandry prevails, considerable quantities of tobacco and hops. Potatoes and fruits are largely grown; and cyder, perry, and wine are made in considerable quantities. The timber trees of the grand-duchy consist principally of the fir, pine, oak, beech, birch, alder, aspen, and ash.

Among the mineral productions we may enumerate the garnet, crystal, jasper, chalcedony, and onyx; marble, alabaster, gypsum, chalk, porcelain earth, and potter's clay. Silver, copper, and lead are found along the valley of the Kinzig and Münster, and in the neighbourhood of Kork and Pforzheim. Iron ore is obtained from the mines at Stockach, Kandern, the Black Forest, Hauenstein, &c. Inconsiderable quantities of Cobalt, manganese, zinc, snlphur, coals, alum, vitriol, and bismuth, are likewise raised. Salt is procured in great abundance in the Black Forest.

The manufacturing industry of the grand-duchy does not rank high, either for its extent, or for the variety or superiority of its productions. Pforzheim, Carlsruhe, and Mannheim are the chief places. The government possesses eight iron-works; and there are others in private hands, but the produce is small. Fire-arms, iron wire, copper ware, nails, alum, vitriol, saltpetre, linen, woollen, cotton, silk, clocks, watches, jewellery, wooden ware, paper, tobacco, potash, white lead, smalt, glass, and earthenware, are manufactured in various parts of the duchy—mostly in small quantities.

The position of the country on the Rhine, Main, Neckar, and other streams, and the access which they give it to Switzerland, France, and Germany, have rendered Baden a country of extensive transit, and secured to it outlets for its own productions. The imports of Baden consist of French and other wines, colonial produce, drugs and dyes, iron, steel, cottons, silks, fine woollens, horses, cattle, &c., and its exports of timber, grain, meal, oil, skins and hides, wine, hemp, linen, tobacco, iron wares, jewellery, fish, &c.

BADGER. The hide of this animal is not without value; when properly dressed, it makes the best pistol furniture. In some parts of France badger's hides are commonly used as a sort of cover or ornament to the collar and trappings of waggon-horses. The hair is used for painter's brushes, and brushes for other purposes. The hind-quarters, when salted and smoked, make excellent hams. In China, as Bell the traveller assures us, dozens of badgers may be seen hanging for sale, as food, in the meat markets of Pekin.

BAGDAD is the name both of a pashalic and of a city, in the Tigris region of Asia. The pashalic produces the tamarisk shrub, the liquorice plant, the willow, the poplar, the castor-oil plant, the carob plant, the crowfoot, the caper, and many others. Grapes, figs, pomegranates, and quinces are largely grown; but the plants best known in England are not much cultivated. The region is not rich either in timber or in minerals.

The city of Bagdad, so famous in oriental story, was formerly a great emporium of eastern commerce. Besides the traffic with its own manufactures, it was the entrepôt for the commodities of eastern aud western Asia. But the political and commercial events of recent years have greatly reduced this commerce. The manufactures are not very numerous or extensive. The red and yellow leathers are excellent, and are held in high estimation throughout Turkey. Another principal manufacture consists of pieces of a sort of plush, in shawl patterns, often very rich and beautiful, and used by the Turks for covering the cushions which form their divans or sofas. A few other manufactures in wool and silk are carried on.

BAGPIPE, a musical instrument, which consists of a leathern bag, inflated by a port-vent fixed in it, which has a valve. It has three pipes, the first and second called the great and little drone, each giving but one note, the third, a kind of oboe having eight ventages, or holes, on which the tune is played by the fingers. The wind is communicated to the pipes by compressing the bag under the arm, the mouth-piece of each pipe being fixed in the bag. The compass of this instrument is three octaves.

A similar instrument was in use among the antients under the name of *tibia utricularis*. The bagpipe is mentioned by Chaucer as the music to which the Canterbury pilgrims performed their journey.

BAHAMAS. These West India Islands

are in general fruitful, and produce several species of trees, as mahogany, satinwood, lignum vitæ, cedars, pines, braziletto, wild cinnamon, fustic, and pimento, with a great variety of esculent vegetables. Cattle are reared in great plenty.

The chief articles of export are sugar, cotton, dyewoods, bark, fustic, salt, with turtle and fruits. The crops of cotton are often destroyed by the chenille and red bug; the latter stains the cotton so as to render it of little value. The cultivation of cotton is no longer the staple. Great numbers of pineapples are grown for sale, principally to North American traders. The islands generally produce sufficient maize and ground provisions for the use of the inhabitants. Turk's Islands afford the principal supply of salt; from one to two thousand 'rakers' visit them annually, beginning their operations in February. The Bahamas took British produce and manufactures to the value of 24,709*l.* in 1849.

BAHAR, one of the provinces of Northern India, yields large quantities of saltpetre, which is produced in artificial beds, consisting of the refuse of vegetable and animal matters in a state of decomposition, mixed with calcareous and other earths. Opium is produced very abundantly; but wheat of excellent quality is the chief produce. Rice, sugar, indigo, cotton, castor-oil, and essences, particularly the attar of roses, are among the ordinary productions of the province.

BAHAWU'LPOOR, in the province of Mooltan, is deserving of our notice in this place—not so much for its products as for the commercial energy which marks its inhabitants. The manufactures carried on by them are of silken girdles and turbans, and some species of cotton cloths called coongees, which are celebrated for the fineness of their texture: the weavers are chiefly Hindoos. The merchants of Bahawulpoor are also Hindoos; they have a great deal of commercial enterprise, and deal extensively in goods of European manufacture, which they receive from Pallee in Marwar, by way of Bicaneer and the desert of Ajmeer, and conveyed them by land-carriage through Mooltan and Lahore, crossing the Indus at Kaheree. These Bahawulpoor merchants often travel to Balk and Bokhara, and sometimes to Astrakhan, for commercial purposes.

BAHI'A, one of the maritime provinces of Brazil, is distinguished rather for commerce than for manufactures. The metals, which once formed a considerablo portion of the wealth of this province, are now of very little importance. Gold has long ago ceased to be worked: silver is found, but it would not pay the expense of working. Iron is abundant, but neglected. Copper is still worked in the northern district, but not to any great amount. The largest piece of native copper perhaps in the world (excepting one recently found on the shores of Lake Superior) was found about two miles to the east of the town of Cochocira; it weighed 1666 pounds, and is now in the Royal Museum at Lisbon. Armenian bole, antimony, saltpetre, and rock-salt, are among the mineral produce.

The chief cultivated plants are cotton, sugar, coffee, tobacco, and corn; while among the spontaneous products of the soil, possessing commercial value, are ipecacuanha, Jesuits' bark, jalap, tamarinds, Brazil root, curcuma or turmeric, betony, copal, dragon's blood, mastic, copaiba, Brazil-wood, bow-wood, iron-wood, oil-wood, cachew nut, nayha, palm, and numerous timber trees for carpentry and cabinet work.

BAHREIN is the name of a bay and an island on the Arabian coast. The chief town of the island, called Manama, is at the north-east extremity, and is large and populous, being supposed to contain upwards of 40,000 inhabitants. The bazaar is well supplied with cattle, sheep, poultry, fish and vegetables; and a very considerable trade is carried on. Upwards of 140 vessels of various sizes are employed in trading; but the pearl fishery is of the greatest importanco to tho island, which in the season employs 2,400 boats, each containing from eight to twenty men. The annual produce of these fisheries amounts, it is said, to sixteen or twenty lacs of dollars.

BAIGORRY, a valley in the south of France, has rich copper and iron mines, and large copper and iron works for smelting and refining the ores.

BAIKAL. The mineral productions on the shores of this extensive Asiatic lake are noticed under ALTAI MOUNTAINS.

BAIREUTH, in Bavaria, has tan-yards, manufactories for making tobacco-pipes, parchment, linen, porcelain and earthenware, cottons, and stockings; and the inhabitants carry on considerable trade in grain and flour.

BAKEWELL, is situated in the middle of that part of Derbyshire which is so rich in mineral produce. There are stone and marble quarries at Ashford, and lead mines at some little distance from Bakewell, which afford employment to numerous labourers belonging to the town and its vicinity. The marble, a very beautiful black kind, is wrought here into a great variety of useful and ornamental objects; and the inlaying of it with a species of mosaic is carried on with great skill. Those who are familiar with the contents of the

British Museum will remember two beautiful tables in the Mineralogical Gallery made of Bakewell marble. Near the town is a cotton manufactory established by Arkwright; but during the last ten years it has only been worked occasionally.

In the parish of Bakewell there is one building which will ever be associated with the recollection of Mr. Paxton's Crystal Palace in Hyde Park—we mean *Chatsworth.* The unequalled conservatory which Mr. Paxton constructed for the Duke of Devonshire in the grounds of that palatial residence was the forerunner of the building now being erected for the Exhibition of Industry. This building, and the relation between it and the Hyde Park structure, will be found described a few pages later [CONSERVATORY].

BAKING. [BREAD.]

BAKU. This peninsula, which juts into the west side of the Caspian Sea, is celebrated for its numerous volcanoes, which discharge volumes of mud; but still more for the superabundance of naphtha with which its soil is charged, particularly in the neighbourhood of the capital. It not only issues spontaneously through the surface, but rises wherever a hole is bored. It is of two descriptions, black and white; and its principal sources are situated at a spot called Balegan, about 6 miles from Baku. The whole of these naphtha springs belong to the government, and are farmed at a rental of about 9000*l*.

BALAGHAUTS, a district near the Madras coast of India, exports indigo and cotton in considerable quantities. The central and eastern divisions contain several diamond mines; and it is from these, and not from mines in their own district, that the diamond merchants of Golconda have been supplied.

BALANCE. The instrument most commonly known by the term balance is a superior sort of scales, executed with all the precision necessary for the nicest operations of physics, and particularly of chemistry.

A balance should be so sensible that, when equipoised, a very small additional weight in either scale may overcome the friction and adherence of the pivot by which it rests; and the diminution of friction to the utmost possible extent is accomplished by giving the supports a high polish and attaching a knife-edge pivot to each side of the beam. The knife-edges must not be so sharp as to cut the supports; and, to prevent them from becoming too blunt, they are in some balances removed from the supports, when the instruments are not in use, by an apparatus for the purpose.

The sensibility of a balance is estimated by the angular deviation of the beam from a horizontal position when a very small weight is placed in one scale: thus, if one grain placed in a scale of each of two balances should make the beam of the first incline two degrees, and that of the second four degrees, the latter balance would be twice as sensible as the former. The quantities weighed in delicate balances are usually small. A balance made by Ramsden for the Royal Society, weighing ten pounds altogether, turned with the ten-millionth of that quantity, or with about the thousandth part of a grain.

A balance should be made as much as possible of brass. Steel and iron are apt to acquire magnetic properties. It should also be enclosed in a glass case, with doors for communication.

Mr. Cotton's beautiful apparatus, employed at the Bank for weighing sovereigns, is described under GOLD-WEIGHING MACHINE. The more ordinary balances for commercial purposes are noticed under STEELYARD; WEIGHING MACHINES.

BALASO'RE, a large town, not far from Calcutta, affords an instructive example of the mode in which British manufactures become spread among the islands of the east. The trade carried on here is principally with the Maldives' islanders, whose boats, constructed of the trunks of cocoa-nut trees, arrive at Balasore in the months of June and July, during the south-west monsoon. Their import cargoes consist of coir, cocoa-nut oil, and other products of the cocoa-nut tree, which is their grand staple; cowries, tortoise-shell, and salted fish. These articles they exchange for rice, sugar, broad-cloths, stuffs of silk and cotton, hardwares, and cutlery; and with these they return home during the month of December, favoured by the north-east monsoon. Some trade is likewise carried on in salt, which is made on the sea-shore a few miles from the town, by lixiviating the mud in the manner practised in the Sunderbunds of Bengal.

BALAS RUBY, a term used by lapidaries to designate the rose-red varieties of Spinel. It should be carefully distinguished from oriental ruby (the sapphire), a gem of much greater rarity and value.

BALCONY. Balconies are much employed in edifices of modern date. They are formed nearly on a level with the floors of rooms, and supported on cantilevers or brackets, and sometimes, though more rarely, on columns of wood or stone. The floor of the balcony is laid on the cantilevers, and the sides are enclosed with a rail of iron, or a balustrade of stone. Since the introduction of Grecian architecture some balconies have been inclosed with small Greek columns, instead of the baluster used by the Italian architects. In Venice there are very magnificent balconies in the Gothic taste, remarkable for their richness. Elizabethan architecture shows some very elaborately designed balconies; but perhaps the nearest example to the *palco* of the Italians will be found in some of the colleges of Oxford. Magdalen College contains an example of such a balcony in a pulpit supported on corbels.

BA'LDACHIN, a kind of canopy, either supported on columns, or suspended from and used to cover an altar in a Roman Catholic church. The form, for the most part, is square, and the top covered with cloth with a hanging fringe: sometimes the fringe is formed of pieces of cloth cut out after the fashion of a banner. The baldachin in St. Peter's at Rome, made by Bernini, is the most celebrated, and is the largest known work of the kind in bronze.

BALEA'RIC ISLANDS. These Mediterranean islands, comprising Majorca, Minorca, and three others, yield granite, marble, jasper, porphyry, slate, and pit-coal, also lead and iron. The soil is generally good, and chiefly cultivated with vines, olives, and other fruit-trees: corn is not produced in sufficient quantities for home consumption. This article and cattle form the principal imports, in exchange for wines and brandies of an inferior quality, coarse woollen cloths, and dried fruits; the pottery made in these islands is much esteemed.

BALIZE, or BELIZE. [HONDURAS.]

BALKAN. The natural riches of this extensive Turkish mountain system are very imperfectly known. The silver and gold mines worked by the ancients are not now known. Yet, in some parts, mines of this description are worked, as at Kostendil, or Guistendil, not far from the sources of the Karasa Struma, in the Egrisu Dagh. In the same range, farther to the west, are considerable mines of copper, which are also found in the Emineh Dagh, near Shumla, and probably in other places. Iron seems also to be abundant, and is got from the Dupishna Dagh, near the place which has given to this range its name. In many parts there are mines of lead, and in others rock-salt in great abundance. Marble is abundant in the southern ranges.

BALKH. This once celebrated Asiatic city has sunk into insignificance. Its commerce and manufactures have been superseded by those of Bokhara.

BALLAST, a term used to denote any heavy material placed in a ship's hold with the object of sinking her deeper in the water, and of thereby rendering her capable of carrying sail without danger of being overset. Ships are said to be in ballast when they sail without a cargo, having on board only the stores and other articles requisite for the use of the vessel and crew, as well as of any passengers who may be proceeding with her upon the voyage. In favour of vessels thus circumstanced it is usual to dispense with many formalities at the custom-houses of the ports of departure and entry, and to remit the payment of certain dues and port charges which are levied upon ships having cargoes on board.

A foreign vessel proceeding from a British port may take on board chalk as ballast. Regulations have at various times been made in different ports and countries determining the modes in which ships may be supplied with ballast, and in what manner they may discharge the same; such regulations being necessary to prevent injury to harbours.

Iron weights are sometimes used as ballast, but sand is more extensively employed. All the empty Newcastle coal ships carry river-sand ballast on their return voyages to the north; and the hoisting and shipping of this ballast in the Thames amounts to 10,000 tons per week.

BALLISTIC PENDULUM, a rectangular block of elm weighing from 600 to 2800 lbs., and suspended by an iron stem from a horizontal axle, which rests upon the upper part of a strong frame of timber standing on the ground, or, for the sake of greater stability, inserted in the wall of a building. It is used for determining the velocities of shot discharged from a gun by given quantities of powder. The shot being made to strike the block in the direction of its fibres, and entering it to a certain distance, causes it to vibrate on the horizontal axis of the machine, when, by the extent of the vibrations, measured from a vertical plane passing through the axis, the velocities at the instant of striking are found.

The block is strongly bound by bars of iron, and, in order to obtain the extent of a vibration, a tongue of iron terminating below in a point projects from the lowest surface of the block; and this tongue makes a mark which indicates the extent of the vibration.

By the Ballistic Pendulum has been obtained almost all the information we possess respecting the velocities of cannon balls and the resistance of the air in the case of bodies in rapid motion.

BA'LLIUM. This term antiently meant an outer bulwark; but was afterwards adopted for the area or court-yard contained within one. In towns, the appellation of ballium was given to a work fenced with palisades, and sometimes masonry, covering the suburbs. When there was a double enclosure of walls, the areas between the walls and within the interior wall were styled respectively the outer and inner ballia.

The name Bailey, as the Old Bailey, in London, and the church of St. Peter in the Bailey, in Oxford, seems to have been derived from ballium.

BALLOON. A balloon generally consists of a bag of silk, or other light material, inflated with gas or heated air, so that, being lighter than an equal bulk of common air, it will rise from the earth with sufficient force to lift a car, in which persons may perform an aërial voyage.

The notion of flying or sailing through the air, evidently suggested by the flight of birds, is very ancient; but passing over the early fables or traditions on the subject, we find the first idea of a real balloon suggested by the Jesuit Francis Lana, in a work published in 1670. The actual invention of balloons, however, is of much later date, and is due to Stephen and Joseph de Montgolfier, paper-manufacturers at Annonay, near Lyon. They first tried to confine hydrogen in paper. Failing in this, in consequence of the escape of the gas through the pores of the paper, they succeeded in raising a small balloon by heating and thereby rarefying the air within it. The balloon was made of large pieces of paper 110 feet in circumference, fixed to a frame, the whole weighing about 500 pounds, and containing 22,000 cubic feet (French measure). On the application of fire underneath, the mass gradually unfolded and assumed the form of a large globe, striving at the same time to burst from the arms which held it. At length it rose with great rapidity, and in less than ten minutes was at 1000 toises of elevation. It then described a horizontal line of 7,200 feet, and gradually sank. This balloon contained nothing but heated air, maintained in a state of rarefaction by a fire, the receptacle of which was attached underneath the globe of paper, which had an orifice opening downwards. This occurred in 1783.

Very soon afterwards balloons were made of varnished silk, and small animals were caused to ascend in them, or suspended from them.

In November M. Pilâtre de Rozier made the first aeronautical voyage attempted with a free balloon. The balloon used was a Montgolfier (fire balloon), 70 feet high, and 46 feet in diameter. It ascended from the Château de la Muette, near Passey, gained an elevation of at least 3000 feet, and, after catching fire, which was easily extinguished by the intrepid voyagers, descended safely, after a journey of 5000 toises (about 6 miles), which was performed in from twenty to twenty-five minutes. On the 1st of December M. Charles ascended to the height of 1500 toises (nearly 2 miles), in a hydrogen balloon of 26 feet diameter, from the Tuileries; and on the 19th of January seven persons ascended in a Montgolfier 126 feet high, and 102 feet in diameter. To reduce the above measures, which are French, to the English standard, it should be remembered that the French foot was equal to 12.7892 English inches.

On the 22nd of February, 1784, a small balloon, launched by itself from Sandwich, crossed the Channel; and in the course of that year several personal ascents were made with both kinds of balloon. M. Blanchard, in his first ascent from Paris on the 2nd of March, with a hydrogen balloon, added wings and a rudder, but found them useless. He also first attached a parachute, or open umbrella, above the car, to break his fall in case of becoming accidentally separated from the balloon. In one of the French ascents of this year the use of oars was tried, with, it was thought, some effect. In England a hydrogen balloon of 10 feet in diameter was launched from the Artillery Ground, London, by Count Zambeccari, on the 25th of November, 1783; but the first personal ascent was made by Vincentio Lunardi, from the same place, on the 15th of September, 1784. On the 7th of January, 1785, M. Blanchard and Dr. Jeffries crossed the Channel from Dover; and on the 15th of June following M. Pilâtre de Rozier and M. Romain ascended from Boulogne with the same object, with a Montgolfier, which caught fire, and precipitated them from a height of 1000 yards. Among the more memorable subsequent ascents may be mentioned that of M. Garnerin in 1802, from London, on which occasion he descended successfully by means of a parachute; that of the same person from Paris, in 1807, in which, after encountering great risks, he landed at, or rather was dashed against, Mount Tonnerre, at a distance of 300 miles from his starting-point; that of MM. Gay Lussac and Biot, from Paris, in 1804, to the height of 13,000 feet, for the purpose of making scientific observations; the subsequent ascent of M. Gay Lussac alone, in the same year, to the height of 23,000 feet; and the attempt made in 1806, by Carlo Brioschi, astronomer royal at Naples, and Signor

Andreani, to attain a yet greater elevation; when they reached an atmosphere so rarefied that the balloon burst, its remains proving, however, sufficient to break their fall so that their lives were saved.

Although much has been suggested, very little has been accomplished towards rendering balloons available for any practical use. Little has been done towards guiding a balloon. Many of the schemes which have been proposed for the purpose evince a singular disregard of the essential difference between a ship and a balloon. The former sails in two fluids of very different density, and the action of the water, the denser of the two, upon the rudder is a guide to the impelling power derived from the air, or lighter or less dense element; but no such regulator can be applied to the balloon, which is sustained, as well as impelled, by the air.

Mr. Green has been the most successful of our æronauts. He was the first to introduce the use of common coal gas instead of hydrogen gas for the purpose of inflation, by which an immense saving of cost is effected, and the buoyancy of the balloon may be longer maintained, as it is far less liable to escape. Mr. Green, accompanied by Messrs. Holland and Monck Mason, made the remarkable voyage undertaken on the 7th of November, 1836, with the Great Nassau balloon. Intending to cross over to the continent, these voyagers started from Vauxhall Gardens, London, at half-past one on the above-named day, crossed the Channel, continued their voyage through the night, and descended at half-past seven the following morning in the valley of Elbern, about two leagues from Weilburg, in the duchy of Nassau. The balloon with which this feat was performed is of silk, more than 60 feet high, and about 50 feet in diameter, and will contain, when fully distended, more than 85,000 cubic feet of gas.

We can hardly avoid an expression of regret that so much ingenuity should be still unprofitably wasted on ballooning. Year after year contrivances are brought forward which have before been shown to be unsound in theory. In 1840 Messrs. Marsh and Ranwell suggested a complicated machine, consisting of a light metallic frame, to which about twenty small balloons were attached. Sir George Cayley has proposed a light kind of frame, exposing about 500 square feet of surface, to which some sort of steering apparatus is to be attached. Mr. Partridge has drawn attention to a machine which had somewhat the appearance of an ovoid balloon; with a complicated apparatus of sails and vanes; and a steam engine fed with liquid fuel! M. Eubriot, in 1839, made an oblong balloon, with a car provided with sails; he expected that the car and sails would guide the balloon; but when the machine was tried at Paris, the balloon guided the car, as it is the wont of balloons to do. Mr. Green himself, in 1840, exhibited a model at the Polytechnic Institution, of an apparatus which he expected would suffice to guide a balloon; but we may conclude that nothing satisfactory has resulted. About ten years ago, Dr. Polli, of Milan, suggested that the structure of a fish should form a model for an aerial locomotive; but he was forestalled in this obvious but fallacious idea, by other parties in England. In 1842 Mr. Henson took out his patent for that "aerial machine" which lived its little day of popularity, and then went out of sight; a small steam-engine, in a car, was to propel a light framework 150 feet long; and a tail 50 feet long was to serve as a rudder at one end; but whether the machine could raise itself to a height, or could propel itself by the engine, or could steer itself by the tail, were enquiries never satisfactorily answered. Next came M. Monge's copper balloon, constructed at Paris in 1844; it was about 30 feet diameter, formed of sheet copper $\frac{1}{200}$th of an inch thick, weighed 300 lbs., and was capable of containing 100 lb. of hydrogen; but of its success we have heard nothing. The egg-shape, the fish-shape, the fan-shape, the kite-shape, all have been proposed, time after time, within the last few years; one of the latest being that of Mr. Bell, who recently patented two machines—a *balloon motor*, having both a sustaining and a propelling power; and a *parachute motor*, having a propelling power which constituted its own sustaining power. The plan looked ingenious upon paper, but this is not very high praise.

Occasionally balloons are made subsidiary to science; but very seldom. The British Association has more than once directed its attention to this matter, but with very little result. In 1843 Mr. Green made observations with meteorological instruments, at five different elevations, varying from 2591 to 6758 feet; while Mr. Jones, the instrument maker, was making similar observations at the surface of the earth at the same time—such observations as these might perhaps be multiplied with advantage. Mr. Rush communicated to the British Association, in 1849, a series of thermometrical and barometrical observations, made during five balloon ascents, in 1847-8-9, at various altitudes ranging up to 20,000 feet. One of the latest suggestions, for making balloons useful, was that recently made by the unfortunate Lieutenant Gale, for rendering assistance in the search of Sir John Franklin.

During the recent ballooning season, it was stated that the number of recorded ascents exceeds 3000, of which the elder Green has made nearly 500; and that the ascertained fatal accidents do not amount to 20.

Of the sad foolery of ascending on the backs of horses, ponies, and other animals, nothing can be said but in condemnation. The last example was that in which Madame Poitevin, decked in white muslin and purple velvet, with a crown of roses on her head, ascended from the Champ de Mars on the back of a *bullock!*

BALSAMODE'NDRON, a genus of Oriental trees, is deserving of our notice here as producing *Myrrh*, and *Balsam of Gilead.* Myrrh exudes from the bark, and is at first soft, oily, and of a yellowish-white colour, then acquires the consistence of butter, and by exposure to the air becomes harder, and changes to a reddish hue. As met with in commerce, it is of two kinds, that which is called *myrrh in tears*, and that called *myrrh in sorts.* The smell is peculiar and rather disagreeable, the taste is bitter and very unpleasant.

The alcoholic tincture of the best myrrh, mixed with equal parts of nitric acid, becomes red or violet. The tincture of the false myrrh (of Bonastre) so treated becomes turbid and yellow, but not red. The taste of this false myrrh is very bitter, but the smell is that of turpentine.

The produce of the *Balsamodendron Gileadense*, though called a balsam, and denominated Balsam of Mecca and Balsam of Gilead, is not entitled chemically to rank as such, being an oleo-resin. It is of two kinds, that obtained by spontaneous exudation, and that which is obtained by boiling the branches. The former is so highly prized in the East and so expensive, that it is never brought to Europe. It is said that even in Constantinople there are only two shops whence it can be procured genuine, and where it costs about 1*s.* per grain English. That which is obtained by boiling is of different qualities and value, according as the boiling is continued for a short or long time. When for a short time only, the substance which floats on the surface is highly esteemed, and almost all of this quality is consumed in Asiatic Turkey and Egypt. The variety procured by long-continued boiling is sent to Europe in small conical leaden bottles, the mouth of which is closed with a leaden stopper, and covered over with bladder. It is, however, frequently adulterated on account of its high price; and the cheaper kinds ordinarily sold contain not an atom of the real balsam.

BALSAMS. The substances commonly included under this title are of various natures. There are natural balsams exuding from trees, as those of Peru and Tolu, &c., which contain benzoic acid and resin. There are also the balsams of Copaiba, Gilead, &c., which contain no benzoic acid, but are turpentines containing a volatile oil and resin. There were in former pharmacopœias sundry very different preparations ranked together as balsams, such as balsam of sulphur, traumatic balsam, &c.: these, when retained in modern pharmacopœias, are arranged under other forms.

Balsams are obtained from certain vegetables, chiefly of the *Leguminosæ*, or pea tribe, the *Styraceæ*, or Storax tribe, and that section of *Amentaceæ* called *Salicineæ.* Numerous substances of a resinous nature were formerly designated *balsams*, and turpentines and balsams are still popularly confounded with each other. The term balsam, however, should be limited to such articles as contain *benzoic acid* along with a volatile oil and resin. The others, which contain only volatile oil and resin, should be called turpentines, or oleo-resins. The true balsams appear to be only five, viz. balsam of Peru and balsam of Tolu, benzoin, storax, and liquidamber.

Balsams command very varied prices in the wholesale market, from 1*s.* to 6*s.* per lb.

BALTIC SEA. The countries surrounding this very important sea supply timber, grain of different kinds, hides, tallow, &c., in the greatest abundance and of the first quality. If we except the seas contiguous to the British islands, and that which incloses the maritime tracts of the Chinese empire, no portion of the ocean is so much frequented by ships as the Baltic; and this in spite of the difficulties of the navigation. From 13,000 to 15,000 ships enter and leave the Baltic every year, of which about one-fourth are British. It is thought that 2 per cent. of the vessels which visit the Baltic are annually lost, while the commerce between Great Britain and America is carried on with the loss of 1 per cent. Besides this, the harbours of the Baltic are shut up for three or four months by the ice, and thus the navigation is interrupted for nearly one-third of the year. Another disadvantage is the shallowness of the harbours on the southern coast, and the complete want of tides. These difficulties render it necessary that the vessels employed in the Baltic trade should be of comparatively small burthen, averaging from 200 to 300 tons.

BALTIMORE. This important American city has great trade. The exports consist principally of tobacco, wheat, wheat-flour, maize, hemp, and flax; and its imports, of colonial produce and the principal European products and manufactures. Its export trade has of late years been greatly increased by the railroads which connect the town with Philadelphia, Washington, Ohio, York in Pennsylvania, &c.; by these the products of the interior, including even the valley of the Mississippi, find a rapid transit to Baltimore, whence they are shipped to various parts of the United States and of Europe. There are lines of steam-packets to Philadelphia and to Norfolk, and other packets to New York and various parts of the Atlantic. The water power of the Jones' Falls and of the Patapsco, which has a fall of 800 feet in a course of 30 miles, is made available in the numerous flour mills, cotton factories, and other manufactories of cloth, paper, iron, copper, glass, steam-engines, tobacco, chemicals, powder, &c., in the environs of the city. In the city itself there are cotton factories, tanneries, distilleries, breweries, sugar refineries, potteries, saw-mills, glass-works, rope-walks, tobacco manufactories, printing-offices, &c.

BALUSTER, or BALLISTER, a peculiar kind of column employed in balustrades. The baluster has also of late years been formed after the model of Greek and Roman columns. Balusters are placed on a plinth, and are surmounted with a cornice.

BALUSTRADE, the termination of a modern edifice. Balustrades are most commonly placed over the cornices of large edifices, after the manner of a parapet, as at the Banqueting House at Whitehall, and St. Paul's Cathedral. Balustrades are not only employed in large edifices, above the orders of architecture, but also to inclose stairs, terraces, altars, fonts, and the balconies of houses. The balusters forming a balustrade are placed on a plinth, at equal distances from one another, with a small opening between them: they support a cornice, and are divided at intervals by a pedestal.

BAMBARRA. The chief mineral wealth of this African region is iron: it abounds in many districts, and the inhabitants make utensils of this metal, which are exported to the neighbouring nations. Gold is also found. Salt is imported in large quantitities from the Sahara and the coasts of Guinea. Dried fish is a considerable article of commerce.

Bambarra carries on a very active commerce though it is limited to a small number of commodities. The principal trading places are Jennée, Sansanding, Sego, Yamina, Bammaku, and Boure, all of which are on the Joliba. The last, which lies to the south-west of Bammaku, is the principal market for gold. Besides gold, the principal articles of exchange are slaves, ivory, and coarse cotton cloth made by the natives; they are exchanged for salt brought from the desert, for tobacco, and European merchandise. In their way to the northern countries they pass through Timbuctu, which is the general dépôt for them. There seems also to exist some trade with the coast of Guinea, from which salt is imported.

BAMBERG, in Bavaria, has many points of interest as a commercial town. Among the numerous incorporations in this town is that of the gardeners, which consists of 508 masters, 70 apprentices, and upwards of 250 workmen. The highest prize which it gives —and it is given but once in three years—is for the cultivation of officinal plants, particularly the liquorice root, of which above 50,000 lbs. are annually exported. Very considerable quantities of vegetable seeds are raised and exported by the Bamberg growers. There are sixty brewers here, whose beer is in much demand in some of the German states. The other manufactures consist of tobacco, porcelain, musical instruments, marble wares, starch, sealing-wax, gold and silver plate, gloves, &c. Two annual fairs give life to the trade of the town, the situation of which enables it to share largely in the traffic of central Germany.

BAMBOO, or BAMBUSA. This very useful genus of grass is distinguished by its *stems*, which are hard externally and coated with flint; in the inside they are hollow, except at the nodes, where strong partitions stretch across the inside, and cut off the interior into a number of closed up cylinders.

The purposes to which different species of bamboo are applied are so numerous, that it would be difficult to point out an object in which strength and elasticity are requisite, and for which lightness is no objection, to which the stems are not adapted in the countries where they grow. The young shoots of some species are cut when tender, and eaten like asparagus. The full grown stems, while green, form elegant cases, exhaling a perpetual moisture, and capable of transporting fresh flowers for hundreds of miles: when ripe and hard, they are converted into bows, arrows, and quivers, lance-shafts, the masts of vessels, bed-posts, walking-sticks, the poles of palanquins, the floors and supporters of rustic bridges, and a variety of similar purposes. In a growing state the spiny kinds are formed into stockades, which are impenetrable to any but regular infantry, aided by artillery. By notching their sides, the Malays make wonderfully light scaling-ladders which can be conveyed with facility where heavier machines could not be transported. Bruised and crushed in water, the leaves and stems form Chinese paper, the finer qualities of which are improved by a mixture of raw cotton and by more careful pounding. The leaves of a small species are the material used by the Chinese for the lining of their tea chests. Cut into lengths and the partitions knocked out, they form durable water-pipes, or, by a little contrivance, are made into excellent cases for holding rolls of papers. Slit into strips, they afford a most durable material for weaving into mats, baskets, window-blinds, and even the sails of boats. Finally, the larger and thicker truncheons are exquisitely carved by the Chinese into beautiful ornaments. It is however more especially for building purposes that the bamboo is important. In Sumatra the frame-work of the houses of the natives is chiefly composed of this material. In the floorings, whole stems, four or five inches in diameter, are laid close to each other, and across these laths of split bamboo about an inch wide, are fastened down with filaments of the rattan-cane. The sides of the houses are closed in with the bamboo opened and rendered flat by splitting or notching the circular joints on the outside, chipping away the corresponding divisions within, and laying it in the sun to dry, pressed down with weights. Whole bamboos often form the upupright timbers, and the house is generally roofed in with a thatch of narrow split bamboos, six feet long, placed in regular layers, each reaching within two feet of the extremity of that beneath it, by which a treble covering is formed. Another and most ingenious roof is also formed by cutting large straight bamboos of sufficient length to reach from the ridge to the eaves, then splitting them exactly in two, knocking out the partitions, and arranging them in close order with the hollow or inner sides uppermost; after which a second layer, with the outer or convex sides up, is placed upon the other in such a manner that each of the convex falls into the two contiguous concave pieces, covering their edges; the latter serving as gutters to carry off the rain that falls upon the upper or convex layer.

BAMBOUK, in Northern Africa, is a country which yields silver and iron of excellent quality, and also a great quantity of gold. The principal gold mines of Bambouk are situated to the south of the city of Bambouk, in the mountains of Tambaoura; but a greater quantity seems to be obtained by washing the sand which tho rivers havo carried down from the mountains and imbedded along their courses in the alluvial soil.

Part of the gold is converted into ornaments for the women. When a lady of consequence is in full dress, her gold ornaments may be worth altogether from 50*l.* to 80*l.* sterling. But the greater part of this metal is annually carried away by the Moors, who take it to Timbuctu, whence it finds its way to the northern coast of Africa, to Egypt, and to Asia. It is exchanged for other commodities, but chiefly for salt, the value of which article is very great in these mountainous countries of Africa. One slab, about two feet and a half in length, fourteen inches in breadth, and two inches in thickness, will sometimes sell for 2*l.* 10*s.* sterling; and from 1*l.* 15*s.* to 2*l.* may be considered as the common price. This salt is brought from tho Desert of Sahara. The European merchandise brought from the coast, has till lately been generally paid for with slaves.

BANBURY, in Oxfordshire, has long been noted as a thriving place of trade. The neighbourhood is very thickly covered with villages. The trade chiefly depends on the agricultural neighbourhood; but there is a considerable manufacture of plush, shag, and girth and other webbing, carried on at Banbury, which employs within the parish above a hundred men, besides women and children, in some branches of the manufacture; and many others are engaged in the same manufacture in some of the adjacent villages. A manufacture of linen-weaving, formerly carried on at Banbury, has been abandoned. There is also a manufactory of agricultural implements.

The Banbury Cakes, which have been celebrated from the time of Ben Jonson, are still in high repute; and are not only sold in the town and neighbourhood but sent to considerable distances. They have been exported to America, Australia, and India. The Banbury cheese, which Shakspere and Burton mention, is believed to be no longer made; though a peculiar kind of rich cream cheese is still made in the neighbourhood of Banbury at a late season of the year, whence it is known as 'latter made cheese,' and fetches a high price.

Banbury agricultural implements, and Banbury cakes are to take part in the Exhibition of Industry in 1851.

BANCA, an island in the Indian Ocean lying off the north coast of Sumatra, derives all its importance in a commercial point of view, from its tin-mines, which were first discovered in 1710 or 1711, and have since yielded immense quantities of ore: they appear in fact to be inexhaustible. The ore (an oxide), after being washed in the nearest mountain stream, is smelted, and yields in various proportions from thirty to seventy pounds of tin, for every hundred pounds of ore; the more usual proportion is about sixty of metal to one hundred of ore. If the ore should yield less than twenty-five per cent. of metal, the mine is abandoned as unprofitable. The proportion of metal partly depends upon the quality of the charcoal used in smelting.

From the time of their first discovery, the tin-mines of Banca have been worked by Chinese, whose numbers have been annually recruited. The quantity of tin procured was about 3,000,000 lbs. annually, at the time of cession to the Dutch; since which time it has largely increased; so largely, indeed, that after fully supplying the markets of China and India, a large quantity is annually brought to Europe, where it has consequently lessened the demand for the tin of Cornwall.

BAND, in architecture, a flat moulding, with a vertical face slightly projecting beyond the vertical or curved face of any moulding or parts of an edifice to which it is attached. It is very extensively employed, and is used to give an appearance of binding parts of buildings together.

BANDA ISLANDS, a small group of islands in the Malay Archipelago. These islands produce the nutmeg almost exclusively, whence they are frequently called the Nutmeg Islands, in contradistinction to the Amboynas, which yield the clove.

BANDANAS, or BANDANNAS, a name originally applied to a peculiar kind of silk handkerchief made by the Hindoos, is now given to silk and cotton handkerchiefs manufactured in this country, decorated with patterns of similar character, though by a very different process. A bandana handkerchief has a dyed ground, usually of a bright red or blue, ornamented with circular, lozenge-shaped, or other simple figures, either white, or in some cases of a yellow colour. These spots are said to be produced, in real Indian bandanas, by tying up the parts intended to be white or yellow with bits of thread before exposing the handkerchief to the action of the dye, and thus protecting them from it. In the process followed by British manufacturers, which was invented in 1810 by M. Köchlin of Mühlhausen, the whole surface of the handkerchief is dyed of one uniform colour; a number of pieces thus dyed are laid between two leaden plates perforated with holes wherever white spots are intended to be, and while the several thicknesses of cloth are compressed in this manner by the power of a hydraulic press, a fluid capable of discharging the dye is made to percolate through the holes in the leaden plates, removing, in its passage, the dye from such parts of the cloth as are exposed to its action. By varying the discharging fluid the spots may be made yellow instead of white; and arrangements are sometimes made for combining white and yellow spots in the same handkerchief.

Messrs. Monteith's Bandanna Works, near Glasgow, are among the finest of our factory establishments.

BANGALORE, in the Mysore territory, is a busy commercial place. Its merchants carry on dealings with every part of the south of India. The principal articles which enter into this commerce are salt, sugar, betel-nut, spices, metals, dyeing-stuffs, raw silk, and cotton wool. Many of these articles are imported for the use of its manufacturers. The tissues woven here, both of silk and cotton, are almost entirely retained for the use of the district. The spinning of cotton is all performed by women, who carry their yarn to a weekly market for sale to the weavers.

BANGKOK, the capital of the kingdom of Siam, is a place of considerable trade. The most active commerce is carried on with the ports of the Chinese empire; but the trade between Singapore and other places of the neighbourhood has greatly increased of late years. The internal commerce with the extensive countries drained by the river Menam is also very important.

BANGOR. This Welsh city owes its trade almost entirely to slates, which are brought to Port Penrhyn from the quarries of Llandegai, a place about 8 miles distant, by means of a railway made for the purpose. These quarries give constant employment to upwards of 2000 workmen, and they produce a large revenue to the proprietor. It is stated by Mr. Parry, 'Cambrian Mirror,' p. 152, that '90 years ago these quarries brought only 80*l*. a year to the pocket of the proprietor; and now it is said that the present honourable and fortunate possessor receives the enormous and almost incredible sum of 250,000*l*. a year.' But this no doubt means the produce of the quarries, from which all working expenses have to be deducted. The greater part of the slates are exported, but many are manufactured in Bangor into billiard tables, chimney-piers, and a great variety of objects. One slate manufactory is on a very extensive scale, and there are several less extensive. All of them have been established within a few years; indeed the application of slate to these purposes is quite recent. In addition to the dock and wharfs at Port Penryhn, a new shipping place has just been erected at Garth for shipping slates from another quarry.

BANISTER. [BALUSTER.]

BANJARMASSIN, a town on the south coast of the island of Borneo, carries on a considerable trade with China. The imports of the town are principally of piece goods, cutlery, opium, gunpowder, and fire-arms. The produce exported in return consists of pepper, diamonds, gold dust, wax, camphor, spices, rattans, and edible birds' nests. Some steel of very superior quality is also manufactured at this place.

BANK — BANKER — BANKING. Important as the principle of banking is to the development of manufactures and commerce, it would be impossible so to treat the subject as to bring it within the limits of the present work. There is, however, one aspect of the subject, of much moment to the operative classes, treated under SAVINGS BANKS.

BANK NOTE MACHINERY. Considerable mechanical ingenuity has been shewn in devising the best mode of manufacturing bank notes, so that they shall be light, durable, and not easily imitated by forgers. The making of the paper, the engraving of the steel-plate, and the numbering of the notes, have all called forth this ingenuity.

It was stated some short time ago in the public journals that many of the banks in the United States have adopted the use of a peculiar kind of paper made expressly for bank-notes. There are introduced into the body of the piece of paper for each note as many cotton threads as will shew the value of the note in dollars, up to certain limits; or at least, that a definite number of threads shall represent a definite value in the note; so that no chemical or mechanical tampering with the printed part of the note will prevent the paper from revealing the true original value.

In respect to the plates from which bank-notes are printed, they used to be formed of copper; but as this material soon wears away, a mode of using steel plates was devised by Messrs. Perkins and Heath, by which a surprising number of copies may be taken. A block or thick plate of steel is softened on the upper side; the device is engraved on this softened surface; the block is hardened by a very careful process after the engraving; the device is transferred from the hardened block to the convex surface of a small soft steel roller, by intense pressure; the roller is hardened, and the device is transferred from it to any number of softened steel plates; these plates are hardened after the transfer, and are then in a state to be printed from. By this beautiful train of operations one originally engraved block is made to suffice for an almost endless number of printings.

The mode in which the writing, the emblems, and the ornaments are combined in a bank-note, is so planned as to render forgery difficult. The *numbering* is a remarkable process, as now performed. In 1809, the bank adopted a numbering press invented by Mr. Bramah, by which the expense and uncertainty of finishing annually a large number of bank notes with a pen was materially diminished, and forgery rendered more difficult. The machine was, however, so far incomplete that it produced only units, the tens and hundreds requiring to be brought forward by hand. In 1813 a machine invented by Mr. John Oldham, and used at the Bank of Ireland, had the additional power of effecting numerical progression, from 1 to 100,000 by its own operation; one of these machines was subsequently attached to each press for printing the body of the notes, in order to register and check the number of notes passing through the press.

In 1819 Mr. Bryan Donkin invented a counting machine, applicable to the numbering of notes. Like most others of the kind, its action depended on the relative motion of a series of ratchet wheels with projecting rims, having notches cut in them; so that when the first wheel counted units, the second wheel indicated tens, and so on progressively. When Mr. Thomas Oldham succeeded his father, Mr. John Oldham, as engineer to the Bank of England, he endeavoured to improve on the instruments previously constructed, and devised the form of apparatus now employed, which is as follows:—Four wheels each divided by ten notches, leaving a facet between each pair, engraved with consecutive numbers from 1 to 0, are placed upon a shaft; a portion of their breadth being turned down about one-half of their depth, having a boss or collar between every two. Upon these bosses, and filling up the spaces, rest latches; and over each wheel is a pall, the width of the first being equal to that of the unit wheel, and the breadth of the others equalling that of the wheel and latch. The palls are driven by a crank; by each revolution of which the first wheel is moved through a space equal to one tenth of its entire circumference, bringing regularly forward the numbers from 1 to 0. When the figure 0 is reached, the latch of the second wheel is depressed, and the wheel moves forward one division marking the tens. The same process is repeated with regard to the other wheels, and thus any amount of numbers can be registered, by simply increasing the number of wheels in proportion. Machines of this kind are extensively adopted in the Bank of England; with, of course, an inking apparatus to apply to the types.

A patent was taken out in 1844 for a mode of printing bank-notes intended to obviate the liability to forgery. The surface is covered with two designs, one geometrically regular, and the other very irregular; the two designs are engraved on different plates, and are printed with different inks, the one with visible and the other with invisible ink. Both of the inks are delible or removeable by chemical means; and the usual engraving of a bank-note is printed on paper so prepared. The rationale of the suggestion is this: that whatever means a forger might take to alter by chemical agency the letters or figures, or to transfer them by lithographic or anastatic processes, the state of the paper would betray him: for he would remove some parts of the design in the one case, and fail to transfer it in the other.

BANKS, SIR JOSEPH, was a great contributor to industry and science in the latter half of the last century. Besides his own voyages and travels, all the voyages of discovery which were made under the auspices of Government for the last thirty years of Sir Joseph Banks's life had either been suggested by him, or had received his approbation and support. In the affairs of the Board of Trade, of the Board of Agriculture, and of the Mint, he was constantly consulted, and he took a leading part in the management of the Royal Gardens at Kew. He was a distinguished promoter also of the interests of the Horticultural Society founded in 1804. His influence was frequently directed to soften to men of science the inconveniences of the long war which followed the French Revolution; to alleviate their sufferings in captivity; or to procure the restoration of their papers and collections when taken by an enemy. Baron Cuvier, in his 'Eloge' upon Sir Joseph Banks, mentions that no less than ten times collections addressed to the Jardin du Roi at Paris, and captured by the English, were restored, by his intercession, to their original destination. His purse was always open to promote the cause of science, and his library of natural history always accessible to those who desired to consult it. During the two-and-forty years in which he continued President of the Royal Society, he was indefatigable as an official trustee in the management of the British Museum; to which institution, after innumerable gifts, he made a contingent bequest of his scientific library, together with his foreign correspondence, where both are now deposited.

BANNER, a piece of drapery attached to the upper part of a pole or staff, generally hanging loose, but sometimes fixed in a slight framework of wood.

BANQUETTE, in fortification, is a step formed of earth at the foot of the interior slope of a parapet, and extending along its whole length, except where intervals are left for placing artillery to fire through the embrazures.

BANYAN-TREE, or *ficus indicus* is a native of most parts of India, both on the islands and the main land. The wood is light, white, porous, and of no value. Brahmins use the leaves as plates to eat off; birdlime is manufactured from the tenacious milky juice. The branches spread to a great extent, dropping their roots here and there, which as soon as they reach the ground rapidly increase in size till they become as large as and similar to the parent trunk, by which means the quantity of ground they cover is almost incredible. Roxburgh says that he has seen such trees full five hundred yards round the circumference of the branches, and a hundred feet high, the principal trunk being more than twenty-five feet to the branches, and eight or nine feet in diameter.

BAPTISTERY, an ancient building, in which Christians performed the ceremony of baptism. The most celebrated existing baptisteries are those of Rome, Florence, and Pisa; the most ancient is the baptistery of S. Giovanni in Fonte, near the church of S. Giovanni Laterano at Rome, commonly said to have been erected by Constantine the Great. The plan of this building is an octagon, with a small portico at the entrance; the interior is decorated with eight most beautiful porphyry columns, the finest of the kind in Rome. The diameter of this structure is about 75 feet.

The Baptistery of Florence, which is octangular, with a diameter of about 100 feet, stands opposite to the principal entrance of the Cathedral. The three great bronze doors are celebrated for the beauty of their bas-reliefs, and for the marble and bronze figures above them.

The Baptistery of Pisa, erected between the years 1152 and 1160, by Diotisalvi, is a singular design. The plan is circular, with a diameter of 116 feet; the building is raised on three steps, and surmounted with a dome in the shape of a pear. The external elevation is divided into three stories.

BAR-LE-DUC, is a busy town in the eastern part of France. Its manufactures consist of cotton and woollen goods, cotton yarn, hosiery, handkerchiefs, and leather. The town is celebrated for its sweetmeats, and contains several breweries. The Ornain is navigable below Bar, which has thus a ready means of transit for its industrial products, and for the other items of its trade, namely, wine, iron, fir and oak planks, and firewood for the supply of Paris. There are extensive iron-works and stone-quarries in the neighbourhood.

BA'RBACAN, or BARBICAN, in ancient fortification, was usually a small round tower for the station of an advanced guard, placed just before the outward gate of the castle-yard, or ballium. In cities or towns the barbacan was a watch-tower, placed at some important point of the circumvallation. It had sometimes a ditch and drawbridge of its own. The street of London called Barbican received its appellation from its vicinity to a tower of this sort attached to the city wall, the remains of which were visible within the last half-century.

BARBADOES is one of our West India Sugar Islands. Like others of the same group which have lost a monopoly, it has suffered from the recent change in the sugar duties. There are about 106,000 acres of surface, of which 20,000 were under sugar cultivation in 1848. The sugar exported in that year was about 33,000 hogsheads, and the molasses 13,000 hogsheads. The shipping that belonged to Barbadoes in 1848 amounted to 43 vessels, of 1716 tons, with 255 men. The entire imports for that year were valued at 430,000*l.* and the exports 600,000*l.* In 1849 the island imported British and Irish produce and manufactures to the value of 319,958*l.*

Governor Colebrooke, in a letter to Earl Grey in the spring of 1850, expressed an intention to encourage by every means in his power the cultivation of cotton in Barbadoes. He stated that 'at a former period, and especially in seasons when the sugar crops had failed, or were unproductive, cotton was extensively cultivated.'

BA'RBARY. The products and industry of this great African region are briefly noticed under the names of the countries which comprise it. [ALGIERS; MAROCCO; TRIPOLI; TUNIS.]

BARBERINI VASE. [PORTLAND VASE.]

BARCELONA is the most important manufacturing and trading town in Spain. The staple manufactures are cotton and silk. The commerce of Barcelona, owing to a variety of causes, but principally to oppressive restrictions on the importation of foreign goods, to the independence of South American states, and to the civil wars, has greatly fallen off from its former prosperity. The imports are cotton, sugar, coffee, cocoa, indigo, and other colonial products, chiefly from Cuba and Puerto Rico, hemp, coals, corn, deals, salt fish, hides, iron, hardware, &c. The trade with the Levant, the colonies, and France, as well as the coasting trade, is pretty active. The exports are wrought silks, soap, fire-arms, paper, hats, ribands, wine, brandy, oil, vermicelli, cork, bark, fruits, &c. The so-called Barcelona nuts are shipped to England from Tarragona. The exports and imports of Barcelona each amount to three to four millions sterling annually. From the 'Mercado,' or Price Current, of Barcelona, we are enabled to give the quantities of the principal imports into Barcelona for the year 1846. They are as follows:—8,000,000 lbs. of sugar, 115,000 cwts. of salt fish, 114,000 hides, 3,250,000 lbs. of cocoa, 2,000,000 lbs. of coffee, 50,000 tons of coal, 16,000,000 lbs. of cotton, and 280,000 lbs. of indigo. In the year 1846 the export of wine amounted to 30,000 pipes, nearly all of which went to the West Indies.

BARGE COURSE, a term applied to that part of the tiling of a roof which projects over the gable end of a building; the under part of which is stuccoed. To protect this stucco from the weather, two boards, called *barge-boards*, following the inclination of the roof, are often attached to the gables of old English houses, fixed near the extremity of the barge-course, and carved in the gothic style.

BARI, TERRA DI, a province in the kingdom of Naples, is rich in grain. Two kinds of it are cultivated, the common wheat for bread, and a small-grained hard wheat (grano duro) which is preferred for maccaroni, and is exported to Naples and elsewhere under the name of Barletta corn, from the harbour of Barletta where it is shipped. The principal farmers of this part of the province have formed themselves into a company, so that the corn trade of Barletta is entirely in their hands. The other crops are olives, tobacco, cotton, flax, almonds, and other fruits. Capers, liquorice, and the soda plant are also abundantly grown. The best wines are those of Trani, Bitonto, and Terlizzi. A little silk is produced. The fisheries and saltworks along the coast are very valuable. The province has no manufactures of importance; but shipbuilding is carried on in most of the towns along the coast. The trade is chiefly carried on by sea with Naples, Venice, Trieste, and the coast of Dalmatia, and consists of the agricultural products mentioned above.

BARILLA is the commercial name given to the impure carbonate of soda imported into this country, principally from Spain, the Canary Islands, and Sicily. The best is brought from Alicante, in the neighbourhood of which place it is prepared chiefly from the *Salsola soda.* The plants are usually gathered in September, and, after they have been allowed to become heated by being thrown together in heaps, are dried in the sun. In October

KNIGHTS CYCLOPÆDIA OF THE Industry of all Nations.

No. 9.

the plants are burned in a hemispherical kiln dug in the earth; the soda contained in them is fused and collected in masses, which have a hard and spongy consistence; and this soda, when broken into fragments, is ready for shipment.

The carbonate of soda is largely used in the manufacture of soap and glass, and for other purposes. From 1829 to 1834, the average annual importation of barilla into Great Britain was 252,000 cwts.; and at the present time it is hardly imported at all: in 1848 the import was only 2349 cwts. This change has been occasioned by the production of carbonate of soda from common salt through the agency of sulphuric acid: salt having become much cheaper from the repeal of the duty, and sulphuric acid also, from improvements in the manufacture. The quantity of carbonate of soda now consumed annually is calculated to be seven times as much as the largest importation of barilla in any single year. Barilla at present sells at 9*l.* to 10*l.* per cwt.

BA'RIUM, a peculiar metal, discovered by Davy in 1807: it is the basis of the alkaline oxide or earth *barytes*, from which it is obtained by various chemical processes. It resembles silver in appearance: it is much heavier than water. By exposure to the air it is slightly covered with a crust of barytes. It fuses before it becomes red hot, and at this temperature it acts upon glass, without being volatilized; when exposed to the air, and moderately heated, it burns with a deep red light. It may be flattened a little, so that it is to a certain extent a malleable metal. Barium has, however, as yet been obtained only in small quantities, and consequently its properties are but imperfectly known.

The protoxide is met with combined with sulphuric acid, forming *heavy spar*, or *cawk*, termed chemically sulphate of barytes, and with carbonic acid, constituting the mineral termed *witherite*, or carbonate of barytes; it may be procured by decomposing either of these native compounds. It is of a grayish white colour; when moistened with water it becomes very hot, and in a short time falls into a fine white powder; if more water is added, it becomes a crystalline and very hard mass. It is extremely poisonous, has an acrid, alkaline, caustic taste, and requires a high temperature to fuse it.

Barium combines with many substances to produce chemical compounds. One of the best known is *sulphate of barytes*, which occurs largely in many parts of the earth, especially in the lead mines of the north of England; it occurs both amorphous and crystallized. In the former state it is sometimes colourless and transparent, and frequently opaque. The crystals are often very large. It is extremely heavy, its specific gravity being about 4.7. It is unalterable by air or by water, and is scarcely affected by heat. When sulphate of barytes is only moderately heated with carbonaceous matter, a solar phosphorus is formed, which is called the *Bolognian Phosphorus*.

BARK. Several kinds of bark, being used for processes in the arts or for medicine, enter largely into commerce. Of the former class are oak bark, cork bark, mimosa or wattle bark, and quercitron bark; and the most important among the latter is Jesuits' or Peruvian bark. [CINCHONA.] Some others, such as CINNAMON and CASSIA, are noticed elsewhere.

Oak bark is extensively, and was formerly almost exclusively, used in tanning, for which it is valuable on account of the large proportion which it contains of the peculiar astringent called *tannin*. Sir H. Davy has shown that 8½ lbs. of oak bark are equal in efficiency to 2¼ lbs. of galls, 3 lbs. of Sumach, 7½ lbs. of the bark of the Leicester willow, 11 lbs. of the bark of the Spanish chestnut, 18 lbs. of elm bark, or 21 lbs. of common willow bark. The quantity of tannin, however, varies both with the age of the trees, and with the season in which they are cut; being more abundant in the bark of young than of old trees, while if taken in the spring the bark has four and a half times the quantity, in a given weight, that it would have in the winter.

Cork bark, or *Cork*, is the outer bark of an evergreen oak (*Quercus suber*), which grows abundantly in Portugal, Spain, the south of France, and Italy. Most of the cork bark used in Europe is supplied by Spain and Portugal, but that of the best quality by France. As the cork is really dead bark, it may be carefully removed without injuring the tree, which may be stripped every eight or ten years, beginning when it is fifteen years old. At each successive stripping the produce becomes greater in quantity, and better in quality. The inner bark, which contains much tannin, cannot be removed without destroying the tree. Cork bark is usually charred lightly when taken from the tree, to improve the texture by closing the pores; but this process, which is liable to impart a disagreeable flavour to liquors stopped with cork so treated, is not required for the thinner but closer layers of young bark. The lightness of cork recommends its use as floats for fishing-nets, for life-preservers, for insuring the buoyancy of life-boats, and for similar purposes; while its compressibility and elasticity, being combined with a closeness of pore which prevents the passage of liquids, render it valuable for stopping bottles and casks. [CORK-MANUFACTURE.]

Mimosa, or *wattle bark*, is collected from two species of Mimosa which abound in New South Wales, Van Diemen's Land, and New Zealand, where it is employed in tanning. It contains about 150 lbs. of pure tannin in a ton of bark, which is about three fifths of the proportion yielded by the best white oak bark; and it imparts a reddish colour to the leather.

Quercitron bark is the produce of the *Quercus nigra*, or *tinctoria*, a North American oak, and is used as a yellow dye. The colouring matter resides wholly in the inner bark; and care is needful in extracting it to avoid any admixture of the tannin of the bark, which would give a brown tinge.

The imports of bark for tanning in 1849 amounted to the very large quantity of 365,755 cwt., of which more than two-thirds were supplied by Holland and Belgium. Oak bark sells at present from 90*s.* to 130*s.* per ton.

BARK-BED, in Horticulture, is a bed formed of the spent bark used by tanners, placed in the inside of a brick pit in a glazed house, constructed for forcing, or for the growth of tender plants.

BARKER, ROBERT, deserves notice in this place as the inventor and patentee of panoramas. He practised originally as a portrait-painter in Dublin and in Edinburgh. The first picture of the kind which he painted was a view of Edinburgh, exhibited in Edinburgh in 1788, and in London in 1789, but with indifferent success. His second panorama was a view of London from the Albion Mills, and it was exhibited, with complete success, in Castle-street, Leicester-square, and afterwards in Germany. He built, and opened in 1793, with a panorama of Spithead, the present panorama exhibition-rooms in Leicester-square. He died in London, in 1806.

The chief characteristics of Dioramas and Panoramas are briefly noticed in later articles. [DIORAMA; PANORAMA.]

BARLEY is a grain too generally known to require a minute description. It is readily distinguished from other grain by its pointed extremities, and by the rough appearance of its outer skin, which is the corolla of the flower closely enveloping the seed, and. in most varieties, adhering strongly to it.

Of all the cultivated grains, barley is perhaps that which comes to perfection in the greatest variety of climates, and is consequently found over the greatest extent of the habitable world. It bears the heat and drought of tropical regions, and ripens in the short summers of those which verge on the frigid zone. In genial climates, such as Egypt, Barbary, and the south of Spain, two crops of barley may be reaped in the same year, one in spring from seed sown the preceding autumn, and one in autumn from a spring sowing.

Winter barley is mostly sown in those countries where the winters are mild, and the springs dry, as in the south of France, Italy, and Spain; or in those where the snow lies deep all the winter, and where the sun is powerful immediately after the melting of the snow in spring, as is the case in parts of Russia, Poland, and some parts of North America. In most climates, where the winter consists of alternate frost and thaws, and the early part of the spring is usually wet, as is the case in England, Scotland, and Ireland, the young barley is too apt to suffer from these vicissitudes, and the spring-sown barley gives the more certain prospect of a good crop.

The barley most commonly cultivated in England is that which has only two rows. It is almost universally sown in spring. The cultivation of all the varieties is nearly the same, and is best understood in the counties of Essex, Norfolk, and Suffolk, in which a great quantity of excellent barley is produced and malted for the London market.

The quantity of barley sown formerly was four or five bushels per acre: but, if the land is duly prepared and the seed good, from two to three bushels is an ample allowance. The best practical rule is, to sow as soon after the middle of March as the ground is dry. The practice of sowing clover, rye grass, or other seeds, with the barley, is almost universal, and is considered as one of the great modern improvements in agriculture.

The principal use of barley in this country, and wherever the climate does not permit the vine to thrive, and no wine is made, is to convert it into malt for brewing and distilling. The best and heaviest grain is chosen for this purpose, and, as it must have its germinating power unimpaired, the least discoloration, from rain or heating in the stack, renders it suspected, and consequently not so saleable. It is, however, still fit for being ground into meal, for feeding cattle and pigs, when it is not used for human food; or it may be made into pot barley by the process of shelling.

The produce of barley on land well prepared is from 30 to 50 bushels, and more, per statute acre, weighing from 45 to 55 lbs. per bushel, according to the quality. It is said to contain 65 per cent. of nutritive matter; wheat contains 78 per cent. A bushel of barley weighing 50 lbs. will therefore contain about 32 lbs. of nutriment; while a bushel of wheat weighing 60 lbs. contains 47 lbs. Good oats weighing 40 lbs. contain about 24 lbs. of nutritive substance; so that the comparative value of wheat, barley, and oats, in feeding cattle, may be represented by 47, 32, and 24, the measure being the same.

1,389,858 quarters of barley were imported in 1849; average price 27*s.* 9*d.*

BARLEY, PEARL, is the small round kernel which remains after the skin and a considerable portion of the barley have been ground off. Barley from which only the outer husk or skin has been removed is called *Pot Barley*.

Both these preparations of barley are made by means of mills constructed for the purpose, and differ only in the degree of grinding which the grain undergoes. In the mill originally used, and still common in Germany and France, the barley is rubbed between a pair of small mill-stones, the upper one of which has several grooves in its lower surface, mounted at such a distance from one another, that they rub without breaking the grains. This is *pot-barley;* and *pearl-barley* is produced by continuing the process until a further portion of the outside of the grain is rubbed off. The powder or meal which flies off through the perforated case forms excellent food for cattle, pigs, and poultry.

In another kind of mill, originally introduced from Holland, and generally used in Scotland, an ordinary grindstone of about three feet in diameter is made to revolve upon an horizontal axis, while a perforated case, similar to that above described, surrounds it, and revolves in the same direction, but with a much slower motion. The barley is admitted at an opening in the circumference of the case, and the effect is produced by the violent tossing which it receives between the stone and the case. This kind of mill is much more easily constructed and kept in order than the former, and is well adapted for use with hand-labour.

Pot and pearl-barley are very wholesome and nutritious, and it is to be regretted that they are not more used as food by the labouring classes of England, as they are in Scotland, Germany, and Holland. The essential oil of barley, which gives it its peculiar taste, resides chiefly in the skin and adjacent parts of the grain; the interior is a purer farina, more nearly resembling that of wheat. This farina, obtained by grinding pearl-barley in a common mill, is called *patent barley* and is used extensively for making barley-water; but if the essential oil possesses any medicinal properties, it is evident from what was observed before, that common pot-barley would be preferable for making a decoction of barley when prescribed as a remedy. The great use of pot and pearl-barley is in broths, stews, and puddings, as a substitute for rice. It swells, and unites well with the fat and oily matter extracted from meat in boiling. Even the bran, having been steeped in water, and allowed to ferment till it becomes acid, is relished by the humbler orders in the mess called *sowens.* In Holland, pot-barley, boiled in butter-milk and sweetened with treacle, is a common mess for children and servants.

BARM. [YEAST.]

BARMEN, a town in Rhenish Prussia, is a busy centre of industry. It is literally studded with cloth factories, cotton and silk mills, bleaching-establishments, dye-houses, soaperies, tobacco-factories, potteries, warehouses, and a variety of other buildings for the manufacture of linen, ironmongery, metal and plated goods, chemical products, &c. The annual value of the industrial products of this busy district are stated to be nearly a million sterling.

BARN, a building in which agricultural produce is stored, to protect it from the weather and keep it in safety. The thrashing-floor, which is required even where thrashing-machines are used for thrashing out the smaller seeds, is usually in the middle of the barn, and made of stone, brick, oak, or tempered earth; those of oak, formed of planks two inches and a half thick, dowelled or ploughed and tongued together, being considered the best; and it is often so arranged that a loaded waggon may be drawn in upon it, so as to throw the corn at once into the *bays*, or ends of the barn. Free circulation of air is important in all parts of a barn.

Barns are built of stone, brick, timber, or, in some places, of dry rammed earth in the manner termed *pisé.* If roofed with tiles, they should be bedded in coarse hay, which is more effectual than mortar in preventing the drifting of snow; and, if with thatch, reeds are to be preferred to any other material, because they afford no lodgment for vermin, and afford an excellent protection against the weather.

Hay is now seldom put in a close barn, experience having shown that it keeps much better in the open air in ricks. But where a considerable quantity of hay is tied up in trusses for the market, it is extremely useful to have a building with a roof to protect them from the wet, and to load the carts under shelter. For this purpose a kind of barn is contrived, which some call a *Dutch barn*, but which may very properly be called a *skeleton barn*, being the frame of a barn without the boarding. Another contrivance of similar character is used in Holland, in which a pentagonal thatched roof is made to slide up and down a series of vertical poles, on which it may be secured by pins at any required elevation. The lower ends of the poles are well braced together by a timber framing, which rests upon a brick foundation. Its chief use is for hay, which may be deposited safely in either large or small quantities, the roof being raised when additions are made, and lowered as the hay is taken off the top for use.

BARNARD CASTLE. This is among the busiest towns in Durham. The inhabitants are chiefly employed in the manufacture of carpets and shoemakers' thread. There are four large carpet manufactories and two thread mills, which employ several hundred hands. Many persons are engaged in the tanning business, producing a leather formerly highly esteemed in the manufacture of white leather breeches.

BARNSLEY, owes all its importance to its manufactures. Wire-works were in existence here in the time of James I., and the town had for a long period the reputation of producing the best wire in the kingdom. This manufacture has, however, greatly declined; and but little wire is now made in the town. Barnsley has lost its ancient trade, and has acquired a new one, to which its present prosperity is entirely owing; viz., the linen trade. Its fabrics are linen cloth, damasks, diapers, drills, ducks, checks, and ticks. The great improvements which Barnsley has made during a very recent period in the production of these articles, is a main cause of the prosperous state of the town. In damasks and drills it is said that Barnsley stands unrivalled. Some of tho above goods are technically called *unions*, from both linen and cotton being united in their production. Much of the flax which is spun in the large flax-mills of Leeds is sent to Barnsley to be woven: there are, however, two flax-spinning mills in Barnsley. Weavers in this town are not generally employed in factories, but the manufacturers give out the yarn to them, which they weave at their own houses.

There are extensive bleaching works and dye-houses connected with the staple commodity of the town. The numerous coal-mines, and tho iron-works in the immediate neighbourhood find occupation for hundreds of people; there are also several iron-foundries and a glass-house. The coal-mines became a subject of painful interest in 1847, when by an explosion at the Oaks Colliery 72 lives were lost.

All the varieties of Barnsley linen and flax manufactures will be illustrated by specimens at the Hyde Park Exhibition in 1851.

BARNSTAPLE, in Devonshire, enjoys the advantage of being the port for an extensive and improving inland district, and carries on a steady trade. There are lace-manufactories in the town, and also establishments for the manufacture of baizes, shalloons, tammies, hose, pottery, and fishing-nets, which afford employment to a considerable number of persons.

BAROACH, a city on the Bombay side of India, maintains a considerable trade with Bombay and Surat, to which places it sends cotton, grain, and seeds. This traffic is carried on in boats which draw little water, and which are impelled by large lateen sails.

BARO'METER, is the name applied to those instruments in which a column of air is weighed against a column of mercury.

Galileo, Torricelli, and Pascal, in the 17th century, successively made those experiments and observations on the pressure of the air, which led to the invention of the barometer. It was first found that the pressure of a column of the entire atmosphere is equal to that of a column of water (of tho same diameter) about 33 feet high; it was next found that the pressure is equal to that of a column of mercury about 30 inches high; and it was afterwards ascertained that on a mountain the pressure will sustain a less height of mercury than at the earth's surface. These facts proved the existence of atmospheric pressure, and also the law of diminution in this pressure at different altitudes.

If a tube, closed at one end, be deprived of air, and the open end be immersed in mercury, the mercury will rise in the tube to the height of 28 or 30 inches, by the pressure of the atmosphere on the mercury in the vessel. Descartes, Huyghens and Dr. Hooke, devised barometers in which the use of one or more fluids of different specific gravity in connection with mercury was tried as a means of obtaining more distinct indications of very small changes of level; and many other forms of simple mercurial barometers have been constructed. One contrived by Amontons, consisting of a conical tube of glass closed at the smaller end, partially filled with mercury, and then inverted, is more simple and elegant in principle than any other; but the obtaining of a tube of the requisite accuracy is almost an ideal supposition. One contrived by Gay-Lussac for portable purposes permits the access of air to the mercury only by a holo too minute to allow the escape of mercury. Fortin's is a Torricellian barometer with a contrivance for raising or lowering the bottom of the cistern by a screw, so as to adjust the lower level of the mercury exactly to the zero point before commencing an observation. Hooke's *wheel barometer*, though too inaccurate for scientific use, is very much used as a weather-glass; for which it may answer well enough, if it be remembered that it is not the *state* of the barometer which furnishes any probable test of the weather, but the *change* which is taking place for the time being. This change is indicated by it pretty distinctly, though it cannot be trusted for showing either the exact amount of the change, or the exact height of the column of mercury. In this contrivance, a weight is placed on the mercury of a siphon barometer, and nearly counterpoised by another weight connected with it by a string, which passes over a pulley. The movement of the mercury causes this floating weight to rise and fall, and consequently the pulley, which carries an index, to turn more or less on its axis. The form of barometer invented by Gay-Lussac has been recently much employed in determining the heights of the mountains along the Anglo-American frontier in New Brunswick.

To observe the temperature of the mercury, which, by altering its bulk, affects the indications of the barometer, a thermometer is attached to the best instruments, the bulb of which is in the cistern.

In using the barometer as a weather-glass, it must be remembered that no rule which can be given will always hold true. The rising of the mercury usually presages fair weather, and its falling foul weather, as rain, snow, high winds, and storms, the lowest fall being found in great winds, though unaccompanied by rain. In very hot weather the falling of the mercury usually foreshows thunder; in winter, the rising presages frost; in frosty weather a continued fall foretells a thaw, and, in a continued frost, a rise indicates the approach of snow. If a change of weather follows very close upon a change in the barometer, it may be expected to last but for a short time, and *vice versâ;* and where the motion of the mercury is unsettled, changeable weather may be anticipated.

The mountain barometer, used for determining the altitude of mountains, is the most scientific form which the instrument assumes. All the resources of the instrument maker are here brought into requisition; and many of our distinguished philosophers have devised forms of the instrument known by their names. Among the more recent changes in this instrument are two for which Mr. Bursill obtained patents in 1841, intended to obviate certain slight inaccuracies in the ordinary forms. Another kind of mountain barometer was patented by Mr. Readman, in 1842. Mr. David Napier, in 1848, patented a barometer of such ingenious construction, that it can not only mark the entire course of atmospheric pressure for a continuous period of 24 hours, but can register its own observations on a piece of paper.

Sir John Robinson has contrived a simple substitute for the complex mountain barometer. It consists of a wooden box, containing a thermometer and a number of tubes, of a bore somewhat wider than those of self-registering thermometers, open at one end, and blown into bulbs at the other; there is also a small vessel of mercury. The observer notes the thermometer at each station on the mountain and immerses the end of one of the tubes in the mercury. When the observer descends to a lower level, mercury will be found to have entered each tube, to a greater height according to the height of the station to which each tube refers. By exposing each tube to an air-pump, exhausted till the mercury stands at the same height as at the station, the atmospheric pressure at that station becomes determined.

The making of barometer and thermometer tubes is among the curiosities of the glass-manufacture. Few manipulative processes are more striking. The workman collects a quantity of melted glass on the end of a tube, rolls it into a cylindrical form, blows through the tube to hollow the glass within, and holds it up to enable another man to attach a rod to the other end of the glass; the two men then walk backwards in opposite directions, to a distance of forty or fifty feet, elongating the glass as they go, or rather allowing it to elongate itself; until that which was a short thick cylinder, becomes a long thin tube, with an equable bore throughout its whole length. The tube so made sinks gently to the floor of the glass-house; and when cold it is cut or broken into convenient lengths.

The filling of the tubes with mercury, and the adjustment of the scales, are delicate processes in the manufacture of a good barometer.

A remarkable modern form of this instrument has been already described. [ANEROID BAROMETER.]

BARREL. In the old English measures a barrel was used to denote

31½ gallons of wine,

32 gallons of ale,
36 gallons of beer.

But these measures were altered in the reign of William and Mary, and of Anne; and when the imperial measures were introduced (1835) the contents of a barrel were thus determined :—

	Imp. Galls.
Wine barrel	26¼
Ale ditto (London)............	$32\frac{32}{59}$
Ale and beer ditto (England)....	$34\frac{34}{59}$
Beer ditto (London)	$36\frac{36}{59}$

Many other barrels have been in use to denote certain quantities of goods usually sold in barrels; thus the barrel of salmon or eels = 42 gallons, that of soap 256 lbs., &c.

The word barrel means, in common use, also any hollow cylinder, such as the barrel of a gun, a jack, or a hand organ.

BARREN LAND, in Agriculture, is that in which the plants generally cultivated do not prosper or arrive at maturity. This barrenness may arise from various causes. The texture of the soil may be such that the moisture essential to vegetation cannot be retained; or that the fibres of the roots cannot penetrate in search of food. In either case it is seldom that the soil can be rendered productive, so as to repay the expense of cultivation. There are, however, in all countries tracts of land which are barren and waste in their present state, but which, for want of better soils to employ and feed an increasing population, are well worth improving, and will ultimately repay the labour bestowed on them. The relative acreage of cultivated and uncultivated land in the British Islands is estimated as follows :—

	Cultivated. Acres.	Uncultivated. Acres.	Total. Acres.
England .	26,632,000	6,710,400	33,342,400
Wales . .	3,117,000	1,635,000	4,752,000
Scotland .	5,265,000	14,473,930	19,738,930
Ireland .	12,125,280	7,316,664	19,441,944
British Islands	383,690	735,469	1,119,159
Total .	4 522,970	30,871,463	78,394,433

Looking at this table, it is impossible not to ask whether so very large a proportion of the surface of the British dominions in Europe may not remain uncultivated, more from want of industry and skill than from insuperable barrenness?

The most prevalent causes of barrenness in land are a deficiency or an excess of water: the methods of remedying these are explained under IRRIGATION and DRAINING. Supposing that the moisture has been regulated, and that the land is to be brought into cultivation, the first thing to be done is to remove obstructions and impediments, whether they be rocks, stones, trees, or shrubs, or only the heath and coarse grasses which generally cover waste lands. When the surface is very uneven, so as to form hillocks and hollows, in which the water is apt to stagnate, levelling is a necessary process. The most effectual way of doing this is by the wheelbarrow and shovel; but, if the soil is loose and sandy, it may be best done by means of the *mollebart*, a Flemish instrument, consisting of a kind of large shovel, drawn along by a horse, and guided by a man. The small fields of Flanders are often levelled by this means. In France a somewhat more complex kind of mollebart has been patented.

The land being thus so far prepared the skill of the agriculturist is made available to determine on the crop, and to suit the soil for that crop. Some soils in this condition, require only exposure to the air; others require manure; others marling and ploughing; others a course of turnip husbandry; others a season of pasturing; &c.

The unproductive state of waste lands in many populous countries has suggested the employment of the poor and friendless on their improvement; and it has been thought a more enlightened charity to expend the money, which would otherwise be given in simple temporary relief, in such a manner as to make the labour of paupers available to their future comfort and independence. It is near increasing manufactures, where land acquires a greater value, that barren land is soon converted into fertile fields. It is there also that the improvement of waste lands is most profitable. The neighbourhoods of Aberdeen, Birmingham, Manchester, and Sheffield, among many others, furnish examples of the greatest industry and perseverance in overcoming the natural barrenness of the soil.

BAR-IRON. This important material of manufactures is noticed under IRON-MANUFACTURE.

BARTER is the exchange of one thing for another. The term is properly applied only to the exchange of movable things. Barter is simply the giving of one movable thing for another, without reference to any standard of value.

If two persons exchange things with reference to a money value, as if one man gives one hundred pounds' worth of wheat at the current price for one hundred pounds' worth of cotton wool at the current price, the transaction is still exchange or barter: the price has only been used as a means of making the exchange a fair transaction. If two persons exchange things on which they have agreed to put a money value, and the two things have an unequal money value, so that one party has also to give a sum of money to another, the transaction may be considered a *sale*.

Pure barter only takes place among barbarous nations, or between barbarous people and the traders of civilized nations. The exchanges of civilized nations are effected in the form of sale, which is more convenient for all parties.

BARYTES. [BARIUM.]

BASALT, a hard dark-coloured rock of igneous origin. It can only be considered as a variety (and a comparatively recent variety) of that mass of melted rock which has been ejected at various periods from beneath the crust of the globe, and to which various names have been assigned, according to the characters which circumstances have impressed upon different portions of it. Basalt is a rock of very extensive occurrence on the surface of the earth, and is very frequently found in the vicinity of volcanoes, both extinct and active. The greatest mass yet observed is that noticed by Colonel Sykes in the Deccan, constituting the surface of many thousand square miles of that part of India. When basalt occurs in horizontal tabular masses, and is columnar, the columns are generally perpendicular. When basalt forms the substance of a perpendicular dyke, cutting through other rocks, and is columnar, the columns are usually horizontal. Basaltic columns are sometimes also curved, and of this mode of occurrence there is a beautiful example in the island of Staffa.

When basaltic columns are jointed, and exposed to the destructive action of breakers on a coast, they often present the appearance of some great ruined work of art. Such deceptive appearances are, however, not confined to coasts, for in some countries, and especially in India, masses of basalt rise suddenly from the plains, and the broken columns, shooting upwards, may readily at a distance be mistaken for buildings. When viewed from above, the heads of a number of basaltic columns, if unbroken, appear like a pavement composed of numerous polygonal pieces of stone fitted into each other.

BASCINET, BASINET, or BASNET, was a light helmet, so called from its resemblance to a basin, generally without a visor, though it appears that the visor occasionally accompanied it.

BASE, or BASS, a name sometimes given to the VIOLONCELLO.

BASEL, BASLE, or BALE. The chief manufacture of this important town and canton is silk ribands; which are exported to the amount of 12,000,000 francs annually, principally to America. The transit trade also employs many hands. Business in Bills of exchange, and the wine and book trade are also considerable. There are likewise large tanneries, tobacco manufactories, &c. Basel stands at the termination of three great lines of railway.

BASEMENT, in Architecture, is the lowest story of a building, forming the base of a private house or public edifice. In edifices used as dwellings the basement is high; but in churches and other public buildings it is usually kept low. In basements the masonry is usually rusticated and set upon a plinth, on which there is sometimes a moulded base; the upper part of the basement is surrounded with a broad band, under which, at times, mouldings are employed. A cornice is also used occasionally instead of the band.

BASI'LICA. The Romans gave the name of Basilicæ to those public buildings with spacious halls, often surrounded with wide porticoes, many of which were built at different times in the various Fora of Rome. They were usually called after the person who caused them to be built.

The principal feature of the Basilica was a large roofed building, supported on columns. The roof, which was called the *testudo*, rose high above the other part of the structure, which consisted of two galleries, called *porticus* placed one above the other, and round the internal sides of the central building. The porticus was covered with a lean-to roof, the upper part of which commenced below the capitals of the columns which supported the testudo. The light was admitted between the spaces formed by the under line of the architrave of the testudo, the upper line of the lean-to roof, and the perpendicular lines of the columns. At the end of the central part of the interior a raised platform formed the tribunal for a magistrate.

It is probable that Rome possessed Basilicæ in all the different Fora of the city. Of these the Basilica Ulpia, which formed a part of the Forum Trajanum is the only one of which there are considerable remains left. Another Basilica, of the Corinthian order, was discovered on the Palatine Hill. A large edifice in the Forum, called the Temple of Peace, has also been named the Basilica of Constantine.

The most perfect Basilica of antiquity exists in Pompeii, constructed on the south-west, and consequently the warm side of the Forum. This edifice is 220 feet by 80. The testudo rose to the height of about 60 feet, judging from the diameter of the portions of the columns still remaining.

The early Christian churches of Rome may be considered as the best resemblances of the Roman Basilicæ. Not only the apsis, but the general form of the nave and aisles, of our ancient cathedrals is evidently borrowed from the Italian church Basilica.

BASIN is a geographical term which is used in such expressions as the basin of a sea, the basin of a lake, the basin of a river; and it includes all the countries drained by the waters that run into such sea, lake, or river.

If the basin of a sea runs far inland, and comprehends a great extent of country, it commonly contains large and fertile plains, maintains a numerous population, and at some period of history civilization has made considerable progress within its limits. Thus the basin of the Bay of Bengal comprehends countries not much less than half of Europe in extent. Accordingly we find, not only that it is, and ever has been, much frequented by vessels, but also that at a very early period civilization made considerable progress, and that at all times the arts of peace have been greatly cultivated within the limits of this basin.

On the other hand, if the basin of a sea is of small extent, the surrounding country is poor, its inhabitants backward in civilization, and its ports only occasionally resorted to by vessels. Such is the case with the Arabian Gulf, of which the basin commonly coincides with its shores, and in no place probably extends more than twenty miles inland.

The basins of lakes offer likewise several varieties. Those which are commonly called mountain-lakes, but with more propriety valley-lakes, have in general a very narrow basin, being inclosed on all sides by mountains. Many of them receive a river at one extremity, in which case their basin runs up such river to its source. The lakes of plains have in general a much larger basin, as they receive the drainage of a more extensive country, as the lakes of North America, and those of Russia.

In its geological sense, a basin indicates a depression or concavity of strata. Thus, the tertiary basins of London, Hampshire, and Paris, resting on chalk; the coal-basin of South Wales, resting on old red sandstone; and, in a larger sense, the European basins between the Ural, the Scandinavian chains, and the Pyrenees, Alps, &c. Some of these basins are due to the original circumstances of deposition, others have acquired their configuration from elevations and depressions of particular geographical areas.

BASKET-MAKING. Baskets have been made from the earliest ages, in most countries where pliant willows, reeds, or grasses are to be met with. In England the osier or willow is chiefly used for this purpose; and many of the specimens produced are exceedingly elegant. The willow twigs or other materials are prepared in various ways, according to the costliness of the basket to be made; and the manufacture consists in a kind of interlacing, very simple in its character, and requiring the aid of but few tools. Any of our excellent Blind Asylums, where industrial pursuits are carried on, will afford a pleasing exemplification of the ease with which basket-making can be carried on by blind persons.

A very large per-centage of the baskets bought by the middle and working classes in London, are made by poor persons, whose wives and children hawk them about the streets for sale. It is precisely one of those trades likely to put on such a commercial aspect—easy to learn, and requiring little or no capital to carry it on.

Foreign baskets are imported to a considerable amount—about 30,000*l.* in the year 1849.

BASQUE PROVINCES. The inhabitants of these Spanish provinces are very industrious. Most of them are engaged in agriculture, which is better understood than in most parts of Spain. Oxen are used in ploughing, but spade husbandry is the system chiefly adopted. The peasantry live generally in *caserios*, or hamlets of six or eight houses. Each farmer is the proprietor of the land he tills. The chief crops raised are wheat, barley, oats, maize, fruits, hemp, flax, and pulse. Some poor wine called *chacoli* is made; but the common beverage is cider, apples being very abundant. The chief iron mines and smelting furnaces of Spain are in these provinces. The ores are very rich; those of Somorrostro yield 33 per cent., those of Mondragon 40 per cent. of metal. Copper, tin, marble of different colours, and jasper, are also found. The preparation of charcoal, and the important fishery on their long extent of seaboard afford employment to those not engaged in tillage of the soil, or in the iron works. The number of corn-mills for grinding flour, which is one of the principal exports, is very great. Somorrostro, one of the towns, is celebrated for its iron-mines and iron-works, in which about 6000 tons of iron are annually made.

BASRA, BASSORA, or BUSSORA, the chief town of the Turkish district of Basra, is the chief inlet by which the products of Hindustan and the eastern countries are introduced into the Turkish empire. Its commerce is therefore considerable. Six or eight British ships arrive annually, but the chief part of the commerce is carried on in Arabian vessels, which belong to the merchants of Muscat. The imports consist of indigo, sugar, spices, &c., from Hindustan, tin from Banca, shawls from Persia, pearls from Bahrein, and cotton and woollen goods and cutlery from Europe; the exports, of bullion, copper, dates, raw silk, horses, and drugs. The export of dates has sometimes exceeded 10,000 tons in a year. The trade in the interior is chiefly carried on by caravans to Aleppo and Bagdad.

BASSA'NO, a town in the delegation of Vicenza, in Austrian Italy, is a place of great trade: it has manufactures of woollen cloths, straw hats, and tanneries; and it exports a great quantity of silk, the produce of its own territory.

BASSET-HORN, is a clarinet of enlarged dimensions, and the bell end is wider. On account of its length, the tube, which consists of five pieces, is bent inwards, forming a very obtuse angle. The scale of this instrument embraces nearly four octaves—from C, the second space in the base, to G in altissimo, including every semitone; but its real notes, in relation to its use in the orchestra, are from F below the base staff, to C, the second leger line above the treble.

BA'SSIA, is a genus of tropical plants, which yields many valuable substances. The *Bassia butyracea*, the Indian butter-tree, yields a fat-like substance, which is a kind of vegetable butter. The *Bassia longifolia*, the Indian oil-tree, has a yellowish fruit, from which is obtained by pressure a valuable oil, used by the poorer natives of India, for their lamps, for soap, and, instead of better oil, for cookery. The flowers also are roasted and eaten by the Indian peasants, or bruised and boiled to a jelly, and made into small balls, which are sold or exchanged for fish, rice, and various sorts of small grain. The wood is as hard and durable as teak, so that this is one of the most generally useful trees found on the continent of India. The *Bassia latifolia* has hard and strong wood, flowers which yield a spirit by distillation, and seeds from which a considerable quantity of greenish yellow oil is obtained, which is found useful for the supply of lamps. The *Shea tree*, another species, is the *butter tree*, so very important an article of African internal commerce.

BASSO DI CA'MERA, a double base, or *contrabasso*, reduced in size and power, but not in compass, and thus adapted to small or private rooms. It has four strings; two of gut, and two covered with silver wire, all proportionably thicker than those of the violoncello, and tuned in 5ths, to the same literal notes as the violin, but two octaves lower than the latter.

BASSO-RILIEVO. The Italian term basso-rilievo, or the French bas-relief, is commonly applied to any work of sculpture connected more or less with a plane surface or background, and in this general sense is opposed to insulated detached figures, or sculpture in the round. In its more particular meaning basso-rilievo, low or flat relief, is usually appropriated to figures which have a very slight projection from the ground. *Alto-rilievo*, on the other hand, is not only rounded to the full bulk, but has generally some portions of the figures quite detached; and *mezzo-rilievo*, a style between the two, although sometimes rounded to a considerable bulk, has no part entirely unconnected with the plane surface or ground.

The British Museum contains unquestionably the finest existing specimens of this branch of sculpture in the rilievi which decorated the Parthenon, or Temple of Minerva, at Athens.

BASSOON, a musical instrument blown through a reed. It consists of four tubes of wood, bound together and pierced for ventages, of a brass craned neck, in which the reed is inserted, and of several keys. The whole length of the tubes is 6½ feet, but by doubling up this is reduced to four. It may be considered as a base oboe, and its compass is from B flat, below the base staff, to B flat, in the treble staff.

The *double-bassoon* is a bassoon of increased dimensions, the scale of which is an octave below that of the ordinary bassoon. The Serpent and the Ophicleide now supply the place which it was meant to fill.

BASTENNES, a village in the French department of Landes, is noted for a rich asphalte mine, which is said to yield more bitumen than the mines at Seyssel. The bitumen at Bastennes is very much used as cement for stone or wood; and when mixed with pebbles it forms an excellent pavement. Its adhesiveness is so great, that stones cemented with it cannot be separated by a less force than is sufficient to break them.

BASTI'A, the most populous and most commercial town in the island of Corsica, has manufactures of shoes, glove-leather, soap, wax candles, and liquors. The exports consist of wine, oil, hides, timber, and cattle. Fishing gives employment to a large part of the population. Steamers ply regularly every week between Bastia and Marseille.

BATAVIA, a city on the north coast of

Java, is an important place, from its excellent bay and its advantageous position for European commerce. It is the chief Dutch settlement in the east, and is a place of much trade. The Chinese carry on much traffic there. The town is unhealthy; but the country around is very beautiful and fertile, producing pine-apples, oranges, shaddocks, lemons, limes, mangoes, bananas, grapes, melons, pomegranates, custard-apples, papaws, mangosteens, and rombusteens, with many others mostly unknown in Europe. The chief imports are opium and piece goods; the exports, sugar, coffee, and spices: salt also forms an important article of colonial commerce. Near Batavia there are some very extensive works for making salt from sea-water.

BATHS AND WASHHOUSES. The practice of bathing is one which is too much neglected in this country. In the east, and at Rome in ancient times, the arrangements for bathing show much completeness. Some of the finest buildings at Rome were Baths. There were sixteen public baths at Rome in the time of Augustus, besides many sumptuous private baths; the public baths named after or by Agrippa, Nero, Titus, Domitian, Caracalla, and Diocletian, have acquired quite a European celebrity for their vastness and splendour.

In England domestic bathing is far too little practised. As metal-work becomes cheapened, the means of so doing are placed more and more within reach of the middle class. The *shower-bath*, especially, is becoming more and more efficient and economical. One form, recently introduced, is a kind of funnel turned upside down, with a colander or perforated plate placed over the open surface of the funnel; the small end is held in the hand; and as long as that exit is closed so as to prevent the admission of air, no water can flow from the colander; but as soon as the small end is opened, water flows through the perforations. The bather therefore keeps his finger on the small end of the machine until ready for the flow of water. Another bath has been more recently introduced, in which there are two holes stopped by the two thumbs at the lower part of the apparatus; it is more convenient than the other, inasmuch that the hand has not to be held so high above the head.

An ingenious improvement on the common shower-bath was made in 1844 by Messrs. Lewis, who registered their invention. It consists in making the water flow out at various heights and in various directions; and it is designated by its inventors by the somewhat learned name of *omni-directive*. Water is in the first instance poured into a reservoir at the bottom, whence a small hand-pump forces it to a reservoir at the top. From this upper reservoir it is made to descend in a great variety of ways. By pulling one particular string, the water descends perpendicularly, as in the common shower-bath. By pulling another string, it descends along five tubes which extend the whole height of the bath, round the outer circumference; and as these tubes have small orifices on the side next the bather, he can have a number of little streams pouring upon him from all directions. By moving one or more slides, he can close any number of these orifices in the tubes so as to limit the streams of water to particular directions. By turning a handle, and holding a small leathern pipe in the hand, the bather can discharge a more copious stream in any required direction; and by moving another handle at the bottom of the bath, he can obtain an upward stream. The apparatus is somewhat complex; but it certainly is 'omni-directive.'

The public baths in England are very few in number; and being also too high-charged to meet the wants of the operative classes, a happy suggestion was made to combine cheap public *baths* with public *laundries*. It was in 1844 that an association was formed in London, for 'Promoting cleanliness amongst the Poor;' and this association has been the forerunner of an amount of good which can hardly be calculated. At first it was a *charitable* undertaking, supported by the benevolent; then it was regarded as a *commercial* undertaking, planned so as to support itself; and at last it has assumed the form of a *corporate* undertaking, supported by parish or borough funds. All three varieties do, indeed, exist at the present time; but it is the last of the three which will probably be developed to the greatest extent. Public washhouses and laundries were formed in Glasshouse Yard, in Whitechapel, and in George Street, Hampstead Road; and these having been found very advantageous, an Act of Parliament was passed in 1846 empowering parishes and boroughs to construct baths and washhouses, under certain regulations. Few recent statutes have worked so much good, silently and unostentatiously. Baths and washhouses have been formed, and are now being formed, not only in various parts of the metropolis, but in most of the populous towns in England.

In the George Street Baths, in the six months from March to September, 1850, there were 63,000 persons who used the baths, and 36,000 who used the washhouses.

It is gratifying to learn that the French National Assembly has just voted 600,000 francs for the establishment of Baths and Washhouses.

BATTENS are pieces of timber 6 feet or more in length, 7 inches in width, and usually from 2 to 2¾ inches in thickness. *Deals* differ from battens in being always above 7 inches wide, and *batten-ends* in being under 6 feet long. These are merely technical distinctions used in the timber trade.

BATTERIES, ELECTRICAL AND GALVANIC. All that need be said on this head in the present work, will be found under ELECTRO-METALLURGY and GALVANISM.

BATTLE-AXE, a military weapon of offence used in different countries from the remotest times. The introduction of the battle-axe into this country has been attributed to the Danes: but proofs of an earlier use of it in our islands are deducible. That it was used in England in the Saxon times appears from several MSS. of the ninth century; and the English are represented as using it, in the Bayeux tapestry. The pole-axe, with an edge on one side and a sharp point on the other, is believed to have come in with the Normans. The use of the battle-axe declined during the middle period of English history.

BATTLEMENT, a parapet wall, commonly employed in castellated and in ecclesiastical edifices of that kind which are distinguished by the general name of Gothic. The battlement was originally designed for the protection of the besieged, but afterwards became merely an ornament to the edifice. The battlement is generally indented, with a coping inclined both ways from about the centre; the lower part between the coping and the cornice of the building is often pierced and decorated. Mr. Rickman has described the characteristic features of the Norman, Early English, Decorated English, and Perpendicular English styles of battlements.

Castellated battlements have the embrasures between the battlements sometimes nearly equal to the width of the battlements themselves; sometimes the embrasures are narrow, and the battlements wide, with the coping moulding placed horizontally and the sides cut plain. Another battlement consists of a moulding running round the battlement and the embrasure, while a capping is set upon the horizontal part of the embrasure and battlement, as at York Minster.

BAVARIA. This important country, like most others which have mountain ranges as well as wide plains and river valleys, is rich in varied produce. Few countries possess a more productive soil than Bavaria. Agricultural industry is principally directed to the cultivation of wheat, rye, barley, and oats. The grape is much cultivated in Bavaria, especially for the Franconian, the Steinwein, and the Leistenwein varieties. About 20,000,000 English gallons are supposed to be an average produce of Bavarian wines. Among other articles of Bavarian vegetable produce are hops, tobacco, flax, hemp, linseed, rapeseed, mulberry-trees for silk rearing, fruits of many kinds, coriander and other seeds, madder, the potato, and fodder for cattle. Most of the mountains are finely wooded.

The principal mineral products are iron, coal, and salt; gold and silver are found in small quantities, only in the waters of the Inn, Rhine, Danube, and Isar; quicksilver, in the circle of the Rhine; and copper, which was formerly raised in several quarters, is now confined to the works at Kahl and Kaulsdorf, in the circle of the Upper Main. There are two mines of cobalt also on the latter spot, from which small quantities of tin, lead, and antimony have occasionally been obtained. The Upper Main, Rhenish Bavaria, Regen, Lower Danube, and Isar territories are the chief mining districts in Bavaria. Among the other mineral produce may be named black lead, sulphur, porcelain earth, marble, alabaster, rock crystal, asbestos, and many of the gems.

In Bavaria, as in many other German states, the profits arising from vast establishments, and the concentration of productive powers, are comparatively unknown; manufacturing industry is mostly diffused over a multitude of adventures on a small scale. The manufacture of linens, which is the chief, is not confined to a few large establishments, but is scattered over the whole state, and in many districts the agricultural population partly maintain themselves by weaving linen. Linen-yarn is also spun in some districts, but not to any great extent, and chiefly for exportation. The manufacture of woollens and worsted hose is carried on principally in Ausbach, Baireuth, Lindau, Munich, and the Upper Palatinate; but this branch of industry is in the hands of individuals, and not carried on in large factories. The supply is very inadequate to the consumption of the country, and sometimes the excess of imports over exports has amounted to 40,000*l.* per annum. There is a similar deficiency in the domestic supply of manufactured cottons; the use of improved machinery, however, is gradually increasing in many quarters, and additions are constantly making to the number of spinning-mills. The districts about Augsburg, Kaufbeueren, and Hof are the most important seats of this branch of Bavarian industry, and numbers are also employed in hand-spinning. The leather manufactories are of considerable importance, but mostly carried ou by numbers of small manufacturers. Bavarian calf-skins are in great repute and largely exported, but sole leathers are not produced in sufficient quantity for the home demand. The supply of paper, of which Aschaffenburg, Nürnberg, Fürth, Augsburg, and Schwabach furnish many fancy sorts, is beyond the domestic consumption. Schweinfurt and Mainberg possess largo manufactories of paper-hangings, which aro of excellent quality, and in much demand in other German states. Straw-platting has increased considerably of late years. The manufacture of looking-glasses and of glass for optical purposes is in a high state of efficiency in Bavaria; and the glass manufactures generally are very extensive. The manufacture of articles in wood, and the felling, hewing, and general manufacture of timber occupy thousands of hands. There are nearly 2000 sawing-mills in Bavaria for the preparation of boards, deals, and laths; and almost as many families are wholly supported in Ammergau and Berchtesgaden by the manufacture of articles in carved wood, some of which are very beautiful. There are several porcelain manufactories at work; that at Nymphenburg, not far from Munich, produces china which may bear comparison with tho finest in Europe. The potteries and the slate-works are numerous. The working of the metals chiefly consists in extensive manufactories of iron-ware, especially nails and needles, the export of which is considerable. There is a manufactory of arms at Amberg which supplies the army. The gold and silver smiths of Munich, Würzburg, Nürnberg, and Augsburg, are in great repute. Fire-arms, fowling-pieces, cannon, brass-ware, gold and silver leaf, employ a large number of workmen. The brewing of beer, in many respects the most important branch of manufacture in Bavaria, employs upwards of 5000 establishments, or taxed brewers, by whom about one hundred million gallons of beer are annually made. Many establishments aud institutions exist in Bavaria tending to the encouragement of manufactures.

Though Bavaria is an inland country, its trade is greatly favoured by its geographical position, which has rendered it in some degree a central point between the Mediterranean, the Baltic, and the German Ocean, and a medium of intercourse between the west and the east of Europe. Its excellent roads, rivers, and railways, have tended to the same result. The principal articles of export are grain, salt, timber, potashes, fruit, liquorice-root, seeds, hops, cattle, sheep, swine, fish, flax, yarn, coarse linens, glass, leather, beer, &c. The imports are principally wines, cotton, coffee, sugar, rice, tobacco, drugs, sea-fish, copper, oil, hides and skins, hemp and flax, silk and silk goods, woollens, lead, furs, honey, and cheese.

Bavaria being an inland country, all British goods reach there by indirect means; so that the amount can hardly be stated.

To the extent of her means, Bavaria is making preparations to occupy a place in the Industrial Exhibition of 1851. All the chief towns will be contributors, and many of the articles contributed will be of a peculiar character.

BAYEUX, a town in the French department of Calvados, is famous for its manufacture of lace. There is a manufactory for producing large lace-pieces, such as dresses, scarfs, shawls, mantillas, &c. These laces are exported to Spain, Mexico, the United States, and elsewhere. The porcelain of Bayeux maintains a very high repute. Muslins, serges, calicoes, table-linen, cotton yarn, leather, and hats are also manufactured.

BAYEUX TAPESTRY, a web or roll of linen cloth or canvass, preserved at Bayeux, upon which a continuous represeutation of the events connected with the invasion and conquest of England by the Normans is worked in coloured woollen thread, after the manner of a sampler. It is 20 inches wide, and 214 feet long; and is divided into 72 compartments, each of which bears an explanatory Latin inscription. It is stated traditionally to have been worked by or under the superintendence of Matilda, the Conqueror's queen, and presented by her to the cathedral of Bayeux, of which Odo, the Conqueror's half-brother, was bishop. It represents the minutest manners and customs of the earliest Norman lines in England, and was evidently designed while the particulars of the contest, of many of which it affords the only record known, were fresh in recollection. A curious illustration of its minute accuracy of detail occurs in the compartment representing the funeral of Edward the Confessor, where a person is represented placing a weathercock upon the spire of Westminster Abbey; indicating that the building was scarcely finished at the time of his decease.

BAYO'NNE, a town in France, on the confines of Spain, has extensive rope-walks, glass bottle factories, sugar refineries, ship building yards, and establishments for fitting out ships for tho whale fishery. It is famous for its hams, for its liqueur-brandies, and for its chocolate. Tho trade of the town is very considerable. The exports consist of broad cloth, linen, silks, and other manufactured articles, wine, brandy, timber, planks, pitch and tar, drugs, &c. The imports are chiefly Spanish wool, saffron, liquorice, bullion, &c. The coasting trade employs the greater part of the vessels which enter or leave the port of Bayonne.

BAZAAR. In Turkey, Egypt, Persia, and India, this term distinguishes those parts of towns which are exclusively appropriated to trade. In this exclusive appropriation they resemble our markets; but in other respects they approximate more nearly to our retail shops.

The regular bazaars consist of a connected series of streets and lanes; and, when of a superior description, they are vaulted with high brick roofs. The domes or cupolas which surmount the vaulting admit of a subdued daylight. In the best specimens of the vaulted bazaar the passages are lined on each side with a uniform series of shops, the floor of which is a platform raised from two to three feet above the level of the ground, and faced with brick. As the vault springs from the front of the line of shops, they seem like a series of recesses, and the partition-walls between them appear like piers supporting the arch. These recesses are entirely open in front, in all their height and breadth; they are scarcely more than very small closets, seldom exceeding six feet in breadth, rarely so deep as wide, but generally from eight to ten feet in height, and occasionally more. But in the more respectable parts of large bazaars, there is generally a little door in the back wall which conducts to another small and dark closet, which serves the purpose of a store-room. The front cell is the shop, on the floor of which the master sits with his goods all around him.

The peculiar principle of the oriental bazaars is that all the shops of a city are there collected, instead of being dispersed in different streets as in Europe; and that in this collected form the different trades and occupations are severally associated in different parts of the bazaar, instead of being indiscriminately mingled as in our streets.

An English Bazaar, in which many different kinds of manufacture are assembled under the same roof, is not a good imitation of its eastern original.

BDELLIUM is a gum-resin, the produce of a species of amyris, or rather balsamodendron, a native of India. This substance occurs in masses sometimes as large as a walnut, in oblong or angular pieces of a yellow, red, or brownish colour. The clearest pieces are transparent; the odour is weak and peculiar; the taste bitter, balsamic, and resembling myrrh, or Venice turpentine. It is tolerably brittle at the ordinary temperature of the atmosphere, but with a slight increase of heat the finer kinds may be kneaded between the fingers.

Resembling myrrh in appearance, it also resembles it in its effects upon the human system, and is often fraudulently substituted for it: it is however weaker, while it is more disagreeable and acrid. It is now disused in Britain, but is found intermixed with gum Arabic.

BEACON, a sign ordinarily raised upon some foreland or high ground as a sea-mark. It is also the term used for the fire-signal which was formerly set up to alarm the country upon the approach of a foreign enemy. The power of erecting beacons as sea-marks was originally in the king, and was usually delegated to the lord high admiral. Many sea-marks, signal-posts, and substitutes for light-houses, are still called beacons.

BEADS. The manufacture of Glass Beads is carried on in the following manner, at Murano near Venice. Tubes of glass of various colours are drawn out to great length, in a gallery adjoining the glass house; in the same way as barometer and thermometer tubes are drawn out in an English glass house. The tubes are then cut into very small pieces of nearly uniform length, on the edge of a fixed chisel. These small pieces are put in a heap into a mixture of fine sand and wood ashes, and stirred about with an iron spatula till their cavities get filled. The mixture is transferred to an iron pan suspended over a moderate fire and continually stirred until the cylindrical bits assume a smooth rounded form. When removed from the fire, and cleared out in the bore, they constitute beads.

Foreign beads are imported to the value of 8,000*l.* to 10,000*l.* annually.

BEAN. There are two distinct kinds of beans cultivated; the one is our common garden or field bean: the other is the French bean, haricot, or kidney-bean.

The common bean, of which there are several varieties, bears a pod containing several oblong rounded seeds, which are used in the soft young state for the table, and in the hard dry state for domestic animals chiefly, either whole or ground into meal. The *Windsor* bean and the *horse* bean are the two chief varieties. The usual mode of sowing is to drill them by a machine, at the distance of from twenty to thirty inches, according to the richness of the soil; or to dibble them by hand. The soil best adapted for beans is a rich strong loam, such as produces good wheat. In such a soil the produce is sometimes fifty or sixty bushels per acre, but an average crop, on moderate land, is about half that quantity. The wheat which follows beans is generally good and heavy, and seldom runs to straw. In cold wet soils beans require great care to ensure good crops. Although the nutritious matter in a good crop of beans is great, and almost equal to that obtained from a crop of wheat, it exhausts the soil much less; and thus there is perhaps no crop bearing seed which gives so great a return with so small an expenditure of the nutritive juices of the soil.

The principal use of beans is to feed horses, for which purpose they are admirably adapted, and far more nourishing than oats. They should be bruised or split in a mill, and given to horses mixed with hay and straw cut into chaff. Great quantities of beans are consumed in fatting hogs, to which they are given whole at first, and afterwards ground into meal. Bacon hogs may be fatted almost entirely on beans and bean-meal. Bean-meal given to oxen soon makes them fat. All but the very best wheaten flour is adulterated with bean-meal.

The French bean, kidney bean, or haricot bean, is chiefly cultivated for its tender and succulent pod, being one of the most esteemed vegetables for the table. The dried seeds are also boiled after being soaked in water for some time, and are thus used very extensively by the French.

The imports of beans for three years were—

1846	..	255,047	Qrs.
1847	..	443,675	of
1848	..	490,353	beans.

BEAR. Many species of bear contribute in various ways to the arts and to domestic economy. In the Arctic countries the *brown bear* is hunted and taken in pitfalls and traps of various kinds; and in some countries, as Lapland and Kamtchatka, there is no part of the animal which is not turned to some useful purpose. The fur of the brown bear in youth is of a yellowish colour, excepting on the feet, where it is of a deep black. The *black bear* inhabits every wooded district of the American continent, from the Atlantic to the Pacific, and from Carolina to the shores of the Arctic Sea. Every where however its numbers have been greatly thinned, partly owing to the value of the animal's skin in commerce, and partly to the tide of European colonization. It must not, however, be imagined that 'bear's skin' gloves or other articles of dress are necessarily made from the skin of the animal whose name they assume. No part is useless to the American bear-hunter: the flesh, the fat, and the skin are peculiarly esteemed; and a feast of bear's flesh is conducted with many observances. Of the *Syrian bear*, the gall is in great esteem; the skins are sold, and so is the dung, which is used as medicine for diseases of the eye in Syria and Egypt. The fur is woolly beneath, with long straight or but slightly curled hair externally. Many other species of bear are occasionally captured for the sake of their furs. The bear-skins imported into this country in 1848 amounted in number to 9712, of which about two-thirds were from the Hudson's Bay Company's territories.

It is perhaps scarcely necessary to inform any reader of average intelligence, that the *bear's grease* so profusely advertised has, for the most part, had little indeed to do with the life or the death of bears. More is used every year in England than could be procured from the carcases of all the obtainable bears in all countries. Large quantities of the so-called bear's grease are made of hog's lard, palm oil, and flowers of benzoin.

BEARING, the direction of the line drawn from one point to another, is a term usually applied to the points of the compass. To take *bearings* is to ascertain the points of the compass on which objects lie. The distances of a ship from a headland may be found by observing its bearings at two different hours of the day, knowing the course or bearing of the ship's path and the distance sailed in the intermediate time.

BEAUCAIRE, a town in the department of Gard in France, is very advantageously situated for trade; whereby it has long been an entrepôt of the trade of France with Spain, Africa, Italy, and the Levant. One of the great old fairs of Europe is held here every year; when Greek, Armenian, Turkish, Egyptian, Arabian, Italian, Spanish, and Moorish merchants arrive to sell the merchandise of their respective countries and take away in return the manufactures of France. The concourse of people at this fair in ordinary times is said to exceed 100,000. For their accommodation a supplemental town, regularly laid out in streets, is built of tents in a vast meadow bordered with elm and plane trees, which extends between the Rhône and the ruins of the old castle. Here articles of every kind, whether of convenience or luxury, may be found; and in this city of canvas the main business of the fair is transacted. A tribunal consisting of twelve members settles any disputes between the buyers and sellers during the continuance of the fair. The prefect of Gard always attends and entertains the principal merchants and strangers. The transactions at this fair, which lasts two or three weeks, are said to cause an outlay of above 150 millions of francs, and to be so profitable to the good folks of Beaucaire, that when it terminates they resume the *far niente* habits of the south, having gained in one month wherewith to take their ease during the rest of the year.

The ordinary commerce of the town consists of corn, flour, provision stores, wine, oak planks, &c. The principal manufactures are hosiery, serge, silk stuffs, olive oil, pottery, and leather. The Arles and Lyon steamboats land and take up passengers at Beaucaire.

BEAUNE, an old Burgundian town in the department of Côte-d'-Or, in France, has manufactures of broad-cloth, serge, druggets, and great numbers of wine-casks. There are beet-root sugar-refineries, vinegar-works, dye-houses, breweries, and tanneries in the town, the trade of which consists in the products named, and in corn, cattle, and provisions. Beaune exports annually about 40,000 butts of wine.

BEAUVAIS, an ancient episcopal city of Picardy, has some very important manufactures. It has long been famous for its silk tapestries; broad cloths of every quality and colour, flannels, swansdowns, shawls, hosiery, cotton and woollen yarn, ribands, black lace, china, and chemical products, are also extensively manufactured. The greater part of the cloth worn by the French army is made at Beauvais. There are also several establishments for bleaching linen, besides tanneries, and dye houses. The commerce of the town consists of its industrial products and corn.

BEAVER. The beaver is almost as interesting to us as an *artificer*, in the formation of his retreat, as in respect to the valuable fur which he yields, and which has in past years been so largely used for hats (though less now than formerly). It is not only for its fur that the beaver is prized, but for a product called *castor*, found in certain glandular sacs, and used in medicine and perfumery. The fur of the beaver varies from glossy brown to almost black; the tail, or caudal paddle, used as a rudder in diving or ascending, is flat, scaled, and oarlike.

The beaver-skins imported in 1848 amounted in number to 41,132; almost entirely from the Hudson's Bay Company's Territories.

BEDFORD LEVEL. The Bedford Level is an instructive example of energy overcoming natural difficulties. The level comprises about 400,000 acres of flat country in the fen-district of Lincolnshire, Cambridgeshire, &c. There is abundant evidence that it was once a forest, and then a stagnant morass; and to bring the morass into the state of fertile corn-fields, has been the object of the Bedford Level Drainage. This drainage has been in progress, at intervals, for four centuries: the principal works being the construction of canals or artificial rivers to carry off the stagnant water to the sea. These rivers or 'cuts,' are several miles long, and of various widths.

One of the great works is that called the Nene Outfall, which includes a cut six miles long by 200 feet wide, and which was made at the cost of 200,000*l.*

At the present time very extensive operations are in progress. A fine bridge is being constructed over the Nene at Sutton Wash; the cuts and embankments in the northern part of the Level are undergoing improvements; and the whole of Whittlesea Mere is being drained. The public spirit and the private munificence which have marked the encouragement given to this useful enterprise by the successive Dukes of Bedford, well justify the name given to the Level.

BEDFORDSHIRE is the most purely agricultural county in England, having the smallest proportional number of inhabitants engaged in manufactures and trade. Indeed, it can hardly be said that the county contains any persons engaged in manufactures; the comparatively few persons so employed might with equal propriety have been included among the class engaged in trade or handicraft, their employment being for the most part that of straw-plaiting.

BEDSTEAD, the frame employed to support a bed. Bedsteads of iron and brass, of very light and simple construction, occupying little space, easily taken to pieces and put together, and affording the best security against the harbouring of vermin, have been much used of late years, and may be highly recommended as favourable to health and cleanliness. Mr. Winfield, the eminent brass manufacturer of Birmingham, patented many valuable improvements in metallic bedsteads, in 1848. In the next following year Messrs. Sturges and Harlow, also of Birmingham, patented other improvements in bedsteads, calculated to impart elasticity to various parts. The metallic bedsteads of Birmingham manufacture, and probably others from the continent, will occupy a place in the Industrial Exhibition of 1851.

Invalid bedsteads have been contrived, in which, besides offering facilities for performing surgical operations, dressing wounds, &c., ingenious mechanism has been applied to enable the patient to vary his position with very little labour or trouble; but all contrivances of this character fall short of Dr. Arnott's hydrostatic bed, or water-bed, in which a very soft feather-bed or mattress is laid upon a waterproof sheet floating upon the surface of a tank or vessel partly filled with water. The support offered by such a bed is so perfectly equable as to afford comfortable rest under circumstances where the unequal pressure of the body upon the softest ordinary bed would be painful and injurious; while its yielding character will in many cases allow the application of poultices, or the performance of other offices of the sick-chamber, without any alteration of the patient's position.

BEE. We can only notice this small but important insect, in so far as regards the *honey* and *wax* of the honey-bee. A colony of bees is termed a swarm, or a hive, and consists of three sorts, viz. males or drones, neuters or workers, and the queen or reigning female. A hive of bees, besides males, workers, and queen, consists also of eggs and larvæ, destined to form a future brood. The number of workers in a well-stocked hive varies from 15,000 to 20,000. The number of males, or drones is irregular; sometimes they amount to 1000, sometimes only to 600 or 700.

To the labours of the workers are due various products, as *honey*, *bee-bread*, *wax*, and *própolis*.

Honey.—Honey is the nectar of flowers, lapped out of the nectary by the tongue, and conveyed to the crop or honey-bag. Here it undergoes but little alteration (for honey extracted from some plants is poisonous), and is disgorged into the cells destined to receive it. Of these some are store-cells, others are filled for daily use. A single cell will contain the contents of many honey-bags; and though the cell is horizontal the honey will not escape, for a thick cream arises, and forms a glutinous film obliquely placed, keeping in the treasure. The store cells, when filled, are covered with a waxed lid.

Bee-Bread.—While the bee is extracting the sweets of the flowers, it becomes covered with the pollen of the anthers; this pollen it wipes off from its body with the brushes of its legs, collects every particle together, and kneads it into two little masses, which are each placed in a sort of basket on the broad surface of the tibia or middle joint of the leg, where a fringe of elastic hair over-arches a concavity, and acts as a sort of lid or covering. Thus burdened, off the insect flies to the hive; first the honey is safely lodged, then the bee-bread, or kneaded pollen, is disposed of as circumstances may require. Sometimes it is eaten by several bees, called by a peculiar sort of hum to their repast, and if more is collected than required for present use it is deposited in some of the empty cells as a future provision.

Wax.—Wax is a peculiar secretion in little pouches or cells, beneath the scales of the abdomen. Of these pouches there are generally four on each side, at the base of each intermediate segment on the under surface, and concealed by the overlapping of the preceding segment. It would appear that by some internal process wax is elaborated from honey, as the wax-workers retain the honey when wax is required, which they would otherwise disgorge into the cells. The wax oozes out between the abdominal rings in the form of little laminæ; it is then worked with the mouth, and kneaded with saliva, that it may acquire the requisite degree of ductility for the construction of the comb.

Própolis.—This is a glutinous or gummy matter, employed for smearing or varnishing the waxen cells. It is procured from the buds of various trees, as the birch, &c. The bees procure this gum by means of their mouth, prepare it, load each hind leg with it, and so carry it to the hive. It is employed, not only in varnishing the cells, but in stopping up crevices, for coating the sticks which support the combs, and for mixing with wax, and patching up weak parts. Often it is spread interiorly over the dome of the hive, and it is mixed up with the wax forming the cells.

The marvellous instinct which impels the bee to construct its beautiful honey-comb, we do not touch upon here.

BEECH. The common beech, known in America as the *white* beech, is the most useful species of this valuable tree. The timber is hard, and is employed for a great variety of purposes. It is used for the keels and side planking of ships; for ringing mill-wheels; for making piles, weirs, sluices, flood-gates, and other constructions exposed to the action of water; for cogs of wooden wheels; for making bedsteads and chairs; for panels of carriages: for various articles in joinery, cabinet-making, and turnery; for numberless small articles of household furniture; for railway-sleepers; for barn-floors; for herring barrels; for wooden shovels and peels; for wooden-screws and sieves. In Germany beech-wood is used for many of the purposes above-named; and also for gun-carriages, wheel-felloes, bowls, porringers, salt boxes, spindles, rollers, spinning-wheels, pestles, presses, bellows, and numerous other articles; while, sawn into thin boards, it is used for boxes, packing cases, sword scabbards, and even the boards of books (instead of millboard). In France, besides other purposes, beech is used for gun-stocks, plough socks, cricket bats, cheap knife-handles, and cheap *sabots* or wooden shoes.

Beech is used to an enormous extent in France and Germany for fuel. The bark is used in tanning. The dried leaves are said to form an excellent substitute for feathers in beds, and to be largely employed in such a way in some districts. The dried catkins of the leaves are used to stuff cushions. The *mast* or fruit is eaten by many animals; and from this fruit an oil useful for lamps and for cooking is obtained. A *Beech-Oil Company* was one of the most noted commercial speculations of Queen Anne's reign.

BEER-MACHINE. In the ordinary Beer Machine, each handle has a single action, that is, draws from one cask only; but in many respects it would be useful if two pumps could be worked at once by the same handle. From the rapid fluctuations which malt-liquor undergoes in quality, owing to changes in the weather, it is frequently necessary for the retailer to mix old and new beer together, in order to maintain a uniform quality. This is done either by drawing from two butts, by two pumps and two handles, or by mixing beer of two ages in the same butt, by which a liability to a new fermentation is incurred. To obviate these inconveniences was the purpose of Ernest's Beer Engines, patented a few years ago. The arrangement of this machine is very ingenious. One handle works the levers, rods, and pistons of two pumps, which may be connected with the beer in two butts. In the usual perpendicular position of the handle it works both pumps at once; but if drawn a little on one side, by a slight movement of the hand, it works one pump only; and it is optional with the drawer whether to work one or the other pump, or both, and whether to draw equally or unequally from both.

BEET. There are two distinct species of beet commonly cultivated, each containing several varieties, the one called *Beta cicla*, which produces succulent leaves only, the other *Beta vulgaris*, distinguished by its large fleshy root. The cicla is chiefly cultivated in gardens as a culinary vegetable, and forms one of the principal vegetables used by agricultural labourers and small occupiers of land in many parts of Germany, France, and Switzerland. The second species, the *Beta vulgaris*, or Beet-Root, has been long cultivated, especially that variety called the *red beet*, which, when boiled and sliced, makes such an excellent addition to salads.

The common field-beet for cattle, or *mangel wurzel*, which has been long known in Germany, was introduced into England at the latter end of the last century. There are few crops so valuable for winter food for cattle as the beet; Swedish turnips exceed them in the quantity of nourishment, weight for weight, but on good light soils the produce of the beet per acre is much greater. The *white beet* has been chiefly cultivated for the extraction of sugar from its juice. It is smaller than the mangel-wurzel, and more compact, and appears in its texture to be more like the Swedish turnip. The beet-root sugar manufacture sprang up in France in consequence of Bonaparte's scheme for destroying the colonial prosperity of Great Britain by excluding British colonial produce. It having been found that from the juice of the beet-root a crystallizable sugar could be obtained, he encouraged the establishment of the manufacture by every advantage which monopoly and premiums could give it. According to Chaptal, the process is thus conducted. The roots, after being cleansed by washing and scraping, are rasped and reduced to a pulp in a rasping machine. When ground, the pulp is powerfully squeezed by a press, in canvass bags, to expel the juice, which is received in a copper. In this copper the beet-juice is heated to about 178° Fah.; lime-water is then added, and stirred up with it. Having been mixed with animal charcoal it is made to boil, by which both a scum and a sediment are separated from it. The clear liquor is drawn off, and is evaporated in shallow vessels; the process is continued till the juice becomes a thick syrup, which is then strained through a linen bag. The syrup is again boiled and skimmed and then transferred to a cooler, where it remains for a short time. It is next transferred to sugar moulds, and treated pretty much in the same way as the sugar-cane juice, described under SUGAR.

The beet-root sugar manufacture is said to be difficult to manage well; but the sugar when produced is equal to cane-sugar. Five tons of clean roots produce about 4½ cwt. of coarse sugar, which give about 160 lbs. of double-refined sugar, and 60 lbs. of inferior lump sugar. There is also a quantity of molasses, fitted to yield spirit, and the pressed refuse, which is good food for sheep and cattle. As a question of commercial enterprise, however, the manufacture of sugar from beet is not found profitable, wherever colonial cane-sugar is admitted at a reasonable rate of duty. There are beet-root sugar manufactories in Russia, France, Prussia, and many of the other German States.

BEIRUT, or BAIROUT, the Syrian port for Damascus, is the channel through which British goods find their way to Bagdad and Mesopotamia. There are about 400 laden vessels enter the port yearly. The imports consist of cambrics, cotton twist, calicoes, indigo, shawls, printed goods, shirtings, handkerchiefs, &c.: the exports are chiefly raw silk and cotton, skins, hides, madder, gum, galls, fruit, tobacco, sponges, &c.

BELFAST is the principal place of trade in Ireland, and has increased in wealth and population with great rapidity. In 1758 the number of looms was 399. The spinning of cotton by machinery was introduced in 1777, and of linen in 1808. In 1838 there were 50 steam-engines of an aggregate of 1274 horse-power engaged in the spinning of linen and cotton yarns. In 1841 the number of steam-mills for spinning linen yarn was 25; one of which employed 800 persons; and since then the number and extent of the mills has greatly increased. In 1792 ship-building was first commenced here: there are now four large ship yards in full employment. The registry of shipping belonging to the port, the arrival and departure of laden ships, the quantity of imports and exports, and the amount of customs' revenue, have all increased with great rapidity during the last few years.

The manufacture of linens, damasks, and diapers is carried on in all its branches with great activity. In the ornamental wrappers alone in which the linens are made up for the foreign market, a sum of 80,000*l*. a year is said to be expended. In cottons the principal articles manufactured are velvets, fustians, jeans, ticking, ginghams, quiltings, calico muslins. Calico printing is carried on extensively at Whitehouse, and there are in the town and vicinity numerous dye-works, bleach-works, and print fields. The total number of spindles employed in the linen and cotton factories was computed in 1837 at 982,000. Since that time the number has probably increased more than half. There is also a very large trade in cured provisions. In the town and vicinity are several extensive foundries and machine-making establishments, where all kinds of steam-engines and mill machinery are made. Orders have recently been executed at the iron-works of Messrs. MacAdam for St. Petersburg and Cairo.

The Royal Society for the Promotion and Improvement of the growth of Flax in Ireland has its office in Belfast. It was established in 1841 by some Belfast merchants, who perceived the great importance of providing the market in Ireland and Great Britain, with a home-grown article, instead of purchasing it as heretofore from abroad at an annual average cost of 6,000,000*l*. A staff of agriculturists trained in the most approved methods of management is retained by the society, and sent to give instructions to all parts of Ireland where there are farming societies or landed proprietors subscribing to the society's funds. The cultivation of the flax-plant has by this means been largely introduced into many parts of the country where it was previously unknown. The recent important experiments concerning the growth and manufacture of flax are likely to be of great moment to Belfast. The School of Design, at Belfast, is one of the most flourishing in the three kingdoms. In the middle of 1850 the number of pupils was no less than 148, many of whom are designers for damask weavers and muslin embroiderers.

Few towns in the empire have entered with more earnestness than Belfast into the principle and details of the Industrial Exhibition of 1851. A managing committee has been chosen, and local juries are to be formed for selecting the specimens to be exhibited. The flax fabrics generally are to be divided by the Belfast Committee into three classes. 1st. Plain linens, and lawns. 2nd. Damasks, diapers, drills, and other twilled linens. 3rd. Cambrics, printed linens and cambrics, and handkerchiefs—plain, bordered, embroidered, printed, and dyed. Each class is to contain specimens bleached, unbleached, and dyed. There will also be a very rich exhibition of Irish produce from Belfast.

BELI'ZE, or BALIZE. [HONDURAS.]

BELFRY, that part of a church-tower or steeple in which the bells are hung. In constructing a belfry, the frame-work is placed either on stone corbels, or is made to bear on a recess formed in the wall. The higher the bells are placed in the tower, the more does the vibration, caused by ringing them, affect the masonry.

BELGIUM. The coal-fields of this important country are in the provinces of Limbourg, Liége, Namur, and Hainault; and many of them are very rich in produce. The other varieties of mineral produce include iron, calamine, and building stone.

The soil, which in each of the provinces consists almost entirely of clay and sand, has for the most part been rendered fertile by a due admixture of both these elements. Agricultural industry is carried to a great extent in the kingdom, and the cultivators have availed themselves of every advantage within their reach for increasing their productions. The most general objects of cultivation are wheat, rye, barley, oats, meslin, buck-wheat, hemp, flax, madder, hops, chicory, colza, and the artificial grasses, clover, trefoil, lucerne, and sainfoin. The ruta baga, or Swedish turnip, turnips, carrots, parsnips, and potatoes are raised to a considerable amount by field culture. Tobacco is grown in some situations, and everywhere fruits of the kinds grown in England are objects of careful cultivation. Turf-ashes and drainage refuse are much more largely and advantageously used as manure in Belgium than in England. Among the timber trees are the oak, chestnut, horse-chestnut, beech, elm, horn-beam, ash, walnut, fir, and different descriptions of poplars.

The manufacturing industry of Belgium has declined in modern times as compared with the extent to which it was carried on in the 14th century. The making of thread-lace, originated in Flanders, and up to a comparatively recent period Brussels and Mechlin carried on a large trade in that article: in the former city more than 12,000 persons were once employed for its production. Early in the 14th century, Louvain contained 4,000 looms for woollens; and Brussels and Antwerp had together as large a number. At a date not quite so remote, Ghent employed between 30,000 and 40,000 looms for the weaving of woollen and linen goods. It is mentioned that the weavers of that city once mustered 16,000 men in arms under the banners of their respective trades. The woollen manufacture is now prosecuted at Verviers, Charleroy, Tournay, Mons, and some other towns. Cotton-spinning and weaving are carried on in some of the larger towns. Liége and Maastricht contain large tanneries. At Antwerp, Ostend, and Ghent, there are some sugar refineries; cutlery is made at Namur; and fire-arms in considerable quantities at Liége. Breweries are numerous and extensive in most of the principal towns throughout the kingdom. Earthenware is made of good quality in several places; and the manufacture of nails has been carried on for a very long period in the provinces of Liége and Hainault.

The articles which Belgium supplies to England are oak-bark, flax, madder, clover seed, spelter, and sheep's wool; in return for which we send various kinds of East India and West India produce, tobacco, and cotton wool, besides British and Irish produce and manufactures, consisting principally of brass and copper manufactures, cotton manufactures and yarn, hardware, earthenware, salt, sheep's wool, woollen and worsted yarn, and woollen manufactures. The exports of British produce and manufactures to Belgium have averaged about one million sterling annually for the last six or eight years; but in 1849 they reached nearly a million and a half.

In no continental country, except France, are such extensive preparations being made to assume a creditable position at the Great Exhibition of 1851, as in Belgium. The whole of the great towns will contribute their choicest productions. Of the industrial exhibitions of Belgium, we have spoken in the INTRODUCTION.

BELGOROD, or BJELGOROD, the chief town of a circle in the Russian province of Kursk, has several manufactories for refining and pressing wax, and for spinning and weaving; and it carries on a considerable trade in hemp, bristles, honey, wax, leather, soap, &c.

BELGRADE, the capital of the principality of Servia in Turkey, is the principal entrepôt of the trade between Constantinople and Saloniki on one side, and Vienna and Pesth on the other. The exports consist of wool, dressed skins, buffalo and cow hides, wax, honey, tan-bark, silk, oxen and cows, immense numbers of pigs, and firewood. From Hungary, hardware, delft, porcelain, pottery, and salt are imported; and from Semlin the city is supplied with wheat, flour, oats, meat, vegetables, and fruits. There is considerable manufacturing industry among the inhabitants. Carpets, silk and cotton stuffs, arms, and leather are manufactured, and there are several bell foundries in the town.

BELL. Bells of a small size are undoubtedly very ancient; the Hebrews, the Greeks, and the Romans used them. The large bells now used in churches are said to have been invented by Paulinus, bishop of Nola in Campania, about the year 400; and they were probably introduced into England very soon after their invention.

The city of Nankin in China was anciently famous for the largeness of its bells, but they were afterwards far exceeded in size by those of the churches in Moscow. A bell given by the czar Boris Godunof to the cathedral of Moscow weighed 288,000 pounds, and another given by the Empress Anne, probably the largest in the known world, weighed 432,000 pounds. According to Coxe the height of this last bell was 19 feet, the circumference at the bottom 63 feet 11 inches, and its greatest thickness 23 inches. The great bell of St. Paul's weighs between 11,000 and 12,000 pounds. The new 'Great Tom of Lincoln,' cast in 1835, weighs 12,000 pounds; the 'Great Tom of Oxford,' 17,000 pounds; and the great bell cast in 1845 for York Minster, the heaviest in the United Kingdom, upwards of twelve tons, or about 27,000 pounds. The most ponderous bell ever cast in this country was, we believe, that made by Messrs. Mears in 1843 for the Roman catholic cathedral at Montreal.

The tone of a bell depends conjointly on the diameter and the thickness; a small bell or a thick bell giving, relatively, a more acute tone than one which is either larger or thinner. Hence the founder regulates the diameter and thickness according to the musical pitch of the tone which the bell is to yield; but, as this cannot be rigidly attained by casting only, the bells (say a set to form chimes) are attuned by chipping away some of the metal with a sharp-pointed hammer; reducing the diameter at the lower edge when the tone is too low, and reducing the thickness at the part where the hammer strikes when the tone is too acute.

Some of the recent parlour or table bells are not only convenient but very elegant productions. In Mr. Furlong's registered table-bell, which is quite ornamental enough to take its place among other adornments of the table, we have only to press down a little button or knob at the top, when a sound is produced loud enough to be heard in a distant room. The knob acts upon a small spring which moves a hammer.

It has been suggested that a single bar of well-made cast steel would be the cheapest of all bells for small churches, on account of its sonorous quality. There remains the consideration, however, how far such a substance would bear blows without fracture.

The casting of large church-bells is a process requiring great care and attention. Messrs. Mears, of Whitechapel, have for many years manufactured nearly all those made in this country of large dimensions. The operations are briefly described in a later article. [FOUNDING.]

BELL-METAL. [ALLOY.]

BELPER, Derbyshire, is one of those towns which owe their rise and importance to the cotton manufacture. Its prosperity is of modern date, and is to be principally ascribed to the establishment of the cotton works of Messrs. Strutt. It is now one of the most flourishing towns in Derbyshire. The chief manufacturing establishments are Messrs. Strutt's, who employ upwards of 2000 persons in the various departments of the cotton manufacture; Messrs. Ward, Sturt, and Sharp, manufacturing hosiers; and Messrs. Brettle, also manufacturing hosiers. This hosiery work is mostly carried on at the houses of the operatives. The manufacture of nails is carried on to some extent at Belper. There is also an extensive manufactory of brown earthenware near the town. Seams of coal are worked in the neighbourhood.

BELVEDERE, in Architecture, is a small building constructed at the top of a house or palace, and open to the air, at least on one side, and often on all. The term is an Italian compound, signifying 'a fine view;' and in Italy it is constructed expressly for that purpose, combined with the object of enjoying the cool evening breeze. The most celebrated construction of this kind at Rome, which is in the Vatican, was built by Bramante in that part called the Court of the Belvedere. Belvederes are not uncommon in France; but the term is applied rather to a summer-house in a park or garden, than to the constructions on the tops of houses.

BENCOOLEN, a settlement in the possession of the Dutch on the Island of Sumatra, has many spice plantations, which are cultivated by slaves under the superintendence of the Dutch. Bencoolen trades with Batavia, Bengal, the Coromandel coast, and the more northern ports of Sumatra. The imports are chiefly cloths, rice, salt, opium, tobacco, sugar, and European manufactures.

BENGAL. The province of Bengal is poor in mineral productions. The hills in Silhet produce iron ore. Iron is made at Punduah by a curious process, which at once smelts the ore and renders it malleable. Granular iron ore of the fineness of sand is washed clean and mixed with water into a soft mass; bits of reed, sticks, or leaves are then dipped in it, and take up as much as they will hold, and these, when pretty dry, are thrown into the top of a small clay cupola furnace and melted. It appears from this detail that the ore must possess a great degree of purity. The ore might be collected in large quantities, and as limestone of good quality and coal are found in the same range of hills the smelting might be easily effected. Some petroleum springs exist in the same district. Coal is abundant also in the Jungle Mahals, whence it can be easily conveyed to Calcutta in the rainy season, down the Dummoodah river. Coal and iron ore are both of them procured in Birbhoom, and iron works have long been carried on there by the natives. Extensive forests occur in the neighbourhood of these works, and the smelting is performed by means of charcoal.

The external commerce of Bengal is of great magnitude In the year 1831-2, under the regulated commerce during the existence of the trading privileges of the East India Company, the amount of the imports into Bengal (exclusive of the trade with China) was close upon two millions sterling; of the exports about 3,380,000*l.* The imports, by the year 1842, rose to nearly 6,000,000*l.*, and the exports to more than 8,000,000*l.* In 1846 the number of British ships entered inwards at Calcutta was 1080, of foreign ships only 99; in the same year there cleared outward 725 British ships, and 114 foreign ships.

The whole of these vessels had an average tonnage of about 300 tons.

A considerable part of the trade between Bengal and China is carried on from Calcutta. The most valuable part of this trade as regards its amount, is the shipment of opium. It formed more than one half of the value of the cargoes sent from the different presidencies to China, but the recent treaties with that country have considerably altered the trade in that article. The present value of opium exported from India amounts to upwards of 3,500,000*l*. The other principal articles shipped from Bengal to China are saltpetre, pearls, carnelians, coral, woollen and cotton manufactures of Europe, and rice.

The trade of Bengal with England comprehends an immense variety of objects. The principal articles of import are various metals, foreign wine and spirits, beer, woollen and cotton cloths, cotton yarn, glass, and hardware; in return for which the exports are, silk and silk manufactures, indigo, sugar, saltpetre, and lac-dye. Of these articles indigo is by far the most important, its value being equal to nearly one-half the total exports to Europe from the province. It is principally cultivated in Moorshedabad, Nuddea, and Jessore in Bengal, and Tirhoot in Bahar, where there are altogether from 300 to 400 factories in operation. The cotton exported is not so much from Bengal as from other provinces. With the exception of the districts on the eastern frontier, silk is grown in every part of the province of Bengal, and forms a considerable part of its exports; nearly the whole quantity of raw silk that is shipped is sent to England, which likewise receives more than half of the silk fabrics exported from the province. Saltpetre is another article of importance. Nearly seven-eighths of the whole quantity shipped from the province come to Great Britain. This branch of trade is valuable, from its furnishing a material part of the freight of homeward bound ships, the weight and bulk of saltpetre being great in proportion to its money value, while the opposite condition holds with regard to the greater part of the productions of India.

From France Bengal receives wine and brandy; the returns are principally made in saltpetre and indigo. To Portugal cotton piece-goods form the principal export; the imports consist almost wholly of bullion and wine. A large part of the trade of Portugal with China has been carried on intermediately through Calcutta, where the Portuguese traders take in opium and cotton, the returns for which go direct from Canton to Portugal, or to the transatlantic possessions of that country. A trade nearly similar in its character has been kept up between Bengal and Brazil, since the political separation of the latter country from Portugal. The United States of America take from Bengal silk, piece-goods, and indigo, with some other articles of Indian produce to a small amount; and send in exchange specie, metals, manufactured goods, and ice.

Bengal exports to Java piece-goods and opium, and receives in return copper, Banca tin, pepper and spices. To Manilla cotton piece-goods are sent; the returns are copper and silver from the South American mines, and a few trifling articles of fragrant woods and spices, the produce of the Philippine isles. From the Coromandel coast chank shells are brought, to a considerable value. These shells are employed by the Hindoos in their religious worship, and are cut into bracelets or worn round the ancle: payment for them is usually made in rice, and European goods. Ceylon supplies Bengal with cocoa-nut oil, coir, a few pearls, some spices, and chank-shells; in return for piece-goods, sugar, silk, and rice. Teak timber, sandal-wood, coir, cocoa-nuts, and drugs, are received from Malabar; which takes in payment piece-goods, metals and British woollens, with dates, raisins, coral and pearls. From the shores of the Persian Gulf Bengal receives Persian copper, almonds, dates, coffee, gums, pearls, coir, cocoa-nuts, pepper, and bullion; the returns are made in cotton piece-goods, silk goods, indigo, sugar, and grain. With the Mauritius, Bengal exchanges rice for pepper and spices. With the Moluccas and other eastern islands Bengal carries on a considerable trade. From the Burmese empire Bengal imports timber, gold and silver treasure, wax, sapan-wood, ivory, and drugs; and exports thither British cotton goods, grain, indigo, sugar, and opium.

It is expected that a few productions from this far distant region will grace the Industrial Exhibition of 1851.

BENZO'IC ACID. This acid, as its name imports, is usually obtained from the resinous substance called *gum benzoin* or *benjamin;* it occurs also in some other vegetable bodies, as the balsam of Peru and of Tolu, storax, and the flowers of the *trifolium melilotus officinalis.* It is found also in the urine of some animals.

The properties of benzoic acid are, that when pure it is colourless; it crystallizes in soft and rather elastic crystals, which have scarcely any smell; its taste is rather aromatic and penetrating than sour; by exposure to the air it undergoes no change; it combines readily with alkalies, and earthy and metallic oxides, forming salts which are called *benzoates;* it fuses and sublimes at a gentle heat, but a part of it is decomposed by the process; if strongly heated, it takes fire and burns with a bright yellow flame.

The saline compounds of benzoic acid are not very important. In its medical uses, the sublimed acid is the best form. It occurs in white needle-like prisms, with a silky lustre, a peculiar odour, and a pungent taste. It enters into the composition of the *Tinctura Camphoræ Composita* of the 'London Pharmacopœia,' and the *Tinctura Opii Ammoniata* of the 'Edinburgh Pharmacopœia,' two preparations long known under the name of *paregoric elixir.*

BENZOIN, or BENJAMIN, a resinous substance commonly but improperly termed a gum. It is extracted from the *Styrax Benzoin*, which grows in Sumatra, by making incisions in the trunk. It hardens very quickly, and is imported in the state of brittle masses, which when fractured present a mixture of white, brown, and red grains, frequently as large as an almond. Its smell is agreeable, resembling that of vanilla. It melts at a moderate heat, and yields benzoic acid, of which it contains about eighteen per cent. It contains, besides benzoic acid and a little volatile oil, three different resins, the separation of which requires complicated chemical processes.

In its medicinal action benzoin resembles the other balsamic resins, being stimulant and exciting. It is chiefly employed to yield benzoic acid, and as an ingredient in pastiles, or to burn in censers in Roman Catholic churches. It enters into the composition of the *Tinctura Benzoini Composita.* A solution of benzoin in alcohol, added to twenty parts of rose water, forms the cosmetic called *Virgin's milk.*

Gum benzoin is rather an expensive article. Its present price is about 50*l.* per cwt.

BENZOLE LIGHT. The Benzole light, introduced in 1849 by Mr. Mansfield, is founded on an ingenious mode of combining air with the vapour of a volatile liquid. Benzole is a compound of hydrogen and carbon, procured in considerable quantity from coal tar. Mr. Mansfield's plan consists in conducting a stream of atmospheric air or of common gas through a reservoir charged with benzole. The benzole vaporizes very rapidly; and in so doing, it combines with the air or gas, and produces a mixture well fitted for artificial illumination. Benzole and other hydro-carbons, when used in lamps in the usual way, contain too much carbon to burn satisfactorily; and means have long been sought to obviate the difficulty, by mixing the vapour of these substances with any gas or air which contains less carbon, or by mixing two liquids together before the vaporization of the hydro-carbon. A gallon of benzole is said to be equal in light-giving power to a thousand cubic feet of coal gas. The method is intended to be applied both on a large and on a small scale.

BE'RBERIS, a genus of plants containing many useful species. The fruit of the *Berberis aristata* and *B. Nepalensis* is dried by the mountaineers of India as raisins, and sent to the plains for sale. The bitterness and astringency of the bark has caused them to be received into the list of useful medicinal plants. The *Berberis vulgaris*, or Common Barberry, appears to inhabit equally the north of Europe, Asia, and America, in woods and thickets, especially in limestone countries. It is usually a bush from four to six foot high; but in Italy it becomes as large as a plum tree, living a couple of centuries or more. The wood is hard, but brittle, and is chiefly employed by the dyers for staining yellow.

BERBICE. [GUYANA.]

BERGAMO, a province of Austrian Italy, is in many parts very fertile; and the system of irrigation is extensively applied. The vine, the olive, and the walnut are cultivated, and there are large plantations of mulberry-trees, raising silk, which constitute the chief wealth of the country. There are also valuable iron mines, large iron-works, and several woollen and silk-factories in the province. In the chief town, Bergamo, is *La Fiera*, a vast quadrangular building, with three gates on each side, courts and streets within, and contains 600 shops, in which the various manufactures of Lombardy and other provinces of Austria are exposed for sale, at an annual autumnal fair. Goods are sold at this fair to the amount of 1,000,000*l.*, about one-third of which is laid out for silks.

BERGAMOT, ESSENCE OF, an essential oil, obtained both by pressure and distillation from the rind of the Bergamot, the ripe fruit of the *Citrus Bergamium:* it is limpid, yellowish, and fluid. The kind procured by pressure is not so fluid as that yielded by distillation, but its odour is more agreeable. The smell resembles that of oranges, and it is used as perfume.

About 22,000 lbs. of Bergamot oil was imported in 1848.

BERGEN, a town in the kingdom of Norway, on the sea-coast, has a commerce of

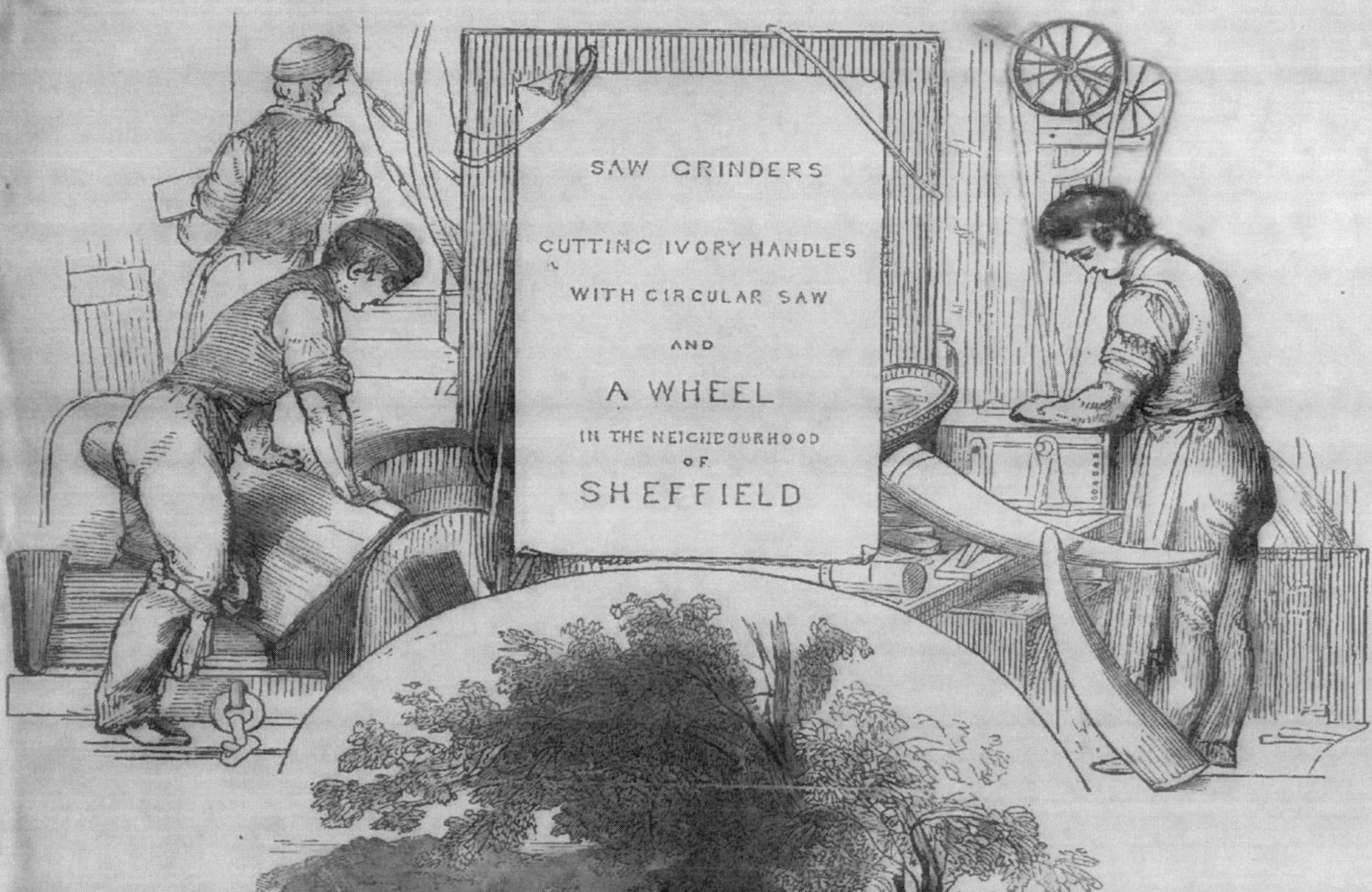

KNIGHTS CYCLOPÆDIA
OF THE
INDUSTRY OF ALL NATIONS

much magnitude. The northern provinces receive from Bergen the greater part both of the necessaries and the luxuries of life. In return, Bergen receives from these provinces large quantities of fish, herrings, roes, fish-oil, tallow, skins, feathers, &c., all which articles are brought by the Nordlandmen themselves in their own vessels to Bergen. They come to Bergen twice a year with their own yachts, which form a peculiar class of merchant vessels. The arrival at Bergen of the fishing-vessels from the Lofoden winter fisheries occasions extraordinary life in the port and on the quays; the harbour is almost blocked up with vessels; frequently the whole night is employed in transporting, packing, and preparing goods; so that this season may be considered as a continual fair.

The trade of Bergen with the other parts of Norway is by no means so important as that with Nordland. From the interior of the country Bergen receives iron-manufactures, glass, tiles, &c.; from the towns in the diocese of Trondjem, some copper, with millstones and grindstones.

Of foreign trade, that with the Baltic is very considerable. Bergen exports thither large quantities of herrings and other fish, and skins, receiving in return hemp, glue, hops, canvas, linen, &c. The trade with Denmark, Hamburg, Holland, England, Sweden, France, and the Mediterranean, is extensive: the produce and manufactures of those countries being received in exchange for the fish and other produce of Norway. Bergen is, in fact, the Liverpool of Norway.

BERLIN, the metropolis of the Prussian monarchy, and the largest and finest town in Germany, (Vienna only excepted) cannot be otherwise than an important commercial and industrial centre. Among the six *quartiers*, or quarters, and the five suburbs, of which the city consists, are many manufacturing establishments of great magnitude. In the Berlin Quarter are the *Lager* house and the royal *Gewerb* house, where several royal manufactories are conducted on a large scale. In the new Cologne Quarter is the Royal Salt Magazine. In the Friedrichswerder Quarter is the Royal Foundry. In the Friedrichstadt Quarter is the Royal Porcelain Manufactory; and the royal manufactory of gold and silver work. The celebrated Berlin iron trinkets are manufactured near the Oranienburg Gate.

Berlin is one of the first manufacturing towns in the Prussian dominions. Its chief productions are the celebrated Berlin china, silks, silks and cottons mixed, woollens, cottons, stockings, and ribands; and next in order are gunpowder, cast-iron ware, silk hats, paper, oils, refined sugars, and tobacco and snuff.

If war should not unhappily step in to check industry, Berlin will be well represented at the Hyde Park Exhibition of 1851. Its iron, porcelain, terra cotta, silks, woollens, linens, paper, and machinery, are all to be illustrated by choice specimens. The Berlin castings are especially looked forward to with interest. Casting in zinc, an art not much practised in England, is carried to much perfection in Berlin; cast groups in this material, the size of life, are to be forwarded to England. In terra-cotta and earthenware the Berlin manufacturers are endeavouring not merely to attain high artistic excellence, but also to produce good and cheap articles for every day use.

A very interesting feature, in relation to the Industrial Exhibition, is the formation of a committee at Berlin, for facilitating the visit of a large number of Prussians to London in 1851. Contracts are to be made with railway companies, and with steam-boat and omnibus proprietors; dwelling-houses and a dining-hall are to be engaged; and all expenses from Berlin to London, in London, and from London back to Berlin, are to be charged to each visitor in one sum.

BERLIN WORK. [EMBROIDERY.]

BERMUDAS. These islands grow the palm-tree, the leaves of which are exported to be made up as ladies' fans. Coffee, cotton, indigo, and tobacco, are no longer cultivated, with the exception of a little indigo; the soil appears to have become less suitable than formerly for the production of these articles. The principal employment is the building of vessels, which are generally small, swift, and very durable, being constructed of cedar. Plaiting of straw, and of the mid-rib of the palmetto leaf, is also carried on; and a beautiful species of white freestone, easily cut, is exported to the West Indies for ornamental architecture. Vessels annually visit the Bahamas for salt.

Bermuda is one of the naval and military depôts of Britain. Plans have been recently drawn up for a new steam factory, storehouses, hospitals, workmen's dwellings, &c. Upwards of 300,000*l.* were spent in the public works between 1838 and 1848; of this 157,000*l.* were for a breakwater. The Government are about to build a hauling-up slip. The new victualling-office is planned to contain one year's stores for 5000 men. The new steam factory has been formed in order to facilitate the repairs when needed of the Atlantic steamers. The vessels belonging to the Bermudas in 1848 were 56, of 3645 tons burden. The imports in 1848 were of the value of 149,000*l.*; the exports 18,000*l.* The British produce and manufactures sent to Bermuda in 1849 were valued at 47,138*l.*

BERN, the largest and most populous canton of Switzerland, produces corn, though not sufficient for the consumption of the population, and fruit in abundance, especially apples, pears, plums, nuts, and cherries. From the cherries the spirit called *kirschwasser* is made, which, as well as the extract from absinth, or wormwood, are articles of common use, as in the rest of Switzerland. Beer and cider are made in the country. The vine thrives in a few districts, chiefly in that of Nidau near the lake of Bienne, where wine is made. Hemp and flax are also among the products of the soil; but cattle and the products of the dairy constitute the chief wealth of the country; cheese is made in abundance for exportation, especially in the valleys of Emmenthal, Simmenthal, and Gessenai or Saanen.

The canton of Bern is, to a moderate extent, a manufacturing country. Linen is made in many places, sufficient for the internal consumption: there are tanneries at Bern, as well as a few manufactories of silks, coarse woollens, and paper. Mathematical instruments, watches, and jewellery, muskets, and other arms, are made at Bern, Porentrui, &c. The Bernese gunpowder is excellent, and far superior in quality to the French: the manufacturing of it is free, and not subject to monopoly as in France. At Correndelin, Untervilier, and other places in the valleys of the Jura, there are iron-works and foundries, the iron ore being found in abundance in the mountains. Timber for building and fuel are supplied by the mountain forests, and from other woods in several parts of the lowlands.

The chief town, Bern, is rather a centre for the general commerce of the country, than a manufacturing place.

BERTHOLLET, CLAUDE LOUIS, must be briefly noticed in this place, for the services which his chemical discoveries rendered to manufactures. Shortly before the first French revolution, he was appointed superintendent of dyeing processes, which office had been occupied by Macquer. To this appointment chemistry was indebted for his work on dyeing, which contains a better account both of the theory and practice of the art than any work which had before made its appearance. When the French Revolution broke out, and that country became involved in war, many of the requisites for carrying it on which had previously been imported could no longer be obtained through this channel. This was especially the case with saltpetre for the manufacture of gunpowder. In this emergency Berthollet visited almost every part of the country, for the purpose of pointing out the means of extracting and purifying this salt; he was also employed with some other men of science, in the processes of smelting iron and converting it into steel. In the year 1792, being appointed one of the commissioners of the mint, he introduced considerable improvements into the processes employed in that establishment.

BERWICK-UPON-TWEED. From the reign of Edward I. to that of Elizabeth, the principal export trade of Berwick was wool, wool fells, hides, and salmon: but the trade of the place has suffered some modification in later times. The principal manufactures are those connected with shipping; but there are also iron-foundries, and steam-engines; sacking, cotton hosiery, damask, diaper, carpets, hats, and shoes are made. Until within the last thirty-five years, a highly lucrative trade was carried on in the export of pork and eggs to London, the annual value of the eggs shipped being at least 30,000*l.*, and of pork about 10,000*l.*; but since the peace this trade has totally ceased, and the metropolis is supplied from Ireland and the Continent. Berwick is now a bonding port. The existing trade of the town is principally confined to the exporting of salmon, corn, and coals to London, to various ports in Scotland, and to foreign countries. Of late considerable quantities of ale and whiskey have been shipped to London. The smacks and small brigs which formerly carried on the trade of the place have been superseded by large and well fitted schooners, and clipper ships. There are regular traders between Berwick, London, Kingston-upon-Hull, Newcastle-upon-Tyne, and Leith. About 70 vessels belong to the port.

The salmon fisheries in the Tweed have for many centuries been very productive. Until about the year 1790 the salmon sent from Berwick were either salted and dried, or boiled and pickled with salt and vinegar, except salmon-trout, which were occasionally kept alive in wells or tanks in the ship's hold. The exports were principally to London, but considerable quantities of salted salmon were also sent to the Mediterranean. At present the whole are sent fresh to London packed in ice. About 800 of the inhabitants of Berwick are now (1850) employed in the fisheries.

BERYL, a mineral species, among the varieties of which are found two of the most beautiful and costly gems with which we are acquainted, namely, the *emerald* and the *precious beryl.* The species belongs to the rhombohedral system of crystallization, usually occurring in regular hexagonal prisms. Its constituents are silica, alumina, glucina, lime, and oxides of iron, columbium, and chromium, in proportions which differ in different specimens.

The two chief varieties, emerald and aquamarine or precious beryl, differ chiefly in colour; the term emerald being applied to those possessing the peculiar rich deep green so well known as the emerald green; while all the other varieties are comprehended under the name of beryl: those which are clear, transparent, possess a good colour, and present various shades of sky-blue or mountain-green, being the aquamarine or precious beryl. The colour of the emerald is attributed to a small quantity of green oxide of chromium; while the varieties in the tints of beryl may be considered to be produced by admixtures of the oxides of iron, the yellow being the colour of the peroxides of iron, and the mountain-green and the various shades of blue being the effect of varying quantities of the protoxide.

Emeralds, for the last two centuries, have rarely been found, except in Peru, where they occur in Santa Fé and in the valley of Tunca. Those met with in modern times seldom exceed the size of a walnut. Beryls are procured from Siberia, Brazil, Sweden, Saxony, Bohemia, and Iceland. The beryl sometimes occurs in crystals of very large size. The value of the emerald depends not only on its size, colour, and brilliancy, but also on its being free from flaws, by which this gem is frequently greatly deteriorated in the eye of the jeweller.

BESANCON, the capital formerly of Franche-Comté, is a place of considerable manufacturing industry; its position on the Doubs, which is navigable, and on the canal which unites the Rhone and the Rhine, makes it the centre of an important trade. The chief manufacture is that of the works of watches and clocks, in which 2000 men are employed. Hosiery, coarse woollens and cottons, carpets, room-paper, hardware, stoves, liqueurs, and artificial flowers, are manufactured. There are also iron-foundries, china-works, tanneries, several large breweries, and establishments for bleaching wax. The trade of the town consists in its industrial products, and in wine, brandy, broad-cloth, groceries, iron, and coal.

BETEL-NUTS. These nuts are procured from the *Areca Catechu*, a palm which grows in India. They have an astringent flavour; but when mixed with lime, and with the leaf of the betel pepper, they become milder, and are chewed by the natives of India.

BEVEL, or BEVIL, is the name applied both to the oblique angle formed by two surfaces which meet at either more or less than a right angle, and to the instrument employed by carpenters and joiners for taking and transferring such angles. The common carpenter's bevel consists of a straight wooden stock, mortised at one end to receive a thin blade, which is usually formed of steel, and attached to the stock by a pin in such a way that it may be turned to any required angle, and secured by a tightening screw. Where many articles have to be worked to the same angle, it is desirable to use a fixed bevel, made to the required angle, especially where one or both of the limbs are curved.

BIDEFORD. This town, one of the most active in Devonshire, has long had a considerable foreign trade. The principal imports are timber from North America; timber, hemp, and tallow, from Russia and Norway; fruits, wines, and brandies, from Spain, Portugal, and the Mediterranean; and general goods from Ireland. The exports are oak-bark, which is shipped in considerable quantities to Scotland and Ireland; earthenware, tiles, &c., to Wales, Guernsey, and Jersey; linen and woollen goods, cordage, iron, naval stores, provisions, &c., to the North American colonies. Corn is largely exported to the Metropolis, and to the ports along the coast. About 150 vessels belong to the port. In recent years there have been about 800 arrivals and departures of vessels annually. Ship building is carried on at Bideford to a considerable extent. There are several potteries, principally for the manufacture of flower-pots. A manufactory of coarse china and earthenware has been lately established at a short distance from the town. Clay of a good quality is found on land in the neighbourhood belonging to Lord Clinton. Anthracite or culm is found in the vicinity in sufficient quantity to be worked for economical purposes.

BIGA, a chariot or car drawn by two horses. The Romans had also their quadrigæ, and sometimes their sejuges, septim-juges, &c.; and Suetonius says that Nero, when he was a performer in the Olympic games, made use of a decem-jugis, a chariot drawn by ten horses.

BILBA'O, one of the chief towns of Spain on the Biscayan coast, has an active population, who are employed in agriculture, commerce, and the manufacturing of iron. There are also manufactures of paper, hats, soap, leather, earthenware, and cigars.

The principal articles of exportation are wool and wheat to foreign countries, and iron to other parts of the Peninsula.

BILL OF LADING, is an acknowledgment

signed usually by the master of a trading ship, but occasionally by some person authorised to act on his behalf, certifying the receipt of merchandise on board the ship, and engaging under certain conditions and with certain exceptions, such as 'the act of God,' the 'king's enemies,' &c., to deliver the said merchandise safely at the port to which the ship is bound, either to the shipper, or to such other person as he may signify by a written assignment upon the Bill of Lading.

BILLON, in coinage, is a composition of precious and base metal, consisting of gold or silver alloyed with copper, in the mixture of which the copper predominates. The word came to us from the French.

BILSTON, Staffordshire, owes all its importance to the introduction of the iron works. It previously consisted of only a few private houses; but standing in a district which possesses considerable mines of coal, iron-stone, quarry-stone, and clay, it has rapidly increased in extent and population. The manufacturing industry is very great. There are numerous furnaces for smelting iron-ore, with foundries, forges, slitting-mills, steam engines, and the various works necessary for the preparation of iron. The manufacture of tin, and of every kind of japanned and enamelled wares, with that of iron, from nails and wire to the heaviest and bulkiest articles, is largely carried on at Bilston. At night there are upwards of fifty furnace fires and coke heaps sending forth their bodies of flame in and near the town. Coarse pottery is made with the clay which is found in the neighbourhood in much abundance. There is also here a deep orange-coloured and almost impalpable sand, which is much used in the casting of metals; the neighbourhood is likewise noted for a stone quarry.

BINGLEY is one of the remarkable clothing towns of West Yorkshire. The manufacture of worsted yarn is carried on to a considerable extent in the town and neighbourhood, besides which there are very extensive cotton-mills; there are also paper manufactories; and there is some trade in malt. Altogether Bingley has become a place of much manufacturing and commercial importance.

BINNACLE, a kind of box used on board ship to contain the compass. *Bittacle*, an abbreviation of the French word *habitacle*, a small habitation, was the original form of the word. Many improvements have been made in the binnacle within the last few years; chiefly in relation to the mode of throwing light upon the compass card in the night.

BIRCH. The birch is extremely valuable among our forest trees, from the variety of materials which it furnishes to the manufacturing arts. The common birch is one of the hardiest of known trees, and flourishes best in cold countries. The timber, without possessing any one quality in an eminent degree, possesses many qualities in a very useful degree. It is employed in France for the felloes of wheels; and in Russia for the construction of small rustic carriages. On many parts of the continent it is used for many articles of furniture, cooperage, and turnery, and sabots or wooden shoes. The Highlanders of Scotland use birch for so many purposes that they are said to, 'make everything of it;' they build their houses of it; make their beds, chairs, tables, dishes and spoons of it; construct their mills of it; make their carts, ploughs, barrows, gates, and fences of it; and even manufacture ropes of it. The above uses apply to the *white* birch. The *black* or *canoe* birch is also of great value; it flourishes in North America, and is there applied to numerous purposes: some specimens of the timber are so beautifully grained that they are cut into veneers and used in cabinet work. The wood of the *tall* or *American* birch is used in the United States and Nova Scotia for yokes of cattle and frames of sledges, for hoops of casks, for articles of furniture, and for many other purposes. The wood of the *pliant* birch has a fine and close grain, a considerable degree of strength, and takes a brilliant polish. It is used in the United States for tables, bedsteads, arm-chairs, sofas, coach-panels, shoe-lasts, and a great variety of purposes.

The *bark* of all the species of birch is of very considerable value, especially in cold northern countries, where it is applied to a great variety of uses. It is very durable, and little acted on by air or water. In some countries it is used as a coping for walls and a covering for roofs. The bark of large trees is cut by the Laplanders into pieces large enough to form capes or short cloaks. It is also employed for boots, shoes, baskets, boxes, mats, cordage, harness, and thread. In Kamtschatka the inner bark is dried and ground, and mixed with oatmeal to form an article of food; and the same people eat the bark in small pieces with the roe of fish. It is much used for tanning leather; and a yellowish brown dye which it yields is employed in some countries for dyeing woollens and rein-deer skins. The bark of the *canoe* birch is used in America for roof coverings, baskets, boxes, portfolios, paper, and inner soles of shoes; but it is more extensively employed in making the canoes of the *voyageurs*, engaged in the fur-trade of Canada: such a canoe, capable of accommodating four persons will weigh no more than forty lbs. Tents are also made of this bark. The bark of the *tall* birch is used in tanning; that of the *pliant* birch is stripped white in the green state, by the Kamtschatkadales, cut into narrow strips like vermicelli, and stewed with caviare.

The *branches* and young *shoots* are also of much value. They are made into hoops, brooms, faggot-ties, baskets, hurdles, cream-whisks, and similar articles—including the well-known rod of our old-fashioned school-masters. The Alpine mountaineers make torches of them. The Laplanders construct tents with birch branches covered with turf. In the Scottish highlands the branches are employed as fuel in the distillation of whiskey, being found to impart a flavour to it which enhances its value; they are similarly employed for smoking hams and herrings. The young branches of the *dwarf* birch furnish beds and fuel to the Laplanders; and those of the *black* birch are employed in the United States for making hoops for rice-casks.

The *leaves*, *catkins*, and other green parts, have also their value. The leaves are eaten by goats and rabbits. A yellow colour is obtained from them, useful in painting and dyeing. The Finlanders use the dried leaves as tea. The buds and catkins afford a substitute for bees' wax. A bed stuffed with birch leaves is said to be useful to rheumatic persons by promoting perspiration. The leaves of the dwarf birch yield a peculiar kind of fungus, from which the *moxa* or *amadou* is prepared, and which the Laplanders employ as a medicine in many painful diseases; and its seeds afford nourishment to the ptarmigan or white partridge, a very important bird in Lapland.

The *sap* of the birch is made to yield beer, wine, spirit, vinegar, and sugar, according to the mode of treatment; the tree being tapped to allow the sap to flow or ooze out. Birch beer is made by fermenting the sap with yeast, hot-water, and hops; birch wine is made by boiling the sap with sugar or honey, and fermenting, clarifying and flavouring in various ways; but spirit is made by distillation; birch vinegar by allowing the acetous fermentation to supervene on the vinous; and birch sugar by boiling and evaporating the sap.

To complete the catalogue of the use of the birch we have to mention the *fuel*, the *ashes*, and the *oil*. The wood gives a bright and ardent flame, and is much employed for smelting iron in France, Russia, and Sweden—its charcoal burns a long time, and is in much demand for making gunpowder and black crayons. The ashes are rich in potash. An oil, much used in Russia, is obtained by burning birch bark in close receptacles.

BIRD'S-EYE VIEW, a mode of perspective representation, in which the objects are drawn as seen from above. Thus, if a hole were bored through the ceiling of a lofty room, a person looking down through it would have a proper bird's-eye view of the apartment and its furniture. But the most common mode of giving a bird's-eye view differs from ordinary perspective only in the horizontal line, and consequently the point of sight, being placed considerably above the objects represented. The scene is thus shown as it would appear from some lofty station, as a tower or other eminence.

BIRD-LIME, a glutinous vegetable product, obtained principally from the inner bark of the holly, or from the berries of the misletoe, but also from other plants. It is prepared from the holly bark by bruising, long boiling in water, and fermentation; the mass is again boiled in water, and evaporated to a proper consistence. In different countries various processes are employed. When properly prepared from the holly it is of a greenish colour; its smell resembles that of linseed oil; its taste is bitter; it is adhesive, tenacious, and may be drawn out into threads.

BIRKBECK, GEORGE, M.D., one of the warmest friends and kindest instructors of the operative classes, was born in 1776, at Settle, in Yorkshire, where his father was a merchant and banker. He displayed an early predilection for mechanical and scientific subjects, which led him to select the medical profession as his pursuit. While at Edinburgh, he was put in nomination for the professorship of the Andersonian Institution at Glasgow, and his election was carried by a considerable majority. In November 1799 he commenced his first course of lectures at Glasgow on Natural and Experimental Philosophy. Some time afterwards he commenced a gratuitous course of lectures, which he continued until 1804, when he relinquished the professorship, and was succeeded by Dr. Ure.

While in active practice in London as a physician, Dr. Birkbeck had few opportunities of following up the labours which he had commenced at Glasgow for the advancement of scientific knowledge amongst artisans; but it was a subject which he had always at heart. In 1820 he gave a gratuitous course of seventeen lectures at the London Institution. In 1827 he was the chief means of promoting the first *Mechanics' Institution*. He presided at a public meeting at the Crown and Anchor, which was attended, amongst others, by Dr. Lushington, Jeremy Bentham, David Wilkie, and Cobbett; and after another meeting, on the 2nd of December, the first officers of the 'London Mechanics' Institution' were appointed on the 15th of December. Dr. Birkbeck was elected president, which office he filled till his death; and his son has since been annually elected to the same post. At the formation of the institution, Dr. Birkbeck generously lent the sum of 3,700*l.*, for the purpose of building a lecture-room, &c.

Dr. Birkbeck's professional and scientific pursuits, and his services in various ways, in connection with objects of public utility, were continued to the last; and those who attended the lectures at the London Mechanics' Institution, in its best days, will well remember those of Dr. Birkbeck as among the most instructive and the most attractive. He died December 1, 1841, at his residence in Finsbury-square, London.

BIRKENHEAD. The grand undertakings at this town are among the most remarkable commercial phenomena of our age. The overflowings of Liverpool commerce are to form the basis of Birkenhead commerce.

The rapid growth of Birkenhead is entirely owing to the formation of commodious docks. In 1842 the town commissioners were empowered by act of parliament to purchase the manorial rights, &c., pertaining to the ancient ferry at Woodside, which is the nearest ferry to Liverpool; and in 1844, under another act, they purchased Monk's Ferry. In 1844 they obtained an act of still greater importance, under which a tidal basin, docks, and other extensive accommodations for trade and shipping are now in progress. The magnitude of these works may be inferred from the following abstract of their cost, which is taken from the estimates: New market, 20,000*l.*; town-hall, 10,000*l.*; park, 25,000*l.*; docks in Wallasey Pool, 400,000*l.*; dock warehouses (by a private company), 600,000*l.* The design of converting Wallasey Pool, on which Birkenhead is situated, into docks, was entertained several years ago, and originated with the late Mr. Laird; but it was not until 1844 that an act, as already mentioned, was obtained for effecting this object. The first stone of the proposed docks was laid on the 23rd of October, 1844. The area of the principal or floating dock will be 120 acres, a space exceeding that of all the docks in Liverpool, and it will have 19 feet depth of water. It will be surrounded with quays, warehouses, and other conveniences for shipping and discharging cargoes. There will also be a tidal harbour of about 40 acres, accessible at all times by the largest steamers employed in the coasting trade, and by all vessels whose draught does not exceed 15 feet; a harbour of refuge with an area of 10 acres; and beaching-ground of 4 or 5 acres, for the free use of the river craft.

A certain clashing of interests between different governing bodies at Birkenhead, has rendered new arrangements frequently necessary. Besides the act of 1844, a second was obtained in 1845 for the formation of dock and wharf walls; and another in 1847 for new powers in respect to these constructions. In 1848 an act was passed for the formation of a board of trustees of the Birkenhead docks, which board (in order to represent and reconcile conflicting interests) is to be formed as follows:—Four trustees chosen by the bondholders, with whose funds the docks were in part constructed; four chosen by the Birkenhead commissioners; and three by the Wallasey commissioners.

There has recently (1850) been an act passed, which relieves the commissioners from a very onerous engagement with the Woods and Forests department; and the dock-works have recommenced (after some delay) with great vigour. Three thousand men are now employed; forty-five acres of dock are nearly ready for the reception of shipping; and the whole are expected to be finished in 1851.

Birkenhead is connected by railway with Chester, and thence with all parts of England; and a branch to Warrington, recently opened, has shortened the distance between Birkenhead and Manchester. The rails are brought round all the quays of the docks. Hitherto the trade of Birkenhead has not reached the point which had been anticipated, and the hope of which had led to such extensive and costly works; but whenever a large traffic shall grow up there, it will be well accommodated by the railway, the docks, and the warehouses, all of which are admirably planned to work together in one system. It is expected that the coasting trade and the steam-packet trade will be those which will first seek accommodation at Birkenhead.

BIRMAH. The Birman empire is rich in mines of gold, silver, copper, tin, lead, antimony, and iron, but they are much neglected by the natives. Many kinds of precious stones are obtained by digging and washing the gravel in the beds of rivulets or small brooks. The varieties said to exist are, the oriental sapphire, the oriental ruby, the opalescent ruby, the star ruby; the green, the yellow, and the white sapphire; and the oriental amethyst. Noble serpentine or green-stone, is found in most of the upper branches of the Irawaddi, and exported in considerable quantities by the Chinese to their own country, where it is used for rings and amulets. Mines of amber are found on the branches of the Kyan-Duayn, and in the vicinity of the Bhanmò. Coal seems to be plentiful, but it is not used. Limestone exists in great abundance in the mountains near the capital; and statuary marble is also met with. Nitre, natron, and culinary salt, are found in many of the arid and calcareous tracts in the upper provinces, and chiefly in the neighbourhood of the capital. Natron, in an impure state, is used by the natives instead of soap, a preparation with which they seem to be unacquainted. Salt is extracted from some lakes in the upper provinces, especially near Monchabo, and from the sea water in the lower provinces.

Among the vegetable productions of the Birman forests the teak holds the first place. The plants which become articles of commerce in the country include bamboo, catechu, sugar, tea, cocoa, tobacco, cotton, indigo, and betel.

The progress of the Birmans in the useful arts has not been great. All their cotton fabrics are coarse and high-priced, and British piece-goods are imported in considerable quantity. Silk articles, coarse and unglazed earthenware, iron implements, muskets and swords, and gold and silver ornaments, are manufactured, mostly in a rude style.

The commerce carried on in the interior of the country is considerable; the different portions of the empire producing several things which are not found in others. The inhabitants of the sea-coast and the lower country carry to the capital and the upper provinces rice, salt, dried fish, and foreign commodities; which are paid for by the produce of the interior. The foreign commerce, chiefly with China, is conducted principally at two annual fairs, at Bhanmò and Midé. The Chinese arrive with laden horses, mules, and asses; bringing with them an immense assortment of goods.

BIRMINGHAM, is in many respects the most remarkable of our manufacturing towns. It dates its productive industry from early times. Being situated at a moderate distance from the Staffordshire iron mines, which were unquestionably worked at a very early date, and placed in a district which was distinguished as woody (the northern or Arden division of Warwickshire), it offered great facilities for smelting the ore of iron, which, before the introduction of the steam-engine, could only be effected by means of charcoal. The iron being prepared on the spot, it is natural to suppose that a colony of artificers would settle here, and that they would early acquire skill in the use of the material. In the time of Leland, Birmingham was inhabited by 'smiths, that use to make knives and all manner of cutting-tools; and many lorimers that make bitts, and a great many nailors.' A place thus characterised by the industry and ingenuity of its inhabitants, waited only for more favourable circumstances to increase its wealth. This change appears to have taken place in the 17th century, when, on the restoration of Charles II., a fondness for metal ornaments was introduced from France, where the exiled king and his adherents had long resided, and Birmingham took the lead in the manufacture of the glittering trifles which the taste of the age demanded.

Camden, who travelled through England in the 16th century, a few years after Leland, says of Birmingham, in his 'Britannia,' that 'most of the inhabitants be smiths;' to which Bishop Gibson, in his edition of Camden, published in 1722, adds, 'and other artificers in iron and steel, whose performances are greatly admired both at home and abroad.' The editor was, however, scarcely correct if he meant it to be understood that the manufactures of the town were in his time confined to iron and steel goods. Various fancy articles in other materials were then regularly made, and the manufacture of brass goods had commenced. The use of this valuable compound metal has continually increased during the last hundred years, and the talent of the designer has been tasked in the invention of new forms, and in the adaptation of classical models to the purposes of modern domestic comfort and ornament. The introduction of the stamp especially, which was first applied to the multiplication of copies of smaller wares, as buttons, buckles, and cloak pins, and which was at length adapted, by increasing its power, to the production of large forms, has caused the greatest change in this branch of manufacture. There are establishments in Birmingham which have from two to three hundred thousand dies employed in stamping

In plated wares the style and form were long deficient in grace, but the taste and spirit of Messrs. Boulton and Watt were instrumental in improving the forms of the articles usually produced; and an increasing familiarity with antient models, and with the florid and playful style of the age of Louis XIV., continues to give new impetus to this manufacture. The introduction of the new mixture called Albata, or British plate, was the forerunner of a very large branch of manufacture at Birmingham. The convenient material called Britannia metal is also largely manufactured here.

Tho founding of iron is rapidly improving and extending itself in this town. A comparatively few years ago the principal cast articles of this material were heavy kitchen articles grates and stoves; but increased care in the selection of the metal, and a desire to produce elegant forms at a cheap rate, have caused cast iron articles to be manufactured of small size and of light and tasteful patterns, which, when coloured by bronzing, almost equal the moro expensive brass wares; and in hollow vessels such perfection in thinness and lightness is attained, that tho use of beaten copper is almost forgotten. The iron-work of Mr. Paxton's Palace of Industry has been prepared under the direction of the eminent Birmingham firm of Fox and Henderson.

The manufacture of guns was introduced at the commencement of the last century, and has been carried on to an immense extent; nearly 5,000,000 of fire arms were supplied from Birmingham between the years 1804 and 1818 inclusive, to meet the demands of government and of private trade. A proof-house, under the conduct of a master, wardens, and trustees, was established by act of parliament in 1813 where the fabric of all guns and pistol barrels is tried by a heavy charge: all those which sustain the explosion receive a stamp, to counterfeit which is felony; and to sell such barrels without the stamp is punishable by heavy fines. There is also a government proof-house for the ordnance department, a comprehensive and interesting establishment near the Walsall Road, at the northern end of the town.

Buttons and buckles, so far as they are articles of ornament, almost took their rise in Birmingham, and this town witnessed all tho fluctuations of these manufactures, from the small plain buckle, and the horn or bone button coated with metal foil, through all the capricious and almost innumerable varieties of form and ornament which prevailed during the age of powder, embroidery, and gold lace, or which the still more fantastic taste of foreign markets demanded. At length the buckle has been completely supplanted by shoe-strings, and the button has undergone great changes: moulds of wood or horn being now very generally covered with silk or some other woven material, as a substitute for the metal button. The button factories are among the largest establishments in Birmingham. The denomination of 'The toyshop of Europe,' given to Birmingham by Burke, was correct at the time, but the extensive application of powerful mechanical forces has now raised tho character of the staple productions of the place. All articles of metallic ornament, such as polished steel toys, gold and gilt jewellery, chains, snuff-boxes, &c., are still manufactured, but not to such an amount as to form a preponderant part of the industry of Birmingham.

The quantity of silver used in the manufacture of pencil-cases, boxes, chains, thimbles, &c., and in the numerous fittings and mountings attached to glass and other wares, is considerable, and an assay office is established in the town, where all articles in this metal being above five dwt. are examined, and if found to be of the proper standard, are marked with the government stamp. The use of gold and silver has greatly increased in Birmingham in recent years. The process of electro plating has given rise to a wholly new department of manufacture, of which Birmingham is the chief seat.

Japanning in all its varieties, is another extensive branch of manufacture. It commenced with the varnished boxes and small articles, which were coarse imitations of the Oriental toys, but the art was gradually improved by John Taylor, who gavo elegance to the devices on the surface; and still further by Baskerville, who introduced tho light and highly polished but firm and durable *papier mâché*, which he adorned with paintings in a style before unknown. This branch of industry has called forth great talent; and some of those who have taken rank among the painters of their age have commenced their career by executing the ornamental designs on the trays and waiters of Birmingham. Articles of this kind are susceptible of great elegance, and when produced in perfection are beautiful specimens of the pictorial art. In all the recent Exhibitions of Manufactures in this country the *papier mâché* of Messrs. Jennens and Bettridge and other manufacturers at Birmingham, has been remarkable for its artistic beauty.

Glass making has long been carried on in Birmingham. This manufacturo is not now confined, in its higher branches, to cut vessels for the table, nor to the sparkling drops which decorate girandoles and chandeliers; but glass for ornamental purposes is cast into forms of scrolls, foliage, busts, and well-formed complete figures of small size. Window-glass is also mado in large quantities. Messrs. Chance's glass works, among tho largest in the world, are at Birmingham; it is here that the glass for the Industrial Palace has been made.

An apparently trivial article, the steel-pen, has latterly grown into such extensive use as to form a considerable branch of manufacture. The price has been perpetually diminishing, and the article itself, at the same time, continually improving. This manufacture was first established in Birmingham in 1821, before which time the article was scarcely known in the market. Shortly after this date they sold for 12*s.* per dozen, but the price rapidly fell to 2*s.* per dozen, or 1*l.* 4*s.* per gross. The increasing facilities of production, and the consequent abundant supply, added to the competition of the numerous manufacturers, has since gradually lowered the price to 6*d.* a gross, or even less. There is one establishment in Birmingham (besides others of less extent) where many hundred millions of pens are made annually, and where 300 persons are employed.

The cutlers, lorimers, and makers of wrought nails, who in Leland's time formed the bulk of the industrious population of Birmingham, have thus been gradually driven away by the increasing demand for articles requiring more taste and skill in design and execution. Agricultural and manufacturing steel and edge tools, including files and saws, are however still made, and numerous new manufactures have been introduced during the present century, which owed their origin to the facilities afforded by the newly created mechanical forces, that gave a spur to invention by almost insuring its success. Among these are wire-drawing, cut-nail, screw, and pin manufacturing. Fine turnery naturally arose from the increasing use of the lathe. Die-sinkers, modellers, and designers were required by those who used stamps and casting-moulds; and engravers were called for to represent in the books of patterns exhibited by the merchants the forms of the numerous articles prepared by brass and iron-founders and other manufacturers. Artists in these several lines have been thus drawn to the place, and the arts themselves are here cultivated to a degree of perfection before unknown out of the metropolis.

The establishment of gas companies gave an impetus to the manufacture of tubes of various descriptions, as well as to the taste of the designer in forming graceful combinations. One of the most complete establishments in the town, the Cambridge Works, comprising long ranges of newly-built premises, is devoted to the making of all kinds of furniture in which brass tubing can be employed.

Some branches of the cotton manufacture have been localized in Birmingham, such as those of webbing for braces and girths, cords, lines, &c., probably on account of the facility with which the requisite machinery can be procured.

The umbrella trade arose from the demand for the brass furniture of these useful contrivances, which led to an attempt to execute orders for the articles complete. This attempt has been so successful that many thousand operatives are now engaged in the Birmingham umbrella trade.

In the nail manufacture as carried on in Birmingham, machinery is used by which well-formed nails are cut out of sheet-iron, with a rapidity which leaves far behind the swiftest motion of the muscles in snipping paper with scissors. There is one very large establishment, filled with machines for making nails by steam-power, where from one to two thousand millions of nails are made in a year. Screws are also formed with beautiful precision without heat, and by a series of mechanical contrivances which remove the severity of the labour, and render the attention and superintendence of women and children nearly sufficient.

Steam-engines are now very numerous in Birmingham. Their number was estimated in 1840 at 5,400 horses' power, consuming about 380 tons of coal per day, and equalling the labour of 86,400 men.

There are few large factories, properly so called, in which an article goes through the entire range of manufacturing processes; but there is a vast number of workshops, more or less extensive, in each of which portions of the work are done. One manufactured article, which is sold retail for a penny, may go through 20 workshops before it is finished; some having 40 or 50 workmen, some 4 or 5, while some are simply the garrets of workmen, who ply their trade each by his own fireside. With the exception of the metropolis, there is perhaps no town in England where there are so many persons combining in themselves the characters of master and workman, as Birmingham, and none in which there is more observable a chain of links connecting one with another.

The School of Design is rendering much service in Birmingham. The classes have been well filled from the time of their establishment; and it is found that boys who have attended those classes are sought after by manufacturers in preference to those who have not had such training. During 1850 there have been about thirty pupils in the modelling class alone: a branch of study peculiarly important in a town where so much metal casting is carried on. Some time elapsed before the Birmingham manufacturers fully appreciated the necessity of cultivating the arts of design, as a means of competing with France in productions of taste; but this necessity is now well understood, and rapid advances are being made in the right direction.

Near Birmingham were the celebrated Soho Works. These works were built by a native of Birmingham, Matthew Boulton, and ten years afterwards, in 1774, Watt entered into partnership with him. During the remainder of the century, the Soho Works produced those numerous steam-engines which became the marvel of all Europe. But it was not merely the making of steam-engines and other large pieces of machinery that made these works famous; other manufacturing processes were introduced; or, more properly speaking, other manufactures preceded that of steam-engines by a few years. Buttons, buckles, watch-chains, and trinkets, were the first objects of manufacture; then plated ware; then or-molu vases, candelabra, clock cases, and watch stands; then pure silver plate of the highest order of excellence. Among the various processes carried on at Soho, perhaps none has attained a more extended celebrity than the application of steam to coining; the engine for this purpose was erected by Boulton in 1783, but subsequently received great improvements. The Soho factory has been recently abandoned; and the Soho or Aston estate has been offered for sale to the town authorities, to form a People's Park for Birmingham.

Of all the towns in England, perhaps, excepting the metropolis, Birmingham could present the greatest variety of manufactures to the Exhibition of 1851; and it is on all accounts to be hoped that that town will be worthily represented. There are understood to be about 300 Exhibitors from Birmingham, who will illustrate between 40 and 50 different branches of manufacture, and will occupy about 25,000 square feet of exhibition space. All the chief departments of Birmingham industry will be represented.

BISCAY. The commerce carried on in the harbours of the Bay of Biscay is considerable. Spain, however, furnishes only a small portion of the exports, owing to the difficulty of transporting heavy commodities to the coast from the interior. From the inland provinces only wool is brought to the ports of Santander and Bilbao; the produce of the coast itself is not considerable, and consists chiefly of fruits. But more than half the products of the soil of France, and nearly the same portion of its manufactures, are exported from the harbours of Bayonne, Bordeaux, Rochelle, Nantes, Vannes, and Orient; and large quantities of foreign merchandise are received by the same ports.

BISCUIT, a kind of bread usually made in the form of flat cakes, and pierced with holes, to insure the complete evaporation of moisture in the baking, which is necessary for preserving it during long voyages. Biscuits are used on land as a kind of luxury, but at sea they are an article of the first necessity, since bread, in the more ordinary form in which it is used on shore, would speedily become mouldy and unfit for food. The name biscuit (twice-baked), is evidently derived from the nature of the processes to which this kind of bread was formerly subjected. The two bakings then used are no longer found necessary; but the name, although thus rendered inappropriate, has been continued. The same name is applied, inappropriately also, to several articles made by confectioners, such as sponge biscuits, Naples biscuits, &c., which are sweetened with sugar, and are not reduced by baking to the state of dryness which is a necessary quality of biscuits in their ordinary form. Biscuits for use as ship-bread are usually made of the meal of wheat from which only the coarsest bran has been separated. The process of mixing, kneading, stamping, and baking by hand were brought to an almost machine-like degree of rapidity and regularity in the great biscuit-manufactories established by government for supplying the British navy; but of late years they have been still further perfected and facilitated by the introduction of machinery, by which the dough is thoroughly mixed and rolled out into sheets about two yards long and one wide, which are stamped at one stroke, into about sixty hexagonal biscuits of about six to the pound, in such a manner as to leave the sheet sufficiently coherent to be put into the oven as one piece, though when baked the biscuits are easily separated. The hexagonal shape has been substituted for the circular, because it effects a saving of time and material, and also of space in packing.

At the ship-biscuit bakery of Mr. Harrison, at Liverpool, an apparatus has been constructed which exceeds in automatic completeness even that employed at the government establishments; for the made biscuits travel into the oven without the aid of any *peel* or other hand-worked tool. The flour and water are placed in a cylinder, mixed well together by revolving bars, kneaded by a large iron cylinder, and spread like a large sheet on an endless cloth. As this cloth travels along, a nicely adjusted piece of mechanism cuts the dough into the shape of six-sided biscuits, and stamps them. Passing along the endless cloth, the biscuits are received by a kind of gridiron and enter the oven. This oven is 26 feet long; it is heated by hot water, and bakes the biscuits as they slowly travel through it. The mechanism was patented by Mr. Harrison in 1849.

BISCUIT, in pottery, is a term applied to articles which have been only once baked or burnt, and have not yet received the glaze or vitreous coat, with which most articles of porcelain or earthenware are covered. The name appears to be given on account of the resemblance of such wares in colour and texture to ship-bread. Biscuit-ware is permeable to water, which, however, it imbibes without undergoing any alteration of texture; and owing to this quality it is used for vessels in which fluids are cooled by evaporation from the outer surface. Statuettes of great delicacy are now made of this material.

BISMUTH. The minerals in which this metal constitutes the principal ingredient are comparatively few in number. *Native or Octahedral Bismuth* occurs in opaque crystals, having a metallic lustre, and a reddish silver-white fracture. *Bismuth-ochre* is a straw-coloured mineral, consisting of an oxide of the metal. *Bismuth-glance* is a lead-gray-coloured mineral, occurring in four-sided prisms, having a metallic lustre; it is a sulphuret of the metal.

The pure metal, bismuth, was first shown to be a peculiar one by Stahl and Dufay: this metal generally occurs native, sometimes combined with sulphur, but rarely with oxygen, in Saxony, Bohemia, and Transylvania. It is largely produced at Schneeberg, in Saxony, to the extent of 10,000 lbs. per annum. Bismuth is of a reddish-white colour; its lustre is considerable, and its structure lamellated: it is so brittle as to be easily reducible to powder when cold; it melts at about 470° or 480°. At a high temperature this metal is volatilised, may be distilled in close vessels, and solidifies in foliated crystals; if it be merely melted in a crucible and cautiously cooled, it crystallises in well-defined cubes.

Bismuth and the metals generally combine to form alloys, and it frequently renders the metal with which it unites more fusible. Potassium, sodium, arsenic, antimony, and tellurium, all form alloys with bismuth. It imparts brittleness to copper, silver, tungsten, palladium, rhodium, gold, and platinum, when alloyed with them. With mercury it forms a very fluid alloy. Newton's fusible metal is composed of eight parts of bismuth, five of lead, three of tin; this alloy melts at 212°. Rose's alloy is still more fusible; it is made of two parts bismuth, one lead, and one tin; it fuses at about 201°.

Bismuth and Acids combine to form salts of bismuth, many of which are used in medicine and the arts. Bismuth is principally employed for the purpose of making fusible alloys and as an ingredient in solders. It is often called in the arts *tin-glass*. For medicinal purposes, the subnitrate or *magistery* of bismuth is sometimes employed. The cosmetic termed *pearl white*, or *Spanish white*, is subnitrate of bismuth.

BISON. This fine animal is much valued by the North American Indians: among whom the flesh is in great request, and is prepared in various ways. The tongue is accounted an especial delicacy; and the hump, or rather the flesh on the long spinous processes of the anterior dorsal vertebra, forming the withers, is accounted excellent. Much of the bison meat is made into *pemmican* for keeping, and a good bison cow furnishes dried flesh and fat sufficient to make a bag weighing ninety pounds. A fat bull has yielded a hundred and fifty pounds weight of tallow. The Indians dress the skins generally with the hair on; they serve as blankets and warm wrappers, and are sold for a considerable sum. The fleece is also useful, and is spun and woven into various articles. Dr. Richardson informs us that some of the bison wool has been manufactured in England into a remarkably fine and beautiful cloth; in the colony of Osnaboya on the Red River, a warm and durable cloth is formed of it. The horns are converted into powder-flasks.

BISTRE, a brown pigment made of the soot of different kinds of wood, but that of beech is generally preferred. The soot of the burned wood is sifted, steeped in water, decanted, and dried, to obtain a pure clean powder. Bistre is not used in oil painting, but produces the same effect in water-colours as brown pink does in oil.

BITTERS, a collective term applied to those vegetable substances the most prominent sensible quality of which is *bitterness*. It was at one time attempted to refer this quality to an hypothetical principle, which was termed *bitter principle;* but it was soon perceived that sbustances having a bitter taste were indebted for it to very different sources. A certain quantity of bitter matter seems to promote the digestion of all food; hence bitter substances are found abundantly distributed in the vegetable kingdom. Where there is a deficiency of bitter matter, and the food is of a very watery kind, such as grows in wet pastures, cattle are known to suffer from various diseases, especially from the rot. The best known bitters, perhaps, are quassia, wormwood, aloes, chamomile, colocynth, gentian, hop, rhubarb, rue, trefoil, and briony. *Bitters* is also the name for a class of beverages. The Swiss peasant, inhabiting high stations on the Alps, which are almost constantly wrapped in a thick and penetrating mist, uses a spirit distilled from gentian, called *bitter snaps*. In the West Indies, where languor of the system, with weakness of the digestive organs, is produced by the excessive heat, the appetite is restored and the stomach invigorated by taking before dinner a few drops in a glass of water of an elixir made of gentian, serpentaria, orange-peel, and sweet flag-root; and in America the infusion or tincture of serpentaria is sometimes taken every morning in damp aguish situations to prevent intermittents. In England, the "bitters" of the spirit shops are made of brandy, orange-peel, gentian, cassia, cloves or some other spice, sugar, and one or two other ingredients.

BITTERSPAR is a crystallized mineral, sometimes colourless, but frequently presents tints of pink, yellow, brown, and green, derived from the presence of iron and manganese. It possesses various degrees of transparency, and has a somewhat pearly lustre, whence it has been called pearlspar.

BITUMEN. A considerable number of combustible mineral substances are sometimes arranged under the head of bitumens; but their properties vary greatly in some respects, as, for example, with regard to solidity, fluidity, and colour. The term bitumen is however usually applied to two varieties, a harder kind called asphaltum [ASPHALTUM], and a softer kind called elastic bitumen. Naphtha is a fluid kind, and petroleum semi-fluid.

Elastic bitumen, sometimes called fossil caoutchouc, is a rare mineral product. It is found in the Odin mine, near Castleton, in Derbyshire; in a coal-mine of Montrelais, a few leagues from Angers, in France; and in a coal-mine near South Bury, in Massachusets, United States.

Elastic bitumen is brown or blackish brown, translucent in small portions, soft and elastic like caoutchouc, but sometimes hard as leather. Its density varies from 0.9053 to 1.233. It fuses readily, and at a higher temperature it takes fire and burns with a sooty flame. It is but slightly soluble in alcohol, but readily in potash.

According to the analysis of M. Henry, jun., the elastic bitumen consists of

	English.	French.
Carbon . .	52.250	58.260
Hydrogen . .	7.496	4.890
Azote . .	0.154	0.104
Oxygen . .	40.100	36.746
	100.	100.

In Texas there has recently been discovered a bituminous lake very similar to that of Trinidad. It is situated in Jefferson county, about 100 miles from Houston. It is about a quarter of a mile in circumference. In the summer months there is a spring near the middle of the lake where an oily liquid like petroleum continually boils up from the bottom; this liquid gradually hardens on exposure to the air, and forms a black pitchy substance. It burns, when lighted, with a clear bright light, but gives out a very pungent odour. During the winter the bitumen in the lake presents a hard surface, and is covered with water having a somewhat sour taste.

BLACK LEAD. [PLUMBAGO.]

BLACKBURN. This is one of the great cotton manufacturing towns of Lancashire. As far back as 1650, one particular article of the staple trade of the county was produced here with better success than in any other place. It was known by the name of 'Blackburn checks,' and was a species of cloth consisting of a linen warp and cotton woof, one or both of which being dyed in the thread, gave to the piece when woven a striped or checked appearance. This fabric was afterwards superseded by another, 'the Blackburn grays,' so called because the materials of which it was composed were not dyed, but sent to the printers unbleached, or as it is technically described, in the gray state, in order to have the patterns stamped upon them. In the history of the improvements by which the manufacture of cotton has been brought to its present state of perfection, it appears that several improvements of considerable importance owe their discovery to the ingenuity and talent of natives of this town. Among others the invention of the crank and comb for taking the carding from the cylinder of the carding-engine, undoubtedly belongs to James Hargrave, a working carpenter of Blackburn. His patent was one of the earliest that was taken out for the construction of the spinning-jenny. But, for a long period, the chief article manufactured here was calicoes, for which the Blackburn weavers were celebrated. This branch of trade is now transferred to the power looms, and the remnant of hand-loom weavers are chiefly employed in making low-priced muslins.

According to statistics recently furnished to us, there are now (1850) from 50,000 to 60,000 pieces of cotton goods manufactured each week in Blackburn and the vicinity, on which above 10,000 persons are employed. The annual value of the goods produced is supposed to exceed 2,000,000*l*. About 100,000 spindles are employed in cotton-spinning, producing about 100,000 pounds of yarn weekly, at 40 hanks to the pound. The power-looms and woven fabrics of Blackburn will be illustrated at the Industrial Exhibition.

BLACK SEA. This important sea was an emporium of commerce in very early times. The Greeks, and more especially the Ionian Greeks of Milétus, formed numerous establishments along its shores, from which they exported slaves, cattle, and corn in great quantities. The shores were pretty well known to the Romans. In the times of the Byzantine emperors, Constantinople drew from it a considerable part of its provision; and in the twelfth century the Genoese formed some establishments on its north-eastern coast, and carried on a very active commerce overland with India. When the Turks acquired power in this quarter, the trade of this sea declined, but the rise of Russian power on the northern shore gave a new impulse to it. At the present time the number of Greek vessels is by far the greatest in this sea. They export the corn, hides, timber, iron, and furs of Russia, and import wine, fruits, and the manufactures of England and France. Between the northern and southern shores of the Black Sea the commercial intercourse is not great, the produce of the Anatolian shores, which consists of grain, timber, and copper, not being in demand in Russia, which exports the same commodities. There are very few fisheries carried on in this sea.

BLADDERS, when brought to a clean and prepared state, are especially useful to druggists, oilmen, colourmen, and other manufacturers, as coverings for various kinds of vessels; they derive their value from their thinness, toughness, and impermeability to water. The bladders of the ox and other animals, when deprived of bits of loose membrane and other impurities, are washed in a weak solution of chloride of lime; then rinsed in clean water; then blown out and submitted to pressure by rolling them under the arm, which stretches and enlarges them; then blown out quite tight, and fastened and dried.

BLASTING has long been practised as the most efficient mode of removing or detaching heavy masses of rock in mining operations, and, by reason of recent improvements, has become one of the most important resources of the civil engineer. The old method of blasting rocks consisted in drilling or boring a hole to a considerable depth with suitable instruments, depositing a charge of gunpowder at the lower or farther end of the hole, and then filling up, or 'tamping,' the remainder of the hole with clay, or some other soft mineral substance, well rammed, to make it as tight as possible. A wire laid in the hole during this operation was subsequently withdrawn, and a train of gunpowder inserted in its place; and this train, and consequently the blast itself, was fired by a slow match (often consisting simply of brown paper smeared with grease), intended to burn long enough to allow the person who fired it to reach a place of safety. Many accidents have arisen from the uncertainty of this process, the risk of which has however been lessened by the substitution of copper for iron in the 'needle' by which a passage for the train is formed. Beckford's 'safety fuse,' too, is a great improvement; it consists of a small train of powder inserted in a water-proof cord, which burns at so steady and uniform a rate, that by cutting it to a suitable length any desired interval may be secured between the lighting and the explosion.

The great improvement of modern times however consists in the employment of a galvanic current to ignite the powder,—an arrangement which renders premature explosion next to impossible. A galvanic current, so long as it passes along an uninterrupted wire, is perfectly harmless; but if its course be interrupted by breaking the continuity of the wire, intense heat, sufficient to ignite powder, is produced. In addition to the superior safety and certainty of this mode of firing, it has the advantage of being applicable under water as well as on land, and, by its perfectly instantaneous action, of enabling the engineer to fire as many blasts as he may desire at one operation, so as to accomplish, by their joint action, effects otherwise unattainable.

Colonel (now General) Pasley first employed galvanism in submarine blasting in 1839, in his successful operations on the wreck of the Royal George at Spithead. Shortly afterwards galvanic blasting, both on land and under water, was practised both in America and in Scotland; but it was in January 1843 that Mr. William Cubitt commenced, on the works of the South-Eastern Railway, the stupendous operations which established its capabilities on a scale never before attempted. He began by throwing down, by three simultaneous blasts, consuming together about 18,000 lbs. or more than eight tons of gunpowder, a bulky promontory called the Round Down Cliff, between the Abbot's Cliff and Shakspere tunnels, near Dover. By this operation, which was attended with very little noise, a cliff nearly 400 feet high was thrown down, and no less than 400,000 cubic yards of chalk were distributed over the beach, covering an area of 18 acres to an average depth of 14 feet; and it was computed that 7000*l.* and six months' time were saved to the company. Several smaller operations followed this great experiment, in one of which twenty-eight blasts were arranged to explode simultaneously, although from some derangement of the wires a few failed. The same agency has since been extensively employed elsewhere, especially at Seaford in 1850.

The latest invention relating to blasting which requires notice is the substitution of gun-cotton for gunpowder, which bids fair still further to diminish danger and to increase the certainty of the operation. From experiments tried early in 1847, at the Standege tunnel, on the Huddersfield and Manchester Railway, and on the works of the Birmingham, Wolverhampton, and Stour Valley Railway at Birmingham, it appears that the effects of the gun cotton is, weight for weight, from three to five times as great as that of gunpowder; so that a much smaller bore will suffice for the blast, and it may be, with equal labour, carried down much deeper into the rock. A still more important difference is, that the gun-cotton produces no smoke, so that the workmen may resume their labours immediately after the explosion, instead of having to wait several hours, and sometimes a whole day, as when gunpowder is used. The cotton also produces much less noise and vibration, and is considered far less liable to accident in removal from place to place than gunpowder.

BLAST FURNACE. [FURNACE.]

BLEACHING is the whitening of fibrous materials used as clothing. Wool and silk, cotton and flax, the substances most usually submitted to this process, contain certain colouring matters which, though natural, are not essential constituents; and these colouring matters are more readily acted upon by chemical agents, and suffer decomposition with greater facility than the animal and vegetable substances with which they are combined; so that they may be removed with little or no injury to the texture of the articles, thereby increasing their beauty, and fitting them for the processes of the dyer and calico-printer.

Bleaching is a very ancient process, and was practised especially in Egypt, but probably in a very simple and tedious way; the process, perhaps, consisting of little more than exposure to air, light, and moisture. The art was scarcely known in Great Britain until about a century since, it having formerly been usual to send brown Scotch linen to Holland to be bleached, where it was done by steeping several days in a solution of potash, and subsequently for nearly a week in butter-milk, and then spreading it out upon grass for some months. One of the first improvements on this tedious process was the introduction, about the middle of the last century, by Dr. Home, of Edinburgh, of dilute sulphuric acid in lieu of sour milk, by which the process, which formerly occupied from six to eight months, was reduced to four months, the acid being as effectual in one day's application as the milk in six or eight weeks. This improvement was eclipsed by the application of chlorine, formerly called dephlogisticated marine acid, or oxymuriatic acid, which was discovered by Scheele about 1774. Berthollet suggested its application to bleaching in 1785, in a paper read before the Academy of Sciences at Paris; and from him the process was shortly afterwards introduced into Scotland by Watt. About the same time Mr. Thomas Henry, of Manchester, introduced the process in Lancashire; and to these two gentlemen belongs the credit of perfecting and applying in this country a process whereby as much bleaching is as well performed in a few hours, within a space a few hundred yards square, as on the old process would have required weeks of exposure upon a hundred acres of land. The chlorine was first used in a state of simple solution in water; but chloride of lime, commonly called *bleaching powder*, for the manufacture of which Mr. Tennant, of Glasgow, obtained a patent in 1799, is now almost universally employed, especially in the bleaching of cotton. Sulphurous acid gas, or the fumes of burning sulphur, is also often employed in bleaching wool and silk, as well as straw and feathers. Wax is usually bleached simply by exposure to air, light, and moisture.

Scarcely a year elapses without developing some new processes or apparatus for bleaching, which are made the subjects of patents, though not always with advantage to the patentees. M. David, of Paris, took out a patent in 1849 for a peculiar mode of applying chlorine to the goods to be bleached. The chemical materials for making the gas are to be provided by the bleacher; and as the gas is generated, it is conveyed by pipes into a close chamber. The woven goods are to be laid on perforated shelves in this chamber, and thus be acted on by the chlorine. A fan or blowing machine is used to clear the chamber of gas before the goods are removed from it; and glass windows are provided to the chamber, through which the process may be watched. Messrs. Cocksey and Nightingale, in the same year patented an apparatus to be used in bleaching, dyeing, or sizing; it consists in a peculiar way of conducting the cloth into and through a vessel of liquid, and beating it on both surfaces immediately after its emersion; so that the fibres become impregnated, and the superfluous liquid driven off. A third patent in the same year, by Mr. Thom, relates to a mode of causing the woven goods to pass over two rollers, one above another, in a close chamber filled with chlorine or sulphurous acid gas.

The bleach-works of Lancashire and Glasgow are among the largest and finest of our manufacturing establishments; exhibiting mechanical contrivance, chemical knowledge, and those powers of combination and classification so remarkably developed where many hundred persons are employed.

BLEIBERG, is the seat of one of the Austrian mining departments, and its neighbourhood contains valuable lead mines, which produce annually about 2000 tons of metal. About 80 tons of red lead also are annually produced. There are besides valuable copper mines and marble quarries in the neighbourhood.

BLIND, MECHANISM FOR THE. There are many ingenious mechanical contrivances for assisting in the instruction of the blind.

In the infancy of the art of teaching the blind, *raised music* was invented, in order that they might be enabled to acquire their lessons independent of a master. In 1827 the Society of Arts gave the large silver medal for a contrivance by Don Jaime Isern, the object of which is to enable a blind composer to transfer his thoughts to paper in the usual musical notation, without the necessity of employing an amanuensis. Embossed music, and maps and globes for teaching geography, would naturally be suggested to those persons who were engaged in teaching reading to the blind by raised figures. M. Weissembourg, a blind man of Mannheim, appears to have been the first person who made relief-maps; up to which time the instruction given to the blind on geography was merely oral. Various methods for producing maps of this character were employed, but at first without success; after a time, however, the chief difficulties were conquered, and a process which is minutely described by Dr. Guillié has supplied all the maps which have been in use at the Parisian Institution to the present time. The map of a country is pasted upon thick pasteboard, a wire is then bent round the curves of the coast, and along the courses of the rivers; these wires are fastened down, and a second map in every respect similar to the first is pasted over it; when this is pressed, the windings of the wire will be easily traced by the touch. Another plan consists in having a metal plate engraved with all the lines, elevations, boundary marks, positions of towns, &c.; from this plate impressions are struck in pasteboard, which produce a perfect embossed map. There is an elementary treatise on mathematics, by the Rev. William Taylor, of York, called 'The Diagrams of Euclid's Elements of Geometry, arranged according to Simpson's edition, in an embossed or tangible form, for the use of blind persons who wish to enter upon the study of that noble science,' York, 1828.

The intellectual education of the blind has made great advances within the last few years. The interest connected with the question of 'Types for the Blind,' to which considerable impetus was given by the Society of Arts for Scotland at Edinburgh, who offered their gold medal for the best alphabet for the blind, has tended greatly to bring about this change. The late Mr. John Alston, the treasurer of the Glasgow Asylum, adopted the plain Roman characters deprived of their small extremities —the *sans-serif* of type-founders; and, finding that it could be easily read, that it would also enable any seeing person who could read to be a teacher of the blind, he at once procured founts of type, and published several works in raised letters; the success of these for their special object established the pre-eminence of his alphabet. He also brought out some beautiful embossed music and maps; and he published the Old and New Testaments in 19 vols., super-royal 4to. The paper used for these works is strongly sized, to retain the impression. In order to account for the great extent of the Bible, it must be borne in mind that the paper can only be printed on one side, and that the letters require to be of considerable size in order to be distinct to the touch. The printing is effected by a copper-plate press. The types being strongly relieved, and liable frequently to give way under the heavy pressure required, it was necessary to have them re-cast four times during the progress of the work. The whole of the works have been completed within the walls of the Glasgow Asylum, a man and a boy acting as compositors, there being one pressman, and the ordinary teacher acting as corrector of the press.

The different kinds of industrial works executed by the blind are nearly the same in all the asylums, varying slightly with the requirements of the district: at Glasgow they are house baskets of all kinds, mill baskets and hampers, door-mats, twines, mattresses, hair-friction gloves, curled hair for upholsterers, hearth and door rugs, table rugs, fringed rugs, articles of needle-work, stockings and pan-soufles, nets, sacks and sacking.

BLOCK MACHINERY. The vast number of blocks constantly required for the use of the English navy and the mercantile marine of this country may be understood from the fact, that upwards of 1400 blocks of all sorts are needed for fitting one ship of 74 guns; while for smaller vessels, although the sizes may be different, the number will not materially vary from what is here stated. These blocks are a kind of pulley, for fastening and guiding the rigging. It was long a matter of considerable moment to devise means for simplifying the mode of manufacture, which requires great accuracy, and thus diminishing the cost. In 1781 a large manufactory was established at Southampton by Mr. Taylor, who had secured a patent for an improved method of making sheaves, and who further adapted machinery for cutting the timber and shaping the shells of the blocks. Mr. Taylor for some time supplied all the blocks required for the navy; but shortly after the expiration of his patent machinery was introduced into the dock-yard at Portsmouth, and the government undertook the manufacture, with the double object of economy, and of being independent of any individual for the supply of an article of first necessity for the equipment of ships.

About this time (1801) the late Sir M. I. Brunel succeeded in completing a perfect working model for constructing both the shells and sheaves of blocks. This model being submitted to the inspection of the Lords of the Admiralty, the invention was at once adopted by government, and the inventor was engaged to superintend the construction of the requisite machinery upon a scale sufficiently large for making blocks to supply the whole naval service of the country. The completion of this machinery occupied nearly six years, and was not brought into full operation until September 1808, since which time it has been found to work without requiring any alteration. It is a truly beautiful combination of mechanism. It consists mainly of an assemblage of saws and lathes, forming an extensive series of machines all of which are set in motion by one steam-engine. By some of these the logs of elm from which the shells are to be formed are cut up into pieces of suitable dimensions; others bore the holes for the pins or axles, and cut the mortices into which the sheaves are to be placed; others cut off the corners and complete the rounding and shaping of the shell by very ingenious arrangements; and another, the scoring-machine, cuts the grooves intended to receive the rope by which the block is to be suspended. Another series of apparatus is provided for cutting the lignum-vitæ of which the sheaves are made into slices, sawing them to a circular shape and cutting a round hole in the centre, fixing in the centre hole a metal *coak*, or ring, through which the axis is to pass, forming the groove in the edge of the sheave, and turning and polishing the iron pins for the axles. It is found that with this machinery ten men can perform the work that previously required one hundred and ten, and can easily produce 140,000 blocks per annum. Sir M. I. Brunel received 20,000*l.* from government as a reward for his ingenuity; yet it is said that the *savings* of four years, as compared with the cost of blocks made in the former manner, were sufficient to defray this sum and the whole cost of erecting the buildings and machinery. So important has this mechanism been regarded, in a national point of view, that duplicate machines have been constructed in the Chatham dock-yard, to be used in case of accident to those at Portsmouth.

Ship's blocks for the mercantile navy are still made by hand, and improvements are frequently made therein.

Among many recent patents relating to ship's blocks, one by Mr. Stowe, of Bermuda, describes the use of a metal fork which contains the block, and which has a hole drilled in the lower part of each leg; through this pair of holes is passed the spindle on which the spear revolves. Another patent, taken out by Capt. Chamier in 1849, relates to improvements in the strapping, the cheeks, and the sheaves. Instead of the ordinary rope strapping, a coil of strands of iron wire is used, coated or painted for preservation; the cheeks are formed of two thin metallic sheets, one flat and one convex, filled up by soft metal between them; the sheave is formed of three metal discs—the outer ones bent, and having their ends turned over to form the groove for the rope, while the centre one is kept straight.

BLOOD is useful for many purposes in the Arts. The blood of the bullock is employed for the clarification of wines and spirits; for the preparation of adhesive cements; for mixing with coarse paint for out-door work; as an ingredient in some modes of bleaching; and as a manure. Dried or powdered blood is prepared for export to the West Indies, where it is used in clarifying sugar; the drying is effected by exposing the bullock's blood to currents of warm air. Dried bullock's blood is said to be much used in adulterating musk.

BLOW-PIPE. This instrument, in the simple form in which it has long been employed by jewellers and others in soldering upon a small scale, is a metallic tube seven or eight inches long, about a quarter of an inch in diameter at one end, and gradually tapering to a fine point, pierced by an extremely minute orifice at the other. The tube is bent to a right angle about an inch or an inch and a half from its smaller extremity; and, the larger end being inserted in the mouth of the operator, it is used to direct the flame of a lamp upon the solder or other substance to be heated. The substance thus operated upon is laid upon a piece of charcoal held in the left hand of the operator, and a steady gentle current of air is impelled through the pipe by contracting the muscles of the cheek, the mouth having been previously inflated with air. The power of thus producing a blast without the aid of the lungs, and of respiring during the operation, is an important accomplishment, as without it the health may be injured by the use of the blow-pipe; and experience is necessary to enable the operator to regulate the strength of the blast, which if too great will diminish the heat by throwing too much air into the flame, and if too weak will produce a feeble flame.

In the simplest form of blow-pipe, the collection of water from the condensed moisture of the breath prevents the continuance of the blast for any length of time. This inconvenience is avoided by making the blow-pipe in two pieces, and interposing between them a receptacle for retaining the water, and preventing its entrance to the finer portion of the pipe.

The application of the blow-pipe to scientific purposes appears to have originated about 1738, when Antony Swab, a Swedish bergrath, or counsellor of mines, employed it in the examination of ores and minerals. Cronstedt, whose system of mineralogy, based upon the chemical composition of the minerals, was published in 1758, by the employment of fluxes in the experiments performed with this instrument, may be considered the founder of a new department of chemical science; Bergman published a Latin treatise embodying the results of his researches with it in 1779; and Gahn, though he left no work on the subject, far exceeded any of his predecessors in experiments with this instrument, the results of which were subsequently given to the world by J. J. Berzelius, in a treatise, of which English, French, and German translations have appeared.

Modifications of the common blow-pipe have been contrived with jets of hydrogen or oxygen, or of the two gases combined in definite proportions. By the oxyhydrogen blow-pipe, which, though highly dangerous in the form in which it was originally contrived by Dr. Hare, of Philadelphia, early in the present century, has by successive improvements, been rendered a safe apparatus, the hardest and most refractory substances, including all kinds of jewels and other stones, metals, rock crystal, and every description of porcelain, may be fused or sublimed, and the most brilliant effects of combustion may be produced.

BLOWING MACHINES. Bellows, or machines for directing a current of air upon a fire, to excite the requisite intensity of combustion for metallurgical and other operations, are of very early origin. Rosellini represents an Egyptian painting in which a man is engaged in working two pairs of bellows with his feet, having strings to assist in raising the boards of the exhausted pair to admit a fresh supply of air. Bellows consist, essentially, of an air-tight chamber capable of alternate expansion and contraction, and furnished with two valves, one opening inwards to admit air while the chamber is expanding, and the other opening outwards into a pipe or muzzle, to allow the air to escape when the chamber is compressed. In some of the recent Expositions of Manufactures, bellows have been exhibited which show great beauty in form and ornament.

The blast from common bellows being necessarily intermittent, and variable in intensity, it is necessary, when a continuous blast is required, either to employ two or more separate bellows or pairs of bellows, working alternately; or, where more perfect equability is required, to direct the air expelled from the bellows into a second chamber of variable dimensions, which is kept under a constant and uniform pressure, and from which the blast is directed into the nozzle. In forge-bellows of this construction three boards are used, connected by leather sides, which are kept in regular folds by hoops of cane. The middle board, to the upper side of which the nozzle is attached, is fixed in a horizontal position, and the upper and lower boards are moveable, forming two chambers, of which the lower one is kept distended by weights excepting when the board is raised by a lever and chains, and forms the part analagous to ordinary bellows; while the upper one, which is constantly compressed by weights attached to the top board, constitutes the air-chamber or reservoir. In the best smith's bellows the boards are circular, instead of being pear-shaped like the domestic machine, and in some helical springs are used instead of weights. Very simple and efficient bellows may be made of wood alone, on the model of common bellows, by the use of two boxes sliding upon one another so as to constitute, jointly, a chamber of variable dimensions; and the missionary Williams, in the absence of leather for ordinary bellows, constructed an efficient blowing-machine of wood, consisting of two square boxes with pistons arranged to rise and fall alternately. Wooden bellows are sometimes used in large organs.

The *trombe*, or *trompe*, is a blowing engine often referred to by old writers, in which a shower of water, in its fall down a large vertical tube, draws with it so much air as to produce a powerful current, which is conducted from the bottom of the tube, where it is separated from the water, to the furnace. The most important blowing-machines however for metallurgical operations, are those in which the air is alternately drawn into and expelled from large cylinders resembling those of a steam-engine, by the action of pistons impelled either by water wheels or by steam-engines. The first machines of this character were constructed by Smeaton for the Carron Foundry about 1760. The cylinders, of which any number may be employed, usually force the air into large air-chests, or chambers of iron or masonry, from which it is conducted to the blast-pipes, which are called *tuyeres* or *tweers*. The force of the blast may be regulated either by a contrivance resembling a safety-valve, allowing the air to escape when the pressure exceeds a given degree, or by connecting with the air-chest an apparatus similar to a gasometer.

One of the largest blast-engines or blowing-machines ever constructed is now in use at the Coltness Iron Works in Scotland. The high pressure cylinder is 54 inches in diameter, 9 feet stroke, and weighs 10 tons; the blowing cylinder is 122 inches in diameter, 9 feet stroke, and weighs 31 tons. The beam is 36 feet long, 6 feet broad in the centre, and weighs 36 tons. The connecting rod gives 14 strokes per minute, with a stroke of 12 feet. The fly-wheel is 30 feet in diameter, and with its shaft weighs 35 tons. The steam pipes are 21 inches in diameter. The working mechanism is supported on two columns and entablature, weighing 22½ tons. The pedestals on which the machine stands are composed of 1900 tons of solid masonry. This gigantic machine was constructed to supply a blast to ten iron furnaces.

BLUE, as a pigment. The substances used for this purpose are of different natures, and derived from various sources: they are all compound bodies, some natural and others artificial.

Prussian Blue.—This beautiful pigment was discovered in 1710 by Diesbach, a manufacturer of Berlin. It is a compound of cyanogen and iron, is inodorous, tasteless, insoluble in water, alcohol, æther, and oils. It is hygrometric, attracting water strongly from the air, which it retains until heated to nearly 280°. Prussian blue is employed both as a water colour and in oil; in the latter case, on account of the deficiency of what is termed *body*, it is usually mixed with white lead, and it will bear admixture with a large portion of this on account of the intensity of its colour. Its stability is very considerable, and it is not only used as a pigment, but also as a dye.

Indigo.—This fine blue is extracted from different species of *indigofera* in the East Indies, and Guatimala in North America, of which the latter is most esteemed. [INDIGO.]

Blue Verditer.—This pigment is used as a water-colour, and chiefly in the manufacture of paper-hanging. It is a gritty powder of a very fine light blue. It is a carbonate of copper.

Ultramarine.—This splendid and permanent blue pigment was originally, and indeed until within a few years exclusively, prepared from a mineral called Azure Stone, or Lapis Lazuli; but it is now prepared by artificial means. It has hitherto, on account of its high price, been used almost exclusively by artists, both as a water-colour and in oil; but on account of the reduced charge at which it will probably be hereafter obtained, it will doubtless be rendered much more extensively useful.

Cobalt Blue.—This was proposed as a substitute for ultra-marine before the invention above described had rendered this latter colour easily obtainable at a moderate price; it is of great permanence, but is not so fine as the ultra-marine, and will hereafter be probably little employed.

Smalt is a blue colour also prepared from cobalt, but is generally used rather to diminish the yellow tint of writing paper and of linen, and to give a bluish colour to starch, than strictly speaking as a pigment; it is merely glass rendered blue by oxide of cobalt, and this, when reduced to a very fine powder, is commonly called *powder blue*.

BOAT. [LIFE-BOAT; SHIP-BUILDING.]

BOBBIN NET. [LACE.]

BOG. The name of bog has been given indiscriminately to very different kinds of substances. In all cases the expression signifies an earthy substance wanting in firmness or consistency. In some cases, where springs of water, or the drainage from an extensive area are pent up near the surface of the soil, they simply render it soft or boggy, and in this state the land is perhaps more properly called a quagmire. A second state of bog is where in addition to the condition just described, a formation of vegetable matter is induced, which, dying, and being reproduced on the surface, assumes the state of a spongy mass of sufficient consistence to bear a considerable weight. Bogs of this description are numerous and extensive in Ireland, where they are valuable, from the use made of the solid vegetable matter both as fuel and as a principal ingredient in composts for manures. Where the turf has been cut away for these purposes, several bogs have been reclaimed by draining; and the subsoil is then readily brought into cultivation. Bogs also occur in Cornwall, and other parts of Great Britain, where the form of the surface and the nature of the earth favour the general condition under which bog is formed. The bogs of Ireland are estimated in the whole to exceed in extent 2,800,000 English acres.

When bogs become consolidated or compressed, they are called peat-mosses. An extensive tract of peat-moss (Chatmoss) in the county of Lancaster has attracted public attention from the circumstance of the Liverpool and Manchester Railway having been carried through it. Chatmoss (6 miles long by 3 broad) has a depth of 30 feet of spongy moss, which Mr. Stephenson succeeded in making fit to bear a railway, by filling it with an enormous mass of solid earth. The late Mr. Roscoe brought part of Chatmoss into a state fit for cultivation by marling and manuring.

Many of the Irish bogs contain wood of a peculiar kind, called bog-oak, bog-yew, &c.; of which statuettes, models, and ornaments are carved; beautiful specimens of this kind were displayed at the 'Dublin' Exhibition of Manufactures in 1850.

The present attempts to give commercial value to the peat of Dartmoor are noticed elsewhere. [PEAT.]

BOHEMIA. The productive and industrial resources of this important country have been briefly noticed in connexion with the Empire of which it forms a part. [AUSTRIA.]

BOILER. This name is now most commonly applied to the close vessels used for the generation of steam. Such boilers, to lessen the danger of explosion, are almost invariably made of wrought metal, which, if burst, will tear rather than fly to pieces, as cast metal would do; and the plates made for the purpose are formed of the best and toughest metal, and rolled or wrought with peculiar care. Engineers differ as to the comparative merits of iron and copper as a material for steam-engine boilers. Most however admit that iron, when of good quality, has the greatest cohesive strength, although the greater uniformity of texture in sheet-copper renders it safe to construct copper boilers of less thickness than those of iron, to withstand a given pressure. Further than this, supposing an explosion to occur with a copper boiler, it is likely only to produce a rent or tear in the metal, while an iron boiler, even though wholly of wrought plates, is frequently blown to pieces.

Dr. Ritterbandt's plan of removing from steam-engine boilers the incrustations with which they become coated, is a valuable recent improvement. All the fresh water employed in boilers contains lime, in the form of a soluble bi-carbonate. The heat converts this into an insoluble carbonate, which falls to the bottom of the boiler, and carries with it any floating masses of other insoluble matter. When salt water is used the same results occur, but in addition to this, the carbonate forms nuclei for the accrescence of sulphate of magnesia, chloride of sodium, and other saline compounds, which crystallize and precipitate much sooner than would otherwise be the case. The incrustations so formed within the boiler thicken its substance, occasion a greater expenditure of fuel for the heat to reach the water, and renders the boiler liable to burst; because as the incrustation is not so good a conductor of heat as the metal, the latter becomes burnt and weakened before the heat of the furnace can penetrate through the incrustation to the water, and thus explosion may occur. Dr. Ritterbandt's method is a chemical one. He introduces into the water of the boiler some ammoniacal salt, the acid of which, mixing with the lime, will form a soluble salt instead of an insoluble carbonate of lime. It is not therefore simply a cure for a disease; it is a prevention of the disease from taking place at all, and is on that account a very scientific method. There are many ammoniacal salts to choose from, such as the muriate, the acetate, and the nitrate. The quantity of ammoniacal salt used must depend on the quantity of lime in the water.

The *Times* gave valuable testimony, in 1847, to the efficacy of Ritterbandt's process in the following paragraph;—" The invention has been tried for nearly twelve months upon the boilers of the engines printing the *Times*, working on an average seventeen hours *per diem* throughout the year. Not only have the boilers been kept perfectly free from deposit, but an incrustation which was formed previously to the application of the invention has been completely removed. We can further state, that neither the boilers nor any part of the machinery, has been in any, even the slightest degree acted upon or injured by the action of the remedy in question."

The patented improvements in steam-engine boilers, introduced within the last few years, are so varied that we cannot even enumerate them.

BOILING OF FLUIDS. When fluids are heated to such a degree as to be strongly agitated and produce much vapour, they are said to boil, or be in a state of ebullition. Under similar circumstances, the temperature at which this occurs is always the same in the same fluid, and is called its *boiling point*, being the greatest heat which the fluid is capable of acquiring. When the vapour which arises from a boiling fluid is condensed, the resulting liquid is perfectly similar to that from which its vapour was produced, having suffered no chemical change. Most metals, though rendered fluid by melting, never boil, and many oils become decomposed before reaching a temperature at which they would otherwise boil.

When water is heated, there is a point, just before it has acquired it highest temperature, at which a slight noise, or rather a succession of noises, is heard, usually called simmering. This is occasioned by the formation of minute bubbles of vapour, at the bottom of the vessel, and nearest the source of heat, which, being specifically lighter than the water in which they are formed, rise into the upper and cooler part of it, and are then condensed. Soon after this and when the whole of the water has acquired its highest temperature, the bubbles of vapour rise to the surface, and there bursting constitute steam, which, being transparent and colourless, is consequently invisible, but when it comes into contact with the cold air it undergoes partial condensation, and is then visible and appears as a mist. This temperature, under average circumstances, is about 212° Fah.; but, with variations in the density of the air, it varies as follows:—

Barometer.	Boiling point.
26 inches	204.91
26.5	205.79
27	206.67
27.5	207.55
28	208.43
28.5	209.31
29	210.19
29.5	211.07
30	212.00
30.5	212.88
31	213.76

On ascending mountains, by the consequent diminution of atmospheric pressure, and in proportion to it, water is found to boil at a lower temperature. Thus, on the summit of Mont Blanc, which is about 15,000 feet above the level of the sea, Saussure found water to boil at 178° of Fah., or 34° below its usual temperature. Fluids boil at 140° less in vacuo than under ordinary atmospheric pressure; so that water in vacuo boils at about 72°. On the other hand, if the pressure of air be increased, the boiling point becomes higher. Thus, Southern established the following relation between the barometric pressure and the boiling point of water:—

Atmospheres.	Inches of Mercury.	Temperature.
1	29.8	212°
2	59.6	250.3
3	89.4	275
4	119.2	293.4
5	149	309.2
6	178.8	322.7
7	208.6	334.4
8	238.4	343.6

It is to be observed, that the temperature of the steam is always equal to that of the water from which it is generated. The boiling point of any one liquid, as above stated, depends mainly on the pressure to which it is exposed; but it is also slightly affected by the substance of the vessel containing it, and the contiguity or immersion of other bodies.

The following are the boiling points of a few liquids under the same atmospheric pressure:—

	Boiling point.
Muriatic æther	52°
Sulphuric æther (sp. gr. 0.7365 at 48°)	113
Bisulphuret of carbon	113
Acetic æther	160
Nitric acid (sp. gr. 1.5)	210
Oil of turpentine	314
Naphtha	320
Phosphorus	554
Sulphur	570
Sulphuric acid (sp. gr. 1.848)	600
Mercury	662

BOKHA'RA, a country situated in Central Asia, exhibits the industry of its inhabitants in the cultivation of their lands. The larger and the smaller canals, both of which are numerous, must have required a good deal of labour when they were first made; and they are still kept up at a considerable expense. Cotton, hemp, sesamum, tobacco, and a few dye-stuffs are cultivated.

Gold is found among the sands of the Amoo, and collected from it in many places along its banks. All other metals are imported from Russia. Salt is dug out in masses in some parts of the desert, and on the banks of the Amoo, below Chardjooee. Alum and brimstone are got in the neighbourhood of Samarcand, and sal-ammoniac in its native state occurs in the mountainous district.

The mechanical arts are not neglected, and some commodities are even made for exportation. The most extensive manufactures are those of cotton and silk; and some kinds of cloth, in which both materials are combined, are in great demand in Russia for morning dresses of the rich nobility. The dye of all their manufactured goods is excellent. The Bokharians do not understand the art of tanning so well as the Russians, but they make excellent Marocco leather. Their swords are good, but much inferior to those of Persia.

The chief city, also called Bokhara, is a place of much commercial importance. There are six commercial routes radiating from it. One of these leads to Samarcand, Khokand, and Kashgar; another to Khiva and Astrakhan; a third through the Kirghis region between the Sea of Aral and the Caspian; a fourth to Merve and Meshed; a fifth to the Oxus and Herat; and a sixth to Balkh, Khooloom, Bameean, and Cabul. Most of the commodities of Asia and Europe find their way along one or other of these six routes.

BOLE, an earthy mineral which occurs in amorphous masses in various countries, as in Armenia, Saxony, Tuscany, Siena, Ireland, and the Isle of Skye. The colour of Bole is various, either yellow, brown, red, or brownish, and pitch black; it is dull, has a greasy feel, and adheres to the tongue. Its fracture is conchoidal, yields to the nail, and the streak is shining. The chief varieties are the Armenian and the Lemnian bole, both of which consist mainly of silica and alumina. They are used to a small extent as pigments, and also in medicine: but not to so great an extent as formerly.

BOLETUS, an extensive genus of fungi, consisting, according to the old botanists, of leathery masses, which are sometimes of considerable thickness, and having the spores lodged in tubes which occupy the same situation as the plates in the gills (or hymenium) of the common mushroom.

The true Boleti are generally found growing on the ground in woods and meadows, especially in pine woods. Some are eatable; some are used in medicine; while one variety, when dried and sliced, furnishes the German tinder, or AMADOU.

BOLSOVER STONE. The yellow limestone of Bolsover, in Derbyshire, is used in the construction of the New Houses of Parliament, in London. It was selected for its durability, strength, fitness for ornamental work, and colour. It is a combination of carbonate of magnesia with carbonate of lime, in small granular crystals, without flinty nodules or other blemishes.

BOLTHEAD, a chemical vessel, usually of green glass, and of a globular form, with a narrow neck. It is chiefly employed in the process of sublimation.

BOLTON. This important Lancashire town has maintained an eminent position in manufactures for many centuries. Leland speaks of its being a market for cottons and coarse yarns; and another writer (Blome), who wrote somewhat later, describes it as 'a fair well-built town, with broad streets, with a market on Mondays, which is very good for clothing and provisions; and it is a place of great trade for fustians.' There seems to be little doubt that the making of woollens was introduced by some Flemish clothiers who came over in the 14th century; that other branches of trade were introduced by the French refugee manufacturers, who were attracted by the prosperity of the neighbourhood; and that the manufacture of cotton cloth was improved, and in many of its kinds originated, by some emigrant weavers, who came from the palatinate of the Rhine.

Bolton made no great advances in population until the improvements in the machinery for spinning cotton gave an impetus to the trade, which has been gradually increasing ever since. Almost the first invention of importance originated in this town. It was a machine which combined the principles of the spinning-jenny and the water-frame, and was called a *mule*, by its inventor, Samuel Crompton. This ingenious man lived at 'Hall in the Wood,' near Bolton, and had to struggle for an existence, while his invention was enriching others. 'Hall in the Wood' still exists, a memento of the rise of the cotton manufacture.

While Crompton's invention was enriching others, Sir Richard Arkwright, another native of Bolton, who had risen from a very obscure condition, had established large factories in Derbyshire, where he carried the cotton machinery to the greatest perfection. The opposition made by the labouring classes in Bolton to the improvements in machinery has, at various times, driven the most lucrative branches of employment from that town to other places. The introduction of the mule and of the power-loom was not accomplished until they had enriched other communities for some time. After a while cotton factories, filled with machinery upon the best principle, began to rise up in various parts of the town. Foundries and machine manufactories followed them, and a great extension was immediately given to the trading interests of the place.

The cotton mills of Bolton are very numerous; and some of them are among the largest in the county, employing more than 100,000 spindles each. The weavers of Bolton produce a great variety of fabrics, probably a greater variety than any other single place in the county. Plain and fancy muslins, quiltings, counterpanes, and dimities, are the chief kinds of cloth; but cambrics, ginghams, &c.,

are also woven. Formerly, fustians, jeans, thicksetts, and similar fabrics, were the principal articles made in the town; but these descriptions of cloth are now chiefly produced in the power-loom, as well as calicoes and dimities. The bleach and dye-works, especially the former, in the town and neighbourhood are among the largest in the kingdom; and there are likewise a few print-works. A great proportion of the cotton goods manufactured here are sold in Manchester, where the manufacturers have warehouses for the storing and sale of their cloths; they meet their customers there from all parts of the country, one, two, or three days of each week.

Mr. Harris, superintendent of the Bolton Police, in his Police Report for 1849, made to the Corporation, gives the following interesting details respecting the manufactures of Bolton, in the year just named; these details relate to the borough only, and do not include the other townships of the parish.

	No.	Steam Horse-power.	Hands Employed.
Cotton Mills	53	2200	9759
Foundries and Forges	22	590	3043
Bleach Works	8	628	937
Paper Mills	1	124	118
Coal Mines	5	85	64
Gas Works	1	...	43
	90	3627	13,964

Many of the above items fluctuate so much, that the table can be regarded only as a useful approximation. Several new cotton mills have since that date been built at Bolton. The attempts occasionally made to introduce the silk manufacture into Bolton have only been partially successful. The manufacture of steam-engines and machines is carried on to a large extent. The town is abundantly supplied with coal, which lies beneath and around it.

Counterpanes and other products of Bolton industry will be exhibited at the grand display of 1851; and many of the workmen in the factories have subscribed to the general fund for the Exhibition.

BOMB, the original name of what is now called a *shell*, is a hollow globe of iron, which, when charged with a certain quantity of gunpowder, is projected from a mortar or howitzer, generally at a considerable angle with the horizon, in order that, by the momentum acquired in its descent, it may crush the roofs, and, by exploding, destroy the buildings on which it may fall.

In 1688 there was cast in France an enormous bomb, which is said to have been in the shape of an egg, and to have been capable of containing 7000 or 8000 pounds of powder; it was to have been discharged against the Algerines, but it was not employed, probably in consequence of an opinion that it would not have had the intended effect; and no attempt has since been made to project such an immense mass of metal. While the citadel of Antwerp was besieged by the French army in 1832, shells twenty-four inches in diameter were thrown from the largest mortar which has been employed in modern warfare; the shell or bomb was capable of containing ninety-nine pounds of powder, and when charged weighed 1015 pounds.

BOMB-PROOF. This name is given to a military magazine, or other building, when its roof has sufficient thickness to resist the shock of shells falling on it.

BOMB-VESSEL, a ship of about 350 tons burthen, usually forming part of a fleet intended by a bombardment to destroy or compel the surrender of some town situated on the sea-coast. It carries one 13-inch and one 10-inch mortar, besides two 6-pounder guns, one 12-pounder, and eight 24-pounder carronades. The mortars are placed on traversing platforms in the middle of the gun-deck, and they may be fired over either side of the ship at elevations never less than 45°.

BOMBAX. The wood of this genus of trees is soft and spongy, and is frequently used for making canoes. One species, the *silk-cotton tree*, is very large; the down, which is contained ln the seed vessel, is soft, but is too short to be used in the manufacture of cloth. It is made into hats and bonnets, and used for stuffing chairs and pillows by the poor people in the districts in which it grows. It is not made into beds, as it is reputed unwholesome to lie upon. The trunks of the largest are made into canoes, and some of them will carry from 15 to 20 hogsheads of sugar. The bark of another species is used in making ropes.

BOMBAY. This great and important city is more distinguished for commerce than for manufactures: for exchanging the produce of India for that of England, than for producing on its own account. Yet there must necessarily be much manufacturing carried on. The property is principally in the Parsee inhabitants, who are also the principal merchants; and it is usual for every European house of commerce to contain one or more Parsee partners, who supply a great part of the capital. The shops and warehouses belonging both to European and to native merchants and traders are upon a large scale.

The docks within the fort, although the property of the East India Company, are entirely under the management of Parsees, by whom merchant-vessels of 1000 to 1200 tons

KNIGHTS CYCLOPÆDIA
OF THE
Industry of all Nations.

No. 11.

burden, frigates, and even line-of-battle ships are built. These docks were about forty years ago enlarged and improved under the superintendence of Major Cooper of the Engineers. The buildings are greatly admired for their architectural beauty; and the slips and basins are calculated for vessels of any size. Bombay being situated between the forests of Malabar and Gujerat, receives supplies of timber with every wind that blows. Ships built of teak-wood are much more durable than those built with European timber; they have been known to last more than 50 years. From the cheapness of labour, ships were formerly built at Bombay for three-fourths of the cost in England; but recent experience has shown that ships can be built cheaper in England. The Minden, a 74 gun ship, launched at Bombay, in 1810, was constructed entirely by Parsees, without any assistance from Europeans; and since that time several frigates and line-of-battle ships have been built at these docks.

In addition to its trade with Europe and with China, a very great traffic is carried on by coasting-vessels with all the ports on the western side of India, from Cape Comorin to the Gulf of Cutch. The vessels thus employed vary in size from 10 to near 200 tons burden, and nearly 800 of them are registered as belonging to the port. The articles which form the principal part of this trade from Bombay are European manufactures, and the produce of Bengal and China, the returns being made in cotton-wool and cloths, timber, oil, and grain from the northern ports, and from the south, cotton, hemp, coir, timber, pepper, rice, and cocoa-nuts.

The merchandise thus brought to Bombay is in great part re-exported in larger ships to different parts of Europe, to North and South America, to Canton, to the Arabian and Persian Gulfs, and to the Bay of Bengal. The goods sent from India to China comprise principally cotton wool, opium, metals, spices, dye-woods, and woollen goods. From the Arabian and Persian Gulfs, Bombay receives raw silk, copper, pearls, galls, coffee, gum-arabic, copal, myrrh, olibanum, bdellium, assafœtida, dried fruits, horses, and bullion. The returns are grain, Bengal and China sugar, British manufactured goods, cotton and woollen, and spices. The merchandise sent to Calcutta from Bombay, in return for sugar, indigo, and rice, are timber, coir, cocoa-nuts, sandal-wood, and cotton.

Cotton forms the most important article of export from Bombay. It is received from the provinces of Gujerat and the Concan, from Malabar, Cutch, and Sinde. Bombay has exported more than 100 millions of pounds of cotton in one year, besides exports to other places.

The following were the imports into and exports from Bombay during the years stated:—

Years.		Imports.		Exports.
1834	..	£3,653,319	..	£3,303,515
1836	..	4,429,127	..	5,451,554
1838	..	4,444,693	..	4,236,027
1840	..	4,831,558	..	5,018,335
1842	..	5,542,578	..	5,273,986

Bombay has been the chief Indian port connected with the establishment of steam communication with England. The route between Suez and Bombay is still in the hands of the East India Company; but the other portions of the great overland route are managed by the Peninsular and Oriental Steam Navigation Company; and if the present discussions concerning the Australian mails should result in the Singapore route being chosen, Bombay will have an enlarged field for its commercial enterprise.

BOMBAZINE is a woven fabric in which the warp is formed of silk, and the weft, or shoot, of worsted. The worsted is thrown on the right side, which has a twill upon it. The manufacture originated in Norwich, among the Dutch who were settled in that city, about 1575. Bombazines were formerly made of various colours, but owing to changes of fashion they are now manufactured in black only, for use as mourning.

BOMBYX. [Silk.]

BONA, is the principal rendezvous of the vessels employed in the coral fishery, which extends along the coast as far as the island of Tabarkah, which belongs to Tunis.

BONES have been of late years very extensively used as a manure, especially on poor and dry sands and gravels. When crushed and used judiciously, the advantage of bones as a manure, in distant and uncultivated spots, where the carriage of common stable or yard manure would have been too expensive, and where it could not be made for want of food for cattle, is incalculable. By means of bones large tracts of barren sands and heaths have been converted into fertile fields.

The bruising or grinding of bones has become a distinct business, and they may be bought in London and at the principal ports ready to put upon the land. They are broken into different sizes, and are accordingly called *inch bones, half-inch bones* and *bone-dust.* Most of the bones procured from London and the manufacturing towns have undergone the process of boiling, by which the oil and a great part of the gelatine which they contain have been extracted. The German agriculturists instead of using bone-manure on their own land, now export it to England, on account of the good price here obtainable. No less than 29,424 tons of foreign bones were imported in 1849.

Bones consist of about one-half animal matter: the rest being phosphates of lime and magnesia, and carbonate of lime. They derive their fertilising property mainly from the phosphate of lime; but in part also from the mechanical texture of the bones, and their power of absorbing and retaining moisture, which enables the plants to feed on the decomposed gelatine of the bones.

The mode of applying bone manure to the land is either by sowing from twenty to forty bushels of them per acre by the hand broadcast, as is done with corn, and harrowing them in with the seed; or by putting them into the drills by a machine made for the purpose, which is an addition to the common drilling machine.

The mill which is used to break and grind bones consists of two iron or steel cylinders, with grooves running round their circumference, the projections being cut so as to form strong teeth. These turn upon one another by means of machinery, so that the teeth of one run in the groove between the teeth of the other. The bones are put into a hopper, whence they pass between the two cylinders, where they are crushed during the passage. The bones from Germany are sometimes ground before importation, sometimes afterwards.

The uses of bones (besides as a manure) are very numerous. *Bone-ash* is prepared by calcining bones to whiteness, and reducing them to a powder; it is used for burnt hartshorn, and for making cupels. *Bone-black*, or *ivory* black, is made by a careful preparation of the *soot* of clean bones, when burned in a peculiar manner. There are successive stages in the manufacturing uses of bones; first the bones are boiled, and the grease sold to the candle and soap makers; then the larger pieces are selected for making knife-handles, &c.; then the best pieces are laid aside for bone-black; and finally the worst pieces are appropriated as manure. The coarser kind of bone-black is made into *animal charcoal*, used by sugar refiners; while the finer kind is employed in making black paint and colours, inks, dyes, &c.

Bone, as a material for knife handles and other articles, may be dyed red, black, green, purple, yellow, blue, or other colours, by the same dyes as are used for ivory. Bone is easily wrought by the saw and lathe.

BOOK-BINDING. This interesting art includes not only the fastening together of the leaves of a book; but also the preliminary operations of folding each sheet so that the several pages of which it consists may follow one another in due order, and of *gathering* or collecting together in proper sequence the several sheets, and *collating* or examining them, to see that no error has been made in the arrangement. To aid these operations certain letters or figures, called *signatures*, are placed at the bottom of the first page and one or two other pages of each sheet.

In the subsequent processes it is necessary to distinguish between the comparatively slight and loose mode of binding in cloth or paper covers, which is technically called *boarding*, and the more solid kind of binding in leather, to which, among the trade, the application of the term *binding* is limited.

If the book is to be simply boarded, the sewing of the sheets, individually, to a series of strings called *bands*, stretched in a machino called a sewing-press, is the next operation after folding and collating; but, if it is to be bound, the sheets are previously either beaten upon a smooth stone, or passed in small parcels through a rolling-press, to make them close and smooth. The bands run across the back of the book, and are often rendered invisible by cutting with a saw, in the back of the collected parcel of sheets, a series of grooves to receive them. After the sheets are thus sewn to the bands, and also connected together here and there by a *ketch-stitch*, the bands are cut so as to leave about an inch projecting beyond the book on each side, and the back is smeared over with melted glue, which further unites the back edges of the several sheets. The back is then rounded in a curious manner by a process of hammering, before the glue is fully set; and the book is compressed firmly between two boards, with the back projecting a little, while the back is further beaten so as to make it spread out a little over the edges of the boards. If for binding, the edges of the sheets are then *ploughed* or cut with a machine to a perfectly flat and smooth surface, the convexity of the back being temporarily destroyed while the front edges are cut, so that they may be cut flat, and afterwards restored, so as to draw them into a corresponding concavity. If the book is only to be boarded, it is not usual to cut the top edges, which, being folded, are pretty smooth and regular; and the front and bottom edges, if cut at all, are only pared sufficiently to remove the principal irregularities.

The *boards* or pieces of millboard (which is

a kind of strong and smooth brown paste-board, of different degrees of thickness to suit the different sizes of books), which constitute what in ordinary language are the covers of the volume, are cut a little larger than the leaves, and, when the volume is to be bound, are laid on the sides of the book, with their back edges against the projecting or overlapping edges of the glued back, and secured to the book by passing the ends of the strings or bands, which are previously scraped thin, through holes near their back edges, from the outside, and glueing them down firmly and smoothly on the inside. In boarding, however, it is the more usual practice to paste the boards to the paper or cloth cover, leaving a space between their back edges sufficient for the back of the book, and to connect the boards with the book simply by pasting down to them the *end-papers*, or blank leaves which are applied in sewing at the beginning and end of the book. In binding, on the contrary, the leather is put on after the boards are attached to the book in the manner above described. Books are often so boarded or bound as to leave the back of the cover detached from the glued back of the book itself, which is done by interposing a double layer of paper or cloth between the back and the cover, glueing one layer to the cloth or leather cover, and the other to the back, and connecting the two layers with one another at their edges only.

Half-binding is that style of binding in which only the back and corners are covered with leather, and the sides with paper or cloth.

In the *finishing* or ornamenting of a bound book much taste may be displayed. The cut edges of the leaves are usually either sprinkled with colour, smeared over uniformly with a sponge dipped in colour, marbled, or gilt with leaf-gold; the edges being, for the last-mentioned process, previously coloured with red chalk and water, and then moistened with white of egg mixed with water, and subsequently burnished with a smooth hard stone, which polishes, but does not disturb the gold. The covers are sometimes coloured or sprinkled by the binder, and are impressed, both at the sides and back, with ornamental devices and inscriptions, by the application of heated stamps or dies, either with or without leaf-gold; such impressed devices as are not gilt being distinguished by the name of *blind-tooling*. When gold is used, the surface of the leather is prepared to receive it by the successive application of parchment-size, white of egg, and a little oil. In ordinary hand-work the patterns are produced by the separate application of a number of small dies, and engraved rollers for lines and long narrow patterns; but sometimes a number of dies are fitted together, and applied simultaneously by means of a press. This process is called *blocking*.

Much ingenuity and taste have been devoted of late years to the perfection of cloth-binding or boarding. By peculiarities in the mode of weaving the cotton cloth used for the purpose, and of subsequently stamping or embossing it between steel rollers, the textile appearance is destroyed, and a surface is sometimes produced very nearly resembling morocco leather.

The peculiarity of *india-rubber binding* (which has been imitated with an artificial cement) consists in the entire absence of sewing. The back as well as the other edges are ploughed, so as to reduce the book to a collection of single leaves, to the back edges of which a layer of caoutchouc or cement is applied. This mode of binding is well adapted for maps, music, ledgers, and manuscript books generally, as it allows the book to lie open with equal facility at any place, and the inner margin to be used, if needful, close to the edge of the paper.

Mr. Richards, a bookbinder, patented a few years ago a method of stitching the sheets by machinery; but we are not aware that it has come much into practice.

The book-binding trade has gradually assumed many of the features of the factory system. Some of the principal London firms, such as that of Messrs. Westley, have immense buildings planned expressly for that species of combination and subdivision which mark the larger departments of manufactures. Tier after tier of stories, each lighted from end to end with numerous windows; each story or range under the supervision of one foreman, and devoted to one department of binding; separate warehouses for the mill-board, the leather, and the cloth; powerful machines for embossing cloth and stamping leather; a department where females are employed in folding, collating, and sewing; another department where men are engaged in glueing, pasting, cutting, hammering, and pressing the 'boarded' books; another department for the 'roan' or 'sheep' binding; a fourth entirely devoted to those school books which (whatever be their merit), have a sale so enormous and continuous that the process of binding them is always going on; a fifth occupied by the 'extra' workmen employed in the costlier kinds of binding—such are the features of the establishments in question: establishments where many hundreds of workpeople are employed under one roof.

We may reasonably hope that our bookbinders, as well as those of foreign countries, will not be slow to contribute to the grand Industrial Congress of 1851. It is profitable, too, to glance once now and then at the curious specimens of bookbinding belonging to the 15th, 16th, and 17th centuries: many beautiful examples of such work were placed in the Mediæval Exhibition of 1850.

BOOK TRADE. The publisher of the 'Cyclopædia of Industry' has made various computations, from time to time, of the produce of the Press in this country. The data for such estimates must necessarily be inexact, and the results can only be considered as approximations to truth. They are, however, abundantly sufficient to show the prodigious increase of readers.

We may exhibit the rapid growth of the publication of *new* books, by examining the catalogues of the latter part of the eighteenth century, passing over the earlier years of the reign of George III. In the 'Modern Catalogue of Books,' from 1792 to the end of 1802, eleven years, we find that 4,096 *new* works were published, exclusive of reprints not altered in price, and also exclusive of pamphlets: we have thus an average of 372 new books per year.

The number of new publications issued from 1800 to 1827, including reprints altered in size and price, but excluding pamphlets, was, according to the London catalogue, 19,860, showing an average of 735 new books per year, being an increase of 363 per year over the last eleven years of the previous century. The demand for new books, even at the very high cost of those days, was principally maintained by Reading Societies and Circulating Libraries. When these new modes of diffusing knowledge were first established, it was predicted that they would destroy the trade of publishing. But the Reading Societies and the Circulating Libraries, by enabling many to read new books at a small expense, created a much larger market than the desires of individual purchasers for ephemeral works could have formed; and a very large class of books were expressly produced for this market.

But a much larger class of book-buyers had sprung up, principally out of the middle ranks. For these a new species of literature had to be produced,—that of books conveying sterling information in a popular form, and published at a very cheap rate. In the year 1827 'Constable's Miscellany' led the way in this novel attempt; the Society for the Diffusion of Useful Knowledge commenced its operations; and several publishers of eminence soon directed their capital into the same channels. Subsequently editions of our great writers have been multiplied at very reasonable prices. This circumstance will explain how the number of works published of late years does not exhibit a proportionate increase in the number of volumes. One compact volume may now contain as much matter as three octavos of the beginning of the century.

The 'London Catalogue of Books published in Great Britain' from 1814 to 1846—a period of thirty-three years—contains about 36,500 titles of works, shewing an average of 1106 new books per year, being an increase of 371 over the number in the former catalogue.

The Catalogue of New Books for 1849, arranged from 'Bent's Literary Advertiser,' exhibits the titles of above 2000 works—an enormous number for the issue of one year, and that not particularly favourable to publishing enterprise. In looking over this catalogue we cannot help remarking that the range of *price* is perhaps more extreme than at any former period, from the Shilling Railway Volume to the Five Guinea Illustrated Book. Luxurious and expensive books, for a few purchasers, are not less frequent than in times when dear books formed the greater portion of the Book Trade. Taking the cheap and the dear we find that a single copy of each of these 2000 books would amount to about 1000*l*.

But the most remarkable characteristic of the Press of this country is its Periodical Literature. The number of *weekly periodical works* (not newspapers) issued in London on Saturday December 21, 1850, was 87; in this number we include the 'Athenæum,' 'Builder,' 'Chambers' Journal' and 'Papers,' 'Church of England Magazine,' 'Eliza Cook's Journal,' 'Dickens's Household Words,' 'Expositor,' 'Family Herald,' 'Hogg's Instructor,' 'Home Circle,' 'Knight's Half-Hours,' 'London' and 'Industry,' 'Lady's Companion,' 'Lamp,' 'Lancet,' 'London Journal,' 'London Labour,' 'Mechanics' Magazine,' 'Punch,' 'Working Man's Friend,' &c.; the total issue of the 87 is fully 400,000 weekly, or upwards of 20,000,000 yearly.

Of these 87 weekly publications the prices vary, being 1*d*., 1½*d*., 2*d*., 3*d*., 4*d*., 7*d*.; the total retail value of their sale, independent of the supply of them in monthly parts, we assume, upon the authority of an experienced bookseller, to be 2,500*l*. per week or 130,000*l*. per annum. Other authorities would set the number higher. A minute analysis of these Weekly Periodicals is, to some extent, satisfactory; for it shows that of the low publications—including those which may be called 'Guides to Newgate,'—the number sold is about an eighth of the innoxious publications.

The issue of *monthly* periodical publications from London is unequalled by any similar commercial operation in Europe. 287 monthly periodical works were sent out of London on the last day of December, 1850, to all parts of the United Kingdom, the bulk of them departing from Paternoster-row; to which must also be added 41 periodical works published quarterly, making a total of 328.

A wholesale bookseller, who has been thirty years an attentive observer of the progress of periodical literature, and has been nearly all that time in the midst of it in Paternoster-row, has made a variety of computations of the work of the great literary hive of industry in London on 'Magazine-day;' the results of his examinations are as follow:—

The total of the new numbers of the monthly and quarterly periodical works sold in London on December 31, 1850, was about 600,000. The total retail price of these works was 38,000*l*.

Three thousand five hundred parcels were despatched into the country by the various wholesale agents in London on this day. The total returns of these monthly and quarterly periodical works must exceed annually 1,000,000*l*., the selling prices varying from ½d. to 7*s*. 6*d*. It must be observed that the sale on 'Magazine-day' does not by any means represent the total sale.

In addition to the monthly periodical works issued through the regular booksellers—'the Trade'—an amount quite unequalled at any former period is circulated throughout the country by a class of persons known as 'canvassers.' We are induced to think that the annual returns of such works cannot be less than 150,000*l*.

The number of *newspapers* published in the United Kingdom in 1849 was 603. They consumed nearly 79 millions of stamps at one penny, besides halfpenny stamps for supplements. At fivepence each their annual returns would be nearly 1,500,000*l*.

We recapitulate the estimated annual returns of the commerce of the press:—

1. New books and reprints—one set 1,000*l*. .. .. .. Estimated average number sold of each work 750		£750,000
2. Weekly periodicals ..	£130,000	
Monthly periodicals	1,000,000	
Canvassers' numbers	150,000	
		1,280,000
3. Newspapers		1,500,000
		£3,530,000

The English books exported in 1849 were returned as entitled to drawback of duty on 12,000 cwts.—in value 190,000*l*.

The foreign books imported in 1849 paid a duty of 7,751*l*.

The writer of this article considers that the *paper duty* enters into the selling price of books, &c., in the following proportions:—

1. New books—4 per cent. ..	£30,000
2. Periodicals—8 per cent. ..	102,400
3. Newspapers	56,250
Estimated total of duty on printing paper	£188,650

BOOT AND SHOE MANUFACTURE.

Scarcely any handicraft employment engages the attention of so many persons in this country as boot and shoe making. From the artist of aristocratic circles to the cobbler who rolls himself up in a stall under a pot-house, is a wide interval; and this interval is filled up by numerous grades. At Northampton boots and shoes are made on a very large scale for the London market; they include chiefly the cheap varieties; but at some of the recent Exhibitions of Manufactures the Northampton boot-makers have exhibited specimens of workmanship which are considered to fall in no way behind those of London or Paris. At Edenbridge in Kent, and at other places, the strong coarse 'hob-nailed' shoes are made, which are so much worn by waggoners and others. The London makers import from Paris very large quantities of boot *fronts*, which when combined with other parts of English manufacture, constitute many of the 'French boots' which now glitter in the windows.

Of the circumstances of the trade, so far as regard the relations between masters and workmen, the most ample and interesting, perhaps, are those prepared a few months ago by Mr. H. Mayhew, for the 'Morning Chronicle.' The London work, and the more wretched features of it, are at any rate here depicted with much vividness.

The mechanical details of the manufacture have been well described by Mr. Devlin; who, in his 'Shoemaker,' forming one of the 'Guides to Trade,' has contrived to throw a general interest into that which would otherwise be merely technical.

Of the improvements or suggested improvements recently introduced into the manufacture, our patent records contain many examples. One inventor has suggested that the different parts of a boot or shoe should be sewn together with wire-thread instead of hempen thread. Another has proposed the use of revolving circular heels, which may be turned round in order that every part may receive equal wear. A third proposes heels to be made of an iron rim, with the vacuity filled up with gutta percha. A fourth has directed his attention to a mode of introducing a layer of gutta percha between the outer and inner soles. A fifth has introduced elastic pieces into the side of the boot to ensure a close fit round the instep. A sixth has invented a simple apparatus to assist in 'blocking' the fronts of boots. With respect to making boots and shoes by machinery, Sir M. I. Brunel invented a comprehensive plan, to be adopted for soldiers' shoes in the time of the war; but it has not acquired a permanent utility.

It has often seemed strange to persons not engaged in those trades, that boot and shoe makers should adopt such a cramped attitude as those to which we see them accustomed. In most cases of this kind there is a good reason for the adoption of that which has become very general. But be this as it may, a contrivance was introduced a few years ago, with a view to enabling a shoe-maker to ply his avocation either sitting or standing, without necessitating the stooping position which appears to be (and perhaps is) so painful. Mr. Warne, practically engaged in the craft, registered the contrivance in question. It consists of a kind of high stool, something like a desk stool, covered with a hard leather cushion. Another round cushion is placed upon the lower. There is a hole through both cushions, through which a strap passes down to an axle, wheel, and ratchet beneath. A last being placed upon the upper cushion, can be instantly bound tightly by the strap; while the last and the upper cushion can easily be moved round horizontally. A hinged seat is attached to the frame. The inventor states that every operation of boot and shoe making can derive aid from this contrivance.

Notwithstanding the large number of persons employed in these avocations in England, and the abundant supply of leather, there is still a considerable import of boots and shoes from abroad, chiefly France. In 1849 these imports amounted to 160,000 pairs of boots and shoes, and no less than 540,000 pairs of boot-fronts. The clue to this difference is, that boot fronts pay a much smaller import duty than boots and shoes.

We may expect to see a rich supply of these commodities at the forthcoming Exhibition. The boots of All Nations are worthy of comparison one with another.

BORACIC ACID, formerly called *Homberg's sedative salt* and *sedative salt of borax*, is a compound of the elementary body *boron* and oxygen. It exists not only in the form of boracic acid, but also in large quantity in the East Indies, in combination with soda, forming *borax*, or the borate of soda. Boracic acid is usually obtained from borax. It has the form of small, scaly, brilliant, colourless crystals, which have a greasy feel. This acid is inodorous; its taste is not strong, and scarcely at all acid. Dr. Bowring ('Report on the Statistics of Tuscany') describes a remarkable boracic acid lagoon, or system of lagoons, in Tuscany. They are spread over a surface of 30 square miles, and send out dense and stinking odours. The peasants long deemed the district an entrance to the infernal regions, and regarded it with great superstition. The lagoons are now the property of an enterprising manufacturer, who derives a considerable revenue from the boracic acid which he obtains from them.

Borax, or borate of soda, consists of boracic acid and soda. A crude kind of borax, imported from the East Indies, is called *tincal;* which is found crystallised on the edges and shallows of a brackish lake. Tincal is in the form of bluish or greenish white crystals, which are dissolved and recrystallised to form borax. Borax has an alkaline and sweetish taste, and effervesces slowly in the air.

Boracic Acid and Borax are largely employed as a flux for metals, as an aid in soldering, as an ingredient in cosmetics, and as a medicine. No less than 30,000 cwts., (chiefly boracic acid) were imported in 1848.

BORA'SSUS, a kind of palm-tree, which grows all over India both on the continent and in the islands, where it is esteemed of the greatest use on account of the vinous sap and the sugar which are extracted from it. The mode of obtaining the sap of this palm is by crushing the young inflorescence, and amputating the upper half; the lower half is then tied to a leaf-stalk, and has a vessel, usually of bamboo, attached to its end. The vessel gradually fills with sap, and is removed every morning; when replaced, a fresh slice is cut from the wounded end of the inflorescence,—an operation which is repeated daily until the whole of the raceme is sliced away. In procuring the sugar, exactly the same process is followed: but the inside of the receiver is powdered with lime, which prevents fermentation taking place: the juice is afterwards boiled down and finally dried by exposure to smoke in little baskets.

BORDEAUX. This celebrated city, one of the most important in France, has great facilities both for foreign and internal commerce. Wine, brandy, and fruits are the chief articles of export. The Médoc or claret wines are sent chiefly to England; the inferior sorts to Holland and Germany. England was among the best customers for Médoc wines as far back as the time of our Norman kings. The produce of this famous district of the Gironde is about 165,000 hogsheads annually. One half of the total produce of the three best vineyards, viz. Chateau Margaux, Chateau Lafitte, and Chateau Latour, comes to England. Large quantities of wine are also shipped to America; but this trade is chiefly in the hands of European and American Spaniards who are settled at Bordeaux. Other articles of commerce are, all kinds of bread-stuffs, hemp, flax, pitch and tar, cork, oil, salt provisions, hardware, metals, cotton yarn, ship timber, and rigging. Ships are fitted out at Bordeaux for the whale and cod fisheries. The manufactures of the town are jewellery and plated goods, linen, muslin, woollen stuffs, calicoes, hosiery, gloves, corks, soap, chemical products, musical instruments, &c. The town also has several distilleries, sugar-refineries, breweries, gas-works, glass and china works, tobacco-factories, rope-walks and dockyards. Colonial products, cotton, dye-stuffs, pepper, hides, tobacco, and rice, are the principal imports. There is a regular service of packets from Bordeaux to the Havanna and the coast of Mexico. The custom duties paid at Bordeaux amount to the large sum of 12,000,000 francs a year,—nearly half a million sterling.

BORING. Whether the vertical cavity for an Artesian Well is made, or the cavity of a cannon formed, or the cavity of a cylinder or barrel perfected, or a hole simply made in wood—the term *boring* is equally applied to all these operations.

Cannon are usually cast solid, and bored by machinery; and in an accommodated sense the term is applied to the similar operations by which musket-barrels, the cylinders of steam-engines, and other articles which are originally made hollow, have their inner surfaces turned to a perfectly smooth surface and cylindrical shape. The boring instruments of the carpenter consist of *awls*, which are put into soft wood, with a rotatory motion, without removing or bringing away its substance; *gimlets* and *augers*, which are supplied with cutting edges, and are partially hollowed, to allow of the escape from the hole of the detached particles of wood; and *bits* of various kinds, which also remove the wood, and are applied with greater power and precision by means of a crank-shaped instrument called a *brace*. Small holes in metals are usually bored with *drills*, which are formed with scraping rather than cutting edges, and are used either in a brace, a drill-stock capable of imparting an alternating rotatory motion by means of a bow worked by hand, or some other contrivance, or in a lathe. Boring machines of the lathe character are too various and complex to be described here. Suffice it to say, that the perfection to which they have been brought has rendered most essential service to science and manufactures, and removed one of the greatest difficulties experienced by early improvers of the steam-engine.

Of the various boring operations of the miner, that of boring Artesian wells is unquestionably the most interesting. It is performed with various kinds of chisels or *jumpers*, augers, and instruments suitable for extracting the detached fragments, attached to the lower end of an iron rod formed of many lengths screwed into one another; these instruments are either turned round, or jumped up and down, or worked with a combination of these two motions by suitable mechanism, the kind of tool employed, and the mode of working, being varied from time to time as the several strata are met with. By such means the interesting works noticed in ARTESIAN WELLS were completed.

Beart's boring tools, patented in 1844, are intended to be used in circumstances where the hole made by the borer can be kept constantly full of water. The borer itself is attached to a hollow tube instead of a solid rod, and acts as one leg of a syphon; the other leg being an excavated channel prepared for the purpose, and kept full of water. The arrangement of the several parts is such, that as fast as the fragments of rock or soil are loosened by the borer, they are drawn up with the water by which they become saturated, through the tube which forms the stem or vertical rod of the borer: this, at least, is the theory on which the inventor has founded his patent.

At the meeting of the British Association in 1846, Mr. Vignolles communicated an account of a method of boring Artesian wells, invented by M. Fauvel of Perpignan. M. Fauvel had observed that in several cases of success in boring for water with solid iron rods, so soon as the spring was tapped all the triturated particles were brought up without the use of the auger. He inferred that if the boring could be effected by a hollow tube about two inches less in diameter than the width of the auger, communicating with an injecting force-pump by a flexible tube from the surface, a result would follow similar to that which resulted from the natural power of the rising column of water. Having tested the hypothesis, he found that the well could be bored in much less time than by the former method. The plan has since been largely adopted, in some cases to very great depths.

An attempt was made by Mr. Gard, of Calstock, in 1848, to produce an improved boring machine, to effect in another way the objects intended by Mr. Beart in England, and M. Fauvel in France. His boring machine consists of a hollow cylinder to the bottom of which the boring-bit is attached in a peculiar way; and as the rock or earth is bored, the fragments force themselves up into the cylinder, where they are retained by a valve. The cylinder does not reach to the top of the bore, but requires to be raised when full, in order that it may be emptied; it however will contain so large a quantity, that the necessity of raising it will occur much less frequently than under the usual system. Instead of joining successive lengths of rod to the boring tool, the latter is raised and lowered by a chain.

At a meeting of the Cornwall Polytechnic Society, a few years ago, Mr. Prideaux proposed the adoption of a chemical means of facilitating the process of boring. He found that a stream of hydro-oxygen gas applied to a piece of granite stone produced heat; and that on the application of cold water the stone became soft, and yielded to the tool. Oxygen might be superseded by common air from a pair of double bellows; and common coal-gas might be used instead of hydrogen.

A very instructive illustration of the apparatus employed in well-boring may be studied at the Museum of Economic Geology.

BORNEO is likely, at some future time, to become an important commercial emporium. When the Dutch made an exploratory Expedition into the island in 1823, they found it rich in many materials of manufactures; and since Sir James Brooke has acquired power in those regions, the natural riches have become still further known. Diamonds, gold, antimony, tin, iron, copper, lead, and coal, are all known to exist in Borneo or its neighbouring island Labuan; and the vegetable produce is also rich and varied. If the time should arrive (and we may hope it is not far distant) when Australia will be placed in steam communication with India and China, Borneo will be in the route, and the commercial advantages of the island will become developed.

BORON is an elementary body, and one of the constituents of boracic acid, oxygen being the other. This substance was first obtained by Davy in 1807. It is always procured either from boracic acid or from one of its salts.

Boron is a powder of a deep brown colour with a shade of green. It is devoid of smell and taste. It is not altered by exposure to the air or to oxygen gas at the usual temperatures; but when heated to about 600° it absorbs oxygen, and burning with considerable brilliancy it is converted into boracic acid. It combines with most of the elementary bodies and forms compounds which are noticed under the names of those bodies.

Minerals containing boron or any of its compounds as an essential component part are comparatively few in number, and only found in a few spots. They comprise sassoline, or native boracic acid; borax, or borate of soda; boracite, or borate of magnesia; datholite, or borate and silicate of lime; botryolite; axinite; and tourmaline. The presence of boron in any mineral may be readily detected with the blow-pipe, owing to the beautiful green tint communicated to the flame by the boracic acid.

BOSNIA, one of the provinces of Turkey, has a fair amount of natural produce, if the industry of the inhabitants would do it and themselves justice. Gold, silver, iron, quicksilver, lead, and coal, are known to exist in many districts: some of the mines are indeed rich, but are poorly worked. Among the articles manufactured are leather, coarse woollens, worsted coverlets, cannon balls, saltpetre, gunpowder, iron ware, and weapons; but the extent of the manufactures is very limited.

The exports comprise wool, honey, wax, goats' hair, hides, morocco and other leather, timber and other articles of wood, worsted coverlids, &c., horses, horned cattle, sheep, goats, swine, poultry, dried fish, pitch, and other domestic produce: and the imports consist of linens, woollens, silks, cotton goods, glass-ware, flax, steel-ware, tin, lead, copper, and iron-wares, indigo, colonial produce, &c.

BOSTON is the chief port of Lincolnshire, and a place of considerable trade. The foreign trade is chiefly with the Baltic, whence are imported hemp, iron, timber, tar, and other commodities. The chief exports consist of corn, particularly oats, large cargoes of which are sent to London. The gross receipts of customs in 1847 amounted to 40,555*l*. The vessels registered at the port in 1849 were 159: and the ships which entered and cleared the port amounted in number, in that year, to 1,833. The manufactures carried on within and around the town consist chiefly of ships, sails, canvas, sacking, iron and brass work, cooperage, ropes and cordage, leather, hats, bricks, whiting; there are also breweries and malt-houses.

BOSTON, in the United States, is one of the most important commercial cities in the republic. Several large steam-vessels form a regular line of communication between Boston and Great Britain, stopping at Halifax, and performing their voyages in 11 to 13 days; they start once a fortnight from Liverpool. Other lines of steam-packets communicate with every port of importance in the United States. The foreign commerce is very large, amounting to six or seven millions sterling annually, and employing a vast number of fine vessels. The manufactures, too, are important; but Boston is a trading rather than a manufacturing city.

BOTANY. It scarcely needs to be observed that, though botany as a science cannot be treated in this work, a knowledge of it is most important to the arts and manufactures: every increase in our knowledge of the principles which govern the vegetable kingdom, increases our store of materials for industrial pursuits.

BOTHNIA. This frigid region of Sweden and Russia cannot be expected to yield many materials of industry. Rye is the principal grain cultivated, and potatoes are largely grown. Butter and hides, which are the principal articles of export, are sent to Stockholm. The Laplanders have considerable herds of reindeer, and live upon their flesh and other produce. Fish is very abundant. The forests yield abundance of timber, including birch, pine, fir, alder, and aspen. Some of the trees yield tar and pitch.

BÖTTICHER WARE. All the collectors of old china are glad to obtain specimens of Bötticher ware. Bötticher was a chemist and druggist in Saxony, who after failing in various attempts at alchemy, tried the much more rational art of pottery. He produced, in 1703, a kind of red-stone ware; and in 1709 he succeeded in making a beautiful white porcelain—the first European example of that which had before been limited to China. He found that the proper materials were procurable in Saxony; and he established the famous manufactory at Meissena, which has since produced the well-known Dresden china.

The Bötticher ware which finds a place in our cabinets of rarities, and of which many specimens were to be seen at the Mediæval Exhibition of 1850, is generally a kind of brown or reddish brown pottery, polished in a lathe, and covered with a black or iron varnish, enriched with painting and gilding, but not fixed by fire.

BOTTLES, GLASS. The curious mode of making glass bottles is briefly described in a later article [Glass]. We will here merely state that the making of bottles is one of the most extensive departments of the glass manufacture in this country. Besides the immense quantity used for home purposes, no less than 233,108 cwts. of glass bottles were exported in 1849.

BOTTOMRY, as a contract in commercial transactions, is a pledge of the ship as a security of the repayment of money advanced to an owner for the purpose of enabling him to carry on the voyage. This contract is usually in the form of a bond, called a Bottomry Bond, and the condition is that, if the ship be lost on the voyage, the lender loses the whole of his money; but, if the ship and tackle reach the destined port, they become immediately liable, as well as the person of the borrower, for the money lent, and also the premium or interest agreed to be paid upon the loan.

BOUCHES-DU-RHONE. This department of France is chiefly deserving of a word of mention here on account of its wine produce. Nearly 100,000 acres are devoted to vineyards. In 1846 the quantity of wine produced in the department amounted to 13,750,000 gallons, about one half of which was used for home consumption, and the remainder exported or converted into brandy. The white wines of Cassis and Ciotat, the red wines of Séon and St. Louis, and those of Château-Regnard and Saintes-Maries are the most esteemed sorts. The number of Mulberry-trees for the production of silk exceeds a million. The olive is extensively cultivated, and the oils of this department are the best in France. The manufacturing industry of the department, too, is great. The most important products are brandy, soap, vinegar, soda, chemical products, broad cloth, leather, hats, and perfumes. There are several sugar refineries, glass-works, tile and brick-fields, silk, cotton, and tobacco factories, and important salt-works along the coast and on the several lagunes. The commerce of the department is very active with all the southern departments, with the Levant, the coasts of Africa and Spain, and the West Indies. The exports consist of the industrial products named, and dried fruits, cork, and colonial produce. Mines of coal, marble, slate, plaster of Paris, chalk, alabaster, and potters' clay, are successfully worked. Iron and lead-mines have been discovered, but they are not worked. The chief commercial town is noticed elsewhere. [Marseille.]

BOULOGNE, in a commercial point of view, is gradually becoming an important place. The connection by railway of Boulogne with Paris, and of Folkestone with London, has given rise to a large passenger-transit through Boulogne; and goods-traffic is now beginning to follow the same route. The trade of the town is considerable. The herring and mackerel fisheries call into employment a considerable capital, and several vessels are fitted out for the Newfoundland cod fishery. Coarse woollens, sailcloths, pottery, nets, and tulles, are manufactured. There are also a linen-yarn factory which contains 3,000 spindles, glass-bottle works, rope-walks, gin distilleries, sugar refineries, tan-yards, tile and brick works.

BOULTON, MATTHEW, has left a name which will live in all records of mechanical art. He was born in 1728, at Birmingham, where his father carried on the business of a hardwareman. He received an ordinary education, and also acquired a knowledge of drawing and mathematics. The death of his father left him in possession of considerable property; and, in order to extend his commercial operations, he purchased, about 1762, a lease of Soho, near Handsworth, two miles from Birmingham. In 1769 Mr. Boulton having entered into communication with Watt, who had obtained a patent for some improvements in the steam-engine, Watt was induced to settle at Soho; and on his entering into partnership with Mr. Boulton, the Soho works soon became famous for their excellent engines. The manufacture of plated wares, of works in bronze and *or molu*, such as vases, candelabra, and other ornamental articles, was successively introduced at Soho. Artists and men of taste were warmly encouraged, and their talents called forth by Mr. Boulton's liberal spirit. Boulton expended about 47,000*l.* in the course of experiments on the steam-engine, before Watt perfected the construction and occasioned any return of profit. Mr. Boulton died in 1809.

BOURGEOIS, SIR FRANCIS, is noticeable here as the bequeather of the Bourgeois collection to the custody of Dulwich college, for the use of the public. The collection was formed by Noel Desenfans, an eminent picture-dealer, who left it to Sir Francis. He at his death, left it to the widow of his friend, with the greater part of his property, for life; bequeathing 2,000*l.* to Dulwich college for the purpose of building a gallery for the pictures, the reversion of which they were to have. The Dulwich Gallery, as it is generally termed, comprises upwards of 300 pictures.

BOW, an instrument used in producing the sounds from violins, &c. It consists of a stick of Brazil wood, 80 or 100 horse hairs, and a nut to tighten these hairs in the bow. The violin bow was very short in Corelli's time, but gradually increased in length, till Viotti fixed it at 28 inches. The violincello bow is larger and stronger. That for the double-bass is short and strong, and the stick is bent, forming something like the segment of a circle, of which the hairs when stretched are the chord.

BOWS. The common bow and arrow have been known as weapons of offence in almost every country. Among the ancients the bows were made from reeds, the spath of the palm, and various kinds of elastic and tough wood; while the arrows, made of reeds or light wood, were often pointed at the ends with sharp stone instead of iron. At the present day the bow and arrow-makers have an extensive choice of materials, as well for the bow and the arrow as for the string. The cross-bow has been noticed elsewhere. [ARBALEST.]

BOX-WOOD. This remarkably close-grained wood is the produce of the *Buxus* genus of trees. The *Buxus Sempervirens* is the species which yields this valuable wood. It is a small tree common to the south of Europe; but in England it is only found on warm chalky hills, such as Boxhill in Surrey. England is supplied with box-wood chiefly from Turkey; while France receives her supply mainly from Spain. In 1815 there were box-trees cut down on Boxhill which produced 10,000*l.* For the turner, the mathematical instrument-maker, the carver, and especially for the uses of the wood-engraver, box-wood is extremely valuable. The French employ it for making coat-buttons.

At the Mediæval Exhibition of 1850 opportunity was afforded for witnessing the exquisite skill of some of the old carvers in box-wood.

BRABANT. The chief features which render Brabant interesting, in an industrial point of view, are briefly noticed under BELGIUM; BRUSSELS; NETHERLANDS.

BRADFORD. It is curious that both of the well-known towns of Bradford owe their importance to the woollen manufacture. Bradford in Wiltshire has for many centuries been noted for its fine broad-cloths, which have at all times formed its principal manufacture. 'The toune of Bradford stondith by clooth making,' Leland said three centuries ago; and this is still true.

Bradford, in the West Riding, is however the greater town of the two; for its recent progress in wealth and importance has been astonishingly rapid. The chief manufacture of Bradford and the neighbourhood is of worsted stuffs. The spinning of worsted yarn employs many thousands of workpeople, in some of the largest mills of Yorkshire, and the stuffs are woven from the yarn. Woollen yarn for the manufacture of cloths, broad and narrow, is also spun and woven at Bradford in considerable quantities; but the worsted manufacture is the staple employment of the place, Leeds and its dependencies being the more immediate seat of the woollen manufacture. The piece hall, which is the mart for stuff goods, is 144 feet long by 36 feet broad, and has a lower and an upper chamber. The business which is transacted in the piece hall at the Thursday's market is very great, and forms one of the most animated commercial scenes in the kingdom. Many proprietors of worsted mills supply the small manufacturers with yarn, besides employing a great number of looms themselves. Machinery, worked by steam, has almost superseded manual labour in the stuff manufacture, the weaving being now generally done by power-looms. The stuffs manufactured in Bradford are chiefly dyed in Leeds, the proprietors of the dye-houses being among the largest purchasers in the Bradford market. It is however understood that at the present time (1851) Bradford is rapidly rising at the expense of Leeds. Many of the woollen and wool merchants have lately left Leeds, and opened warehouses in Bradford. Several of the large firms of Manchester and Huddersfield have also recently opened warehouses in this flourishing town. Several new worsted mills have been erected between 1846 and 1850, and others are now in course of erection. The central situation of Bradford, with reference to the other clothing towns, has probably been a chief cause of this recent advancement.

The iron trade has long flourished in the neighbourhood of Bradford; indeed it is supposed that the Romans worked iron mines near this spot. There is an abundant supply of iron-ore and coal, both of excellent quality; and the well-known ironworks at Bowling and Low Moor are only a short distance from Bradford. At these foundries some of the most ponderous works in cast-iron are executed. Vast numbers of workmen are employed in different departments of the establishments—from the raising of the ore and coal, to the various marketable states of the metal. These ironworks have the reputation of being carried on with great skill; the improvements of modern times having been successfully introduced in the different branches of the manufacture.

The principal merchants and manufacturers in the trades of Bradford are wool-staplers, wool-combers, worsted-spinnners and manufacturers, worsted-stuff manufacturers, and woollen-cloth manufacturers. Several of the trades which are carried on are dependent upon the woollen and worsted trade; among them are the manufactures for combs, shuttles, and machinery.

Bradford is preparing with much vigour to take part in the Industrial Exhibition of 1851. The manufacturers require 2,000 square feet of space for their appropriation; and they have appointed a committee by whom the articles to be exhibited are grouped in five classes: viz., worsted stuffs, cotton stuffs, iron, machinery, and miscellaneous. One indefatigable weaver, it is said, has woven the four Gospels on cloth, to exhibit as a specimen of his skill.

BRAKE, or BREAK. This name is given by machinists to a contrivance for retarding or arresting motion, by creating an amount of friction too great for the moving power, or for the momentum of the machine, in cases where the moving power is suspended, to overcome. Brakes generally consist of blocks of wood so connected with a system of levers or screws that they may be pressed firmly against the periphery of a wheel mounted upon the main axle of the machine; but in some cases, instead of a block of wood, a strap or belt of iron, of sufficient length to embrace one-half of the periphery of the brake-wheel, or a series of small blocks of wood attached to the concave surface of such a strap is used.

Among the many contrivances for attaining safety in railway travelling, self-acting brakes have been devised, which would begin to act as soon as the buffers of two adjacent carriages were pressed together, and would arrest the revolution of the wheels with a force directly proportionate to the force with which the carriages ran together; but it is doubtful whether the inconvenience of such an apparatus under certain circumstances would not more than counterbalance the anticipated advantages. It is however a fair field for invention, and many patents have recently been obtained in relation to this matter.

BRAMAH, JOSEPH, occupies a distinguished rank as the maker of delicate pieces of mechanism. He was born in 1749. He established himself as a cabinet-maker in London, and afterwards obtained celebrity as the inventor of important improvements in water-closets, and of an ingenious lock, which yet maintains its character as one of the most inviolable ever contrived. [Lock.] This invention was patented in 1784. He also contrived improvements in water-cocks, pumps, and fire-engines, and in 1796 patented the invaluable machine known as the Bramah press, or hydraulic press. Among his other inventions were the beer-machine, commonly used in taverns for drawing beer in the bar from barrels deposited in the cellar; improved planing-machinery; paper-making machinery; an instrument for making quill-pen nibs; and the beautiful contrivance [BANK-NOTE MACHINERY] by which bank notes are numbered with a regular succession of numbers, without the possibility of twice producing the same number. By the introduction of this last-named machine into the Bank of England the labour of 100 clerks out of 120 was dispensed with. Bramah died in 1814.

BRAMAH'S PRESS. [HYDRAULICS.]

BRANDENBURG, a province of Prussia, possesses considerable manufactures in many of the towns. The first manufactures were established by the Huguenot refugees, who received cordial assistance from the government, and were liberally seconded by it in their outset. The woollen manufactures, which are the most important, are established in most of the towns; those for the finer sorts of goods are at Luckenwalde, Züllichau, Kottbus, and Guben; kerseymeres and merino cloths are made in Berlin, where woollen yarns are spun on a large scale by steam-machinery. The manufactures of linens, chiefly of the middling and coarser sorts, is extensively carried on in the Lusatian districts and the circle of Frankfort. Tanneries, paper-mills, sugar-refineries, and manufactures of tobacco, glass, porcelain, earthenware, iron, steel, copper and gunpowder, are among the industrial establishments of the province. The Berlin iron ornaments have become particularly celebrated.

BRANDY. This well known liquid is the alcoholic or spirituous portion of wine, separated from the aqueous part, the colouring matter, &c., by distillation. The word is of German origin, and in its German form, *brantwein*, signifies burnt wine, or wine that has undergone the action of fire. Brandies, however, have been made from potatoes, carrots, beet root, pears, and other vegetable substances; but they are all inferior to true brandy. Brandy is prepared in most wine countries, but that of France is the most esteemed. It is procured not only by distilling the wine itself, but also by fermenting and distilling the *marc* or residue of the pressings of the grape. It is procured indifferently from red or white wine; and different wines yield very different proportions of it, the strongest of course giving the largest quantity. Brandy obtained from marc has a more acrid flavour than that from wine, which appears to be occasioned by an oil contained in the skin of the grapo, which when separated proves so acrid that a single drop would deteriorate several gallons of good brandy. The celebrated brandy of Cognac, a town in the department of Charente, and that brought from Andraye, seem to owe their excellence to being made from white wine, so fermented as not to be impregnated with this oil. Like other spirit, brandy is colourless when recently distilled. By mere keeping however, owing probably to some change in the soluble matter contained in it, it acquires a slight colour, which is much increased by keeping in casks, and is made of the required intensity by the addition of burnt sugar, or other colouring matter.

The production of brandy, so far as obtaining the alcoholic principle is concerned, is described under DISTILLATION.

Although brandy drinkers despise or affect to despise patent or British brandy, yet it is a question whether this may not be quite as pure and strong as much that goes by the name of foreign brandy. So enormous is the duty paid on foreign brandy, that the French manufacturers are induced to strengthen it artificially by spirits of wine, and the English dealers to increase its bulk by water and other additions. Foreign brandy ought to be a little 'over proof;' but it is frequently 12 to 15 degrees below proof. Dr. Normandy, in his recent work on adulteration, has the following remarks on the worst or really fraudulent brandy:—

'Brandy, when newly distilled, is white, but that met with in commerce is always of a yellowish, brown, or dark brown colour, which is due to the presence of some extractive matter, and of tannic acid, which it has dissolved from the oak casks in which it has been kept for a long time. But in order to simulate this colour of genuine brandy, the brandy of commerce is nothing else than new brandy or alcohol, at once converted apparently into old brandy by means of caramel, or burnt sugar.'

British brandy, for which patents have been obtained by many English distillers, is the result of numerous attempts to produce, from malt-spirit, a liquor that shall bear much resemblance to foreign brandy. The best malt-spirit is the basis of all the British brandies; and the flavour, colour, and degree of strength, are brought about by the addition of some among the following long list of ingredients: water, red tartar, acetic ether, French vinegar, French plums, wine-bottoms, tincture of catechu, oak shavings, bitter almonds, burnt sugar, tincture of vanilla, oil of cassia, rum, &c.: each manufacturer having a favourite recipe of his own. It is said that where black tea is cheap, as in America, it is often employed to give an imitative brandy-roughness to coloured spirits.

Whatever may be the quantity of imitative brandy made in England, the importation of foreign brandy still continues very large. In 1849 it amounted to no less than 4,480,306 gallons.

Brandy is an ingredient in a large number of cordials and liqueurs; such as cherry-brandy, carraway brandy, lemon brandy, orange brandy, peach brandy, raspberry brandy, and the like. They all bear a family resemblance in so far as they consist of brandy, flavoured by the fruits or seeds whose name they bear, sweetened with sugar, and rendered fragrant with spices.

BRASS. This very valuable metal is an alloy of copper and zinc, which, from the remotest antiquity, has been extensively applied to useful and ornamental purposes. It was made long before zinc was obtained in its metallic form, by exposing grain or bean copper, which was produced by pouring melted copper into water, or copper clippings, to great heat in crucibles with calcined and powdered calamine, a native carbonate of zinc and charcoal; but in 1781 James Emerson obtained a patent for making brass in a more direct way, by melting together its constituent metals; and this mode is now generally practised. The proportions of the two metals vary much in different kinds of brass, but nearly two-thirds copper and one-third zinc appears to be best for ordinary purposes. M. Machts, of Vienna, has recently found that brass made in a peculiar way from 60 per cent of copper, and 40 of zinc possesses a valuable degree of malleability. Prince's, or Prince Rupert's metal, tombac, or tombak, pinchbeck, similor, Mannheim gold, and several other alloys of similar character, are only varieties of brass, the several proportions of which however are variously given by different writers.

The general properties of brass are, a fine yellow colour, susceptibility of a high polish, and being only superficially acted upon by the air. It is brittle at a high temperature, but very malleable and ductile when cold. Its specific gravity is greater than that deducible from the specific gravities of its constituent metals. It is more fusible, a worse conductor of heat, and harder than copper. The facility with which it may be cast, and turned in a lathe, or otherwise worked, renders it peculiarly useful in the construction of mathematical instruments, and the smaller parts of machinery. Brass wire is extensively used in pin-making, and for various other purposes. *Latten* is a name sometimes given to thin sheets of rolled brass; and *Dutch metal* or *Dutch gold* is brass beaten out into very thin leaves.

It has been much contested whether brass is a true chemical compound of copper and zinc, or merely a mechanical mixture. Since the rise of electro-metallurgy, many experimenters have stated that they have precipitated or deposited brass from liquid solution, which, it is calculated, could not occur if the two component metals were merely an alloy, and not a chemical compound. The subject has not yet been definitely settled.

A mode of using sheet brass or other metal for ornamental purposes was introduced a few years ago, in which the appearance of solid metal might be obtained without the weight, by using a wooden core to place the sheet metal upon. The method is useful for making cornice-poles, mouldings, or other articles of continuous form and pattern. The wood is first shaped, by planes and other tools, to the required pattern; the sheet metal is placed upon it; and the two together are drawn through a suitable die, which unites them by driving the edges of the metal into the substance of the wood. If the pattern be a plain one, it is struck down upon the wood by the die through which it passes; but if the pattern be full and complicated, it is imparted to the sheet metal by swaging tools and dies, previous to the application of the metal to the surface of the wood.

The brass manufacture is one of the most important of the Birmingham branches of industry. No less than thirty manufacturers of that town have announced their intention to present specimens at the forthcoming grand Exhibition, in the departments of brass bedsteads, lamps, gas furniture, tubing, ornaments, &c.

Brass work was exported in 1849 to the value of 114,000*l*.

BRAZIL. This vast country is rich in products useful in the arts and manufactures. Besides the ordinary kinds of vegetable food, the natives cultivate the cocoa-plant, the maté-plant, coffee, sugar, cotton, tobacco, indigo, ginger, pepper, cinnamon, cloves, vanilla, sarsaparilla, caoutchouc, copaiva, copal, various fruits and also various dye-plants and timber-trees. The herds of horned cattle are immense; and their produce, consisting, besides live stock, of hides, jerked beef, tallow, horns, and horn tips, is exported in great quantities. As soon as the animals are skinned, the hides are spread on the ground, slightly salted, and dried in the sun. The flesh is cut into thin slices, salted, and dried in the air, for consumption in the northern provinces. A little butter and cheese is made.

The Brazilians produce many useful substances from the animals by which they are surrounded. They prepare spermaceti and oil from some of their fish; they salt and dry many of their larger fish, to serve as a store of provisions; they make sausages from the flesh of the manati, a peculiar kind of fish; they produce a fatty substance from the eggs of turtles by roasting; and they fry one species of ant as an article of food.

The mineral wealth of Brazil is considerable, but limited to a few articles, of which the chief are gold and iron, diamonds and topazes, and salt. Before the beginning of the last century the quantity of gold obtained was inconsiderable, but it increased rapidly. The greatest quantity was found between 1753 and 1763, but it afterwards decreased. The grains of gold in the sand being nearly exhausted, and capital being wanted to work the veins in the mountains, the produce fell off; but, since the introduction of British capital into some of the provinces, the produce of the mines has increased. Iron is very abundant: in some places there are whole mountains of ore; but up to the present time it has been worked on an extensive scale only in two or three places. In 1843 a government iron-foundry was abandoned as an unprofitable speculation. No *silver* has been found, and only slight indications of *copper*, *tin*, and *quicksilver*. *Platinum* occurs in some places. *Lead* and *cobalt* are more common.

No country probably is richer in diamonds than Brazil, but hitherto they have only been found in the rivers. The diamond district, or the district of Tejuco, where by far the greatest quantity of diamonds has been found, is situated under 18° S. lat.; and here many hundreds of persons are employed by the government in searching for diamonds. In about a century from 1730 to 1830, it is supposed that the diamonds found must have been worth three millions sterling. In another diamond district, that of Abaeté, was found in 1791 the great diamond weighing 138½ carats, one of the largest in the world. Diamonds are also found in other districts of Brazil.

The Brazilians obtain their salt from salt steppes or plains. There are here and there patches of salt efflorescence on the surface of the ground. There are also salt springs, and salt steppes which yield salt after a shower of rain.

Internal communication in Brazil is in a very imperfect state. The roads are few, and mostly bad. The rivers offer a fine field for traffic enterprise, but the country is not in a state to develope its own advantages. Steam transit has been partially introduced on one or two of the rivers.

The foreign commerce of Brazil is very large. The vessels of all nations are admitted on the same conditions, and their cargoes pay the same duties. The most important articles of exportation are sugar, coffee, and cotton. The exportation of cocoa, hides, tobacco, rice, horns and horn-tips, dye-woods, sarsaparilla, and indian-rubber is also considerable. The smaller articles are isinglass, indigo, castor beans, castor-oil, and different drugs. The chief ports visited by European vessels are S. Pedro, Santos, Rio Janeiro, Bahia, Pernambuco, Maranhao, Parà, Aracaty, Seara, and Parahyba. Rio Janeiro is the chief place of export for coffee, Bahia for sugar, and Pernambuco for cotton.

The British produce and manufactures sent to Brazil in 1849 exceeded 2,000,000*l.* in value. The exports from Brazil amount to four or five millions sterling per annum; they are sent to almost every part of Europe and America, and to many African and Asiatic ports.

BRAZIL NUTS. There is in the vast forests on the banks of the Orinoco, a genus of trees, of large size, called *Bertholletia.* Its stem averages a hundred feet in height, and two feet in diameter, not branching till near the top, whence its boughs hang down in a graceful manner. The fruit is figured and described by Humboldt as a spherical case, as big as a man's head, with four cells, in each of which are six or eight nuts; its shell is rugged and furrowed, and covered with a rind of a green colour. The nuts are irregularly triangular bodies, having a hard shell, which is very much wrinkled, and which is fixed to a central placenta by their lower end. The seed is a firm oily almond, of a pure white colour. 'The Portuguese of Para,' says Humboldt, 'have for a long time driven a great trade with the nuts of this tree, which the Spaniards call *almendron;* they send cargoes to French Guiana, whence they are shipped for England and Lisbon. The kernels yield a large quantity of oil, well suited for lamps.' They are sold in England under the name of Brazil Nuts.

BRAZIL WOOD, is much used in dyeing. A decoction is made from the wood by the action of hot water; and this decoction, by various modes of using, is made to impart a beautiful red-dye to cottons, linens, silks, and woollens.

Another name for this wood is *sapan.* It is brought from Brazil and is the wood of the *cæsalpinia crista.* From 3,000 to 4,000 tons are imported annually.

BREAD and BAKING. There is a marked characteristic which separates bread into two kinds:— *biscuit* bread, which is made without fermentation, and is compact, heavy, and hard; and *loaf* bread, which is fermented, and thereby rendered porous, light, and soft. The flour of barley, oats, and rye, is used as well as that of wheat for making bread; but our brief details will apply more especially to wheaten bread, which is the most extensively used in England, and in which the properties of perfect bread are most distinctly exhibited.

In making biscuit bread [BISCUIT], no chemical change is effected: the operation being the merely mechanical one of moistening particles of flour so as to cause them to adhere together, and to remain in one mass by the subsequent process of baking. The operation of making fermented bread is far less simple.

Wheat flour consists of *starch* and *gluten*, with a very small proportion of other substances: and the relative proportions of these constituents vary in different kinds of corn. A mode of comparing the qualities of flour in this respect has been already described. [ALEUROMETER.]

When flour is mixed with water, it forms the well-known paste called *dough*, which ferments if left in a moderately warm place. During this fermentation, carbonic acid gas is evolved; and this gas, in its natural tendency to escape into the air, is arrested in its progress through the dough by the adhesiveness of the gluten, and consequently forms the numerous cavities we see in fermented bread. These are more numerous, and consequently the bread is lighter, when wheat flour is used than when the flour of oats or rye, which contains less gluten, is employed. This natural process of fermentation however is slow and tedious, and is liable to impart a disagreeable flavour to the bread; to remedy which, the custom of accelerating the fermentation by adding a small quantity of dough in a state of strong fermentation, called *leaven*, was introduced. The substitution of *yest* (the frothy scum which rises on the surface of beer during its fermentation,) for this leaven is a further improvement.

In the ordinary mode of making bread the water is used at a temperature of from 90° to 100°, a little salt and yest is mixed with it, and then a quantity of flour. The substance thus produced is covered up and set aside in a warm situation: this part of the process being called *setting the sponge*. Within an hour the progress of fermentation is manifested by the swelling and heaving of the sponge; and this process is allowed to proceed, with the occasional dropping or sinking of the dough when the confined gas becomes so powerful as to force a way for escape, until a period dictated by experience as that beyond which further fermentation would be hazardous. The baker then adds the remaining flour, water, and salt, and incorporates all the materials thoroughly together by long and laborious kneading. When this has been continued until the dough will receive a smart pressure of the hand without adhering to it, it is again left to ferment for a few hours, and afterwards kneaded more gently, in order so to distribute the gas engendered within it as to make the bread equally light and porous throughout. It is then formed into loaves, which being set aside for an hour or two, expand to about double their original volume: and these loaves are finally baked in the oven, by which process they enlarge still more in bulk, not by the continuance of fermentation, but by the expansion of the gas already formed, through the effect of heat. The result is a loaf composed of an infinite number of cellules filled with carbonic acid gas, and lined with a glutinous membrane.

When flour is converted into bread, it is found on leaving the oven to have increased from 28 to 34 per cent. in weight; but bread which has gained 28lbs. will lose about 4lbs. within thirty-six hours after leaving the oven. The season of growth, the age of the flour, and other circumstances, affect the quantity of bread obtainable from a given weight of flour; but generally speaking the better the flour is, and the older, within certain limits, the greater will be the quantity of bread.

The *panary* fermentation, or the fermentation which dough undergoes, is nearly identical with *vinous* fermentation; a little alcohol being produced by it. Hence arose a notable project, a few years ago, for *saving the spirit* produced in bread making; a sum of 20,000*l.* was spent in establishing a bakery at Chelsea but it was soon found that the projectors had totally misconceived the chemistry of their subject; while neighbouring bakers, by advertising '*bread with the gin in it*,' contrived to throw the gin-less bread quite out of popular favour.

Under ordinary circumstances, no machinery is employed in bread making in England. About 20 years ago Mr. Clayton obtained a patent for a rotatory kneading machine: in the interior of which knives were placed diagonally; and other mixing and kneading machines have since been invented; but the hand method remains still almost exclusively in force in this country. Our French neighbours understand these things better: they apply more science to the chemistry of eating and drinking. The mixing and kneading are generally effected by hand: but they are more carefully attended to than in England. There is, however, a machine-bakery, patented at Paris by M. Mouchot, of which Dumas gives a description: the lifting of the flour into the troughs, the admission of water, the mixing, the kneading, the baking—all are effected by the aid of efficient machinery.

A machine for baking bread by steam was introduced into France about five years ago. It consists principally of two concentric cylinders, the inner one of which has numerous perforations. The dough is placed in the inner cylinder, and steam is admitted to the space between the two cylinders. Half an hour is said to be sufficient for the heat of the steam to bake the bread; but it would appear that there ought to be some mode of drying the bread after this process.

An ingenious mode of baking biscuits is described in the 'Mechanics Magazine' (No. 981) as having been invented by Mr. Deucale, an American, and practised in New York. A brick oven stands in the middle of the bakehouse, 12 feet long, 6 feet wide, and 4 feet high. The top has no opening whatever. The front has an opening near the ground, with a metal door, through which the fuel is introduced and made to cover the entire area of the floor of the oven. About a foot above the furnace door is an opening six or eight inches high and the whole width of the oven; a similar opening exists at the back of the oven. Near each opening is a wooden cylinder; and round both cylinders a wire lattice-work is tightly coiled, so as to form an endless cloth stretching horizontally within and across the oven, over the fire. The dough and biscuits being ranged in a row along the front edge of the wire-cloth, the baker turns a winch hand and winds them into the oven; this he does row after row, until, by the time the first row has reached the back of the oven, the biscuits in that row are properly baked. This method presents a good deal of analogy to that described under BISCUIT.

In respect to *ovens*, considerable improvements have been introduced within the last few years; instead of placing fuel *in* the oven, it is placed on one side, and flues are so arranged as to heat the oven with less waste, more quickly, and with more cleanliness than on the old method.

Of the condition of the *bakers* much has been said lately which tends to show that there is sad want of improvement; Dr. Guy's Report on this subject gives a gloomy picture of the effects of night work on the journeymen bakers. Nor is the genuineness of the bread produced quite so undeniable as one might wish. Indeed the public has been a little scared at the long list of objectionables used to adulterate bread—damaged wheat, beans, peas, carbonate of ammonia, potatoes, plaster of Paris, chalk, pipeclay, burnt bones, are all said occasionally to take part in the manufacture of what ought to be wheaten bread. There is a double mischief in all this: it is a robbery in itself; and it leads to the honest as well as the dishonest being suspected by those whose suspicions are aroused, but who have neither inclination nor skill to analyse their bread.

The varieties of bread used only in a small degree are numerous. There are bran bread, French soup bread, grain bread, household bread, Iceland moss bread, leavened bread, potato bread, &c.—all of which have peculiarities either in the ingredients or in the mode of making.

BREAD FRUIT. A Bread-Fruit is a fig turned inside out, and much larger in all its parts; that is to say, the flowers which form the bread-fruit and fig grow, in both cases, upon a fleshy receptacle; but in the former the receptacle is solid and bears its flowers externally, while in the latter it is hollow and bears its flowers internally.

The bread-fruit (*Artocarpus incisa*) is a native of the South Sea Islands, and of many parts of the Indian Archipelago. The fruit is green and of considerable size, equalling a melon of the larger kind in dimensions, and is of many different forms. The nuts, when roasted, are said to be as good as the best chesnuts; but it is principally for the fleshy receptacle that it is valued. When roasted it becomes soft, tender, and white, resembling the crumb of a loaf; but it must be eaten new, or it becomes hard and difficult to swallow. It forms so important a part of the support of the South Sea Islanders that it was introduced by the British Government into the West Indies, where it is still cultivated, and whence it has been carried to the continent of America. It does not appear, however, equal to the plantain as an article of human food.

BREAKWATER. The Plymouth breakwater is a public work on which we justly pride ourselves. It was commenced in 1812, and is formed of stone procured from the shores of the harbour. The quarrying of the stone, the conveyance into the vessels by a railway, the dropping of the stones into the sea by opening trap doors in the vessels, the gradual accumulation of the vast heap, and the dressing of the surface to the required form, are all remarkable operations. The works are not even yet completed; for so late as August, 1850, the admiralty advertised for 130,000 cubic feet of dressed limestone, to be supplied during 1851. The breakwater is a straight line of stone-work with two wings inclined a little towards the north; the straight portion is about 1000 yards in length, and the wings 350 yards each. The width at the bed of the sea is 300 to 400 feet; but only 50 at high water level. The upper surface is horizontal, and about 2 feet above high water spring tide. The inner face has a slope of 2 to 1, and the outer face a slope of 5 to 1. The coarse rubble contained in the structure, up to the present time, exceeds 3,600,000 tons; the dressed masonry 2,500,000 tons. Upwards of 330,000 tons were deposited in one year (1816). The works (which were under the late John Rennie until 1821, and since under the present Sir John) have cost about 1,500,000*l.*; and seldom has public money been more advantageously expended.

The breakwater at Cherbourg, which is so honourable to our French neighbours, and which attracted so much the attention of our naval officers on a recent occasion, is briefly described in another article. [CHERBOURG.]

The breakwater at Portland, now being constructed by Mr. Rendel, will shelter an area of 1822 acres. From the eastern point of the island of Portland, it will run out 1,500 feet in an easterly direction, and then 6,000 feet north-eastward; but at the angle between these two portions will be an opening about 500 feet wide, for the entrance of steamers and small craft. More than 7,000 feet of the entire length will be built in 5 to 8½ fathoms depth at low water. From the large store of stone in the island, the facility of transport, and the employment of convict labour, it is estimated that this great work may be completed for 560,000*l.* A railway, with three inclines, drums, wire-ropes, &c., are employed to raise and lower the waggons, and to carry stones from the top of the island to the spot where they are dropped into the sea.

The determination of the government to construct harbours of refuge has led to the promulgation of many plans for breakwaters. A few of these we shall briefly glance at, as well as others suggested somewhat earlier.

Captain Tayler's Floating Breakwater was introduced to public notice in 1838. It consists of a frame-work or caisson of timber, moored and shackled, so as to yield to the violence of the sea, and to admit the water to pass under, over, and through it. The circumstances which, to the inventor's mind, seem to point out this as a useful form, are the following: 1st. It divides and breaks the waves, and reduces them to a harmless state; converting all that happens to lie within a crescent of such breakwaters to still or smooth water. 2nd. It is free from the objections which often pertain to solid breakwaters, in so far as they tend to the filling up or obstructing of harbours and channels by accumulation of sand and mud. 3rd. It can be laid down on any part of the coast, so as to form a harbour where none can be formed by ordinary means. 4th. It can be constructed and kept in repair at a mere fraction of the cost of an ordinary breakwater. These are high claims, but they have not yet met with a favourable reception. According to the specification of the patent, the timber-framed caissons are to vary in shape and form according to the depth and nature of the sea wherein they are to be moored; but, as a general rule, about one-third of the mass is above water. As it is optional to make the structure of any convenient dimensions, many such may be chained or otherwise fastened end to end, so as to form a lengthened straight or curved breakwater.

Another plan recently proposed consists in placing a number of spars upright in the sea, three or four feet apart: the spars being five or six inches square, and of a length (about 24 feet) sufficient to reach the whole depth of the deepest waves. A heavy stone or any kind of mooring anchor is lowered to the bottom of the sea beneath each spar, and the spar is connected with this by a chain. Each spar yields easily to any forcible pressure from the sea, since the small chain at bottom acts as a hinge; but it will soon recover its vertical direction, which it maintains by virtue of the wood being of less specific gravity than sea-water. How many rows of such spars would be necessary to check the force of a sea, would in all probability depend on the nature of the locality.

Captain Vetch (in Weale's *Quarterly Papers*, 1843) advocates a vertical construction of breakwaters, instead of a sloping face towards the sea. His plan consists in a peculiar application of wrought iron rods, which pass vertically through the water, and are supported by horizontal iron frames, through orifices in which the rods pass. The frames and rods receive lateral support by other rods placed in a sloping position, in a double row on the two faces of the breakwater.

In 1848 Mr. W. H. Smith published a small pamphlet relating to Harbours of Refuge, in which he recommends the use of a peculiar kind of breakwater. It consists of a hollow framework of timber, which is secured to the ground by screw-piles, such as those employed in Mitchell's screw-pile lighthouses; the framework is free to oscillate on these piles, within certain limits, which are determined by mooring blocks, and counterbalance weights.

Captain Sleigh's proposed breakwater consists of a series of sloping or oblique platforms supported by floating hollow vessels or caissons; by which the platforms are always maintained in an oblique position, and are enabled to rise and fall with the tide. These floating vessels and sloping platforms are to be so arranged as to form sea and wind barriers for sheltering ships, pier-heads, and bridges; they may be made of any dimensions, and any convenient number of them may be ranged end to end, so as to form either a straight or a curved line, according to the size and shape of the spot to be sheltered.

A singular form of Breakwater was suggested by Captain Norton a few years ago. He had observed, that where the *lotus* plant grows on a lake or pond, if a strong wind ruffles the water on one side of the leaf, the water is comparatively smooth on the other side: resulting from the wind having no hold on the broad expanse of the leaves. He had also observed, after a storm at sea, the solid timbers of a wrecked vessel splintered in pieces by being driven against the shore; while a wicker basket escaped uninjured. These two facts suggested the idea of constructing a floating breakwater of *osiers*. A model of such a machine was exhibited at the Polytechnic Institution in 1843.

Engineers of eminence, both military and civil, are at present engaged in a discussion whether *vertical* or *sloped* faces are best for sea walls and breakwaters. So much is this an undecided question, that the recent injury to the new works at Dover Harbour is appealed to, to afford evidence on one side or the other.

BREMEN, one of the free Hanseatic towns, owes its prosperity to the navigable river (the Weser) on which it stands. It is the entrepôt for imports of all the countries bordering on the Weser, and especially for Hanover, Oldenburg, and Hesse-Cassel. A railroad from Bremen to Hanover was opened in Dec. 1847. Large vessels go up the river only as far as Bremerlehe, 28 miles below Bremen; there they discharge their cargoes in a new harbour called Bremerhaven. Ships of 200 to 250 tons unload at Vegesack, 13 miles below Bremen; and vessels of seven or eight feet draft go quite up to the town. Cargoes brought to Bremerhaven and Vegesack are forwarded to Bremen by lighters and boats. Bremen is a place of great resort for the warehousing and transit of foreign and German goods; it has a bank, discount office, and several insurance companies. The ships of Bremen have been largely engaged of late years in carrying out German emigrants to America. The chief imports are raw cotton, cotton yarn, sugar, coffee, tea, tobacco, dye-stuffs, and other colonial produce. The exports consist of these same items, and linens, grain, oak-bark, salt meat, hides, seeds, rags, wool, woollen goods, and wine. The vessels which arrive annually are 1100 or 1200 in number, many of them of large tonnage; and they bring to the city an immense quantity of merchandize. The town has several sugar-refineries, above 100 distilleries, tanyards, soaperies, cordage and canvas factories, cotton-mills, bleach-works, tobacco factories, &c.

BRE'SCIA is rich in most of those articles of produce, such as silk, oil, wine, and fruit, which will come under our notice in the article LOMBARDY.

BRESLAU, the capital of the Prussian province of Silesia, is highly favoured by nature for a trading depôt; its central position among the manufacturing districts of Silesia, its facilities for trade by means of internal navigation, and by railroads which connect it with Vienna, Prague, Dresden, Leipzig, Hanover, Hamburg, Berlin, and Stettin, render it one of the most thriving manufacturing and commercial cities of Europe. It is an entrepôt for the fine and coarse woollens, cottons, linens, silks, hardwares, glass, wools, hemp, and flax of Silesia; for the wines of Hungary and all kinds of colonial produce. The oxen of the Ukraine and Moldavia, the corn and cattle of Silesia, and the produce of its own distilleries, tanyards, typefoundries, and all those manufactures which it has in common with other large towns, find a regular sale at Breslau. Four fairs are held in the year, those for wool are held in the early part of June and October. The average quantity of wool sold at the June fairs amounts to 7,000,000 lbs.

It is interesting to note, as a proof of the tendency of trade to penetrate in all directions, that at the Michaelmas wool-fair at Breslau, in 1850, more than 300 bales of *Australian* wool were sold, and were readily bought by the manufacturers of the Zollverein or Customs' Union district of Germany.

BREST is a fortress and naval station of the first class. There are handsome quays, ship-building yards, extensive storehouses, rope-walks, and barracks; but as its works relate wholly to defence and not to commerce, we need not describe them here.

BREWING and BREWERIES. Whether ale or beer be the object of the brewer's attention, the *chemistry* of the manufacture is pretty nearly the same. It consists in the process of extracting a saccharine solution from grain, and in converting that solution into a fermented and spirituous beverage. This art, although a perfectly chemical one in nearly all its stages, has not until recent times been indebted to chemistry for any of the improvements which have been made in its details.

In brewing the various beers, as ale, porter, and table-ale, two kinds of malt are employed, the *pale* and the *brown*. The first is used for ales, and for the finer qualities the malt is dried very pale indeed; the brown malt is used for porters and stouts. Roasted or black malt is used as a colouring material, in place of burnt sugar.

The malt is first ground or crushed; and the grist or ground malt being prepared, the next part of the process is the mashing. The *mash-tun*, or vessel in which this operation is carried on, is usually of wood, varying in size according to the quantity of malt to be wetted, and having two or more taps in the bottom. From one to two inches above this bottom is a false bottom pierced full of small holes, on which the grist is placed; the hot water is then admitted, and the grist is intimately mixed with the water. For this purpose machinery is used to stir it about, and cause it to assume a homogeneous consistence. The whole is then allowed to stand at rest for a certain time; and the taps being opened, the infusion, or sweet wort, is allowed to run off into a vessel called the *underback*, whence it is pumped or otherwise conveyed to the copper for boiling. When the wort has run off, the taps are closed, and a fresh quantity of hot water is run on for a second mash. When the whole of the wort is pumped into the copper, the hops are thrown in, and the boiling commences. For large coppers machinery is used to prevent the hops from settling down and burning. When the boiling is complete, the whole contents of the copper are turned into the *hop-back*, which is a large square or oblong vessel of wood or iron, having a false bottom for large brewings, and a sieve partition at the corner for small ones.

As the boiled wort drains from the hops it is allowed to run, or is pumped, into the *coolers*. These hops, when sufficiently drained, may be again boiled with a second copper of wort, or with the return wort or table-beer. The coolers are large shallow vessels, placed in as open a part of the brewery as possible, so as to command a free current of air over the whole of their surface: they may be constructed of either wood or iron. Fans and blowers are sometimes used to assist the rapidity of this part of the process. When sufficiently cool, the wort is allowed to run into the fermenting tun.

The wort is next fermented in a large vessel called a *gyle*, or fermenting *tun*. As soon as the wort begins to run from the coolers, and when a sufficient quantity is in the tun, the yest is added. When the fermentation has arrived at a certain point of attenuation, that is, when a certain quantity of the saccharine matter of the wort has been converted into alcohol or spirit, it is cleansed from the yest; for this purpose it is either run into smaller vessels, such as casks or rounds, or the yesty head is skimmed off from the top; and this is repeated at intervals until the beer is clean. This operation of skimming is generally confined to the cleansing of ales. The *casks* are simply filled with the fermenting beer, and so arranged as to be always kept quite full, with a trough or stillion to catch the yest as it works out at the orifice of these vessels. The beer, being thus cleansed from all the yest, is now either racked directly into casks as for ale, or run into vats prepared for it. On the large scale a large vessel is first used, into which the beer intended to be vatted is allowed to run so as to be perfectly well mixed, and also to deposit a further portion of yest by standing. The beer is by this means also rendered flat, which is necessary for stock or store beer that is to be kept some time before coming into use.

The last operation the beer has to undergo is the fining, or clearing, which is sometimes done by the brewer, sometimes by the publican. The fining material consists of isinglass, or other gelatinous matter, dissolved in acid beer, or sours, which, having been added to the ale or beer, agglutinates or collects together all the lighter floating matters which render the beer thick, and ultimately falls to the bottom of the vessel with them, leaving the beer clear and transparent.

Such is a simple outline of the processes, whether bitter or mild, strong or weak beverage is to be brewed, and whether the scale of operations be large or small. The reader will have no difficulty in conceiving that the mechanism and details of the processes must vary greatly, although the chemical principles may remain the same. In Bavaria the brewing of beer is one of the chief, perhaps *the* chief, manufacture; for the Germans are resolute beer drinkers. They have black beer, white beer, brown beer, thin beer, strong beer, double beer, bitter beer—differences which we attempt, though not very successfully, to indicate by our names *ale*, *beer*, *porter*, *stout*, &c. Bavarian beer and Scotch ale differ from English beers and ales in being fermented at lower temperatures. *Ale*, in England, is brewed from paler malt than *beer*; *porter* is brewed from pale malt coloured with burnt malt; *stout* is only a superior kind of porter; *table-beer* is simply poor or weak beer. Malt is the proper material for yielding beer; but imitative beers are brewed from bran, potatoes, spruce, sugar, and treacle.

A few flavouring and sweetening ingredients are recognized and allowable in brewing; but the world knows very little of the adulterations to which beer is too often subjected. Quassia, gentian, wormwood, broom-top, to impart bitterness; capsicum, ginger, coriander, orange peel, caraway, to give pungency; opium, cocculus indicus, nux vomica, tobacco, poppy, henbane, to intoxicate; molasses, sugar, treacle, as substitutes for malt; sulphuric acid, alum, vitriol, salt, to impart various properties —all are suspected, and more than suspected, of playing a part in the manufacture of some of those beverages which occasionally go by the name of beer. The Excise have battled hard against these difficulties; but with only partial success.

Mr. Tizard, a brewer of Birmingham, has suggested a remarkable arrangement for fermenting the beer. He proposes the use of a subterranean fermenting room, sunk to such a depth as to have a uniform temperature from 45° to 52° at all hours and seasons. This, in our country would be a depth of about 70 or 80 feet. The fermenting vessels are surrounded with cold water in this subterranean chamber. The cooled wort is conveyed by a pipe down into the vessel; and after the processes of fermenting, cleansing, and fining, it is drawn up again through racking taps, which only just dip below the surface of the liquid, so as not to disturb the lees of the liquor.

A cooler for brewing, introduced by Mr. Davidson, acts in the following way. The wort is pumped up at a slow and regulated speed into a recipient at the top of the machine; it there divides into a series of thin films or streams, and trickles down the inside of a number of thin metallic tubes, set vertically. An upward current of air passes through these tubes, meeting and cooling the hot wort.

Various other improvements are frequently being introduced or suggested; but we must hasten to say a few words of the vast establishments wherein brewing is sometimes conducted, and of which Messrs. Barclay and Perkins' Porter Brewery is the most notable specimen.

This large establishment covers many acres, and contains so many court yards and buildings surrounding them, that it almost requires a map to render the arrangement intelligible. Here is the vast 'tun-room' or fermenting house; north-east of this, on the river side, is the wharf for landing the malt and for shipping the beer; westward of the wharf are the immense malt warehouses; nearer at hand are the steam-engine apparatus, the water reservoir, the cooperage, the ale and porter brewhouses, the fining house, the store vaults, the splendid stables for the dray-horses.—Such are the objects which present themselves, over an area of eight or nine acres. And when we examine them more closely, the details themselves are vast. Everything is on a large scale. The water cisterns are 30 feet long by 20 wide; the malt-bins, two dozen in number, are each large enough to contain an ordinary three-storied house; the great brewhouse is nearly as large as Westminster Hall; the copper vessels for boiling contain 12,000 gallons each; the store of beer always on hand requires 150 vats, of an average capacity of 30,000 gallons each; one particular vat contains 100,000 gallons, and weighs when full 500 tons; the number of butts, puncheons, and barrels, belonging to the establishment exceeds 60,000; about 200 horses are kept, who have stables arranged with all scientific appliances, and a veterinary surgeon on their especial behoof.

BRICK. The ancients used bricks both baked and simply dried in the sun. Those found in the ruins of Babylon [BABYLON] are among the oldest specimens existing. The Egyptians used sun-dried bricks, and the process of making them is represented in their paintings. The Greek bricks appear to have been used simply dried. Roman bricks were very thin in proportion to their length and breadth, and were well burnt.

In making ordinary English bricks, the top soil, or *encallow*, is first removed from the clay, which is dug and turned over in the winter. Exposure to wet and frost prepares it for use by the spring, when fine ashes are added to it in the proportion of one-fifth ashes to four-fifths clay, or 60 chaldrons to 240 cubic yards, which will make 100,000 bricks. When much sand is mixed with the clay, forming what is called a mild earth, a smaller proportion of ashes may be used. This quantity requires also the addition of about 15 chaldrons, or, if mild, of about 12 chaldrons of *breeze*, which is a kind of coarse coal ash, separated by sifting, to aid the burning. The clay and ashes being well mixed by digging, watering, and raking backwards and forwards with a pronged hoe, the mass is removed in barrows to the *pug-mill*, which consists of an upright barrel in which a series of strong iron knives and teeth are caused to revolve by the power of a horse walking in a circular path, so as to cut and masticate the clay very thoroughly as it passes from the top of the barrel to an aperture provided for its exit at the bottom. As the clay oozes out of the mill, it is removed with a *cuckhold*, or concave shovel, and covered with sacks to prevent its drying too fast. A person called the feeder takes from the stock of clay thus prepared a piece about the size of a brick, covers it with sand, and passes it to the moulder, who throws it with some force into a wooden mould of the size and shape of the brick, which mould is previously sanded. Having filled the mould, the moulder cuts off any superfluous clay with a stick kept in a bowl of water by his side, and then removes the back and sides of the mould, after which the soft brick is carefully transferred from the bottom board of the mould to a pallet-board, and, when a sufficient number have been moulded, is conveyed with others to the *hacks*, which are long level lines raised about 4 inches from the surface of the field, and formed about 2 feet 6 inches wide. The upper surfaces of the bricks are previously sanded, and great care is taken to avoid twisting or otherwise injuring their shape in transferring them to the hacks, on which they are laid in two rows, with a little space between each to allow the free circulation of air. One double row being completed, another is put upon them, and this is continued until the bricks are piled from seven to ten high. In putting them down the workman counts them, and makes a dot with a stick in every thousandth brick. The hacks are covered with straw at night and showery weather; and in some brick-fields sheds are erected over them; but this plan is expensive, and retards the drying. When partially dried, the bricks are removed, placed diagonally, with wider apertures, and with the bottom bricks brought to the top; and after this process, which is called *skintling*, they are removed to the *kiln* or *clamp*, which is a vast pile of bricks, laid together as closely as possible, on a slightly concave foundation of brick rubbish, the raised ends of which face the north and south. On this foundation the new bricks are built up in lots or *necks*, of which the centre one, which is first erected, is vertical, while the others, owing to the concavity of the foundation, have a slight inclination towards it. Small spaces, filled with breeze, are left among the lowest courses of bricks, and flues, or *live-holes*, about the width of a brick, and from 6 to 9 feet apart, are also formed to aid the lighting of the clamp, and filled with dry bavins or wood. When full, the clamp is surrounded by old bricks, or by the driest of those newly made, and a thick layer of breeze is spread on the top. The external bricks are coated with a thin plastering of clay; and, if the weather prove wet, the kiln is protected by *loos*, or hurdles interwoven with rushes. The fire is lighted at the mouths of the flues or live-holes, which are closed when it burns well; and in favourable weather the bricks will be completely burnt in about twenty-five or thirty days, in the course of which time the cindery matter dispersed through their substance becomes gradually ignited and consumed. Such bricks as are found to be imperfectly burnt, are put into the next clamp to be burned again. Those which are sufficiently burnt are separated, according to quality, into—hard sound *stocks; place*, or inferior soft red bricks; and *burrs* or *clinkers*, which are black-looking masses of vitrified brick, of very inferior value.

Ordinary bricks are moulded in this country 10 inches long, 5 inches wide, and three inches thick, and are reduced by drying and burning to about 9 inches long, 4½ inches wide, and a proportionate thickness.

Kiln-burnt bricks, are, as their name implies, burnt in a kiln or oven instead of a clamp, and have no ashes mixed with the clay. Marl or malm stocks, which are either baked or burnt, take their name from the marl originally used in them, which has now given place to chalk. Dutch clinkers are a kind of small, hard, yellow bricks. Fire-bricks, also called Windsor bricks, are 1½ inch thick, and of a quality to resist the action of fire. Paving bricks, draining bricks, capping or coping bricks, coggin bricks, compass bricks for wells and circular works, feather-edged or thin bricks for the external parts of wooden buildings, and many other varieties of form, size, and quality, are also made. In some cases, a smooth or glazed surface is produced in the burning.

Much ingenuity has been directed, and of late years with great success, to the substitution of machinery for hand-labour in many of the processes of brick-making. The contrivances for this purpose are necessarily too complicated for description within our limits; but as a general remark it may be observed, that the increased solidity and closeness of texture obtained in bricks so made recommend them for use in the brick-work of railway arches and tunnels, which has been found in some cases subject to decay from the alternations of temperature and moisture. The comparative costliness of machine-made bricks has hitherto impeded their general use; but machinery is already very extensively employed in the manufacture of draining and other tiles and other superior articles of the brick character.

It is known that the ancients were in possession of a method of making bricks which, though having considerable strength, and a remarkable power of resisting heat, were yet of such small specific gravity that they floated on the surface of water. About the year 1790 M. Fabbroni, an Italian, suggested that these bricks were probably made of a kind of earth found in Sicily, called *mountain meal*, containing 55 per cent. of silica, 15 of magnesia, 12 of clay, 3 of lime, 1 of iron, and 14 of water. Bricks formed of this material were found to be very slow conductors of heat, and to be so light as to float in water. They are not quite so strong as common bricks, but can be made so by the addition of a little more pure clay. They unite well with lime, and resist the action of mortar. These various qualities render such a material very serviceable for the construction of various parts of ships liable to be exposed to great heat; such as stoves, cooking arrangements, steam-engine furnaces, &c.; where lightness and incombustibility are wanted. Such bricks also might be used for constructing floating-houses on ornamental waters.

The recent repeal of the brick duty has already begun to produce beneficial effects, by allowing scope for the exercise of inventive talent. The duty, which was 5*s.* 10*d.* per thousand on ordinary bricks, increased largely if the bricks were either larger in size or of superior quality; so that the maker was deterred from any departure from ordinary size and quality. The number of bricks charged with duty during the last few years, has varied from 1,200 to 1,900 millions. Since the repeal of the duty, measures have been taken to introduce brick ornaments in architecture. Messrs. Bowers of Tunstall have patented a method of making brick ornaments by which the substance assumes a much more vitrified appearance than ordinary brick. A hydraulic press is used to force the prepared clay into moulds; and the ornament is produced with a degree of sharpness equal to fine carving. It is intended to apply such bricks to the formation of cornices, mouldings, skirting-boards, finger-plates for doors, pilaster facings, ornamental archivolts, picture frames, upholsterers' fittings, &c. The surface is so hard and smooth, that it is capable of being painted, grained, or gilt.

Mr. Robert's *hollow* bricks, introduced in 1849, are valuable for many purposes where dry, warm, and light brickwork is required.

BRICKWORK. The art of the bricklayer is shown, not merely in laying and cementing his bricks, but in making them to mutually support each other. This object, which is termed *bonding*, is accomplished by breaking or distributing the joints; so that two may never come immediately over each other; and by laying some of the bricks as *stretchers*, or stretching courses, with their length in the direction of that of the wall, and others, which are called *headers*, with their length running across, or in the direction of the breadth or thickness of the wall. The bonds in most common use are *English bond*, consisting of alternate layers or courses of headers and stretchers; *Flemish bond*, in which headers and stretchers are laid alternately in the same course, the headers of one course being laid across the middle of the stretchers of the course below it; *garden-wall bond*, consisting of three stretchers and one header in the same course; and *herring-bone bond*, which is sometimes used in very thick walls, and is produced by laying the bricks at an angle of 45° with the direction of the wall, and reversing the inclination of each successive course. Whenever it is necessary, in order to prevent the *perpends*, or vertical joints, coming immediately over each other, a half, quarter, or three-quarter brick, or *bat*, is used to commence or finish a course. Walls, the thickness of which is nine inches, or equal to the length of one brick, are called single brick; those half that thickness, half-brick; and others brick and a half, two bricks, two bricks and a half, &c.

Arched and groined work requires peculiar care, and in many cases the cutting of the bricks to fit each to its particular bed; and in ordinary house-building great neatness is called for in the formation of the flat arches over doorways and windows.

Mortar, the cement usually employed for brickwork, is composed of either gray or white lime, and river, sea, or road sand mixed with water in the proportion of one part of gray lime to two and a half of sand, or one of white or chalk lime to two of sand. The dipping of the bricks in water as they are laid makes them adhere more firmly to the mortar. *Putty* is a very fine kind of mortar, made of lime and water only, used for delicate purposes, and such as the setting of rubbed or gauged arches, where the joints are visible.

The foundations of a wall are always laid broader than the superstructure, and the broader courses are termed *footings*, the projections themselves being called *set-offs*. Garden-walls are usually strengthened with piers or buttresses projecting 4½ inches, at intervals of 10 or 12 feet. When new walls are joined on to old, it is usual to take out a brick or part of a brick from every alternate corner of the old work, in order to *tooth in* the new work; and these toothings are left in the first building when it is intended to join new work to it. In many cases, also, strips of iron

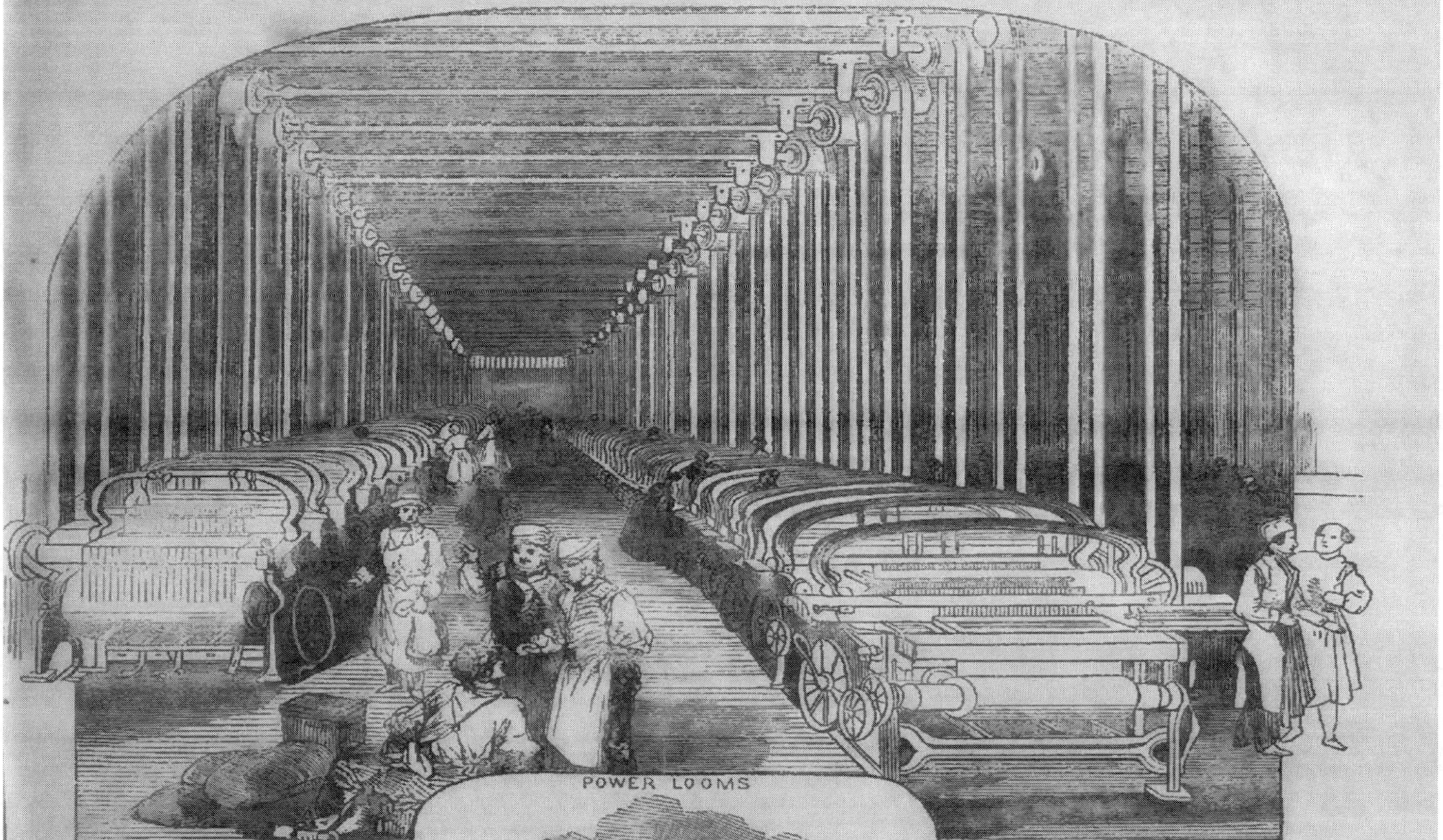

POWER LOOMS

MANCHESTER

MULE

ROVING

KNIGHTS CYCLOPÆDIA OF THE Industry of all Nations

No. 12.

hooping are laid in the horizontal joints, to afford a further bond or tie between the old and new brickwork. Brickwork is measured by the *rod* of 272 superficial feet.

Mr. Kennedy, in his 'Campaign of the Indus,' states that no brickwork he had ever seen in Europe equalled the perfection of that exhibited in the ancient tombs near Tatta. The most beautifully-chiselled stone could not surpass the sharpness of edge and angle, or the accuracy of form; whilst the substance was so perfectly homogeneous and skilfully burned, that each brick had a metallic ringing sound, and fractured with a clear surface like breaking freestone.

BRIDGE. Most countries can exhibit specimens of bridge-building. The Chinese lay claim to high antiquity in the construction of arched bridges. One at Fou-tcheou-fou is 400 yards long, about 12 yards wide, and had formerly ranges of shops upon it; and one at the æstuary of Suen-tcheou-fou is 2500 Chinese feet in length, 20 in width, and has 252 stone piers, on which is laid a roadway of huge stone blocks. Chinese bridges have pointed, semi-circular, polygonal, and semi-elliptical arches. The Romans executed many good specimens of bridge-building, some of which remain in use to the present time. Trajan's bridge over the Danube, the most stupendous work of the kind constructed by the Romans, had 20 stone piers, 60 Roman feet broad, and 150 feet, without the foundations, above the bed of the river. The Pont du Gard, near Nismes, is a remarkable example of their bridge-aqueducts. It consists at the base of a series of six arches, forming a bridge of 465 feet long; this is surmounted by a longer series of arches, extending 780 feet, to the slope of the mountains on each side; and above these is a third series, of 35 smaller arches, extending to the length of 850 feet, on the top of which is the aqueduct or channel for water. The entire height is 190 feet.

The bridges erected by the Romans in the provinces under their sway afforded models from which the art of constructing bridges extended throughout the north and west of Europe. No country possesses finer or more numerous examples than our own; in which, even before the extraordinary impulse given to this department of civil engineering by the introduction of the railway system, it has been carried to the utmost perfection. The oldest bridge now existing in England is the triangular bridge at Croyland, in Lincolnshire, which is said to have been erected about A.D., 860; it consists of three semi or half-arches, whose bases stand equidistant from each other, in the circumference of a circle, and unite at the top. Old London Bridge, which, with numerous alterations and patchings-up, remained in use until 1831, was begun in 1176, and was for several centuries covered with houses. The modern bridges across the Thames at the metropolis form noble specimens of bridge architecture and engineering; but those constructed in the last century, Westminster and Blackfriars bridges, have entailed heavy subsequent charges on account of the insufficiency of the foundations. New London Bridge is of granite, 928 feet long between the abutments, and consists of five semi-elliptical arches, of which the centre one has a span of 152 feet, while the next pair and the abutment arches are 140 and 130 feet respectively. It was commenced in 1824, and completed in 1831. Southwark Bridge is 718 feet between the abutments, and consists of three cast-iron arches each forming a segment of a very large circle; the span of the centre one being 250 feet, and of the others 210 feet each; they are supported by granite piers. Waterloo Bridge is a fine example of a flat or level bridge, with a horizontal roadway, supported by a series of arches of equal elevation. It is of granite, has nine elliptical arches of 120 feet span, and is approached by elevated roads, supported upon brick arches. The length between the abutments is 1380 feet, the river being wider at this point than it is lower down; but, including the arched approaches, the total length is 2456 feet. The cost was upwards of 1,000,000*l*. Some very fine specimens of equal-arched bridges have been erected by French engineers, of which the Pont de Neuilly, built by M. Perronnet, between 1768 and 1780, over the Seine, has five arches of 128 feet span.

The first iron bridge in England was erected in 1779 over the Severn at Coalbrook-dale; it consists of a single arch of about 100 feet span. Bishop-Wearmouth iron bridge, completed in 1796, is a single arch of 240 feet span; and Sunderland iron bridge, built about the the same time, is an arch of 236 feet span, and has a clear height from low water of 60 feet to the spring and 94 feet to the centre of the arch, so that ships of 300 tons pass under it by lowering their top-gallant masts. The very important class of iron bridges in which the suspension principle is adopted are treated of under SUSPENSION-BRIDGE. Swing-bridges, and other contrivances for removing the roadway when it is necessary to allow a passage for masted vessels, constitute another class of iron bridges on which much ingenuity has been expended. In many cases such a bridgo consists of two parts, which when closed meet in the centre, and which are either raised or turned aside out of the way when the waterway has to be opened. Another curious contrivance for a similar purpose is the *telescope bridge* introduced by Mr. Rastrick, on the Brighton and Chichester Railway; in which a massive platform, more than twice as long as the water way is broad, is so mounted on wheels as to be capable of having one half either projected across the river Arun, or drawn back out of the way; an adjoining portion of the railway being laid on another moveable platform which may be rolled to one side to make way for the larger platform when it is thus pushed back from the river.

Timber bridges, which are in many cases advantageous from their cheapness, are frequently preferred by modern engineers for their peculiar fitness in cases where an imperfect foundation, or some other circumstance, renders bridges of stone, brick, or iron unsuitable; while the introduction of various methods for preserving wood from decay obviates one of the principal objections to them. By the due application of trussing, timber bridges of extraordinary span may be constructed with safety. Some such are called *pendent* or *philosophical bridges*, and many examples of this kind of structure are found in America. The Upper and Lower Schuylkill bridges, near Philadelphia, and that across the Delaware at Trenton, are among the most remarkable. The Upper Schuylkill bridge, which is also called the Colossus, consists of one very flat arch of 340 feet span. The Lower Schuylkill bridge has three arches, one of 195 and the others 150 feet span, resting on stone piers. The Trenton bridge, erected in 1819, has five arches, one of 200, two of 180, and two of 160 feet span, resting upon light stone piers. *Lattice bridges*, so called from their structure resembling lattice-work, are much used in the United States, and have been introduced in English railway engineering.

The securing of a good foundation for the piers is the point of primary importance in bridge-building. Where the ground is soft, this must be done by *piling*, or driving whole trunks of timber, pointed and shod with iron, into the earth; it is in this kind of work that Nasmyth's steam pile-driver shows its great power; and still more, perhaps, Dr. Pott's mode of sinking hollow piles by pneumatic pressure. In order to exclude the water while laying the foundations and constructing the masonry of the piers, it is usual to form in the bed of the river a *coffer-dam*, or water-tight enclosure of piling, from the interior of which the water is pumped out. To save the enormous expense of this plan *caissons* were invented; they may be compared to great tubs or flat-bottomed boats, with very strong vertical sides. One of these being floated to the spot where a pier is to be founded, a few courses of masonry are built within it, and it is sunk into the required position. The vertical sides are subsequently removed, leaving the flat bottom beneath the masonry, as a kind of floor or foundation.

An ingenious modern contrivance is the *floating bridge* contrived by Mr. Rendel in lieu of an ordinary steam ferry-boat, for which the current was found to be too strong, as a means of communication between Torpoint and the Cornwall shore, at the mouth of Plymouth harbour, and which has since been applied also to the harbours of Dartmouth, Portsmouth, and Southampton. It consists of a large flat-bottomed vessel, the deck of which is adapted to receive horses and carriages as well as foot passengers, and which is propelled by means of wheels turned by a steam-engine mounted in the vessel. These wheels, however, instead of propelling the vessel by their action upon the water, do so by taking hold, by means of protuberances formed on their circumference, of chains which are extended from shore to shore, secured at each end, but allowed to hang under water in a festoon or curve of sufficient depth to allow ships to pass over them without danger. The chains, which are not absolutely fixed at the ends, but are attached to very heavy balance weights, are lifted up by the vessel as it proceeds, and serve not only as an abutment to secure the progress of the vessel, but also to keep it in its right course.

The *high-level bridge* at Newcastle is one of the finest examples of modern bridge building. It accommodates the York and Berwick Railway, and also the ordinary road traffic. It is a double bridge, with the railway road 22 feet above the horse road. The total length is about 1,400 feet. The extreme height is 112½ feet above high water mark. There are 6 arches, each of 125 feet span, besides several land arches. The piers are of masonry; but the arches, pillars, braces, girders, and balustrades are of iron. The carriage roadway is 20 feet wide, with two foot pavements of 6 feet each. The bridge piers are no less than 131 feet high from the foundation; they are 48 feet by 16½ in the square; they are built on piles, some of which penetrate to a depth of 50 feet in the ground. The road bridge is suspended from the arches of the upper or railway bridge; thus affording a very remarkable example of the combination of two distinct principles in bridge building.

The border bridge over the Tweed at Berwick is another fine example of railway work; constituting one of the finest stone bridges in existence. The still more extraordinary Britannia tubular bridge over the Menai will come for notice in a later article. [MENAI BRIDGES.] The *hollow girder* principle, so scientifically applied in the Britannia bridge, is now much used for small railway bridges over roads and streets.

Mr. Gladstone has recently suggested the employment of wrought iron bars as a material for bridges. The astonishing strength of the angle irons and other parts of the Britannia tubular bridge, is leading engineers to the consideration of further employment of similar materials. Mr. Gladstone proposes the use of malleable iron bars, of the double T shape, to form almost the only material of the bridge. These bars are to be either rivetted at their flanges, or fastened together by nuts and screws. All the bars are to be placed horizontally; and, at spots where additional strength is required, such as near the abutments or piers, they might be rivetted side by side, so as to form a solid mass; while near the centre of the water way or arch they might be so extended as to form an open iron-work of elegant character. The engineer who suggests this plan points out four advantages which he thinks would accompany its adoption—it would enable a span of almost any length to be made; it would render a nearly flat roadway practicable; it would give a higher water-way than an arch springing from piers in the usual manner; and it would render the use of expensive centering unnecessary.

The fall of an iron railway bridge over the Dee, at Chester, belonging to the Chester and Holyhead Railway Company, in 1847, has led to many enquiries on the nature of such bridges. Mr. Locke, who has constructed so many bridges of stone, brick, and timber, stated in the evidence which he gave in relation to that catastrophe, that he thinks cast-iron to be wholly unfitted for the construction of bridges for railways, unless under special circumstances.

In 1839 a bridge had to be constructed at Grisoles, over the branch canal of Garonne, in France; and as building stone is scarce in that district, M. Lebrun determined to construct it of *béton* or *concrete*. This he accomplished, and the bridge was finished in 1841. Both the French *béton* and the English *concrete* are formed of lime, sand, and pebbles; but there are slight differences in the mode of preparation. The *béton* was laid on course after course; and only as much was made each day as could be laid on in that day. The entire mass of the abutments, and the greater part of the arch, was made of béton: bricks being used only in a few places, to increase the strength.

Mr. Remington's *ærial bridge*, familiar to the visitors at the Surrey Zoological Gardens, has obtained its name from its extreme lightness. It is entirely formed of thin pieces of wood: so thin and light as to excite general surprise that it should be able to bear the weight of many persons at one time. In 1848 Earl Talbot caused a bridge to be built on this system by Mr. Remington, over the river Trent, as part of an accommodation road on the earl's estate near Ingestre. The bridge is 150 feet span; and yet, remarkable to observe, the beams or stringers, six in number, which extend from end to end, are only five inches square at each end, and diminish to 2¼ inches square at the centre of the bridge; they are formed of pieces of timber, 20 to 25 feet long, scarped together at the ends. They rest, at either shore, on a light abutment formed of posts of oak, 6 inches square, framed together with iron clasps. The stringers hang into a slight curve, depressed about two feet in the centre; and the extreme lightness at the centre prevents the structure from being borne down by its own weight. The planks which form the bridge are placed crosswise upon the stringers. The bridge, although strong enough to bear a carriage and horses, cost only 200*l.*; and the timber of which it is formed was growing on the earl's estate six weeks before the completion of the bridge. A similar bridge has been since thrown over the lake in Birkenhead Park, and others have been built in Birmingham and elsewhere.

BRIDGEWATER. Much of the foreign and coasting trade of Somersetshire centres at Bridgewater, which lies nearly at the mouth of the river Parret. The principal imports are grain, coals, tallow, and timber. Coals are imported from Wales, and conveyed into the interior of the country by means of the river Parret and a canal. The foreign trade is principally with Russia, the United States, Canada, Newfoundland, and the West Indies. More than 4,000 vessels, large and small, enter and clear at Bridgewater in the course of a year.

A manufacture peculiar to, and constituting the staple trade of Bridgewater, is the fabrication of that kind of white brick known as *Bath Brick*, so largely used in knife-cleaning; this branch of industry gives employment to many of the inhabitants. These bricks are formed of the sediment or sand of the river Parret, cast into moulds and dried. These

Bath (or more justly Bridgewater) bricks will have the honour of a place in the grand display of 1851; for it is quite fitting that the staple manufacture of a town, however apparently humble, should be there represented. Various manufactures in clay and brick will also be exhibited from Bridgewater.

BRIDGEWATER, FRANCIS EGERTON, DUKE OF, is indissolubly associated with the history of canal engineering in this country. One of the estates which he inherited, situated at Worsley, near Manchester, contained a rich bed of coal; but was comparatively of little value, in consequence of the heavy expense of land carriage and the inadequate means of communication afforded by the Irwell; and this led him to conceive the plan of a navigable canal, for which, in 1758-9, he obtained an act of parliament. From this circumstance he is frequently styled 'the Father of British Inland Navigation.' He chose BRINDLEY for his engineer, and on his plans, and under his superintendence, the work was completed in spite of many difficulties. The length of the main line is above 27 miles, all on the same level, which has rendered great embankments necessary, as the canal crosses several depressions. One of these embankments is 900 yards long, 17 feet high, and 112 feet wide at the base. With the exception of that part between Worsley and Leigh, every part of the canal was executed, under the direction of Brindley, in about five years.

The Duke of Bridgewater died March 8, 1803, without children, and his great wealth was distributed among the collateral branches of his family. The canal property, with the Lancashire, Cheshire, and Brackley estates, he left to his nephew, the late Duke of Sutherland. They are now in the possession of the Earl of Ellesmere.

BRIDPORT is one of the few commercial towns in Dorsetshire; having a safe and busy harbour. It once had a considerable coasting trade in coal and grain; but this trade has been almost entirely lost in consequence of the superior facilities for transmission of goods afforded by railways. Hemp, flax, tallow, timber, and wheat are imported from Russia and the Baltic; and timber from Norway and America. Wines, spirits, skins, coals, culm, and slates are also imported. The exports consist chiefly of the manufactures of the town, and of cheese and butter for which the neighbourhood is celebrated. The manufactures of Bridport are principally of twine, shoe-thread, cordage, sailcloth, and fishing nets. The antiquity of the hemp trade in Bridport has long since dignified a halter with the name of a 'Bridport dagger.'

The townsmen of Bridport very properly intend to illustrate the industry, which has given them their manufacturing title, at the forthcoming exhibition. Specimens of hemp and flax twine, netting, yarn, canvas, girth, webbing, bags, and sacking—for all of which Bridport has been noted ever since the time of Henry VIII—are to be exhibited.

BRIMSTONE. [SULPHUR.]

BRINDLEY, JAMES, shared with the Duke of Bridgewater in the honour of introducing canal navigation into this country. He was born in 1716, and was apprenticed in his 17th year to a millwright near Macclesfield. When the period of his apprenticeship had expired, Brindley engaged in business on his own account; but he did not confine himself to the making of mill machinery. His reputation as a man of skill and ingenuity steadily increased; in 1755 he executed the machinery for a silk-mill at Congleton; and in 1756 he erected a steam-engine at Newcastle-under-Lyne.

Shortly after this time, Brindley was consulted by the Duke of Bridgewater on the practicability of constructing a canal from Worsley to Manchester. His success in this undertaking was the means of fully awakening public attention to the advantages of canals. Within forty-two years after the Duke's canal was opened, application had been made to Parliament for 165 acts for cutting canals in Great Britain, at an expense of above thirteen millions. In 1766 the Trent and Mersey Canal was commenced under Brindley's superintendence. It is 93 miles long, and unites the navigation of the Mersey with that of the Trent and the Humber. It was called by Brindley the 'Grand Trunk Navigation,' owing to the probability, from its great commercial importance, of many other canals being made to join it. Brindley next designed a canal 46 miles in length, called the Staffordshire and Worcestershire Canal, for the purpose of connecting the Grand Trunk with the Severn. He also planned the Coventry Canal, but did not superintend its execution. He, however, superintended the execution of the Oxford Canal. The canal from the Trent at Stockwith to Chesterfield, 46 miles long, was Brindley's last public undertaking. He also surveyed and gave his opinion on many other lines for navigable canals besides those mentioned. Brindley died in 1772, aged 56.

BRISTOL. This famous old city has been an emporium of commerce for a longer period than almost any other sea-port in the kingdom. It long preceded its great rival Liverpool, which has now so signally overtaken it. The commercial buildings of Bristol are mostly connected more or less closely with the docks. These docks were formed by excavating a new course for the Avon south of the city, and converting the whole of the old channel, through the city, into one floating harbour, about 3 miles in length. By subsequent changes and enlargements, the harbour and docks have gradually been made capable of accommodating a large amount of shipping. The dock rates on vessels and goods, until 1848, far exceeded the corresponding rates at the ports of London, Liverpool, Hull, and Gloucester; but a gradual decline in the commerce of Bristol has led the inhabitants generally to see the necessity of modifying the port charges, in order to invite shipping to bring their cargoes thither.

By a special Act obtained in 1848 the docks are transferred from a private company to the corporation; and new dock charges have been established, much more calculated to attract shipping to the port. On November 13, 1848, a grand procession paraded through Bristol to commemorate this important alteration. It has been found that arrivals and departures of shipping have considerably increased since the new system was adopted. There were in 1849 about 300 vessels registered at the port, some of very large tonnage. The tonnage of merchandize brought into Bristol is always much greater than that shipped from thence; on account of Bristol being one of the chief places of import of West India produce.

The foreign trade of Bristol principally consists in imports of sugar, rum, wine, brandy, colonial and Baltic timber, tallow, hemp, turpentine, barilla, dye-woods, fruits, wheat, and tea. The principal articles of export are iron, tin, bricks, refined sugar, glass bottles, Irish linen, and manufactured goods. Bristol derives a considerable portion of her supply of foreign produce coastwise under bond principally from London and Liverpool, but also from the minor ports of Gloucester, Newport, Bridgewater, Exeter, Barnstable, and Bideford. The coasting trade is very considerable, particularly with Ireland. The imports principally consist of iron, tin, coal, salt, Irish linens, and agricultural produce; the exports of articles of foreign and colonial produce, particularly groceries, tea, wines, and spirits, and of the manufactures of the place. The quantity of live stock imported into Bristol from Ireland in three successive years was as follows:—

	Pigs.	Sheep.	Cattle.	Horses.
1845	32,926	1,603	1,015	38
1846	46,811	3,590	4,925	19
1847	33,673	46,465	13,602	381

The existing manufactures of Bristol are glass bottles, crown and flint glass, brass wire, pins, sheet lead, zinc, spelter, chain cables, anchors, machinery, drugs, colours, dyes, painted floor cloth, earthenware, refined sugar, starch, soap, British spirits, tin, copper and brass wares, bricks, beer, porter, pipes, tobacco, and hats. Most of these manufactures are either carried on within the city or in its immediate neighbourhood; but the manufacturing circuit may be considered to extend 6 miles around. The principal factories are those for glass, sugar, iron, brass, floor-cloth, and earthenware. In addition to these there has been established a very large joint-stock cotton factory in the parish of St. Philip, under the title of the Great Western Cotton Works. The building was commenced in 1837. It consists of an immense range of spinning, weaving, bleaching, and repairing shops, with all the appliances for employing 2000 hands. In May, 1850, this building suffered extensively by an accidental fire.

As a specimen of engineering work we must not omit mention of the suspension bridge over the Avon. The original act for the construction of the bridge was obtained so far back as 1831; but as it appeared likely to be a failure from the exhaustion of the funds, four subsequent acts have been obtained for permitting the postponement of the works. The last of these postponing acts was passed in 1848, by which the powers of the Bridge Company are extended to 1853. A sum of 45,000*l.* has been collected, partly by the accumulation at compound interest of a sum of money left for this purpose in 1754, and partly by private subscription; and this sum has been expended in erecting the abutments and piers on both sides of the river, the excavation of the rock for the roads of approach, and the purchase of a portion of the iron-work. The estimate for the future cost is 30,000*l.*, towards which there is nothing forthcoming; but it is said that there are negociations now on foot which will render the finishing of this remarkable bridge a probability. [SUSPENSION BRIDGE.]

Among the contributions from Bristol to the Industrial Exhibition will be one of a peculiarly interesting character; viz., a few specimens of native African manufacture, consigned by the black king of Dahomey to the care of Messrs. King, African merchants at Bristol. Nothing can better show how widely spread is the fame of this Exhibition.

BRISTLES. The bristles so largely used in brush making are brought almost entirely from Russia. The importation in 1849 exceeded 2,000,000 lbs.

BRITANNIA BRIDGE. The two splendid

works over the Menai, by Telford and Stephenson, will be best described in conjunction. [MENAI BRIDGES.]

BRITISH AMERICA. The commercial and industrial features of this vast country are noticed under the names of the territories which compose it [CANADA; NOVA SCOTIA; &c.] We may here briefly state that the British produce and manufactures, exported to the whole of those colonies in 1849, amounted in value to 2,279,193*l*.

BRITISH ASSOCIATION. Those who appreciate the intimate connexion between theory and practice, will be ready to expect that an Association 'for the advancement of science,' ought to advance industrial art likewise. This has been most undeniably the case in respect to the distinguished body here under notice. From the first meeting in 1831 to the twentieth meeting in 1850, every year has contributed something to the improvement of manufacturing industry through its medium. Mr. Eaton Hodgkinson's researches on the strength of iron and other materials; Mr. Scott Russell's very remarkable investigations on waves, and on the best form of ships to accommodate themselves to the waves; the long and patient observations of Dr. Whewell and Mr. Burt on tides; Baron Liebig's labours in the fruitful field of organic chemistry—such are a few among the numerous services, fostered by the Association, which have been found to be directly beneficial to some among the many departments of art. And the British Association has shown, too, that Art can aid Science, as Science can aid Art; for many beautiful pieces of mechanism have been brought forward under the auspices of the Association, which have rendered important services to scientific investigations.

BRITISH MUSEUM. This valuable establishment so instructively illustrates Art—fine art in respect to its best specimens, and industrial art in respect to its minerals, &c., that we must not pass it over without a few words of notice. The establishment of a national Museum was suggested by the will of Sir Hans Sloane, who, during a long period of eminent practice in physic, had accumulated, in addition to a numerous library of books and MSS., a large collection of objects of natural history and works of art; these he directed should be offered after his death, which took place in 1753, to the British Parliament for the sum of 20,000*l*., the collection having cost him 50,000*l*. From that period to the present, valuable donations of books, manuscripts, sculptures, bronzes, coins, prints, minerals, &c., have been made; and Parliament has appropriated large annual sums to the same object. Hence has gradually accumulated the present most valuable collection.

The buildings forming the New British Museum are arranged in a hollow square, facing the cardinal points of the compass. The southern or Russell-street front is the principal one, and presents to view a columnar façade of the Ionic order. At the extreme west end is a detached building, and another one at the east end; these are dwelling-houses and offices for the librarians and chief officers of the establishment.

There are two stories of galleries and rooms round the greater part of the building, to some of which the general public are not admitted. All the ground-floor between the portico-entrance and the south-east angle is occupied as a depository for manuscripts, and as apartments for receiving, sorting, and reading manuscripts. The ground-floor of the greater part of the east side is occupied by the King's Library, a magnificent apartment, 300 feet long. The entire ground-floor of the north side is closed from general visitors, being devoted to literature and study; there are two large reading-rooms, together about 120 feet in length, and a library for books, extending 200 feet. At the north-west angle of the building, and in one or two other parts, are collections which are not thrown open to the public generally; such as the prints, the botanical collection, the coins, and the gems.

The door in the centre of the portico gives entrance to the new hall or vestibule. This is a fine large apartment, worthy of the building to which it gives access. On the right are the two statues of Sir Joseph Banks and Shakspere, on each side of the door leading to the manuscript department; and on the left is the statue of the Hon. Mrs. Damer, the lady sculptor, who left the attractions and fascinations of gay life for the mallet and chisel. In front is a glazed door opening to the central quadrangle, the buildings on three sides of which can be well seen from this point; and at present, until other arrangements are completed, the extraordinary Lion and Bull brought by Mr. Layard from Nineveh are placed near this door. The hall is lofty, and the ceiling is richly painted in encaustic colours, formed into square compartments of divers tints. On the left, close to the front wall of the building, is a passage leading to the various sculpture galleries; and northward of this is the grand staircase, a noble feature of the building. The ascent of nearly seventy stone stairs, half of them westward and then the other half eastward, the elegant balustrade, and the encaustic work of the ceiling, come with freshness and welcome upon the eyes of those who for many years have been accustomed to the dingy entrances to the Museum.

Arrived at the top of the stairs, a range of rooms extends eastward along the building. By the side of the upper part of the staircase, over the passage leading to the sculptures, is an antiquarian or ethnographical room, in which the dresses and ornaments, the industry and implements, of all nations, are illustrated in a highly interesting manner. The room at the head of the stairs, and immediately over the entrance-hall, is devoted to zoology. Beyond this room, towards the east, are two others, devoted like it to zoological specimens. The Mammalia Saloon forms the upper story of the south-east angle of the Museum; and from thence proceed a magnificent suite of rooms, called the Eastern Zoological Gallery, extending along the whole eastern side of the building from south to north, and filled with specimens illustrating the natural history of animals. Arrived at the north-east angle of the building, we find a double range of galleries almost as beautiful as the former: they are side by side, and occupy the upper floor of the whole northern side of the Museum, from end to end. One of these ranges is the Northern Zoological Gallery, and the other the Mineralogical Gallery.

At the north-west angle is a staircase leading down to the lower story; but turning to the left, a range of rooms leading along the west side of the building is devoted to the reception of Egyptian and Etruscan antiquities. There are portions of this west side lately opened to visitors, but not yet filled with specimens: they lead to the western entrance of the Ethnographical Room; so that the entire circuit of the building may now be made. The staircase conducts the visitor down to an ante-room at the northern extremity of the great Egyptian gallery; from which ante-room proceeds an entrance to another smaller Egyptian room, and also doors leading to the library not open to the public. Traversing the Egyptian Gallery southward, we come to a kind of large central saloon; westward, and projecting from this range, is the Phigaleian sculpture-room; and beyond this the Elgin Saloon, where the valuable sculptures from the Parthenon are placed.

All the rooms from the Egyptian Saloon back to the entrance are of recent construction, and many of them are not yet occupied: they will contain the Townley, the Xanthian, the Nineveh, and other collections of sculptures.

Such is a sketch of the important building which is silently and healthfully educating thousands of persons; for every visit is an educational lesson, in some form or other. Of the 1,062,218 visits made to the British Museum in 1849; of the 19,000 visits made on the 'boxing-day' of 1850; it may safely be said that they were visits in a proper direction, having a germ of good in them.

BRIXHAM. The prosperity of this seaport of Devonshire is chiefly dependent on its fishery, which is said to be the largest in England. More than 200 sail of vessels, comprising 20,000 tons of shipping, and employing 1,500 seamen, belong to this town, most of which are engaged in the fishing trade. The average amount received for fish is said to be 600*l*. per week. The best of the fish are sent to Exeter, Bath, Bristol, and London. The cost for carriage alone has been calculated to average 1000*l*. per annum. Turbot, soles, whiting, plaice, mullet, mackerel, and other kinds of fish are taken in considerable numbers. During the London season about 50 of the decked trawl boats are usually absent from Brixham, being employed in supplying the London market with soles, turbots, &c., from Hull and Ramsgate, fishing over all the intermediate space between those places. Several of the vessels belonging to Brixham are employed in the Mediterranean, Spanish, and coasting trade.

BROKER. In relation to ordinary commercial dealings, a broker is a person employed in the negotiation of mercantile transactions between other parties, and generally engaged in the interest of one of the principals, either the buyer or the seller, but sometimes acting as the agent of both. As it usually happens that brokers apply themselves to negotiations for the purchase and sale of some particular article or articles, they acquire an intimate knowledge of the qualities and market value of the goods in which they deal, and obtain an acquaintance with the sellers and buyers as well as with the state of supply and demand, and are thus enabled to bring the dealers together, and to negotiate between them on equitable terms. There are separate brokers in London for nearly all the great articles of consumption; and there are also ship-brokers, exchange-brokers, stock-brokers, share-brokers, &c., to conduct the transactions indicated by their names. Custom-house brokers, or agents, are licensed by the Commissioner of Customs; and no person without such licence can transact business at the Custom-house or in the port of London relative to the entrance or clearance of ships, &c.

BROMINE, an elementary fluid body, was discovered in 1826 by M. Balard, and named from *βρῶμος* (stink), on account of its strong and disagreeable odour. It is found in sea water, in salt springs, in mineral waters, in many marine plants, and in some marine animals. Balard first procured it from a salt spring; but it is now obtained from various sources.

Bromine is liquid at the usual temperature of the air. Its specific gravity is 2.996. It is poisonous. In considerable bulk its colour is a deep brownish red; in small quantities it is of a hyacinthine red. Its odour is extremely strong, greatly resembling that of chlorine; its taste is disagreeable. When exposed to a temperature between zero and 4° of Fahrenheit, it becomes solid, crystalline, brittle, and hard enough to be powdered. It boils at about 116° Fahrenheit, and its volatility is great. It suffers no change by the agency of light, heat, or electricity, and, having never been decomposed, it is regarded as an elementary or simple substance. It is very corrosive.

The various combinations of bromine with other substances have been hitherto but little used in the arts.

BROMSGROVE. In this Worcestershire town the linen manufacture was formerly carried on to a considerable extent, but has been entirely abandoned. Nail-making is now the principal trade, but there is also an extensive manufactory for patent buttons.

In the parish of Stoke Prior, and closely adjoining that of Bromsgrove, are situated the extensive salt and alkali works of the British Alkali Company. The manufacture of salt has been carried on for centuries in the adjoining borough of Droitwich, where it is prepared from rich springs of native brine. The only situations where rock-salt had been met with in this island were in Cheshire, previously to its being discovered at Stoke Prior, where it was obtained in 1829, in the course of sinking a pit in search of brine. The beds of salt were of great thickness, and were excavated to a considerable extent; but at present the supplies for making refined salt are derived from a natural brine spring, which has communicated with the excavations. Immediately after making this discovery, the proprietors erected extensive works for the manufacture of salt, and for the preparation of British alkali, by the decomposition of this substance, which very speedily changed the green fields and retired lanes into an active manufactory and a lively village. The works have become very extensive and the centre of a considerable population.

BROMWICH, WEST, or West Bromwich, in Staffordshire, affords a remarkable instance of the growth of population and wealth through mining and manufacturing industry. A few years ago it was little else than a barren heath lying on either side of the road from Birmingham to Wolverhampton; but it has gradually grown up to a town nearly three miles in length, which takes the name of the parish in which it is situated. The existence of iron and coal beneath the surface of the whole parish is the cause of the growth of the town. The manufacture of iron goods is carried on to an immense extent at Bromwich: guns, gun-locks, swords, bayonets, saddlers' ironmongery, fire-irons, coach ironmongery, chains, bolts, nails, and agricultural implements, are among the kinds of iron goods made here.

BRONZE is essentially a compound of copper and tin, which metals appear to have been among the earliest known. Copper is not unfrequently found in its metallic state, and fit for immediate use; and tin, though not so met with, often occurs near the surface, and its ore is easily reduced. These metals, though neither of them possesses the hardness requisite for making instruments either for domestic or warlike purposes, appear to have been early found capable of hardening each other by combination; the bronze, which is the result of this combination, consisting of different proportions of them, according to the purposes to which it is to be applied.

Bronze is always harder and more fusible than copper; it is highly malleable when it contains 85 to 90 per cent. of copper; tempering increases its malleability; it oxidises very slowly even in moist air, and hence its application to so many purposes. The density of bronze is always greater than that of the mean of the metals which compose it: for example, an alloy of 100 parts of copper and 12 parts of tin is of specific gravity 8.80, whereas by calculation it would be only 8.63.

The green hue that distinguishes ancient bronzes is acquired by oxidation and the combination with carbonic acid; and the moderns, to imitate the effect of the finer antique works, sometimes advance that process by artificial means, usually by washing the surface with an acid. Vasari alludes to this practice among the artists of his time, and to the means they adopted to produce a brown, a black, or a green colour in their bronze.

Bronze was well known to the ancients. Among the remains of bronze works of art found in Egypt none are of large dimensions. Many specimens of bronze works found in India are doubtless very ancient. In the time of Homer, arms, offensive and defensive, are always described as being made of bronze, or perhaps copper alone, which it is possible they had some means of tempering and hardening. The art of casting statues seems to have been first practised in Asia Minor, Greece, properly so called, being then probably too uncivilised to undertake such works. The first and most simple process, among the Greeks, appears to havo been *hammer-work;* in which lumps of the material were beaten into the proposed form; and, when the work was too large to be made of one piece, several were shaped, and tho different parts fitted and fastened together by means of pins or keys.

The art of metal-casting in regular moulds was undoubtedly known very early, though its adoption in European Greece is probably of a comparatively late date. Its progress was evidently marked by three distinct stages. The first was beating out the metal, either as solid hammer-work or in plates. The next was casting it into a mould or form, the statue being of course made solid. The last stage was casting it into a mould, with a centre or core to limit the thickness of the metal. Bronze-casting seems to have reached its perfection in Greece about the time of Alexander the Great. The ancient statuaries seem to have been extremely choice in their selection and composition of bronze; and they seem also to have had a method of running or welding various metals together, by which they were enabled to produce more or less the effect of natural colour. Some works are described that were remarkable for the success which attended this curious and, to us, unattainable process. They also tinted or painted their bronze with the same view of more closely imitating nature. Pliny states that there were three sorts of the Corinthian bronze; the first, called candidum, received its name from the effect of silver which was mixed with the copper; the second had a greater proportion of gold; the third was composed of equal quantities of the different metals.

The Romans never attained any great eminence in the arts of design. Their earliest statues were executed for them by Etruscan artists. Rome, however, was afterwards filled with a prodigious number of works of the best schools of Greece; and artists of that country, unable to meet with employment at home, settled at Rome. Zenodorus executed some magnificent works in the time of Nero. But Pliny, who lived in the reign of Vespasian, laments the decline of the art, and the want of skill of the artists, in his time. The practice of gilding bronze statues does not seem to have prevailed till taste had much deteriorated. The practice of art among the Romans declining rapidly, and with but few interruptions, ceases to interest us about A.D. 200. In the beginning of the thirteenth century, at the taking of Constantinople, we read that some of the finest works of the ancient masters were destroyed for the mero value of the metal. Among the few works saved are tho celebrated bronze horses, which now decorate the exterior of the church of St. Mark at Venice.

Passing over the intermediate age of barbarism, we arrive at the epoch of the revival of art in Italy, under the Pisani and others, about the fourteenth and fifteenth centuries. The celebrated bronze gates of the Baptistery at Florence, by Ghiberti, which M. Angelo said were fit to be the gates of Paradise, are among the more remarkable works of the time. In the succeeding century wo find Guglielmo della Porta practising the art with great success; and he is distinguished by Vasari for adopting a mode of casting that was considered quite original, in executing his colossal statue of Paul III. The metal when run from the furnace, was carried downwards by a duct, and then admitted to the under side or bottom of the mould, and thus, acted upon by a superior pressure, as in a common fountain, was forced upwards till the mould was entirely filled. It is necessary in this process that the mould should be kept in a state of great heat, in order that the metal may not cool before the whole is run. But among the artists who are celebrated for their skill in bronze-casting, Benvenuto Cellini holds a distinguished rank: there are few collections that cannot boast somo specimens of his smaller productions, while the larger works that remain, particularly at Florence, prove that his high reputation was not undeserved. In his process the metal was allowed to flow at once from the furnace into the channels or ducts of the moulds.

The modern practice of the English, French, Italian, and German artists does not differ materially in its principle, from that of the earlier Italians. The process is described under FOUNDING.

Bronze for cannon in England is composed of 90 copper and 10 tin. Bronze for cymbals and tamtans is composed of 78 copper and 22 tin; in France, of 100 copper and 11 tin. English bell-metal consists of copper 80, tin 10.1, zinc 5.6, lead 4.3, = 100. Reflectors for telescopes consist of 66 parts of copper and 33 parts of tin; they resemble steel in colour, are very hard and brittle, and susceptible of a fine polish. Bronze for medals is formed of 100 copper, and 7 to 11 of tin and zinc.

At the Mediæval Exhibition of 1850, there were many bronzes of great beauty displayed. Vases, chains, keys, fibulæ, lamps, busts, statuettes, censers, fountains, inkstands, ewers, —these were among the specimens exhibited.

The articles of bronze imported are classed by the customs' authorities under three groups —1st. works of art, 2nd. other articles in bronze, and 3rd. bronze powder: the first group is stated at from 200 to 300 cwts. annually; the second and third groups have a value of about 2000*l.* annually.

BRONZING; BRONZE POWDER. Much ingenuity is displayed in imitating the colour of ancient bronzes—both the greenish and the rich golden tints. Metals, wood, and plaster, are all subject to surface-processes having this object in view.

Captain Pidding states that the Chinese exercise the art of bronzing in a very superior manner. After having rubbed the vase or other ornament with coal-ashes and vinegar, they dry it in the sun, and then coat it with a composition of which the following are the ingredients—two parts of verdigris, two of cinnabar, two of sal ammoniac, two of the beak and liver of duck, and five of pounded alum, —moistened to the consistency of a paste. When the article is thus prepared, it is passed through the fire, and washed when cold; again it is coated with the composition, again fired, and again washed; and so on for several times in succession.

Becquerel introduced to the notice of the Académie des Sciences, a few years ago, a method of bronzing, in which a thin layer of bronze is applied to the surface of any article of iron, steel, lead, zinc, tin, or other metal. It is effected by precipitation from a solution, through the agency of a galvanic battery in the usual manner of electro-metallurgy; but the difficulty surmounted consists in the discovery of a proper solution. The solution described by Becquerel consists of carbonate of potash, chloride of copper, sulphate of zinc, and nitrate of ammonia; with a plate of brass or bronze as a positive decomposing plate.

A process of bronzing on paper is now frequently adopted for ornamental purposes. Thin plates of copper, or of copper alloyed with some other metal, are beaten out into thin leaves, and these leaves are ground or worked to powder. A pattern is printed on the surface of paper with an adhesive and rapidly-drying varnish; and just before this varnish is dry, the bronze powder is rubbed on with a piece of soft cotton, whereby a metallic lustre is produced, varying in its tint from a bright gold to a deep red colour, according to the metallic constituents of the bronze powder. Sheets of paper, thus bronzed after having been glazed and printed, in various colours, now form the highly adorned coverings for albums and many other kinds of books.

BRU'CIA, a vegetable alkali, found in the bark of the *strychnos nux vomica*, and in some other kinds of bark. It is a non-crystallised substance, resembling wax in appearance; but it crystallises under certain circumstances in colourless oblique four-sided prisms. It combines with the principal acids to form *Nitrate*, *Muriate*, *Sulphate*, *Oxalate*, *Phosphate*, and *Acetate of Brucia:* most of which are crystallised, and have a bitter taste.

Brucia acts on the human system as a violent poison, and in precisely the same manner as strychnia, but more gently, being much less powerful.

BRUGES (*Brugge*), capital of the Belgian province of West Flanders, has considerable manufactures of linens, lace, woollen and cotton goods, salt, refined sugar, earthenware, paper, distilled liquors, and other minor branches of industry.

Many of the Bruges manufactures will be illustrated at the Exhibition of 1851.

BRUNEL, MARK ISAMBERT. So long as engineering genius and mechanical invention are honoured, so long will the name of Brunel occupy a niche among the worthies of industry.

The late Sir M. I. Brunel was born at Hacqueville in Normandy, in 1768. He studied first for the church, and then for the navy; but the natural bent of his mind marked out another career for him. He was obliged to flee to the United States during the French Revolution, and here he commenced his engineering career; but feeling that England was a better sphere for him, he crossed the Atlantic about the year 1800, and devoted the rest of his life to mechanism and engineering in the country of his adoption. His first great work was the Block Machinery at Portsmouth, which occupied him till 1806. [BLOCK MACHINERY.] He next constructed the Royal Saw Mills at Chatham and Woolwich. Soon after this he invented a beautiful little machine for winding cotton thread into balls. In 1813 he contrived an extensive series of machines for making shoes for the army; but these machines have not been used since the war. He was engaged in building one of the early steamboats, and introduced many improvements in marine engines. After numerous minor works he projected the Thames Tunnel: having previously proposed to the Emperor Alexander the construction of a tunnel under the Neva at St. Petersburg, to obviate the evils occasioned by the freezing of the river in winter. The Thames Tunnel was commenced in 1824, but was not finished (so far even as it may yet be deemed finished) until 1843, under an amount of difficulty which would have crushed any but an indomitable mind. [THAMES TUNNEL.]

During the later years of his life, Sir Mark (who received the honour of knighthood during the Melbourne administration) did not engage in any great enterprizes, but lived quietly and respected to a good old age. He died in Dec. 1849; leaving a worthy successor in his son, the present Mr. I. K. Brunel, engineer of the Great Western Railway and of other extensive works.

BRUNN, the capital of the Austrian province of Moravia and Silesia, is the principal seat of the woollen manufactures of Austria. Its fine woollen cloths and kerseymeres are in great repute. It also manufactures largely silks, ribbons, yarns, machinery, leather, cotton prints, soap, and vinegar. It has four wholesale markets in the year, which are each of fourteen days' duration, and to which manufacturers from all parts of Austria resort in considerable numbers.

BRUNSWICK. The duchy of Brunswick is rich in mines, which are of two classes; one class comprising such as are worked in conjunction with the Hanoverian government, and the other independently of it. The annual produce of the first class, which includes the mines on the Rammelsberge, in the Upper Harz, has ever since the year 1788 been divided into seven shares, of which Hanover takes four and Brunswick three. These mines are under the direction of a joint board at Goslar, and consist of one of gold, three of silver, copper, and lead, and three copper and sulphur works. The independent mines lie on the Lower Harz, in the principality of Blankenburg, near Seesen, and the district of the Weser; their principal produce is iron.

Brunswick produces marble, alabaster, limestone, gypsum, potter's clay, asbestos, serpentine-stone, agate, jasper, chalcedony, garnets, porphyry, sandstone, freestone, coal, and alum. There are salt-works at Salzdahlum, Schöningen, Salzliebenhall, and Juliushall.

The chief manufactures of the Duchy are metals, yarn and linen, stockings, cloth made of a mixture of woollen and linen, oil, paper, gypsum, earthenware, tobacco pipes, glass, soap, and beer. The export and import trade is small, on account of the want of sea-coasts.

BRUSA or BRUSSA, a city in Asia Minor, about 60 miles from Constantinople, is one of the most flourishing towns in the Turkish empire. Its satins and tapestry are of the best quality. Gauzes, taffetas, and cottons, are also manufactured. The trade with the interior is carried on by the caravans which pass through the town between Constantinople and Smyrna. Brusa is the centre of a district in which a great quantity of raw silk is produced, to the amount of about half a million lbs. annually; and the cultivation of the mulberry is yearly on the increase. Grapes, melons, and fruits of all kinds, are abundant. Meerschaum clay is dug in the neighbouring mountain. British long-cloths, dyed sarcenets, cotton shirtings, cambrics, *chalès* or thin figured woollen dresses, cotton twist, Paisley shawls, and printed calicoes, find a ready market at Brusa.

BRUSH-MAKING. Brushes and brooms may be classified into simple brushes, or such as consist of a single tuft of hairs, be it large or small; and compound brushes, or such as have many tufts. The former may be subdivided into such as are inserted in a handle, or in a tube which serves to connect them with a handle, as the several varieties of *hair pencils*, mounted in quills, and painters' *tools*, which are similarly inserted in tubes or flattened cases of tin, or put into the cleft end of a wooden handle, and bound round with twine or thread, smeared over with glue; and the larger and coarser brushes, in which the end of the handle is inserted and bound up in the midst of the tuft, such as the large painting and dusting *brushes* (technically so called), used by house-painters, and the much larger *carpet brooms* and *besoms* or *birch-brooms*. *Stock-brushes* form an intermediate kind, in which several simple tufts or brushes are separately attached, side by side, to the thin edge of a flat board-like stock or handle: such are used for whitewash and distemper. Compound brushes, consisting of several tufts or *knots*, inserted in a stock or handle, range under two principal kinds: *set-work* or *pan-work*, and *drawn work*. For both the wooden stock is bored, usually in a lathe, with holes varying in size, depth, and direction, according to the kind of brush. In *pan-work*, the tufts or knots are formed by gathering together as many bristles or hairs as may be needed, striking one end even, dipping it in melted pitch, binding it round with thread, and, having dipped it again in the pitch, *setting* it in one of the holes in the stock with a peculiar twisting motion. Common house-brooms of most kinds, and some *dusters*, are made in this way. In *drawn* brushes the boring of the stock is more carefully performed, and a small hole is carried through from the extremity of each knot-hole to the back of the stock; and the brushmaker, taking in one hand about half as many bristles as will fill the knot-hole, passes their root ends through the bight or loop of a fine flexible wire which, with the other hand, he has passed double through the hole from the back of the stock. He then pulls the wire smartly, the effect of which is to draw the tuft into a bight or double, and to force it as far as possible into the knot-hole. After proceeding thus from hole to hole, he cuts the ends of the bristles evenly to the required length with shears. Brushes of this character comprise scrubbing, shoe, clothes, tooth, and nail brushes. In such the stiffness of the root end of the bristles is mostly desirable; while in such as are used for laying on colour, dusting, or sweeping, the softness of the *flag* or taper ends, which are cut as little as possible, is preferable. The stocks of drawn brushes are usually covered at the back with a veneer, which conceals and protects the wires; but small brushes set in bone or ivory are often drawn with silver wire, which is either left visible or sunk in fine grooves which are subsequently filled with hard red cement. The best are *trepanned*, or have the drawing holes so contrived as to come out, not through the back, but at some unconspicuous part of the stock, where they may be filled up with small plugs after the drawing, which is done with silk instead of wire. Mr. Hancock has patented a brush in which leather is used instead of wood or other unyielding material for the stock.

The brush manufacture is chiefly a domestic one, and is well adapted for the employment of females and children. The chief materials employed are *bristles*, many of which are imported from Russia and Poland, and are sorted into black, gray, yellow, white, and *lillies*, the lightest of all; horse-hair, goat's hair, and other kinds of hair; fibres of whalebone; a dark-coloured vegetable fibre called *bass*, used for stable and other coarse brooms; and *wisk*, a light-coloured vegetable substance of much finer quality, used for carpet-brooms, and a very fine variety for velvet-brushes; woods of various kinds for the stocks and veneers; and wire, usually of brass, but sometimes of a superior compound, looking much like copper, called red brass wire.

Mr. Cole, a brush-manufacturer, took out a patent in 1842 for numerous improvements in brush-making. In the general modes of making brushes the bristles are fixed in their places either by some kind of cement or by wire; but in Mr. Cole's new method the knot of bristles is kept in each hole by the hole being made of a conical shape, with the smaller end of the cone at the face or hair side of the brush: the knot is so shaped that it maintains its place in the brush without either cement or wire. A second improvement consists in steeping in a preservative solution the string with which some brushes are bound round, so as to enable them to be placed in water without loosening. A third consists in a new mode of fastening wedge-shaped handles into various kinds of brushes. A fourth consists in the manufacture of a new kind of brush for delicate purposes, by making a covering of plush to a foundation of white flock. A fifth consists in making brushes or pencils of spun glass, by which aquafortis and other corrosive acids can be applied by silversmiths and jewellers with more delicacy and safety than by any of the usual means. A sixth improvement is in the construction of brushes intended for cleansing decanters and bottles. A seventh relates to brushes for cleaning cruets and small phials.

Various patents have been taken out for making flexible backs to brushes.

A recent project, the subject of a patent, is to make brushes and brooms of the branches of the cabbage-palmetto tree, in such a way that the handle shall form one piece with the brush.

In Mr. Cocker's brushes, registered in 1849, the bristles are set diagonally, by which more of them are brought into action at once, and the surface of the brush is firmer.

BRUSSELS, the capital of Belgium, is a place of considerable manufacturing activity. The manufacture of lace is carried on to a considerable extent; the quality is very superior, and the finest sorts fetch from 3,000 to 4,000 francs a pound. A few facts concerning the lace manufacture of Brussels, in connection with the Exhibition of Industry, are given in the *Introduction* to this work. Many other manufactures are also prosecuted, among which are carpets, silk hats, cutlery and surgical instruments, hosiery, calicoes, gold and silver lace, paper-hangings, upholstery, porcelain, hardware, and chemical products. Vast numbers of books are printed in Brussels, a large number of which are cheap reprints of foreign works, chiefly French.

BRYO'NIA, the wild Bryony of our hedges, *Bryonia dioica*, is a plant formerly much employed in rural pharmacy, but now disused. It was chiefly employed on account of the powerful drastic properties of its root. Overdoses are extremely dangerous, and sometimes even fatal. The peculiar principle of Bryony-root is called *bryonin*. It is a yellowish white substance, sometimes with a red or brownish tint. Its taste is at first rather sweet, then styptic, and extremely bitter. It is a drastic purgative, and poisonous in too large doses.

BUC'CINA, a military instrument of the shrill horn or cornet kind, in use among the ancients, and by some supposed to have been formed of the horn of the bull or goat. According to others it was the shell of the buccinum, a fish. Vegetius says that it was made of brass, and bent in a circle. The probability is, that in its primitive state it was a simple horn, and that subsequently it was formed of a more durable material.

BUCHAREST, the capital of Wallachia, is the grand commercial mart for the principality, and the inhabitants carry on an extensive trade in grain, wool, honey, wax, tallow, and cattle. There are no large manufactures; but small quantities of woollen cloths, carpets, brandy, &c., are made.

BUCK-WHEAT. The cultivation of buck-wheat has never been very extensive in the variable climate of Britain. It is not so well adapted to cold wet soils as to warm sands; nor is it so certain a crop as oats or barley on lands which are suited to the growth of these grains. For countries where there are very poor light lands with a hot dry climate, unfavourable to the growth of oats and not rich enough for barley, buck-wheat is a great resource. Under particular circumstances, it might be introduced with advantage into many parts of England where it is now unknown. It is sown tolerably thick, and when the plant is in its greatest vigour and in full blossom a roller is passed over the crop to lay it level with the ground. Manure is seldom or never laid upon land in which buck-wheat is sown, because even where manure is abundant it is reserved for other crops supposed to require it more.

Buck-wheat is sometimes cut in its tender state for soiling cattle. It is said to increase the milk of cows, and is occasionally pastured by sheep. It may be given to horses instead of oats, or mixed with them. No grain seems so eagerly eaten by poultry, or makes them lay eggs so soon and so abundantly. The meal, when it is ground, is excellent for fattening cattle or pigs. The flour is fine and white, but, from a deficiency in gluten, does not make good fermented bread. It serves well however for pastry and cakes; crumpets made of buck-wheat flour, eaten with butter, are a favourite dainty with children in Holland. A hasty pudding is also made of the flour, with water or milk, and eaten with butter or sugar.

Out of nearly 11,000,000 quarters of corn and meal imported in 1849, only 627 quarters were buck-wheat.

BUCKINGHAMSHIRE. A little cheese is made in this county; but the quantity of butter is much larger. It is chiefly sent to London made up in the form of oblong rolls weighing two pounds each. It is sent in baskets called from their shape *flats*, which hold from 20 to 40 rolls. Their depth is uniformly 11 inches. Each flat is marked with the initials of the dairyman who sends the butter, and the carrier who conveys it, to whom also the flat belongs. Many of the calves in the dairy farms are fattened for veal, for the London market. The rearing and fattening of ducks for the early London season is carried on to a large extent. It is said that ducks to the value of 4,000*l* are sent annually from Aylesbury alone, and 20,000*l*. worth from the whole county.

BUDA, or OFEN, is that half of the metropolis of Hungary which stands on the left bank of the Danube; the other half, Pesth, being on the right bank. Buda manufactures a little silk and velvet, leather, some cottons, and woollens. It possesses also a cannon-foundry, copper foundries, a gunpowder manufactory, a silk-spinning mill, and a tobacco manufactory. The trade of the town principally consists in the wines produced by the vineyards in the environs, to the annual amount of about 4,500,000 gallons. This wine, which is well known under the name of 'Ofener-wein,' comes from the extensive vineyards belonging to the town itself, which are said to cover an area of 70 square miles. But Buda is now perhaps more interesting to us since the magnificent suspension-bridge over the Danube has been built by our countryman, Mr. Tierney Clark: perhaps the finest engineering work on the Danube.

BUDDING is an operation in horticulture, by means of which the branches of one kind of plant are often made to grow upon the stem of another kind. It is adopted for the purpose of artificial propagation, either by planting the separate buds in earth, or by introducing them into the branches of other plants. The former is called propagation by eyes; the latter only is technically named budding.

There are several modes of budding, such as *reversed budding* and *scallop-budding*, which are occasionally practised. Roses, plums, peaches, nectarines, cherries, and many other plants are chiefly propagated thus, and there is no theoretical reason why it should not be extended to all species. In practice however it is occasionally found impracticable, as in heaths, in vines, &c., owing to specific causes which vary in different instances.

Budding is usually performed in the months of July and August, because at that season the bark separates freely from the wood, and the young buds are fully formed; but, whenever the two latter conditions can be satisfied, the operation may take place equally well.

BUDE-LIGHT is the name given by its

inventor Mr. Gurney to a vivid flame, employed in lighting churches and other buildings. Originally it was obtained from an oil-lamp, the flame from which was acted on by a current of oxygen gas; subsequently oil gas was substituted for the liquid oil; but now the gas which is made for lighting the streets of towns is employed to produce the flame, and the brilliancy is increased by a current of air ingeniously introduced. The mode of admitting fresh air, and carrying off the products of combustion, constitute the difference between this and the common gas-light. It is found to be a cheap mode of producing a bright light; but as a similar effect may be produced by other means, the distinctive name of bude-light is not now much employed.

BUENOS AYRES, the capital of the republic of La Plata, carries on a large trade with France, importing from thence linen, wearing apparel, toilet articles, shoes, dressed leather, woollen and silk goods, &c. The imports from England and Germany are smaller in amount. The imports from France in 1844 amounted to 769,280*l.*; the exports to France to 411,168*l.* The total exports from Buenos Ayres in 1843 were valued at 1,659,206*l.* Buenos Ayres is the outlet for the produce of the vast herds of cattle which roam over the Pampas of La Plata; from this source we imported in 1848 about 115,000 hides, 13,000 lamb skins, and 80,000 cwts. of tallow.

BUILDING. In the practice of civil architecture, the builder is the individual who comes between the architect who designs and the artisans who execute the work; and building is essentially a manufacture. Referring to such articles as BRICKWORK, CARPENTRY, FLOOR, FOUNDATION, HOUSE, JOINERY, PLASTERING, ROOF, &c., for a few details relating to the art of building, a few words of a general nature may be here introduced.

The article BRICKWORK relates simply to the modes of arranging the separate bricks or component parts into a solid and adhesive wall. The builder must further combine the several portions of a wall broken or separated by openings for doorways and windows, and tho several walls of a house, into a self-sustaining structure, every part of which should, as far as possible, lend support to every other part. The effect of openings, for example, must be counteracted by *inverts* or *inverted arches* beneath them, and *discharging arches* over them; these being either left visible or concealed by a facing of other brickwork, according to circumstances. *Wood bricks*, or blocks of seasoned wood, must be inserted in the walls to facilitate the fixing of door and window frames, or other woodwork. *Lintels*, or bars of wood surmounting square-headed apertures, are sometimes used in lieu of arches, but should always be surmounted by discharging arches. *Templates* are pieces of wood larger than wood bricks, inserted to support and distribute the pressure of the ends of beams, &c., and *wall-plates* are still longer pieces let into the brickwork to support the floor-timbers. *Bond-timbers* are sometimes inserted to distribute and equalise strain; but the liability of timber to shrink and swell, to rot and to be destroyed by fire, render it desirable to insert it in brickwork as little as possible, and that under such circumstances that its total destruction may not affect the stability of the walls. The plans recently introduced for preserving timber [TIMBER, PRESERVATION OF] somewhat lessen the objections to its use.

In the erection of any building it is desirablo to carry up all the walls as equally as possible, to avoid the risk of unequal settlement. Interior partition walls are often formed of lath and plaster, on a timber framing; but, where weight is not an objection, of *brick-nogging*, or brickwork 4½ or 3 inches thick, strengthened by timber framing. Some use half-brick walls, built in cement, and strengthened with iron hooping laid in a few of the joints. The tops of brick walls are protected by COPING, which should be so formed as to throw off water.

Other modes of building than with brick are noticed elsewhere. [MASONRY.] *Flints* and *earth* are also advantageously employed in certain districts. Buildings of flint depend much for their strength upon the quality of the mortar or cement employed, and upon the judicious introduction of bonding-courses and quoins or angles of brick or of larger stone. Building with compressed earth, or building *en pisé*, is a very cheap mode, long used in some parts of France, but less known in this country than it deserves to be. Another mode of building well adapted for cottages in which no great strength is required in the walls, is with *hollow walls* of brick laid on edge, but otherwise arranged like ordinary Flemish bond. In this plan a space of 3 inches is left in the middle of the wall between each pair of stretchers. Walls thus constructed exclude damp and cold far better than solid walls. For modes of constructing FIRE-PROOF BUILDINGS, see that article.

BULKHEADS, which divide the hull of a ship into several water-tight compartments, are formed with the view of preventing the whole hull from being filled with water in case of a fracture or leak. Mr. C. W. Williams, in a paper communicated to a parliamentary committee on steam vessels, states that it has been found impracticable to make bulkheads of timber, on account of the liability of timber to shrinkage and leakage. Bulkheads of iron plates obviate this objection. Vessels are divided into two, three, four, or five water-tight compartments, by one, two, three, or four bulkheads; the more there are the greater the safety; but as they interfere with free passage from one end to another of the vessel, and as they entail greater expense and consumption of material, there soon arises a practical limit to the number. Mr. Williams recommends four bulkheads and five compartments for a steam-boat. The central compartment would hold the engine, boiler, and other machinery; the two compartments next to the centre would form the fore and after cabins or the fore and after holds, according as the steamer is a passenger or a trading vessel; while the two end compartments need not come up so high as the main-deck, on account of the deck at these parts being lifted higher up above the water than near the waist or middle of the ship.

BULLETS. The general mode of making bullets is noticed under SHOT-MANUFACTURE. We may, however, here state that a patent for making bullets was taken out in America in 1849, in which the bullet is formed by punching. The end of the punch has a hemispherical cavity, and a die is used which has a similar cavity. A strip of sheet lead is laid on the die, and the punch is brought down upon it with a force sufficient to sever a small piece of lead, and to form it into a globular shape by means of the two hemi-spherical cavities.

Several years before, however, in 1840, Mr. David Napier had patented a method, somewhat similar in principle, but more comprehensive, for making bullets in which great accuracy of form may be required. The machinery consists of two sliding plungers, placed horizontally and opposite to each other; each carrying a hemispherical die. The meeting and closing of the two dies give a perfectly spherical form to any substance compressed between them. In the centres of these plungers are two sliding plugs, which, in the retrocession of the plungers, are urged forward by a spring placed behind them, and drive out the compressed ball. An alternating motion backwards and forwards is given to the plungers. Strips of lead having projections, prepared either by rolling or casting, are supplied to the machine, the continuous pressing of which converts the projecting pieces of lead into perfect spheres, held together by a thin film of lead. The strips are then taken to a small hemispherical punch, working vertically into a circular bed the same size as the balls; and on bringing down this punch by means of a foot treadle, the balls are cut out, fall through the bed, and roll down a trough into a proper receptacle. This method of making bullets by compression was, we believe, at one time adopted by the government at Woolwich, the apparatus being worked by steam.

BULLION. This term is strictly applicable only to uncoined gold and silver, but it is frequently used in discussions relating to subjects of public economy to denote those metals both in a coined and in an uncoined state. At the Bank of England, all persons may demand of the issue department notes in exchange for gold bullion at the rate of *3l. 17s. 9d.* per ounce of standard gold, to be melted and assayed by persons appointed by the Bank, at the expense of the persons who tender the bullion.

Bullion is also applied as a distinctive name of particular kinds of fringe.

BU'NIUM. The *pig-nut* of the rural districts is the nearly globular root of the bunium plant, of a black or chesnut colour on the outside, and white inside. It has an aromatic sweet taste, and is frequently dug up and eaten by children. Pigs are very fond of these nuts, and get fat when allowed to feed on them. When boiled, they are a pleasant and nutritious food. Roasted, they are preferred by some people to chesnuts, and are often in this country and on the continent added to soup or broth.

BUOYANCY is the power which certain materials have of being supported at the surface of a fluid, so as to sink in it as much only as a part of their depth or thickness. Thus ice, some woods, &c., are said to have buoyancy in water, and almost all solid bodies have the power of floating on mercury. The term is frequently used to designate the weight which a solid mass of wood, or a vessel of wood or metal, will support in water. A brief explanation of the principle of buoyancy is given under HYDRAULICS. The propositions relating to it are useful in determining the amount of volume which would have buoyancy sufficient to raise a sunken ship; or in determining the dimensions of a floating bridge which may support a given weight of troops or artillery.

BUOYS are vessels formed of wood, cork, or some other substance which is specifically lighter than water. They are moored so as to float on the water at some certain spot, in order to point out the course or channel that a vessel should follow. Buoys are also used for the purpose of marking the situation of ships' anchors to which they are attached, and thus facilitating the future recovery of the anchor and cable in cases where the latter has been broken, or where it has been cut, in order to provide on emergencies for the safety of the ship, when circumstances do not admit of the anchor being weighed into the vessel. The first description of buoys are denominated public buoys, and the last private buoys. Another kind of buoys are those placed in harbours to mark the situation of mooring-chains to which ships frequenting the port are made fast.

Until the reign of Queen Elizabeth all public buoys in this kingdom were under the management of the Lord High Admiral; but since 1594 they have been under the control of the Trinity House. The amount of revenue annually collected for the use of buoys by the Trinity House corporation is between 11,000*l.* and 12,000*l.* The charge made is according to the tonnage of the vessels frequenting the ports in or leading to which buoys are placed: the rates vary according to circumstances, and are highest in the port of London, where British and foreign *privileged* vessels (those belonging to countries with which we have 'reciprocity treaties') pay one penny per ton; and foreign vessels not privileged pay two pence per ton.

The buoys which are sometimes used as life-preservers are noticed elsewhere [LIFE-BUOYS.]

BURETTE, is an instrument invented by M. Gay-Lussac, for the purpose of dividing a given portion of any liquid into 100 or 1,000 equal parts. It consists of a measure of definite capacity, a graduated tube, and another tube of smaller bore attached to the former. It is much used in French chemical factories, but is scarcely known in England.

BURNING GLASSES AND MIRRORS. A convex lens or a concave mirror, by collecting a quantity of light within a small space at the focus, will also, if the lens or mirror be of considerable size and the light very strong, as that of the sun, collect a quantity of heat sufficient to destroy almost any substance. This property has been long known. Among the earliest attempts to produce considerable effects by burning instruments is that of Tschirnhausen, who, about the year 1700, made a glass lens 33 inches diameter and 7 feet focal length, by which the concentrated light of the sun, in a short time, burnt wood, melted small pieces of metal, vitrified slate, &c. In the year 1747 M. Buffon constructed an apparatus which, on a concave surface, carried 220 plane mirrors; with this the sun's light burnt wood at the distance of 200 feet, and melted metals at 50 feet. About the year 1800 Mr. Parker, in London, executed a burning lens of flint glass 3 feet diameter and 6 feet 8 inches focal length, with which, by concentrating the sun's light, he fused gold in three seconds, steel in 12 seconds, and limestone in 55 seconds; and, by the heat thus produced, a diamond weighing 10 grains was reduced to six grains.

As a source of heat, the burning glass has not yet been made available in manufactures, except in a few trifling instances: but there is nothing irrational in supposing that it may one day subserve useful purposes.

BURNLEY is one of the busy cotton-spinning towns of Lancashire. The trade of the town was formerly confined to woollens: but the cotton manufacture is now the staple. At the present time (1850) there are about 30 cotton spinning and weaving mills; there are no cotton bleaching or dye works; but there are two calico printing establishments. There are also three worsted mills. Besides the above, Burnley contains four corn mills (one of them very large), iron foundries, machine-making works, brass foundries, roperies, tanneries, breweries, and collieries.

The Leeds and Liverpool canal, and the East Lancashire and other railways, afford media for the conveyance of goods through tho whole line of country, from the German Ocean to the Irish Sea. Besides its manufactures Burnley sends coal, freestone, and slate from the vicinity.

BURNT-EAR, in corn, is a disease in which the fructification of the plant is destroyed and as it were *burnt* up: hence its English name and the corresponding names of *charbon* in French and *brand* in German. In *burnt-ear* the black powder which appears in the ear is external, and the grain has either never been formed, or its coat has been destroyed, so that the whole ear appears black or burnt. The powder also has no smell, and, being easily blown away by the wind, or shaken off in the reaping, little of it adheres to the corn or is mixed with it when ground; and, except the loss of so much grain as would have been contained in the sound ears, no great detriment arises to the quality of the corn. Microscopic observations show that the black powder consists of the minute germs or sporules of a parasitical fungus, which are developed in the growing ears and live on its substance. The best preservative against this disease is to drain the land well and keep it in good heart.

BURSLEM, in Staffordshire, often receives the name of tho 'Mother of Potteries,' having been the first, and for a long period the chief of the pottery towns. From an early period it has been distinguished for the variety and excellence of the clays in its vicinity. All the subsoil of the town is clay, varying from two to ten feet in thickness; it is called in the neighbourhood *tough Tom*, and is employed in the manufacture of red, brown, and yellow wares. Below the subsoil is a very thick stratum of fire clay, of which the saggers or baking vessels for the pottery kilns are made. Below the fire-clay is coal. Most of the early improvements in the pottery manufacture were made at Burslem; and the town took the lead in this art, until Wedgwood removed thence to Etruria. Longport is now so closely united to Burslem, that the two form in effect one large town, every part of which is occupied by the pottery works, the houses of the work-people and employers, or the shopkeepers. No town in England, perhaps, is more dependent on one particular branch of manufacture than Burslem is on that of porcelain and earthenware. There are at the present time in the whole parish nearly forty pottery establishments; besides glass-works at Longport.

BURY is one of the active manufacturing towns of Lancashire. The manufacture of woollen cloth became a staple article of trade in this place so far back as the fourteenth century, and flourished to such an extent that in the reign of Elizabeth one of her aulnagers was stationed in the town to stamp the cloth. Up to a much later date woollens were almost the sole manufacture of the place; but upon the introduction of the cotton trade into the county many of the inhabitants became weavers of cotton fabrics, and the woollen trade has been gradually retiring into Yorkshire and other parts of the country where the cotton manufacture is less paramount. The different branches of the cotton manufacture, owing to the vicinity of Bury to the Manchester market, and the abundant supply of coal and water, are carried on to a considerable and increasing extent in this and the adjoining township.

Several important improvements in the cotton manufacture took their rise in this place. A new method of throwing the shuttle by means of the picking-peg instead of the hand, and thence called the fly-shuttle, was invented by John Kay, a native of the town: and in 1760 his son, Robert Kay, invented the drop-box, by means of which the weaver can at will use any one of three shuttles—an invention which led to the introduction of various colours into the same fabric, and made it almost as easy to produce a fabric consisting of different colours as a common cloth of only one. Bury is indebted for one branch of its present trade to the father of the late Sir Robert Peel, who established his extensive print-works on the banks of the Irwell, near this town; he resided at Chamber Hall, in the immediate vicinity, where, or at a smaller house close by it, the late Sir Robert Peel was born.

There are at the present time in Bury more than a dozen large factories for spinning and manufacturing cotton, several large woollen manufactories, two calico-printing and bleaching establishments, and two dye-works. Besides the different branches of cotton and woollen manufactures, there are three large foundries, several smaller ones, and manufactories of hats and other articles.

BUSHEL. By the act of 1824 the standard gallon contains 10 pounds avoirdupois of pure water. Eight such gallons make a bushel, and eight bushels a quarter. This, by the other provisions of the act, made it contain 2218.2 cubic inches very nearly.

BUST, in sculpture, means a statue truncated below the breast. As a question of fine art, the production of a bust depends on the same exercise of taste and refined judgment as that of a statue. As a question of mechanical execution, we shall have occasion in a later article to describe Mr. Cheverton's remarkable mode of carving busts by machinery. Busts in bronze or other metal, in biscuit or other kinds of porcelain, and in plaster, are produced by casting.

BUTTER is the fat or oleaginous parts of the milk of various animals, principally of the domestic cow. The milk of the cow consists of curd, whey, and butter, and is esteemed chiefly in proportion to the amount of butter, which differs much in that of different breeds.

For the making of butter, the milk, brought into the dairy from the milking-shed, is strained through a fine sieve or cloth into shallow pans, or troughs lined with lead, which are filled to the depth of four or five inches. These should be in a place sheltered from the sun, but having a thorough draught of air by means of opposite wire windows. The floor should be kept moist in summer, to produce coolness by evaporation; but in winter a small stove is an advantage, provided smoke and smell be avoided. After standing twelve hours the finest parts of the cream will be found to have risen to the surface; and this, if skimmed off, will furnish a very delicate butter. More generally however the milk is allowed to stand twenty-four hours, and then the cream is collected, either by skimming or by letting off the thin milk from beneath it by opening plugs in the troughs. The cream is put in a deep earthen or stone-ware jar, which should be glazed, but not with lead; and more is added every day until there is sufficient to churn. The cream is usually stirred from time to time, to promote a slight acidity, which facilitates the process of churning.

There are many varieties of churn [CHURN]; but most of them have a beater or fan which agitates the cream. The barrel of the churn should not be more than two-thirds full of cream. In the course of an hour's agitation or churning, small kernels of butter are found among the cream, and these become gradually united into a solid mass, leaving a fluid residue called *butter-milk*, which is set aside for domestic use, or for feeding pigs. The butter is then removed to a shallow tub, well beaten with the hand or a flat wooden spoon, and repeatedly washed with clear spring water, until all the remaining butter-milk is removed from it; after which, if intended to be sold fresh, it is made up in rolls or cakes for the market, or salted and put into casks if intended for keeping. Cakes or pats of fresh butter are often impressed with some device from a carved wooden print, resembling a large seal. In Cambridgeshire butter is made up into rolls a yard long, and passed through a ring of a certain diameter, for the convenience of dividing it into small portions without weighing. In salting butter the quality of the salt is of great importance; and some, instead of simple salt, use half an ounce of dry salt, pounded fine, two drams of sugar, and two drams of saltpetre, to every pound of butter. As a cask is gradually filled up, every addition is carefully incorporated with the preceding portion. Should it shrink in the cask, melted butter may be poured round it to fill up the interstices.

Butter may be preserved for domestic use, without salt, by melting it very gently, without boiling; which causes the watery particles to evaporate, and the curd, which is always present in small quantity and is a principal cause of rancidity, to fall to the bottom. The clear butter is then poured into an earthen vessel, and covered with paper; and a piece of bladder or leather is tied over it to exclude the air. Butter thus prepared resembles lard in appearance, loses some of its flavour, but is much superior to salt butter for ordinary purposes.

In Devonshire, instead of the ordinary mode of raising cream in shallow pans, the milk is, after standing twelve hours, exposed to heat, without boiling, by which a thick scum called *clotted cream*, more solid than cream, but not so solid as butter, is thrown up. A very slight agitation converts it into butter, another mode, which is followed in parts of Holland, Scotland, and Ireland, is to churn the milk and cream together, by which, it is said, more butter is produced.

Much attention is paid to the most minute circumstances in the manufacture of butter, especially in all that relates to cleanliness. In Switzerland men are chiefly employed in milking and in making butter and cheese; the women only cleaning the utensils and carrying green food to the cows when kept in the stable. The gradually extending use of the thermometer is an important improvement in dairy practice; and probably the electrometer may be found similarly useful, as the state of the atmosphere in reference to electricity evidently has a powerful influence on the making of butter. The nature of the pasture is also important. The best butter is produced from cows fed in rich natural meadows; and some plants which grow in poor and marshy soils impart a disagreeable flavour to the butter, as also do turnips and other roots, and most cut grasses. This may be in some measure obviated by adding a little water and saltpetre to the milk, or, it is said, by giving salt to the cows with their food. The best winter butter is made where the cows are fed with good meadow hay, or aftermath hay, which contains few seedstalks. The colour varies much from different cows, and from the same at different times. Arnotto or the juice of carrots is sometimes mixed with the cream to impart a deeper yellow.

Upon an average, four gallons of milk produce sixteen ounces of butter; and, to be profitable, a good dairy cow in England should produce six pounds of butter per week in summer, and three pounds in winter, allowing from six weeks to two months for her being dry before calving. This makes 120 lbs. in twenty weeks after calving, and 80 lbs. in the remaining time, or 200 lbs. in the year.

Whey Butter is an inferior kind made in some cheese dairies from the oily portion of the milk skimmed from the whey; it is sold chiefly to labourers, seldom comes to market, and is totally unfit for salting and keeping. *Ghee*, or fluid butter, forms one of the staple productions of many districts in India.

All the butter that is produced in England is consumed at home, and a large quantity is imported from Ireland, Holland, and other countries. The consumption of butter in London is estimated by M'Culloch at 15,000 to 16,000 tons annually, of which 2000 tons are supplied to shipping. At 10*d*. per lb. for 34,400,000 lbs., the value consumed of this article amounts to 1,433,333*l*. The consumption per head in this estimate is assumed to be 5 oz. weekly, or 16 lbs. per annum. In 1835 the imports from Ireland were 827,009 cwts., valued at 3,316,306*l.*; but since that date the imports of Irish butter do not appear in the Government tables.

Almost all the butter exported is derived from Ireland. In 1849 the exports of this commodity amounted in value to 210,604*l.*, of which the largest quantities were sent to Brazil, West Indies, and Portugal. The importations of foreign butter, in 1849, amounted to 282,501 cwts., of which two-thirds came from Holland.

A few interesting details concerning the Irish butter-trade will be found under CORK.

BUTTERS, VEGETABLE, the name given to the concrete oil of certain vegetables, from its resemblance to the butter obtained from the milk of animals, and from being employed for similar purposes. The chief vegetable butters are produced by the *Bassia butyracea* and other species of the genus Bassia. [BASSIA.]

BUTTERS, (in pharmacy), is an obsolete name for the hydrochlorates of the metals, such as antimony, arsenic, bismuth, tin, and zinc.

BUTTON MANUFACTURE. Gold, silver, brass, copper, pewter, mother-of-pearl, hard wood, bone, ivory, horn, leather, paper, glass, silk, wool, cotton, linen, thread, are all formed into buttons, and the manufacture is carried on to a very great extent. Metal buttons with shanks are stamped out of a plate of the material; and each circular piece or 'blank' is trimmed and smoothed. The shanks are made of wire by an ingenious machine and are soldered on to the blanks. After a little further preparation, the buttons (if of the common gilt kind) receive a coating of gold [GILDING], which is now often effected by the electro process. White metal buttons, such as those on soldiers' dresses, are cast in moulds containing ten or twelve dozen, and the shanks are placed in the moulds previously to casting, so that when the buttons are cast the shanks are fixed at the same time. Mother-of-pearl buttons are cut out of the pearl shell by a cylindrical saw; and the shanks are fixed by a kind of dove-tailed projection of the wire in a hole drilled in the shell through one-half its thickness.

Buttons without shanks are made of mother-of-pearl, wood, bone, metal, &c., the metal ones being stamped, and the rest turned. They have four holes through which the thread is passed to fix them on the garment. These holes are stamped in metal buttons, but they are drilled in those which are made of other materials. The holes are drilled while the buttons are in the lathe: four long drills are made to converge towards the button, and thus the four holes are all drilled at once. The buttons most extensively used at present are those covered with cloth or silk, the manufacture of which has arrived at great perfection. Most varieties of coat-button now consist of two circular blanks of iron, one of thick pasteboard, one of thick canvas, and one of silk or florentine. All these are cut out separately with great rapidity, by a stamping press from sheets of the respective materials. Into a kind of die or cell is placed, first, the silk or florentine, then a disc or 'blank' of iron, then the pasteboard, then the canvas, then the other piece of iron—all superposed. A stamping-press, of beautiful construction, fixes all these together, without the aid of any other mode of fastening.

Buttons made of wire rings covered with thread or with linen, and metal buttons made iridescent of minute grooves, are among the varieties of the manufacture.

A singular method was introduced a few years ago, of imitating covered cloth buttons by a layer of flock, such as is used in paper hangings. In the first place, thin sheets of metal are coated on one side with copal varnish thinned with turpentine, and coloured according to the colour of the flock to be employed. After being heated in an oven to 150° Fahr., and then allowed to cool, the surface is coated with a kind of paint formed of white-lead, linseed oil, gold size, and colouring matter. While in this wet state, a quantity of flock is sifted over the surface, and allowed to remain on it twelve hours, by which time a film of flock will have adhered firmly to the metal. The loose flock being shaken off, the sheet is fitted to be cut up into collets or discs for the backs of buttons, to be made in the usual way.

Mr. Prosser's method of making buttons and other small articles of compressed clay was patented in 1840. Clay, clayey earth, or clay combined with a small portion of flint or felspar to give it hardness, is thoroughly dried and ground to a fine powder. The powder is passed through a sieve having about two thousand perforations in a square inch: all particles too large to pass through the perforations being rejected. For some coarser purposes a coarser sieve may be used. Buttons and other small articles are made of this powder by dies, or moulds and a fly-press. The fly-press is firmly secured to a strong bed or frame; and a die, carrying on its under face the form in reverse (i. e. hollow instead of relief,) proposed to be given to the top of the button, is screwed to the follower of the press. A second tool or die of a kind of T shape, with an impress of the back of the button, fits loosely into a corresponding recess in the bolster. Below the press there is a treadle supported on a fulcrum near its centre, from one end of which a rod passes up through a small hole in the bolster to the lower die or tool. The hollow or recess in the bolster in which this tool rises and falls is of such a depth as to be an exact measure of the quantity of powder necessary for the formation of a button. The hollow in the mould being filled with powder, and the powder squared off to an exact level with the top of the mould, such power is applied to the press as will bring down the tool with a force of about 200 lbs. on the square inch, upon the powder lying in the mould. The powder is by this means compressed into a very dense, hard, and durable substance, having on its surface the device imparted to it by the die. If the button is to have a metallic shank attached to it, a recess is formed at the back of the button for its reception, by a corresponding projection on the face of the lower die. If the button is to have holes similar to a brace-button, the dies must have such projections as will form these holes while the powder is being pressed into the mould.

In the course of a year or two after this patent was obtained, no less than 5000 gross of these buttons were made weekly, at Minton's porcelain works in Staffordshire.

The Vicomte de Scrionne took out a patent in 1850, for a somewhat complicated mode of making buttons, which should have a sort of crystalline appearance. They are made of felspar, basalt, lava pumice, granite, or flint. These minerals, or the one to be adopted, is reduced to powder, and made into a paste with salt and flour; the paste is pressed into a mould, of which the upper and under parts give the device to the button; and by subsequent modes of treating the surface, the button assumes either a transparency, or an agate-like opacity.

Birmingham is the great seat of the Button manufacture in this country. [BIRMINGHAM.] It is supposed that at the present time (1851) there are upwards of 5000 persons employed at Birmingham in making buttons, of whom rather more than half are women and children.

BUTTRESS, a projecting support to a wall, most commonly applied to churches in the Gothic style. Buttresses are usually finished with a sloping top, and divided into several heights, each of which projects less from the wall as they ascend. The buttresses of Gothic buildings are variously decorated. The most superb buttresses ever executed in this country belong to Henry VII's chapel at Westminster Abbey.

BUTY'RIC ACID, a colourless acid liquid, which exists in butter. It combines with water, and evaporates readily in the open air. It consists of carbon 8, oxygen 3, hydrogen 6. It combines with different bases to form salts, called *butyrates*, few of which are of importance. In intimate relation with this substance is *butyrine*, a yellow liquid procurable from butter.

BYSSUS. Recent investigations have determined that byssus is linen: at least so far as the term has been applied by Greek and Roman writers to mummy-cloth. Herodotus states, that the Egyptians wrapped their dead in the cloth of the byssus; and it has been shown, by microscopic observations, that every specimen of mummy-cloth yet examined is made of linen fibre.

Byssus is also a name given to the long silky fasciculus of filaments by which some of the bivalve shell-fish (such as mussels, hammer oysters, &c.), are moored to submarine rocks. Some authors have regarded these threads as a peculiar secretion spun as it were by the animal. De Blainville, however, asserts them to be an assemblage of muscular fibres, dried up in one part of their extent, but contractile and living at their origin, as they were throughout at the period of their first attachment. The Byssus in the great *Pinna* of the Mediterranean is largely developed. It is manufactured in Italy into various articles, as gloves, &c., of which specimens are preserved in many museums. The *byssus* or *beard* of the mussel is familiar to all.

C

CABBAGE. The cabbage is not only valuable as a food for man, but it is an important aid to the operations of the grazier. When given to cattle or sheep, cabbages should be sliced in the same manner as turnips or beet-root. When milch cows are fed with them, all the decayed leaves should be carefully taken off and given to store cattle or pigs; for these are the chief cause of the bad taste which the milk and butter acquire from this food. For bullocks, cabbages and oil-cakes are excellent food, and increase their flesh rapidly. For sheep, cabbages should be sliced, and given to them in troughs in the field where the cabbages grow, or on grass land which requires to be manured.

In Germany there is an immense consumption of the large white cabbage in the form of the national mess, called *sauer kraut*. This is prepared by slicing the cabbage, and placing them in a tub with alternate layers of salt and allowing them to ferment. This preparation, when washed with soft water and stewed with bacon or salted meat, is a very wholesome dish, and much relished by those who have been early accustomed to it. In long voyages it has been found to be an admirable preservative from the sea-scurvy.

CABIN, is an apartment or room in a ship. In large vessels, the admiral's and captain's cabins extend across the ship near her stern, and are usually divided into two, termed the fore-cabin and after-cabin. Those belonging to the junior commissioned and warrant officers are ranged along the side of the ship, having an area of from 5 to 6 feet in width, and from 6 to 7 feet in length.

In frigates the captain's cabin is on the main-deck; and the gun-room, or after part of the lower deck, is given to the officers; but in two-decked line-of-battle ships the captain takes the cabin under the poop, and the officers the great cabin on the upper gun-deck, which is called the ward-room. In three-deckers this large apartment is appropriated to the admiral, and the officers take the corresponding one on the middle gun-deck. The partitions by which all these cabins are inclosed are called *bulk-heads*, which are instantly removeable when the decks are ordered to be cleared for action.

CABINET MAKING. [FURNITURE MANUFACTURE.]

CABLE. [CHAIN-CABLE; ROPE.]

CABUL, or CAUBUL. The industry and commerce of this country have been already briefly described. [AFGHANISTAN.]

CACAO, the bruised seed of the *Theobroma*, is more familiarly known as COCOA, under which name we shall describe it.

CACTUS. Some kinds of cactus render useful services to man. In most of those found in tropical America, the stems are filled with an abundant insipid wholesome fluid, and their fruit is succulent, and in many cases superior to that of European gooseberries. In cases of fever in their native countries they are freely administered as a cooling drink; and being bruised they are esteemed a valuable means of curing ulcers.

Opuntia Tuna is the species of cactus which nourishes the cochineal insect. According to Humboldt it is in much esteem in Peru as the food of that valuable insect.

CADIZ, a large commercial town on the S. W. coast of Spain, enjoyed for a long time a high degree of prosperity, arising from its trade with the Spanish American colonies. In 1792 the imports from Spanish America were to the amount of 7,295,833*l.*; in 1791, the amount of gold and silver, coined and uncoined, received from the same quarter exceeded 5,300,000*l.* This commercial activity was wholly destroyed by the defection of the Spanish possessions in America. The foreign trade of Cadiz, which is now in a state of great depression, consists of the importation, in Spanish bottoms, of colonial produce from Cuba, Puerto-Rico, and the Philippine Islands; cocoa, hides, cochineal, indigo, and other produce from South America. Salt-fish is imported from Newfoundland in English vessels. Linens, silks, and woollen cloths, iron hoops, tin, glass, hardware, and earthenware, butter and cheese, are imported from England, Germany, and France, mostly in Spanish ships; staves are supplied by the United States in vessels belonging to those states; and timber is imported from Russia and Sweden, in foreign bottoms. The chief articles of export are wine, salt, fruit, oil, wood, cork, and quicksilver, which are usually shipped in vessels bearing the flag of the country to which the shipments are made. The manufactures carried on in the city consist of soap, glass-ware, coarse woollens and linens, cotton and silk fabrics, and hats; there are likewise some sugar refineries and tanneries.

CA'DMIUM, is one of the recently discovered metals. It occurs in ores of zinc, from which it is usually obtained. It has the colour of tin, is brilliant, and susceptible of a fine polish. Its fracture is fibrous, and it crystallizes readily in regular octahedrons; while solidifying its surface is covered with arborations like fern leaves. It is soft, easily bent, filed, and cut; it stains substances upon which it is rubbed, like lead. When bent, it gives a peculiar crackling noise, like tin. It is very ductile, easily drawn into wire and beaten into thin leaves. Its specific gravity after fusion is 8·604, but when beaten 8·694. Cadmium melts below a red heat; and, at a temperature a little above that of boiling mercury, it boils and distils in drops. The vapour of cadmium has no particular odour. Like tin, it is slowly acted upon by the air, but is eventually tarnished by it.

Cadmium combines with several other elements; but these compounds have not yet become extensively valuable in the arts.

CAEN, in Normandy, is famous for the manufacture of lace, angola gloves, and cutlery; linen, woollen and cotton stuffs, hosiery, porcelain, oil, paper, and leather, are also made. The town is a depôt for salt, and has large timber and ship-building yards. About 800 vessels arrive annually, of which 160 are freighted with salt. The other articles of commerce are corn, wine, brandy, cider, clover-seed, hemp, horses, fat cattle, butter, iron, hardware, mill-stones, building stone, and granite for paving.

CAERMARTHENSHIRE. The southern part of this county, bordering upon Glamorganshire and the sea, forms part of the great coal-field of South Wales. The coal is chiefly what is called stone coal; the large coal of this quality is used for drying hops and malt; the small coal, called culm, for burning limestone. Towards the coast the coal is more bituminous. The coal-field of South Wales lies in a basin of mountain or carboniferous limestone, and the northern outcrop of this limestone crosses Caermarthenshire in a waving line E. and W. From this limestone is obtained marble for chimney-pieces, stone for tomb-stones, and lime for manure.

CAERNARVONSHIRE, in North Wales, is rich in minerals. There are copper-mines at Great Orme's Head, in the vale of Conwy a little west of Llanrwst, in the vale of Llanberis, and near Pont Aberglasllyn. Lead and calamine are obtained in the vale of Conwy near the junction of the Llugwy with the Conwy, and in that part of the county which lies east of the Conwy. Mill-stones are dug in the vale of Conwy. Slates are found in various parts of the county, and form one of the chief articles of export. The finest are those on the west side of the ridge of the Snowdonian mountains, and they become finer as they descend towards the sea. Not only roofing-slates and writing-slates are procured from these mines, but inkstands and other fancy articles are made. Slabs are procured large enough for tomb-stones and paving-slabs.

CAFEIC ACID exists in coffee, which owes to it a part of its odour. It is combined with lime, magnesia, alumina, and iron, forming salts or *cafeates* of those bases. The alkaline cafeates are of a pure brown colour without any admixture of green, and by evaporating the solutions they are obtained in the state of brown horny masses. *Cafeine* is another peculiar substance obtained from coffee, in soft, silky fibres, which have a very bitter taste.

CAIRN, or CARN, a heap of stones thrown together in a conical form. Lhuyd, in his 'Additions to Camden's Britannia, in Radnorshire,' asserts that in the Cambro-Britannic *Kaern* is a primitive word appropriated to signify such heaps of stones. Cairns and tumuli of earth were the common monuments which the ancient Britons erected in honour of their great men. Pausinius mentions monuments of collected stones, especially near Orchomenus, in Arcadia, for persons who had fallen in battle.

CAIRO. The industry and commerce of this important city are noticed under EGYPT.

CAJEPUT OIL, is produced chiefly from the *Melaleuca Cajuputi*, a native of Amboyna, and other East India islands. The oil is obtained by distillation of the leaves and branches, which are collected the night before they are subjected to this process. It is very limpid, pellucid, and of a light or yellowish green colour. In its action on the human frame Cajeput Oil participates in the properties of other volatile oils, and is rubefacient externally; stimulant, and anti-spasmodic, when taken internally.

The Cajeput Tree, a native of the East India Islands, was at one time supposed to yield the oil of commerce. Roxburgh asserts that it possesses little or no fragrance in its leaves, and that it is seldom or never used for the distillation of the oil which is used in the European markets.

CALIMINE. [ZINC.]

CA'LAMUS is the genus of palms whose different species constitute the *rattan canes* of commerce.

The species are principally found in the hotter parts of the East Indies, where they grow in the forests, climbing over trees and

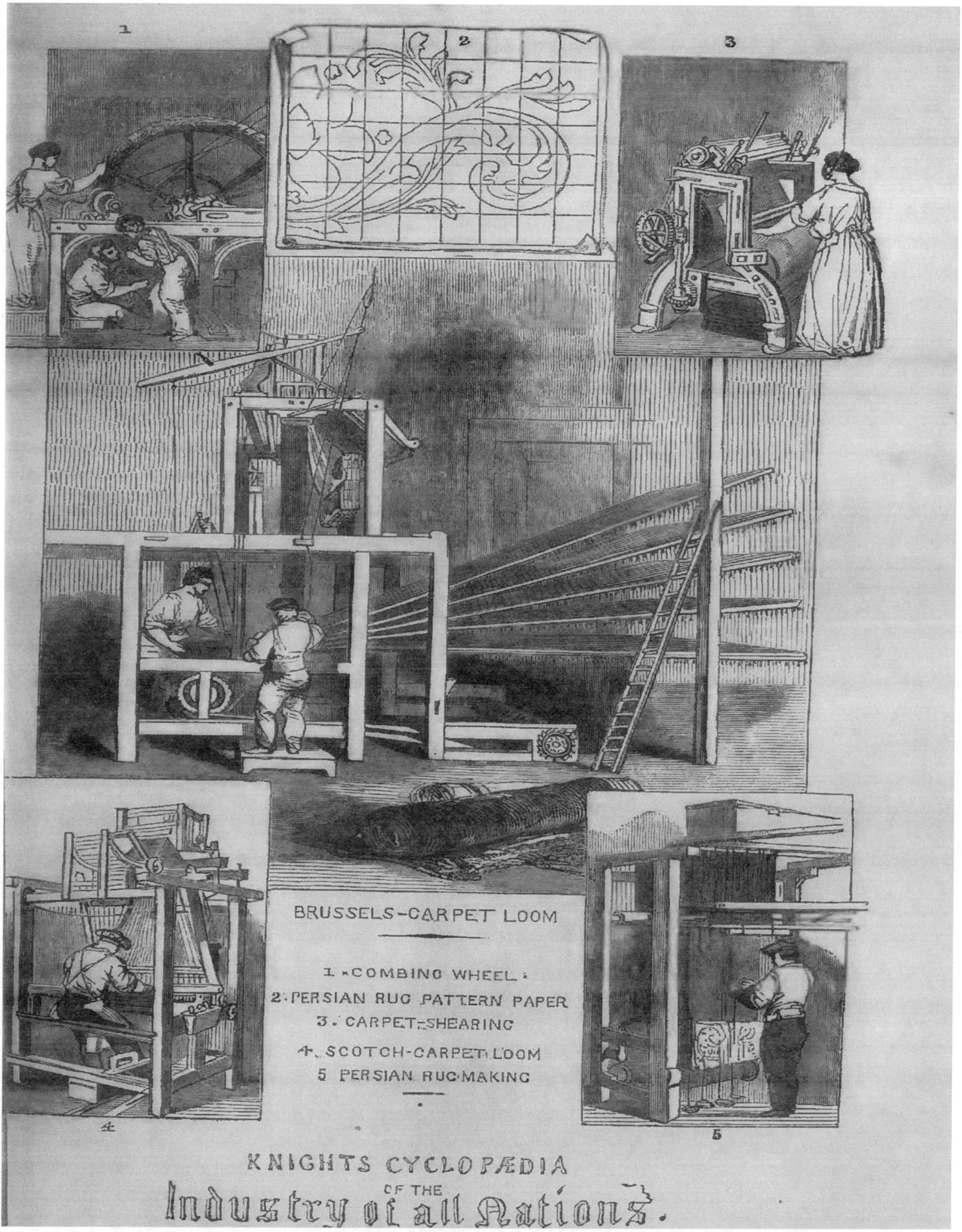

KNIGHTS CYCLOPÆDIA
OF THE
Industry of all Nations.

bushes to a greater extent than any other known plants. The stem of *Calamus verus* is described as being 100 feet long; that of *C. oblongus* 300 to 400, of *C. rudentum* upwards of 500, and of *C. extensus* as much as 600 feet; Rumphius even states that one kind of Calamus attains the extraordinary length of 1,200 feet. It is closely covered over by the tubular bases of the leaves, through which it is drawn by the cane-gatherers when green; afterwards it is dried in the sun, and then is ready for market. From three to four millions of these canes are imported into this country annually. They are extensively used for the sake of the hard flinty coating of their stems, which are readily split into strips, from which the bottoms of chairs and similar articles are manufactured. It is not possible to say from what particular species the canes of the shops are obtained, it being probable that many are gathered indiscriminately. The flesh that surrounds the seeds is a delicate article of food; and the young shoots of some of the species while still tender, are roasted or boiled, chopped small, and, being fried with pepper and gravy, are said to furnish a very delicate dish.

The greater part of the *Dragon's Blood* now met with in commerce is obtained from several species of this genus. They are natives only of Hindustan, Cochin China, and the Moluccas. The ripe fruits are covered with a reddish-brown, dry, resinous substance. In this state they are collected, and allowed to remain till the resin drops off. The resin is afterwards melted, either by the natural warmth of the air or by artificial heat, and then moulded into the different forms in which it occurs in commerce. Dragon's Blood possesses no astringent properties, as was once supposed to be the case, owing to *kino* being confounded with it. It is now seldom used internally, but it is added to tooth-powders. It is however employed as a colouring matter and an ingredient in varnishes.

CALCAREOUS SPAR is one of the names given to the rhombohedral crystals of carbonate of lime. The specific gravity of the purest crystals of this mineral is 2·721; and the hardness is between gyps and fluor spar. It is of itself colourless, but frequently occurs of various tints of yellow, green, red, brown, and even black, from the admixture of impurities. Its glance is mostly vitreous. The lead mines of Derbyshire and Cumberland, and of Andreasberg in the Harz, are noted as affording the most beautiful crystals, and the greatest diversity of forms.

Every visitor to the British Museum has opportunities of inspecting exquisite specimens of calcareous spar.

CALCEDONY. [AGATE.]

CALCINATION, is the separation of the volatile from the more fixed parts of a body: thus bones which are heated till they become black are termed *burnt bones;* but when, by the further operation of heat, they become white, they are called *calcined bones.* But what were formerly termed metallic calces or calcined metals are now described as metallic oxides.

CAL'CIUM, a peculiar metal, of which *lime* is the well-known oxide. It was first obtained by Davy, in 1808, by the action of voltaic electricity on a small mass of chalk. That calcium is a white combustible metal is nearly all that is known respecting it; but many of its compounds with other elements have been long known and extensively employed. [LIME.]

CALCULATING MACHINES. Before computers had attained great proficiency in performing arithmetical operations by the pen, machines by which the results of such operations could be obtained by inspection were in almost constant use. The principal of these were the Roman *abacus*, which continued to be employed in the south of Europe till the end of the 15th century, and in England to a later period; and the *Schwan-pan*, which in China has long been the principal means of making computations. [ABACUS.] For the operations of multiplication and division the ivory rods of Napier, commonly called *Napier's Bones*, were for a time used; and, for solving trigonometrical problems, *Gunter's Scale* or the *Logarithmic Scales* were once very generally employed by navigators.

The celebrated Pascal constructed, it is said, when only 19 years of age a machine for executing the ordinary operations of arithmetic. Subsequently to the time of Pascal, Leibnitz invented a machine by which arithmetical computations could be made; but no account of it appears to have been published.

All former contrivances for performing such operations may be said to have been cast in the shade by the machine invented by Mr. Babbage, which, should it be completed, will constitute one of the most superb monuments of human ingenuity. Not only are its operations accomplished with certainty, but the results may be transferred to copperplates, from which any number of copies may be printed without a possibility of error. A very brief notice however of the manner of using it, and of the principles on which it is constructed, can be here given.

In any series of numbers arranged in line

or column, if the difference between the first and second, between the second and third, and so on, be taken, there will be formed a line or column of what are called *first differences*; if the difference between the first and second, between the second and third, and so on, of these last numbers be taken, there will be formed a line or column of what are called *second differences.* Proceeding in like manner to form third, fourth, &c., orders of differences, there will at length be found a series of differences which are either constant, or to a great extent are nearly so. Then having any one of the numbers in the first column, and the numbers corresponding to it in the several columns of differences, all the succeeding numbers of the series may be found by mere additions or subtractions, and the latter process may be avoided by using arithmetical complements.

The machine accomplishes these additions by the movements of a number of cylinders having on the convex surface of each the series of numbers 1, 2, 3, 4, 5, 6, 7, 8, 9, 0; and the operations are of two kinds: by the first, the additions are made; and by the second, there is introduced the 1 which should be carried to the *ten's* place every time that the sum of two numbers is greater than 10.

Let it be imagined that there are side by side several vertical axles, on each of which are several cylinders one above another; and that these axles with their cylinders are capable of being turned by wheelwork, so that any one of the ten figures may be made to stand on the face of the machine, and immediately under a fixed index. Let it be further imagined that the figures composing a given number are under the indices in front of the cylinders on the first vertical axis towards the left hand; and the figures composing the several orders of differences in front of the cylinders on the other axis successively towards the right. Then, the general axle of the machine being, by a winch, turned one quarter of a revolution, only the first, third, fifth, &c. axles turn, and every cylinder on each of these axles turns, at the same time, through as many tenths of a revolution as are expressed by the figure in front of the cylinder immediately on its right hand.

There is thus brought to the front of each turning cylinder the unit's figure in the sum of the figure previously in front of that cylinder, and the figure in front of the cylinder on its right. When any of these sums exceed 10, a turn of the general axle through a second quarter revolution causes each of those cylinders, whose number should be increased by the 1 *carried* to describe one-tenth of a revolution, and thus the number in its front becomes greater by 1 than before.

Now, on turning the general axle through a third quarter revolution, the second, fourth, &c. axles only turn, and every cylinder on each turns at the same time through as many tenths of a revolution as are expressed by the figure in front of the cylinder immediately on its right hand; there is thus made, as before, an addition of the figure previously in front of the turning cylinder and the figure on its right. A turn of the general axle through a fourth quarter revolution performs also, as before, the operation of *carrying* where necessary; and now the cylinders on the first axle towards the left present to the front the figures constituting the number which, in the required series, follows the given number. The like operations are to be performed for all the succeeding numbers.

We have it not in our power to do more than give the following very general notion of the mechanism by which these remarkable movements are produced. Behind each column of the cylinders on whose convex surfaces are the nine numerals with zero is a vertical axle, carrying as many pairs of wheels, one above another, as there are cylinders. The upper wheel in each pair acts as a driving wheel to the cylinder, and has besides, on its circumference, teeth like those of an inverted crown wheel, and both wheels are capable of being connected with or disconnected from their common axle; the lower wheel carries on its upper surface an inclined plane, and between the two wheels is a bolt with two pins which project from it, one above and the other below. By the revolution of that wheel, the inclined plane is carried under the lower pin, and thus the upper pin is enabled to enter between two teeth in the crown wheel or to disengage itself from them. Another axle, in a vertical position behind the former, carries projecting bars which, when the axle is turned by the moving power, press upon the bolts and cause the pins to move up or down as above mentioned. This engagement and release of the inverted crown wheel are the means by which the cylinder is made to describe such part of a revolution as is required; and when the cylinder is to remain at rest while those on other axles turn round, an apparatus provided for the purpose removes out of its place the bar which should press against the end of the bolt. The process of *carrying* is accomplished by a bar on the axis of a cylinder, which at a proper time comes against the extremity of a claw; and this then engages itself between the teeth of a ratchet wheel connected with the next cylinder.

In order to transfer to copper-plates the results obtained from the machine, a curvilinear bar of metal is to act on an arm of a lever so as to raise it to ten different heights, corresponding to the ten figures on the surface of each cylinder, and the opposite arm of a lever is to move an arch carrying ten punches having on them in relief, the ten characters, 1, 2, 3, &c. to 0. A bent lever is to press the punch upon the copper-plate and produce the impressions of the figure.

Various circumstances, concerning which there has been much discussion in Parliament and among men of science, have led to the suspension of the construction of this superb machine: a subject of great regret. The portion which has been already executed is now in the library of King's College, London; and it is capable of producing tables of the powers and roots of numbers not extending beyond eight places of figures.

Edmondson's Railway Ticket Machine consists of a series of multiplying wheels, with a stamping and cutting instrument in the interior. There is an index wheel whose disc is engraved with letters and numbers corresponding with those on an inner wheel. When the pasteboard material is introduced, and the machine set in motion by hand, the cards ready printed, numbered, and dated are ejected with great rapidity into a receiving box, ready packed and sorted for delivery; and the machine itself tells with unerring accuracy the number of tickets it has struck off. Machines of this kind are now extensively used at railway stations. Nothing can be more beautiful than the arithmetical accuracy with which this machine delivers and tells off an immense number of tickets in a brief period.

Baranowski's calculating or registering machine, recently introduced, is intended to facilitate many commercial operations. One form of the machine is adapted to the prompt calculation of goods per ton, cwt., or lb., or for the calculation of monies per day, month, or year. By adjusting a slide displaying the given sum, and turning a wheel, the amount per year, or week, or month is given in a marginal slide, which is developed by the operation. Mr. Baranowski has patented various modifications of his machine, adapted for numbering, stamping, and registering.

At the meeting of the British Association in 1840, the Astronomer Royal described a new calculating machine which had been invented by Mr. Fowler, to facilitate the labours of the guardians of a Poor Law district in Devonshire, in calculating the proportions in which the several divisions were to be assessed. The mechanism was much the same as in many other machines of a similar character: but there was a peculiarity in the notation adopted for the special object held in view. Instead of the common *decimal* notation, it had a *ternary* notation; that is, the digits became not tenfold but threefold more valuable in their course from right to left. Thus, in such a notation, 1 and 2 express one and two as in the common system; but 10 express (not ten, but) three, 11 express four, 12 express five, and so on. The relative number of teeth in some of the wheels of the machine would depend on which notational system is employed.

Dr. Roth's Automaton Calculator, introduced about the year 1841, has many modifications suited to the performance of different calculations. The machine for performing addition, subtraction and multiplication consists of a narrow oblong box, with a metal plate on the top, which is divided into nine indexes and semicircular notches. The first six, from left to right, serve for the numbers from hundred thousands to units: the last three are appropriated to shillings, pence, and farthings. Round each index are engraved figures, from 0 to 9; and the semicircular notches contain teeth which correspond with the figures. Under each notch is a circular hole, in which the result of the calculation appears at the end of the operation. In using the instrument, a metal point is inserted in the teeth of such figures in the indexes as are required to be brought into action, and each point is brought down to 0; the result is then read off from the circular opening in which it appears recorded. The interior mechanism consists chiefly of a simple combination of toothed wheels and springs. This machine has been used in some offices to facilitate calculations; and also as a register of the number of strokes or of rotations in machines.

A new calculating or rather numbering machine was invented and patented by Mr. Lewthwaite in 1847; for numbering railway tickets and pawnbrokers tickets, paging books, and similar purposes, and printing numbers in any consecutive or serial form. The mechanism is complicated but ingenious. The chief parts consist of figure-wheels, driving-wheels, and key-stops. The figure-wheel is a wheel with ten teeth, the outer facets or ends of which are stamped or typed with the ten digits from 0 to 9; the driving-wheel is also a wheel with ten teeth, which work between the teeth of the figure-wheel; and the key-stop is a kind of lever, one end of which catches successively in the teeth of the figure driving-wheel. If the machine were only required to number up to 9, comprising only one digit or place of figures, only one figure-wheel would be required; but if two, three, four, or five places of figures be necessary, expressing tens, hundreds, thousands, and tens of thousands, then two, three, four, or five figure-wheels would be required. There are one driving-wheel and one key-stop to each figure-wheel. All the figure-wheels are placed upon one axis, on which they revolve independently of each other; the same may be said of all the driving-wheels; and all the key-stops: each driving-wheel moving its appropriate figure-wheel, and each key-stop being similarly limited. By working a crank handle all the ten facets of the units' figure-wheel come in succession downwards, and stamp or impress their device by a small inking apparatus. When figure 9 is produced, the key-stop catches into the wheel so as to bring the tens' figure-wheel also into action; and two wheels then work together, producing the numbers 10, 11, 12, &c. At every complete revolution of the units' wheel, the tens' wheel makes one tenth of a revolution; at every complete revolution of the tens' wheel, the hundreds' wheel makes one-tenth of a revolution: and so on consecutively. It is obviously a sort of clock-work mechanism; with figures at the ends of the cogs capable of being brought into such a position as to print their results upon paper.

In 1849 a Calculating Machine was introduced before the British Association, invented by M. Slovinski, a Pole. It consists of a thin box covered by a metal plate, in which are ten circular apertures; the digits from 0 to 9 are marked near these holes, and toothed wheels are placed behind them. The upper part of the instrument is used for addition and the lower for subtraction; and the processes are performed by causing a rotation of the wheels which correspond to the digits to be added or subtracted. The multiplication instrument consists of a shallow rectangular box, containing cylinders which are made to revolve by knobs that protrude through the box. The cylinders have printed tables of figures on their circumference, and there are also index figures which appear through small holes over the axes of the cylinders. Besides these index holes there are nine other rows of holes, eight in a row, at which appear the results of the multiplication. The instrument can perform all sums up to millions multiplied by millions.

A principle of numerical reckoning is adopted in Whiffen's Registering machine, patented in 1850. It consists of a dial-plate and a system of wheel-work, to be attached to the trap-door of ship's coal weighing machines. The object is to determine the number of times that the door is opened for the discharge of coals. The same object, it is conceived, may be attained in respect to the filling of grain measures; but there is nothing essentially new in this: it is but an application of the principle of the WEIGHING MACHINE.

A remarkable apparatus for registering votes by ballot is described under VOTING MACHINE.

CALCUTTA, the seat of the supreme government of Great Britain in the East Indies, possesses great advantages for inland navigation. All kinds of foreign produce are transported on the Ganges and its affluents with great facility to the north-western parts of Hindustán over a distance of at least 1,000 miles, while the productions of the interior are received at Calcutta by the same channel. Operations have lately commenced for the construction of a railroad from Calcutta to Delhi, a distance of more than 1,000 miles, of which so much as can be constructed for 3,000,000*l.* is to be proceeded with forthwith.

The chief articles of export from Calcutta are indigo, opium, sugar, raw silk, and silk piece-goods, saltpetre, rice, hides, cotton, and cotton piece-goods. The chief articles of import are British cotton manufactures and cotton twist, bullion, copper, tin, lead, zinc, iron, and other metals; woollens, wines and spirits; hardware and cutlery; jewellery, watches, &c.; coffee, tea, books, and stationery.

The present system of communication between London and Calcutta by steam-vessels (the 'overland route') was established in 1845; but it is hoped that the time is not far distant when Calcutta will also have communication with China and with the Australian colonies. The foreign commerce of Calcutta has been already noticed under BENGAL.

CALENDERING, in the manufacturing districts, is a general name applied to the processes of smoothing, dressing, and glazing cotton and linen goods; the object being either to prepare them for the operations of the calico-printer, or to impart the last finish to the goods before they are folded and packed for the market. The earlier calenders, or calendering machines, closely resembled a common mangle in their action, but were very large and heavy, and worked by a horse-wheel, or other sufficient power; but the process was greatly improved by the invention of a machine in which the pressure is produced between cylinders, instead of between cylinders and flat surfaces, and in which, consequently, the alternating motion is got rid of, and, also, it is easier to give a uniform and equal pressure. The rollers or cylinders were formerly made of wood; they are now usually made either of paper or of cast-iron. The paper cylinders are formed by packing a great number of circular pieces of stout pasteboard upon an iron axis, and compressing them very tightly by means of iron bolts passed through them, acting upon circular end-plates of cast-iron. The surface is brought to a perfectly even and polished state by turning in a lathe. Iron rollers are made hollow, and, when necessary, heated from the inside. Where a glazed or polished surface is required on the goods to be calendered, mechanism is employed to cause two adjacent rollers to revolve with different velocities, so as to produce a rubbing action.

CALF. The rearing and fattening of calves is an important part of rural economy. In dairy districts the milk is so valuable, that the calves are got rid of as early as possible, and are purchased by the calf-dealers, who fatten them and prepare them for sale to the butcher. Calves should be fat by eight or nine weeks old; it is seldom advisable to keep them above twelve weeks, as they then consume a greater quantity of milk than can be afforded. In some countries calves are killed when only a few days old; the flesh is then soft and tasteless. In France and Switzerland no calf is allowed to be killed for sale under the age of ten days. Calves intended to be reared for grazing or the dairy are suckled for three or four days, then brought up by the pail, and gradually educted from their milk diet to one of a vegetable nature. About 30,000 calves are sold annually at Smithfield. About 14,000 calves were imported from foreign countries in 1849; this import commenced in 1842. Calf-skins form the material for one of the most valuable kinds of leather.

CALIBRE, CALIPER, or CALLIPER. The first of these words is French, and was a technical term signifying the internal diameter or *bore* of any piece of ordnance. In England it has come to signify generally the diameter of any round substance. Caliper compasses, or callipers, are compasses intended to measure the calibre or diameter of round bodies, and are formed with curved legs.

CALICO. [COTTON.]

CALICUT, a sea-port town in Hindustan, is worthy of notice as exemplifying a remarkable fact in the history of manufactures. It used to be an extensive cotton manufacturing town: our word *calico* being derived from it; but, notwithstanding Indian cotton and Hindoo labour being so cheap, cotton goods are now mostly imported. The present exports consist principally of cocoa-nuts, betel-nuts, pepper, ginger, turmeric, teak-wood, sandal-wood, cardamoms, and wax.

CALIFORNIA. There is, perhaps, no parallel in the history of nations to the rapid growth of a community in California. That which was almost a desert country four or five years ago is now a busy mart of commerce and mining.

The whole region of California comprises the wide stretch of Pacific coast from Oregon in the north to Mexico in the south; but that portion which now attracts commercial attention is the river district, whereof the outlet is at San Francisco, in 38° N. lat., 122° W. long. Here, about the time that California was assigned by treaty from Mexico to the United States, gold was first discovered—unless, indeed, as is supposed, the Jesuits were aware of its existence there some generations back. The gold is so loosely mixed up with sand and sediment in the bed and the banks of the Sacramento and other rivers, that the grains and small particles are without difficulty separated from the impurities. For a short time the secret was retained by a few; but no sooner did the news spread abroad than a gold mania sprang up. The Mexicans, from the hitherto insignificant town of St. Francisco, the native Indians of the country, and the hardy trappers and backwoodsmen from the United States, all rushed to seize the golden treasure. After a time the Sandwich Islanders heard the news, and steered over the Pacific to get a share of the riches. Vessels came to St. Francisco from different ports; and the seamen, abandoning their vessels to the mercy of chance, ran off to the 'diggings' and became gold-hunters. Soon the tidings reached the United States, and parties and companies set forth to El Dorado, the golden land. Some took the perilous inland route across the Rocky Mountains; some adopted the tedious sail round Cape Horn; but the majority have availed themselves of the Panama route. The tens of thousands who thus went, having no other object than to get gold, had neither means nor inclination to grow their own food nor to manufacture their own necessaries; and hence arose a field of enterprise which the merchants of England and of the United States did not neglect. Valuable cargoes were transmited to St. Francisco to be there sold in exchange for the gold-dust; and as such transactions could not be carried on without some kind of commercial machinery, St. Francisco speedily put on those features which distinguish a busy port.

So rapid have been these transactions that they have scarcely yet been narrated in an authentic form. It would not be safe to say how much gold-dust has left California, nor how many adventurers have arrived there, for both have been exaggerated. St. Francisco has been nearly destroyed by fire three or four times during its brief existence; yet it rises from the ashes, after each conflagration, with increased vigour and importance. We may simply jot down two or three facts which serve to illustrate the present position of this remarkable place.

During one week in 1850 gold-dust to the value of three million dollars was shipped and exported from St. Francisco. In August of the same year the monthly shipment was about 8,000,000 dollars, of which gold-dust to the value of 3,000,000 dollars was transmitted to England, the rest being consigned chiefly to the United States. On September 15, 1850, there were in that port no less than 684 vessels of 181,021 tons, belonging to twenty-one different nations; 496 vessels belonged to the United States, 86 to England, all other countries much smaller numbers; some of the vessels, small in size, had crossed the whole breadth of the Pacific from Australia and New Zealand, with the view of exchanging their produce for gold-dust. In the first two weeks of October, in the same year, 94 vessels arrived at St. Francisco, besides the mail steamers which ply between that town and Panama, and besides 10 other steamers which now ply between St. Francisco and the smaller Californian ports. Between 40,000 and 50,000 letters now cross the isthmus of Panama every month *en route* from the Atlantic nations to California, and an equal number in the opposite direction.

As might reasonably be expected under such circumstances, recklessness and mad speculation have done much injury at California; but the United States government has shown energy in establishing steady and useful laws and institutions in its newly-acquired territory; and, whatever may be said of the *Industry* of all nations, the *Commerce* of all nations is likely to be instructively illustrated at California.

CALLAO, a small sea-port town in Peru, derives all its commercial importance from being the port for Lima, which is seven miles distant. The Peruvian ships in 1840 amounted to 57 (6637 tons); in the same year the custom duties on British goods, chiefly cottons and linens, amounted to 240,000*l.*; and the total value of British manufactures sent to Peru through Callao and Valparaiso was 1,230,000*l.* The exports from Callao consist of bark, bullion, specie, copper in ore and in bars, raw cotton, hides, &c. The value of the exports to Europe and the United States in 1840 was 948,346*l.*, being an increase of 315,476*l.* on the preceding year. There has since been a small annual increase in these quantities.

CALOMEL. [MERCURY.]

CALOPHYLLUM is the name of a genus of trees from which much useful oil is procured. The *Calophyllum Inophyllum* is a native of the East Indies, and often attains a height of 90 or 100 feet. It has large handsome leaves like those of a water-lily, snow-white fragrant flowers, and a fruit about the size of a walnut. The nuts afford a fixed oil, which is expressed and used for burning in lamps. Another species, the *Calaba-tree*, attains a height of 60 feet, and is a native of the Caribee Islands. It has white sweet-scented flowers, and a green fruit something like the Cornelian cherry, which contains a white solid kernel. An oil is expressed from the seed for domestic uses and for burning in lamps. The timber is used for various purposes, especially for staves and cask-headings.

CALOTYPE. The patent for Mr. Fox Talbot's Calotype, obtained in 1841, contained specifications relating to many departments of photographic operation; but the proper calotypic process is what we are here concerned with. The operation comprises three stages—to prepare the paper; to produce the negative picture; and to produce the positive picture. The best and smoothest writing-paper is washed on one side with a camel-hair pencil dipped in a solution of 100 grains of crystallised nitrate of silver in six ounces of distilled water. The paper is dried slowly, and then dipped for a minute or two in a solution of 500 grains of iodide of potassium in a pint of water; it is then dipped in water and dried. Immediately before using, this paper is washed on the prepared side with a solution of 100 grains of nitrate of silver in two ounces of distilled water, combined with one-fourth of its volume of acetic acid, and an equal quantity of tincture of galls or of a saturated solution of crystallised gallic acid. The paper is dried a third time, and is then ready for use. In taking the calotype picture, the paper is placed in a camera obscura, where it speedily receives the image, which sometimes requires to be brought out by a wash of gallo-nitrate of silver. To fix the image, the paper is dipped into water, partly dried with blotting-paper, and washed with a solution of 100 grains of bromide of potassium in 8 or 10 ounces of water, after which it is again washed and dried. The image or picture thus produced is a *negative* one, the lights and darks being reversed. To produce a *positive* picture from this, a second sheet of calotype paper, or of common photographic paper, is placed in contact with the picture; a board is placed beneath, and a plate of glass above them, and all are screwed closely together. On placing them in the sunshine for some time, a picture with the lights and shadows in their natural position is produced on the second paper; and this duplicate is to be fixed in the same manner as the original picture. Many calotype positive pictures may be taken from one negative picture.

In another method, Mr. Talbot produces a positive calotype at once, without the intervention of a negative one. A sheet of calotype paper is exposed to the daylight until its surface is slightly browned. It is then dipped into a solution of iodide of potassium; on being taken out of this solution the paper is dipped into water and partially dried. It is next placed in the camera, where, in the course of five or ten minutes, the image becomes impressed upon it. The paper, when removed from the camera, is washed with gallo-nitrate of silver, and warmed. A positive picture then makes its appearance on the surface.

CALUMET, the name given by the North American Indians to a pipe for smoking tobacco. The calumet, or pipe of peace, is a large tobacco pipe, with a bowl of polished marble, and a stem two feet and a half long, made of strong reed, adorned with feathers and locks of women's hair. When it is used in treaties and embassies, the Indians fill the calumet with the best tobacco, and, presenting it to those with whom they have concluded any great affair, smoke out of it after them.

CALVADOS, a department in France, which formerly constituted part of Normandy, is a great cider district, the annual produce being about 30,000,000 gallons. The best kind is that made in the Auge district; it will keep for years and contains a large proportion of alcohol. Melons, haricots, onions, &c., are extensively cultivated. The department contains about 1,000 wind and water mills, 150 foundries and furnaces, and about as many factories. Building stone, marble, slate, brick, potter's clay, and iron, are found. Marl abounds in the arrondissement of Lisieux and Pont-l'Evêque, and is used for manure. Coal mines are worked at Littry, in which several steam engines are employed.

The chief industrial products of the department are cotton and woollen yarn, fine and coarse woollen cloths, linen, flannel, blankets, shawls, calicoes, lace, porcelain and cutlery. Throughout the department the manufacture of lace alone gives employment to 50,000 persons, and the value of the lace annually exported amounts to many millions of francs. The department contains several paper-mills, sugar refineries, tanneries, oil-mills, and establishments for the manufacture of chemical products and bleaching linen. The commerce consists of its industrial products, together with horses, fat cattle, butter, cheese, poultry, cider, honey, spirits distilled from cider, clover seed, hemp, wood, oil, &c. The imports are iron, wool, raw cotton, hides, and colonial produce. Great quantities of lobsters, oysters, and other fish, are taken along the coast and conveyed to the markets of Paris and of the interior.

CAMBOGE, or GAMBOGE. This gum-resin was introduced into Europe by Clusius about 1603. From the bruised leaves and young branches of *Stalagmites cambogioides* flows a yellow juice, which is received in cocoanut shells or earthen vessels; it is then allowed to thicken, and afterwards formed into rolls; this is the finest sort called the *Pipe Camboge* of Siam. A portion is formed into round cakes, which are either entire or have a hole in the centre; this is the *Cake Camboge* of Siam.

At the ordinary temperature of the air, camboge, from whatever source obtained, has little smell, but when heated gives out a very peculiar one. Taken into the mouth it has scarcely any perceptible taste, but upon being chewed for some time it causes a sharp and somewhat acrid feeling, ending in a sweet sensation, accompanied with dryness in the mouth. It excites afterwards a flow of saliva, which is coloured yellow. It is almost entirely soluble in alcohol, and is not precipitated from solution by the addition of water. With water it forms an emulsion, in which the resin is kept suspended by the gum. It is soluble in the alkalies. The resin, which forms three-fourths of its weight, may be considered its active principle.

Camboge is much used in medicine, especially in quack medicines; but it is more extensively used as a pigment.

CAMBRIC. This is one of the numerous varieties of flax or linen manufactures, which derived its name from having been first made at Cambray. It bears much the same relation to linen that muslin does to calico, being a very fine and thin fabric. Scotch cambric, now largely manufactured, is a kind of imitation cambric, made from fine hard-twisted cotton. The French material called *batiste* is a sort of Scotch cambric, to which dyes and printed colours are applied.

In 1848 about 33,000 pieces of French cambric and lawn were imported. In 1849 the quantity sank to 29,000 pieces.

CAMBRIDGE is so much more closely

associated with education than with trade, that we can have little to say concerning it in this place. It has however a considerable trade in coals and grain; and a large quantity of butter is conveyed from Norfolk and the Isle of Ely to London, where it obtains the name of Cambridge butter.

CAMBRIDGESHIRE is so purely an agricultural county (except in relation to the straw-plait manufacture, and one or two others), that we need merely say a few words concerning its fens. When these fens are drained [Bedford Level], the first operation is to pare, by means of a paring plough, the surface on which coarse grass and sedge are growing in a matted state. The sods are then burnt, and reduced to a carbonised mass, which, when cool, is spread over the ground. This is immediately ploughed in, and the land is sown with cole-seed or rape, of which an abundant crop is invariably produced. The cole is fed off with sheep, the land ploughed once, and oats are sown, which produce astonishing crops; after which the land is available for the rotation culture. Rape-cake is much used as manure. The uncultivated fens yield turf, reeds, and osiers.

CAMEL. The camel is an important adjunct to trade and commerce in tropical sandy regions. The organization of this animal proves its adaptation for the arid deserts over which it is destined to travel. The pads, or sole-cushions of the spreading feet, divided into two toes without being externally separated, which buoy up, as it were, the whole bulk with their expansive elasticity from sinking in the sand, on which the animal advances with silent step—the nostrils so formed that the animal can close them at will, so as to exclude the drift sand and the parching simoom—the beetling brow, and long lashes which fringe the upper lid, so as to screen the eyes from the glare of the sun—the cleft prehensile upper lip, and the powerful upper incisor teeth, for browsing on the dry tough prickly shrubs of the desert—the hunch acting as a reservoir of nutriment against a time of long abstinence—and the assemblage of water tanks in the stomach—these are characteristics without which the 'ship of the desert' could not render his invaluable services to man.

The Bactrian, or *two-humped* camel, occurs throughout Central Asia; it is the patient, laborious, and willing slave of the Turcomans, travelling over sandy deserts, and administering to the wants of a wandering people. The Arabian, or *single-humped* camel, or dromedary, is spread through Egypt, Arabia, Syria, North Africa, Persia, India, &c., and its history is interwoven with that of the patriarchs of old, nor is it now less important than in those early days. Caravans of camels still traverse the desert, conveying merchandise. The load of a camel is from 500 to 600 lbs., and it will move at the rate of nearly 3 miles an hour, regularly as clock-work, day after day, for eight hours daily. It lies down resting on the callosities of its breast and limbs, to be loaded and unloaded. In the oriental caravans some of the animals are loaded with water skins, some with merchandise, others carry the food and necessaries of the pilgrims and their own provender, and others are mounted by riders.

The camel is not only serviceable as a beast of burden; its milk and flesh are both in requisition, especially the former. Of its hair the Arab weaves clothing, and even tents; his belt and sandals are the produce of its hide; and the dung affords him fuel. From the soot, sublimated in closed vessels, is procured sal ammoniac, formerly imported into this country from Egypt. Camel's hair is imported into this country for the manufacture of pencils for the painter; that from Persia is the best. There are three qualities, black, red, and gray; the black is most valuable, next the red; the gray is very inferior.

CAMEO, or CAMAIEU, is a gem worked in *rilievo*. The art of engraving on stone is of high antiquity; but it was for the most part confined to *intaglio*, or indenting. It has been supposed that the Etruscans had the art of engraving hard stones before it was known to the Greeks; many engraved stones, however, that are called Etruscan are doubtless early Greek, as may be inferred from their subjects.

The age of Augustus is remarkable for the excellence of the gem-engravers who were then living. One of the finest camei preserved in the collections of Europe is the Apotheósis of Augustus, in the collection at Vienna. In the French collection, the sardonyx of Tiberius is one of the best known. We possess in this country some camei of first-rate excellence, but they are chiefly in private collections.

The workers in cameo not only exercised their skill in the cutting or engraving, but also in so arranging their subject and the composition of its details as to make the different colours or zones of the stones answer for parts of the design. The ancients were so partial to this variously coloured work, that they even imitated the material in glass; and we possess in this country one of the most beautiful specimens of their ability in the Barberini, or Portland Vase, now in the British Museum.

At the decline of the Roman Empire, gem-engraving fell with the other arts; and it was not till a late period that the taste and munificence of the Florentine family of Medici caused its revival in Italy. It was much encouraged in the fifteenth century, and the sixteenth century can also boast of several very distinguished artists in this class. In the succeeding century there was a considerable falling off, but in the eighteenth the art again rose.

Rome is now the chief seat of the art of cameo-cutting. There are two kinds: those cut in *pietra dura*, or hard stone, and those cut in shell. The stones most prized for this purpose are oriental onyx and sardonyx—provided they have at least two different colours in parallel layers. The value of the stone is greatly increased if it has four or five differently coloured parallel layers, provided that the layers are so thin as to assist in marking the device of the cameo. For example, a specimen of stone which had four parallel layers might be useful for a cameo of Minerva; where the ground would be (say) dark gray, the face light, the bust and helmet black, and the crest over the helmet brown or gray. All such camei are wrought by a lapidary's lathe with pointed instruments of steel, and by means of diamond dust. Shell cameos are cut from large shells found on the African and Brazilian coasts, and generally show two layers, one white, and the other either pale coffee colour or deep reddish orange. The subject is cut with small steel chisels out of the white portion of the shell. The gem camei are far more costly than those made of shells.

At the Mediæval Exhibition of 1850, very beautiful specimens of the cameo were exhibited in sardonyx and blood stone.

Camei to the value of 6,502*l.* were imported from France in 1847.

CA'MERA LU'CIDA and CAMERA OBSCU'RA (*light and dark chambers*) are names given to two methods, very like in principle, of throwing images of external objects upon a plane or curved surface, for the purpose of drawing or amusement.

The *Camera Obscura* now in use has, occasionally, the form of a box. In front is a sliding tube, carrying a convex lens, through which the light from distant objects passes to a mirror at the opposite extremity of the box: the mirror is inclined to the horizon at an angle of 45 degrees, and from thence the light is reflected upwards to a glass plate in a horizontal position. The rays in the pencils converge at the upper surface of this plate, which, on that surface only, is ground rough, and thus the images of distant objects are visible upon it, a shade over the plate preventing the direct light from interfering with them.

A camera obscura for exhibition is generally made in a room with a conical roof and an aperture at the top. Above this aperture is a revolving plane mirror inclined at 45°, and reflecting pencils downwards. A convex lens causes these pencils to converge upon a surface of plaster of Paris, properly curved. The mirror revolves about a vertical axis, thus allowing all the compass points of a landscape to be successively thrown on the surface.

Portable camera obscuras are often made in a similar manner, the mirror and lens being in a sliding case at the top of a pyramidal box, and the image being received on paper laid at the bottom. Apertures on one side of the box allow the spectator to see the image and introduce a hand for the purpose of drawing on the paper.

A camera obscura is an indispensable aid in most forms of photographic operation.

The *Camera Lucida* was invented by Dr. Wollaston. It consists of a metal stand supporting a glass prism, of which one angle is 135°. The action of the instrument is such, that when rays of light fall horizontally on one side of the prism, they suffer reflection within the glass, and are thrown upwards to the eye through an opening in a plate which excludes all except the end of the prism, and a part of a sheet of paper or other flat surface placed beneath the prism. Hence the image of an object is thrown towards the visible part of the paper, and, the eye viewing both the image and the sheet of paper (with different parts of the pupil, however, which creates a difficulty in using this instrument), the observer is enabled to trace the object upon the paper.

The image of the distant object must be made to coincide with that of the paper; and, for this purpose, since, except when the object is very remote, the rays in the pencil are in a divergent state, a convex lens is interposed between the prism and the paper.

CAMP, ROMAN. In a Roman camp the standard was fixed in the centre, and around this, within a space of 200 feet each way, was the prætorium or place of the general's quarters, on one side of which was the forum, and on the other the space allotted to the stores of the army, with the quarters of the Quæstor, or officer who had charge of the military chest. Further, towards the right and left were the cavalry and infantry, forming the general's body-guard, and the volunteers in his service. This line, which in length may be estimated at 1650 feet, constituted the breadth of the camp. In front of the line were the tents of the legionary tribunes and of those officers among the allies who had corresponding rank. Before the tribunes' tents was the principal street, 100 feet wide, stretching across the camp; and beyond this, extending about 1050 feet towards the front, were the quarters of the soldiers. These were divided into two parts by a street 50 feet wide, which ran from the prætorium to the head of the camp. The streets divided the various bodies of soldiers.

Such was the order of encampment for a consular army, consisting of two legions besides the allies; its whole depth might be about 1700 feet; and there was round the encampment a clear interval 200 feet broad, between the tents and the entrenchments. These consisted of a rampart of earth and stones, and a ditch, through which were four gates or entrances: the Prætorian gate, in front of the camp, opposite the Prætorium; the Decuman gate, at the back of the camp, and a gate at each end of the Principia or principal street.

CAMPANI'LE, an Italian term signifying a tower for bells. The word is derived from *campána*, 'a bell.' Many of the Italian churches have these towers or campanili separated from the body of the church. Among the most remarkable are those of Cremona, Florence, Ravenna, Padua, Bologna, and Pisa. The leaning tower of Pisa is a campanile; it is 150 feet high, and 13 feet out of the perpendicular. The campanile of Cremona is the highest in Italy, having an elevation of 395 feet. The campanile of Florence, which is 267 feet high, was constructed by Giotto in 1324, and is considered the most elegant campanile in Italy; the façade of the tower is in the Gothic style, mixed with somewhat of the Italian taste in architecture, which soon after prevailed over the Gothic. The cathedral at Seville has a fine campanile 350 feet high, which was built in 1568 by Guever the Moor.

CAMPA'NULA. Many plants belonging to this genus are usefully applied. The *campanula edúlis* is a native of Arabia Felix; its root is thick and sapid, and contains a considerable quantity of starch; it is on this account frequently eaten by children, as are the roots of many other species. Of the *campanula rotundifolia*, or *blue-bell*, the juice of the flowers makes a very good blue ink, and when mixed with alum a green one. The roots of this species also may be eaten. The *campanula rapunculus* is much cultivated in France and Italy, and sometimes in Britain, for the sake of the roots, which are boiled tender, and eaten hot with sauce, or cold with vinegar and pepper.

CAMPHINE LAMPS. Camphine is very pure spirit of turpentine, obtained by the distillation of common turpentine. Turpentine is very cheap in the United States, and camphine is there much used for lighting; and when the duty on turpentine was reduced in England a few years ago, the use of camphine became familiarized among us—one of the many proofs how much influence fiscal laws have upon manufactures.

The light produced from camphine is very pure and brilliant; and the modes of applying the liquid to this purpose have given rise to various forms of lamp which are now familiar; such as the 'Vesta,' the 'Imperial,' the 'Victoria,' the 'Gem,' the 'Paragon,' and many others. All lamp-oils contain some oxygen, which neutralizes a part of the hydrogen and carbon; and also some oxide or other substance which damps the brilliancy of the flame; whereas rectified camphine, being composed almost wholly of hydrogen and carbon, contains nothing but what is susceptible of combustion. The best camphine is obtained, as stated, from turpentine; but tar and naphtha, if subjected to careful distillation and rectification, will yield very fair camphine.

In using camphine for lamps, certain precautions are necessary. Camphine is so extremely inflammable, that the arrangements of a common oil-lamp would not be available without danger of accident. All the camphine lamps present in common a reservoir, generally of glass, placed between the supporting pillar and the burner; the spirit is contained in this reservoir, and a cotton wick dips down into it. The chief points in which the various camphine lamps differ are in the arrangement for admitting air to the flame. In Young's 'Vesta' lamp, the cotton wick hangs down from the burner into the camphine, so as to supply itself by capillary attraction, without the intervention of any metallic or heat-conducting substance.

As a question of art-manufactures, many camphine lamps are now made of very elegant forms. The last Birmingham Exposition was rich in specimens; and we may reasonably expect that the Great Exhibition of 1851 will not be deficient in this respect.

A very elegant application has been made of the gas produced from camphine. The gas can be made with a small apparatus, and with little difficulty; and the jet which it produces is very pure and brilliant. The camphine is heated in a retort set in a small furnace; and the gas, escaping from the retort, is purified by passing through certain liquids. This gas has been found useful for lighting railway stations and other buildings, too far distant from ordinary gas-works.

CAMPHOR is the stearopten (or one of the principles arising from the separation of the volatile oil) of two trees—the one *Cinnamomum camphora*, a native of Japan, China, and Cochin China; the other, *Dipterocarpus camphora*, a native of Borneo and Sumatra. From these it is procured by different processes. It exists in every part—root, stem, branches, and leaves—of the Cinnamomum camphora, which is chopped into pieces sufficiently small to be thrown into iron vessels: these vessels are afterwards covered with earthern hoods, in which are placed rice-straw and rushes, heat being subsequently gradually applied. The camphor is volatilised, and afterwards condenses on the straws, rushes, &c. This, after being purified from the intermixture of straws, is found in commerce under the name of crude camphor.

From the Dipterocarpus camphora it is not procured by distillation, but exists in a solid form in the stem of the tree. In that part of the stem which should be occupied by the pith it is found along with camphor-oil, and on the trunk being split open the camphor is found in the centre, in pieces about a foot long, which is much prized and used in the East, but is not sent to Europe.

Camphor is an organic substance of a peculiar kind, representing the volatile oils in a solid state. It is so volatile, that on exposure to the air it is entirely volatilised, and leaves no residuum. It is insoluble in water, but is easily dissolved in spirit, is inflammable, and has an aromatic smell and taste. It is much employed in medicine.

Two substances, called *camphor oil* and *camphoric acid*, are obtained from camphor: they are not much employed.

CAMWOOD, is a red wood, the colouring matter of which is similar to that of Nicaragua or peach wood. It is used in dyeing, and also in cabinet work. It is brought chiefly from Sierra Leone.

CANADA. This large country, with its magnificent lakes, cannot fail to rise steadily in commercial importance. The mineral resources are immense, but till very recently they have been almost wholly neglected. Marbles and serpentine are quite common. Plumbago, ores of antimony, lead, iron, and copper are frequently met with. The mountains north of the Saguenay abound in iron to such an extent as to influence the mariner's compass. The iron mines of St. Maurice have long been celebrated for the excellence of their yield, and metal not at all inferior is cheaply produced at Charlotteville near Lake Erie, and at the Marmora works about 32 miles N. of the Bay of Quinté. The dreary wastes northward of Lake Superior contain stores of copper, perhaps unsurpassed any where in the world. At the Coppermine river 300 miles from the Sault de St. Marie the metal occurs in great masses in a pure state. Gold, silver, and tin have also been discovered in the same region. The northern and western shores of Ontario abound in salt springs, some of which (Stony Creek and St. Catherine's) are very productive. The north shore of Lake Erie exhibits immense beds of gypsum which are quarried for agricultural purposes.

Copper mining is now being prosecuted with great energy on the banks of Lake Superior. If the accounts recently received should prove correct, Canada will far excel every other part of the world in the richness of the copper ore; indeed it seems as if the produce should scarcely be termed ore: it is almost pure native copper.

The variety of trees found in the vast Canadian forests is astonishing, and it is supposed that many kinds still remain unknown. Of all these none is more beautiful and useful than the maple, the adopted emblem of Canadian nationality. Its timber is valuable for many purposes, and large quantities of excellent sugar are made from its sap. The other forest trees most prevalent are beech, birch, elm, bass, ash, oak, pine, hickory, butternut, balsam, hazel, hemlock, cherry, cedar, cypress, fir, poplar, sycamore, whitewood, willow, and spruce. Timber and ashes, the raw produce of the forests, constitute the chief exports of the province. An immense quantity of oak and pine is annually sent down to Montreal and Quebec. The American ashes contain a larger proportion of pure potash than those of Dantzic or Russia.

The total breadth of land under culture in Lower Canada in 1844 was 2,802,317 acres. The number of inhabited houses in Lower Canada in the same year was 108,794; the number building 1652; vacant 4115. The following particulars, given in the returns of that year, throw some further light upon the habits and occupations of the people:—Lbs. of maple sugar 2,272,457; number of taverns, 1052; stores where spirituous liquors are sold, 808; grist mills, 422; oatmeal mills, 108; barley mills, 45; saw mills, 911; oil mills, 14; fulling mills, 153; carding mills, 169; threshing mills, 469; paper mills, 8; iron works, 99; triphammers, 18; nail factories, 6; distilleries, 36; breweries, 30; tanneries, 335; pot and pearl ash factories, 540; other factories,

86. There were in Lower Canada in 1844, 469,851 cattle, 146,729 horses, 602,821 sheep, and 197,985 swine.

In Upper Canada in 1848 the number of acres occupied was 8,613,591. The lands returned as under cultivation were 1,780,152 acres arable, and 766,768 pasture, or 2,546,920 in all. The crops of Upper Canada in 1847 were—Wheat, 7,558,773 bushels, (an increase of more than 50 per cent. in five years): barley, rye, and buckwheat, 1,394,593; oats, 7,055,730; maize, 1,137,555; potatoes, 4,751,331; peas, 1,753,846. In 1848 there were in Upper Canada 565,845 neat cattle, 151,389 horses. 484,241 hogs, 833,807 sheep. The average annual yield of maple sugar in Upper Canada is 4,140,667 lbs., which is very nearly 6 lbs. for each inhabitant, no portion of this produce being exported. There were sent to market in 1848—butter, 3,380,406 lbs.; cheese, 668,357 lbs.; beef or pork, 99,231 barrels. In the census returns of 1848 are enumerated 553 grist mills, 96 oat and barley mills, 1584 saw mills, 239 fulling mills, 138 distilleries, 100 breweries, 354 tanneries, 1,200 asheries, 67 woollen factories, 10 shingle factories, 105 foundries.

From the United Kingdom Canada receives coals, metals, cordage, East India produce, and the various kinds of British manufactures; from the British West Indies, sugar, molasses, coffee, rum, and hard woods; from the United States, beef and pork, biscuit, rice, and tobacco. The exports of Canada are—to the United Kingdom, pot and pearl ashes, wheat and flour, and timber; to the West Indies, beef and pork, beer, grain, and flour; to the United States, forest produce, wheat, flour, butter, wool, live stock, &c. The total exports of the colony in 1847 amounted to 2,612,852*l*.

The exports of British and Irish produce and manufactures to Canada, in 1849, amounted to the large sum of 1,324,031*l*. It may be interesting to note some of the chief items:—

Apparel	£111,772.
Cotton goods	357,626.
Hardware and cutlery ...	64,470.
Iron and steel	208,391.
Linen goods	52,527.
Silk goods	50,624.
Woollen goods	219,630.

The commercial prosperity of Canada will be greatly increased by the Great Western Railway, now being constructed from Detroit to Niagara: a portion of 75 miles, from Hamilton to London, is under contract; and the works have been pushed forward with great energy during 1850.

In no part of our colonies has the Great Exhibition of 1851 been welcomed with more heartiness than in Canada. As a sort of test of their manufacturing ability, the colonists held an Industrial Exhibition of their own at Montreal, in October 1850, at which the manufactures filled two vast rooms. Hardware, cutlery, cottons, woollens, linens, silks, earthenware, and other goods of Canadian manufacture; corn, beef, pork, butter, cheese, maple-sugar, honey, hams, of Canadian growth; a veneer of bird's-eye maple, 100 feet long, sawn from a single log; soft and beautiful leather made from porpoise-skins; clear and bright oil obtained from the same animal—these were some of the specimens in the Montreal Exhibition. Mr. Logan, a Canadian geologist, has been employed to classify specimens of all the principal minerals found in that country. Household furniture, of Canadian forest-wood, is to be transmitted to London. During the last week in 1850 the ship *Pearl* arrived in London, bringing the first consignment of Canadian specimens for the Great Exhibition, in 107 packages.

CANAL. Ancient Egypt was intersected with canals, which were used both for navigation and irrigation; and in China they have been in use from before the Christian æra. The first made in Europe appears to have been that cut by Xerxes across the low isthmus of Athos. The Romans made canals in Italy and in the Low Countries, about the outlets of the Rhine, and probably also in Britain. In modern Europe canal making commenced in Lombardy between the 11th and 13th centuries, and in Holland, where they may be compared for number with the public roads of this country, in the 12th century.

The origin of canal navigation in this country dates from 1755, when an act of parliament was passed for constructing a canal about 11 miles long from the mouth of Sankey-brook, on the Mersey, to Gerrard's Bridge and St. Helen's. The next works of this kind are noticed under BRIDGEWATER, DUKE OF; and BRINDLEY.

During the remainder of the 18th and the earlier years of the 19th centuries, the construction of navigable canals was carried on with vigour, until they were made in England alone to an aggregate length of more than 2200 miles. In conjunction with new canals, many rivers have been artificially rendered navigable, so that it has been asserted that no spot in England, south of Durham, is more than 15 miles distant from water communication. The introduction and rapid extension of railways has almost entirely put a stop to the construction of canals, and in several instances canals either have been, or are about to be, drained and converted into railways; but it is by no means indisputably proved that the newer and more rapid mode of transit can compete with canals in the transit of heavy goods, especially as competition has led to a very great reduction in canal charges, and to improved modes of conducting the carrying trade.

In cutting a canal where the soil consists of sand, gravel, loose rock, or other matter through which the water will percolate, the floor and sides of the canal must be covered with an impervious lining, called *puddling*, which generally consists of light loam and coarse sand or fine gravel, well mixed with water, and applied, in a semi-fluid state, in three or more successive strata, each carefully worked into the preceding, to the thickness of about three feet. The puddling is then covered with common soil to the depth of 18 or 24 inches. Strong clay is not suitable for puddling, on account of its tendency to shrink and crack, nor is any soil containing roots or other organic matter which would decay and leave cavities. As a further security against the escape of water, *mud* or *puddle-ditches* or *gutters* are sometimes formed along the sides of the canal. They are ditches about three feet wide, dug perpendicularly to a depth below the bottom of the canal, and gradually filled with puddling stuff to a few inches above the top water-line. When the banks are raised above the natural level, if the soil be of a porous nature, their stability will be aided by covering them with turf.

Canals are supplied with water from springs and rivulets, and reservoirs are occasionally necessary. Steam-engines may in some cases be indispensable for raising water to supply these reservoirs; and many arrangements are necessary with the owners of mills and others affected by any interference with the waters from which a supply may be taken. Puddling, embanking, and other engineering operations may be needed in improving the streams adopted as feeders; and in some cases brick culverts or iron pipes may have to be used to conduct the supply. Where the feeders have to be conveyed across a valley or another stream, cast-iron pipes may be found very advantageous.

When the canal passes through an uneven country it must frequently be conducted in a very tortuous course to maintain the level; and deep cuttings, tunnels, embankments and arched or iron aqueducts must be introduced where the level of the canal is unavoidably much below or above the natural surface. Canal tunnels are usually of smaller transverse dimensions than those found on railways, though this is not invariably the case; but many are of great length. That at Blisworth, on the Grand Junction Canal, is 3080 yards, or a mile and three quarters long; that on the Thames and Medway Canal, which has been recently converted into a railway tunnel, is about two miles and one-eighth; one on the Leominster Canal at Pensax is 3850 yards, or nearly two miles and a quarter; and the Marsden tunnel, on the Huddersfield Canal, is 5451 yards, or upwards of three miles long. The tunnels or excavations on the Duke of Bridgewater's Canal, which is conducted by several channels into the heart of a coal mine, are said to be altogether eighteen miles long. Telford introduced, for situations where a canal is greatly elevated above the surface, aqueducts formed of cast-iron plates screwed together by means of flanches, and supported upon piers or pillars of masonry. The first aqueduct of this kind was that for carrying the Shrewsbury Canal across the Fern valley at Long Mill; but the most extensive and remarkable is the Pont-y Cysylte, which carries the Ellesmere and Chester Canal over the Dee at an elevation of about 125 feet above the bed of the river. The trough or aqueduct is 988 feet long, 20 feet wide, and 6 feet deep, and it is supported by 19 pairs of stone pillars, 52 feet apart.

Unavoidable changes of level are usually overcome by *locks*, the invention of which has been disputed by the Dutch and the Venetians. Leonardo da Vinci is said to have applied them in 1497 to the Milanese canals. A lock is a chamber of masonry constituting the bed of the canal between the upper and lower levels, at the point where it is desired to transfer boats from one to the other, and is furnished with gates at each end, and with sluices communicating with both the levels. When a boat is to be passed from the lower to the upper level, the water is suffered to escape from the lock until its surface coincides with the lower level. The gates at the lower end are then opened, and the boat is floated into the lock. The sluices which communicate with the upper level being then opened, the level of the water in the lock is raised until it coincides with the upper level of the canal. The upper gates are then opened, and the boat is floated out of the lock. The operation of lowering a boat is precisely the reverse. Every time the operation is performed, a quantity of water, equal to the contents of the lock, is lost from the upper level. To make this loss as small as possible, locks are made only just wide enough to admit the widest boats used on the canal; and in some cases two are formed side by side, with a communication between them, so that, whenever one has to be emptied, one-half of its contents may be transferred to the adjoining one, and saved for a future occasion. This arrangement also saves time. Inclined planes, up and down which the boats may be conveyed on trucks or sledges, have in a few cases been used as substitutes for locks.

The usual mode of moving boats upon a canal is to *tow* or draw them by means of a long rope, by horses driven along a raised *towing-path* formed along one bank of the canal. To save expense, the older canal bridges were made so small that it was necessary to detach the horses on coming to them, and to get the boats through by manual labour, or by mere impetus; but on the best modern canals the arches are made large enough to include a towing-path as well as a water-way. The same remark applies to tunnels. In several of the older tunnels the boats were forced through by the laborious and dangerous process of *legging*, which was performed by men lying upon their backs on the boat, and thrusting their feet against the sides or roof of the tunnel. In some cases, ropes or chains worked by steam-engines have been used for hauling boats through. The attempts made to propel canal-boats by steam-power, have been of questionable success. Paddle-wheels of every kind disturb the water so much as to injure the banks. In 1844 screw propellers were for the first time used on canals in Scotland, on the Union Canal. The steamer was a tug-boat, capable of drawing eight or ten heavily laden barges: it had two Archimedean screws on either side of the bow. A steam tug was tried on the Grand Junction Canal in 1845, provided with a submerged propeller invented by Captain W. H. Taylor, differing somewhat from the screw-propeller. It produced scarcely any wave when going four miles through the water, and gave promise of being a useful means of traction for goods traffic. On the Glasgow, Paisley, and Androssan Canal fly-boats for passengers, drawn by horses at a considerable speed, have been run successfully: but, amidst conflicting statements, it is difficult to decide whether in any case the ordinary walking pace of a horse can be exceeded on a canal without a greater loss of power than would attend the like increase of speed upon a railway or perfect road. From experiments made while railways were yet in their infancy, it would appear that, while at a very slow pace heavy goods may be conveyed much more economically on a canal than in any other way, the economy turns in favour of a railway where the velocity exceeds four miles per hour, while at high velocities the economy of the canal disappears even as compared with an ordinary road.

Mr. Watson patented in 1839 a form of canal boat which could be lengthened or shortened according to the length of the lock which it had to pass through. It was divided into two or more separate and independent water-tight portions, connected together by means of hinges or coupling links and bolts; so that they might either be separated and placed side by side, or the ends turned round and doubled back without being unhinged or uncoupled.

A singular mode of ascending and descending canals was proposed by the late Mr. Smith of Deanston, as a means of saving expense in locks and gates at changes of level. He proposed to divide the canal into a series of basins, the water levels of which should be from 12 to 18 inches above each other. The extremity of each basin is so contracted as to permit only the free passage of a boat; and at this spot is placed a single gate, hinged to a sill across the bottom; the head pointing at a given angle across the stream, and the lateral faces pressing against rabbits in the masonry. The gate is constructed of buoyant materials, or made hollow so as to float and be held up by the pressure of the water in the higher level. On the top of the gate is a roller to precipitate the passage of boats. When a boat is required to pass from a higher to a lower level, the bow end, which must be armed with an inclined projection, depresses the gate to as great a degree as the depth of the immersion of the boat, and as much water escapes as can pass between its sides and the walls of the contracted part of the basin. The same action takes place in ascending, except that a certain additional amount of power must be expended to enable the boat to surmount the difference of level between the basins.

The canals which have been commenced and completed in the United Kingdom, since the year 1800, are thirty in number, and extend about 600 miles. Mr. M'Culloch gives a list of British canals, with the numbers of shareholders in the proprietary of each, the amount and cost of shares, and the price on the 27th of June, 1843. The Erewash, with 231 shares, each 100*l.*, returned a dividend of 40*l.*, each share being then worth 675*l.* The Loughborough, with only seventy 100*l.* shares, the average cost of each share having been 142*l.* 17*s.*, had a dividend of 80*l.*, and a selling price per share of 1,400*l.* The Stroudwater, with two hundred shares of 150*l.*, returned a dividend of 24*l.*, with a price in the market of 490*l.* On the other hand, the 50*l.* shares of the Crinan were then selling at 2*l.* The 50*l.* shares of the North Walsham and Dillon were of the same almost nominal value in the market; and the shares of the Thames and Medway, with an average cost of 34*l.* 4*s.* 3*d.* were worth but 1*l.* Of the cost expended in the construction of the canals of England, there is no means of giving a precise account, but the following calculation seems sufficiently accurate. In round numbers, the 250,000 shares of the forty principal canals averaged an expenditure of 100*l.* per share, the result would be 25,000,000*l.*, and perhaps we may estimate the canals of the United Kingdom to have cost 35,000,000*l.*, or one-tenth as much as the railways already sanctioned.

In 1846 a canal was opened, under the name of Ludwig's Kanal, from Bamberg to Khleim, in Bavaria. It unites the Rhine with the Danube; so that a vessel could cross Europe from Rotterdam to the Black Sea; and in so far it carries out an idea which had been suggested in early times by Charlemagne.

One of the most interesting features at the present time, in respect to canals, is the project for a ship-canal over the isthmus which connects North and South America. A convention was signed at Washington in April 1850, between the British and United States governments; by which both governments promise their protection, though no pecuniary support, to a company formed for cutting the Nicaragua ship-canal.

There has also recently been a revival of the very ancient plan for cutting a ship-canal through the isthmus of Suez, to connect the Mediterranean with the Red Sea.

CANARIES. These islands are fruitful in produce. On an average of the last few years they have produced wheat, maize, barley, millet, and rye, 170,000 quarters; wine, 54,000 pipes; barilla, 300,000 quintals; and potatoes, 500,000 barrels. The chief foreign trade is with England, the United States, and Hamburg: there is also an active trade between the islands. The number of foreign vessels which visit the islands annually is about 120. The principal ports are Santa-Cruz and Orotava in Teneriffe, and Palmas in Gran-Canaria. The exports consist of wine, fruits, corn, barilla, honey, orchilla, moss, fish, cochineal, raw silk, &c.; the imports are woollen and cotton cloths, linen, silks, colonial produce, brandy, paper, oil, glass, hardware, &c. There are important fisheries along the coast of Africa.

The exports of British and Irish manufactures to the Canaries have varied, during the last twenty years, from 20,000*l.* to 60,000*l.* per annum. In 1848 they were 45,832*l.*

In the chief island, Teneriffe, the quantity of wine annually made amounts to 3,000,000 gallons; the best sort, called Vidonia, which resembles Madeira, is exported to England. Coffee has been cultivated with success; iron ore is found, and sulphur abounds on the Peak of Teyde. Linen and woollen stuffs are manufactured by each family generally for its own use. Some silk stuffs, earthenware, soap, vermicelli, leather, brandy, ropes from the agave, hats, baskets, and mats of palm leaves, are the other chief articles of manufacture.

CANDELA'BRUM, was an article of furniture used by the Romans both in their public edifices and private dwellings. The candelabra used in public edifices were usually of a greater size than those for private dwellings, and were made with a large cup at the top to receive a lamp or sufficient unctuous material to feed a large flame.

In the Townley collection, in the British Museum, there are several bronze candelabra from 12 inches in height to upwards of 5 feet, and of various patterns. They are mostly flat on the top, although some are formed with a cup-like top, as if for a large flame. One has a spike to receive a clay lamp, with a hole in the centre. Two exquisite works of candelabra, carved in marble, are preserved in the Radcliffe Library, Oxford.

CANDIA. This once-celebrated island is still rich in produce, though fallen from its high position. It contains extensive woods, pastures, and meadows; and produces corn, wine, oil, opium, liquorice, flax, cotton, silk, carobs, oranges, lemons, dates, and other southern produce. Besides the common domestic animals, game, wild sheep, chamois, goats, bees, and fish are very numerous and abundant. About 600,000 sheep and goats are fed on the mountains; their wool is coarse, their milk is made into cheese. There are in the island about 50,000 horned cattle, which are used chiefly for ploughing: the milk of cows is not used, there being a prejudice against it. The habitations of the peasantry are rude in the extreme, and their clothing consists of coarse cottons, linens or woollens, manufactured by each household. The chief manufacture is soap, which is highly esteemed all through the Levant. The principal exports are oil and soap; the imports are some British and Austrian manufactured goods and metals, colonial produce and corn. Every article produced on the island pays one-seventh to the government. In lieu of a tax on silk, the mulberry trees are rated.

CANDLES AND CANDLESTICKS. Candles are commonly made of tallow; but wax, spermaceti, stearine, palm oil, and other materials are also employed. A wick, mostly formed of cotton fibres, passes through the candle. The action of this wick is merely mechanical, serving in the first instance by the heat given out during its combustion to fuse that portion of the tallow or wax to which it is more nearly applied, and then to take up through its fibres the fluid matter, which is thus prepared by minute division for decomposition and combustion. In order to ensure the proper burning of the candle, the wick requires to bear a given relation to the thickness of the candle.

There are two ways of making candles, which are distinguished as *dipped* or *mould* candles, according to the method employed. Dipped candles are made as follows:—Wicks made of spun cotton are selected of a size proper for the intended diameter of the candle, and are cut into the requisite lengths by a simple and convenient machine, being first doubled and twisted so as to leave a loop at one end. Into this loop a smooth cylindrical stick half an inch in diameter and about three feet long is inserted, and several of the cottons or wicks, being so treated and disposed at regular intervals on the stick, are ready to receive their external coating of tallow. The number of cottons ranged upon each stick varies according to the size of the candles to be made. The tallow, being previously melted and strained, is placed in a kind of trough, into which the wicks are dipped three times for the first 'lay;' after being kept a short time over the trough for the wicks to drain, the sticks are placed on a rack from which the candles hang freely, and are thus allowed to harden. The same process is repeated a second and a third time and oftener, according to the required weight of the candles. Where large quantities are to be made, several sticks are placed together in a kind of frame, and are lowered into the melted tallow and raised again by machinery, a counter-weight being used in order to indicate when the wicks have taken up the required quantity of tallow.

Mould candles are made in cylindrical moulds of pewter, one end of which is smaller than the other to allow of the easy removal of the candles.

From 10 to 16 of these moulds are placed together in a wooden frame, so that their larger ends terminate in a kind of trough common to the whole; the wicks are inserted and kept firmly in their proper places in the centre of each cylinder by strong wires. The frame being then placed with the trough uppermost, the moulds are filled with melted tallow and are placed in the air to cool, after which the wires by which the wicks are fixed are withdrawn, the superfluous tallow is removed from the trough, and the candles are pulled out of the moulds.

The process used in making wax candles is different. The wicks being cut and twisted in the manner above described, a set of them is suspended over a basin of melted wax, which is taken up by a large ladle and poured from time to time on the tops of the wicks, and the melted wax running downwards adheres to and covers the wicks throughout their length. This is repeated until a sufficient weight of wax has been gathered upon each. After the candles are sufficiently cooled, they are rolled upon a smooth table in order to give them a perfectly cylindrical form, and they are then polished.

The candle manufacture is distinguished by many interesting features. In most cases the processes are little other than of a handicraft character; but in large establishments machinery is more and more introduced. At the great soap and candle works in London, and at other establishments of magnitude elsewhere, store or dip candles are made by dipping as at other places; but a greater number are dipped at one time. Twenty to twenty-four candles, for instance, are hung on one broach or stick; thirty broaches are ranged side by side to form a frame; and thirty six frames are suspended from a machine which is capable of being brought over the vat of melted tallow. There may thus be twenty to five and twenty thousand candle wicks suspended from one machine, and all the candles made by one man and a boy in less than a day.

At several of the larger and more important establishments, a beautiful machine is now employed for making mould candles. The wick is wound on a reel in lengths of 100 feet, of which there are as many as there are moulds. In a kind of frame are enclosed a certain number of moulds, with a reel of cotton attached to each. A portion of cotton is unwound from each wheel, and made to pass through a mould, the lower end of which is only large enough to admit of the passage of the wick. The frames are then so arranged that the melted tallow can be made to flow into them; and when the tallow has solidified, the frames are laid on their side, and by a beautiful adaptation of mechanism, the candles are forced out of the moulds, and thrown on a table in parallel lines; after which the wicks are cut to a proper length.

The novelties in the manufacture of candles,

and in candlesticks adapted to them, have been very numerous within the last few years. Patents have been obtained for candles made of palm oil, which is solid in our climate, though liquid in Africa. Stearine and margarine are also employed for this purpose. *Palmer's* candles are distinguished chiefly by the use of a wick which, bending out to the hottest part of the flame as it burns, consumes without the necessity of snuffing. But the chief feature in Palmer's patents is the use of a candlestick which maintains the candle always at the same height; there is a spring beneath the candle, which presses it upwards with such force, that the top of the candle is always maintained on a level with the top of the candlestick, the wick alone protruding. The construction of candles with wicks so contrived as to require no snuffing, has often engaged the ingenuity of practical men; but in most cases the attempts have failed. A kind of candle lamp was introduced a few years ago, in which solid tallow is placed within a lamp, and melted as it is required for burning.

One of the patents obtained by Mr. Palmer in 1849, relates to several improvements in the manufacture of wicks for candles. The first is the formation of helical or spiral wicks, consisting of a number of strands bound together by cross gymp; with one strand stiffer than the rest, to retain the wick in its proper position. The second form consists of cotton cord, twisted hard and firm. The third is the formation of wicks plaited on a wire, which wire is afterwards withdrawn to leave a space for capillary action of the melted tallow. The fourth is for coating one of the strands of a wick in a metallic envelope, by dipping it in melted bismuth.

Mr. Maudslay patented a remarkable machine in 1847, for making candles by a sort of tube-drawing process, something akin to the Italian mode of making maccaroni. The tallow or composition is brought to a soft warm paste-like state, and in that state is forced through a tube kept cold by immersion in water; it gradually solidifies during its passage through the tube (which is of considerable length, and is coiled round a circular vessel), and is discharged into water, where it at once assumes a solid form. At one particular point before the tallow has solidified, an end of cotton wick is introduced into the tube, and is drawn in and enveloped by the tallow as it passes. The theory of the machine is such that it could produce an *endless* candle, which may be cut by simple machinery to any given length. The machine is remarkably novel and ingenious in its arrangements.

The Patent Candle Company's works at Vauxhall and Battersea are interesting, as showing the application of chemistry and of mechanism on a large scale to this manufacture. Besides the steam-engines and hydraulic presses, 700 men are employed, and 4,000 tons of palm and cocoa-nut oil are used per annum. The cocoa-nut oil is chiefly procured from Ceylon, but the palm-oil (which is the chief ingredient in the patent candles) from Africa. The palm-oil reaches this country in a semi-solid state. It is first liquified by passing a steam-pipe through it, then converted by chemical processes into a colourless concrete mass; then cut by a rotatory machine into slices, which are placed one upon another, with cocoa-fibre mats between them, and iron plates between the mats. These bundles are taken to a room where are forty-two powerful hydraulic presses, worked by steam power; and this immense pressure is applied, first cold and then hot, to force out the oleic acid from the palm-oil, leaving the solid stearine behind. This stearine, after being again liquefied, is in a fit state for use in making candles, which is effected by the patent moulding machine. The company spin their own wicks (29 miles of which form the preliminary "cottoning" of one machine), and conduct several other subsidiary arrangements on a large scale, involving the combustion of 100 tons of coals per week.

There are many curious little pieces of mechanism, patented within the last few years, having for their principal object the mode of adjusting candles in candlesticks. One consists of a candle shade constructed in a circular ring, which ring is suspended from a conical cap resting on the top of the candle; as the candle burns this cap sinks with it, and by that means, the shade maintains a constant level relatively to the flame of the candle. Another little piece of apparatus consists of a wire-frame for supporting a shade, and which is itself supported by having a sort of circular spring hoop, which clasps the candle. Many varieties of wedges and springs have been devised for fixing candles into the candlesticks. An ingenious self-acting extinguisher for candles was invented a few years ago, but we believe not patented. A steel spring clasps the candle firmly within its jaws: and the extinguisher is hinged to the handle of this spring by a bent arm. A wire projects from the arm of the extinguisher, and thrusts into the solid part of the tallow of the candle. When the candle has burned down so as to soften the tallow around the wire, the latter slips aside by being no longer able to maintain its position; and the extinguisher falls over the flame of the candle. By adjusting the wire to any particular distance below the wick, the candle can be extinguished after any given amount of time.

Among the almost endless variety of new candlesticks is one patented in 1849 by Mr. Sturges of Birmingham. Where the general character and pattern of a candlestick are such as ill fit it to be finished in a lathe, Mr. Sturges proposed to cast it with melted metal in moulds, which moulds are kept slowly rotating during the casting.

The export of candles for the first nine months of 1850 amounted to 2,033,280 lbs.

CANE. [Calamus.]

CA'NNABIS. [Hemp.]

CANNON. The invention of cannon is noticed under Artillery, and matters relating to their use under Gunnery. Cannon are not cast hollow, it being found that if so cast they would not, owing to the irregular cooling of the metal, be equally strong in every part. Being cast solid, the outside cools first, with a close sound grain, and all the porous or spongy parts of the metal are found in the centre. This is subsequently turned or bored out in an engine-lathe, which leaves the inner surface perfectly true, and the bore of the requisite diameter.

Mr. Maudslay has recently proposed to the government the use of cannon having a peculiar form of breech. Under ordinary circumstances, cannon are loaded, and sponged after firing, at the mouth; but it has long been felt that if these operations could be performed at or near the remote end of the cannon, the change would be accompanied by greater rapidity of firing, less exposure to the enemy, and a diminution in the number of hands employed. According to Mr. Maudslay's plan, the cannon is bored quite through; but a moveable breech is provided, which is fixed after the cannon is loaded, but is removed for the sponging and re-loading. A lever, rack, and pinion are provided for fixing and unfixing the moveable breech.

CANOPUS is the name of an Egyptian jar of a big-bellied form, with a cover or top representing a human head or that of some animal. These vessels are generally made of baked earth, sometimes of alabaster, and even of green basalt. Some have hieroglyphics on them, and are painted and glazed. Bodies of sacred animals are sometimes found in these vessels. Earthen jars of this form seem to have been used for keeping water cool, as they still are in Egypt.

CANOPY, the covering over a niche used in Gothic architecture. They are usually elaborately carved, being intended not merely as a covering, but also as a mark of distinction. The various Gothic edifices in England present numerous examples of canopies; of which Henry the Seventh's chapel at Westminster Abbey is perhaps one of the most striking.

CANTAL, one of the southern departments of France, is rich in pastures. The number of horned cattle reared for exportation and for the purpose of making butter and cheese is immense. As much as 50,000 quintals of cheese is annually made. In mineral wealth the department is also rich; copper, iron, lead, sulphur, alum, antimony, coal, limestone, slate, granite, &c., are found, but the only mine worked is one of coal. The manufacturing industry of the department is of little importance; it is confined to the making of lace, copper vessels, coarse stuffs, glue, and leather. At the end of autumn many of the population emigrate to Paris and other parts of France, where they find employment as porters, water-carriers, tinkers, and handicraftsmen, returning home in the spring of the following year, or in some instances after an interval of several years, for the inhabitants are strongly att ched to their poor, wild, but highly picturesque country.

CANTEEN, a small wooden vessel capable of containing three pints, which is carried by each soldier on the march on foreign service or in the field. The use of them has been for some time general in the British army. Another kind of canteen is a square box fitted up with compartments, in which officers on foreign service pack a variety of articles.

CA'NTHARIS, or *Spanish Fly*, is largely imported for medical use, on account of a pungent volatile principle contained in the insect. The insects are killed in vinegar, dried on hurdles, and packed for use. Though bearing the name of Spanish Blistering Flies, the greatest quantity is obtained from St. Petersburg; and the Russian insects are superior to those from Sicily or France. When good, they are of a shining yellowish green colour; the odour is strong and disagreeable; and the taste acrid and caustic.

The active principle of these insects is a white substance, which may be obtained in the form of small crystalline plates. To this principle the name of *cantharidin* has been given. Cantharidin may be extracted in various ways. It is so powerful, that one-hundredth part of a grain applied to the skin will excite vesication.

CANTILEVER, or bracket, a projecting piece of wood, stone, or iron, which supports a cornice, balcony, &c.

CANTON. The trading and manufacturing features of this city are highly interesting.

The shops are commonly quite open towards the street, that is, those appropriated to Chinese customers; for the few streets devoted to European trade are rather on a different plan, the shops being of a closer structure, and less exposed to external observation. The several streets are commonly devoted to distinct trades. By the side of each shop is suspended from on high a huge ornamental tablet of wood, varnished and gilded, on which are described the particular calling of the tenant and the goods in which he deals. Some of the shops, which are pretty richly supplied, are much exposed towards the street; but the inhabitants of each division generally combine into a system of watch and ward for common protection, and during the night the streets are closed at each end by doors, which are guarded by the regular police.

No inconsiderable part of the population lives upon the river, in the junks, barges, and small boats. The space opposite to Canton and its suburbs resembles a floating city. By far the largest part consists of boats which are generally not more than 10 or 12 feet long, about 6 broad, and so low that a person can scarcely stand up in them. Their covering consists of a bamboo or mat tilt, shaped like that of a waggon, which is very light, and serves tolerably as a defence against the weather. Whole families live in these boats, and are considered as a distinct part of the population, being under a separate regulation, and not allowed to intermarry with those on shore.

The whole frontage of the buildings in which foreigners of all nations are shut up together for the prosecution of their trading business at Canton does not exceed between seven and eight hundred feet. Each front, of which there are about thirteen, extends backwards a hundred and thirty yards into a long narrow lane, on each side of which, as well as over arches that cross it, are the confined abodes of the English, French, Dutch, Americans, Parsees, and others.

The European factories are called by the Chinese *Hongs*, this word hong being always used by them to denote a commercial establishment or warehouse. Near the factories are the warehouses of the several Hong merchants, all of them communicating with the river by wooden stairs, from which the tea and other goods are shipped. The shops, instead of being set out with the showy and sometimes expensive front of an English or French shop, are closed in by gloomy black shutters, and very ill lit by a small sky-light, or rather a hole in the roof.

Canton is one of the five ports of China, at which, according to the treaty with the Chinese of August 29, 1842, British subjects are permitted to trade. The principal stipulations in that treaty have since been very fully carried into effect, under a series of general regulations, subject to occasional interruptions.

By far the largest article of export from Canton is tea. The other chief exports consist of silver, silks, and china-ware. Exports have frequently exceeded 4,000,000*l.* annually. The imports consist of woollen goods, cotton, cotton-yarn, long cloths, and various other articles of British manufacture.

Canton has few native manufactures or products suitable for deposit in the Great Exhibition of 1851; but its merchants have contributed towards the subscribed funds.

CANVAS. As exemplifications of hempen canvas, we cannot do better than refer to those important uses of it described under FLOOR-CLOTH MANUFACTURE; and SAIL-MAKING.

CAOUTCHOUC. This remarkable substance is produced by the *Siphonia elastica*, the *Ficus elastica*, the *Urceola elastica*, and many other American and Asiatic plants. It is often termed *India rubber*, from its use in removing pencil traces from paper. It was in the year 1735 that this substance was first discovered by De La Condamine to be the inspissated juice of a tree. In a pure state, it is insipid and scentless, white, extremely elastic, inflammable, not altered by exposure to the air, insoluble in water and in alcohol, soluble in æther and in the essential oils, acted upon by alkalies, and decomposed by concentrated sulphuric and nitric acids.

In order to obtain caoutchouc, the trees which produce it are pierced in the rainy season, upon which a thick juice of a yellowish white colour exudes, which becomes darker by exposure to the air. If this juice be kept in well-corked bottles, it may be preserved for some time without undergoing much change, and it has been imported in this state; but, however perfectly the atmosphere may be excluded, it will ultimately solidify. Heat coagulates the juice and separates the caoutchouc: alcohol and acids produce the same effect. If exposed to the air in thin films, it soon dries, losing from one-third to one-half of its weight: and leaving caoutchouc of the usual appearance. By the natives of South America it is applied in successive coats to the surface of clay models of bottles and of animals, and dried over fires, the smoke of which communicates to it a dark colour. While the caoutchouc is still soft, various lines are drawn upon it with a blunt tool, which remain permanently impressed. When the whole has become dry, the clay is crushed and shaken out of the bottles.

The import of caoutchouc in 1849 amounted to 5328 cwts., and in the first nine months of 1850 to 4800 cwts.

The varied useful purposes to which this singular substance is applied are noticed under INDIA RUBBER MANUFACTURES.

CAPE OF GOOD HOPE. This colony will probably play an important part in the future industrial history of nations. The immigrants have yet been too few to place the colony in a high position; but Cape Town, Graham Town, Port Elizabeth, &c., are rapidly growing in commercial importance, and the inner country is year by year producing more and more of the raw materials of manufacture.

The exports of British and Irish produce and manufactures to the Cape of Good Hope at several periods five years apart, were as follow:—

1830	..	£330.036
1835	..	326,921
1840	..	417,091
1845	..	648,749

In 1848 they amounted to 645,718*l.*; but in 1849 they lessened to 520,896*l.*

During the first seven months of 1850, 206 vessels arrived at the Cape with cargoes; against 275 in the same period of 1845. Port Elizabeth (Algoa Bay) exported produce to the value of 80,000*l.* during three months only of 1850; the exports included 1,167,273 lbs. of wool, and 228,335 lbs. of gum. Graham's Town is also rapidly rising as a place of export.

A sub-committee is arranging the details of a transmission of South African produce, to the Great Exhibition of 1851.

CAPE VERDE. The Cape Verde Islands are rich in plants. Maize and rice, the chief food of the people, oranges, melons, pomegranates, bananas, lemons, figs, guavas, are the chief products. The fruits are of the best quality. Sweet potatoes are grown; the sugar-cane and the vine are cultivated, but it is prohibited to make wine. The palm, tamarind, and adansonia are the principal trees. Turtles are abundant in the neighbouring seas. Salt is made from sea water by solar evaporation, and is an important article of export to America and the coast of Africa. Orchilla is gathered for the government. Besides salt and the products above named, the principal exports are goat skins and asses to the West Indies.

The exports from this country to the Cape Verde Islands are but small: seldom above 2000*l.* per annum; in 1848 they were however 3,324*l.*

CAPERS, are the flower-buds of a plant which grows naturally upon rocks and ruins all over the south of France and Italy, rendering them inconceivably gay with its large white blossoms, from the centre of each of which there springs a long tassel of deep lilac stamens. The quality depends exclusively upon the age at which they are gathered, the smallest and youngest being the dearest and most delicate, and the largest and oldest the coarsest and cheapest. On an average each plant of the Caper-bush gives a pound of buds: The consumption of capers in this country is inconsiderable.

CAPILLARY ATTRACTION and REPULSION. If a tube of very small diameter be plunged into a fluid, the fluid in the tube either rises above or sinks below the level of that on the exterior, and at the same time is slightly curved at its upper surface. In cases where the fluid stands higher within the tube than without, as is the case with water and glass, its upper surface is always concave; but when the fluid is lower within the tube, as with mercury and glass, it is convex. These phenomena are the results of what are termed *capillary attraction* and *repulsion*.

The laws according to which a fluid thus rises or falls are as follow:—1. When a tube of dry glass is plunged in a vessel of water, the attraction of the glass does not extend beyond the depth of the very thin film of water which would adhere to the interior surface if the tube were drawn out. 2. If the tube previously moistened by such film were plunged in water, the rise would be much less than in the other case; and, whatever be the substance of the tube so moistened, the elevation of the water in it is found to be the same. 3. When cylindrical tubes of different diameters are compared, the elevation is inversely proportional to the diameter. 4. If the interior of the tube be conical, the elevation or depression in it is found to depend on the diameter at the upper part only of the elevation; and to be the same as in a cylindrical tube of that diameter. 5. If the tube be double (one tube within another), the fluid rises to the same height in the interval between the two tubes, as it would do in a tube with that interval for its radius. 6. Between two parallel plates immersed at a very small interval, the fluid rises as high as in a tube with that interval for its radius. 7. Between two plates vertically placed, but inclined at a very small angle (like a double screen nearly closed), the fluid rises higher and higher as we proceed towards the upright line of junction; and the curve of the upper surface of the fluid is an hyperbola.

As an example of capillary action exemplifying itself in every-day processes, we may mention the wick of a candle or lamp, in which oil or melted tallow rises solely by virtue of this power.

CAPITAL is a term used in commerce to express the stock of the merchant, manufacturer, or trader, used in carrying on his business, in the purchase or manufacture of commodities, and in the payment of the wages of labour; and is understood not only of money, but of buildings, machinery, and all other material objects which facilitate his operations in trade. The term itself and the practical qualities and uses of capital are sufficiently understood in this its commercial sense. But capital, in a more extended form, embraces not only the capital of particular individuals, but the entire capital of a country. In this latter sense capital may be defined as the products of industry possessed by the community, and still available for use only, or for further production.

Capital is first called into existence by the natural foresight of man, who even in a savage state discerns the advantage of not immediately consuming the whole produce of his exertions in present gratification, and stores up a part for his future subsistence. The greater proportion of mankind possess this quality, and those who do not are admonished of its value by privation. A desire to accumulate some portion of the produce of industry being natural to mankind and nearly universal, the growth of capital may be expected wherever the means of accumulation exist; or, in other words, wherever men are not obliged to consume the whole products of their labour in their own subsistence. From the moment at which a man produces more than he consumes he is creating a capital; and the accumulated surplus of production over the consumption of the whole community is the capital of a country.

The relation of capital to manufacturing industry forms one of the most important departments of study in political economy.

CAPRIFICATION is the process by which the maturation of the fig is accelerated in the Levant. It is well known that fruits which have been bitten by insects ripen sooner than others, the wound appearing to act as a stimulant to the local action of the parenchyma. This is turned to account by the Greeks in the following manner, which is called Caprification. When the cultivated fig is preparing for becoming ripe, a quantity of the branches of wild fig trees are brought into the fig orchards and placed upon the cultivated plants. The wild figs bring with them a great number of a small insect called *Cynips Psenes*, or *Dipollepis Ficus Caricæ*, which fly among the cultivated figs and pierce their fruit for the purpose of laying eggs. This not only brings about an earlier ripening of the fig crop than would otherwise be obtained, but enables the cultivator to obtain two harvests a year. It is however said that the practice deteriorates the quality of the fruit. Caprification has been artificially imitated by puncturing a fig with an awl, and introducing a little oil into the wound, for the purpose of preventing its healing too soon.

CAPS, PERCUSSION. It is explained in ARMS how the earlier kind of fire-arms were discharged. The percussion-cap is a modern contrivance for this purpose. It depends on the property possessed by several chemical substances of exploding by a blow or percussion. Fulminating mercury was the first substance employed in this way; but as soon as it became known that a slight blow would explode certain powders, and that this explosion would ignite gunpowder, numerous improvements were introduced by degrees. Various salts and other chemical compounds, such as some of the chlorates, nitrates, and fulminates, will explode in this way, the most familiar example of which is afforded by the 'lucifers' or 'congreves' now sold so cheaply in the streets, and which ignite so readily by friction (in effect a series of minute percussions).

When the method was first introduced, there was some difficulty in causing the explosion of the mixture to ignite the gunpowder. But this is now effected by putting the detonating mixture into a little copper box or cell called a *cap*, which is adjusted over the touch-hole, and so arranged that a smart blow bursts the cap and explodes its contents: the little cell itself is destroyed, so that a new one is required for each firing. The size of the cell, or 'percussion-cap,' the nature of the mixture, the quantity employed with each charge, and the mechanism for firing it, have been the subjects of many improvements within the last few years, some of which are patented. The caps are now made in large numbers at Birmingham, in much the same manner as metal buttons, blanks being cut out of sheet copper or mixed metal, and stamped or pressed into the proper shape. One of the recent inventions has been to make the cap double, or one cap within another, with the mixture between the two, and a small hole in the inner one to communicate with the gunpowder.

Many contrivances have also been suggested for applying these caps under a modified form to larger guns; and the detonating compounds themselves have been brought into use for exploding the contents of bombs and shells.

CA'PSICUM, or Bird-Pepper. The shell

of the fruit of this plant is fleshy and coloured, and contains a pungent principle, which also exists in its seed in great activity. On this account both the fruit and seeds of different species of capsicum are in request as a condiment, and either in the unprepared state or ground into *Cayenne pepper*, form a considerable part of the stimulating vegetables used by man. In Europe the capsicum enters largely into the seasoning of food and the preparation of pickles; and in warmer countries it constitutes one of the first necessaries of life, either green or ripe. The species from which the fresh capsicums used in Europe are principally obtained is the *Capsicum annuum*, a weedy plant found wild in South America and the West Indies. A much hotter species is the *Capsicum fruticosum* or Goat-Pepper, a native of the East Indies, which differs from the *Capsicum annuum* in being a shrub, and in its fruit being very small.

The capsicum is easily brought to perfection in this country. Its seeds are sown in a hot-bed in the beginning of April; the young plants are managed like other tender annuals; and about the end of May they are planted in the open air under a south wall. They will readily ripen their fruit in such a situation.

CAPSTAN. [WINDLASS.]

CARAT, KARAT. The karatium was originally the twenty-fourth part of the *marc*, or half-pound among the French, from whom the word came: so that three carats made an ounce. The carat was a small weight used for gold and jewels, and varied greatly in different countries. At last however it went out of use, except only in the sense in which it still exists, namely, that a carat means the twenty-fourth part of any weight of gold or gold alloy. If such a weight be all gold, it is said to be twenty-four carats fine; if one-third only be gold, it is said to be eight carats fine.

CARAVAN, a travelling body of merchants or pilgrims, who join company for safety and convenience. The term, which is of Persian origin, is confined to journeys in the East, and applies more particularly to those made in Arabia, Nubia, Syria, Persia, and Asia Minor; but the practice obtains, though mostly on a smaller scale, in many other countries where the roads are insecure, and where deserts and desolate tracts of land are to be crossed.

In the East the caravans have a commercial or a religious character, and very frequently both; the greatest of them all, or those which proceed annually to the holy city of Mecca, have always trade as well as prayers in view.

Besides these large annual caravans, others on a smaller scale are constantly occurring in the East, where merchants and travellers going the same road wait for one another until they can form a caravan, when they generally appoint one of their voluntary association to regulate the order of march. But the caravan trade is not limited to Southern Asia. The great trade between China and Russia is a caravan trade. The road runs from Peking to Kiachta, the great border-market for the barter of Chinese and European articles: the journey is from 70 to 90 days. Other similar lines of route exist in Russia and the countries to the east of the Caspian Sea.

CARAWAYS, the ripe fruit of a plant called *Carum Carui*. The seeds, as they are vulgarly called, which are the furrowed halves of the ripe fruit, have a peculiar aromatic flavour, and are used as an agreeable carminative by confectioners: the roots themselves are eaten in the north of Europe.

Caraways are used in medicine as a carminative. The chief English cultivation of the plant is in Essex and Suffolk, upon old grass land broken up for the purpose. As it is a biennial, it is generally sown with another plant of the same tribe called coriander; and sometimes a crop of teazles (*Carduus Fullónum*) is raised on the same land. The three give a very valuable return during two or three years.

It would hardly be supposed, considering the minor uses to which they are applied, that caraways would be imported to so large an extent as the Board of Trade tables indicate In 1848 the importation amounted to 7,266 cwts.

CARBON, a non-metallic elementary solid body, which is widely diffused throughout nature. The purest and at the same time the rarest form in which it occurs is that of the *diamond*; the more common states in which it is met with are those of anthracite, graphite, and coal; but in these cases it is not free from admixture. Another well-known form of carbon, but still impure, is *charcoal*. Carbon is the chief element in three groups of substances:—the mineral forms, such as diamond, anthracite, &c.; the carbonates; and the vegetable series, as coal, asphaltum, peat, amber, &c.

Charcoal consists mainly of carbon procured from the decomposition of wood by burning. This operation is generally conducted in pits made in the ground; sometimes however it is carried on in iron cylinders. Wood is essentially composed of carbon, oxygen, and hydrogen. By the action of the heat it is decomposed the oxygen and hydrogen are ex-

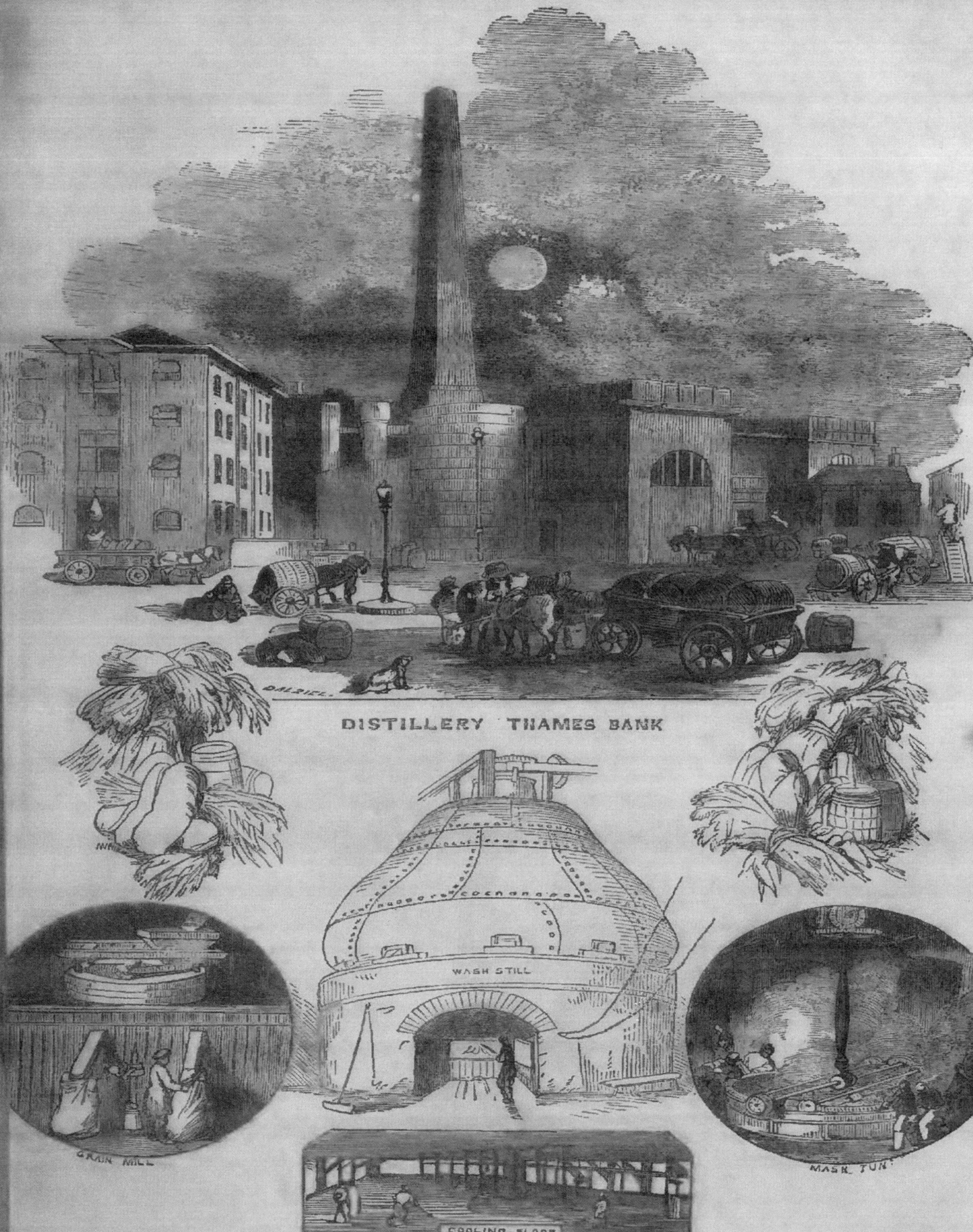

DISTILLERY THAMES BANK

pelled, and uniting in certain proportions form water; and also with carbon various gaseous and other compounds are formed. Among the latter are *acetic acid*, sometimes called *pyroligneous acid*, and a peculiar inflammable fluid known by the name of *pyroxilic spirit*, and *tar*.

Charcoal has the following properties. It is black, lighter than water, and full of pores, occasioned by the expulsion of the bodies volatilised. Charcoal, from whatever source procured, is absolutely infusible by any degree of heat however great; neither that of a mirror, the oxhydrogen blow pipe, nor the voltaic discharge, being sufficient to produce fusion. In its common state it is one of the worst conductors of heat known, but its power is increased after being strongly heated. Charcoal is a conductor of electricity, which is so far from being the case with the diamond, that it may be rendered electrical by friction.

Charcoal is tasteless, inodorous, and insoluble in water. It possesses the property of destroying colouring matter, especially the charcoal procured by burning bones, which is usually called *animal charcoal*. It is largely used for this purpose in sugar refining. It has the power of condensing gaseous bodies to a greater degree than most or perhaps any other substances. Charcoal is highly combustible; it burns in the air when strongly heated, though not very rapidly. During this combustion carbonic acid is formed by the union of the oxygen of the air with carbon.

It has been mentioned that charcoal is not pure carbon; when a quantity is burnt there always remains a portion of ashes containing a considerable quantity of carbonate of potash and some other alkaline and earthy salts, which have been taken up from the soil in which the tree grew that furnished the charcoal.

Charcoal is used not merely for combustion, but also for the important purpose of making gunpowder. It is also applied to other various well-known uses. Its power of absorbing gases and moisture renders it useful in some cases, while in other cases it seems to act by some power exerted on the vital energies of the system. Charcoal, especially animal charcoal, possesses the power of destroying the colour, smell, and taste of a great variety of vegetable and animal substances, particularly of mucilages and oils, and of matters in which *extractive* abounds. Meat and game too far decomposed may be restored to a condition fit for use by the employment of finely powdered charcoal, assisted by sulphuric acid. Water also may be restored from a tainted state by filtering it through charcoal. Charcoal, both from its antiseptic and vital properties, is useful in many forms of disease.

CARBONIC ACID. There are three compounds of carbon and oxygen, *Carbonic Oxide*, *Carbonic Acid*, and *Oxalic Acid*. Carbonic acid is the most important of the three. It exists largely in nature. It is in comparatively small quantity in the gaseous state in the atmosphere; it is in solution in most spring water, and in some called mineral waters to a considerable degree; but it is in solid combination that it is found in the largest quantity, forming nearly 44 per cent. of all limestones and marbles, besides occurring in less quantity united with other earths and metallic oxides. Carbonic acid is produced by fermentation; by the process of respiration; by animal and vegetable putrefaction; and by combustion, whether of oil, wax, tallow, vegetable matter, or coal.

In its uncombined state carbonic acid is a gas, colourless and transparent, and therefore invisible; it has an acid and slightly astringent taste; it extinguishes burning bodies, and is fatal to animals. On account of its great density, it diffuses slowly in the air, and hence it is apt to remain long in fermenting vats, old wells, &c., and has frequently produced fatal effects upon persons descending into them. Atmospheric air may however contain 1-20th of its volume of this gas, and be respired without becoming hurtful. On account of its great weight, it may be poured from vessel to vessel, as is shown by its extinguishing a taper repeatedly. Though gaseous at common temperatures, Faraday has showed that carbonic acid can be brought to the liquid state by intense cold and pressure: it is then a limpid colourless fluid, which M. Thilorier rendered even solid, in which state it is one of the most powerful refrigerating substances known. Carbonic acid is an ingredient in many mineral waters, to which it imparts effervescing qualities.

Carbonic acid gas is apt to be formed and accumulate in mines, particularly coal-mines, where it is termed *choke-damp*, and whence have arisen fearful colliery accidents; it is also found in old draw-wells.

Carbonic acid plays so important a part in medicine, in chemical manufactures, and in every day life, that it would be impossible even to enumerate its characteristic functions.

CARBONIFEROUS SYSTEM is the geological name for the great group of strata which includes nearly all the valuable coal yet discovered. We are concerned with it here only in respect to Coal.

CARCASS, a shell, or hollow ball of iron, perforated in three places at equal distances from each other within one hemisphere of the shell, and filled with a composition which burns with violence during eight or ten minutes. When discharged from a mortar or howitzer, the flames issuing from the perforations set fire to any building on which the carcass may happen to fall.

CARDAMOMS are the aromatic capsules of different species of a genus of plants called *Amomum*. The Malabar cardamoms are the best, and are in most extensive use. The Madagascar cardamoms are strong-flavoured. The *Grains of Paradise* are the fruit of one species of cardamoms.

CARDIFF is one of the busiest and most rapidly growing towns in South Wales. The population rose from 2,000 to upwards of 10,000 between 1801 and 1841; this increase has been chiefly owing to the shipment of the coal and iron from Merthyr Tydfil and its neighbourhood. The Glamorganshire canal, finished in 1798, was for many years the channel by which this produce reached the coast; but in 1840 the Taff railway was opened as an additional means of conveyance. The river, the canal, and the railway run nearly side by side, and terminate at Cardiff. While the railway was under construction, the late Marquess of Bute, the owner of a large amount of property in this neighbourhood, conceived the project of forming a large harbour or dock between the town and the Bristol Channel on a piece of waste ground belonging to himself. The dock, called the Bute Dock, and a ship canal leading thence to the sea, were opened about the same time as the railway. They form a work of great magnitude, on which a sum of 300,000*l.* has been expended. The entrance into the floating harbour from the sea is through sea-gates 45 feet in width; the harbour or basin has an area of an acre and a half, and is fitted for the reception of large vessels. The main entrance lock is at the north end of this outer basin, and is 152 feet long by 36 feet wide. On passing this lock the ship canal is entered, which extends to Cardiff, 1,400 yards in length and 200 feet in width, comprising a great extent of fine wharfage, and varying in depth from 13 feet to 19 feet.

Since these facilities were afforded, the trade of the port has increased rapidly. The coals shipped coastwise in 1848 were 544,196 tons, and to foreign ports 115,604—being five times as large a quantity in 1848 as in 1838. The value of the exports in 1848 was 729,094*l.* Few ports in Great Britain have increased more rapidly in the extent of their export trade than Cardiff. The number and tonnage of vessels registered as belonging to the port of Cardiff on the 31st of December, 1849, were 77 vessels, of 6,287 tons. The number and tonnage of vessels that entered and cleared at the port during the year 1849 were 9,064 vessels, of 695,022 tons.

CARDIGAN carries on a respectable amount of commerce. The number and tonnage of vessels registered as belonging to the port of Cardigan on 31st December 1849 were 249 vessels, of 14,368 tons. Many of these vessels are engaged in the Irish, colonial, and coasting trade. The number and tonnage of vessels entered and cleared at the port during 1849 were 777 vessels, of 20,170 tons.

The imports are chiefly coal, culm, limestone, and deals; the exports, oats, butter, and slates. No manufacture of any importance is carried on here. Salmon fishing is productive, and the herring fishery is of some importance.

CARDIGANSHIRE has a little mineral wealth. Veins of copper ore, lead, and sulphate of zinc occur. The mines were in the 16th and 17th centuries worked extensively and profitably. They afterwards became unproductive, and were almost wholly neglected; but within the last 12 or 14 years the spirit of mining enterprise has led to the re-opening some of the old mines and to the commencing of new ones. The lead mines are said to be most successful. The lead contains silver, varying from 14 to 80 ozs. to the ton: at Llanvair mine specimens have occurred which yielded 100 ozs. to the ton. There are slate quarries in the neighbourhood of Aberystwith, but the slate is not of good quality.

Cardiganshire is chiefly an agricultural county. The manufactures are unimportant, being confined to the weaving of a small quantity of flannel and coarse woollen stuffs. Gloves are made in the neighbourhood of Aberystwith and Tregaron. Oats, butter, and slates are exported. The decks of some of the vessels engaged during the summer in the coasting trade, are taken off in autumn, and they are used as fishing-boats. The principal imports are coal from Liverpool, culm from South Wales, Pembroke limestone, and Memel and American deals.

CARDS, CARD-MAKING MACHINE, an arrangement of wires used in the manner explained in COTTON MANUFACTURE, for disentangling the fibres of cotton preparatory to spinning. These cards are now made by a very beautiful machine. The wires are inserted in rows in strips of leather; and, by various movements of the machine, the strips of leather are pierced with holes; the wire is unwound from a coil, straightened, and cut off to the proper lengths; each wire is bent to a definite form, and then driven into the hole. One steam engine can set 100 of these machines at work at once; and each machine can form and fix 400 or 500 teeth in a minute.

CARDS, PLAYING. The manufacture of playing cards involves several processes of much nicety. The preparation of the material, the cutting into quadrangular pieces, and the stamping with the coloured device, all require careful operations. The card-board is made by many successive processes of pasting and pressing. In Mr. Dickinson's patented method, damp paper is wound over certain rollers; a paste trough with circular brushes are placed near the rollers; and during the transfer of the paper from one set of rollers to another, these circular brushes coat the surfaces of two or more papers with paste. Roller-pressure completes the operation.

Several patents have been taken out for cutting the pasteboard into strips, preparatory to a further cutting into card-pieces; of these patents, one by Mr. Dickinson will illustrate the principle generally. The machine consists of a pair of rollers, each roller having a number of circular revolving cutters; the pasteboard is passed between the rollers, where the cutters act upon it in the manner of shears, and cut it into strips, which strips are afterwards cut into card pieces.

The printing and colouring of the cards have exercised much ingenuity. In the ordinary mode of manufacture, the device is partly produced by copperplate printing and partly by stencilling in water-colours. Mr. De la Rue has patented a method of using oil-colours, and of printing in a mode very similar to that of calico-printing. The pips (hearts, spades, &c.) are set up by blocks or types, and printed at a press—the black with lamp-black ground in oil, and the red with vermilion ground in oil. The 'court cards' are printed by a series of impressions in different colours, almost precisely in the same way as that described under FLOOR CLOTH MANUFACTURE. Mr. De la Rue also employs the system of lithography, in which case there must be as many stones as there are colours, each having one particular part of the device.

The same ingenious inventor has contrived a mode of introducing gold or silver among the colours of the device. In this case all the portions of surface which are to be thus adorned are printed with gold-size instead of ink; and while this gold-size is yet moist, gold or silver-powder is sprinkled over the card: it adheres to the moistened parts, and may be lightly brushed from other places; and when all is dry, the gold will bear a careful polishing.

Some playing cards have a surface of such exquisite whiteness and smoothness as to resemble ivory; this is produced by coating them with a composition of fine French white, drying-oil, and size.

CAREX is the name of a genus of plants which render a few useful purposes to man. In the hop-grounds of Great Britain the leaves of some of the species are used for tying the bines of the hops to the poles. In Italy they are used for placing between the staves of wine-casks, are woven over Florence flasks, and occasionally employed for making chair bottoms. The leaves of the *Carex sylvatica*, according to Linnæus, are combed and dressed, and used as a warm lining for gloves and shoes; and, thus protected, the Laplanders seldom suffer from being frost-bitten.

CA'RICA, a remarkable tree found in various parts of South America, having a simple trunk, from 12 to 20 feet high, and abounding in a milky juice. The fruit is called the *papaw*, and is singularly useful in many ways to the natives where it grows. The fruit is eaten ripe, and when unripe is boiled and used as a vegetable. The juice forms a cosmetic, and the leaves are employed in washing instead of soap. It is also much used in medicine. The milky juice of the fruit is spoken of as a vermifuge; but the most extraordinary property of the papaw tree is, that animals which are fed upon the fruit are found, when killed, to be peculiarly tender.

CARLISLE. Till about a century ago, no trade or manufacture of any importance appears to have been carried on within this city: but it is now gradually rising in importance. The principal business of Carlisle arises from its manufactures of cotton goods and ginghams, and its coasting trade, which is somewhat extensive. The distance of the city from Port Carlisle, at the mouth of the river Eden, on the Solway Frith, is about nine miles; a ship canal, eleven miles in length, which was completed in 1823, connects Carlisle with Bowness on the Solway Frith. By this canal vessels of 100 tons burden can ascend to the town. A steamer plies twice a week between Liverpool and Port Carlisle. One of the principal stations on the line of railway from London to the Scottish districts by the North Western and Caledonian railways is at Carlisle. The town also possesses railway communication with Newcastle-on-Tyne and South Shields on the eastern coast, and with Maryport on the western coast. The vessels registered as belonging to Carlisle on the 31st of December, 1849, were 42, of 2107 tons. The number and tonnage of vessels entered and cleared during the year 1849 were 883 vessels of 108,115 tons.

The products of Carlisle industry will be exhibited to a limited extent at the Grand Display of 1851. Cottons, furniture chintzes, woollens, checks, and mixed fabrics, will occupy a place.

CARMINE, one of the most beautiful of the red colours used by painters. It is obtained from cochineal; and its colouring matter, called *carmin*, may be extracted by the aid of ammonia. [COCHINEAL.]

Carmine has been obtained from *dahlias*, by M. Rupprecht of Vienna. It is only the deep clear purple dahlia that will yield it; but from this variety he has obtained 235 lbs. of carmine from 200 square fathoms of dahlia beds. The carmine is said to be too fleeting for silk or cotton dyeing, but to be fitted for staining confectionary, artificial flowers, fancy paper leather, and rouge powder.

CARNELIAN, or CORNELIAN. [AGATE.]

CAROLINA. North and South Carolina supply varied produce for the commercial markets. In *North* Carolina Indian corn is raised throughout the State, and in some parts cotton. In the upper country, oak, walnut, lime, and cherry-trees of large size abound. The principal minerals are gold and iron; the gold region is on both sides of the Blue Ridge; and here the gold is found in grains, in small lumps, and in veins. The exports consist of live cattle, tar, pitch, and turpentine, lumber, Indian corn, cotton, tobacco, pork, lard, tallow, &c. Most of these are sent to South Carolina and Virginia to be exported thence.

In *South* Carolina, the principal objects of agriculture in the low plains are rice and cotton, the latter being also cultivated in some districts farther inland. The sugar-cane is only grown with advantage in the most southern part of the state. The fruits of the seacoast are oranges, lemons, pomegranates, olives, and figs. In the upper country all the grains and vegetables of England are grown, with Indian corn in addition. The forests contain fine timber trees, especially oak, beech, and hickory. No metal abounds, except iron, which is met with in several places in the upper country. A little gold is found, and some copper and lead are wrought. To facilitate internal commerce a few short canals have been cut, especially to avoid the rapids of the rivers. The exports consist of cotton, rice, tobacco, and hides, and the imports of manufactured goods, and the productions of the East and West Indies, with wines from the countries of southern Europe.

CARPENTRY is the art of framing timber generally, and especially the chief timbers in house-building. The neater wood-work of doors, window-frames, the planking of floors, skirtings, and stairs, more properly belong to JOINERY.

Carpentry requires a knowledge of the properties of timber, and of its strength when exposed to various strains. [MATERIALS, STRENGTH OF.] This will teach the peculiar fitness of each kind of timber for its own peculiar purpose. It will show, for example, that while oak greatly exceeds fir in hardness and durability, it may be inferior to it under certain circumstances; because, while the fibres of a sawn beam of fir are so straight as to run in unbroken lines from end to end, those of a sawn beam of oak are often so tortuous as to be repeatedly divided by the saw. Seasoning, by long exposure to a current of air, is necessary to prepare timber for use in carpentry; but as the best seasoning will not entirely prevent subsequent warping, shrinking, and splitting or flying, timbers should be so fitted together as to counteract as far as may be the effect of such changes. When it is required to bend timbers, they may be softened by boiling or steaming, and then brought to and secured at the desired curvature, which, when cold and dry, they will retain with very little variation.

Illustrations of a few details of carpentry will be found under FLOOR, ROOF, SCARFING, TRUSSING, &c. The most gigantic examples of timber-work in modern times, are to be found, perhaps, in the scaffolding for the Britannia tubular bridge. In respect to one continuous flooring, the Palace of Industry in Hyde Park furnishes, perhaps, the largest known example.

CARPET. The following kinds of carpets are now made in Great Britain:—Axminster, Venetian, Kidderminster or Scotch, British or damask Venetian, Brussels, and Wilton or Pile carpeting. These names do not always denote either the present or original place of manufacture. Brussels carpets were introduced into Kidderminster from Tournay in 1745: and it is doubtful whether Venetians were ever made at Venice. Wiltons (which are in fact Brussels carpets) were made on the continent before they were introduced at Wilton; and what are called Kidderminster are made in the greatest quantities in Scotland or Yorkshire.

Axminster Carpets are usually made in one piece, according to the dimensions of the room for which they are required. The warp or chain is of strong linen, placed perpendicularly between two rolls, or beams which turn round and enable the chain to be rolled from off one beam and on to the other as the weaving of the carpet proceeds. Small tufts or bunches of different coloured worsted or woollen are tied to or fastened under the warp; and when one row of these tufts has been completed, the shoot of linen is also thrown in and firmly rammed down. Another row of tufts is then arranged in such a manner as, by a change of the colours, to form a further portion of the pattern. To guide the weaver as to the position of the colours, a small paper design or drawing constantly hangs before him, from which he works. The tufts wholly conceal the linen threads. Real Turkey carpets are manufactured in a similar manner, and they are regularly imported, though not in very large quantities. Finger or Town-made and Stormont rugs are also formed with tufts put in as they are in Axminster carpets, but with a different arrangement of apparatus.

Venetian Carpets.—Here the warp or chain which is of worsted, and generally arranged in stripes of different colours, is alone visible; the shoot, which is of a dark colour and usually black, is concealed between the upper and under surface. By using shoot of different sizes these carpets are sometimes made to assume the appearance of plaids, checks, or twills.

Kidderminster or *Scotch Carpets* are formed by the intersection of two or more cloths of different colours; but as these cloths may be woven in stripes of different shades, by introducing at intervals shoots of different colours, the carpet is usually made to assume a great variety of colours. These carpets are sometimes 'three-ply,' or have three thicknesses of cloth; but for the most part they are 'two-ply.' Each cloth is perfect in itself, so that, if one cloth were carefully cut away, the other would remain perfect, and be in appearance like a very coarse baize. The process of weaving both cloths is carried on at the same time, and in each part of the carpet that cloth is brought to the surface which is required to produce that portion of the pattern. The back of the carpet will necessarily be of exactly the same pattern as the front, but the colours will be reversed. A complicated variety of the jacquard loom is employed in weaving these carpets.

British or *damask Venetian Carpets* partake both of the character of Venetian and Kidderminster, though more of the former than the latter. The warp, as in the Venetian, is the only part seen, whereas in Kidderminsters the shoot forms by far the greatest portion of what is visible.

Brussels Carpets form by far the most important and increasing portion of the carpet trade. Brussels are composed of linen and worsted, the cloth or reticulated part of the structure being entirely of linen, which is formed into a kind of very coarse sampler cloth, with two threads of linen for the shoot (one above, and the other below the worsted). The mode of bringing up to the surface the particular worsted thread which gives the pattern requires much ingenuity in the arrangement of the Brussels loom.

Wilton or *Pile Carpets* differ from Brussels only in this: that the loops of worsted are all cut through, and the carpet assumes a velvety appearance. At Glasgow a beautiful kind of velvet carpet is manufactured, in which coloured chenille is thrown in as a shoot, and afterwards cut at the surface. The manufacture of Brussels carpet was introduced into Wilton soon after its introduction into Kidderminster; the Wilton carpets being originally a better description of goods, were distinguished by the name of Cut or Wilton Carpets.

The chief export trade for carpets is to the United States of America; but they are also sent to most parts of the continents of Europe and America. By far the greatest quantity of Brussels is made in Kidderminster: what are called Kidderminster or Scotch are made in the largest quantities in different parts of Scotland and the north of England.

Mr. Wood, of Darwen, patented in 1850 an ingenious mode of making looped or piled (or what may perhaps be termed velvet) carpets. Under the ordinary circumstances of making velvet [VELVET] wires are inserted at intervals to assist in forming the loops; and these wires have to be inserted and removed by hand. In Mr. Wood's plan of carpet making, however, wires are thrown in among the warp-threads, and removed when the weft is formed, by ingenious mechanism attached to the loom.

There is a mode of imparting colour to carpets, patented by Mr. Henshall, a carpet manufacturer of Huddersfield, in which something like the principle of calico-printing is applied to carpet-work. The object is to produce differently coloured spots, squares, or stripes, independent of the mere weaving process. The warp threads are arranged side by side in a peculiar frame, so as to form an even horizontal layer; and in that state they are drawn tightly over a printing table, and printed in colours by blocks in the usual way. When these warp threads (or they may just as conveniently be weft-threads) are applied to weaving, a pattern is produced by the variation of the colour in each thread, in addition to the primary pattern which results from the weaving process.

In a communication to the *Times* in 1845, a correspondent suggests the manufacture of cheap carpets from coarse cotton. 'There are many kinds of carpets made of cotton in India—stout, serviceable, handsome things; generally they are termed *serriyce.* These are of all sizes, from the small one, seven feet by three, which every man possesses; to enormous ones for rooms and halls. These are generally striped, red and blue, or three shades of blue, sometimes woven into patterns; and I have often thought how useful they would be in England, these coarse kinds, for the poorer classes, for bed-rooms, &c. Again, what beautiful designs might not be manufactured by the skill of English workmen,—how large a quantity of small ones for individuals, or large for halls, might not be made for exportation to Africa, South America, and even India! At Warungole, in the Nizam's country, beautiful carpets of the same description as Turkey—that is, with a nap raised—are made of cotton.

A patent has been taken out within the last few years, for a mode of manufacturing carpets by a felting process.

A carpet of a very remarkable kind is now being prepared for the Great Exhibition, by a committee of ladies of Westminster. It will be thirty feet long by twenty wide, and will consist of 150 pieces two feet square. For each piece a design has been drawn by Mr. Papworth and Mr. Simpson, the full size; and each lady, on payment of a guinea, has one design placed at her disposal, to work up into a piece of the carpet; the work is to be executed by hand in Berlin wool, which is supplied by the committee. There are to be 340 threads in each direction, in each piece; and when completed, the whole of the pieces are to be joined edge to edge to form a carpet. The whole carpet will form — not a repetition of designs—but one comprehensive design, which it is supposed could not be imitated in the loom for less than 1000*l*.

CARPOBA'LSAMUM, a kind of volatile aromatic oil, said by Bruce to be furnished by the *Balsamodendron Gileadense.* It is produced by the nuts, which have a fleshy kernel yielding the balsam by simple expression. It should be employed while recent, otherwise it loses its odour and becomes inert.

CARRIER, in a commercial sense, is one who for hire undertakes the conveyance of goods or persons for any one who employs him. In a legal sense, it extends not only to those who convey goods by land, but also to the owners and masters of ships, mail-contractors, and even to wharfingers who undertake to convey goods for hire from their wharfs to the vessel in their own lighters, but not to mere hackney coachmen. A common carrier of goods for hire is not only bound to take goods tendered to him, if he has room in his conveyance, and he is informed of their quality and value, but he is liable for their loss, except in three cases:—1, Loss arising from the king's *public* enemies; 2, Loss arising from the act of God, such as storm, lightning, or tempest; 3, Loss arising from the owner's own fault, as by imperfect packing. A carrier can refuse to deliver up goods which have come into his possession *as a carrier,* until his reasonable charges for the carriage are paid.

CARRONADES are short iron guns, differing from other guns, and from howitzers, only in their dimensions and in the manner of attaching them to their carriages, which is by a joint and bolt underneath the piece, instead of trunnions. They derive their name from the village of Carron, in Stirlingshire, where they were first made.

When fired at point-blank, their range is about 150 yards; and, at an elevation of three degrees, it varies from 660 to 750 yards. They are extremely serviceable on land for breaching ramparts of earth, or for enfilading the faces of works; and at sea, in engagements at close quarters.

CARROT. The principal use of carrots is as food for cattle. The orange carrot and its varieties are the most common in England; but the large white and yellow carrots are more esteemed on the continent; they are supposed to contain more saccharine matter, and to produce a greater bulk of nutriment on the same extent of ground. The best method of taking up the carrots, to store them for winter use, is by means of three-pronged forks, such as are used in digging asparagus beds. The plough is sometimes used after the coulter has been removed; but, with all the care of the ploughman, the plough and the horses will cut and bruise many of the finest carrots. Carrots may be kept all winter in dry cellars, if they are protected against the frost. The more common way is to store them in straw in long trenches. The produce of carrots on good light land is nearly double that of potatoes, and they do not impoverish the land so much. From twenty to forty pounds of carrots, with a small quantity of oats, is a sufficient allowance for a hard-working horse for twenty-four hours. Where hay is scarce, it is a most economical substitute; and where the value of urine is known carrots are much prized, as they greatly tend to its increase.

If carrots are cut in pieces and steamed, they become more nutritious, and the expressed juice made to ferment affords by distillation a very good and wholesome spirit.

Sugar may also be extracted; but the carrot is inferior to the beet in this respect.

Carrot seed to the amount of 22,000 lbs. was imported from France in 1847.

CART. The drag-cart without wheels, which is used in some mountainous districts, is one of the simplest contrivances for transporting heavy weights. It consists of two strong poles, connected by cross-pieces fixed at right angles to them, the ends resting on the ground. The other ends of the poles form the shafts for the horse to draw by. The Irish car may be considered as the next step towards a better construction. This car consists of a bed or platform and two shafts. The wheels, in the simplest form, are round disks of wood, fixed on a square axle of wood at the distance of three or four feet from each other. To the under part of the bed of the cart two blocks of wood are fixed, which raise it so that the wheels may go under the cart, and in these blocks are two round holes to admit the ends of the axle. This is the simple old Irish car. The only difference in the construction of the most improved modern cars is the substitution of neat wheels and iron axles for those described above, and a railing or box fixed on the platform.

The common cart differs from the car in that the body rests on a fixed axle between the wheels, which turn upon the axle by means of boxes in the centre of the naves. The simplest cart is that used by carriers in France and Germany. It consists of two strong poles of ash or beech, resembling those of the drag-cart described above. One end forms the shafts, and the whole is equally poised on the axle. The wheels are often nearly six feet in diameter, and narrow at the tire; they are slightly dished, but run nearly perpendicularly to the road. On these carts very great weights are transported, so as to require five or six horses to draw them. Where the roads are level and hard, waggons are much to be preferred to carts; but in hilly countries and bad roads carts have many advantages. For agricultural purposes various kinds of carts have been invented. The capacious tumbril for carting earth and dung, with broad wheels to prevent their sinking in soft ground, is too generally known to require description. The light Scotch cart, drawn by one horse, is justly considered as the most advantageous for transporting earth, lime, or dung, especially in hilly countries. It is low and short, so that the horse draws very near the centre of gravity; and there is little power lost by obliquity. It is made to carry hay and straw by means of a light frame, which is laid on it, and projects over the body and the wheels in every direction.

To avoid the weight resting on the back of the horse, carts have been invented with three wheels, the small additional wheel being made to turn in front. The addition of springs to carts and waggons is a very great improvement, and should be adopted in every case where they are much used on the roads. The additional weight of the springs and their cost are greatly overbalanced by their advantage: they lessen the draught, and, by preventing jolting and shaking, add to the durability of the vehicles.

Our agricultural machine makers have made many improvements in carts within the last few years. Croskill's one-horse cart is formed to carry a considerable load, with less weight on the horse than ordinary carts; it is now much used in agricultural counties, to carry (say) five quarters of wheat 10 or 12 miles to market and return with a solid load of 30 cwt. Among other varieties are the Norwich cart, the Norwich pair-horse waggon, the Exeter cart, the Scotch cart, the Newcastle cart, &c. Many of these carts are now provided with Croskill's patent wheels and axles, made wholly by machinery, and consisting principally of iron.

CARTHAMIN and CARTHAMEIN. The yellow colouring matter of carthamus is to be extracted by water, and it is then to be sprinkled with a very dilute solution of carbonate of soda, which dissolves the carthamin; this is to be precipitated by a salt of lead, and the oxide of lead separated by hydrosulphuric acid. By this treatment a yellow solution is obtained, which by spontaneous evaporation yields small prismatic crystals of pure *carthamin*. When exposed over mercury to oxygen gas, it becomes after some days merely yellowish; but, if a little alkali be added to it, it becomes immediately yellow, and then passes rapidly to a rose colour, which is employed by dyers as the source of some of the more delicate rose colours and the rich scarlet called *ponceau*. It also constitutes the basis of the cosmetic known by the name of *rouge*. The acids, and particularly citric acid, precipitate it from the alkali in the state of the well-known fine rose colour, which is called by M. Preisser *carthamein*.

CARTOON, is a word used by artists to signify the full-sized drawings or studies made in chalks, or body colour (*tempera*, as it is called in Italy), preparatory to executing any great work either in oil colour or fresco. Cartoons are also made when the design is to be copied in tapestry. The great masters seldom commenced any extensive picture without first making studies or cartoons in *chiaro 'scuro*. Many of those by Raffaelle, Andrea Mantegna,

Domenichino, the Caracci, and others, remain to attest the laborious diligence and care with which their great works were accomplished. By this means the composition, drawing, expression, and light and shade, were all perfected before the colouring of the picture was attempted.

The finest specimens of cartoons that are known are those executed by Raffaelle d'Urbino, which were sent to Flanders, in the reign of Pope Leo X., to be copied in tapestry, in two sets. The tapestries (only shadows of Raffaelle's exquisite designs) were finished, and one set is now in Rome. The cartoons, originally twenty-five in number, were left neglected at Brussels, and most of them seem to have been lost or destroyed. A few, however, escaped this fate, and seven are now in England in the royal collection at Hampton Court. Their history ever since their arrival in England is eventful. They were bought in Flanders by Rubens for King Charles I. At the dispersion and sale of the royal collection, the cartoons were secured to the country by purchase, by Cromwell's particular command; at which time, we are told, the Triumphs of Julius Cæsar, by Andrea Mantegna (still preserved at Hampton Court) were valued at 2000*l.*, while the cartoons of Raffaelle were estimated at only 300*l.* In the reign of Charles II. they were again consigned to neglect. They had been sent to Mortlake to be copied in tapestry, where they were seriously injured. William III. had them repaired, and built a gallery at Hampton Court for their reception. George III. removed them to Buckingham Palace, and subsequently to Windsor Castle. They were again removed to Hampton Court, where they now are.

The subjects of these seven Cartoons are as follow :—

1. Paul preaching at Athens.
2. Death of Ananias.
3. Elimas the Sorcerer.
4. Christ delivering the keys.
5. Sacrifice at Lystra.
6. Apostles healing the Sick.
7. Miraculous draught of Fishes.

CARTRIDGE, is a cylindrical case containing a charge of gunpowder or shot, or of powder and ball, for fire-arms. Those used for loading muskets, carbines, and pistols, are formed of paper, and are styled ball or blank cartridges according as they contain both powder and ball, or powder only; while the larger cartridges for cannon and mortars, which always consist of powder only, are usually cased with flannel, though sometimes pasteboard, tin, or even wood, is employed. The North Americans, during their last war with England, are said to have employed very thin sheets of lead, resembling those used for lining tea-chests, for this purpose, thereby avoiding the danger of burning fragments of the cartridge-case remaining in the piece after firing.

Wire cartridges, for containing a charge of small shot, without powder, have been introduced for sporting purposes within the last few years. They consist of an inner case of wire network inclosed in a thin paper case, to the outer end of which a wadding is attached. The shot, with which it is usual to mix bone-dust or some other substance to fill up the interstices, is put within this case, which is rammed down upon the charge of powder. When the gun is fired, the paper case is torn to pieces as soon as the cartridge leaves the gun, and the shot immediately begins to quit the cartridge by passing through the meshes of the iron net-work, which is carried forward with the charge until it is quite empty, when it falls to the ground. By this contrivance the heating of the gun is avoided, and the recoil produced by the discharge is lessened, the charge leaving the barrel like a bullet. The shot are also carried so much more closely than when loose, that lighter charges, and consequently a lighter gun, may be used; much time is saved in loading, especially as no separate wadding is required; and, as the cartridge has no inclination to move before it is impelled by the explosion of the powder, the danger arising from the accidental shifting or rising of loose charges is avoided.

Mr. Berney patented a few years ago a new kind of cartridge. The shot is enclosed in a spiral wire case, tapered towards the end, and provided with a cushion at bottom of wool, moss, tow, or any other soft elastic substance, to prevent by its elasticity the sudden explosion of the powder from breaking the case or jamming the shot. The case expands after its discharge from the gun, and according as the coils are more or less apart, so does the distance vary to which the bulk of the shot may be carried before escaping through the coils. The object intended by this cartridge is to convey a greater number of shot to a given mark, without diverging or separating, than can be done by the use of the ordinary cartridges; and experiments made near Chalk Farm in 1840, with this object in view, seem to have borne out the intention of the patentee.

Another new form of cartridge was patented in 1840 by Mr. Bush. It is made by taking a circular disc of wood, or two card-board boxes, like two pill-box lids fitted one within the other, having a hole in the centre in which a percussion cap is placed, and held there by being covered with a piece of calico or canvas.

Around this as a base the paper cylinder or case is formed and filled up with the proper charge of gunpowder, and shots or a ball as the case may be. This invention is intended to be used in conjunction with a peculiar mode of constructing muskets so as to be loaded at the breech.

Dr. Jager invented a new kind of cartridge in 1847, intended to be used with a new kind of musket also invented by him. There is neither priming nor percussion cap needed in the firing; but a kind of percussion cap, or nipple filled with fulminating powder, is formed in the cartridge itself; and the gun is so formed, that a small hammer, moved by the trigger, strikes on the nipple, which projects a little way into an aperture in the side of the gun.

From a return presented to the Committee of the House of Commons on the Ordnance Estimates, in 1849, it appears that the store of cartridges kept on hand by the Ordnance is immense. On the 1st January, 1849, the store in the United Kingdom and the colonies was as follows:—

Musket Ball Cartridges . . .	48,727,366
„ Blank „	8,527,159
Carbine Ball „ . . .	8,188,288
„ Blank „ . . .	4,335,087
Pistol Ball „ . . .	4,077,722
„ Blank „ . . .	946,023
Rifle Ball „ . . .	3,802,584
Musketoon Ball „ . . .	58,326
	78,662,555

When percussion muskets were introduced into the army, the old cartridges became useless. Most of the cartridges are made up by boys, in the Royal Laboratory at Woolwich; there are about 180 boys so employed, each of whom can make 600 ball cartridges or 900 blank cartridges in a day; but sometimes artillery men make them up in the colonies from powder sent from England in barrels.

CARTWRIGHT, EDMUND, though a graduate and a clergyman, comes before us for notice here as a mechanical inventor. In the year 1784 his attention was accidentally called to the subject of mechanical weaving. Dr. Cartwright's attention had never been directed to mechanical inventions, but by the April of 1785 he was enabled to produce his first power-loom, which, though an extremely rude machine, soon received many valuable improvements. Its first introduction was opposed both by manufacturers and their workmen, owing to various prejudices; and a mill containing 500 of his looms, the first which had been erected, was wilfully burnt down. With various improvements however it continued to force its way into use. In April 1790, Dr. Cartwright took out a patent for combing wool; altogether he obtained ten different patents for inventions and improvements of various kinds. In 1809 Parliament granted to Dr. Cartwright, who had hitherto derived little advantage from his inventions, the sum of 10,000*l.* for 'the good service he had rendered the public by his invention of weaving.' This was less than he had expended on his projects, but it enabled him to pass the remainder of his days in ease and comfort. He died in 1823, in his 81st year.

CARVING is usually understood to refer exclusively to works in ivory or wood, to distinguish it from carving in marble or stone, which comes under the term *sculpture;* or in metals, when it is called *chasing.* The ancients used ivory to a great extent in works of art, and its union with gold, called by the Greeks *chrys-elephantine* sculpture, was adopted by the greatest artists. In later times carving in ivory has been confined to smaller objects. Wood of almost every description was a favourite material for carving among the ancients, and, after clay, was doubtless, from the facility of cutting it, the first substance used for imitative art.

For a long period in modern times, there was a great demand for fine wood-carvings. The elaborately worked Gothic screens, choir seats, and desks, in most of our cathedrals and colleges, canopies, frames for doors and pictures, cabinets, and indeed every description of furniture, are evidences of the extent to which it was employed, and of the skill of the artists. One of the most eminent modern carvers in wood was Grinling Gibbons, a native of England. In London, the choir of St. Paul's may be instanced as a work of this artist. The German and Flemish carvers in ivory and wood were also much distinguished.

In Jordan's carving machinery, now at work at Messrs. Taylor, Williams and Jordan's establishment in the Belvedere Road, the wood has movement given to it, while the tools remain nearly stationary. A pattern of the work to be carved is first modelled by the artist, and afterwards copied by the machine in wood with perfect accuracy, and in such a manner that two or three copies are made simultaneously; the carving thus prepared by the machine is then sent back to the artist, who introduces by hand the finishing touches. A very large amount of the carving in the new Houses of Parliament has been effected by this machine. The more delicate work for the same building requiring hand-processes, is entrusted to Mr. Rogers, whose exquisite productions have done much towards the revival of a taste for this art.

About five years ago Mr. Pratt patented a carving machine, which was based on another patent machine, invented by Mr. Irving, for preparing the materials for inlaying. According to a description given of it before the Institute of British Architects, Mr. Pratt's Machine combines the principle of the lathe, the drill, and the pantograph. The material on which the design is to be carved is fixed on a table which turns on a centre. The tool, acting in the manner of a centre-bit, is attached to an arm, also working on a centre, and is made to revolve with great velocity. Guided by a pattern of cast-iron, the tool, by a double movement of the arm and the table, can be made to pass through any combination of curves, drilling out the material as it passes over it. The lines of the design are determined by the iron pattern, and the depth and form of the sinking by the shape and position of the tool; and if a double moulding is required, two patterns and two tools and a double operation are necessary. The tool and its position at the end of the arm being once adapted to the section of the moulding to be produced, the rest is purely mechanical; the workman guides the tool with one hand, and the table with the other, and the design comes out with great rapidity. The tool revolves three thousand times in a minute; and the wood is cut away in the form of very fine fragments, like sawdust, leaving a smooth surface behind it. The machine will cut stone with nearly the same facility as wood.

A kind of imitative carving was introduced a few years ago, in which a hot iron is employed instead of a cutting tool. An iron mould is prepared corresponding to the pattern to be produced; and this mould, being heated to redness, is applied with great force to the surface of a piece of damped wood; and this process is repeated until the required form is produced, by burning away the surface of the wood. The char is then removed; and any requisite undercutting is done by hand. When finished, the work has somewhat the appearance of old oak; and the surface may be brought to a high polish.

The recent exhibitions of manufactures, both modern and mediæval, have been rich in specimens of carving, showing to how high a degree of excellence this art may be carried. It is a pleasing feature in the history of taste that this art, after a long period of decline, has now again worked itself into favour.

CARYA'TIDES, female figures employed in architecture in place of columns. Like many other forms of art, they were most probably drawn from Egypt. Six beautiful Caryatid figures were employed in the Pandrosion, one of the buildings on the Acropolis of Athens. The northern portico of the Pandrosion had six Ionic columns, four in front, and one on each flank: the southern portico was supported by six Caryatid figures, four in front, and one on each flank. They were placed upon a basement, and supported an enriched entablature. One of the figures is now in the British Museum, among the Elgin collection. The execution of this figure is very fine; its height is 7 feet 9 inches. Caryatides may be seen at the side porches of St. Pancras Church.

CARYO'TA, a genus of palms which grows in tropical Asia. Its wood is so hard as to be cut with some difficulty, and is consequently of considerable value, provided the soft sapwood in the centre is scraped away. Roxburgh describes the tree as being highly valuable to the natives of the countries where it grows in plenty: it yields them, during the hot season, an immense quantity of toddy, or palm-wine. The pith, or farinaceous part, of the trunk of old trees is said to be equal to the best sago; the natives make it into bread, and boil it into thick gruel.

CASAN is one of the busiest cities of European Russia. It has a great cloth manufactory, in which 1000 work-people are employed. Cottons, morocco and other leather, soap, steel, iron, and earthenware, tiles, gunpowder, spirits, and beer are the other chief manufactures. It carries on an extensive trade by means of the Volga in these products, and in tea and other Asiatic imports.

CASE-HARDENING. This is a process by which the surface of a piece of iron has a quality imparted to it very much allied to that of steel; so as to superadd the hardness of a steel surface to the toughness of an iron foundation. It is applied to various kinds of tools and utensils; and is brought about by the action of heat and charcoal, as in the conversion of steel. [Steel Manufacture.]

CASE-SHOT are bullets contained in a cylindrical tin canister, or in a spherical shell of iron, which are discharged from a piece of ordnance. The first of these kinds of cases burst immediately on leaving the gun, and the bullets, which at first take diverging rectilinear directions, soon lose all regularity of motion; their effective range does not exceed 500 yards. The spherical case-shot, which were formerly called Shrapnell's Shells from the name of the inventor, are fired like common shells, and, the length of the fuse being properly regulated, they only burst at the required spot; consequently the scattered balls and the fragments of the shell may be made to take full effect in a column of an enemy's troops at 800 or 1200 yards' distance.

CASEIN is the basis of the various kinds of cheese, and closely resembles albumen in many properties. It is a curdy white substance, insoluble in water or alcohol, but soluble by water containing an alkali or its carbonate. It is coagulable, and is separated from the milk in making cheese.

CASEMATE, is a vault of stone or brick-work, frequently built in the thickness of the rampart of a fortress for the reception of artillery which is to fire through embrasures pierced for the purpose in the front of the vault.

CASHMERE. This very interesting mountain region of India has produce and manufactures of a peculiar character. The lower classes live partly on the *singhara*, or water-tun, which, during eight or nine months in the year, is fished from the bottom of the lake Wulur. Of this article, 60,000 tons are procured annually, sufficient for the support of 20,000 persons. The mucilaginous pith of the water-lily also supports a considerable number of people during eight months. Among the cultivated plants the crocus is the only one which furnishes an article of export, the saffron of Cashmere being known in all parts of Western Asia. A sort of grape, called *sungut*, yields, by distillation, a beverage which, in the opinion of the Chinese, is not inferior to that of the ordinary grape. Common grapes also abound, and the wine which is made resembles Madeira. No trees are cultivated with any care except the walnut, of which there are three different kinds; the kernel is eaten, and used for making oil; and the husks of the fruit are employed in dyeing black. Cashmere is famous for its flowers, especially roses, which are cultivated with care, and from them *attar* is extracted. [ATTAR OF ROSES.] Bees are very numerous, and each farmer has several bee-hives in the walls of his house,—sometimes as many as ten; these hives are of a cylindrical form, and extend quite through the wall. Silk-worms are reared, but less than formerly, when silk was an article of export. The metals are iron, which is abundant, copper, plumbago, and lead exist, but are not worked.

The Cashmerians are very industrious, which is shown in the excellence of their cultivation, and the perfection which their manufactures have attained. The principal branch of industry is shawl-making, in which 60,000 individuals are employed, though the number of looms, which two hundred years ago amounted to 40,000, has been greatly reduced. Two weavers work at each loom, when the shawls are simple; but when they are of a superior kind, four persons are required. According to one authority, 80,000 shawls are annually made, but the number is constantly fluctuating, so that no correct estimate can possibly be formed. Paper is also manufactured, and though less is now exported than formerly, it is still considered as the best made in Western Asia. The Cashmerians work with great skill and taste different objects in wood, which, as well as lacker-work, are exported to the neighbouring countries. The commerce of the country seems to be limited to the exportation of the manufactured goods, and the importation of wool from Tibet, and of metals from India, and perhaps from Persia. The transport of goods over the high mountains is chiefly effected by men, who carry them on their backs. Between Cashmere and Ladak sheep are used to carry burdens.

CASHMERE, is a peculiar textile fabric formed of the fine downy wool found about the roots of the hair of the Tibet goat, and so called from the original seat of the manufacture, in the valley of Cashmere. Shawls of exceedingly delicate quality are the principal articles manufactured of this material; but a cloth woven in imitation of them is also made, and called by the same name, or by corruption, Cassimere. *Kerseymere*, which resembles cassimere in sound, is a different fabric. [WOOLLEN AND WORSTED MANUFACTURES.]

An interesting description of the manufacture of Cashmere shawls is given in 'Vigne's Travels in Kashmir.' The process is exceedingly slow, the weaving of a pair of shawls, or, as some writers have it, of a single shawl, often employing three men with a clumsy old-fashioned loom for a period of six months; and, owing to the numerous heavy duties charged upon the shawls between leaving the loom and reaching a purchaser in this country, the price of real Cashmere shawls of the best quality is very high. They have frequently been sold in London at from 100 to 400 guineas each, and at one time, when the import duty, which has since been greatly reduced, amounted to 80 per cent. on the value, as much as 500 guineas has been demanded for a single shawl.

Various attempts have been made to naturalise the Cashmere shawl goat in this and other European countries; but, as the peculiarities of its wool appear to be dependent upon climate, the perfect success of any such attempt is problematical. The wool itself has also been imported as a raw material. In 1830, at which time the weaving of shawls from Cashmere yarn imported from France, had become an important branch of manufacture, a premium of 300*l*. was offered by the

Board of Trustees for the Encouragement of Arts and Manufactures in Scotland, to the person who should first establish the spinning of Cashmere wool upon the French principle. In consequence of this offer, Captain C. S. Cochrane devoted himself to the subject, and having succeeded, after some difficulty, in obtaining a knowledge of the secret, he patented the plan, and subsequently sold his patent to the Messrs. Holdsworth, of Glasgow, who established the manufacture successfully, and obtained the offered reward in 1832.

CASKS; COOPERAGE. The making of casks, barrels, butts, hogsheads, tubs, &c., is, up to the present time, almost wholly a handicraft employment. The peculiar shaping of the pieces of wood, the fitting them together, and the mode of binding them with iron hoops, —are all effected without the aid of anything which deserves the name of machinery. Yet when we consider how mathematically exact all the angles and curves must be, it would seem to be a branch of manufacture peculiarly fitted for the application of machinery.

Accordingly, we find that patents are frequently taken out for cask-making machinery. One such patent, by Mr. Brown, obtained twenty or thirty years ago, relates to a system of machinery, of which one part cuts the edges of the staves; another part cuts the groove or chine for receiving the head; a third part cuts the head into a circular shape: a fourth bevels the edge of the head; and a fifth gives a smooth circular surface to the exterior of the cask.

Davison and Symington's patent respecting casks, taken out in 1844, relates to the value of a rapid current of heated air, not only in drying wood, but in removing fungous impurities which often accompany damp-wood. They recommend that, in making a cask, instead of drying the wood in the ordinary way before using, by which it is difficult to bend without blistering, it should be cut up quite green, and shaped into staves and heads—due allowance being made for shrinkage. The pieces are easily bent in this state; and being temporarily fastened together, they are exposed to a rapid current of heated air, which carries off all the moisture, and shrinks the pieces to the proper size.

The same patentees also uso hot air to cleanso casks after using: a method which they consider to be more effectual and cheaper than the use of steam, which is ordinarily employed in the great breweries. In order to remove from tho interior of the cask any fungus or impurity which cannot be removed by the heated air, the patentees use a peculiar kind of chain, which enters at the bung-hole, and is worked about by means of machinery.

Mr. Robertson, a cooper of Liverpool, took out a patent in 1849 for a series of machines of rather complicated character, for making casks and similar vessels. One piece of apparatus is intended to plane, at one time, both sides of the staves which are to form the curved part of the cask; giving a convexity to one surface and a concavity to the other surface of each piece of wood. A second piece of apparatus planes the edges of the staves, giving to each edge the particular slope necessary for the staves to assume a circular arrangement when placed edge to edge. A third machine compresses all tho staves together in a circular form, and forces the ends within the hoops which are to bind them together. Another machine presses together the pieces of wood which are to form the head of the cask, cuts them into a circular form, and bevels the edges. A fifth piece of apparatus cuts the groovo in which the head is fitted to the cask; and another punches the holes in the iron hoops. Thus, according to the patentee's plans, every part of a cask is made by machinery.

Mr. Samuel Brown patented in 1840 a modo of making metallic casks. The cask is formed of a parallelogram of sheet iron or other metal, turned up into a cylindrical form, with an ordinary lap joint. The head of the cask is formed of a circular piece of metal, cut out and turned up all round the edge; this being forcibly driven into the cylindrical barrel, has rivets placed at intervals of four or five inches all round, which are rivetted through the barrel and through the turned up edge of the head. The other end of the cask, called the moveable head, is made like the first, but attached in a different manner; in this case projecting ears of metal are rivetted at proper intervals around the cylinder; and the heads of these rivets being within the cylinder, serve as stops to prevent the head of the cask from being driven in too far. This second head being forced into its place, the ears are bent down upon the edge of the cylinder and over the raised edge of the head, thereby retaining it firmly in its place. The joints are to be made fluid-tight with any of the ordinary paints or cements.

CASPIAN SEA. The depth of this inland sea in some places reaches to 600 feet; but, as the sea is mostly shallow near the coasts, it is unfavourable for navigation by large ships. The water is salt, but less so than that of the ocean. The navigation is confined to the countries lying on the west shores between the mouth of the Volga and the town of Asterabad. The Russians of Astrakhan use brigs of from 150 to 200 tons; but the Persians only small vessels, from 50 to 70 tons. The fisheries give employment to the inhabitants of the adjacent countries, who capture vast numbers of sturgeon, belugas, sterlets, salmon, and seals. On the shores, much naphtha is met with.

CASSA'VA, or Manioc, a nutritious fecula obtained from the roots of Jatropha or Janipha Manihot, and some allied species. This plant abounds in a highly poisonous juice, very small doses of which produce the most dangerous consequences; it is however of so volatile a nature as to be entirely driven off by heat, and consequently there is no practical difficulty in procuring the nutritious substance in a pure state. In order to effect this the roots are peeled, well washed, and then ground between millstones till they are reduced to a state of paste. This is subjected to pressuro for the purpose of depriving it, as far as possible, of the juice; the residue is placed in vessels over a brisk and regular fire, and continually stirred, until it becomes dry; it then acquires a granular appearance, is gradually cooled, and afterwards packed in barrels, when it may be preserved for a great length of time. *Tapioca* is a preparation of Cassava.

CA'SSIA, is a genus of leguminous plants, consisting of a large number of species, chiefly inhabiting the tropical or temperate parts of the world, and including among them the plants that produce the *Senna* leaves of the apothecaries.

Cassia fistula is a small tree, with largo yellow flowers growing in long loose racemes, having the aspect of a laburnum, and is found wild in India and the tropical parts of Africa. The leaves, flowers and pulp of this plant are purgative, but they are not now much used. *Cassia acutifolia*, a small under shrub, is found wild in Egypt, Sennaar, and Abyssinia, and forms an important article in the commerce of those countries. It is chiefly sent to Alexandria for shipment, whence it has gained the name of *Alexandrian Senna* among the drug-merchants. It is considered the most valuable of all the sennas. *Cassia lanceolata* is found wild in Arabia, whence it is exported under the name of *Senna of Mecca*.

Of the species of Cassia mentioned above either the pulp or leaves are used in medicine.

The quantity of Cassia imported in 1849, amounted to no less than 472,693 lbs.; and in six months, from April to October 1850, to the enormous quantity of 940,395 lbs.

CASSIA BUDS. The unexpanded flowers of a species of *Cinnamomum*, when they have attained about a fourth of their complete size, are collected and sold under this name. The taste and odour resemble cinnamon, and they are used for similar purposes. By distillation they yield a heavy yellowish-coloured oil.

CASTILE. New and Old Castile are richly favoured provinces in Spain. The plains of New Castile are among the finest wheat districts in the world; in La Mancha and Toledo the annual produce of wheat amounts to about 2,000,000 quarters. The want of roads, canals, and navigable rivers, is however severely felt. Almost the only means of transport for all kinds of produce is by mule-back. The principal objects of cultivation besides wheat are saffron, oil, fruits, wines, hemp, silk, and *garbanzos*, a sort of pea much used for food. The province is rich in minerals; but mines of iron, salt, and quicksilver are the only ones worked. The manufactures are confined principally to articles of common use. The province contains three or four important towns which call for notice elsewhere. [ALMADEN; MADRID; TOLEDO.]

The other province, *Old* Castile, nearly resembles New Castile in general character. In the department of Santander the high lands contain fine pasturage, and in many places are covered with forests of chestnuts, oak, pine, and fir. A great deal of butter is made. Goats are very numerous. Iron of the best quality is obtained. In summer the mountain pastures of the sierras are frequented by countless numbers of migratory sheep, which remain here till the beginning of October, when they commence their return to Andalusia for the winter. The manufactures are confined to coarse woollens, cotton, linen, leather and glass. Though agriculture is in a very backward state in all the departments, yet a good deal of wheat is exported from the province. The chief sea-port, Santander, is a place of considerable commercial activity, and carries on an extensive trade with Cuba, to which it exports flour ground at the large mills in the neighbourhood. Wool is exported to England and other countries. The imports consist chiefly of colonial produce. San Ildefonso, on the northern slope of the Sierra de Guadarrama, is famous for its manufacture of glass.

CASTING. [FOUNDING.]

CASTLE, from the Latin *castellum*, a diminutive of *castrum*, an encampment, is a walled inclosure with a tower or towers, strongly constructed and intended as a place of safety. Numerous castles, many of which are in ruins, still remain in various parts of Great Britain, France, Germany, Italy, and in the East. The castles of England consist of those erected by the Romans; of British and Saxon castles erected previous to the Norman conquest, and Norman castles erected after it; and also of the more modern stone and brick castles, erected from about the reign of Edward I. to the time of Henry VII. The Roman castles in this country are numerous, and some of them still in very perfect condition, such as Burgh Castle and Richborough. The Saxons most probably adapted the Roman inclosures to their modes of defence, and it appears that they often raised a mound on one side of the walls, on which they erected a keep or citadel. Roman castles were probably sometimes formed on the sites of British works; and Saxon castle-building was probably borrowed from the Romanised Britons, who had acquired a taste and knowledge of the arts from the Romans.

Norman castles, as fortifications, are the strongest. They consisted of mounds and ditches, or moats, with walls on the mounds surmounted with battlements: the walls were also fortified at the top with small projecting towers called bastions. In the walls were entrance gate towers, with bridges either of stone or wood, which were made to draw up and down. The entrances were also guarded with thick doors and portcullises, or gates which dropped down through grooves at the side of the masonry. All apertures, except the gateway, were usually very small. Platforms were made behind the parapets. The gateway was sometimes defended by a barbican and also flanked by towers, as well as the outer walls. The keep was usually in or near the centre of the castle, and it had sometimes a chapel within it. Rochester Castle, which stands on a small eminence near the bridge over the Medway, is a fine example of a Norman castle.

William the Conqueror was a great builder of castles. Forty-nine castles are mentioned in Domesday Book, which notices Arundel as the only one named in the time of the Confessor. It is said that in the nineteen years of Stephen's reign 1115 castles were erected. Every feudal chieftain had his stronghold, round which his immediate retainers rallied, for the purpose of mutual defence or to annoy and plunder their neighbours. A very considerable number of old towns of Europe gradually arose around these baronial fortifications; and it is interesting to trace, in the history of many of these communities, the progress by which the town, originally a miserable dependence on the castle, gradually attained privileges, and charters, and wealth, and increased in strength and importance exactly in proportion as the owner of the fortress lost both, till finally the castle, from being neglected and deserted, was either levelled with the ground and furnished materials for house-building, or remained in ruins, an enduring monument of the slow but certain victory of the once subject townsmen over their lords.

CASTOR is a secretion formed within the body of the beaver. The secretion is at first in a liquid state about the consistence of syrup, but it ultimately becomes solid, losing some of its odour and activity. As met with in commerce it is of two kinds, the Russian, and Canadian or English, of which the Russian is the rarest and most esteemed: it is more carefully managed from the time of its excision, being first dried in smoke, and often wrapped in swine's bladder. The odour is peculiar, very penetrating and unpleasant; the taste is also peculiar, bitterish, somewhat acrid or aromatic, and enduring. *Castorine* may be obtained by boiling one part of castor in six of alcohol, and leaving the filtered liquid to cool, when it falls to the bottom. It is very combustible, and is neither acid nor alkaline; it has a copperish taste.

Castor is used to a considerable extent in medicine.

CASTOR-OIL is procured from the *Ricinus Communis*, or Castor-oil plant, which was known from very ancient times both to the Egyptians and to the Greeks. The native country of the *Ricinus communis* is unknown, though it is conjectured to be originally from Barbary. The entire plant is possessed of active properties, but the oil extracted from the seeds is only employed in Europe. The ancients administered the seeds entire, but their variable action, occasionally even producing fatal effects, led to their disuse, and the oil is of comparatively recent introduction. The seeds, of which three are found in each capsule, are about the size of a small bean. They were formerly known in the shops as *Semina Ricini*. Various procedures have been adopted to extract the oil, and these have much influence on its qualities in respect of colour, acridity, and freedom from rancidity. Both in India and America, whence the first supplies were brought, much heat was employed, and during the process a volatile principle was either liberated or produced, which was so irritating as to require the workmen to protect their faces by masks. Even in the present day some heat is used to obtain what is termed the *cold drawn* castor-oil, but it is quite unnecessary, and should always be avoided.

Castor-Oil of good quality is a thickish fluid, of a very pale yellow colour, almost limpid, with a slightly nauseous odour, and an oily taste, mild at first, but causing a feeling in the back of the throat, which is more or less intense in proportion to the freshness of the specimen. Old or badly-prepared oil is rancid and disagreeable. It can be solidified only by a very low temperature.

Castor Oil is a valuable and well-known medicine, of which considerable quantities are used. The quantity imported in 1848 was no less than 4588 cwts.

CASTRES, a town in the department of Tarn in France, is a place of great manufacturing industry; for their care and skill, and the finish given to their productions, its artisans are considered the best in the south of France. It is particularly celebrated for its fine wool-dyed cloths, called *cuirs de laine;* but all other sorts of woollen stuffs are manufactured, as well as linen, soap, leather, glue, and paper. There are also several bleaching, dyeing, and silk-weaving establishments, and iron and copper foundries. The commerce of the town is very considerable.

CATALONIA, one of the provinces of Spain, is deficient in corn and cattle, but a good deal of wine is produced. Other articles of produce are oil, hemp, nuts, almonds, fruits, silks, &c. The forests abound with cork-trees, the bark of which is a considerable article of commerce. Catalonia abounds in mineral wealth, coal, copper, lead, zinc, manganese, cobalt, nitre, salt, marble, &c., being found. It is the chief manufacturing province of Spain, the principal products being woollens, cottons, silks, lace, leather, paper, iron, brandy, and liqueurs. The coasts abound with fish. Since the loss of the Spanish American colonies the trade of Catalonia has greatly declined.

Besides BARCELONA, the principal town, there are *Tortosa*. with its salt pits and quarries of jasper; *Tarragona*, with its manufactories of silks, trade by sea, and exports of oil, nuts, wine, brandy, cork, &c.; *Reus*, with its manufactories of brandy and liqueurs; *Manresa*, with its manufactures of silks and gunpowder. *Mataró* has manufactories of cottons, silks, lace, and glass, and ship-building yards. *Vich* has manufactories of woollens and cottons; coal and copper mines are worked in the neighbourhood, in which also are found amethysts, topazes, and coloured crystals, which are worked by the jewellers of Barcelona. *Ripoll* is north of Vich, and has manufactories of firelocks, swords, and bayonets.

CATAMARAN is a name given both in the East and West Indies to some kinds of rafts which are used in short navigations along the sea-shore. Those used at Madras, where the coast is shallow and shelving and the surf very great, consist of three cocoa-tree logs lashed together, and only large enough to carry one or at most two persons. On the coast of South America the rafts are from 70 to 80 feet long, and from 20 to 25 feet wide.

CATECHI'NUM. This peculiar principle is obtained not merely from Catechu, strictly so called, but also from gambir and some kinds of cinchona bark. The best mode of procuring it is to digest catechu in sulphuric æther, then evaporate the æther, wash the residuum in cold water, repeatedly dissolve it in boiling water, and by renewed evaporation procure it pure. It is persistent at the ordinary temperature of the air; but by long exposure to damp it resolves into a mould-like mass: at a moderate heat it melts into a transparent fluid; by a strong heat it becomes brown. Catechin is valuable as an application to check the flow of blood from leech-bites, scarification of the gums, &c.

CATECHU. [ACACIA.]

CATENARY (from *caténa*, a chain) is the curve in which a string of perfect flexibility and uniform thickness and density will hang from two points, which we may suppose to be in the same horizontal line, as the nature and properties of the curve will be the same from whatever points it may hang. And all catenaries are similar curves; that is to say, let there be any number of such curves formed by chains of different lengths, then each of them will be a picture, on a reduced or enlarged scale, of some portion of the longest.

In Bridge-building, great attention is paid to the natural tendency of materials to assume a catenary curve under certain circumstances.

CATGUT. Several useful articles, manufactured from the intestines of the sheep, are for some explained reason denominated catgut. Catgut is generally in the form of cord, string, or twine. The chief purposes to which such cord is applied are musical strings, for harps, violins, and guitars; hatters' bowstrings, for the bowing of fur and wool; clockmakers' cord; and thongs or cords for whips. Gold-beaters' skin is formed from a membrane covering the intestine of the ox.

CATTLE. A few of the commercial features relating to cattle are all that need be touched on in this work.

The British and Irish breeds of cattle have been resolved into Long-horns, Middle-horns, and Short-horns. The *Long-horns* were formerly coarse and heavy beasts; they had, however, good points; the hide was thick and mellow, and the milk, though not abundant, was rich. The great improver of this breed was Mr. Robert Bakewell, of Dishley, who founded what was called the New Leicester or Dishley Stock. But of late years this breed has fallen behind the improvéd Short-horns;

and, though good Long-horned cattle may occasionally be seen in the midland counties, the fame of the New Leicesters is extinguished. To the *Middle-horned* race belong the breeds of Devonshire, Herefordshire, Gloucestershire, Sussex, Wales, and the Scottish Highlands. The horns are of moderate size, fine, well turned, and sharp pointed; the limbs are clean; the figure is compact, and the expression animated; the oxen readily fatten, and the cows yield rich milk. In hardiness, and in the excellence of the meat they yield, the Middle-horns claim a high rank. Devons, Herefords, and Scots, whether horned or polled, sell well in the London markets. The *Short-horns* had long been known in the counties of Durham and York, before the time of their great improver, Mr. Collings. The cows were held in reputation as milkers, but the oxen were indifferent feeders, coarse, and ill formed, and produced meat of inferior quality. In the improved breed, however, while the milking properties are preserved, the tendency to fatten is brought to a high degree; and these qualities are combined with size, a magnificent figure, and the production of beef of the highest excellence.

The present leading breeds are the Middle-horns, and the Durham, Yorkshire, and Teeswater improved Short-horns. It is from the latter stocks that the great London dairies are supplied with milch cows. While in milk they yield abundantly, and when dry may be fattened off for the market with rapidity.

The great day for the sale of cattle in London is on the Monday in the week before Christmas. On this day, in six following years, the numbers brought to Smithfield have been as follows:—

1845	..	..	5320
1846	..	..	5470
1847	..	..	4250
1848	..	..	5940
1849	..	..	5758
1850	..	..	6720

The cattle exhibited for prizes at the Smithfield Cattle Show increased in number from 83 in 1845 to 180 in 1850.

The foreign cattle (including calves), imported into the ports of London and Hull, in forty-six weeks of the year 1850, amounted to 51,572.

The cattle sold at Smithfield amount at the present time to about 220,000 annually.

Of the uses which cattle render to the arts of life, in respect to milk, butter, cheese, leather, bladder, gold-beater's skin, horn, blood for clarifying, bone for handles and for manure, &c., the details given in this work afford much evidence.

CAVIAR, an article of food, which consists of the roes of large fish, salted and dried, especially of the sturgeon caught in the Volga. Large quantities are made in the neighbourhood of Astrakhan, as many as 30,000 casks having been exported from that city in a single season.

CAXTON, WILLIAM, to whom England owes the introduction of printing, was born probably in 1412, in the Weald of Kent. He was put apprentice to one Robert Large, a mercer or merchant of considerable eminence; and afterwards he travelled in the Low Countries for a short time. In 1471 Caxton describes himself as leading a life of ease, when, 'having no great charge or occupation,' he set about finishing the translation of Raoul le Fevre's 'Recueil des Histoires de Troye,' which he had commenced two years before. The original was the first book he printed, and this translation the third. In the Low Countries he entered into the service, or at least the household, of Margaret, duchess of Burgundy, who encouraged him to finish his translation of Le Fevre's 'History of Troy.' From the prologues and epilogues of this work we discover that he was now somewhat advanced in years, and that he had learnt to exercise the art of printing; but by what steps he had acquired this knowledge cannot be discovered; his types, however, show that he acquired it in the Low Countries. The time of his return to his native country is not known with certainty; but the usual supposition has been that he brought the art of printing into England in 1474. In 1477 he had undoubtedly quitted the Low Countries, and had taken up his residence in the vicinity of Westminster Abbey, where and in which year he printed his 'Dictes and Sayings of the Philosophers.' Stowe says he first exercised his business in an old chapel near the entrance of the Abbey; but a very curious placard, a copy of which, in Caxton's largest type, is now at Oxford in the late Mr. Douce's library, shows that he printed in the Almonry. His death took place in 1491 or 1492.

Caxton, Mr. Warton observes, by translating, or procuring to be translated, a great number of books from the French, greatly contributed to promote the state of literature in England. The known productions of his press amount to 64, and are enumerated with their titles in the 'Penny Cyclopædia.' Lists are also given by Dibdin, Lewis, and others.

The two largest assemblages of the productions from Caxton's press now known are those in the British Museum and in Earl Spencer's library at Althorpe.

CAYENNE PEPPER, is capsicum in a ground state. [CAPSICUM.]

CEDAR. The Cedar of Lebanon *(abies cedrus)* is described under ABIES, p. 6. The name of *Red Cedar* is sometimes given to the *Juniperus Bermudiana*, a tree from whose wood cedar pencils are made. About 1700 tons of this wood were imported in 1847.

CE'LEBES, a large island in the Eastern Seas, grows cotton, coffee, tobacco, and other merchantable produce. There are mines of iron, which yield metal of excellent quality, and some gold is obtained. Very large quantities of turtle are taken on the coast.

The population of Celebes is composed of several distinct races, of which the Bugis are considered to be the first in enterprise and intelligence; they engross nearly all the carrying trade of the Indian Archipelago, the trading of other tribes being almost entirely confined to coasting voyages.

CELLI'NI, BENVENUTO, born at Florence in 1500, was one who combined metallurgic skill with artistic genius to a degree perhaps never paralleled. His works may be divided into two classes. The first, for which he was most celebrated, comprises his smaller productions in metal, the embossed decorations of shields, cups, salvers, ornamented sword and dagger hilts, clasps, medals, and coins, in which he showed great skill in composition, and excellence in the details of execution. The second includes his large works, as a sculptor; and a reference to his bronze group of Perseus, with the head of Medusa, in the Piazza del Gran' Duca, in Florence, will be sufficient to illustrate his merit in the higher walk of his art. He also executed some fine portraits. His far-famed Shield of Achilles was displayed at the Mediæval Exhibition of 1850

CEMENT. Various cements are described under GLUE; LUTES; MASTICH; MORTAR; SOLDER. Another cement, used for fixing pieces of glass while being ground for optical purposes, is made of resin, bees' wax, and whiting. Metal chasers often use a cement made of pitch, resin, tallow and brickdust. A cement for alabaster or spar may be formed of resin, bees' wax, and plaster of Paris. For various purposes in the arts, the following are used as cements:—Shell-lac; melted sulphur; a mixture of lime and white of egg; a mixture of gum arabic, gum ammoniac, and alcohol; gum ammoniac, isinglass, and alcohol; rice paste; sal ammoniac, flowers of sulphur, and iron filings; red lead, white lead, and linseed oil; quicklime and ox-blood.

Benson's metallic cement is a mixture of blue lias lime with a sort of metallic sand very much like the Italian *puzzuolano*, but containing rather more iron. It is very durable both as a concrete and as a cement. It has been used at the Houses of Parliament, at the London Bridge Station, at the Alfred Life Office, and at other large buildings—sometimes as a concrete for foundations, but more frequently as a stucco for surfaces.

The recipes given in practical works, for making cements, are exceedingly numerous.

Mr. Swindells, a manufacturing chemist of Manchester, has recently introduced a cement made from the refuse of the manufacture of chromates of potash and soda—useful for no other purpose.

CENSUS. The general subject of a census of population is beyond the scope of the present work; but we may give from the census of 1841, the number of persons engaged in productive industry, under the headings of commerce, trade, manufactures, agriculture, and unskilled labour, in Great Britain.

CLASSES.	ENGLAND.	WALES.	SCOTLAND	ISLES in the BRITISH SEAS.	GREAT. BRITAIN.
	Total of Persons.	Total of Persons.	Total of Persons.	Total of Persons.	Total of Persons.
Commerce, Trade, and Manufacture	2,529,073	90,133	473,581	17,589	3,110,376
Agriculture	1,157,816	103,632	229,337	8,493	1,499,278
Labourers	620,492	53,430	84,573	3,373	761,868
	4,307,381	247,195	787,491	29,455	5,371,522

The approaching census, to be made on March 30, 1851, will afford materials for a useful comparison with the above.

CENTIGRADE means divided into one hundred degrees. The centigrade thermometer of Celsius, which is much used on the continent, divides the interval between the freezing and boiling points into 100 degrees. Thus 100 centigrade degrees are equivalent to 180 of Fahrenheit.

CENTRE, CENTER. This word is used with many different applications, in manufactures and machines dependent on dynamics and statics:—*Centre of gravity* is the point at which, the weight of a body being collected, the equilibrium of the body and of the system, if any, of which it forms a part, will not be disturbed. *Centre of gyration* is the point at which, if the whole of the matter in a body were collected, given forces would produce the same angular velocity of rotation in a given time as they would do if the particles of the body were distributed in their proper places. *Centre of percussion* is that point of a revolving body which would strike an obstacle with the same force as if the whole of the matter were collected in it. *Centre of oscillation* is the point in which the whole of the matter must be collected, in order that the time of oscillation may be the same as when it is distributed. *Centre of pressure* is the point at which the whole amount of pressure may be applied with the same effect as it has when distributed.

CENTRIFUGAL FORCE. Centrifugal force is very usefully applied in the action of DRYING MACHINES, and many other pieces of mechanism employed in manufactures. The nature of the force may be thus illustrated:— Let us suppose a small bullet attached to a string, which string is fastened to a point upon a table, friction and the resistance of the air not being supposed to exist. Let the bullet be placed in a state of revolution round the fixed point, by means of the string, and with a given velocity. It will continue to revolve round with the same velocity, and the string will be stretched by a pressure depending upon the mass of the bullet and its velocity.

This pressure of the string is caused by an effort to escape on the part of the bullet, arising from its tendency to continue its motion in the direction of the tangent. This is the *centrifugal* (or centre-avoiding) force, which is thus measured: suppose, for instance, the velocity of revolution in the circle to be 8 feet per second, and the radius 10 feet. Divide the square of the velocity by the radius, or divide 64 by 10, which gives 6.4. Then the pressure is such, that were it to take the place of the earth's attraction, the bullet, being allowed to fall, would, at the end of one second, have acquired a velocity of $6\frac{4}{10}$ feet per second, instead of $32\frac{1}{6}$, which is the case with bodies falling freely to the earth.

CERATES are mixtures made by druggists, in which wax is always a component. They are of a consistence between that of plasters and ointments, and are used as external applications in many surgical cases. There are not less than thirty different varieties of cerate employed by medical practitioners.

CERIUM, a peculiar metal, discovered in 1804, is pulverulent, chocolate-coloured, inflammable in gaseous chlorine and the vapour of sulphur. It decomposes water readily. When heated it burns long before redness. With oxygen and other simple substances it unites to form many compounds; but these are not yet much employed in the arts.

CETINE, is the cystallisable matter which forms the greater part of the substance called *spermaceti*. It is white, crystalline, soft to the touch, and friable; it is nearly inodorous, and tasteless; it fuses at 120° Fahr.

CEYLON. This fine island is particularly rich in natural produce; and preparations are being made to exhibit a most extensive collection of such produce at Hyde Park in the present year. Among the vegetable produce are cotton, tamarinds, gamboge, coir, cocoanuts, coffee, rice, nutmegs, ginger, mandioca, arrow-root, a great variety of vegetable fibres fitted for cordage, and a fair variety of timber wood. Of animal products there are being collected ivory, buffalo and deer horns, honey, wax, hides, hoofs, and musk. Among dye materials are madder, jack-wood, sapan-wood, and turmeric. The sea shores will yield pearls, mosses, sponge, cowries, and salt, minerals, medicinal substances, gums, and resins—are all in rich variety.

Mr. Capper, secretary to a committee for managing the transmission of specimens to England, in a letter to Lord Torrington, remarks: "Without placing the Cingalese carvers and workers in the fine metals, on an exact par with other nations famed for such works, they may yet be fairly entitled to an honourable place. The specimens now preparing of carvings in ebony, calamander, ivory, shells, &c. will, it is believed, earn a reputation for the island workmen, which has not yet been accorded them in England. The committee is doing all in its power to procure the best specimens of silver ornaments."

An important arrangement for Ceylon is that which makes it a central point for the Oriental Mail Packets. A mail which leaves Southampton every month, viâ Alexandria and the Red Sea, stops at Ceylon whence two branch mails issue, one to Madras and Calcutta, the other to Penang, Singapore, and Hong Kong; and it is probable that another branch mail to Australia, Van Diemen's Land, and New Zealand, will be made part of this monthly system — all conducted by steam navigation.

A good deal of weaving is carried on at Ceylon. The pressure of oil from numerous varieties of seed is also largely conducted. Ceylon takes British goods to the value of about a million sterling annually, and sells in return large quantities of cinnamon, coffee, and cocoa-nut oil.

CHAFF MACHINES. The machines for cutting chaff for cattle and horses present many varieties. At the recent Smithfield cattle show (1850) many forms were exhibited. Gillet's Guillotine Chaff Engine acts either by hand or by steam power; by hand it will cut 30 bushels per hour; by steam 200 bushels. It has a knife with two edges so as to cut both up and down during its motion, which is communicated by a crank. Samuelson's chaff cutter has a large wheel, rotated by a lever handle, and having a knife edge forming one radius to the wheel. Wedlake's machine is somewhat similar, but has two radial knives instead of one. The more common chaff-cutter or chaff box consists of an oblong box, in which the hay or straw is laid: and a long knife cuts the ends which protrude beyond the box; the knife has a double lever action, which assists the labour of the cutter. Messrs. Cottam's chaff-cutting machine, patented in 1849, is a complicated piece of apparatus in which the hay or straw is led between rollers to the spot where the cutters can act upon it.

CHAGRES. Under PANAMA is given a slight sketch of the important travelling routes across the American isthmus, of one of which Chagres is the Atlantic port.

CHAIN (in Surveying) is a measuring chain of 100 links, altogether 4 poles, or 66 feet, or 22 yards in length, so that ten square chains make an acre. It is commonly called Gunter's Chain, having been first used by him, and described in his treatise on the Cross Staff, &c.

The chain is of universal use in modern surveying; but care must be taken to verify its length from time to time, since the material is very extensible, and the apparatus must necessarily be roughly used.

CHAIN-CABLES are iron chains used in lieu of hemp cables for anchoring vessels. The liability of hemp cables to be destroyed by the alternate action of air and water, and especially by chafing in rocky anchorage ground, led M. Bougainville to suggest the idea of substituting iron as early as 1771; but the idea was not taken up till 1808, when Mr. Slater, a surgeon in the navy, obtained a patent for a chain-cable. Even after this many years elapsed before their advantages wree generally recognised. Chain cables are usually furnished with bolts at the distance of one or two fathoms from each other, by withdrawing one of which a ship may slip her anchor in case of emergency in less time than would be required to cut a hemp cable. The weight of a chain-cable is an advantage while the ship is at anchor, as the strain is exerted on the cable rather than on the ship, and must be excessive before it can draw the cable straight.

Mr. Frearson, of Birmingham, patented in 1848 a method of making chains (for cables and other purposes). The rod of iron is grasped while red-hot by tongs or pinchers, and drawn between two grooved rollers; these rollers have so peculiar a movement imparted to them by machinery, that the bar is forced round a die or mandril, into a form fitted to produce a link; while arrangements are at the same time made for connecting this link with the one last made.

A new cable-proving machine was introduced in 1848 by Messrs. Dunn and Elliot, of Manchester. It consists mainly of a horizontal iron cylinder, with a piston working to and fro. The chain-cable is attached to one end of the piston-rod; and beyond this rod is a long iron trough, in a right line with the cylinder, and continuing to a considerable length, depending on the length of chain to be tested at one time. At the remote end of this trough a pair of claws grasp the other end of the chain; so that the chain extends from the piston to the claws, through the cylinders and the trough; and any force which tends to move the piston backwards will stretch the chain. The end of the cylinder next the trough is made watertight; and water is forced by a double hydraulic pump into the hollow space between the piston and this closed end of the cylinder: the cylinder is thus forced backward, and the chain becomes severely stretched. A water ram and scale-beam are so placed in connection with the cylinder as to measure the amount of force exerted on the chain. The same machine can test strengths between the wide limits of ½ cwt. and 100 tons.

CHAIN-SHOT. Two iron balls linked together by a chain eight or ten inches long are so called. They are used in naval actions.

CHAIRS. It is a remarkable fact that the handsome chairs of a modern drawing-room are very little other in shape than fac-similes of the chairs made by the Etruscans twenty-five centuries ago. The chair of Bede, the Saxon bishop and historian, was simply a long narrow box without a lid, formed of rough boards, nailed together and set upright, with a shelf near the lower end as a seat. King Edmund Ironside had a gala chair formed of two carved beams of oak, crossed like the letter X, with a cushion-seat at the place where the beams crossed. The chair appears to have been more used in England than on the continent in past ages; for it did not come into customary use among the nobility of France and Italy till about the reign of Francis I.

In reference to chair making in London at the present time, a few details are given under Furniture Manufacture.

Modern ingenuity has devised a mode of making chairs which shall also serve as sofas and bedsteads. A piece of furniture recently patented by Messrs. Key and Mitchell is of this kind. The *suspension* chair, patented by Messrs. Brown, is a remarkable contrivance consisting simply of eight wrought iron bars, and a piece of strong canvas or damask; although capable of forming either a chair or a sort of couch-bed, it can be unscrewed, and packed in a box 52 inches long by about 2 inches square.

CHALK forms the higher part of the geological series or group termed cretaceous. It is composed of nearly 44 parts of carbonic acid and 56 parts of lime. It is extensively used in agriculture, to improve various soils: the soils most improved being the strong wet clays which contain a portion of iron. Chalk acts as an absorbent, corrects astringency, and prevents clay from becoming a solid mass. On loose sands it acts chiefly as a cement, binding the silicious particles together. In districts where chalk is much used, it is generally put on the land in autumn, and not ploughed in till it has been exposed to the frost.

It is of advantage to throw chalk into ponds used by cattle: it corrects any acidity which may arise from stagnation. In fattening calves chalk is of great use; it may be laid in the calf-pens for them to lick, or it may be scraped and mixed with a small quantity of salt, and laid in a small manger within the reach of each calf.

Chalk is used in preparing crayons, and for a few other purposes in the arts.

CHAMOMILE. This useful plant is frequent in a wild state on many of the commons near London. The flowers are much used as a tonic.

CHAMPAGNE WINE is the produce of the vineyards of the departments of the Marne, Haute-Marne, Ardennes, and Aube, which were comprehended in the ancient French province of Champagne. Of the various growths of Champagne, that made on the banks of the Marne has the highest reputation, and forms the greater part of what is sent to foreign countries. Champagne wine is light in body: it is of various colours, white, straw-colour, pink, and red: and these are divided into sparkling, creaming, and still, or, as they are called in France, *mousseux*, *crêmant*, and *non-mousseux*. The red wines of good quality are, for the most part, exported to Belgium, and the white to England, Russia, Germany, the Levant, Greece, and the French West India colonies; some portion of the shipments to England are reshipped to India and other parts. The details of the vintage are given under Wine.

CHAPTAL, JEAN ANTOINE, was one of those experimental chemists whose labours bring great and immediate aid to the manufacturing arts. He was born in 1750; and inheriting a large fortune from his uncle, he established some important chemical manufactories in Montpellier, and thus bestowed upon France several valuable products which were previously obtained from foreigners. In 1793 Chaptal was called to the capital by the Committee of Public Safety, to manage the manufactory of salt-petre, which substance could no longer be obtained from abroad, and the want of which was pressing. He was one of the first professors of the Polytechnic School, and in 1798 was elected a member of the Institute. While he was in office under Napoleon, he established chambers of commerce, and consulting councils of arts and manufactures; the School of Arts and the Conservatory at Paris are monuments of his enlightened solicitude for increasing the opportunities and means of instruction. He published useful processes, visited the manufactories, conversed with the workmen, offered them his advice, applauded their discoveries, and encouraged the importation of processes and apparatus from abroad. In fact, during the whole course of his active life, he extended his views and his care to every substance and circumstance which he considered favourable to the improvement of arts and manufactures. He died at Paris in 1832.

CHARCOAL. The relation which charcoal bears to carbon has been already explained. [Carbon]. As now conducted, charcoal is prepared by two different methods. One is that of piling the wood in a heap, which is covered with turfs and sand, to allow of the entrance of such a portion only of atmospheric air as is sufficient to carry on the imperfect combustion required. The heap is fired at several holes left near the bottom, and a draught of air is obtained by at first leaving an orifice at the top of the heap; this is afterwards covered, and, when it is found that the flame has prevaded the heap entirely, the bottom holes are also closed. In the other method, the wood is put into iron cylinders, which are set in brick-work, and surrounded by fire: the wood in the cylinders has no communication with the external air, and they have only a small opening to allow of the escape of the residual products, which consist chiefly of water, pyroligneous acid, creosote, pyroxylic spirit, and empyreumatic oil.

M. Violette communicated an important paper to the French Academy of Sciences in 1848, on the manufacture of charcoal for gunpowder. He found that when wood is exposed to heat in close vessels, it does not become charred till near 500° F., when it produces an imperfect charcoal; at near 600° it yields a brown charcoal; while the best black charcoal requires a temperature of nearly 700° F. He also invented a remarkable mode of making charcoal by the heat of steam. The wood is put into a horizontal cylinder, round which is coiled a steam-pipe, and through this pipe is sent a constant flow of steam of a determinate temperature, according as a greater or lesser degree of charring is required. M. Violette has found that fuel is saved, and better charcoal produced by this method; he has adopted it at the powder mills of Esquerdes, which are under his charge.

CHASING OF METALS. Metallic goods are generally made in one of three ways—by casting in moulds, by forging or turning in masses, or by pressing or stamping out of thin sheets. The last of these three has been greatly developed at Birmingham within the last few years. Either the entire article receives its form from the sheet by stamping, or, when roughly formed, it receives an ornamental device by a process of chasing. For the latter variety of work, steel blocks, punches, or bosses are provided, each one presenting at the end a definite form, such as curved, angular, square, &c.; and these are fixed or held with the finished end uppermost. The article to be ornamented, which is always of a thin, hollow kind, is placed face uppermost on the punch: a pattern or design is drawn on the face of the article, and the adjustment is so made that the punch beneath shall follow the course of the lines in the device. A fine hammer is then employed to strike the piece of thin metal; the effect of which is, that the metal is forced upwards in a fine burr or protuberance at every place where there is a punch beneath it. By shifting the piece of metal so that different parts of its lower surface may in succession be brought over the punch, and by changing the form of the punch when necessary, a protuberant design or pattern in relief is formed on the article of metal.

At the Mediæval Exhibition of 1850 the specimens of chased metal were numerous and beautiful.

CHATHAM ARSENAL. Chatham is worthy of our attention for the government works there established. The naval and military establishments consist of a dockyard, nearly a mile in length, which has four wet docks capable of receiving vessels of the largest size, and several building-slips; metal mills: an extensive arsenal; barracks on a large scale for artillery and engineers, infantry and royal marines; a park of artillery; magazines and storehouses; besides a handsome dock-chapel and a number of habitations for the civilians who are employed. The principal mast-house is 240 feet long by 120 feet wide. The rope house is 1,128 feet in length, and 47½ feet wide: in it cables 101 fathoms in length and 25 inches in circumference are made. The machinery used in all the departments is of the very best kind. A duplicate of Brunel's block-making machine is kept here, ready for use in case the machine at Portsmouth should get out of order. The engineer barracks are built in a plain and simple style, and are extensive and convenient. Near the dock-yard gate is a large naval hospital, which was erected at the suggestion of William IV. when lord high admiral.

In 1848 a committee of the House of Commons inquired into the navy estimates and the works and expenditure for which they were required. Chatham dock-yard was included among the naval establishments investigated. The estimates included salaries 17,459*l.*; and wages 101,300*l.* The authorised or established workmen were 1,727 in number, and the hired workmen 233. There were said, in the Report, to be four docks, viz.: two for first rates, and two for frigates; and nine slips, of which six were for first rates. After the fire at Devonport dock-yard in 1840, which was greatly extended owing to the tarred wooden and paper roofs which covered the building slips, the admiralty began gradually to replace such roofs with others made of metal. Of these three have been constructed for Chatham, and placed over the slips Nos. 1, 2, and 3, at a cost of 32,590*l.* Nearly all the slips have been recently either rebuilt or strengthened and repaired. The metal mills at Chatham are more extensive than at any other of the dock-yards. At the time of the inquiry (1848) the metal mills produced 700 tons of sheet copper, 400 tons of bolt copper, and 800 tons of remanufactured iron per annum. All the old copper sheeting from the various dock-yards is re-melted here into sheets.

There are saw-mills at Woolwich, Chatham,

and Sheerness: but those at Chatham are the most complete. The Chatham mills could, indeed, it is said, cut timber enough for most of the yards. It is merely straight cutting: the machinery employed is not fitted for cutting the curved pieces required in a ship, which are still cut by hand.

CHECK, a species of chequered cloth, in which coloured lines or stripes cross each other rectangularly, like a chess-board. This manner of beautifying webs is very antient; for many of the figures in Rosellini's 'Egypt' are dressed in chequered cloths. The compartments of a checked pattern are sometimes formed by differently coloured threads, and sometimes by threads of different quality. Cotton handkerchiefs checked of various colours have been manufactured in India, probably from time immemorial, under the name of *pullicates.* The ground of these has usually a pale buff colour, and is woven with the nankin yellow cotton. Checks in this country are mostly manufactured for the coarser purposes of seamen's shirts, aprons, &c., and the demand is very large.

Mr. Robert Kay, of Bury, son of the ingenious but persecuted inventor of the fly shuttle, invented the drop box, for making checks, by means of which the weaver could at pleasure use any one of three shuttles without rising from his seat, each shuttle containing a differently coloured weft.

CHEESE. Milk consists of three distinct substances, which begin to separate from one another as soon as it is exposed to the air. The oily part rises to the surface by its less specific gravity, and, when it is collected into a solid mass by agitation, it forms *butter*; the caseum coagulated by the action of any acid is called *curd,* and when pressed becomes *cheese.* The fluid which remains is the serum, or *whey.*

The first process in making cheese is to separate the curd from the whey, which may be done by allowing the milk to become sour; but it is better to bring about this result by artificial means, by the addition either of certain vegetable acids, or of a substance called *rennet,* which is the gastric juice of the stomach of a sucking calf. The calf stomach is very carefully prepared, and brought to a dry state like parchment; and at the time of making cheese, a piece of this substance, called *vell,* is cut off and soaked for some hours in water or whey, and the whole is added to the warm milk, or else pieces of vell are put into a linen bag, and soaked in warm water until the water has acquired sufficient strength. Soft and rich cheeses are not intended to be kept long; hard and dry cheeses are adapted to be kept and stored for provisions. Of the first kind are all cream cheeses, and those soft cheeses called Bath cheeses and Yorkshire cheeses, which are sold as soon as made, and if kept too long become soft and putrid. Stilton and Gruyère cheeses are intermediate; Parmesan, Dutch, Cheshire, Gloucestershire, and similar cheeses are intended for longer keeping. The poorer the cheese is the longer it will keep; and all cheese that is well cleared from whey and sufficiently salted will keep for years. The Gruyère and Parmesan cheeses differ only in the nature of the milk, and in the degree of heat given to the curd in different parts of the process. Gruyère cheese is entirely made from new milk, and Parmesan from skimmed milk. In the first nothing is added to give flavour; in the latter saffron gives both colour and flavour: the process in both is exactly similar.

In making cheese the milk is heated to about blood-heat (95° to 100° Fahr.), and the solution of rennet is well mixed with it. The coagulum, or curd, having been formed, which may be in about half an hour, it is cut into slices, the heat raised to about 135°, and after remaining about an hour at that temperature, and being stirred with a staff, the curd is found to be broken into small pieces. It is then collected on a cloth woven with wide interstices, or a sieve, to allow the whey to drain from it. When sufficiently drained, the curd is put into a wide hoop, shallow barrel, box, or something of the kind, and subjected to the action of the cheese-press. Sometimes the curd is mixed with salt, and sometimes salt is rubbed on the cheese after it is made.

In Cheshire the making of cheese is carried on in great perfection, and the greatest pains are taken to extract every particle of whey. For this purpose, the curd is repeatedly broken and mixed, the cheeses are much pressed, and placed in wooden boxes which have holes bored into them. Through these holes sharp skewers are stuck into the cheese in every direction, so that no particle of whey can remain in the curd. The elastic matter formed also escapes through these channels, and the whole cheese is a solid mass without holes, which in this cheese would be looked upon as a great defect. The salt is intimately mixed with the curd, and not merely rubbed on the outside. This checks internal fermentation and prevents the formation of elastic matter.

Gloucester and Somersetshire cheeses are similarly made—with this difference, that the curd is not so often broken or the cheese skewered, and a portion of the cream is generally abstracted to make butter.

Stilton cheese is made by adding the cream

WASHING BY DASH-WHEELS

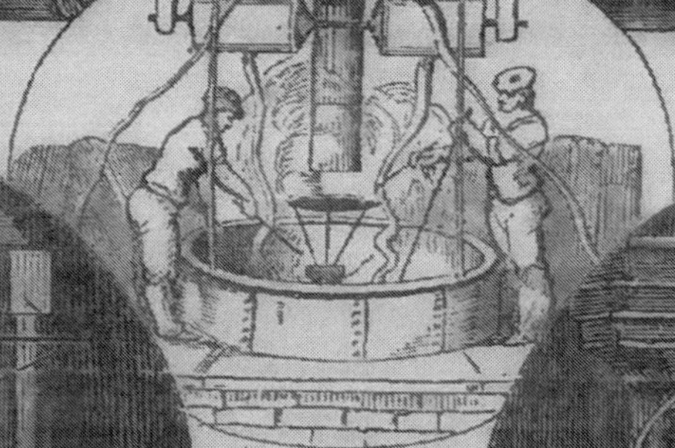

KEIR OR BOILER

SINGEING

BANDANA PRESS

YARN-WRINGING

BLEACHING-GROUND

KNIGHT'S CYCLOPÆDIA OF THE INDUSTRY OF ALL NATIONS.

15.

of the preceding evening's milk to the morning's milking. It is generally preferred when a green mould appears in its texture. To accelerate this, pieces of a mouldy cheese are sometimes inserted into holes made for the purpose by the scoop called a *taster*, and wine or ale is poured over for the same purpose; but the best cheeses do not require this, and are in perfection when the inside becomes soft like butter, without any appearance of mouldiness.

Cheeses are frequently coloured, a practice which probably arose from the notion of making the cheese look richer; but now it deceives no one. Yet, if some cheeses were not coloured they would not be so marketable, owing to the association which subsists between the colour and the quality of the cheese. The substance used for colouring is most commonly *arnotto*, which is ground fine on a stone, and mixed with the milk at the time the rennet is put in. The juice of the orange carrot and marygold-flowers are also used for this purpose; this last gives a more natural tint than the arnotto, which is too red. Cheddar, Stilton, Derby, and some other cheeses are never coloured; Cheshire slightly; but Gloucester and North Wiltshire deeply. Foreign cheeses are only coloured very slightly, if at all. Dutch cheeses are made in a very similar manner to the Gloucester cheeses, but the milk is generally curdled by means of muriatic acid. Before the curd is made up into the round shape in which it is usually sold, it is well soaked in a strong solution of common salt in water; this diffuses the salt throughout the whole mass, and effectually checks fermentation. When the cheeses are finally pressed, all the whey which may remain is washed out with the brine; salt is likewise rubbed over the outside, and they are set to dry on shelves in a cool place. The flavour of the cheese is perhaps impaired by the stoppage of the fermentation; but it never heaves, and it acquires the valuable quality of keeping well even in warm climates. The little cheeses made from cream, and folded in paper, and called Neufchâtel cheeses, are imported from France as a delicacy. They can be easily imitated, being nothing more than cream thickened by heat, and pressed in a small mould. They undergo a rapid change, first becoming sour and then mellow, in which state they must be eaten.

When a cheese which has been much salted and kept very dry is washed several times in soft water, and then laid in a cloth moistened with wine or vinegar, it gradually loses its saltness, and from being hard and dry becomes soft and mellow, provided it be a rich cheese. This simple method of improving cheese is worth knowing. A dry Stilton cheese may thus be much improved.

No less than 379,648 cwts. of foreign cheese were imported in 1849. The quantity of English cheese exported is extremely small, so much does the consumption in England exceed the manufacture.

CHEMISTRY. Under this heading, as under BOTANY and many others relating to large bodies of scientific knowledge, no systematic details can be given in this work; but the practical application of chemical principles to manufactures is illustrated in an immense range of industrial art. ALUM, BLEACHING, DYEING, COTTON PRINTING, and other articles, furnish evidence of this important application, and show how it arises that the manufacturer is so intimately dependent on the scientific chemist. Nothing that the Fourcroys, the Berthollets, the Davys, the Faradays, the Liebigs discover, but may one day be of value to the manufacturer. The connection of science with practical application is in no case more striking or more instructive.

CHERBOURG. This important French sea-port and naval station is distinguished for its great engineering works. The naval harbour is cut out of the solid rock; it has a depth of 52 feet at high water, and is large enough to contain fifteen vessels of the line. To the south of the harbour are dry docks, and round these four slips for building the largest ships, two slips for frigates, forges, furnaces, workshops, a large timber shed, and various other establishments necessary to a naval arsenal. To protect the roadstead from winds, as well as to defend that part of it which is beyond the range of the guns of the forts, a breakwater (*digue*) was commenced about two miles north of the town, in 1784, and after many failures, disasters, interruptions, and an enormous expense, this gigantic undertaking is now all but accomplished. It extends between Isle Pélée on the east and Querqueville on the west for a length of 2 miles 593 yards, leaving an opening of 1,093 yards at the eastern end, and of 1 mile 830 yards on the west. Its width at the base is 99 yards, on the summit 33 yards; and the depth of water about it varies from 36 feet to 45 feet. In the central fort of the breakwater there is a lighthouse 65 feet high.

Cherbourg is also a place of considerable commercial activity. The principal industrial articles are cotton-yarn; hosiery; refined sugar to the amount of 12,000 cwts. a year; soda, of which 12,000 tons are produced annually in the neighbourhood; chemical products, and leather.

CHERRY. The cherry-tree includes many varieties. Of the *Wild Cherry*, the wood is remarkable for the large size of its medullary processes, which give its longitudinal section a bright satiny lustre, and render it well suited for ornamental cabinet work. The *Common Cherry* is found wild in the woods of Asia Minor, where it attains a very large size; from the time of the Romans it has ever since formed one of the most esteemed varieties of dessert fruit. The *Black American Cherry* is rather a handsome tree, of which the fruit is as large as a moderately-sized cherry. The *Choke Cherry* is a large tree growing in the United States, from 80 to 100 feet high; its fruit is not very edible in a recent state, but when dried and bruised it forms an esteemed addition to pemmican. The timber is among the best in the United States for cabinet makers' work. The *Broad-leaved Laurel Cherry* is remarkable for the abundance of hydrocyanic acid secreted in its leaves.

CHESHIRE. The most important mineral productions of this county are fossil or rock-salt, and coal. The rock-salt is obtained near the banks of the Weaver and its tributary streams. It was first discovered near Northwich, in 1670, in searching for coal; it has since been found very abundantly in the townships of Witton, Wincham, Winnington, and Marston, near Northwich. There are salt-works also at Nantwich, Middlewich, and Winsford. The salt is of two kinds, the one white and transparent, the other of a reddish brown. The former has been found by analysis to be an almost pure muriate of soda: the latter contains a small portion of oxide of iron, from which its colour is derived.

The principal salt-works are in the neighbourhood of Northwich, where there are mines in addition to brine-springs. The rock-salt is found from 28 to 48 yards beneath the surface of the earth. The first stratum is from 15 to 25 yards in thickness, extremely solid and hard, and resembling brown sugar-candy. Many tons at a time are loosened by blasting with gunpowder. The second stratum is of hard stone, from 25 to 35 yards in thickness. The salt lies beneath the stratum in a bed above 40 yards thick, generally quite white and clear as crystal. The external surface above these strata is of whitish clay and gypsum. The quantity of salt annually taken from the pits around Northwich, amounts to many thousand tons; besides this quantity of fossil salt, many thousand tons are annually manufactured at the same place from brine-springs, which are from 20 to 40 yards in depth.

Coal of a good quality is found abundantly in the north-east part of the county, especially in the townships of Worth and Poynton, where there are very extensive collieries, which supply the manufactories of Stockport. At Denwell, in the hundred of Wirral, there is also coal. Copper and lead are found at Alderley Edge and the Peckforton Hills; the former place supplies a considerable quantity of cobalt. There are several quarries of excellent freestone in this county, of which those at Runcorn, Manley, and Great Bebington, are the most important. Limestone is found only at Newbold Astbury. Mowcop Hill, or Molecop, which is partly in Staffordshire, has long been famous for its mill stones. Marl is found in almost every part of the county, and is generally used for manure.

Cheshire is famous for its dairy husbandry. Dairy farms require considerable buildings; and some have been erected by wealthy proprietors in the best and most substantial manner. Although butter is made in considerable quantity, cheese is the main produce of these dairies. The making of Cheshire cheese is described in another article [CHEESE.]

Excepting at Stockport, and at other towns which share in the cotton manufacture of the neighbouring county of Lancashire, Cheshire can hardly be termed a manufacturing county. Ship-building, rope-making, sail-making, shot-making, and fringe-making, are, to some extent, carried on at Chester, where there are also tanneries, chemical works, soap works, and quarries.

CHESNUT, or CHESTNUT. This tree is available for a great variety of uses in the arts and domestic economy. There are two kinds—the *Sweet Chesnut* and the *Horse Chesnut*.

The *Sweet Chesnut* is in most cases cultivated more for its fruit than for any other purpose. In England the chesnut is eaten in many ways—raw, roasted, stewed with cream, made into soup either with milk or gravy, stewed with salt-fish, or used as a stuffing for fowls and turkey. Evelyn speaks of the chesnut as being 'a lusty and masculine food for rustics at all times, and of better nourishment for husbandmen than kale or rusty bacon; yea, or beans to boot.' In the south of France and the north of Italy, chesnuts serve in a great measure as a substitute for bread and potatoes. The nuts laid by for winter vegetable are those which fall off the trees; while those which are beaten off are carried to Paris and other large towns for immediate use. As a means of depriving the nuts of their husks, they are trodden under foot by men wearing *sabots* or wooden shoes. Chesnuts are dried in France, and preserved for many years; they are dried by the air, by the sun's heat, by a kiln, or by partial boiling, according to the mode in which they are to be used. The French make many dishes from chesnuts. *Galette* is a thick flat cake made with chesnut-meal, milk, salt, and sometimes a little butter and eggs, and baked on a hot stone or iron plate; *polenta* is a thick porridge made by boiling the chesnut-meal in water or milk, and stirring it till it forms a thick paste, something like the oatmeal parritch of the Scotch; *chatigna* is made by boiling the nuts whole, without their skins, in water with a little salt, till they become soft, and then mixing them up like mashed potatoes; *marrow-glace* is made by dipping the nuts into clarified sugar, and then drying them. The nuts are also frequently cooked by boiling them in water containing the leaves of celery or sage.

The timber of the sweet or Spanish chesnut is much used for posts, fences, stakes, hoops, &c. The wood is more fitted for such purposes than for beams or planks, as it is liable to become rent with fissures. It is used in France for making wine-casks; and for many purposes where most other woods would decay, chesnut timber is found very desirable.

In respect to the *Horse-Chesnut*, the fruit is eaten by animals; the meal is used in some places to whiten flaxen cloth, in others to strengthen bookbinders' paste; and in France attempts have been made to produce sugar and spirit from it. The timber is used for flooring, cart-linings, sabots, packing-cases, and water-pipes; on being burned it yields good charcoal and potash. The bark is used in tanning, in dyeing, and as a drug.

There were 63,033 bushels of Spanish chesnuts (as the fruit of the sweet chesnut is called) imported in 1848.

CHICORY is a perennial plant, the whole of which is bitter and aromatic; the leaves, as well as the root, have been used in medicine, in the form of a decoction, as a tonic bitter, and diuretic. It is frequently used as a salad, especially when blanched. The luxuriant growth of the leaves of the chicory, and their speedy reproduction after they have been cut, suggested the more extensive cultivation of this plant as food for cattle and sheep. But, notwithstanding its abundant produce, it has not been found so much superior to other green food as to make its cultivation general.

Chicory is now chiefly cultivated in Belgium and Germany, for the purpose of preparing from the root a powder which can be substituted for coffee. The roots, when taken up in September, are cleaned by scraping and washing, split where they are thickest, and cut across in pieces about two or three inches long. These pieces are dried by means of a slow oven or a kiln. In this state it is sold to the merchants, packed in bags. It is afterwards cut or chopped into small pieces, and roasted exactly as coffee, ground in a mill, and packed in papers in pounds and half-pounds for retail sale.

Chicory was brought into use long before the once-celebrated *Roasted Corn* of Henry Hunt. This latter was simply roasted rye; and, although used in large quantity, and sweetened with much sugar, it had but a flat and insipid taste. Chicory bears a much closer resemblance to coffee of middling quality. It was about the year 1808 that chicory became generally known in England, when Napoleon's anti-commercial policy led the nations of Europe to look around them for various substitutes for articles no longer obtainable with the same ease as before. The Germans and the French used chicory before the English; and the Germans still use it largely, often without any admixture with coffee. They even, as a question of economy, use the leaves of the plant in the same way.

There has been much said and written lately about the admixture of chicory with coffee. Many persons prefer coffee which has a little chicory added to it, as it is said that body, colour, and a soft pleasant aroma are imparted thereby. From one to two ounces to a pound of coffee is stated to be a proper proportion. It is however known that this proportion is enormously increased; for as chicory is much cheaper than coffee, fraudulent dealers do not fail to avail themselves of the circumstance. It is known that the very low-priced coffee of such vendors sometimes contains as much as two-thirds chicory to one-third pure coffee. If purchasers bought their coffee *whole*, and ground it at home, they might at once defeat this fraud.

Chicory imported from Germany pays a small import duty, and English farmers have therefore begun to grow it. Hence has arisen alarm in two quarters—the Chancellor of the Exchequer fears for his customs revenue, and the Colonial coffee-growers fear a competition against their produce. It is said that 12,000,000 lbs. of chicory are now used annually in England.

CHILE is famous for its herds of cattle. Single proprietors sometimes possess from 10,000 to 20,000 head of cattle. Live stock, jerked beef, tallow, and hides are large articles of export. Cheese is made on the banks of the Rio Maule, and sent to Peru; and butter is made in the neighbourhood of the larger towns.

Gold dust is found in the sand of nearly all the rivers which come down from the Andes, as in the Rio de Aconcagua, Rio Maule and Biobio. Silver is still more abundant, but the ore is not very rich. In 1832 however very rich silver mines were discovered, about sixty miles south of the town of Copiapò. The copper mines are very numerous, especially in the northern districts. Ores of lead, tin, and iron, are said to exist, but they are not worked. There are considerable stores of coal, but it is of bad quality. A little salt is met with, but not sufficient for the demand.

The British exports to Chile amounted in value to about a million sterling in 1849.

CHIMES. These are bells tuned to the modern musical scale, and struck by hammers acted on by a pinned cylinder or barrel, which revolves by means of clock-work. Chimes differ from *Carillons* (as the last word is commonly understood in England), inasmuch as the bells of the former are acted on by clock-work, those of the latter by keys struck by the hand. But the French apply the term *carillon* to the tune played, and, generally, to the series of bells, whether sounded by machinery or by hand, though the most accurate writers distinguish the latter kind as *le carillon à clavier.* The *carillons à clavier* comprise three octaves of bells, sounded by means of keys, similar to the pedals of an organ, which the performer strikes forcibly with hands clenched and sideways, the little fingers being guarded by a thick covering of leather. These keyed carillons are found in many towns of Holland and the Netherlands.

In Mr. Payne's musical chime clocks, for which a patent was taken out a year or two ago, the sounds are emitted by steel springs instead of bells, and elicited by pins instead of hammers. In the general arrangement of hammers and bells, the mechanism is complex and takes up much room; and it was to lessen these inconveniences that Mr. Payne introduced his new arrangement. The principle of action is almost precisely that of the musical snuff-box. Steel springs emit sounds not only equal but superior to those of bells.

CHIMNEY. In modern English houses chimney-flues are often formed within the substance of the party-wall, leaving the width and projection of the jambs entirely to the taste of the architect; and, where two adjoining houses are built with the fire-places back to back, two sets of flues are introduced in the same party-wall. Where this is not done, the flues are carried up in the projecting jambs, which are necessarily made large. In some of the best houses all the flues are so constructed as to be swept from openings in the basement story, without entering the rooms into which the fire-places open.

The chimneys, flues, or *stalks,* (as they are often termed) of our great chemical works, are among the most remarkable examples of construction. The gaseous exhalations from such works are so noxious, that an attempt is made to discharge them into the atmosphere at as great a height as possible; and a great height also increases the *draught* of the furnaces below. Hence the enormous chimneys which have been constructed within the last few years. Cotton factories have also occasionally chimneys of enormous height. At Messrs. Dewhirst's factory, at Manchester, a chimney has lately been built 243 feet high; it has a circular shaft, resting on a rectangular base 21 feet square by 45 feet high; and is wholly built of stone, of which it contains 1,700 tons. The chimney to Messrs. Dixon's cotton factory, at Carlisle, is 305 feet high; and it is octangular, and built of brick with stone angles. The chimney to Messrs. Muspratt's chemical works at Newton is 397 feet high. At Messrs. Blinkhorn's chemical works near Little Bolton is a chimney 368 feet high; it consumed in its construction 800,000 bricks and 120 tons of stone. The chimney at the great St. Rollox chemical works, near Glasgow, is 430 feet high, 50 feet in diameter at the foundation, 40 feet at the level of the ground, and 14 feet at the top. It has an inner chimney, disconnected from the outer, 260 feet in height by 16 feet in diameter. This fine chimney, being on a hill, forms a fine object for many miles; but it has needed repairs of a very troublesome and difficult kind. A great chimney was finished at Wigan in 1847, after four years of construction, in connexion with an extensive chemical work. It exceeded 400 feet in height. Almost immediately after its completion, an indentation was observed near the top, and an eminent engineer of Manchester recommended the removal of a portion of the top. About 80 feet was thus gradually removed; but the base continued to sink and displace during this period, until at length the whole ponderous structure fell in one mass, and stretched its huge mass across the Leeds and Liverpool Canal.

The chimney belonging to Messrs. Cubitt's building establishment at Pimlico, is a remarkable one. An attempt has been here made to give architectural character to that which is too often unsightly. The chimney shaft is entirely enclosed within a square tower, which presents much the appearance of an Italian campanile. The shaft is circular, 120 feet high, 5 feet internal diameter, and varying in thickness from 14 to 6 inches. The square tower envelopes the shaft without touching it. The upper portion of the tower, besides a belfry and a clock-room, affords space for a capacious cistern, useful in many exigencies. These advantages, and a saving of fuel from the shaft being kept shielded from the external cool air, are considered to pay an ample return for the increased outlay, independently of the architectural ornament thus produced.

The chimneys or flues connected with some of our mines are more remarkable than any yet described. At the great *Cwm Avon* mining and smelting works in South Wales, a chimney has been built at the top of a mountain; and flues are carried up the sides of this mountain from the works below to the chimney above. At the Tamer lead mine, on the confines of Cornwall and Devon, a steam engine has lately been set to work at a depth of 800 feet below the level of the river Tamer; and in order to give an outlet for the smoke of this engine, flues extend from it, in horizontal galleries and vertical shafts, like a flight of steps, until they reach the surface on the opposite side of the river. This united flue is nearly two miles in length.

CHIMNEY PIECE. As soon as some degree of architectural refinement began to be introduced into the habitations of noblemen, external dressings, constituting a chimney-piece, were added to the fire-place. Some of these, in which the Gothic style was employed, are marked by a fitness and propriety of character, and a happy union of simplicity with richness. Some examples—one from Tattershall Castle, Lincolnshire, and two from Windsor Castle—are given in Pugin's 'Gothic Specimens,' all of which, in regard to compactness and simplicity of composition, accord much more nearly with modern taste, and have a much less 'Gothic' air than the cumbrous and extravagantly ornamented chimney-pieces in the Renaissance style of the Continent, and our own Elizabethan. In these the design was carried quite up to the ceiling, so as to form a sort of architectural frontispiece, composed of two or more stages piled upon each other, and adorned with columns, pilasters, caryatides, termini, niches, &c., presenting an overloaded mass of carving and sculpture. But, though such compositions were generally exceedingly capricious, and equally fantastic and coarse in detail, some were real works of art—truly admirable for artistic beauty of design and masterly execution; such as were in the palace of Fontainebleau; two noted ones in the Hôtel de Ville at Courtrai; and one of matchless beauty for its exquisite carvings in chestnut-wood, in the Palais du Franc de Bruges. In our own country, chimney-pieces of the time of Elizabeth and James I. are by no means uncommon: many are remaining, not only in mansions of that period which are still kept up, but in houses which have been almost completely modernized in all other respects.

As the more regular Italian style gained ground, the fashion of chimney pieces greatly changed. The chimney-piece and fire-place were reduced to nearly their modern proportions and dimensions, whereas the opening or fire-place had previously been of such size that a person might stand within it. Marble is now the usual material for chimney-pieces even in ordinary houses.

CHINA. Whatever may be the actual antiquity of the Chinese people, no doubt seems now to exist of their having been the authors of what are justly considered in Europe as three of the most important inventions or discoveries of modern times: the art of block-printing, the composition of gunpowder, and the magnetic compass. To these may be added two very remarkable manufactures, of which they were unquestionably the first inventors, those of silk and of porcelain. It is curious to contrast inventions of such high utility and importance with the very small progress which the Chinese have made in the sciences, as astronomy, geography, and mathematics, for which they were not ashamed to be indebted to the European missionaries. With regard to the fine arts, the Chinese have not made much progress. In painting, their colours are beautiful, but their perspective is very erroneous. In music, their instruments are numerous, consisting of different species of lutes and guitars; flutes and other wind-instruments; an harmonicon of wires, touched with two slender slips of bamboo: bells and pieces of sonorous metal; drums; and a sort of clarionet, which emits as nearly as possible the tones of the Scottish bagpipe.

Through the plain which constitutes the north-east part of China runs the Imperial Canal 700 miles long. Its width, depth, embankments, cuttings, flood-gates, and bridges are on a large scale. It serves partly for navigation, partly for draining, and partly for irrigation. This canal, together with the rivers, gives a very extensive system of inland navigation in China. The plain watered by the canal is perhaps the most populous country upon earth. It contained, in 1813, 177,000,000 of inhabitants. To protect this rich plain the Great Wall was erected, which incloses China on the northern boundary, and extends over mountains and rivers for about 1,400 miles. This great work was constructed about 200 years before the Christian æra, as a defence against the nomadic tribes of Tartars. The main substance of the wall is earth or rubbish, retained on each side by a thick casing of stone and brick, and terraced by a platform of square tiles. From its eastern extremity there is an extensive stockade of wooden piles, inclosing the country of Mougden. The total height of the wall is about 20 feet, on a basis of stone projecting 2 feet under the brickwork, and about the same in height. The thickness of the whole wall at the base is 25 feet, diminishing to 23 feet at the platform. The towers are 40 feet square at the base, diminishing to 30 at the top, and about 37 feet in height.

Of the produce of this remarkable empire, tea is that with which England is most interested [TEA]. Coal, lime, gold, silver, and other minerals are met with.

Of the mechanical ingenuity of the Chinese we have spoken in the *Introduction* (p. xi). There seems no reason, however, to expect that the Chinese will take part in the Industrial Exhibition of the 'barbarians' of Europe; although the European residents at Hong Kong and Canton have contributed towards the funds of the Exhibition.

The materials employed by the Chinese in house-building are wood, of which that most in use is the nan-mon, a kind of cedar: stone, marble, bricks, bamboo, and glazed or porcelain tiles are also employed. The construction of houses is directed by a public functionary, whom we may not inaptly designate a district surveyor. Every one is obliged to build his house according to his rank, and for every house a certain size and details are fixed. The ordinary habitations have one floor. The houses called heon, that is, of many floors, were once very much the fashion, and some were built about 211 feet high. Wooden columns, so placed as to support the roof, are common, and are from eight to ten diameters in height. They are fixed on stone or marble bases, but have no capitals. The roofs, which are slightly constructed of bamboo, are often double, and resemble one roof rising out of the other: they turn up at the eaves, at the angles of which are hung grotesque figures of dragons, &c. Not the least singular appearance in a Chinese house is the door, which is often a complete circle; the window frames and sashes are formed of small pannels of various forms moulded out of clay, and neatly joined together. The sills of doors are of stone. The palace of Pekin is on an immense scale, 2,513 feet by 3,235 feet. It is divided into a number of courts, is composed of towers, galleries, porticoes, halls, and immense buildings, and, as a whole, has an imposing appearance.

CHINA WARE. [PORCELAIN.]

CHINCHILLA. This small animal, a native of South America, is in request for the sake of its fur. That which comes from Peru is rougher than that brought from Chile, but not always so beautiful. Great numbers of these animals are caught in the neighbourhood of Coquimbo and Copiapó, generally by boys with dogs, who bring them to Santiago and Valparaiso, whence they are exported. The Peruvian skins are either brought to Buenos Ayres from the eastern parts of the Andes, or are sent to Lima. The extensive demand in Europe for this fur has occasioned a very large destruction of these animals.

CHLORINE is an elementary gaseous body discovered by Scheele, in 1774. It has a very powerful and disagreeable odour, is very suffocating, even when considerably diluted with air, and its taste is astringent. Faraday has shown that, when this gas is subjected to a pressure of about four atmospheres, and kept cool, it is condensed into a yellow limpid fluid, which is extremely volatile, and, when the pressure is removed, rapidly reassumes the gaseous form. Neither light, heat, nor electricity produces any change in the properties of chlorine gas, provided it be dry; but, if it be moist, then light causes it to decompose the water.

One of the most curious and important properties of chlorine is the power which it possesses of destroying the colour of animal and vegetable matter in general, and hence its extensive application to the purpose of bleaching. [BLEACHING.] This is effected however not by dry chlorine, but when moisture is present. Chlorine is a powerful supporter of combustion: if certain metals, and especially antimony, in the state of powder, be thrown into chlorine gas, they burn spontaneously; phosphorus also exhibits similar phenomena. Chlorine is a powerful disinfectant; Sir William Burnett's 'Disinfecting Fluid' consists of chloride of zinc. Mr. F. Smith has recently (1847) introduced a small apparatus for making chlorine, to be used in hospitals, or houses, or rooms, where the air is likely to be tainted.

Many of the compounds of chlorine with other substances are highly important. The most so perhaps is *Muriatic* or *Hydro-chloric Acid*, which consists of chlorine and hydrogen; it is a colourless gas, with a pungent odour and an acrid taste; it extinguishes burning bodies, and excites coughing; it is expanded by heat, and decomposed by electricity; it readily absorbs atmospheric moisture, and then becomes liquid muriatic acid, which has the smell and acid properties of the gas.

Muriatic acid is largely used in chemistry and the arts. When it is mixed with nitric acid, it is decomposed, and a solution of chlorine is obtained, which, under the old name of *aqua regia* or modern name of nitro-muriatic acid, is used for dissolving gold and platinum.

The manufacture of chlorine at the Felling Chemical Works, near Newcastle, according to the patent obtained by Mr. Lee in 1842, is conducted as follows:—Each of the chambers for the manufacture is covered by an arch, over which the furnace flue is led, so that the heat may be transmitted downward through the arches to the materials placed within the chambers. In each chamber is a stone trough, such as is used for the condensers and flues of alkali works. One side of each chamber is furnished with a leaden door, and at the opposite side is a pipe of lead or of earthenware for the escape of the chlorine. Tho fire being kindled, and the chamber sufficiently heated, lumps of manganese are placed in the troughs, and the doors closed; muriatic acid is then introduced through glass tubes, conveniently placed for that purpose. The chlorine is speedily given off, and passes into another chamber; and the muriate of manganese is drawn off from tho troughs on the completion of the process by means of syphons.

CHLOROFORM is a peculiar compound limpid fluid, which is soluble in alcohol and æther, and dissolves iodine, phosphorus, and sulphur. Although mankind had for a long time had recourse to various narcotic agents for relieving pain in disease, it was not till the discovery by Drs. Jackson and Norton, in America, of the narcotising powers of the vapour of æther, that such agents were employed for the purpose of relieving the dreadful suffering endured in surgical operations. This discovery can only be regarded as second in importance to that of vaccination, as a preventive of small-pox, by Dr. Jenner. Scarcely had it been generally known that æther possessed the power we have mentioned than, in the latter end of the year 1847, Dr. Simpson, of Edinburgh, discovered that the vapour of chloroform possesses the same powers. The discovery that the vapour of chloroform produced the same effect as that of æther produced scarcely less sensation than the discovery of the powers of æther itself. For it possesses many advantages over æther in its application to the production of insensibility. These are—1. A smaller quantity of chloroform than of æther is required to produce the same effect; for thirty or forty drops upon a handkerchief or sponge, and applied to the nostrils, are sufficient to produce the desired effect. 2. The action of chloroform is more rapid and complete, and more persistent than that of æther. 3. Frequently after taking the vapour of æther, sickness and headache come on; but, although these effects sometimes take place with chloroform, they are not so frequent. 4. The expense of chloroform is much less than that of æther, from the small quantity required.

Chloroform is obtained by distilling a mixture of chloride of lime, water, and spirit.

CHOCOLATE. [COCOA.]

CHORLEY is one of the busy cotton-manufacturing towns of Lancashire. The chief articles of manufacture are calicoes, muslins, and ginghams. Eight cotton factories, two print works, two weaving sheds, bleaching works, a paper-mill, coal-mines, and stone-quarries, afford employment to many of the inhabitants. Another large cotton factory has been just completed. A new patent brick and draining-tile manufactory has been recently established. Four miles from Chorley, lead and carbonate of barytes are found. The Leeds and Liverpool canal, and the Lancashire and Yorkshire Railway, are of great benefit to Chorley in affording facilities for the carriage of goods. A very large increase has taken place in the population and prosperity of the town owing to the great increase of calico-printing.

CHROMATYPE is the name given by Mr. Robert Hunt to a variety of the photographic process discovered by him in 1842. It derives its name from some of the chromates, especially the chromates of mercury and copper, employed in preparing the photographic paper.

CHROMATIC THERMOMETER is the name given by Sir David Brewster to an instrument consisting of several rectangular plates of glass placed with their surfaces in contact, and intended to measuro the difference between the temperature of the glass and of any body, solid or fluid, which may be applied to it. The temperature induced in the glass must however be below that at which the glass would become red hot. The heated body, solid or fluid, being in contact with the edges of the glass plates, the inequality of action caused by differences of temperature in the parts of each plate of glass gives rise to differences of tint in the polarized light of the glass, which differences are made to measuro (scientifically though not practically) differences of temperature.

CHROMIUM, a metal discovered by Vauquelin in the year 1797, is pulverulent, of a yellowish white colour, and metallic lustre. It suffers but little change by exposure to the air, and acids act upon it but slightly. Chromium combines with many of the elementary substances. One of the oxides of chromium has a green colour, and is the colouring matter of the emerald; it is employed to give a green colour to glass and porcelain. The chromate of lead and other compounds of the metal are of great value in the arts.

CHRONOMETER. Such time-keepers as are used for determining the longitude at sea, or for other purposes where great accuracy is required, combined with portability, are called by this name. Some are made for the pocket, resemble ordinary watches in appearance, and, like them, are made to go thirty hours with once winding up. Marine chronometers are usually larger, with dial-plates three or four inches in diameter, and made to go from two to eight, or, by some recent improvements, even as many as thirty-two days with once winding up. They indicate hours (from I. to XXIV., to avoid the possibility of an error of twelve hours), minutes, and seconds, often on separate circles; and they are furnished with a small hand to indicate the days which have elapsed since the winding up. The mechanism is enclosed in a brass box, mounted on gimbals, so as to preserve one uniform position, and inclosed in a mahogany case.

The greater part of the mechanism of a chronometer resembles that of a common watch, but is constructed with every possible provision to ensure accuracy. They differ from the common watch chiefly in the *detached escapement* and the *compensation balance*. The former is a contrivance by which the balance, the vibrations of which constitute the actual measure of time, is, during the greater part of its movement, entirely detached from, and consequently unaffected by, the train of wheel-work from which its impulse is derived; the wheels, in fact, standing still through the greater part of each vibration. The *compensation-balance* is a beautiful contrivance for counteracting the effect of changes of temperature, which, by causing an ordinary balance to expand and contract, occasion a variation in the extent of its vibration, and consequently in the rate of going of the time-piece of which it forms the essential feature. This correction, in the ordinary compensation-balance, is effected by forming the rim of the balance of two semicircular slips of metal, fixed at one end only, and each consisting of a very narrow riband of steel joined to an outer rim of brass. Each of these semicircular slips, consisting thus of two metals differently affected by heat, is capable of altering its shape with every change in the temperature to which the chronometer is exposed, in such a way as to keep the vibrations of the balance always the same. In the first marine chronometers, constructed by Harrison, this object was attained by applying such a compensating apparatus to the balance-spring. Arnold, following, probably unconsciously, in the track of the great French watch-maker, Le Roy, applied it to the balance itself. Many other improvements have been made in the chronometer, rendering it almost as perfect as any thing from the hand of man can be expected to be; and of late years very ingenious contrivances have been devised by Messrs. Dent, Eiffe, and Molyneux, for correcting certain irregularities of action in the ordinary compensation-balance and producing a balance surpassing it in accuracy of movement as it surpasses the balance of a common watch.

The wonderful accuracy of modern chronometers was made the means in 1839 of determining the longitude of New York, as compared with Greenwich. The first experiment was made on the occasion of the first trip across the Atlantic by the *British Queen.* The longitude determined by that mode differed 2·63 seconds from that determined by the usual astronomical means. Mr. Dent was dissatisfied with a discrepancy—marvellously small to the minds of others—but large in the estimation of one accustomed to the performances of chronometers; and he determined to made a second attempt. He placed four chronometers under the care of Captain Roberts, the rates of which had been previously ascertained. The chronometers made a voyage out and home in the *British Queen,* showing, of course, *Greenwich time* all the while; and on being compared in America with other chronometers which marked *New York time,* the difference of longitude was measured by this difference of chronometer time. So astounding was the accuracy of those instruments, that while the difference of longitude between the observatory at Greenwich and the City Hall at New York is found by the best astronomical methods to be 4 h. 56 m. 0·72 s., it was measured by the chronometers to be 4 h. 56 m. 0·24 s.,—a difference of less than half a second! It was found that the chronometers were able to withstand the shaking of the vessel, and all other disturbances incidental to a steam-ship, without perceptibly marring their action.

Mr. Dent, shortly afterwards, determined

by chronometric means the difference of longitude between Greenwich and Devonport. As ascertained by the Trigonometrical Survey, the difference of longitude, between the Observatory at Greenwich and the flag-staff on Mount Wise, near Devonport, is 16 m. 38·1 s.; while the difference given by a mean of four chronometers was 16 m. 39·8 s.—a difference of less than two seconds.

During the last five years, there have been 219 Admiralty chronometers at Greenwich Observatory. It is curious that in these successive years, 1845-6-7-8-9, five different makers stood successively first on the list, in respect to the accuracy of the chronometers made by them; showing how closely the spirit of honourable scientific competition has brought them on a level one with another. Of the whole number 70 were purchased for the public use; the highest price paid was 68*l.* 5*s.* [CLOCK AND WATCH MAKING.]

CHURCH. The principal type of a complete church, as an architectural structure, is a cathedral. Almost every cathedral is varied in plan, although the leading features, the nave and choir, are found in almost all. The plan usually consists of a galilee, or chapel, at the principal entrance; the nave, or main body of the church; the side aisles, which do not rise so high as the nave, and are placed on each side of the nave, sometimes with chapels, at other times without, between the openings formed by the windows; the choir, or place for the ceremonies of the church; the transept, or division at right angles to the end of the nave next the choir, which projects on each side, and forms a cross on the plan. Some cathedrals have a double transept, and the transepts have often aisles. At the end of the choir is the high altar, behind which is occasionally a lady chapel, or chapel to the Virgin. The choir end of a cathedral is sometimes terminated by an apsis or semicircular end. Along the sides of the choir are ranged richly carved seats, ornamented with arches, pinnacles, and tracery, carved in oak. The bishop's seat, richer than the others and raised above them, is on one side, at the eastern end. The choir has also side aisles. Cloisters and a chapter-house are usually attached to English cathedrals. The minor parts of a cathedral are the muniment room, the library, the consistory court, the vestries of the dean and chapter, minstrels' chapels, a font, and a minstrels' gallery. Beneath the body of the cathedral there is usually a crypt, or low basement, supported on arches springing from thick columns, as in Canterbury Cathedral and others. At the point of intersection of the transept with the nave there is usually a tower, sometimes surmounted by a spire. The nave of a Gothic cathedral is supported by clustered columns, arched from one to the other, over which there is usually a row of small arches forming a gallery, which is called the triforium, and above are windows called clere-story windows. The chapter-house and cloister are large and important features in many of our cathedrals. The finest chapter-houses in England are of a polygonal form, and have in some cases a column, or cluster of columns, in the centre, to support the vaulted roof. The cloistures are rectangular inclosures, with a richly ornamented and arched gallery running round the sides. Such are the leading features of the cathedrals and large churches of Europe. The numerous cathedrals of France, Italy, and Germany present beautiful specimens of architecture, not only in the Gothic style, but also in the Italian style. St. Peter's at Rome is the largest cathedral in Europe. Vienna and Strasburg have the highest spires; the former is 465 feet, the latter 456 feet high.

CHURN. The common churn for making butter is a wooden cask rather wider at bottom than at top, covered with a round lid having a hole in the centre. Through this hole passes a round stick about four feet long, inserted in the centre of a round flat board having holes in it; the diameter of this board is a little less than that of the top of the churn. The milk is churned by giving a vertical movement to the board immersed in it.

There is obviously a great waste of power in such a contrivance; and many forms have been devised to render the work of the churner more efficacious. One of the most recent is the *atmospheric churn*, made by Mr. Samuelson. It consists of a square box, inside which are four vanes or boards, made to rotate round a central horizontal axis, the handle of which projects through one side of the box. Two of the vanes are perforated, and two are solid; the former break the cream and separate the butter from the butter-milk; while the latter cause air to be forced into the milk. These churns are made of various sizes, to churn from 4 to 96 quarts, and are sold from 25*s.* to to 115*s.* each.

CIDER, or CYDER. There are two cider districts in this country. The Hereford cider district is comprised in the four counties of Hereford, Gloucester, Worcester, and Monmouth; the Devonshire cider district in those of Devon, Dorset, Somerset, and Cornwall.

The principal kinds of apple used in these districts for cider are the New Foxwhelp, the Wilding, the Cherry Pearmain, and the Yellow and Red Norman. In the Devonshire district, the situations chosen for orchards are generally hollow dells or shelving banks, in the neighbourhood of the farm-houses, the land on which they are planted being put to little other use; while in the Hereford district the choice is determined chiefly by the quality of the soil, without reference to the position of the farm-house. Very little attention is paid to enriching the soil round the trees when once they have been planted. In by far the largest proportion of orchards, with the exception of gathering the fruit, nothing is done to the trees from the beginning of the year to the end. The fruit of the different varieties of apple ripen at different times of the year, earlier or later, according to the season. The customary method of picking the fruit is by striking the trees with poles, provincially called 'poulting,' and then gathering the fallen apples; but it is better economy to pay a small extra price for collecting the fruit which falls at several times. When the apples have been gathered, each sort by itself is collected into heaps, about ten inches deep, where they remain for a month, or more, until they become mellow; they are then ready for the mill.

Cider is manufactured with very rude machinery, by the following process:—The apples are thrown into a circular stone trough, usually about eighteen feet in diameter, called the *chase*, round which the *runner*, a heavy circular stone, is turned by one or two horses. The crushed pulp or *must* is pressed between horsehair cloths, and the juice expelled. This juice is poured into casks, placed either out of doors, or in sheds where there is a free current of air. In about three or four days the liquor ferments; the thick heavier parts subside as a sediment at the bottom of the cask, and the lighter becomes bright clear cider. This is then *racked*, or drawn off into another cask.

The fermentation of cider is a process requiring great care and skill. *Slight* fermentation will leave the liquor thick and unpalatable; *rapid* fermentation will impair both its strength and durability; *excessive* fermentation will make it sour, harsh, and thin. It is not the habit of the farmer to add sugar, treacle, brandy, or any colouring matter to the liquor; it is only adulterated in the hands of cider dealers and publicans, who often 'doctor' up sour cider to make it palatable.

At the beginning of January the cider is moved into cellars, where by large growers it is frequently stored in casks of great capacity, containing 1000, 1500, or even 2000 gallons. In March the liquor is bunged down; it is then fit for sale, and may be used soon afterwards, though it will greatly improve by keeping.

Cider of good quality is made in Ireland, in the counties of Waterford and Cork; in Normandy, whence we have many of our best apples; in Belgium; and of inferior quality in Germany. It is also made in abundance, and of excellent quality, in many parts of the United States of North America.

CIGAR. The manufacture of cigars is exceedingly simple. A boy, with a quantity of unstripped leaves before him, takes them one by one, strips them, and then passes them to the cigar-maker, who is seated in front of a low work-bench, which has raised ledges on every side excepting that nearest to him. He takes a leaf of tobacco, spreads it smoothly before him on the bench, and cuts it to a form resembling one of the gores or stripes of a balloon. He then lays a few fragments of tobacco leaf in its centre, and rolls the whole up into a form nearly resembling that of a cigar. The next operation is to place the partially-formed cigar in an iron guage, which cuts it to a given length. The maker then lays a narrow strip of leaf upon the bench, and rolls the cigar spirally in it. All this is done with great rapidity, a few seconds being sufficient for the production of a cigar. The cigars are finally dried for sale.

The following account of the cigar manufacture at Havannah appeared in some of the London journals in 1841:—The greatest manufacturers of Havannah cigars are Cabanas, Hernandez, Silva, and Rencareiul; there are a hundred others of less note, who make from 10,000 to 100,000 a day. The cigar is composed of two distinct parts, the inside and the cover. For these, two different kinds of leaves are used; of which that for the cover is generally finer in texture and more pliant. These leaves are damped the night previous to their being made up; when rolled, they are placed on a large table, where they are divided into the various qualities of first, second, third, &c., and priced accordingly. Those which are most carefully rolled are called *Regalias*, and are sold at 22 to 26 dollars per thousand; while the second best, which are of the very same tobacco, and made by the same man, only with less care, are sold at 14 dollars; and others are done so low as 6 dollars. D. Hernandez employs about fifty men in his manufactory. Of the best common cigars, a workman can make a thousand a day; of the Regalias six hundred. The daily issues from that immense *fabrica* are about 30,000 cigars; which at 14 dollars per thousand would give nearly 100*l.* per day. They pay an export duty of half a dollar per thousand, and an import duty in England of nine shillings. The very best in quality do not find their way to Europe, because they are not fashionable here: they are generally dark coloured; whereas a light coloured and smoothly rolled cigar is preferred to the strong and highly flavoured rough ones, which are the best.

CI'NCHONA; *Jesuits'* or *Peruvian Bark.* By whom the important properties of the various species of this genus was first made known to Europeans is unrecorded. The native Peruvians attached no febrifugal importance to the bark. Its introduction to Europe took place through the Spaniards in the year 1640. Little was known of the tree producing this substance till the voyage of La Condamine, who, in 1738, first printed a detailed account of *Quinquina*, as it was then called.

The manner of collecting the Cinchona bark of commerce is thus described:—In the month of April the preparations for an expedition commence; and in May the people start for the forest, whence the last green bales are transmitted home in November. They fell the trees close to the root, sparing those trunks which appear too young, as, till they have attained maturity, the bark is of no value. The next process is to divide the stems into pieces of uniform length, rejecting only the very smallest branches. The bark is then cut lengthwise, so as to remove the rind without injuring the wood or severing any of the fibres. In a few days the bark is taken off in strips as broad as possible. In the market the value of the bark depends on the celerity with which it is dried. In the dense forests it is impossible to perform this operation properly, and therefore the bundles of green bark are dispatched with all speed to the nearest inhabited place, where the person appointed to take charge of them is stationed. They are laid in a spot exposed to the full action of the sun, and the greatest care is requisite to protect them from the wet.

Cinchona barks, in England, are classed under three heads — pale, yellow, and red barks. Of each there are several varieties. Of the *Pale Barks*, three varieties are known in English commerce:—1, Crown or Loxa Bark; 2, Gray, Silver, or Huanuco Bark; 3, Ash Bark. These are always quilled, and never in flat pieces. The powder, which gives the name, varies from gray to fawn colour. The Crown Bark occurs in pieces from 6 to 14 inches long, the quills varying in diameter from the fourth or even smaller part of an inch to nearly half an inch. The colour of the exterior is marked dark gray, in some specimens verging to brown. The odour resembles that of tan. The taste at first is slightly astringent, and faintly acid; afterwards very astringent, somewhat bitter, but not acrid. The Gray and Ash Barks differ from the Crown chiefly in tint.

The *Yellow Barks* also present three varieties. The variety best known in England occurs in two forms—quills and flat pieces; the quills were formerly most prized, but all well-informed persons now prefer the flat pieces as much richer in quinia. The external surface is generally grayish brown, inclining to blackish, yellow, or whitish, according to the kind of lichen by which it is beset. The flat Yellow Bark, or that in splints, occurs either with the epidermis or divested of it.

The *Red Bark*, of which one kind only is known in English trade, was not much used in Europe till 1779. It occurs in quills and flat pieces, most frequently in the latter form.

The various forms of Cinchona Bark are justly considered the most valuable tonic and febrifugal medicines we possess; and the commerce in them has thereby become important.

CINCHONIA, is a vegetable alkali contained in all the varieties of Cinchona, but principally in the *Cinchona lancifolia*, or pale bark. Cinchonia has a peculiar bitter taste; and combines with many of the acids to produce a peculiar class of salts.

CINNABAR. [MERCURY.]

CINNAMON has been known to European nations from very high antiquity. That which is now chiefly consumed in England is the aromatic bark of a small tree found in the island of Ceylon. The time for stripping off the bark is from May to October. The bark, after being removed from the branches, is tied up in bundles for twenty-four hours, during which time a sort of fermentation takes place, which greatly facilitates the separation of the outer part of the bark from the cuticle and the epidermis, which is very carefully scraped off the Ceylon cinnamon. It is then rolled up into quills, or pipes, about three feet in length, the thinner or smaller quills being surrounded by larger ones, a mark which always distinguishes cinnamon from cassia. It is then conveyed to Colombo, where it is sorted by government inspectors into three kinds, of which the two finest alone are allowed to be exported to Europe, while the third, or inferior kind, is reserved to be distilled, along with the broken pieces of the other two, for the purpose of obtaining the oil of cinnamon. The select cinnamon is formed into bales of about 92½ lbs. weight, containing some pepper or coffee, and wrapped in double cloths made of hemp.

This fine cinnamon occurs in pieces about forty inches in length, generally containing from six to eight rolls or quills in each, one within the other, of the thickness of vellum paper, of a dull golden yellow colour. It is very fragrant, agreeably aromatic, taste pleasant, warm, aromatic, slightly astringent. Analysed by Vauquelin, it yielded volatile oil, tannin in large quantity, an azotised colouring matter, a peculiar acid, mucilage, and feculum.

The root of the cinnamon tree yields a kind of camphor, and the leaves yield an oil which resembles oil of cloves, which it is often used to adulterate. This is quite distinct from the oil of cinnamon obtained from the bark. The ripe berries yield by decoction a solid volatile oil, similar to the oil of junipers.

Cassia is often mistaken for cinnamon; but they differ in the following particulars: The bales in which Cassia arrives are much smaller, containing only from two to four pounds, bound together by portions of the bark of a tree. The quills are thicker, rolled once or twice only, and never contain thinner pieces within; the diameter of the bark is much thicker than that of cinnamon, and harder, and the outer rind less carefully removed. It has the odour of cinnamon, but fainter and less grateful; the taste more acridly aromatic, pungent, less sweet, at the same time more powerfully astringent, yet mucilaginous.

Oil of Cinnamon is obtained chiefly from the fragments which fall from the quills during the inspection and sorting at Colombo. These fragments are coarsely powdered, and, after being immersed for forty-eight hours in sea-water, are distilled, when a milky fluid comes over, which separates into two parts, a light oil which floats on the water, and a heavy one which sinks. In time a spontaneous separation takes place, and there are formed transparent crystals of *stearopten*, or cinnamon camphor. *Oil of Cassia* is also obtained by distillation; at first it is whiter than oil of cinnamon, afterwards it becomes yellow, but never of such a fiery yellow as cinnamon-oil. The odour is agreeable, but not so delicate; the taste, acrid, burning, but different from cinnamon.

Oil of cinnamon, as a costly article, is often adulterated with oil of cassia; with the oil of cassia-buds; with the oil of the *Cérasus lauro-cerasus*, or cherry-laurel; and it is also said with oil of bitter almonds, an exceedingly dangerous intermixture.

Cinnamon is an extremely valuable aromatic stimulant, useful both in cookery and in medicine. Cassia has similar properties in a less degree.

347,368 lbs. of cinnamon were imported in 1848.

CIPOLIN is a variety of green marble with white zones, found in the vicinities of Rome and Autun.

CIRCLE. The following rules respecting the circle are of constant application in mechanical operations. To find the circumference of a circle (with more than sufficient nearness for practical purposes) take the 113th part of 355 times the diameter, or 3.14159 times the diameter. To find the area in *square* units, multiply the number of units in the radius by itself, and take the 113th part of 355 times the result (or multiply by 3.14159).

CIRCUMFERENTOR. This instrument is a species of surveying compass, consisting of one circular plate of brass, graduated, and of another turning on the same axis, which carries a vernier; these are supported on a tripod stand, and may be rendered horizontal by means of small spirit-levels. The upper plate carries two sight-vanes or perforated plates in vertical positions, at the opposite extremities of a diameter, and through these an object is seen when the *bearing* of a station line from the magnetic meridian is to be found.

Such an instrument, being far inferior to a theodolite in respect of the accuracy with which by its means a survey may be made, is not much used in Europe; but in the United States of America, and in the British Colonies, where land is less valuable, it is almost the only instrument employed.

CI'THARA was an ancient stringed instrument, supposed to have been somewhat like the modern guitar.

CITRIC ACID. This acid exists in numerous fruits, particularly those of the orange tribe, such as the lemon and lime, either alone or with malic and other acids; sugar, mucilage, and extractive are also present. It is colourless, inodorous, and extremely sour. When decomposed, it yields pyrocitric acid, and several other compounds. The citric acid is separated and purified on a large scale. Citric acid, when crystallised, has scarcely any odour, but a very distinct acid taste. It is soluble in cold and still more in warm water. It is used as a discharge in calico printing.

Citric acid combines with ammonia, potash, soda, iron, zinc, copper, silver, lead, and other bases, to form salts.

Concentrated citric acid is somewhat caustic, but lemon juice is gratefully acid. To imitate the natural state, citric acid is only given largely diluted. In this state it proves a pleasant drink in fevers and diseases where the temperature of the body rises above the natural standard. According to Broussais, it agrees better than any other acid with the stomach when affected with acute inflammation. It is not so pleasant as lemonade prepared from new fresh lemons; and, according to the statement of Sir G. Blane, the solution of citric acid is not so efficacious in the prevention and cure of sea-scurvy as the recent lemon-juice. This is attributable to the absence of the volatile oil and the bitter principle of the rind, which are valuable adjuncts to the citric acid in its action on the stomach. The utility of lemon-juice in promoting the digestion of gelatinous meats, such as veal and turtle, is well known. Fresh lemon juice may be preserved in bottles in the same way as ripe fruits, by boiling the bottles in which it is contained for half an hour, first placing them in cold water and gradually heating it, and, as soon as the contents of the bottles have fallen to the temperature of the air, closing them hermetically. Where lemon juice so preserved, or fresh lemons, cannot be obtained by ships on long voyages, the dissolved citric acid, to which a portion of an alcoholic extract of lemon peel may be added at the time of using, is sometimes used when apprehensions of scurvy are entertained.

Citric acid, as well as lemon juice, is much employed to decompose alkaline carbonates, forming therewith pleasant effervescing solutions.

CITRON, is one species of that important kind of fruit which includes the LEMON and ORANGE.

CIVET is a perfume obtained from an animal bearing the same name. The animal is a native of North Africa, and is two to three feet in length. The perfume is procured by scraping the inside of the pouch with an iron spatula, at intervals of three or four days; about a drachm may be obtained each time.

As civet sells at rather a high price, that which goes by the name in the market is too often adulterated with suet or oil.

CLACKMANNANSHIRE. This Scottish county presents a fair amount of produce and manufacturing industry. In the parish of Alloa are distilleries, breweries, manufactures of yarns, plaidings, shawls, tartans, druggets, and blankets, corn and flour mills, besides a glass work, a foundry, a brick and tile work and pottery, and a tan work. There are salmon fishings in the Forth. The manufacture of Scotch blankets and serge was formerly carried on at Tillicoultry, but shawls and tartans have been found more lucrative, and have engrossed much of the industry of this populous village. Small quarries of sandstone and limestone are wrought in various parts of the county, but the most important branch of industry pursued is the working of the extensive coal fields in Alloa and Clackmannan parishes, which form that part of the county lying on the banks of the Forth. Coal has been wrought here for 200 years, and there is an immense annual exportation of that article from Alloa. The occupation next and almost equal in importance is the iron manufacture, at Devon iron works, on the banks of the stream of that name, and in Clackmannan parish. Small railways connect these several works with Alloa harbour and Clackmannan Pow, and they will soon be brought into ready communication with all the great markets by the Stirling and Dunfermline line of railway.

CLARET, a name used in England to denote the red wine of Medoc, or, more correctly a mixture of that wine with some other more full-bodied. The word *clairet*, from which the name is derived, is used in France to signify those wines which are red or rose-coloured; but the name, as understood by us, is not known in that country. [BORDEAUX; WINE MANUFACTURE.]

CLARIFICATION, the process of rendering a fluid clear by separating the substances which, being suspended in it, render it turbid. Isinglass, gelatine, bullocks' blood, and white of eggs, are employed for the purpose. In the great London porter-breweries, a liquid solution is prepared, of which isinglass is one ingredient; and a very small portion of this 'fining-liquor' is put into every butt of beer.

CLARINET, a musical instrument made of wood, similar in shape to the oboe, but of rather larger dimensions, and having a fixed mouth-piece containing a reed, which forms the upper joint of the instrument. In the orchestra three instruments are employed, of different dimensions, namely, a C, a B, and an A clarinet, to play in different modes or keys. The compass is from E in the base to G in altissimo. The clarinet was invented about a century and a half ago, by Denner of Nürnberg. The *Base Clarinet*, and the *Contra-Base Clarinet*, invented by Streitwolf, about twenty years ago, are longer, larger, and deeper-toned instruments than the above.

CLARION, was the name of a shrill kind of trumpet, not now in use.

CLAVICHORD, was the name of a musical instrument which preceded the pianoforte. The strings were struck by brass pins, projecting from the remote ends of the keys, instead of by hammers; but the tone was one which would now be deemed intolerably harsh and wiry.

CLAY. Any natural mixture of earths which breaks down or disintegrates in water, and affords a plastic ductile mixture may be called a clay. *Pipe-Clay* is of a grayish-white colour, has an earthy fracture, and a smooth greasy feel. *Potter's Clay* disintegrates by exposure to the air; when mixed with sand it is made into bricks and tiles. *Stourbridge Clay* is of a dark colour; it is extensively employed in the manufacture of crucibles. *Brick-Clay* or loam varies much in appearance; texture, and composition; it lies in abundance upon the London clay, and frequently rests upon an interposed bed of sand. *London Clay* is a blueish deposit, often including beds of sandstone. *Plastic Clay* consists of a variable number of sand, clay, and pebble beds, irregularly alternating, lying immediately upon the chalk. *Porcelain Clay* is of various shades of white; it is dull and opaque; occurs friable or compact; feels soft to the fingers, and adheres to the tongue.

Clay is an essential component part of all fertile soils. A clay soil consists of a large proportion of alumina united to silica of various degrees of fineness, and frequently also a portion of carbonate of lime. In rich wheat soils the silica is very fine, and intimately mixed with the alumina; but English clays are not usually of this character, and are not so much approved for wheat crops as lighter soils. Clay land will bear a repetition of the same crops much oftener than lighter lands. The great disadvantage of clay soils in a moist climate like that of Great Britain arises from an excess of water, and the obvious remedy is perfect draining of the subsoil. [DRAINING.] Clay is extensively used in many parts of England to improve light land, by being carried on the surface in considerable quantities. Burnt clay is used as manure. Clay by burning alters its nature; it becomes insoluble in water, and loses its attraction for it; it then resembles silicious sand, and may greatly improve a very strong retentive clay, tempering it and rendering it more porous.

The Newcastle district will furnish many specimens of clays used in the Arts, for exhibition at the approaching industrial festival. The manufacture of fire clay into bricks, &c., is carried on very extensively in the neighbourhood of this town; and among the articles exhibited, formed of clay, will be fire-bricks, vases, pedestals, and ornaments of various kinds. Stourbridge will in like manner send specimens of those clays and clay-manufactures which have given celebrity to that town.

CLEPSYDRA. Before the invention of pendulum clocks, it was not unusual in astronomical observations to measure time by the flowing of water, upon a principle which, in its most simple application, resembled that of the hour-glass, but which was varied by contrivances for accuracy or ornament. Such a contrivance was called a *clepsydra* or water-clock. The Chaldeans divided the day into twelve equal parts by a Clepsydra. Water-clocks were used in Egypt, Greece, and Rome; and there is evidence that they were used in India in the twelfth century. Many fanciful forms of Clepsydræ are given in old works on Hydraulics; but modern clock and watch work has rendered them quite obsolete.

CLICHÉE MEDALLIONS. Large medallions are sometimes made in France by a process called *en clichée.* The metal of which the medallion is formed is used while in a pasty state, between solid and liquid. Such medallions, unlike more elaborately wrought coins and medals, have a device on one side only, on which side alone they are intended to be seen; they appear to have been devised in France, where large and cheap medallions are more prized, and are more extensively produced, than in England. In the time of Napoleon, it was customary to make large medallions *en clichée*, bronze them, mount them into the lids of snuff-boxes, and protect them with convex glasses.

The medallions are made in the following way. The metal employed is *fusible metal,* [ALLOY] which melts at a very low temperature. This being melted in an iron vessel, a little is taken up in a ladle, and agitated until it assumes a pasty consistency. Sufficient to form one medallion is poured on a piece of clean paper, placed in the bottom of a box enclosed on all; a stamper is made to fall suddenly on the mass, and impress a device upon it, which device remains when the metal cools. The device is produced in one of two ways. In one case the original medallion, which is to serve as a copy for those to be made, is used as a model from which a *mould* en clichéo is made, and this mould is fixed, face downwards, to the bottom of the stamper; while in the other case a die is engraved, and this die itself is fixed to the stamper. It is obvious that the same results are produced by both means. The box contains a little simple mechanism for regulating the descent of the stamper, and to prevent the semi-liquid metal from splashing about. The medallions are made one by one, and removed as fast as made.

The medallions are generally finished by bronzing. The back and edge are brought true by turning in a lathe; and the medallion is then subjected to some one of many different routines of processes, any of which will impart a bronze-like colour to the surface.

The dies or moulds for clichée medallions may be formed of iron, brass, copper, wood, sulphur, or plaster. The Italian figure casters often employ a kind of clichée method in producing moulds for small casts.

CLITHEROE, in Lancashire, was, until recently, a place of little trade; but extensive print works and cotton manufactories have been established, which, along with the lime-kilns, provide ample employment for the increasing population. The neighbourhood abounds with limestone, for which there is a great demand, as it can now be conveyed by water to any part of the kingdom. The chief establishment in the town is the celebrated print-works of Messrs. Thomson at Primrose Lodge, on the south-west margin of the town. A dam has been thrown across the valley of Mearley Brook, to form a reservoir for working the great water-wheel of these works. At the beginning of the present year, 765 males and 121 females were employed at the Primrose works. Attached to the works is a farm of 80 acres, supplied with manure by means of sewage refuse, which would otherwise contaminate the streams. The chief proprietor of these works is one of our most accomplished manufacturers. No calico-printer in this country has done more to study the chemistry of colours, and the application of taste to the production of designs.

There are four cotton factories at Clitheroe, which at the beginning of 1850 employed 556 males and 1,117 females. Nearly one third of the total population of Clitheroe, adults and children, are employed at the five large establishments.

The Bolton and Blackburn Railway has recently (June 1850) been extended to Clitheroe.

CLOA'CÆ, were large arched drains or sewers, formed under the streets of some ancient Roman cities. The most remarkable were the cloacæ of Rome, large portions of which still remain, and which were doubtless of high antiquity.

The cloacæ of Rome consisted of several branches, which ran in the low parts between the hills; these branches fell into one very large arched drain, constructed of solid blocks of stone, called the Cloaca Maxima. A portion of this cloaca is visible near the arch of Janus. The arched drain of the Cloaca Maxima is fifteen feet wide, and thirty high (these dimensions include the masonry), with three arches in contact one within another: in some parts there are raised paths along the sides of the cloaca; and in the walls are stone brackets to support the ends of the waste pipes of the fountain. The only cloacæ or drains for a city, which can be compared with the cloacæ of Rome, are the sewers of London.

The maintenance of the Roman cloacæ was originally the business of the censors, but afterwards belonged to the ædiles. Agrippa, during the ædileship, made numerous large cloacæ. The city of Pompeii had cloacæ on a smaller scale.

CLOCK AND WATCH MAKING. The first author who has introduced the term *horologium* as applicable to a clock that struck the hours appears to be Dante, who was born in 1265 and died in 1321. It would appear from this, that striking clocks were known in Italy as early as the latter part of the thirteenth or beginning of the fourteenth century. There is known to have been some such kind of clock at quite as early a period in England; but it is considered probable that the next following century produced the first clock properly so called, the term *horologium* having previously included many kind of time measurers. Many allusions to celebrated clocks, in France, Italy, Germany, and Holland, are to be met with, belonging to the fourteenth and fifteenth centuries. It is now believed that a regulated clock was not the invention of one man, but a compound of successive inventions, each worthy of a separate contriver.

There was a clock made in 1364 by De Wyck, for the Emperor of Germany, which had two pallets worked by a crown-wheel, and two weights on a lever to regulate the movement to time. In 1484 Walthus made a balance-clock for astronomical observations. In 1560 Tycho Brahé had four clocks which indicated hours, minutes, and seconds; the largest of which had only three wheels, one having 1200 teeth. In 1577 Moestlin had a clock whose beats enabled him to determine approximately the apparent diameter of the sun. At what time *watches* or small clocks were introduced, by the use of a mainspring instead of a weight as the moving power, is not known; but it is supposed to have been in the early part of the sixteenth century. Galileo's discovery of the isochronism of the pendulum paved the way for the introduction of pendulum clocks; and it is probable that both Galileo and Huyghens had constructed pendulum clocks before 1648, though some writers say that Richard Harris made a pendulum clock a few years earlier, viz. in 1641. In 1676 Barlow, a London clock-maker, invented the repeating mechanism by which the hour last struck may be known by pulling a string. Several artists followed in the same line, particularly Quare, in London, and Julien le Roy, Collier, Larçay, Thiout, &c., on the Continent.

Clocks were soon after this made to show not only mean but apparent time.

A London clockmaker named Clement invented in 1680 the anchor-escapement, which was a great improvement on the crown-wheel before in use; he also introduced the practice of suspending the pendulum by a thin and flexible spring. The next important improvement was the adjustment of the length of the pendulum to the varied effects of heat and cold. In 1715 George Graham, by substituting a jar of mercury for the pendulum-ball, succeeded in retaining the point of suspension and the centre of oscillation at the same distance from each other. The principal objection to this pendulum is its liability to breakage, of which its author felt the full force, and in consequence suggested the idea of the opposite expansions of different metals as a compensation for a pendulum. John Harrison immediately turned his attention to the subject, and, by dint of perseverance, overcoming all the difficulties of his humble and retired situation, not only astonished the world by his improvements in horological machines, but absolutely constructed with his own hands a timekeeper which determined the longitude within such limits as to procure him the parliamentary reward of 20,000*l*. Although the anchor escapement previously mentioned was a great improvement upon all that had preceded it, still it was subject to objections, not one of the least of which was that at every vibration a considerable recoil took place. The inconveniences of this escapement were however removed (about the same time with the invention of Harrison's pendulum) by Graham, who introduced what is called the dead-beat escapement, which is both simple and effective.

Eight-Day Clocks.—In an eight-day clock there are two barrels containing springs, one to give motion to the train of wheels called the *going* train, and the other to the *striking* train. The first of these springs gives motion to a wheel called the main wheel, which in its turn acts upon several other wheels, the time of rotation of which corresponds with that of the minute and hour hand. The last wheel of this system acts upon two little levers or pallets, which give an alternating motion to the pendulum of the clock. A *fusee*, which is a kind of spiral system of grooves, is fitted to the main wheel, and enables the main wheel to maintain an equable motion during the varying pulling force of the spring. All the above-named wheels belong to the *going* train. There is a somewhat similar train belonging to the *striking* action; but the teeth of the wheels, instead of being so cut as to facilitate the movement of two index hands, act upon certain pins and levers which move the hammer belonging to the bell; this part of the mechanism is exceedingly beautiful, especially when the clock strikes the quarters.

Once in eight days the clock is 'wound up,' which consists in coiling up the going spring very tightly in its barrel. In its efforts to uncoil itself, the spring forcibly pulls round the main wheel with which it is placed in connection; and the fusee causes this motion to go on pretty steadily and equably. As the main-wheel cannot rotate without moving the train of wheels to which it is connected, all these latter also rotate, with a velocity depending on the number of teeth which act on each other. In two of the wheels these numbers are so regulated that the wheels revolve in one hour and twelve hours respectively; and the axes of these wheels serve as axes for the minute and hour hands. Meanwhile the second spring gives motion to the second train of wheels, which are so connected with the going wheels as to enable the bell-hammer to be moved at the proper time. One of the many kinds of pendulum, concealed behind or within the clock, is set in motion by one of the wheels, and, by its isochronous or 'equal-timed' vibrations, tends to give regularity to the movements of the wheels generally.

Large Pendulum Clocks.—Turret clocks differ from other machines employed for measuring time, not only in their greatly superior size, but because such a clock is frequently required to indicate the time upon as many as four different dials, on the four external faces of the tower in which it is mounted. This is accomplished by placing the clock near the centre of an apartment, and causing the motion of the axis which under ordinary circumstances would carry the minute hand (which revolves once in an hour), to be transmitted by bevil-gear to a vertical rod, the opposite end of which carries a horizontal bevil-wheel nearly on a level with, and situated centrically with reference to, the four external dials. The motion of this central wheel is communicated by four vertical bevil-wheels of the same size and number of teeth, ranged round its circumference, to four horizontal rods, the opposite ends of which, passing through the several dials, carry the four minute-hands. At the back of each dial is a series of wheels and pinions, by which motion is imparted to the hour-hand, which revolves once in twelve hours. In a turret-clock, the moving power is supplied by the descent of a weight, regulated in the case of the movement, or going-train, by the oscillations of a large pendulum, and in that of the striking train by the resistance of the air to the rapid revolutions of a fly or fan set in motion by the wheelwork. Owing to the necessity for using a very heavy hammer to strike the hours in a church clock, the power required for working the striking-train considerably exceeds that of the going train.

Musical Chimes.—These require the addition of another train of mechanism, somewhat like that which constitutes the striking train. The mechanism of the chimes very nearly resembles, on a large scale, that of a musical snuff-box: levers, connected with hammers which strike upon a series of bells, being substituted for the springs which in the musical snuff-box are caused to vibrate by the projecting pins on the revolving barrel.

In the new Royal Exchange clock, made by Mr. Dent, many improvements have been introduced. There is a simple but strong cast-iron framing, which enables the several parts of the clock to be put together with less strain than usual. The wheels for the striking train are made of cast iron; more durable and less costly than the usual gun-metal wheels. The wheels of the going train, smaller and requiring to be more nicely adjusted than those of the striking train, are made of hammered brass. Hollow iron drums are used instead of wooden cylinders for the driving barrels, and wire instead of hemp or ropes for suspending the weights. It was required, by the terms of contract, that this most admirable clock should have a compensation-pendulum, and that it should be so constructed as not only to show perfectly correct time upon the dials, but also to tell it with accuracy by making the first stroke of the hour upon the bell true to a second. This object is attained by a beautiful arrangement of mechanism. In this clock has also been introduced a beautiful contrivance for maintaining the motion of the wheels during the time of winding up, which was invented a few years since by Professor Airy for the clock-work of the great Northumberland telescope at the University of Cambridge.

Pocket Watches.—A pocket-watch is very similar in principle to a good clock, except that the regulation of the former is by a balance and spring, and that of the latter by a pendulum. It would be a matter of some difficulty to determine what artist first reduced the portable spring-clock to the dimensions of a watch to be worn in the pocket. The small clocks prior to the time of Huyghens and Hooke were very imperfect machines; they did not even profess to subdivide the hours into minutes and seconds until the invention of the balance-spring, which is to the balance what gravity is to the pendulum, and its introduction has contributed as much to the improvement of watches as did that of the pendulum to clocks. The honour of this invention was warmly contested by the last-named individuals previous to 1658; but, so far as priority of publication is concerned, the honour is due to Hooke.

When clocks and watches had acquired a certain degree of accuracy in their performance, the time lost in winding up (especially when it had to be done every twenty-four hours) became a matter of importance, and there have been several inventions to remedy this evil. By Huyghens the clock was kept going while winding up by means of an endless cord. The *forcing spring* gives another plan, in which a lever is so adjusted as to allow the wheels free movement, while the spring barrel is being acted on by the key. But Harrison's contrivance for the same purpose is the one now in general use, both in clocks and watches, and is admirably adapted to the purpose, as it requires no attention from the person who has to wind up the machine, but is always in its place, and ready for action the moment the operation of winding is commenced. It is generally called the *going fusee*, but a better name for it is *maintaining power*. The principle of its action depends on the mode in which the fusee is fixed into a socket connected with the main wheel, so as to allow the wheel and the fusee to rotate independently of each other when required.

The word *escapement* is a term applied to a combination of parts in a clock or watch, which has for its object the conversion of the circular motion of the wheels into a vibratory motion, as exhibited in the pendulum. The component parts include the scape-wheel, the pallets with their arbor or axis, and a bent lever attached thereto, called the crutch, which last piece maintains the motion of the pendulum. In a watch this combination consists of the scape-wheel, together with all those parts lying between it and the balance, and which are concerned in converting the circular motion of the wheels into the alternating one of the balance. The pallets act upon or between the pointed teeth of the scape-wheel by a reciprocal or oscillatory motion.

In a common *Vertical Watch*, the barrel containing the spring is near one edge; and next to it is the fusee. The spring within the barrel, formed by a narrow strip of highly tempered steel, is fastened at one end to the interior of the barrel, and at the other to the axis or arbor of the barrel. A fine steel chain runs from the exterior of the barrel to the exterior of the fusee; and, when the watch is wound up by the application of the watch-key to the arbor of the fusee, the chain is drawn from off the cylindrical surface of the barrel, and wound on the grooved surface of the fusee. In this process the spring within the barrel becomes coiled round very tightly; and, it is the recoil or resistance of the spring which slowly pulls the chain back again to the barrel, and causes the fusee to rotate. The fusee is concentric with a toothed wheel, whose teeth act upon those of a second wheel, and those upon a third, and so on throughout the delicate machine: one wheel rotating with such a velocity as to enable an index hand upon its axis to mark hours, another minutes, another (in a seconds-watch) seconds, and another to act upon the regulating or pendulum apparatus.

One of the chief distinctive features in watches, and the one by which the name or designation is often determined, is the nature of the escapement. The *duplex* escapement so named from a French watchmaker, is much more intricate than the escapement of a common vertical watch. A *vertical watch* has the escapement perpendicular to the face of the watch, while a *horizontal watch* has the escapement so formed parallel to the face of the watch. A *lever watch* has an escapement differing from all the others, which is preferred to those of either the vertical or horizontal watch. Earnshaw's *detached escapement*, intended chiefly for chronometers, is considered to excel all others for the accuracy of its performance.

The term *repeater*, or *repeating watch*, is applied to those watches which, in addition to showing the time on the dial, are supplied with mechanism for giving audible indication of the time when required. In an eight day spring clock, the number of blows given by the hammer to the bell corresponds with the hour denoted by the hand of the clock; and there is an arrangement by which the pulling of a string may be made to denote the hour *last* struck. But, from the peculiar mechanism involved, there are about ten minutes in every hour during which this repeating could not be produced. The filling up of this deficiency is an object in a repeating watch or clock. Some of these watches strike only the hours and quarters; while others, called minute repeaters, strike the minutes also. In a common watch, the wheels and pinions which are placed between the frame-plates constitute the *going train;* while the wheels and pinions placed between the uppermost frame-plate and the dial, serving to communicate the motion from the centre wheel to the index hands, constitute the *motion-work;* but, in addition to these a repeating watch has another system of mechanism, called the *repeating train*, for the purpose of transmitting the movement from motion-work to the hammers which are to strike the hours and quarters.

Many interesting novelties have been introduced within the last few years, in respect to clocks and watches.

Trinity Church at Hull is believed to have the largest clock in the world with four dials or faces. Each dial is 13 feet in diameter, and each pair of hands weighs 56 lbs.

A useful kind of kitchen clock was described a few years ago by the late Mr. Loudon. It had a bell which called the attention of the cook at certain prescribed periods. Whether it were to boil an egg, or to perform any other kind of cooking which required a certain definite number of minutes, the cook moved an index hand on the face of a dial; and when the allotted time had expired, an alarum or bell rang to announce the fact.

Many of our churches and public buildings have clocks of which the faces are illuminated at night. The Horse Guards' clock was thus first illuminated in 1839, by the rays from a bude-light falling on the surface. It has, however, been frequently felt that the mode of illuminating public clocks is not such as to enable the hands to be visible for any considerable distance; the direction of the hands is the one important point in the indications of a clock; and if this be made distinct, the illumination of the clock generally may be in considerable part dispensed with. Mr. Hughes of Liverpool introduced a new method in that town in 1844, and published a small pamphlet relating to it. His plan consists in illuminating three points only; viz. the centre of the clock, and the outer extremity of each of the two hands. A stream of gas is conveyed into the spindle or shaft on which the hands are fixed, and thence to the hands themselves; and there are three orifices or jets where this gas is ignited. In the centre is a red light; at the outer extremity of the short hand is a green light; and at the outer extremity of the long hand a white light. The white and the green lights revolve with the hands round the dial plate: the white being always the farthest distant from the central stationary red light. A little consideration will show that this is quite sufficient to make the time intelligiblo; for in looking at an ordinary clock or watch, we are moro guided by the *direction* taken by the two hands, with respect to tho centre, than the figures towards which the ends of the hands point. It can be seen from a much greater distance than the ordinary kinds of illuminated clocks; and if it be at first not quite so intelligible, it might easily be made so by a few illuminated markings or figures round the circumference of the dial.

A curious circumstance is observable at nearly all our railway stations. If a train proceeds eastward or westward, the change of longitude produces a change in the proper time at the successive stations. If the station clocks show time corresponding to their longitudes, it would make the time-tables very confused; and the pocket watch carried by a passenger would never correspond with the station clocks, except at the town from which his watch is adjusted. But if, on the other hand, all the station-clocks shew Greenwich time (which is the plan adopted throughout Great Britain), then those clocks will not and do not correspond with the church-clocks and pocket-watches of the several towns, and much miscalculation of time results. Mr. Pilbrow has suggested an ingenious mode of obviating these difficulties, by having a clock which shall shew double time; and a clock so suggested has been constructed by Mr. Fairer of Tottenham. The arrangement is very simple: differing from the common clock only in the construction of the long or minute hand. This hand is shaped like the sector of a circle, corresponding in size or the number of degrees to the number of minutes in the difference between Greenwich time and the time at any particular station. The curved part of the hand is made of glass, so that the figures can be read through it. One edge or corner of the sector will mark Greenwich time, and the other edge the time at the station; so that the relation between the two will be instantly observable.

A singular kind of clock was registered in 1849 by Mr. Tanner, for shewing time adapted to places in five different longitudes. There is one large dial plate, with four smaller dials disposed equidistant upon it. The large dial has hour and minute hands, figures, &c., like an ordinary clock; while each small dial has its own set of figures and hands. The large dial shews Greenwich time; while the four small dials may be made to shew the time at four different places in any part of the world: differing from Greenwich time according to the differences of longitude. The mechanism of the clock is so adjusted as to shew Greenwich time on the large dial, while a train of toothed wheels and pinions transmits motion from the central clock to each one of the four small dials: the index hands being arranged 'fast' or 'slow,' according as the place to which the small dial refers lies east or west of the meridian of Greenwich.

An ingenious clock was made by Ratrenhofer of Vienna, in 1840, which shewed the time for 73 towns in different parts of the world, according to their longitudes. It had a dial-plate 14 inches in diameter, in the centre of which was the dial for Vienna; and around this dial were arranged 72 very small dials for the other towns; the Vienna dial or clock was set to work by the descent of a 4 lb. weight; and the other 72 dials were moved by wheels connected with the Vienna dial; so that one winding up set the whole in motion. All the 73 dials shewed different time, according to the longitudes of the towns to which they were respectively adjusted.

From a Report made by M. Francœur to a committee on the Mechanic Arts of the So-Societé d'Encouragement, in 1839, it appears that the French clock makers have endeavoured to produce church clocks at a much lower rate than they could be constructed in former times, by the adoption of the manufacturing system rather than the handicraft system: that is, by making considerable numbers of each kind at once. There is at Moret a manufactory of what are called *Jura Clocks*, in which all the pieces of the mechanism are made in the large way and all made to fit; wheels, weights, bells, dial plates, hands, hammers, &c., are made, set up, and delivered in the market for about forty francs the set. One of these low-priced clocks is taken, and a few changes made in it to fit for the tower of a church, by using larger hammer, bell, dial, and hands. According to the report of M. Francœur, as quoted in the *Annales des Mines*, the result is much cheaper than if a single clock were made throughout on the usual system.

French clocks, many of which exhibit great beauty of form (though we believe they are scarcely considered to equal English clocks in solidity and durability of construction) were imported in 1849 to the value of 65,000*l*.

The Clock and Watch Manufacture exhibits many remarkable features. The large clocks for public buildings are made by a very small number of firms, on account of the demand being limited and the duration of the clocks considerable. Nearly all the watch-makers of London live in one district—Clerkenwell; but even these, great as is their number, do not make the wheel-work for the watches; these works, or *movements*, as they are called, are nearly all manufactured in Lancashire, where they can be produced cheaper than in London. There are no watch-factories in Clerkenwell; but there are thirty or forty distinct classes of tradesmen, comprising perhaps three times that number of minor subdivisions, all living and working at their own homes, most of them having aid from apprentices or journeymen, and all employed at some one or other of the numerous parts of a watch. A *Watch Manufacturer*, in the Clerkenwell sense of the term, makes none of these parts, but puts them all together when others have made them.

CLONMEL is one of those towns to which Ireland may fairly look as seats of her future prosperity, whenever that prosperity shall arrive. For the last 20 years Clonmel has been steadily advancing in prosperity. 'It is,' says Mr. Inglis,' writing in 1834, 'the great point of export for Tipperary, which is one great granary, as well as for parts of other counties, for it is the first point at which water-carriage commences.' The exports are chiefly corn, bacon, and butter; of wheat from two to three hundred thousand barrels are annually brought into the town. The flour mills are very numerous and extensive. They are chiefly situated on Suir island. The bacon trade was also very extensive until within a few years. The butter trade, though large, has also lately been on the decline. Another considerable source of employment is the great posting establishment of Mr. Bianconi, of which Clonmel is the depôt. There are also several breweries, and an extensive distillery in the vicinity; and a cotton manufactory, which employs about 200 persons. There is consequently little want of employment. The carrying trade of the town is conducted by barges of from 20 to 40 tons which ply on the Suir to Waterford: of these there are about 120 on the river. The northern bank of the Suir, between the two lower bridges, is quayed in. The Waterford and Limerick Railway now in progress passes through Clonmel.

CLOVER was introduced into the agriculture of Great Britain about the 16th century, from the Low Countries, where it had been long cultivated as green food for cattle in situations where natural pastures were scarce. The species of clover are annual, biennial, or perennial plants. The most approved variety of the biennial clovers is the common *red* or *broad clover*, which is usually sown with barley or oats, or sometimes among wheat or rye in spring. In Scotland clover is often sown among wheat, in Norfolk invariably with barley, and in Belgium among rye. It is usual to sow *rye-grass* in a small proportion with clover seed, especially where clover, having been often repeated on the same land, is apt to fail. A very extensive use of clover-hay in London is to cut it into chaff, and to mix this with oats and beans for dray horses, which have little or no hay given them in any other way; but the most profitable use of clover is to cut it green for horses and cattle. The *white* or *Dutch clover*, the *cow-grass*, the *yellow trefoil*, and the *hop trefoil* are all usefully employed as fodder. The only annual clover which is cultivated is the *French clover*, a most valuable addition to the plants usually sold for fodder, from the short time in which it arrives at perfection if sown in spring; so that, where clover has failed, this may be sown to fill up the bare places.

On good land, an acre of clover will produce as much as three tons and a half of dry hay; that is, two tons the first cutting, and one and a half the second. Greater crops are obtained on very highly manured land.

Clover seed was imported to the extent of 99,813 cwts. in 1848.

CLOVES. The cloves of the spice-shops are the flower-buds of the *Caryophyllus Aromaticus*, gathered before they open, and dried in the sun. The tree is a native of the Molucca, whence it has been carried to other tropical countries. The name *clove* is a corruption of the French word *clou*, a nail, a name that has been suggested by the resemblance of the dried clove to a nail. The aromatic stimulating effects of cloves are well known.

By distillation a thickish oil is obtained, which is at first colourless, but by time becomes yellow and brown. Its taste is very fiery and aromatic; it reacts as an acid. In time there separates from it a stearopten, or clove-camphor, called *caryophyllin*.

Cloves are employed in medicine, and also more extensively for culinary purposes. When received into the stomach they are powerfully stimulant, and promote digestion when taken along with food which is insipid or difficult of digestion. Oil of cloves is used much in medicine.

Cloves were imported in 1849 to the extent of 274,712 lb.

CLYDE. Below Glasgow the Clyde has been made the scene of astonishing engineering works. About 80 years ago, only vessels of 3¼ feet draught could come up to Glasgow Bridge; in 1775 the whole river from Glasgow to Dumbarton was deepened so as to receive vessels of 6 feet draught: this depth was increased by 1831 to 13½ feet; by 1847 to 15 feet; and works now in progress will carry the depth to 20 feet at neap tides. The river for 12 miles is being widened, straightened and deepened.

A suggestion of a singular kind has been recently thrown out, in the pages of the *Glasgow Advertiser*, concerning the forthcoming Industrial Exhibition. "There is at the present day in Glasgow, we believe, in the hands of Messrs. Claud, Girdwood, and Co., or their successors, the very identical steam-engine that Henry Bell fitted on board the *Comet*, the first steamer that ever sailed on the Clyde —the vessel, in fact, which may be called the precursor of the splendid steamers that now circumnavigate the globe, and bring the antipodes, as it were, to our very threshold. This steam-engine has on several occasions been exhibited in Glasgow, and has always been an object of much attraction, as properly it should be, to those who know the value of such a wonderful invention as that of the marine steam-engine. Mr. John Wood, of Port Glasgow, the veteran ship-builder who laid the keel of the first passsage steamer that navigated the Clyde—the father of all the wonderful steamships that now exist—possesses the draft, and, if required, could even at the present day produce an exact counterpart of the Comet. Now, what we would propose as a source of attraction at the Exhibition of 1851, is that an exact duplicate of the Comet should be built by Mr. Wood, and that it should be fitted with the original steam-engine of that vessel, so as to present an exact counterpart to that eventful steamer as she sailed on the river Clyde in the year 1812. The expense of such an undertaking would be a mere bagatelle."

COACHES AND COACH-MAKING. It is stated by Stow, that in '1564, Boonen, a Dutchman, became the queen's coachman, and was the first that brought the use of coaches into England.'

A long time elapsed before this luxury was attained by more than a few very rich and distinguished individuals, and a very much longer time before coaches became general. Coaches let for hire were first established in England in 1625; they did not stand in the streets, but at the principal inns. In 1637 there were, in London and Westminster, 50 hackney-coaches. Stage-coaches were first used in England soon after the introduction of hired carriages. The first mail coach travelled from London to Edinburgh about 1785, and to Glasgow in 1788.

The use of stage-coaches rapidly extended itself; and from the latter part of the last century, until the establishment of railways, there was scarcely any small town through which some stage-coach did not pass, and no considerable road which was not travelled by many. In this country the best stage-coaches were very perfect machines, and the arrangements by which they were conducted, when the number of persons and animals that were engaged is considered, were extremely complete. The principal stage-coaches ran with four horses, and the rate of travelling among the *fast* coaches was rapid. In 1833, the distance between London and Shrewsbury (154 miles), Exeter (171 miles), and Manchester (187 miles), was done in a day. The mail to Holyhead did the 261 miles in 27 hours, and that to Liverpool, 203 miles, in 21 hours. The coaches were on springs, and, though strong, were light and elegant.

The omnibus, a sort of long-bodied coach, was introduced into London in 1831. We shall have some details to give in a later article, concerning the hired vehicles of London. [OMNIBUSES AND CABS.]

The coaches which form the trains upon railroads are of very different construction from those used on common roads; they are stronger, larger, and heavier: they are fastened together with links of chain, and there is attached to the back and front of each a 'fender' by which concussion is prevented when the train is stopped.

Upon the Continent, travelling in public carriages was never so rapid or so commodious as in England. In France the diligences were, and those which still exist are, clumsy carriages, generally consisting of three bodies, and are drawn by five or six horses, usually driven by one postilion from his saddle. The first body, called the 'coupé,' formed like a chariot, contains three people; the second, which is like a coach, the 'intérieur,' holds six persons; the third, which is similar to a coach turned sidewise, carries six or eight passengers, and is called the 'rotonde.' In addition to these, there is on the roof, before the place appropriated to the luggage, the 'banquette,' a bench sometimes furnished with a hood for the accommodation of four passengers. But every where the use of the railroad is superseding the old stage-coach on all the great lines of road in all highly civilised countries.

In the making of coaches or carriages, as a highly skilled department of manufacture; the timber, the iron, the leather, the brass and plated metals, the trimmings, and other materials, are wrought by wholly distinct bodies of operatives; and there are many minor divisions of each class. The 'body-makers' produce the vehicle or body itself, while the 'carriage-makers' are employed on the stouter and stronger timbers beneath and around the body. The chief kinds of wood employed are ash, beech, elm, oak, mahogany, cedar, pine, deal, fustic, birch, and larch—each kind appropriated to the purpose for which its fibrous nature best fits it. In working up these varieties of timber, tools and processes are employed similar to those in cabinet-making, together with others peculiar to coach-making.

The various forms of the coach, gig, dennet, curricle, tilbury, stanhope, &c., lead to the exercise of much ingenuity in fashioning the wood-work to the requisite curved forms. The axles on which the wheels work, the springs which protect the carriage from concussion, and the iron perch which is sometimes used instead of wood, are the work of the 'coach-smith,' one of the most highly paid classes of London workmen. The coating of the body of the coach with leather is a most difficult and delicate art; and the subsequent painting, trimming, and decorating, all rank among the highest kinds in their respective classes. Coach-axles have been made the subject of patents; and so indeed have many other improvements in the manufacture of parts of coaches. So far as regards workmanship and processes, carts and waggons bear almost the same relation to coaches that carpentry does to cabinet-making; similar in character, but coarser.

COAGULATION is the solidification of a liquid produced without evaporation and without crystallisation.

COALS AND COAL MINING. We shall here treat in succession of the *formation of coal*, the *coal fields*, *coal mining*, and the *coal trade*,—giving a few brief details under each heading.

Formation of Coal.—From the presence of tree-ferns, and palms, and other plants which now grow in tropical climates, in coal, it has been inferred that at the period at which the coal-beds were deposited the temperature of these parts of the world at least was much greater than it is at present. If the facts we actually possess are soberly examined, they amount to these :—

1. That coal is of vegetable origin.

2. That at the period of its deposit the earth was covered with a rich vegetation, of which only a small portion has been preserved, and that of this portion all the species and several of the races are totally unknown at the present day.

3. That the climate may possibly have been something milder than it now is, but that there is no evidence in the vegetable kingdom to show that it was materially different from that of the present day.

From these data it is assumed that coal is the result of vegetable substances which have been pressed down through unknown ages into a compact mass, which has passed through the intermediate stage of peat or bog, and become gradually consolidated into coal.

The report of Sir H. De la Beche and Dr. Lyon Playfair, on the quality of coal best suited for the steam navy, contains much valuable information on the different kinds of coal, and their heating effect. One kind will raise steam very quickly; another is slower in its action, but generates a greater abundance of steam. Two kinds may be equal in these respects, yet one would speedily crumble by stowage, while the other would remain unbroken. Some kinds occupy much less bulk for a given weight than others. All these points being of importance, it has been the desire of the Admiralty to ascertain which kind of coal possesses the greatest number of advantages, and the fewest disadvantages, in respect to steam navigation. The commissioners constructed apparatus, especially calculated to further the enquiry; and experimented on thirty varieties of coal. Among the data ascertained were — the number of pounds of water evaporated from an initial temperature of 212°, by one pound of coal; weight of one cubic foot of the coal, as used for fuel, and as calculated from the specific gravity; space in cubic feet occupied by one ton; cohesive power of the coal; weight of water evaporated from 212° by one cubic foot; rate of evaporation, or weight of water evaporated in one hour; chemical constituents of the coal, in carbon, hydrogen, nitrogen, sulphur, oxygen, and ash; per centage of coke after coking; weight of water that can be raised from 32° to 212° by the heat of one pound of coal; per centage of the various products of combustion, in coke, tar, water, ammonia, carbonic acid, sulphuretted hydrogen, olefiant gas, &c.; and the force generated or weight that could be raised to the height of one foot by the combustion of one pound of coal.

The commissioners show that fuel for war-steamers ought to raise steam quickly; to possess high evaporative powers; to contain but little bitumen; to possess considerable cohesion among the particles; to have density and closeness of structure; to contain but little sulphur; and to have no liability to decay during storage. The kinds brought to the test of experiment shewed, as might be expected, very different results under these several headings; insomuch that no one kind stood first on the list in respect to more than two or three of the above qualities. Three kinds of patent fuel, formed by admixtures of coal dust with bituminous and other substances, were included among the varieties examined; and it was found that Warlich's patent fuel stood higher than any kinds of coal in respect to many qualities. The commissioners expressed an opinion that it might be practicable to produce a composite coal, or

KNIGHT'S CYCLOPÆDIA OF THE INDUSTRY OF ALL NATIONS.

No. 16.

a mixture of many kinds of coal, which would possess a more useful aggregate of qualities than those possessed by any one sort of coal *per se;* and they recommend further experiments as a means of putting this plan to the test. As an example of their mode of stating the evidence for and against any one species of coal, we may take Anthracite:—"It has a very high evaporative power; but not being easily ignited, it is not suited for quick action. It has great cohesion in its particles, and is not easily broken up by attrition; but it is not a caking coal, and therefore would not cohere in the furnace when the ship rolled in a gale of wind. It emits no smoke; but from the intensity of its combustion it causes the iron of the bars and boilers to oxidate or wear away rapidly."

Coal Fields.—These are large accumulations of coal which exist in various parts of the world. Coal is found in these fields in strata of various thickness, alternating with slate-clay and sandstone; the alternations being frequently and indefinitely repeated. The coal beds, which are of various qualities, are principally distinguished by the proportion of bitumen in the coal. The coal-seams, together with their alternating strata, called the *coal-measures*, usually lie on beds of millstone grit and shale (hard coarse-grained sandstone and slate clay), which sometimes exceed 120 fathoms in thickness. Under this series is the mountain or carboniferous limestone, an assemblage of calcareous strata, of variable thickness, sometimes exceeding 900 feet. The carboniferous limestone rests on a bed of old red sandstone, varying in thickness from 200 to 2000 feet. These four different series of strata are usually comprehended under the term 'coal-formation.'

The coal-fields of Great Britain are very numerous and deserve to be studied somewhat in detail. The Northumberland and Durham coal-field commences near the mouth of the river Coquet on the north, and extends nearly to the Tees on the south. Its greatest length is 58 miles, and its greatest breadth about 24. The beds of coal in some places appear at the surface, while in the opposite direction they are at great depths. The beds of these coal-measures are about 80 in number, and consist of alternating beds of coal, sandstone, and slate-clay; making an aggregate thickness of 1620 feet, which varies however in different parts. The aggregate thickness of coal is supposed to be about 44 feet, of which about 30 feet are workable. This coal is shipped in immense quantities from the Tyne, the Wear, and the Tees. There is another coal-formation, which extends through parts of Durham, Northumberland, and Cumberland, independent of the former.

In Yorkshire there are detached coal-fields, very limited in extent, being small insulated coal-basins, lying in hollows in the gritstone. They occur near Middleham, Leyburne, Thorpefell, near Burnsell, and as far west as Kettlewell. Southward of these is an extensive coal-field, which occupies an area extending north and south from a little to the north-east of Leeds nearly to Derby, a distance of more than 65 miles; its greatest width, 23 miles, is on the north, reaching nearly as far as Halifax to the west. The strata of this coal-formation are very numerous; the coal-seams are about 30 in number, varying from 6 inches to 11 feet in thickness. Since the opening of the Midland Railway, which traverses this coal-field, the working of the collieries has been vastly extended by the facilities for inland carriage. In north Staffordshire there are two detached coal-fields: the one situated on the N. E. of Newcastle-under-Lyme, distinguished as the Pottery Coal Field; the other at Cheadle, to the east of the first. The first measures from 6 to 10 miles in every direction; the second, from 3 to 5 miles. Thirty-two beds of coal have been met with, from 3 to 10 feet thick, and at depths from 50 to 400 yards. The South Lancashire coal-field forms an area somewhat in the shape of a crescent, having Manchester nearly in the centre; and northward of this are the North Lancashire and the Whitehaven beds; in the latter, some of the seams are very thick and of the finest quality; the shafts are very deep, and some of the mines are worked under the sea.

The South Staffordshire coal-field is about 20 miles long by 7 broad. Many coal-seams, of eight, six, and four feet in thickness, are worked in the northern portion of this field; but the southern portion is of much more importance, as it contains seams from 30 to 45 feet in thickness. This enormous thickness is however not one continuous seam, but a number of seams, divided by layers of what the miners call *band*, which are very thin beds of clay-slate. The working of these thick seams is not so profitable as might be supposed. The pillars left standing in order to support the high roof are estimated at about one-third of the whole coal in the bed, and the small coal left in the mine is about equal to another third, so that only one third of the whole is at present taken out of the mine. This district supplies coal to the numerous iron-works in the immediate neighbourhood, and the manufactories of Birmingham and its vicinity; besides which, all the neighbouring counties, as far south as Reading and Gloucester, are supplied by means of inland navigation. Leicestershire and Warwickshire have small coal fields, independent of the one here noticed.

In North Wales, a valley crosses the Isle of Anglesea, parallel to the Menai Straits, and is flanked on both sides by parallel bands of carboniferous limestone. Coal of good quality exists here, and a few mines have been successfully opened. In Flintshire a coal-field exists, extending north and south from the Dee to Oswestry, about 30 miles: not continuously however, but in patches. It is supposed that the seams pass under the Dee, and join those of Lancashire. The Coalbrook Dale coal-field is composed of the usual alternating strata, and comprises nearly 90 alternations; the seams vary from a few inches to 5 feet in thickness; they occur at depths from 100 to 700 feet.

The coal-field of South Wales is upwards of 100 miles in length, and the average breadth in the counties of Monmouth, Glamorgan, Caermarthen, and part of Brecon, is from 18 to 20 miles; it becomes much narrower in Pembrokeshire, being there only from 3 to 5 miles. This area extends from Pontypool on the east, to St. Bride's Bay on the west, and forms a vast basin of limestone, in which all the strata of coal and ironstone are deposited. The lowest bed is 700 fathoms deep at the centre, and all the principal strata lie from 500 fathoms deep to this depth. But this district is intersected by deep valleys, which generally run in a north and south direction, intersecting the coal. By driving levels in the hills, the beds of coal are found without the labour and expense of sinking shafts; there are also many pits in the low valleys. The seams vary from a few inches to 9 feet in thickness; and their aggregate thickness is about 100 feet. On the south side of the basin, the coal is principally of a bituminous nature; on the north-east it is a coking coal; on the north-west, stone coal. The occurrence of rich iron ore with or near the coal has led to the establishment of vast ironworks in South Wales.

The Gloucester and Somerset coal-field is about 25 miles long by 11 wide. The seams of coal are very thin in comparison with those which are worked in the principal coal-fields of England, and in most of those would be rejected as not worth the working. The Forest of Dean contains a coal-field about 10 miles long by 6 wide.

The principal coal-district of Scotland occupies the tract which forms the great central lowland of Scotland, and lies between the great transition chain on the south, and the still loftier primitive mountains of the Highlands on the north. In the county of Haddington are three seams of good workable coal. There are a few mines in Fifeshire and Mid-Lothian. In Lanark the coal-fields are numerous and extensive. Throughout this district seven seams of coal are usually found within 415 feet of the surface; five of these seams are of sufficient thickness to be wrought, and of good quality. Coal is found in various other parts of Scotland.

Coal has been discovered in more or less quantity in seventeen counties of Ireland. The Munster coal-district occupies a considerable portion of the counties of Limerick and Kerry, and a large part of the county of Cork; it is by much the most extensive in Ireland. Coal and culm have been raised for near a century in the neighbourhood of Kanturk, in the county of Cork. At Dromagh colliery the work has been carried on to a very considerable extent; and the beds found in it are of four kinds, the *Coal-Bed*, the *Rock Coal*, the *Bulk-Bed*, and *Bath's Bed*. The greatest depth of the Munster collieries is about 80 yards.

On the continent of Europe coal-fields are very irregularly scattered. They occur abundantly in Belgium. In Saxony and Bohemia coal is found; and in less quantity in Russia, Sweden, and Spain. France has many coal-fields, but the produce is not enough for her consumption. There were 425 coal mines in France in 1844, of which however only 252 were worked, employing 30,000 persons.

Asia contains a little coal in China, Birmah, India, and Persia. Coal has been found abundantly both in Australia and Van Diemen's Land. America, according to recent discoveries, seems to be richer in coal than any other part of the world.

Mr. Taylor, in his valuable 'Statistics of Coal,' says that the ascertained areas of the coal-fields of various countries are as follows:—

United States	133,132 sq. m.
British America	18,000
Great Britain	11,859
Spain	3,408
France	1,719
Belgium	518

But the actual yearly production, and bringing to market, form a remarkably different series:—

Great Britain	31,500,000 tons.
Belgium	4,960,000
United States	4,400,000
France	4,140,000
Prussia	3,500,000
Austria	700,000

Coal Mining.—The thickness of workable beds of coal may be said generally to vary from three or four to eight or nine feet, although sometimes, when several seams come together without any intervening layers of rock, they may expand to twenty or thirty feet, of which we have an example in the 'ten yard coal' of Staffordshire. In every coal-field there are many seams of coal at greater or less intervals, one below another, of which as many as three or four are frequently worked in the same mine.

When the position of the beds of coal has been discovered, the first process is to sink a perpendicular shaft from the surface so as to intersect the various strata containing the coal, and of course as many of the beds of coal as are considered to be worth working. The upper portion, as far down as the solid rock, is either bricked or walled, and where the ground is weak this casing may be continued throughout. On reaching the first workable seam of coal, the sinking of the pit is for a time suspended, and a broad straight passage termed a 'bord' or 'gate' is driven from it upon the seam of coal in opposite directions. The breadth of this passage is usually twelve or fourteen feet, and it is formed the whole height of the seam of coal, so as to expose the stratum above, which is called the 'roof,' and the one below, which is termed the 'thill,' and its direction is always arranged so as to follow the cleavage of the coal which forms its sides, which thus presents a clean uniform surface. When the principal bord has proceeded some distance on both sides of the pit, narrow passages, termed 'headways,' are driven from it at regular intervals, and exactly at right angles; and when these have proceeded eight or ten yards, they are made to communicate with another bord, which is opened parallel to the first and on each side of it. Thus the operations continue, until the mine resembles a town of streets rectangularly arranged. The water encountered in the above operations is drawn to the surface by a steam-engine erected at the top of the shaft, which is so arranged as also to raise the coal and rubbish, for which purpose either 'corves' or baskets are commonly employed. In small coal mines the ventilation is managed by separating a portion of the shaft from the larger part by an air-tight boarding, which is carried down to the bottom; but in large coal-mines another shaft is sunk at some distance from the first, and when the communication between them has been effected, the one being made downcast and the other upcast, the air is made to pass through the whole of the passages.

While the workings on the first seam of coal are thus going on, the shaft may be sunk to a second or third seam, where similar operations will be commenced, small underground pits or 'staples' being sunk at intervals from the workings on the upper seam to those on the seam below, by which ventilation will be promoted.

The mode in which the pitman proceeds in excavating the coal is by cutting a narrow fissure on the seam on each side of the bord with his pick-axe, and undermining the coal between, and then cutting into and forcing down the isolated portion of coal, or, where the seam is thick, by detaching the great cubical mass thus prepared by blasting, two or three shots being sometimes simultaneously fired at the top of the seam. From 60 to 80 or 100 tons of coal may thus be brought down at once, when it is put into corves, drawn along a tram-road to the shaft, and thence raised by a steam-engine to the surface, where it is often passed over gratings or 'screens' in order to separate the small pulverised coal from the larger masses.

In mines which are not endangered by explosive gases or 'fire-damp,' the coal-miner or 'pit-man' is guided in his operations by the usual subterranean light—a small candle stuck into a piece of moist clay; but where the fire-damp is apprehended the safety-lamp is used. [Lamp, Safety.]

The frequency of colliery accidents has recently drawn the attention of scientific men to the subject; and the Institute of Civil Engineers is at the present time engaged in the discussion of schemes for improved systems of ventilation.

Coal Trade.—It was long considered politic to check the exportation of coals to other countries, both through fear of exhausting the mines, and because it was imagined that our superiority as manufacturers might be endangered. A heavy export duty was accordingly levied; but this was gradually lessened in 1831, 1835, and 1842, and abolished altogether in 1845. There was formerly a revenue on coals carried coastwise, but this was abolished in 1831.

A very peculiar regulation was established by the coal owners of the northern coal-field, called the 'limitation of the vend.' It was a systematic combination among the owners of collieries having their outlets by the Tyne, the Wear, and the Tees, to raise the price to consumers by a self-imposed restriction as to the quantity supplied. When the coal duty was abandoned in 1845 the coal-owners gave up the 'limitation of the vend.'

A regulation which affects the coal trade from the Tyne and the Wear has been established by act of parliament (1826), under the provisions of which every ship must be loaded in her turn; and, if any colliery refuse to sell, a penalty is imposed of 100*l.*; but this regulation may be and has been evaded by the coal-owners by an easily concocted pretext. Regulations have also been made as to the unloading of coal-vessels in the Thames: the number being guided by the price of coal in such a way as to keep up the monopoly.

In May 1844, the harbour-master of the port of London presented a return to the lord mayor, which shows the operation of the regulations established by the coal-owners in the port of London for keeping up the price of coal. On the first of May there were 260 vessels laden with coal, detained in sections waiting their 'turn' of sale. On one day in the same month, ten colliers had been detained, with their captains and crews, for 46 days, and two had been detained above 50 days. On the 27th of May, 109 coal-laden ships were detained in sections, and the price of the best coal had advanced to 24*s.* and 25*s.* per ton, or about 34*s.* per ton to the consumer.

The railways now in progress will have an important and most beneficial effect in reducing the price of coal in all districts lying far away from the collieries; indeed such influence has already been felt, since the year just named. The York and Berwick Railway, and the York and North Midland Railway, carry an immense quantity of coal; and the Great Northern Company have lately commenced to do the same.

In 1845, the collieries of Northumberland and Durham were 129 in number; the steam-engines employed were 19,204 horse-power; the actual production was 6,790,993 tons. In 1844 there were 16,515 persons employed at the Tyne collieries; 13,173 at those of the Wear; and 4211 at those of the Tees; making 33,899 in all. The largest number at any one colliery was 1403 at Lambton. The colliery proprietorships are ranged under four classes, according to the scale of the operations. The 1st class comprises four great concerns, headed respectively by the Marquis of Londonderry, the Earl of Durham, Lord Ravensworth, and the Hetton Coal Company. The capital sunk in each of these concerns is supposed to be not less than half a million sterling; they each comprise from six to twelve separate mines, and all the necessary engines, waggons, horses, &c.; and they are believed to realise a profit on an average from 35,000*l.* to 45,000*l.* per year each. The 2nd class comprises companies or partnerships whose sunk capital ranges from one to two hundred thousand pounds. The 3rd class includes those concerns which have only a single pit each, and whose capitals are from forty to sixty thousand pounds. The 4th class, humbler but more numerous than any of the others, comprises those which have a capital ranging from eight to thirty thousand pounds. In South Staffordshire, the 'Butty' system of employing miners is extensively acted on. This consists in the miners being the servants, not of the proprietor or lessee of a colliery, but of a contractor called a 'butty,' who engages with the proprietor of the mine to deliver the coal at so much per ton; hiring the labourers himself, using his own horses, and supplying all the tools necessary for working the mines. These butties have in general been working miners, who, by the accumulation of some little capital, or by the assistance of relations, are enabled to engage a pit, with or without partnership with other persons, and to enter into a bond to raise the coal at a given price per ton. But in the Northumberland and Durham district the relation between the proprietors and the miners is more direct and intimate. No middlemen or contractors are employed; the overseers, viewers, and other intermediate officers are paid by regular salaries; and the working colliers receive in cash from the proprietors, once a fortnight, the amount of their earnings.

The coal trade of England is one of great magnitude. The coal exported from the United Kingdom to foreign countries in 1849 amounted to 2,730,507 tons. The coal brought to London in the same year amounted to 3,380,786 tons. Of the quantity brought to London, about two-fifths are shipped at the Tyne, and nearly the whole of the remaining three-fifths at the Durham ports. Of the coal sent to foreign countries, about 600,000 tons, or more than one-fifth of the whole, is sent to France: our next best customers being Germany and Prussia, who together take about 450,000 tons.

The great towns of Lancashire, Yorkshire, Nottinghamshire, Derbyshire, Leicestershire, Warwickshire, and Staffordshire, are supplied by canals or by land-carriage from collieries in the respective counties here enumerated. It has been estimated that the iron-works of Great Britain, most of which are situated in spots were coal is found, require every year, for smelting the ore and converting the raw material into bars, plates, &c., nearly seven millions of tons. There is good reason for believing that the annual consumption of coal within the United Kingdom is not far short of 35,000,000 tons. In 1841 the number of persons in Great Britain employed in coal-mines was 118,233. In Durham there were in that year, on an exact enumeration, more persons employed under ground in coal-mines than in cultivating the surface.

Coal and the collieries will not be neglected at the forthcoming Exhibition of Industry. The coal-owners of Northumberland and Durham have deputed to a number of intelligent colliery viewers the preparation of a map of the coal district, showing the extent and outcrop of the different coal-beds, together with the faults and other remarkable interruptions —a section of a coal-field, from and to given points, north and south, and a similar section from east to west—a model in pieces showing the structure of a given portion of the coal-field—a synopsis of the coal-seams in illustration of the map and sections—a collection of the fossils found in the coal-strata—working plan of a colliery, exhibiting the system of working and ventilation—a model showing the system of ventilation—specimens of the strata properly arranged—materials, &c., employed in coal-mining—models of machinery, underground railways, engines, shafts, lamps, loading machinery, drops, &c.

A block of coal, of gigantic dimensions, has been raised from Hange Colliery, near Tipton, to be sent to the Exhibition. It is six feet high by eighteen feet in circumference, and weighs about five tons. It is supposed to be the greatest weight ever attempted to be drawn out of a coal-mine in one piece; and it is also a general opinion that no coal-field in Great Britain could yield such a large mass, except the 30 foot seam of South Staffordshire. The specimen is said to be remarkably fine, bright, and clear.

COALBROOK DALE. This small spot, situated in the eastern part of Shropshire, has acquired a manufacturing celebrity for the iron goods cast there; and this as a manufacture has depended in part on the existence of coal at the spot. The coal-field of the Dale is about 6 miles long by 2 broad, and contains 86 alternations of coal and other strata, which have been penetrated to a depth of more than 700 feet.

The Coalbrook Dale Iron Works have belonged to the family of Messrs. Darby for more than 200 years. Some of the earliest castings of great magnitude in this country—indeed we believe the earliest, were made here; and the works have ever since been celebrated for the delicacy and beauty of the smaller castings in iron. On a pleasant festive occasion in 1850, planned in compliment to the chief proprietor, the colliers, miners, and workmen of the Coalbrook Dale district generally, to the number of nearly 4,000, walked in procession through Horsehay, Ironbridge, Madeley, and Dawley, and ended the day with some of those displays of kindly feeling which are always so valuable in the relation between employers and the employed.

COBALT. This metal was discovered by Brandt in 1733, associated with arsenic and other metals. It has a reddish gray colour, and a weak metallic lustre; it fuses at a high temperature, and crystallises in cooling.

Cobalt is extensively employed in the Arts. Its oxide gives an intense and beautiful blue colour to glass, and is hence much employed in painting glass and porcelain; while the blue glass thus produced, when reduced to a fine powder, is called *Smalts* or *powder blue*, and is used for correcting the yellowish tint of paper and linen.

The nitrate of cobalt, when dissolved in water, forms a *sympathetic* ink, the traces of which become blue when heated, or green if iron be present. The acetate forms a sympathetic ink which becomes blue when heated. The phosphate of cobalt, combined with alumina, produces a blue colour almost as intense and beautiful as that of ultramarine: it is called *Thenard's* or *cobalt blue*.

Cobalt forms alloys with arsenic, antimony, tin, zinc, lead, gold, and platinum.

COCA, the dried leaf of *Erythroxylon coca*, is one of those stimulating narcotics which belong to the same class with tobacco and opium, but is more remarkable than either of them in its effects upon the human system. The plant is found wild in Peru, according to Pöppig, in the environs of Cuchero, and on the stony summit of Cerro de San Cristobal. It is cultivated extensively in the mild but very moist climate of the Andes of Peru, at from 2000 to 5000 feet above the sea: in colder situations it is apt to be killed, and in warmer districts the leaf loses its flavour.

The effects of this drug are said to be of the most pernicious nature, exceeding even opium in the destruction of mental and bodily powers. The coca leaf is chewed by the Peruvian, mixed with finely powdered chalk, and brings on a state of apathy and indifference to all surrounding objects. The desire for this drug increases so much with indulgence in it, that a confirmed coca-chewer is said never to have been reclaimed.

The immoderate addiction of the Peruvians to the use of this drug is such that their forests have long since ceased to be able to supply their wants; and the cultivation of the plant has been carried to a very great extent, not only under the Incas but beneath the local government of the Spaniards, who seem to have been no more able to resist the temptation of a large revenue from the monopoly of this article than European nations from the consumption of ardent spirits. The cultivation of coca is therefore an important feature in Peruvian husbandry.

The exciting principle of the coca has so very volatile a nature that leaves only twelve months old become perfectly inert and good for nothing. Large heaps of the freshly dried leaves, particularly while the warm rays of the sun are upon them, diffuse a very strong smell resembling that of hay in which there is a quantity of melilot.

CO'CCULUS. Many species of this plant are usefully applied, chiefly in medicine; but that which is best known is the *Cocculus Indicus*, a native of East Africa. *Cocculus Indicus Berries* are the fruit of the *Cocculus suberosus*, or *Menispermum cocculus.* Besides being occasionally used in medicine, it is a poison which is used for destroying fish, and has also been extensively used by brewers as a substitute for hops—an adulteration which is prohibited in Britain by severe statutes. Cocculus Indicus is never used internally in the practice of medicine; but an ointment formed of the powdered berries is very efficacious in some cutaneous diseases.

Columba is the root of the *Cocculus palmatus*, a native of the forests on the east coast of Africa, whence it is sent to Ceylon, and thence to Europe. It occurs in the form of transverse sections, the bark of which is thick and easily separable: the woody portion is spongy, of a yellow colour, and when old much perforated by worms. The odour is faintly aromatic, the taste bitter and slightly acrid. It contains much starch, a yellow azotised matter, a yellow bitter principle, traces of a volatile oil, woody fibre, salts (chiefly of lime and potassa), oxide of iron, and silex. The active principle is *Columbine*, which may be obtained either by alcohol or æther. Columba is much used in medicine. Other roots are often fraudulently substituted for it; and slices of Bryony root are often employed to adulterate it.

COCHINEAL is extremely rich in the finest red colouring matter, and has been long employed in scarlet dyeing, and in the manufacture of carmine. It consists of a colouring matter, a peculiar animal matter, a fatty substance, and several salts. The chief use of cochineal is the dyeing of scarlet. The fine colour which it yields is converted to this tint by means of chloride or muriate of tin.

The insect which constitutes cochineal feeds chiefly upon *Cactus cochenillifera* and *C. opuntia.* The female insect only is collected. Several varieties are distinguished in commerce, and have different degrees of value attached to them, dependent chiefly upon the different methods employed to kill and dry the insects. When dried, they resemble small grains, scarcely so large as a pepper-corn, ovate, convex above, plane below, transversely furrowed, externally blackish brown, but as if dusted with a white powder, light, friable, the internal substance consisting of extremely small grains, obscurely purple, but when reduced to powder of a rich purple. They are inodorous, but with a bitter sweet acrid taste. They impart to water or alcohol by digestion an intensely red colour.

Cochineal has hitherto been employed mostly as a colouring material, either of tinctures, or of other things, the nature of which it is wished to disguise; but it is also used to a small extent in medicine.

Previous to the revolt of the Spanish American provinces, almost all the trade in cochineal with the different markets of Europe was carried on through Spain, and chiefly through Cadiz; but since that event the markets of consumption are supplied with cochineal either direct from the places of production, or from neighbouring stations, to which the article has found its way in the natural course of commerce. Representing a considerable value in a small bulk, cochineal is frequently used, with great convenience to merchants, as a medium for making remittances, and hence the comparatively circuitous route by which the greater part of it reaches the places of ultimate consumption. The quantity of cochineal imported into Great Britain in 1848 was 18,380 cwt; of which Honduras yielded 9139 cwt., and Mexico 6054 cwt.

COCK, or STOP-COCK. The stop-cocks in most common use consist of a short tube of brass, intersected by a nearly cylindrical plug, capable of being turned on its axis at pleasure, and so perforated or cut that, while in one position it completely prevents the passage of fluid through the pipe, it may be so turned as to permit the fluid to pass through it, and consequently to flow through the pipe. The kind of cock usually employed, under the name of a *tap*, for drawing off the contents of barrels, usually terminates in a curved *nose*, or spout, from which the liquor may be conveniently received in a jug or other open vessel; but, where it is desired to transfer the liquor from the cask immediately to bottles, the nose is prolonged into a long slender tube, which will enter the neck of a bottle, and obviate the necessity for a funnel. Other cocks are adapted for insertion in metallic cisterns or boilers, and fitted with a flange to bear against the outer face of the cistern, and a nut, wormed on to the portion of the tube of the cock which passes into the cistern, by which they may be screwed up firmly. Others again are adapted for soldering to the end of a leaden pipe, such as the service-pipe for laying water on to a house. Some stop-cocks, again, have no nose or spout, but are made alike at each end, for the purpose of being soldered between two lengths of leaden pipe.

In some cocks the plug is so contrived as either to contain a piece of cork, which may be turned so as to close the pipe, or to revolve within a hollow cylinder of cork, with arrangements for opening or closing a passage through it at pleasure. In others the principle of the revolving plug is entirely departed from, and the pipe is closed by means of a flat disc of metal, covered with a leather washer, and screwed up firmly against the end of the pipe, or by a conical or globular valve similarly applied. In such cocks caoutchouc forms an excellent substitute for leather. Another ingenious class of cocks comprises those furnished with contrivances for admitting air to a barrel as fast as the liquor is drawn off, and thereby superseding the use of a vent-peg. Another class are furnished with apparatus for *locking* the cock.

Cocks are most commonly made of *tap-metal,* a peculiar alloy of inferior brass, or rather copper saturated with lead. Fine brass is sometimes used; as also a white alloy made to resist the action of vinegar and other corrosive liquors. For such liquors, however, cocks of porcelain or stoneware are to be preferred. Even wood is occasionally employed; and attempts have been made to manufacture cocks of cast-iron.

The *four-way cock* consists of a plug perforated with two distinct passages, and mounted in a barrel into which four separate pipes or channels open. Its object is to connect the four passages with each other in alternate couples, either by a continuous revolution upon its axis, or by an alternating motion through one-fourth part of a revolution; and it has frequently been applied to steam engines as a means of alternately admitting steam to and allowing it to escape from each end of the engine-cylinder.

COCOA AND CHOCOLATE. *Cocoa* is the more familiar name of the article, the proper name of which is *cacao ;* just a reversal of the vowels. It is the cotyledon of the seeds of the cacao plant, which is extensively cultivated in many tropical countries. The Mexicans call the tree *chocolalt*, and hence our name for the seed in a prepared state. The capsules of the fruit each contain about twenty-five seeds. The quality varies greatly; and the Mexicans are accustomed, to improve the flavour of the inferior sorts, to bury them in the earth in heaps, and allow them to ferment for nearly a month. The kinds produced in different countries vary much in the quantity of the oil or butter of cacao which they contain; a product to which much of the nutritious quality is due.

The simplest and best form of using cocoa is that of *cocoa-nibs*, consisting of the seeds roughly crushed. *Flake cocoa* is merely the seeds crushed between rollers. Common cocoa is usually the seeds pressed into cakes, or reduced to a paste.

Chocolate is cocoa brought to a further state of preparation. The seeds or beans, after being carefully picked, are gently roasted in an iron cylinder; and when the aroma begins to be well developed, they are turned out, cooled, and sifted. They are then mixed into a paste, and put into moulds, and when dry they form the ordinary chocolate of the shops, especially in England; but on the continent the chocolate is more frequently sold in a flavoured state, having had vanilla, cloves, cinnamon, almonds, starch, or sugar mixed with it. Lard, sago, and red lead are said to be used in the compounding of some of the cheap kinds of chocolate. The various 'patent' chocolates presented to our notice in the shops, are simply various modes of preparing the cocoa seeds.

The imports of cocoa are now becoming large. In 1848 they amounted to :—

British colonial cocoa	2,602,309 lbs.
Foreign	3,848,677
Hucks and shells	1,208,282
Chocolate and cocoa paste ..	13,016
	7,672,284

COCOA NUT. The cocoa-nut tree is found all over the tropical parts of the world, especially in the vicinity of the sea, growing within reach of salt water, and establishing itself upon reefs and sand-banks as soon as they emerge from the ocean. Its great importance to man has caused it to be cultivated wherever the climate is favourable to its growth; the whole Brazilian coast from the river San Francisco to the bar of Mamanguape, a distance of 280 miles, is, with few breaks, thus occupied; and it was estimated that in the year 1813 no fewer than 10,000,000 trees were growing on the south-west coast of Ceylon. The cocoa-nut palm rises like a slender column to from 60 to 90 feet in height.

In hot countries the uses to which the cocoa-nut tree is applicable are innumerable. The roots are chewed in place of the areca-nut; gutters, drains, and the posts of huts are formed from the trunk; the young buds are a delicate vegetable; shade is furnished by the leaves when growing, and after separation from the tree their large size and hard texture render them invaluable as thatch for cottages; they are, moreover, manufactured into baskets, buckets, lanterns, articles of head-dress, and even books, upon which writing is traced with an iron stylus. Their ashes yield potash in abundance; their midrib forms oars; and brushes are formed by bruising the end of a leaf with a portion of the midrib adhering to it. From the juice of the stem, a kind of palm wine, and subsequently an ardent spirit, are prepared; the farinaceous matter contained in the stem is a good substitute for sago; and a coarse dark-coloured sugar, called jagghery, is obtained from inspissating the sap. This jagghery, mixed with lime, forms a powerful cement, which resists moisture, endures great solar heat, and will take a fine polish. The ripe fruit is a wholesome food, and the milk it contains, a grateful cooling beverage; indeed these together constitute the principal sustenance of the poorer Indians in many countries. The fibrous bark is used to polish furniture, as brushes, and to form a valuable elastic cordage called *coir;* the fibrous matter of the husk is also employed to stuff mattresses, and a manufacture of it into cordage, mats, sacking, &c., has lately sprung up in Great Britain. The shell is manufactured into drinking-vessels and vessels of measure; and, fi-finally, the albumen, or white solid matter contained within the shell, yields by pressure or decoction an excellent oil; pressure is the method usually employed. This oil is not only employed for burning, but in the manufacture of torches, and in the composition of pharmaceutical preparations; and mixed with dammer (the resin of *Shorea robusta*) it forms the substance used in India for covering the seams of boats and ships.

Cocoa-nuts are brought to Europe as wedges to set fast the casks and other round packages in the cargo of vessels; their freight therefore costs nothing.

It is a curious circumstance that in commerce there are two kinds of *Cocoa-Oil* or *Oil of Cocoa*, entirely different in origin. The Cacao or cocoa seeds, described in the last article, yield a butter or solid oil which is usefully employed in making candles, soaps, and pomatums—chiefly in France. But that substance which is quoted in our market-lists as *Cocoa-nut Oil* is produced from the cocoa-nut, now under notice. So much has this substance now come into demand, that no less than 64,451 cwts. were imported in 1840.

CODEIA, an alkali discovered by Robiquet in opium, is a bitter, alkaline, crystalline substance, used to a small extent in medicine.

COFFEE. The *Coffee-Tree* or *Coffea Arabica* is an evergreen shrub, with oblong pulpy berries, which are at first of a bright red, but afterwards become purple. It is stated by Niebuhr to have been brought from Abyssinia to Yemen by the Arabs, from a country similar to their own plains and mountains. By that people it has for ages been cultivated in the hilly range of Jabal, in a healthy temperate climate, watered by frequent rains, and abounding in wells and water-tanks. A combination of circumstances seems to favour the cultivation of coffee in Arabia, which can hardly be attained elsewhere. Frequent rains, and a pure and cloudless sky causing an almost uninterrupted flood of light, communicate an excessive stimulus to all the functions of vegetation, and are causes of the perfect elaboration of those delicate principles on which the aroma of the coffee is dependent.

The seed consists of much horny albumen and a peculiar principle or alkaloid, termed *cafeine*, which is identical with the active principle of tea, *theine*, as well as with *paraguaine*, the alkaloid of the Paraguay Tea. The seed is used in a raw state in medicine; but when roasted, it forms the well-known coffee of commerce. The coffee-plant begins to produce fruit when two or two and a half years old; but the quality of the seeds from young stems is not so good as that from stems four or five years old. The size and colour of the bean (as the inner part of the seed is called) vary considerably, those from the West Indies being larger than those from the East.

Much more depends upon the manner of roasting and making the coffee than upon the quality of the bean. The superiority of French coffee, in the preparation of which little or no Mocha coffee is used, proves this position. The taste of raw coffee is somewhat sweetish; but the application of heat in the process of roasting produces important changes. The bean increases to nearly twice the original size, while it loses about a third of its weight: a powerful and agreeable odour is evolved, and a large quantity of empyreumatic oil, which appears in small drops on the surface, is formed along with a bitter principle, probably by an alteration in the cafeine and of the saccharine matter. The roasting should take place in a close revolving iron cylinder, over a clear but moderate fire, and should not be carried too far: when the beans have acquired a light chestnut colour, the roasting should be discontinued. The beans are then to be cooled quickly by being tossed up into the air, and the grinding, or rather rough pounding, should be performed in a covered mortar or mill. The drink should be prepared from it as soon as possible, by infusion, which is preferable, unless some apparatus be employed by which a kind of decoction is made in a close vessel. About half an ounce of coffee powder should be used for every eight ounces (half a pint) of water. In Britain the roasting is generally carried too far; and the subsequent parts of the process, instead of being performed immediately, are often postponed for days or even weeks, by which the aroma is dissipated: when made, the liquid is generally deficient in strength and clearness. The employment of white of egg or fish-skin to clarify is decidedly objectionable: clearness is thus purchased, but at the expense of the strength.

It was an endeavour to establish an improved mode of roasting coffee that led to the death of Mr. Dakin, of St. Paul's Churchyard, in 1848. His plan consisted in placing the coffee in a cylinder lined with silver, and in enclosing this cylinder within a cellular steam oven, or cylinder, patented by other parties. The heat attained within the oven was very great, and the metal of the oven was not sound enough to resist its action: an explosion ensued, with a fatal result. The silver or silvered cylinder was an intended means of retaining the fine qualities of the coffee, without acquiring any defective qualities during the roasting.

The addition of milk (which should always be hot) and of sugar heighten the nourishing qualities of coffee, and in the morning render it a more substantial article for breakfast. When taken after dinner to promote digestion, it should be without milk, and, where the palate can be reconciled to it, without sugar.

The coffee-trade has been wholly created since the beginning of the eighteenth century. Nearly all the coffee which now comes to Europe is the produce of trees propagated from a single plant, which, having been raised from seed procured from Mocha in Arabia, by Van Hoorn, governor of Batavia, was sent by him to the Botanical Garden at Amsterdam, and the progeny of which was, in the year 1718, twenty years after its reception from Java, sent to Surinam.

The coffee imported in 1849 amounted to the following quantities:—

British	...	...	40,334,630 lbs.
Foreign	...	...	22,985,876 lbs.
			63,320,506 lbs.

Of this quantity nearly 37,000,000 lbs. were brought from Ceylon alone.

The use of chicory in coffee has already been adverted to. [CHICORY.]

COFFEE APPARATUS. Considerable ingenuity has been displayed in devising apparatus for preparing coffee for the table. The ordinary coffee pot is the plainest and simplest of all; there is no contrivance for filtering the coffee. In Dresden and other parts of G-many, a thick piece of flannel or some other woven material, is laid in a funnel; the ground coffee is placed on the flannel; and the boiling water filters through the coffee, the flannel, and the funnel, to a vessel below—carrying with it the flavour of the coffee without the grounds or sediment.

Platow's Automaton Coffee Pot has for its object to make coffee in less time and in a better manner than by the ordinary method. The machine consists of of two parts. There is at the top a glass vase which screws off and on by means of wooden handles, and is furnished with a long narrow straight tube, resembling the pipe of a common funnel, and reaching nearly to the bottom of a metallic urn placed beneath the vase. Boiling water is poured into the vase in quantity sufficient for the coffee to be made; and this is allowed to descend into the urn. The ground coffee is then placed within the vase, on a small perforated silver plate. A lamp containing spirit or naphtha is placed beneath the urn; and in a short time the peculiar action of the apparatus developes itself. The steam formed on the surface of the water in the urn forces, by its elasticity, the water up the tube into the glass vase; where it acts upon the coffee in the usual way for extracting the qualities of the berry. When the coffee is so far prepared and is required to be *fined*, the lamp is removed, the formation of steam ceases, a partial vacuum is formed in the urn, and the external atmosphere, pressing on the open vase, presses or strains the coffee, first through the grounds and then through the perforated silver plate; so that it trickles into the urn in the state of a pure bright decoction. It is thus seen that the liquid makes two descents and one ascent between the vase and the urn, during the process. In a cheaper form of the apparatus, a common fire or a lamp is used instead of a spirit lamp.

A coffee pot of rather complicated structure was patented by Mr. Andrews of Wolverhampton in 1842. This coffee-pot had no less an adjunct than a small forcing-pump, placed near the handle. The boiling water was poured in the forcing-pump, while the ground coffee was put in a perforated vessel in the middle of the coffee-pot; and the hot water, being forced by the pump, was made to saturate the ground coffee in a way which (we presume) was supposed to produce a result adequate to the costliness of the apparatus.

Waller's Coffee Pot, patented in 1847, differs in many particulars from all the others. A horizontal partition, perforated near the centre with fine holes, divides the vessel into two equal chambers; an open pipe leads nearly from the top of the upper chamber to near the bottom of the lower chamber; and another pipe leads from the perforations some way down the lower chamber, with a tap or cock which can be worked by a handle protruding through the side of the coffee-pot. The requisite quantity of water, either hot or cold, is poured into the upper chamber, and allowed to flow through the perforations and small pipe into the lower chamber; the ground coffee is placed on the perforated plate; the spout is closed with a cork or plug; and the vessel is placed on the fire. As the water becomes heated, the steam generated has no outlet upwards or sideways, and it therefore presses on the water, and forces it up the long pipe, whence it falls into the upper chamber, upon the ground coffee. When all the water is thus forced up, the coffee-pot is removed from the fire, the vacuum in the lower chamber is condensed, the plug is removed from the spout, the top of the short pipe is opened, and the water trickles through the ground coffee and through the perforations into the lower vessel, imbibing all the soluble and aromatic properties of the coffee as it descends.

COFFERDAM, called by the French a *batardeau*, is a wooden inclosure formed in a river, in order to obtain a firm and dry foundation for the piers of a bridge. It usually consists of a double wall of piles, with intervening space between the inner and outer wall filled with clay or chalk rammed down hard. This done, the water is pumped out from the interior of the cofferdam.

COHESION means the adherence or coherence of particles of matter, by which they form collective masses, requiring the application of more or less force to separate the parts. The gaseous, fluid, and solid states of matter show the most sensible effects of the variations produced by the action of heat in the forces existing between the particles of bodies. In the first state, the particles absolutely repel one another; in the second, a repulsive force is almost exactly counterbalanced by an attractive force, so that there results only that weak degree of cohesion which exists in fluids; while, in the third, the particles absolutely attract each other. Again, two plates of a solid material may be pressed together till the particles at their nearest surfaces are brought close enough to attract one another, so that the plates will remain in cohesion even in a vacuum; and they may be hammered together till the cohesion is as strong as if they had been naturally united. In the force of cohesion we have therefore indications of a real physical attraction: and it follows that there must exist in the intervals between the particles of bodies a repulsive power, having its sphere of action interior to that of the cohesive force; from which we are led to conclude that the particles of bodies really act on one another at a distance.

A few practical considerations connected with cohesive forces, in relation to mechanism and manufactures, are treated of under STRENGTH OF MATERIALS.

COINS AND COINING. The production of coins, as a branch of manufacture, is briefly described under MINT.

COIRE, consists of the fibres of the cocoanut. The rind of the nut is soaked in water for several months, then beaten upon a stone with a piece of heavy wood, and afterwards rubbed with the hand until the intermediate substance is completely separated from the fibrous portion. The rind of forty average nuts supplies about six pounds' weight of the fibre. This fibre constitutes the coire, which is then ready for use in the same way as hemp or other fibrous materials, for cordage, matting, canvas, &c. Besides the actual weaving or plaiting of this material into textile fabrics of a coarse kind, it is used as a stuffing for mattresses, pillows, and cushions. The availability of coire for such a purpose seems to depend upon these qualities:—that the coire is very indestructible; that it does not harbour vermin, as horse hair would in a warm climate; and that it is free from offensive smell.

COKE is coal divested of its gaseous and more volatile constituents by partial combustion in close chambers, or in heaps from which the free access of air is excluded. The simplest mode of coking coal, which is still occasionally followed, is to lay the coal in large flattened heaps, often containing thirty or forty tons each, in the open air; and to cover it with ashes and earth to confine the heat, so that the mass of coal may be slowly burnt in a smothered manner: men being employed during the process to renew the covering wherever the fire may begin to burn too fiercely. But the best mode of making coke is by means of ovens. These are of different forms; but in principle they consist of an inclosed chamber, in which the coal is burned without access of air: the volatile ingredients are driven off, but the carbon remains. Coke is also made, in the process of making gas, in all gas-works: the coal which is put into the cylinders to make the gas being removed as coke after the volatile matter has been carried off to the gasometer. Coke is much preferable to coal where pure fuel is required in many smelting operations, and where smoke is wished to be avoided. An immense quantity is now used for locomotives; and the principal railway companies have established coke-ovens at their depôts. From a given quantity of coal, the produce of coke is about 20 per cent. less in respect to weight, but 20 per cent. more in respect to bulk.

There has recently been established a company at Alloa, for supplying coke to the railway companies of Scotland. Coke-ovens have been built at a spot which lies near the Forth, and also near the Alloa branch of the Scottish Midland Railway; so that there are great facilities both for receiving coal and sending out coke.

Mr. Church's method of making coke, introduced in 1846, has many peculiarities. The coke oven is much more complicated than those usually made, and the process altogether more carefully conducted. The coal is thrown into the oven so as to form a layer about two feet thick over the whole area. A slight depression is made in the middle of the surface of the layer; and in this depression is thrown a little burning coal. All apertures are then closed, except a few for admitting air for combustion, and these are gradually more and more closed as the coking advances. When the cessation of flame shows that the coal is wholly converted into coke, the last aperture is closed. In ordinary coke-making, the coke is cooled by cold water being applied to it; but by Mr. Church's method, two air passages are opened, which allow a stream of cold air to enter a series of passages which run under and around the oven, without communicating with the interior; these passages end in a chimney or flue; so that the air cools the oven as it passes, becomes itself heated, and finally escapes. Not until the oven and the contents are thoroughly cold is the coke removed. The professed object of this method (which, regarded in a scientific point of view is much more complete than the ordinary method) is to produce coke which shall be purer, denser, harder, of more powerful heating quality, and more abundant in quantity, than was before producible from a given amount of coal. Of course a long and strict trial could alone test the existence of these superior qualities.

Mr. Fisher patented a new form of coke-oven in 1849, intended to produce a better ingress and egress of air to the burning mass beneath the coke retorts, than in the ordinary construction.

It has been recently discovered, that although coke is apparently a loose spongy substance, the particles of which it is formed are intensely hard—so hard indeed as to cut glass like a diamond, which no other mineral will effect so well. This is deemed a striking confirmation of the well known chemical fact, that the diamond is nothing more than pure carbon in a crystalline state. It is expected that coke, carefully prepared for the purpose, will gradually come into use as a substitute for the diamond in the ordinary cutting of plate and window glass. Mr. Nasmyth stated at the Swansea meeting of the British Association, that the eminent firm of Messrs. Chance at Birmingham, by whom all the glass for the Crystal Palace has been since made, looked forward to a saving of 400*l.* a year, in respect to this apparently simple discovery.

COLBERT, JEAN BAPTISTE, is worthy of a meed of admiration from all who advocate the advancement of manufactures and commerce. Louis XIV. appointed Colbert contrôleur-général des finances; and Colbert's most strenuous and effective efforts were directed to the encouragement of commerce and manufactures. He succeeded in giving a great impulse to French industry; he roused and directed the national mind towards a new and useful exercise of its faculties. Woollens, silks, glass, pottery, leather, and iron manufactures were either created by him, or greatly enlarged and improved. He founded Quebec and Cayenne, made new settlements in India and on the coast of Africa, and favoured the colonies of Martinique and St. Domingo. He caused the first statistical tables of the population to be made out, and advanced the interests of his country, in industry and commerce, in many ways. Colbert was born in 1619, and died in 1683.

CO'LCHICUM, or *Meadow Saffron*, is a plant with a solid rootstock or cormus, found wild in various parts of Europe and in Great Britain, forming a gay carpet in the autumn in the fields, where its lively purple crocus-like flowers spring up. Its corms and its seeds abound in an acrid, stimulating, deleterious principle, which has been carefully examined by modern chemists, and forms an important plant in the Materia Medica, large quantities of both corms and seeds being annually consumed in the manufacture of *Eau Médicinale*, and other medicinal preparations.

COLLISION. When a body in motion strikes another, whether at rest or in movement, the particles of the first body, at the place of contact, have their forward motions retarded, in consequence of which the particles immediately behind approach closer to those in front than they were before the impact, and thus a condensation takes place. This condensation gives rise to an exertion of the force of elasticity, which acts against the succeeding particles, retarding the motions of these last and giving rise to a new condensation and a new exertion of elasticity against the next succeeding particles; and so on. The like actions must be understood to take place in the body struck; and these actions continue in both bodies till the bodies have attained the state of greatest compression, when, for a moment, both may be conceived to move with a common velocity. After this, the force of elasticity overcoming the force of compression, the particles of both bodies gradually return to a permanent state, which, if the elasticity were perfect, would be the same as that in which they were before the impact, the force of restitution thus causing the bodies to separate as if repelled from each other. A certain interval of time elapses between the instants of first contact and separation, but this is so short as to be scarcely sensible.

If the bodies have different degrees of hardness, an indentation may take place in that which is the least hard, the other penetrating to a certain distance in it. When the bodies are soft, like balls of wet clay, the change of figure produced by collision is manifest. When the hardness is very great, a vast resistance arising from friction will be overcome by the percussion arising from the descent of a comparatively small rammer. It has been observed that a sledge-hammer, in driving hard pegs, produces an effect equivalent to the pressure of 70 tons. It is from this circumstance that collision or percussion is a very valuable mode of applying force, in many of the manufacturing arts connected with machinery.

COLOGNE. This important city has the manufactures and commerce belonging to a sort of metropolis, rather than one distinguishing manufacture. The manufactures are cotton yarns, cotton goods, hosiery, woollens, silks, velvets, tobacco, brandy and spirits, Eau de Cologne, of which above a million bottles are annually exported, &c. Being a free port and having communication by railway with Belgium and various parts of Germany, Cologne has an important transit trade in home and foreign produce. In the vicinity of the city are several coal-mines, and abundance of a particularly fine sort of porcelain-earth and potter's clay. Steamers ply regularly between Cologne and the towns along the Rhine.

COLONIES. The British Colonies exert a most important influence on our National Manufactures. So varied are the climate and productions of those colonies, scattered as they are in every part of the world, that the talent of our manufacturers is repeatedly brought into play to supply the every-day wants of the colonists: especially as it is the policy of England—wise or unwise—to confine her colonial trade pretty nearly to her own manufacturers, merchants, and ship-owners.

In a parliamentary paper published in 1850 the whole of the British Colonies and dependencies, including British India, are placed under 48 headings; and the value of all the British and Irish produce and manufactures, exported to those 48 possessions in the year 1849, is stated. These exports are arranged under 48 headings, according to the kinds of goods exported. Without entering into this degree of minuteness, it may yet be interesting to give the total values to each of the colonies, which we do as follow:—

Colony.	Exports.
Heligoland	357*l*.
Channel Islands	634,125
Gibraltar	533,481
Malta	387,744
Ionian Islands	165,805
River Gambia Settlements ..	35,770
Sierra Leone	60,290
Gold Coast Settlements ..	134,591
Fernando Po	3,197
Cape of Good Hope ..	520,896
Ascension Island	4,997
St. Helena	18,315
Mauritius	234,022
Aden	14,564
East Indies	6,149,784
Ceylon	159,351
Singapore	494,080
Hong Kong	651,969
Western Australia	12,518
South Australia	315,652
New South Wales	1,330,839
Van Diemen's Land	315,021
New Zealand	106,334
Hudson's Bay Territories ..	61,795
Newfoundland and Labrador	297,349
Canada	1,324,931
New Brunswick	277,591
Prince Edward Island ..	41,421
Nova Scotia and Cape Breton	276,106
Antigua	70,194
Barbadoes	319,958
Dominica	22,484
Grenada	28,348
Jamaica	624,568
Montserrat	402
Nevis	1,093
St. Christopher	45,408
St. Lucia	16,672
St. Vincent	58,268
Tobago	14,887

Colony.	Exports.
Tortola	46*l*.
Trinidad	247,779
Bahamas	24,709
Bermudas	47,138
Demerara	279,002
Berbice	17,819
Honduras	206,244
Falkland Isles	6,173
	£16,594,087

It is no less interesting to see which among our manufactures are exported in greatest value to these numerous possessions. Cottons take the lead; in their various forms of piece-goods, hosiery, lace, small wares, twist, and yarn, their value is no less than 7,204,469*l*. Iron, steel, and machinery, amount in value to 1,056,901*l*. All other metal goods (gold, silver, tin, pewter, brass, and copper) give an aggregate of 1,374,316*l*. Woollen and worsted goods amount to 1,275,833*l*. Linen and hempen goods, 710,951*l*. Glass and earthenware. 291,652*l*. Apparel, slops, haberdashery, and hats, 1,281,927*l*. Leather and harness, 349,937*l*. Beer and ale, 294,991*l*. Soap and candles, 202,077*l*. Books and stationery, 309,422*l*.—Out of the sixteen millions sterling, about eleven millions relate to the materials for dress.

The imports from the Colonies to Great Britain consist chiefly in the raw materials of manufactures, and vegetable substances used for food. Their value is not given with the same degree of minuteness in the government tables; but they are less in value than the exports.

Canada, Ceylon, the Cape of Good Hope, and several other of these colonies, will be represented at the Industrial Exhibition.

COLOURS. The word Colour is used in many different ways. Besides its original meaning, in relation to the tints of rays of light, it has gradually come to be applied to the substances by which those tints are imitated.

Painter's Colours, for house-painting and similar purposes, are mostly prepared from mineral substances (white lead, red lead, umber, ochre, &c.) ground up with linseed oil and turpentine to the state of a thick liquid. It would, perhaps, scarcely be supposed that 'Painters' Colours' appear in the Board of Trade tables, as an article of export to the value of about 170,000*l*. annually.

The oil colours for artists are more carefully prepared than those for house painting. They used to be sold tied up in small bladders; but an ingenious and more convenient arrangement is now adopted. Mr. Winsor's envelopes for colours, patented in 1840, consist of small metal or glass tubes, open at both ends, and provided with elastic pistons or plugs of cork or some similar material. The piston has a worm or nut in its centre, which corresponds to a screw attached to a handle rather larger than the tube. The open ends of the tube are covered with small metallic plates having holes in their centres. When the colour is placed in the tube, the arrangement of the apparatus is such as to keep the air from acting on it; and when any is required to be used, the screw is turned round, the piston is pressed down and a little colour exudes from the lower end. Mr. Rand's Collapsible Colour-tubes, so useful to artists, were the subject of a later patent in 1842; the objects of which were, to introduce a mode of punching out by dies the thin pieces of tin of which the tubes are made; and to make a screw cap at the mouth of the tube, to prevent leakage. These little tubes, by a gentle squeeze, are made to yield the colour at one end just in sufficient quantity for use.

Water-Colours for artists include both vegetable and animal as well as mineral substances, and are prepared with very great care.

Mr. Smith of Blackford has lately communicated to the Royal Scottish Society of Arts, a paper showing that when chromate of lead is mixed with muriate of ammonia, and subjected to the action of heat, a substance is obtained of a different colour from either of the matters used. If the proportions of the substances be varied, and different degrees of heat applied, distinct colours and tints will be the result. Thus, when five parts of chromate of lead, and one part of muriate of ammonia, are heated to redness in a crucible, a red colour is obtained; a blue colour is formed by heating 10 parts of muriate of ammonia, and 1 part of chromate of lead to ebullition; and a green is produced when the last mixture is heated nearly to redness. By employing various proportions of the substances, and different degrees of heat, a great variety of tints are formed—scarlets, oranges, browns, blues, purples, greens, yellows, and others. It is conceived that these properties may lead to useful applications in the arts.

COLU'MBIUM, a metal discovered in 1801 by Mr. Hatchett in a ferruginous mineral from North America, is a black powder which by the burnisher acquires the colour and lustre of iron. It is nearly insoluble in acids and in chlorine. When heated in the air, it is oxidised, and converted into columbic acid. Its combinations with other bodies are very little used, or even known.

COLUMBUS. This truly great man exerted such immense influence on the industry and commerce of the last three centuries by his discoveries in America, that it is desirable here to note down the extent and dates of his researches. Born at Genoa in or about 1445, he acquired a taste for a maritime life; and towards the close of the century he conceived the idea of crossing the Atlantic, and reaching Asia on the opposite side from that which it had already presented to European travellers: the intervening Continent of America being then unknown. After many difficulties Ferdinand and Isabella of Spain authorized an Expedition by him in 1492.

On Friday, August 3, 1492, Columbus, as admiral of the seas and lands which he expected to discover, set sail from the bar of Saltes, near Palos, with three vessels and 120 men, who were full of doubts and fears, and were partly pressed into the service. With great difficulty he succeeded in inducing his crew to persevere through a tedious voyage, till on October 11, 1492, the manifestations of land were such as to convince the most dejected. Accordingly, after the evening prayer, Columbus ordered a careful look out, and himself remained on the high stern of his vessel from ten o'clock, when he had observed glimmerings of light, as he supposed on shore, till two in the morning, when the foremost vessel fired a gun as a signal of land having been discovered. Not an eye was closed that night, and on October 12, with tears of joy, after fervid thanksgivings, Columbus kissed the earth on which he landed, and with great solemnity planted the cross in the new world, at Guanahani, or San Salvador, one of the Gucayos, Lucayan, or Bahama Islands. Those who had lately been most in despair were now the most extravagant in their joy.

On the 24th Columbus set out in quest of gold and Cipango (Japan). After discovering Concepcion, Exuma, and Isla Larga, Cuba broke upon him like an elysium; he no longer doubted that this beautiful land was the real Cipango. When this delusion was over, he fancied Cuba, which to the day of his death he took for part of the main land of India, to be not far from Mango and Cathay. He next took Hayti or Santo Domingo for the ancient Ophir, the source of the riches of Solomon, but he gave it the Latin diminutive of Hispaniola, from its resembling the fairest tracts of Spain. Leaving here the germ of a future colony, he set sail homeward January 4, 1493. After weathering a dreadful storm, he at last landed triumphantly at Palos, March 15, 1493. He proceeded to Barcelona, where Ferdinand and Isabella received him seated in state, rose as he approached, raised him as he kneeled to kiss their hands, and ordered him to be seated in their presence.

On September 25, 1493, Columbus left Cadiz on a second expedition, with seventeen ships and 1500 men. He discovered the Caribbee Islands, Puerto Rico, and Jamaica; and after repeated mutinies of his colonists, and great hardships, he returned against the trade-winds to Cadiz, June 11, 1496. Having dispelled various calumnies that had been accumulated upon him, Columbus embarked on May 30, 1498, at San Lucar de Barrameda, on a third expedition, with only six vessels. In this voyage he discovered Trinidad, the mouths of the Orinoco, the coast of Paria, and the Margarita and Cubagua Islands. On August 14 he bore away for Hispaniola to recruit his health. While here the intrigues of his enemies induced Ferdinand, in July 1500, to despatch Francisco Bovadilla to supersede Columbus, and bring him back in chains. Vallejo, the officer who had him in charge, would have taken his chains off; but Columbus proudly refused. The general burst of indignation at Cadiz, which was echoed throughout Spain, on the arrival of Columbus in fetters, compelled Ferdinand himself to disclaim all knowledge of the shameful transaction. With restricted powers and a broken frame, but with his ever-soaring and irrepressible enthusiasm, Columbus sailed from Cadiz again on May 9, 1502, with four caravels and 150 men, in search of a passage to the East Indies near the Isthmus of Darien, which should supersede that of Vasco de Gama. The mutiny of his crew compelled him to return to Hispaniola after coasting the Mosquito Coast, Costa Rica, and Veragua to the point called El Retrete. He reached Santo Domingo August 13, 1503. Sailing homewards on September 12, he anchored his tempest-tossed and shattered bark at San Lucar on November 7, 1504. From San Lucar he proceeded to Sevilla, where he soon after received the news of the death of his patroness Isabella. He was detained by illness till the spring of 1505, when he arrived at Segovia, to have only another courtly denial of his redress, and to linger a year longer in neglect, poverty, and pain, till death gave him relief at Valladolid on the 20th of May, 1506.

COLUMN. The column, in architecture, is a shaft of wood, stone, or iron, in the form of a truncated cone, a little swelled from the straight line at about one-third its height from the lower extremity: this swelling is called the éntasis. Columns are of various proportions and kinds: circular on the plan, and rarely polygonal. The Romans had five models of columns, which were called orders;

but the Greeks, from whom the Romans appear to have derived their architecture, only three. The Egyptians used columns, but they were very different in their form and proportions from both the Roman and Greek examples.

It seems not at all improbable, that the admirable construction of the Palace of Industry by Messrs. Fox and Henderson, in which light and graceful columns of iron form so notable a feature, will go far to bring into vogue a new kind of architecture, in which unexpected resources may gradually develope themselves.

COMB-CUTTING. The old method of forming the teeth of combs is by means of a double saw, which consists of two separate fine saws, placed parallel with each other, and adjusted to such a distance from each other as to embrace a tooth of the required fineness between them. These two saws are so arranged that, while one cuts into the comb to the full depth required, the other cuts only about half that depth, and by this contrivance the uniformity of the comb is secured, because, while the deeper saw is completing the first cut, the shallower one is forming the commencement of the second, and when, on the completion of the first cut, the deep saw is put into the second cut to complete it, the shallower one immediately commences a third The cuts thus formed are subsequently enlarged and rendered smoother by means of a very thin wedge-shaped file, which also points the teeth. Though this method of comb-cutting is still practised, a much quicker mode of performing the same operations by means of circular saws and revolving cutters for pointing the teeth has been long in use.

By the above described modes of comb-cutting all the material of the interstices between the teeth is lost or destroyed, but by the operation known as the *parting* of combs such loss or waste of material may be avoided in the manufacture of combs of tortoiseshell, horn, or any tough material. Two combs are by this process, made out of one piece, the teeth of one being cut, by the pressure of chisel-like instruments, out of the interstices of the other.

An American patent was taken out in 1839, by Mr. Ives of Connecticut, for making metallic combs by the following method. A strip of sheet metal is prepared, of a width equal to that of the intended comb, and of a thickness equal to that of the intended teeth. The piece of metal is bent or plaited in a zig-zag manner crosswise: the bends being of such width only as shall adapt them to the forming of a single tooth. The bending is effected by a sort of crimping rollers; and these plaits or bent portions are placed up together, being kept separated by a distance equal to the interval between the teeth of the intended comb. Ribs are soldered to make the back of the comb; and the two surfaces are smoothed or cut away, so as to separate the several plaits, and make each one stand singly as a tooth of the comb.

COMBINATION LAWS. These laws, which were an object of much solicitude to manufacturers and artizans, were repealed in 1824. Till then any combination of any two or more masters, or any two or more workmen, to lower or raise wages, or to increase or diminish the number of hours of work, or quantity of work to be done, was punishable at common law as a misdemeanour; and there were also thirty-five statutes in existence, most of them applying to particular trades, prohibiting combinations of workmen against masters. The act passed in 1824 repealed all the statute and common law against combinations of masters and of workmen, provided a summary mode of conviction, and a punishment not exceeding two months' imprisonment, for violent interference with workmen or masters, and for combinations for violent interference; and it contained a proviso, with regard to combinations for violent interference, that no law in force with regard to them should be altered or affected by the act. But, all the common law against combinations being repealed by the act, this proviso was considered as of no force; and the act also went beyond the intentions of the framers in legalising combinations unattended with violence for the purpose of controlling masters in the mode of carrying on their trades and manufactures, as well as peaceable combinations to procure advance of wages or reduction of hours of work.

Immediately after the passing of this act a number of widely-organised and formidable combinations arose in various trades and manufactures for the purpose of controlling the masters as to the way in which they should conduct their business; and the extent to which the act had repealed the common law being doubtful, and the act having clearly gone beyond the resolutions on which it was grounded in legalising combinations, the act of 1825 was passed, which is the act now in force relative to combinations. It relieved from all prosecution and punishment persons meeting solely to consult upon rate of wages or hours of work, or entering into any agreement, verbal or written, on these points. And it provided a punishment of not more than three months' imprisonment, with or without hard labour, for any one using violence or threats to make a workman leave his hiring, or return work unfinished, or refuse to accept work, or belong to any club, or contribute to any common fund, or pay any fine for not be-longing to a club, or contributing to a common fund, or refusing to conform to any rules made for advance of wages or lessening of the hours of work, or regulations of the mode of carrying on any business, and for any one using violence to make any master alter his mode of carrying on his business. By this act therefore, combinations of masters and workmen to settle as to rate of wages and hours of labour are made legal: but the common law remains as it was as to combinations for otherwise controlling masters. This enactment does not necessarily interfere with plans for joint enterprises among workmen. [CO-OPERATIVE SYSTEMS.]

COMBUSTION, a process in which both light and heat are emitted by chemical agency. When a piece of charcoal is ignited and put into oxygen gas, combustion commences and continues with increasing brilliancy until the charcoal disappears, or the oxygen has undergone a change which renders it incapable of further action as a supporter of combustion. This is an example in which a gas (carbonic acid) is the result of the combustion; but in other examples, such as burning iron in oxygen gas, a solid oxide is produced. *Ignition* differs from combustion in this, that the heated body gives out light and heat without undergoing decomposition. In all common cases of combustion, the heat which is generated by it is accompanied by flame, but not necessarily so. Some idea of the difference may be formed by observing the circumstances under which bituminous coal and anthracite burn; the former burns with flame, and the latter with scarcely any.

COMPASS, AZIMUTH. This instrument used by astronomers and by surveyors, is a compass with a telescope, or with plain sights (generally vertical wires) attached to it in such a manner as to be moveable round a vertical axis independently of the needle or of the card to which the needle is affixed. A pointer shows the angle which the position of the telescope, or sights, marks out on the card, that is, the *bearing* of the object towards which the sights are directed. This angle is the true azimuth of the object.

COMPASS, THE MARINER'S. This invaluable instrument is a cylindrical box, generally of brass, in the centre of which is fixed vertically a steel pin terminating in a fine conical point, and on this is accurately balanced a magnetised needle, or a circular card to the underside of which such a needle is attached in the direction of a diameter. In the centre of the needle is usually inserted a piece of agate in the lower part of which is sunk a conical hole to receive the point of the pin; and the needle with the card is supported on that point so as to *traverse* freely in a horizontal position. The rim of the compass-box, or the circumference of the card, is divided into thirty-two equal parts called *points*, which have symmetrical designations on opposite sides of each of the four cardinal points as they are called, namely, the north, the east, the south, and the west. In some compasses the points are subdivided into *quarters* of $11\frac{1}{4}$ degrees each, and sometimes into single degrees.

When the needle is attached to a card, the north point on the card is directly over the northern extremity or pole of the needle. To insure the horizontality of the compass-card the cylindrical box in which it is enclosed is supported in a hoop at opposite points by pins projecting from it, so as to allow the box to revolve inside the hoop. This hoop is supported in the same manner on pivots, the line of which is at right angles to the first pivots; so that, between the rotation of the compass-box in the hoop and the hoop itself, the former can always find its position of equilibrium, which is the horizontal position. The small oscillations of the apparatus are immediately destroyed by the friction. The apparatus is then said to be supported on gimbles, or gimbals.

The Mariner's Compass still remains, in principle, what it has been for ages; but there have not been wanting attempts to improve it in minor details. Mr. David Napier included in his patent of 1848 a kind of compass-box having an analogous movement to that of his barometer [BAROMETER]. There is ordinary clock-work machinery placed at the bottom of the compass-box. Connected with this are a lever and a pricker, which rise and fall at certain regular intervals of time. Within the compass-box is placed a ruled circular piece of paper containing 24 concentric circles, and a number of radiating lines corresponding to the points of the compass in a compass card. The vertical pricker is made to travel over the surface of the paper from the inner concentric circle to the outer one, and in a line parallel with the keel of the vessel, once in 24 hours. The pricker punctures the paper at certain regular intervals of time; while the paper follows the movements of the magnet and compass card; the consequence of which is that the direction of the ship's course will be indicated by the punctures on the radiating lines, while the hours of the day which correspond to these directions will be marked by the punctures on the concentric circles. A new paper has to be used every day: each paper being a record of one day's proceedings.

The Admiralty have recently bestowed a good deal of attention on the *storm compasses* of Mr. Walker, which are becoming extensively used in the navy. During a storm the ordinary compasses are liable to great derangement by the violent commotion; and Mr. Walker has sought to devise such an adjustment of the apparatus as will bring this evil to a minimum.

COMPASSES. There are many varieties of these useful instruments. The *Common Compasses*, or *Dividers*, are simply two pointed legs on a common pivot, for transferring distances. For drawing a circle the lower end of one of the legs is removed, and its place supplied by a holder for a pencil, or by a steel pen. In the *Hair Compasses*, one of the legs has a part attached to the upper part by a spring, so that by means of a screw a very small motion may be given to the lower end; the instrument is convenient for very accurate dividing, but must be used with care. *Triangular Compasses* have three legs and two pivots, so that the three points of a triangle can be at once transferred; the instrument is useful only in rough work, as it is difficult to handle. *Proportional Compasses* consist of two dividing compasses with a common pivot, which, when open, present vertically opposite angles; consequently, the intervals between the points of one and the other are in the same proportion as the legs of one to the legs of the other. The pivot is a clamping screw, which can be transferred along the interval between the pairs of points; and a scale points out how to adjust the instrument to alter any line, or surface, or solid, in a given proportion. These compasses sometimes have an apparatus for slight adjustment. *Beam Compasses* consist of a cylindrical bar, perpendicular to which, with clamping screws, slide a point and a pencil. The use of it is to describe large circles, or measure large distances, the common compasses being very liable to slip when opened very wide. It is a very safe and sure construction.

A machine used as a substitute for compasses, in describing a curve passing through three or more points nearly in a straight line is made as follows:—An elastic rod of metal is furnished with a rigid bar on which it can be drawn up by screws, so that the rod shall form an arc, the chord of which is a part of the bar. This may be adjusted so as to pass through the given points when the curve is to be traced along the front of the rod. This is sometimes called a Shipwrights' Bow.

COMPOSING MACHINES. In ordinary typography [PRINTING] the types are collected one by one, by the fingers of the compositor, from little cells or compartments, and arranged in the proper order for printing. About ten years ago however two very ingenious attempts were made, by Messrs. Young and Delcambre in one case, and by Captain Rosenberg in the other, to perform this work by the aid of a machine.

Messrs. Young and Delcambre's first composing machine was patented in 1840; but by the year 1842 considerable improvements had been introduced in its mechanism. Considered in its latest form, it does not set up types in a state fit for printing from; but it is intended so to facilitate the process of composition as to enable that to be done by females and children which now requires the services of highly paid men, and to do the work more quickly.

The mechanism for carrying out this intended object may be described as follows. The general appearance of the machine somewhat resembles that of a cottage piano forte, without its case. There is a row of keys which are played upon by the fingers of the compositor, who is seated in front of the machine. There is one key to each letter, stop, numeral, space, &c., required in printing; so that the number of keys must be very considerable. Each key is marked with its particular letter or other type, and each type is placed in a receptacle containing many duplicates of that character. These receptacles are all filled with types by boys; and one compositor can use the types as fast as two boys can supply them. The compositor seats himself in front of the instrument, with the author's MS. placed before him. We will suppose the first word to be *The*. He places his finger on the key marked with a capital T; the key moves an upright steel lever, the upper end of which pushes a type out of its receptacle or channel; this type is a T, which slides down an inclined plane, in a little hollow or groove, until it reaches a sort of spout at the bottom; thence it passes to the justifying-box, where the automatic action of the machine terminates. Here another compositor takes up the type and arranges it in the composing stick, as in ordinary printing. While the T has been thus travelling downwards, the *h* and the *e* have been made to follow, and are treated exactly in the same way; and so on throughout the MS. The number of persons required to work the machine is five; viz. two to distribute the type used in previous printing and to supply the types to the receptacles, one to play the keys, one to work an excentric wheel which forces the arranged types into the justifying-box, and one to justify or place the types in the composing stick. Two of the persons are females, and three boys; and these five are said by the inventor to be able, after six months practice, to compose and distribute 6000 types in an hour; 1,500 per hour being an ordinary compositor's work, including corrections.

It is singular that two machines were in progress for the same object about the same time. Rosenberg's Type Composing Machine was patented in 1841, shortly after the first patent of Messrs. Young and Delcambre. The two machines bear a strong general likeness; but there are sufficient points of difference to mark the ingenuity which has been shewn in each. Rosenberg's Machine is rather more compact of the two, and effects more by automatic means—requiring the aid of fewer persons. In Captain Rosenberg's own statement of the capabilities of his machine, he claims for it the the power of composing 10,800 types in an hour; of requiring only three persons instead of five; and of distributing the type as well as composing it, instead of composing only as in Young and Delcambre's machine.

The compositor, pressing on the keys in succession, forces down the several types from a series of vertical racks in which they had been placed. The types arrange themselves in proper order upon an endless belt or chain, which is constantly passing through the middle of the machine from right to left. The types travel along this endless band till they come to a receiver, where they rank themselves closely side by side until enough are so arranged to form one line of the book to be printed. The compositor is warned by the striking of a little bell that the line is full; and by turning a handle close to him, he removes the finished line from its place, and leaves room for the next line. An assistant compositor then takes up the finished line, in a small apparatus into which it falls, reads it, corrects any mistakes, and places it in the page of type ready for printing. All the *leads* for 'spacing' the type are applied by hand by this assistant compositor. The arrangement of the types in their original receptacles is so peculiar, that the compositor can sometimes compose or bring down four or five types at one time, by pressing four or five keys at once, as a pianoforte player can do. This may be done whenever the letters of a word succeed each other in the order which they follow in the alphabet. For instance, in the word *adopt* each letter has a later alphabetical rank than the one which precedes it; so that if the five corresponding keys be pressed down at one time, the five types will be found ranged in their proper order on the endless band: it is true that they will be unequally distant apart; but they all become pressed together closely at a later stage of the operations. The word *accentuation* is given as an example wherein three pressures on the keys will suffice instead of twelve; thus, *accentu—at—ion*, in which each of the three groups consists of letters which take rank in their proper alphabetical order.

The *Distributing* Machine is quite detached from the *Composing* Machine. When the printing is completed, a line of type is lowered from the galley [PRINTING] into a sort of travelling carriage, by means of a slider with a handle. The distributor reads over the line, and puts his finger successively on a row of keys, each key corresponding to a particular letter; the key is raised by the touch, and he moves the carriage sideways until it is stopped by the key which has been thus raised. The type contained in the carriage is by this movement forced out of the line in which it had previously held a place, and falling down through a recess, it is deposited in a small receptacle. By the time the whole line has been thus distributed, by touching the keys as many times as there are types in the line, all the *a*'s are found in one receptacle, all the *b*'s in another, and so on. By means of a 'feeding-stick,' 200 or 300 of these types of one letter may be lifted up and transferred from the distributing machine to the composing machine, ready to be used over again.

There is considerable mechanical beauty in these two machines, especially Rosenberg's; and the leading printers would certainly by this time have adopted them had the statements of the respective patentees been borne out. It seems however now fully decided that a book cannot be printed so quickly or cheaply by the aid of these machines as by the ordinary means.

CONCAVE and CONVEX. A curve or surface is concave on the side on which straight lines drawn from point to point in it fall between the curve or surface and the spectator; that side is convex on which the curve or surface falls between such lines and the spectator. A surface may be either entirely concave, as the inside of a sphere, or entirely convex, as the outside; or concave in some directions and convex in others, as the surface of a dice box.

CONCENTRIC, means having the same centre; thus concentric circles are those described about the same point.

CONCERTI'NA, a musical instrument recently invented by Professor Wheatstone, the principle of which is explained under the word ACCORDION. One variety is called the Double-Action Concertina, because two springs are given to each note, in order that the same sound may be produced whether the bellows be pressed in or drawn out. The Single Action Concertina has but one spring or tongue for each note, yielding a sound only when the bellows are moved inwards; that is, pressed. There are treble, tenor, and base concertinas, embracing different portions of the musical scale. The concertina is far more complete as an instrument than the accordion.

CONCRETE. This name is given to a very useful kind of cement or rather rough earth, largely used in the foundation of buildings. It usually consists of crushed pebbles, rough sand, and lime. The Palace of Industry affords an example of the useful application of concrete, as a means of preserving wood and iron from damp. The columns and the flooring joists are shielded from the damp soil by layers of concrete.

CONDENSER, is the general name for a vessel employed to facilitate the liquefaction of aqueous or spirituous vapours, by exposing them to the cooling effect of a current of water, which may be either injected immediately upon or among the vapour, or, where it is required to keep the condensing water and the product of condensation distinct, separated from the vapour by a thin partition of metal. In the latter case, copper is the metal most generally employed, on account of the rapidity with which it conducts heat, and the facility with which it may be fashioned into thin sheets adapted for the purpose. Mr. Siemens described before the Society of Arts in 1850 a remarkable condenser, so contrived as to save or render available the heat developed during the process of condensation. [BREWING; DISTILLATION; STEAM ENGINE; STEAM VESSEL.]

CONDIMENTS are substances taken with food, either to impart flavour or to promote digestion: such as salt, vinegar, lemon-juice, aromatic herbs, oil, butter, sugar, honey, and sauces.

CONE. The following measurements relating to the cone are often useful. The *surface* of a cone is one-half the circumference of its base multiplied by the distance from the vertex to the circumference of the base (called the *slant side*). The *solidity* of a cone is one-third of the product of the area of the base and the perpendicular distance of the vertex from the axis.

CONFECTIONS, called also *Conserves* and *Electuaries*, are formed of fresh, generally succulent, vegetable substances, in a few instances with prepared chalk, as in the aromatic confection, preserved by means of sugar or honey. These were formerly much more numerous than at present.

When astringent substances, such as roses, are to be pounded, this process must be conducted in marble, not iron, mortars. The conserves should be put into several small pots, rather than one large pot, which should be glazed with salt, as in Bristol ware, not lead. They should then be well closed, and kept in a dry cool place. Patent jars, of a very useful kind, are now manufactured for this purpose.

There are more than twenty varieties of confections, whose names find place in books of receipts.

CONGELATION. [FREEZING MIXTURES.]

CONGLETON. At one period the chief manufactures of Congleton were gloves, and tagged-leather laces called Congleton points; but for nearly a century the silk manufacture has been the principal occupation of the inhabitants of the town. A number of mills for the manufacture of silk (chiefly black silk), for silk throwing, silk spinning, &c., are situated in Congleton and its immediate vicinity. The making of silk ribbons has of late years grown into an important branch of industry, in which females as well as males find employment. In the neighbourhood are several extensive coal mines. The Congleton viaduct of the North Staffordshire Railway, about half a mile from the station, is a fine work of ten arches. It is constructed of blue brick with stone bastions and stone parapet. The arches are 50 feet in span. The height from the bed of the stream to the rails is 114 feet; the length of the viaduct, exclusive of the embankments, is 231 feet.

CONGREVE LIGHTS. [MATCHES.]

CONGREVE ROCKETS. [ROCKETS.]

CONIA, is an alkali obtained from hemlock (*Conium maculatum*). It is procured from the seeds or fresh leaves of the plant by distillation with water holding some potash in solution. It has the appearance of a colourless volatile oil, and is lighter than water, its specific gravity being 0.89. Its odour is powerful, diffusible, and repulsive, somewhat like that of hemlock itself. It is intensely acrid to the taste, and is strongly alkaline. By exposure to the air it quickly becomes of a dark colour, and spontaneously decomposes with the evolution of ammonia.

Conia is an awfully-rapid poison; but when greatly diluted it is used in medicine.

CONNAUGHT. This, the north-western province of Ireland, is almost shut out from industrial connection with England. It is very poor, and the potato failure of 1847 rendered it still poorer. There have been lately, however, numerous projects formed for the improvement of this province, and the development of its great resources. Of these the chief is the extension, now in progress, of the

Great Midland Railway from Mullingar by Athlone to Galway. Another is the establishment of a packet station for the conveyance of the mails from that port to Halifax. The Viceroy steam-ship was placed on the station in 1850, but was not of sufficient dimensions to perform the voyage with the requisite speed; and having been wrecked on the return passage from New York to Halifax, has not as yet been replaced. The merchants of Galway are at the present time strenuously endeavouring to have that port selected as a mail-packet station. The improvement of the navigation of the Shannon has given a continuous line of water carriage along the eastern boundary of the province. It has also been in contemplation to connect the lakes of Galway and Mayo, so as to form a line of navigation from Galway to Killala, through Loughs Corrib, Mask, Carra, Castlebar, Cullin, Conn, and the river Moy to Ballina, a distance of 80 miles, through a district susceptible of immense improvement. To connect these lakes it would require a series of cuts only 17 miles in length.

Perhaps the most useful of the various efforts made for the improvement of Connaught has been the introduction or revival of the culture of flax. The quantity grown in 1847 was 10,866 cwt. and the cultivation of flax crops is since then much increased. The system of farming has been greatly improved in these districts which have passed through the transition attendant on the recent change of proprietary and occupants.

CONSERVE. A conserve differs from a *confection* in having a more definite relation to some particular vegetable substance. All conserves are pasty mixtures of sugar with some recent or fresh vegetable, whether fruit, flowers, or leaves. Their number is considerable.

CONSERVATORY, properly so called, is a building heated by artificial means, having its whole southern part closed by large glazed sashes, which may be opened or shut at pleasure. Its floor is generally of stone, and a part of it is occupied by a stage on which plants in pots can be placed. Plants when in a growing state require an abundant supply of light: a conservatory is ill calculated, on account of its solid roof and sides, for the admission of light, and consequently a conservatory is not suitable for plants in a growing state; but plants when torpid, as in the winter season, require a very moderate supply of light, and this a conservatory is sufficiently calculated to admit.

A house of this kind is best suited for gardens of considerable extent, where a large number of plants is required during the summer for the ornament of the flower garden and shrubbery. Under such circumstances the erection of conservatories is the cheapest, the most efficient, and the most ornamental mode of preserving in a healthy state during winter not only oranges, myrtles, and similar plants, but in general all the species which are natives of countries that, without experiencing severe frost, are cold enough during winter to suspend the vital energies of vegetation.

A most important change has recently been introduced by Mr. Paxton in the principle of construction in conservatories, by the substitution of iron and glass for brickwork. The Duke of Devonshire's magnificent conservatory at Chatsworth, planned by Mr. Paxton, is composed entirely of iron and glass. The length is nearly 300 feet, the width 150, and the height 70. It covers nearly an acre of ground, and has a carriage drive through it. The tubes for the hot water which regulate the temperature are six miles in length. A light but beautiful gallery extends round the upper part of the interior of the building; while around the foundation is a tunnel, which gives access to the stoves and pipes.

The new Palm House in Kew Gardens is another beautiful example of the same kind of construction. It is 362 feet long, 100 feet wide by 66 high at the centre, and 50 feet wide by 30 high at the wings or ends. The curves which the glassy surface is made to assume are exceedingly graceful. A gallery runs round the lofty central portion, which is reached by an elegant iron spiral staircase. The glass employed has had a pale yellowish green tint imparted to it, to temper the heat of the solar rays. The structure is heated from beneath by stoves, the chimney of which, made somewhat ornamental, is at a considerable distance.

That triumph of constructive skill, the Palace of Industry in Hyde Park, was suggested by Mr. Paxton on the strength of the experience which his conservatory-building has afforded him; and Messrs Fox and Henderson have worked out the idea with masterly results. This palace will be described in another part of the present work.

CONSTANTINOPLE. This capital of the once great Turkish Empire is commercial rather than manufacturing. The harbour formed by the strait called the Golden Horn is deep, commodious, well sheltered, and capable of containing above 1000 large ships, which may load and unload alongside the quays. The number of vessels that enter yearly is from 5000 to 6000; and the departures about the same. About 2000 tons of coffee, 1,200,000 lbs. of sugar, 300,000 lbs. of spices, 2000 puncheons of rum, and very large quantities of cheap cottons, are annually imported. Other articles of import are dye-stuffs, woollens, cotton-twist, cutlery, coals, iron, furniture, nails, butter, cheese, flour, paper, glass, watches, jewellery, &c. The exports are wool, silk, opium, otto of roses, wax, hides, bullion, diamonds, goat's hair and skins, valonia, box-wood, mohair, yarn, &c. Steamboats ply regularly to Trieste, Smyrna, Odessa, the Danube, and Trebisond, under the management of an Austrian company; and to Malta, Gibraltar, and Southampton, under the Peninsular and Oriental company.

Among the earliest continental arrivals of products of industry for the Exhibition in Hyde Park, has been a consignment from Constantinople, transmitted at the expence of the Sultan. It comprises both natural products and manufactured specimens, from various parts of Turkey.

CONTENT, or CAPACITY. The content, or quantity of space contained within any given boundary, is calculated by certain rules. The solid content of a *parallelopiped* (or figure like a box) is found by multiplying together the units in the lengths of its three dimensions. Thus, 3 feet of length, 2½ feet of breadth, and 4 feet of height, give $3 \times 2\frac{1}{2} \times 4$, or 30 cubic feet. The solid content of any *cylinder* or *prism* is found by multiplying together the number of square units in the base and the number of linear units in the altitude; and one-third of a similar product is the content of a pyramid or a cone. The content of any irregular solid bounded by planes must be found by dividing it into pyramids.

COOKING APPARATUS. If cookery be raised to the dignity of a chemical art (and there is no good reason why it should not) we ought to regard cooking vessels as chemical apparatus. It is, however, chiefly in the mode of applying and economising heat, that such apparatus calls forth the exercise of ingenuity.

Of the ordinary cooking vessels we need say nothing; their simplicity has rendered them familiar to all; but of the modern cooking stoves and apparatus, many examples evince skilful arrangement.

In the so-called 'bachelor's kettles,' of which Spiller's is a recent specimen, the problem seems to be to determine in how short a space of time, and with how little trouble, can a frugal meal for one person be prepared. Spiller's apparatus consists of a kind of saucepan, with a small opening on one side to admit air, and a flue fixed in the opposite side to let off smoke. A very shallow tea-kettle forms the cover to this saucepan. In the middle of the saucepan is a small iron grating, and on this grating is placed one of those small net-work arrangements of sticks which constitute 'patent firewood' and which are now sold so cheaply at one farthing each. This wood being kindled, and the kettle placed over it, the heat is so confined as to make the water in the kettle boil by the time the wood is consumed. With some of these contrivances a kind of small frying-pan is sold; and by using a larger piece of patent firewood, time is allowed for a small dish of savory cookery after the water has boiled: the kettle being quickly replaced by the pan. There is a certain amount of usefulness in the contrivance, which makes it available for others besides the 'bachelors' whom the patentee seems to have had in his thoughts.

Many varieties of gas cooking-stoves have been introduced, in which gas jets are made to yield heat sufficient for the processes of boiling, stewing, roasting, baking, frying, &c. Among other varieties is Defries' 'Economic Gas Cooking-stove,' which is made to suit either large or small culinary wants. Mr. Boggett's gas stoves, for which a patent was taken out in 1850, comprise many varieties, which differ from each other chiefly in the mode of making the heat practically available. There is one form called the Liverpool Gas stove, in which separate departments are provided for roasting, baking, broiling, frying, boiling, stewing and steaming. For many of these purposes the gas is supplied in a ring of jets. On a recent festive occasion at Exeter, M. Soyer cooked a monster joint of meat by means of this apparatus. The meat weighed 565 lbs., and was cooked in a gas oven in five hours, with an expenditure of about five shillings worth of gas.

The kitchen ranges, and other stoves and grates in which coal or coke is burned, are for the most part contrived both for warming apartments and for cooking; but some are designed especially for cooking. The Cottager's stove, designed by Mr. Grant, and manufactured by Messrs. Bailey of Holborn, consists of a square iron case supported on four legs. Inside this case, and near one end, is a fire-pot, the top of which opens into a flue to carry off the smoke; the rest of the vacant space constitutes an oven; while the top, being flat, is available for many cooking processes. In some of these stoves a boiler is attached to that end which is nearest to the fire.

The cooking apparatus of Messrs. Burbidge and Healy is founded on the plans of heating developed by Mr. Sylvester. There are, as in many other similar kinds of apparatus, a large range, an oven, a boiler, a hot-plate, and various subsidiary parts; but its chief features consist in the economising of fuel, and in lessening the amount of radiation sent into the middle of the room. This radiation is an annoyance to the persons present, and involves a loss of some of the heat produced; and it is unquestionably an improvement, other things being equal, if nearly the whole of the heat produced can be applied to the purposes for which it is primarily intended.

Among the many forms of cooking apparatus, that of Mr. Brown is distinguished by having the whole kitchen range, with its oven boiler, hot-plate, &c., set in a frame-work which may be placed in any sized fire-place, however large, without setting. The throat, or opening to the flue, is formed in the iron-work of the range itself, so as to be at once determinate in shape and size. With this range is used an Automaton Roasting jack, arranged in a singular way. In front of the range is placed a sort of semi-cylindrical oven, with the usual hooks and dripping pans for roasting. A hollow tube projects from the lower part of the oven; and when the oven and range are arranged for cooking, this tube is thrust into an opening beneath the fire-place of the range. While the contents of the oven are exposed to the action of the fire, a current of air is continually drawn through the tube into the oven; and this current sets in rotation a vane-wheel to which the suspended hooks are attached.

Remington's Roasting apparatus, recently introduced, is, as the name imports, adapted to roasting only. The meat is suspended and roasted by a jack. There are concave reflectors above and below, which reflect the heat so as to act on the upper and under surfaces of the meat. The centre of both reflectors is perforated; the fat which drips from the meat passes through the perforation in the lower reflector into a small vessel beneath, and is from time to time poured into another vessel, which is perforated and placed over the perforations in the upper reflector. The inventor hence calls his apparatus not only a roaster, but a 'self-acting baster.'

M. Soyer, whose gastronomic skill has acquired some notoriety, has devised a very pretty and scientific cooking stove, in which spirit is the fuel used. A lamp is so placed as, by its heat, to boil spirit placed in a vessel above; the steam or vapour of this boiling spirit has no outlet, except through a tube which gradually becomes so narrow as to resemble a blow-pipe; this blow-pipe is placed opposite to a second spirit-flame, and the blowpipe wafts such a constant stream of spirit-vapour into this flame as to heat it greatly, and to make it act rapidly on small cooking vessels placed above it. There is a good deal of chemical ingenuity shewn in thus feeding one spirit-flame by vapour derived from another.

COOLER. For cooling wine, wort, &c., the hot liquor is sometimes exposed in shallow wooden vessels, and stirred with fans to keep the liquor in motion, and thus expose fresh surfaces to the air. Sometimes cold spring water is allowed to pass through metal pipes placed in the liquor which is to be cooled. In Spain and Egypt, wine is cooled by placing it in porous earthenware vessels, called by the Spaniards *Alcarrazas:* the vessels are wetted externally, and the consequent evaporation occasions cold within.

A remarkable mode of cooling liquids was introduced in 1848 by Mr. Lillie of Manchester. It depends on centrifugal force. The liquid is placed in a bowl or colander, either pierced with minute holes all round the sides, or having sides made of wire gauze. Through the intervention of a vertical shaft, this bowl is made to rotate rapidly. The water first rises all round the sides, and then rushes out through the perforations or meshes in a multitude of small streams; these streams, coming in contact either with the ordinary atmosphere in an outer vessel, or still more effectively with artificial currents of air, become rapidly cooled.

Professor Smyth, of Edinburgh University, has recently suggested a method of cooling the air of rooms in sultry weather. It depends on the principle that air when compressed shows a higher temperature than it had before, but resumes its initial temperature on the pressure being removed. Professor Smyth proposes to compress air, and cool it while under pressure; so that on regaining its original bulk, the temperature shall be less than that of the external air.

CO-OPERATIVE SYSTEMS. There seems to be a longing in modern society for the discovery of some new mode of remunerating the workman for the skill and labour which he bestows on manufacturing operations. Under the usual arrangements the employer agrees with the workman for a certain money payment, determined either on the quantity of work done or on the number of hours engaged: in other words, by 'piece-work' or by 'day-work.' The relative supply and demand of work to be done and of persons to do the work, is almost the only condition which determines the amount of wages to be paid for labour. It is wished at the present day, and

SECTION OF A RETORT-HOUSE

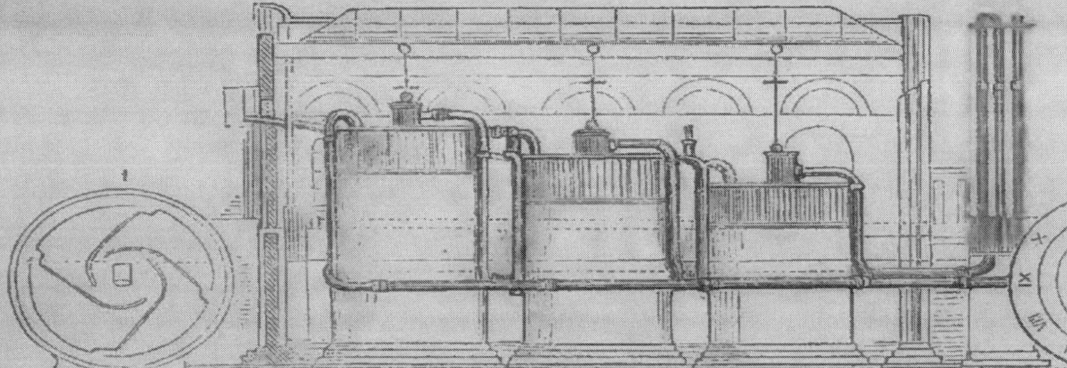

PURIFIERS AND CONDENSERS

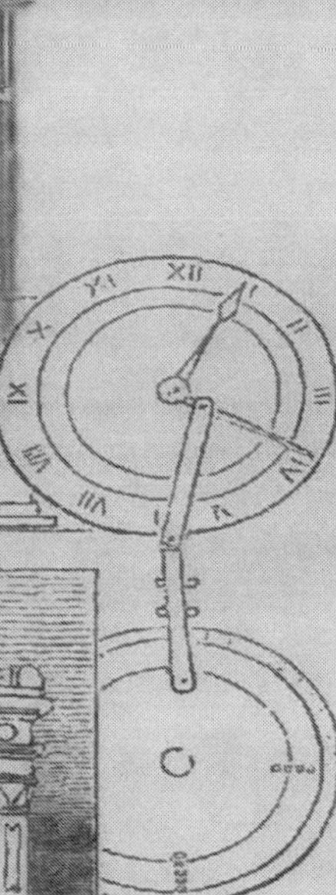

TELL-TALE

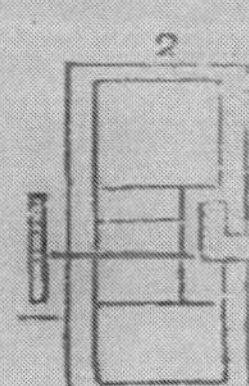

METER

RETORT (END)

METER

GASOMETERS

KNIGHT'S CYCLOPÆDIA OF THE INDUSTRY OF ALL NATIONS.

No. 17.

it has often been wished in former periods, that some mode could be devised by which the workman would have a deeper personal interest in the success of the firm for which he works, than he now has ; that some sort of partnership system could be introduced, which would make the workman a partner on a humble scale, and yet leave to the capitalist and to the skilled superintendent a proper degree of liberty and of remuneration. Something of this kind is observable in the system on which the Cornish miners work ; and many earnest persons are endeavouring to test the practicability of applying a similar system to manufactures generally.

If any clear and undoubted result had yet developed itself, we would briefly review the subject in this place ; but the attempts hitherto made are too much in their infancy for us to do more than point out a few sources where the reader can obtain information on both sides of the question. Among the works we would name are Mr. Babbage's "*Economy of Machinery and Manufactures*"; Mr. Mill's "*Political Economy ;*" "*Companion to the British Almanac,*" *for* 1851 ; "*Report of the Committee of the House of Commons* on the Savings of the Middle and Working Classes," in 1850 ; "*Edinburgh Review,*" January 1851 ; and the *Reports* of various co-operative associations.

COPAIBA or COPAIVA, is a resin or turpentine produced from several species of a tree grown in South America and the West Indies. It varies in appearance and qualities according to the species from which it has been procured, and likewise according to the age of the tree and the time of the year. Incisions are made in the tree, from which flows a liquid differing little in consistence from thick sap. It is collected in calabashes, after which the incisions are closed with wax or clay. The incisions are repeated in general three times each season. The fluid is brighter or darker in colour, more or less rich in volatile oil, more acrid or more bitter, according to circumstances. It is mostly of a light yellow colour, clear and transparent, seldom turbid or cloudy; odour peculiar, volatile ; taste oily, mild, slightly aromatic, at last acridly bitter. In a state of purity, it consists of a volatile oil, in the proportion of 40 to 45 per cent., and 50 per cent. of an acid crystallisable resin. It is frequently adulterated with castor-oil, almond, poppy, nut-oil, and the finer sorts of turpentines. Good copaiva should be perfectly soluble in alcohol of the strength of 90 per cent. It is soluble in all known æthers, and in the volatile and fixed oils.

Copaiva is a valuable ingredient in many medicines. It is imported in casks containing 100 to 150 lbs. each, in large bottles, or in cylindrical tin boxes.

COPAL, a resin, the produce of the *Rhus copallinum*, a native of Mexico ; it is in rounded masses, smooth and brittle, nearly transparent and colourless ; it has but little taste, and is nearly inodorous ; it is insoluble in water, fusible, and inflammable.

Copal varnish is prepared from copal and oil of turpentine. It is exceedingly durable and brilliant ; it resists scratches, and is susceptible of a fine polish. There are several modifications of this varnish used for particular purposes.

COPENHAGEN. The trade of Copenhagen is considerable, but stationary rather than improving. The imports are chiefly sugar, coffee, cotton, rice, tobacco, potash, train oil and blubber, iron, salt, wool, dry and salt fish, pitch and tar, flax, hemp, oranges and other fruits, wine, brandy, rum, coals, &c. The exports consist of corn, flour, rape and other seeds, butter, cheese, beef, pork, cattle, wool, hides, bones, spirits distilled from corn, peas, beans, &c. A foreigner cannot trade as a merchant without becoming a burgher, which costs 100*l*. The industrial establishments of the city are numerous ; they consist of brandy distilleries, breweries, vinegar distilleries, sugar refineries, soaperies, tanneries, iron foundries ; cloth, cotton, silk, linen, aud tobacco factories ; besides ropewalks and extensive workshops for the making of hats, gloves, &c.

Copenhagen is preparing a collection of its produce and manufactures for the Hyde Park Exhibition.

A few details illustrative of the commerce of Copenhagen are given under DENMARK.

COPING. This name is applied to the stone or brick covering of a wall, intended to protect it from the weather. Flat coping is called *parallel coping*, and is used upon inclined surfaces, as on the gables and parapets of houses, and also on the tops of garden and other walls. *Feather-edged* coping has one edge thinner than the other. *Saddle-back* coping is thicker in the middle than at the edges. Coping-stones should project over the walls which they cover, and should have a groove or *throating* underneath the projected part to throw off the water. The coping of Gothic battlements, and the walls of churches, castles, and dwellings in the Gothic style of architecture, have a deep throating in the form of a bold cavetto in front, and are sometimes decorated with mouldings.

In South Wales, near the copper-smelting town of Swansea, very durable coping, of a semi-cylindrical shape, is made from the hard slag of the copper-works, cast into moulds.

COPPER AND ITS MANUFACTURES. Copper is one of the metals with which the Greeks were acquainted; it was used by them, alloyed with tin, for cutting and warlike instruments, before iron was known, or at any rate before it was common.

Copper has a red colour, and is capable of receiving a good polish; when warmed or rubbed, it emits a disagreeable smell, and it imparts a nauseous taste: all its preparations are poisonous. It is both malleable and ductile, and is so tenacious, that a wire $\frac{78}{1000}$ of an inch in diameter supports a weight of 302 pounds without breaking; it is extremely sonorous, and is a good conductor of heat and electricity. It melts at a temperature about 1196° Fahr.

This metal is one of those which occur in the greatest number of places and in the largest quantity. It is found in small proportion in a metallic state, both crystallised and non-crystallised. Its ores are very numerous, the chief being sulphuret of copper and iron (Copper Pyrites), and sulphuret of copper (Nitreous Copper Ore). It occurs also naturally in some oxides and salts.

Copper pyrites occurs in the north of Europe, in England, especially in Cornwall, Devonshire, and Anglesey, and in many parts of Asia and Africa, and the American continents.

In 1844, a vein of very productive copper ore was discovered in South Australia. In 1846 the owners of the Capunda mine shipped to England 1200 tons of copper-ore, which sold for 25*l.* a ton, while English copper ore brought only 19*l.* But the Burra-Burra mine is perhaps the richest in the world. It contains a layer 17 feet high and very wide, which is worked like a quarry. The ore is a pure oxide of copper, and fit to be put at once into the smelting-forge, and yielded in 1846 from 35 to 75 per cent. of pure metal. In July 1846, several tons of ore from this mine were sold at Swansea for 31*l.* 11*s.* a ton; and during the six months preceding May 1847, 2700 tons were raised from the same mine, which yielded 87 per cent. of pure copper, and sold for 31*l.* a ton. The shares in this mining company, on which only 5*l.* have been paid, now command a price of more than 200*l.*; and even at that price they yield a very large dividend. Such is the facility of working the Burra-Burra mine, that in 30 days 8 miners dug out 80 tons of ore. The copper ore exported from South Australia in six years was as follows:—

1843............ 20 tons.
1844............ 422 „
1845............ 1158 tons.
1846............ 6609 „
1847............ 9301 „
1848............ 17006 „

There seems to be remarkable evidence of the existence of large masses of native copper around the shores of Lake Superior. One such piece was met with a few years ago, at Outanagon, which weighed two tons; but a Toronto newspaper, in 1846, gave an account of a mass of copper, far exceeding in bulk any piece of native metal, probably, yet seen in the world. The miners had excavated 90 feet horizontally without coming to the end of its length; they had sunk 4 feet without finding the limit of its depth; but the thickness was about 1½ feet. The part exposed to view was estimated to weigh 80 tons, and to be worth 25,000 dollars. It was stated that machinery was about to be erected for sawing the block into moderate pieces, as the only mode of removing it from its bed. Since that time further indications of the richness of this store have been obtained; but the country is so scantily supplied with roads, that some time will elapse before mining operations can be regularly carried on.

The copper of England is chiefly produced from copper pyrites, yielded by the mines of Cornwall and Devonshire. As coal is scarce in those counties and plentiful in South Wales, the ore is conveyed to the latter district for smelting.

The first process in smelting copper is to calcine the ore; this is done by heating it in a calcining oven, which expels the arsenic and the sulphur contained in the ore, oxidises the copper and the iron, and reduces them to a black powdery state. This powder is then melted in a highly heated oven; and when liquid the mass is well stirred, to allow the metallic sulphuret to separate from the earthy matter. This metallic sulphuret is drawn off into a vessel of water and granulates into *coarse metal*, which is, weight for weight, four times as rich in copper as the original ore. The coarse metal is again calcined, and again melted; if drawn off into water, it obtains the name of *fine metal*, but if into sand, *blue metal*: it now contains 60 per cent. of copper (the coarse metal having about 33 per cent.). Another calcination and another melting bring it to the state of *coarse copper*, which contains 80 to 90 per cent. of pure copper. This coarse copper is exposed to a high heat in a roasting furnace, by which volatile matters are expelled, and the metals become oxidised; it is kept in a melted state for many hours, and is drawn forth from the furnace as *blistered copper*, almost wholly free from sulphur, iron, and other impurities. The blistered copper is transferred to a refining furnace, covered with charcoal, and is brought to a liquid state. It is thus rendered tough and malleable, and fit for subsequent manufacturing processes.

Attention has for some years been directed to the commercial advantage of smelting copper-ore by electric agency. Several years ago, Messrs. Claubry and Dechaud submitted to the French Academy of Sciences a plan in which the ore was first to be converted into a sulphate of copper by ordinary chemical means, and then the copper precipitated from a solution of this salt by electricity. In 1843 and 1844 Mr. Wall took out patents; and Mr. Ritchie, in 1844, took out another patent, having similar objects in view, namely, to separate the pure copper from the impurities of the ore, while in either a melted or a liquid state, by electric agency. Electro-smelting however has not yet been practised to any considerable extent.

Various important applications are made of copper in the state of sheets or rolled copper. Copper, like most of the unmixed metals, is generally rolled hot, being malleable at all degrees of heat till it approaches its melting point. Most of its alloys with zinc, forming brass, are malleable only when cold, with the exception of one or two lately brought into use, which are extremely malleable at a certain high temperature. Copper for the purpose of rolling leaves the smelting works in cakes about 12 × 18¼ inches, each weighing about 90 lbs. The cakes are put into *muffles*, where they are uniformly heated; and the heated copper is drawn between cast-iron rollers. This double process of heating and rolling is repeated until the cake of copper is reduced to the form of a sheet. An oxide forms on the surface during these operations; but this is easily removed by the application of a saline liquid, aided by heat. The edges are then trimmed, and the sheet copper is fit for application to manufacturing purposes.

Copper forms valuable alloys with other metals. Those which result from its union with tin and with zinc are the most important, such as *Bronze*, *Bell-Metal*, and *Brass*. *Tutenag* is an alloy of copper, zinc, and a little iron. *Tombac*, *Dutch Gold*, *Similor*, *Prince Rupert's Metal*, and *Pinchbeck*, are alloys containing more copper than exists in common brass. *Manheim Gold* is a peculiar alloy of copper and zinc, which is said to consist of three parts of copper and one part of zinc. *Packfong*, or the white copper of China, is an alloy of copper, nickel, and zinc, now extensively employed in this country under the name of *German Silver*.

The compounds of copper with non-metallic substances are numerous and important. The *oxides* are often employed to give a blue colour to other substances. The *sulphuret* constitutes one of the most valuable ores of copper. *Acetate of Copper*, more commonly known as *verdigris*, is much employed in painting, dyeing, and calico-printing. The *Arsenite of Copper* forms *Scheele's Green*, a well known valuable pigment. *Green Verditer* and *Refiners' Verditer* are obtained from *Carbonate of Copper*, and *Blue Verditer* from the *Nitrate*. *Sulphate of Copper*, under the name of *Blue Vitriol*, is largely employed by colour makers, dyers, and others.

The principal peculiarity of manufactures in copper arises from the facility with which it may be fashioned by the hammer. The processes of casting and rolling, both of which are extensively practised in the manufacture of copper goods, so closely resemble the like operations upon other metals, that they do not require further notice; but the operations of the coppersmith are very distinct from any other branch of metallic manufactures. For example, in the manufacture of the lower half or hemisphere of the large vessels called *sugar-pans*, used in sugar-refining, the copper is in the first place cast into a form resembling that of a double convex lens, or spectacle-glass, thickest in the middle, and diminishing gradually towards the edges. This lens is then subjected to the powerful blows of a tilt-hammer, directed more continuously near the centre than near the edges. This hammering while it reduces the thickness of the copper, makes it curl up at the edges, and assume a dished or hollow form. Another process no less peculiar to the manufacture of copper is the hammering, technically called *planishing*, by which the metal is rendered dense and firm, and its toughness is increased. Any one who examines a large copper vessel will perceive, both in the hammer-marks and in the density and close grain of the surface, evidences of the planishing process.

It is by the combined operations of casting, rolling, hammering, and planishing, aided by the fastening processes of riveting and soldering, that nearly all articles of copper are made. There are five different modes of forming copper piping out of sheet metal; in the first the edges of the sheet, which is curved round a mandril, are made to meet without overlapping, and united by a hard solder; in the second they overlap, and are united by soft solder; in the third they overlap, and are secured by rivets: in the fourth the edges are folded one over another, and made close and firm by hammering; while in the fifth both edges of the pipe are turned back, and covered with a strip of sheet metal, the two edges of which are turned in and hammered down.

Copper was at first obtained in this country in small quantities in working the tin mines in Cornwall; but about the close of the 17th century mines were set at work purposely for copper. Improvements in the art of smelting have greatly increased the products of the mines, and ores which produce only three or four per cent. of metal are now smelted. The average annual produce of the Cornish mines was only about 3,300 tons in 1780; the later produce we shall presently have to mention. The value of the produce of all the British copper-mines is in good years about 1,500,000*l*. Four-fifths of the whole quantity is raised from the Cornish mines; the rest being derived from Devonshire, Staffordshire, Anglesey, and the Isle of Man.

The duty on foreign copper ore, previous to 1842, was 12*l*. a ton, and on smelted but unwrought copper 27*l*. a ton; these rates were greatly lowered in 1842, and were reduced to merely nominal amounts in 1848.

The Cornish copper-ore sent to Swansea to be smelted, from 1820 to 1850, has varied from 100,000 to 160,000 tons annually. The quantity has gradually increased, but the quality of the ore has deteriorated. The selling value of this ore for the last few years has been from 800,000*l*. to 900,000*l*. Between 1844 and 1848 the foreign copper ore smelted at Swansea varied from 36,000 to 47,000 tons annually. The whole of the ore, British and Foreign, smelted at Swansea during the sixteen years from 1833 to 1848, has yielded the following averages:—

Average quantity smelted ..	194,142 tons.
Average price per ton	£7 7*s*.
Average money value	£1,424,818
Average produce of copper ..	18,567 tons.
Average richness of ore ..	10¼ per cent.

In 1848 four firms at Swansea purchased and smelted no less than four-fifths of all the British and foreign ore smelted in Great Britain; the firms were those of Messrs. Williams and Foster, Messrs. Vivian, Messrs. Simms and Willyams, and Messrs. Grenfell; and the value of the ore purchased by them exceeded 1,100,000*l*.

COPPERAS. The sulphate of copper is frequently called *Blue Copperas*, the sulphate of iron *Green Copperas*, and the sulphate of zinc *White Copperas*.

COPYING MACHINES. Copying Machines are extensively used in mercantile establishments for producing duplicates of letters, invoices, and other manuscript papers. The most simple contrivance acts by transferring, by means of a rolling or screw press, a portion of the ink with which a letter is written to the surface of a sheet of blank paper prepared to receive it by damping. The transfer thus obtained is of course the reverse of the original letter, and, unless it be taken on paper so thin and transparent that it may be read through it, it must be read backwards. Watt's copying-press was a contrivance for obtaining transfers of this kind upon thin unsized paper, wetted, and then placed between two woollen cloths, which absorbed all unnecessary moisture. Elegant screw presses of iron are manufactured for this purpose; some having the power applied solely by means of a screw, turned by a transverse bar or lever, or by a cross or wheel-shaped handle; while others have also a contrivance for increasing the pressure beyond what can be conveniently applied by the simple turning of the screw. In some cases, letters intended for transferring by the copying-press are written with an ink made for the purpose; and when common ink is used it may be thickened by adding a little sugar to it. Transfers are also taken from the pages of a manuscript book prepared for the purpose, a sheet of dry oiled paper being placed over the damp sheet to prevent the transmission of the moisture.

Contrivances for enabling a person to write with two pens or pencils at once, on different sheets of paper, on the principle of the PANTOGRAPH, have been tried as copying-machines, but they are too complicated for ordinary use. All such machines, and perhaps even the copying press, are far surpassed in convenience by the *Manifold Writer*. In this apparatus a sheet of paper blackened on both sides with printers' ink, and dried for five or six weeks between sheets of blotting-paper, or covered with some other black composition which will come off when pressed hard, but will not move with a slight degree of pressure or friction, is laid between two sheets of thin writing-paper, and the whole is placed upon a smooth copper or pewter plate. The letter is then written firmly on the upper sheet of paper with an agate style or point, the pressure of which causes the blackened paper to produce two impressions of the writing, one, which is read through the paper, upon the under side of the sheet directly acted upon by the style, and the other upon the upper side of the lower sheet. More than two impressions of the writing may be obtained by using two or more sheets of blackened paper, interposed between several sheets of thin white paper. This apparatus is conveniently fitted up in a small portfolio, and occupies no more room than an ordinary writing-case.

In a machine recently registered by Messrs. Mordan, a stamping press is combined with an ordinary copying machine. When worked in the customary way, the platten rises with the screw, leaving a space beneath it for the copying process; but by a little adjustment the screw is raised without the platten, leaving a die and counterdie in proper position for stamping any device on letters, envelopes, or papers.

COPYRIGHT OF DESIGNS. [DESIGNS, COPYRIGHT AND REGISTRATION.]

CORAL AND THE CORAL FISHERY. Coral consists of the cells or habitations of minute animals, so built up as to form a tree-like structure. Being beautiful in form and colour, it is sought after for purposes of ornament; and its fishery or gathering gives employment to many persons in the Red Sea, the Persian Gulf, the Mediterranean, and other places. In the Straits of Messina, the rocks which yield coral are from about 350 to 650 feet below the surface of the water. The coral here grows to about the height or length of twelve inches, and requires eight or ten years to come to perfection. In the general mode of fishing for coral, the instrument used consists of two heavy beams of wood, secured together at right angles, and loaded with stones to sink them. Hemp and netting are attached to the under side of the beams, to the middle of which is secured one end of a strong rope, by which the apparatus is let down from a boat, and guided to the spots where the coral is most abundant. The branching form of the coral causes it to become entangled in the hemp and network, by which means it is broken off from the rock, and drawn up with the apparatus to the surface of the water.

CORBEL, in building, is a projecting piece of stone, wood, or iron, placed so as to support a weight of materials. Corbels are sometimes in the form of the modillion or mutule employed in entablatures, and also like the console of a window. The machicolations of towers are almost always supported on corbel stones, as may be observed in the old gates of Southampton, Canterbury, and York. In Norman architecture the cornice is supported by a row of corbel stones, the ends of which are carved. In old English castles the main beams of the floors were frequently carried on large corbel stones, as at Porchester Castle. The term bracket is sometimes used for a corbel.

CORDIALS. A cordial is generally one of the many kinds of spirit, flavoured with sweetening and aromatic substances. A distiller who produces raw spirits from corn or malt, is not allowed by the excise laws of this country to give any additional or artificial flavour to his spirit; he must sell it in the crude ardent state in which it leaves the still. This is not done out of any consideration in which the consumers are concerned, but simply as a matter of revenue. The distillers rarely if ever sell spirit to the public generally. It is sold to the *rectifiers*, who re-distil it, and impart flavour to it by various means. Cordials are among the liquors which are so treated. Some are made simply by adding essential oils and syrup to diluted spirit; while others are made by adding aromatics to the spirit, boiling and re-distilling it, and sweetening the re-distilled liquor. Some cordials are made from raw spirit, but the best from rectified spirit of wine.

The various cordials are known by the names of the vegetable substance to which they chiefly owe their distinguishing flavours. Hence we hear of Aniseed, Caraway, Cedrat, Cinnamon, Citron, Clove, Coriander, Lemon, Lovage, Orange, Peppermint, and other cordials.

CORFU. A few details illustrative of the industry and commerce of this island will be found in connexion with the group of which it forms a part [IONIAN ISLANDS.]

CORIANDER, is an annual umbelliferous plant, inhabiting the southern parts of Europe and yielding a globular dry fruit, with slight carminative stomachic properties and a powerful smell.

Coriander fruit, or *seeds* as they are incorrectly called, are used in sweetmeats, in certain stomachic liquers, and in some countries in cookery.

CORK. The county and city of Cork are both worthy of attention, in respect to natural products and commercial pursuits. The principal copper-mines in Ireland are situated at Allahies in this county. They were first worked in 1814. The ore contains from 55 to 65 per cent. of copper. In the same neighbourhood the ashes of a bog impregnated with copper yielded a considerable return until burned out. A deposit of manganese is worked with good profit on the same coast. Veins of sulphate of barytes occur in the neighbourhood of Bantry, and specimens of asbestos have been procured at Beerhaven. The iron-ore is abundant, and when timber was plentiful, many iron-works were carried on. There is good anthracite coal in the Blackwater district; but it is so difficult of access, that it has not yet been made available for the smelting of iron. The principal trade of the county is the export of agricultural produce, such as grain and butter. The linen and woollen manufactures at one time flourished in several towns of this county; but trade in these branches has for many years back been languishing.

In the city of Cork, the manufactures are of little importance compared with the trade and commerce. There are tanneries, iron-foundries, glass-houses, distilleries, and breweries. The export trade consists principally of grain, butter, and other provisions, and cattle; the import trade of timber and the various articles required for the use of the city and the surrounding neighbourhood. Steamers ply daily between Cork and the harbour at Cove; and large steamers trade regularly with Dublin, Belfast, Liverpool, Bristol, and Glasgow.

The principal harbour of Cork is at Cove, about 9 miles below the city, but lighters of 30 tons' burthen come up to Patrick's Bridge, on the north branch of the river, where there is a fine line of quays. Merchant-vessels unload into the lighters at Passage, about 6 miles down the river. The harbour at Cove is 3 miles long and 2 miles wide, completely sheltered and protected by forts on various points. The entrance is 2 miles long and 1 mile wide. 600 merchant-ships have been at anchor in it at once, and 400 have left it under convoy in one day. The colonial trade is chiefly with Canada; the foreign with Portugal, the Baltic, and the Mediterranean.

The butter trade of Cork is very extensive, and is conducted on a remarkable system. There is a committee of members to superintend all the dealings between buyers and sellers. All the butter brought to market is inspected and branded by orders of the committee, and is divided into four classes, according to its quality. A sub-committee each morning fixes the price at which each kind of butter shall be sold on that day; the four kinds differ in value about 5*s.* per cwt. from each other. The number of firkins branded in certain years was as follow:—

1770..........	105,809	firkins.
1800..........	183,249	„
1830..........	277,947	„
1850.. (about)	400,000	„

The butter buyers are in the habit of advancing money before-hand to the dairy farmers; so that sometimes a whole season's produce is thus paid for before any of tho butter is made.

CORK CUTTING. The nature of cork is explained in an earlier article [BARK]. In the making of ordinary corks, the material is entirely shaped by very sharp, smooth-edged broad knives, without the aid of any machinery; it is one of those employments in which everything depends on the manual skill gradually acquired by the workman.

The attempts to make corks by machinery have been very numerous. In one among several American patents for this purpose the quadrangular pieces of cork, cut to proper lengths, are held between two revolving spindles which grip them; and as they revolve, the cork is cut round by a revolving cutter-wheel, the arbor of which is horizontal and has its bearings in a sliding frame. Other apparatus allows the spindles to disengage the cork when cut. The edge of the cutter-wheel is kept sharp during the operation by means of two rotating discs, one acting on each face, and each covered with leather and emery. The blocks or pieces of cork are placed in a box, from which they are taken by a jaw which slides forward and places them between the grips of the revolving spindles.

Another plan was patented a few years ago by Messrs. Cutler and Hancock. A horizontal spindle, running in suitable bearings, carries a hollow conical cutter at each end. The largest end of the cone, which is outwards, is made very sharp; and a small opening lengthwise of the cutter has also a cutting edge, for reducing the cork to a proper size and shape, as it enters the cone. A convenient number of these spindles are mounted in a frame, to which a traversing motion can be given by means of a screw and handle. A rapid motion is communicated to the spindles by a number of belts from a large drum moved by a steam engine or other source of power. Pieces of cork are placed in a holder; and the holder being placed in front of the cutters, with a proper support behind, they are urged forward by the hand screw until the cork has been cut through. The corks, as they are made, are pushed out by rods, which slide within the spindles.

A 'Patent Cork Cutting Company' has been lately established, for the manufacture of corks by machinery. The patentees assert that the corks so made are both cheaper and better than those made by hand,—a matter which will soon be determined by the purchasers. The same company manufacturo cork gun-wadding, used in military services.

Many substitutes for cork have from time to time been introduced, as stoppers for bottles. Mr. Brockedon has invented bottle-stoppers made of india rubber. The core of the stopper is made of cotton twisted into strands; several of the strands, lapped with flax thread, are laid together longitudinally, with looso fine cotton roving laid between them. They are then lapped in a cylindrical form with flax thread, and the india-rubber solution applied to it while warm. It is only for peculiar purposes that these stoppers can be used as substitutes for corks; when applied, they must be slightly wetted to make them slide down the inner surface of the neck of the bottle.

Mr. Betts, the distiller, has introduced a patent capsule, for stopping bottles containing patented and other liquors. The material employed consists of thin plates of metal, formed of a layer of tin united to a layer of lead; and this material is brought to a shape which enables it entirely to cover the corked mouth of the bottle.

One of many modes suggested of employing cork for stuffing beds and cushions is that patented a few years ago by M. Bachelard. According to this suggestion, the cork is used in the state of saw-dust or shreds, instead of in bulk. Any mode of preparing it may be adopted, provided it be in very small fragments. It may be used alone, or combined with wool or horsehair. The patentee states that if a substratum of the cork be covered with a layer of horse-hair or wool, we shall have all the smoothness of a horse-hair or wool mattrass, combined with the lightness and elasticity of cork. When used at sea, such a mattrass might be light enough to act as a life-preserver, in case of exigency.

The unmanufactured cork imported in 1848 amounted to 3,028 tons. The French corks imported in a manufactured state amounted in 1849 to 151,861 lb.

CORKSCREW. The common corkscrew is too simple in its action to require any description; but that which goes by the name of its inventor, and is called the *Shrapnell Corkscrew*, deserves a little notice.

The Shrapnell Corkscrew, though specially adapted for the Shrapnell bottle, is also useful for other bottles. This corkscrew has three spikes, which press down vertically on the upper surface of the cork soon after the screw has entered. As soon as the spikes touch the cork, they are prevented from turning round with the screw, and they thus enter the cork as the screw rotates. When the cork is about to be extracted, a slight twist given to the instrument enables the extraction to take place with much ease. The Shrapnell bottle is intended to obviate the necessity of using wire or string for fastening down the corks of bottles which contain effervescing drinks. The inside of the neck of the bottle is cut or cast with an internal screw; so that the cork, driven in in tho usual way, expands in the screw, and holds so tightly that nothing but a circular or screw-like movement, such as that of the Shrapnell corkscrew, can remove it.

CORN TRADE. The name of *corn* is sometimes given to grain only, while at other times it is made to include meal or flour as well as grain. The American merchants, and some in our own country, give the name of *breadstuffs* to grain and meal collectively. We shall give a few entries illustrative of the consumption of foreign corn in this country.

The wheat and wheat flour imported into Great Britain between the years 1825 and 1849, varied from 66,905 qrs. in 1835, to 4,835,280 qrs. in 1849. Of the quantity in this last mentioned year, which exceeded that of any previous year, the imports from the chief sources of supply were in round numbers:—

France	750,000 qrs.
United States	600,000 „
Russia	600,000 „
Prussia	600,000 „

The average importation of wheat and wheat flour, from 1828 to 1849, was 1,771,067 qrs. annually; of which Prussia supplied 435,791, United States 242,094, Germany 232,034, and Russia 209,237.

The quantities of all kinds of grain and meal imported in 1849, were as follow:—

Wheat and wheat-meal	4,835,280
Barley and barley-meal	1,389,858
Oats and oat-meal	1,307,904
Rye and rye-meal	246,843
Peas and pea-meal	236,525
Beans and bean-meal	458,651
Indian corn and meal	2,277,224
Buckwheat and meal	627
Beer or Bigg	843
	10,753 755

The average prices paid for six of these varieties of foreign corn and pulse in that year were—wheat 44*s.* 3*d.*, barley 27*s.* 9*d.*, oats 17*s.* 6*d.*, rye 25*s.* 8*d.*, peas 31*s.* 2*d.*, beans 30*s.* 2*d.* per quarter.

The wheat, barley, and oats, sold in the towns from which the averages given by the corn inspectors are obtained, in three consecutive years, amounted to the following quantities:—

	Wheat.	Barley.	Oats.
1847	4,637,616	2,041,129	960,334
1848	5,399,833	2,401,736	1,022,875
1849	4,453,982	2,099,820	851,079

In the year 1850, the following enormous quantities of 'bread-stuff' were brought into the port of London, from the agricultural counties and from abroad:—

Wheat	874,410 quarters.
Barley	455,475 ,,
Oats	1,141,398 ,,
Beans..........	122,226 ,,
Peas	76,255 ,,
Flour	399,123 sacks and 66,463 barrels.

More than three-fourths of this entire quantity was brought from foreign countries. In 1849 the quantities of wheat, barley, and oats, exceeded those of 1850.

CORNELIAN, or CARNELIAN. [AGATE.]

CORNET was an ancient wind instrument formed of wood; it was superseded in the latter part of the 17th century by the oboe.

CORNET-STOP, in the organ, is an imitative treble-stop, consisting of five ranks of pipes, each key of the instrument causing all the five pipes to sound at once; they are tuned to a given note and its 8th, 12th, 15th, and 17th.

CORNWALL. Copper and tin are the most important minerals of Cornwall. The extent of the metalliferous veins is unknown, as well as the depth to which they extend: no miner has yet seen the end or bottom of a vein. Their width varies much, from the thickness of a sheet of paper to 30 feet; but they are usually from 1 to 3 feet in thickness. The ores of copper or tin do not often occur together in the same vein at any great depth. If tin be discovered first, it sometimes disappears, after sinking 100 feet more, and is succeeded by copper; in others, tin is found at the depth of 1000 feet beneath the surface, almost without a trace of copper; if copper be first discovered, it is very rarely, if ever, succeeded by tin. It is seldom that either ore is found nearer to the surface than 80 or 100 feet.

The copper and tin mines, excepting a few near Callington, are south-west of the rivers Alan and Fowey. The chief mining district extends from St. Agnes on the north coast by Redruth to the neighbourhood of Helston and Marazion; and some mines are worked west of Marazion. St. Austell is in the centre of another but less extensive mining district near the south coast.

The lead mines of Cornwall are not numerous, though the ore has been discovered in many parts of the county. Silver ores have been obtained from several mines in Cornwall, chiefly in lodes or cross courses in the graywacké. Gold has been found in the tin streams. Iron ore is also obtained, and shipped to Wales. Zinc, antimony, cobalt, and arsenic are procured, as well as some other of the semi-metals. Freestone of different qualities is quarried.

During the 30 years from 1815 to 1845, there were 220 copper mines in the county, the produce of which was sold at the public ticketings. In the year 1845, 35 of these mines had been worked upwards of 20 years; 40 had been worked between 10 and 20 years; 31 had been worked between 5 and 10 years; and 114 had been worked less than 5 years. The average per-centage of copper from all the mines during the 30 years was $7\frac{1}{4}$; the highest average from any one mine was $26\frac{1}{4}$; and the lowest average from any mine was $2\frac{3}{4}$. The quantity and value of Cornish ores are briefly alluded to in another article [COPPER].

The following demands for space at the Great Exhibition, whether fully adhered to or not, will serve to illustrate the products and resources of Cornwall:—In the first section (raw materials and produce) for the mineral kingdom will be required—for ores, 398 superficial feet; for models of machinery, illustrating the preparation of the ore for the smelter and tin smelting, 70 feet; ochres, clays, and china stone, including a model of a claywork, 94 feet; building and road stones, sand, hone stones, &c., 171 feet; ornamental stones and slates, 202 feet. Animal and vegetable kingdoms—for hides, 100 feet; pilchards, 4 feet; Normal guano, 3 feet; wheat, 2 feet—109 feet; for nets illustrating the Cornish fisheries, 150 feet; making a total required in section 1, 1,194 feet. In the second section (machinery) are required for steam-engines and instruments connected with steam machinery, 784 superficial feet; miscellaneous machines, models, and tools, 204 superficial feet; naval architecture, 70 superficial feet; total in second section, 1,058 superficial feet. For the display of manufactures 412 feet of space have been demanded, 336 feet of which are required for ornamental manufactures in granite, porphyry, serpentine, riband slate, &c., the remainder being wanted for crucibles, safety fuze, chairs, embroidery, &c. Making a total of space required for the county of 2,664 superficial feet.

CORRIDOR signifies a gallery or passageway leading to apartments independent of each other. In all large buildings containing numerons apartments corridors are necessary, either closed or open. The corridor round the great cortile, or open court, of the Cancellarea at Rome, designed by Bramante, consists of an open gallery supported by columns.

CORSICA. About 25,000 acres in this island are planted with vines. The yearly produce of wine is 6,000,000 to 7,000,000 gallons, some of which, especially that of Cap Corso, is of good quality; but in general it is carelessly made, ripe and unripe grapes being put indiscriminately into the wine-press. Of chestnuts, an important article of food, the produce is about 50,000 quarters; the chestnut-tree is one of the most magnificent vegetable productions of the island. The mulberry is cultivated for the production of silk. The cotton-shrub, sugar-cane, indigo, tobacco, and madder are also cultivated. The orange, citron, fig, almond, pomegranate, date-palm, and other fruit-trees, flourish, and their produce is largely exported. The chestnuts and walnuts of the island are of the best quality and of the largest size. A good deal of excellent honey and wax is gathered.

Iron, lead, antimony, black manganese, granite, varying in colour from gray to red, porphyry, white marble, limestone, jaspar, emerald, amianthus, &c., are found. Of manufacturing industry there is little. A little iron is manufactured from ore brought from the island of Elba, for no mines are worked by the Corsicans. The island has several oil and flour mills, tanneries, and brick-works; 2 establishments for the manufacture of soap, and 1 for making glass. These articles, together with turnery, pitch and tar, and bad cheese, are almost the only industrial products. The commerce consists of the agricultural produce, and brandy, olive oil, dried fruits, wax, salt fish, coral, ship-timber, myrtle leaves, orange flowers, lichen, tanned hides, goat-skins, deals, &c.

CORUNDUM. Several substances differing considerably in colour, and sometimes in form, but nearly agreeing in composition, are classed together under the name of *corundum*, which is that given to the common variety by the natives of India. The *sapphire* is one of these substances; its chief varieties are the *white*, transparent or translucent; the *oriental*, blue; *oriental amethyst*, purple; *oriental topaz*, yellow; *oriental emerald*, green. The sapphire occurs in rolled masses and crystallised; it possesses double refraction, and is inferior in hardness only to the diamond. *Ruby* is of a rose-red colour, and generally occurs in six-sided prisms. *Common corundum*, or *adamantine spar*, is sometimes nearly colourless, and rather translucent; it presents great variety of colour, but is most commonly greenish or grayish, occasionally brown or red, rarely blue; it is used in the East Indies for cutting and polishing precious stones, and also granite and other hard rocks. *Emery* is regarded as amorphous corundum; its colour is usually gray; its lustre is somewhat glistening; when ground to powder, it is used in polishing hard bodies. Alumina forms about nine-tenths of all varieties of Corundum.

COSMETICS. The chemistry of the toilet-table has provided many preparations under the name of *Cosmetics*, for external adornment or artificial beautifying. *Hair dyes, pomatums, pomades, depilatories, dentifrices, tooth-powders*, &c., may all be deemed more or less as belonging to the class of cosmetics; but the name is usually confined to those preparations which are applied to the skin.

The best cosmetic is plain soap and water. To soften the skin, however, many substances are used, such as almond soap, Naples soap, Castile soap, milk of roses, cold cream, or almond paste. Sometimes it is desired to harden the cuticle or outer skin, and this is done by spirit, astringents, and acids. For removing or hiding freckles, various lotions and washes are employed. To give an artificial tint or bloom to the skin is the chief work of the cosmetic artist. Rouge and carmine are much employed to give a red tint: starch and magnesia to impart a delicate whiteness. Several of the salts of bismuth and of lead, under the various fine names of *pearl white, flake white, cream of roses*, &c., are often employed as cosmetics; but they have an injurious effect on the skin, and sometimes produce a sort of skin-poisoning.

A want of attention to the chemical action of colours has sometimes led ladies into an embarrassing predicament. Bismuth-powder, sometimes sold as a substitute for genuine pearl-powder, has the property of turning black when in contact with fumes of sulphur, or with sulphuretted hydrogen gas. A lady who painted with this cosmetic, happened to bathe in a mineral water impregnated with this gas; and the consequence was, that the artificially whitened skin turned nearly black, and so remained for several weeks. Another lady, who used the same cosmetic, attended a lecture at Harrogate on mineral waters; and the lecturer handed round a bottle containing sulphuretted water, that its odour might illustrate the point on which he was directing attention; the lady did as others did—smolt at the bottle; and the result was that she became, not merely figuratively, but literally 'black in the face.' Even the coals of a common English fire often contain enough sulphur to produce in a slighter degree an analogous effect. Instances have been known in which a lady, seated near a large fire at Christmas time, has had one side of her white neck tinged with a darkness which puzzled all, except those who were aware of the effect of sulphur fumes upon bismuth-cosmetics.

COTE-D'OR. This department of France

is famous for its wines. The favoured district is divided into two parts—the Côte-de-Nuits, extending from Dijon to Nuits; and the Côte-Beaunoise, from Nuits to the Dheune. The former is famous for its red wines, the most renowned of which are those called Romanée, Vougeot, Chambertin, Richebourg, and Nuits; while the latter produces both red and white wines, which for flavour, delicacy, and perfume, are not surpassed in the world; but they do not bear transport so well as those grown on the Nuitonne slope. Among the red wines of the Beaune slope, the most famous are those called Volnay, Pomard, Beaune, La Peyrieure; and among the white, Meursault, Montrachet, and Goutte-d'Or. Besides these famous Burgundy wines, a good deal of wine resembling Champagne is manufactured in the department, and sold as such. The annual produce of all the vineyards of the department amounts to about 12,000,000 gallons.

The department ranks the first in France with respect to the extent of its forests, in which oak, beech, and elm are the principal trees.

Iron, coal, marble, millstones, limestone, plaster of Paris, potter's clay, &c. are found. The iron mines, which lie chiefly in the mountains in the north-east of the department, are amongst the most productive in France; the ore is converted into malleable iron and steel at nearly 100 blast furnaces and foundries by means of charcoal near the mine-mouth. There are about 300 factories of various kinds in the department, the products being linen, woollen cloth, blankets, cotton and woollen yarn, beet-root sugar, brandy, vinegar, paper, seed-oil, beer, leather, and earthenware. The commerce of the department consists in the agricultural and industrial products already named, and in wool, hides, timber, oak staves, hay, fuel-wood, nails, and whetstones.

COTTON CULTURE AND TRADE. Cotton is a filamentous substance produced by the surface of the seeds of various species of *Gossypium*. It consists of vegetable hairs, of considerable length, springing from the surface of the seed-coat, and filling up the cavity of the seed vessel in which the seeds lie. These hairs are long weak tubes, formed from cells which have grown together, and which, when immersed in water and examined under the microscope by transmitted light, look like flat narrow transparent ribands, presenting at short intervals a spiral twist, by means of which their surface is roughened, so that cotton goods are less soft than linen.

The genus *Gossypium* is common to both continents. There is no record of the first cultivation of the cotton plant in Asia or America: it being indigenous to both, so far as our present knowledge extends. Africa and Europe are supposed to have first become acquainted with cotton by the exportation of muslin from India by way of the Red Sea. The various species occupy naturally a belt probably exceeding the torrid zone in breadth, but in a cultivated state we have cotton now extending on one hand to the south of Europe, and Lower Virginia, and even Maryland, in the United States of America; while, on the other, we have it as far south as the Cape of Good Hope, and in America to the southern parts of Brazil. Within these limits it may also be seen cultivated at considerable elevations. Baron Humboldt mentions having seen it even at 9000 feet of elevation in the Equinoctial Andes; and in Mexico, at 5500 feet. Dr. Royle states it as being cultivated in small quantities at 4000 feet of elevation in 30° N. lat. in the Himalayas. The localities suited to the production of cotton depend as much upon the climate as the soil, and also upon the specific peculiarities of the different kinds of cotton plants.

The distinctive names by which cotton is known in commerce are mostly derived from the countries of their production: the exceptions are Sea Island Cotton and Upland Cotton. The former of these was first cultivated in the low sandy islands near the coast of Charleston in America; while the latter is grown in the inner or upland country. The Sea Island Cotton is the finest of all the varieties of cotton. The Upland is often called Bowed Cotton.

In India and many of the islands of the Indian Ocean, the cotton-plant has been cultivated, and its filaments spun and woven, from time immemorial. In Mexico the Spaniards found cotton in common use at the time of their conquest of the country. The Egyptians were acquainted in the time of Pliny with the use of cotton. The cotton-plant was very early known in China, and cultivated as an ornamental garden shrub; but its filaments were not brought into use until about the 13th century. The Saracens cultivated cotton in Spain and Sicily in the 10th century. The manufacture of cotton did not rise in other countries till a much later period. It was not until the 17th century that cotton goods were made in England; and even of these the warp was composed of linen and only the weft of cotton, until the invention of Arkwright afforded the means of producing good fabrics of cotton only. From that date (1769), the trade in cotton in this country has gone on increasing with astonishing rapidity. The quantity of cotton brought to this country in 1744 was about 4,000,000 lbs.; in 1780, about 7,000,000 lbs.; in 1790, about 30,000,000 lbs.; and in 1800, about 50,000,000 lbs. The imports did not increase very rapidly during the war; but since that time they have augmented in the following manner, taking an interval of five years between the respective dates :—

Years.	Pounds.
1815	99,000,000
1820	152,000,000
1825	229,000,000
1830	264,000,000
1835	364,000,000
1840	592,000,000
1845	722,000,000
1849	775,000,000

Mr. Woodbury, the Secretary of the United States Treasury, has estimated the entire produce of cotton in all countries, at various periods, as follows :—

Years.	Pounds.
1791	490,000,000
1801	520,000,000
1811	555,000,000
1821	630,000,000
1831	820,000,000
1834	900,000,000

In 1791 the United States produced only $\frac{1}{25}$th of the entire quantity; in 1834 its share exceeded one-half; and in 1844 its produce was nearly double of that in 1834. More than half in value of the entire exports from the United States now consist in cotton wool. More than four-fifths of the entire cotton produce of the United States is purchased by Great Britain. In the Mississippi valley land fresh brought under cultivation will yield on an average from 1000 to 1200 lbs. per acre of cotton with the seed, which will yield 250 or 300 lbs. of cleaned cotton.

As there are frequently doubts entertained concerning the capability of the United States to supply us regularly with cotton, and concerning the prudence of depending mainly on one country for a supply, attempts are now being made to encourage the growth of cotton in the West Indies and Port Natal, and an increased growth in the East Indies. Many of these attempts seem likely to be attended with success. The experiments now being made in respect to flax [FLAX] were in like manner suggested by uncertainty concerning the American supply of cotton.

The imports of cotton in the years 1845-6-7-8 and 9, and placed under the names of the countries whence imported, were as follow, in bales :—

	1845—49.		Yearly average.
United States ..	6,188,144	..	1,237,619
Brazil	495,685	..	99,137
Egypt	224,579	..	44,018
East Indies ..	899,213	..	179,852
Miscellaneous ..	44,833	..	8,966
	7,852,454	..	1,570,492

A bale or bag of cotton has become a gradually increasing quantity. In 1820 it averaged about 250 lbs.; at present the average is somewhat above 400 lbs. Our imports, in lbs., were 717 millions in 1848, and 775 millions in 1849.

Nearly all the cotton used on the continent of Europe is grown in the United States. The average United States produce for the years 1844-50 has been about 2,200,000 bales—nearly a thousand million lbs.!

COTTON MANUFACTURE. Cotton was woven by the Hindoos and Chinese many centuries before the Christian æra. The Egyptians are supposed to have imported woven cotton before the plant had begun to be cultivated in their country; and the Romans received woven cotton from India long before the cotton-plant was known in Europe. The first Europeans who spun and wove cotton were the Italians of the commercial republics, who had become familiar with the material while exercising their trade as merchants between Europe and the East. From the 10th to the 13th centuries, cotton goods were manufactured to a large extent by rhe Moors of Spain, especially a coarse variety to which they gave the name of *fuste*, whence our 'fustian.' The other nations of Europe learned the manufacture of cotton, not from the Moors of Spain, but from the Christians of Italy. The art travelled from Italy to the Netherlands, and thence to England, where it was first practised in the beginning of the 17th century.

The extension of this manufacture has been far more rapid in England than in any other country. Before Arkwright's time, it was the custom for the weavers, who were dispersed in cottages throughout the manufacturing districts, to purchase the material with which they worked, and, having converted it into cloth, to carry their wares to market, and sell them on their own account to the dealers; but about 1760 the merchants of Manchester began to employ the weavers, furnishing them with yarn for warp, and with raw cotton, which was spun by the weaver's family for the weft, and paying a fixed price for the labour bestowed in weaving. The Factory System, now so closely connected with the cotton manufacture, arose out of the invention of complicated pieces of machinery which could not be worked in the cottages of the weavers. About 1760 James Hargreaves invented a carding-engine, to assist in straightening the fibres of cotton. In 1767 the same ingenious man invented the Spinning Jenny, by which a number of threads could be spun as easily as one thread by the old spinning wheel. The saving of labour which this machine effected roused the jealousy of the spinners, who for a time prevented the new machine from coming into general use. This opposition however being overcome, the Spinning Jenny became generally used for spinning weft threads in the manufacture of cloth, wherein linen thread formed the warp. Arkwright patented in 1769 his Spinning Frame, by which cotton yarn could be woven strong enough for warp threads. All attempts to produce fine muslin, although India-spun yarn was used as weft, were for many years fruitless; but in 1786 Samuel Crompton invented the Mule Jenny, by which yarn could be produced much finer and softer than any before wrought in this country.

This train of inventions led to an astonishing increase of manufacture. But the manufacturers were for a time subjected to much discouragement from the determination of the revenue officers to charge for cloth composed wholly of cotton double the duty payable upon calicoes woven with linen warp and printed for exportation, and also by prohibiting their use at home. With some difficulty an act of Parliament was obtained for removing these obstacles to the development of the maufacture, which from that time was prosecuted with a great and continually accelerated rate of increase. Of the inventors who gave the spur to this industry, Hargreaves and Crompton died comparatively poor, while Arkwright was enabled to accumulate enormous wealth. Some of Crompton's finest yarns were sold by him at 20 guineas per lb.: they can now be produced of the same fineness for 15 shillings!

Arkwright brought out a succession of improvements in the various processes of the manufacture; and since his time every year has added to the number, until the preparing and spinning machinery has reached an extraordinary degree of perfection. The first successful attempt to *weave* by machinery was made in 1785 by Dr. Cartwright; and Mr. Monteith of Glasgow was the first person to make use of the new method on a large scale. Radcliffe added efficiency to the power looms by the invention in 1804 of the Dressing or Starching Machine.

The processes connected with the preparation and spinning of the cotton fibres are described under ARKWRIGHT; COTTON SPINNING; and THREAD. The weaving of the yarn into piece-goods is described under FUSTIAN; VELVET; and WEAVING. The imparting of colour and design to the woven cloth is treated under BANDANA; COTTON or CALICO PRINTING; and DYEING. The statistics of the manufacture, in respect to the number of factories, power-looms, work-people, &c., are given under FACTORIES. Mr. McCulloch estimates that, allowing for old persons and children dependent upon those actually employed in the various departments of the cotton manufacture, and in the construction and repairs of the machinery and buildings required to carry it on, the entire manufacture in Great Britain must furnish subsistence for at least 1,250,000 persons.

Mr. Kennedy estimated the value of the cotton manufactures produced in Great Britain in 1832 at about 25,000,000*l.* Mr. Baines made the estimate for 1833 at about 31,000,000*l.* Mr. McCulloch's estimate for 1836 was about 34,000,000*l.* Mr. Porter's estimate for 1841 was about 49,000,000*l.* It is admitted that there are no exact data for determining these quantities; but the above are approximately correct. The capital invested is supposed to amount to 30,000,000*l.* or 35,000,000*l.*

The real or declared value of manufactured cotton goods exported from this country in various years was as follows:—

Years.	£
1820	16,516,748
1825	18,359,526
1830	19,428,664
1835	22,128,304
1840	24,668,618
1845	26,119,331
1849	26,890,794

The exports for 1849 were thus divided:—

	£
Piece goods	18,834,601
Lace and net	487,300
Thread	427,422
Hosiery	118,418
Yarn	6,701,920
Sundries	321,133
	£26,890,794

Of this enormous value the portion sent to the British colonies amounted to 7,264,469*l.*

The cotton manufacture is now largely conducted in the United States, France, Belgium, Germany, and other countries; and specimens from all those countries will be found in the forthcoming Industrial Exhibition.

COTTON SPINNING. The spinning of cotton into the form of yarn, or thread, requires many preparatory processes. The first of these consists in mixing the contents of different bags together, to equalise the quality. This is done by spreading out the contents of each bag in a horizontal layer of uniform thickness, the contents of the several bags forming separate layers and resting one upon the other, so that the number of layers corresponds to the number of bags. The cotton of which this heap is composed is then torn down by a rake from top to bottom. It is evident that in its progress a portion of each horizontal layer will be brought away, and that thus, if the work be skilfully done, the contents of the different bags must be collected together in a mass of uniform quality. The mode of conducting the mixing depends on the quality of yarn required.

The *scutching-machine* is used to open the locks of cotton and separate its fibres, while at the same time it separates from it any sand or seeds which it may contain. This machine consists of feeding rollers made of wood, and placed at a short distance from each other, through which the cotton is made to pass slowly. After passing through the rollers the cotton is struck by a set of beaters made to revolve 1000 or more times in a minute. The cotton is passed through two sets of rollers, and subjected to two sets of beaters.

Up to this stage the fibres of the cotton cross each other in every direction. The use of the *carding-engine* is to disentangle them, to draw them out, and to lay them parallel to each other. The card is a species of brush made of short wires passed through a sheet of leather and pointing all in one direction. In the early period of cotton-spinning in this country, these cards were nailed on small pieces of board with handles, and two of them were used together, one held in each hand. Hargreaves invented an improved arrangement of cards in 1760; but this gave way to the cylinder machine, now universally employed. This consists of a horizontal cylinder covered with narrow fillet cards, studded with wires. Over the cylinder is a concave frame, the interior surface of which is lined with cards, and the form of which corresponds to that of the cylinder. When the cylinder is made to revolve, the cards on it and on the frame work against each other, by which means the fibres of cotton are disentangled and properly arranged, as already mentioned. The cotton is spread out into a sheet of given length and breadth, and placed so that the teeth of the carding-engine can catch it and draw it in. A sort of comb draws the fibres of cotton off the teeth when the carding is effected; and the cotton passes through two rollers into a tin can, where it assumes a light fleecy form called a *sliver*.

The next operation, that of *drawing*, has for its object the arranging of the fibres of cotton longitudinally, in a uniform and parallel direction, and to remedy all existing inequalities in the thickness of the sliver. The *drawing-frame* acts upon the same principle as Arkwright's spinning-frame, two sets of rollers being employed moving with unequal velocities. The cotton is drawn several times, to attain the utmost regularity.

Roving, the next step in the process, is a continuation of the drawing, with this only difference, that the cord, now called a *rove* or *slub*, being so much reduced in thickness that it will not otherwise hold together, a slight twist is given to it by passing it into a conical can, which, while receiving it, is made to revolve with great velocity. The rove, thus slightly twisted, is wound upon bobbins by children, and is then ready for the spinning-frame. The *fly-frame* and the *tubeframe* are two machines employed in this process.

The principle of Arkwright's *spinning-frame* has been already explained. [ARKWRIGHT.] The *throstle-frame* is the same in principle as Arkwright's invention, but the movement of the parts is simplified. A throstle-frame now contains from 70 to 150 spindles on each side; and one young woman can manage the double set, from 140 to 300 spindles. The Mule Jenny, invented by Samuel Crompton, combines the essential principle of Arkwright's frame with the property of stretching possessed by Hargreave's Jenny. By means of the mule-jenny, the roving is first drawn and then stretched. The effect of this improvement is to make the yarn finer, and of a more uniform tenuity. The spindles in this machine are regularly arranged on a carriage, which, when put in motion, recedes from the rollers with a velocity somewhat greater than that at which the reduced rovings are delivered from them; during this time the yarn is receiving its twist by the rapid revolving of the spindles, and when the rollers are made to cease giving out the rovings, the mule-jenny still continues to recede, but with a slower motion, and its spindles to revolve, and thus the stretching is effected. When the drawing, stretching, and twisting of the thread are thus accomplished, the mule disengages itself from the parts of the machine by which it has been driven, and then the attendant spinner returns the carriage to the rollers, again to perform its task. While returning to the roller, the thread which has been spun is wound or built on the spindle in a conical form, and is called a cop. The mule-jenny has become a 'self-acting machine,' by some beautiful inventions of Messrs. Sharp and Roberts, at Manchester. Some of the modern double self-acting mules contain 2200 spindles, all managed by one man.

The spun yarn is reeled into hanks containing 840 yards. Yarn of *low* numbers, or below 40 hanks to the lb., is generally spun by the throstle; but *high* numbers, or fine yarn, is more frequently spun by the mule. At Houldsworth's Mill, at Manchester, yarn was spun a few years ago to the astonishing degree of fineness of No. 460; that is, 460 × by 840, or 386,400 yards, or nearly 220 miles in length, from 1 lb. of cotton. This yarn was worth five times its weight in silver, and was spun for a muslin dress for her Majesty. But even this triumph of skill is about to be exceeded. A Manchester manufacturer is spinning a pound of cotton for the Great Exhibition of 1851, in length 238 miles and 1120 yards, being the finest ever yet produced. Those most conversant with the details of cotton-spinning can best appreciate the value of the machinery and the talent displayed in so wonderful a production. The cotton was, we believe, from Egypt, and is considered the finest specimen that was ever imported into this country.

COTTON or CALICO PRINTING. This art has been practised from time immemorial in India. Pliny describes a mode which was adopted by the Egyptians in staining cotton cloth, evidently similar to the modern process of employing wood-cuts. In India, not only is the art of using wood printing-blocks well known, but also that of applying resist-pastes, in order to preserve the cloth from the action of the dye-bath in any desired figures or spots. Processes of printing, similar to the Indian, have been long practised in Asia Minor and in the Levant; but they were not attempted in Europe till about the middle of the 17th century. The first print-ground in England was established near Richmond, in Surrey, in 1696; but it was not till the year 1768 that the business was carried into Lancashire, where it now constitutes one of the most interesting and productive branches of English manufactures. From its outset the printing of cotton goods encountered the keenest hostility from the silk weavers of Spitalfields; and it was not till 1831 that printed cottons were relieved from the burdens thrown on them by protection.

Calicoes, muslins, &c., intended for printing are first of all freed from their fibrous down by the action of the *singeing machine*. This consists either of a semi-cylinder of iron or copper, laid horizontally, and kept at a bright red heat by a furnace, or by a horizontal range of gas-jet flames: over one of these the plain of cloth is drawn with a steady continuous motion, and at a rate suited to its texture. The cotton cloth is next well bleached [BLEACHING], because, the whiter it is, the more light it will reflect from its surface, and the more brilliant will be the colour of its dyes. The goods are next rinsed, dried, and sometimes smoothed under the calender. If they are not calendered, they are run through a machine called in Lancashire the *candroy*, which spreads them smoothly in the act of rolling them upon a cylinder.

There are four mechanical modes of printing calicoes: first, by small wooden blocks, worked by hand; second, by large wooden blocks, set in a frame, and worked by a machine called the *Perrotine;* third, by flat copper plates (a method now nearly obsolete); and fourth, by copper cylinders.

The blocks are made of sycamore wood, or of deal faced with sycamore. They are about ten inches long and five broad, with an arched handle on the back for convenience of holding. The face is either cut in relief into the design required, or the same object is obtained by the insertion edgewise into the wood of narrow slips of flattened copper wire in the desired configurations. These narrow fillets have one edge inserted into the wood, are fixed by the taps of a light hammer, and are all filed down and polished into one horizontal plain, to secure equality of impression in the several lines. The interstices between the copper ridges are filled up with felt-stuff. Occasionally both the wood-cutting and insertion plan are combined in one block.

Calico-printing by hand is performed by applying the face of the block to a piece of woollen cloth stretched over one end of a sieve-hoop, and imbued with a colouring matter of a thin pasty consistence by means of a flat brush. The block is then applied to the surface of the cotton cloth while extended upon a flat table covered with a blanket, and the impression is transferred to it by striking the back of the block with a light mallet. This method, besides the great cost of labour which it involves, has the inconvenience of causing many irregularities in the execution of the work. It has been superseded to a considerable extent, both in France and Belgium, by the Perrotine. Three thin wooden blocks, engraved in relief, about three feet long, and from two to five inches broad, are successively brought to bear on three of the four faces of a prismatic roller of iron, round which the cloth is successively wound. Each block rests on springs, which enable it to press with the delicacy of a skilful arm; and each receives its peculiar-coloured paste from a woollen surface imbued by a mechanical brush in rapid alternation. In England a machine has been introduced in which three or more oblong blocks are laid side by side, and are imbued with different colours all at the same time, from a trough arranged for the purpose.

The *cylinder-machine* consists of a hollow cylinder of copper about three feet long and three or four inches in diameter, whose surface is engraved, not by the hand-graver, but by the mechanical pressure of a steel roller from one to two inches in diameter, and three inches long, which transfers the figures engraved on it to the relatively softer copper. The first steel roller, called the die, is softened before being engraved in intaglio; it is then hardened, and made, by a powerful press, to transfer its design in relief to a similar die called the mill, which is the one used for transferring the design to the copper cylinder. The process of etching is also sometimes had recourse to for covering the cylinder with various figures.

The engraved cylinders are mounted upon a strong iron shaft or arbor, carrying a toothed wheel at its end, in order to put it in train with the rotatory printing machine, for one, two, or more colours. On a roller, at the upper part of this apparatus, are wound whole calico webs stitched together, the end of which is then introduced between the engraved copper cylinder and a large central cylinder covered with blanket, against which it is made to bear with regulated pressure. The engraved cylinder turns on the top of another cylinder covered with woollen cloth, which revolves with the former while its under part is plunged in an oblong trough containing the dyeing matter, which is of a pasty consistence. The engraved cylinder is thus supplied with an abundance of impressible colour, and is cleared from the superfluity by the thin edge of a flat ruler made of bronze, called vulgarly the doctor, which is applied obliquely to it with a gentle force. The cylinder, after its escape from this wiping tool, acts upon the calico, and rolls it onwards with its revolution, imparting its figured design with great precision. One single machine will print calico at the rate of a mile an hour.

Dye-stuffs, capable alone of imparting fast colours to calico, have been called *substantive;* and such as require the intervention of a mordant, *adjective.* Indigo, catechu, and certain metallic oxides belong to the former class; madder, cochineal, and Persian berries to the latter. There are five general styles of work in calico printing:—1, The fast colour or chintz style, in which the mordants are applied to the white cloth, and the colours of the design are afterwards brought up in the dye-bath. 2, Where the whole surface receives a uniform tint from one colouring matter, and figures of other colours are afterwards brought up by chemical discharges and reactions; this is called the Rongeant style in France. 3, Where the white surface is impressed with figures in a resist-paste, and is afterwards subjected to a general dye, such as the indigo-vat. 4, Steam-colours, in which a mixture of the mordants and dye-extracts is applied to the cloth, and the chemical combination is effected by the agency of steam. 5, Spirit-colours, consisting of mixtures of dye-extracts with nitro-muriate of tin; these cannot be exposed to a steam heat without corroding the cloth: this style is brilliant, but fugitive.

The tint or shade of colour produced in the dyeing-bath is proportional to the strength of the mordant previously applied to the cloth. The thickening of mordants is one of the most important operations in calico-printing; for the permanence and beauty of the impression depend not a little on the consistence and quality of the inspissating substance. The substances usually employed in thickening are flour starch; flour; roasted starch; gum Senegal; gum tragacansh; salep; pige-clay mixed with gum Senegal; potato starch; sulphate of lead and gum; sugar; treacle; glue.

In the printing of yellows, greens, purples, pinks, and browns, different colouring substances are used, and different processes adopted for causing the colours to combine permanently with the cloth; but they all possess a common character, inasmuch as mordants are applied to the white cloth, and the colours of the design are afterwards brought up in the dye-bath.

In almost all the modes of calico-printing, the processes are very numerous, to ensure the beauty and the permanence of the colours. In what is called the *steam-colour* printing, the agency of steam is applied to aid in fixing the colours to the cloth. The cloth is first steeped in a mordant liquor; then printed by the cylinder with various colours, which for their peculiar properties are called steam-colours. The cloth is hung up to dry, and when dry it is exposed to the action of dry steam. This is done by five different kinds of apparatus—the column, the lantern, the cask, the steam-chest, and the chamber. The first of these, which is most frequently used, is a hollow copper cylinder about 45 inches long by 2 to 6 in diameter, perforated along its whole surface with small holes one quarter of an inch apart. To the lower end of the column a circular plate is soldered, which serves to prevent the cloth coiled round the cylinder from falling down from it. The bottom of the hollow cylinder is terminated by a tube one inch wide, which fits tight into the socket of an iron chest beneath it, into whose side the steam pipe of supply enters. The goods printed with the steam-colours and properly dried are lapped tight round this hollow cylinder, and covered exteriorly with an envelope of strong cotton cloth, blanket-stuff, or flannel. The steam is then let on, and continued for 20 or 30 minntes, according to the nature of the dyes. The steam being stopped, the printed goods are rapidly unrolled from the column while still hot, lest any condensation of vapour should take place to stain them.

A pretty and ingenious method of producing the 'rainbow' pattern is as follows: a number of sieves, containing the different shades of colour, are placed nearly under each other, over each sieve a disc revolves, having projections of copper wire, which dip into the colours. These discs are supported on pedestals which admit of easy adjustment, and are so regulated, that as they revolve the projecting wires give colour to the cylinder in successively lighter shades.

The designs for calico printing are very costly. A copper cylinder is worth from 5*l.* to 7*l.*; and the engraving costs from 5*l.* to 10*l.* more. A constant succession of new patterns must be kept up by the manufacturer to produce 'novelties' for the season. Some of the Lancashire firms expend as much as 5000*l.* a year in designing and engraving new patterns. Property in these designs is secured by law. [DESIGNS, COPYRIGHT, AND REGISTRATION.] The art of designing now receives encouragement from the government. [DESIGN, SCHOOLS OF.]

In the year ending June 1846, the printed and dyed cotton goods exported from this country amounted to 327,465,580 yards.

COUNTERPOISE is, generally, a mass of brass or iron so disposed as to keep a part of some instrument or machine in equilibrio. Large astronomical instruments are generally mounted so that their centres of gravity are supported, in which case they require no counterpoise; but a reflecting circle is sometimes so placed as to require a heavy counterpoise on the other side of the pillar which sustains it. A transit instrument or mural circle, whose pivots would press heavily on their supports, is sometimes provided with counterpoises, one for each point which is to be relieved. Lord Rosse's great telescope has two counterpoises to assist in the requisite adjustments. A drawbridge usually has its weight relieved, or almost wholly removed, by a counterpoise, so that the machinery employed to raise it has little except the resistance arising from friction to overcome.

COUPLING, in machinery, is the name given to various arrangements by which the parts of a machine may be connected or disconnected at pleasure, or by which a machine may be disengaged from, or re-engaged with, a revolving wheel or shaft, through which it receives motion from a steam-engine, water-wheel, or other prime mover. Coupling-boxes, clutches or glands, a solid conical wheel working in a hollow cone, friction-wheels whoso peripheries act in contact, and Hook's universal joint, are different forms of apparatus for effecting this adjustment.

COURTRAI, a town in West Flanders, is famous for the manufacture of damask and other linen textures, which are exported to all parts of Europe. Flax of the finest quality is produced in large quantities in the vicinity, which contains a great number of bleaching establishments, The dyers of Courtray imitate with success the colour known as Turkey red. Thread and silk lace are among the branches of industry pursued.

COVENTRY. In the time of the Edwards and Henries, the tradesmen of Coventry were famed for their affluence. In 1448 they equipped 600 armed men for the public service. Until the war between England and France in 1694, the staple manufacture was woollens, broad-cloths and caps; and previous to 1580 there existed a famous manufacture of blue thread; the water of the small river Sherbourne, which passes through the city, being an excellent menstruum for dyeing this colour. During the 18th century there was a flourishing manufacture of tammies, camlets, shalloons, calimancoes, gauzes, &c., but it is no longer continued. At present the staple manufactures are ribbons and watches. The ribbon manufacture was introduced about 1730, and is supposed now to give employment to about 6,000 persons in the city; it is said that 20,000 are employed in ribbon weaving in Coventry and the vicinity. The weaving has hitherto been almost entirely performed by the hand-loom, and the weavers are in general a poor class; but steam factories have been of late increasing, and are probably superseding the loom at the workmen's dwellings. The leaders of the trade are not the manufacturers, but a comparatively small number of wholesale firms in London and Manchester, whose agents attend at Coventry. Gimp and other trimmings are also made in Coventry, and there are large establishments for dyeing silk. The making of watches has been carried on here probably as long as the ribbon manufacture, and is now so extensive that as many watches are said to be made in Coventry as in London.

The Report on the Government Schools of Design for 1850 contains a statement relating to the branch school of Coventry well worthy of attention. 'Of the beneficial influence of the school on the manufactures of the town, the manufacturers entertain a strong and increasing conviction; for the employment of designers in the strict sense of the term, the ribbon manufacture affords but a narrow basis; and until the prejudices of the public in favour of French ribbons is removed, there can be but little production in England of that description of goods upon which designs of the highest class can be exhibited; but it is certain that during the last five years there has been a marked improvement in the Coventry patterns, accompanied by improved quality and closeness of texture in the fabric, and that a superior class of Coventry goods, to some extent, under the name of French, is gaining ground in the market. These results the manufacturers unhesitatingly ascribe to the superiority which the rising generation of pattern draughters have attained through their education in the school. Nor is it only in the greater refinement and better execution of the patterns that an advantage has been obtained; they are also drawn and draughted at a much less expense than formerly, an evidence that it is the young hands and apprentices who excel in the art.'

There are several guilds, or incorporated trading companies, some of which are possessed of considerable property, which they spend in charity and festivities.

The local position of Coventry is favourable for commercial operations, being nearly central between the four greatest ports of England —London, Bristol, Liverpool, and Hull; possessing great facilities of water communication by the Coventry and Oxford Canal, which opens into the Grand Trunk navigation, and having one of the main roads from London to Birmingham passing through its streets. The London and North Western Railway passes close to the town; and there are two branch lines, one turning northward to Leamington and Warwick, and another (not yet finished) to Nuneaton.

COWRY SHELLS are called by conchologists *Cypræœ*. Their beauty has procured them a place among the ornaments of our chimney-pieces, and they have been in demand among civilised and uncivilised nations time out of memory. Cowries are used as small coin in many parts of Southern Asia, as in India, the Burmese Empire, Siam, &c., and especially on the coast of Guinea in Africa. In 1740 a rupee in Bengal was worth 2400 cowries; in 1766, 2560 cowries; and now, we believe, 3200 may be had for it.

COYPOU or COYPU is one of the numerous fur-bearing animals of South America. Like the beaver it has two kinds of fur; an outer coat of long ruddy hairs, and an under garment of fine brownish wool, much used in the manufacture of hats. In France the skins of this animal are sold under the name of Racoonda. M. Geoffroy mentions that in certain years a single French furrier, M. Bechem, has received from 15,000 to 20,000 skins. They are imported into Great Britain to a large amount; from 600,000 to 800,000 have been stated as the importation of one year, principally from the Rio de la Plata. They are here known under the name of Neutria or Nutria, an appellation derived from some supposed similarity in the habits and appearance of the animal to those of the otter, the Spanish name of which is Nutria.

CRAB is a kind of portable windlass, or machine for raising weights, or otherwise exerting force, by winding a rope or chain round a horizontal barrel. Crabs are usually mounted in a strong heavy framework of wood or iron; and, when employed for a temporary purpose, but one which involves considerable strain, they are either bolted down to a temporary foundation, or loaded with heavy weights put upon the framework.

CRACOW. The little which can be said concerning the produce and industry of Cracow will be found under POLAND.

CRADLING, is a name given to the slight timber-framing constructed under floors in order to form arched or coved ceilings.

CRAMP, or CRAMPERN, is a piece of metal bent at each end and let into the upper surface of two pieces of stone when their perpendicular faces are joined together. Cramps are employed in the masonry of all solid structures. Iron is mostly used, but copper is more durable. The Greeks used cramps in the construction of their temples, and wooden cramps were sometimes used by the Egyptians.

CRANE, is a machine employed for raising weights vertically by means of a rope or chain acted upon by a windlass, but carried over a pulley or wheels attached to the extremity of a projecting arm or jib. The common warehouse crane, which is usually formed of iron, may be compared to an inverted L, the vertical portion of which is so mounted as to form a pivot or axis upon which the whole may be swung round; so that the horizontal arm, which is strengthed by diagonal struts, may extend in any direction. The rope or chain of such a crane is conducted along the horizontal arm, and connected with a kind of windlass or crab, which is usually provided with two sets of gearing for working at different velocities, so that in raising light goods a much greater speed may be given to the chain with the same motion of the winch-handles than when the load is very heavy. Wharf-cranes are frequently of somewhat different construction, owing to the circumstance that they usually stand alone, that is to say, that they are self-supported, instead of being attached to and supported by a wall or a post secured to a wall. There is a vertical pillar of iron or wood, the lower end of which is firmly secured to a foundation of masonry, while the upper end terminates in a pointed or conical pin, upon which, as a pivot, the revolving part of the crane rests and turns. The arm or jib projects obliquely from the pillar, and is strengthened by diagonal braces. The windlass or crab for working the crane is attached to the central pillar. Some cranes are worked by a tread-mill moved by men; some by horses or oxen; some by the surplus power of a steam engine; some by the compression of air in a strong vessel; some by hydrostatic pressure; but the customary mode is by a winch-handle. Many of the cranes at the principal docks and quays are capable of raising immense weights.

Mr. W. G. Amstrong, who has introduced many ingenious applications of water power, has recently patented a singular method of working a crane by means of the pressure of the water in the common water pipes of a town. One such hydraulic crane was set up and worked on the quay at Newcastle in 1846. The machinery for working the crane is all underground. There is a sort of dial plate visible, with handles or indicators for guiding all the movements of the machine, such as raising, lowering, stopping, &c., these indicators act upon valves which regulate the water-pressure beneath, so that the movements produced can be made exactly proportionate to the work to be done.

Mr. Henderson's derrick crane, which has been so largely used by Messrs. Fox and Henderson at the Industrial Palace in Hyde Park, is especially adapted for circumstances where the crane is required to be moved from place to place during the progress of the works. This kind of crane has a derrick or jib, rising nearly from the ground, and hinged at its lower extremity to the upright post of the crane. This hinge enables the derrick to be moved to any required angle, so that the upper extremity may be near or far from the central post, according to the position of the load to be raised. While the derrick can thus move vertically on a horizontal hinge, the post can rotate horizontally on a vertical pivot; so that the crane has a wide extended area of action.

CRANK, in machinery, is a bend in an axle by which a reciprocating motion in a rod is made to produce a revolving motion of the axle and of a wheel which may be connected with it.

CRAPE is a light transparent fabric composed of silk, from which, by the mode of its preparation, all the gloss has been taken, and which, when dyed, as it usually is, of a black colour, is worn as a material for mourning-dresses. For thin crape, the only preparation which the filaments of silk undergo previous to the weaving is the simple twisting, which forms the first process of the throwing mill, and in which state the thread is technically called *singles.* When it is intended to make a more substantial fabric, the warp is made of two and sometimes three filaments twisted together, which in that state are called *tram:* the weft is still composed of singles. The wrinkled appearance of crape is produced by the application of a viscid solution of gum.

In the Custom House returns, crape goods are entered distinct from other varieties of silk. In 1848 crape shawls, scarfs, and handkerchiefs were imported to the value of 15,490*l.*; partly from France, but chiefly from India.

CRAYONS are a useful kind of material for drawing. Black chalk found in Italy, white chalk found in France, and red chalk, form three of the best varieties of crayons; each has its own peculiar value as a drawing material. Artificial crayons are composed of different coloured earths and other pigments, rolled into solid sticks with some tenacious stuff such as milk, common gin, or beer wort; the best are procured from Switzerland. A new kind called Athenian crayons has recently been introduced; they are sold at the London colour-shops at three to four shillings per dozen. The native crayons are the legitimate materials for the artist in the study of drawing, and in tracing the first thoughts of design. Some of the sketches of Raphel, Michael Angelo, the Caracci, and others of the great painters are in this material.

An instrument called a portcrayon is employed to hold the crayon. It is a metal tube split at each end, so as to admit the crayon; a sliding ring embraces the tube, and assists in retaining the crayon. A stump made of leather, cork, or paper, closely rolled, or cut into a short round stick more or less sharply pointed at each end, is used to soften and spread the chalk or crayon in the shaded parts of the drawing.

Messrs. Wolff have recently introduced what they call crayon-paper; its surface has a fine nap similar to that of cloth, which renders it capable of receiving the marks of the crayon with great readiness.

The following materials are said to form a kind of crayon fitted for drawing on glass. Equal quantities of asphaltum and yellow wax, melted together, thickened with lamp black, and poured into moulds to form crayons. These crayons may be bevelled to a fine point, and will mark well on a perfectly clean piece of glass.

CREAM. [BUTTER; MILK.]

There are various preparations which pass by the name of *creams*, and which for the most part consist of cream combined with syrups, spices, fruits, &c.; but sometimes there is no milk-cream contained in them; the name being derived from the consistency rather than from the ingredient.

The French *crémes* are cordials or liqueurs, which have a cream-like smoothness in their taste. Such are the Créme d'Anise, Créme d'Orange, &c.

CREASOTE or KREASOTE is a fluid compound of oxygen, hydrogen, and carbon, obtained from oil of tar. It is colourless, transparent, and has a strong odour which greatly resembles that of smoked meat, with a caustic and burning taste. It is highly antiseptic, and combines both with acids and with alkalies; but it is decomposed by strong nitric and sulphuric acid.

Creasote coagulates albumen, even when much diluted, and it also coagulates serum. Meat and fish are preserved after having been brushed over with creasote and dried in the sun; the antiseptic power of pyroligneous acid and wood smoke is supposed to be derived from its presence. A few drops added to ink are said effectually to prevent its becoming mouldy.

Creasote, from its extraordinary antiseptic qualities, is becoming employed in various ways for the preservation of animal and vegetable food. A joint of uncooked meat, in hot weather, may be preserved pure for many days by the use of this remarkable agent. There are many ways in which this may be done. The meat may be exposed to the smoke produced by the burning of the wood which contains or yields creasote; or the meat may be soaked for a short time in water which contains a few drops of creasote; or it may be hung up in a larder or safe, with a dish beneath it containing a little creasote, the slow evaporation of which gradually affects the meat. The first two of these methods are in some respects objectionable, inasmuch as a peculiar smell and taste are imparted to the meat; but in the third method, especially if both the dish and the meat are covered with cloths, the antiseptic effect is said to be produced without the accompaniment of the odour and taste.

CREDITON. On the rise of the woollen manufacture in the west of England, Crediton became one of the most important seats of that branch of industry. Little cloth is now made in the town; but hand-loom weavers are employed in their own houses by manufacturers at Exeter and North Tawton. The principal occupation in the town at present is shoe-making, which employs several hundred people. At Fordton, south of the town, is a manufactory for coarse linens, dowlasses, sail-cloth, &c. Early in 1848 a railway was completed from Exeter to Crediton, and it was about to be opened in connection with the Great Western Railway, when the South Western Company obtained a majority in the direction, and altered it from the broad to the narrow guage, with a view to open it in connection with a projected line from Exeter to Yeovil and Salisbury. This led to litigation, and the consequence has been that the Crediton railway has not been opened to the present time (February 1851).

CREFELD, a town in Rhenish Prussia, is a place of great manufacturing activity; the principal fabrics are silks and velvets, which are woven chiefly by hand, and give employment to 6000 workpeople. The articles of manufacture are calicoes, woollens, tape, ribands, linen, hosiery, glass, refined sugar, soap, iron, and cotton wares, &c.

CREMONA. The produce and industry of this beautiful city and district are similar to those of the country in which they are situated. [LOMBARDY.]

CRETA LEVIS. This name has been recently given to a kind of drawing pencils, intermediate in character between lead pencils and crayons. Being formed of very fine chalk, they somewhat resemble crayons; but they are put into handles or hollowed sticks like pencils. The pencils can be cut to a fine point; and as they are made of every variety of colour, they form a convenient means of imitating, in a rough but expeditious way, the effects of a water-colour drawing. They are sold at six to twelve shillings per dozen according to the colours.

CREWE, in Cheshire, is one of the most remarkable instances of a thriving and populous town springing into existence in connection with the system of railway communication. It owes its erection entirely to the formation of the London and North Western line of railway. The inhabitants consist almost wholly of persons in the employment of the railway company, with their families, and the tradesmen and shopkeepers required to supply them with the necessaries and conveniences of life. The houses and shops in the town are, of course, nearly all new, and they are well built; the streets are wide, and the footpaths are laid with asphalte. The town is lighted with gas, and well supplied with water; a powerful steam-pump supplying at once the engines in the extensive workshops of the company, the locomotive engines, and the houses in the town. This pump raises from 80,000 to 90,000 gallons of water daily; the portion intended to be used by the inhabitants passes through two filtering processes before reaching the houses. Baths are also provided at a cheap rate. The town of Crewe has a council for the management of the affairs of the community: two-thirds of the council are elected by the workmen and inhabitants, and one-third by the directors of the railway company. Medical attendance and medicine are secured for the workmen and their families on payment of a small weekly rate, the highest charge (that for a married man with a family) being 2*d.* per week. A field in the neighbourhood is used for cricket-playing.

The railway station at Crewe is very spacious and splendid. From this place branch off five lines of railway, affording ready means of communication with all parts of the country. The workshops and machinery of the North Western Railway Company at Crewe are on a very extensive scale. Railway carriages and locomotive engines are manufactured and repaired. The number of carriages of all kinds maintained at Crewe amounts to nearly 700, of which 100 at a time are usually under repair.

CRIMPING MACHINE. Hughes's crimping machine, patented in 1844, is intended to produce all those varied forms in woven goods called crimping, fluting, quilling, and goffering, for ruffs or *rouches.* A female worker employed at this process can goffer about 288 yards of blonde in twelve hours; the new machine will do about eight times that quantity in the same time. The machine consists essentially of a series of rods, laid parallel, and revolving on their axes in contact with one another. The muslin or other material is drawn between the rods, and receives in its passage a series of flutings or other wavy forms, the precise arrangement of which depends on the shape and arrangement of the rods. The machine acts on a principle nearly analogous to that employed in many departments of the sheet metal manufacture; such, for example, as the preparation of corrugated sheet iron for roofs.

CRINAN CANAL, in Argyleshire, was constructed for the purpose of enabling vessels of small burden to dispense with the rather dangerous passage round the Mull of Cantyre, from Lochfyne to the Sound of Jura. The project of forming this canal was first started about 60 years back under the auspices of the then Duke of Argyle. Sir John Rennie, the civil engineer, having surveyed the ground and reported favourably, an act of parliament was obtained, and a company formed in 1793, and the works were forthwith commenced. The canal was opened in 1801. Engineering difficulties in constructing the works, and alterations in the original plans, added considerably to the estimated expense, and parliamentary grants have been more than once made in aid of the company. The canal, although not more than 9 miles in length, has been of great service to the coasting trade of the west of Scotland and the Highlands. The number of locks in the Crinan Canal is 15; the average breadth is 24 feet, and the depth of water 10 feet: if found necessary, 12 feet depth of water could be maintained. Since 1818 the canal has been under the management of the Commissioners of the Caledonian Canal, with the navigation of which it is intimately connected; together these canals form an important portion of the inland passage between Glasgow and Inverness. In 1848 the dues on vessels and merchandise were somewhat reduced, and an increase of traffic is anticipated. Vessels of 200 tons burden can pass through the canal.

CROCKET, is an ornament of frequent use in Gothic architecture. It consists of leafy buds growing out of the angular sides of pinnacles and the label moulding of windows and doors.

CRONSTADT, or KRONSTADT. There are two important commercial towns of this name, one in Transylvania and the other in Russia. Cronstadt in Transylvania manufactures cloth, linens, cottons, coarse woollens, hosiery, woollen yarn, &c., flasks of maple wood, &c. There is a paper-mill, and two grounds for bleaching wax. Cronstadt was the first place in Transylvania where a printing-press was established. The town has a very important commerce in manufactured goods, Austrian and Turkish produce, salt, &c., which is chiefly in the hands of a Greek trading company.

Cronstadt in Russia is the harbour of St. Petersburg, and the principal naval station of Russia. There are three harbours, one of which, capable of containing 600 ships, is allotted to merchantmen. The imperial naval harbour is formed by a mole, and can accommodate 35 ships of the line besides smaller vessels. Adjacent to it are slips for building ships, a powder magazine, a manufactory of pitch, tar, &c. Vessels are repaired and built in the large canal of Peter the Great, which runs directly into the town between the middle and merchant's harbour. Near it are the various docks for repairing ships; the foundry, which supplies annually 1200 tons of bombs, balls, &c.; the admiralty rope walk, tar works, and excellent wet docks. By the Catherine Canal vessels are enabled to take their stores, munition, &c., directly from the store houses. Large vessels load and unload at Cronstadt, and the cargoes are conveyed to and from St. Petersburg by lighters; but vessels drawing not more than 8½ feet water can get over the bar of the Neva.

CROTON AQUEDUCT. [AQUEDUCT.]

CROTON, is the name of a plant which is largely used in medicine. Cascarilla bark is yielded by the *Croton cascarilla*, a tree or shrub growing in the vicinity of Jalapa. It occurs in pieces about a foot long. The colour externally is yellowish, ash-gray, or varying to reddish brown: this last colour is mostly owing to the presence of lichens. The inner surface is a dirty or rusty brown colour. The odour is faintly aromatic: taste bitter, not unpleasant, and stimulating. One pound of bark yields one drachm and a half of volatile oil. This bark is sometimes mixed with cinchona barks, being called *Gray Fever Bark*. *Croton tiglium*, an inhabitant of the Moluccas, Ceylon, and other parts of the East Indies, is a powerful drug; every part, wood, leaves, and fruit, seems to participate equally in the energy. The *Molucca grains*, formerly used in medicine, were the seeds of this species. *Croton lacciferum* is a native of the East Indies. This species is said to furnish the finest of all the sorts of lac, but scarcely ever to find its way to England; it is very pure, of a bright red, and furnishes a brilliant varnish in Ceylon. From the *Croton balsamiferum*, the liqueur called *Eau de Mantes* is distilled.

CRUCIBLE, is a chemical vessel in which substances are exposed to high temperatures. Earthen crucibles are used in assaying ores: for these purposes the refractory kind, called Hessian or Cornish crucibles, are prepared. Black lead crucibles, formed of about three parts of plumbago and one of good clay, are much employed, especially in melting metals. Glass-makers' crucibles are usually made of Stourbridge clay. Crucibles of silver and of platinum are employed in various chemical processes.

CRUTH, or CRWTH, a musical instrument of the violin kind, was formerly much used in Wales. It had six strings and was somewhat of the lute form.

CRYO'PHORUS. Dr. Wollaston gave this name to an instrument invented for the purpose of exhibiting the congelation of water in consequence of evaporation. It consists of two glass bulbs connected by a bent stem. One of the bulbs, if cooled when empty, causes water to freeze in the other, the stem being in vacuo.

CRYPT, is the name given by architects to a low-vaulted chamber, the vaulting of which is supported on columns and the basement walls of a church or cathedral. Some crypts have become the receptacle of the monuments of the dead, as at the abbey of St. Denis. Crypts are far from being common to all churches and cathedrals.

CRYSTALS; CRYSTALLOGRAPHY. Although the study of crystals as a science, apart from their practical applications in the arts, does not belong to the present work, it may be useful to explain certain terms and properties, which are constantly in use when crystals are spoken of. Mineralogists have adopted certain groups of *primary* and *secondary* forms, as a means of classifying crystals. The primary forms, according to one system of crystallography (for there are more systems than one), consist of the *cube*, the *square prism*, the *right rhombic prism*, the *oblique rhombic prism*, the *doubly oblique prism*, and the *rhomboid* or *rhombohedron*. The nature of these forms may be best explained by showing the relations between them. The *cube* has the well-known form of a die, with six equal surfaces. If the lateral edges of the cube be supposed to be longer or shorter than the terminal edges, a *square prism* would be produced; if two opposite lateral edges of a square prism could be pressed towards each other, the parallelism being kept, a *right rhombic prism* would be formed; if this prism could be pressed in the direction of either of the diagonals of its terminal plane, so as to make the figure overhang the base in that direction, an *oblique rhombic prism* would be represented; and if again pressed in the direction of the other diagonal, so that it should overhang the base in both directions, a *doubly oblique prism* would be formed. If a cube be made to stand on one of its angles by placing the fingers on an opposite one, and if, while held in this position, the two angles could be pressed nearer together or drawn further apart, the altered cube would become a *rhomboid*.

The *secondary* forms of crystals are supposed to be occasioned by some natural influence operating upon the first germ of the crystal, and continuing during the period of its increase in size. The number of known secondary forms belonging to each system is already very great; in one mineral, carbonate of lime, they amount to many hundreds. Crystals occur more frequently in the secondary than the primary forms. *Twin crystals* are produced by the union of two or more crystals according to some regular plan, so that, if any number of twin crystals of the same kind of mineral should be found they would be fashioned in the same manner.

The crystallisation of salts from solution in fluids generally takes place when the solutions are considerably evaporated, but the degree of evaporation is very different for different substances. Some salts begin to crystallise at the surface very soon after evaporation commences; and others (for example sugar) must be evaporated to the consistence of a thick syrup before any crystals will be formed. Hot fluids will generally dissolve more matter than cold ones, and crystals are frequently produced during the cooling of the hot solution. Some soluble substances however cannot be brought to crystallise under any circumstances hitherto tried; but, on the solvent evaporating, a thick pasty matter is left, which by further evaporation becomes a hard solid mass. Camphor affords an instance of the formation of crystals by volatilization. The slags of furnaces will frequently be found to contain crystallised matter; and the common rolls of sulphur when broken will frequently present small cavities lined with thin needle-like crystals. Becquerel, Crosse, Fox, and others, by the electrical induction of chemical action, have effected the crystallisation of mineral bodies which are wholly insoluble in any fluid which does not subject them to immediate chemical change.

CUBA is the largest of the islands which constitute the Columbian Archipelago, in the foreign West Indies. The objects raised for consumption and exportation are sugar, coffee, tobacco, cotton, cocoa, and indigo; but the last three on a very small scale. As immense tracts are not cultivated, but only used as pasture ground, the number of cattle is very great, and hides form an article of exportation. About 2,000,000 acres, or one-fourteenth of the whole surface of the island, is under cultivation. The uncultivated part contains large prairies of great fertility, on which great numbers of cattle pasture; but the greatest part is overgrown with large forest-trees, some of which supply excellent timber for ship-building. Gold and copper have been found in the Sierra del Cobre.

In few countries has commerce increased so rapidly as in Cuba. About 1780 the exportation of its own produce amounted to little more than two millions of Spanish dollars in value: in 1760 the produce of sugar and coffee together amounted to 5,000,000 lbs.; in 1800, to above 40,000,000 lbs. In 1820 the exports of these articles reached 100,000,000 lbs.; and in 1847 the quantity of sugar alone exported had advanced to 256,800 tons, or 575,232,000 lbs. In 1842 the exports of Cuba amounted to 26,000,000 dollars. Havana is by far the largest port for foreign trade. The chief articles of importation are provisions, particularly flour, rice, and maize, butter, cheese, candles, tallow, jerked beef and hams, and salted fish and cod. Brandy and the wines of Spain, France, Portugal, and Germany, also form a considerable branch of importation. As Cuba has no manufactures, cotton stuffs, woollen goods, linens, hardwares, and silk stuffs, are imported to a large amount. Of the whole exports, rather more than one-third are to England, and one-fifth to the United States. Of the whole imports about one-eighth are from England, and one-fourth from the United States. The recent change in the sugar duties has largely increased the English consumption of Cuba sugar.

The exports from Great Britain to Cuba, in 1848, amounted in value to 733,169*l*. The chief items were:—

	£
Brass and copper manufactures	19,452
Coals	14,469
Cotton manufactures	228,986
Earthenware	24,411
Hardware and cutlery	38,578
Iron and steel goods	83,250
Linen manufactures	218,121
Woollen manufactures	41,207

Among the articles imported from Cuba in 1848 were:—

Coffee	596,250 lbs.
Molasses	42,511 cwts.
Rum	158,817 gals.
Sugar	734,862 cwts.
Tobacco	512,984 lbs.

The internal traffic, formerly impeded by the badness of the roads, is much facilitated by the introduction of railroads, of which there were 800 miles open in 1847; the coasting-

KNIGHT'S CYCLOPÆDIA OF THE INDUSTRY OF ALL NATIONS.

No. 18

trade is active, 4,000 small vessels being used to bring the produce of the neighbourhood to Havana alone.

CUDDAPAH DIAMONDS. [DIAMOND.]

CUIRASS or CUIRASSE. The cuirass, in former days, was a piece of defensive armour, made of metal, and serving to cover the body from the neck to the girdle, both before and behind; the front, called the breast-plate, and the hinder part or back plate were fastened to each other by straps, buckles, hooks, or some other contrivance. The Egyptians are said to have been the inventors of such armour, but among that people it consisted of folds of linen. Cuirasses of brass or steel, and occasionally of gold or silver highly ornamented, were used by the Greeks and Romans. After having been long disused, the cuirass was revived in Europe about the middle of the fourteenth century. In the Mediæval Exhibition of 1850 many curious specimens of these old cuirasses were collected. In the English service the cuirass was again disused after the reign of George II. Since the year 1820, however, it has been revived as part of the accoutrements of the life-guards.

CULTIVATOR. The names of *Cultivator* and *Scarifier* are sometimes given to an agricultural machine on three wheels, which has five arms or vertical bars, the lower ends of which are shaped something like ploughshares. These points or rather blades project forward, and act to a slight depth upon the earth as the machine proceeds. They are adapted for strong retentive clay soils. A Cultivator was exhibited at the Smithfield Cattle Show, 1850, by Mr. Smith of Uxbridge; similar in principle to some now in use at the royal farms in Windsor Forest.

Harris's Annular Cultivator, registered in 1850, has seven shares or cutters ranged round a circle, intended to ensure a more equable action on the soil than when they are arranged in right lines

CUMBERLAND. This county is rich in minerals; comprising silver, copper, lead, iron, plumbago, limestone, and coal. The principal lead mines are situated at Alston, and are almost exclusively the property of Greenwich Hospital, to which institution they were appropriated by act of parliament on the attainder of the Earl of Derwentwater. Silver and copper are found in some of the mines in the same veins with the lead ore. Silver and lead are got in abundance at Greenside and Eagle-crag in Patterdale. Veins of lead-ore have been found and worked between Skiddaw and Saddleback, in Buttermere, Newlands, and Thornthwaite. There are copper mines at Alston, Caldbeck, and at Wythburn. There is one also below the level of Derwent-water, and another in the parish of Lowes-water. A very rich vein of gold is said to have been discovered at Newlands by a German, in the time of Queen Elizabeth; but the working was discontinued in consequence of a law-suit between that queen and the Earl of Northumberland, then the lord of the manor of Derwent-fells. Iron-ore is raised in great abundance near Egremont; the thickness of the band of ore, which is hard solid metal, is said to be between twenty-four and twenty-five feet. The quantity of iron ore shipped from Ulverston and Barrow is very great: 300 carts of ore are taken daily from Lindale to Barrow for exportation. The ore of this county produces upwards of double the quantity of metal that is got from iron ore in general; and it is often mixed in the smelting furnaces with the South Wales ore to produce a particular quality of iron. Coal is worked to a large amount at Whitehaven, Workington, and in the vicinity of Maryport, from whence it is exported to Ireland and the west of Scotland. The eastern part of the county also abounds in coal, particularly Tindale-fell, Talkin, and Blenkinsop, which produce the chief supply for Carlisle, Brampton, Penrith, and the intermediate country. Some of this coal is now exported at Port Carlisle to Ireland and Scotland. There are collieries at Gilcrux, Arkleby, Oughterside, Bolton, and Hewer-hill. Limestone is very abundant in many parts of the county. In some places it is burnt in great quantities for exportation, particularly to the west of Scotland. At Catlands the limestone is overlaid by the coal measures on all sides. Plumbago, or black lead, is found, in irregular masses, in a rock of gray felspar porphyry at Borrowdale near Keswick. A little cobalt has been got at Newlands; and antimony near Bassenthwaite; but this is not, we believe, now worked. Lapis calaminaris, small quantities of manganese, galena, iron pyrites, and spar of various kinds and of different colours and forms are found in several places. Slate of a pale blue colour and of the finest quality is plentiful in Cumberland.

The agriculture of the county has improved considerably of late years, and great quantities of corn and produce of various kinds are now exported. The chief exports are from Port Carlisle, Whitehaven, Workington, and Maryport, and consist of cattle, sheep, poultry, grain, potatoes, butter, bacon, &c. The land being divided into small farms, the dairies are necessarily on a small scale, though their produce is excellent, and bears a high price in the market.

The cotton and woollen manufactures are

carried on to a small extent in Cumberland, and there are manufactures connected with the mining products; but it can scarcely be called a manufacturing county.

CUMIN, or CUMMIN, is the fruit (miscalled the seed) of a plant cultivated in the East. Externally it is of a grayish yellow colour, and is larger than that of caraway or anise. The odour is strongly aromatic and rather unpleasant; the taste is warm, bitter, and disagreeable. The odour and taste are mainly due to a volatile oil which is more abundant in this fruit than in most umbelliferous plants: one pound yields half an ounce of this oil, according to some authorities; while ten pounds yield only three ounces and a half, according to others. Notwithstanding this large quantity of oil, the fruits are frequently eaten by insects.

The disagreeable odour of Cumin seems to have gradually discarded it from medicine for man, and restricted its use to veterinary medicine. Its employment in this way may be a relic of its ancient repute, for the Israelites esteemed it highly as a remedy for cattle after the bites of insects. Still it is a valuable drug; it enters into the composition of many curry-powders, but should be introduced into these in very small quantity.

CUMNOCK, in Ayrshire, affords an illustration of the effect even of a trifling manufacture to give a sort of celebrity to a town. Weaving and hand-sewing employ a portion of the population; threshing mills are made here, and pottery was formerly extensively made; but the manufacture which has rendered the village somewhat celebrated is that of the well known wooden snuff-boxes, which are so generally admired.

CURRANT, a well known hardy fruit, produced by two species of the genus *Ribes*. The red currant is remarkable for the mixture of sweet and acid in its fruit, and for the beauty of its semitransparent red or yellow berries. In the fruit of the black currant, a powerful and agreeable aromatic principle takes the place of acidity. The currants of the grocers' shops are the dried berries of a small kind of grape, chiefly cultivated in the Morea and the Ionian Islands, Corfu, Zante, &c. Of these dried currants no less than 429,729 cwts. were imported in 1850. A machine has been lately registered by Mr. Weatherley for cleaning dried currants. In the ordinary method, the currants are cleaned by rubbing them in a sieve or cloth. But in Mr. Weatherley's machine, there is a hollow case made of wire gauze; within this is a cylinder or axle, from which radiate bundles of split whalebone. When the currants are put into the case, and the cylinder made to rotate, the whalebone brushes clean them from dirt, and the dirt falls through the meshes of the wire gauze.

CUSCO-CHINA. This bark comes from Cuzco in Peru; but the tree which yields it is altogether unknown. The alkaloid is procured by the same process as is used for cinchonia, which it resembles in its physical qualities, but differs from in its chemical properties. The taste is more bitter, rather heating, and subastringent. It is equally insoluble in water, but easily so in alcohol and in sulphuric æther. It forms with acids salts which resemble those of cinchonia, but have a more bitter taste.

CUSTOMS-DUTIES consist for the most part of taxes levied upon goods and produce brought for consumption from foreign countries; but such duties are also sometimes collected upon exports made to foreign countries, and upon goods and produce passing from one port to another of the same country. Since the abolition of the export duty on coal in 1845, the only duties outwards consist of an *ad valorem* duty of one-half per cent. on the shipment of some articles of British production.

Shortly before Sir Robert Peel's fiscal reforms, there were customs' duties levied on considerably more than a thousand different articles; he reduced this number to 813 in 1842, and to 382 in 1845; and further reductions have still taken place.

The net amount of duties collected in the United Kingdom on imported articles, after the deduction of drawbacks, repayments, &c., in the several years from 1830 to 1850 was as follows:—

1830	£21,622,683
1831	21,272,263
1832	21,714,524
1833	20,892,902
1834	21,282,060
1835	21,873,814
1836	22,758,369
1837	21,849,109
1838	22,121,038
1839	22,958,254
1840	23,153,958
1841	23,302,152
1842	22,356,324
1843	22,450,074
1844	23,864,494
1845	20,196,856
1846	22,168,735
1847	21,539,775
1848	22,477,609
1849	22,194,600
1850	21,904,566

CUTCH, a principality in the west of India, is one of those in which cotton is grown. The cultivation is carried on extensively, and the produce exported in return for grain, of which a sufficiency is not grown for consumption, and which is procured from Gujerat and Sinde. Iron ore occurs generally throughout the country, and in most parts coal is found in abundance. The wool of the Cutch sheep is of long staple but coarse, answering well for the manufacture of blankets and carpeting: the weight of the fleece averages from four and a half to five pounds. Coarse woollen cloths are made and used by the inhabitants.

Mandavee, the principal sea-port of Cutch, is situated on the shore of the Indian Ocean, and is the most populous place in the principality. The port is an open roadstead with a creek; there are 250 vessels belonging to the place, by means of which a very considerable trade is carried on with Zanguebar and the whole east coast of Africa, with the Red Sea and Arabia, with the Persian Gulf, Mekran and Sinde, and with India as far as Ceylon. The vessels employed in this traffic vary from 25 to 200 tons burden; they carry a large lateen sail, and have two masts, but are never decked; they are navigated by native pilots, who have acquired the use of the quadrant, and steer by charts. The most valuable branch of the trade of Mandavee is that carried on with the eastern coast of Africa, a distance of 3000 miles, whence the merchants of Cutch procure ivory, rhinoceros hides, and other valuable articles. The principal article of export is cotton.

CUTLERY. Nearly all the cutlery used in this country, and a vast quantity of that which is met with in other parts of the world, is made at Sheffield. It is one of those curious examples which the history of manufactures often presents, of the settlement of a particular branch of industry in one spot, where the skill of the inhabitants becomes habituated to that particular manufacture.

Cutlery is generally considered to comprise most steel cutting instruments, such as table knives, pen and pocket knives, lancets, razors, scythes, saws, scissors, shears, spades, edge tools, &c. Swords would also come under this classification; but it is remarkable that swords are made principally at Birmingham, and not at Sheffield. The number of processes to make each kind of cutting instrument depends on various circumstances. In making a *table-knife*, for example, a piece of bar steel is cut off; it is forged to a rough blade shape; a small piece of iron is welded to it, and forged to form the tang; the shoulder, between the tang and the blade, is fashioned into shape by swaging or hammering it with a die; and the knife thus far finished, is tempered, ground, sharpened, and polished.

In making a *fork*, the end of a steel bar is first made red hot; it is hammered so as to give a rough approximation to the shape of the shank or tang; it is again heated, and a blow from a die or stamp gives the proper contour; the prongs are cut out by a powerful blow from a stamp of peculiar form; and the fork is finally annealed, hardened, ground, and polished. It is this process of fork-grinding which has so often been made a subject for comment; the fork is ground *dry* upon a stone wheel, and the particles of steel and grit are constantly entering the lungs of the workmen, thereby ruining the health and shortening the duration of life. Many contrivances have been devised for obviating this evil; but the fork-grinders have not seconded these efforts so zealously as might have been anticipated.

In making *pen* and *pocket* knives, a slender rod of steel is heated at the end, hammered to the form of a blade, and carried through many subsequent processes. But the putting together of these hinged knives requires more time than the making of the blades, and affords a curious example of minute detail. When the pieces of ivory, pearl, tortoiseshell, horn, bone, or other substance, which are to form the outer surface of the handle, are roughly cut to shape; when the blade has been forged and ground; and when the steel for the spring is procured—the whole are placed in the hands of a workman, who proceeds to build up a clasp knife from the little fragments placed at his disposal. So many are the details to be attended to, that a common two-bladed knife has to pass through his hands seventy or eighty times before it is finished.

In making a *razor*, more care is required than in most kinds of knife making. A piece of steel is heated and hammered at the end; it is again hammered on a round anvil to make the blade concave; by cutting and forging it is brought to the peculiar shape which a razor-blade often presents; it is ground upon a small grindstone, to give the concavity without which it could not be sharpened to the requisite degree; it is tempered with very great care, and is finally polished. The recently-patented *Guard* razors are somewhat complicated contrivances for shielding the skin of a clumsy user from being cut.

The making of *handles* for cutlery is a very large department of Sheffield industry. Mother o' pearl, ivory, ebony, bone, horn, &c., are purchased in large quantities; and the making of each kind of handle or haft constitutes a distinct employment.

A method was introduced a few years ago of ornamenting cutlery by transferring the impression of an engraving to the surface of the steel. The engraving may be from a copper plate or from a wood cut, printed in the one case by the roller-press and in the other by the printing-press. The ink is a composition of asphaltum and bees-wax. The impressions on paper are applied to the steel, and an acid liquor fixes the device.

Solingen, in Germany, is designated the Sheffield of that country; and it is expected that at the forthcoming Exhibition a trial of skill will be made in this as in other departments of manufacture.

CYANOGEN, or bicarburet of nitrogen, is a gaseous compound, discovered by Gay Lussac in 1815. It is colourless, and has a peculiar and pungent odour. It is inflammable, and burns with a purple flame; but a taper immersed in it is extinguished. It is not readily decomposed by heat. It is an essential ingredient of *Prussian Blue*. Combined with oxygen it forms *Cyanic Acid*, a sour liquid.

CYANOMETER, is an instrument which was invented by M. de Saussure for the purpose of enabling an observer to ascertain the intensity of colour in the sky. It consists of a circular plate or ring, of metal or pasteboard, on the surface of which, about the circumference, is a band divided by radii into fifty-three equal compartments. One of these is white, and those which follow in succession are coloured with blue of different degrees of intensity from the most faint to the deepest which can be produced; the rest of the compartments are coloured with mixtures of Prussian Blue and Ivory Black, and gradually increase in darkness to the last division, which is quite black. The colours laid on are such, that at equal distances from the eye the tint in each compartment cannot be distinguished from that of the next inferior to it, when the latter is near the eye. The white space being zero, the others are marked, in succession from thence, with the numbers 1, 2, 3, &c.

In using the instrument, the observer, who should be in the open air, holds it up between himself and that part of the sky at which he intends to ascertain the colour, when the compartment which, to the eye, appears to be exactly equal to it in tint expresses by its number the required intensity of the blue colour in that part of the sky. Such an instrument is useful in meteorological observations.

CYCLOGRAPH, or ARCOGRAPH, is an instrument for drawing arcs of circles without centres, used in architectural and engineering drawing when the centres are too distant to be conveniently accessible. Bricklayers and masons when they wish to strike an arc upon the face of a wall, have recourse to a very simple but perfect mode of accomplishing the object, by driving a nail into the wall at each extremity of the intended arc, and then nailing two straight laths or rods together at such an angle, that while their external sides or edges are in contact with the nails driven in the wall, their apex or meeting point shall touch the crown of the required arc or arch. When secured to each other at the required angle, the laths are so moved that, while they remain in contact with the nails, the apex may traverse the whole distance from one nail to another, in doing which it will describe the required curve, which may be marked on the wall by a piece of chalk carried round with it. The same plan may be adopted in drawing on paper, substituting pins for the nails, and a piece of stout cardboard, cut to the required angle, for the laths. Mr. Rotch's *Arcograph*, Mr. Alderson's *Curvilinead*, Mr. Warcup's *Curvograph*, and Mr. Peter Nicholson's *Centrolinead*, all described in the 'Transactions' of the Society of Arts, are instruments for producing somewhat similar results. The centrolinead may be compared to a T-rule, in which the transom consists of two pieces adjustible to any required angle with each other, and the centre of which, answering to the apex of the cyclographs above described, is precisely on a line with the fiducial or drawing edge of the stem or long limb of the rule. The instrument being once adjusted to the required angles, and having its angular transom laid against two fixed pins, just like the angle of a cyclograph, any number of converging lines may be drawn by it as readily as parallel lines are drawn by a common T-rule.

CYLINDER. The manufacture of cylinders for steam engines and other purposes is noticed under BORING and FOUNDING.

CYLINDRICAL LENSES are made by grinding each of the opposite surfaces of a plate of glass in the form of the segment obtained on cutting a cylinder by a plane parallel to its axis. Two segments thus obtained being placed with their plane surfaces in contact, and so disposed that straight lines parallel to the axis of the cylinder drawn on the convex surface of one may be at right angles to lines similarly drawn on the other, would constitute a lens of the kind here indicated.

Lenses of this kind were devised and executed soon after the commencement of the present century by an optician of Paris, who introduced them as eye-glasses in spectacles in place of the usual spherical lenses. This person afterwards, conceiving that in such lenses the chromatic aberration was destroyed, attempted to employ them as simple object-glasses for telescopes; but they have since been found unfitted for this purpose.

CYMAMETER. Mr. Fenn registered under this title, in 1850, an ingenious contrivance for making copies of the outlines of capitals, cornices, mouldings, and other architectural figures. It consists, essentially, of a large number of very thin laths or plates, all of equal length and placed one on another; when one end of these laths is pressed against a moulding or other device, the other end is driven out, the laths which press against a convex surface being driven out further than those pressing against a concave surface; so that the outer extremities of all the laths form collectively a type of the moulding or device.

This is simply a new application of a principle practised long ago for other purposes.

CYMBALS. These musical instruments are traceable to the remotest ages of antiquity, and, with no great change in form, are still used by the moderns. They are always in pairs, are made of brass, and are nearly flat, about twelve inches in diameter, the central part sunk in; and at the back of the sunken poition is a strap by which each instrument is held.

CYPRUS. This fine island, which has remained in the hands of the Turks for nearly three centuries, is naturally fertile. Cotton of the finest quality, excellent wine, and all kinds of fruit are produced; but agriculture is in a most backward state. Besides the productions already named, madder, opium, oranges, lemons, pomegranates, &c., are grown. The carob-tree abounds in some districts; its succulent pods are exported to Egypt and Syria, while the fruit called St. John's Bread is used as an article of food. On the mountains are forests of fine timber. Sheep and cattle thrive. Copper, asbestos, talc, rock-crystal, and various other minerals are found. Salt is made on the sea-shore. Game and fish are plentiful. But these natural advantages are made of little account; for under the Turkish rule the inhabitants are oppressed and miserable, and show little industry, either productive or commercial.

D

DACCA, in Bengal, is principally known in Europe for its manufactures of cotton goods. The striped and figured muslins of Dacca were long celebrated throughout the world. The beauty and delicacy of these fabrics were once unrivalled; but of late years the weavers of Paisley and Manchester have so successfully competed with those of Dacca, that a large proportion of the families in that district, who have for many generations employed themselves in their production, have been compelled to adopt other pursuits. Another reason for this change may be found in the altered condition of the former lords of the country, among whom the curious fabrics of Dacca were held in the highest estimation, and who are now unable to gratify their taste for costly apparel.

DADO, a term for the die or plane face of a pedestal. The dado employed in the interiors of buildings is a continuous pedestal, with a plinth and base-moulding, and a cornice or dado moulding surmounting the die. This continuous pedestal, with its moulding, is constructed of wood, and is usually about the height of a chair-back, and is now used to protect the stucco-work or paper of the wall. Some dados are panelled.

DAIRY; DAIRY FARMS. A dairy-house should be situated on a dry spot somewhat elevated, on the side of a gentle declivity, and on a porous soil. It should be on the west or north-west side of a hill if possible, or at least sheltered from the north, east, and south, by high trees. Coolness in summer, and an equable temperature in winter, are essential requisites in a dairy.

The following description of a Netherland cow-house and dairy under one roof combines all that is useful, with considerable neatness internally and externally:—It is a building about sixty feet long by thirty wide, with a verandah running round three sides of it. The dairy-room is sunk below the level of the soil, and is paved with brick. The sides are covered with Dutch-tiles, and the arched roof with hard cement. The cow-house, like all in Holland, has a broad passage in the middle, and the cows stand with their heads towards this passage, which is paved with clinkers, or bricks set on edge. Their tails are towards the wall, along which runs a broad gutter sunk six or eight inches below the level of the place on which the cows stand. The cows stand or lie on a sloping brick floor, and have but a small quantity of litter allowed them, which is removed every day and carried to the dung-heap or to the pig-sties. Whenever the litter is removed, the bricks are swept clean; and in summer they are washed with water. In Holland the cows' tails are kept up by a cord tied to the end of them, which passes over a pulley with a weight at the other end, as we see practised with horses that have been nicked; thus they cannot hit themselves, or the person who milks them. The cows are fastened in a way so as to give them freedom of movement without striking their neighbours with their horns. The mangers or troughs are of wood, or of bricks cemented together, and are kept as clean as all the rest of the cow-house. In Switzerland the cow-houses are similar, but there is also a rack, the back of which towards the passage shuts up with a board on hinges.

The utensils of the dairy, such as pails, churns, vats, &c., are usually made of white wood, and are easily kept clean by scalding and scouring. Leaden troughs are used in large dairies. Brass pans have the advantage of being readily warmed on a chafing-dish in winter. In Devonshire tin or brass pans are frequently used instead of earthenware. In Holland the milk is invariably carried in brass vessels. Cast-iron pans have been invented, which are tinned inside. Glass and white ware are used for the same purpose; especially owing to the repeal of the glass duties, since which time glass has become extensively used in dairies.

The dairy farms of England are chiefly in Gloucestershire, Devonshire, and Cheshire. They require a smaller capital than arable farms of the same extent. The chief outlay is in the purchase of cows.

The principal duties of the dairy are noticed under BUTTER; CHEESE; CHURN; MILK.

DALAGO'A or DELAGOA BAY, on the eastern coast of Southern Africa, is much frequented by whalers, as the bay abounds in whales. The Portuguese have a small fort on the western shore of the bay. Supplies are abundant and cheap; piece-goods, buttons, beads, cutlery, brass wire, old clothes, iron, copper pipes, spirits, sugar, &c., are readily taken for bullocks, fowls, vegetables, fish, hippopotami teeth, gold dust, ambergris, &c.

DALMATIA. As a part of the Austrian dominions, the produce and industry of Dalmatia have been briefly noticed under AUSTRIA.

DAMASCENE WORK. The damask, damascene, or damascus work, so often met with in choice specimens of metal manufacture, especially on the old Damascus sword-blades, is a method of producing a pattern or design by encrusting one metal with another. It was introduced into Europe from the Levant, where it was much practised in the middle ages, especially at Damascus. The metals usually employed were silver or gold on iron or copper, gold on silver, or silver on gold; but any other combination would equally come within the principle of the art.

There were several different modes of damascening. If the metal to be damascened were hard, its surface was wrought into fine lines crossing each other, and the designs were afterwards traced upon it; the design marks were filled in with the metal inlay, which was fixed by a strong pressure or by hammering; and the entire work was then burnished, by which the lines uncovered by the incrustation were erased, and a fine polish given to the surface. Another method was that of hatching the incised lines only, and of fixing the incrustation as before. In a third method, when the incrusting metal was of a ductile nature, the pattern was simply incised in outline, and the body of the design left on the same level as the rest of the surface; a thin sheet of metal was then laid upon these designs, and fixed by the insertion of its edges into the exterior incisions; the incrustation was thus in relief, and was afterwards occasionally engraved. A fourth kind of damascene work partook of the nature of *picqué*, or a design formed by small pins or studs, much in vogue in England in the seventeenth century.

Various European cities had artists who practised damascening; but Venice and Milan were the chief.

At the Mediæval Exhibition of 1850, several beautiful specimens of damascene-work were collected, including candlesticks, tankards, inkstands, shields, etuis, swords, &c.; but the most exquisite was Cellini's far-famed shield, presented by Francis I. to Henry VIII., and now the property of Her Majesty. It is made of embossed steel, damascened with gold and silver. It has represented upon it in compartments, scenes from the history of Julius Cæsar, each consisting of numerous figures in relief of the most highly finished execution.

DAMASCUS is the chief emporium of the trade in European manufactures with Bagdad, Bassora, Persia, and the neighbouring countries, whither goods are conveyed by camels; it is also a place of great manufacturing industry, and contains silk factories, cotton printing and dyeing establishments, tobacco factories, copper and iron foundries, glassworks, soaperies, &c. There are nearly 800 merchants engaged in the sale of damask cloths alone. The manufacture of Damascus blades, once so famous, no longer exists. Saddles and bridles, both rich and highly finished, fine cabinet-work, and rich jewellery are among the articles of Damascus industry.

DAMASK, a peculiar kind of woven cloths composed both of flax and of silk, which are believed to have been originally brought from Damascus. Silk damask weaving was introduced into England from Flanders in the latter half of the 16th century, and linen damask weaving in the latter half of the 18th. Damask cloths are of thick texture, but fine in quality, and the weaving of them puts into requisition all the skill of the weaver for the production of the elaborate patterns which they bear.

DAMSON, or DAMASCENE, is the well-known name of a kind of plums, cultivated in this country for the sake of their hardiness and prolific habits. They are a mere form of the domestic plum, from which there are no certain characters to distinguish them, except the abundance of their late oval fruit, and the property they possess of propagating by suckers. All the varieties are used for kitchen purposes principally, and are generally confined to the gardens of cottages or farm-houses where the quantity of produce is more valued than its quality. Much the finest variety of this sort of plum is that called the Shropshire Damson, which is extensively multiplied in the nurseries by grafting.

DANUBE, called by the Germans the *Donau*, and by the Hungarians tho *Duna*, is a river of the first rank, and the second of European rivers, being inferior only to the Volga. Its course is calculated to be about 1770 miles, and the surface drained by it and its numerous tributaries probably exceeds 300,000 square miles. Steam navigation is established on the Danube. The voyage is divided into several *strecke* or portions — Donauwörth to Ratisbon, Ratisbon to Linz, Linz to Vienna, Vienna to Pesth, Pesth to Orsova. From Orsova, or rather from a station below it called Drenkova, to Skela Gladova, a distance of 54 miles, the river is not navigable except for light cutters, owing to the rapids, whirlpools, and dangerous ledges that occur in this interval. Passengers are conveyed between these stations in carriages along a splendid road cut in the rocks that line the river. The remaining portions of the voyage are from Gladova to Galatz, Galatz to Odessa, Odessa to Constantinople. In consequence of the melting of the snows the Danube rises from June to the middle of July, and does not begin to sink till the middle of August. This period is very favourable to the navigation of the river from the increased depth of water.

DANZIG. This important Prussian city owes its commerce and prosperity to its harbour, and to the extensive inland navigation afforded by the Vistula and its numerous tributaries, by which the corn, timber, and other products of Poland and the Ukraine are conveyed to Danzig. The town is traversed by the Radaune and Motlau, feeders of the Vistula.

There are yards and slips for ship-building; sugar refineries, spirit and liqueur distilleries, breweries, and copperworks; and manufactories of silks, woollens, linens, leathers, hats, and gloves, soap and starch, earthenware, arms, steel-ware, hats, tobacco, &c. The town has a very considerable export trade, consisting of corn, timber, flour, linseed, rapeseed, deals, staves, ashes, quills, spirits, black beer, spelter, wool, flax, hemp, &c. The imports aro composed of wine, brandy, rum, raw cotton, coffee, herrings, iron and steel wares, indigo, lime and plaster, sugar, salt, tobacco, &c. The gross value of the imports is about 400,000*l.* annually; about one-fourth of the imports in value are brought from England. The gross value of the exports nearly reaches two millions sterling annually, of which England takes nearly three-fourths.

DARIEN. The projects for making a railroad or a canal over this isthmus will be better noticed under PANAMA.

DARLINGTON. The trade of Darlington is considerable: for a long period the principal manufactures were of camlets and other woollens; sixty years ago moreens and similar stuffs were made: the woollen manufacture was superseded in a great degree by that of linens, as huckabacks, diapers, sheetings, and checks; but this branch of industry has also declined, and the chief occupation of the inhabitants now is combing wool and making woollen yarn (which is used for imitation India shawls, Brussels carpets, &c.), spinning flax, grinding optical glasses, and the manufacture of brass and iron. There are very extensive worsted mills.

DARTFORD. The first paper-mill erected in this country is usually stated to have been at Dartford on the site of the powder-mills; but this has lately been disproved in 'Notes and Queries.' The first mill established in England for rolling and slitting iron is also said to have been near Dartford. The trade of Dartford is considerable. There are chalk-pits near the town; oil, powder, and paper mills in the neighbourhood on the river Darent; two corn-mills on a large scale worked by water-power and steam; also a large iron foundry and manufactory of machinery. At a short distance from the town are a cotton-mill and silk printing works.

DAVY, SIR HUMPHRY, must be regarded as one whose discoveries have afforded important aid to manufacturing industry, although relating in the first instance to scientific chemistry. He was born at Penzance in 1778. His father was a carver in wood. In the year 1795 he was apprenticed to Mr. Borlase, a surgeon and apothecary of Penzance, where he appears to have laid down an extensive plan of study, not merely of the sciences which related to his profession, but the learned languages, mathematics, history, &c. In 1798 he was considered competent by Dr. Beddoes to take charge of an establishment which he had founded at Bristol under the name of the Pneumatic Institution. In the next two years he wrote several essays on chemical subjects; and in 1801 he came to London, and on the 25th of April he gave his first lecture at the Royal Institution. He began with the history of galvanism, detailed the successive discoveries, and described the different methods of accumulating it; and on the 31st of May, 1802, he was appointed professor. From the year 1800 to 1807 a great variety of subjects attracted his attention, especially galvanism and electro chemical science; the examination of astringent vegetable matter in connection with the art of tanning; and the analysis of rocks and minerals with relation to geology and to agricultural chemistry. In November 1807, his second Bakerian Lecture was read, in which he announced the most important and unexpected discovery of the decomposition of the fixed alkalies by galvanism, and of the metallic nature of their bases, to which he gave the names of potassium and sodium. From the year 1808 to 1814, twelve papers by Davy were read before the Royal Society, and published in their 'Transactions,' relating to various chemical and electro-chemical subjects, and all containing details of original and important researches. He showed that the earths barytes, strontian, lime, and magnesia, are oxides of metals, and he laid the foundation which has enabled other chemists to prove the same thing in respect to other earths. He made important additions to the existing knowledge concerning sulphur, phosphorus, carbon, chlorine, and alkalies, and indeed extended almost every department of chemical science. In 1810 he published the first volume of his 'Elements of Chemical Philosophy,' which, although it bears marks of haste, contains much interesting matter: no further portion of this work was printed. His elements of Agricultural Chemistry,' which appeared soon after, is a work containing much useful matter, and replete with sound and practical views of the subject. One of his greatest inventions was that of the miner's safety-lamp, the first paper in relation to which appeared in the 'Philosophical Transactions' for 1815, and the last in 1817.

All Davy's discoveries have since been turned to account in industrial processes, especially in manufacturing chemistry. This great chemist died in 1829.

DEALS are boards of fir above 7 inches in width, and of various lengths exceeding 6 feet. If less than 7 inches wide, they are called battens. The duty on deals or boards since April 5, 1848, is 1*l.* the load, if imported from a foreign country; but if from a British possession it is 2*s.* the load.

DECOCTIONS are formed by subjecting the harder parts of plants, which are not easily penetrated by liquids, or are insoluble in water of a low temperature, to the process of boiling, generally in water, but sometimes in oil. By this means much of the substance is dissolved, and the active principles of the plant are imbibed by the fluid, which is then used medicinally, either internally or externally. This method of extracting the medicinal properties of plants is inadmissible when their powers depend upon any aromatic or volatile principle, such as essential oils, which are dissipated by the high temperature. In many other instances this process is not only unnecessary, but injurious, being employed when infusion is sufficient, even when cold water is used for the purpose of infusion. The heat is apt to destroy the very principles which are desired to be obtained in many cases; and this process is most suitable to those substances which are both nutritious and medicinal, such as Iceland Moss. Many principles which are dissolved by the water at a boiling temperature are deposited by it on cooling; on which account the liquid should always be strained while hot, and the contents of the bottle shaken up before each dose be poured out. Aromatic liquids are frequently added to the fluid after it is strained; or the aromatic substance may be placed at the bottom of the vessel into which the hot decoction is strained, and, after being allowing to infuse for a few hours, may then be applied to the use intended. A better method however is to add some aromatic tincture after the straining, as the spirit retards the tendency to decomposition, while it imparts the flavour and qualities of the substances from which it had been prepared.

The decoctions employed in medicine are so numerous, that a mere list of them would occupy considerable space. They are prepared from bark, berries, rind, root, stems, seeds, pods, kernels, &c.

DEER SKINS, are tanned into leather for various purposes. From 40,000 to 80,000 are imported annually.

DELFT, a large town in the province of South Holland, was formerly famous for its pottery, to which it gave its name; but this manufacture has been supplanted even in Holland by the superior pottery of England; the earthenware of Delft is now of the coarser kind, and not more than 200 persons are employed in the manufacture. Manufactures of woollen cloths and tobacco-pipes are carried on. The blue Delft ware, and carpeting from the same town, will find a place in the Industrial Exhibition of 1851.

DELHI. This once-celebrated Indian city retains something of its former manufacturing and trading eminence. The commerce is still extensive, particularly in shawls, of which it is a great mart. They are brought from Cashmere in large quantities, some plain, to have borders sewn upon them, and to be embroidered in gold and silk. The goldsmiths are much celebrated for the elegance and delicacy of the jewellery which they produce.

The following announcement in the public journals is interesting, in connection with the forthcoming Exhibition of Industry. "The renowned Delhi seal-cutters have nearly finished the seals which are being cut for the Queen and Prince Albert, under the superintendence of Budi-oo-deen Ulee Khan. The seal for the Queen is described as a cornelian, with the corners cut off, on which is engraved an inscription in Hindostanee. Prince Albert's seal is cut on a blood-stone. The inscriptions are in the true grandiose style of the East. Besides these, Budi-oo-deen has prepared two beautiful emeralds for seal rings, to be presented by himself as specimens of his skill; one for the Queen, three eighths of an inch in length, by two-eighths in breadth."

DEMULCENTS are medicinal agents which have the property of protecting sensible surfaces from the action of irritating matter, by hindering it from coming in direct contact with them. When much water is present in any demulcent liquid, the action is partly that of a diluent, but the chief benefit results from the bland nature of the substance, or from its viscidity. Demulcents are either solutions, such as mucilage of gum arabic, or certain substances mechanically diffused through water or milk, such as wax, spermaceti, or suet.

DEMURRAGE, in shipping affairs, is the term used to denote the money payable to the owner of a ship on the part of the shippers or consignees of goods, as compensation for detention beyond the time stipulated for her loading or discharge, as the same is expressed in the charter-party or bills of lading.

DENMARK is principally an agricultural country. The most fertile parts are the islands of Laaland and Falster, and next to them Seeland and Funen; but agriculture is most skilfully carried on in the Baltic districts of Holstein. The Danes however are not generally good agriculturalists. Of the whole area, about two-thirds are appropriated to arable land; one-twelfth to pasture and meadow; and one-twentieth to woods and forests. The average yearly produce is stated at about 8,000,000 quarters of corn: 2,000,000 tons of potatoes; and a proportionate quantity of other produce. Peas and pears, rapeseed, flax, hemp, and tobacco are grown: fruits and table vegetables are comparatively small in produce. The fine forests once possessed by Denmark have been allowed so to decay, that the inhabitants are obliged to import wood from other countries. The chief timber-trees are pine, beech, oak, and birch.

Denmark possesses no mines or metals whatever; nor any minerals of importance, except coals, freestone, and salt. Amber is collected on the Hitze, a sandbank on the western coast of Jutland. Potters' and porcelain earths are also obtained. Peat is got wherever there are swamps, and every village in those parts has bog lands assigned for its supply.

Manufactures are but slightly developed in Denmark. Altona produces silk, woollen, and cotton goods, leather, soap, refined sugar, and tobacco. Lace is made on a very extensive scale in and about Tondern. There are large tobacco manufactures, but they are said not to produce more than one-eighth of the quantity consumed. The woollen and cotton manufactures are small in amount. There are a few establishments for linen, gloves, paper, and ironware. Straw hats, sail-cloth, glass, soap, leather, saltpetre, gunpowder, and arms, plated goods, china, and earthenware, beer and spirits, thread, refined sugar, soda, and potashes are among the productions of Danish industry. The brandy distilleries are rather numerous. The peasants' families make their own woollen clothing in general, which is composed of a coarse stuff termed wadmel; and indeed there are few articles of domestic use, whether utensils or for apparel, which are not made by their own hands.

There is probably no country in Europe better adapted or more favourably situated in many respects for commerce than Denmark. It is the key of the Baltic, and possesses peculiar advantages for a ready and cheap intercourse with all the maritime nations of Europe. Copenhagen, the capital, is the central point of the Danish foreign trade, which has been greatly favoured by the neutral policy which the government has endeavoured to pursue during the last hundred years and more. Navigation, in which about 50,000 hands are employed, is a great source of profit to the country, for the Danes navigate their vessels on cheaper terms than many of their competitors, and are excellent mariners, on which account they are the carriers for other countries, particularly to the Mediterranean and Levant. There is a brisk intercourse by sea between the several ports. The chief places of trade are Copenhagen, Altona, Kiel, Koersoer, Helsingor, Odensee, Viborg, Randers, Flensberg, Schleswig, Aalborg, Rendsburg, Tondern, Aarhus, Gluckstadt, Neustedt, and Itzehoe. Railways have been recently formed from Altona to Gluckstadt, Rendsburg, and Kiel.

Denmark exports grain, butter, cheese, brandy, salted and smoked meats, horned cattle, horses, skins and hides, oil, eider-down, fish, tallow, bristles, &c., and imports wines, salt, silk, wool, cotton, timber, coals, colonial produce, brandy, spirits, glass, drugs, &c.

The British produce and manufactures exported to Denmark in 1846-7-8 were of the following values:—

1846	..	..	£340,318
1847	..	..	253,701
1848	..	..	296,466

Of the articles thus exported, cotton, coals, and iron manufacture comprises the largest items.

The imports from Denmark into Great Britain in 1848, comprised, among other items, butter 8,056 cwts, corn about 1,000,000 qrs., flax 9,000 cwts., flax and other seeds, 45,000 qrs., seal skins, 14,000, wool 1,500,000 cwts.

The Danish vessels which left British ports in 1849 amounted to 1708, and those which entered were 1885. These vessels are small, however, the average tonnage being under 80 tons.

DENSITY, properly speaking, has no absolute meaning, but it is a term which may be considered as representing the number of material particles in a body. Thus gold is more dense than air, because probably, under equal volumes, gold contains a greater number of particles than air. The measure of the density of any body is called its specific gravity. [SPECIFIC GRAVITY.]

DERBY. The principal manufactures of this interesting town are of silk and cotton goods, porcelain, jewellery, and ornamental articles made of the various kinds of spar found in the county, red and white lead, lead pipe, sheet lead, cast iron, ribbed stockings, and bobbin-net, and other lace. Silk hosiery is extensively made. There is a considerable printing and publishing establishment, besides several printing offices.

In the early part of the 18th century the art of spinning or 'throwing' silk, which had been exclusively possessed by the Italians, was introduced into Derby by a Mr. Crotchet, who did not succeed in business. In 1717 Mr. John Lombe, who had obtained access to the machinery of the silk throwsters of Piedmont in Italy, agreed with the corporation of Derby to rent an island or swamp in the river Derwent, 500 feet long and 52 feet wide. Here he erected, at a cost of 30,000*l*., an immense silk-mill, now the property of the corporation, the lease having expired. In 1718 Lombe took out a patent, and was proceeding successfully in his business when he died. He was succeeded in his mill by his brother William, and afterwards by his cousin, Sir Thomas Lombe. The accounts of the machinery of this immense mill have been much exaggerated: the wheels have been said to amount to 26,000; Hutton, who served an apprenticeship of seven years in the mill, states that the number of wheels was 13,384. The whole machinery was moved by one water wheel. Many throwing mills have since been erected at Derby, and this branch of industry may be regarded as the staple of the town. The cotton manufacture is of later introduction and of smaller extent. The spars of the county, especially the fluor spar, or 'blue John,' are wrought into vases and other ornaments, and the black marble of Ashford into vases, columns, chimney-pieces, &c.

The Derby Arboretum is an honour to the town, both or its own beauty, and for the circumstances under which it was formed. This Arboretum is a piece of ground of about 16 acres in extent, well laid out and arranged with trees and shrubs, so as to combine instruction with recreation. The original Arboretum, a piece of ground about 11 acres in extent, carefully arranged by the late Mr. London, was given to the town by Joseph Strutt Esq.;

an adjoining portion of about 5 acres has since been purchased and laid out in a similar manner. The inhabitants are admitted to the grounds on payment of an admission fee, the proceeds of which defray the expenses of maintaining the establishment.

DERBYSHIRE. This county is rich in mineral strata. The coal-measures underlie the magnesian limestone, and crop out from beneath it on the west. These coal measures form part of that important coal field which occupies a considerable part of the west riding of Yorkshire, and extends into Nottinghamshire and Derbyshire, being bounded on the east by the magnesian limestone, and on the south by the red marl. The strata range from north to south, and dip to the east. The Derbyshire portion of this coal field is east of a line drawn from between Hathersage and Sheffield to Little Eaton, near Derby. Every variety of coal seems to be found in this field, hard stone coal, cannel, peacock, and caking coal. The coal-pits in Derbyshire are dispersed over the coal field, and are very numerous, especially about Chesterfield and Alfreton, and in the district south and west of the Cromford and Erewash canals. The beds which lie between the seams of coal are worked for various purposes. The workings of the ironstone are generally begun at the surface, and pursued until they become dangerous from the loose nature of the stratum in which they lie. The ironstone which is marked with impressions of mussel shells (called the mussel band) is worked as an ornamental marble. From the gritstone beds are quarried grindstones for cutlers; the binds, where they are hard and black, are used as black chalk; others, when decomposed, make good brick earth; the clunch is sometimes of that kind which is used for fire-bricks; where it crops out to the surface it becomes soft clay. Potter's clay, of various colours and qualities, occurs in this coal-field.

Black marble is quarried for ornamental purposes. One of the beds of limestone contains white chert or china stone, which is extensively used in the Staffordshire potteries. The beautiful fluor spar called 'Blue John,' from which vases and other ornaments are made, is found in a mountain of limestone. Numerous veins of lead, zinc, iron, manganese and copper, also occur.

A large proportion of the land of this county is in permanent pastures, of which some are very rich. Derbyshire cheese is noted as of good quality, and the best is often sold for Cheshire or Gloucester when made of the shape and colour of these cheeses. The common Derbyshire cheese is not generally coloured; it resembles some kinds of Dutch cheeses, and keeps well.

At Cromford, in this county, the late Sir Richard Arkwright erected a spacious cotton-mill on the left bank of the Derwent; it is now occupied by the Messrs. Arkwright, his grandsons, who employ in these mills and those at Masson, a little higher up the Derwent, several hundred persons. Lead mines are worked in the neighbourhood; lapis calaminaris is ground and prepared, and red lead manufactured. At Dronfield manufactures are carried on in iron goods, such as railway wheels, cast iron chains and nails, axes, chisels, and other edge tools, and agricultural implements. At Heanor are manufactories for cotton goods, hosiery, and bobbin-net lace. In and near Ashford there are extensive marble works where the black and coloured marbles which are quarried in the neighbourhood are wrought into chimney-pieces, tables, slabs, &c; there are also quarries of lime-stone; and lead mines. Scythes and reaping hooks are largely manufactured at Beighton and at Hackington. At Clay Cross and in its immediate vicinity are extensive collieries and iron works. At Codnor the Butterly Iron Company have extensive iron works and collieries; and iron, lead, limestone, and coal are abundant. At Long Eaton, paper mills and stone quarries give employment to many of the inhabitants. Needles, pins, edgetools and mill stones are manufactured at Hathersage. Ironville is a busy and populous district; the inhabitants are employed in the iron works, smelting, &c.; a national school (in which divine service is performed on Sundays) was erected in 1841, at a cost of 3000*l*., by the Butterly Iron Company, and an infant school has been since erected by the same company; there is also a mechanics institute. At Milford, six miles from Derby, schools have been founded by the Messrs Strutt, who have extensive cotton and bleaching works here, employing 1,000 hands; they have also an iron foundry here, in which all their machinery is cast and made, and gas works at Milford which supply the town of Belper.

Many other towns and villages in Derbyshire carry on some or other of the industrial pursuits noticed in the above sketch.

Derbyshire has some peculiar laws and regulations connected with the working of the lead mines. These laws and regulations are of very high antiquity. The principal part of the county where lead ore is found in any considerable quantity is called 'the King's Field,' and comprehends nearly all the wapentake of Wirksworth and a considerable part of the High Peak hundred. 'The King's Field' has been from time immemorial let on lease. The lessees have each in his respective district a steward and bar-masters. The steward presides as judge in the barmote courts, and with 24 jurymen, chosen every half year, determines all disputes which arise respecting the working of the mines. Debts incurred in working the mines are cognizable in these courts. These courts meet twice a year, or oftener if need be. The court for the High Peak district meets at Monyash, that for the wapentake district at the town of Wirksworth. The office of the barmaster is principally to put miners into the possession of veins that they have discovered, and to collect the proportion of ore to which the lessee of the crown or the lord of the manor has a claim. When a miner has discovered a new vein of ore in 'the King's Field,' he may acquire a title to the exclusive possession of it, provided it be not in a garden, orchard, or high road, by a proper application to the barmaster of the liberty. Should the miner neglect to work the vein, the barmaster may, after a certain time, dispose of it to any one who is willing to try it.

The cottons, the silks, the hosiery, the bobbing net, the iron, the marbles, the pottery, &c. of Derbyshire will all be represented at the Great Exhibition. The quarries in North Derbyshire possessed by the Dukes of Devonshire and Rutland, will be represented in their several products by Messrs. Lomas and Oldfield, the lessees respectively of the marble works of Bakewell and Ashford-in-the-Water; while the splendid amethystine fluor spar, locally designated 'Blue John,' and found exclusively at Castleton in the Peak, will find its way to the Crystal Palace in the elegant form of a colossal Grecian vase, the finest and most important article ever produced from this material. The vase was manufactured at Matlock by Mr. Vallance, who is preparing a number of inlaid black marble tables, vases, candelabra, and other articles peculiar to the county. It is also the intention of Mr. Vallance to exhibit such a collection as will illustrate the peculiar mineralogical and geological character of Derbyshire, as well as the applicability of its products to ornamental purposes.

DESICCATION is the chemical operation of drying bodies. It is sometimes effected by simple drying in the air; sometimes in warm chambers; at others, by paper filters, by the air-pump, by the action of deliquescent salts placed near the body to be dried, and by many other modes.

DESIGN. In the fine arts the word design is employed in two very different significations: in the first place, it is used merely to signify the act of drawing, or representing in lines the form of any object; in the next place it expresses that combination of invention and purpose which enables the artist to compose a picture or a group, without reference to the material in which it is executed. The accurate conception of form and beauty is displayed in the most masterly degree in the ancient Greek sculptures; and in the invention of appropriate attitudes and perfection of physical form the design of the best Greek sculptures cannot be surpassed. But, of all the existing specimens of art, the paintings of the Italian masters display the most consummate excellence in design, especially the Florentine and Roman schools, and among them Raphael's in particular.

In architecture, the design or scheme for a building is shown by means of a series of diagrams or drawings, which, taken one with another, convey a much more exact and complete notion of the whole, both internally and externally, than can be obtained by any other mode of delineation. Such drawings consist of *plan*, *elevation*, and *section*, besides others of *details*, or *parts at large;* and their number will depend, either upon the nature of the building, that is, on its being more or less complex, or as it is intended to show it more or less fully.

DESIGNS, COPYRIGHT AND REGISTRATION. Intermediate in character between the *copyright* of literary productions, and *patents* for mechanical inventions, is the registration of designs in which fine art is more or less exhibited. An act of parliament in 1735 gave a copyright for fourteen years in the arts of designing, engraving, and etching prints: enforcing the right by fine and forfeiture. An act of 1767 extended this right to a period of twenty-eight years, and made it to include the designing of maps, charts, and plans. An act in 1777 increased the power of designers to enforce the observance of the right. Three acts, passed respectively in 1787, 1789, and 1794, gave a copyright for securing the use of new patterns in the printing of linens, cottons, calicoes, and muslins, for a period of three months. An act of 1798 gave a copyright for fourteen years in respect to models, casts, and other sculptures; and another act in 1814 strengthened this right. An act in 1830 extended many of the above copyrights to Ireland. An act in 1838 secured copyright for printing designs in other woven goods, in addition to cottons and linens.

These were the statutes which governed the

copyright of designs, down to the time of passing the Registration Act of 1839. This Act declared the existence of copyright in respect to the following productions—patterns to be painted, printed, or worked upon any material; modelling, casting, embossing, chasing, or engraving any new design; a new shape or configuration of a manufactured article. The Board of Trade was empowered to appoint a registrar, deputy registrar, and six clerks, to manage the registration of such designs; and any person so registered had a copyright in his design for three years.

A more comprehensive act was passed in 1842, which gave a copyright for any new and original design, whether applicable to the ornamenting of any article of manufacture, or to the employment of any new material for manufactures. The right was made applicable for the pattern, the shape, or the ornament; and was equally valid whether the pattern were worked by printing, painting, embroidering, weaving, sewing, modelling, casting, embossing, engraving, staining, or dyeing. Arrangements were made for registering the designs, for transferring property in them, and for enforcing penalties in cases of infringement. All designs were classed under one or other of thirteen headings; and the period of copyright was declared to be three years, one year, or nine months, according to the class to which the design belonged.

By another act in 1843 the copyright was extended to designs which, though not actually ornamental, have reference to some purpose of utility in respect to shape or form. All such articles are to be stamped with the word 'registered,' and the copyright in them exists for three years. The registrar is to prepare an index of all such non-ornamental designs; and at the expiration of the copyright, the designs may be copied by any person at the registrar's office, on payment of a fee.

These two acts, in conjunction, guided the proceedings in respect to the copyright of designs for several years; but a statute passed in 1850 has introduced—not so much a change —as an extension of the right. When it was found that the proposal for an Exhibition of the world's Industry was likely to be liberally responded to, it was felt that something ought to be done to secure the copyright of any new designs which might be made public at the Exhibition; and it was mainly to secure this end, that the act was passed which received the royal assent in August 1850. By this act any new design may be *provisionally* registered for twelve months; during this period the proprietor may exhibit his design, and describe it in catalogues, without vitiating his copyright; and at any time during the twelve months he, and he alone, may register the design in the fuller manner set forth in the former acts; but if during this provisional period he should *sell* any of the articles to which this design is applied, he loses the power of completing the registration. Several other clauses are introduced, tending to secure the right of Exhibitors at the Industrial Exhibition of 1851.

The Commissioners have made arrangements for this provisional registration, in respect to new designs to be exhibited in Hyde Park. Until February 1, 1851, the designs were registered at Somerset House, on payment of a small fee; but after that date they are to be registered in the 'Palace of Industry,' free of charge. The Commissioners have issued minute instructions to guide those who are about to register their designs; the designs themselves being placed in two great groups, in respect to *ornamenting* and to *shape*, and each group being divided into classes. The Registrar of Designs has also issued full instructions, explanatory of the operation of the three acts of 1842, 1843, and 1850, and applicable to other purposes besides those of the Great Exhibition.

DESIGN, SCHOOLS OF. In France and in several of the German States, schools in which drawing and the principles of design are taught have been long established. In Prussia there are many elementary schools at Berlin and several provincial towns, in which drawing and modelling from the antique, and geometrical and architectural drawing are taught at an average fee of 12*s.* per year. From these schools the more promising of the pupils are removed to the 'Gewerb Institut' (Manufacturing Institute), and the 'Bau Akademie' (Architectural Academy.) In the former of these two, the studies have reference to all the branches of science or art bearing upon manufactures: in the second, all matters which bear in any way on building, civil engineering, or surveying: in these schools the instruction is gratuitous. The highest class, in which the fine arts are embraced in their widest range, is the Royal Academy at Berlin.

In Bavaria, education in art is mixed up with general education, but it is made to occupy a prominent place. The earliest stages are taught at the elementary schools; the next stage at the gymnasia, of which there is one in each large town; and the last stage at the lycea, of which there are three in the kingdom, at Munich, Nürnberg, and Augsburg; that at Munich being chiefly for architecture and the application of the fine arts to manufactures, that at Nürnberg to metal casting and wood carving, and that at Augsburg to textile manufactures.

In France there are, intermediate between the elementary schools and the royal academies, several others which treat of art in its relation either to manufactures or to science, and which are either supported partly by the state and partly by municipalities, or are private establishments assisted by municipalities; and in most of them a very extensive system of studies is pursued, bearing in various ways on the science and the fine arts of manufactures. The school of art at Lyon, in particular, is an important one in connection with the silk manufacture carried on in that city; and every endeavour is there made to foster taste in manufactures.

The advantages which resulted to the manufactures of the countries in every department requiring the display of taste was so obvious, particularly as displayed in the silk manufactures of France, that a strong desire was felt by the manufacturers and merchants of England to secure similar advantages for this country. Accordingly, in 1836, a school of design was established at Somerset House in connection with the Board of Trade, but under the control of a council and director, with masters in several departments. The school continued to make progress; but the management was not on the whole satisfactory, and early in 1848 the Board of Trade resumed the direct control, and the director and the council were dispensed with. The schools are now under the management of a committee, consisting of the principal officials of the Board of Trade, assisted by three eminent artists in the departments of painting, sculpture, and architecture. The general business arrangements and management of details are assigned to the resident secretary. Admission to students is granted on the recommendation of two respectable persons, for a probationary period of three months, but no instance of rejection has occurred since the alteration in the management of the schools. The terms and hours of attendance have varied more than once since the opening of the school. There are two classes; one in the morning from ten till two, the other in the evening from half past six till nine, on every week day except Saturday. The payment is two shillings per month for morning or evening attendance. Lectures are occasionally delivered by the teachers. There is also a morning school for females, established in 1842, to which the payment is of the same amount. The instruction given is of a character to enable the student to apply the principles of high art to the purposes of the manufacturer and the decorator. The primary classes at the school are three—form, colour, and ornament; and it is said to be purposed to blend colour and ornament into one class. Choice specimens have been obtained from Italy of arabesques, mosaic pavements, terra-cottas, &c. M. Guizot has presented to the school casts from the celebrated gates of the Baptistery at Florence, and there is also a large collection of other casts from the antique, and of Gothic, and other styles of ornament. Specimens of paper hanging, silk, glass, porcelain, bronze, wax ornaments, and other objects have been provided by government for the use of the schools. Books, many of them expensively illustrated, have been purchased, forming a library of reference in matters relating to art and decoration; and some of these books are, under certain regulations, lent out to the students. Books, casts, and other examples of art are supplied by the committee to all the branch schools.

In connection with the School of Design at Somerset House, there are several branch schools. One is established in Spitalfields; and others at Manchester, Birmingham, Coventry, Nottingham, Sheffield, York, Leeds, Huddersfield, Newcastle-on-Tyne, Norwich, Stoke-upon-Trent, Hanley, Glasgow, Paisley, &c.; all of which are well attended, and have been productive of much good. Some of the students have already become teachers in the schools, and many have successfully applied their talents to the improvement of our native manufactures.

There is one other school, that at Edinburgh, which is not in connection with Somerset House. It was established some years previous to that at Somerset House, under the sanction of the Board for the Improvement of Manufactures and the Herring Fishery. It has been well attended, and two of the early conductors at Somerset House were formerly masters there. Its object is nearly the same; the chief distinction is, that in Edinburgh it is the only school of art, while in London there is the Royal Academy for the more aspiring and ambitious.

Under Belfast, Birmingham, Coventry, Nottingham, &c., a few details will be found illustrative of the present state of the Schools of Design in those towns. There are circumstances connected with the Belfast school so interesting that we will quote a portion of the Annual Report for 1850 relating to it, showing how important the mere *wrappers* for woven goods are regarded. After stating that some among the 148 students in 1850 were designers for sewed muslin, and others designers for damasks, the report goes on to say;—'Eleven of the pupils are entered as engravers, and of these several are draughtsmen and designers for the paper bands and envelopes used in tying up the rolls of linen. The value attached to these ornaments in preparing the packets of linen for the foreign markets, the decoration which is lavished upon them, the taste and care with which it is thought necessary to get them up, and the extent to which they are imported into Belfast from London and Paris, render them no unimportant article of trade. In the year 1847, when the establishment of the School of Design at Belfast was first taken into consideration, one stationer at Belfast had made a beginning in the manufacture of these articles, and had a press at work in embossing them. The same stationer has now nine presses at work, and others of the trade have taken up the business. Most of the bands yet made are of an inferior sort, but there are attempts to improve the quality; some are taking the place of the more simple French patterns, and the sale is increasing. The establishment of the school has been happily timed for the encouragement of a branch of trade so favourable to the development of artistic skill, and there is every prospect that by the help of the school the "linen band" will become a home manufacture, and secure to the town of Belfast an annual expenditure of 60,000*l.*, now paid to strangers and foreigners."

There is at the present time an active movement in Belfast with respect to ornamental design. The production of specimens for the Exhibition of 1851 is one stimulus, and French workwomen have been engaged, not to supersede, but to instruct the native embroiderers of muslin.'

DETONATION is a chemical term employed to express combination or decomposition which occurs with noise and frequently with combustion. It occurs when oxygen and hydrogen, in certain proportions, are fired; when hydrogen and chlorine are heated by the sun's rays; when certain salts and oxides are struck or rubbed; and in some other cases.

DEVONPORT DOCK YARD. [PLYMOUTH.]

DEVONSHIRE. This fine county is rich in minerals available in the manufacturing arts. Slate rocks are very predominant. These rocks are quarried for roofing-slates: they are metalliferous, affording iron-stone, and veins of tin, copper, and lead: the veins or lodes which yield tin or copper, run, as in Cornwall, from N. E. to S. W. (approaching more or less to E. and W.), and those which afford lead run nearly at right angles to these. The strata in the mining field about Tavistock which yields tin, copper, lead, and manganese, are traversed by porphyritic (elvan) beds, bearing nearly east and west. A few lead and copper mines are wrought in North Devon: the lead is combined with silver. The limestone is quarried for building and burnt for manure: beautifully veined marble is worked in different places. Imperfect coal or lignite, called Bovey coal, occurs at Bovey Heathfield, on the right or south west bank of the West Teign or Bovey river in a plain where the strata of it rise to the surface. It lies in parallel seams from four to sixteen feet thick, at six or eight feet distance from each other, to the depth of sixty feet, and exhibits a gradation from the most perfect ligneous texture to a substance nearly approaching the character of pit coal. Potters' clay and pipe clay are found in the same neighbourhood. The Bovey coal is used for fuel in the potteries on Bovey heath, and by the poorer people of the neighbourhood: but its difficult and imperfect combustion, and fetid gas, render it unfit for domestic use. The Dartmoor granite is remarkable for the size of the felspar crystals which it contains: it is much valued for its durability, fineness of texture, and the size of the blocks: it is quarried and exported to a considerable extent, especially to London. It is metalliferous; containing veins of tin, even the rock itself being sometimes impregnated with this metal.

Grass land being far more abundant in Devonshire than arable, butter, cheese, and live stock may be considered as the chief agricultural produce for exportation. The clouted or clotted cream of Devonshire is a well-known delicacy; it is made by heating the milk on the hearth, or by means of a stove, to a degree a little below the boiling point, when the clouted cream ries to the top like a thick scum, and is taken off when cooled. This cream being merely stirred briskly with the hand or a stick, is converted into butter. The chief beverage of the Devonshire people is cider, which is here superior to any other in England. The soil on the slopes of the hills is peculiarly adapted to the growth of fruit trees, especially on a loose rocky bottom, where the roots may insinuate themselves and find moisture at all times. The wood grown in Devonshire is chiefly oak, but beech, ash, and elder are interspersed, according to the soil and situation.

A few towns are briefly noticed in separate articles; such as EXETER, CREDITON, HONITON, &c. We may here state that at Prince

Town, on Dartmoor, is a building which was formerly a prison, but which has lately been leased to a company who were engaged in extracting naptha from peat. Considerable interest is just now attached to this place from its being the field of an important experiment on the application of convict labour. In the autumn of 1850, a number of convicts were sent down here to be employed in the reclamation of a portion of the moor and other useful works. The prison is of such extent, and so well constructed, as to afford abundance of room, security, and facility of supervision, and the situation, though bleak and dreary, is very healthy, while it is sufficiently removed from any populous neighbourhood, thus permitting the experiment to be made under very favourable conditions. At present the number of convicts at Dartmoor is limited, but it is understood that it will be increased if the experiment succeeds.

Mining, quarrying, and lace-making are the chief industrial pursuits of Devonshire. Specimens from many of the chief towns will be displayed at the Great Exhibition.

DEWSBURY is one of the busy manufacturing towns of the West Riding district. Many extensive establishments are here in operation for the production of woollen fabrics chiefly of the heavy and useful kinds, such as blankets, carpets, and inferior descriptions of woollen cloth. There are also worsted yarn manufactories, and wool carding establishments; and wool-stapling, iron-founding, tanning, malting, and nail-making are extensively carried on. Several corn mills and lime-works are in the neighbourhood.

DEXTRINE, is a modification of starch procured by boiling common starch in dilute sulphuric acid and also in some other acids: by this treatment the starch soon loses its consistence and becomes thin and limpid, being converted into dextrine. When the ebullition is continued after the formation of the dextrine, this substance is converted into grape sugar, and this effect is produced with great readiness.

DIAGONAL SCALE. Equidistant parallel lines cut all lines drawn across them into equal parts. Consequently a set of equidistant parallels laid down upon a ruler, with oblique lines of various lengths drawn across them, give with the compasses the means of immediately taking off various proportions of those lines. The common diagonal scale is so formed as to facilitate the laying down of the hundredths of units in a scale of equal parts; and when well made it will shew $\frac{1}{100}$th of an inch with tolerable accuracy.

DIAMOND. This crystalline gem, on account of its high lustre and extreme hardness has always been regarded as the most valuable of the precious stones. The diamond usually occurs in imbedded octahedral crystals in alluvial ground, in the East Indies, Brazil, and the Ural mountains. It is commonly colourless or grayish, but sometimes green, yellow, red, brown, blue, and black: the two last-mentioned colours are the rarest. Its lustre is adamantine; refraction single; transparent, but sometimes rendered opaque by foreign matter. It is harder than any other substance, and can be cut or worn down only by rubbing one diamond against another; and it is polished by the friction of portions of the gem itself reduced to powder. It is broken without difficulty. The specific gravity of the diamond is 3.52. When rubbed, it phosphorises and becomes positively electrical. When heated, without the contact of air, it suffers no change; but, if ignited in contact with it, it is totally converted into carbonic acid gas.

For ornamental purposes diamonds are cut into two shapes, namely, *rose diamonds* and *brilliants*. The weight and consequently the value of diamonds is estimated in carats, each of which is equal to 3.166 grains.

It was conjectured by Newton that the diamond is a combustible body; but the proof of its being absolute carbon in a crystalline form was developed by slow degrees by the Florentine Academicians in the seventeenth century, by Lavoisier a century later, and by many chemists in the present century.

The pencil diamond used in cutting glass is a small fractured piece of diamond. The part of the diamond used is of a trapezoidal shape, weighing about the sixtieth part of a carat, and is set in a wooden handle.

The diamond-mines of Cuddapah in the East Indies, near Madras, instructively shew the mode in which these gems are procured. These mines have, it is said, been worked for several hundred years with various success. The places in which diamonds have hitherto been found consist either of alluvial soil or of rocks of the latest formation. The mines are pits of small depth. The diamonds are not scattered through the whole of the mine from the surface to the greatest depth, but occur in beds always harder than the adjacent soil, and usually not exceeding one or two feet in thickness. Dr. Heyne, who carefully examined these mines, has given in his statistical tracts the following description of one: 'The uppermost, or superficial stratum, consists of sand or gravel, mixed with a small proportion of loam. Its thickness scarcely exceeds a foot and a half. Immediately under it is a bed of stiff blueish or black mud, similar to what are seen in places that have been inundated; it is about five feet thick, and contains no stones. The diamond bed comes next, and is easily distinguished from the incumbent bed by the great number of large rounded stones which it contains. It is about two feet or two and a half feet thick, and is composed of large round stones, pebbles, and gravel connected together by clay.' The contents of this bed are put into a cistern about eight feet square and three feet deep, when water is poured into it, which separates the clay and loamy particles, leaving the gravel and small stones at the bottom. These being removed are thinly spread upon a smooth surface, about twenty feet square, of hardened clay, and six or seven people examine the whole carefully several times. At first they pick out the large stones; at the second and subsequent examinations the smaller gravel is carefully turned over by hand, while they 'watch for the spark from the diamond, which invariably strikes the eye.'

In 1845 the public journals gave frequent extracts from Brazilian correspondence relating to the discovery of a new diamond mine in that country. The locality was the Assuara, a desert part of the province of Bahia. At this spot gold was found a few years earlier; and among the many hundreds who flocked to work the gold veins, some discovered the presence of diamonds. No sooner was the discovery made, than the gold was abandoned, and the more precious diamonds sought for; and the accounts seem to convey the information that the store of these gems was very large. One ship is said to have carried to Europe diamonds to the value of 100,000*l*.

The commercial value of diamonds is a very curious feature. In the first place they are estimated by weight. A weight called a *carat* (equal to rather more than three grains troy) is taken as an unit, and is divided into halves, quarters, eighths, and sixteenths, to give fractional parts. Then the quality and form of the diamond are examined, and a price per carat fixed from all these circumstances. The larger the diamond the greater is the price per carat given for it. Under five carats, the price varies from thirty shillings to thirty guineas per carat: but very large diamonds, like *chefs d'œuvre* among pictures, obtain a price limited only by the competition of the small number of persons able to purchase them. The Russian diamond, the Pitt diamond, and the Pigott diamond, are gems which have obtained notoriety on account of their large size and enormous value. The celebrated *Koh-i-noor*, or *Mountain of Light*, is an Indian diamond which has lately fallen into the hands of the English at Lahore, and has been brought to this country as the property of Queen Victoria. It weighed 900 carats when rough, but this is reduced to 279 by cutting and polishing. As to its value, guesses have varied from half a million to three millions and a half sterling: shewing how vague are all attempts to estimate such rarities. It is said that Her Majesty intends to deposit this gem at the Industrial Exhibition.

DIAPER, is a kind of linen or cotton cloth, upon the face of which a figured pattern is produced by a peculiar mode of weaving. Diapers are chiefly used for table linen, fine towels, &c.

In decorative painting the term *diapering* is sometimes applied to a small pattern introduced to diminish the appearance of baldness where a considerable space is covered with one colour.

DIASTASE, is a substance formed during germination. It is prepared by reducing freshly germinated barley into a pulp, with half its weight of water, and then pressing out the liquor strongly. It is afterwards treated repeatedly with alcohol, purified, and precipitated. The precipitate is at last dried in thin layers upon glass at a temperature between 104° and 122° Fahrenheit. Diastase is solid, white, not crystalline, soluble in water, but insoluble in alcohol unless it be weak. Common malt is stated in general not to contain more than 1-500th of its weight of diastase; one part of it is sufficient to convert 2000 parts of starch, thickened with water, into a mixture consisting of much dextrine and a little sugar.

DIDYMIUM is a metal recently discovered in cerite. Cerite eventually yields, by treatment with sulphuric acid, large red crystals, which are sulphite of didymium, from which, by treatment with potash and exposure to a red heat, the oxide of didymium is obtained in small lumps of a brown or blackish colour; the powder is light brown. It has no alkaline reaction, and is dissolved pretty readily even by dilute acids, and they yield salts of an amethystine red colour. By the blowpipe the oxide mixed with the salt of phosphorus becomes amethystine red with a tint of violet; when heated with carbonate of soda or platina foil, it melts into a grayish white mass. It does not appear to have been reduced to the metallic state.

DIE-SINKING. In the preparation of coined money and of medals the most important feature is the engraving of the 'die' which is to form the stamp. The piece of steel is prepared with the utmost care, and is brought to a soft state when about to be submitted to the hands of the engraver. By the aid of small, fine, hardened steel tools, the engraver cuts away the steel until he has produced, in cavity or 'intaglio,' an exact reverse of the design for the medal or coin. The steel, in a soft state while being engraved, requires hardening before being applied to use. When further prepared so as to be rendered more durable, it obtains the name of the *matrix*, and might be used in that state to stamp coins or medals; but as such a matrix is very costly, and might be spoiled by fracture, arrangements are made for producing multiplied copies of it. A small block of soft steel is by immense pressure, made to receive an impress, *in relief*, from this matrix; and from this second piece, which obtains the name of the *puncheon*, after being hardened and retouched by the graver, *dies* or duplications of the original matrix are produced. In the use of dies by means of the stamping-press, the number of blows required to transfer the device to a blank piece of metal depends upon the depth of the intaglio.

A method sometimes adopted of producing medals from a die by means of stamping upon metal which is in a semi-liquid instead of a cold and solid state has been already described [CLICHE' MEDALLIONS]; the method is called *en cliché*, and has been much practised in France.

DIEPPE is among the busiest of the seacoast towns of France. The population of the suburb of Pollet, to the east of the town, are all engaged in the herring, oyster, and cod fisheries. The quantity of herrings cured has in some years amounted to 36,000 barrels, and of mackerel to 12,000 barrels. There are sugar-refineries, rope-walks, paper-mills, and ship-building yards in the town. Fine linen, lace, and articles of ornament in bone, horn, shellwork, and ivory, are made. Wine, brandy, vinegar, salt, nails, iron, steel, millstones, colonial produce also enter into the commerce of the town. The coasting trade is active.

DIGESTION, in Chemistry, is the exposure of any substance to partial or total solution in a fluid, either at common temperatures or with a gentle heat, as in the preparation of tinctures. It is commonly performed in a glass matrass, which is half filled with the fluid, and covered with a piece of wet bladder at the mouth.

DIORA'MA is the name given to a mode of painting and scenic exhibition invented by two French artists, Daguerre and Bouton. The peculiar and almost magical effect of the diorama arises, in a considerable measure, from the contrivance employed in exhibiting the painting, which is viewed through a large aperture or proscenium. Beyond this opening the picture is placed at such a distance that the light is thrown upon it, at a proper angle, from the roof, which is glazed with ground glass, and cannot be seen by the spectator. The light may be diminished or increased at pleasure, and that either gradually or suddenly, so as to represent the change from ordinary daylight to sunshine, and from sunshine to cloudy weather, or to the obscurity of twilight; also the difference of atmospheric tone attending them. Some parts of the painting are transparent, and on them the light can occasionally be admitted from behind, thereby producing a brilliancy far exceeding that of the highest lights of a picture upon an opaque ground. The combination of transparent, semi-transparent, and opaque colouring, still further assisted by the power of varying both the effects and the degree of light and shade, renders the diorama the most perfect scenic representation of nature. The principle forms the basis of an attractive exhibition in the Regent's Park, London; but it is also capable of being applied to the embellishments of corridors, &c.

DISTEMPER, is an inferior kind of colouring, used as a cheap substitute for oil colours. It is composed of whitening mixed with size, to which the colouring is added to form the necessary tint. Coarser colours are used for distemper than are employed in oil-painting. Scene-painting and paper-staining are executed in distemper.

DISTILLATION is a chemical process for applying a regulated heat to fluid substances in covered vessels, in order to separate their more volatile constituents in vapour: and for condensing them immediately by cold into the liquid state. The distillation of aromatic waters was known to the Greeks and Romans, and to the Arabians from very remote times. Arnoldus de Villa Nova and Raymond Lully both noticed in the 13th century, a mode of producing intoxicating spirits by distillation. The alchemists of those days imagined that spirit derives its ardent qualities from the fire employed to heat the vessels.

The only substances employed in this country in the manufacture of ardent spirits upon the great scale (which is the chief example of distillation) are different kinds of corn, such as barley, rye, wheat, oats, buckwheat, and maize. Peas and beans also have been occasionally used in small quantity. The principles in these grains from which the spirits are indirectly produced are starch and a little sweet mucilage, which, by a peculiar process called *mashing*, are converted into a species of sugar. It is the sugar so formed which is the immediate generator of alcohol, by the process of fermentation. In mashing one or more kinds of corn, a greater or smaller proportion of malt is always mixed with the raw grain, and sometimes malt alone is used, as in the production of malt-whiskey.

The manufacture of ardent spirits consists of three distinct operations: first, mashing; second, fermentation; third, distillation.

Mashing.—Either malt alone, or malt mixed with other grain, and coarsely ground, is put into the mash-tun, along with a proper proportion of hot water, and the mixture is subjected to agitation by a mechanical revolving apparatus. The water is applied at a temperature varying from 145° to 165° Fahr. After two or three hours' agitation, the whole is left to repose for an hour and a half, and then the worts (as the liquor is called) are drawn off to about one-third the volume of water employed, the rest being entangled in a pasty state among the farina. About two-thirds of the first quantity of water is now let into the tun, but at a temperature somewhat higher, and the mashing motion is renewed for nearly half an hour. A second period of infusion or repose ensues, after which these second worts are drawn off. Both infusions must be cooled as quickly as possible down to about 75° Fahr.: this is usually effected by exposing the wort for some time in large shallow cisterns, called coolers, freely exposed to aerial currents; but the liquor is sometimes cooled by being passed through serpentine tubes surrounded with cold water, or by the agency of ventilators blowing over its surface in extensive cisterns only three or four inches deep. A third mashing is conducted with a fresh portion of water in order to extract the remaining saccharine matter from the grain.

The specific gravity of the first and second worts, when mixed, is about 1.060; and the liquor contains about 60 lbs. of saccharine extract per barrel of 36 gallons. The three mashings employ about 27 gallons of water to every bushel of ground meal.

Fermentation.—This consists in bringing the worts to a fermented state. The worts are drawn off into a fermenting vessel; and yeast or ferment is added, sufficient to decompose the sugar in the liquor. The process is commenced at a temperature between 60° and 70° which soon afterwards rises to 85° or 90°. The first appearance of fermentation shows itself by a ring of froth round the edge of the vat usually within an hour after the addition of the yeast; and in the course of five hours the extrication of carbonic acid from the particles throughout the whole body of the liquor causes frothy bubbles to cover its entire surface. The yeasty froth begins to subside in about 36 hours, and, when the attenuation gets more advanced, the greater part of it falls to the bottom on account of its density relatively to the subjacent fluid. In from forty-eight to sixty hours the liquor begins to grow clear, and becomes comparatively tranquil. The liquor is stirred up occasionally during the fermentation, and the vessel is kept mostly closed after the first violence of the action. The specific gravity of the liquor diminishes as the process advances; the fermentation converts the sugar into alcohol or spirit; and, as the alcohol is lighter than water, it diminishes the specific gravity of the whole. The liquor itself is now called *wash*. 100 gallons of this wash contain about 12 gallons of proof spirit; if the whole of the sugar were decomposed (which it never is in practice), the produce of spirit would be greater. In the great distilleries, where the quantity of liquor operated on at once is very large, the duration of the fermenting process is longer than that above named.

Distillation.—Great distilleries are usually mounted with two stills, a larger and a smaller. The former is the *wash* still, and serves to distil from the fermented worts a weak crude spirit called *low-wines;* the latter is the *low-wine* still, and rectifies by a second process the product of the first distillation. In these successive distillations a quantity of fetid oil, derived from the corn, comes over along with the first and last portions received, and constitutes by its combination what is styled the strong and weak *faints*. These milky faints are carefully separated from the limpid spirit, by turning them as they begin to flow from the still into distinct channels, which lead to separate *receivers*. From these receivers the various qualities of spirit, low wines, and faints are, for the purpose of redistillation, pumped up into charging backs, from which they are run in guaged quantities into the low-wine and spirit stills.

The distilling apparatus, in one of the large establishments near London, is thus arranged. The wash is conveyed through pipes from the fermenting vessel to the wash-charger, which is a closed iron cistern, capable of containing 30,000 gallons. From this vessel the wash flows into the wash-still, a copper vessel holding 20,000 gallons; it is heated by a fire beneath, and is terminated at the top by a cover, which gradually decreases in diameter, and at length joins the worm, in another vessel. The wash is made to boil: and as alcohol boils and passes off in vapour at a temperature of 180°

Fahr., while water requires a temperature of 212°, the heating is so managed as never to reach 212°; and the alcohol vapour passes off with only a small portion of water vapour: if the process were perfectly conducted, there would be no water pass off with the spirit; but in practice there always is a small quantity, and to this extent the spirit is weakened by the mixture. The alcohol-vapour passes off into the worm, which is a copper tube curved spirally round the inside of a vessel thirty feet high, called the worm-tub: the tube is two feet in diameter at the upper part of the vessel, and diminishes down to two inches near the bottom. The worm-tub is filled with constantly flowing cold water, which keeps the copper worm at such a low temperature that the vapour in the worm is condensed into a liquid. This liquid, forming the *low-wines*, flows out of the narrow end of the worm into the low-wines receiver, from which it again flows into the spirit-still. Another distillation occurs, and sometimes a third, until so much of the water is driven off as to leave the spirit of a proper strength. Standard or 'proof spirit' consists of one half absolute or pure alcohol and one half water: if a given bulk of distilled water weighs 13 ounces, an equal bulk of proof spirit will weigh exactly 12 ounces. This difference of specific gravity gives rise to the construction and use of the HYDROMETER. There are certain stages or degrees of strength, 'above' or 'below proof,' according to circumstances: thus, the strongest spirit produced by distillation is 70° above proof, spirit of wine is not less than 43° above proof, raw spirits sold by the distiller to the rectifier are at 25° and 11° above proof, gin is about 17° below proof. The rectifying, or giving a modified strength and a peculiar flavour to spirit, is effected in totally distinct establishments from those in which the spirit is produced from grain. Scotch and Irish *whiskey* are distilled spirit without artificial flavour. English *gin* is flavoured with juniper berries, sugar, and other substances.

A large revenue is derived from distilled spirits; and the revenue officers exercise a most rigorous supervision over all the operations of a distillery.

The total number of proof gallons of spirits distilled and charged with excise duty, in 1849, was as follow:—

England	..	5,318,526 gallons
Scotland	..	10,444,709 „
Ireland	..	8,117,844 „
		23,881,079 gallons.

In looking at these numbers, we cannot fail to be struck with the circumstance that Ireland, with half the number of inhabitants, manufactures 50 per cent. more spirit than England: and (more striking still) that Scotland, with one-fifth of the population, manufactures twice as much spirit as England.

The Excise duty (7*s.* 10*d.* per gallon in England, 3*s.* 8*d.* in Scotland, and 2*s.* 8*d.* in Ireland) realised 4,847,217*l.* in 1849.

A few additional details respecting distilled spirits will be found under BRANDY, RUM, &c.

DIVING BELL. Much ingenuity has been devoted from an early period to the contrivance of apparatus for enabling men to descend beneath the surface of water, to a greater depth, for a longer space of time, and with less exertion and danger, than is possible by the unassisted powers of the body. Machines which in some degree included the principle of the Diving-Bell were suggested, contrived, and sometimes used for the purpose of obtaining property sunk in the sea or in rivers. At length, in the 16th century, the Diving Bell itself was invented and used; and Halley, in No. 349 of the 'Philosophical Transactions,' describes its defects, and suggests a remedy for them. In its simplest form the diving bell is a strong heavy vessel of wood or metal, made perfectly air and water tight at the top and sides, but open at the bottom. If such a vessel be gradually lowered into the water, in a perfectly horizontal position, the air which it contains cannot escape, and therefore the vessel cannot become full of water. Where the diving-bell is used for descending to a very small depth, as the pressure of the water is small, it will not rise in the bell to a sufficient height to be inconvenient; but at the depth of thirty-three feet the pressure is so great as to compress the air into one half its original volume, so that the bell will become half full of water; and at a greater depth the air will be still more compressed, and the water will rise proportionately higher in the bell. The unpleasant pressure of the condensed air on the ear, the difficulty of breathing, and the confinement of space within the bell, have all led to various improvements, by Dr. Halley and others.

The diving-bell used by Dr. Halley was of wood, in the form of a truncated cone, five feet in diameter at the bottom, and three feet at the top, and containing about sixty cubic feet. This was coated with lead, and so weighted about the lower part that it would sink while empty, and would always remain in its proper position; that is, with the large open end downwards, having its rim parallel with the horizon. In the top of the bell was a very strong glass window, and a cock, by opening which the foul air might be allowed to escape.

About a yard below the mouth of the bell was suspended a stage, so weighted that it might hang steadily. The apparatus for conveying air to the diving-bell consisted of two barrels, holding thirty-six gallons each, weighted with lead to make them sink readily. Each of these had an open bung-hole in the lower end, to allow water to enter during their descent, so as to condense the air; there was also a hole in the upper end of each, to which was fitted an air-tight leathern hose, long enough to fall below the bottom of the barrel, and having its loose end so weighted that it would fall naturally into that position. When the open end of the hose was turned up by the attendant, so as to be above the level of the water in the barrels, the air rushed out with great force into the bell, the barrels becoming at the same time full of water. By sending down these air-barrels in rapid succession, the air in the diving-bell was kept in so pure a state that five persons remained in it, at a depth of nine or ten fathoms, for more than an hour and a half at a time, without injurious consequences. When the sea was clear, and especially when the sun shone, sufficient light was transmitted to allow a person in the bell to write or read; and when the sea was troubled and thick, which occasioned the bell to be as dark as night, a candle was burnt in it. Halley sometimes sent up orders with the empty barrels, writing them with an iron pen on plates of lead.

The credit of having been the first to apply the diving-bell in aid of civil engineering operations is usually attributed to Smeaton, who used it in 1779 in repairing the foundations of Hexham Bridge. The bell used on this occasion was an oblong box of wood, four feet high, two wide, and three and a half long; and it was supplied with air by a pump fixed on the top. The river being shallow, the bell was not covered with water. In 1788 the diving-bell was used in a much more important work, Ramsgate harbour, by the same engineer. The depth here being considerable, an apparatus was employed for sending in a supply of air through a flexible pipe, by means of a forcing-pump. The bell used was of cast-iron, similar in form to that at Hexham, but four feet and a half high, four and a half long, and three wide. Its weight was 50 cwts., and the thickness was so adjusted that it would, without the addition of any weights, sink in the proper position. In levelling foundations under water by this machine the surface of the water at the bottom of the bell formed a convenient and unerring level to work to; and in this, as well as in the subsequent operation of building, every necessary motion was given to the bell by the tackle by which it was suspended; signals being made from below by striking one, two, three, or more blows upon the side of the bell with a hammer.

Since the time of Smeaton the diving-bell has been frequently, and with great advantage, employed in submarine works; sometimes in situations in which it would have been impossible to construct a coffer-dam, or to perform the required operations by any other means. The diving bells used in such works are usually formed on the model of that made for the works of Ramsgate Harbour; but the mode of suspension differs according to circumstances. The bell may be suspended over the side or end of a vessel; or through an opening in the centre of a barge; or from frame-work resting upon two barges, placed parallel with each other, but at such a distance apart as to allow the bell to descend between them; or from a scaffolding supported by piles. Of the use of this important machine in recovering property from wrecks, the operations upon that of the Royal George afford a familiar example. Smeaton's method of supplying air to the bell is that most commonly employed; but that of Halley may, in some cases, have the advantage.

One of the largest diving-bells ever constructed is that at the Polytechnic Institution. This machine is made of cast-iron, and weighs three tons. It has twelve glazed openings, six at the sides and six at the top: the glass being half an inch thick. It is 5 feet high, 4 feet 8 inches diameter at the bottom, and from 1½ to 2½ inches thick. Air is supplied to the bell by two air-pumps, with 8 inch barrels.

Many plans have been proposed for enabling a man to walk beneath the surface of water in such a manner as to assist in the recovery of property from wrecks, by means of waterproof coverings for the head and upper part of the body, or of strong vessels in which every part but the arms should be encased; a supply of air being either transmitted from above by a flexible pipe, or contained in the cavities of the protecting armour. Dr. Halley devised such an apparatus. The diver's head was covered by a heavy leaden cap, supplied with air by a flexible tube extending from the large bell. The diver was to coil this tube round his arm, and unwind it as he left the bell; and to use it as a clue to direct him to the bell in returning. This pipe was formed of leather soaked in oil and hot wax, and was held open by a spiral coil of brass-wire; its internal diameter being about one-sixth of an inch. The front of the helmet was glazed; and the diver, who was clothed in a thick woollen dress fitting close to the body, to diminish the effect of the coldness of the water, was enabled to walk by means of a weighted girdle and weighted clogs. The invention of water-proof India-rubber cloth, which has been applied in various ways to diving-apparatus, affords great facilities for the manufacture of water-tight tubes for such a purpose. Many varieties of diving-dresses have been since employed. Mr. Thornthwaite introduced a few years ago a contrivance for facilitating the descent and ascent of a diver. It consists of a hollow belt of India-rubber cloth, to which is attached a small but strong copper vessel. Into this vessel air is to be forced by a condensing-syringe until it has a pressure of thirty or forty atmospheres. The belt is then put on, in a collapsed state, so that it has no buoyancy, and does not impede the descent of the diver; but when he desires to rise, he opens a valve, by which the condensed air escapes from the copper vessel into the belt. As it expands the belt, it affords sufficient buoyancy to raise the diver immediately to the surface.

A few years ago Dr. Payerne attracted a good deal of public attention by his attempts to dispense with an air-pump to supply air to diving-bells. He made his experiments in 1842, first at Paris, and then at the Polytechnic Institution in London. The ordinary air-tube was removed from the diving bell; and he remained under water three or four hours without any connection with the external air. The experimenter took down with him a small box, containing some chemical agent which will absorb carbonic acid gas as fast as it is generated, and another agent which will evolve pure oxygen gas rapidly; and as he vitiated the air in the bell by his breathing, the one chemical substance absorbed the carbonic acid from it, while the other furnished a fresh supply of oxygen. Many such chemical agents are known; but we believe Dr. Payerne professed to keep his method secret. He made one or two descents at Spithead, near the wreck of the Royal George.

DNIEPER and DNIESTER. These two rivers of European Russia are made the media of conveying much merchandize and produce to the Black Sea. The entire length of the *Dnieper*, with its windings, is about 1000 miles. Its basin comprises fourteen of the finest provinces of Russia, with all of which it has communication by its navigable branches and by canals. The river is navigable almost from its source to its mouth; even the obstructions presented by the cataracts have been removed by the magnificent hydraulic works of the Russian government; several of the ledges of rocks having been entirely removed, and channels formed which are protected from winds by lofty dikes of granite. Produce is generally conveyed down the river to the cities on the Black Sea; but fleets of large barks also pass annually by the canals to Riga and St. Petersburg. The freights consist chiefly of timber, corn, iron, linen, hemp, salt, &c. The *Dniester* which is about 600 miles long, carries cargoes of timber, grain, and other produce to Odessa, on the Black Sea: much of which is brought to England.

DOCKS AND DOCK-YARDS. A dock is a place artificially formed for the reception of ships, the entrance of which is generally closed by gates. There are two kinds of docks, dry-docks and wet-docks. The former are used for receiving ships in order to their being inspected and repaired. For this purpose the dock is so contrived that the water may be admitted or excluded at pleasure, so that a vessel can be floated in when the tide is high, and the water run out with the fall of the tide, or be pumped out, the closing of the gates preventing its return. Wet docks are formed for the purpose of keeping vessels always afloat. Dock yards belonging to the government usually consist of dry docks for repairing ships, and of *slips* on which new vessels are built; besides which they comprise various workshops and storehouses.

The first wet dock for commercial purposes made in this kingdom was formed in the year 1708 at Liverpool. Since that time others have been added at different periods; and at present the margin of the Mersey along the whole extent of the town, for about three miles, is occupied by docks. They comprise the *Northern*, the *Clarence*, the *Victoria*, the *Waterloo*, the *Prince's*, the *George's*, the *Canning*, the *Manchester*, the *Salthouse*, the *Duke's*, the *King's*, the *Queen's*, the *Albert*, the *Union*, the *Brunswick*, the *Herculaneum*, and the *Harrington* docks. They cover more than 100 acres, and have an extent of quay ten or twelve miles in length.

At Birkenhead are docks noticed in a former article [BIRKENHEAD]. Fleetwood, Hull, Bristol, and other commercial towns, have convenient docks.

The first commercial wet dock constructed in the port of London was for the accommodation of vessels employed in the Greenland whale fishery. This dock, which is now known as the *Commercial Dock*, is situated at Rotherhithe; it occupies altogether 49 acres, about four-fifths of which are water: it is now used mainly for the timber and corn trade. Adjoining it is the *East Country Dock*, used for the timber trade.

Up to the end of the last century, nearly all

FLOOR CLOTH
PRINTING
TROWEL PAINTING
PREPARING
RED
BLUE
BLACK
COMBD COLOURS
YELLOW
GREEN

ships arriving in London discharged their cargoes into lighters in the river. To remedy this inconvenience, a plan was sanctioned in 1799 for constructing wet docks for the reception of ships employed in the West India trade. The *West India Docks* extend across the Isle of Dogs. The import dock is 879 yards long and 166 yards wide; the export dock is of the same length and 135 yards wide; there are besides two basins, one at each entrance, that at Blackwall being 5 acres, and that at Limehouse 2 acres in extent. A canal cut across the Isle of Dogs has been also appropriated as a dock or basin. The *London Docks*, situated in Wapping, and finished in 1805, consist of the western dock of 20 acres, the eastern dock of 7 acres, and the tobacco dock, between the other two, of more than 1 acre. The space included within the dock walls exceeds 71 acres. The warehouses, especially those for tobacco and wine, are of vast extent. The *St. Katharine's Docks*, situated between the London Docks and the Tower, were opened in 1828; the outer wall encloses an area of 24 acres, of which 11 acres are water, the remainder being occupied by quays and warehouses. There are two docks each capable of receiving vessels of 800 tons burden.

The Commercial Dock Company propose, in 1851, to purchase the East Country or Greenland Dock, and to expend 200,000*l.* in enlargements and improvements.

In the half year from June to November 1850, the laden ships which entered the London Docks from foreign countries were 685, measuring 186,517 tons. The stock of goods in the warehouses, on Nov. 30 in that year, amounted to 124,825 tons. A new stack of warehouses has just been constructed by the company on the West Quay.

At the St. Katharine's Docks the goods received during the year 1850 amounted to 119,149 tons. The ships which entered with cargoes were 703, of 152,046 tons; and those which entered to load were 259. The goods in warehouse on December 31, 1850, were 68,121 tons.

Collier docks are about to be formed opposite Woolwich, near the North Woolwich station of the Eastern Counties Railway. A dock of 70 acres is planned, available not only for collier ships but for passenger steamers.

The construction of *floating dry docks* is now engaging the attention of engineers: the principle being, to adopt a means of buoying up a ship on some kind of floating support, so as to leave it high and dry. There are now being constructed for the United States Government, at Philadelphia, docks of a remarkable kind on this principle. There are ten closed compartments, called sections, capable of being exhausted of water by means of pumps; and when so exhausted, each section can buoy up a weight of 800 tons. Six of them together would bear up a ship of the line, while four would bear a frigate. There is a stone basin or dock, 350 feet long by 226 wide. When a ship is to be dry-docked, some of the sections are filled with water sufficiently for the vessel to be floated in on the top of them; and when brought into the basin, the water is pumped out of the sections, and the vessel thus buoyed up. There is a railway, also, by which the vessel may be brought up completely on dry land. These remarkable works are expected to be finished during the year 1851. Other works of a similar kind are being constructed in other parts of the United States.

The largest gates ever made for docks, perhaps, are those which Messrs. Rennie have recently made for the Russian government, to be fitted up at Sevastopol on the Black Sea. On account of the peculiar locality of the town with respect to the depth of the shores, three locks were made so as to raise a ship of war to a height of 30 feet above the sea level. These locks have nine pairs of gates, varying from 21 to 34 feet in height, and from 47 to 64 feet in width. On account of the ravages of a peculiar worm, the use of wood was determined against, and iron substituted. The gates consist of wrought iron plates in cast iron frames; and so enormous are some of the masses, that the engineers had to erect large and costly machinery for planing and punching them.

Our Government Dock Yards are briefly described under the names of the towns where they are situated. [CHATHAM; PLYMOUTH, &c.]

DOLL MANUFACTURE. Let not any one suppose that the making of dolls is too trifling an employment to merit notice in a work devoted to industrial pursuits. It affords bread to numerous persons, and is subjected to as many divisions and subdivisions as other manufactures. A glass manufacturer of Birmingham, some years ago, astonished a Committee of the House of Commons by stating that he had received, at one time, an order for 500*l.* worth of dolls' eyes!

There are two classes of dolls—*wooden* and *sewed;* the former cheap, and the latter more expensive. The wooden dolls make but little approach to anatomical correctness; whereas the sewed dolls are the results of more ambitious skill. The wooden doll passes through few hands in the process of making; but the sewed doll is the work of many distinct classes of artificers—such as the doll sewer and stuffer, the dolls' head maker, the dolls' arm and leg maker, the dolls' wig maker, the dolls' eye maker, and the doll dresser.

In wooden dolls the body is turned in a lathe, thereby giving to the human bust a form which nature never gave—an equal rotundity on all sides. They are carved or cut by hand to impart certain improvements; and the legs are made—with calves or without calves—according to the price. A composition is laid on the face; and the painter's pencil is employed to supply lips, eyebrows, &c. Every doll, except in the humblest station of life, has jointed legs, which are fixed to the body by a kind of wooden hinge. Unless the doll have painted ringlets, real ringlets are purchased from the dolls' wig maker. The arms are usually made of stuffed leather.

The *sewed* dolls go through a larger number of processes, and employ more persons. The maker cuts out the calico which is to form the outer surface, and gives it together with sawdust or wool to the doll sewer and stuffer, by whom the structure of the doll is built up. The composition heads for these dolls are usually made of *papier maché*; but they have a superficial coating of wax; they are painted flesh colour, and then dipped into melted wax. The mould for the papier maché is made from a wax model, and the substance itself is a kind of sugar paper, reduced to a pulp. The arms and legs, and the wig, are made by other persons.

Dolls' eyes seem to form the most curious department of this curious manufacture. They are of two kinds, the cheap and the expensive. The more cheaply constructed eyes are simply small hollow glass beads or spheres, made of white enamel, and coloured either black or blue, but without any attempt at diverse colouring. The better kind of eyes, called by the makers natural eyes, are made in the same manner so far as concerns the glass or enamel, but the iris is represented by a painted or stained ring.

In one of the interesting papers recently published in the *Morning Chronicle*, some curious statistical facts are given respecting the doll manufacture. The commonest wooden dolls were formerly sold at a penny each, but now (competition having affected dolls as well as more important commodities) command a price of only one farthing. Some of the sewed dolls are stuffed with sawdust and sewed for half a crown per gross. The commonest dolls' eyes sell from five to six shillings per twelve dozen pairs; while the best or *natural* eyes obtain a price of fourpence per pair. Dolls' eyes are largely exported; in Spanish America *black* eyes only will find a sale, while in this country *blue* eyes are the favourites.

Gutta percha is now employed as a material for some dolls; and various costly novelties are from time to time introduced. The *speaking* doll is an object of great admiration to doll buyers; but the six guineas' price limits the sale to a small number. It was the invention of a London doll maker, who, after nine years of experimental trial and failure, succeeded in making his doll speak the two favourite nursery words 'mama' and 'papa.' One of these was sent to St. Petersburg; it became injured on the way, and lost its speech, which no Russian doll-maker was found able to restore.

DOLLOND, JOHN, as an eminent practical optician, calls for a few words of notice in this place. He was descended from a French refugee family, settled in Spitalfields, and was born in 1706. His father was an operative silk-weaver, and his own boyhood was spent in the drudgery of a manufactory; he found time however to make considerable progress in the study of mathematics and natural philosophy; besides which he cultivated anatomy, and devoted his leisure moments to ecclesiastical history and to languages. About the year 1755 he commenced a series of experiments on the dispersion of light, and in 1757 he made the decisive experiment which showed the error of Newton's conclusion respecting the proportional refrangibility of light in all media. In consequence of the discovery, Mr. Dollond was enabled to construct what are called achromatic telescopes, or such as afford images of objects almost wholly free from coloured fringes. The discovery was rewarded, by the Council of the Royal Society, with the Copley Medal. After this he became eminent as the first optical instrument maker of his day, and communicated many papers to the Royal Society.

Mr. Dollond died in 1761; but his establishment has ever since maintained its high character, under various members of his family.

DOLOMITE. This rock, having the aspect and general geological history of limestone, but composed of carbonate of magnesia united to carbonate of lime, usually atom to atom, occurs as a part of the oolitic system of the Alps and Apennines, and of the German Jurakalk; and it is perhaps proper to call by the same name the crystallised magnesian limestone of Nottinghamshire, Derbyshire, Yorkshire, and Durham. The best example of this English dolomite is at Bolsover, in Derbyshire, whence the stone is taken to build the new Houses of Parliament.

DOME, a term applied to a covering of the

whole or part of a building. The word *dome* is strictly applied to the external part of the spherical or polygonal roof, and *cupola* to the internal part.

The most magnificent dome of antiquity is that of the Pantheon, supposed to be a chamber of the great baths of Agrippa. Internally it is divided into five rows of square compartments, which are supposed to have been decorated with plates of silver. The external part of the dome appears also to have been decorated with bands of bronze. The base of the dome externally consists of a large plinth with six smaller plinths or steps above it; and in the curve of the dome a flight of steps is formed which leads to the opening at the top. The dome is constructed of bricks and rubble. The thickness is about 17 feet at the base, 5 feet 1½ inches at the top of the highest step, and 4 feet 7 inches at the top of the dome. The circular wall which supports the dome is 20 feet thick.

The Thermæ, or baths, of Caracalla, Titus, Constantine, and Diocletian, were all surmounted by domes. Near Pozzuoli there is a very perfect circular building with a dome 96 feet in diameter, built of volcanic tufo and pumice stone. The temple of Minerva Medica, without the walls of Rome, had a dome of ten sides built of brick and pumice stone. The dome of Santa Sophia, at Constantinople, built in the reign of Justinian, rests on the square formed at the intersection of the arms of a Greek cross. The dome is supported by four corbellings placed in the angles of the square, surmounted by a kind of cornice which supports a circular gallery. Externally the dome is divided by projecting ribs, rounded and covered with lead. The top is surmounted by a lantern or finishing like a baluster, on which is a cross. The dome of San Vitale at Ravenna, is curiously constructed. The lower part of the plan is a regular octagon, which is supported by eight piers placed at the angles of the dome; in the spaces between the piers are seven niches, divided into two stories. The wall above the niches sustains a hemispherical dome, the plan being a circle described within a regular octagon. The dome is built of a double row of pipes, hollow at one end and pointed at the other, the point of one being placed in the hollow of the preceding; it is covered with mortar both within and without. The church of San Marco at Venice, built in the tenth century, is decorated with five domes. One of these, placed in the centre of the church, is much larger than the others. Each dome is enclosed within four pieces of semi-cylindrical vaulting, forming together a square, in the angles of which are four corbels, which gather in the circular base of each dome. The dome of Santa Maria del Fiore, at Florence, built by Bruneleschi, stands upon an octagon tower 175 feet high; it is double, being the first of the kind that is known. The internal dome is connected only at the angles to the external one, and forms a species of gothic vault. The first modern dome constructed in Rome was that of the church of Our Lady of Loretto, built in 1507; it is double, and circular in plan, and is constructed on double consoles.

The dome of St. Peter's at Rome, as planned by Michael Angelo, and executed by himself and succeeding architects, is thus constructed. It stands upon four piers 62 feet high. From the arches spring corbellings, which are finished by an entablature; upon this is a plinth, octagonal within and circular without; upon this is a circular stylobate, 12 feet high. Above the stylobate is the drum of the dome, built of rubble and fragments of brick, and pierced by sixteen lofty windows: the height of the drum is about 52 feet. On this is placed a circular attic story, 19 feet high, and then comes the double dome. The space between the two domes varies from three to ten feet in width. The thickness of the inner dome is about six feet; the outer dome is of less thickness: the two are joined together by sixteen strong walls or spurs. Above the dome are a lofty lantern and cross: the dome is about 102 feet high above the drum, and the lantern and cross 90 feet above the dome.

The dome of St. Paul's Cathedral, London, is placed over the intersection of the four naves. The ground plan is a regular octagon: four of the sides are formed by the four great arches of the naves; the other four sides are formed by false arches of the same size. The corbellings gather in a circle, and are surmounted by a complete entablature decorated with consoles. The drum, which surmounts the entablature, is 62 feet in height; and from the summit of this rises the double dome. The inner dome is much less lofty than the outer: the outer one is constructed of wood, covered with lead.

The dome of the Invalides at Paris is raised on the centre of a Greek cross, on an octagonal base with four large and four small sides A circular entablature is placed over the corbellings, and on the entablature is raised the drum of the dome. The dome, which is double, rises from a springing common to both. The lower or internal dome, constructed with masonry, is spherical; whereas the outer dome is of a spheroidal form, and constructed of stone at the base, and of brick above. The dome of the Pantheon at Paris is constructed entirely of stone, and is placed in the centre of a Greek cross. It is supported by four triangular piers, pierced above with arched openings, and between the piers with the openings are large arches. Between these arches rise the corbellings, which are gathered in to form the circular plan of the drum. Tho arches and the corbellings are crowned with a large entablature about 13 feet high, and above this is the circular drum, 55 feet high. There are three domes one within another; one forming the interior vault or roof, a second forming the exterior, and a third shaped like the small end of an egg, and intermediate between the other two, for supporting the lantern.

The following admeasurements of most of the principal domes of Europe are from Mr. Ware's 'Tracts on Vaults and Bridges.'

	Feet in diameter externally.	High from the ground line.
Dome of the Pantheon	142	143
,, Minerva Medica	78	97
,, Baths of Caracalla ..	112	116
,, Baths of Diocletian ..	74	83
Temple of Mercury	68	
,, Diana	98	78
,, Apollo	120	
,, Proserpine and Venus	87	77
Santa Sophia at Constantinople	115	201
Mosque of Achmet, ditto	92	120
San Vitale at Ravenna	55	91
San Marco at Venice	44	
Santa Maria del Fiore	139	310
The Chapel of the Medici ...	91	199
Baptistry at Florence	86	110
St. Peter's at Rome	139	330
Ch. of the Madonna at Venice	70	133
,, Superga at Turin ..	64	128
,, Invalides at Paris,	80	173
,, Val de Grace, Paris,	55	133
,, Sorbonne, Paris ..	40	110
Pantheon, Paris	67	190
St. Paul's London	112	215

DONEGAL. This Irish county is rich in quarries of fine stone. The white marble of Dunlewy, near the mountain Erigal, is stated to be of an excellent quality, and its bed very extensive; it has been traced over a space of half a mile square, and is so finely granular, that it may be employed in the nicest works of sculpture. 'Its texture and whiteness,' says Mr. Griffith, 'approach more to those of the Parian than of the Carrara marble. It is very well known that perfect blocks of the Carrara marble are procured with great difficulty, and I firmly believe that the marble of Dunlewy is free from mica, quartz grains, and other substances interfering with the chisel, which so frequently disappoint the artists who work upon the marble from Carrara.' A large supply of fine siliceous sand was formerly drawn from the mountain of Muckish by the glass-houses of Belfast, and considerable quantities have been exported to Dumbarton for the manufacture of plate and crown glass.

The linen manufacture is carried on to a very considerable extent, and is increasing in the cultivated country about Raphoe and Lifford, and also in the neighbourhood of Ballyshannon. Bleachgreens are numerous in the neighbourhood of Stranorlar. Strabane, in the county of Tyrone, within two miles of Lifford, is the principal linen market for the southern district. Londonderry and Letterkenny are the markets for the district to the north. Burning kelp continues to be a profitable occupation along the coast. About the beginning of the present century private distillation was carried on to an immense extent all over this county, particularly in the baronies of Inishowen and Kilmacrenan: repeated baronial fines and the vigilance of the authorities have latterly checked the practice, but it still exists to some extent in the mountain districts. Considerable numbers of whales have from time to time been taken off this coast; but this, as well as the herring fishery, is now neglected. In 1802 there were but two flour mills in this county. There was a few years back an export of 3000 to 4000 tons of corn annually from Letterkenny, and the remaining export of the county is from Londonderry; but it has suffered in the recent general depression of Ireland.

DORSETSHIRE. This county yields many mineral substances useful in the arts. The eastern parts of the county are mostly occupied by the plastic clay. Potters' clay in beds of various thickness and at different depths alternates with loose sand in this formation in the Trough of Poole; it is sent to Staffordshire, where it is mixed with ground flints, and employed in the finer kinds of pottery. Beneath the potters' clay lies a seam of very friable earthy brown coal, somewhat like Bovey coal. The Purbeck strata, belonging to the upper series of the oolitic formation, consist of argillaceous limestone alternating with schistose marl; they crop out from under the iron-sand in the Isle of Purbeck. A variety of the Purbeck stone, known as Purbeck marble, was formerly much used in building. The Portland oolite, another member of the same series, which succeeds the Purbeck stone, occupies the remainder of the Isle of Purbeck and the whole of that of Portland. It consists of a number of beds of a yellowish white calcareons freestone, generally mixed with a small quantity of siliceous sand. The varieties of this formation afford the greater part of the stone used for architectural purposes in London. In the Portland quarries, the saleable stone occupies layers of strata situated several feet beneath the surface; and the quarrymen have to exert great labour in the removal of the superincumbent rubbish, before they can reach the stone. The thickness of workable stone varies from 7 to 16 feet, and the works proceed at the rate of about an acre of good stone per annnm. Almost the entire mass of Portland Isle consists of the Purbeck series.

The Dorset butter is in good repute in London and Portsmouth for ship provision as well as domestic use: it is not so salt as the Irish, and is therefore preferred, although the Irish is richer when it is of the best quality. Dorset salt butter, when well washed, is very commonly sold in London for fresh butter. The butter is made from the cream, and the skimmed milk is made into cheese. The Dorsetshire skim-milk cheese is preferred on account of streaks of blue mould which frequently run through it.

In 1847 an act was passed for the formation of a harbour of refuge off the Isle of Portland by the construction of a breakwater, extending northward from the north-eastern point of the island for 2¼ miles, so as to include a large part of Portland Road. Owing to the facilities afforded by the presence of an abundant supply of suitable stone on the island, it is estimated that the cost will not exceed 500,000*l*. The works are now steadily advancing.

Dorsetshire contains very few towns of a manufacturing character, and will only to a limited extent take part in the Industrial Exhibition.

DOUAI. The inhabitants of this ancient French city are engaged in the manufacture of linen, lace, thread, gauze, cotton, soap, glass, leather, beer, gin, pottery, paper, oil, chemical products, and refined sugar. A considerable trade is carried on also in corn, wine, brandy, chicory, wool, hops, flax, woollen cloth, and cattle. Exhibitions of the industrial products take place every two years. The commerce of the town is more active than formerly, in consequence of its connection by railroads with the chief towns of France and Belgium. Douai has also extensive communication by means of the Scarpe, which falls into the Schelde, and by numerous canals that connect it with the principal trading towns of France, Belgium, and Holland.

DOUBLE-BASE, or *Contra-Basso*, is the largest musical instrument of the viol kind. In England, Italy, and France, it has three strings: in Germany a fourth is added. From the body and firmness of its tone, it is considered to be the foundation of an orchestral band.

DOVER HARBOUR. [HARBOURS OF REFUGE.]

DOVETAIL is the end of a piece of wood fashioned into the fan-like form of a dove's tail, and let into a corresponding hollow of another piece of wood.

DOWN. In this Irish county the linen manufacture is the staple trade, and gives employment to a greater number of operatives, in proportion to the population, than in any other part of Ireland. It has been estimated that the linen trade gives employment, in various ways, to 10,000 persons in the county. Much of the flax employed is grown in the county; and seed for this flax is imported from Flanders. The new impetus now being given to the flax manufacture will probably lead to favourable results in this county. Machine-spun yarn is now mostly used for the warp-thread of linen, but hand-spun yarn is preferred for the weft. The weaving is mostly done in cottages, by persons who devote a part of their time to farming. There are about a dozen towns in Downshire where linen markets are held. The bleaching of the woven linen is a large branch of manufacture, conducted in bleach fields on the banks of the river Bann. The remaining articles of manufacture in the county are chiefly muslin, leather, salt, glass, and vitriol. The fisheries on the coast are rather extensive. The chief exports of the county are shipped at Belfast and Newry.

At Ardglass, Banbridge, Downpatrick, Portaferry, Newtownards, &c., much manufacturing is carried on. Belfast, though the principal port for this county, is in Antrim. Newry ranks high in exports, and the imports are very considerable. Steamers sail regularly to Liverpool and Glasgow, and many vessels trade to America, the Baltic, the Levant, and various parts of England. Besides flour and oatmeal mills, there are various manufactures carried on connected with ship-building, and the retail trade of the town is extensive.

DRACHM, or DRAM. There are two drachms or drams remaining in our system of weights. The first is the sixteenth part of the ounce, which is the sixteenth part of the pound avoirdupois of 7000 grains. In the national standard, the troy pound of 5760 grains, there is no dram; but this weight occurs in that particular division of the troy pound which is used by apothecaries, in which the dram is the eighth part of the ounce, which is the twelfth part of tne pound of 5760 grains. The *drachma* was a Greek silver coin, the weight of which was abont 61 grains.

DRACI'NA, or *draconin*, is the colouring matter of Dragon's Blood gum. It is of a fine red colour, and very fusible; it may be worked between the fingers, and drawn into threads. It melts at about 130°

DRAINING. As a certain quantity of moisture is essential to vegetation, so an excess of it is highly detrimental. In the removal of this excess consists the art of *Draining*, which presents three principal features:—1. To drain land which is flooded by water coming over it from a higher level, and having no adequate outlet below. 2. To drain land where springs rise to the surface, and where there are no natural channels for the water to run off. 3. To drain land which is wet from its impervious nature, and where the evaporation is not sufficient to carry off all the water.

The first branch includes all those extensive operations where large tracts of land are reclaimed by means of embankments, canals, sluices, and tunnels. Such works are generally undertaken by associations under the sanction of the government, or by the government itself: the BEDFORD LEVEL is an example of them. In Switzerland many marshes have been laid dry by tunnelling through solid rocky obstructions; and in Holland vast tracts are protected from flooding by embankments.

Where the land is below the level of the sea at high water, it requires a constant removal of the water which percolates through the banks or accumulates by rains; and this can only be effected by sluices and mills, as is the case in the fens in England. The water is collected in numerous ditches and canals, and led to the points where it can most conveniently be discharged over the banks. In hilly countries it sometimes happens that the waters which run down the slopes of the hills collect in the bottoms where there is no outlet, and where the soil is impervious. In that case, it may sometimes be laid dry by cutting a sufficient channel all round, to intercept the waters as they flow down, and to carry them over or through the lowest part of the surrounding barrier. In draining a great extent of land, it is often necessary to widen and deepen rivers, and alter their courses; and not unfrequently the water cannot be let off without being carried by means of tunnels under the bed of some river, the level of which is above that of the land.

The draining of land which is rendered wet by springs arising from under the soil is a branch of more general application. The object is to find the readiest channels by which the superfluous water may be carried off; and for this purpose an accurate knowledge of the strata through which the springs rise is indispensable. Abundant springs which flow continually generally proceed from the outbreaking of some porous stratum in which the waters were confined, or through natural crevices in rocks or impervious earth; and these, as well as land-springs, are traced by geological means. Wherever water springs, there must be a pervious and an impervious stratum to cause it, and the water either runs over the impervious surface, or rises through the crevices in it. When the line of the springs is found, the obvious remedy is to cut a channel with a sufficient declivity to take off the water in a direction across this line, and sunk through the porous soil at the surface into the lower impervious earth. The place for this channel is where the porous soil is the shallowest above the breaking out, so as to require the least depth of drain; but the solid stratum must be reached, or the draining will be imperfect. When there is a great variation in the soil, and it is difficult to find any main line of springs, it is best to proceed experimentally by boring in various parts; whereby it will generally be easy to ascertain whence the water arises, and how it may be let off. When the drains cannot be carried to a sufficient depth to take the water out of the porous stratum, it is often useful to bore numerous holes with an auger in the bottom of the drain through the stiffer soil, and the water will either rise through these bores into the drains and be carried off, or it will sink down through them if it lies above. This method is often advantageous in the draining of peat mosses. If the soil, whatever be its nature, can be drained to a certain depth, it is of no consequence what water may be lodged below it. It is only when it rises so as to stagnate about the roots of plants that it is hurtful.

The third branch in the art of draining is by far the most expensive operation, in consequence of the number of drains required to lay the surface dry, and the necessity of filling them with porous substances, through which the surface water can penetrate. There is often a layer of light earth immediately over a substratum of clay, and after continued rains this soil becomes filled with water, like a sponge, and no healthy vegetation can take place. In this case numerous drains must be made in the subsoil, and over the draining tiles or bushes which may be laid at the bottom of the drains loose gravel or broken stones must be laid to within a foot of the surface, so that the plough shall not reach them. The water will gradually sink into these drains, and be carried off, and the loose wet soil will become firm and dry. The slope of the field and the fall which can be obtained for the drains, their size and depth below the surface, the angles at which they intersect each other, and their number—all are circumstances which require the drainer's best attention. In draining clay land, where there is only a layer of a few inches of loose soil over a solid clay which the plough never stirs, the drains need not be deeper than two feet in the solid clay, nor wider than they can be made without the sides falling in. The common draining tile, which is a flat tile bent in the form of half a cylinder, is the best for extensive surface draining. In solid clay it requires no flat tile under it; it is merely an arch to carry the loose stones or earth with which the drain is filled up. In grass land the sod may be laid over the drain after it has been filled up, so as to form a slight ridge over it. Sometimes a drain is covered with a sod, without any tile whatever; and at ether times a twisted rope of straw is thrust into the drain. Draining tiles are now made of various shapes and sizes.

As the draining of wet clay soils is the only means by which they can be rendered profitable as arable land, and the expense is great, various instruments and ploughs have been contrived to diminish manual labour and expedite the work. Among these are the common mole plough, the draining-plough, Smith's subsoil plough, tapering spades, and hollow spades. Weir's improved draining level is one of the instruments now often employed in these works.

The draining of Haarlem Lake is one of the greatest hydraulic enterprises ever conducted. We have nothing in this conntry that can give an adequate idea of this lake, or the necessity of its being drained. Three centuries ago there were several small lakes in the flat district which lies between the towns of Amsterdam, Leyden, and Haarlem, in Holland; but by the gradual wearing away of the soft ground between them, many of these became converted into one large lake; and the shores continued to be washed away so extensively, that by the beginning of the 18th century a lake was formed covering an area of 45,000 acres. As the level was 13 feet below the level of the neighbouring sea, there was no outlet for the water; and although the Dutch incurred heavy expenses to endeavour to arrest the enlargement of the lake, they had no means of diminishing it. At length, in 1836, two inundations occurred of so serious a character, as to determine the Dutch government to drain the lake at any cost; one inundation covered 10,000 acres of low land near Amsterdam, while another covered 10,000 acres near Leyden. The first work was to dig a canal entirely around the lake, 38 miles long, 120 feet wide, and 9 feet deep; this canal was to accommodate the immense water traffic which was conducted on the lake, and to serve as a receptacle for the water of the lake. The next point was, to close with large earthen dams all inlets into the lake, so that it should have no increase, except from rain water. Other hydraulic works were executed in other places, to facilitate the flow of water into the sea as soon as it was raised from the lake. These preliminary works occupied the time from the year 1840, when the enterprise was determined on, till 1845, when the steam-engines were set to work. These engines are the largest that have ever been constructed; they were made by Cornish engineers, who have acquired great skill in the manufacture of steam-engines which shall perform a great amount of work with a small amount of fuel. Each steam engine has an enormous cylinder 12 feet in diameter, with an annular or ring-shaped piston; and within this piston cylinder is another cylinder and piston 7 feet in diameter. Eleven pumps, more than 5 feet in diameter of barrel, are ranged around a sort of tower, on which the steam engine is placed; and all these enormous pumps are worked at once by the steam engine. The water is lifted by the pumps from the lake into the canal, whence it flows by sluices into the sea. It was calculated that about a thousand million tons of water would have to be lifted from the lake; and that after it was drained, there would regularly be about fifty millions of tons that would require to be annually removed, the result of drainage and rain. It will servo to convey some idea of the enormous power of the engines employed, that each engine raises 112 tons of water 10 feet high at one stroke.

A draining operation of great magnitude is about to be commenced at the æstuary called the *Wash*. This æstuary forms a sort of bay between Norfolk and Lincolnshire, and into it flow the rivers Witham, Nene, Welland, and Ouse. It has become so silted up, that a large area is utterly useless—too shallow to be available for navigation, and too wet to be used for agricultural purposes. To deepen the mouths of all the rivers, and to reclaim many thousand acres of marshy useless land, are the great objects of the Wash Drainage enterprise. All the rivers will be greatly improved by these works; while it is estimated that the reclaimed land, as an agricultural estate or estates, will pay for the operation, and yield an adequate profit. The towns of Lynn, Wisbeach, Spalding, and Boston, situated respectively on the four rivers, will all be benefited by the operation, as vessels of larger tonnage will be enabled to reach those towns than can ascend the present partially-choked streams.

DRAWBRIDGE is a bridge used in ancient castles and in modern fortresses over a ditch or fosse, and capable of being raised up at one end, so as to cut off the means of access. Drawbridges are usually formed of boards nailed to a frame constituting a platform, which is furnished at one end with hinges fastened to a beam placed parallel to one end of the frame. The bridge is raised by means of chains passed through the masonry of the gate, and these chains are worked either by wheels or by hand.

DRAWING, in its strict meaning, is the art of representing objects on a flat surface by lines describing their forms and contours alone, independently of colour or even shadow, although the latter is closely allied with drawing, both in practice and in theory. Although drawing embraces all objects and their forms, in its more restricted technical sense it is usually understood to imply the drawing of the human figure, as that species of it which is the most scientific in itself and the most important in art. Perspective, which is generally treated of separately, and is therefore ordinarily considered a distinct study, is neverless a most essential part of drawing—in fact, its very grammar, all objects being subject to its laws, although they do not admit of being delineated according to the processes employed for drawing buildings, furniture, and such things as consist of strict geometrical forms.

There are various manipulations or modes of drawing, distinguished according to the materials or implements made use of, such as chalk, black lead pencil, sepia or other tinted drawings, which last-mentioned class are sometimes called washed drawings, in which some indication of colouring is occasionally introduced. But what is termed water-colour drawing, as now practised, is altogether a species of painting, although the process is totally different from that of oil colours, or even distemper. Pen and ink drawings, in the style of etchings, either with or without the addition of wash or shadow, are capable of producing considerable effect.

The invention of Lithography has been applied with great success to making fac-similes of such drawings; it also enables artists to make drawings at once upon stone, from which impressions may afterwards be taken that are equivalent to autograph delineations.

Our Schools of Design are becoming every year more and more the means of diffusing a knowledge of drawing among artisans and pattern designers; a knowledge, the fruits of which will be shown at the forthcoming Exhibition.

DREDGING-MACHINES are employed for clearing away deposited matter from the beds of rivers, canals, harbours, and basins. Some machines for this purpose may be compared to harrows or shovels, which loosen the deposit preparatory to its removal either by the action of the tide or by sluicing. But, for the most part, they remove as well as loosen the deposit. The spoon dredging machine consists of a strong hoop of iron, about two feet in diameter, attached to a pole thirty or forty feet long, and carrying a large bag of perforated bullock's hide. This apparatus is connected by ropes with a barge, from the side of which it is let down and manœuvred in such a manner that the edge of the hoop cuts into the soft bottom, and scoops a large quantity of silt into the bag, which is then drawn up to the surface. The bucket dredging machine is a long massive framework with a wheel at each end, over which a series of endless chains is placed; so that by turning one of the wheels the whole chain is set in motion. Attached to the chain is a series of perforated iron buckets. By means of tackle the bucket-frame is let down until it reaches the bottom, when, the steam-engine being set to work, the chain of buckets begins to perform its circuit, by which every bucket is, in succession, made to scoop up a quantity of silt, which it carries up to the top of the oblique frame, and pours out its contents into a barge.

Dredging machines are constantly in use in the Thames, to deepen those parts which have become too much shallowed by mud and sand.

DRESDEN. However interesting the capital of Saxony may be as a repository of works of art, it has no external trade or manufactures of much importance. It is a place of transit for colonial and other foreign produce from Magdeburg, Hamburg, &c., and has six general fairs. Its mechanics have obtained some note in Germany for the manufacture of mathematical, mechanical, and musical instruments, engraving on steel and stone, the making of gloves, carpets, turnery ware, jewellery, straw hats, painters' colours, &c. These mechanics are incorporated into 60 fraternities. Morocco and other leather, refined sugar, tobacco, white lead, tin ware, glass, stockings, cotton goods, &c., are also manufactured.

The part which Dresden will take in the

approaching display of the world's industry, will have its leading feature in the celebrated Dresden China, of so great celebrity. This, however, is not a Dresden manufacture; it is made at Meissen, a town several miles distant from that metropolis. We shall notice the factory and the manufacture in a later article. Among the articles to be sent from Dresden is a beautiful model of that city, in porcelain, large enough to admit of accurate models of the principal churches and buildings. A porcelain vase of great size and artistic beauty is also said to be in preparation. These works are being prepared at the Royal Porcelain Manufactory.

DRILL. [Boring.]

DRILLING is a mode of sowing by which the seed is deposited in regular equidistant rows, at such a depth as each kind requires for its most perfect vegetation. It has been practised by gardeners from time immemorial, and from the garden it has gradually extended to the field. The drill husbandry, by combining the advantages of continued tillage with those of manure and a judicious rotation of crops, is a decided improvement on the old methods of sowing all seeds broadcast. The crops which are now most generally drilled are potatoes, turnips, beans, peas, beet-root, cole-seed, and carrots; and in general all plants which require room to spread, whether above or under the ground. The distance between the rows in these crops is generally such as to allow the use of a light plough or horse-hoe to be drawn by a horse between them. The most common distance is twenty-seven inches. The Northumberland mode of cultivating turnips, which is adopted by most scientific farmers, consists in placing the manure in rows immediately under the line in which the seed is to be drilled, and keeping the intervals in a mellow and pulverised state by repeated stirring.

The instrument used for sowing seeds in single rows is sometimes a small light wheel-barrow, which a man pushes before him; hence called a *drill-barrow*. It has a box in which the seed is put, with a slide to regulate the quantity. This is allowed to fall on a wooden or metal cylinder below. In the circumference of this cylinder are several cavities where the seed lodges, and is carried down into a tin funnel below; the remainder is prevented from falling through by small brushes in which the cylinder turns. The motion is communicated from the wheel which runs on the ground to the cylinder by means of a chain and pulleys. The improved drills, of which there are many patented varieties, are complex but very efficient machines, which sow several rows at once.

At the Smithfield cattle shows, and at the annual exhibitions of the Royal Agricultural Society, the variety of ingenious drills displayed every year is very considerable. One machine, exhibited at the Smithfield show in 1850, is Hensman's eight-row corn and turnip drill, for which a prize was awarded by the Agricultural Society at the York meeting in 1848. It is adapted for all sorts of corn and seeds; the hopper into which the grain or seed is put is self-acting; tho axles slide, to give a shifting movement to the drills; and there is a steering lever behind to guide the action of the drills. Another useful apparatus is Wedlake's corn and seed drill. Smith's Uxbridge drill is another kind, which has been introduced within the last few years. Some drills are formed so as to deposit manure only without seed or grain; the hoppers are filled with soot, lime, ground bones, or some other manure brought to a fine state.

DROGHEDA, although not strictly a manufacturing town, contains iron foundries, cotton spinning mills, flax spinning mills, corn mills, salt works, tanneries, soap works, and breweries. Drogheda carries on a considerable trade, particularly in grain. Vessels of 250 tons can discharge at the quay; and goods are carried inland by the Boyne navigation, in barges of 50 tons, to Navan. There are several steamers which ply constantly between Drogheda and Liverpool.

DROITWICH, in Worcestershire, owes its present commercial importance to the vast store of salt embosomed in the earth in its immediate vicinity. This, and the mode of obtaining table-salt therefrom, will be noticed in a later article. [Salt Manufacture.]

DRUGS; DRUGGISTS. The difference between drugs and chemicals is vague and indeterminate; and the professions of the chemist and druggist and the apothecary are in like manner generally confounded together in popular estimation. The rules established by the medical corporations, such as the College of Physicians, the College of Surgeons, and the Apothecaries' Company, have had much to do in producing this uncertainty. The acids, alkalies, salts, and oxides, used in largest quantity, are made on a scale which requires complete manufacturing arrangements, with large furnaces, stills, and other apparatus. Such is the case in respect to sulphuric and nitric acids, chlorides of lime and of sodium, alum, &c.; such articles are made by manufacturing chemists, at the vast chemical works which are met with at Glasgow, Liverpool, Newcastle, Hull, and Bristol. A retail shopkeeper who calls himself a chemist and druggist, is a chemist in so far as he retails, and understands the general character of, the chemicals made on a large scale by others; while he may be regarded as a druggist to the extent that he understands, and sells by retail, the substances used in medicine. If he can himself prepare, on a small scale, a considerable number of the substances which he sells, it is now customary to term him a pharmaceutist or pharmaceutical chemist.

The druggists of the metropolis have agreed to send a very extensive and valuable collection to the Exhibition of 1851, illustrative of the chemical and pharmaceutical productions of the country. The towns of Manchester, Glasgow, and Newcastle-upon-Tyne have also taken very active steps in order to secure a complete representation of the chemical manufactures of the country.

Dr. Normandy has recently published a valuable work on drugs and chemicals, under the name of 'The Commercial Handbook of Chemical Analysis.' It is especially designed to afford aid in the detection of fraud in the manufacture of food, drugs, and chemicals. The list of articles of which the processes of adulteration, and the means of detection, are given, is very comprehensive; including not only ordinary viands, as bread, porter, tea, coffee, chocolate, and cocoa, spirits, liquors, and wines, but the drugs used in medicine, and a great variety of miscellaneous substances. They are alphabetically arranged, for convenience of reference.

'Country druggists,' it has been remarked, 'form a class of persons to whom this book would be very serviceable; for, although there are of course highly creditable exceptions, particularly in great provincial towns, the bulk of them are not distinguished for chemical or even pharmaceutical knowledge. Few are capable of conducting an analysis or organic research, and they are frequently imposed upon by wholesale dealers, who send them damaged or spurious drugs, which, if administered in dangerous maladies, might induce aggravation of disease, and very probably cause death.'

DRUM. Of this musical instrument there are three kinds,—the *Side Drum;* the *Base* or *Turkish Drum;* and the *Double Drum.* The first is a cylinder, made of brass, on each end of which is a hoop covered with vellum or parchment. The second is formed like the first, but of oak, on a much larger scale. The third is made of copper, nearly hemispherical, covered with a strong head of calf's skin, and stands on three iron legs. The Double Drums vary in dimensions, from nineteen inches to three feet in diameter. They are always in pairs, and are tuned by means of many screws (or of a lever and hooks in the patent drum) which tighten the head to the key-note and the fourth below.

DRUMMOND'S LIGHT. The difficulty of distinguishing the stations chosen for the angular points of the triangles in a geodetical survey, such as the Ordnance Survey of the United Kingdom, when those stations are many miles asunder, renders it necessary to have recourse to illumination even in the day-time; and the late Captain Drummond, of the Royal Engineers, invented a heliostat which reflected the sun's rays in sufficient abundance to render visible the station which was to be observed.

This was a plane mirror of a rectangular form and mounted on a stand with joints by which it could be fixed at any angle with the horizon. On the stand was a telescope which was capable of being moved horizontally, with the mirror, and directed to the distant station while another telescope was directed to the sun. The adjustments of the mirror were such that, when the telescopes were directed as has been said, the face of the mirror reflected the rays of the sun on the distant station, and illumined it sufficiently to render a mark there visible in the telescope of the theodolite by which the required angle was to be taken.

In order to observe the angles subtended between distant stations at night, Captain Drummond employed a light which has been found to exceed in brilliancy any before used. This is produced by placing a ball or disk of lime, about a quarter of an inch in diameter, in the focus of a parabolic mirror, at the station to be rendered visible, and directing upon it, through a flame arising from alcohol, a stream of oxygen gas.

The cistern containing the alcohol is supported on a stand, behind the reflector, and is connected by a tube of caoutchouc with the lower part of a hollow stem supporting the upright wire at the top of which is fixed the ball of lime on a level nearly with the cistern: the spirit ascends in the stem, and afterwards through three or more tubes to the ball. The vessel containing the oxygen gas is connected, by a flexible tube, with an orifice in a cylindrical box on the same stem, from which it ascends through three flexible caoutchouc tubes to the ball, after passing with friction through three small cylinders. The whole apparatus is attached to a stand which carries the mirror; and adjustments are provided by which the ball may be placed exactly in the focus of the mirror. The intensity of the flame is from sixty to ninety times as great as that of an argand burner, while the expense is only about ten times as great. The lime made from chalk is preferred to any other; and such is the brilliancy, that stations above sixty miles from one another have been very distinctly visible even in hazy weather.

Captain Drummond suggested that burning lime should be employed for lighthouses; and he proposed that, instead of alcohol, hydrogen gas should be employed with the oxygen gas. The gases are to proceed from separate vessels, or gasometers, and enter a chamber through a series of small apertures: the united gases are then to pass through two or three pieces of wire gauze, and issue in two streams against the ball or disk of lime. To prevent the latter from wasting too rapidly in one place, it is made to revolve once in a minute; and in order to keep up a constant light, it is proposed to have an apparatus by which a number of balls may be successively made to fall in the focus of the mirror.

A light of this kind may also be employed as a signal in determining the difference between the longitudes of stations.

The *Electric* light, brought under public notice since Captain Drummond's death, has not yet, we believe, been applied to geodetical purposes.

DRYING MACHINES. A valuable improvement has been made within the last few years in the mode of drying woven cloth which has been bleached or otherwise wetted. In the ordinary mode of drying by exposure to the open air, the moisture gradually evaporates; in a hot room this evaporation is expedited; but in the drying machine the mechanical principle of centrifugal force is brought into use in a singular way.

A drying machine was brought into use in Paris in 1839, by Messrs. Penzolt and Levesque. It acted on the centrifugal system. It consisted of two drums or cylinders, one within the other; the inner one being pierced with holes. The textile goods, wetted by the process of washing, scouring, or bleaching, were placed within the inner cylinder, which was then made to revolve with a rapidity of 4000 turns in a minute; the cloth was driven forcibly against the perforated surface, and the water driven through the holes with such irresistible force that the cloth became nearly dry in three or four minutes.

In 1844 Messrs. Keeley and Alliot, of Nottingham, patented a very elaborate machine to facilitate the scouring, bleaching, or dyeing of cloth. The same inventors had before introduced a machine very similar in principle to that of Messrs. Penzolt and Levesque; but in the new machine, the cloth is put into a certain compartment, the bleaching or dyeing liquid into another compartment, and the machine is made to revolve rapidly; when the centrifugal force generated by the movement drives the liquid speedily and effectually through every pore of the cloth—leaving the cloth instantly afterwards almost in a state of dryness, and bleached likewise.

DRY ROT. This is the name given to a disease affecting timber, and particularly the oak, employed for naval purposes. When dry rot is produced by the attacks of fungi, the first sign of it consists in the appearance of small white points, from which a filamentous substance radiates parallel with the surface of the timber. This is the first stage of growth of the seeds of the fungus, and the filamentous matter is their thallus, or spawn. As the thallus gathers strength it insinuates its filaments into any crevice of the wood, and they, being of excessive fineness, readily pass down and between the tubes from which the wood is organised, forcing them asunder, and completely destroying the cohesion of the tissue. When the thalli of many fungi interlace, the radiating appearance can no longer be remarked; but a thick tough leathery white stratum is formed wherever there is room for its development, and from this a fresh supply of the destructive filamentous thallus is emitted with such constantly increasing rapidity and force, that the total ruin of timber speedily ensues where circumstances are favourable for the growth of the fungi.

There is reason to believe that any of the fungi that are commonly found upon decaying trees in woods are capable of producing dry rot. The circumstances that are most favourable to the development of the dry rot fungi are damp unventilated situations, and a subacid state of the wood. Whatever other causes may combine to promote the decomposition of wood by dry-rot, or other forms of decay, there can be no doubt that imperfect seasoning, by leaving in the pores of the timber a large portion of the fermentable juices always found in recently-felled timber, is one of the most important, and therefore that good seasoning is as essential in promoting the durability of wood as it is in lessening the tendency to those changes of form and bulk which so greatly increase the difficulties of the carpenter and joiner. The process of seasoning usually consists simply in the exposure of the timber to the action of air in a dry situation, in stacks or piles so constructed as to allow the free circulation of air in contact with as much as possible of the surface of each piece of timber, until the sap or vegetable juices shall have dried up so far as to offer no facility for the germination of the microscopic fungi which constitute various kinds of rot. In order to the success of this operation it is important that the pile of timber be so far elevated from the ground as to allow the circulation of air beneath as well as through and around it; and also that, if exposure to rain be not entirely avoided, care be taken to prevent the lodgment of moisture in any place where it would be likely to remain long.

The protecting power of metallic oxides, when applied to the surface of wood in the form of paint, is well known; and many abortive schemes for the preservation of timber have been devised to act upon the same principle, which is that of excluding such external influences as might promote decay. To imperfectly-seasoned timber, however, such applications are worse than useless, because by filling up the pores they impede the natural drying of the vegetable juices, and therefore rather promote than check internal decay. Far more efficient than these are the numerous modes of protection which involve the impregnation of the timber with some antiseptic substance, or with such matters as, by preoccupying the pores, may render the reception and germination of destructive fungi mechanically impossible.

Of plans for protecting timber by impregnation, perhaps none has attained such general celebrity as Mr. Kyan's, which was patented in 1832, and has since been very extensively used. The preservative agent in this process is bi-chloride of mercury, commonly called corrosive sublimate, which is dissolved in water, and forced into the pores of the timber, in closed tanks, by means of forcing-pumps, and which combines with the albumen of the wood, and converts it into a compound capable of resisting the ordinary chemical changes of vegetable matter. Chloride of zinc, creasote obtained from the distillation of tar, oil of tar, and other bituminous matters containing creasote, and pyrolignite of iron, have all been successfully used. Coal-tar is stated to be very superior to vegetable tar, and its efficacy in resisting the worm is attributed to its containing sulphocyanic or sulpho-prussic acid, which is highly destructive to animal and vegetable life. Piles protected with coal-oil are stated to have resisted the attacks of the terédo better than those protected by Kyan's process. It is necessary however to observe that the coal must be deprived of its ammonia, which would produce immediate decay if thrown into the timber.

Another process, called *Paynising*, from the name of the inventor, consists in first filling the pores of the wood with a solution of chloride of lime, and next forcing in a solution of sulphate of iron, by which an insoluble sulphate of iron is formed in the body of the wood, rendering the latter extremely hard. Timber so prepared has been recently much used.

DUBLIN. This large and populous city resembles a great metropolis in this respect, that its manufactures are of a general kind, adapted to the varied wants of its inhabitants, rather than belonging to any particular group of manufactures. At the exhibition of manufactures at Dublin in 1850, noticed in the *Introduction*, the manufactures of the citizens were surprisingly varied, comprising a very full collection both of the useful and the ornamental, in house fittings, furniture, dress, implements and machines, vessels and apparatus, &c.

Dublin is to be the general place of collection for the specimens to be forwarded to the Industrial Exhibition in Hyde Park. The extent of the collection will be found noticed under IRELAND. It is understood that the Dublin manufacturers intend to put forth all their skill in certain branches of industry which are largely carried on by them.

DUCTILITY is the property of bodies which admits of their being drawn out in length, while their diameter is diminished, without any actual fracture. Gold, silver, platinum, iron, copper, zinc, tin, lead, nickle, are ductile in the order here given. Wire-drawing depends on ductility.

DUDLEY. This is one of the great iron manufacturing towns of the South Staffordshire district. It is, in truth, in one corner of Worcestershire; but it lies over that valuable bed of coal and iron which is independent of mere topographical names, and which includes within its range parts of the counties of Stafford, Worcester, Warwick, and Shropshire. Iron is cast and forged in large quantities at Dudley; innumerable articles are there manufactured of iron; and the nailers, or makers of nails by hand, congregate in and about Dudley to the number of many thousands. Useful stone is quarried near the town; and there are all the indications of a busy manufacturing population.

Dudley is at present accommodated only by the South Staffordshire Railway; but it will shortly be connected by railway with towns in various directions.

A few specimens of Dudley manufactures will have a place at the Industrial Exhibition.

DULCIMER is the name of a very ancient musical instrument, supposed to be the psaltery of the Hebrews. In the modern form, it is a trapezium in shape, has many strings, two to each note, and is struck by a pair of sticks with wooden or metallic knobs.

DUMBARTON. This Scottish town has some extensive manufactures in glass.. In the county to which it belongs, the principal mineral production is coal, of which there is a large field, but of inferior quality, which is wrought at Langfauld, in the southern extremity of the county. In the eastern division of the county iron-stone is dug, and conveyed on the Clyde and Forth Canal to the great iron-foundry at Carron. Some large quarries of limestone and of freestone are worked. There are also several slate quarries.

On the banks of the Leven are numerous and very extensive works for cotton printing, and bleaching fields, the pureness of the Leven water being peculiarly adapted for this process. Some large iron works are established at Dalnotter.

DUMFRIES. The Nith, near the mouth of which Dumfries is situated, has been deepened within these few years, and vessels of a good size can discharge their cargoes close to the town. There is also a quay at the bend of the river near Castledykes; one for vessels of greater burthen a mile and a half farther down; and another near the mouth of the river for vessels of still larger size. The foreign trade is in timber from America. The coasting trade is with Liverpool, Whitehaven, Maryport, and other places on the west coast of England. A steam-boat plies once a week in the summer months between Whitehaven and Dumfries, in connection with one between Whitehaven and Liverpool.

The county of Dumfries contains coals only at Sanquhar and Canobie; a great portion of the county being supplied with coal from Cumberland, and from Lanarkshire and Ayrshire. At Wanlockhead, near Leadhills, are extensive lead mines. From this lead silver is extracted in the proportion of six to twelve ounces in the ton. Gold is occasionally found in the mountains at Wanlockhead, in veins of quartz, or washed down into the sand of the rivulets. Gypsum occurs in thin veins.

A great quantity of hams and bacon of the very best quality are cured in this county, and sent off to the Liverpool, London, and Newcastle markets. A great number of pigs are kept by the farmers and cottars, and bacon may be considered a staple commodity of the county.

Annan has a small import and export trade; and there are a few other places where commerce is pretty well kept up.

DUNDEE. This important town, the third in rank among the manufacturing towns of Scotland, has deep shipping-quays on the Tay which accommodate a large amount of export and import trade. In 1815 the renovation and extension of the harbour gave an impulse to its manufactures and commerce, which has led to its present state of prosperity. The harbour now consists of three wet docks, two tide-harbours of large extent, a graving-dock, a patent slip, yards for ship-building, &c.

The chief manufactures of Dundee consist of the spinning of flax, the weaving of linen, and the making of cordage and ropes. Besides the fine linen, a large quantity of sail-cloth is woven.

Steam-vessels ply regularly between Dundee and Perth, Newport, Leith, Glasgow, London, and other places. About 350 vessels belong to the town, some of large tonnage; and about 4000 vessels enter and leave the port yearly, engaged in coasting and foreign commerce.

From a return recently laid before Parliament, it appears that in 1850 the following were the statistics of the factories for flax and linen goods in the county of Forfar, in which Dundee is the chief manufacturing town. There were 85 flax-spinning factories, with 135,311 spindles, 2559 horse-power for moving machinery, and 12,365 persons employed, of whom about 9000 were females; there were 11 factories for flax-weaving, with 1347 power-looms, 219 horse-power moving-force, and 1888 persons employed, of whom 1500 were females: and 5 factories both for spinning and weaving flax, with 22,686 spindles, 240 power-looms, 345 horse-power, and 2011 persons employed, of whom nearly 1400 were females. The cotton, woollen, and mill factories in Dundee are but small in number.

All the chief varieties of Dundee manufactures in flax will be represented at the Industrial Exhibition.

DURA'MEN is the name sometimes given to the central wood or heart-wood in the trunk of a tree. It is the oldest part of the wood, and is filled by the secretions of the tree, so that fluid can no longer ascend through its tubes, which are choked up by the deposition of solid matter; otherwise it is of the same nature as the alburnum. It is only where plants form solid hard secretions that heart-wood is distinguished from sap-wood: in the poplar, willow, lime, &c., no secretions of this kind are formed; the two parts of the wood are both nearly alike, and consequently the timber of such trees is uniformly perishable.

DURERTYPE. Mr. Dicks, in 1845, proposed a new mode of copying engravings, to which he gave the name of *Durertype*, for the somewhat insufficient reason that it enables a person to copy Albert Durer's prints, and others of a similar kind. To effect this, a clean flat piece of glass is coated on one side with a thin smooth film of pure white bees'-wax: the glass being first washed with spirits of turpentine, and then warmed; and the wax being applied in a melted state to one side of the glass. When laid upon a print, the lines can be seen through the thin film; and those lines are traced or etched on the waxen surface by a pointer of ivory or steel. The design is thus marked over the wax surface in a series of cavities or depressions; and a cast from this is then taken in copper, by the common electrotype process.

DURHAM COLLIERIES. The colliery operations which form so large a part of the industrial and commercial enterprises of Durham are noticed in an earlier article [COAL AND COAL MINING].

DÜSSELDORF is one of the most manufacturing districts in Rhenish Prussia. There are extensive manufactures of woollens, silks, cotton, thread, leather, steel, iron, ironware, and cutlery, tobacco, soap, &c. Iron, coals, and potters' clay, are among the native products. At Duisberg there is a large vitriol factory, steam cloth mills, slips for building steam and sailing vessels, and several other industrial establishments. Lennep has important cloth factories, and dye-houses, and trades in wines, hats, iron ware, &c. Mühlheim has large silk and cotton factories, zinc, and iron works, and establishments for the manufacture of steam machinery. Neuss, Ronsdorf, and Ruhrort are busy manufacturing towns. Solingen, sometimes called the German Sheffield, is famous for the manufacture of sword blades, foils, cutlery, and iron ware. At Wesel the inhabitants manufacture woollen and cotton cloths, soap, hats, cordage, leather, beer, &c., and carry on a considerable trade with Holland by the Rhine, and with Westphalia by the Lippe, which has been made navigable; the chief articles of commerce are corn, timber, coals, salt, wine, brandy, and colonial produce. Düsseldorf, the chief town of the district, has manufactories of woollens, cotton, leather, hats, tobacco, jewellery, mirrors, stockings, &c., and carries on a considerable trade in cotton, wool, wines and spirits, colonial produce, coals, timber, slates and other commodities. It has been a free port since 1829. The growing importance of Düsseldorf as a commercial port is seen from the following table of the quantity of merchandise imported and exported in the years stated:—

	Imported. Cwts.	Exported. Cwts.
1836....	855,533	113,144
1840....	1,160,952	135,825
1843....	1,332,465	219,647
1844....	1,311,310	193,773
1845....	1,535,926	206,370

The manufacturers of this part of Prussia are about to take an active part in the approaching great Exhibition.

DYEING is the art of staining textile substances with permanent colours. It was an art known and practised to a considerable extent by the ancient Egyptians, Phœnicians, Greeks, and Romans. The moderns have obtained from the New World several dye-drugs unknown to the ancients; such as cochineal, quercitron, Brazil wood, logwood, arnotto; and they have discovered the art of using indigo as a dye, which the Romans knew only as a pigment. But the vast superiority of our dyes over those of former times must be ascribed principally to the employment of pure alum and solution of tin as mordants, either alone or mixed with other bases; substances which give to our common dye-stuffs remarkable depth, durability, and lustre. Another improvement in dyeing of more recent date is the application to textile substances of metallic compounds, such as Prussian blue, chrome yellow, manganese brown, &c.

Bergman appears to have been the first who referred to chemical affinities the phenomena of dyeing. Having plunged wool and silk into two separate vessels containing solution of indigo in sulphuric acid diluted with a great deal of water, he observed that the wool abstracted much of the colouring matter, and took a deep blue tint, but that the silk was hardly changed. He ascribed this difference to the greater affinity subsisting between the particles of sulphate of indigo and wool, than between these and silk; and he showed that the affinity of the wool is sufficiently energetic to render the solution colourless by attracting the whole of the indigo, while that of the silk can separate only a little of it. He thence concluded that dyes owed both their permanence and their depth to the intensity of that attractive force. We have therefore to consider in dyeing the play of affinities between the liquid medium in which the dye is dissolved and the fibrous substance to be dyed. By studying these differences of affinity, and by varying the preparations and processes, with the same or different dye-stuffs, we may obtain an indefinite variety of colours of variable solidity and depth of shade.

Dye-stuffs, whether of vegetable or animal

origin, though susceptible of solution in water, and, in this state, of penetrating the pores of fibrous bodies, seldom possess alone the power of fixing their particles so durably as to be capable of resisting the action of water, light, and air. For this purpose they require to be aided by another class of bodies, *mordants*, which bodies may not possess any colour in themselves, but serve in this case merely as a bond of union between the dye and the substance to be dyed. Mordants may be regarded in general as not only fixing but also occasionally modifying the dye, by forming with the colouring particles an insoluble compound, which is deposited within the textile fibres. Such dyes as are capable of passing from the soluble into the insoluble state, and of thus becoming permanent, without the addition of a mordant, have been called substantive, and all the others have been called adjective colours. The first principle of dyeing fast colours consists in causing the colouring matter to undergo such a change, when deposited upon the wool or other stuffs, as to become insoluble in the liquor of the dye-bath. The more powerfully it resists the action of other external agents, the more solid or durable is the dye.

In the following details concerning the art of dyeing we shall consider principally its application to wool and silk, having already treated, in the article COTTON OR CALICO PRINTING, of what is peculiar to cotton and linen.

The operations to which wool and silk are subjected preparatory to being dyed are intended, 1, to separate certain foreign matters from the animal fibre; 2, to render it more apt to unite with such colouring particles as the dyer wishes to fix upon it, and also to take therefrom a more lively and agreeable tint, as well as to be less liable to soil in use.

Silk is scoured by means of boiling in soap and water, whereby it is freed from a sort of varnish: if intended to be very white, it is bleached by humid sulphurous acid. Wool is first washed in running water to separate its coarser impurities; it is then deprived of its *yolk* (a species of animal soap secreted from the skin of the sheep) either by the action of ammoniacal urine, by soap and water, or by a weak lye of carbonate of soda. It receives its final bleaching by the fumes of burning sulphur, or by aqueous sulphurous acid.

Tinctorial colours are either simple or compound. The simple are black, brown or dun, blue, yellow, and red; the compound are gray, purple, green, orange, and others. Gall-nuts, pyrolignite of iron, logwood, copperas, and verdigris, are the chief materials for producing black. Walnuts, sumach, madder, cochineal, cudbear, acetate of iron, catechu, Brazil wood, arnotto, are all employed in producing brown. Indigo, Prussian blue, and woad, are employed for blue. Fustic, Persian berries, quercitron, turmeric, and weld, for yellow. Cudbear, Brazil wood, cochineal, kermes, lac, logwood, madder, safflower, for red; and various compounds for purple, green, orange, &c.

The black dye for hats is communicated by logwood, copperas, and verdigris, mixed in certain proportions in the bath. The ordinary proportions used by the English black dyers for 100 pounds of cloth, previously treated in the indigo vat, are about 5 pounds of copperas, as much nut-galls bruised, and 30 pounds of logwood. They first gall the cloth, and then pass it through the decoction of logwood in which the copperas has been dissolved. A finish of weld is often given after fulling.

Silk is dyed black in two methods, according to the market for which it is made. When sold by weight, it is an object with the dyer to load it with as much colouring or other matter as possible. When silk is sold by superficial measure, on the other hand, it becomes the dyer's object to give it a black colour with as little weight of materials as possible. Hence the distinction well known in trade of heavy and light silks. The silk dyers keep up from year to year a black vat, often of very complex composition. The essential constituents of the vat are sulphate of iron and gum; but many vegetable matters, as well as filings of iron, are usually added.

The infusion of walnuts, as used by the continental dyers, affords very agreeable and permanent brown tints without any mordant, while it preserves the downy softness of the wool, and requires but a simple and economical process in applying it. Sumach is usually employed in this country to dye fawns, and some browns; but more beautiful browns may be given to woollen stuffs by boiling them first with one-fourth their weight of alum and some tartar and copperas; washing, and afterwards dyeing them in a madder bath. The shade of colour depends upon the proportion which the copperas bears to the alum. The finest browns are produced by boiling each pound of the wool with two ounces of alum, dyeing it in a cochineal bath, and then transferring it into a bath containing a little cochineal darkened with acetate of iron.

Silk may receive a ground of arnotto, and then be dyed in a bath of logwood or Brazil wood, whereby a fine brown tint is obtained. Catechu is used for giving a bronze and brown to cotton goods.

Additional details are given under the

names of the colours and of the dye-materials, such as ANNOTTO, COCHINEAL, INDIGO, MADDER, &c.

The dye-materials imported from foreign countries which find a place among the Customs Returns prepared by the Board of Trade are chiefly the following:—Cochineal, fustic, gum arabic, gum Senegal, gum animi, gum copal, gum tragacanth, indigo, lac dye, shell lac, logwood, madder, Nicaragua wood, safflower, sumach, smalts, valonia, yellow berries, and zaffre. Of these nineteen substances, about 4000 cwts. were imported in 1848.

There are few manufacturing arts in which the English may more profitably study the productions of the French than dyeing. The French chemists have studied the production of colour more than those of our own country; and the French dyers have availed themselves of every aid which science has been able to afford. It is one of the good features in the Exhibition which is about to take place, that the dyes of various nations will fairly be brought into comparison. If the French are really our superiors in this art, it will be just to acknowledge, graceful to commend, and profitable to imitate their skill.

DYNAM; DYNAMOMETER. In estimating the effect of mechanical labour, it is desirable to have some idea of a simple unit well fixed in the mind. All who have studied know how much advantage there is in referring every kind of pressure to weight, and measuring it by the weight which will balance it. Thus if one hundred pounds weight will bend a spring into a certain position, we have no difficulty in substituting an opposite force to the weight for the recoil of the spring at the point of application. It is equally convenient to arrive at a distinct notion of a unit of useful effect in the workmanship of machines. We may consider any machine as simply applied to raising a weight, and look upon the weight raised as a dynamical equivalent for any possible effect that the machine could have produced; observing that the useful effect of any application of power varies jointly as the weight raised and the height to which it is raised. Accordingly, the product of the number of pounds raised, is a *relative* measure of the quantity of power.

We can convert the above relative measurement into an absolute form by assuming as a unit one pound raised through one foot: let this be called a *dynam*, or dynamical unit. Thus, what is commonly called a horse power is meant by our engineers to signify 550 dynams in a second; a steam-engine which can raise one pound through 550 feet in every second is said to be of one-horse power.

This term was introduced by French writers, who called the effect of a cubic metre of water raised through one metre, a *dynamie* or *dyname*. Dr. Whewell in his 'Mechanics of Engineering,' has proposed to naturalise the term dynam, as applied to our most convenient units, the pound and the foot. Mr. Watt was really the first who assumed, as a dynamic unit, the simple notion of one pound raised one foot: but he did not venture on a name, though the now common term, the *duty* of an engine, first used by him, has reference to the number of such simple units as may be obtained from the engine.

The name of *dynamometer* has been applied to an instrument which measures anything to which the name of power has been given, whether that of an animal, (or to take a very different instance) of a telescope.

A dynamometer, registered in 1849, by Messrs. Elce, is used to ascertain the power required to drive, or the power exerted by, any machine. The differential qualities of oil may also, the inventors state, be detected; and when a machine requires too much driving power owing to a strained shaft, or some other radical defect, the loss of power may be ascertained. The difference in the power required to drive similar descriptions of machines by different makers can be estimated; or when any improvement is introduced into a machine by which it is proposed to gain power, such gain, if there be any, can be ascertained.

E

EAGLE-WOOD. This is a highly fragrant wood, much esteemed by Asiatics for burning as incense, and known in Europe by its present designation ever since the Portuguese visited and imported the substance direct from the Malayan islands and the kingdom of Siam, where it has always been abundant, and long established as an article of commerce. The Malayan name is *Agila*, whence the wood was called *Pao d'Agila* by the Portuguese, and has since been converted into *Pao d'Aguila*, and *Pao d'Aquila*, *Bois d'Aigle*, and *Eagle Wood*. The term eagle wood is also applied to the wood known to the ancients by the name of *Agallochum*.

Of the two kinds of agallochum which are most valued, and both considered genuine, one is distinguished by the name of Calambac, and the other as the Garo of Malacca. Calambac appears, as far as hitherto known, to be a native of Cochin China only, growing on the mountains of that country in about 13° of N. lat. It has been described as a lofty tree with erect stem and branches, long lanceolate shining leaves, and terminal bunches of flowers. The other kind, Garo, to which the name of Eagle Wood is more frequently applied, has long been an article of export from Malacca and the kingdom of Siam. Specimens of the tree which yield this were first obtained by M. Sonnerat in his second voyage to India, from which probably have been given the figure and description by Lamarck. The fragrant nature of genuine agila or eagle wood is well known, and that it has from very early periods been employed both by the natives of India and of China as incense. Mr. Finlayson, in his visit to Siam, says, that the consumption of this highly odoriferous wood is very considerable in Siam, but that the greatest part is exported to China. In China it is used in a very economical manner. The wood being reduced to a fine powder, and mixed with a gummy substance, is laid over a small slip of wood, about the size of a bullrush, so as to form a pretty thick coating. This is lighted, and gives out a feeble but grateful perfume. Eagle wood was burned as a perfume by Napoleon in the imperial palace.

EAR-TRUMPET. We may refer on this subject to ACOUSTICS and SPEAKING TUBES, under which latter title the recent remarkable applications of gutta percha are noticed.

EARTHS. The old chemists imagined that all material substances were ultimately resolveable into four simple bodies, viz., air, fire, water, and earth, which were therefore called the four elements. It is now universally admitted that the bodies called earths are compounds of oxygen and a base, and in fact they are mostly metallic oxides. The principal earths are *alumina*, *barytes*, *glucina*, *lime*, *magnesia*, *silica*, *strontia*, *yttria*, *zirconia*.

EARTHENWARE. [POTTERY.]

EAST INDIES. This immense and important country is deeply interesting to us in an industrial and commercial point of view, both for its natural riches, and for the influence which an English company has so long exerted in that quarter. We shall touch briefly on both these characteristics, so far as is consistent with the scope of the present volume.

The East Indies are usually considered to include the peninsula of Hindustan lying to the east of the river Indus, and thence eastward as far as the boundary of the Chinese empire, by which empire, and by Tartary, India is also bounded on the north. The East Indies include also the islands of the Indian Ocean which lie between Hindustan and Australia as far north as the Philippine Islands, and as far east as Papua, but without including either the Philippines or Papua. It is not in so wide a sense that the term is used when speaking of the operations of the East India Company; but in truth the names India, East Indies, British India, and Hindustan, are all vague in their geographical limits.

Our power in those regions has wholly risen through the intermedium of the East India Company. This association—the most remarkable which commerce has yet known—was first formed in London in 1599, when its capital, amounting to 30,000*l*., was divided into 101 shares. In 1600 the adventurers obtained a charter from the crown, under which they enjoyed certain privileges, and were formed into a corporation for fifteen years, with the title of 'The Governor and Company of Merchants of London trading to the East Indies.' The first adventure of the association was commenced in 1601; and this, as well as seven or eight subsequent voyages, yielded a commercial profit of 100 to 200 per cent. The charter was renewed for an indefinite period in 1609, subject to dissolution on the part of the government upon giving three years notice to that effect. In 1611 the Company obtained permission from the Mogul to establish factories at Surat, Ahmedabad, Cambaya, and Goga. The capital was increased by a new fund of 1,600,000*l*. in 1617. The functions of government were first exercised by the Company in 1624, when authority was given to it by the king to punish its servants abroad either by civil or by martial law, embracing even the power of taking life. In 1632 a third fund of 420,700*l*. was raised. The king encouraged the formation of a rival company in 1636, but the rivals coalesced to form a joint company in 1650.

In 1652 the Company obtained from the Mogul, through the influence of a medical gentleman, Mr. Broughton, the grant of a licence for carrying on an unlimited trade throughout the province of Bengal, without payment of duties. An increase of capital, an extended charter, and a successful attempt to keep down a new rival company, marked the next ten years. Factories were established at Bantam in 1602, Surat in 1612, Madras in 1639, Bengal in 1652, and Bombay in 1668.

The first occasion on which the Company was brought into collision with any of the native powers of India occurred in 1664, when Sevajee, the founder of the Mahratta States, attacked the city of Surat. The aid which the Company's servants gave on this occasion to the inhabitants won for them the good will of the Mogul; and the Company gradually obtained increased power, both from the Mogul and from Parliament. In 1693 the Company obtained a new charter by gross bribery of the highest officers of state; but the House of Commons refused to sanction it. Another new company was formed about the same time, and another amalgamation took place, which left the United Company on the footing which it maintained from 1702 till 1833. The capital has been gradually increased to 6,000,000*l.*, on which dividends are paid.

The home government of the Company consists of the Court of Proprietors, the Court of Directors, and the Board of Control, between whom it has been sometimes difficult to maintain harmonious relations. The act of Queen Anne gave the Company exclusive trading powers to the East, which lasted with little alteration till 1813. In this year much of the trade was thrown open by a new charter for twenty years: that with China being however retained as a monopoly. In 1833 another renewal for 20 years was granted, which took away from the Company the right of trading either to its own territories or the dominions of any native power in India or in China, and threw the whole completely open to the enterprise of individual merchants. The time is now rapidly approaching when another charter will be applied for, and its terms canvassed.

The Company's nominal profits in the 18th century were very high; but as their trade was conducted in a costly way, and was burdened with military charges, it yielded little real profit. Private traders have always been able to outbid the Company, when allowed to compete. Thus, in the 20 years from 1813 to 1833, the value of goods exported by the private trade increased from about 1,000,000*l.* sterling to 3,979,972*l.*, while the Company's trade fell from 826,558*l.* to 149,193*l.* The impossibility, as thus shewn, of the Company's entering into competition with private merchants had a powerful influence with parliament; and in the charter of 1833 the Company was confined altogether to the territorial and political management of its vast empire. The dividend guaranteed by the act of 1833 is 650,000*l.*, being 10½ per cent. on a nominal capital of 6,000,000*l.* The dividends are chargeable on the revenues of India, and are redeemable by parliament after 1847.

The following table is given, in the deficiency of official returns, merely as an approximation, in order to afford such a general view as may be useful, though not accurate, of the areas and population of the territories of Hindustan:—

British Possessions.	Sq. Miles.	Inhabitants.
Bengal Presidency ..	220,000	47,000,000
North West Provinces	100,000	20,000,000
Madras Presidency..	140,000	14,000,000
Bombay Presidency	70,000	7,500,000
Sinde..............	70,000	1,500,000
Lahore	60,000	3,000,000
	660,000	93,000,000
Dependent States.		
Hydrabad	95,000	9,000,000
Berar, or Nagpoor ..	45,000	2,200,000
Mysore	27,000	3,500,000
Gwalior and Malwa..	34,000	4,000,000
Gujerat	25,000	2,000,000
Oude	20,000	4,0000,00
Balwulpoor	12,000	500,000
Cashmere States	20,000	1,000,000
Sikh Hill States	20,000	1,000,000
Bundelcund States ..	8,000	1,000,000
Rewah	7,000	600,000
Bhopal	6,000	500,000
Indore	8,000	600,000
Dhar	500	30,000
Sattara	8,000	1,000,000
Colapoor	3,000	600,000
Sawunt Warree	1,000	30,000
Bhurtpoor	2,000	500,000
Travancore	5,000	600,000
Cochin	1,500	200,000
Sikim	2,000	140,000
Rajpoot States: Bikaneer	14,000	12,000,000 (Rajpoot States together)
Jessulmeer	9,000	
Joudpoor......	25,000	
Jypoor	14,000	
Oodipoor	10,000	
Cutch	7,000	
Sirohi	3,000	
Kotah	4,000	
Boodee	2,000	
Dholpoor, &c...	2,000	
	500,000	48,000,000

Independent States.	Sq. Miles.	Inhabitants.
Nepaul	45,000	1,500,000
Bootan	25,000	500,000
	70,000	2,000,000
Total.		
British Possessions..	600,000	90,000,000
Dependent States ..	500,000	48,000,000
Independent States..	70,000	2,000,000
	1,170,000	140,000,000

Such is the immense territory whch is vaguely known to us as the East Indies. Commerce between India and the western nations of Asia appears to have been carried on from the earliest historical times. The spicery, which the company of Ishmaelites mentioned in Genesis were carrying into Egypt, must in all probability have been the produce of India; and in the 30th chapter of Exodus, where an enumeration is made of various spices and perfumes, cinnamon and cassia are expressly mentioned, which must have come from India or the islands in the Indian Archipelago. This trade appears to have been carried on by means of the Arabs. Indian articles were also brought from the Persian Gulf to Phœnicia, and Europe was thus supplied with the produce of India.

The produce of India was also imported into Greece by the Phœnicians in very early times. Many of the Greek names of the Indian articles are evidently derived from the Sanskrit. The western nations of Asia appear to have had no connection with India, except in the way of commerce, till the time of Darius Hystaspes. The expedition of Alexander into India first gave the Greeks a correct idea of the western parts of India, and paved the way for a further extension of Indian commerce. After the foundation of Alexandria in Egypt, the Indian trade was almost entirely carried on by the merchants of that city. We may form some idea of the magnitude of the Indian trade under the emperors by the account of Pliny, who informs us that the Roman world was drained every year of at least fifty millions of sesterces (upwards of 400,000*l.*) for the purchase of Indian commodities. The articles imported by the Alexandrian merchants were chiefly precious stones, spices and perfumes, and silk. Alexandria supplied the nations of Europe with Indian articles till the discovery of the passage round the Cape of Good Hope by Vasco de Gama in 1498. But the western nations of Asia were principally supplied by the merchants of Basra, which was founded by the caliph Omar, near the mouth of the Euphrates, and soon became one of the most flourishing commercial cities in the East. In addition to this, a land trade, conducted by means of caravans which passed through the central countries of Asia, existed from very early times between India and the western nations of Asia.

The modern commerce of India has taken many fresh directions. Nearly all that depends on the East India Company is transacted at the three ports of Calcutta, Madras, and Bombay. The native merchants in the north west of India carry on a large inland trade to Persia, Bokhara, Siberia, and other Asiatic countries. In respect to Great Britain, the exports of British manufactures to India in 1849 amounted in value to nearly 7,000,000*l.* In respect to the imports from India into Great Britain in 1848, the following will give an idea of the principal commodities and quantities :—

Cassia	40,000 lbs.
Cloves	60,000 lbs.
Coffee	33,000,000 lbs.
Indian cottons ..	120,000 pieces
Gums	30,000 cwts.
Hemp	260,000 cwts.
Hides	70,000 cwts.
Indigo	60,000 cwts.
Mace	40,000 lbs.
Senna	800,000 lbs.
Silk	800,000 lbs.
Silk goods	300,000 pieces
Skins and Furs ..	60,000
Rum	900,000 gallons.
Sugar	1,400,000 cwts.

Cotton has hitherto been exported from India only in small quantity; but strenuous exertions are now being made to extend the culture. The other chief products are noticed in the above list. Other commercial and industrial details will be found under the names of the chief countries and cities, such as BENGAL, BOMBAY, CALCUTTA, DELHI, &c.

Ceylon, although close to India, does not belong to the Company. That territory is about to take up a worthy position at the approaching exhibition [CEYLON]; but in India the preparations do not seem to have been on so complete and well-organised a scale. There will however be many individual specimens of great interest. For example, the Maharajah Goolab Singh has arranged to send a magnificent collection of shawls from Cashmere, to the Great Exhibition. They are said to be worth nearly 100,000 rupees (10,000*l.*), and to be of the most exquisite kind. Various other articles have been forwarded to Bombay from Lahore and its principal towns; including papier maché articles (which it will be interesting to compare with those now made at Birmingham), a carpet of large dimensions, a gold-inlaid suit of armour, cotton and silk manufactures, firearms, agricultural implements, and other articles.

EBONY is well known as a hard black-coloured wood, brought from tropical regions. From its hardness, durability, susceptibility of a fine polish, and colour, (which has almost become another name for blackness,) ebony has always been in high estimation, and in the present day is much used for mosaic work and ornamental inlayings, though cheaper woods dyed black are frequently substituted. Several trees yield this kind of wood, but all belong to the genus *Diospyrus.* The species are found chiefly in the tropical parts both of Asia and America, as in the Malayan archipelago and peninsula, and in almost every part of India.

The species called *Diospyrus ebenus*, the true ebony, and that which is considered to be of the best quality, is a large tree, a native of the Mauritius, Ceylon, and Madagascar. Large quantities of the ebony of this species have been sometimes imported into Europe.

One of the most remarkable productions in which ebony takes a part, is perhaps the ebony and satinwood bridge in Ceylon. It is at Paradina, about five miles from Kandy, and forms part of the coach-road from Kandy to Colombo. It consists of a single arch, resting on stone abutments. The timbers are all light and simple in form; and it affords a proof of the abundance and cheapness of these kinds of wood in Ceylon, that ebony and satinwood should be employed for such a purpose.

ECUADOR. This South American republic has a soil and climate which yields sweet potatoes, mandioca, yams, bananas, rice, Indian corn, sugar, cocoa, cotton, tobacco, fruits, and numerous other plants and roots. Sheep and cattle are reared in great numbers; horses, asses, and mules to a smaller extent. Gold, silver, lead, and quicksilver mines are worked, but not so largely as in other parts of South America.

The traffic between England and Ecuador is not considerable, owing mainly to the circumstance that Guayaquil, the only port, is on the Pacific shore, and therefore not to be reached without a voyage round Cape Horn. In 1848 the total value of our exports to Ecuador amounted only to about 6000*l.* Cocoa is the commodity with which Ecuador supplies us in largest quantity, the import in 1848 amounting to more than 1,100,000 lbs.

EDDYSTONE LIGHTHOUSE. [LIGHTHOUSES.]

EDINBURGH. Important and interesting as the Scottish metropolis may be in many particulars, it is not in respect to manufactures or commerce that it appeals to our notice. Its maritime commerce is all conducted at Leith; while its manufactures of paper, types, and other commodities, are of the miscellaneous kind which belong to a large metropolitan city, rather than partaking of any one distinctive character. The same may be said of Dublin, except that Dublin has no such great rival to its industry as Edinburgh has in Glasgow.

It is in the aid which the educational and literary talent of Edinburgh affords towards the study of all sciences, and their application to the arts, that we are to look for the chief link which connects Edinburgh with the industry of the age. The Scottish Society of Arts, among other institutions, has rendered valuable aid in this direction.

The county to which Edinburgh belongs has a few industrial towns. Dalkeith contains a large iron-foundry, a gas-work, and there are manufactures of felt and beaver hats, straw hats, and woollen stuffs. At Musselburgh, besides a small coasting-trade, there are manufactures of sail-cloth and hair-cloth; and there are coal mines in the neighbourhood. Leith claims a word of notice elsewhere. [LEITH.]

The number of parties who have come forward at Edinburgh as exhibitors at the Great Industrial Exhibition amounts to 163. Of these, 14 will be in the section for raw materials and produce, 68 in the section for machinery, 62 in the section for manufactures, and 19 in the section for sculpture, models, and the plastic art. The entire space which will be required extends to 10,143 square feet, of which 3,558 is floor space, 1,939 table space, 4,646 wall space. The articles that are proposed to be exhibited are very miscellaneous.

EFFERVESCENCE is the rapid disengagement of a gas, which takes place in a liquid in consequence of chemical action and decomposition.

EFFLORESCENCE is the property by which certain salts containing water of crystallization lose it, and become opaque by exposure to the air.

EGG TRADE. The egg trade is now one of great magnitude. What the number of English eggs produced and eaten may be, it is impossible even to guess; for there are no returns which can apply to this subject; but of foreign eggs we find that there have been imported the following quantities in four recent years:—

1847	77,485,487
1848	88,012,585
1849	97,903,151
1850	105,761,995

These are principally obtained from France.

Eggs are largely employed in the leather manufacture, in the preparation of kid skins into leather for gloves and shoes. In one process of the manufacture, yolk of egg is mixed with alum, salt, and flour in a barrel, and the skins are agitated with this mixture for some time. Much of the softness of good kid leather is due to this use of egg-yolk. There is one leather-factory in Bermondsey where 60,000 to 80,000 eggs are used for this purpose every year; they are imported from France in the spring, and are kept good throughout the year in lime-water.

EGYPT. This remarkable country is possessed of very little mineral treasure. It depends more upon the alluvial subsoil left by the Nile than upon the metal and stone found in the rocks. On the west of the Nile however, above the Delta, the mountain range which bounds the valley contains limestone, sandstone, slate, and quartz; while the eastern range contains the famous granite quarries which furnished material for the great works of the ancient Egyptians. In the mountainous region between the Nile and the Red Sea are found mines of various metals, and quarries of porphyry and other valuable stone.

The agriculture of Egypt depends on the annual inundation of the Nile. This inundation, occasioned by the periodical rains of Central Africa, begins in June about the summer solstice, and it continues to increase till September, overflowing the lowlands along its course. The Delta, or Lower Egypt, then looks like an immense marsh, interspersed with numerous islands, with villages, towns, and plantations of trees just above the water. The inundations, having remained stationary for a few days, begin to subside, and about the end of November most of the fields are left dry, and covered with a fresh layer of rich brown slime: this is the time when the lands are put under culture. From thence till the next inundation, the Delta goes through the alternatives of a delightful spring and a fiercely hot summer.

The agricultural produce of Egypt consists of the following winter plants, which are sown when the inundation has ceased, and reaped in three or four months after: wheat, barley, beans, peas, lentils, vetches, lupins, clover, flax, coleseed, lettuce, hemp, cummin, coriander, poppy, tobacco, water-melons, and cucumbers; and of the following summer plants, which are raised by artificial irrigation by means of water-wheels and other machinery: doorah, Indian corn, onions, millet, henneh, sugar-cane, cotton, coffee, indigo, madder. Rice and numerous fruits are also cultivated. Mehemet Ali pensioned off the landed proprietors, and seized the land himself; so that the poor fellah farmers became his immediate tenants, and a wretched life they seem to have led.

In regard to constructive and mechanical arts, Egypt is more distinguished for its ancient than its modern works. The wondrous pyramids, the temples, the statues, the obelisks, the sphinxes, are among the most striking antiquities of any nation. In respect to modern industry, Mehemet Ali strove zealously to establish the cotton manufacture and other branches of industry in Egypt; and to a certain extent he succeeded.

Of the towns of Egypt, there are only four of commercial importance. *Alexandria* has been already briefly noticed [ALEXANDRIA]. *Cairo* or *Kahira* carries on a number of manufactures connected with the wants of a large metropolis; but as it is not a sea-port town, and is distant a mile from the Nile, it has no shipping. *Rosetta* and *Damietta* are sea-ports, having considerable trade.

Engineers are now, and have long been, impressed with the desirability of establishing some better mode of communication between the Mediterranean and the Red Sea, across Egypt. The India mail, after being landed at Alexandria, has to be navigated up the Mahmoudieh Canal to Boulak, then carried one mile to Cairo, and then transferred across the desert to Suez. A ship canal across the isthmus, from Pelusium to Suez, is one of the schemes under discussion. Mr. Robert Stephenson, the eminent engineer, has lately been to Egypt. A recent correspondent at Alexandria of one of the London journals says, 'He (Mr. Stephenson) seems impressed with the advantages Egypt and the trade with our Indian and Eastern possessions would derive from the establishment of railway communication between the two great trading cities of Alexandria and Cairo. The cumbrous navigation of the Nile at the best seasons, and impracticability at others, for laden boats, render the advantage of such a highway so palpable, that men of less discernment have been recently agitating the question, and urging it on the viceroy's attention. Produce of the value of 15,000,000 of piastres is annually brought down the river in native craft, subject to the delays of navigation, the danger and neglect of those charged with it, and the uncertainty of arrival to meet the engagements or the wants of the trader."

The exports and imports at Alexandria in 1849 amounted to,

Exports	£1,661,000
Imports	1,474,000

The export of cotton in that year was 183,878 bales, valued at 515,000*l.* The corn exported was of the value of 460,000*l.* of which Great Britain took 325,000*l.* worth. The total exports to Great Britain were 808,000*l.*; and the imports thence were 607,000*l.* There were 3200 ships sailed and arrived during the year, of which 708 were English. The chief articles of export, besides corn and cotton, consist of gums, incense, ivory, senna, coffee, tamarinds, rice,flax, flax-seed, sesame, mother-of-pearl, tobacco. Those of import consist of cotton, woollen, hardware, silk and glass manufactures, machinery, drugs, spices, sugar, oil, candles, soap, tar, timber, wines, cordage, &c.

The trade formerly carried on through Egypt from the Red Sea is now quite inconsiderable. The imposition of heavy transit duties, and the monopoly of certain articles by the government, have given a new direction to it, and created markets elsewhere.

EIDOGRAPH, is an instrument invented in the year 1821, by the late Professor Wallace of Edinburgh. It is a species of pantograph, and, like the latter, it is used for the purpose of copying plans or other drawings on the same or on different scales.

EIDER DOWN. This beautiful substance is obtained from one species of the duck, called the eider duck, found extensively in the icy seas of the north. There are two kinds of eider down, the live and the dead. The live down consists of the exquisitely light feathers which the duck strips off from herself to keep her progeny warm in the eggs. Its lightness and elasticity are such that two or three pounds of it, squeezed into a ball which may be held in the hand, will swell out to such an extent as to fill a case large enough for the foot-covering of a bed. The quantity of down afforded by one duck during the whole period of laying is about a pound. The down-gatherers are obliged to be cautious not to carry their somewhat cruel robbery too far, or the ducks will not again return to the same spot. Any district in which the eider duck is willing to locate itself is regarded as a valuable property in Norway and Iceland, and the landowners do their best to enconrage the location. The *dead* down is that which is taken from the dead duck; it is inferior to the live down.

ELASTICITY. When the form of a body is affected by the pressure of another extraneous to it, the reacting force by which it sustains or tends to remove that pressure is its elasticity. Amongst bodies whose elasticity is very apparent, we may enumerate glass, ivory, caoutchouc, gutta percha, sponges, and fibrous substances, as beams, muscles, and artificial webs, some gums, steel, and all the gases and vapours. In gases and vapours its effects may be produced to any extent, but they are limited in solids by their softness and facility of fusion, as in wax, lead, &c.; by their absorption of moisture, as in clay, feathers, catgut, straw; or by their friability, as in glass, dry resins, and copper or iron which have been exposed to a stream of ammoniacal gas.

The elastic force of steam is found to increase nearly in a geometrical progression when the temperature is increased in an arithmetical progression; from which property steam has now become a great mechanical agent.

ELATERIN, a vegetable principle extracted from the wild cucumber (*Momordica elaterium*). Elaterin has a bitter and somewhat styptic taste. It is insoluble in water, and in diluted and alkaline solutions. It melts at a few degrees above 212°, and at a higher temperature it is volatilised in very acrid white vapours. It is a powerful medicinal agent.

ELBERFELD is a large manufacturing town in Rhenish Prussia. The waters of the Wupper river are said to possess most valuable bleaching properties, and to this circumstance Elberfeld is indebted for its origin and prosperity. The town is the seat of an extensive cotton and silk manufacture, but is more important still for its dyeing, printing, and bleaching establishments. The cotton printers and silk-dyers consume a large quantity of piece-goods that are woven by hand in the surrounding districts; their patterns, which are very superior, are designed on the premises of the large printers, who keep French artists at high salaries in their employ. Merinos and fancy woollen goods are also manufactured here. The town has about 70 dyeing establishments, 10 bleaching-grounds, 6 cotton-spinning factories, 1 large woollen mill, with machine-makers, and colour-works; it has also block-pattern cutting, printing, engraving, and lithographic printing establishments. Tapes and ribands are an important article of manufacture, with which this town and Barmen (which touches Elberfeld on the north extremity) supply all Germany. The colour called Turkey red is produced in Elberfeld more cheaply and of better hue than in any other place of Europe.

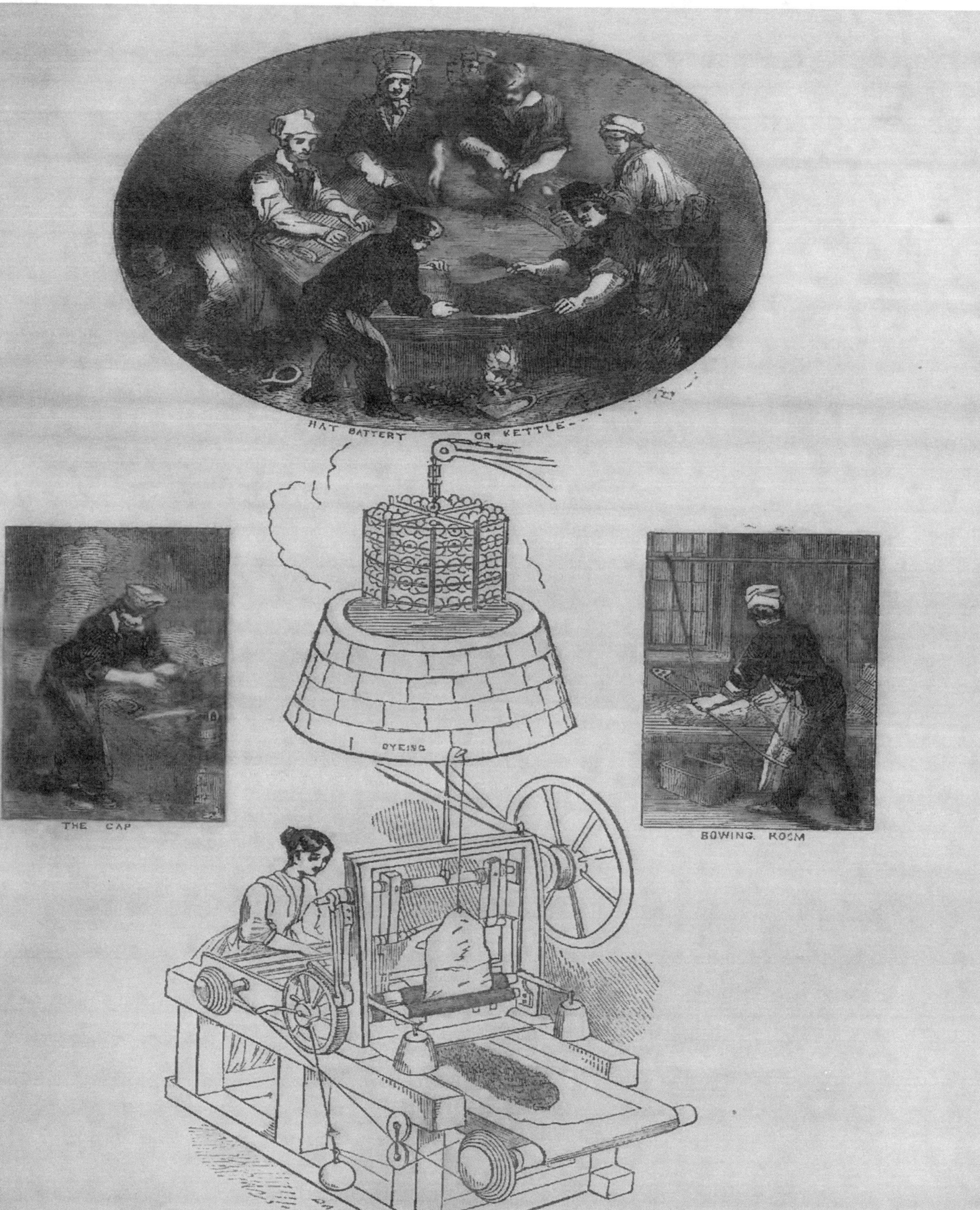

KNIGHT'S CYCLOPÆDIA OF THE INDUSTRY OF ALL NATIONS.

No. 20.

Elberfeld will supply a notable part of the Prussian contribution to the Industrial Exhibition.

ELBEUF, a large manufacturing town in France, has had many extensive factories built within the last few years. It has a *conseil des prud'hommes*, or council of experienced men, for the settlement of questions between manufacturers and their workmen. The factories of the town and neighbourhood, which exceed 200 in number, and are mostly worked by steam power, produce a great quantity of woollen cloths; the descriptions are various, and include double-milled and waterproof cloths, zephyrs, and fancy cloths of all colours. From 60,000 to 70,000 pieces of 60 yards each, at from 10 to 20 francs a yard, are produced annually. The cloth is purchased of the manufacturers by large commission houses, of which there are about 70 in the town, and by them it is sent to various parts of France. This town is also celebrated for the manufacture of billiard-table cloth and flannel. It contains several dye-houses, fulling-mills, and large wool-stores, besides establishments for washing wool, which lie along the Seine and the Puchot, a small winding stream that traverses the town.

ELECTRIC LIGHT. Among the numerous practical applications of electric power, not the least curious is that of maintaining a steady light for public streets. The scheme has not yet assumed a fully satisfactory position; but it is not improbable that it may do so ere long.

In 1846 Messrs. Greener and Staite patented the electric light, as a means of illuminating public thoroughfares and buildings. The plan described by the patentees involves the use of small lumps of pure carbon, enclosed in air-tight vessels, and rendered luminous by currents of galvanic electricity; pieces of platinum are also mentioned as being fitting substitutes for the carbon. The idea was not new; but the patentees claimed to have placed it in a more practical form than it had before assumed. During the year 1847 Mr. Staite exhibited his electric light in many parts of the country; and in a lecture on the subject at Newcastle, he gave the following statistical estimate of its capabilities:—'With a battery consisting of 40 small cells in series, the light was equal to 380 tallow candles, 300 wax candles, or 64 cubic feet of gas: this being effected by the consumption of little more than ¾ of a lb. of zinc per hour. The relative cost was by the electric light 1*d.*, gas 6*d.* or 8*d.*, tallow candles 7*s.* 6*d.*, and wax candles 12*s.* 6*d.* per hour.' We may remark however that this mode of comparison is open to many fallacies.

In 1848 the electric light was exhibited very frequently in different parts of London. The general arrangement is as follows:—Two small cylinders of carbon are placed with their ends nearly in contact, being distant apart some fraction of an inch, which is made to depend for its amount on the size and purpose of the apparatus. A train of wheels is attached to the machine to keep these carbon-points always at the same distance apart during their slow combustion. There are also the galvanic apparatus and the wires; and the principle of action depends on the fact that the galvanic circuit is not completed unless the fluid can traverse the small distance from one piece of carbon to the other: the resistance which the carbon offers to the transit occasions the evolution of a most intense light. The mechanism by which the points are kept at such a distance as to give *continuous* instead of an *intermitting* light, is very ingenious, and such as had not previously been applied.

In the same year an electric light of somewhat similar character, but differing in many working details, was introduced at Paris, and was afterwards exhibited also in London, by MM. Achereau and Fourcault. During 1849, in a lecture by Mr. Grove at the Royal Institution, and at the meeting of the British Association in Birmingham, as well as in scientific and practical papers in the public journals, the merits and demerits of the electric light were discussed at considerable length.

In Mr. Allman's electric light, brought under public notice in 1850, the mechanism differs from that of the older form in maintaining the carbon points always at a proper distance apart. When more of the electric fluid is passing than is necessary to maintain the required intensity of light, the mechanism so adjusts itself as to bring the carbon points farther apart; whereas, when the electric force is below its proper limit, the points approach more closely. The apparatus possesses therefore something of the self-governing or self-adjusting power which is so admirably exemplified in modern steam-engines. There are many circumstances which seem to indicate that we are not far removed from the period when light produced by electric agency will be rendered practically available in manufactures and the arts of life.

ELECTRIC TELEGRAPH. The marvels of this admirable contrivance will be better appreciated if viewed in connection with telegraphic agency in general. [TELEGRAPH.]

ELECTRO-METALLURGY. In this beautiful modern department of manufacture, articles in gold, silver, and other metals are made chiefly by galvanic agency. When a galvanic current is passing through a solution of metallic salt, it separates the metal from the other chemical elements, and precipitates it in a fine layer, which solidifies into a film or sheet. When an ornament of white metal is to be coated with silver by this means, the metal foundation, properly prepared, is dipped into a chemical solution of silver, and a galvanic current is passed through it. The result of this action is, that the solution is decomposed, and a fine film of metallic silver becomes deposited on the surface of the article suspended in the liquid; the thickness of the deposited layer being determined conjointly by the duration of the immersion, the strength of the solution, and the strength of the current. In the progress of the operation the solution becomes exhausted of its silver; and, to keep up the supply, plates of pure silver are suspended in it; the silver dissolves in the liquid as rapidly as the deposition on the articles takes place, atom for atom. If the article—whether a piece of table-plate, a button, or a trinket, is to be coated with gold instead of silver, a process generally similar to the above is followed; the nature of the solution being the chief point of difference.

Articles of solid metal are sometimes wholly made in a similar way. A wax model, exactly representing the article to be made, after being properly prepared, is suspended in a tank containing a chemical solution of copper. Galvanic agency is then resorted to, to deposit a layer of copper on the surface of the model, and this layer is made of such a thickness that when the waxen model is melted from within it, the copper may be able to retain its shape unsupported. The inside of the copper shell represents a mould of the outside of the article to be manufactured. The exterior of the copper is protected by a resisting composition, and it is then suspended in a tank containg a solution of silver (or gold, as the case may be); the galvanic current causes the deposition of the gold or silver on the inside of the copper mould, deposition on the outside being prevented by the resisting composition. When a sufficient thickness of the precious metal is thus obtained, the copper mould is exposed to the action of an acid which gradually eats it away without injuring the gold or silver beneath. The article then consists solely of pure gold or silver, wholly deposited by galvanic action. The atoms of metal cohere so well together, that the article has a sonorous vibration when struck, and is capable of being hammered, burnished, &c.

Mr. Dent has coated the balance springs of chronometers with gold, by the electro-metallurgic process, to protect them from damp. Professor Christie has proposed the same treatment for magnetic needles. Medallions are sometimes coated with copper as a means of preservation or of beautifying. The medallion is first coated with black-lead, and then exposed to a solution of copper (in the state of sulphate or some other salt), the metal of which is precipitated on the medallion by a galvanic current. Fruit, small twigs, leaves, seeds, and other vegetable specimens, may be similarly coated with copper; either for ornament or for the purpose of illustrating the size and form of the object. Insects too, such as butterflies, may be thus coated with a metallic film; and it is a striking proof of the equability with which the particles of metal arrange themselves, that the exquisite framework of the insect's wings is exhibited almost as distinctly as in the natural state. Ornamental baskets, whether made of wicker or of wire, are coated in a similar manner. So likewise are lace and other articles made of woven fibres.

Patents have been taken out for smelting metallic ores by electricity; and the most sanguine expectations have been entertained as to the results. There can be no doubt that, scientifically speaking, the method is practicable; but it has not yet reached the commercial stage of being profitably applicable.

Soon after the first application of electro-metallurgy to the manufacturing arts, Mr. Alexander Jones took out a patent for a mode of making copper tubes and vessels by this means. Moulds are made of some one among many different substances applicable to the purpose, and coated with a non-conducting material. The mould is placed in a solution of nitrate or sulphate of copper, and surrounded with a cylinder of sheet copper, or of copper turnings enclosed in a wicker basket. The mould is next connected by a wire with the positive end of a galvanic battery, and the surrounding copper with the opposite end; and the apparatus is allowed to remain in this state for four or five days. During this period the electric action has been going on, and copper has become deposited upon or within the mould, according to the shape of the article to be made. The mould or core is lastly removed, in a way which must depend partly on the substance of which it is made, and the form of the article.

One of the grandest applications of electricity to the arts is that exhibited in the cathedral of St. Isaac, at St. Petersburg, where the sculptures and ornamental details have been formed by electro-metallurgy. The architect was led to the adoption of this plan not only because these electrotypes would be cheaper than bronze castings—but for reasons of a more artistic character; the sculptures can be copied from the models without chiselling; the lightness of the material enables the sculptor to give bolder relief to his ornamental designs, and to suspend pieces from the vaultings which would be too ponderous if cast in bronze. There are seven enormous doors to the cathedral, three of which are 30 feet high by 44 wide; they are of bronze, and all the adornments are formed by electro-metallurgy; they contain 51 bas-reliefs, 63 statues, and 84 alto-relievo busts. All the gilding on the metallic portions of the building have been effected by the same process.

Electro-metallurgy has arrived at a high state of excellence in England. The establishment of Messrs. Elkington produces works of great beauty; and we may look forward to the exhibition of some splendid productions at the forthcoming Industrial Display.

ELECTRO-MOTIVE POWER. Can electricity move machinery? This is a question that is now occupying the attention of scientific and practical men. The powerful force possessed by an electro-magnet is a store which may one day be made available for moving machinery.

In 1833 Mr. Sturgeon exhibited a small magnetic contrivance for moving machinery; it was capable of pumping water, sawing wood, and drawing weights along the floor; it was a mere toy, but it shewed the operation of the principle. Since that time every year has witnessed the bringing forward of new plans for electro-motive agency. Dr. M'Connell of Pennsylvania made in 1837 a small machine which caused a driving wheel to rotate 70 times in a minute, carrying a load of 40 lbs. through a space of 300 feet per minute. In 1842 a locomotive carriage was driven on the Edinburgh and Glasgow Railway, at the rate of four miles an hour, by an electro-motive apparatus invented by Mr. Davidson. Shortly before this, Professor Jacobi of St. Petersburg navigated a small vessel on the Neva by electric agency; the vessel was 28 feet long, 7¼ broad, drew 3 feet of water, and carried 14 persons: it was impelled at a rate of three miles an hour by a battery contained within the boat.

Many inventors have thought that, as a 'feed of coke' now supersedes a 'feed of corn' in long journeys on land, a 'feed of zinc and water' will perhaps ere long supersede a feed of coke. But the system has yet many ordeals to go through before its true applicability can become established.

In the early part of the year 1849 M. Hjorth, a Dane, succeeded in bringing the electro-motive engine to a greater stage of completeness than it had before exhibited. He had at that time an engine in course of construction in London, which he supposed would possess a 10-horse power; one of the electro-magnets was shewn to be able to support a weight of 5000 lbs.; and even at a distance of one-eighth of an inch its attractive force was equal to 1500 lbs.

Professor Locke, of the United States, has invented a form of instrument which he calls the *chronograph*, and which was ordered to be placed by the Government in the National Observatory at Washington, in 1849. It is employed to *print* instead of merely *record* the dates of astronomical events, on the running paper-fillet of Morse's Telegraph Register. An Astronomical Clock of delicate construction has an apparatus attached to the arbor of the seconds' hand, so as to make and break the galvanic circuit every second. By putting it in connexion with Morse's Telegraph line at any spot, the paper becomes graduated automatically with the hours, minutes, and seconds; the paper thus graduated is called the automatic clock register. Each second of time is represented on the paper by a line nearly one inch in length. If an astronomer wish to mark the transit of any heavenly body across the meridian, or any similar astronomical phenomenon, he touches a key at that instant, which breaks the galvanic circuit and makes a particular mark (or rather a particular vacancy) at a certain graduated spot on the paper. There is thus produced a permanent record of the event, which requires no writing down to make it significant.

In Shepherd's Magnetic Striking Clock, patented in 1849, the vibrations of the pendulum are caused by the repeated impulses of a fine spring, the attraction of the electro-magnet being solely employed to relieve the pendulum from the action of the spring during the return of vibration. Thus a variation in the power of the battery does not affect the going of the clock. The hands are moved by separate electro-magnets, the circuit of the wires being completed and broken by the pendulum as it swings. The number to be struck is regulated by a locking plate, divided as usual, the hammer being moved by the direct action of an electro-magnet.

A new interest is now given to the subject of the Electric clock, by the adoption of this remarkable contrivance at the Crystal Palace in Hyde Park. The apparatus is entrusted to the inventive care of Mr. Shepherd; while Mr. Owen Jones has planned the decorative arrangements. There will be three dials, in the middle of the east, west, and south fronts respectively, all worked by an electro-magnetic apparatus. The south dial is a remarkable one; it is a semicircle, instead of a circle, with hours marked from 6 in the morning to 6 in the evening. There will be two hands, a minute hand, 16 feet in length, and an hour hand somewhat shorter; each hand will be double pointed, or have the pivot in the middle of its length; and that half which happens to be at any time above the horizontal line will mark the hour on the semicircular dial. The hour figures tend to decorate the south transept end of the building.

An Electric Gun was exhibited in London in 1845, and described in the public journals at the time. It was invented by Mr. Benningfield; but as he had not secured his invention by a patent, the mechanism was not made known; but it was understood that the motive power was derived from a galvanic battery. The gun was capable of discharging balls five-eighths of an inch in diameter; and 1000 of these could be propelled in a minute. The barrel was supplied with shot from two chambers; and these chambers, as well as the gun and the electro-motive apparatus, were placed upon a single-horse carriage.

ELECTROTYPE. Besides the larger works produced by Electro-metallurgy, many exquisite copies of delicate works of art are produced by a modification of the same process, called *Electrotype.*

Let the object to be copied be a small bas-relief of about six inches by four, executed in a material such as marble, ivory, or plaster of Paris. A wax mould is made from the bas-relief; and this wax is made a conductor of electricity by being brushed over with powdered plumbago. The mould and a plate of copper are placed parallel, in a convenient vessel containing a solution of sulphate of copper. The copper plate must have a wire soldered to its upper edge, for the purpose of connecting it with that of the battery; and the wax mould must be similarly connected with the zinc element of the battery. The mould and the copper plate being thus placed in the metal and connected by wires with the battery and the solution being poured in, the whole is left undisturbed from 24 to 36 hours; at the end of which time, the mould, being detached from the battery and withdrawn, will be found covered over with pure bright metallic copper, rough on the outer surface; but when separated from the wax by gently heating, it will, if the operation has been successful, present a perfect copy of the bas-relief, every line of which, to the most delicate markings, will be found transferred to the metal with more precision and delicacy than could have been produced by a cast made with the copper in a state of fusion. Perhaps few facts connected with the laws of aggregation of homogeneous matter are more striking than this, and few facts indirectly afford a more remarkable instance of the chemical divisibility of matter.

The copying of coins, medals, seals, and plaster casts, is extensively practised by the process above described. The production of copper busts, made entirely by deposition from solution, is also an example of the application of this process. Stiglmayer, the sculptor, devised a mode of coating colossal plaster statues with copper by the electro-process in the short space of two or three hours. Daguerreotype pictures are capable of being copied in electrotype, by a kind of etching by galvanism; and Mr. Smee has suggested the employment of a plan somewhat similar for etching in general.

The terms *Electrotint* and *Glyphography* have been applied to two methods of etching by electricity, in which the device is produced in rather a peculiar way. The methods are adapted, one for plate-printing, in which the design is in intaglio: and the other for surface printing, as in common typography. Both have been partially brought into use, but not to any considerable extent.

A most curious instance of the extensive applicability of the art of electrotyping, is the fact of calico having been printed by means of it. The linen, steeped in proper liquids, is made to pass between rollers, one of which has patterns formed in it of different metals inserted into its substance, and connected with the zinc of a battery: the other roller is a simple metallic conductor: the current between these surfaces produces different colours by the difference in their action on the common fluid, and thus the pattern is imparted to the calico.

The electrotype process has been recommended not only for copying engravings, but for making the copper-plate itself on which an engraving is to be executed. The copper-plates prepared for engravers generally contain a small portion of other metals, which render both the engraving and the etching somewhat uncertain. By the substitution, therefore, of plates produced by electro-deposition, in which the copper is quite uncontaminated with other metals, an advantage is anticipated. To produce these plates, a copper-plate is prepared in the usual way and suspended in a copper solution, by which a film of any desired thickness may be produced; and by a previous adjustment of the plate, the new portion may be separated from the old in the form of a distinct plate, susceptible of after-preparation for the engraver. Or, the copper-plate, instead of being made by deposition upon another plate of the same material, may be produced on a flat surface of wax or plaster properly prepared.

ELEMI, is a resin obtained from the *Amyris zeylanica*, *Eleagnus Hortensis*, and other trees, in the East Indies and elsewhere. It occurs in irregular-shaped small pieces, which run into masses, of a yellowish colour and agreeable odour. Elemi is recommended as an ointment, but is chiefly used to form pastiles, or to burn as incense.

ELGIN MARBLES. Among the choicest treasures of the British Museum are the Elgin Marbles, a collection of ancient sculptures, chiefly from the Acropolis of Athens, whence they were obtained by the Earl of Elgin (who had been the English ambassador to Turkey) between the years 1801 and 1812. This collection was purchased in pursuance of an act of the legislature, dated July 1st, 1816, for the sum of 35,000*l*., and is now deposited in the British Museum, in a room built for its reception.

The Parthenon, or Temple of Minerva, at Athens, whence the more important of these sculptures were obtained, was built during the administration of Pericles, about the year B.C. 448. It was constructed entirely of white marble from Mount Pentelicus; Callicrates and Ictinus were the architects: and the sculptures were produced partly by the hand and partly under the direction of Phidias. Two models of the Parthenon have been placed in the Elgin Saloon at the British Museum, one of which represents the building in its ruined state, and the other restored to its perfect state, with the sculptures occupying their proper places.

The sculptures of the Parthenon in the Elgin collection contain the Metopes, most of which represent the combats of the Centaurs and Lapithæ; a portion of the Frieze of the cella, which represents the Panathenaic procession; and the Statues, or parts of them, from the tympana of the pediments.

The possession of the Elgin collection has established a national school of sculpture in our country, founded on the noblest models which human art has ever produced. A tribute of thanks is due to the nobleman to whose exertions the nation is indebted for it. If Lord Elgin had not removed them the greater part would long since have been totally destroyed. In the last siege of Athens the Parthenon suffered additional damage.

ELLIPTIC COMPASSES, the name given to any machine for describing an ellipse. A simple method of forming the curve is to fasten a pin in the paper at each of the two foci, and to attach to the pins the opposite ends of a thread whose length is equal to the major axis of the ellipse. Then, if a pencil move in such a way as to keep the thread always stretched, it will describe an ellipse.

The ordinary machine consists of two bars of metal at right angles to one another, in each of which is a groove: two pins in a ruler, of which one extremity carries a pencil, are made to travel in the grooves, when the motion of the ruler causes the pencil to describe an ellipse. The distances of the pencil from the two pins are made equal to the semi-axes of the curve.

ELM. The elm-tree frequently grows to a very large size; and the timber thus yielded has a scantling sufficient to adapt it for use in the keels of ships. The wood of the elm is of a brownish colour, hard, and fine-grained. Besides the keel, it is used for blocks, dead-eyes, and other parts of a ship's fittings. It is frequently used for the naves of wheels; and in London for coffins. It is used for the brine pipes or tubes in salt works. Many specimens of elm are so beautifully grained and knotted, that this wood is largely used in the form of polished veneers.

As fuel and as charcoal the elm is not quite equal to the beech. The ashes are rich in alkali. The leaves and young shoots are employed in France as food for cattle, and they are boiled as food for pigs. In some parts of Russia the leaves are used as tea. The outer bark is sometimes prepared into an astringent medicine; the inner bark is made into nets and cordage; and both are made to yield a substance which serves as glue. In Norway the bark is kiln-dried and ground with corn as a material for bread.

Most of the above details refer to the common or English elm. The mountain or Scotch elm is likewise useful to the ship and boat builder, the pump and block maker, the cart-wright, the coachmaker, the cabinet-maker, and other manufacturers. Floor-timbers of ships; naves, poles, and shafts of carriages; swingle trees for gun-carriages; dyers' and printers' rollers—all are frequently made of Scotch elm.

ELSINORE, a seaport town in the Danish island of Seeland, at the narrowest part of the Sound, is remarkable for being so placed that all ships entering the Baltic must pass it. Ships passing the Sound pay duties to the Danish government at Elsinore. The number of vessels which passed the Sound during the first nine months of 1847 was 17,404, which was an increase of 2,843 over the same period of 1846; of this number 9,100 came from the North Sea, and 8,304 from the Baltic.

ELUTRIATION, the process of separating substances reduced to powder, when of different specific gravities, by means of water. It is also employed as a method of reducing any one substance to a fine powder.

EMBANKMENT. It is often necessary to raise mounds or dykes along the course of rivers to keep them within their channels, and prevent their flooding the lands which lie near them. Many parts of Holland could not be inhabited if the sea were not kept out by strong embankments: and the destruction of a dyke frequently desolates great tracts of country.

The first thing attended to in forming embankments is to enable them to resist the pressure of the highest floods which are likely to occur, and to prevent the effect of the waves and currents in washing them away. When it is the mere pressure of a column of water which is to be withstood, a simple earthen bank made of the soil immediately at hand, provided it be not of a porous nature, is sufficient. Its form should be a very broad base with sloping sides, and with a flat top, which may serve as a path or even a carriage road. When the dykes are only intended to check the waters at the time when they flow over their natural banks, it is best to raise them at some distance from the river on each side, and parallel to its course; because, in sudden floods, the water, having a greater space to flow through, will not rise so high, and will sooner recede.

Where embankments are made against the sea, greater skill is required to resist the force of the waves. If there are materials at hand to lay a bank of stones imbedded in clay, with a broad base, and the sides sloping very gradually upwards, a very safe barrier may be opposed to the waters. It is not the direct impulse which is the most destructive; waves striking against a sloping surface lose their force and rise over it; but it is in returning that they draw the materials with them, and scoop out the foundations. In a place where shingles were usually thrown up by the waves, and the bottom was a strong clay, their retreat has been intercepted by rows of strong piles driven in a line along and parallel to the shore, and covered with boards nailed to them on the land side; in one night the shingles have been thrown over the piles; and being retained by the boarding, have formed a perfect wall. In other cases several rows of piles are driven in, and stones thrown into the spaces between them.

Where the land lies very flat for a considerable distance from the shore, it is of advantage to have two complete banks, one within the other; so that if the outer bank is broken through, the second will keep back the waters until the first can be repaired. The water which accumulates within the banks, and is collected in the internal ditch and those which divide the marshes, must be let off occasionally by means of channels and sluices at the time when the tide is out, and the water outside the bank is lower than that which is within it.

EMBOSSING is the art of producing raised figures upon wood or other materials, by means of pressure, either applied by a sudden blow, as in a stamping press, or in a more gradual manner, as by an ordinary screw or hydraulic press, or by revolving cylinders. The pattern is usually produced by forcing the face of the material against an engraved die in which the design is cut; and sometimes, when the article to be embossed is in the form of a thin sheet, a counterpart to the die is applied at the back to aid the process. In many cases heat is employed during the operation with great effect.

Mr. Straker has proposed a method of embossing, by pressing a device forcibly on a surface of wood, planing down the rest of the surface, and bringing up again into relief the pressed portion, by exposing it to the action of water. Leather is capable of being embossed in a beautiful manner, by being pressed into metallic moulds while in a very moist, soft, and pliable state.

At the Mediæval Exhibition in 1850, many beautiful specimens of this art were exhibited, in metal, in leather, and in other materials.

EMBROIDERY, is a mode of working devices on woven substances. In some examples of this kind a rich effect is produced by inserting slips of parchment cut to suit the devices, between the fabric upon which the embroidery is executed and the threads of silk or other material of which the pattern is formed, so that the embroidery may be raised considerably above the surface. Gold and silver thread are often used in embroidery with good effect, and spangles or tinsel are occasionally mixed with the needlework. The fabric to be embroidered is usually stretched in a kind of frame or loom, and the pattern is drawn either upon its surface, or upon a piece of paper applied underneath it.

Although embroidery has, until within a few years, been a purely handicraft employment, it has latterly assumed the character of a manufacture, a most ingenious machine for executing it having been invented by M. Heilmann of Mühlhausen, and brought into use in France, Germany, Switzerland, and England. Attended by one grown person and two children, each machine does as much work as fifteen embroiderers. The machine is figured and minutely described in Ure's 'Dictionary of Arts.' The embroidery of the middle ages is noticed under TAPESTRY.

Embroidery has its periods of success and decline, like other arts. At present there is a disposition towards its revival; and it is pleasing to find that Ireland is doing her share towards bringing about this result. At the Dublin Exhibition of Manufactures in 1850, many exquisite specimens of Irish Embroidery were displayed, mostly contributed by Messrs. McGee of Belfast. They were principally waistcoatings or vestings, of velvet, satin, and other rich materials, embroidered with gold, silver, silk, &c., in a variety of tasteful designs. Many of the designs or patterns were made by pupils of the Belfast School of Design, and all the embroidery was done by young females at Belfast. Arrangements are being made to teach this beautiful art to poor and industrious females in Dublin.

What is now called *Berlin Work*, though not exactly embroidery, may be briefly touched on here. Miss Lambert, in her 'Handbook of Needlework,' gives some interesting details concerning the origin of Berlin work. The kind of work itself is, of course, old enough; the only novelty consists in the care bestowed on the production of patterns. About the year 1805 a Mr. Phillipson published some patterns, which, being badly executed and devoid of taste, did not meet with encouragement. In 1810 Madame Wittich, a lady of great taste and an accomplished needlewoman, justly appreciating the advantages which the art would derive from the production of superior patterns, prevailed upon her husband, a printseller of note at Berlin, to undertake the publication of a series of designs. He did so; and the designs were got up in so superior a manner, that many of the first patterns which were issued from his establishment have had a continued demand almost to the present time. The designer and engraver of these designs are paid as *artists*, in proportion to their talents. The cost of the first coloured design on point paper, (divided into small squares) varies from three to thirty or forty guineas; but in some instances, such as the large patterns of Bolton Abbey, Boccaccio's Garden, &c., it is considerably more. The colouring affords employment for men, women, and children. A dozen or so of copies are given to each person at a time, with the original design as a guide. The earnings are from sixpence to three shillings a day, according to the age and skill of the persons employed.

Berlin workers have had their work facilitated by an ingenious frame, registered by Mr. Lisle in 1843. From a flat horizontal stand rise two pillars, which support the frame somewhat in the same way as a toilet looking-glass is supported, so that the frame may be placed and secured in any convenient position. The canvass or other woven material is wound on rollers, which turn easily on their axes; all the canvas is wound on one roller in the first instance, and is unwound to the other roller as fast as the work proceeds: the space between the two rollers being occupied by a smooth well-stretched portion of the canvas. The rollers are worked by small handles, and there are crotchet wheels to prevent them from slipping backwards. The side or selvage edges of the canvas are kept stretched by two rods. By this apparatus the Berlin worker or embroidress can work on a piece of canvas of almost any length.

Embroidery and needlework were imported to the following amount in four recent years, viz.—65,345*l.* in 1846, 82,889*l.* in 1847, 96,449*l.* in 1848, and 104,699*l.* in 1849.

EMDEN, the principal seaport of Hanover, has been a free port ever since the year 1751. Ship-building is carried on to a considerable extent; the herring fishery, which is a source of great profit, is carried on by four companies who send out between fifty and sixty ships. Emden has brandy distilleries, sawing and oil crushing mills, manufactures of fustians, cottons, stockings, sail-cloth, cordage, needles, leather, soap, tobacco, &c. It has considerable trade in linens, thread, grain, butter, and cheese.

EMERALD. [BERYL.]

EMERY. The nature of emery is noticed under CORUNDUM. Emery-paper consists chiefly of powdered emery secured by glue or some other cement to paper. In 1849 Mr. Day took out a patent for a mode of making emery paper or emery cloth which should resist damp. He coats the paper or cloth on one side with a composition formed of boiled linseed oil, African copal, Venice turpentine, Venetian red, Prussian blue, and litharge; the pounded emery is sifted on this moistened surface, and the other surface is afterwards treated in a similar way.

EMPYREUMA, is the name given to the peculiar smell and taste resulting from the action of heat upon organic substances in close vessels. Destructive distillation goes on so as to produce an oil which has a strong empyreumatic smell and taste.

EMULSION is a term applied to mixtures

which generally have a milky appearance, and which, in some cases, are partial solutions, in others merely mechanical suspensions, of oily or resinous substances: thus oil of almonds may be for a time diffused through water by trituration, but will ultimately separate and float on the surface. Emulsions should be used soon after being formed, as in a few hours the constituent parts separate or become acrid.

ENAMELS and ENAMELLING. There exists evidence that the Egyptians practised this beautiful art; but this cannot be affirmed of the Greeks. The Romans, however, have bequeathed abundant evidence that they were acquainted with the art, and practised it extensively, at least in the time of the Lower Empire.

Enamels are vitrifiable substances, and may be divided into two kinds, transparent and opaque. The basis of all enamel is a white transparent glass. The addition of some of those metallic oxides which merely impart colour, as gold, silver, copper, cobalt, &c., convert this into a transparent enamel; while those of tin and antimony, which render it opaque without imparting colour, form a white opaque enamel. There is also a material, of which the commercial name is glass enamel, the opacity of which arises from the presence of arsenic. This substance is very glassy, brittle, easily scratched, readily fusible, and very white: it is used for making the common kinds of watch and clock dials, ornaments for the mantel shelf, the toilet, &c.

Enamel is made in some of the English glass houses, but the best is imported from Italy. This is in the form of circular cakes, measuring from about three to about seven inches in diameter, and half or three quarters of an inch in thickness. It is cream coloured, heavy, less brittle than glass, is sufficiently hard to scratch crown glass; its fracture is conchoidal, and exhibits a resinous lustre, and it fuses at a temperature a little below that which melts gold. It is sold at from 12*s*. to 20*s*. per lb.

Enamelling divides itself into two branches —transparent and opaque. The first is employed for the purpose of ornamenting gold and silver snuff-boxes, watch cases, and various articles of jewellery. Previously to the application of the enamel, various patterns and devices are *bright-cut* with the graver or the rose-engine, when the cuts reflecting the rays of light from their bright and numerous surfaces exhibit through the richly coloured enamels with which they are encrusted a beautiful play of colours. Sometimes this enamelled bijouterie is further adorned with paintings in enamel executed on rich transparent grounds.

Opaque enamelling is employed in the manufacture of watch and clock dials and of plates for pictures. For this purpose the enamel is first broken with a hammer into small pieces, and then ground with a pestle and mortar formed of agate. It is then spread evenly on a plate of copper, which has been prepared for its reception, and, being passed through the furnace, the enamel is melted, and adhering firmly to the metal, thus forms an enamel plate. For the best kind of dials, a second coat of enamel is laid over the first, and for pictures a third is added. The figures are painted on the dials in a vitrifiable colour, when they are again subjected to the heat of the furnace, which melting the colour and softening the enamel at the same time, incorporates the two into one body, and thus permanently fixes the painting. Gold is frequently used instead of copper for small enamel pictures. When the enamel plate is prepared, the artist proceeds to paint his picture in a similar manner to that which is pursued by the painter in oil or water colours; a principal difference being, that instead of waiting for the colours to dry before proceeding to lay on another coat of colour, he has his work passed through the fire, by which process the colours are imperishably and immoveably fixed. Paintings in enamel are usually subjected to the furnace ten or twelve times, and in some cases oftener. The colours are composed of a colourless glass as a base, the colouring matters being metallic oxides. Thus silica, borax, and the red oxide of lead, form a base or flux for some colours. The habitudes of the various oxides, however, require that each should be treated with reference to its peculiar properties: for instance, the flux which, employed with gold, is best adapted for the production of a useful and beautiful colour, is wholly inefficient if used with cobalt.

In a lecture on Ancient and Modern Enamels, delivered by Mr. Digby Wyatt to the Society of Arts in 1848, attention was drawn to six different kinds of enamel-work, which marked six different periods from the time of Justinian to modern dates. The Byzantine process consisted in the formation of cavities of gold filagree, filled with enamel. The Early Limoges style, instead of having a framework of filagree, had the enamel fixed into cavities scooped from thick copper plate by the graver. The Early Italian method consisted in engraving silver after the manner of medallic relief, and then floating over it with variously-coloured transparent pastes. In the Later Italian method, small gold or silver objects were covered with glass powder mixed with water in which the pips of pears had been steeped; this held the paste in its place until vitrification took place, and was yet so delicate a cement as in no degree to interfere with the purity of the enamel. The Later Limoges style consisted in covering entirely the surface of the metal with an opaque paste, and then painting with transparent colours: regaining the effect of a translucent ground by applying silver leaf in particular situations fastened with a glaze of colourless enamel, and then tinting over it. The sixth style is the modern miniature painting on enamel.

The nature of the material and the expense attendant upon attempts to produce large works in enamel, have tended to restrict the dimensions of enamel paintings. Until the time of the late H. Bone, R. A., but few attempts had been made to extend their size beyond that adapted for trinkets. This artist, with amazing perseverance and industry, overcame innumerable difficulties, and exhibited for a long series of years enamels of large dimensions. The largest works which have been executed in enamel are, 'Bacchus and Ariadne,' after Titian, by H. Bone, R. A.; and a 'Holy Family,' after Parmigiano, by Charles Muss. The former measures 16½ inches by 18; and the latter 15¼ inches by 20½. George Bowles, Esq., purchased the Bacchus and Ariadne for 2200 guineas, and His Majesty George IV. gave 1500 for the Holy Family. This last now forms part of the collection in Buckingham Palace.

The power of resisting decay renders enamel a valuable medium for preserving for ages the likenesses of celebrated individuals. The artists who practise this durable and beautiful style of painting have not at any time been numerous.

At the Mediæval Exhibition in 1850, enamels of exquisite beauty were displayed, chiefly of French and Italian workmanship.

Another kind of enamelling, much humbler in rank, but practically of great usefulness, is that of enamelling the interior of cast-iron and other hollow articles, such as saucepans and other culinary and domestic utensils. The superior cleanliness of such articles, and the security which they afford against any metallic taint, render them peculiarly valuable for some delicate operations in cookery and confectionary, and for the preparing of pharmaceutical decoctions, extracts, &c. The enamel used for this purpose may be stated, in general terms, to consist of silica, soda, borax, and potter's clay. Until within the last few years, enamelled iron saucepans were imported from Germany; but they may now be regarded as a home manufacture rapidly extending.

ENCAUSTIC PAINTING is a kind of painting in which, by heating or burning in, the colours were rendered permanent in all their original splendour. It was not, however enamelling, but a mode of painting with heated or burnt wax, which was practised by the ancients. Pliny describes three modes of encaustic painting. In the first mode, the wax was melted, mixed with as much earth colour finely powdered as it could imbibe, and then this mass spread on wood, or on a wall, with a hot spatula. When it became cold it was the ground, in which the designer cut the lines with a cold pointed tool (style, cestrum). In the second mode, ivory tablets were covered with red or black wax, and the design cut into it with the style, the object being to use the clear and smooth surface of the ivory for the lines, that they might look the more beautiful. The third kind was the applying the colours with the pencil; the wax was dissolved, the colours mixed with it, and laid on with the pencil, and the painting then finished by careful approximation to the fire: for this purpose a hot iron (cauterium) was used. When painting had been greatly improved by the invention of the pencil, a new method of encaustic was attempted. Encaustic wax painting had hitherto been designing on a coloured ground; it now became painting with wax colours burnt in. When the artist had laid on the wax ground, and traced the outlines with the style, he proceeded to the colouring. From the wax mixed with the colours he separated with the hot style as much as he wanted to cover a certain space, and spread it over the ground, put a second, third, &c., colour next the first, so that he had local tint, half tint, and shade together, which he softened into each other with the hot style.

This art, having been long lost, was revived by French and German artists in the 18th century, and is now occasionally practised.

ENDOSMOSE and EXOSMOSE. These names are given to a remarkable filtering process which takes place through membranes. Endosmose is the attraction through an animal or vegetable membrane of thin fluid by a denser fluid. M. Dutrochet found that if he filled the swimming bladder of a carp with thin mucilage and placed it in water, the bladder gained weight by attracting water through its sides: to this phenomenon he gave the name of *Endosmose*. He also found that if he filled the same bladder with water and placed it in thin mucilage, it lost weight, its contents being partially attracted through its sides into the surrounding mucilage: this counter-phenomenon he named *Exosmose*. The same circumstances occur in the transmission of fluids through the tissue of plants. The parts of vegetables may be gorged with fluid by merely placing them in water, and may be emptied again by rendering the fluid in which they are placed more dense than that which they contain. This phenomenon takes place with considerable force. Water thickened with sugar in the proportion of 1 sugar to 2 water, is productive of a power of endosmose capable of sustaining a column of mercury of 127 inches, or the weight of 4½ atmospheres.

Dutrochet considers endosmose to be owing to what he calls intercapillary electricity, grounding his opinion partly upon the experiment of Porret, who found that when two liquids of different levels are separated by a membrane, they may be brought to a level by establishing an electrical current between the two, thus rendering the membrane permeable; and partly upon experiments of his own. But M. Poisson, on the contrary, has demonstrated that endosmose may be the result of capillary attraction joined to differences in the affinity of heterogeneous substances.

A few applications of this principle have been made in the arts; but it still remains chiefly in the domain of science.

ENGINEERING (from the French word *engin*) is properly the art of constructing and using engines or machines; but the term is also applied to that of executing such works as are the objects of civil and military architecture, in which machinery is in general extensively employed.

A distinction has long been made between the civil and military engineer; and since every thing relating to the service of artillery is now confided to a particular corps, the duty of the military engineer may be said to comprehend the construction of fortifications, both permanent and temporary, including the trenches and batteries required in besieging places; also of barracks, magazines, and other works connected with warlike affairs.

The profession of the civil engineer comprehends the design and execution of every great work by which commerce and the practice of the useful arts may be facilitated. Thus, in creating or improving the communications of a country, he would be called upon to form a road through hills, or over valleys or rivers, or to excavate a canal in connection with the waters by which it may be supplied, and to build the locks for retaining the surface at different levels, in different places, when the inequalities of the ground are considerable. He raises embankments to resist the encroachments of the sea or to reclaim the land which it may have covered, and dams to break the force of its waves at the mouths of natural harbours. He renders rivers navigable when their course is obstructed by rocks or banks; he forms docks or artificial harbours where ships may remain in security; he is required to penetrate by mines to vast depths for the purpose of seeking the mineral treasures contained within the bosom of the earth; and the formation of iron roads or railways is now a most important branch of the profession. Such are the occupations of this class of men; and it is necessary to observe that they frequently, in addition, practise the avocation of the machinist in executing the presses, mills, looms, and other great machines employed in the arts and manufactures; particularly in constructing steam-engines and the apparatus by which they are rendered available for giving motion to ships, carriages, or machinery.

In France the title of engineer is extended to persons who are employed for the public service in trigonometrical surveying in the interior of a country or on the coasts, and in the practice of naval architecture. The French have thus a corps of ingénieurs géographes, of ingénieurs d'hydrographie, and of ingénieurs de marine.

Of the national works executed by the ancients, and which are to be considered as properly falling within the province of the engineer, one of the first of which we have any intimation is the canal uniting the Red Sea and the Nile, which, according to Pliny, was begun by Sesostris, or, according to Herodotus, by Necos, the son of Psammetichus, and finished by Darius the First. The canal of Xerxes across the isthmus of the peninsula of Athos is another example of works of this kind. The introduction of arches in works of magnitude may be said to have constituted an epoch in the profession of the architectural engineer, since the idea of giving to blocks of stone a form which would enable them to sustain themselves in balanced rest by their mutual pressures, the discovery of the means of arranging them on a curve surface, and the determination of the magnitudes of the piers or abutments so that the lateral pressure of the vault might be adequately resisted, imply a higher degree of intellectual power than is exhibited in covering a space with a horizontal roof. The Cloaca Maxima [CLOACÆ] at Rome is probably the most ancient example in Europe of this scientific construction. The dome of the Pantheon, and the various arches of the Thermæ and of other public buildings, both at Rome and in the provinces, such as aqueducts and bridges, attest the grandeur of design, combined with purposes of public utility, which characterised the architects who lived under the early emperors.

Previously to the commencement of the eighteenth century, the most celebrated practical engineers were Brunelleschi, who built the dome of St. Mary at Florence; Peruzzi, San Gallo, and Michel Angelo, who executed that of St. Peter at Rome; San Micheli, the supposed inventor of the bastion system of fortification; and to these may be added Sir Christopher Wren, the architect of St. Paul's Cathedral in London.

But the extension of the manufactures of this country, and the consequent augmentation both of its internal and foreign commerce, have, in more recent times, called forth all the energies of the people, who, in the works performed for facilitating the means of communicating between one place and another, and in the practice of the useful arts, have risen to an eminence which other nations have not been able to attain. Among the former may be mentioned the numerous canals and railways which intersect the country; the majestic bridges executed in stone over the Thames; in cast iron over the Avon, the Thames, &c.; those on the suspension principle at the Menai Strait, and across the Thames at Hammersmith and Hungerford Market; and those on the tubular principle over the Menai and the Conway. Among the men to whose talents in this branch of engineering the nation is indebted, may be named Brindley, Smeaton, Jessop, Telford, the Rennies, Walker, the Brunels, and the Stephensons.

The course of education by which a student may qualify himself to become an engineer, whether civil or military, must necessarily comprehend a greater extent both of the pure and physical sciences than would be required for a person who is to follow any other profession. It will be, perhaps for ever, a matter of opinion how much mathematics should enter a school course of engineering; and there are no doubt some persons who contend that no more is required than would serve to compute the cost of materials and the wages of labour; this and the observation of existing examples being supposed sufficient to enable a man to enter upon the practice of the profession. It is not, however, with such knowledge only that an engineer is qualified to design an important work which it may be required to conduct under new and difficult circumstances. On the other hand, mere diligence in observing the results of practical operations will never raise a man to proficiency in art unless he is gifted with very extraordinary powers. A judicious combination of theory and practice is indispensable, and such a combination can only be made by a man in whom great natural talent is blended with all the aids that the sciences can afford.

Of the military engineer it may be said that a greater knowledge of the more minute details of construction is required than would suffice in the civil practitioner; because it may happen that the former is called upon to exercise his profession in some colony where workmen adequately skilled in the mechanical operations may be wanting. The accomplishment of the work may then become impossible, should the officer not be qualified to give the necessary instructions to those who are placed under his direction.

There is now near the metropolis a college for the education of young persons who are destined to act as civil engineers, where the science and practice of the profession are effectively taught; while the military seminaries at Woolwich, Sandhurst, and Addiscombe, afford corresponding advantages for those who have adopted the military service.

The *Institution of Civil Engineers*, formed at London in 1828, cannot fail, by the publication of its transactions, to be the means of greatly assisting such persons as may hereafter enter the profession; and, through them, of rendering service to society itself. Even established practitioners may occasionally derive benefit from the theoretical investigations and the practical details of construction which are the subjects of the papers read at the meetings of the members.

An *Institute of Mechanical Engineers* was established at Birmingham in 1847, for encouraging experiments and essays relating to engineering subjects. It is under the presidency of Mr. Robert Stephenson, and seems to be a sort of miniature Institute of Civil Engineers.

ENGLISH MANUFACTURES AND TRADE. We retain an entry under this heading, simply to explain how the subjects of English manufactures and trade are treated in the present volume. All the principal *substances* employed in the arts, organic or inorganic, are briefly described under their proper headings, the commercial name being retained rather than the scientific name. All the principal *processes* employed in the arts and manufactures are set forth in simple form, without any attempt at minute or technical detail. All the important *machines* are described in a similarly brief and simple way. Nearly all the *counties* are glanced at, with a view to show what productive and industrial resources they exhibit. All the principal *towns* are similarly noticed, in so far as they are connected with manufacturing or shipping operations. A few commercial *principles* are touched upon which bear closely on manufactures. Lastly, a few *persons* are made the subjects of biographical sketches, in cases were they were especially connected with mechanical or manufacturing celebrity.

In respect to foreign countries, a smaller degree of the same system is acted upon. An attempt is made to show what are the chief natural products of each country, what are the chief manufactures of the countries and their large towns, and what are the chief imports and exports at their shipping ports. As such elements are really the elements of the 'Industry of all Nations,' they form a fitting part of the present work. All merely geographical detail is beyond the scope of this volume.

Besides the minor statistical details scattered through the work, larger illustrations of commercial and manufacturing statistics will be met with under such articles as CUSTOMS DUTIES, EXCISE DUTIES, FACTORIES, IMPORTS AND EXPORTS, SHIPS AND SHIPPING.

ENGRAVING. From the book of Exodus we learn that when Moses had liberated the Jews from Egyptian bondage, he was commanded to 'make a plate of pure gold, and grave upon it, like the engravings of a signet, holiness to the Lord.' He was also commanded 'to take two onyx stones, and grave on them the names of the children of Israel according to their birth, with the work of an engraver on stone, like the engravings of a signet.' Both these passages distinctly imply the practice of gem and seal engraving, and also of engraving on metal plates. From Herodotus we learn that one of the earliest uses to which engraving was applied among the Greeks was the delineation of maps on metal plates. Some of the Egyptian hieroglyphic inscriptions are evidently executed with instruments similar to those now in use. Some of the lines narrowing downwards have clearly been cut with the lozenge-shaped graver now chiefly used; but other lines, being of the same width through their whole depth, must have been produced with that species of graver called a scooper, still used for effecting broad incisions. It is believed that some of the relics of Etruscan art in the British Museum are of as high antiquity as any existing specimens of engraving. In India, also, the art of engraving on plates of copper appears to have been practised long before the Christian æra. It would appear that it was there customary to ratify grants of land by deeds of transfer actually engraven on plates of copper, as we now write them on skins of parchment.

In England, before the Conquest, many of the buckles, clasps, rings, and military accoutrements were engraved. In the museum of Oxford is preserved a finely engraved gold jewel, which belonged to Alfred the Great. About the 12th century was introduced the art of engraving sepulchral brasses. They are executed entirely with the graver, and in the same manner that a copper plate is now engraved.

We now approach the period when the invention of *printing* gave to engraving a new direction. The first prints were obtained from engraved wood blocks. The earliest print with a date attached to it is one known as the St. Christopher, which is from a wood block, and dated 1423; but no impression from an engraved *plate* has been found with a date anterior to 1461. The art of engraving on metal plates for taking impressions on paper was first practised by Tommaso Fineguerra, a Florentine goldsmith, about the year 1460. Some writers have claimed the invention for Germany; but it is generally considered that the art was first practised in Italy, and had its origin in the workshops of the goldsmiths. Many of these goldsmiths were *niellatori*, or workers in *niello*—a mode of ornamental engraving usually performed on silver plates—the design engraved on which was afterwards filled in with a black composition.

An accident is said to have suggested to Fineguerra the possibility of taking an impression from the engraved design with ink on moistened paper. When once established, the new art was eagerly taken up by Baldini, Botticelli, Pollajuoli, and Mantegna; and in Germany by Martin Schoen, Israel van Mecheln, Leydenwurf, and Wolgemut. The first *book* printed at *Rome* (an edition of Ptolemæus's Geography) was illustrated by the first *plate engravings*, twenty-seven in number, which were maps, and were executed there by two Germans, Sweynheym and Buckink. This work is dated 1478, but was commenced in 1472. Another early work was an edition of Dante's 'Inferno,' published at Florence in 1481, and embellished with engravings by Baccio Baldini, after the designs of Botticelli.

One of the best engravers in Italy in the early part of the 16th century was Raimondi, who studied under Francia and Raffaelle. His great merit lay in the correctness and beauty of his outline. He engraved many of Raffaelle's pictures, which he copied with great truth, although defective in respect to light and shade. He was succeeded in Italy by Agostino de Musis, Marc de Ravenna, Caraglio, Giulio Bonasoni, and Enea Vico, all pupils of Raimondi; Georgi Ghisi of Mantua, and his relatives Diana and Adam Ghisi, Cornelius Cort, &c. The principal painters who have practised engraving in Italy are Agostino

Carracci, Stefano della Bella, Spagnoletto, Guercino, Salvator Rosa, Claude Lorraine, Swaneveldt, Canaletto, Piranesi, &c.

In Germany engraving made more rapid strides towards excellence, in the mechanical parts of it; and at the commencement of the 16th century appeared Albert Dürer, a man whose universality of talent extended the boundaries of every department of art; and carried all to a degree of perfection previously unknown in that country. He had great command of the graver, and carried his plates to a much higher degree of finish than his Italian contemporaries. He is also believed to have invented the art of etching by corrosion: three of his specimens are dated 1515, 1516, and 1518 respectively. On examining the etchings of Albert Dürer, we see that they have all been corroded at one biting-in; which sufficiently explains their monotonous appearance, and proves that 'stopping out' was not then understood. The principal German engravers, after Albert Dürer, are Aldegraver, the Behams, Altdorfer, Bink, Penz, Solis, &c.

Lucas Jacobs, best known by the name of Lucas van Leyden, was the father of the Dutch and Flemish schools, and the contemporary and friend of Albert Dürer. After Van Leyden the art was maintained in the Low Countries by the Wierinxes, the Sadelers, whose works are multifarious, and embrace every class of subject; the elder and younger Jode, Cornelius, Theodore and Philip Galle, Abraham and Cornelius Bloemart, Goltzius, Spranghèr, Müller, Lucas Killian, Matham, Saenredam, and the two brothers Bolswert. Many of these introduced improvements in the art. To mention the artists of this school from whose hands we have etchings, would be to name nearly all the most eminent painters belonging to it: Rembrandt, Berghem, Cuyp, Karel du Jardin, Paul Potter, Ruysdael, Ostade, Waterloo, Adrian Vandervelde, with many others.

In France engraving has been practised with pre-eminent success in the departments of history and portraiture. The celebrity of the school dates from the time of Louis XIV. The family of the Audrans produced six eminent engravers; but of those the most distinguished was Gerard Audran, who was the first engraver who successfully united, to any extent, the use of the graver and the etching point. Gerard Edelinck, although born at Antwerp, may be fairly considered of the French school, and was an engraver of the highest order. In portrait Nanteuil is no less celebrated than his contemporaries. The Drevets, John Louis Roulett, Le Clerc, Simoneau, Chereau, Cochin, Dupuis, Beauvais, Balechou, Le Bas, John George Wille, are among the best of the French engravers.

The English school of engraving dates only from about the middle of the eighteenth century, previous to which those who practised the art in England were chiefly foreigners.

Hogarth engraved many of his own designs. Francis Vivares introduced the favourite art of landscape etching; he, Woollet, and Browne, produced some of the finest landscape engravings extant. Sir Robert Strange excelled in portrait engraving. Mezzotinto engraving, although not strictly born among us, has been in no other country practised with a degree of success at all approaching that attained by M'Ardell, Earlom, Smith, Valentine Green, and others. Bartolozzi, Ryland, Sharpe, Paul Sandby, Middiman, Milton, Fitler, and Raimbach, are among the most eminent of deceased engravers.

A modern engraving is usually the result of two processes, namely, of direct incision with the graver or the dry point, and of etching by corrosion. The principal instrument is the *graver*, or *burin*, which is usually of the form of a quadrangular prism, fitted into a short handle. The square graver is used in cutting broad lines, and the lozenge-shaped for more delicate ones. In making the incision, it is pushed forward in the direction of the line required, being held by the handle at an angle very slightly inclined to the plane of the copper. An instrument called a *scraper* is required to scrape off the barb or burr which is formed by the action of the graver and dry point. A roll of cloth dipped in oil, called the *rubber*, is also used to make the surface smooth. The *burnisher* is used to polish the plate and to erase any scratches which it may accidentally receive, and also to make lighter any part of the work which may have been made too dark. *Etching-points*, or *needles*, are nearly similar in appearance to sewing-needles, but fixed into handles four or five inches long; some are made of an oval form, to produce broader lines. The *dry point* does not, like the graver, cut the copper clean out, but throws it up on each side of the line produced by its progress through the metal.

Etching is the superaddition of the chemical process of corrosion to drawing, when performed on a plate of copper over which a substance called *etching-ground* is laid. This etching-ground is a substance composed of wax, asphaltum, gum mastic, resin, &c., incorporated by melting over a fire, and capable of resisting the action of aquafortis; it is applied by the aid of heat, so as to lie in a thin stratum on the copper. To transfer the design to the copper, an outline is made with a black lead pencil on a piece of paper, and laid with the face downwards on the etching-ground; the whole is then passed through a rolling-press, the effect of which is to transfer an impression of the outline on to the prepared ground. After this the design is completed with the etching-needles, which remove the ground from the copper wherever they pass, and expose it to the action of the acid during the process of biting-in. The aquafortis continues on the plate until the fainter parts are supposed to be corroded sufficiently deep; after which it is poured off, the plate washed with water, and left to dry. The parts which are bitten-in enough are now to be covered with what is called *stopping-ground*, which is a mixture of lamp-black and Venice turpentine; this is applied with a camel-hair pencil, and allowed to dry. After this the acid is again poured on, and this process of *stopping-out* and *biting-in* is repeated till the darkest parts are sufficiently corroded.

Engraving in stipple is performed with the graver, which is so managed as to produce the tints by small dots, rather than by lines, as in the ordinary method.

Engraving and *etching on steel* are performed in the same manner as on copper, for which steel has of late years been often substituted on account of its yielding a greater number of perfect impressions, owing to its superior hardness.

Medallic engraving is a species of etching introduced by M. Collas and Mr. Bate. By this mode very beautiful representations are obtained of medals, &c., by means of a machine of peculiar construction.

Etching on glass is performed by laying on the glass a ground of bees' wax, and drawing the designs thereon with the needle, as in etching upon copper. Sulphuric acid is then poured on, and fluor spar, or fluoric acid, sprinkled on it. After four or five hours it is taken off, and the work cleaned with oil of turpentine.

[AQUATINTA; ELECTROTYPE; LITHOGRAPHY; MEZZOTINT.]

ENHARMONIC ORGAN. It is familiar to all who have observed the construction of a pianoforte or an organ, that the same black key serves as the sharp of one note and the flat of the note next above it. This is convenient, but it is not strictly accurate; the sharp of one note is *not* in strictness the flat of the note next above it; it differs from it by some small fraction of a semitone. Hence it has been an object with some persons of refined musical ear to increase the keys to such a degree as to provide a series for the flats, differing from that which constitutes the sharps. But there are two inconveniences attending such a plan; the keys become embarrassingly numerous, and unless the instrument be tuned with most delicate precision, the nicety of the double system is wholly lost. An organ with such an arrangement of parts is called an *enharmonic organ*; at one time the subject attracted much attention, but the plan is now pretty nearly abandoned. A violin player with a correct ear can produce enharmonic intervals easily, as the strings can be stopped at any part of their length.

ENTRE-DOURO-E-MINHO is the most fertile province in Portugal. The principal productions are wine, oil, flax, Indian corn, wheat, oats, vegetables, and fruit of all sorts. Pastures are rather scarce, yet a considerable quantity of cattle, both large and small, are reared. The principal article of exportation is wine, which is made chiefly from the vineyards in the valley of the Douro, and is shipped at Oporto under the name of port-wine. There are fisheries along the coast, which occupy a great number of hands. The commerce is briefly noticed under OPORTO and PORTUGAL.

ENTRESOL, a French term used to signify a floor between other floors. The entresol consists of a low apartment or apartments, usually placed above the first floor. There is a very good example of an entresol over the shops of the Quadrant in London, just beneath the terrace of the colonnade (lately removed). In continental cities the entresol is frequently employed.

ENVELOPES. Before the introduction of the Penny Postage, the number of written letters put into envelopes was comparatively small; but since that period the use of envelopes has increased to an astonishing extent. The cutting out has been for some years performed by machinery; but the folding, until within the last three or four years, has been done by hand. An ingenious machine, however, patented by Messrs. Hill and De la Rue, now folds envelopes with great celerity. From a description of this folding machine given by Mr. Faraday at the Royal Institution in 1849, it appears that it can fold 42 envelopes in a minute. There is a flat metallic surface on which the piece of paper is laid; a sort of hollow frame descends and creases the paper at the four edges: and four levers or folders press down the four flaps of the envelope. There are two finger-shaped projections, made of caoutchouc, which, owing to their property of adhering slightly to a paper surface, never fail to carry off each envelope as fast as it is folded. Though there are twenty-two movements for folding each envelope, all succeeding each other with great rapidity, there is no blow or jar of any kind in the working of the machine.

Mr. Worsdell's patent for making envelopes, enrolled in 1850, relates to mechanism of a very complicated construction. Under the usual methods envelopes are made partly by hand and partly by machinery, with certain intervals of time between the several processes. Mr. Worsdell has sought to carry on two or more of the processes simultaneously, and to make other processes succeed them uninterruptedly. There are shaping, cutting, stamping, gumming, creasing, pasting, and applying processes. A web of paper is unrolled, laid upon a bed or plate, and a series of fine knife edges descend and cut out a piece the proper size and shape for an envelope; this same piece of paper, before it is removed, is creased into an oblong quadrangular form, and the four corners turned up. The roughly-shaped envelope falls out of this machine, and is placed in another where the subsequent processes are carried on. By one movement a die is brought down, and made to stamp a device on the seal-flap; by another movement two bits of sponge, moistened with some kind of gum or cement, and held at the ends of small cylinders, are passed lightly over the edges of the two end flaps; by a third movement the sponges are brought back again; by a fourth movement another bit of sponge, moistened with adhesive composition, is made to touch the inside of the seal flap; by a fifth movement the three flaps are pressed down, leaving the seal flap, with its adhesive composition, untouched; and by a sixth movement the finished envelope is thrust out of the machine. Considerable mechanical ingenuity is displayed in this apparatus.

It is supposed that there are upwards of a million envelopes manufactured *daily* in this country.

EPROUVETTE is an apparatus consisting of a gun or mortar suspended from a horizontal axis for the purpose of determining the strength of gunpowder by the recoil of the piece when a charge is fired in it. Mr. Robins ('New Principles of Gunnery') first proposed the employment of such a machine, but Dr. Hutton, of Woolwich, afterwards considerably improved its construction.

A gun suspended in the manner above described has been employed, instead of the ballistic pendulum, to determine, by its recoil, the initial velocity of the shot fired from it with a given charge of powder.

EPSOM SALTS. This valuable medicine is sulphate of magnesia. It obtained its common commercial name from having been first obtained from a spring at Epsom. The mode of obtaining it first adopted when it became a popular medicine was by evaporating and crystallising the bitter deposit remaining after preparing common salt from sea-water; but the late Dr. Henry invented a much superior mode of preparing it from magnesian limestone. Epsom salts are not only valuable as a medicine, but a source whence common magnesia is largely obtained.

EQUATORIAL INSTRUMENT. This name is generally given to astronomical instruments having their principal axis of rotation in the direction of the poles of the heavens. When the purpose of a machine of this nature is simply to carry a telescope, it has been called a *machine parallactique* or *parallatique* by the French, and sometimes *Polar Axis* by English writers.

It results from the general form of the management, that if a telescope is fixed equatorially, it always points to some spot or other of the celestial equator. These instruments are described with great fulness and completeness in the PENNY CYCLOPÆDIA. Some of the largest telescopes in this country are equatorial.

ERBIUM, is the name given to a metal discovered by Mosander associated with yttria. Its properties are little known. Some of them are as follows:—Its oxide becomes of a dark orange colour when heated in contact with the air, which colour it loses with a little weight when heated in hydrogen gas. It is to the presence of this oxide that yttria owes its yellow colour, when prepared as hitherto directed. The sulphate and nitrate of erbium are free from colour. It does not appear to have been reduced to the metallic state.

ERECTHEIUM, is the name of one of those buildings in Greece which have acquired a world-wide celebrity. It is a beautiful Ionic temple dedicated to Erectheus, built near the western brow of the Acropolis at Athens, and at the time when Stuart visited the place forming part of the modern fortress of the Acropolis. Connected with this building, and placed on one side of it at the end of the cella, is a tetrastyle Ionic portico, in the same style as the portico of the Erectheium, forming a small temple which was dedicated to Minerva Pólias; and on the opposite side is a small roofed building supported by caryátides placed on an elevated basement, forming another small temple dedicated to Pandrosos, and called the Pandrosium. It would appear from the regularity of the plan of the Temple of Erectheus, that it was constructed before the other buildings, and was of that regular parallelopipedal figure most commonly employed in such edifices: and that at a later period the Pandrosium was constructed, with the portico on the opposite side forming the entrance or vestibule to the cella of the temple, which was formed from a part of the cella of the Temple of Erectheus, cut off from the end of that cella, which was either at that time or previously lighted with windows.

Mr. Inwood, the architect, has imitated the Erectheium and Pandrosium in the external design of part of new St. Pancras Church, London.

EREMECAUSIS is the name given by Liebig and other chemists to the act of gradual combination of the combustible elements of a body with the oxygen of the air. This process is constantly going on in combustible bodies exposed to the atmosphere, and one of the first changes which take place during the decomposition of animal and vegetable substances, is the union of one or more of their elements with oxygen, The changes in colour, consistence, and other properties which vegetable juices, saw-dust, leaves of trees, blood, &c., undergo when exposed to the atmosphere, are owing to the same cause. Eremecausis differs from fermentation and putrefaction in the fact that it cannot take place without the access of atmospheric air, through which means the oxygen is supplied to the decaying body. Eremecausis must precede any decomposition of an organised substance; and it is by virtue of this law that animal food may be kept from putrefaction by being heated to the temperature of boiling water, and then secured in air-tight vessels. Food thus prepared has been kept for fifteen years, and when the vessels were opened in which it was contained, it has been found as fresh as when first secured.

ERFURT is a busy province or government of Prussian Saxony. The chief products are grain, flax, tobacco, hops, oil, and salt. Great numbers of horses, horned cattle, sheep, goats, and swine are reared. In the circles of Weissensee and Schleusingen there are mines of iron, lead, and copper. Marble and gypsum, as well as sulphur, are also among its mineral productions. Erfurt is likewise distinguished for its manufactures of iron and steelware, tin plates, seed-oil, woollen yarns, cloths, flannels, and carpets, linens, silks, cottons, stockings, paper, porcelain, glass, brandy, wooden clocks, &c.

Erfurt, the chief town, has considerable manufactures of cottons and woollens, besides less extensive ones of linens, ribbons, leather, soap, earthenware, meal, seed-oil, stockings, gloves, tobacco, &c., and it carries on a brisk trade in fruits, seeds, grocery and drugs, grain, &c. *Mühlhausen*, an antient walled town, has manufactures of woollen cloth, calicoes, beer, tobacco, spirits, leather, oil, glue, starch, &c.; it has also several dyeing and fulling mills. *Nordhausen*, an old fashioned place girt with walls and towers, has very large distilleries, and manufactures woollen cloths, flannels, chemical products, rape-oil, and leather; great numbers of oxen and swine are fattened on grains and pressed rapeseed. *Suhl*, a thriving manufacturing town, produces large quantities of ticking and dimity, and fire-arms, swords, bayonets, ramrods, surgical instruments, &c.; the iron and steel (7000 cwts.) for these last are furnished by 9 forges in the neighbourhood. Suhl stands in a district of the Thüringerwald, entirely separated from the rest of the Prussian territory.

ERGOT is a name bestowed upon a peculiar state of the seed of several cereal grains, but most frequently of the rye, which resembles a spur, or horn; hence, likewise, termed *Secale cornutum*, or Spurred Rye. The spur is of variable length, from a fraction of an inch to two inches, and is from a sixth to a fourth of an inch in thickness; when large, only a few grains in each ear are affected; when small, in general all of them are diseased. In colour the exterior or husk is of a blueish-black or violet hue, with two or three streaks of dotted gray; the interior is of a dull whitish or gray tint. It is specifically lighter than water, which affords a criterion for distinguishing sound from tainted grain. When fresh it is tough and flexible, but brittle and easily pulverised when dry. The powder is apt to attract moisture, which impairs its properties; and time destroys them.

Spurred rye occurs more frequently in some countries and districts than in others, and more abundantly in some seasons than in others. Rye raised in poor soil, and in a humid close air, such as that of the district of Sologne in France, is most liable to be infected; but, according to the experiments of Willdenow, it may be brought on at any time, by sowing the rye in a rich damp soil, and watering the plants freely in warm weather. A very rainy season, such as was that of 1816, is apt to produce it.

Bread prepared from grain which has a large admixture of the spur, occasions very distressing and often fatal effects, which are shown more or less rapidly according to the quantity present in the food, and the circumstances in which those who use it are placed. Ergot of rye is sometimes employed in medicinal practice. The Ergot is produced by a fungus.

ERMINE. This beautiful substance is the fur of the *stoat*, one among many species of *weasel*. It is a native of the northern parts of Europe and Asia, and the finest furs, both as to colour and quality, are brought from the northernmost regions. Ermine-skins formed part of the Canada exports in the time of Charlevoix; but they have since sunk so much in value, that they are said not to repay the Hudson Bay Company the expense of collecting them; and very few are now obtained from that quarter. Our chief supply is obtained from Norway and Siberia. In Siberia ermines are taken in traps baited with flesh. In Norway they are either shot with short arrows, or taken in traps made of two flat stones, one being propped up with a stick, to which is fastened a baited string; the animal nibbles at the bait, and the stone falls and captures him. In Lapland two logs of wood are used for this purpose, and in the same way.

There were 183,547 ermine furs imported in 1848.

ERZERU'M, in Turkish Armenia, is important as a commercial town. Besides the produce of its manufactures it exports corn, cattle, sheep, and dried meats. But it derives other commercial advantages from its being situated on one of the most frequented caravan roads of Western Asia, which leads from Persia and Georgia to the great commercial towns of Asia Minor.

ERZGEBIRGE (the Ore Mountains) is a mountain-range in Germany, which derives its name from the rich mineral treasures embosomed in the mountains. The surrounding district abounds in mines of silver, tin, lead, iron, cobalt, copper, &c., which afford employment to upwards of 200,000 persons. The silver mines are at Schneeberg, Schwarzenberg, Annaberg, and Marienberg. The most considerable tin mines are at Altenberg, Geier, and Schneeberg. The most productive iron mines are those of Johann-Georgenstadt. Near Aue and Bockau, to the south of Schneeberg, lie the largest cobalt mines and smalt works in Germany; of these smalts the yearly produce is between 9000 and 10,000 cwts., besides large quantities of arsenic, &c. The white porcelain earth used in the royal china manufactory at Meissen is procured and prepared in this district. Sulphur and vitriol are made at and near Beierfeld and Geier: magnesia and porcelain earth are obtained at Elterlein; and there are coal mines of importance at Planitz, and other spots near Zwickau. Gold is found in some places, but no mines are worked.

Besides considerable manufactures of iron, tin, steel, and copper ware, the province has extensive manufactuaes of thread, twist, linen, cotton goods, woollen cloths, flannel, woollen stockings, bobbinet, tape, ribbons, &c.

ESPALIER is a trellis for training fruit trees or bushes upon, instead of nailing them to walls. The stakes which form the espalier are made of different materials, some of wood, others of wire and wood, and some of cast iron. The first of these is by far the most simple, and is composed of stakes, five or six feet in height, driven into the ground from one to two feet apart; along the top a bar, which is nailed to each, connects the whole together. The wire and wood rail is formed by strong vertical wires, strained from two wooden horizontal rails, which are connected and held fast by wooden posts fixed in the ground. The iron rail is constructed like a common street railing.

The best wood for this purpose is young larch, the thinning of plantations.

ESSENCES. This name is given to a large variety of pharmaceutical preparations; but there is a good deal of vagueness in the designation, Concentrated infusions, decoctions, tinctures, and liquors, are often termed essences; and it is by no means easy to distinguish the limits of each kind of preparation. Some essences are made by digesting vegetable substances for a long time in spirit. The essences of lavender, of musk, of ginger, and some others, are made by simply dissolving the essential oils of those substances in spirit. Many of the fragrant essences prepared by the perfumer and the druggist, in which the aromatic and volatile principles are alone wanted, are made by digesting the ingredients in spirit for a few days, and then distilling. In preparing the essences used for perfuming and flavouring, spirit is employed which is perfectly tasteless, scentless, and colourless.

The delicate substance called *Essence d' Orient* is made from the scales of the fish called the blay or bleak, and is used as a paint for the inside of glass beads, to make artificial pearls. A few other essences are used in the manufacturing arts, and a few in medicine; but most of them are employed either as perfumes or for flavouring food and beverages.

ESSEX is almost entirely an agricultural county. The feeding of oxen in winter is now extensively practised by all good farmers in Essex, whether of strong or light loams. In those farms which have marshes attached to them a great number of cattle is constantly kept. Along the Thames the salt marshes are extensive, and are profitable from the number of horses which are sent to feed there from London. Besides the common crops usually cultivated, considerable quantities of cole or rape-seed, caraway, coriander, and teasels are raised. In that part of Essex which lies within a few miles of London, the cultivation of the soil partakes more of the garden culture. Vegetables, especially cabbages, are raised in great quantities, and very extensive fields are almost entirely devoted to the raising of potatoes. The cows and horses in Essex are chiefly reared in Suffolk, and Scotland supplies the oxen to fatten. Many calves are fatted, which are killed in the county, or go to London by railway. Essex is not a sheep-breeding county, although many fine lambs are reared; but they are generally bought from the breeders in Wiltshire or Sussex in autumn, and sold fat to the butcher in the succeeding spring.

In Barking, many of the inhabitants are fishermen, or employed in conveying coals and other necessaries from London for the supply of Barking and other places in the neighbourhood. At Coggeshall manufactures of silk have nearly superseded the former manufactures of woollen. At Harwich, Malden, Romford, and other towns, manufactures are carried on to a limited extent; but Essex can by no means be considered a manufacturing county. Women's stays and shoes, and small wares in silk, are made to some considerable extent in the neighbourhood of Stratford.

ESTHONIA one of the Baltic provinces of Russia, produces large crops of rye, barley, and oats; wheat, Indian corn, hemp, flax, hops, and tobacco are also raised. The produce of corn exceeds the consumption; the surplus is chiefly used for distillation. As the harvest season is attended by heavy rains, the farmers have subterranean kilns in most parts, into which the moist grain is carried for the purpose of being dried. Esthonia has large meadows, and produces abundance of hay; it has likewise good grazing grounds. The woods and forests, composed of the fir, pine, elm, birch, larch, and beech, occasionally intermixed with the oak, alder, linden, crab-apple, &c., are abundant. Next to agriculture, the rearing of cattle is the most important branch of rural industry. The fisheries along the coast and in lake Peipus are very productive. On the islands ship and boat building is a source of employment. The mineral products are building stone, potter's clay, and gypsum; there is abundance of peat.

The manufactures of Esthonia are extremely limited; the peasantry are clothed with linen and coarse woollen cloth woven in their own houses, or else with sheep-skins. There are about 400 distilleries scattered through the province.

ESTREMADU'RA, a province of Spain, is rich in pastures. About four millions of sheep come to graze, during the winter, from the other provinces on the open pastures of Estremadura. Other tracts are covered with underwood and wild odoriferous herbs. There are also forests of oak, beech, chestnut, and pine trees, where numerous herds of swine feed. Bacon and pork form the most important articles of commerce with the other provinces of Spain. Game of every sort is plentiful. The cultivated parts produce wheat, oats, Indian corn, flax, hemp, and the vine, olive, mulberry, and lemon trees. Excellent honey and wax are also gathered. There are mines of copper, lead, iron, and silver. The manufactures are few, consisting chiefly of leather and hats at Badajoz, Zafra, and Caceres.

There is also a province of the same name in Portugal, which is fertile and salubrious. The rivers, as well as the sea-coast, abound with fish. The principal products of the country are wine, oil, maize, fruits of every sort, and cattle. Wheat and oats are also raised, but in no great qnantity. At Belem there are iron foundries. At Alhandra lime and brick kilns. At Alemquer a paper manufactory. At Thomar there is a large manufactory for spinning cotton, and manufactories of hats and worsted stuffs. Setubal exports large quantities of salt made from sea-water in the neighbourhood, and also wine and fruits, especially oranges. It is, next to Lisbon and Oporto, the most commercial place in the kingdom.

ETHAL is a substance separated from spermaceti. It is a solid, fusible at nearly the same point as spermaceti, and on cooling crystallises in plates. It is susceptible of union with various bases, with which it forms salts or soaps.

ETHER. [ÆTHER.]

ETHIOPS, a term now obsolete, was formerly used by the old chemists to denote various dark-coloured metallic preparations; as *Ethiops Martialis*, which is a black oxide of iron: *Ethiops Mineralis*, which is a black mixture of mercury and sulphur, &c.

E'TIENNE, ST., a large manufacturing town in the department of Loire, stands in the centre of one of the most important coal fields in France, from which about 500,000 tons of coal are exported annually. It is especially famous for the manufacture of silk ribbons and fire-arms. Its ribbons, which are exported to all parts of the world, are unequalled for richness of colour and beauty of pattern, and of the quantity manufactured an idea may be formed from the statement that their value amounts annually to upwards of 40,000,000 francs. Government orders for fire-arms having considerably fallen off since 1834, the workmen have turned their attention to making fowling-pieces, of which 30,000 a year are disposed of, besides a great number of pistols, &c. The manufacture next in importance is that of hardware and cutlery. To these leading articles of industry are to be added the manufactures of scythes, nails of all kinds, saw blades, foils, anvils, vices, files, silk and cotton velvets, &c., &c. The town has also many dye-houses and tanyards; and in the suburb of Terre-Noire there are important iron-forges and furnaces.

Many manufactured products from this important town will have a place in the approaching Exhibition.

ETRUSCAN WARE. The ancient Etrurians produced pottery ware, specimens of which still remain to illustrate the ingenuity of that very ancient people after a period of twenty-five or thirty centuries.

The Etruscan vases belong to three different periods of art, each exhibiting its peculiar style. The most ancient are those which resemble the Egyptian style: indeed it has been asserted that they were imported from Egypt; but it is more probable that they were manufactured in Etruria, from Egyptian models. They are partly coloured of black and red upon a pale yellow ground; and harpies, sphynxes, griffins, &c., are depicted on them. The next in order are those with black figures on a red ground, in stiff and ungraceful outline, while the form of the vase itself is very elegant. The third and most modern style exhibits a more graceful form of vase, and graceful and spirited figures; the designs, in red figures, represent stories of gods and heroes, as well as incidents of domestic life.

The Etruscan Room at the British Museum is well worth a study; the specimens of ancient pottery are numerous and highly curious.

EUDIO'METER, an instrument invented by Dr. Priestley, and originally employed by him in ascertaining the goodness of atmospheric air obtained from various places and under different circumstances. The use of the eudiometer, termed eudiometry, has, since its original contrivance, been extended to all gaseous mixtures, but especially to determining the quantity of oxygen which they contain when resulting from the operations of analysis.

The principle upon which the use of the eudiometer depends, so far as atmospheric air and oxygen gas are concerned, is that of exposing them to the action of some substance, whether solid, fluid, or gaseous, which, on account of its affinity for oxygen, combines with it and leaves the gas with which it is mixed unacted upon.

The eudiometer invented by Dr. Priestley was extremely simple. He filled a phial with water, and displaced the water with the gaseous mixture to be examined; the volume of this being noted, it was transferred into an air-jar. An equal volume of nitric oxide was added to it, and they remained together a few minutes. When this part of the process was over, the gas was transferred to a graduated glass tube. After noting the volume of the gas, the result was expressed in measures and decimal parts; thus, when equal volumes of common air and nitric oxide were mixed, and they afterwards occupied the space of one volume and two-tenths, Dr. Priestley, in speaking of the air so tried, said the measures of the test were 1.2, or the standard of the air was 1.2.

Numerous attempts have been made to render the eudiometrical application exact and certain by Cavendish, Fontana, Ingenhouz, Sardiniani, Dalton, Gay Lussac, Henry, Thomson, Davy, and others. The eudiometer of Scheele was a graduated glass tube containing a certain volume of air, which was exposed to a mixture of sulphur and iron-filings made into a paste with water. De Marté, instead of using sulphur and iron, employed a solution of sulphuret of potassium prepared by dissolving sulphur in a solution of potash. Guyton employed sulphuret of potassium also in his eudiometer, but he used it in a solid state, and applied heat to expedite its action. The eudiometer of Seguin is a glass tube, filled with and inverted in mercury; a small piece of phosphorus is put under the open end of the tube, and by its lightness it immediately rises to the top of it, where it is melted by the approach of red-hot iron. A measured portion of the gas to be examined is then passed into the tube; the phosphorus inflames on each addition of the gas, and the mercury rises, owing to the condensation of the oxygen. The quantity of the residual gas is determined by transferring it into a graduated tube, and the difference between the quantity submitted to experiment and that left after it indicates that of the oxygen absorbed. Berthollet also employed phosphorus in his eudiometer, but instead of heating it, as in the above-described method, he allowed combination to take place between it and the oxygen by slow combustion. Dr. Hope, Dr.

Henry, and Mr. Pepys, employed a eudiometer, in which the test liquid was either a solution of iron impregnated with nitric oxide, or a solution of sulphuret of potassium. Volta's method of determining the quantity of oxygen contained in gaseous mixtures is by means of combustion with a known volume of hydrogen gas; for it having been ascertained that when a mixture of oxygen and hydrogen gas is fired, one-third of the diminution is owing to the condensation of oxygen, we have only to observe the measure of the contraction of volume to ascertain that of the oxygen which was present. Various modes of effecting this have been devised by Volta, Mitscherlich, Dr. Ure, and others.

Dobereiner has suggested a eudiometrical process, founded on his curious discovery of the property which spongy platinum possesses of causing the combination of oxygen and hydrogen gases. In this eudiometer the combination occurs without explosion, and yields results of great accuracy. Dobereiner found that when the spongy platinum was mixed with certain substances, so as to prevent its immediato and explosive action, it caused the oxygen and hydrogen to combine with moderate rapidity. Dr. Henry and Dr. Turner employed modifications of this process.

EUPHO'RBIUM, improperly called a gum, or gum-resin, since it is entirely destitute of any gum in its composition, is the concrete juice of several species of *Euphorbia*, either exuding naturally or from incisions made in the bark. Much of the article found in British commerce is obtained from the *Euphorbia Canariensis*, while that which occurs on the continent is obtained from *Euphorbia officinarum*, and other African species, particularly from an undescribed species, called by the Arabs *Dergmuse*. The branches of this plant are used in tanning, and to it, according to Mr. Jackson, the morocco leather owes its peculiarities. By the most recent chemical analysis, euphorbium seems to consist of resin, wax, and saline matter (mostly malates). The resin is the active principle, and differs in some respects from most other resins.

Euphorbium is a powerful acrid substance, causing irritation and inflammation of the parts with which it comes in contact. It is less used in medicine now than formerly.

EU'PION is the name given to a liquid obtained from animal tar, especially that of bones or horns. It is very limpid, colourless, inodorous, and tasteless; it boils at about 340° Fahr.

EURE. This department is one of the cider districts of France; about 30,000,000 gallons are produced annually. The department is rich in iron ore; building stone, millstones, and paving granite are quarried; fullers' earth and potters' clay are found. The manufactures consist of fine and coarse woollen cloths, linen, thread, calico, paper, printed cottons, ,cotton yarn, cutlery, tape, cotton hosiery, blankets, carpets, wind instruments, horn and boxwood combs, glue, nails, pins, hardware, &c. There are numerous furnaces and foundries for the manufacture of iron, glass-works, numerous flour and paper-mills, dye-houses, fulling-mills, marble-sawing works, sugar-refineries, bleaching-grounds, important copper foundries, zinc-works, and a great number of tan-yards. The factories of various kinds are about eight hundred in number. The exports are composed of the various agricultural and industrial products named; the imports chiefly of the raw material required in the numerous manufactures, and of colonial produce.

Louviers, in this department, is one of the chief seats of the cloth manufacture in France; it has upwards of 40 factories, in which from 7000 to 8000 hands are employed. It has been long famous for the finest description of cloths (for uniforms &c.), which range from 30 to 65 francs an ell. Of late years coarser cloths, cassimeres, fancy goods for trousers, mantles, &c., are also made. There are also several woollen-yarn factories, large tan-yards, bleaching establishments, card factories, steam-engino and mill-work factories, dye-houses, brick-works, &c., and a brisk trade in corn, wood, charcoal, flax, wool, teazels, &c.

This department must not be confounded with that of *Eure-et-Loir*, which bounds it on the south. Eure-et-Loir is one of the cider districts of France. Besides wheat, rye, barley, oats, leguminous plants, teazels, weld, flax, hemp, &c., are grown. Hops grow spontaneously in some districts of this department. The number of wind and water mills for the manufacture of flour is about seven hundred. Along the course of the Avre or Aure there are important paper-mills belonging to the Messrs. Firmin Didot. There are also numerous other paper-mills, tanning and fulling-mills, cotton-spinning factories, iron forges and furnaces (which are supplied with ore partly from the mines of the department, and partly from those of Eure), and from 500 to 600 factories and workshops of different kinds. Besides the articles indicated, flannels, serges, druggets, blankets, linen, sieves, and woollen hosiery, are manufactured and exported. A great number of caps are knitted of the fine wool of Beauce or of Spain, and sent to Orleans, where they aro dyed of different colours, and form an important article of export. The imports are wine, brandy, timber, wool, cloth, colonial produce, &c. Stone, marble, granite, and gypsum are quarried. Marl is very abundant, and is used for manure. Brick-clay and potters' clay are found.

EUROPE. All the countries of Europe are briefly noticed in other parts of this volume, in respect to their products, manufacturing industry, and commerce. We will here give, therefore, simply a few statistical details, covenient for reference.

Europe has an area of about 3,900,000 square miles. This area is drained by rivers which flow into five seas, or directly into the Atlantic, in the following proportion:—Into the Caspian 850,000 square miles; into the Baltic 900,000; into the Mediterranean 250,000; into the Atlantic direct 600,000; and into the Northern Ocean and White Sea 400,000. The areas of the seas themselves are—

Mediterranean	760,000
Black Sea	190,000
Baltic	180,000
Caspian	160,000
White Sea	40,000

The longest straight line that can be drawn through Europe is about 3000 miles, from Cape St. Vincent to the river Kara on the Frozen Ocean. The coast-line of Europe extends about 20,000 miles. The sovereign states of Europe are about 60 in number, and the population about 250 millions. Nearly one-half of the population profess the Roman Catholic religion, nearly a quarter Protestantism, and nearly a quarter the Greek church; the remainder comprise miscellaneous sects.

In mineral produce, Europe contains a supply of most of the chief kinds. In animal products, applicable to the arts, Europe contains a largo number, but is deficient in many others. The botany exhibits the following features:—The southern districts exhibit a strong resemblance to the vegetation of Africa and its adjacent islands. The vine, the date, the pisang, the prickly pear, the castor-oil plant, the American aloe, rice, the sugar-cane, the cotton-plant, maize, Guinea corn, the fig, the olive, the orange—all are met with in different parts of the south of Europe. At about the parallel of the south of France, a marked change occurs in vegetation: most of the southern equinoctial forms of vegetation either disappear or become uncommon. Still more to the north, where the vine begins to languish, its place is better occupied by broad plains of wheat and other corn; the hardy trees of England, elms, limes, oaks, ashes, alders, beeches, birches, willows, and poplars, are found everywhere, with rich pastures, and verdant fields, unknown in the land of oranges and myrtles. At last, in the more northern districts of the continent, aspens, bird-cherries, birches, lime-trees, alders, junipers, spruce-firs, and pines, are the principal trees that remain; barley and oats are the only corn-plants, but potatoes continue to be reared in the short cold summer.

EVAPORATION is the transformation of a liquid into a gaseous state by the action of heat. If any liquid be placed in an open vessel, it gradually diminishes in quantity by evaporation, and at length disappears. The quantity of vapour produced in a given time is proportional to the area of the exposed surface; but, with equal temperatures, the escapo of vapour from different liquids varies in rapidity. Over the surface of an ocean the aqueous vapour held in the atmosphere amounts to an enormous quantity. The quantity of vapour which rises from a liquid depends mainly upon the temperature; but it is influenced by the state of the atmosphere with respect to dryness or moisture, a dry and warm atmosphere being favourable to it. At equal temperatures, in a close vessel, the evaporation is the same in quantity whether the vessel containing the liquid contain also air, or have the air exhausted from it, but more rapid in the latter case.

It was found by Dalton, that at 212° Fahr., the evaporation of water from one square inch of surface is equal to 4.244 grains per minute; and at 138° Fahr., one grain per minute. Dalton and Gay Lussac have found that the evaporation from ice is equal to that from water at the same temperature. Dalton also determined that the quantity of vapour raised from a given surface of any liquid, at a given temperature, is directly proportional to the elastic force of the vapour at that temperature. Solid substances and liquids of great specific gravity have vapours of small elastic force. When, by evaporation, a liquid is transformed into a vapour, heat is abstracted from the liquid, and a thermometer in it indicates a depression of temperature.

EXCENTRIC, or ECCENTRIC, in machinery, is a kind of wheel in which the axis or centre of motion does not coincide with the geometrical centre, or in which the periphery is not circular. Eccentrics form an important class of mechanical expedients for converting one kind of motion into another. They also furnish means for producing, from the uniform speed of one revolving shaft, rotatory motion of continually varying speed in shafts placed in connection with it.

EXCISE DUTIES. This name is given to taxes or duties levied upon articles of consumption which are produced within the kingdom; and also upon licences to permit persons to carry on certain trades, the post-horse duties, and others of a similar kind.

Excise duties are said to have had their origin in this country in the reign of Charles I., when a tax was laid upon beer, cider, perry, of home production, by the Long Parliament in 1643. This act contains also a list of foreign articles upon which excise duties were imposed in addition to duties of customs already chargeable. This act was adopted and enforced under the protectorate of Oliver Cromwell; and under Charles II. the duties of excise were granted to the crown as part of its revenue.

In every highly taxed country, where consumption duties form part of the public revenue, it would seem to be hardly possible to avoid the adoption of this class of duties. In England a drawback is allowed on the exportation of domestic articles which are subject to excise duty.

Excise duties are liable to this among other very serious objections, that the regulations under which they are collected interfere with processes of manufacture, so as to prevent the adoption of improvements. Upon the same premises, with the same capital and the same amount of labour, double the quantity of cloths has been printed which could have been printed previous to the repeal of the duty and the consequent abolition of the excise regulations. The abolition of the excise duty on glass in 1845 was made principally with the object of facilitating improvements in the manufacture; and this result has been most remarkably apparent. The Crystal Palace, as it is termed, could not have been built six years ago, before the glass duties were removed; neither the market price of glass nor the manufacturing arrangements would have permitted its construction. The excise regulations respecting the manufacture of soap have prevented our soap manufacturers from entering into competition with the manufacturers of other countries. The effect of the paper duty has been already adverted to. [BOOK TRADE.] Another great objection to excise duties is, the facilities which they offer for the commission of frauds against the revenue.

In 1797 the number of articles subject to excise duties was 28; 15 in 1833; 10 in 1835; and in 1845 there were only 9, including sugar. The post-horse duty is under the management of the Board of Excise, and in Ireland the duty on game certificates. The brick duty was repealed in 1850. The eight following articles are still subject to these duties, and with sugar made here constitute all the articles on which the excise duty is now collected: — Hops, Licences, Malt, Pepper, Soap, British Spirits, Vinegar. All such imposts as the window tax come under the designation of assessed taxes, and not excise duties.

In 1822 the excise duties yielded for the United Kingdom more than twice as much as the customs duties. In 1821 the excise duties reached to 27,400,300*l.*, which is the highest sum they ever attained. In 1845 they were again reduced to the amount at which they stood in 1797, a little above 11,000,000*l.*

In 1835 the number of traders in the United Kingdom who were surveyed periodically by excise officers was 588,000. The cost of these surveys in England alone amounted to 533,902*l.*; but since 1835 several of these surveys have been abolished.

The net produce of the excise duties, in the year ending October 10, 1850, was 12,913,102*l.* Under the names of the exciseable articles are given in this work a few statistical details concerning the duties.

Prior to 1823 there were separate and independent Boards of Excise for England, Scotland, and Ireland, and the total number of the excise commissioners was twenty-one. The business is now better conducted by seven commissioners, and by one board in London. The commissioners hold courts and decide summarily in case of the infraction of the excise laws. The number of persons employed at the chief excise office in London is about five hundred, while those employed in different parts of the country are about four thousand

For the management of the business of the excise department the whole of the United Kingdom is divided into collections, and these are subdivided into districts, rides, and divisions. There are fifty five collections in England and Wales, exclusive of the London collection, and at the head of each is a collector, who visits the principal towns in his circuit eight times a year to receive the duties and transact other business connected with the department; besides which he is required to have an eye generally upon the discipline and efficiency of the service. The number of officers in a collection varies from forty to ninety. The next subdivision of a collection is the district, at the head of which is a supervisor. Next come the subdivisions of the districts into rides and divisions, or foot-walks. Where the traders are scattered, the officer is obliged to keep a horse, and his circuit is called a ride; but, if a large number of traders reside

KNIGHT'S CYCLOPÆDIA OF THE INDUSTRY OF ALL NATIONS.

No. 21.

London: Charles Knight, 90, Fleet Street. Price Twopence

in a smaller circuit, they are visited by the officer on foot, and then each portion is termed a division or footwalk. Before going out each day, the officer leaves a memorandum at his home which states the places he intends to survey, and the order in which he will visit them; and the exact time at which he commences each must be entered in his journal. The supervisor resurveys some of the officer's surveys; but which they will be the officer is of course ignorant; and if errors are discovered they must be entered in the supervisor's diary. These diaries are transmitted to the chief office every two months, and no officer is promoted unless the diaries show him to be efficient. The periodical removal of officers from one part of the country to another was Mr. Pitt's suggestion, and is still acted upon: about 1100 officers change their residence yearly. At the chief office in London there is a department of Surveying-General Examiners, who are despatched to any district without previous intimation, as a check upon the accuracy and integrity of the supervisors. Promotions take place in the excise department after a certain fixed period in each grade, and only then when the officer petitions for advancement. This involves a rigid examination into his qualifications, which is termed 'taking out a character.'

EXETER is a sort of western metropolis. Its manufactures are very miscellaneous, and such as befit the centre of a large agricultural district. Its contributions to an exhibition of manufactures must necessarily be of the same miscellaneous character as its products generally. Its importance depends mainly on its being a cathedral city, and the focus for a large and fruitful district of country.

EXPLOSION is the sudden displacement of gaseous particles, accompanied by a loud report. The bursting of a bladder under the air-pump, the bursting of a steam-boiler, and the firing of gunpowder are examples. The explosions which, in the atmosphere, accompany a flash of lightning, are ascribed to the rush of air into the vacua produced when the aqueous vapours in large portions of space become rapidly condensed. DETONATION is a species of explosion.

The bursting of steam-boilers is sometimes occasioned by the formation of an incrustation on the interior, which prevents the heat from radiating freely through the metal.

EXPORTS. [IMPORTS AND EXPORTS.]

EXTRACTS are medicinal preparations of vegetable principles, obtained in various ways. Sometimes they are merely the juices expressed from the fresh plants, brought by careful evaporation to the consistence of honey, and then more properly denominated *inspissated juices*; at other times they consist of certain principles of the fresh or dried plant extracted by some menstruum in which they are soluble, such as water, proof spirit, or vinegar, and afterwards evaporated, as in the former case. According to the nature of the menstruum employed the extract is called *aqueous*, *alcoholic*, or *acetous*.

The preparation of extracts requires the greatest care. The plants must be in every respect of the best quality, as regards the place of their growth, season when collected, &c., and the evaporation must be conducted rapidly, yet at a low temperature. Extracts are simple or compound, according as they are prepared from one plant or from several different kinds.

A well-prepared extract should possess in a great degree the odour, and especially the taste, of the plant from which it is obtained; it should not have either an empyreumatic smell or taste, and it should have a proper and uniform consistence. It is necessary to preserve extracts in a dry situation. To assist in keeping aqueous extracts, it is customary to sprinkle a little alcohol over the surface before covering them up; but such extracts, if made with cold water and with due care, rarely require this precaution. It is proper to examine the condition of all extracts very frequently, both during very warm and very wet weather: any portion which seems spoiled should be immediately thrown out.

F

FAÇADE, is a French term of modern introduction into the English language. It expresses the face or front view of an edifice, and is often used in speaking of architectural buildings, as the façade of the Louvre, or the façade of St. Peter's at Rome.

FACTOR is a mercantile agent, who buys and sells the goods of others, and transacts their business on commission. He is intrusted with the management and disposal of the goods, and he buys and sells in his own name, in which particulars consists the main difference between factors and brokers. The chief part of the foreign trade of a country is carried on through the medium of factors, who generally reside at a distance from the merchants or manufacturers who employ them. The common duty of a factor is to receive consignments of goods, to sell them, and to make remittances either in money, bills, or purchased goods, in return; and he is paid by a commission upon the money which passes through his hands. It is usual for a factor to make advances upon the goods consigned to him, for which, and for his commission, he has a general lien upon all the property of his employer which may at any time be in his hands.

It is the duty of a factor to keep the goods with which he is intrusted free from injury, to keep a clear account of his dealings, and at proper times to transmit it to his employer, with information of all the transactions and liabilities which he has entered into and incurred in the course of his employment, by which his principal can be affected; also to send him advice of all bills accepted or drawn upon his credit, and generally to act with fidelity to him.

There is another description of factor, who acts under what is called a *del credere* commission, where, for an additional per centage he engages for the solvency of the purchasers of the goods consigned to him. In this case, the factor stands in the relation of a surety for the persons with whom he deals on account of the employer, and he is liable to his employer only in case of their default.

FACTORIES; FACTORY-SYSTEM. The word factory has had two different meanings. It formerly meant an establishment of merchants and factors resident in foreign countries, who were governed by certain regulations adopted for their mutual support and assistance against the undue encroachments or interference of the government of the countries in which they resided. In modern times these factories have, in a great measure, ceased to exist, because of the greater degree of security which merchants feel as regards both the justice of those governments and the protection, when needed, of their own country. The Venetians, Genoese, Portuguese, Dutch, French, and English have all had establishments of the nature of factories. In China the Portuguese established a factory at Macao, and the English at Canton. In most instances factories have at first obtained the privilege of trading, and afterwards procured for the precinct assigned to them some exemption from the jurisdiction of the native courts. In this state of things the supreme government of the country whose subjects have established the factory prepare laws for its control and administration, and treat it in fact as if it were its dependency, though the sovereignty of the native government is undisputed.

But in its usual acceptation, the word factory has now a different meaning. By the Factory Act of 1844, a factory means any building wherein steam, water, or other mechanical power is used to work any machinery employed in the manufacture of cotton, wool, hair, silk, flax, hemp, jute, or tow.

What is called the Factory System owes its origin to the invention and skill of Arkwright; and it is probable that but for the invention of spinning machinery, and the consequent necessary aggregation of large numbers of workmen in cotton-mills, the name would never have been thus applied. It is in the cotton-mills that the factory system has been brought to its highest state of perfection. The power of subdivision of employment according to strength and skill, and that of bringing to bear upon every distinct process exactly as much force as is necessary, without waste, are the two great and valuable advantages of the factory system.

The legislature has interfered to prevent children in factories being tasked beyond their strength, to the permanent injury of their constitutions. This abuse was the more to be apprehended, because a large proportion of the children engaged in cotton-spinning are not directly employed by the masters, but are under the control of the spinners, a highly paid class of workmen, whose earnings greatly depend upon the length of time during which they can keep their young assistants at work. A parliamentary committee sat for the investigation of this subject in 1832, and subsequently a commission was issued by the crown for ascertaining, by examinations at the factories themselves, the kind and degree of abuses that prevailed, and for suggesting the proper remedies. In consequence of these inquiries, an act was passed in 1833 for regulating factories. This act was amended by that of 1844.

On January 1, 1846, a new act came into operation, which brought print-works, or calico-printing establishments, within the operation of the factory regulations. By the terms of another act, passed in 1847, 'no children' or 'young persons' are to work in a factory more than 11 hours a day, from July 1, 1847; nor more than 10 hours a day from May 1, 1848. The same provisions were made in respect to all women of whatever age; so that at the present time the work-hours of women, boys, and girls, are limited: those of men unlimited by any enactment. By an act passed in 1850, a few minor changes were made, chiefly with a view to prevent night-work in factories. The 'Ten Hours' Bill,' advocated by many persons, would, if passed, limit the working hours of males in factories.

The United Kingdom is divided into four factory districts, presided over by four inspectors and several sub-inspectors. Each inspector presents a report half yearly to the Home Secretary, respecting the state of the factories within his district. These reports occasionally give such information as will show the number of factories and work-people. In 1845, Mr. Horner, whose district is very nearly coextensive with the county of Lancashire, gave the following as the stato of his district in that year :—

	Mills.	Workers under 18.	Workers 18 & above.	Power Looms.
Cotton Mills	1,724	69,155	128,305	138,717
Woollen do.	241	5,456	6,485	3,237
Flax do.	71	2,255	3,336	„
Silk do.	32	3,121	3,324	995
	2,068	79,987	141,450	142,949

The great strength of the woollen and worsted trades lay in another district, concerning which similar returns were not made.

In September 1848 tho mills and works within the limits of the town of Manchester, subject to the factory laws, were as follow:

	Mills.	Hands.
Cotton . .	96	26,809
Silk . . .	8	2,850
Worsted . .	3	169
Small Wares	17	1,752
Print Works	4	1,172
Dye Works .	23	1,847

In 1850 a return was made to the House of Commons respecting factories, more detailed and instructive than any beforo prepared. We will give a few of the results, calculated to illustrate different aspects of the subject.

First, in respect to different parts of the United Kingdom we have :—

	Factories.	Spindles.	Power Looms.	Horse Power.	Children Employed.	Total Employed.
England and Wales	3,689	22,850,010	272,588	109,824	34,155	495,707
Scotland	550	2,256,403	23,811	19,861	929	75,688
Ireland	91	532,303	2,517	4,532	38	24,687
	4,330	25,638,716	298,916	134,217	35,122	596,082

In this table, the *horse-power* includes both steam engines and water-wheels employed in working the machinery in the factories; they are nearly in the ratio of four-fifths steam power to one-fifth water power. The term *children* is applied to those at and under 13 years of age; from 13 to 18 the term applied is *young persons.*

Taking the whole of the United Kingdom in one entry, and regarding only the ages and sexes of the persons employed, we find the following numbers :—

	Males.	Females.
Under 13 .	19,400	15,722 = 35,122
13 to 18 .	67,864	329,577 = 555,307
Abovo 18 .	157,866	
	245,130	345,299 = 590,429

In respect to females, one entry includes *young persons* and *adults*, as the same laws now apply to both classes. Of 100 persons working in factories 58 are females and 42 males. About 6 per cent of the workers are under 13 years old.

The next classification we shall notice is that which depends on the kind of operations carried on. There are four classes, as follows :—

Spinning factories	2,636
Weaving factories	454
Spinning and weaving factories ..	1,005
Not specified	505
	4,600

Next in regard to the five principal kinds of

materials employed, we find the factories to be distributed as follows:—

Cotton factories	..	1,932	330,024
Woollen ,,	..	1,497	74,443
Worsted ,,	..	501	79,737
Flax ,,	..	393	68,434
Silk ,,	..	277	42,544
		4,600	596,082

The number of factories here given (4,600) is in excess of that given in the first table (4330); this probably arises from some of the factories being entered twice, in cases where they work *mixed fabrics* of cotton and woollen, or cotton and silk, or woollen and silk. The cotton factories are rather less than half the whole number, but employ more than half the entire number of operatives. The average number of operatives in cotton factories is 120; the average in all factories is 75. Out of the 1932 cotton factories, no less than 1235 are in Lancashire; out of the 1998 woollen and worsted factories, no less than 1298 are in Yorkshire. It will be seen that a remarkable parallelism exists in these numbers; 64 per cent of all the cotton factories are in Lancashire, and 65 per cent of all the woollen and worsted factories are in Yorkshire.

FAHRENHEIT, GABRIEL DANIEL, is noticeable here on account of one particular invention. He was born at Danzig, near the end of the 17th century, but the precise year of his birth is unknown. His taste inclined strongly to scientific pursuits, and having travelled through different parts of Germany in order to acquire information respecting the subjects of his studies, he came to Holland, and established himself at Amsterdam as a maker of philosophical instruments. He is chiefly distinguished for the invention of that particular scale which he applied to thermometers [THERMOMETER], and which has ever since been generally in use in this country. He was elected a Fellow of the Royal Society of London in 1724, and wrote some papers in the 'Philosophical Transactions' for that year. He died in 1740.

FAIR. Anciently, before any flourishing towns were established, and the necessaries or ornaments of life, from the convenience of communication and the increase of provincial towns, could be procured in various places, goods and commodities of every kind were chiefly sold at fairs; to which, as to one universal mart, the people resorted periodically, and supplied most of their wants for the ensuing year. Wharton, in his 'History of English Poetry,' has given us a curious account of that of St. Giles's hill or down, near Winchester. It was instituted by William the Conqueror, at first for three days, which were afterwards extended to sixteen. Its jurisdiction extended seven miles round, and comprehended even Southampton, then a capital trading town; and all merchants who sold wares within that circuit, unless at the fair, forfeited them to the bishop. As late as 1512, as we learn from the Northumberland Household-book, fairs still continued to be the principal marts for purchasing necessaries in large quantities, which are now supplied by the numerous trading towns.

The fairs of Frankfort-on-the-Main and Leipzig are still pre-eminent in Europe. A very large part of the book-trade of Germany is centered in the Easter fair at Leipzig.

The fair at Nischnei Novgorod, in Russia, between the river Oka and the river Volga, is the largest at the present day: 200,000 visitors are said to attend it, and commodities to the amount of 4,000,000*l.* sterling to be disposed of. There is also a singular fair held at Berbera, on the coast of Adel, in Eastern Africa. Throughout nearly the whole of the year the place is abandoned to the hyena and the jackall, and the huts are left open; but as the period of the fair approaches, caravans of camels, horses, mules, asses, and troops of warriors continue to arrive, and in a short time the desert is animated by the presence of many thousands of persons, who, having transacted their business, disperse, and the place resumes its desolate solitude. The great commercial fair at Beaucaire in France has been already described. [BEAUCAIRE.]

FALKLAND ISLANDS. These remote islands will in time acquire commercial importance. They are situated in the South Atlantic, and consist of two islands of considerable size, and many smaller ones. East Falkland is about 90 miles long, and on an average 40 miles wide; West Falkland is about 80 miles long, with a mean width of about 25 miles. The smaller islands, about two hundred in number, vary considerably, from 16 miles in length and 8 in width, to mere islets of half a mile in diameter. The area of the whole is about 6000 square miles.

The Falklands are moderately fertile, and contain several good harbours. Small colonies were formed there by the French and the English in the last century, but afterwards abandoned. When, however, it was found that the islands formed a convenient halting-place for southern whalers, the Republic of Buenos Ayres took possession of them in 1820. England protested against this step in 1829. Meanwhile the government of Buenos Ayres had formed a settlement at Port Louis in

1823, but Great Britain asserted its rights, and the colony was given up to the English in 1833. The islands have since assumed the condition of a regular British colony, and in 1844 a new town was laid out on the southern shore of Stanley Harbour, a land-locked inlet sheltered from every wind.

In a recent letter from Falkland it is said: 'The number of wild cattle now upon East Falkland is estimated at over 150,000 head, in addition to which there are herds of several thousand tame stock, and about 3000 wild horses, with several troops of tamed horses, some imported from South America, and some of the native breed, trained to assist in capturing and managing the cattle. This latter work is chiefly performed by a class of men called Guachos, natives of the Pampas of La Plata, whose occupation, from childhood upwards, is the pursuit and subjection of the wild herds which, in countless numbers, cover those vast plains; but latterly several English and Irish men have been initiated in the arts of the Guachos, and have proved themselves quite as skilful as the South American hunters, whilst they conduct their perilous occupation with more humanity and consequently with greater profit to their employers. It is found that all esculent vegetables, particularly carrots, parsneps, and turnips, thrive and grow to great perfection in these islands, the climate of which is remarkably salubrious. As a naval station, there can be no question that the Falklands are, at the present juncture, more than at any former period, a most important possession of the crown.'

FALLOW is a portion of land in which no seed is sown for a whole year, in order that the soil may be left exposed to the influence of the atmosphere, the weeds destroyed by repeated ploughings and harrowings, and the fertility improved at a less expense of manure than it would be if a crop had been raised upon it.

The practice of fallowing land is as old as the Roman Empire. It appears that, whereever the Romans extended their conquests and planted colonies, they introduced this mode of restoring land to a certain degree of fertility when exhausted by bearing grain. The attention of agriculturists has in later times been turned to lessen the necessity of fallows, and to substitute some other means of restoring fertility. It is acknowledged by all experienced farmers that manure alone is not sufficient for this purpose. The ground must be tilled and noxious weeds destroyed; and the only efficacious mode of doing so is to stir the ground at the time when their seeds have vegetated, their roots have made shoots, and before any new seed can ripen. Light sandy soils require only cleansing from weeds; and if this can be done without leaving them fallow for a whole summer, a great advantage will be obtained. This has been effected completely by the cultivation of turnips and clover, which was first practised in the light soils of Flanders, and afterwards introduced into the similar soils of Norfolk, from whence it has spread all over Great Britain, and is beginning to be adopted more generally in Ireland. On light lands the preparation for the turnips, the abundant manuring and subsequent hoeing, are as effectual in cleansing the land and bringing it into a fertile state as any complete fallow could ever be; and the clover smothers and destroys the weeds which may have come up amongst the barley or oats sown after the turnips. On heavy soils it is often impossible to keep the land clear of weeds, in wet climates and unfavourable seasons, without a complete fallow, and when this is the case it is best to do the thing effectually. Upon cold wet soils, which should always first of all be well underdrained, no pains should be spared to get the land perfectly clean.

The advice given by the late Mr. Rham was —Avoid fallows if you can keep your land clean; but, when you fallow, do it effectually, and improve the soil at the same time by chalk, lime, or marl, according to circumstances. Do not spare either ploughs or harrows in dry weather. In short, neither ploughing nor manuring alone will keep a soil in a good fertile state. There must be an occasional fallow for some soils, and turnips or similar husbandry for others.

FALMOUTH. The harbour of this Cornish seaport is an extensive bay, well protected by the surrounding highlands, and so conveniently situated, that vessels have frequently been able to proceed on their voyage from this port, while those from Plymouth and Portsmouth have been forced back by contrary winds before they could reach the mouth of the Channel. The exports consist principally of the produce of the tin and copper mines. The number of sailing vessels registered at the port is about 120.

Unfortunately for Falmouth, the non-existence of a railway through Cornwall has nearly deprived this town of its former importance as a packet station. Southampton has risen in its stead, on account of its admirable position in respect to communication with the metropolis. Nothing but a complete line of railway will restore Falmouth as a packet station; and even that could only occur after the expiration of existing contracts between the Government and the various steam-packet companies.

FALUN, a town in Sweden, the capital of the province of Dalecarlia, is celebrated for the great mine of copper, which is in the middle of the town, and which also yields small quantities of gold, silver, and lead, besides vitriol, ochre, and brimstone. There are a few manufactures of tobacco, linen, cotton, and wool.

FAN. This name is given to an instrument or machine for agitating the air by the wafting or revolving motion of a broad surface for the purpose of producing artificial currents. Large revolving fans, driven by machinery, are frequently used either to facilitate the cooling of fluids or the process of winnowing, or as blowing machines to urge the combustion of a fire, or to assist in ventilation. Another application of such an apparatus is for the purpose of regulating or checking, by the resistance of air to its rapid motion, the velocity of light machinery. A familiar example of such an use is afforded by the revolving fans of a musical snuff-box.

FAN MANUFACTURE. The manufacture of ladies' fans is a larger department of industry than many persons would suppose. After a considerable interval, during which fans were little used, they have lately come again into favour; and the manufacture is conducted in France on a considerable scale. The firm of M. Duvelleroy at Paris are preparing some magnificent specimens for the Great Exhibition. From an account of that establishment recently given in the 'Expositor,' we learn that M. Duvelleroy has prepared a whole set of fans displaying the stories of the 'Arabian Nights,' intended by the Grand Sultan as presents for the ladies of his harem; they are to be submitted to the lady of the Turkish Ambassador at Paris, before being transmitted to Constantinople. M. Duvelleroy manufactures fans for the courts not only of European countries, but for those even of Africa and Asia. It is said that we shall have submitted to our inspection at the Exhibition a fan now being made for the Emperor of Morocco, at a cost of more than 1000*l.* Another is now in progress for the Empress of Russia.

From the source above referred to we gather some curious details concerning the fan manufacture. Fans were known in the East from remote ages; but they are not supposed to have been introduced into western Europe until the time of the crusaders. About the 16th century fans came into very general use; generally made by fixing peacock or ostrich feathers in a handle of gold, silver, or ivory. As early as 1522 the fan manufacturers formed one of the industrial guilds of Paris. In the time of Louis XIV. the Jesuits who returned from China brought over specimens of the Chinese folding-fan, which at once superseded the former shape. When the Edict of Nantes drove so many artisans out of France, fan makers were among the number; they came to England, where the trade became established on a firm footing. Just a century afterwards, the French Revolution crushed the remains of the manufacture in France, and England became the chief emporium of fans. At the termination of the war the manufacture revived in France; and so congenial is it to the taste of that nation, that France now almost entirely monopolises the manufacture, very few fans being made in England.

It is said that Duvelleroy employs 2000 persons—a statement scarcely credible; he has made it a point to grasp the two extremes of the scale in costliness as well as all intermediate degrees, for he makes fans from one halfpenny each to one thousand guineas. Every halfpenny fan goes through no less than fifteen hands: a proof that the factory system must be thoroughly carried out in that establishment. Duvelleroy's fans are sent to all parts of the world, and are now competing in the East with those of China. Spain is trying to maintain a home manufacture, but all the best specimens come from Paris. America affords the best markets, for while the ladies of North America closely imitate the fashions of Paris, those of South and tropical America are passionately fond of gorgeous fans, on which the most exciting scenes are painted in the most dazzling colours. Duvelleroy has a large corps of intelligent artists, who study the peculiar tastes of every nation in respect to pictures and colours.

In the manufacture of fans, the chief parts are called the *handle*, the *brins*, the *panaches*, the *end*, and the *leaf*. The *handle* is the part at which all the rest of the fan is hinged together, and which is made of ivory, wood, or any hard material. The *brins*, or radiants, from twelve to twenty-four in number, radiate from the handle; they are about four inches long. The *ends* are elastic pieces which connect the brins with the handle, and which form with them the skeleton of the fan; they are made of mother-o'-pearl, tortoise-shell, ivory, horn, ebony, bone, citron-wood, sandal-wood, or plain wood, and are rivetted with diamonds, gold, pearls, or more cheap material, according to the price. The *panaches* are the two outermost brins, made wider and stronger than the rest for security. The *leaf* is the surface of the fan, cut into the form of the segment of a circle. It is made of paper, of cabretille (very delicate kid-skin), vellum, parchment, satin, tulle, gauze, or crêpe, according to circumstances. There are as many folds or plaits given to this leaf as there are brins; and the brins govern the opening and closing of the leaf.

It is in the painting and decorating of the leaf that the costliness of the best fans chiefly consists. Duvelleroy has a number of highly paid and accomplished artists engaged in this department.

The Chinese workmen are not permitted by the Emperor, it is said, to send goods to England for the approaching Exhibition; but M. Duvelleroy is about to send some choice specimens of Chinese fans, as well as others of his own manufacture.

FARM. In the present state of agriculture, a man who takes a farm of 200 acres of arable land, or land partly arable and partly good pasture, will require from 1600*l.* to 2000*l.*; and it is not the interest either of the landlord or the tenant that he should take the farm unless he can command that sum. The amount of capital required depends in a great degree also on the quality of the land; very rich land requires less capital in proportion to the rent than poor land. Besides the quality of the soil, many other circumstances determine the value of a farm. The roads, especially those which lead to the neighbouring towns, whence manure may be obtained, are a most important object; and, if there is water-carriage, it greatly enhances the value of the farm. The roads to the fields, and the distance from these to the farm-yard; the convenience of having good pasture, or land easily laid down in grass, near the homestead; and especially the situation of the farm buildings with respect to the land, and the abundance of good water—are all circumstances which must be well considered, and which will greatly influence the probable profits, and consequently the rent which may be fairly offered.

Large straggling farm-buildings are inconvenient, and cost much in repairs. The yard or yards in a large farm should be sheltered on the north side by the barns, which need not be so extensive as used formerly to be thought necessary. Every farm which is so extensive as to require more than one floor to thrash the corn on ought always to have a thrashing-mill attached to it. A small yard, distinct from the other, with sheds for the cattle to shelter themselves under in wet and stormy weather, is a great advantage. The cart-sheds should be in the stack-yard, which properly occupies a space north of the barn. There should be a sufficient number of stands with proper pillars and frames to build stacks on. On each side of tho yard should be placed the stables, cow-houses, and feeding-stalls, with a pump of good water near the last, and convenient places to put hay, straw, and turnips in, with a machine to cut them. An under-ground cistern near the cow-house and stables, into which the urine and washings of the cow-house may run by means of a sink or drain, is a most useful appendage. Light thatched roofs are sufficient for the sheds and smaller buildings, and even for the cow-houses and stables.

In the old system of agriculture a third of the gross average produce was considered as a fair rent for a farm, including all the direct payments for the occupation of the land, such as tithes, rates, and taxes; another third was supposed to cover the labour and expenses of the farm and interest of capital; and tho remaining third was appropriated to the maintenance of the farmer and his family, out of which he had to save whatever he laid by as a clear profit. But this calculation is no longer applicable to the present state of agriculture. The expenses are greatly increased, and the produce is also greater. Rents in Scotland are higher than in England, not only for small occupations, but for extensive farms; and yet the tenants have complained less of the times than their neighbours in the south. One cause for this difference is, that the Scotch farm-labourer is more advantageously kept as a sort of in-door servant than in England; another is that the horses are better managed on a Scotch farm; and a third is that Scotch farmers are generally more alive to scientific improvements than those of England.

In the accounts of a farm there are many separate items to be taken into consideration. There may be a separate account kept for every field. There should always bo one for every crop of which the rotation consists. There is an account of the labour of men and horses; of the produce of the dairy; of the stock purchased to be fatted, or sold again in an improved state. In short, the divisions of the general account may be increased without limit. M. de Dombasle, at his celebrated farm of Roville, in France, has all his principal servants and his apprentices assembled every evening after the day's work is over. Each man gives an account of the work done by him or under his superintendence, which is written down by the clerk. The orders for the next day are then given, and every one rereturns to his lodging or his home. In the course of the next day the clerk enters all that is in the journal into a book, where every person employed has an account: every field has ono; every servant and domestic animal has one; and every item which can be separated from the rest is entered, both as adding to the account or taking from it.

FAT is of two different kinds, which differ as to their melting point: these are termed *olein* (or *elain*) and *stearin*. The substances to which these names are given are not however in all cases absolutely identical: they vary as to smell, taste, solubility in alcohol, &c.; but all fats agree in being insoluble in water, and in not containing any nitrogen, which is a common constituent of most other animal matter.

Human Fat varies a little according to the part of the body producing it; that from the region of the kidneys, after it has been melted, is yellowish and inodorous; it begins to concrete at 76° Fahr., and is solid at 64°. The *Olein* of human fat is a colourless, oily, sweetish fluid, and remains so at 40°. *Ox Fat*, when melted, begins to solidify at 98°, and the temperature then rises to 102°; it contains about three-fourths of its weight of stearin, which is solid, hard, colourless, not greasy, and of a granular crystalline texture. The olein of ox fat is colourless and nearly inodorous. *Sheep's Fat* (or *Mutton Suet*), by exposure to the air acquires a peculiar odour; after fusion it congeals at a temperature varying between 98° and 102°; the stearin is white, translucent, and after fusion but imperfectly crystalline. *Hog's Fat*, or *Hog's Lard*, is a soft colourless solid, which fuses between 78° and 86°; the stearin is inodorous, solid, and granular. *Goat's Fat* contains a peculiar fat, termed by Chevreul *Hircin*, to the presence of which its peculiar odour is owing. *Goose Fat* is colourless, and of a peculiar taste and smell.

The fluid fats, whether of animal or vegetable origin, are usually termed *oils*. [OILS.]

The olein and stearin of animal fats are highly useful and important substances in the manufacture of soap and candles; for the latter purpose stearin has been of late very advantageously employed, and to a considerable extent, as a substitute for wax. [CANDLE; SOAP.]

FEATHERS. The principal uses to which feathers are applied are for personal decoration, as plumes for ladies' head-dresses, or for the hats of military officers; as a soft and highly elastic material for filling beds, cushions and pillows; or, in the case of the larger quill-feathers, as writing-pens, or small tubes for the manufacture of hair-pencils, or similar purposes.

Of the various kinds of feathers employed as plumes for head-dresses the most important are those of the ostrich. They are first washed in a lather of white soap and water, and subsequently in warm clear water. They are bleached by three successive operations: first with water only, then with a little indigo, and then a little sulphur. The feathers are then dried by hanging upon cords, during which they are shaken from time to time to separate their fibres. To increase their pliancy, the ribs are scraped with a bit of glass cut circularly; and, to impart the requisite curly form to the filaments or fibres, the edge of a blunt knife is drawn over them.

Feathers have long been used as a stuffing for beds and pillows; goose feathers especially. Goose feathers are divided into white and gray, the former being deemed the most valuable. The less valuable kind of feathers, known by the general name of *poultry feathers*, are obtained from turkeys, ducks, and fowls. Wild duck feathers are both soft and elastic, but their value is impaired by the great difficulty of removing the disagreeable odour of the animal oil which they contain. Various methods are practised of cleansing feathers from their oil, principally by the use of lime or lime-water; but Mr. Herring has introduced a method of purifying feathers by steam, which is said to be very efficacious. The softest and finest kind of feathers employed for bedding are those from the breast of the eider-duck. [EIDER-DOWN.]

Of the quills of feathers employed for pens, those from the goose are most used. One among many modes of preparing them is the following:—A workman sits before a small stove fire, into which he thrusts the barrel of the quill for about a second. Immediately upon withdrawing it from the fire, he draws it under the edge of a large blunt edged knife, called a hook, by which it is forcibly compressed against a block or plate of iron heated to about 350° Fahr. By this process the barrel, which is rendered soft and elastic by the heat, is pressed flat, and stripped of its outer membrane, without danger of splitting. It springs back to its natural form, and the dressing is completed by scrubbing with a piece of rough dog-fish skin. The principal workman employed in this operation can pass 2000 quills through his hands in a day of ten hours. By whatever process the external membrane is removed, that inside the quill remains, shrivelled up in the centre of the barrel, until it is cut open to convert it into a pen.

Foreign feathers were imported to the following values, in four recent years, viz.:—5,279*l*. in 1846, 4,237*l*. in 1847, 4,680*l*. in 1848, and 5,096*l*. in 1849.

FELSPAR is a mineral which occurs both crystalline and massive. The primary form of the crystal is an oblique rhombic prism. Both the colour and the degree of transparency vary greatly. Felspar, which is a component of all granites, consists mainly of silica and alumina.

FELT; FELTING. Under HAT MANUFACTURE will be found a description of that peculiar process whereby woollen and fur fibres are felted into a material fitted for hats.

Woollen fibres are sometimes combined by the felting instead of the weaving process for carpets and various kinds of cloth. Among other manufacturing firms for the purpose, there is the 'Patent Felted Woollen Cloth Company;' by whom is made felt carpets, embossed and printed felt table-covers, felt polishing cloth for plate and other purposes, felt for veterinary purposes, felt waistcoatings, felt coach-cloths and railway carriage-linings, upholsterers' felt, and felt for pianofortes.

A material called *Asphalted Roofing Felt* has come rather extensively into use. The two principal kinds are Croggon's and McNeill's. The qualities of this material are stated by the patentees to be imperviousness to rain and snow, non-conductibility of heat, elasticity, lightness, durability, economy, and easy application. It may not perhaps possess all these desirable qualities, but it certainly possesses many of them. It is used for roofing churches, houses, cottages, verandahs, farm-buildings, cattle sheds, and other buildings; for lining granaries and stores; for protecting ceilings from damp; for lining the insides or outsides of wooden buildings; for covering conservatories and garden-frames; for thatching corn and hay ricks; and for many other purposes.

The felt for the above purposes is sold in large sheets at the rate of about a penny per square foot. Another kind, called Inodorous Felt, is saturated with waterproof material free from the smell of the ordinary felt, and is used to prevent wall-paper from being injured by damp. There is also a patent Felted Sheathing, for covering ships' bottoms; it is a felted mixture of hair and vegetable fibre, and is not intended as a substitute for copper sheathing, but to be used as a layer beneath it. Another variety, the Non-conducting Felt, is used as a covering for boilers and steam-pipes, on account of its power of confining the heat within the vessel enclosed by it; it is used for fixed, locomotive, and marine steam-engines, and in breweries and distilleries: it is said also to be a good protective of water pipes from frost.

The Asphalted Felt is made in long pieces, 32 inches wide by about 30 yards long, and is sold in any smaller or larger quantities. The fibrous material of which it is formed is saturated with asphalte or bitumen. Many sheds and other buildings at Devonport and Woolwich Dock Yards, Isle of Portland, and elsewhere, are now covered with this material.

FELUCCA is the name of a vessel or small craft used in the Mediterranean for coasting voyages, being propelled both by oars and sails. The feluccas carry two masts, main and fore, with lateen sails.

FENCES. When a park is inclosed to keep in deer and game, the best fence is a stone or brick wall, well built with lime mortar; but, as this is expensive where stone and lime are not at hand, the common *park paling* is more frequently met with. This is composed of posts and rails of oak morticed and pinned together, and split pales of the same material nailed upon these in an upright position. Sometimes the pales are nailed at a distance from each other, which makes the *open paled fence*, and the pales are then generally cut to a point at top. Wood fences on the continent are generally of ruder construction.

In wild mountain passes in Scotland and Ireland it is usual to separate the properties of different individuals or that of parishes by rough stone walls put together without any mortar. The materials are generally at hand, and a rough and efficient fence is made without much labour. Where stones are not at hand, a high bank of earth faced with sods of grass is substituted for a wall. Furze seed is often sown on it, and soon forms an excellent fence, which, by proper care and clipping, will last a long time. But the most common kind of fence for fields is the hedge and ditch, the bank being raised with the sods and earth taken out of the ditch, and the hedge planted in the side of the bank towards the ditch, or on the top. Where they are not required as drains, it is a great waste of land to have any ditches, and a simple hedge planted on the surface of the soil is much to be preferred. Of all fences, a live hedge, which is carefully planted, and kept properly cut and trimmed when it is grown up, is by far the best.

When a fence is required within sight of a dwelling, a deep ditch is sometimes dug, and a fence placed at the bottom of it. This is called a *sunk fence*. Sometimes a wall is built against a perpendicular side of a ditch, and some very light fence is placed obliquely outwards near the top of it, and level with the ground. This is called a *ha-ha fence*, a name given to it from the surprise excited in a person unacquainted with it, when he suddenly finds himself on the top of a wall with a deep ditch before him. A variety of *light fences of iron* have been invented for the same purpose: some of these are fixed, and others moveable: some have upright pieces of cast iron as posts let into oak blocks sunk in the ground, and rods of wrought iron passing through holes in the uprights: some have wire for the same purpose. But the most common iron fence is composed of separate wrought-iron hurdles, which may be moved at pleasure, and are kept together by screwed pins and nuts.

FERMENTATION. This is a general name for certain changes which occur in vegetable and animal matters, and by which there are produced new fluids and gaseous compounds. Fermentation is of three kinds: the *vinous*, producing alcohol; the *acetous*, yielding vinegar; and the *putrefactive*, of which the products are very variable, and usually fetid.

When the expressed juice of grapes is exposed in warm weather to the air, it soon becomes turbid; its temperature rises a few degrees, a motion occurs in the fluid, and minute bubbles of air form and break. As the process goes on, a thick froth, consisting of these bubbles and viscid matter, rises to the surface, and, when these bubbles have burst, a viscid substance falls to the bottom of the vessel: this possesses the property of causing fermentation to take place in other fluids which, without its presence, would not undergo such a change: this substance is called *yest*. The sugar of the grape has undergone by this fermentation a decomposition into alcohol and carbonic acid.

Although sugar yields alcohol by its decomposition, yet pure sugar suffers no fermentation. In the juice of the grape, there is some accompanying matter which acts as a ferment; and when yest is thus spontaneously produced it causes fermentation in sugar, without, as far as appears, adding anything important.

The fermentation of malt-extract is noticed under BREWING and DISTILLATION. Acetous fermentation is treated under ACETIC ACID and VINEGAR. The putrefactive fermentation is the spontaneous decomposition of vegetable and animal matter, which is unaccompanied with the production of alcohol or acetic acid. In vegetable putrefactive fermentation the principal product is carbonic acid, and probably water, both derived from the absorption of the oxygen of the air, which unites with the hydrogen and carbon of the vegetable matter. In the putrefactive fermentation of animal matter ammonia is formed by the union of the hydrogen and nitrogen of the substance.

FERNS. The properties and uses of the ferns are numerous. Many of them deposit starch in their rizomata, from which food may be prepared. The roots of *Nephrodium esculentum* are eaten in Nepaul; those of *Angiopteris evecta* are used in the same manner in the Sandwich Islands. *Diplazium esculentum*, *Cyathea medullaris*, *Pteris esculenta*, and *Gleichenia dichotoma*, all yield starch, and are employed as food in different countries. The *Adiantum Capillus Veneris* yields astringent and aromatic secretions. Some of the American polypodiums are said to possess powerful medicinal effects. The *Angiopteris evecta* yields an aromatic oil, which is used in the Sandwich Islands to perfume the fixed oils, as cocoa-nut oil. The stems of many species contain bitter principles, and have hence been used as tonics. Species of *Aspidium* and *Asplenium* have been used in European medicine. The Brazilian negroes form tubes for their pipes from the stems of *Mertensia dichotoma*. *Osmunda regalis* had once a great reputation in medicine.

FERO'NIA. The Elephant or Wood Apple of the Coromandel coast, is a species of the *Feronia* genus of plants. The fruit is fleshy, and extremely acid before it arrives at maturity; but, when ripe, it contains a dark brown agreeable sub-acid pulp. In appearance the fruit is large, spheroidal, rugged, and often warted externally. A transparent oily fluid exudes from the trunk of this tree when an incision is made into it, which is used by painters for mixing their colours. A clear white gum may also be obtained from the tree very much resembling gum arabic. The wood is likewise valuable on account of its durability, whiteness, and hardness.

FERROCYANIC ACID is composed of hydrocyanic acid, cyanide of iron, and water. It contains 23.27 per cent. of iron. This acid is decomposed by long exposure to the air, Prussian blue being formed and precipitated; this is also produced by adding it to a persalt of iron.

FERRO'L, a seaport town of Gallicia in Spain, has some manufactures of hats, and carries on a considerable fishery of herrings, and sardines, which are pickled and exported. It also carries on some trade with America, exporting wine, brandy, and corn.

FE'RULA. The drugs called *Sagapenum* and *Assafœtida* are yielded by species of the Ferula plant.

Assafœtida is said to be found only in two districts of Persia, that is, the fields and mountains round Herat, the capital of Khorassan, and the range of mountains in the province of Lar. The plant is said to arrive at as great an age as man himself, and in consequence its roots sometimes attain a considerable size. It is from wounds in this part that the drug is obtained. The roots are not wounded before they are four years old; the greater their age, the better the quality of their produce. There were four operations each year when Kæmpfer visited the country; the first in the middle of

April, the second at the latter end of May, the third ten days later, and the fourth in the beginning of July. The gatherers on the first occasion only clear the hard sandy or stony soil away from the root to the depth of a span or so, pulling off the leaves, replacing the earth about the roots, and then heaping the leaves on them, and pressing them down with a stone. On the subsequent occasions they slice the roots transversely, beginning a little below the top, and collecting the juice that flows from the wounds. After every operation they cover the root with the old leaves, to screen it from the sun. After the last gathering the roots are left to perish.

Various useful substances are yielded by other species of this genus of plants.

FIBRE, is one of the most elementary forms of vegetable tissue. It consists of excessively delicate threads twisted spirally in the interior of a cell or tube. The fibre is solid. It is this elementary fibre which, being turned spirally round a long delicate tube with its spires in contact, forms the elastic spiral vessel.

Without entering into minor differences, fibre is a general name for the cotton, flaxen, and hempen material which forms so important a class of our textile manufactures.

FIBRIN, is a substance contained in the bodies of animals both in a fluid and in a solid state; in the fluid state it exists in the blood, and in the solid state in muscular fibre, but the fibrin of venous blood differs from that of arterial blood. When separated from the other constituents of the blood, fibrin appears in the form of long white elastic filaments; it is inodorous, tasteless, and insoluble in water whether cold or hot, but by long-continued boiling a portion is dissolved. When dried at a gentle heat, it loses about four-fifths of its weight, which loss is water, and it becomes then horny and translucent, and very much resembles albumen which has been coagulated. Acetic acid and fresh fibrin, when kept for some hours in contact, form a transparent gelatinous mass which is soluble in water. Solution of potash dissolves fibrin. Its composition is precisely similar to that of coagulated albumen, and they have several properties in common.

That variety of fibrin which constitutes muscular fibre is so interwoven with nerves, vessels, and cellular and adipose tissue, that its properties are probably always more or less modified by foreign matters. To obtain the fibrin of a muscle, it must be finely minced, and washed in repeated portions of water at 60° or 70° till all colouring and soluble substances are withdrawn, and till the residue is colourless, insipid and inodorous. It is then strongly pressed between folds of linen, by which it is rendered semitransparent and pulverulent.

There is also a substance called *Vegetable Fibrin*, which is obtained from wheat flour by the following process :—Make the flour into a paste, and wash it on a fine sieve with a small stream of water. The gluten of the flour will remain, and a milky liquid will pass through the sieve, which when suffered to rest will in a few hours become clear by depositing the starch by which it was rendered turbid. If this clear liquor be boiled, a flocculent precipitate is formed in it, which, when washed, dried, and purified by boiling æther, has the same composition as animal fibrin. When heated, it coagulates, and possesses the properties of coagulated albumen.

FIFE, a very small flute giving acute piercing sounds. It is an octave higher than the flute, and in compass comprises two octaves. Fifes are of three sizes, named by the letters A, B, and C. The first is the lowest; the last, which is that in common use, is the highest.

FIFESHIRE is one of the best cultivated counties in Scotland. The soil is of various kinds. In the most fertile districts it consists principally of a rich loam: in the poorer tracts it is mostly a wet clay, resting on a cold bed of till. A level tract of deep, rich, and very fertile loam extends from east to west along the whole southern side, varying in width from three miles to one mile from the shore of the Frith of Forth; and there are in other parts very rich tracts of land. The extensive water-boundary gives the county many excellent ports and small harbours, from which steam communication is kept up with Edinburgh, Dundee, Perth, and other places. Most of the chief towns of the county will be shortly linked together by railways. Coal and limestone of the best description are found in abundance in almost every part of the county south of the Eden; but they are not found in the upper division, north of this river. The collieries are numerous, and some are very extensive, and employ a large number of hands. Limestone quarries are numerous in various parts of the southern district. Ironstone is plentifully obtained in several parts of the coal fields, especially near Dysart, and in the parish of Balgonie. Lead mines have been worked in the Lomond Hills. Freestone, whinstone, and many of the primitive rocks are abundantly met with. There are beds of rich marl, brick-clay, and peat. Gems are sometimes picked up in the beds of the rivers.

There are a few patches of natural wood in

Fife. The plantations are numerous, and the timber in them, which is mostly aged and valuable, consists of ash, elm, beech, fir of different kinds, limes, chestnut, sycomore, and oak. Flax is grown to a considerable extent, and is used in the linen manufacture at Dunfermline and elsewhere. The county of Fife has been long distinguished for the excellence of its breed of black cattle; when fat, they bring a much higher price at Smithfield market than any other kind. The Fife cows are also of high repute in the dairy.

Small breweries and distilleries for the manufacture of malt liquor and malt spirits, flour mills and pot-barley mills, salt-works and coal-works, tan-works and soap-works, and brick and tile works, are among the industrial establishments of the county. But the linen manufacture is by far the largest; it occupies a great number of hands, who spin and weave flax into damasks, diapers, checks, ticks, coarse sheeting, and many other kinds of linen fabrics. There are fisheries of salmon, cod, turbot, haddock, &c., off the coasts. There are a good many trading vessels belonging to the county.

At Dunfermline fine linens are largely manufactured. At Kirkaldy an excellent harbour has been formed, from which about 50,000 tons are annually shipped, chiefly to places on the coast of Scotland. Corn, potatoes, sheep, and pigs also form large items of exportation to London and various other ports. There are several flax-mills, extensive manufactures of coarse linen fabrics, an iron-foundry, tanneries, &c.

The factory-statistics of Fifeshire in 1850 presented the following results:—There were 2 factories for spinning and weaving woollens, with 26 power-looms and 1480 spindles. There were 40 factories for spinning flax, having 52,344 spindles, 1353 horse power for moving machinery, and employing 3980 persons. There were 3 factories for weaving flax, with 104 power-looms, and having 42-horse power.

FIGS. Figs belong to the *Ficus* genus of plants. The number of species of ficus is very considerable, perhaps as great as that of any arborescent genus. They are all either tropical or inhabitants of warm countries. Some are small plants creeping upon the surface of rocks and walls, or clinging to the trunks of trees like ivy; others are among the largest trees in the forest. They abound in a milky juice containing caoutchouc; and there is every reason to believe that the specimens of this substance which come from Java are exclusively procured by tapping different species of Ficus. The best known on the continent of India is yielded by *Ficus elastica*.

Although the fruit of *Ficus carica* (the common fig) and some others is eatable, yet the whole genus abounds in an acrid, highly dangerous principle, diffused among the milky secretion. This is perceptible even in the common fig, whose milk produces a burning sensation on the tongue and throat; but, when the fruit of that species is ripe, the acridity is destroyed by the chemical elements entering into new combinations. The common fig is a small tree, naturally inhabiting the temperate parts of Asia, and now commonly cultivated in Europe for the sake of its fruit. In the fertile islands of the Mediterranean, in Spain, Italy, and Greece, and even so far north as the south of France, the fruit is so well ripened as to form a valuable article of exportation in a dried state. The fruit is grown with some success even in the southern and milder parts of England, but it is seldom found in the northern parts or in Scotland, except under glass. The fig-tree is very apt to throw off its fruit before it ripens, and various methods have been suggested to prevent this. In the Levant, to insure a crop, the process of caprification is resorted to. [CAPRIFICATION.]

The figs imported in 1849 amounted to 39,516 cwts.; and in 1850, to 33,964 cwts.

FILBERT. This term was originally applied to those kinds of nuts which have very long husks; but, owing to the number of varieties that have of late years been obtained, this distinction, which was never scientific, appears to be nearly disregarded, and *nut* and *filbert* are almost synonymous terms, excepting that the wild uncultivated fruit, and those varieties which most nearly approach it, are never called filberts. The best sorts are the Frizzled Filbert, Red Filbert, White Filbert, Cob-Nut, Bond-Nut, Downton, and Northamptonshire.

About Maidstone, and in other parts of Kent, the management of the filbert is better understood than in any other part of this country; and, as the soil and other circumstances seem to suit its growth, immense quantities are grown for the London market. In order to preserve filberts in a fresh and plump state, it is only necessary to prevent their parting with their moisture by evaporation. Burying them in heaps in the earth, putting them in earthen jars in a wine-cellar, covering them with dry sand, are all very good plans, and many others equally efficient will suggest themselves.

FILE MANUFACTURE. A file, as every one knows, is a steel instrument having flat or curved surfaces so notched or serrated as to produce a series of fine teeth or cutting edges, which are employed for the abrasion of metal, ivory, wood, &c.

Steel for making files, being required to be of unusual hardness, is more highly converted than for other purposes, and is sometimes said to be *double converted.* Small files are mostly made of cast steel. The very large files, called smiths' rubbers, are generally forged immediately from the converted bars. Smaller files are forged from bars which are wrought to the required form and size by the action of tilt-hammers, either from blistered bars or from ingots of cast steel. These bars are cut into pieces suitable for making one file each, which are heated in a forge fire, and then wrought to the required shape on an anvil by two men, one of whom superintends the work, while the other acts as general assistant.

The next operation upon the blanks which are to be converted into files is that of softening or 'lightening,' to render the steel capable of being cut with the toothing instruments. This is effected by a gradual heating and a gradual cooling. The surface is then rendered flat and smooth, either by filing or by grinding.

The cutting of the teeth is usually performed by workmen sitting astride upon a board or saddle-shaped seat, in front of a bench, upon which is fixed a kind of small anvil. Laying the blank file across the anvil, the cutter secures it from moving by a strap which passes over each end and under his feet, like the stirrup of the shoemaker. He then takes in his left hand a very carefully ground chisel made of the best steel, and in his right a peculiarly-shaped hammer. If the file be flat, or have one or more flat surfaces, the operator places the steel chisel upon it at a particular angle or inclination, and with one blow of the hammer cuts an indentation or furrow completely across its face from side to side, and then moves the chisel to the requisite positions for making other similar and parallel cuts. If it be a half round file, as a straight-edged chisel is still used, a number of small cuts are necessary to extend across the file from edge to edge. So minute are these cuts in some kinds of files, that in one specimen about ten inches long, flat on one side and round on the other, there are more than 20,000 cuts, each made with a separate blow of the hammer, and the cutting-tool being shifted after each blow. The range of manufactures afford few examples more striking of the peculiar manual tact acquired by long practice.

Several highly ingenious machines have been contrived for superseding the tedious operation of file-cutting by hand; but, suited as the process may appear to be for the use of machinery, it has been found to present such great difficulties, that we believe no file-cutting engine has been brought successfully or extensively into operation. One very serious difficulty arises from the circumstance that, if one part of the file be either a little softer than the adjacent parts, or narrower, so as to present less resistance to the blow of the hammer, a machine would, owing to the perfect uniformity of its stroke, make a deeper cut there than elsewhere.

After the files have been cut, the steel is brought to a state of great hardness; this is effected in various ways, according to the purpose to which the file is to be applied: they are generally coated with a sort of temporary varnish, then heated in a stove, and then suddenly quenched. After hardening, the files are scoured, washed, dried, and tested.

We will here give, from a Sheffield newspaper, a description of a file intended for the Great Exhibition, the most elaborate perhaps ever produced. It was wholly made by a file-forger named Hiram Younge, in the employ of Messrs. Carr of Sheffield. The length is 54 inches, breadth 3½ inches, thickness ⅝ of an inch, weight 28 lbs. With some small exceptions, the whole surface is covered with ornamental designs, all cut by hand with hammer and chisel. The tangs (it is a double-tanged file)—are sunk by filing, and are ornamented on one side with the national arms and the words "God save the Queen," on a shield; a front view of the cutlers' hall on the other, with the motto 'Pour parvenir a Bonne foy.' The other tang represents Atlas bearing the globe, with two lions couchant: beneath are the Sheffield arms, and a cornucopia on each side. On the reverse side appear the cutlers' arms with the emblem of industry—beehives and bees on the wing—on each side. On the moulding these words appear: 'Cut, designed, and executed by Hiram Younge, a member of the Sheffield file trade.' The centre or body of the file is ornamented on one side with an accurate, full-length view of the Great Palace of Industry, in perspective, forming an elegant and spirited sketch. The reverse side is occupied by a view of the Sheffield Infirmary; while on the ends, between the centre and the tangs, are four views, illustrating the processes of file manufacturing. 1. A file-forger's shop, exhibiting bellows and other appointments, and a file-forger and striker in working costume. 2. The interior of a wheel: grinders at work. 3. A file-cutting shop: three men cutting files, and one grinding his chisel. 4. A hardening shop:

hardeners at work, and two women scouring files. The edges of the file are occupied with an inscription. The remaining space is filled up with chequered work, half diamonds, &c. This unique file revolves on pivots, so that every part can be inspected in succession with ease, and the position varied to bring out the innumerable effects which light produces. The lighter parts possess that peculiar bright richness observable on highly ornamented silver plate. But the most remarkable feature in this elaborate ornamentation is a number of trees in full foliage, luxuriant as the work of the pencil. Each separate shade is effected by a distinct style of perfect tooth. Those practised in the delicate art of file-cutting can best appreciate this wonderful piece of work; but the uninitiated may judge of its merit by bearing in mind that if a single tooth were cut too deep or too shallow, too narrow or too broad, or the least awry, it would destroy the uniformity of the shade, and that nowhere is there such a defect discernible.

FILLET, a flat rectangular moulding, of very frequent occurrence in architecture. It is used to terminate or divide other mouldings, as in the cavetto, which is surmounted with a fillet, and in the flutings of columns, which are divided by a fillet. The fillet is much used in entablatures.

FILTER. The smaller kinds of filters are strainers used in chemical operations for rendering fluids transparent by separating the suspended impurities which make them turbid; or for separating and washing the precipitates resulting from chemical analysis. They are usually made of unsized or blotting paper; and they are used either spread out upon cloth stretched on a wooden frame, or folded and placed in funnels, and having consequently the form of an inverted cone. They are either single or double, according to the purposes to which they are to be applied.

Various forms of filter are employed for the purpose of filtering water, either for drinking or culinary purposes. These filters generally depend upon passing water through sand or small pebbles and charcoal. It is well known that the Thames water, though it contains but little saline matter in solution, is frequently turbid, owing to mechanical admixture of earthy matter, which the filters in question are well calculated to remove, so as to render the water, though not so agreeable as spring-water for drinking on account of its flatness, yet well adapted for other purposes.

A considerable portion of the river-water of Paris is filtered in large establishments where it is employed. The filters employed are small boxes, many in number, lined with lead, open at top, and having at the bottom a layer of charcoal between two layers of sand. If the water is foul, the upper layer of sand requires to be renewed daily. At the Hôtel Dieu the boxes are hermetically sealed, and the water is forced through the filtering layers by artificial pressure.

A very simple water-filter may be made of a common garden-pot, or similar vessel, with a bottom pierced with holes. Fill the lower part with round pebbles, then place a layer of smaller pebbles, then coarse sand, and lastly a layer three or four inches in depth of well-made pounded charcoal. The water, in percolating through these various strata, loses nearly all its mechanical impurities.

Murray's 'Self-cleansing Domestic Tubular Filter,' registered in 1850, is to be soldered to the end of the service-pipe. The enlarged part of the pipe contains a perforated tube with several folds of flannel and linen wrapped round it. The smaller tap communicates only with the outer casing, so that no water can reach it that has not passed through the filtering tube. The larger tap communicates with the interior of the tube; and by allowing it to run, the filter will clean itself.

In 'Bird's Hydrostatic Syphon Water Purifier,' also registered in 1850, the filtration is performed in two inverted cones containing filtering media, situated in the cylinder. When used, the instrument is immersed in the water to be filtered, and the pipe uncoiled so as to hang with its stop-cock below the bottom of the instrument. On drawing out the air from the pipe, it acts as a syphon and a stream of pure water flows.

Foster's Pressure Filter, recently patented at Liverpool, and recommended for use by the Sanitary Board of that town, consists of a porous stone, hollow in the inside, and contained in a metal jacket. This apparatus, when screwed on to the service-pipe, causes the water, forced through the stone by the pressure of the main, to lose all its pollutions, and come out pure and clear in the extreme. There are two taps, one of which draws the filtered water from the interior of the stone globe; the other the unfiltered from the exterior; and the apparatus is so arranged that the drawing of the unfiltered water cleanses the stone and increases its powers of filtration.

FINISTÈRE. This department of France, in Brittany or Bretagne, produces, besides the usual kinds of crops, flax, hemp, tobacco, and cider fruits. The cider produce is about 1,500,000 gallons annually. Eels, trout, salmon, lobsters, and oysters are plentiful; but the pilchard fisheries along the coast afford the most profitable occupation to the Breton fishermen. In this pursuit more than 1000 vessels of small size, and about 4000 men, are employed, and a gross annual value of 2,000,000 francs is obtained. This includes the value of the enormous quantities of the common pilchard (4,400,000 lbs.), the anchovy pilchard, caught off Concarneau in Forêt Bay (1,100,000 lbs.), and a large quantity of oil pressed from fish which are not cured. These fisheries form an excellent nursery for the French navy, which draws its best seamen from Bretagne.

Iron, coal, lead, bismuth, and zinc mines are worked. An excellent stone, easily worked, and capable of resisting the action of the weather, is found at Daoulas and one or two other places near the Brest Roads: it is of a light green colour, and when worked presents the appearance of bronze; it is called *Kersanton* stone, and of it several of the churches in the department are built. Granite, marble, building stone, and slates are quarried; potters' clay, kaolin, and whetstones are found. The manufactures consist of sailcloth, linen, soda, soap, seed oil, candles, ropes, pottery, paper, leather, refined sugar, litharge, and tobacco. Ship-building is carried on at Brest and in most of the large towns on the coast. The commerce of the department is composed of the various products already named, and of wine, brandy, beer, Dutch cheese, butter, salt, and colonial produce.

FINLAND. This cold Russian province, lying north-east of the Baltic, has extensive forests of firs and pines in the south, interspersed with oaks, elms, &c. In northern Lapland these trees are replaced by the birch, until, in the coldest districts, trees cease altogether. The chief crops are barley, rye, oats, wheat, peas, beans, hemp, flax, potatoes, carrots, parsnips, onions, hops, and tobacco; but the produce is seldom large. Of fruit there is scarcely any. The forests yield much timber, pitch, and potash. The streams are well provided with fish, which form the chief food of the people. The mineral produce met with is chiefly bog-iron, lead, copper, marble, slate, and chalk.

Agriculture, the breeding of cattle, and in some parts the fisheries constitute the principal occupations of the people. There are few manufactures except in the large towns, and these are principally of iron-ware, sailcloth, and stockings. The navigation and trade are inconsiderable.

FIR. [Abies; Pine-Tree.]

FIRE-ENGINE. In Rome under the emperors there were bands of trained firemen kept. Ctesibius is believed to have invented some engine for the extinction of fires in the time of the Ptolemies; and a few indications of similar inventions are met with in other quarters. But the first fire-engine which has been distinctly described was made by Hautsch of Nürnberg about 1657. Duperrier received a patent for making fire-engines for France in 1699. None of these earlier engines had either a flexible hose or an air-chamber: the first of these was introduced by Jan Vanderheide in 1672; and the latter by Leupold in 1720. It was about the beginning of the same century that fire-engines came generally into use in England.

A fire-engine of the common construction consists of an oblong wooden chest or cistern, along the lower part of which runs a metallic pipe, into which the water flows from a feed-pipe connected at the other end with the street plug. The water having entered the interior pipe is elevated and forced into an upright air vessel by two pumps which are worked by manual power, by means of long handles or levers on the outside. From the air-vessel the water is forced into a pipe connected with the leather hose; and from the latter it is forcibly impelled on the burning buildings. If there were no air-vessel the water would not flow out in an equable continuous stream, but would gush forth at intervals at every successive movement of the pump-handles; but by the aid of the air-vessel the stream is rendered continuous by the elastic pressure of air within the vessel.

Numerous improvements have been introduced in almost every part of the fire-engine, whereby it has been rendered much more efficient than formerly. In 1830 Mr. Braithwaite introduced an ingeniously constructed steam fire-engine, which has occasionally been employed. The same engineer has also introduced a steam floating fire-engine, in which the power of the engine can be transferred from propelling the vessel to working the pumps when requisite.

Mr. Tilley, the fire engine maker, has recently contrived a small fire-pump, calculated to be useful before the larger engines arrive. It is well suited for warehouses and shops, as it can be worked from a single bucket of water. It consists of a sort of double cylinder, one within another, the inner one being the barrel, and the outer the air-vessel. In the barrel works a piston, the rod of which ends at the top in a nob, which serves as a handle. The lower end of the instrument being placed in a bucket of water, and the piston being worked vertically, water is drawn into the barrel, and is forced by the air pressure through a hose screwed to one side of the air-vessel. The pump can discharge six gallons of water per minute, to a height of thirty feet.

Down to the year 1825 all the Fire Insurance Companies of London had their separate establishments of fire-engines; but in that year the Sun, the Union, and the Royal Exchange Companies joined their fire-engine establishments, which were placed under one superintendence. Soon afterwards the Atlas and the Phœnix Companies joined the association. The advantage of this combined system of action having been proved, most of the remaining companies joined in 1833, and formed a new association, which was to be managed by a committee, formed of one member from each of the associated companies. London was divided into a certain number of districts, in each of which were two or more stations, provided with engines.

The plan has worked well: more companies have joined the association; and it is found that all are benefited. The firemen are formed into a corps, called the *fire-brigade*, which is under the efficient control of Mr. Braidwood, superintendent of the establishment. The men are clothed in a uniform; and a certain number of them at each station are ready at all hours of day or night. Each company pays its quota towards the expenses of the fire-engine establishment.

A fire engine of great power was made for the London Docks a few years ago, with working barrels eight inches diameter. It would throw a jet perpendicularly to a height of eighty feet; at an angle of 45° the jet would reach to a distance of 130 feet.

The West India Dock Company employ a steam tug to move the vessels using the docks; and their assistant engineer, Mr. P. Clark, has designed a simple method of making the power of the engines of the boat available in case of fire. A large Downton's pump is fixed on deck, and connected by gearing to the engines, so that they can be readily disconnected from the paddle-wheels, and their power applied to the pump. The power of the engines is 30 horses, which, nominally, would be equal to 240 men, or 10 of the ordinary fire-engines, but in reality to a much greater number. Without using the whole power of the engines, a stream of water equal to 600 gallons, or 3 tons, per minute, is projected 20 feet higher than the highest warehouse in the docks. As the fires in the boilers are never allowed to go out entirely, this machine is always in readiness, and in the event of a ship taking fire could tow her out of danger, and extinguish the fire at the same time.

In the year 1850 there were 247 premises totally destroyed by fire in the metropolis, 621 partially destroyed, and 18 lives lost. Nearly 100 houses were more or less injured by explosions of fire-works.

The employment of saline substances for extinguishing fires has been long known. Dr. Clanny suggested, a few years ago, the employment of water for fire-engines, containing five ounces of muriate of ammonia to each gallon of water. Mr. Phillips's apparatus, now occupying a good deal of public attention, is briefly noticed under the heading of ANNIHILATOR, FIRE.

The engines employed in gardening and agriculture partake a good deal of the character of fire-engines in their construction. [GARDEN ENGINE.]

FIRE-ESCAPE. Numerous contrivances have been brought before public notice from time to time for saving the lives of persons who may be in a building while it is burning. Mr. Meseres devised a kind of chair of straps, by which a person could lower himself from the window. Mr. Davis proposed the use of three ladders, which might draw out like a telescope, and might reach from the ground to the upper windows of a house. Mr. Young contrived a sort of rope-ladder, with iron rounds of very flexible construction. Mr. Braby invented a sort of a long pole, down which a car or chair might travel from a window to the ground. Mr. Witly introduced a sort of bag or case, which may be lowered from the sill of a window by ropes governed by the person who might be seated in the bag. Mr. Ford recommended the use of a long pole, at the upper end of which is tackle for lowering persons from a window. Mr. Merryweather has contrived a series of short ladders, which fit on to each other end to end, and can be elevated to a considerable height quickly.

But the fire-escape which has come most into use in London is a wheel-carriage supporting a lofty canvas shoot or trunk, attached to a ladder or frame; when placed up against a house, a person can get into this trunk from a window, and slide safely down to the bottom, with the aid of some ingenious mechanism attached to the frame. Many such machines are kept in public places in London during the night, attended by men whose business it is to wheel these machines to any spot where life is endangered by fire.

A Report was presented to the city corporation in 1840 from the police commissioners, descriptive of thirty plans for fire-escapes, which had been proposed by different parties. They were of three classes: 1st. Machines intended for domestic use only, to be resorted to by inmates of houses in cases of fire; 2nd. Machines to be used from the outside, and made to combine the security of property with the protection of persons; 3rd. Machines exclusively for the protection of life from fire, to be used out of doors under the responsible direction of the police. Among the thirty were Davies's effective but rather ponderous machine; Wivell's, with the canvas trunk; and Gregory's sliding ladders on a carriage. Whichever may be the best form in wide thoroughfares, it is thought that the common fire ladders of the London Brigade are the most generally useful in courts and confined situations.

FIRE, GREEK, an invention of the middle ages which was often employed in the wars of the Christians and Saracens. According to Gibbon, this combustible was used at the sieges of Constantinople in the 7th and 8th centuries. It was afterwards employed by the caliphs against the Crusaders; but the invention of gunpowder changed the nature of military tactics. There is much uncertainty as to the nature of this Greek Fire. It is supposed to have been a compound of naptha, sulphur, and pitch; and Gibbon thus describes its effects :—'From this mixture, which produced a thick smoke and a loud explosion, proceeded a fierce and obstinate flame, which not only rose in perpendicular ascent, but likewise burnt with equal vehemence in descent or lateral progress; instead of being extinguished, it was nourished and quickened by the element of water; and sand, urine, or vinegar, were the only remedies that could damp the fury of this powerful agent, which was justly denominated by the Greeks the liquid or the Maritime Fire. For the annoyance of the enemy it was employed with equal effect by sea and by land, in battles or in sieges. It was either poured from the ramparts in large boilers, or launched in red-hot balls of stone and iron, or darted in arrows and javelins, twisted round with flax and tow which had deeply imbibed the inflammable oil: sometimes it was deposited in fire-ships, the victims and instruments of a more ample revenge, and was most commonly blown through long tubes of copper, planted on the prow of a galley, and fancifully shaped into the mouths of savage monsters, that seemed to vomit a stream of liquid and consuming fire.'

FIRE-PROOF BUILDINGS. The most obvious method of rendering houses and other buildings indestructible by fire is to construct them entirely of incombustible materials, such as stone, brick, and iron. Such a mode of construction, however, is of very limited application. The use of iron, and especially of cast iron, in buildings, has indeed increased very much, and many plans for the construction of dwelling-houses almost entirely of that material have been brought forward.

Brickwork forms in this country the chief material of the external walls of houses, and it is occasionally employed without any admixture of timber for the partition walls also,—a plan which, in conjunction with other precautions, tends greatly to limit the damage done by a fire to the apartment in which it may happen to break out. Cast-iron pillars and brest-summers are very extensively employed in modern London shops and warehouses, where the whole front on the ground floor is left open for shop-windows and doors. Fire-proof floors are now often adopted, not only in public buildings, but also in the larger and better sort of private houses; the beams being either of cast or wrought iron, and the brick vaultings, which abut upon the ledges of the beams, being often only half a brick thick. In Farrow's patent method of fire-proof building, the floors are supported upon joists of wrought iron, formed with a projecting flange on each side, upon which are laid, stretching from joist to joist, a series of flat stones the upper surfaces of which lie flush with the upper edges of the joists. These produce a level stone floor, interlined with iron, which may either be used as such or be covered with planks. Mr. Frost has invented a mode of constructing floors and roofs of hollow square earthenware tubes, laid in strata crossing each other in direction, and united with cement in such a way that the whole floor becomes one solid flagstone. In one mode of construction, hollow earthen pots are employed to form a sort of vaulted roof.

The great use of timber in building renders very important any method by which it may be rendered incombustible. Solutions of muriate of ammonia, muriate of soda, salammoniac, borax, alum, and several other salts and alkalies, with which wood may be impregnated, or which may be applied to its surface, possess this quality in a limited degree; and by Payne's wood-preserving process timber is made, for all practical purposes, completely incombustible. The non-conducting power of earth and sand, or of a layer of sand placed over timber, has been the basis of many plans for preventing fires.

FIRE-SHIP is a vessel laden with combustible materials, which is sent or left in a burning state among the ships of a hostile fleet for the purpose of setting them on fire. Such vessels have been used in various countries, at different times. Those now constructed have between decks, on both sides, a stage containing a groove, in which the train of powder for firing the combustibles is deposited in a hose or tube. The stage is covered with a tarpaulin on which is strewed loose powder; and on this are placed faggots of wood and bundles of hemp steeped in a mixture of resin, turpentine, saltpetre, and mealed gunpowder, billets of wood dipped in saltpetre and pitch, casks filled with chips of wood mixed with pitch and turpentine, and loaded shells and carcasses. Faggots soaked in pitch are also fastened to the sides of the ship; and around the ship are grappling-irons to enable it to cling to the ill-fated vessel to be destroyed. When the crew has brought the fire-ship close to its prey, they fire the combustibles, and escape by a boat as quickly as possible.

FIRE-WOOD MANUFACTURE. The manufacture of such an article as fire-wood would only be thought of in a large and populous city, far distant from woodland and copses. The neat appearance of our London bundles and net-works and wheels of fire-wood has to this day an air of strangeness to country people.

The bundles of fire-wood, largely used in London, and having a cylindrical shape, are made with simple apparatus. The pieces of wood, well dried, are cut by saws into blocks about six inches long, and these blocks are chopped up to the requisite degree of thinness. A sufficient number of small sticks to form one bundle are placed within a kind of hoop, and confined there until a piece of tarred string is firmly bound round them.

The *Patent* fire-wood of recent times assumes two forms—the *wheel* and the *gridiron*. In the first form a number of small pieces are arranged somewhat like a wheel, and bound into that form by string. In the gridiron form the pieces are first notched or dovetailed, by a machine, and made to fit very tightly into each other. Both forms have a few fragments of shavings, and a slight coating of resin on one side, to facilitate their ignition.

The manufacture of the cylindrical bundles of fire-wood is deemed sufficiently important to warrant the erection of an extensive factory at Bow, where steam-power is employed to work an ingenious series of machines recently patented by Messrs. Thompson and Elms. There are two machines, for cutting and for binding. The cutting-machine has a large wheel, on the periphery of which are eight equi-distant cutters. An endless band passing over the rollers, acts as a feeder to these cutters. The billets of wood are cut by the saw into blocks, about six inches long; and these blocks are ranged, side by side, on the feeding-band, with the grain of the wood perpendicular. As the feeding band travels on, these blocks are brought one by one to a spot where the cutters may act upon them: and they are speedily cut up into slices or flat pieces. These slices are re-arranged on the feeding-band, side by side, but in such a position that they may be cut up into splints or square sticks. These splints are much more regular in form than those produced by the old method of chopping. The splints are next taken to the binding-machine. They are placed in a kind of hopper, through which they descend into a horizontal cylinder, and a plunger or piston here compresses them, retains them at one end while the bundle is being bound with string, and then forces the bundle out of the cylinder.

FIRKIN is a measure of ale, beer, and some dry commodities, now disused. Eight gallons of ale, soap, or herrings, made a firkin, and nine gallons of beer made a firkin.

FISH. Of the varieties of fish eaten in this country, those that are the whitest and most flaky when cooked, such as whiting, cod, flounders, sole, haddock, turbot, hake, &c. are the most easily digestible; but those which abound in oily matter, such as salmon, eels, herrings, &c., contain more nourishment.

Fish may be preserved in a dry state, Mr. Cooley informs us, by sugar alone. Fresh fish may be thus kept for some days, so as to remain as good as when first caught. The sugar gives no disagreeable taste. This process is very useful in making what is called *Kippered Salmon*. A few table-spoonfuls of brown sugar are sufficient for a salmon of five or six pounds weight: and a little salt or saltpetre may be added. Salmon kippered in this way preserves its natural flavour better than if salted or smoked.

FISHERIES are localities frequented at certain seasons by great numbers of fish, where they are taken upon a large scale. Of the British fisheries, some are carried on in rivers or their æstuaries, and others in the bays or along the coasts. Our principal cod fishery is on the banks of Newfoundland: and for whales our ships frequent the shores of Greenland, Davis's Straits, and the South Seas. Of late, whale fisheries have also been carried on near the shores of Australia, New Zealand, and the Cape of Good Hope.

In the reign of Queen Elizabeth and afterwards, various associations were formed and orders in council issued, having for object the encouragement of British fisheries; but the trade did not flourish under these protections. Every attempt to encourage the fisheries by means of bounties failed, and the impolicy of granting these bounties was at length seen and acknowledged. In 1821 the tonnage bounty of 60*s.* per ton on fishing vessels was repealed; the bounty of 4*s.* per barrel, which was paid up to the 5th of April, 1826, was thereafter reduced 1*s.* per barrel each succeeding year; so that, in April 1830, the bounty ceased altogether. This alteration of the system was not productive of any serious evil to the herring fishery.

In 1849 the white herrings *cured* in Great Britain amounted to 770,698 barrels; the number *branded* by the commissioners was 213,286 barrels; and the number *exported* 340,256 barrels. Including those cured and those sold for immediate consumption, the number was 1,151,979 barrels. In the cod and ling department, there were 98,903 cwt. cured dried, and 6,580 barrels cured in pickle. In that year there were 14,962 boats and 59,792 fishermen under the control of the commissioners.

The removal of the bounty has been attended with an improvement in the condition of the fishermen generally, and in Scotland the fishermen have been able, from the fair profits of their business, to replace the small boats they formerly used by new boats of larger dimensions, and to provide themselves with fishing materials of superior value.

The facilities of communication with populous inland districts have greatly extended the market for fish, and the rapid means of transport by railways enables the inhabitants of Birmingham and London to consume cod and other fish caught in the Atlantic by the fishermen of Galway and Donegal. The fishermen who supply the London market, instead of returning to Gravesend or other ports of the Thames and Medway, put their cargoes, already packed in hampers, on board the steam-boats which pass along the whole eastern coast as far north as Aberdeen: or they sometimes make for Hull or some other port in the neighbourhood of the fishing-ground, and there land their cargoes, which are conveyed rapidly inland per railway. Fast-sailing cutters are sometimes employed to take provisions to the boats on the fishing-ground, and to bring back the fish taken by each.

One branch of fishing wholly different in its object from all other branches is the *Stow-Boat Fishery.* This fishery prevails principally upon the Kentish, Norfolk, and Essex coasts; and the object is the catching of sprats as manure for the land, for which there is a constant demand.. This branch of fishing gives employment on the Kentish coast alone to from 400 to 500 boats.

Vessels and boats employed in fishing are licensed by the Commissioners of Customs; and they are required to be painted or tarred entirely black, except the name and place to which such vessel or boat belongs. The licenses thus granted specify the limits beyond which fishing vessels must not be employed: this distance is usually four leagues from the English coast.

The *Pilchard Fishery,* which is carried on upon parts of the Devon and Cornish coasts, employs about 1000 boats, 3500 men at sea, and about 5000 men and women on shore. As soon as caught the pilchards are salted or pickled and exported to foreign markets, chiefly to the Mediterranean: the average exports amounts to 30,000 hogsheads per year.

Our chief *Salmon Fisheries* are carried on in the rivers and æstuaries of Scotland, but the annual value of this fishery is not exactly known. The produce of the fishings in the rivers Tay, Dee, Don, Spey, Findhorn, Beauly, Borriedale, Langwell, and Thurso, and of the coasts adjacent, are conveyed in steam-boats and small sailing-vessels to Aberdeen, where they are packed with ice in boxes and sent to the London market. London is the great market to which Scotch salmon are sent. The quantity which arrives during one season is about 2500 tons, and the average price is from 10*d.* to 1*s.* per lb.

Mackerel visit every part of our coasts in the spring and early part of the summer, and are taken in great abundance. As mackerel will not keep, it may be hawked about on Sunday for Sale.

The fisheries of Ireland, by the Act of 1842 have been placed under the regulation of the Board of Public Works, the commissioners of which prepare an annual report concerning them. In 1845 the commissioners registered 19,883 vessels and boats, and 93,073 men and boys as engaged in the Irish fisheries. The whole coast of Ireland is divided into 28 fishing districts.

The *Cod Fishery* at Newfoundland was carried on as early as 1500 by the Portuguese, Biscayans, and French, but it was not until 1585 that the English ventured to interfere with them. The French and English have still continued to fish there. The principal fisheries of Newfoundland are prosecuted on the banks which nearly surround that island: the object of these fisheries is solely cod-fish. These fisheries may be said to be the sole pursuit of the settlers in Newfoundland, and of the traders who frequent the island.

In 1818 a convention was concluded between the United States' government and that of

Great Britain for regulating the fisheries on the coasts of the British American provinces. Conventions are also in force relating to the British and French fisheries in the English Channel.

The *Whale Fishery* will form the subject of a separate article. [WHALE FISHERY.]

The fish imported in 1848, and paying import duty, were

Anchovies......	161,100 lbs.
Eels	76 ship loads.
Salmon	1,344 cwts.
Turbots and soles	41 cwts.
" " of British taking	99,147 cwts.

FLA'GEOLET, a small musical instrument, played on by means of a mouth-piece. Its compass is two octaves, from F, the first space in the treble clef, to F in altissimo. The scale of the *Quadrille Flageolet* is rather more limited; and that of the *Patent Octave Flageolet* is an octave higher than the ordinary instruments. The *Double Flageolet* consists of two instruments, united by one mouth-piece, and producing double notes.

FLAME is the combustion of gaseous or of volatilized matter. It is attended with great heat, and sometimes with the evolution of much light; but the temperature may be intense when the light is feeble: this is the case with the flame of burning hydrogen gas, it being scarcely visible by day-light, though its heat is intense.

In the burning of a candle, the wax or tallow being first rendered fluid by heat, rises in the wick, and although the wick supplies some hydrogen and carbon, by far the greater portion of these is yielded by the wax or tallow, which burn by the assistance of the oxygen of the air. The supply of hot vapour diminishes as it ascends, and eventually fails, and hence the flame of a candle gradually tapers to a point, and then ceases.

That flame is merely a thin film of white hot vapour, and that this combustion is entirely superficial, while inflammable matter is contained within which cannot burn for want of oxygen, is proved by inserting one end of a small glass tube into the dark central portion of a flame; the inferior unburnt vapour or gas will escape through it, and may be lighted at the other end of the tube. For various illustrations of flame, see BUDE LIGHT; DRUMMOND'S LIGHT; LAMP, SAFETY.

FLANDERS. There are two provinces of this name in Belgium, East and West.

East Flanders, is low and level. In many parts of the province there are beds of peat. The chief productions of the earth are wheat, rye, barley, oats, potatoes, flax, hemp, hops, madder, and tobacco. There is but little wood of large growth in the province. The chief manufactures are lace, linen and woollen cloths, bobbin net, silk, cordage, bricks, hats, soap; and there are also cotton-factories, potteries, sugar-refineries, distilleries, and breweries. GHENT is the chief town. The manufactures are carried on chiefly at Ghent, Eecloo, Grammont, Lokeren, St. Nicholas, Ninove, Oudenarde, and Renaix.

West Flanders is admirably accommodated by inland navigation; the most important of these are the canals between Ghent and Bruges, Bruges and Ostend, Dunkirk, Furnes, and Nieuport. The production and industrial occupations of the people are similar to those of East Flanders. The agriculture of this province, as well as that of East Flanders, is of the most perfect kind. The chief manufacturing towns are BRUGES and COURTRAI; and besides these, various branches of industry are carried on at Iseghem, Menin, Poperingen, Roulers, Thielt, Thourout, Ypres, and other towns.

The most fertile land, in both provinces of Flanders, is that of the low districts which have been reclaimed from the sea by embankments: it is chiefly composed of a muddy deposit mixed with fragments of marine shells and fine sea-sand. These lands are called *polders*, and their great natural fertility causes them to be cultivated with less art and industry than those lands which are much inferior. The usual rotation of crops in the polders consists of—1, Winter barley after a fallow;—2, Beans;—3, Wheat;—4, Flax;—5, Clover;—6, Potatoes. The polder farmer seldom thinks of purchasing manure; and even the ashes made by burning weeds are usually sold, to be sent to the poorer sandy soils, where their effects are more perceptible. In the tillage of the land the Flemings use few and very simple instruments. The common plough for light lands is a small light foot plough, which has no wheels and is drawn by one or two horses. In the stiffer soils the turn-wrest plough is sometimes used, made much smaller and lighter than the heavy Walloon plough. An instrument peculiarly Flemish is the *traineau*; this is a wooden frame of a triangular shape, covered with boards, which is drawn over the ground to smooth the surface and press in the seed. The *mollebaert* is another Flemish instrument for levelling ground. The Hainault scythe and hook are generally used for reaping corn. The most important instrument in Flemish agriculture is the spade, which is used to a much greater extent than in England, and in some instances is the only instrument of tillage. Flax is everywhere a most important crop, for it much exceeds all other crops in value. In most agricultural crops, the Flemish farmers contrive to do with a smaller amount of seed than the English.

In respect to the Industrial Exhibition of 1851, out of 509 intending exhibitors from the nine provinces of Belgium, 138 are from East and West Flanders. The products and manufactures to be exhibited comprise almost every possible variety.

FLANNEL. [WOOLLEN MANUFACTURES.]

FLAX MANUFACTURE. Flax is an annual plant, cultivated from time immemorial for its textile fibres, which are spun into thread and woven into linen cloth. It has a green stem from a foot and a half to two feet high, and a blue flower, which is succeeded by a capsule containing ten flat oblong seeds of a brown colour, from which an oil is expressed, which is extensively used in manufactures and in painting. There are several varieties of flax cultivated. The best seed comes from Riga and from Holland. There is a very fine long variety which is cultivated in the neighbourhood of Courtrai, in Flanders. The most common variety of flax is of a moderate length with a stronger stem. There is a small variety which does not rise above a foot, grows fast, and ripens its seed sooner. Another variety has a perennial root, and shoots out stems to a considerable height.

The soil best adapted to the growth of flax is a deep rich loam in which there is much humus or vegetable mould. It thrives well in the rich alluvial land of Zeeland and the polders. It is also raised with great success in the light sands of Flanders, but much more careful tillage and manuring are required. The land on which flax is sown must be very free from weeds, the weeding of this crop being a very important part of the expense of cultivation. In southern climates flax is sown before winter, because too great heat would destroy it. It is then pulled before the heat of summer. In northern climates the frost, and especially the alternation of frost and thaw in the early part of spring, would cause the flax to perish; it is consequently sown as early in spring as may be, so as to avoid the effect of hard frost. In Flanders the ground is prepared for flax more carefully than in any other country. The seed which is used is generally obtained from Riga, it being found that the flax raised from home-grown seed is inferior after the first year.

When the flax is full grown (and this depends on whether coarse or fine fibres or seeds for oil are the chief commercial object), the pulling begins, which is done carefully by small handfuls at a time. These are laid upon the ground to dry, two and two obliquely across each other. Soon after this, they are collected in larger bundles and placed with the root end on the ground, the bundles being slightly tied near the seed end; the other end is spread out that the air may have access, and the rain may not damage the flax. When sufficiently dry, they are tied more firmly in the middle, and stacked in long narrow stacks on the ground. This is the method adopted by those who defer the steeping till another season. Some carry the flax as soon as it is dry under a shed, and take off the capsules with the seed by *rippling*, which is drawing the flax through an iron comb fixed in a block of wood. The flax is then immediately steeped: but the most experienced flax-steepers defer this operation till the next season. In this case it is put in barns, and the seed is beat out at leisure in winter.

Steeping the flax is a very important process. The object is to separate the bark from the woody part of the stem, by dissolving a glutinous matter which causes it to adhere. The usual mode of steeping is to place the bundles of flax horizontally in shallow pools or ditches of stagnant water, keeping them under water by means of poles or boards with stones or weights laid upon them. The method adopted by the steepers of Courtrai, where steeping flax is a distinct trade, is different. The bundles of flax are placed alternately with the seed end of the one to the root end of the other, the latter projecting a few inches: as many of these are tied together near both ends as form a thick bundle about a foot in diameter, and these are placed in an oblong wooden frame. The frame is sunk in the river Lys, low enough to keep all the flax under water, and is kept there till the steeping is effected. The bundles are now untied, and the flax is spread evenly in rows slightly overlapping each other on a piece of clean smooth grass which has been mown or fed off close. It is occasionally turned over, and is allowed to remain spread out upon the grass till the woody part becomes brittle. It is then taken up, and as soon as it is quite dry it is tied up again in bundles, and carried into the barn.

In the domestic manufactures the flax is broken or scutched at home, when the weather prevents out-door work. The common brake consists of four wooden swords fixed in a frame, and another frame with three swords, which play in the interstices of the first by means of a joint at one end. The flax is taken in the left hand, and placed between the two frames, and the upper frame is pushed down briskly upon it. It breaks the flax in four places, and by moving the left hand, and rapidly repeating the strokes with the right, the whole handful is soon broken. It is then scutched by means of a board set upright in a block of wood so as to stand steady, in which is a horizontal slit about three feet from the ground, the edge of which is thin. The broken flax held in handfuls in the left hand is inserted in this slit, so as to project to the right and a flat wooden sword of a peculiar shape is held in the right hand; with this the flax is repeatedly struck close to the upright board, while the part which lies in the slit is continually changed by a motion of the left hand. This operation beats off all the pieces of the wood which still adhere to the fibre, without breaking it, and after a short time the flax is cleared of it and fit to be heckled. On a larger scale the breaking, scutching, and, and subsequent heckling, are effected by more efficient machines.

Flax is found in every quarter of the globe, and has been cultivated for its fibrous stalk from the very earliest period of which we have any record. England has never grown a sufficient quantity of flax for its own use, although it has been attempted to give encouragement to the cultivation by public rewards or bounties. A considerable quantity of land is now sown with flax seed every year in Somersetshire, Lancashire, and Yorkshire: it is largely grown in Scotland, and still more so in Ireland.

There has perhaps never been a period when the flax culture and manufacture occupied a larger share of public attention than at present. Many circumstances have combined to bring about this state of things. We will briefly glance at the chief aspects which the subject presents.

Cotton forms a larger item of our textile manufactures than all other fibrous materials combined: and the United States supply an overwhelming proportion of the cotton which we work up. We imported 775 million lbs. of cotton in 1849, of which four-fifths were brought from the United States. Hence our manufactures are almost wholly at the mercy of any fluctuations of crop which may occur in America; for the market-price depends chiefly in the abundance or scarcity of the United States supply.

If therefore we could increase the quantity of any fibrous material capable of being grown in our own country, and use it as a partial substitute for cotton, it would give our manufactures greater independence of America. Besides this, Great Britain and Ireland would be benefited if a good sale were commanded for home grown flax. Ireland and the Highlands of Scotland since the failure of the potato crops, and England since the repeal of the Corn Laws, have been in a position to seize eagerly on any new culture which promises moderate success; and landowners in all three countries are at the present time encouraging their tenants to direct attention to the flax culture.

Mr. G. R. Porter, in an able paper read at the Edinburgh Meeting of the British Association in 1850, said—'Hitherto we have in this country been greatly dependent upon our foreign importation for supplies of flax. While the law imposed restrictions upon the importation of grain for human food, there existed a kind of impediment in the way of increasing our home growth of articles for any purpose not of equal primary necessity. That impediment is now removed; and there can be no reason given why our fields should not be henceforth used for the production of any article that promises an adequate profit to the farmer.' These words have had considerable effect in urging agriculturists to attend to this matter.

It is admitted that much has yet to be learned before the English and Irish farmers will equal those of Belgium in the flax culture. Great care must be shewn in selecting the seed; and Sir Robert Kane has lately shewn how, by applying the steep-water to purposes of manure, and the woody or stalky refuse to purposes of fuel, greater profit may be realized than heretofore. It is not only the flax fibre which we largely import, but flax-seed for sowing, flax seed for making linseed oil, and flax oil-cake for feeding our cattle. In addition to many minor improvements recently suggested, Mr. Donlan has introduced a mode of pickling or chemically preparing the seed before sowing; which (unless the accounts are greatly exaggerated) seems to be a very important improvement.

But improvements in *culture* are not the only object of attention; improvements in *manufacture* are equally undergoing enquiry. The reader will have observed, in the earlier paragraphs of this article, that whatever the mode of steeping may be, *cold* water is always employed. Now it has occurred to Mr. Schenk that if *hot* water were substituted, the process might be expedited. The method has been tried by the Royal Flax Society of Belfast, who placed the flax in long troughs, filled the troughs with cold water, and heated the water by steam. The experiments tried seem to bear out the assertion that the process is not only more quickly conducted by the new method than by the old, but that more flax fibre can be obtained from a given weight of flax plant.

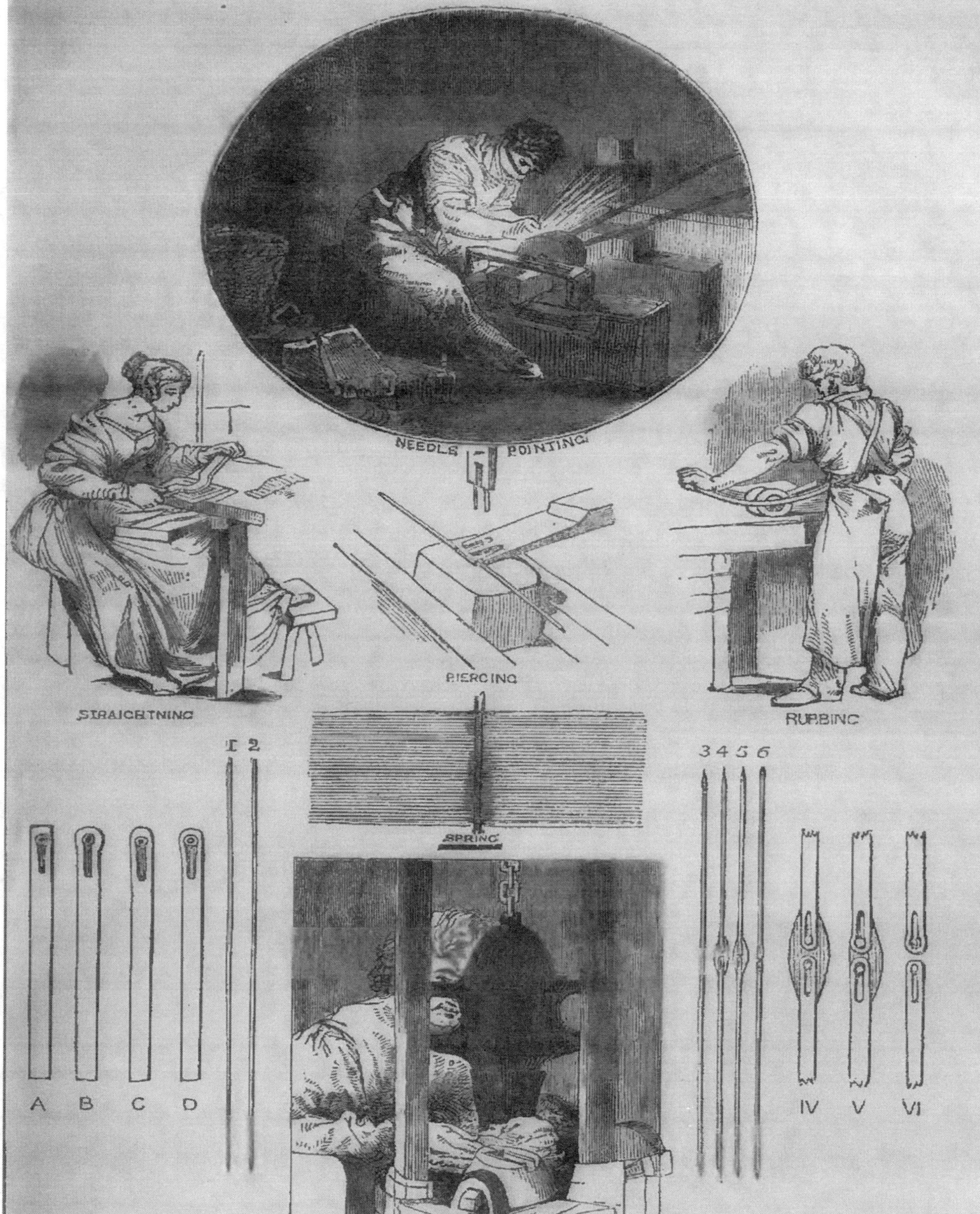

NIGHT'S CYCLOPÆDIA OF THE INDUSTRY OF ALL NATIONS.

No. 22.

While this hot water process has been under examination, Mr. Donlan has introduced a *dry* process, by which the fibre is separated from the stalk without any steeping whatever. The mode of proceeding is not yet made public, as it is not yet patented; but its advocates assert that it is as much superior to the hot water process as that is to the old mode of steeping in cold water. The experiments which are now being carried on will speedily determine the relative merits of all the three systems.

To shew how remarkably this subject is calling forth the energies of different persons, we need only state that the Chevalier Claussen is carrying out improvements in a direction differing from all those hitherto noticed. He takes the flax fibre after it has been prepared to a certain stage, and so modifies its substance as to make it susceptible of being spun by the usual cotton machinery. It is known that flax or linen goods have a *coldness* which other textile fabrics have not. M. Claussen has tried to give to flax, instead of this coldness, the *warmth* of woollens, the *softness* of cottons, and the *glossiness* of silks; and hence he has prepared four kinds, which he calls *flax fibre*, *flax cotton*, *flax wool*, and *flax silk*. The flax fibre is fit to be spun into beautiful linen thread or yarn; the flax cotton is intended to be combined with cotton, and to be spun with it into a mixed yarn; and so in like manner the flax wool with wool, and the flax silk with silk. The processes comprise, among others, the bursting or opening of the cylindrical tubes which form the minute fibres of flax, by exposing them to carbonic acid gas.

Application has been made to the Crown for a trading charter to a Flax Company; by the terms of which, the company engage to give for Irish flax a price better than can now be obtained under any other arrangement; which flax is to be prepared up to a certain stage by Donlan's process, ready to be carried forward to its ultimate results by Claussen's process. This charter has not yet been granted; but the application is receiving the favourable consideration of the government.

The reader will hence see that flax culture and manufacture are now in a highly interesting phase of their history. In Ireland especially the subject is being favourably taken up. Besides the culture, the spinning is there on the increase. There were 41 flax mills in Ireland in 1841, and 73 in 1850.

Further details will be found under LINEN MANUFACTURES. The flax imported in 1850 amounted to 97,982 cwts., of which more than two-thirds were from Russia. The flax seed imported in the same year amounted to 132,343 quarters.

FLEXIBILITY; FLEXURE. Flexibility is a property of bodies by which they yield transversely, on the application of some power: this property is distinct from elasticity, as it does not necessarily follow that the bodies acted on recover their original figures when the power is removed. [MATERIALS, STRENGTH OF; ROPES.]

In intimate connection with this subject is the flexure of columns, which has undergone much investigation since the prevalent use of iron for columns. The fibres of wooden pillars are generally of serpentine forms, and they adhere together laterally, with comparatively a small force: hence, when such a pillar is compressed longitudinally by a weight, the latter acts obliquely on the fibres; and thus a pillar of wood becomes bent sooner than one formed of the other materials.

The valuable series of experiments carried on by Mr. Hodgkinson, and of which a full account is given in the Philosophical Transactions for 1840, have thrown much light on the flexure and strength of columns. In these experiments the columns, which were placed in vertical positions, were of various lengths, from a few inches to seven feet six inches, and all were subjected to pressures acting vertically; some were cylindrical and others were rectangular prisms, and the former were either solid or hollow: in some cases the ends of the columns were planes perpendicular to the lengths, in order that the pressure might be diffused uniformly over those ends; and, in the others, the ends were hemispherical, in order that the pressure might be transmitted almost wholly in the direction of the axis. From his experiments Mr. Hodgkinson has obtained the following conclusions:—All the pillars whose lengths exceeded four times their diameters became bent before they broke; and, when the pillars were of uniform dimensions, both ends being plane or both hemispherical, the greatest flexure was near the middle of the length, and the fracture was at that place; but when one end was plane and the other hemispherical, the fracture was at a distance from the rounded end equal to about one-third of the whole length. Pillars of cast-iron with plane ends, and having their lengths about thirty times their diameters, were broken by weights equal to one-third or one-fourth of those which would crush them if they had been made short enough to be crushed without bending. In some of the experiments the cast-iron columns were formed with discs at their ends, the diameters of the discs being about twice as great as those of the columns; and it was found that these sustained a greater pressure before breaking than the simple columns. When the columns were thicker in the middle than at either end, their strength was thereby increased, if compared with cylindrical columns, by about one-eighth. In the prismatic pillars, the flexure always took place in the direction of a diagonal.

In all such buildings as the Crystal Palace, where the entire weight is supported on iron columns, the due appreciation of these various properties of columns is of the highest degree of importance.

FLINT. The true native place of this well-known mineral is the upper bed of the chalk formation, where it occurs in regular beds. Gravel consists principally of flints which have been rounded by attrition, and, by exposure to air and moisture, have acquired a yellowish red colour.

Flint is usually of a gray colour. It is rather harder than quartz; thin fragments of the black varieties are translucent; it is fragile, and, being rarely laminated, it is broken with equal facility in almost every direction. Specific gravity, 2.594. It is infusible, but becomes opaque and white by the action of heat. Flint is almost wholly pure silica.

The true origin of flint—as it occurs in the chalk of Europe especially—has been, and still is, the subject of much discussion among microscopists and geologists. Mr. Bowerbank believes generally in the origin of flints (and some allied minerals) from sponges. Ehrenberg, finding in some flints abundance of infusorial animalculæ, suggests the origin of flint from aggregations of these silicious-shielded microzoaria.

Flint is an important article in many departments of manufactures. In the making of glass and porcelain it is almost indispensable; it is the ingredient which gives hardness and strength to those substances. Flint glass, called by the French *crystal*, owes its English name to the large proportion of flint which it always contains.

Since percussion caps have been largely used in the army, gun-flints have been to the same extent abandoned; but they used in former years to be an object of some importance. The best chalk-flints were selected: those which occur in nodules from 2 lbs. to 20 lbs. each. Hammers of various shapes were employed in the manufacture. The workman began by holding a flint on his left thigh, and breaking it with a hammer into several broad flattish pieces. He next held one of the pieces in his left hand, and chipped off the white envelope by a pointed hammer. By means of other hammers and a peculiar form of chisel he brought the pieces to the requisite size and shape for gun-flints. The gun-flint makers prided themselves on keeping their modes of proceeding secret, at least in France and Germany.

FLINTSHIRE. In this Welsh county, coal-measures occupy the coast of the æstuary of the Dee, and the coal-field, which has several seams of various thickness, extends across the county. Many pits are worked. Extensive lead mines are worked in the limestone, especially in the neighbourhood of Holywell. Copper, iron, zinc, and calamine are also found. At the town of *Flint* the neighbouring lead and coal mines, and the works for smelting the lead, give employment to a great number of persons, and furnish the principal articles for export. *Holywell* was formerly an inconsiderable village, but the minerals of the neighbouring country, and the manufactures connected with them, have rendered it a flourishing town. The mines supply lead, copper, calamine, and other ores, and there are smelting furnaces, copper works, brass works, wire works, &c. Steam power is used as well as the stream which issues from the well of St. Winifrede, from which the town derives its name.

FLINTY-SLATE, or *Silicious Schistus*, is a substance which is found of various colours, gray, blueish gray, and red; its structure is rather slaty; it contains about 75 per cent. of silica, the remainder being lime, magnesia, and oxide of iron. It is employed, when polished, for trying gold by a comparison of colours, and has thence obtained the name of *Touchstone*.

FLOOR-CLOTH MANUFACTURE. This useful production is made partly of hemp and partly of flax, the former being the cheaper of the two, but the latter better fitted to retain the oil and paint on the surface. As a means of avoiding the necessity for seams or joinings in the cloth, looms are constructed expressly for the weaving of the canvas of the greatest width likely to be required. As brought to the floor-cloth factories, the pieces of canvas have generally one of these scales of dimensions: a hundred yards long by six wide, a hundred and eight yards by seven, a hundred and thirteen yards by eight. The flax and hemp are spun, and the canvas woven, almost entirely in Scotland, chiefly at Dundee; and the degree of fineness is generally such as to present about 16 threads to the inch.

The canvas is cut into pieces varying from sixty to a hundred feet long: each of these pieces is stretched over a frame in a vertical position; and in most of the factories there is a large number of such frames, some a hundred feet long by eighteen or twenty high, others sixty feet long by twenty-four high. A wash of melted size is applied by means of a brush to each surface; and, while this is yet wet, the surface is well rubbed with a flat piece of pumice-stone, whereby the little irregularities of the canvas are worn down, and a foundation is laid for the oil and colour afterwards to be applied. The paint employed consists of the same mineral colours as those used in house-painting, and, like them, mixed with linseed oil; but it is much stiffer or thicker in consistence, and has very little turpentine added to it. The canvas receives many coatings on the back as well as the front, and is well dried and smoothed at intervals.

The printing of floor-cloth is conducted much on the same principle as that of paper-hangings for rooms, and that of 'colour-printing,' viz., the successive application of two or more blocks or engraved surfaces, each one giving a different part of the device from the others, and being supplied with paint of a different colour. As at present conducted, the pattern is engraved or cut upon blocks of wood, formed of pear-tree on one side and deal on the other: they are about fifteen inches square; and each block is to give the portion of the device which is to be in one particular colour.

The blocks (which we will suppose to be four for one pattern, red, yellow, blue, and green) being ready, and the prepared canvas spread out on a flat table, the printing commences. The paint (say red) is applied with a brush to the surface of a pad or cushion formed of flannel covered with floor-cloth; the block, held by a handle at the back, is placed face downwards on this cushion, and the layer of paint thus obtained is transferred to the surface of the canvas by pressing the block smartly down on the latter. A second impression is made in a similar way by the side of and close to the first; and so on throughout the length and breadth of the canvas; each impression being about fifteen inches square. The proper junction, or 'register,' of the successive impressions is aided by pins at the corners of the blocks. When the whole surface is thus printed with one colour, all the other three are similarly applied in succession. Such would likewise be the case if the number of colours was more than four: but the greater the number the greater would be the care necessary in adjusting the numerous partial impressions so as to insure a proper arrangement of the whole.

There will be some splendid specimens of floor-cloth at the approaching Exhibition; some made on the usual commercial principles, and some as curiosities.

FLORENCE. This beautiful city is more distinguished in fine arts than in industrial arts. In the province of Tuscany to which it belongs, the valleys produce corn, wine, oil, silk, and abundance of fruit; and the mountains are adorned with chestnut trees, and timber trees. The chief manufacture is straw plat. The other manufactures are pottery and china-ware, cloth, paper, leather, &c., mostly for home consumption.

A few details bearing indirectly on the industry of Florence, will be found under LEGHORN and TUSCANY.

FLO'RIDA. The productive and commercial features of Florida will be briefly noticed under UNITED STATES.

FLOTSAM, or FLOATSAM, in relation to the laws of shipping, are barbarous terms for such portion of the wreck of a ship and the cargo as continues floating on the surface of the water. *Jetsam* is goods which are cast into the sea, and there sink and remain under water. *Ligan* is goods sunk in the sea, but tied to a cork or buoy, in order that they may be found again. Flotsam, jetsam, and ligan belong to the king, or his grantee, if no owner appears to claim within a year after they are taken possession of by the persons otherwise entitled. They are accounted so far distinct from legal wreck, that by the king's grant of wreck, floatsam, jetsam, and ligan will not pass. Wreck is frequently granted by the king to lords of manors, as a royal franchise; but, if the king's goods are wrecked, he can claim them at any time, even after a year and a day.

FLOUR; FLOUR DRESSING. When corn is ground to the state of a powder, it becomes *meal;* and the particular kind of meal which is produced from wheat constitutes *flour*. The term flour is sometimes applied to other kinds of meal, but not usually.

The mode in which wheat is ground into flour by the crushing action of two circular stones is explained under WINDMILL; but we may here briefly speak of the mode of *dressing* flour by a smaller machine. Nearly all the flour dressing machines used in farm houses and for domestic purposes, comprise either a revolving fan or a perforated cylinder; a handle protrudes through the machine; and ground corn being placed inside, the centrifugal action occasioned by the rotation separates the flour from the husk or bran.

In the Board of Trade returns, wheat flour is converted from cwts. into qrs. at the rate of 392 lbs. per qr. In most of those returns the wheat and wheat flour are entered under one heading, so that we cannot separate them. [CORN TRADE.]

Dr. Normandy, in his recent work on adulteration, tells us that 'The physical characteristics of wheat flour of good quality are the following:—It has a dull white colour somewhat inclining to yellow; it should exhibit to the eye no trace of bran, even when pressed smooth, either with the hand, or with a polished surface. It should have a homogeneous appearance, and not lose more than from 6 to 12 per cent. after drying it in a stove. The less it loses by drying the better it is.' But it is often adulterated. The substances generally employed in the adulteration are potato starch, bean flour, Indian corn flour, and rice flour. These are innocuous, and the roguery consists only in selling them at wheat flour price; but wheat flour is also adulterated by alum, chalk, bone dust, and plaster. All these can be detected. The spurious substances introduced in making up the flour into bread are even more numerous. Some, however, are not commonly used, and others (as sulphate of copper) not resorted to in this country.

A singular mode of filling and weighing barrels of flour was made the subject of a patent in America a year or two ago. It is intended that the filling and weighing should both be effected by one operation. A trough is suspended on an axis; and beneath one end of the trough is a pair of scales, or rather the flour-pan of a pair of scales. The barrel is placed on the scale pan, and flour flows through the trough into the barrel. When the proper quantity has thus been precipitated, and the scale pan and barrel have descended by their weight, a small piece of apparatus catches to the trough, and tilts it into the contrary direction, so that no more flour can flow through it into the barrel.

FLOWERS, ARTIFICIAL. [ARTIFICIAL FLOWERS.]

FLUID, FLUIDITY, are terms applied to substances of which the parts possess perfect mobility amongst themselves. Fluids or liquids have been generally treated as incompressible bodies, but this is not strictly correct; for it is found that all to a certain degree yield to pressure. The term fluid has been extended to the supposed media through which the forces of electricity, galvanism, and magnetism act: but little that can be relied upon has been deduced from their supposed analogy with material fluids.

All ponderable matter exists either in the gaseous, fluid, or solid state; and most solids, when heat is applied to them, may be rendered fluid, or converted into liquids, under which circumstances mutual repulsion of particles takes the place of cohesion. As most solid bodies may be rendered fluid by heat, so many gaseous and fluid bodies are converted into solids by diminishing their temperature.

Those liquids which present an æriform state are often termed *elastic fluids*. Among the æriform fluids, however, those which are usually considered as permanently elastic are called gases; and the term elastic fluid is frequently confined to atmospherical air and the vapours which are produced from solids or liquids by the action of heat. Many of the gases, on being combined with one another and with other substances, form solids or liquids: thus, oxygen gas unites with metals and becomes solid; ammoniacal gas and muriatic gas unite and form the solid called muriate of ammonia; while oxygen and hydrogen gas unite to form water. Almost all gases are invisible; but several which are so when they exist alone, become visible on being mixed with one another.

The temperatures at which liquids become elastic fluids by the action of heat are very various; muriatic and nitric æthers boil, under the usual pressure of the atmosphere, at about 70° (Fahr.); sulphuric æther boils at 98°, and acetic æther at 160°; water boils at 212°, while mercury can be made to boil only at a temperature of 670°.

FLUOR SPAR, *Fluor, Fluate of Lime*, is a fluoride of calcium. It occurs colourless, and of almost every colour, as gray, purple, black, brown, red, yellow, green, and blue; in Derbyshire the last is the prevailing tint, and the massive fluor of that county is termed by the miners *Blue John*. It is frequently transparent, but more commonly only translucent. The massive varieties are nodular or amorphous. The blue and variegated fluor spar of Derbyshire is turned into various ornamental forms, candlesticks, &c.; that of Cornwall is used as a flux in the reduction of copper ore. Some very fine specimens are being wrought into the form of vases, &c., in Derbyshire for the approaching Exhibition. Pieces of fluor spar of great magnitude and beauty are to be seen in the British Museum.

FLUORIC ACID. [HYDROFLUORIC ACID.]

FLUORINE is a gas of a yellowish brown colour; its odour resembles that of a mixture of chlorine and burnt sugar, and, like chlorine, it has the power of destroying colour: it does not act upon glass. Like chlorine and oxygen, it appears to have a powerful affinity for metallic bodies, and for hydrogen; with this latter it forms hydrofluoric acid. The compounds which contain fluorine, when they do not possess acid properties, are termed *fluorides*. Many of the fluates and fluorides are employed in the arts

FLUTE. The use of this well-known musical instrument under different forms and names may be traced to the remotest periods of antiquity. The ancient flute had some sort of mouth-piece; it was double as well as single—that is, was often composed of two tubes, both played together. The old English flute was not unfrequently called the Flute à Bec; it had a mouth-piece, and was held in the manner of the clarionet. It had seven finger-holes, and no keys. The Flute à Bec was gradually superseded by that now in use, the German flute. This, at first simple in construction, in length about a foot and a half, and having only one key, has by dgrees been extended to twenty-seven inches, and has sometimes as many as a dozen keys, but usually eight; so that every kind of music within its compass, and adapted to the nature of a tube, may now be executed on this instrument. It is formed of any kind of hard wood, of ivory, and even of glass. The middle tones of the flute are the finest.

The *Octave Flute* is a small instrument an octave higher than the common flute. The best of these are provided with four keys.

Several patents for improvements, or supposed improvements, in the flute have been taken out within the last few years. In Mr. Dawson's patent, obtained in 1848, the flute is described as being constructed of two tubes, sliding air-tight one within the other. The outer tube is furnished with small lateral cells, each provided with two holes, one to be stopped by a key or finger, and the other to open communication with the inner tube, which is perforated with corresponding holes. The outer tube slides easily up and down over the inner one. The object of this arrangement is to vary the *pitch* or register of tone in the instrument. Another proposed arrangement by the same patentee is an elastic gutta percha valve to cover a long slit in the flute; the pressure of the finger on any part of the valve being equivalent to the action of a finger-key or a finger-hole in a common flute.

Mr. Clinton's patent, also obtained in 1848, describes a flute in which facilities are afforded for acting on some of the keys; when a key is far distant from the embouchure or mouth-hole, motion is given to it by means of a connecting rod, carried along the edges of some of the finger-holes; in such a way that whenever any of these holes is stopped by the fingers tho rod will be depressed, and the key to which it is connected acted upon. There is also a new arrangement for producing the notes B and C, under certain difficult combinations of notes.

Mr. Carté patented several improvements in the construction of flutes in 1850. They do not involve any change in the general form of the instrument; but relate to new arrangements of the metallic keys, which facilitate the performance of rapid passages and 'shakes,' under circumstances which are somewhat difficult in the ordinary flutes.

FLUTE-STOP, on the organ, is a range of wooden pipes, tuned in unison with the diapason. It generally produces a very successful imitation of the instrument whence its name is derived.

FLUX, in chemistry and metallurgy, is any substance employed to assist the reduction of ores or metallic compounds to their metallic state. Limestone is employed as a flux for clay-iron ore, and fluor spar for copper ore. The alkaline substance called Black Flux is doubly useful in smelting ores; the carbonate of potash combines with the earthy parts of the ore; while the charcoal unites with the oxygen of the metallic oxides, and, carbonic acid being formed and expelled, the metal is reduced and melts. White Flux, or carbonate of potash, disintegrates stony matter, as alumina and silica, separates acids and sulphur from metals, and dissolves many metallic oxides. Argol, or bitartrate of potash, is much used as a flux. Charcoal, glass, wax, tar, pitch, fat, oil, gum, sugar, and starch, are all occasionally employed for this purpose.

FLYING BRIDGE. This consists usually of a boat or other vessel, which, being attached by a rope to a buoy moored in the middle of a river, is made by the action of the current to move across on an arc of a circle of which the buoy is the centre. The buoy being securely anchored in the middle of the river, a rope or chain leads from thence to the mast of the boat, which is at a distance from the head equal to one-third of the vessel's length; then, the keel of the boat being kept at a certain angle with the direction of the current, a resolved part of the pressure of the water against one side of the boat will cause the latter to describe an arc of a circle across the river. In a rapid current it may be impossible to make the boat move up the ascending arc of its path; in which case a boat near one bank may, by means of a cable made fast at a point directly opposite on the other bank, be allowed to describe a descending arc quite across the river. A triangular raft having its front parallel to the direction of the current, and being connected by a ring with a rope stretched tightly across the river, may, by a resolved force of the current, be impelled directly to the opposite bank; and, on reversing its position, the raft may be impelled across in a contrary direction. A boat running by a ring at one end on a rope may, by being kept in an oblique position, in like manner be *sheered* across the river.

On broad rivers, and when objects of great bulk and weight, as horses, carriages, or artillery, are to be conveyed across, two boats or barges placed in parallel positions, and carrying a platform extending between their exterior gunwales, are employed. Each vessel is provided with a mast, which may be from 20 to 30 feet in height.

In military manœuvres, flying bridges will continue to be frequently useful; but for general inland purposes steam-bridges are now coming into use over broad rivers.

FLYING MACHINES. All that need be said in this work on these hitherto futile contrivances, will be found under BALLOON.

FOILS. Very thin leaves of metal are often called by this name; they are placed under artificial gems to heighten the brilliancy. They are made of tin, copper, tinned copper, or silvered copper. They are left white for imitation diamonds, but are coloured for imitation rubies, sapphires, &c. The coloured foils are prepared by coating the white foil with coloured varnish. The best white foil is made by coating a plate of copper with a layer of silver, and then rolling it into sheets in the flatting mill. The principal colours used by artists are employed, mixed with mastic, spirit, and drying oil, to form the coloured varnishes.

FONT. The form of the font in churches is usually hexagonal, similar to the form of the baptistery, in which fonts were originally placed. Fonts also occur both of a circular and a square form. They are usually shaped like a cup, with a solid stem, or supported on columns; the top is hollowed out for the water, and the sides and stem are often highly enriched with ornaments, sculptured figures, and with colour and gilding. In many instances a flight of steps forms a base, and even the sides of these steps are carved with pannels, having quatrefoils and rosettes sunk within them. It was usual to cover the basin of the font with a wooden lid, and there are some of these remaining of a pyramidal or spire-like form, richly carved and designed, with a profusion of shafts, buttresses, and tracery piled up to the apex.

Among the fonts especially worthy of note may be mentioned those of Porchester church, which is like the circular stone mouth of the well in the atrium of a Roman house; of Lincoln cathedral, which is square, on five columns, one being in the centre: of Lowestoff in Suffolk, and Loddor in Norfolk, both remarkable for their richness of decoration; of Winchester cathedral, very curious and ancient; and of East Dereham in Norfolk.

FOOD. All organized bodies are nourished by the introduction into their internal structures of materials from without, which form the numerous kinds of *food* so familiar to us. Although man derives his food from both the vegetable and animal kingdoms, it is found that the animals which are consumed by man derive their nourishment from the vegetable kingdom alone, so that plants are the true source of all the food both of man and the lower animals. The principal constituents of the human body, as well as all other animal bodies, are the organic elements, carbon, hydrogen, oxygen, and nitrogen; and it is the waste of these substances which is constantly going on that it is the object of food to supply. Plants, however, do not supply the animal with carbon, hydrogen, oxygen, and nitrogen, in a simple form, but as secretions of the vegetable tissues known to chemists under the names of gluten, fibrin, albumen, casein, &c. The plant itself does not derive its food from the organic elements in a pure form, but combined with each other: thus, carbonic acid gas, consisting of carbon and oxygen; water, composed of oxygen and hydrogen; and ammonia, of hydrogen and nitrogen, are the great sources of vegetable nutrition, and consequently of the various secretions used as the food of man and animals. Not only do these secretions serve to build up the fabric of the human body, and to supply the daily waste of tissue which is going on, but they also supply materials for keeping up animal heat within the system.

The reader will find a familiar exposition of this subject, and of the relative value of albumen, fibrin, casein, starch, sugar, fat, oils, acids, spices, condiments, &c., in Dr. Lankester's 'Food of Man.'

FORCE, in mechanical and scientific matters, is a term employed to denote the unknown cause of any mechanical effect. Thus the cause of motion and the cause of pressure are both *forces:* again, difference of effects must be attributed to difference in the producing causes: thus, greater or less velocity, and greater or less pressure, are both attributed to differences in the causes of velocity or pressure. But, on the other hand, effects which are the same in one point of view may differ in another; thus, bodies of different weights, let fall from the same heights above the ground, will strike the ground with the same velocities, but with different degrees of effect upon the substance which they strike.

When force, in the sense of pressure, is considered as the cause of motion, we must take into account both the element *time*, and also the *quantity of matter* which is moved. The connection of pressure, velocity created by pressure, and time which pressure takes to create velocity, as deduced from experiment, are contained in the following results:

1. The same pressure continually acting upon a given mass for different times produces velocities which are proportional to the times, and augments velocity by equal portions in equal times.

2. The same pressure applied to different masses of matter (that is to different weights of matter), during the same time, produces velocities which are inversely proportional to those masses.

3. The velocities of falling bodies is accelerated by 32.19 feet in every second: and in that proportion for all other times.

Very exact calculations and experiments on all these points are of great importance to machinists and engineers, who have to provide force adequate to the kind and quantity of the work to be done.

FORESTS; FOREST-SCIENCE. A forest is a large tract of ground overgrown with trees and underwood. As civilization and population advance, forests lessen in every country. It has been notably so in Great Britain. Ireland has few forests. In Norway the mountains are covered with wood; birch, maple, pine, and fir, forming immense forests. The fir sometimes attaining a height of 160 feet, is in great estimation for masts and building timber. In the regions of moderate elevation are aspens. The good lands have some fine forests of oaks. The forests of Sweden are similar to those of Norway. In Denmark the existing forests cover but a small area. The timber of Holland consists of beech, fir, poplar, and ash; willow grows along the canals, and the coppices are of maple, ash, hornbeam, birch, and beech, with a slight portion of oak-bushes. In Germany the forests are estimated to cover nearly one-third of the whole surface; they comprise most of the usual varieties of timber-trees. Switzerland is abundantly wooded, particularly with the cone-bearing trees. France has many fine forests, though hardly sufficient for the consumption of a country where wood is the chief combustible. Italy, Spain, and Portugal, are all rather deficient in forests. European Turkey has fine forests of oak, elm, pine, plum, apple, pear, cherry, apricot, maple, sycamore, walnut, chestnut, and beech trees.

Of all the countries of Europe, Russia is the most abundantly provided with timber; and her forests would be an almost inexhaustible source of wealth, if it were possible for the government effectually to protect them from destruction. In 1802 regulations for the preservation of the forests were established; but such is their extent and that of the country, that it is next to impossible wholly to prevent the waste of wood. There are 200,000,000 of acres exclusively covered with pine and other cone-bearing trees, without counting oaks, maples, beech, poplar, hornbeam, and birch. Poland is, for its size, nearly as well supplied with forests as Russia.

In Asia Minor, Mount Taurus is covered with forests of cypress, juniper, and savines. Oaks and fir abound in the forests along the Black Sea. Trees of all these kinds occur in the Caucasus. Persia has few forests, except amongst the mountains near the Caspian. Arabia has none. Central Asia is too little known to yield us much information respecting its forests. Siberia has some vast forests of the harder kinds of trees. China, Japan, and Corea, all possess immense forests in their more mountainous districts. India, both within and beyond the Ganges, is rich in wood. There are whole forests of the bamboo, which sometimes attain a height of 60 feet. Cocoa-nut and palms of all kinds cover large tracts. Here are woods of oak, fir, cypress, and poplar; there of mangoes, banyan-trees, uvarias, robinias, sandal-wood, &c. Nearly all the eastern islands seem to be tolerably rich in forests, Australia perhaps excepted.

In Africa there are some spots in which vegetation is rich beyond description. Thus Senegambia, Guinea, and Congo, are covered with forests, which consist of the baobab, of palms, robinias, sycamores, sandal-wood, tamarinds, bananas, oranges, limes, and pomegranates; there are also cocoa-nut trees in great abundance. The tamarind and cedar, which grow in the greatest profusion on the borders of the Congo, furnish timber of the finest quality. Abyssinia has abundant woods. The Atlas Mountains are covered with magnificent forests, producing a variety of oaks, the mastic tree, the cypress, &c. The kingdom of Bornou has immense forests, and the date-palm abounds there.

America is, of all parts of the world, the most thickly covered with wood. Canada contains immense forests, as do most of the British North American territories. The United States are abundantly wooded, the cleared land even in some of the Atlantic states being inconsiderable when compared with that still covered with the primitive forests. Oregon, Mexico, and Texas, have all splendid forests. The West India islands are for the most part only moderately wooded. In South America the Caracas possesses inexhaustible forests; and so indeed do most of the South American states. The forest region of the river Amazon and of the upper Orinoco, according to Humboldt, covers an area of about 719,000 square miles.

There are no laws respecting the forests of England among the laws attributed to the Conqueror; but after the Norman Conquest the royal forests were guarded with much greater strictness. In later times these forests gradually sunk in importance; and our government department of 'Woods and Forests' shews how little benefit the royal forests produce to the state generally.

In Germany a distinct branch of education has become established, called 'Forest Science.' In the Forest Academies are taught botany generally, including vegetable physiology, mineralogy, zoology, chemistry, surveying, mensuration, mechanics, the methods of resisting the encroachments of sands, draining and embanking, together with the care and chase of game; and also the laws and regulations of forest administration. In Prussia and other German states, in France, and in Russia, similar studies are carried on. The wood from forests is applied to the various purposes of house-building, ship-building, mill and wheel work, turnery, ornaments, fuel, &c.; and the study of its fitness for these purposes forms a part of forest science.

In England, where no such schools exist, knowledge has accumulated from out-door experience, rather than school education. In English timber plantations, as crooked pieces of large oaks are of value in ship-building, the side branches are not taken off higher than fifteen or twenty feet from the ground, and where trees have plenty of room, as in hedge-rows or parks, this may be judicious, but in close plantations it is of advantage to have a long stem without branches. In France and Germany the branches are always cut off to the height of 30 or 40 feet.

FORFARSHIRE. The Grampian Hills, in this Scottish county, are of granite, having frequently topazes and rock crystal in its cavities and fissures. There are also limestone slate, porphyry, and lead ore. In the Strathmore district there is a shell-marl, which is procured in large quantities from beneath beds of peat-moss at the bottom of several ancient lochs which have been drained chiefly for this purpose; it is dragged up by means of iron scoops, worked from boats, and is used for manure. Iron and pipe-clay occur in this district. The maritime district contains beds of sandstone and extensive quarries of limestone. Fragments of granite from the Grampians lie strewed about the lower ground. Coal of an inferior quality has been traced a little to the west of Aberbrothwick. The poor, who cannot obtain coal without difficulty, procure for fuel peat, brushwood, broom, and furze.

It may in general be stated that almost every useful improvement has been adopted in the modes and implements of agriculture in this county. Inclosures are made chiefly by stone dykes in the highlands, and by quick thorn hedges in the plains of Strathmore and towards the sea. The chief crops are oats, barley, and wheat. Much of the oat crop is consumed by horses and exported from the county. Oatmeal porridge, eaten with milk or beer, forms the breakfast and supper of the labouring classes, among whom oat cakes are still much used as bread. Considerable quantities of wheat are annually exported to London and other ports, and some American, Danzig, and other foreign wheats are imported to mix with that produced in the county. Barley is much used in the county for broth, porridge, and cakes. There are about 40,000 acres of natural pasture. The grazing and stall feeding of cattle are prosecuted to a much greater extent than the rearing, large numbers being brought into the county to be fed and prepared for the butcher.

The deep-sea fishing off the eastern coast is very productive, and large quantities of salmon and smaller fish are taken in the Frith of Tay, and at the mouths of several streams from thence to the North Esk. Cod, ling, herring, haddocks, turbots, sole, skate, sprats, smelts, lobsters, crabs, mussels, and fresh water fish are all abundant. The chief manufactures of the county are represented by those of its busiest town. [DUNDEE.]

FORK. The manufacture of this useful implement is briefly noticed under CUTLERY.

FOSSIL COPAL occurs in irregular pieces in clayey soils. Its colour is yellowish or dull brown; nearly opaque; specific gravity 1.046. When heated it yields an aromatic odour, and melts into a limpid fluid.

FOSSILS. The time may arrive when fossils or organic remains will be largely employed in the arts. At present they are chiefly objects of scientific geological investigation, and as such they do not come within the range of this work.

FOUNDATION, the lower part or courses of the basement walls or piers of a building. In foundations it is of the utmost importance to prevent the settlement of the walls in an unequal manner; this can only be done by making the earth on which the foundation is set equally solid throughout its whole extent. Concrete composed of gravel or shingle and hot lime is often used to form a solid bearing for the footings of foundations. The greatest care and judgment are required in making foundations for heavy superstructures, for if the piles should be of a bad quality, and the ground in which they are driven of a very loose and boggy nature, the same catastrophe which occurred at the New Custom House in London may be expected to take place. In this building it was found necessary to remove the piles and loose earth, and form a solid concrete foundation.

FOUNDING. This important mechanical art embraces all the operations of reducing ores, and of smelting and casting metals. There are various branches of the art, and some difference prevails in the minor details of the processes, as in iron, brass, and bronze founding, in casting guns and cannon, types for printing, and bell founding. The art has been known and practised from the earliest ages.

The preparation of the principal ores is described under the names of their metals, such as COPPER, IRON, &c. The furnaces are described under FURNACE.

Founding is practised either in casting any quantity of metal in the solid, or with a core (by means of which the metal is preserved of a determined thickness or substance), or in plain casting. Before any article can be cast in metal it is necessary that a *model* of it be prepared. The models must be made of various substances; clay or wax, or sand with clay, are those usually employed, but they may also be made of wood, stone, or any other material. Upon those models *moulds* must be made. These are commonly composed of plaster of Paris, mixed with brick-dust, sometimes sand, or sand with a mixture of cow-hair. For moulds for iron and brass work a yellowish sharp sand is preferred, which is prepared by mixing it with water and then rolling it on a flat board till it is well kneaded and fit for use. If the article is cylindrical, or of a form that admits of it, it is moulded and cast in two pieces; these two parts are then carefully joined together, and the edges or seams carefully cleaned. For the smaller class of works, instead of running the metal at once from a large furnace, earthen crucibles are used, into which the metal is thrown in small pieces: the crucible is placed in a strong heat in a close stove, and as the metal is melted and sinks more is added till the vessel is full. It is then lifted out by means of iron instruments adapted to the purpose, and the metal is poured from it into the moulds, in which channels or ducts for receiving it have been previously made.

In noticing the different ways of casting, mention has been made of one in which a core is used. The *core*, as its name denotes, is a part or portion situated within the body of the cast; and its purpose is to form a centre to the work by which the thickness or substance of the metal may be regulated. In coring, the mould is first made complete; into this, clay or wax, or any other fit substance or material, is then squeezed or pressed in a layer of uniform thickness; in large works it is usually from half an inch to an inch thick. This layer represents the metal. The mould, if in parts, is then put together, the above-mentioned layer being left within it, and into the open space in the centre a composition (usually of plaster of Paris with other substances mixed with it) is introduced, and made to adhere to the clay or wax, or rather is filled up to it. This is the core, and it is often made to occupy the whole interior of the mould. When this is *set*, or dry, the mould is taken to pieces, and the material which has been made to represent the metal removed. The mould is then again put carefully together ronnd its core or nucleus, the two portions being secured from contact by stops and keys properly arranged for that purpose. The mould and core are dried to dissipate moisture; and large moulds are strengthened with iron hoops. Channels or ducts are made for the entrance of the melted metal; and others are also made for allowing the air to escape as the melted metal enters the mould; these are called vents. With respect to placing the mould, it is only important to secure a sufficient inclination of plane from the mouth of the furnace to the mould that the metal may run easily and uninterruptedly, and not have time to grow cool and therefore sluggish. The usual method in bronze works of large size is to bury the mould in a pit a little below the level of the furnace, and by ramming sand firmly round it to ensure its not being affected by any sudden or violent shock, or by the weight of the metal running into it. When everything is ready and the metal found to be in a state fit for running, the orifice or mouth of the furnace (which is usually plugged with clay and sand) is opened, when the metal descends, and in a few minutes the mould is filled. The metal is allowed to run till it overflows the mouths of the channels into the mould. The work is then left to cool, after which the mould is scraped or knocked off and the cast undergoes the necessary processes (such as cleaning, chasing, &c.) to render it fit for the purpose designed.

Large bells and *statues* are cast in the way first described. *Brass ordnance* is always cast solid. The model is made round a nucleus of wood called a spindle, and the mould of loam and sand made over it. When this is perfectly dry, the model and spindle within are removed, and the mould is well dried or baked. When ready for casting, it is placed upright in the pit, and the metal is allowed to run into it till filled. What is called a dead head is left at the upper and smaller or mouth end of the gun, which presses the metal down, and prevents its becoming porous as it settles and cools. After a few days the mould is knocked off, and the gun is ready for finishing. The dead head is turned off, and the boring, which is an operation requiring great care is effected. [BORING.]

After the founding, the metal cast is often finished by chasing, burnishing, lacquering, plating, or gilding.

One of the largest cylinders, cast and bored in iron, is that employed at the Mostyn colliery in Flintshire. It was made at the Haigh Foundry at Wigan in 1848. It is 17 feet long, by 8 feet 4 inches in diameter; it weighs 22 tons; and the quantity of metal brought to a liquid state for the purpose of casting was 30 tons.

A silver statue was cast at Paris in 1850. In the preceding year M. Pradier exhibited at the Luxembourg a bronze statue of Sappho, which was much admired for its beauty; and a silver copy of this statue was prepared in 1850, as a prize for a sort of Art Union lottery. The founding was entrusted to M. Simonet, who has produced many beautiful specimens in this department of Art. The weight of silver used was about four thousand ounces.

The largest cast statue of recent times is the allegorical figure of *Bavaria*, placed in front of the Rühmeshalle on the Theresien meadow near Munich. The figure is 63 feet high, and stands on a granite base 30 feet high; so that the wreath held in the uplifted hand of the figure is nearly 100 feet from the ground. A winding staircase leads entirely up the interior of the statue. It is said that no fewer than 26 musicians were placed within the head of the statue, on the occasion of the inauguration. The length of the forefinger, 38 inches, will give an idea of the size of the statue. The statue was modelled by the great sculptor Schwanthaler, who hastened his death by his intense application to it. The founding or casting was entrusted to Stiglmayer; but as he also died, the work was carried out to a successful completion by his pupil Ferdinand Miller. The statue was cast in many pieces, one of which required 380 cwt. of molten bronze!

FOUNTAIN. A fountain is a jet or jets of water, flowing either naturally out of the earth, or from structures formed by art. Artificial fountains consist of water flowing from statues, vases, or architectural buildings combined with sculptured figures and other ornamental decorations. At Pompeii not only the streets but even the private houses were decorated with fountains. At Rome, the proper distribution of the rivers which flowed through her aqueducts was a matter of great importance, intrusted to the care of an officer of very high rank. The aqueducts were each charged with a certain number of pipes of supply; and no new pipe could be inserted without a special application to the emperor. Those whose means of interest were insufficient to obtain a private pipe, were obliged to fetch water from the public fountains.

Some of the cities of Italy and the East are adorned with fountains, which are no less agreeable to the eye than useful to the inhabitants. Many of the fountains of Rome are highly decorated, of great magnitude, and very varied in their mode of ejecting the waters with which they are supplied from the existing aqueducts.

The city of Paris is well supplied with fountains, many of which are elegantly designed. The fountains of Versailles and St. Cloud in France, and the fountains at Wilhelmshöhe near Cassel, are the largest in Europe. London has no fountains worthy of notice except the two large ones in Trafalgar Square, which are supplied from a very deep artesian well; and these have been severely criticised as works of art.

The great fountain, planned by Mr. Paxton for the Duke of Devonshire at Chatsworth, is in all probability the loftiest in the world. It presents one single jet that rises to a perpendicular height of 270 feet. The pressure is derived from a previous descent of water from a height of 380 feet. A reservoir has been formed at that height, in some hills which bound the eastern side of the park; and more than half a mile of piping is employed to convey the water from the reservoir to the fountain.

FOURCROY, ANTOINE-FRANCOIS DE. This eminent French chemist deserves our grateful notice for the aid which his discoveries afforded to many practical arts. He was born in 1755, and died in 1809, after having filled many important offices. Among his other discoveries, Fourcroy shewed that the salts of magnesia and ammonia have the property of uniting together and forming double salts. His dissertation on the sulphate of mercury contains some good observations. The same remark applies to his paper on the action of ammonia on the sulphate, nitrate, and muriate of mercury; and he first described the double salts which are formed. We may mention the process of Fourcroy and Vauquelin for obtaining pure barytes, by exposing nitrate of barytes to a red heat, as a good one. They discovered the existence of phosphate of magnesia in the bones, of phosphorus in the brain, and in the milts of fishes, and a considerable quantity of saccharine matter in the bulb of the common onion, which, by undergoing a kind of spontaneous fermentation, was converted into manna.

FRAMEWORK KNITTERS. [Hosiery Manufacture.]

FRANCE. This important country has a varied though perhaps not very rich supply of mineral wealth. Granite, sienite, porphyry, variolites, and serpentine are quarried in some of the departments; lava in others; marble, limestone, and slate in others; while various parts of France yield lithographic stone, porcelain clay, brick clay, pipe clay, gypsum, chalk, millstones, and sandstone. Of metals, the chief ores are those of iron, manganese, antimony, lead, and copper. Minute traces of gold and silver are met with. Thirty-three of the departments contain excellent coal. Anthracite, asphaltum, bitumen, petroleum, alum, rock-salt, and lime, are also obtained. There are about 500 coal-pits in France, from which four to five million tons of coal are annually extracted.

France has always been considered one of the most agricultural countries in Europe, chiefly on account of the numerous publications relating to this subject; but in most parts of the country, the progress towards a general adoption of improved methods of cultivation is very slow. The northern part of France, on the confines of Belgium, and the part in the immediate neighbourhood of Paris, are the best cultivated. In most other parts, except where maize is cultivated, the old system of two or three crops of corn and a fallow is generally adopted.

The arable land of France is now estimated at 23,000,000 hectares, which (taking the hectare =2.47 acres nearly) are about equal to 56,810,000 acres English measure. In recent years there have been about 14,000,000 hectares under corn culture, yielding 180,000,000 hectolitres (a hectolitre = about 22 gallons, or 2¾ bushels) of wheat, oats, rye, meslim, and maize; the wheat being ⅗ and oats ¼. The corn culture has not increased much during the present century; but the cultivation of the vine, of the artificial grasses, of pulse, and, above all, of potatoes, has much increased. Beet-root is extensively grown for the manufacture of sugar. The esculent roots and table vegetables are common. Flax and hemp are cultivated in various parts of the country, and to a considerable extent; hops, tobacco, and madder, in a small degree; and colza and rape, for oil, are grown in the north.

The vine is one of the most important objects of cultivation in France. The amount of land occupied by this culture is about 5,000,000 English acres. The average yearly produce is nearly 1,000,000,000 of English gallons, of which about one-sixth is converted into brandy. The annual produce of the vineyards is estimated at about 30,000,000*l.* sterling, of which at least nine-tenths are consumed in France. Of fruits and of timber-trees France has a very fair supply.

The coasts abound in fish of various kinds, the taking of which occupies a number of hands: the oyster, the herring, the mackerel, and especially the sardine or pilchard, are the chief objects of attention to the fishermen of the coasts of the Channel and the Atlantic: the tunny and the anchovy to the fishermen of the Mediterranean.

Every branch of industry in France has undergone vast improvement since the peace of 1815. The energies of the nation being turned from war to domestic employments, speedily repaired the evils which France had suffered from so long a struggle. The woollen manufacture has increased materially: the increased quantity of wool used is partly furnished by the increased number of sheep bred, partly by the importation of foreign wool. The quality of the home-grown wool has been improved by the introduction of foreign breeds, and the Cashmere goat has been naturalized on the slopes of the Pyrenees. The cotton manufacture has increased since 1812 in a greater proportion than that of wool, and the process of manufacture and the fineness and excellence of the fabrics have undergone great improvements. The north and east of France are the chief seats of this manufacture. Printed calicoes are made at Rouen and Bauvais; but especially at Colmar, Mühlhausen, and other places in the department of Haut Rhin, the printed cottons of which are much approved in the German markets for the vividness of their colours (especially the Turkey red), and their other qualities. The silk manufacture is carried on chiefly in the south. The brilliancy of the French silks has been increased by the substitution of Prussian-blue for indigo as a dye.

A part of the raw silk required for these various fabrics is grown in France. Linens, damasks, sail-cloth, and lace, are made to some considerable extent.

The working of the metals has much increased, especially iron. The quality and appearance of the steel and wrought-iron goods have much improved; yet the quality of the French iron is inferior, and it maintains its ground against the Russian and Swedish iron only by means of protecting duties. In the manufacture of clocks and watches France is almost equal to Switzerland; and for chronometers and instruments for scientific purposes it is not surpassed by any country. The inventions of the French chemists and the improvement of chemical science have done much in producing with economy and expedition the many chemical agents employed in the various branches of manufacture, and particularly dyeing. The commoner sort of French earthenware has much improved in beauty of design. Fine porcelain is made at Sèvres, Paris, and Limoges. The cut-glass is nearly equal to that of England in beauty of workmanship, and it is perhaps superior in elegance of form.

The means of internal communication in France are much inferior to those of Great Britain. The roads are divisible into those maintained by the central government, and designated *Routes Royales* and those which are kept up at the cost of the several departments to which they belong, and designated *Routes Départementales.* Besides these there are *Chemins Vicinaux*, or bye-roads. The *Routes Royales* extend about 22,000 miles. Posting and the mail service along these roads are under the control of the government. Diligences run on all these roads. The departmental roads are rather greater in length than the royal, but are mostly in bad condition. The inland water communication is carried on by means of the great rivers and by the canals which have been formed. Many of the rivers have been improved for navigation; and the artificial canals are rather numerous. The canals present a united length of about 1,600 miles. The railway system of communication has not made considerable progress in France; but lines have been laid out along most of the great travelling routes in the kingdom.

The following important statistics of French commerce, shipping, and manufactures have recently appeared — mostly referring to the year 1850. There exist in France 5,607 manufactories of various denominations in which steam machinery is employed. This machinery is worked by means of boilers, the number of which is 9,288, and of which 8,776 were made in French establishments. These boilers represent a force of 65,120 horses' power, calculating the horse power as 75 kilogrammes (180 lb.) raised one metre (1 yard) per second; they represent the force that would be produced by 195,361 draught horses and 1,367,530 labourers. The length of railway now open for traffic is 2,171 kilometres (1,300 miles), on which are employed 725 locomotives. The number of steam trading vessels is 279; their tonnage amounts to 40,098 tons; and they are propelled by 502 engines, constituting a total power of 22,893 horses. The merchandise transported by these vessels amounted to 730,948 tons. The progress of steam navigation in France is indicated in the following facts:—In 1835 there were 75 steamers, by which 1,038,916 passengers were carried, and 88.140 tons of merchandise; in 1840 there were 211 steamers, 2,547,116 passengers, and 485,539 tons; in 1845, there were 259 steamers, 3,461,336 passengers, and 696,066 tons; and in the last year there were 279 steamers, 2,808,886 passengers, and 730,948 tons. The total number of steam engines employed by land or sea in France amounts to nearly 7,000, and they constitute together a force of 110,178 steam horses, or 330,535 draught horses.

In 1850 there were 12,335 vessels engaged in the import trade, and 11,587 in the export. About 513 kilometres of new railway are expected to be opened in 1851. In 1849 the iron foundries produced 700,000 tons of iron.

In 1848 we imported the following among other commodities from France:—

Corn	390,000	qrs.
Flour and meal	370,000	cwts.
Gloves ..	3,000,000	pairs.
Madder ..	54,000	cwts.
Prunes ..	34,000	cwts.
Clover seed ..	29,000	cwts.
Silk	1,350,000	lbs.
Silk goods ..	720,000	lbs.
Skins and furs	640,000	
Brandy ..	2,360,000	gallons.
Wine ..	660,000	gallons.

In the same year Great Britain sold to France:—

Brass and copper goods ..	150,000*l.*
Coals	570,000 tons.
Hardware and cutlery ..	51,000*l.*
Machinery	35,000*l.*
Silk goods	57,000*l.*
Wool and woollens ..	194,000*l.*

and other goods to the aggregate value of 1,024,521*l.* The amount was more than double this in 1846 and 1847; for 1848, being a year of revolution, presented unfavourable commercial results.

Of the important Expositions of Industry which have been held in France in past years, a brief account has been given in the INTRODUCTION. Everything affords ground for believing that France will hold a distinguished position at the approaching display in Hyde Park. All the goods from all the departments have been collected at one spot in Paris, where they have been inspected by a jury, who would not suffer any specimens to be exhibited but such as will reflect credit on the manufacturers. From Paris they have been forwarded by railway to Dunkirk, and thence by sea to London. The following has been announced to be the number and distribution of the exhibitors. Of the eighty-six departments of France nine only are without intended exhibitors. In the department of the Seine there are 1,730 exhibitors; Rhone, 96; Nord, 56; Seine Inférieure, 53; Marne, 47; Loire Inférieure, 33; Gard, 25; Bas Rhin, 23; Haut Rhin, 22; Ardennes, 20; Gironde, 18; Oise, 18; Seine et Oise, 18; Haute Vienne, 17; Pas de Calais, 16; Loire, 14; Seine et Marne, 14; Ardêche, 12; Aube, 12; Haute Garonne, 12; Hérault, 12; Jura, 12; Maine et Loire, 10; Sarthe, 10. The following is the analysis, according to the classification decided on by the English committee, of the 2,481 persons declaring an intention to exhibit above mentioned:—Section 1. Raw materials, 485; 2. Machinery and tools, 554; 3. Manufactured productions, 1,088; 4. Plastic arts and models 354. Even Algeria will take part in this industrial display.

FRANKFORT. With the exception of Sachsenhausen and its 5000 inhabitants, who are principally agriculturists, gardeners, and day-labourers, the citizens of Frankfort-on-the Main derive their subsistence from commerce, money operations, and manufactures. It is a place of considerable transit for German and foreign produce. The chief articles of trade are wines, English, French, and Italian goods, Bavarian timber, German wools, colonial produce, and German manufactures. The chief manufactures are carpets, galloon, tobacco, cards, cottons, silks, printer's black, &c.

An establishment formed here for the sale of Bohemian glass, contains some of the best examples of that manufacture. The works which supply the stock are situated at Hayda, and the activity with which they are conducted here and elsewhere is necessarily a means of many improvements and novelties. Some of the examples of verre perruche are very beautiful; this is a production in which glass of different colours is joined together. There are also many examples of enamel on colourless glass, presenting forms and designs of much taste. There is in this city an establishment for the extensive sale of the productions of the iron-foundry of Hanau, comprehending a very extensive assortment of objects of utility and ornament—as candlesticks, branches, paper-weights; vases, tazzas, and every other ornamental object which the French artists and manufacturers produce in bronze. The finest manufacture, that in gray iron, is also brought to a high degree of excellence; this class of productions comprehends every ornamental article in which iron filligree is in anywise available, and so fine is the workmanship in this hair wire material, that iron, equivalent in value to 1*l.* sterling, may be manufactured into a variety of articles amounting in value to 1000*l.*

Many curiosities from Frankfort will appear at the forthcoming Exhibition.

There is another Frankfort, called *Frankfort on the Oder.* The manufactures of the town consist of wines, mustard, brandy, tobacco, sugar, gloves, stockings, linen, leather, &c.: its trade is extensive, and the three periodical fairs, instituted in 1253, are well frequented, particularly by Polish dealers.

FRANKINCENSE is the produce of the *Abies excelsa*, *Pinus abies*, or common Spruce Fir, from which it either exudes spontaneously or more abundantly from incisions in the bark. When it first flows out it is liquid, but on exposure to the air concretes, and is collected during autumn and winter. It occurs in two states, in tears, and in large irregular lumps or compressed cakes. When recent, the colour should be white, or only inclining to yellow, subdiaphonous, soft, tenacious, and glutinous: by the action of time it becomes hard, and even friable, the colour having deepened into an orange hue. By the heat of the hand it softens, and by a higher temperature liquefies. It possesses a turpentine-like odour and taste. It is insoluble in water, but completely soluble in alcohol with the aid of heat. Frankincense consists of two kinds of resin mixed with oil of turpentine. By melting it in water, and straining it through strong cloths, it is deprived of much of its oil, when it is termed *Pix arida* or Burgundy Pitch.

It is scarcely now used internally, but is irritant and diuretic. Externally it is useful in the composition of plasters.

FRAXININ is a neutral principle obtained from the bark of the *Fraxinus excelsior.* It is obtained in slender hexagonal prisms, which are unalterable in the air. Fraxinin is very soluble in water and in alcohol, and only slightly so in æther. It has a very bitter taste and has neither an alkaline nor acid reaction.

FREEZING MIXTURES. Freezing is the solidification of fluid bodies by the abstraction of the heat necessary to their fluid form. Freezing mixtures are such as produce cold by the liquefaction of their solid ingredient. Such mixtures reduce the temperature of substances immersed in them on the principle of the transfer of heat, which always takes place from hotter to colder bodies when exposed to each other.

The process used by confectioners for producing cold is by the mixture of ice and common salt, both of which in liquefying absorb so much heat, or, in other words, produce as much cold, as will reduce the thermometer from the usual temperature to zero of Fahrenheit, or even rather below it. If however freshly fallen snow be used instead of ice, then the fluidity is more suddenly produced, and the cold is more intense. It is found that ice or snow, though exceedingly convenient substances for the production of artificial cold, are by no means necessary to it. Any salts which dissolve rapidly in water, finely powdered, are powerful freezing mixtures. Mixtures of muriate of ammonia and nitrate of potash, and of these with phosphate of soda, act strongly in this way; and so do various other salts.

The following are useful freezing mixtures, with the temperature which they produce:—

—Salt 1 part, snow 2 parts...... — 5° Fahr.
—Salt 2, mur. of ammonia 1, snow 5—12° „
—Salt 10, snow 24, mur. of ammonia 5, nit. of pot. 5 .... —18° „
—Snow 3, dilute sulph. acid 2 .. —23° „
—Snow 5, concen. mur. acid 8 .. —27° „
—Snow 4, concent. nit. acid 7 .. —30° „
—Snow 5, chloride of calcium 4 . —40° „
—Snow 2, chloride of calcium 3 . —50° „
—Snow 3, fused potash 4...... —51° „
—Snow 8, dilute sulphuric acid 10—91° „

These negative temperatures indicate so many degrees below zero of Fahrenheit. In some cases they depend on the temperature of the substance before the freezing process. Solid carbonic acid is an agent in producing still greater degrees of cold.

In order to produce the congelation of water by a rapid evaporation from its own surface under the exhausted receiver of an air-pump, Sir John Leslie introduced in the receiver a shallow vessel containing highly concentrated sulphuric acid, above which was placed the vessel containing the water. The air being extracted as quickly as possible, the vapour, which, in consequence of the removal of the pressure, escaped continually from the water, was absorbed by the acid as fast as it rose; and the remainder of the water was speedily frozen. Dry potash, muriate of lime, or powder of basalt, will do instead of sulphuric acid. Leslie succeeded in freezing mercury by the absorption of caloric from a coating of ice in which the bulb of a thermometer was immersed.

FREIGHT, in commercial matters, is the charge made for the carriage of merchandise in a ship. The amount of the freight is generally specified in the bill of lading. It frequently happens that the whole ship is hired by a merchant for a voyage, and a certain amount is paid without reference to the quantity of goods put on board. In such cases the mode of payment is part of the matter of agreement between the shipowner and the merchant, and the terms of the agreement are stated in an instrument called a *charter-party*. Where the shipper of goods does not stipulate for the use of the whole ship, the amount of the freight, as well as the mode of payment, may be inserted in the bill of lading. Where this is not done, the freight is due from the merchant on the delivery of the goods, and the owner or master of the ship may demand payment of the same, package by package, as the same are delivered. In London where the greater part of the merchandise brought from foreign countries is delivered into the custody of one or other of the incorporated dock-companies, there is a custom of arresting the goods in their hands, so that they cannot pass away from the original importer until the shipowner, or some person acting on his behalf, has signified in writing that the freight has been paid. If goods are damaged on board the ship, through the carelessness or neglect of those in whose charge she and her cargo are placed, so that the owner of the ship is liable for the amount of the damage, this cannot, without the consent of the owner or master, be set off against the amount of the freight, which must under all circumstances be paid, and the merchant must afterwards substantiate his claim to compensation for the amount of the damage.

FRENCH BERRIES are the berries of the *Rhamnus infectorius*, which are gathered before they are ripe. They afford a pretty but fugitive yellow dye.

FRESCO PAINTING. A painting is said to be a *fresco*, or painted in fresco (*sul fresco intonaco*, upon the fresh coat), when it is executed in water-colours upon wet plaster. Fresco is the most noble and imposing of all methods of painting. *Colouring* in fresco was practised by the ancients, though it has not yet been shown that they *painted frescoes*. Vitruvius explains the mode of preparing the walls for this species of colouring, and describes a method of varnishing them when coloured to preserve them. The earliest Italian frescoes are in the church of Assissi, in the cathedrals of Orvieto and Siena, in the Campo Santo at Pisa, and in San Miniato and Santo Spirito at Florence. These and other later frescoes are painted on different kinds of walls: in the old Gothic buildings, on ashlar walls covered with a thin coat of plaster; in more recent buildings, on brick and rubble walls; and, in some of the most recent edifices, on lath covered with various thicknesses of plaster. The best preserved of these frescoes are on brick. There are many frescoes at Pisa, Florence, and Venice, on lath, and all are in tolerable preservation.

The method of plastering the walls for painting has been nearly uniform in most ages. The walls of the baths of Titus at Rome are covered first with a layer about half an inch thick of coarse sand and lime; above this, a thick layer of lime and pozzolana with an admixture of sand and pounded brick; the third and upper coat is of lime and pounded marble. The third loggia of the Vatican, painted by Giovanni da Udine, is much the same as this. Cennino Cennini, Alberti, and various other Italian writers, give instruction as to the mode of preparing the walls and the materials for them. The selection of the limestone to be employed in fresco-painting, both for the ground and for the white, is a matter of great importance; it should be nearly pure carbonate of lime, and should contain as few foreign materials as possible. Modern fresco-painters recommend the lime to be kept a much longer period than Cennini and other early writers direct. If it is used too fresh, it blisters, and sometimes turns the colours to a brownish red. The lime for the *intonaco* in fresco painting must not be entirely carbonated, or it would not set; a certain degree of causticity is necessary. The picture must be executed while the *intonaco* is wet or soft; no more work therefore ought to be commenced than can be completed within the time (a few hours) that the plaster requires to harden. Numerous joints are thus necessary in a large fresco; and a judicious painter contrives that these joints shall be identical with the inner outlines of the parts of the figures and their draperies, or any other object, so as to be no disfigurement to the work. Before laying on the *intonaco* the prepared ground is repeatedly wetted, until it will absorb no more; then a thin moderately rough coat of plaster of sand and lime, is laid over as much of the wet surface as can be painted in one day; as soon as this coat begins to set, in about ten minutes or so, another thin coat is laid on with a wooden trowel, both layers together being scarcely a quarter of an inch thick. Upon this coat the fresco is painted. This *intonaco* will be fit to paint upon in about a quarter of an hour.

The colours used in fresco painting are all ground and mixed in water, boiled or distilled; they are chiefly earths. Lime, ochres, siena, vitriol, Verona green, cobalt, chrome, ultra marine, and vermilion are the chief colouring substances employed. Sufficient of each tint is kept ready for the whole picture. The brushes and pencils are made of hog's hair and otter's hair.

The method of *fresco-secco*, or dry fresco, is thus practised:—The plastering of the wall having been completed, the whole is allowed to dry thoroughly. Before painting, the surface of the *intonaco* is rubbed with pumice-stone, and on the evening of the day before the painting is to be commenced it is thoroughly washed with water mixed with a little lime; it is wetted again the next morning, and is then ready for pouncing or tracing the outline, and painting; the wall must be kept constantly moist by means of a syringe.

Frescoes are sometimes cleaned by dry bread; sometimes by pure water, by vinegar, and by wine. Ingenious modes have been devised of removing frescoes from walls, and transferring them to canvas.

FRET, in musical instruments of the stringed kind, is a wire or ridge so placed as to mark the exact part of the finger-board to be pressed for the purpose of producing certain sounds. Frets are now never applied to any instruments except guitars, lutes, &c.

FREYBERG, the centre of administration for the Saxon mines, stands about 20 miles from Dresden. The Berg Academie or Mining Academy was opened in 1767, and comprises class and lecture rooms, a museum, in which are rich collections in mineralogy, &c., a geographical and a geognostic cabinet, a museum of models of mining machines and philosophical and chemical apparatus, and an extensive library. The manufactures consist principally of articles in imitation of gold and silver ware, brass wares, white lead, gunpowder, iron and copper wares, linen, woollens, gold and silver lace, ribands and tape, leather and laces.

FRICTION. All surfaces have certain degrees of roughness arising from the innumerable small asperities with which they are covered; and from these, when two surfaces move upon one another, there arises a force acting in a direction opposite to that in which the surfaces move. This is *friction*, which is therefore a retarding force capable of destroying but incapable of generating motion, and capable of acting powerfully as a mechanical force, of which the tendency is to bestow stability.

The following are a few of the laws which govern friction, useful in all considerations respecting moving machinery:—1, Friction is increased by *time;* thus it requires the application of a greater force to move a weight along a horizontal plane from its position of rest than to keep it afterwards moving on the same plane. 2, Between substances of the same nature the friction is proportional to the *pressure;* thus, if a block of oak be double the weight of another, and both, having equal surfaces of contact, are placed on one plane of uniform nature, the force necessary to move the first will be double of that requisite for the second. 3, The amount of friction is independent for one and the same body of the extent of the surface of contact. 4, When the fibres of two substances are parallel, friction has a tendency to increase; thus, when a rectangular block of oak is placed on an oak table so that the fibres in both lie parallel, the friction is greater than in the case where the fibres of the block lie transversely to those of the table. 5, The friction is independent of the velocity, at least when the velocity is neither very small nor very great.

Mr. Rennie made many valuable experiments on friction a few years ago, with various substances drawn on a horizontal plane. He found that metals moving upon each other produced friction in the following order:—

Brass on wrought iron.
Steel upon steel.
Brass upon cast iron.
Brass upon steel.
Hard brass upon cast iron.
Wrought iron upon wrought iron.
Cast iron upon cast iron.
Cast iron upon steel.
Cast iron upon wrought iron.
Brass upon brass.
Tin upon tin.

Amongst the conclusions which Mr. Rennie draws, the following are perhaps the most important. With fibrous substances, such as cloth, &c., friction is increased by surface and time, and diminished by pressure and velocity. With harder substances, such as woods, metals and stones, the amount of friction is simply as the pressure, without regard to surface, time, or velocity. Friction is greatest with soft, and least with hard substances. The diminution of friction by unguents depends on the nature of the unguents, without reference to the substances moving over them.

M. Coulomb and M. Morin have made valuable experiments on the friction produced by one kind of wood moving over another.

FUEL is any combustible matter employed for the purpose of creating and maintaining heat. In the early ages of the world, *wood* must have constituted, as indeed in many countries it does to this day, the principal fuel employed. *Charcoal*, another kind of fuel, is merely wood that has undergone imperfect combustion, so as to expel its hydrogen and oxygen, and to leave the greater part of the carbon. *Peat*, or *turf*, which is a congeries of vegetable matter, in which the remains of organisation are more or less visible, is used in many countries as fuel. In this country *coal* furnishes the great supply of fuel. *Coke* bears nearly the same relation to coal that charcoal does to wood. In the East, dried camel's dung is often used for fuel.

The number of substitutes for coal introduced within the last few years has been surprisingly large. Oram's patent fuel was planned with a view to make use of the small coal which is so extensively left to waste at the mouths of the pits; this coal to be mixed with earthy substances, such as sand, marl, clay, or alluvial deposit; or with some bituminous substance, such as mineral tar, coal tar, gas tar, pitch, resin, or asphaltum; or with saw dust, coke dust, or breeze. In short this was one of those vague patents which defeat their own purpose by the wideness of their grasp.

Mr. C. W. Williams, managing director of the Dublin Steam Packet Company, has patented three or four inventions for artificial fuel in which peat shall be one of the ingredients. The peat, after being dried, is pressed with great force, to expel the moisture with which it is saturated; and it is then mixed with some bituminous substance. By different modes of treatment Mr. Williams produced a very dense brown combustible solid, a charcoal twice as compact as hard wood charcoal, an artificial coal, and an artificial coke.

All the more recent patent fuels consist of various combinations of the substances noticed above. Bessemer's, Buckwell's, Cowper's, Snowden's, Reece's, Green's—all have a certain family resemblance, however they may differ in details. Warlich's patent fuel has been found to possess certain favourable qualities for use in steam-boats. See also CARBON; CHARCOAL; COAL; COKE; PEAT.

FULGURITES are vitrified sand-tubes, supposed to have originated from the action of lightning. These tubes are nearly all hollow, and vary in diameter from a fraction of an inch to two or three inches. All the evidence goes to show that they are produced by the action of lightning on the silicious particles of sand. They serve to illustrate in a pleasing manner how sand or flinty particles may be converted into a kind of glass by intense heat

FULLERS' EARTH, a mineral product, was formerly much used in the fulling of cloth. It occurs massive, and is usually of a greenish brown or dull gray colour; sometimes it is nearly of a slate colour. It occurs in many parts of England, between beds of sand or sandstone.

FULLING. [WOOLLEN MANUFACTURE.]

FULTON, ROBERT, the first to establish steam navigation on the American seas and rivers, was born in 1765, in Pennsylvania. In 1786 he embarked for England, and projects for the improvement of canals began to occupy the chief share of his attention. In 1794 he took out a patent for an inclined plane, which was intended to set aside the use of locks; he invented a machine to facilitate excavation, and wrote a work on canals, in which he first styled himself a civil engineer. He also invented a mill for sawing marble, and took out patents for spinning flax and making ropes. These projects failed to enrich him; and he went to Paris, where he studied languages, invented a sub-marine boat, projected a panorama, and made experiments in the Seine with small steam-boats. After trying in vain to introduce his sub-marine boat into England, he went to America in 1806, and soon afterwards commenced the construction of a steam-vessel of considerable size, which began to navigate the Hudson in 1807. He afterwards built others of large dimensions, one of them a frigate, which bore his name. His reputation became established; but law-suits in reference to certain patents kept him poor, and anxiety and excessive application shortened his days. He died in 1815.

Henry Bell in Scotland, and Robert Fulton in America, both died poor; after enriching —each his own country—by the decisive introduction of steam-navigation.

FUMIGATION. The vapours of hot vinegar, burning sulphur, and of aromatic vegetable matters, have been long used to counteract unpleasant or unwholesome smells: this is effected chiefly by the formation of such as are stronger. The most important kind of fumigation is that which consists in the employment of such vapours or gases as do not merely destroy unhealthy odours by exciting such as are more powerful, but which by their chemical action prevent the decomposition of animal and vegetable matters. The fumigation of the first kind, that which is intended to produce a healing effect, is now much less employed than formerly. In the last kind of fumigation several substances have been employed in the gaseous state; such as the vapour of burning sulphur, or sulphurous acid gas, muriatic acid gas, nitric acid gas, and chlorine gas. Chlorine which is undoubtedly preferable to any disinfectant, was first recommended by Dr. Rollo, the gas being liberated by the usual method of mixing sulphuric acid, binoxide of manganese, and common salt. When it is desirable to produce a great effect in a short time, this is still unquestionably the best mode of proceeding.

Where unpleasant smells or effluvia are produced only in small quantities, the chloride of lime or soda, and especially of the former, has been within a few years successfully employed. The chloride of lime is a substance well known and extensively employed under the name of bleaching powder. It is used in solution, and is obtained by dissolving one part of Bleaching Powder in about 100 times its weight of water, and allowing the solution to become clear. This is to be exposed to infected air, or, in rooms which have any unpleasant odour, in flat vessels, in order that a sufficient surface may be acted upon. If it should be required, the operation may be quickened by the addition of a little vinegar, or of muriatic acid largely diluted.

Where it is necessary to diffuse a gas, vapour, or smoke over a given space, the usual plan is to place some easily evaporable substance on or near the spot; but in fumigating plants some difficulty arises. To remove this difficulty is the object of Brown's *Fumigator*, an ingenious apparatus patented in 1840. It comprises a cylinder, a fan, a funnel, a handle, a winch, and a spout. The cylinder is a metallic chamber, across the centre of which an axle extends; and to the middle of this axle a fan of several vanes is attached. The winch, outside the cylinder, affords the means of giving a rapid rotatory movement to the vanes; while a handle on one side of the cylinder enables the apparatus to be conveniently held in any desired position. The funnel is fixed into the top of the cylinder, and has a diaphragm of perforated metal about its centre. The action of the apparatus is simply as follows. Tobacco or other substance whose fumes are required, is put in the funnel and ignited, and the top of the funnel closed; the winch is turned, and the draught thereby occasioned within the cylinder sucks in the smoke, and then forces it out through the spout. This spout is so formed as to act easily on any part of a plant.

FUNGIN, the fleshy substance of mushrooms, purified by digestion in a hot weak solution of alkali: it is whitish, soft, insipid, and but little elastic. It is a highly nutritious substance, and in many of its properties it strongly resembles lignin.

FUNICULAR MACHINE is a name given by some mechanicians to a cord or chain attached at one extremity to an immoveable point, the other end passing over a fixed pulley or friction wheel, and having a weight suspended from it; a weight being also suspended from the cord or chain in some part of its length between the fixed extremity and the pulley. The cord or chain becomes thus a mechanical agent, since unequal weights, applied as has been said, may be in equilibrio.

FUNNEL is a hollow conical vessel with a small pipe issuing from its apex, much used in domestic life for conveying fluids into vessels of small apertures, and in chemical operations not only for this purpose but for that of filtering.

FUR TRADE; FUR DRESSING. The use of furs appears to have been introduced into civilised Europe by the northern conquerors.

The fur trade was taken up by the French colonists of Canada; and, through the ignorance of the Indians, the traders at first made very great profits. When the hunting season was over, the Indians came down the Ottawa in their canoes, with the furs, and encamped outside the town of Montreal, where a kind of fair was held until the furs were all exchanged for trinkets, &c. At a later period, European settlers under the name of *Coureurs des Bois*, or wood-rangers, set out at the proper season from Montreal in canoes loaded with various articles, and proceeded up the river to the hunting grounds, where they conducted their traffic with the hunters, and returned with the furs or peltries.

The Hudson's Bay Company, established for the express object of procuring furs, was chartered by Charles II. in 1670. This association founded several establishments. In 1783 a rival association, called the North West Company, was established by some British settlers in Canada; and from that time till 1821 great jealousy and enmity existed between the agents in the two companies. An amalgamation took place in 1821: and the Company have recently added Vancouver Island to their territories. The clerks, agents, &c., of the United Company are very numerous. All the furs collected by the Hudson's Bay Company are shipped to London, some from their factories of York Fort, and on Moose River, in Hudson's Bay; other portions from Montreal, and the remainder from the Columbia River.

The fur trade is prosecuted in the north-western territories of the United States by an association called the North American Fur Company, the principal managers of which reside in New York. The Company employs steam-boats for ascending the rivers, which penetrate with ease to regions which could formerly be explored only through the most painful exertions in keel boats and barges, or by small parties on horseback or on foot. There is also a Russian Fur Company, in the extreme north-west of America.

The following are the principal skins taken for the sake of the fur:—The *ermine*, called by way of pre-eminence 'the precious ermines is found almost exclusively in the cold region,' of Europe and Asia. The fur of the ermine is of a pure whiteness throughout, with the exception of the tip of the tail, which is black; and the spotted appearance of ermine skins, by which they are peculiarly known, is produced by fastening these black tips at intervals on the skins. The *stoat* is an inferior kind of ermine. The *sable* is a native of Northern Europe and Siberia; those of the darkest colour are the most esteemed. *Martens* are found in North America as well as in Northern Asia; the American skins are generally the least valued, but many among them are rich and of a beautiful dark brown olive colour. The *fiery fox*, so called from its brilliant red colour, is taken near the north-east coast of Asia, and its fur is much valued, both for its colour and fineness, in that quarter of the world. *Nutria* skins are chiefly used by hat-manufacturers as a substitute for beaver. *Sea-Otter* fur, of the young animal, is of a beautiful brown colour, but when older the colour becomes jet black. The fur is exceedingly fine, soft, and close, and bears a silky gloss. *Fur-Seals* are found in great numbers in the colder latitudes of the southern hemisphere. Bears, foxes, beavers, racoons, badgers, minks, lynxes, musk-rats, rabbits, hares, and squirrels are procured in North America.

Furs may be classed as *felting furs* and *dressed furs*. The first includes all such as are employed in hat-making, and are principally the skins of the hare, the rabbit, the beaver, and the neutria.

The mode of preparing beaver fur for the hatter will sufficiently illustrate the treatment of furs generally. The pelt or skin is so greasy, that it requires to be scoured with fuller's earth and whiting before it attains a sufficient state of cleanness. The coarse hairs are pulled out by the knife and thumb, and, being of no use to the hatter, they are sold as a stuffing for cushions. Then comes the cutting or cropping, which is at the present day, and in the largest establishments, effected by a very beautiful machine. There is a long broad and sharp blade, so adjusted as to fall rapidly with a chopping action against or near the edge of another blade beneath. The fur falls down in a light flocculent layer on an endless apron beneath, whence it is removed when the pelt has been shorn. [HAT MANUFACTURE.]

The term *dressed furs* is given to those furs which are retained on the original pelt, and in that state worn as garments or trimmings, in the forms of cloaks, tippets, cuffs, collars, &c. The fur-hunters, when they have captured a beaver or other fur-bearing animal, strip off the skin, and hang it up to dry, either in the open air or in a dry and cool room. When the skins are brought to England and placed in the hands of the furrier, he examines them minutely to see that the drying has been properly effected, and the pelt in a firm state. He then washes the skin, to extract all greasiness from the fur, and gives the pelt a sort of slight tanning, or tawing, by means of alum or other ingredients. The skins are then ready to be worked up into materials for garments. In order to give the surface of the fur a uniform length and colour of fibre, it is often necessary to cut up many skins, and sew them edge to edge; for it is rarely if ever the case that every part of the same skin is of one uniform colour.

FURNACE. The common grate is the most familiar example of a furnace; and in the smaller chemical operations various contrivances are used, midway in character between a grate and a furnace; but the furnaces usually so called are the following:—

The *Wind Furnace* gives a very high temperature by the aid of a powerful draught. It is from 12 to 15 inches square, and is furnished with moveable bars and a cover. The air is conveyed by pipes directly from without doors to the ash-pit, and the chimney is narrow and high. Such a furnace is much employed in the reduction of metals, and in the assaying of copper and various other ores. The fuel used is either coke or a mixture of coke and charcoal.

The *Assay* or *Cupelling Furnace* is a small furnace made of iron, lined with refractory clay, and containing a muffle; it is used principally for the cupellation of gold and silver, which is placed upon a cupel in the muffle, previously heated to redness. The interior of the furnace contains merely the muffle resting upon two bars of iron; it is put about two-thirds into the furnace, and there is consequently left a space between it and the back part of the furnace. Charcoal is used in this furnace.

For metallurgic operations on a large scale, as well as in making alkalies, red lead, &c., the *Reverberatory Furnace* is much used. There is a space furnished with a grate or bars, to contain the fuel, which is either coal, coke, or wood, according to circumstances. Beyond and behind this is a large low vacant space, so shaped that the flame may reverberate from the brick roof, and strike down upon the substance to be heated, which is placed upon a flat brick surface. There is a very high chimney that produces the draught, and which may be closed by a damper.

The *Smelting Furnace*, for iron works, is a large structure of brick, having a small square receptacle for the fuel beneath, a large interior space for the ore to be smelted, a wide-mouthed chimney at the top, and air-holes at the bottom to admit either the hot or cold blast. Some of the South Wales furnaces have an internal cavity of 5000 cubic feet.

In scarcely any department of machinery or manufacturing apparatus are there more numerous patented inventions than in the construction of furnaces. Newton, Grist, Jukes, Pollock, Burrows, Holcroft, Baker, Coad, Clarke, Bramwell, Homersham, Barker, Deeley, Williams, Newcome, Hall, Mackintosh, White, Howard, Wilson, Pidding, Robinson, Lee, Knowlys, Prideaux, Bessemer, Galloway, Johnson, Cliffe, Dalton—all these names, and many others, are connected with improvements in furnaces within the last two or three years. Some of these improvements relate to the furnaces of locomotives, some to those of marine engines, some to those of stationary engines, and some to furnaces in general. In one case the patentee seeks to economize space, in another fuel, in another to avoid the 'smoke nuisance.' Some relate to metallic furnaces, some to fire-brick furnaces. In some the object is to raise steam in great quantity; while in others it is to substitute rapidity for quantity.

An important principle has just been put in operation by the Ebbw Vale Iron Company of South Wales. It is no less than the application of blast-furnace gases to heating purposes. After a furnace has performed the work for which it is intended, various gases escape with the smoke, at the upper orifice; and these gases carry with them a large amount of valuable heat. If the heat could be abstracted and usefully applied, without lessening the power of the furnace, an economical benefit would result. The above named company have 11 blast furnaces, five engines to produce the blast, and twenty-five boilers to supply the engines with steam. The greater number of these boilers are wholly heated by the waste heat from the blast furnaces; and various ovens and stoves in the Works are heated by similar means. It is said that 1000 tons of coal per week are saved by this admirable contrivance. The heated gases are arrested near the top of the furnace, carried out by a horizontal tube, mixed with atmospheric air which enters in thin sheets or layers, and ignited by a small fire. It forms a true gas-light; and this gas-light heats a large flue, which is surrounded by a boiler containing water; and thus is a supply of steam obtained.

FURNITURE MANUFACTURE. It is supposed that there are about 50,000 workers in wood in the metropolis, and 350,000 in the kingdom, of whom a very large number are employed in making articles of household furniture. There has also been a rough estimate that about 160,000 average timber trees are required to make the furniture for the new houses built annually in England and Wales. There are about 30,000 sawyers in England, to cut up timber for various purposes. The carpenters and joiners are about 180,000; carpenters construct all the rough portions, and joiners all the more finished details, in the timber-work of houses. The cabinet-maker engages on such timber-work only as is connected with household furniture; but there are many departments, such as the chair maker, the bedstead maker, the carver, the general cabinet maker (who makes tables, drawers, sideboards, wardrobes, &c.), the fancy cabinet maker (who uses veneers of costly woods, and makes workboxes, teacaddies, desks, dressing cases, and other highly finished articles). The upholsterer does what is called the 'soft work,' that is, all that relates to curtains, hangings, cushions, and so forth; he is also responsible for the due finishing and fittings of carpets and beds.

The general furniture or cabinet makers require tools which cost from 30*l.* to 40*l.* per set. A portion of the journeymen in this trade in London belong to trade societies, by whom the rate of wages is to a considerable extent determined. Those employed at the west end of London generally receive higher wages than those of the east; but a much larger number are free of the trade-societies, and make their own bargains with employers concerning the rate of wages. There has been a large increase, in this trade, in what are termed 'garret masters,' who bear in manufactures a position analagous to that which 'peasant proprietors' bear in agriculture: that is, they supply both capital and labour. The garret master buys just so much wood as he can pay for at a time, works it up into tables and other articles of household furniture, and takes those articles to furniture dealers, to whom he sells them for the best prices he can obtain. A very large per-centage of the showy French-polished furniture now to be seen marked at low prices in the London shops, is manufactured in this way; and on a Saturday evening, in the busy districts, the garret masters and their apprentices may be seen carrying such commodities to the shops of the dealers, or conveying them in a hired vehicle.

It is one of the features attendant on any extra demand for accommodation for visitors, that furniture makers share in the increased activity. It is known that the cabinet or furniture makers of London, both garret masters and others, are at present busily engaged in making furniture for houses about to be finished for our expected visitors to the Great Exhibition.

FUSTIAN is a cotton fabric similar in the mode of manufacture to velvet, having in addition to the warp and weft, common to all woven goods, a *pile* consisting of other threads doubled under the weft, and 'thrown in' at intervals so close together that when the goods are finished the interlacing of the warp and weft are concealed by them. While in the loom, the pile forms a series of loops, which are afterwards cut and sheared; the shearing is effected by very beautiful machinery.

There are different varieties of fustians, known by the names of cotton velvets, velveteens, beaverteens, moleskin, corduroy, and cords. Different patterns are produced by different dispositions of the pile threads.

Ingenious machines have been patented within the last two or three years, for facilitating the production of the nap in fustians.

FUSTIC is the name of two kinds of yellow dye-wood. *Young Fustic* is the produce of *Rhus Cotinus*, a native of Italy, France, and Greece. The root and the wood of this shrub are both imported, deprived of their bark, and employed for dyeing a yellow colour approaching to orange, upon wool or cottons. *Old Fustic*, the 'bois jaune' of the French, is the produce of *Morus tinctoria*, a native of tropical America and the West India Islands. The wood is yellow, hard, and strong, but easily splintered, and is imported in the form of large logs or blocks. The yellow colour which it affords with an aluminous base, though durable is not very bright.

FUZE, is a short tube made of metal or of well-seasoned beech, and fixed in the bore of a shell. It is filled with a composition, which is fired by means of a small piece of quick-match inserted for the purpose. The length of a fuze is regulated by the intended range of the shell or by the intended time of its flight.

Mr. Loam, mining engineer in Cornwall, patented in 1849 a new kind of fuze for blasting. It is made of calico or some similar material. In making the fuze, a strip of calico is unwound from a reel, and made to assume the shape of a trough; it passes under a hopper filled with gunpowder, and a train of powder becomes deposited on it during the passage. The calico is then drawn through a hollow axis, whereby the trough-like form is exchanged for that of a tube. The tube passes through another piece of apparatus, by which it becomes closely bound round with yarn or thread. When the tube has been thus far completed, it is coated with any of the usual water-proofing materials.

G

GABION, a hollow cylinder of wicker-work, resembling a basket, but having no bottom. It is formed by planting slender stakes vertically in the ground, at intervals from each other, on the circumference of a circle, and interweaving with them osiers or other flexible twigs. The most usual kind of gabion is about two feet in diameter, and two feet nine inches in height, but the stakes, whose extremities are pointed, project beyond the basket work about three or four inches at each end. Such gabions are used during a siege in executing trenches by the process of sapping.

GA'LBANUM. The plant usually believed to yield this medicinal gum resin is *Bubon Galbanum*, a native of the Cape of Good Hope; but there is some doubt on this point. Three sorts of Galbanum are distinguished:—1, galbanum in grains or tears; 2, galbanum in masses; and 3, Persian galbanum. The first two come from Africa, especially from Ethiopia; the third sort from Persia. *Galbanum in tears* is most likely the spontaneous exudation from the plant; and that in masses, obtained by incision. The first occurs in irregular generally oblong grains, mostly distinct, but sometimes agglutinated together, about the size of a lentil or small pea, of a colour verging from whitish into yellowish brown, more or less diaphanous, opaque, or shining with a resinous lustre. The odour is strongly balsamic and disagreeable. The taste is resinous, sharp, bitter, and disagreeable. *Galbanum in masses* consists of irregular pieces of a yellowish or dark brown colour: the odour is stronger than that of the preceding kind, which, in its general characters, it much resembles, except that it can be powdered only during the low temperature of winter. *Persian galbanum*, being very soft and tenacious, is sent in skins or chests; it often contains many fragments of plants.

Galbanum is largely employed in making pills, plasters, and other medicinal preparations.

GALI'CIA, a province in the north-west of Spain, produces wine, fruits, flax, wheat, barley, maize; good pastures, which feed a vast quantity of cattle; and abundance of chestnuts, which constitute a common food of the peasantry. The forests supply plenty of fuel and timber. The principal manufacture of the country is linen. The town of *Betanzos* has a few manufactories, and some trade in wine and pickled anchovies and pilchards, which are taken all along this coast. *Vigo*, on the Bay of Vigo, which forms one of the largest and safest natural harbours in Spain, carries on a considerable trade with America, exporting wines, sardines, linen cloth, and stockings, and other articles of native industry.

GALIPE'A is the name of the plant which yields *Angostura Bark*. It is found in the neighbourhood of Angostura. Angostura Bark is obtained both from the stem and branches. The specimens from the stem are flat, while those from the branches are often quilled. Some specimens have the surface covered with a thick, fungus-like, whitish yellow or clay-coloured crust, which may be more or less easily scraped off, and beneath which is a yellowish red smooth bark, often exhibiting small cracks. Other specimens have this covering much thinner and closely adhering to the bark. The internal surface is generally smooth, of a tawny or reddish yellow colour. The bark is easily broken, and the recent fracture is of a brownish red colour, smooth, with a resiny shining surface. The shining appearance is best seen when a transverse section is made with a sharp knife. The smell is disagreeable: the taste pleasantly bitter, warm, aromatic, and causing a flow of saliva. The powder has the colour of rhubarb. The infusion is of an orange-yellow colour; the decoction, a clear light brown.

Angostura Bark is a valuable medicinal agent; but there is a spurious kind which requires to be guarded against.

GALIUM is the botanical name for a genus of plants which comprises many useful species. One, called *Wild Madder*, is a native almost throughout Europe and the Caucasus, and is found in Britain. The roots are creeping, and yield a red dye like the true madder, but of a brighter colour; they also have the property of colouring the bones of animals red that feed upon them. This plant has been extolled as an effectual cure for epilepsy. The *Dyer's Bedstraw* is another species. From the roots of a third species the Indians extract the red dye with which they colour their feathers and the ornaments of their dress. The Cree women use the roots of the *Northern Bedstraw* to dye red. Of the *Ladies' Bedstraw* or *cheese rennet*, the stalks and flowers have been used in the cheese counties for the purpose of curdling milk, and also for colouring it. Mathiolus says it produces an agreeable flavour, and makes the cheese 'eat sweeter.' The French formerly used to prescribe the flowers in hysteria and epilepsy. The roots afford a rich red dye, superior in colour to madder. All the other species yield a red dye.

GALIZIA. The produce and industry of this country have been briefly glanced at in connection with the empire to which it belongs. [AUSTRIA.]

GALLERY, in its most extended sense, is used synonymously with corridor. In England however it is understood to be either a long narrow passage-way, or an open space, generally longer than wide, raised above the floor of a building, and usually supported by columns. Such galleries are met with (among other places) in English churches, in some courts of justice, and in theatres. The long external wooden passage-ways, formed something like a balcony, such as are occasionally seen in old inns, are called galleries.

Gallery is also a name of distinction given to a room either on account of its extent and proportions, or to one or more rooms especially appropriated to pictures and other works of art, whence the term Gallery is extended to the collection itself, without any reference to the building.

In mining operations, a gallery is a horizontal passage, excavated to facilitate the progress of the miners.

GALLEY; GALLEON; GALLIOT. These are the names of three kinds of vessels. The *Galley*, a large-sized long and narrow vessel propelled by oars and sails, was much in use in the Mediterranean until the end of the 18th century for coast navigation, and for making the shore in shallow water. The oars were a great advantage in the dead calms so frequent in the Mediterranean, until the introduction of the steamboat. The largest galleys were 166 feet long, and about 32 wide, with 52 oars. The rowers, who were generally convicts or Turkish prisoners, with chains to their feet, sat on benches on the deck. The ship carried a 24 pounder and two 8-pounders. The Venetians had a sort of large galleys, with a very lofty poop, called 'Galeazza.'

The *Galleon* was the name given to very large ships, with three or four decks, which the court of Spain used to send to the coasts of Mexico and Peru, to receive on board the gold and silver bullion extracted from the mines, and bring it to Spain.

The *Galliot*, is a strong-built flat-bottomed vessel of a peculiar construction, used as a bomb-ship to fire against forts or batteries on the coast. Galliot is also a kind of small galley or large fellucca, used chiefly in the Mediterranean. The Dutch, Swedes, and other northern nations have a sort of merchant ship which they call Galliot, rounded both fore and aft, heavily and clumsily built, but strongly timbered, and of the burthen of from 200 to 300 tons.

GALLIC ACID exists in most astringent vegetables, but principally in the gall-nut, and hence its name. When obtained from the plants, it appears as slender prismatic colourless crystals. The taste is slightly sour and astringent. Gallic acid, in the form of *tincture of galls*, is much employed as a chemical reagent.

GALLON. Distinct gallons for wine, ale and beer, and corn and dry goods, continued in use until the act of 1825. By statutes of 1689 and 1697, the wine gallon was declared to contain 231 cubic inches. The ale gallon was measured in 1700 or thereabouts, and found to contain 282 cubic inches. The corn gallon was thought, in the middle of the last century, to contain exactly 272¼ cubic inches: but the statute of 1697, which declares that a round corn-bushel must be 8 inches deep and 18½ inches wide, had in fact fixed the gallon at 268 $\frac{4}{5}$ cubic inches. The imperial gallon, as settled by the Act of 1825 is to contain 10 pounds avoirdupois of distilled water, of which it is declared that 252.458 grains fill a cubic inch; consequently the imperial gallon contains 277.274 cubic inches.

GALLS are the result of a morbid action excited in the leaf-buds of several species of

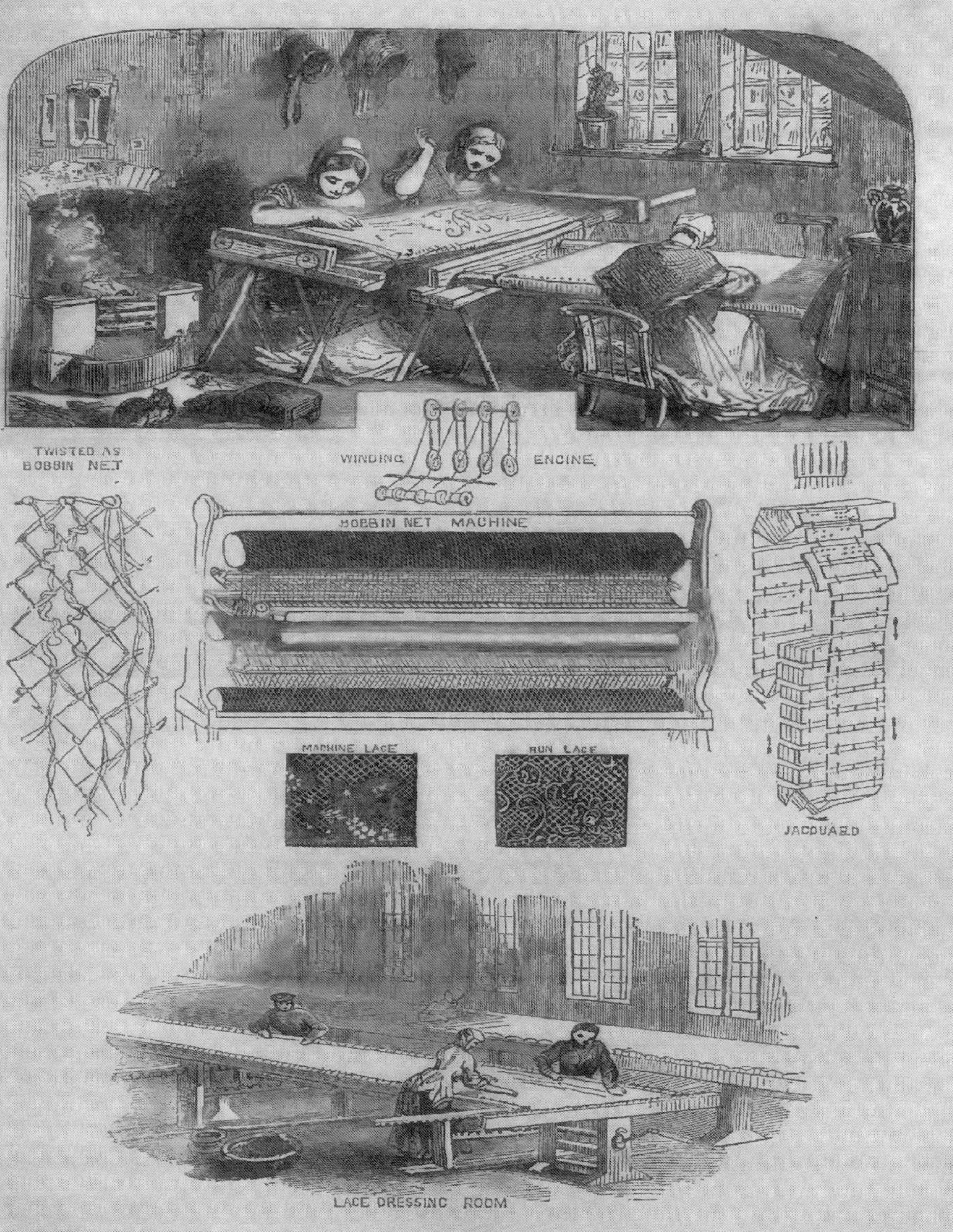

KNIGHT'S CYCLOPÆDIA OF THE INDUSTRY OF ALL NATIONS.

No. 23.

the oak, occasioned by an insect depositing its ova in the bud. Such buds, instead of elongating and becoming branches, undergo a peculiar transformation, and enlarge into a globular figure, so as to constitute a fit nidus for the future larva. The galls of commerce are chiefly those which occur on the *Quercus infectoria*. They vary in size, from that of a pea to that of a nutmeg. The surface has irregular elevations or lines, with the interspaces generally smooth. The colour is white or yellow in one variety; green, gray, or black in another. The white variety, which is the largest, often has a hole in the substance of the shell, by which the larva has escaped. This kind is the least powerful and least esteemed. The best galls come from Aleppo and Smyrna, but are often mixed with those from Syria and Cypress.

The infusion and other preparations of galls are used in medicine. But the most extensive use is made of them in the arts, and as a chemical test.

Gall is also the name given to the bitter fluid secreted by the liver. Ox-gall is largely employed in scouring cloth, and in other manufacturing arts. Refined ox-gall is used by artists to fix chalk and pencil drawings before tinting them, and to remove tho greasiness from ivory and tracing paper.

GALVANISM. The chiet points of interest which connect galvanic or electric agency with the arts of life are noticed under ELECTRO-METALLURGY, ELECTROTYPE, &c.

GALWAY. The greater part of this Irish county is comparatively flat, and much of it encumbered with bogs. The whole district west of Lough Corrib and Lough Mask is known by the general name of Connamara, and has of late years attracted much attention by its capabilities of improvement. Westward from the town of Galway, and round the entire coast of Iar-Connaught and Connamara to the boundary of Mayo, there is a succession of harbours for vessels of the largest class, unequalled perhaps on any similar extent of coast in Europe. These harbours are at Galway, Costello Bay, Casheen Bay, Greatman's Bay, Kilkerran Bay, Birterbuy Bay, Roundstone Harbour, Mannin Bay, Clifden Bay, Cleggan Roadstead, Ballynakill Harbour, and Killeries Bay. Some of these harbours have piers or jetties. On the whole, there is no part of this district more than four miles from existing means of navigation. The harbours fit for vessels of any burthen are upwards of twenty in number. There are twenty-five navigable lakes of a mile or more in length, and hundreds of smaller size. Lough Corrib and Lough Mask alone have upwards of seventy miles of navigable coast; and all these waters abound with fish. The sea-shore affords a constant supply of red and black sea-weed, which can be used either as manure or in the manufacture of kelp. Banks of calcareous sand and beds of limestone are of frequent occurrence, and there is an inexhaustible supply of peat fuel and of water power.

The attempts made to improve the fisheries on the coast of Galway have been beneficial to the county generally; and roads have been gradually formed from the interior to the coast. There is an extension of the Grand Canal from Shannon Harbour to Ballinasloe. A railway from Dublin to Galway is rapidly approaching completion.

In respect to geology, the mountains of the primitive district are highly metalliferous. Copper, lead, iron, and manganese are met with; and there are also abundant quarries of black, green, and variegated marbles, millstone grit, yellow ochre, and potter's clay. In 1847 the land under culture was thus appropriated:—Corn and beans, 141,318 acres; potatoes, 12,876; turnips, 14,788; meadow and clover, 37,146; all other crops, 3460; total under crops, 209,588 acres. The fisheries off the coast yield a very considerable produce. Nearly 100 million herrings have been caught in one year. Besides the herring fishery, there is an excellent take of cod, ling, whiting, and turbot, from December to March; and of gurnet, mackerel, bream, and pollock, from May to August, together with a copious supply of oysters, lobsters, and crabs. The sun-fish deep-sea fishery is peculiar to this coast. The manufactures comprise scarcely any but a few coarse friezes, linens, and hosiery.

In the chief town, *Galway*, there are many flour-mills, and other mills driven by the water-power of the river. Wheat, oats, and flour are exported, and a good deal of black marble from the neighbourhood. Timber, iron, slates, wines, &c., are imported. Tho retail trade is large. A wet-dock, comprising 9 acres, and admitting vessels drawing 14 feet of water, has been formed on the south side of the town. At *Ballinasloe* a very large sheep, cattle, and horse fair is held annually.

The Galway merchants are making praiseworthy exertions to have their port selected as a mail-packet station for the American route.

The beautiful black marble of Connemara will, it is to be hoped, find a place in the approaching Exhibition.

GAMBOGE. [CAMBOGE.]

GARD. In this department of the South of France, iron, coal, and silver-lead mines are worked. Silver, copper, and calamine are found; but the working of the mines has been abandoned. Sulphate of iron, manganese, kaolin, antimony, fuller's and potter's clay, plaster of Paris, building stone, &c., are also found. The sheltered hills and the plains are devoted to the cultivation of the vine, the olive, the mulberry, and the almond. The vine is extensively cultivated all through the department, which yields annually 25 to 30 million gallons of good strong wine, one-fourth of which is consumed at home, one-sixth is distilled into brandy, and the remainder is exported through Cette, chiefly for the purpose of mixing with the poorer wines of more northern departments. The olive, too, is carefully cultivated in sheltered spots, and on the southern slopes of the hills; the oil of the department is in high repute. The cultivation of the mulberry, which here becomes a large and beautiful tree, is very extensive.

The industrial products of the department are varied and important. The principal are silk textures of all kinds, the chief seat of which is Nîmes; cashmere shawls, made of a mixture of Tibet wool, silk, and cotton; silk and cotton hosiery of every description; table-covers, carpets, &c.; woollen cloth, swanskins, blankets, shoe and glove leather; silk hats; ribbons and gloves; iron, steam machinery, wine casks; pottery, tiles, and bricks; glass, paper, cards; nails, plaster, and lime; cotton and woollen yarn; salt, soda. The commerce of the department consists of the various products already mentioned. The number of wind-mills and water-mills amounts to nearly 800; iron forges and furnaces about 150; factories and workshops, of different kinds, 500 to 600.

At *Calvisson* a good deal of cream of tartar is made, and the town gives name to a delicious claret. *Roquemaure* has silk-reeling factories, brandy distilleries, hydraulic saw-mills, and a great manufacture of wine-casks, of which 20,000 are made annually.

GARDENS. A garden, as distinguished from a farm, is a piece of ground designed for the cultivation of plants not actually indispensable to man for food. While corn for flour, various roots and herbs for the sustenance of cattle, or tracts of pasture land on which animals destined for slaughter are maintained, constitute the essential features of a farm,—a garden, even when exclusively occupied by culinary vegetables, is still a source of objects of luxury, not of first necessity; in a more extended sense, and as it usually exists at the present day, it is chiefly intended to gratify the senses, and to minister to the more refined enjoyments of social life. The possession of a garden is one of the earliest indications of civilization in man: it may be fairly considered that the taste for gardens has been at all times commensurate with the wealth of nations generally, their peaceful habits, and advance in the social relations of life.

The first great step that was made by gardeners to advance their art beyond mere mechanical operations was the invention of glass-houses, in which plants might be grown in an artificial climate, and protected from the inclemency of weather. Until this was effected, it is obvious that the cultivation of exotic plants in Europe, especially its northern kingdoms, must have been much circumscribed. Mr. Loudon, in his 'Encyclopædia of Gardening,' gives valuable descriptions of all the most famous gardens in the world. The repeal of the glass duties in England is likely to be very beneficial to gardening, in respect to the construction of green-houses, hot-houses, palm-houses, &c.

A little information on the supply of London with vegetables and fruit will be found under MARKET GARDENING.

GARDEN ENGINES. The engines employed for watering plants in gardens are very similar in principle to fire-engines. The water is either poured into them from buckets, or drawn in by a suction-pump; while it is expelled in a continuous stream by a forcing-pump, easily worked by one or two handles.

At the various agricultural and cattle shows, garden-engines are usually exhibited among other apparatus. One such, exhibited at the Smithfield cattle show in 1850, is placed on a light platform drawn on four low wheels; it is worked by six men, and will discharge 60 gallons per minute; it is therefore fitted to act as a fire-engine, and as a garden-engine on a large scale. Read's patent garden-engine has two wheels and two handles; it will contain 28 gallons, and a jet can be forced by one man to a distance of 50 feet; it is adapted for watering both wall trees and standard plants. A slight modification in an instrument of this kind renders it workable by two men, with a power to force a large stream of water on any distant object. Mr. Warner has lately registered an ingenious *spreader*, by which the jet from a garden-engine can be readily spread out into a fan-like form. The same inventor has introduced a 'fire-engine, force-pump, drainer, and irrigator,' for farming purposes. It consists of an engine supported by a kind of barrow with two wheels and two handles; it can be worked by one or two men; it draws in its own water from a tank or reservoir, and it forces out a stream of considerable power.

GARNET. There are many varieties of

this well-known precious stone. Some of them are probably distinct species; but, agreeing in form and some other properties, they are classed together. This mineral occurs crystallised, massive, and granular. The primary form is a cube, but it occurs in the form of a rhombic dodecahedron. The crystalline varieties, according generally to their colour, have received various names. Precious garnet, *Almandine*; black, *Melanite*; *Pyreneite*; greenish yellow, *Grossularia*; yellow, crystallised, *Topazolite*; granular, *Succinite*; brownish yellow, granular, *Colophonite*; greenish, compact, *Allochroite*; red, *Pyrope*, *Carbuncle*; reddish brown, *Essonite*, *Cinnamon-stone*, *Romanzovite*; magnesian, *Rothoffite*.

GARONNE. The mineral treasures of this French department are iron, copper, lead, antimony, bismuth, zinc, coal, rock-crystal, slates, gypsum, marble, jet, and granite. Gold is found in the sands of the Garonne and the Salat. There is a salt-spring at Salies. Mineral waters are found at various places; those of Bagnères-de-Luchon are the most celebrated.

The quantity of wine grown in the department annually is 14 to 15 million gallons, one-third of which is used for home consumption; the quality is generally inferior. The commerce of the department is composed of its agricultural products and of its manufactures, the chief of which are scythes, files, copper utensils, mathematical instruments, porcelain, pottery, tiles, coarse woollens, canvas, blankets, calico, tape, brandy, tin-ware, and leather of various kinds. There are about 80 iron furnaces, and about 350 factories of different kinds, including glass works, copper foundries, cannon foundries, gunpowder mills, tobacco factories, distilleries, marble sawing works, &c.; together with more than 1000 wind and water mills. The department has considerable commercial intercourse with Spain, whither many handicraftsmen annually emigrate to exercise their callings.

The commerce and industry of the chief town, TOULOUSE, are briefly noticed elsewhere.

GAS. The main difference between *vapours* and *gases* is, that vapours are reduced to solids or liquids when the heat is withdrawn; while gases preserve their aëriform state at common temperatures. This difference is one of degree only, but it is usefully retained. The number of gaseous bodies is great, and they possess in many respects such different properties that it would be impossible to give a general description of them.

Gay-Lussac found that, when 100 volumes of gas or air are heated from 32° to 212° F., they become 137½ volumes; or the increase is $\frac{1}{480}$ for each degree of Fahrenheit. This law has supplied a simple rule for determining what the known bulk of a gas at any temperature will be at any other temperature. Suppose, for example, it is desired to know what the bulk of 100 cubic inches of air at 32° will be at 60°: subtract 32 from 480, the remainder is 448; to which add the degrees above zero indicating the temperature of the air; these are 32° and 60°, making 480 and 508. Then say 480 : 508 :: 100 : 105.832 the volume of the air at 60°.

Air suffers diminution of volume in proportion to the pressure to which it is subjected, and the same law holds good with all the more incondensible gases.

The solubility of gases in water is extremely various. Dr. Henry ascertained that the volume of each gas absorbed by water is the same, whatever be the pressure to which the gas is previously subjected. 100 volumes of water will absorb 450 volumes of cyanogen; whereas the absorption of hydrogen is only 2 volumes. In general, the more easily a gas is condensable by cold and pressure, the more soluble it is in water. Gases are also absorbed by charcoal and other porous bodies, the absorption being in ammonia 90 times the volume of the absorbent, and in hydrogen 1.75 times.

Some gases are more soluble in water than others; and some are more readily absorbed than others by porous substances. Dr. Faraday has liquefied some gases and solidified others. The method which he employed consisted in combining the condensing powers of mechanical compression with that of very considerable depression of temperature. The first object was attained by the successive action of two air-pumps. The tubes into which the air, thus condensed, was made to pass were of green bottle-glass, and had a curvature at one portion of their length adapted to immersion in a cooling mixture: they were provided with suitable stopcocks, screws, connecting pieces, and terminal caps, sufficiently air-tight to sustain a pressure of 50 atmospheres. Cold was applied to the curved portions of the tube by their immersion in a bath of Thirolier's mixture of solid carbonic acid and ether. The degree of cold thus produced, when the mixture was surrounded by the air, was — 106° Fah., by an alcohol thermometer; but when placed in vacuo, the thermometer indicated 166° below zero. Without the aid of mechanical pressure, Faraday liquefied sulphurous acid gas, cyanogen, chlorine, ammoniacal gas, hydro-sulphuric acid gas, carbonic acid, hydrochloric acid, and nitrous oxide. With the combined aid of cold and pressure he liquefied sulphuretted hydrogen, arseniuretted hydrogen, hydriodic acid, hyrobromic acid, nitric oxide, fluosilicon, and olefiant gas. Alcohol, ether, and chlorine have not yet been solidified; oxygen, hydrogen, nitrogen, and carbonic oxide have neither been solidified nor liquefied.

GAS-LIGHTING. When coal, oil, wax, wood, or any other organic inflammable substance is exposed to destructive distillation in close vessels, an inflammable gas is the result. This gas is some compound of hydrogen and carbon: more or less brilliant when ignited, according to its constitution. That the gas obtainable from coal is inflammable has been known for more than 200 years; and so long ago as 1691 Dr. Clayton made and used inflammable gas as a philosophical experiment. In 1733 Sir James Lowther brought before the notice of the Royal Society the existence of inflammable gas in one of the Whitehaven collieries; and some years afterwards Dr. Watson further drew public attention to the subject.

But, although the properties of coal gas were known to so many persons, no one thought of applying it to a useful object until the year 1792, when Mr. Murdoch, an engineer, residing at Redruth in Cornwall, erected a little gasometer and apparatus, which produced gas enough to light his own house and offices. In 1797 he erected a similar apparatus in Ayrshire, where he then resided. In the following year he was engaged to put up a gas-work at the manufactory of Boulton and Watt, at Soho. This was the first application of gas in the large way; but, excepting in manufactories or among scientific men, it excited little attention until the year 1802, when the front of the great Soho manufactory was brilliantly illuminated with it on the occasion of the public rejoicings at the peace. Soon after this, several manufacturers, whose works required light and heat, adopted the use of gas. Mr. Winsor, a German, brought the subject forward in London, and formed a 'National Light and Heat Company,' in 1804, which failed. In 1807 however he lighted up Pall Mall, and this continued for some years to be the only street in London in which gas was used. In a few years afterwards a Gas Company was chartered; and London gradually became better lighted. The business of the company steadily increased; and in the year 1823 it was shown that this company alone consumed annually 20,678 chaldrons of coals, which produced on an average 680,000 cubic feet of gas every night; this was distributed by means of 122 miles of pipe, which supplied more than 30,000 burners, giving a light equal to as many pounds of tallow candles. Several other companies were established in London. The provincial towns followed the example, and continental cities one by one availed themselves of this useful system, until at length it has become one of the best known and extensively used of modern improvements.

Various substitutes for coal in gas-making have been proposed from time to time, such as resin, wood, and peat, but with little success. Oil yields a brilliant gas, which is easily manufactured; but coal excels them all in cheapness, and is almost universally employed.

Although in the large way there are many practical difficulties to be surmounted in the manufacture of coal gas, the operation is easily understood; it is merely a process of distillation. A quantity of coal is put into a retort, which is well closed, and placed upon the fire; the temperature is raised to redness, which decomposes the coal, and drives the gas resulting from the decomposition through a pipe leading from the retort to the receptacle prepared for it. A mass of coke remains, of greater bulk though less weight, than the coal first put in. Such is the theory of gas-making; the manner of putting it into practice remains to be described.

The *retorts* now in use are generally long cast-iron vessels, semi-cylindrical in shape, with the flat side placed lowermost, and each holding from two to three bushels of coals. They are placed in ovens, in groups of three, five, seven, or more; and their mouths, where the coal is put in, stand out in front of the ovens. Just behind the mouth of the retort a pipe leads from it perpendicularly several feet; then, taking a sudden turn, it descends again, and enters a much larger pipe technically called the *hydraulic main*, which runs through the whole building, and receives the gas produced from all the retorts. This great main is generally about half full of the tar and water which leave the coal with the heated gas, and rise with it in the state of vapour, but are condensed by the coldness of the main. Into this mixture the end of the pipe dips, and is thus closed against a return of gas, which would take place if the supply should slacken. The gas is now made; but it is very impure, being mixed with water, tar, sulphuretted hydrogen, and other impurities. The tar and water are easily got rid of, little more being required for this purpose than to cool the gas and to allow the deposit to run off. The separation of the sulphuretted hydrogen can only be effected by some substance for which it has a chemical attraction, but which has no influence on coal gas. Such a substance is lime. The lime is used by being mixed up with water into a thin pasty mass, which is placed in a cylindrical vessel, and is constantly stirred by machinery. The gas as it comes from the condenser passes into the lime, and comes from it partially purified; it then enters another purifier, made and furnished precisely in a similar way; after that another; and often a fourth, in large works. When it leaves the last vessel, it may be considered pure.

In the manufacture of oil gas it is only necessary to project a small stream of oil into a red-hot retort, in which pieces of brick or coke are inclosed; the gas immediately passes off through another pipe, and may be at once received into the gasometer.

The *gasometer* employed in gas-works is a very large cylindrical vessel, closed at the top and open at bottom; it is suspended by a rope or chain, and weight, in a tank filled with water, in which it rises and falls freely, being kept in its place by guide-wheels. Two tubes pass under and through the water, reaching above its surface into the hollow of the gasometer; one of them comes from the purifiers to admit the gas into the gasometer, the other carries it off when wanted for use. The action of this part of the apparatus is simple; when the gasometer is near the top of the water, it is full of gas, which has no communication with the air, because the edge of the gasometer is under water. If now it be pressed downwards, which is effected by lessening the counterbalancing weight, the gas will be forced through the pipe which is to convey the gas out, and which must be left open for the purpose. When the gasometer reaches the bottom, it will be full of water, and ready to receive gas again, which is admitted through the other tube; the gasometer then rises to the top as the gas goes in, and may be pressed down again. In this way it is alternately filled and emptied. In most establishments there are many gasometers, some filling and others emptying. Some gasometers are now made so large as to have a capacity of 100,000 cubic feet. Some of them have the telescope construction; that is, there are two gas-holders, one within another, and both within the tank; the inner gas-holder is filled first, and then, by an ingenious contrivance, it elevates the outer one as the gas continues to enter.

Many other contrivances are used before the gas is carried to its destination: a *meter*, to measure it; a *governor*, to equalise the flow; a *pressure-gauge*, to indicate the resistance offered to its passage; and a *tell-tale*, to show the quantity manufactured during every hour.

The tubes which convey the gas to the streets are of course larger or smaller, according to the number of burners which they supply. The largest in use are about 18 inches in diameter, the smallest about a quarter of an inch. The street gas-pipes are laid in slightly inclined planes, and a vessel is placed at the bottom of each descent to receive and carry off any deposition which would otherwise clog the pipes.

The burners are of many different forms, and each has its technical name; such as the argand, the fan, the cock-spur, and the bat's wing. The arrangement and management of the burners in practical use are exceedingly varied.

It was estimated in 1848 that at that time there were 6,000,000 tons of coal consumed in England for gas-making; that one-twelfth of this, or 500,000 tons were used in London alone; that the production in London was 500,000 cwts. of coke, and 4,500,000 cubic feet of gas; and that the length of the gas-mains in London was upwards of 1500 miles. The length of gas mains must now be much greater, owing to the operations of rival companies.

The Western Gas Light Company has recently erected extensive works near Kensal Green. The gas is here made from Cannel coal, on a principle patented by Mr. Palmer. The retort-house is a remarkable building. It is a polygon of twelve sides, 166 feet in diameter, and contains 360 retorts. The processes, after the making of the gas in the retorts, differ in many respects from those usually adopted; principally in the mode of purifying the gas. The largest gas-holder or gasometer is of great magnitude; it is 135 feet in diameter by 25 feet deep, and will contain more than 350,000 cubic feet of gas.

The recent agitation of the gas question in London has led to the formation of a new company, by whom mains have been laid down through the principal streets, and a much lower rate of charge introduced than was before known. The mode of charge per cubic feet, as estimated by one among the many varieties of *meter*, is gradually superseding the old mode of charge per burner.

There have been some singular projects lately brought before public notice, relating to gas-lighting. One is White's *Water and Resin Gas;* which is proposed to be formed by heating small coal and fragments of iron in a retort; dropping water on the burning materials; and mixing the gases thus evolved with carburetted hydrogen formed by decomposing resin or fat. M. Jeannery's *Soap-suds Gas* was devised by him as an economical mode of using the soap-suds or scouring water of a woollen-factory at Mulhausen; the sediment from the suds is strained, mixed into a paste with quicksilver, dried, and distilled in a retort. A *Portable Gas* apparatus has been recently introduced, capable of making gas on a small scale for isolated buildings, workshops, &c. The furnace, retort, and purifying vessel can all be comprised within a space of eight or nine square feet. The fuel used is any kind of fat or grease; and on this account it is conceived that such an apparatus might be valuable for emigrants and other residents in sheep or ox-farming countries. Another novelty is Holliday's *Self-generating Gas-lamp*, which, according to the comprehensive eulogy of the inventor, is 'smokeless, portable, safe, durable, clean, of intense light, simple, requiring no attention when once lighted; no fixings, pipes, or meters, consequent on the old gas plan; nor liable to derangement; and is applicable to every purpose.' It comprises a cotton-wick through which naphtha flows; and this naphtha becomes converted into gas or vapour before it reaches the burner: it is a sort of medium between a spirit-lamp and a gas-lamp. An invention, which is now attracting much attention in America, is Payne's *Water-Gas;* this is a plan by which water is decomposed through the agency of an electro-magnet; and the hydrogen is carbonised by being passed through spirits of turpentine, whereby it is converted into carburetted hydrogen—all this is scientifically possible; but whether it is commercially advantageous remains to be seen.

Gas works have recently been constructed in Mexico; and as there were difficulties in procuring the usual sheet-iron gasometers, Mr. Hancock has ingeniously contrived a gasometer made of canvas saturated with india-rubber. These gasometers are cylindrical bags, 12 feet diameter by 15 feet high, formed by two thicknesses of strong canvas cemented together by indai-rubber solution. Iron rings are placed at intervals to keep the bags in shape; and the whole can be flattened to the form of a circular disc a few inches in depth for convenience of transport. The cost of each of these gasometers was about 55*l.*

In Mr. Rutter's recent Treatise on Gas-Lighting, it is stated that there are 560 proprietary gas-works in England and Wales, and 170 in Scotland and Ireland; that these represent a capital of ten and a half millions sterling; that they all, taking one with another, pay a dividend of about five per cent. (a remarkable approximation to that which railway companies show a tendency to converge to); that the quantity of gas produced is about 9000 millions of cubic feet annually; that the coal consumed to produce this gas is about 1,125,000 tons; that the cost of mould candles to produce a light equal to all this gas would be eleven millions sterling; that the cost of sperm oil for the same purpose would be thirteen millions sterling; that the price at which the gas is sold is about 1,600,000*l.*; and that the number of persons constantly engaged in various ways in the manufacture and its subsidiaries is about 20,000.

There is a constant supply of new patents relating to the manufacture of gas, to the forms of burners for consuming it, and to the construction of meters for measuring its quantity.

GASTRIC JUICE. This term is applied to the fluid, secreted from the interior of the stomach, which is the principal agent in digestion. The gastric juice is a transparent slightly viscid liquid, which, when obtained from the stomach of an animal while fasting, possesses neither acid nor alkaline reaction, but has a saline taste. During the process of digestion, on the contrary, it is distinctly acid. Gastric juice possesses strong antiseptic properties, suspending putrefaction, and restoring the freshness of the tainted meat: it also coagulates milk, which property is independent of the presence of any acid. But the most remarkable quality of the secretion of the stomach is its solvent effect, which will even act on nutritive substances out of the body.

GAUGING is the method of determining by actual measurement the number of gallons contained in any vessel intended to hold goods.

The books which relate to this subject give rules and formulæ, according to the shape of the vessel to be gauged.

GAUZE, is a light transparent cloth made of fine silken threads. The texture is different from that of plain weaving, in which the warp, or longitudinal threads, are always parallel to each other. The essential character of gauze-weaving is, that between each cast of the shuttle a crossing of the warp thread shall ensue, and thus the weft (which forms the cross-threads interlaced by the warp) is not brought into absolute contact with the the cross-thread immediately preceding. The intervals left between the interlacings cause that degree of transparency which, without such arrangement, could only result from a looseness of texture, incompatible with beauty and utility.

GEARING, or GEERING, in machinery, is a term somewhat indefinitely applied to a train of toothed wheels, or other similar contrivance, for transmitting motion. Couplings [COUPLING] may in some cases be considered a kind of gearing; and the expression 'to throw machinery *into* or *out of gear*' is commonly applied to the act of engaging or disengaging such connections.

GELATINE is the jelly of animals separate from the other constituents of the body. It is procured by the action of boiling water from bones, tendons, ligaments, membranes, and skin. *Glue-size* and *isinglass* are all varieties of gelatine. In France the gelatine of bones is extracted and employed as a part of the diet in hospitals, with excellent effect.

The substance sold in the shops as *animal gelatine* is obtained from bones, skins, or inferior isinglass. Gelatine has even been obtained from *fossil* bones: those of the mastadon. *French gelatine* is done up in small thin cakes and coloured with beet-juice, spinack-juice, or some other vegetable juice. Very pleasing specimens of gold-printing are now effected on thin and carefully-prepared sheets of coloured gelatine.

GEMS; JEWELS. Besides mere purposes of ornament, the hard and beautiful stones or crystals which constitute gems are applied to many useful purposes.

The application of Gems in watches is noticed elsewhere [JEWELLING OF WATCHES.] A well-known application of the *diamond* is in cutting glass [DIAMOND]. Gems are occasionally employed for the nibs of pens; thus, pens made of gold, with small *rubies* at the nibs, have been known to bear constant use for many years without any appreciable wearing. Many years ago Messrs. Hawkins and Mordan patented a new pen, of which the barrel was made of horn or tortoiseshell, and the nib of a small fragment of diamond or ruby, imbedded into the horn by pressure. From the high refractive power of the diamond, it is employed to form minute and exquisitely accurate lenses for the best kinds of microscope; Mr. Pritchard succeeded in forming such lenses, after the professed diamond makers had pronounced it to be impossible; and Sir David Brewster has had similar lenses made of rubies and garnets. In respect to the general operations of the lapidary or jewel-cutter, they could hardly be conducted without the aid of diamond-dust; for the general mode of cutting and shaping precious stones is to hold them against a very small metallic disc or wheel, which is rotating with great velocity, and to moisten the edge of this disc with oil and diamond dust; the exceedingly hard particles of diamond enable the disc to cut the stone or jewel.

The manufacture of *factitious* or *artificial* gems is a very curious department of art. Any one who glances round a shop containing cheap jewellery, will at once see that no inconsiderable portion of the glittering store is of this nature. Where pence instead of shillings are charged—or in some cases pence instead of pounds—it is easy to see that such must be the case. The brilliant transparency of the diamond, the purple of the ruby, the blue of the sapphire, the green of the emerald, the orange tint of the hyacinth, the transparent blood-red of the garnet, the variegated tints of agate and porphyry, the delicate subdued whiteness of the pearl — all are imitated. Most of these imitative gems are made of glass, called *paste* in this country and *strass* in France; it is of this substance that most artificial diamonds are formed; and by mixing various metallic oxides with the strass, the colours of other gems are imitated. The strass is not common glass, but is carefully made from a mixture of rock-crystal, potash, borax, and oxide of lead. The oxides of iron, antimony, arsenic, manganese, copper, chromium, cobalt, &c., are employed to give to the strass the requisite colour for other gems.

Many artificial gems are *doublets*, and deceive the eye by a curious contrivance. Two little fragments of glass, previously shaped, are cemented together with Venice turpentine and mastich, coloured with carmine, lake, Prussian blue, verdigris, or some other pigment; a humble sort of imitative gem is thus produced. A still humbler method, and the cheapest of all, consists in simply placing a bit of coloured metal foil behind the fragment of transparent glass.

The manufacture of artificial *pearls* is more remarkable perhaps than that of any other gem. They are made of glass beads, coated on the inside with a peculiar substance. A fine and narrow glass tube is held in a lamp at one end, while the workman blows through it from the other; the heated end is blown out into a globular form: and the workman breaks off the bead thus made and proceeds to form another. So rapidly is this done, that a workman can make 5000 or 6000 in a day. The pearl-liquor, or *Essence d'Orient*, is made by steeping in water the scales of the bleak or blay fish; and a single drop is dexterously blown into every bead by means of a little tube; the bead is shaken, to equalize the contact of the liquid with the interior surface. Each bead is then filled with wax, to strengthen it, and a hole is made through the wax to receive a string.—Artificial pearls are chiefly made in Paris.

GENE'VA, the smallest of the Swiss cantons, except Zug, is rendered productive by the industry of the inhabitants: about one-third of it is sown with corn, another third is pasture-land, a much smaller proportion is planted with vines, which yield an indifferent sort of wine; the rest consists of woods, orchards, and gardens. The number of cattle is small. Manufactures and commercial speculations form the principal sources of wealth of the Genevese. Watches and jewellery are now the principal manufactures; they are exported to France, Italy, the Levant, and other countries.

In the chief town, also called Geneva, the staple manufactures of the town are watches, musical boxes, and jewellery: of watches about 20,000 are made annually. All these manufactures will be illustrated by specimens at the approaching Exhibition.

GENEVA. This spirituous liquor is frequently confounded with *gin*. It is procured by the fermentation of the berries of the *Juniperus communis*. From the quantity of sugar which they contain they can easily be caused to ferment and yield a spirit. Geneva is a very powerfully stimulating liquor, containing a large proportion of alcohol: 337,042 gallons of proof Geneva were imported in 1850.

The more common English liquor, *gin*, for which *geneva* is a polite but incorrect name, is malt-spirit flavoured by a variety of herbs, fruits, seeds, sugar, &c.

GENOA. In the province of Genoa, in the Sardinian dominions, the industry of the inhabitants has turned to advantage every spot capable of cultivation; but the produce is not equal to the consumption. The chief products are wine, chesnuts, oil, silk, cotton, hemp, citrons, oranges, lemons, figs, pomegranates, almonds, and other excellent fruits. Marble, alabaster, slate, limestone, asbestos, and coal are found: and a good deal of salt is made along the coast. The principal occupations, besides those indicated above, are trading by sea, fishing, and manufactures of jewellery, velvet, embroidered cambrics and muslins, cloth, furniture, both plain and ornamental, &c.

The town of *Chiavari* is famous for the manufacture of light willow chairs. *Borzonasca*, a large village inland among the Apennines, is important for its cloth manufactures. *Lavagna* has extensive slate quarries. *Rapallo*, a flourishing town, has manufactures of lace and oil. But the chief place in the province is *Genoa*, the famous old Italian city. At Genoa there is regular communication by steamers with Marseille, Barcelona, Leghorn, Civita Vecchia, &c.; and Genoese vessels trade to the Levant, the Black Sea, the Baltic, to America, and even to the coasts of the Pacific. The yearly importations amount to nearly three millions sterling, the exports to somewhat above two millions. The principal articles of export are silk, rice, hemp, oil, and paper. There are at Genoa manufactories of silk stuffs and velvet, woollens, surgical and optical instruments, jewellery and fancy articles, musical instruments, canvas, cordage, paper, and cotton.

GENTIAN. This useful plant is one among many species of *Gentiana*, common in the mountainous and sub-alpine districts of Switzerland, Germany, &c. Though the whole plant is bitter, yet, as this property is most concentrated in the root, that part only is used in medicine. This should be taken up in autumn, and is best when the plant is only one year old. It is generally cylindrical, often an inch thick at the summit, but below rather branched, of a dark or brown colour externally; internally fleshy and yellow. In commerce it is met with in pieces, cut longitudinally, from half a foot to a foot in length. The greater portion is procured from Germany; the specimens from Switzerland are generally thicker and darker coloured. When fresh it has some smell, which is almost entirely lost by drying. The taste is at first somewhat sweet, then purely and strongly bitter. Yellow Gentian-Root is often confounded with the roots of other species of this genus. Gentian-Root is a pure and excellent bitter tonic: it yields its properties to water, particularly when warm, to alcohol, and to wine.

GEOLOGICAL STRATA. Geology as a science is beyond the scope of the present work; but the connection between geology and manufactures is illustrated in such articles as ALUM; COAL; COPPER; GRANITE; IRON; MINING; SLATE; &c.

GEORGIA. The chief vegetable productions of this little-known province of the Russian dominions are grapes, cotton, madder, rice and saffron. There is every reason to believe that great mineral wealth is concealed in the mountains, but hitherto nothing of any importance has been discovered. The present commerce of these countries by the Caspian Sea is carried on from the ports of Derbend, Baku, Shamakhi, and Lencoran, to Persia, and to Astrakan. The overland trade is with Russia and Persia, as well as with Asiatic Turkey. The commerce by the Black Sea is carried on from the mouth of the Rion with Odessa and other Russian ports, as well as with Constantinople; and there is a small traffic with the highlanders of the Caucasus.

GEORGIA is also the name of one of the

United States. The cotton grown in a number of islands off the coast, known by the name of Sea-Island Cotton, fetches a higher price in the market than any other. In the southern districts of Georgia the temperature is suitable to the sugar-cane, orange, olive, fig, pomegranate, &c. The chief products are cotton and rice, of which large quantities are exported, but tobacco, as well as Indian corn, wheat, and other kinds of grain are also grown. The hilly region resembles, in climate as well as in products, the countries of Middle Europe, and much of it is covered with pines, and some of it with oak, hickory, cedar, and other trees. Iron and copper occur in several places in the hilly country, and the ore is said to be rich. Gold is found in the northern part of the state in considerable quantity. A few other industrial statistics of Georgia will be found under UNITED STATES.

GERMANY. This large and important country, including the states which form the ZOLLVEREIN or German Customs Union, will occupy an important position at the Exhibition of the Industry of all Nations. In addition to the brief details given under the heads of the component countries, [BADEN; PRUSSIA; SAXONY, &c.], we will give the following abstract, relating chiefly to the arrangements for the Exhibition.

To carry out the intentions of the English commissioners it became necessary to establish special commissions in Berlin and the leading points of the Prussian monarchy—in Munich, Stutgardt, Dresden, Brunswick, Wiesbaden, and Frankfort, in order to digest and arrange the applications for space in the Crystal Palace. The results of the collective labours of these several commissions have been transmitted to Berlin, to be from thence forwarded to London. By these it appears that there have been 1,572 applications from the artistic and industrial producers within the Customs Union. Of this number 455 belong to the eastern, and 430 to the western provinces of the Prussian monarchy; 197 to the southern states, Bavaria, Wurtemberg, and Baden; 339 to the central German States, Saxony, Brunswick, the Anhalt, and Thuringian territories; and 151 to the states of western Germany, viz., the two Hesses, Frankfort, Luxemburg, Nassau, Birkenfield, and the principality of Lippe.

In a long and valuable report which the Prussian commission has issued a review is taken of the industrial resources of Germany, and of the power which she possesses to occupy a distinguished place in any Exhibition of produce and manufactures. Germany is the great store-house for zinc; in 1849 she produced 452,546 cwts. In the Rhenish provinces more than 1,800,000 cwts. of iron were made in that year. Anhalt, Westphalia, and the Rhenish provinces can produce specimens of lead and antimony; Prussia and Saxony can contribute copper; cobalt and smalt are found and abundantly used in Bavaria; coal is found in various parts of the Zollverein; salt is abundant; aluminous clays, pottery clays, building stones—in short almost every kind of mineral produce useful in the arts is to be met with in one or other of the German states; and the Prussian Commissioners have striven so far as lay within their authority, to have all these varieties represented at the Great Exhibition. The same may be said of vegetable and animal produce used in the arts. In the section of manufactures Germany is in a condition to produce a most varied assemblage, if her manufacturers put forth their best powers; while in machinery and in the fine arts, there is no reason why she should not equally maintain a high reputation.

As an example of the admirable way in which a systematic arrangement enables the Zollverein to contribute from each state what it can best contribute, we may take the department of *Drugs, Perfumery, Dyeing and Tanning materials* and *Printing materials*. Here we find that balsams and mountain herbs will be exhibited from Hirschberg. Perfumes by Farina (the elder and younger of Cologne), by other houses in that city, and in Dusseldorf. Specimens of woad—an article which was once of great commercial importance—will be sent from Erfurt, where the last remnant of its cultivation has been still preserved. Madder and madder dyes will be sent from Mulhausen; indigo carmine from Cologne; printing ink from Markttift (in Lower Franconia), and from Mayence; ink for copperplate printing from Frankfort-on-the-Maine; extract of gall-nuts from Ratisbon; alkaloid and Peruvian bark from Rhenish Hessen; printing colours from Leipsic; aquarell, Indian ink, and paints from Saalfeld, in Meiningen.

In respect to textile materials, fleeces will be sent from Limmenau, Dombran, Zwerbrodt, Hennersdorf, and Oberberg, all in Silesia; from several places in the Grand Dukedom Posen, Prussia proper, Brandenberg, and Saxony. Raw silk will be exhibited from Berlin and the Grand Dukedom Posen. Bristles of peculiarly good quality will be sent from Alach, in the neighbourhood of Erfurt. And so likewise in respect to tanned leather. Hides will be sent from Neckarsteinach (exhibiting a novel and peculiar process of tanning); from St. With, Muhlheim, Trier,

Bingen, and Mayence. The eastern provinces, Berlin, Magdeburg, Stettin, Weissenfels, Mühlhausen, and Gera, will send samples. Lacquered leather, skins, &c., will be sent from Palgorsheim in Bavaria, Bingen, Offenbach, Frankfurt, Worms, and Mekenheim. Sheep skins and morocco leather will be sent from Wäldin, on the Lahr, in Baden; parchment and drumskins from Erfurt; instrument leather from Altenburg; saddlery, harness, Russian and strop-leather will be forwarded from Trier, Barmen, and the Marches. String-gut will be sent from Tilsit and Brüel; animal glue from Cologne, Mühlhausen, and Stralsund; grainy and fine-ground animal charcoal from Tilsit; carmine, and other animal dye-stuffs, from Elberfeld, Berlin, Liegnitz, and Schweinfurt.

Nearly all the other departments are equally rich in examples.

The shipping trade between Great Britain on the one hand, and the entire of Germany on the other (including both Austria and Prussia) exhibited the following results in 1850.—The vessels which entered British ports were 3,147, of 464,770 tons; while those which left British ports were 2914, of 405,218 tons.

GERMINATION is the first growth of a seed, the act by which it exchanges the condition of an embryo for that of a young plant. Attempts have been made to expedite the process of germination by steeping seeds in a weak solution of chlorine, but no practical advantage has been derived from the experiment. A more effectual plan has been found for hard-shelled seeds, such as those of the Acacia, namely, boiling the seeds for a period between one and five minutes.

GERS. In this department of France, wheat, maize, peas, beans, oats, and rye are grown in quantity more than sufficient for the consumption. Marble, building-stone, plaster-of-Paris, marl, potters' clay, and a fusible spar used in glass and china works are found. Some mineral springs, but no metals, are found in the department. Of manufacturing industry there is little. Coarse woollens, bricks, glass, pottery, and other articles of common necessity are made for home use. The quantity of leather tanned is in excess of the consumption, and some of it is exported. The other exports are brandy, wine, corn, flour, wool, poultry, and cattle. The quantity of wine produced in this department yearly is about 25 millions of gallons, about one-fourth of which is used for home consumption, and the greater part of the remainder is distilled into brandy, known by the name of Armagnac, from the former name of the district. In quantity of alcohol, the Armagnac brandies bear to the Cognac the ratio of about 8 to 9. Until lately, all brandies paid in France the same duty, whence came the general preference for Cognac, as it contained a greater quantity of alcohol. But for mildness and delicacy of flavour, and for a peculiarly agreeable aroma, both of which qualities improve with age, the Armagnac is a very superior spirit; and it has this advantage over Cognac, that it comes from the still at a strength ready for consumption, whereas Cognac requires reduction of strength, which process, it need not be said, endangers, and may mar, the peculiar excellencies of that spirit. The best qualities of Armagnac are distilled from two varieties of white grape, called *piquepoul* and *clairet*, in the cantons of Montréal, Eauze, Cazaubon, Manciet, and Nogaro.

GHEE, is a species of butter used by the natives of India. The milk, when first taken from the animal, is boiled in earthen pots for an hour or two; it is then allowed to cool, and a little curdled milk, called Tyre, is added to promote its coagulation. By the next morning the whole mass has been converted into tyre, or coagulated acid milk. This milk, well churned and boiled with water, produces the ghee, which is rather distasteful to Europeans.

GHENT, the capital of East Flanders, in Belgium, was formerly one of the most famous manufacturing and commercial cities in Europe. By the prosperity consequent on its manufacturing industry, the city increased so rapidly, that towards the end of the thirteenth century it exceeded Paris in extent and population. At the beginning of the fifteenth century, the number of its citizens employed in the manufacture of woollens is said to have amounted to 40,000. Ghent afterwards sank in commercial importance; but it has nevertheless continued to be a place of considerable note.

About 19,000 persons are employed in spinning, weaving, bleaching, and printing cotton. Sugar refining is carried on to a large extent in several establishments. Among the various other manufactures are those of lace, silk-weaving, salt-refining, paper making, woollen cloths, tanning, bleaching, soap-boiling, and pin-making.

GIBBONS, GRINLING. At a time when the beautiful art of carving is undergoing such a judicious revival, and is about being applied so largely to decorative purposes, it is right to pay a tribute of admiration to Grinling Gibbons, whose taste produced such exquisite specimens of the art nearly two centuries ago. Having been recommended by Evelyn to Charles II., he was employed by that monarch on the ornamental carving of the chapel at Windsor; he produced such emblematical objects as doves, pelicans, palm-branches, &c. For the choir of St. Paul's he carved much of the foliage and festoons belonging to the stall work, and those in lime-tree which decorate the side aisles of the choir. Much of his choicest work is at Chatsworth: mere ornament, indeed, such as foliage, flowers, feathers, &c.; but finished with such exceeding delicacy and truth, that the workmanship not only confers value on the material, but also on the subject. Occasionally he exerted his skill on subjects altogether trivial in themselves, and merely curiosities in art; such as feathers and pens, that might be mistaken for real ones. He presented to the Duke of Devonshire, on completing his labours at Chatsworth, a point-lace cravat, wrought up in wood. At Southwick, in Hants, he carved the embellishments of an entire gallery; and also those of a room at Petworth, which has generally been deemed one of his chief performances. Gibbons died in 1721.

GIBRALTAR. This celebrated rock-fortress is so much more important in a military than an industrial point of view, that we need say little of it in this place. The natural productions are wild rabbits, woodcocks, teal, and partridges. The trade of Gibraltar is not large. The British produce exported thither in 1849 amounted to 533,481*l.* The principal imports thence to Great Britain in the same year consisted of bark for tanning, gum Arabic, raw silk, and brandy. Mail steamers call at Gibraltar three times a month, from Southampton; these steamers keep up a communication between Gibraltar and Vigo, Oporto, Cadiz, Malta, Alexandria, and Constantinople. In fact, Gibraltar is a kind of half-way station on the overland route.

GILDING. In the gilding of articles of metal, pure gold is first combined or amalgamated with quicksilver, by boiling the gold in five or six times its weight of quicksilver. The boiling mixture is poured into cold water, by which it loses a great deal of its fluidity; and it is then squeezed through chamois leather. The amalgam has now the consistence of a stiff clay, has a greasy and gritty feel, and is in the most convenient state for being weighed out into portions requisite for each respective quantity of work. The main object of bringing the amalgam to this consistence and these proportions is to have it in a form convenient for division and apportionment, as well as for the sake of having a uniform standard by which to ascertain the quantity and value of the gold employed.

On the application, however, of this amalgam to the surfaces of metal, it is found that, as there is no chemical affinity between the substances thus brought into contact, the direct union of them is impossible. Nor can it be effected by allowing them to remain in contact for any length of time. The intervention of a solution of nitrate of mercury is therefore used. The solution is, by the operatives, termed 'quick-water.' When a piece of copper or brass is immersed in or brought in contact with this solution, its surface is immediately converted into an amalgam. To this amalgamated surface mercury and gold amalgam closely adheres, by means of the molecular attraction of the particles of the fluid metals for each other.

The manner in which this agent is applied in practice varies according to the description of articles to be gilt. If they are small, strong, and to be gilt all over, as copper buttons, buckles, and rings, a quantity of them, three or four pounds in weight, is put into a deep glazed earthen pan, or 'jowl;' to these are added about three or four tea-spoonfuls of the 'quick-water,' together with the requisite portion of amalgam. The whole is then thoroughly stirred with a brush or stick, till the amalgam entirely covers the surface of every article. When they are completely covered, they are by some gilders rinsed in cold water and dried by shaking in a bag of warm sawdust; while by others this part of the process is postponed to a later period of the operation, and they are put in their wet state, with the generated nitrate of copper still hanging about them, into the cage.

The 'gilding-cage' is made in a cylindrical form, and is generally about 18 inches in length by 9 or 10 in diameter. It is formed of coarse iron-wire gauze, supported by an external framework of iron, and furnished with a solid iron door at one extremity. It is provided with an axle, which extends to a length of about three feet from the end at which the door is placed, and is then terminated by a winch, and to a distance of five or six inches in the opposite direction. The articles under process of gilding are placed in this cage, and the door of it securely fastened; it is then suspended by its axle on two supports in an iron cylinder. The cylinder being previously heated by a coal fire beneath it, to such a degree as to be red-hot over a large proportion of its inferior surface, the cage is introduced, and the doors of the cylinder closed. The heated air contained within the cylinder soon raises the temperature of the substances immersed in it, and, as the cage is kept continually revolving, they have all an equable share of heat, and allow of a nearly equal evaporation of the mercury from all their surfaces. The hinder part of the cylinder is connected with a chamber and flue so constructed as to carry off the deleterious fumes of the mercury.

After the cage, with its contents, has been in the cylinder for a length of time, varying, according to the temperature at which it has been kept, from five minutes to a quarter of an hour, the mercury will be found to have entirely evaporated from the gilt surfaces. Another application of 'quick-water,' and another heating in the cage, are sometimes necessary to bring the surface to a proper state. The gilt articles are then 'heightened,' which is done by continuing to revolve them at the same high temperature within the cylinder, occasionally taking out the cage and shaking them together, that they may all have an equal share of the heat. The end intended to be effected is a partial oxidation of the surface of the gold. This partial oxidation occasions a slight difference of colour, which is perceptible by an experienced eye, and confers on the gold a degree of that orange colour which is so generally admired in golden and gilt articles.

Buttons and articles of a similar description are often gilt only on their tops, or on some other portion of their surfaces, while the remainder is left uncovered with gold, and of the native colour of the metal of which they are manufactured. This is accomplished by brushing them over the part to be gilt with a hard brush wetted with 'quick-water,' or by rubbing it with a piece of chamois leather similarly moistened. They are afterwards briskly rubbed with a dry brush. They are then put into the 'gilding-cap,' which is a white felt hat of a peculiar sort and shape. The amalgam is put into the gilding-cap along with them. The whole is then well shaken together for a few minutes, when the amalgam will be perceived clinging to the amalgamated parts of the goods, but leaving the remainder in their original state. They are then put into the cage, the mercury is evaporated, and they are afterwards heightened in the manner already described.

For larger goods, and where considerable portions of hidden surface are not required to be gilt, there are two modes of preventing the amalgam from adhering to those parts. One is to lacquer those parts, and, after the spirit of wine is thoroughly evaporated, to immerse them in the quick-water, and afterwards apply the amalgam. The other mode of applying the gold is to distribute the quick-water over the parts requiring it by a small brush or camel's hair pencil, and these then have the amalgam applied as before. If, as is sometimes the case, the goods are to be entirely covered, they are immersed at once in the quick-water. If the articles are of a kind which would be injured by revolving in the cage, the heating is effected by other means. Gilt articles are afterwards coloured to a deeper orange tint by the application of several chemical mixtures aided by heat.

Most gilt articles are burnished by a stone burnisher, formed of a polished piece of black hæmatite. This is fixed into a proper handle. Small articles, as buttons, &c., are placed in a lathe, and the stone applied to them as they revolve; and those that do not admit of this are burnished by hand on a table or bench.

Steel and iron are gilt by being immersed in a mixture of the nitro-muriate of gold with sulphuric ether or alcohol. By combining these liquids together, an alcoholic solution of gold is formed, from which the metal is precipitated by the iron or steel.

Ivory may be gilt by immersing it first in a solution of sulphate of iron, and afterwards in one of nitro-muriate of gold.

The edges of the leaves of books are gilt by applying to them, when squeezed in a press, a composition of four parts Armenian bole and one part sugar-candy, ground together with the white of eggs. Gold leaf is then laid on, and is afterwards burnished by rubbing with a polished piece of agate.

The gilding of porcelain is accomplished by the application of gold-leaf during the process of its manufacture, which is fixed by that intense heat which confers on this substance its enamel or glaze, and is afterwards burnished by a stone as above described.

Carved wood or wood-mouldings are gilt by laying on a foundation of whiting and size, and a further series of layers of gold-size, to which leaf-gold is made to adhere by wetting the surface underneath it: this is 'burnish-gilding.' In 'oil-gilding,' the gold is made to adhere by using oil-gold-size, instead of burnish-gold-size wetted with water. The former kind of gilding admits of being burnished with a smooth piece of agate, but not the latter.

Glass may be gilt by applying leaf-gold to the glass when wetted with a solution of isinglass.

For the process of Electro-Plating, which is now much employed as a substitute for metal-gilding, see ELECTRO-METALLURGY.

GIN, or GYN, a machine employed instead of a crane, chiefly by artillerymen, for the purpose of raising guns, howitzers, &c. on their carriages. It consists of three round poles, placed up in a pyramidal form, within which a windlass and tackle afford the means of raising weights. A similar contrivance is often used in the coarser kinds of Engineering.

Gin is also the name of a machine employed in the United States for cleaning cotton; in which a number of revolving spikes disentangle the cotton fibres.

GINGER. This useful condiment is the rootstock of a plant which grows extensively in the East and West Indies, and other hot countries; it is one among many species of the genus *Zingibera*. The ginger-plant is propagated either by seeds or by cuttings of the root. When the cuttings are planted out in spring, which is the mode generally pursued in its cultivation, in the course of three or four months the rootstocks have a mild aromatic flavour; and it is in this state they are used for the preparation of what is called *preserved ginger*. At the end of the same year, or the beginning of the next, they are considered fit to yield the ginger of commerce. The rootstocks are then prepared in two ways: either by scalding them in boiling water, and drying them with artificial heat; or by peeling, and drying them in sunshine. The former method produces the *black ginger* of commerce, and the latter the *white ginger*.

About 14,000 cwts. of Ginger were imported in 1848.

GINSENG, is a root found in China, to which extraordinary properties have been ascribed. It is not only considered a universal remedy for all maladies, but is spoken of in the highest terms as a specific in particular circumstances. European botanists have, however, some doubts concerning the identification of the plant.

GIRONDE, the largest department of France, is rendered remarkable, in an agricultural point of view, by the district called the *Landes*. These landes are sandy heaths, of which only a small part has been brought into cultivation, and which occupy nearly half of the department, extending from the sea to the valley of the Garonne. The sands of the downs along the sea-shore, driven inland by the winds, gradually overspread a considerable tract of country, encroaching yearly from 70 to 80 feet along the whole extent of the coast. The increasing devastation has however been checked by planting broom and other shrubs, by means of which the sand has in most parts become fixed.

The department produces wheat, rye, maize, and millet. The rye and millet are raised in such parts of the Landes as have by dint of manure been brought into cultivation. Excellent fruits and a large quantity of hemp are grown. But the staple produce of the department is wine, of which 40 to 50 millions of gallons are produced annually. The finest clarets are from this part of France, as the growths of Lafitte, Latour, Château-Margaux, (these are in the Médoc district, on the left of the Garonne and Gironde, between Bordeaux and the sea) Haut-Brion, Sauterne, Barsac, and the Vins de Grave. The extensive woods which skirt the sea-coast, or pervade the Landes, consist chiefly of the pine (*Pinus maritima*), from which turpentine, pitch, and charcoal are procured, as well as timber for building and masts for vessels. The cork-tree is abundant. The inhabitants of the Landes make charcoal, or tend the numerous flocks, which obtain scanty food amid these sandy wilds. The chief manufactures of the department are calico, muslin, soap, chemical products, pottery, paper, vinegar, brandy, sugar, beer, leather, glass, &c. Ship-building is extensively carried on in Bordeaux. There are several tobacco factories, dyehouses, rope-walks; and a great deal of salt is made along the coast. The department contains upwards of 1,600 wind-mills and water-mills, about 50 iron-foundries, and 350 to 400 factories of different kinds.

The most important commercial town is BORDEAUX. Next to this is *Blaye*, which has linen and woollen factories, glass-works, potteries, ship-building yards, and a considerable commerce in wines, brandies, spirits, oil, soap, fruits, ship-timber, staves, &c. Vessels put into the port of Blaye to complete their cargoes, and to supply themselves with provisions. *St. Vivien* has a great trade in salt, of which 6,000,000 bushels are annually produced from the neighbouring salt-works. At *Libourne* the manufactures are of cotton yarn, iron, leather, ropes, and nails; ship-building is also carried on. The trade is in wine and brandy, oak staves, iron, coal, and salt. *Castillon* has cotton factories, tan yards, rope yards, and cooperages, and nails are manufactured to a considerable extent.

GLAMORGANSHIRE. This is the most commercial and manufacturing county in Wales. It has all the elements of increasing greatness. Its canals, its railways, its mines, its manufactures, its shipping, are all important. The chief rivers, such as the Taff, the Daw, the Ogmore, the Avon, the Neath, the Tawe, the Loughor, and the Cynon, are all made the media of bringing mining produce to the sea, or have been so until canals and railways were made. The Cardiff Canal extends from Merthyr Tydvil to a point a mile and a half below Cardiff; about 25 miles. The Aberdare Canal runs from the Cardiff Canal to near Aberdare;

about 6½ miles. The Neath Canal makes a short cut between two points on the Neath River; about 14 miles long. The Swansea Canal extends from Swansea Harbour into Brecknockshire; about 17 miles. The Penclawd Canal has a short course of 4 miles into the æstuary of the Burry. There are many railways for conveying minerals, among which are the Duffryn, Llynvi, and Porth Cawl; the Bridgend; the Aberdulais; the Oystermouth; and the Aberavon railways. The Tâf Vale Railway is both for passengers and goods; and so is the South Wales Railway, which now traverses the county from east to west.

The coal-measures occupy all the northern part of the county. The miner finds coal without any considerable descent; for the whole county is intersected with deep valleys in a north and south direction; and the miner, taking advantage of this, drives levels into the adjacent hills and obtains ironstone and coal. There are however many mines in valleys and low places. The coal which occurs in the county is of very varied quality and applicable to many different purposes. Ironstone is found in the valley of the Neath, but most abundantly near Aberdare and Merthyr, which last may be considered as the capital of the iron district of South Wales. There are some lead mines in the district occupied by the carboniferous limestone, near Cowbridge and Llantrisaint. Limestone is quarried in various places.

A few details illustrative of the produce and industry of this busy county will be met with under CARDIFF, MERTHYR, and SWANSEA. All the chief towns will contribute towards the Industrial Exhibition.

GLASGOW. This city and its river are among the wonders of our empire. Until 1775 the Clyde was only navigable by vessels of very small burthen; but since that time large sums have been expended in its improvement, the banks have been widened, the bed deepened, and the numerous sand banks and other obstructions to the navigation have been removed. There are now quays on both banks nearly a mile in length. Vessels drawing 14 feet of water can come up close to the lowest bridge. The revenue derived from the harbour in 1847 was 54,000*l*. Port Glasgow, situated 14 miles down the Clyde, belongs to Glasgow, and is governed wholly by the Glasgow magistrates.

Prior to the union in 1707, the commerce of Glasgow was limited to France and Holland, and consisted principally in the curing and exportation of salmon; but after that Glasgow entered so extensively into the trade with Virginia and Maryland, that before the commencement of the American War in 1776, which suspended the tobacco trade, the annual imports exceeded 50,000 hogsheads. At the present time the trade with the United States and the West Indies, and the timber trade with North America, are carried on upon a very large scale. There are about 80,000 tons of iron, and 130,000 tons of coal exported annually from the Clyde. The ships which are owned by Glasgow houses amount to about 600, with a tonnage of 150,000 tons.

Glasgow is also quite as much a manufacturing as a commercial town. With the exception of some large establishments near Aberdeen and Stirling, almost the entire cotton manufacture of Scotland is confined to Glasgow and the country surrounding it to the extent of 25 miles. The manufacture of linens, cambrics, &c., was first introduced into Glasgow about 1725, the power-loom in 1793, and at the present time the numerous establishments for weaving and spinning are on the most splendid scale. The School of Design at Glasgow is rendering valuable service in respect to the artistic department of textile manufacture. But, although the cotton manufactures have hitherto constituted the staple trade of Glasgow, those of iron become annually of greater extent; and from the peculiarly advantageous position of the town, in a mineralogical point of view, Glasgow is becoming more and more the centre of an iron district, especially since the introduction of the hot-blast in the iron manufacture. Shipping and steam engines are among the important manufactures of Glasgow.

Glasgow is the centre of a very extensive system of railways, which radiate from it in every direction.

The population of Glasgow has increased at a very rapid rate. It was only 14,000 in 1651; in 1811 it had increased to 112,330; in 1821 to 150,818; in 1831 to 207,393; in 1841 to 274,533; and it is supposed that the present population is more than 370,000.

In a series of papers recently given in 'Chambers' Edinburgh Journal,' and founded on personal researches, are some valuable statistics of the industry of Glasgow in 1850. We will note down a few of the more prominent features.

Glasgow itself was estimated in 1849 to contain 367,000 inhabitants; but it is the centre and metropolis of a district which now contains not less than 600,000. It is the metropolis for Paisley and its shawls; for the shipping of Greenock and Port Glasgow; for Kilmarnock and its carpets; for Pollockshaws, Barrhead, and Johnston, and their cotton spinning and weaving mills; for the vale of Leven and its bleach works; for the cotton manufacturing district of Lanark, Blantyre, and Campsie; and for the great iron mining and smelting district of Airdrie and Coatbridge.

The harbour of Glasgow is now fitted to accommodate vessels of 1,000 tons burden, and exhibits not less than 10,000 feet of quays. The largest merchant ships, from all parts of the world, can come almost into the very heart of Glasgow; and the finest mail steamships receive their engines from the quays within the limits of the town.

The following is given, by the authority alluded to above, as the result of a very careful enquiry into the textile factories, and those immediately dependent on textile manufactures, in Glasgow in 1850; giving the number of firms, and the number of operatives employed:—

	Firms.	Operatives.
Cotton and thread spinners	76	25,000
Power loom weavers ..	24	3,640
Hand loom weavers ..	..	3,200
Calico manufacturers ..	240	4,000
Gingham „	37	1,840
Muslin „	40	920
Silk „	22	720
Lace „	16	140
Carpet „	5	260
Shawl „	10	64
Woollen and worsted „ ..	14	1,570
Rope and sail makers ..	45	840
Calico printers & bleachers	64	1,860
Dyers	50	1,400
Calenders and packers ..	48	500
Designers and block cutters	35	520
Cylinder engravers ..	6	750
Miscellaneous	150	700
	882	47,924

These numbers, even supposing them to be strictly correct, could only apply to one particular week; but they afford a useful approximation. Besides the operatives employed by these firms, there are many thousand clerks, packers, and porters. These numbers refer to Glasgow alone; the textile factories in Paisley and the other towns of the Glasgow district form a wholly distinct series.

Vast as these textile manufactures are, they only employ two-thirds of the regular operatives of the Glasgow district, the other third being employed chiefly in the mineral and chemical manufactures. On the east and south of Glasgow the district is bristled with iron furnaces. There are in this district about 100 firms engaged in the smelting and casting operations, by whom 600,000 tons of iron are now annually manufactured. At the Govan and Calder works alone (Messrs. Dixon's) are no less than 13 blast furnaces; at Gartsherrie (Messrs. Baird's) 16; at Dundyvan (Messrs. Wilson's) 10; at Tollcross (Messrs. Dunlop's) 9; at the Monkland works 6.

The customs' receipts at Glasgow in 1850 were 645,669*l.*; and those of Greenock (which in many respects may be deemed a second port for Glasgow commerce) 383,487*l.*; making a total of upwards of a million sterling for the Clyde ports.

The chemical works are another mighty element of Glasgow industry. At the St. Rollox works of Messrs. Tennant chemical manufactures are conducted on a scale which no other establishment in the world, we believe, equals; and there are many others of considerable magnitude.

Glasgow is well fitted to take a commanding position in any Exhibition of the World's Industry.

GLASS MANUFACTURE. This transparent and beautiful substance, though exceedingly brittle while cold, is rendered so flexible and tenacious by a high degree of heat that it may with the utmost facility be moulded into any form. It is so ductile while heated, that it may be spun into filaments of the greatest conceivable fineness, and these when cold are pliant and elastic in a high degree.

The time at which glass was invented is very uncertain. The ancient Egyptians were certainly acquainted with the art of glass making. The manufacture was long carried on at Alexandria, from which city the Romans were supplied with that material; but before the time of Pliny the manufacture had been introduced into Italy, France, and Spain. Glass utensils have been found among the ruins of Herculaneum. The application of glass to the glazing of windows is of comparatively modern introduction. The earliest manufacture of flint glass in England was begun in 1557, and that of plate glass in 1673. The principal seat of the manufacture in England is at Newcastle-upon-Tyne and the neighbouring town of Shields; next in importance is Stourbridge; then the works in and near Liverpool, including the Plate-glass Company's establishment at Ravenhead; next follow Bristol, Warrington, Birmingham. Leeds, and London. There are several manufactories in Scotland and Ireland.

There are five distinct kinds of glass, which differ from each other in regard to some of the ingredients of which they are made, and in the processes of manufacture. These kinds are *flint glass*, or *crystal*; *crown glass*, or

German sheet glass; broad glass, or *common window glass; bottle glass;* and *plate glass.*

The principal ingredients used for the production of each of these kinds of glass are silex, or flint, or sea sand, and an alkali. The differences in the various kinds result from the description of alkali employed, and from the addition of certain accessory materials, usually metallic oxides. The alkali employed for making fine flint glass is purified pearlash. Barilla, kelp, and wood ashes, combined with many impurities, are used for making inferior kinds of glass: the impurities even assist towards fusing the silex. Coarse alkaline substances all contain iron in some degree, and it is to the presence of this metal that the green colour of common glass is owing.

Flint Glass, known in other countries under the name of crystal, is the most generally useful, the most brilliant, and the heaviest description of glass. The following is one among many ratios of ingredients:—

120 parts fine clean white sand,
40 ,, well purified pearlash,
35 ,, litharge, or minium,
13 ,, nitre; and a small quantity of the black oxide of manganese. The litharge is employed to assist the sand to melt; nitre is used to dissipate carbon, and manganese to dissipate colour. The ingredients are intimately mixed together before they are put into the crucibles or pots, which are previously placed in the furnace. A very strong and long continued heat is necessary, not only for the perfect fusion and amalgamation of the materials, but also for the discharge of the impurities which they contain. The glass is cooled down to a pasty mass, and then wrought. There is perhaps no process of manufacture which excites so much the surprise and admiration of a stranger as that of fashioning flint glass into all the various objects of convenience and ornament for which it is employed. To see a substance, proverbially brittle, blown by the human breath, pulled, twisted, cut, and then joined again with the greatest facility, never fails to strike with astonishment those who are unaccustomed to the sight. The tools with which all these operations are performed are of the most inartificial description, and do not appear to have received any notable improvement from the earliest records of the manufacture.

Crown Glass.—This is the best description of window glass; and one recipe for it is:—

120 parts of white sand,
60 ,, purified pearlash,
30 ,, saltpetre,
2 ,, borax,
1 ,, arsenic,

with the addition of a minute quantity of manganese. Crown glass is made by blowing, in the form of circular plates of 50 to 60 inches diameter. A quantity of glass in the pasty state is collected upon the end of a hollow iron tube; and this glass is then converted, by blowing through the tube, into a hollow globe of the requisite thickness. This globe is transferred to the end of the rod, and after several re-heatings it is twirled round by the workman somewhat in the manner that a mop is twirled to drive off the moisture; with this twirling the softened material is continually driven off from the centre by the centrifugal force, until at length the whole substance is converted into a flat disc of circular form, and, except at the centre, where it is attached to the rod, of a uniform thickness.

Broad Glass is an inferior kind of window-glass, made with a cheaper kind of alkali. It is blown to a cylindrical form, cut open, and spread into a flat plate.

Bottle Glass is still inferior in quality to broad glass, the alkali employed being the cheapest that can be procured, with the addition of a portion of lime to assist fusion. Bottle glass is fashioned by blowing into hollow moulds.

Plate Glass is both blown and cast. The following proportions and ingredients are given by Parkes:—

Lynn sand, well washed and dried	720 parts.
Alkaline salt, containing 40 per cent. of soda . . .	450 ,,
Lime, slaked and sifted .	80 ,,
Nitre	25 ,,
Broken plate glass . .	425 ,,
	1700 parts.

It requires 40 hours' exposure to the full heat of the furnace to reduce the materials to the proper state of fusion and vitrification. When this is accomplished, the glass is transferred from the melting pot to a large vessel called a *cuvette*, and from this to a large casting table, where it is distributed by means of a roller over the whole surface of the table, bars of metal being placed at each side along its entire length, and across the bottom, in order to prevent the glass from running upon the floor. The casting of large plates of glass is one of the most beautiful processes in the arts: the large mass of melted glass, rendered in a high degree luminous by heat, exhibits changing colours in the sheet after the roller has been passed over it.

When annealed, which all glass requires to be before using [ANNEALING], the plates of glass are ground with powdered flints, and then with emery powder, and are afterwards polished with oxide of iron laid upon woollen pads. Plate glass is silvered for looking glasses with an amalgam of mercury and tinfoil.

There has perhaps never been known a more signal effect produced on a manufacture by fiscal arrangements, than that which has resulted from the removal of the glass duty in 1846. What is the amount of this effect, it would be difficult to say, as there is no account now kept by the excise of the quantity of glass manufactured. Until 1846 the excise regulations were most vexatious to the glass manufacturer. The annealing ovens were under lock and key, and no glass could be put in or taken out of them without the presence and sanction of the excise officers. The efforts of the manufacturers to improve their wares were paralysed; for they could not even institute experiments without paying duty for the glass wasted in so doing. The sum realised to the revenue in 1845 amounted to 115,000*l.* The export has very largely increased since the remission of the excise duty; in 1850 it amounted to 336,614 cwts. of flint, window, and bottle glass, besides plate glass, which is estimated by measure and not by weight: the value of all the four kinds was 308,346*l.*

It may be safely asserted, that without the remission of the glass duty in 1846, the Palace of Industry in Hyde Park could not have been constructed on Mr. Paxton's plan; whatever the building might else have been, it would not have been a 'crystal' palace. Until the duty was removed, the successful experiments in making large sheets on the *broad glass* method would hardly have been made; and it is only on this method, and at the cheap prices which now prevail, that the acres of glass could have been provided for this beautiful structure. The vast establishment of Messrs. Chance at Birmingham is now one of the most interesting centres of industry in the country: the many hundreds of men employed; the surprising skill with which the workmen (Englishmen and Frenchmen working in harmony) make the cylinders which afterwards become sheets of broad glass; and the rapidity with which the immense supply for the Hyde Park building has been furnished—all have tended to render these works lately well worthy of study.

Nor are there wanting examples of the beneficial results of the fiscal change in other directions. *Dairy* glass is now an important article; and we find that in London and other large towns establishments have been opened for the sale of glass—coarse but strong—fashioned into an amazing variety of utensils and implements. Rough plate for skylights and conservatories, and rough plate for floors (as much as an inch and a half in thickness); glass tiles and slates; perforated glass for ventilation; glass milk pans, cream pots, lactometers, preserve jars, pastry slabs, rolling pins, glass syringes, leech glasses, and pill-making slabs; bee glasses, propagating glasses, wasp traps, cucumber glasses, hyacinth cups, flower dishes, crocus glasses, peach and grape protecting glasses, and fern shades; glass cornice poles; glass churns, glass syphons—these are some among the many articles now made of this beautiful and useful substance.

An important modern application of glass is as a material for pipes, in cases where iron, stone, and wood would be less efficient. Several hundred feet of glass pipes have been recently laid down on the estate of the Earl of Zetland.

A very remarkable and brilliant effect is now produced in cut glass by coating parts of the interior with silver, on a plan recently patented. A brief notice of this, and of the ordinary mode of silvering looking glasses, will be found under SILVERING.

The glass manufacturers of the Tyne district are expected to make a worthy display of their art at the approaching Exhibition. They will send specimens of plate glass in all the stages of progress, some of them almost unparalleled in size; and the other kinds of glass will be fittingly illustrated. From St. Helen's we are promised other specimens; and there can be little doubt that this department of our national manufacture will be well represented. Our manufacturers, in return, will be eager to see what Bohemia and Bavaria and France can produce, in this beautiful branch of industry.

GLASS PAINTING, or STAINING, is practised as follows:—The design having been first drawn on paper, the glass is laid thereon, and the outline traced with a coloured fusible glass. The parts intended to be yellow, orange, or red, are then coated, either on one or both sides, according to the tint required, with a mixture composed of silver, antimony, and oxide of iron. The glass is then exposed to a red heat, in which process the tracing colour is fused, and adheres permanently to the glass. The mixture of silver and antimony stains the glass, but does not melt, so that the oxide of iron, which is in the state of dry powder, may be brushed off, leaving the glass coloured, but as transparent as before. The other colours, composed, as for enamel [ENAMEL], of a very fusible glass coloured with metallic oxides, are then added, and the glass is again fired. In subjects which are too large to be executed in one piece, the joinings are carefully arranged to run in the outline; and for draperies, &c., the artist avails himself of glass already coloured in the manufacture (pot metal), and which requires shadowing, diapering, &c.

In *painting* glass, the colours applied remain on the surface of the glass, and interfere with its transparency. In *staining* glass, the colour sinks into the glass a very small distance, but leaves it as transparent as before. The only colours which modern artists are able to produce by staining are yellow, orange, and red. There are two modifications of painting or staining on glass, called melting and embossing, produced by special chemical means.

The glass stainers of St. Helen's, Newcastle, and other towns, are preparing large and fine specimens of their art for the Great Exhibition.

GLAUBER SALT occurs as a mineral body. It is found as an efflorescence, and also crystallised; whitish, translucent, and having a cool bitter taste. It is a hydrated sulphate of soda.

GLAZE; GLAZING. One of the modes in which the word *glazing* is employed is to designate the fixing of panes of glass into windows. As a manipulative art, glazing is very simple; the putty with which the glass is fixed is a mixture of whiting and linseed oil; and the glass itself is cut by a diamond—though (see COKE) it seems as if a much less costly material may be made available for this purpose. The largest and most interesting specimen of glazing ever yet executed is perhaps the Glass Palace in Hyde Park: the contrivances for enabling the workmen to pursue their avocations in the most difficult positions have been truly admirable for their simplicity and efficiency.

In the earthenware and china-ware manufacture *glaze* is the name of the vitrified gloss or varnish applied to the ware. The nature of this kind of glazing is noticed under POTTERY and PORCELAIN.

GLIADINE, is a peculiar azotised vegetable matter which exists in small quantity with the gluten of wheat, and to which its adhesive properties are owing. It may be separated by boiling alcohol, together with a thick fluid oil which is separable by ether. Gliadine is adhesive, and is insoluble in water. When dried, it is hard and translucent like horn; it dissolves in acetic acid and solution of potash.

GLOBE-MAKING. This is in many respects a remarkable branch of art. It is said that there are only four globe-makers in England and one in Scotland; and that the annual sale of globes is only about a thousand pair. The price of a pair of globes varies from six shillings to fifty pounds. But from the smallest 2-inch, to the largest 36-inch globe, a systematic process is carried on at every step of its formation. The following account of the manufacture is condensed from Dickens' 'Household Words.'

Globes are made of paper and plaster, shaped upon a model or mould. This mould is turned out of a piece of wood, and has for an axis a piece of iron wire at each pole. On this mould a boy will in a very short time form a pasteboard globe. He first covers it entirely with strips of strong paper, thoroughly wet, which are in a tub of water at his side. The slight inequalities produced by the over-lapping of the strips are immaterial. The saturated paper is not suffered to dry; but is imediately covered over with a layer of pasted paper, also cut in long narrow slips. A third layer of similarly pasted paper—brown paper and white being used alternately—is applied; and then a fourth, a fifth, and a sixth. Here the pasting process ends for globes of moderate size. For the large ones it is carried farther. This wet pasteboard ball has now to be dried,—placed upon its axis in a rack. The extrication of the wooden mould from its prison then takes place. The wooden ball, with its solid paper covering, is placed on its axis. A sharp cutting instrument, fixed on a bench, is brought into contact with the surface of the sphere, which is made to revolve; and the pasteboard ball is quickly cut in half. Within every globe there is a piece of wood—we may liken it to a round ruler—of the exact length of the inner surface of the sphere from pole to pole. A thick wire runs through this wood, and originally projected some two or three inches at each end. This stick is placed upright in a vice. The semi-globe is nailed to one end of the stick, upon which it rests, when the wire is passed through its centre. It is now reversed, and the edges of the card rapidly covered with glue. The edges of the other semi-globe are instantly brought into contact, the other end of the wire passing through its centre in the same way, and a similar nailing to the stick taking place. We have now a paper globe, with its own axis.

The paper globe is next placed on its axis in a frame, of which one side is a semi-circular piece of metal. The workman applies to the surface of the globe a coating of whiting, glue, and oil; and this is repeated five or six times, with intervening periods of drying. The globe is therefore by this time a paper sphere enveloped in another sphere of plaster. If it does not revolve quite equably on its axis a few shot are introduced into the too-buoyant portions.

What may be called the artistical portion of globe-making here commences, in which the intelligent labour of females is available. The workwoman takes the polished globe in her lap, for the purpose of marking it with lines of direction for covering it with engraved strips; which lines are those of latitudes and longitudes. These lines are struck with great rapidity, and with mathematical truth, by an instrument called a 'beam compass.' The sphere is now ready for receiving the map, which is engraved in fourteen distinct pieces. The arctic and antarctic poles form two circular pieces, from which the lines of longitude radiate. These having been fitted and pasted, one of the remaining twelve pieces, containing 30 degrees of longitude and 133 degrees of latitude, is also pasted on the sphere, in the precise space where the lines of longitude have been previously marked; its lines of latitude corresponding in a similar manner. The paper upon which these portions of the earth's surface are engraved is thin and extremely tough. It is rubbed down with the greatest care, through all the stages of this pasting process. We have at length a globe covered with a plain map, so perfectly joined that every line and every letter fit together as if they had been engraved in one piece,—which, of course, would be absolutely impossible for the purpose of covering a ball.

The artist who thus covers the globe, called a paster, is also a colourer. By long experience the artist knows how the various boundaries are to be defined, with pink continents, and blue islands, and the green oceans, connecting the most distant regions. The globe has now to be varnished with a preparation technically known as 'white hard,' to which some softening matter is added to prevent the varnish cracking. Four coats of varnish complete the work.

The globe has to be mounted. The brass meridian ring has been previously accurately graduated; this operation is comparatively rapid; but for the largest globes it involves considerable expense. After great trouble Messrs. Malby have succeeded in producing cast-iron rings, with the degrees and figures perfectly distinct; and these applied to 36-inch globes, instead of the engraved meridians, make a difference of ten guineas in their price. For furniture they are not so beautiful: for use they are quite as valuable. The axis of the globe revolves on the meridian ring, and of course it is absolutely necessary that the poles should be exactly parallel; this is effected by a little machine which drills each extremity at one and the same instant; and the operation is termed poleing the meridian. The mounting of the globe,—the completion of a pair of globes,—is now handed over to the cabinet-maker.

Globes have occasionally been constructed of very large size. Such a one was designed in 1823 by an ingenious mechanician, M. Delangard. The spectator reached a circular gallery in the centre of the globe by a winding stair. The sea was represented by transparencies coloured and varnished; the land being opaque and tinted, as in ordinary globes. Another was constructed in 1844 by M. Charles Guérin, who constructed another in the Champs-Elysées. It was placed within an ornamental house of wood; the globe was more than 30 feet in diameter, was viewed by the spectators from a central gallery, reached by a double-winding stair; an iron framework representing the lines of latitude and longitude, gave the outline of the globe, and supported the varnished calico which stretched over the entire surface, and upon which the map was painted. This exhibition was called the Géorama.

But Mr. Wyld, the eminent map publisher, is about to eclipse all previous attempts in this direction. He has paid 3000*l.* for the lease, for a definite period, of the central area in Leicester Square; and on this area he will construct a building for exhibiting an immense globe, 60 feet in diameter. There will be two galleries within it for spectators, at different elevations. The countries, oceans, &c. will not be merely coloured: they will exhibit many of the features of physical geography. The mountains will be in relief. The globe will be formed of ribs of zinc, in the direction of the meridians, and will be covered with some convenient woven material, on which the lines and colours will be depicted.

GLOUCESTERSHIRE. The commerce of this county is greatly aided by canals. The Thames and Severn Canal connects those two great navigable rivers; it commences at Lechlade, and joins the Stroudwater Canal at Wallbridge, near Stroud; its length is about 30 miles; it has a tunnel at Sapperton 2⅜ miles long. The Stroudwater Canal commences at the Severn, near Framiload, and terminates in the Thames and Severn Canal at Wallbridge; its length is 8 miles. The Hereford and Gloucester Canal is open from Gloucester to Ledbury, 18 miles. The Gloucester and Berkeley Canal, by which the navigation up to Gloucester is shortened 11½ miles, extends from Gloucester to the Severn near Berkeley, 16½ miles. Portions of the Midland Railway and of the Great Western Railway pass through this county.

The south-west corner of the county is occupied by the coal field of the Forest of Dean. Iron appears to have been wrought here during the Roman occupation; and we find it recorded in the reign of Edward I. that there were then 72 furnaces for smelting iron in the Forest. The iron ore here is not very rich in metal, and it is now therefore comparatively little worked. Two hundred pits have been opened for the coal in different parts of the Forest, but the coal is not considered so good as that of Staffordshire. Lead ore is found in many parts of the county, but not in sufficient quantities to defray the expense of working. Pyrites, or sulphuret of iron, has been found in great abundance. Lapis calaminaris, petrosilex, barytes, quartz crystals, gypsum, limestone and freestone are met with in the county.

The manufactures are numerous and important. The cloth manufacture is extensively carried on at Wotton-under-Edge, Stroud, Minchinhampton, Bisley, Uley, Norsley, Cam, Painswick, Rodborough, and King's Stanley. At Frampton, Cotterell, Winterbourn, Bitton, and Westerleigh, there are considerable hat and felt manufactories, and some persons are also engaged in stocking-making. The last-mentioned manufacture is extensively pursued at Tewkesbury, where frame making likewise gives employment to some of the inhabitants; some of them are also engaged in lace-making. In Gloucester and in the suburbs of Bristol there are pin manufactories. At Newland and English Bicknor tin plates are made. Edge-tools are made at Cooley; and glass bottles in the suburbs of Bristol. At Moreton and a few other places cheese cloths and other articles of linen are made. The large commercial city of Bristol has also several manufactories, and works in brass, iron, floor-cloths, lace, hats, soap, vinegar, &c.

Flax was formerly cultivated to some extent in the Vale of Gloucester, but the belief that it was a very scourging crop, and returned nothing to the land, has led to the prohibition of it in leases. Teasels are raised for the use of the manufacturers of woollen cloth, but not to such an extent as they were once. Gloucestershire is essentially a dairy country, and has been always renowned for its butter and cheese. There are fine orchards in different parts of the Vale and Forest districts, and some very good cider and perry are made in the county. *Gloucester*, the chief town, (if we except Bristol, half of which is in this county) is a flourishing commercial place, which has water communication with most parts of the kingdom. In the year 1850 there were 491 vessels arrived at the port of Gloucester, with cargoes from foreign countries; and the customs revenues at the port amounted to 94,082*l*. *Cheltenham* is more notable for its fashion than for its manufactures. At *Lechlade* commences the Thames and Severn Canal, and the Thames first becomes navigable for barges of 70 or 80 tons' burden; in consequence of these favourable circumstances, the place has much traffic in the produce of the country and in London goods. At *Marshfield* a considerable quantity of malt is made for the supply of the Bath and Bristol brewers. The borough of *Stroud* comprehends an important part of the west of England clothing district. The peculiar features of this district are, the situation of the mills on streams in deep ravines, the scattered and irregular manner in which the houses are built on the hill sides, and the contrast between the high land, in many cases with few inhabitants, and the valleys, studded with houses and thickly peopled. This district comprehends the market-towns of Stroud, Minchinhampton, Painswick, and several other places. The site of Stroud was early chosen by clothiers and dyers, and the town has been improving of late years. At *Tewkesbury* the chief manufacture is of cotton and lambs'-wool hosiery.

There were in the county of Gloucester, in 1850, one cotton factory, 49 woollen spinning factories, 11 woollen weaving factories, 20 factories for mixed woollen goods, 3 flax factories, and 7 silk factories—the whole employing 8618 persons.

GLOVE-MAKING. The great seats of the leather glove manufacture in England at present are—Worcester, Woodstock, Yeovil, Leominster, Ludlow, and London. The number made every year in the town and immediate neighbourhood of Worcester has been estimated to exceed 6,000,000 pairs. It is almost entirely a hand manufacture. Worsted gloves are made chiefly in and near Leicester, cotton gloves in Nottingham, and silk gloves in Derby. The manufacture of these three kinds is closely connected with that of stockings, and will be found briefly noticed under HOSIERY MANUFACTURE.

In the year 1850 there were 3,261,061 pairs of leather gloves imported, chiefly from France. Very few English-made gloves are exported.

GLUCI'NIUM is the metallic base of an earth or oxide (*Glucina*) discovered by Vauquelin in 1798. It is a fine powder of a deep gray colour, very difficult of fusion. When burnished, it acquires the metallic lustre. It suffers no change by exposure to air or water, at common temperatures; but when heated to redness it burns, combines with oxygen, and is converted into glucina. *Glucina*, the only known oxide of the metal, is a light white powder, inodorous, tasteless, infusible, insoluble in water. *Chloride of Glucinium* is colourless, sweet, very fusible and volatile, and sublimes readily in white brilliant needles; it deliquesces in the air. Glucinium combines also with bromine, iodine, and sulphur. The salts which glucina forms with acids are not important. They are all colourless, except the chromate, which is yellow; the taste is sweet, and hence the name of the earth, and slightly astringent. This rare metal has not yet been of much practical value in the arts.

GLUE. This useful substance is prepared from the clippings of hides, hoofs, &c., by washing in lime-water, boiling in water, skimming, straining, evaporating, cooling, and drying. When properly prepared, glue is of a deep brown colour, translucent, and free from spots and clouds. When required for use, it is broken into pieces, and steeped for about 24 hours in cold water, by which it swells and softens; after this it is heated in a glue-pot, which is a water-bath made for the purpose.

Another variety of glue, which is much softer and called *size*, is obtained from parchment cuttings and several animal membranes.

Jeffery's *Marine Glue*, introduced within the last few years, and so remarkably adhesive for many purposes, is not strictly glue: it is a cement.

GLYCERIN is a nearly colourless viscid liquid, obtained from olive oil; it cannot be made to crystallise. Its taste is extremely sweet. It mixes with water in all proportions, and is not fermentable.

GOAT-SKINS. Goat-skins, both with respect to the *felt* which forms the foundation and the *hair* which forms the surface, are useful materials of manufactures. There were 241,333 goat-skins imported in 1848: while there were foreign manufactures of goat's hair imported to the value of 57,994*l.* in 1848, and 93,306*l.* in 1849.

GOLD. This costly and beautiful metal has been known from the remotest antiquity, and has been un versally employed as a medium of exchange. Although the quantity of gold which is found, when compared with that of other metals, is small, yet it occurs in greater or less abundance in almost every part of the globe. It occurs in the native state, and combined with silver, and frequently mixed with metallic sulphurets and arseniurets. The greatest quantity of gold, next to that recently discovered in California, is the produce of South America; the richest mines of Europe are those in Hungary, and of Asia, in Siberia; it has been found also in the sands of the Rhône, the Rhine, and the Danube; small quantities are occasionally found in the stream tin-works of Cornwall, in Wicklow in Ireland, and in the Lead Hills in Scotland. In 1826 one piece of native gold was found in Siberia weighing 26 lbs.

Native gold occurs crystallised, capillary, and massive; the primary form is a cube. Gold not unfrequently occurs alloyed with silver, and this compound, where the quantity of silver is considerable, is known by the name of *electrum*. Gold is separated from the various substances with which it is mixed by the process of *amalgamation;* this consists in combining it with mercury, and heating the amalgam formed, so as to distil the mercury, which is thus repeatedly used for the same purpose.

Gold is of a fine yellow colour, and is susceptible of a high degree of polish. It is nearly as soft as lead. For its malleability, see GOLD-BEATING. It is also exceedingly ductile; a single grain may be drawn out into 500 feet of wire. Gold suffers no change by exposure to air or moisture, even when heated. It melts at about 2016° of Fahr., according to Daniell's pyrometer; when in fusion, it appears of a brilliant green colour.

Most metals are susceptible of combining with gold to form *alloys*, of which the following are the chief. *Arsenic* and gold form a brittle gray substance. *Tellurium* and gold, but mixed also with a considerable portion of lead, occur in combination, constituting three varieties known as *graphic tellurium*, *yellow tellurium*, and *black tellurium*. *Antimony* and gold form a pale yellow finely grained substance. *Manganese* and gold form a pale brittle alloy. *Zinc* and gold yield a pale green alloy, very brittle. *Tin* and gold form a pale yellow alloy, slightly flexible. *Iron* and gold form an alloy of a pale yellowish-gray colour; it is very ductile, and may be rolled from the thickness of three-quarters of an inch to that of a guinea. *Nickel* and gold form a brittle yellow alloy; as do *Cobalt* and gold. *Copper* and gold combine in all proportions, with little alteration of the colour of the gold; the density is diminished, but the hardness is increased. *Bismuth* and gold form a brittle yellow alloy. *Silver* and gold combine well; the resulting alloys are very ductile. Silver and copper are both used as alloys in gold coin. *Lead* and gold yield a very brittle alloy. *Mercury* and gold form an *amalgam* much used in the arts [AMALGAM; GILDING]. *Platinum* and gold form an alloy in which the colour of the gold is destroyed.

The *Salts* of Gold, formed by the combination of the metal with acids, are not much employed in the arts, and are mostly of an unstable character. A compound of gold with peroxide of tin forms the beautiful *purple powder of Cassius*.

GOLD-BEATING; GOLD-BEATERS' SKIN. The peculiar substance called *Gold Beaters' Skin* is prepared from the outer or peritoneal membrane of the large intestine of the ox, by successive processes of soaking, scraping, washing, alkalising, &c. The manufacture, called in France (where it is chiefly carried on) *boyauderie*, is an exceedingly dirty and offensive one; but the resulting product is a remarkably fine and beautiful kind of membrane.

Gold beating is a process whereby gold is brought to the state of very fine leaves, for use in various kinds of gilding. The remarkable ductility of gold—a quality possessed by it to a greater degree than by any other known substance—is here taken advantage of to the fullest extent, as a means of limiting the quantity of this costly material required on a given surface.

It is by a combined process of rolling and hammering that the attenuation of the gold is produced. An ingot of gold is milled or rolled, to a thickness of about $\frac{1}{800}$ of an inch; and this riband is then hammered. The hammering does not take place on the gold itself; but thin membranes are interposed between the hammer and the gold. These membranes are of three kinds: an outside covering of common parchment: a set of leaves made of very fine and smooth calf-skin vellum; and another set made of gold-beaters' skin. The riband of gold is cut up into small pieces, each measuring exactly an inch square; and 150 of these are beaten or hammered at once, interleaved between the membranes, until they are expanded to nearly four inches square. They are removed, cut into quarters, replaced between new membranes of gold-beaters'-skin, and beaten again; they again expand to nearly four inches square and are again removed, cut into quarters, and replaced between the skins. A third beating expands them nearly as before. The thickness of the film of gold, by this time, varies from $\frac{1}{200,000}$ to $\frac{1}{300,000}$ of an inch, according to the purpose to which it is to be applied. The attenuation may be rendered more intelligible by stating that 100 square feet of the leaf gold weighs no more than an ounce—a result nearly as surprising as anything presented in the mechanical arts. A certain greasiness which comes upon the interleaved membranes is removed by beating them between pieces of white paper. The beating of the gold is effected by hammers weighing from 10 to 16 lbs., on a smooth block of marble: 150 small squares of gold form the group or bundle for the first beating, 600 for the second, and 800 for the third.

Two other metals, silver and copper, have sufficient malleability to be brought into the state of thin leaves by hammering; and both are used to a limited extent in this state in the arts. But these metals would fracture long before such a degree of thinness could be obtained as in the case of gold; consequently leaf-silver and leaf-copper are thicker than leaf gold.

GOLD-WEIGHING MACHINE. In 1843 Mr. Oldham described before the Institution of Civil Engineers the beautiful Gold-weighing Balance, invented by Mr. Cotton, at that time Governor of the Bank of England. In the transactions between the Mint and the Bank on the one hand, and between the Bank and the public on the other, scrupulous accuracy is requisite in weighing the sovereigns and half-sovereigns. When there is a coinage of new gold, the gold is conveyed from the Mint to the Bank in parcels called 'journeys,' each journey weighing 15 lbs., and containing 701 sovereigns. A group of 200 sovereigns is accurately weighed, and other groups are then balanced against them, so that the pieces are not counted. The officers of the Mint are allowed an overplus called the 'remedy,' amounting to twelve grains in every lb. weight, but they generally work to within one-half of this amount: that is, in two bundles of 50 new sovereigns each, the total weight will not differ so much as six grains.

But it is in the circulation of the gold coins between the bank and the public that the varieties of weighing arise. It is computed that, at a rough average, 30,000 sovereigns pass over the bank counter every day; and it is necessary—either as a regular system, or at stated periods—to ascertain how much the coins have lost in weight by the friction of usage. With the old bullion-scales, 4000 sovereigns could be weighed in six hours, and a deficiency amounting only to $\frac{1}{000}$ of a grain could be detected; but the agitation of the air by the sudden opening of a door, the breathing of persons near the apparatus, and many other minute circumstances, were sufficient to disturb this delicate instrument; while the eyes of the teller or weigher became wearied and dimmed, by constantly watching the indicator of the balance, after weighing three or four thousand sovereigns. Mr. Cotton therefore, endeavoured to plan an instrument which while it should be still more accurate than the bullion-balance, might at the same time be easier and more expeditious in use; and with the aid of Mr. Napier, the Engineer of Lambeth, he completely succeeded.

LEATHER-FACTORY, BERMONDSEY.

DRAWING GOAT-SKINS.

STAKING.

SUMACH TAN-TUB.

UNHAIRING.

LEATHER-SPLITTING.

FULLING-STOCKS.

KNIGHT'S CYCLOPÆDIA OF THE INDUSTRY OF ALL NATIONS.

No. 24.

The exterior of Mr. Cotton's apparatus presents a plain brass case, with a small hopper tube on the top plate. About four inches from the hopper there is an opening in the top plate, through which is seen a platform in the shape of a quadrant, suspended above one end of a balanced beam. On one side of the case is a till, to receive the sovereigns as they are weighed; it is partitioned so that one division is left for standard coin, and the other for such as are light; and each division has a sliding door, for removing the coins. The hopper being filled with gold coins, a system of clock-work within the machine places a sovereign on the little platform; if the sovereign is of standard weight, a small tongue comes rapidly forward and pushes it into that side of the till allotted to such coin; if light, another tongue pushes the sovereign into the other side of the till. These tongues act at right angles to each other. While one sovereign is being thus weighed, a succeeding one is on its way from the hopper to the platform; and the moment the preceding sovereign is disposed of, another supplies its place. All that the attendant has to do, when the machine is wound up for action, is to keep the hopper supplied with sovereigns, and to remove the weighed sovereigns from the till from time to time. The machine can weigh 10,000 sovereigns in six hours. It can separate into two groups sovereigns which differ in weight by a fraction of a grain so inconceivably small as to be scarcely credible to those who are not acquainted with the high excellence of this delicate branch of art.

During the investigation of the Royal Mint Commission, in 1848, it appeared by the evidence of Mr. Miller, weighing clerk in the Bank of England, that Mr. Cotton was led to the invention of his machine by an injustice which the bank unconsciously inflicted on the public. Sovereigns which were issued from one counter at the bank as being full weight, were refused at another counter as being light; and when this matter was investigated it was found that numerous causes rendered the attainment of uniformity in the action of the bank scales quite hopeless, however small the actual amount of error might be in each individual case. Between 1844 and 1848 there were 48,000,000 gold coins weighed by Mr. Cotton's machines at the Bank of England; and the bankers, who pay and receive more coin at the bank than private persons, place undoubting reliance on the accuracy of the machines. Every sovereign now paid over the counter of the bank, has been passed through the machine before being so paid. The bank, according to the evidence of Mr. Miller, has six of these machines in action, five for sovereigns and one for half-sovereigns; each of which will weigh 33 coins per minute! The machines require cleaning once a week—an easy hour's work to each machine. The machines cost about 200*l*. each, and have never yet needed repair. The bank saves about 1000*l*. per annum in wages to weighers, and the public is shielded from unintentional wrong on the part of the bank, by the use of these truly wonderful little machines.

GOLD-WORKING. We are in the habit of associating our ideas of mines of gold with a few favoured spots; but in truth this precious metal is very widely diffused throughout the world. Spain has gold among the sands of the Tagus, but in too small quantity to be worth collecting. France, Piedmont, and Tuscany, also present a few traces. In the territory of Salzburg gold occurs in sufficient quantity to attract attention. Ireland has a little gold among the Wicklow mountains. But it is in Hungary and Transylvania that the greatest European deposit is met with; at Konigsberg, Borson, Schemnitz, Felsobanya, Telkebanya, Kapink, Vorospatak, Offenbanya, Zalatua, and Nagy-ag, in those countries, gold mines are worked, and gold obtained to the extent of one to two thousand lbs. annually. Asia presents numerous gold mines at Breezof and other places on the Ural, and especially in Siberia; in Tibet, Lydia, Japan, and Ceylon. The Eastern Archipelago presents traces of gold in Formosa, Java, Sumatra, Borneo, and the Philippines. Africa presents its store of gold dust, in greater or less quantity, in Kordofan, Sofala, and the wide region which bounds the Sahara desert on the south. America is, however, the richest part of the globe for gold. In Brazil, Chili, Peru, Ecuador, New Grenada, Mexico, North Carolina, and—last, though not least—California, this precious metal is found. Perhaps we may name California, Siberia, and Brazil, as at present the three richest gold-producing countries. From all the countries and districts named, the gold brought to market is mostly derived from alluvial sand, and is extracted by washing.

Under CALIFORNIA and RUSSIA will be found a little notice of the quantities of gold procured from those countries; but we may here say in addition, in respect to California, that it has lately been ascertained that during the year 1850, gold was shipped as freight from St. Francisco, to the value of nearly 30 million dollars; besides an estimated amount, for gold brought away by returning adventurers, and gold retained in California as a circulating medium, of 18 millions more making 48 million dollars' worth as the produce of one year.

The gold obtained from the sand of river valleys is separated from the sandy particles by repeated processes of washing; but the smaller grains of gold, which cannot easily be so separated, are subjected to the process of amalgamation by means of quicksilver. Sometimes the gold is found mixed with sulphurets of copper, silver, arsenic, or other metals; and to separate these sulphurets requires the combined processes of washing and amalgamation. The recent furor concerning California has led to the invention of a number of new machines to facilitate the separation of the gold from the sands. A *gold winnowing machine*, recently introduced at Paris, is intended for emigrants to California. Leaving out the separate lumps of gold, it is said that the auriferous sands yield about one ounce of gold in 500 lbs. of sand; so that this weight of sand must be washed, before the gold can be procured. The new winnowing machine is intended by its inventors to separate much more gold from the sand than by the ordinary washing, and to do it much more quickly. The machine acts by keeping up a constant agitation among the particles, with a provision to allow the escape of the earthy matter. The sand is put into a kind of hopper, whence it descends into a receptacle where a rotating fan or winnow works; the winch which works this fan at the same time pumps up water from a river through a hole; the sand and water flow down a trough into the river, while the gold is left in the machine. It is said that one of these machines is to be sent to the Great Exhibition.

The working of gold into purposes of use and ornament gives rise to many important and interesting branches of manufacture. The coining of gold into money is noticed under MINT; and the making of thin leaves under GOLD BEATING. Gold and silver plate is an important branch of manufacture. By mechanical means (pressure between steel rollers) a thin layer of gold or silver may be made to adhere to a thicker plate of some cheaper metal; but true gold plate has no such inferior layer. The processes of rolling, casting, punching, chasing, hammering, stamping, soldering, riveting, all come into requisition in the manufacture of a piece of gold plate. The approaching Exhibition will contain many magnificent specimens of this art, especially from London and Paris; some of the works from Paris will be of great value. The Goldsmith's Company of London, in order to encourage an art with which they are so intimately connected, have offered rewards to the amount of 1000*l.* for the best specimens prepared for the Exhibition. The prizes are to be one of 200*l.*, three of 100*l.*, three of 50*l.*, three of 30*l.*, six of 25*l.*, three of 20*l.*, two of 15*l.* and two of 10*l.* The articles are to be the modelling and manufacture of British artists; they are to bear the London Hall-mark of 1850-1; and they may be of silver, silver-gilt, or gilt in part. The articles named are groups of figures, table candelabra, shields, salvers, sideboard and altar dishes, dessert services, sideboard ewers, ornamental cups, entrée dishes, candlesticks and light-branches, tea and coffee services, communion services, salt cellars, claret jugs, bread or cake baskets, tea or coffee salvers, tea kettles, inkstands, spoons, and forks.

A considerable quantity of gold is used in the manufacture of watch-cases; but much more is consumed in the numerous trifles which come under the general name of jewellery. Pencil cases, pen-holders, thimbles, bodkins, toothpicks, tweezers, broaches, finger-rings, watch-rings, ear-rings, chains, bracelets, buckles, clasps, &c.—these lead to a large consumption of gold in London and Birmingham, and to the employment of a considerable number of persons. Some of these small trinkets are made of solid gold, some with a thin film of gold on a substratum of silver or copper. Most of these articles are made by persons who receive the material from manufacturers or wholesale dealers, and who employ a few apprentices and assistants to make up the trinkets. Lathes, vices, rollers, hammers, punches, files, draw-plates, wire-drawing apparatus—all these, on generally a small scale, are employed in working up the gold to the required form.

GO'NDOLA is the name given to the pleasure-boats at Venice, which are very numerous, and serve, on its canals, for persons of all classes to proceed from one district to another. The gondola is shallow, long, and narrow, looking, as Byron describes it, like a coffin in a canoe, owing to the black curtains, &c., of the cabin in the centre. The gondolieri once formed an important corporation, several thousands in number, and distinguished for their wit as well as for their skill and honesty. The number of gondolas has greatly decreased in consequence of the decline of the prosperity of Venice.

GONG, is a Chinese musical instrument of percussion, made of a mixed metal of copper and tin, in form much like the cover of a large culinary chaldron, being circular, varying from about fifteen to twenty inches in diameter, and having a rim of from two to three inches in depth. It is struck by a kind of drum-stick, the head of which is of hard leather. It is a very sonorous and powerful instrument.

GONIO'METER is an instrument employed to determine the angle at which the planes of crystals are inclined to each other. The common goniometer consists of two arms of metal, like the letter X, turning on a joint at the intersection. Two contiguous planes of the crystal are placed between the shorter arms, and a graduated arc between the longer arms serves to measure the inclination of the planes. As this instrument is incapable of affording results sufficiently accurate to determine the species to which a crystal belongs, we proceed to describe the more perfect instrument invented by Dr. Wollaston, and called the *reflective goniometer*. This instrument consists of a graduated circle mounted upon a horizontal axis, to one extremity of which is attached a moveable pin, having a slit for the purpose of receiving a small brass plate. To this plate the crystal is attached by means of a piece of wax, so that it may project beyond the edge of the plate. The pin (which is provided with a vertical and horizontal movement) is then raised or lowered until the reflection of any convenient object above appears to coincide with some other object beneath. The instrument being thus adjusted, the graduated circle is turned until a similar reflection is obtained from the contiguous side of the crystal. The arc which the circle will then have described will be equal to the supplement of the inclination of the crystalline planes; but, the margin of the circle being graduated in an inverted order, the true inclination is given without further computation, and may be read off with considerable accuracy. In turning the crystal, the direction of the edge common to its two planes should not be altered, and the rays in both instances should be reflected from that portion of the planes which is nearest to their common edge, otherwise the observation will be affected by parallax. By this instrument the inclination of planes, whose area is less than the 100,000th part of a square inch, may be determined, by means of a vernier, within a minute of a degree.

GOOSE-FEATHERS. The product which chiefly renders the goose valuable in the Arts, is noticed under FEATHERS.

GOOSEBERRY. In the manufacturing districts of Lancashire, and the adjoining counties, the cultivation of the gooseberry has been brought to surprising perfection, at least as regards the size of the fruit; and this chiefly by the manufacturing classes, in consequence of prizes being awarded to successful competitors at the gooseberry-show meetings. Judging from the quality of the varieties grown for competition in this way, it appears that weight is the only qualification required.

GÖTHEBORG, or GOTHENBURG, a town in Sweden, is in a very thriving state. Its commerce is extensive and very active, especially with England. About 600 vessels are engaged in its trade with foreign countries, and nearly as many in that with other Swedish harbours. Its exports consist chiefly of iron and steel, timber, tar, and pitch. Many vessels are built here. The manufactures, though numerous, are on a small scale.

GOTHIC ARCHITECTURE. We can only touch on this large subject in the present work so far as regards brief descriptions, under their several headings, of the mechanical structure involved in the chief parts of a gothic building.

GÖTTINGEN, a principality of the kingdom of Hanover, has large forests and good pastures. The mineral products are iron, salt, basalt, freestone, millstones, potter's and porcelain clays, coals, and alum. The manufactures consist of linen yarn and linens, iron and copper ware, deals, mirrors, glass, pottery, woollens, leather, paper, &c. The chief town also called Göttingen, is more famous for its University than for its industry and commerce. The expenditure of those connected with the university forms the principal means of subsistence to the inhabitants; but they have however considerable manufactures of woollens, tobacco, leather, soap and candles, musical and scientific instruments, stockings, &c.

GOURD, a kind of fruit obtained from various plants of the natural order *Cucurbitaceæ*. In countries having hot and dry summers the different kinds of this fruit are held in high estimation, and are a valuable article of consumption, acquiring a very large size, abounding in nutritious matter, and being moreover very wholesome. The largest is the kind called Potiron Jaune by the French, which sometimes weighs above 2 cwts.

GRADUATING INSTRUMENTS. The name of graduation is given to the marking of degrees and fractions of a degree, on mathematical and astronomical instruments. This graduation, or, as the workmen more generally style it, *dividing*, is performed in two ways, by making a *copy* of a system of divisions already existing, or by *original* dividing. The straight scales and rules which are in common use in cases of drawing instruments, are divided thus:—The original pattern, and the scale on which the copy is to be laid, are placed side by side; a straight edge, with a shoulder at right angles, like a carpenter's square, is made to slide along the original, stopping at each division, when a corresponding stroke is cut by the dividing knife on the copy. With care and practice, this method admits of considerable accuracy. By making the straight edge turn on the centre of a divided circle, the divisions of that circle may be copied upon any concentric circle. Common protractors are thus divided, and scales upon circular limbs. The original circle, which may have several orders of divisions for different purposes, is called a *dividing plate.*

Theodolites and ordinary circular instruments were thus divided, previous to the invention by Ramsden of his *dividing engine.* The general principle of this engine may perhaps be understood by the following description:—A horizontal circle of four feet diameter turns upon a vertical axis; the outer edge is ratched, or notched, by an endless screw, one revolution of which carries the circle round 10′, or one-sixth of a degree; the pressure of the foot upon a treadle turns the screw forward, and there is a series of very ingenious contrivances which enable the divider to turn the screw through any portion of its revolution at each descent of the treadle, and which restores the position of the parts, when the foot is taken off, without allowing any return motion to the screw. The circle to be divided is fixed upon the dividing engine, and made concentric with it, and a division cut after each pressure of the foot. The Board of Longitude gave Ramsden a reward of 300*l.* for the invention of this machine, and 315*l.* for the machine itself, leaving it, during pleasure, in his possession, on condition that he would divide sextants at six shillings and octants at three, for other mathematical instrument makers. Machines of a similar kind, with some alterations and improvements have since been constructed by John Troughton, Edward Troughton, and others, and these are still employed in all instruments which are not large enough, or not sufficiently valuable, to require original dividing.

Dividing engines have been constructed somewhat differently by Reichenbach and others in Germany, and by Gambey in Paris. Much of the German division is excellent, and probably superior to any English engine-dividing. It is understood to be performed by copying. A large circle having been divided originally with great care, the copy is placed upon it, and concentric with it. A microscope is fixed independently over the divided circle, the divisions are brought in succession under the wires of the micrometer, and a line is cut in the copy after each bisection. This process is much more tedious than the English engine dividing, but it admits of the greatest accuracy when the workman is careful and expert.

Original dividing, by which the dividing engines themselves are graduated, and which is employed for the highest class of astronomical instruments, is a process requiring all the resources of delicate mechanical and mathematical art.

GRAIN. In the common weights and measures of this country, a *grain* is the smallest weight now in use. It is of about the weight of a seed of wheat corn, and must therefore be considered rather as a theoretical aliquot part of a larger weight than as itself a proper standard of weight. By a statute of 1266, it was enacted that 32 grains of wheat, taken out of the middle of the ear, and well dried, should weigh a pennyweight, of which 20 should make an ounce, of which 12 should make a pound. Consequently the pound (troy) of this period consisted of 7680 grains, whereas that afterwards in use had only 5760. The reason was, that it became usual to divide the same pennyweight into 24 instead of 32 grains. The grain lost much of its importance by the introduction of the averdupois pound, of which it is not a constituent aliquot part. The ancient averdupois pound is variously stated at from 7009 grains to less than 7000, at which latter number it is now fixed by law.

The weight of one grain is obtained, for practical purposes, without difficulty, by weighing a thin plate of metal of uniform thickness, and cutting out by measurement such a proportion of the whole plate as should give one grain. But a much better plan is to draw a given weight of ductile metal into very thin wire, and to cut from the wire that length which is the same proportion of the whole length as a grain is of the whole weight. In this way pieces of wire are obtained for chemical purposes which weigh only the thousandth part of a grain; and even less weights might be obtained, if it were necessary.

Another popular use of the word *grain* is as a synonyme of *corn;* for a few statistical details concerning which we may refer to CORN TRADE.—Adding here, however, a later item, concerning the Corn Trade of 1850. In that year the grain or corn imported into Great Britain amounted to 7,969,435 quarters; while the various kinds of flour and meal imported were 3,873,908 cwts. Nearly half of the grain imported was wheat; and nearly all the meal was wheat-meal or flour.

GRAINS OF PARADISE are hot, acrid, aromatic seeds, obtained from the coast of

Guinea, and used for medicinal and other purposes as stomachic and cordial stimulants. They are produced by the *Amomum Grana-Paradisi* of Linnæus, and *Amomum grandiflorum* of Smith.

GRANADA. This beautiful Spanish province is covered with a luxuriant vegetation. The sumach and the cork trees, the oak bearing the edible fruit, and many other valuable trees and shrubs, form the extensive thickets of the Sierras. The soil is very productive and the agriculture good. Metals are abundant in the mountains. Near Cangajar alone there are 117 lead mines. Copper ore lies on the surface in many places; antimony and quicksilver are found near Malaga, and molybdenum at Ronda. Coal is found on the margins of the Beiro and of the Alfacar, near the capital. Exquisite marbles, jaspers, and alabaster, are abundant.

The famous city of Granada, the capital of the province, has fallen from its ancient grandeur. It still has, however, a royal manufactory for saltpetre and gunpowder, and several manufactories of silk stuffs, such as velvet, taffetas, satin, handkerchiefs, and ribands. The sewing silk of Granada is preferred to all others.

There is yet another Granada — the New Granada of South America, one of the lately formed republics of that continent. The productions of New Granada include cacao, cotton, coffee, tobacco, indigo, rice, and sugar. The forests furnish Nicaragua and Brasiletto wood, fustic, and logwood. To these may be added the Cinchona, or Peruvian bark. The numerous herds which pasture on the Llanos furnish hides and tasajo, or dried meat; horses, mules, and horned cattle are exported to the West Indies. The mineral riches are considerable, and mostly occur on the western declivity of the three chains of the Andes. They consist of gold, silver, platinum, mercury, copper, lead, iron, and rock-salt. The produce of gold seems to be on the increase, but has not yet attained the quantity which was got before the war of independence. Iron and coal are found in the mountains bordering on the table land of Bogotà: some attempts have been made to work the iron-mines, and the coal is used in the smithies and for the steamboats. Rock salt and salt springs occur. The manufacturing industry is not important. It is limited to woollen and cotton stuffs of a coarse texture, only adapted for the use of the lower classes, and mostly made by the consumers. British produce and manufactures were exported to New Granada in 1848 to the value of 247,916*l.*: the chief port of debarkation being Cartagena.

GRANULATION. This term is applied to a process by which metal is reduced to the state of small fragments. While the metal, such as silver or copper, is in a melted state, it is forced into an iron vessel filled with holes; it passes through these holes, into a pool of water, or upon a bundle of twigs soaked in water, and becomes thus solidified into small globular fragments like shot: indeed the making of shot is thus conducted. [SHOT MANUFACTURE]. Silver alloys are granulated previous to refining; and copper is brought to the state called bean shot, by granulation.

GRANITE. This is one of the most abundant rocks seen at or near the surface of the earth. It underlies the stratified rocks, and appears at some remote geological æra to have been in a fluid state from the effect of intense heat.

Granite is one of the most beautiful of rocks, and viewed mineralogically its composition is remarkable. Mica, felspar, and quartz, in distinct crystals, or else filling interstices between crystals, constitute the typical varieties; but other minerals, such as hornblende, actinolite, chlorite, talc, compact felspar, steatite, garnet, zircon, &c., enter into and sometimes considerably modify the aspect of granite, especially in colour, which varies much. Except in a few cases, granite, as its name implies, shows the grains of its component parts; the size of these varies extremely. Granite is indeed rather a name for a mode of aggregation than for a definite chemical or even mineralogical structure; and the varieties are thus too numerous to be distinctly named.

Granite is largely employed in building, especially in the more important engineering works. New London Bridge affords a beautiful instance of its use. It is also much employed in paving the London streets. When polished it presents a fine appearance; but the polishing is a work of great labour, on account of the hardness of the stone. Aberdeenshire, Devon, and Cornwall, furnish our chief supplies of granite.

A very large block of granite, upwards of 20 feet long, and of the finest quality and colour, has lately been raised by the Cheesewring Granite Company, at their quarries, on the Cheesewring-hill, near Liskeard, which is intended to be sent to the Great Exhibition of 1851. The mass of stone, of which this formed a portion of the quarry, contained by measurement the extraordinary quantity of above 4,000 cubic feet, or about 300 tons in weight.

A fine specimen of Irish granite is also to be exhibited, obtained from the Ballyholland quarries near Newry.

GRAPE-SHOT is an assemblage, in the form of a column, of nine balls resting on a circular plate, through which passes a pin serving as an axis. The ball are contained in a strong canvass bag, and are bound together on the exterior of the latter by a cord disposed about the column in the manner of a net.

GRAPES; GRAPE-VINE. The delicious and well-known fruit of the vine is used as an article of diet in several ways. Its agreeable sweet acid flavour when ripe has always rendered it a very desirable food when fresh. The ancients also, there can be little doubt, were in the habit of drinking the expressed juice of the grape before fermentation. Grapes are also dried and used under the name of *Raisins.* The drying is generally effected by cutting half through the fruit-stalk whilst they are suspended on the tree. Grapes thus dried are called Muscatel Raisins, and are principally brought from Spain and the Levant. The most extensive use of the grape is for the purpose of making wine. [WINE.]

Although our climate does not permit of the grape attaining its greatest perfection in the open air, yet in the forcing system of cultivating grapes by heat, Great Britain probably produces the most delicious grapes in the world. But even in the open air in the southern counties of England, if proper care is taken, very good fruit may be obtained.

Grapes may be kept by packing them in jars, each branch separately wrapped in paper. The bunches and layers of fruit are to be separated by well-dried bran; bran is also laid above and below the grapes; and there are finally laid over the top a piece of paper, a stretched piece of bladder, and a well fitting cover to the jar.

Sugar is obtained from grapes, by saturating the juice with chalk, decanting the clear liquid, evaporating to a syrup, clarifying with white of egg, and then evaporating. It is less sweetening than al-sugar.

Grapes to the value of 30,000*l.* to 40,000*l.* are annually imported.

GRASS LAND includes water-meadows, upland pastures, and artificial meadows. The first are briefly treated of under IRRIGATION. *Upland pastures* are portions of land on which the natural grasses grow spontaneously, varying in quantity and quality with the soil and situation. When a pasture is naturally rich, the only care required is to stock it judiciously, to move the cattle frequently from one spot to another, and to eradicate certain plants which are useless or noxious. The urine of the cattle is the manure which chiefly keeps up the fertility of grass land. A poor arid soil is not fitted for grass, nor one which is too wet from the abundance of springs and the want o outlet for the water. These defects can only be remedied by expensive improvements.

When an arable field is sown with the seeds of grasses and other plants which give herbage for cattle, it is called an *artificial meadow.* The introduction of the artificial meadows in districts where the soil seemed not well adapted for pasture has greatly increased the number of cattle and sheep reared and fattened, and has caused greater attention to be paid to the means of improving the breeds of both. In the neighbourhood of large towns there are many meadows, which, without being irrigated, are mown every year, and only fed between hay harvest and the next spring. The management of this grass land is well understood in Middlesex. An acre of good grazing land, worth 40*s.* rent, is supposed to produce 200 lbs. of meat in the year.

GRASSES. There is a great difference between the value of grasses for pasture; certain kinds suit the meadows, others marshes, others upland fields, and others bleak and sterile hills, where they furnish valuable food for sheep: these kinds will not grow indiscriminately, or are not equally suitable for different soils and situations, and it is therefore essential for the husbandman that he should be capable of discriminating between them. Some indicate the quantity of soil. The same remarks are applicable to the grasses used for various purposes in the manufacturing arts. The principal grasses useful to man are described in this work under their usual commercial names.

GRAVEL. This name is usually given to the small fragments of rocks which have been drifted by any force of water over the surface of the earth. Whether the gravel observed at any spot was transported along the natural drainage hollows of the surface; and whether the waters descending these valleys performed the effects while flowing at higher levels, under the influence of dams, lakes, or other peculiarities; become interesting questions in connection with the past history of the earth's surface. But in relation to the industrial arts, gravel is not much used except as a material for roads, paths, terraces, &c.

GRAVITY, CENTRE OF. If a lever were balanced by means of two solid spheres of uniform density hung at the ends, the equilibrium would still remain if all the matter of either of the spheres could be concentrated at its centre; the centre of the sphere is then its *centre of gravity.* When a body is suspended by a string, and allowed to find its position of rest, the centre of gravity is in the line of continuation of the string.

In every kind of machinery this important law, by which the centre of gravity always tends to assume the lowest place, is kept constantly in view in arranging the weight of different parts of a machine or engine.

GRAVITY, SPECIFIC. [SPECIFIC GRAVITY.]

GREAT BRITAIN. The industrial statistics of Great Britain are briefly glanced at under the headings—ENGLAND, SCOTLAND, WALES, the names of counties, and the names of the chief towns and rivers; as well as under such headings as CUSTOMS DUTIES, EXCISE DUTIES, FACTORIES, IMPORTS AND EXPORTS, SHIPPING, &c. Beyond the features which illustrate produce, industry, and commerce, we have nothing to do with geography in this work. A few data under our present heading will suffice.

Great Britain has about 84,000 square miles of surface, and about 4000 miles of coast-line. There are seven rivers 100 miles or more in length, viz., Thames 200, Severn 190, Tay 150, Trent 144, Ouse 120, Wye 120, and Tweed 100; these seven rivers, with their tributaries, drain about 24,000 square miles of surface. There were in 1827 (since which year new inclosures and cultivation have gradually increased) about 14 million acres of farms and gardens, 21 million acres of meadows, pastures, and marshes, 10 million acres of improveable wastes, and 13 million acres of unimproveable wastes. It is a useful fact to bear in mind, (with sufficient accuracy for general comparison) that Ireland and Scotland have about equal areas, and that Ireland and Scotland united have an area about equal to that of England and Wales united. In respect to population these ratios altogether fail, for England is more populous than the other three combined.

GREECE. This once celebrated country has little to interest us in respect to its present industry and commerce. In the plains of the Morea the peasantry are not proprietors, all the land belonging either to the state or to the wealthy families of the primates or archontes. In the mountains there is a great number of small proprietors, generally thrifty and industrious husbandmen. The resources of the continental part of the kingdom are derived chiefly from agriculture. There are about 120,000 families of cultivators of the soil, of which 20,000 are proprietors. The vineyards are almost all private property. There are also about 215,000 olive trees, chiefly in Attica, Megaris, and the eparchy of Salona, a great part of which is national property. Greece produces about two-thirds of the corn required for its consumption. Wheat, barley, and Indian corn are the species cultivated; oats and rye are not in use. Tobacco thrives, especially near Argos and Calamata, and cotton grows also in considerable quantity. The wine made is enough for the home consumption; it is generally good-bodied, but for want of proper management in making it, and of cellars, it does not keep beyond a year or two. Currants are cultivated in various districts, especially in the eparchies of Patras and Vostitza, and are of excellent quality. The olives are of good quality, but the art of pressing and refining the oil is very imperfectly understood, and the oil is inferior to that of Provence. Silk is made in Messenia and Laconica, and also at Tinos, and in other islands, but is inferior to the Italian silk. The almond, the fig, the chestnut, the orange, and the lemon thrive well. Horned cattle are not numerous, nor sufficient for the labours of the field, for which they are almost exclusively used, and oxen are imported for that purpose from Thessaly and Asia Minor. There, are, however, numerous flocks of sheep and goats, which migrate to the mountains in the spring, and return to the plains after the harvest. The produce of wool is considerable, but of a coarse kind, and is used chiefly for home manufacture. Pigs are scarce, except in Arcadia. The only milk used is that of ewes and goats, and the butter and cheese made of it is very inferior. The fine forests with which the mountains were once clothed have been sadly wasted, and for the most part entirely destroyed.

The commerce and navigation of Greece are centered in the ports of Nauplia, Mesolonghi, Patras, Galaxidi, and the islands of Hydra, Spezia, and, above all, Syra. The number of Greek merchant vessels is somewhat over 1000, exclusive of small craft, or coasting boats. The extensive line of coast and the numerous islands supply a multitude of good sailors. The principal traffic of the Greek vessels is the carrying trade between the ports of the Mediterranean and the Black Sea. The Exports from Great Britain to Greece in 1848 amounted in value to 284,834*l*. Among the imports from Greece in the same year were 225,175 cwts. of currants, being more than half of our consumption.

GREEN. In dyeing green, the usual custom is to impart a blue dye first, and then change this to a proper tint by a yellow dye. The same principle is followed in many kinds of painting; a lively green being produced by a mixture of blue and yellow pigments; and a dingy green by a mixture of blue with orange or with yellowish brown. There are, however, many green pigments produced without this admixture. *Green bice* is a carbonate of copper. *Brunswick green* is a carbonate of copper, mixed with chalk, white lead, alumina, or magnesia. *Friesland green* is an oxychloride of copper. *Scheele's green* is an arsenite of copper. *Prussian green* is a modification of Prussian blue. *Sap green* is prepared from the juice of buckthorn berries. *Iris green* is prepared from the juice of the petals of the blue flag plant. *Verditer* is a mixture of oxide of copper with whiting.

GREENHOUSE. Structures of this kind were formerly erected with slated roofs, like dwelling-houses, and with large upright windows in front, divided and supported by pillars; examples of which may yet be seen in several of the royal gardens about London, and also in different parts of the country. It was soon found that handsome specimens of plants could not be grown in houses of this description, and the only purpose to which they are now applied is the growing of orange or lemon trees, and protecting other plants in winter. The best kinds of greenhouses are those with span-roofs, which are often built in the following manner: a neat wall, about three feet high, is built round the front and ends; the back wall being about two-thirds of the height of the roof. Along the top of the front wall a row of glass sashes, eighteen inches in height, is placed upon the brickwork, which will raise the front to 4½ feet. The span-roof will then be supported upon this in front, and its back sashes will rest upon the back wall. A greenhouse should always, if possible, front the south.

To what extent the increased use of glass, noticed under CONSERVATORY, will be available for greenhouses, it rests with gardeners to decide.

GREENOCK. This busy Clyde port has a harbour which, at the beginning of the last century, was only fit for the reception of fishing boats; but ten acres were afterwards enclosed between two circular quays; and subsequent improvements have rendered the outer harbour available for ships of large burden. This has been the means of raising the place to an important position as a sea-port. The number of vessels belonging to the port is about 450. Ship building is extensively carried on in and near the town; and great commercial activity is observable. The large Customs' returns at Greenock are noticed under GLASGOW. Greenock is, in many particulars, a port for Glasgow.

GRENADE, frequently called hand-grenade, is a shell or hollow ball of iron, 2½ inches in diameter, which, being charged with powder and provided with a fuze, is thrown as a missile during sieges. As soon as the composition in the fuze is consumed, the fire communicates with the powder, and the ball is burst in fragments.

GRENOBLE. In this ancient town, formerly the capital of Dauphine, in the south of France, the chief manufactures are kid gloves, of which about two million francs' worth are exported to England and America annually; liqueurs, chamois and other leather. The dressing of hemp gives employment to about 1000 workmen. The trade of the place is much promoted by the navigation of the Isère; other articles of trade are wrought iron, marble, and timber.

GRIMSBY. This Lincolnshire port has hitherto been a place of little importance; but the extensive works now progressing under Mr. Rendel, will render it a commercial emporium of considerable rank. There is already a dock at Grimsby, but it is wholly above the level of high water mark, and is supplied with water by land streams. Between that level and low water mark is an unsightly mass of muddy shore; and it is this useless expanse which Mr. Rendel is bringing into requisition by forming magnificent docks. About 130 acres are to be enclosed, of which part will form a dock, and the rest will afford sites for wharfs and warehouses. The water area of the dock will be 27 acres; there will be 5000 feet of dock wharfage, and 6000 feet of river wall. There will be a basin of 11 acres, to connect the dock with the Humber; and two piers of 600 feet long each will bound the basin on the east and west. Such is the full scope of the plan proposed by Mr. Rendel, part of which is now being carried out by the Sheffield and Lincolnshire Railway Company, to whom the works belong.

GRINDSTONES. The stones used for sharpening cutting instruments vary greatly in texture, from the roughest grindstones to the smoothest hones. The sizes are equally varied; some of the stones used by the saw-grinders of Sheffield are as much as seven feet in diameter. The grindstones for table-knives are from three to four feet in diameter, and six inches thick; they are formed of a species of sandstone. In one of the large grinding establishments in that town, where cutlery from pen-knives to saws are ground, the grindstones are of all sizes, from four inches to seven feet in diameter. There are many quarries in England from which stone fitted for such purposes may be obtained. Some grinding wheels have a surface of crocus or of emery applied to them, to aid in particular kinds of grinding.

The grinding and sharpening stones prepared by Mr. Meinig, present a remarkable variety. He has natural grindstones, from quarries belonging to himself, of ninety-seven different diameters, from 1½ to 24 inches; and of thirteen degrees of thickness, from an eighth of an inch to 3 inches. The same sandstone is cut into other shapes, for various abrading processes. German hones are prepared for sharpening fine tools; whereas a kind called green-water hones are used for giving an edge to razors and lancets. Turkey oil-stone presents five different degrees of hardness and texture to suit different modes of application. Petrified wood is employed as a material for whetstones or hones; it can be cut into the form of wheels, up to three or four inches in diameter.

GRIT. Hard sandstones are called grits in the north of England, and indeed many soft sandstones are so termed. In particular districts some distinctive terms are applied, as millstone grit, red grit, white grit, grindstone grit, &c. Almost universally in the north of England the term Freestone belongs to such gritstones as will work easily and to a good face.

GRITS or GROATS. This useful material for gruel is made of oat seeds deprived of their husks. When bruised, ready for use, they are denominated Embden grits, or prepared or patent groats or grits. A greater or smaller quantity of these are to be used to a pint of water, according to the object in view. When employed for an article of nourishment, the gruel may be made thick; when required as a demulcent or diluent, to promote perspiration at the commencement of a cold, it should be thin. This is regarded as a light and digestible article for invalids. The husks are frequently steeped in water for a few days, and then drained off. The liquid when boiled stiffens into a dish called sowens in Scotland. This is slightly acid, and forms with milk a favourite food of the peasantry for supper.

GRODNO, a government of Russia in Europe, produces quantities of barley, rye, oats, hops, hemp, and flax. The crown holds a great number of the forests, which abound chiefly in pine. Horned cattle and sheep are numerous. Much wax and honey are made. The minerals consist of iron, limestone, clay, chalk, and saltpetre. The manufactures of the province are woollen cloths, hats, leather, paper, and spirits. There is a good export trade in grain, wool, cattle, and timber, with Memel, Riga, and Königsberg.

GROINS are the lines formed by the intersection of arched vaultings. Such intersections are called 'groinings,' and the vaultings 'groined arches.' Groins, which arose in the first instance out of the simple intersection of arches, were in later times the foundation of an extensive system of decoration. This system is exemplified in the elaborately groined ceilings of many of our ecclesiastical buildings. Groined arches are constructed of stone, brick, and wood and plaster. When constructed with stone or brick, a centering of wood is used to turn the arch and form its groins. Great nicety is required in the execution of the groined work, and the best workmen among bricklayers and masons are always selected.

GUAIACUM. This is the name of a genus of small crooked trees inhabiting several of the West India Islands, in low places near the sea. The most remarkable species yields the hard, compact, black-green wood called *Lignum Vitæ*, which is so heavy that it sinks in water, and from which pestles, ship-blocks, rollers, castors, &c., are turned. The same species also produces the gum-resin known in medicine under the name of *Gum Guaiacum*. For medicinal purposes, the wood should be procured from the central part of the trunk, as being the richest in the active principle. This wood is very dense, heavier than water, of an obscure greenish fawn colour; but the recent fracture is yellowish, exhibiting an unequal cleavage, with a fatty shining appearance, if the specimen be good. The wood of the circumference is lighter, both in colour and weight, pale fawn, and opake. Genuine guaiac-wood or lignum vitæ is destitute of smell, but if rubbed, and still more if set on fire, it evolves an agreeable aromatic odour. If long chewed, the taste is peculiar, guttural and bitterish. The wood is less used than the resin. Guaiac-resin exudes spontaneously, or in consequence of incisions, and hardens on the bark. Resin obtained in this way is generally in spherical or long tear-shaped pieces.

Guaiac possesses the property of stimulating the system generally. It is not prized now so highly as on its introduction into European practice in the sixteenth century, when it bore a most extravagant price, four ducats being often given for a pound of the wood. It is however a useful medicine, and the wood is applied to many purposes in the arts.

GUANO. This valuable manure is the excrement of sea-fowl, and appears to have been used as a manure long before Peru was visited by the Spaniards. A recent German traveller, Meyer, says, 'Along almost the whole coast of Peru this excrementitious matter covers the small islands and cliffs near the coast, and on some spots lies in such enormous beds as could only be produced by the accumulation of thousands of years.' About the commencement of 1843 guano was discovered on the island of Ichaboe, about two miles and a half from the main land of Africa, in 26° 13′ S. lat., and 14° 15′ E. long. The place soon attracted notice, and by the end of 1844 the whole of the guano had been carried away. As many as 350 ships have been anchored off the island at the same time. The guano was from 35 to 38 feet in depth, and the deposit extended to a length of about 1100 feet, with an average width of 400 feet. Towards the close of 1844 another guano island (Malagas) was discovered at the entrance of Saldanha Bay. The guano covers an extent of about eight miles, and the thickness is from about four yards to eight yards. It has been supposed that the excrement of the sea-fowl which swarm on some parts of the coast of Great Britain might be used as a fertiliser with the same results as Peruvian or African guano; but the quantity which could be collected is comparatively small, as the animal accumulation is in most cases washed away by the rains, and the valuable properties of that which remains are dissipated by the changeable nature of our climate.

The value of guano is to be estimated according to the proportions which it contains of—1, ammonia; 2, phosphates; 3, organic matter. African guano has the largest proportion of soluble matter, and that from Peru is remarkable for the quantity of uric acid that it contains, an element which dissolves very slowly. It is said that 4 cwts. of guano, which is the usual quantity applied to one acre, are equal in effect to fifteen tons of farm-yard dung. It is usually mixed with pulverised earth to prevent it from coming in contact with the seeds. For small allotments or gardens it is often most convenient to use guano in a liquid state, in which case 4 lbs. of guano may be mixed with twelve gallons of water, and used after it has stood twelve hours, and the proportion per acre may be from a half to one cwt. of guano to 100 gallons of water.

The quantity of guano imported in the last four years has been very considerable:—

1847	.. ..	82,134 tons.
1848	.. ..	71,414 ,,
1849	.. ..	83,438 ,,
1850	.. ..	116,926 ,,

GUERNSEY. In this member of the Channel Islands group, the pursuits of agriculture are carefully attended to; as much as 54 Winchester bushels of wheat have been raised per acre. The ashes of sea-weed are the manure chiefly used for corn crops. Red-wheat is the chief of these crops. Neither sheep nor horses are carefully reared; but the breeding of cattle, especially of cows, is an object of great attention. The dairy is on all farms of any size the principal object of attention, and the chief source of the farmer's profit. The butter that is made is in high repute. English fruits, and fruits of more southern climates, are much cultivated. The shores are abundantly supplied with fish. The manufacturing industry of Guernsey is but small; and the same may be said of the little islands near it —*Alderney*, *Serk*, *Herm*, and *Jethou*. There is steam communication to Guernsey from Southampton, Plymouth, Torquay, St. Malo, and Granville.

GUINEA. Many parts of the region of West Africa, known by the name of Guinea, are rich in produce which gives rise to much commerce. Thus, in the country called the *Grain Coast*, the valleys produce rich crops of rice, which is exported to a large amount. Cattle, sheep, pigs, goats, poultry, rice, pepper, camwood, and ivory are abundant. The *Ivory Coast* and the *Slave Coast* are the names of other portions of Guinea, the produce of which is exported to various countries. *Sierra Leone* will call for a word of notice elsewhere, in respect to its produce and commerce. [SIERRA LEONE.]

GUITAR. This musical instrument, in various shapes, may be traced to the remotest periods of antiquity. It was often called *Cittern* and *Gittern* by the old English poets. The English and French guitar of the last century was wide and thin in body, short in the neck, and strung with wire. The modern guitar, which is of the Spanish kind, and differing little from the lute, consists of a body from seventeen to eighteen inches in length, four in depth, and of a neck of about sixteen inches, the latter carrying a finger-board divided by seventeen frets. It has six strings, three being of silk covered with silvered wire, and three of catgut. The compass of this elegant instrument is from E below the base staff to A above the treble staff, including all the intermediate tones and semitones. The best and cheapest guitars are made in Germany.

GUM. This vegetable juice is of more universal occurrence than any other secretion by plants. It is the material generally prepared by them for their own nourishment, and is at first in a state of solution; but when it escapes to the exterior of the bark it frequently becomes thickened, and even solid and pulverisable. The purest gum (arabic) consists of a principle termed *arabin*, and is soluble in water, forming with it a mucilage. Other gums contain *bassorine*, either alone or with arabin and other matters. The term gum is sometimes erroneously applied to gum-resins, such as assafœtida, &c.

Most of the commercial gums are obtained by incisions made in the bark of several species of acacia growing in Arabia, India, Upper Egypt, Senegal, &c. The specimens differ considerably in colour, even when obtained from the same species. Genuine gum-arabic occurs in pieces from the size of a pea to that of a walnut, or larger, which are irregular in shape, or roundish or angular; either white, yellowish, or dark wine-yellow; scarcely any odour; taste mawkish, glutinous. Gum, when in powder, is often adulterated with starch, the presence of which is detected by tincture of iodine; or, when cold water is used for the solution of the gum, the starch will remain undissolved. The mucilage made with cold water is not only purer, but keeps better, and for all purposes for which it can be used is preferable to that made with warm water, which is the common method.

Gum is highly nutritive, six ounces in twenty-four hours being deemed sufficient to sustain the life of an adult; yet it is not very easily digested when taken alone. Gum will often pass through the stomach nearly unchanged, if not associated with some bitter or astringent principle. This property however renders it demulcent in affections both of the throat and also of the intestines, by sheathing the membrane from air or the irritation of acrid secretions. Hence allowing a portion to dissolve is also used to suspend many insoluble matters in water. Its agglutinating properties render it valuable in many of the arts.

Of four kinds of gum which are enumerated in the Board of Trade tables, the quantities imported in 1848 were—

	Cwts.
Gum-arabic	24,022
Gum-Senegal	7,404
Gum-copal	2,958
Gum-tragacanth	234

GUM-RESINS are secretions of plants, which are produced in the greatest quantity, and most perfectly elaborated, in warm countries. They are obtained chiefly from trees and shrubs of particular tribes of plants. They either exude spontaneously, or are procured by incisions of the stem and branches. When they first escape to the surface they are fluid, and of a light colour, but gradually harden, and become of a deeper hue, either by the evaporation of some of their volatile oil, or by the absorption of oxygen from the air, and the conversion of the oil into a resin. Some remain in a semi-liquid viscid state, such as *sagapenum* and *galbanum*, which are only pulverisable in winter. Most gum-resins possess a strong odour, which in many instances is disagreeable, such as that of assafœtida, with a warm acrid taste, and by application to the skin for any considerable time they cause redness and inflammation.

Gum-resins, which are largely employed in medicine, should be kept in cool well-closed places, to prevent the evaporation of their volatile principles.

GUN-COTTON was first discovered by M. Schönbein of Basel, and made known in the year 1846. It is prepared with cotton wool, and explodes at 400° Fahr. Gunpowder explodes at 600°. In consequence of this, gun-cotton may be fired on gunpowder without igniting it. This peculiarity results from the minute division of the cotton fibres; for mealed powder, or gunpowder dust, will explode at a much lower temperature than grained powder.

Gun cotton may be prepared in various ways. Mr. Taylor made it by saturating cotton wool in a mixture consisting of equal quantities of nitric and sulphuric acids. This must be done as rapidly as possible by pressing the cotton in the mixture with a glass rod. When this is done, it is taken out, and as much as possible of the mixture is squeezed out of it. The cotton is then washed in successive portions of water until it loses all taste of acid. It is then pressed in a linen cloth and dried. Sawdust, wood-shavings, and any body consisting principally of carbon, may be rendered explosive by preparation in a similar way.

The manufacture and use of these preparations are however dangerous, and they have in consequence been prohibited generally in France. Gun cotton is more powerful than gunpowder, *i.e.*, with equal quantities by weight a much greater effect is produced by the cotton; in consequence of which there is every probability that it will supersede powder for the purposes of blasting, for which it possesses the important advantage that it does not generate smoke. It remains however to be proved whether it will answer for military purposes. The experiments of the French government are against it, in consequence of the production of an inconvenient quantity of moisture by its explosion. M. Schönbein has secured the patent for his preparation in England, and it is manufactured on his account by agents appointed by him. So extremely explosive is this material, that many serious accidents have happened in connection with its manufacture.

GUN MAKING. The manufacture of muskets and fowling-pieces is carried on to a very large extent at Birmingham. More than five million pieces of fire-arms were made in that town between 1804 and 1818. Yet there are no gun-factories properly so called. The same gun travels about from factory to factory, from shop to shop, before it is finished.

The most essential part of a gun is the *barrel.* The interior of the barrel is usually a smooth cylinder, but the exterior is made slightly conical by thickening the metal at the *brèech* or hinder end. The commoner barrels are formed of tenacious soft iron, which is rolled into the form of flat bars, called *skelps*, each of which is sufficient to form a single barrel. The length of a skelp is usually about three feet, and the breadth about four inches at one end, and two and a half at the other. In welding these skelps into barrels, the thicker end is heated to redness, and hammered upon a hollow cavity in an anvil until the edges are turned up. A mandril being then inserted in the concavity between them, the edges are turned over and welded together. The skelp is thus gradually converted into a tube or barrel, after many beatings and hammerings. This laborious process of welding is now to a great extent superseded by improved methods. In one of these methods, the barrels, instead of being formed of skelps forged to the length of the barrel, are made from slabs of refined bar-iron, ten or twelve inches long, and weighing from 10 to 11 lbs. Each slab, by being heated and passed between rollers of a peculiar shape, is bent round into a tubular form; and repeated drawings between other rollers weld the two edges firmly together, and at the same time elongate the tube to the proper dimensions, a mandril being placed inside to preserve the bore of the barrel. The above processes are for *plain* barrels. *Twisted* barrels are made of long and very narrow strips of iron; one of which, being moderately heated to increase its pliancy, is wrapped spirally round a cylindrical mandril, in such a way as to form a tube, which may be slipped off the mandril at pleasure. As the rods are not usually made of sufficient length for one to form a barrel, several are usually joined end to end, those which form the breech being thicker than those at the muzzle end. By heating and hammering, these pieces are welded into a continuous and very strong and tough tube. Partially worn or 'scrap' iron is preferred for these purposes. The twisted barrels, technically termed *wire-twist*, are formed of narrow rods of compound metal, composed of alternate bars of iron and steel forged into one body, and then rolled out to the requisite tenuity. *Damascus* barrels are composed of similar metal, but the rods are twisted upon their own axes until their component fibres have from twelve to fourteen turns in an inch, and the rods are thereby doubled in thickness and proportionately reduced in length. Two such rods are welded together side by side, their respective twists being reversed. The varieties in the modes of making twisted barrels are very numerous.

After welding, the barrels are carefully examined, and, if needful, straightened by a few blows of the hammer. They are then bored in a machine with an angular plug of tempered steel, which is caused to revolve rapidly within the barrel, a stream of cold water being directed upon the outside to check the heat generated by the excessive friction of the tool. The outside is brought to a smooth surface either by grinding on a large grindstone or turning in a lathe. The breech end of the barrel is tapped with a screw-thread, to receive the breech-plug, which closes it at that end.

The barrels are then ready for *proving*, which consists in firing them in a building in which their explosion can do no harm, with a charge four or five times as great as they will have to bear when in use. A great number of barrels are fired at once, by laying them upon a strong framework of wood, with their touch-holes downwards, and connected with a train of powder which is conducted outside the building, within which is laid a heap of sand to receive the bullets. They are then carefully examined, and such as show any defect are returned to be reforged, after which they must be proved again, while such as have stood the test satisfactorily are stamped with a distinguishing mark.

Sporting guns are often made with two barrels fixed side by side upon one stock. Such barrels are made separately, and have their adjacent sides filed flat, in order that they may lie close together. They are secured together by ribs running between them from end to end.

The wooden *stock* upon which the barrel is mounted is most commonly made of walnut-tree. When the shaping of the stock is completed, it is shod with brass, the trigger-guard and other metallic fittings and ornaments are let into the wood, and every part is fitted with suitable screws and fastenings, after which the whole is taken to pieces; the woodwork is finished by staining and polishing, the brass-work is filed and polished, and the barrels are sent to be finished, which is done in various ways. Most barrels are now *bronzed*, by the application of some chemical liquid aided by heat. Until a comparatively recent period all military guns, and most of those used for sporting purposes, were made with flint locks, in which the ignition of the priming-powder was effected by the sudden stroke of a wedge-shaped flint against a piece of steel, by which a stream of sparks was directed into the pan containing the priming. But *percussion caps*, containing an explosive powder, are now generally used. The fulminating substance is usually placed in a small copper capsule resembling a thimble in shape, which fits on to the nipple of the touch-hole, and if not blown to pieces by the explosion, is removed previous to reloading. The hammer is provided with a shield to prevent any fragments of the copper cap from flying against the face of the shooter.

In the manufacture of common infantry guns, Birmingham is beginning to feel the competition of Liége, in Belgium; but in the better kinds of fowling-pieces she has no competitor but London.

Of the hand guns used in past ages, the variety was greater than many readers would suppose. The following are the names of most of them:—*Arquebus*, *haquebut*, *demi-haque*, *musquet*, *wheel-lock*, *currier*, *snaphaunce*, *caliver*, *carabine*, *esclopetta*, *fusil*, *musketoon*, *petronel*, *blunderbus*, *dragon*, *hand-mortar*, *dag*, *pistol*, *trickerlock*, *firelock*, *&c.* Of those whose names are best known at the present day, the *musquet* was a Spanish invention, originally very clumsy; the *carabine* is a short gun, about forty inches long; the *fusil*, a French invention, was as long as the musquet, but much lighter; the *blunderbus* is shorter than the carabine, and has a wide barrel; the *pistol* was invented at Pistoia in Tuscany, in the time of Henry VIII.

At Vincennes in France, specimens of all the fire-arms in Europe have been lately tried by the government authorities, with a view to determine the relative efficiency of different forms and different manufactures.

GUNPOWDER. The date of invention of this explosive composition is involved in obscurity. It has been said that it was used in China as early as the year A. D. 85, and that the knowledge of it was conveyed to us from the Arabs on the return of the Crusaders to Europe; that the Arabs made use of it at the siege of Mecca in 690; and that they derived it from the Indians. Roger Bacon has been supposed to allude, in an enigmatic way, to the composition of explosive force of gunpowder; and about 1336 Berthold Schwartz, a monk, is said to have also discovered the mode of manufacturing it.

Whatever may have been the history of its origin, gunpowder at the present day consists of a very intimate mixture of nitre, or nitrate of potash, charcoal, and sulphur. The proportions vary; but they generally consist of about 6 parts of nitre to 1 of charcoal and 1 of sulphur. According to a comparative table which has been published, gunpowder for sporting contains the largest ratio of nitre, gunpowder for blasting the largest ratio of sulphur, and the Austrian gunpowder the largest ratio of charcoal; but the range of difference is only small—chiefly observable in the sulphur. The ingredients must be of the greatest attainable purity; and the nitre is fused before use. The charcoal, either of alder, willow, or dog-wood, is prepared in iron retorts; and the sulphur is the volcanic kind imported from Sicily, and is refined by melting or subliming.

When the ingredients are prepared, they are separately ground to a fine powder, and mixed in the proper proportions. The composition is sent to the gunpowder mill, which consists of two stones vertically placed, and running on a bed-stone. On this bed-stone the composition is spread, wetted, and ground, and is then taken off and taken to the corning-house to be corned or grained; here it is first pressed into a hard and firm body, broken into small lumps, and the powder grained by these lumps being put into sieves in each of which is a flat circular piece of lignum vitæ. The sieves are made of parchment skins, having round holes punched through them; several of these sieves are fixed in a frame, which by machinery has such a motion given to it as to make the runner in each sieve go round with velocity sufficient to break the lumps of powder, and force them through the sieves, forming grains of several sizes. The grains are separated from the dust by proper sieves and reels; they are then hardened, and the rougher edges taken off by being run a sufficient length of time in a close reel, which has a proper circular motion given to it.

The gunpowder, thus corned, dusted, aud reeled, is sent to the stove and dried, care being taken not to raise the heat so as to dissipate the sulphur. The heat is regulated by a thermometer.

The theory of the action of gunpowder is this: that particle on which a spark falls is immediately heated to the temperature of ignition; the nitre is decomposed, and its oxygen combines with the charcoal and sulphur, which are also heated; this combination extricates as much heat as is sufficient to inflame successively, though rapidly, the remaining mass. The cause of the expansive force of gunpowder is the production of carbonic acid, carbonic oxide, and nitrogen; and, these being liberated at a very high temperature, the effect is greatly increased. The firing may be effected by the electric spark, and also under some circumstances by percussion.

In ascertaining the goodness of gunpowder, which is done by determining its strength, an *éprouvette* is employed to measure its projectile force. This is a small strong barrel, in which a given quantity of the powder is fired, and the comparative expansive force is measured by the action exerted on a spring or weight.

The principal gunpowder works near London are at Waltham Abbey, Dartford, and Hounslow. The magazines require very cautious management, to obviate danger of explosion.

GUNTER'S SCALE. [SLIDING RULE.]

GUTTA PERCHA. This lately-discovered and very useful substance exudes from a tree grown in Singapore, Borneo, and other of the eastern islands. The first specimen seen in England was sent to the Society of Arts, London, in 1843, by Dr. Montgomerie. The first articles made of this substance in England were a lathe-band, a short piece of pipe, and a bottle case, which were presented to the Society of Arts in 1844.

There seem to be three varieties of this substance, named Gutta Girek, Gutta Tuban, and Gutta Percha. The word gutta means a gum which exudes from a tree; while percha (pronounced pertsha) is the Malayan name for tho tree which principally yields this gum. The trees are forest trees, and the natives appear to tap the bark when and how they think they may obtain the largest supplies. The gum is brought to England in shapeless lumps, and is then wrought into the secondary forms of rods, tubes, blocks, sheets, strings, &c., preparatory to being manufactured for various useful purposes.

The articles now made of gutta percha are numerous and varied. The toughness of the material (differing somewhat from the elasticity of caoutchouc), and the facility with which it may be softened by heat, render it peculiarly apt to receive, and maintain permanently, any form that may be imparted to it. Pressure in moulds, while the gutta percha is in a warm and plastic state, is one of the most convenient modes of giving it a determinate form. Whether wet or dry, its uses are confined to cold purposes, as it is very readily affected and thrown out of shape by heat. For many purposes, naphtha and other inflammable liquids act as cements and even solvents for the gutta percha. In its usual condition it is a brown substance, and not much unlike very tough leather, but having a peculiar odour; its surface is, however, capable of being prepared so as to receive paint, gilding, japanning, bronzing, and other ornamental modifications. The crude substance, as brought to England, is reduced to a pulp by macerating machines, purified by water, combined with many different substances according to the purpose to which it is to be applied, and pressed into sheets or other forms by rollers; and familiar mechanical processes are then sufficient to work up this prepared material to the required forms.

It was reasonable to expect that, after gutta percha came into general use, it would be employed in some of the processes of bookbinding. Accordingly, in 1845, Mr. Nickels patented a method of using gutta percha for cementing together the leaves of books, exactly in the same way as in caoutchouc binding. The cement is a solution made by dissolving gutta percha in rectified naphtha, rectified oil of turpentine, or some other essential oil. The solution also is used for pasting down the end-papers, attaching vellum or leather to the boards, sizing the exterior for marbling and gilding, and for mixing with the colour for colouring and marbling edges, &c. Sheets of gutta percha are used as a substitute for vellum, leather, cloth, or paper, in covering books; or a covering is made by coating a piece of cloth with gutta percha solution. The same material is used as a substitute for paste-board for binding: the flexible boards being made of a composition, in which gutta percha is mixed with paper, pulp, leather dust, wool, or cotton. When for any of the above purposes a little more elasticity is required than belongs to gutta percha, a little caoutchouc is combined with it.

Lieut. Rouse, Superintendent of the Greenwich Hospital Schools, has lately caused 800 pairs of boys' shoes to be soled with gutta percha; he states that they are more economical than leather, and that the waterproof quality is fully determined. Gutta percha water-pipes are being gradually substituted for lead. At the Bristol Vitriol Works gutta percha pump-buckets are used. It is employed as a lining for muriatic acid casks at the Patent Candle Works. From its power of resisting the most potent chemicals, it is of the greatest service to the chemical manufacturer, as he is enabled to use it in many operations instead of glass or metal. The most concentrated alkalies do not affect it, nor any of the acids used in pharmacy or the arts, with the exception of the strongest sulphuric and nitric acids. Messrs. Muspratts have had carboys made and wine pipes lined with it, for the conveyance of muriatic acid by railway, instead of glass; and so successful has been the experiment, reducing the carriage, and obviating all danger of breakage, that they are now using nothing else. For the conveyance and stowage of water—entirely preventing the injurious effects arising from drinking water contaminated with lead—it is peculiarly well adapted, as it is not in the least acted upon by the carbonic acid and fixed air which in some waters so readily attack lead. Its applicability to many other chemical purposes, such as funnels, syphons, &c., and for strapping for diseased joints, stopping for decayed teeth, balsam for cuts, catheters, bougies, and stethescopes, is very important. In electrical processes the insulating power of gutta percha is most valuable. Gutta percha was first employed as a cover to the wires in damp tunnels, and its perfect success there suggested the idea of laying down within its protecting folds telegraphic lines between England and the Continent.

The best illustration of the uses of this remarkable substance is perhaps furnished by a list of the articles now made by the Gutta Percha Company in the City Road:—*Domestic, &c.*—Soles for boots and shoes; lining for cisterns; picture frames; looking-glass frames; ornamental mouldings; bowls; drinking cups; jars; soap dishes; ornamental inkstands; vases; noiseless curtain rings; card, fruit, pin, and pen trays; tooth brush trays; shaving brush trays; window blind cord; clothes line; nursing aprons; coloured material for amateur modelling; ornamental flower stands and pots; sheet for damp walls and floors; drain and soil pipes; gutta percha domestic telegraphs; watering tubes for gardens; lining for bonnets; jar covers; sponge bags; watch stands; shells; foot baths; balsam for cuts, chilblains, &c.; lighter stands; water and gas pipes. *Surgical*—Splints; thin sheet for bandages; stethescopes; ear trumpets; liquid gutta percha for wounds; bed straps. *Chemical*—Carboys; vessels for acids, &c.; syphons; tubing for conveying oils, acids, alkalies, &c.; flasks; bottles; lining for tanks; funnels. *Manufacturing*—Buckets; mill bands; pump buckets, valves, clacks, &c.; felt edging for paper makers; bosses for woollen manufacturers; flax holders; shuttle beds for looms; washers; bowls for goldsmiths; bobbins; covers for rollers; round bands and cord; breasts for water wheels; oil cans. *For offices, &c.*—Wafer holders; inkstands; ink cups; pen trays; cash bowls; washing basins; tubes for conveying messages; canvas for covering books, &c.; architects' and surveyors' plan cases. *Agricultural*—Tubing for conveying liquid manure; lining for manure tanks; driving bands for thrashing machines, &c.; traces; whips; buckets, bowls, &c. *Electrical, &c.*—Covering for electric telegraph wire; insulating stools; battery cells; handles for discharging rods, &c.; electrotype moulds. *Ornamental*—Medallions; brackets; cornices; console tables; mouldings in imitation of carved wood. *Uses on Shipboard*—Sou'-wester hats; pilots' hats; life buoys; buckets; pump buckets; speaking trumpets and tubes; drinking cups; powder flasks; fishing net floats; sheathing for ships; waterproof canvas; air-tight life boat cells; tubes for pumping water from the hold to the deck; round and twisted cords; lining for boxes; tiller ropes. *Miscellaneous*—Suction pipes for fire engines; fire buckets; stable buckets; lining for coffins; sounding boards for pulpits; tap ferules; communion trays; tubing for ventilation; hearing apparatus in churches and chapels for deaf persons; cricket balls; bouncing balls; golf balls; fencing sticks; portmanteaus; police staves; life preservers; embossed book backs; embossed globes and maps for the blind; railway conversation tubes; miners' caps; beds for paper cutting machine knives; fringe for mourning coaches; fine and coarse thread; alarum tubes for mines, &c.; official seals, &c.; envelope boxes; bible backs; prayer book backs; powder flasks; box lids.

The great seal of Ireland, attached to patents and similar documents, has hitherto been made of a soft, easily-melted wax; but it is now stamped in gutta percha.

An ingenious method has been devised by Dr. Branson of Sheffield, of producing engraved plates of ferns, sea-weeds, &c., by means of gutta percha. The ferns are pressed upon a carefully prepared sheet of this material, while warm; and the delicate markings are left in *intaglio* or cavity on the gutta percha surface. A cast in brass may be taken from this intaglio; and impressions may be printed from the brass.

The advance in the trade in gutta percha has been astonishingly rapid, as will be shown by the amount exported from Singapore to Great Britain:—

1844	.. ..	230 lbs.
1845	.. ..	22,000 lbs.
1846	.. ..	710,000 lbs.
1847	.. ..	1,200,000 lbs.
1848	.. ..	1,700,000 lbs.

It was computed that 300,000 trees were destroyed to obtain the above quantities.

GUYA'NA, GUAYA'NA, or GUIANA, is the north-eastern portion of South America, extending from the banks of the river Orinoco southward to those of the river Amazon. Few countries on the surface of the globe can be compared with it for luxuriance of vegetation, which shows itself especially in the great number of indigenous plants and the large forest trees which cover perhaps not less than one-half of its surface. Timber, furniture-wood, and dye-wood are afforded in abundance. Indian corn, rice, mandioca, yams, sweet potatoes, arrow root, bananas, pineapples, cocoa-nuts, sugar, coffee, cotton, tobacco, ginger, pepper, clover, nutmegs—all are grown in Guyana. Wheat does not thrive well. Black cattle grow to a greater size than in Europe, but their flesh is not so tender nor of so fine a flavour. The wool of the sheep is converted into hair. Among the ferocious animals are the jaguar and couguar. Other animals are the armadillo, agouti, and bear, sloth, monkeys, lizards, iguana, alligators, bats, and snakes. The birds and insects are very numerous.

In that portion of Guyana which belongs to Great Britain, an interesting commercial feature has displayed itself. In the year 1846, about seventy creole field labourers clubbed their savings together to buy an estate on the west bank of the Demerara River, for which they gave 25,000 dollars: an instance which Governor Light, in a despatch to Earl Grey, adduces to show the rising character of many of the working population. In 1838 there were 308 coffee and sugar estates in cultivation; in 1846 the number had fallen to 251, owing to the disasters attending the sugar trade. In 1846 there were 641 vessels entered the port of Demerara, with a tonnage of 107,820; those at the port of Berbice were 170, with a burthen of 2000 tons. The imports from the United Kingdom in 1849 amounted in value to 326,821*l*. These numbers relate to *British* Guyana. *Dutch* and *French* Guyana have commerce chiefly with the mother countries.

The postal arrangements established by England, France, and Holland, with the three Guyanian colonies, are all managed by the Royal West India Mail Packet Company, and will be shortly improved by the new contract entered into by that company.

GYPSUM, or sulphate of lime, is a mineral which is found in a compact and crystallised state, as alabaster [ALABASTER] and selenite, or in the form of a soft chalky stone, which in a very moderate heat gives out its water of crystallisation, and becomes a very fine white powder extensively used under the name of Plaster of Paris. [MANURE.]

The principal demand for pure white gypsum is by the Staffordshire potters, who form their moulds with it. Fine blocks of gypsum are selected for making alabaster ornaments. The plaster stone of Paris, mixed with water, forms an adhesive cement or mortar much used in building. Coloured stuccoes for walls are made of gypsum, ghee, and some colouring matter.

H

HAARLEM. In the southern suburbs of this fine old Dutch city are the famous nursery flower-gardens, which formerly supplied a great part of Europe with tulips, hyacinths, and other flowers. There are extensive bleaching establishments here, which formerly supplied large quantities of linen to England, whence the article came to get the name of *Holland*, as coming from that country. Silk, cotton, velvet, ribands, linen, and thread are among the principal manufactures.

The lake of Haarlem, which lies south east of the town, is 14 miles long, 10 broad, and 14 feet deep, between water and mud. The mud of the lake is manufactured into valuable bricks called clinkers. The project of draining this lake has been briefly adverted to under DRAINING; and we give here a few additional details concerning the progress of the works. The area of the lake is between 400,000 and 500,000 acres, and it is intended to leave not more than 700 under water. The drainage is now about two-thirds completed. The area of the lake is expected to sell for above 7*l*. per acre, subject to the land-tax of about 7*s*. per acre. The soil is a peaty loam, and the whole is to be kept dry, after the present operations are completed, by a canal through the middle and smaller inlets into the lake.

HADDINGTONSHIRE. Several attempts have been made to introduce manufactures into this Scottish county. Pot-barley mills, flax mills, cotton mills, paper mills, and starch works have been tried at different times, but from various causes they have failed; and the manufactures at present carried on in the county are very unimportant. A good deal of fishing is carried on near the coast. From Haddingtonshire the improved system of agriculture has been diffused over Scotland, and this county continues to hold a high rank in respect of agriculture and produce. The smaller farms are on the most productive soils. Wheat is the principal grain cultivated, though large crops of beans and oats are likewise raised. The turnip crops are very large. Barley is not much cultivated. Since the increase of pasture land the breeding of sheep and cattle has been extended; but breeding in the lowland and midland districts is carried on upon a very limited scale, the more usual practice being to purchase and fatten for the Edinburgh market. In the Lammermuir district, however, the breeding of live stock is the chief business of the farmer. The town of Haddington carries on a considerable trade in wool, in tanning, and in preparing bones and rape cake for manure. It is also one of the largest wheat-markets in Scotland.

HAGUE. This large and beautiful Dutch city, though neither manufacturing nor commercial in its general features, is preparing for the Great Exhibition carved rosewood furniture, silver embroidery, chased silver cups, and other specimens of workmanship.

HAINAULT, is a very fertile, busy, and prosperous province of Belgium. The chief crops are wheat, rye, oats, barley, beans, rape, flax, hops, and potatoes; tobacco and chicory are also grown. Much of the land near the rivers is laid out in meadow; in other parts trefoil, lucern, and sainfoin are cultivated. Horned cattle, horses and sheep of excellent breed are numerous; poultry, game, and bees abound. The province is traversed by several good roads and numerous canals, by which communication was much facilitated, even before the making of railways; and, like every other part of Belgium, it is well supplied with this new and rapid means of transit. The commerce of the province is composed of its varied industrial products—glass, porcelain, pottery, salt, spirits distilled from grain, beer, machinery, woollen stuffs, linen, lace, Brussels carpets (the great manufacture of which is in Tournay), &c. The most considerable articles of export are coal, iron, and lime, which are transported by canals and railroads to France and the neighbouring countries. Slates, marble, and building stone are quarried.

Charleroi is one of the manufacturing towns; glass, salt, sugar, leather, nails, woollen yarn, &c., are among its products. The town stands in a most extensive coal field, which gives employment to 10,000 men, and yields annually 3,000,000 tons of coal. The number of smelting furnaces, iron foundries, and nail factories in the surrounding district is very great. At *Chimay* are numerous breweries, iron works, and coal mines. *Lessines* is a place of much trade; the neighbouring quarries furnish large quantities of paving and building stone. There are salt refineries, distilleries, and chicory-factories; and there is much trade in coal, wood, and oil. There are many other large manufacturing towns in the province, several of which are on the list of those who will contribute to the Industrial Exhibition.

HAIR; HAIR-WORKING. The hairy coverings of animals are composed of long delicate processes of a horny substance, which grow from bulbs situated in or beneath the skin. Human hair is more or less flattened, so that a transverse section presents an elliptical form, or sometimes, from one side being grooved, has the shape of a bean. The hair of the whiskers, beard, and mustachios, and in general all short curly hair is most flattened. In most instances flatness and curliness are directly proportionate, and both attain their maximum in the crisp woolly hairs of the negro, which are sometimes as much as two thirds broader in one direction than in the other. Except at their base the hairs are perfectly solid, and in most animals their substance is similar throughout. The hair of the head is sometimes known to have attained a length of seven or eight feet.

Hairs are very elastic; they admit of being stretched nearly one third of their length, and regain their original length almost completely; in proportion to their size they are very tough and firm. In chemical properties hair resembles horn, nails, &c. It is soluble in water at a very high temperature, as in a Papin's digester, leaving a large quantity of oil mixed with sulphuret of iron, and some sulphuretted hydrogen. It is this oil, with the sulphuret of iron, which gives the colour to the hair, and by whose absorption grayness is produced. The iron is most abundant in the darkest hair, and the sulphur is the ingredient on which the action of the various black dyes for red or gray hair depends.

In the manufacture of hair into various articles of use and ornament, the hair of different animals is employed; but the most singular feature connected with the manufacture is the *hair harvest* in France. Young women in England, who have beautiful tresses, are often urged by poverty to part with them for money to the hair-workers; but in France it is a regular system. There are hair merchants in Paris, who send agents in the spring of each year into the country districts to purchase the tresses of young women, who seek to obtain an annual crop with the same care as a farmer would a field crop. The agents frequent fairs and markets; and have with them a stock of handkerchiefs, muslins, ribbons, &c., which they give in exchange for the hair. So sensitive a barometer is commerce, of slight changes in the value of exchangeable goods, that the agents know the hair of a particular district to be worth a few sous more per pound than that of a district thirty or forty miles away: a fact which naturalists would have been long in finding out. It is estimated that 200,000 lbs. of hair is purchased at each spring harvest. The price paid is about five francs per lb. The agents send the hair to their employers, by whom it is dressed and sorted, and sold to the hair workers in the chief towns at about ten francs per lb. That which is to be made into perukes is purchased by a particular class of persons, by whom it is cleaned, curled, prepared to a certain stage, and sold to the peruke maker at twenty to eighty francs per lb. The peruke maker gives it the form which, as is well known, commands a very high price; a peruke is often sold for double its weight in silver.

In respect both to the hair itself, and to perukes and other articles made of hair, France supplies a considerable quantity to England and the United States. The importations of hair, and of manufactured goods in which hair is the only or chief material, have lately been to the value of about 20,000*l.* annually.

Differences are observed in manufactures from *curly* or from *straight* hair; the former is spun into a kind of elastic cord; while the latter is woven into cloth for sieves, or damask hair chair bottoms. The hair here spoken of is horse hair, obtained chiefly from the tail. It may be dyed of various tints. The mode of weaving horse hair cloth does not differ essentially from other kinds of weaving: there are a few minor adjustments of the loom necessary, to accommodate the rigidity of the material. In many kinds of such cloth the warp is made of black linen thread or yarn. The cloth is hot calendered after weaving to give it a gloss. The manufacture of hair pencils is noticed in a later article. [PENCILS.]

HALEB, or ALEPPO, is one of the busiest cities of Syria, or of the east generally. Before the earthquake of 1822 Haleb was supposed to possess 12,000 artisans, and was celebrated for its gold and silver lace, its manufactures of silk and cotton goods, shawls, &c. It carries on a great caravan trade with Persia, and the eastern parts of Asia. The goods destined for the European market are shipped from the port of Latakia. Consuls from all the commercial states of Europe reside at Haleb. The inhabitants of the district around Haleb only cultivate the land in the mountainous districts, which produce wheat and other sorts of corn, melons, olives, cotton, tobacco, figs, &c.: the level parts of the country are abandoned to the Kurds and Arabs.

HALIFAX takes a high rank among the clothing towns of the West Riding. The chief articles at present manufactured at Halifax are worsted stuffs, including shalloons, tammies, calamancoes, duroys, everlastings, moreens, shags, serges, merinos; also baizes, narrow and broad cloths, and kerseymeres. Bombasins, crapes, and other fabrics, composed of silk and worsted, are also manufactured here, and the cotton trade is carried on to a considerable extent. Halifax has joined with the other West Riding towns to furnish a combined series of specimens for the Great Exhibition: a mode well calculated to illustrate the resources of this highly interesting district.

HAMBURG. This large city, the most important centre of commerce in Germany, is the main channel of communication between North Germany and foreign countries. The number of vessels that enter from the sea is about 4000 annually, with an average tonnage of about 150 tons per vessel. In 1845 the entries from the sea were 3990 ships, as follows:—

435 from Transatlantic ports;
1566 from British ports
1989 from other European ports;

and these numbers will afford a tolerably correct ratio for later years. Of the values of the commodities imported by this mass of shipping we have no specific returns; but, taking imports and exports together, the sea-borne trade of that year was about 22½ millions sterling.

The imports are composed chiefly of sugar, coffee, raw and manufactured cotton, cotton yarn, tobacco, hides, dye-stuffs, wine, brandy, tea, rum, spices, &c. The exports comprise grain of all sorts, wool, seeds, bark, spelter, butter, salt provisions, rags, wooden clocks, linens, all kinds of German manufactures, Rhenish wines, &c. Hamburg possesses about 600 ships, including a few steamers. It has regular steam communication with London, Amsterdam, &c.; steamers daily ascend the Elbe to Magdeburg.

A very large model of St. Stephen's Church, the chief church in Hamburg, is to be deposited at the Great Exhibition; the former church was destroyed at the great Hamburg fire in 1842; and the present structure has been built from the designs of an English architect. Some beautiful specimens of ivory carving are said to have been prepared at Hamburg.

HAMPSHIRE. The New Forest in this county has varied in area from time to time: at present it includes 64,000 acres, and is the property of the crown, subject to rights of common and other ancient claims. Much of the oak and beech timber for the navy is grown here. Alice Holt Forest also contains much valuable timber. The northern part of the county is naturally very unproductive, and till within a few years was almost entirely covered with a brown heath, on which some hardy forest sheep and a few miserable cattle were reared, and contrived to pick up a scanty living; but a good deal of heath has recently been brought into cultivation. South of this district the chalk prevails, better adapted for pasture than for corn culture. In the valleys and along the lower slopes of the chalk-hills the soil is of a tough tenacious nature, very difficult to cultivate; but it can be made to yield good crops of beans, wheat, and oats. Hampshire, although it cannot be compared with some eastern and northern counties for agricultural improvements, is not far behind them; and there are some farms as well managed as any in England. The farm-buildings and the agricultural implements are gradually improving. The native hogs, which live on the acorns and beech-mast of the New Forest, although the flavour of their flesh may be good, are coarse, raw-boned, flat-sided animals, and are now seldom met with. The improved breeds produced by crosses of the Berkshire, the Suffolk, Essex, and Chinese pigs, are those from which the Hampshire bacon is usually prepared. The excellence of this bacon is mainly due to the care with which the curing is effected.

Hampshire cannot be deemed a manufacturing county; although there are several bustling towns. Alton is celebrated for its ale breweries, and for the hop-plantations near it. At Andover the chief business consists in malting, and in the manufacture of silk. The malting and corn trades constitute the principal business of Basingstoke. At Fareham considerable trade in corn and coal is carried on. At Fordingbridge there are some manufactures of sail-cloth and bed-ticking. Winchester depends more on its ecclesiastical antiquities than on its trade and commerce. PORTSMOUTH and SOUTHAMPTON call for a word of notice elsewhere.

HAMS. Hams are usually prepared from the legs of pigs; but those of the sheep are also sometimes prepared. They are salted either by immersion in the pickle, or by having salt rubbed over them. A little powdered saltpetre is sometimes rubbed over them before salting; and moist sugar or treacle is frequently employed for flavouring. About three weeks are required for wet-salting, and four for dry-salting; mutton hams do not require so long. When properly salted, the hams are ready for smoking.

There were 11,751 cwts. of hams imported in 1849; and 16,268 cwts. in 1850.

HAND-GLASS is a name given by gardeners to a portable glazed cover which they place over certain plants for one of two purposes; either to screen them from the effects of cold and wet without depriving them of much light, or to maintain around them an atmosphere of uniform humidity. Bell-glasses differ from hand-glasses in no respect with regard to the purpose they are intended to serve, but are blown from a single piece of glass instead of being composed of many pieces fastened together. Glasses of this description are principally used to assist cuttings of plants in the process of striking root, or newly planted individuals in establishing themselves in the soil.

HANOVER. The mountains in the southern part of this kingdom abound in mineral wealth, and are covered with forests of red pine and fir, with some oaks and other timber. Agriculture is the chief source of subsistence to the inhabitants, which is much favoured by the facilities for exportation when the harvest is abundant, as well as by the transit trade, and the consumption of the neighbouring maritime towns. In the marsh-land the breeding of cattle is more followed than agriculture. The county produces flax, tobacco, hops, fruit, pulse, potatoes, &c. Timber is abundant, and considerable quantities are exported.

Manufactures are not carried on to any considerable extent. Thread, linens, woollens, and calicoes are manufactured to a small extent. The commerce is not of large amount. The principal commercial port is Embden; and Münden, at the junction of the Werra and the Fulda, has an active trade with the interior of Germany.

The Hanoverian produce imported into Great Britain in 1849 was valued at 185,287*l.*; and the British produce and manufactures exported to Hanover 150,927*l.*

It has been stated that the manufacturers of Hanover have not received from their sovereign, in respect to contributions towards the Industrial Exhibition, that countenance and assistance which most continental sovereigns have afforded in their respective countries; and that the specimens transmitted to England will be limited by this circumstance.

HANSEATIC LEAGUE. This was a very remarkable commercial association, which took its name from the ancient German word 'Hanse,' signifying an association for mutual support. The cities of Hamburg, Lübeck, and Bremen were, in the middle ages, the depositories of the manufactures of Italy and Germany, with which they supplied the northern countries of Europe in exchange for their raw produce. The wealth which they acquired excited the envy and the rapacity of the princes and nobles; the imposition of new and the augmentation of old tolls were great impediments to trade, which was likewise rendered unsafe by numerous banditti and pirates who infested the roads and the neighbouring seas and rivers. Hamburg and Lübeck concluded an alliance in 1241 by which they engaged to maintain ships and soldiers for the purpose of protecting their commerce. The city of Brunswick joined the alliance in 1247. In course of time most of the trading towns in Europe joined this association, which included London, Rouen, Bordeaux, St. Malo, Bayonne, Marseille, Barcelona, Seville, Cadiz, Lisbon, Antwerp, Danzig, Dort, Amsterdam, Bruges, Rotterdam, Ostend, Dunkirk, Leghorn, Messina, Naples, Bergen, Novgorod, all the towns on the Baltic, the Elbe, and the Weser, Embden, Cologne, and other towns, to the number of eighty-five. Their principal factories were Bruges, London, Novgorod, and Bergen. All the towns sent deputies to a congress which usually met in Lübeck. The Hanse Towns became so powerful, that in 1348 they defeated the kings of Norway and Denmark, deposed Magnus, king of Sweden, and gave his crown to his nephew Albert; they equipped in 1428, 40 ships of war and raised 12,000 troops, exclusive of seamen, in a war with Erick, king of Denmark; and in the same century they compelled Edward IV. to restore all their privileges and property in England, which he had attempted to withhold. That part of the city of London called the Steelyard was their exclusive property, and Bishops-Gate, one of the principal entrances to London, was intrusted to them to guard. But when the roads and seas were no longer insecure, when America was discovered, and India was reached by doubling the Cape of Good Hope, the Hanseatic League gradually declined, and at the last general assembly at Lübeck, in 1630, the deputies from the several cities appeared merely to declare their secession from the League. Hamburg, Lübeck, and Bremen, formed an association in 1641, and remained free republics till December 1810, when they were incorporated with the French empire, but in 1813 they were again separated from France, and with Frankfort-am-Main are now called the Free Hanseatic Cities of the Germanic Confederation.

HARBOURS OF REFUGE. Among the engineering works now in progress, in the southern half of our island, the formation of harbours of refuge is not the least important. Numerous as are our ports, harbours, bays, and æstuaries, fitted to receive and despatch merchant shipping, there is a deficiency of harbours into which fleets could go to find shelter during a storm, and which would serve as general places of rendezvous for shipping.

Dover is in many respects one of the most important harbours on the coast: chiefly from its proximity to the continent. Yet is it only a tidal harbour, and has a shallow entrance even when the tide is in. Many a merchantman would be glad to avoid the perils of the Goodwin Sands by a temporary anchorage in Dover Harbour, if it were better suited as a refuge. In 1844 a Government Commission was appointed to consider this subject, in relation to the forming of harbours of refuge for merchant ships, and stations for war ships. The commissioners recommended extensive works at Dover, Portland, Seaford, and Harwich, with this object in view: to be proceeded with in the order here specified if all could not be advanced simultaneously. The recommendation was adopted, in its main features, by the Government. The harbour of refuge at Dover is being constructed; there is to be a harbour of 520 acres up to high water mark, or 380 acres at low water; there is to be an entrance 700 feet wide on the south side, and another 150 feet wide on the east. The first work will be a pier, running out from the point called Cheeseman's Head into seven fathoms water; it will protect the existing harbour during south-west gales, and will form the first link in the great wall of masonry which will enclose the harbour. The eastern boundary of the harbour will be far beyond the limits of the present inhabited town of Dover; the harbour will be a mile and a quarter from east to west, and three quarters of a mile from north to south. The existing contract for a part of the works was taken in July 1847; the works were commenced in October of the same year; in 1848 the masonry was carried out 270 feet from the shore; in 1849 this length was increased to 460 feet; in 1850 the works were proceeding steadily, until a terrific storm on the night of the 7th of October, produced very disastrous results on the masonry and scaffolding. Much of the subsequent labour has been in repair of this disaster.

The operations at Portland are briefly noticed in another article. [DORSETSHIRE.] See also the article BREAKWATER.

HARDNESS. In distributing crystals and minerals into classes, an attempt is made to determine their relative hardness. The following are the gradations, from soft to hard:—

Talc, white or greenish; rock salt and uncrystallised gypsum; calcareous spar, cleavable; fluor spar, which cleaves perfectly; apatite, from Salzburg; adularia; rock crystal, transparent; topaz; corundum, from Bengal; diamond.

HARP. This is one of the most ancient as well as most beautiful of all musical instruments. The Welsh triple-stringed harp of the present day extends from G an octave below the first line in the base, to G, or A in altissimo on the *right* side; and from G, the first line in the base, to the same upper notes on the *left* side; the middle row consists of the semitones of the outward rows. Hence, if the outside rows be tuned in the diatonic scale of G, each parallel note being in perfect unison, the notes of the middle row are tuned a semitone higher.

The harp, as a generally useful instrument, may be said to date its existence from the time when pedals were added to it, by the invention of Sebastian Erard. With these it is possible to modulate into all keys, and to execute any music suited to keyed instruments. In the *single action*, the pedals raise the tone of every string half a note; in the *double action*, the instrument is tuned in C flat; and by fixing the pedals in the first groove the instrument is at once transposed into C natural: whereas by fixing them in the second groove it is transposed another semitone higher, into the key of C sharp. The compass of the harp thus improved is from double E below the base to E in altissimo.

HARPSICHORD. This keyed musical instrument, in form the same as the grand pianoforte, but smaller, was strung with steel and brass wires, two to each note; these were struck by *jacks* armed with small pieces of quill, acting as plectrums, and thus made to render a brilliant but somewhat harsh sound, wholly unlike that produced by the hammers of the pianoforte. *Stops, swells*, and double rows of keys were occasionally employed to modify the power of the wires. The harpsichord came into use in England in the seventeenth century; but it is now entirely superseded by the PIANOFORTE.

HARROWS. The well-known agricultural implement, the *harrow*, which is drawn over the land when the seed has been sown after the last ploughing, is a frame set full of spikes. The *bush-harrow*, which is drawn over the ground after the seed has been sown by the dibble, is without spikes, but has thorns or rough bushes fitted into it.

At the various agricultural and cattle shows improved forms of harrow are constantly making their appearance. Among those of recent introduction is Uley's drag harrow, or Scarifier and Cultivator; it has two small wheels in front, two larger behind, and five or seven tines or spikes, according to the width. Smith's Iron Harrow comprises three frames linked together at certain spots, and having about sixty tines or spikes arranged in such a way that each tine leaves its scarified mark or line in the ground independent of the others. Crosskill's Norwegian Harrow is used immediately after ploughing, and leaves three or four inches depth of finely pulverised mould, well prepared for sowing; the instrument acting by a rotatory motion given to barrels loaded with spikes, which scratch along the ground as the machine proceeds. Numerous other forms are frequently brought before public notice.

HARTSHORN. The horn of the common stag contains less earthy matter, and more gelatine, than other bones, and is on this account very useful in medicine. It is kept in the form of shavings, of which a sufficient quantity boiled in water yields a jelly suitable to convalescents, which may be flavoured with lemon-juice or wine, &c.

The liquid which is called *Spirits of Hartshorn*, and which is obtained from hartshorn and other kinds of horn, is carbonate of ammonia combined with a peculiar oil.

HARTZ FOREST. The mineral treasures of this district are noticed under GERMANY.

HAT MANUFACTURE. English hats, in the present day, are mostly made of straw, wool and fur, or silk. The first are noticed under STRAW PLAIT. Beaver hats of the finest quality are made with lamb's wool and the fur of English rabbits. To form the body of the hat, the wool and rabbit's fur are separately *bowed* in the manner employed for freeing cotton from its seeds. The two substances are next bowed together until they are intimately mixed; after which the mass is spread evenly, covered with an oil-cloth, and pressed to the state of an imperfectly tangled felt. The next process is to cover the felt with a triangular piece of damp brown paper, and then to fold it in a damp cloth and work it well with the hand, pressing and bending, rolling and unrolling it, until the interlacing or felting is much more perfect, and the mass is compact. The felt thus prepared is next taken to the wide brim of a boiler charged with hot water and beer-grounds and a small quantity of sulphuric acid; it is wetted, rubbed, and rolled, until it no longer contracts. The felt is next stiffened with shell-lac, a solution of which is applied by means of a brush to one or to both sides of the felt; after which it is heated in a stove, and by this means the whole substance becomes duly impregnated with the resin: this renders the hat nearly waterproof. To form the nap of a hat, one-half or three-fourths of an ounce of beaver, and some other less costly fur, are bowed together and imperfectly felted in the manner already described, and shaped the same as the body to which it is to be applied; that body is then softened by immersing it in the boiler, when the nap is applied and worked as in felting, until the required union is effected between the two bodies.

The felt thus covered is brought to the proper shape by working it on a wooden block, and is then dyed black. The hat is softened by steam, the crown is strengthened by placing in it a disc of scale-board, and linen is pasted over this. The nap is raised, and a uniform direction given to its fibres by means of warm irons and hair brushes. The last processes are binding and lining, when the hat is ready to be worn. In the low-priced hats of the present day, commoner wool and fur, and smaller quantities of each, are used.

Silk hats consist of a cover or exterior part made of silk plush, which is laid upon a foundation of chip, stiffened linen, or some other light material, previously blocked into shape. The so-called *Velvet* hats and *Satin* hats deserve those titles only so far as the plush resembles those materials. The plush is mostly woven in the north of England. *Paris* hats are for the most part made in England, the silk plush being imported from France, where it is made better than our weavers seem able to equal.

The hats exported in 1848 amounted in number only to 8,768 dozens, and in value to 27,455*l.*: so little demand is there abroad for English hats; the exports are almost entirely to our own colonies. Silk-plush for covering *Paris hats* was imported in 1850 to the extent of 138,909 lbs.

HATCHING APPARATUS. The method, strange to those who do not understand it, of hatching chickens by artificial means, is nothing more than a mode of applying warmth to the eggs. If a hen for any reason does not 'sit' upon her brood, an *artificial* mother is sometimes provided, which will rear several broods at once; it is a board or box lined with soft lambskin, covered with a wicker, and placed near a heated wall in such a way that the young chicks may receive warmth sufficient for their tender condition. These artificial mothers are, however, only a sort of house for chickens newly hatched: they are not hatching-machines. The Egyptians have long been in the habit of applying heat and moisture artificially to the hatching of chickens. Mr. Bucknell some years ago invented a hatching-machine under the somewhat learned name of the *Eccalcobion;* and more recently Mr. Cantelo's *HydroIncubator* has attracted public attention. In this apparatus heat is applied to the upper surface of the eggs as they are ranged in layers. A current of warm water flows over a waterproof cloth, beneath which the eggs are placed. A tank of water is kept continually at a temperature of 109° Fahr., with the surface so arranged that the heated water may flow over the waterproof cloth: a return pipe being so placed as to connect the outer end of the cloth with the bottom of the tank. There is thus a continual flow of water over the cloth, at one uniform temperature. The eggs are placed in drawers having perforated bottoms, with a layer of woollen cloth between; the upper surface of the eggs can just touch the under surface of the warmed waterproof cloth; but the arrangement is such that air can freely circulate between the eggs and the cloth. The water is heated by slowly burning charcoal fires.

Although there is much ingenuity displayed in this apparatus, it seems doubtful whether the method will be a commercially prosperous one.

HAVANNAH. This flourishing commercial town, with the best harbour in the West Indies, or perhaps in the world, has been already mentioned under CUBA. Its magnificent harbour is capable of accommodating 1000 ships of the largest size, vessels of the greatest draught coming close up to the quays. Among the commercial cities of the western hemisphere Havannah ranks inferior only to New York, and for a long period it engrossed the whole foreign trade of Cuba. The principal articles of export are sugar, copper ore, coffee, raw tobacco and cigars of the best quality, molasses, and the precious metals; other exports are mahogany, cedar, rum, cocoa, cotton, wax, hides, fruits and preserves, honey, dye-stuffs, &c. In consequence of the relaxation of the English tariff in 1842, and of the sugar act of 1846, the exports are said to have greatly increased, and this is in part proved by the quantity of sugar exported in 1847, which from Havannah and Matanzas amounted to 1,004,496 boxes. The imports are composed of flour, corn, provisions, cotton goods, wine, linen, hardware and metals, silk, gold and silver from Mexico, spices, leather, butter, lard, cheese, fish, deals, casks, hoops, &c. The trade of Havannah extends to all countries of Europe and America, but chiefly to Spain, the United States, and England. In the nine months from January to September 1850, no fewer than 1262 ships entered the

KNIGHT'S CYCLOPÆDIA OF THE INDUSTRY OF ALL NATIONS.

No. 25.

port of Havannah, with a tonnage of 418,388 tons.

HAVRE. The harbour of this important French seaport consists of three wet docks, and an outer port separated by locks, and capable of containing 450 ships. A fourth dock is in course of formation for steamers. The fine quays which border the docks are always lined with vessels, and present great activity of business. The trade of Havre produces in ordinary years customs duties amounting to about a million sterling, representing a total movement of merchandise to the value of over 20,000,000*l*. Besides vast quantities of foreign and colonial produce for the supply of Paris and the north of France, such as coffee, sugar, spices, the imports consist of raw cotton for the manufacturing districts of Rouen, St. Quentin, &c., of indigo, dyewoods, tobacco, rice, hides, timber, iron, tin, tea, &c. The principal exports are silks, broadcloth, cotton manufactures, lace, gloves, shoes, trinkets, plated and tin wares, perfumery, wine, brandy, glass, furniture, books, &c. Above 450 vessels belong to the port, including 50 of 400 to 500 tons engaged in the whale fishery, and 40 large and small steamers. There is regular communication by powerful steamers with Rouen, London, Southampton, Bayonne, Hamburg, Lisbon, &c., and by packet ships with New York, Bahia, Vera Cruz, New Orleans. Small steamers ply to Honfleur, Caen, Rouen, and Paris. The manufactures comprise vitriol, pottery, lace, paper, oil, carpenters' tools, bricks and tiles, ship cordage, tobacco, furniture, &c. There are also several sugar refineries, and breweries. Outside the town and close to the shore there are five ship-building yards, which have constructed some of the best sailing vessels and swiftest steamers belonging to France.

HAY-MAKING MACHINE. The grasses which form the material of a field of hay are of several kinds. The *sweet-scented vernal grass* gives the delightful odour to newly mown hay; the *cock's foot grass*, a coarser but valuable herbage; the *fox tail grass*, greatly relished by cattle; the *meadow fox tail grass*, liked by sheep; the *meadow fescue*, and many other kinds. All these are alike cut down by the mower's *scythe;* which is a long thin blade of steel, well tempered, and having a rim of iron along the back to within a few inches of the point; the handle is of wood, and is adjusted at a particular angle to the plane of the blade; two short projecting handles are fixed to the principal handle, to facilitate the using.

There is no machine, we believe, to supersede hand labour in cutting hay; and therefore the so-called hay-making machines must be understood as applying to a later process. Under ordinary circumstances, the cut grass is collected into heaps by *rakes*, worked by hand; but on large farms a *horse rake* is sometimes used; there are twenty or more teeth or tines, which are drawn over the field until they have collected as much as the interstices can contain; and then the driver, by lifting up a pair of handles, raises the teeth from the ground, so as to throw out the contents of the rake. The *hay making* or *hay tedding machine*, however, turns the hay over and over in the field; it is chiefly valuable for meadow-hay, which requires more turning and scattering than hay from clover or rye-grass. There is a cylinder, or framework of wheels, with rows of prongs projecting from the surface; the cylinder revolves on the same axis as the driving-wheels, and with the same speed as those wheels. As the cylinder revolves, the hay is caught up by the prongs, and thoroughly *tedded* or spread abroad. Various minor improvements have from time to time been made in the construction of these machines.

HEAT. The fundamental laws of heat, so far as they have yet been discovered, form a very subtle and difficult department of science. Only a few words respecting the action of heat can be admissible in this work.

It is found that *expansion*, *fusion*, *evaporation*, *thermo-electric currents*, and various *physiological* phenomena, are effects of heat or at least accompany its absorption. Besides the solar rays, heat may be produced artificially by any means which propagate agitations internally in bodies; hence friction, hammering, percussion, sudden condensation, chemical combination, and electrical discharges are all proper to produce or rather to develope heat.

The spread of heat throughout a liquid is marked by curious effects. If we place a heated plate on the surface of water in a vessel, but so as not to touch the edges, a thermometer placed in the water will indicate little or no alteration of temperature; and, if the bottom of a vessel of water be heated, the heat will be distributed through the liquid only by currents ascending from the heated part. Liquids indeed conduct heat very slowly; and it is only by the rising of heated particles of water, through their lightness, that a vessel of water is quickly heated.

The agency of heat in promoting chemical action is important and extensive; in some cases no combination can take place without it, and in others it greatly facilitates chemical combinations, while in some instances it decomposes compound bodies, and resolves them either into simpler or elementary forms of matter. In the solution of salt in water, an increase of heat, by increasing the affinity between the solid and the liquid, increases the solvent power. Heat has also great power in modifying as well as in causing chemical action, and different degrees of it produce very opposite effects in some cases. The dilatation of substances by heat is nearly proportional to the increase of temperature, except when they are about to change their physical or chemical states; thus water near the freezing point expands when the temperature is diminished. The following table gives the relative dilatation of different solids from the freezing to the boiling point:—

Glass tube	.00083	Copper	.0017
Crown glass	.00089	Brass	.0018
Platinum	.00093	Silver	.0020
Palladium	.001	Tin	.0022
Cast Iron	.0011	Pewter	.0023
Steel	.0012	Grain tin	.0025
Do. tempered	.0013	Lead	.0028
Gold	.0015	Zinc	.0030

Several instruments have been constructed to measure heat; the most important of which are noticed under PYROMETER and THERMOMETER.

HEDGE. Hedges are made of various kinds of shrubs and trees, trained so as to throw out numerous branches along the stem from the surface of the earth upwards; this is done by judicious pruning when they are young. Holly, which bears prickles on the edges of the leaves, is on this account by far the best shrub to form a hedge; but yew, box, thorn, hornbeam, elder, sweet briar, prickly pear, and privet are all employed for hedges, each having its particular excellencies, and requiring a particular kind of culture. There is a method of repairing hedges which is called *plashing*. It consists in cutting half through some of the stems near the ground, and then bending the upper parts down in a horizontal or oblique position, keeping them so by means of hooked sticks driven into the bank. Thus a live hedge is made, which fills up the gaps in the same manner as a dead hedge would have done, and the bent stems soon throw out shoots.

HELENA, ST. This lonely island, situated in the Atlantic Ocean, 1200 miles west of the coast of Benguela, in South Africa, has one of the healthiest climates under the tropics, and is found beneficial to invalids from India and even from Europe. Viewed from the sea, the island appears barren; but the interior is covered with a rich verdure, and is watered by abundant springs. Horned cattle, sheep, and goats feed on the rich pastures. As an English settlement it is of little importance; it is visited by ships returning from India, who there take in fresh provisions and water.

The British produce and manufactures exported to St. Helena in 1849 amounted in value to 18,315*l*.

HE'LIOSCOPE is the name given to a kind of telescope adapted for making observations upon the sun without the eye being injured by the intense brightness of the solar rays. A coloured glass placed before the lens nearest to the eye, in a telescope, has long been the means used to prevent such injury.

HE'LIOSTAT is an instrument employed in making experiments on light. The instrument consists of a plain metallic mirror, from the back of which projects a rod perpendicularly to its plane. The extremity of the rod is connected with the index of a clock, the plane of whose face is parallel to the equator; and, as the index is turned by the wheel-work, the motion of the rod causes the mirror to turn about a vertical axis, and also about a horizontal axis, so that a pencil of the sun's light reflected from the mirror is always in the same position.

HELLEBORE. *White Hellebore*, a valuable medicine, is prepared by triturating the roots of a plant of the same name, called by botanists the *Veratrum Album*. There are also *black hellebore* and *oriental hellebore*, both used medicinally, but derived from plants of different genera from that which yields the white.

HEMP; HEMP-SEED. The plant which yields this most valuable fibre is the *Cannabis sativa*, nearly allied in many of its botanical features to the nettle. It is said to be a native of Persia, but is now known throughout northern Europe. The hemp plant possesses a remarkably tough kind of woody tissue, capable of being manufactured into canvas and cordage; and its value in this respect has given rise to manufactures and commerce of great magnitude. [ROPE-MAKING; SAIL-MAKING.]

The extraction of the fibre from the plant is so similar to that of flax, that we may refer to FLAX for a brief description. Hemp-seed is made to yield a useful oil by pressure; and the hemp plant is useful in many ways for medicine.

Nearly all our hemp is procured from Russia. During the war, the demand was so large (for ship's cordage), and the supply so precarious, that the price sometimes rose to 118*l*. per ton; in recent years the average price has been about one quarter this amount.

The quantities of hemp, imported in the last four years have been as follow :—

1847	..	811,565 cwts.
1848	..	845,771 „
1849	..	1,061,893 „
1850	..	1,048,635 „

Of these quantities, the supply from Russia has been nearly two thirds.

HENBANE, is one of the species of the plants belonging to the *hyoscyamus* genus. The leaves and seeds contain a powerful principle called *hyoscyamia*, on which the deadly as well as the medical effects of henbane depend.

HERAULT, one of the departments of France, produces corn in quantity more than sufficient for the consumption. There is a considerable breadth of artificial meadows; and large crops of lucern, sainfoin, and clover are grown. For quantity of wine produced, Hérault stands at the head of the wine growing departments of France, the annual produce being nearly 50 million gallons. The red wines of St. Georges, St. Christol, and St. Drézéry, the muscadel wines of Frontignan, Lunel, and Béziers, and the white wines of Marseillan and Pinet, are considered the best. Fruits, especially raisins, olives, almonds, figs, and chestnuts, and all kinds of pulse are grown. The mulberry is cultivated for the production of silk; aromatic and medicinal herbs, and plants used for dye stuffs, are gathered. The principal material of the woods are the chestnut and green and white oak. The industrial products comprise woollen cloths, silks, hosiery, calico, muslin, flannel, blankets, brandy, chemical products, pottery, tiles, honey, perfumes, leather, oil, beer, paper, &c. There are also numerous dye houses, and establishments for the rearing of silkworms. Ship building is carried on at Cette and other towns on the coast. Mines of coal and copper, quarries of marble, building and mill stone, slate, gypsum, and granite are worked. A vast deal of salt is made by evaporation on the lagunes and on the shore of the Mediterranean, this department being one of the chief sources for the supply of that article to France. The exports consists of most of the articles enumerated, but chiefly of wine, dry fruits, and brandy. The imports are wool, cotton bales, staves, colonial produce, raw hides, cork, &c.

HEREFORDSHIRE. The soil of this county is very favourable to the growth of trees, especially the apple tree and oak. In the neighbourhood of towns the land is cultivated chiefly as meadow or pasture. The high lands are generally occupied by oak coppices, which are numerous and extensive; these are felled at periods of from 16 to 20 years, and fetch a price of from 18*l.* to 20*l.* an acre. In the lower lands, crops are raised in the following succession: wheat, turnips, barley, clover, and peas or vetches. Hop yards are common in the middle and eastern portions of the county. Orchards are numerous, and produce large quantities of cyder.

Few of our counties possess so little mineral wealth as Herefordshire; nor are its manufactures or general commerce considerable. There is an iron foundry and a little manufacture of gloves, at Hereford; and miscellaneous manufactures at Bromyard, Ledbury, Kington, Leominster, Ross, and Weobly.

HERRING FISHERIES. A brief notice of the herring fishery, as a department of commerce, is given under FISHERIES.

HERTFORDSHIRE. This county has no minerals of any value. The loams are generally well cultivated, but the heavy clays are capable of much improvement. Wherever the turnip husbandry prevails, the superiority of the crops is striking. Wheat, beans, oats, and fallows are the only varieties. Clover is much less in quantity than might be desired. The old heavy plough with four horses in a line may still be seen. The county is remarkable for its high banks and hedges; in many of the lanes, where two carriages could scarcely pass one another, it is difficult for a man standing on a waggon to see over the hedge; but wherever the old high banks have been levelled, and neat quick hedges have been planted in their stead, the ground which has been gained has soon paid the expense. A species of rough garden husbandry has been introduced on the best soils nearest to London for the growth of early potatoes, cabbages, peas, and other culinary vegetables, which are succeeded in the same year by other crops, the whole being forced by an abundance of manure. The plough is used, but a great portion of the labour is done by the spade and the hoe. There are many orchards chiefly for apples and cherries, which are sold in London.

Very little manufacturing is carried on in the county. The country around Barnet is celebrated for its hay, and a great deal of business is done at the market. At Bishop's Stortford a great deal of corn is accumulated, and the malting trade carried on to a great extent. At Hemel Hempstead the females are much engaged in making straw plat, and there are corn and paper mills in the neighbourhood. At Hertford a good deal of business is done in malting, and there are many corn mills on the Lea, the Mimram, and the Beane. At Hitchin much straw-plat is made;

there are some breweries, and also a silk mill. At Rickmansworth there are several paper and flour mills near the town; and some straw platting and horsehair weaving is carried on. There is considerable trade at Ware; the market is one of the greatest in the county for corn. At Watford there are considerable silk mills, and also a paper mill.

HESSE. The small German principalities under this name do not occupy a very high rank in industry or commerce. In *Hesse Cassel* flax and timber are the staple articles: tobacco, hemp, madder, a few hops, and rape-seed are also among the products. The vine is cultivated only in some parts of Hanau. Garden produce of excellent quality is raised about Cassel and Hanau. Hesse abounds in mineral wealth, producing silver, copper, lead, iron, quicksilver, cobalt, salt (from saline springs and in great quantities), saltpetre, vitriol, and alum. There are also coals, marble, very fine white alabaster, porcelain, potter's clay, and pipe clay, &c. The manufactures are insufficient for home consumption. The principal are linen, mostly coarse, which is exported to the value of 300,000*l.* sterling annually; fine linen is made in Cassel and Herzberg. Cotton spinning is pretty general. Schmalkalden manufactures almost all the steel and iron of the country; Grossalmerode is celebrated for its crucibles, which are exported to all parts of the world.

In *Hesse Darmstadt* the chief productions are corn of all kinds, likewise maize and spelt —wheat and rye, flax, hemp, hops, tobacco, pulse, potatoes, wines, both white and red, garden vegetables and fruit, and timber. Mining is not carried on to any great extent: it is confined to copper, iron, coals, salt, and brown coal. Cobalt, basalt, lime, sandstone, marble, and slate are found in different parts of the grand duchy. The chief manufactures are of woollens, cottons, and linen, leather, and hardware. Wine is produced chiefly in Rhenish Hesse. The most considerable manufacturing and trading town is Offenbach, which has two annual fairs. Mainz is the principal place for the transit trade. The exports consist of the natural productions of the country and of some manufactures.

These two Hessian principalities will contribute to the extent of the resources to the Great Industrial Exhibition. There are two or three other Hesses, very small and unimportant.

HEXACHORD, was a name given by the ancient Greeks to a lyre of six strings; also to a scale of six sounds. The term hexachord was also applied to a system of musical scales now disused.

HIBISCUS. Many plants of this genus yield very useful fibre for rope making and similar purposes; this fibre is yielded by the bark. The *hibiscus cannabinus* is cultivated everywhere in India in the rainy season for this purpose; and its fibre is often imported into Europe, as a substitute for hemp. In the island of Tahiti rope and string are manufactured from the bark of the *hibiscus tiliaceous*, which is also made into matting of a white colour, and of different degrees of fineness. Almost all the species possess sufficient tenacity of fibre to be used for cordage, whips, &c. They also abound in mucilage, which renders them serviceable as articles of diet; the calyces are often employed in making tarts, and a decoction of them, sweetened and fermented, is used in the West Indies as a cool and refreshing drink. The seeds of the *hibiscus abelmoschus* are said to be added to coffee in Arabia, and are in India employed as a cordial medicine.

HICKORY. This tree is applied to many useful purposes in North America. The wood is coarse grained, very heavy, exceedingly tough and strong, and red at the heart; but it is not very durable. It is employed for the shafts and springs of carriages, for large screws for presses, for bows, chair backs, whip handles, wooden cogged wheels, cask-hoops, and a variety of other purposes. It is one of the most economical kinds of wood fuel. The nuts of a species called the pecan hickory, are eaten in North America; and so, to some extent, are those of most of the species.

HINDOO MANUFACTURES. Under EAST INDIA COMPANY we have glanced at the commercial relations which exist between India and other countries. We have here to speak of the native skill of the Hindoos. It is evident from the most ancient Sanskrit works, as well as from the testimony of the Greeks who visited the country, that the useful and fine arts had attained a considerable degree of perfection among the Hindoos in very early times. The Ramayana (a Sanskrit manuscript of great antiquity) contains numerous proofs of the progress they had made in working metals. The art of smelting iron ore and of manufacturing steel is undoubtedly of great antiquity; and their skill in the manufacture of gold and silver ornaments is evident from the descriptions of the Ramayana. The degree of perfection to which the Hindoos carried the art of weaving in ancient as well as modern times is well known. Their country has always been distinguished for the number and excellence of the substances which it contains for dyeing colours, and the beauty and brilliancy, as well as durability, of their colours were as celebrated among the Greeks and Romans as among ourselves. Silk was probably manufactured in India in very early times. The art of obtaining intoxicating liquors by distillation is mentioned in the Ramayana and the laws of Manu.

In painting the Hindoos have not attained much proficiency: their artists draw with great accuracy, but they have no knowledge of perspective. With regard to music their instruments are numerous; but their compositions are confined to a few simple melodies.

With respect to the present state of the arts among the Hindoos, Bishop Heber remarks, 'Nor is it true that in the mechanic arts they are inferior to the general run of European nations. Where they fall short of us (which is chiefly in agricultural instruments and the mechanics of common life), they are not, so far as I have understood of Italy and the South of France, surpassed in any great degree by the people of those countries. Their goldsmiths and weavers produce as beautiful fabrics as our own; and it is so far from true that they are obstinately wedded to their old patterns, that they show an anxiety to imitate our models, and do imitate them very successfully. The ships built by native artists at Bombay are notoriously as good as any which sail from London or Liverpool. The carriages and gigs which they supply at Calcutta are as handsome, though not so durable, as those of Long Acre. In the little town of Monghyr, three hundred miles from Calcutta, I had pistols, double-barrelled guns, and different pieces of cabinet work brought down to my boat for sale, which in outward form nobody could detect to be of Hindoo origin; and at Delhi, in the shop of a native wealthy jeweller, I found brooches, ear-rings, snuff boxes, &c., of the latest models, and ornamented with French devices and mottoes.'

Architecture.—The architecture of the Hindoos has hitherto been little studied by professional men. On examining the Hindoo works of construction, or edifices erected above ground, we can hardly avoid being struck by the prevalence of pyramidal masses and forms, as exhibited in pagodas or towers. The Egyptian structures of this kind bear a much closer resemblance to natural or rudely constructed prototypes than do those of the Hindoos. The gopuras, or pagoda towers erected over the gateways leading to temples are indeed pyramidal in their general form, but infinitely more complex than, not the pyramidal alone, but anything else we meet with in Egyptian architecture. Neither do they terminate in a point or mere platform; but have generally a great deal of ornament bestowed on their summit, which sometimes assumes, not inelegantly, the form of a crown. Besides this, they differ from the pyramid in being of far loftier proportions. Of a domical termination, if not exactly a dome, we have an example in the great pagoda at Tanjore, which is considered one of the finest specimens of the kind in India.

HINGE. Hinges are constructed in a great variety of forms; but in most of the commoner kinds the action is that of a hollow cylinder working round a fixed central pin. In Collinge's patent hinges, which are peculiarly adapted for hanging large heavy doors and gates, the principal rubbing action is between a hollow cap and an accurately turned sphere, formed, as it were, upon the end of the pin, a cavity being provided for the reception of a supply of oil to lubricate the rubbing surfaces. Mr. Redmund is the inventor of the rising hinges so frequently used for hanging room doors in houses of superior character. In ordinary door hinges the hollow cylinder which works round the axis or central pin is divided transversely into two or more portions; but in the rising hinges, instead of the hollow cylinder being divided transversely at right angles, it is divided by spiral or rather helical lines. The result of this contrivance is, that when the door is opened it is lifted up a little from the floor by the sliding upon one another of the inclined helical surfaces; so that, although the door may shut very close to the floor, it rises, when opened, to a sufficient height above the floor to allow its lower edge to clear the carpet. Other forms of hinges are very numerous.

HISPANIO'LA, known also under the names of SAINT DOMINGO and HAITI, is one of the larger islands of the West Indies, and is the most fertile of the whole. At the end of the last century Hispaniola was noted for its extensive plantations of sugar, coffee, and cotton, but they have now almost entirely disappeared, except those of coffee, which are much reduced. The principal commercial wealth of the island is derived from the forests which cover the greatest part of the mountains. The timber consists chiefly of mahogany trees and different kinds of dye-woods. The capital, Port-au-Prince, has considerable commerce with the United States and with Jamaica.

HOBART TOWN. A few details concerning the commerce and industry of Hobart Town will be found under VAN DIEMEN'S LAND.

HOE; HORSE-HOE. The hoe is an instrument used in gardens and fields for loosening the earth, and destroying the weeds between plants. It has various forms. The most common hoe consists of a blade or flat piece of iron, with an eye in which an handle is inserted at an acute angle with the plane of the blade. This hoe is used by striking the edge of it down into the ground, and the earth is moved by drawing the handle towards the workman. Another hoe has the handle at a very obtuse angle, and is used by pushing it forward and cutting off the weeds an inch or less under the surface of the ground. Hoes are made of different sizes and shapes, according to the work which is to be done. When the earth is to be stirred between plants which are very near each other, the hoe is narrow and pointed, so that the smallest weed may be taken out close to the growing plant. When the distance is considerable, the hoe is wide, and sometimes compounded of several hoes, in order to stir a greater width of earth at once.

One of the greatest improvements in practical agriculture has been the introduction of the hoe into the field for every kind of crop, consequent on the sowing of seeds in parallel rows. Hand-hoeing not having been found sufficiently expeditious on a large scale, a hoe has been invented of a larger form, to be drawn by a horse. The rows have in consequence been widened, and this has introduced the horse-hoeing husbandry, which half a century ago was thought so important a discovery as to receive the name of the New Husbandry, from its great improver, Jethro Tull. The simple horse-hoe is an instrument with a beam like a plough, and two stilts or handles, but much lighter; in this beam is inserted, instead of a coulter, the end of an iron hoe, of the proper breadth to stir the whole surface between the rows. A small wheel is generally added to keep the hoe at a proper depth in the soil. Many varieties of horse-hoes have been invented of more or less complicated forms; but the object of them all is the same, viz., to stir the ground between the rows, and destroy the weeds as fast as they appear. The horse-hoe is now chiefly used in the cultivation of peas, beans, potatoes, cabbage, turnips and carrots.

One recent variety of this instrument is the Uxbridge Expanding Horse-hoe, made of wrought iron. There are two small wheels behind, one in front, two handles, and seven hoes. These hoes are arranged in a peculiar manner. The frame to which the hoes are fixed is expansive, that is, its outside bars are moveable farther or nearer apart; and by adjusting these bars, the cutting edges of the hoes are made to present different angles, according as circumstances may require.

HOFWYL. The name of this estate will always have an industrial interest connected with it, on account of the educational institution of Mons. de Fellenberg. It is situated in a valley about three leagues from Berne, in Switzerland, and consists of a number of distinct buildings surrounded by about 250 acres of land. The founder had for his object the improvement of the condition and character of all classes of society by means of an education adapted to their respective wants. To effect this, he divided the institution into classes, of which the higher, the sons of wealthy parents, paid a large yearly sum; the second class, a smaller sum; and the lowest class were received without payment. All were instructed in agriculture, and the trades connected therewith, all of which were practised on the estate. All the classes also were instructed in the usual branches of school education, and the lower class in the sciences connected with agriculture; but these were carried farther in the second class, and the highest class had a still wider range. The upper class was commenced in 1808, the lowest was added in 1810, and the middle class was not introduced till 1830. Fellenberg was enthusiastic, and succeeded in imparting much knowledge to his pupils, of whom he had usually about 100 who paid stipends, and 100 who were boarded, clothed, and educated for their labour. Fellenberg died in 1844, lamented and respected. The school is still carried on, and has about 40 scholars of the first class, and 70 of the second, many scholars of these classes being English; of the third class the number is still continued at 100. It was Fellenberg's wish to have his institution adopted by the state, but this has not been done.

HOG. The commerce and consumption of these animals, and the useful purposes to which they are applied, are noticed under PIGS.

HOGSHEAD. This ancient measure of liquids, not being mentioned in the Act of 1825, cannot now be considered as having any legal existence, although it is familiarly used. The hogshead of wine was 2 wine barrels, or 63 old wine gallons; the London hogshead of ale was 1½ ale barrels, or 48 ale gallons; the London hogshead of beer was 1½ beer barrels, or 54 beer gallons; and the ale and beer hogsheads for the rest of England was 1½ barrels, or 51 gallons. All Excise measurements being now made in gallons, the term hogs-dead remains in use only as the name of a large cask.

HOLLAND. Although we are in the habit of giving this name to a kingdom, it is in strictness the name of one of the provinces of the Netherlands. Under this restricted meaning, Holland may be described as being flat, and in many parts below the level of the sea, against which it is protected by the sandy downs on the west coast, and by stupendous dykes built along the shores of the Zuider-zee, the Haarlem-meer, and the banks of the principal rivers. The country is traversed by canals in all directions. A railroad passing from Rotterdam through the Hague, Leyden, Haarlem, Amsterdam, Utrecht, and thence to Rotterdam, incloses a very important part of the province. Gardens and orchards are carefully cultivated; some barley, oats, peas, beans, mustard, and other seeds are the chief crops in the northern part of the province; in the southern part more corn is produced. But pasturage prevails much more than arable cultivation: the produce of the dairy farms, butter and cheese, constituting the chief wealth of the landholder. The drained districts called *polders* have been before noticed [FLANDERS]; as well as the great drainage of Haarlem Lake. [DRAINING; HAARLEM.] Flowers are cultivated in the tract between Alkmaar and the Hague, but especially about Haarlem. Hemp, flax, and madder are grown. Wood, both for construction and for fuel, is scarce. The manufactures, which are chiefly carried on in the towns, are important; they are linen, paper, woollen cloths (for which Leyden is famous), silk, leather, tobacco, sugar, &c. The gin distilleries of Schiedam are very extensive, and have been long celebrated. Large quantities of fine lime are made from the shells gathered on the coast of the German Ocean. The fisheries on the coasts are important, and most industriously plied.

Besides the two most notable commercial towns [AMSTERDAM; HAARLEM] there are other busy spots. From *Edam* the export trade in sweet milk cheese is important; the chief industrial products are salt and fish oil. *Helder* is notable for the great *Helder-Dyke*, which protects the extremity of north Holland from the fury of the storms to which it is exposed, and is one of the most astonishing monuments of Dutch industry, perseverance, and skill. It is nearly 6 miles in length, 40 feet broad on the summit, along which there is a good road; it presents to the sea a slant side of 200 feet, inclined at an angle of 40°, the whole constructed of granite blocks brought from Norway. *Naarden* forms the key of all the water communication of Holland, and is important for the defence of Amsterdam, with which it is connected by a fine canal. *Zaanden* has a most singular appearance; it seems to consist of a line of windmills, some of which are of gigantic size, and have houses attached to them, extending along the Zaan, and forming a street nearly 5 miles in length. The number of these mills is variously stated, but it seems to amount to about 700; they are applied to the various purposes of grinding corn, draining the land, sawing timber, making paper, grinding tobacco into snuff, crushing rapeseed to express the oil, grinding colours for painters, grinding stones into sand for the floors of the Dutch housewife, and grinding the volcanic substance called trass into dust in order to form a cement, which hardens under water and is much used in Holland. *Gonda* has tobacco pipe factories that give employment to 6000 men, brickworks (the clay for the supply of which is taken from the bed of the Yssel), rope walks, gin distilleries, and breweries. Gonda numbers also among its industrial products woollen cloth and sailcloth; it is famous as a cheese market. *Schiedam* has glass works, rope walks, white lead works, above 200 distilleries for the manufacture of gin, for which it is universally celebrated. It has a large trade in pigs, 30,000 of which are said to be annually fattened on the grains from the distilleries.

A few of the towns of Holland will be represented at the Great Exhibition.

HOLLY. The common holly or *Ilex aquifolium* is chiefly valued as an ornamental tree, but its fine-grained, heavy, compact timber is used for a great number of useful purposes, especially by the turner and mathematical instrument maker. The berries are poisonous.

HOLYHEAD. [MENAI BRIDGES.]

HONDURAS. British Honduras, in central America, owed its origin to Mahogany cutters. Mahogany trees of great size and beauty grow in this colony; and the first establishment of the English in this quarter was made by mahogany cutters from Jamaica, in the 17th century. Logwood is also largely grown and cut; and the English cutters of these woods had many contests with the Spaniards, before they were permitted to settle finally in their new colony.

Most of the mahogany and logwood trade of Honduras is conducted by five or six firms, established at Belize. The cutters are employed by these firms; and these firms also ship the wood to other countries. The colony took British produce and manufactures in the year 1849, to the amount of about 200,000*l.*

The exports from Honduras are larger than the imports; they consist of mahogany, logwood, rosewood, hides, tortoiseshell, fustic, cochineal, indigo, sarsaparilla, and cocoa-nuts. In 1848 no less than eight million cubic feet of mahogany were exported.

HONEY is a fluid or semi-fluid substance, the materials of which are collected by different kinds of bees, in Europe chiefly by the hive-bee, and solely by the neuter or working bees, from the nectariferous glands in the cup or chalice of flowers. It cannot be said to be a purely vegetable production, for, after being collected by the proboscis of the insect, it is transmitted to that distension of the œsophagus termed the crop, sucking stomach, or honey bag, where it is elaborated, and again disgorged, to be deposited in the cell of the honey-comb. It undergoes less change when the bees are very young, remaining nearly white, and is then denominated virgin honey. At all times it retains qualities derived from the kind of plant whence it has been procured; as is manifest not only by the peculiar odour of the honey, but by the effects which follow the use of honey obtained from certain plants.

Honey is sweet, faintly aromatic, granular, soluble in water, and capable of undergoing the vinous fermentation.

The finest honey in Europe is said to be that of Narbonne, which is supposed to derive its excellence from the rosemary which grows in the neighbourhood. When honey is taken from the honey-comb it is fluid, but gradually thickens by age; and in cold weather a firm and solid mass of honey forms.

Honey is used as a substitute, sometimes for sugar and sometimes for butter. Honey is an ingredient in the useful medicine *Oxymel of Squills. Mel boracis* is borate of soda mixed with honey; *mel rosæ* is made of honey and red rose petals; *oxymel simplex* consists of clarified honey boiled in dilute acetic acid. When fermented, honey water obtains the name of *mead*, and is in fact honey wine, which is the name given to it in Germany (*honigwein*). Mead was formerly drunk to a considerable extent in England, and in most parts of northern Europe. Real mead or Metheglin is a fermented wine; but many drinks made from honey are little else than honey water or *hydromel*. Such is the *sbitene* of Russia, which consists of honey mixed with boiling water and boiling milk, and seasoned with pepper.

HONITON LACE. [LACE MANUFACTURE.]

HOPS. This useful plant, the *Humulus lupulus* of Linnæus, is extensively cultivated for the flowers or seed-vessels, which give flavour and permanence to beer by being boiled with the wort in brewing. Hops were introduced into England from Flanders about the year 1524. The most extensive plantations are in Kent, Sussex, and Herefordshire; but they are also cultivated in Worcestershire, Wiltshire, Hampshire, Glo-cestershire, Surrey, and several other counties.

The hop is a slender climbing plant, which requires a very rich mellow soil and careful cultivation. The soil of a hop garden must be rich to a considerable depth, or made so artificially. The young plants are raised in beds, and may be raised from seed; but it is more usual to plant the young shoots which rise from the bottom of the stems of old plants. The varieties most esteemed are the Grape Hop, the White Vine, and the Golden Hop. The young plants are placed in groups of three each, about six inches asunder, in the midst of prepared masses of soil about a yard asunder. A watering with liquid manure greatly assists their taking root, and they soon begin to show bines. A stick three or four feet long is then stuck in the middle of the three plants, and the bines are tied to this stick with twine or the shreds of Russia mats, till they lay hold and twine round it. During their growth the ground is well hoed and forked up around the roots, and some of the fine mould is thrown around the stems. In favourable seasons a few hops may be picked from these young plants in the autumn, but in general there is nothing the first year. Early in November the ground is carefully dug with the spade, and the earth, being turned towards the plants, is left so all the winter.

In the second year, early in spring, the hillocks around the plants are opened and the roots examined. The last year's shoots are cut off within an inch of the main stem, and all the suckers quite close to it. A pole about twelve feet long is then firmly stuck into the ground near the plants; to this the bines are led and tied as they shoot, till they have taken hold of it. The ground being well hoed and the earth raised round the plants, the produce this year will average 4 cwt. per acre if the season is favourable. In September the flower containing the seed will be of a fine straw colour, turning to a brown; it is then in perfection. No time should now be lost in picking them. The hops when picked are dried on a hair cloth in a kiln. They are then laid in heaps on the floor, where they undergo a very slight heating. As soon as this is observed, they are bagged. This is done by pressing them into large bags suspended below a hole in the floor; when sewed close and tight, the bag is stored in a dry place till the hops are wanted for sale. The crop of the third year will average 8 cwt. per acre, but will in some cases reach 15.

The occupation of hop-picking is a remarkable one. There is not available labour enough in Kent and the other hop districts to pick all the hops in the requisite time; and hundreds of poor persons arrive from other parts of the country, to sojourn for a few days or weeks in the hop districts, during which time they are employed in picking the hops.

The poles are an expensive article; those of chestnut are the most durable, and also the dearest. They should be put into a shed during winter; or else be placed on end in the form of a cone, leaning against each other.

Besides the use of hops in brewing, they produce a bitter infusion and a tincture which are valuable in medicine for complaints in the stomach.

The number of acres of Hops in England in 1849 was 42,798; the weight of hops charged with duty was 16,650,915 lbs., the duty on which was 145,693*l.* In that year 274,811 lbs. of hops were exported. The excise duty on British hops is 18*s.* 8*d.* per cwt., and 5 per cent. additional; the customs duty on imported foreign hops is 45*s.* per cwt. The produce in 1848 and in 1850 was very much larger than in 1849; in the former year the duty was 394,923*l.*, and in the latter 426,194*l.*

HORN. This musical wind-instrument is of very ancient origin, and of various forms. The *French horn* is a tube of about ten feet, very narrow at top, widening considerably at the bottom, and bent in rings for the convenience of the performer. It is not provided with holes, as the flute, &c.; the production of the various sounds depending upon the lips of the player, the more or less pressure of his breath, and the insertion of the hand in the bell, or wide end, of the instrument. Crooks and shifting pieces are provided to adjust the instrument to different keys or fundamental notes. The *Bugle Horn* is a tube of three feet ten inches in length, doubled up in a small compass. The *Keyed Bugle*, or a Bugle horn with keys, is that now in common use, the scale of which comprehends about two octaves, with the semitones. The *Cornopean* and the *Cornet-à-Pistons* are improved modern forms of this instrument. The *Russian Horn* is an unbent brass tube, conical in shape, of various dimensions: the deepest toned is eight feet long, and nine inches in diameter at the wide end, and the highest is two inches and a half in length by one at the wide end. The former gives A, an octave below the first space in the base; the latter gives E, the third additional line above the treble. Some of these horns have keys, producing one or two semitones, but generally every note has its separate horn; and a band of Russian Horns counts almost as many individuals as diatonic notes in a scale of between four and five octaves. The *English Horn*, or *Corno Inglese*, is a deep-toned oboe, of large dimensions, somewhat bent, the lower end very open, and is to the oboe what the basset horn is to the clarinet, or what the viola is to the violin. The tone of this instrument is extremely pathetic, and by the Italians is thought so much to resemble the human voice, that they sometimes call it the *voce umána*.

HORN MANUFACTURE. The horns of the ox, antelope, goat, and sheep may be described as a number of conical sheaths inserted into one another, the innermost of which lies upon the vascular membrane which covers the bony core. The tip, or that portion of the point of the horn which projects beyond the core, is very dense, and the several layers of which it is composed are scarcely distinguishable; while towards the base the layers may be readily distinguished, owing to their successive terminations forming prominent rings. There are many points of resemblance between the substance of horns, nails, claws, hoofs, scales, hair, feathers, and even skin.

The principal kinds of horn employed in manufacturing operations are those of oxen. The first process is to remove the bony core or pith, which is accomplished by steeping the horns in water for several weeks, by which operation the membrane which lies between the core and the horny sheath is so destroyed or softened by putrefaction that the cores may be easily extracted. These are applied to many useful purposes. The solid tip of the horn is sawn off with a frame-saw, and is employed for making knife-handles, umbrella-handles, the tops of whips, buttons, and various other articles. The remainder of the horn, which is employed for purposes for which thin laminæ are required, may either be left entire or sawn into two or more lengths, according to the use to which it is to be applied. When divided, the lower part, or that next the root of the horn, is frequently employed for making combs; while the portion which has formed the middle of the horn is used for lanterns and for other articles where a thin plate of horn is required. To prepare the horn for use it is softened in boiling water; and, while hot from this operation, it is held in the flame of a fire until it acquires about the temperature of melting lead, and becomes so soft as to be semi-fluid. The slitting is performed while it is in the semi-fluid state, by a strong pointed knife resembling a pruning-knife; and, by the application of two pairs of pincers, one to each edge of the slit, the cylinder or cone of horn is opened until it is nearly flat. Several such pieces are then exposed to pressure between alternate plates of iron until they are flattened. The thin sheets of iron are then scraped, rubbed, and polished.

The various articles made of horn require manufacturing processes differing in different cases. The making of combs is noticed elsewhere. [COMB-CUTTING.] Umbrella handles, snuff-boxes, knife-handles, bell-pulls, drawer-knobs, &c., are made by softening the horn to such a degree that it may be pressed into moulds. Horn is easily dyed of various colours; but in this country it is usually coloured of a rich reddish brown, and spotted to imitate tortoiseshell, by a mixture of pearl-ash, quick-lime and litharge, or red lead, with water and a little pounded dragon's blood.

No part of the refuse of the horn manufacture is without its value. When exposed to a decomposing heat in close vessels, horn produces a large quantity of the gaseous compound which forms the base of prussic acid, on which account hoofs and horn cuttings are in great request among the manufacturers of Prussian blue, and of the beautiful yellow prussiate of potash. The clippings of the comb-maker and of the lantern maker are also used as manure.

HORSE SHOES. This invaluable animal, the horse, subserves many useful purposes to man, after his career as a beast of burden is at an end. The hair of the tail and mane is much employed for weaving into a tough cloth, and for other purposes. [HAIR MANUFACTURE.] The hide is tanned into a valuable kind of leather; the hoof is useful as a horny material; and various parts of the dead animal are employed as materials in different manufactures.

Horse Shoes are implements on which much attention have been bestowed. Nature has given to the foot of the horse a certain degree of expansive or spreading power, which lessens the shock received by placing the foot suddenly to the ground; but the material of the hoof is such that friction will gradually wear it away; and the difficulty arises, how to protect the hoof from wear without destroying or rendering nugatory the elasticity of the hoof. Various contrivances are employed in rude countries to shield the hoof; a covering of strong ox-leather, a wrapper of woven strips of tough fibres, a wisp of straw fastened with a cord—all are used in various countries.

The ordinary English horse shoe is (or ought to be) made of the best iron; and small pieces of steel are occasionally attached to a part which is more than usually worn. The width and thickness vary according to the strength and age of the horse, the purpose for which he is employed, and the particular opinions of the person who has the direction of shoeing the horse. The horse shoe is formed from a bar of iron about an inch and a quarter wide and three quarters of an inch in thickness; and is forged into its proper form by two men. The shoe is fastened on by eight or nine nails, to receive which holes are made in the iron. A sunken groove is also forged, to admit the heads of the nails: this groove is forged by the hammer. It has been proposed to give the necessary grooved surface by drawing the bar of iron between two rollers whose surfaces have pins and ridges inserted, by which the groove and the nail holes are made; it has also been proposed to cast the horse shoes in plaster moulds, and afterwards anneal them. The shoes are fastened to the foot by driving nails into the hoof, but as this has a tendency to break away the substance of the hoof, modes have been devised for fastening with sandals and straps; none of these contrivances, however, have been permanently successful. For heavy draught horses two points or projections stand out from the back of the shoe and are turned downwards; these assist the animal in obtaining a sure footing. Horse shoes vary from twelve ounces to seven pounds weight, according to the service required of them.

Within the cavity of a horse's hoof is a wedge-shaped substance called the *frog*. Farriers used to shoe horses in such a way as to shield this from the ground; but it is now believed that Nature intended this substance to assist the movements of the animal, by its elasticity.

The subject of the proper shoeing of the horse, in relation to the anatomy of the foot, has been treated with much clearness by Mr. Clarendon of Dublin, in his 'Treatise on the Foot of the Horse;' this forms a sequel to another work on the 'Powers of the Horse;' and both are intended to show the means by which the structure of the horse may point out the best modes of practically applying the muscular power. The result of modern enquiries has been to show that the horse shoe ought not to be rigid; that it ought to allow the frog of the foot to come into action. Mr. Bracy Clark has invented a shoe with a joint at the toe; the design being that it should open at each step, with that joint as a centre. Mr. Rogers' horse shoe has a slit near the front, which gives a yielding elasticity something like that of a steel pen. Another horse shoe has been invented with two joints, one on either side. Mr. Turner has devised a mode of nailing the shoe on one side only, so as to leave an expansive action to the foot. Mr. Clarendon has patented a shoe, in which elasticity is afforded by a singular contrivance; the shoe does not differ much from others in shape, and is nailed near the point in the usual way; but all the other nail holes are made large enough to admit of a spreading action of the foot. Specimens of this horse shoe will be sent to the Exhibition.

HOSIERY MANUFACTURE. The principal seat of this manufacture in England is in the three counties of Leicester, Nottingham, and Derby. In the first of these, worsted hosiery forms the principal branch of the manufacture, while in Nottinghamshire the material chiefly used is cotton, and in Derbyshire silk goods are mostly made.

The stocking-frame, by means of which this manufacture is carried on, is, next to the common warp and weft loom, the oldest machine in existence applicable to textile fabrics. It was invented about the close of the 16th century by the Rev. William Lea, of St. John's College, Cambridge, but a considerable time elapsed before the produce of this frame took the place of the trunk hose then worn by all who could afford such an article of dress. For this reason Mr. Lea settled at Rouen, in Normandy, where his manufacture was carried on under the patronage of Henri IV.; but the assassination of the king and the political troubles brought on by that event caused the abandonment of Mr. Lea's establishment, and that gentleman shortly after died in a state of poverty at Paris. From the time of its first invention the stocking-frame has not received any considerable improvement in respect to its principle; but the details have been improved by a long series of patented inventions.

The principal seat of the cotton hosiery manufacture abroad is at Chemnitz, in Saxony, where, owing to the low rate of wages, goods are made, with yarns imported from Lancashire, at prices which have excluded English goods from many foreign markets.

The hosiery or frame-work manufacture is a peculiar kind of interlacing. Instead of being a series of cross threads woven in a loom, it is a series of loops or links, so connected as to possess both strength and elasticity in a remarkable degree. It is a continuous thread which is thus linked around itself; in a way which bears a good deal of resemblance to many kinds of ladies' netting and crochet work. The article made in the stocking frame is not a stocking, but a piece of knitwork cloth, which is afterwards sown up into the form of a stocking by needle and thread. Hence, there are three kinds of operatives engaged; the *winders*, who put the thread into or on the machine; the *frame-work knitters*, who work the thread up into a knitted fabric; and the *seamers*, who make the stockings out of the pieces thus produced. The winders are generally children, who can each wind thread enough for half a dozen machines; the knitters are men, women, and youths, who hire both the winders and the seamers; and the seamers are women. Some of the stocking-frames are owned by the frame-work knitters; some are let out to the men by the owners, at so much per week for each frame; while other persons are the renters of what is termed a 'shop of frames,' containing eight or ten frames; these, with standing-room to work in, they let to the workmen, at so much per frame per week. The master manufacturer gives out his thread, and the workman returns this thread in the form of stockings, the work being paid for at so much per dozen pair.

We have spoken only of hosiery, but many other articles besides stockings are made of this linked fabric. Gloves, waistcoat-pieces, mitts, pantaloons, drawers, braces, webs, comforters, caps, jackets, leggings, and various other articles—are made nearly in the same way, and of the same material. The processes for worsted, cotton, and silk are nearly analogous; those for silk requiring, however, the greatest care. Some progress has been made towards the manufacture of hosiery by means of steam-power; but the extreme lowness of wages in this department of labour has hitherto kept it nearly in the position of hand-loom work.

It is pleasing to find that Ireland is gradually advancing in this as in many other branches of manufacture. At Balbriggan there is a hosiery manufacture, from which specimens of cotton hosiery are to be sent to the Great Exhibition, of a degree of fineness such as has never perhaps been equalled; one dozen pairs of ladies' full sized stockings will weigh only nine ounces. Cotton stockings of a peculiar kind of open work are also manufactured in the same town.

The exports of stockings in 1850 amounted to the following quantities:—

Cotton	234,163	dozen pairs.
Silk..........	4,482	,, ,,
Worsted......	119,873	,, ,,

HOT-BED; HOT-HOUSE. A hot-bed is a heap of fresh stable litter in a state of fermentation, upon which a glazed box is placed for the cultivation of certain plants requiring heat and moisture in greater quantity than those agents exist in the external air. For the growth of cucumbers and melons, raising seeds of tender annuals, and of other plants, either culinary or ornamental, hot-beds are advantageously employed. They may be formed of various substances, such as rotting dung, tan, leaves, or a mixture of these with moist litter; in short, any substance capable of producing and retaining fermentation, and which will admit of being built up so as to support a frame with sashes.

A *hot-house* is a structure in which exotic plants are cultivated under circumstances approximating as closely as possible to those under which they naturally exist; or it is used for accelerating the production of flowers and fruits of either indigenous or exotic plants. Hot-houses appropriated to the latter purposes are very frequently termed *forcing-houses*.

The principles by which the construction of hot houses must be governed have reference to the three great agents in vegetation—*heat*, *moisture* and *light*. There must be means for varying all these to a wide extent. With regard to the means of supplying artificial heat, the old system of using brick flues is now rapidly being superseded by that of hot water. The glass for admitting light to hot-houses is found to be better fitted for its object if it has a slight green tint.

Hot-houses may be classed under four different heads, namely, the *dry stove*, the *damp stove*, the *bark stove*, and the *forcing house*. The *Dry Stove*, as the name implies, is used for the cultivation of plants which do not require much water: such as the different species of Cacti, some Euphorbias, and other succulents of like habits. The temperature of such a house during the winter months should never exceed 55° of Fahr. The *Damp Stove* requires treatment of an opposite description. Instead of being kept dry like the last, its atmosphere should be always excessively humid, except in the winter season; the temperature is made to vary from 55° to 70° according to the season. The beautiful *Palm House* at Kew may be regarded as a damp stove. The *Bark Stove*, when it is of large dimensions, consists of a pit in the middle of the house, surrounded by a brick wall, leaving as much room round the sides as will form a passage to walk in. The pit is filled with bark, and, after being allowed to sink a little and ferment, the pots containing the plants are plunged more or less deep as prudence may suggest. The *Forcing House* is a contrivance of frames and pits, heated with dung, to accelerate the growth and maturation of flowers, fruits, and vegetables.

There are also *hot walls*, or walls with flues in them, constructed in cold countries, in order to afford warmth to trees placed against them. One furnace is allowed for heating about 40 feet of wall, that is, 20 feet on each side of the place where the fire is situated. The flues on either side are made to take four courses, or two returns; the first course being a little above the surface of the ground, and the upper 1½ or 2 feet below the coping. Instead of flues, hot water pipes might be introduced into the cavity of a common hollow wall, a little above the level of the border.

HOUSE. The houses of this country have undergone many changes of form and construction. Three centuries ago they were constructed in a very different manner from the houses of the present century. The chief materials were wood and plaster, and a common but peculiar feature was the projecting upper floors. The internal arrangement was adapted to the wants of that day, and the external architecture had often a picturesque appearance. After the great fire of London the advantage of building in cities with brick or stone became so apparent, as well as the adoption of some regularity, that a great change took place in house-building in the metropolis, which extended by degrees to the houses which were from time to time rebuilt throughout the country. In this gradual change have almost entirely disappeared the projecting floors with large bow windows, the wooden galleries round the quadrangular courts, the boldly projecting dripping eaves, and the high-pitched roofs with their large windows. In London and other large towns, the basement story is for the most part built below the level of the ground, the earth being excavated for that purpose; this floor usually contains the kitchen and the rooms for the use of the domestics. English houses are in general well provided with means for carrying off water and all impurities which require to be removed from the premises; that is, the better houses in the large towns are so provided; but many improvements must be yet introduced before the same can be said of the mass of dwellings. The houses of the poorer classes are too often negligently constructed. In their construction, economy, convenience, and a wholesome ventilation, should be mainly kept in view, and these may be united with as much picturesque beauty as the nature of the materials will admit of without increasing the expense.

The English and Scotch cottages differ in their external appearance and arrangement. The best English cottages of recent construction are built of brick and covered with slate.

The use of these materials has changed the character of this class of dwellings. In many cottages the chimney-stack forms the principal bearing of the floors and roof. The Scotch cottage has not only a different appearance when compared with the English, but, from its being so much wider, it admits of two apartments being formed on the ground floor; this is also a matter of necessity, as they are seldom raised more than one story. The material for the walls is most commonly stone; the roof is large and heavy in appearance, and has but a small projection beyond the walls; the gable walls also run up frequently above the roof, forming a parapet, which is sometimes notched so as to resemble steps, or has a battlement appearance. As the French and Italians of the middle classes do not generally live in separate houses like the English, but on floors containing a series of rooms, it follows that the arrangement of their houses differs from that of the English. The staircase, as in public chambers, is common to each floor. The rooms communicate with each other, and generally with a passage or balcony on one side; chimneys are rare, stoves being most commonly used to heat the rooms. French and Italian houses are mostly built of rough stone and stuccoed; the floors are seldom boarded, being paved with glazed tiles or unglazed bricks. The Spanish houses are very spacious; they have large courts in the interior, and are formed with galleries round the inside of the quadrangular courts: families occupy the separate floors. The houses in many parts of Germany approach nearer to the English in their arrangement than the French and Italian houses. In many places the houses are a framework of wood, and the interstices are filled with unbaked bricks, and are plastered with clay. The city architecture of Russian houses, both in its effect and arrangement, resembles the architecture of Italian and French houses, except that the roofs are covered with sheet-iron painted with vivid colours, mostly green and red. The windows are double.

Many details connected with the building of houses will be found scattered under various headings in this work. With regard to the present state of things in this country, one of the most interesting social features is the attention now being made to the construction of healthy dwellings (at a moderate rent) for the working classes.

HOWITZER, is a short but broad-mouthed cannon. It is employed to project solid and hollow shot, loaded shells, carcasses, and case shot, either in the point-blank direction or at angles of elevation, which hitherto have not exceeded fifteen degrees. It is used against troops in the field, in the attack of redoubts or villages, and both in the attack and defence of regular fortresses.' About the year 1820, Colonel Paixhans, in France, constructed what were denominated canons obusiers, for the purpose of projecting solid or hollow shot of great diameter: and in 1824 and 1836 the late General Millar, in this country, executed for the like purpose iron shell-guns, or naval howitzers as they are called, whose calibres are 10 inches and 8 inches respectively. Besides these, 24-pounder and 12-pounder howitzers are employed in the British service.

HUDDERSFIELD, is one of the most notable of the West Riding towns. The manufactures of Huddersfield and the adjacent villages are principally woollens and waistcoatings; indeed fancy productions in which wool is mixed with silk or cotton now form a very large department of the industry of the town. The cotton manufactures are also carried on, though not to a very great extent. In 1765 a commodious cloth-hall was erected for the buyers and sellers of the Huddersfield manufactures by Sir John Ramsden. The trade derives great advantages from its inland navigation, by means of the Ramsden and Huddersfield canals, both eastward and westward, and by the railways which now connect it with the neighbouring towns.

At the Industrial Exhibition, Huddersfield will display specimens of all the leading products of the town.

HUDSON'S BAY COMPANY. This remarkable trading company obtains its name from the great inland sea which lies westward of Labrador in North America. The countries which inclose Hudson's Bay on all sides constitute by far the greatest portion of the British dominions in North America. The area cannot be given, as considerable tracts of the coast are still unknown, but it probably does not fall much short of 3,000,000 square miles. This immense country may be divided into four natural regions. The most eastern is the *Sterile Region*, which lies along the shores of the sea, and extends far inland. The second or *Wooded Region*, extends on both shores of James's Bay, and along the southern shores of Hudson's Bay, as far westward as Cape Churchill. It is generally well wooded, and produces fur-bearing animals. Beyond this is the *Savannah Region*, which extends to the foot of the Rocky Mountains, and northward to the Lake of Athabasca and the Peace River: its surface stretches out in extensive plains, intersected only by the beds of several rivers, which are considerably below the plains. The fourth region, the *Mackenzie Valley*, comprehends the country between the Sterile Region and the Rocky Mountains, north of Lake Athabasca.

The present wealth of the country consists in its animals, especially rein-deer, musk-ox, moose-deer or elk, other kinds of deer, bears, wolves, wolverines, foxes, beavers, otters, racoons, and several smaller animals. Iron, copper, and lead are known to exist, though not yet worked to any extent; and coal has been found at various places, Vancouver's Island being one. The settlements of the Hudson's Bay Company are divided into two districts; the southern comprehends the settlements on the west coast of Labrador, together with the more numerous establishments in the countries inclosing James's Bay, and as far as the banks of the Albany River. The principal depôt is at Moose Fort, near the mouth of Moose River. The northern district comprehends all the others as far north as Fort Good Hope on the Mackenzie River, north of the Polar Circle. Its chief settlement is York, on the Hayes River.

The circumstances which led to the establishment of a trading company in these regions have been noticed under FURS; FUR TRADE. Vancouver Island, on the coast of the North Pacific Ocean, was granted by the British government to the Hudson's Bay Company in August 1848.

HULL. This seaport is the greatest shipping emporium on the east coast next to London. The exports formerly were chiefly wool, woolfells, and leather; its imports, wine and timber. At present the coasting trade is one of its chief branches of profit. It has also an extensive commerce with the Baltic, with the north of Germany, Holland, and Denmark. The Greenland fishery owed its revival, about 1766, and its subsequent importance, to the mercantile enterprise of Hull. The facilities of communication between Hull and the interior of the kingdom are numerous; the Ouse, Trent, Aire, and Calder, all communicate with the Humber, and these means of internal communication are extended by the York, Newcastle and Berwick Railway, the York and North Midland Railway, and the Hull, Selby and Leeds Railway. The prosperity of Hull has been greatly increased by the progress of steam-navigation, and it may be considered as the second great centre of this mode of transit on the eastern coast.

There are large docks and extensive quays. The number of sailing vessels registered at Hull in 1848, was 462 (64,951 tons). The number of steam-vessels was 28 (5658 tons).

The manufactures of Hull are varied. The expressing and refining of oil from linseed is effected by wind-mills and steam-mills; the residue of the seed is prepared as food for cattle. There is a large sugar-house, a soap manufactory, several white-lead works, shipbuilders' yards, turpentine and sail-cloth manufactories, extensive ropewalks, and several breweries. There are also two large joint-stock cotton mills.

Hull is the great port of the Humber, and the outlet for the vast produce of the district watered by that river and its tributaries. Hull is especially the port at which Baltic timber, Russia hemp, and Belgium flax are imported; and at which the Lancashire and Yorkshire manufactures are exported to the continent of Europe.

At the ensuing Exhibition, the Hull manufactures, of oil, oil-cake, tar, turpentine, &c., will be illustrated. There will also be every variety of English and foreign wood in the form of books, showing the grain, quality, and perhaps the bark, with the name of each engraved or sculptured on the back: and a complete series of the imports of the port, which will be arranged by the local committee, and will give a statistical account of the quantity of each imported during a series of years.

HUMIDITY is that property of a substance by which it communicates to a body in contact with it some of a liquid which it may have absorbed. The humidity of the atmosphere is caused in a great measure by the evaporation of water from the seas, lakes, &c., of the earth; and the quantity of moisture which a volume of air is capable of containing depends upon the temperature. Dr. Dalton found by experiment that a body of earth one foot in depth, when saturated with moisture, contains seven inches in depth of water, and that it may lose one-fourth or one-half of that quantity without becoming incapable of supporting vegetation. The effects of humidity on the dimensions of bodies are various: when a watery vapour penetrates between the twisted fibres of cordage which are vegetable materials, the cordage swells out transversely, and thus becomes shortened; while cords made of animal substances become relaxed by humidity and increase in length. Most salts absorb water, and thereby increase in weight.

HUNGARY. The produce and manufactures of this interesting country are briefly glanced at in connection with the Empire of which it forms a part [AUSTRIA].

HUNTINGDONSHIRE. Only a small portion of the county is unproductive. Peat is found in many parts. The farms are mostly of considerable extent. The expense of cultivation on the fen-land, when it is once drained, is small in proportion to the produce. Paring and burning the surface is the general practice. Rape seed is sown, which is fed off with sheep the first year, and left to ripen its seeds the next. The straw of the rape is burned on the land, after the seed has been thrashed out; and this is all the manure required to produce a good crop of wheat. Oats, barley, and beans are also grown. Mustard-seed is grown to some extent, and in good soils gives a good return. On the borders of the Ouse and Nene are some very rich meadows. A great part of the county is still in pasture, although much has been broken up and converted into arable land. In the marshy parts willows grow rapidly, and are profitable, although not ornamental. Although Stiltón is in this county, and it is asserted that the cheese which bears that name was originally made there, none of that kind is now produced in any of the dairies; all such cheeses are made in Leicestershire and Lincolnshire.

Huntingdon, the chief town, has a considerable trade in wool and corn. At St. Ives, brewing and malting are carried on, but there are no manufactures. There are a few other towns, but none of manufacturing importance.

HUSBANDRY. The land in England consisted originally for the most part of woods, and of extensive pastures, in which sheep and cattle were bred, which constituted the chief wealth. A very small proportion of the soil was cultivated; and, while the population was thin, there was no difficulty in obtaining land which had never before been broken up, and which with little trouble or manuring produced moderate crops of corn. When the husbandmen began to congregate in villages for mutual defence, the best land nearest to the habitations was cultivated, and the common pastures fed the cattle without much trouble or expense. Manure was seldom made; four times the seed was an average corn crop; and fields were fallowed every second year. Wheat was little cultivated; barley, rye, and oats were the principal produce. Many hogs were fed on acorns and beech-mast in the woods. Bread made of rye, barley, peas, or beans, was the food of the labourers who were attached to the soil. The immediate tenants of the lord cultivated a portion of the lands which they held for their own use, and let the remainder to smaller tenants, who, although born free, were little above the condition of the labourers, and lived much in the same manner. The live stock was frequently hired from the landlord. Oxen drew the ploughs; horses carried the produce to mill and market; and the implements were of the rudest kind.

From these beginnings various systems of husbandry have brought the land of this country into the state briefly noticed under the names of the counties and the chief crops.

HYDRACIDS are such acids as contain hydrogen instead of oxygen as the acidifying power: hydrobromic and hydrochloric acids are examples. Their acidity is in general very strongly marked. All the hydracids are gaseous, and are easily combined with water, forming solutions which possess the well-known and strongly marked properties of sourness, acting upon carbonate, and reddening vegetable blue colours. They are all artificial products. They have not hitherto been of much value in the arts.

HYDRATES, are compounds which contain water in definite proportion, but which do not assume the crystalline form. Thus, when water is added to potash, it may form with it either water of solution, water of crystallisation, or water which constitutes it an hydrate; and it is observable that, while water of solution has comparatively little affinity for the substance with which it is combined, water of crystallisation has more, and water with which the body constitutes an hydrate has the greatest affinity of all.

HYDRAULIC MACHINES. The art of constructing docks, quays, or any buildings whose foundations are laid under water, is denominated *hydraulic architecture;* and all machines in which water is employed as a moving power, or by which water is put in motion, may be termed *hydraulic machines.* No countries in Europe possess more advantages with respect to naval power than Great Britain and Ireland. The islands and headlands on their coasts form excellent natural ports; and these, where necessary, have been converted into secure harbours by every means which the science of the hydraulic engineer could devise. The Breakwater at Plymouth, the lighthouses which have been raised in the ocean, and the vast docks at the principal sea-port towns, are so many practical examples which render the British Isles a complete school for the study, in detail, of every subject connected with this branch of art.

Hydraulic architecture chiefly now involves the construction of masses of masonry whose foundations are laid in the beds of rivers or æstuaries, or in that of the sea, such as the piers of bridges, quays, jetties, and breakwaters; also the formation of artificial harbours and docks for shipping, and locks at the falls on rivers or canals. In the articles BREAKWATER, BRIDGE, CANAL, DOCK, HARBOUR, &c., these matters have been briefly touched upon.

Hydraulic machinery has been brought to its present efficient state by many successive improvements. It may be remarked however that, on account of the high degree of perfection which, within a few years past, the steam engine has attained, the employment of hydraulic machines for raising great quantities of water, or as first movers with respect to extensive works of any kind, has of late considerably diminished. Yet, where the circumstances are favourable, as when a supply of water for working the machine can be readily obtained; the latter, from being less expensive in their construction, are still preferred to the former.

The principal hydraulic machines which are in use for domestic or general purposes are the *Siphon*, the *Screw of Archimedes*, the various kinds of *Pumps*, the *Hydraulic Press*, and *Wheels* turned by water. For the first two see SIPHON and SCREW PROPELLER. The others will be now briefly described.

The common pump is a machine for raising water by the pressure of the atmosphere. It consists of a cylindrical body, or barrel, from the lower part of which a tube descends into the water contained in the well or reservoir. In the interior of the cylinder is a moveable piston, surrounded with leather, in order that it may be water-tight, yet capable of moving up and down with freedom. The piston is perforated, and the orifice is covered above by a valve which opens upwards: a similar valve at the bottom of the cylinder or barrel covers the upper extremity of the tube which leads to the well. The piston being raised by means of the handle, the air contained in the tube tends by its elasticity to occupy the lower part of the cylinder, which it enters by forcing up the last-mentioned valve; and its elasticity diminishes in consequence of its occupying a greater space than before. Hence the air exerts on the surface of the water within the tube a less pressure than that which the external air exerts upon the water in the well; and the water consequently rises in the tube to a certain height. The valve then falls over the orifice, and, the piston being depressed, the air contained between it and the bottom of the cylinder will be condensed; in which state it will force up the piston valve, and escape at the top of the pump. The valve then falls; and, if the piston be again elevated, the water will rise higher in the tube, for the same reason as before. The operation of raising and depressing the piston being repeated a few times, the water will at length enter into the cylinder through the valves; after which it will, at each stroke of the piston, be forced through the spout.

The *lifting pump* is frequently similar in construction to the common pump above described; but the lower valve is always below the surface of the water in the reservoir, and the piston is so when depressed to the bottom of the cylinder or barrel. On raising the piston, the water above it is lifted up, and the pressure of the external atmosphere forces the water of the reservoir to enter into the cylinder. Then, by successive depressions and elevations of the piston, the water is at length raised to the top of the pump, and discharged by the spout.

The *forcing pump* is one in which the water, when raised in the barrel, is driven through an orifice in its side by the depression of the piston, which is solid, or without a perforation; it is also, in general, provided with an air-vessel, into which the water is forced, and whence, by the elasticity of the condensed air, it is made to issue through a pipe inserted in the upper extremity.

In the *chain pump* a chain, carrying a number of flat circular pistons, passes round a wheel at the upper, and sometimes also at the lower extremity; each piston, as it goes over the wheels, being in part received in the intervals between the radii. The wheel being put in motion, the pistons descend in a barrel on one side, and enter from below into another on the ascending side, when pushing the water before them, they raise it into the reservoir, from whence it escapes by a pipe. Pumps of this kind are frequently fixed in inclined positions; and it is when the inclination of the barrel is about 24 degrees, the distance of the pistons from one another being equal to their diameter, that the greatest quantity of water is raised.

The *Hydraulic Press* was invented by Mr. Bramah, and is a machine of very great power in compressing bodies or lifting weights; or, again, in drawing up trees by the roots, or piles from the beds of rivers. There is an iron cylinder in which a piston works. At the bottom of the former is inserted a tube, whose aperture, under the piston, is covered by a valve. The other end of the tube communicates with a small forcing pump, by which water is driven through the said valve into the lower part of the cylinder, where its hydrostatical action is exerted to raise up the piston. Now suppose the diameter of the cylinder to be 10 inches, and that of the piston in the forcing pump to be one quarter of an inch, then the proportion between the surfaces of the pistons will be that of 1600 to 1; and, on the principle of the equal pressure of fluids in every direction, the force with which the larger piston is raised bears the same proportion to the resistance against the lower surface of that in the forcing pump.

The largest and finest hydraulic presses ever constructed, were those made by Messrs. Easton and Amos, and employed in raising the ponderous tubes of the Britannia Bridge. The ram or larger piston is 22 inches in diameter; the cylinder in which it worked is 9 feet long by six inches thickness of metal; and one of the castings for making the largest press required 21 tons of melted iron.

In *water wheels*, water is made to act as a moving power against wheels by its weight, its momentum, or by both combined. In the first case the wheel is provided with a number of buckets, or troughs, into which the water is received near the level of the axle of the wheel; the vessels thus filled becoming heavier than those on the other side, the wheel is made to revolve by that excess of weight merely. But if the water fall into the troughs from a channel on a level with the top of the wheel, or at least above the axle, the wheel will revolve both by the weight and by the momentum which the water acquires by its fall. This is called an *overshot* wheel. If the lower part of the wheel be placed in a stream of water which is made to act on float-boards fixed on the circumference, the machine has the name of an *undershot* wheel. Lastly, when the wheel is placed in a sort of channel, or *race*, as it is called, which is formed between two projections of masonry below the bed of the upper portion of the stream, and so as to coincide very nearly with the lower quadrant of the wheel's circumference on that side, the water descending from the stream upon float-boards, or troughs, and thus acting both by its momentum and weight, the machine is called a *breast* wheel. It has been determined by experiment that the effect of the wheel is the greatest when its velocity is about half the velocity of the stream; and it is asserted that the efficacy of an overshot wheel is more than double that of an undershot wheel of equal magnitude.

A remarkable application of water power has been recently made in the United States, to work the printing press of a daily paper in Boston. Through a two inch lead pipe, a stream of water is introduced into a meter, which only occupies twenty-four square inches. The fall of water between the Boston reservoir and this meter is about a hundred feet. This two-inch stream will discharge eighty gallons of water each minute, and in passing through the meter will give a motive power equal to what is called three-horse power. This is more than sufficient for driving the press.

HYDROFLUORIC ACID. The properties of this acid (which is a compound of fluorine and hydrogen) are, that it is fluid, clear, colourless, and volatile; and, when it escapes into the air, which it does at about 60°, it forms with the moisture of it white fumes. Its vapour is extremely pungent and irritating, and it acts strongly on vegetable blues. It acts upon and decomposes glass with great facility, on account of its affinity for the silica which it contains. And hence it has, to a certain though not to a very great extent, been employed to engrave on glass

HYDROFUGAL MACHINE. Under DRYING MACHINE a description is given of certain contrivances, by which drying is effected through the agency of centrifugal force, engendered during the rapid rotation of the articles to be dried. In France much progress has lately been made in applying similar machines to other purposes; and the name of *hydrofugal machines* has been proposed as applicable to them. Sugar has been clarified by rotating in such a machine. Beer has been cooled by a similar rotation. Attempts have been made to produce a sufficiently low temperature by this means to permit the formation of ice; but these have not hitherto succeeded. In Alsace a hydrofugal machine is employed in making starch; the starch particles are separated from the other components of flour by the centrifugal action. It is also conceived that this machine may be advantageously employed in classifying and sorting different qualities or sizes of grain, seed, or ores; since the heaviest particles are driven farthest from the centre of the machine.

HYDROGEN. This remarkable gas is the lightest of all known bodies. It may be obtained in several modes, but it is usually procured by the decomposition of water, by causing some substance to act upon it which has affinity for its oxygen and none for the hydrogen, so that this element is separated, and asumes the elastic or gaseous state. Hydrogen is colourless, inodorous, insipid, and it has resisted all attempts which have been made to condense it by the united agency of cold and pressure. 100 cubic inches weigh only 2.15 grains. This gas extinguishes flame by itself; but when it meets with a supporter of combustion, as oxygen, it burns readily, and with a continuous but feeble flame, and much heat. When mixed with oxygen, a taper causes immediate and loud explosion attended with the formation of water by the combination of the gases. When mixed with oxygen gas, and the mixture gradually burned into a small jet, intense heat is generated. When a very small jet is burned, the flickering nature of the flame causes musical sounds when a tube of glass or metal or even of paper is held over it.

Hydrogen unites with all other elementary gaseous bodies, and forms with them compounds of vast importance and utility: thus with oxygen it forms *water;* with nitrogen, *ammonia;* with chlorine, *hydrochloric* or *muriatic* acid; with fluorine, *hydrofluoric* acid; with bromine, *hydrobromic* acid; with carbon it forms the *fire-damp* of coal mines, the liquid *naphtha*, and the solid *caoutchouc*, according to the proportions and the mode of combination.

It is needless to expatiate on the utility of hydrogen in the arts and manufactures, since scarcely any process goes on without its presence and immediate action.

HYDRO'METER. The principle of the hydrometer is this:—When a body is immersed in a fluid it loses as much of its weight as is equal to the weight of that portion of the fluid which it displaces. Hence, if the same body be immersed successively in two different fluids, the portions of weight which it will thereby lose will be directly proportional to the specific gravities of those fluids. The body in this case is supposed to be specifically heavier than the fluid. If it be lighter it will float upon the surface, so that its tendency to descend, or its weight, will then be entirely counteracted by the fluid; from which it appears that, when a body floats upon the surface of a fluid, the weight of the portion of fluid displaced is equal to the entire weight of the body. Now, since the weight of the fluid displaced by a floating body is constant (being always equal to the weight of the body), whatever may be the density of that fluid, it is obvious that if we can determine how much of the body is immersed we may immediately deduce the specific gravity of the fluid; because, when the weight is constant, the specific gravity varies inversely as the bulk.

Upon this principle is constructed the well-known instrument called Sykes's *Hydrometer*, which is now employed in the collection of the spirit revenue of Great Britain. It consists of a thin brass stem about six inches in length, passing through and soldered to a hollow ball of the same material, and about one inch and a half in diameter. To the inferior extremity of the stem, from which the hollow ball is about one inch distant, a permanent pear-shaped weight is attached; so that, when the instrument is placed in a fluid, the other extremity may float perpendicularly to the surface. There are also ten weights of different magnitudes, nine of which are circular, and one in the form of a parallelopiped. By the successive application of these weights the instrument may be sunk so as to obtain the complete range of specific gravity, from that of pure alcohol to that of distilled water.

See further under ALCOHOMETER and SPECIFIC GRAVITY.

HYDROSTATIC BED. [ARNOTT BEDSTEAD.]

HYDROSTATICS. The laws of hydrostatics and hydrodynamics, or the pressure and motion of fluids, belong to the physical sciences, and not to the object of the present volume. The practical applications of those laws are noticed under HYDRAULIC MACHINES and other headings.

HYGRO'METER. This is an instrument serving to determine the quantity of aqueous vapour in the atmosphere or other gas under examination. M. De Luc employed for this purpose a thin slip of whalebone, the contractions of which indicated the variations of moisture; and De Saussure had recourse to a human hair, by means of which he constructed a far more delicate instrument. Leslie's hygrometer consists of a glass tube, bent so as to form two equal branches parallel to one another, and each terminating with a hollow ball, in which is introduced sulphuric acid coloured. One of the balls is covered with cambric, which is kept constantly moist by water from a neighbouring vessel; and the evaporation of the water, by cooling that ball, allows the air in the other, by its superior elasticity, to depress the acid in the tube below. This depression, being measured by a convenient scale, affords an indication of the relative dryness of the atmosphere.

All these instruments have however been nearly superseded by the hygrometer invented by the late Professor Daniell. It consists of two thin glass balls one inch and a quarter in diameter, connected by a glass tube about 7 inches in length. The tube is bent in two places at right angles, so as to form three arms of unequal length, the longest of which contains a small thermometer, whose bulb descends into the lower of the two glass balls. This ball, after being filled about two-thirds with æther, is placed over a spirit-lamp until the vapour of the æther has expelled the contained air through a capillary tube which is left open for the purpose, and afterwards hermetically sealed. The other ball is then covered with a piece of muslin, and the instrument thus adjusted is placed upon a stand, to which is attached a small thermometer, indicating the temperature of the external air. When about to be used, a small portion of æther is poured upon the muslin, which, by evaporating, lowers the temperature of the glass ball, and thereby occasions a rapid condensation of the æthereal vapour contained within the instrument. The condensation of the vapour within the tube produces a continuous evaporation from the surface of the æther in the lower ball, whereby the temperature of the included æther is continually reduced until a deposit of moisture from the surrounding atmosphere is observed to take place upon the exterior of the glass. At this instant the inner thermometer, which always indicates the temperature of the æther, is observed, and thus the dew point, or that at which the precipitation of atmospheric moisture takes place, is determined with considerable accuracy.

As an illustration of the facts brought out by the use of the hygrometer, we may state that in Great Britain the mean evaporation per minute from each square inch of the surface of water, one inch deep, is 0.01155 grains.

HYPONITROUS ACID. This liquid at common temperatures is green, but at 0° it is colourless; it is very volatile, so that when exposed to the air it is rapidly converted into an orange vapour.

I

ICE-HOUSE. One of the simplest modes of preserving ice consists in enveloping it in a great quantity of straw, above the surface of the ground, in such a position that moisture, which is even more injurious than heat, may drain off freely. But to preserve ice in larger quantity and for a longer period, and to obtain a cool temperature for meat and fish, an *ice-house* is requisite.

Such an ice-house may be simply a large cellar, with hollow or double walls, floor, roof, and doors, and furnished with a trapped drain to allow the escape of such water as may be produced by a partial thaw, without admitting any air. Mr. Loudon gives a ground plan and section of a complete ice-house of approved construction, of the inverted conical shape, with an arched roof, which it is proposed to cover with two or three feet of earth, or more in hot climates, over which he suggests the propriety of training ivy, for the sake of excluding solar heat. In this design a small pump is shown communicating with a well in the drain of the ice-house, for the purpose of raising the thaw-water for drinking or other use. Dr. Ure, in his 'Dictionary of Arts,' gives a section of a similar structure, but with solid walls and a conical roof of timber, which may be simply thatched, or covered with brick-work and thatched, and which should have a gutter round it to collect and conduct to a distance all rain that falls upon it, that the circumjacent ground may be kept dry. Many other forms of ice-house have been proposed by different writers.

ICE TRADE. A remarkable traffic has sprung up within the last few years; viz., the transport of ice from America to various parts of the world. In the East Indies the artificial formation of ice has been long carried on, as the only means of cooling beverages and food. The ground near Hoogley, about 40 miles from Calcutta, is formed into shallow troughs; into these troughs, on a layer of straw, are placed pans of porous earthenware. Shortly before midnight in the winter months, and when the wind happens to be blowing from the north-west, a little water is poured into each vessel or pan; and if all the circumstances are favourable, a film of ice is found in each pan on the following morning; and this ice is collected and stored with the utmost care. The selling price of this ice at Calcutta is about sixpence per pound; but the Calcutta inhabitants were surprised by the arrival, in 1833, of a ship from the United States, laden entirely with ice, which was offered for sale at three-pence per pound, and was understood to yield a good profit even after paying all the expences of a long voyage. Since then the price has been much lowered; and ice has become a regular article of shipment from America.

This remarkable trade is in the hands of the Wenham Lake Company. The company purchased a lake of pure water, and the surrounding land, at Wenham, about 18 miles from Boston; they built storehouses, and formed a railway from Wenham to Boston. The lake is very deep, and is supplied solely by springs, which issue from its bed. During winter the ice which forms on it is very thick, clear, and compact. When the ice is about a foot thick, a number of men, horses, and machines are set to work. The surface is first swept scrupulously clean; an *ice-plane* is drawn over it, to cut away a layer of loose or imperfect ice; an *ice-plough* is drawn over it, to cut a groove across the lake; and other machines are successively employed, until the ice is removed from the lake, in solid blocks weighing from one to two cwts. each. They take two acres of lake surface into operation at one time; this will yield, at the average thickness, about two thousand tons of ice; and forty men, assisted by twelve horses, will cut and stow four hundred tons of this in a day. The company's store-house, near the lake, is built of wood, and has double walls two feet apart: the intervening space being filled with saw-dust: twenty thousand tons of ice can be stored in this building at one time. The company bring the ice to Boston on their own railway, and thence transmit it to various parts of the world. Large store-houses have been formed in many parts of the United States, as well as in London and Liverpool.

Whether procured from Wenham, or from our own streams and ponds, ice may be conveniently kept in *portable ice-houses* or *refrigerators*, which are now much used in England and America. This consists of a box with two lids, and with perforated sliding shelves; ice is placed under the shelves, meat or other provisions is laid on the shelves, and the box is closed; being air-tight, it allows the ice to cool the other contents of the box with great rapidity. A new form of apparatus has been recently patented by Mr. Ling, under the name of *ice-safe*. The ice is placed in a distinct chamber, in a way that is intended to economize that material. The smaller size, for families, is planned so as to cool two gallons of water at a time, besides meat, &c.

ICELAND. The best inhabited spots on this lonely island are near the *fiords* or creeks, where establishments are kept up for the sake of trade and shipping. Corn is cultivated to a limited extent. Hay is the great harvest of Iceland. Those who live on the coast attend to fishing, which is very productive; and those a little further inland rear cattle. The common food of the people is butter, milk, and fish; fresh meat and rye bread are holiday fare. The exports consist of cod and other dried fish, whale oil, salted mutton, eider-down and sulphur, which is abundant. Turf is the common fuel of the inhabitants; fossil wood, iron, and copper are found. In the northern district there is a kind of town or village, called Eyafiordur, and a factory called Husavik, on the Skialfianda-fiord, from which sulphur from the neighbouring mines is shipped. Other factories are scattered about the coast, especially in the west.

ICELAND MOSS. This lichen, though a native of the higher mountains of the northern part of Britain, is procured mostly from Norway and Iceland, on the lava of the west coast of which latter country it abounds and attains a large size. It is imported through Hamburg. When dry it has scarcely any odour, and the taste is bitter and unpleasant. The powder or flower is of a whitish gray. When the bitter principle is removed, the starchy matter differs from wheat-flour in nutritive properties, though some authorities assert that a soup prepared with it is twice as nutritious as one made with flour. Certain it is that the inhabitants of Norway, Lapland, and, above all, of Iceland, use it extensively as an alimentary substance, the latter regarding it as the gift of 'a bountiful Providence, which sends them bread out of the very stones.' Dr. Henderson ('Tour in Iceland') says that a porridge made of this lichen flour is to a foreigner not only the most wholesome but the most palatable of all the articles of Icelandic diet. It is submitted to no other preparation than repeated steepings in cold water, drying, and powdering; after which it is either made into cakes or boiled in milk. The excellence of Iceland Moss depends upon its freshness and freedom from accidental impurities, which should be carefully removed before it is used.

IDOCRASE, is the name of a gem which is sometimes called *Pyramidal Garnet*. The colour exhibits various shades of brown, black, gray, blue, green, and yellow.

ILLE-ET-VILAINE. The soil of this department of France is made to produce all kinds of breadstuffs, in quantity more than enough for the wants of the population. In the rich soils, wheat of excellent quality is raised; tobacco is grown near St. Malo; rye, barley, oats, buckwheat, and mixed grain are produced in the middling and poorer soils. The cultivation of flax and hemp for the manufactures of the department is very extensive; the flax and hemp in the dressed state, as also the seeds, are important objects of commerce. The apple and the pear are extensively cultivated for making cider and perry, the chief drinks of the population; the cider is strong enough to keep for two years, and is considered the best made in France. Excellent butter and cheese are made. The forests of the department contain fine timber: the prevailing kinds are oak and beech; next come chestnut, poplar, and birch. Several iron mines are worked: roofing and clay slate, white quartz for the glass factories, limestone, and granite are quarried: lead and copper ore are found.

The most important manufactures are linen, sailcloth of the best quality, Russia duck, canvas, and shoe and morocco leather; felt and straw hats, sewing thread, thread stockings, ship cordage and ropes, fishing nets, hooks and lines, pottery, cotton and woollen yarn, are also made. There are besides, several bleaching establishments, brandy distilleries, paper mills, iron forges and smelting furnaces, and flour-mills; in the towns on the coast shipbuilding is carried on to some extent. Salt is made in some of the marshes on the coast. The commerce is composed of the various articles named, and of groats, chestnuts, salt pork, hides, oak staves, firewood, &c.

ILLINOIS. A few commercial features relating to this rapidly-advancing state will be found under UNITED STATES.

ILLYRIA, a kingdom and province of the Austrian empire, is slightly noticed in respect to its produce and manufactures, under AUSTRIA. We may here state in addition that the most important town is *Idria*, famous for its quicksilver mines. It is situated at the bottom of a narrow valley surrounded by high mountains, on the banks of the little river Idria, and has 5000 inhabitants, who subsist partly by lace making and straw platting; but the greater part are employed in the mines and in the quicksilver works and cinnabar factories in the neighbourhood. The entrance to the mine is nearly in the middle of the town, by a large iron gate, which opens to a horizontal passage leading to a flight of 757 steps cut in the limestone rock.

IMPORTS AND EXPORTS. Until a time comparatively recent, our official trade accounts were not furnished in such a manner as to allow of any certain deductions being made from them; but the monthly and yearly accounts of the Board of Trade now furnish very complete information on these points. The list of our imports from foreign countries and the colonies comprises almost every article of use and of luxury which cannot be profitably produced within the kingdom; while our exports comprise chiefly mineral produce, and manufactured goods of a very varied description.

We find that in the last five years, the value of British and Irish produce and manufactures exported has been as follows:—

Year.	Total Exports.
1846	£57,786,876
1847	58,842,377
1848	52,849,445
1849	58,910,883
1850	65,756,032

Taking the year 1848 as an example, we find that the largest customers for our manufactures were the following:—

United States	£9,564,909
Germany	5,263,588
East Indies	5,077,247
Holland	2,823,258
Turkey	2,664,281
Brazil	2,067,302
British America	1,990,592
West Indies	1,434,477

The Board of Trade returns respecting Imports give *quantities* of each kind of commodity, rather than *values*; and it is therefore not easy to present an abstract of them. We will however take the year 1850, and show what were the most notable items, both of export and import. First for Export:—

Candles	2,723,531 lbs.
Coals	3,347,607 tons.
Cotton Goods	1,358,238,837 yards.
Cotton Lace	114,095,554 yards.
Cotton Yarn	131,433,168 lbs.
Earthenware	76,952,735 pieces.
Glass	336,614 cwts.
Linen	122,397,457 yards.
Linen Yarn	18,559,318 lbs.
Metals and Machinery (about)	10,000,000*l*.
Oil	3,292,266 gallons.
Salt	15,824,780 bushels.
Silk Manufactures (about)	1,300,000*l*.
Soap	124,038 cwts.
Soda	888,146 cwts.
Wool and Woollens (about)	11,000,000*l*.

Among the items of Import, the following were the most considerable:—

Brimstone	664,630 cwts.
Coffee	50,809,521 lbs.
Corn	7,969,435 quarters.
Corn-meal	3,873,908 cwts.
Cotton	5,934,793 cwts.
Cured or Salted Meat	687,199 cwts.
Hemp	1,048,635 cwts.
Live Stock	217,247 head.
Metals	117,148 tons.
Rice	785,692 cwts.
Saltpetre	529,012 cwts.
Silks (about)	6,000,000 lbs.
Spices (about)	13,000,000 lbs.
Spirits	7,763,279 gallons.
Sugar	1,250,441 cwts.
Tallow	1,241,781 cwts.
Tea	50,513,003 lbs.
Tobacco	35,427,335 lbs.
Wine	9,267,573 gallons.
Wool	74,326,778 lbs.

INCLINED PLANE. In mechanical and mathematical considerations an *inclined plane* is a plane surface making any angle with the horizon. A body placed on it is capable of being moved upwards along it with more facility than it can be raised in a vertical direction. The principle on which it constitutes a mechanical power was first introduced by Stevinus in the sixteenth century.

Among the useful rules ascertained on this subject are the following:—A weight placed upon an inclined plane is propelled down the plane by such a fraction of the whole pressure of the weight as the height of any section of the plane is of its length. The velocity acquired by a body in descending from the top to the foot of a plane, whatever be its inclination, is the same as in falling vertically from the top to a horizontal plane passing through the foot.

INCLOSURES. The amount of common land (land in a state of nature or waste) in England is not known, but it is conjectured that it may be about 8,000,000 of acres; the total area of England and Wales being supposed to be about 37,000,000 acres. There is another class called *commonable lands*, which is commonable or open to all the parishioners during a part only of each year. As common and commonable lands produce relatively little on account of insufficient culture, *Inclosures* of land have now been going on for many years. It is stated that since 1800 about 2000 inclosure acts have passed; and prior to that time about 1600 or 1700. These inclosure acts (with certain exceptions) are private acts, and the expense of obtaining them and the trouble attendant on the carrying their provisions into effect have often prevented the inclosure of commons. In 1836 an act was passed for facilitating the inclosure of open and arable fields in England and Wales. In pursuance of the recommendation of a Committee of the House of Commons, which sat in 1844, an act of parliament was passed in 1845, the object of which is thus stated in the preamble:—'To facilitate the inclosure and improvement of commons and other lands now subject to the rights of property which obstruct cultivation and the productive employment of labour, and to facilitate such exchanges of lands, and such divisions of lands intermixed or divided into inconvenient parcels as may be beneficial to the respective owners.'

Although the local rights of parishioners are somewhat interfered with by these inclosures, there can be little doubt that the general culture of the land, and the wealth of the community, are increased thereby.

INDIA. [EAST INDIA COMPANY.]

INDIA RUBBER MANUFACTURES. A description of this singular substance, and of the mode in which it is obtained in the East, will be found under CAOUTCHOUC. When the gum became known in England, its elasticity and its imperviousness to water pointed it out as a valuable material for manufactures; and it has gradually come into very extensive use.

Before Caoutchouc can be practically applied, it requires to be brought from its first crude state to that of a cake, a thread, or a liquid, according to its mode of application. The crude substance is cut into shreds, washed, heated, and kneaded by rollers until it assumes a homogeneous consistency; it is then pressed into moulds, which bring it to the form of large rectangular masses. From these masses sheets are cut by machinery to any required thickness; and from these sheets threads or any of the other countless forms of the material are prepared. By the use of petroleum, naphtha, oil of turpentine, or a few other liquids, caoutchouc may be dissolved; and in that dissolved state is an admirable varnish for rendering porous substances water-proof.

As a solid substance, as a woven material (with or without any fibrous ingredient), and as a varnish, caoutchouc is now applied to countless purposes, in dress, in machinery, and in other ways. Every reader will be able to verify this assertion.

Mr. Hancock, who has probably done more than any other person to vary the modes in which caoutchouc may be employed in manufactures, took out a patent in 1845 for removing three inconveniences which are often presented by this substance. These inconveniences are, a clammy adhesiveness; a tendency to stiffen and harden by cold; and a tendency to become softened or even decomposed by heat or by oil. To remove the clammy adhesiveness, Mr. Hancock brings the caoutchouc to the state of a sheet by the pressure of iron rollers, and forces into this sheet twice its weight of powdered French chalk, or silicate of magnesia, by repeated pressure. Other processes then incorporate the two substances completely; and the compound is ready to be applied to varied purposes. For some purposes powdered black lead, or powdered dry asphalte, are used instead of the silicate.

To enable caoutchouc to resist heat, cold, air, grease, oil, and various solvents, is the purport of Mr. Hancock's Vulcanized India Rubber. This is a compound of caoutchouc and sulphur. The sulphur is either pounded and pressed into the sheets of caoutchouc in the same manner as the silicate; or the sheets are steeped in melted sulphur until they become thoroughly impregnated with it. The compound is then made into a paste, or a so-

KNIGHT'S CYCLOPÆDIA OF THE INDUSTRY OF ALL NATIONS.

No. 26.

lution, or thin sheets or threads, or any of the numerous forms in which it is employed. The caoutchouc loses some of its extent of elasticity, but acquires more perfect elasticity, the longer it remains in the melted sulphur; that is, it becomes less easily stretched, on account of its increasing toughness, but its elasticity is more intense so far as it goes. Some of the Vulcanised India Rubber now used is wonderfully elastic.

In 1846 Mr. Parkes patented many improvements in the caoutchouc manufacture. One of these is a new kind of vulcanised India rubber. The change which has obtained this name is produced, according to this patent, by immersing thin sheets of caoutchouc in a solution of chloride of sulphur or bisulphuret of carbon, heating them to a temperature of 80 Fahr., boiling them in a caustic ley, and drying. Vulcanising in the dry way, Mr. Parkes effects by kneading or pressing fine chloride of sulphur into the substance of the soft caoutchouc. Another part of the patent relates to the dyeing of caoutchouc. The following are the ingredients named, for forming the various dyeing liquids:—For black; sulphate of copper and caustic ammonia. For green; sulphate of copper, muriate of ammonia, and caustic lime. For purple; sulphates of copper and of potash, and sulphate of indigo. For merely colouring the surface, without dyeing the substance, many ingredients may be employed, and many tints produced.

It would carry us beyond our limits even to name the various patents which have been brought out for india rubber manufactures, and the improvements suggested therein. We may however briefly glance at a few.

Mr. Lorimer, in 1848, among other novelties patented a waterproofing material, made of caoutchouc combined with oxide of copper and slaked lime acidulated with oxalic acid. Another patent in the same year was for imparting certain qualities to caoutchouc by combining it with carbonate of magnesia. Mr. Nickells in 1849 introduced a mode of combining sulphur with caoutchouc. The caoutchouc is placed in what is called a masticating machine, flowers of sulphur are added, heat is applied, and a roller passes to and fro over these substances, until they are kneaded into a uniform mass. Simpson and Foster's patent, in the same year, was for a mode of dissolving caoutchouc by the use of bisulphuret of carbon combined with pentachlorido of antimony. Burke's patent, about the same time, was for giving permanent elasticity to caoutchouc by the application of antimony and carbonate of soda. Newton's patent, in 1850, is for combining caoutchouc with gum lac, as a means of removing its odour.

Notwithstanding the large use of caoutchouc, it must be admitted that Gutta Percha has lately been outstripping it in public favour.

INDIANA. A few industrial statistics of this State will be found under UNITED STATES.

INDIGO. This well-known and beautiful blue vegetable colour is extensively employed in dyeing and calico printing. The plants from which it is mostly obtained belong to the genus *indigofera*, of which the chief species grow in India. When the plant is in full flower, it contains most colouring matter. After being cut, it is put into vats, and covered with water; fermentation takes place, accompanied with the evolution of carbonic acid and probably other gaseous products, and the yellow liquor is covered with a froth which in a little time becomes of a violet colour, and a substance is dissolved which is rendered blue by absorbing the oxygen of the air, and being then rendered insoluble it is precipitated; and this, when collected and dried, is indigo.

The usual appearance of indigo as it occurs in commerce is that of nearly cubical cakes of an intense blue colour and earthy fracture. Indigo seldom contains more than about half its weight of pure colouring matter, and frequently much less.

When common indigo has been treated with dilute acids, alkalis, and alcohol, the remainder is *indigotin*, or indigo, nearly in a state of purity.

The quantity of indigo imported into Great Britain in 1850 was 70,482 cwts.

INDRE. This department of France produces corn in quantity more than enough for the consumption; buck-wheat, hemp, flax, chestnuts, and fruits are also grown. The annual produce of wine is six to seven million gallons, about one-half of which is exported. Sheep are a source of great profit to the farmers, on account of the fineness of their wool: the quality of the wool of the *Champagne* district especially is very superior. Several iron mines are worked; marble, millstone, limestone, mica, flint, lithographic stones, granite, quartz, spar, marl, potter's clay, variegated marbles, &c., are found. The cloth manufactures of Châteauroux and some other places are important; linen, hosiery, scythes, paper, porcelain, and earthenware are made. There are also numerous establishments for the manufacture of woollen yarn, leather, beer, parchment, &c. The most important iron-works are those of Clavières. The commerce of the department is composed of the various agricultural and industrial products named.

There is another department, called *Indre-*

et-Loire, one of the most important products of which is wine; of which 14 or 15 million gallons are made yearly; next come hemp, walnuts for making oil, plums, beans, leguminous plants, liquorice, anise, and coriander; citrons, melons, almonds, apples, pears, truffles, &c. Bees and silkworms are carefully tended. Iron mines are worked; stone, especially a tufaceous sandstone, of which most of the houses are built, is quarried out of the hills near the Loire, and excavations thus formed are occupied as dwelling places by the poorer inhabitants. Millstone grit, marl, potter's clay, and brick-earth are found. Copper ore is met with, but no mines are worked. The chief industrial products are bar iron, powder, and files; woollen cloth, of which manufacture Tours is the centre; silk, leather, paper, and pottery, are also made, but the manufacture of these articles is not so important as formerly. The exports consist mostly of agricultural products, the imports of colonial produce, glass, cotton stuffs, fine linen and woollen cloth, furniture, haberdashery, &c.

INFUSIONS are solutions of some of the principles of vegetables, generally in water, but occasionally in other vehicles. When water is employed it may either be hot or cold. It is customary to use warm water, but in many instances cold is preferable. Sometimes alcohol is added, after straining, to assist in keeping the infusion, or to increase its powers. Hard water should, if possible, be avoided in the preparation of infusions.

INK. The writing ink of the ancients was essentially different from that which is now employed. Its basis was finely divided charcoal, mixed with some mucilaginous or adhesive fluid: it was much less destructible than modern writing ink, and somewhat more resembled printer's ink. Writing ink is now a chemical compound, and not a mere mechanical mixture. Its basis is proto-gallate and proto-tannate of iron, which by oxidisement become per-gallate and per-tannate; and it is owing to the oxygen of the air effecting this change gradually that recent writing is of a comparatively light colour, and that it subsequently becomes black. Many processes have been given for preparing writing ink. The common ingredients are galls and sulphate of iron; in fact, while printers' ink may be considered as a black paint, writing ink may be regarded as a black dye. The following, which is recommended by Mr. Brande, gives, he says, an excellent ink, and it possesses the merit of greater simplicity than most others: —Aleppo galls, bruised, 6 ounces; sulphate of iron, 4 ounces; gum arabic, 4 ounces; water, 6 pints. Boil the galls in the water, then add the other ingredients, and keep the whole in a well-stopped bottle, occasionally shaking it. In two months strain and pour off the ink into glass bottles, to be well corked. To prevent mould, add one grain of corrosive sublimate, or three drops of creosote, to each pint of ink. Modern writing ink, unlike the ancient, is readily destroyed by chlorine, acids, and alkalis. Red, blue, and other coloured inks have nearly the same chemical properties as black ink, and depend for their colour on the kind of ingredients employed. A *Magic Sand* has been recently introduced, to 'write without ink,' and to avoid spilling and spotting. The magic consists probably in sand being saturated with ink.

Indian Ink.—The cakes of this ink are made of lamp-black and size, or animal glue, with the addition of perfumes or other substances not essential to its quality as an ink. It is used in China with a brush, both for writing and for painting upon paper of Chinese manufacture. It is used in Europe for designs in black and white, in which it possesses the advantage of affording various depths of shade, according to the degree of dilution with water.

Printers' Ink is of two kinds: for letter-press printing and for copper plate printing. Printers' ink is prepared by boiling linseed or nut oil in an iron pot; and, if it does not take fire of itself, it is kindled, and suffered to burn for about half an hour; the flame is then extinguished by closely covering the vessel, and the oil is by this operation found to have acquired the necessary drying quality, after being again boiled. It is then mixed with a proper quantity of lamp-black, when black ink is required; if red ink be required, the colouring matter employed is vermilion for finer works. Copper-plate printers' ink is made with oil which is less boiled, and the charcoal used is Frankfort black, made from vine twigs.

Marking Ink is employed for marking linen: it is a solution of nitrate of silver, written with a pen upon the fabric to be marked after it has been moistened with an alkaline solution, as potash or soda. By this process oxide of silver is precipitated upon and combines with the cloth so as to be scarcely removeable by any reagent which does not also destroy its texture. There are other chemical preparations used for this purpose.

Sympathetic Inks are such as are invisible until heat is applied, and then, by the chemical change induced, the writing becomes visible. The most remarkable of these is that prepared from cobalt, called Hellot's Sympathetic Ink, which is a chloride of the metal. When the written paper is held to the fire so as to evaporate the water, the letters become green.

INTA'GLIO. This name is given to small works of the gem class, in which the design is indented or engraved, to distinguish them from those in which the subject or device is raised, called *Cameos*. The Greeks carried this branch of the fine arts to the same perfection which their genius and feeling for the beautiful enabled them to reach in all others to which they devoted their attention; but we do not trace its existence among them to a very remote date. We have no information respecting the process by which the ancient intagliatori (or sculptores) executed works which are now justly referred to as the best examples of the art. The modern practice of cutting stones in intaglio is by an apparatus similar in principle to the turning lathe, which gives the cutting tool, placed horizontally, a quick rotatory motion, and, the stone on which the design is to be engraved being brought in contact with it, the surface is ground away or indented, till the effect required is produced. Instruments of various sizes are used, which can easily be removed and replaced, and it is usual, during the process of engraving, to supply the points of the tools with diamond dust mixed with a little sweet oil. As the work proceeds, proofs are occasionally taken in wax.

Die-Sinking or the engraving of dies is an important branch of the art of intaglio, and requires great care and skill for its perfection. The die is made of finely prepared and tempered steel. When the first intaglio, or original die, is executed, it forms a *matrix* (or mould), into which a conically formed block of softer steel is compressed, the matrix first undergoing a process by which it is hardened. An impression taken in this way is called a *puncheon*. When this is completed (and frequent annealing and restriking are necessary before it is perfected), the engraver retouches the work, now in relief, and gives it all the delicacy of the original model; the metal is then hardened, and, by pressing this puncheon into other steel which is soft (by almost a repetition indeed of the before-mentioned process), it serves for the purpose of making the dies for coining.

INVENTIONS. A few words on the present state of the law respecting patents (or what may be termed copyright) for mechanical inventions, will be found under PATENT LAWS.

INVERNESSHIRE. By far the greater part of the surface of this Scotch county is covered with heath; but a good deal of the heathy ground is arable, and a considerable extent of it has been brought into cultivation during the present century. Limestone is found in several districts, and in some districts approaches to the nature of marble. Sandstone is also frequently met with. Some veins of lead and silver have been discovered, and also iron ore in small quantities. The soil is for the most part light and sandy, with a subsoil of gravel or clay: but in the neighbourhood of the town of Inverness it is enriched by a fine loam deposited by the waters which fall into the adjoining firth. Formerly there were a great number of small arable farms only a few acres in extent; but these have much decreased since the introduction of sheep-farming. The attention of the farmers is chiefly directed to the rearing of sheep and cattle. The fir woods in Glenmore and those of Strathspey in the adjoining county of Elgin are supposed to be more extensive than all the other natural woods in Scotland together. Glen Morrison, which opens into Glenmore, also contains much fine timber. Those which grow naturally are the oak, fir, birch, ash, mountain ash, holly, elm, hazel and the Scotch poplar. Those which are planted are the larch, spruce fir, silver fir, beech, plane, and fruit-trees. Formerly a good deal of hemp, worsted, and linen yarn was made in this county; but this has greatly declined since the establishment of the large manufactories of the south.

The only important town in the county, Inverness, is noticeable rather in a picturesque than an industrial point of view; there is a small import of hemp, timber, and tar, and an export of oats.

IODINE. This remarkable non-metallic elementary body was discovered by M. Courtois in 1812. Iodine exists in the water of the ocean and mineral springs, and in marine molluscous animals and sea-weeds; but it is principally obtained from kelp, or sea-weed which has been burnt for the purpose of obtaining alkali. It is a soft opaque solid, of a blueish black colour and metallic lustre. When moderately heated, it rises in vapour of a violet colour, and hence its name from the Greek word for violet. On cooling, it again crystallises unchanged, nor is it decomposed or altered by being subjected to very high temperatures; and it has resisted all attempts to decompose it.

Iodine has a strong disagreeable odour and taste; it stains the skin of a brownish colour, but not permanently. It is readily dissolved by alcohol, but scarcely at all by water. It is very poisonous. Its characteristic property is that of giving an intense blue colour when added to a solution of starch. It unites with metals to form compounds, which are termed *Iodides;* and, like chlorine and bromine, it forms acids both with hydrogen and oxygen.

Iodine, though only obtained in an isolated state of late years, has been long employed as the efficient principle of other preparations and therapeutic agents, namely, burnt sponge and certain mineral waters. It is only since it has been procured as a distinct principle that its action has been ascertained with precision. In the present day it is administered rather in some artificial compound than as pure iodine, owing to its very sparing solubility in water. Its value in medicine is very great. In photographic processes and in other processes connected with the arts, iodine is also very useful.

At the Dublin Exhibition of manufactures in 1850, the Messrs. Bullock, manufacturing chemists of Galway, exhibited specimens of Irish iodine. It appears that iodine is found in large quantities in the sea-weed which covers the rocks for miles round the west coast of Ireland; it has been hitherto collected by the peasatns for manure; but Messrs. Bullock have found that it will yield iodine in sufficient quantity to pay for the extraction. This affords one among many exemplars of the advancing spirit of manufactures in Ireland.

IONIAN ISLANDS. This name is given to the islands of Corfu, Cephalonia, Zante, Santa-Maura, Theaki, Paxo, Cerigo, and some small islets, all situated in the Ionian Sea, off the west coast of Albania and the coast of Greece. Oil, wine, corn, cotton, the small species of grape called currants, and other fruits, and flax, are the chief productions; the olive is extensively cultivated in all the islands; the currant is grown in the greatest perfection in Cephalonia and Zante, but of late years the cultivation of this fruit is diminishing in the islands and increasing on the main land of Greece. Earthenware, salt, soap, and some coarse woven goods, are the principal industrial products; ship-building and the fisheries give employment to a considerable number of hands. The coasting trade is important. The imports, consisting of sugar, coffee, and drugs, raw and manufactured cotton and silk; wool and woollen cloth, glass, hardware, staves and hoops; iron, timber, wheat, Indian corn, rice, cheese, flour, fish, cattle, sheep, tobacco, &c., average in value about 630,000*l.* a year. The import and export is almost entirely carried on in British ships.

The British produce and manufactures imported into the Ionian Islands in 1849 amounted in value to 165,805*l.*; those from other countries amounted to three or four times this value, but mostly in British shipping.

Of these several islands *Cephalonia* depends chiefly on its culture of currants, of which there are about 6000 acres planted. *Corfu* produces oil, wine, cotton, fruit, flax, and corn; oil is the chief produce, the annual produce being about 200,000 barrels. *Cerigo* and all the other islands produce nearly the same crops, varying a little in richness.

IOWA. This member of the United States confederacy, which attained to that honour only so late as 1846, is too young a state to present us yet with any marked industrial developments.

IPECACUANHA. This emetic substance is the root of several plants growing in South America. All the kinds have nearly the same ingredients, but differ in the amount of the active principle which they respectively contain, termed *emeta.* The best is the annulated, yielded by the *Cephaëlis Ipecacuanha*, a small shrubby plant, native of Brazil and of New Granada. Of this sort there are three varieties, namely, the brown, red, and gray, or gray-white, called also greater annulated ipecacuan. As this is the only sort sent from Rio Janeiro, it is sometimes called Brazilian or Lisbon ipecacuanha. It is sent in bales and barrels.

IRELAND. This beautiful and naturally rich portion of our Empire contains six coal districts: the Leinster, or Castlecomer district; the Slieve Arda, or Tipperary district; the Munster district; the Lough Allen district, round the source of the Shannon; and the Monaghan and Tyrone districts; there is also a coal district of small extent in Antrim. The coal raised in the southern districts is anthracite, or blind-coal; that raised in the districts north of Dublin is bituminous. In addition to these the central district of Ireland contains upwards of one million acres of bog, comprehended for the most part within that portion which would be embraced by lines drawn from Wicklow to Galway, and from Howth-head to Sligo. In respect to lakes and rivers, it has been estimated that the water power afforded by the different rivers and natural dams of Ireland is greater than in any equal extent of accessible country in Europe: this is a very important feature in connection with the future industrial progress of Ireland.

Of the 20 millions of acres of land in Ireland, it has been estimated that 5¼ are arable and garden ground; 6¾ meadows, pastures, and marshes; 5 improveable wastes; and the rest unimproveable wastes. In 1841 there were about 350,000 acres of plantations in Ireland. In 1847, about one-fourth of the whole area of Ireland was under crop, comprising about 5,000,000 acres; of which two-thirds were under corn-crops, and one-third under crops of beans, potatoes, turnips, clover, flax, &c. The corn produce in that year was about 16,000,000 quarters; comprising wheat, oats, barley, bere, and rye; and giving about

5 quarters average per acre. The Irish fisheries are carried on upon a considerable scale, under the management of the Board of Works. The whole coast of Ireland has been divided by the commissioners into 28 fishery districts, in which are registered about 20,000 vessels and boats, and about 100,000 fishermen and boys.

Among the manufactures of Ireland, that of linen takes the lead; it gives a flourishing character to the district around Belfast and Coleraine. Cotton spinning and weaving, and calico bleaching and printing, also occupy many hands. The woollen and silk manufactures, once carried on to a respectable extent, have greatly declined within the last few years. In grinding, malting, brewing, and distilling, a considerable trado is carried on. The malt made in Ireland in 1850 was 1,682,102 bushels. The quantity of spirits charged with duty in Ireland in the same year was 7,408,086 gallons. There are numerous paper-mills, glass-works, and tobacco manufactories.

The inland traffic is kept up by tolerably good roads, rivers, canals, and railways. The chief canals are the Grand Canal, Royal Canal, Shannon Navigation, Limerick Navigation, Lagan Navigation, Newry Navigation, Tyrone Navigation, Boyne Navigation, Slaney Navigation, Barrow Navigation, and Ulster Canal, giving about 620 miles of available navigation. Railways will very shortly cross the island from east to west and from north to south. The external traffic is greatly aided by steam power; steam vessels of large size run from London, Plymouth, Bristol, Holyhead, Liverpool, Fleetwood, Greenock, and Glasgow, to Cork, Waterford, Wexford, Dublin, Belfast, Londonderry, and other Irish ports.

Every one at all interested in the welfare of Ireland is anxious to see her great industrial capabilities developed. That her manufacturers can produce manifold and excellent specimens of skill was sufficiently shewn at the Dublin Exhibition of Manufactures in 1850, noticed in our '*Introduction*.' That Ireland is not insufficiently supplied with mineral wealth is exemplified in the black and white marbles of Galway, the slates of various districts, the coal of her various beds, and the peat which—though now an incumbrance and an eyesore—may yet become a mine of resources. That the Ulster cultivators and manufacturers are not blind to improvements is shewn by the eagerness with which the investigations concerning flax are now being regarded. That the merchants of Ireland aro alive to the energy of commercial enterprise, let Cork and Limerick, Waterford and Dublin, Belfast and Derry, bear witness. The castings for an iron bridge for the South Wales Railway have just been made at Dublin—a feature which has excited well-merited attention. When we find that 19 Irish counties contain iron, 17 copper, 18 lead, and 16 coal, we cannot but hope that a brighter future is in store for that country.

At the forthcoming Industrial Exhibition, Ireland will occupy about 10,000 square feet of floor and counter, and 14,000 of wall space. In the section relating to manufactures there are more exhibitors than in the other three combined. From Cork the contributions will comprise marble, pottery clay, fine sand and silex for glassmaking, wool, leather, friezes, blankets, ginghams, models of inventions in machinery, and cabinet work. From Clonmel—cutlery, ivory turning, crochet and other work; woollens, models of agricultural implements. From Tipperary—coal, copper ore, &c. From Kilkenny—the marbles for which it is so celebrated, Kellymont flags, anthracite coal, hunting breeches, and friezes, and specimens of the leather used in making them; together with an interesting cabinet of the materials used in the manufacture of artificial flies for angling, flies and fishing tackle. From Wexford—porphyry, sand for glass, clay, the herring nets made by the fishermen of that locality, models of machinery, architectural models, and philosophical instruments. From Limerick—the beautiful Limerick lace, gloves, brushes, cutlery, army clothing, fishing tackle, worsted work, leather, and tobacco; in raw materials, alumina, silex, pottery clay, fire-clay slates, flagstones, building stone, marbles, copper and iron ore; in fancy woods, bog oak, bog yew, and arbutus; and in the mechanical section, models of machinery and inventions; and from Mountmellick, the bits and stirrups for which it is famous. These are from the south and west of Ireland; the north and east will contribute yet more largely.

IRI'DIUM. This rare metal is found combined with platinum in the ores of the latter metal, from which it may be separated by a complex chemical process. A few minute grains of native iridium have been found, but it is rarely so met with. Iridium is brittle, and when carefully polished has the appearance of platinum. When heated to redness in the air, if in a state of fine division (which is obtained by precipitation), it is oxidised, but not if in mass. Iridium is with difficulty acted upon by acids. It combines chemically with many simpler substances; but its usefulness has not yet become very great.

IRON AND ITS ORES. Of all the metals iron is the most widely diffused, the most abundant, and the most useful. It is found not only intermixed with soils, and contained in rocks and minerals, but it is even met with in some animal and vegetable bodies, and also in mineral waters. It occurs rarely in nature in the metallic state, for almost the whole of it that has been found occurs as meteoric iron containing nickel, or in meteoric stones. It is mostly found either combined with oxygen, oxygen and carbonic acid, or sulphur. The best iron ores are oxides, which occur in primitive countries, where they generally form very large beds; such are those of Sweden: but the greater part of the iron ore of Britain is an impure carbonate.

When separated from its ores, the colour of iron is grayish white with a tint of blue. It is extremely ductile, so that it may be drawn into wire finer than the human hair, but it cannot be beaten into very thin leaves. It is of all metals the most tenacious, for a wire $\frac{1}{15}$th of an inch in diameter is capable of supporting a weight of about 550 lbs. It is susceptible of a high polish. It is combustible when minutely divided, as in the state of filings. It is very hard at common temperatures, and this property may be increased by its being heated and then suddenly cooled; it then however becomes brittle. It requires a most intense heat to melt it; but when heated to redness it becomes soft and pliable, and possesses the valuable property of *welding*, that is, two pieces of red-hot iron may be made to unite by hammering. Its texture is fibrous. Its specific gravity is about 7.77; but this varies in some degree according to the extent to which it has been drawn, rolled, or hammered, and it is increased by fusion. Iron, or rather steel, is capable of being rendered permanently magnetic. Iron has great affinity for oxygen and sulphur, and some other elementary bodies, and combines with them in various proportions.

The chief ores of iron are the following:—*Oxydulous* or *Magnetic*; *Specular* or *Micaceous*; *Goethite*; *Iron Froth*; *Red Hematite*; *Brown Hematite*; *Carbonate of Iron*, or *Spathose Iron Ore*; and *Clay Iron Stone*. The last named is the most abundant in this country.

Of the valuable chemical substances in which iron forms an ingredient, it is difficult to give even a list: so numerous and varied are they. *Steel* and *black lead* consist of iron and carbon; *green vitriol* is sulphate of iron. The presence of phosphorus in iron is said to give it what iron manufacturers call the *cold short* quality. The *acetate of iron* is much used in calico printing.

The *Alloys of Iron* are much less useful than might be expected from the extreme utility of the metal itself. *Potassium* and iron, and *sodium* and iron, combine when heat is applied to them: the alloys are more fusible than pure iron, especially when in contact with the air; and they are decomposed by air and water. *Silicium* and iron form an alloy which is ductile or brittle according to the quantity of charcoal which it contains. *Arsenic* and iron form an alloy which has a grayish white colour, does not obey the magnet, is very brittle, and much more fusible than iron. *Chromium* and iron form an alloy very little known. With *columbium* a hard brown alloy is formed. *Zinc* gives a white and brittle alloy with iron. *Tin* and iron form the alloy seen on tin-plate ware. *Antimony* and iron unite when heated together in close vessels: the alloy is white, hard, brittle, and its specific gravity is less than that of the mean of the two metals. No metal appears to deprive iron more of its magnetic property than antimony. *Cobalt* and iron form a hard magnetic alloy. *Nickel* and iron form the meteoric alloy. *Bismuth* combines with difficulty with iron. *Molybdenum* forms with it a blueish gray brittle alloy. The alloy of *copper* and iron is magnetic. *Silver* combines readily with iron when they are fused together, but they separate on solidification, and globules of silver appear on the surface of the alloy. With *mercury* a white tenacious alloy is formed. *Lead* and iron combine with difficulty. *Rhodium*, *iridium*, *tungsten*, and *platinum* may all be made to form alloys with iron. *Gold* and iron combine with facility; a compound of eleven parts of gold and one part of iron is nearly white, and very ductile.

IRON MANUFACTURE. The art of smelting iron was practised in this country during the time of the Roman occupation, and in many ancient beds of cinders, the refuse of iron-works, Roman coins have been found. The principal ancient seats of the iron manufacture in this country appear to have been Sussex and the Forest of Dean, or Arden, as it was then called. Remains of ancient iron-furnaces have been noticed in Lancashire, Staffordshire, and Yorkshire. The art of working in iron and steel was much practised in this island before the Norman Conquest. At the present day the chief iron manufacturing districts in this country are the Lanark district of Scotland, South Wales, and South Staffordshire; the works distributed in other parts of the kingdom are much less extensive, though many even of these are of great importance.

There are two distinct qualities into which this metal is commonly divided, viz. *pig-iron* and *malleable* or *bar iron*, the second being the result of an extension of the processes necessary for the production of the first kind.

The first process is that of reducing the iron-stone or ore, or, as it is technically called, the *mine*, into a metallic state by means of fusion. This operation is conducted in a *blast-furnace* or *smelting-furnace*. [FURNACE.] The furnace is charged from the top with certain proportions of iron ore, coke, and limestone. The ore is previously roasted in a kiln, in order to drive off the water, sulphur, and arsenic, with which it is more or less combined in its native state: by this process it loses one sixth part of its weight. A furnace of the size commonly used in Wales will produce from 5 to 6 tons of pig-iron in twelve hours. For the largest quantity the furnace is charged progressively with 15 tons of roasted iron ore, 22½ tons of coke, and about 6 tons of limestone. These ingredients are supplied at 50 charges, and are intimately mixed together in the furnace. The limestone is broken into small pieces, and is used to act as a flux to the ore and promote its fusion. The heat that would be produced in any furnace by merely setting fire to the fuel which is contained in it would be altogether insufficient for the fusion of the ore, if its intensity were not promoted by the forcing in of a current or blast of air. For this purpose it is necessary to use a strong mechanical force, and of late years the agency of steam has been most commonly employed for this purpose. The blast is carried into an intermediate chamber of a spherical or cylindrical shape, called a regulator; and, as the air is in a state of condensation when admitted, its effort to expand itself again to its natural volume causes the continuous and regular supply to the furnace which is necessary. The air thus forced into the furnace keeps the heat at a degree of intenseness which is indispensable for the smelting of the ore. A most important improvement was made by Mr. Neilson, some years ago, in using the *hot blast* instead of the *cold*, that is, drying and highly heating the air before it is forced into the furnace. This has proved to be the most valuable and economical of all modern inventions in the iron manufacture.

The iron is run from the furnace every twelve hours, by tapping the front of the furnace on a level with the bottom of the hearth. When the furnace is tapped, the metal is allowed to run into channels formed in the sand of the smelting-house floor. The names of *sow-metal* and *pig-metal*, which were originally given by the workmen, signify in one case the blocks of iron which are formed in the large main channels, and in the other case the smaller blocks which are formed in smaller side channels communicating with the larger ones.

The quality of pig-iron varies according to the purposes for which it is intended, and depends not only upon the quality of the ore, but also upon that of the fuel. The principal division is into *foundry-iron* and *forge-iron*, the former being used for castings, the latter for conversion into malleable iron. Foundry-iron is further divided into three qualities, distinguished by the numbers 1, 2, and 3, and differing in the amount of carbon combined, the fluidity when melted, and the hardness when cooled. Forge iron is divided also into three qualities, and is distinguished as *bright iron*, *mottled iron*, and *white iron*, which names are indicative of the appearance which each quality presents to the eye; they have less carbon, less fluidity, and more hardness, than foundry iron.

Forge or bar iron is pig-iron freed from carbon and oxygen. The first operation for producing this change is called *refining*, and is performed in small low furnaces, about three feet square at the base, having the bottom, or hearth, of fire-bricks, and the sides of cast iron, made hollow to allow a stream of water to pass constantly through, which prevents their being quickly burnt away; near the top are holes for the insertion of blast-pipes. The iron is kept in a state of fusion in the refinery for some time exposed to an intense heat produced by a strong blast, and is then run out into a flat mould twenty feet long by two wide, placed over a cistern of water, where it speedily cools into a bright brittle state.

The first process employed for making bars is called *puddling*, and is performed in a *reverberatory* or *puddling furnace*. [FURNACE.] The quantity of refined metal put into this puddling-furnace at each charge is from 3½ to 4 cwt. In about half an hour from the charging of the furnace the metal begins to melt. The puddler then observes, through a small hole provided for that purpose and for the introduction of his tools, the progress of the work. The business of the puddler is so to dispose of the pieces of metal, moving them by means of his tools, as to ensure an equable application of heat to the mass. When the whole quantity is fully melted, the puddler stirs the metal about briskly, changing his tools continually, that they may not be melted. By means of this agitation the metal gives off an elastic fluid, and after a time becomes thick, and grows increasingly so, until it loses all fluidity and forms into lumps. The contents of the furnace are then divided into five or six portions by the puddler, and each is made up by means of his tools into a spherical form. These balls are technically called *blooms*. Being taken from the puddling-furnace, they are subjected each to ten or twenty blows from a heavy hammer (called shingling), or to an intense pressure by a machine called a *squeezer*, which makes them more compact and gives them a shape more convenient for going through the rollers. These rollers consist of two cylinders working in contact, and having on their surfaces a series of grooves, varying in size. The iron is passed through all these grooves in succession, until it is reduced to the requisite width and thickness. It is thus converted from a fusible, hard, and brittle substance, to a tough and elastic bar which is hardly fusible, and which, from its property of yielding and altering its form under the hammer, has acquired the name of malleable iron.

The bars, when they have been passed through these rollers, and while yet hot, are cut into convenient lengths and taken to the balling-furnace, the shape and construction of which resemble those of the puddling furnace. In this balling furnace the bars are piled evenly, so that one bar does not project beyond another. Several of these piles, each of which is composed of five or six bars, are placed at once in the furnace, and when sufficiently heated, so that they will weld together, the piles are taken out separately, and are passed again through rollers similar in construction to those described above, but differing from each other in the form of their orifices and grooves, so that either round or flat or square rods and bars may be produced at the pleasure of the maker, and these, when weighed and put up into bundles, are ready for sale.

The progress of the Iron Manufacture in this country has been astonishing. The quantity of iron made in different years presents the following results :—

1740	..	17,300 tons.
1750	..	22,000 „
1788	..	68,000 „
1796	..	125,000 „
1806	..	250,000 „
1820	..	400,000 „
1830	..	677,417 „
1840	..	1,396,400 „
1848	..	1,998,568 „

The quantity of nearly two million tons in 1848 was thus made up :—

England	..	735,800 tons.
Wales	..	722,800 „
Scotland	..	539,968 „
		1,998,568 tons.

The near approach of Wales to England in produce is remarkable, and shews how rapidly the iron manufacture of South Wales must have been extending.

In 1796 each furnace throughout the kingdom yielded an average produce of about 1000 tons of iron annually; in 1840 the average yield was about 6000 tons: so great have been the improvements in the manufacture. In 1848 the total number of furnaces, in and out of blast, was 623. The price of *bar iron*, at the close of ten successive years, was as follows :—1840, £8½; '41, £6½; '42, £6; '43, £5; '44, £6⅛; '45, £10; '46, £8½; '47, 9½; '48, £5½; '49, £5¼. Best iron, angle iron, rail iron, sheet iron, and hoop iron, all exceed the above prices by 5*s.* to 40*s.* per ton. The highest price of *pig iron* for the last twenty years has been £6¾ per ton; and the lowest about £2.

A few further details of the iron districts will be found under GLASGOW, MERTHYR, STAFFORDSHIRE, WALES, &c.

Our Exports of iron are very large. In 1849 the quantity of Bar, Pig, Bolt, Rod, Wire, Cast, and Wrought iron exported was 772,865 tons; besides iron in the forms of steel, cutlery, hard ware and machinery, to the value of 4,077,151*l.*; making altogether a value of about nine millions sterling.

The various manufactures in which iron or steel are employed to considerable extent are noticed under their proper headings in this work; such as CUTLERY, FILES, NAILS, NEEDLES, SAWS, &c.; see also STEEL MANUFACTURE. We may notice here the modern and very useful form of *galvanized tinned iron*, as prepared under the patent of Messrs. Morewood and Rogers. The sheets are rolled in the usual way, to any required degree of thinness; some are kept in the original flat state; while others are *corrugated*, or brought to the form of alternate ridges and hollows. Both surfaces are covered with a layer of tin by the galvanic process, analogous to those noticed under ELECTRO-METALLURGY. This material, either in the flat or the corrugated form, is used for roofing, ships' bolts and sheathing, carriage roofs, tunnel linings, gutters, pipes, cisterns, chimney pots, cowls, baths, cans, buckets, coal-boxes, stove pipes, and numerous other articles. Temporary houses and stores, made of corrugated iron, are sent out to the colonies and California.

It is to be hoped, and reasonably expected, that every department of a manufacture on which so much of the prosperity of England depends, will be well represented at the approaching Exhibition. Nor is it less to be desired that foreign countries should shew their strength in the same direction.

IRRIGATION. In China and in India, as well as in Egypt, ingenious modes of watering lands have been adopted from the most remote ages. No expense has been thought too great to secure a supply of water, and to distribute it in the most advantageous manner.

The whole art of irrigation may be deduced from two simple rules: first, to give a sufficient supply of water during all the time the plants are growing; and, secondly, never to allow it to accumulate so long as to stagnate. The supply of water must come from natural lakes and rivers, or from artificial wells and ponds, in which it is collected in sufficient quantity to disperse it over a certain surface. As the water must flow over the land, or in channels through it, the supply must be above the level of the land to be irrigated. But there must also be a ready exit for the water, and therefore the land must not be so low as the natural level of the common receptacle of the waters, whether it be a lake or the sea, to which they run.

When there is a considerable fall and a sufficient supply of water, a series of channels may be made, so situated below each other, that the second collects the water which the first has supplied, and in its turn becomes a feeder to irrigate the lower parts of the declivity: a third channel receives the water and distributes it lower down, until the last pours it into the river. This is called *catch-work*, because the water is caught from one channel to another. When the surface to be irrigated is very flat and nearly level, it is necessary to form artificial slopes for the water to run over; the whole of the ground is laid in broad beds, undulating like the waves of the sea; and the water, carried along the ridge of each bed, is allowed to flow down the slopes. When it is intended to form a water-meadow on a surface which is nearly level, the whole of the land is laid in beds about 20 or 30 feet wide, the middle or crown of these beds being on a level with the main feeders, and the bottoms or drains on a level with the lower exit of the water, or a little above it. Grass-seed being sown over these beds, the water may be let on for a very short time, to make them spring. As soon as the grass is two or three inches above ground, a regular flooding may be given and in a very short time the sward will be complete. Instead of sowing seed, tufts of grass cut from old sward may be spread over the newly formed beds, and they will soon cover the ground.

The rules for adjusting the time and mode of irrigation to the growth of the plants are among the studies of practical agriculture.

ISÈRE. This French department has a more than usually varied produce, including wheat, rye, barley, maize, buckwheat, peas and beans, potatoes, fruit of all kind, walnuts, mulberries, almonds, medicinal plants, hemp, &c. Vines are mostly grown in the fertile valleys, trained either to greenwood supports of maple or cherry-tree, or to dry tall poles of chestnut wood; vines thus grown are called high vines (hautins). But on the hill slopes in favourable situations and in the Rhône district, the low vines, as they are called when unsupported, produce a stronger better-keeping wine, and more fitted for transport. The produce of wine in ordinary years is 5 to 6 million gallons, the best of which is produced in the neighbourhood of the Rhône. The mulberry grounds are extensive; the number of trees exceeds a million.

In mineral wealth the department is very rich. Iron, lead, copper, and coal mines are worked; gold and silver mines have been worked, but are now abandoned. In the year 1837 a vein of platina was discovered in the valley of the Drac. Marble, granite, porphyry, gypsum, slate are quarried. Antimony, zinc, cobalt, rock-crystal, vitriol, sulphur are found.

The industrial products consist of sailcloth, table and household linen, gloves, soldiers' uniforms, calicoes, printed cottons, oil, turpentine, liqueurs, and mineral acids. There are iron, copper, and lead foundries, steel works, zinc and copper rolling factories, marble sawing mills, paper and vellum works, naileries, dyehouses, glass-works, cotton yarn manufactories, magnaneries, and silk throwing establishments.

Of the manufacturing towns of this department, *Vienne* is among the most conspicuous. It is one of the principal seats of the woollen manufactures in the south of France; common cloth, pasteboard, soap, leather, glass bottles, paper, chemical products, &c., are also made; and there are establishments for reeling and throwing silk, dye-houses, iron furnaces, steel works, sheet copper and lead works, copper and brass foundries.

ISINGLASS. This remarkable substance, one of the purest kinds of glue, or animal gelatin, is made chiefly in Russia, from the dense membrane which forms the air-bladder of the sturgeon and other fishes of the same family.

1591 cwts. of isinglass were imported in 1848.

ITALY. Brief sketches (for they can only be brief in this work) illustrative of the produce, manufactures, and commerce of this beautiful country, will be found under the names of the chief states and cities which compose the Italian peninsula; such as LOMBARDY, NAPLES, VENICE, &c.

IVORY. This delicate substance, derived from the tusks of elephants, is extensively used for the handles of knives and forks, and for making or embellishing numberless small articles in general use. The principal supplies of elephants' tusks to this country are from the west coast of Africa and from Ceylon. The remaining imports are from the coast of Barbary, the Cape of Good Hope, Madagascar, and Siam. The quantity imported annually is about 5500 cwts., of which about 4500 cwts. are retained for consumption.

The demand for ivory has much increased within the last few years, and the supply can scarcely keep up with it. A great quantity is now brought over by the Peninsular Company's steamers from Alexandria, sometimes as much as 20,000*l.* worth in one cargo. This portion of the trade consists chiefly of wild elephants' tusks which have been shed in the deserts of Arabia, and bought up by the Pacha of Egypt for sale to English buyers.

The teeth and tusks of the elephant, hippopotamus, wild boar, and narwahl, all form ivory of various kinds; though the tusk of the elephant is that which usually goes by the name. Ivory was used for some of the colossal statues of the ancients, especially the far-famed statue of Jupiter by Phidias. Among the moderns, the Chinese show great skill in working ivory, especially in the production of elaborate carvings. Ivory is used for billiard and bagatelle boards; for veneers; for scales connected with mathematical instruments; for artificial teeth; for miniature tablets; for combs; for flutes; and for numerous other purposes. Ivory is worked into form by saws, files, and edge-tools, used with great care and delicacy. It may be etched by using an etching ground of nearly the same kind as that employed by engravers; and it may be stained or dyed of various colours.

Mr. Cheverton in 1850 patented a mode of making what he terms artificial ivory. It consists in giving an ivory-like surface to gypsum or alabaster. The ornaments or other articles made of this material, are exposed for forty-eight hours to a temperature of 300° Fah., by which the moisture is driven off. They are then immersed till saturated in olive oil or in white hard varnish; and after being steeped several times in warm water, they are polished with whiting or putty powder, by which they obtain an ivory-like surface.

J

JACQUARD LOOM. The Jacquard Loom, or more correctly Jacquard appendage to the loom, is the most beautiful of all contrivances connected with weaving. We will say a few words of the inventor and of the machine.

Joseph Marie Jacquard was born at Lyon in 1752, of humble parents, both of whom were employed in operations connected with weaving. His parents died, leaving him a small property, which he employed in the attempt to establish a business in the weaving of figured fabrics. The undertaking failed, and he was compelled to sell his looms in order to pay his debts. He subsequently married, and occupied himself with ingenious schemes for improvements in weaving, cutlery, and type-founding, which produced nothing for the support of his family. In 1792 he assisted in the defence of Lyon against the army of the Convention. Being denounced after the reduction of Lyon, he was compelled to fly. When he was enabled to return, and Lyon began to rise from its ruins, Jacquard applied himself with renewed energy to the perfection of the beautiful apparatus for figured weaving which bears his name. He had conceived the idea of such an apparatus as early as 1790, and he now succeeded, though but imperfectly, in accomplishing his end. His machine was presented, in September 1801, to the national exposition of the products of industry, the jury of which awarded him a bronze medal for its invention. In the same year he obtained a patent, or 'brevet d'invention,' for a term of ten years. About the same time his attention was accidentally directed to the construction of a machine for weaving nets for fishing and maritime purposes. He accomplished the desired object, but, having amused himself and his friends with his contrivance, he threw it aside. His machine-made net however fell into the hands of the préfet at Lyon, and the result was that, according to the arbitrary fashion of the time, he and his machine were placed under arrest and conveyed to Paris, where the invention was submitted to inspectors, amongst whom were Napoleon and Carnot, and a gold medal was awarded to him in February 1804. In 1804 Jacquard returned to Lyon, where he was long engaged in superintending the introduction of his inventions for figured weaving and for making nets, in which he was powerfully aided by Camille Pernon, a rich manufacturer. For some years Jacquard had to struggle against much opposition and prejudice on the part of the Lyonese weavers; but before his death, in 1834, he had the pleasure of knowing that his ingenious invention had become extensively employed.

The apparatus which cost Jacquard so much thought and anxiety is intended to facilitate the weaving of figured patterns on cloth of any kind. In plain weaving the weft or cross threads pass alternately under and over the warp threads, forming a perfectly regular interlacing; but in pattern or figure weaving, the device is made by irregularities in these alternations; sometimes two or more threads are crossed over at one time, without any intermediate under-crossing. When the shuttle with the weft thread has to be thrown from edge to edge of the warp or web, some of the warp threads have to be lifted up to allow it to pass; and the Jacquard apparatus assists in this elevation, which depends (in every throw of the shuttle) on the pattern to be woven. There are numerous cards (as many as 500 for a complicated pattern), formed of pasteboard, and pierced with holes. Every card has a certain relation to one throw of the weft-thread; and the number and arrangement of the holes determine which warp threads shall be drawn up to let the weft pass. The cards are linked together into an endless chain, which is passed over a hollow box at the top of the loom. The chain is made to rotate slowly, one movement for every weft thread thrown; and each card in turn acts upon a series of levers by which the warp threads are raised: the blank part of each card acts upon the levers; while the perforated parts allow the levers to pass into the holes without being affected.

Mr. Mackenzie has recently patented a machine for punching the holes in the Jacquard cards. Hitherto this operation has required two workmen; one to 'read the pattern,' as it is termed, and one to arrange the punches; but in Mr. Mackenzie's arrangement, the person who reads off the pattern plays at the same time on a set of keys, each of which inserts a punch into its proper place.

An ingenious variation of the Jacquard apparatus has lately been patented, in which the device is marked by pins on a rotating barrel, instead of by holes in a chain of cards. The principle is the same as that of the barrel organ and the musical snuff-box; and there would seem to be no reason why it should not apply efficiently to the weaving apparatus.

JAGGERY. This is the name given to various kinds of sugar, made and used in the east. It is procured by evaporating and granulating cocoa-nut toddy, Palmyra toddy, Malabar toddy, and Mysore toddy—toddy being a general name for the fermented juice of the palm. Ten gallons of the toddy yield nearly thirty lbs. of jaggery.

JALAP, is obtained from the *Convolvulus Jalappa*, an American plant. It is chiefly shipped from Vera Cruz, and takes its name from the town of Xalapa, or Jalapa, in the interior. The large root, which often weighs 50 pounds, is divided into portions, which are hung in nets over a fire, and dried in ten or twelve days. It occurs in commerce in irregular round or pear-shaped masses, which, when good, are dry, hard, with a brown shining fracture, resinous, not light, somewhat tough. It is often adulterated with portions of the root of white bryony, which however are white, or when old, gray, not heavy, very brittle, fracture not resinous, spongy, without smell, but with a very bitter taste. Dried pears are also often substituted for it; but they may be detected by being laid open, when the core will be seen, containing the seeds.

Jalap is a well-known and powerful medicine; but it is not used, so far as we are aware, in other arts. 68,829 lbs. of Jalap were imported in 1848.

JAMAICA. The staple produce of this the most important of our West India Islands, are sugar, rum, and molasses, which form by far the most important articles of export. The sugar plantations are very numerous and extensive, especially in the lower and warmer tracts of the island. On the hills and their declivities coffee is cultivated to a great extent. Next to these the pimento plantations supply the most important article of export. Arrowroot, indigo, (which formerly was much more cultivated than at present,) ginger, turmeric, and cacao are also cultivated, as also a little tobacco. Indian corn is universally cultivated, and yields an abundant produce; two and even three crops of it can be raised within the year. Guinea corn is cultivated, as are also yams, cassava, sweet potatoes, a few grasses, and a great variety of delicious fruits. The forests contain mahogany, satinwood, cedar, fustic, logwood, bamboo, cocoa, and various other trees.

The horned cattle are very numerous. The horses are of a middle size, hardy and active, but only fitted for the saddle and harness. Mules are numerous, and employed on the sugar estates. Sheep, goats, and hogs abound.

All kinds of poultry are raised in the greatest abundance, excepting geese and ducks.

The greatest part of the produce of the southern districts is sent to *Kingston*, the chief town, and hence exported to Europe or America. A railway from Kingston to Spanish Town was completed and opened in 1846.

The abolition of slavery, and (twelve years afterwards) the change in the sugar duties, have greatly shaken the prosperity of Jamaica. It was so essentially a protected slave-holding state, that, being now left to its own resources, it is found wanting in the energy which free labour and free competition engender. Its sugar plantations have fallen away, and much of its commerce has gone to Cuba. Attempts are, however, now being made to establish, or rather to increase, the cotton culture. Specimens have been sent to England within the last twelve months, illustrating the kind of cotton which Jamaica is capable of growing. The great experiment has, however, yet to be made: can free-grown cotton be raised as cheaply as slave-grown? Almost the whole of the cotton (nine-tenths at least) used in this country, is slave-grown: if Jamaica can raise good cotton by free labour, and derive a remunerating profit therefrom, it would be a great result.

The British Produce and Manufactures exported to Jamaica in 1849 amounted in value to 624,568*l*.

JANEIRO, RIO DE, the capital of the empire of Brazil, has perhaps the finest, safest, and most capacious harbour in the world. Most of the inhabitants are engaged in commerce. There are numerous sugar refineries, tanneries, cotton factories, rum distilleries, train-oil factories, and diamond-cutting establishments. The commerce is extensive, and on the increase. The principal exports are coffee, sugar, hides, rice, tobacco, rum, tapioca, ipecacuanha, manioc flour, gold, diamonds, &c. The quantity of coffee exported is immense: amounting in some years to nearly 200 million of lbs. The imports, more than one-half of which in value are derived from Great Britain, include cotton, woollen, linen, and silk manufactures, wines, ironmongery, flour, meat, fish, butter, spirits, earthenware, paper, &c.

JAPAN. This remote Asiatic Empire is almost unknown to us. It is certain, however, from the scanty information obtained, that agriculture is carried to a high degree of perfection in Japan. Nearly all the declivities of the hills are formed into terraces, and these terraces are cultivated with the utmost care. The produce comprises rice, wheat, barley, rye, maize, millet, batatas, potatoes, cotton, silk, hemp, and a very great variety of fruits and esculent vegetables. Japan abounds in mineral wealth. Gold seems to be very plentiful in several provinces, but is only partially worked. Silver, iron, and tin exist in small quantities; copper is more plentiful. Salt and porcelain clay abound. The Japanese, in manufacturing industry and in scientific knowledge, seem to be nearly equal to the Chinese, and in some articles the Japanese are superior. Their manufactures in metals, silk, cotton, china, glass, and paper, and their cabinet-work, are highly esteemed. The inland trade is very considerable. The coasting trade is much favoured by the great number of small harbours, and the interior communication by well-planned and well-maintained roads, which are always thronged with carriages and people. The foreign commerce is chiefly with the Chinese.

How many ages will elapse before Japan will take part in any Exhibition of Industry, where other nations (not to say all nations) will be represented, it would be difficult to surmise. At present the Japanese go beyond even the Chinese, in rejecting intercourse with foreigners.

JAPANNING is the art of producing a highly varnished surface on wood, metal, or other hard substance, sometimes of one colour only, but more commonly figured and ornamented. The process has received its name from that of the island of Japan, whence articles so varnished were first brought to Europe; though the manufacture is also extensively practised by the Chinese, Siamese, Birmese, and other nations of eastern Asia, among whom it was suggested most probably by the possession of a tree, which affords with little preparation a beautiful varnish, exceedingly well adapted for the purpose, and which hardens better than those prepared in Europe.

The appearance of japanned work is as various as the taste and fancy of the artists employed in it. Sometimes it is a plain black or red, with a gilded or painted border; or it is an imitation of marble, of fine grained or rare wood, or of tortoise-shell; sometimes a drawing, with high finish, brilliant colour, and showy patterns; and occasionally fine copperplate engravings are applied to a japanned surface with good effect. In all cases the work is highly polished and varnished. Japanning is applied to ladies' work-boxes and work-tables, to toilet-boxes, cabinets, tea-caddies, fire-screens, tea-trays, bread-baskets, snuffers and trays, candlesticks, and a variety of other articles.

Three processes are usually required in

japanning: laying the ground, painting, and finishing. In addition to these processes, whenever the article to be japanned is not sufficiently smooth to receive the varnish, or when it is too soft or coarse, it is sometimes prepared or primed before any of the proper japanning processes are applied. Almost every workman has his own peculiar modes of working, and his own receipts for making and mixing his varnishes. In whatever manner the work has been painted or printed, or if all addition to the plain colour of the ground has been dispensed with, nothing now remains but the finishing. This is a very simple process: the workman chooses a suitable varnish, and passes it over the work with a brush several times, until he judges the coating to be thick enough to bear the polish.

JASPAR. [Quartz.]

JAVA. This large and important island, in the Eastern Archipelago, yields abundantly the yam, the sweet potato, the Java potato, arrowroot, the common potato, artichokes, cabbages, and peas. The Javanese also cultivate cucumbers, onions, capsicums, cocoa-nuts, ground-nuts, Areca palm, betel, tobacco, coffee, sugar, pepper, cardamom, ginger, cotton, and great varieties of dye-stuffs, and fruits. They procure oil from many of their trees, and make toddy from the palm. Few minerals are known to exist in Java; but iron, sulphur, salt, and saltpetre are obtained.

Java is extremely well adapted for an extensive commerce. The island itself is rich in productions, and its northern coasts, which are accessible to vessels all the year round, lie opposite the richest countries of Asia. Besides this, the Dutch government has made it the centre of all the trade which Holland carries on with its extensive settlements in the Indian Archipelago. Hence the transmission of native produce to other countries, and the importation of foreign commodities, are both very large. The exports of British produce and manufactures to Java, in 1848 amounted to 336,843*l*., of which by far the largest items were cotton and linen goods. The produce of the Dutch possessions in Java was in 1848—coffee 144,861,372 lbs., sugar 112,000 tons, indigo 1,151,368 lbs., cochineal 146,000 lbs., tea 988,529 lbs., pepper 461,680 lbs., cinnamon 250,550 lbs., tobacco 1,500,000 lbs. In the year 1828, the island supplied Great Britain with only 15,000 tons of sugar; in 1847, the quantity of sugar imported from Java into Great Britain amounted to 75,000 tons.

JERSEY. The agriculture of Jersey is backward, which is partly owing to the minute subdivision of property, arising from the custom of gavelkind. Wheat is the principal grain crop; barley is grown, and some oats, parsnips are extensively grown and used for fattening hogs and bullocks. Potatoes for exportation are widely and increasingly cultivated. Lucerne is one of the most valued crops. A considerable portion of the land is laid out in orchards. The trade of Jersey, owing to the privileges possessed by the islanders, is very considerable. The agricultural produce of the island, potatoes, apples, cider, butter, cows, and other live stock, are sent to England; the articles required for the consumption of the island are in a considerable degree supplied from France.

JEWELLING OF WATCHES is the art of setting diamonds, rubies, sapphires, chrysolites, or other hard stones, in the frame-plates and other parts of watches, in such a manner that the pivots of the watch may act in holes made in these stones. The province of the watch-jeweller is to select the stones, and (except in the case of diamonds) to grind, polish, turn, drill, and set them into the frames or other parts of the watch in such a manner that the holes in the stones may correspond exactly in position with holes previously made by the watch-finisher or escapement-maker. Jewelling is an operation which, when well performed, adds materially to the durability, and not a little to the elegance of the machine. The apparatus necessary for the jeweller to carry on his business are, a small lathe: small gravers for turning brass and steel; a quantity of rough diamond in fragments, technically termed *bort;* small mills or circular disks of metal (usually copper) for grinding the stones into shape; diamond-powder of various degrees of fineness for polishing; and turning-tools, made by cementing small pieces of bort into a notch made in the end of small brass wires and fixed in proper handles.

JEW'S-HARP. This simple musical instrument consists of an iron frame, resembling in form the handle part of an old fashioned corkscrew, in the centre of the upper and wide part of which is riveted at one end an elastic steel tongue. The extremity of this tongue, at the free end, is bent outwards to a right angle, so as to allow the finger easily to strike it when the instrument is placed to the mouth and firmly supported by the pressure of the parallel extremities of the frame against the teeth. The action of this instrument is very remarkable; the elastic spring gives the sound by its vibrations; but this sound undergoes musical modifications by varying the cavity of the mouth of the performer, which he does by slight movements of the lips and jaws. The late M. Eulenstein produced exquisite music from this instrument.

JOINERY. This name is given to the handicraft of joining pieces of wood together, for the interior fittings of buildings, for making articles of furniture, and for numerous purposes requiring greater neatness of workmanship than the operations of the carpenter. As carpentry and joinery are in many cases carried on in the same establishment, and even by the same workmen, it would be difficult accurately to define the limits of these two kindred arts. The proper object of carpenter's work in a building is to give firmness and stability to the structure; and within its proper range may be embraced all the rough timber-work necessary for the support, division, or connection of the several parts of a building. Carpentry thus includes the construction of the framing of floors, partitions, and roofs. Joinery has for its object the addition of all the fixed woodwork necessary for convenience or ornament. Cabinet-making, or that department of woodwork which relates to the making of furniture, has little affinity with joinery, although the same materials and tools are employed in both descriptions of work. The line of demarcation, however, between joinery and cabinet-making seems to be even more difficult to define than that between carpentry and joinery; and, with the exception of such matters as veneering and polishing, which relate only to the use of the harder and more valuable woods, the operations of the cabinet-maker and the joiner are nearly identical, the same means being adopted by both for the production of heat and strong joints, and for evading the injurious effects of shrinkage and warping in the material operated upon. A few details on these subjects will be found under CARPENTRY; FURNITURE MANUFACTURE.

JUNIPER. There are about twenty species of this plant, three or four of which are valuable in the arts and in medicine. The *Common Juniper* grows wild in all the northern parts of Europe. The fruit is used in considerable quantities in the preparation of gin, and in medicine. *Oil of Juniper* is said to be the most powerful of all diuretics in doses of four drops. The *Juniperus Sabina*, or *Savin*, is found wild in the middle of Europe and the west of Asia, inhabiting the most sterile soil, and is frequently met with in this country in shrubberies. The *Oil of Savin*, and other preparations of the plant, are powerful medicines. The *Juniperus Bermudiana*, or *Bermuda Red Cedar*, is very little known in Great Britain, in consequence of its not bearing the climate without protection. It is a native of the Bermudas, where it becomes a large tree, with a soft fragrant wood, the value of which is well known from its use in cabinet work and the manufacture of pencils.

JURA. On the more elevated parts of this mountainous department of France, there is abundant pasture, on which during summer, from June to October, great numbers of cattle and horses are fed. During that season the châlets, or solidly constructed huts, on the heights, serve as habitations for the herds, stores for the dairy produce, and as sheds for the cattle; in these the cows are milked, butter and cheese are make. There is one herdsman for every 20 cows, and one cheese-maker for every 80. The agricultural produce of the department is barely enough for the consumption. The produce of wine amounts to about 8,000,000 gallons annually, the best growths being those of the districts about Arbois, Château-Chalon, and Lons-le-Saulnier. Several iron mines are worked; gold, copper, lead, and coal are found; the peat beds are dug for fuel; marble, alabaster, and lithographic stone are quarried. There are important salt-works at Salins and Montmorot. The manufacture of iron and iron wares, carried on in about a hundred smelting furnaces, forges, and foundries, is the most important object of industrial activity. The other manufactures are paper, watch and clock works; turnery in wood, bone, ivory, and horn; coarse woollens, linen, mineral acids, salt, casks, steel, scythes, nails of all kinds, tiles and leather.

K

KALEIDOSCOPE. This beautiful optical instrument was invented by Dr. (Sir David) Brewster, and made public in 1817. The essential parts of the instrument consist of two plane mirrors of glass, having their hinder surfaces blackened in order to prevent any reflection of light from thence. Each mirror is from six to ten inches long, and of a trapezoidal form; the larger end about an inch and a half wide, and the shorter end about three quarters of an inch; and the two are placed in contact with one another at the wide end of each, so as to form a dihedral angle, the like ends being placed together. The object to be viewed is disposed contiguously to the larger ends, and the eye should be near the opposite extremity, but a little above the line of contact. The effect produced by the reflections of the light from the two surfaces is singularly beautiful; the objects viewed undergo multiplied reflections, and assume graceful symmetrical forms. Sir David Brewster found means to obtain multiplied images of such objects as flowers, trees, and even persons or things in motion: and thus the importance of the instrument was greatly increased. Some kaleidoscopes have been executed in such a manner that the two mirrors may be placed at any required angle with one another; by which means the images in the visible field of view may be varied at pleasure. The instrument is capable also of being constructed so that the multiplied image may be projected on a screen, and thus made visible at one time to many spectators. Again, Dr. Roget has shown that the properties of the instrument may be greatly extended by employing, instead of two, three and even four plain mirrors, united together at their edges so as to form a hollow prism, or a frustum of a pyramid, the reflecting surfaces being towards the interior. These are called polycentral kaleidoscopes.

KAMTCHATKA. In this remote corner of Asia there are a few spots which yield rye, barley, buckwheat, potatoes, white cabbages, turnips, radishes, and cucumbers, but these articles are only cultivated by the Russian settlers. The natives formerly lived chiefly on the produce of the chase; but since the number of wild animals has considerably decreased fishing is more attended to. Fish is very abundant on the coasts. The forests contain many fine timber-trees, which are little used, but might be employed in ship-building. The mineral wealth is little known: in some places there is iron ore, and sulphur in immense beds is found in the vicinity of the volcanoes. The manufactures and commerce of such a country are of course extremely limited.

KAOLIN. This is the Chinese *porcelain clay*. It occurs massive and disseminated in disintegrating granite rocks, and is generally supposed to be derived from the decomposition of the felspar which they contain. Its colour is either white, yellowish, or reddish-white. Kaolin is found in China, France, Saxony, &c.; and in England a large tract of this substance occurs near St. Austle in Cornwall, on the south side of the granite range. It contains crystals of felspar, quartz, and mica. From this source the porcelain manufactory of Worcester is supplied.

KELP. [Ashes; Soda.]

KENT. This fruitful county is well circumstanced in respect both to commerce and its productions. It has a most abundant steam traffic from Dover, Deal, Ramsgate, Margate, Herne Bay, Sheerness, Gravesend, Greenhithe, Erith, Woolwich, Charlton, and Greenwich, to London; from Rochester to Sheerness; from Ramsgate and Dover to Ostend; from Dover to Calais and Boulogne; and from Folkestone to Boulogne. The whole of the railways of the county belong to one company—the South-Eastern. They comprise lines from Red Hill to Ashford; Ashford to Hastings; Ashford to Dover; Ashford to Canterbury; Canterbury to Ramsgate and Margate; Canterbury to Whitstable; Minster to Deal; Paddock Wood to Maidstone; Tunbridge to Tunbridge Wells (now being extended to Hastings); the Greenwich and Bricklayers' Arms' Branches; and the North Kent line (London to the Medway).

Kent produces several crops which are peculiar to it, such as canary and radish seed. Other seeds are likewise raised for the London seedsmen, such as spinach, cresses, and white mustard. Kidney beans are cultivated to a considerable amount in the neighbourhood of Sandwich, and produce from ten to twenty bushels per acre. Woad and madder were formerly much cultivated. The marshes produce most of the hay consumed in winter. Romney Marsh, which is well known for the richness of its grass, contains about 44,000 acres; on the borders of the Stour are 27,000; and along the Medway, Thames, and Swale, about 11,500 more. A great many sheep are reared and fattened in these marshes. Hops are grown to a very great extent in this county, and, with the exception of those which are raised at Farnham in Surrey, are the most esteemed of any in England. Near London there are many extensive gardens; and about Deptford hundreds of acres are laid out in asparagus beds. Great quantities of peas are also raised for the London market on the line of road from London to Rochester. Apples, pears, plums, and cherries are raised in orchards, and the produce sent to London markets. The cultivation of filberts is peculiar to Kent, and well managed, especially in the neighbourhood of Maidstone. The Kentish woods are diminishing every year; and the produce of bark and timber is much reduced from what it formerly was.

Ashford is becoming an important town in this county, on account of it being the depôt of the South-Eastern Company. CHATHAM, DARTFORD, and DOVER are briefly alluded to elsewhere. *Folkestone* harbour, owing to the accumulation of shingle, is not capable of affording anchorage to many vessels, but has been considerably improved by the engineers of the South-Eastern Railway Company, who purchased it when they extended the line of railway from Folkestone to Dover. Steam-packets ply between Folkestone and the opposite ports of France; and the town is acquiring commercial importance. *Gravesend* and *Greenwich* are both important for their steamboat traffic. *Maidstone*, the assize-town of the county, is situated on a declivity on the west bank of the Medway. A lock has been made at Allington, about a mile below Maidstone, to improve the navigation of the river, previous to the formation of which the tide ascended to Maidstone. There is much traffic on the river, in coals, timber, iron, groceries, &c., upwards, and in Kentish ragstone, paper, hops, fruit, &c., downwards. *Margate* and *Ramsgate* have much active commerce arising out of their pleasure-traffic. *Milton* has considerable trade, arising from its oyster fishery, and from its being the port of communication with London for the surrounding agricultural district. At *Sheerness* the dockyard is sufficiently capacious to receive ships of war of the largest size. There are large storehouses, a mast-house, rigging-house, sail-loft, &c. At *Tunbridge Wells* there are considerable manufactures in turned wood. At *Whitstable* the inhabitants are engaged in the oyster fishery. *Woolwich* derives its main importance from its dockyard, from the government foundry for cannon having been established there, and from its having been made a great depôt for naval and military stores. The Royal Dockyard contains two large dry docks, a basin 400 feet by 300 feet, capable of receiving the largest vessels, together with extensive storehouses, mast-houses, &c. The foundry for cannon forms one of the principal departments of the Royal Arsenal. In the Rope-yard, at the east end of the town, cables of the largest size are made.

KENTUCKY. The produce and manufactures of this important American state receive a few illustrations under UNITED STATES.

KERMES MINERAL is a peculiar sulphuret of antimony, formerly much but now little used in medicine. It is obtained in the form of a brownish red powder.

KERRY. Mountain ridges, bounding valleys of greater or less width, form the distinguishing features over the greater part of this Irish county. The whole coast line, from the Shannon to the Kenmare, contains many good harbours, of which that of Valentia might be made of high commercial value. The roads in the south-western parts of Kerry up to the year 1820 were scarcely passable for wheel-carriages, and there are some parts of the coast between Kenmare and Cahirciveen still inaccessible, except on foot or horseback. But great exertions have been made to establish good roads across the county; and these roads have been very instrumental in developing the resources of the district. The mountains of Glanbehy abound with iron-ore, which was formerly smelted in considerable quantities at Blackstones, in works erected by Sir William Petty; but, the supply of timber having failed, these works were given up about the year 1750. Iron has been worked in other parts, and copper and lead also exist in the county. The slate quarry in Valentia produces flags and slates to a large amount; the flagging, which is of a very superior description, is transported to London.

Cider is made in the county in considerable quantity. The chief trade consists in exports of agricultural produce, chiefly oats and butter. The manufacture of linen is carried on with some activity in the neighbourhood of Dingle. There is also a general manufacture of coarse woollens throughout the county for home consumption. Fishing is carried on extensively on the coasts.

Situated in the south-west corner of Ireland, it may yet be a long time before Kerry rises into commercial importance; it has however many of the requisite elements, when more propitious days for Ireland shall arrive.

KERSEYMERE. In the woollen manufacture, *broad-cloth* is an example of plain weaving, followed by the process of fulling; while the name of *kerseymere* is given to a fulled cloth which is woven into the peculiar *twill* pattern. These differences are explained under WEAVING.

KETCHUP. This well-known preparation from the mushroom and other plants used as a condiment for flavouring, differs greatly in its ingredients and manufacture, according to the chief substance which gives it its name. There are camp ketchup, cucumber ketchup, sea ketchup, mushroom ketchup, Pontac ketchup, Tomato ketchup, walnut ketchup, wine ketchup, and two or three others. Mushroom ketchup is prepared (according to one among many recipes) from mushroom juice, pimento, cloves, pepper, mustard, ginger, salt, and shalots.

KEY. [LOCKS and KEYS.]

KHERSON. In this province of Asiatic Russia agriculture is in a backward state; the breeding of cattle and sheep is the chief occupation of the population. Corn, hemp, flax, tobacco, liquorice, saffron, and mustard are grown. The vine is cultivated, and much attention is paid to horticulture. Oxen and buffaloes are numerous, and used for draught. The fisheries on the sea-coast and in the rivers are important. The minerals are—fine potter's clay, freestone, slate, chalk, talc, saltpetre, agates, and garnets. The province is well situated for trade; and the foreign commerce of the country is very important and rapidly increasing.

KIACHTA, a town in Siberia, is commercially very important on account of the traffic of this place with *Maimaitchin*, the Chinese emporium, which is less than a mile from the town. The Russians bring to Kiachta furs of the sable, black fox, and ermine; hides, woollen cloth, and other coarse woollen fabrics; glass, looking-glasses, and cattle. They receive in return from the Chinese, manufactured silk and cottons, tobacco, china, furniture, and several kinds of toys; but the principal commodity taken in exchange is tea.

KIDDERMINSTER CARPETS. The relation which the carpets so called bear to other varieties is explained under CARPET MANUFACTURE. Kidderminster mostly depends on its carpet trade; and the manufacturers have sent specimens of their skill to the Great Exhibition, of carpets, tapestry, and rugs.

KILDARE. This Irish county, in the districts near the Liffey, is in a high state of cultivation, and much of it in demesne. The Grand Canal, which crosses the Liffey by an aqueduct near Naas, is carried through a tract of bog which comprises about 40,000 statute acres of peat-moss, in some places 40 feet deep, reposing on limestone gravel, which rises in low cultivable ridges between the principal fields of morass. The north-western part of the county, extending from the Bog of Allen to the Boyne, is open and chiefly in pasture. Portions of the Great Southern and Western Railway, and the Midland Great Western Railway, pass through this county. The soil of the county is generally a rich loam, resting on limestone or clay-slate. There are rich fattening lands in the baronies of Carberry, Clane, and North and South Salt, which occupy the north western and north eastern portions of the county. An improved system of agriculture has been introduced by the resident proprietors, and is practised to some extent by the smaller farmers. Oxen are in general use both for draught and the plough. There are many corn-mills in the county. The only manufactures carried on within the county are of cottons and woollens, but to a very limited extent.

KILKENNY. We here have another Irish county, which, like Kildare, is wholly inland. The surface of Kilkenny is mostly occupied by the limestone of the central plain, overlaid in the hilly districts north of Kilkenny city by shale and sandstone. The coal formations are nearly co-extensive with the hilly districts. These coal-beds would be of great commercial value, if the natural resources of Ireland were better developed. The general colour of the limestone is a blueish gray. Near Kilkenny it passes into a fine black marble, containing a great variety of shelly impressions. These beds are extensively quarried, and the blocks dressed on the spot by a saw-mill driven by the Nore. The marble, which is sometimes procured of a jet black, is manufactured into chimney-pieces, tombstones, &c.; it bears a very high polish, and can be raised in large blocks. In the coal-tract the soil is a moory turf lying over a stiff whitish clay, which is the poorest district out of the mountain region; but many districts have deep rich soils. Some of the best wheat and meadow lands in the south of Ireland are situated in the level tract along the Suir. About one-third of the level districts is in tillage. There are two districts almost wholly occupied by dairy-farmers, the Walsh Mountains and the southern part of the Castlecomer tract. In the southern dairy district the sour milk is used for fattening pigs for the Waterford market: in the northern district the milk is sold, there being no convenient market for pork.

The manufacture of carpets, diapers, and tapestry was introduced into the county by the Countess of Ormonde in 1359. James, Duke of Ormonde, about the middle of the 17th century, established and encouraged, at a great expense, both linen and woollen manufactures; and about the close of the same century the Bessborough family introduced the manufacture of linen into the southern parts of the county. None of these branches of trade, however, nor that of blankets, introduced about a century ago, have continued on anything like an extensive scale. A coarse frieze for home consumption is made among the peasantry. There are many flour-mills in the county.

KINIC ACID, sometimes called Cinchonic Acid, is obtained from cinchona bark. It has a very sour taste; it reddens litmus paper strongly, is unalterable in the air, dissolves in 2½ times its weight of water at 48°, and is also soluble in alcohol. It combines with many of the alkalies and metals to form salts, which are more used in medicine than in the manufacturing arts.

KINO. This astringent substance is the concrete juice of one or more plants, the identification of which is a matter of dispute among botanists. From India, Africa, Australia, and the West Indies, concrete juices are brought, which, correctly or not, obtain the name of Kino. These different extracts differ in their chemical habitudes with reagents, but they all agree in possessing a strong astringent power. Kino most commonly occurs in grains of a shining aspect and rich ruby-red colour; they are easily reduced to powder. It is nearly entirely soluble in water and in alcohol.

KNIFE MACHINES. The manufacture of knives is noticed under CUTLERY. It affords a curious illustration of the extent to which the saving of labour by mechanical aid has been carried, that a machine has been invented to perform the operation of cleaning table-knives; in which the cleaner has simply to turn a handle, instead of bestowing arm-movement in a somewhat laborious way. There are two rival patented machines for this purpose, Kent's and Masters'; both relate to a machine which was invented by an American, and was introduced into this country, under certain arrangements, by the parties above-named. The machine consists of a flat cylinder, or drum, in the inside of which are brushes placed in contact; holes are made round the drum, in which are placed from four to twelve knives, according to the size of the machine. The blades of the knives pass between the brushes; and when the brushes are made to rotate by a handle worked from without, the blades of the knives are exposed to an amount of friction sufficient to clean their surfaces. The machines are sold from about two guineas upwards.

KÖNIGSBERG, one of the two governments into which the province of East Prussia is divided, is a place of considerable commercial enterprise. *Memel*, the most northern town in Prussia, is well situated for commerce: the exports consist of timber, hemp, flax, corn, hides, tallow, bristles, &c., most of which are brought from Poland and Russia; the imports are chiefly salt, colonial produce, and manufactured goods. The number of ships that frequent the port amounts to between 700 and 800. In the town there are several breweries, distilleries, soap factories, oil and saw mills, &c. *Tilsit* has a trade in corn, linseed, timber, beer, spirits, leather, &c. *Insterburg* has manufactures of cloth, linen, woollen stockings, and spirits, and trades extensively in corn and flax. *Gumbinnen* has woollen and linen factories, distilleries, and tanyards; the trade in corn and flax-seed is important. *Königsberg*, the capital of the province, has communication by the Friedrichs-Gruben Canal with the Memel, by which river, the Oginski Canal, and the Dnieper, it has the advantage of a complete interior navigation into Poland, Lithuania, and even to the Black Sea. The manufactures consist of woollen cloth, linen, silk, leather, tobacco, sugar, beer, and spirits. The exports are composed of corn, flax-seed, flax, hemp, linen yarn, linen cloth, oil cakes, bristles, feathers, and hides. The imports are chiefly sugar, coffee, spices, dyewoods, tobacco, salt, various raw materials and manufactured goods.

L

LABORATORY. This name is given to the room in which chemical operations are performed. The requisites for the proper arrangement of and the necessary instruments for a laboratory may be seen at length in Professor Faraday's 'Chemical Manipulation.'

LAC, is a resinous substance, which in the East Indies flows from certain trees in the state of a milky fluid, on account of the puncture made by a small insect, the *Coccus ficus*, in their branches, in order to deposit its ova. The trees are principally the *Ficus indica*, *Ficus religiosa*, and *Rhamnus jujuba*. There are three kinds of lac known in commerce, distinguished by the names of *Stick Lac*, *Seed Lac*, and *Shell Lac*. Stick Lac is the substance in its natural state; it is of a reddish colour, and incrusts small twigs; when broken off and boiled in water, it loses its red colour, and is then termed Seed Lac; and, when melted and reduced to the state of thin plates, it is called Shell Lac, which has a yellowish brown colour.

Several chemical substances are produced from Lac. *Laccin* is the substance which remains after the lac has been repeatedly digested in alcohol and water. It is insoluble in water, alcohol or ether. *Laccic Acid* separates from solution in water, by spontaneous evaporation, in crystalline grains. With the alkalies and with lime it forms salts which are soluble in alcohol and in water, and are deliquescent. *Cochinellin*, or the colouring matter of stick-lac is similar to that of cochineal, is used for the same purposes, and yields a scarlet colour little inferior to it.

Lac Dye and *Lac Lake*, two preparations of lac which are manufactured in the East Indies are used to a very considerable extent in scarlet dyeing.

LACE MANUFACTURE. This very pleasing branch of industry exhibits instructive features in respect to the application of machinery to what was before mere hand-labour. We must glance at the subject in its two aspects of *pillow-lace* and *bobbin-net*.

Pillow Lace:—Real lace, such as that which often obtains so high a price, is mostly made of flax thread, and is produced in the following way. The lace-worker sits on a stool or chair, and places a hard cushion on her lap. The desired pattern is sketched upon a piece of parchment, which is then laid down upon the cushion; and she inserts a number of pins through the parchment into the cushion, in places determined by the pattern. She is also provided with a number of small bobbins, on which threads are wound; fine thread being used for making the meshes or net; and a coarser kind, called gymp, for working the device. The work is begun at the upper part of the cushion by tying together the threads in pairs, and each pair is attached to one of the pins. The threads are then twisted one round another in various ways, according to the pattern; the bobbins serving as handles as well as for a store of material, and the pins serving as knots or fixed centres around which the threads may be twisted. The pins inserted in the cushion at the commencement are merely to hold the threads; but as fast as each little mesh is made in the progress of the working, other pins are inserted, to prevent the thread from untwisting; and the device on the parchment shews where these insertions are to occur.

The kinds of lace which have obtained different names have certain peculiarities in the character of the mesh. *Brussels point* has a network made by the pillow and bobbins, and a pattern of sprigs worked with the needle. *Brussels ground* has a six-sided mesh, formed by twisting four flaxen threads to a perpendicular line of mesh. *Brussels wire-ground* is of silk; the meshes are partly straight and partly arched, and the pattern is wrought separately by the needle. *Mechlin lace* has a six-sided mesh formed of three flax threads twisted and plaited to a perpendicular line: the pattern being worked in the net. *Valenciennes lace* has a six-sided mesh formed of two threads, partly twisted and plaited: the pattern being worked in the net. *Lisle lace* has a diamond-shaped mesh, formed of two threads plaited to a perpendicular line. *Alençon lace* has a six sided mesh of two threads. *Alençon point* is formed of two threads to a perpendicular line, with octagonal and square meshes alternately. *Honiton* lace is distinguished by the beauty of the devices, worked by the needle. *Buckingham* lace is mostly of a commoner description, and somewhat resembles that of Alençon.

Pillow lace, such as we have just described, is supposed to have been first made in Saxony in the 16th century: the earlier Italian lace having been wrought by the needle. From Saxony it extended to Flanders and France. In Brussels alone there were 10,000 females employed at lace-making at the close of the last century. The art was introduced into England soon after its invention in Saxony; and it is curious that Honiton has produced the best kinds from that time to this. Throughout the midland counties, especially Bedford, Buckingham, and Northampton, almost every town and village exhibits this manufacture; but hand-made lace has suffered severely from the invention next to be noticed.

Bobbin-net:—About 1770 a stocking weaver at Nottingham, named Hammond, made the first attempt to imitate lace by a slight adaptation of his stocking-frame; and many other persons gradually introduced improvements in the art; but it was Mr. Heathcoat who, early in the present century, gave the chief impulse to the trade by the invention of his bobbin frame, which gave the name of *bobbin-net* to machine-made lace. The manufacture sprang up into wonderful activity in and around Nottingham; and though it has suffered many fluctuations since it still constitutes a very notable department of Nottingham industry.

The cotton used in making bobbin net is mostly spun in Lancashire. The machines are very costly and are seldom or never owned by the actual worker. They are among the most complicated apparatus employed in manufactures; and when adapted for steam-power, and provided with the Jacquard apparatus for the production of figured net, the machines are sometimes worth 1000*l.* a piece. One set of threads, which we may call the warp, is stretched in parallel lines up and down the machines; another set, equivalent to the weft, is wound round small bobbins; and the meshes of the net-work are produced by these bobbins twisting in and around and among the vertical threads. After being woven or made, the net is gassed or singed to remove the little hairy filaments; then embroidered or 'run' by females, if the better kind of net; then mended if any of the meshes have given way; then bleached; then dyed, if it be black net; then dressed or stiffened with gum or starch; and finally rolled and pressed.

Besides the specimens from Belgium, lace will form an important item in the number of things sent over from France to the Great Exhibition. The greatest in amount, and most remarkable for beauty, will be contributed from Nancy. Besides several pieces of minor importance, one especially is intended to attract great attention. It is a counterpane, three yards long and two and a half broad. In the middle is embroidered a bouquet of roses and poppies, and a garland all round of the same flowers, of a large size, all embroidered *au lancé* with cotton of size No. 120, the appearance created being that of a white satin texture. The leaves are embroidered on what is termed a sanded ground. The tracery cost three months of labour.

LACQUERING. [JAPANNING.]

LACTIC ACID. This substance exists in milk, and in larger proportion when it has become sour; it also exists in various other animal fluids, and in many vegetable juices. Lactic Acid is colourless, inodorous, and very sour; it attracts moisture from the air, and dissolves in water and alcohol in all proportions. The combinations which it makes with alkalies and oxides are not of much importance in the arts.

LACTUCA'RIUM is obtained from the *Lactuca virosa*, or Acrid Lettuce, being the inspissated milky juice of the plant, and which is at first white, but afterwards, by exposure to the air and sun, concretes and becomes brownish. The juice of the leaves only should be collected before the flowering has begun; puncturing the leaves is the best mode of procuring it. The inspissated concrete juice resembles opium in its action, and is used in medicine.

LAKE. This is a general name for an animal or vegetable colouring substance, precipitated in combination with oxides of tin or alumina. Most persons consider a beautiful crimson to be the proper colour of lake; but according to the chemical definition, it includes pigments of various colours. Most of these are prepared by causing alum to act in an infusion or decoction of the substance employed. *Blue Lake* is prepared from Indigo, and from the blue flowers of some plants; *Brazil-wood Lake* from Brazil-wood; *Florentine Lake* from cochineal; *Madder Lake* from madder; *Green Lake* from a mixture of blue and yellow lakes; *Orange Lake* from arnotto; *Red Lake* from cochineal, differently employed from that required for Florence lake; *Yellow Lake* from quercitron or turmeric; and there are a few others, presenting other tints.

LAMP-BLACK, is a fine charcoal prepared from certain kinds of fir containing much resin, and the refuse and residuary resin left by the distillation of turpentine. The furnace chimney is long, and the greater part of it nearly horizontal, and its exit is covered with old sacking; or the smoke containing the charcoal is carried into chambers, where it is deposited on coarse cloths. The purest lamp-black is procured by the combustion of oils, but that is much too expensive for common use. Lamp-black is extensively employed as a black colour, and mixed with other pigments.

LAMP, SAFETY. It has been long known that coal mines, and especially such as are deep, are occasionally infested with carburetted hydrogen, known to the miners as *fire-damp*. Several contrivances have been proposed for safely lighting coal mines subject to the visitations of this gas; but the safety-lamp of Sir H. Davy is the only one which has ever been judged safe, and been extensively employed.

Davy found that this gas requires an admixture of a large quantity of atmospheric air to render it explosive; that explosions of inflammable gases are incapable of being passed through long narrow metallic tubes; and that this principle of security is still obtained by diminishing their length and diameter at the same time, and likewise diminishing their length and increasing their number, so that a great number of small apertures will not pass explosion when their depth is equal to their diameter. This led to trials upon sieves made of wire gauze: and he found that, if a piece of wire gauze was held over the flame of a lamp, or of coal gas, it prevented the flame from passing; and he ascertained that a flame confined in a cylinder of very fine wire gauze did not explode even a mixture of oxygen and hydrogen, but that the gases burnt in it with great vivacity.

These experiments enabled Davy to determine the principles of a new safety-lamp. It consists of a cylinder of wire gauze, formed of iron wire about $\frac{1}{50}$ of an inch in diameter, the meshes being about $\frac{1}{24}$ of an inch. The wire cylinder is strongly jointed, and is defended by three upright strong wires, which meet at the top, and to them a ring is fixed, from which the instrument is suspended. The lamp is screwed on to the bottom of the wire gauze, and is supplied with oil by the pipe projecting from it, when the top is unscrewed and removed. A wire, bent at the upper end, is passed through the bottom of the lamp for raising, lowering, or trimming the wick.

When the lamp is lighted and introduced into an atmosphere gradually mixed with fire-damp, the first effect of the fire-damp is to increase the size and length of the flame. When the inflammable gas forms as much as $\frac{1}{12}$ of the volume of the air, the cylinder becomes filled with a feeble blue flame, but the flame of the wick appears burning brightly within the blue flame, and the light of the wick continues till the fire-damp increases to one-sixth, or one-fifth, when it is lost in the flame of the fire-damp, which in this case fills the cylinder with a pretty strong light; and, when the foul air constitutes one-third of the atmosphere, it is no longer fit for respiration.

The operation of the wire gauze in preventing the communication of flame is thus explained:—Flame is gaseous matter so intensely heated as to be luminous, and the temperature requisite for producing it exceeds that of the white heat of solids. When the flame comes into contact with wire gauze, it loses so much heat in consequence of the conducting power of the metal which conveys it to the surrounding air, that it is cooled below the point at which gaseous matter can remain luminous, and consequently the flame of the gaseous matter burning within the lamp is incapable of passing through it so as to set fire to and explode the mixture of fire-damp and air by which it is surrounded; and this cooling power is exerted, even though the wire gauze, by effecting it, is rendered and remains red-hot.

Much discussion has arisen concerning the safety of this instrument; it is admitted that there are situations where it would not be danger-proof; but it is also admitted that no other invention is yet equal to it in respect to safety. A form of the instrument devised by Dr. Clanny is that which is now most frequently employed.

The original model of the safety lamp, made by Sir Humphrey Davy's own hands, has been lately placed among the collection of scientific instruments belonging to the Royal Society.

LAMPS. The chief varieties of artificial lights are noticed in earlier articles [ARGAND LAMP; BENZOLE LIGHT; BUDE LIGHT; CAMPHINE LAMP; CANDLE MANUFACTURE; DRUMMOND LIGHT; ELECTRIC LIGHT; GAS MANUFACTURE; LAMP, SAFETY]. Most of the oil-lamps are now on the argand principle, that is, having a ring-formed wick, so as to admit air within and without. Some lamps have been formed for burning solid instead of liquid fuel; such as the *Soho* lamp, which is adapted for burning tallow or fat. One variety of lamp is the *Carcel lamp*, in which the oil is raised through tubes by clock-work, so as continually to overflow at the bottom of the wick, and thus keeping the wick thoroughly soaked. In Parker's *hot oil lamp* the oil is kept between two concentric tubes near the flame, so as to become heated before it reaches the wick. The *meteor lamp* is intended to burn rape oil. The *camphine lamps* are described in an earlier article. In the 'Peerless Self-generating Gas Lamp,' registered by Mr. Holliday in 1840, the arrangement is such that the oil is heated and converted into vapour before it reaches the burner.

The manufacture of brass-work for lamps and chandeliers forms one of the most important departments of Birmingham. The brass tubing is drawn, and the ornaments cast, on a scale of great magnitude; and the various processes of stamping, planishing, lacquering, burnishing, &c., all employ a large number of hands in the lamp trade. All our exhibitions of manufactures contain specimens of Birmingham lamps. Many of those which are ordinarily considered to be made in London are of Birmingham manufacture, put together in London.

LANARKSHIRE. The wonderful energy of this iron-smelting, cotton-spinning county has already engaged a little of our attention [GLASGOW]. In addition to the industrial statistics there given, we may state that there were in Lanarkshire, in 1850, 94 cotton factories, 9 woollen and worsted factories, 4 flax factories, and 4 silk factories; that these contained about 930,000 spindles, and about 10,000 power looms; that the steam and water power employed to work these factories was equal to about 6,300 horse-power; that the number of persons employed in the factories was about 25,000; and that of these persons, nearly 20,000 were females.

LANCASHIRE. To the coal-field of South Lancashire this county owes its manufacturing pre-eminence. It occupies a large irregular tract between the Ribble and the Mersey. The pits in the northern coal field are chiefly in the neighbourhood of Hornby. The principal mineral production of Lancashire is coal. Lead and iron occur to some extent, copper in small quantity, slate, flag-stones, freestone, scythe-stones, brick clay, and pipeclay are among the mineral products of the county.

The county of Lancashire is richly provided with those highways of commerce—canals. The Sankey Canal was the first executed in England; it extends from St. Helens to Warrington, about 12 miles. The Duke of Bridgewater's Canal, one of the most celebrated of Brindley's works, extends from Leigh to Manchester, with extensive tunnels and underground works at Worsley. The Leeds and Liverpool Canal, one of the most extensive in the kingdom, connects those two important towns, and passes near Colne, Burnley, Blackburn, Wigan and Ormskirk. The Lancaster canal begins near Kendal in Westmoreland, and runs to Wigan. The Ashton Canal commences on the eastern side of the town of Manchester, and runs to Fairfield, about 4 miles from Manchester; it has branches to Stockport; to the Huddersfield Canal at Dukinfield; to the collieries at Hollingwood, near Oldham; and to the Rochdale Canal. The Huddersfield and Peak Forest canals belong rather to Yorkshire and to Derbyshire respectively than to Lancashire. The Rochdale Canal commences in the Calder and Hebble Navigation in Yorkshire, and proceeds by Todmorden and Rochdale to Manchester. The Manchester, Bolton, and Bury Canal commences in the Mersey and Irwell Navigation at Manchester, and runs to Bolton, with a branch to Bury.

Nor is Lancashire less richly provided with railways. The first locomotive line in England was the Liverpool and Manchester. Since the opening of that railway in 1830, the railways of Lancashire have taken the lead of those in every other county. The lines open are the following:—Liverpool to Manchester; Warrington to Newton; Warrington to Heyton; Runcorn to St. Helens; Runcorn to Heyton; Liverpool to Bury; Liverpool to Preston; Manchester to Preston; Newton to Preston; Kenyon to Bolton; Bolton to Clitheroe; Clifton to Colne; Manchester to Todmorden; Manchester to Stockport, to Ashton, and to Oldham; Preston to Accrington; Preston to Fleetwood; Preston to Lancaster; and many minor branches. They form a complete network, the proprietorship of which we need not here disentangle.

From the moist nature of the climate, Lancashire is more productive in grass than in corn. Oats are more cultivated than wheat. Potatoes were early cultivated in the fields in Lancashire, and they retain their celebrity. Meadows and pastures are very extensive. Even the extent of grass which is kept for the purpose of bleaching linen on is very considerable, especially in the neighbourhood of Manchester, of Bolton, and other manufacturing towns. A great quantity of new milk is required in the manufacturing towns, and much butter and cheese are also made in the county.

Lancashire is the most important manufacturing county in England. Not only is the cotton manufacture the largest branch of industry, but it has probably no parallel in any other country. The cotton factories are exceedingly numerous, and are spread over most parts of the county. Silk, woollen, and flax manufactures are also carried on, but to a much smaller extent than cotton. Engineering of every description, and ship-building, are other branches of Lancashire industry. Iron and brass manufactures; hat factories; glass,

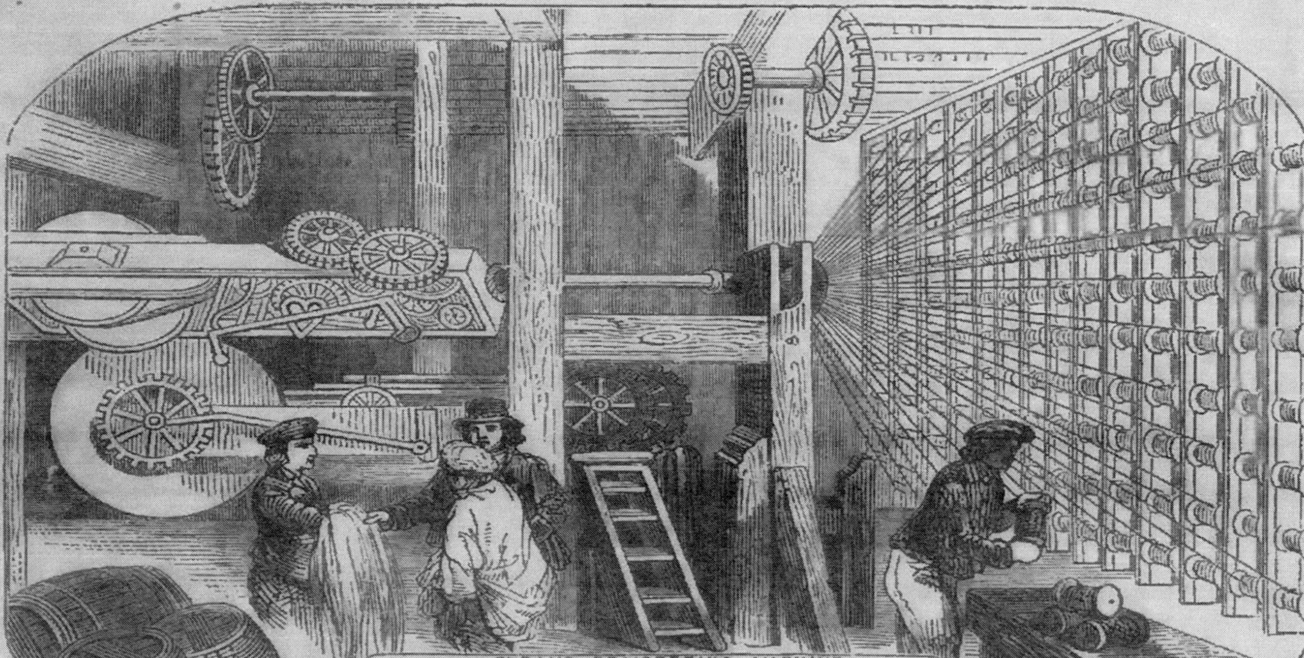

STRAND REGISTERING MACHINE.

LAYING

ANALYSIS OF A ROPE.

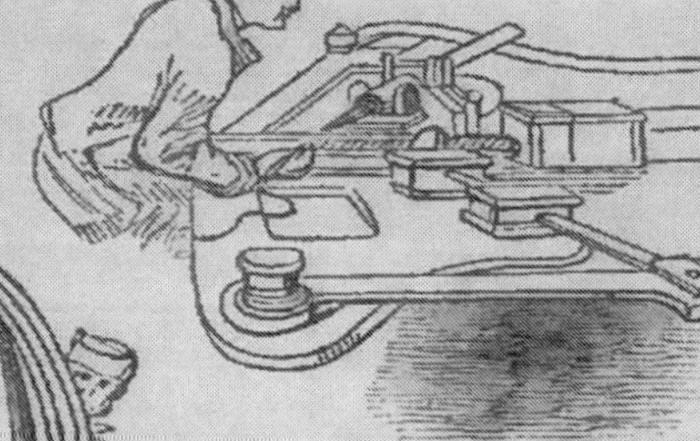

FLAT-ROPE MAKING.

SPINNING.

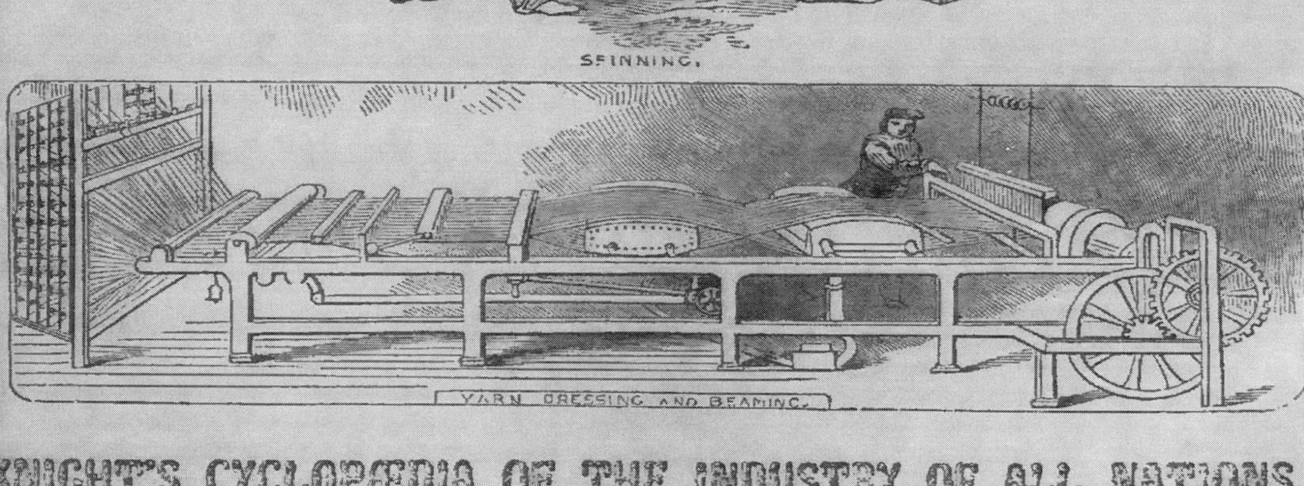

YARN DRESSING AND BEAMING.

bottle, and pottery works; alkali, soap, and chemical works; pin manufactories; watch movement manufactories—are among the numerous branches of Lancashire industry.

The commerce of Lancashire consists mainly in the immense trade carried on at Liverpool: the shipping at Lancaster and Fleetwood is of no great amount. The canals and railways conduct a vast inland traffic with other parts of England.

Many of the great towns occupy some of our attention in separate articles, in respect to their industry and produce [ACCRINGTON; ASHTON; BLACKBURN; BOLTON; BURY; CLITHEROE; LIVERPOOL; MANCHESTER; PRESTON]. *Fleetwood* stands at the mouth of the æstuary of the Wyre. The town, harbour, docks, warehouses, and pier were planned under the auspices of Sir Hesketh Fleetwood, about the year 1836, on ground which before that time was little else than a rabbit-warren. It was expected that this port would attract a large amount of traffic to and from Belfast, Londonderry, Drogheda, and other Irish ports; and to and from Glasgow and Ardrossan; but Liverpool still commands nearly all the Irish traffic. The port of *Lancaster* formerly had a considerable share of the West India trade, which is now in a great degree transferred to Liverpool; but it still possesses a portion of foreign commerce, and a considerable coasting trade. The cotton manufacture was introduced not many years ago into the town and neighbourhood, where it has considerably increased. At *Leigh* the townspeople are engaged in the manufacture of cambrics and fustians; there are collieries and stone quarries in the parish. *Oldham* has rapidly risen in prosperity, mainly owing to its being in the neighbourhood of extensive coal mines, which give employment to a large portion of its population, and to the great increase of cotton manufactures since the middle of tho last century. The manufacture of fustians, cotton, and woollen and silk goods is very extensive; and there are more hats produced here than in any other part of England. *Prescot* is celebrated for its manufactures of small files, and the movements and other parts of watches. In *Rochdale* the manufactures are very important. In the time of Edward III. some Flemings introduced the woollen manufacture into the town; it has continued to flourish, and now forms its staple commodity. Calico, cotton yarn, and hats are also manufactured. Coal is dug, and slates, flagstone, and freestone are abundantly quarried in the parish; and there are also iron-works. *St. Helens* has risen into importance chiefly by means of the large establishments of the British Plate-Glass Company at Ravenhead, in the adjacent township of Sutton, and of the copper-works belonging to the proprietors of the Parys Mine, in Anglesea, who brought their ore here to be smelted. In *Todmorden* the inhabitants are engaged in the cotton and woollen manufactures, both of which have greatly increased. The principal branches of industry in *Warrington*, are cotton-spinning, the manufacture of flint glass and glass bottles, machinery and mill-work, and many branches of iron manufactures. There are steam flour-mills, tanyards, malt-houses, one or more paper-mills, and several breweries. *Wigan* from its situation on the Lancashire coal-field, has increased with the development of manufacturing industry. The manufactures of the place comprise linens, calico, checks, fustians, the spinning of cotton yarn, and other branches of the cotton manufacture.

In addition to the details under COTTON and FACTORIES, we give the following statistics of Lancashire factories in 1850. In that year there were in the county 1,235 cotton factories, 37 woollen and worsted factories, 9 flax factories, and 29 silk factories. In these factories were about 15,000,000 spindles, and about 185,000 power looms. The machinery was moved by steam-power equivalent to about 50,000 horse power, and by water power to the extent of 4,000 horse power. The persons employed at the 1,310 factories were about 240,000 in number, of whom 130,000 were females. Of the persons so employed, about 12,000 were children under 13 years of age.

LANDES. This department of France calls for a little notice here on account of the extraordinary mode in which some of the inhabitants are obliged to pursue their industrial avocations. Much of the department consists of a loose ashen-gray sandy soil. Numerous flocks of wretched half-starved sheep wander over this desert waste, tended by shepherds who walk on high stilts to enable them to pass dry-footed over the marshes that occur in all directions. Clothed in sheepskins, perched on his lofty stilts, and seated on a high staff with a flat broad end, the shepherd of the Landes watching his sheep, and knitting woollen stockings, his constant occupation, presents to the stranger unprepared for the sight an extraordinary appearance. Not only the shepherds, but the charcoal burners, aud almost all the scanty population of the Landes, are accustomed to the use of stilts, on which they walk with astonishing rapidity. The most important produce of the Landes are the pine forests which cover nearly one-fourth of the surface, and which, besides the value of the timber, yield a great quantity of resin. The more fertile districts of the department yield wheat, maize, millet, hemp, flax, madder, saffron, &c. About 10,000,000 gallons of wine are produced annually, of which about a third goes to supply the home consumption; the rest is exported, or distilled and sold as Armagnac brandy. Mines of iron and bitumen are worked; mica, coal, marble, granite, lithographic stones, chalk, ochre, potters' clay of superior quality, crucible earth, &c., are found. Peat fuel is dug. The industrial produce is composed of coarse woollens, pottery, liqueurs, bar iron and ironware, resin, pitch, tar, glass, paper, leather, brandy, beer, oil, &c. There is also a considerable trade in timber, deals, linseed oil, fruits, wool, pork, &c.

LANTERNS. It is said that we are indebted to Alfred the Great for the invention of lanterns, or lanthorns. Before the invention of clocks, Alfred caused six tapers to be made for his daily use; each taper contained twelve pennyweights of wax, and was twelve inches long. The whole length was divided into twelve parts or inches, of which three would burn for one hour; so that each taper would be consumed in four hours, and the six tapers, being lighted one after another, lasted twenty-four hours. But the wind, blowing through the windows and doors and chinks of the chapel, or through the cloth of his tent, in which they were burning, wasted the tapers, and caused them to burn irregularly. He therefore designed a lantern, made of ox or cow horn cut into thin plates, in which he enclosed the tapers; and being thus protected from the wind, the period of their burning became a matter of comparative certainty.

The translucent part of a lantern is made of cow-horn. The horn is softened and separated into thin leaves, by following the natural layers of the substance. The thin leaves are flattened, scraped with a blunt-edged knife, smoothed with a woollen rag dipped in charcoal dust, and finally polished with horn shavings.

LAPIDARY. The work of the lapidary is the shaping, cutting, and polishing of precious stones. He uses mortars for crushing and grinding diamond powder; cutting instruments for reducing stones to thin layers; instruments for giving flat and curved surfaces to gems; lathes for turning, and drills for piercing holes; apparatus for making the facets of brilliants, &c. A few details bearing on this subject will be found under CAMEO; DIAMOND; GEMS; INTAGLIO.

LAPIS LAZULI. [ULTRAMARINE.]

LARCH. A few words have been said concerning this valuable tree, in connection with the genus to which it belongs [ABIES]; and we will here add a little detail concerning the uses of the tree in the arts.

Larch wood seems to be more and more valued as its qualities become known: and it will probably supersede others which have hitherto been held in greater repute. The Germans find larch wood almost indestructible for wine-casks. In many parts of France houses are built of larch, and water-pipes made of the same material. In Switzerland it is used for vine props. In all cases where timber is exposed to alternations of wet and dry, larch is particularly valuable. As naval timber the larch is rising rapidly into note. As sleepers for railways, axles for mill work, hop poles, stakes for plants, and numerous other useful articles, larch is a most valuable material. It is rather too difficult to work to be used much in the carpentry of English houses.

The qualities which render larch so serviceable for the above purposes are the following:—It is much clearer of knots than fir-wood; it is more durable than fir; it is much less liable to shrink than common deal; it will not crack with any moderate degree of heat, when in the form of planks or boards; it is more tough than foreign deal; as an ornamental wood it often presents a very beautiful colour, and will receive a high polish.

LASER, was the name given by the ancients to a gum-resin highly esteemed by them, and which was sometimes called *Silphium*. It is supposed to have been procured from certain species of the genus *Loderpitium;* the root of which is extremely bitter, and yields an aromatic resinous substance. The gum-resin was employed medicinally by the ancients, and was an article of some commercial value.

LATA'NIA, is a genus of Palms. The leaves, like those of other palms, are employed by the natives of the Isle of France for covering their huts, as well as for making fans and umbrellas. The leaf-stalks are split, and employed for making baskets, sieves, &c.

LATHE. [POTTERY; TURNING.]

LAUDANUM. [OPIUM.]

LAUREL. The fruit of the laurel or *Sweet Bay* is endowed with aromatic properties as well as the leaves, whence both, as well as a fatty oil expressed from the seed, have long been used in medicine as stimulants and carminatives.

From the laurel is obtained *laurine*, an acrid and bitter principle contained in the berries; its smell resembles that of laurel oil.

LAVAL, the capital of the French department of Mayenne, is the centre of a large manufacture of table and household linen and linen-yarn, for the sale of which there are weekly markets; calico, flannel, cotton handkerchiefs, serge, soap, leather, &c., are also made; and there is a good business done in flax, wine, brandy, clover-seed, timber, iron, marble, &c.

LAVENDER. Lavender plants are hoary, narrow-leaved, fragrant bushes, inhabiting the south of Europe, the Canaries, Barbary, Egypt, Persia, and the west of India, with generally blue flowers. Twelve species are described, of which two only are of general interest, namely, the common lavender and Spike Lavender, both natives of sterile hills in the south of Europe and Barbary. The common lavender yields the *Oil of Lavender*, so extensively employed in the preparation of perfumes; and its flowers are employed in medicine. The spike lavender yields the *Oil of Spike*, or foreign oil of lavender; this is less fragrant than the other oil, and is used to adulterate it, and also as a material in painting.

LEAD. This very useful metal has a blueish gray colour, and considerable brilliancy when fresh surfaces are formed by cutting. If it has not been cooled too rapidly, it is so soft that, even when in pieces of considerable thickness, it may be easily bent. It soils slightly, and leaves on paper or cloth a mark after friction resembling that of plumbago. Its specific gravity is 11.4. Lead may be reduced to thin laminæ; but its tenacity is extremely slight, so that a wire about $\frac{1}{10}$th of an inch in diameter breaks with a weight of 30 pounds. It fuses at about 612°, and crystallises when slowly cooled. It is not a volatile metal, for in close vessels it may be heated to whiteness without subliming. When exposed to the air, it absorbs oxygen and carbonic acid slowly, and acquires a superficial coating of carbonate of lead. If it be exposed to air and water, it is oxidised and converted into carbonate of lead with considerable rapidity; this carbonate has the appearance of minute shining brilliant scales. Though at common temperatures lead is slowly acted upon by the oxygen of the air, it is readily oxidised when the heat is raised.

The ores of lead, strictly speaking, are few in number. Indeed the only one which can properly be considered as a working ore is the *Sulphuret*, or *Galena*. This almost universally diffused ore occurs in attached crystals and massive. The crystals are opaque and leaden gray. The massive varieties have a granular structure. By the blowpipe on charcoal the sulphur is first dissipated, and then metallic lead is obtained. In Cornwall and Scotland the veins of this ore traverse primary rocks; in Derbyshire it occurs in veins or beds in transition rocks. It very commonly contains a considerable portion of silver. There are many minerals in which lead forms a component ingredient, but most of the lead of commerce is procured from the sulphuret.

Lead forms many useful substances in combination with other bodies. Protoxide of lead is *massicot*, and the deutoxide is *Minium*, both used as colours. Oxychloride of lead forms *patent yellow*. Carbonate of lead forms *White Lead*. Acetate of lead is *Sugar of Lead*. Di-acetate of lead forms *Goulard's Extract*. Chromate of lead is a beautiful yellow pigment. The manufacture of RED LEAD and WHITE LEAD will be noticed in separate articles.

Of the *alloys* of lead, three are of some importance. Alloyed with antimony, lead forms *Type-metal*. *Pewter* consists of about 80 parts tin and 20 lead. Equal parts of tin and lead form *Plumber's Solder*.

LEAD MANUFACTURE. Lead was known to and used by the Greeks and Romans for various purposes. Among others it was employed for pipes to convey water, just as it is now. The lead-mines of this island were worked by the Romans. The chief of them are in Cornwall, Devonshire, Somersetshire, Derbyshire, Durham, Lancashire, Cumberland, Westmoreland, Shropshire, Flintshire, Denbighshire, Merionethshire, and Montgomeryshire; in Scotland, in Dumfriesshire, Lanarkshire, Ayrshire, and Argyleshire. Lead is also found in Ireland, in the counties of Armagh, Wexford, Wicklow, Waterford, Clare, and Down.

The ore of lead, when extracted from the mine, is called *Galena*, and is combined with various earthy matters. The first processes subsequent to its extraction are those of crushing or pounding and washing the ore. The ore is then smelted, sometimes in a common smelting furnace and sometimes in a reverberatory furnace; and the melted metal is allowed to run into a large iron pan, from which it is ladled into cast-iron moulds. It then constitutes what is called *Pig-Lead*. In this state lead always contains more or less of silver. The proportion is sometimes exceedingly minute, varying from 1 to 30 ounces in a ton of lead. The extraction of the silver is always performed when it exists in a proportion sufficient to pay the expense of the process, which varies in different localities according to the cost of fuel. The process of extraction, which is called refining, depends upon the well known circumstance, that lead, when heated to redness, absorbs a large portion of oxygen from the air, and is converted into an oxide; while silver does not undergo any such change, but retains its metallic form at almost any temperature. Mr. Pattinson, of Newcastle, has introduced an improved process, in which the crystallising properties of melted lead are brought into requisition.

The most extensive use of lead is in the forms of sheets and pipes. To make sheet-lead, the pigs are brought to a state of fusion in a large pot or cistern, near which is placed the table on which the sheet is to be cast. This table, which is usually from 18 to 20 feet long and 6 feet wide, is made either of wood or cast iron. The wooden table has its surface protected by a layer of fine sand, which is wetted and spread evenly and firmly over it before the melted lead is poured on. To prevent the lead from running over the sides, a ledge is provided, two or three inches thick, and two inches high, which forms the margin of the table. An instrument called a strike is also provided to regulate the thickness of the sheet, and to spread the melted metal evenly over the table. In casting the sheet the fused metal is taken from the cistern with an iron ladle, and put into a triangular-shaped iron shovel or peel, placed at the head of the table, which peel being raised so as to pour out the lead upon the table, the strike is brought into use to spread it evenly over the whole surface: the surplus, if any, falling into a vessel placed for its reception at the foot of the table. A sheet of lead weighs 9 cwts., so that its length and breadth will be greater in proportion to the diminution of its thickness. The thickness of sheets of lead is frequently reduced by means of heavy rollers worked by steam power. Rolled sheet-lead is made by the repeated compression, between steel rollers, of a block of lead several inches in thickness.

Lead pipes are sometimes made, when great exactness of shape is not required, by bending a length of sheet lead of the necessary width over a mandril, and soldering the edges together; but the more usual method of manufacture is by casting and drawing. The casting-box employed is an iron cylinder made in two parts, and put together longitudinally with flanges; inside of this cylinder is placed an iron rod or core, which is so fixed as to be concentric to the cylinder, without touching it; a space is thus left, into which the melted lead is poured. When this is set, the core is removed, and the cylinder opened, so as to withdraw the pipe, which is much thicker than is needed, and must be lengthened, while its substance is reduced, by drawing it through a succession of holes in steel plates, diminishing gradually in diameter. The making of lead shot is described elsewhere [SHOT MANUFACTURE.]

In a purely metallic state, lead produces no action on the human system except such as arises from its mechanical properties; but, as soon as it becomes oxidised, it can combine with the contents of the stomach, and produce different effects, according to the nature of the substances it meets with. Painters are exposed to a distressing disease from the use of white lead, called *Painter's Colic.* The lid or cover of cisterns should never be made of lead, as the vapour which condenses on it possesses all the solvent power of distilled water. It is also unsafe to use water which has flowed over leaden roofs, more particularly in towns, as the surface of the lead is almost invariably coated with some soluble salt. No kind of adulteration or impregnation with lead, from accident or ignorance, is more common than that of wine or cyder. Even a single shot of lead left by accident in a bottle after cleaning has produced severe colic; and the more extensive use of the salts of lead to *fine* wines, as it is termed, that is, to remove their acid taste and make them sweet, has occasioned most serious consequences.

In the year 1848 lead ore was raised from sixteen counties in England and Wales; viz., Cornwall, Devon, Cumberland, Durham, Northumberland, Westmoreland, Derbyshire, Shropshire, Somerset, Yorkshire, Cardigan, Caernarvon, Caermarthen, Flint, Montgomery, and Merioneth. The quantity of ore raised in that year, and of lead smelted from the ore, in the United Kingdom, was as follows:

	Ore.	Lead.
England	55,638 tons.	39,142 tons.
Wales	16,305 ,,	11,122 ,,
Scotland	2,588 ,,	1,736 ,,
Ireland	1,912 ,,	1,188 ,,
Isle of Man..	2,521 ,,	1,665 ,,
	78,964	54,853

From this we learn that three tons of ore produce about two tons of metallic lead. The richest English mines are in Durham. The richest Welsh in Flintshire.

The pig and sheet lead imported in the three years 1848, 1849, and 1850, were 3,789, 7,216, and 11,977 tons, respectively. The quantities exported in the same three years were 6,129, 170,27, and 22,083 tons, respectively.

LEAGUE. In modern English a league means the 20th part of a degree of latitude, or three geographical miles, each of which is the 60th part of a degree. The league of our sailors may be described and easily remembered as 3.456 statute miles of 1,760 yards each. The same marine league is used by the French and other nations: besides which, the French have among their itinerary land measures, two distinct leagues (or *lieues;* in some of the provinces *lègues*), the first of 2000 toises, or 2.42 English miles, which is the legal posting measure; the second of 25 to the degree, or 2.77 English miles.

LEATHER MANUFACTURE. This remarkable substance, which is universally employed throughout the civilised world, is prepared from the skins of animals, or, it would perhaps be more correct to say, consists of that substance after it has been chemically changed by the process of tanning. This change is effected by means of a substance residing in several vegetable matters, to which the name of *tannin* has been given. When this tannin, which is soluble in water, is applied to the hides of animals from which the hair, epidermis, and any fleshy or fatty parts adhering to them are removed, and which hides then consist wholly of *gelatin*, also soluble in water, these two soluble substances so unite chemically as to form the wholly insoluble substance called leather. Of the ox-hides which are converted into leather, those supplied by bulls are thicker, stronger, and coarser in the grain than those of cows; while the hides of bullocks are intermediate between those of the bull and the cow. Such leather is employed for the soles of boots and shoes; for most parts of harness and sadlery; for making leather trunks, buckets, hose for fire-engines, and pump-valves; for the thick belts used in military accoutrements; and for the gloves of cavalry. The thick *buff-leather*, formerly used as armour, and which was pistol proof, and would resist the edge of a sword, was made from the hide of the urus or wild bull. The skins of *calves*, though thinner than those of cows, are thicker than most other kinds of skin which are converted into leather.

The process necessary to convert hides into the thick hard leather used for the soles of boots and shoes is as follows:—The horns are removed from the hides; and the latter are scraped, steeped, and sweated, and the hair removed. The hides are then immersed for a few days in a liquid which opens the pores and fits them for the action of the tanning ingredients. In the old method of tanning, which is not yet entirely abandoned, the hides and powdered bark were laid in alternate layers in the tan-pit, which was then filled with water to the brim. After some months the pit was emptied and re-filled with fresh bark and water, and this process was repeated whenever the strength of the bark was exhausted. In this way the time required for impregnating the hides varied, according to their thickness and other circumstances, from one to four years. The process has been expedited by the use of a concentrated solution of bark instead of mere layers of bark in water. The variations of practice among different tanners extend to the substance used as an astringent, as well as to the manner of applying it. Ground oak-bark, which was formerly the only material in common use, and is still the most general, produces good leather of a light fawn-colour. Valonia, of which considerable quantities are imported for the use of tanners, produces leather of great solidity and weight, the colour of which is inclined to gray, and which is more impervious to water than that made with oak-bark. Catechu, or Terra Japonica, the inspissated extract of the *Acacia Catechu*, produces leather of a dark reddish fawn colour, which is light, spongy, and very pervious to water. Another substance which has been used of late years is a kind of bean-pod called *divi-divi.* These substances may be used either individually or in various combinations; and they are prepared with plain water or with ooze, with hot water or with cold, according to the judgment of the tanner. In whichever way the tanning is effected, the hide is subjected to the action of solutions increasing progressively in strength, until it is so perfectly penetrated, that when cut through it presents a uniform brown colour; any appearance of a light streak in the middle of its thickness being an indication of imperfect tanning. When the process is complete, the hides are hung up in a shed, and allowed to dry slowly, and, while they are drying, they are compressed by heating or rubbing, or by passing them between rollers, to give them firmness and density.

Several schemes have been devised for forcing a tanning solution through the pores of the hide by mechanical pressure. Mr. Spilsbury patented a method of forcing the tan liquor into the pores of the hide by hydrostatic pressure, but in a mode which was found to produce leather of unequal quality. Another process, by Mr. Drake, consisted in sewing two skins together (after they had received a slight tanning in the ordinary way), so as to form a water-tight bag, which was filled with tan-liquor, and compressed so as to force the liquor through the skin. In another plan, which has been tried under several forms, the tanning liquid is applied to both sides of the hides, which are placed in an air-tight vessel, and is forced into their pores by hydrostatic pressure, the air being previously pumped out. In the plan patented by Messrs. Herapath and Cox of Bristol, a number of hides are connected together by strings, so as to form a continuous belt, and passed between rollers turned by steam or other power; there are several pairs of rollers, each pair erected over a pit. The pits contain tanning liquors of different degrees of strength. The hides are dipped first in the weakest liquor and so on to the strongest, passing between and being compressed by the rollers after each dipping. This process is said greatly to expedite the conversion of hide into leather; but it is not yet settled whether the leather is of quality equal to that prepared by the old method.

The thinner hides or skins for the upper leathers of boots and shoes are tanned with the same materials as the thicker, but by a quicker and less elaborate process.

Of the thin skins prepared for ornamental purposes, many are tanned with a substance called *sumach*, prepared from a plant of the same name. After a preparatory cleansing, &c., the goat-skins for morocco leather are sewed up into the form of a bag, with the grain or hair-side outwards; they are nearly filled with a solution of sumach, inflated with air, the aperture tied up, and the bags then thrown into a cistern of hot sumach liquor. Being thus acted on, both within and without, the skins are soon impregnated with sumach. The bags are then opened, the liquor removed, and the skins washed, rubbed, dried, dyed, and wrinkled by pressure with a grooved instrument. Cheap or imitation morocco is made of sheep-skins.

Tawing is the name applied to the process by which the skins of sheep, lambs, and kids, are converted into soft leather by the action of alum. Of this kind of leather gloves are usually made. Skins intended for tawing pass through a series of operations resembling those by which skins are prepared for tanning; but the tawing materials consist of alum, salt, flour, and yolk of eggs (chiefly the first two), which are applied in various ways. The skins require a great deal of stretching and rubbing after the steeping, to give them the requisite softness.

In making *Chamois Leather* or *Shamoyed Leather*, of which wash-leather is a cheap example, the skins of deer, goats, and sheep, are impregnated with oil instead of with the ingredients hitherto mentioned. After a certain preparation, the skins are beaten for many hours with heavy wooden machines, and cod-oil is forced into the pores.

Sheep-skins, when simply tanned, are employed for inferior bookbinding, for leathering bellows, and for various other purposes for which a cheap leather is required. All the *whit-leather*, as it is termed, which is used for whip-lashes, bags, aprons, &c., is of sheep-skin; as are also the cheaper kinds of *wash-leather*, of which gloves, under-waistcoats, and other articles of dress, are made. Mock or imitation morocco, and most of the other coloured and dyed leathers used for women's and children's shoes, carriage-linings, and the covering of stools, chairs, sofas, writing-tables, &c. are also made of sheepskin. *Lamb-skins* are mostly dressed white or coloured for gloves; and those of *goats* and *kids* supply the best qualities of light leather, the former being the material of the best morocco, while kid leather affords the finest material for gloves and ladies' shoes. Leather from goat-skins, ornamented and sometimes gilt, was formerly used as a hanging or covering for walls. *Deer* and *antelope* skins, shamoyed or dressed in oil, are used chiefly for riding breeches. *Horse-hides*, which, considering their size, are thin, are tanned and curried, and are used by the harness-maker, especially for collars; and occasionally, when pared thin, for the upper leathers of ladies' walking shoes. *Dog-skins* are thick and tough, and make excellent leather. *Seal-skins* produce a leather similar but inferior to that supplied by dog-skins; and *hog-skins* afford a thin but dense leather, which is used mostly for covering the seats of saddles.

Currying is the general name given to the various operations of dressing leather after the tanning is completed, by which the requisite smoothness, lustre, colour, and suppleness are imparted. The processes of the currier are various. The first is styled *dipping* the leather. It consists in moistening with water, and beating upon a trellis-work of wooden spars, with a mallet or mace. After this beating, by which the stiffness of the hide or skin is destroyed, it is laid over an inclined board, and scraped and cleaned, and, wherever it is too thick, pared or shaved down on the flesh side, by the careful application of various two-handled knives; and then thrown again into water, and well scoured by rubbing the grain or hair side with pumice-stone, or with a piece of slaty grit, by which means the *bloom*, a whitish matter which is found upon the surface in tanning, is removed. The leather is then rubbed with the *pommel*, a rectangular piece of hard wood, about twelve inches long by five broad, grooved on the under surface, and fastened to the hand. The currier uses several of these instruments, with grooves of various degrees of fineness, and also, for some purposes, pommels of cork which are not grooved at all. The object of this rubbing is to give grain and pliancy to the leather. The leather is then scraped with tools applied nearly perpendicular to its surface, and worked forcibly with both hands, to reduce such parts as may yet be left too thick to a uniform substance. After this, it is dressed with the *round knife*, a singular instrument which pares off the coarser fleshy parts of the skin. In addition to these operations, the currier uses occasionally polishers of smooth wood or glass for rubbing the surface of the leather; and, when the leather is intended for the use of the shoemaker, he applies to it some kind of greasy composition called *dubbing* or *stuffing*.

Leather is occasionally dressed 'black on the grain,' or having the hair or grain side instead of the flesh side coloured. The currying operations in such a case are similar to those above described, but the finishing processes are somewhat modified. The leather is rubbed with a gritstone, to remove any wrinkles and smooth down the coarse grain. The grain is finally raised by repeatedly rubbing over the surface, in different directions, with the pommel or graining board.

Japanned Leather of various kinds is used in coach-making, harness-making, and for various other purposes. *Patent Leather* is covered with a coat of elastic japan, which gives a surface like polished glass, impermeable to water; and hides prepared in a more perfectly elastic mode of japanning, which will permit folding without cracking the surface, are called *Enamelled Leather*. Such leather has the japan annealed, something in the same mode as glass: the hides are laid between blankets, and subjected to the heat of an oven at a particular temperature during several hours.

In making *Russia leather*, the skins are freed from the hair or fleece by steeping them in an ash-lye, then rinced, fulled, fermented, and cleaned. They are then soaked for forty-eight hours in a bath composed of water mixed with a paste of rye-flour. The skins, when taken out of the bath, are left in tubs for fifteen days, then washed, and immersed in a boiler containing a hot decoction of willow bark, in which they are handled and pressed for half an hour. This manipulation is repeated twice a day for a week, after which the tanning infusion is renewed, and the process is repeated on the same skins for another week, after which they are exposed to the air to dry, and are then dyed and curried.

Shagreen, a peculiar kind of leather, or rather of prepared skin, formerly much used for the covers of watch-cases, mathematical-instrument cases, &c., is produced by soaking, scraping, rubbing, softening, salting, and dyeing. The unevenness of surface is produced in a singular way. The grain side of the skin is strewed with the hard round seeds of the Goose-Foot (*Chenopodium album*). A felt being laid over these, they are trodden deeply into the soft-yielding skin; and when dried, the seeds may be shaken out without violence, leaving the skin in a hard horny state, covered with deep indentations.

It has been recently stated that Dr. Burnland, of Vienna, has discovered a method of making leather out of certain refuse animal substances; and that the substance is at one stage of its process in a state of fluidity, and can be *cast* into boots and shoes and other articles.

Leather-splitting machines, by which even very thin skins may be divided into two thicknesses, each of which is capable of being dressed as a perfect skin, have called forth much ingenuity of contrivance. In one machine of this kind, the skin is drawn between two revolving rollers, and presented, as it emerges from their grasp, to the edge of a long and very sharp knife, which is kept continually moving a little backwards and forwards with great velocity

As there are attempts now being made to revive the beautiful art of carving, in its higher artistic branches; so does the art of embossing and gilding leather seem likely to meet with some revival. Embossed leather, ornamented in gold, silver, and colours, was largely manufactured some centuries ago, first in Spain, Italy, and Flanders, and then in Germany, France, and England. It was much used as tapestry for rooms; and some of our old English mansions still present specimens of it. The Alhambra in Spain still contains some very rich examples. The leathers so employed were made of calf, goat, and sheep-skins. Mr. Leake has recently introduced machinery which bids fair to produce embossed leathers in high relief, and presenting patterns of great beauty.

The untanned hides imported into this country in 1850 amounted to 591,920 cwts. The leather manufactures imported in the same year, comprised about 3,260,000 pairs of gloves, and about 780,000 pairs of boots, shoes, and boot fronts. The English-tanned leather, and English made leather goods exported in

1850, comprising saddles, harness, gloves, and other articles, had an aggregate value of 608,656*l*.

LEECH TRADE. The traffic in leeches is a remarkable one, alike for the gatherer and the dealer. The leech is met with more abundantly in the south than the north of Europe. The country about La Brienno in France is famous for its supply of leechos; and here is exhibited the wretched nature of the employment of a leech-gatherer. He has his arms and legs bare, and walks about in the marshes where the leeches abound. They attach themselves to his legs as he moves along, and he picks them off from time to time; he seeks for them also about the roots of the bullrushes and sea-weeds. He can on some days gather a gross in three or four hours; and he puts them into a small bag suspended round his neck. Such is the leech-fishery in spring; but in summer it is still worse. The leeches then go into deeper water; and the gatherer strips naked to go after them. These poor fellows are exposed to fogs, mists, and fœtid vapours, and are subject to agues, catarrhs, and rheumatisms; but the trade is tolerably lucrative, and thus there is no scarcity of leech gatherers.

A large portion of our leeches are imported from Hamburg, to which port the dealers bring them from different countries. They are sometimes imported in bags, but more usually in small barrels containing about 2000 cach; tho head being made of stout canvas to admit the air. Some years ago it was stated that four principal dealers in London imported about 7,000,000 leeches annually. It is estimated that the consumption in Paris is about 3,000,000 annually.

LEEDS, the principal emporium of the woollen manufactures in the West Riding of Yorkshire, is one of the most important of our northern towns. Though the spinning of worsted and the manufacture of worsted stuffs is not extensively followed at Leeds, vast quantities of these goods are brought there to be dyed and finished. The dye-houses and dressing-shops at Leeds are very extensive. In these establishments both the woollen and worsted goods are finished, after being purchased in the rough at the cloth-halls and piece-halls of the clothing towns. The mills at Leeds for the spinning of flax for canvas, linen, sacking, thread, &c., are very extensive. There are also large manufactories of glass, earthenware, steam-engines, locomotives, and all kinds of machinery. These and the other operations of the district are facilitated by the abundant supply of coal, produced from the mines in the vicinity of the town.

The largest commercial buildings in Leeds are the cloth-halls. The Coloured Cloth Hall was built in 1578; the White-Cloth Hall in 1775. In the cloth-halls, the principal sales of woollen cloths in their rough state from the country manufacturers to the merchants are effected. The cloth markets are held on Tuesdays and Saturdays, and last only one hour and a quarter at each hall.

There is a School of Design at Leeds, to improve the taste of the workmen. Some exquisite specimens of communion cloths, made of silk warp and flax weft, elaborately damasked have recently been woven at Leeds.

LEGHORN. This enterprising free port in Tuscany is, in the western district, intersected with canals, by which goods are carried in boats from the shipping in the harbour and landed before the warehouses of the merchants. Many of the private houses are handsome. The outer mole is about a mile in length. The harbour is tolerably large, but not sufficiently deep for large vessels, which lie in the roads, where the anchorage is safe and good. The Darsena, or interior harbour or dock, is only fit for smaller vessels. Leghorn is rather a commercial than a manufacturing town; it has however tan yards, rope-walks, soap and candle factories, glass-works, establishments for the manufacture of coral ornaments, woollen caps, cream of tartar, borax, and sulphur. Steamers and sailing vessels are built. A railroad connects the town with Pisa, Pontedera, Empoli, and Florence.

The imports into Leghorn are either for consumption or for deposit. They consist of corn, tissues of cotton, hemp, and wool, sugar, raw and manufactured silk, bronze work and jewellery, salt fish, hides, hemp and flax, coffee, raw cotton and cotton yarn, wool, spices and drugs, dye-stuffs, porcelain, gum, wine, brandy, rum, spirits, tobacco, &c., to the value of about 3,000,000*l*. annually. Many of these articles of course enter into the exports, for the transit trade is very extensive. Other exported articles are—oil, anchovies, paper and rags, straw hats, marble and alabaster, works of art, timber, cork, coral, tallow, potash, &c. The total value of the exports amounts to about 2,000,000*l*. a year. The number of vessels that enter the harbour annually is over 4000, with about 400,000 tons cargo. The number of ships that clear out annually are about the same in number, but the freights are somewhat less. About 2000 of these vessels are Tuscan. Steamers ply regularly to Cività-Vecchia, Naples, Sicily, Genoa, Nice, and Marseille.

LEGU'MIN, is a peculiar vegetable product obtained by Braconnot from peas, and which he considers as a vegetable alkali. It appears to be a substance intermediate between gluten and vegetable albumen; it differs from the first in being insoluble in alcohol, and from the last in readily dissolving in the alkaline carbonates. It contains some sulphur and also azote, but less than animal albumen. It exists in peas and beans, to the amount of about 18 per cent.

LEICESTERSHIRE. This county has coal-fields near Ashby, which furnish a cheap supply of fuel; and there are also procured within the county coarse slate, gypsum, limestone, freestone, and brick-clay. The county is supplied with canals and railways, in amount quite adequate to its traffic. In respect to agriculture, the most fertile soils are almost invariably kept in pasture, for which this county is pre-eminent. Out of above 500,000 acres of surface, fully one-half is in permanent grass. Grazing and breeding cattle and sheep are the chief objects of the Leicestershire farmers, and they have succeeded admirably both with oxen and sheep. Most of the improved modern instruments, such as scarifiers, spiked rollers and drills, have been introduced and are used in the larger farms, which are chiefly in the hands of the proprietors. The county contains many large dairies, and produces excellent cheese, especially the Stilton cheese.

Leicestershire is the centre of the worsted hosiery manufacture, nearly all of which is conducted within this county. Leicester is the chief town both of the county and of the manufacture. Most of the principal manufacturers are connected with the hosiery or wool trades. Some of the larger firms employ 2000 to 3000 hands; and one or two spinning mills recently built would rival those of Lancashire. There are worsted spinners, lambs' wool spinners, wool staplers, &c., to supply the raw material; there are frame-smiths, needle-makers, sinker makers, &c., to supply the working apparatus; and there are thousands of persons to weave and sew the stockings. Market Harborough, Lutterworth, Hinckley, Market Bosworth, Loughborough, and most of the villages between these towns, and between them and Leicester, are inhabited by the stockingers (as they are often called). See farther on this subject under Hosiery Manufacture. The other departments of industry in Leicestershire are not very extensive. There were 35 spinning mills in this county in 1850.

LEIPZIG. This busy city, the second in rank but the first in commerce in Saxony, has extensive manufactures in oil, paper, musical and optical instruments, bronzed articles, hats, leather, hardware, &c. The town has a tribunal of commerce, an exchange, savings' bank, a discount bank, and several assurance companies. There is a considerable trade in American and Russian furs; and the wool fairs, especially that held in June, are very important. Leipzig, though comparatively small, has become one of the most important cities in Europe, owing to its university, its fairs, and its book trade. These fairs have laid the foundation of the prosperity and wealth of Leipzig. The concourse of merchants from various countries is very great, and the value of the manufactured goods of all kinds sold annually is estimated at upwards of three millions sterling.

The singular concentration of the German book-trade in Leipzig has been a main cause of the celebrity and wealth of that city. The first two booksellers, who were also printers, that settled in Leipzig were Steiger and Boskopf, in 1545. There are now 110 publishing establishments, and 23 great printing houses, with 14 printing machines and 260 presses. Above 40 millions of sheets are annually printed at Leipzig, and the bales of books brought thither every year amount on an average to 30,000 cwt. For the transaction of business, and settlement of accounts, there is a handsome building called the Booksellers' Exchange, which was opened in 1836.

At the Leipzig fairs of 1850 it was remarked that the attendance of great buyers had somewhat slackened: the increased facilities for travelling having enabled merchants to visit the manufacturing towns, and make some of their purchases there.

LEITH. The chief manufactures of this important Scotch seaport are ropes, cordage, sailcloth, bottles, soap, and candles. There are several breweries, ship-building yards, and a distillery.

There are two commodious dry docks for the repairing and building of ships, and two wet docks, each of which is 300 feet wide and between 700 and 800 feet long, and of sufficient depth to admit vessels of from 200 to 250 tons' burthen. They are surrounded by well-constructed quays, upon which are erected appropriate warehouses for the reception of merchandise. Extensive additional wet docks are now being constructed, to accommodate increasing traffic. Steamers ply to and from Leith; but the new pier at Granton is found to be more available for this kind of traffic. Leith is the most important naval station on the east coast of Scotland, and its commerce is large. The gross customs receipts in 1848 were 563,452*l.*, ranking next after London,

Liverpool, Dublin, Bristol, and Glasgow. The vessels which entered the port of Leith in 1848 were 1028 with an aggregate tonnage of 122,675 tons. 386 boats, and 2064 persons, were engaged in the Leith and Burntisland fisheries in 1846.

LEMBERG, the capital of the kingdom of Galizia, has manufactures of woollen cloth and linen. Lemberg has an important commerce with Russia and Turkey. The commission trade is very extensive, and an immense amount of business is done at the annual fair; it commences on Jan. 6, and for some weeks afterwards a vast concourse of strangers resort to this place.

LEMNIAN EARTH is an earthy substance soft, dull, opaque, yellowish white, and falls to pieces when put into water. It was formerly used in medicine under the name of *Terra Sigillata*. Two-thirds of its weight consist of silica.

LEMON. For a few details relating to this fruit, see the article ORANGE.

LENS. This name is given to a glass, or other transparent medium, ground with two spherical surfaces. If one side is flat and one convex, it is called *plano-convex;* if both are convex, it is *double convex;* if one is flat and one concave, it is *plano-concave;* if both are concave, it is *double concave;* if one is convex and one concave, it is *meniscus*, or concavo-convex. All these lenses, for optical purposes, are ground to the proper curve by revolving wheels.

LEVELLING. The relative heights of a series of points on the ground are obtained by means of their vertical distances from others which, on the supposition of the earth being a sphere, are equally distant from its centre; and these, which are called level-points, must be found by an instrument constructed for the purpose. [SPIRIT LEVEL; THEODOLITE.] In general, a choice is made of any convenient stations on the line of operation, and the distances between them are determined by actual admeasurement. The instrument is then set up at or near the middle of the interval between every two such points in succession. When the telescope thus placed has been rendered horizontal by means of the adjusting screws, an assistant at each of the adjoining stations, holding what is called a station staff in a vertical position, moves a vane or index along the staff, upwards or downwards according to the directions of the observer at the telescope, till it appears to coincide with the intersection of two wires in the telescope. The points thus determined on the staves are level points or points equally distant from the centre of the earth; and the difference between the height of the index on the two staves will give the relative height of the ground at the two stations.

It is frequently the practice to execute a sort of double-levelling; which consists in placing the instruments successively at each of the stations, a staff being held up vertically at the other, when, the axis of the telescope being at equal heights from the ground at both stations, half the difference between the heights read on the staves will express the difference in the height of the stations.

The profile of the ground is usually expressed on paper, in portions of any convenient length, for the purpose of enabling the engineer to determine the depths of his excavations, or the heights of the masses of earth to be raised, when it is proposed to execute a canal or road. A right line being drawn to represent one parallel to the horizon, and passing through the highest or the lowest point of the natural ground; the heights and depressions of the remarkable points, with respect to such line, are obtained by additions or subtractions from the numbers in the field-book, and are, by a proper scale, set out from that line on others drawn perpendicularly to it at intervals equal to the horizontal distances between the same points. The series of points thus obtained, being joined by hand or otherwise, give the figure of the required vertical section of the ground.

LEVER. This simple but invaluable mechanical instrument consists merely of a bar of wood or metal, by fixing one point of which called the *fulcrum*, a pressure at the end more distant from the fulcrum is made to counterbalance a larger pressure at the nearer end; or, if both ends be equally distant from the fulcrum, equal pressures are made to balance each other.

The first explanation of the lever was given by Archimedes, and in a simple and correct form. It assumes two principles; firstly, that when a system is in equilibrium, the state of rest will not be disturbed if additional pressures, such as compensate each other, and would by themselves produce no motion, be introduced or removed; secondly, that, when a weight is made to rest by being attached to an immoveable point (say it is suspended by a string), the point or pivot of suspension undergoes a pressure equal to the weight of the system, whatever may be the form of that system, or the dispositions of its parts. Thus, a cylindrical or prismatic bar of uniform material will necessarily rest if a pivot be passed through a section in the middle of its length, since there is no reason why it should preponderate on either side; now, divide the bar into any two parts, and, from their middle points, suspend weights equal to the weights of the parts; also apply counterpoises of equal weights at the same points, by means of strings passing over pulleys; the equilibrium will then be undisturbed; take away from the system the parts of the bar and the counterpoises (which are equal and opposite to one another), and the equilibrium will subsist between the remaining weights, which are those first suspended. The points of suspension being in the middle of the lengths of the two parts are at distances from the pivot (at the middle of the whole length of the bar), which are inversely proportional to the suspended weights.

This may be briefly illustrated thus. When a straight and uniform bar is supported on a central pivot, if weights on either side of the pivot keep the bar exactly horizontal; then the weight on one side, multiplied by its distance from the pivot will be equal to the other weight similarly multiplied by its distance. If a weight of eight lb. balances another of sixteen, the former must be twice as far from the pivot as the latter. It is on this principle that the *Steelyard*, and other kinds of weighing machines, act.

In English treatises on mechanics it is customary to call one of the pressures which balance on a lever, the *power*, and the other the *weight*. Levers are thus distinguished as of the first, second, or third kind, according as the fulcrum, the weight, or the power, is in the middle.

LEYDEN. In this Dutch city the manufactures of linen and woollens have declined considerably, but are still the most important in Holland. The woollen manufacturers are especially famed for the production of very soft blankets with scarlet borders. A great wool fair is held annually. There are likewise extensive manufactories of soap and indigo, tanneries, salt-works, &c.

LI'BER, the inner bark of a plant, is a layer consisting of woody tissue, cellular substance, and vessels, forming a compact zone immediately applied to the wood. The woody tissue of which it is composed quickly becomes thick-sided, by the addition of internal ligneous strata, the consequence of which is, that such tissue in this part is more tough than elsewhere. Hence it is usually from the liber that are extracted the fibres employed in making cordage or linen thread: this at least is its source in hemp, flax, the lime tree, the lace-bark, and many other exogens which furnish thread; but in endogens, which have no liber, as the cocoa-nut, it is the ordinary woody bundles of the leaves, stem, and husks of the fruit from which the fibre used for ropes is procured. In many plants a new layer of liber is formed annually, contemporaneously with a new layer of wood; but this is by no means universal; on the contrary, the oak and the elm increase their liber slowly and irregularly.

LI'CHENS. This large and important natural order of imperfectly organised plants contains numerous species employed in the arts as pigments, and as articles of food. It is principally in the former respect that they are of economical interest, in consequence of the great consumption of orchal, or archil [ARCHIL], Cudbear (*Lecidea tartarea*), and others by the dyer. Lichens are distributed over all parts of the world, forming in the polar and similar regions a food for animals and man. *Cladonia rangiferina* supports the reindeer; *Cetraria islandica* furnishes the nutritious Iceland moss of the druggists' shops; and various species of *Gyrophera*, under the name of Tripe de Roche, form a part of the supply of food scantily furnished by nature for the Canadian hunter. In warmer countries they acquire a firmer consistence, and appear to form secretions of a peculiar kind in much greater abundance than in the northern parts of the world.

LIEGE. This very important Belgian province produces hops, corn, and a little wine; the pastures are good, and maintain great numbers of horned cattle and sheep. The mineral wealth of the country is considerable; there are mines of calamine, alum, lead, and iron ore; but more important than all these together are the numerous coal mines of the province. The manufactures, which are conducted on a large scale, consist of all kinds of steam-machinery for railroads and factories, mil castings, fine woollens, merinoes, linen, cotton stuffs, cutlery and surgical instruments, fire arms, glass, hardware, &c. The number of steam-engines of different kinds in the province is between 400 and 500.

The manufacturing towns are numerous. *Glons* is the centre of a great straw-hat manufacture, which gives occupation to upwards of 6000 people. *Herstal*, or *Heristal*, has important coal-mines, iron and steel works, and iron-foundries. *Herve* has manufactures in woollen cloth, stockings, and shoes. At *Huy*, beer, spirits, paper, leather, linen, and cast iron are manufactured. *Seraing* has coal-mines, important iron-foundries, and glass-works. *Spa*, famous for its mineral springs and baths, exports about 150,000 bottles of mineral water annually from the Pouhon spring, which is the strongest. Spa is famous also for the manufacture of elegant wooden toys, workboxes, writing-desks, &c. *Verviers* is famous for the manufacture of fine and ordinary woollen cloths and kerseymeres, giving employment to 40,000 hands in the town and neighbourhood; the Belgian army is clothed principally from the looms of Verviers, the total produce of which is estimated at 1,000,000*l.* sterling annually. Flannels, serges, tickings, coverlets, mouselines de laine, merino, &c., are also manufactured. The dyes of Verviers are said not to be surpassed in Europe. There are also establishments for the manufacture of steam machinery, ironmongery, soap, beer, &c.

But the most important town in the province is *Liège*, from which the province itself has been named. The extensive coal-mines near the town; its numerous iron-works, royal cannon foundry, and establishments for the manufacture of fire-arms, hardware, broadcloth, glass, and leather; its engine-factories, zinc-rolling mills, and naileries; its linen and cotton factories, steel-works, and breweries; together with a flourishing commerce in colonial produce and manufactured goods,—render it one of the most important towns in Belgium, and one of the most industrial spots in Europe.

LIFE-BOAT; LIFE-PRESERVER. Many ingenious plans, more or less practicable, have been proposed for saving from drowning those who may be in peril by shipwreck or otherwise. These contrivances may be classed as *Life Boats*, *Life Buoys*, and *Life Dresses*.

Life Boats.—A life boat is a boat constructed with great strength to resist violent shocks, and at the same time possessing sufficient buoyancy to enable it to float, though loaded with men and filled with water. Such boats are maintained at most of the ports of this kingdom, always ready to put to sea when vessels are seen in danger of shipwreck, and provided with means for being conveyed to the shore, and launched as rapidly as possible. As early as the year 1785, a patent was granted to Mr. Lukin for a life boat with projecting gunwales and hollow cases or double sides under them, as well as air-tight lockers or inclosures under the thwarts: these contrivances increased the buoyancy of the boat, and the air-tight cases under the gunwales, by their weight when raised above the surface of the sea, and their resistance when depressed beneath, greatly prevented rolling. Mr. Lukin's boat was strong and buoyant, but it was liable to be disabled by having the sides staved in. This defect was obviated in Mr. Greathead's boat, which was invented soon after; its prevailing feature is that the boat is lined inside and outside with cork. Mr. Greathead's boat was instrumental in saving the lives of 300 persons in five years, near Tynemouth.

In 1839 Mr. Mackintosh of New York took out a patent for a sort of temporary life boat. It consists of canvas rendered impervious to water by being saturated with a solution of caoutchouc. A square piece of this canvas is so hemmed at the edges as to leave a hollow tube or channel, which, when filled with air, may act as a buoyant cell or air-chamber. The opposite edges of the piece of canvas are partially sewn together, so as to give to it the semblance of a boat, the sewn edges being cemented with caoutchouc to render them air and water tight. Mr. Adams shortly afterwards contrived a boat lined with cork in the inside, and having air-vessels under the decks or seats. Holcroft's pontoon, or safety boat, also of recent origin, has some peculiarities about it, on account of its portability. It is formed of a skeleton frame, easily detached and folded into one-sixth of the space which it occupies as a boat. The frame is covered with layers or folds of strong canvas saturated with India-rubber; and in various parts are cases or air-cells, partitioned off one from another. The portability of the boat is brought about by having the framework hinged to the keel, so that the sides close together like a portfolio. Captain Smith's paddle-box boats, for steam-vessels, originated from that officer having observed that there is room, upon such paddle boxes, for a life boat, without encumbering the ship in any way; and builders of steamers have devised a mode of making the inverted boat a covering for the paddle box.

Every year brings forward some new projects relating to life boats. There was a singular suggestion made a year or two ago by Mr. Bateman, for the construction of a wooden boat, having as many vertical cylinders as there were to be persons accommodated; each cylinder was to be 36 inches deep by 16 in diameter. Each cylinder was to have a cover when not in use; but when the cover was removed, a man was to get into each cylinder, and thus seek for safety. The interstices were to be filled up with cork, and other arrangements made for lightening, strengthening, and rowing the boat.

The Duke of Northumberland has recently offered a prize for the invention of the most efficient form of life boat; and this offer has led to the exercise of much ingenuity on the subject. One of the inventions proposed to compete for the prize is that by Messrs. Russell and Oswald of the Isle of Man. The boat is on the double or twin principle; both boats being divided into ten air-tight compartments, and completely decked over, by which arrangement they cannot be swamped. The boats are placed three feet apart; and upon them is fixed a framing, with seats and row-locks for eight rowers. The bottom of each boat is a curve, rising up at both ends to a considerable height above the water. There are arrangements for masts and sails. This boat is, we believe, to be exhibited at Hyde Park.

Life Buoys.—Besides those life boats which have been constructed for the especial purpose, there have been several inventions for converting ordinary ships' boats into life boats upon a sudden emergency, which may be applied by the crew of a ship in distress. Mr. Bremmer, about the year 1800, proposed that empty casks should be strongly fixed in ships' boats upon a plan described by him, which on trial was found to answer perfectly. Captain Gordon's life buoy consists of a series of bamboos of different lengths fastened together; the uppermost piece is the longest, the others diminish gradually to the lowest, which is the shortest of all; thus forming a triangle, which is covered with pieces of sound cork, strongly fixed to the bamboo rods. Two of these triangles are intended to be fastened to a boat, one on each side, the long pieces being close to the gunwale, the shortest near the keel. Well-tarred sheepskin bags, inflated with air; air-tight copper tubing fitted under the seats of boats; and many other contrivances have been partially used. Cork mattresses have been found useful, but it was alleged that they gave sailors facilities to desert, and they were discontinued; floating ropes lined with cork have also been suggested, but, like fire-escapes, these contrivances are never at hand when most wanted. Boyce's life buoy is intended to be kept suspended at a ship's stern, to be dropped into the water in case a man falls overboard. It is composed of two hollow wooden cylinders, either made air-tight or else filled with cork, and connected by a wooden grating so as to form a sort of raft. It has been suggested to convert the warping buoys which abound in our harbours into a sort of life buoys, by fitting them up with wooden battens placed lengthwise from end to end upon their circumference. Cooke's life buoy is formed of two hollow copper spheres, connected by a horizontal rod; and from the middle of the rod rises a vertical stem containing a fuse at the top. The fuse is lighted, the buoy is lowered, and the person in the water, attracted towards the buoy by the light (if at night), seeks safety by clinging to the floating mass. Captain Beadon's buoy consists of a metal tube, eight feet long by one foot in diameter, tapered at its after end; it is divided into water-tight compartments, and has a keel ten or twelve inches deep. There is a kind of saddle across the cylinder, on which a man may sit; a staff, on which a light may be kindled; and a paddle to work the buoy, or two oars hinged to it. Irvine's safety-portmanteau, which will support two persons clinging to it in the water; Henvey's cork float; and Taylor's deck chair, are among the numberless modern contrivances for a similar object.

Safety Dresses.—Among these contrivances is the life hat. The upper part of the crown of the hat is made air-tight and water-proof, so that, in the event of the wearer falling into the water, its buoyancy may (according to the intention of the inventor) save him from being drowned. The lining of the hat is capable of being loosened, and the vacant space expanded by air being blown into it, so as to form a buoy capable of being grasped by any one immersed in the water, instead of being worn like a hat. Macintosh's life cape is a waterproof garment, which is capable, by the introduction of air through a stop-cock into a vacancy formed by a double thickness of cloth, of being converted into a life-buoy. Air tight jackets, belts, pads, cushions, &c., have been devised in many forms.

Besides all the above contrivances, may be mentioned those, such as Captain Manby's, in which a rope is propelled by a cannon from the shore to a ship in distress.

LIGHT-BALLS, for military purposes, are hollow cases, either spherical, or in the form of cylinders terminated at each extremity by a hemisphere: they are filled with a combustible composition, and being thrown, by night, in a burning state from mortars, or in some cases from the hand, they serve to discover the working parties or troops of the enemy. The composition consists of pulverised saltpetre (6¼ lbs.), pulverised rosin (1⅞ lbs.), ground sulphur (2¼ lbs.), and linseed oil (¼ lb.) The balls are propelled from mortars varying from 4⅖ to 10 inches calibre, and correspond to the size of the mortar employed. Spherical cases of pasteboard or canvas, filled with a composition which while burning emits a great quantity of smoke, are frequently discharged from mortars in order to conceal a movement of troops from the view of the enemy, or to suffocate the enemy: these are called *smoke-balls*.

LIGHTHOUSES. These important buildings are erected along the sea-shore, or upon rocks, from which lights are exhibited at night for the direction of mariners. Floating lights perform a similar office, being shown from the masts of vessels moored in certain positions, generally as beacons to enable ships to avoid shoals or sunken rocks in the æstuaries of great rivers.

The erection of lighthouses in this country has not proceeded upon any systematic plan, but in every instance they have been constructed simply because of the disastrous losses that had occurred for want of them. From this cause it arises that our lighthouse establishments in the several parts of the United Kingdom have until recently been conducted under entirely different systems, different as regards the constitution of the management, the rates or amount of the light-dues, and the principle on which they are levied. Under the operation of recent acts of parliament, all the public or general lighthouses around the coast of England are under the management of the Trinity House; those around Scotland under the Commissioners of Northern Lights; and those around Ireland under the Ballast Board of Dublin. There is a second class of lighthouses, consisting of local or harbour lights, which are managed by corporations and local trustees, under powers given for that purpose; but even these local lights are being brought more and more under general central authority. There are at the present time about 320 lighthouses round the several coasts of the United Kingdom. These lighthouses are maintained by dues levied on all vessels which leave the harbours of the United Kingdom, at so much per ton per vessel, according to the number of lighthouses which the vessels pass. These dues, which have amounted in some years to nearly 400,000*l.*, are in some instances very oppressive; but gradual improvements are being introduced in the whole system.

A principal object in the establishment of these buildings is to give intimation to vessels approaching the coast during the night as to the place in which they are. It is therefore of importance that the lights exhibited on the same line of coast should have some essential differences, so as to be readily distinguished by mariners. The different appearances thus required are given by having two lights placed either vertically or horizontally with respect to each other, or three lights, as at the Casket rocks, or by causing the lights to revolve or to appear only at certain intervals, and to remain in sight only for a given number of seconds at each appearance; or by the employment of lamps of different colours, as in some of the harbour-lights, which do not require to be seen at a great distance.

The mode of lighting now generally used in this country is that of placing an argand burner in the focus of a parabolic reflector. This instrument is made of silver strengthened with copper, and is about 3 or 4 inches in focal length, and 21 inches in diameter. The number and the arrangement of reflectors in each lighthouse depend upon the light being fixed or revolving, and upon other circumstances connected with the situation and importance of the lighthouse. The mode in use in the lighthouses of France consists in placing a large argand lamp, having four concentric wicks, and giving a very powerful light, in the centre of the upper part of the building, and placing around the lamp a series of glass lenses of a peculiar construction; thus using a refracting instead of a reflecting instrument to collect the light, and only one lamp instead of a greater number. The lens employed is about 30 inches square, plano-convex, and formed of separate rings or zones, whose common surfaces preserve nearly the same curvature as if they constituted portions of one complete lens, the interior and useless part of the glass being removed.

Of the fixed lights of England and Scotland, in 1844, 76 were *catoptric*, or reflecting lights; while 18 were *dioptric*, or lens lights. The reflecting lights had, on an average, about 15 burners each; and the one burner of each lens light was about equal in efficiency to 14 burners on the reflecting principle. The English floating lights had an average power of about 12 burners each. The Irish lights are powerful; they presented an average power of 21 burners to each fixed light. The average annual cost for keeping up the fixed public lights is about 450*l.* per lighthouse.

In France, the lighthouses and harbour-lights are all under a public board; and the expenses are paid out of the treasury, and met by levying a port charge of 10*d.* per ton upon shipping generally. In 1845 there were 52 general coast lighthouses, and 101 harbour-lights. In America, as in France, the lighthouses are maintained by the government.

We will here briefly describe the three most notable lighthouses of modern times; viz., the *Eddystone*, the *Bell-rock*, and the *Skerryvore*.

Eddystone.—The Eddystone is the name of a rock which lies about 12 miles south-west of Plymouth Sound, in a position peculiarly dangerous for ships entering the Sound. A lighthouse was built on this rock in 1696, but blown down by a storm in 1703. A second was built in 1706, and burned down in 1755. The present lighthouse was planned by Smeaton in 1756, and finished a few years afterwards. It is a circular tower of stone, sweeping up with a gentle curve from the base, and gradually diminishing to the top. The upper extremity is finished with a cornice, and surmounted by a gallery and lantern. The tower is furnished with a door and windows, and an interior staircase and ladders. The granite Eddystone rock was partly wrought to form a foundation; and the dressed stones (granite at bottom and limestone at top) were dovetailed to the rock in a manner calculated to give immense strength. These stones were generally from one to two tons weight each. The base of the lighthouse is about 27 feet in diameter, and the entire height is about 80 feet.

Bell Rock.—About twelve miles from Arbroath, on the Forfarshire coast, is a dangerous rock called the Bell or the Inchcape Rock. On this rock Mr. Stevenson built a beautiful lighthouse, which was finished in 1811. The foundation is 42 feet in diameter, and is built solid to a height of nearly 40 feet, every stone being dovetailed into those which surround it. The higher or hollow part of the building is divided into six rooms, used as a fuel room, an oil room, a kitchen, a bedroom, a library, and the light-room. There are two large bells belonging to the building, to be rung when the weather is too foggy to permit the lights to be seen from a distance.

Skerryvore.—In the Atlantic Ocean, between the Hebrides and Ireland, are many dangerous half-hidden rocks, which have occasioned numerous shipwrecks. On one of these rocks, called Skerryvore, a lighthouse has been built in recent years, under circumstances of immense difficulty. Mr. Alan Stevenson undertook the work in 1834, but it was not till 1844 that the lights were exhibited. The rock is 12 miles from a small island called Tirree; and Tirree is two or three days' sail from any part of the coast whence supplies could be obtained; hence the difficulties encountered by the engineers and workmen were most harassing. It was at all times difficult to approach the rock; and when there, the number of working days in a year was very small; the rock itself is excessively hard, and the difficulty great of transporting stones thither. But all difficulties gradually gave way to the skill and perseverance of the engineer, and the structure was at length completed. It is 138 feet high, curving inwards from a basis of of 42 feet. It contains 9 stories or apartments in height. More than 4000 tons of material were used in its construction. The lighting apparatus consists of eight annular lenses revolving round a lamp of four concentric wicks, and producing every minute a bright blaze visible to a distance of 18 miles.

Among modern contrivances for lighthouses is that of forming the body of the building of iron. Such was the lighthouse constructed by Mr. Alexander Gordon, in 1842, for Jamaica; and many others have since been made. These structures are formed of cast-iron plates or in some cases of sheet iron, riveted together and braced in various ways, and having provision made for the contraction and expansion of the metal. Mr. Bush for many years advocated the use of a peculiar kind of floating light or lighthouse on the Goodwin Sands, but after the expenditure of much time, money, and ingenuity, the project has failed. Another scheme due to Captain Bullock, has for its object the construction of a safety beacon on the same perilous locality; and many other contrivances have been experimentally tried for the same purpose; but we believe none of these well-meant schemes have shown indications of permanent success. One of the most remarkable of modern lighthouses or beacons is the *screw-pile* lighthouse of Mr. Mitchell. This lighthouse is constructed on spots where a sandy soil would render a fixed structure unavailable. It consists of a light timber edifice, supported on eight or more very long and powerful piles, which are separately screwed down firmly in the sand by a screw formed at their lower extremity. One such lighthouse was constructed on the Maplin Sand at the mouth of the Thames, another at Fleetwood, and another at Carrickfergus. More recently, Dr. Potts has devised a mode of forming a foundation for a lighthouse on sand, by the sinking of hollow cylinders, through the aid of an air-pump, which pumps out the air from within the cylinder, so that the cylinder is forced down by atmospheric pressure.

LIGNIN, or vegetable fibre, is the substance which remains after a plant has had its soluble matter dissolved out of it. Lignin, properly speaking, constitutes the skeleton of the trunk and branches of the tree. It varies in different kinds, as to its colour, hardness, texture, and specific gravity. The texture of lignin is always porous; these pores, when fresh, contain the juices of different substances; during the drying of lignin the water evaporates, and leaves the matters dry which it held dissolved. When dry, lignin is a non-conductor of electricity. When exhausted of air in its pores, it is much heavier than water. When kept entirely dry, or entirely immersed in water, it resists decay for centuries; but, when alternately wet and dry, it gradually decomposes. The wood inclosing Egyptian mummies is found in good preservation, although some of it must be about 3000 years old. When wood (or lignin) is heated in iron cylinders, a great variety of important substances are obtained, besides charcoal, such as pyroligneous acid, pyroxilic spirit, creasote, and tarry matter.

LIGNITE, consists of fossil wood carbonised to a certain degree, but retaining distinctly its woody texture. A greater degree of change constitutes *cannel* and *common coal*, in which the original structure of the constituent plants can only with difficulty be traced; a less change belongs to *peat*, so that lignite occupies a place between coal and peat. *Jet*, *Surturbrand*, *moor coal*, *Bovey coal*, *Cologne earth*, and *basaltic coal* are considered to be varieties of lignite. Lignite often occurs in beds of considerable thickness and extent, and supplies to particular districts a bad substitute for coal. In general, lignite is most plentiful in the tertiary strata, and coal among the older rocks of the secondary series. Lignite is found in various parts of England, France, Italy, and Switzerland.

LIGNUM VITÆ. [GUAIACUM.]

LILLE. The manufactures of this town, which has been transferred from Flanders to France, are very important; they consist of all kinds of cotton goods; linen and linen thread, lace, blankets, and other woollen stuffs; paper, leather, beetroot sugar; steam machinery and ironmongery; gin, beer, and great quantities of oil, which is expressed in 300 windmills near the town; glass, soap, tape, hats, carpets, chemical products, &c. There are also iron and copper foundries, dye-houses, bleaching establishments, and sugar refineries. The trade in these various products and in colonial produce, wool, hides, hops, coal, tobacco, chicory, &c., is extensive. The town is lighted with gas, and has communication by railway and by canal with all parts of France and Belgium.

LIME. This substance, which is an oxide of Calcium, has been known from the remotest antiquity, and is most abundantly diffused in nature. It is never found pure, but always combined with other earths or with acids. It is easily obtained in a pure state, by applying heat to drive off the carbonic acid from carbonate of lime, leaving pure lime or *quick-lime*. Lime is white, opaque, and inodorous; its taste is acrid and alkaline. It cannot be burned in the strongest furnace. When exposed to the air it falls to powder. It readily combines with water, to form a *hydrate* and *lime-water*. A hydrate is formed when quick lime is slaked by the addition of water. Lime-water is prepared by dissolving the hydrate in water.

Lime is employed for a vast number of purposes, in common life, in agriculture, and in the arts and manufactures. Among its most important applications are the making of mortar, and the amelioration of certain soils. It is extensively used also in soap-making, leather-dressing, dyeing, and for various medicinal purposes.

LIME TREE. The lime tree is applied to many useful purposes. It is known in many foreign countries as the linden tree. The wood is of a pale yellow or white colour, close-grained, soft, white, smooth, and not liable to be attacked by insects. It is used by pianoforte makers for sounding boards, and by cabinet makers for a variety of purposes. It is turned into domestic utensils, and into small boxes for apothecaries. It is carved into toys, and is the material for some of the most exquisite carvings in our old English mansions. The blocks employed by Hollar for his wood engravings were of lime tree. The wood makes excellent charcoal for gunpowder. Baskets and cradles were formerly made from the twigs. Shoemakers and glovers use planks of lime tree upon which to cut the finer kinds of leather.

Lime-bark is used in making twine, ropes, baskets, mats, shoes, fishing nets, roof-coverings, and many other articles in various European countries; and in Carniola the peasants make a kind of coarse cloth from it. The leaves are used as food for cattle. The sap will yield sugar of very good quality. The fruit and flowers have been prepared into a kind of cocoa, pleasant in taste, but not fit for keeping. The flowers yield very delicate honey, especially in the Ukraine, where the bees who feed in the lime forests produce honey of great value.

LIMERICK. This Irish county has tracts of great fertility; especially one called the Golden Vein, which occupies the greater part of the eastern plain of Limerick. The soil is a rich, mellow, crumbling loam, and is equally suited to grazing or tillage: it is chiefly in pasture. A still richer soil is that of the 'Corcasses,' which extend for fifteen miles along the southern bank of the Shannon, from a little below Limerick to the embouchure of the Deel. They yield the greatest wheat-crops raised in Ireland; and their produce of potatoes is also large. Pasture and dairy farming are the staple occupations of the people. Great quantities of butter are made. Pigs of a very superior description are bred in great numbers by the dairy farmers.

There is a small manufacture of coarse woollens for home consumption, and the bleaching of linen is carried on, but on a contracted scale. There are paper-mills, and large and powerful mills for the grinding of corn.

The chief town of the county, *Limerick*, is the fourth town in importance in Ireland, and is the capital of the western part of the island as Dublin is of the east, Belfast of the north, and Cork of the south.

There are distilleries, breweries, tanneries, foundries, flour-mills, and ship-yards. Vessels of 1000 tons' burthen can approach within five miles of the city, and those of 400 tons can unload at the quays. By the inland navigation of the Upper Shannon, and the Grand Canal and Royal Canal, the city has communication with Dublin, as well as by one of the branches of the Great Southern and Western Railway. The number of ships registered at the port of Limerick is about 120. About a thousand vessels leave the port annually; and an equal number enter.

Limerick has a reputation for its lace, its gloves, and its fish-hooks; and the marble and slate of the neighbouring districts have considerable value.

LIMESTONE. In regard to the chemical composition of limestones, some, as statuary marble, are nearly pure carbonate of lime; others, as the dolomitic rocks of the Alps, contain a certain proportion of carbonate of magnesia; and some are penetrated by bituminous matter, as the black marbles of Yorkshire. Limestones also vary in quality, and become debased by admixture with sand, clay, oxide of iron, pyrites, &c.; so that there is in fact a real gradation from limestone to schist, to sandstone, to shale, to ironstone, &c. Limestones have a crystalline aggregation, as statuary marble, and generally the limestones mixed with primary systems of strata; or they are composed of small crystalline grains, as the magnesian limestone of Mansfield in Nottinghamshire; full of round concretionary parts, as the oolites of Portland, Bath, and Oxford; earthy, as chalk, and some magnesian limestones; or compact, as the lithographic stone of Solenhofen. The beds of calcareous rocks are of every thickness, from a mere lamina to some yards thick. The colours of limestone vary indefinitely; and the different kinds have very different degrees of value as building stone.

LINCOLNSHIRE. This county is famous for its fens. A general account of the great fen district of England, and of the changes which it has undergone, is given elsewhere. [BEDFORD LEVEL.] The artificial cuts or drains are very numerous; they are called by the several names of 'cuts,' 'drains,' 'leams,' 'droves,' 'becks,' 'eans,' and 'dykes.' The chief among them, in this county, are the Car Dyke, the South Forty-Foot, the North Forty-Foot, the East Fen Drain, the West Fen Drain, the Old and New Hammond Becks, and the Shire Drain. Of navigable canals, besides the Ancholme, Louth, Horncastle, Sleaford, Bourn, and other navigations, there are only two; viz, the Foss Dyke, and the Stainforth and Keadby Canal. When the works of the Great Northern Company are finished, Lincolnshire will be well supplied with railways.

The grazing land in this county cannot be surpassed in its capabilities for fattening cattle; and some of the drained fens and warp-lands along the rivers possess a high degree of fertility when cultivated. The lands which have been reclaimed from the sea by banking and draining are mostly laid in large farms, which require a considerable capital. In other parts of the county there are many small properties, cultivated by the owners, and kept with great neatness. Fish is much used as a manure. Ground bones are used very abundantly on the light sands. The grass-lands of Lincolnshire are some of the best feeding lands in the kingdom. Some of the finest pastures are fed off by horses which are fatted for the markets. Several parts of Lincolnshire have been improved by *warping*. The warping is effected by letting in the water of the rivers, which have a muddy current, by artificial channels and sluices, and retaining it there till low water. The river Humber carries off, in its course over various soils, all the finer particles which are too light to be immediately deposited. These consist of every kind of earth and portions of vegetable and animal matter, and are in such quantity that a layer one-tenth of an inch in thickness is often deposited between one tide and the next. Thus in a very short time a new soil is formed of any depth that may be desired, provided the land lies below the level of the river at high tides. Besides creating a soil, the warping fills up all inequalities, and a perfectly level surface is produced. The soil thus produced is of extreme fertility.

Lincolnshire is an agricultural county; but a few manufactures are carried on in the towns. At *Barton* a considerable trade in corn is carried on; and bricks, tiles, ropes, and sacking are extensively manufactured. BOSTON and GRIMSBY have been noticed in earlier articles. At *Bourn* wool-stapling and tanning are carried on, and the town has some trade in leather and wool. *Gainsborough* has a busy trade. By means of the Trent, which falls into the Humber about 20 miles below the town, vessels of 200 tons' burthen can came up to the wharfs. *Grantham* has a trade in corn, malt, and coals. *Lincoln* the county town has a large trade in flour, and there are some extensive breweries noted for their ale.

LINE. The French used to divide their inch into twelve *lines*, and the line into twelve *points*, which measures are out of date, since in all scientific investigations the metrical system is adopted. Sometimes, but rarely, the line has been divided into ten points, thus giving 1440 points to the foot. The French line is .0888 of an English inch, and is also two millimetres and a quarter. It is sometimes given in English books translated from the French; and on that account its meaning is worth bearing in mind.

LINEN MANUFACTURE. The woven goods in which flax is the chief material comprise *linens* as the principal; but also numerous others; such as *duck, check, drabbet, tick, huckaback, damask, diaper, drill, towelling, shirting, sheeting, sacking, sail-cloth, dowlas, canvas, &c.* Barnsley is the centre of the English flax manufactures, mostly conducted on the hand-loom system, but partly on the factory system. Dundee is the centre of the Scotch flax manufacture for coarse goods, and Dunfermline for fine, mostly conducted on the hand-loom system. *Belfast* is the centre of the Irish flax manufacture, one of the most important for the interests of that country.

The preparation of the flax for the spinners and weavers has been described under FLAX MANUFACTURE. We will here give a few statistics to illustrate the extent of the manufacture.

The flax factories in the United Kingdom in 1850 were as follows:—

	Factories.	Steam power.	Water power.
England and Wales	135	3,616	871
Scotland	189	5,004	1,421
Ireland	69	2,285	1,095
	393	10,905	3,387

From this we learn that the flax machinery was moved by an aggregate of 14,292 horse-power. These factories contained 965,031 spindles, and 1141 power looms. The persons employed in them numbered 68,434, of whom 47,617 were females. The children under 13 years of age were 1,581.

The exports of linen manufactures in 1850 comprised the following entries:—

Linen goods	122,397,457	yards.
Thread lace	464,164	,,
Sewing thread	3,361,922	lbs.
Linen yarn	18,559,318	lbs.
Miscellaneous	£ 17,728	value.

LINSEED, the seed of *Linum usitatissimum*, or flax plant, contains a mealy albumen of so oleaginous a nature that it yields by pressure in great abundance the oil of linseed. The seed of the flax-plant is harvested, not merely with a view to the reproduction of the plant, but also because of the oil which it yields by compression. For both these purposes, of sowing and crushing, linseed is largely imported into the United Kingdom. Linseed is also much used as food for small birds. Some of the imported seed goes to Ireland, and is chiefly used for sowing. The best seed for this purpose is brought from Holland. The residuum of linseed from which the oil has been expressed is used, under the name of *oil-cake*, for fattening cattle. For the import of linseed or flaxseed, see FLAX.

LINSEED OIL may be procured by cold expression of the seeds, a process which makes the oil clearer; or the bruised seeds are roasted in the oil mills, in which case it is brownish yellow, and easily becomes rancid, probably from attracting oxygen. Linseed oil is pellucid, with a faint but peculiar odour and taste. By long boiling it becomes dark brown, tenacious, and thickened, but dries more easily, and in this state is used for printer's ink; by still longer boiling it becomes black, almost solid, and elastically tenacious, like caoutchouc, and in this state it serves for bird-lime.

Linseed-oil is used to form liniments, of which the most common is that with lime-water, as an application to burns. But it is much more extensively used in the arts, particularly for painting.

LINTING MACHINE. The lint used by surgeons has until lately always been made by hand; but linting or lint making machines have recently been invented. One such was patented by Mr. Taylor in 1850. A committee of the Army Medical Board was appointed a short time ago to report on the quality of machine-made lint; and their report being favourable, the substance is coming extensively into use in hospitals and in private practice.

In the linting machine, the cloth which is to be scraped into lint is wound on a roller, from which it unwinds as the operation proceeds. During its progress its surface comes within the action of a knife or scraper, which has a sort of chopping or vertical motion; this cuts to a small extent into the warp and weft threads; and the cloth being immediately afterwards drawn forcibly beneath the edge of the knife, a nap or pile is raised over the whole surface of the cloth. This constitutes lint.

LIQUATION, or ELIQUATION, was one of the processes (now almost disused) for separating silver from copper.

LIQUIDAMBAR. This is the name of some fine trees which occur in Java, the Levant, and North America. *Liquidambar styraciflua* is the species found in Mexico and the United States, in the latter of which it is called Sweet Gum, and forms a large and fine tree. The wood is of a hard texture and fine grain, and makes handsome furniture; but the tree is more noted for the fragrant liquid resin which exudes from incisions in the stem, though not very copiously. This is called *Liquidambar*, or Oil of Liquidambar, which has a pleasant balsamic odour aud an aromatic bitter taste. This, becoming dry and opaque, forms what is called Soft or White Liquidambar, which resembles very thick turpentine, has a feebler odour than the liquid balsam, and contains less volatile oil.

LISBON. The trade of this interesting city, though much diminished since the loss of Brazil, is still considerable. It exports wine, fruits, and oil; and it imports corn, salt fish, salt butter, cheese, timber, iron, lead, tin, copper, coals, tar, and all sorts of foreign manufactures, with which it supplies the whole southern part of the kingdom. Lisbon has some manufactories of silks, paper, soap, and leather; its goldsmiths and jewellers are very expert; and there are also sugar refineries and potteries.

LITHARGE. [RED LEAD.]

LI'THIUM, a metal, the oxide of which is one of the earths, and is called *lithia*: it occurs in a few minerals, combined with silica. When separated, the metal resembles sodium in whiteness; but it has not been much examined. None of the chemical compounds of lithium have yet been applied to much use in the arts.

LITHOGRAPHY. In printing from an engraving on a copper or steel plate, the ink is delivered from the incisions made therein with the graver or etching needle. An engraving on wood gives its results from the projecting surface of the block, or those parts which are not cut away by the graver. The lithographic process differs from both these modes, the impressions being obtained (by strict attention to chemical affinity) from a level surface.

There are various styles of lithography, but the principle of the art is uniformly the same.

The stone best calculated for lithographic purposes is a sort of calcareous slate, found in large quantities on the banks of the Danube in Bavaria. Stones much resembling the German have been found in some parts of Devonshire and Somersetshire, and also in Ireland; but they want some of the most essential qualities of those brought from Germany, which are therefore almost exclusively used. Even these vary much in quality, all the strata not being equally good. A good stone is porous yet brittle, of a pale yellowish drab, and sometimes of a gray neutral tint. The stones split into slabs varying from 1½ to 2½ inches in thickness, which are then cut or squared into the different sizes necessary for use, and the face or upper surface of each is made level. In this state the stones are sent from the quarry; but further preparation is yet necessary to fit them for the immediate use of the artist, and they are either grained or polished, according to the nature of the work they are intended to receive. Grained stones are used for drawings in the chalk manner, or for imitations of those produced with the black-lead pencil. Writings, imitations of etchings, pen and ink sketches, &c., require the face of the stone to be polished, which is effected by rubbing it with pumice-stone and water, or pumice-stone dust and water, applied with rags.

The two principal agents used for making designs, writings, &c., on stone, are called lithographic chalk and lithographic ink. They are composed of tallow, virgin-wax, soap, shell-lac, and enough lamp-black to impart a colour to the mass. These are incorporated by a peculiar process of burning in a closely covered saucepan over a fire, and the whole is ultimately cast into a mould, and receives the form calculated to fit it for use. The ingredients are the same in the chalk and the ink, but the proportions are varied. The chalk is used as it comes from the mould in a dry state; but the ink is dissolved by rubbing, like Indian ink, in water, and is used in a pen or camel-hair pencil. It is the presence of the soap in this greasy material which renders it soluble in water.

To render the lithographic process intelligible, let it be supposed that the artist completes a drawing with the chemical chalk just described, upon a grained stone. If, while in this state, a sponge filled with water were passed over the face of the stone, the drawing would wash out, the chalk with which it is made being, as we have seen, soluble in water, by reason of the soap which it contains. Before, therefore, it is capable of yielding impressions, a weak solution of nitrous acid is poured over it, which unites with and neutralises the alkali or soap contained in the chalk, and renders it insoluble in water. After this, the usual course is to float a solution of gum over the whole face of the stone; and when this is removed, if a sponge and water be applied to its surface, as before supposed, the drawing is found to be no longer removeable, because the chalk with which it is executed is now no longer soluble in water. In this state the work is ready for the printer, who obtains impressions by the following process.

Having thrown with the ends of his fingers a few drops of water on the stone, and spread them with a sponge, so as to wet, or rather damp, the whole surface equally, the printer finds that the water has been imbibed by the stone only on those parts not occupied by the drawing, which, being greasy, repels the water and remains dry. A roller properly covered with printing ink is now passed over the whole stone, which will not even be soiled where it is wet, from the antipathy of oil and water. But the parts occupied by the drawing, being, as we have seen, dry and greasy, have an affinity for the printing ink, which therefore passes from the roller, and attaches itself to the drawing. In this state it is said to be charged, or rolled in. Damped paper is then put over it, and the whole being passed through a press, the printing ink is transferred from the stone to the paper, and this constitutes the impression. By repeating in this manner the operations of damping the stone and rolling in the drawing, an almost unlimited number of impressions may be obtained.

The modes of lithography are, as we have said, various, but the illustration just given will explain the principle of them all. It consists in the mutual antipathy of oil and water, and the affinity which the stone has for both, *i. e.* in its power of imbibing either with equal avidity. Some of the coloured lithographs now produced are exquisite productions.

To insure complete success, great nicety is requisite in the preparation of all the agents employed in this art. Those who wish to study or practice the art in its full extent will do well to consult 'A Complete Course of Lithography,' by its discoverer, M. Senefelder, or 'A Manual of Lithography,' by M. Raucourt, both translated into English.

Plates of zinc have lately been much used as substitutes for the German stones, in chemical printing, and the practice is then called *zincography :* but, excepting the difference of the material on which the work is performed, it is precisely the same art as lithography.

LITMUS, or LACMUS, is a fine blue but fugitive colour prepared from the *Lecomora tartarea*, a lichen which grows in the Canary and Cape Verd Islands. In order to extract the colouring matter, the lichen is cleaned and reduced to powder; this is then mixed with urine and lime, and in a few days the blue colour is developed. The litmus is imported in small cubical cakes of dusky blue colour, which are light and easily reducible to powder.

Litmus is used as a chemical test for detecting the presence of acids, by which it is turned red, and the blue is restored by alkalis, so that when slightly reddened it may also be employed to detect alkalis. It will detect the presence of sulphuric acid, even when diluted with 100,000 times its weight of water.

LIVE STOCK. The animals necessary for the stocking and cultivation of a farm, and those which are kept on it for profit, or for the sake of their dung, are called the *live stock* of the farm, in contradistinction to the *dead stock*, which consists of the implements of husbandry and the produce stored up for use. To have the exact number of animals which will give the greatest profit is one of the most important problems which a farmer has to solve; and it also requires much experience and nice calculations to ascertain what stock is most profitable on different kinds of land and in various situations.

The following are the numbers of animals comprised among live stock, imported in the last two years :—

	1849.	1850.
Oxen and Bulls........	1,678	2,316
Cows	965	1,810
Calves................	1,002	1,345
Sheep	9,491	16,251
Lambs................	12	10
Swine and Hogs	199	675

LIVERPOOL. The advance of this most important commercial town has had few parallels in the world's history. In 1650 it is said there were only 15 ships belonging to the port. Towards the middle of the next century three docks were constructed for the convenience of the shipping employed in the African and West Indian trades. In 1764 more than half the African slave trade was carried on by the merchants of Liverpool. From the settlement of the cotton manufacture in Lancashire, Liverpool has become the port where the great bulk of the raw material of the manufacture is received, and whence the exports of manufactured goods are chiefly made to all parts of the world. The cotton imported into Liverpool is more than six-sevenths of the whole quantity imported into Great Britain. Still more recently, and especially since the employment of steam-vessels for the conveyance of merchandize, this port has enjoyed a very large proportion of the trade between England and Ireland, for the prosecution of which it is particularly well situated.

The magnificent docks of Liverpool, unequalled perhaps in the world, are noticed under DOCKS. The full number is now 21 docks, 2 half-tide docks, 8 graving docks and 4 basins. They are capable of containing 1500 sail. The annual income of the docks is about 300,000*l.*, and the charge about 280,000*l.*

The receipt of customs duties in 1850 was 3,366,284*l.*, against 3,472,202*l.* in 1849.

The growth of the trade of Liverpool has been very rapid. In 1816 there were 6,888 vessels entered the docks, of 774,243 tons burden, and paying in dock dues 92,500*l.*; whereas in 1850 there were 20,457 vessels entered Liverpool, of 3,500,000 tons burden, and paying 211,000*l.* dock dues.

Eight parts out of nine of all the American cotton brought to this country are shipped to Liverpool. There have often, in recent years, been 50,000 hogsheads of sugar, 20,000 barrels and bags of coffee, and 10,000 puncheons of rum, brought to Liverpool in one year. It has been estimated that 50,000,000 cwts. of goods have been shipped at the Liverpool docks in one year. As one among numberless illustrations, which might be given of the extent of Liverpool commerce, it has been stated that 27,000 cubic feet of logs of cedar for *pencils* have been in the docks at one time.

About two-fifths of the tonnage inwards and outwards are engaged in the trade with the United States of America. Liverpool keeps up a larger intercourse with Ireland than all the other English ports combined, and it has benefited more than any port in the kingdom (London alone excepted) from the application of steam power to navigation. Besides those which proceed to the United States and other foreign countries, steam ships of the first class proceed to and arrive from Dubiin daily; and it has communication more or less frequently with Drogheda, Belfast, Waterford, Newry, Londonderry, Glasgow, the Isle of Man, Whitehaven, Beaumaris, Bangor, Menai Bridge, and Carnarvon. Most of the Irish emigrants come to Liverpool to embark.

The inland trade of Liverpool is much assisted by means of canals, the most important of which in extent is the Leeds and Liverpool Canal, 128 miles long. The Mersey and Irwell navigation, the Duke of Bridgewater's Canal, and the Ellesmere Canal also connect Liverpool with the inland counties. Besides the various ramifications of the London and North Western Railway, there are now also the Liverpool and Bury Railway, and the Liverpool and Preston Railway.

One of the most interesting productions intended for the Great Exhibition, is a model of the commercial part of Liverpool, comprising the whole of the docks, and the great foci of trade and commerce in the town. The frontage of the town is almost five miles long, from north to sonth. The scale of the model is eight feet to the mile. There is also, associated in some respects with this model, a collection formed (or forming) of all the chief products imported into Liverpool; comprising a variety scarcely paralleled in any other British port. These two memorials of Liverpool greatness—the model and the collection of imports—will each occupy several hundred feet of space, and are intended to form a permanent exhibition at Liverpool after the grand but temporary display in London.

LIVONIA, one of the Baltic provinces of Russia, is a somewhat barren country. The chief occupations of the inhabitants are agriculture and the distillation of spirits. The country produces rye and barley, flax, hops, hemp, and linseed. The fruit, such as apples, plums, and cherries, is very indifferent. There are no minerals of importance nor manufactures, except in Riga. The exports are corn, hemp, flax, and linseed; the imports are salt, iron, lead, colonial produce, wine, manufactured goods, and articles of luxury.

LLAMA. This valuable South American animal was found by the Spaniards, when they conquered Peru, to be employed in bringing down ore from the mines among the mountains. Its ordinary load was 80 or 100 pounds, and its average rate of travelling with this burden was from 12 to 15 miles a day over rugged paths and through mountain passes; but, like the camel, if too heavily laden, it would lie down, and obstinately refuse to proceed; nor would it bear to be urged beyond its accustomed pace. Gregory de Bolivar estimated that in his day 300,000 were employed in bearing the produce of the mines of Potosia alone, and 4,000,000 annually killed for food.

As a beast of burden in its native mountains, whether of Peru or Chili, the Llama has yielded to the mule. But it is still most important on account of one of its qualities which attracted the attention of the ancient Peruvians; it is a wool-bearer, and that of no ordinary kind, the wool approximating in its character to silk. Large quantities of this material are imported into Europe for the manufacture of shawls and other delicate fabrics, and the improvement of this material has been made a subject of earnest consideration and trial. The *Alpaca* and the *Vicunu* seem to be species of Llama.

LOAM, is the name given to a soil compounded of various earths, of which the chief are silicious sand, clay, and carbonate of lime, or chalk. The other substances which are occasionally found in loams, such as iron, magnesia, and various salts, are seldom in such proportions as materially to alter their nature. Decayed vegetable and animal matter, in the form of humus, is often found in loams in considerable quantities, and the soil is fertile in proportion.

LOBSTER FISHERY. The lobster is found in great abundance on the rocky coasts of Great Britain, in clear water at no very great depth. Pennant mentions the great quantities supplied to the London markets, in his time, from the Orkneys and the eastern coast of Scotland; and states the number annually brought in well-boats from the neighbourhood of Montrose alone at sixty or seventy thousand. Lobsters being very voracious, the fishery for them is carried on sometimes by means of traps or pots made of twigs, baited with garbage, lowered into the sea, and marked by a buoy; sometimes by nets baited with the same materials; and in some countries, by torchlight, with the aid of a wooden instrument which acts like a forceps or a pair of tongs.

LOCKS AND KEYS. Great ingenuity is shewn in the numerous modes of shooting or working the bolt, in locks. In some locks the bolt is projected by the action of a spring; in others there are two or more bolts, one of which only is under the control of the key, the others being moved by handles; while in another class of locks two or more bolts are shot or projected by the action of the key alone. *Padlocks* are a kind of detached lock in which a curved bar of iron, pivoted to the lock at one end, may be passed through a staple, and then so secured by shooting the bolt into a cavity in its free end, which is inserted into the lock for the purpose, that it cannot be removed from the staples or links through which it has been passed.

By far the greater part of the almost innumerable ingenious contrivances for rendering locks inviolable may be classed under one of two systems of security. The first consists in the insertion in the lock of fixed obstacles, commonly called *wards*, which prevent the entrance of any key which is not formed with corresponding openings, so as to thread its way among them, and thus render the bolt inaccessible to any but the proper key. The second consists in the use of moveable impediments (which in their most general form are called *tumblers*) to the motion of the bolt itself, the security arising from the difficulty of bringing these moveable impediments, by the use of any but the proper key, to the actual and relative positions necessary to allow free motion to the bolt. In many locks both of the above means of security are used.

The key of an ordinary lock consists of a cylindrical shank with a loop-shaped handle at one end, and a piece called the *bit* projecting from it at a right angle at or near the other end. The bit end of the shank is hollow or solid, according as the lock may be opened from one side only, or from two. The projecting bit, after being introduced into the body of the lock through the key-hole, is turned round within the lock until it comes in contact with a part of the bolt which is so shaped that the bit of the key cannot pass it, to conplete its revolution, without shooting the bolt either backwards or forwards, as the case may be. When thus moved, the bolt is retained in its position by a spring, or some other means, until it is again moved by the reverse action of the key.

The varied and highly ingenious inventions of Chubb, Bramah, Mordan, and other lockmakers, depend on various combinations of the above two contrivances, the *ward* and the *tumbler*, aided by peculiarities in the form of the key.

As a means of security somewhat differing from any of the above, and affording certain advantages peculiar to itself, we may notice the *permutation* or *combination* principle, of which the simplest application is in a kind of padlock often termed a puzzle-lock, which opens without a key, but is regarded rather as an ingenious toy than as an available substitute for locks of the more usual construction.

Some locks have been made in which tho action depends on the key being a powerful magnet. In others the difficulty of opening is increased by requiring a peculiar method of applying the key; but, in addition to the circumstance that the secret must be known to several persons, these contrivances have the disadvantage of being very inconvenient in use. In one invention a key with two bits, and requiring eight or nine distinct movements in the act of unlocking, is used with a double lock, capable of shooting two distinct bolts. Many contrivances have been effected for attaching an alarum to locks, by which tho introduction of a false key should ring a bell or fire a pistol. But most of these contrivances are curiosities rather than conveniences. In the compound-locks for iron safes, which often throw out two or three bolts in every direction, that is to say, on each side, and towards the top and bottom of the door, these are usually but so many branches of four massive pieces of iron, capable of being simultaneously projected by a handle in the centre of the door, the actual lock being but small, and merely intended to move an apparatus by which the great bolts are themselves locked or held fast; so that the key need not bear

NIGHT'S CYCLOPÆDIA OF THE INDUSTRY OF ALL NATIONS.

o. 28.

any proportion to the magnitude of the bolts by which the door is secured.

A most complete series of locks was constructed, some years ago, by the late Mr. Chubb, for the Westminster Bridewell. It consists of about eleven hundred locks, forming one series, with keys for the master, sub-master, and warders. At any time the governor has the power of stopping out the under keys, and in case of any surreptitious attempt being made to open a lock, and the detector being thrown, none of the under keys will regulate it, but the governor must be made acquainted with the circumstance, as he alone has the power, with his key, to replace the lock in its original state. These locks, although they have been in constant wear for sixteen years, are still in perfect condition.

Mr. Chubb, in an interesting work on this subject, remarks, 'The manufacture of locks and keys is carried on, principally, at Wolverhampton, and the adjacent towns in Staffordshire, as well as in Birmingham and in London, and gives employment to thousands of persons. Besides the home consumption, a large export trade is also carried on; and it is gratifying to know, that the use of the best locks, on which a great amount of labour is expended, is increasing, whilst greater attention has lately been paid to the style and character of the ornamental parts of both locks and keys."

Mr. Chubb has lately produced a remarkable specimen of lock-making. It is a gold finger-ring which instead of a stone contains a perfect padlock, on Chubb's patent principle, opening with its miniature key, all made of gold, and capable of locking and unlocking; the lock and key only weigh ten grains.

LOG AND LOG'LINE. This is the apparatus by which the velocity of a ship's motion through the water is measured. The log is a flat piece of wood, loaded with lead at one of its edges to make it float upright; and to this is attached a line about 150 fathoms long, divided into equal lengths by little pieces of knotted twine rove into it. These divisions begin about twenty or thirty yards from the log, where a piece of red rag is usually fastened, in order to show the place readily. From the lee quarter of the vessel the log is thrown into the sea, where it is supposed to remain stationary during the operation, and the line is veered out at least as fast as the ship sails. As soon as the red rag leaves the reel, a half-minute glass is turned, and, when the sand is all run down, the reel is stopped. Then, by measuring the quantity of line run out, the distance sailed by the vessel in half a minute is known, and by calculation its rate of going per hour. The usual way of dividing the line is to place the knots at distances of fifty feet from each other. Now, as 120 times half a minute make an hour, and 120 times fifty feet make almost a geographical mile, so many knots will run from the reel in one experiment as the vessel sails miles in the hour; from this comes the expression of a vessel's sailing so many knots an hour—meaning miles.

Mr. Berthon's log, patented in 1850, registers the speed of ships out at sea by the height of a column of water raised by the resistance. There are two tubes which project beyond the bottom of the vessel; those tubes have small apertures through which the water enters, the height of ascent being greater as the speed of the vessel increases. There are various minor contrivances to measure the speed by the indications obtained.

LOGWOOD, OR CAMPEACHY WOOD, imported from the West Indies for the purposes of the dyer, is the wood of a low tree called *Hæmatoxylon Campechianum*. The wood is hard enough to take a fine polish, and is very durable. Its colouring matter is dissolved both by water and alcohol, and it is principally derived from the presence of a peculiar body, to which Chevreul, who discovered it, gave the name of *hematin* or *hæmatoxyline*. Logwood is employed by the calico-painter to give a black or brown colour, the cloth being always first impregnated with alum mordant, and thus black is obtained. Iron mordant and logwood also yield a black, but it is not so good as with the alum mordant. Cloth with the alum mordant, dyed in a mixture of logwood and madder, has a fine brown colour fixed upon it. Logwood is also employed in the preparation of lake-colours. The logwood imported into Great Britain in 1850 amounted to 34,690 tons.

LOIRE. This important river, whose length is between 500 and 600 miles, constitutes the great outlet for the produce of central and western France. The Loire is connected with the Saône by the Canal du Centre, with the Seine by the Canals de Briare, d'Orléans, and du Loing, and with Brest harbour by the canal from Nantes to Brest; and it has many important commercial towns built on its banks.

The river also gives name to a department, which contains extensive forests of pine, fir, beech, and oak; on Mont Pilat, near St.-Étienne, an immense number of deals are made, saw-mills being established on every available stream of water. But much of the finest pine timber is made into charcoal, in consequence of the great difficulty of transport from the mountain-heights on which it grows. Great quantities of chestnuts are grown; these enter largely into the food of the people. The department contains one of the richest coal-beds in France, which, besides feeding the numerous factories and furnaces of St.-Étienne, and other places in the department, furnishes large quantities for exportation to Lyon and the towns on the Rhône. The quantity of coal annually furnished by the mines of Loire amounts to one-third of all the coal raised in France. Lead and iron mines are also worked; building stone, granite, potters' clay, &c., are found; mineral springs are numerous. The manufactures of the department are of the greatest variety and importance, and give rise to a very extensive commerce. The chief products are fire-arms, ironmongery, and machinery of all kinds, silks, ribands, crape, velvet, plush, laces, linen, cotton, glass, bricks, steel, iron, scythes, hardware, canvas, mill-castings, files and tools of all descriptions, cotton and linen yarn, lace, cutlery, earthenware, tiles, lime, &c. &c. Great numbers of coal barges and canal boats are built at Roanne and St.-Rambert. The great centre of manufacturing industry is St.-Étienne.

There are four other departments of France, whose names bear some resemblance to that of Loire; viz. *Loire-et-Cher*, *Loire Haute*, *Loire Inférieure*, and *Loiret*. They present varied aspects in respect to produce and manufactures; but are not so important in those respects as the department of the *Loire*.

LOMBARDY. The administration of the Austrian government in Lombardy has paid peculiar attention to the material improvements of roads, bridges, canals, dykes, and other public works. Among the most useful enterprises have been, constructing or repairing the dykes in the province of Mantua; completing the great canal called Naviglio; making roads in the mountainous districts of Bergamo, the great commercial road of the Splugen, and the road over the Stilfer Joch to Como and Lecco; and building the splendid bridge at Buffalora on the Ticino. Railways have also been constructed from Milan to Monza, 12 miles, Milan to Trevilio, 18¼ miles, and Venice to Vicenza, through Padua; and others are in progress.

The Lombardo-Venetian kingdom is generally one of the most fertile countries of Europe; and the industry of the inhabitants, and the extensive system of irrigation, increase the natural fertility of the soil. Lombardy produces in abundance every thing that is necessary for the sustenance of its population—corn, wine, rice, fruits, cheese, and excellent meat. The chief articles of export are silk, rice, cheese, and hemp. The chief manufactures are silk, glass, paper, bronze works, and straw hats; but Lombardy is essentially an agricultural country, and receives most of the manufactured goods which it uses from the other parts of the Austrian monarchy. The bookselling and publishing trade, although subject to the censorship, is (in peaceable times) more flourishing at Milan than in all the rest of Italy put together.

A little further information concerning the industrial statistics of this beautiful country will be found under the names of some of the provinces and cities.

LONDON. To present a few industrial statistics of this, the greatest commercial city in the world, is of course all that can be attempted in a work like the present.

In the City of London there are 89 companies or guilds connected with trades or employments, eight of which are practically extinct; and one other, that of Parish Clerks, is not connected with the municipal institutions of the city. Most of the companies possess what is called a *livery*; that is, a part of their body, under the name of liverymen, if they be freemen of the corporation, enjoy privileges which other freemen do not possess—such as voting for mayor, sheriffs, chamberlain, &c. Most of the guilds have long ceased to be practically beneficial to the crafts to which they relate. Most of them are in possession of real property and money in the public funds, both for their own use and on various trusts. The Irish Society is a corporation connected in a peculiar manner with the corporation of London; its property is chiefly in the county of Londonderry, in Ireland.

That London is not commonly considered as a manufacturing town is owing to the more important aspects under which it presents itself, and not because of the absence of manufacturing industry. Manufactures of almost every kind are in fact carried on in the metropolis, and upon a scale of great magnitude. The largest breweries, distilleries, and sugar-refineries in the kingdom are in the metropolis. The manufacture of metals in almost every branch is carried on to a vast extent. Almost every kind of machinery, from the smallest wheels required by the watch-maker to the most powerful steam-engines, are made in London. The making of gold and silver articles, of optical and surgical and other instruments, tools of the best quality, and musical instruments, gives employment to numerous hands. Ship-building, with all its accessories, rope-making, mast-making, block-making, anchor-making, &c., has always been actively prosecuted. There are also numerous chemical works on a large scale, tanneries, soap-manufactories, potteries, and dye-houses. Male and female clothing of all descriptions is made, not merely for the use of the inhabitants of the metropolis, but for the supply of wealthy persons in various parts of the kingdom and even in the British colonies. There are not much fewer than 1500 separate trades or occupations carried on in the metropolis. The metropolis is also the great workshop of literature, science, and the arts. The number of books printed and published in all other parts of England is small in comparison with what is produced in London.

It is not possible to state with any pretensions to accuracy the amount of consumption in London of any except a very few articles of general use, because such commodities are becoming less and less under Excise and Customs regulations. The cattle sold in Smithfield amount to nearly 200,000 annually; sheep, 1,600,000; calves, 25,000; and pigs, 250,000. But, besides these, a large amount of slaughtered meat is now brought to the metropolis by railway and steamers. There are 5000 licensed publichouses, besides beer retailers, and exclusive of inns, hotels, and wine merchants. There are 1600 butchers' shops, 2400 bakers' shops, and 2800 grocers and tea dealers. The coffee shops are now very numerous. Concerning the recent arrivals of COAL and CORN in London, see those articles. See also MARKET-GARDENS.

The relative proportion of the foreign and colonial trade enjoyed by the merchants of London, as compared with those of other ports, may be shown from the fact, that out of the gross receipt of customs at all the ports of the United Kingdom, usually about 22,000,000*l.* sterling, that of London about equals all the other ports combined. The shipping entries vary; but on the whole there is a constant progressivo increase. In 1848 the amount was :—

	Vessels.	Tons.
From Foreign Countries .	7,686	1,267,875
From the Colonies	1,843	546,195
Coastwise	22,584	3,242,572
	32,113	5,056,642

The vessels which left London with cargoes we may presume to be about equal in number. The ships which entered the port of London from Foreign Countries alone, in 1850, amounted to 9,910, of 1,903,407 tons.

There are about 50 wharfs on the north and south banks of the Thames, within the limits of the metropolis, besides the canal wharfs and the docks for the shipping destined to foreign countries.

The facilities for accommodating shipping are noticed under DOCKS. The railways from the metropolis are mainly accommodated at six large stations: viz. Euston Square, King's Cross, Paddington, Waterloo Bridge, London Bridge, and Shoreditch; besides a smaller station in Fenchurch Street, and separate goods' stations at Camden Town, Vauxhall, and Bricklayer's Arms. The chief canal of London is the Regent's Canal, which curves round the northern part of the metropolis from Limehouse to Paddington (whence it communicates with the northern and western parts of the kingdom), and has several basins and wharfs: the remaining canals are all short, and comparatively unimportant.

There is no port in the kingdom which has profited more than London through the application of steam to navigation. A great part of the steam vessels that arrive and depart carry passengers only, and are therefore not required to make entry at the custom house, and with regard to such as carry goods no distinction is made at the custom house between them and sailing vessels; for which reasons no accurate account of the number of this class of ships that enter and leave the port can be given. Steam passage-boats are passing and repassing daily between London, and Chelsea, Kew and Richmond, and in summer some go up to Hampton Court; and between London and Greenwich, Woolwich, Gravesend, and other places, downwards; while, at less frequent intervals, steamers start from the Thames to nearly all the principal ports in the United Kingdom and throughout Europe.

That such a gigantic focus of industry will take up a worthy position in the Great Exhibition of All Nations, may well be expected and believed.

LONDONDERRY. In this county railways are in progress from Londonderry to Enniskillen, and from Londonderry to Coleraine. A remarkable feature of the last-named scheme is, that the railway is to cross Loch Foyle on an embankment 19 miles long, as a means of inclosing and reclaiming 18,000 acres of land. The best improved portions of the county are the district of Loch Neagh, the valley of the Roe, the valley of the Faughan, and the immediate vicinity of Londonderry on both sides of the Foyle. There is a very general scarcity of timber. The progress of agriculture in this county has been materially forwarded by the establishment of an agricultural school near Muff by the Company of Grocers of London, who here hold large estates under the crown. Oats and barley are the principal grain crops.

The manufacture and bleaching of linens is the staple trade of the county. The most extensive bleach-greens lie along the rivers Roe and Faughan, on the latter of which there is abundant water-power and numerous sites admirably calculated for this branch of manufacture. The weavers and flax-dressers are numerous. The export and import trade of the county is carried on at the ports of Londonderry city and Portrush, the latter being the seaport of Coleraine.

LOOM. [WEAVING.]

LOT. There are two departments of France which take their names from the river Lot. One, the department of Lot, is very fruitful. The hill-slopes along the rivers are generally laid out in vineyards, which yield annually 13 to 14 million gallons of wine, the best kinds being those of Cahors and Grand-Constant. About two-thirds of the whole produce is exported or distilled into brandy. The white mulberry is extensively cultivated for the production of silk. A few iron and coal mines are worked; lead, calamine, marble, millstone grit, granite, limestone, potters' and fullers' earth, &c., are found. Of manufacturing activity there is little; a little bar and cast iron, coarse cotton and woollen stuffs, brandy, and paper, are made. The corn-mills, which are about 1000 in number, are the only important manufacturing establishments in the department. The commerce is composed of the articles already indicated, and of hides, salt, oak-staves, groceries, small wares, broad cloth, &c.

The other department, that of Lot et Garonne, produces 14 to 15 million gallons of wine yearly, half of which goes for the home consumption; part of the surplus is distilled into brandy, and the remainder is exported to Bordeaux. Immense numbers of geese are reared, and form an important article of export. Iron mines are worked; good building stone, calcareous spar, gypsum, and marl are found. The chief manufactures are cork, sailcloth, linen, swanskins, pottery, linen and cotton yarn, iron, glass, paper, lime, ropes, leather, tobacco. The commerce is composed of the various industrial and agricultural articles enumerated, and of pitch and tar made from the pines of the Landes.

LOUISIANA. A few industrial statistics relating to this fruitful portion of America, will be found under UNITED STATES and NEW ORLEANS.

LOUTH, a maritime county of the province of Leinster in Ireland, is not rich in minerals. Iron and lead ore are the only minerals which have been observed, but nowhere in sufficient quantity to warrant mining operations. The soil of the southern division of the county is well calculated for every kind of grain crop. Farming in general is carried on in a superior manner. Green crops are grown by almost all the gentlemen farmers. The fences are usually of quickset, and the lands well drained. The linen manufacture is carried on with some activity at Ravensdale and Collon, where there are large bleach greens, but chiefly in Drogheda and its neighbourhood, where the trade is generally very brisk. The fisheries off the coast give occasional employment to several hundred persons.

Dundalk carries on a brisk trade, chiefly in the exportation of grain, cattle, and other agricultural produce, and in the importation of groceries and goods in boxes and bales for the supply of the counties of Louth, Monaghan, and Cavan. Steamers ply regularly to Liverpool twice a week. Drogheda is briefly noticed in respect to its commerce elsewhere. —[DROGHEDA.]

LÜBECK. The commerce of this celebrated city is of considerable importance. Lübeck has 80 ships of its own, and the arrivals are about 800 annually. The principal export and import trade is with Russia, Sweden, and Denmark; vessels of 9 feet draught can come up to Lübeck, where they enter a spacious basin lined with quays; larger ships discharge their cargoes by lighters at *Travemünde*, which is situated at the entrance of the Travo into the Baltic, and has a fine secure harbour. Steamers ply from Travemünde to St. Petersburg, Copenhagen, Hamburg, Amsterdam, and Stockholm. Small steamers convey passengers up the river to Lübeck. Lübeck was one of the most famous of the HANSE TOWNS.

LUCERNAL MICROSCOPE, is an optical instrument invented by Mr. Adams. It consists of a hollow pyramidal box, at the smaller extremity of which is a tube carrying the usual system of lenses for magnifying objects. At the larger end, which is towards the observer, there are two lenses in frames, their axes, as well as those of the small lenses at the opposite extremity, being coincident with the axis of the box; and between the exterior of the two lenses and the eye of the observer there is usually placed a plate of glass, rough-ground on one side, which serves as a screen to receive the rays of light proceeding from the object whose representation is to be viewed. The object is fixed in a small frame, as usual, and is placed in a groove made for the purpose immediately beyond the tube containing the system of lenses at the small end of the box. Instead of the plate of ground glass, a board painted white is frequently placed, to serve as a screen, at the distance of 6 or 8 feet from the instrument. Such a screen should have the form of a segment of a hollow sphere, the light being received on its concave surface. An Argand lamp, or an oxy-hydrogen light, is placed beyond the object. The light, after passing through a hemisphere of glass, is, when an opaque object is to be viewed, made to fall in a convergent state upon a small concave mirror, which is so inclined as to reflect the light back upon the object; and from the different points on the surface of the latter the pencils of rays proceed through the object-lenses and the box to the glass screen.

By the refraction of the light in passing through the lenses a highly magnified image of the object is formed; and several persons may then place themselves so as to see the image on the screen at the same time; or, by placing the eye at the small aperture in the produced axis of the instrument, one person may, with a pencil, draw on the glass, or on tracing-paper laid over it, the figure of the object, it being understood that the instrument is used by night or in a darkened room.

When the object to be viewed is transparent, the light is made to fall in a condensed state upon it, after having been transmitted through a convex lens, or two such; and from the object the rays proceed as before to the screen through the system of lenses which constitute the compound object-glass of the microscope, and through those at the opposite extremity of the box.

LUPULIN, is a substance extracted from hops, and containing from 8 to 12 per cent. of the vegetable matter to which hops owe their power, and to which the name of *lupulite* has been given. Lupulite is nearly colourless, but sometimes of an orange colour: in the former case it is opaque, but in the latter transparent; it has no smell till it is heated, and then it has the odour of hops; its taste is bitter.

LUTE, is a musical stringed instrument with frets, one of the numerous varieties of the ancient *Cithara*. Till towards the end of the 17th century its practice formed an essential part of a good education, but it has since been partially superseded by the guitar. The lute consists of three parts: the table, made of fir; the body or belly, of the same wood or cedar, constructed of nine convex ribs joined; and the neck, on which was fixed the finger-board, of hard wood, having nine frets made of catgut. To these is to be added the head or cross, in which the pegs or screws were placed. The lute had at first six strings, or rather eleven, for the five largest were doubled; but the number was gradually increased till it reached twenty-four.

LUTES, in chemistry, are substances employed in various operations for closing the joints of apparatus, and especially for connecting retorts and receivers so as to prevent the escape either of the vapour or gases generated during distillation or sublimation. The term lute is also applied to the external coating of clay and sand, or other substances applied to glass retorts, in order that they may support a high temperature without fusing or cracking. Common plastic clay answers sufficiently well in some cases, but in some small distillations, as of nitric acid, the Fat Lute is used, which is prepared by mixing dried and powdered pipe-clay into a paste with linseed oil; and the joint is further secured, both where this lute is used and in many other cases, by tying it over with moistened bladder. In luting common stills, in which oils or water are merely distilled, linseed meal and water made into a paste, form an effectual lute.

In luting, or rather coating, glass retorts, in order to enable them to sustain high temperatures, Stourbridge clay or Windsor loam mixed with tow have been used; but they require long drying, and are apt to crack. The simplest mode is that of brushing the retort over with a paste of pipe-clay and water, sifting sand upon it, drying it quickly in the ash-pit of the sand-heat, then covering it again with clay and sand, and repeating the alternate applications and drying till the coating is judged sufficiently thick.

LYNX FUR. The lynx skins imported for furriery purposes in 1847 amounted to 32,540 and in 1848 to 47,317.

LYON or LYONS. This most important French town is very advantageously situated on the line of railway from Paris to Marseille, now in course of construction, and on two navigable rivers the Rhône and the Saône, in the fork between which the greater part of the town is built.

Lyon is a flourishing manufacturing town. The staple articles of industrial produce are silk stuffs of all descriptions, which for solidity of texture, richness and permanence of dye, and beauty of design, are not equalled elsewhere. In this manufacture about 100,000 of the population are directly or indirectly concerned. Cashmere and silk shawls, ribands, cotton cloth, hosiery, hats, printed calico, jewellery, liqueurs, chemical products, gold and silver lace, crapes, tulle, glue, sheet lead, musical strings, ornamental paper, &c., are also made. There are, besides, numerous printing establishments, dye-houses, metal foundries, glass works, potteries, tan-yards, breweries, boat building yards, &c.

Lyon is also, from its advantageous position, a place of great commerce. The products imported into the town, for its own consumption, or for re-exportation, are wine, brandy, oil, hemp, flax, soap, rice, chestnuts, salt, raw cotton, coffee, indigo, sulphur, lead, teazels, madder and other dye-stuffs, &c. Timber, firewood, building stone, and asphalte are the chief articles brought down the Rhône to this city. Down the Saône are brought timber of all kinds, oak staves, fire wood, charcoal, tanning bark, iron and iron ore, gypsum, hay, straw, corn, building stone, bricks, tiles, &c. Steamers ply on the Saône to Châlon-sur-Saône, and on the Rhône to Avignon and Arles. The town has communication with the Rhine by the Canal du-Rhône-au-Rhin; and with Paris by the Saône and the canals that join it to the Seine. A railroad, 35 miles in length, unites Lyon to the great manufacturing town of St. Etienne and the extensive coal fields of the department of Loire.

LYRE. This musical instrument has been known under various names, from the earliest historical period. Some of the Greeks ascribe its invention to Mercury, some to Apollo; but it is possible they may have had it from the Egyptians, and the Egyptians from Asia. Of many instruments, figured or described in early writings, it is difficult to decide whether they should be termed lyres, lutes, harps, or guitars. The most ancient Grecian lyre had only three strings. That of Terpander had seven. Timotheus increased the number to eleven; and others were gradually added, till they reached sixteen, fifteen of which rendered the principal sounds in the Greek scale, and the sixteenth was the added or supernumerary sound.

M

MACCLESFIELD, is one of the silk manufacturing towns of the north. The various factories are situated on the Bollin. One of the cotton factories cost 30,000*l*., and some of the silk factories 14,000*l*. The silk trade of Macclesfield progressively advanced from 1808 to 1825, when it attained its greatest prosperity. It has since been less prosperous, but is still large. Every variety of silk article is produced here, from the narrowest riband to the different kinds of sarsnets, plain and figured gros de Naples, satin, silk, vestings, and velvets. It is likewise the chief place for the manufacture of silk handkerchiefs of every description.

MACE. [NUTMEG.]

MACERATION is the steeping of substances in cold liquids, either merely to soften the parts of the substance operated on, or to dissolve the aromatic parts of a substance when *digestion* would not merely dissolve but dissipate them.

MACHINE; MACHINERY. The advantage which any machine affords for overcoming resistance consists in the reaction by which it supports a certain portion of the weight producing that resistance, so that the motive power has only to counteract the remainder. This may be immediately observed in those simple machines called the *mechanical powers*. For example, in the lever, the wheel and axle, and the pulley, any convenient portion of the resistance may be made to rest on the point of support, or the point of suspension. Again, in the inclined plane, the wedge, and the screw, the motive power, the resistance and the reaction of the support, being, in the case of equilibrium, represented by the three sides of a triangle, the ratio of the first to either of the others may be varied at pleasure by the construction of the machine.

The powers employed to give motion, through machinery, to any object, are produced by the muscular strength of men or animals; the actions of weights, springs, wind, water, steam, or fired gunpowder; and these powers may generally be considered as pressures exerted during certain portions of time. Even that power which is produced by a sudden impulse, as when a rammer descending by its weight falls on the head of a pile, is only a pressure existing during an indefinitely short interval of time. The point in any machine to which the moving power is applied is called the impelled point, and that against which the resistance acts is called the working point.

In the classification proposed by Dr. Lyon Playfair, and adopted by the Commissioners at the Great Industrial Exhibition, *machinery* forms one of the four great divisions into which the specimens exhibited are to be disposed; and this division is subdivided into six classes; viz. 1. Machines for direct use, including carriages, and railway and naval mechanism; 2. Manufacturing machines and tools; 3. Mechanical, civil engineering, architectural and building contrivances; 4. Naval architecture, military engineering and structure, ordnance, armour, and accoutrements; 5. Agricultural and horticultural machines and implements; 6. Philosophical, musical, horological, acoustical, and miscellaneous instruments. This classification is doubtless convenient for the immediate object in view; but it gives to the word 'machinery' a much wider application than is ordinarily adopted.

Our exports of machinery and mill-work in 1850 amounted in value to 1,043,764*l*.

MACKEREL FISHERY. [Fisheries.]

MADDER. This useful dye-drug is procured from one of the many species of the plant *Rubia*, a name derived from *ruber* (red), in allusion to the red colour yielded by many of the species. Amongst the numerous species several are employed in medicine and in the arts; in the latter for the sake of the colouring matter which is contained in the roots. *Rubia tinctorum*, Madder, has been long known, and was employed in medicine even in the time of Hippocrates, but is valued chiefly as a dye. It is a native of Europe and Asia Minor, but is now extensively cultivated in Holland and France; the culture has likewise been attempted, and successfully, in this country; but the English madder could not be sold so cheap as the foreign; it is therefore still largely imported, chiefly from Holland, France, Italy, Turkey; though cochineal, since it has become cheaper, is much used for the same purposes. It is employed by dyers and calico-printers as a red and scarlet dye. It has also the singular property of turning red the bones and secretions of fowls and other animals fed on it. *Rubia cordifolia*, the *Munjeet* of India, a native of Nepaul, &c., possesses similar properties, and is imported into England from Calcutta.

About 254,722 cwts. of madder and madder root were imported in 1849, and 261,841 in 1850.

MADEIRA. This beautiful and fruitful island produces many tropical plants near the sea-shore. Above this region, to a height of from 750 to 2,500 or 2,800 feet, the fruits and grain of Europe, especially wheat and maize, are raised; and in this region are also the extensive vineyards, which till recently furnished the most important article of exportation. Then follows a tract covered with high trees, which rises to 3,200 feet and higher, where many plants and trees are found which do not occur in Europe; and above this level is a region of grass, fern, and heath. The commerce of Madeira is considerable. The exports consist chiefly of Madeira and Malvasia de Madera wines. Minor articles of export are, fruits, dragon's blood, honey, wax, orchil, and tobacco, besides provisions for the vessels bound to more remote places. The imports consist of manufactured goods, corn, fish (herrings and cod), oil, salt-beef, salt, and some tropical productions. The imports into Great Britain from Madeira consist mainly of wine and nutmegs. The wine imported thence in 1847 amounted to 154,701 gallons.

MADRAS. A few commercial statistics of this city and presidency will be found under East India Company.

MADRID, has no commercial or industrial features to call for notice here, further than such as are described under Castile and Spain.

MAGAZINE, is a strong building, constructed generally of brick or stone within a fortified place, or in the neighbourhood of a military or naval station, in order to contain in security gunpowder or other warlike stores. The buildings in which gunpowder is contained are constructed with every precaution necessary to insure dryness. They are generally in places remote from other buildings; they are furnished with metallic conductors, in order to avert danger from lightning; and, for security against the attempts of ill-disposed persons, they are surrounded by a wall and ditch. The great magazines which have been constructed in this country consist of several parallel vaults, separated from each other by brick partition-walls, in which are doorways for affording lateral communication. Each vault is about 90 feet long, 19 feet wide internally, and from the floor to the crown of the arch 19 feet high. The side walls are from 8 to 10 feet thick, and are strengthened by buttresses built at intervals against them. The thickness of the brickwork forming the vaulted roof is 7 or 8 feet at the crown, and about 3 feet at the hances.

MAGDEBURG. The industry and commerce of this portion of the Prussian dominions receive a few illustrations under Prussia.

MAGIC LANTERN. The object of this remarkable optical instrument is to obtain an enlarged representation of figures on a screen in a darkened room, by means of the pencils of light issuing from a lamp or candle and passing through a convex lens.

The instrument consists of a lantern generally of tin, and of a cubical form, in the interior of which is the light; and at a perforation in one of the sides is applied a tube, projecting horizontally from it, which carries two glass lenses. A groove in front of the lantern and parallel to that front receives a rectangular frame containing the glass plates on which are painted, with transparent colours, the objects of which an enlarged view is to be obtained. A remarkable improvement in the manner of employing the magic lantern was first exhibited in London in the year 1802. The lantern itself is similar to but larger than that which serves for more general purposes, and the images are represented on a transparent screen, which is stretched in a vertical position across a theatre or an apartment; and, this being made quite dark, the spectators occupy the space in front of the screen, while the apparatus is disposed on the opposite side. All light is excluded both before and behind the screen, except that which, in proceeding from the lantern, produces the image to be observed; and, the screen being itself invisible, the spectators can scarcely divest themselves of the idea that they are looking into a dark cavern, in which the objects appear to be gradually advancing towards or receding from them. The allusions produced have caused the name of *Phantasmagoria* to be applied to the apparatus.

The magic lantern and the phantasmagoria are used only for purposes of amusement; whereas the CAMERA OBSCURA has been made available in photography.

MAGNESIA. This name, derived from a province in Asia Minor, has been applied to several useful substances which contains the metal *magnesium* as a basis. Oxide of Magnesium, termed also, from the mode of procuring it, *Calcined Magnesia*, is an alkaline earth, possessing the usual qualities of alkalies in their habitudes with acids, and likewise very valuable properties as a medicine. Sulphate of Magnesia, or *Epsom Salts*, in the ordinary form, as met with in the shops, are small acicular crystals. [EPSOM SALTS]. *Magnesia Alum*, *Magnesia Pharmacolite*, and *Magnesite*, are three naturally formed minerals, in which magnesia is a chief element. *Magnesian limestone* is a valuable building stone. *Magnesium*, the base of all these substances, is of a white colour, like silver; its lustre is metallic and brilliant; it is very malleable, and fuses at a red heat. When heated to redness in the air or in oxygen gas, it burns brilliantly, and, combining with oxygen becomes magnesia. *Chloride of Magnesium* forms a transparent colourless mass: it is inodorous, intensely bitter, very deliquescent, and soluble both in water and alcohol. This salt is one of the saline ingredients of sea-water. Carbonate of magnesia constitutes the *Common Magnesia* of the druggists.

MAGNETIC POWER. The combination of Magnetic power with galvanic power, in several recent mechanical contrivances, are briefly noticed under ELECTRO-MOTION and TELEGRAPH.

MAGNOLIA. This genus of American and Asiatic plants includes many species which are applied to useful purposes. Of the *Swamp Magnolia*, the bark has a bitter and aromatic odour resembling sassafras. On this account it has been used in America as a substitute for other aromatic bitter barks, as Cascarilla, Canella, &c., and, it is said with great success. Although not much used in Europe, very favourable reports of its efficacy in chronic rheumatism, ague, and remittent fever have been given. Of the *Cucumber-tree*, another species, a tincture is made of the fruit, and is used in cases of rheumatism. Other species are applied to useful purposes, chiefly in North America.

MAHOGANY. There are many species of trees belonging to the genus *Sweetenia*, which include among them the mahogany. One of the species yields the *African Mahogany*, brought from Sierra Leone; the timber is hard, but is liable to warp; it is employed where a hard cheap timber of large scantling is needed; the negroes employ an infusion of the bark in medicine. Another species yields the beautiful East Indian *Satin-wood*, which is of a deep yellow colour, close grained, heavy, and durable. The most useful and well-known species, however, is the *Campeachy Mahogany;* the timber of which is so familiar to us as to need no description. It appears to have been first imported into this country about the year 1724. From the elevated parts of the country the wood is closer grained and darker coloured than that grown near the coast; the former is termed *Spanish* and the latter *Honduras* mahogany. Spanish mahogany is imported in logs about ten feet long, and from twenty to twenty-six inches square; whereas Honduras mahogany can be procured in logs of larger size. When the grain of mahogany is more than usually beautiful, it will obtain a price for fancy cabinet-work far beyond the usual market standard. On one occasion Messrs. Broadwood, the eminent piano forte manufacturers, gave 3,000*l.* for three logs of mahogany, which were each about 15 feet long by 38 inches square; it was of exquisite beauty and closeness, and was cut up into thin veneers for the more costly pianofortes.

Since the abolition of the duty on mahogany, the import has largely increased. In 1848 the import was 32,000 tons. The attention of ship-builders is being attracted towards the fitness of mahogany for building vessels.

MAILS. A few words concerning the Post Office Mails, as a remarkable commercial feature of our age, will be found under POST OFFICE.

MAINE. The productions and industry of Maine claim a little of our attention under UNITED STATES.

MAINE-ET-LOIRE. In this department of France about 11,000,000 gallons of white and red wine are made annually, some of which is of good quality. Since 1838 a good deal of effervescing wine, resembling the true champagne, and rivalling it in quality, has been manufactured. The department is famous for its melons. A considerable quantity of cider is also made. Iron and coal mines are worked; and marble, granite, building and lime-stone, slate, and potters' clay are quarried. The slate quarries of the department, especially those of Angers, are vast and frightful excavations, worked right from the surface of the ground. They give employment to about 3000 men, who raise about 80,000,000 slates annually. The number of factories and workshops of different kinds in the department is about 200, in which sail-cloth, linen, cotton handkerchiefs, flannels, paper, oil, cotton and woollen yarn, &c. are made. There are also numerous tanyards, sugar-refineries, distilleries, bleach-mills, and dye-houses.

MAIZE, or *Indian Corn*, is a plant commonly cultivated in the warmer parts of the world, where it answers a purpose similar to that of wheat in more northern countries. It is the *Zea Mays* of botanists, of vigorous growth, with stems of not more than two feet high in some varieties, and reaching the height of eight or even ten feet in others. Each grain has a long thread-like style, which projects beyond the enveloping sheaths; and as there are some hundreds of them upon each spike, the whole form a long tassel, which looks as if made of silk. A plant generally bears two full ears, the grains of which vary greatly in number: some of the largest ears in America contain at least 800 grains.

This plant in its wild state is met with in Paraguay, in Chili, and in North America. The bread made from maize is not so palatable to some as wheat bread, but, by mixing it in certain proportions with wheat, it makes a very pleasant food. In the United States of North America, Indian corn forms almost the only bread eaten by many of the people; and in the slave states it is the only bread that the negroes eat. It is not, however, in the shape of baked bread that maize is most generally used in Europe, but in boiled messes and soups, as peas are with us.

A light, moist, and warm soil suits this plant best. It thrives well on land broken up from grass. The time for sowing maize in the south of France is the month of April; farther north, it is sown later. When the maize is fully ripe, the ears are twisted off by hand and laid in a dry place; they are turned occasionally, that the sheath may not become musty, and are then stored in a dry place. The leaves are gathered for fodder a short time before the ears are pulled. In America and in Italy mattresses are stuffed with the dry sheath, which makes a cool and elastic bed. Horses, pigs, and poultry are fond of maize; it gives the flesh of the last two a peculiarly fine flavour. One of the most important uses of maize in Europe is to sow it thick, to be cut green as food for cows, oxen, and sheep. In a proper climate there is no plant which gives so great a mass of green food as maize. The produce is most abundant and nutritive.

Since the repeal of the Corn Laws, maize has been imported in considerable quantity into this country. The importations for the last three years were as follows:—

1848	1,575,521	qrs.
1849	2,224,459	„
1850	1,286,264	„

About 230,000 cwts. of maize-flour were imported in 1848; but the quantities in the next two years were much smaller.

MALAGA. From the earliest ages, under all the nations who have possessed it, this Spanish sea-port has been renowned for its commerce. Its imports are colonial produce, broad cloths, cottons, laces, spices, hardware, and cutlery. Its exports amount to about 1,000,000*l.* sterling annually. They consist of wine, grapes, muscadel raisins, almonds, figs, lemons, olive oil, brandy, anchovies, and lead. The harbour is spacious enough to accommodate a large fleet; it is protected on the east by a massy stone mole, five furlongs in length, and terminated by a handsome light-house.

MALIC ACID was discovered in 1785 by Scheele. It received its name from having been first obtained from the juice of apples, in which it exists in considerable quantity; but it also exists in many other fruits. Malic acid is colourless, inodorous, very sour to the taste, and acts strongly on vegetable blues; in a moist air it is deliquescent; it is very soluble both in water and in alcohol. Nitric acid converts it into oxalic acid. Its saline compounds are called malates, some of which exist in nature. They are not an important class of salts.

MALLEABILITY is that property of certain metals which admits of their being extended by the blows of a hammer or by pressure. In this quality gold exceeds all other metals: thus the gold-leaf sold in books is so extremely thin, that less than 5 grains cover about 270 square inches, and the thickness of each leaf does not exceed $\frac{1}{300000}$th part of an inch. Metals which are malleable are also ductile, that is, they may be drawn into wire. Iron which has been made hot by hammering loses its malleability, and cannot be again hammered till it has been annealed.

MALLOW. The common or *Marsh mallow* belongs to the *Malva* genus of plants. It grows in waste places and road sides; and the whole plant, but especially the root and the leaves, yield by boiling a mucilage which is very useful in medicine.

MALMSEY. This luscious and high-flavoured wine is made in the island of Madeira from grapes of a peculiar kind, which are suffered to attain the last stage of ripeness before they are gathered. Malmsey wine has much body, and will retain its good qualities for a long time. When newly made, Malmsey Madeira is of the same golden hue as the ordinary wine of the island, but its colour is materially deepened by age. Malmsey wine is also made in the island of Teneriffe, but the quality is greatly inferior to that of Madeira.

MALT AND MALTING. Malt is grain, usually barley, which has become sweet and more soluble in water, from the conversion of its starch into sugar by artificial germination to a certain extent, after which the process is stopped by the application of heat. The making of malt, called *Malting*, is conducted as follows—The barley is steeped in cold water for a period which (as regulated by law) must not be less than 40 hours; but beyond that period the steeping may be continued as long as it is thought proper. Here it imbibes moisture, and increases in bulk; at the same time a quantity of carbonic acid is emitted, and a part of the substance of the barley is dissolved by the steep-water. 100 bushels of grain, after being steeped, swell to the bulk of 120 bushels; and the quantity of matter which the steep-water holds in solution varies from $\frac{1}{50}$th to $\frac{1}{100}$th of the weight of barley. It consists chiefly of an extractive matter of a yellow colour and disagreeable bitter taste. After the grain has remained a sufficient time in the steep, the water is drained off, and the barley thrown out of the cistern upon the malt-floor, where it is collected into a heap called the *couch*, about 16 inches deep. In this situation it is allowed to remain about 26 hours. It is then turned by means of wooden shovels, and is diminished a little in depth. This turning is repeated twice a day or oftener, and the grain is spread thinner and thinner, till at last its depth does not exceed a few inches.

When placed in a couch, it begins gradually to absorb oxygen from the atmosphere, and to convert it into carbonic acid, at first very slowly, but afterwerds more rapidly. The temperature, at first the same with that of the external air, begins slowly to increase; and in about 96 hours the grain is at an average about 10° hotter than the surrounding atmosphere. At this time the grain, which had become dry on the surface, becomes again so moist that it will wet the hand, and exhales at the same time an agreeable odour, not unlike that of apples. At the time of this moistening, which is called *sweating*, the roots of the grains begin to appear, at first like a small white prominence at the bottom of each seed, which soon divides itself into three rootlets, and increases in length with very great rapidity, unless checked by turning the malt. About a day after the sprouting of the roots, the rudiments of the future stem, called *acrospire*, may be seen to lengthen. It rises from the same extremity of the seed with the root, and, advancing within the husk, at last issues from the opposite end; but the process of malting is stopped before it has made such progres.

As the acrospire shoots along the grain, the appearance of the kernel, or mealy part of the corn, undergoes a considerable change. The glutinous and mucilaginous matter is taken up and removed, the colour becomes white, and the texture so loose that it crumbles to powder between the fingers. The object of malting is to produce this change: when it is accomplished, which takes place when the acrospire has come near to the end of the seed, the process is stopped by drying the malt upon a kiln. The temperature at first does not exceed 90°; but it is raised very slowly up to 140° or higher, according to circumstances. The malt is then cleared, to separate the rootlets, which are considered injurious. In familiar language, malting may be considered as a change of the *starch* of grain into *sugar*, preparatory to a further change into *spirit*.

The subsequent processes of BREWING and DISTILLATION are described in previous articles.

The quantity of malt charged with excise duty in the last three years was as follows:—

1848.............. 37,545,912 bushels.
1849.............. 38,935,460 „
1850.............. 40,745,050 „

MALTA. The Maltese harbour is about 3,400 yards in length, with an entrance 450 yards wide, defended by a strong fort. The harbour varies in width from 700 to 450 yards, and is surrounded by all the requisite buildings for a naval arsenal: it is one of the finest harbours and naval stations in the Mediterranean. Of the surface of Malta about two-thirds are cultivated, and the remaining third is bare rock. There is much good native earth in the valleys, which has been converted into productive fields; but a great portion of the land has been brought to its present state of culture by the industrious native, who with great labour and expense cuts away the hard surface of the rock, and frequently finds a quantity of earth lying inert in the crevices and interstices beneath. The produce of Malta is cotton (which is its staple), wheat, barley, pulse, potatoes, barilla, cumminseed, and sulla, or the French honeysuckle, which is used as fodder. As there is no meadow-land, much barley is cut when green for draught animals; and the straw (which is very fine) is a good substitute for hay. The natives of Malta are hardy and industrious. The great bulk of the people who are not employed in field-labour are stone-cutters.

The British produce and manufactures exported to Malta in 1849 amounted in value to 387,744*l.*

MANCHE, LA. In this department of France, apple and pear trees are extensively cultivated for making cider and perry, the favourite beverages of the country. Of cider above 22,000,000 gallons are made annually; some of it, especially that made near Avranches, is of excellent quality. Hemp and flax are grown in considerable quantity on the eastern slopes of Cotentin. Fruits of various kinds are sedulously cultivated in the arrondissement of Avranches. Excellent butter is made, and large quantities of it are exported from Isigny. The department is rich in minerals. Iron, lead, and coal mines are worked; granite and building stone are quarried; marble, slate, potters' clay, and limestone are found. Manufacturing industry is actively exerted in the making of iron, the working of zinc and copper, the fabrication of plate glass, serge, calico, drugget, cutlery, woollen stuffs, lace, tape, hair-cloth, porcelain, oil, hardware, cotton yarn, paper, leather, soda made from kelp, basket-work, &c. Ship-building is actively carried on at Cherbourg and other towns on the coast. The articles enumerated, and the products of the soil, support an active commerce and coasting trade. The chief exports are fresh and salt fish, corn, cattle, horses, poultry, wax, honey, salt butter, feathers, salt, salt provisions, soda, &c.

The great engineering works at CHERBOURG are noticed elsewhere.

MANCHESTER. This most important town, the centre of the largest cotton-manufacturing operations in the world, is situated in a district which contains some excellent coal strata, a circumstance to which the place is in no small degree indebted for its prosperity. It has the credit of having given an impulse to our means of internal communication, and has reaped an ample reward. The achievements of Brindley were prompted by the desire which the Duke of Bridgewater had of sending his coal from Worsley to Manchester at a small expense; and Manchester now possesses the means of water-communication with almost every part of the country. In the railroad enterprises Manchester has held a prominent station. It furnished its full share of the capital employed in the formation of the Manchester and Liverpool Railway; and it is now the centre of a system of railways radiating in six different directions. There are two magnificent viaducts across the town, for connecting the Liverpool line with the Yorkshire and the London lines.

The commercial spirit dates back to a very early period. At first the woollen was the only branch of trade, but since the middle of the last century the cotton business has nearly superseded the former fabric. The series of brilliant inventions and discoveries, applied, improved, or originated in the district of Manchester, which comprise the steam-engine, the spinning-jenny, the mule jenny, the fly-frame, the tube-frame, the mule, &c., have proved most effective instruments in aiding the development of the cotton manufactures. Several hundred millions of pounds of cotton are brought into Manchester from Liverpool every year; and the cotton factories are by far the most important buildings in the town: there are more than two hundred of them within the precincts of the town and parish. Some of them are only spinning factories; others are both spinning and weaving. Bleach-works, dye-works, and print-works, all connected with the cotton manufacture, exist on a large scale in and near Manchester.

The processes of throwing and weaving silk were extensively carried on at Macclesfield several years before they reached Manchester. The silk-mill of Mr. Vernon

Royle, erected in 1819-20, was the first brought into operation in the latter town. Since then the trade has rapidly increased. Printing is another branch of the silk business, chiefly, if not exclusively, carried on at Manchester. Dyeing of silk is also extensively pursued, and in fact the town is becoming the centre of transactions in the silk trade. Besides the manufactures in cottons, silks, and woollens Manchester carries on large manufactures in hats, umbrellas, and small wares. Machinery of the finest kind is also made there to a large extent.

The warehouses of Manchester are on a vast scale; they contain not only the woven products of the town's factories, but the produce of most of the other cotton towns is brought to Manchester, as a central exchange for the manufacturer and the dealer. It was calculated in 1837, that 700,000 tons of goods were carried by canal alone from Manchester to the south, yearly; besides that which passed north, east, and west, and besides the railway goods' traffic. In 1851 the amount is vastly greater, especially in respect to railways.

Manchester, as a centre of the calico-printing trade, presents a fair field for the exercise of taste in designing; and a School of Design is gradually producing important results in the town. The report of the Schools of Design for 1850 states:—'The Manchester school is in a flourishing condition. The greatest number of pupils on the books at any former period was 217, reduced to 90 when the present master undertook the re-establishment of the school. There are now about 350, the average attendance being the full amount which the premises can accommodate, although additional space has lately been taken into occupation. The students are also of a better class than at any former period. There is a large proportion of adults, and about 50 of the advanced students are actively engaged in the production of designs, principally as pattern draughtsmen.'

The report proceeds:—'The school is undoubtedly gaining in the estimation of the manufacturers. In fact, the practical effects of the school upon the manufactures of the town are making themselves manifest in a way which may waken the interest of the most indifferent, by showing that good art possesses a money value. In the case of those manufacturers who produce goods to compete with the French manufactures in the American markets, attention to design has at all times been indispensable; and previously to the establishment of the schools they were under the necessity of employing foreigners, not only to sketch their designs, but also to draw out their patterns, at great expense, and under the disadvantage of much uncertainty. Those manufacturers who have had the intelligence to understand the manner in which the schools would become available, are now able to produce with certainty better patterns, at far less cost, by means of their own apprentices pursuing their studies in the school; the apprentices at the same time obtaining higher wages than were ever paid to artisans of the same class before. Many of these young men, as they acquire experience and knowledge of their business, are exhibiting much talent, as designers, in the strict sense of the term.'

Mr. Annersley, the principal of this school, has lately given notice that the sum of 110*l.* has been placed in his hands by a calico-printer of Manchester, for the purpose of being divided into prizes for the best designs suited for printing on calico or delaine, as follows;—20*l.*, for the best set of six three-colour patterns; 10*l.* for the second ditto; 5*l.* for the third ditto; and similar prizes for the best, second, and third best four and five colour patterns, which make up the sum thus offered.

The prize patterns are sent to the Great Exhibition, where about 14,000 square feet of counter space is occupied by Manchester contributions.

MANDIOC. The names of *Mandioc*, *Cassava*, and *Jatropha Manihot*, are given to an American plant, and to a wholesome food prepared from it. Bread is made from a kind of meal procured from the root or tuber which is somewhat parsnip shaped. The tuber is dug up, washed clean, peeled, and ground or grated. In Brazil where mandioc bread is made more largely than in any other country, many persons are employed together in peeling the tubers, which are then applied to and pressed against the face of a wheel made to revolve with great rapidity; and in this way the tubers are ground, the pulp falling into a trough beneath. The pulp is then placed in bags, which are exposed to a pressure sufficient to force out the juice which is of an unwholesome character. The pulp is then poured out upon a hot iron hearth, where it becomes baked into thin cakes. Though deemed somewhat harsh flavoured by persons accustomed to corn bread, these mandioc cakes are highly relished in Brazil. It is only the *bitter cassava* which requires to have the juice expelled; that of the *sweet cassava* is wholesome. When fermented with molasses, the juice yields an ardent spirit.

Tapioca, which is capable of being made into excellent puddings, and into light food for invalids, is a kind of starch prepared from the farina of cassava tubers. A considerable quantity of tapioca is brought annually from Brazil to Europe.

MANDOLINE, is a musical instrument of the lute kind, but smaller, having four strings, which are tuned in the same manner as those of the violin. The mandoline is still met with occasionally in Italy, but has fallen into disuse in most other parts of Europe.

MANGANESE. This metal was first discovered by Scheele and Gahn, about 1775. Its natural compounds are very numerous, and the metal is easily separated from them. Manganese has a grayish white colour, and resembles white cast iron in appearance; it is hard, brittle, and has a fasciculated crystalline structure; its specific gravity is 7.05; it is inodorous and tasteless, but when breathed upon, emits a smell somewhat resembling that of hydrogen gas. By exposure to the air, manganese readily tarnishes by oxidisement, and even in a very short time attracts sufficient oxygen to lose its metallic lustre, and falls to a reddish brown powder; hence the necessity for preserving it immersed in naptha. Even at common temperatures it slowly decomposes water; and at a red heat the decomposition is rapidly effected, and in both cases hydrogen gas is evolved, and oxide of manganese formed.

The ores of manganese are chiefly oxides, and are very numerous. There are no fewer than five oxides of the metals, of which the protoxide gives an amethystine colour to glass. *Manganic acid* has not hitherto been obtained in a separate state; but manganate of potash is easily prepared. It is of a green colour, and has long been known by the name of *mineral chameleon*, on account of the change of colour which the solution undergoes during the process. *Hypermanganic acid* has a fine red colour, and is rapidly decomposed by organic matter, as paper or linen. It bleaches coloured matter. Manganese combines with chloride and with sulphur. It also combines with several other metals, as gold, silver, copper, tin, and iron; with the last-mentioned, combination takes place readily, and the iron is rendered harder, whiter, and more brittle by it; and it is stated that iron which contains manganese is best adapted for making steel. A small quantity of iron causes manganese to obey the magnet, and renders it less oxidable. The oxides of manganese, and especially the binoxide, as containing most oxygen, are largely employed in the preparation of chlorine, for the manufacture of bleaching powder, or chloride of lime. It is employed in glass-making to correct the yellow colour which oxide of iron is apt to impart to the glass; it is used also in making the black enamel of pottery. Sulphuret of manganese has also been used within a few years to give a brown colour in calico-printing. The binoxide, the sulphate, and the hydrochlorate of manganese, are all employed in medicine.

MANGEL WURZEL. [BEET.]

MANGLE. [CALENDERING.]

MANGROVE. The Mangrove trees are found on tropical shores, where they form extensive forests. The wood of the *Red Mangrove* is heavy, of a deep red, and takes a fine polish. The bark is used in dyeing red, and is used in the West Indies as a fever medicine. The *gymnorhiza* species of Mangrove produces yellow, hard, durable wood; it has a sulphureous smell and burns with a vivid light. It is chiefly used by the natives for fire-wood, and for making posts for constructing their houses. The pith of the wood, boiled in palm wine or with fish, is used as food.

MANIFOLD WRITER. [COPYING MACHINE.]

MANIPULATION, in chemistry, embraces every part of the subject which is of a mechanical nature, such as the operations of weighing, measuring, the application of heat and electricity, the various modes of effecting solution, precipitation, distillation, and sublimation, and in fact every step in chemical research includes manipulation. The whole subject is treated in Faraday's 'Chemical Manipulation.'

MANNA, is the concrete juice of the *Ornus Europæa*, a species of ash which is a native of the south of Europe, growing abundantly in Sicily, Apulia, &c. The juice exudes spontaneously in warm dry weather, and concretes upon the bark of the tree; the finest manna is however procured by making longitudinal incisions of about three inches long. The manna flows at first in the form of a thick juice, which gradually concretes. The finest kind is called *Calabrian* or *flake manna;* it is in pieces of a pale yellowish white colour, is light, rather dry, and brittle, and it bears frequently the impression of the branch on which it concretes. It has a slight peculiar odour, and a sweetish taste, mixed with a slight degree of bitterness, and altogether leaves a disagreeable impression. Although it has a composition not unlike sugar it is not fermentable.

Besides the genuine manna above described, other sweetish secretions are exuded by some other plants which are usually considered to be kinds of manna. These appear to be all produced in warm and dry parts of the world, and are the produce of various species of plants. Manna belongs to the same series of vegetable bodies as sugar, and like that compound is widely distributed in the vegetable kingdom. It is a mild and useful medicine.

MANTUA. The territory of Mantua, one of the provinces of Austrian Italy, is noted for its fertility. It contains numerous fine meadows well adapted for the grazing of cattle, and irrigated by numerous streams and canals; vines and mulberry trees also abound. Landed property is very valuable in this district, which labours however under two disadvantages, namely, the danger of the inundations of the Po, to prevent which the dykes and sluices are kept in constant repair at a great expense, and the unwholesomeness of the air in summer. Neither in the province generally, nor within the city of Mantua, are much manufactures or commerce carried on; Mantua depends on its fine Arts rather than on its productive industry.

MANURE. Every substance which has been used to improve the natural soil, or to restore to it the fertility which is diminished by the crops annually carried away, has been included in the name of manure. There are some substances which evidently belong to both classes of manure. Of these *lime*, either in its caustic state of quick lime, or its milder form of a carbonate or chalk, is the principal. Lime, being an earth less porous than sand, and more so than clay, has an improving effect on soils in which either sand or clay prevails; but it has also a chemical effect as an alkaline earth.

Perhaps the most important class of manures are the excrements of animals. From the most ancient times of which there are any records, the dunging of a field has been an important part of cultivation. The preparing of the dung of animals, so as to render it more efficacious, is a later improvement, which however has not yet attained the perfection of which it is capable. A mixture of the dung of all the different animals kept on a farm, with all the straw that can be afforded, will give a manure of an average strength, which may be used upon all kinds of land. The great use of *liquid* manure on light soils is to impregnate them with soluble matter, which, being diffused through their substance, supplies nourishment to the roots of plants, wherever they may shoot out. It may be applied to the land at any time before the seed is sown, and soon after, when the blade springs up or the seed begins to form. The great effect of liquid manure has set farmers on finding some artificial substitute for it. Such substitutes are obtained by mixing all kinds of refuse animal matter (such as the refuse from oil mills and other manufactories) with water, and inducing putrefaction. This becomes a branch of trade in those countries where nothing will grow without manure. The increase of manure by the formation of *composts* is well known in many parts of Britain, and by their means the land has in many districts been rendered much more productive.

BONES and GUANO are important substances for manuring. The various substances which are generally enumerated as occasionally used for manure, are chiefly the refuse of manufactures, consisting of earths, salts, and organic substances. Soapers' waste is chiefly lime with a small portion of alkali. The scrapings of leather, horn, bones, and the refuse of the shambles, the hair or wool of animals, and rags made of these, may be all classed together. They must be distinguished as acting in a twofold manner: they absorb and retain moisture, at the same time that they afford nourishment by their gradual decomposition. One substance has been highly extolled as a manure. This is called *urate*, being a compound of urine and plaster of Paris. It is formed by mixing sand and burnt gypsum with urine, and forming a hard compound, which is afterwards reduced to powder. The ashes of vegetable substances which have been burnt in the open air contain a great portion of potash, with some fine earths. The refuse ashes from bleachers' and soap-boilers' premises have still some portion of alkali in them, and as they contain lime and other earths in a very divided state, their effect on the soil is very perceptible.

Mr. Blachfield took out a patent in 1849, for an artificial manure, composed of the following substances:—1100 cwt. of river sand saturated with sulphuric acid, 400 cwt. of superphosphate of lime, 300 cwt. of sulphate of ammonia, 100 cwt. of sulphate of soda, 100 cwt. of sulphate of potash.

MAP-MAKING. The mechanical execution of a map is simply an example of engraving on steel, copper, stone, wood, or zinc; but there are a few expressions relating to the projection or planning of a map which it is useful to know.

The methods adopted in the construction of maps are as various as the taste and judgment of the geographers themselves, but they may all be referred to two principles, viz. *Projection* and *Development*. By *Projection* is is meant the representation of the surface of a sphere on a plane, according to the laws of perspective. By *Development* is to be understood the unfolding or spreading out of the spherical surface on a plane. This however first supposes the sphere to be converted into a cone or a cylinder—these being the forms, portions of which most resemble portions of a sphere, and which, at the same time, are susceptible of the required development.

The *Gnomonic* or *Central Projection* supposes the eye to be placed in the centre of the sphere, and that the various objects to be delineated are transferred from a sphere to a plane, which is a tangent to its surface. The Maps of the Stars, prepared by the Society for the Diffusion of Useful Knowledge, are on this projection. In the *Orthographic Projection*, the eye is supposed to be at an infinite distance, so that the visual rays leave the sphere in parallel lines; the representation will decrease in accuracy with the increase of distance from the centre; the parts near the circumference being much foreshortened and distorted. In the *Stereographic Projection*, the eye is supposed to be placed at the surface of the sphere, and to view the concave of the opposite hemisphere through the plane of that circle, in the pole of which the eye is placed. It is especially calculated for maps of the world, as usually made in two hemispheres, from the circumstance of the representation being less distorted, and also on account of the meridians and parallels intersecting each other at right angles, as they do on the globe. In the *Globular Projection*, the eye is supposed to be placed at a distance from the sphere equal to the sine of 45°; that is, if the diameter of the sphere be equal to 200, the distance of the eye from the nearest point of the circumference would be $70\frac{7}{10}$. Some modification was subsequently deemed desirable, in order that the meridians might intersect the equator at equal distances. This condition is nearly fulfilled when the distance of the eye is $59\frac{1}{2}$, the diameter being 200. This projection is also much used in maps of the world. In the *Conical Projection*, the sphere is supposed to be circumscribed by a cone, which touches the sphere at the circle intended to represent the middle parallel of the map; the points on the sphere being projected on the cone, the latter is then conceived to be unrolled or developed on a plane surface. In the *Cylindrical Projection*, the sphere is supposed to be circumscribed by a cylinder instead of a cone. The peculiarity of this method is, that the meridians, as well as the latitude circles, are projected in parallel straight lines. In *Mercator's Projection*, so largely used by mariners, the degrees of latitude on the chart are made to increase towards the poles, in the same ratio as they decrease on the globe; by which means the course which a ship steers by the mariner's compass becomes on the chart a straight line; the various regions of the map, however distorted, preserve their true relative bearing, and the distances between them can be accurately measured.

MAPLE. The useful purposes to which the Maple-tree is applied are noticed under ACER.

MARBLE. A limestone which will admit of being worked equally in all directions, and is capable of taking a good polish, deserves the title of marble; when it is granular and of a white colour, it may be useful in statuary.

The varieties of marble are exceedingly numerous. Taking them in respect to colour, we find the following among others:—*Black Marbles.* Most of these contain bitumen, and are fœtid when bruised. They include the Namur marble, the marble of Ashford in Derbyshire, Dent in Yorkshire, near Crickhowell, Tenby, Kilkenny, &c.; the marble anciently called Marmor Luculleum, and now Nero Antico. *White Marbles* comprise the marble of Paros; the Carrara marble, of finer grain, much used in modern sculpture; the Skye marble, that of Inverary, Assynt, Blair-Athol, &c. *Ash* and *Gray Marbles* include a beautiful marble, of compact oolitic texture, at Orleton, near the Clee Hills in Shropshire. *Brown* and *Red Marbles* comprise the Rosso Antico; a marble on the estate of the Duke of Devonshire, near Buxton. The mottled brown marble of Betham Fell, near Milnthorp, is of good quality. Among *Yellow Marbles* are the Giallo Antico; Siena marble. That used in ancient Rome is said to have been from Numidia. *Blue Marbles.* Of these there is one example near St. Pons in Languedoc. *Green Marbles* present as an example the Marmor Lacedæmonicum of Pliny, dug near Verona. *Black Marbles* variegated with other colours; *White Marbles* variegated with other colours; *Ash* and *Gray Marbles* variegated with other colours; and similar variegated varieties of *Brown, Red, Yellow* and *Green Marbles*, are abundant. The British Islands contain numerous examples of marbles containing shells and corals. Some of the Plymouth, Ashburton, and other Devonian limestones are extremely beautiful, from the abundance of fine corals exquisitely preserved in them; the crinoidal marbles of Flintshire, Derbyshire, and Garsdale in Yorkshire, are elegant examples of the carboniferous limestone; the shell marbles of Buckingham, Whichwood Forest, Stamford, Yeovil, may be noticed, from the oolitic rocks. That of Petworth and Purbeck, from the Wealden strata, has been extensively used by the architects of the middle ages.

The mechanical working of Marble does not

differ much from that of stone. [SCULPTURE; STONE MASONRY.] Beautiful specimens of English and Irish marble have been sent to the great Exhibition.

MARBLING. There are many processes in the Arts by which an attempt is made to imitate the veins and markings of marble. Marble itself may be stained or dyed of any required colour. Litmus or indigo for blue; logwood for brown; alkanet root for crimson; alkanet and wax for flesh colour; sal ammoniac, verdigris, and white vitriol, for gold colour; sap green or verdigris for green; dragon's blood or cochineal for red; gamboge, turmeric, or saffron for yellow—these are the colouring matters employed, used when hot.

The marbling of books or papers is effected by applying to them a coloured preparation of the required tint. The pigments employed are Prussian blue, indigo, rose pink, or any of the well known colours, chiefly mineral. These are ground up with a little ox-gall and small beer to a proper consistence. Linseed and water are boiled in a copper pan to a mucilaginous consistence, and are poured into a trough to cool. The colours are then successively sprinkled on the surface of the mucilage in the trough with a brush, and are waved or drawn about with a quill or stick, according to taste. When the design is thus formed, the book, tied tightly together between cutting boards of the same size, is lightly pressed with its edge on the surface of the liquid pattern, and then withdrawn and dried. It will be found to have taken up a thin layer of colour. This illustrates one only among many ways of marbling paper. Ordinary book edges are simply sprinkled with colours, from a brush dipped into it.

The marbling of wood is simply an attempt to imitate the tints and markings of marble by ordinary painters' colours.

MARGARIC ACID, is prepared from soap made with olive-oil and potash. It crystallises in pearly needles; it is insoluble in water. It has an acid reaction; and its salts, except those of the alkalis, are very sparingly soluble in water. Its saline compounds are termed *margarates*. The *Margarate of Potash* presents the varied forms of brilliant scales, a solution, and a jelly, according to its mode of preparation. A substance nearly allied to this acid, and called *Margarin*, is a peculiar fatty matter contained in vegetable oils, and also in animal fats, as mutton suet and hog's lard. This substance is very soluble in cold æther, which distinguishes it from stearin. *Margaron* is a solid white fatty matter which crystallises in pearly scales, and is obtained by distilling margaric acid with excess of lime.—The whole of these substances obtain their characteristic designation from the Greek name for a *pearl*.

MARJORAM, is an aromatic potherb used in cookery, especially among the French. It is a native of Barbary and the Himalaya mountains. In gardens it is little better than an annual.

MARKET GARDENS. The market gardens near London, which chiefly supply Covent Garden market, have a soil which is a moist alluvial loom deposited from repeated overflowings of the Thames, which are now prevented by banks or dykes. The gardener's year properly begins in autumn, when the land is dug, or rather trenched, and well manured. Various vegetables which will be required in winter are now sown, and especially those which are to produce plants to be set out in spring; spinach, onions, radishes, and winter salads are sown, and, when the weather is severe, are protected by a slight covering of straw or mats. In February, the cauliflowers which have been raised in frames or under hand-glasses are planted out. The cabbage plants are pricked out. The radishes, onions, and salads go to market as soon as they are of sufficient size, and sugar-loaf cabbages succeed them. As the cauliflowers are taken off, they are succeeded by endive and celery, and the same is the case with the cabbages. Thus there is a constant succession of vegetables, without one moment's respite to the ground.

The principle on which the gardens are cultivated is that of forcing vegetation by means of an abundant supply of dung, constant tillage, and occasional watering. The whole surface is converted into a species of hotbed; and crop succeeds crop with a rapidity which is truly astonishing. Those vegetables which arrive at a marketable state in the least time are always the most profitable, and those also for which there is a constant demand at all times of the year. With an abundant supply of manure, the market-gardeners have no fear of exhausting the soil; and dissimilar vegetables may grow together on the same ground. Raspberries, gooseberries, and currants are planted in the rows between fruit trees; which rows being thirty or forty feet apart, leave ample room for vegetables. The market gardeners near London do not raise many peas or beans, except such as are forced and require glass frames to protect them. The chief supply of peas in the season comes from a greater distance, and is the produce of whole fields sown for that purpose by the farmers within a moderate distance of London. An acre of the richest garden ground near London is said to yield produce valued at 220*l.* in a year.

An abundant supply of manure is indispensable in a market garden, and this can generally be obtained in large towns at a trifling expense. The neighbourhood of a town is therefore a necessary circumstance towards the production of the crop, as well as its sale. The profits of a garden near London, of the extent of ten or twelve acres, are as great as that of a farm of ten times the extent cultivated in the best manner, without the help of purchased manure.

The *Morning Chronicle* has lately given some interesting statistical details respecting the supply of London from the market gardens. The *Green Markets* are the Covent Garden, the Borough, Spitalfields, Farringdon, Portman and Hungerford Markets. Of these Covent Garden is not only the largest, but is said to be the largest in the world. It is divided into six sections, for fruit stands, flower stands, potato stands, casual cart stands, yearly cart stands, and yearly pitching stands, all of which pay a rental according to the kind of commodity sold, and the conveniences required for the sale. The following is given as one recent year's amount of sales at Covent Garden market, all of home-grown produce:—

Apples	360,000	bushels.
Pears	230,000	„
Cherries	90,000	„
Plums	93,000	„
Gooseberries	140,000	„
Currants	90,000	sieves.
Strawberries	638,000	pottles.
Raspberries	30,000	sieves.
Filberts	1,000	tons.
Walnuts	25,000	bushels.
Cabbages	16,000	loads.
Turnips	10,000	„
Carrots	5,000	„
Onions	500,000	bushels.
Brocoli, Cauliflowers	1,000	loads.
Peas	270,000	bushels.
Beans	100,000	„
Celery	18 million	heads.
Asparagus	60	„
Endive	150,000	scores.
French Beans	140,000	bushels.
Potatoes	83,000	tons.
Watercresses	23,000	cwt.

All the other vegetable markets of London united, present but a small aggregate, compared with this of Covent Garden.

MARL is an earthy substance found at various depths under the soil, and extensively used for the improvement of land. It consists of calcareous and argillaceous earth in various proportions, and as the former or the latter prevails, so it is beneficially employed on clays or sands. There are several distinct sorts of marl—*clay marl, shell marl, slate marl,* and *stone marl.* The effect of marl is the same as that of clay and chalk upon sandy soils; on heavy soils its effect is proportioned to the quantity of calcareous earth which it contains. The peculiar advantage of marl is its readily crumbling to powder by the effect of air and moisture. An excellent use of marl is in forming composts with dung and peat earth. It is laid in layers with the dung and peat, and if the heap is well soaked with urine or the washings of stable-yards, it will in a short time become a most valuable manure for all kinds of soils.

MARMALADE. Marmalade is properly a conserve made of quinces and sugar, and is named from the Portuguese name for a quince. Marmalades are, however, now made of orange, citrons, apricot, hips, apples, pears, plums, and other fruits. It is by using the cheaper varieties of these fruits, that Marmalade is now sold at such a low price. Marmalade is made either by pounding the pulped fruit in a mortar with white sugar; or by mixing them together by heat, passing them through a hair sieve while hot, and then putting them into pots or glasses. The fruit pulps are obtained by rubbing the fruit through a fine hair sieve either at once, or after it has been softened by boiling.

MARNE. There are two French departments thus named, which present a fair amount of productive and commercial industry.

In *Marne* the vine for the production of the famous Champagne wines is the chief object of the landholder's care all through the department, more especially in the arondissement of Reims and Épernay, wherein the white wines of Sillery, Aï, Mareuil, Pierry, Épernay, and Dizy; and the pink wines of Verzenay, Verzy, Bouzy, Taissy, Cumières, Aï, Hautvilliers, Mareuil, Dizy, and Pierry, all of the first class. The Champagne vintage is noticed under WINE MANUFACTURE. The quantity of wine of all kinds made in the department annually amounts to 15 or 16 million gallons. In this department, chalk, flint, millstone of the best quality, building-stone, potters' and brick clay, and turf, are the chief mineral productions. The chief manufactures are woollen stuffs of all kinds, and cotton hosiery, which centre chiefly at Reims. There are also several tan-yards, dye-houses, paper mills, glass works, potteries, rope-walks, oil mills, soaperies, and establishments for the making of Spanish white. The most important article of commerce is Champagne wine, the great marts for which are Reims and Epernay. Other articles of trade are corn, flour, brandy, the articles previously named, together with timber, hides, and firewood, of which great quantities are sent for the supply of Paris.

Haute Marne, the other of these two departments, is also a wine country. The vine is extensively cultivated in favourable situations, and about 13,000,000 gallons of wine annually made, two-thirds of which are consumed on the spot, and the rest is exported to Switzerland and to the departments of Vosges and Haut-Rhin. The department is rich in iron ore; several mines are worked; the metal is smelted and manufactured into bars, utensils, and tools in numerous furnaces and foundries, in which wood charcoal is the fuel exclusively used. Building stone, marble, alabaster, gypsum, &c., are quarried. Marl, brick earth, fuller's earth, and turf are dug. Besides ironmongery and cutlery, the industrial products include brandy, vinegar, cotton and woollen yarn, drugget, woollen stockings, leather gloves, cast-iron tubes, paper, leather, beer, &c. The commerce in the products before named, and in timber, planks, fire-wood, oak-staves, oil, honey, &c., is considerable.

MAROCCO. In this large country of Northern Africa are cultivated wheat, barley, rice, Indian corn, and holcus sorghum, or dhurra. Other objects of cultivation are cotton, tobacco, sesamum, hemp, saffron, henna, and different kinds of peas and beans. The plantations of date trees, olive trees, and almond trees are very extensive. The fruit-trees of southern Europe are also common, especially the fig and the pomegranate. Forest trees are numerous on the northern slope of the Atlas. The Marocco sheep produce a wool not inferior to any for softness, fineness, and whiteness. Goat-skins constitute one of the most important articles of export. The mineral wealth of Marocco is very imperfectly known, but is supposed to include gold, silver, copper, lead, iron, rock salt, and fuller's earth.

As the inhabitants dress chiefly in wool, the manufacture of woollen cloth is general, but the material is usually coarse. In some places however there are manufactories on a large scale, which supply articles of export. A few silk goods are also woven. The inhabitants of Fez are distinguished as goldsmiths, jewellers, and cutters of precious stones; many of them are also occupied in making Marocco leather, and different kinds of earthenware. Tanning and leather dressing are carried on extensively; and carpet weaving is also much practised.

The Moghribins carry on a very active commerce with Soudan or the interior of Africa, and with Egypt and Arabia, by caravans, and with several parts of Europe by sea. From Timbuctoo, as a central point, the merchants traverse the adjacent countries, exchanging their goods for those of Soudan. The caravans which go to Mecca are chiefly composed of pilgrims, and are much more numerous than the trading caravans. They depart only once in the year, and follow two routes.

European vessels visit the harbours of Tetuan, Rabatt, Saffi, and Mogadore, and export the produce of the empire to Italy, France, Spain, England, and Holland, bringing in return the produce of European and other countries.

MARSEILLE. This influential French city is the chief port of the Mediterranean; and the steam-packet station for Italy, the Peninsula, and the East. It is likewise one of the stations for the Anglo-Indian Overland Mail; although in this respect Trieste may possibly interfere with it at some future day. A railway is in course of construction direct from Paris, through Dijon, Lyon, and Avignon, to Marseille.

Marseille depends entirely upon its commerce, which is extensive; and, since the conquest of Algeria by the French, has been rapidly on the increase. Within the last few years an artificial basin has been made in the roadstead near Marseille by the construction of a dyke between the small fortified islands of Ratonneau and Pomègue, in which vessels of the line may anchor with perfect safety, and on the shores of which ship-building is extensively carried on. The number of vessels which enter the port of Marseille annually is estimated at 5000 or 6000; the custom-house and other dues collected exceed 1,100,000*l*. annually; and the municipal revenue is about 110,000*l*. The French trade with the Levant is entirely carried on from Marseille. The chief imports are of raw cotton, sugar, dye-woods, and divers articles from the Levant; exports, of wines, brandy, corn, dried fruits, oil, soap, hosiery, damask, and other linens, woollens, silks, leather, hides, &c. The local manufactures consist of soap, morocco and other leather, glass, porcelain, hats, gunpowder, alum, sulphur, vitriol, and cutlery. The refining of sugar and salt, calico printing, the distillation of brandy, essences, and liqueurs, cork-cutting, and the preparation of anchovies, dried fruits, olives and wine for exportation are carried on.

MARTELLO TOWER, is the name given to a circular building of masonry, generally two stories high. The lower story is divided into chambers for the reception of stores, and the upper serves as a casemate for troops. The roofs are vaulted, and that of the upper story is shell-proof. On the terreplein of the roof are placed pieces of artillery, which rest on platforms of timber traversing on pivots, so that the guns are capable of being fired in any direction. The whole work is generally surrounded by a ditch and glacis.

There are several of these Martello towers on the south coast, near Hastings; but not being wanted for military purposes, they are occupied by the Revenue Coast Guard.

MARTIN SKINS. The skin or fur of the martin is used to a considerable extent in this country for furriery and other purposes. The number imported in 1847 was 259,032, and in 1848 it was 219,195.

MARYLAND. A few industrial statistics of Maryland are given under UNITED STATES.

MASONRY. [STONE MASONRY.]

MASSACHUSETTS. [UNITED STATES.]

MASTICH, is a resin which is extracted from the trunk and branches of the *Pistacia lentiscus* by incision. This tree grows in the Levant, and particularly in the island of Chios. Mastich is composed of two resins, one of which is soluble in dilute alcohol, and the other is not; this last constitutes from $\frac{1}{8}$th to $\frac{1}{12}$th of the whole weight of the mastich, and possesses very nearly the characters of copal, it being soluble in absolute alcohol, æther, and oil of turpentine; these liquids also dissolve mastich without leaving any residue. Mastich is principally employed as an ingredient in varnish, and as a temporary stopping for carious teeth.

MATCH, is a material employed in firing military mines or in discharging pieces of ordnance. Before the invention of fire-locks, hand-guns or small arms were fired by matches, which the soldiers carried with them when on service; and matchlock fire-arms are still used in some parts of Asia. What is called *slow-match* is only a piece of slightly twisted hemp which has been well soaked in a strong solution of saltpetre with boiling water. The materials employed in the formation of *quick-match* consist of a wick of cotton steeped in a mixture of saltpetre and mealed gunpowder with spirit of wine and rain water.

MATCHES; CONGREVES; LUCIFERS. The manufacture of these humble and marvellously cheap articles marks a curious stage in the progress of civilization, where luxuries become conveniencies, and then become necessaries. The friction of two pieces of dry wood we now regard as a barbarous mode of procuring light; yet it is a scientific one, where the materials for a quicker process are wanting. The flint and steel had a long reign in this country; the tinder box formed an item in Wolverhampton manufactures; and the sulphur-tipped matches, arranged in bunches spread out in fan-like manner formed the stock in trade of many an itinerant dealer. As mechanical ingenuity supplied the flint and steel and tinder box to supersede the rubbing sticks, so has chemical ingenuity made a wide step in advance, by showing how to tip the little splints or matches with a composition which will kindle by slight friction.

Whether called *Congreves*, *Lucifers*, or *Instantaneous Lights*, these small but valuable articles are now made in almost inconceivable quantities. Hand cutting has long been unable to produce the splints in sufficient quantity; nothing less than steam power can do this. At one among many saw mills in London, these matches are made in the following way. The wood employed is American yellow pine. It is first sawn into blocks about 12 inches long, 5 or 6 wide, and 3 thick. Several of these blocks are placed in a machine where a number of revolving cutters, worked with great rapidity, slice the blocks up into layers, and cut the layers into splints. One machine will cut up two million splints in a day. The splints, as liberated from the machine, slide down into another room, where women and girls tie them up in boxes, the boxes in parcels, and the parcels in bundles. These splints are sold by the *hogshead* to the lucifer match makers, each hogshead containing perhaps two million splints. At one saw mill alone, it is estimated that the timber of four hundred large pine trees is cut up yearly for lucifer matches!

The chemical composition which gives to the matches their easy-igniting power, can now be bought at a very low price; and as children are chiefly employed in the manufacture, the matches can be sold extremely cheap. Whether the colour be red, yellow, brown, blue, or green, the composition possesses the requisite quality in respect to ignition by friction; and chemists are now acquainted with many such. There are many processes and compositions adopted. In one, the matches are dipped into a mixture of phosphorus, oil of turpentine, and flowers of sulphur; and afterwards into a mixture of gum arabic, chlorate of potash, and soot. In a second method the composition consists of chlorate of potash, phosphorus, gum arabic, and gelatine; the matches being dipped into melted sulphur before being dipped in this composition. In a third method, the composition consists of gum arabic, vermilion, phosphorus, and saltpetre. What are called *chlorate matches* are dipped into a mixture of chlorate of potash, flowers of sulphur, powdered lump sugar, gum arabic, and vermilion; these matches were originally lighted by dipping their ends into sulphuric acid; and it was in endeavouring to avoid the necessity of using this dangerous acid that the manufacturers hit upon the composition requisite for *lucifers*, which in turn gave way to the equally efficient and less noisy *congreves*. The lucifers here spoken of were dipped into a mixture of sulphuret of antimony and chlorate of potash, made into a paste with a solution of gum.

The dipping, drying, packing in boxes, pasting, &c., are of course very simple operations; but they are far from being safe, for among the fires of London during the last few years, a considerable number have occurred at the premises of lucifer match makers.

MATERIALS, STRENGTH OF. The strength of any material object, as a rod, bar, beam, chain, or rope, is that power by which the substance resists an effort to destroy the cohesion of its parts. If a rod or bar be suspended vertically, and a weight fixed to the lower end, that weight would tear asunder the bar, fibre from fibre, or particle from particle, if increased beyond a certain limit. Supposing the bar to be one inch square, the following weights would suffice to tear it asunder, according to the material of which it is made:—

English oak . .	8,000 to 12,000 lbs.
Fir	11,000 to 13,488 lbs.
Beech	11,500
Mahogany . . .	8,000
Teak	15,000
Cast-steel . . .	134,256
Iron-wire . . .	93,964
Swedish bar-iron .	72,064
Cast-iron . . .	18,656 to 19,488 lbs.
Wrought-copper .	33,792
Platinum-wire . .	52,987
Silver do. . .	38,257
Gold do. .	30,888
Zinc do. .	22,551
Tin do. .	7,129
Lead do. .	3,146

Rope, line, and cables range from 5000 to 12,000, according to the material and the mode of twisting.

According to the experiments of Mr. Barlow it appears that a bar of malleable iron is extended one ten-thousandth part of its length by a direct strain equal to one ton for each square inch in the area of the transverse section: when stretched with ten tons per inch its elasticity was injured, or the bar did not return to its original state.

In relation to the power of bearing a *crushing* pressure; various materials have been found to take rank as follows:—Iron, granite, limestone, oak, Portland stone, white deal, elm, red brick, and chalk.

Since the strengths of beams attached at one end or supported on props, the other dimensions being the same, vary as the squares of the vertical depths, it follows that the most advantageous position, when the areas of the transverse sections are equal, is that in which the broadest surface is in a vertical position. In this manner girders and joists in edifices are invariably placed.

When a beam or bar is attached at one end to a wall, or when it turns upon its middle point like the great lever of a steam-engine, if it be required that the beam should be equally strong in its whole length, it should be made to taper towards its extremities. If a weight be applied at any point in the length of a beam which is supported on two props, the strain produced by it will be the greatest when it is placed in the middle.

Such machines as capstans and windlasses, also axles which revolve with their wheels, are, when in action, subject to be twisted, so that their fibres tend to become curved in oblique directions: the strain thus produced is called that of *torsion*, and the strength of a solid cylinder to resist this kind of strain is found to be proportional to the cube of the diameter. Since the strain of torsion depends on the diameter of the cylinder, it is evident that a hollow cylinder must be stronger than a solid one containing the same amount of material.

We may remark that in testing the stability of the Palace of Industry in Hyde Park, a number of ingenious contrivances have been employed, to determine the strength of the materials to render the service required of them; especially in respect to the columns and girders.

MATRASS, is a glass chemical vessel, employed for the purpose of digesting, boiling, and distillation.

MAURITIUS. This British colony, formerly called the Isle of France, was once covered with woods, and even now a considerable part of the native forest is allowed to remain for ornament round the plantations. Many tropical and a few European plants are cultivated. The culture of the sugar-cane has spread rapidly since the English obtained possession of the island. The quantity of sugar it supplied to England, in 1828, was 40,320,000 lbs.; in 1847, 133,679,952 lbs.; but in 1848 the entire crop of the island yielded only 99,234,352 lbs. This diminution is no doubt in some measure, if not entirely, owing to the fact that a fatal disease has lately made its appearance among the cane plants of the island; and to such an extent that, in 1848, 10,000 plants of a different species of cane were introduced from Ceylon, but it is said with little success, as the insect (a species of coccus) which preyed upon the old plants seeks its food on all plants of the same genus as the sugar-cane. In consequence of this disaster, and perhaps also of the effect of the act of 1846 on the sugar trade of the island, much attention is now given to extend the cultivation of the mulberry for the production of silk, which cultivation had been previously introduced with great success in those parts of the island that were least adapted for the growth of the sugar cane. Coffee and pepper are also cultivated to some extent. The trade of the island is carried on not only with England, but with the countries around the Indian Ocean. There is packet communication monthly between Mauritius and Ceylon.

In the three months ending Oct. 10, 1850, the imports into Mauritius in British vessels amounted in value to 296,951*l.*, and in Foreign vessels to 22,301*l.*; being larger amounts than in the corresponding period of 1848 and 1849. The exports in the same three months were 121,287*l.*: being somewhat smaller than in the corresponding three months of 1848 and 1849. The yield of sugar in Mauritius in 1850 has been estimated at about 55,000 tons, or 120 million pounds.

MAYO. The geological structure of Mayo resembles, in its general features, that of Galway, exhibiting an arrangement of primary and secondary rocks skirting a limestone basin. As usual, the cultivated district and the field of limestone are co-extensive. Indications of coal are said to have been observed in Slieve Carnon, and deposits of manganese occur near Westport, but at present there are no mining operations carried on in this county beyond the quarrying of slates. Marble susceptible of a good polish has been quarried in several parts of the barony of Murrisk. Generally speaking, cultivation occurs only in detached patches. In 1847 out of the 1,363,882 acres which Mayo contains, there were only 122,567 under crops. The coast fishery, which might be rendered very productive, gives employment to about 4,000 fishermen. Turbot, sole, cod, ling, hake, haddock, plaice, oysters, lobsters, and herrings, are caught.

The manufacture of linens is carried on to a considerable extent by the country people: the cloth is generally sold in the rough state by the small manufacturers, and bleached in other counties. There is also throughout the county the usual home manufacture of friezes and coarse woollens.

The 'Castlebar Telegraph,' in a recent article concerning the products which will be forwarded to the Exhibition from Mayo, states that 'It is an undoubted fact that no equal extent of country in Ireland—ay, in Great Britain—can excel Mayo in her minerals of copper, lead, tin, iron, metal, marble, coal. We have also seen silver and gold extracted by a chemical process, by Dr. Atkinson of this town, upon whose authority we state that the country around us, for miles, abounds in minerals sufficient to enrich thousands of our population if they but possessed the knowledge of acquiring it. Recently, we are informed, a rich coal mine was discovered on the estate of Lord Kilmaine, in the neighbourhood of Castlebar.'

MEADOWS are properly low grounds on the banks of rivers, which, being kept moist by their situation, and also occasionally flooded by the rise of the waters, are best adapted for the growth of grass, and are generally mown for hay. Some meadows of great extent, belonging to a community or district, in which every inhabitant has a right to send his cattle to graze, under certain regulations, are never mown. The herbage of low wet meadows is generally coarser and less nutritious than that of those which lie higher; hence upland hay, as it is called, is preferred for the better sort of cattle. Upland meadows are very valuable wherever there is a demand for good hay. Of late years the practice of *soiling* has been extensively adopted; that is, all the grass is mown and carried every day in a green state, to cows or horses tied up in a stable. When a natural meadow has been neglected, and the grass is of an inferior quality, and mixed with rank weeds and moss, it requires much care to restore it to its original fertility.

MEATH. This county has very few mountain wastes, and the proportion of the bog is small. The land is flat rich pasture-land. The soil is for the most part a loam of the richest character, and in many places of such depth that the turning up of a fresh portion of the soil by ploughing deeper than usual is considered as an efficient substitute for manuring. The farms are on the average larger than in most other parts of Ireland; the grazing farms average about 150 acres; and tillage farms 20 to 50. The mode of farming, though very slovenly and defective, bears some resemblance to that of England. The whole quantity of land devoted to green crops is small, in consequence of the abundance of the natural pastures, which are of unequalled richness, and have led the farmers to give their chief attention to grazing. The quantity of cattle fattened in the pastures of the county is considerable, and the breeds fattened are numerous. The grazing is carried on on a large scale. Many persons fatten from 300 to 500 cows in a season, besides bullocks and sheep. Oxen are frequently employed in the plough. There are large flocks of sheep kept by the more extensive farmers.

The only home manufactures are a little coarse linen, sometimes, though rarely, a little coarse frieze coating, and the knitting of coarse worsted stockings, which last branch of industry is pretty commonly done by girls, widows, and old women. Spinning and weaving, from the cheapness of manufactured goods, have almost entirely ceased.

There is another Meath, called ***West Meath***, or ***Westmeath***, the soil of which comprises heavy loam, light loam, hilly sheepwalks, and a great deal of bog. The chief crops raised by the farmer are oats and potatoes; a very little wheat, some barley, flax, rape, and clover are grown. Dairy farming is practised to some extent in this county. The manufactures of the county are not important; they consist chiefly of the most necessary articles, such as coarse linens, woollens, and cottons.

The Shannon is navigable for steam-boats conveying goods and passengers. The Royal Canal crosses this county from east to north-west. The principal roads are good. The Midland Great Western Railway passes through the county.

MECHANICAL POWERS. This name is given to certain simple machines or engines, either of which is occasionally used by itself in moving bodies or raising weights, or any of which are combined together in the formation of the complex constructions which are employed in manufactures and the arts.

The several machines to which the name of mechanical powers is applied are the LEVER, the WHEEL AND AXLE, the INCLINED PLANE, the WEDGE, the SCREW, and the FUNICULAR MACHINE.

The object proposed in every machine is to transmit a force from the point at which it is immediately applied to that at which some resistance is to be overcome or some operation to be performed; and, in the transmission, the intensity of the motive power is to be increased so that effects may be produced which could not be accomplished by that power alone. The increase of the power is obtained by causing part of the resistance which is to be overcome to rest on the machine or on the fixed points which serve for its support, so that only the part which remains is opposed to the motive force. Thus a heavy body may be raised to a certain height from the ground by means of an inclined plane, on which part of the weight is destroyed by the reaction of the plane.

This manner of overcoming a resistance will serve to illustrate the fact that in every application of a mechanical contrivance to overcome a resistance, as much advantage is lost in respect of time or space as is gained in respect of power. For it is evident that, in order to raise the object vertically through a space equal to the height of the plane, it would be necessary to move it over a space equal to the length of the plane: that is, through a space which bears the same ratio to the vertical height as the weight of the object bears to the power required to move it up the plane.

All the familiar tools, implements, instruments, machines, and engines, exhibit the operation of some one or more of the mechanical powers.

MECHLIN. The industry of this ancient town is briefly adverted to under BELGIUM.

MECKLENBURG. In this member of the German confederation, agriculture forms the chief employment of the inhabitants; wheat, rye, barley, and oats are raised in large quantities for exportation. The forests produce some excellent timber. The breeds of horses, cattle, and sheep, are good, and the geese of Mecklenburg are celebrated for their size and flavour. Fish abound on the coast and in the lakes. The manufactures, though at present inconsiderable are extending. *Rostock*, is the principal trading port of Mecklenburg, and possesses about 150 ships. The chief exports are corn and wool: imports, colonial produce, wine and bay salt. There are manufactories of linen, soap, &c. In *Schwerin* there are manufactures of vinegar, cloth, pottery, and tobacco. *Wismar* has a harbour considered to be the safest in the Baltic. Wismar possesses from 60 to 70 vessels, and the entries into the harbour average 300 ships annually. The exports consist chiefly of corn; the imports are mostly Swedish productions. Fishing, agriculture, and the manufacture of tobacco and linen employ a large portion of the population. *Ratzeburg* is bounded on the west by the lake of Ratzeburg, by means of which timber, corn, pulse, flax, and cattle are sent to Lübeck for exportation. The inhabitants also carry on considerable fisheries.

MECONIC ACID, is a substance found only in opium, in which it exists in combination with the alkali Morphia. It is a crystal-

KNIGHT'S CYCLOPÆDIA OF THE INDUSTRY OF ALL NATIONS.

No. 29.

line substance, which acts on litmus paper, and has a sour taste; it is soluble in four times its weight of water, and also in alcohol. The salts which contain this acid are called *meconates*. The chief among them are combinations of the acid with Ammonia, Potash, Soda, Lime, Magnesia, Barytes, and Iron: the whole of these crystallise. It forms many curious compounds with other substances, but they are not yet of much value in the arts.

MEDAL: MEDALLION. Some account of the mode of executing these works will be found under CLICHÉ MEDALLIONS, and INTAGLIO. See also MINT.

MEERSCHAUM PIPES. Whether smoking be a good or an evil practice, it leads at the present day to a wide system of commercial enterprise. The *meerschaum* pipe is one among many manufactures connected with it. Meerschaum means in German *sea foam;* and the equivalent French name of *écume de mer* is applied to the same substance. It is a silicated magnesian mineral, found in Greece, Turkey, and a few other countries. It is used by the Tartars for washing linen, somewhat in the same manner as pearl ash or fullers' earth. The mineral is principally used however as a material for tobacco pipes, which, when made, are soaked in melted tallow, then in white wax, and finally polished with shave-grass. If genuine, a meerschaum pipe acquires a beautiful brown colour after being smoked for some time, the oil of the tobacco being absorbed by the clay; and this is a point to which connoisseurs in smoking attach much importance.

Dr. E. D. Clarke gives some interesting details on this subject. In the Crimea the meerschaum clay is called *keff-kil*, and forms a stratum about two feet thick, beneath a much thicker stratum of marl. 'The first rude form is given to the pipes upon the spot where the mineral is found; here they are pressed within a mould, and laid in the sun to harden; afterwards they are baked in an oven, boiled in milk, and rubbed with soft leather. In this state they go to Constantinople, where there is a peculiar bazaar or khan for the sale of them; they are then bought up by merchants, and sent by caravans to Pesth in Hungary. Still the form of the pipe is large and rude. At Pesth a manufacturer begins to fit them for the German markets. They are there soaked for twenty-four hours in water, and then turned in a lathe. In this process many of them, proving porous, are rejected. Sometimes only two or three out of ten are deemed worthy of further labour. From Pesth they are conveyed to Vienna, and frequently mounted in silver. After this they are carried to the fairs of Leipsic, Frankfort, Mannheim, and other towns upon the Rhine, where the best sell from three to five and even seven pounds sterling. When the oil of tobacco, after long smoking, has given them a fine porcelain yellow, or which is more prized, a dark tortoise-shell hue, they have been known to sell for forty or fifty pounds of our money.'

Dr. Clarke's description refers to a period many years back; but it will serve to illustrate the subject.

MEISSEN. It is in this town in Saxony, about 18 miles from Dresden, that the celebrated *Dresden China* is made. There is a large factory supported by the government, where all the processes of the porcelain manufacture are conducted on a very complete scale. Some specimens of a highly curious character are displayed at the Great Exhibition.

MELON. In regions where most cooling vegetables disappear on the approach of great summer heat and drought, the melon, together with the water-melon, become essential substitutes. The antiquity of the cultivation of melons being so remote, and their dispersion over large portions of Asia and Africa so extensive, their indigenous locality cannot be traced at the present day. So far as moisture is concerned, the melon will bear a tropical heat; and, generally speaking, it will not succeed perfectly in the open air beyond the 43rd parallel of latitude. Its range of atmospheric temperature may be estimated at between 70° and 80°. Light is so essential, that unless the plants are kept near the glass, no tolerable degree of flavour will be acquired. A free admission of the air is also to be recommended, so far as it is consistent with the mainterance of a high temperature.

MELTING. The temperatures at which solids melt are also their freezing points; the freezing of water and the melting of ice, for instance, both occur at 32° F. In addition to the list given under FREEZING, are the following melting points:—

Tallow	92° to 127° F.
Phosphorus	108°
Stearin, from hog's lard	109°
Spermaceti	112°
Margaric acid	134°
Potassium	136°
Yellow wax	142° to 149°
White wax	156°
Sodium	190°
Sulphur	218° to 234°
Tin	442°
Cadmium, about	442°
Bismuth	497°

Lead . . . . 612° F.
Zinc . . . . 773°
Antimony . . . . 809°
Silver . . . . 1873°
Copper . . . . 1996°
Gold . . . . 2016°
Iron, Cast . . . . 2786°

MEMBRANE. The thin membranes which exist so largely in animals are applied to many useful purposes. The bladders used for covering vessels, the thin substance called goldbeaters' skin, the strings of catgut used for musical instruments—all are examples of this kind. They are briefly noticed under appropriate headings in this work.

MENAI BRIDGES. The Menai Strait is the locality of two of the finest engineering works of our country; viz., the *Suspension Bridge* of Telford, and the *Tubular Bridge* of Stephenson.

This narrow channel, about 17 miles in length, which separates the island of Anglesey from the mainland of Wales, intervenes on the great mail-route from England, by way of Holyhead, to the eastern coast of Ireland. Telford's bridge was commenced Aug. 10, 1819, and the mail-coaches drove over it for the first time Jan. 30, 1826. The distance between the supporting pyramids or points of suspension is 560 feet, and the height of the carriage way above high water in the Strait is 100 feet. The roadway of the bridge is divided into two carriage ways, each 12 feet wide, with a footpath 4 feet wide between them. The main chains are 16 in number, with a deflection of 37 feet, their ends being secured in a mass of masonry built over stone arches between each of the supporting piers. The weight of the chains, plates, screw-pins, wedges, and transverse ties is 398 tons; that of the suspending rods and platforms is 246 tons; making a total suspended weight of 644 tons. It is estimated that the bridge will bear 732 tons more than its own weight.

Notwithstanding the excellence of this bridge, it was deemed inadequate to bear the trains of the Chester and Holyhead Railway; and hence arose Mr. Stephenson's grand project for the *Tubular Bridge*. This unequalled structure, called the Britannia Bridge, consists of two tubes of iron placed side by side, through which the up and down trains of the Chester and Holyhead Railway respectively pass. The entire length of each tube is 1516 feet, and the height above high water 102 feet. Each tube consists of four pieces, the ends of which rest upon and are joined together on a central pier built on the Britannia Rock in the middle of the Menai Strait, on two towers on the shores of Anglesey and Caernarvonshire respectively, and on two abutments farther inland on each coast. There are therefore eight tubes in all. The clear length of each tube reaching from the side-towers to the central tower is 460 feet, so that the entire length of tube across the Strait is 920 feet, leaving 596 feet for the entire length of the side tubes. The top of each tube forms a regular arch of slight curvature; the bottom is quite straight and horizontal. The interior height is 26 feet in the centre, and 18 feet 9 inches at the ends. The internal width is 14 feet from side to side. The tubes are formed of plates of wrought iron strongly riveted together. The weight of each tube is about 5000 tons, or 10,000 tons for the whole of the double tube of iron.

The lifting of these tubes was the grandest mechanical operation, perhaps, that the world ever saw. The hydraulic presses with which the lift was effected are displayed at the Great Exhibition; they ought to be preserved, as a memento of this great engineering work. It may be interesting to add a record of the *dates* which marked the progress of the work. On June 30, 1845, the bill sanctioning the construction of the Britannia Bridge was passed by Parliament. In July the preliminary experiments to determine the form of structure commenced; April 13, 1846, the first workmen were engaged on the bridge; April 21, first stone of the Britannia tower was laid; June 13, 1847, the first vessels arrived with iron at the Strait; August 10, the first rivet was inserted; February 22, 1849, the Caernarvon and Anglesey towers were completed; April, 1849, the pontoons were brought to bear; May 4, first tube was completed and platform cut away; June 20, first tube floated; June 22, last stone in Britannia tower laid; November 9, first tube deposited in permanent bed; December 4, second tube floated; February 7, 1850, second tube deposited on permanent bed; March 3, Caernarvon small tube lowered; March 5, first engine passed through tube, and last rivet inserted; March 18, single line of tube opened for public traffic: June 10, third tube of second line floated; July 11, third tube deposited; July 25, last tube floated; October 21, second line of tube opened for public traffic.

Holyhead, at which the railway terminates, is a market-town with a good harbour, and is situated on the northern coast of Holyhead Island. Holyhead harbour is formed by a pier faced with hewn limestone 900 feet in length, at the head of which the water is 14 feet deep at low tides; but the government and the company are about to incur a large expenditure in forming a magnificent harbour.

The direct distance across from Holyhead to Kingstown Harbour in the Bay of Dublin is 64 miles.

MENTHA, is the name of many useful species of plants. *Mentha piperita* is the common *peppermint*, which, when dried, yields a peculiar aromatic odour, and a pleasant camphor-like taste; the dried herb is used for the preparation of a distilled water and of a volatile oil; and from the oil, of which there are three varieties, the essence of peppermint is prepared. *Mentha pulegium* is the *pennyroyal*, which, besides being medicinal in its natural state, is made to yield a distilled water, a spirit, and a volatile oil. Analogous products are also obtained from a third species, the *Mentha viridis* or *spearmint*.

MERCATOR'S PROJECTION. The nature of this useful variety of chart is briefly noticed under MAP-MAKING.

MERCURY, or QUICKSILVER. This metal, which possesses the remarkable property of being fluid at usual temperatures, has been known from the remotest ages. Although it is met with in very large quantity, yet the mines occur in comparatively few places; those of Almaden in Spain, and Idria in Carniola, are the most important. There are however mines of this metal in Hungary, Transylvania, and the district of Zweibrücken in Germany. Mercury has been obtained for a very long time in China and Japan, and although the amount of the produce is unknown, there is every reason to think it is considerable; it is also found at Huancavelica in Peru. The average yearly produce is estimated at about 2000 tons, of which about two-thirds come from Almaden. The quantity brought to England in 1848 was 1,562,663 lbs. and in 1849 it rose to 2,682,592 lbs; in 1850 it was very much smaller, owing to monopoly arrangements.

Mercury is always obtained from cinnabar, which is a bisulphuret of the metal; it is found in the red sandstone associated with coal at Almaden; sometimes, as in the district of Zweibrücken, the cinnabar occurs in the subordinate porphyries; and at Idria in the subordinate bituminous schist, but rarely in limestone itself.

Various processes are adopted for the purpose of separating the mercury from the ore, all of which depend upon the volatility of the metal, its conversion into vapour in distilling vessels or retorts, and its condensation by cold. In order to separate the sulphur from the metal, either iron or lime may be employed; the first forms sulphuret of iron, and the latter of calcium, with the sulphur, and the metal is thus set free, volatilised, and condensed. The retorts employed are made of cast or sheet iron or earthenware.

Mercury is fluid at ordinary temperatures, is of a silvery white colour, and possesses a high degree of lustre; it is inodorous, tasteless, unacted upon or very slightly by exposure to air at common temperatures, and not at all by water at any temperature. The specific gravity of mercury is about 13·568. It boils at 670°. At 40° below zero, mercury becomes solid, crystallises in octahedrons, and gives a dull sound like lead; at the moment of congelation it contracts considerably; when in this state it is malleable, and may be cut with a knife. It is only on some few rare occasions that our Arctic explorers have encountered a cold so intense as to freeze mercury; in such case a *spirit* thermometer is the only one available, for spirit has never yet been frozen or solidified.

The number of valuable compounds which mercury forms with other substances is very considerable. The *binoxide* is a dark red crystal used in medicine. The protochloride constitutes *calomel*, and the bichloride *corrosive sublimate*. The bi-sulphuret yields *cinnabar* or *vermillion*; and another combination of mercury and sulphur forms *Ethiop's mineral*. The sulphate of mercury is *Turbeth mineral*. The fulminate of mercury forms *detonating powder*. All the alloys of mercury, or combinations of mercury with other metals, are called *amalgams*, and are noticed elsewhere. [AMALGAM.]

The uses of mercury in the arts are most varied and abundant. A few among them will be found briefly noticed under BAROMETER, BUTTON MANUFACTURE, GILDING, PENDULUM, PHOTOGRAPHY, SILVERING, THERMOMETER. All these relate to mercury in its liquid or metallic form; the chemical compounds of mercury with other substances have a still more extensive range of usefulness. The *medical* use of mercury lies beyond the scope of this volume.

MERTHYR TYDVIL. This town, one of the most important in South Wales, is the centre of the great iron smelting operations of that country. The stores of iron and coal in the immediate neighbourhood are most abundant; and the smelting is carried on upon a larger scale than at any other spot in the kingdom. In the immediate vicinity of Merthyr are the Dowlais works of Sir John Guest, the Cyfarthfa works of Messrs. Crawshay, the Plymouth works of Messrs. Hill, the Pen-y-darren works of Messrs. Thompson, and two or three of smaller rank. At no great distance from Merthyr are the large iron-works of Hirwain, Aberdare, Pentwain, Varteg, Blaenavon, Bryn-Mawr, Nant-y-Glo, Ebbw Vale,

Beaufort, Sirhowy, Rhimney, and many more. At the Dowlais works (the largest in the world) there are 18 blast furnaces, 77 puddling furnaces, 66 balling furnaces, besides a number of refining furnaces. About 1000 tons of coals per day are used at the works; and in busy times from 5000 to 6000 persons are employed. The quantities of iron and coal sent down the Taff Valley, by railway and canal, from the Merthyr district to Cardiff, are immense.

MESSINA. The produce and industry of Messina receive a little illustration under SICILY.

MESTA. The Mesta is a very peculiar kind of right of pasturage in Spain. Spain has vast tracts of unclaimed pasture-land on which the wealthy owners of flocks claim prescriptive right to pasture their sheep at the proper seasons.

The number of migratory sheep at the beginning of the present century amounted to about five millions. In the month of April the flocks leave the plains of Andalucia and Estremadura for the cooler pastures of Leon, the two Castilles, and Aragon, whence they begin to return southwards in October; for the lands depastured during the winter months a low price is paid, regulated by usage, and on which no advance is allowed. The sheep are divided into flocks of 10,000, each managed by a conductor, who has under him 50 shepherds and as many dogs. They pass unmolested, and feed over the pastures and commons that lie on their road; they are not allowed to traverse cultivated lands, but the proprietors of such lands are obliged to leave a clear space, 85 yards wide on each side of the road, for the passage of the flocks. At night they are penned in with nettings made of the esparto rush. The different routes and the length of each day's journey in these migrations are fixed by immemorial usage. Lambing takes place during the winter sojourn in the south. The sheep-shearing commences in May on the northward journey, and is effected in vast buildings by the roadside, called *Esquileos*, capable of containing 50,000, and some of them 60,000 sheep; the principal of these buildings are in the environs of Segovia.

The wool of the sheep belonging to the *Mesta* is celebrated for its fineness, length of fibre, and silky softness: this excellence is said to be owing to the habits of the sheep, whereby they are led to live in almost always the same temperature. The meat of these sheep is however of inferior quality.

The mesta is very unpopular in Spain, for the following among other reasons—the number of persons (40,000 or 50,000) whom it takes from the cultivation of the soil; the immense extent of valuable land kept out of cultivation; the continual trespass on the cultivated lands near the route taken by the flocks in their migration; the scarcity of food for the stationary sheep in the line of march; the loss in an agricultural point of view (in respect to manure) of the sheep never being penned on arable land; and the despotic behaviour of the shepherds, who are protected in their improper privileges and conduct by the tribunal of the mesta. All attempts to abolish the mesta have, however, failed.

METALS; METALLURGY. The metals form a numerous and highly important class of simple or elementary bodies. They amount in number to upwards of forty. They are, given alphabetically, as follows:—*Aluminum, antimony, arsenic, barium, bismuth, cadmium, calcium, cerium, chromium, cobalt, columbium, copper, gulcinium, gold, iridium, iron, latanium, lead, lithium, magnesium, manganese, mercury, molybden, nickel, osmium, palladium, platina, potassium, rhodium, silver, sodium, strontium, tellurium, thorium, tin, titanium, tungsten, uranium, vanadium, yttrium, zinc, zirconium.* Some chemists rank *selenium* and *silicium* also among the metals, and a few newly discovered metals are now undergoing examination.

With the exception of mercury all metals are solid at the usual temperature of the air, and the colour of most of them is grayish-white. The lustre of metals is great and peculiar, and is well known by the name of the metallic lustre; they differ however very considerably in the degree in which they possess this property. When reduced to a state of minute division, the metallic lustre is lost but the colour remains. The metals are generally reckoned perfectly opaque, even when reduced to thin leaves; but it is found that gold-leaf which is $\frac{1}{200000}$ part of an inch thick, suffers light to pass through it, and it has a green colour; it is therefore extremely probable that all metals, if they could be rendered equally thin, would also be translucent. There are some metals, such as lead, tin, copper, and iron, which, when rubbed, emit a peculiar and disagreeable smell; and others, such as arsenic and antimony, which emit an odour when heated. All the metals are heavier than water, except sodium and potassium. Platinum is the heaviest. About one half of them are ductile or malleable, and the other half brittle. Gold is the most ductile and the most malleable, iron is the most tenacious, and titanium the hardest, in their native state. The elasticity and sonorousness of metals are generally associated with their degree of hardness. There are not however any metals which are by themselves either very elastic or sonorous; but there are alloys which possess these properties in a high degree, as for example those of copper and tin.

Metals are sometimes lamellar, sometimes granular, and frequently crystalline: indeed, some of them, and more especially copper, occur crystallised in the form of the cube and its varieties. Bismuth is a metal which may be artificially crystallised in cubes with great facility.

No particular effect has been attributed to the agency of light upon metals. The metals are good conductors of heat; some of them rank in the following order in this respect—gold, silver, platina, copper, iron, zinc, tin, lead. Their capacity for heat ranges them in a different order, bismuth and lead taking the lead. Immediately that heat pervades the metals, and before it fuses them, it expands them in all directions. This dilatation is different in different metals; it varies also in the same metal with every degree of the thermometric scale; but from the freezing to the boiling point of water it may however be regarded as nearly constant. The fusing point of metals varies extremely. [FREEZING; MELTING.]

Some metals are volatilised at moderate degrees of heat: among these are mercury, cadmium, arsenic, tellurium, zinc, potassium, and sodium; but there are others which may be exposed to the most intense heat of a wind furnace without being at all vaporised.

The relative conducting powers of the principal metals for electricity are as follow:—copper, gold, silver, zinc, platina, iron, tin, lead, mercury, potassium. Each of the following metals is positive with relation to those which follow it:—zinc, lead, tin, iron, antimony, bismuth, copper, mercury, silver, gold, tellurium, palladium, platina. There are two metals only which are capable of being rendered permanently magnetic, namely, iron and nickel; the former of these only is met with possessing this property in nature; it is an oxide of iron, and commonly called the *loadstone*. Most of the metals combine with each other and form compounds differing very materially in properties from their constituent metals. [ALLOYS.] All metals unite with oxygen, but with different degrees of facility and affinity; most of them combine with more than one proportion of oxygen and some of them with several proportions. A few of these compounds form acids, but most of them oxides. Hydrogen, chlorine, bromine, sulphur, iodine, and phosphorus, all combine with some or other of the metals. Some metals, as potassium, sodium, and manganese, decompose water even at common temperatures, combining with its oxygen and evolving the hydrogen; others, as iron and zinc, require to be strongly heated, or the presence of an acid, to effect this decomposition.

Although most metals are dissolved by acids, yet platina and gold are exceptions to it, these and some others requiring chlorine, and generally in the nascent state called *aqua regia*.

Metallurgy, or the separation of metals from their ores and from other compounds, varies in its processes according to the metal; for which see COPPER, GOLD, IRON, LEAD, &c. The working of metals into useful forms constitutes the basis of such numberless mechanical arts that we cannot here even enumerate them; the principal among them will be found under their proper headings.

In relation to commerce, the metals form a very important section of our Exports and Imports. Among our Imports for 1849 and 1850 we find the following:—

	1849.	1850.
Copper and copper ore,	47,433 tons	45,930
Wrought copper .	51,808 cwts.	97,706
Iron in bars	29,396 tons	34,066
Steel	1,012 tons	49
Lead	7,216 tons	11,977
Zinc	15,915 tons	18,626
Tin	35,827 cwts.	33,332
Mercury	23,952 cwts.	3,170
Watches	86,305*l.*	97,245*l.*

Our Exports of metals in the same two years included the following:—

	1849.	1850.
Iron, pig, bar, and wire . . .	567,417 tons	615,150
Iron, cast	16,549 tons	21,201
Iron, wrought . .	117,431 tons	136,514
Steel, unwrought .	8,097 tons	10,587
Brass	23,811 cwts.	25,899
Copper	409,603 cwts.	422,309
Lead	17,027 tons	22,083
Tin, unwrought .	35,292 cwts.	31,663
Tin plates	709,788*l.*	928,181*l.*
Machinery	700,631*l.*	1,043,764*l.*
Cutlery and hardware . . .	2,201,315*l.*	2,639,728*l.*

In respect to Exhibitions of Manufactures, such as that which so largely attracts public attention in 1851, the metals form by far the most bulky of the specimens.

METEORIC STONES. [STONES, METEORIC.]

METERS. The increased use of gas for lighting streets and buildings has led to the invention of a number of *gas-meters*. In the early stage of the system, gas was charged for at so much per light, according to the number of holes in the ring of the burner; but it has become gradually admitted that a more equitable principle would be to charge for the quantity actually consumed. This is done by measure; and a gas-meter determines the number of cubic feet consumed. The meter is placed at some spot between the main and the burner, so that all the gas must pass through the meter before reaching the burner. The meter is a hollow box, and in most cases contains water in some of the interior compartments; but whether so or not, the progress of the gas through the meter moves a system of wheel-work, by which index hands shew the amount which has passed.

METRONOME. This ingenious instrument was introduced about the year 1814, by John Maelzel (civil engineer and mechanician to the Emperor of Austria), for the purpose of determining the movement, *i.e.* the quickness or slowness, of musical compositions. Of Maelzel's Metronome there are two kinds. The one is a pendulum kept in motion by a spring and wheelwork, and which ticks the vibrations:—the other is also a pendulum, but without any machinery, and acting only so long as the force of the impulse given shall last. The former, therefore, it will be obvious, is complicated and expensive; the latter is simple and cheap.

Much opposition was made to the use of this excellent instrument, when first introduced; but it is gradually coming into extensive use.

Mr. Greaves of Sheffield has lately registered a very simple and cheap metronome. In size and form it resembles a small watch, and can be carried in the waistcoat pocket. It consists of a case containing a tape 40 inches long, which can be drawn out to any required length, and be there retained by a stop. The extreme end of the tape being held by the finger and thumb, the case forms the bob of a pendulum, which may be swung to and fro. Instead of holding it between the finger and thumb, a small spring affords the means of attaching it to a pianoforte or a music stand. As all pendulums oscillate a certain number of times in a minute according to the length, the tape is drawn out more or less according as the oscillations are to be slow or quick; and this depends upon the tune of the piece of music. The tape has marks to indicate any number of oscillations per minute from 60 to 160; and it is also marked with those Italian words which serve to point out the quickness or slowness of a piece of music: such as *presto, spiritoso, vivace, allegro, poco allegro, moderato, allegretto, andante, andantino, larghetto, lento, largo, grave, adagio.*

MEURTHE. In this department of France a very large quantity of wine is made; in ordinary years the produce is 20 to 21 million gallons. The surplus over the home consumption is sold into Alsace and the department of Vosges. In the arrondissement of Sarrebourg, where the climate, owing to the proximity of the Vosges mountains, is colder than in the rest of the department, the vine is not cultivated at all. Rape is extensively grown, both for green food and for making oil. Hay is abundantly produced along all the river bottoms. Potatoes, potherbs of all kinds, and fruits are largely cultivated. Iron ore is found, but too poor to be worth digging for. Building stone, marble, and limestone are quarried; lithographic stone, red and gray granite, grindstone grit, glass sand, potter's clay, &c., are found. A mine of salt-rock at Vic, and several salt-springs, are the most valuable mineral treasures of the department.

The industrial activity of the department has been greatly developed within the last few years, and is exerted on a great variety of products, among which are—woollen cloth, calico, canvas, embroidered muslins and cambrics, playing cards, room paper, cut and plate glass, tobacco pipes, oil, mineral acids, cotton twist, gloves, beet-root sugar, candles, basket and wood work, &c. There are also some iron and bell foundries, numerous glass-works, tanyards, paper mills, dye houses, and potteries. Of the articles just enumerated and of its agricultural produce the commerce of the department is composed.

MEUSE. This is another of the French departments, deriving its name from an important and busy river. The lower part of the basin of the Meuse includes a good deal of fertile flat land, with not a few marshes and peat bogs; the upper part of it is in general fertile, and presents some pretty and some bold scenery. The basin of the Meuse communicates with those of the Rhine, the Seine, and the Schelde, by means of canals.

In the department, hemp, flax, and oleaginous seeds are cultivated. Cattle, swine, and goats are numerous; horses are small. Gooseberries and strawberries are grown in very large quantities in the neighbourhood of Bar-le-Duc and Ligny, whence they are largely exported in the preserved state. Gruyère and cream cheese are made in the arondissement of Commercy. About 20 to 24 million gallons of wine are made annually, two-thirds of which are consumed on the spot, and the remainder is exported to Belgium.

Several iron mines are worked; good building stone, marl, potters' clay, and slates are found. Fossils of great variety, and some of large dimensions, are met with. The chief manufactures are—iron, made in about forty forges and furnaces, cotton cloth and twist, hosiery, oil, glass, paper, pottery, beer, leather, inferior brandy, &c. The commerce of the department is fed by the articles already enumerated, and by timber, oak staves, clover seed, butter, fat pork, hides, wool, confectionary, &c.

MEXICO. Humboldt asserts that within these states almost all the vegetable productions may be grown which are found between the equator and the polar circle. Any enumeration of them here would therefore be unnecessary. The agriculture of the table-lands does not supply any article for exportation. Cotton is grown along the shores of the Pacific, and in the valley of the Rio Nasas, in a deep depression of the northern table land; and coffee on the eastern coast, west of the town of Vera Cruz; sugar is cultivated in many places, and a considerable quantity is exported; cocoa is collected in the low country along the river Huasacualco; and indigo along the southern coast, but only for home consumption. Tobacco, which in many parts succeeds very well, is only permitted to be grown in certain places.

The domestic animals, brought over from Europe by the Spaniards, have multiplied greatly in Mexico, owing to the wide tracts which are not or cannot be cultivated, and which afford pasture-ground for nine or ten months of the year. Cattle is abundant, both on the table-lands and the lower tracts. Jerked beef and horns are exported. Sheep are numerous on the table-lands, especially on the northern, which are much drier; and wool is an article of exportation. Horses abound generally. Horses and mules are exported in great numbers to the United States. On the great plains bordering on the Red River and the Arkansas the American buffalo abounds. Game is abundant, especially deer and hares. The cochineal insect is reared with great care on the table-land of Mixtecapan, whence by far the greatest part is brought to the markets of the world.

Mexico is noted for its mines of gold and silver. The gold mines occur chiefly on the western side of the Sierra Madre, north of 24° N. lat.: the silver mines are richest on the mountains which rise on the table-lands, and in those which border their margin. Besides the precious metals, Mexico has abundance of copper, iron, and lead, which are worked. The iron mines, however, have only been opened since the year 1825. A quicksilver mine is worked at S. Onofre, on the northern declivity of the Sierra Madre. The carbonate of soda, which is necessary for the smelting of the silver ore, is collected in several lakes, where it is found crystallised on the surface in great abundance.

Before the Mexican Revolution in 1810, there were many flourishing manufactures in Mexico, the annual produce of which amounted to from eight to ten millions of Spanish dollars, or about two millions of English money. The most considerable were those of cotton and wool in the towns of Puebla, Cholula, Tlascala, Queretaro, Lagos, Guadalaxara, and Tezcuco. The manufactures of soap, leather, and saddlery were also considerable. The manufacturers owed their prosperity to the high price at which, under a system of monopoly, European goods were sold in that country. After the harbours were thrown open to a free trade (in 1820) the manufactures began to decline, and are now much diminished.

The commercial intercourse between the coast and the table-lands is difficult on account of the steep ascent to the table-lands from the coast. Even in those parts where there is no obstacle to the use of carriages, the goods are commonly carried by mules, on account of the great number of these animals, and the low price at which they are bought.

The maritime commerce is considerable; but it is carried on chiefly in foreign vessels, Mexico possessing few vessels of her own. In the beginning of the present century the exports, according to Humboldt, amounted to 22,000,000 of Spanish dollars, and the imports to 15,000,000 of dollars. Between 1820 and 1830, however, the exports considerably diminished, on account of the comparatively small produce of the mines, the precious metals constituting the principal article of exportation. The coinage of gold and silver in Mexico in 1845 amounted to 15,141,816 dollars. The amount of gold coined in Mexico in the 18 months ending June, 1849, was 1,351,416 dollars, and of silver, 27,003,989 dollars; which, with nine or ten million dollars' worth left uncoined, present a total of about 38,000,000 dollars' worth raised in 18 months. It is understood that, but for the high price of quicksilver for smelting or amalgamating, the produce would have been larger.

The total Mexican exports are estimated at about 20,000,000 dollars, of which 18,000,000 are in precious metals. The British and Irish produce exported to Mexico in 1848 was valued at 945,937*l.* Our imports from Mexico consist chiefly of cochineal and logwood.

The aboriginal architecture of Mexico resembles that of Egypt, not only in the vast scale and massiveness of its monuments, but in the application of the pyramid, or of forms composed of it. Pyramids not inferior to those of Egypt, and some of even still larger dimensions in their plan or base, exist in the Mexican territories; and examples of the second class occur in pyramid towers, consisting of a series of truncated pyramids placed one above another, each successive one being smaller than the one on which it immediately rests, so that it stands upon a platform or terrace. At Teotihuacan, about eight leagues to the north-east of the city of Mexico, are an immense number of pyramids, several hundred small ones ranged in files or lines, and two larger ones consecrated to the sun and moon. Besides monuments which are chiefly works of magnificence, others exist which attest the high degree of civilization attained by the aboriginal nations of Mexico, such as Cyclopean roads and bridges. The former of these were constructed of huge blocks of stone, and frequently carried on a continued level, so as to be viaducts across valleys.

MEZZOTINTO is a peculiar mode of engraving designs of any description upon plates of copper or steel. In this style of engraving, which essentially differs from every other, the surface of the plate is first indented or hacked all over by the action of an instrument something like a chisel, with a toothed or serrated edge, called a *cradle*, or mezzotinto *grounder*. This tool, being rocked to and fro in many directions, indents or barbs the plate uniformly over its face, and produces what is called the mezzotinto grain or ground. The barb or nap thus produced retains the printing-ink; and if in this state of preparation an impression were taken from the plate upon paper, it would be uniformly of a deep black colour.

The mezzotinto ground having been laid, the business of the artist properly commences. Having traced or drawn, with a pencil or other instrument, his outline upon the paper (unless, indeed, as is sometimes the case, this should have been etched by the ordinary process previous to the mezzotinto ground having been laid), he proceeds to cut away the nap or ground, in conformity with the design, from all those parts which are not intended to be perfectly black in the impression. The instruments required for this purpose are *scrapers* and *burnishers*. With the former he scrapes away more and more of the ground in proportion to the brightness of the light, and the burnishers are used to produce perfect whiteness where it is required, as the high lights on the forehead or tip of the nose, or white linen in a portrait, &c. As the work proceeds it may be blackened with ink, applied with a printer's ball or otherwise, to ascertain the effect; after which the scraping may be again proceeded with, the artist taking care always to commence where the strongest lights are intended to appear.

The great facility with which mezzotintos are executed, as compared with line engravings, will be obvious, seeing that it is much easier to scrape or burnish away parts of a dark ground corresponding with any design sketched upon it than it is to form shades upon a white ground by an infinite number of strokes, hatches, or points, made with the graver or etching needle. Herein consists the leading difference between this and all other modes of engraving; for, while the process in each of these is invariably from light to dark, in mezzotinto it is from dark to light; and even the very deepest shades are produced, as we have seen, before the design is commenced. The characteristic or distinguishing excellence of mezzotinto engraving would seem to consist in the rich profundity of its shadows, and its chief defect seems to be a corresponding poverty in the lights. Lithography has of late years, in a great degree, superseded mezzotint.

MICA is a mineral which usually occurs in thin plates, semi-transparent, and of a peculiar lustre. It consists chiefly of silica and alumina, with small proportions of potash, lithia, and other substances. It is very useful for many optical purposes, since it is easily separable into very thin plates, and is in that state almost transparent.

Mica gives the name of *mica schist* to one of the earliest groups of stratified rocks known to geologists, and very extensively distributed throughout the mountain regions of the globe, often in contact with granite, but more frequently superposed on gneiss. It is frequently interstratified with gneiss, primary limestone, quartz rock, chloritic schist, and clay slate. It differs from gneiss by the absence of felspar. In respect of the magnitude, relative abundance, and crystalline aspect of the ingredients of mica schist, there is every possible variation, so that some specimens approach obscurely to granite, others to well defined gneiss, and others to clay slate.

MICHIGAN. A few industrial statistics of this American state will be found under UNITED STATES.

MICROMER. These ingenious contrivances for measuring small spaces or angles with great accuracy or convenience, present many varieties.

Wire Micrometer.—This frequently consists of two fine wires or spider's threads, of which one is fixed and the other moveable, in the eye-tube of a telescope at the place where the image is formed. The moveable wire is in a sliding plate which, by a screw, is moved parallel to the other, and perpendicularly to the axis of the telescope, till the object appears to be comprehended between the wires; and a graduated scale is provided for the measurement of the angle. Each division is equal to the extent of space moved by the wire during one revolution of the screw, and the head of the screw is graduated, in order to subdivide the scale. The instrument was invented by Mr. Gascoigne in the seventeenth century, but it appears to have been afterwards neglected, and was re-invented by M. Auzout. The micrometer microscope, for reading off the divisions of graduated circles, is an instrument of this kind.

The *Position Wire Micrometer* has lately come very much into use for observations of double stars, and is the wire micrometer proper for equatorials. In this construction there are two wires parallel to each other, each moveable by its own screw: the whole apparatus can also be turned round in the plane of the wires, so as to place the wires in any direction, the angle round which it is turned being read off by two verniers upon a small circle called the position circle. The mode of measuring double stars by this instrument is a very refined problem in practical astronomy.

The *Divided Object-Glass Micrometer.* If an object-glass be cut across so as to form two semicircles, and the semilenses be separated by sliding one beyond the other, each portion will form its proper image, and these will retreat from each other as the semilenses are moved. The semilenses are mounted on slides, and the quantity of separation read off upon a scale.

The *Divided Eye-Glass Micrometer.* This consists of a convex lens bisected in the direction of a diameter, and placed either at the end of a telescope nearest the eye, or between some of the other lenses of the eye-piece; it acts as a micrometer by separating the two halves of the lens, as in the former case.

The *Reticule Micrometer* is employed where less accurate measurement is required. The reticule, or diaphragm, as it is sometimes called, is any fixed arrangement of wires or bars which can be applied to a telescope for the purpose of measurement. Suppose, for example, a cross like an X to be cut out of brass plate, and inserted in the principal focus of a telescope. A star, in passing through the field of the instrument, is occulted at its passage behind each of the bars, and the time noted. The *interval* will show, by an easy calculation, how far it passes from the vertex; and the *mean* of the times, the moment when it passes the axis of the diaphragm. This reticule is very convenient for mapping, if placed in the meridian, or for cometary observation, if the telescope is mounted as an equatorial, however rudely.

The *Circular Micrometer.* A metal ring is set in the centre of a perforated glass plate, and the outer and inner edge of the ring is turned true. The plate is fixed in the focus of a telescope, and the observer notes the time when a star disappears at the outer ring, reappears on the inner ring, disappears again, and finally reappears. These data afford the means for measuring small angles.

It need hardly be stated that manufacture of such apparatus as the above must take a high rank in philosophical instrument making.

MICROSCOPE. As the *micrometer* enables the man of science to measure very small spaces, so does the *microscope* afford the means for seeing smaller objects than would otherwise be visible. The scientific principles of the microscope are beyond the present work; it is only as a work of *construction* that it is treated here.

By the term *Simple Microscope* is meant one in which the object is viewed directly through a lens or combination of lenses. When, however, the magnifying power of the glass is considerable, it requires to be placed at the proper distance from the object with great precision: it cannot therefore be held with sufficient accuracy and steadiness by the unassisted hand, but must be mounted in a frame having a rack or screw to move it towards or from another frame or stage which holds the object. The lens is then called a *microscope;* and it is furnished, according to circumstances, with lenses and mirrors to collect and reflect the light upon the object, and with other conveniences.

The *Compound Microscope* has two lenses which have totally different functions; the first receives the rays from the object, and, bringing them to new foci, forms an image, which the second lens treats as an original object, and magnifies it just as the single microscope magnified the object itself. Each of these purposes is further carried out by an increase in the number of lenses. By means of successive improvements, the Compound Microscope now holds a very high rank among philosophical implements; while the transcendant beauties of form, colour, and organization which it reveals to us in the minute works of nature, render it subservient to the most delightful and instructive pursuits.

The *Solar Microscope* consists of a conical tube fixed by its base to a frame of wood, which is screwed to a closed window-shutter, at an aperture purposely made in the shutter: the tube projects into the room, which, when the observations are to be made, is rendered quite dark, and is sometimes lined with black cloth. The magnifying power is produced by a system of lenses contained in the tube, as in other microscopes. On the exterior of the window is a frame carrying a rectangular piece of looking-glass, which, by turning on a hinge, is capable of being fixed at any angle with the wall of the building, while, by means of a ring and a rack and pinion, it can be made to turn on tho horizontal axis of the instrument, so as to permit the rays of the sun, whatever be the position of the latter, to be reflected into the tube. These rays are made to converge on the object; and from thence, after refraction through the system of object-glasses, they proceed to a screen, on which they depict the magnified image. The solar microscope is now nearly superseded by the *Oxyhydrogen Microscope*. [LUCERNAL MICROSCOPE.]

MIDDLESEX. The interest in this small county is so absorbed by that of the gigantic metropolis which it contains, that we need not enter upon its industrial and commercial features here. It would be but a very slight deviation from accuracy to say, that the whole county is occupied either by persons whose daily avocations are centred in London, or by persons who supply the various markets of the metropolis with produce. There are malting, brewing, distilling, and other processes carried on upon a considerable scale in the extra-metropolitan parts of Middlesex, but chiefly looking to London as a centre.

MILAN is a gay thriving city: its markets are abundantly supplied with every luxury. Numerous coffee-houses, splendid hotels, abundance of handsome carriages, several theatres (among which is La Scala, one of the largest in Europe), well supplied with actors and singers,—all attest the habits of a luxurious capital. It is also a famous seat of learning and of the fine arts. But whatever may be its attractions in these directions, Milan can hardly be called a commercial city. Its manufactures consist chiefly of silks, printed cottons, plate-glass, jewellery, artificial flowers, soap, and leather.

MILE. The connection between measures of length and commercial matters renders it useful to have at hand a comparison of the different lengths of a mile, in different parts of Europe. The English statute mile is 8 furlongs, each of 220 yards, or 40 poles of 5½ yards or 16½ feet each. It is also 80 surveying chains of 22 yards each. It is therefore 1760 yards, or 5280 feet. The square mile is 6400 square chains, or 640 acres.

	Yards.	Stat. miles.
Ancient Roman mile....	1614	.917
Modern Roman mile....	1628	.925
English statute mile	1760	1.000
Tuscan mile	1808	1.027
Ancient Scottish mile ...	1984	1.127
Irish mile............	2240	1.273
French posting league ..	4263	2.422
Spanish judicial league..	4635	2.634
French league of 25 to the degree	4860	2.761
Portugal league........	6760	3.841
German short mile	6859	3.897
Flanders league	6864	3.900
Spanish common league.	7416	4.214
Prussian mile..........	8237	4.680
Danish mile	8244	4.684
Danzig mile	8475	4.815
Hungarian mile........	9113	5.178
Swiss mile............	9153	5.201
German long mile......	10126	5.753
Hanoverian mile	11559	6.568
Swedish mile	11700	6.648

MILK. This remarkable and valuable liquid consists, in addition to the watery portion, serum, &c., of globular particles, having a diameter of about one ten-thousandth of an inch. They are composed of a fatty matter (butter) and a coagulable substance, which in many points resembles albumen, termod *caseine*, or the matter of cheese. Milk is a compound fluid, chiefly consisting of oil, sugar, and protein.

Milk may be brought to a dry state, and powdered, in which condition it keeps for a length of time; and by dissolving it in tepid water an artificial milk may be formed, capable of being used at sea, particularly for children during long voyages. Of the valuable use of milk in dairy husbandry, see BUTTER; CHEESE; DAIRY. Milk is also used as an antidote in cases of poisoning by some metallic salts, such as corrosive sublimate, perchloride of tin, sulphate of copper, &c.

There is too much reason to believe that the milk sold in busy towns is far from pure; water is often added to increase the quantity, and strange compounds (according to chemical tests) are added to imitate the quality. Until dealers learn to be commercially honest, there is no cure but the vigilant observation of the buyers; for it is doubtful whether legislation could meet the evil.

MILLET, is cultivated largely in the southern parts of Europe—in Spain, Italy, the south of France, Switzerland, and southern Germany; but it is grown most extensively in the East Indies, China, Arabia, Syria, Egypt, and

Nubia. It has also been introduced into the West Indies, where it is called *Guinea Corn*. In the East millet is used as food for man; but in Europe, though it is sometimes made into loaves and cakes, and frequently into puddings, it is mostly used for feeding poultry and domestic animals. The leaves and panicles are given, both green and dried, as fodder to cattle.

MILLS; MILL WORK. The name of mill is employed rather indefinitely in machinery. A cotton factory is called a mill; a windmill is a mill; a coffee-grinder is a mill; and many agricultural implements are called mills. Without extending the application too widely, we will notice a few of the mills connected with agricultural pursuits.

All the machines for grinding corn and seeds are mills, whatever may be their particular application. At the Smithfield Cattle Show, and similar agricultural exhibitions, such mills are numerous. One prevalent form is that of an iron machine supported on four legs, having a winch handle on one side, a fly wheel on another, a hopper at the top, and a crushing apparatus in the centre. The grain or seed is put into the hopper, the winch handle is turned, the grain becomes crushed to powder, and falls out at the bottom of the apparatus. Sometimes the mill is made chiefly of wood, but with iron wheel and crushing apparatus. Lloyd's wheat mill, in addition to the usual mill apparatus, has a chest which acts as a flour dressing machine. Some mills are adapted for crushing beans rather than seeds.

Crosskill's patent mill has a somewhat higher class of action, since it is adapted either for hand, horse, or steam power. In addition to the grinding of corn and seed, it will hull rice, coffee, and olives; crush bones and metallic ores; and grind colours, drugs, charcoal and various other substances.

The crushing apparatus in mills is of two kinds, either one stone working round in contact with another; or two metallic surfaces between which the substance is forced, but between which it cannot pass except in a fine state.

MILLSTONES. The millstones employed in grinding corn require to be made of a peculiar kind of stone. The greater proportion of our millstones are procured from a particular spot in Western Germany. At about ten miles from Coblenz is a small town called Andernach, the chief trade of which is in millstones procured from the neighbouring quarries of Nieder-Mendig. There are several quarries, averaging about 50 feet in depth, each quarry shaped like an inverted cone, down the sides of which the quarry men descend by a spiral path. The quarry men have to cut away through a superincumbent layer of soft porous stone, till they come to a layer of hard, blackish, heavy stone, regularly porous, and yielding sparks when struck with iron. This is the mill-stone, and requires good and well prepared tools to work it; it is supposed to be a compact lava from some extinct volcano; and as there are fissures or gaps at intervals, these facilitate the separation of the stone into blocks suitable for millstones. All round the bottom of the conical cavities, the stone has been excavated in galleries or horizontal passages. The stones are brought to shape by means of hammers and chisels. A deep socket is cut through the middle of such stones as are intended for *runners*, or upper stones. The furrows on the surfaces of the stones are produced by means of a double edged hammer, about 14 lbs. weight.

The hard volcanic stratum from whence the millstones are cut, extends five miles in length by three in breadth; so that the supply may for all practical purposes be deemed inexhaustible. It is known that millstones have been procured from this spot during a period of 2,000 years. Four or five families usually unite in the labour of sinking a shaft and working the stone; all assisting in the labour according to their strength and ability. The workers divide themselves into four groups —the miners, the lifters, the cutters, and the loaders. When the millstones are properly shaped, they are sent down the Rhine upon the immense timber rafts which navigate that river. When the rafts arrive at Holland, they are broken up for the sale of the timber; and the millstones are distributed in various quarters according to the demand.

MINARET in Turkish and Eastern architecture, is a very slender and lofty turret, having one or more projecting balconies around it, that divide it externally into two or more stories. They are used in Mohammedan countries for the purpose of calling the people to prayers, and therefore serve the purpose of belfries; but they are also frequently added merely for ornament.

MINERALS. Various methods of arrangement of minerals have been proposed by different authors. According to Werner, minerals were divided into the four classes of earthy minerals, saline minerals, inflammables, and metals: Karsten classed them under the heads of earths, salts, combustibles, and metals: Haüy divided minerals into acidiferous earthy substances, earthy substances, non-metallic combustible bodies, metallic bodies, substances not sufficiently known to admit of classification, rocks and volcanic products; Phillips's classes are, earthy minerals, alkaline-earthy minerals, acids, acidiferous earthy minerals, acidiferous alkaline minerals, native metals, metalliferous minerals, and combustible minerals; Berzelius made a chemical classification. Various modes of classifying minerals have depended on the relative *structure*, *fracture*, *hardness*, *specific gravity*, *transparency* and *lustre* of the minerals. The study of this subject in a systematic form constitutes the science of *Mineralogy*.

MINIATURE PAINTING. Miniature painting, properly so named, is in water-colours, though it is not at all similar in its process to that employed in water-colour drawings in general. Instead of being applied in washes, or by different tints laid over each other, the colours are entirely dotted, stippled, or hatched upon the surface; though sometimes only the face and other flesh parts are so executed, as requiring greater finish and delicacy, while the drapery and background are either partially or wholly executed according to the usual mode of water-colour drawing. The material employed for painting upon is generally ivory (the surface of which is first prepared for receiving the colours), or vellum; sometimes Bristol-board, or other drawing-paper of that sort. Ivory however is preferred, as not only more durable, but bearing out the colours with greater brilliancy.

MINING. The use of the metals, and consequently some process for the extraction and separation of them, may be traced to the most remote antiquity. In respect to our own country, mines were worked in Britain by the Romans; but during the Saxon period they were much neglected; and subsequently to this period they were chiefly worked by Jews. In the reign of Elizabeth the art of mining had fallen into so much decay that an importation of foreign skill was found necessary to revive them; and the Germans, long and justly celebrated as skilful miners, received every encouragement to settle in this country and turn their attention to them. In the 17th century the use of gunpowder in mines was introduced; and early in the next century the rich copper mines of Cornwall were first worked. The invention of the steam-engine was early rendered applicable to mining in this country, and contributed to the present perfect state of the art. After the invention by Savery and Newcomen, the steam engine became a most useful auxiliary in the hands of the miner; and the improvements of Watt were still more beneficial. The Cornish steam engines are now among the most powerful in the world. The use of iron pumps instead of wooden in the shafts, and the laying down of tramroads in the galleries of a mine, were two other great improvements. Great improvements, too, have been made in the mechanical treatment of the ores after they have been extracted.

There are four principal classes into which mineral deposits may be divided; *veins*, *beds*, *masses*, and *fragmentary deposits*. *Veins* are generally long, narrow, and irregular fissures, traversing the rocky crust of the globe, which they penetrate to an unknown depth, and at a high angle of inclination. They are for the most part filled with sparry and stony substances called the 'veinstone,' or the 'gangue,' of the vein, but contain here and there irregular masses or 'bunches' of the metallic ores, often of immense size and value, and which it is the principal business of the miner to discover and extract. Most of the metals are of common occurrence in veins. *Beds* are layers of mineral substances interposed between the strata of solid rock, which, except in their containing valuable matter, they very much resemble. Several of the metals, especially lead, are occasionally found in beds; coal, clay-ironstone, and rock-salt, exclusively so. *Masses* or *Pipe-Veins*, are irregular branching cavities descending either vertically or obliquely into the rock, and filled up with metalliferous matter. They usually contain copper, lead, or oxides of iron. *Fragmentary Deposits* occur associated with many of the loose superficial beds of sand and gravel which occur in the valleys of mineral districts, consisting of the detritus of the neighbouring mountains, which has been washed down from thence at remote geological epochs. Tin and gold are the chief metals found in this form. Each kind of metallic ore is found to prevail in some one geological formation rather than others.

Most metals are found in the state of *Ores*, that is, chemically combined with certain mineralizing substances. The most important of these mineralizing bodies are oxygen and sulphur; the next in rank are chlorine, and the sulphuric, carbonic, and phosphoric acids. These elements require to be separated by the processes of metallurgy; but there are also other mechanical impurities scarcely less important, which require to be partially separated in the mine, and which therefore fall entirely within the province of the miner. It frequently happens too that ores of a worthless character are mixed up with the more valuable ones; thus copper and lead are very generally accompanied by iron pyrites and blende, both of which must be regarded as impurities, and therefore separated as far as possible previous to any process in the furnace.

Veins or beds are seldom visible at the surface of the ground, being generally concealed by the soil. As the deposits usually present no trace of their existence at the surface, certain general indications must be had recourse to for their discovery; the number of indications which guide the miner is considerable, and increases as science and experience advances. When a new vein or mineral deposit has been by any process discovered, the most usual step, after obtaining the consent of the proprietor, is the formation of a company; for companies are generally found to work mines better than individuals. The company agree with the proprietor as to the extent of ground within which operations may be carried on, the proportion of the gross mineral produce or its equivalent in money which the owner is to receive free of all expense in raising and making it marketable, and other matters.

In commencing the mining operations, the usual system is, to dig down from the surface until the vein or bed is reached. A spot is selected as the site of a shaft, which is frequently sunk in an inclined direction upon the course of the vein, or if intended to be perpendicular, it is commenced upon that side towards which the vein inclines or underlies, and at such a distance from its 'back' or outcrop, as to come down upon it at a given depth, say 10, 20, or 30 fathoms. On cutting the vein, the shaft is for a time suspended, and two horizontal passages, often termed 'galleries,' but by the miner 'levels,' are excavated or 'driven' upon the vein in both directions. These passages are usually about six feet in height and three or four in breadth, and rather smaller above than below. They are the principal means of exploring the contents of veins. If the shaft is deep, 'cross-cuts' and other levels are made at different heights, so as to explore the vein at different parts. After cutting the vein, there are two modes of proceeding — continuing the shaft perpendicularly through the vein, or obliquely upon the vein; the choice between these two plans depends on a number of practical circumstances. Supposing the shaft to proceed perpendicularly after cutting the vein, on reaching the depth of ten fathoms or thereabouts below the point of intersection another cross-cut will be driven to it. In this manner the shaft proceeds indefinitely, cross-cuts being driven at every ten fathoms or whatever distance is most convenient, and levels extended from each upon the course of the vein, the nature and value of which are thus thoroughly explored.

The mining operations are soon affected by the impurity of the air. It is chiefly in the ends of the levels that the evil of imperfect ventilation begins to be felt, the air here gradually becoming close and unfit for respiration, as the levels advance further from the shaft, especially when from the hardness of the ground frequent blasting is necessary. As soon as this is found to be the case, a remedy of a very simple nature is applied, which consists in sinking a small pit, termed a 'winze,' upon the vein, from the upper level to the extremity of the one below it. This communication having been effected, the two levels became perfectly ventilated, each having a double communication with the atmosphere by which both an ascending and descending current is produced. The winzes are generally made at intervals of 20 or 30 fathoms apart, and from each level to those above and below it: they serve not only for ventilating the galleries, but also assist the exploring and working of the vein.

The various operations may proceed indefinitely, according to the richness of the vein The shaft will continue to be sunk, cross-cuts driven to the vein at every ten fathoms or thereabouts, levels extended in both directions from them, and the ground between them subdivided by winzes. The excavations will now have assumed a regular form, and become what is properly termed a *mine*. In mining operations, where the vein is not very hard, the ore may be broken down with the 'pick' only, but it is generally necessary to blast it with powder, by which process large quantities are detached from the vein by every shot. The ore having been detached is carried in tram-waggons to the shaft, and thence raised to the surface. When the levels have been extended to a considerable distance from the shaft, the ventilation will again become defective, notwithstanding their communication by winzes. The expense of the transport of ore and masses of rock and rubbish to the shaft also becomes considerable; and if the prospects of the mine continue such as to warrant the expense, a new shaft must now be sunk on one or both sides of the former. This new shaft will be so placed as to intersect the vein much deeper than the former, and this point will be so arranged as to correspond either with one of the deepest levels, or some proposed level deeper still. By accurate measurements, mining engineers are able to work a second shaft from many different depths at one time. At the Consolidated Mines in Cornwall, a perpendicular shaft, 204 fathoms in depth, was worked from fifteen different points at once. Mining shafts are generally about eight feet by six in area.

As veins are generally found to run nearly parallel, and often at no great distance from each other, and as the neighbourhood of a productive vein is a favourable indication of the contents of others in its vicinity, transverse levels or 'cross-cuts' are frequently driven from mines at various depths, with a view to discover side-veins or to make trial of branches which diverge from the main lode. Metalliferous veins are often traversed by other veins crossing them at nearly right angles, which seldom contain ore, except perhaps near the points of intersection: they are termed 'cross-courses,' or 'cross-veins.'

Where a vein has been worked by driving a level towards it from a valley or other convenient point on the surface, the drainage to the point of intersection is, of course complete; and hence in mountainous countries, where deep ravines occur, levels may be made for draining at a much smaller expense than where engines are required to pump the water up from a great depth.

The tools and processes employed by the miner in the excavation of the rock or the vein are simple. As his work is chiefly of two kinds, simly *excavating* the ground when soft, and *blasting* it when hard, his tools are suited to each process, the 'pick' and 'gad' being used for the former; the 'borer' or 'jumper,' and the hammer used to propel it, for the latter, with several minor accessories for firing the shots, when the hole has been completed to its proper depth. The *pick* resembles a common pickaxe, but is smaller and more convenient, the iron head being sharp and pointed at one end, and very short and hammer-shaped at the other. The wedge or 'gad' is sometimes used in conjunction with the pick; it is made of wrought iron, and often with curved sides. The 'borer' or jumper' is an iron rod or circular bar, usually about two feet in length, steeled, and formed into a flat sharp edge at the end; it is driven into the rock by one man with a heavy hammer, while the other continually turns it round so as to expose the cutting edge to fresh surfaces of the rock. The pulverised matter is drawn out from time to time by a tool called a 'scraper;' and in the hole so formed are placed the powder and fuse for blasting.

When the influx of water in a mine becomes at all considerable, recourse must be had to the power either of a water-wheel or a steam-engine to discharge it to the surface. If a water-wheel is used instead of horse-power, pumps are in that case fixed in the shaft, proportioned in size to the quantity of water to be drawn, 10 or 12 inches in diameter being a very common size where there is only a moderate influx. The pumps used in mines do not act like common household pumps; they are arranged in 'lifts' or columns, of considerable height, often indeed from 20 to 30 fathoms, the water being discharged into cisterns placed at the foot of each. The pumps are now commonly made of iron. The whole column of pumps in a shaft is commonly worked by a single pump-rod, which goes down the middle of it and communicates with each column by a rod attached to its side. The steam-engine has long been the great auxiliary of the English miner, both for drawing up the minerals and for discharging the water.

The mode of support used in mines is of three kinds—by leaving pillars of the vein, for which purpose the poorer masses are of course selected; by timbering; and by walling either with brick or stone. Timbering is a very common and convenient plan, and consists of timber frame-work and boards. Shafts and levels are sometimes also supported by walling.

The ventilation of mines is most generally and most effectually accomplished rather by a judicious arrangement of the works and frequent communication with the surface than by mechanical means, although it sometimes becomes necessary to resort to the latter. The general mode of working and ventilating coal-mines is noticed under COAL.

The ore raised to the surface is enormous in some mines. At the Consolidated Mines in Cornwall it has sometimes amounted to 200 tons a day, of which three-fourths is earth or rubbish. To remove this rubbish is the object of *dressing*, for which purpose the lumps are taken to the 'dressing floors,' near the mouths of the principal shafts and levels, and are there broken with hammers. The ore is then picked out by boys and women, and further subjected to various processes of crushing, stamping, and washing. When the metallic portions are as far separated as it is possible for them to be by these processes, they are roasted in furnaces, to drive off the oxygen and all other chemical substances that may be combined with them.

During the year 1850, a number of new English mines were opened, and many old mines were brought more prominently than before into notice. As a field of investment and speculation, English mines, after a long period of depression, have lately revived; and there are not wanting indications that something of the recklessness of railway speculation will soon be observable in mining transactions. There are public manias of this kind which seem to supervene at intervals of a few years. There were dividends, to the amount of 213,570*l.*, paid in 42 Devon and Cornwall mines in 1850; being larger in amount than in the four preceding years. The Devon Great Consols Mine, near Tavistock, is at the present time the richest in the United Kingdom; no other mine yields so large a return for the capital sunk in working it; and the value of the shares, in respect to premium on the original price, excels any thing that the railway ferment has presented to us, either in England or elsewhere. Most of the best mines in Devon and Cornwall yield both tin and copper, the copper being generally found below the tin.

Various details relating to English mining will be found under COPPER; CORNWALL; DERBYSHIRE; IRON; LEAD; &c.

MINT; COINING. The mode of coining English money in early times, was rude and inartificial; the sole expedient employed being to fix one die firmly in a wooden block, and to hold the other in the hand as a puncheon; then, by striking the latter forcibly and repeatedly with a hammer, the impression required was at length worked up. Scarcely any improvement was made in this method until about the middle of the 16th century, when the power of the screw was applied to coinage at the French mint.

When bullion or ingots of gold or silver are sent to the mint to be coined, the weight and quality are ascertained with scrupulous exactness, in order that an equivalent in coin may be returned for it. They are melted in pots, with such proportion of alloy as shall give the requisite standard of quality. The melted and alloyed metal is cast into bars, and these bars are rolled into plates of the proper thickness, whether for sovereigns, half sovereigns, shillings, or any other coins. The plates or sheets are cut up into circular pieces by a cutting-out press, each scrupulously accurate as to weight and size.

Then come the processes for impressing a device on each surface of the coin. The coining press consists of a screw, to which the upper die is connected; this is worked by a fly, and forces that die which is attached to it with considerable force upon the other die, which is firmly fixed below. The circular form of the piece admits of some addition to the impression, to preserve the outer edge. This was first attempted by placing a graining so as to form a regular circle on the outside of the legend, quite to the edge of the coin. Afterwards a legend was imprinted upon the edge of the larger pieces; such an impression is given to the edge of the coin by passing it between two plates, so that when the coin has been carried by the moveable plate to the end of that which is fixed, it has become marked upon the whole of the edge. As it is difficult to impress a legend upon the rim of the smaller coins, a graining has been devised for the protection of their outer edge; this, which is called *milling*, has at different times been rectangular and diagonal to the thickness of the piece, according to the views entertained as to the best mode of preventing coin-clipping.

From the money, when finished, two pieces are taken for every 15 lb. weight of gold, and two at least for every 60 lbs. weight of silver. These selected pieces (which are presumed to be an average of the whole) are subjected to rigorous assayings—one called the *private assay* within the mint; and the other the *trial of the pix*, at which some of the great officers of the government are always present.

At the London Mint the melting pots will each hold 400 lbs. of gold. The ingots into which the gold is cast are 10 inches long, 7 broad, $\times$ 0·6 thick. The press-room has eight stamping presses, which will together strike nearly 20,000 coins in an hour. In standard coins, the pure gold is alloyed with a little silver, and the pure silver with a little copper. A sovereign weighs 123·274 grains, of which 113·001 grains are pure gold; a shilling weighs 87·27 grains, of which 80·727 grains are pure silver.

MIRROR. This term is nearly equivalent to *looking glass*, in ordinary application; it applies to flat silvered looking glasses, as well as to the convex and concave mirrors which used to form articles of ornamental furniture. But it is, or ought to be, equally correct a name for any polished plate of silver, steel, or other substance which yields a clear optical reflection. A few details concerning silvered glass mirrors will be found under SILVERING.

MISSISSIPPI (or the Great Water, as the term signifies in the native language), is one of the largest rivers on the globe, which drains with its numerous branches, a surface of about 1,100,000 square miles. It falls into the Gulf of Mexico by six mouths, after a course of more than 3200 miles; but if we consider the Missouri as the principal river, the whole course is at least 4400 miles. Several of its other affluents would, considered singly, be deemed grand and mighty rivers, especially the Ohio, the Wisconsin, and the Illinois.

The rivers Mississippi and Missouri each give name to a state of America, a few industrial statistics of which will be found under UNITED STATES. Perhaps no region in the world is increasing more rapidly in production and commerce than the rich valley of the Mississippi. Steamers now carry heavy freights for a distance of many hundred miles along this great river, in the midst of a valley of almost unparalleled productiveness.

MIST, is the vapour of water rendered visible by the temperature of the air being reduced below that of the vapour. When the mist is very thick it is called a fog. Water, in the state of vapour, is continually rising into the atmosphere at all the usual temperatures; but in very hot weather the air is not easily saturated with vapour, and in cold weather evaporation is slow: thus there is more vapour in the air in summer than in winter, and in hot countries than in temperate climates, in all cases where similar surfaces of water are exposed to the sun's rays. Indeed, it has been found that the quantity of vapour in the air diminishes nearly uniformly with the temperature from the equator to the poles.

MODELLING. Modelling in clay requires the aid of a few tools; but no tool is more useful than the finger; indeed tools have been invented as mere aids to the fingers, and are designed only to do what they cannot perform. Wire tools are the most useful, being fashioned into loops of various shapes and sizes, round and angular, and fixed into wooden handles. The wooden tools are made of box and ebony, of various shapes and sizes—curved, straight, pointed, rounded, and flat and broad; the broad tools being notched, and designed chiefly for working the large convex masses, or large folds in drapery.

The clay used is common potter's clay, but of the best quality. It must be so wet that it will not stand in a mass much higher than its own width without support. The supports for the clay are a most important consideration; for if not properly attended to, the finished work, the fruits of months of labour, might suddenly fall to pieces by its own weight. Sculptors generally model figures of the ordinary size upon a bench or stand called a banker, about 30 inches high, and about 30 inches square,—for a bust it must of course be much higher; above this a solid circular plinth is fixed on a wooden box, and is revolved upon six or more wheels, or what are better, short slightly conical rollers, fixed to the plinth near the circumference. A revolving plinth is necessary to enable the sculptor to see his work on all sides in any light, and it enables him to work on all parts, in one spot, or in the same light. On the centre of the plinth is built up a skeleton frame-work of iron and wood, projecting in various directions to support the various parts of the figure.

Another essential part of modelling is preserving the moisture of the clay, which should be always uniform if possible; it must never be allowed to dry, and it can be kept moist with very little trouble. While the modeller is at work, and the figure is exposed, especially in warm weather, he should repeatedly sprinkle it with water. A plasterer's brush is the best instrument for this purpose. When the model is complete, the next process is to take the cast, to work the marble from, or to make other casts from. The ancient sculptors used to bake their models, but this is not so good a plan as making plaster casts from them, though less troublesome and much cheaper.

MODILLION is an architectural ornament in the Corinthian cornice, resembling a small bracket placed horizontally, that is, with its back against the soffit of the part it supports, in which respect it differs from the Console. Modillions are placed beneath the corona of the cornice, and although sometimes omitted out of parsimony, are indispensable to the character of the order.

MOIRÉ METALLIQUE. There is a singular and often elegant way of ornamenting metallic surfaces, called by the French *Moiré Metallique,* equivalent to *clouded* or *watered* metal. The metal has a sort of crystallised appearance, somewhat resembling a frosted window on a winter's day, but far more brilliant and diversified. It was first introduced at Paris in 1817, by M. Allard, and was much used soon afterwards as an ornamental covering for Kaleidoscopes and other articles.

The moiré metallique is tinned iron plate, the tinned surface of which has been exposed to a peculiar chemical action from acid. Tin plate consists of sheet iron coated with melted tin; and it is believed that the clouded or watered appearance is produced by inequality of action between the tin and the iron at different parts; but the results are not visible through the whole thickness of the tin; and the art consists in removing so much of the tin as to lay bare the thin film which exists at the junction of the two metals. This is a point of much nicety, for if the acid employed for this purpose be allowed to penetrate too deeply, it will lay bare some of the iron, and there will result dark spots instead of the silvery lustre and pearly appearance of the moiré. Dilute nitro-muriatic acid is one among many acids and corroding liquids employed for the purpose. The plate is exposed to the action of the acid for a few minutes, while heated; then carefully washed, and finally coated with varnish, by which the moiré is preserved.

MOLASSES, is the name given to the uncrystallised syrup produced in the manufacture of sugar and which is suffered to drain from the casks into a cistern, in what is called the curing-house, before the sugar is sent away from the plantation. [SUGAR.] Part of the molasses is fermented and distilled for rum in the West Indies, and part is made to yield a little sugar by crystallisation: the residue constitutes *Treacle.*

The molasses imported during the last three years amounted to the following quantities:—

1848..............	517,535 cwts.
1849..............	1,062,837 ,,
1850..............	905,054 ,,

MOLYBDE'NUM, a metal discovered by Scheele, in 1778, is a mineral which resembles and had been confounded with plumbago. This metal is obtained as a porous mass or in globules, and has not yet been procured in the state of a button or bar. The grains are somewhat crystalline; sometimes they are of a silver-white colour. When obtained by the reduction of the oxide, this metal has not much lustre, but acquires it by burnishing. When long exposed to the air at ordinary temperatures, it appears to tarnish, but the oxidation is superficial. Oxide of molybdenum occurs encrusting the sulphuret of molybdenum, and also between its laminæ in thin layers. Its structure is thin, fibrous, earthy, friable, and pulverulent; and its colour is pale yellow or greenish.

Molybdenum combines with many other substances; but neither in its simple nor its compound state has it yet been applied to many useful purposes: it still remains in the domain of scientific chemistry.

MONAGHAN. This Irish county contains a valuable deposit of gypsum; and near this is a small coal-field. Limestone of great variety and excellent quality is quarried; also fine marble, and valuable freestone for building. A fine white sandstone, dug in the Slieve Beagh Mountains, is extensively used for architectural purposes. Ironstone, slate, and lead-ore, exist in small quantities.

The soil of the county varies much. The wheat grown is generally red wheat, and of inferior quality; but the flax crop is important. Clover, vetches, and other green crops, are more attended to than turnips or mangel wurzel. A good deal of butter is made, and sent to England. The population of the county is very dense; the number of labourers has increased; and the decline of the linen manufacture, which once furnished them with employment, has left the great majority with little other work than that which they bestow on the small spot of land which they occupy. Some of the worst features of Irish poverty and improvidence are to be found in Monaghan.

MONEY. At a time when industry has caused the assembling in London of visitors from so many countries, it would not be an inconsistent feature in this work to present a Table of the values of some of the best known European coins. Kelly's *Cambist* is our authority.

Bajocchio; copper coin at Rome and Bologna; worth rather more than one halfpenny.

Batzen; a Swiss coin of inferior silver about 1½*d.*

Carline; Piedmont gold coin; about 5*l.* 12*s.* 3*d.*

Cash; Chinese coin of copper and lead; about 120 to a penny.

Cent; United States' copper coin; about 0½*d.* In France a *cent* or *centime* is not a coin, but a money of account, one-hundredth of a franc.

Cowries; shells used for money in the east; about 120 to a penny.

Crown; the crown coins in foreign countries have been mostly superseded by other denominations.

Crusado; Portuguese coins, both gold and silver; about 2*s.* 6*d.*

Dime; United States' silver coin; 5¼*d.*

Doit; Dutch copper coin; half a farthing.

Dollar; United States' silver coin, 4*s.* 4*d.* Also a Spanish silver coin, 4*s.* 3½*d.* See also *Thaler* and *Rix-thaler.*

Doubloon; Spanish gold coin; about 3*l.* 6*s.*

Ducat; there are gold ducats in Russia, Sweden, Holland, and Germany, varying in value from 8*s.* 4*d.* to 9*s.* 5*d.* There are silver ducats in Italy; about 3*s.* 6*d.*

Eagle; United States' gold coin; about 2*l.* 4*s.*

Florin; there are both gold and silver florins in Germany; worth respectively about 7*s.* and 1*s.* 8*d.* to 2*s.*

Franc; French silver coin, 9½*d.* Also a Swiss silver coin; 1*s.* 2*d.*

Frederick; Prussian gold coin; 16*s.* 4*d.*

Guilder; another name for *Florin.*

Groschen; German silver coin; 1*d.* to 1½*d.*

Imperial; Russian gold coin; 33*s.* 4*d.*

Kopeck; Russian copper coin; rather less than 1*d.*

Kreutzer; German copper coin; three to one penny

Mark; Hamburg silver coin; about 1*s.* 3*d.*

Milree; Portuguese gold coin; about 5*s.*

Mohur; East Indies gold coin; about 33*s.*

Napoleon; French gold coin; 15*s.* 10*d.*

Paolo or *Paul;* Italian silver coin; 5¼*d.*

Pfenning; Prussian copper coin; ten to a penny.

Piastre; Levant silver coin; rather over 1*s.*

Pistole; German gold coin; about 21*s.* Also an Italian gold coin, variable in value in different states.

Real; Spanish silver coin; 5*d.* The *Real vellon* is a smaller coin; 2½*d.*

Rix-thaler; German silver coin; about 4*s.* 2*d.* The Danish *Rigsbank thaler* is about 2*s.* 3*d.*

Rouble; Russian silver coin; 3*s.* 1*d.* There are platinum coins of three and six roubles.

Rupee; East Indian silver coin; about 2*s.*

Schilling; German coin of inferior silver; about 1¼*d.*

Scudo; Italian silver coin; about 4*s.* 4*d.*

Sechsling; Hamburg copper or base silver coin; rather more than 0½*d.*

Sequin; Italian gold coin; about 9*s.* 5*d.* The Turkish sequin varies much in value.

Sou; French copper coin, $\frac{1}{20}$th of a franc; about 0¼*d.*

Stiver; Dutch copper coin; about 1*d.*

Thaler; the ordinary name in Germany for the *Rix-thaler* or *Rix-dollar.*

The weights of English gold and silver coins are as follow:—

	Dwt.	Grains.
Sovereign	5	3.274
Half sovereign ..	2	13.637
Crown	18	4.4 - elevenths.
Half crown	9	2.2 - elevenths.
Shilling	3	15.3 - elevenths.
Sixpence	1	19.7 - elevenths.
Fourpence	1	5.1 - eleventh.

MONMOUTHSHIRE. In the north-west part of this county iron and coal are found in considerable abundance; and these form the main elements of the wealth of Monmouthshire. In respect to agriculture, the soil is various, but generally fertile. The agriculture has been a good deal improved of late years. In the north-west a little wheat is grown, but oats and barley are the principal crops. The southern tract bordering on the Bristol Channel is an alluvial soil, which in parts would be overflowed if not protected by great dykes. There are numerous small orchards.

Monmouth, the county town, has a considerable commerce with Bristol, by means of the Wye. There are large iron-foundries in the neighbourhood. *Newport*, near the mouth of the Usk, is the outlet for a large amount of coal, and a still larger amount of iron, which are brought down the Blaenavon, the Ebbw, the Sirhowy, the Rhimney, and other valleys from the mountain district where the mines are situated. Newport has been much improved of late years. Ship building is carried on, the river being so situated that vessels of great burthen can be launched from the docks into deep water. The docks and the river are always crowded with vessels waiting for cargoes of coal and iron. At *Pontypool* most of the inhabitants are employed in the coal mines and iron works.

MONOCHORD, an instrument of one string, is used by scientific musicians for the purpose of ascertaining and demonstrating the relative proportions of musical sounds. It is composed of a board, or rule, divided and subdivided into various parts, and of a string distended between two bridges, one of which is placed at each end of the rule. In Dr. Crotch's 'Elements of Musical Composition' will be found a simple and cheap method of constructing a monochord.

Mr. Higgs's monochord, described before the Society of Arts in 1843, is a single string stretched over a bridge, and tuned to the middle C of the pianoforte; but it is provided with other stops or bridges which enable it to yield all the notes of the diatonic, chromatic and enharmonic scales of the octave. It is calculated to educate the ear of a singer to appreciate musical intervals, and to aid in the tuning of pianofortes and other instruments.

MONTPELLIER, capital of the French department of Hérault, has a very extensive system of commerce and manufactures. Liqueurs, perfumery, preserves, dried fruits, verdigris, alum, cream of tartar, vitriol and aquafortis, woollen cloth, muslins, printed cottons, calicoes, table linen, blankets, hosiery, hats, leather, corks, and paper, are manufactured; these articles, with wool, wine, brandy, oranges, citrons and other fruits, and the oil of the surrounding districts, furnish the chief articles of trade. There are several printing-offices, sugar refineries, potteries, oil-mills, paper-mills, and saw-mills. In the central prison, which receives convicts from 20 departments, several articles of silk and cotton are manufactured.

MONTREAL, the capital of Lower Canada, set the first example of an Exposition of manufactures in America; it was at Montreal that the Canadian Industrial Exhibition of 1850 was held, an exhibition which prepared the Canadians to take part in the far greater Exhibition of 1851.

In respect to commerce, the harbour of Montreal, which is formed by an arm of the St. Lawrence, is small but secure; the difficulty of approach, which the rapid of St. Mary formerly presented to sailing vessels, has been overcome by the employment of steam-tugs. The shipping trade of Montreal is very active whilst the navigation is open. The repeal of the Navigation Laws, and the uninterrupted steam navigation by the Rideau and Welland Canals and the great lakes westwards, as far as Chicago on the south-western shore of Lake Michigan, whereby the produce of Illinois and the western states will find a ready vent to Europe, promises to add greatly to the trade of Montreal. Steamers ply regularly during the season to Quebec.

MOORS. A Moor is an extensive waste covered with heath, and the soil of which consists of poor light earth, mixed generally with a considerable portion of peat. The want of fertility in moors arises chiefly from a deficiency or superabundance of moisture, the subsoil being either too porous to retain it, or too impervious to allow it to escape. Both extremes occur in some moors, which are parched up in dry weather, and converted into a dark mud by any continuance of rain. When the moor consists of a loose peaty earth of little depth incumbent on a rock, as is the case in many mountainous countries, no art can fertilise it. In the valleys, where the waters have brought various earths mixed with decayed vegetable matter from the surrounding hills, the substance deposited is mostly peat; this soil, by careful management, may be made productive. Sometimes extensive moors have been converted into flourishing farms of arable and grass land, as in many parts of Scotland and the north of England; sometimes they have been most advantageously planted with forest-trees, and, where there is a great extent of waste and a scanty population; this is generally the most certain mode of improving a property, although the return is slow and distant.

MORAVIA is one of the richest provinces of the Austrian empire in respect to produce. Agriculture is in an improved condition. Large quantities of very fine wheat, rye, barley, and oats are grown. Flax and hemp are very extensively grown; but the consumption of these articles is so great, that large quantities of them are imported. Fruit is plentiful and good. The vine flourishes. The forests furnish vast quantities of timber. The pastures are extensive. Formerly mines of gold and silver were worked. At present iron, sulphur, vitriol, alum, coals, marble, pipeclay, and precious stones, particularly topazes, are the chief mineral products.

The woollen, linen, and cotton manufactures are very flourishing, and on a large scale, and furnish supplies for an extensive export trade. The manufacture of thread is likewise considerable. Dyeing is carried on at Brünn, which is particularly celebrated for dyeing Turkey red. Moravia enjoys also the benefit of a great transit trade. The imports are colonial produce, wool, Vienna silks, Russian furs, tallow, wine, oil, porcelain, glass, &c.

MORDANTS. [DYEING.]

MOREA. The produce and industry of the Morea are briefly noticed under GREECE.

MO'RPHIA, the first discovered of a numerous and important class of vegetable products, or alkalies, sometimes termed *alkaloids.* It was obtained in 1803 by Sertuerner, a German chemist, from opium, in which it exists in combination with a peculiar vegetable acid, the meconic acid, and probably also with sulphuric acid. Morphia is a colourless crystalline substance, with a bitter taste. When heated strongly, it emits a resinous smell, smokes, and burns with a lively red flame, and leaves charcoal. Morphia is probably the most active principle of opium, but being very slightly soluble in water, is never used alone medicinally. Having, however, like other alkalies, affinity for acids, it readily combines with them and forms salts, which are now extensively used in medicine. The acetate and hydrochlorate of morphia are those salts which are usually employed medicinally.

The uses of morphia and the other alkaloids are almost exclusively, up to the present time, medicinal.

MORTAR. Common mortar is the substance placed between the stones or bricks of a building to cement them together. Mortar is essentially composed of slacked lime and siliceous sand. The hardness which mortar acquires is owing to the gradual conversion of the lime into carbonate of lime, which takes place very slowly by the absorption of carbonic acid gas from the atmosphere. In this state it adheres very firmly to the particles of silica diffused through it, and both are strongly united with the material employed in the building. When limestones contain considerable portions of silica and alumina, they form what has been termed *Hydraulic Lime*, and the mortars made with them are called *Hydraulic Mortars.* Of these, Parker's cement is a well-known kind: it will *set*, as it is termed, or become solid, in a quarter of an hour, either in the air or under water. In France artificial hydraulic lime has been prepared, and appears to answer the purpose extremely well.

A second application of the name *Mortar* is to a vessel in which substances are either reduced to fragments, pulverised, or dissolved, by beating or trituration with a pestle. Mortars are made of cast-iron, stone-ware, glass, agate, flint, or porphyry, according to the use to which they are to be applied.

It is not very easy to shew why such should be the case; but the same name has a third and wholly different signification, as applied to a gun or cannon. A mortar is a piece of ordnance which, compared with guns, is very short, and is employed to throw shells or carcasses at considerable elevations (generally at 45°). Mortars are either of iron or brass; they rest upon solid beds, and the trunnions or cylinders upon which they turn, in giving the required elevation, are placed at the lower extremity of the piece. The calibres of mortars in the British service are 4⅖, 5½, 8, 10, and 13 inches. All these different kinds of mortars are used on land, and the two last are also employed in the navy; but in this latter service the pieces are about 16 inches longer than the land-service pieces of the same calibre. The first two are sometimes called royal mortars. The Dutch engineer Coehorn invented small mortars for throwing grenades. They were capable of being carried about and served by one man; consequently they could be readily brought up to a convenient spot, and rapidly fired.

MORTICING MACHINE. The cutting of a mortice in wood-work, for joining or framing the pieces together, is under ordinary circumstances performed by hand; but in the remarkable operations at the Palace of Industry, a morticing machine has been employed, patented by Messrs. Furness and Lanton. It consists of an upright frame, with ledges and supports suitable to retain in a proper position the piece of wood to be morticed. The morticing chisel is fixed to the lower end of a vertical rod; and its mode of adjustment is such that it can be turned round in any direction, and may be made to cut a deep or a shallow mortice at the discretion of the workman. The machine is not wholly automatic, but may be compared to a lathe; the workman puts his foot upon a treadle, by which the morticing chisel is brought down to the wood; and in that position it is retained until the mortice is cut. There are many ingenious minor appendages, to facilitate the action of the machine.

MOSAIC. This very elegant production is a species of inlaid or tessellated work, made with minute pieces of coloured substances, generally either marble or other coloured stones, or else glass more or less opaque, and of every variety of hue which the subject may require. The former mode was that chiefly employed by the Romans for their costly tessellated pavements, many of which have at various times been discovered in England. Mosaics of this description, that is, for pavements, generally consist only of a series of ornamental borders inclosing one or more compartments containing some figure or device, or occasionally a group or subject. Others consist entirely of a pattern, generally in two colours, sometimes in three—black, white, and red. Examples of pavement mosaics in each of these modes have been discovered at Pompeii. Mosaic continued to be used both for pavements and ornamenting walls to a late period in the middle ages, and was greatly practised in Byzantine buildings, and by Byzantine artists who were also employed in Italy.

A kind of mosaic or coloured inlaid work was occasionally employed in Italy during the middle ages for external decorations also; as an instance of which the façade of the Duomo at Pisa may be mentioned, where, though the pattern is chiefly in black and white, brilliant reds and blues are intermixed at intervals.

Although nearly similar as to their process, mosaic pictures, especially some of those of later times, may be considered as a distinct branch of the art. Whether actually employed as pavements or inserted in walls, mosaics of this class consist chiefly of ornament and pattern, executed in few and simple colours, with hardly any attempt at variety of tints and due graduation of tones, even in the figures, human or animal, occasionally introduced in them. For a long period after the decline of the arts, mosaic painting continued to be employed in Italy, both externally and internally, for the decoration of churches, as for instance, on the façade as well as within the basilica of St. Mark at Venice. Some have supposed that such productions were entirely the work of Byzantine or Greek artists, but the contrary opinion is maintained by Cicognara, who asserts that mosaic was practised by native Italians, and that it was well known to the earliest Venetians.

Copies of celebrated works by Raphael and other masters have been executed in mosaic, and have the effect of paintings produced in the usual way, though they are attended with infinitely greater cost, and are beyond all comparison more laborious and tedious in their process. As each separate piece of glass is of the same colour throughout, the graduation of tints, the melting off of any one colour from its highest light to its darkest shadow, can be obtained only by an immense number of small pieces, of which those contiguous to each other exhibit scarcely any perceptible difference to the eye. The sole advantage, in any degree proportionate to the cost attending it, is the extreme durability of the work when once accomplished.

Similar mosaic is employed sometimes on a miniature scale, for pictures on the lids of snuff-boxes and articles of that kind, or tablets in chimney-pieces, which are at the best mere curiosities and very laborious trifles. *Florentine Work* may also be mentioned as a species of mosaic, chiefly used for inlaying or veneering marble slabs for tables and decorative purposes of that sort, upon a moderate scale.

The Mediæval Exhibition of 1850 presented many beautiful specimens of mosaic, mostly on a small scale. In our own day, the chief mosaic work produced is in the form of tesselated tiles for pavements.

MOSCOW. In this important Russian province, agriculture is the chief occupation of the inhabitants, and Moscow is one of the best cultivated as well as one of the most populous provinces of the whole empire. Flax, hemp, and hops are cultivated. Horticulture is carried on to a great extent, and the produce is nearly adequate to the consumption. Timber and wood-fuel are plentiful. Horses, cattle, calves, and poultry are reared. The minerals are freestone, potters' clay, brick-clay, lime, gypsum, alabaster, and bog-iron.

Manufactures of various kinds are carried on to a great extent, both by the country-people for their own supply as well as for sale, and also in the villages and towns, and especially in the capital. The province has an extensive inland trade.

Of the far-famed city of Moscow we need not speak in this work; for it is rather a political metropolis than an emporium of manufactures. It is, however, the centre of an immense inland trade, by which the produce of Europe and Asia is interchanged; for there is no city in which the luxuries of the East and West meet in more singular proximity than Moscow.

MOSELLE. This is an interesting department of France, in respect to produce and commercial industry. The valleys and hill-sides are covered in general with a rich soil, and are carefully cultivated so as to yield great quantities of wheat, rye, and oats, of which a considerable surplus over the home consumption is sold for exportation in the great corn-market of Metz. Other crops raised are vetches, millet, peas, beans, and lentils. Several Champagne wine merchants, settled at Metz, purchase Moselle wine, and manufacture from it what they call champagne wine for the German and Russian markets. Pears, peaches, and other fruits are grown in large quantities, and exported in the form of dry, liquid, and crystallised conserves from Metz, where preserved fruits form an important article of commerce. Flax is extensively grown, both for the sake of the fibre and of the seed, which is pressed for oil; rape and turnips are also grown. The forests consist of oak, beech, hazel, &c. Bees are very numerous, and much honey is gathered.

Several iron mines are worked, and the ore is smelted and made into malleable iron. Lead and copper are found, but no mines are worked. Building stone, quartz, gypsum, crucible and pottery earth are quarried. Marl is found in great masses in the north and north-west of the department, and is extensively used in manure. Plaster-of-Paris is also much used as a top-dressing for meadow land. The industrial products consist of sheet and bar iron, block-tin, nails, glass, unbleached and table-linen, embroidered muslin, canvas, paper, beer, tobacco, oil, starch, room paper, beet-root sugar, tiles, pipes, pottery, leather, hosiery, and common woollen and cotton stuffs. These articles, together with timber, and the products previously mentioned, support an active commerce. *Metz*, the chief town of the department, is a place of considerable manufacturing and commercial enterprise.

MOTHER OF PEARL. The nature of this singular and beautiful substance is illustrated under PEARLS; SHELL.

MOULDINGS are any assemblage of narrow surfaces projecting from the face of a wall or other surface, and advancing one beyond the other. They are bounded by straight lines, either horizontal or vertical, according to their situation, but the surfaces themselves are plane or curved, and if the latter, concave or convex, or else compounded of both forms; and again are either plane or curved. The *Fillet*, *Tænia*, *Band*, are all plane or flat mouldings. The *Corona* is also a mere plain band, except that it is occasionally enriched in Roman architecture. Lesser convex mouldings are termed *Beads*, but the longer mouldings of the same kind in the bases of columns are termed *Tori* or Torusses. The *Cyma Recta*, or *Cymatium*, is a compound moulding, concave above and convex below; while the *Cyma Reversa*, is convex below and concave above. The *Cavetto* is a mere hollow or sweep intervening between and serving to connect two mouldings, one of which projects beyond the other. The *Ovolo* is a simple convex moulding, so called because it is generally carved into *Ova*, or ornaments in the shape of eggs, within hollows. All the other mouldings may be carved or enriched, except the cavetto and fillet; the pattern being accommodated to the surface of the moulding. The cyma recta, or *Talon*, as it is sometimes called, is cut with a peculiar kind of tongued or arrow-headed ornament.

MOVING POWERS. The means employed to give motion to machinery, (independently of the cases in which the force of gravity is applied directly, as in turning the cylinder of a clock,) are chiefly the following:—the *strength of men and animals*, the *pressure of the atmosphere*, the *expansive force of steam*, and the *action of wind or water*. It is even probable that the recently proposed actions of the galvanic fluid and of fired gunpowder or guncotton, will in time be numbered among motive forces for impelling carriages, vessels, or machines.

Originally the larger kind of engines, except such as were impelled by wind or water, were moved by the power of horses; and when other agents were employed, the gross effect of the engine was estimated by the number of horses to whose action it was equivalent. A strong horse being able to draw 125 lbs. at the rate of 3 miles per hour during 8 hours; the product of these numbers, multiplied by the number of feet in a mile, and divided by the number of minutes in 8 hours, gives 33,000 lbs. for the weight carried or raised 1 foot per minute continually. This last number is the usual representation of the power of a horse; but the 'horse power' of engineers' estimates is felt to be a vague standard, and will probably give way to something more scientific. The force of steam-engines is estimated according to the volume of water evaporated, the pressure of the steam, the length of the stroke, &c.

Wind and water are employed as prime movers by means of the momentum arising from their velocity; and the latter, occasionally, by the pressure arising from its weight. The force of wind is made to act on sails in giving motion to vessels on the surface of water, and also in producing the revolutions of windmill sails. The velocity of a vessel impelled by steam, in which paddle-wheels are employed, might easily be found if it were possible to determine, nearly, the number of square feet of paddle which, on both sides of the vessel, are at every moment acting efficiently against the water. To determine the exact amount of moving power available at any given time and place, and under any given circumstances, is one of the most important duties of the engineer; since upon it must depend the power of his machinery.

In 1850 Mr. Cottam patented an apparatus for ascertaining the amount of motive power employed in working machinery. It is composed of a plate, to which a circular spring is attached by one end, while the other end is made fast to a lever. The lever is also attached to a pointer which moves over a scale, whereby the power exerted will be indicated. The pointer also carries a pencil, which travels over the top of one of a pair of cylinders, round which a roll of paper is wound. The curve described on the roll of paper indicate the force applied. The cylinders are made to revolve by toothed gearing.

MUFFLE is the name given to a vaulted flat-bottomed earthen vessel in which substances may be strongly heated, and at the same time protected from the contact of the fuel. In the muffle smaller vessels are placed, containing the substances to be acted upon. Muffles are used in chemical operations, in glass-staining, in enamel-painting, and in a few other processes.

MÜHLHAUSEN, a large manufacturing town in the French department of Haut-Rhin, has obtained deserved celebrity for its printed cottons, for the manufacture of which there are several important establishments. The other manufactures are cotton and woollen yarn, muslin, silk, woollen cloth, hosiery, straw hats, morocco leather, soap, damask, linen thread, &c. There are dye-houses, tan-yards, metal-foundries, and large establishments for making steam machinery. There is also a considerable commerce in corn, wine, brandy, groceries, hardware, iron, &c. The canal which unites the Rhône to the Rhine, passes by the town. A railroad, 13 miles in length, runs westward from Mühlhausen to the busy little manufacturing town of Thann.

MULBERRY. The black or common mulberry is the fruit of *Morus nigra*. It is a native of Persia, and its indigenous range appears to be extensive. Its introduction to this country dates about the middle of the 16th century. Under great vicissitudes it proves very tenacious of life; and under ordinary circumstances it attains, even in this climate, a considerable age, for some trees planted in 1548 are still alive. The fruit is used in medicine. It contains much mucilage, with an astringent resin, and is sweetish and subacid, owing to the presence of some malic or tartaric acid. As the cooling properties depend on the acid, the fruit should be gathered before it is quite ripe. It may either be formed into a syrup, or a vinegar may be made with it similar to raspberry vinegar.

But a more important species is the *Morus alba*, or White Mulberry. This is a native of China, where it forms a small tree, and whence it has been gradually carried westward, till it has become a common plant in most of the temperate parts of the Old World, forming in the south of Europe a pollard-tree by road sides. It is on this species that the silkworm is chiefly fed; and in silk countries many varieties are cultivated for the purpose, some of which are said to be much better than others. Some years since a mulberry was introduced into France from Manilla, whence it has gained the name of the Philippine Mul-

STEEL CASTING FURNACE —— FILE CUTTING

FORGING AND STRIKING

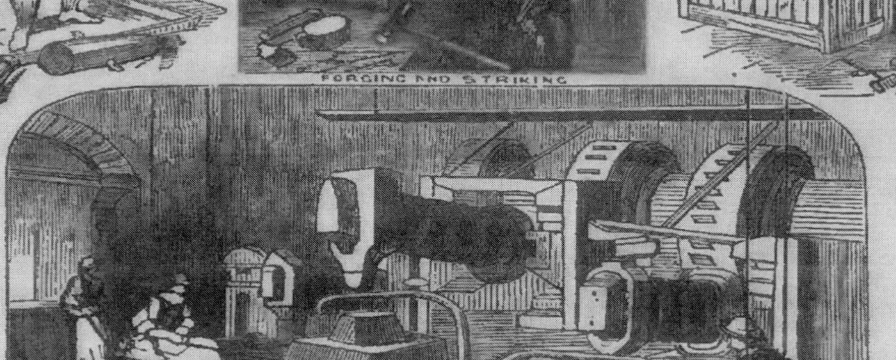

SHEAR AND TILT HAMMERS

KNIGHT'S CYCLOPÆDIA OF THE INDUSTRY OF ALL NATIONS.

No. 30.

berry, the great excellence of which seems universally acknowledged. It grows much faster than the white mulberry, and strikes from cuttings as freely as a willow, which is not the case with the white mulberry. The abundance of its leaves is much greater than in any other known variety, and it is not only freely eaten by the silkworms, but perfectly agrees with them. Its culture is now superseding that of all others in the south of Europe, and it is even taken as a stock on which to graft the common white mulberry, when the latter is wished for.

MULE; MULE-JENNY. The purpose of this oddly-named machine is described under COTTON SPINNING.

MULLION. In gothic architecture mullions are the upright bars, or rather stone shafts, dividing the general aperture of a window into secondary openings, which are again frequently subdivided by a similar shaft crossing the mullions horizontally, and therefore called a *Transom;* whereby the whole space beneath the head of a window (supposing it to be an arched one) is formed into a series of panels in which the glass is fixed, and which are sometimes technically distinguished as *lights*. For instance, the façade of York Cathedral is divided into eight lights or compartments by seven mullions, while that above the entrance to Westminster Hall has eight mullions.

MUMMY CLOTH. At one period there was much discussion as to the nature of the woven material in which Egyptian mummies are found to be enveloped. The early history of the cotton and flax manufactures is interested in this question. The bandaging, to which all the Egyptian mummies were subjected, was one of the most remarkable parts of the process of embalming. Their envelopes are composed of numerous bands, each several feet long, applied one over the other fifteen or twenty times, and surrounding first each limb, and then the whole body. They are applied and interlaced so accurately, that one might suppose they were intended to restore to the dry shrivelled body its original form and size. The only difference in the bandages of the different kinds of mummies is in their greater or less fineness of texture; they are applied on all in nearly the same manner. The bandages and wrappings have been examined with the microscope within the last few years; and in every instance they are found to be made of flax or linen; this has set at rest an opinion formerly held, that cotton was employed by the Egyptians for such purposes.

MUNICH, the capital of the kingdom of Bavaria, owes its present beauty and celebrity as a seat of the fine arts, chiefly to the late Ludwig I. Architecture, sculpture, and painting have been most munificently patronized; and the arts of painting in fresco, in encaustic, and on glass, have been revived and carried to their former perfection. The treasures of the Glyptothek, the Pinacothek, the Königsbau, the Festbau, the Chapel Royal, and other buildings in Munich, deserve the attentive study of the admirers of high art; but we have here only to do with the industrial features of that town. The manufactures of Munich are of many different kinds, chiefly for the consumption of the city and neighbourhood; the articles made are linen, woollen cloth, calicoes, damask, silk, ribands, household furniture, piano-fortes, playing-cards, articles of gold and silver, coaches, excellent mathematical, surgical, optical, and astronomical instruments. There are likewise breweries, distilleries, tanneries, paper-mills, snuff-mills, and the celebrated Fraunhöfer's (now Utzschneider's) manufactory of astronomical and optical instruments.

A magnificent figure of a lion, by Frederick Miller, of Munich, adorns the Exhibition of 1851. The lion forms one of a *quadriga*, or group of four, to surmount a new town gate at Munich. It is 14 feet long by 8 feet high. Two lions of this enormous size were cast at one melting—among the largest casting operations ever known. Of the private manufacturing establishments, there are a few which have sent to the Exposition works of much beauty. By one establishment for the manufacture of glass, has been contributed an enamelled vase of large size and extraordinary workmanship. The design of the vase is Moresque, and made expressly for this production. The articles of furniture manufactured in inlaid work at Munich are extensively known and appreciated.

MURCIA. In this province of Spain sandstone, marl, lignite, and gypsum are found. Porphyry, slates, fine marble, rock-crystal, freestone, bole, alum, and nitre, are also met with. Near Hellin is a mine of sulphur, at Villena a saltpit, and saltpetre abounds in the neighbourhood of Cartagena. Several argentiferous lead mines are worked; iron and copper are found. The most commonly cultivated trees are the mulberry, the date-palm, and the olive; evergreen and other oaks, poplars, and carobs are in some parts numerous. The sugar-cane thrives, but is not cultivated to any extent. The pines on the Sierra de Segura form the largest forest in the south of Spain. Great quantities of barilla are produced on the sea-coast; silk and oil are extensively produced, and also saffron and wine. The manufactures are few and unimportant. Agriculture and mining give employment to all the disposable industry of Murcia. Corn and wine are exported when the harvest or vintage is good, otherwise they are imported from Valencia. Raw silk, barilla, some cutlery, saffron, and articles made of the esparto-rush, are the principal exports. The imports are vegetables from Valencia, beef and mutton, oil, spices, ironware, linen and woollen goods, and silk stuffs; for there is not industry enough in the province to manufacture the raw silk produced. In the city of Murcia there are several potteries, cloth-factories, tanneries, oil-mills, establishments for the spinning of silk and for the manufacture of soap and white lead. There are also royal factories of gunpowder and saltpetre. There are important glass works in the environs of the town. Wine and provisions of all kinds are exceedingly cheap. The manufacture of the esparto-rush into baskets, cordage, sandals, &c., employs many hands.

MURIATIC ACID. Under CHLORINE the chemical nature of this valuable acid has been described; but it will be instructive to trace the mode of manufacturing the acid, as conducted at the great chemical works of St. Rollox, near Glasgow.

The same chemical operation which produces *soda* will also produce *muriatic acid.* Common salt is *chloride of sodium;* and by a certain train of operations, the chloride combines with hydrogen to form muriatic acid, while the sodium combines with oxygen to form soda, and with carbonic acid to form carbonate of soda. Common Cheshire salt is put into a pan in a reverberatory furnace, and sulphuric acid is slowly dropped upon it through a leaden pipe passing through the roof of the furnace. The action of the acid on the heated salt generates a new product, muriatic acid gas, by bringing into play the various degrees of chemical affinity between the substances employed. The substance then remaining in the furnace is, by further treatment, converted into soda. In the infancy of the manufacture, when the soda was the chief object of attention, the muriatic acid gas was a source of infinite trouble to the manufacturer. It is so deleterious, that if allowed to mingle with the atmosphere near the ground it would do great mischief: hence we have a clue to the history of the lofty chimneys which distinguish chemical works. But after a time it was found that this deleterious gas might be made a valuable commercial article, by changing it into liquid muriatic acid, or *spirit of salt,* as it is somewhat expressively termed, in familiar use. This change has been brought about as follows: all the soda furnaces discharge their muriatic acid gas into a bulky stone tower, about 40 feet high, by 8 feet square; this tower is filled with coke, upon which a stream of water is constantly falling from above; and the gas, ascending the tower from the flues of the furnaces, meeting with an innumerable series of little streams of water trickling through the coke, becomes absorbed by the water, and thus gives rise to the formation of liquid muriatic acid, which falls to the bottom of the tower.

The tendency of modern chemistry has been to change the name of *Muriatic* to *Hydrochloric* acid, since the latter name expresses the composition of the acid (hydrogen and chlorine). In the same way the salts formed by the combination of the acid with gases are gradually changing their names; instead of the *muriates* of soda, potash, ammonia, tin, &c., we have the *hydrochlorates* of those substances.

MURRHINE (sometimes written *Myrrhine*) VASES, vessels used by the ancients, were made of the stone or hard substance, whatever it might be, termed *murrha (μυρρα).* They are frequently noticed by the classic writers, and usually described as transparent, though sometimes spotted or clouded, like our cups of agate. Pliny speaks of them as coming from the East, from Parthia and Carmania; but there is very little now known concerning them.

MUSHROOM. A few details concerning the uses of the mushroom will be found under AGARICUS.

MUSICAL INSTRUMENTS. All the principal musical instruments are described under their proper headings in this work. Music, as a science and a fine art, is of course beyond the range of the present volume.

Musical instruments occupy from 3000 to 4000 feet at the Great Exhibition. There are various specimens of organs from the various London builders; among the rest, especially to be noticed, is a gigantic church organ, containing upwards of eighty stops, with an independent pedal organ upon the largest scale. The cost of this instrument has been several thousand pounds. There is also an interesting instrument, designed by Col. P. Thompson, M. P.—an enharmonic organ—the object of which is, by minute subdivision of the scale, to attain a perfect intonation; there is also an enharmonic guitar. No class of musical instruments is left unrepresented. As might be expected, pianofortes are most numerous. In this department the most eminent manufacturers have exerted their utmost powers to exemplify the superiority of native instruments. There are several improvements exhibited, both as regards tone and mechanism.

MUSK. This very powerful perfume is the odorous secretion contained in a peculiar abdominal sac, in the Male Musk Deer. This species is a native of Tonquin, Tibet, Nepaul, the mountain regions of Siberia and China, &c. By the analysis of Geizar and Reiman musk appears to consist of a peculiar volatile principle, which can exist in a free state; ammonia; a peculiar fixed uncrystallisable acid; stearine and oleine; chloresterine; a peculiar bitter resin; osmazome, with several salts; a mouldy-like substance, in part combined with ammonia and several salts; sand; water, acid, &c., with some volatile odorous matter.

The name of *pod musk* is given to the bag in its natural state containing the musk; while *grain musk* is the musk without its bag.

The musk of the shops is said to be rarely pure; it is adulterated either with dried bullock's blood or with chocolate, under ordinary circumstances; but a multitude of other substances are occasionally employed. The Chinese are said to be skilful adepts in this nefarious practice.

Taken in the dose of a few grains, musk rouses the energy of the digestive organs; and it soon afterwards produces sympathetic phenomena, the powers of the whole animal system appearing suddenly increased.

MUSLIN is a thin cloth made of cotton. The name is supposed to be derived from Massalia, since called Masulipatam, from which place such fabrics were first imported into Europe. Until the early part of the present century all the muslin used in Europe was of the manufacture of India. Some of the muslins of India, and especially those of Dacca, are of the most astonishing degree of fineness, so as to justify their poetical description as 'webs of woven wind.' Such however has been the result of the mechanical inventions of England in this branch of industry, that not only are muslins of British manufacture now used at home, to the exclusion of those woven in India, but large quantities are exported to all parts of the world, and find their way even far into the interior of India.

There is essentially no other difference between *muslin* and *calico* than in the fineness of the fabric; but the spinning, the weaving, and the dressing, are all concerned in the production of this fineness. The embroidering of muslin is becoming an extensively diffused employment for females in Ireland [EMBROIDERY.] The 'Armagh Gazette' lately stated:—'According to the statement of a respectable agent, there are in Armagh and its vicinity about 1,800 girls and young women engaged in this occupation. Agencies have been established in Keady and other rural towns in this county. The demand for the sewed or embroidered muslin would appear to be unlimited. In many cases, where the heads of poor families are out of employment, the average earnings of their daughters protect all from that last refuge of poverty—the workhouse.'

MUSQUASH FUR. The *Musquash* or *Musk-rat* is a small North-American animal, the fur of which is employed in hat-making and for other purposes. The number of musquash furs imported in 1847 was 420,946; the number for 1848 increased to 766,764. Some of these are re-exported to various European countries, but most of them are worked up in England.

MUSTARD. This name is given to two species of *Sinapis*, the *black* and the *white*. The black mustard plant is most used, and is extensively cultivated in Durham and Yorkshire; it is this which yields the powerful condiment for the table; whereas the white species, when a young plant, is eaten with water-cress as a salad.

The seeds of the black mustard are an intricate compound of myrosine, fixed oil, a fatty matter, a gummy matter, sugar, colouring matter, and many other substances. By bruising the seeds a fixed oil may be obtained; and by distilling the *marc* or refuse from this process, a volatile oil results. The fixed oil is very bland; but the volatile oil is stimulant and irritating. About 28 per cent of the black mustard-seed consists of fixed oil; to obtain it the seeds are crushed in a mill or between rollers; the skins being subjected to pressure as well as the farina or flour. The remaining cake is sifted and reduced to a fine powder, which retains all the pungent qualities of mustard. The fixed oil is a good fuel for lamps, and it forms a firm and useful soap with alkalies.

Flour of mustard, mixed with water, forms the well-known condiment of the dinner table. *French* mustards and *patent* mustards have, however, usually something else added to them —vinegar, parsley, cherril, celery, tarragon, garlic, anchovies, sugar, ginger, salt, horse radish, and cayenne, being among the list of addenda so employed.

Mustard, like too many other commodities at the present day, is often adulterated; flour and salt are employed to increase the bulk, turmeric to colour, and cayenne to season it.

N

NAIL MANUFACTURE. Until a comparatively recent period almost every kind of nail was produced by hand-labour: each nail, however minute, was separately forged from a thin rod of iron, a process which is still followed in the production of what are technically known as *wrought* nails. As nails so formed possess certain advantages, for particular kinds of work, over those formed either by casting, or by cutting or stamping out of rolled sheet metal, there is no reason to anticipate the total abandonment of this process, notwithstanding the continual improvement of nail-making machinery.

For some purposes nails formed by the much cheaper process of *casting* have been long used. Common cast nails are, however, so clumsy and so brittle that they can only be used for a few coarse purposes, as in plasterer's work, and in the nailing up of fruit trees. By the introduction of great improvements in the manufacture, however, a very useful kind of cast nail, of an exceedingly pure malleable cast iron, has been successfully introduced for certain descriptions of woodwork. Nails of this kind are very neat and regular in their appearance, being cast with great accuracy; and they are annealed to such perfection that the metal will bear far more bending than ordinary wrought-iron without injury. This extraordinary degree of tenacity is, however, obtained at the expense of rigidity, such nails being often nearly as soft as copper, and therefore quite unsuitable for use in hard woods.

In the making of cut-nails, the nails are cut from sheet-iron of suitable thickness, which is first reduced by cutting transversely, into strips or ribands of a breadth equal to the intended length of the nails. These strips are then applied to a machine in which a chisel-shaped cutter descends with sufficient force to cut off from the end of the strip, at each downward stroke, a narrow piece sufficient to form one nail. As the nails are required to be of a tapering form, the cutter must be so fixed as to form a slightly oblique angle to the direction in which the strip is pushed into the machine, and this obliquity must be reversed or varied after each stroke, by means similar to those adopted in comb-cutting machinery.

Nail making is conducted upon a very extensive scale in Birmingham. Within the town itself, *cut* nails are made by the aid of machinery; whereas in the neighbouring villages *wrought* nails are made by hand. There is one particular establishment at Birmingham, the machinery of which was, a few years ago, adequate to the manufacture of two thousand millions of nails annually. The machines so employed are the following:—Sheets of iron are cut up into strips, each strip as wide as the length of the nail to be made; this cutting is effected by a kind of enormous shears, worked by steam power. The strips are then cut up into nails. In one kind of cutting machine, the cutter or blade vibrates up and down, cutting off a piece of iron from the strip at each descent; and it has also a swinging motion horizontally, so as to make the cuts at an acute angle with each other instead of parallel; the consequence of this is that the cuts, being alternately oblique in different directions, give a wedge shape to the pieces of iron cut off, and these pieces thereupon constitute the nails. In another form of machine the blade has not a swinging movement; but after each cut the strip of iron is turned over, so as to present the other side uppermost for the next cut; an arrangement which brings about the same wedge-shape to the cut nail, but by different means. In a third form of machine, the piece of iron, after being cut from the strip, is caught by a kind of clasp, and exposed to a pressure which gives a head to it. *Spike* nails are made by machinery in a different way. A square rod of iron, of the proper thickness, is cut into lengths; and each length or piece is exposed to such powerful pressure as to squeeze it into the form of a nail: this more resembles a *wrought* than a *cut* nail. All cut nails are annealed before being fit for use.

A newspaper paragraph has lately stated, 'William Laugher, a nail-maker, of Bromsgrove, has received orders to make a thousand gold, a thousand silver, and a thousand iron 'tacks,' for exhibition in the Crystal Palace, the whole three thousand not to weigh more than three grains. They will be the smallest nails ever produced.'

NAMUR is one of the busiest provinces of Belgium. The iron mines which lie between the Sambre and the Maas, are very productive, and give employment to a large portion of the population. Lead-mines are worked near the city of Namur. A great number of coal-mines are worked. Marble is quarried in different parts of the province; it is of various colours, red, gray, blue, and black; the greatest part of what is raised is exported to France. Potters' clay is found.

Namur, the capital, being situated at the confluence of two navigable rivers, is favourably circumstanced in relation to commerce. The chief manufactures are—superior cutlery, surgical instruments, tin and brass ware, copper utensils, tools of all kinds, agricultural instruments, ironmongery, and leather. The iron, lead, and coal mines and marble quarries of the neighbourhood give employment to a large portion of the population.

NANKEEN is a kind of cotton cloth, usually of a yellow colour, imported from China, and taking its name from the city of Nanking, in which great quantities are made. The peculiar colour of these cloths is natural to the cotton-wool of which they are made, and not the effect of any dye. An imitation of nankeen was largely manufactured in England twenty or thirty years ago; but it has now almost entirely ceased.

NANKING. This famous Chinese city has a great number of manufactures, especially silk, nankeen, paper, and Indian ink, and also carries on a very considerable commerce, being situated in the most populous part of the empire, about half-way between Canton and Peking. Through the ports of Soo-Cheou and Shang-Hae it receives great quantities of corn and other articles. They are brought by water to Nanking, as there are several canals which connect the town with the river.

NANTES, a large seaport town in France, is admirably situated for commerce, having communication with the interior by railway, and by steam boats up the Loire, which forms the harbour of Nantes, and admits at high water vessels of 200 tons up to the quays which line its banks. Vessels of larger size unload at Paimbœuf. Besides these facilities for traffic, Nantes has communication by canal with Brest. The industrial products of Nantes are, white and printed cottons, cotton twist, refined sugar, ship cordage, glue, chemical products, blankets, serge, flannel, ship biscuits, &c. There are several ship-building yards, copper foundries, tan-yards, brandy distilleries, bleach-mills, and dye-houses. Vessels are fitted out for the whale and cod fisheries. The foreign and coasting trade is active. The chief articles of export are wine, brandy, woollen cloths, silk, paper, linen, gold and silver lace, hardware, prepared meats, provisions, furniture, small wares, books, &c.; the imports are composed of ship timber, planks, hemp, pitch and tar, steel, copper, lead, wool, raw cotton, oil, Spanish wine, cochineal, dye-stuffs, gum, ivory, perfumes and colonial produce. Other articles of commerce are salt, butter, coal, building stone, hoops, flour, vinegar, and agricultural implements.

NAPHTHA. This remarkable substance is a volatile oil, which issues from the ground in various parts of the world, and is on that account called *rock-oil* or *stone-oil*. Colourless naphtha issues at Baku near the Caspian Sea, where the vapours which arise from it are kindled, and the flame applied to domestic and manufacturing purposes. In ultra-Gangetic India there is a spot where no fewer than 500 naphtha springs are met with; each spring yields nearly 150,000 lbs. of naphtha yearly. The city of Parma is said to be lighted with naphtha. Naphtha possesses a penetrating odour and generally a yellow colour; but it may be deprived of colour by distillation. It boils at about 160° and is very inflammable. It mixes easily with alcohol and with oils, but not with water; and it dissolves a great variety of substances. It forms with caoutchouc a gelatinous varnish. Naphtha is chiefly employed for purposes of illumination, as a solvent for caoutchouc, and in the preparation of a very superior black pigment.

NAPLES. The productions of the soil, in this rich region of southern Italy, are various. The staple products are corn, wine, oil, wool, and silk. The plains of Apulia produce vast quantities of corn and wool for exportation. Gallipoli is the great oil mart. Silk is made in Calabria, in Abruzzo Citra, Terra di Lavoro, and Principato. Cotton is produced in the provinces of Bari, Principato, near Castellamare, and other places. Wine is made all over the kingdom, and in great abundance and variety, but most of it is consumed in the country and within the year. Some brandy is made and exported to America. The country produces most kinds of fruit, such as figs, chestnuts, almonds, oranges, lemons, pomegranates, melons, peaches, and apricots. Tobacco is cultivated chiefly near Lecce, saffron in Abruzzo, and the sugar-cane in Calabria. Flax, hemp, and rice are also raised in considerable quantity in the low grounds. Indian corn is also much cultivated. Cheese is made chiefly in Abruzzo and Apulia. In some favoured spots, such as in the neigbourhood of Naples, at the foot of Mount Vesuvius, near Monteleone and Reggio in Calabria, the fertility of the soil seems inexhaustible. A little coal and iron are found. The forests have been much neglected.

The city of Naples has manufactures of hats, straw-hats, gloves, leather, earthenware, coral, and jewellery; but the kingdom generally is far from being a manufacturing or commercial one.

The British produce and manufactures exported to Naples and Sicily in 1848 amounted in value to 695,660*l*. The imports thence into Great Britain in 1848 comprised among the larger items sulphur (625,032 cwts.), olive oil (3455 tons), oranges (57,283 packages), silk (54,193 lbs.), wine (589,369 gallons), wool (641,608 lbs.).

NARCOTI'NA is an alkaline principle found in opium. It is procured in light white flocks, or in pearly acicular crystals. It is insoluble in cold water and very sparingly soluble in hot water; its taste is not bitter.

NARWHAL IVORY. The teeth and tusks of the narwhal form one of the best kinds of this beautiful substance. [IVORY.]

NASMYTH'S HAMMER. This mighty engine, one of the most remarkable inventions of the last few years, is described under STEAM HAMMER.

NATAL. The time is probably approaching when this new colony will present interesting commercial and industrial features. The settlement lies eastward, and is within the territorial limits, of Cape Colony; but it has many of the elements of a distinct settlement. Mr. Christopher, a settler at Natal, has lately published a description of the settlement, in which he states that nine kinds of cotton have been grown there, and that *all* kinds may probably be cultivated. There were exported from the colony 1740 lbs. of cotton in 1846, 5821 lbs. in 1847, and 13,931 lbs. in 1848; these are small beginnings, certainly; but they *are* beginnings, and of an interesting character. Besides cotton, the colony already produces Indian corn, aloes, columbo root, castor oil, gum acacia, coffee, honey, bees' wax, wild olive, ivory, tallow, hides, mimosa bark for tanning, wheat, beans, butter, tobacco, and many varieties of timber and dye woods. The principal towns yet established in the new settlement are D'Urban and Pieter Maritzburg. Accounts from the colony to December 1850, report very favourably of its progress and prosperity. The markets at D'Urban were beginning to show the effects of the skill and labour of the settlers by an abundant supply of vegetables of all kinds. The cabbages, turnips, lettuces, spinach, and cauliflowers are said to be as fine as any Covent-garden can boast of. Among the new towns which are springing up the most flourishing are Richmond, on the Illovi; Pine Town, near New Germany; and Lady Smith, on the Klip-river. Several others are in progress or projected.

NATRON LAKES. These lakes are in a valley in the western desert which borders on Lower Egypt. The Natron valley contains six shallow lakes, remarkable for the great quantity of salt which they produce. The crystallisations are both of muriate of soda, or common salt, and of carbonate of soda, called natron or trona. The lakes occupy a total length of about 16 miles; they vary in size according to the season; the bottom is muddy, of mixed sand and clay. The lakes are supplied by water which oozes out of the banks chiefly on the side which is towards the Nile. It appears that the water flows abundantly when the Nile is high, and decreases with its decrease, until some of the lakes become quite dry. The natron is collected once a year, and is used both in Egypt and Syria, as also in Europe, for manufacturing glass and soap, and for bleaching linen.

NAVARRE. In this Spanish province the mountains contain jasper and marble. There are many mines of iron and one of copper; one also of rock salt near Valtierra, and several hot springs. Forests of pine cover the slopes of the Pyrenees, and much timber is cut, and sent down by the mountain streams to the Ebro, by which it is floated onward to Aragon and Cataluna. The other principal forest trees are the oak, the olive, the chestnut, the beech, and the box. Wine, cider, and olive oil are among the products of the province. The annual produce of sheep's wool is about 1,500,000 lbs. The manufactures are coarse linen, some woollen cloth, leather, soap, iron, and brandy, of which the quantity annually distilled averages 2,000,000 gallons. There are also some potteries, a royal shot and shell foundry, and some manufactories of Spanish liquorice. The exports are corn, oil, wine, wool, and iron; the imports consist of cottons and silks, cutlery, tobacco, sugar, spices, and other luxuries, which are imported, principally from France.

NAVIGATION LAWS. The recent change in the Navigation Laws is already producing such important results in the commerce of England with foreign nations (and consequently in the industry of all nations) that it will be desirable briefly to notice the subject here.

The system of the Navigation Act, as it is termed, had its foundation during the Protectorate; but the act so called was that of 1672. This act declared that no produce of Asia, Africa, or America, should be imported into Great Britain except in British ships, navigated by a British subject, and having at least three-fourths of their crew composed of British seamen. It also laid higher duties on all goods imported from Europe, than if they were imported in British ships. To this act many persons have attributed the great growth of British shipping. When the American colonies became independent, their ships lost the advantage which they had when the States were colonies, and their shipping was placed on the same footing as other foreign ships. The consequence was that American ships sailing to Great Britain came in ballast, while British ships carried merchandise both ways; and accordingly the United States placed British shipping under the same disadvantages in their ports that American shipping was under in British ports. The consequence of this was that British ships sailed to America in ballast when they went to the United States to get a cargo, and American ships came to Great Britain in ballast when they wanted a British cargo. The consumer of the foreign produce in both countries accordingly paid double freight for it. This lasted till 1815, when it was agreed by treaty between Great Britain and the United States that the ships of the respective countries should be placed on the same footing in the ports of Great Britain and the United States; and all the discriminating duties were mutually repealed. In 1822 Mr. Wallace, president of the Board of Trade, introduced five bills, which were passed into laws, and which made other important alterations; one repealed certain statutes relating to foreign commerce, which were passed before the Navigation Act; a second repealed various laws that had been passed since the Navigation Act, and also that part of the Navigation Act which enacted that goods of the growth, produce, or manufacture of Asia, Africa, and America should only be imported in British ships, and that no goods of foreign growth, production, or manufacture, should be brought into Great Britain from Europe in any foreign ship, except from the place of their production or from the ports from which they were usually brought, and in ships belonging to the country of production or accustomed shipment; a third permitted certain goods then enumerated to be brought to Great Britain from any port in Europe in ships belonging to the port of shipment; a fourth permitted the importation, subject to certain duties, into certain ports, of various articles from any foreign country in America or port in the West Indies either in British vessels or in vessels belonging to the country or place of shipment, and such goods might be again imported to any other colony or the United Kingdom; and a fifth permitted the exportation in British ships from any West India colony to any foreign port in Europe and Africa, of any goods that had been legally imported into the colony, or which were of its growth or manufacture; and it permitted the exportation of certain articles, enumerated in the act, in British ships to any such colony from any foreign port in Europe or Africa.

In 1823 Prussia retaliated, as the United States had done, which led Mr. Huskisson to propose the passing of what are called the Reciprocity Acts, in 1824 and 1825. These acts empowered the king, by order in council, to authorise the importation and exportation of goods in foreign ships, from the United Kingdom, or from any other of his majesty's dominions, on the same terms as in British ships, provided it shall first be proved to his majesty and the privy council that the foreign country in whose favour such order shall be made shall have placed British ships in its ports on the same footing as its own ships. Since that time reciprocal treaties of navigation have been made with the following countries: Prussia, Denmark, Hanover, Oldenburg, Mecklenburg, Greece, Bremen, Hamburg, Lübeck, States of La Plata, Colombia, Holland, France, Sweden and Norway, Mexico, Brazil, Austria, Russia, and Portugal. That with the United States of North America, as already observed, dates from 1815.

An act was passed in 1849, entitled 'An act to amend the Laws in force for the encouragement of British Shipping and Navigation.' The full meaning of this act can only be understood by referring to the acts and parts of acts which it repeals, and to its provisions. It repeals a part of the act of 1824, and the whole of that of 1825. The general purpose is to diminish the restraint on the freedom of navigation. British shipping has already derived great advantages from the enactments above mentioned, and the Reciprocity Acts.

There seems every probability that as British shipping is now fairly brought into competition with foreign, great improvements will be made in ship building: indeed such improvements have already commenced.

NEEDLE MANUFACTURE. This is one of the most remarkable industrial pursuits of our country, both technically and locally. In a technical point of view it is striking for tho number of processes which every individual needle passes through; while it is not less noteworthy on account of the grouping of the manufacture in and around the town of Redditch in Worcestershire; where it has been calculated there are 60 to 70 millions of needles made every week!

In commencing the manufacture of a needle, soft steel wire of the required thickness is first cut into lengths of about five inches, and these lengths being placed together in a bundle, are bound together by means of iron rings, five inches in diameter, placed at each end of the bundle. This bundle is then placed on a cast-iron table, and rolled to and fro upon it, under the pressure of a flat bar of iron, by which means the wires are made perfectly straight. About a dozen and a half or two dozens of these wires are then taken by the grinder, and together are pointed on a small dry grindstone. This, like the dry grinding of the Sheffield cutlers, is a very deleterious employment, towards the amelioration of which the workmen render very little assistance, unfortunately for themselves.

When the pointing is finished, the wires are cut into the required lengths, and the holes or eyes are perforated. This operation is usually performed by females. The tools employed are, a small anvil fixed on the work-bench, a hammer, a finely-pointed and well-tempered steel punch, a pair of pliers, a file, and a block of lead. The woman first slightly flattens the unpointed end by a stroke of the hammer, then makes an indentation on one side by means of the punch and hammer; the needle is then taken from off the anvil, and being placed with the indented side downwards on the block of lead, the perforation is completed by striking with the punch and hammer on the opposite side of the needle. Holding then the needle in the pliers, the head is somewhat bent, and with the file the *guttering* is performed, which is the forming of the channel that may be seen on each side where the perforation is made. The head is then smoothed by passing the file over it. Needles to which the name *drilled-eyed* is applied are perforated in the manner here described, but the additional process is used of smoothing the eye by means of a drill after it is perforated.

For making the eyes and gutters in large needles, machinery is employed. The wires used for making these needles are pointed at both ends, and the channels and eyes are formed in the middle, when the two needles thus made are cut asunder, and their heads smoothed with a file.

These operations being performed when the steel wires are in a soft state, they are more or less bent, and must be straightened, which is done by rolling them on one plate of metal under the weight of another. The needles are then placed, many thousands together, in a kind of crucible, and covered over with ashes, when they are put into a close furnace and exposed to a cherry-red heat. When this degree of heat has been obtained, the crucible is withdrawn, and the needles are dropped into cold water, from which they are taken out and put upon an iron plate almost red hot, where they are turned about so as to cause the heat to apply equally to all, and as fast as the needles become of a blue colour, they are removed as being of a proper temper.

Such of the needles as now appear crooked are straightened on a small anvil by blows from a hammer.

The needles are next ranged in parallel rows upon a coarse cloth, which has been smeared with a mixture of oil, soft soap, and fine emery powder. In this cloth from 40,000 to 50,000 needles are rolled up, and several of these rolls are placed together in a machine like a mangle. The rolling to which they are here subjected is continued, by means of steam or water power, for two and sometimes three days, during which time the cloth wrappers, being worn out, require to be once or twice replaced by new ones. When taken out, after this rolling, the needles are perfectly bright. They are finally sorted, packed, and papered.

NEPAUL. This remote country of India, situated close to the Himalaya Mountains, yields a fair supply of vegetable produce in the river valleys. It also contains several metals in abundance, especially iron, lead, copper, and zinc; the first three are worked rather extensively. Gold is found in the sand of some rivers. Of the inhabitants of the country, the Newars are mostly cultivators of the soil, and exercise many arts and trades. They make coarse cotton-cloth, and work very well in iron, copper and brass, and are particularly ingenious in carpentry. The trade with Tibet is mostly in the hands of the tribe called the Bhot, who transport their goods on the backs of sheep or men over the mountain passes. They bring from Tibet to Nepaul sheep, musk, skins of the musk-deer, chowry-tails, quicksilver, borax, sal ammoniac, Chinese silk stuffs, paper, drugs, gold and silver; and they carry back rice, wheat, oil, iron, copper, cotton cloth, catechu, juniper boards (which are used in fine cabinet-work), pepper, spices, indigo, tobacco, otter-skins, sugar, and some smaller articles. Nepaul exports to British India elephants' teeth, timber, hides, ginger, turmeric, wax, honey, oranges, long pepper, ghee, bastard cinnamon, large cardamums, and some smaller articles. It imports from the British dominions in Bengal cottons and muslins, silks of various sorts, raw silk, gold and silver, laces, carpets, English cutlery, saffron, spices, sandal-wood, quicksilver, cotton, tin, zinc, lead, soap, camphor, tobacco, pepper, and coral.

NET; BOBBIN-NET. [LACE MANUFACTURE.]

NETHERLANDS. In England the *Nether-*

lands and *Holland* imply pretty nearly the same thing, viz. the territory which, after the separation of Belgium, in 1830, remained to the King of Holland. In this remarkably flat country, sufficient corn for home consumption is not raised; hemp and flax are grown in great abundance. There are no minerals except a little bog-iron in Overyssel and Guelderland: there are brick-earth, potters' clay, fullers' earth, and a little sea-salt.

The history of the commerce of the Netherlands properly begins with Bruges in Flanders, in the 14th century. From Bruges the trade was for the most part transferred at the end of the 15th century to Antwerp, which became the greatest emporium in the world. But the ravages of the war with Spain and the capture of the city after the memorable siege in 1585 drove the wealthiest inhabitants to the northern provinces, especially to Amsterdam. The Dutch East India Company conquered kingdoms and islands in the east; and Amsterdam became the first commercial city in the world. From 1795 to 1813 the trade of Holland was much depressed by French domination; but since that period it has partially recovered, though it has not attained its former extent. The inland trade employs 6000 of the vessels called *trekschuyts*, and 15,000 boats.

The exports from the Netherlands consist of colonial produce from the East and West Indies, coffee, sugar, spices, tea, silks, and other articles from China and Japan; together with the home produce of butter, cheese, flax, hemp, tobacco, madder, flowers, cattle, horses, and fish. The chief articles of importation are corn, salt, wine, timber, stone, marble, and various manufactured goods; besides colonial produce of every kind from the possessions in Asia, Africa, and the West Indies. The value of the British and Irish produce and manufactures exported to Holland in 1848 was 2,823,258*l*. The produce imported into Great Britain from Holland is chiefly butter, cheese, flax, madder, and Dutch colonial produce.

The principal manufactures are linen of the best quality; woollens, once the most celebrated in the world; silks, and leather. Sugar refineries, tobacco-pipe manufactories, distilleries, and cotton mills, are numerous. As has been noticed in HOLLAND and other articles, many of the chief towns of the Netherlands take part in the Industrial Exhibition.

NEUTRAL SALTS. Formerly this term included such salts as did not obviously contain an excess either of acid or alkali; but at present the term Neutral Salt includes such compounds as are composed of one equivalent of each of their constituents: thus the subcarbonates of potash and of soda are now termed carbonates, notwithstanding their alkaline reaction, because they consist of one equivalent of acid and one of base. Chemists apply the term *Neutralization* to the decomposition of the alkaline carbonates, by the gradual addition of some acid more powerful than the carbonic, and which of course expels it from the alkaline bases with effervescence.

NEW BRUNSWICK. The great commercial wealth of this North American colony consists in its extensive forests, which are composed of pine, fur, spruce, hemlock, birch, beech, maple, ash, elm, and poplar. Wheat, rye, oats, barley, beans, peas, buckwheat, flax, Indian corn, and common vegetables are cultivated. On the alluvial grounds which occur along the banks of the numerous rivers there are fine meadows and pasture-grounds. The mineral riches are imperfectly known; but they comprise iron, coal, marble, and gypsum. The exports of the province are almost wholly confined to the produce of the forests and the fisheries; they amount to nearly a million sterling annually. Ship-building forms a considerable branch of industry in the province.

The Exports from Great Britain to New Brunswick in 1849 amounted in value to 277,591*l*.

NEW HAMPSHIRE. A few commercial statistics of this American state will be found under UNITED STATES.

The same may be said also in respect to *New Jersey.*

NEW ORLEANS. This American city is one of those which are rising into importance with a rapidity which can scarcely be understood in Europe. Situated near the mouth of the Mississippi, it is the outlet for an immense amount of produce—timber from the north, grain from the centre, cotton and sugar from the south. From New Orleans this produce is diffused to every part of the globe. More cotton is shipped at New Orleans for England than from any other port. From New Orleans the numerous, large, and powerful steamers start, which navigate the great Mississippi for upwards of a thousand miles. From New Orleans to St. Louis the busy traffic of the Mississippi is mainly concentrated; while at St. Louis, which stands at the junction of the Missouri with the Mississippi, commences the commerce of the western prairies, and the emigrant routes over the Rocky Mountains to Oregon and California. At New Orleans the river is too much encumbered with sand banks to enable large ships to sail up to the quays; but they are drawn up by tug-boats. The ships lie in tiers alongside an embankment or quay, called the *Levee*, sometimes three or four deep, presenting the appearance of a forest of masts.

Some years ago the exports from New Orleans were estimated at twelve million dollars annually; but they now greatly exceed this amount. In the environs of the city are large plantations of sugar, cotton, indigo, and rice, which are cultivated in a very perfect manner.

NEW YORK. This most famous portion of the United States is the name both of a state and of a city. In the state of New York, maize, wheat, rye, barley, oats, buckwheat, potatoes, turnips, peas, beans, and numerous fruits, are generally cultivated. In some parts flax and hemp are grown, especially in the Lake Country. A considerable part of the state is still covered with forests, which consist of oak, ash, walnut, pine, maple, beech, chestnut, birch, poplar, elm, cedar, hemlock, and hickory. Several minerals occur in abundance, but only iron, salt, limestone, and marble are worked. Coal is imported from various places, especially from Nova Scotia. The canals and railroads are numerous; the former extend 600 to 700 miles; while the railways are forming a complete network over the state. In 1840 there were 323 woollen manufactories, 890 fulling mills, 186 iron furnaces, 120 forges, 77 paper mills, 1216 tanneries, and a great variety of other works; and in the subsequent eleven years these numbers must have vastly increased. The commerce greatly exceeds that of any other of the States.

But it is the city of New York which appeals most to our notice in respect to commercial and industrial features. The situation of New York as a commercial port is admirable. New York Bay, which is completely landlocked, is about 8 miles long and from 1½ to 5 miles wide, and affords a perfectly safe anchorage. It is easy of approach, and is very rarely closed by ice. The entrance between Long Island and Staten Island, by a channel called the Narrows, is protected by forts, while the approach to it is facilitated by lighthouses. The bay contains several small islands, on which fortifications have been constructed. There is sufficient depth of water, both in the Hudson and East River, for ships of large burden to load and unload at the wharfs. The commercial intercourse with the interior and with the western States of the Union is provided for by means of the Hudson, and the system of canals connected with it.

The most expensive and useful public work undertaken by the city is the aqueduct called the Croton Water-Works, noticed in a previous article. [AQUEDUCT.]

No fewer than 3,341 vessels, of 1,247,860 tons burden, and manned by 46,158 seamen, entered the port of New York in 1850; and the shipping which left the port presented corresponding numbers. About one half of the shipping was American, one-third British, and the remainder belonging to various countries. The tonnage of the arrivals at four nearly equidistant periods presents the following remarkable differences:—

1821	171,963 tons.
1830	314,716 „
1840	527,594 „
1850	1,247,860 „

The number of persons who arrive every year at New York by sea, chiefly from Europe, is immense. In the ten years, 1841 to 1850, the number averaged 123,784 yearly; in 1849 it reached the high figure of 221,799. A very large proportion of these are emigrants, who land at New York as a convenient point whence to start farther westward. There is, perhaps, no other city in the world which, at the present time, equals New York as a centre of transit, or as a temporary abode for thousands who make it a mere resting point on a journey: this circumstance gives it a peculiar character both in its commercial and its social features. In the single month of September 1850, the exports from New York amounted to five millions and a half of dollars, considerably more than one million sterling. Very nearly one-half of this value of commodities was sent to Great Britain. Half a million went to Panama, *en route* to California, with which an immense commerce is now conducted from New York. In the first nine months of 1850, no fewer than 37 ships were launched at New York, averaging 1150 tons each; and at the end of September in that year there were 31 more building, of about the same average tonnage. Of the whole 68 vessels, 38 were steamers.

The mail steam ships which now run between England and New York are among the finest which the world has yet seen.

NEWCASTLE UPON TYNE. This busy and important town is very well provided with railway accommodation. The Newcastle and Carlisle Railway extends across the island nearly from one sea to the other; the North Shields line passes through North Shields to Tynemouth; the Newcastle and Berwick Railway establishes a communication with Scotland; lastly, the Durham railways, which, taking their departure from Gateshead, open up a communication with South Shields, Sunderland, Durham, York, and the south of England generally. A station near the centre of the town, which is to form a junction with all these lines by means of viaducts, has for some time been in progress. The most important part of this work is a bridge across the Tyne, undertaken by the railway companies, and one of the finest engineering works in England.

It is a double bridge, the lower one at an elevation of 90 feet above the river, for carriages and foot passengers, and a railway bridge at a further elevation of 25 feet. The whole length of the structure is nearly 1400 feet. It has two piers at the margin of the river, and fonr others in the stream itself, besides smaller piers to support the land arches. The *High Level Bridge*, as it is termed, is one of those creations which will give lasting fame to Robert Stephenson.

The commercial importance of Newcastle arises from its situation on a river navigable thus far by sea-borne vessels of 400 tons. The Tyne forms the haven, and is under the care of the corporation. The river side is lined with warehouses and extensive quays. The chief business is in the shipment of coals, the produce of the surrounding coal-pits. The coals were formerly brought down the river in barges called keels, bnt vessels are now chiefly loaded from staiths. Coal is exported very considerably; also lead, cast and wronght iron, glass and pottery, copperas and other chemical productions, soap, colours, grindstones, salt, and pickled salmon. The imports are wine, spirituous liquors, and fruit, from the south of Europe; corn, timber, flax, tallow, and hides, from the Baltic; and tobacco and various other articles from North America. The number of sailing vessels registered at the port is about 1500, besides about 200 steamers.

The chief manufactures are of glass bottles and plate and crown glass, steam engines, mill work, and other machinery. A number of persons are engaged in ship and boat building, block, mast, and sail making, flax-dressing, rope making, &c. There are several malthouses, breweries, flour-mills, iron and lead works, and chemical works.

Newcastle takes up a worthy position at the Great Exhibition. In mineral produce, in machinery, and in manufactures, the town and neighbourhood are well fitted to occupy a high rank.

NEWSPAPERS. Considered in its relation to produce, industry, and commerce, it is scarcely possible to place a limit to the importance of a newspaper. It meets us at every turn, as an example either of the aid which newspapers render to commerce, or of that which commerce renders to newspapers. As a question of paper-making, of taxation on paper, of type founding, of steam-press machinery, of rapid printing, of the advertising system, of the tax on advertisements, of the reporting system, of the statistical tabulating system, of the postage system, of the express travelling system, of the ocean mail system—in all these respects a modern London newspaper is a marvel.

Under the head of PRINTING will be found a little information concerning the vast scale on which the great newspapers are printed in London and in New York. In the present article we shall take a newspaper as the representative of rapid transport, showing how it reaches Dublin at a period of urgent demand. Let it be the Queen's speech of February, 1851, as printed in the morning journals of the next day; and let us trace the mode adopted by Messrs. Smith (who conduct vast operations of this kind), to convey those journals and that speech to Dublin, to Liverpool, and to Manchester. A special engine left Euston station at 6·22 A.M., and after some slight detention for water, &c., amounting altogether to 20 minutes, it reached Crewe at 10·8, the distance of 166 miles having been performed in 3¾ hours, or a running rate averaging 50 miles an hour. From Crewe an engine proceeded to Manchester, 32 miles, in 40 minutes, and another to Liverpool, 44 miles, in 75 minutes. The express to Ireland started from Crewe at the same moment as the Liverpool and Manchester expresses; it proceeded by Chester, where the superintendent of the Chester and Holyhead Railway joined it. Under his management the special engine reached Holyhead at 12·45, having travelled over a great portion of the distance between Chester and Bangor at the rate of 60 miles an hour. At Holyhead the Chester and Holyhead Company's steamer Scotia, commanded by Captain Hirste, was lying ready to start with the express, but in consequence of the violence of the gale she was unable to get clear of the harbour for some minutes. Notwithstanding the delay and the heavy sea, she made Kingstown Harbonr by 5·30 P.M., and the morning papers were distributed in Dublin by a little after six o'clock. The mail trains carried them into the provinces —the same mails which conveyed the London letters and papers of the previous evening. It is now proved that the entire distance from London *via* Holyhead and Dublin to Cork—upwards of 500 miles—can be accomplished in 16 hours. The Queen's speech was forwarded by Messrs. Smith on the afternoon of its delivery, by telegraph to Crewe, and thence by special engine to Holyhead, and by steamer to Dublin. It was printed in Dublin within eight hours and a half after its delivery, and reached Cork, by special engine engaged by Messrs. Smith, in four hours and a half from Dnblin.

NIAGARA BRIDGE. The suspension bridge thrown over the Niagara Falls may be considered, under the extraordinary circumstances of its position, as one of the most remarkable of its kind. The first transit across from bank to bank was made by a kite. A kite being raised on one bank, when the wind was in a particular position, was so manœuvred as to be made to fall on the opposite bank; the string was secured, and was made the means of dragging over a larger string, then a rope, then a cable of 36 iron wires. Several persons crossed the perilous chasm in a car suspended from this wire cable. The bridge was next proceeded with. On each bank is a wooden tower 50 feet high, over which pass 14 cables; viz., 5 of 36 wires each, 5 of 72, 1 of 125, and 3 of 150 wires each, making 1115 wires in all. These wire cables, hanging in the usual curve, support the platform of the bridge, which is capable of withstanding a pressure of 1000 tons, and is traversed by passengers, teams, and droves of cattle. There is however now being constructed a far mightier work over the Falls, to connect the United States railways on one bank with the Canadian railways on the other. A locomotive defying the Falls of Niagara will picture the grandeur of art and the grandeur of nature in singular proximity! The railway bridge will have 16 wire cables, each containing the enormous number of 6000 iron wires,—not twisted round each other, but laid straight, and bound round with smaller wire. It is calculated that the bridge will be able to maintain 6000 tons besides its own weight.

NICHE is a small recess, or concavity in the face of a wall for the purpose of containing a statue. The use of niches seems to have originated with the Romans, for scarcely anything of the kind occurs in the architecture of the Greeks. In Italian architecture niches are of very frequent occurrence. They are usually semicircular in plan, and round-headed, that is, covered by the quarter of a hollow sphere, owing to which the shadow within the concavity produces a highly beautiful curve. Niches exhibit great diversity in the modes of decorating them; but in this country it has usually been the fashion to leave them plain.

NICKEL. This metal was first described by Cronstadt in 1751. It is usually procured from the sulphuret. It has a white colour with a yellowish tint; its lustre is considerable, and it is both malleable and ductile. Like iron, it is attracted by the magnet, and may, like it, be rendered magnetic at common temperatures, but it loses this power when heated to 630° Fahrenheit. The specific gravity varies from 8·28 to 9·0. Nickel is nearly as hard as iron. It suffers little or no change by exposure to the air and moisture at common temperatures. It is very difficult of fusion, but melts at a lower temperature than iron. At a red heat it absorbs oxygen gradually from the air, and also decomposes water at this temperature. Nitric acid is the only acid which readily acts upon nickel. Nickel occurs in meteoric iron and aërolites.

The uses of nickel are very limited, and until within a few years it was scarcely employed at all; but it is now very usefully employed, and to a considerable extent, in forming an alloy with copper and zinc, known by the name of German silver. Its oxides impart a green colour to glass and porcelain. Nickel forms alloys with arsenic, potassium, antimony, zinc, tin, iron, cobalt, mercury, and copper.

NICOTINA is an alkali which exists in the different species of tobacco. It crystallises in small plates, which, by exposure to the air, absorb moisture sufficient to become a transparent colourless liquid. When cold it is nearly inodorous, but when heated it has a disagreeable odour and taste. It boils at 375°; its specific gravity is 1·048. The salts which it forms with alkalies are colourless. There is also a substance called *Nicotianin*, which is concrete oil having a smell of tobacco and a bitterish taste; it is the principle which gives the characteristic odour to tobacco.

NIELLO-INLAYING. This name is given by the Italians to a peculiar kind of ornamental metal-work. Niello is composed of an alloy of silver and lead, or silver and copper, blackened by the action of sulphur. It was first called *nigellum*, but afterwards *niello*. The use of it is occasionally mentioned in documents from the 7th to the 13th centuries, at which latter period it had arrived at a state of great excellence. The process used in working the niello was somewhat similar to that of enamel incrustation. The object intended to be ornamented with niello had incised or cut into its surface the required design, into which niello was inlaid in small grains, and afterwards fused by the action of the fire, and polished. Originally, the channels in the metal were cut broadly, and of an equal depth; giving to the entire work, after the introduction of the niello, the appearance of a rude picture, the outlines only of which were formed, sometimes by the niello and sometimes by the metal; but afterwards the designs on the metal were engraved with great delicacy, and occasionally were carefully shaded by lines. The origin of taking impressions on paper from metal plates is ascribed to the practice of Finiguerra, a Florentine goldsmith, who, in the middle of the 15th century, was in the habit of taking impressions from plates he had engraved for the purpose of ascertaining their fitness to receive the niello. Some few of these old impressions still exist, and equally with the plates themselves are called *nielli.* The metal which was engraved to receive the niello was usually either gold, silver, or copper.

Many beautiful specimens of niello were collected at the Mediæval Exhibition in 1850; including a silver super-altare, a copper-gilt ciborium, a silver brooch, statuettes of saints, silver plates, and a pax.

NILE. The influence of this far-famed river on the industry and commerce of the neighbouring countries has been briefly adverted to under EGYPT.

NIMES or NISMES, the capital of the French department of Gard, has long been an important manufacturing town. Its importance has been lately on the increase in consequence of its being the centre from which the railways diverge that connect the town with Alais, Montpellier, Cette, Arles, Avignon, and Marseille. The principal manufactures are fancy silk goods, silk stockings and caps, hosiery of all kinds, velvet, small wares, printed cottons, shawls, handkerchiefs, chintzes, &c. There are several dye-houses, potteries, brandy distilleries, vinegar-works, and tan-yards; and the town is the great market for the raw silks of the surrounding district. Nimes carries on considerable trade in these productions; and in wine, spices, drugs, oleaginous seeds, medicinal plants, and dye stuffs.

NISCHNEI-NOVGOROD FAIR. This famous fair has already been adverted to [FAIRS]; but it may be well to notice it a little more in detail, as a means of shewing its important influence on trade and commerce. Nischnei-Novgorod is a town in the heart of the Russian empire. The inhabitants carry on various manufactures; but the great and annually increasing importance of the town arises from its fair. This fair, which is opened on June 29 in each year, is one of the greatest in the world. It is held in a group of buildings, formed into a large oblong parallelogram, surrounded with shops, before an edifice adorned with three rows of columns, which is the hotel of the governor, in which the local authorities reside during the fair. Forty-eight blocks of buildings, separated by streets which intersect each other at right angles, extend behind this parallelogram. The number of the shops is about 2524, and over each there is a small apartment, in which the merchant may reside. During the fair, all the streets and warehouses are filled with a countless multitude, who have flocked thither from the two Russian capitals, from various other towns of Russia, from the shores of the Baltic and the Caspian, from Bokhara, Khiva, Kokand, and Taschkend, from Asia Minor, from the mountains of Turkistan and the frontiers of China, and, of late years, from different parts of Western Europe. All these magazines and booths are filled with the produce of the most diverse countries, and thousands of boats are employed in landing the goods, or in taking them on board to convey them to the seas which wash the northern and southern shores of the empire. Other goods, such as wooden wares, are piled up even in the open country, and farther on are long lines of carts with their horses, which serve both as magazines and lodgings for the country-people. From 4000 to 5000 warehouses and booths are let during the fair. The goods sold amount to 10,000,000*l.* to 12,000,000*l.* annually.

NITRE. [POTASSIUM.]

NITRIC ACID was formerly called *Spirit of Nitre*, or Glauber's Spirit of Nitre; and when much diluted with water, it is called *Aquafortis.* When pure, it is a colourless liquid, but is usually yellowish. Its smell is strong and disagreeable, and it emits white fumes. It is so acrid that it cannot be safely tasted without being much diluted, and is even then very sour. In its concentrated state it stains the skin of a yellow colour, and eventually the skin is destroyed and peels off. When mixed with water it gives out considerable heat. When colourless nitric acid is exposed to the action of the light, it undergoes partial decomposition.

Nitric acid is used for numerous purposes; such as the refining of gold and silver, in preparing various metallic and saline solutions for medicinal purposes, and the use of the dyer and calico-printer; in scientific chemical researches it is most extensively employed. Its saline compounds are termed *Nitrates*; and both the acid itself and the nitrates are used in medicine.

The gas called *nitric oxide*, which contains less oxygen than nitric acid, has not yet been much applied to useful purposes. The same may be said of *nitrous acid* and *nitrous oxide*, which differ from each other and from the two nitric compounds chiefly in the amount of oxygen contained.

NITROGEN, or AZOTE, one of the most abundant and extensively diffused of the gases, is transparent, colourless, inodorous, and insipid. It is lighter than atmospheric air. Its refractive power and its specific heat are both lower than those of common air. Water dissolves but a very small quantity of this gas. It is fatal to animals when respired by itself, as is implied by the term *azote;* it extinguishes flame immediately. No degree of cold and pressure to which this gas has been subjected has condensed it to a fluid form. It resembles all other elementary bodies in being destitute of acid or alkaline powers. It enters into the composition of a great number of important compounds. Thus it constitutes $\frac{80}{100}$ of the volume of *atmospheric air.* With oxygen it forms five definite compounds, viz., *nitrous oxide, nitric oxide, nitrous acid, hyponitrous acid,* and *nitric acid.* With hydrogen it constitutes the alkali *ammonia;* with chlorine and iodine it gives rise to *detonating* compounds; with carbon it forms *cyanogen;* and with phosphorus a *phosphuret.* It enters into the composition of most animal matter except fat and bone; and, though not a constituent of the vegetable acids, it forms a part of most of the vegetable alkalies. Although by itself fatal to animals, yet it is a most important constituent of the air, as serving to moderate the action of oxygen during combustion, and the too great excitement which that gas, respired unmixed, would produce on the animal system. It appears also from the experiments of Majendie that animals will not live on food that contains no azote.

NORD, the most northern department of France, raised the following quantities of agricultural produce in 1848: 2,124,549 quarters of corn; 2,960,264 bushels of potatoes; 13,330 hogsheads of flax seed; 352,429 cwt. of flax fibre; 142,398 tons of hay; 612,401 tons of straw; besides a fair average of vegetable crops and fruits. Authority was given to plant 2498 acres with tobacco in the year 1849, calculated to furnish 63,070 cwt. of leaf. A good deal of the barley grown in the department is used for malting, beer being the common beverage; other grain and potatoes are also used in the gin and other spirit distilleries.

The mineral wealth of the department consists chiefly of its coal and iron mines; of the former, 19, all situated in the valley of the Escaut, were worked in 1848, and of the latter, 3 were worked in the arrondissement of Avesnes. Steam-engines are used for draining the mines. Marble, paving-stones, brick-earth, potter's clay, peat, and fossil ashes, which are used as manure, are found. There are mineral waters and baths at St. Amand. The industrial products are of the most varied description, including all kinds of woollen, cotton, and linen manufactures, ticking, duck, velveteen, printed cottons, and handkerchiefs, woollen, flaxen, cotton, and hempen yarn, lace, tulle, cambric and lawn, soap, refined sugar and salt, beer, oil, nails, glass, paper, tiles, bricks, earthenware, ropes, leather, toys, small wares, cannon, small arms, saltpetre, &c. These numerous products form the items of a large home and foreign commerce. The imports are chiefly raw cotton, wool, flax, colonial produce, wine, brandy, and timber. At the principal points on the Belgian frontier, custom-house officers are stationed, who are under the direction of the custom-houses of Dunkerque and Valenciennes.

The manufactures of this department give rise to great activity in the towns of *Lille, Auzin, Roubaix, Tourcoing, Douai, Dunkerque, Valenciennes,* and *Cambrai,* all of which are distinguished for their industry and commerce.

NORFOLK. This agricultural county contains little of what may be designated mineral wealth. Chalk is dug for lime in many places; excellent sand for glass-making is procured between Snettisham and Castle Rising; some potter's earth is found and excellent brick-earth; marl is dug in the valley of the Bure; and the Fen districts of the west furnish peat for fuel and manure. The district in which the true Norfolk system of cultivation was first adopted, and where turnips and clover were introduced in the regular rotations, was that on the north-west, where the better kinds of sand prevail; from this district it has gradually spread; and there are now few soils in Norfolk which are considered too heavy to bear turnips, especially after having been well underdrained. The crop which is raised in the greatest perfection in Norfolk is barley.

Among the towns of Norfolk there are but few which present a manufacturing character. At *Lynn,* rope and sailcloth are almost the only articles of manufacture in the town; but the trade of the place is considerable, owing to the harbour. The exports are principally corn and agricultural produce, sent coastwise, and a fine white sand ground near the town, and used for making glass. A vast quantity of shrimps, caught on the shores of the Wash, are sent to London. The imports are corn and coal; timber from America, timber, deals, hemp, and tallow from the Baltic; wine from France, Spain, Portugal, &c. There are about 180 vessels belonging to the port. *Thetford* has few manufactures; but there is a good deal of malting, and the trade of the place is favoured by the river Ouse being navigable up to the town; by means of which an export of agricultural produce and an import of coal are carried on. At *North Walsham* the silk manufacture is prosecuted to some extent. In *Norwich* the most important trade consists of the manufacture of silk and worsted into shawls, crapes, bombazines, damasks, camlets, and imitations of the Irish and French stuffs. A School of Design has been established to aid in the production of elegant woven goods; but the textile manufactures are in a declining state at Norwich; and there is a want of enterprise and spirit observable in the manufacturing operations.

In 1850 the county of Norfolk contained 2 cotton factories, and 11 worsted factories, employing altogether about 1700 persons.

NORTHAMPTONSHIRE. Although this county presents some remarkable features in respect to the boot and shoe manufacture, it must be regarded as an agricultural county. The soil is generally adapted to produce both corn and pasture of a superior quality. The pastures are both rich and sound, and the cattle grazed in them in summer repay the capital laid out on them with good interest. The fattening of cattle is a principal object of the Northamptonshire farmer.

Among the towns there are a few in which manufactures are carried on. At *Kettering* wool-stapling and wool-combing are carried on; there is a considerable manufacture of shoes; and that of silk shag for hats has been also introduced. At *Northampton* the principal branch of trade carried on is boot and shoe-making; the articles are sent to London and other parts of England, or are exported; and considerable business is also done in currying leather. Stockings and lace are made. There are iron foundries. The trade of *Wellingborough*, and of other towns in this county, is dependent mainly on the boot and shoe manufacture. The only reasonable explanation of the settlement of this branch of industry in this county seems to be that Northamptonshire is a grazing county, and yields hides fit for tanning; but whether this be the correct explanation or not, it is a well-known fact that the ready-made boots and shoes of the London shops are supplied to a very large extent by the county of Northamptonshire. The work is done on the *piece-work* system. There are not large factories where men are employed at weekly wages; but the manufacturers give out leather cut to the proper shapes to the workmen, who return the finished or partially finished boots and shoes, and receive so much per dozen pairs for their labour. Competition between these workmen has brought down the wages to a very low average.

NORTHUMBERLAND. The south-eastern part of this county, bounded by a line drawn from Warkworth, at the mouth of the Coquet, by the head of the river Blyth, to the Tyne, and thence southward to the bank of the Derwent, is included in the great coal-field of the counties of Northumberland and Durham. [COAL-FIELDS.] This coal-field is the great source of wealth to the county, and gives it a high rank among the shires of Britain. The salmon fishery of the Tweed is very important, and a considerable number of boxes of that fish packed in ice are sent from that river to the London market, besides what is salted. The county of Northumberland has been one of the foremost of the English counties in adopting the improved system of agriculture, the chief feature of which is the cultivation of turnips for the rearing and fattening of cattle. So great has been the advantage derived from this change from the old triennial system, that many fields now yield heavy crops of this useful root, which in most other parts of England would be considered as totally unfit for its cultivation. The instruments of tillage are mostly of improved make. The ploughs are generally iron swing-ploughs, on the principle of the old Rotherham plough, which was originally copied from the Belgian plough, and afterwards improved. The harrows, rollers, scarifiers, &c., are as in other counties. Threshing-machines, moved by water, wind, or horses, are thought essential on the larger Northumberland farms.

The manufactures of the county are noticed in connection with its chief industrial centre [NEWCASTLE]; but there are other busy towns worthy of note. *Allendale* lies near the lead mines, and has establishments for the smelting of that metal. *Alnmouth* has a considerable export of wool to the West Riding, and of corn to the metropolis. *Blythe* has ship-building yards for small vessels. *North Shields* has a great trade in coal, and a very active shipping commerce, by which it is becoming every year a place of more and more importance. All along the Tyne, but especially from Newcastle to the German Ocean, the number of manufacturing establishments is very great. Besides the enormous shipment of coals, there are very extensive chemical and alkali works, soap works, lead and shot works, white and red lead works, potteries, plate and window glass works, oil mills, starch mills, &c.

NOTTINGHAMSHIRE. This county, as noticed in a former article [COAL] contains a portion of one of the midland coal-fields. It contains also a small supply of gypsum, building stone, and paving stone; but the county can hardly be deemed rich in minerals. There are many hop plantations in the county, which in some years give a good profit to the grower. There are excellent market gardens in the neighbourhood of Newark, Nottingham, and other towns, the sandy soil being very favourable to the cultivation of roots and vegetables.

There are also some good orchards on the heavier soils.

In respect to manufactures, Nottinghamshire derives importance from being the centre of the cotton hosiery and bobbin-net trades. [HOSIERY MANUFACTURE; LACE MANUFACTURE]. Not only in the town of Nottingham itself, but in all the towns and villages in the southern half of the county, these manufactures are carried on. Nottingham itself is the focus of these trades, where the wholesale manufacturers and dealers reside. The bobbin net is mostly made in factories; but the hosiery is made at the houses of the operatives, with cotton yarn supplied by the manufacturers: the workpeople being paid so much per dozen pairs for their labour, out of which they for the most part have to pay a frame-rent for the machines.

In 1850 the county of Nottingham contained 19 cotton factories, 4 silk factories, and 1 worsted factory; these 24 factories employed about 2200 persons.

A School of Design has been established at Nottingham; and it is stated in the annual report of the Inspector of these schools for 1850, that the effect of the school in improving the taste of designers in the lace trade is becoming very evident. It will be gratifying if the Great Exhibition should verify this improvement.

NOYAU, or *Crème de Noyau*, is a favourite liqueur or cordial in France. It is formed of bitter almonds, proof spirits, coriander seed, lump sugar, cinnamon, ginger, and mace. One variety, called *Crème de Noyau de Martinique*, is said to consist of the following ingredients:—

Loaf sugar............	24	lbs.
Water	2½	gallons.
Proof spirit...........	5	gallons.
Orange-flower water	3	pints.
Bitter almonds.........	1	lb.
Essence of lemon	2	drachms.

NUMBERING MACHINE. Different forms of apparatus for recording or marking numbers are described under CALCULATING MACHINES; REGISTERING MACHINES.

NUTMEGS. The two favourite spices of *nutmeg* and *mace* are derived from the same plant. This plant is the *Myristica Moschata*, a tree native of the Molucca Islands, especially of Banda, but cultivated in Java, Sumatra, and elsewhere in the East, and of late years in Guiana and several of the West India Islands; but the best are produced in the first-mentioned islands. The fruit is of the size and form of a peach, and when ripe the fleshy part separates into two nearly equal halves, exposing the kernel surrounded by an arillus, the former being the *nutmeg*, the latter the *mace*. The odour of the mace is strongly aromatic; the taste aromatic, but sharp and acrid. It contains both a fixed oil (in small quantity) and a volatile oil. One pound of mace yields by distillation one ounce of volatile oil. The fixed oil is not an article of European commerce, and what is termed the *expressed oil of mace* is obtained from the nutmeg, and should bear its name. An inferior mace is obtained from various species of *Myristica*. The properties of mace are similar to those of the nutmeg.

Two or three gatherings of the nutmegs are made in the year, generally in July, or August, in December, and in April. The third period yields the best nutmegs. The collected nuts are dried in the sun or by the heat of a moderate fire till the shells split: they are then sorted and dipped in lime-water, to preserve them from the attack of insects. Those of good quality should be heavy, each weighing on an average 90 grains.

The quantities of these spices imported in the last three years were as follow:—

	Mace.	Nutmegs.
1848	47,572 lbs.	336,420 lbs.
1849	45,986 ,,	224,021 ,,
1850	76,365 ,,	312,418 ,,

NUTS. A few words concerning the chief varieties of nuts are given under the proper names; and an instance of the large consumption of hazel nuts in London will be found under MARKET GARDENS. In respect to the commerce in nuts, the following were the quantities of the three best known kinds, imported in 1848:—

Hazel Nuts.....	150,022	bushels.
Chestnuts.......	63,033	,,
Walnuts........	29,604	,,

Of the quantities grown in England, there are no means of forming an estimate.

NUX VOMICA. This very powerful medicine is one among many products of the plant *Strychnos*. Among these products is *strychnia*, a vegetable alkali which exists in the plant combined with *strychnic acid*; it is colourless, inodorous, crystalline, unalterable by exposure to the air, and extremely bitter; it is extremely poisonous; one-eighth of a grain is sufficient to kill a dog, and a quarter of a grain produces a dangerous effect upon a man. The *strychnos* itself is a kind of *nightshade*, of which there are several species. The best known is *strychnos nux vomica*, or *poison nut*, or *ratsbane*. The wood of this plant is very hard and durable, and on that account is applied to many purposes by the natives on the coast of Coromandel and other places where it grows. The fruit is about the size of a St. Michael's orange, with a bitter astringent pulp, and containing from three to five seeds. The pulp may be eaten, but the seeds are poisonous and officinal. Another remarkable species is the *strychnos toxifera*, *Wooraly*, *Urari*, or poison plant of Guiana, a native of Guiana. It had long been suspected that the poison used by the American Indians for their arrows was a species of Strychnos, but such is the secrecy with which they gather the plant and prepare the poison, that all enquiries have been frustrated. Sir R. Schomburgk's long stay in Guiana has enabled him to decide this point: by bribing some of the natives, he induced them to guide him to a spot where their famous Urari flourished, and on arriving at the place, found it to be the species of Strychnos above described. In the preparation of the poison, the Urari is not the only ingredient, but forms about half of the bulk of the ingredient used.

As a medicinal agent, nux vomica possesses valuable qualities; but it is so extremely poisonous except in very minute doses, and much diluted, that its use is deemed dangerous except under great precautions.

O

OAK. The oak is perhaps the most celebrated and the most valuable of all timber trees; no others are applied to so many useful purposes. The timber is more durable than any other of extensive growth in Europe. It is hard, tough, tolerably flexible, strong without being too heavy, not easily splintered, and not readily penetrated by water. When the grain is twisted, no other timber is so well adapted for posts, piles, shingles, palings, laths, casks, and all articles exposed to the action of moisture may fittingly be made of oak. It is extensively employed for the spokes of wheels, and for all kinds of poles. The young tree yields slender rods, well calculated for hoops, walking sticks, and whip handles. Old specimens produce a very beautiful effect when carved, as is well shewn in many of our churches and ancient mansions. Of all other modes of application, however, *ship building* is that to which oak is most extensively devoted in this country, and in which it renders the most important services. During the height of the last maritime war, it was calculated that the ships of the Royal Navy existing at one time contained more than eleven hundred thousand loads of oak. Fifty acres of oak plantation are required to produce the timber for a 74-gun ship; and the consumption must therefore have been enormous during the war. Specimens of oak of magnificent dimensions are to be met with in some English mansions. At Dudley Castle is (or was) an oak table 75 feet long by 3 feet wide, formed of one plank of oak. At Goodrich Castle is a beam of oak 66 feet long by 2 feet square throughout its whole length. The mainmast of the Royal Sovereign, built in the reign of Charles I. was 99 feet long by 3 feet diameter at the lower end, and formed out of one piece of oak.

The *root* of the oak is applied to ornamental rather than useful purposes. Evelyn says that of the root of the oak were formerly made handles to daggers and knives, tobacco boxes, mathematical instruments, panels for pictures, and various minor articles. At the present day the root of oak is cut into veneers which, when polished, shew exceedingly beautiful veins and markings.

The leaves of oak, gathered green and dried, furnish in some places a winter fodder for sheep, goats, deer, &c. They are also used as a substitute for tanners' bark in hothouses, hotbeds, &c. Concerning the acorns of the oak, we have spoken elsewhere [ACORNS].

The *bark* of the oak is a valuable tanning ingredient, as noticed under BARK. The stripping of the bark is effected by women in the following way. The barkers are each furnished with a light short handled wooden mallet, sharpened at one edge like a wedge. With this edge an incision is made all along the bark; and cross-cuts are then made with an instrument called the barking-bill, so as to separate the bark into pieces two or three feet long. A shovel-shaped instrument is then thrust beneath the bark, so as to force it off in sheets or pieces. These pieces are carefully dried for two or three weeks, and piled in large stacks until sold to the tanner.

The substance called *nut-galls* is yielded by a species called the Gall Oak. The gall is a morbid excrescence, produced in it by the puncture of an insect. There are two kinds of gall nuts known in commerce; those which still contain the insect, and which are known under the names of *black* or *blue* galls; and those from which the insect has escaped, called white galls. Both are used extensively in dyeing; but the dark contain much more astringent matter than the white. The English oak yields galls, but not so valuable as those of the east. Most of them known in commerce are from Syria and Asia Minor.

OAKUM. When the various cables, stays, shrouds, ropes, &c., belonging to a ship have gone through their term of service, and are no longer strong enough to be used, they are cut up into pieces, and then pulled asunder, all the hempen threads being loosened and disentangled one from another. In this state the hempen threads are called *oakum*, which varies in quality according to the kind of rope from which it is produced. The old ropes of a ship are sold to dealers; and when picked into oakum they are again sold to ship-builders. The work of oakum-picking is a kind of forced employment in many prisons. The oakum is sold to the ship-builders in large bundles, and is then spun into loose threads. These threads are of a very primitive kind; a small bundle of fibres is rolled by the hand on a sloping board, till it assumes the form of a loose irregular kind of rope, from half an inch to an inch in thickness. These oakum ropes are used for driving into the crevices or seams in the outside of a ship, to prevent the entrance of sea-water. This process is called *caulking*, and is effected by the aid of a large mallet or hammer and a caulking chisel; by which a dense layer of oakum is forced into the crevice—afterwards to be well tarred.

OATS. The great use of oats, and the ease with which they are raised on almost every kind of soil, from the heaviest loam to the lightest sand, have made them occupy a place in almost every rotation of crops. The best oats are raised in Scotland and in Friesland, and in both countries the land is carefully cultivated. In Scotland, oats are generally sown on a grass layer which has been in that state for some years, and sometimes on old pastures, which are broken up for the purpose. A heavy loam is best suited for oats: they require a certain degree of moisture, and a deep soil is very favourable to their growth. On poor moist land oats are more profitable than barley. Clover and grass seeds may be sown among them with equal advantage, as they will seldom grow so high as to be laid and smother the young clover; and barley is very apt to fail on land subject to retain the water. Six bushels of oats are often sown on an acre; but if they are drilled, four bushels are sufficient, and when dibbled, which is sometimes the case in Norfolk and Suffolk, much less seed is used. The produce of an acre of oats varies according to the soil and preparation, from four to eight and even ten quarters.

In respect to the use of oats, they are given in some countries to horses in the straw without thrashing them; and where the quantity can be regulated the practice is good. The horses masticate the corn better in the chaff, and the straw is wholesome; but where horses do hard work, they would be too long in eating a sufficient quantity, and it is better to give them oats thrashed and cleaned, with clover hay cut into chaff. It is estimated that a pound of good oats gives as much nourishment to a horse as two pounds of the best clover, or sainfoin hay. A truss of hay of 56 pounds is therefore equal to 28 pounds of oats; or a bushel of the best oats will go as far as one truss and a half of hay; and if this quantity is worth four shillings, which is at the rate of 4*l.* 16*s.* per load of thirty-six trusses, the equivalent price of oats is 32*s.* per quarter.

The oats and oatmeal imported in 1849 amounted to 1,292,707 quarters, at an average price of 17*s.* 6*d.* per quarter. The imports were almost entirely from Northern Europe—Russia, Sweden, Norway, Denmark, Prussia, Hanover, and Holland. The quantity imported in 1850 was rather less than that in 1849.

OBELISK. An obelisk is a lofty monumental four-sided shaft diminishing upwards with the sides gently inclined, but not so as to terminate in an apex at the top. Small obelisks were sometimes of sandstone or granite, but the larger Egyptian obelisks are all of the red granite of Syene; and it is certainly astonishing how such enormous masses of that material could be quarried out and afterwards removed and placed in their position. When the Romans became masters of Egypt, they removed many of these monuments to their own capital, among others that now known as the Obelisk of the Lateran. This is the largest obelisk now known, its shaft being 105 feet (although it has been reduced, a portion at the lower part having been cut off in consequence of being fractured), and two of its sides 9 feet 8½ inches, the other two 9 feet; it weighs about 445 tons. In the present century, the labour of bringing away and re-erecting an obelisk nearly equal to some of the largest removed by the Romans has been accomplished by the French. The raising of this obelisk upon a granite platform prepared for it in the Place de la Concorde at Paris was a remarkable operation. An inclined plane leading from the river Seine up to a platform of rough masonry level with the top of the pedestal was formed, and the obelisk, having been placed on a kind of timber car or sledge, was dragged up by means of ropes and capstans. One edge of its base having been brought to the edge of the pedestal, it was reared perpendicularly by ropes and pulleys attached to the heads of ten masts, five on each side; and within about three hours the operations were completed.

The largest Egyptian obelisk hitherto brought over to England is that which was removed from the island of Philæ by Belzoni, and which is now erected at Kingston Hall, Dorsetshire. It is a monolith or single stone of red Egyptian granite, 22 feet 1 inch in length, and its larger end or base 2 feet 2 inches square, the other being 1 foot 5¾ inches.

OBOE, is a musical instrument blown through a reed, like a clarionet. It is a tube of boxwood 22 inches in length, slender in the upper part, but spreads out conically at the lower end. It consists of three joints or pieces, besides the reed. Its compass is usually two octaves and a fifth, from C below the treble clef, to G, the fourth added line above it. The instrument, which has been in use since the time of Edward III., was long known only by its French name of *Hautbois*.

OBSIDIAN, is a mineral which occurs in beds, in large and rolled masses and in small grains. Its structure is compact, colour greenish or grayish, and before the blow-pipe it swells up strongly and fuses into a transparent glass. It occurs in veins and beds traversing rocks, and consists chiefly of silica and alumina.

OCHRE. This earthy substance is somewhat complex in its nature. It consists of silica and alumina, coloured by oxide of iron and occasionally by other oxides. It generally occurs in beds several feet in thickness, which overlie the oolite, and underlie sandstones and iron sands. The ochre obtains commercially the names of *yellow* and *brown*, according to its tint; and it is used by painters and colour makers. It is prepared for use by grinding and washing. The yellow ochre may be reddened in tint by calcination. Native red ochre is called *red chalk;* it is more strongly impregnated with oxide of iron than either of the others. At Shotover Hill, near Oxford, there is an ochre bed, about six inches in thickness, at a depth of twenty feet below the surface. *Armenian bole*, obtained in a few places in Greece and Italy, is a kind of ochre; the pigment called *terra di Sienna* is obtained from it.

About 7184 cwts. of ochre were imported from France in 1847.

ODESSA, is one of the most famous commercial cities of the Russian empire. It is on the borders of the Black Sea; and in the year 1817 it was declared a free port for thirty years. Though not situated at the mouth of any great river, Odessa, in consequence of its excellent harbour and convenient situation, is the emporium where the surplus produce of southern Russia is collected for exportation, and where foreign products required for the interior are imported. The products brought down the Dniester, the Bug, and the Dnieper, are all exported from Odessa; but because of the difficulties of the river navigation, a vast quantity of the corn brought to the town from the neighbouring provinces is conveyed on carts drawn by oxen. The trade of Odessa extends to all parts of the Mediterranean and western Europe. The chief exports are—corn, tallow, linseed, wool, iron, hides, copper, wax, caviar, potash, beef, furs, cordage, sailcloth, tar, butter, isinglass, &c. The imports consist of coffee, sugar, and other colonial products; cotton, silk, and woollen goods; oil, wine, brandy, spices, dyestuffs, tobacco, fruits, raw cotton, tin, cutlery, timber, &c. In ordinary years about 800 foreign ships enter and leave the harbour; the value of the imports is close upon a million sterling, that of the exports is nearly two millions annually. The trade of Odessa has increased greatly within the last few years—a circumstance which is no doubt in a great measure, but not altogether, owing to the failure of the crops in western Europe, and the consequent demand for foreign supplies. In the first six months of 1847, 709 foreign ships arrived with imports worth 893,917*l.*; and 734 sailed with 1,056,493 quarters of corn, and a total value of exports amounting to 2,716,969*l.* The exports are usually more important during the last six months of the year. The privileges of a free harbour are continued to Odessa till 1854, by an imperial ukase issued in 1849; this freedom of the port has an immense influence on the nature and extent of the trade. Odessa has considerable breweries, distilleries, and manufactories of woollens, silks, tobacco, soap, and candles.

OHIO. A few industrial statistics of this rapidly rising state will be found under UNITED STATES.

OIL COLOURS. The colours used by house-painters are chiefly mineral or vegetable; seldom of animal origin. They are purchased from the colour merchants, mostly in the state of powder or of crystal; and after being ground as fine as possible, are mixed to the requisite degree of liquidity with turpentine and linseed oil. Other liquids besides these are occasionally employed; but the two here named constitute the principal.

The oil colours for artists comprise a more extensive range than those used by house-painters, and are prepared with more care. Such colours are sometimes prepared in the form of *cakes.* To prepare these cakes, the colours are ground with oil of turpentine, in which has been dissolved about one-sixth of its weight of powdered mastic. The mixture is left to dry, and is then exposed to the action of a slow charcoal fire until the mixture is softened. It is then made into a paste by the addition of a warm solution of spermaceti dissolved in half its weight of poppy oil. The whole mass is worked up together until it is stiff enough to be pressed into cake-moulds. When used by artists, the cakes are ground up with oil of turpentine and poppy or some other oil. The oil colours which are sold in bottles or bladders are prepared to a certain stage like the cake colours, but they are thinned with pale drying oil before being put in the cases.

The principal colouring substances employed by painters are described under their proper headings. See also COLOURS.

OIL MILL. The extraction of oil from seeds—such as linseed, hempseed, rapeseed, &c.—requires considerable pressure. The mode of obtaining linseed oil from lin or flax seed includes many singular processes.

When the flax plants have grown to that stage which imparts to the seed the greatest amount of oleaginous quality, they are pulled, and partially dried in the air; and the capsules which contain the seed are stripped off by a kind of comb called a ripple. The capsules are dried, thrashed, and winnowed, to separate the seeds from the husks or capsules. The seeds are exceedingly hard and smooth, and require one of two kinds of press to crush them; one the *wedge press,* and the other the *hydraulic press.* In the wedge press, a wedge is driven very forcibly between two bags of seed; and it is found that the oil is driven out of the seed by this process more readily than by the use of a mill-stone. But in modern oil mills the hydraulic press is gradually superseding the wedge press. In preparing the seed for the hydraulic press, the following is the routine of processes. The seed is bruised by two crushing-rollers, so placed side by side that the seed, introduced between them from a hopper at the top, becomes crushed by the rotation, and falls into a chest beneath. The seeds are further ground or crushed by ordinary edge-stones, and assume the state of an oily pulp. The pulp is heated, and put into oblong flannel bags. These bags are flattened slightly by the hand, and piled one on another in cast-iron cases, which are placed in the hydraulic presses. The presses are then worked, and the oil speedily begins to ooze from the pulp through the bags. When as much oil has been obtained as will flow by these means, the press is loosened, the bags removed, and the pressed cake of pulp taken out of each bag; and this cake is ground, re-heated, re-bagged, and re-pressed, to yield more oil. The refuse pulp now forms valuable manure, and commands a good price as *oil-cake.* What is called *cold-drawn* linseed oil is obtained by pressing the seed immediately after it has been crushed, without any intermediate heating; it is obtained in small quantity, but of very fine quality. Flax-seed varies from 48 to 52 lbs. per bushel, or about 400lbs. per quarter; the seed yields 13 to 19 gallons (98lbs. to 122lbs.) of oil per quarter, the average being about 16 gallons.

No other kind of vegetable oil requires so heavy a pressure as that procured from flax and similar seeds. In Italy and other northern countries where *olives* grow abundantly, the produce is crushed beneath an edge-mill-stone, and then pressed, to force out the oil, in a screw-press. *Oil of almonds* is procured by shaking the almond kernels in bags, so as to separate the brown skins, and then grinding and pressing them. *Palm oil* is procured from the fruit of many species of palm, which the Africans collect into a heap, and steep in hot water, by which the oil is liberated and made to swim on the surface of the water, from which it is afterwards removed. *Nut oil* is procured from walnuts and hazel-nuts, which in the south of Europe contain sufficient oil to be worth the process of pressing.

OILS. These useful substances are obtained from very different sources and under various circumstances. First, animal fats are to be regarded as varieties of oil. There are also animal oils more properly so called, as *whale* and *spermaceti* oil. Secondly, there are the oils of vegetable origin, as those of *olives* and *linseed,* obtained by pressure, and called fat, fixed, or expressed oils, and those procured by distillation, termed volatile, essential, or ætherial oils. Thirdly, there are various oils produced by heat from animal, mineral, and other bodies, such as *Dippel's oil* and *naphtha.* Lastly, there are certain oils produced by chemical action, as *oil of wine,* &c. Most fats and expressed oils consist of *olein,* by some chemists called *margarin* and *stearin.*

Animal Oils.—One of the best known and most extensively used of these is common whale or train oil, obtained by melting the blubber of the animal. As met with in commerce it is of a brownish colour, rather viscid, and has a disagreeable fishy smell and taste. Like other oils, it is very combustible, and it is largely employed for the purpose of giving light. *Spermaceti Oil* is obtained from an oily matter lodged in a bony cavity of the head of the Spermaceti Whale. When this substance is subjected to pressure in bags, a quantity of pure limpid oil is expressed; and the residue after being melted, strained, and boiled with a weak solution of potash, is well known by the name of *spermaceti*. The other animal oils are of less importance.

Fluid Oils.—The *Vegetable Expressed Oils* vary in their properties. *Olive Oil* is yellowish, the odour and taste but slight. *Linseed Oil* is expressed from the seeds of the common flax. When no heat is employed in the pressing, it is more viscid and has a greenish-yellow colour; it is then called in commerce *cold drawn* linseed oil. Its smell and taste are stronger and more disagreeable than those of olive oil. Linseed oil is largely employed in oil painting and in varnish-making. *Almond Oil* is of a light yellowish colour, more fluid than olive or linseed oil; its odour and taste are very slight. It is employed sometimes in soap making, and also in medicine. *Castor Oil* is the expressed oil of the seeds of the *Ricinus communis.* When expressed without the assistance of heat, it is transparent and nearly colourless. It is very considerably viscid, and becomes solid when exposed to about 0° Fah.

Solid Oils.—One of the chief of these is *Cocoa Nut Oil.* It is white, has a slight pleasant smell, and its taste is rather agreeable; it melts at 122° Fahr., and of late years it has been employed in soap making. *Palm Oil* is of the consistence of butter, and of on orange yellow colour; its smell is agreeable. It melts at about 103° Fahr.

Volatile or *Essential Oils.*—These oils are fluid at the usual temperature, and with few exceptions are obtained by distillation. Essential oils are distinguished principally from the expressed oils by the following properties:—Usually they are more perfectly fluid, more combustible, have an aromatic or fragrant odour, and an acrid taste; they are volatile *per se* without decomposition, and may be distilled with water at 212°, although their boiling-point is much higher. In some instances the volatile oils are obtained by pressure, without the application of heat: this is the case with the oils of lemons, oranges, and bergamot. In general however they are procurable only by distillation, and this is effected by putting the herb or bark into a still with water, when the oil and water are volatilized and condensed together. Like the fixed oils they appear to contain a harder and a softer principle; the former has been called *stearopten*, the latter *eleopten.* The most important oils of this class are those of *Turpentine, Lemons, Marjoram, Cinnamon, Cloves,* and *Almonds.*

Both volatile and fixed oils are very extensively diffused through vegetables; the former in almost every part of a plant except the cotyledons of the seed, and the latter in the seeds chiefly, but also in their fleshy covering as in the olive, some palms, and other plants. Some families of plants abound especially in fixed oil. Among the *Cruciferæ* are mustard seed, rape seed, and colza seed oils, with other species especially cultivated in Europe, India, and Japan, of which some have of late years been imported into this country. Several of the family of *Compositæ* secrete oil in quantities large enough to render it desirable to cultivate them for this purpose alone, as the Sun Flower and Jerusalem Artichoke; also some species of *Carthamus* or Bastard Saffron, and also the *Verbesina sativa* of India. *Madia sativa* yields Madi Oil, and its seeds are said to contain more oil than any plant introduced into Europe. Most of the *Cucurbitaceæ* also, as the melon, gourd, cucumber, and the numerous varieties, cultivated especially in India, contain a large proportion of oil, which is expressed in the east as it formerly was in Europe. The *Rosaceæ* also store up a large proportion of oil in the kernels of their fruit, as in the almond, the apricot, as well as the Briançon apricot, and other species of *Prunus.* In the Himalayas oil is also expressed from the apricot kernel, and has been sent to this country, of a fine quality. Among the *Amentaceæ* several species yield oil of good quality, and in sufficient quantity to repay the expense of expression, as hazel-nut oil, beech-nut oil, and walnut oil. Besides these poppy oil, Bennut oil (*Hyperanthera*), ground-nut oil (*Arachis*), physic-nut oil (*Jatropha*), are well-known. The cotton seed yields oil, and also the seeds of the tea plant, especially of the species called *Thea oleifera*, and some of the Camellias.

The imports of the principal oils and of oil cake for the last two years have amounted to the following quantities:—

	1849.		1850.
Whale Oil . .	20,001	tuns.	21,328
Olive Oil . . .	16,064	,,	20,783
Palm Oil . . .	493,331	cwts.	448,589
Cocoa Nut Oil .	64,452	,,	98,040
Oil Cake . . .	59,462	tons.	65,055

The linseed, hempseed, and rapeseed oil exported in 1850 amounted to 3,292,266 gallons.

OINTMENTS. In their mechanical preparation, ointments differ slightly in consistency; some being very stiff, while others are softer in substance. They are mixed and used in the same manner as cerates, but are of different consistence; in this respect cerates occupy a middle place between plasters and ointments. [CERATES.] Ointments have in general the consistence of good butter in an average temperature. The active ingredient which gives name to the ointment is sometimes a powder, sometimes a liquid; if the former, it is usually mixed with lard; if the latter, it is mixed with suet and lard, with occasionally a little wax. Ointments may be preserved from rancidity by adding to them a little gum-benzoin or benjamin.

OLEIN, or ELAIN, is one of the two constituents of most fats and expressed oils: the other being *Stearin*. Olein has scarcely any taste or smell when procured from oils which possess these properties only in a slight degree. It solidifies at 27° Fahr., and crystallises in needles. On account of the very low temperature at which olein congeals, it is well adapted for lubricating the wheels of watches, and its value in this respect is enhanced by its not readily becoming rancid by the action of the air.

The very pure olein or liquid oil used by watchmakers is thus prepared. Almond or olive oil is mixed with eight parts its weight of proof spirit, and heated nearly to boiling; it is then agitated, allowed to settle, and the clear upper stratum decanted off; it is cooled, filtered, and all the spirit driven off by distillation. Oil so prepared will not thicken or freeze at any ordinary temperatures, and is thus well fitted for the delicate work of the watchmaker. Oil prepared in this way has sometimes been sold so high as 1*s.* 6*d.* per drachm. Watchmakers' oil of a cheaper kind is prepared by placing a clean strip of lead in a small white glass bottle filled with olive oil, and exposing it to the sun's rays for some time; the action between the lead and the oil, aided by the solar rays, throws down a curdy matter, and leaves the rest of the oil limpid and colourless.

OLIBANUM. It appears that the gum resin called *Olibanum* is the *frankincense* that was used by the ancients in their religious ceremonies. The Greeks obtained their frankincense from Arabia. The Arabians call olibanum both *Lubán* and *Cundur;* but, as benzoin is most used at the present day for religious purposes, the Mohammedan writers of India on materia medica apply only the term *Cundur* to olibanum. This *Cundur* has been ascertained by Messrs. Colebrooke, Hunter, and Roxburgh to bo the *Boswellia thurifera*, as botanists call it, a large timber-tree found in the mountainous parts of India, yielding a most fragrant resin from wounds made in the bark. From this Roxburgh distinguishes, as a different species, *Boswellia glabra*, a plant also yielding a resin which is used for incense, and as pitch in some parts of India. A substance analogous to olibanum, and used in a similar way in various parts of the world, is procured from several different trees. Olibanum occurs in commerce of two kinds, the Arabian and East Indian: the former kind is now seldom met with; the latter is obtained from the *Boswellia thurifera*. There are two varieties of it. Olibanum is now seldom used in medicine; it is principally employed as incense in Roman Catholic churches.

OLIVES; OLIVE OIL. In most plants which yield fixed oil, the oil is obtained from the seed; but in the olive it is yielded by the pericarp. Olive trees sometimes attain a great age. There is one near Nice, the lower part of the trunk of which measures 38 feet in circumference.

The oil which is expressed from the ripo fruit immediately after being gathered is most esteemed, and is called *virgin oil.* When the oil is extracted by a stronger pressure, or by the aid of heat or of slight fermentation, it forms the common *olive oil,* the properties of which vary in proportion to the mode adopted. An oil of still inferior quality is obtained when the husk of the olive, after the former treatment, is boiled in water; this inferior oil is used in making soap. Virgin oil is a very pale yellow, limpid, and inodorous; common olive oil is darker, thicker, and less pure in smell. Olive oil is frequently adulterated with rape oil, a cheaper product.

Olive oil is used by watchmakers; by the manufacturers of soap; as a substitute for whale oil in lamps; as a salad oil; and to form cerates and plasters in medicine. A few additional details concerning olive oil will be found under OILS.

OMNIBUS AND CAB. The street travelling of London is ono of the most remarkable commercial features of our age. It would be impossible to estimate the value of the *time* saved (and consequently *money* saved), by the use of these vehicles; but there can be no question that it is enormous.

In respect to *coaches* or *cabs*, the changes have been remarkable. A few years ago every vehicle on a coach stand was drawn by two horses: there is now not such a thing to be seen (we here speak of the Metropolis). Hackney coaches first began to ply in 1625; their number had increased to 200 in 1652, to 400 in 1661, to 800 in the beginning of the following century. This number has gradually increased to about 3000. In 1813 a

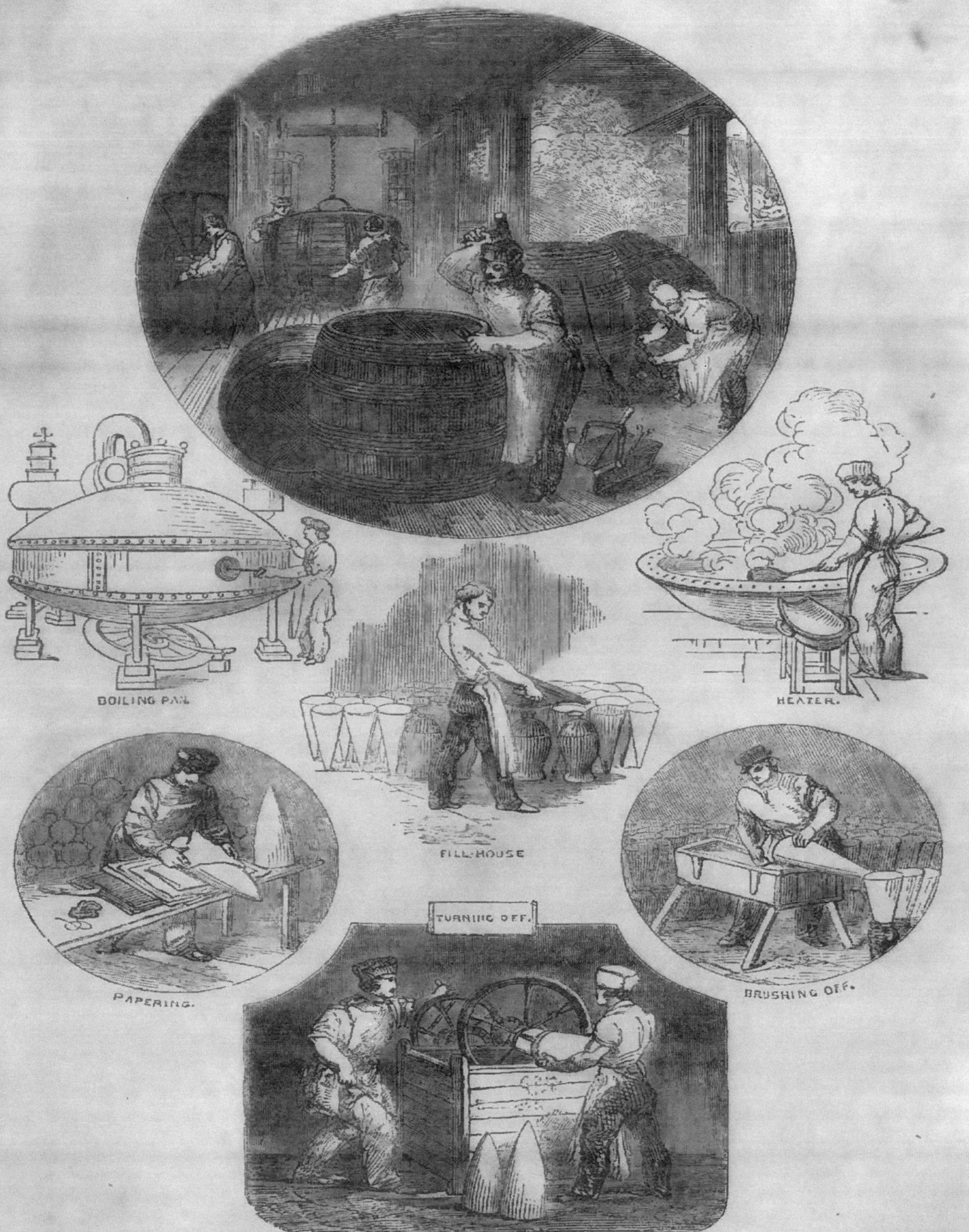

KNIGHT'S CYCLOPÆDIA OF THE INDUSTRY OF ALL NATIONS.

No. 31.

lighter kind of vehicle, drawn by one horse, was brought into use in Paris. In 1823 licences were obtained in London for eight *cabriolets*, which were started at fares one-third lower than those of hackney coaches; the 'vested interest' of the old hackney coachmen was made the groundwork of a strenuous opposition; but the convenience of the new vehicles gradually bore down all difficulties. A limit was made to the number of each kind until the year 1832, when all restriction was removed, and any one could obtain a licence (under proper regulations), by paying for it.

It is curious to mark the gradual improvements in cabs, or cabriolets, as the system established itself. They were at first hooded chaises, in which a liveried driver sat on the same seat with the person who had hired the cab. Then came an alteration by which two persons could be accommodated; the driver having a little seat fitted for him at the right hand of the body of the vehicle. Next came the boxed-up vehicle, which presented the appearance of a slice off an omnibus; it was on two wheels, with a door at the back. After a few minor changes, the four-wheeled cab presented itself, and has ever since remained the type of the class generally; it is well built, and will contain four persons. Lastly came the dashing *Hansom's* patent; a two-wheeled vehicle, very low, opening in the front, having a seat for the driver behind the top, and having large wheels, which enable it to rattle on at a great speed.

It is believed that the returns which a cab brings to its proprietor average about half a guinea a day, besides that portion which goes to the driver for his wages. Many attempts have been made to provide means for testing the honesty of the drivers by some mechanical arrangement connected with the vehicle; either a sort of tell-tale, to shew how often persons have entered or left the vehicle, or how many miles the wheels have rotated; but hitherto nothing of this kind has been found available. A company is, we believe, in process of formation, for constructing cabs which shall admit of equitable arrangements for the proprietors, the drivers, and the public; there is to be some kind of passenger-index, which will afford means for determining the distance run.

The *Omnibus* system is still more remarkable than that of cabs. It is only about twenty or twenty-five years ago that one stage coach, and one only, ran from Paddington to the Bank. All the villages round London had in like manner their small array of slow coaches. In 1829 Mr. Shillibeer introduced the omnibus, a Parisian invention, in London, under an amount of opposition which nearly ruined the projector, while he was benefiting the public. His first omnibus ran from Charing Cross to Greenwich, and was drawn by three horses abreast; but the number two was soon adopted; and the stage-coach proprietors, unable to beat the omnibuses off the road, adopted them, and the system became firmly established. It was soon found that an omnibus, with its easy means of entrance and exit, is a very convenient vehicle in the public streets, where passengers enter and alight at various points along the route; and hence omnibuses have effected what the old stage coaches never did or could effect, viz., the establishment of cheap routes through all the principal commercial arteries of London. The fares became gradually settled at sixpence per passenger for any distance in and near London; but the last few years have witnessed a reduction to 3*d.* (recently 4*d.*), in respect to short distances.

The principle of competition has led to an instructive result in respect to metropolitan omnibuses. When each proprietor had only a few vehicles, he opposed, and was opposed by, his neighbours on all sides; and a scene of recklessness ensued which endangered the lives and limbs of passengers as well as pedestrians. But this has given way to large combinations or associations, in which each proprietor brings his contribution of vehicles and horses to the common stock, and agrees to obey certain rules laid down for the guidance of all. The result has been admirable. With a few exceptions here and there, the omnibus system is now conducted with a regularity, a precision, a civility, and a safety, which was never before equalled. Through the main avenues of London, especially the New Road, Holborn, and the Strand, omnibuses proceed every two or three minutes throughout the day. There have lately been omnibus maps published, in which there appears a surprising number of routes. There are at least two Associations or Companies, each of which possesses a hundred omnibuses, with considerably more than a thousand horses to work them. It has been found by experience, that to buy good horses, and to treat them well, is a more economical practice than the opposite system. Most of the horses employed in the Paddington and City trade (we believe about three thousand in number), make but one journey each a day in each direction.

Mr. Pownall has lately invented a *passenger-index* for omnibuses. It consists of an electric battery placed in the bottom framing of the vehicle, near the door. Every passenger on entering the omnibus steps upon an elastic spring, which acts upon the battery, and this in its turn acts upon an index or dial. At the end of a day's work, the machinery of the dial will shew how many times persons have entered and left the vehicle. Such is the theory of the apparatus; but there seem at first sight to be many difficulties in the way of its practical use. A new kind of omnibus has also been recently started, in which each passenger has a separate and distinct seat, and in which there are increased facilities for ascending to the roof of the vehicle.

ONYX. [AGATE.]

OOLITE is the characteristic rock of one of the great systems of secondary strata. The fine yellow *freestone* of Kettering, the *Bath freestone*, and the *Portland stone* are good examples of oolite; and these serve to illustrate the economic uses of the strata.

OPACITY is a condition of bodies by which they are incapable of transmitting light through them. According to Newton, it may arise from the unequal densities of the particles of certain substances, in consequence of which the rays of light on entering those substances suffer such refractions and reflexions as cause them to be finally absorbed. The scientific determination of this question, however, does not concern us here. As a circumstance of relative opacity or transparency, the quality of manufactured goods is often affected by it.

OPAL. Of this mineral, which is essentially a hydrate of silica, there are nearly a dozen varieties, named *Precious Opal*, *Fire Opal*, *Hydrophane*, *Common Opal*, *Semi-Opal*, *Wood Opal*, *Cacholong*, *Opal Jasper*, *Menilite*, *Hyalite* or *Muller's Glass*, and *Geyserite*. The varieties differ greatly in colour and transparency. The *Precious Opal* exhibits a beautiful play of colours.

OPHICLEIDE. This powerful musical instrument is made of brass or copper, and is intended to supersede the *Serpent*—of which it is a decided improvement—in the orchestra and in military bands. It is a conical tube, the longest nearly nine feet in length, terminating in a bell, like the horn. It has ten ventages, or holes, all of which are stopped by keys, similar to those of the bassoon, only of larger dimensions, and is furnished with the same kind of mouth-piece as the Serpent. The scale of the base Ophicleide is from B, the third space below the base staff, to C, the fifth added space above it, including every tone and semitone within this compass of three octaves and one note. The volume of sound it emits is immense, but the tone is rich and round, and blends well with the voices in choruses.

OPISOMETER. This name has been given to a recently-invented apparatus by Mr. Elliott, for measuring the length of roads, rivers, walls, &c., on maps and plans. There is a horizontal steel axle, which is cut with a screw-worm from end to end. On this is placed a wheel, which works along the screw like a nut. The axle is fixed to a convenient handle for holding. When a map or plan is laid down flat on a table, and a road or river is to be measured, the wheel is made to traverse carefully over the whole length of the tortuous line, following the windings as carefully as may be. This movement causes the wheel to shift its position on the screw; if it be at one end of the axle when the movement begins, it will have advanced a certain distance towards the other end by the time it is finished. If the wheel be now applied to a scale of miles or yards, or any other units on the map, and made to rotate in a *reverse* direction until it is brought back to its original position on the axial screw, it will determine the length of the road or river. The principle is strictly correct, and requires nothing but careful application.

OPIUM. This remarkable substance, which has had so much influence both on the commerce and the wars between England and China, is yielded by one species of plants of the genus *Papaver*. Of the 25 species of this genus, the *papaver somniferum*, or *white poppy*, which produces opium, is the most important. It is a native probably of Asia Minor, but, having been so long cultivated, it is found wild in many parts of Europe. There are two varieties of this species, both of which yield opium. The juice of the poppy seems to have been used on account of its narcotic powers from a very early period, first in the East, of which it is a native, and afterwards in the West.

The mode of collecting the opium in Asia Minor, is by puncturing the green capsule, and allowing the juice to exude, which is then scraped off, and deposited in small earthen vessels, and beat up with saliva. It is afterwards enveloped in dry leaves, and in this state is sold. In India the juice is mixed with oil obtained from the seed of the poppy, to hinder the rapid drying of the juice. The produce of the first incisions is of a light yellow colour; the others are fainter in odour and darker coloured. In general all three gatherings are mixed together, and sent to market in small baskets. The quantity obtained varies not only with the soil and mode of cultivation, but also with the season and the time of collecting. In wet, gloomy seasons, not only is the quantity less, but it does not keep well; in such a case the proportion of *morphia*, the active principle of the opium, is also less. The quantity of morphia depends likewise very much on the time of gathering; if the harvest be postponed till the capsules begin to turn white and hard, it is greatly deficient; and by the time the capsules are mature and the seeds ripe, it has entirely disappeared. It is not, as in the case of many of the vegetable alkaloids, transferred to the seeds, as they are altogether devoid of any narcotic principle, the oil which is obtained from them being bland and wholesome, and abundantly used as food.

The varieties of opium met with in commerce are—*Smyrna* or *Levant* opium; *Constantinople* opium; *Egyptian* or *Alexandrian* opium; *Trebizond* or *Persian* opium; *Indian* opium; and *English* opium. The chemical or organic constituents are extremely numerous, the most important being morphia. Good opium is not perfectly soluble in water; $\frac{1}{12}$th generally remains undissolved, consisting of the caoutchouc and resin. Constantinople opium however leaves no residuum of caoutchouc. It is very inflammable, and burns with a clear flame, and forms a transparent alcoholic solution: opium from the bruised capsules is not inflammable, and forms a turbid alcoholic solution.

The poppy is cultivated in many parts of Europe on account of its seeds, which yield a bland oil much esteemed in France. In England it is cultivated chiefly for the capsules, which are used medicinally. In India the cultivation takes place in the cold weather, that is, during the winter of Europe. The collecting of the opium is commenced very soon after the flowers fall, as the capsules rapidly enlarge.

It forms no part of our object here to trace the extraordinary effects of opium on the human system, nor the modes of preparation by which opium is converted into a valuable medicine. As an article of international commerce, there can be no question that opium caused the late war between England and China, however it might be disguised by other circumstances. India produces large quantities of opium, which the Chinese are willing to purchase for eating or smoking, or both; but the Chinese Government has never willingly sanctioned the purchase, and has often strictly prohibited it. By about the year 1831 the purchase of opium had become so large, that the sale of *tea* was insufficient to pay for it, and Chinese silver had to be paid to settle the balance. The Chinese authorities commenced a series of petty insults towards the English merchants at Canton, with a view to expel them altogether, if possible; and these insults gradually brought the attention of the British Government to that quarter. So matters continued for some years; the merchants persisted in bringing opium, which the Chinese people were ready to buy; the Emperor effected all he could to prevent the import; and the British Consul tried to hold the balance even between all parties. At length, in May 1839, the European factors were expelled from Canton, and all the opium in the ports, amounting to 20,283 chests, was seized by the Chinese authorities and destroyed. This gave rise to a war which lasted, on and off, for three years. The Chinese Emperor was compelled to pay the value of the opium destroyed.—There is a *moral* aspect in this opium war, which can never be quite satisfactory.

The consumption of opium in this country is comparatively small. The imports in the last three years were as follow:—

1848............200,019 lbs.
1849............105,724 ,,
1850............126,318 ,,

And of these quantities, about two-thirds were re-exported to other countries.

OPORTO. The principal trade of this Portuguese city is in port wine, which takes its distinctive name from the town. Oil, sumach, lemons, oranges, wool, refined sugar, cream of tartar, salt, leather, cork, &c., are also exported. The imports are—corn, rice, beef, woollen, cotton, iron, and hardware manufactures; salt fish, hemp, and flax; sugar, coffee, deals, &c. There are at Oporto some manufactories of hats, silks, linen stuffs, and pottery, besides ropewalks and dockyards, none of which however are in a thriving condition. The wine and brandy trade is a monopoly of the Oporto Wine Company. The export of wine is from 30,000 to 35,000 pipes annually; of this quantity four-fifths go to England. The customs duties of Oporto for the year ending June 30, 1849, amounted to 1,891,347 dollars.

OPTICAL INSTRUMENTS. Optics, as a science, forms no part of the subject of this volume. The chief among those delicate instruments, by which the science is brought within the range of practical operations, are briefly noticed under their proper headings [CAMERA LUCIDA; KALEIDOSCOPE; LENS; MAGIC LANTERN, MICROSCOPE; TELESCOPE; &c.] It is believed that one of the happy consequences of the removal of the duty on glass will be to enable manufacturers to produce glass better fitted than before for optical purposes; not that the amount of duty is of much importance in an expensive lens, but that the manufacturer was deterred from making experiments by the interference of the Excise with his freedom of operations.

ORANGES, LEMONS, CITRONS. There are several beautiful fruits belonging to the genus *Citrus*. Among these are the *sweet orange*, the *bitter orange*, the *lime*, the *shaddock*, the *lemon*, and the *citron;* and these again are divided into many varieties. Of the sweet orange there are the *China*, the *pear-shaped*, the *Nice*, the *blood-red*, the *ribbed*, the *sweet-skinned*, the *Mandarin*, the *St. Michael*, and several other kinds. Of the bitter orange there are also many kinds: such as the *horned*, the *curled leaf*, the *purple*, the *double flowered*, the *Seville*, and the *Bizarre* orange. The *China* orange is the common sort of our English markets, and of the Portuguese. The *sweet-skinned* orange is the *Pomme d' Adam*, or *forbidden fruit*, of the Paris shops. The *Mandarin* orange, in which the ripe pulp is completely loosened from the rind, is much cultivated in China and in Malta. The *St. Michael's* orange has small, round, pale yellow, seedless fruit, with a thin rind and an extremely sweet pulp. This, when in a state of perfection, is perhaps the most delicious of all the oranges, and it is by far the most productive. Great quantities are imported from the Azores, where it appears to be exclusively cultivated as an object of trade. It is said that 20,000 of these oranges have been picked from a single tree, exclusively of the large quantity which were blown down or rejected as unfit for sale. The *Seville* orange has an exceedingly bitter rind; in England it is employed in the manufacture of bitter tinctures, and in the preparation of candied orange peel; the bitter aromatic principle gives flavour to the liqueur called *Curaçoa*. The *bergamot* orange has a remarkable fragrance, and is employed in making an essence of delicious quality.

The *lime* has different varieties, according to the thickness of the rind; it is employed chiefly in flavouring punch, sherbet, and other drinks. The *shaddock* is among the largest fruits which are known, and is commonly cultivated both in the East and West Indies, for the sake of the delicate subacid juicy pulp in which it abounds. When shaddocks arrive at their greatest size they are called *pompoleons*, or *pompelmousses*. When at the smallest, they form the *forbidden fruit* of the English markets. Another small variety, with the shaddocks growing in clusters, forms a larger tree than any other citrus; the fruit is about as large as the fist; it is what the West Indians call the *grape-fruit*. The *lemon* does not present many varieties; its appearance and use are well known. The *citron*, grown chiefly in the east, is noticeable for the fragrance of the rind, from which a delicate sweetmeat is prepared.

Of the invaluable use of lemon juice or lime juice in the navy, due to the citric acid contained in the fruit, a little has been said under CITRIC ACID. In a commercial point of view, the orange trade has greatly benefitted by the introduction of steam-boats and railways. Oranges are brought in large quantities to Southampton, whence they are transmitted very quickly to London. During the last three years (1848, 1849, 1850) about 400,000 boxes or chests of oranges and lemons have been annually imported into this country.

ORCHARD. Apples, pears, and cherries are the fruits principally cultivated in orchards. The term orchard is likewise used to signify inclosures in which filberts or walnuts are grown. Orchards of apples and pears are more numerous, because more productive, on the old and new red sandstone formations than on any other strata. A very large proportion of all the cider and perry that is manufactured is grown upon these soils. The principal orchards of England are in Devonshire, Somersetshire, Gloucestershire, Herefordshire, and Worcestershire. For an orchard of apple-trees, a deep unctuous soil is selected, in a situation sheltered from the north and north-west winds, and open to the south and south-east; and a bank is preferable to a low spot. For pear orchards a lighter soil is desirable than for apples; the same rules may be observed for their planting and preservation. The principal cherry-orchards in England are in Buckinghamshire and Kent; from the latter county a large supply is sent to the London markets.

ORCHIL, or ORCHELLA, also written *Archil*, is the name of a dye as well as of the plant (one of the tribe of Lichens, or Rock-moss) which yields it. [ARCHIL.] It is often corrupted in commerce into *Rochilla Weed*. Several kinds are employed for the same purpose, which are distinguished according to the country from whence they are imported, and also by manufacturers into *Weed* and *Moss*, the former name being applied to the filiform lichens of botanists belonging to the genus *Roccella*, while the terms Moss and Rock-Moss are applied to the crustaceous lichens belonging to the genus *Lecanora*, which include the *Cudbear* and *Parelle* of dyers. *Dyers' Roccella*, or *Orchil*, and *Flat-Leaved Orchil*, are both found on maritime rocks, as well on the coast of England as of other parts of Europe, and also of Asia, Africa, and America. They are also found on dry stone walls exposed to the influence of the sea-breeze. The more arid the situation the better is the quality of the lichens. The presence of the colouring matter is ascertained by steeping the weed broken up in small pieces in diluted solution of ammonia, in a bottle half filled with liquid, which should be kept corked, but frequently opened in a temperature not exceeding 150° Fahrenheit.

ORDNANCE. All great guns used in war, such as cannons, carronades, howitzers, and mortars, are called by the general name of *ordnance.* The materials of which ordnance is formed are iron and brass, properly bronze, the latter metal being composed of copper and tin, in the proportion of from 8 to 12 parts of tin to 100 parts of copper. Iron guns are stronger than those made of brass, and consequently they are better able to resist the effects of the long-continued firing which takes place at the sieges of fortresses. Brass guns, on the other hand, being lighter, are more conveniently transported from place to place with troops in the field. Ordnance is now cast either in loam or in dry sand; a model, or pattern, of the gun being made of wood or brass, about which the mould is formed. In twelve hours after being cast the mould may be removed and the gun may be bored. Iron guns are cast from pig-metal of different qualities, which are melted together in order to produce a composition possessing only that degree of hardness which will permit the boring to be effected. Ordnance formed of cast-iron and of gun-metal being apt to run at the vent in consequence of the heat produced by rapid firing, the vent in guns of cast-iron is drilled in a bolt of wrought-iron, and in those of gun-metal in a bolt of pure copper; the bolts are then screwed into the pieces for which they were intended.

The length of a cannon is divided into six parts:—That which is behind the base ring (the ring of greatest diameter) at the larger end is called the *cascable;* and from the base ring to the next mouldings towards the smaller end, is the *vent-field.* The two succeeding portions, separated from one another by a moulding, are called the first and second *reinforce;* and near the extremity of the latter are situated the *trunnions,* two cylinders at right angles to the axis of the gun, and by which it rests on its carriage. From the second reinforce moulding to another near the smaller extremity of the gun is the *chase,* and the last portion is called the *muzzle.* The hollow of the gun is called the *bore,* and the diameter of the bore is designated the *calibre* of the piece. It has of late been found practicable to diminish considerably the quantity of metal in iron guns; and for this purpose some of the ordnance then existing was *reamed-up* (scraped out), so as to bring each kind of gun to the next highest calibre. Thus the old iron 6-pounders have been converted into 9-pounders; 18-pounders into 24-pounders, and so on. The application of locks to naval ordnance was introduced by Sir Charles Douglas, and their efficiency has since been fully recognised. A lock carrying two flints, invented by Lieut.-Gen. Sir Howard Douglas, in 1818, was afterwards introduced, and percussion locks are now much used in the British service.

The following are the lengths and weights of different kinds of iron and brass ordnance, known by particular names :—

Iron Ordnance.	Length.		Weight.
	ft.	in.	cwt.
13-inch mortar, sea-service	3	$0\frac{1}{2}$	$36\frac{1}{3}$
10-inch do. land-service	2	4	$16\frac{1}{2}$
8-inch do. do.	1	$10\frac{1}{2}$	$8\frac{3}{4}$
$5\frac{1}{2}$-inch do. do.	1	3	$2\frac{1}{2}$
$4\frac{2}{5}$-inch do. do.	1	$0\frac{1}{4}$	$1\frac{1}{2}$
10-inch howitzer do.	5	0	41
8-inch do. do.	4	9	21
Monk's 56-pr. gun do.	11	0	97
Millar's 10-inch gun do.	9	4	84
8-inch gun, sea-service	9	0	65
32-pr. gun, land-service	9	6	56
24-pr. do. do.	9	6	48
18-pr. do. do.	9	0	42
12-pr. do. do.	9	0	34
32-pr. carronade, sea-service	4	0	17
24-pr. do. do.	3	7	13
18-pr. do. do.	3	4	10
12-pr. do. do.	2	8	$6\frac{3}{4}$
Brass Ordnance.			
9-pr. gun, land-service	8	0	$13\frac{1}{2}$
6-pr. do. do.	5	0	6
3-pr. do. mountain-service	3	0	$2\frac{1}{2}$

The *carriages* for ordnance are of several kinds, according to the nature of the gun or the manner in which it is employed. Field *gun-carriages* consist of two cheeks, or side pieces, of elm, firmly attached together by transoms, and resting on the axle-tree of the wheels; the trail, consisting of a solid piece of oak, is firmly attached at one end to the side pieces, near the axle, and its other extremity rests on the ground when the gun is in a state for action. The limber is a bed, with shafts, mounted on two wheels, and carrying two ammunition boxes for the service of the gun; the horses are harnessed to the limber, and the gun with its carriage is drawn after the limber. An ammunition waggon also accompanies each piece of ordnance, and there are others always in reserve. Field *howitzer-carriages* and their limbers are similar to those just mentioned, but stronger, and the cheeks of the carriage are farther asunder. The travelling carriages for *siege-ordnance* are made wholly of oak, and the limber carries no ammunition. Carriages for *garrison service* and for the *navy* consist of two short cheeks or brackets, connected by transoms, and they move on four truck-wheels. *Mortars* are placed upon solid beds of wood or iron, which are made as heavy as is consistent with the power of transporting them from place to place, for the sake of obtaining steadiness when the piece is fired.

OREGRUND IRON. A little information concerning the valuable oregrund or Swedish iron will be found under STEEL MANUFACTURE.

ORES. The ores of the principal metals, and the processes whereby the extraction of the valuable constituent is managed, are described under the names of the metals themselves. [COPPER, IRON, LEAD, MERCURY, &c.]

ORGAN. This is incontestibly the noblest of musical instruments, whether considered in regard to the grandeur and beauty of its sounds, the variety of its powers, or the sacred purposes to which it is usually dedicated. It consists of a vast number of metallic and wooden pipes, divided into different *stops*, the wind being admitted into the pipes from a bellows. It is played on by means of a keyboard.

It must have been early discovered that air may be forced into a closed cavity, and then distributed at will into one or more tubes; and pursuing the contrivance a little further, something like a modern organ was likely to be produced. That an instrument similar in principle, though not in details, to the modern organ, was known in very early times, there is abundant evidence to show. The period when the organ was introduced into the churches of Western Europe is very uncertain. Pope Vitalian is supposed to have been the first to admit the instrument, about the year 670; but the earliest account, to be at all relied on, of the introduction of this instrument in the West is, that about the year 755 the Greek emperor Copronymus sent one as a present to Pepin, King of France. In the time of Charlemagne however organs became common in Europe. Before the 10th century they were not only common in England, but of large size. They were however very rude in construction, and extremely limited in means. The keys were four or five inches broad, and must have been struck by the clenched hand, in the manner of the carrilons: the pipes were of brass, harsh in sound, and the compass did not exceed a dozen or fifteen notes in the 12th century; and to accompany the plain-chant no more were required. About that time half notes were introduced at Venice, where also the important addition of pedals or foot-keys, was made in 1470.

Most of the early English organs were destroyed by the Puritans. The tone of the pipes of the old builders—depending on what is technically called the *voicing*—has never been excelled by later makers; but in point of *touch*, and mechanism generally, the moderns are much superior to their predecessors. In mechanical skill and delicate finishing the English organ-builders far surpass their continental rivals, while in tone they at least equal them.

The following are some of the largest foreign organs:—

	Stops.	Pipes.
Seville cathedral	100	5330
Goerlitz, in Upper Lusatia	82	3270
Hamburg, St. Michael's..	67	
Amsterdam, the old church	64	
Weingarten, in Suabia ...	60	6666
Rotterdam (150 feet high)		5500
Tours cathedral	60	
Haarlem...............	60	5000

Among the principal organs in England are those of York Minster, Birmingham Town-hall, St. Paul's Cathedral, Westminster Abbey, Exeter Hall, Christ's Hospital, and Mr. Willis's noble organ at the Great Exhibition. See also APOLLONICON.

The mechanism of the organ is complicated. The *principle* of it is—that when the finger of the player presses down a key, or the foot presses down a pedal, a valve opens the lower end of a pipe or pipes, into which air rushes from a chamber wherein it has been condensed by bellows. The length and form of each pipe are so arranged that it may yield a certain definite note. Each *stop* is a particular set of pipes, differing in pitch, but all having the same character of sound. Some stops imitate the flute sound, some the trumpet sound, and so on. It is the combination of many stops with many octaves of notes that gives rise to the large number of pipes in an organ.

The *barrel-organ* is an instrument by which most of the effects of a small keyed-organ are produced by certain machinery. Instead of keys for the fingers, the keys, if so they may be called, are inside the organ, and acted on by means of a cylinder, or barrel, *pinned*, or studded, in a particular and singularly curious manner. This barrel is made to revolve by a winch, and in those of an expensive kind by wheel-work, moved by a spring.

Under AUTOPHON, it is stated that Mr. Dawson's ingenious contrivance called by that name is an appendage to the barrel organ; whereas it should have mentioned that the autophon is the complete instrument itself.

It is a self-acting organ, in which a handle regulates—not the motion of a barrel with pins on its surface—but the admission of air through holes in a perforated card. It will play as many tunes as there are cards provided, without limit; and as the cards are sold at 6*d*. each, a player with no more skill than is required to turn a handle regularly can play a range of music, either sacred or secular, to which there is (or need be) no assignable limit.

The organ builders of England and the Continent justly think that the present is a fitting opportunity for showing the power of the noblest of instruments in the noblest of exhibition rooms. The east and west ends of the Palace of Industry each contains one of the finest specimens of modern organ-building—the one English and the other foreign; while the north and south transepts have organs of somewhat smaller dimensions.

ORIEL. This term is applied to that particular kind of bay-window which is made to project from the upper story of a building. The distinction therefore between a *bay* and an *oriel* is this: by the former is understood a projecting window, or rather a projection pierced with window openings in its entire width, and rising immediately from the ground, whether it be confined to the lower part of the building or carried up through one or more stories above the ground-floor; whereas an oriel is a bay which does not descend to the ground, but is suspended over the face of the wall beneath it. Bays generally terminate in either a plain or embattled parapet; but oriels are for the most part made to show some sort of roof, either rising behind or resting upon the mouldings which serve as their cornice. Occasionally this roof or crown is rendered an ornamental part of the design, and terminated by some kind of finish.

ORLÉANS is one of the old manufacturing towns of France. The chief manufactures are—hosiery for exportation to the Levant, refined sugar, vinegar, bleached wax, blankets, and counterpanes. To these articles of manufacture must be added cotton and woollen yarn, fine woollen cloths, flannels, hats, files, rasps, and other tools, glue, leather, tin ware, and earthenware. There are numerous breweries and dyehouses. Trade is carried on in the above articles, and in wine, brandy, corn, flour, wool, hides, iron, salt, hoops, dye-stuffs, saffron, fire-wood, timber, oak planks, coals, groceries, and spices. Its situation on the Loire, which is navigated by small steamers, and communicates with the Seine by means of canals, and on the railway, to which the lines connecting Bourdeaux, Nantes, and the centre and South of France with Paris converge,—renders Orléans the centre of a very considerable commerce and of a large transit trade.

ORPIMENT is a yellow *sulphuret of arsenic*. The finest specimens come from Persia, in brilliant yellow masses, of a lamellar structure. Artificial orpiment is manufactured in Saxony by subliming a mixture of sulphur and white arsenic; it is a yellow compact opaque mass, of a glassy aspect; it affords a pale yellow powder. The finest kind of orpiment is prepared into a yellow pigment for artists, while the coarser varieties are used as a colouring substance for house-painting and other purposes.

ORRERY. This name has been applied to four different kinds of machines for representing the phenomena of the solar system. A *planetarium* exhibits the orbital motion of the planets about the sun; a *tellurian* and *lunarian*, when combined, exhibit, respectively, the motion of the earth about the sun, and of the moon about the earth; and a *satellite machine* exhibits the motion of Jupiter's satellites about their primary. Planetary machines were in use at a very remote period, and appear to have consisted for many centuries of moveable spheres having the earth in their centre. In the 17th century Huyghens and Roemer employed themselves in the construction of planetary machines in conformity with the Copernican doctrine. Roemer also invented a satellite machine prior to the year 1679. In England, about the year 1700, Mr. George Graham constructed a machine which exhibited the motion of the earth about the sun, while the moon revolved about the earth; one of these machines was made for the Earl of Orrery, from which circumstance the term Orrery originated. A large planetarium was, in 1801, made for the Royal Institution of London, and a more complete instrument was constructed by Dr. Pearson in 1813.

To produce the revolution of the planetary bodies about the sun, a system of vertical concentric tubes is usually employed, which are adjusted very near to each other, but yet so far removed as not to influence each other's motion. These tubes are of different lengths, the innermost being the longest, and to the superior extremity of each a radius or projecting wire is attached, and thereby made to revolve once during each revolution of the tube. The lower extremities of the tubes form the arbors or axes of as many toothed-wheels, which are either immediately driven by pinions adjusted to a verticle axle called the "annual arbor," or derive their motions indirectly from those pinions by means of an interposed train of wheels. The determination of the relative number of teeth which must be given to the wheels and pinions, in order to produce the required motion, depends upon the relative velocities of the motion to be imitated; and here the machinist must depend upon the astronomer. As an aid to astronomical studies, orreries are less highly estimated than they formerly were.

OSIER is the name given to various species of *Salix* or *Willow*, employed in basket-making on account of their tough flexible shoots. [BASKET-MAKING; WILLOW.]

OSMAZOME. This name has been given to a spirituous extract of meat. According to the experiments of Chevreul, osmazome contains a peculiar substance, to which he has given the name of *créatin;* but the chemistry of this subject is yet very little known.

O'SMIUM. This metal was discovered by Mr. Tennant, in the year 1803, in the grains of native platinum. It is white, with a bluish gray tint. It may be reduced to leaves. Its specific gravity is 10. It is unalterable in the air at common temperatures, but if strongly heated it oxidizes. This very peculiar metal forms several compounds with oxygen, chlorine, and sulphur; but none of them are of much importance.

OSTRICH FEATHERS. There are many uses which this noble bird renders to man, in the hot countries which the ostrich inhabits. The flesh when young is good and palatable. The eggs are considered a great delicacy, especially when eaten with butter. In the luxurious suppers of the wealthy Romans, in the time of the Emperors, the brains of Ostriches formed a favourite dish.

But it is for the feathers that these birds are chiefly valued. [FEATHERS]. The Africans who hunt the ostrich for the sake of the feathers proceed systematically to their work. They hunt on horseback, and begin the pursuit by a gentle gallop; for should they, at the outset, be rashly eager, the ostrich would start off at such a speed as would carry him wholly beyond reach of his hunter; but when the pace is more steady, the ostrich makes no particular effort to escape. It does not go in a direct line, but wavers from one side to the other; and this enables the hunter to save distance. The chase often continues several days, at the end of which time the strength of the ostrich becomes exhausted, and he yields. The feathers on which value is placed are chiefly those of the tail; and the hunters are careful not to disfigure these in the process of capture.

OTTER SKINS, are employed, but only to a small extent, in this country; or rather they are imported by the Hudson's Bay Company, and re-exported to the Continent. About 15,000 were so imported in 1848.

OVENS. The general character of ovens will be found sufficiently explained under BREAD, FURNACE, and STOVES.

OXALIC ACID. This acid was discovered by Scheele, in 1776, in the *Wood Sorrel*, *Common Sorrel*, and other plants. The crystals of oxalic acid are prismatic, colourless, and transparent; the primary form is a right rhombic prism. The taste is extremely sour; and the crystals are very poisonous. Oxalic acid is the most highly oxygenated of all the vegetable acids, and is also the most rapid and certainly fatal of any which are capable of being crystallised. As the crystals are not unlike those of the Sulphate of Magnesia, or Epsom Salts, mistakes between the two are of very frequent occurrence. Being likewise much used in the arts, and commonly known by the name of *Acid of Sugar*, it is taken either accidentally, or under the supposition that it is akin to sugar, and therefore pleasant and innocent. This acid, and the salts obtained by its combination with bases, are employed to a limited extent in the arts.

OXFORDSHIRE. This county may be reckoned amongst the most productive agricultural counties of England; and some of the land is of a quality which can scarcely be surpassed anywhere. The red land is partly in old grass, in which state it is very valuable, and partly cultivated as arable land. The low lands in the valleys through which the rivers flow are in many places covered with the finest herbage, and maintain much cattle. The course of crops on the light loams is based on the Norfolk rotation, but generally with the addition of an extra crop or two after the wheat, such as beans and oats. The cultivation of sainfoin on the chalky loams is one of the great resources of the farmers on such soils, and is much appreciated in this county. The meadows in this county which lie along the banks of the rivers are productive of excellent herbage; and the hay of some of the upland meadows cannot be surpassed.

Oxfordshire is not a manufacturing county. In the city of *Oxford* itself, such manufactures alone are carried on as are indispensable to the daily wants of a somewhat wealthy and luxurious city. *Burford* has diminished in wealth and importance from the decay of the coarse woollen manufacture and the malting business, which once flourished there, and from the diminished traffic along the line of road which passes through the town. At *Witney* wool-stapling is extensively carried on, and there is a considerable malt trade. The manufacture of blankets—for which the place has been long celebrated—still continues to flourish. At *Woodstock* the only manufacture is that of gloves, which, though it has declined of late years, is still carried on to a considerable extent.

OXYGEN. The properties of this most remarkable elementary body are best known in its elastic or aëriform state, in which it is termed *Oxygen Gas*. The discovery of this important substance was made by Dr. Priestley in 1774, and somewhat later independently by Scheele. To this gas Dr. Priestley gave the name of *dephlogisticated air*, Scheele called it *empyreal air*, and Condorcet *vital air*. Lavoisier gave it the name of *oxygen*, which it still retains. Dr. Priestley first procured this gaseous body by heating the binoxide of mercury in an air-jar over mercury, by means of a lens, and he afterwards obtained it from other substances. It is now prepared in various ways, according to the purposes to which it is intended to be applied.

Oxygen possesses great power of combination with other elementary bodies, there being scarcely one with which it is not known to combine either by direct union or indirect chemical action. The compounds to which it gives rise by combining, for example, with certain metals, and also indeed with some other bodies, may be classed under the three heads of *Oxides*, *Acids*, and *Alkalies*. There are many bodies which, by a moderate degree of oxidation, become first oxides, and by an increased degree, acids; such substances are charcoal, phosphorus, chromium, &c.

Oxygen Gas is devoid of colour, taste, or smell. It is transparent and invisible. It possesses the mechanical properties of common air. It is capable of being respired, and a given volume of it will support life much longer than an equal bulk of common air. It is heavier than atmospheric air, 100 cubic inches at a medium temperature and pressure weighing 34·4 grains, whereas an equal volume of atmospheric air weighs 31 grains. It is but slightly soluble in water, requiring about 27 times its bulk for solution. Light has no effect upon this gas. By heat, like all gaseous bodies, it is merely expanded. The most remarkable property of oxygen gas is the facility and splendour with which bodies, when previously ignited, burn in it; substances which do not undergo combustion in the air, will readily do so, and with great brilliancy, in oxygen gas. Iron, for example, burns very readily in it when previously made red-hot.

Until after the discovery of oxygen nothing was or could be known respecting the nature of the air, of water, or of earth, all of which, formerly reckoned as elementary bodies, are now known to be compound, and to contain oxygen as one of their constituents. It has also thrown great and unexpected light on the nature of combustion and respiration.

The principal compounds which oxygen forms with metals and other elementary bodies, are briefly treated under their respective heads. To notice the useful purposes subserved in the arts by oxygen is neither necessary nor possible; since it takes part, in some way or other, with every combination and every process.

OYSTER TRADE. The management of the oyster fishery presents many peculiar features. The best kind of oysters in this country are the small variety called *Natives*; they are found in the rivers Colne, Medway, and Swale; or rather, they are really French oysters, the produce of the coast of Normandy, whence the spat or spawn is gathered, and laid down on the oyster beds in the Essex and Kent rivers. The spawn, when first cast, somewhat resembles in appearance a drop of suet; it is composed of an immense number of minute oysters, each of which becomes about a quarter of an inch long in three days, as large as a shilling in three months, as a half crown in six months, and as a crown in twelve months. The oyster is found in the seas of most countries, but never at any great depth, and seldom far from the mouth of a river. The fishing for oysters is permitted from the first of September to the end of April.

So far as regards the London supply, the oysters are brought principally from the Essex coast and rivers; but the Milton oysters are most highly esteemed. None are sent from the north of England; but broods are sent from thence to be fattened in Kent and Sussex. The sale at Billingsgate is enormous; it is estimated to average, in ordinary years, about 300,000 bushels, of 4 pecks to a bushel, and 400 oysters to a peck; amounting to nearly five hundred million oysters. A remarkable feature is now being developed in the oyster trade. At Southampton there is a wide margin of muddy shore at low water. A Company has leased part of this shore as an oyster bed. Oysters are brought from the Jersey fishery, laid down on those beds to fatten, turned and attended to every day, taken up when wanted, opened, placed in tin cans, and sent up to London by railway. These oysters are used for pickles and sauces, and not eaten in the ordinary way. A tramway extends from the South-Western Railway to the oyster beach, so that the dispatch of the oysters is very rapidly managed. An electro-telegraphic message can be sent at any hour, and a supply of filled oyster-cans transmitted to London with a rapidity which sets all former doings at defiance. The oysters are sent without their shells, to save freight; there is a corps of oyster-openers in the service of the company.

The opening of an oyster, like many other simple operations, has been brought within the scope of machinery. M. Picault, of Paris, invented an oyster-opener in 1849. It consists of an apparatus something like an ordinary pair of sugar nippers; but pointed together at the top of the curved part instead of the bottom. One of the curved parts is made hollow, or indented, to receive the front edge of the oyster, which is placed therein with the flat shell uppermost; while the other part is fitted with a curved knife, which, when the handles are brought together, enters the hinge of the shells, separates them, and, severs the oyster from the flat shell, which then falls into the deep one. One of the sides may be made a fixture, supported on a standard, if deemed necessary.

P

PACKING. It is worthy of note, as it illustrates the immensity of the manufacturing operations in Lancashire and the West Riding (especially the former), that the trade of a packer is one for which there is constant demand, and which is conducted on a large scale. The packing of bales of goods for the London and provincial markets, and for shipment to foreign parts, requires great skill, to enclose the greatest mass in the smallest space, and to enable the bale to bear any ordinary amount of rough usage without yielding. The cases or wrappers are of strong canvas, and the bands for binding are often strips of hoop-iron instead of rope. The case, the bands, and the goods are placed in their proper position upon or within a peculiarly shaped hydraulic press; and when the mass has been brought by intense pressure into a cubical form, the fastenings are secured before the pressure is removed. In the earlier stages of this system, the hydraulic presses were worked by hand; but on such a scale of magnitude are the operations of the Manchester packers now conducted, that this is too slow a method; steam-power is applied. There are perhaps few operations conducted in our manufacturing districts more illustrative of economy of power, than this employment of hydraulic presses to supersede the old screw presses; and the working of the hydraulic presses by steam instead of manual power.

PADLOCK. [Locks and Keys.]

PADUA, is one of those rich provinces, the produce and industry of which are briefly noticed under Lombardy.

PAGODA is a name applied by Europeans to temples in the East, from China to Hindustan. These structures generally consist of a porch, a vestibule or ante-sanctuary for the priests, and an inner sanctuary, containing the principal idol. Some of the Chinese pagodas are elevated upon a terrace, and consist of two stories, the lowermost surrounded by a peristyle of columns. Others are lofty towers in several stories, diminishing in height and width as they ascend. The Hindoo pagodas are of a pyramidal form.

PAINTING. As a question of high art, of genius, of expression, or even as a means of copying the every day scenes of nature, painting is beyond the province of this volume. And as a mechanical operation we have very little to say concerning it. The preparation of the canvas and the panels is simple; and the management of the colours and the brushes is superior only in degree, not in nature, to that of mere house-painting. A few words are said concerning different kinds of painting, in respect to technical differences, under Enamels, Encaustic, Fresco, and Miniatures; while the chief working materials are adverted to under Brush, Colours, Crayons, Oil Colours, Pencils, and the names of the chief colouring substances.

In respect to *house-painting*, it is executed either in *oil* or *distemper*. In *oil* the principal tools employed are brushes, made of hogs' bristles for large surfaces, and sash tools made of finer hair for small work, as mouldings, window-bars, &c. White lead is used for white colour; it is also the basis of all ordinary colours. The colouring substances in general use are earths, umber, ochre, Siena, Venetian red, purple, brown, &c. The first three are sometimes burnt, a process which reddens and darkens them. Metallic compounds are red lead, vermillion, Prussian blue, chrome yellow, verdigris, Brunswick green, verditer, &c., &c. Animal and vegetable colours are lakes, indigo, ivory black, and lamp-black. The liquids in use are linseed oil (sometimes boiled with litharge to render it drying, and hence called *boiled oil*), and oil or spirits of turpentine, called *turps*. These are combined for use in various proportions, according to circumstances: when the paint is required to bear a gloss, or is intended for outside work, most oil is used; and for black, chocolate colour, green, &c., outside, boiled oil alone, or with a very little turps, is best. For *flatting*, which has no gloss, turps alone is requisite. To all paint a little sugar of lead, or litharge, is added to make it dry quickly.

In painting in *distemper*, the brushes for large surfaces differ from those used in oil: they are wider and flatter, and are termed distemper-brushes; but the tools for small work are similar. Whiting takes the same place in this branch that white lead holds in oil; the colouring substances are similar, but ground in water, and the fluids are water and melted size.

PAISLEY, though far from being a handsome town, ranks the third in Scotland in respect to population and commercial importance, solely on account of its manufactures. In 1707 the principal articles made in the town were coarse linen, chequered cloths, and Bengals, to which succeeded chequered linen handkerchiefs, and goods of a lighter texture, such as lawns. About 1725 the machinery for making white sewing or ounce thread was introduced from Holland. About 1760 the manufacture of silk gauze was introduced upon the plan practised by the Spitalfields houses, and, during the greater part of the following 30 years, was carried on upon a very extensive scale. The reduction in the cost of cotton goods, consequent upon the invention of Arkwright's spinning machinery, lessened the demand for silken fabrics, the manufacture of which at Paisley has since then greatly declined.

Many of the principal establishments of Paisley are now exclusively engaged in the various branches of the cotton manufacture, among which the muslin branch may be particularly mentioned as that of which Paisley is regarded as the chief seat. A considerable portion of the yarn used in making the finer qualities of muslins is imported from Lancashire. Crape dresses and damask and embroidered shawls are also manufactured to a great extent. There are also brass and iron foundries, breweries, distilleries, bleach-fields, &c.

In the report of the School of Design for 1850 it is stated that the branch school at Paisley is gradually shewing beneficial results in the muslin and shawl departments. In the patterns for embroidered muslins a more correct and graceful style of drawing is visible in those executed by pupils of the school.

A few details concerning the shawl trade of Paisley, now one of the most important—perhaps *the* most important—in the town, will be found under SHAWL MANUFACTURE.

PALANQUIN is a kind of covered litter carried, by means of poles, upon the shoulders of men, which forms the principal vehical for personal transport in Hindustan.

The system of *dâk* travelling in India is by means of palanquins. The palanquin bearers are provided by the government postmasters. When Bishop Heber was travelling from Calcutta to Benares he hired a set of palanquin bearers, twelve in number; his clothes and writing-desk were placed in two wicker boxes, which one man carried slung on a bamboo across his shoulders. So cheap is human labour in India, that the bishop paid only twelve shillings for the services of the twelve men for each stage, a distance of eight or ten miles. Only four men put their shoulders to a palanquin at a time; but the services of the others are often required on the wretched roads of India.

PALIMPSEST MANUSCRIPTS illustrate in a remarkable way the money value of paper and printing, as shewn by the want of them in past times. Palimpsest manuscripts are manuscripts from which the original writing has been erased or washed out, and which have been then written on again. This practice is as old as the time of Cicero, as appears from a letter of his to Trebatius in which he praises his friend for having been so economical as to write on a palimpsest, but says that he should like to know what those writings could have been which were considered of less importance than a letter. The scarcity and expense of parchment, and the demand for the writings of the fathers and books of devotion in the middle ages, frequently induced the monks to erase or wash out the writings of the classical authors to make room for those of the fathers. In many cases however they did not obliterate entirely the ancient writing; aud a careful examination of some of these palimpsest MSS. has led to the discovery of valuable works and fragments of the classical authors; among the rest one of the works of Cicero.

PALLA'DIUM. This metal was discovered by the late Dr. Wollaston in the grains of native platinum, in the year 1803. Palladium is of a grayish white colour; it is very malleable, and slightly elastic. It is almost as difficult of fusion as platinum, and does not oxidize by exposure to the air.

This metal forms alloys, most of which are brittle, with arsenic, iron, bismuth, lead, tin, copper, silver, platinum and gold; the alloy with nickel is ductile. Palladium, when fused with six parts of gold, destroys its colour; and this alloy was proposed by Dr. Wollaston for the graduated part of the mural circle of the Greenwich Observatory. Palladium combines with most of the simple substances; and its oxide forms salts with acids; but only a few of these compounds have become practically useful.

PALMS: PALM OIL. There is scarcely a species of palm in which some useful property is not found. The cocoa-nut, the date, and others are valued for their fruit; the fan-palm and many more, for their foliage, whose hardness and durability render it an excellent material for thatching; the sweet juice of the palmyra when fermented yields wine; the centre of the sago-palm abounds in nutritive starch; the trunk of the *Iriartea* or *Ceroxylon* exudes a valuable vegetable wax; oil is expressed in abundance from the oil-palm; an astringent matter resembling dragon's blood is produced by *Calamus Draco*; many of the species contain within their leaves a kind of fibrous matter, so hard and tough that it is manufactured into cordage; and finally, their trunks are in some cases valued for their strength and used as timber, or for their elasticity, or their flexibility, as in the cane-palm.

Of these varied products, *palm-oil* is that, perhaps, which has of late acquired most commercial importance in this country. It is obtained from the oil-palm of Guinea, cultivated in the western part of Africa. The fruit of this tree is about the size of a pigeon's egg, with its outer fleshy covering of a golden yellow colour. The oil is obtained by bruising the fleshy part of the fruit and subjecting the bruised paste to boiling water in wooden mortars; an oil of an orange yellow colour separates, which cools to the consistence of butter, and has, when fresh, the smell of violets. Africans use this oil in cooking, and for anointing the body. When imported into England, palm-oil is used in soap making, candle making, perfumery and medicine. Although liquid in the warm climate of Africa, it is solid in our climate; and the mode adopted for extracting it from the casks is to place the cask over a trough with the bunghole downwards, and to pass a steam pipe into it, by which means the palm-oil is brought to a liquid state. The large imports of palm-oil are noticed under OILS.

PANAMA TRANSIT. One of the most interesting and important enquiries now in progress, concerning the formation of a highway of nations, is the choice of a route across the Isthmus of Panama from the Atlantic to the Pacific. This isthmus connects North with South America. Since the acquisition of portions of Oregon and California by the United States, it has become a matter of high importance to obtain easy access to those far distant regions. The only ship route is round Cape Horn; and this carries the traveller so far southward, that the distance is far more than double what it would be if a passage across the isthmus could be made. Washington and San Francisco are about in the same latitude; but in the ship-route from one to the other, the mariner has to go 95 degrees of latitude southward along the Atlantic, and then 95 degrees northward along the Pacific; whereas if the isthmus could be cut across near Panama, the southing and northing would each be less than 30 degrees. Whether from England, from New York, or from New Orleans, the saving of distance by the Panama route to Oregon and California would be enormous.

But it is not simply in relation to those two regions that the Panama route would become important. The wide spreading Pacific, with its islands and coasts, would be brought within easier reach of the Anglo-Saxon race. The Sandwich Islands, New Zealand, Borneo, Australia, China—all are becoming every year more commercially important; all would be nearer to the United States by the Panama route than any other; and some would be nearer to England than by the existing routes. The same West India Mail which now renders so much service would be available for the ocean mail of the Pacific.

The desirability of a Panama passage being conceded, it became a matter of importance to decide on the best mode of effecting it. In the long string of land which connects North with South America, there are three or four places where the land from ocean to ocean is less in distance than at any other points. The narrowest part is from Chagres to Panama, near South America; a little farther north is a spot where the Lake of Nicaragua occupies the middle of the isthmus, with a river flowing from it into the Atlantic; while still farther north, at Tehuantepec, a river which flows into the Atlantic springs from a point very near another river which flows into the Pacific. All these three have been proposed as sites for canal or railway communication. The Panama route is to have a railway; it was commenced in 1849, and is now in process of formation. The Tehuantepec route is also to have a railway; or rather, the Mexican government is endeavouring to foster a company having this object in view; but there are many reasons for doubting whether this will be carried out. Meanwhile the Nicaragua route is that in which most energy is being displayed. At the Atlantic mouth of the river St. Juan de Nicaragua is Greytown, held by the British as a sort of guardianship over the black King of Mosquito; from this steamers ascend to a certain point up the St. Juan; after which a short land passage brings the traveller to the Lake, whence two routes are marked out to the Pacific. Whether the engineering and commercial difficulties will ever permit a ship canal to be constructed, through which a laden vessel from England or the United States might pass across the isthmus, time alone can shew. Probabilities seem to be against such a supposition. If the Panama Railway be finished, with a tolerable harbour at each extremity, two sets of steamers, an Atlantic line and a Pacific line, would be formed, and there would be two shiftings of mails and luggage (a debarkation and an embarkation) at the isthmus. This great enterprise would be intended, in the first instance for mails and passengers: merchant cargoes will long continue to use the old ocean-routes.

PANORA'MA. This name is given to a picture showing a view completely around the spectator. This ingenious pictorial contrivance was first devised by an English artist, Robert Barker, about the year 1794; and is not so much a new mode of painting—the process itself being similar to scene-painting or in distemper—as a novel application of it. Contrary to the diorama [DIORAMA], the panorama forms the surface of a hollow cylinder or rotunda, in the centre of which is a detached circular platform for the spectators, covered overhead to conceal the skylight, and thereby increase the illusion and give greater effect to the painting itself. The view is not painted on the walls but upon canvas, like the scenes of a theatre, and afterwards fixed up, in order that the picture may be changed. The subjects generally chosen are views of cities, or interesting sites, whose entire locality and buildings may thus be vividly placed before the eye, in a manner no less instructive than interesting.

PANTHE'ON. This celebrated monument of Roman art consists of a rotunda with a noble Corinthian octastyle portico attached to it, and resembles in its general mass the Colosseum in the Regent's Park, London, except that the body of the latter building is a polygon of sixteen sides, and its portico (a Grecian Doric hexastyle) is only a single intercolumn in depth. After being robbed of its rich ornaments, gilded bronze-work, and statues, it was consecrated as a Christian church in the seventh century. It is by far the largest circular structure of ancient times, the external diameter being 188 feet; and the height of the summit of the upper cornice 102 feet, exclusive of the flat dome, which makes the entire height about 148 feet. The portico, 103 feet wide, is octastyle, but there are in all 16 columns. The columns are 47 English feet high, with bases and capitals of white marble, and granite shafts, each formed of a single piece. The interior diameter is 142 feet, the thickness of the wall being 23 feet through the piers, between the exhedræ or recesses, which, including that of the entrance, are eight in number. The dome has a circular opening in the centre, 23 feet in diameter, which lights the interior completely.

PANTOGRAPH, sometimes improperly written *Pentograph*, is an instrument for copying maps, plans, and other drawings. It is formed of certain rules or bars jointed to each other, with tubes, in which may be fitted a tracer and a pencil. The copy may be made of the same size as the original or smaller, as one fourth, one half, or in any other proportion. There are different forms of the instrument.

PAPER HANGINGS. The word *Hangings* was originally and properly applied to the woven or embroidered tapestry with which the walls of apartments were covered. From the time necessary for their production, these were too costly for any classes but the wealthy. About 200 years ago, however, a mode was devised of printing or painting a pattern on sheets of paper, and pasting them against the walls of a room. These are Paper-Hangings, and they have greatly contributed to the comfort and cleanliness of domestic apartments.

There are three modes of producing the required device:—1. Wooden blocks are carved representing in relief the outlines of the figure; an impression is taken from these blocks, and the device is completed by painting with a pencil. 2. A sheet of paper, leather, tin, or copper, is cut out into the required device, and laid on the paper to be stained; a brush, dipped in a coloured pigment, and worked over the surface of the perforated plate, conveys the pigment through all the perforations, and forms a pattern on the paper. 3. A block is carved for each of the colours to be employed, and an impression from all the blocks in succession fills up the design on the paper. The first of these modes is too slow and costly for ordinary use; the second produces imperfect outlines, and is now chiefly employed, under the name of *Stencilling*, to paint a pattern on the plaster walls of a room, without using paper-hangings; the third is the mode almost exclusively employed at the present day. Each block is furnished with small pins at the corners, by the aid of which the successive impressions are made to correspond properly. As many as seven or eight colours are sometimes employed in one pattern, and, generally speaking, there must be as many blocks as there are colours.

Progress is, however, now being made towards the application of cylinder-printing to paper hangings. Hitherto these papers have not vied in beauty with block-prints; but some of the London houses have recently succeeded in producing beautiful specimens by the cylinder, in which six or eight colours are printed by one passage through the machine. A single machine is capable of printing in one hour 200 pieces of paper, each 12 yards long; or 18,000 yards per day. It serves to illustrate the advance both of paper making and of paper-staining, that the paper upon which the patterns are printed by cylinder is manufactured in lengths of 2880 feet; each length is, after printing, cut into 80 pieces of 12 yards long each.

A reduction of the duty charged on all kinds of paper has had a considerable effect in extending the use and improving the manufacture of paper-hangings.

PAPER MANUFACTURE. In early times the materials used for writing upon were chiefly such as only required some little mechanical fashioning to fit them for that purpose. Smooth flat stones, clay afterwards burnt, waxed boards, plates of iron or metal, leaves and bark, skins and intestines, papyrus, and parchment, were all employed. The art of making paper from fibrous matter reduced to a pulp in water appears to have been first discovered by the Chinese about the year 95 A.D. In the time of Confucius they wrote with a style, or bodkin, on the inner bark of the bamboo. The Chinese paper is made from the inner bark of the bamboo, but the Chinese also make paper from cotton and linen rags, and a coarse yellow sort for wrappers is made from rice straw.

In respect to the rise of this manufacture in England, a Mr. Tate is said to have had a paper-mill at Hertford early in the 16th century: and another mill is stated to have been established in 1588 at Dartford in Kent, by a German, who was knighted by Queen Elizabeth. Great improvements were introduced in the manufacture by Thomas Watson, in 1713; but it was not till recent times that the manufacture reached any high degree of excellence.

In the making of paper any fibrous vegetable substance may be used, such as bark, stalks, tendrils, hop-bine, and wheat-straw. Nothing however has yet been found to answer so well as linen, hempen, or cotton rags. The sweepings of the cotton-mills are also much used.

In all kinds of paper-making, whether from the bark of trees or other fibrous matter, or from rags, the general process is the same. The fibrous material is cut and bruised in water till it is separated into fine and short filaments, and becomes a sort of pulp. This pulp is taken up in a thin and even layer upon a mould of wire cloth, or something similar, which allows the water to drain off, but retains the fibrous matter, the filaments of which are, by the process of reduction to pulp and subsequent drying and pressing, so interwoven or felted together, that they cannot be separated without tearing, and thus form paper. The rags of our country do not constitute a fourth part of the quantity which we use in making paper: Italy and Germany furnish the principal supplies.

In every paper-mill the first business is to sort the rags and cut them into small pieces. This is done by women, each of whom is provided with a large knife to cut the rags. Threads and seams are carefully put by themselves: if ground with the cloth they would form specks in the paper. The rags, when cut, are thrown into five or six different compartments of a large chest, according to their qualities. Only the finest linen rags are used for the best writing paper, but cotton as well as linen rags are now used for printing-paper. Hempen rags are used for coarse paper, and old cordage and tarred ropes for brown wrapping papers.

The rags are now to be washed, which is done either with hot water in a fulling-mill, or they are subjected for some hours to the action of steam. The colour is taken out of them by a careful use of chlorine. The rags, after being washed, are subjected to the action of a revolving cylinder, the surface of which is furnished with a number of sharp teeth or cutters, which are so placed as to act against other cutters fixed beneath the cylinder. The rags are kept immersed in water, and subjected to the action of the cutters for several hours, till they are minutely divided and reduced to a thin pulp.

The pulp, or *stuff*, as it is technically called, is now ready to be made into paper, which is done either by hand or by machine. In the hand method, the stuff is put into a large vat, and is kept at a proper temperature either by a stove or steam-pipe, and the fibrous matter is held in suspension by stirring. The paper is made with a *mould* and *deckle*. The mould is a shallow square frame covered with wire-cloth, and a little larger than the sheet intended to be made upon it. The deckle is a very thin frame of wood which fits close upon the mould, and is required to retain the stuff on the mould, and to limit the size of the sheet. The dipper, or *vatman*, inclining the mould a little towards him, dips it into the vat with the deckle upon it, and lifts it up again horizontally. He shakes it to distribute the stuff equally, and the water drains through the wire. He lays the mould on the edge of the vat, and takes off the deckle, which he requires to apply to another mould. After remaining two or three seconds to drain the mould is taken by another workman, the *coucher*, who, having deposited the sheet of paper upon a piece of woollen cloth, returns the mould to the dipper, who in the meantime has made another sheet, which stands on the vat ready to be couched upon another felt spread over the former sheet. Thus they proceed till they have made a pile of sheets, called a *post*, consisting of six or eight quires. This post, with its felts, is placed in the *vat-press*, and subjected to a strong pressure to force out the superfluous water, and to give firmness and solidity to the paper. The pile is then removed from the vat-press, the felts taken out, and the sheets are pressed again by themselves. They are then taken from the press and hung up, five or six together, in the drying-room.

Writing-paper is dipped, five or six sheets together, into a tub of size, and afterwards pressed to force out the superfluity. It is then hung up again in the drying-room. Printing paper is sized in the stuff. Every sheet is now examined, imperfections removed, and bad sheets taken out. A large pile of paper is then made, and pressed with great force, to render the sheets quite flat and smooth. The pile is then taken down, sheet by sheet, and another made, by which new surfaces are brought in contact with each other, and the pile again pressed strongly. This operation, which is called *parting*, is done two or three times for the best papers. The paper is now counted into quires, folded, and packed up into reams.

Various wire-marks, or water-marks, as they are called, were formerly applied to paper to distinguish it. Hand-made paper is now commonly marked with the name of the maker, and the date of the year when it was made.

The paper making machine, invented by Fourdrinier, and improved by Dickinson and others, is a very beautiful combination of mechanism. The pulp is first made to flow from the vat upon a wire frame or sifter, which moves rapidly up and down so as to force the fine filaments of pulp through the wire whilst it retains any knots and lumps. The pulp then flows over a ledge in a regular and even stream, and is received upon an endless web of wire gauze, which presents a surface of five or six feet long. The wire web moves forward with a motion so regulated as to determine the thickness of the paper; at the same time a lateral motion is given to the wire web, which assists to spread the pulp evenly, and also to facilitate the separation of the water; by which means the pulp solidifies as it advances, and is at the same time prevented from flowing over the sides by straps which regulate the width of the paper. Before the thickened pulp leaves the wire web, it is pressed by a roller covered with felt, and is then taken up by an endless web of felt which forms an inclined plane; the web absorbs a further portion of the moisture. The pulp is now seized by a pair of rollers, between which it is pressed, and then it passes upon another inclined plane of felt, which conducts it to another pair of pressing rollers. The pulp is now paper, and only requires to be made dry and smooth. To effect these objects the machinery conducts it over the polished surface of a large cylinder heated by steam; from this cylinder it passes to a second, larger and hotter; and then to a third, which is still hotter than the second. After this it is subjected to the pressure of a woollen cloth, which confines it on one side while the cylinder smooths it on the other. It is then conducted by another roller to a reel, on which it is wound, perfectly dry and smooth, and ready to be cut into sheets for use. In two or three minutes the pulp, which is introduced upon the wire web at one extremity of the machine, is delivered at the other in the state of perfect paper. In many of the paper machines, a partial vacuum is produced under the endless wire web by means of large air-pumps or of revolving fans; and the atmosphere is thus made to press upon the pulp, whereby the moisture is forced through the wire.

Machines for cutting paper into sheets of any required size have been invented, in many varieties: they are separate from the paper making machine, and are beautiful contrivances. One recently introduced by Messrs.

Metcalf, and called the Industrial Cutting Machine, has a sharp blade which works upon a horizontal table. One end of the blade is connected with a lever moved by wheel-work; and as the wheels revolve, the blade is brought down with a cutting action. The machine may be worked either by steam or by hand power; and it is calculated not only for paper makers, but for all trades in which papers or pasteboard have to be cut.

In respect to commercial and fiscal regulations, the paper trade is now deservedly attracting public attention, with a view to the removal of a duty which is found not only to be financially oppressive, but to be hurtful in a literary point of view. The publisher of the present work, and other publishers concerned in the issue of low-priced but carefully prepared publications, have shewn that a premium is paid to inferior literature, to 'literary garbage,' by the existing duty on paper; and that many well planned but not profitable works would have yielded a sufficient profit had not this duty exerted its repressing influence.

The quantity of paper charged with excise duty in the United Kingdom in the last three years was :—

1848	121,820,229 lbs.
1849	132,132,600 ,,
1850	141,032,474 ,,

The quantities exported to foreign countries were as follows:

1848	5,180,286 lbs.
1849	5,966,319 ,,
1850	7,764,534 ,,

In other words, our exports of paper amount to only four or five per cent of our manufacture.

PAPIER-MACHÉ, is the French term for a preparation of moistened paper, of which many articles are manufactured in England, France, and Germany. Two modes are adopted of making articles of this kind: 1, by glueing or pasting different thicknesses of paper together; 2, by mixing the substance of the paper into a pulp and pressing it into moulds. The first mode is adopted principally for those articles, such as trays, &c., in which a tolerably plain and flat surface is to be produced. Common millboard, such as forms the covers of books, may convey some idea of this sort of manufacture. Sheets of strong paper are glued together, and then so powerfully pressed that the different strata of paper become as one. Slight curvatures may be given to such pasteboard when damp by the use of presses and moulds. Papier-Maché properly so called, however is that which is pressed into moulds in the state of a pulp. This pulp is either paper-maker's pulp, or is more generally made of cuttings of coarse paper boiled in water, and beaten in a mortar till they assume the consistence of a paste, which is boiled in a solution of gum-arabic or of size, to give it tenacity. The moulds are carved in the usual way and the pulp poured into them, a counter-mould being employed to make the cast nothing more than a crust or shell, as in plaster casts.

Our recent Exhibitions of manufactures have presented few articles more beautiful than those formed of papier-maché. The firm of Messrs. Jennens and Bettridge, at Birmingham, is pre-eminent for productions in this department of industry.

PARACHUTE. Under BALLOON a brief account is given of aëronautic ascents; we will here say a few words concerning the attempts to *descend* from a balloon. A parachute is a machine attached to a balloon, and is intended to convey the aëronaut gently to the earth, in case of an accident happening to the balloon. It is in shape like an umbrella, with ropes or stays fastened to the extremities of the whalebones, and brought down to the handle, where they must be fixed, so as to prevent the umbrella from turning inside outwards. Instead of the stick, suppose a metal tube to be fixed in the centre, with a rope passing through it, attached by its upper extremity to the balloon and by the lower end to a tub or car. This machine is a parachute. While ascending it will be like a closed umbrella, but it may at any moment be detached from the balloon by cutting the end of the rope which ties it to the car; the resistance of the air will then cause it to expand, and will at the same time retard the velocity of the descent.

Machines like umbrellas, to break the fall from a high place, were used in Siam two centuries since: but the first experiment in Europe with such a machine was made at Paris in 1783 by M. le Normand, who leaped safely from a window of a house with a stout umbrella of thirty inches in diameter in his hand. M. Blanchard several times caused dogs to descend from great heights by means of parachutes; and, in 1802, M. Garnerin, who five years before had made a like descent at Paris, repeated the experiment in London. The parachute of this gentleman was 23 feet in diameter; and at the height of 8000 feet, he cut the rope which attached him to the balloon. The descent was at first very rapid; but, the machine at length expanding, he came to the ground without serious injury. Madlle. Garnerin, his daughter, descended twice in 1816, from great elevations, apparently without being in the least discomposed

In 1837 Mr. Cocking descended near London, from a balloon, by a parachute constructed in the form of an umbrella turned upside down. The parachute was 34 feet in diameter, and it was kept open by a wooden hoop. As soon as it was cut away, it fell with rapidity; its vibrations were violent, the hoop broke, and the unfortunate aëronaut fell, dreadfully mutilated, to the ground. Other parachute descents have since been made.

PARAPET, is a low or breast-high wall or fence, to serve as a protection on bridges, terraces, platform-roofs, &c. In Italian architecture parapets are generally balustrades. In gothic architecture the parapet is merely a continuation of the wall carried up above the edge of the roof, and finished by a coping; unless machicolated, in which case it projects and overhangs the walls below. In the Lombardic buildings of Italy there is seldom any parapet, the eaves of the roof finishing the elevation. The same is frequently the case in the Norman style. In Elizabethan buildings open-work parapets, forming various fantastical devices, are common. In engineering and in fortification a low wall is often, in like manner, called a parapet.

PARCHMENT is the skin of the sheep, lamb, goat, pig, or calf, prepared for writing upon. When the skin is divested of its hair, or wool, it is placed for some time in a lime-pit, and then stretched on a square wooden frame drawn tight by pegs. When in the frame, it is first scraped on the flesh side with a blunt iron, then wetted with a moist rag, covered with pounded chalk, and rubbed well with pumice-stone. After a short pause these operations are repeated, but without chalk. The skin is then turned, and scraped on the hair side once only. The flesh side is scraped once more, and again rubbed over with chalk. All this is done by the skinner, who allows the skin to dry in the frame, and then cuts it out and sends it to the parchment-maker, who repeats the operations with a sharper tool, using a sack stuffed with flocks to lay the skin upon instead of stretching it in a frame.

The relation which parchment-making bears to tanning is noticed under LEATHER MANUFACTURE. The costliness of parchment in the middle ages is illustrated by the PALIMPSEST MANUSCRIPTS.

PARING AND BURNING, are the two processes of a combined operation in agriculture, which consists in cutting a thin slice from the surface of land which is overgrown with grass, heath, fern, or any other plants which form a sward by the matting together of their roots. The sods are allowed to dry in the sun to a certain degree, after which they are arranged in heaps, and burnt slowly, without flame or violent heat. The result is a mixture of burnt earth, charred vegetable fibre, and the ashes of that part which is entirely consumed. The object of this operation is two-fold: first, to kill insects and destroy useless or noxious weeds completely; and secondly, to obtain a powerful manure, impregnated with alkaline salts and carbonaceous matter, which experience has shown to be a very powerful promoter of vegetation. The instruments by which this is effected are, either a common plough with a very flat share, which may be used when the surface is very level without being encumbered with stones or large roots, as in low moist meadows, or in most other cases a paring-iron used by hand, the cross-bar of which is held with both hands; and the upper parts of the thighs, being protected by two small slips of board, push the instrument into the ground, so as to cut a slice of the required thickness, which is then turned over by moving the cross handle. The labour is severe, and a good workman can scarcely pare more than one-sixth of an acre in a day.

PARIS. This most important city, besides its distinguishing features in other respects, has a considerable manufacturing population; for in the variety and extent of its productions of industry, Paris may vie with most cities of the world. The carpets of the manufactory of La Savonnerie and the tapestry of the Gobelins are well known. Cashmere, silk, and woollen shawls; light woollens, cotton goods, hosiery, gloves, hats, embroidery, lace, and other articles of fashionable attire; jewellery, gold and silver plate and trinkets, clocks and watches, bronzes, and musical, mathematical, and philosophical instruments; paper-hangings, houshold furniture, carriages, sadlery, leather, glue, cutlery, fire-arms, liqueurs, and confectionary, are made. Dyeing, printing, engraving, and lithography; the manufacture of salts, acids, oxides, and other chemicals; the refining of sugar, tallow-melting, the distillation of brandy from potatoes, brewing, and the manufacture of potato-starch,—all are carried on with considerable activity. The Seine furnishes the principal means of water-carriage: it is navigable for barges and other small craft. The canals of the Ourcq, St. Denis, and St. Martin, give to Paris water communication with many parts of the vicinity. The timber brought into Paris is immense. Wood is the principal fuel consumed at present, but the consumption of coal is gaining ground. The markets for the sale of provisions are numerous and generally well arranged.

There are some curious industrial statistics in which London and Paris are compared, contained in a recently published report to the French government, by M. Darcy, divisional inspector of the Ponts et Chaussées, who has been to England to obtain information relative to the macadamized roads. The total surface of London is said to be 210,000,000 square metres; its population, 1,924,000; number of houses 260,000; length of the streets, 1,126,000 metres; surface of the streets, not including the foot pavement, 6,000,000 metres; length of the sewers, 639,000 metres. The total surface of Paris is 34,379,016 square metres; population, 1,053,879; number of houses, 20,526; length of the streets, 425,000 metres; surface of the streets, exclusive of the foot pavement, 3,600,000 square metres; length of the sewers, 135,000 metres; surface of the foot pavement, 888,000 metres. Thus in London every inhabitant corresponds to a surface of more than 100 square metres; at Paris to only 34 metres; which shews that Paris is much more densely populated than London. In London the average of inhabitants for each house is 7½; at Paris, 34. The Boulevards of Paris is the part where the greatest traffic takes place, and the following are the results of the observations of M. Darcy on the subject:—On the Boulevard des Capucines there pass every 24 hours 9,070 horses drawing carriages; Boulevard des Italiens, 10,750; Boulevard Poissonnière, 7,720; Boulevard St. Denis, 9,609; Boulevard des Filles du Calvaire, 5,859; general average of the above, 8,600. Rue du Faubourg St. Antoine, 4,300; Avenue des Champs Elysées, 8,959. Other items are given respecting the traffic in the London streets; but these seem to be of doubtful accuracy.

The numerous Industrial Exhibitions at Paris have been noticed in the *Introduction*.

PAR'THENON. This far-famed structure, the temple of Minerva, is situated on the Acrópolis of Athens. It was erected in the time of Pericles (about B.C. 448). This temple has always been considered the most refined example of the Grecian Doric style, and one of the noblest monuments of antiquity. Yet its grandeur is by no means owing to its extraordinary dimensions, since in point of size it falls far short of many other structures, modern as well as ancient, its extreme length being only 228 feet, and its breadth 100, and the interior of the cella only 145 feet by 63 feet. This temple had columns along its sides and at both ends, viz., eight beneath each pediment, making in all 46 columns, there being, including those at the angles, 17 on each side, or 16 inter-columns. Besides these external columns, there was likewise a range of inner columns at each end. The cella or body of the temple was hypæthral, that is, the central space between the columns along each side was open to the sky. Even in its present shattered and mangled state, the temple is the admiration of all travellers and artists who have beheld it. The chief portion of the sculptures of the edifice were removed by Lord Elgin. [ELGIN MARBLES.] One object of art that originally decorated the interior or shrine was the chryselephantine (gold and ivory) statue of Minerva, 39 feet high, which was the work of Phidias. Since the establishment of King Otho's government (1833), excavations have been made on the Acropolis and around the Parthenon, and a great number of fragments of sculpture and architecture have been brought to light. Some of the fallen columns have also been replaced, and measures taken to restore the structure as far as circumstances will permit. In the British Museum are two models of the Parthenon, on a large scale, one in its ruinous state, and the other a restoration with the sculptures in their respective situations.

PASTILES. These are used either to diffuse an agreeable odour, or more usually to hide some offensive odour. They are made somewhat cone-shaped, so as to burn slowly. Many different combinations of odiriferous substances are employed in their manufacture. One kind is made of gum benzoin, tolu balsam, sandal wood, charcoal, tragacanth, labdanum, nitre, gum arabic, and cinnamon-water. Other kinds resemble this nearly in the solid ingredients, but substitute rose water, essence of orange, essence of vanilla, or oil of cloves, for the cinnamon water.

PASTES. The pastes or vitrifiable materials which are employed to imitate gems for cheap jewellery are noticed under GEMS and GLASS MANUFACTURE.

PASTURE LAND. The pasturage of cattle is now a part of regular husbandry. The land which affords the herbage for cattle forms part of private possessions, and a rent is paid for its use. Pastures are now fenced and protected, and pains are taken to improve them, so as to maintain many more cattle and sheep than they would in their natural state. Whenever pastures are hired, the rent is always reckoned, not by the extent of surface, but by the stock which can be maintained upon it. Thus, in Switzerland, the mountain pastures are divided into portions of twenty, forty or more cows. In Scotland they reckon sometimes by the number of bullocks which can be reared, and sometimes by the number of sheep which can be kept. In many places pasturing has been found much more productive than cultivation; and some large proprietors have converted great tracts of land from arable into pasture farms. Pastures are seldom improved with manure, which is generally reserved for arable land, or grass land intended to be mown for hay: but if richness is valuable in a pasture, it will well repay the expense of manuring.

PATENTS; PATENT LAWS. The object of patents is to encourage useful inventions. Before applying for a patent for an invention, two considerations are necessary: first, what is entitled to a patent; and next, whether the invention has the requisite conditions. In the first place, the machine, operation, or substance produced, for which a patent is solicited, must be new to public use, either the original invention of the patentee, or imported by him and first made public here. A patent may be obtained for England, Ireland, or Scotland, although the subject of it may have been publicly known and in use in either or in both of the other two countries. In the second place, the subject of the invention must be useful to the public, something applicable to the production of a vendible article. The discovery of a philosophical principle is not entitled to such protection: such principle must be applied, and the manner of such application is a fit subject for a patent.

An invention entitled to patent may be a new combination of mechanical parts, whereby a new machine is produced, although each of the parts separately be old and well known; or an improvement on any machine, whereby such machine is rendered capable of performing better or more beneficially; or when the vendible substance is the thing produced either by chemical or other processes, such as medicines or fabrics; or where an old substance is improved by some new working, the means of producing the improvement is in most cases patentable. If the inventor think that the machine, operation, or substance produced comes under any of these enumerations, and that it is new, and likely to be useful to the public, he must proceed in the form required by law to obtain the letters patent.

The chief clause in a patent grants the sole use of the invention to the inventor for fourteen years, whereby all other persons are restrained from using the invention without a licence in writing from the patentee; and persons are restricted from imitating the invention, or making any addition thereunto or subtraction therefrom, with intent to make themselves appear the inventors. Another clause declares that the patent shall be void, if contrary to law or prejudicial and inconvenient to the public in general, or not the invention of the patentee, or not first introduced by him into this country. A patent may be shared among any number of persons up to twelve. The specification of a patent must show exactly in what the invention consists for which a patent has been granted, and it must give a detailed account of the manner of effecting the object set forth in the title; it must describe exactly what is new and what is old, and must claim exclusive right to the former; the introduction of any part that is old, or the omission of any part that is new, equally vitiates the patent. The patent is granted on condition that such full and accurate information shall be given in the specification as will enable any workman or other qualified person to make or produce the object of the patent at the expiration of that term, without any further instructions.

If a patentee finds that the time allowed him by the patent is not sufficient to remunerate him for the trouble and expense of his invention and patent, he may apply for an extension of the term. Any person wishing to oppose the extension, must enter a *caveat* at the Privy Council Office, and the petitioner and enterer of the caveat are heard by their counsel before the Judicial Committee, which reports to the crown; and the crown is authorised, if it shall think fit, to grant new letters patent for the same invention for a term not exceeding seven years after the expiration of the first term.

The assemblage in London, in 1851, of a larger amount of manufactured articles than were ever before collected in one place, has led to anxious discussions concerning the patent laws. It has been long felt that these laws are clumsy, tedious, costly, and unjust: a constant source of vexation to those whose ingenuity has developed new machines or processes, and who wish to receive a fair commercial advantage from that ingenuity. Foreigners are still more anxious that any new combinations or inventions which they may exhibit in England should not be copied by dishonest persons in this country, without some recognized means of securing a right and property to the real inventors. The government, the legislature, the legal profession, and the Commissioners for the Industrial Exhibition, have all felt that changes in the existing patent laws are necessary; and committees have been appointed, by different bodies, to investigate the subject. So far as relates to *designs* rather than to *inventions*, certain improvements have been introduced which are noticed under DESIGNS. A bill is now before the legislature, intended to meet some of the evils of the system generally, and to apply specially in some clauses to the Great Exhibition; but so much diversity of opinion prevails concerning the best mode of carrying out the improvements, that little can be said respecting the probable character of the future regulations on this important subject.

PAVEMENTS. [ROADS; TESSELATED FLOORS.]

PEARLASH. [POTASSIUM.]

PEARLS; PEARL FISHERY. A pearl is a small concretion which is formed within the hard envelope of a shell-fish. The pearl oyster nearly resembles in shape the common English oyster, but is larger, being usually about three inches in diameter. The pearls are most commonly contained in the shell; but sometimes they are found in the thickest and most fleshy part of the oyster. A single oyster will frequently contain several pearls; and it is on record that one has been known to contain a hundred and fifty. The pearl itself is supposed to be the result of some accidental deposit or extravasation of the liquor secreted by the animal in the gradual enlargement of its shell—very small in the first instance, but increased by successive layers of pearly matter.

The beautiful substance called (somewhat expressively) *mother of pearl*, is the hard silvery, brilliant internal layer of shells, especially oyster shells, and more particularly the pearl oyster. In English oysters this substance is too thin to be workable for manufacturing purposes; but the oysters of the eastern seas yield it of considerable thickness. The brilliant hues which distinguish mother of pearl do not depend upon the nature of the substance, but on an exquisitely fine series of furrows upon the surface, which shed a brilliant reflexion of colours according to the angle at which the light falls on them. Much care is required in working this delicate substance; but it may be cut by saws, files, and drills, with the corrosive aid of sulphuric or muriatic acid. It is polished by colcothar of vitriol. In all those ornamental manufactures where *pearl* is said to be used for flat surfaces, such as inlaying, mosaics, buttons, knife-handles, &c., it is not real pearl, but mother of pearl, that is employed.

The *Pearl Fishery*, or the fishing for pearl oysters, is an important employment on coasts where this particular kind of fish abounds. The chief fisheries are on the west coast of Ceylon, on the Coromandel coast, on the shores of the Persian Gulf, on the coast of Algiers, on the shores of the Sooloo Islands, in the Bay of Panama, and on the Pacific coast of some of the South American States. The Ceylon fishery is a monopoly of the British government, and the Coromandel fishery is a monopoly of the East India Company; but the rent at which the fisheries are let out seldom pays more than the expense of superintendance. In the Persian Gulf the fishery often yields nearly 100,000*l*. of pearls in two months. The oysters are procured by diving. In the Ceylon fishery about 1200 or 1400 divers are usually employed. The share of profits gives each individual 5*s*. to 6*s*. per day for the time he is employed; the price of ordinary labour being 6*d*. per day. But each bank being available only for one period, of about 20 days in every 7 years, sometimes the fishery is smaller, and sometimes there is none at all; and in no season does it last for more than 30 or 35 days, commencing with the calm weather about the 5th of March. The divers, in 6 or 7 fathoms water, remain immersed from 50 to 55 seconds, very rarely longer. A reward being offered to him who should remain the longest under water, it was gained by one who remained 87 seconds. The diver's sack is not fastened round his neck, but is attached to a cord held by the man in the boat above; and it is pulled up when full at the signal of the diver, who, if he choose, is drawn up with it. So far from the occupation being unhealthy, it is the belief of the natives that divers live longer than other labourers; and its short season is held as a gainful holiday by the divers themselves, who at other times are engaged in ordinary labour. If the oyster is taken before seven years old, its pearls are imperfectly developed.

When the oysters are brought to land, they are thrown into a pit and allowed to rot, whereby the pearls can be extracted without injury to their delicate structure. The pearls do not undergo much preparation to fit them for ornament, as an irregularly shaped pearl is regarded as being but little inferior to a symmetrical one. Various kinds of drills are employed to bore holes through the pearls; and the powder of ground pearls is sometimes employed to polish them.

A vessel arrived at London in the early part of 1851 from Panama, with no fewer than 2,104,000 pearl shells; to be used, we may presume, as mother of pearl. This was the largest importation ever known.

The mode of imitating pearls is described under GEMS.

PEAT is a substance of vegetable origin, found wherever the soil has been long soaked with water which has no outlet and does not completely evaporate by the heat of the sun. When dried peat is examined, it is found to consist of roots and fibres in every stage of decomposition, from the natural wood to the completely black vegetable mould. From the nature of its formation under the surface of the water, it acquires a portion of tannin, which has the property of preserving animal and vegetable matter from decomposition. Hence large branches and trunks of trees are found imbedded in peat, which have no mark of decomposition, except what may have taken place before the wood was completely immersed in the peat. Peat contains all the elements of the richest manure, and may by an easy process be converted into humus: for this purpose the agency of alkalies is the most effectual. If the tannin be decomposed, that of the vegetable fibre will go on, and soluble humus will be formed. When peat is newly dug up, if caustic lime be added to it before it is dry, the moisture of the peat slakes the lime, which acts on the gallic acid in the peat and neutralises it. If this mixture be then excited to fermentation by the addition of animal matter, such as urine or dung, oxygen is absorbed and carbonic acid evolved; and the residue is converted into an excellent manure, containing much soluble humus. The same may be effected more slowly by mixing peat with clay or marl, and allowing the mixture to remain exposed to the atmosphere for a considerable time, frequently turning it. But nothing accelerates this process like the addition of putrescent animal matter, which acts as a ferment and greatly hastens the decomposition.

The soils for which peat forms the best manure are the chalky and clayey. Sand has too little tenacity; it lets the gases produced by the decomposition escape, instead of attracting them, as clay and chalk do, and thus preventing their escape.

Coincident with the present Flax movement is an enterprise for converting the peat of Ireland into charcoal. The Irish Amelioration Society has already made a good beginning in this work. The charcoal thus obtained is not only highly valuable in the smelting of iron and other metals, but comes into action as a most useful ally in the sanitary and economical measures that are now making such progress. As a deodoriser, it is the best substance yet discovered, and by its agency the most offensive matter is converted into perfectly inoffensive and highly nutritious manure. It has already been largely contracted for, to purify the sewerage of the metropolis, and to convert its nuisances into a source of profit. As the manufacture of this charcoal increases, the inducement to reclaim land will be multiplied. Already round each charcoal factory a rim of cottage gardens spreads, and the land, relieved from the load of otherwise unprofitable peat, produces the crops of a virgin soil.

A British and Irish Peat Company, too, is in process of formation, in which English capitalists propose to assist in the work. This company was suggested with reference rather to Dartmoor peat than to Irish peat; but if available for one, it would also for the other. The company profess to be able to obtain naphtha, paraffine, fixed oil, volatile oil, acetate of lime, and sulphate of ammonia, from peat, at profitable prices; but the correctness of the calculations requires the test of experience.

PEDAL. In musical instruments pedals are of two kinds:—1., those keys which are acted on by the feet of the performer; 2, the levers acting on the swell of the organ, and on the stops; and also those of the pianoforte and harp. The foot pedals of the organ play certain keys; the stop-pedals or levers of the same instrument bring into play distinct groups of pipes; the foot pedal of the pianoforte raises the dampers from certain strings; the foot pedals of the harp raise the tone of the strings half a note.

PEDOMETER. This ingenious instrument, in the shape of a small watch, enables a person to tell what space of ground he has walked or ridden over. The instrument is so constructed that when the body of the traveller is raised, either by the spring of his foot, or the motion of his horse, a lever is made to act upon the wheel-work of the instrument, and an index or hand on the dial-plate points to the figures which denote the number of miles passed over.

PE'KEA is the name of a plant inhabiting Guiana, and furnishing the *Saouari Nuts* of the shops. The shell is brownish and rugged, and contains a kernel of a soft consistence, and of the most delicate buttery quality. It is by far the best of the South American nuts that are brought to England, and much superior to our own walnuts and filberts.

PEMBROKESHIRE. In this Welsh county, forming the south-west projection of the principality, much useful mineral produce is found. The anthracite or stone coal tract bisects the county; it is a continuation of the great coal-basin of South Wales, which extends over the whole coast of Caermarthen Bay. Copper-ore has been found in small quantities in the neighbourhood of St. David's, but not sufficient to repay the cost of working. Slate-quarries are opened in the Precelli Mountains and near St. David's; the quality of the slates is inferior to those of North Wales. Coal is the only mineral besides slate which is worked in Pembrokeshire: it is of that description called anthracite, or stone-coal. The best coal is raised at Landshipping, on the shore of Milford Haven. A considerable quantity of good coal is also raised at Kinsmoor and Kilgetty, whence it is conveyed by a railway to the sea at Saundersfoot, where a dock has been built.

The soil in different quarters is very varied; and the state of agriculture is as various as the soil. Considerable advances have been made of late years, but a general want of capital among the farmers prevents any rapid progress.

Pembrokeshire has not much pretensions to the character of a manufacturing county. *Fishguard* is remarkable for little besides a fine fishing ground near the bay, frequented by small craft from Liverpool. The port is capable of accommodating 100 sail of merchantmen. The principal exports are corn and butter; the imports, coal, culm, limestone, &c. If, however, the South Wales Railway should be carried to Fishguard as originally planned, it would become a place of commercial importance. *Haverfordwest* is principally occupied by shopkeepers, mechanics, and persons of moderate independent fortune, for whom the cheapness of the place is an attraction. The river Cleddy is navigable at spring tides to Haverfordwest, for vessels of 100 tons burthen. *Milford* was a highly prosperous town till the removal of the dockyard and packet establishment.

Pembroke Dockyard is the most important establishment in the county. It is situated at Pater, about two miles from Pembroke, on the shores of Milford Haven. The naval dockyard and arsenal were removed from Milford to this spot in 1814. The two together occupy about 60 acres; the dockyard is one of the most complete in the kingdom, capable of building five or six first-rates and many smaller vessels at the same time. In respect to ropes, anchors, machinery, it is not so celebrated as some of the other royal dockyards. Steamers ply regularly from Bristol to Pater; and the neighbourhood of the dockyard is gradually becoming flourishing.

Milford Haven, near and beyond the dockyard, is being strongly fortified. Towers, forts, and batteries are being constructed at different spots. These works have been commenced because it has been felt that the shipping and dockyard were in a somewhat unprotected state.

PEN MANUFACTURE. Among the small articles of daily use, few are more important than pens, and few exhibit more remarkably the application of the factory system to the production of cheap implements.

Under FEATHERS, the reader will find an account of the mode of preparing goose-quills for pens. Of the common method of making pens by hand it is not necessary to speak; we shall therefore only say a few words upon the manufacture of *quill nibs*. The barrel of the quill in the first place has both ends cut off, and is divided down the centre; the halves are then laid on their convex side and the edges shaved smooth; after this they are divided into three or four lengths each, and the end of each length is made into a pen by a small machine, which at one time makes the slit and cuts the shoulders; they are then finished by being nibbed by hand. Pens are shaped differently according to the kind of writing for which they are intended.

Owing to the constant necessity for mending quill pens, the loss of time consequent thereon, and the inequality of the writing, an immense amount of labour and ingenuity has been employed to produce some more durable substitute. The only substitute which has attained to anything like general use is the steel pen; but long before their general introduction, metallic pens of other kinds were tried; sometimes silver, when intended for presents; sometimes brass, when intended to accompany cheap brass inkstands that used to be made some years ago. One of the first attempts to combine the elasticity of quill pens with increased durability consisted in arming the points with metallic nibs; but the improvement was not adequate to the increased cost. Another class of improvements, or suggested improvements, was the introduction of pens whose nibs should be formed of precious stones. One kind consisted of a tortoiseshell tube or barrel, with small fragments of diamond or ruby imbedded in the nib. Another kind contained a nib of ruby set in fine gold, and such pens have been said to last six years without injury. Some have also been formed of rhodium nibs set in gold. Pens of gold, of silver, and of gold alloyed with silver, are occasionally made.

But, as we have said, steel is the only material which has successfully competed with the quill. The present generation has witnessed a descent from sixpence a piece to sixpence a gross. Steel pens are now manufactured to an amount in quantity and at a

CUTTING AND PUNCHING ENGINE

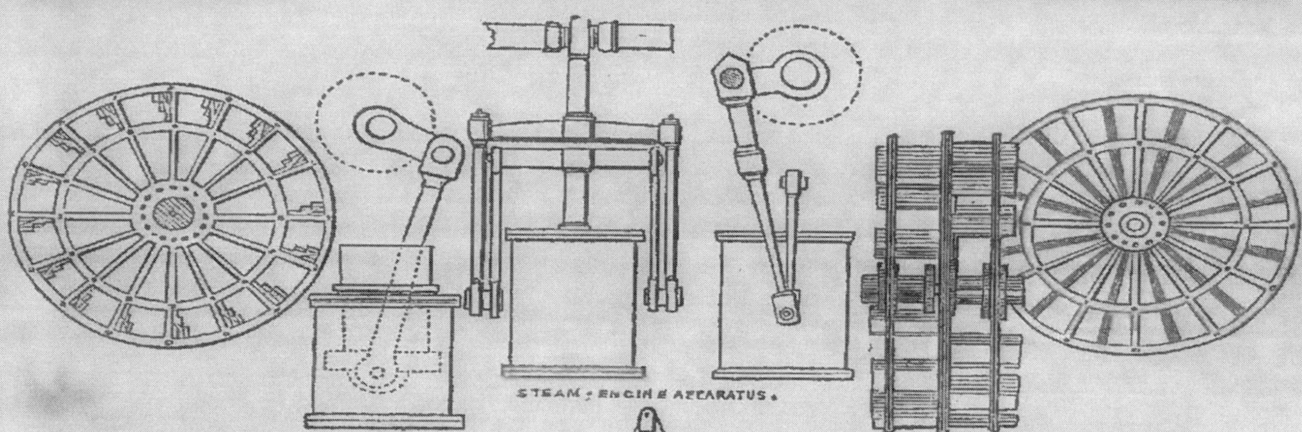

STEAM ENGINE APPARATUS.

BORING

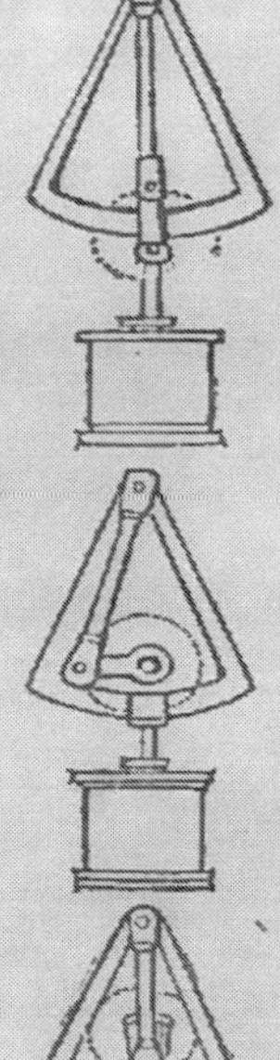

PLANEING.

KNIGHT'S CYCLOPÆDIA OF THE INDUSTRY OF ALL NATIONS.

No. 32.

cost so small as hardly to be credible. Different makers have different modes of operation, but the following will give a general idea of the method employed. In the first place flat pieces of steel are cut out, of the shape required, by a stamping-press; they are then placed under another press, which pierces the holes and cuts the slits; and they are struck into their convex shape by a third press. They are then polished and tempered. The polishing is managed in rather a curious manner; a quantity of pens are shut up in an iron cylinder, leaving a considerable space unoccupied; this cylinder is attached at each end to a crank, the axes of which are connected by a wheel and set in motion by a handle or by machinery. Thus by being rubbed against each other the pens come out well polished, and with all the burrs or sharp angles left by the cutting-presses rubbed smooth. Birmingham is the great seat of the steel pen manufacture; some of the manufacturers have fine manufacturing establishments, and make several hundred millions of pens annually. Mr. Albert Smith in his "Month at Constantinople," gives us a curious instance of the spread of English manufactures all over the world. At Constantinople he saw a Turk, seated on the wall of a cemetery, and exhibiting a tray of Birmingham steel pens for sale.

Fountain pens are so made as to hold a reservoir of ink. Music-pens are formed so as to make large dots as well as strokes. The geometric-pen is an ingenious mathematical instrument for drawing curves.

PENCILS. The well-known *black-lead pencil* is made by cutting black-lead, or plumbago, into thin plates with a saw, and again into strips as wide as the plate is thick. These strips are then laid in a groove in a piece of cedar, upon which is glued another and thinner piece: the whole is afterwards rounded by a plane adapted to that purpose. The finest plumbago is obtained from a mine in Cumberland. [PLUMBAGO.] Some pencils are filled with coloured chalk instead of black-lead.

The *ever-pointed pencil* is an instrument for using cylindrical pieces of black-lead, which are forced forward in the pencil just so far as to allow them to be used without breaking. The leads are manufactured of different thicknesses, and the pencil-cases are marked with a letter to correspond with the lead required for it.

The pencils for using liquid colours or paints are of course wholly different from those just described. They are made of hog's bristles, camel's hair, fitch, sable, &c. Those of a large and common kind are described under BRUSH MAKING. The soft pencils for artists are made as follows:—The tail of the animal (sable, badger, marten, &c.) is scoured in a solution of alum; then steeped for several hours in luke-warm water; then dried in linen cloths; and finally combed out regularly. The hairs are seized with pincers, and cut off near the skin; and the little parcels of hair are sorted into groups according to their length. A few hairs are then taken enough for one pencil, and placed in a little receptacle which holds them while a thread is bound round near the roots. The base of the pencil is them trimmed flat by scissors. The hairs thus prepared are fitted either into quills or into tin tubes. The quills are those of swans, geese, ducks, lapwings, pigeons, or larks, according to the size of the pencil. Each quill is softened and swelled in hot water: and the bunch of hairs is introduced at the larger end, and pulled forward by a simple apparatus to the smaller end, where the shrinking of the quill binds the hairs closely. The great art in pencil making is so to arrange the hairs that their ends may be made to converge to a fine point when moistened and drawn between the lips; and it is said that females are more successful then men in preparing the small and delicate pencils.

PENNSYLVANIA. This is one of the most busy and commercial states of the American Union. It abounds in minerals. From the western declivity of the Alleghany Mountains the bituminous coal-fields of Pennsylvania extend into Maryland and Virginia, and occupy many thousands of square miles; this coal is mostly wrought in the neighbourhood of Pittsburg, where it is used for manufacturing purposes. The anthracite coal-field, which lies to the east of the Blue Ridge, is also of great extent, and is wrought to some extent. Iron-ore is in abundance, and limestone occurs in all parts of the state.

The most important manufactures of Pennsylvania are those of iron. So far back even as 1840 there were 213 furnaces, which produced 98,395 tons of cast-iron, and 169 forges, &c., which produced 87,244 tons of bar-iron. There were 235 woollen manufactories, 337 fulling-mills, and 106 cotton manufactories. The quantity of bituminous coal obtained was 11,620,654 bushels. Steam-engines are manufactured to a large amount, chiefly at Pittsburg; and there are numerous other manufactures. The most important canal in Pennsylvania extends from Philadelphia, including a railroad of 37 miles, over the Alleghany Mountains, to Pittsburg, 400 miles. There are several other large canals and numerous small ones. The railroads are still more numerous; from Columbia to Philadelphia, 81 miles; Philadelphia to Reading, 95 miles; Tamaqua to Williamsport, 106 miles; and many others. Pennsylvania is, in short, one of the most enterprising of the sstates; and Pittsburg (the largest town next to Philadelphia), is a great centre of manufactures. As to the monetary credit of the State, in respect to loans and bonds, we have nothing to do with it here.

PEPPER. This powerful condiment is obtained from an Asiatic plant called *Piper Nigrum.* The best comes from Malabar; the worst from Java and Sumatra. The plant is allowed to grow, trained to the stems of other trees, for four years before the fruit can be collected. The fruit or berries are gathered when yet green, before they are perfectly ripe, and are quickly dried on mats, by which they turn black; and this constitutes *black pepper.*

White pepper is the same fruit freed from the outer rind; for this purpose the ripe berries are steeped in water, which allows the rind to be easily removed.

Black pepper contains a great variety of proximate chemical principles; such as an acid resin, a volatile oil, extractive matter, gum, malic and tartaric acids, piperin, bassorin, and several salts. The white pepper has a less powerful odour and taste than the black. The odour of pepper is attributed to the volatile oil, and the pungent taste to the resin. Pepper is used to some small extent in medicine, but much more as a stimulant or condiment with food. Notwithstanding the large consumption in Europe, the Chinese are the great consumers; for among them it appears to hold a more important place than among European nations.

Cayenne pepper is obtained from CAPSICUM.

The importation of pepper into the United Kingdom during the last three years amounted to the following quantities:—

1848	8,125,545 lbs.
1849	4,796,042 „
1850	8,082,518 „

The smallness of the import in 1849 is not explained in the government tables.

PERAMBULATOR, is an instrument for measuring distances on roads. It consists principally of a wheel upon which it runs, and an index which shows the number of turns of the wheel reduced into miles, furlongs, poles, and yards. The carriage or stock, which is divided in order to receive the wheel, is made of wood, and is about three feet long. At one end is a handle for the person who uses it, and the other is furnished with sockets in which the axle of the wheels turns. Upon the stock and just in front of the handle is the dial-plate, with its two hands by which the distance is registered. The wheel is 8¼ feet, or ½ pole, in circumference; and upon one end of its axis is a small pinion, which works into a similar pinion at the end of a rod passing up the stock or carriage to the works beneath the dial-plate. Motion is communicated by means of this rod to a worm or micrometer-screw, which turns once round for each revolution of the carriage-wheel of the perambulator. This worm works into a wheel of 80 teeth, which is moved forward one tooth for every ½ pole, and carries a hand or index, which makes one revolution for 40 poles or one furlong. On the axis of this wheel is a pinion of 8 teeth, which moves a wheel of 160 teeth. This last wheel carries another hand, which makes one revolution for 80 of the former, that is for ten miles. The movements of the two index-hands thus shew the miles and furlongs passed over.

There are other instruments for the same or similar purposes, bearing different names, as *Waywiser* and *Odometer;* but the construction of all of them is very similar. *Waywiser* is the name generally given to that form of the instrument which is applied to a carriage, in which, by a slight adaptation to one of the wheels of the carriage, the instrument is made to register the number of turns of such wheel, in the same manner as the Perambulator.

PERCH, or POLE. This measure, though now mostly used as a square measure (a perch usually meaning a square perch, or a square of a perch in length and breadth), was originally a measure of length, arising out of the custom of measuring small portions of land by a staff or pole. A perch is the quarter of a chain, and a square perch contains 30¼ square yards.

PERCUSSION CAPS. [CAPS, PERCUSSION.]

PERFUMERY. The pomatums, essential oils, distilled spirits, pastes, pastilles, essences, &c., which make up the fragrant store of the perfumer, require different chemical processes for their manufacture. Distilling in some cases, infusion in others, decoction in a third, pressure in a fourth, evaporation in a fifth, and so on. The reader will find a few details on these subjects under ESSENCE, OIL, PASTILLE, POMATUM, &c.

PERSIA. This ancient and celebrated country is neither in industry nor commerce so important as nature has fitted it to be. The slothful despotism of an Asiatic country is a sad bar to advancement. Agriculture is, however, well understood and carefully attended to, as is evident from the means of irrigation employed, and especially the subterraneous aqueducts. Rice, wheat, and barley are the most usual crops; but there are also millet, maize, tel, or sesamum, dal, a species of vetch, and several kinds of beans and peas. Cotton, indigo, sugar, tobacco, and madder, are raised in many places, but especially in Mazanderan. Fruit trees and garden vegetables are cultivated in great plenty.

Iron is abundant in many places, but it is not much worked. Lead, copper, antimony, rock-salt, and bitumen, are among the mineral products of the country.

Among the commercial towns of Persia, *Tabriz* has fallen from its once flourishing condition. *Kermanshah* carries on a considerable commerce. *Dorak* is celebrated for its manufacture of Arabian cloaks. At *Shuster* there is a considerable manufacture of woollen stuffs. *Shiraz* carries on a considerable trade with Yezd, Ispahan, and Bushire; and has manufactures of cotton, glass, iron, gunpowder, swords, and wine. It is also distinguished for the otto of roses procured from the rose-gardens in the neighbourhood. *Lar* in Laristan, is celebrated for the manufacture of swords, muskets, and cotton cloth. The bazar is the noblest structure of that kind in Persia. At *Kerman* trade and manufactures are considerable. The bazar, which is extensive and well built, is abundantly supplied with articles of every description; and there are nine large caravanserais within the walls, and a number of inferior ones both within and without. *Herat* and *Mushed* are among the most commercial towns of Persia. Near *Nishapoor* are the famous turquoise mines. *Yezd* is remarkable as a commercial and manufacturing town. Its commercial importance arises from the caravan routes, which here cross one another, and thus connect it with all parts of Asia.

The manufactures of Persia, though not adequate to so large an Empire, are still numerous and of various kinds. In the manufacture of some articles the Persians are still distinguished, as in several kinds of silk stuffs, especially brocades, and sword-blades, leather, carpets, felt of camel-hair, and jewellery. No machinery being used in the Persian manufactures, the cotton and silk goods introduced by the British have obtained a ready sale owing to their cheapness.

The internal commerce of Persia is very considerable, though managed in a slow and clumsy manner. The different regions which compose this extensive empire differ considerably in their natural productions, and the transport alone of commodities gives occupation to a great number of merchants and other people. To this must be added the produce of the manufactures, and the numerous articles which are brought into Persia from the neighbouring countries, especially from India, and are distributed all over the country. This commerce is entirely carried on by caravans; which usually comprise a very large number of persons and animals of burden, and have regular defined routes across the empire in various directions.

So completely is Persia shut out from direct intercourse with European countries, that the export of British commodities to that country is extremely trifling; it is only through indirect channels that commercial intercourse is maintained between the two countries.

PERSPECTIVE is the name given to the branch of art in which the rules for correct drawing are laid down. It is usually divided into *Linear Perspective*, in which form and outline alone are considered; and *Aerial Perspective*, in which the effects of the atmosphere, &c., on distinctness are considered. But what is commonly meant by the word is that which appertains to linear perspective. The rules of perspective exhibit a curious combination of principles derived from the science of optics, with others depending on pictorial or artistic principles.

PERTHSHIRE. In this Scottish county the plantations have been much extended of late years, and many districts have been covered with them. Oak, ash, birch, beech, elm, lime, alder, plane, and larch trees, are planted, though not so extensively as the fir tribe. The most valuable tract is the Carse of Gowrie, the district watered by the Isla and its tributaries the Ericht and the Airdle, and comprehending a portion both of Forfarshire and Perthshire. The Carse of Gowrie, Strathearn, and the valleys of the Teith and the Forth, yield good crops of wheat; but in the midland districts oats and barley are the principal grain crops. Turnip cultivation is carried on to a considerable extent. The chief article of agricultural produce is, however, the potato, of which great quantities are yearly shipped for London.

The cotton and linen manufactures are very extensively carried on in this county: Stanley is the principal seat of the one, Dundee of the other, Woollens and silks are also woven, the latter at Perth. It was the cheapness of labour which led to the establishment of the cotton manufacture in this part of Scotland; for it is not so well suited as the Glasgow district, in respect either to the supply of coal or to convenience of shipment, to a manufacture on the factory system.

PERU. In this once celebrated and still interesting country the forests supply, besides timber, vanilla, sarsaparilla, copaiva, caoutchouc, dye-woods, medicinal bark, resins and gums, indigo, and a number of other useful products. The cultivated lands yield, according to their latitude and elevation, olives, sugar, bananas, yams, mandioc, grain, and many other useful plants.

The Peruvian Indians consume a very small quantity of European manufactured articles. Only the creoles dress in European stuffs. There are some manufactures of cordovan leather, and some tanneries and soap-houses. The iron utensils, such as hatchets, scissors, &c., made in Caxamarca, are highly valued. In the large towns many persons are occupied with making vessels, utensils, and ornaments of gold and silver. The country is too mountainous to admit the making of carriage-roads in the interior. Mules and llamas are generally used by travellers and for the transport of merchandise. Six great roads traverse the country from west to east; and the goods imported from foreign countries are sent by these roads into the interior of Peru. The goods exported are chiefly gold, sugar, and saltpetre. The principal harbours from which the exports are made, are—Payta, Lambayeque, Callao, Pisco, Islay, Arica, and Yquique. Peru is beginning to share the advantage of steam navigation on the Pacific.

The British produce and manufactures exported to Peru in 1849 amounted in value to 878,251*l*. The imports from Peru into Great Britain amounted in the same year to (official value) 1,037,903*l*.

PERUVIAN BARK. [CINCHONA.]

PESTH. This, the greatest city in Hungary, has considerable industrial and commercial activity. The manufactures are silk, cotton, leather, jewellery, and musical instruments; that of tobacco is a government monopoly. Pesth has, next to Vienna, the greatest trade of any city on the Danube. It has four fairs, each of which lasts a fortnight. The principal articles sold are manufactures, colonial produce, cattle, wine, wool, tobacco, and raw hides, honey, wax, &c. The disasters of this interesting city during the lamentable war of 1848-9 form no part of our present subject. The relations between Pesth and its sister town are noticed elsewhere. [BUDA.]

PETERSBURGH, ST. This celebrated city is not only the capital but the greatest manufacturing city of the Russian empire. There are above two hundred manufactories of different descriptions, some carried on by private individuals, of silk, cotton, woollen, leather, glass, gold and silver articles, watches, surgical instruments, paper, snuff and tobacco, sugar, &c. There are others which the government has considered it advisable to carry on upon its own account; such are the great manufactory of tapestry, a large manufactory of aqua fortis, an assay-office and a mint, a plate-glass manufactory, a porcelain manufactory, a great manufactory of cotton and linen, and a cannon-foundry and powder-mills.

The commerce of St. Petersburgh is very considerable. Cronstadt is the harbour. The exports are hemp, flax, tallow, leather, iron, tobacco, canvas, coarse linen, bees'-wax, linseed, linseed-oil, tar, potash, &c. The imports are colonial produce of all kinds, manufactures of silk, cotton, hardware, French wines, jewellery, and all articles of luxury and fashion. The trade with England is greater than with any other country. A few industrial statistics will be found under RUSSIA.

PETRO'LEUM is a viscid variety of bitumen, found in many parts of Europe and America, but chiefly in Asia, flowing from beds associated with coal strata. It has a dark reddish-brown colour; it is slightly translucent, and its odour is bituminous. When petroleum is heated to nearly 450°, drops of an oily fluid come over, though very slowly; this oily body has a brown colour, and is very liquid. *Petrolene* is the name given by Boussingault to this oil; it has a pale yellow colour, slight taste, and a bituminous smell. *Asphaltene* is the solid portion of petroleum. Its colour is black, and it has a great deal of lustre. It breaks with a conchoidal fracture, and is heavier than water. There is an intimate chemical relation between petroleum and several other inflammable substances. [ASPHALTE; BITUMEN; NAPHTHA.]

PETUNTZE is the Chinese name for a white earth used with kaolin in the manufacture of porcelain. Kaolin is said to be derived from the decomposition of the felspar of granitic rocks. Petuntze is the same mineral which has not suffered decomposition, and on account of its fusibility is employed in glazing the porcelain. The English manufacturers of porcelain have sought for and found certain varieties of stone and clay which greatly resemble petuntze and kaolin.

PEWTER is a compound metal, extensively employed, especially in the manufacture of those drinking vessels called *pewter pots*. The finest pewter is said to consist of 12 parts of tin, 1 part of antimony, and a very little copper; while common pewter consists of about 80 parts of tin and 20 of lead. Pewter was formerly much more employed that at present, especially in the manufacture of plates and dishes.

PHILIPPINES. These islands, among the most important in the Indian seas, are rich both in produce and in commerce. The staple articles for the European market are sugar, indigo, rum, and tobacco; and for the Chinese market, sapan-wood, rice, edible birds' nests, and trepang. A small quantity of coffee, ebony, sulphur, cotton, pearls, mother-of pearl shells, tortoise shells, and cordage, are also exported. Cordage is made from the fibres of a species of banana. The principal food of the inhabitants consists of rice and fish. They also cultivate millet, and several kinds of beans and other pulse. The fruit-trees include the cocoa-nut, bread-fruit, mango, orange, fig, areca-nut, and plantain. Gold, iron, and copper, are said to exist in Luzon and Magindanao, but at present none of these metals are worked. Salt and brimstone are procured in several places.

The Malays use very few manufactured goods exported from other countries, and they have applied themselves to some branches of manufacture with success, including earthenware, cotton stuffs, straw and chip hats, mats, and especially cigars and cheroots.

The commerce of the Philippines was formerly limited to the mother country and the Spanish colonies in America. The most important and lucrative branch was the commerce with Mexico, which was conducted by means of galleons that sailed once a year between Acapulco, in Mexico, and Manila, in the Philippines. They chiefly carried to America silk manufactures, and other goods, obtained from the Chinese, and brought in return the produce of the Mexican silver-mines. But since the Spanish colonies in America have obtained their independence, the port of Manila has been thrown open to all commercial nations, and the increase of the exports has been very rapid. Manila now carries on commerce with a great number of nations. The value of British merchandise exported to the Philippines averages about 100,000*l.* annually.

PHLOGISTON. Before the agency of oxygen in leading to the phenomena of combustion and flame was discovered, the name of *phlogiston* was given to an hypothetical substance, by supposing the existence of which Stahl explained the nature of combustion. He imagined that by combination with phlogiston a body was rendered combustible, and that its disengagement occasioned combustion, and after its evolution there remained either an acid or an earth: thus sulphur was by this theory supposed to be composed of phlogiston and sulphuric acid; and lead, of the calx of lead and phlogiston, &c. The doctrine proposed by Stahl maintained its ground for about half a century. Soon after the discovery of oxygen gas by Dr. Priestley, the experiments which others had made on the calcination of the metals were repeated with great accuracy by Lavoisier; the consequence was, that the phlogistic theory gave way to the antiphlogistic; for the combustion, which had been attributed to the extrication of phlogiston, was known in all common cases to be derived from the absorption of oxygen, and this explained the increase of weight which bodies acquired by combustion, whereas on the phlogistic theory they ought to have suffered a diminution by the process.

PHŒNIX OR DATE TREE. The date tree (*Phœnix dactylifera*) is one of the most valuable among eastern plants. A considerable part of the inhabitants of Egypt, Arabia, and Persia subsist almost entirely on its fruit. They make a conserve of it with sugar, and even grind the hard stones in their hand-mills for their camels. In Barbary they form handsome beads for paternosters of these stones. From the leaves they make couches, baskets, bags, mats, brushes, and fly-traps; the trunk is split and used in small buildings, also for fences to gardens, and the stalks of the leaves for making cages for their poultry. The threads of the web-like integument at the bases of the leaves are twisted into ropes, which are employed in rigging small vessels. The sap is obtained by cutting off the head of the palm and scooping out a hollow in the top of the stem, where, in ascending, it lodges itself. Three or four quarts of sap may be obtained daily from a single palm, for ten days or a fortnight, after which the quantity lessens, until at the end of six weeks or two months, the stem is exhausted, becomes dry, and is used for firewood. This liquor is sweetish when first collected, and may be drunk as a mild beverage, but fermentation soon takes place, and a spirit is produced, which is distilled, and forms one of the kinds of arrack. Such being the importance and various uses of the date-tree, it is not surprising that in an arid and barren country it should form so prominent a subject of allusion and description in the works of Arab authors, and that it should be said to have 300 names in their language. Many of these are, however, applied to different parts of the plant, as well as to plants of different ages.

Another kind, called the *Phœnix sylvestris*, is a species common in the arid parts of India. It yields, by incision, tarri, or palm wine, commonly called toddy. Mats and baskets are made of the leaves. Sugar is made from this species.

PHOSPHORUS. This elementary body was discovered in 1669, by Brandt, an alchymist of Hamburg. It is contained in many substances of animal origin, but it is usually procured from bones. Phosphorus is solid, translucent, and nearly colourless, but sometimes it has a yellow reddish tint; it is so soft that it may be indented by the nail, and it is very readily cut. When heated to about 108° it fuses, and at 550° it is converted into vapour. It has a peculiar smell when exposed to the air, but this is probably derived from the action of the oxygen of the air upon it. Neither water nor alchohol dissolves phosphorus, but it is dissolved by æther and by oils. It emits light when exposed to the air in the dark. It is extremely inflammable, and has been known to take fire spontaneously in the atmosphere when its temperature was not above 60°.

Phosphorus combines with a great many other substances, to form oxides, acids, phosphurets, salts, &c.; several of which are useful in the arts and in medicine.

PHOTOGRAPHY. *Photographic pictures* are facsimile representations of objects, produced by the chemical action of light on a prepared tablet, upon which the images of the objects are thrown by a camera-obscura. Such a process has been named after its inventor the *Daguerreotype;* but other methods have received the names of *Calotype*, *Talbotype*, *Chrysotype*, &c. The process generally may be termed photography (light-drawing), or heliography (sun-drawing). The invention was first formally communicated to the public by M. Arago, who read an account of the Daguerreotype process before the Academy of Sciences, January 7, 1839. From that moment Daguerre (who was afterwards rewarded by a pension by the government) and his invention engrossed general attention. The discovery was spoken of as little short of miraculous; and though it does not realise all the sanguine hopes of its early inventors, the invention is unquestionably highly valuable, because it not only ensures perfect fidelity of likeness where it is most essential, and where it is hardly attainable by the most practised and patient hand and eye, but also gives us the minutest details—those which are imperceptible to the naked eye, and of course cannot possibly be represented upon paper, yet become visible in a photographic drawing when it is examined with a magnifying-glass.

In Daguerre's original process, the photographic drawings were produced upon plates of copper coated over with silver. After being washed with a solution of nitric acid, the plate was put into a well-closed box, where it was exposed to the action of iodine, a small quantity of the latter being placed at the bottom of the box with a thin gauze between it and the plate. A layer of ioduret of silver was thus formed on the surface of the plate, and manifested itself by the yellow hue produced on the silver, which shows that the process of giving the plate the sensitive coating on which the action of light delineates objects is completed. Thus prepared, the plate was next placed within a camera-obscura of particular construction; and the delineation of the object was then effected in a very short space of time, but had to be afterwards brought out and rendered distinct by another operation, namely, submitting the plate to the action of vapour of mercury. Even then the process was not completed, for the plate had to be plunged into a solution of hyposulphate of soda, and afterwards washed in distilled water, which being done, the impression was fixed, and the plate could be exposed to light with perfect safety.

Mr. Fox Talbot, and other experimenters, were engaged upon somewhat similar researches about the same time as M. Daguerre; and within the last twelve years numerous improvements have been introduced by Herschel, Talbot, Hunt, Claudet, Beard, Kilburn, and others.

By the experiments of these individuals much has been done to render Daguerreotype portraits more pleasing, by improved management of the light, and by placing behind the sitters painted screens, to relieve the head, and to form artificial backgrounds. One of the greatest difficulties in the original process arose from the circumstance, that, as the image produced in the camera-obscura was totally invisible until brought out by a subsequent exposure to the vapour of mercury, it was impossible to tell precisely at what moment the action of the light should be stopped, to avoid, on the one hand, an image imperfectly developed, and, on the other, the misty undefined appearance occasioned by the unavoidable motion of the object to be copied (whenever it is an animate object), and the discoloured or burnt appearance of an image which has been exposed too long to tho chemical action of light. This inconvenience has been remedied by many ingenious devices. One important class of improvements has reference to the means of fixing and securing from injury by the subsequent action of light or other means, the Daguerreotype image. Considerable progress has been made towards transferring the colours of natural objects to the Daguerreotypes; but in the ordinary coloured Daguerreotypes, some of which mako a tolerably near approach to the effect which might be expected if colours could be fixed in the camera-obscura, the tinting is produced by the application of finely powdered colours to the surface of the photographic impression, which is previously coated with an alcoholic solution of copal, and nearly dried; so that the colouring, which is so delicately performed as not to impair the distinctness of the impression, is not in any degree the result of the action of light.

Most of the numerous patented or proposed improvements in the art depend chiefly on the mode of producing the pictures. The Chromatype, Chrysotype, Calotype, Cyanotype, Amphitype, and Ferrotype, all are so many modes of producing and fixing the impressions. Some of the improvements, however, relate to the mechanism of the camera-obscura, in which the sensitive surface is placed. See further on this point under AMPHITYPE; CALOTYPE; CHROMATYPE.

Mr. Brunel has lately registered an apparatus called a *Photographotrope*, comprising all the necessary materials for taking and fixing a photographic picture, packed up so as to stand upon a tripod or simple support. There is at the top of the apparatus a camera for producing the focal image of the object; and there are the proper means for impressing this image upon a metal plate. Below this is a spirit lamp in a tube, and a recess in which the plate is to be placed to be acted on by heated mercurial vapour. Below this again, is a small galvanic battery, which expedites the photographic process.

PHOTOMETER is the name given to instruments constructed for the purpose of measuring the relative illuminating powers of different sources of light. Photometers have been constructed by Professor Leslie, and by Mr. Ritchie, late professor of natural philosophy in London University College; but a mode of comparing the illuminating powers of two lights was suggested by Count Rumford, which is remarkable for the facility with which it may be applied, and the simplicity of the requisite apparatus, nothing more being needed than a smooth surface of small extent and of a light uniform colour, and a blackened stick for throwing a shadow. The surface is illuminated by the two lights experimented upon, which are to be so placed, that when the stick is interposed between them and the surface, the two shadows may be nearly in contact, which will enable the eye to decide whether they are of equal depth, and will at the same time ensure the intercepting of rays equally inclined to the surface. So long as the shadows are of unequal depth, one of the lights must be brought nearer to or retired farther from the surface till an equality of depth is obtained, and then the squares of the perpendicular distances of the lights from the surface give the ratio of their intensities. If an equality between the inclinations of the intercepted rays to the surface cannot be obtained, then, when the two shadows are of the same depth, the intensities of the lights will be directly proportional to the squares of their perpendicular distances from the surface, and inversely proportional to the sines of the inclinations of the intercepted rays to the surface. This method is theoretically perfect when applied to lights of the same colour.

PIANO-FORTE. This musical instrument is variously formed, and receives different designations, such as *grand*, *square*, *semi-grand*, *cabinet*, *cottage*, and *piccolo*. The first notion of the square piano forte was taken from the clavichord by a German mechanic of the name of Viator, about a hundred years ago; but, for want of friends or funds, he never became known as a maker. The invention, however, was followed up by other musical instrument makers of the same nation, who all left their clavichords and harpsichords for the new instrument, the piano-forte. The grand piano-forte is supposed to be of earlier date than the square piano-forte, and is said to have been the invention of a German musician of the name of Schröder, or, as others say, of Christofali, a harpsichord-maker of Padua. The first maker at all known in this country was a German of the name of Backers, but we are not aware that success attended his exertions in comparison with the solid advantages which were enjoyed by his contemporary, Zumpe, who realised an ample fortune, and retired.

The grand piano-forte retains the shape of the instrument from which it was taken, the harpsichord. Here we have two instruments alike in form, but unlike in almost every other circumstance; for their action, their tones, and the style in which they are played upon, are all entirely different. The action of the harpsichord was simply a key and what was called a *jack*, which was a piece of pear-tree with a small moveable tongue of holly, through which a cutting of crow-quill was passed to touch the string when the jack was in action; the tone produced by this contrivance was a kind of scratch with a sound at the end of it. The action of a grand piano-forte consisted of a *key*, a *lever*, a *hammer*, a *button*, a *check*, and a *damper*, with rails and sockets to connect them. By this combination of parts, every musical effect known or desired at that time was perfectly attainable, and with admirable results by Mozart, Haydn, Cramer, and others. But modern music requires greater powers in the instruments; and for the last half century, the Broadwoods, Erards, Collards, and other celebrated makers, have introduced a succession of singular and most delicate contrivances, to give all possible perfection to the tones and the means of their production.

The *square* piano-forte was taken from the clavichord, but it retains only its shape, with the same disposition of the strings and keys: their actions have no similarity. It may be necessary to state that the 'action' of a piano-forte is the technical name for the whole of the mechanism which intervenes between the pressure on the key and the striking of the string. The action of the clavichord was simply a piece of brass pin-wire, which was placed vertically at a point where it could be struck or pressed against its proper string, the right-hand division of which was free to vibrate, whilst the left-hand was muffled by a piece of cloth, the object of which was to damp or stop the string, which it did the instant the finger was taken off the key. The touch of the clavichord was peculiar, partaking both of the harpsichord and the organ; in other words, both *struck* and *pressed*, and the pressure could be so varied as to produce a kind of tremblant effect. The tones were feeble, soft, and melancholy, and better suited to the student, the composer, or the solitary, than any purposes of social amusement.

The action of the square piano forte, on its first introduction, consisted of a *key*, a *lifter*, a *hammer*, and a *damper*. The key was the same as that of the clavichord. The lifter was a brass wire, with a piece of hide leather as a head, which was covered with a piece of soft leather as a finish. This lifter, when in motion, struck the hammer against the string, and thus produced the tone of the instrument. The damper followed the performer, and stopped the vibrations as quickly as the finger was removed from the key. The tone of this piano-forte was thin and wiry, the hammer having only one slight covering of sheep-skin leather upon it. The subsequent improvements in the square piano-forte down to the present day have consisted chiefly in the application of sundry small pieces of mechanism, called the *hopper*, the *under-hammer*, and the *check*, to improve the tone.

Some piano-fortes have seven octaves; but the usual number in the best instruments is six and a-half; in others six, or five and a half. The strings of the early piano-fortes were partly of steel and partly of brass, the treble notes of steel, and the lower notes of brass; a few of which, in the bass, were over-lapped or covered, rather open, with plated copper wire, to give them more gravity, according to the length attainable in the instrument. But modern piano-fortes have steel wire throughout with about an octave in the bass closely lapped with unplated copper wire. The strings which are now used in piano-fortes are considerably larger than those which were formerly used; the advantages of which are durability and firmness. Almost all the wire employed for this purpose in England is made by one firm near Birmingham: it requires especial care in the manufacture. *Stops* and *pedals* are used in various degrees in piano-fortes; the stops are moved by hand, to alter the position of the dampers used against the strings; the pedals are moved by the feet for an analogous purpose.

The upright piano-forte was, doubtless, taken from the upright harpsichord; it was invented by Mr. Hancock. The next novelty was the invention of Mr. Hawkins, who constructed an upright instrument with a detached sound-board in an iron frame, and the whole was so arranged as to be able to meet the atmosphere with compensating powers. In the bass, it had spiral or helical strings, by which length was gained; and, in the treble, three octaves of equal tension were accomplished by a uniform size of wire. The cabinet piano-forte and the piccolo piano-forte were two other forms in which the strings were placed vertically: the minor changes in these two varieties have been very numerous.

A laudable attempt has been made within the last year or two to construct piano-fortes which, while well made and of good tune, shall be comparatively cheap on account of being made of plain materials. No efforts, however, can make this a cheap instrument; the mechanism is too intricate and delicate for us to hope to realise "piano-fortes for the million," so far as price is concerned.

PIAZZA. Although in the Italian language a piazza signifies merely an open place, it is employed by us to denote a covered ambulatory, whether formed by columns or arches, in the lower part of a building; such cloistered walks being very common in the *piazze*, or public squares, of Italian cities, as that of St. Mark's at Venice, &c.

PIER, is the general name for the solid spaces between a series of openings in a wall, whether windows or arches; but in its technical meaning the term is more particularly applied to the pillar-like masses of masonry or brickwork from which arches spring, rising from the impost capping the pier, and which generally consists of a series of mouldings, although sometimes it is merely a plat-band, and occasionally the impost is omitted altogether, especially in rusticated basements. In many instances columns are substituted for piers, placed either singly or in pairs; and the arches spring either immediately from their capitals or from an entablature over them. There are again many examples in which both piers and a lesser order or sub-order of columns are employed, the latter being insulated on each side of the pier, and their entablature forming the impost from which the arches spring.

The term pier is also applied to the solid masses supporting the arches of a bridge; with the exception of the extreme ones, which are distinguished by the name of abutments. The term is also applied to a mole or jetty carried out into the sea, whether intended to serve as an embankment to protect vessels from the open sea, or merely as a landing-place; for which latter purpose suspension chain-bridges are now frequently employed.

PIGS. The commercial value of swine is very considerable; for besides the flesh considered as an article of food, the skin, the bristles, and other parts of the animal are applied to many useful purposes. In 'Frazer's Magazine' for October, 1850, is given a lively account of the traffic which these animals occasion in one of the newly-formed cities of the United States; the paper has the usual rattling tone of a Magazine article; but there is internal evidence that the statements are trustworthy respecting the varied purposes to which the slaughtered animals can be applied, in a district where the supply is abundant.

That Ireland depends greatly on pigs 'to pay the rent' is well known. A very large proportion of the pigs reared in Ireland find their way either alive or cured into the English market. This transit has increased to an astonishing extent since the Union. In 1801 there were only 2000 pigs sent from Ireland to England; in 1805 it was 6383; in 1813 it was 14,521; in 1821 it was 104,501. In this last named year steam navigation began to tell in the matter, by lessening the expense of freight. By the year 1837 the number rose to 700,000. It is difficult now to form a judgment of the number, for the trade between the two countries is in most cases assimilated to a coasting trade. The small farmers of Ireland mostly sell their pigs to jobbers or dealers who go round the country, and who either drive the pigs at once to the shipping ports, or sell them to third parties who fatten, slaughter and cure the pigs for the bacon market. The year 1847 was not a good year for taking any averages in Ireland; but in that year it was found there were, living in all the farms of Ireland, 622,459 pigs. Pigs are plentiful in Ireland in good years; and it was well ascertained that the number in the calamitous 1847 was far below the average.

The swine and hogs imported into Great Britain from foreign countries in the last three years were:—

Year.	No. Imported.
1848	2,119
1849	2,653
1850	7,287

In fact, we are almost exclusively dependent on Ireland for such of our pigs, pork, and bacon as is not the produce of our own island.

The pigs sold at Smithfield yearly average about 40,000; the selling price presenting a usual average of about 30*s*. The dead pigs sold in Newgate Market annually give an aggregate weight of about 110,000 to 120,000 stone of 8 lbs., besides 15,000 sucking pigs. At Leadenhall Market the weight amounts to the large quantity of 500,000 stone. The Leadenhall butchers also slaughter about 30,000 pigs annually.

PILE ENGINE is a machine by which a heavy mass of iron is raised to a considerable height in the air; the mass being then allowed to fall by gravity on the head of a pile, the momentum acquired by the descent forces the pile into the ground.

Such an engine is employed in driving piles for the support of the sleepers or horizontal timbers on which are built the piers of bridges, the revetments of the ramparts of fortresses, or any other heavy mass of brick-work or stone-work when the soil is not sufficiently firm to carry the structure. Piles are also thus driven in order to form cofferdams in rivers, preparatory to the construction of piers or the faces of quays, basins, &c.

The most important improvement in pile-engines is the steam-hammer of Mr. Nasmyth. The principle of this most powerful instrument consists in having a small steam engine so connected with the ram or hammer, that after the latter has fallen by its own gravity, it is raised again by the action of steam. The saving of the time by the use of this machine is very great, and the invention is one of singular importance in engineering. It is applicable to the forging of anchors, and other works, where powerful blows are to be given.

A very remarkable principle has been introduced within the last few years in pile-driving; it was invented by Dr. Potts, and has been extensively applied by Stephenson, Brunel, and other engineers. In the ordinary process the power is applied to the pile; but in Potts' method the power is applied to the ground itself. The pile is hollow, and is placed perpendicularly over the spot where it is to be sunk; it is made air-tight on the top by fixing a cast iron plate upon it. A tube passes through this plate or cover, and connects the hollow of the pile with an air-pump. When the air is drawn out of the hollow centre, the sand or gravel is sucked up into it, by atmospheric pressure, and the metallic pile is facilitated in its descent. In some cases this operation has been conducted on an enormous scale. A bridge has lately been built by Messrs. Fox and Henderson over the Shannon for one of the Irish railways. It is supported on Dr. Potts' hollow piles. Each pile is ten feet in diameter; and these enormous masses were sunk into a clay soil with astonishing rapidity, by withdrawing the air from the interior of the pile.

PIMENTO, is the produce of *Eugenia Pimenta*, a tree native of the West Indies, but cultivated almost exclusively in Jamaica, thence called Jamaica Pepper. The unripe two-seeded berries, which are about the size of a pea, are dried by frequent turning in the sun, by which their colour is changed from green to brown or grayish-brown. The shell is very brittle, about the thickness of a card, and encloses two seeds, which are roundish, dark brown, somewhat shining, and having a weak aromatic taste. The shell possesses an agreeable clove-like taste and smell. Two kinds are met with in commerce, English and Spanish, of which the former is the better. About 20,000 cwts. of Pimento are imported yearly.

PIN MANUFACTURE. The first thing to be done in the manufacture of pins by the hand method is to reduce a quantity of brass wire to the requisite size. This is generally done in the pin factory, as the wire is received of larger diameter than necessary. It is performed in the usual manner of wire drawing; and the wire is then made up into coils of six inches diameter, and any dirt or crust which may be attached to the surface is got rid of by first soaking the coils in a diluted solution of sulphuric acid and water, and then beating them on stones. The next process is to straighten the wire; after which it is cut into pieces, each about long enough for six pins. These latter pieces are then pointed at each end, in the following manner—The person so employed sits in front of a small machine, which has two steel wheels or mills turning rapidly; of which the rims are cut somewhat after the manner of a file, one coarse, for the rough formation of the points, and the other fine for finishing them. Several of these pieces are taken in the hand, and by a dexterous movement of the thumb and fore-finger are kept continually presenting a different face to the mill against which they are pressed. The points are then finished off by being applied in the same manner to the fine mill. After both ends of the pieces have been pointed, one pin's length is cut off from each end, when they are repointed, and so on until each length is converted into six pointed pieces. The stems of the pins are then complete. The next step is to form the head, which is effected by a piece of wire called the mould, the same size as that used for the stems, being attached to a small axis or lathe At the end of the wire nearest the axis is a hole, in which is placed the end of a smaller wire, which is to form the heading. While the mould wire is turned round by one hand, the head wire is guided by the other, until it is wound in a spiral coil along the entire length of the former. It is then cut off close to the hole where it was commenced, and the coil taken off the mould. When a quantity of these coils are prepared, a workman takes a dozen or more of them at a time in his left hand, while with a pair of shears in his right he cuts them up into pieces of two coils each. The heads, when cut off, are annealed by being made hot and then thrown into water. When annealed, they are ready to be fixed on the stems. In order to do this, the operator is provided with a small stake, upon which is fixed a steel die, containing a hollow the exact shape of half the head. Above this die, and attached to a lever, is the corresponding die for the other half of the head, which, when at rest, remains suspended about two inches above the lower one. The workman takes one of the stems between his fingers, and dipping the pointed end into a bowl containing a number of the heads, catches one upon it and slides it to the other end; he then places it in the lower die, and moving a treadle brings down the upper one four or five times upon the head, which fastens it upon the stem, and also gives it the required figure. There is a small channel leading from the outside to the centre of the dies, to allow room for the stem. The pins are now finished as regards shape, and it only remains to tin or whiten them. A quantity of them are boiled in a pickle, either a solution of sulphuric acid or tartar, to remove any dirt or grease, and also to produce a slight roughness upon their surfaces, which facilitates the adhesion of the tin. After being boiled for half an hour, they are washed and then placed in a copper vessel with a quantity of grain tin and a solution of tartar; in about two hours and a half they are taken out, and after being separated from the undissolved tin by sifting are again washed; they are then dried by being well shaken in a bag with a quantity of bran, which is afterwards separated by shaking them up and down in open wooden trays, when the bran flies off and leaves the pins perfectly dry and clean. The pins are then papered for sale.

The drawing and cutting the wire, the cutting of the heads from the coils, and the tinning, are performed by men; the other operations by women and children.

Machines have been invented, and partially employed for some of the processes; but most pins are made by the hand method.

PINE TREE. Under ABIES is given a brief description of some among the many varieties of Fir trees. We will here glance at some of the more prominent uses of the Pine, which has many points of similarity to the fir.

In respect to food the pine and fir do not render much service, at least in European countries. The *pine apple* is a misnomer; it is the fruit of another kind of plant, and has obtained its name from a certain resemblance to the cone of a pine tree. The Romans used the pine cones to flavour their wine; and some modern nations do the same. The Laplanders grind the inner bark of the Scotch pine into a kind of coarse flour, to make bread. Pine meal and oatmeal, mixed into a dough, and baked in a pan or plate, are said to make tolerable cakes. The young shoots are eaten in Siberia. Chips of pine have sometimes been used as a substitute for hops. The kernels of the fruit of the stone pine are pleasant eating, and are dished up in various ways in France and Italy. Of the Cembra pine, the kernels yield an oil, and the shell of the kernel yields a red dye. *Spruce* and *spruce beer* are made in the following way:—Twigs of the spruce fir are fastened into a bundle, and boiled in a copper until the bark separates. While this is doing, a given weight of oats is roasted on a hot plate, with sea biscuits or slices of bread. These ingredients are then boiled with the twigs for some time. Sugar or molasses is added; and the liquid is tunned off, leaving all the solid ingredients behind; a little yeast is added, and spruce beer is the result. In England spruce beer is made from *essence of spruce*, which is prepared in America from the young twigs.

As a timber tree, it is scarcely possible to enumerate all the uses of the pine and fir. Many of them are mentioned under ABIES. One species yields long straight timbers for the masts of ships; another is available for part of the hull; a third for flooring boards in a house. It is of white pine that the three magnificent American bridges are constructed, at Philadelphia, Trenton, and Boston.

It would suffice to take the Norway spruce fir as an example of the numerous uses which these trees subserve, in addition to those in which the timber is employed. When burned it yields valuable fuel and charcoal; the ashes furnish potash; the bark is used in tanning; the buds and young shoots yield spruce beer; the cones, boiled in whey, are used as a remedy against the scurvy; the young shoots are used as fodder for live stock in many countries; the floors of rooms and the pathways to churchyards are strewed with the young green tops in Sweden; the inner bark is made into baskets in Sweden and Norway; the long and slender rootlets are used as cords.

The pine and fir yield many remarkable substances derived from the juice or sap of the tree. Among these are *resin*, *turpentine*, *tar*, *pitch*, *lamp black*, &c. Their relation to each other may be stated as follows:—turpentine is the juice of the living tree; resin is a solid residue obtained from the turpentine; spirit of turpentine is the clear liquid which results when the resin is removed from turpentine; tar is the juice of the dead tree; and lampblack is the soot obtained by burning the above. These substances are described under their proper headings.

PINK. There are many varieties of pink colour employed as pigments by artists and painters; but there are also some which, though bearing this name, have not the tint which is usually known by the name of pink. *Brown pink* is a yellow pigment, prepared from French berries, pearlash, fustic, and alum. *Dutch pink* has a golden yellow colour; it is prepared from French berries, turmeric, alum, and whiting or starch. *Rose pink*, which has a roseate hue, is obtained by mixing whiting with a decoction of Brazil wood and pearlash. *Pink dye*, used as a cosmetic and for tinting silk stockings, is made from safflower, subcarbonate of potash, spirit of wine, and lemon juice. *Pink saucers* used by artists, are small saucers on the interior surface of which a layer of pink colour or paint is deposited; the colour is made from safflower, carbonate of soda, French chalk, and solution of tartaric acid; a red powder is produced, which is applied to the saucer with gum.

PIPES. Pipes, tubes, or cylinders are made in various ways, according to their size and material. The large iron cylinders for steam engines, hydraulic machines, and other engineering works, are cast in sand moulds, in the manner described in FOUNDING. Stone cylinders and pipes are cut by the aid of machinery, as noticed under STONE WORKING. Glass pipes are coming extensively into use for draining and for other purposes; they are produced by a combined process of blowing and drawing, something like that by which barometer tubes are made [BAROMETER]. Lead pipes are made in three or four different ways [LEAD]; and those of copper in two or three [COPPER MANUFACTURE]. Wooden water pipes (now almost superseded by iron) are made by boring out the centre of a tree-trunk; and some other kinds of tubes are bored out of the solid [BORING]. TOBACCO PIPES are described in a later article.

PISTON. [AIR-PUMP; HYDRAULICS; STEAM ENGINE.]

PITCH. [TAR.]

PIX, TRIAL OF THE. As a security for the integrity of the coinage, it is required that, before the master of the mint can receive his 'discharge,' or an admission that his duties have been properly performed, the coins should be submitted to a trial by jury. This final examination is technically called the *Trial of the Pix*, from the box in which the coins, which have been selected for that purpose, are contained. They are secured by three locks, the keys of which are respectively in the custody of the warden, master, and comptroller of the Mint. Newspaper readers may have remarked that there was a trial of the pix in March, 1851. The important operation of coining is briefly described under MINT.

PLANE TREE. This Asiatic tree is most valued for its ornamental appearance; but it is not without its economical uses. Its timber is fine-grained, hard, and well suited to such kinds of joiners' work as do not require strength; for which its brittleness renders it ill suited. The *occidental* or western plane, as distinguished from the *oriental* or eastern plane, is a less beautiful tree, and the timber less valuable.

PLANING MACHINERY. The first attempt to economise labour by means of planing machinery was made by General Bentham, who obtained a patent in 1791 for a contrivance by which large planes, wide enough to take the whole width of a plank at one stroke, and supplied with apparatus for directing their course, regulating the depth to which they could cut, and, generally speaking, for superseding the necessity of skill and judgment on the part of the operator, might be worked either by mechanical power or by manual labour. The improved principle, now generally adopted, was introduced in Bramah's patent of 1802. In a beautiful machine which he constructed for the Woolwich Arsenal, the wood is placed upon a carriage, and drawn by hydraulic power under the lower surface of a rapidly revolving disk or mill, to the face of which a series of planes or cutting instruments are attached, which, acting upon the wood in quick succession, bring it to a very smooth and even surface.

Immense saving of labour, accompanied with a corresponding improvement in accuracy has been effected by the application of planing machinery to the levelling of iron and other metals, in lieu of the cold chisel and the file, worked by hand. In some instances this has been done on the principle of Bramah's machine above referred to; but more generally the planing of iron is effected by a stationary cutter, the iron being brought under it by a rectilinear motion. For this purpose it is not usual to employ wide cutting instruments, as for wood; but a narrow tool, cutting a mere line of the surface at once, is brought into contact with all parts of the surface to be levelled in succession.

PLANISPHERE. A planisphere, as now usually constructed, is an instrument for finding the position of the heavens at any one moment, much more easily used than the celestial globe, and very much less expensive. A circular disk of pasteboard, on which the stars visible in our latitude are laid down, turns on a second disk, round which are the days of the year on one circle, and the hours of the day on another. A third and hollow disk turns upon the same pivot, the hollow part being so cut that the portion of the heavens which it shows is precisely that which is visible at one time in the latitude of the instrument: the points of the compass are marked round the rim of the hollow disk or of the horizon. The effect is that by setting the disk which contains the stars to the day of the year, and the hollow disk to the hour of the day, the part of the heavens visible at that day and hour is distinctly shown. The time at which any star rises, culminates, and sets can be found.

PLANTAIN. The plantain is the fruit of the *musa sapientum*, and is eaten to a most remarkable extent by the inhabitants of the torrid zone. From its nutritious qualities and general use, it may, whether used in a raw or dressed form, be regarded rather as a necessary article of food than as an occasional luxury. In tropical countries the plantain is one of the most interesting objects of cultivation for the subsistence of man. Three dozen fruits will maintain a person, instead of bread, for a week, and appears better suited to him in warm countries than that kind of food. Indeed the plantain is often the whole support of an Indian family. The fruit is produced from among the immense leaves in bunches, weighing 30, 60, and 80 lbs., of various colours, and of great diversity of form. It usually is long and narrow, of a pale yellow or dark red colour, with a yellow farinaceous flesh. But in form it varies to oblong and nearly spherical; and in colour it offers all the shades and variations of tints that the combination of yellow and red, in different proportions, can produce. Some sorts are said always to be of a bright green colour. In general, the character of the fruit to an European palate is that of mild insipidity; some sorts are even so coarse as not to be edible without preparation. The greater number however are used in their raw state, and some varieties acquire by cultivation a very exquisite flavour, even surpassing the finest pear. In the better sorts the flesh has the colour of the finest yellow butter, is of a delicate taste, and melts in the mouth like marmalade. In the West Indies, plantains appear to be even more extensively employed than in the Eastern world. The modes of eating them are various. The best sorts are served up raw at table, as in the East Indies, and have been compared for flavour to an excellent reinette apple after its sweetness has been condensed by keeping through the winter. Sometimes they are baked in their skins, and then they taste like the best stewed pears of Europe. They are also the principal ingredient in a variety of dishes.

The *Banana* of hot countries is a mere variety of the plantain, distinguished by being dwarf, with a spotted stem. Botanists call it *Musa Paradisiaca*, in allusion to an old notion that it was the Forbidden Fruit of Scripture.

PLANTING and PLANTATIONS. Planting is the operation of placing in the soil the roots of a plant which has been previously removed. The manner of performing the operation may be reduced to one general principle; that of placing the roots in the soil so as to imitate as closely as possible the position which they occupy when growing naturally. The excavation for the reception of the roots of a plant should be considerably larger than those roots will traverse when extended at the time of planting. It should be as wide at bottom as at top. The bottom should be more or less convex, and the depth such as to admit of the roots being covered to the extent observed in undisturbed seedling plants of the same species; that is to say, the upper part of the root should only be just covered. The lower roots should be regularly disposed over the convex bottom of the excavation, and carefully strewed with some of the finer portion of soil, over which the other roots may be spread. More soil should then be carefully rather than forcibly introduced. A plentiful watering should be given when the soil is nearly all filled in; and after the water has subsided, so as not to stand above the surface, the latter should be covered with the rest of the soil.

Plantations are generally planted thick in the first instance, and with various species of trees. Larch, Scotch fir or pine, mountain ash, &c., are interspersed amongst the hard wood for shelter, or as nurses. Too close planting produces weak drawn-up timber, in consequence of the tops only receiving a due share of light. If, on the contrary, trees are planted at too great a distance from each other they are inclined to ramify into large limbs and spreading tops, with a stem short but much thicker than where the space admits of less expansion of foliage. If therefore very thick timber of no great length be required, wide planting is proper; but if tall timber be the object, the plantation must be moderately thick. The proper season for felling trees is when the sap is most at rest; the operation ought not to be performed at any other time, unless for firewood. With respect to oaks, the practice of barking in the spring and felling in the succeeding autumn is by no means unobjectionable, and on some accounts is decidedly inferior to felling in autumn or very early in winter without previous disbarking.

PLASTER OF PARIS. [CALCIUM; LIME.]

PLASTERING. The business of the plasterer, besides forming plain plastered ceilings and walls, also embraces the formation and fixing of ornamental cornices, centre pieces, and other similar ornaments.

In plastering a brick wall, the first thing observed is to secure a rough and porous surface to which the composition may adhere readily. In applying the plaster, the surface is first brushed free from dust, then wetted with water, and covered with a first coat of fluid stucco, applied with a coarse bristle brush; after which, before it is quite dry, the first coat of coarse mortar-like composition is applied. In plastering upon quarter partitions or upon the under surface of timber floors to form ceilings, a very different process is adopted. In both of these cases a surface is formed to receive the first coat of plaster by nailing to the timber quarterings, or to the joists in the case of a floor, narrow slips of wood called *laths*. This done, the first coat of plaster, consisting of what is called *coarse stuff*, which is a mortar of lime and sand mixed with ox or horse hair, to give it consistency, is applied with a peculiar kind of trowel, in such a way as to force the mortar through the narrow openings between the laths, behind which in consequence of its soft and wet state, it swells in such a way that, as it sets or hardens, it becomes firmly *keyed* to the laths, so that it could only be broken away in little bits, and by the application of considerable violence. This groundwork serves to receive any kind of plastering that may afterwards be applied.

PLATA, RIO DE LA. This noble South American river has one of the broadest æstuaries in the world. Through this æstuary the commercial produce of about one-fourth of South America is brought to the market of the world. It is therefore a great advantage to the countries from which the æstuary of the Plata receives its waters, that the rivers which flow into it offer less obstruction to navigation than is usual in large streams. These rivers are many of them large; the chief are the Paraná, Uruguay, Paraguay, Pilcomayo, Vermejo, Lavayen, Tarija, and Salado.

The same name of *La Plata* is given to a republic which covers an immense area, and the commerce of which finds an outlet at Buenos Ayres on the south shore of the æstuary. In respect to agricultural produce the republic may be divided into two regions, which are separated from each other by the Gran Salina. On the north of it they partake of the intertropical productions: mandioc, rice, Indian corn, and the cocoa plant are cultivated in most of the lower valleys; while in the more elevated tracts, tobacco and cotton succeed well, and are cultivated on a large scale. South of the Gran Salina the agriculture resembles that of southern Europe, except that no rice is raised; wheat and Indian corn are the principal crops, but barley and lucerne are also extensively grown, especially near Mendoza. The principal exchangeable wealth of the republic is derived from the herds of cattle. The number of heads is above 4,000,000, of which the province of Buenos Ayres alone is said to possess 3,000,000; they wander about in the pampas nearly in a wild state. The largest items in the list of exports consist of hides, hair, horns, tallow, and jerked beef.

Gold and silver occur in the Andes, and also in the Sierra de Cordova. Iron and lead are met with in small quantities. There is little coal; but salt is most abundant.

The most important branch of manufactures is that of *ponchos*, or oblong square pieces of woollen cloth, with a hole in the middle, to pass the head through; they are used by the gauchos and other people as cloaks; the finest are made of vicuna skins, in the town of Santiago del Estero. Some woollen fabrics for men and women's dresses are also made, as well as saddle-cloths. In some parts some coarse cotton-cloth was formerly made by the country-people for their own use, but this branch of domestic industry has been nearly abandoned since the introduction of British manufacture.

The internal commerce of the states is considerable, as most of them have some products which are either not at all or only to a small amount raised in the neighbouring states. The external commerce under Spain was very small; but it has greatly increased within the last few years. Trade is now carried on with all the principal countries of Europe, and with various parts of America. The value of the British and Irish produce and merchandise exported to the Argentine States, between 1836 and 1846, varied from 590,000*l.* to 990,000*l.* annually; and in 1849 it amounted to no less than 1,362,904*l.* The imports from the republic to Great Britain in the same year amounted to 1,392,445*l.*

The exports of the principal articles of produce from January to the end of November, 1850, were as follows, in 402 vessels of 88,762 tons:—Hides, ox and cow, salted, 687,367; ditto, dry, 1,514,965; ditto horse, dry, 47,194; ditto, salted, 127,619; Horns, ox and cow, 1,717,632; Tallow, 11,966 pipes, 24,738 boxes, and 80 serons; Wool, 16,414 bales, 3,262 serons, and 180 arrobas; Beef, jerked, 339,654 quintals.

PLA'TINA, or PLA'TINUM, is an important metal, which was first made known in Europe by Mr. Wood, assay-master in Jamaica, who met with its ore in 1741. Platina is separated from the sand and other matters with which it is mixed, by washing with a great quantity of water, from which the heavier parts of course subside, and these contain the ore in question. The ore of platina is composed of irregular rounded grains, which are sometimes flattened; they are of various sizes, often very small, and occasionally they exhibit traces of crystallisation; but these are probably derived from the presence of some other metal. The ore, which has a specific gravity of 17·33, contains traces of six or seven other metals; and the process of separation is one of great complication. The pure platinum has a grayish white colour, intermediate between silver and tin. When it is free from iridium, it is so very ductilo that it may be drawn into very fine wire, not exceeding the 2000th part of an inch in diameter; it is also very malleable, and may be beaten into thin leaves. When perfectly pure, it is softer than silver, and it is susceptible of receiving a fine polish. Of all metals it is the least expansible. Its density varies from 19½ to 21½ times that of water. It suffers no change by exposure to the air, nor is it oxidized when heated in it. It does not under any circumstances decompose water.

It is infusible in the strongest heat of a smith's forge, but it may be melted by voltaic electricity or by the oxyhydrogen blowpipe. Of all metals, except iron and copper, it is the most tenacious: a wire of the diameter of $\frac{1}{18}$th of an inch, is capable of sustaining a weight of 274 pounds. Like iron, platina possesses the very valuable property of welding at a high temperature, and this enables us to form it into chemical vessels of great and daily use.

The uses of platina are numerous and important; but it is especially employed for forming vessels, not merely for chemical operations on a small scale, but for the concentration of sulphuric acid by manufactures. Some years ago as much as 1000*l.* was paid for a platina still for making certain acrid chemicals; the price being about a guinea an ounce; but it is now lower in value.

PLATING. [ELECTRO-METALLURGY; TIN MANUFACTURE.]

PLOUGH. The oldest forms of plough of which we have any description in ancient authors, or which are represented on monuments or coins, are very simple; a mere wedge with a crooked handle to guide it, and a short beam by which it was drawn, form the whole instrument. The light Hindoo plough, now in use in many parts of India, seems to differ little from the old model.

The different essential parts of a plough have certain names usually given to them. The *Body* of a plough is that part to which all the other parts are attached. The bottom of it is called the *Sole* or *Slade*, to the fore part of which is affixed the *Point* or *Share;* the hind part of the sole is called the *Heel.* The *Beam*, which advances forward from the body, serves to keep the plough in its proper direction, and to the end of it are attached the oxen or horses, which are employed to draw it. Fixed in the beam in a vertical position, before the point of the share, with its point a little forward, is the *Coulter*, which serves to cut a vertical section in the ground; while the point of the share, expanding into a *Fin*, separates a slice by the horizontal cut from the subsoil or solid ground under it. The *Mould-Board*, or *TurnFurrow*, is placed obliquely behind the fin, to the right or left, in order to push aside and turn over the slice of earth which the coulter and share have cut off: it thus leaves a regular furrow wherever the plough has passed, which furrow is intended to be filled up by the slice cut off from the land by the side of it, when the plough returns. The *Stilts*, or handles, of which there may be either one or two, as is thought more convenient, direct the plough by keeping it in the line required and at a regular depth in the ground. The single stilt appears to be the most ancient form.

Wheels are a modern invention in comparison with the other parts. They support the end of the beam, and prevent it from going too deep into the ground or rising out of it while the plough is going on. The greatest improvements introduced into modern ploughs are in the shape of the mould-board or turn-furrow, and the contrivances for regulating the line of draught so as to make the plough go at an equal depth, and cut off a regular slice of equal breadth, without any great force being applied by the ploughman who holds the stilts. The mould-board is either fixed on one side, or made so as to be shifted from one side to the other; in the first case half the furrow-slices lie on one side and half on the other, and there is of necessity a double furrow where they join. When it is desirable that the surface should be quite flat, and the furrow-slices all in one direction, the mould-board must be shifted at every turn, and a plough which admits of this is called a *Turn-Wrest Plough.*

Ploughs were formerly made of wood, having those parts covered with iron where the greatest friction takes place, the share and coulter only being of iron; but in consequence of the greater facility of casting iron in modern times, most of the parts are now made of this metal. The beam and stilts are still usually of wood, but even these are now sometimes made of wrought iron. The advantages of iron are, its durability and the smaller friction it occasions when once polished by use. The inconveniences are the additional weight of the instrument, and consequent greater friction of the sole. Recent experiments have proved this to be greater than was generally suspected. A great improvement has been introduced by making the points of the shares of cast-iron, which, by a mode of casting the lower surface on a plate of metal, makes one surface much harder than the other; and as the softer surface wears more rapidly, a sharp edge is always preserved. The different parts of a plough are now usually cast so that if any one fails or wears out, it can be instantly replaced, by moving a few screws or bolts. There is another advantage in having the essential parts of cast-iron. If any particular shape has been once discovered to be the best for any part, that shape is preserved without deviation in every plough made on the same pattern, and with respect to the turn-furrow this is of great importance. The stilts of the plough are mostly of wood; one will suffice for a light soil, but two are required for a heavy soil.

The shape of a plough must vary with the nature of the soil which it is to turn up. A light soil must be shovelled up; a mellow one may be turned over with any kind of mouldboard; a very stiff tenacious soil which adheres to any surface pressed against it, will be more easily turned over by a few points of contact which do not allow of adhesion. Hence the point and turn-furrow have been made of all imaginable shapes, and while one man contends for a very concave form, another will admit of nothing which is not very convex. The lighter the plough is, consistently with sufficient strength, the less draught it requires, all other circumstances remaining the same.

It does not fall within the province of this work to trace the circumstances which call for the varied modes of ploughing. They are numerous, depending both on the crop and on the soil. For some purposes the clod requires to be turned right over; for others, to be turned to a certain angle. Very little attention was formerly paid to the straightness of the furrows; but it is evident that every deviation from parallelism causes a defect in the contact of the slices, and a loss of force by the obliquity of the draught. Hence equal and straight furrows are a sign of good ploughing. One of the most useful operations in ploughing land is to cross the former furrows, by which means the whole soil is much more completely stirred; and if any part has been left solid without being moved by the plough-share, which is called a Balk, it is now necessarily moved.

As a means to enable the farmer to save hands and expedite the tillage of the land, ploughs have been contrived which make two or more furrows at once. When they are well constructed, they are very useful on light soils. If it is not required to go deep, and two horses can draw a double plough, there is a decided saving of power; but if it requires four horses nothing is gained. The double ploughs are therefore not much in use.

Deep ploughing is generally acknowledged to accord with the best husbandry, where the subsoil is dry naturally, or has been artificially drained; but some inconvenience may arise from bringing a barren subsoil to the surface, in trench-ploughing by two ploughs following each other in the same furrow. It has therefore been suggested to take off the turn-furrow from the plough which follows the first, so as to stir the subsoil without bringing it to the surface. This idea has been improved upon by constructing a *Subsoil-plough* of great strength, which will go very deep into the ground and stir the subsoil a foot or more below the bottom of the usual furrow.

The instruments which have been invented to save the time and labour required by repeated ploughings are very numerous. New ones are daily invented, and some are supported by wheels, which render them both lighter and more convenient. One of the most important of these instruments is the *Cultivator*, or *Scarifier*. [CULTIVATOR.]

It would be in vain to enumerate the various ploughs which have been invented and which are exhibited at the annual cattle and agricultural shows. The Essex plough, the Gold hanger plough, the Subsoil plough, the Surface plough; as well as those which are designated by the names of their makers, Ransome, Crosskill, Wedlake, Garratt, &c.—all have their respective points of excellence. There has recently been introduced a *hill-side* plough. Several forms of *steam plough*, also, have been introduced; in which steam-power takes the place of horse power. A steam plough has been recently patented by Messrs. Calloway and Purkis of Putney. There are two ploughs attached to an endless chain which passes over two wheels; and these wheels are moved whenever the locomotive movement of the steam-engine takes place. The ploughing is effected transversely to the movement of the machine; and this movement is only just rapid enough to enable the plough to act upon new portions of ground when necessary.

PLUMBA'GO.—*Graphite, Black Lead.* This substance occurs both crystallised and massive; but mostly in irregular nodules. It is found in various parts of the world. That of Borrowdale in Cumberland is of the best quality for what are called *black-lead pencils*; while the commoner sorts are used for making melting-pots, for diminishing the friction of machinery, and for protecting iron from rusting. That which is imported from the East Indies is remarkably soft. Plumbago conducts electricity, is infusible, and very difficult of combustion. It was at one time supposed that plumbago was a carburet of iron, but, in the opinion of Berzelius, it is a peculiar form of carbon, and that the substances which it contains are in a state of mixture merely and not of chemical combination.

Plumbago is found usually in primary or transition rocks. At Borrowdale it occurs in nests in a greenstone rock, which constitutes a bed in clay-slate. In Inverness-shire it occurs in gneiss; at Arendal in Norway, in quartz rock; and in the United states, in felspar and mica-slate, but always in primary rocks.

The Borrowdale mine is interesting, and till lately supplied most of the material for English pencils. It is about six miles from Keswick. It is about half way up a mountain two thousand feet high, somewhat difficult of access. Some of the nodules procured are pure plumbago; while others have particles of iron ore adhering to them. From the small supply of the material, and the high price which it commands in the market, the mining operations are conducted with much precaution and even secrecy. In the last century persons contrived to rob the mine of much treasure with impunity; and this led to a very stringent set of rules for working. The mine is now nearly exhausted.

The manufacture of black-lead pencils from this substance is noticed under PENCILS. The cedar of which the cases are formed is sawed into long planks, and subsequently into smaller rods; grooves are cut out by means of a fly-wheel, of such a size as to receive the black-lead. The pieces of mineral are cut into thin slabs, and then into rods; these rods are inserted in the grooves, and the two halves of the case are glued together.

A material for pencils is very much used, especially in France, made of plumbago mixed up with very fine clay. Any required degree of hardness can be given to the composition by varying the proportion of the ingredients. Wolff's "purified black-lead pencils," sold in London, have thirteen different degrees of hardness. Mr. Brockedon and other persons also manufacture pencils in which the *hardness* and the *blackness* vary in any desired degree.

PLUMBLINE. When a heavy body suspended by a flexible string is at rest, the line passing through the point of suspension and the centre of gravity of the weight is in the direction in which gravity acts. The *Horizon* is a plane perpendicular to this line, and the *Zenith* is that point of the heavens marked out by the continuation of the line upwards. If the string be perfectly flexible, it will coincide with the theoretical line above described.

The plumbline is used in the arts. In levelling and in astronomical instruments, it has in most cases been superseded by the spirit level or observation by reflection.

PLUSH. This is a kind of velvet, having a *nap* or *shag* on one surface. It consists of a double warp and a single weft: one of the warps being so thrown up to the surface as to form the loose nap. Very frequently the upper warp is made of goat's or camel's hair; so that when woven and cut the surface presents something of a fur like appearance. The mode of producing fabrics of this kind, whatever may be the materials employed, is noticed under VELVET.

PLYMOUTH DOCK YARD. Plymouth is one of the most important towns in the west of England, in an engineering and commercial point of view. The Breakwater, the Eddystone lighthouse, and the Royal Dock Yard, all tend to give importance to the place. The first two of these are briefly described in earlier articles. [BREAKWATER; LIGHTHOUSES.]

The dockyard is more properly at Devonport; but the two towns form one for all practical purposes. The dock yard extends about half a mile from north to south, by a quarter of a mile from east to west, and in it are employed about 3000 persons. There are six building slips for vessels of various dimensions; three docks for fitting and repairing first-rate vessels; and two for smaller vessels. The building slips are covered with immense roofs of iron, copper, or zinc. On these slips 27 war ships were built between 1828 and 1848. There have been lately about 6000 loads of timber used annually in the dock yard. A new basin is now being constructed, blasted out of the solid rock, at an estimated expenditure of 345,000*l.* There are two rope houses, 1200 feet long. A chain cable storehouse has lately been built, at a cost of 40,000*l.* About 2000 tons of hemp are annually used in the dock yard, for ropes and other purposes. The rigging-house is an extensive building, 500 feet in length. The Smithery is an extensive building, in which Nasmyth's steam-hammer performs wonders in anchor-forging. In the engineering or mill-wright establishment, the planing, turning, punching, drilling, and cutting of metal is carried on. In the saw-mill timber is cut into various forms and sizes by steam-power. There are mast-houses, boat houses, sail lofts, storehouses, and all the works of a great naval yard.

At Keyham Point, a short distance northward of the dock yard, new steam docks are now being constructed on a magnificent scale. They will comprise large basins and docks for the reception of steamers, and factories for conducting every kind of repair which the steamers may require. There will be three-quarters of a mile of granite quays to the basins. Up to the present time the sum expended in these works has been about 700,000*l.*; and at least half a million more will be required to finish them.

There are many other government establishments at Plymouth and Devonport which give rise to much industrial and commercial activity. But there is also much trade and commerce independent of those establishments. Considerable trade is carried on with the West Indies, the Baltic, and the Mediterranean; and coastwise with London and other places. There is an active fishery of hake and whiting. Granite, limestone, slate, and marble, are quarried in the neighbourhood.

The Plymouth Dock Company are forming basins, docks, and quays, to accommodate the steamers on various mail routes which are proposed to be established there. The Cape mail steamers already start from Plymouth. The dock will be placed in immediate connection with the broad guage railway to London.

POLAND. Whether regarded as a kingdom, or as a mere province of the Russian Empire, Poland demands only a few words respecting its produce and commercial industry.

Though Poland is not distinguished by fertility, it produces more grain, hemp, flax, and tobacco, than are required for its consumption, and it exports these articles to other countries. Wheat is only abundant in the hilly southern region: the principal species of grain which are cultivated in the other parts of the kingdom are rye, oats, and buckwheat; barley is also raised, but less extensively. Leguminous vegetables are much valued and their cultivation attended to. As a considerable part of the country is still covered with forests, timber constitutes an important article of export. The forests consist of oak, ash, lime-trees and birch, but chiefly of pine and fir. Several metals and minerals are abundant in the hilly region. Among the metallic ores are those of silver, iron, copper, lead, and zinc. Rock-salt, marble, and a little coal, are met with.

In the city of *Cracow* there are no manufactures of any importance except a few in cloth and woollens. Cracow is the chief depôt in Poland for Hungarian wines, salt, and wax, and is the central point of commerce between Poland and Hungary; but its trade, which is principally in the hands of Jews, is not extensive. At *Warsaw* the manufactures are of many different kinds, and the trade of the city is considerable, the vicinity of the Vistula being favourable to its developement. It is felt, however, that the mouth of the Vistula being in another country (Prussia), is a circumstance which greatly checks the commerce of Warsaw, owing to the restrictions in international commerce between Russia and Prussia. All the other towns in Poland are less in commercial and trading importance than Cracow and Warsaw.

POLARISCOPE. The phenomena of the Polarization of light are of so refined and delicate a character, that any description of a polariscope would be of little value, without such a notice of the phenomena as would carry us beyond the province of the present work. We will therefore merely state that a polarising apparatus, whether called a polariscope or by any other name, is a contrivance for exposing crystals and other translucent bodies to the action of light, with a power of giving rotatory movement to one or more parts of the apparatus.

POLYCHRO'MY is a modern term used to express the ancient practice of colouring statues and the exteriors of buildings. In Egypt it was at all times a universal custom to have recourse to colours in the decoration of architecture. As to the practice in Greece, it appears, from the remains of colour found upon antient monuments, that the colouring was strictly confined to the ornamental parts —to the friezes, the metopes, and the tympana of the pediments. In later times amongst the Romans, in the times of Vitruvius and Pliny, the practice seems to have degenerated into a mere taste for gaudy colours, and to have been very general, as we see in the ruins of Pompeii, where however, occasionally, the Arabesque decorations upon the walls of the courts in the larger houses are very elegant.

Polychrome sculpture was quite as general amongst the Greeks as polychrome architecture. The *acrolithic* and the *chryselephantine* statues both come under this head. In the latter style were many of the most remarkable productions of ancient art: the *Jupiter* at Olympia, and the *Minerva* at Athens, by Phidias; the *Juno*, at Argos, by Polyclétus, and the *Æsculapius*, at Epidaurus, by Thrasymédes; and others described by Pausanias. In the flourishing period of Grecian art, custom seems also to have defined limits to this practice, for, except in the rudest ages, the figure itself was never painted, although it appears to have been sometimes covered with an encaustic varnish. The naked marble of the works of the greatest sculptors was not coloured; the colouring was confined to the lips, the eyes, the hair, the drapery, and the ornaments of the dress.

At the present day polychromy in architecture is advocated by many persons of taste. The encaustic painting of some of our interiors and the gorgeous splendour of the new House of Lords, are examples. The much discussed choice of colours by Mr. Owen Jones in the Palace of Industry bears on the subject of polychromic decoration.

POMATUM. The pomatums or *pommades* as they are called by the French, are so named because they were originally made of apples and lard. They are now made of various ingredients, and in various ways. For a considerable number of pomatums hogs' lard and beef suet are brought to a very fine state, melted and scented by causing odoriferous flowers to remain in the mixture for many hours. In another method the pomatum is spread into a layer upon which the leaves of scented flowers are placed, and removed daily until the mass is scented. Another mode is by adding fragrant essences to the pomatum. All these are manufactured on a very large scale in France; and the variety of flowers employed is considerable.

PONTINE MARSHES is the name of a low marshy plain in the Papal State, about 24 miles long by 10 broad. It is remarkable from the attempts made to drain it; somewhat analogous in character to those of the BEDFORD LEVEL. There is every appearance that this district, which is a basin nearly surrounded by hills, was once a gulf of the sea, which has been gradually filled up by alluvium from the mountains. Within the historical period it was a fertile district, containing towns, and a considerable population. Both under the Republic and the Empire great works were undertaken for the draining of these marshes; and the Appian Road traversed part of them to Terracina. Something has been done in modern times by the popes, from Boniface VIII. to Pius VI., and by Napoleon during the French occupation of the Roman States. Since that time all that has been done for the Pontine Marshes has been to maintain the drainage in the state in which Pius VI. left it, by keeping the canals clear and the dykes in repair. The greater part of the plain is covered with rich pastures, in which are fed numerous herds of horned cattle, and other parts of it are sown with rice, wheat and Indian corn, and afford rich crops. In the spring, before the great heat renders the atmosphere unwholesome, it has the appearance of a most delightful region. But, except the post stations along the high road, and some scattered huts here and there, there is no permanent population throughout the whole of the plain.

PONTOONS are vessels used in the formation of floating-bridges for military purposes. General Pasley has constructed pontoons in the form of canoes, with decks, each end being shaped like the head of a boat. They consist of light timber frames, covered, except the deck, with sheet copper; and each vessel is formed in two equal parts by transverse partitions, so that the demi-pontoons may be separated from each other when the bridge is to be conveyed on carriages by land with the army. When in the water, the parts are connected together by a rope, which passes through two perforations in the keel, near the place of junction, and by a rectangular frame of wood, which is laid along the deck, and attached to it by lashings.

Sir James Colleton, some years since, invented pontoons of wood of a cylindrical form, some of which have been occasionally employed in experimental operations; and cylindrical pontoons of tin, which were subsequently invented by Colonel Blanchard, have lately been introduced into the service. These last have hemispherical or conical ends. They possess the advantages of great lightness and buoyancy. The diameter of one of the cylinders is 2 ft. 6 in., and its length 22 ft. A rectangular frame, rather greater in length than the breadth of the intended bridge, is made fast, by ropes, longitudinally, on the surface of each of two cylinders placed parallel to one another at about 10 ft. asunder; and on these frames rest the baulks carrying the chesses, or planks, which form the road. Two pontoons, with their platform, constitute a raft; which, when the bridge is to be formed, are rowed to their stations in a line across the river, the lengths of the pontoons being parallel to the banks, and there anchored; the distances between the nearest pontoons in two rafts being equal to that between the two pontoons in each raft. Then each raft carrying the materials which are to make a platform over the water between itself and the next, such platform is laid down in a manner similar to that which is employed in laying down the platform of the raft; and from each of the extreme pontoons a like platform is extended to the shore of the river.

POPLAR TREE. There are several varieties of poplar tree, which render useful service to man, though not in so great a degree as many other trees. The timber of the *white* poplar is very light coloured, and is used in France and Germany for a variety of minor purposes. It makes excellent packing cases, because nails may be driven into it without causing it to split. It is used extensively by turners and cabinet-makers. The boards and rollers around which pieces of silk are wrapped in merchant's warehouses and in shops are made of this wood, which is adopted on account of its lightness lessening the expense of freight. It is much used for flooring-boards, for large folding-doors for barns, and for other building purposes. It is used as a substitute for lime-tree in musical instruments. Wooden dishes and casks are occasionally made of it. The timber of the *black* poplar is used for much the same purposes as the white. It is yellow, soft, and easy to work; and is preferred by cabinet-makers for many purposes. It is used for clogs, the soles of wooden shoes, bowls and other turner's ware, and in cart building. The *Lombardy poplar* produces wood less serviceable than that from the other varieties; but rafters, small beams, boards, &c., made of this wood and afterwards coated with tar, are found to be durable. The wood of the *Trembling poplar* or *Aspen* is white and tender; and is employed by turners; by coopers for herring casks, milk pails, &c.; by sculptors and engravers; by joiners and cabinet-makers; and by the makers of clogs, wooden shoes, butcher's trays, pack saddles, and a number of other articles.

As fuel, poplar wood is of inferior heating power; but it gives out its heat very quickly; the ovens of nearly all the Paris bakers are heated by this wood. The bark of the black poplar is employed in tanning leather; when pulverised it is eaten by sheep; and being very thick, light, and corky, it is used by fishermen to support their nets, and even as corks for bottles. The bark of the aspen forms the principal food of the beaver; it is also usefully employed in medicine.

In Sweden the leaves of the white poplar are eaten by cattle. The buds of the black poplar, macerated in boiling water, and afterwards bruised in a mortar and pressed, yield a fat substance which burns like wax and exhales a fine odour. The balsamic sap with which the buds are covered forms the basis of an ointment which was much prized in former times. The young shoots may be used in basket-making; and the shoots with the leaves on are sometimes used as brooms. The cottony substance or flock which surrounds the seed has been used in Germany and France as wadding; and it has also been occasionally manufactured into cloths, hats, and paper. The *Balsam poplar* yields a balsam from the buds; it is collected from the trees in spring, at which season it collects into drops on the points of the buds. In Siberia a medicated wine is prepared from the buds.

POPLIN. Among the varieties of woven goods in which silk and worsted or silk and woollen are used in combination, poplin is one of the best and most esteemed. *Tabinet* is one form of this material; and Ireland has been distinguished for the excellence of its poplins and tabinets. The demand is now small, as other kinds of textile fabrics have lately been more in favour; but the rich Irish poplins and tabinets, though employing only a small number of persons in their manufacture, maintain their high character.

POPPY. [OPIUM.]

PORCELAIN. [POTTERY AND PORCELAIN.]

PORCH is a general term for any projection forming a covered space immediately before the entrance to a building, open in front, and more or less inclosed at its sides. The distinction between a porch and a portico is, that, however important it may be as a feature, the former appears only a subordinate part of the building to which it is attached; whereas the other may be the whole of a front. In Norman architecture, the porches or portals are little more than a modification of the similar features in Byzantine and Lombardic architecture. Of porches, strictly so called, there are few instances, either in Norman or Gothic architecture; there are often however spacious portals, which do not advance beyond the general plan of the building in front, but form entrances, deeply recessed and inclosed within the lower part of the structure. In ancient English domestic architecture, porches, properly so called, are frequent.

POROSITY is a property common to all the bodies of nature, at least we know none in which the particles are contiguous to one another. In some, as sponge and cork, the pores are visible to the eye, and in others they may be rendered so by the aid of a microscope. In bodies whose pores are not thus manifest, the existence of the intervals between the molecules is proved by various circumstances. Thus water or mercury being contained in an open vessel of wood over the exhausted receiver of an air-pump will, by the pressure of the atmosphere, be forced through the wood, and fall thence in a shower: liquids also are frequently filtered by being made to pass through the pores of paper; and in the Florentine experiment, for determining whether or not water is compressible, the fluid was by pressure forced through the pores of the vessel of gold in which it was contained. Again, the porosity of bodies is inferred from their elasticity, and the sounds which are heard when the molecules are in a state of vibration: also, in transparent bodies (and the most dense metals are, when rendered sufficiently thin, found to be transparent), it is inferred from the fact that the particles of light pass through them, or that the vibrations of an æthereal fluid take place among the molecules. Finally, the porosity of bodies is proved from the fact that they suffer contraction of volume by being exposed to cold and by mechanical compression, since such contractions can only take place in consequence of the particles being forced closer together than they are in the usual states of the bodies.

PORPHYRY. A large number of rocks of igneous origin, both very ancient and comparatively modern, are thus designated; but properly speaking, a particular structure is indicated by it, and not a definite rock or family of rocks. Felspar of a granular texture, without crystals imbedded, is claystone; with imbedded crystals of felspar it is porphyry. Hornblende, mixed with uncrystallised felspar, makes some greenstones; with imbedded crystals of felspar this becomes greenstone porphyry. Hence, by this mode of designation, we have pitchstone-porphyry, greenstone-porphyry, basaltic-porphyry, felspar-porphyry, and even so vague a term as trap-porphyry; and on the other hand, more correctly, porphyritic pitchstone, porphyritic claystone, porphyritic greenstone, porphyritic basalt, and porphyritic granite.

PORTCULLIS is an assemblage of several large pieces of wood, joined across one another like a harrow, and each pointed with iron at the bottom. They are sometimes hung over the gateways of old fortified towns, ready to let down in case of a surprise, when the gates could not be shut.

PORTFIRE is a composition consisting of saltpetre, sulphur, and mealed gunpowder, in the proportion of 6, 2, and 1, respectively, mixed together, and rammed or driven into a paper case of a cylindrical or conical form, and less than an inch in diameter. Portfire is used for firing artillery or mines; and a piece sixteen inches long will burn from twelve to fifteen minutes.

PORTICO. Originally applied without distinction to colonnades and covered ambulatories, this term is now limited to signify a sheltered space inclosed by columns at the entrance to a building; and unless otherwise expressed, roofed with a pediment, like the end or front of a Grecian temple. The term as now restricted, answers to the *Prondos* of such a temple. Porticos are described according to the number of columns in front, viz., tetrastyle, hexastyle, octastyle, &c. They are called prostyle when, as generally happens, they project from the main building. Such as are *in antis*, and recessed within tho front of the building, are technically called *loggias*.

PORTLAND STONE. [DORSETSHIRE; STONE FOR BUILDING.]

PORTLAND VASE. This beautiful specimen of ancient art is one of the choicest treasures deposited in the British Museum. The time of its production is now unknown; but it is presumed to be the work of a Grecian artist. The first information we have respecting it is that about the middle of the 16th century the vase was found enclosed in a marble sarcophagus, within a sepulchral chamber, under the eminence called the Monte del Grano, about two miles and a half from Rome on the road to Frascati. This sepulchral chamber appears to have been the tomb of the Emperor Alexander Severus and of his mother Julia Mammæa; and the vase was probably a cinerary urn belonging to the sepulchre. The elegance of form and the admirable workmanship of the vase procured for it a place in the palace of the Barberini family at Rome, where it remained more than two centuries; after which it became the property of Sir William Hamilton, from whom it passed to the Duchess of Portland. In 1810 it was deposited in the British Museum by the Duke of Portland. On Feb. 7, 1845, a young man, a visitor at the museum, wilfully broke the vase into several pieces by throwing a stone at it. The offender was secured, and punished by imprisonment. He seemed to be influenced by no other motive than a morbid desire for notoriety. The fragments of the vase were afterwards joined together, and the work restored far more successfully than might have been anticipated.

This vase was said by Montfaucon to be formed of a precious stone; but subsequent examinations has shown the material to be dark blue glass, relieved by figures and devices in white enamel. It is about ten inches in height.

PORTSMOUTH DOCKYARD. The excellence of Portsmouth Harbour attracted the notice of the Romans, who established a station at Porchester on its northern shore. Portsmouth was a place of importance in the time of Henry I., and there was a naval station there in the reign of John. The dockyard is the largest in the kingdom, covering from 115 to 120 acres. It includes a rope-house, anchor wharfs, an anchor forge, a copper-sheathing foundry and mills; block, mast, sail and rigging, and other store-houses; a grand basin, in which vessels are received with all their standing and running rigging to be repaired; building slips, docks for repairing—in a word, all that is requisite for the construction, equipment, armament, and repair of vessels. There are also residences for the port-admiral, the admiral superintendent, and other officers of the yard, a chapel, a school for naval architecture, and other buildings. The block-machinery, invented by the late Sir M. Isambert Brunel, is an admirable manifestation of mechanical skill; it is impelled by steam. [BLOCK-MACHINERY.] Adjacent to the dockyard is the spacious and well furnished gun wharf and its connected buildings. It is the grand depôt for cannon, shot, and every description of ordnance stores.

The trade of Portsmouth, which is considerable at all times, but especially in time of war, depends much upon the expenditure connected with or caused by the naval station and dockyard, and is of a very miscellaneous character. There is a considerable import of cattle from the Isle of Wight and from the west of England. Corn and provisions are brought in from Ireland, eggs from France, timber from the Baltic, and wine is imported direct from the Continent. Steam communication is kept up with the Isle of Wight, Southampton, Plymouth, and Havre. The number of vessels registered at the port is about 150.

PORTUGAL. The agricultural produce of this country includes corn, Indian corn, rice, hemp, flax, honey, wax, plenty of fruit, especially excellent oranges and lemons, almonds, and abundance of good wine. The sea along the coasts and the rivers abound with fish, which is a great article of food with all classes. Sea-salt is collected in various places, particularly in the lagoon of Setubal. The sheep supply abundance of wool, of which some is equal to that of the Spanish merinos in fineness. Portugal has mines of copper, tin, and iron, of which only some of iron are worked. The manufactured articles are coarse woollen cloths in Alentejo and Beira; linens in Minho, Beira, and Tras os Montes; silks at Campo Grande, near Lisbon, and also at Oporto and Braganza; jewellery at Lisbon and Oporto. There are glass-works at Marinha Grande; paper manufactories at Alemquer, Lisbon, and Guimaraens; potteries at Lisbon, Oporto, Coimbra, Beja, Estremoz, and Caldes; cotton manufactories at Alcobaça and Thomar; and tanneries in various parts.

The foreign trade is principally in the hands of English merchants. Most of the Portuguese wines and other produce are consumed in England; especially the wines, of which no less than nine-tenths of the quantity sold to European countries are sent to England; this results from the prevalent taste for Port wine in England. The quantity of wine exported to England in the year 1847 was 2,883,806 gallons. The wine-produce of 1850 has been lately stated to amount to:—

First class wines	....	34,226 pipes.
Second „ „	....	18,908 „
Third „ „	....	19,864 „
Fourth „ „	....	12,346 „
		85,344 pipes.

Portugal holds a very humble position in respect to industry and commerce. There are no railways or canals; the roads are bad; and the rivers are navigable only in certain parts of the year. Yet there are not wanting indications of some revival of commercial spirit. The English Industrial Exhibition has called forth the dormant energies of many manufacturers; the articles of Portuguese manufacture were exhibited at Lisbon before being sent to England; the Government voted a sum to defray the expences of transport; and a spirit of fair emulation was excited. A communication from Portugal to one of the London journals, if correct in its statements, will shew that the last ten years have been years of progress in Portuguese industry:—"Oporto, the depôt of our best wines, has likewise become the chief seat of our manufacturing industry. It is now a vast workshop, distinguished not only by the great power of its machinery, but by the humanizing occupation of its people. A district almost wholly industrial adjoins Lisbon on the side next to the entrance of the port. Cavilha, in a few years, has raised twenty new factories. Portaligue thrives admirably in its industry. The credit of our Torres Novas linens improves unquestionably. Wool, both Portuguese and foreign, is woven and dyed in different manners in our factories. The brightness of the colours we use enhances the productions which in this process receive their perfecting finish. Our cotton printing establishments are advancing rapidly to perfection. The expensive and colossal industry of cotton spinning and weaving is already founded in Portugal. Our iron foundries produce machinery capable of presenting in the market solid and well-finished productions. The first steam boilers, of Portuguese manufacture, are constructing in one of the Lisbon workshops. Cabinet-making, cutlery, and other applications of labour to the raw material, are generally improving very greatly, and all this progress has been made within little more than ten years."

POST; MAILS; LETTERS. To trace the influence of the postage system on the industry and commerce of the country is quite beyond our present bounds. Whether as regards the internal machinery of the great establishment in St. Martin's-le-Grand; the wonderful effect of the penny postage rate; the rapid transit of letters by railway; the establishment of ocean mails; or the surprising results of money orders—the subject is indeed a vast one. We can give only a few figures in reference to it.

The increase of letters has been at least eight fold since the reduction in the rate of postage. On the 5th of December, 1839, the

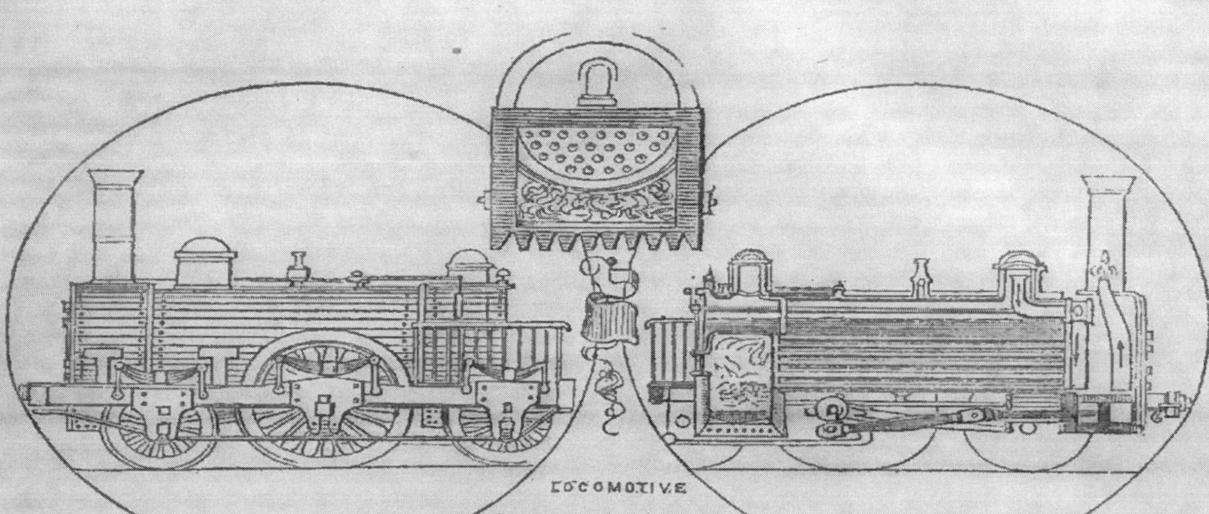

LOCOMOTIVE

SECTION OF DITTO AND FIRE BOX

LOCVMOTIVE FACTORY

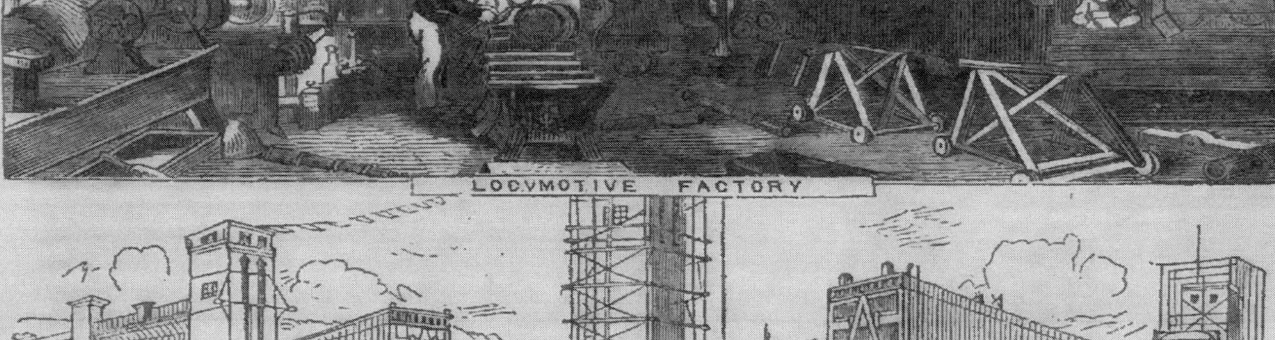

BRITTANNIA BRIDGE

change was made from distance-rates to a fourpenny rate; and on the 10th of December following a further change to the penny-rate was made. The following are the total numbers of letters which passed through the post-offices of the United Kingdom in the last twelve years, beginning with the year when the first partial change was made:—

Year.	Number of Letters.
1839	76,000,000
1840	169,000,000
1841	196,500,000
1842	208,500,000
1843	220,500,000
1844	242,000,000
1845	271,500,000
1846	299,500,000
1847	322,000,000
1848	329,000,000
1849	337,500,000
1850	347,000,000

In the year 1851 we may take one million letters per day, Sundays included, as a very near approximation to the probable number. In the year before the alteration (1838) the gross receipts of the post-office were 2,467,216*l.*; the net receipts were 1,676,522*l.* In 1849, the gross receipts were 2,213,149; and the net receipts 840,787*l.*

The conveyance of the letters from one part of the kingdom to another is effected by contract between the postmaster-general and the coach and railway proprietors. In the year 1839 the number of miles travelled by mail coaches was 7,377,851, at an average speed of about nine miles an hour. At the present time all the mails from London are conveyed by railway, with the aid of branch coaches to convey them beyond the reach of the railways. Contracts are entered into with the various companies and the rates determined partly on the probable number of letters, and partly on the length of line. In 1849, the General Post-Office paid to the Railway Companies for conveying letters and newspapers the sum of 253,586*l.* The mileage performed by the trains which conveyed the letters and newspapers was upwards of 20,000,000 miles.

Among the many admirable contrivances for facilitating the post-office business of railways, is Mr. Dicker's apparatus for giving and receiving the bags at each station. The apparatus is used by many of the great companies, and is about being used by more. The *post* stations are more numerous than the *passenger* stations; or, more correctly, the mail trains do not stop at certain minor stations, which must yet have their regular bags of letters; and as the throwing of the bags to or from the platform during a speed of 30 miles an hour would be very uncertain work, another plan is adopted. The station keeper adjusts the bag which is to go *from* the station; and the mail-guard adjusts that which is to go *to* the station. The station has a *delivery standard*, and the mail-carriage has a *receiving net;* the two bags are hung loosely, respectively, on the standard and on the edge of the net; and while the train is passing rapidly by the station, the edge of the net catches against the station-bag, whisks it off a kind of hook, and deposits it in the net which is spread open at the side of the carriage; at the same instant the carriage-bag is caught against the standard, and thrown down upon the platform, or else enclosed in a net.

In respect to foreign countries, there are contracts in force with steam-packet companies for the conveyance of mails from England to various parts of the world. The amount paid for this service in 1849 was 748,296*l.*

The principle of cheap postage has been applied to the transmission of money through the post-office by means of money-orders. A few years ago the cost of sending 10*s.* to a person 160 miles from London would have been 2*s.* 2*d.*, whereas the expense would now be only 4*d.*, including the postage. In November, 1840, the commission on money-orders was reduced from 1*s.* 6*d.* to 6*d.* for sums above 2*l.* and not exceeding 5*l.*; and from 6*d.* to 3*d.* for sums not exceeding 2*l.* The number of offices empowered to grant money-orders has been increased, and other facilities have been granted. The consequence of these successive changes have been as follows:—

Number and amount of money-orders issued in England and Wales in the quarters ending—

	No.	Amount.
5 April, 1839	28,838	£49,406
5 Jan., 1840	40,763	67,411
5 Jan., 1841	189,984	334,652
5 Jan., 1849	4,203,727	8,151,295
5 Jan., 1850	4,248,891	8,152,643

POTA'SSIUM; POTASH. The remarkable metal *Potassium* was discovered by Sir H. Davy in the year 1807. Its properties are the following:—In colour and lustre it strongly resembles mercury; it is solid at the usual temperature of the air: at 50° it is soft and malleable, and yields like wax to moderate pressure, and at 32° it becomes brittle; at 70° it is somewhat fluid, but not perfectly so till the temperature reaches 150°; if heated to low redness, out of the contact of the air, it sublimes, and condenses on cooling, unchanged. Its texture when brittle is crystalline. Its specific gravity at 60° is only 0·865, thereby presenting a remarkable contrast to mercury. It is opaque, and a good conductor of heat and electricity.

The most remarkable chemical property of potassium is its great affinity for oxygen, which at common temperatures exceeds that of any other body for this elementary substance. It tarnishes rapidly and visibly by mere exposure to the air, and the more rapidly as the air contains moisture, which it decomposes, and by combining with its oxygen becomes oxide of potassium, or potash. On account of its powerful affinity for oxygen, it must be kept either in small glass tubes hermetically sealed, or in a fluid, such as naphtha, which contains no oxygen. When heated in the air it takes fire, burns with a purple flame, the evolution of much heat, and is converted either into potash or peroxide of potash, or a mixture of them. It takes the oxygen from any mixture of gases containing it, and indeed from almost every substance with which that element happens to be combined; so that when thrown upon water it decomposes it, burning vividly.

Oxygen and *Potassium* form two compounds, of which the chief is the well known substance *Potash*. This is white, solid, extremely caustic, and readily attracts moisture and carbonic acid from the air; it fuses when heated, but bears a high temperature without being volatilised or decomposed. The *hydrate of potash* is formed whenever an aqueous solution of potash is evaporated to dryness; it is white, hard, and brittle, extremely caustic, very deliquescent, and very soluble both in water and in alcohol. Potash is most extensively employed in manufactures, and is an extremely valuable alkali. From a combination of cyanogen with potassium *Prussian Blue* is obtained. *Nitrate of Potash*, *Nitre*, or *Saltpetre*, is colourless, inodorous, has a cooling, sharp saline taste, and is readily soluble both in cold and in hot water. At about 616° of Fahr. nitre fuses, and at a high temperature it suffers decomposition. Nitre possesses powerful antiseptic properties. It is largely employed in the manufacture of gunpowder and of nitric acid, and also in numerous processes in the chemical arts and manufactures. *Chlorate of Potash* is colourless, inodorous, and has a cooling austere taste. When triturated with certain inflammable bodies, as sulphur and phosphorus, combustion or explosion, or both, are produced. This salt is employed in chemical investigations on account of the purity of the oxygen gas which it yields; it is also employed in the manufacture of matches which are fired by means of friction. [MATCHES.]

Carbonate of Potash is known in its impure state by the name of *Pearl Ash*; when pure, it is colourless and inodorous, its taste is strong and disagreeable, it does not readily crystallise, and is never kept in crystals; it is largely employed in the arts, and also in medicine. *Bicarbonate of Potash* is inodorous, colourless, and crystalline; has scarcely any alkaline taste, and is largely employed in medicine and in chemical investigations. *Sulphate of Potash* is colourless, inodorous, bitter, and rather hard; it is employed to a small extent in medicine and manufactures. *Bitartrate of Potash*, *Cream of Tartar*, or *Tartar*, is colourless, rather hard, inodorous, and has a sour taste. It is very largely employed in the preparation of tartaric acid, in medicine, and some chemical arts. When an equivalent of potash is added to this salt, it becomes *neutral tartrate of potash;* this salt is used in medicine, and being much more soluble in water than the bitartrate, was formerly called Soluble Tartar. *Oxalic Acid* forms three different compounds with potash, the *oxalate*, *quadroxalate*, and *binoxalate;* this last is a natural product obtained from sorrel, and is commonly known by the name of *salt of sorrel*. It is a colourless crystalline salt, and has a sour bitterish taste. There are many other valuable substances obtained from potassium.

POTATO. The potato was first brought to this country from Virginia by Sir Walter Raleigh, and was first planted in his garden at Youghal, in Ireland. But the potato had been known in Spain and Portugal at an earlier period, and it is from them that we most directly derive the name by which we know it. The inhabitants of Quito called it by some name which the Spaniards corrupted into battata, to which potato is a close approximation. The potato was limited to the garden for at least a century and a half after it was first planted at Youghal, and it was not until 1732 cultivated as a field crop in Scotland.

The farina of the potato, properly granulated and dried, is sold in our shops as *tapioca*, to which it bears the closest resemblance both in appearance and essential properties. For confectionary the flour is so delicately white, and it is so digestible and nutritious, that it ought to be in more general use, among the children of the poor especially, in the winter season, when they so rarely enjoy the luxury of milk; and the cost is not more than a sixth or seventh of the price of tapioca or arrow-root, if it be made at home. Few housewives are ignorant of the method of obtaining it by the use of a common hand-grater and sieve; but for yielding larger supplies some machinery is necessary.

The misery of Ireland, consequent on the failure of the potato crop, is too well known to require notice here. In 1847, the Earl of Clarendon, wishing to know the exact amount of vegetable food grown in the country, caused an accurate enumeration to be made. It was found that there were 284,116 acres of land under potato-crop in 1847; the produce of which was estimated at 2,046,195 tons of potatoes. No means are at hand for determining the ratio which these numbers bear to those of former years; but it is well known that the quantity was greatly diminished during and immediately after the disastrous year 1846

It has been lately estimated that the potatoes sold in Covent Garden market annually amount to about 6,600 tons, or about 14,000,000 lbs.

POTOSI' MINE. Potosi, a town in South America, in the republic of Bolivia, has near it the mountain or Cerro de Potosi, 16,037 feet high. It contains one of the richest silver mines in the world; the mine has yielded since 1556 an amount of silver worth nearly 200,000,000*l.* sterling. Potosi contains about 30,000 inhabitants.

POTTERIES. The name of *The Potteries* is given to a remarkable district in Staffordshire, in which the greater part of the English pottery and porcelain is made. It is a row of seven or eight towns, lying along the same turnpike road, and having the intervals between them every year more and more filled up by more than twenty hamlets and chapelries. It may be characterised as a street eight miles in length, with shorter streets branching out on either side. Over the whole of this space the characteristics of a pottery district are observable; especially the bulky and somewhat ugly *Kilns* which every establishment possesses. The chief towns among the group are Tunstall, Burslem, Longport, Hanley, Shelton, Stoke, Fenton, and Lane End; the smaller places are too numerous for enumeration here. *Etruria*, the celebrated establishment where Wedgewood obtained his fame and his wealth, is not so much a town as a factory, with the mansion of the proprietor and the houses of the workpeople. There are not less than a hundred and twenty pottery and porcelain establishments in the district, some of which employ six or eight hundred persons each. The names of Copeland, Minton, Ridgway, Davenport, and Wood, are among the most celebrated of the manufacturers; and it is among these we are to look for those gradual improvements which will leave us nothing to wish for in emulating the production of China, Sèvres, and Dresden. The Exhibition of 1851 will tell its own tale on this subject.

In the last annual report of the School of Design, the following interesting remarks are made on the progress of the branch Schools in the Pottery district:—'The schools at Stoke and Hanley continue to be conducted in the most satisfactory manner, and are exercising a marked influence on the manufactures of those places. The proportion of the students actually engaged in the manufactories is unusually large, amounting to three fourths of the whole number; and about thirty are established modellers and painters. Several of the young pupils have advanced to the study of colour, but the difficulty of forming or maintaining a class, in the absence of proper examples, is extreme. A life class is established at Hanley. The modelling classes have now assumed their proper importance in the schools, with reference not only to their numbers, but to the quality of the pupils, many of whom are modellers of long standing, established in the manufactories, who come to the schools already skilled in the handicraft of their business. Their practice in the schools is to study the figure, and to model after the finest examples of ornament, and afterwards to exercise their knowledge of form and relief by reproducing specimens of the like character, from the engravings of Albertolli and others. No plan can be better adapted for spreading among the modellers, who are also to a great extent the designers, that in which their previous education has been deficient, that is to say, a knowledge of the best forms, and taste to prefer them. There are also several pupils in the modelling classes who have begun at the beginning, and worked through the elementary studies of the school. One of the principal modellers in the Potteries is stated to have drawn his first line in the Hanley school.'

POTTERY AND PORCELAIN. The pottery art appears to have been practised in the earliest ages, and undoubtedly has been known amongst the rudest nations. The most ancient records allude to the *potter's wheel*, and we have proof that great skill had been acquired in the manufacture of porcelain of a superior quality in China and in Japan at a very remote date. The little figures, covered with a fine deep-blue glaze, which are deposited with Egyptian mummies, and numerous jars, some specimens of which may be seen in the British Museum, show that in Egypt, likewise, the art was anciently practised. Vestiges of considerable Roman potteries have been discovered in many parts of this island. In newly-discovered countries it has been found that the use of earthen vessels is familiar among people otherwise little acquainted with the arts of civilised life.

Although *Earthenware* may be considered as a general term applicable to all utensils composed of earthen materials, it is usual to distinguish such utensils more particularly into three different kinds, namely, *Pottery*, *Earthenware*, and *Porcelain*. Under Pottery are classed the brown stoneware made into jugs, &c., red pans and pots, porous vessels, &c. Earthenware consists of the white, blue and white, and yellow ware, which is so extensively used in this country. Porcelain is distinguished from earthenware as being a semi-vitrified compound, in which one portion remains infusible at the greatest heat to which it can be exposed, while the other portion vitrifies at a certain heat, and thus intimately combines with and envelopes the infusible part, producing a smooth, compact, shining, and semi-transparent substance, well known as the characteristic of true porcelain.

Until the beginning of the 18th century, the manufacture of earthenware in this country was confined to a few objects of the coarsest description, and till nearly the close of the same century, the porcelain of China was still in common use on the tables of the wealthy, the home manufacture being confined to articles of the commonest domestic use. Earthenware was likewise largely imported from Holland, and superior kinds from Germany and France. English earthenware and porcelain are now not only brought into general use in this country, to the exclusion of all foreign goods, but earthenware is also largely exported to almost every part of the known world, and even to those countries where the art was previously prosecuted. England is mainly indebted to Mr. Wedgwood for the extraordinary improvement and rapid extension of this branch of industry. Before his time our potteries produced only inferior fabrics, easily broken or injured, and totally devoid of taste as to form and ornaments. Wedgwood's success was not the result of any fortunate discovery accidentally made, but was due to patient investigation and unremitting efforts. He called upon a higher class of men than had usually been employed in this manufacture to assist in his labours, and in prosecuting his experiments he was guided by sound scientific principles; and signal success,which crowned his first exertions, only served as an additional motive for continuing his pursuit. One of the principal inventions of Mr. Wedgwood was his *table ware*, known at present as *Queen's Ware*. It is characterised as a dense and durable substance, covered with a brilliant glaze, and capable of bearing uninjured sudden alternations of heat and cold. Mr. Wedgwood's more beautiful inventions were—a *terra cotta*, which could be made to resemble porphyry, granite, Egyptian pebble, and other beautiful stones of the silicious or crystalline kind; a black porcelainous biscuit, very much resembling basalt in its properties, and therefore called Basaltes; a white and a cane-coloured porcelain biscuit, both smooth and of a wax-like appearance; and another white porcelainous biscuit, distinguished as jasper, having in general all the properties of the basaltes, with a very important addition, the capability of receiving through its whole substance from the admixture of metallic oxides, the same colours as those oxides communicate to glass or enamel in fusion. This peculiar property renders it applicable to the production of cameos and all subjects required to be shown in bas-relief, as the ground can be made of any colour, while the raised figures are of the purest white. Mr. Wedgwood likewise invented a porcelain biscuit, nearly as hard as agate, which will resist the action of all corrosive substances, and is consequently peculiarly well adapted for mortars in the chemist's laboratory.

Since porcelain is only a finer kind of pottery, the following description, in its earlier portion at least, will comprehend the mode of manufacturing both kinds of ware.

The materials for earthenware are reduced to the consistence of cream, in which state they are called *slip;* this fluidity is necessary to insure the perfect mixture of all the ingredients, and their mutual chemical action in the fire. The basis of the composition is a clay from the plastic clay formation in Devonshire or Dorsetshire, to which is added ground flint, which gives whiteness and solidity to the goods. For the better kinds, a portion of China-clay, or decomposed felspar from Corn wall, is added, together with a small quantity of ground white granite. By this means the density of the ware is increased, greater purity of whiteness is obtained, and also a degree of vitrification which makes the ware sonorous when struck. The flints employed are burned in a kiln, slaked to destroy their coherence, and ground to powder in a mill. The powder is then sifted in water, until reduced to a fit state for combination with the other substances. The clays are thrown into their several vats sunk in the ground, where they are blended with water, and sifted through fine silk lawns into other receptacles, and then diluted with water. The mingled flint and clay, in the state of a creamy liquid, is then pumped into a boiler, or slip-kiln, the bottom of which is formed of large flat fire-bricks, under which four or five parallel flues pass from the fire-place to a high chimney. The water is evaporated, until the boiling mass is brought to a proper consistency for working; but the steam having given it a cellular and porous texture, it requires to be beaten or wedged until the air is driven out, and a section of the mass, when cut, is smooth and compact.

All the various kinds of ware, such as *cream ware, drab ware, drab body, brown body, Egyptian black, blue body, jasper body, turquoise body*, &c., are formed of different kinds and proportions of flint and clay, with small additions of colouring materials. Round articles, which may be turned upon a lathe, have their form given upon the thrower's wheel, which is a lathe with a vertical spindle, having a small round table on the top, at which the thrower sits. He receives the clay prepared to the proper size by a woman, and throws it upon the whirling-table between his knees, which is put in motion by the wheel-woman, whose eye watches every motion of the thrower, and regulates the velocity of the work with perfect accuracy. The thrower first draws the clay up into a pillar, then depresses it into a flat cake, until the whole mass has been drawn into a circular arrangement of all its parts. He then opens the hollow of the vessel with his thumbs, and continues to draw out the clay, or press it inwards, until the desired shape is given to it. It is then cut from the table by a brass wire, and placed on a board, which, when full, is carried into a stove-room to harden.

When a number of vessels of the same size are to be thrown, a gauge is fixed so that its point just touches the top edge of the article when it is revolving; this fixes both the height and diameter of all that are made in that pattern.

When the vessels are sufficiently hardened, they are turned upon a lathe similar to that used by wood-turners. The turner dexterously shaves away the clay to the proper thickness, and works the mouldings, &c., polishing the whole with a steel burnisher. He frequently ornaments bowls, jugs, &c., with a coating of various coloured clays, which are sometimes blended with each other, so as to give a marbled surface; by these earthy pigments he produces an infinite variety of patterns. This kind is called *Dipped Ware.*

Such articles as require handles and spouts are then passed to the handler, who makes those appendages in plaster moulds, and sticks them to the vessels with liquid clay. Plain handles are pressed by a syringe through a hole of the proper size and form, and as the clay comes through in long strings, it is cut off, and bent into the desired shape for the handle.

Thrown and turned goods are sometimes ornamented with figures in relief, which are made out of flat moulds by children, and fixed upon the ware by workmen, who, having carefully adjusted each figure to its place, run a little water under it with a camel-hair pencil, which unites it to the surface of the pot. Goods of an oval or angular shape, which cannot be turned, are made by pressing clay into plaster moulds, which give the outside form to the vessel: this is called *Hollow-Ware Pressing.* Another kind, called *Flat-Ware Pressing*, is performed by giving the shape to the goods by moulds which fit the inside of the vessel; plates, dishes, saucers, cups, and hand-basins are made on this principle.

Casting is resorted to when a mould is so intricate as to be difficult for the workmen to fill by pressing. Slip clay is poured into the mould, which rapidly absorbs the water; and a coating of clay is deposited upon the inside; the remaining fluid is then poured out or drawn with a syringe, and a thicker mixture is put in, and left rather longer than the first before it is withdrawn. The mould is then put into a stove to dry.

When completed by the workman, the goods are placed on boards to dry, before going to the biscuit-oven, in which they receive the first fire. The ware to be thus burnt is placed in *Saggers* made of crucible clay; in shape they resemble hat-boxes, and being piled in columns, each sagger covers the one beneath it, and protects the goods from the immediate contact of smoke and flame. When the baking is finished and the oven cooled, the doorway is opened, the saggers brought out, and their contents submitted to a rigid scrutiny: all cracked and crooked pieces are rejected and thrown away. The ware is now called *Biscuit*, and in this state goes to the printer or biscuit-painter to be ornamented.

The printing of earthenware is effected by transfer-papers from engraved copper-plates. The ink used in printing is made of linseed-oil boiled with litharge, rosin, balsam of sulphur, or Barbadoes tar, and is tinted with any of the usual mineral colours—blue being the principal, and formed of oxide of cobalt. The colour having been ground very fine, the printer blends it with his oil upon a hot stove, and filling the engraved plate with it, takes off the impression by the common rolling-press. The tissue-paper used for this purpose is first prepared with a solution of soap. As soon as the print is taken, a girl cuts out the engraving with scissors, and hands it to the transferer, who carefully places the print upon the biscuit-ware, which being absorbent, holds it with great tenacity. The transferer then passes it to her assistant, who with the end of a cylinder of flannel, tightly rolled and bound with twine, rubs the print with such force as to work the ink into close contact with the biscuit. The goods thus coated with paper are then put into a tub of water, and the paper being wiped off with a sponge, every minute point of the engraving is found accurately transferred to the earthenware. When dry, the goods are packed close in a large muffle, or kiln, round which a fire circulates, and brings the whole to a low red heat. By this means the oil is burned out of the colour, which would be injurious to the process of glazing which follows. Some patterns are executed on biscuit by painters, who lay on the colours in gum-water.

The biscuit-ware, thus ornamented, is carried to the dipper, who dips each piece into the tub containing the finely-ground mixture which, when melted, forms the glassy coating to the ware. This glaze is blended in water, which, being absorbed by the biscuit, leaves a thin cover of glazing-powder upon the surface; a dexterous shake of each piece in a circular motion, as it emerges from the fluid, prevents the glaze from setting unequally, and throws off all that is superflous. The material of the glaze differs according to the kind of ware: white lead is a general ingredient.

When the goods have been dipped in the glazing mixture, they are dried, and placed in saggers, which are washed on the inside with a compound of glaze with lime and clay. Every piece is carefully placed so as not to touch another; otherwise, when the glaze melts, they would stick together. When drawn from the oven, the ware is carried in baskets to the glossed warehouse, where it is again subjected to a close examination.

Porcelain is a finer species of pottery, in which the ingredients are so selected that they act chemically upon each other, and are brought to a state of vitrification; the fracture has a dense or greasy surface, like that of a flint stone, and is therefore not liable to be acted upon by acids. When the porcelain is coloured by metallic matter, it is called stoneware; jasper and some drab-ware are of this description: but when it is perfectly free from colouring matter and is translucent, it is called China; of which there are two species, hard and soft china.

Hard China is formed chiefly of Kaolin or Cornish clay, felspar, sand, and selenite; but Soft China, which is more frequently made in England, has a different composition. Bones calcined and ground are largely used in the manufacture of English china, combined with aluminous and silicious earths in such proportions that they will vitrify together. The mode of mixing the materials, and the general processes of manufacture, are nearly the same as for earthenware.

The decoration of china by enamel colours and gold affords employment to a great number of persons, some of whom attain great excellence in their beautiful art. The colours used are all prepared from metallic oxides, which are ground with fluxes, or fusible glasses of various degrees of softness, suited to the peculiar colours with which they are used. When painted, the goods are placed in the enamel-kiln, where the fluxed colours melt, and fasten to the glazed surface, forming coloured glasses. The gold, which is applied in the form of an amalgam ground in turpentine, is afterwards burnished with steel burnishers.

Pottery, comprising the coarsest and commonest wares, involves the use of clay only, and requires much less careful processes than porcelain or earthenware.

The porcelain manufacture has made great advances within the last few years. The Exhibitions of manufactures in this country have afforded room for the honourable emulation of manufacturers from different districts; while the excellence of Sèvres, Dresden, and other foreign manufactures of porcelain, have shewn our native artists what are the points in which we are still excelled by our neighbours. The production of statuettes in biscuit and parian has lately reached a high degree of beauty; especially in those specimens which, under the name of Art Manufactures, have called forth the inventive skill of Bell, Marshall, and other sculptors, and the practical skill of Minton, Copeland, and other distinguished manufacturers. Slabs of highly decorated porcelain are now much used in fire-places, and in many forms of house-decoration. The mode of pressing dry porcelain powder into various forms has given rise to many new productions [BUTTON MANUFACTURE]; and the combination of parti-coloured clays has enabled the manufacturers to imitate many of the pavements and floors of the Romans [TESSELATED FLOORS.]

In respect to the commerce in these articles, it is the plain, neat, well made, and well glazed *earthenware*, for which the greatest demand exists in foreign countries; for no where are such things so excellently produced as in England. The export in the last three years has been

1848........53,286,076 pieces.
1849........61,528,196 „
1850........76,952,735 „

Two-thirds of these quantities go to the United States. The more costly porcelain, and the rough stone-ware, are not so largely exported as earthenware.

POULTRY. The mechanical arrangements for facilitating the hatching of poultry have been noticed under HATCHING. In respect to the commerce in this variety of farm produce, the only enumeration or estimate which we have met with is that which was made in Ireland in 1847. The poultry then alive in all the farms in Ireland numbered as follows:—

Leinster	1,674,039
Munster	1,684,775
Ulster	1,567,587
Connaught	764,654
	5,691,055

In one of the recent valuable papers in the *Morning Chronicle*, it is stated that the average yearly sale of tame birds, or *poultry*, at Newgate Market, is about 900,000; while that of wild birds, or *game*, is about 400,000; making 1,300,000 in all. But Leadenhall Market is said to be the largest poultry and game market in the world; the numbers are given, by the above authority, at 2,700,000 poultry, and 1,300,000 game, making together 4,000,000.

POWER is a term applied to any cause which is capable of producing motion, or of resisting motion; but the word has a merely technical meaning in treatises of mechanics. From among the numerous combinations which occur in machinery, the *Lever*, *Inclined Plane*, *Wheel and Axle*, *Pulley*, *Wedge*, and *Screw*, have been selected, and named *Mechanical Powers*, apparently because they are the simplest objects by which are produced such effects as could not be produced by the unassisted or unadapted operations of a motive agent, as gravitation, muscular strength, &c. The word Power here may be conceived to signify that which produces a mechanical advantage; but the same word may be used to signify a beneficial effect, as when a thing is done quicker or better at an equal expense of labour or time.

The mechanical advantages of simple machines are shown under the words LEVER, WHEEL AND AXLE, &c.; see also MECHANICAL POWERS. Beneficial effect may be produced in various ways without mechanical advantage:—for example, in the division of labour there is not only the moral benefit, namely, the making a human agent fitter for his work by giving him a more limited range of operations, but the actual saving of the labour of laying down one tool and taking up another.

PRAGUE, the capital of Bohemia, is a place of some industrial and commercial importance. The manufactures consist of cotton, hosiery, silk, leather, hats, gloves, earthenware, jewellery, and plated goods, mathematical and musical instruments, glass, buttons, snuff and tobacco, paper and paper-hangings. There are also breweries, saltpetre works, and many other industrial establishments. Prague has a very flourishing commerce: the transit trade is considerable, and there are three great annual fairs.

PRESS. [HYDRAULICS; PRINTING; SCREW-PRESS.]

PRESTON. This is one of our busy Lancashire towns. The staple trade of Preston, till within the last half century, was in linens; but this trade has given place to that of cotton, which is now manufactured very extensively. There are several iron foundries, chiefly for making the machinery used in the cotton manufactures. Leather is extensively made. The Ribble is navigable at spring-tides for vessels of 150 tons; but it is ill adapted for trade. The Lancaster canal passes on the west side of the town, and connects it with the great canal system of the manufacturing districts; while the town is still better connected by railways with the great centres of commerce.

PRINCE'S METAL, or *Prince Rupert's Metal*, is an alloy of copper and zinc, which contains more copper than brass does, and is prepared by adding this metal to the alloy.

PRINCIPAL is the name of a stop or row of metal pipes in an organ, tuned an octave higher than the diapason, an octave lower than the fifteenth, and serving to blend the two, as well as to augment the volume of sound.

PRINTING. The art of printing from blocks has been known in China since the middle of the 10th century, and that mode of printing is still practised there. Even in Europe, although writing, unlike that of the Chinese, is alphabetic, printing from blocks was the method first practised. Some have even supposed that the knowledge of the art was originally obtained from China; but, as far as we can trace, it was not till fully a century after Marco Polo returned from that country that even this simplest kind of printing began to be practised in Europe. It appears to have been first applied to the fabrication of playing cards and manuals of popular devotion. The æra of these block prints and books, as they are called, may be stated to be the first half of the 15th century: one in Lord Spencer's collection bears the date of 1423, and there is reason to believe that other specimens were executed almost as late as 1450. Of the block-books of any considerable magnitude the two most remarkable are—the 'Biblia Pauperum,' a small folio of forty leaves, each containing a picture, with a text of scripture or some other illustrative sentence under it, which is supposed to have been produced some time between 1430 and 1450; and the 'Speculum Humanæ Salvationis,' consisting of sixty-three leaves of the same small folio size, containing in all fifty-eight pictures, with two lines of Latin rhyme under each. With regard however to this last block-book there has been a great deal of disputation, some denying altogether its claim to be reckoned a specimen of block-printing, in so far as the legends are concerned. The probability is that at first the 'Speculum' was entirely a block-book, but that in subsequent editions the block-printing was mixed with printing from moveable types. These block-books are, like the Chinese books at this day, printed only on one side of the leaf; and they all appear to have been produced in the Low Countries.

The art of printing, in its essential principles the same as now practised, had certainly been discovered before the middle of the 15th century; but when, where, and by whom, each successive improvement of the original pigment-printing by means of engraved blocks was discovered and first put in practice, is not so easily settled. The employment of moveable types, the production of such types by the process of casting them in metal, and the cutting of the punch, or stamp of hardened steel, with which the face of the type is impressed in copper to be afterwards used in the matrix, or mould, in casting—these may be considered as the three great mechanical changes, by which block-printing was transformed into the art as it now exists.

Four names have principally figured in the controversy that has been raised about the invention of printing:—John Gutenberg (paternally Gensfleisch), of Strasburg; John Fust (or Faust), of Mainz; Peter Schoeffer (in Latin, Opilio), of Gernsheim; and Lawrence Coster (or Janszoon), of Haarlem. The probability is, that Coster was one of the early block-printers, whose art, there is every reason to believe, was first practised in Holland. The use of separate letters, or types, at first of wood and afterwards of metal, and the various improvements in the manner of casting them, are all to be attributed to Gutenberg, Fust, and Schoeffer. Gutenberg, it is now generally supposed, first began to print at Strasburg with moveable types of wood some time between 1436 and 1442. Having then established himself in Mainz, which was his native town, he there, in 1445, entered into partnership with Fust, who seems to have assisted Gutenberg in devising or carrying into effect his subsequent great improvement of the art, by casting the types of metal. But to Schoeffer, who was in the service of Gutenberg and Fust, and had married Fust's daughter, is assigned the credit of having facilitated and (as far as the principle was concerned) brought to perfection the process of founding by the contrivance of the punch. The knowledge of the art was first made public and carried into other countries by the dispersion of many of the workmen on the storming of Mainz by Adolphus of Nassau, in 1462. Printing was first practised in Italy, in the town of Subiaco, in the Roman territory, in 1465; in France, at Paris, in 1469; in England, at Westminster, in 1474; and in Spain, at Barcelona, in 1475. It is said that by the year 1530 there were already about 200 printing-presses in Europe. The name of William Caxton is indissolubly connected with the introduction of printing into England.

The date of the invention of the *printing-press* is unknown, but some contrivance for this purpose must have been used as soon as printing by blocks or types was introduced. The increased force requisite to make an impression, the size of the surface to be printed from being increased, would soon suggest recourse to some of the simple machines or mechanical powers for the modification of the power requisite to obtain the necessary pressure. The screw, as applied in the common screw-press, would obviously suggest itself; and accordingly, in all the earlier printing-presses, the screw alone is used.

The operations to be performed in the process of printing will point out the essential parts of a printing-press. The types, being set up and arranged in a chase (or iron frame) of suitable dimensions, which is then called a *form*, have to be inked; this is effected by passing across them a cylinder, or roller, covered with an elastic composition of molasses and glue, which has been first rolled in a thick ink made of lamp-black and burnt oil. The paper to be printed has to be laid on the type when inked, and then the requisite pressure for making the impression has to be applied.

Screw Press. The earliest form of printing-press very closely resembled the common screw-press, as the cheese or napkin-press, with some contrivance for running the form of type, when inked, under the pressure, and back again when the impression was made. This rude and inconvenient form of press was superseded by the invention of Blew, a printer of Amsterdam. Other improvements were from time to time introduced; but they were all superseded, about the commencement of the present century, by an invention of Lord Stanhope's.

In the *Stanhope Press*, as in the common wooden screw-press, the form of type is laid upon a table which has a horizontal traversing motion. To the carriage on which the form moves are attached the tympans, which are light frames covered with parchment, so constructed that the inner tympan just lies within the outer tympan. Some blanketing is placed between the tympans, so as to equalise the pressure upon the surface of the types. To the outer tympan is attached a skeleton frame called the frisket. The sheet of paper to be printed being placed on the outer tympan, the frisket is turned down upon it; and then the frisket and tympans are turned down upon the form of type. The frisket is covered with paper, cut out so that the sheet to be printed, when placed between the tympan and frisket, and folded down together on the form, may be in contact with the surface of the type, while the remainder of the frisket-sheet preserves the margin from being soiled. The form of type being inked, and the tympans and frisket, with the sheet of paper between them, folded down on the form, the whole is made to traverse, by means of a crank-handle, until it comes beneath the platten, which is a massive plate of cast-iron, moveable up and down perpendicularly. The principal improvement of the Stanhope Press consists in the manner in which the descending motion is given to the screw. The carriage is then run back, the frisket and tympans unfolded, and the printed sheet being taken out, the same operation is repeated.

The principle of the Stanhope press has been followed out by several subsequent inventors, and improvements of mechanical detail introduced, tending to the economy of time and labour, and to precision of workmanship. In the *Ruthven Press*, the form of type remains stationary, and the platten is removed to permit the type to be inked: and in this, as well as the *Columbian Press*, the pressure is produced by a combination of levers alone, without the use of any portion of a screw or inclined plane.

Copper Plate Press. The press for copper-plate printing consists of two cylinders or rollers of wood, supported in a strong wooden frame, and moveable about their axes, one placed just above and another just below the level of the table upon which the plate to be printed is laid. The upper roller is turned round by the arms of a cross fixed to its axis. The copper-plate being inked, the paper on which the impression is to be taken, and two or three folds of soft material, as blanketing, are placed upon it. The plate so prepared is moved along the table to the junction of the two rollers, and the upper roller being turned by the arms of the cross, the plate, with its furniture, is passed through the press. The rollers may be placed nearer to or farther from each other, according to the amount of pressure requisite for making a good impression, that is, according to the depth of the engraving and the degree of blackness which the impression is required to have.

Printing Machine. The printing-press, though much improved during the last half century by the ingenuity of Lord Stanhope and others, is quite inadequate to a rate of production equal to the present demand. The attention of practical men was consequently directed to some more rapid means of production; and as early as 1790, even before the Stanhope Press was generally known, Mr. W. Nicholson had letters-patent for a machine similar in many respects to those which have now come into use. Subsequently, Mr. König, a German, conceived nearly the same idea, and meeting with the encouragement in this country which he failed to obtain on the Continent, constructed a Printing Machine. On the 28th November, 1814, the readers of the 'Times' were informed that they were then for the first time reading a newspaper printed by machinery driven by steam-power. This printing-machine, though highly ingenious, was very complicated; and the machine of König was superseded by that of Messrs. Applegath and Cowper, the novel features of which were accuracy in the register, an improved method of inking the type, and great simplicity in parts previously very complicated.

Printing-machines are either single or double; the single being that in which only one side of the sheet of paper is printed; the double that in which both sides are printed before the sheet leaves the machine. The single machine is used for most newspapers and that kind of printing in which it is not necessary for the two sides of the sheet to 'register,' that is, for the printing on one side to be exactly at the back of the other; the double machine for books, in which it is essential that the printing on one page should correspond with the printing on the other when the sheets are folded. This important object of the register is effected by causing the parts to move at precisely the same speed. This being the principle of the register, its success will depend on great accuracy of workmanship in the mechanical parts. In the double printing-machines now in use, the sheet of paper is laid on the feeder, which consists of girths of linen tightly stretched by being passed round two cylinders. By the motion of this feeder the sheet is placed between two systems of tapes, which lie two and two over each other on a series of cylinders and rollers. The sheet of paper grasped between them is kept clean at the places in which it is in contact with them, and by the motion of the various parts is conducted under the first printing-cylinder, and receives an impression from the first set of types; thence by means of two other cylinders to the second printing-cylinder, where it receives an impression on the other side from the second set of types. Thus printed on both sides, it is taken out by an attendant. An inking apparatus is placed at each end of the table which carries the types, and which traverses backwards and forwards under the printing-cylinders and inking-rollers. The ink, received from a reservoir by two rollers, is transferred from them to the surface of the inking-table; the surface of the table inks two other rollers, and these, in their turn, ink the types as they pass backwards and forwards for each impression. The excellence of the printing depends in a great measure on the type being properly inked. The machines commonly used for printing books will print from seven hundred to one thousand per hour in perfect register; and for newspapers, printed on one side only, from four thousand to six thousand per hour.

König's machine printed 1,800 copies of the 'Times' per hour. Messrs. Cowper and Applegath's machine of 1827 printed 5000 in an hour. In May, 1848, Mr. Applegath erected a printing-machine for obtaining the enormous number of 10,000 impressions of the 'Times' in an hour. According to a paper on this subject by Mr. Cowper, read before the *Institution of Civil Engineers*, this beautiful machine consists of a vertical cylinder, about 65 inches in diameter, on which the type is fixed, surrounded by eight other cylinders, each about thirteen inches in diameter, covered with cloth, and round which the sheets of paper are conveyed by means of tapes; each paper cylinder being furnished with a feeding apparatus, having one boy to lay on the sheets and another to take them off. The inking rollers are also placed in a vertical position, against the large cylinder, upon a portion of the surface of which they distribute the ink. The ink is held in a vertical reservoir, formed of a ductor-roller, against which rest two 'straight edges,' connected at the back, so as to prevent the ink from running out: it is conveyed from the ductor-roller by one of the inking rollers, against which it is occasionally pushed. The type used is of the ordinary kind, and the form is placed upon a portion of the large cylinder, being fixed to it in a very plain but ingenious manner: a slab of iron is curved on its under side, so as to fit the large cylinder, whilst its upper surface is filed into facets or flat parts, corresponding in width and number to the width and number of the columns of the newspaper. Between each column there is a strip of steel, with a thin edge, to print the 'rule'—the body of it being wedge-shaped, so as to fill up the angular space left between the columns of type, and to press the type together sideways, or in the direction of the lines; the type is pressed together in the other direction by means of screws, and firmly held together. The surface of the type thus forms a portion of a polygon; and the regularity of the impression was obtained by pasting slips of paper on the paper cylinders. The operation of the machine is very simple: the 'layer-on' draws forward a sheet of paper on the feeding-board until its edge is under a roller, furnished with tapes, which drops down and draws the sheet forward and downward, into a vertical position, when other rollers and tapes carry it round the paper cylinder, where it meets the type, which has been inked by passing in contact with the inking rollers; the sheet then continues its progress until it reaches the 'taker-off.'

A few statistics, relative to the printing of the 'Times,' were mentioned by Mr. Cowper, from which it appears, that on the 7th of May, 1850, the 'Times' and 'Supplement' contained 72 columns, or 17,500 lines, made up of upwards of a million pieces of type, of which matter about two-fifths were written, composed, and corrected, after 7 o'clock in the evening. The 'Supplement' was sent to press at 7 50 P.M., the first form of the paper at 4 15 A.M., and the second form at 4 45 A.M.; on this occasion, 7,000 papers were published before 6 15 A.M., 21,000 papers before 7 30 A.M., and 34,000 before 8 45 A.M., or in about four hours. The greatest number of copies ever printed in one day was 54,000, and the greatest quantity of printing in one day's publication was on the 1st of March, 1848, when the paper used weighed 7 tons, the weight usually required being 4½ tons. The surface to be printed every night, including the 'Supplement, is 30 acres; the weight of the fount of type in constant use is 7 tons; and 110 compositors and 25 pressmen are constantly employed. The whole of the printing at the 'Times' office is performed by three of Applegath and Cowper's four-cylinder machines, and two of Applegath's new vertical cylinder machines.

According to recent accounts, it would appear that some of the New York newspapers are now printed with machines still more gigantic and complete than those employed on the 'Times,' and that the rapidity of printing is still greater. There is not the slightest reason to doubt, however, that if the sale of the 'Times' were to largely increase, machines would be invented to increase the rapidity of printing to any required degree. At present, the paper duty, the stamp duty, and the advertisement duty, keep the price of English newspapers much above that of the American, and unquestionably limit the demand.

A few further details illustrative of printing will be found under STEREOTYPE, and TYPE FOUNDING.

PROGNOSTICATOR. This name has been given by Dr. Merryweather to an apparatus recently contrived by him for foretelling probable changes in the weather. It is founded on a curious fact, that *leeches* shew great sensitiveness to approaching changes in the electrical state of the air; and the apparatus is so contrived as to bring these weather-wise animals into use as meteorological instruments. Twelve leeches are placed in a circle, each in a separate glass bottle; every leech tries to get up to the mouth of his bottle when the atmosphere is in such a state as to forewarn an approaching storm; and Dr. Merryweather has contrived sundry small pieces of apparatus, which register any attempts of the leeches to climb through the narrow necks of the bottles. The whole apparatus is contained within a mahogany box. In so novel a contrivance, nothing less than a long course of observation will test the validity of the arrangement.

PROPORTIONAL COMPASS. [COMPASSES.]

PROTEIN is a substance obtained by Mülder from albumen, casein, horn, and animal and vegetable fibrin. When any one of these is dissolved in a solution of potash, and the filtered solution is mixed with a slight excess of acid, a copious grayish-white flocculent precipitate is formed, and a slight smell of hydrosulphuric acid is perceived. This white substance is *protein*, so called from its occupying the first or most important place in relation to the albuminous principles. It is found that all food which sustains animal life, and promotes growth and strength, must contain protein.

PROTRACTOR. Any instrument for laying down angles is thus called; such as the graduated semicircle which is found in cases of instruments, the rectangular ruler with graduated edges, and various other more expensive contrivances. But the truth is, that the easiest and safest protractor is a table of chords, a scale of equal parts, and a pair of compasses. Even the scale of chords laid down on the rulers, used in the usual manner, is a better protractor than the graduated semicircle, which is worthless, except for very rough work.

PRUD'HOMMES. *Prudentes Homines*, experienced men. This name relates to a remarkable kind of commercial or manufacturing council, well known in France, but to which we have nothing exactly parallel in England. In 1452, King René established at Marseille a council of Prud'Hommes, with summary jurisdiction in disputes between the fishermen of that port: this institution has since been frequently confirmed, and still exists. In 1464, Louis XI. granted power to the citizens of Lyon to appoint a Prud'Homme to decide summarily upon disputes that might arise between merchants attending the fair. By a decree of Napoleon, dated March 18, 1806, a council of Prud'Hommes, consisting of nine members (five manufacturers and four master weavers), elected annually, was established in Lyon to settle disputes between manufacturers and their workmen, and between masters and apprentices. The council acted chiefly as a court of conciliation, but was also vested with power to decide, without appeal or expense, cases involving an amount not exceeding 60 francs. This institution has been recognised and confirmed by succeeding governments. Councils of Prud'Hommes with increased numbers, with powers of summons, seizure, and imprisonment not exceeding three days, and with summary jurisdiction to the amount of 100 francs, are now established in all the great manufacturing towns of France, with the exception, we believe, of Paris. If the amount exceeds 100 francs, an appeal lies to the Tribunal of Commerce. The sittings of these councils are held in the evening, when the workmen have given over their labour for the day. Lawyers are not suffered to plead in their courts. The council of Prud'Hommes is perhaps the most extensively-useful institution in France; in Lyon alone, the cases decided annually exceed 5000; appeals are rare, and a reversal of the decree of the council very much rarer still.

PRUSSIA. This important kingdom does not possess a great variety of natural productions; but it has all those the cultivation of which has been gradually introduced into central Europe; and the most indispensable of them in sufficient abundance for its own consumption, and for the obtaining of foreign luxuries and comforts. Agriculture is the chief source of the national wealth, and is carried on with great care in most of the provinces. Wheat, rye, oats, and barley, are raised both for home consumption and exportation; there are likewise peas, beans, vetches, millet, maize, rape-seed, and linseed. Potatoes are cultivated in all the provinces. Flax, hemp, hops, tobacco, succory, beet-root, and garden vegetables of all kinds are raised, but of the first three articles not enough for home consumption. The vineyards of Rhenish Prussia are extensive and valuable. There is abundance of timber. The mineral products are salt from salt-springs, of excellent quality, and in great abundance; amber and coals in large quantities; alum, vitriol, saltpetre, alabaster, basalt, granite, porphyry, marble, slate, freestone, chalk, lime, porcelain-clay, pipe-clay, &c. The metallic products are silver, copper, lead, iron, zinc, cobalt, arsenic, and calamine. The precious stones are the onyx, agate, jasper, and carnelian.

The principal manufactures are:—Linen in all the provinces, but chiefly in Silesia; woollen cloths and cotton goods, especially in the province of the Rhine, at Elberfield, Barmen, Crefeld, &c.; silk, leather, iron, and copper ware, cutlery, articles of gold and silver, succory, paper, china, glass, earthenware, snuff and tobacco, beet-root sugar, gunpowder, &c. The breweries and brandy distilleries are very considerable.

The abundance of products of various kinds, and the active industry of the people, give occasion to an extensive commerce, which is highly favoured by the advantageous position of the country in the centre of Europe, the great extent of coast on the Baltic, and by the great rivers (the Rhine, the Elbe, the Oder, and the Vistula,) which traverse the country, and are connected by navigable tributary streams and numerous canals. In 1831 the Prussian or Commercial League (Zollverein) commenced, and has since been gradually joined by almost all the German states. The object is to establish an entire freedom of trade among the German states, and to subject foreign trade to such restrictions only as the protection of national manufactures or the financial circumstances of the state may render necessary. The Prussian harbours are:—Memel, Pillau, Neufahrwasser near Danzig, Stolpermünde, Rügenwald, Kammin, Schweinemünde, Peenemünde, Griefswald, Stralsund, and Barth. The most considerable commercial towns are:—Berlin, Königsberg, Danzig, Breslau, Stettin, Magdeburg, Cologne, Elberfeld, and Aix-la-Chapelle. The great fairs are those of Breslau, Frankfort-on-the Oder, and Magdeburg. At present there are in Prussia about 1400 miles of railway open for traffic.

In the year 1849 the imports into Great Britain from Prussia were valued at 2,805,040*l.*, and the exports of British and Irish produce and manufactures to Prussia were 428,748*l.* These sums may mislead, unless accompanied by a little explanation. The value of the imports is *official*, that of the exports is *declared. Official* value means a certain hypothetical value which was fixed for each kind of commodity by the Custom-house authorities many generations since, and has been retained to this day, without any reference to present prices; whereas *declared* value is the actual marketable value at the time. Another circumstance is, that besides the British and Irish produce, England exports largely of foreign and colonial produce to Prussia.

The contributions of Prussia to the Great Exhibition are very numerous, and of a high degree of importance. They comprise almost every variety of manufactured goods, and natural produce to the extent of the country's resources.

PRUSSIAN BLUE is a pigment of pure dark-blue colour, discovered accidentally by a colour-manufacturer of Berlin, in 1704. It is a prussiate of iron, consisting of 52 parts of red oxide of iron combined with 48 parts of prussic acid, to which is added a certain proportion of alum, in order to give more body and greater brightness to the colour.

PRUSSIC ACID, or *Hydrocyanic Acid.* This powerful acid exists ready-formed in several vegetable products, as the leaves of the cherry-laurel and the peach-tree; but it is generally prepared by the action of hydrochloric acid on bi-cyanide of mercury. It is a colourless liquid, with a strong and peculiar odour; its taste is at first cooling and afterwards burning, and it is extremely poisonous. It boils at about 80°, becomes solid at about 5° Fahr., and then crystallises in fibres. As an acid, its powers are but feeble. It is so very volatile that, when dropped on paper, the sudden evaporation of a portion of it renders the remainder so cold that it solidifies; and this effect is produced even when the temperature of the atmosphere is nearly 70°.

Prussic acid is one of the most deadly of all poisons. In the hands of an experienced practitioner it becomes a valuable medicine in some cases. It is of little direct use in the arts; but its combinations with bases produce many useful substances, of which *Prussian-blue* is an instance.

PSALTERY was an ancient musical instrument of the harp kind, in use among the Jews, and supposed to have been tho *nebel* mentioned in several of the Psalms. Whether this instrument was square or triangular, whether played on by the finger or struck by a plectrum, seems doubtful; the probability is that it took many forms, and was played in both ways. According to some authorities this instrument was in shape a trapezium, and similar to, if uot the same as, the dulcimer. [DULCIMER.]

PUERTO RICO. The soil of this Spanish West India island is of the richest and most varied description. The produce of sugar is very abundant, and tropical productions in general are plentiful. The island exported in the first 10 months of 1849—98,000,000 lbs. of sugar, 4,475,000 lbs. of molasses, 6,703,161 lbs. of coffee, and 1,702,000 lbs. of tobacco. The industry and commerce of the inhabitants are exhibited chiefly in connexion with these products.

PUG-MILL. [BRICK.]

PULLEY. The pulley is one of the simple machines or mechanical powers employed in the construction of machinery and in the transmission and modification of force. The kinds of pulley in use are very numerous; but they all consist of combinations of a grooved wheel, moveable on an axis, and a rope lying in the groove; and the manner in which this rope passes over and under a system of these wheels, so as to connect the force with the resistance, or the power with the weight, determines the species or kind of pulley. The following are the combinations by which the principle of the pulley is made available:—

The single fixed pulley possesses no mechanical advantage, the power and the weight being equal to each other. The single moveable pulley consists of one wheel fixed and the other moveable; the power acts at one end of the rope, and the other end is fixed to an immoveable obstacle; the weight or resistance is attached to the sheave, or block, of the moveable wheel. In this the power is one-half the resistance when thero is equilibrium. The first system of pulleys consists of an upper and lower set of wheels, called the upper and lower block; the upper being fixed, and the lower, to which the resistance or weight is attached, being moveable. The power is to the weight or resistance as unity to twice the number of wheels in the lower block. A system consisting of one fixed and two moveable pullies is called a Spanish Barton. *Smeaton's Tack*, so called after the celebrated engineer of that name, contains two tiers of wheels, one above the other, in each block. This arrangement is ingenious, but it is attended with great friction and inequality of wear. *White's Pulley* consists of a single wheel in each of the two blocks. The wheel has a conical form, with grooves on its convex surface; and the diameters of the grooves are in arithmetical progression, by which they revolve with velocities equal to that of the line passing over them. The advantage is that the friction is reduced to that of the pivot and the two lateral faces.

There are two systems in which each block contains a single pulley, and has a separate string. In one system the string is made fast at one end to the block next above it, and at the other to an immoveable object. In the other system each string is attached to the weight. These are superior to the other systems, with respect to the ratio of the resistance to the moving power, but they are of no practical use.

PULPIT. Great cost, both of material and workmanship, was frequently bestowed on pulpits in early times; and some of them rank among the most celebrated monuments of art of their period, and for a long time appear to have been treated as an architectural feature of the interior, being constructed, if not of marble, of the same material as the rest of the building. Of stone pulpits we have few early specimens remaining in this country; but there is one in Bristol cathedral, and another in Worcester. The pulpits of the present day are for the most part, in respect to design, mere carpenter's and joiner's work.

PUMICE STONE. This remarkably light and porous stone is a true *lava*. It is vomited forth by the volcanoes which are distributed in different parts of the earth. That which we employ is obtained from Etna and Vesuvius. It is used for many purposes of rubbing and smoothing.

PUMP. [AIR PUMP; HYDRAULIC MACHINES.]

PURBECK STONE. [DORSETSHIRE; STONE FOR BUILDING.]

PUTCHUK is the name by which a fragrant root is designated in the price-currents of Calcutta and Bombay, whence it is exported to Canton, being highly esteemed by the Chinese as an incense. From the places of export this would appear to be a product of India, but neither the plant which yields it nor the place where it grows has been discovered until very recently. The discovery is interesting, as the putchuk is a substance which was known to the ancients. Dr. Royle, while in the north-western provinces of India, obtained a root which formed a considerable article of commerce, and which was said to be brought from Lahore. It was warm and aromatic in taste, fragrant, and frequently called Orris (Iris)-Root by Europeans in India. On comparing specimens of this root, which he obtained in northern India, with what was called putchuk in Calcutta, he found that they were identical, and he was subsequently informed by Mr. Beckett, who had been long settled as a merchant in northern India, that what he purchased from Umritsir under the name of Kooth, he sold in Calcutta by that of putchuk, so that there can be no doubt of the identity of the two substances; but all that has been ascertained with respect to the place where it was produced, was that it seemed to be to the north of the river Sutlege.

PUTTY, the useful cement used by glaziers for fastening the glass in the frames of windows, is composed of linseed oil and whiting. The whiting should be well dried, and then pounded and sifted till it becomes a fine powder and is quite free from grit. The whiting, a little warm, should be gradually added to the oil, and well mixed by means of a piece of stick or a spatula. When it is sufficiently stiff, it should be well worked with the hand on a table, and afterwards beaten on a stone with a wooden mallet, till it becomes a soft, smooth, tenacious mass. Putty by exposure to the air gradually hardens till it becomes almost like stone. A ball of putty, when left some days, becomes somewhat hard, but may be easily softened by beating.

The most extensive employment of this substance for glazing has perhaps been in the recent operations in the Glass Palace.

PYRAMIDS. The pyramids of Egypt, especially the two largest of the pyramids of Jizeh, are the most stupendous masses of building in stone that human labour has ever been known to accomplish. The Egyptian pyramids, of which, large and small, and in different states of preservation, the number is very considerable, are all situated on the west side of the Nile, and they extend, in an irregular line and in groups, at some distance from each other, for a length between 60 and 70 miles. All the pyramids have square bases, and their sides face the cardinal points.

Herodotus was informed by the priests of Memphis that the great pyramid was built by Cheops, king of Egypt, about 900 B.C., or about 450 years before Herodotus visited Egypt. He says that 100,000 men were employed twenty years in building it. Whether this were or not the true origin of the great pyramid, the vast structure, as at present standing, consists of a series of platforms, each of which is smaller than the one on which it rests, and consequently presents the appearance of steps, which diminish in length from the bottom to the top. Of these steps there are 203, and the height of them decreases, but not regularly, from the bottom to the top; the greatest height being about 55 inches, and the least about 20 inches. The horizontal lines of the platforms are perfectly straight, and the stones are cut and fitted to each other with the greatest nicety, and joined by a cement of lime with little or no sand in it. It has been ascertained that a bed, eight inches deep, has been cut in the rock to receive the lowest external course of stones. The vertical height, measured from this base in the rock to the top of the highest platform now remaining, is 456 feet. This platform has an area of about 1067 square feet, each side being 32 feet 8 inches. If to this were added what is necessary to complete the apex of the pyramid, the total height would be about 479 feet. Each side of the base, measured round the stones let into the rock, is rather more than 763 feet, and the perimeter of the base is therefore 3053 feet. The area of the base, measured along the outside of the stones let into the rock, is 64,753 square yards, or about 13¼ acres. This area is about the same as Lincoln's Inn Fields, London, measured by the wall of Lincoln's Inn Garden and the sides of the houses within the court-yards. The surface of each face, not including the base let into the rock, is 25,493 square yards; and that of the four faces is consequently 101,972 square yards, or more than 21 acres. The solid content of the pyramid is about 3,394,307 cubic yards, which (not making any deductions for chambers and passages in it) has been estimated to be six times the mass of stone in the Plymouth breakwater. Reckoning the total height at 479 feet, the pyramid would be 15 feet higher than St. Peter's at Rome, and 119 higher than St. Paul's, London.

These measurements, relating to the Great Pyramid, will serve to convey an idea of all of them; we need not notice them particularly here, nor need the internal cavities and passages be here dwelt upon. The materials of all the pyramids are limestone; and Belzoni is of opinion that part of the stone for the second pyramid was procured immediately on the spot, judging from the manner in which the rock has been cut away round the pyramid. Herodotus certainly understood that all the stone was brought from the mountains near Cairo, where there are indeed ancient quarries of great extent; but it seems probable that the greatest part of the materials came from the west side of the Nile. The blocks of granite were brought from Syene, which is nearly 500 miles higher up the Nile. The rock on which the great pyramid stands has been found to project at least as high as 80 feet into the body of it. The stones of which it is built rarely exceed 9 feet in length and 6½ in breadth; the thickness has been already stated.

At Thebes there are some small pyramids of sun-dried brick, in which the central chambers have vaulted roofs. There are numerous pyramids in Nubia, perhaps eighty or more, but they are generally small. Next to those of Egypt the most extraordinary pyramids now existing are those of Mexico.

PYRENEES. The lofty chain of the Pyrenees gives name to three departments of France. In the mountains themselves iron, copper, and lead mines are worked, and fine statuary and other marble, including some of the most beautiful varieties, is quarried.

In the department of *Basses Pyrenees* the annual produce of wine is about 7,000,000 gallons, the best kinds being those of Jurançon and Gan. The high mountains are to a great extent covered with forests of pine, fir, and oak, which afford good ship timber. The growing of flax and hemp, the trade in hams with Pau and Bayonne, and the traffic in mules and cattle with Spain, are the most important sources of wealth to the agriculturist. Silver, copper, iron, lead, coal, salt, cobalt, and sulphur, are found. Slate, marble of all colours, granite, alabaster, rotten-stone, and marl, are quarried. The manufactures include linen, calico, coloured handkerchiefs, flannel, drugget, capes, hosiery, Bearnese caps, carpets, chocolate, liqueurs and common brandy, paper, leather, pottery, and some iron. Ships are built on the Adour and on the coast. The commerce is composed of the various products already named, and of wine, liquorice, rosin, prepared skins, wool, hides, deal planks, colonial produce, salt, &c.

In the department of *Hautes Pyrenees* about 6,000,000 gallons of good white and red wines are made annually. Horned cattle and sheep are very numerous; good butter and cheese are made; mules, asses, and horses are reared, and also pigs and large numbers of poultry, especially geese, the legs of which are salted for export. Bees are carefully tended, and honey and wax are abundant. Iron, copper, zinc, lead, manganese, nickel, and cobalt, are found, but no mines are worked; marble of different colours, building stone, slate, granite, amianth, kaolin, marl, fullers' earth, and potters' clay, are raised. The commerce of the department is limited to cattle, corn, mules and horses for Spain, timber, oak staves, hoops, the agricultural products before named some linen, cotton and woollen stuffs, cutlery, nails, hides, &c.

In the third of these departments, *Pyrenees Orientales*, about 7,000,000 gallons of wine are made annually. The red wines of Roussillon are in general of excellent quality, agreeable taste, strong body, and well adapted for transport; they are used for giving colour and body to the lighter growths of Cahors and Auvergne. The wines of Collioure and Port-Vendres have the highest repute; they fine themselves and become of a golden hue with age; in this state they take the name of *Rancio de Rousillon*. The sweet wines of Rivesaltes hold the first rank among the dessert wines of France. The mountains of the department are in many parts clothed with fine forests of oak, beech, pine, and fir, and abound with aromatic and medicinal plants. The cork tree grows naturally, and is also an object of careful cultivation. Bees and silkworms are carefully attended. Many iron mines are worked, and the ore is smelted, and converted into malleable iron at about 180 forges and furnaces, by means of charcoal prepared on the spot. Copper, lead, bismuth, and alum, are found. A coal mine is worked near Estavar; marble, alabaster, granite, and steatite, are quarried. Besides wine and iron, the industrial products include coarse woollen cloths, leather, corks, knit stockings and caps, brandy, whip-handles, common pottery, tiles and bricks. The fisheries on the coast are actively plied, and large quantities of sardines and anchovies are preserved. The coasting trade in the leading articles named, and in wool, oil, honey, &c., is active.

PYRMONT WATER. Pyrmont is the name of a small county belonging to the Prince of Waldeck in North Germany. It derives its chief revenue and importance from a mineral spring in the town of Pyrmont. The great bathing house which contains 140 apartments, tastefully fitted up, and handsome spacious baths, is the most important structure in the place. Above 300,000 bottles of the water from the principal chalybeate spring are exported annually.

PYROGRAPHY. This name has been recently proposed for a peculiar kind of painting or rather delineation, in which *heat* is the chief agent employed. The homely phrase of *poker painting* is that by which it is generally known; since a red-hot poker might be the substitute for the painter's brush in producing the pictures; but homely English is often made to give way to learned Greek, in scientific and artistic designations.

These pyrographs are pictures produced on the surface of wood by heated irons. Some curious specimens of this art were produced by Dr. Griffiths, Master of University College, Oxford, about thirty or forty years ago. The altar piece in the college chapel, and one or two heads in the Taylor Gallery, are still existing; they are said to have very much the appearance of mezzo-tinto engravings, or of crayon drawings; but, from their very nature are much more durable than any engravings or drawings, and are considered to be well fitted to ornament panels. The wood is either sycamore or plane-tree; which are not liable to warp, and which present large surfaces. The delineations are produced by solid pieces of thick iron, shaped somewhat like the heater of an Italian iron.

This art has a renewed interest imparted to it, by the circumstance that the Committee of the Great Exhibition has allotted 30 feet of wall space to the productions of a lady, Mrs. Mills, who has lately introduced many improvements in the preparation of the wood and in the form of the iron implements. The specimens to be exhibited are fitted by their general character to adorn collegiate, corporate, or baronial apartments. The effect in Dr. Griffiths' pictures is produced mainly by broad shadows; while the more recent productions have somewhat the character of etchings. Representations of animals, such as those which almost live and breathe on the canvas of Edwin Landseer, are said to be those for which the art shows peculiar aptitude.

By the rules of the committee, no *paintings* are admitted at the Exhibition; but it would appear that these curious specimens partake of the durability and surface quality of *carvings*, and are on that ground admissible.

PYROLIGNEOUS ACID. [ACETIC ACID.]

PYRO'METER. This instrument was invented by Musschenbroek for measuring the effects produced in the dimensions of solid bodies by the application of heat; but the signification of the term has since been extended so as to include those instruments the object of which is to measure all gradations of temperature above those which can be indicated by the mercurial thermometer. We will briefly describe five or six varieties.

Musschenbroek's Pyrometer consisted of a metallic bar, about six inches in length, one extremity of which was fixed, while the other was left free to advance as the metal elongated from the effect of several spirit lamps placed beneath, which, at each experiment, were charged with the same quantity of highly rectified spirit of wine. The advance of the moveable extremity gave motion to a pinion and wheel, the latter of which drove an index over a graduated circle, each degree of which corresponded to a linear expansion of some determinate fraction of an inch. Desaguliers afterwards substituted fine cords and friction rollers for the wheel and pinion.

Borda's Pyrometer.—The rods employed by Borda in measuring the base-line of the great French Survey consisted of a rule of brass laid upon a somewhat longer rule of platinum and attached at one extremity. The portion of the platinum rule not covered by the one of brass was divided into millionths of its entire length, and further subdivided by means of a vernier and microscope adjusted to the extremity of the brass rule. The value of each of these divisions having been previously ascertained, by first surrounding the compound rule with melting ice, and then immersing it in boiling water, it was only necessary to observe the indications of the vernier in order to apply the requisite correction for reducing the length of the rod to the standard temperature.

Ramsden's Pyrometer.—For low temperatures, the contrivance of Ramsden was employed by General Roy in determining the expansion of the rods used in measuring the base on Hounslow Heath for the Trigonometrical Survey. The rod was immersed in a trough of water, and over each extremity was placed a microscope, to which a slow motion could be given in the direction of the length of the rod by means of a fine micrometer screw. The temperature of the water was then gradually raised, till a thermometer placed in the trough indicated an advance of 10°, 20°, 30°, or any required number of degrees. The consequent elongation of the rod destroyed the coincidence of its extremities with the lines of collimation of the microscopes, which was re-established by turning the micrometer screws, and carefully noting the number of turns and fractions of a turn necessary for that purpose; when, the value in parts of an inch in each turn being previously known, a direct measure of the expansion was obtained, free from the errors of a system of levers or of a train of wheels and pinions.

Wedgwood's Pyrometer.—The property of alumina whereby it undergoes a diminution of bulk when heated, was employed by Wedgwood as a measure of high temperatures. His pyrometer consisted of cylinders of fine white clay, and an apparatus for accurately measuring their length. This apparatus consisted of a metallic plate, upon which were fixed two brass rules slightly inclined to each other. The rules used by Wedgwood were 24 inches long, and divided into 240 equal parts. The distance between the rules at one extremity was three-tenths and at the other five-tenths of an inch; consequently the difference between their distances at any two consecutive divisions was the 1200th part of an inch. The clay cylinders were first baked at a red heat (about 947° Fahr.), and then reduced to exactly five-tenths of an inch in length, so as to fit the first division of the scale. When afterwards exposed to a greater heat they underwent contraction, and the amount of this contraction was determined by observing the division of the scale corresponding to their diminished length.

Dulong and Petit's Pyrometer was constructed for measuring the *cubical expansions* of various substances. By observing the difference of altitude at which mercury of different temperatures stood in the two arms of an inverted glass siphon, they determined the absolute expansion of the mercury; and by comparing this with the apparent expansion of mercury in a glass tube, they deduced the absolute expansion of the glass. A cylinder of the metal whose expansion was sought was then placed within a glass tube, closed at one extremity and terminating at the other in a capillary opening, and the rest of the tube occupied with mercury. Upon the whole being heated a portion of the mercury was expelled equal to the excess of the absolute expansions of the mercury and metal above that of the glass; and as the expansions of the mercury and glass were previously known, the weight of the expelled mercury determined the expansion of the metal.

Prinsep's Pyrometer.—The unoxidable metals (gold, silver, and platina) present three marked temperatures, from the low melting-point of silver to the high ignition of platina; and many intermediate links may be made by alloying the three metals together in different proportions. When such a series has been once prepared, the heat of any furnace may be expressed by the alloy of least fusibility which it is capable of melting. As the melting points of silver and gold are comparatively near to each other, Mr. Prinsep assumed only ten intermediate gradations of heat, the lowest of which corresponded to the fusing point of pure silver, and the others to the fusing points of silver alloyed with 10, 20, 30, &c., per cent. of gold. From the melting point of gold to that of platina, he assumed one hundred gradations of heat, which were the melting points of pure gold and of gold alloyed with 1, 2, 3, &c., per cent. of platina. Among the advantages of this mode of identifying temperatures are:—the smallness of the requisite apparatus, nothing more being needed than a small cupel, containing in separate cells eight or ten pyrometric alloys, each of the size of a pin's head; the indestructibility of the specimens, since those melted in one experiment need only to be flattened under a hammer, when they will be again ready for use; and the facility of notation, since two letters and the decimal of alloy will express the maximum heat.

Daniell's Pyrometer is a complex apparatus depending on the small expansibility of black lead compared with that of metals. A bar of black lead is bored nearly from end to end like a gun; and into this bore is placed a rod of the metal to be experimented on. When both are exposed to a great heat, the metal expands more than the black lead, and causes a small cylinder of porcelain to protrude from the top of the tube or bore. This cylinder is connected with an index or hand which moves round a graduated arc; and the degrees on this arc are so calculated as to indicate the temperature to which the metal has been exposed.

PYROTECHNY. The art of making fire-works is essentially a chemical one. It takes advantage of the chemical affinity between substances, of the power of ready ignition, of the rapid and slow combustion produced by different proportions of the ingredients, and of the production of exquisite colours by the substances while burning. The revolving of stars, &c., is partly a mechanical arrangement arising out of the resistance or inertia of the air when a burning material is forcing its way out of a tube. The three chief ingredients are nitre, sulphur, and charcoal; the secondary ingredients are filings of iron, steel, copper, zinc, and other materials; while various oxides, acids, alkalies, and salts, tend to produce varied colours by different modes of combination. The coloured fires are the most interesting results, and require much care in the choice and preparation of the materials. One familiar kind of fire-work is noticed under ROCKETS.

PYROXYLIC SPIRIT, or *Pyroligneous Æther*, obtained by distillation from wood, is a colourless liquid, has a peculiar penetrating smell, partaking both of alcohol and æther, and its taste is pungent. It is lighter than water, and boils at about 150° Fahr. It is an extremely inflammable liquid, and burns without residue; and being cheaper than spirit of wine, it is advantageously substituted for it in many manufacturing arts. It is capable of combining with chlorine, iodine, and other elementary bodies; it unites also with acids to form various compounds.

Q

QUADRANT. [Sextant.]

QUARANTINE LAWS. Quarantine laws are the result of imperfect knowledge on a subject which is of great importance to commerce. They are regulations chiefly of a restrictive nature, for the purpose of preventing the communication from one country to another of contagious diseases, by means of men, animals, goods, or letters. The term Quarantine originally signified a period of forty days, during which a person was subject to the regulations in question. The regulations consist in the interruption of intercourse with the country in which a contagious disease is supposed to prevail, and in the employment of certain precautionary measures respecting men, animals, goods, and letters, coming from or otherwise communicating with it. Men and animals are subjected to a probationary confinement, and goods and letters to a process of depuration, in order to ascertain that the contagious poison is not latent in the former; and to expel it, if it be present, in the latter. Quarantine lines may either be drawn round a coast, as is the case in France, Italy, and Greece, with respect to the Levant; or they may be drawn along a land frontier, as on the frontier between Austria and Turkey.

Goods carried in ships or by land are subject to quarantine, according as they belong to the class of susceptible or non-susceptible goods. Goods which are supposed to be capable of containing and transmitting the poison of the plague, are called *susceptible*. Goods which are supposed to be incapable of containing and transmitting the poison of the plague, are called *non-susceptible*. All animal substances, such as wool, silk, and leather, and many vegetable substances, such as cotton, linen, and paper, are deemed susceptible. On the other hand, wood, metal, and fruits, are deemed non-susceptible. Every ship is furnished by the consul or other sanitary authority at the last port where it touched, with a document styled a *Bill of Health*, declaring the state of health in that country. If the ship brings a *clean bill* of health, the passengers and goods are not subject to any quarantine. If she brings a *foul bill*, they are subject to quarantines of different durations, according as the plague is known or only suspected to have existed in the country at the ship's departure. On account of the prevalence of plague in the countries on the Levant, they are considered as permanently in a state of suspicion; and no ship sailing from any of them is considered to bring a clean bill. The periods of quarantine vary from two or three to forty days; the usual periods are from ten to twenty days. The building in which passengers usually perform their quarantine, and in which goods are depurated, is called a Lazaretto. The most spacious and best appointed lazarettoes in the Mediterranean are those at Malta and Marseille.

The laws of quarantine depend directly on the contagion or non-contagion of certain diseases; and on the difference between *susceptible* and *non-susceptible* commodities, if the contagion-theory be true. It becomes therefore a medical question; and the opinions of medical men throughout Europe are gradually tending to such a result as will either abolish quarantine altogether, or greatly modify and limit it: a result of very great importance to the commerce and industry of Europe.

QUARRYING is the operation of extracting from the ground, or detaching from the sides of rocks, marble, stone, or other minerals in considerable masses. When the material to be excavated lies vertically below the surface of the ground, the work commences by removing the earth to a depth sufficient to lay that material bare, in order that it may be separated into blocks, and removed; but when the stone, &c., is in the interior, and near the side of a mountain or hill, the workmen proceed as in the operation of mining, running galleries into the ground, and leaving pillars of the material for the support of the mass above them.

A quarry of small extent is opened by sinking vertically in the ground a shaft, into which the men descend by ladders; and the blocks of stone, being separated from the mass, are drawn up by means of cranes, which are worked by a windlass or other machine. In working the larger quarries, the vegetable mould forming the upper surface is removed by the spade; and the beds immediately underneath, generally consisting of rag, or stone of an inferior quality, are broken up by gunpowder or otherwise, and conveyed to a distance. The stones intended for sale, and which are generally in beds much below the surface, are sometimes also detached from the mass by blasting; but as by this process the blocks are broken irregularly and the stone wasted, a different method is generally employed. The large mass of stone, as it exists in the quarry, consists of strata contiguous to one another, and the surfaces in contact form planes of *cleavage;* in lines parallel to which the stones being more easily divided than in any other direction, these lines constitute what is called the *cleaving* grain of the material. In order therefore to separate a large block from the mass, a series of iron wedges, placed in line a few inches asunder, on the natural face of the rock and in the direction of the cleaving grain, are driven into the stone till a part is loosened: a channel is then cut in the direction of the length of the intended block, and at a distance from the natural edge of the stone equal to its required breadth; and wedges being planted in the channel, they are driven by repeated strokes till the stone is split in that direction also. In the hardest stones, the wedges are placed not in the channels, but in what are called *pool* holes sunk in the direction in which the block is to be severed from the mass. A similar operation is then performed in the direction of the breadth of the block; and thus a large portion is detached from the original mass.

The natural strata of the stone in different quarries are in different positions; frequently they are horizontal, but generally they are inclined to that plane, and sometimes they are vertical: occasionally also both the first and last of these positions are assumed by the stone in the same quarry. It is evident that the separation of the blocks from a mass must be most easily effected when the natural strata are in vertical positions; cutting the stone in directions perpendicular to the line of the grain is always a work of difficulty, and the operations are attended with some danger to the quarry-men when the latter are obliged to work in galleries under ground.

After the blocks have been severed from the mass, they are reduced as nearly as possible to a rectangular form; and this is done by means of a tool called a *kevel*, pointed at one end and flat at the other, with which the irregular parts are knocked off. The blocks are then usually, by means of cranes which are capable of being moved from place to place, raised upon trucks or low carriages; and these are drawn, generally on iron railways, to the quays or wharfs where the stone is put on ship-board. At the slate quarries in Caernarvonshire the slabs are placed on sledges, which, by an engine, are drawn up an inclined plane; and, from the summit of this plane, the stone is drawn by horses to the Menai.

QUARTZ, is the mineralogical name of numerous varieties of rock crystal, the native oxide of silicium [SILEX], called also siliceous or flint earth, and silicic acid. Quartz occurs crystallised and massive, and in both states it is widely diffused throughout nature, especially as one of the constituents of granitic and the older rocks. Quartz is hard enough to strike fire with steel; it becomes luminous and electrical by friction; it is of various colours; it is infusible; insoluble in acids, in general. but acted on by hydrofluoric acid. *Hornston*, and *chert* are varieties of compact quartz. Cavernous quartz is termed *spongiform quartz* or *swimming stone*. Among the numerous varieties of quartz are *brown* or *smoky quartz*, *purple quartz*, or *amethyst*, *blue quartz*, *green quartz*, *yellow quartz*, and *red quartz*. Among the minerals in which quartz is the chief ingredient, are *agate*, *avanturine*, *flint*, *flinty slate*, *opal*, *chalcedony*, *heliotrope*, *onyx*, *plasma*, *sard*, *sardonyx*, and *jasper*.

QUA'SSIA, is a genus of plants consisting of trees inhabiting the tropical parts of South America, particularly Surinam and the adjoining countries.

Quassia amara, the true Quassia of modern botanists, is a small tree inhabiting the woods of Surinam, Demerara, and probably the greater part of Central America. The wood of the root of this plant was formerly in great repute as a stomachic and as a remedy for the malignant endemic fevers of Surinam. The flowers also were, and still are, in that country infused in wine or spirits, and form a bitter beverage; but the wood is out of use, in consequence partly of its being less easily procured than that of the next species, and partly from an opinion being entertained of some bad properties existing in connection with the intense bitter. *Quassia excelsa* is a large tree inhabiting Jamaica. The wood is white, and scentless, but most intensely bitter; it is one of the ingredients employed by fraudulent brewers in adulterating beer. *Quassia Simaruba* is the plant which furnishes the bark called Simarouba, which comes from Jamaica in bales, and is used as a tonic, although it also appears to act as an emetic.

Quassia is imported in billets, sometimes a foot in diameter, and several feet long; but before being used for medicinal purposes, they are cut into chips, which are of a light gray colour, or, by long exposure to the air, of a yellow or brownish hue. The active principle of Quassia seems to be *quassite*, a neutral substance, which crystallises in white prisms, and is readily soluble in alcohol.

QUERCITRON BARK. This valuable dye-drug is described under BARK. Chevreul has given the name *Quercitrin* to the colouring principle of the Quercitron Bark. It crystallises in colourless acicular crystals, which have a slightly sweet taste, and subsequently a bitter one. They are very soluble in water, in alcohol, and in æther. On boiling a solution of Quercitrin, it becomes turbid, and deposits a quantity of small acicular crystals of *Quercitrein*, less soluble in water, and which forms with hydrate of lead a beautiful yellow lake of lead.

QUERCUS. [BARK; CORK; OAK.]

QUICKSILVER. [MERCURY.]

QUINA or QUINIA, is a very important vegetable alkali, contained in the three well-known varieties of Cinchona, or Bark, but principally in the Yellow Bark. This alkali is colourless, inodorous, and extremely bitter. It fuses at about 300° Fahr., and when cold is yellow, translucent, friable, and somewhat like resin. When subjected to a strong heat, with access of air, it is totally dissipated, with the formation of the vapour of the carbonate of ammonia. The only one of the salts of quina extensively employed is the *Disulphate*, the *Quinæ Disulphas* of the London Pharmacopœia, and the *Quinæ Sulphas* of the Edinburgh. The crystals of this salt are colourless, acicular, have a pearly lustre, a bitter taste, and effloresce when exposed to the air.

R

RADIATION OF HEAT. There are certain experiments on the radiation of heat which possess great practical value, in so far as they show what substances should be employed, and what avoided, when heat is required to be retained in any vessel or other body. In the jackets or envelopes for boilers and steam pipes this matter is always attended to.

Sir John Leslie placed a tin canister filled with hot water in the focus of a parabolic mirror of the same metal, and a differential thermometer in the focus of another such mirror, which was placed opposite to it. The four sides of the canister were covered with the substances whose radiating powers were required. When three of the sides were covered respectively with lamp black, paper, and ground glass, and then turned so as to radiate directly on one speculum, the heat reflected by the other raised the thermometer to 100°, 98° and 90°; but when the fourth side, which was uncovered, was similarly directed, the thermometer fell to 12°. Thus it appears that polished metallic substances are bad radiators, which may be attributed to the internal reflection of the heat from their surfaces. A similar apparatus served to measure the absorptive power of different substances, the bulb of the thermometer being covered with an envelope of the substance to be examined; and this power is thus found to be nearly in proportion to that of radiation. In another experiment Leslie filled a canister with ice or snow, and found that the cold apparently emitted from the varnished side was the greatest, and that from the polished side the least; he observed also that the cold like the radiant heat, varied with changes in the absorbent power of the thermometer and of the surface of the mirror.

Count Rumford laid down, as a rule justified by numerous experiments, that if we would confine heated substances, solid or fluid, in a vessel, the surface of the latter should be highly polished; on the other hand, if the object be to cool the substances, the surface should be painted or varnished, or be covered with a soft coating which is not metallic. Also, in warming apartments by steam, the intention being to promote radiation as much as possible, the tubes conveying the steam should be unpolished or painted.

The colours of bodies have some effect on the velocity of radiation and on the absorption of heat. Dr. Stark of Edinburgh surrounded the bulb of a thermometer successively with equal weights of black, red, and white wool, and placed it in a glass tube, which was heated to the temperature of 180° by immersion in hot water; the tube was then cooled down to 50° by immersion in cold water, and the several times of cooling were respectively 21, 26, and 27 minutes.

Those phenomena of radiation which are still the subject of scientific enquiry, and which are not yet applied in the arts, do not come under our notice here.

RAGS. Paper, it is well known to most persons, is made chiefly from the rags or worn fragments of woven materials—linen being the best adapted. The rags of our country do not constitute a fourth, perhaps not a fifth, of the quantity which we use in making paper. Italy and Germany furnish the principal supplies; and it is a curious illustration of national habits that English rags are known from all others by being *cleaner*, while those of Italy are wretchedly dirty. The rags and other materials imported for making paper in 1848 amounted to 7191 tons.

RAILWAYS. If cotton spinning were the greatest commercial phenomenon of the first quarter of the present century, railways may unquestionably be said to be so for the second. Nothing else has been attended by such vast (and in many respects beneficial) results.

Wooden railways or tramways were introduced in the collieries of the north of England in the early part of the seventeenth century. They were adopted in order to reduce the labour of drawing coals from the pits to the places of shipment in the neighbourhood of Newcastle-upon-Tyne. They consisted, in the first instance, simply of pieces of wood imbedded in the ordinary road, in such a manner as to form wheel-tracks for the carts or waggons employed. An improved form was afterwards adopted, by laying the wooden rails on transverse sleepers. The vehicles used upon these wooden railways were generally waggons, containing from two to three tons of coal, mounted upon small wheels. The wheels were provided with a flange or projecting rim, which, by coming in contact with the side of the rail, retained the waggon upon the railroad.

About the year 1767 iron plates were laid upon the wooden rails on a railway at the Colebrook Dale iron works. Some time after the experiment at Colebrook Dale, cast-iron rails, with an upright flange, were brought into use at the colliery of the Duke of Norfolk, near Sheffield, in 1776. Originally they were fixed upon cross sleepers of wood, like those used to support wooden rails; but about the year 1793 blocks of stone were introduced as supports, instead of the wooden sleepers. Various inconveniences attendant on these *plate-railways* led to the use of *edge-railways*, which have now almost entirely superseded the previous form. The first edge-railway of any considerable extent was completed in 1801 for the conveyance of slate from the quarries of Lord Penrhyn. The decided advantages of edge-rails were so well appreciated by the coal owners of Northumberland and Durham, that they were adopted extensively by them within a few years after the successful experiment at Penrhyn. Many successive varieties have been introduced in the form of the rails; but the greatest improvement was the invention, in 1820, of an efficient and cheap method of rolling iron bars suitable for rails and similar purposes. The fibrous texture of wrought-iron makes it far less likely to break when subjected to concussion than cast-iron, and the sectional form used is such as to render bending improbable.

The application of the steam-engine to the purposes of locomotion was suggested in one of the patents of Watt: but it does not appear that either he or any other inventor carried their ideas into practice until about 1802, when Messrs. Trevithick and Vivian patented a high-pressure engine, which, by its simplicity and compactness, was admirably adapted for locomotive purposes. Within a few years they built several carriages, one of which, at least, was for use on a common road. In 1805 they made some interesting experiments with a locomotive on a tramway near Merthyr Tydvil, and thereby proved the practicability of their plan. Engineers at first thought that the wheels would not hold or *bite* on the rails, without some other contrivances; but those fears have been dissipated.

Shortly before the completion of the Liverpool and Manchester railway, the directors decided that horse traction would be too slow for the requirements of the traffic; and they determined to try locomotives. They offered a premium of 500*l*. for the best to be produced which would fulfil certain conditions, of which some were that it should not emit smoke, should draw three times its own weight at the rate of ten miles per hour, should be supported on springs, not exceed six tons weight, or four tons and a half if on only four wheels, and should not cost more than 550*l*. The trial was fixed for October, 1829, when four steam locomotives were produced, one of which was withdrawn at the commencement of the experiment. Of the other three, the *Novelty*, by Messrs. Braithwaite and Ericson, and the *Sans Pareil*, by Mr. Hackworth, failed in some of the conditions. The remaining engine, the *Rocket*, was constructed by Robert Stephenson and Mr. Booth, of the Liverpool and Manchester Railway, and succeeded in performing more than was stipulated for. The most marked improvement in Stephenson's locomotive was the use of a tubular boiler instead of a large flue.

From the opening of that railway, the success of the great system was at once decided. Nothing could check the spread of so vast an improvement; and we have since seen such a twenty years of commercial energy as the world never saw before.

In the laying down and construction of a railway, the engineer so adjusts his inclinations or *gradients* as to make the nearest practicable approach to a level, avoiding if possible any loss of power from undulations of surface, by making all the inclinations on one side of the summit, or highest point to be passed over, rise towards it, and all on the opposite side descend from it. Curves on a main line of railway being objectionable, the engineer so adjusts his line as to avoid them when possible, and to make those which are inevitable of as large a radius as circumstances will admit. The works of a railway consist chiefly of *tunneling, excavation, embankment, arching, viaducts, bridges;* concerning each of which a few words may be said.

Tunnels are, in general, the most formidable works, and the time and expense of forming them can be least accurately calculated, because unforeseen circumstances often arise to retard their progress. Being objectionable also on other accounts, tunnels are avoided as much as possible in the more recently-designed railways. *Excavations* of great depth and extent are of frequent occurrence where the railway passes through high ground, but not at such a depth from the surface as to require a tunnel. The depth of cuttings is frequently from fifty to a hundred feet; and the slope of the sides depends on the nature of the rock or soil. *Embankments* are the artificial ridges of earth formed to support the railway on a higher level than the natural surface of the ground. Their dimensions are often fully commensurate with those of cuttings, from which their materials are mostly procured. In the ordinary mode of proceeding, an embankment is formed simultaneously with a cutting, the earth waggons proceeding filled from the excavation along a temporary railway to the embankment, where they are tipped up to discharge their contents. *Arching* of almost every kind is more or less required in viaducts, bridges, culverts, and drains; and simpler work in the retaining walls, station buildings, and other necessary erections. *Viaducts* of great magnitude are often executed for the purpose of crossing valleys at an elevation greater than could be conveniently obtained by embankment, and also for entering or passing through towns. They are usually of stone or brick, but sometimes of wood or iron. *Bridges* are required occasionally for crossing rivers, and very frequently at the intersection of roads, and as communications between severed property. They are formed of stone, brick, wood, iron, or combinations of two or more of these.

In order to obtain a firm dry foundation for the blocks or sleepers on which the rails rest, a layer or stratum of broken stone, technically called *ballast*, is spread over the road to the thickness of a foot or more, varying according to the construction adopted and other circumstances. The rails used to be spiked down to stone blocks; but it is found better either to rest them on sleepers placed at intervals, or on continuous timber bearings, as on the Great Western line. Mr. Barlow has recently invented cast iron bearings for the rails, which are found to be a valuable improvement. He has also introduced a very broad wrought iron rail which requires no sleepers, the broad bottom of the rail being laid upon the ballast itself. The rails now used vary from 70 to 90 lbs. per yard. In the old colliery tramways, four feet was not an uncommon width for the *gauge* of the rails, but many lines were less. Some of the colliery railways of Northumberland are four feet eight inches and a half; and from these the Stockton and Darlington, Liverpool and Manchester, and other lines, took their gauge. The advantage of uniformity has led most companies to follow this example. The ordinary width being considered by him inconveniently limited, Mr. Brunel fixed upon seven feet as the gauge of the Great Western and its tributary lines; and hence has arisen the late 'battle of the gauges,' which may be truly said to have cost the respective companies millions of money, in law and legislation.

Wherever there is a uniform gauge, the *clearing-house system* is acted upon by the railway companies, to the obvious advantage of all parties. The principle of the system is, that passengers shall be booked through at all principal stations, and conveyed to their destination without change of carriage; that horses and cattle be in like manner carried through without change of conveyance, and goods without being shifted or re-assorted; that the companies respectively shall pay a fixed rate per mile for such carriages and waggons, not their own property, as they may use, and a further sum per day by way of fine or demurrage for detention, if kept beyond a prescribed length of time; and that all traffic accounts between the several companies shall pass through the Clearing-House.

The carriages used on railways we need not stop to describe; every one has had more or less opportunities of noticing the gradual improvements introduced. The wonder-working *locomotive*, however, must engage a little of our attention.

In a modern locomotive, the tubes through the boiler, for the passage of flame and heated air, are now always made of brass, which is found much more durable than copper. They vary in number in different engines from about ninety to a hundred and fifty or upwards,

KNIGHT'S CYCLOPÆDIA OF THE INDUSTRY OF ALL NATIONS.

No. 34

being frequently less than an inch and a half in diameter. The power of generating steam, which is the measure of efficiency in a locomotive engine, depends much upon judicious tubing. Boilers are frequently tubed to such an extent that from four to six hundred square feet of heated metal is exposed to the water, in addition to the area of the fire box itself. An important feature in a locomotive boiler is its security from bursting, because as the tubes are much weaker than the external casing of the boiler, they are almost certain to give way first; and the bursting of one or two tubes is rarely productive of more serious consequence than extinguishing the fire, and thereby causing a gradual stoppage of the machine. In the old engines the cylinders were placed at the bottom of the smoke-box, and the machinery under the boiler; but there is a growing preference for those in which the cylinders are fixed outside the framing, and the power is conveyed to the wheels by external cranks and connecting-rods. The 'long-boiler' engines of the narrow gauge are very large; but those of the Great Western Company are still more so. One of the engines of this company has about 1750 square feet of heating surface in the boiler; has cylinders of 18 inches diameter and 24 inches stroke; driving-wheels of 8 feet diameter; and two pair of bearing-wheels of 4 feet 6 inches in diameter. The total length is 24 feet; the distance between the supporting wheels 16 feet; the weight of the engine alone, without fuel or water 28½ tons, and of the tender, 10 tons; and the total weight of engine and tender when loaded, about 56 tons. These engines, in the express train between London and Exeter, go at a speed, in some parts, of 60 miles an hour.

Small and light locomotives have been recently introduced, fitted for the traffic of branch lines.

Taking one line of railway with another, main lines with branch lines, and passenger traffic with goods traffic, it is found that one locomotive is required for about every two miles of railway; to work all the traffic effectively, and to have a sufficient reserve store for contingencies. We are thus enabled to form a rough estimate of the number of locomotives in the United Kingdom.

Rope traction on railways is becoming gradually abandoned; and the once highly extolled *Atmospheric traction* is only applied on two miles of the Dublin and Kingstown Railway.

We will next take a rapid glance at the *statistics* of railways. The first railway established in this country as a distinct undertaking, and intended for public use, was the Surrey Iron Railway, the company for which was incorporated in 1801. In the following twenty years only twenty new railway companies were incorporated; but the Stockton and Darlington Railway, the act for which passed, after much opposition, in 1821, gave an impulse to this kind of enterprise. Between 1801 and 1840 there were 299 acts passed relating to railways. These sanctioned the construction of about 3000 miles of railway; but many of the schemes were afterwards abandoned. Down to 1840 about 1100 miles of railway were finished and open, and about 60,000,000*l.* had been expended on them. Between 1840 and 1850, railway legislation presented the following results:—

Year.	Acts.	Length.
1841	19	14 miles.
1842	22	67 ,,
1843	24	91 ,,
1844	48	797 ,,
1845	120	2883 ,,
1846	270	4790 ,,
1847	184	1663 ,,
1848	83	300 ,,
1849	35	50? ,,
1850	36	50? ,,
	841	10,705

Taking the earlier acts at 299, and mileage at 3000, we have a total of 1140 acts of parliament sanctioning railways, and about 13,700 miles of railway so sanctioned. This includes the lines which have been abandoned.

At the end of 1849 the length of railway open for traffic in the United Kingdom was 5996 miles; at the end of 1850 it was 6621 miles. This last amount is made up as follows:—

England and Wales	5132 miles.
Scotland	951 ,,
Ireland	538 ,,
	6621

The average receipts per mile in England and Wales, during 1850, for passengers was 1218*l.*, and for goods 1110*l.*; this shows that the goods traffic has nearly reached the level of the passenger traffic. The passengers conveyed in the year ending June, 1850 were 66,840,175; who paid fares amounting to 6,465,575*l.* It is a curious fact that the average paid by *all* passengers, of *all* classes, for *all* journeys, on *all* the railways, remains every year pretty nearly equal in amount, viz. two shillings per journey; this is much smaller than most persons would have expected, and it shows how much the short or local traffic preponderates over the long or through traffic. The goods traffic in the same twelve months brought 5,042,277*l.*; giving with the passengers' receipts the astonishing sum of 12,407,852*l.*—exceeding one million sterling per month. There is every reason to believe that the year 1851 will show a very notable increase on these numbers.

Among foreign countries, America, Prussia, Germany, Belgium, and France have not been slow to imitate the railway proceedings of England. On the first day of 1851, the United States had 8797 miles of railway, which cost about 60,000,000*l.* On the continent of Europe the system is making rapid strides, but not comparable to that of the United States.

It is satisfactory to know that the Great Exhibition contains specimens of the latest and finest constructions relating to railway machinery.

RAIN-GAUGE, or *Pluviometer*, is a vessel for measuring the quantity of rain which falls on any particular part of the earth's surface, the quantity being indicated by the depth of the precipitated water which would cover the ground about the spot, supposing the ground to be horizontal, and that the water could neither flow off nor penetrate into the soil. The instrument generally consists of a conical funnel, open both at top and bottom, the lower extremity entering into a cylinder below, which thus receives the rain from the funnel. A graduated rod passes through a perforation in a bar fixed in the direction of a diameter of the cone at its upper surface, and is attached, at the lower extremity, to a circular piston, which has nearly the same diameter as the interior of the cylinder: the weight of the piston and rod is such as to allow the former to float with its upper surface on a level with the surface of the water. A rim, of a cylindrical form, rises a little way above the upper extremity of the conical part of the funnel, in order to prevent the rain-water, which would strike the interior of the latter near that extremity, from being thrown out in consequence of the shock.

The diameter of the funnel at the top may be 12 inches, and that of the cylinder 6 inches; in which case the area of the horizontal section on which the rain falls will be to that of the cylinder in the ratio of four to one. Hence a depth of water equal to one inch at the horizontal section will be expressed by a space equal to 4 inches on the length of the rod; and, each of such spaces being divided into 100 parts, the depth of water at the said section will be indicated in hundredths of an inch. The height of the cylindrical vessel below the funnel may be from 25 to 30 inches. For the sake of diminishing the evaporation and of measuring small quantities of rain with greater precision, the diameter of the cylinder is sometimes reduced to 2 inches, and the collected water is, by means of a small pipe, inserted in the bottom of the cylinder, and furnished with a cock made to pass into a glass tube whose interior diameter is half an inch. In this case the diameter of the upper extremity of the funnel being the same, a shower of rain whose depth on the ground might be one-hundredth part of an inch, would be indicated by 5·76 inches in the tube.

RAISINS. The dried fruits of several varieties of the vine are called *raisins*. They are named after the countries where they are produced, or the places whence they are imported; as *Malaga*, *Valencia*, and *Smyrna*. The peculiar small and generally seedless grapes, formerly called *Corinths*, are now better known as the dried or Zante *Currants* of the shops.

There are many modes of preparing the raisins. One is to dry the grapes, after being cut when fully ripe, by exposure to the heat of the sun on a floor of hard earth or of stone. Another method is to cut the stalk half-way through when the grapes are nearly ripe, and leave them suspended till the watery part is evaporated; the flow of sap is in a great measure prevented from entering the fruit, in consequence of the incision, and whilst evaporation continues to go on undiminished, desiccation must take place. The currant-grapes are gathered in the end of August and beginning of September. Rains often spoil the crop when they occur at the timo of gathering or drying. The fruit, when sufficiently dry, is separated from the stalks by small rakes, and afterwards stored in magazines, 'seraglie,' constructed somewhat like a lime-kiln, having an opening at top, where the fruit is put in, and a door at bottom, opened only at the time of sale. The fruit is rendered so compact by its own weight, that considerable force is requisite to break it up for the purpose of being packed in the large casks in which it is exported.

The Malaga raisins are esteemed the finest; and the muscatels from thence exceed all others in price. The black Smyrna raisins are those of least value. The white grape of Alexandria furnishes very fine raisins. An oil exists in the seeds of the grape, in the proportion of 12 pounds of oil to 100 pounds of seeds. Though it is not obtained without difficulty, it is extracted in Italy in large quantity. When heat is used it has a harsh taste, and is mostly used for burning; but when cold-drawn, it may be used for food. *Tannin* of the purest kind may be obtained from the seeds of the grape.

Nearly all the raisins imported into this country are from Spain and Turkey. Of the total quantity imported, 99 per cent. is from these countries, namely, 64 per cent. from Spain, and 35 per cent. from Turkey. A small supply is received from Portugal, Italy, and the Cape of Good Hope. The raisins imported in the last three years amounted to—

1848	239,668 cwts.
1849	209,180 „
1850	276,312 „

RAMPART. The ramparts of ancient fortresses were walls of stone or brick, frequently from 60 to 100 feet high and 20 feet broad, including the galleries formed in them; and round or angular towers were constructed at intervals along the walls. A modern rampart is surmounted by a parapet of earth, on the interior side of which, towards the town, is a nearly level space, varying in breadth from 35 to 40 feet, called the terreplein; and on this the artillery is placed. The exterior and interior sides of the rampart are formed with slopes making angles of about 45 degrees with the horizon: or they are retained by revetments, or walls of brick or stone, nearly upright, the exterior face of the rampart constituting the *escarp* of the ditch in front.

RAMSDEN, JESSE, will always occupy a distinguished position in the history of mechanism by his beautiful optical and astronomical instruments. He was born in 1735. At the age of 20 we find him engaged as a clerk in a cloth warehouse in London, in which capacity he continued till 1757-8, when his predilection for other pursuits led him to bind himself for four years to a working mathematical and philosophical instrument maker. He commenced working on his own account, and his skill as an engraver and divider gradually recommended him to the employ of the leading instrument-makers. Ramsden subsequently married Dollond's daughter, and he received with her part of Mr. Dollond's patent right in achromatic telescopes. His occupation afforded him frequent opportunities of observing the defective construction of the sextants then in use, the indications of which, as had been pointed out by Lalande, could not be relied on within five minutes of a degree, and might therefore leave a doubt in the determination of the longitude amounting to fifty nautical leagues. The improvements introduced by Ramsden are said by Piazzi to have reduced the limits of error to thirty seconds. This circumstance, added to the cheapness of his instruments, which were sold for about two-thirds the price charged by other makers, soon produced a demand which, even with the assistance of numerous hands, he found difficulty in supplying. In his workshops the principle of the division of labour was carried out to a considerable extent, and a proportionate dexterity was acquired by the workmen; but it is asserted that in none of these, even the most subordinate, and least of all in the higher departments did the skill of the workmen surpass that of Ramsden himself. His attention was incessantly directed to new improvements and further simplification, the result of which was the invention of a dividing-machine. From this time his fame was fully established as the first instrument-maker of his day. He died in 1800.

RAPE-SEED. The *Brassica napus*, the plant which produces the rape-seed, and which is of the cabbage tribe, is cultivated like Cole, or Colza (*Brassica napus sativa*), for the sake of its seeds, from which oil is extracted by grinding and pressure. It is also extensively cultivated in England for the succulent food which its thick and fleshy stem and leaves supply to sheep when other fodder is scarce. The mode of cultivation of the colza and rape for seed is nearly the same. The colza takes a longer time to come to maturity, and produces more seed. The rape grows on less fertile soils, and may be sown in spring as well as in autumn. Both are hardy, and resist the winter's frost.

The rape-seed imported in the last three years amounted to:—

1848	79,970 quarters.
1849	29,480 „
1850	107,029 „

RAREFACTION is an augmentation of the intervals between the particles of aeriform fluids, so that the same number of particles are made to occupy a volume greater than that under which they were previously contained. The term is used in opposition to *condensation*, and in the same sense as *dilatation*, which last is applied both to fluids and solids. From the experiments of Gay-Lussac and Dalton it has been ascertained that, under equal external pressures, the rarefactions of all dry gases and of the aëriform substances produced by the evaporation of liquids are equal at equal temperatures, between the points of freezing and boiling water, and that they vary in volume proportionally to the increments of heat expressed by the expansions of mercury in the thermometer. Between the temperatures of freezing and of boiling water, the dilatations of all metals and of the fluids called non-elastic are constantly proportional to the increments of temperature;

but, beyond the temperature of boiling water, the dilatations increase in a higher ratio. A remarkable circumstance is observed in the state of water when near congelation. On being cooled to a temperature within the limits of 33·9° and 34·5° (Fahrenheit), its volume remains stationary, and in this state water seems to have attained its maximum of density; for on continuing the cooling process, the water begins to expand, and it continues to do so until it is converted into ice.

RATAFIA, is a liqueur prepared by flavouring sweetened spirit with various kinds of fruit. There are many varieties, generally named after the fruit which is employed. *Ratafia de Cassio* has cherries, *Ratafia de Curaçoa* has the peels of Portugal oranges; *Ratafia d' Angelique* has Angelica seeds; *Ratafia d' Anis* has aniseed; and so on. There are ratafias not only of fruits but of seeds, berries, flowers, balsams, and other vegetable products. There are ratafias, for instance, of cherries, quinces, raspberry, juniper, walnuts, peach and apricot kernels, coffee, cocoa, clovepinks, Seville orange peel, orange flowers, violets, Tolu balsam, &c. All these ratafias have spice and sugar added to them. The French liqueurists are the most skilled in this as in most other branches of delicate distillation and making of essences.

RAZOR MAKING. [Cutlery.]

READING. The trade of this town is considerable. There was anciently a large manufacture of woollen cloth, but it has become extinct. Silk ribands and galloons are woven, and floor-cloth and sail-cloth are made. There are iron foundries, breweries, and yards for boat-building. Trade is carried on in corn, seeds, malt, timber, bark, hoops, wool, cheese, and beer. The Kennet is navigable to the Thames, and the Kennet and Avon Canal affords a water communication with the west of England.

REALEJO, a seaport on the Pacific, in the republic of Nicaragua, is fast rising into commercial importance. The inhabitants are chiefly merchants and persons occupied in ship-building, for which the neighbouring forests supply abundance of timber. Ship-building is a large branch of industry, and there are docks for that purpose. The commerce with the other republics of South America is considerable. The principal articles of trade are cacao, indigo, sugar, timber, mahogany, cedar-wood, tar and pitch, sail-cloth, and hides. The activity along the western coasts of America, consequent upon the discovery of gold in California, and the position of the town at the western terminus of the projected ship-canal between the Atlantic and the Pacific oceans, are likely to render Realejo a place of considerable importance.

REALGER. [Arsenic.]

REAPING. The common *Reaping Hook*, or *Sickle*, with which corn is usually cut, is one of the oldest instruments of husbandry. In reaping with the sickle, a portion of the stems is collected with the left hand, and held fast, while the sickle in the right hand is inserted below the left, taking the stems in its semicircular blade, and cutting them through by drawing the sickle so as to act as a saw, for which purpose the edge is finely serrated in a direction from the point to the handle. The heads of the corn, with the upper part of the straw, are then laid on the ground in quantities which may readily be collected into a sheaf. The division of labour is introduced with advantage amongst a band of reapers. A certain number cut the corn, while others follow to gather the sheaves; some only preparing the bands, and others tying them and setting up the sheaves into stooks or shocks, which usually consist of ten or twelve sheaves. In many places there is a regular measure for the circumference of a sheaf, which should never exceed thirty inches. The bands are made by taking two small handfuls of the cut corn, and crossing them just below the ears into a knot; the sheaf is then pressed with the knee, and the band drawn tightly around it; the ends are twisted together like a rope, and inserted under the band, which effectually fastens it.

Wherever the sickle is used for reaping, the straw is cut at a certain height from the ground, and the remainder forms a stubble, which is sometimes mown at leisure after harvest, and carried into the farm-yard for litter; but in the neighbourhood of large towns, where straw is sold at a good price, or exchanged for stable dung, it is important that as much as possible of it should be cut with the corn. This has introduced the practice called *fagging*, or *bagging*. The instrument used for this purpose partakes of the nature of a scythe, as well as of a reaping-hook. It is shaped like a sickle, but is much larger and broader; and instead of being indented like a saw, it has a sharp edge like a scythe, which is renewed when blunt by means of a stone or bat. The Fagging-Hook cuts the straw close to the ground by a stroke of the hand; and its curved form is only useful in collecting stray stems, and holding a certain quantity of them between it and the left hand of the reaper when he makes up a sheaf. The *Hainault Scythe*, which has been described in most agricultural works, does the work better and with less fatigue; it is in fact a fagging hook, but is not quite so much curved; the handle is longer, and placed at an angle with the plane of the blade. A better instrument however on extensive farms is the *Cradle-Scythe*, which, in the hands of an expert mower, will do more work and more effectually secure all the straw than any other instrument.

Mr. Whitworth, the eminent machinist of Manchester, patented a new reaping machine in 1849. It is a circular disc or scythe (for cutting grass or reaping corn), placed upon the side of a four-wheeled machine; motion being given to the disc by wheel-gearing attached to one of the wheels of the machine.

REBEC was a musical instrument (now disused) of the violin kind, which had three strings tuned in fifths, played on by a bow. It was somewhat smaller than the violin.

RECTIFYING. Under DISTILLATION it is explained that raw spirit, as produced by the distiller, is a very different liquid from those which are retailed in the shops, and consumed in such large quantities. Gin, British brandy, spirits of wine, whiskey, (except the purest Irish and Scotch, and such cordials as aniseed, peppermint, &c.),—are all produced by the *rectifier*, from raw spirit made by the *distiller*. In accordance with the Excise laws of this country, rectifying must not be carried on in the same building, nor at less than a certain defined distance from the same building, as distilling; because the distilled spirit pays duty, the rectified spirit none. Throughout England there are scarcely a dozen distilleries, properly so called; all the others being *rectifying* establishments, where the spirit is redistilled, purified, and flavoured with various vegetable substances. The raw spirit is sold by the distiller to the rectifier in two different strengths, technically known as 25° and 17° 'over proof;' and the transfer from one establishment to the other must be known to and sanctioned by the Excise officers. The spirit is redistilled, by which a certain portion of essential oil is removed from it; and a third distillation then takes place, in which the spirit in the still has the addition of various fruits, herbs, berries, or seeds, according to the liquor to be produced. The distillation is carried on until the spirit becomes very much weaker than crude spirit, (except in the case of spirit of wine), and until it has imbibed the fragrant, the sweetening, and the flavouring properties of the vegetable substances placed in the still.

RED LEAD. Red lead or *minium* is an oxide of the metal; *litharge* being another oxide. Litharge is produced in the process of cupellation, or the separation of the minute quantity of silver which most lead ores contain; it is a refuse, so far as the immediate process is concerned; but it is afterwards used in making flint glass, or as a material whence many of the salts of lead, useful in the arts, are prepared.

Red Lead, however, is purposely manufactured, and the furnaces are adapted expressly for this purpose. It is one of the wonders of chemistry, to see this red powder produced simply by the action of the common air on melted metallic lead: it baffles all our usual conceptions concerning the production of colour. Pigs of lead, to the weight of about 30 cwt., are put into a reverberating furnace, and exposed to a melting heat. A man then stands before the open mouth of the furnace, and keeps the molten lead continually moved by a sort of rake. This movement causes all parts of the metal to come successively in contact with the air, which enters at the open mouth of the furnace. In five or six hours the lead thickens, and acquires the look of a grayish yellow powder; it has become a mixture of oxidized lead with lead which has not yet had sufficient contact of air to have become oxidized. The contents of the furnace are then raked out, and when cold are ground in a mill to a fine state, and steeped in water. The lead particles sink, while particles of yellow oxide remain diffused in the water. The water is poured off, and allowed to settle, and the yellow oxide precipitates. This oxide, when collected and dried, constitutes *Massicot*; and by again exposing it to the heat of a furnace, and allowing it to absorb more oxygen, the oxide changes its colour from yellow to red, and changes from Massicot to Red Lead.

This manufacture is carried on, among other places, at the lead works of Newcastle.

REFINING is a term applied to various processes in the useful arts, and especially in metallurgy, whereby the substances acted upon are purified by the chemical separation of dross and impurities, and of such foreign matters as may be in combination with them. [ASSAYING; IRON MANUFACTURE; LEAD; STEEL MANUFACTURE; SUGAR.] Some of the furnaces employed in these operations are called *refineries* or *refining furnaces*.

REFLECTORS. The reflectors employed for conveying rays of light to a focus, or for throwing them into a different direction, are of varied forms and application. They may be flat, convex, concave, spherical, parabolic or elliptic, according to the purposes required; and they may be made of glass silvered on the back, or of polished silver, or of one among many alloys which yield a bright white surface capable of being beautifully polished.

A few details concerning the reflection from silvered glass, for ornamental purposes, will be found under SILVERING; the aid which a small metallic reflector may render in microscopic observations, is noticed under MICROSCOPE; the larger reflectors for distant view, are noticed under SPECULUM and TELESCOPE; while the reflectors for lighthouses are noticed under LIGHTHOUSE.

REFRIGERATORS. There are many processes in what may be termed chemical manufactures, in which a liquid is required to be cooled with as much rapidity as possible. In the practical modes of effecting this, the caloric of the heated liquid is carried off either by a current of cold water near it, or by a current of air. Exemplifications of these processes will be found under BREWING; DISTILLATION; VINEGAR MANUFACTURE.

REFUGE HARBOURS. A few details on this subject will be found in the articles BREAKWATER, DOVER, HARBOUR, and PORTLAND.

REGA'LIA is the name given to the costly specimens of jewellery belonging to the crown. In England, the regalia properly so called are the crown, the sceptre royal, the virge, or rod with the dove, St. Edward's staff, the orb or mound, the sword of mercy, called Curtana, the two swords of spiritual and temporal justice, the ring of alliance with the kingdom, the armillæ or bracelets, the spurs of chivalry, and sundry royal vestments. The regalia here enumerated, all but the vestments, are preserved in the Jewel-Office in the Tower of London.

REGISTERING MACHINES. Under CALCULATING MACHINES, is given a brief description of many contrivances for registering and numbering by automatic means. Under BANK NOTE MACHINERY, and VOTING MACHINE, also, other similar contrivances are noticed. Some years ago, a machine was invented by Mr. Walker, a cloth manufacturer of Leeds, to which he gave the name of *Opera Meter*, and of which the object was to measure or register the amount of work done by certain machines. The apparatus had a shaft which could be connected with the gig-mill, the shearing machine, or other machines employed in the cloth manufacture. This shaft rotated as fast as the machine to which it was applied; and the shaft gave motion to a train of wheel-work, with a dial face and index hands to denote the number of revolutions made in a given time. The index hands thus became a measure and recorder of the amount of work done.

A piece of mechanism called a *Counter* is often used in cotton factories, to count or reckon how many revolutions the main shaft of the machinery has made in a given time; this number becomes, under certain conditions, a measure of the amount of work which the machinery has effected.

Under OMNIBUS is noticed a recent contrivance for registering the number of persons who enter a vehicle. Whether practically applicable or not, the apparatus is theoretically fitted for supplying a similar register at the entrances of public gardens and places of amusement generally.

REGISTRATION OF INVENTIONS. [DESIGNS, COPYRIGHT AND REGISTRATION; PATENT LAWS.]

REICHENHALL, a town in the circle of the Isar in Bavaria, is a place of great importance, as being the central point of the four great salt-works of Bavaria. The salt springs seem to have been turned to profit ever since the eighth century. As the great consumption of wood for so many years made fuel too scarce to boil all the brine on the spot, a very ingenious system of hydraulic machinery was contrived in 1618 to carry the brine in iron pipes from Reichenhall to Traunstein, over an elevation of 828 feet perpendicular height, and extending 21 miles in length. A similar conduit, 42 miles long, to Rosenheim on the Inn, where there is abundance of wood, was made in 1809; so that now all the springs which formerly ran to waste for want of wood are turned to account. In 1817, the salt springs of Reichenhall, Traunstein, and Rosenheim were connected by hydraulic works of great power and ingenious contrivance with the salt-mines of Berchtesgaden. The salt produced yearly is 16,000 tons.

REIMS, or RHEIMS, a city in the French department of Marne, is noticeable in a commercial point of view, besides the attractions of its famous cathedral. The manufactures are extensive; they consist of woollen cloths, kerseymeres, light stuffs for summer coats and trousers, swanskins, camlets, merinos, cashmere shawls, flannels, blankets, carpets, hosiery, bolting-cloth, cordage, candles, soap, and leather. Wax and wool bleaching, dyeing, wool-combing, brewing, and the making of machinery, are carried on. The spiced bread and biscuits of the town are in great repute. The chief trade is in the above-named articles of manufacture, corn, flour, champagne wines, brandy, spices, colonial produce, wool, cotton-yarn, flax, hemp, raw hides. A railway in course of construction will join Reims to the Paris-Strasbourg line, on which it abuts a little east of Épernay.

RENAISSANCE. The term *Renaissance* indicates the period of the *Revival*, in respect to architectural and decorative matters, when the classic began to be re-introduced after the mediæval styles. It is often used as synonymous with the term *Cinque-Cento*, which literally means five hundred, whereas it is used as equivalent to mille cinque-cento, the *mille* being understood though not expressed, therefore it stands for fifteen hundred. In its technical sense among artists, the term renaissance may be considered to mean the style of architecture and general decoration which prevailed during the 16th century, or rather the earlier part of it; nor is it so restricted, for without exact reference to date, it is also applied to what belongs to the style so denoted though it may happen to be *before* the year 1500, which period may be taken as the line of demarcation laid down by the historians of art.

RENFREWSHIRE. The south-eastern part of this Scottish county is included in the great coal district of the west of Scotland. The chief coal works are at Quarrelton near Johnstone; and at Hurlet and Househill near Paisley: the mines here are very productive. Limestone, sandstone, ironstone, granite, and secondary trap-rocks, are found in considerable abundance. Good freestone for building is quarried; limestone is also wrought for burning; and the mines of coal and ironstone give employment to many persons. The hilly parts of the county on the west and south are chiefly devoted to pasture. Owing to the demand for meat, vegetables, milk, butter, &c., by the large and crowded populations of Greenock, Glasgow, and Paisley, a large part of the cultivated land is meadow-land or garden-ground. Dairy farming is very extensively practised.

Renfrewshire possesses a considerable amount of manufacturing and commercial industry in some of the towns. *Greenock* has been already alluded to in connection with the great city of GLASGOW. At the beginning of the last century, the harbour, which was then only fit for the reception of fishing boats, was enlarged: more than ten acres were enclosed between two circular quays; and subsequent improvements have rendered the outer harbour available for ships of large burthen. This has been the means of raising the place to an important position as a sea-port. The Newfoundland and Nova Scotia fisheries are carried on extensively. The number of vessels belonging to the port is nearly 500. *Johnstone*, near Paisley, contains cotton mills and some other manufactories. The parish of *Neilston* contains several villages; most of the inhabitants, amounting altogether to about 10,000, are employed in various branches of silk and cotton manufactures, the river Levern affording excellent water power for driving machinery. There is also abundance of clear water suitable for bleaching. PAISLEY industry has been noticed elsewhere. *Pollockshaws* is a tolerably large place, depending almost entirely on the cotton manufacture; spinning, weaving, bleaching, and printing are actively carried on. In *Renfrew* the manufactures are various: muslin weaving is by far the most important. Many females are employed in clipping, tambouring, and flowering. A few small vessels carrying coal, manure, &c., on the Clyde, belong to the burgh; but a considerable number of vessels, chiefly laden with grain from Ireland, or with dye-stuffs for Paisley, discharge their cargoes here.

The following were the factory statistics of Renfrewshire in 1850: Paisley being the chief town to which those statistics relate. There were 51 cotton factories, being a much larger number than in any other Scottish county except Lanark; these factories had about 500,000 spindles: 2000 power looms; water and steam power equal to 2742 horse-power; and 7884 factory operatives, of whom no less than 5717 were females. There were 3 woollen factories, 1 worsted factory, 4 flax factories, and 1 silk factory—the whole nine employing about 1500 persons.

RENNIE, JOHN, is a member of a family well worthy of admiration in all that respects mechanical and engineering skill. He was born in 1761 in Haddingtonshire. He appears to have very early devoted his attention to the subjects of machinery and architecture, and he attended at Edinburgh the lectures given by Dr. Robinson and Dr. Black, on mechanical philosophy and chemistry. About 1780 he left his native place, and shortly afterwards established himself as a mechanist in London, where he obtained immediate employment. From this period he continued to be occupied in the construction of steam-engines, or of the different kinds of machinery to which, as a first mover, steam is applied; and at the same time he was almost constantly engaged in designing or superintending those public works which have given him so just a claim to celebrity. Between 1799 and 1803 he constructed the stone bridge at Kelso, below the junction of the Tweed and Teviot. He also built stone bridges at Musselburgh and other places in Scotland; but his masterpiece of this kind is the Waterloo Bridge over the Thames. The Southwark Bridge, over the same river, is an iron bridge, and was also constructed by him. He superintended the formation of several canals. But his chief work in connection with inland navigation is the Kennet and Avon Canal, which extends from Bath to Newbury. He also gave a plan for draining the fens at Witham in Lincolnshire, which was executed in 1812. The London Docks and the East and West India Docks at Blackwall are among the great works which are executed from the plans and under the direction of Mr. Rennie. He formed the new docks at Hull (where also he constructed the first dredging machine used in this country), the Prince's Dock at Liverpool, and the docks of Dublin, Greenock, and Leith. To these must be added the Plymouth Breakwater. Mr. Rennie also gave plans for improving the harbours of Berwick, Newhaven, and other places, and the dockyards of Portsmouth, Plymouth, Pembroke, and Chatham: he also built the pier at Holyhead. Before his death he had given plans for improving the docks at Sheerness; which have since been executed by his first and second sons, Messrs. George and John (now Sir John) Rennie. To Sir John Rennie was also confided the charge of the construction of the present London Bridge, from the design of his father.

Mr. Rennie died in 1821, and was buried in St. Paul's Cathedral. His sons are worthily following in his steps in engineering works.

REPULSION. Both attraction and repulsion exist in all the particles of material substances, and seem to be properties by which those particles act upon one another when not in contact. The reality of a substance between the particles of bodies, whether solid, fluid, or gaseous, admits of no question; for the difference in the densities of these classes of bodies, as well as the different contractions of the bodies in the process of cooling, can only be conceived to arise from the different extent of the intervals between the particles. It is right however to observe, that the word repulsion is often applied to phenomena which are in reality the results of attraction. For example, a small quantity of quicksilver being laid on a glass plate assumes a spherical form, instead of spreading over it in a thin surface; and this was once supposed to arise from a repulsive power in the glass, whereas it is owing to the attraction of the particles of quicksilver for one another being greater than the attraction of the glass for the quicksilver. The expansions of solids and fluids by heat, and the elastic powers of gas at different temperatures, are consequences of the repulsions residing in the particles of caloric, or induced by the latter in those of the bodies with which they are combined. The repulsive power existing in the air which is condensed in nitre, produces, on being combined with heat, a velocity of expansion equal to about 7000 feet per second; and the force of pressure resulting from it is thought to be equal to 2000 times the pressure of the atmosphere. It is this which gives such force to the explosion of gunpowder.

The scientific theories whereby the phenomena of expulsion are sought to be explained, and the experiments made to test the theories, are beyond our present scope.

RESINS are secretions of plants, which are probably all in a fluid state, but become solid either by the evaporation of their more volatile parts, or by the absorption of oxygen. They are distinguished from true Balsams by the absence of benzoic acid, and from Gum-Resins by the absence of gum, their complete insolubility in water, and their requiring alcohol for perfect solution. Some are soluble in cold alcohol, and these are termed *resins;* others are soluble only in boiling alcohol, and termed *sub-resins;* but the two are often also associated in the same substance. Many volatile oils, by long exposure to the air, or merely by a reduction of temperature, deposit a substance termed *stearopten,* which is analagous to resin. Where a considerable quantity of volatile oil co-exists with a resin, a honey-like consistence is preserved, and the resin is termed *soft resin.* When a very large portion of oil is present, a fluid condition exists, and *turpentine* is the proper designation.

The manufacture of common resin is described under TURPENTINE.

RESISTANCE is a power by which motion, or a tendency to motion, in any body is impeded or prevented. When a weight or pressure acts upon a beam or bar in any direction, the tenacity by which the particles of such material oppose that action constitutes a resistance of one kind. [MATERIALS, STRENGTH OF.] Again, when a body is made to move on another, the inequalities of the surfaces of both create a resistance of a different kind. [FRICTION.] When a body moves in a fluid, the inertia of the fluid particles displaced by it produces a third kind of resistance. It is computed that a 24-pounder ball experiences a resistance equal to 800 lbs. when its velocity is equal to 2000 feet per second. Like effects take place in the movement of boats or ships; when the velocity is great, the water accumulates in front, and flowing off from thence obliquely, it carries away some from the sides, and, causing the surface of that which is near the stern to be rather lower than the general level, it there produces a diminution of pressure, while there is an excess in front on account of the accumulation.

From the experiments of Mr. Telford, the following values of the resistances experienced by loaded carriages on level roads have been determined. On a good pavement the resistance is $\frac{1}{70}$ of the weight of the carriage and load; on a broken surface of old flint, $\frac{1}{35}$; on gravel, $\frac{1}{15}$; and on a well-constructed railway, from $\frac{1}{300}$ to $\frac{1}{250}$. Mr. Barlow has found that, with small velocities, the force of traction on canals is less than on railways; and when the velocity is equal to four miles per hour, the forces are equal. Beyond this velocity the advantage is in favour of the railway.

All these enquiries are of great importance in ship building, railway making, and other engineering works, where *motion* is to be provided for.

RESPIRATOR, or breath-warmer, is a singular instrument invented some years ago for giving warmth to the air drawn into the lungs in breathing, and thereby enabling invalids to whom cold air is injurious to enjoy the benefits of exercise in the open air without injury or inconvenience.

The apparatus usually consists of from eight to twelve frames of sheet-silver or other metal, about three inches and a half long, one inch and a half wide, and $\frac{1}{200}$th part of an inch thick; the metal of which is pierced away by machinery so as to leave merely a narrow frame containing six vertical bars of $\frac{1}{30}$th and five horizontal bars $\frac{1}{80}$th of an inch wide. On both sides of each of these frames a layer of wires an inch and a half long and $\frac{1}{450}$th of an inch thick is soldered, care being taken to connect each wire, not only with the top and bottom bars of the frame, but also with each of the five horizontal bars. The wires are laid about $\frac{1}{200}$th part of an inch apart, and are so numerous that a large respirator of high power contains 2000 feet of wire, divided into about 12,000 pieces, and soldered to the frames at more than 80,000 distinct points. The frames or lattices of wire-work are fixed parallel to each other, and kept a short distance apart by small studs of a substance which is a slow conductor of heat, so that the inner layer is always kept, as nearly as possible, at the temperature of the air expelled from the lungs, and each successive layer diminishes in warmth, till the outer one is nearly as cold as the external air. The curious and philosophical application of a non-conducting medium between the metallic screens is essential to the perfect action of the instrument, as without it the heat would be equally diffused, and no part of the metal-work could retain more than half the temperature of the breath. By this arrangement the air inhaled, finding each layer of wire warmer than the preceding, is gradually raised, in respirators of the highest power, to the greatest attainable temperature. These instruments are more especially useful in diseases of the lungs.

RETINASPHALTUM occurs in irregular opaque masses of a pale brownish-yellow colour, having a glistening lustre and imperfect conchoidal fracture. It is soft and brittle, melts when placed on hot iron, smokes, and afterwards burns with a bright flame, emitting a fragrant odour. Partly soluble in alcohol, leaving an unctuous residue. It consists chiefly of resin and bitumen.

RETORT, is the name of a chemical vessel in which distillation or decomposition is effected by the application of heat. For different purposes retorts are made of glass, earthenware, and metal; and the form varies according to the mode in which the retort is to be used. In general, when the application of the higher temperatures is required for distillation or decomposition, earthen retorts are employed. In preparing hydrofluoric acid, lead is used; and in concentrating sulphuric acid, platina retorts are now largely employed, and would be universally so, were it not for their very high price. In the distillation of coal [Gas Lighting] iron retorts are used; and also, on the small scale, for obtaining oxygen from the peroxide of manganese; and in various other chemical operations.

REVETMENT. This name was originally applied to brick and stone walls used in a particular way in fortification; but it is now also used by civil engineers. A revetment, as constructed by the latter, is a kind of retaining wall. The exterior and interior faces of the revetment or retaining wall of a dock, have in a vertical section the form of concentric arcs of circles, with their convexities towards the land; and this form is given them that the stones may be able to resist the hydrostatical pressure of any water which, when the dock is full, may get behind the wall, and which may be prevented from escaping when the dock is made dry.

RHAMNUS, or Buckthorn, is the name of a genus of plants, many species of which are valuable in the arts. The berries of one species, the *Rhamnus catharticus*, have long been known for their medicinal properties, and still continue to hold a place in several Pharmacopœias. This property is participated in by those of other species, as well as by their inner bark. The berries of several species of Rhamnus form articles of commerce from the Mediterranean, under the name of *French, Turkey*, and *Persian Berries, Grains d'Avignon*, &c., being valued on account of the colouring-matter which they yield, and which varies from yellow to green. This M. Brongniart supposes to be owing rather to different degrees of ripeness than to essential differences in nature. *Sap-green* is a mixture of the juice of these berries with those of some others. *Rhamnus infectorius, saxatilis, amygdalinus, catharticus*, and *Clusii* are the species generally employed; some for dyeing morocco leather of a yellow colour, others for dyeing wool, and the bark of some for striking a black with the salts of iron. The *Lycium* of the ancients is supposed to have been a species of Rhamnus; hence also one species has been called *Rhamnus Lycioides:* it has a hard yellow wood.

RHENISH PRUSSIA. This portion of the Prussian dominions, situated near the Rhine, is very important for its produce and manufactures. The natural productions are equally numerous and valuable Some parts of the mountains are crowned with forests, and the declivities are covered with vineyards where the exposure is favourable. The mineral kingdom yields silver, iron, copper, lead, calamine, marble, slate, freestone, millstones, basalt, porphyry, alum, manganese, sulphur, coal, and salt. In the level parts of the north there are productive corn fields and rich pastures; between the mountains there are fertile valleys, where flax, hemp, hops, and tobacco are grown, and fruit and garden produce of every kind are cultivated in great abundance. Game is plentiful, and all the domestic animals are bred in sufficient numbers. The Rhine passes through this province for 180 miles, and is navigated by steamers. The small rivers and streams are applied to turn mills and to work manufacturing machinery of every kind. The trade of the province is very extensive. The province had, at the end of 1846, 41 cotton factories with 109,547 spindles. When we state that the province contains the important towns of *Cologne, Coblentz, Elberfeld, Düsseldorf, Aix-la-Chapelle* and *Treves*, it will be seen how rich a portion it must constitute of the Prussian dominions, in manufactures and commerce.

RHEO'METER, is an instrument by which the force of an electric or magnetic current may be measured. The word was first proposed by M. Peclet as a synonym for galvanometer; and it has since been employed by Professor Wheatstone in a general sense, together with *Rheoscope*, denoting an instrument by which the existence of an electric, &c. current may be ascertained; and *Rheomotor*, expressing any apparatus, as an electrical or galvanic battery, by which a current of that kind is orignated. The Rheometer or Galvanometer employed by Mr. Wheatstone is a glass cylinder resting on a stand, and containing within it a magnetised needle, which is suspended from the cover. A graduated circle serves to show the deviations of the needle from the zero of the graduations, and the amount of deviation is read by means of a microscrope. For forces or resistances which are considerable, there are placed below the circle numerous coils of fine wire; but for small forces a thick plate of wire making but one coil is used.

RHINE. The Rhine is certainly the most commercial river of continental Europe. From Basel to Mainz the Rhine is navigable for barges of 100 tons; from Mainz to Cologne, for vessels of 200 tons; and lower down, for vessels of 300 tons. The river is connected by canals with the Saône and Rhône, the Schelde, the Meuse, and the Danube. A very important trade in colonial produce, manufactured goods, timber, coal, iron, corn, wine, and other agricultural products, is carried on by the Rhine, and its chief navigable feeders, the Moselle, the Main, and the Neckar. This trade has been greatly increased by the policy of Prussia, which has rendered most of the large towns on her part of the river free ports; and the resolution of the government of the Netherlands, in February, 1850, to abolish the Rhine duties altogether, is likely to add a great stimulus to this traffic. The river is now navigated by the steam-vessels of three companies—those of the Cologne Company, plying between Arnheim in Holland and Strasbourg; the Düsseldorf Company, between Rotterdam and Mannheim; and the Dutch Company's boats from Rotterdam to Mainz. From Basel a railroad runs along the right bank of the river to Wiesbaden, and another runs along the left to Strasbourg, whence a line, now nearly completed, passes to Paris. A short line joins Bonn with Cologne, and from Deutz, a suburb of the latter, a line runs through Düsseldorf into the great railway system of North Germany.

This important river gives name to two of the busiest districts of the continent; viz., *Haut Rhin* and *Bas Rhin*, in France, and *Rhein Provinz*, in Prussia; these are described, in respect to their industrial features, under ALSACE, and RHENISH PRUSSIA.

RHODE ISLAND. A few details illustrative of the produce and industry of this portion of the American Union, will be found under UNITED STATES.

RHO'DIUM. This rare metal exists in combination with platinum, and was discovered by Dr. Wollaston. Rhodium is white, has a metallic lustre, is brittle, extremely hard, and its specific gravity is about 11. It suffers no change by exposure to air, either dry or moist. Rhodium forms very hard alloys with other metals, which are sometimes used for the nibs of pens; but neither the metal nor its combinations have yet been very extensively applied in the arts.

RHÔNE. The Rhône is perhaps the most commercial of the rivers of France. The river is navigable *downwards,* from near Seyssel to its mouth, a distance of 330 miles; for some miles higher up it is available for floating timber. Steamers ply between Lyon and the Mediterranean; owing however to the rapidity of the current, the *up* navigation is very slow. The Rhône is a most important highway for the transfer of the produce of this part of France; and it is connected by the Saône, which is navigable for steamers up to Châlon, and by canals with the Bay of Biscay, the Rhine, the Seine, and the Loire. Its basin includes the Swiss cantons of Valais, Vaud, and Geneva, the duchy of Savoy, and fourteen French departments, most of which are famous for their corn, wine, silk, and oil. In the lower part of its course its waters are turned to great advantage in fertilising the land near its banks by irrigation.

The Rhône gives name to one of the departments of France, fruitful and commercially important. In the extreme south of this department are the famous chestnut forests which yield the favourite large chestnuts sold in Paris by the name of *marrons de Lyon.* The valleys, plains, and accessible slopes are carefully cultivated, the products comprising almost everything that grows in France, except the orange and the olive. The mulberry is cultivated for the production of silk. The lower slopes of the hills are almost everywhere planted with vines; this is especially the case with the slopes along the Saône and the Rhône, from the neighbourhood of Belleville to Condrieu. This region, which includes the *Mont-d'Or,* so called from its rich wine products, contains some of the finest vineyards in France. The annual produce is about 17,000,000 gallons; the best sorts are those called Côte-Rôtie, Romanèche, Condrieu, and Sainte-Foy. The department contains important copper-mines and works at St. Bel near Arbresle, and at Chessy, a small place on the Azergue. Coal mines are worked. Lead, gold, manganese, rock-crystal, porphyry, granite, marble, talc, asbestos, gypsum, fuller's earth, potter's-clay, excellent building-stone, and various other minerals are found. The Mont-d'Or contains excellent stone quarries, and is noted for the great number of fossils it contains.

The department is the most famous spot in Europe for all kinds of silk manufactures, including satins, taffeta, lutestrings, velvets, gold and silver brocade, crape, gauze, shawls, ribands, hosiery, &c. This trade centres at LYON. There are also important manufactures of plain and figured muslins, handkerchiefs, silk hats, calicoes, cotton yarn and twist, blankets, gold and silver lace, small wares, straw hats, mineral acids, machinery and mill work, and liqueurs. There are besides several dye houses, bleach-works, type-foundries and printing offices, breweries, paper-mills, glass-works, potteries, and plaster-mills. The various products named or indicated, together with corn, wool, brandy, raw silk, broad cloth, linen, lace, hardware, hides, bar and sheet iron, ironmongery, timber, planks, staves, &c., form items of an extensive commerce, which is still further increased by the important transit trade carried on by means of the navigable waters of the department, and by the railway to St. Étienne.

RHUBARB. Long as this valuable medicine has been known, it is remarkable that the species of *Rheum* yielding it, and of which the stalks and roots consist, is yet unknown; this is in consequence of the best species, *Turkey* Rhubarb, being only obtained by the Russians at Kiachta from the Chinese. The different species of rhubarb are important plants, not only on account of the roots being so extensively employed, and so valuable for their medicinal qualities, but also on account of the stalks of the leaves being now so much employed, from their agreeable acidity, in making tarts, &c. As the species are all indigenous in cold parts of the world, that is, in the southern parts of Russia, Siberia, Tibet, the north of China, and the Himalayas, so they may all be grown in the open air of this country, and several are cultivated on account of their stalks. Some also, both in England and France, are cultivated on account of the root, which is sold as Turkey Rhubarb.

As the particular species which yields the officinal rhubarb, and even the precise place of its growth, are not known, we can only speak of the drug as it is brought to market. There are six well marked varieties, viz. Russian or Turkey, Dutch Trimmed, Chinese, Himalayan, English, and French. Of the first sort the greater portion at present comes from St. Petersburg, and is denominated Muscovite, Bokharian, or Siberian rhubarb; while a part has always formed one of the imports from China into Bokhara, whence passing to Smyrna, it is known in Europe as *Turkey Rhubarb*, which name it commonly bears in the shops. This kind varies much in size and appearance, the pieces being cylindrical, spherical, flat, or irregular, from two to three inches long, one to three broad, and one to three thick. The smaller pieces are picked out, being preferred, while the larger pieces and the dust are employed for powdering. Holes are remarked in many of the pieces, of which one occasionally extends entirely through, the others only partially; the former having been made in order to suspend the piece in drying, the others in examining the quality. This kind, and probably the other sorts, is frequently worm-eaten, owing to the ravages of a small beetle. *Dutch Trimmed Rhubarb*, called also by some writers *Persian Rhubarb*, and *Batavian*, occurs in flat or round pieces, and is not much different in appearance from the preceding, but it reaches Europe through Canton and Singapore. *Chinese* or *East Indian Rhubarb*, termed in commerce *half-trimmed* or *untrimmed* rhubarb, rarely presents an angular character, but occurs in rounds or flats. The best pieces are heavier and more compact than those of the Russian kind, and the odour is much less powerful and less aromatic. *Himalayan Rhubarb* is not known as a commercial article in this country, nor is it even an article of large consumption in India, where it sells for only one tenth of the best rhubarb, resembling in quality the Russian, and which is found in India. *English Rhubarb* occurs in two states, *dressed* or *trimmed* so as to resemble the Russian kind, and *stick* rhubarb. The first is grown at Banbury in Oxfordshire, and is frequently used for the show-bottles in druggists' windows, and often sold in the streets of London for Turkey Rhubarb, by persons dressed up as Turks. Stick Rhubarb is sold in the herb shops, and is in long pieces. *French Rhubarb* is not brought into this country.

About 300,000 lbs. of rhubarb are imported annually.

RIBBON MANUFACTURE. *Ribbon*, or *Riband*, is the well known name for a long narrow web of silk worn for ornament and use. Ribbons of linen, worsted, and gold or silver thread were formerly included in the term, but it is now generally confined to those made of silk. Paris, Tours, Lyon, and Avignon, were originally the chief seats of the ribbon trade; the two last cities were rivals until the year 1723, when, partly owing to the regulations which the jealous Lyonnese had prevailed upon the government to make in their favour, and partly to a plague of two years' continuance, the trade of Avignon was ruined, and in great measure transferred to Lyon. At Paris the master ribbon-weavers were incorporated into a company, under the designation of *tissutiers rubaniers* of the town and suburbs of Paris. Figured ribbons were made chiefly at Paris. The ribbons called *double lisse* (double warp), which were considered the richest and best, were made at Tours. Before the revocation of the Edict of Nantes, the ribbon-looms of Tours amounted to 3000; but this measure, which banished the Protestants, banished with them their trade, and both Tours and Lyon suffered severely from its effects; but the trade of Lyon afterwards revived. In 1831 the number of ribbon manufacturers at St. Étienne and St. Chamond was 200. The number of ribbon looms in these towns and the surrounding district, which in 1812 was 9000, had increased to 23,000. Their daily produce was 350,000 ells. There are three kinds of looms in use in that district; 1st, the old unimproved single-hand loom called *basselisse*, employed for plain satins and sarsenets. 2nd, the single hand loom called *hautelisse*, generally applied to produce large patterns. 3rd, the *à-la-bar*, or *bar loom*, employed in sarsenets, velvets, sarsenet galoons, stout and light satin, and striped gauzes. There are now few ribbons made at Lyon, many of the ribbon-looms being now employed in weaving shawls. The best ribbons made in France are chiefly for the English market; the home consumption being of the less costly kind.

The making of ribbons and small articles in silk long preceded in England that of broad silk. The trade was principally in the hands of women; and, like a sickly plant of foreign growth, it appears to have constantly demanded props and support, which have however been removed by recent reforms of the tariff. Coventry has become the principal seat of the ribbon manufacture in this country.

The weaving is done on several systems. We shall describe these somewhat in detail, as the ribbon trade illustrates the chief points in the silk manufacture generally. The *Undertaking System* applies now only to the single-hand trade in the country districts,—Bedworth, Nuneaton, Hartshill, &c.: it is the same that the French have employed since the days of Colbert. According to this plan, the undertaker, or master-weaver, receives the silk dyed in the hank from the manufacturer, and returns it in finished ribbons to his order;

all the intermediate operations being included in the price of weaving—two-thirds of which are paid to the journey-hand for his labour. Three-fourths of the single-hand weavers are women, and nearly one half of the remainder are youths under 20. Boys and girls are considered competent weavers at 16 or 17. On the *Journey-Work System*, by which the great proportion of the engine-looms in Coventry and its neighbourhood are worked, the manufacturer gives the silk, already wound and warped, to the 'first-hand journeyman,' who is also the owner of the looms. The shoot silk is given in hank, for the winding of which the manufacturer allows 1*d.* per oz., besides the price for weaving, in which is included 'the filling,' or the winding of the shoot on the small revolving pins within the shuttles. About one-fourth of the hands employed on this system are women. On the *Hand-Factory System* the manufacturer is the owner of the looms. The 'journey-hands work them in the 'loom-shop' of the proprietor, who gets the winding and warping done at his own charge, leaving only the filling to the weaver, which is included in the price of his work, and is often done by very young children. A modern innovation, encouraged by the last system, is the employment of two hands to a loom, the one being occupied uninterruptedly in 'shooting-down,' or passing the shuttle and making the ribbon; the other in 'picking up,' or fastening broken threads, picking out knots, &c. On the *Steam-Factory System* the manufacturer gets every preparatory process done; and by the steam-power one half of the weaving process itself —the shooting down; all that is left to the weaver being the picking up and superintendence.

The *Dutch Engine-Loom*, for weaving ribbons, was introduced about eighty years ago. In this loom, instead of one piece of ribbon only, several are woven at once, four of the broadest width, or as many as twenty-four of the narrowest. Each warp has a separate shuttle. The batten extends across the whole width of the loom; the shuttles slide within grooves made in the batten; the driver is worked horizontally backwards and forwards by a handle. At each motion the shuttles are propelled by the cross bars of the driver across their proper warps in the corresponding direction. The loom is worked by the hands, and with treadles for the feet, like the single-hand. The *à-la-bar* or *Bar-Loom*, was invented and introduced into St. Étienne by two Swiss brothers about seventy years ago. It is a hand power-loom worked by means of a long transverse handle or bar, which extends along the front of the loom, and is connected with wheels on each side, which communicate the motion. The shuttles are driven by means of a rack and pinion across the warps. Figures on ribbons, as in other fabrics, are chiefly formed by omitting the regular crossing of the warp and shoot in such a manner that a difference of texture shall occur in the web so as to mark out any pattern. This is effected in the single-hand loom by a multiplication of treadles connected with the lisses by which the different portions of warp are alternately raised. Forty treadles have been sometimes required to form an intricate pattern. Small figures produced in this manner are called *Leys*. To execute more complicated patterns, an intricate arrangement of the loom is necessary.

Ribbons are made according to a fixed standard of widths designated by different numbers of pence, which once no doubt denoted the price of the article, but at present have reference only to its breadth. The French distinguish their widths by simple numbers. All dressed ribbons, as satins, gauzes, &c., are made in the loom one-twelfth of an inch wider than sarsenets, in order to allow for the diminution of breadth which results from the lengthwise stretching which they receive in the operation of dressing. Fine gauzes require an allowance of two-twelfths. French fancy ribbons are generally made and sold in *garnitures*, that is, a broad and narrow piece taken together of the same pattern. *Sarsenet and Lutestring* ribbons are made by the simple and regular alternation of the warp and shoot, as in plain cloth, called technically *ground.* By *Grogram* (French *gros-grains*) is meant a variation in the texture caused by the warp threads passing over two of the shoots at once, taking up one only: this often finishes the edge of a ribbon.

The figures are frequently produced in a different colour from the ground by the mixture of colours in the warp; the colours being warped separately. In the intervals of the figures the coloured threads are carried along the under side of the ribbon; and it is said to have a double or treble figure, according to the number of colours passing through each dent. A change of colour in the shoot is effected by the use of different shuttles. In brocades the figure is made by small additional shuttles, thrown in partially across the ribbon as the pattern may require; the connecting threads of shoot being clipped off. By *Damask* is meant the laying of the warp over the shoot to form the figure in the manner of satin. Some fancy ribbons are of plain texture, but varied in colouring; they are shot or woven in shades, stripes, bars, or cheques, called in the trade *Plaids;* these last, which require the shuttle to be changed very frequently, are still made in the single-hand loom. In *Shot* Ribbons the warp and the shoot are of different colours. *Clouding* is a peculiar management in the dyeing by which a change of hue is produced in the same thread of silk. In *Chiné* ribbons the figures are printed or painted on the warp after it is prepared for the loom, and afterwards woven in by the shuttle. Ribbons are *watered* by passing two pieces together between two cylinders, one of which has a heater within it. *Galloons* and *Doubles* are strong thick ribbons, principally black, used for bindings, shoe-strings &c. The narrow widths are called Galloons; the broader, Doubles. *Ferrets* are coarse narrow ribbons shot with cotton, used for similar purposes. In *gold* and *silver* ribbons a silk thread of similar colour is wound round by a flattened wire of the metal, and afterwards woven. Lyon was particularly celebrated for its fabrics of this kind.

The number of persons employed in ribbon-making in Coventry, including winders and warpers, was estimated, in 1838, at 6000 or 7000; and in the rural parishes, at 10,000 or 11,000. It has since varied considerably, according to the fluctuations of the ribbon-trade.

The ribbons imported into Great Britain in 1850 amounted to the following quantities:—

Silk or Satin Ribbons . .	282,799 lbs.
Gauze or Crape Ribbons . .	44,531 lbs.
Velvet Ribbons	16,675 lbs.

Most of these are imported from France. Very few English ribbons are exported.

RICE. The important rice plant is a native of India, whence it has been introduced into various parts of the world. It is extensively cultivated in India, in the south of Europe, and in the southern United States; and less largely in many other countries. It requires so much heat combined with moisture that it cannot be profitably cultivated in northern climates. The cultivation in India and China depends either upon the rainy seasons, or upon irrigation; the tanks for irrigation are in some cases quite enormous, being bounded by embankments many miles in length. The best rice-fields are never manured, and yet they yield 30 to 100 fold. They are usually exensive open plains through which large rivers pass. They more frequently depend on rain for irrigation than on tanks. There are many kinds of rice, which require different modes of cultivation. One of the principal kinds is sown in June or July, and transplanted in about forty days, when the plants are from 9 to 18 inches high. The fields are then kept constantly wet. When the grain is ripe the water is drained off, and the crop is cut down with the sickle; it is either stacked or trodden out by cattle. The grain is preserved in pits dug in high ground and lined with the rice straw. There are usually two crops in a year; but as the produce is very uncertain, the growers look chiefly to the first.

Of the kinds of rice imported into England, the *Carolina* is the best; the grains are shorter, broader, and boil softer than the *Patna* rice, which is the best Indian kind brought to this country.

Rice is no doubt the grain which yields food for the largest portion of the human race, but even in Hindustan great numbers do not eat rice. In fact in all the north-western provinces wheat is the principal crop, and the natives eat wheaten cakes. It abounds however in nourishment, being composed almost entirely of fecula, that is, 96 per cent., and therefore cannot be baked into bread; but it is more easily cooked. It is light and wholesome, and easily digested, and might form a much larger portion of the diet in Europe than it does. Europeans in India eat it at breakfast as well as at other meals, and with fish as frequently as with their curries.

About 976,196 cwts. of rice were imported in 1849, and 785,692 cwts. in 1850.

RICE-MILL. When rice has been cultivated and gathered, some sort of mechanism is requisite for the removal of the husk. The Chinese and Hindoos beat the grain in a kind of rude mortar of stone or earthenware, with a conical stone attached to a lever worked by the hand or foot. Sometimes several such levers are moved by arms projecting from the axis of a water-wheel. This process being uncertain and tedious, the preference has been given of late to a mill in which the stones are placed at such a distance asunder as to detach the shell without crushing the grain; the stones being inclosed in a case which prevents the dispersion of the rice by the rapid rotation of the machine. The rice is thrown out of the case by an opening in its side, and conducted over a sieve that separates the dust; after which it is made to fall in a gentle stream exposed to a current of air produced by revolving fanners, and is thereby separated from the husk. After the removal of the husk, the grain is exposed to the action of a whitening machine, which removes the inner cuticle, or red skin, remaining on the surface of the grain.

One of the English methods consists in breaking the husk by mill-stones, and removing the red cuticle by beating or titurating in mortars; the latter operation being aided by mixing a quantity of the husks, well dried, with the grain, which obviates an inconvenience occasioned by the glutinous character of the red coating. The refuse matter and the broken grains are then separated by a peculiar kind of screen, and the rice is finally cleansed and polished by rotating in a machine. In another method, the first operation is performed between one millstone and a piece of wood of precisely similar shape, and the subsequent removal of the dark pellicle is effected by rubbing between flat wooden surfaces covered with sheepskin. In a third method, the rice is allowed to enter the upper end of an inclined cylinder by a hopper, and the mutual attrition of the grains, as they pass between bars which are revolving in the opposite direction, causes the separation of the husks, which are removed by a current of air as the grain falls into a bin under the lower extremity of the cylinder.

RICK VENTILATOR. The formation of a rick of harvested produce is comparatively an easy matter; but the preservation of the rick from injuries by heating, rotting, and spontaneous combustion, is an important and difficult subject for the farmer's attention. The destruction of ricks by natural heating is, we believe, not covered by fire-insurance; so that the farmer is left to his own resources. In the case of barley ricks, the grain is frequently discoloured and deteriorated in value, by the too great heat of the interior of the rick. In the case of hay ricks, a large portion is frequently cut away and destroyed or injured, to prevent the rest from taking fire.

It has been lately proposed to obviate these evils by *ventilating* the rick; and an instrument has been invented for effecting it, and patented. The instrument makes a ventilating *chimney* or *flue* in the rick in any part where it is suspected of being too much heated. A hole is bored from the top to the middle or the bottom of the rick, forming a clear circular aperture, which tends to carry rapidly off the heat from the surrounding hay or corn. The instrument has a long shaft, with a cross end for working; and at the lower end of the shaft is an apparatus somewhat like a patent corkscrew, or one of the many sorts of boring tools, by which a hole is bored and the loose material cleared away.

RIFLE, or RIFLED, is a term applied to muskets or pieces of ordnance when their bores are furrowed with spiral grooves; the grooves or channels being formed by a machine which scrapes away the substance of the barrel interiorly in parallel and serpentine directions.

The object to be attained by this grooving may be thus explained. A bullet made of lead cast in a spherical form, according to the practice till lately followed, having unavoidably some irregularities on its surface, and frequently, from unequal expansion, a cavity in the interior; it follows that, when such bullet is discharged from a common musket, it deviates continually from the direction which it should take by gravity and the impulse of the fired gunpowder. The intention therefore in forming spiral grooves within the barrel of a musket or piece of ordnance, is, to produce a rotatory motion of the shot about an axis which shall coincide with the line of its path, in order that the unequal pressure of the atmosphere in its front, on account of any irregularity in its form or density, may correct itself at every half-revolution of the shot on such axis. The number of spiral channels in a rifle-musket is, in general, two; and one revolution of the spiral, in the whole length of the barrel (=30 inches) is considered sufficient.

The most general practice of late has been to press the bullets (by means of the ramrod) into the barrel upon a piece of greased cloth or leather (called the *plaster*). But, at present, rifle-bullets are made with a projecting zone which surrounds them on the circumference of what may be called a great circle. The pieces are loaded at the muzzle, and the parts of the zone which are diametrically opposite to one another are those which pass along the two grooves in the barrel.

Bullets for common muskets, as well as for rifle-barrels, are not now cast in their actual forms, but are made from lead which has been previously cast in cylindrical rods. The bullets are then formed by compressing the rods between two revolving cylinders. The pressure, by forcing the particles together, fills up any vacuities which may form themselves in the rods during the cooling process, and probably renders the density of the ball nearly uniform. Bullets and balls have occasionally been made of other than a spherical form, as experimental means of determining the best form for ensuring a direct course.

RIGA is a very important commercial town, one of the principal indeed in Russia. The numerous ships in the river Düna, the bustle in the streets, and the well-stocked warehouses and shops, are indications of the extensive trade of which Riga is the centre; it is in fact, next to St. Petersburg, the greatest emporium of foreign commerce in the empire. The exports consist of the great staple articles of Russian produce, corn, timber, flax, hemp, linseed, tallow, Russian leather, and sail-cloth. The total value of the exports in 1849 was 2,730,000*l.* against 2,120,000*l.* in 1848. In these were included 44,700 tons of flax; 15,250 tons of hemp; 81,703 barrels of sowing, and 255,000 quarters of crushing, linseed; 11,500 quarters of hemp-seed; 274,260 quarters of corn, chiefly barley, oats, and rye; 35 tons of quills; 410 cargoes of timber and staves; and 1700 tons of hempen and flaxen tow. The sale of linseed or flax-seed for sowing in other countries forms a remarkably large item in Riga commerce. Between 1841 and 1850 the quantity so sold varied from 55,000 to 177,000 barrels. The largest sale is to England which took 50,000 barrels in 1850. In the previous year 1849, 1729 vessels arrived, and 1677 left the harbour.

The value of the imports, consisting of colonial produce, woollens, calicos, silks, wine, &c., is not above one-third of the value of the exports. About two-thirds of the ships that enter the port arrive in ballast. Riga has now considerable manufactories of woollens, cotton goods, tobacco, starch, looking-glasses, and iron wares; it has also sugar-refining houses.

RIGGING. This is the name given to the whole of the ropes and cordage of a ship. It is divided into two kinds—the *standing* and the *running* rigging. The standing rigging comprises all the *shrouds*, *stays*, *back-stays*, and other ropes which are employed to maintain the masts and bowsprit in their proper position, and which remain pretty nearly in a constant state, whether the ship is in full sail or all the sails are furled. The running rigging comprises the various ropes called *braces*, *sheets*, *tacks*, *halyards*, *buntlines*, &c., which are attached to different parts of the masts, yards, sails, and shrouds; and are employed principally in furling and unfurling the sails for the purposes of navigation. The ropes are called *cables*, *ropes*, or *lines*, according to their diameter; but every rope in a ship has besides this its own distinctive name.

The occupation of a *Rigger* is intermediate between those of a rope-maker and a ship-builder, and distinct from both; he takes the coils of rope as prepared by the former, and adapts them to the various requirements of a ship. A *rigging-house* (such as may be seen in most large ship yards) is a place provided with tackle for stretching the ropes, and with the necessary instruments for attaching the blocks, rings, &c. The cordage employed for a large East Indiaman weighs several tons, and some of the ropes are four inches in diameter: the bending and fixing of such ropes, therefore, require the aid of powerful implements. Much of the cordage undergoes a process called *serving*, which consists in binding a small rope very tightly round a larger one, to preserve it both from rotting and from any friction to which it may be exposed. The substance thus bound round the rope is not necessarily a made-rope, but is sometimes made of old canvas, mat, plat, hide, or spun-yarn, according to circumstances: all these substances, when thus employed, receive the name of *service*, and the larger rope is said to be *served* with them.

The rigging of the ship is applied in its proper places at the time when each rope is wanted to serve its destined purpose. Each mast, each yard, the bowsprit, and various other parts of the ship, requires its own particular ropes; and the parts—the wood and the hemp—are built up into form simultaneously.

Other matters bearing on this subject are noticed under ROPE MAKING and SHIP BUILDING.

RIGIDITY OF ROPES. When a stiff rope is bent over the upper part of a wheel or pulley, in a vertical plane for example, the weights or powers applied at its extremities are not always sufficient to draw the descending portions into the positions of two vertical lines; and the experiments of Coulomb have shown, that, with ropes consisting of 30 threads and 2¼ inches in circumference, the weights requisite to overcome the rigidity, when the ropes passed over a pulley 4 inches diameter, and were strained by weights equal to 25 lbs., 125 lbs., and 425 lbs., were 5 lbs., 8¼ lbs., and 23 lbs. respectively. White ropes when wet are more stiff than those which are dry, and the rigidity of ropes is greatly increased by tarring them. In general the weights necessary to overcome the resistance of tarred ropes is proportional to the number of the threads of which they are composed. This rigidity has to be allowed for in the use of thick ropes in engineering works.

RIVETS. The rivets which fasten together plates of iron and other parts of mechanism are usually short thick pieces of iron or copper, forged or drawn into the shape of a rod, and then cut off to the proper lengths. These are used either cold or red hot, according to circumstances; and when placed in a hole, the two ends of each rivet are exposed to such powerful blows (or blows on one end with pressure on the other) as to form a burr or head which clasps the plate tightly. The two millions of rivets in the Britannia Bridge present perhaps the most remarkable example of rivetting yet known. [MENAI BRIDGES.]

ROADS. The Romans were distinguished by the vast extent and solid construction of their roads, of which several thousand miles were made in Italy alone; while every country which was brought under their sway was more or less intersected by these excellent highways. The solidity of their construction was fully equal to the boldness of their design, a fact proved by the existence of many that have borne the traffic of nearly two thousand years without material injury. The Romans always gave a firm foundation to their roads, by ramming down a layer of small stones and broken brick; on this layer a pavement of large stones was laid, either squared to fit closely around one another, or cemented into a hard and firm causeway.

In this country very little was done towards a sound and scientific construction of roads until the beginning of the present century. The *Highland* roads have been made under a commission issued in 1803, and have been of incalculable benefit in opening districts which were before placed almost beyond the reach of commercial enterprise. The commissioners have constructed about 1000 miles of excellent road, and much more than that number of bridges. The *Holyhead* road improvements were commenced in 1815, under Mr. Telford; these comprise the establishment between London and Holyhead of the best coach-road in England, in which principles of sound construction have been more attended to than in any other examples. The greatest angle or ascent allowed in this road is 1 in 35: a slope which may be ascended at a good rate of speed, and descended at twelve miles an hour without risk.

The *Macadamised* roads, named from the inventor, exhibit a particular mode of applying small stones to the surface. Under the old method, stones of irregular sizes and shapes were thrown down upon the soft earth of a road, and became mixed up with it in such a way as to form a very irregular road. Mr. M'Adam conceived that if small stones of nearly uniform size were used, they would tend to lock together into a hard and compact mass, forming a sort of crust nearly impervious to water. He objected to any kind of chalk or earth being mixed with the stone; but the quantity of stone must depend on the quality of the ground beneath; in many cases a layer three feet thick has been required. Mr. Telford employed the still more durable system of placing a layer of hand-laid larger stones beneath the smaller, so as to form, in fact, a sort of two-fold paving.

It has been found by experiment, that a layer of hard broken stone on a substratum of stone affords easier draught for horses than where the substratum is of earth; and that a gravel surface is more trying to horses than a broken stone surface. As a general rule, the hardest stone—such as basalt, granite, quartz, sienite, or porphyry—is found to be the best for road-metal, or the broken stones for the surface; but this is not invariably the case, as some hard stones are found to wear more rapidly than softer but tougher stone. Limestone, slaty stone, and sandstone, are all unfitted for roads. On some parts of the Holyhead road small cubes of iron, about an inch square, are placed at intervals of four inches among the stones, and well packed round with small chips of stone; they have been found to produce a remarkably durable road.

Stone tramways have occasionally been applied to common roads with great advantage. They consist of wheel-tracks formed of large blocks of stone, usually granite, over which the wheels roll smoothly, while there is an intermediate broken stone road for the horses. Iron tramways are sometimes used for a similar purpose. The saving of horse-labour by these tramways is remarkable. Sir John Macneill stated in 1839:—"If a tramway were constructed of iron plates the whole way from Leeds to Birmingham, a coach carrying sixteen passengers might be drawn at the rate of ten miles an hour with only two horses; and one horse would be able to draw a post-chaise more easily than two now can."

The pavements of towns require a different mode of construction from the roads of open districts. They must afford the means of sweeping or cleaning, and there must be pavements besides those which are traversed by vehicles. Of the granite paving, the wood paving, the asphaltic paving, the inhabitants of London have had abundant means of forming a judgment within the last few years, for they have been renewed and repaired to a wearisome degree.

It is supposed by many persons, that if stone or iron tramways were laid down, locomotives on common roads would have had much more success than has hitherto attended them. Such locomotives have been constructed in considerable variety within the last thirty years; but although mechanically correct in principle they have not come into use—owing partly to the imperfect state of the roads. The public journals have recently noticed a new road-locomotive at St. Etienne, in France, which excited much attention on its first appearance. It was invented by M. Verpilleux. On its first journey it went through all the streets of the town with the greatest facility, under the most perfect control of the man sitting in front, turning it to the right or left, or sending it backward or forward, as he pleased. Two cabriolets, filled with some of the friends of the inventor, were attached to the carriage, as was afterwards a heavy cart of coals. The carriage weighs two tons, and is of four horse power. It runs on three wheels, and its speed is 10 English miles an hour. Its consumption of coke per hour is from 20 to 25 kilogrammes. It had left the same morning Rive-de-Gier, and arrived at St. Etienne by the old Sorbiers road, which is badly kept and full of ruts. The carriage, however, did not suffer. A new vehicle on the same principle, but of a 12-horse power, is now in course of construction: it will be able, it is said, to move four coal-waggons with a weight of 12,000 kilogrammes. It is intended shortly to employ this mode of locomotion for carrying the coals of Bessège to the Rhône, and those of Firminy to the Lyon Railway. The cost for doing this will not, it is calculated, be more than one-half of that of the ordinary mode of conveyance.

ROASTING. There is a little chemistry in the art of cooking, which, while it has engaged the philosophic mind of a Liebig, cannot be beneath the notice of others. The familiar modes of preparing animal food, for instance, deserve a little study. In the process of broiling meat, the heat is applied immediately and suddenly to the surface, by which it is hardened, so that the juices of the meat are greatly retained, evaporation being thereby prevented; while in roasting, the heat is applied gradually, the watery portion is evaporated, as well as the fat melted out to a considerable extent, till the progressive browning and hardening of the surface prevent the further escape of the juices. The loss of weight in roasting meat is much greater than by boiling, much of the fat being melted out and water evaporated, but the nutritious matter remains condensed in the cooked solid; whereas, in boiling, the gelatine is partly abstracted. Roasted meat is therefore more nutritive than boiled meat, and also more digestible.

ROCKET is a cylindrical vessel or case, of pasteboard or iron, attached to one end of a light rod of wood, and containing a composition which, being fired, the vessel and rod are projected through the air by a force arising from the combustion.

Rockets have long been used as a means of making signals for the purpose of communication when the parties have been invisible from distance or darkness; and they have occasionally served the important purpose of determining the difference of longitude between two places. Rockets have also been constructed for the purpose of being used in warfare, and such missiles were so employed for the first time at the battle of Copenhagen, in 1807. Signal rockets are made to weigh half a pound, one pound, or two pounds; and the one pound rocket is about 16 inches long. The rod is generally attached near the base, on one side of the rocket, and its length is about 8 feet. The composition with which the cylinder is filled consists generally of saltpetre, sulphur, and charcoal or gunpowder, and the composition which produces what are called the stars, consists of saltpetre, sulphur, antimony, mealed powder, and isinglass. The latter is dissolved in one quart of vinegar, after which one pint of spirit of wine is added, and then the mealed composition is mixed with the liquid till the whole becomes like a stiff paste. The burning composition acting at the head, and at the opposite end of the rocket, produces impulsive forces in opposite directions; but sundry perforations at the lower extremity, by allowing the fire to escape there, nearly destroys the pressure against the lower end, and thus the pressure at the head is almost wholly effective in giving a forward motion to the rocket. The rod serves to guide it in its flight, the resistance of the air perpendicularly to its length checking any vibrations which may be caused by inequalities in the action of the burning composition.

Rockets whose diameters vary from 1 to 2 inches have been found to ascend vertically to the height of about 500 yards, and those whose diameters vary from 2 to 3 inches have ascended to the height of 1200 yards. The distances at which rockets can be seen vary from 35 to 40 miles; and the times of ascent, from 7 to 10 seconds. Rockets, to be employed as military projectiles, were invented by Sir William Congreve, and, in the British artillery service, a body of men, called the Rocket Troop, has been organised expressly for their management. From their form they penetrate to a considerable depth when fired against timber or earth: 12-pounder rockets, after a range of 1260 yards, have been found to enter the ground obliquely as far as 22 feet. As used in pyrotechnic exhibitions, rockets always have pasteboard cases.

ROLLERS. Cylindrical rollers are used for very many purposes in the arts, especially where two are employed in contact. If one roller is rotating on its axis, and if another be brought close to it, surface to surface, with the axes parallel, the second roller will be made to rotate in an opposite direction from the first; this property is often made use of in transmitting and reversing motion. In *cylinder printing*, at the cotton print works, the passing of the cloth between two cylinders, one of which is engraved and supplied with colour, suffices to print the cloth. In bookbinding, or rather in pressing the sheets for the bookbinders, a roller-press affords an immense power: this consists, in principle, of two rollers rotating nearly in contact, and pressing between them the quire of leaves. In all kinds of metal working the pressure of two rollers is employed to flatten a mass of metal into slabs, sheets, or ribbons. If the surface of one or both rollers be grooved in a direction transverse to the axis, any substance passed between the rollers will assume a form corresponding with those grooves. It is in this way that railway bars are made; the iron is first passed between rollers grooved so as to produce a square bar, and then through other rollers so grooved as to give the contour of a railway bar. All such modes of compression have a tendency to increase the length of bars according as the width and thickness are diminished.

In agricultural matters the roller is often used singly, and generally as a weight. In the common garden and road roller a heavy cylindrical mass is employed to press the earth or gravel of a path smooth or level; it is sometimes made of stone; but sometimes a hollow iron cylinder, weighted, if necessary, with stones. A roller is sometimes used over corn fields, whose surface is covered with teeth. Such is Crosskill's Patent Serrated Roller and Clod Crusher. This roller is very heavy, and requires three horses abreast to work it over a newly ploughed field; the surface of the roller presents angular teeth in every part, and these teeth tend to break up the clods of earth which have been turned up by the plough. It also tends to give solidity to loose soil, one of the advantages ordinarily produced by sheep-treading.

ROOF. In order to cover in a building in which the space to be spanned is greater than can be covered by single blocks of stone extending from one point of support to another, it is necessary either to have recourse to the principle of the arch, as in vaults and domes of stone or brick, or to form a framework of timber to support the covering. [ARCH; DOME.] Roofs formed of one level plane, which are extensively used in eastern countries, are not adapted for our climate; and a single inclined plane carries up the roof to too great a height.

The best figure for a simple roof is that formed of two inclined planes, rising from the two opposite walls that approach nearest to each other, and meeting over the centre of the edifice, so as to form a ridge: this is called a *common* or *gable-ended* roof. Frequently four inclined planes are used, disposed as a *hipped roof*, which takes its name from the hips, or inclined ridges formed by the meeting of the sides and ends. Sometimes the inclined faces are not continued upwards till they meet, but the roof is completed by a horizontal plane. Such a roof is called a *truncated*, *terrace*, or *cut roof*, and may have two, three, or four inclined faces. A similar saving of height is frequently obtained by means of a roof in which each sloping face consists of two planes of different degrees of inclination. This form, which is denominated a *curb roof* (or, from its inventor, a *Mansarde roof*), is very common in London, because it affords more space for the formation of bed-rooms in the roof than the simpler forms. These various kinds of roof require many modifications to suit irregularities of shape, or combinations of rectangular forms. Thus, in the junction of different roofs or portions of roofing at right angles with each other, there are inclined lines or *valleys*, which, at the junction of two planes, form hollows the reverse of hips. When two faces of a roof join, so as to form an angle similar to a valley, but in an horizontal instead of an inclined position, the term *gutter* is applied instead of valley. A further distinction is that between roofs with dripping eaves, and those in which the water is collected in gutters. In the former case the roof projects several inches, or even feet, beyond the walls, and the water running from the roof either drops at once on the ground, or is collected in troughs fixed under the margin of the eaves, and conducted by them to descending pipes. In gutter roofs the timbers do not extend to the outside of the walls, which are carried up as parapets, of a reduced thickness, to such a height as to conceal the roof either wholly or partially. The gutters, which are troughs of wood, covered with lead or other metal, are laid at the bottom of the slopes, just within the parapets, and have a gentle inclination (usually about an inch in ten feet), to cause water to run freely towards the pipes.

The timbers of a roof have various names to them, according to their position and purpose. Thus, those which join the wall are the *wall-plates;* that at the meeting of two faces, parallel to the wall-plates, is the *ridge-piece;* and the inclined bars extending from the wall-plates to the ridge-piece are *rafters*, those which form the salient angles in hipped roofs being distinguished as *hip-rafters*. In a hipped roof, the rafters near the ends are called *jack-rafters*. Additional support is supplied by horizontal rectangular bars called *purlins*, and these are supported by a series of bars called *principals*. The lower ends of the principals are mortised into the ends of the *tie-beam*, which stretches across the building, and rests upon the wall-plates. The triangular frame formed by the two principals and a tie-beam, with any bars it may comprise for additional strength, is called a *truss*, and such frames being placed at regular intervals, the timber work between any two of them is called a *bay of roofing*. The lower extremities of the common rafters, being elevated by this arrangement above the wall-plates, are supported by *pole-plates*, or pieces of timber parallel to the wall-plates, resting on the ends of the tie-beams. The supporting frame-work altogether is called a *carcass-roof*. The outward thrust against the wall is counteracted by a horizontal *tie-beam*, and the sinking is prevented by a vertical bar called the *king-post*. Sometimes the king-post is dispensed with, and its office performed by two similar posts, called *queen-posts*, at equal distances from the centre of the truss. In order to keep these in their right position, a short horizontal beam, called a *collar-beam*, is inserted between their upper extremities, and another, termed a *straining-sill*, between their lower ends. *Cushion rafters* are pieces occasionally added, in large roofs, to strengthen the principals. In curb roofs the upper rows of rafters are called *curb-rafters*, and the horizontal bars that receive the upper ends of the lower rafters, and the feet of the curb-rafters, are known as *curb-plates*.

In roofs of very large span it is often desirable, in order to avoid running up to a great height, to form two or more ridges. Roofs without ties may be greatly strengthened by the use of parabolic curves of iron, notched into the rafters of each inclined face, and abutting on the wall-plates, which in such a case are firmly bolted together. Wrought iron straps of various forms are very useful, when judiciously applied, in strengthening the joints of a roof. The *Norman roof* is an ingenious contrivance for the construction of roofs of large span with small pieces of wood; in this arrangement all the rafters abut on joggled king-posts, of which there are several, their relative position being maintained by diagonal braces. Domes of wood, of great size, have been made without trussing, simply by forming the timbers into curved ribs abutting on the wall-plates, which then form a circle, and are kept in their proper positions by horizontal circles framed with them at intervals. The wooden dome formerly existing at the Halle aux Blés, at Paris, was a remarkably bold example of this kind, being 200 feet in diameter, and having a large opening in the centre.

All the different kinds of roof-coverings require certain fitting arrangements of the timber beneath, according to weight, angle of slope, &c. Cast iron, wrought iron, yellow fir, thatch, tiles, pantiles, plain tiles, slates, shingles (thin boards shaped like slates), slabs of thin stone, plaster, asphalte and other cements, tarred paper, sheets of lead, copper, iron, tinned iron, and galvanized zinc iron—all are used for roof coverings.

One of the largest roofs in existence is that over the Riding-school at Moscow; it is 235 feet span, with a slope of 19°; and the external dimensions of the building are 1920 feet by 319. But the most remarkable roof, all things considered, is that which Messrs. Fox and Henderson have recently erected over the Exhibition Building in Hyde Park. The slender appearance of the many hundred columns which support it; the elegant lightness of the girders which brace the columns together; the ridge-and-furrow principle by which drainage is secured; the matchless waggon-vaulted transept, upwards of 400 feet long by 72 in diameter; and the acres of glass which form the roofing material—all serve to distinguish this roof from any before constructed.

The same engineers have recently constructed a magnificent iron roof at the Liverpool terminus of the Lancashire and Yorkshire Railway. It covers five lines of rails and three platforms, and a carriage road twelve yards wide, in one span, having no columns nor supports besides the outside walls; the span varies from 136 feet to 128 feet, and the total length is 631 feet. The total area thus covered is 83,457 feet. The material used in the construction of this roof is entirely iron. The framing consists of a series of trussed principals, placed at intervals of eleven feet from centre to centre; and immediately over the principals are fixed wrought iron purlines, which support the covering; this covering is of corrugated sheet iron, galvanized. The roof is both lighted and ventilated along the ridge by four continuous rows of large skylights, and two rows of louvres; half the light is distributed along the ridge, and the remaining half is equally distributed at the eaves; the total area of light admitted being equal to one-fourth of the entire area of the roof.

ROPE-MAKING. The name *Rope* is generally confined to the larger descriptions of cordage, such as exceed an inch in circumference, though the principles of formation are much the same for cordage of every size; the smaller sizes are known by various names.

In rope-making, whether for large or small ropes, the first process consists in twisting the hemp into thick threads, called *Rope-Yarns*.

This process, which resembles ordinary spinning, is performed with various kinds of machinery. The common mode of spinning rope-yarns by hand is performed in the rope-ground or rope-walk, an inclosed slip of level ground, sometimes 600 feet or more in length. At one end of this ground a spinning-wheel is set up, which gives motion by a band to several small rollers or *whirls.* Each whirl had a small hook formed on the end of its axis next the walk. Each of the spinners is provided with a bundle of dressed hemp, laid round his waist, with the bight or double in front, and the ends passing each other at his back, from which he draws out a sufficient number of fibres to form a rope-yarn of the required size; and, after slightly twisting them together with his fingers, he attaches them to the hook of a whirl. The whirl being now set in motion by turning the wheel, the skein is twisted into a rope-yarn, the spinner walking backwards down the rope-walk, supporting the yarn with one hand, which is protected by a wetted piece of coarse cloth or flannel, while with the other he regulates the quantity of fibres drawn from the bundle of hemp by the revolution of the yarn. The degree of twist depends on the velocity with which the wheel is turned, combined with the retrograde pace of the spinner. When the spinner has traversed the whole length of the rope-walk (or sooner, if the yarns are not required to be so long), he calls out, and another spinner detaches the yarn from the whirl, and gives it to a person who carries it aside to a reel, while the second spinner attaches his own hemp to the whirl-hook. The hemp, being dry and elastic, would instantly untwist if the yarn were now set at liberty. The first spinner, therefore, keeps fast hold of it all the while that the reeler winds it up, walking slowly up the walk, so as to keep the yarn equally tight all the way. When it is all wound up, the spinner holds it till another is ready to follow it on the reel. Sometimes, instead of being wound on a reel as they are made, the yarns are laid together in large hooks attached to posts at the side of the walk, until about four hundred are collected together, when they are coiled up in a *haul*, or skein, in which state they are ready for tarring. In some roperies machines have been introduced, especially one invented by Mr. Lang of Greenock, for spinning yarns.

The yarns being thus spun, they are warped or stretched to a given length, in order that they may, when formed into a strand, bear the strain equally. When the rope is to be tarred, that operation is usually performed upon the yarns immediately after their being warped, as the application of tar to the yarns previous to their combination is necessary to the complete penetration of the whole substance of the rope. The most common method of tarring the yarns is to draw them in hauls or skeins through the tar-kettle by a capstan; but sometimes the yarns are passed singly through the tar, being wound off one reel on to another, and the superfluous tar being taken off by passing the yarn through a hole surrounded with spongy oakum.

In making large cordage, from fifteen to twenty yarns are formed into a *strand*, and three or more such strands are afterwards combined into a rope. The twist of the strand is in an opposite direction to that of the yarns. In *closing* or *laying* the rope, three strands are stretched at length along the walk, and attached at one end to separate but contiguous hooks, and at the other to a single hook; and they are twisted together by turning the single hook in a direction contrary to that of the other three; a piece of wood called a *top*, in the form of a truncated cone, being placed between the strands, and kept during the whole operation gently forced into the angle formed by the strands, where they are united by the closing or twisting of the rope. As the rope shortens in closing, one end only of the apparatus is fixed, the other being on a moveable sledge, whose motion up the rope-walk is capable of regulation by suitable tackle attached to it, or by loading it with weights. The top also is mounted on a sledge, for closing large cordage, and its rate of motion may be retarded, in order to give greater firmness to the twist of the rope. Ropes formed in this manner are said to be *shroud-laid*, or *hawser-laid.*

Those large ropes which are said to be *cable-laid* are formed by the combination of smaller ropes twisted round their common axis, just as shroud-laid ropes are composed of strands twisted round their common axis. As cable-laid ropes are harder and more compact than others, this mode of formation is adopted for ropes to be exposed to the action of water, even though their thickness may not be very great. Originally all the yarns (from $\frac{1}{12}$ to $\frac{1}{8}$ of an inch in thickness) composing a strand were of the same length; but Captain Huddart showed that in such an arrangement the outermost yarns must be more strained than the inner: he accordingly, in 1793, patented his *register* cordage, in which the strain is equalised throughout. The same gentleman invented machinery for almost every department of rope-making.

Ropes formed by plaiting instead of twisting are made use of for some purposes in which pliability is especially needed, they being more supple and less liable to entanglement than those of the ordinary make. Such ropes are preferred for sash-lines, clock-lines, &c., and generally where the rope has to pass over pulleys of small diameter. Flat ropes, which are much used for mining purposes, are either formed of two or more small ropes placed side by side, and united by sewing, lapping, or interlacing with thread or smaller ropes, or of a number of strands of shroud-laid rope similarly united. In either case it is necessary that the component ropes or strands be alternately of a right hand and left hand twist, that the rope may remain in a quiescent state.

Many experiments were made by Réaumur, Knowles, and others, to test the loss of strength by the ordinary twist given to ropes. Duhamel prepared the following statement, to show the comparative strength of ropes formed of the same hemp, and the same weight per fathom, but twisted respectively to two-thirds, three-fourths, and four-fifths of the length of their component yarns:—

Degree of twist.	Weight borne in two experiments.	
$\frac{2}{3}$	4098 lbs.	4250 lbs.
$\frac{3}{4}$	4850	6753
$\frac{4}{5}$	6205	7397

The result of these experiments led Duhamel to try the practicability of making ropes without any twist, the yarns being wrapped round to keep them together. These had great strength, but very little durability. In shroud or hawser-laid ropes the usual reduction of length by twisting is one-third; but cable-laid ropes are further shortened, so that 200 fathoms of yarn are required to make 120 fathoms of cable. A hawser-laid rope 6 inches in circumference by 120 fathoms (720 feet) long, weighs about 10 cwts. A cable-laid rope 12 inches in circumference and 120 fathoms long, weighs 36 cwts. A hawser-laid rope 6 inches in circumference will bear a weight of 140 cwts. The tarring of ropes somewhat impairs their strength, but renders them more durable. Oils, fats, and tallow of various kinds have been occasionally used; but tar is found to be the best preservative.

Several other kinds of vegetable fibre besides hemp have been made use of in the manufacture of cordage, and some appear greatly to exceed hemp in strength. The fibres of the aloe, long wool, hemp mixed with threads of caoutchouc, thongs of ox-hide, and several other substances, have been employed; but none are found to combine so many advantages as hemp.

Ropes formed of iron wire have been, within the last few years, introduced to a considerable extent, and have been found to effect a great saving of expense from their durability and superior lightness. Ropes of twisted iron wire were used in the silver mines of the Harz Mountains twenty years ago; they were nearly equal in strength to solid iron bars of equal thickness, and equal to hempen ropes of four times their weight. Wire ropes are now made in England under many patents. They are formed in various ways, according to their intended use. For standing rigging straight untwisted wires are employed, bound round with cloth or small hempen cordage saturated with a solution of caoutchouc, asphaltum, or other preservative from rust. Flat ropes may likewise be made of straight wires, interwoven or wrapped with hempen yarn, or sewed between canvas, &c. Other ropes are formed much in the same way as those of hemp, the wires taking the place of rope-yarns, and being twisted into strands, and combined into ropes, both hawser-laid and cable-laid. The twisting should not be so hard as in hempen cordage; and all the wires must be protected by an anti-corrosive composition, or by coating with tin, zinc, &c. It is sometimes the practice to twist wires round a core, either of wire, hemp-cord, spun yarn, or other material to form a strand, and to lay such strands round a similar core when there are more than three strands in a rope.

The annexed table, showing the comparative size and weight per fathom for equal strength, may serve to show the great superiority of wire ropes over those of hemp, which they surpass even in flexibility:—

Hemp Rope.			Wire Rope.			
Size.	Weight per fathom.		Size.	Weight per fathom.		Equal to a strain of
Inches.	lbs.	oz.	Inches.	lbs.	oz.	cwts.
3	2	4	$1\frac{1}{4}$	1	4	50
4	3	15	$1\frac{1}{2}$	1	9	70
5	6	0	$1\frac{3}{4}$	1	14	135
6	9	0	2	2	2	160
7	12	3	$2\frac{1}{4}$	2	9	171
8	14	3	$2\frac{1}{2}$	4	1	198
9	19	6	3	5	4	306
10	25	0	$3\frac{1}{2}$	7	1	486
11	30	0	4	11	6	585
12	36	8	$4\frac{1}{2}$	15	12	704

Suspension bridges are now occasionally made of wire rope of enormous dimensions and strength.

ROSCOMMON. In this Irish county some of the mountains are composed of shales and sandstones, with three beds of coal resting on beds of the millstone grit series, from which good ironstone is obtained. The coal answers well for smelting iron, and is used in the Arigna iron-works in this county. In many places, good limestone is quarried for building. Potter's clay and pipe-clay are found in various parts of the county. The Royal Canal opens

KNIGHT'S CYCLOPÆDIA OF THE INDUSTRY OF ALL NATIONS.

No. 35.

into the Shannon opposite Tarmonbarry in this county; the Grand Canal just below the junction of the Suck. The traffic on the canals consists chiefly of corn and butter sent to Dublin, and English manufactures and general goods sent in return. The navigation of the Suck commences at Ballinasloe (county of Galway) for light flat-bottomed boats; small row-boats ascend higher. But a canal is cut parallel to it on the Galway side of the river, from Ballinasloe to the Shannon. The soil in the limestone district is commonly fertile; there is, however, a large extent of bog or other wastes. The amount of pasture land is considerable: the natural pastures, which are esteemed to be some of the best ground in the county, are in the limestone districts. The extent of the unimproved mountains and bogs has been estimated at above 130,000 acres; several of those on the uplands are comparatively dry, and afford in their natural state coarse pasturage for young and hardy cattle.

Roscommon has little to boast of in respect to manufactures; its towns are small, and very little is produced there beyond a supply for the immediate wants of the inhabitants.

ROSE ESSENCE. The rose is more frequently cultivated as an ornament than for its applications to medicine or the arts. It has, however, astringent and tonic properties which render it useful in medicine. In the East it is extensively grown for the purpose of procuring, in a variety of ways, the volatile oil which gives it its delicious fragrance. For these purposes the species that are mostly cultivated are the *Musk*, the *Damask*, the *Centifolia*, from all of which the attar, otto, essence, or oil of roses may be procured in considerable quantities. The attar of roses forms an object of considerable commercial importance on the coast of Barbary, in Syria, Persia, India, and various parts of the East. [ATTAR OF ROSES.] Many other perfumes are made from roses, and are consumed in large quantities, as rose-water, vinegar of roses. spirit of roses, honey of roses, &c.

ROSEMARY. Besides the beauty of this plant from its variegated leaves, it is used in medicine and perfumery. The *Oil of Rosemary* is chiefly prepared in Spain and the south of France, by distillation of the leaves and flowers. At first it is nearly transparent and very limpid, but by time it becomes both yellowish and thicker. It possesses the strong penetrating odour of rosemary, with a camphor-like intermixture, and a burning taste. Rosemary possesses valuable stimulant and carminative properties; but it is chiefly employed as a perfume, entering into the composition of *Hungary Water*, *Eau de Cologne*, and aromatic vinegar. It is also said to promote the growth of hair and prevent baldness.

ROSIN. [RESINS.]

ROTATION OF CROPS. As we touch upon Agricultural subjects in this work only so far as relates to the mechanical appliances of the art, and to the economical uses of the crops produced, we will notice the *Rotation of Crops* simply as a means of shewing what the expression means, and how it bears upon practical agriculture. A further developement of the subject must be sought for in other works.

It has been found from experience that a repetition of the same crops in succession has a peculiar effect on the soil, so that if grain of the same nature be sown year after year in the same ground, it will not produce the same return of the seed, even when abundantly manured. It is the formation of the seed which principally causes the deterioration of tho soil; for if the crops be fed off in a green state, or mown before the seed is formed, the same may be safely repeated, and no diminution of the plant is apparent. However judiciously the land may be manured, it is not practicable to raise a crop of wheat or clover, or of many other plants, on a soil which has shown that, as the farmers say, it is *tired* of that crop; but clover grows well after wheat, and wheat after clover, so that the same effect is not produced in the soil by these two crops. In all countries where peculiar attention has been paid to agriculture, the most advantageous succession of crops is generally known; and certain general principles are commonly admitted as fully established.

In order to find the crops which may advantageously succeed each other in rotation, many circumstances must be taken into consideration. First of all the quality of the soil, and its fitness for particular crops; next the wants of the farmer and his family, and the maintenance of the stock required to produce a sufficient supply of manure; and next the particular market which lies open to him. That which forms the food of man is always the principal object in the cultivation; and, excepting rice, which only grows in warm climates, there is no food more universally used than that which is made from wheat. Rye, barley, oats, and pulse, are only substitutes where wheat cannot be raised in sufficient quantities. Next to grain comes meat, chiefly beef, mutton, and pork, of which the consumption increases with the wealth of a nation and the advance of its agriculture. Wheat and fat cattle are therefore primary objects with every good farmer; and he who can raise most wheat and fatten most oxen or sheep or pigs will realise the greatest profit. The rotation adopted depends on all these circumstances combined, and the farmer follows different systems according to the balance of advantages, such as the three-year rotation (a year of fallow, a year of wheat, and a year of barley or oats); or the four-year course (turnips, barley, clover, wheat,) &c.

ROTE, was a musical instrument mentioned by the early French and English writers; it seems to have been similar to what the French call a *vielle*, and the English a Hurdy-Gurdy.

ROTTEN STONE, is a mineral, of a grayish, red, or dark brown colour, soft and earthy, consisting chiefly of alumina. It is employed in polishing metals.

ROTTERDAM, the capital of the Dutch province of South Holland, is intersected by numerous canals connected with the river Rotte, on which the largest merchantmen can come up and unload at the very doors of the warehouses. Along the Maas are many fine quays, the handsomest of which is called the Boomtjes, from the rows of trees with which it is planted. Rotterdam is connected by canals and by railway with the principal towns in Holland. The commerce of Rotterdam extends to all parts of the world, and embraces almost every kind of produce and manufacture. The imports and exports are similar to those of AMSTERDAM, but greater in quantity. The total value of the imports is about 10,000,000*l.* sterling annually; of the exports about 7,000,000*l.* Rotterdam is pre-eminently a commercial town, and is said now far to surpass Amsterdam in trading importance. Steamers ply regularly to Amsterdam, London, Cologne, Antwerp, &c.

ROTUNDA, is a term applied to buildings which are circular in their plan both externally and internally, or else to halls and other apartments of that shape, included within and forming merely a portion of the edifice containing them. The technical application of the term is however restricted to circular buildings whose height does not much exceed their diameter, for we should not describe a lofty cylindrical edifice, such as a round tower, by the term. The Colosseum in the Regent's Park, London, might without any great impropriety be classed among rotundas. The shape is now very seldom adopted, being unsuited to buildings in general, whatever their particular purpose may be, unless it be one for which nothing more than a single spacious hall or area is required internally. In ecclesiastical architecture circular and polygonal structures were by no means uncommon among the early Christians, especially for baptisteries and sepulchral chapels. The rotunda became afterwards in a manner incorporated with or added to the cruciform plan, being raised aloft and placed over that part of it where the transepts intersect the body of the edifice. Nearly all modern cupolas may be described as rotundas elevated above the rest of the building and viewed by looking up into them from below.

ROUEN. This important French city is situated at a point of the Seine where two small islands convert the river into a good harbour for sea-borne vessels of 300 tons. Above the stone bridge on the eastern side of La-Croix islet lie the large river craft and small steamers that ply up the Seine to Paris; between it and the suspension-bridge, and also below the latter, sea-borne vessels load and unload close to spacious well-built quays, extending all along the right bank of the river, and backed by lofty warehouses. The suburbs generally are inhabited by the manufacturing population; they contain numerous cotton factories. But though Rouen resembles many old towns on the continent in presenting a labyrinth of streets, composed of old picturesque timber-framed gable-fronted houses, it is not, like most of them, abandoned by trade, but still swarms with a population engaged in all the bustling activity of commerce and manufacturing industry.

The important manufactures of Rouen comprise striped and checked cottons for women's dresses, called *rouenneries*, calicos, woollen cloth, nankins, muslin, handkerchiefs, shawls, velvet, hosiery, swanskin, flannel, hats, lace, ropes, blankets, combs, preserved meats and confectionary, liqueurs, glue, soap, mineral acids and chemical products of all kinds, porcelain, pottery, room paper, haberdashery and small wares, steam machinery and mill-work, shot and sheet-lead, tin-ware, cotton and woollen yarns, &c. There are numerous cotton-mills, driven by steam and by water power; hand-loom weaving also prevails to a considerable extent. The other industrial establishments include dye-houses, sugar-refineries, bleach-works, tan-yards, breweries, ship-building docks, saw-mills, mills for grinding dye-woods, copper and iron foundries, fulling and pressing-mills.

Advantageously situated for commerce, with a good harbour, in which the influence of the tide is felt, and in rapid communication by railway with Paris, Havre, and Dieppe, Rouen has a very considerable import and export trade in its various industrial products, colonial and foreign produce, corn, flour, wine, brandy, fish, oil, salt provisions, hides, groceries, drugs, raw cotton, hemp, wool, iron, slates, pitch and tar, timber, &c. About 100 vessels, including steamers, belong to the port. The annual value of exports from the city exceeds a million sterling; the imports do not exceed half the amount; this is exclusive of the transit trade. Rouen is a special entrepôt for colonial and foreign produce, and has one of the most important corn-markets in France.

The Rouen journals announce that a good-sized brig, called the Athalie, has lately sailed from that port for Constantinople, and that another is about to follow. They add that it is hoped that a regular service, by means of sailing-vessels, will be established between the two places, and that eventually steamers will be employed; as the improvements recently made in the bed of the river Seine now enables steamers of large burthen to come up to Rouen. Goods from Paris sent to the Levant *viâ* Marseilles cost 130 fr. to 150 fr. the ton, but from Rouen the expense will rarely exceed 60 fr.

ROUGE. The rouge employed as a cosmetic is made in the following way. Safflower is washed in pure water, dried, reduced to powder, and steeped in a weak solution of soda, which thereby assumes a yellow colour. Lemon juice is added; a little cotton wool is steeped in the liquid; and in a short time the yellow colouring matter becomes precipitated upon the cotton. By a curious train of subsequent processes, the yellow precipitate assumes the delicate rose tint which characterises rouge.

The above is said to be the only rouge which does not injure the skin; but many other kinds are occasionally employed. *Rouge Indienne* is the Indian or Persian red imported from Ormuz. *Liquid Rouge* is the red liquid left from the preparation of carmine. *Rouge de Prusse* is burnt yellow ochre. *Vert Rouge d'Athènes* is obtained from Safflower; but by a process different from that above noticed. *Spanish Lady's Rouge* is cotton wool repeatedly wetted with ammoniacal solution of carmine, and dried.

ROXBURGHSHIRE. This Scottish county, though containing no large town, numbers several in which manufactures are carried on. At *Hawick* the manufactures are chiefly of woollen yarns, flannels, and other woollen under-clothing, plaiding, shawls, tartans, druggets, woollen-cloths of various descriptions, blankets, and lamb's-wool hosiery. At *Jedburgh* similar manufactures are carried on; and there are quarries of red and white sandstone in the parish. The manufactures of *Kelso* are not important; they consist of leather, linens, stockings, hats, woollen cloth, and tobacco. The industry of the county, however, is mostly exhibited in grazing operations, the sheep walks being numerous and extensive.

RUDDER. The rudder of a ship is too well known to require detailed description. When it is in a right line with the keel, its movement suffers no resistance from the water, and the direction of the ship's motion is not affected by it; but when the rudder is forced to assume a position oblique to the keel, the surface becomes subjected to a resistance from the water, which affects the position of the stern of the vessel, and gives a new direction to the keel, and to the vessel's movement. Patents are occasionally taken out for improvements in the form or action of rudders; but there is a pretty general adherence to the old kind of rudder. Some rudders are worked by a *tiller* or lever; others by a wheel.

RUE. This useful plant is a native of the south of Europe. Every part of it is marked by transparent dots, filled with volatile oil. The leaves and immature fruits are medicinal, and owe their virtue to the volatile oil and a bitter extractive. The odour is peculiar, strong, and penetrating; the taste intensely bitter, aromatic, and stimulating. Rue possesses powerful stimulant, antispasmodic, and tonic properties. Rue is sometimes called Herb of Grace, and in some parts of England, Ave Grace. This name is said to have been given to it on account of its use in exorcisms. In company with rosemary it has been used from time immemorial as an emblem of remembrance on account of its evergreen foliage.

RULER, PARALLEL. In its usual form, this instrument consists of two rectangular rulers connected by two cross-bars of equal lengths, which move on pivots in the rulers in such manner that the four pivots, two in each ruler, shall be the four points of a parallelogram. One ruler being held fixed, and a line drawn with the edge of the other ruler in any position, then any motion given to the other ruler by the rotation of the cross-bars gives, on the edge of the moving ruler, a line parallel to the first line. To give the instrument more extent, three rulers are sometimes put together, each connected with the next by cross-bars in such manner that the cross-bars connecting the first and second have an opposite revolution to those connecting the second and third.

The rolling parallel ruler consists of an ordinary ruler of rectangular form, both edges of which are bevelled and divided into inches and tenths, or otherwise. Two short rollers of equal diameters, and connected by an axis of nearly the same length as the ruler, are let into perforations made in the latter, so that when the instrument is moved perpendicularly to its length on the paper, lines drawn along either of its bevelled sides are parallel to one smother. Perpendiculars to a given line are drawn by adjusting the ruler so that any division on a bevelled edge may travel on the given line.

RUM. This well known spirit is distilled from cane-juice, or the scummings of the juice from the sugar-boiling-house, or from treacle, or molasses, or from *dunder*, the lees of former distillations. As the entire juice of the cane is not necessary for making rum, the distillation is carried on in conjunction with the manufacture of sugar. The best rum is made from the uncrystallised syrup called molasses. [MOLASSES.] The proportion of molasses made in crystallising a cwt. of sugar varies from 50 to 90 gallons, and depends both upon the climate and the season, being lowest in the Leeward Islands, which have a dry climate, and highest in Demerara and Trinidad, and it is in the latter that in fine seasons the proportion reaches 90 gallons per cwt. Nearly one gallon of proof rum may be made from one gallon of molasses. The best rum is from Jamaica; the worst from the Leeward Islands. The consumption of rum in England is diminishing; its place being filled by gin and British brandy. In the finer qualities of Jamaica rum, slices of pine-apple are put into the hogsheads; and the liquor then obtains the name of *pine apple rum.*

A few statistics relating to Rum will be found under SPIRIT TRADE.

RUSH; DUTCH RUSH. This material, which is used to some small extent in the arts, is the *Equisetum hyemale.* The stem is very rough, with from fourteen to twenty slender furrows. It is a native of England, Scotland, and Ireland, as well as the continent of Europe; but is almost unknown in the middle and southern English counties, and is only sparingly distributed anywhere. It appears to possess tannin, and to act as an astringent. It is supposed to be injurious to cows, and is said to cause their teeth to drop out, but horses eat it with impunity. This plant, more than any other species, is used for the purposes of polishing. Lightfoot says, that in Northumberland the milk-maids scour their pails with it. It is also used for the purposes of polishing wood, bone, ivory, and various metals, particularly brass, and is brought into this country from Holland, where it grows abundantly, and is sold in the shops of London under the name of Dutch Rush.

There are several other specimens of rush or Equisetum, but none so usefully applied as the species just noticed.

RUSHES. The well-known *rushes* of country places belong to a different genus of plants from the Dutch rush. They belong to the Genus *Juncus;* of which one species, the common soft rush, is to be found in most moist pastures, by the sides of streams, and under hedges. In some districts these rushes are used by the poor as a substitute for candles. They are gathered in summer and autumn; the largest and longest being deemed the best. They are kept in water until they are to be peeled; which process consists in divesting the rush of its peel or rind, so as to leave one regular narrow rib from top to bottom, to support the pith. The rushes are then bleached on the dewy grass, and dried in the sun. These rush-piths are finally dipped into any kind of fat or grease, until they acquire a coating analogous to that of a candle. In the bacon districts of Hampshire, hog's fat is employed for this purpose. When White wrote his well-known *Natural History of Selbourne*, he strongly recommended this feature in domestic economy; but it is possible that the cheapening of candles has lessened the relative advantage of the more primitive system.

Rushes are, however, more ordinarily used for plaiting into mats and chair-bottoms, and for constructing small toy baskets. The wicks of rushlights are made of the pith.

RUSSIA. This vast Empire ranks low in respect to produce, manufactures, and commerce, relatively to the vast area which it covers; but still it cannot fail to be important and even mighty when we consider at how many points it comes into near approach to fertile and prosperous lands. The 1,700,000 square miles of area in European Russia are far richer and more populous than the 4,800,000 square miles in Asiatic and American Russia, with the exception, perhaps, of the gold region of Siberia. Its great rivers (Volga, Dwina, Dniester, Don, &c.) place the heart of the Empire in communication with the White, the Black, the Caspian, and the Baltic seas; and as Russia is for the most part a level country, the extent of navigable rivers is most remarkable. The energetic Czars of the Empire have striven to make these water communications still more complete, by cutting canals from river to river at certain points. One such canal, for instance, connects the Volga with the Neva; another connects the Volga with Lake Ladoga; a third connects Lake Onega with the Neva; and a fourth connects the Volga with the Moskwa. The result has been that there is now continuous water communication from the Baltic and White seas in the North, to the Caspian and Black seas in the South; and an immense extension of mercantile traffic has taken place, by which the corn produce of the empire is conveyed to whichever sea will lead to the best market.

In respect to agricultural produce, Russia produces much more grain than is required for the home consumption; and considerable quantities are exported, especially rye. Wheat is the principal object of agriculture in the fertile tracts along the rivers in the southern districts, but especially in the Ukraine. Barley, oats, millet, and maize, are all cultivated. Flax and hemp are more extensively grown than perhaps in any other country in Europe; both the climate and the soil being very favourable to their cultivation. Tobacco is much cultivated in the Ukraine, whence it is exported to the neighbouring countries. The climate is not favourable to the cultivation of fruit-trees; but in the most southern districts there are peaches, apricots, quinces, mulberries, and walnuts; and in the numerous and extensive orchards of the Crimea there are also almonds and pomegranates. Grapes are grown in a few spots. Potatoes, cabbages, turnips, and carrots, are extensively grown; and in some places cucumbers, pumpkins, and radishes. Melons, asparagus, hops, and liquorice, are among the vegetable produce.

The forests constitute one of the principal sources of wealth to Russia; and their produce, consisting of timber, fire-wood, tar, pitch, pearl-ash, and potash, is exported to a large amount. About three-fourths of the countries between 65° N. lat., and the course of the Volga as far east as its great bend near Casan, are covered with forests. In all these countries only pine, fir, larch, alder, and birch are found, with a few lime trees; ash-trees are rare. From these countries is derived the greatest part of the produce of the forests which goes to foreign markets. The central provinces have in most cases no more timber than is required for their own use. West of the Dnieper several extensive forests occur on the banks of the Niemen and in the swamps of Pinsk and Ratnor. South of the swamps there are some forests of beech. The oak forests of Casan, Nischnei-Novgorod, Pensa, and Saratov, have engaged the attention of government, on account of their great importance for the navy. The southern provinces of Russia are almost without trees.

Russia contains minerals in great abundance. Gold is found chiefly in the Ural Mountains, partly on the European side, but mostly on the Siberian side. The produce in 1846 was as follows:—

Private Mining	1490 poods.
Public Mining	187 ,,
	1677 poods.

The total quantity obtained in 1847 was 1779 poods. The produce in the ten years 1837-46 was 8,387 poods of fine gold, which (at 36 lbs. avoirdupois = 1 pood) amounts to 366,931¼ lbs. troy, value nearly 19,000,000*l.* The produce seems, however, to be gradually diminishing; for the gold produce of 1848 was 1726 poods, and that of 1849 was 1587. Platinum was discovered in the Ural in 1823, and has been worked ever since; the produce in 1848 was 213 poods = 7668 lbs. Silver is met with only in the Asiatic governments. The quantity obtained in 1847 was 1190 poods. Copper and iron are extensively worked in the Ural, and in other places. Mercury, arsenic, nickel, cobalt, antimony, and bismuth, are met with, but are not much worked. Salt is found in various lakes, and a salt formation extends along the western declivity of the Ural Mountains, to the source of the Kama, and thence westward on both sides of the Uwalli. In all these districts salt is made from the salt-springs, which are numerous. Coal exists in a few places, but not in large quantities. Other minerals are not much worked, with the exception of marble and granite.

The manufactures of Russia commenced, as in other countries, with the beginning of its political importance, but have been chiefly indebted for their encouragement and progress to the efforts of the government. The czars Ivan I. and II., who in the 15th and 16th centuries had restored Russia to independence, invited artisans and workmen from Germany, the Netherlands, and Italy, and established at Moscow, Yaroslaw, Smolensk, and Kiev manufactures of woollen cloth, linen, arms, &c. But the civil wars before the accession of the house of Romanoff, and the interference of Sweden and Poland, which led to the desolation of the country, checked the infant manufactures, so that in fact nothing was done till the reign of Peter the Great, who in this, as in many other respects, was the founder of the prosperity of Russia.

During the reign of the present Emperor the manufactures of Russia have increased to a remarkable extent. Smelting works, engineering works, cotton factories, woollen factories, tallow-melting works, tanneries, soap factories—all have increased most rapidly. The central part of the empire is the chief theatre of manufacturing industry. Moscow has become the focus of it; in the lesser towns of the government of which it is the capital, the number of manufactories continues to increase. Next to Moscow, in industry, are the governments of Vladimir, Nischnei-Novgorod, Saratov, and St. Petersburg.

The inland trade is carried on in a very great measure by means of annual fairs, the most remarkable of which is that of Nischnei-Novgorod. [FAIRS.] The number of these great commercial fairs is somewhat over twenty; but there is a still larger number of minor fairs and markets. The inland trade, as before remarked, is greatly promoted by the extensive system of inland navigation. The vessels which have arrived from the interior at the ports of Archangel, St. Petersburg, and Riga, have frequently amounted in the year from 2,500 to 3,500 barks. Goods destined for Odessa from the interior are carried down the Dniester or the Dnieper, and from the mouths of those rivers to Odessa by coasting vessels. Kherson, Astrakhan, Taganrog, Nakhitschevan, and Rostow, are the other chief ports.

The ships which enter and clear at the various Russian ports annually have an average tonnage of about 2,000,000 tons; of which those to and from Great Britain amount generally to nearly one half. The British trade at Russian ports in 1848 involved the use of —Inwards, 2,562 vessels; outwards, 1,916 vessels; together 969,572 tonnage, 41,613 men. The declared value of the British and Irish produce and manufactures transmitted to Russia in 1847 was 1,844,543*l.*; the following were the chief items:—Coals, 108,378 tons; woven cottons, 1,541,112 yards; cotton twist and yarn, 12,853,754 lbs.; earthenware, 345,421 pieces; hardware and cutlery, 7,676 cwts.; iron and steel goods, 15,732 tons; lead and shot, 1,764 tons; machinery and mill-work, 226,036*l.*; salt, 2,318,584 bushels; tin, 6,268 cwts.; woollens and worsteds, 57,720*l.*; ditto yarn, 1,727,850 lbs., = 189,014*l.* The value in 1849 was somewhat lower. The nature of the trade between Russia and Great Britain is indicated by the chief exports from the former to the latter in 1847, namely—Bristles, 1,278,570 lbs.; corn, 2,000,000 quarters; flax and tow, 681,167 cwts.; hemp, 542,857 cwts.; linseed, 853,900 quarters; tallow, 939,946 cwts; tar, 9,656 casks; timber, 220,000 loads; wool, 2,919,776 lbs.

The St. Petersburgh and Moscow Railway exhibits some remarkable commercial features. It was at first intended to order all the locomotives and machinery from England, as being the cheapest in the end; but an enterprizing American firm made such offers as induced the Emperor to enter into a contract with them. They were to have the use of certain machine works at Alexandroffsky, which were to be adapted for their purposes; they were to employ their own hands, on their own terms; but they were also to employ 500 serfs belonging to the Alexandroffsky Estate, whose services were to be paid for at a certain stipulated rate: they were to construct, at those works, 200 locomotives, 5,800 trucks, 70 passenger carriages, and other rolling stock, for which they were to be paid at stipulated prices; they had the privilege of importing coal and iron duty free; and they were to be paid once a month till all the works were finished. The whole was finished long before the railway itself was finished; and the Emperor expressed his satisfaction by a distribution of some of those orders and medals which form such a remarkable feature in the imperial proceedings. The Alexandroffsky works covered 160 acres, and at some periods employed nearly 3,000 persons—nearly all of whom were semi-serfs, who worked well if well directed. At the same establishment steam-engines have been made for the Siberian mines.

It is fitting that Russia should shew, at the World's Exhibition, to what point her producing and manufacturing skill has now attained.

RUST, in the common acceptation of the term, is the red pulverulent substance which is formed on the surface of iron when exposed to air and moisture. It is an oxide of iron.

RUSTICATED WORK, in Architecture, is a species of decoration for walls, wherein the joints between the courses, and between the separate stones in each course, are strongly defined by sunk channels or grooves. Rustication gives an appearance of solidity to the surface, and was frequently employed by the Romans. Italian architecture presents many examples of rusticated work, and there are several specimens among the public buildings of London.

RYE. This valuable plant bears naked seeds on a flat ear furnished with awns like barley. The straw is solid, the internal part being filled with a pith, which makes it valuable for litter, and still more so for thatching. The value of the straw is often nearly equal to that of the grain. Rye grows on poor light soils which are altogether unfit for wheat. It was formerly raised in considerable quantities in England, either alone or mixed with wheat, and was then called *Meslin*, from the old French word *meslé*, which means *mixed.* The meslin when ground produced a very wholesome and palatable household bread. Rye is at present raised in very small quantities in England.

In England rye is mostly sown as a green crop, and when fed off early in spring with sheep, the land is invigorated, and will bear excellent potatoes or turnips the same year.

The preparation of the land for rye is the same as for wheat, except that in very light soils no more ploughings are required than will clear the ground of weeds. If rye is sown after harvest, one ploughing only is usually given. It will thrive upon rich wheat soils, as well as upon lighter, and, as it throws out numerous stems in rich land, it is the more profitable as fodder, although the crop of grain might not be so abundant when the plants are too much crowded.

The Rye and Rye-Meal imported in the last three years amounted to the following quantities:—

	Rye.	Rye-Meal.
1848	62,635 qrs.	35,984 cwts.
1849	240,556 ,,	18,468 ,,
1850	94,078 ,,	966 ,,

S

SACBUT, is the name which was formerly given in England to the TROMBONE.

SACCHAROMETER, is an instrument used principally in the operations of brewing and making sugar. It serves to indicate the density of the liquid extracted from malt, or the degree to which the juice expressed from the sugar-cane is concentrated previously to undergoing the process of crystallisation; in other words it is a measurer of the sweetness of, or the amount of saccharine matter contained in, a liquid.

The saccharometer which is most commonly employed is made of copper, and differs in form from the hydrometer in common use only in its stem, which is six inches long, having four equal faces, each less than a quarter of an inch in breadth. Three of these faces are graduated, and the volume and weight of the whole are such that when the instrument is immersed in water it sinks till the top of the stem is but little above the surface. The line at which the surface of the water cuts the stem is marked as the zero of the scale; and the graduations are such that, when the instrument is immersed and floats upright in a vessel containing the saccharine matter, the number of the division at the surface expresses the density of the liquid by the number of pounds avoirdupois which ought to be added to the weight of a barrel of water, in order to show the weight of an equal volume of the liquid.

For the general purpose of determining the specific gravity of fluids, on the principle of the hydrometer and saccharometer, the best instrument is one which consists of a glass cylinder about seven inches long and three-quarters of an inch in diameter. It has at its lower extremity a stirrup, carrying a small cup in the form of an inverted cone, and its opposite part is drawn out so as to form a slender stem or tube, which is terminated at the upper extremity by a small cup. About the middle of the stem a mark is made, and, in order that the instrument may be enabled to float vertically in a vessel containing the liquid whose specific gravity is to be determined, a constant weight, which may be a ball of glass containing mercury, is placed in the lower cup.

SACK, is a Spanish wine of the dry kind; in French, *Vin sec;* and in some old English works it is called *seck.* There is a general opinion that sack was the same wine which is now named Sherry.

SAFETY LAMP. [LAMP, SAFETY.]

SAFFLOWER, or *Bastard Saffron*, is obtained from the *Carthamus tinctorius.* This plant has been cultivated in eastern countries from the earliest times, both on account of the oil expressed from its seed and for the colouring matter procurable from its flowers, which in their dry state form the Safflower of commerce. It is largely used to adulterate saffron. The oil of the seeds of *Carthamus* was valued by the ancients as a laxative medicine, and is still employed by the Asiatics for the same purpose, as well as for external application. It is most extensively used as a lamp-oil. The plant is however chiefly cultivated on account of its flowers, not only in China, India, and Egypt, but also in the south of Europe. The Safflower brought from China is the most valued, and fetches a much higher price than that from Bengal. The quantity imported into Great Britain in 1847 was 1,128 cwts.

SAFFRON consists of the dried stigmas of the *Crocus sativus*, a plant native of Greece and Asia Minor, but extensively cultivated in Austria, France, Spain, and also formerly in England. The Sicilian saffron is said to be the produce of the *Crocus odorus*, but both in ancient and modern times this sort has been little esteemed. England is chiefly supplied from France and Spain; that of Spain being preferred. In Germany however Spanish saffron is not in such repute as the Austrian, great pains being taken in the cultivation of the plant in that country. When the flowers expand, and are thoroughly open under the influence of the sun, the stigmas, of which there are three, are plucked out, a portion of one style remaining attached to them, and spread upon paper, to be dried either by means of portable kilns over which a hair-cloth or fine sieve is stretched, or in a room by the sun. The stigmas have a penetrating, aromatic, and, when in large quantity, stupifying odour, and a bitter aromatic taste; by mastication the mouth and saliva are rendered yellow. By long internal use of them many of the secretions acquire a yellow colour. According to Mr. Pereira, one grain of good saffron contains the stigmata and styles of nine flowers; hence 4320 flowers are required to yield one ounce of saffron. Saffron was formerly met with in two forms, Hay Saffron and Cake Saffron; the former is now alone in demand, the latter being entirely an artificial compound of the florets of the safflower, gum, and some other materials. About 10,000 lbs. of saffron were imported from France in 1847.

SAGAPE'NUM, is a medicinal substance yielded by *Ferula Persica*, which grows in Persia and other regions of the East. It is procured in the same way as assafœtida. It occurs either in tears or irregular masses, of a dirty brownish colour, containing in the interior white or yellowish grains. It is difficult to break (unless when very old), is tenacious, and not easily powdered, except in winter. It has a similar odour to assafœtida, but less powerful, with a nauseously bitter and acrid taste. It consists chiefly of resin, gum, and volatile oil. Its action on the human system is the same as that of assafœtida and other fetid gum-resins.

SAGO. This word signifies, in the language of the Papuas, *bread*, since it constitutes the staple article of food of the inhabitants of the Eastern Archipelago and other parts where the plants which yield it grow. It is not a seed, but the farina from the stem of several palms and palm-like vegetables. Sago is a variety of starch, prepared by the plant for the use of the flowers and fruit, and is most abundant just before the evolution or appearance of the flower-bud, which is known by a whitish dust transuding through and covering the leaves. At this time the stem is cut down near the base, and then divided into pieces of five or six feet in length. A part of the outer hard wood is then sliced off, and the workman, coming to the pith, cuts across the longitudinal fibres and the pith together, leaving a part at each end uncut, so that when it is excavated there remains a trough, into which the pulp is again put, mixed with water, and beaten with a piece of wood; the fibres, being then separated from the pulp, float at the top, and the flour subsides. After being cleared in this manner by several waters, the pulp is put into cylindrical baskets made of the leaves of the tree; and, if it is to be kept some time, those baskets are generally sunk in fresh water to keep it moist, for the pulp will keep long if preserved from the air, but if exposed it presently turns sour.

The quantity yielded by one tree is prodigious. Five or six hundred pounds are not an unusual produce for one tree; and as the vegetation still remains after being felled, a stem again springs up, which goes through the different stages of growth till it is fit for the axe.

The flour or powder is rarely imported, granulated sago being the state in which it is commonly brought to Europe. To bring it into this state from the flour, it must be moistened and passed through a sieve into an iron pot (very shallow) held over a fire, which enables it to assume a globular form. Thus all our grained sago is half baked, and will keep long. Of this granulated sago there are two varieties, the common or *brown* sago, and *pearl* sago. The latter is in small hard horny or semi-transparent grains, about the size of a pin's head; the former are in larger grains, about the size of the grains of pearl barley. Both are inodorous, and with an insipid taste. They swell in cold water, and are almost entirely soluble in boiling water, so as to form a thick starch-like solution, which may be used as a pudding, or prepared in other ways as an article of diet for children and invalids, if a farinaceous diet is required. 65,000 cwts. of sago were imported in 1848.

SAILS; SAIL MAKING. The principal sails of large vessels can be placed at right angles to the direction of the keel of the ship, and this position is given to them when the vessel goes before the wind; in other cases the same sails may, by means of the braces, be placed obliquely to the keel. The sails which are attached to the ship's stays, and the sails of boats or small vessels, are when supine in a vertical plane passing through the keel; a certain degree of obliquity to that plane may, however, be given to them at their lower extremities, if necessary.

When a vessel is in still water, the pressure of the wind against the sails overcomes its inertia, and motion takes place in some direction. The motion goes on increasing by the accelerative power of the wind, as the motion of a descending body is accelerated by the force of gravity; but at the end of a certain time the resistance in an opposite direction, both of the air against the sails and hull of the ship, and of the water against the latter, becoming equal to the accelerative power of the wind, the ship acquires a terminal or uniform velocity, and in this state (neglecting the resistance of the air) there may be said to be an equilibrium between the pressure of the wind against the sails and of the water against the vessel.

The management of a sail in a ship belongs to seamanship; but the manufacture of the sail itself is simply an industrial employment. The canvas used for sails is a very stout material, woven in England or Scotland from Russian hemp, and purchased in the form of rolls called *bolts*, each bolt containing about 40 yards of canvas 24 inches wide. There are six or seven different qualities of this canvas, according to the size and position of the sail to be made; and each quality has a particular number attached to it, and must have a certain weight per square foot. Thus, in the Royal Navy, a bolt of No. 1 canvas, containing 38 yards, must weigh 44 lbs.; whereas No. 7 weighs only about half as much: the intermediate numbers having intermediate weights.

As the canvas is only two feet wide, many breadths are required to form a large sail. The mainsail of an East Indiaman contains nearly 700 yards of canvas: while the whole suit of sails for such a ship requires as much as 9000 yards. As the sails vary much in shape, considerable tact is required in cutting up the canvas so as to avoid waste. The art of the sail maker consists not only in seaming up the numerous breadths, so as to give the requisite dimensions to the sail, but also in strengthening the sail by sewing rope to its edges. The seaming and sewing are effected with large three-sided needles, of seven or eight different kinds, which are threaded with sewing twine having from 200 to 400 fathoms to the lb. The skeins of twine previous to being used are dipped into a trough, containing melted tar, grease, and oil, which is afterwards dried. The sail-maker has a thumb-stall and a palm-thimble, for protecting his right hand. His stitches have a regulated degree of closeness, on which his rate of payment in part depends; there are usually about 100 stitches in a yard. The overlapping of the breadths is an inch or an inch and a half. Besides the seaming, sundry small pieces of canvas are stitched to the sail to strengthen it in various directions; and the edge rope or bolt rope is sewn on with great firmness. So skilfully is the canvas marked out and cut up by a master sail-maker, that in the 9000 yards for the forty sails of a large ship, there will not be more than three or four yards actually wasted.

The *Storm Sails* patented in 1844 by Mr. Archibald Trail are made in the usual manner, but are subsequently strengthened by sewing to their surface a number of canvas bands about an inch broad, with cords woven in them, such bands being secured at their ends into the bolt-ropes, or cords forming the boundaries of the sail, and carried diagonally across the surface of the sail at an angle of 45° with the seams, and at a distance of about three feet from each other. Two sets of bands are used, crossing the sail in opposite directions, one set being attached on each side of the canvas. By this simple contrivance the strain is so equalised as to render tearing less probable than with an ordinary sail; while, if any injury be inflicted, the rent is confined within the narrow limits of one of the diamond-shaped compartments into which the sail is divided by the protecting bands.

SAL AMMONIAC. [AMMONIA.]

SALEP, *Salap*, or *Saloop*, is a nutritious article of diet, much valued in the East for its supposed general stimulant properties, but which is justly esteemed bland and nutritious, and well suited to children and convalescents. Salep consists of the tubers of different species of *Orchideæ*, which have been known in medicine from very early times by the name *Orchis*. All these plants have two tubers, charged with nutritious matter, and while one is nourishing the flower-stem and seeds of the current year, by which it is robbed of its store, the other serves as a reservoir for th flower-stem of the succeeding year. This last alone is fit for use. Both are dug up together, but the solid one only is retained. It is dipped in warm water, after which the fine brown skin is easily removed by means of a coarse cloth or brush. The tubers, being thus cleaned and peeled, are to be arranged on a tin plate, and then placed within an oven heated to the same degree as is necessary for baking bread; here they are to remain for seven or ten minutes, in which time they will exchange their opaque and milky whiteness for a semi-transparent horn-like appearance, and a yellowish colour, retaining their original bulk. Being then withdrawn from the oven, they are exposed during some days to dry and harden in the air; or by the employment of a very gentle heat, they may be brought to the same state in the course of a few hours: all that is then required to adapt the salep for food is to boil it in water (or milk) to the required consistency.

SALINOMETER. An instrument has been patented by Mr. How under this name, for measuring the degree of saltness in the water contained in the boilers of marine steam engines. When this saltness gets beyond a certain limit, it impedes the proper action of the boiler, and the salt water requires to be removed. Mr. How's apparatus consists of a small cylinder, open at the top, and having a stop-cock at the bottom. By means of this stop-cock water from the boiler can be admitted into the cylinder. An instrument on the principle of the hydrometer and saccharometer, but adapted to this especial purposo, is immersed in the saline water; and the degree to which its graduated stem will sink suffices to measure the saltness.

SALMON FISHERY AND TRADE. A few commercial statistics concerning salmon will be found under FISHERIES; and we will here append one or two more.

The London market receives its supply of salmon chiefly from Scotland—three-fourths from the river Tay. The Tay salmon sold at Billingsgate in recent years has been about 15,000*l.* annual value. A small quantity of Irish salmon reaches Billingsgate from Limerick and Cork; and a much smaller quantity of Severn and Wye salmon. A small quantity is also brought over from Holland. There seem to be indications that the salmon fisheries generally are declining, and the supply less than it was formerly—owing, as some persons think, to a somewhat reckless mode of fishing, by which the fish are not allowed time to arrive at maturity. Salmon is brought to Billingsgate in boxes. Of late years there have been sold annually at Billingsgate about 30,000 boxes, each containing seven salmon; or about 200,000 salmon. This is independent of the *pickled* salmon, brought to London in kits.

SALT; SALT TRADE. The chemical nature of this invaluable substance is noticed under SODIUM. We will here speak of its extraction and trade.

The principal part of the salt of England is made in the valley of the Weaver in Cheshire. When the salt duty was repealed in 1824, there were 75 works where salt was raised in a fossil state: 34 were at Northwich, 26 at Winsford, 3 at Middlewich, and 2 at Nantwich, all in Cheshire; 2 were at Shirley Wich in Staffordshire; 6 at Droitwich in Gloucestershire; and 2 in Durham. There were at the same time 35 works at which salt was made by evaporation from sea-water, 29 of which were in Hampshire and the Isle of Wight. In Scotland, at the same time, there were 15 salt works, and in all of them salt was made from sea water. At Droitwich alone 260,000 tons of salt are made annually from the brine springs of that town. A singular feud has recently existed in the town, owing to attempts made to prevent the brine from flowing to certain salt works. Nearly the whole of the salt exported is made in Cheshire, and is sent down the river Weaver, which communicates with the Mersey, to Liverpool. The Staffordshire rock-salt is chiefly exported from Hull, and that of Gloucestershire from the port of Gloucester.

The rock-salt of Cheshire was first discovered near Northwich, while searching for coal. It is found from 28 to 48 yards beneath the surface; the first stratum is from 15 to 25 yards in thickness, extremely solid and hard, and resembling brown sugar candy. Many tons at a time are loosened by blasting with gunpowder. Beneath this comes a stratum of hard stone, 25 to 35 yards in thickness; and then is encountered a bed of perfectly white and pure salt, 40 yards thick. There are also brine springs, which appear to have been formed by springs flowing over the beds of rock-salt, and becoming saturated with the saline particles; this brine is pumped up to the surface. The brine springs are from 20 to 40 yards in depth. Tho English table salt is almost entirely produced by evaporating this brine; but a considerable portion of that which is exported is rock salt. The evaporation was in former times effected by the heat of the sun, but artificial heat is now employed. So far as observation has yet gone, the English supply is practically inexhaustible; no limit is known to the extent of the beds or the springs; and it ought to be regarded as ono of the blessings which we owe to the mineral wealth of our country that the beautiful table salt of England may be obtained at such an extremely low price as that now charged for it. One specimen of Northwich rock salt, weighing two tons, has been forwarded to the Great Exhibition.

About 70,000 tons of Cheshire salt are annually used by the alkali makers on the banks of the Tyne. It used to be conveyed round the Land's End and the south coast by ships; but it is now sent by canal and river to Liverpool, from thence to Maryport by sea, and from thence to Newcastle by railway.

A duty of 10*s.* per bushel was laid on salt in 1798, which in 1805 was increased to 15*s.* In 1823 this duty was reduced to 2*s.*; and in 1825 was wholly repealed. Salt used in the fisheries, in bleaching, or in agriculture, was nearly duty-free. The salt exported in 1849 amounted to 18,539,865 bushels.

The British government in India monopolises both the manufacture and sale of salt. In the ten years 1836-45, the net receipts from this monopoly of home salt, and duty on imported salt, varied from 989,389*l.* to 1,707,287*l.* annually. It is believed that a moderate duty on British salt would yield as large a revenue in the course of a few years, if the monopoly were abolished, while commerce would be benefitted by the interchange of East India sugar and other native commodities for British salt; smuggling in salt, which is extensively carried on, would cease; and in place of arbitrary and harsh restrictions, the consumer would obtain a better article at a cheaper rate.

SALTPETRE. The chemical nature of this valuable substance is explained under POTASSIUM. About 14,000 tons of saltpetre were imported in 1850.

SALTS. The term Salt, originally restricted in its application to common salt, which it still means when used merely by itself, is now applied to a vast number of substances which have in many cases few properties in common. Common salt is the principal of a class composed of a metal and such bodies as chlorine, iodine, bromine, and fluorine, and the radicals of the hydracids. It was formerly believed that common salt was a compound of muriatic acid and of soda; and hence it was very commonly called muriate of soda. But it has been shown by Davy that salt is really chloride of sodium. The *Oxy-Salts* form another numerous and important class of compounds: these are formed when an oxacid is made to combine with an oxidised base; as, for example, when sulphuric acid unites with soda, the result being sulphate of soda. The sulphate of potash, lime, magnesia, &c., are similarly constituted.

In general properties the various classes of salts, and indeed the individuals of the same class, differ as widely as possible; some are crystallisable, others uncrystallisable; they are colourless, and of various colours; sapid and insipid; soluble and insoluble in water, alcohol, and other menstrua; volatile and fixed in the fire; decomposeable or undecomposeable by the same re-agent.

SALVADOR, SAN, or BAHIA, formerly the capital of Brazil, is still one of the greatest commercial ports of that empire. The bay presents a capacious basin with several islands and harbours, a depth of water varying from 8 to 40 fathoms, and ample room and shelter for all the fleets in the world. Three roads lead from Bahia to the interior of Brazil, by which the foreign goods reach the places of consumption, and the produce of the country is brought to market. The exports consist of sugar, cotton, coffee, tobacco, cigars, rice, rum, molasses, tallow, hides, horns, cocoa-nuts, fancy woods, bullion, &c. For the year ending September 30, 1849, Bahia exported 62,000 cases and 9925 bags of sugar; 19,500 bales of cotton; 20,238 bags of coffee; 82,866 hides; 9554 pipes of rum; and 10,901 bales of tobacco. The imports consist of different kinds of cotton fabrics, woollen stuffs and cloth, linen, iron and tin ware, provisions, flour, salt, fish, soap, wines, codfish, leather, furniture, &c.

SAMPHIRE, is a herb in much request in some parts of the country as a salad and pickle. The true samphire is the *Crithmum maritimum*, a plant belonging to the natural order *Umbelliferæ*. It grows on rocks by the sea-side. The species of *Salicornia* are often called samphire, and are used in the same manner, but they are very much inferior to the *Crithmum* as an article of diet.

SANDAL WOOD. This wood, yielded by one or more species of *Santalum*, is well known both in commerce and the arts as a fragrant-smelling wood. It is used as incense, and is also employed in the manufacture of necklaces, fans, elegant boxes, and cabinets. There are three kinds known, the white, the yellow, and the red. The last is the *Sanders' wood* (as it is often called) of commerce, which is used only as a dye wood and as a slight astringent in medicine. The white sandal tree, when felled, is barked, cut into billets, and buried in a dry place; the deeper the colour and the nearer the root, the more fragrant it is. As seen in commerce it is in compact pieces of a white colour and agreeable odour, but with little taste. The Chinese manufacture various articles with the yellow sandal wood, which is the most fragrant; they also burn it in their temples and private houses as an incense, and especially in the form of long slender candles, which are formed by covering the ends of sticks with the sawdust of sandal wood mixed with rice paste.

About 200 tons of sandal wood are annually imported into Calcutta from the Malabar coast, and about twice as much into Canton from the islands of the Indian Archipelago. The red sandal or sanders wood is imported in large billets, which, when fresh, are of a brilliant red colour, but which gradually deepens by exposure to air; it takes a very fine polish, and somewhat resembles Brazil wood.

SANDARAC. Although usually called a gum, sandarac does not possess the requisite characteristics; it consists of a mixture of two different kinds of resin and a little volatile oil. It exudes spontaneously from the bark of certain large trees which grow in Morocco; it concretes in irregular drops or masses on the surface, of a yellowish colour, and semi-transparent. A powder forms on the surface, which constitutes *pounce*. The sandarac easily melts and ignites, and emits a somewhat powerful odour. It is used for the preparation of varnishes; also occasionally for incense or pastiles, plasters, and ointments. Sandarac is sometimes used to adulterate mastic; and it is itself occasionally adulterated with a cheaper substance.

SANDIVER. This name is given to the saline scum that swims on molten glass when the ingredients first combine into a homogeneous mass. It is called by the French *sel de verre*, or *glass salt*. It is occasionally used as a tooth powder.

SAÔNE. The river Saône in France gives name to two departments, each of which presents a few interesting features connected with industry.

In *Saône-et-Loire* about 18,000,000 gallons of wine are made annually; the best kinds are those grown near Romanèche in the arrondissement of Mâcon, near which there is also the richest manganese mine in France. The department contains one of the richest coal fields in France. Fifteen mines are worked; and in their neighbourhood are numerous iron works, the ore used in which is partly mined in this district, but most of it is the produce of distant mines. At Creuzot, where iron and coal mines are worked, is one of the most important iron works in France, and great foundries in which cannon, anchors, steam machinery, mill castings, &c., are manufactured. There are large forests of oak, elm, beech, and fir, in the Morvan and Cévennes ranges, and in several other districts; in the eastern division of the department the forests contain also maple and poplar. To the industrial products of the department already mentioned are to be added steel and steel ware, glass bottles, copper ware, paper, beetroot, sugar, pottery, bricks, cotton cloth and yarn, linen, leather, felt hats, drugget, plaids, wine casks, oil, flour, &c.

In *Haute Saône* the mountainous regions abound in forests of oak, fir, beech, ash, &c., and are covered in many parts with good summer pasture. Minerals are abundant, including red and gray granite, green and violet porphyry, freestone, lithographic stone, grindstone, gypsum, white sand used in glass factories, limestone, marble, and iron. Several iron and coal mines are worked. Vast quantities of cherries for making kirschwasser are cultivated. About 8,000,000 gallons of inferior Burgundy wine, are made annually. The chief industrial product is iron, in the various forms of pig, bar, sheet, tin plates, steel, wire, or articles of ironmongery. This manufacture is carried on in about 60 forges, furnaces, and foundries. The other industrial establishments include glass-works, potteries and brickfields, distilleries, tan-yards, cotton mills, paper-mills, dyehouses, oil mills, &c. Straw and felt hats, hosiery, drugget, and hempen cloth are also made; and there is good trade in corn, flour, hay, timber, oak staves, deals, butter, cheese, salt and cattle.

There is one remarkable establishment in this department which deserves notice. It is the corn mill belonging to M. Tramoy, at Gray. This mill, which is of elegant construction, and the finest establishment of the kind in France, is driven by a current drawn from the Saône. It contains eleven water wheels, which drive eleven pairs of stones and a saw mill; and by ingenious mechanical contrivances, all the various processes in the grinding, sifting, and lifting of the greater part of the surplus corn of five adjacent departments ground in this vast establishment, are performed with the help of only fifteen workmen. The flour from these mills enters largely into the supply of Lyon and Marseille, whither it is conveyed by barges down the Saône and Rhône.

SAPAN-WOOD. This dye-wood is yielded by a species of *Cæsalpinia*, which grows in India and the Indian Archipelago. The wood has been used as a dye-wood from very early times in India, and is described as a medicine in Persian works. It found its way into Europe some time before the discovery of America, and it still continues to be imported. Its colouring matter differs little from that of Brazil Wood; but the best Sapan Wood does not yield more than half the quantity that may be obtained from an equal weight of Brazil Wood, and the colour is not so bright.

SAPINDUS, or *Indian soap*, is a plant, the berries of which are used for soap in many parts of Asia. In the East Indies several species yield berries which in their dried state may be bought in every bazaar, as they are everywhere employed as a substitute for soap. The fleshy part of these berries is viscid, and in drying assumes a shining semi-transparent appearance. When rubbed with water, they form a lather like soap. This is owing to the presence of a principle called by chemists *Saponine*, which is often united with an acrid principle, whence these berries are said to injure cloth which has been much washed with them. The bark and root have similar properties, and have been employed for the same purpose, as well as medicinally, in the countries where they are indigenous. The berries, which are about the size of cherries, enclose black shining nuts. The kernel of these nuts contains an edible oil, which is sometimes employed for burning. The fruits of some species are eaten, and the wood of others, which is close grained and hard, forms valuable timber.

SAPPHIRE. [CORUNDUM.]

SARCO'PHAGUS is the name given to the Egyptian stone coffins. These coffins consist of two parts, a case formed of one piece, and open at the top, in which the mummy was to be deposited, and a lid to cover the top. As these sarcophagi are generally of hard stone, and often extremely hard, the working of them must have been very expensive, and they could only have been made for kings and very rich persons. There are some fine specimens in the British Museum.

SARDINIA. This large Mediterranean island is well provided with forests; the best timber is in the mountainous districts. The cork tree grows very large and in great quantity in the northern part of the island. Timber is very scarce in the plains, and the want of roads prevents the people from making use of that of the mountain forests. Dwarf mulberry-trees grow in abundance. The vine is extensively cultivated, both soil and climate being highly favourable to it; and though the process of making wine is still very imperfect, Sardinia produces some excellent wines. *Malvasia*, or *Malmsey*, and *Muscat* are both Sardinian wines. There are several extensive olive-grounds, but the oil has not yet been largely exported, although this branch of commerce is on the increase. Cheese is a great object of rural economy; it is made chiefly from sheep and goats' milk, and being steeped in brine it has a salt bitter taste. Little butter is made, as the treatment of cows is not well understood, and fodder is scarce. Tobacco is grown in some districts, and is a royal monopoly. Salt is a monopoly of the government, and a profitable branch of the royal revenue. The salterns are round the gulf of Cagliari, at Oristano, Terranova, and on the northern coast west of Porto Torres; they are worked by convicts sentenced to the galleys, but the excavation of the mounds and the carriage of the salt is a labour forced on the adjacent villagers, for which they receive a small compensation. Flax is cultivated to a small extent, and is woven into linen. Wool is coarse, owing to the flocks being neglected, and it is manufactured into coarse cloth for the peasantry. A better quality of cloth and fine flannel are made of lambs' wool.

The fisheries of Sardinia are very productive, especially the establishments for taking the tunny fish, which are on various parts of the coast. The fishery lasts from April to July. Most of the tunnies weigh from 100 to 300 lbs.; and all the parts of the fish are turned to account, most of them being salted. Most of the tunneries are let to foreigners, who ship off the produce to various ports of the Mediterranean, and a comparatively small proportion is used in the island. There are fisheries of anchovies, sardines, coral, and pearls off the coast. The coral is polished and worked into necklaces, earrings, and other ornaments, at Genoa, Leghorn, Marseille, and Naples. The pearls are of inferior quality.

Sardinia was noted in ancient times for its mines, which were worked to a great extent, as is attested by vast excavations and remains of foundries. Gold and silver mines were at one time worked. Mercury, iron, and lead are met with in various parts. In the eastern mountains are found porphyry, basalt, alabaster, and marble. Chalcedonies, jaspers, carnelians, sardonyx, turquoises, and rock crystal, are found in the mountains of the west.

When we speak, in England, of the king of Sardinia, we allude to a kingdom which includes much more than the island of that name; it includes Sardinia, Savoy, Piedmont, Genoa and Nice, all of which are now under one king. The Continental States of the king of Sardinia have several fine carriage roads across the Alps and Apennines, which intersect their Territory. The plains of Piedmont are well supplied with canals, chiefly for the purpose of irrigation. The staple products for exportation are silk, rice, hemp, wine, and oil. The principal manufactures consist of paper, silks, woollens, linen, glass, and cotton yarn. The importation of colonial articles and English manufactures takes place chiefly through the port of Genoa. A considerable trade is carried on with Switzerland and Germany by the Lago Maggiore and the road of Mount St. Bernard leading to the Grisons. The commerce of the three principal ports of the Sardinian States, Nice, Genoa, and Cagliari, is illustrated by the following statement for 1846:—

Ships which entered and declared at

	Vessels.	Tons.	Crews.
Genoa	4692	576,705	39,743
Nice	5192	309,399	32,270
Cagliari	724	79,918	6,711
	10,608	966,022	78,724

The exports of British produce and manufactures to the Sardinian States in 1848, amounted in value to 611,992*l.*; besides the produce and manufactures of other countries. The imports from those states into England consist chiefly, (and indeed almost entirely) of silk.

SARDONYX. [AGATE.]

SASSAFRAS. The species of this genus of plants most known is the Sassafras Laurel, an inhabitant of the woods of North America, from Canada to Florida. It is mostly a small tree or bush, but sometimes attains the height of forty or fifty feet. In America the Sassafras is divided into two varieties, the red and white. Its great use is for medicinal purposes. It is however employed in America for making bedsteads and other articles of furniture, which are not liable to the attacks of insects, and give out a very agreeable odour. The root of the Sassafras Laurel is the officinal part in the London Pharmacopœia; but the whole plant possesses the aromatic odour common to the Laurels; and some assert that the bark of the stem and branches is stronger than that of the root; but this seems to be an error. The taste is sharp, acrid, aromatic, and, as well as the odour, resembles fennel. A kind of chocolate, called *Sassafras Chocolate*, is made from the nuts of the sassafras tree, to form a beverage for invalids.

SATIN. [SILK.]

SATIN SPAR is a whitish, fibrous, translucent mineral, which occurs at Alston Moor in Cumberland, and in North America, in tabular masses of an inch or two in thickness, in veins in slaty clay and shale. It consists chiefly, if not altogether, of carbonate of lime.

SATINWOOD. This beautiful wood is obtained from an East Indian tree called the *Chloroxylon Swietenia.* It is of a deep yellow colour, remarkably close grained, heavy, and durable, and comes nearer to box wood than the produce of any other tree. An essential oil, called *wood oil,* is obtained from the satinwood tree.

SATURATION. When common salt, or indeed most other saline and many vegetable bodies, are added to water until it ceases to dissolve them, the solution so obtained is termed a *saturated solution* of the substance dissolved. Saturation may exist with regard to one body and not to another. Thus water saturated with common salt will still dissolve sulphate of soda, and vice versâ; so also a saturated solution of common salt will dissolve sugar. There are many other cases in which the point of saturation may be determined by the cessation of solution; while there is a third class in which saturation cannot be determined by insolubility; as when both bodies are employed in a fluid state, or when the excess of a solid body is soluble in the water which holds the saturated salt in solution. The saturating power of bodies is in many cases greatly influenced by heat, while in others variation of temperature produces but little effect; thus cold water will take up nearly as much common salt as hot water; but sulphate of soda is more soluble in hot water than in cold.

SAW MANUFACTURE. Saws were used by the ancient Egyptians; a specimen, found among the tombs of Thebes, is deposited in the British Museum. There is a picture among the remains discovered in the ruins of Herculaneum, representing the interior of a carpenter's workshop, with two genii cutting a piece of wood with a frame-saw; and on an altar preserved in the Capitoline Museum at Rome there is a perfect representation of a bow-saw, exactly resembling, in the form of the frame, and the twisted cord for tightening it, those used by modern carpenters.

Saws are of various forms and sizes, according to the purposes to which they are to be applied. The *Cross Cut Saw* is used for dividing logs transversely. The *Pit Saw*, a long blade of steel with large teeth, and a transverse handle at each end, is used for sawing logs into planks or scantlings. The *Frame Saw* is a blade from five to seven feet long, used in a similar manner to the pit saw, but it causes less waste, because the blade, being stretched in a frame, may be made much thinner. The *Ripping Saw*, *Half Ripper*, *Hand Saw*, and *Pannel Saw*, are saws for the use of one person, the blades tapering in width from the handle. *Tenon Saws*, *Sash Saws*, *Dovetail Saws*, &c., are made of very thin blades of steel, of equal width throughout their whole length, and stiffened with stout pieces of iron or brass fixed on their back edges. *Compass Saws* and *Key Hole Saws* are long narrow saws, tapering from about an inch to an eighth of an inch in width, used for making curved cuts. Small *Frame Saws* and *Bow Saws*, in which very thin narrow blades are tightly stretched, are occasionally used for cutting both wood and metal. Saws are made for cutting bone, iron, brass, and many other hard substances.

The very commonest kind of saws are made of iron-plates, hammer-hardened, and planished upon an anvil, to give them some degree of stiffness and elasticity. The more useful saws are made either of shear or cast steel. The steel, reduced to thin sheets, is cut into pieces of suitable size and shape. The edges are perfected by filing, and holding the flat sides of the plates against large grindstones, which process prepares them for the cutting of the teeth. This operation is usually performed by a die-cutter in a fly-press, the motion of the saw-plate being duly regulated, so that the teeth shall be uniform; the larger teeth being cut one at a time; and the smaller, two, three, or more at a time, according to circumstances. The wire edges left on the teeth by the cutting-out press are removed by filing, after which the plates undergo the processes of hardening and tempering. The next operation is planishing by hammers, to make them more even and equally elastic; after which the saws are ground on large grindstones. The plate is held against the circular face of the stone by an interposing board, against which the grinder presses with all his force, in order to grind it as evenly as possible. He stands on tip-toes, stretching over the stone, which revolves with great rapidity; his hands, arms, breast, and knees being all brought into action to produce the desired effect. As this grinding impairs the flatness and elasticity of the saw-plates, they are submitted to a second hammering by the planishers, and their elasticity is restored by heating them over a coke fire until they attain a faint straw colour. The marks of the hammer are removed by again passing the saws lightly over a grindstone, after which the final polish is given by a fine hard stone, a glazing wheel covered with buff-leather and emery, or a wooden wheel, called the *Hard Head.* After being cleaned by women, the saws are handed to the *Setter*, who lays each alternate tooth over the edge of a small anvil, and strikes them so as to bend each uniformly into a slight deviation from the plane of the saw, and then, turning the saw-plate, he sets the remaining teeth in like manner, but in the opposite direction: sometimes peculiar tools are used for this setting. After being set, the saw is placed between two plates of lead, in a vice, and the teeth are sharpened with a triangular file. The size, form, and sharpness of the teeth, vary according to the purpose to which the saw is to be applied. The handles are then fixed on by nuts and screws, and the saws cleaned off, oiled, and packed in brown paper for sale.

Saws for cutting stone are without teeth, although they are sometimes slightly notched upon the cutting edge, that they may collect and retain the particles of sand that are conducted into the cut by a small current of water, and by the attrition of which the effect is mainly produced. The saw plate is tightly stretched in a kind of rectangular frame, of which it forms the lower side; and the frame, being suspended by ropes, is moved backwards and forwards by one or two men.

The saw manufacture is one of the most interesting departments of the industry at Sheffield. Saws are made in that town to an immense extent.

SAW MILLS. Although saw mills have not been very generally introduced till within a few years, they are by no means of recent origin. They were used in England in the 17th century, but not without great opposition. Many of the earlier saw mills were driven by water, and those of North America are still generally worked by that power.

The earliest kind of sawing-machinery was, in its essential features, the same as that still used for sawing logs of timber into planks. In this machine the saws are stretched in a frame which slides up and down on vertical guides; the reciprocating motion being imparted to the frame by a crank upon an axle turned by a connection with the water-wheel or other prime mover. The log is supported on a carriage resting upon rollers, and is made to advance a little at each stroke of the saws, which cut during their descent only. The saws are usually either six or eight in number. Attempts have been made to introduce sawing machines with two sets of saws, one of which should cut upwards; but they do not appear to have succeeded. A similar effect is sometimes produced by connecting two machines with one axle; the cranks being so adjusted that one saw-frame descends while the other rises.

The balks of timber to be divided into planks, of which two are generally operated upon simultaneously, are supported by rollers, and secured at the ends by suitable fastenings to a long iron carriage. This carriage is so connected to the saw frame by wheel and pinion work, that the carriage and balks of timber are propelled forward as fast as the wood is cut. In order to keep the balks of timber steady during the cut, their inner sides slide against polished steel plates fixed to the frame work of the machine, against which they are pressed by rollers.

The loss of power occasioned by the reciprocating motion of a long saw, has led to the adoption of *Circular Saws*, which, by revolving constantly in one direction, require less power, and may be driven with far greater speed than reciprocating saws; while their continuous action not only expedites the operation of sawing, but also makes the motion of the machinery more uniform. Perhaps the most interesting kind of circular saw is that used for cutting logs of hard wood into veneers. The late Sir M. I. Brunel, to whom England is indebted for many valuable improvements in this class of machinery, took out a patent in 1806 for a method of constructing very large circular saws, by attaching several pieces of steel-plate to a flanch of iron turned perfectly true. In this way saws have been made of as much as 18 feet diameter; but such large saws can only be used for cutting veneers or very thin boards, which will easily bend so as to pass the flanch of the saw, which is necessarily of considerable thickness. In the principal room for cutting veneers at the City Saw Mills, London, there are eight saws varying from 8 to 17 feet diameter, and revolving from 70 to 90 times in a minute. By the largest saws logs of mahogany 3 feet square can be cut up into unbroken sheets of veneer, at the rate of about 10 to an inch, and so beautifully smooth as to require scarcely any dressing.

For cutting thinner boards, the circular saw is usually mounted in a bench or table, under which the axle passes, and having a slit or opening through which the upper part of the saw projects. The piece of wood to be cut is laid on the smooth surface of the table, and pushed towards the saw by hand. Small circular saws, so mounted, are often moved by means of a treadle and crank, and by a variety of ingenious modifications may be applied to many useful purposes.

In the beautiful and ingenious block machinery erected at Portsmouth, by Brunel, circular saws are extensively applied. [BLOCK MACHINERY.

Mr. Eastman, of the United States, patented some curious modifications of sawing machinery about 1824. He found that when a circular saw is propelled with great velocity, it will cut much more smoothly and easily if it have only a few teeth placed at equal distances round its circumference than if, as usual, its periphery be full of teeth. He made a saw which had four cutting instruments called section teeth, each consisting of two teeth resembling a hawk's bill in form. The saving of labour as compared with a common saw is estimated at full three-fourths, and it is stated that, when driven at a proper speed (which is from a thousand to twelve hundred revolutions per minute), it will cut nine or ten inches in depth into the hardest white oak timber with the greatest ease. Mr. Eastman contrived these saws for cutting up timber in an ususual way, not through the log, but from the circumference to the centre; so that the cuts form the radii of a circle, and the planks or boards produced are thicker at the outer than the inner edge. The boards cut by this machinery are much used for covering buildings.

SAXE; SAXONY. The numerous German states thus designated, present various degrees of industrial and commercial developement. We will rapidly glance at them in relation to these features.

Saxe Altenburg is hilly, richly wooded, and fertile. Agriculture and grazing are skilfully conducted. There are few minerals; but there are iron-mines in the vicinity of Ronneburg, and the extensive peat-fields near Altenburg yield abundance of fuel. A fine porcelain earth is found in the neighbourhood of Altenburg, which supplies the porcelain manufactory at Gotha. Manufacturing industry is chiefly confined to woollen cloths, stockings, and wooden wares. There are considerable tanneries at Altenburg, Kahla, Eisenberg, and Lukau. The articles of export are corn, cattle, wool, butter, and timber.

Saxe Coburg Gotha is chiefly an agricultural duchy. The forests yield timber, potash, and pitch. The rearing of live-stock is prosecuted with much activity. Iron is found near Friederichsstadt; there are also coals, sandstone, millstones, marble, alabaster, gypsum, lime, potters' clay, porcelain earth, and salt. There is considerable manufacturing industry in Gotha, but little in the other districts. Besides a fair amount of export trade, the duchy has a considerable transit trade, as the high road from Leipzig to Frankfort passes through it.

Saxe Meiningen has salt springs near Friedrichshall and Neusulza. The productions are similar to those of central Germany; the minerals are various and abundant. Agriculture and grazing are the chief employments. In some districts there are many furnaces, mills, and glass-houses. The ordinary manufactures are coarse linens, sail-cloth, woollens, and cottons; there are also distilleries, breweries, and tan-yards. The wooden toys made in this duchy are largely sold in England.

In *Saxe Weimar* the mineral and vegetable productions are similar to those in the other Saxon duchies. The rearing of cattle forms an important branch of industry. Manufactures have made little progress.

Saxony, being a kingdom and of much larger size, has more manufacturing and commercial importance than the duchies just named. The vegetable produce, besides corn, includes rape-seed, hops, flax, hemp, chicory, tobacco, madder, wood, saffron, medicinal herbs, anise, coriander, poppy, &c. Vegetables and fruit are very abundant. A considerable quantity of wine is made. Almost a fourth part of the country is covered with forests, consisting chiefly of pine and fir; other trees are less abundant.

The breed of cattle has been very much improved within the last century; but the most important animal is the Merino sheep, which has since 1765 yielded a supply of the finest wool. The mineral riches consist of gold, copper, iron, lead, tin, cobalt, arsenic, vitriol, bismuth, nickel, zinc, antimony, quicksilver, calamine, rock crystal, various precious stones, potters'-earth, the finest porcelain clay in Europe, basalt, serpentine, granite, marble, alabaster, fluor spar, sandstone, limestone, slate, porphyry, black amber, brimstone, alum, saltpetre, and coals.

Next to England and the Netherlands, Saxony has, in proportion to its population, the most extensive manufactures in Europe. It produces damasks and other linens, lace of great beauty, woollen, cotton, and silk manufactures; and there are paper-mills, tanneries, breweries, distilleries, foundries, and the celebrated porcelain works at Meissen. The centre of the commerce of the country is Leipzig. The inland trade is mostly conducted by the merchants of Leipzig, of which the book fairs are the most remarkable. The principal exports are—fine woollen manufactures to England, Spain, Turkey, and Russia; linen, lace, &c. to Italy, England, Spain, and France; thread, wool, worsted, smalts, porcelain, straw-manufactures, wooden-wares, glass, fruit, timber, and mineral products. The imports are salt, cotton, silk, flax, hemp, colonial produce, salt and dried fish, fancy goods, &c. Saxony is one of the members of the Zollverein or German Customs' Union.

Prussian Saxony, another member of the remarkable Saxe territories, is an active and busy province. The fine wool of the improved breed of sheep supplies not only the extensive woollen manufactures of the province, but furnishes a large overplus for exportation. The mineral products are chiefly copper, antimony, cobalt, and iron. The manufactures are woollens, leather, calico, and linen. There are several sugar-refineries, brandy-distilleries, tobacco-manufactories, and porcelain works. The exports are wool, corn, woollen and cotton manufactures, brandy, copper, iron and steel wares, and salt.

SCAFFOLDING. In ordinary buildings the scaffolding requires very little notice. Poles are erected in a vertical position a few feet from the walls, their lower ends being inserted in the ground. Wherever a platform is required for the workmen, a horizontal pole is tied to the uprights, parallel with the wall; and from this horizontal pole cross-pieces extend to the wall, into which their ends are received, to support a flooring of planks. As the building rises, the scaffold is strengthened by diagonal poles; and the several poles are fastened by ropes.

In the erection of important buildings of stone, a very convenient kind of scaffold has been recently adopted, consisting of large squared timbers well framed together, and terminating at the top in horizontal beams. Such a framing is erected on each side of the wall, unconnected with it, and rails are laid on the top beams, on which runs a carriage, capable of being moved by means of a winch-handle connected with the wheels. The carriage itself consists of a frame supporting another railway at right angles with that on which it runs; and on the upper railway is a smaller carriage, which supports tackle suitable for raising the stones. By this arrangement a stone may be lifted up, and moved, by the combined action of the two railways, to any point required on the wall.

In bridge building and similar works, the *centering* of arches is a peculiar kind of scaffolding; it is the wooden support or mould on which the arch rests while building. A centering usually consists of a number of distinct frames, resembling the trusses of a roof, placed equidistant from each other in vertical planes, and covered with a series of planks or beams of timber called bridging-joists, laid at right angles with the frames or trusses. This boarding or covering of bridgings forms a convexity coinciding with the internal concavity of the intended arch. For small arches the centering is usually covered with planks; but in large works bridging-joists, one laid for each course of arch-stones, are preferred, these being kept at the proper distance apart by blocks placed between them. The whole structure is stiffened by crossbars to keep the trusses equidistant and parallel to each other.

Mr. Hughes has invented a scaffolding, which he used for repairing the interior of a dome at Manchester. It consists of a vertical pole erected in the centre of the dome, to which is connected a framework, supporting a kind of ladder, corresponding with the form of the interior of the dome, and mounted on wheels, so that it may be moved round to any part of it, the vertical pole serving as an axis. Mr. Slacks, a mason, has invented a scaffolding for building an obelisk without scaffolding of the ordinary description. This simple and ingenious machinery was used in erecting an obelisk of sandstone, 100 feet high, not including the foundation, on the summit of a mountain called Whitaw, in Dumfriesshire, in honour of the late Major-General Sir John Malcolm. The Society of Arts rewarded the inventor with their gold Isis medal in 1837.

The finest scaffolding ever invented, perhaps, is that which now surmounts the Victoria tower at the New Houses of Parliament. It is made to travel upwards as the work progresses; and it revolves on a central axis, so that four extended arms of scaffolding may be brought over every part of the tower in turn.

If the scaffolding just mentioned is the most complete, perhaps that by which Messrs. Fox and Henderson have built the Crystal Palace is the most simple—so simple, indeed, that it can hardly be called a scaffolding; it is rather a system of ropes and pulleys.

SCAGLIO'LA, is an incrustation of artificial composition which is applied to columns, and produces the most perfect imitation of marble, from which it can hardly be distinguished either by the eye or the touch, as it takes an equally high polish and feels equally hard and cold. Scagliola has long been in use in Italy; but it was not introduced into this country before the latter half of the last century. The earliest application of it was in the columns of the Pantheon, in Oxford-street, London, built by James Wyatt. The composition or cement itself is prepared from the purest gypsum, which is first broken into small pieces, and after being calcined is reduced to powder. It is then passed through a fine sieve, and mixed with Flanders glue, isinglass, &c. In this state it is mixed up with colouring matter of the hue required.

SCANTLING, is a term used to express the transverse dimensions of a piece of timber; and also, in some cases, as a general name for small timbers, such as the quartering for a partition, rafters, purlins, or pole-plates in a roof, &c. All quartering or squared timber under five inches square is designated scantling. In masonry the same word is used to express the size of stones in length, breadth, and thickness.

SCARFING, is the name which carpenters give to the mode of joining two pieces of timber end to end, in such a manner that they may appear but one, and cannot be pulled asunder by a force applied in the direction of their length, without breaking off part of the wood at the joint. The scarfed pieces are usually bolted together; but there are various modes of forming the junction.

SCARIFIER. There are instruments used in agriculture, to which the names *scarifier*, *scaffler*, and *cultivator* are applied; and indeed other names have been also applied to them, according to slight modifications of form and action. All these instruments have a number of teeth or tines which, when the instrument is drawn forward, furrows and loosens the soil. One such is called the *Thirteen-hoed* scarifier, in which there are two large wheels for the movement of the machine, two handles behind to guide it, and thirteen hoes or tines to enter the soil. Another kind, *Williams' wrought iron scarifier*, has one small wheel in front, two small wheels behind, two handles for guidance, and seven tines.

SCARLET DYE. The finest scarlet dye is obtained from cochineal. [COCHINEAL.] According to Berthollet the dyeing of scarlet is performed at two operations; the first is called the boiling (*bouillon*), and the second the *reddening*.

For a boiling intended to dye about 100 pounds of cloth, six pounds of bitartrate of potash (cream of tartar) are first thrown into water a little more than lukewarm; after the bath has been well stirred, and become a little hotter, half a pound of powdered cochineal is thrown in and well mixed. Immediately afterwards five pounds of clear solution of chloride (muriate) of tin are poured in and carefully mixed. As soon as the bath begins to boil, the cloth is introduced, and made to circulate rapidly two or three times; when it has been subjected to a boiling heat for two hours, it is removed and well washed.

For preparing the second bath, which is the *reddening*, five pounds and a half of powdered cochineal are put into a boiler, as soon as the water which it contains is about to boil, and after being properly mixed, fourteen pounds of solution of chloride of tin are added, and the cloth is thrown in, rapidly whirled for a short time, then boiled for an hour, taken out, cooled, and washed and dried.

SCENE-PAINTING, for the theatre, is executed in *distemper*, that is, with colours mixed up with size, the design being first sketched, and accurately laid down to scale, from which the perspective outlines are transferred to the larger surface. Instead of beginning with dead colouring and then gradually working up his picture, the artist puts in all his effects at once (as in fresco-painting) —the full tone of the lights and shadows finishing as he proceeds, and merely retouching those parts afterwards which require additional depth or brilliancy. It is important that the scene-painter should not only be well skilled in architectural delineation, but also well informed as to the styles of different countries and periods.

Much of the effect of scenery depends upon a skilful mode of lighting it; in which respect considerable improvements have taken place of late years, and the light is now occasionally thrown from above, as well as from the sides and the foot-lights. A variety of mechanical contrivances have also been brought to great perfection so as to imitate particular effects in the most deceptive manner, such as those of moonlight, where the moon breaks through the clouds and gleams upon water, &c.; changes of the sky from clear to stormy, or the contrary; the sudden glare of fire, &c.

With the exception of the Drop-Scene, which is let down between the acts, and is a single picture, the scenes of a theatre generally consist of several parts: of narrow upright pieces called Side-Scenes, or Wings; of Hanging-Scenes, painted to imitate a sky or ceiling; and of the Back-Scenes, which are either rolling scenes, let down from above, or Flats, which are pushed on from the sides, and meet in the centre. There are various other smaller portions of scenery used occasionally for balconies, &c.; and many other contrivances and arrangements in order to produce pictorial effect.

SCHLESWIG and HOLSTEIN. These Danish provinces, which have for the last three years been a scene of so much political contention, present but moderate attractions in respect to industry and commerce.

Schleswig produces corn, pulse, flax, hemp, rape-seed, hay, clover, garden vegetables, and potatoes; and exports much agricultural produce, live stock, and fish. Wood is scarce, both for building and fuel. The country contains limestone, chalk, and slate, but no metallic minerals. The chief occupations of the inhabitants are agriculture, the breeding of cattle, and the fisheries. The manufactures, though varied, are not of large extent. In the town of Schleswig there are manufactures of china, earthenware, lace, cambrics, thread, leather, sailcloth, woollens, starch, and refined sugar.

Holstein is on the whole fertile, especially in the marsh-lands which border on the German Ocean and the Elbe. The mineral products are, in the vicinity of Oldeslohe, salt, lime, and plaster of Paris, and near the Baltic, amber; but there are no metals. The surface is in many parts strewed with boulder stones. The agricultural products are corn, pulse, potatoes, some hops, flax, and hemp. There are no manufactures that need any particular notice. The exports consist of corn, timber, horses, cattle, butter, and turf; the imports, of colonial produce, wines, and manufactures. The herring fishery, and the Greenland whale and sea fishery, are a source of considerable profit. Trade is greatly facilitated by the Holstein or Kiel Canal, made in the years 1777-1784, at the expense of above two millions and a half of dollars, to form a communication between the German Ocean and the Baltic.

SCOTLAND. Under various headings, such as GLASGOW, LANARK, &c., a few industrial statistics relating to Scotland will be found; and we here append a few others which relate to the country as a whole.

The factory statistics of Scotland in 1850 presented the following features. There were 168 cotton factories, in 10 counties; they had 1,683,093 spindles, 23,564 power looms, 7,712 horse power (steam), 2,842 horse power (water wheels), and 36,325 factory operatives, of whom no less than 27,528 were females. There were 182 woollen factories, 6 worsted factories, 189 flax factories, and 5 silk factories. The total numbers for all these five kinds of textile materials, in the whole of Scotland, presented the following results:—

Factories	550	
Spindles	2,256,403	
Power looms	23,811	
Moving power—		
Steam	13,857	19,861 horse power.
Water	6,004	
Operatives—		
Male	22,140	75,688
Female	53,548	

The Iron manufacture in Scotland in 1848 amounted in quantity to 539,962 tons, at 130 blast furnaces. The largest number of furnaces at one establishment was 16, at Messrs. Baird's iron works at Gartsherrie.

The quantities of exciseable articles made in Scotland in 1850 were as follow:—

Bricks	2,679,533 number.
Malt	4,639,159 bushels.
Paper	28,600,019 lbs.
Soap	22,996,251 lbs.
Spirits	7,132,556 gallons.

In 1848 the gross receipt of customs in Scotland was 2,040,840*l.*—rather less than in Ireland. Considerably more than half the amount was taken at the Clyde ports.

SCREEN. Screens are exceedingly beautiful internal features in the Gothic or pointed style of architecture; in which they were employed for a variety of purposes, not in churches alone, but in halls and other buildings. Great diversity is displayed in them as regards both design and material; for we meet with them sometimes solid or nearly so, at others almost entirely of open work; of stone or of timber, and occasionally composed of both; but agreeing in being more or less elaborately decorated. The Organ Screens, Altar Screens, Tomb Screens, &c. in some of our cathedrals and churches, are exquisite specimens of taste and workmanship. Screens of a different character were employed in the halls of domestic and collegiate buildings, for the purpose of cutting off a passage leading to the butteries and offices. Such screens were almost invariably of oak or other wood, and the space over them and the passage behind served as a music gallery. As a revival of mediæval taste, many beautiful examples of screen work have been sent to the Great Exhibition.

SCREW. This mechanical power generally consists of two parts, one of which is a solid cylinder of wood or metal, on whose convex surface is formed a projecting rib or fillet, frequently called a thread, which passes spirally round in such a manner as constantly to make equal angles with lines parallel to the axis of the cylinder. The other is a cylindrical perforation through a block of some material, the surface of the perforation having on it a spiral groove corresponding to the projecting rib or fillet on the solid cylinder. The first of these parts is called a convex screw, and the other a concave screw. When the two parts are in action, the convex screw, being turned round in the other by a power applied at its surface, moves at the same time rectilinearly in the direction of its axis: occasionally however the convex screw is fixed, and then the other being turned about, it acquires at the same time a like rectilinear motion.

As a mechanical power, the screw possesses the property of an inclined plane. In practice, a lever or wheel is always fixed perpendicularly to the axis, and the moving or sustaining power is applied near the outer extremity of the lever, or at the circumference of the wheel.

An *Endless Screw* consists of two or more spiral fillets or threads on a rod which is capable of being turned on its axis by a power applied to the handle of a winch, or to a string passing over the circumference of a pulley attached to the rod. The threads work between teeth on the circumference of a wheel, so that, while the revolution of the rod continues, the wheel turns on its axis. A *Double-Threaded Screw* is one in which a fillet is formed upon each of two continuous spiral lines on the surface of the cylinder; the two making equal angles with lines parallel to the axis. With apparently an equal distance between the threads on both screws, the power of the single-threaded screw is double that of the other. From the high ratio which the resistance bears to the moving power in the screw, the use of this machine for moving or compressing bodies is very great; it is also extensively employed in the construction of philosophical instruments for measuring small angles or distances. [MICROMETER.]

A *Differential Screw* consists of one convex screw which works in the interior of another convex screw. The latter works in a concave screw, which is fixed; and the former is capable of moving in a rectilinear direction only, being prevented from turning on its axis with the rotation of the exterior screw. Also the number of threads in an inch on the convex surface of this last is less by one than the number in an inch on the convex surface of the other. Thus, if the exterior screw have 100 threads in an inch, and the interior screw 101 threads, then one turn of the machine will cause the latter to move through the very minute extent of $\frac{1}{10100}$ inch, and this space may be further subdivided by means of a micrometer head applied to the exterior screw.

SCREW-JACK, is a portable machine for raising great weights by the agency of a screw. The apparatus introduced under the name of the Universal Screw Jack is particularly useful on railways, where it affords a simple means of lifting a carriage or engine that may have run off the rails, and then moving it laterally until the wheels are in their proper position over the rails.

SCREW MANUFACTURE. In the infancy of screw making the thread was formed with a file; but this process has long been superseded by the use of dies and cutters, which are applied in various ways. The cutting of the worm is sometimes performed in a lathe, the blank being fixed in a chuck, and projecting during its revolution between a pair of stationary cutters; the longitudinal motion of the blank, and consequently the size or inclination of the thread, being determined by a regulating or pattern screw attached to the mandril, which must therefore be changed for every different degree of fineness; while the shape of the thread or worm depends on the form and position of the cutters. Small screws are frequently wormed by a similar apparatus turned by a winch-handle attached to the mandril; and sometimes by means of a steel tap-plate. Many patented improvements have been introduced in this manufacture, chiefly in relation to the cutting of the worm. Several attempts have been made to produce screws by casting; but not with much success.

Screw-Bolts and other screws for working in metal are manufactured in a similar manner to common screws when the number required is sufficient to justify the expense of adjusting the machinery. When this is not the case, they are, if small, often cut by hand, without the aid of a lathe. In the screwing of metal work, there are required two portions, the external and the internal screw: these require contrary processes in their manufacture.

In cutting screws in wood, an internal wooden screw is cut by an external screw of iron or steel, and an external wooden screw by an internal screw of iron or steel: the cutter or *tap* being shaped according to the kind of screw to be produced.

The large iron screws used in vices, presses, waggon-jacks, &c., are sometimes formed by means of dies, turned with immense power by very long levers; the thread being made without cutting, by indenting and squeezing up the metal. The very best scrap-iron is required for the screws formed in this manner, on account of the twisting force to which they are subjected.

In the ordinary method of cutting screws in a lathe, the size of the worm, or the distance between the threads, is regulated by a pattern screw, and cannot be varied from it; but an ingenious machine is used in the Woolwich dockyard for cutting a great variety of different screws from one pattern.

Birmingham is the great seat of the screw-manufacture; millions of dozens are made in that town yearly.

SCREW PILES. [Lighthouses].

SCREW-PRESS. In the common Screw-Press the articles to be subjected to compression are laid upon a horizontal bed, forming the base of a strong frame, in the upper cross-bar or *head* of which a nut is firmly secured. The screw works up and down in this nut, and to its lower end is attached the *follower*, or moving piece which presses on the upper surface of the substance operated upon. The connection between the screw and this piece is such that the follower rises and falls, but does not turn round with the point of the screw; and the steady motion of the follower is provided for by making it fit closely to the side-pieces or cheeks of the press, which therefore act as guides. The screw is turned by a long iron lever. The screws of presses were formerly made of wood, but they are now almost uniformly made of iron.

While the diminution of the size of the thread affords the means of increasing the power of a screw-press, by reducing the distance traversed by the point of the screw during each revolution, it is attended with the serious disadvantage of diminishing its strength. This difficulty may be avoided by the use of a double or differential screw. [Screw.]

SCREW PROPELLER. From the time of Archimedes it has been known that a revolving screw may be made the means of raising water; and it has also been known that a peculiar resistance to the motion of a solid in a liquid results from the revolution of a screw. A most important application of this principle has been made within the last few years to steam navigation; the *screw steam ships* wholly depend upon it.

The first vessel fitted with a screw propellor was a yacht, in which the screw was fitted into the dead-wood, between the keel and the stern-post; the screw consisted of a helix, making but one revolution around a horizontal axis passing longitudinally through the ship; and it was put in motion by a steam engine. The absence of the ponderous paddle wheels and paddle boxes of an ordinary steamer greatly improves the sailing qualities of a screw-propelled vessel; while the arrangement of the machinery may be such as to render the vessel far more commodious, and, if desired, to leave the upper decks open from end to end. The usual position of the screw propeller, immediately before the stern post, does not appear either to be disadvantageous to the application of the propelling power, or to interfere with the action of the rudder. An important use to which screw propellers have been advantageously applied, is as an auxiliary power, for occasional use during calms and contrary winds for vessels which are ordinarily moved by sails alone; such auxiliary screws have been supplied to some of the Arctic ships.

The most notable screw steamer ever constructed was the *Great Britain*. It was 320 feet long by 50 broad. The burthen was about 3000 tons; and the engines, consisting of four cylinders of 88 inches diameter by 72 inches stroke, were of 1000 horse power. It had a screw propeller 15½ feet in diameter, with six arms, mounted in the stern, and capable of being turned with great rapidity by the engine. After making four passages across the Atlantic, she was fitted with a new and much stronger propeller, weighing seven tons, of the same diameter as before, but consisting of only four arms or vanes. The subsequent disasters of this noble vessel are well known to most newspaper readers.

After varied experiments and trials a commercial company took up the subject of Screw Steam Navigation; and important results seem likely to follow. The company, formed in 1846, built two screw steamers, of 272 tons each for the Holyhead and Dublin trade. Two other vessels of 320 tons were afterwards added. In 1848 the company was remodelled, and commenced operations on a larger scale. Four screw steamers, from 450 to 560 tons, were built for the trade between England and Constantinople, and performed the service very satisfactorily. In 1850 the company entered upon a contract with the admiralty, for a monthly mail to the Cape of Good Hope; the first screw steamer started on this service on Dec. 18, 1850, and returned to Plymouth on March 12, 1851; and in respect to time and accommodation, the service is considered to have been amply performed. The company are now organizing arrangements for an extension of the system to Mauritius, Ceylon, Madras, and Calcutta; and should this be carried out, it is next contemplated to make a farther extension to the Australian colonies. It is calculated that screw steamers of 1700 tons burden and 300 horse power would reach Sydney from England in 64 days; and such vessels are now being built.—There seems much probability that the recent perplexities concerning an Australian mail will be solved by the success of the screw steamers.

There are also screw steamers in the Royal Navy. Screw steamers have just been started from Glasgow to London—a distance of about 800 miles, whether taken north or south. In April of the present year the first screw steamer started from Glasgow to New York, an entirely new steam route. An American Company are building screw steamers of very large burden, expressly for the emigrant traffic from Liverpool to New York.—Such are the energetic proceedings which the success of the Screw Propeller has engendered.

See further in respect to steam navigation under STEAM VESSEL.

We may here mention that attempts have been made to propel vessels by ejecting water from the stern. A propeller of this curious kind was patented by Mr. Purkis in 1840, and was tried on a boat of large size in the Thames.

SCULPTURE, in its strict sense, is the art of carving or cutting any material into a proposed form or shape. In its more general acceptation it is the art of representing objects by *form;* and is thus applied to carving, modelling (or the plastic art), casting, whether in metal or other materials, and to gem-engraving. Sculpture is practised in various ways; namely, in forming entire or insulated figures, as statues or groups, called, in technical language, 'the round;' or in representing objects more or less raised without their being entirely detached from a background. This latter is termed 'relief,' and the degrees of relief are defined by modern writers and artists by the expression *alto-rilievo,* when the object is so salient as to be nearly round; *basso-rilievo,* when it is slightly raised from the background; and *mezzo-rilievo,* when a medium is preserved between the extremely high and the very flat relief. There is another variety of this manner of working basso-rilievo, which is only or chiefly found in Egyptian sculpture; the outline is sunk into the plane or ground, and the parts are then formed and rounded on the principle of basso-rilievo. By this mode of working there is usually no projection beyond the profile or face of the original ground; to gain effect therefore in this kind of *relieved intaglio,* the Egyptian artists frequently painted the sculpture.

The materials for modelling used by the ancients, were clay, wax, and plaster. The clay model was usually baked, by which it acquired a hardness scarcely inferior to stone. These *terra cotta* works were generally painted. The materials used for carved works comprised every substance, hard or soft, that could by any possibility be employed for the purpose. The Egyptians, whose great objects were to render their works durable, chiefly employed porphyry, basalt, and granite. For casting—gold, silver, copper, lead (and their compounds) wax, and plaster, were all used. [BRONZE; FOUNDING.] *Polylithic Sculpture* was the name given to the combination of different marbles in the same work. When painting or colouring was resorted to it was called *Polychromic Sculpture.*

The consideration of the various schools and far-famed works of sculpture, as productions of genius and high art, lies beyond the range of the present volume; but the *mechanical* operations of sculpture come fittingly under notice here.

The technical or mechanical processes of sculpture are for the most part extremely simple. The sculptor usually begins by making a slight sketch of his subject, either drawing it on paper or at once modelling it on a small scale, in clay or wax. He next proceeds to build up his statue of the desired size. The first thing necessary is to construct a sort of nucleus, or skeleton, by which the clay may be supported. This is made of wood or iron, according to the strength required, and the limbs are usually made moveable by attaching the skeleton parts to the main support, or trunk, by wire joints. The figure is then built up in clay; and whether it is ultimately to be draped or not, it should always be modelled naked, in order that the true forms may be easily distinguished, and the drapery made to fall naturally. In modelling in relief, a plane, or ground as it is called, is prepared, upon which the sculptor carefully draws his design. The clay is then laid and pressed upon this, the outline of the figures being bounded by the lines of the drawing. When the work is completed it is cast in plaster

COLOURED-CLOTH HALL LEEDS.

HAND RAISING.

FIXING TEAZLES.

FULLING-STOCKS

KNIGHT'S CYCLOPÆDIA OF THE INDUSTRY OF ALL NATIONS.

No. 36.

of paris, by means of a mould taken in that material.

In copying a model in marble, the first step is to prepare two stones of the same size, or at least with an exactly corresponding graduated scale marked on the front of each, on which the block of marble and the model are respectively to be placed. The fronts of the two scales are so constructed or fitted up, that a 'pointing instrument' can be applied to them. This instrument is usually composed of a pole or standard, to which a long brass or steel needlo, capable of being extended and withdrawn, loosened or fixed, and moved in every direction by means of ball and socket joints, is attached. This is made to touch a particular part of the model. The whole instrument is then removed to the scale stone on which the rough block is placed, and the marble is cut away till the needle reaches as far into the block as it had been fixed at upon the model. A pencil mark is then made upon the two corresponding parts of the model and block, and thus what is technically called 'a point' is taken. This process is repeated till the uumerous points at fixed depths, corresponding throughout with the surface of the model, are attained, and a rough copy of the sculptor's original work is thus mechanically made. The practice of different sculptors has suggested various changes in detail; but the principle seems to be exactly similar in all. The statue being rudely blocked out or pointed, the marble is in this state put into the hands of a superior workman called a carver, who copies the minuter portions of the work by means of chisels of various sizes, rasps, and files; the pencil marks or points showing him the limits beyond which he is not to penetrate into the marble. When the carver has carried the work as far as the sculptor desires, he proceeds himself to give it the finishing strokes, by retouching and improving the details of form and expression, by producing varieties of texture and surface, and by giving that general quality or appearance to the whole which constitutes what is termed harmony of effect.

SEA WATER. [WATER.]

SEA WEEDS. A few details concerning the uses of various kinds of sea weeds will be found under ALGÆ; ARCHIL; ICELAND MOSS; KELP; LICHENS.

SEAL ENGRAVING. The cutting of the very hard stones or gems used for seals is effected chiefly by the use of small rapidly revolving wheels, the edges of which wear away the substance of the stone applied to them. Under the articles CAMEO; DIAMOND; GEM; INTAGLIO; LAPIDARY—will be found details sufficient to illustrate the general character of seal engraving.

SEALS; SEAL SKINS. These singular animals are captured eagerly, in seas and on coasts where they abound, for the sake of various useful services which they render. The species called the *Elephant Seal*, which is principally met with in the southern hemisphere, is the object of an extensive fishery, maintained for the sake of its skin and oil; and vast numbers are annually destroyed. The skin, though not valued for its fur, is extensively used for carriage and horse harness on account of its thickness and strength. The oil obtained is clear and inodorous, and is said never to become rancid, nor to give out any disagreeable savour in cooking. The quantity afforded by a large seal amounts to 1400 or 1500 lbs., for the blubber is often a foot deep. It is prepared like that of whales, excepting that the operation is performed on shore. This oil is employed in England chiefly in the manufacture of cloth; it is used to a considerable extent in China.

Many other species are valued for the skin, which has a beautiful fur when the animal is young. The *Walrus*, which is a species of seal, is highly valued; the tusks, the skin, and the oil are all commercially valuable; and the flesh is esteemed by the natives of Arctic regions.

Salted seal skins have recently been imported from Northern Europe, under circumstances which could not have occurred before the repeal of the Navigation Laws. Upwards of 45,000 were recently imported in one vessel from Denmark.

There were 753,141 seal skins imported in 1847; and 706,267 in 1848—chiefly from the Hudson's Bay Territories. They are used in making caps, and for various other purposes.

SECTOR (Drawing Instrument), is an apparatus which has the appearance of a small carpenter's rule marked with scales in every part; the greater number of these scales not being laid down parallel to the edges of the rule, but converging towards the pivot on which the moving arm of the rule turns while the instrument is opened. These converging scales only properly belong to the sector; the others are merely laid down for convenience on such blank spaces as are left by the converging or sectorial scales. The sector is, in principle, an aggregate of a large number of pairs of compasses packed up into one; each piece of the ruler being marked with the same scales.

The scales are so graduated as to facilitate many kinds of measurement and calculation, in geometrical and trigonometrical enquiries.

SEDLITZ. This is the name of a village

in the circle of Saaz in Bohemia, containing two bitter salt springs, from which the well-known salts called Sedlitz Powders are obtained. There are several such springs in the neighbourhood, including those at Seidschuz, in the circle of Leitmeritz. Above half a million of bottles of the water of Sedlitz and Seidschuz are annually sent to all parts of Germany.

SEEDS. Of those foreign seeds which are of sufficient importance to find a place in the Board of Trade tables, the following quantities were imported in 1848 :—

Carraway	7,266	Cwts.
Clover	99,813	„
Flax and Linseed ...	799,650	Qrs.
Onion	1,385	Cwts.
Rape	79,970	Qrs.
Tares............	48,929	„

Of most of these, the importation in 1850 was smaller than in 1848.

The economical uses of these seeds are described in other articles.

SEGAR MANUFACTURE. [CIGAR.]

SEINE. This important river of France connects Paris with the sea at Havre. By means of a lateral canal between Marcilly and Troyes, and locks to avoid the fall at Nogent, the river is navigable from Troyes to its mouth, a distauce of 370 miles. From Paris to Rouen it is navigated by small steamers and by barges 150 to 180 feet in length, 30 feet wide, and with a draft of 6 feet. The tide ascends the Seine as far as Rouen, which city is accessible for vessels of 300 tons. Between Caudebec where the Seine begins to widen, and Quillebeuf, the navigation is dangerous, owing to the shoals and shifting sandbanks in the bed of the river. This has led to the undertaking of important works between Villequier and Quillebeuf, the object of which is to confine the river to a narrower bed by means of embankments ; a portion of this undertaking, completed in 1849, gave the satisfactory result of a deepened current, which soon swept its bed clear of sands. The importance of the navigation of the Seine may bo inferred from the fact that about 3500 sea-going ships enter and leave the ports of Havre and Rouen annually, besides a large number of coasters and small craft. Owing to the windings of the river its navigation is tedious. Steamers ply regularly between Havre, Rouen, and several other towns on the lower Seine. The articles of traffic on tho river include almost every description of agricultural, mineral, and industrial products, home, foreign, and colonial.

The river gives name to four of the departments of France; viz. *Seine*, *Seine Inférieure*, *Seine et Marne*, and *Seine et Oise.*

In the department of *Seine*, a large portion of the surface of the department is laid out in gardens, for the growth of kitchen vegetables, fruits, and flowers; wheat, barley, oats, and potatoes are grown in large quantities, considering the smallness of the area of the department; but little wine is made, and that little is all bad. Montmartre and most of the hills consist of accumulations of gypsum; excellent building stone is quarried under the southern quarters of Paris, and at various other points of the department; fine clays for porcelain and pottery, chalk, sand for glass foundries, &c., are raised. The manufactures comprise almost every woven fabric in wool, flax, cotton, and silk ; metallic articles ; jewellery, watches, and clocks ; glass, porcelain, furniture, hats, gloves, ribands, and small wares of all kinds ; scientific instruments, and chemical products of every description, &c. The commerce in these various products, and in agricultural produce, coal, timber, and firewood, raw materials of manufactures, cheoso, metals, salt, drugs, colonial produce, building materials, &c., is most extensive.

In the department of *Seine Inférieure*, hemp and flax are grown, especially along the coast between Fécamp and Havre; the hemp is almost exclusively used for making ropes and fishing nets. The department is remarkable for the vast number of its apple and pear trees. Great attention is paid to the rearing of horses, fat cattle, milch cows, and to the making of butter and cheese, both important articles of export. The Seine is valuable to fishermen for its abundance of salmon, sturgeon, sole, eels, &c. Large fleets of barks of 30 to 90 tons, and with crews varying from 15 to 30 in number, are employed in the mackerel, oyster, and herring fisheries. The minerals comprise marble, building and paving stone, chalk, flint, brickearth, potters' clay, sand used in glass factories, and marl. Iron mines were formerly worked near Forges. Peat is found. The department is famous for its industrial energy, which is exerted upon the spinning, dyeing, and weaving of cotton, wool, and flax; the manufacture of ginghams, cotton cloths, and calicoes of all kinds, broadcloth, flannel, sérge, linen, and mixed cloths of wool and cotton. The cotton manufactures had a great development previous to the revolution of 1848; since then it is said they have received some check. Hand-loom weaving is carried on in almost every hamlet and cottage, and frequently on a pressure of orders the raw material is sent into the neighbouring department to be worked up. The department is famous for its bleach works, which are conducted on the most modern principles, and turn out linen of a purer whiteness than those bleached in any other part of France. The linen woven about Fécamp is of the best quality. Cotton printing has had a great extension during the last thirty years. Among the other manufactured products may be mentioned lace, watch and clock movements, articles of ivory, pottery, window glass, bricks, &c. There are also numerous sugar refineries, silk-mills, manufactories of chemical products, metal foundries, tan-yards, ship-building yards, and other establishments in which industrial and commercial enterprise manifests itself on a large and important scale. The commerce carried on with the interior of France, with its colonies, with the whole of Europe, the West Indies, and America, is most extensive, and includes almost every article of French import and export. Of the manufacturing industry and important commerce of the department other details are given under DIEPPE, HAVRE, and ROUEN.

In the department of *Seine et Marne*, the wine produced is bad, although some of the finest grapes grown in the north of France are gathered in the neighbourhood of Fontainebleau. The forests, which cover more than one-sixth of the whole surface of the department, contain chiefly oak, beech, maple, and birch. Milch cows are numerous; veal calves are fed for the supply of Paris; cheese, known in Paris as *fromage de Brie*, is made in considerable quantity. The quarries of Château-Landon and Nemours furnish very beautiful building stone, of which a very large quantity is raised. Other mineral products are millstone grit, paving flints, alabaster, limestone, gypsum, potters' clay, and white sand. The industrial products include writing and printing paper, pottery and porcelain, cotton yarn and printed calicos, leather, window glass, &c. Glass globes and cylinders of the largest size are made at Bagneaux, near Nemours, and also optical and common glass; in the central prison at Melun various articles are manufactured by the prisoners. The commerce of the department is confined chiefly to agricultural produce, wool, cattle, wood, and charcoal for the supply of Paris.

In the department of *Seine et Oise*, great numbers of milch cows, chiefly house-fed, are kept for the supply of Paris and Versailles with milk. Market gardening is a profitable occupation, and is carried on extensively. Filberts, walnuts, figs, peaches, apricots, grapes, apples, and other common fruits are abundantly grown. About 17,000,000 gallons of poor wine are made annually. In the northwest of the department, where the vine does not flourish, apples and pears are grown for making cider and perry, the common drinks of the inhabitants of that district. The most important forests are those of St. Germain, Rambouillet, Dourdan, Senart, and Montmorency; they contain chiefly oak, birch, and maple, with some beech, chestnut, and hazel. The minerals include only building stone, gypsum, limestone, paving flints, millstone-grit, chalk, marl, and potters' and porcelain clay. The industrial energy of the department has been greatly developed since 1789, when the gunpowder works of Essonne (now established at Bouchet), and the porcelain and glass works of Sèvres, were the only important establishments it possessed. There are now numerous mills and factories at various points of the department, producing cotton, flaxen, silk, and woollen threads, calico, cotton and woollen hosiery, paper, chemical products, woollen cloth, soap, oil, refined sugar, porcelain, glass, saltpetre, beer, toys, crinoline, &c.; besides metal foundries, brick works, and above 800 wind and water mills, the greater number of which are scattered over the arondissements of Corbeil, Etampes, and Pontoise. In the prison of Poissy, various articles of jewellery, cutlery, and furniture are made by the prisoners. The commerce of the department is carried on chiefly with Paris, and consists of the agricultural and industrial products above mentioned.

SELE'NIUM. This non-metallic, solid, elementary body was discovered in 1818 by Berzelius in iron pyrites. It has a metallic lustre, and the appearance of lead when in mass; when reduced to powder it is of a deep brown colour. It is inodorous, moderately hard, may be readily scratched with a knife, is brittle as glass, and easily reduced to powder. Its fracture is conchoidal, and perfectly metallic. Its specific gravity is about 4·30. It is a bad conductor of heat, and a non-conductor of electricity. It softens at 212°, and may be drawn out into fine threads, which are transparent, and of a red colour by transmitted light. When heated above 212° it becomes fluid, and boils at 650°. Selenium is soluble in hot oils and melted wax. It combines with many of the elementary bodies; but none of the compounds have yet been of much use in the arts.

SENEFELDER, ALOIS, deserves to be remembered as the inventor of lithography. He was born at Prague in 1771; and having written two or three plays while yet a youth, he became desirous of procuring the necessary apparatus for printing his own works. Being too poor to gratify this desire, he endeavoured to discover some other mode of printing, but was defeated in several plans by want of means. The result of a variety of experiments, persevered in in spite of every difficulty, was his discovery, through an accident, of the art known as Lithography. [LITHOGRAPHY.] In order to raise money to carry out his idea, Senefelder enlisted as a private in the artillery, as a substitute for a friend, who promised him a premium of two hundred florins; but this plan was frustrated. While at Ingoldstadt, he was led to conceive the peculiar fitness of his new process for printing music. He continued struggling until 1799, when he obtained an exclusive privilege for Bavaria for fifteen years, and carried on a considerable business, employing his two brothers and two apprentices. Mr. André of Offenbach, now became his partner, and they commenced arrangements for obtaining patents and establishing presses in Vienna, London, Paris, and Berlin. While engaged in this project, he visited London, but without succeeding in his object. Unfortunate circumstances led to a hasty dissolution of this promising partnership in 1800; and political events also contributed to his embarrassments. In 1806 however an extensive lithographic establishment was formed at Munich, by Senefelder, in connection with Baron Aretin and others. This partnership lasted about four years, during which period a great number of works were executed; some of them for the government. Several other lithographic establishments were also in successful operation in 1809, when Senefelder obtained an engagement which rewarded him for the vicissitudes of the early part of his career. A royal lithographic office was formed about that time for printing the plans of a new survey of the kingdom, of which a great number were required. In 1809, he was appointed to the office of inspector, with a salary of fifteen hundred florins per annum, and permission to carry on his private business also. The subsequent improvements effected by Senefelder, such as the printing in colours, and upon linen, were attributed by himself to the ease and independence which this honourable engagement afforded.

SENEGAL SETTLEMENTS. On the banks of the Senegal and Gambia rivers in West Africa, different European governments have established settlements. These settlements in Senegambia (as the country is called) differ materially from those in other parts of the world. They are strictly commercial. The settlers have not acquired the property of any land, except the place on which they have settled, and no cultivation is carried on by them or their people, except at a few spots which are rather gardens than plantations. These settlements were originally established for the purpose of procuring negro slaves for the colonies in North America. The country however had other productions which were valued in Europe; and the natives of the interior were desirous of obtaining several articles of European manufacture, partly for their own consumption, and partly to sell them to the nations of Soodan. Accordingly these settlements were not abandoned on the abolition of the slave trade, like those on the coast of Guinea, and they continue in a thriving state. Each of the three European nations which have formed settlements has taken possession as it were of one of the three large rivers; the French of the Senegal, the English of the Gambia, and the Portuguese of the Rio Grande. Each has built a fortress on an island not far from the mouth of the river, which serves as a safe place of deposit for the goods imported, and thence the productions of the country are shipped. The merchants set out from these places in large river boats with their goods at certain seasons of the year, and ascend the rivers as far as they are navigable. They stop at certain points to which the natives bring their productions to exchange for European manufactures. In a few positions on the banks of the rivers small fortresses or blockhouses are erected, in which some black soldiers with two or three European officers are kept for the protection of commerce. Some merchants, particularly English and Portuguese, have formed commercial establishments not far from these fortresses in those villages which are advantageously situated for commerce. The French settlements are chiefly at St. Louis, Podhor, Bakel, and Goree. The English settlements are at Bathurst, Macarthy Island, and Fort St. James. The Portuguese settlements are at Bissao, Jeba, Bolula, Cacheo, and smaller ones in the interior. St. Louis, Bathurst, and Bissao, are flourishing towns.

Nearly all the articles of commerce which are exported from the European settlements in Senegambia are brought from the interior by small caravans or cafilas, which generally stop at certain places where commercial establishments are found, and take European merchandise in exchange for their goods. A considerable commerce is also carried on between Senegambia and the countries further east.

To such of the Senegambia settlements as belong to Great Britain, our exports in 1849 amounted in value to 35,770*l.*; consisting principally of clothing and firearms. These firearms were exchanged with the natives for the produce of the country.

SENNA. [Cassia.]

SENNAAR. In this little-known African country, situated between Egypt and Abyssinia, more industrial activity is displayed than might be expected. The branch of industry in which the Sennaarese are most distinguished is leather, which is of the best quality, and much superior to that made in Egypt or Syria; many useful articles are made of it by the natives. Where dates grow, cords and ropes are made of the fibrous interior bark of the palm date-tree, and in some places of reeds. Cotton cloth is made by the women for domestic use, but it constitutes also a considerable article of trade in Northern Africa, under the name of damour. The workers in gold, silver, and iron, are very skilful, and execute their work neatly with very simple tools. Pottery is made to a considerable extent; and also carved wooden vessels. In some places coloured straw hats are made with great neatness, and they are sent to different countries in the neighbourhood. An extensive foreign commerce is maintained at Sennaar. There is one caravan route to Cairo, two to the Red Sea, one south-westward to Begharmi, and another south-east to Alymuir. Few of the articles imported into Sennaar are brought from European markets; the imports are chiefly from various parts of Africa and Asia. The principal articles of export are slaves, the damour or cotton-stuff of Sennaar and Begharmi, gold, ivory, and ostrich feathers. The inland trade of Sennaar is very active, partly in consequence of the great number of caravans which continually traverse the country, and create a great demand for camels, which are brought to those places through which the caravans pass, and partly on account of the different productions of the several parts of the province.

SERAI is the name for a large building for the accommodation of travellers, common in Eastern countries. The word is Persian, and means 'a palace, the king's court, a large edifice;' hence *karávân-seraï*, a place of rest for caravans. In Turkey these buildings are generally called khans, from *khán*, another Persian word, which has a similar meaning.

SERAPHINE is a musical instrument of the keyed kind, in which very short, thin, and narrow steel bars, or springs, put into vibratory motion by means of a bellows acted on by the foot, are used instead of pipes. The principle on which the sounds are elicited is the same as in the Accordion and the Concertina. The Seraphine is in the form of a chiffonier, about thirty-seven inches high, forty wide, and twenty-two deep. Its compass is five octaves, including all the semitones, and it is played on in the same manner as an organ. In small churches, a Seraphine is often a welcome substitute for a more costly and bulky instrument.

SERPENT. This musical instrument consists of a long conical tube of wood covered with leather, having a mouth-piece, ventages, and keys, and bent in a serpentine form. The compass of the serpent is from B flat below the base staff, to G, the treble clef line, including every tone and semitone between these extremes. Its use is now nearly superseded by the Ophicleide.

SE'SAMUM. This genus of plants is valuable for the oil which it yields. *Simpsea* is the Egyptian and Arabian name of one of the species, remarkable for the quantity and quality of the oil expressed from its seeds. The oil is employed as an article of diet in Eastern nations, on which account the seeds form an article of commerce from India and Egypt in the present day. The oil is bland, of a fine quality, and will keep many years without becoming rancid; it is often used in India as a salad oil. The leaves of the plant are mucilaginous, and are employed for poultices.

SEWERS. Covered drains or sewers of great size, and of very solid construction, still exist under the streets of some ancient Roman cities, and especially of Rome itself. In modern times the sewers of London stand unrivalled for extent and excellent construction, although much yet remains to be done to render them adequate to the necessities of an immense and constantly-increasing population. Full one-third of the sewers in the City of London were made in the ten years preceding 1834. Until 1847 there were seven Boards of Commissioners of Sewers in the metropolis, each having control over a particular district. It was often found that great inconvenience and expense resulted from the want of agreement between these boards; and at length a Metropolitan Commission of Sewers was appointed by Act of Parliament. The Commission commenced its labours in 1847. It has control over the whole of the metropolis except the City; but the City Comission has agreed to act as far as possible in conjunction with it.

All the sewers constructed by the Metropolitan Commissions of late years are of such dimensions as to allow a man to pass through them, for the purpose of inspecting or cleansing them. The smallest sewers in the City of London division are about four feet three inches high by two feet three inches wide, the dimensions being increased according to circumstances, up to ten feet by eight feet. The water brought down by the Fleet River is conducted from Holborn Bridge by two sewers, from twelve to fourteen feet high, and six feet six inches wide, one on each side of Farringdon Street. These sewers unite, towards the mouth, into one passage about eighteen feet by twelve.

The bricks and cement in the London sewers are of the best quality; but the form of the sewers varies greatly; some engineers preferring one form, some another. Nearly all the modern sewers however, have an inverted arch at the bottom; and curved forms are also generally given to the sides and the top. In the metropolitan sewers the inclination varies from a quarter of an inch to an inch and a quarter in ten feet. In some cases it is very difficult to obtain sufficient inclination in a sewer, and still to make it deep enough to drain the basement story of neighbouring houses; which may be readily conceived from the fact that some parts of London are below the level of high water. Wherever it is practicable, new sewers are built at a considerable depth from the surface. The depth of that in Watling Street, in the City of London, which is an extraordinary case, is from thirty-three to thirty-five feet. In many cases however there is a space of not more than three feet between the surface of the roadway and the crown of the arch of the sewer. Where private drains are to be laid into a sewer for the purpose of draining houses, it is necessary that the lowest pavement of the floor of the building be at least four feet above the level of the sewer; because the house would otherwise be liable to be flooded with water from the sewer, when unusually full. Drains leading from private houses are usually of a circular form, and nine inches in diameter, though some are of greater size.

The construction of gulley-holes and shoots for conducting the surface drainage of the streets into the sewers varies considerably in different parts of the metropolis. It has been usual, until very recently, to make apertures, called *Man-Holes*, at convenient distances, to enable persons, when necessary, to enter and cleanse the sewers,; these apertures in some instances, are built in the form of oblong shafts of brickwork, up to within about eighteen inches of the surface of the road, and covered with cast-iron plates, over which the roadway is made good. A later and better plan is that of side entrances. These are passages extending from the side of the sewer to the foot pavement, through which they may at any time be entered by unlocking and opening a cover or trap-door consisting of pieces of flag-stone mounted in an iron frame. When a person enters the sewer by one of these openings the cover is held open by a self-acting catch, and an iron grating which admits light and air rises into its place, and serves to prevent any passenger from accidentally falling in. These entrances greatly facilitate the operation of *flushing* or cleansing the sewers. The necessary body of water for flushing is produced by simply accumulating the ordinary contents of the sewer, which may be done either by a cast-iron grate, fitting closely to a frame-work built into the sewer, and rising to the height that the head is required to be, or by a drop plank or gate of the same material, sliding up and down in nearly vertical grooves. In either case the apparatus may be managed, by means of the side entrances, with the greatest facility. The ordinary run of water in the sewers has hitherto been found sufficient for the purpose; but in case of its proving otherwise, a supply of water for flushing might be readily procured from the water companies.

The subject of the application of sewage refuse to the purposes of manure has recently attracted much attention. Two companies obtained acts of parliament, the one in 1846, and the other in 1847, under the designations of the 'Metropolitan Sewage Manure Company,' and the 'London Sewage Chemical Manure Company.' The plan of the former company was to collect the contents of some of the sewers of Westminster and Pimlico, and convey them by a deep underground channel to Hammersmith, where a steam-engine and other apparatus would distribute the manure in a liquid state to the market-gardens of that neighbourhood. The plan of the second company was to collect the contents of three sewers which now fall into the Thames between Vauxhall Bridge and Westminster Bridge, and, after allowing the liquid part to flow into the Thames, to deprive the refuse of its offensive smell, and sell it as manure in a solid state, Very little has been done, however, towards carrying out either of these plans.

Since the Metropolitan Commissioners of Sewers commenced their operations in 1847 many steps have been taken towards a comprehensive sewerage for the whole of the metropolis. A survey of the metropolis is now being made for the Commissioners by the officers belonging to the Ordnance Survey. The survey will extend to a distance of 8 miles in every direction from St. Paul's, comprising an area of about 201 square miles. On a scale of five feet to a mile, the results of this survey would fill 900 large sheets, and would form a magnificent map of London eighty feet in diameter. While the survey and map are in progress, the Commissioners have invited tenders of plans for a comprehensive sewerage of the metropolis. A very large number of such plans were sent in to the commissioners in the early part of the year 1850; many of these embracing an application of sewage refuse to the purposes of manure.

The Metropolitan Commissioners have not yet begun to develope their great system for the drainage of London; but they executed in 1850 many important works which will be made compatible with their larger scheme. They expended 70,000*l.* during the year in forming 6 miles of brick sewers, 16 miles of pipe sewers, 46 side entrances, 304 air shafts, 565 gullies, 1137 drain mouths, and various repairs. Besides the 21 miles of new sewers executed at the expense of the Commissioners, there were 13 miles constructed for, and paid for by, private parties. About 18,000*l.* had been expended by the end of the year in the survey of London. Of the 900 sheets about 400 are to be engraved, and the rest (the marginal or country district) left simply as drawn plans. Nearly all the 400 are now (April 1851) engraved; they are printed on sheets of double elephant paper, and are sold singly at two shillings each.

The Commissioners determined on the adoption of two comprehensive schemes of drainage for the Metropolis; they directed their engineers to prepare plans, and reports were made in August 1850 and January 1851, respecting the south and north drainages respectively. The general principle of these schemes is understood to be accepted by the Commissioners: the southern to be commenced before the northern, as being more urgently wanted. Without entering into details, it may suffice to say, that the object both of the north and the south drainage is to keep the Thames clear of sewage from Galleon's Reach upwards; to carry the sewers as much as possible under the public streets and places; to make them of dimensions and at gradiants ensuring an unintermittent flow; to secure good house-drainage, and self-cleansing street drainage; to dispense, as far as possible, with periodical flushing; and to provide means for the eventual removal of all open sewers, ditches, and cesspools. A portion of the great scheme for the southern side of the Thames has been already commenced between Kennington and the Old Kent Road. To give some idea of the magnitude of the operations which the Commissioners have under their control, it will suffice to say that 700 miles of existing sewer have been examined north of the Thames, and accurate plans and sections taken of every part of every sewer. It will farther illustrate the scale of these operations to bear in mind that the estimate of expense for the northern drainage alone is nearly a million and a quarter sterling.

SEXTANT. The Sextant is a valuable instrument for measuring angles in navigation and surveying. There were various earlier instruments by Davis, Hooke, Newton, Godfrey and others; but Hadley's Sextant, invented in 1730, superseded all previous contrivances.

The Sextant has a plane glass, called the *Index Glass*, silvered behind, and perpendicular to the face of the instrument. It is fixed on a centre perpendicular to the instrument, and moves with the *Index-Bar*, the end of which slides over a graduated arc. There is another plane glass, the lower half of which, next the instrument, is silvered, and the upper half left clear. It is called the *Horizon Glass* and should be parallel to the index glass when the index points to 0° at the beginning of the arc. The Sextant also has a telescope for viewing the objects observed; whereas in the common quadrants there is merely a plate with a small hole for directing the sight. Suppose a ray of light to proceed from the eye, it will proceed in the direction of the telescope, and if it falls on the upper or unsilvered part of the horizon glass, it will pass forward in a continued straight line until it falls upon some exterior object. But if the ray falls upon the silvered part of the horizon glass, it will be reflected to the index glass (the horizon glass is so placed as to make equal angles with lines from the eye and index glass), and again reflected from the index glass outwards (*i.e.* from the observer), until it meets some external object. Now instead of supposing the rays to pass from the eye, suppose them to come from external objects to the eye; then there will be two images presented at the same time, one formed by the rays which pass through the unsilvered part of the horizon glass, and another formed by the rays which have been previously reflected by the two glasses; and the graduated arc measures the angle between the glasses, and also the angle between the objects observed. The Sextant furnishes the means of measuring the angle between any two well-defined objects, in whatever direction they may be placed (so that the angle does not exceed 140°), and without requiring more steadiness than is necessary for seeing the objects distinctly. There are sets of dark glasses of varying intensity, which may be turned before either the index or horizon glass when the sun's light is too intense.

SHAGREEN, is a sort of leather grained so as to be covered with small round pimples or projections. It is made chiefly of the skin of horses, asses and mules. The skin is soaked in water, scraped, and stretched on frames. While soft, small seeds, such as mustard seeds, are pressed into it, and it is then dried with the seeds in it. The seeds are afterwards beaten out, and the skin has then that pimpled graining which is peculiar to the leather. It is afterwards polished, soaked in a ley, and died of various colours.

SHANG-HAE. By the treaty of Nankin, in 1842, the port of Shang-hae (in the same manner as those of Canton, Amoy, Foochoo, and Ningpo) was thrown open to British merchants; a British consul resides there; and tariffs of imports and exports, as well as inland and transit duties, have been established. The result has been the formation of a large British trade at Shang-hae. In 1846 the vessels which entered and left the port amounted to 148, with an aggregate burden of 42,608 tons. The goods imported in that year were valued at 810,200*l*., and those exported at 1,352,530*l*. The cottons and woollens imported, and the tea and silk exported, in the three years 1844-5-6, were as follow:—

Cottons..	3,001,794 pieces..	1,872,785*l*.
Woollens.	2,359,868 yards ..	424,020*l*.
Tea	21,020,633 lbs.....	967,230*l*.
Silk	30,834 bales ..	2,132,690*l*.

The magnitude of this foreign trade at Shang-hae is accounted for by the circumstance that there is no harbour on the Chinese coast between 30° and 35° N. lat. The Woosung is the first river south of these limits which is deep enough for the purposes of navigation; and hence the whole maritime commerce of this tract is concentrated at Shang-hae, at the mouth of the river. The country which lies at the back of the coast is the most populous part of China, and contains many very large towns. A steamer plies regularly between Shang-hae and Hongkong.

SHAWL MANUFACTURE. The Hindoos have been the instructors of our manufacturers in the production of shawls. There are two modes of working the pattern in an Indian shawl; the one by embroidering it *upon* the material, and the other by working it *into* the web during the process of weaving. The first mode is a sort of needlework, and forms the less valuable kind of Indian shawl. In the production of the most costly kind, a number of skewers made of ivory, and sometimes of wood, about the size of a common packing needle, are used; they are sharpened at both ends, and each skewer is covered with a different coloured wool; and with these simple aids, the pattern is worked stitch by stitch into the web. The backs of these shawls show the effect of this minute and laborious handicraft, and present a totally different appearance from the European shawls, the patterns of which are woven entirely on the loom.

Paisley excels all other towns in the United Kingdom in the manufacture of shawls, in quantity and perhaps in quality. The common kinds are woven in the power loom; while the finer kinds require the more detailed aid of the hand loom weaver. In the common shawls cotton is mixed with the wool; but for the finer articles the best wool of Germany, of Australia, and even of Cashmere, is employed. Some of the finest of these shawls are equal to anything produced in any other country. The Paisley weavers are mainly dependent on French patterns, which they modify in details; but the School of Design in that town is gradually training up a corps of designers whose taste may shortly influence in an important degree the shawl manufacture.

It might seem strange that the paper duty should press injuriously on the shawl manufacture of Paisley; but such is the case. In weaving elaborate patterns it is necessary to employ the Jacquard loom; and in using this loom many hundred perforated pasteboard cards are employed for each pattern. Now the French weavers pay no duty for the paper used in these cards; whereas the English weavers are subject to an impost, the effect of which may be illustrated by one circumstance. In an elaborate Paisley shawl, woven for the Great Exhibition, the preparation of the loom for the intricate design cost 470*l*., of which the mere duty on the card-board comes to 93*l*. A Jacquard loom, when once set up, will weave any number of the same pattern; but as the commercial success of any one pattern is always very precarious, the oppressive duty on the card-board employed may be a serious item even in every individual shawl woven of that pattern.

SHEEP. We shall give in this work a few details on such points, only, of the history of the sheep as relate to industrial uses.

When the Romans had conquered Britain, they turned their attention to the improvement of the country, and among other things they established a woollen manufactory at Winchester. So well did this succeed, that the woollen cloths of Britain soon began to vie with the productions of every other part of the Roman empire. The sheep employed in furnishing the material of these productions were the *Short-woolled Breed.* Winchester was situated in the centre of a country which then, as now, could support short-woolled sheep alone. It would appear to have been some centuries after this that the *Long-woolled Sheep* was introduced. The manufactures of the Winchester mills continued, however, to be duly estimated; and, in point of fact, the cultivation of the various breeds of sheep, and the manufacture of the fleece into many different kinds of cloth, had begun to constitute the chief employment and wealth of the country.

The covering of the original sheep consisted of a mixture of hair and wool; the wool being short and fine, and forming an inner coat, and the hair of greater length, projecting through the wool, and constituting an external covering. When the sheep are neglected or exposed to a considerable degree of cold, this degeneracy is easily traced; it is only by diligent cultivation that the quantity of hair or *kemps*, has been generally diminished, and that of wool increased in our best breeds. The filaments of wool taken from a healthy sheep present a beautifully polished and even glittering appearance. That of the neglected or half-starved animal exhibits a paler hue. This is one valuable indication by which the wool-stapler is enabled to form an accurate opinion of the value of the fleece. Among the qualities which influence the value of the wool, are fineness, and the uniformity of that fineness in the single fibre and in the collected fleece. This fineness, however, differs materially in different parts of the fleece. It is finest on the shoulders, the ribs, and the back; it is less fine on the legs, thighs, and haunch; and is still coarser on the neck, the breast, the belly, and the lower part of the legs. Sheep in a hot climate yield a comparatively coarse wool; in a cold climate they carry a closer and a warmer fleece. The fineness of the fleece is also much influenced by the kind of food. The woolly fibre consists of a central stem or stalk, from which there spring at different distances circlets of leaf-shaped projections, possessing a certain degree of resistance or of entanglement with other fibres, in proportion as these circlets are multiplied and they project from the stalk. They are sharper and more numerous in the felting wools, and in proportion as the felting property exists. They give to the wool the power of felting, and regulate the degree in which that power is possessed.

The South Down sheep supported the first manufactory at Winchester. The South Downs, and the Hampshire and Wiltshire breeds, were formerly of a very small size, and far from possessing a good shape, but the size and shape have been of late years greatly improved, and the wool is short, close, curled, and free from spiry projecting hairs. Mr. Luccock calculated that within a certain distance from the Downs there were 864,000 sheep of this breed, a number which is only to be accounted for by the great quantity of artificial food that is raised on the arable part of every farm. The average dead weight of the South Down wether varies from 8 to 11 stones. The average weight of the fleece used to be 2 lbs.; but from the altered system of management, it is now at least 3 lbs. in the hill sheep, and nearly 4 lbs. in the lowland sheep. This wool has likewise changed its character. It has become a combing instead of a carding wool. Formerly devoted to the manufacture of servants' and army clothing, and being sparingly mixed with other wool, it is now used for flannels and baizes, and worsted goods of almost every description, thus becoming of considerably increased value.

In the 13th century certain Florentine merchants were permitted to export from England to Flanders more than 1000 sacks of combing or long wool. In the 14th century the 1000 had extended to 100,000, and that continued during many years; and in the 15th century Edward IV. permitted his sister Margaret to export annually during her life 2000 rams to Flanders and Holland. There has been a very great improvement in the long-woolled sheep within the last half century, especially that kind called the *New Leicester.* The deficiency of the fleece was formerly objected to in this breed; but the truth seems to be that, with the early breeders, the fleece was a perfectly secondary consideration, and comparatively disregarded. There is now little cause for complaint on this head. The wool has considerably increased in length, and it has improved both in fineness and strength of fibre. It averages from 6 to 7 lbs. the fleece, and the fibre varies from 5 to more than 12 inches in length. Like all other British wools, it is applied to a purpose different from that to which it was formerly devoted, and is mostly used in the manufacture of serges and carpets.

The English wool being, from the increased coarseness of the fibre, rejected by the manufacturer in the construction of fine cloths, recourse was had to foreign wools, and to those chiefly that were derived from the Merino sheep. As early as the commencement of the Christian æra, the wool of the Spanish sheep was in great request for the production of the most costly dresses. In less than half a cen tury afterwards we find Columella busily employed in improving the Spanish sheep, and the effect of his labours remained during the long dark ages that succeeded. The present Merino flocks seem to have been produced by a cross of the native breed with a flock sent from England. [MESTA.] By degrees the Merino sheep found its way to almost every part of the European Continent, and by careful management its fleece rapidly increased in fineness and in usefulness. In Australia the cultivation of the Merino sheep and its fleece has proceeded most rapidly and prosperously.

We may here refer to WOOL for further details concerning the application of the fleece.

In relation to the supply of sheep from foreign countries, the following have been the imports during the last three years:—

1848............128,406.
1849............126,248.
1850............137,646.

The sheep sold at Smithfield during the last ten or twelve years have varied from 1,500,000 to 1,800,000 annually.

SHEERS, or SHEARS. The shears used in masting ships consist of two large poles, the lower ends of which rest upon thick planks laid along the sides of the deck, while their upper ends are lashed together so as to cross each other exactly over the hole in the deck through which the mast is to be dropped, they being sustained in this position by ropes radiating from the top to various parts of the vessel. To this apparatus is attached the tackle necessary for lifting the masts out of the water, when they have been floated to the side of the ship, and lowering them gently into their places. Some ships are masted by the aid of tackle attached to old worn out ships of war called *sheer hulks*, while others are drawn up to the side of a *masting house* on a quay or pier.

SHEFFIELD, in tho beginning of the 17th century, was still only a large village. It now displays all the features of a manufacturing town of the first importance. The principal manufacture is that of cutlery in all its branches, indeed of everything that can be fabricated of iron or of steel. The vast buildings used for the grinding of all kinds of tools and implements by steam power form one of the curiosities of Sheffield. Silver plate and plated goods form also one of the staple manufactures. Brass-foundries are numerous. Articles in Britannia metal and German silver are also manufactured. Brushes, buttons, combs, and optical instruments, are also made here to a considerable extent; and various workmen are employed on manufactures which are connected with the staple commodities of the town, such as cabinet-case makers, haft and scale presssers and cutters, powder-flask and shot-belt makers, silver refiners, wood turners, &c. There are also many mercantile houses, some of which confine themselves to the home markets, while others export to the Continent, to Brazil, the Cape of Good Hope, but especially to the United States of North America. The spring knife makers and table knife makers are the largest classes of artisans. The fork makers are an unfortunate class, owing to the injurious effects of what is called dry grinding: the dust of the stone and metal rises in clouds, and is necessarily inhaled by the workmen, the average duration of whose lives is thus very much shortened. It is to the immense coal bed occupying the surrounding district that Sheffield owes its prosperity; for much of the iron which is there converted into steel comes from Sweden.

It would be difficult to enumerate all the kinds of articles manufactured in this busy town, made principally of steel. They comprise pen, pocket, pallet, table, and other knives, anvils, vices, augurs, gimblets, awls, axletrees, traces and bits, Britannia metal goods, coach springs, razors, edge tools, fenders and fire-irons, files, German silver goods, mathematical instruments, machinery, saws, scales, shears, scissors, scythes, sickles, silver and plated goods, skates, snuffers, spoons, steel plates, steel ornaments, musical instruments, &c.—all of which are represented at the Great Exhibition. Some of the curiosities of Sheffield industry are mentioned under CUTLERY, and FILE; and we may here notice a contribution to the Exhibition, consisting of a clasp knife only three-eighths of an inch in length when open, and so small as to go within the stem of a tobacco pipe. It is not by these trifles, however, that the commercial importance of Sheffield industry is shown; it is in those larger and useful products which are known in every part of the world where English goods penetrate.

There is a School of Design at Sheffield, which is gradually infusing a taste into those who have to determine the patterns to which goods shall be wrought.

SHELL. For various applications of shells to useful and ornamental purposes, see CAMEO; MOTHER OF PEARL; TORTOISESHELL.

SHELL, is also the name of a hollow globe of iron, containing gunpowder, which is introduced at an orifice formed in the ball. In this orifice is driven or screwed the fuze or tube containing the composition by which the powder in the shell is ignited [FUZE]; and the shell, after being discharged from a gun, howitzer, or mortar, is consequently made to burst in pieces when it falls upon or near the object to be destroyed.

SHELLAC. [LAC.]

SHERBET, in Persia, Turkey, and other eastern countries where it is chiefly used, is a beverage composed chiefly of water, lemon-juice, and sugar, with the addition of other ingredients to render it more pleasant to the taste, as the pulp of fruits, perfumed cakes, rose water, &c.

SHIP BUILDING. The most essential conditions in the construction of a ship are, that it be capable of carrying its stores and its artillery or lading; that it be moved by wind or steam with great velocity, and that it readily obey the motion of the rudder; that it have the necessary stability, so as not to be overturned when acted upon by the wind or waves; and finally, that its rolling or pitching be attended with as little strain as possible on the timbers. In merchant ships an ample capacity is frequently of more importance than a great velocity in sailing. In ships of war the number and weight of the guns constitute the basis of the design; for from these the weight of the whole ship, or the volume of the water which it will displace, may be estimated. The draught of water (the depth to which the ship is immersed) may depend on the depth of water in the harbours and roadsteads; but it must also be determined from experience, so that tho ship may be prevented as much as possible from making leeway. Finally, the form of the body must be that which is most favourable for velocity, by causing the least possible resistance of the water at the bows and along the sides; which allows the greatest lateral resistance, and which will permit the rudder to act with most effect in causing the ship to be turned about a vertical axis. Experiments have shown that when the quantity of sail is tho same, the velocity of a ship is increased by increasing the ratio between its length and breadth.

It has been found that ships having the same proportions possess unequal sailing properties; it may be perceived indeed that a small ship built according to the proportions of a large one which is know to sail well, will not possess the like good quality; so that the sailing qualities depend on something more than mere form. That a ship whose hull has been constructed according to the best rules of art does not always fulfil the conditions required, may depend on several causes. The blocks, ropes, &c., may be too heavy, and the sails may be badly formed; or the burden of the vessel may be unskilfully distributed.

In building an ordinary ship the draughtsman draws a plan, analogous to that of an architect in building a house; the drawings represent the intended vessel in many points of view—not only as a whole, but in respect also to the curvatures of the various timbers. Thin pieces of lath are cut and marked so as to assist in determining the proper sizes and shapes of the timbers. For a large East Indiaman there are upwards of 100 of these *moulding pieces* (as they are called) prepared. Tho oak and elm trunks are then cut up to the proper forms for the timbers, by sawing, the moulding pieces serving as guides. All being cut and prepared, the building of the ship commences. Tho *keel*, which is formed of elm, is scarfed together very strongly. The *stem* and *stern-posts*, of oak, are raised and fixed at the two ends of the keel; and various pieces called *transoms, fashion-pieces*, &c., help to give form to the two ends of the ship. Stout timbers, called *floor timbers*, are laid athwart the keel; and around them solid wood, called *dead wood*, is packed in, to form a solid foundation. Then come the *ribs* of the ship, which are tho curved oak timbers bending upwards and outwards from the keel to the top; these are formed of several pieces called *futtocks* or *foothooks*, which are securely bolted together. These various timbers are strengthened with inner timbers, called the *keelson, stemson, sternson, riders*, &c. All the outside is covered with oak planking, varying from three to six inches in thickness, and arranged in parallel rows called *strakes*. The filling up the interstices between these planks has been noticed under RIGGING. The *beams* are timbers of great strength, to support the deck, and to bind the sides of the vessel together; while the *knees* are immense brackets which support the ends of the beams. The *decks* are formed of Dantzig fir or yellow pine, laid in boards from six to ten inches in width, and from two to four in thickness. The *treenails* are the oak pins or bolts by which the planks aro fastened to the timbers of a ship. [TREENAILS.]

The *sheathing* of ships at first consisted of a second covering of planks applied on the exterior of the first, over the bottom and sides as far as they were under water; but this being found to impede the motion of the ship, a sheathing of milled lead (the invention of Sir Philip Howard) was subsequently employed. The application of plates of copper as a covering on the exterior of ships was first tried in 1760; and in 1783 all those belonging to the royal navy were ordered to be covered or sheathed with that metal. By this practice shells and sea-weeds are prevented from adhering to the sides and bottoms; the friction of the water against them is diminished, and the damage which would be caused by worms is avoided. Owing to the great expense of copper sheathing, which has the effect of limiting its use in mercantile shipping, many attempts have been made to substitute for it either other metals, or alloys in which it is mixed with cheaper metals, such as lead, or with such as might increase its durability, as zinc. Iron, protected by the galvanic action of zinc, has been used. Sheathing of brown paper, coated with tar, and a kind of felt, into the composition of which a considerable quantity of cow-hair enters, have also been tried. Copper sheathing is usually applied in sheets about 4 feet long and 14 inches wide, the thickness being such that a square foot weighs from 16 to 32 ounces, but most commonly from 20 to 28 ounces; and the mode of application does not vary materially whether the copper be laid upon the bare planking or upon an interposed layer of tarred paper, felt, or thin boarding. The sheets are pierced with holes, not only round the edges, but also at intervals of 3 or 4 inches over the whole surface; they are laid so as to overlap each other about an inch, and are secured to the ship with flat-headed copper nails. An East Indiaman requires re-coppering after two voyages; and the old copper is found to have lost three or four ounces of its weight in the square foot, by the action of sea-water, friction, and other causes.

The *masts* of ships are built of several pieces selected from the strongest parts of trees, and attached together both in the fore-and-aft and in the athwart-ship directions, the whole being bound together by hoops at intervals. Usually the central piece consists of one log of timber reduced to a many-sided form, and to the sides of this are applied other pieces, which are connected with it either by a longitudinal projection in each, which is let into a corresponding channel made in the central piece, or by blocks of hard wood which are let into both the central and attached pieces.

Vessels of iron are now very frequently constructed both for rivers and for navigation in the open seas, and they have many advantages over ships of wood. They are much lighter, or more buoyant. They are less liable to become arched, and are better able to withstand the effects of striking upon a rock. In the latter case a ship of wood would have its bottom pierced, or it might go to pieces, while the iron one would merely become indented. They are formed with rib frames at intervals, and with longitudinal hoops of iron; and they are covered with iron plates, which are fastened to the ribs by bolts or rivets. The lower part of the interior may be divided into compartments, which can be rendered air-tight; and thus, in the event of the bottom being perforated in any place, the water would be confined within that compartment till the damaged plate could be repaired or replaced.

Ships have different designations, according to the number of their masts or the disposition of their sails. The word *ship* is more particularly applied to those vessels which have a fore, a main, and a mizen mast, with a top-mast and top-gallant-mast to each; and in which the yards, in sailing before the wind, are braced square, that is, in vertical positions perpendicularly to the length of the ship. the mizen-sail alone being usually in a fore-and-aft position, that is, in a vertical plane passing through the keel. A *bark* is a vessel with masts and sails like those of a ship, except that the mizen-mast carries no top-sail or top-gallant sail. A *brig* has a fore and a main mast, with top and top-gallant masts and sails, like those of a ship; but it has no mizen-mast, and the main-sail has a position corresponding to that of the mizen-sail in a ship with three masts. A *snow* is rigged in the same manner as a brig, except that the main-sail is attached to a small mast abaft of and very near the main-mast. A *schooner* has two masts, and the sails attached to them are, in their usual position, in vertical planes passing through the keel: it has small or no top-sails. Lastly, a *sloop* (shaloop) has only one mast, with a main-sail, whose plane is usually in a fore-and-aft position. Each of the different kinds of ships has a bowsprit which carries a fore-stay-sail and a jib-sail.

In the British navy, ships which carry 70 or a greater number of guns are called *line-of-battle ships*. *Frigate* is a term which is supposed to have been first applied to a light galley moved by sails or oars; but it is now applied to ships of war, generally with two decks, and carrying from 36 to 60 guns. These are built narrower than line-of-battle ships in proportion to their length, and sail swiftly. They accompany fleets in order to watch at a distance the movements of the enemy, and they act singly against ships of a like kind. Ships of war of a lower class than frigates have the denominations of *sloops*, *corvettes*, *brigs*, *cutters*, *brigantines*, *ketches*, *schooners*, and *barks*. The sloops of war and corvettes carry from 4 to 20 guns, and some brigs carry 16 guns. The number of guns in a vessel of either of the remaining classes does not exceed 10.

The tonnage of a ship is, properly, an expression for the interior capacity by the number of tons of sea-water which it could contain; therefore, if the interior volume were found in cubic feet, on dividing that volume

35 (the number of cubic feet of sea-water which are equal in weight to one ton), the quotient would be the tonnage required. There have, however, been various modes of estimating ships' tonnage.

There are now employed in tho yearly transit of Great Britain with the world and with her own shores, about 33,700 sailing vessels, and 1150 steam vessels, employing 240,000 seamen. Calculating the value of each ship and cargo, as the value has been estimated before parliament, at 5000*l.*, we have an aggregate value—sailing vessels, steamers, and their cargoes included—of about 174,000,000*l.* Further, supposing that the yearly wages of the seamen, including officers, was 20*l.* per head, the amount paid in wages would be 4,800,000*l.*

Various details bearing more or less closely on the subject of ship-building will be found under ANCHOR; BLOCKS; RIGGING; ROPE MANUFACTURE; SAIL MAKING; SCREW PROPELLER; SHEERS; STEAM VESSEL; &c.

SHOE TRADE. In addition to the few details given under BOOT AND SHOE MANUFACTURE, the following may not be out of place.

In the old statutes a shoemaker is called a cordwainer, apparently a corruption of the French *Cordonnier*, which means a worker of Cordova leather. The companies of shoemakers in our ancient towns were incorporated under this name; and where some of these companies still exist, they still go by the same name. As a legal term, cordwainer is yet in use.

The trade, as now followed in London and other principal places, is subdivided into about twenty branches. The following may be set down as the chief: the shoeman, or maker of the sole part of the shoe; the bootman, or maker of the sole part of the boot; and the boot closer, or joiner together of the leg, vamp, &c. The labour of these is especially directed to what is called the men's line; whilst others make the ladies' shoes or boots. There are many women, too, who get a livelihood by closing the shoe; while others again follow the various sorts of binding.

The mechanical processes, after marking and cutting out the leather, consist chiefly in various kinds of strong needlework, such as the lasting or tacking of the upper leather to the in-sole, the sewing in of the welt, the stitching to this welt of the out or top sole, the building and sewing down of the heel, and the sewing or closing of boot legs. The boot closer is the most skilful of the persons employed, and receives the highest wages.

No other common handicraft is exercised by so large a number of persons as that of the shoemaker. In the metropolis and in many parts of the country, women are extensively employed in the lighter parts of the business. The government contracts for the army and navy, the police, &c., are executed in London and at Northampton and Stafford; and the export market is almost entirely supplied from these quarters. The boots and shoes exported (chiefly to the East and West Indies and tho colonies) are included in the general entry of 'leather wrought and unwrought,' in the parliamentary returns; but it is supposed that the value is about a quarter of a million sterling annually.

In 1850 there were imported, almost entirely from France :—

Women's boots and calashes	22,346	pairs.
Women's shoes	119,420	"
Men's boots and shoes	31,178	"
Children's boots and shoes.	1,698	"
Boot fronts	603,302	"

SHOT are the balls (generally solid) of iron which are discharged from guns, howitzers, or carronades. Solid shot vary in diameter from about two inches, which is that of a one pound ball, to about eight, which is the diameter of a 68-pound ball. For the naval service it has been proposed to discharge from howitzers hollow shot, or unloaded shells, which, having greater diameters than solid shot with equal weights, are capable of producing more destructive effects against shipping.

SHOT MANUFACTURE. The larger kinds of shot, such as pistol bullets and rifle balls, are generally cast in a mould, one at a time. Shot of the next smaller size, such as swan shot, are often produced by casting several at a time; there is a double mould formed something like a pair of nut-crackers, which, when closed, exhibits a range of little moulds into which the melted lead can be poured; and, when open, allows the shot so made to be removed from the mould. A ruder kind is sometimes made by shaking a number of small fragments of lead together in a bag or box, by which the corners or rough edges are worn away. In another mode of manufacture, a piece of thin lead is cut up into litle cubes, and these are placed between two flat stones, the upper of which works over the lower; so that by the combined pressure and movement the cubical fragments are worn to a cubical shape.

But the most remarkable mode of making shot is by *granulation*, which is the plan now adopted for the larger portion of shot now used. The shot are made either over the mouth of a deep well or shaft, or at the top of a lofty tower, so as to provide a vertical descent of one or two hundred feet. The elegant tower (intended originally as a shot-tower, but now applied to other purposes) near the foot of Waterloo Bridge, illustrates the latter of the two methods. In some of the shot works on the banks of the Tyne, an abandoned coal shaft is employed. There are about fifteen sizes of shot made by the granulation method, varying from $\frac{1}{5}$ to $\frac{1}{50}$ of an inch in diameter.

The lead has a little arsenic added to it, and is melted in a furnace or pot. Over the vertical shaft is placed a tripod or stand, and upon this a kind of colander, pierced with holes suitable in size to the shot to be made. A layer of dross from the surface of the melted lead is laid over the holes in the colander, to act as a kind of sieve or strainer, and to separate the liquid lead into small trickling streams before it reaches the holes. The melted lead is poured into the colander by a ladle; and it speedily falls as a sort of silvery rain down the shaft, into a vessel of cold water at the bottom; the lead is found to separate into almost perfectly spherical drops or shots; and these shots when cold, are brought up from the vessel below, dried on steam heated plates, and separated into sizes by sifting. The irregular or ill-shaped shot are separated from the others by a beautiful contrivance; they are made to roll down an inclined plane of smooth iron; and when they get to the bottom, the well-shaped shot have acquired an impetus which sends them into a box or cell, several inches distant; whereas the ill-shaped shot, having descended the inclined plane in an irregular way, have acquired very little velocity, and fall into a cell or box not so far distant as the other. By carefully adjusting the slope of the inclined plane, this separation of good from bad shot is effected with surprising accuracy. The shot are then placed in a kind of churn or revolving barrel, into which a little black lead is also placed: and they are revolved in the churn until they become polished and black leaded. They are lastly tied up in bags containing 28 lbs. each.

SHROPSHIRE. The coal-field of Coalbrook-Dale is the most extensive and most productive part of the carboniferous system of this county. It extends from near Wenlock, on the right bank of the Severn, across that river to Wellington on the N.W., and is prolongated in a N.E. direction to Lilleshall. The most productive portion of this field includes Broseley on the south, and stretches north of the Severn in a large triangular-shaped mass, having Lilleshall for its apex. In several places the seams of coal are numerous and of considerable thickness. At Hadley the number of seams is 10, and the total thickness of coal 15 yards; at Madeley, the seams are 24, and the thickness of coal 10½ yards. The ironstone of this field is both concretionary and flat-bedded, and the various courses of it are known under various local names. The ores of iron are peroxides in sandstone, argillaceous carbonates in shale, and sulphurets in the coal. The sulphuret of iron is the most abundant mineral, and next to it is the sulphuret of zinc, or blende. Petroleum occurs in great abundance in both the upper and lower measures, and some of the beds of shale of the latter afford excellent fire-clay, which is used in the manufacture of pipes and pottery. The Shrewsbury coal-field extends from the Severn at the Breidden Hills on the west, to Shrewsbury on the east. The strata of this coal-field belong to the upper or youngest series of coal-measures. It varies in thickness from three to eight feet. The coal-field of Oswestry is situated on the western verge of the county, and is quite distinct. It contains only two seams of coal worthy of extraction, the upper being four feet thick; the lower, which is six feet thick, is a very inferior coal. The other coal-fields of Shropshire are situated on the south side of the county.

The farms in Shropshire are for the most part arable, but some are for grazing, for hay, for the dairy, and for rearing and feeding. The crops in general cultivation are wheat, barley, oats, peas, vetches, turnips, potatoes, and beans. The meadows adjoining the Severn, and other rivers and streams, are rich, and are often overflowed, and the water lies on them, especially near the Severn, for a considerable time. The rich coal-formations of this county and the iron-stone associated with them give employment to several thousand persons. The greater portion of these are engaged in raising coal, ironstone, and lime, and in the manufacture of iron, and a few in the lead mines on the western side of the county. Near Coalport china of every description and of exquisite workmanship is made; and at Caughley, in the neighbourhood of Broseley, there is another china manufactory, which is chiefly confined to the blue and white, and blue, white, and gold sorts. At Coalport there is a manufactory of earthenware, similar to the Etrurian or Wedgwood ware. There are flannel manufactories at Shrewsbury, Oswestry, Church Stretton, and Worthen. Carpets are made at Bridgnorth. Gloves are made at Ludlow, but not in such quantities as formerly. There are mills for dyeing woollen cloth at Le Botwood, &c., and there are paper-mills at Ludlow, Bridgnorth, Cleobury-Mortimer, Drayton, &c.

SIAM. This portion of south-eastern Asia is rich in natural productions. Rice is most extensively cultivated. On the alluvial soil of the Menam it generally yields forty fold. Maize, several leguminous plants, sweet potatoes, cocoa, and areca palms, are cultivated. Siam is noted for a great variety and abundance of fruit-trees, and their produce surpasses that of all other parts of India in flavour. Several plants are cultivated as articles of foreign trade. The most important is the sugar-cane, which indeed has been grown in Siam from time immemorial; but its culture for the foreign market has now become very large. Tobacco, cotton, and black pepper, are also exported. The forests, which cover nearly all the mountain ranges of this country, yield several articles of trade; among which are cardamums, gamboge, aquila-wood, sapan-wood, gum trees, and a great variety of timber trees. The elephant exists in the greatest perfection, and the ivory, hides, and bones are largely exported to China.

Gold is found in the mountains of the Malay peninsula, and at the southern extremity of those of Siam, and is worked in some places. Tin, iron, copper, lead, zinc, and antimony are met with in many places. The only precious stones which are known to exist in Siam are the sapphire, the oriental ruby, and the oriental topaz. Salt is made in the low wooded and uninhabited country which extends between the mouths of the Menam along the sea.

The Siamese do not distinguish themselves in any of the useful arts, and are much behind the Hindoos and Chinese. Even their vessels and trinkets of gold and silver are imported from China. Considerable manufactures are carried on: but they are mostly in the hands of Chinese who have settled in Siam.

Siam in a commercial point of view is considered the most important of the three empires which divide among them the countries between the Gulf of Bengal and China. As all the provinces of the empire produce some articles which are in demand in foreign countries, and nearly all the foreign commerce is at present concentrated in the town of Bangkok, the inland and coasting trade is very considerable. Large quantities of produce are brought down to Bangkok from the inland districts, by the rivers, especially the Menam. The most important branch of the foreign trade is that with China. It is partly carried on by Chinese vessels, but mostly in vessels built in Siam and navigated by Chinese. Very little if any commercial intercourse exists between Siam and the Birman empire. With Cochin-China there is much commerce. The most important trade, next to that with China, is with the European establishments on the Malay peninsula, and the Sunda Islands, especially with the British colonies of Singapore, Malacca, and Pulo Penang, and with the Dutch establishments of Batavia, Cheribon, and Samarang in Java, Pontianac in Borneo, and Rio in Bintang. Formerly the commodities of Hindustan and Europe reached the capital of Siam by being transported across the isthmus of Kraw and the Malay peninsula; but at the present day Singapore is a better emporium for procuring the goods, and the conveyance by this route is less expensive.

SIBERIA. This vast but little known region is very rich in metals. There are three extensive mining districts. The most western comprehends the mines of the Ural Mountains; which are rich in gold, silver, and copper; and they contain also iron, silver, and platinum in smaller quantities. The second mining-district is that of Bernaul, which yields much silver and copper, but less gold and lead. The mines from which these metals are obtained lie mostly in the Altai Mountains and in those valleys which open to the Irtish River. The third mining-district is that of Nertshinsk, which is situated on the east of the Yablonoï Khrebet, in the basin of the river Amur. These mines contain gold, lead, silver, iron, antimony, and arsenic. The western parts of Siberia get the salt which is required for their consumption from the salt lakes in the steppes of Ishim and Barabinsk, in some of which the salt crystallises spontaneously. The countries bordering on the river Lena obtain salt partly from some salt-springs which occur in the vicinity of the town of Ust Kutsk, and partly from the river Vilui. Da-Uria obtains its salt from one of the lakes of the Gobi, called Dabassuneï Lake, not far from that of Khara. Several kinds of precious stones occur in Siberia, and diamonds have been found along the eastern declivity of the Uralian range. The amethysts, topazes, emeralds, and red tourmalines, are of great beauty; zircons of extraordinary size have been found near Miask, south of Ekatarinburg. Lapis lazuli and talc of fine quality are met with. The tusks of the fossil elephant constitute an article of commerce, and many persons make the discovery of them the business of their life.

Siberia possesses tanneries, iron foundries, glass works, and manufactures of coarse woollens and linens; but their number is inconsiderable. There are smelting and refining works connected with the mines.

Siberia carries on an extensive commerce with Russia, Bokhara, Tashkend, and China.

The most important is the trade with Russia. The transport of the goods is effected by a road which leads from Perm in Russia to Ekatarinburg and Tobolsk. The commerce which is carried on at Kiachta with the Chinese has been noticed under KIACHTA. The goods from Irkutsk to Kiachta, and from Kiachta to Irkutsk, are conveyed from May to November, by large vessels which navigate the Lake of Baïkal and the river Selenga, and in November and December by carts on a mountain road. The inhabitants of Siberia have also some commerce with Tartary.

SICILY. The mineral productions of this island consist of copper, silver, cinnabar, and sulphur, of which last a large quantity is exported to Great Britain, marble, alabaster, and rock salt. A great deal of wine is made in Sicily of which the Marsala is best known in England. Dried raisins are exported from Messina. Messina is also the depôt for the currants of the Lipari Islands, of which about 12,000 barrels are yearly sold and exported to Trieste, England, and America. Oranges and lemons are fine and plentiful. Olive oil and linseed oil, lemon juice, as well as essences of lemon and other fruits, are made for exportation. A little silk is produced. Liquorice-juice is made in large quantities. Manna, almonds, pistachio nuts, sumach, and figs, are among the produce exported. Kid and lamb skins are dressed for exportation. The cattle, sheep, and horses, are mostly of inferior breeds, and not in good condition.

The manufactories of Sicily are neither numerous nor on a large scale. Cotton-cloth is manufactured at Messina, Catania, Palermo, and Caltagirone; silks at Palermo, Catania, and Nicolosi; leather at Messina; gloves, soap, artificial flowers, and paper at Palermo; coral from the coast of Africa is wrought at Trapani.

Concerning the chief commerce of Sicily, a few details will be found under SULPHUR.

SIERRA LEONE. This British colony was established in 1787, by some philanthropists, who intended to show that colonial productions could be obtained without the labour of slaves. In that year 470 negroes, then living in a state of destitution in London, were removed to it, and in 1790 their number was increased by 1196 individuals of the same race, who had been settled in Nova Scotia, but could not bear the severity of that climate. Ten years later 550 Maroons were transported from Jamaica to Sierra Leone; and in 1819, when a black regiment in the West Indies was disbanded, 1222 black soldiers and their families were settled there likewise. In 1820 the population amounted to 12,000 individuals. Since the abolition of the slave-trade (1807), the slaves captured by the British cruisers have been settled in the colony: and the population has increased so that in 1848 it amounted to 46,511. The towns, or rather villages in the settlement, besides Freetown, the capital (which has nearly 20,000 inhabitants), are—Kent, York, Calmont, Waterloo, Hastings, and Wellington. About 20,000 of the inhabitants are liberated Africans, and about an equal number are descendants of liberated Africans, born in the colony. The number of Europeans is very small. The chief article of export is ground nuts, from which is expressed an oil largely used in lubricating machinery: in 1846 the quantity amounted to 8697 tons, valued at 92,049*l*. The other chief articles of export are—ginger, teak timber, hides, palm oil, and camwood. Nearly one-third of the imports consist of British cotton goods. The vessels which arrived at Freetown in 1847 were 185. There are about 120 fishing boats belonging to the settlement.

Sierra Leone, like our other colonies, is gradually reaping the benefits attendant on steam navigation. The new mail screw steamers, which have lately begun to ply between Plymouth and the Cape of Good Hope, call at Sierra Leone going and returning; thereby placing the colony in advantageous connexion both with the mother country and with another colony.

The imports in 1848 amounted in value to 89,174*l*.; and the exports to 95,617*l*. In 1849 the imports from Great Britain were 60,290*l*.

SIGGAR, SEGGAR, or SAGGER. This name, the origin of which does not seem to be well known, is given to the oval vessels in which articles of pottery or porcelain are placed, to protect them from flame and smoke while exposed to the heat of the kiln. [POTTERY.]

SIGNALS. [TELEGRAPH.]

SIGNATURE, in Printing, is the name given to the letters or figures which are placed at the bottom of certain pages in each sheet of a book, to facilitate the gathering, folding, collating, and binding of it. [BOOKBINDING.]

SILESIA. This important Prussian province produces flax, tobacco, hops, madder, woad, teazle, and timber. The minerals are copper, lead, cobalt, arsenic, iron, zinc, sulphur, marble, alum, lime and coal. The linen manufacture of Silesia is of great importance; it is carried on with little aid from machinery, and chiefly by the country people, though this branch of industry affords them but a scanty subsistence; it is however their chief occupation. Woollen cloths are manufactured in some towns, and cottons at Reichenbach. There are sugar refineries in several places; woollen-cloth factories, tanneries, breweries, and brandy distilleries in most of the towns. The cotton manufactures are extending; steam machinery has been introduced into the manufactories; at the end of 1846 the province had three large and eight smaller cotton factories, with 35,524 spindles, and 1749 workpeople.

SILHOUETTE. This name is frequently applied to the black profile portraits commonly known simply as *Profiles*, or *Shades*. The latter name indicates the origin of this simple class of pictorial representations, they having been probably suggested by the shadow thrown upon a wall. Silhouettes are executed in various ways. One of the simplest is that of tracing the outlines of a shadow thrown on a sheet of paper, and then reducing them to the required size, either by the eye or by means of a pantograph. [PANTOGRAPH.] Another mode is tracing the outline upon a glass supported in a suitable position, and either coated with a solution of gum-arabic in water, in order to enable a lead pencil to mark upon it, or covered with a sheet of very thin tracing-paper.

SILEX or FLINT. This valuable substance is an oxide of *Silicium* or *Silicon*, which is regarded by some chemists as a metal, and hence the termination of its name in *um;* while others consider it as non-metallic, and more allied to boron, and these adopt the term *Silicon*. Sir H. Davy was the first to separate this substance from Silica. Silicium is of a dark brown colour, has no lustre, and is a non-conductor of electricity. It is insoluble in water, and incombustible in air or in oxygen gas; it neither fuses nor undergoes any other change when heated in the flame of the blow-pipe.

Oxygen and *Silicon* form only one compound, namely, *silex* or *silica*. Silica exists very largely in nature: it is indeed probably the most abundant of all substances whatever. Many of the forms under which it occurs are mentioned elsewhere. [FLINT; QUARTZ.] Rock-crystal is silica nearly or quite pure; and flints, or white sand, are but slightly intermixed with other bodies. Pure dry silica is an opaque white powder, inodorous, insipid, and gritty. It is infusible by the heat of ordinary furnaces, but by the oxy-hydrogen blowpipe it is more readily fused than lime or magnesia. Silica is a substance of the utmost importance in many respects; it enters largely into the constitution of minerals, rocks, and fossils, and is employed in the manufacture of glass, porcelain, pottery, bricks, tiles, and mortar.

SILK MANUFACTURE. China was undoubtedly the country in which men first availed themselves of the labours of the silk worm. Aristotle was the first Greek author who mentions the silk-worm; and he states that silk was first spun in the island of Cos, but the raw material was still an oriental product. For many centuries it was not known in Europe from what source silk was produced. It was not indeed until the sixth century that the obscurity which enveloped this subject was cleared up, by the successful result of a journey made by two Nestorian monks to China to unravel the mystery. The breeding of silk-worms in Europe was for six centuries confined to the Greeks of the Lower Empire. In the 12th century the art was transferred to Sicily; in the 13th century the rearing of silk-worms and the manufacture of silk were introduced into Italy, whence it was successively introduced into Spain and France, and in the 15th century the manufacture was established in England.

James I. was extremely solicitous to promote the breeding and rearing of silk worms in England; but all attempts of this kind have failed both here and in the United States, partly from the unfitness of the climate, and partly from the high-rate of wages, which renders this employment better adapted to the social condition of China, Italy, the south of France, and Malta, where the wages of labour have nearly reached their minimum. Mrs. Whitby, a lady who has made praiseworthy attempts to foster the growth of silk in England, communicated the results of her partially successful labours to the *Royal Agricultural Society*, in 1844, and to the Birmingham meeting of the *British Association* in 1849. The production of raw silk is fast extending in British India, and the quality has been for some years gradually improving. The countries in which silk is produced are now very numerous.

But although English silk-culture has been hitherto a commercial failure, there are from time to time attempts made which merit attention. To the Great Exhibition has been contributed a scarf woven by the wife of a clergyman, from silk reared by herself; and although such a production is a family curiosity rather than a commercial result, it may be interesting to read her own account of it. 'Having resided for about three years in a vicarage in Hertfordshire, the garden of which possessed a remarkably fine mulberry tree, I wished to give my family an idea of the habits and natural history of the silkworm, and the method by which silk is produced. With this view I procured a quantity of eggs early in the spring of 1847, which were hatched about May, and I placed the worms, 2000 or rather more in number, in an outhouse in the garden. There they were attended and fed by myself and some of the juvenile members of my family, and in due time they spun; and much wishing to turn the produce of their industry to some use, I directed my attention towards making the scarf which I have the pleasure to lay before you. The silk was wound from the cocoons by my daughter and myself on a winding machine, and afterwards I wove it into its present form. It has consequently never been in the hands of any manufacturer, and presents the same colour and quality as when taken from the cocoon. I may add, that the outhouse in which the worms lived had no windows to protect them from the weather, which was unusually cold for the season of the year; as I think this point may illustrate the fact that our English climate presents no insuperable obstacle to the cultivation of silk. The mulberry tree was the common kind.'

The silk is produced from that species of silkworm which, when in the moth state, is called the *Bombyx Mori*. This species, which was originally from China, is of a white or cream colour, with a brown fascia and two or more waved lines of a deeper colour crossing the upper wings. In this country the eggs of this moth are hatched early in May. The caterpillar, or silkworm, is at first of a dark colour, but soon becomes light, and in its tints much resembles the perfect insect,—a circumstance common in caterpillars. Its proper food is the mulberry, though it will likewise eat the lettuce and some few other plants; on these plants, however, it does not thrive equally well, and the silk yielded is of a poor quality. The silkworm is about eight weeks in arriving at maturity, during which period it changes its skin four or five times. When about to cast its skin it ceases to eat, raises the fore-part of the body slightly, and remains in perfect repose. In this state it is necessary that it should continue for some little time , in order that the new skin, which is at this time forming, may become sufficiently mature to enable the caterpillar to burst through the old one. This operation, which is apparently one of considerable difficulty, is performed thus:—The fore part of the old skin is burst; the silkworm then by continually writhing its body (but not moving from the spot) contrives to thrust the skin back to the tail, and ultimately to disengage itself altogether: this last part of the operation however is the most difficult, since it is no uncommon occurrence for them to die, from not being able to disengage the last segment of the body from the old skin.

When full grown the silkworm commences spinning its web in some convenient spot; and as it does not change the position of the hinder portion of its body much, but continues drawing its thread from various points and attaching it to others, it follows that after a time its body becomes in a great measure inclosed by the thread. The work is then continued from one thread to another, the silkworm moving its head and spinning in a zigzag way, bending the fore part of the body back to spin in all directions within reach, and shifting the body only, to cover with silk the part which was beneath it. As the silkworm spins its web by thus bending the fore part of the body back, and moves the hinder part of the body in such a way only as to enable it to reach the farther back with the fore part, it follows that it incloses itself in a cocoon much shorter than its own body ; for soon after the beginning the whole is continued with the body in a bent position. From the foregoing account it appears that with the most simple instinctive principles all the ends necessary are gained. If the silkworm were gifted with a desire for shifting its position much at the beginning of the work it could never inclose itself in a cocoon; but by its mode of proceeding, as above explained, it incloses itself in a cocoon which only consumes as much silk as is necessary to hold the chrysalis. During the time of spinning the cocoon, the silkworm decreases in length very considerably, and after it is completed it is not half its original length; at this time it becomes quite torpid, soon changes its skin, and appears in the form of a chrysalis. The time required to complete the cocoon is about five days. In the chrysalis state the animal remains from a fortnight to three weeks; it then bursts its case, and comes forth in the imago state, the moth having previously dissolved a portion of the cocoon by means of a fluid which it ejects.

Silk is obtained also from the spider; not from the cobweb, but the silky thread which the female spider spins round her eggs. The silken fibres of the pinna form a strong and beautiful fabric; and some species of moths form cocoons which may be spun for curiosity, but not with a view to commercial profit.

Reeling from the cocoons is only performed in countries where the silk is produced. Silk reaches the weaver in three different states, in which it is called *single*, *tram*, and *organzine*, the preparation of which is the business of the throwster. In plain silk-weaving the process is much the same as in weaving woollen or linen; but the weaver is assisted by a machine for the even distribution of the warp, which frequently consists of eight thousand separate threads in a breadth of twenty inches. The Jacquard-Loom has been the means of facilitating and cheapening the production of fancy or figured silks to an extraordinary extent. Patterns which required the greatest degree of skill and the most painful labour are produced by this machine by weavers of ordinary skill, and with but little more labour than that required in weaving plain silks. [JACQUARD]. The power-loom has been only partially employed in the silk manufacture; and excepting for the commonest goods, it does not possess any great advantage over the hand-loom, as the delicacy of the material to be worked, and the attention which must be given to the process of the weft, frequently render it necessary to stop the machine.

The general processes of the silk manufacture have been treated at some length under RIBAND; and some other articles of silk manufacture are noticed under their proper names. *Brocade* and *damask*, the most sumptuous articles of silk manufacture a century ago, are now comparatively unknown. *Persian*, *sarsnet*, *gros-de-Naples*, *ducapes*, *satin*, and *levantines*, are the names given to plain silks, which vary from one another only in texture, quality, or softness. *Satin* derives its lustre from the great proportion of the threads of the warp being left visible, and the piece being afterwards passed over heated cylinders. Other varieties of silk goods are produced by mechanical arrangements of the loom, such as using different shuttles with threads of various substances, &c. The pile which constitutes the peculiarity of *velvet* is produced by the insertion of short pieces of silk thread, which cover the surface so entirely as to conceal the interlacings of the warp and woof. The process of weaving velvet is slow, and it is paid for at five times the rate of plain silks. There are several sorts of goods in which silk is employed with woollen materials, as *poplins* and *bombazines*.

A few of the circumstances which have marked the progress of the silk manufacture in England are noticed under SPITALFIELDS. Ten or twelve years ago, one half of the silk manufactories were in Cheshire, next to which stood Lancashire, Derbyshire, and Staffordshire; but Lancashire has recently advanced more than the other counties in this department of industry. The following were the statistics of silk factories in the year 1850:

Factories in England	272
Spindles	1,188,908
Power looms	6,092
Steam and water-power	3,571 horse power.
Male operatives ..	12,513
Female operatives	29,190

Of the 272 silk factories, 97 were in Cheshire (chiefly at Macclesfield and Congleton). There were only five silk factories in Scotland, employing 841 persons. There was no silk factory either in Ireland or in Wales.

The silk imported in 1850 amounted to:—

Raw..................	4,942,417 lbs.
Waste and husks	14,600 cwts.
Thrown	460,526 lbs.

The manufactured silk goods imported in 1850, including broad silk, satin, ribbons, gauze, crape, velvet, and plush, amounted in weight to 826,650 lbs.; together with 715,739 pieces of Bandanna and other silk handkerchiefs. Our exports were 260,085 lbs., together with 410,473 pieces of silk handkerchiefs —mostly to the colonies.

SILVER. This beautiful metal has been well known and highly valued from the remotest period—circumstances which are readily explained by the facts of its occurring frequently native, and possessing great lustre and fitness for immediate use without being subjected to any metallurgic process.

Ores of silver.—The ores of silver are extremely numerous. Besides the *Native silver*, the chief ores are the following:—*Antimonial silver*, *telluric silver*, *native amalgam*, *auriferous native silver*, *arsenical antimonial silver*, *horn silver*, *earthy corneous silver*, *silver glance*, *earthy silver glance*, *light red silver*, *ruby silver*, *miargyrite*, *biegsamer silberglanz*, *flexible sulphuret*, *brittle sulphuret*, *silberkupferglanz*, *romelite*, *brittle silver*, *selensilver*, *cukairite*, *selbite*, and *ganzekothig-erz*. Most of these are known by two or three names each; some occur only in irregular masses, the rest in crystals. The ores which yield silver most readily and most abundantly are native silver, horn silver (chloride), and silver glance (sulphuret). Silver is also procured by cupellation. [LEAD.]

Silver has a purer white colour than any other metal; it has great brilliancy; and is susceptible of a high polish. Its specific gravity is about 10½. It is sufficiently soft to be cut with a knife; and is very malleable and ductile, so that it may be beaten into leaves about 1—10,000th of an inch in thickness, and drawn into wire much finer than a human hair. It does not rust or oxidise by exposure to the air, but when the air contains sulphureous vapours it tarnishes, becoming first yellowish and afterwards black. Three metals only, viz. iron, copper, and platinum, exceed silver in tenacity; a wire $\frac{1}{12}$ of an inch in diameter supports rather more than 187 pounds without breaking. When exposed to a bright red heat silver melts; on fusion its appearance is extremely brilliant, and during this it absorbs oxygen from the air to the amount of about twenty-two times its volume, and this it gives out either by cooling or being poured into water. When leaf-silver, or fine silver wire, is heated by voltaic electricity, it burns with a fine green flame; if intensely heated in the open fire it boils, and a portion is vapourised.

Oxide of silver gives a yellow colour to glass and porcelain, and is the oxide which is the basis of all the common salts of silver. The chloride of silver is perfectly white, but by exposure to daylight it becomes slowly blueish-white, and eventually almost black. The direct rays of the sun produce this effect almost instantaneously. On this property is founded its use in photogenic drawing. By mere heat it undergoes no change except fusion, and when it has solidified on cooling it has the appearance of horn; hence the name of *horn silver* for the native chloride. It is largely and advantageously used in experimental chemistry. The protoxide forms with ammonia a compound called *fulminating silver*, on account of the facility and violence with which it explodes; in exploding it forms water, sets free nitrogen, and metallic silver remains. A very gentle heat or slight friction causes it to explode sometimes even before it is dry. Nitrate of silver, when moderately heated, fuses, and being then cast in a mould in small cylindrical sticks, it constitutes the Argenti Nitras of the Pharmacopœias, commonly called *lunar caustic*. When sulphur, phosphorus, or charcoal, is mixed with nitrate of silver, and struck on an anvil, detonation ensues, and metallic silver is obtained. Nitrate of silver is employed by precipitation with carbonate of soda, &c., for writing on linen: it is commonly called *Indelible Ink*.

Iron and silver combine with difficulty; they separate on cooling, the iron retaining about one-eightieth of silver, and the silver about one-thirtieth of iron. According to Faraday and Stodart, steel containing about one five-hundredth of silver forms a good alloy for cutting instruments. Iron and silver form a blueish-white granular alloy; tin and silver a white, hard, brittle alloy. When cobalt and silver are fused together, they separate during cooling, each retaining a portion of the other. Lead and silver give a dull brittle alloy; antimony and silver a white brittle alloy; arsenic and silver form a gray, brittle granular compound, containing about 14 per cent. of the former metal. Bismuth and silver give a yellowish-white, brittle, lamellar alloy; molybdenum forms a compact, brittle, gray, granular compound with silver; and tungsten a brown, slightly malleable button: copper and silver readily combine, and the silver is rendered harder by it without much deterioration of colour; the standard silver of this country is composed of 11·10 silver and 0·90 copper. Mercury and silver amalgamate readily, and this compound is sometimes employed for plating, but this operation is now most advantageously carried on by precipitation by means of voltaic electricity.

Silver ores are found chiefly in veins which traverse the primary and the older of the secondary stratified rocks, but especially the former; and also the unstratified rocks, such as granite and porphyry, which are associated with the above. In some of the mines in Peru, and in those of Kongsberg in Norway and Freiburg in Saxony, silver has been discovered in masses weighing from 100 to 800 lbs. In the mines of Europe the veins are numerous and slender. In some of the mines in the Harz Mountains and in the Hungarian mines the veins occur in a small number of spots, and are of considerable dimensions. In three of the richest districts of Mexico there is only one principal vein, which is worked in different places. One of these veins, in the district of Guanaxuato, is from 130 to 148 feet wide, and it has been traced and worked to an extent of nearly eight miles.

In Mexico there were 500 mining establishments, called *Reales*, at the time of Humboldt's visit, and from 3000 to 4000 veins or masses were worked. The average richness of all the ores in Mexico is from 3 to 4 ounces per quintal of 102 lbs. In one of the Mexican mines a working of one hundred feet in length yielded in six months 432,274 lbs. troy of silver, equal in value to about 1,000,000*l*. In Chili some of the mines yield only 8 ounces in 5000 lbs. of ore; but in the rich mine of Copiapo, discovered in 1832, the ore frequently contains 60 or 70 per cent. of silver. The average produce of the mines of Saxony is from 3 to 4 ounces in the quintal. The lead mines of Craven in Yorkshire contained 230 ounces per ton; and those of Cardiganshire, worked in the reign of Charles I., yielded 80 ounces. The average proportion of the lead mines of the north of England is 12 ounces per ton. Even when the proportion of silver is so low as 8 ounces, or one grain per ½ lb., it has been found profitable to separate it. The produce of the Mexican mines averaged annually 4,800,000*l.* from 1793 to 1803, of which nineteen-twentieths were silver. In the first ten years of the present century the average annual value was about 5,000,000*l.*, the quantity of pure silver annually produced in that time being 1,440,650 troy lbs. The mines of Potosi in Peru are the most famous in South America. [POTOSI.] The produce of the Chilian mines in 1832 was about 1,000,000 ounces. At the commencement of the present century Humboldt estimated the annual produce of the silver-mines of Chili, Peru, Buenos Ayres, and New Grenada, at nearly 700,000 lbs. troy, valued at 2,074,476*l.* sterling. The proportion of silver to gold produced from all the American mines was, early in tho present century, as 62 to 1; and from the mines of all countries as 52 to 1.

The most productive mines in Europe are those in Saxony, Austria, Hungary, Norway, Russia and Spain; but nearly all of these are less productive than they have been in former ages. The quantity found in Great Britain is extremely small. Silver has ceased to be abundant in Asia, except perhaps in China. In Africa none is met with.

The silver mines of Copiapo aro those which are now attracting the most attention. In 1824 they produced only 310 lbs. of silver; about 1830 tho yearly produce was 3000 lbs.; after the discovery of new veins in 1832 the production rose to 16,000 lbs.; and during the last eight years the following results have been exhibited:—

1843	39,599	lbs.
1844	61,497	„
1845	76,723	„
1846	80,397	„
1847	102,052	„
1848	130,552	„
1849	171,119	„
1850 (about)	200,000	„

The proportional value of gold to silver was 12 and 10 to 1 from the Anglo-Saxon times to the discovery of America; it is at present 14·28 to 1. In ancient Greece the proportion varied from 15 and 10 to 1, and in Rome from 12 and 7 to 1. Herodotus estimates it at 13 to 1. Since the discovery of America the proportion throughout the world has been between 17 and 14 to 1. The English silver coinage from 1600 to 1800 amounted to about 26,000,000*l.*; from 1800 to 1840 about 11,000,000*l.*

There are nine mints in Mexico, at which the coinage was as follows in the years named.

	Dollars.	£
1842	984,427	196,885
1843	620,532	124,106
1844	726,762	145,352
1845	783,910	156,782
1846	915,752	183,150

When silver is issued for coin, it is always alloyed with copper: the maximum of hardness is produced by one-fifth of copper. One lb. of standard silver of the English coinage contains 11 oz. 2 dwts. of silver and 18 dwts. alloy, or 925 parts of pure silver in 1000 parts of standard silver. For purposes connected with the manufacture of various articles of use and ornament, the alloy is greater. At Birmingham rolled sheets are made which do not contain more than 3 or 4 dwts. of silver to each lb. of the inferior metal.

Mr. Jacob estimates the annual consumption of silver in the United Kingdom at 3,282,046 oz., valued at 820,511*l.* He distributes it as follows:—

That paying duty	1,375,316 oz.
That used in watch-cases	506,730
That used in plating	900,000
That for other minor purposes	500,000
	3,282,046

The value of the stock of silver in the hands of the manufacturers and dealers is estimated by the same authority at 3,280,000*l.* The value of ornaments and utensils of the precious metals in Europe and America, if brought to the crucible, Mr. Jacob values at 400,000,000*l.*, one fourth more than the value of the coined metals; but Mr. M'Culloch thinks these estimates too high; and as they were made before the recent discovery of gold at California, some of them are likely to be modified by the abundance of gold.

SILVERING. A few illustrations of the mechanical working of silver will be found under BIRMINGHAM, ELECTRO-METALLURGY, and GOLD-WORKING; but we are here speaking of the singular operation of silvering one surface of glass.

In an ordinary looking-glass, the reflexion is derived from a film of mercury or quicksilver, in contact with the hinder surface of the glass, and rendered fixed by amalgamating with a sheet of tin foil. Silvering is here not a correct term, for there is no silver employed; the process is nevertheless a highly curious one. In the first place a large sheet of tin foil is unrolled, and laid down on a perfectly flat and very smooth stone table. Liquid mercury is poured on the foil, from the iron bottles in which it is imported, and made to float over the entire surface. The glass, brought perfectly clean, is laid upon the mercury with a peculiar sliding movement, which suffices to remove the slight film of oxide which soon forms upon the surface. The glass is then entirely covered with heavy leaden weights, which could not be done with safety unless the glass and the stone were perfectly flat. After remaining a day or two in this state, with the stone slightly inclined, it is found that all the superfluous mercury has been pressed out from between the glass and the foil; and moreover the mercury has chemically combined with the foil, in such a way that both adhere firmly to the back of the glass. So great is the tact shewn in this process that in a well silvered glass there will not be found the smallest spot which has not its due share of reflective amalgam behind it.

Mr. Drayton patented a new mode of silvering glass, a few years ago. It is not only nominally but really silvering. Nitrate of silver is combined with spirit and certain liquids, and is poured on the clean surface of the glass; a border of putty or some other substance being laid round the glass to retain the liquid. After remaining thus a few hours, the liquid is poured off, and a sediment of silver is found to be left adhering to the glass. This sediment or film is secured in its place by a varnish of bees' wax and tallow.

A recent novelty is Kidd's Embroidered Glass, by which any pattern or device can be embroidered on glass, and thus fixed and rendered conspicuous by a subsequent silvering. The peculiarity of the process is that the patterns have the appearance of being in relief, or embossed on the exterior surface, and illuminated in frosted and burnished silver; whereas the whole of the processes are effected on the under surface. The engraving or embroidering is effected by peculiar tools; a peculiar composition is laid on the embroidered glass before the silver is applied; and the silver itself is applied in a way different from that adopted in any other process.

Another new production is Mr. Thomson's silvered vessels, which display wonderful brilliancy and beauty. Glass vessels of any shape, and made of glass of any colour, are silvered within in such a way as to yield a reflexion of great lustre. Some of the specimens in which green and ruby glass are thus silvered produce an effect which for gorgeousness can hardly be paralleled in any other manufacture. The surface is often richly cut and diversified; and the silvering may be made to appear at any spots selected by the workman. The silvering agent is one of the salts or compounds of silver, as in Drayton's process; but arrangements of a novel and intricate kind are requisite to the due production of the required effects.

These graceful novelties in the glass manufacture appropriately find a place in the Great Exhibition.

SINDE. This portion of India is rich in productions. Though its botanical wealth is not great, the agricultural products are numerous; all the grains and pulse common to India are grown. Rice is the staple in the delta and in the country between the Western Narra and the Indus, but in the other parts wheat and maize are most extensively cultivated. Barley is grown in some districts. Indigo is largely grown in the north-eastern districts, but it is inferior to that of Bengal. Opium is cultivated near Shikarpoor, and in some other districts. The sugar-cane is pretty generally grown throughout the whole of the province, but its produce is inferior to that of Northern Hindustan and the Panjab. Cotton is cultivated everywhere, but the best is grown in the northern districts. Tobacco of good quality is grown in the vicinity of Khyrpoor. Hemp, cucumbers, water-melons, and musk-melons, are extensively cultivated. The gardens produce carrots, turnips, radishes, onions, and several kinds of pumpkins. Among the fruits are the date, mango, pomegranate, apple, grape, lime, citron, fig, and a variety of other fruits. Ghee and hides constitute important articles of export. Sheep and goats are met with almost everywhere in upper Sinde, and wool is exported from that tract which lies west of the Indus and north of Shikarpoor.

The manufactures of Sinde are not numerous; but they may be considered extensive, when the scantiness of the population is considered. Cotton-cloth of a coarse description is manufactured in the principal towns and villages, chiefly for home consumption, and a little is exported to Afghanistan and Persia. Among the silk manufactures those of Tatta have acquired a repute in India, especially a rich fabric of silk, cotton, and gold, variegated in pattern and of close texture.

SINGAPORE. The commercial history of Singapore is remarkable. Singapore is the name of a town, of an island in which that town is situated, and of a settlement, in which the town is the chief feature. It occupies the extreme south of the Malayan peninsula, and is the most southern point in Asia. If the commerce of Singapore were limited to the produce of the place, it would hardly give employment to more than two or three vessels. But Singapore has become the London of southern Asia in the Indian Archipelago. All the nations that inhabit the countries border-

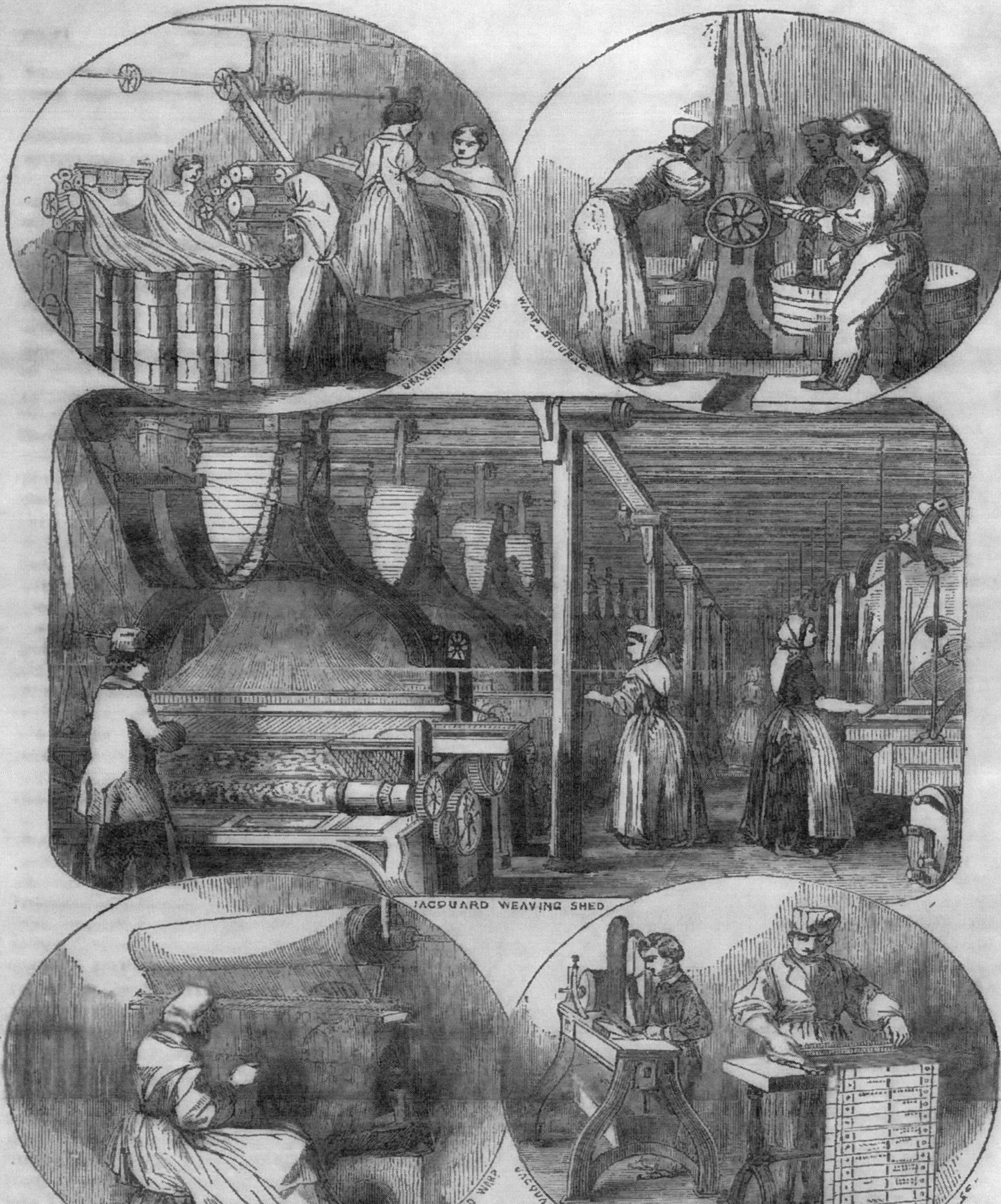

KNIGHT'S CYCLOPÆDIA OF THE INDUSTRY OF ALL NATIONS

No. 37.

ing on the Indian Ocean resort to it with the produce of their agriculture and manufacturing industry, and take in exchange such goods as are not grown or produced in their own countries. All of thom find there a ready market, which at the same time is well stocked with European goods. This effect has partly been produced by the wise policy of declaring the harbour of Singapore a free port, in which no export or import duties, nor any anchorage, harbour, nor lighthouse fees, are levied.

The commerce of Singapore may be divided into the eastern trade, the Straits trade, and the western trade. The eastern trade, or that which is carried on with the countries east and south-east of Singapore, comprehends the commerce with China, the Spanish settlement of Manilla, the independent tribes of the Indian Archipelago, the Dutch settlements on the island of Java and at Rhio, the new settlements at Sarawak and Labuan, the Australian and New Zealand colonies, and the countries of the Peninsula beyond the Ganges which lie east of the Malay Peninsula. The most important branches of this commerce are those with China, Java, and Siam.

The commerce of the Straits is carried on with the Malay Peninsula and with the island of Sumatra. The harbours on the eastern side of the peninsula, which trade with Singapore, are Pahang, Tringanu, and Calantan, and this trade is rather active. The trade with the western coast of the peninsula is not important, and is almost entirely limited to the harbour of Salangore. The commerce between Singapore and the island of Sumatra is almost entirely limited to the ports along the eastern coast of the island. There is hardly any commercial intercourse with the Dutch settlements of Bencoolen, Padang, and Tappanuli, which are on the western coast. The commerce of the eastern coast is divided between Singapore and Penang.

The western trade of Singapore comprehends that with Calcutta, Madras, Bombay, the island of Ceylon, and Arabia, with the Cape of Good Hope, Mauritius, and Australia, and with Europe and America. To enumerate the articles which constitute the materials of these three great streams of commerce would be to name almost all that Europe sells to Asia or Asia to Europe; or which are interchanged among the nations of eastern Asia

It is estimated that 300,000 tons of shipping now enter Singapore annually. The British and Irish produce and manufactures exported to Singapore in 1849 amounted in value to 494,088*l*.

SIPHON is a bent tube whose arms are of unequal length. The shorter of these arms being immersed in a liquid which is to be drawn from a vessel or a reservoir, and the air being removed by suction, or by means of a syringe, the liquid immediately rises in the immersed arm in consequence of the pressure of the atmosphere on that which surrounds the tube; it then passes over the bend and flows through the open orifice at the lower extremity of the other arm. The length of the column of fluid in this arm being greater than in the other, its superior weight causes the flow to be continuous.

The phenomena presented by springs of water are explained by supposing that the rain which is absorbed in the earth occasionally finds its way by small channels to some interior cavity, and from thence by other channels, which may be considered as natural siphons, to an orifice on a lower level at the surface of the ground. At this orifice it issues in a stream of water, which continues to flow till the surface of the water in the cavity has descended below the tops of the vertical bonds in the channels.

The siphon is used in many operations in which it is required to draw liquids from one vessel to another.

SISTRUM. This ancient musical instrument was constructed of brass, and shaped like the frame and handle of a racket, the head part of which had either three or four horizontal bars placed loosely on it, which were tuned, most probably, by some scale, and allowed to play freely, so that when the instrument was shaken, piercing ringing sounds must have been produced.

SKEW-BRIDGE is a bridge in which the passages over and under the arch intersect each other obliquely. Where space and neatness do not require to be considered, an oblique arch may be avoided, either by building the bridge square with the upper passage, and making the span so wide as to allow the stream to pass under it without being diverted; or by building the arch square with the stream, and of sufficient length to allow the upper passage to take an oblique course over it; but either of these is a clumsy expedient, although well adapted for some situations.

The skew-bridges built by George Stephenson on the Liverpool and Manchester Railway were the first in which the scientific principles of the method were properly applied. On that railway, out of rather more than sixty bridges, about one-fourth were built on the skew; one, built of stone, conducting the turnpike road across the line at Rainhill, being at an angle of only 34 degrees, by which the width of span is increased from 30 feet, the width of the railway from wall to wall, to

54 feet, the width on the oblique face of the arch. In the skew-bridge at Boxmoor, the angle is 32°, the square span 21 feet, and the oblique span 39 feet. The difficulty of building skew-bridges increases with the obliquity of the angle from 90° to 45°, which is supposed to be the most hazardous angle for a semicircular arch; but beyond that point, instead of increasing, it rather diminishes to about 25°, which appears to be about the natural limit for a semi-cylindrical arch. Elliptical oblique arches are deficient in stability, more difficult to execute, and more expensive, than semicircular or segmental arches.

The construction of skew-bridges of iron or timber is comparatively simple, the ribs or girders of which such bridges are composed being of the usual construction, laid parallel with each other, but the end of each being in advance of that next preceding it. The extraordinary iron bridge by which the Manchester and Birmingham Railway is conducted over Fairfield Street, Manchester, at an angle of only 24½°, is a fine example of this kind of skew-bridge. It consists of six ribs, of rather more than 128 feet span, although the width of the street is only 48 feet, resting upon very massive abutments of masonry.

SKINS AND FURS. Under FURS is given a brief account of the fur-trade, and of the uses of furs in manufacture. We will here glance at the extent of the trade in these products, so far as Great Britain is concerned.

The skins and furs imported into Great Britain in 1848 were the following:—

Bear	9,712
Beaver	41,132
Cat	7,752
Coney	61,599
Deer	37,737
Ermine	183,547
Fitch	82,140
Fox	72,939
Goat	241,333
Kid	601,119
Lamb	1,381,524
Lynx	47,317
Marten	219,195
Mink	223,254
Musquash	766,764
Nutria	18,546
Otter	14,684
Racoon	387,313
Seal	706,267
Sheep	259,223
Squirrel	2,674,602

Some portions of these were re-exported, but by far the greater part were worked up in England.

SKY. For the description of an instrument invented in order to measure the intensity of the blue colour of the sky, see CYANOMETER.

SKYLIGHT. Including under this term every mode of admitting light into an apartment through its roof or ceiling, we may here briefly notice that particular fashion of skylight distinguished in gothic architecture by the name of Lantern, though lanterns in gothic buildings were not so much intended to admit light as to supply ventilation and the means of escape to smoke. But the term lantern is also applied to the lower part of a tower placed at the intersection of the transepts with the body of a church, which, being open below, forms a loftier portion of the interior, lighted by windows on each side; and again to an upper open story, that is, one entirely filled with windows, on the summit of a tower, and frequently forming a superstructure different in plan from the rest, as in Fotheringay Church, and that at Boston, Lincolnshire, in both which examples the lantern forms an octagon placed upon a square. The upper portion of the tower of St. Dunstan's, Fleet Street, London, may also be described as a lantern.

Of skylights, however, properly so called (that is, which are nearly in the same plane as the general surface of the ceiling), no examples are to be met with in our ancient architecture; nor does anything of the kind occur in Italian architecture, except it be in the form of a cupola over a central saloon. An example of a church lighted entirely from above, without lateral windows, is furnished by that of St. Peter-le-Poor, Broad Street, London, which is a rotunda, covered by a cove, and a large circular lantern, whose tambour forms a sort of clerestory, consisting of a continuous series of arched windows, while the ceiling makes a very flat or slightly concave dome. Sir John Soane was one of the first who attempted to give importance and decorative character to skylights and ceiling windows, or windowed ceilings, as they may be termed, making them ornamental features in his interiors, varied in their design, and producing great diversity of striking effects, occasionally heightened by the light being transmitted through tinted glass, so as to diffuse a warm sunny glow over the apartment. The offices at the Bank of England afford many studies of the kind, while his own house, in Lincoln's Inn Fields, shows what he accomplished by a similar mode of treatment, upon a very limited scale.

The form of skylights more generally used for picture galleries, libraries, and other apartments of that class, is of the simplest kind, being lanterns, not like those in gothic architecture, of narrow and straight proportions, but spacious and low, and occupying a considerable surface of the ceiling. The light is admitted through the sides of the lantern, which are mostly filled in with panes of glass, so as to form a window continued on every side, without other divisions than the bars in its framework. Of other forms of lanterns and skylights in picture-galleries and sculpture-galleries, examples are furnished by those at the British Museum and the National Gallery, London, and the Fitzwilliam Museum at Cambridge, some of which are double skylights, a smaller skylight being raised over the first one.

There are a variety of other modes of lighting rooms from their ceilings, depending in a great measure on the taste and skill of the architect, and the necessities frequently imposed by the situation or purpose of the building.

The ridge and furrow skylights (if we may thus term them) of the Exhibition Building in Hyde Park, afford the largest and simplest example ever yet constructed; as the roof and the skylight are identical.

SLATE. The slaty cleavage or structure in stone appears to be the result of a general cause acting subsequently to the deposition and disturbance of the strata, capable of pervading and re-arranging the particles so as to systematise their mutual attractions, but not to fuse them together, destroy their original distinctness, or obliterate the evidence of their original condition. This force was so general, that along many miles of country, as, for example, in the whole Snowdonian chain, one particular direction (north-north east), in North Devon and Pembrokeshire another (nearly east and west), is found to prevail more or less distinctly in all the rocks. This dependence of the slaty structure on the nature of the rock is sometimes very positively pronounced, as in some classes of rock the cleavage does change and even reverse its inclination where contortions prevail. Pressure, in some peculiar application seems to be the grand agent in the production of slaty cleavage.

For economical purposes there appears little chance of obtaining in the British Islands good Slate (properly so called) from any but the ancient argillaceous strata superposed on mica schist and gneiss, and covered by old red-sandstone or mountain limestone. From these strata in Scotland, Cumberland, Westmoreland, Yorkshire, Charnwood Forest, North Wales abundantly, South Wales, Devonshire, Cornwall, the north and south of Ireland, slates of various value are dug. The thin flagstone of the coal formation in many parts of England and Wales, the laminated sandy limestone of Stonesfield, Collywiston, &c., which are often called slates, and are extensively used in roofing, are all obtained by natural partings parallel to the stratification. True slate is split by wedges from the apparently solid rock along planes often no more discoverable than those of a real crystal. In colour it is purple, blue, green, yellowish, or almost white, or striped across the planes. In some slates (west of Scotland, Ingleton, &c.) crystals of cubical iron pyrites are scattered. Much of the Cumberland slate (Borrowdale) appears full of fragments.

Some slate quarries are remarkably situated, and are wrought under circumstances of difficulty. At Honister Crag, between Borrowdale and Buttermere, there is a quarry near the top of a mountain whose sides are so steep, that the quarrymen take up a week's provision with them, to avoid the necessity of ascending and descending every day. The slates are lowered by sledges in a mode which would be perilous to any not accustomed to it. In all slate quarries the slate is extracted in large blocks; and the lamellar structure of the slate enables the blocks to be easily separated into thin layers by the use of a chisel and mallet. All the slates in ordinary use, both for roofing and for writing on, are brought to the thin slate so familiar to us by these simple means.

A considerable increase has taken place during the last half of 1850 in the export of slate from the various quarries in North Wales; a circumstance attributed to the repeal of the brick duty causing an impetus to the erection of houses. From the port of Caernarvon alone, the exports for the half year were 61,400 tons, being an increase of 11,000 tons over the prior half year, and for the month of February, 1851, the shipment has been to the extent of 6,200 tons. In other ports a large increase is apparent.

Slate is now used for a variety of purposes as a substitute for stone in some cases, and for lead in others. Pavements, cisterns, walls, partitions, &c., are constructed. A superior production called *enamelled slate* is used for ornamental table-tops, slabs for consoles and pier-tables, wash-stand tops, columns, pilasters, door furniture, mural tables, monuments, &c.

Slate pencils are simply narrow slips of a very soft kind of slate. An ingenious kind of slate pencil has been lately devised, in which the material, brought to a very small thickness, is slid into a groove in a wooden stem, through which it is propelled by a spiral apparatus, somewhat on the principle of the ever-pointed lead pencils. In 1849 Mr. Cohen patented a new kind of slate pencil, made from a mixture of alumina, French chalk, soap-stone, and water.

SLAVONIA. The produce and industry of the Slavonian provinces are briefly noticed under AUSTRIA.

SLIDE (or SLIDING) RULE. The sliding-rule is an instrument for the mechanical performance of addition and subtraction, which is converted into an instrument for the mechanical performance of multiplication and division by the use of logarithmic scales, instead of scales of equal parts. This instrument was invented by Oughtred, about 1630, and is very little known on the Continent.

The following are the principal kinds of sliding rule now in use. The common *engineer's rule* or *carpenter's rule* in its best form, is a double 12-inch rule, a slide of two radii with the same scale on one side, and a scale of one radius of double length on the other, with divisors. Bevan's *engineer's rule*, 12 inches, has slides on both faces (which may be exchanged), and serves for squares, cubes, square roots of cubes, &c. There are scales on the backs of the slides and in the grooves, for sines, tangents, inverted numbers, compound interest and annuities at five per cent. Henderson's *double-slide rule*, 12 inches, has two parallel contiguous slides, with scales of numbers fixed above and below, and solves at one operation most sets of multiplications and divisions not exceeding five operations; at the back are tables of divisors for solids. In Woollgar's Pocket Calculator, 8 inches, the two slides work in either of the grooves: the backs and the grooves have scales of sines, tangents, areas of polygons, circular segments; interest, annuities, certain and for lives, at several rates of interest. An addition may be made by a metal slip, giving the solution of the same questions as the last rule. Woollgar's Pocket-Book Rule, 6 and 8 inches, has two radii, one under the other, a line for sines, and duplicate proportions at the back of the slide. At the bottom of the groove are sometimes inserted lines for finding the relations of right-angled triangles, for cask gauging, and for cuttings and embankments. The Excise-officer's *sliding rule*, is an instrument of which the graduations are adapted to the calculation required by those officers.

SLING is an instrument with which stones or other missiles may be thrown to a great distance. In its simplest form the sling consists of a thong of leather, or a piece of cord or some woven fabric, both ends of which are held in the hand of the slinger. The stone or missile is placed in the fold or double of the thong, which is made wide at that part, and sometimes furnished with a slit or socket for the purpose of holding it; and the sling is then whirled round to gain an impetus. In the hands of an expert slinger, this instrument may be made to project missiles to a great distance, and with surprising accuracy.

The sling was long used, both as an offensive weapon and otherwise, in England. Strutt observes, that 'it is altogether uncertain whether the ancient inhabitants of Britain were acquainted with the use of the sling or not;' but that 'our Saxon ancestors certainly used it, and seem to have been skilful in its management.' Slingers formed a part also of the Anglo-Norman soldiery.

SLUICE is any kind of flood-gate or trap to retain water for a given time, or in a given direction. Sluices are extensively used in most hydraulic works, and vary much in their construction, according to the purposes for which they are required. In mill streams they serve to keep back the water when the mill is at rest, and to regulate the supply when it is going. They also act as 'wasters,' to allow the surplus water of a reservoir to escape. For these purposes many self-acting sluices have been contrived, to avoid the inconvenience and even danger which might arise from neglect, as well as to save the expense of a sluice-keeper. For canal-locks it is necessary to make the large gates meet in an angle in the middle of the stream, in order that they may be able to resist the pressure of the water; and as this pressure would render it impossible to open them against any considerable head of water, small sluices are provided either in the gates or in the masonry of the lock, by which the water may be let in or out at pleasure.

SMALT is a glass coloured of a fine blue, by means of oxide of cobalt. [COBALT.] When reduced to an impalpable powder it is employed to give a blue tint to writing paper and linen. Upwards of 150,000 lbs. of smalt were imported in 1848.

SMEATON, JOHN. Smeaton's name will always be held in respect as long as engineering skill calls forth admiration. He was born near Leeds in 1724; he came to London about 1742, and established himself as a mathematical instrument maker in Great Turnstile, Holborn. In 1751 he constructed a machine for measuring a ship's way at sea; and in 1753 was engaged in a course of experiments 'concerning the natural powers of water and wind to turn mills and other machines depending on circular motion.' The results of these experiments were published in 1759, and obtained for him the Copley gold medal of the Royal Society in that year. Smeaton had in

1753 been made a member of the Royal Society; and had contributed to the 'Transactions' even before that date. In 1754 he visited Holland and the Netherlands. In 1766 he commenced the great work which, more than any other, may be looked upon as a monument of his skill—the Eddystone Lighthouse. [LIGHTHOUSES.]

In 1764 Smeaton was the successful candidate for the office of receiver of the Derwentwater estate, the funds of which were, after its forfeiture in 1715, appropriated to Greenwich Hospital. While holding this office he greatly improved the estate, the mines and mills of which required the superintendence of such a man to make them of their full value. Increasing business induced him, in 1777, to relinquish this engagement. Of the many useful works executed by Smeaton, Ramsgate harbour perhaps holds, next the Eddystone Lighthouse, the most prominent place. This work was commenced in 1749, and was placed under his superintendence in 1774; but was completed by the two Rennies, father and son. Smeaton laid out the line of the great canal connecting the western and eastern shores of Scotland, from the Forth to the Clyde, and superintended the execution of great part of it. The Spurn Lighthouse at the mouth of the Humber, some important bridges in Scotland, and many other works of like character were executed by him.

About 1783 Smeaton's declining health rendered it necessary for him to avoid entering upon many new undertakings. He then devoted much attention to the publication of an account of the Eddystone Lighthouse, which was to have been followed by a 'Treatise on Mills,' and other works embodying his valuable experience as an engineer. He died Oct. 28, 1792; and his numerous professional reports were published after his death by a society of his friends engaged in kindred pursuits, in three quarto volumes, to which a fourth was subsequently added, consisting of his miscellaneous papers communicated to the Royal Society, &c. Besides the works already mentioned, Smeaton introduced many improvements in mathematical apparatus, and had an ardent love for science.

SMELTING. [IRON MANUFACTURE.]

SMOKE. The action of an ordinary chimney in conveying the smoke from a fire situated at its lower extremity is very simple. The air in the chimney, being rarefied by the heat, becomes lighter in proportion to its bulk than the surrounding atmosphere, and therefore rises, its place being supplied by fresh air forced in at the lower end by the pressure of the comparatively heavy cold air outside the chimney. A constant rising current is thus created, the force of which is sufficient to carry up with it any light bodies, such as the particles of soot which escape from the fire. The higher the chimney, and the warmer the air within it, the better will the smoke ascend. Franklin enumerated nine causes for the smoking (as it is termed) of ordinary chimneys:—the want of a free supply of air to the bottom of the chimney; the opening at the lower end of the chimney being too large; the chimney being too short; different chimneys in the same house having different degrees of draught, whereby one overpowers another; the situation of the house near a higher house or a hill; the lower level of a chimney than those which surround it; the injudicious arrangement of the doors of a room; the descent of smoke in a chimney out of use; and the occasional effects of high or contrary winds. He treated all these causes in succession, and proposed such measures as he thought likely to meet the exigencies of each.

The nuisance occasioned by the smoke of coal fires has formed a subject of complaint from the earliest times in which mineral fuel was extensively used; and the great increase of steam-engine and other furnaces, consequent on the extension of manufactures, has afforded, of late years, additional grounds for attempts to abate the nuisance. Such attempts are important, not only for the purification of the air but also for the economy of fuel; since the matter which gives smoke objectionable density and colour is unconsumed fuel in a finely-divided state. It appears thereforo that if a supply of air could be thrown into a fire in such a way as to occasion the combustion of the carbonaceous matter, the result would be that a greater amount of heat would be obtained from a given quantity of fuel, at the same time that the nuisance of smoke would be abated.

The quantity of smoke emitted from furnace chimneys varies much with the state of the fire; being greatest when a mass of fresh fuel is thrown on, and least when the fire has burned clear, or the fuel is fully ignited. Attention to this circumstance, on the part of the stoker, will greatly diminish the nuisance; because if he throw on the fresh fuel in a thin layer, it will the sooner become perfectly ignited; and, by laying it in the fore part of the furnace, the dense smoke arising from it has to pass over that part of the fire which is in a state of more perfect combustion, and is thereby in a great measure consumed. Many of the contrivances introduced or suggested as smoke-consuming furnaces act on these principles; arrangements being adopted to insure the right feeding of the fire without much attention on the part of the firemen. The first important attempt made in this country for the combustion of smoke was that of Watt, who obtained a patent in 1785 for a method of constructing furnaces in such a way as to cause 'the smoke or flame of the fresh fuel, in its way to the flues, or chimney, to pass, together with a current of fresh air, through, over, or among fuel which has already ceased to smoke, or which is converted into coke, charcoal, or cinders, and which is intensely hot; by which means the smoke and grosser parts of the flame, by coming into close contact with, or by being brought near unto, the said intensely hot fuel, and by being mixed with the current of fresh or unburned air, are consumed or converted into heat, or into pure flame, free from smoke.' Since that time innumerable plans have been brought forward for introducing the necessary supply of air to the furnace; but while many of them accomplish the purification of the smoke as completely as could be desired, they are generally found either to increase the consumption of fuel, or to weaken the draught of the furnace. A singular plan has been introduced by Mr. Iveson, of injecting steam into the furnace; the steam being thrown into the fire in several minute jets, from a fan-shaped distributor in the fore part of the furnace. The steam not only destroys the smoke, but also greatly increases the intensity of the fire; so much so, indeed, as to sanction the supposition that the steam is decomposed, and that its component gases are consumed. One drawback to the scheme is the great consumption of steam. A patent was obtained in 1838, by Mr. Chappé, for the use of a stream or shower of hot water thrown into the furnace in the same way.

Besides the numerous plans for the combustion of smoke, various methods have been tried on a limited scale for conducting it to a distance from the buildings in which it is formed, by means of subterraneous channels; and for condensing it by means of a shower of water, so that tho sooty matter might be conveyed away by the sewers.

SMOKE-JACK, is an apparatus believed to be of German origin, and as old as the 14th century, by which the rising current in a chimney, acting upon the inclined vanes of a wheel fixed in the funnel, gives motion, through a train of wheels to any matter which is hung before the fire to roast. This contrivance is now almost superseded by jacks impelled by the descent of a weight or the uncoiling of a spring.

SMYRNA. This is one of the most important commercial cities in Asiatic Turkey. The port is frequented by ships from all nations, freighted with valuable cargoes both outward and inward. The chief imports are—coffee, sugar, indigo, tin, iron, lead, cotton twist, manufactured goods, rum and brandy, spices, cochineal, and a variety of other articles. The principal exports are—silk, opium, drugs and gums, galls, cotton, wool, valonia, and fruit. Besides these exports there are various kinds of skins, goats' wool, olive oil, wax, and a variety of other articles. This large commerce has obviously arisen, not only from the advantageous situation of the port, but from the liberal policy of the Turkish government, which has imposed hardly any restrictive enactments with few duties, and those extremely low. Many of the European states have their consuls at Smyrna, such as England, Sweden, Prussia, France, Venice, &c.

SNUFF MANUFACTURE. Snuff is made from the tobacco stalk alone, from the leaf alone, and from the stalk and leaf mixed, according to the kind to be produced. The purest kind of snuff is that which is known by the name of *Scotch*; it is either made entirely of stalks, or of stalks mixed with a very small proportion of leaf. There are many kinds of snuff called *high-dried*, such as *Welch* and *Lundyfoot* (the latter being named after a celebrated maker); these owe their qualities chiefly to the circumstance that they are dried so much as to acquire a slight flavour of scorching. The snuff called *rappee* is made chiefly from leaf, to which is added the *smalls* or broken fibre of tobacco, which are too small to be smoked conveniently in a pipe. The dark colour is principally produced by wetting the powdered tobacco in a box, and allowing it to remain a considerable time, turned occasionally with a shovel; it undergoes a slight fermentation, the degree of which gives rise to the distinction between *brown* and *black* rappee.

The original quality of the leaf is as much attended to as the subsequent processes. Scotch snuff is made from the stalks of light dry leaves; whereas rappee and the darker snuffs are made from the darker and ranker leaves. A process of scenting has great influence also on the flavour of the snuff; since the manufacturer can introduce any kind of perfume which may please his customers. Thus *prince's mixture*, and many snuffs of higher price, owe no small part of their flavour to the kinds of scent introduced.

A curious example of division of labour is presented by the Snuff Manufacture. The maker does not grind his own snuff, although he may do all else that pertains to the manufacture. Nearly all the snuff made in London is ground in and near Mitcham, by the aid of the water power furnished by the river Wandle. The explanation seems to be this—that no manufacturer makes enough snuff to keep a snuff mill going; but that the mill owner, by grinding for many manufacturers, can afford to do it at a price which renders it prudent for them to adopt this system. The mills are provided with two kinds of grinding machines; in one of these a vertical stone rolls in a circle over the surface of a horizontal stone, and grinds the snuff between them: in the other there is a kind of large pestle and mortar, in which the pestle has a rolling motion given to it instead of a series of blows. The proprietor sends the snuff to the mill after a certain stage of preparation; and after it is returned from the mill in a ground state, it undergoes certain finishing operations. Many of the London manufacturers have small mills on their own establishments, for grinding small quantities of snuff, or for passing through any particular process the various kinds of fancy snuff; but the main bulk of the snuff is ground under the arrangements just described.

SOAP MANUFACTURE. The principal kinds of soap manufactured in England are *white* or *curd soap*, made chiefly from tallow and soda, but for some particular purposes olive-oil and soda; *yellow soap*, composed of tallow, resin, and soda, to which some palm-oil is occasionally added; and *mottled soap*, made from tallow, kitchen stuff, and soda; the mottled appearance is given to this soap by dispersing the lees through it towards the end of the operation. There is also a *brown soap*, made from palm oil and resin. *Soft soap* is generally prepared from fish-oil and potash.

The harder or soda soaps are prepared by boiling the fatty matter with an aqueous solution of caustic soda; when combination has taken place, or in other words, when the soap is formed, a quantity of common salt is added, which, dissolving in the lees, increases their density, and the soap then floats on the surface of the liquid. The fire being then extinguished, the semifluid soap, after a proper interval, but while yet hot, is removed from the lees and put into frames of wood or iron, where it remains until it has become cold and hard, when it is cut into bars for sale. In making soft soap no lees are separated, the whole of the solution of potash, which is made strong on that account, being combined with the oily matter used.

The soaps which have the alkalies for their bases are soluble in water, though the solution is in general milky; they are also soluble in alcohol, and the solution is used frequently as a test of what is called the hardness of water; acids also decompose soaps.

Fancy soaps or scented soaps are made in great variety, and have generally French names attached to them; for the French are the leading manufacturers of such articles. Among *soft toilet* soaps are *Naples soap*, *savon nacré*, and *crème d'amandes*. Among *hard toilet* soaps are *Windsor soap*, *Savon à la rose*, *Savon au bouquet*, *cinnamon soap*, *orange-flower soap*, *musk soap*, *bitter almond soap*, and many others. Most of these are scented by the substances which give them their characteristic names.

The soap manufacture is one of considerable importance. The principal seats in England are Liverpool and Runcorn, London, Brentford, Bristol, and Hull; there are also soap-works of considerable extent at Bromsgrove, Newcastle, Gateshead, Warrington, and Plymouth. In Scotland two-thirds of the total quantity of soap are made at Glasgow and Leith. In Ireland soap is chiefly made at Belfast, Londonderry, Limerick, and Cork.

In 1711 an excise duty of 1*d.* per lb. was first imposed on all soap made in Great Britain, which was raised in 1713 to 1½*d.* per lb. In 1782 the duty was again increased, and a distinction was for the first time made between hard and soft soap, the duty on the former being 2½*d.*, and on the latter 1¾*d.* per lb. In 1816 another increase of duty took place, and hard soap was subjected to a duty of 3*d.* per lb. In 1833 the duty was reduced to 1½*d.* per lb. on hard soap, and 1*d.* per lb. on soft. The present duty is 1½*d.* per lb. and 5 per cent. on hard soap; 1*d.* per lb. and 5 per cent. on soft soap. Notwithstanding the strenuous exertions made for its removal, the soap duty still remains a blot on the excise relations of this country.

The quantity of soap charged with excise duty during the last three years has been as follows:

1848	189,669,263 lbs.
1849	197,632,281 „
1850	204,410,826 „

The quantity exported to foreign countries during the same three years amounted to

1848	10,462,069 lbs.
1849	10,728,342 „
1850	12,555,493 „

SOCIETY OF ARTS. This society has been for so long a period connected with the progress of manufactures in this country, that it will be right to trace briefly its history. The object of this Society is 'to promote the arts manufactures, and commerce of this kingdom, by giving honorary or pecuniary rewards, as may be best adapted to the case, for the communication to the Society, and through the

Society to the public, of all such useful inventions, discoveries, and improvements as tend to that purpose.' It was projected in the year 1753; but the first public meeting took place in March, 1754. The plan was formed by Mr. William Shipley, a drawing-master, who acted for some time as secretary to the Society; and it was carried into effect by a few noblemen and gentlemen, among whom appear the names of Lord Folkstone, Lord Romney, and Dr. Stephen Hales. The services of Mr. Shipley were acknowledged by the Society voting to him, in 1758, a gold medal, 'for his public spirit, which gave rise to the Society;' and subsequently by the publication of his portrait as a frontispiece to the fourth volume of their 'Transactions.' The Society began, immediately after its formation, to advertise premiums for the encouragement of young persons of both sexes in the various departments of the fine arts; for improvements in agriculture and manufactures; for mechanical inventions; and for promoting the cultivation of valuable plants in British colonies.

For several years after the formation of the Society of Arts, there was no authorised publication of the papers communicated to the committees, or for making known the results of its labours. The publication of such information in an annual volume of 'Transactions' was contemplated soon after the commencement of the Society's operations; but the first volume did not appear until the year 1783. Many of the papers however, which would otherwise have appeared in such a work, were published, with the sanction of the Society, in Dossie's 'Memoirs of Agriculture and Œconomical Arts,' of which the first volume appeared in 1768, and the third and last in 1782. Some further particulars respecting the early proceedings of the Society are supplied by a 'Register of the Premiums and Bounties given by the Society instituted in London for the Encouragement of Arts, Manufactures, and Commerce, from the original institution in the year 1754 to the year 1776 inclusive.' This register, which was prepared by a committee of the Society, and is arranged in a tabular form, was printed in folio, in 1778.

The total amount of pecuniary rewards bestowed by the Society down to 1776 was, according to the 'Register' above referred to, 23,551*l.* 18*s.* 2*d.*; or, including the cost of medals, and pallets, 24,616*l.* 4*s.* 8*d.* This register was continued by manuscript additions to the end of 1813; and from these it appears that the pecuniary rewards bestowed from 1777 to 1813 amounted to about 2757*l.* 10*s.*, and that the medals and pallets distributed were 188 in gold and 464 in silver. Later than this there does not appear to be any condensed statement of the operations of the Society; but it has been stated for some years past, in their advertisement to the public, that upwards of 100,000*l.*, derived from voluntary subscriptions and legacies, h[illegible] been expended in pursuance of their plan. It may be briefly remarked, in the words of the secretary's address at the distribution of prizes in 1841, that 'at a time when it stood alone in offering encouragement to the fine arts, it effected much good in that department; and that it can now point with proud satisfaction to the names of Bacon, Nollekens, and Flaxman, Cosway and Lawrence, Sharp and Sherwin, Pingo, Marchant, and Wyon, with many other eminent artists, the early manifestations of whose genius were noticed by the Society in a manner which, there can be no doubt, assisted very materially in its developement.' Still more important perhaps have been the effects of the Society's encouragement of poor operatives, in improving the processes with which they are practically acquainted. The history of those inventions connected with weaving, which have been the objects of their encouragement within the last forty years, was adverted to in the address just quoted, as an illustration of what the Society have effected; about twenty pecuniary rewards having been given, chiefly to Bethnal Green and Spitalfields weavers, for inventions of great utility.

As before stated, the first volume of the Society's 'Transactions' was published in 1783. For forty-seven years from that time a volume appeared annually; but since 1829 the volumes have been biennial. An index to the first twenty-five volumes was published in 1808, and two others, embracing respectively from the twenty-sixth to the fortieth, and from the forty-first to the fiftieth, have since appeared. In 1774 the Society removed from their original premises, opposite Beaufort Buildings, Strand, to their present house in the Adelphi, which was erected purposely for them; and in the years 1777-83 Barry decorated their great room with a series of pictures.

The Society of Arts has taken an active part in encouraging the Great Exhibition of 1851; many of the officers and influential members of the Society are also members of the Commissions and Committees relating to the Exhibition; and there can be no doubt that we are in part indebted for this admirable and honourable display to the proceedings of the Society. It would have been pleasant if this Exhibition had formed a centenary commemoration of the Society, in addition to its other attractions; in 1854 such a centenary period will actually occur.

SODA MANUFACTURE. This branch of manufacturing chemistry is a very interesting one as exemplifying the important advantages which we derive from our inexhaustible stores of salt, and from the numerous useful substances which this salt is made to yield.

What is usually called *soda* is not strictly such; it is *Carbonate of Soda;* but both are produced from common salt. Sulphuric acid is the agent which enables salt to yield these valuable products. In some of the chemical works at Glasgow and Newcastle, sulphuric acid is made by the aid of sulphur; and this acid and salt are used for further processes. When a high excise duty was laid upon common salt, soda was made from *kelp* and *barilla;* but now that salt is purchaseable at so low a price, all our soda is obtained from this source, for employment in soap making, alum making, bleaching, washing, &c.

In manufacturing soda a given weight of salt is placed in a reverberatory furnace, in a leaden pan, and sulphuric acid is dropped down upon it through a leaden pipe brought through the roof of the furnace. The salt liquifies in the acid, and a gaseous vapour ascends; this vapour is *Muriatic acid gas,* which takes away the chlorine from the salt, and which is condensed into a liquid in the way described in a former article [MURIATIC ACID.] The sulphuric acid forms a pasty mass of *sulphate of soda,* with the remaining ingredients in the furnace. The sulphate is taken from the furnace, mixed with fine lime and fire coal, put into another furnace, and heated. The coal kindles, and melts the sulphate and lime into a viscid mass, which after being repeatedly raked and stirred, is removed from the furnace into iron trays. The mass, which is called *ball soda, crude soda,* or *British barilla,* is a mixture of carbonate of soda with sulphuret of calcium. The carbonate is separated from the sulphuret by steeping in water, which dissolves the former but not the latter; there is formed, in fact, a solution of carbonate of soda, which, in being evaporated, yields the solid carbonate almost entirely from sulphur. This is a yellowish earthy substance, called *soda ash* or *soda salt,* largely used in manufactures. But a more pure and crystallised carbonate is required for some purposes; this is produced by dissolving, settling, evaporating, and crystallising, whereby beautiful crystals of *carbonate of soda* are produced. By a further chemical process the carbonic acid is driven off, and *pure* or *caustic soda* results.

SODA WATER MANUFACTURE. A few details on this subject will be found under AERATED WATERS.

SODIUM. This metal is the base of the alkalies soda, natron, and the fossil alkali, in which substances it is combined with oxygen, forming the protoxide of the metal. It was discovered by Sir H. Davy in 1807. The properties of sodium are such as to prevent its occurrence in nature, except in combination, on account of its intense affinity for oxygen. Immense quantities occur combined with chlorine, forming common salt; and a considerable quantity is met with in the state of oxide, or soda, combined with carbonic acid; these are its principal sources. [Sodium] has a colour and lustre resembling those of silver. It remains a soft solid at 32°, so that small portions may be welded together by pressure; it becomes much softer at 122°, fuses at about 190°, and by a white heat is volatilised. Like potassium, it speedily tarnishes by exposure to the air, owing to its great affinity for oxygen, and this occurs more rapidly when the air is moist. When thrown on water it decomposes it with a hissing noise, the results being hydrogen and oxide of sodium, or soda. When however it is placed on a moistened bad conductor of heat, as charcoal, it decomposes water with a vivid combustion. Its specific gravity is 0.972, so that although it is considerably more dense than potassium, it is yet less so than water. It is a good conductor of electricity and heat; but if too strongly heated in the air, it burns with a yellow flame.

Sodium and oxygen combine to form pure *soda,* which is a gray solid, resembling potash in appearance, but it is less fusible and volatile. It is extremely acrid to the taste, and is very caustic. It has a great affinity for water, dissolving readily in it, and in large quantity, and the solution has strongly marked alkaline properties. Sodium and chlorine form the valuable substance *common salt,* formerly called Muriate of Soda, and now Chloride of Sodium. Of all natural soluble salts this occurs in the greatest quantity. It is met with solid, constituting rock-salt, in solution in salt springs and in the ocean, and in small quantity in almost all spring and river water. [SALT.] *Nitrate of Soda* is used largely in making nitric acid and sulphuric acid. The *Carbonate of Soda* is noticed under SODA MANUFACTURE. The *Sulphate of Soda,* formerly called *Glauber's Salt,* is readily soluble in water, and the solution by evaporation yields colourless transparent prismatic crystals. It has a very bitter taste; it effloresces when exposed to the air, by losing water of crystallisation.

Borax, Rochelle Salt and many other useful substances, as well as *soda alum,* are prepared from some of the compounds of Sodium.

SOILS. The agricultural soils which have

been formed from the disintegration and decomposition of the primitive rocks, such as granite, basalt, slate or limestone, and especially those which contain all these minerals minutely divided and intimately mixed, are always naturally fertile, and soon enriched by cultivation; the hard particles of quartz maintain a certain porosity in the soil, which allows air and moisture to circulate, while the alumina prevents its too rapid evaporation or filtration. The soils which have been evidently formed from the rocks which are supposed to be of secondary formation, are fertile according to the proportion of the earths of these rocks which they contain.

Each distinct formation gives rise to a great variety with respect to fertility, even where the basis remains the same; but it is of great importance to the farmer to ascertain the general nature of the rocks and strata on which his farm is incumbent, and no chemical analysis can determine the exact value of the land unless the geological situation of it is distinctly known.

The alluvial soils formed by the deposit of a variety of earths in a state of great division, and mixed with a considerable portion of organic matter, form by far the most productive lands. They will bear crop after crop with little or no additional manure, and with a very slight cultivation. These soils are found along the course of rivers which traverse extensive plains, and which have such a current as to keep very fine earth suspended by a gentle but constant agitation, but not sufficiently rapid to carry along with it coarse gravel or sand.

The simplest process of ascertaining the mechanical texture of soils is by washing with pure water. For this purpose nothing is required but a few flat plates and large cups. Some of the soil is formed into a very thin mud by stirring it in a cup nearly full of water. The finer particles are successively poured off from the sand or grit, which at last remains pure, so that the water added to it is no longer discoloured. This being dried and weighed, gives the coarse sand. The water and earth poured off are allowed to settle. A common soup-plate is found a very convenient vessel for this purpose. On the surface of the deposited earth will be found all the undecomposed vegetable matter, which with a little care is easily taken off, dried, and weighed. The finer portions of the earth can be poured off successively by shaking the whole moderately, till nothing but very fine sand remains. The alumina and impalpable silica will remain long suspended in the water, and allow any sand yet remaining to be deposited. They may be rapidly separated from the water by filtration through stout blotting-paper; but it is preferable to pour them into a glass tube about one inch in internal diameter, with a cork fitted in the lower end. In this tube the earths slowly fall to the bottom, and any variety in the size of the particles causes a line more or less distinct, which can be observed through the glass; and thus a very good idea may be obtained of the proportion of the different earths, as far as regards the size of their particles. In order to ascertain their chemical differences, they should be taken to a chemist and analysed.

The chemical and mechanical modes of treating various kinds of soil are briefly noticed under the names of the soils [CHALK; CLAY; LOAM; MARL; &c.,]; also under MANURE, &c.

SOLDERING is the union of the surfaces of two metals, generally by the intervention of a third. In the ordinary mode of soldering, the alloy used as a solder must be more fusible than the metal or metals which are to be united, and must have a strong affinity for them. The solder usually contains a large proportion of the metal to which it is to be applied, in combination with some more easily fusible metals. To insure perfect metallic union between the solder and the surfaces to which it is applied, it is essential that they be made perfectly clean and free from oxide, and that the atmosphere be excluded during the operation, in order to prevent the formation of any oxide while the process is going on. This is effected in various ways, but most commonly by the use of borax, sal ammoniac, or rosin, either mixed with the solder or applied to the surfaces to be joined.

Various kinds of solders or alloys are used, according to the metal which is to be soldered. Platinum is soldered with gold. Gold is soldered with an alloy of fine gold, silver, and copper. Silver solders usually consist of silver mixed with brass, and sometimes with zinc. Brass, copper, and iron are soldered with an alloy of zinc with copper or brass. Articles of wrought iron, and some qualities of steel also, may be soldered with cast-iron; the cast-iron being repeatedly heated and quenched in water, by which it becomes sufficiently friable to be beaten to a coarse powder with an iron pestle and mortar. Common *plumbers' solder* is made of two parts lead and one part block tin; or of the same metals mixed in nearly equal quantities; bismuth is added when it is desired to make the alloy more fusible. *Soft solder* has two parts tin to one lead; and other alloys of tin, lead, and bismuth, are used for uniting various articles of lead, tin, pewter, and other soft compounds. Such highly fusible solders are usually cast in ingots or strips, and melted as they are used by means of an instrument called a soldering-iron, which is tipped with copper—that metal being preferred for its greater affinity for tin. In soldering tin plates together, their edges are made to overlap; but in almost every other case the edges to be joined are made only to meet, the solder being run between their abutting edges.

A kind of soldering, called *burning-to*, has been long practised in some cases with sheet-lead, where it has been desirable to make a vessel entirely of that material; the junction being effected by pouring melted lead on to the edges to be united, until they fuse together. Somewhat similar to this is the process introduced some years ago under the name of *autogenous soldering*. This process, which is the invention of a French gentleman, M. de Richemont, consists of the union of two pieces of metal without the interposition of any solder, by fusing them at the point of junction by jets of flame from a gas blowpipe. The apparatus used for the purpose contains a hydrogen gas generator, bellows for atmospheric air, and valves for regulating the proportion in which the gas and air are to be mixed.

SOLVENT is that which has the power of rendering other bodies liquid; and chemically, a menstruum. Of all the solvents, water is the most universal and useful; it dissolves a great number of neutral vegetable products, as gum, sugar; and of saline bodies, as common salt, sulphate of soda, &c. The solvent of resinous bodies is alcohol, and of some similarly constituted substances; while caoutchouc is insoluble in it, but is dissolved by naphtha, oil of turpentine, and æther. The metals are insoluble in any solvent until they have suffered some change by its action, or by a similar change otherwise produced.

Heat has great power in altering the solvent power of bodies; in most cases it increases it, and hence, when it is required to crystallise certain salts, they are dissolved in hot water, and the solvent power of the water diminishing as the solution cools, the salt is deposited in crystals. In some cases, however, heat diminishes the solvent power. When any solvent has taken up as much of any particular substance as it is capable of taking up, the solution obtained is termed a Saturated Solution. That the change of form from solid to fluid is the result of chemical affinity, is shown by the fact that water which is saturated with one substance will take up another; thus a saturated solution of common salt will still dissolve sulphate of soda, and vice versâ.

The different solvent powers possessed by different substances are of the utmost consequence in many manufactures, especially those connected with manufacturing chemistry.

SOMERSETSHIRE. The geology of this fine county is rich in products valuable in the arts and manufactures. The great oolitic formation, which furnishes the fine-grained freestone commonly known as *Bath Stone*, has a thickness probably of 130 to 150 feet. Masses of this rock are found scattered on the slopes of the hills which it crowns, covering the subjacent clays and fullers' earth. The inferior oolite is extensively quarried in Dundry Hill, where it yields a good freestone. The coal-measures, mountain limestone, and old red sandstone belong to the carboniferous group of the Somersetshire and South Gloucestershire coal-field, and occupy the northern part of the county extending to the Mendip Hills, though covered in most places by more recent formations; in this field are numerous coal-pits. The mineral treasures of the Mendip Hills are important; zinc is obtained abundantly in the central and western parts of the range. There are numerous coal-pits in the villages which lie north-west of Frome; the coal seams are all thin; hardly any exceed three feet.

Somersetshire possesses a soil and climate well suited to the growth of wheat and all the agricultural produce usually raised in any part of England. In some of the vales, such as the extensive vale of Taunton, the soil is of a rich nature, and the wheat which is produced there is of superior quality. Excellent butter and cheese are made where the land is better adapted to pasture. The Cheddar cheese, which, from its superior quality, gives its name to a great portion of the cheese made in the county, is reckoned by many to be the best cheese made in England from pure milk, without any addition of cream: the real Cheddar cheese is consequently scarce, and bought up as soon as it is made. There are a few hops grown in the county, but no very extensive hop-gardens; nor is there much cider made, although there are some good orchards.

In respect to the external commerce of Somersetshire, a little has been said under BRISTOL and BRIDGEWATER. Considerable manufactures are carried on, especially the clothing trade at Frome and its vicinity, the glove trade at Yeovil, &c.

SOMME. This department of France produces oleaginous seeds, beetroot, pot-herbs, hops, dyeing and medicinal plants, grass-seeds, and apples for making cider and beer, which are the chief beverages of the inhabitants. A great deal of hemp and flax is grown in the north of the department. The minerals are building stone, paving flints, marble, chalk, vitriolic earth, potters' clay, and gypsum; coal has been found near Doullens, but no mines are worked. The manufactures are important, comprising fine and coarse woollen cloths, cotton fabrics of every description; also silks, linen, lawn, cambric, gauze, cashmere shawls, canvas, furniture, cotton, carpets, muslins, hosiery, ropes; locks, hardware, nails, leather, paper, oil, soap, glue, glass, pottery, mineral acids and other chemical products. The department has several bleach works, large cotton mills driven by steam machinery, beet-root sugar refineries, dye-houses, oil and tan mills. The commerce in the agricultural and industrial products named above, and in salt, colonial provisions, wine, brandy, coals, raw cotton, sheep and goats' wool, fish, &c., is very considerable.

SONOMETER. Mr. T. Wakley introduced, in 1849, an ingenious acoustic instrument, not for enabling partially deaf persons to hear, but to *measure* the extent of their power of hearing, so as to enable the aurist to adapt his curative means to the circumstances of each case. The instrument, which is called a *sonometer*, consists of a bell fixed to a table with its mouth uppermost. The hammer or clapper which is to strike the bell is attached to a spring, which catches into notches in a steel bar; and according as the spring is detained in a notch near the end or the middle of the bar, so does the hammer make a small or a considerable movement when released, and so does it elicit a soft or a loud sound from the bell. The aurist determines by experiment which of these sounds can be heard by the patient, and the instrument thus becomes a meter or measure of the auditive power.

SOOT is that portion of fuel which escapes combustion, and which is mechanically carried up and deposited in chimneys. The soot of coal contains sulphate and hydrochlorate of ammonia, a brown bitter extract, and an empyreumatic oil; but its great basis is charcoal in a state in which it is capable of being rendered soluble by the action of oxygen and moisture, and hence, combined with the action of the ammoniacal salts, it is used as a manure, and acts very powerfully as such. The soot of wood contains a greater variety of substances than that of coal, but much less both of carbonaceous matter and of ammoniacal salts.

It is in every way desirable that the formation of soot (unburnt fuel) should be prevented as much as possible, since it both wastes valuable material and contaminates the air. [SMOKE.]

SOUND-BOARD, or SOUNDING-BOARD, is a board placed over a pulpit or other place occupied by a public speaker, to reflect the sound of his voice, and thereby render it more audible. Sounding-boards are usually flat, and placed horizontally over the head of the speaker; but a different form and position, contrived by the Rev. J. Blackburn, of Attercliffe-cum-Darnell, near Sheffield, has been adopted in some cases with great advantage. In this arrangement the sounding-board is a concave parabola, which extends partly over and partly behind the speaker. The gutta percha tubes for the use of partially deaf persons in churches are noticed under SPEAKING TUBES.

SOUNDINGS are properly the depths of water in rivers, harbours, along shores, and even in the open seas; but the term is also applied to the nature of the ground at the bottom of the water. If the depth of the water is comparatively small, a man who is stationed for the purpose in the main or mizen chains, on the windward side, throws out a mass of lead, usually in the form of a frustum of a cone, and weighing 8 or 9 lbs., which is attached to one end of a line between 20 and 30 fathoms in length. On this line are fixed, at intervals of two or three fathoms, pieces of leather or cloth of different colours; and the mark which is next above the surface of the water when the lead strikes the bottom affords an indication of the depth. That which is called the deep-sea lead weighs from 25 to 30 lbs., and is attached to a line of great length, on which, at intervals, are knots indicating the depths. The bottom of the lead is covered with a coating of tallow for the purpose of ascertaining, by the sand, shells, or other matter which may adhere to it, the nature of the ground.

When soundings are to be taken in the survey of a coast, a harbour, or the mouth of a river, the surveying ship and its boats are disposed at convenient distances from each other (suppose from two to five miles); their distances with respect to each other and to remarkable objects on the shore being determined by the usual trigonometrical observations. The boats then row or sail along the directions of the lines joining each other, sounding as they proceed at equal intervals, suppose ten minutes, of time; and thus the outline of the shoal, reef, coast, or river, will be determined, as well as the depth of the water. All the soundings must be afterwards reduced to the depths below the surface of the sea at the level of low water.

SOUTH AUSTRALIA. A few commercial details respecting this colony will be found under ADELAIDE and AUSTRALIA. We will here add, that the imports of the colony in

1850 amounted in value to 632,689*l.*; the exports, 483,475*l.* The tallow exported was 5571 cwt.; the wool, 2,841,131 lbs.; the wheat, 14,498 qrs.; and the meal and flour, 1924 tons.

SOUTHAMPTON. This rising town depends for its importance on its connexion with the sea, and its easy communication with the metropolis. The harbour, which is secure, affords good anchorage. Ship-building is extensively carried on, though the vessels built are chiefly small. Southampton has a large coasting-trade, and a considerable trade to foreign ports and the colonies. The customs generally produce about 60,000*l.* a year, gross receipt. In 1849 the specie imported into Southampton amounted to 6,788,655*l.* The number of sailing-vessels registered Dec. 31, 1850, was 208 (12,843 tons). The number of steam-vessels was 10 under 50 tons, and 14 above 50 tons. Very large and convenient docks have been constructed on the eastern side of the town, chiefly for the service of steam navigation. In Dec., 1841, the mail-packet steam-ships to the West Indies commenced running. Passengers to the East embark here, there being a direct communication to India once a fortnight, as well as weekly, by steamers, to Vigo, Oporto, Lisbon, Cadiz, and Gibraltar, and daily to the Isle of Wight, France, and the Channel Islands. The South Western Railway runs to the very edge of the docks, and the trade of Southampton is also promoted by the Andover Canal, which follows the valley of the Anton, and by the navigation of the Itchen, which extends to Winchester.

The trade of the docks is annually increasing. In 1850, the tonnage of sailing vessels entered inwards at Southampton amounted to 187,435 tons, that of steam vessels to 155,566 tons. The dock and railway authorities have recently attempted to make Southampton the depôt for the new Cape Screw-steamers; but in this instance Plymouth has forestalled Southampton.

One of the largest coach factories in England is at Southampton, whence coaches of the finest build are procured. A sugar factory has lately been built near the docks, at an expenditure of 8,000*l.*

SOWING. The most common mode of sowing seed is by scattering it as evenly as possible over the ploughed surface, as it lies in ridges from the plough. The harrows follow, and crumbling down the ridges, cover the seed which has fallen in the hollows between them. It requires an experienced sower to scatter the exact quantity over a given surface, without crowding the seed in one spot, and allowing too great intervals in another. Hence the farmer who does not himself sow the seed, invariably chooses the most experienced and skilful labourer to perform this work. Notwithstanding every care and attention on the part of the farmer or master, the labourer will often relax and become careless, and the result appears only when it is too late to remedy it. This has given rise to various attempts which have been made to invent machines for sowing the seed, such as should insure perfect regularity. [DRILLING.]

SOY. This favourite Indian sauce is prepared from a plant called *Soja hispida.* The seeds are about the size of those of kidney beans, and the soy is made from them in the following way:—The seeds are boiled until nearly all the water has evaporated, when they are taken from the fire and placed in wide-mouthed jars, exposed to the sun and air; water and molasses or brown sugar are added. The mixture is stirred well every day, and allowed to ferment; it is then strained, salted, boiled, and skimmed until clarified. The shopkeepers at Canton who sell soy have large platforms on the roofs of their houses, where the jars for preparing soy are arranged and exposed to the sun. The use of soy is enormously large in China; it is used as a sauce at almost all meals. The sauce made by the Japanese is said to be the best. The use of soy in England is but limited.

SPAIN. If the inhabitants would do as much *with* their country as nature has done *for it,* Spain would be rich and prosperous; since in climate, in minerals, and in vegetable produce, it has many of the elements of commercial greatness.

The most common kinds of grain which are cultivated in Spain are wheat, maize, barley, and rice. Other objects of agriculture are hemp and flax, especially in the basin of the Ebro, and madder and saffron on the table-land of Cuença. In the southern districts the sugar-cane and cotton are cultivated. The most common vegetables are onions, garlic, pumpkins, cucumbers, melons, water-melons, potatoes, beans, and peas. Many fruit-trees are cultivated, as almonds, figs, pomegranates, lemons, oranges, pistachia nuts, carobas, dates in the southern districts, walnuts, hazel-nuts, and especially chestnut-trees, which in some of the northern districts cover large tracts. Olive-trees occur in all parts, except the northern mountain tracts, and the vineyards are extensive, except on the most elevated regions. Several of the Spanish wines are considerable articles of commerce, as Xeres (Sherry), Malaga, Alicante, Malvasia, Tinto, and Val de Peñas. Brandy and raisins also are articles of export. Among the wild trees are the sweet-acorn oak, the cork-tree, the kermes oak, and the sumach-tree. On the Montañas de Asturias and Aralar, and also on the western offsets of the Pyrenees, there are large forests of fine timber-trees. The liquorice-plant is abundant in the vicinity of Sevilla and near the mouth of the Ebro, and the prepared juice is sent to all parts of Europe.

The sheep are noted for their fine wool, which forms an important article of export. [MESTA.] In no country of Europe, except Italy, is so much silk obtained as in the eastern and southern parts of Spain. The cochineal insect has been reared of late years in Andalusia, Granada, and Estremadura, and thrives well. Bees are very abundant, and much honey and wax are obtained.

Spain abounds in minerals. Gold and silver are known to exist in several places. Platinum and copper are met with. A rich mine of quicksilver is worked near Almaden. [ALMADEN.] Lead is very abundant, especially in the Sierra de Gador. Iron ore is very abundant in the Sierra de Aralar and other places. There are also tin, calamine, bismuth, cobalt, alum, vitriol, and sulphur. In some parts large quantities of saltpetre are collected. Coal occurs in the Montañas de Asturias and in the Sierra Morena, but it is not much worked. Many kinds of marble are got in Catalonia. Several precious stones are found, as rubies, topazes, amethysts, turquoises, and garnets. Salt is got near Cardona in Catalonia, from the lagune called the Albufera de Valencia, and from the sea-water along the coast between Cape Trafalgar and the boundary of Portugal.

Few countries of Europe equal Spain in natural commercial advantages, whether we consider its situation or its products. The coasts are extensive, and the ports numerous and commodious; the inhabitants, inured to a warm climate, visit the tropical regions with comparative safety; yet it is far behind most other countries of Europe in commercial importance. During the 17th century most of the Spanish trade with America was carried on in Dutch or English vessels; and, with the exception of wine, wool, and oil, few if any of the productions of the Peninsula found their way to that market. About the close of the last century, under the enlightened administration of Count Florida Blanca, Spanish commerce revived, and several manufactures were established throughout the country. These, however, were all destroyed during the Peninsular war, and the subsequent separation of the American colonies from the mother country has completely annihilated the maritime trade of Spain. At present Catalonia is almost the only province of Spain where manufacturing is carried on to any extent. The chief exports of Spain consist of wines, dried fruits, corn, oil, wool, quicksilver, lead, and some iron. The silk of Valencia, which is equal to that of Italy, is bought by the French manufacturers.

Cadiz is the chief port in Spain; about 3000 vessels arrived there in 1849. The next in rank are Barcelona, Carthagena, Corunna, and Tarragona.

The British produce and manufactures exported to Spain in 1849 amounted in value to 623,126*l*.

SPAR. This name is given in mineralogy to a great number of crystallised earthy and some metallic substances, but chiefly the former. Thus calcareous spar is crystallised carbonate of lime; fluor-spar, fluoride of calcium; heavy spar, sulphate of barytes, &c. By miners the term is frequently used alone, to express any bright crystalline substance; but in mineralogy, strictly speaking, it is never so employed.

SPEAKING TUBES. Instruments for enabling the human voice to be heard at a great distance appear to have been known to the ancient Chinese. The modern speaking-trumpet appears to have been an invention of Sir Samuel Morland, in the year 1670. This first trumpet was of glass, 2 feet 8 inches long; and he afterwards made one of copper, recurved in the form of a common trumpet. Its total length was 16 feet 8 inches, the large end 19 inches, and the small end 2 inches in diameter. With this the voice was heard about a mile and a half. Morland made another of the same form, still larger, and two others of the straight form, and 5 feet and a half long. With the latter a man could make himself heard a mile and a half; and with one of the largest trumpets, tried at Deal Castle, the voice was conducted a distance of between two and three miles over the sea.

The efficiency of the speaking-trumpet is generally ascribed to the repeated reflection of the sound from side to side in passing through it, and its ultimate reflection from the mouth of the trumpet, in such a way as either to collect the rays of sound into a focus at a distance, or to project them forward in parallel lines, instead of allowing them to diverge in all directions. But Sir John Leslie accounts for its effect in the following manner:—'The tube, by its length and narrowness, detains the efflux of air, and has the same effect as if it diminished the volubility of that fluid, or increased its density.' 'The organs of articulation,' he continues, 'strike with concentrated force; and the pulses, thus vigorously excited, are from the reflected form of the aperture, finally enabled to escape, and to spread themselves along the atmosphere.' The effect of a speaking-trumpet is the same, whether the metal tube be used simply, or wrapped round in such a way as to prevent vibration. It is also heard at the same distance when the inner surface is lined with linen or woollen cloth to diminish reflection; and the range of a cylindrical trumpet is the same as that of a conical one.

The most valuable speaking tubes, however, are not those which are intended to convey sound to a great distance, but those intended to aid persons whose sense of hearing is defective. Something has been said on this subject under ACOUSTICS. The principle of the SONIFERON, described in that article, pervades all instruments of this kind; they collect and concentrate the waves of sound, so as to make them impinge upon the tympanum of the ear with greater force. They are in principle the reverse of the speaking trumpet; for in this the sound proceeds from the small end to the larger, whereas in speaking tubes or ear trumpets it proceeds from the large end to the small. Many varieties are made, under the names of *auricles*, *ear-cornets*, *ear-conches*, *conversation-tubes*, *table-soniferas*, &c., adapted to different requirements of partially deaf persons. See also SONOMETER. . . .

It has lately been found that gutta percha—so invaluable for many other purposes—is the best of all materials for speaking tubes, since it conveys the pulses of sound with surprisingly little diminution of intensity. In churches, in ships, in warehouses and factories, and in various other buildings and places, gutta percha speaking tubes are now used to a considerable extent. The mode of applying these tubes to the assistance of partially deaf persons in a church is curious. A funnel of the material is placed either inside the pulpit, quite out of sight, or, if ornamented, in front of the pulpit, so as to come immediately beneath the desk. A tube from this funnel then passes downwards beneath the floor, and is carried along the aisles, with branches off on each side to the pews occupied by people of defective hearing. The termination of the tube is all that appears in sight, and the ivory ear-piece being applied to the ear, the slightest whisper of the preacher is clearly heard.

SPECIFIC GRAVITY, or more properly Specific Weight, is the weight of any gas, liquid, or solid, under some given volume, as a cubic foot, a cubic inch, &c. Distilled water is the substance usually employed for the purpose of comparing together the weights of all substances except the gases; and because the volume of any substance varies with its temperature, in determining from experiment the specific gravity of any substance, the weight under a given volume is reduced to that which it would become at one constant temperature.

In the Parliamentary Regulations, which were made in 1825, a cubic inch of water is stated to weigh 252.458 troy grains, the temperature being 62° Fahrenheit, and the height of the barometrical column 30 inches; and 7000 troy grains are made equivalent to one pound avoirdupois; hence it follows that a cubic foot of water should weigh 997.136 ounces. This number is sufficiently near 1000 to make it very proper that it should be adopted for the specific gravity of water, since a change in the value of the avoirdupois ounce, which would be scarcely appreciable in the ordinary transactions of commerce, would render the ounce an accurate and convenient unit of weight, while the cubic foot constitutes the unit of volume.

On the Continent, since the employment of the decimal scale of weights and measures has become general, the cubic centimetre (.061028 cubic inches English) is the unit of volume, and the gramme (15.407 troy grains) is the unit of weight; the gramme having been determined by the weight of a cubic centimetre of distilled water of the temperature at which its density is a maximum (38.25° Fahrenheit).

The hydrostatic balance which is employed in determining the specific gravities of bodies is constructed similarly to an ordinary balance, but with as much delicacy as possible; and a particular contrivance is adopted in order to ascertain the weight of any substance within, for example, one-hundredth part of a grain. Thus, from the lower part of the scale containing the substance to be weighed, there is suspended a brass wire, whose volume and weight have been previously determined, and part of its length enters into water which is contained in a vessel underneath the scale. The scales with this wire thus attached to one of them being previously put in equilibrio when the surface of the water is at a certain mark on the wire, the substance to be weighed is introduced into the scale above the wire, and weights are placed in the opposite scale till one grain more would be found too great: then gently raising the whole balance till, by the increase of the weight on the side of the scale containing the substance, in consequence of a greater portion of the wire being out of the water, an equilibrium takes place. The wire being graduated so that 100 divisions correspond to a weight equal to one grain, the number of graduations on it between the surface of the water and the fixed mark before mentioned will enable the experimenter to determine the number of hundredths of a grain by which the weight of the substance in the scale exceeds the number of grains already placed in the opposite scale.

The weighing process varies in its details according to the kind of substance to be weighed. Thus—a solid which is heavier than water, a solid which is lighter than water, a solid which is soluble in water, a solid which will imbibe water without being dissolved, a solid in the form of sand or powder, a liquid, a gas or vapour—all require peculiar methods for determining their specific gravity; methods which are fully described in treatises on Hydrostatics, but which we need not dwell upon here.

The following are the specific gravities of several airs and gases, at a temperature of 60° Fahr., and a barometrical pressure of 30 inches: atmospheric air being taken as a standard, or = 1·000:—

Substance	Specific gravity
Hydrogen	0·070
Ammoniacal gas	0·590
Aqueous vapour	0·625
Do. (in contact with water at 212° Fahrenheit)	0·484
Nitrogen	0·969
Atmospherical air	1·000
Oxygen	1·111
Muriatic acid gas	1·284
Carbonic acid gas	1·519
Nitrous oxide gas (laughing gas)	1·527 to 1·614
Chlorine	2·508
Iodine, vapour of	8·678

The following are the specific gravities of various liquids and solids, at a temperature of 60° Fahr., a pressure of 30 inches, and water being = 1·000:—

Substance	Specific gravity
Naphtha	0·708
Æther, muriatic	0·730
Do., nitric	0·909
Alcohol, pure	0·796
Water, at 212° Fahr.	0·956
Do., at 60°	1·000
Sea-water	1·026
Beer	1·023
Port Wine	0·997
Oil of turpentine	0·870
Whale oil	0·923
Muriatic acid	1·194
Nitric acid	1·217
Sulphuric acid (pure)	1·848
Gums, Animal Substances, &c.	
Indigo	0·769
Butter	0·942
Bees-wax	0·965
Camphor	0·989
Blood	1·028
Milk	1·032
Copal	1·060
Mastic	1·074
Gamboge	1·222
Opium	1·336
Honey	1·450
Gum arabic	1·452
White sugar	1·606
Ivory	1·826
Woods.	
Cork	0·240
Poplar	0·383
Yellow Pine	0·440
Spruce Fir	0·518
Larch	0·530
Willow	0·585
Elm	0·588 to 0·800
Lime or Linden-tree	0·604
Cedar, from Palestine	0·613
Mahogany	0·637 to 1·063
Teak	0·666
Walnut-tree	0·671
Elder	0·695
Oak, English	0·743 to 0·760
Beech	0·853
Box, French	0·912
Olive	0·927
Logwood	0·931
Heart of Oak, 60 years old	1·170
Ebony	1·177
Vine	1·327
Box, Dutch	1·328
Lignum Vitæ	1·333
Earths, Stones, &c.	
Pumice-stone	0·915
Gunpowder (closely shaken)	0·932
Amber	1·078
Cannel Coal	1·270
Slate coal, English	1·250 to 1·370
Phosphorus	1·714
Nitre	1·900
Brick	2·000
Sulphur (native)	2·033
Gypsum (opaque)	2·168
Porcelain (china)	2·385
Stone (paving)	2·416 to 2·460
Flint	2·590
Carnelian	2·600
Glass	2·642 to 2·892
Marble	2·649 to 2·838
Brazil Pebbles	2·653
Granite (red Egyptian)	2·654
Quartz (crystallised)	2·655
Agate	2·667
Slate (common)	2·672
Alabaster	2·762
Emerald (from Peru)	2·775
Chalk (British)	2·657 to 2·784
Talc (Muscovy)	2·792
Basalt	2·864
Hone (white), razor	2·876
Lapis-lazuli	2·767 to 3·054
Limestone (white fluor)	3·156
Diamond	3·444 to 5·531
Beryl	3·549
Adamantine Spar	3·873
Sapphire	3·994
Garnet	4·000
Topaz	4·011
Vermilion	4·230
Ruby	4·283
Metals.	
Sodium	0·865
Potassium	0·972
Antimony	4·064
Molybdena	4·738
Manganese	4·756
Copper (from Cornwall)	5·452
Tungsten	6·066
Uranium	6·440
Zinc	6·862 to 7·191
Iron (cast)	7·157 to 7·248
Tin (pure)	7·291
Iron (forged)	7·600 to 7·788
Copper (native)	7·600 to 7·800
Nickel (molten)	7·807
Cobalt (molten)	7·812
Steel	7·818 to 7·833
Brass	7·824 to 8·544
Mercury (precipitate, red)	8·399
Copper (wire-drawn)	8·878
Bismuth (native)	9·020
Mercury (brown cinnabar)	10·218
Silver (hammered)	10·511
Lead (molten)	11·352
Mercury (fluent)	13·568
Do. (congealed)	15·630
Gold	15·709 to 49·500
Platinum (purified)	19·500 to 22.069

The most convenient method of obtaining the specific gravities of fluids is by means of what chemists call a 'thousand-grain bottle.' This is a bottle of a globular form, with a ground glass stopper, so adjusted as to contain exactly 1000 grains of distilled water, at the temperature of 60° Fahr., and accompanied by a weight, which is an exact counterpoise for the bottle when thus filled. In order to determine the specific gravity of a fluid by this means, it is simply necessary to fill the bottle with that fluid at the temperature of 60°, and place it, together with the adjusted weight, in the opposite scales of a delicate balance; then the number of grains which it will be found necessary to add to one of the scales, in order to produce equilibrium, will be the difference between the specific gravity of the fluid and that of water, taken at 1000.

SPECTACLES. The mention of magnifying-glasses by Roger Bacon, who died about 1292, justifies the supposition that something like what are now called spectacles were in use at least several years earlier. Extensively as these useful instruments are employed, there can be no doubt that, were the subject more generally understood, the amount of advantage obtained from them would be greatly augmented. The eyes of an individual whose sight is much tried often receive the most serious injury from improper delay in the use of spectacles; while the sight of many persons is prematurely worn out by the use of glasses of too high a power, or too short a focal length. The use of a single reading-glass instead of spectacles is very injurious; since, by occasioning one eye to be more used than the other, the focal lengths of the two are rendered unequal. The unsteadiness of the glass is also a disadvantage. Varieties in the conformation of the eyes, and in the manner and degree in which they are affected by use, render it impossible to lay down any rule for the focal length of convex glasses for persons of a given age.

It is very essential that the frame of the spectacles should fit comfortably to the head, and be of such a form as to bring the centre of each lens exactly opposite the centre of the eye it is intended to serve. The endless variations met with in the width between the eyes, the total width of the head, and the form of the nose, render it frequently difficult to suit an individual out of even a very large stock. Convex spectacles, being used for viewing near objects, may generally be placed lower down upon the wearer's nose than those used by short-sighted persons. The oval form is usually preferred for the lenses, because it allows most room for the motion of the eye in a lateral direction, without giving unnecessary weight.

The *Periscopic Spectacles* of Dr. Wollaston were contrived in order to allow considerable latitude of motion to the eyes without fatigue, by conforming the shape of the glasses to that of the eyes. This is effected by the use of lenses either of a meniscus or a concavo-convex form, the concave side being in both cases turned towards the eye. Divided spectacles, each glass consisting of two half-lenses, are sometimes used, the upper half of each glass being occupied by a concave lens, or one of very slight convexity, for seeing distant objects, while the lower half has a strong magnifier, for examining things near the eye. The present Astronomer Royal finds that one of his eyes refracts the rays of light to a nearer focus in the vertical than in the horizontal plane; and this defect he has succeeded in remedying by using a double concave lens, one surface of which is spherical and the other cylindrical.

As an article of manufacture, the best spectacles are made by the leading opticians of London; but the medium and inferior kind are made on a large scale in Birmingham.

SPE'CULUM. This name is frequently given to a mirror used for any scientific purpose, as in a reflecting telescope. If a pencil of rays diverge from a radiant point in the axis of a concave speculum of a spherical form, all the rays will, after reflexion, converge nearly to a certain point in the same axis, at which the image of the radiant point is said to be formed. This point is called the *Focus.* None of the rays are, in strictness, reflected to the focus, but all those which are reflected from the mirror at points very near its intersection with the axis fall extremely near it. The image in a convex mirror is always upright, and in a concave one always inverted, except when the object falls between the principal focus (or middle point of the radius) and the mirror.

The best composition for the metal of reflecting telescopes is a subject which has been much investigated. About 70 different mixtures were tried by the Rev. John Edwards, the particulars of which are stated in the 'Nautical Almanac' for the year 1787; he found copper 32, tin 15, brass 1, silver 1, white oxide of arsenic 1, to form an alloy which was the whitest, hardest, most reflective, and took the highest polish.

In the 'Philosophical Transactions' for 1840, Lord Rosse, then Lord Oxmantown, published an account of a speculum 3 feet diameter which he had then executed; and from this we learn that after many trials to determine what combination of metals were most useful for the purpose, with respect to whiteness, porosity, and hardness, one of copper and tin (the materials employed by Newton in the first reflecting telescope) united in the proportion of 126·4 parts of copper to 58·9 parts of tin, was found the best. It is stated that the compound is of admirable lustre and hardness, and has a specific gravity of 8·8, that of water being 1. Lord Rosse has subsequently cast specula 6 feet in diameter, of the like composition, and each in one piece, with complete success. One of these is mounted at Parsonstown, in Ireland, in a telescope 56 feet long, with which important discoveries have been made in the heavens. These specula were cast in moulds made by binding together layers of hoop-iron; and both the grinding and the polishing were executed by machinery which was put in motion by a small steam-engine. The speculum of the largest telescope, when mounted, rests on a bed consisting of twenty-seven triangular pieces of iron, supported at their centres of gravity on the corners of nine other triangular pieces, which are also supported at their centres of gravity. By this contrivance any change in the form of the box or tube, by warping or otherwise, produces no effect on the speculum.

SPELTER. [Zinc.]

SPERMACETI, is a fatty material which is obtained from the *Physeter macrocephalus*, a species of whale, generally met with in the South Seas, but occasionally also on the coast of Greenland. The spermaceti occurs chiefly in the head. During the life of the animal the spermaceti is in a fluid state; and on the head being opened, has the appearance of an oily clear white liquid. On exposure to the air the spermaceti concretes and deposits from the oil. They are then separated, and put into different barrels. The head of a whale sixty-four feet in length has been found to yield twenty-four barrels of spermaceti, and from seventy to one hundred barrels of oil. When brought to England, the spermaceti has not a white shining silky appearance, but a yellowish colour, owing to the presence of some oil. To separate this it is filtered, pressed, and subjected to various operations. When perfectly pure, it becomes cetine.

Spermaceti possesses the properties common to fatty matters. It is bland and demulcent, with considerable nutritive qualities, when taken internally. It was formerly much used in medicine; but it is now chiefly employed externally as an ingredient in ointments and cerates. It is also largely used in the making of candles. 4,712 tons of spermaceti were imported in 1848.

SPHERELATA. *Spherelata*, or hammered metal-work, has been found in great profusion among the Etruscan monuments of antiquity. Statues, busts, bronzes, tripods, vases, amphoræ, basins, incense vessels, shields, candelabra—all these have been met with, fashioned out of pieces of metal chiefly by the aid of the hammer. This art is supposed to have long preceded metal-casting, as a mode of manufacture. In the works of the earliest Greek poets, these hammered metal productions are repeatedly referred to. Large surfaces of metal were hammered, thin plates were twisted, ornaments were chased, and separate pieces were fastened together by nails or rivets—all without the aid of casting or soldering.

SPICES. The following quantities of the principal spices were imported into Great Britain during 1849 and 1850:—

	1849.	1850.
Cassia Lignea	472,693 lbs.	988,017 lbs.
Cinnamon ..	759,088 „	700,101 „
Cloves	274,713 „	749,625 „
Mace	45,978 „	76,365 „
Nutmegs	224,021 „	312,418 „
Pepper	4,796,042 „	8,082,518 „
Pimento	2,884,144 „	2,290,176 „

SPINET, was a musical instrument of the harpsichord kind, formerly much in use. The Spinet had but one string to each note, which was struck by a quilled jack, the latter being acted on in the usual manner by a key. It was smaller than the harpsichord.

SPINNING. Whatever be the substance operated upon by the spinner, whether cotton, wool, flax, or silk, it is necessary in the first place to lay the fibres or filaments parallel with each other, so as to form them into a soft continuous ribbon or cord, sometimes called a *sliver*. Excepting in the case of flax, this is done by a carding or combing process, the object of which is to disentangle and straighten the tangled filaments. If such a sliver or cord be firmly griped or compressed at two points rather farther apart than the average length of its component filaments, it may be extended or drawn out to a greater length; the filaments sliding upon each other. When two or more such cords have been extended in this way, until they will stretch no longer without separating or being pulled asunder, they may be laid parallel to each other, and combined by being slightly twisted together. The compound cord thus formed may be again extended by stretching or drawing; and the repetition of the processes of doubling, twisting, and stretching will enable the spinner to extend the length and diminish the thickness of the cord until it becomes a fine compact thread or yarn.

The primitive modes of spinning by the spindle and distaff, and by the spinning-wheel, which are still extensively practised in the East, and not entirely superseded in some remote districts of Scotland, only enable the spinner to produce a single thread; but with the almost automatic spinning-machinery which has been called into existence by the cotton manufacture, one individual may produce nearly two thousand threads at the same time. The history of the series of inventions by which this result has been gradually attained is briefly noticed in the articles ARKWRIGHT and COTTON SPINNING. In respect to flax, the preliminary processes are described under FLAX. As the fibres of flax have not the same tendency to mutual entanglement as those of wool and cotton, it is necessary to moisten them with water to make them adhere to each other during the process of spinning, and also to render them more pliable and easy to twist. Until recently, cold water was used for moistening the flax for machine-spinning; but the substitution of hot water for that purpose has been found a great improvement. We must refer to the same article [FLAX] for an account of the present efforts to improve and extend this important manufacture.

The manufacture of yarns or threads of silk is a process essentially different from the spinning of cotton, wool, or flax. Instead of combining a number of short fibres into a long thread, the silk-throwster receives the silk in the form of very long and exceedingly fine filaments, which merely need cleansing and twisting together until the requisite strength is attained. The twisting process is, in this case, called spinning. There is however besides the best portion of the silk, which is wound off from the cocoon, a quantity of loose or *floss* silk, which forms a soft tangled mass enveloping it. This, with the refuse of the superior part of the silk, under the general name of *waste*, is converted into yarns for coarse or inferior articles, by a process very similar to that of spinning other fibrous substances. This waste silk was formerly cut by a machine, to reduce its filaments into short lengths, and then treated much in the same way as cotton wool; but the process of manufacturing it into yarns has been recently much improved by the adoption of contrivances similar to those used in flax-spinning, by which the filaments are heckled or drawn out into a sliver without being cut. The spinning of hempen fibres into cordage is described under ROPE MANUFACTURE. In many of the smaller kinds of ornamental spun-work, caoutchouc or India rubber is now largely used. [INDIA RUBBER MANUFACTURE.]

SPIRIT, in Chemistry. This word, especially when employed by itself, is now almost exclusively applied to spirit of wine, or alcohol. Formerly however the word spirit was given to most substances capable of being vaporised and condensed by distillation, and to some not obtained by distillation. It will be requisite merely to name a few of those compounds to show how extensively it was used, and misapplied to substances of very different origin and composition. Thus nitric acid was called Spirit of Nitre; hydrochloric acid, Spirit of Salt; Sulphuric acid, Spirit of Sulphur; chloride of tin, Spirit of Libavius; solution of ammonia, Spirit of Sal-Ammoniac, and so forth.

SPIRIT-LEVEL, is a tube of glass nearly filled with spirit of wine or distilled water, and hermetically sealed at both ends, so that when held with its axis in a horizontal position, the air which occupies the part not filled with the spirit or water places itself contiguously to the upper surface. The tube being supposed to be perfectly cylindrical, the exact horizontality of its axis is ascertained by the extremities of the air-bubble being at equal distances from the middle point in the length of the glass. The spirit-tube is placed within a brass case having a long opening on the side which is to be uppermost, and is attached to a telescope; the telescope and tube are then fitted to a frame, or cradle, of brass, which is supported on three legs.

The use of the spirit-level in accurate surveying requires great care in the adjustment of the tube and the attached telescope.

The *Levelling-Staff* till lately in general use for finding the relative heights of ground is a rod consisting of two parts, each six feet long, which, by being made to slide on one another, will indicate differences of level nearly as great as twelve feet. The face of the rod is divided into feet, inches, and tenths, or into feet with centesimal subdivisions; and a vane, or cross-piece of wood, perforated through the middle, is moved up or down upon the rod by an assistant till a chamfered edge at the perforation is seen by the observer at the spirit-level to coincide with the horizontal wire in the telescope. The rod proposed by Mr. Gravat is divided into hundredths of a foot by stripes which are alternately black and white, and are numbered at every foot in the usual way with figures large enough to be seen on looking through the telescope; the tenths of a foot are indicated by lines longer than the others. A similar staff has been proposed by Mr. Sopwith and Mr. W. P. Barlow.

SPIRIT TRADE. The manufacture of different kinds of spirits is noticed under BRANDY, DISTILLATION, GIN, RUM, &c.

The duty on foreign spirits is 15*s.* per gallon; on colonial spirits 8*s.* 2*d.* for England, 4*s.* for Scotland, and 3*s.* for Ireland. On British spirits distilled in England the duty is 7*s.* 10*d.*, in Scotland, 3*s.* 8*d.*, and in Ireland, 2*s.* 8*d.* per gallon—all estimated at proof strength.

The quantities of Rum, Brandy, and Geneva, imported into Great Britain in 1849 and 1850 were:—

	1849.	1850.
Rum....	5,306,827 galls.	4,188,639 galls.
Brandy..	4,479,549 „	3,237,598 „
Geneva	471,236 „	337,042 „

The home-made spirits charged with excise duty in the same two years amounted to the following quantities:—

	1849.	1850.
England ..	9,102,472 galls.	9,378,790 galls.
Scotland....	6,935,003 „	7,132,556 „
Ireland	6,973,333 „	7,408,086 „

The English spirit is made from mixtures of malt with grain, molasses, and sugar; in Scotland more than half is made from pure malt; in Ireland nearly all is made from malt and grain mixed.

SPITALFIELDS. No part of London is more remarkably connected with a particular manufacture than Spitalfields is with that of silk. For many generations nearly all the silk-weavers of the metropolis have resided in or near this district.

When the Edict of Nantes was revoked by Louis XIV., in 1685, many thousand silk-weavers were expelled from France, and sought refuge in England. Stow writes:—"Spittlefields and parts adjacent became a great harbour for poor Protestant strangers, Walloons and French; who, as in former days, so of late, have been forced to become exiles from their own country for their religion, and for the avoiding cruel persecution. . . . Great advantage hath accrued to the whole nation by the rich manufacture of weaving silks, and stuffs, and camlets, which art they brought along with them." The refugees introduced the various silk fabrics known by the name of *lustrings*, *alamodes*, *brocades*, *satins*, *mantuas*, *paduasoys*, *ducapes*, and *tabbies*; and the silk manufacture of Spitalfields speedily became important.

From that time to the present, the Spitalfields weavers have been unfavourably distinguished for their perpetual attempts to secure 'protection' for their trade in every possible way, reasonable or not; and the statute book contains numerous enactments bearing more or less closely on this point. Their wages have at most periods been small, and the weavers have been poor; but there is no proof that matters were otherwise when protective measures were resorted to; and there is not wanting evidence that renewed energy is shewn by the Spitalfields manufacturers, now that all hopes of a protective system are abandoned.

All the silk spun or *thrown* in this country is spun in large establishments called silk-mills, situated in different parts of the country, none is spun in Spitalfields: it is only the weaving which is here conducted. The *tram* for the weft or cross-threads is spun in England; but a good deal of the *organzine* for the warp or long threads is imported from Italy. The manufacturer gives out the organzine and tram to the hand-loom weaver, who takes it to his humble abode, weaves it into one of the many kinds of silk goods, and takes it back to the manufacturer, who pays him a certain stipulated price for his labour. There are supposed to be about 16,000 silk-looms in the Spitalfields and Bethnal Green district; and it is further estimated that not less than 60,000 persons are wholly dependent for their daily food on the employment of these looms.

A School of Design has been established at Spitalfields, which, if fostered by the manufacturers, may render much service by improving the taste of the designers employed in preparing patterns for the weavers.

SPONGE. The organic origin of sponge is a matter which lies beyond the scope of the present work to treat; nor do the simple uses of sponge require much comment. The use of sponge by surgeons, in its natural state, to absorb fluids, needs no notice, but it is also employed by them under the name of *Sponge Tent*, when prepared in a particular manner. This consists in dipping the sponge in melted wax, and compressing it between iron plates till it hardens on cooling; it is then cut into cylindrical or other forms. The pieces are introduced into sinuses and other narrow canals, with the intention of dilating them by the expansion of the sponge, when the wax melts by the heat of the part. Sponge Tents are however little used by modern surgeons.

When sponge has been cut into pieces, beaten in order to free it from little stones and shells, and burnt in a closed iron vessel till it is black and friable, it is then called *Burnt Sponge*, and contains a quantity of Iodine. It has been almost completely superseded in the treatment of Bronchocele and Scrophula by Iodine and its preparations.

SPRING, in Mechanics, is an elastic plate or rod, which is employed as a moving-power, or a regulator of the motions of wheel-work; also to ascertain the weights of bodies, or to diminish the effects of concussion. The use of a spring as a moving-power may be best exemplified in its application to watch-work. The main-spring of a watch is a thin and narrow plate of well-tempered steel, which is coiled in a spiral form: one of its extremities is attached to a pivot or axle, and the other to the interior circumference of the cylindrical box in which it is contained. In being wound, the spring closes round the axle, and afterwards, in the effort by its elasticity to recover its former position, it turns the cylinder in a contrary direction: thus the chain which is attached to the exterior circumference of the cylinder and to the fusee causes the latter to revolve.

A slender and highly-elastic spring of a like form is employed to produce a vibratory motion in the balance ring of a watch. One extremity of the spring is attached to the axle of the balance, and the other to some part of its circumference. The elastic power of the spring varies with the tension, and is directly proportional to the angle through which the spring is wound about the axle; and thus the vibrations of a spring, like those of a pendulum in a cycloidal arc, are isochronous. The length of the spring and the diameter of the balance are increased by heat and diminished by cold; consequently, without some compensating power, the times of vibration will vary according to the changes of temperature.

SPRING-BALANCE, is a machine in which the elasticity of a spring of tempered steel is employed as a means of measuring weight or force. One of the simplest kinds of spring-balance is the *Spring Steelyard*, or *Pocket Steelyard*. This instrument consists of a helical spring placed in the interior of a tube of brass or iron, closed at both ends; one end of the spring abutting against the plate which closes the lower end of the tube. A rod, having a hook or loop at its lower extremity, passes through a hole in the bottom of the tube, and up the inside of the spring. At the upper end of this rod is a small plate, which slides up and down like a piston in the tube, and rests upon the upper or free end of the spring; thereby causing it to collapse when a heavy body is attached to the hook at the bottom of the sliding rod. The extent of the motion of the spring, and consequently the weight of the body suspended from it, are indicated by the degree to which the rod is drawn out of the tube; for which purpose a graduated scale is engraved upon the rod.

Many improved varieties of spring-balance are now manufactured; and similar instruments are applied to many useful purposes besides weighing. Marriott's Patent *Weighing Machine* has a spring which is a perfect ellipsis, with its longer axis laid horizontally. The stem to which the ring for holding the apparatus is attached is fastened by a nut and screw to the middle of the upper side of the spring; and the rack, with the hook which holds the article to be weighed, to the corresponding point on the lower side of the spring. The spring, rack, and pinion are inclosed in a circular box at the back of the dial-plate, the periphery of which serves as a stop to prevent the spring from being overstrained. A similar apparatus, contrived by M. Regnier, has been used as a dynamometer, as well as a weighing-machine.

SPRING, CARRIAGE. Various methods are adopted for lessening the concussion occasioned by the rolling of a wheeled carriage over a rough road. One of the simplest means is that often adopted in light carts, of suspending the seat from the sides of the body by leather straps or lashings. Next to this is the use of straps to suspend the body itself, an expedient which seems to have been occasionally resorted to from a very early period. To remedy the defects of the primitive slung carriage, it was desirable to render the pillars from which the straps were suspended somewhat elastic. This could not be readily effected with wood, because the pillars were necessarily short, and therefore stiff. Hence arose the use of elastic steel supports, which have gradually assumed the form now well known as C-Springs. These were formerly used for almost all kinds of carriage-springs; but the great improvement of our roads has made way for the introduction, in all stage coaches, and in many private carriages, of the more compact straight and elliptic springs.

Carriage-springs are usually formed of several thin plates of steel, of various lengths, so laid and fastened together that the spring shall be thick in the centre, or at the end by which it is fixed, and thin, or consisting of only a single plate, at the end or ends where the greatest play is required. The steel used is of coarse quality, and has little carbon in its composition.

Coach-makers apply distinct names to a great many varieties of springs. The straight spring, if single, or acting only on one side of the point at which it is fixed, is technically named the *Single-Elbow Spring*. The *Double-*

Elbow-Spring is a straight spring, acting on both sides of the fixed point. *Elliptic Springs*, which are usually but little curved, are used single in some carriages, between the axle and the framework. Elliptic springs are often used in pairs under the name of *Nut-Cracker Springs*, the two springs being hinged together at each end, so as to form a long pointed ellipsis. *C-Springs*, which are chiefly used in private carriages, usually consist of two-thirds of a circle, lengthened out into a tangent; the tangent being laid horizontally, and bolted down to the framework of the carriage. *Telegraph Springs* are combinations of straight springs in sets of four. *Tilbury-Springs* are another combination of straight springs used for the two-wheeled carriage called a tilbury. *Dennet-Springs* are a combination of three straight springs, two of them placed across the axle, and attached at their fore ends to the shafts or the framing of the body, and the third placed transversely, suspended by shackles from their hinder extremities, and fastened to the body at its centre. To meet the deficiencies of the springs in common use, Mr. Adams contrived one on the principle of the bow, which will yield in any direction, and may be made capable of adjustment, by means of screws, to a light or heavy load.

SPRUCE BEER. This fermented liquor is made from the leaves and small branches of the spruce-fir, with sugar or treacle. There are two kinds of spruce beer—the brown and the white—of which the latter is considered the best. In the manufacture, essence of spruce is fermented much in the same way as grape-juice in wine-making. In places where spruce-firs abound, a simple decoction of the leaves and small branches is used instead of the essence of spruce. This agreeable and wholesome beverage is useful as an anti-scorbutic.

STAFFORDSHIRE. This county is rich in coal. [COAL.] Gypsum is quarried in Needwood Forest and in the adjacent part of the valley of the Dove; the pure white gypsum, or that slightly streaked with red, yields plaster of Paris, which is much used in the potteries for moulds. Near Dudley is a mass of basalt, locally termed Rowley Rag; it is quarried for mending the roads and paving the streets of Birmingham. The coal-works of the county are very numerous and important; in the south they supply the iron and other hardware manufactures of Birmingham, Dudley, Wolverhampton, Wednesbury, Bilston, Walsall, &c.; and in the north they supply the fuel to the Pottery district. Perhaps the neighbourhood of Birmingham is the cheapest district for coals in England, and the consumption is prodigious. Ironstone is abundant in the Dudley coal-field.

The canals of this county are numerous. The most important is the Trent and Mersey Canal, or, as it is sometimes called, the Grand Trunk Canal, which crosses the county. The Birmingham Canal and the Birmingham and Liverpool Junction Canal may be regarded as forming another important line, entering the county near Birmingham, and passing through the iron and coal district, by Dudley and Wolverhampton, and then running into Shropshire. There are several smaller lines which belong to the coal and iron districts of South Staffordshire. The county is also well supplied with railways.

The manufacturing towns of Staffordshire are numerous and important. The pottery towns are noticed under POTTERIES. The iron and coal works of BILSTON and BROMWICH are noticed under those headings. *Cheadle* has manufactures of copper in its vicinity. *Leek* is one of the silk manufacturing towns. *Lichfield* is rather an agricultural centre than a seat of manufactures; and the same may be said of *Tamworth*. *Newcastle-under-Lyne* has a considerable manufacture of hats. *Stafford* is one of the depôts of the shoe manufacture. *Tipton* is situated in the centre of the South Staffordshire iron and coal district, and its present size and importance are quite modern, and have arisen from the rapid extension of the iron manufactures. In *Walsall* the inhabitants are employed largely in manufactures of iron and brass; and there are coal-mines and freestone and limestone quarries in the neighbourhood. *Wednesbury* is also in the heart of the South Staffordshire coal and iron district, and it has considerable manufactures of fire-arms, machinery, edge-tools, files, screws, &c. *Wolverhampton* produces largely manufactures of fire-irons, tinned and japanned iron-ware, locks, guns, files, screws, and a variety of other articles.

STAINED GLASS. [GLASS PAINTING.]

STAIRCASE. It was not till about the time of Elizabeth that staircases began to be planned commodiously in this country, and made a decorative feature in the interior of a mansion. At a later period, staircases in mansions of a superior class were made disproportionably spacious, being upon a scale as to size with which the apartments themselves were not at all in keeping. One of the most simple and effective, yet least common arrangements of a staircase, is that which may be described by the term *Avenue Staircase*, the stairs being continued in a straight line.

though broken by spaces into a succession of flights, within what would else be a level corridor or gallery; and occupying its entire width. Simple as such plan is in itself, it is by no means adapted to general application, because, although it requires only moderate width, it requires considerable length, short flights, and ample spaces between them, and stairs with low risers and broad treads. In public edifices or large mansions, whatever be the plan of the principal staircase, it is generally *branched*, that is, there is first a wide central flight, and then two other narrower flights branching off from it on each side, either at right angles to it, or as return flights parallel to it; and it is hardly necessary to observe that in all such staircases the foot-spaces are large and there are no winders. The staircase at Goldsmiths' Hall, which is parted off from the vestibule by a glazed screen, is an example of more than ordinary splendour, being lighted by a dome. The new staircase at the British Museum is also of this kind.

The grand staircase of the Reform Club House, London, is an example, somewhat unusual in this country, though common enough in Italy, of what may be called an *Enclosed Staircase.* The flights are shut up between walls, and consequently there is no open well, nor can the whole be seen at one view.

The architectural effect of a staircase will greatly depend upon the mode of lighting it. Where it is carried up only one floor, the best mode is to light it entirely from above, either through a dome or lantern in the ceiling, or by making the upper part of the walls, just beneath the ceiling, a continued lantern.

STAMPING PRESS. Many articles of metal manufacture receive their form by stamping. One half of the impress is on the lower surface of the hammer or falling weight; the other half is on the upper surface of the anvil or bed; and a piece of metal being placed between the two, it receives an impress on both sides. In making spoons, ladles, and forks, the impress is given to the handles and to the bowls or prongs by distinct operations of different dies; and the pattern being thus partially produced, the articles are finished by filing and hammering. There is, however, a patented method of stamping spoons with one pair of dies, which produce the handle and the bowl at one time.

Various illustrations of the stamping of metals will be met with under BUTTON MANUFACTURE, CHASING OF METALS, and MINT.

STANDARD MEASURES AND WEIGHTS. Measures are wanted for two distinct objects, the commercial and the scientific. The wants of natural philhsophy have grown up within the last two centuries; while so early as Magna Charta it was one of the concessions to the grievances of the subject, that there should be one weight and one measure throughout the land. But though a few acts of Parliament were sufficient, in process of time, substantially to establish the political rights which that charter was intended to grant, hundreds of them, down to the present time, have been ineffectual in producing the use of one weight and one measure. This unity was for commercial not scientific purposes; and the resemblance of natural objects was supposed to be a sufficient reliance for obtaining it. Some of the old statutes expressly make the inch to be the length of three barleycorns, placed end to end, round and dry, from the middle of the ear. Standards were made no doubt from this definition; or at least it was supposed that if the existing standard should be lost, the barleycorns would enable its restoration to be effected. The average length of three barleycorns, whether we call that length an inch or by any other name, among many thousands, would doubtless always be the same under similar conditions of growth.

A commercial standard might be easily recovered from many different modes of proceeding: for example, the average height of the barometer at a given place throughout any period of five years is so nearly the same from one five years to another, that a commercial standard might be sufficiently well obtained from it. It would be of little consequence if the yard were wrongly recovered by one-hundredth or even one-tenth of an inch, in any matter of buying and selling.

It is the *scientific* standard at which the government has been aiming during the last century. The object here is, first, to measure the old standards to the utmost accuracy of which our senses, assisted by microscopes, are capable; secondly, to discover the means of reconstructing a lost standard. In the more delicate operations of natural philosophy and astronomy, our knowledge cannot go down to posterity unless they know within the thousandth of an inch what it is that we call a yard. The public at large has never understood the reason why so much trouble has been taken; and perhaps the members of different administrations, while trusting such investigations to men of science, and relying on them for the whole conduct of the matter, may have wondered at the great difficulty which there seemed to be in the way of furnishing the shopkeepers of all generations with yard measures and pound weights of the same values.

The following is the existing legal definition of standards according to the act of 1825:—

1. The straight line or distance between the centres of the two points in the gold studs in the straight brass rod now in the custody of the clerk in the House of Commons, whereon the words and figures 'Standard yard, 1760' are engraved, shall be the original and genuine standard of that measure of length or lineal extension called a yard . . . the brass being at the temperature of sixty-two degrees of Fahrenheit's thermometer. The act goes on in many words to say that the pendulum vibrating seconds of mean time in the latitude of London in a vacuum at the level of the sea is 39.1393 inches of the said standard.

2. The standard brass weight of one pound troy weight, made in the year 1758, now in the custody of the clerk of the House of Commons, shall be the original and genuine standard measure of weight. . . . . The act goes on to say that the cubic inch of distilled water, weighed in air by brass weights, at 62° of Fahrenheit, the barometer being at 30 inches, is equal to 252·458 grains.

The last event in the history of this subject was the report (in 1841) of a commission of men of science appointed in 1838. After reciting that the standard yard was rendered absolutely useless by the fire at the House of Commons, and that the standard troy pound was altogether missing, the commissioners begin by recommending the total disuse of all attempts to procure a natural standard, and the return to tho old plan of standards manufactured in metal; that four copies of the best existing representations of the old standards should be made, and carefully compared; that one of these copies should be hermetically sealed, and imbedded in the masonry of some public building, marked by an inscription, and only to be opened by Act of Parliament; that the standard of capacity be defined by that of weight, not by that of length; that various precautions, minutely named, be taken for the preservation and safe custody of the others; that the avoirdupois pound, and not the troy, be the standard; that the government purchase all the known copies of the old standards which have been noted in scientific operations; that no circumstance would contribute so much to the introduction of a decimal scale in weights and measures as the establishment of a decimal coinage, which is strongly recommended; that the old Gunter's Chain be preserved in tho measurement of land; that a measure of 1,000 or 2,000 yards receive a name, and be used co-ordinately with the mile, with a view to the gradual disuse of the latter; &c. Steps have been taken to recover a standard yard, by comparison of the existing scales which had been compared with the last standard.

Although not directly of great importance to manufacturing and trading affairs, the determination of theso standards is indirectly advantageous; and the subject is at any rate worthy of more general public attention than it usually receives.

STANNARY. This term sometimes denotes a tin-mine, sometimes the tin-mines of a district, sometimes the royal rights in respect of tin-mines within such district. But it is more commonly used as including the tin-mines within a particular district, the tinners employed in working them, and the customs and privileges attached to the mines, and to those employed in digging and purifying the ore.

The great stannaries of England are those of Devon and Cornwall, of which the stannary of Cornwall is the more important. The stannaries of Cornwall and Devon were granted by Edward III. to the Black Prince, upon the creation of the duchy of Cornwall, and are perpetually incorporated with that duchy. In general both stannaries are under one duchy-officer, called the lord-warden of the stannaries, with a separate vice-warden for each county. The stannary of Cornwall is subdivided into the stannary of Blackmore, in the eastern parts of the county, and the stannaries of Tywarnhaile, Penwith, and Helston, in the west.

All tin in Cornwall and Devon, whoever might be the owner of the land, appears to have formerly belonged to the king, by a usage peculiar to these counties. King John, in 1201, granted a charter to his tinners in Cornwall and Devonshire, authorising them to dig tin and turves to melt the tin anywhere in the moors and in the fees of bishops, abbots, and earls, as they had been used and accustomed. This charter was confirmed by Edward I., Richard II., and Henry IV. In Cornwall the right of digging in other men's land is now regulated by a peculiar usage, called the custom of *bounding*. This custom attaches only to such land as now is or anciently was *wastrel*, that is, land open or uninclosed.

As part of the stannary rights, the Duke of Cornwall, as guarantee of the crown, has or had the pre-emption of tin throughout the county, a privilege supposed to have been reserved to the crown out of an original right of property in tin mines, but in modern times it is never exercised.

The duties payable to the Duke of Cornwall on the stamping or coinage of tin were abolished by an Act passed in 1838; and the stannary courts were remodelled by other Acts in 1836 and 1839. By that of 1839 a stannary courts' duty of one farthing in the pound sterling was imposed on tin and tin ore.

STAPLE. A staple, or market, was the term applied in the middle ages to indicate those marts both in this country and at Bruges, Antwerp, Calais, &c., on the Continent, where the principal products of a country were sold. The staples were confirmed or appointed in England by the king. All merchandise sold for the purpose of exportation was compelled either to be sold at the staple, or afterwards brought there before exportation. This was done with the double view of accommodating the foreign merchants, and also enabling the duties on exportation to be more conveniently and certainly collected. Afterwards the word staple was applied to the merchandise itself which was sold at the staple. The staple merchandise of England at these early times, when little manufacture was carried on here, is said by Lord Coke to have been wool, woolfells or sheepskins, leather, lead, and tin. Incident to the staple was a court called 'the court of the mayor of the staple.' This court was held for the convenience of the merchants, both native and foreign, attending the staple. Many early enactments exist regulating the proceedings at the staple and the court held there; most of these were passed during the reigns of Edward I. and Edward III. A variety of other statutes were passed in the same and succeeding reigns, in some respects confirming, in others altering, the provisions of the leading statute. As commerce became more extended, the staples appear to have fallen into disuse.

STARCH (called also *Farina* and *Fæculum*) is a proximate principle of plants, chiefly found in the seeds of corn and pulse, in many kinds of tubers, and sometimes in wood, bark, and leaves. In all these instances it is associated with other principles, which are either employed with it, or separated by different processes, according to the use intended to be made of it. In wheat it is associated with variable proportions of gluten, sugar, and gum; in potatoes chiefly with gum and sugar. It is mostly lodged in the cells of the cellular tissue, and consists of granules, always white, generally of a roundish and seldom of an angular figure. The granules differ in size, often in the same seed, being generally smallest near the circumference. They differ also in different plants. The granules are lodged mostly in the cells or compartments of the cellular tissue; and each granule consists of a membrane, containing a transparent colourless material resembling gum.

The insolubility of the membrane in cold water affords a means of separating the starch from the gluten in wheat-flour, and from the fibrous matter in potatoes and other tubers. Wheat-flour is formed into a paste with water, and then kneaded under a stream of water so long as the water runs off of a milky appearance; what remains behind is chiefly gluten, while the water has carried off the starch suspended in it; and gum, sugar, and some phosphatic salts, either dissolved or suspended in it. The water charged with these matters is permitted to stand for a few days in summer, but for a week or two in winter, to allow the acetous fermentation to occur, by which the sugar and other principles are got rid of. The acid liquor termed *sours* is drawn off, and the starch thrown upon sieves, and washed; the bran and other impurities are retained on the sieves, while the starch is carried forward into large vessels called *frames*. In these the starch subsides, and the water, which has become perceptibly sour, drawn off, and the *slimes* removed. The starch is then washed, passed through a sieve, and finally allowed to subside. Thus purified it is put into boxes lined with canvas and perforated with holes, by which the superfluous water escapes. Afterwards it is cut into squares, put on bricks, and exposed to the heat of an oven, where it splits into irregular prisms. When free from any artificial admixture, it is perfectly white, and termed white Starch or French Starch: but in general, azure (smalt) or indigo is added, when it is employed for stiffening linen, to which it imparts a more agreeable hue than the dull white of that material.

Starch, when pure, is nearly devoid of odour and taste. The best bread is formed by flour which contains the greatest proportion of gluten. The relative proportions of starch and gluten differ not only in the different cereal grains, but in the same species or variety, according to the season when they are sown, or the manure which has been applied to the land. Starch exists in larger proportion in Carolina rice than in any other grain. Potatoes yield the purest starch, variable in quantity with the kind of potato used, the mode of cultivation, the time of setting, and, above all, the time of year when the process is applied.

Starch is most extensively used in the arts, but it is little employed in medicine, except for its demulcent properties, and as a vehicle for opiate injections. Some of the calico printers use a kind of stiffening material or starch, which they call *British gum*, and which was brought into use on account of the high price of gum senegal; it is prepared from wheat flour, and is midway in quality between common starch and common flour-paste.

STATUARY. [SCULPTURE; STONE MASONRY.]

STEAM. Water converted into steam occupies more than 1700 times its former space. Steam will be produced at a proportionally lower temperature if we diminish the pressure of the atmosphere on the water, which may be done either by ascending a mountain or by drawing away a portion of the air by means of an air-pump. When we continue to apply heat to ordinary steam, under a constant bulk, its elasticity rapidly increases, and it is then termed *high-pressure;* steam of the ordinary temperature being termed *low-pressure*.

The following table gives the temperature of boiling water and the corresponding pressures of the air, measured in inches of barometrical pressure.

Heat of boiling water.	Corresponding pressure of air.
215°	31.8
212	30.
209	28.2
200	22.8
180	15.2
160	9.45
120	3.27
100	1.97
10	1.03

Calling 30 inches of pressure *one atmosphere*, we have the following pressures for high temperatures:

Atmospheres.	Barometer.	Temperatures.
1	29.8	212°
2	59.6	250.3
4	119.2	293.4
8	238.4	343.6

The following table shews the elastic force of the vapour of water in mercurial inches, with the corresponding temperatures.

Temp.	Elasticity.	Temp.	Elasticity.
32°	0.20	200°	23.60
55	0.42	212	30.00
65	0.63	220	35.54
75	0.86	240	51.70
80	1.01	250	61.90
90	1.36	260	72.30
100	1.86	280	101.90
120	3.30	290	120.15
140	5.77	300	139.70
160	9.60	305	150.56
180	15.16	310	161.30

Steam has lately been employed in a considerable number of novel modes, as an effective agent in the arts. A remarkable employment of steam in charcoal making is noticed under CHARCOAL. M. Violette, in a paper communicated to the Academy of Sciences in 1848, states that bread and biscuits may be well baked by means of a current of steam at a temperature of about 400° Fahrenheit. He also thinks that the cooking of meat may be effected by the same agent. The extraction of wood vinegar (pyroligneous acid) is another process which seems to come within the same range; and as the temperature of the steam, and consequently the heat of the whole process, may be regulated at pleasure, it is thought that the acid may be extracted without the empyreumatic oil which usually accompanies it in the ordinary process. The extraction of wood alcohol (pyroxylic spirit) is attainable by the same means. The drying of wood by highly-heated steam adds another to the list of proposed uses.

STEAM-CARRIAGE. The application of the steam-engine to the purpose of locomotion upon railways, has been noticed elsewhere. [RAILWAY.] In a steam-carriage for use upon a common road, provision must be made for passing over rough, soft, and constantly-varying surfaces, and for surmounting acclivities of considerable steepness; the machine must be provided with a steering apparatus, by which it may be guided with ease and certainty along the sinnuosities of a common road or street, among other vehicles, and round sharp corners; the weight must be kept within the smallest possible limits; and the machinery must be compacted within a small space.

There were various attempts to construct such machines in the last century; but the first invention which claims notice is that patented in 1802 by Messrs. Trevithick and Vivian, and shortly afterwards brought into operation. Their carriage was mounted upon four wheels; the principal weight resting upon the hind wheels, which were of large diameter, while the fore wheels, which were used for guiding the carriage, were small, and nearer together than the others. The boiler and the steam-cylinder were placed at the back of the hind axle, and the cylinder was horizontal. The carriage, shortly after the date of this patent, was exhibited in London with sufficient success to prove the practicability of the invention. The inventors, however, soon gave up their experiments on common-road locomotion, and adapted their machinery to use upon a railway.

For about twenty years after the experiments of Trevithick, no steam-carriages for common roads were constructed; but when the improved state of the turnpike-roads rendered steam-locomotion more practicable upon them, steam-carriage projectors arose in rapid succession. Mr. Griffith's steam-carriage, patented in 1821, had the boiler and machinery suspended from the framework by chains and helical springs. Mr. David Gordon's machine, patented in 1822, had its wheels surrounded by cogs or projecting teeth. Another machine, by the same inventor, had two long propellers or legs, intended to obviate the supposed tendency of wheels to slip, when ascending a slope. Of others who have invented and built steam-carriages between 1824 and the present time, the names of Goldsworthy Gurney, Burstall and Hill, W. H. James, Walter Hancock, Summers and Ogle, Messrs. Heaton, Dr. Church, Dance and Field, Squire and Maccrone, Scott Russell, Hills, and Sir James Anderson, are the most prominent, although many others have appeared upon the field. Several of these inventors have produced carriages capable of maintaining an average speed of from ten to twelve miles per hour for considerable distances, and a much more rapid rate of motion for a short time; and some have succeeded in performing extensive journeys with their steam-carriages. The greatest amount of success yet attained was in a steam-carriage constructed by Mr. Gurney, and brought forward by Mr. Charles Dance, who established a regular steam-conveyance between Gloucester and Cheltenham; but commercial failure has hitherto attended all these attempts.

The forms of apparatus in these carriages are of course various. As to the boiler, the essential requisites are the power of generating steam very rapidly; strength, to secure it from explosion; lightness; and compactness. A great number of contrivances have been tried with the hope of accomplishing the desired union of these qualities; all of them consisting either of small tubes, or of separate chambers. The means adopted for producing a strong draft in the fire are of two kinds; viz., by an air chamber, and by air-fans. Many different arrangements have been adopted for communicating the power of the pistons to the wheels of the carriage; as indeed is also the case in respect to railway locomotives. The operation of steering is usually performed by a hand-wheel in the fore-part of the carriage, giving motion, by means of a rack and pinion, or a chain and pulley, to the fore-axle. The *Brake*, by which the motion of the steam-carriage may be arrested when necessary, usually consists of metallic bands, capable of being pressed against either the nave or the periphery of one or both of the hind-wheels.

STEAM-ENGINE. The earlier steam-engines, even Captain Savery's, which was long employed in this country, were only pumps for raising water; a partial vacuum was formed in close vessels by the condensation of steam within them, and the atmospheric pressure raised the water to a certain height, whence it was forced higher by the elasticity of the steam admitted to act on its surface.

The first steam-engine which formed the connecting link between the steam-pumps and the modern steam-engines, was invented by Newcomen (1705). It contained a cylinder open at the upper end, fitted with a piston; and the upward movement of the piston was occasioned by the pressure of steam beneath it; whereas the downward movement was caused by the pressure of the air. Newcomen's engine was successively improved upon by Smeaton, Brindley, and other engineers, previous to Watt's time; and from its intrinsic merits it remained in general use under the appropriate name of the *Atmospheric Engine* during the greater part of the last century, but was only used for pumping water. Its guiding principle was, that the steam was solely employed to produce a partial vacuum by its condensation, its elastic force at high temperatures not being made use of.

The first and most important of Watt's improvements on the steam-engine consisted in effecting the condensation in a separate vessel, termed the *Condenser*, which communicated with the cylinder; whereas Newcomen condensed his steam by a jet of cold water in the cylinder itself. This condenser being filled with steam from the boiler at the same time with the cylinder, the jet of cold water, admitted into the former only, effected the condensation of the whole volume of steam, both of that in the cylinder as well as of that in the condenser. As the cylinder was thus not coooled by a jet, a vast economy of heat resulted. The second of Watt's improvements consisted in closing the cylinder at top, the piston-rod being made to pass steam-tight through a cylindrical neck in that top, termed a *Stuffing-Box*. The object of this alteration was to admit of the elastic force of the steam being employed to impel the piston downwards, instead of simple atmospheric pressure. For this purpose the steam was admitted from the boiler above the piston at the same moment the condensation took place in the condenser; the steam-passage being made double for the purpose, so that the communication with the condenser could be cut off when that with the cylinder was opened, alternately. Such is the general principle of Watt's *Single-Acting Engine*, which hence became a Steam-Engine, and was no longer an Atmospheric Engine; it became a *Double-Acting Engine* by removing the counterpoise, and producing the upward motion of the piston by admitting steam below as well as above it.

The changes in the engine introduced by Watt created the necessity for two pumps, and commonly three, which are worked by rods attached to the beam. The first of these is the *Hot-Water* or *Air-Pump*, intended to remove the air, condensed water, and steam from the condenser, in which they would otherwise accumulate, and finally stop the action; the second is a *Force-Pump*, required to return the water, drawn from the condenser by the first, back to the boiler; and the third, termed the *Cold-Water Pump*, supplies the cold-water cistern which contains the condenser.

In the mechanism of a steam-engine, the *Piston* is one of the most important parts, as it must be steam-tight, and yet work easily in the cylinder. The better class of engines have now usually what are called *Metallic Pistons*, of which there are different kinds, invented by Cartwright, Jessop, Barton, and others. The body of these pistons is metal, made in pieces or segments, acted on by springs radiating from a centre; so that while the friction is diminished by both surfaces being metallic, the piston, owing to its construction, can adapt itself to the irregularities of the cylinder. The steam is admitted to the cylinder by various ingenious contrivances, among which the *four-passage cock*, the *conical valve*, and the *slide valve* are the chief. For the opening and shutting of the valves, an *Excentric* is now generally used; this is a peculiar contrivance, worked from the fly wheel. This *fly-wheel* is necessary when the engine is employed to drive machinery of any kind; it is a heavy wheel, whose weight tends to equalize the motion of the beam and piston.

When Watt substituted the elastic force of steam for the pressure of the atmosphere, he introduced a source of power which might be increased to an indefinite extent, provided it were found advantageous to employ it. Generally it is more advantageous to employ steam of a comparatively high elastic force; accordingly the pressure was increased, in engines constructed by Watt, from 4 to 8, or even 12 lbs. on the inch. Modern boilers are so skilfully made, that steam of 100 lbs. on the inch may frequently be safely used. In the common engine, if the pressure on the piston continue uniform during the stroke, as it would do if the communication with the boiler remained open, the piston would move with an accelerating velocity till it arrived at the end of the cylinder, by which it would produce mischief; hence the steam is cut off at a particular stage in the descent; and when the steam possesses considerable elastic force, the communication with the boiler is cut off sooner, and the piston is urged forward by the expansive force of the steam, which, although decreasing as the space increases, is yet sufficient to carry the piston to the end of the stroke.

Although the Condensing Engine is very perfect and economises fuel, it is necessarily heavy, and occupies considerable room. For cases where the two last-named particulars are of importance, the *Non-Condensing Engine* was invented. A locomotive for railways is the most important form of non-condensing engine; but such engines are frequently valuable for other purposes. Since the pumps of the condensing-engine are dispensed with in the non-condensing engine, the beam may be so likewise; and a still further simplification results from an oscillating movement given to the cylinder. Such engines are termed *Vibratory Engines*, and are successfully used where space must be economised, as with marine engines. Non-Condensing Engines are frequently termed *High-Pressure Engines*, in contradistinction to *Low-Pressure* or Condensing Engines.

Marine Engines, or those used for propelling vessels, are in this country generally condensing engines, their situation admitting the abundant use of cold water. The principal peculiarity in the arrangement of the marine engine is the position of the beam, which, for the purpose of economising room, is placed lower than the cylinder, and is double, there being one on each side. In all vessels of any magnitude, there are two engines complete, so arranged, that while the rod and crank of one are in their neutral position, those of the other are in that of greatest effect. In steam-vessels of smaller size, the *direct action* is often used; that is, the piston-rod turns the shaft without the intervention of any beam. In American steam-vessels the engines are frequently high-pressure.

Engineers have always been induced, by the obvious advantage of a continuous over an alternating motion, to aim at contriving a steam-engine in which the steam should act directly to produce such a motion. Watt accordingly patented more than one of such *Rotatory Engines*, and many others since have from time to time brought forward arrangements for the purpose; but none have come into permanent and general use. The fact is, that the employment of steam in this way is productive of a greater waste of power, with a greater increase of friction, than can be compensated by any real advantages.

The peculiarities of the *Locomotive Engine* are noticed under RAILWAY.

No part of a steam-engine exhibits more variety, according to the purpose to which it is to be applied, than the *Boiler.* Rapid generation of steam, security, compactness, and lightness, must be aimed at in boilers for marine or locomotive engines, even at the cost of a comparative waste of fuel; while for those intended for pumping or driving machinery, economy of fuel must be the paramount object, the weight, form, and space occupied by the boiler being secondary considerations. As very large boilers are unsafe, it is customary to use two or more small boilers instead of one large one; and the principle, carried to its limit, constitutes that of the *Tubular Boiler*, in which the steam is generated in a series of independent metal pipes of small diameter, all communicating with a common steam-chamber, or reservoir, itself small, and strong enough to resist great pressures. The *safety valve* is a contrivance for letting off some of the steam from the boiler when the elasticity is dangerously high. *Gauges* are employed to measure the quantity of the water, and the pressure of the steam in the boiler.

Whenever the steam-engine is employed to execute any work which is variable in its quantity or intensity, there must be some means of adjusting the force of the engine to this varying resistance it has to overcome. The object of that beautiful piece of mechanism termed the *Governor* is to enable the engine to regulate the supply of steam admitted to the cylinder, or in other words to adapt the force it has to transmit to the resistance it has to overcome. In this apparatus, two balls rotate round a common axis, with a velocity depending on that of the fly-wheel; if this velocity is great, the balls diverge by virtue of the centrifugal force, and this divergence is a means of partially closing a valve, and lessening the amount of steam which enters the cylinder. From different causes the marine engine and the locomotive do not require governors.

A museum of steam-engines would display some of the highest results of human ingenuity ever manifested. Among the toys or curiosities of such a museum might be placed the tiny steam-engine, made by a mechanic of Saddleworth, for the Great Exhibition, and weighing only three-quarters of an ounce.

STEAM-HAMMER. The steam-hammer introduced by Mr. Nasmyth, economises time and labour in a remarkable degree. It is the most efficient and practical machine yet invented for dealing heavy blows rapidly and steadily. In anchor-making, in iron-forging, and in pile-driving, its application is particularly valuable. The mode of applying this powerful machine to the purposes here indicated, is briefly adverted to under ANCHOR, IRON MANUFACTURE, and PILE ENGINE. An American patent has more recently been obtained by Mr. Kirk for another steam hammer, in which the hammer has a long handle something like the beam of a steam engine, with a fulcrum at the centre, and the hammer head at one end; but we do not know whether this invention has been practically worked.

A medium between a steam hammer and a sledge hammer has been devised for the use of blacksmiths, and called by the fanciful name of the *Blacksmith's Apprentice.* The *foot* of the blacksmith works the sledge hammer instead of the apprentice or subordinate who assists him. The foot presses on a treadle, the other end of which has a chain which coils round a horizontal barrel, to which barrel the sledge hammer is attached; the sizes of the different parts are so regulated, that when the foot presses down the treadle, the hammer is whirled round with considerable force upon the anvil, leaving the hands of the workman free to conduct subsidiary operations.

STEAM VESSEL. Papin proposed a kind of steam-boat, but made no attempt to construct one; and after his time several plans for propelling boats by other means than oars or sails were proposed and tried. At length, in 1774, the Comte d'Auxiron, a French nobleman of scientific attainments, constructed a steam-boat, and tried it on the Seine, near Paris. It appears that the engine had not sufficient power to move the wheels efficiently; an error which was also observable in contrivances brought forward shortly afterwards by Perier and others. The Marquis de Jouffroy tried a steam-boat of considerable dimensions on the Saône, in 1782: it had a single paddle-wheel on each side, and the machinery appears to have been constructed with some skill, though it was not sufficiently strong. M. des Blancs in 1796 formed a boat which was propelled by means of paddles or float-boards attached to an endless chain stretched over two wheels projecting from each side of the vessel. In America an inventor named Fitch succeeded as early as 1783 in moving a boat on the Delaware by means of paddles (not paddle-wheels) set in motion by a steam-engine. In 1787 Rumsey made some short voyages on the Potomac, with a boat about fifty feet long, propelled by the reaction of a stream of water drawn in at the bow and forced out at the stern by means of a pump worked by a steam-engine.

While Fitch and Rumsey were making their experiments in America, other experiments were in progress in Scotland, which tended, more than any previous trials, to the useful application of steam to the purpose of propelling vessels. Mr. Miller, of Dalswinton, Mr. James Taylor, and Mr. Symington, were the three persons who had most to do with this important improvement. A very small steam-boat was constructed by them in 1788, and one constructed larger in 1789. In 1801 Symington commenced a satisfactory series of experiments on steam navigation, under the auspices of Lord Dundas. The object immediately aimed at was the introduction of tug-boats instead of horses for drawing boats upon canals. After several minor trials, one of the boats built on this occasion by Symington drew, on the Forth and Clyde Canal, in 1802, two loaded vessels, each of seventy tons burden.

Among the numerous individuals who inspected Symington's vessel with interest was Fulton. After various minor attempts, Fulton procured, in conjunction with Mr. Livingstone, a patent in America for steam navigation, about the year 1805. He built a steam-vessel at New York, and launched it in the spring of 1807. It made its first voyage from New York to Albany, 145 miles, at the rate of five miles an hour. The dimensions of the boat, which was of 160 tons burden, were 133 feet long, 18 feet wide, and 7 feet deep. Her cylinder was two feet in diameter, and of four feet stroke; and the paddle-wheels were fifteen feet in diameter, with paddles four feet long, dipping two feet into the water. Meanwhile Mr. Stevens, of Hoboken, near New York, introduced steam-boats on the Delaware, and made such improvements in the form of the vessels as to enable him to obtain a speed of thirteen miles an hour. Steam navigation thus became finally established in America.

Henry Bell, of Helensburgh, on the Clyde, was the individual by whom steam-vessels were first used in Britain for commercial purposes. He built a small steam-vessel called the Comet, of forty feet keel and ten and a half feet beam; and of about twenty-five tons burden, and three-horse power. The boiler was placed on one side of the vessel, and the funnel or chimney, was bent so as to rise in the centre of the vessel, where it served the purpose of a mast for carrying sail. A single cylinder was used impelling a cranked axle which carried a large toothed wheel; and this wheel, working into two others fixed upon the axles of the paddles, caused them to revolve. Two paddle-wheels, or rather two sets of revolving paddles, each consisting of four paddles of a form resembling malt-shovels, were used on each side of the vessel. The Comet began to run regularly between Glasgow and Helensburgh, in January, 1812, and continued to ply successfully during the following summer; her rate of motion was about five miles an hour. Improvements were soon found advisable, and Bell soon abandoned the peculiar arrangement of paddles by which his first experiment was distinguished, and adopted complete paddle-wheels. This interesting little steamer is further noticed under Clyde. From that time to the present numerous experiments and an uninterrupted succession of improvements have brought steam-navigation to its present high state of perfection.

The proportions of steam-vessels were, originally, like those of sailing-vessels, short and full, their length being only about three or four times their breadth; while now the proportion of six breadths to the length is common in the best sea-going steam-vessels, and many of the fast river boats are still longer, ranging in length from seven to ten times their width. In America the proportion of length to breadth is sometimes made even greater than as ten to one; and boats have been built, the length of which is twelve times their breadth. In larger steamers, the depth of the hull bears a greater ratio to the width than in smaller vessels. Different steam-vessel builders adopt very different forms, according as they wish to obtain a *roomy*, a *safe*, or a *swift* boat; at the present day swiftness is regarded as almost an indispensable quality.

One of the important questions which has of late years attracted much attention in connection with steam navigation, is that of the comparative advantages of iron and wood as materials for steam-vessels. Small vessels of iron have for many years past been used for river and canal navigation; and recently steam vessels of considerable size have been built of the same material. Although different opinions prevail as to the relative advantages of the two materials, it is certain that, owing to the superior strength of iron, and its power of bearing strain in any direction, an iron vessel may be made much lighter than one of wood of equal strength; the saving of weight being sometimes estimated at one-half. Another great advantage of iron consists in the facility with which it may be formed into any shape. An iron hull is also superior to one of wood in its security from fire and its greater cleanliness. Steam-vessels may be greatly strengthened by means of water tight bulk heads or transverse partitions in the hull, the adoption of which is becoming very general in large steamers.

As an ample supply of cold water can always be commanded for the purpose of condensation, there is not much inducement for the use of high-pressure steam in marine engines; and this circumstance, with the unfavourable opinion generally entertained as to the safety of high-pressure boilers, has led to the almost universal adoption of low-pressure, or condensing engines, in European steam-vessels; although many of the steamers of North America are worked at a pressure of 140 lbs. to an inch, or even more. The kind of marine engine most commonly used in this country, is the sde-lever engine, where two distinct engines work separate cranks upon the same axle; but the *steeple-engine*, and other forms, are occasionally employed. The means adopted for condensing the steam is a matter of great importance in sea-going steamers. The most effectual method of condensation is by the injection of cold water into the condenser, or by causing it to fall in a thin sheet, to which the steam is exposed. When sea water is used for this purpose, an incrustation of salt forms inside the boiler, productive of much mischief. This evil can only be avoided by the use of fresh water in the boilers and condenser, and allowing the salt water to act only on the outside of the condenser. Hall's Condenser and Howard's Vapour-Engine are two methods of attaining this object; but neither of them has fully realised its intended purpose.

Notwithstanding the defects commonly imputed to it, and the great number of contrivances which have been devised for avoiding them, the common *Paddle Wheel* continues to be the chief means of propulsion used. It consists of a number of flat boards, called float-boards or paddles, bolted to the radii or arms of a light but strong iron wheel, which is fixed securely upon the crank axis of the engine; and it should be so placed that the lowest float-board is entirely immersed in the water. Several improvements upon the common paddle-wheel have been introduced, which tend to diminish the defects attributed to it.

The substitution of the *screw* for the *paddle wheel*, is noticed under SCREW PROPELLER.

Sub-marine Steam Navigation has more than once attracted the attention of inventors. Dr. Payerne, whose contrivances in relation to sub-marine descent, are noticed under DIVING BELL, has lately (1851) formed a screw steamer which (according to the account given) will work at any depth down to 150 feet below the surface of the water; while the contained air is rendered respirable by chemical means. The invention is said to be under examination by some of the savans of France; if there is anything important or valuable in it, we shall soon hear more concerning it in England.

The steam ships of Great Britain now amount to a formidable number. Those which were registered at all the ports in the United Kingdom on Dec. 31, 1850, were:—

	Vessels.		Tons.
Under 50 tons	520	..	12,885
50 tons and above .	658	..	154,327

The steam vessels that left and entered British ports, to and from foreign ports, in 1850, were as follow:—

	Inwards.		Outwards.
England......	10,782	..	10,447
Scotland......	4,467	..	4,603
Ireland	4,340	..	4,534
Isle of Man...	225	..	172
	19,814		19,756

These numbers include the repeated voyages of each vessel. Besides the above, 399 steamers arrived from, and 369 started for, the British colonies in the same year. Eighteen timber steamers, and fifty iron steamers, were built and registered at British ports during the same year.

STEARIC ACID; STEARIN. Stearic acid is procured from stearin by the action of potash and hydrochloric acid. It has the form of brilliant white scaly crystals; it is inodorous, tasteless, insoluble in water. It melts at about 158° of Fahrenheit, and on cooling it forms a crystalline mass. It is volatile, and may be distilled unaltered in close vessels. In the air it burns like wax. Stearic Acid, besides its use in the manufacture of soap, is now very largely employed in the making of candles. *Stearin* is the harder portion of animal fats; *Olein*, or *Elain*, being the softer part. Stearin has a pearly lustre, is soft to the touch, but not greasy; it melts at about 140° to 145° Fahrenheit; and, on cooling, solidifies into a mass like wax, which is not crystalline in its texture, and is reducible to powder. Stearin is the chief and most important ingredient of the harder kinds of fat, and the harder they are the more they contain. It is separable into two different principles, namely, *stearic acid* and *glycerin*.

STEEL ENGRAVING. The comparative softness of copper occasions copper plates to wear so rapidly in the process of printing, that the beauty of the engraving is very soon impaired, and it is impossible to produce from a single plate, a sufficient number of impressions for the illustration of books of large circulation. The use of steel plates for diminishing this inconvenience, although not extensively resorted to until within the last thirty years, is a measure of which the possibility was conceived at an early period, but which was first put into practice about thirty years ago, in the attempts to protect the Bank of England notes from forgery.

In Messrs. Perkins and Heath's method of steel engraving (which has been the basis of all recent modes of producing large numbers of copies), the engraving is executed upon a plate or block of cast steel, the surface of which has been decarbonised or softened by a careful application of heat. On the plate thus softened the engraving is effected with facility; and, when it is completed, the hardness of the surface is restored by exposing the plate for some hours to a red heat, the surface being thickly covered with animal charcoal, formed of burnt leather or bones, and the whole being, as before, enclosed in a cast iron box. The plate is afterwards cooled and retempered in a very careful manner. From this hardened plate the engraving is transferred to a softened steel roller, of small diameter, which is pressed against the plate with such force that its surface becomes embossed with a perfect transfer or impression of the engraved device. The roller or cylinder is then hardened in a similar manner to the original plate, and is afterwards made to transfer the devices from its surface to any required number of softened or decarbonised plates, which are then hardened for printing from. This beautiful process is not only applicable to transferring engravings from one plate to another; but, in cases where one ornament has to be repeated several times on one plate, the device may, by being once engraved, be impressed as often as necessary upon different parts of the same plate. The power of multiplication is, for all practical purposes, unlimited. It is by such a process that the postage stamps are produced, millions of impressions being obtained from only one originally engraved plate. The perfection which has been reached is almost beyond conception; the finest writing, and the most minute and intricate patterns, being transferred from plate to plate with such precision that the keenest scrutiny cannot detect a difference between the original and the transfer. The plan has been much used for country bank-notes and similar purposes.

The application of steel engraving to works of fine art is, in a great measure, due to the late Mr. Charles Warren. In this method, the steel is softened to receive the graver, and is printed from in this softened state. The surface of a steel plate is not polished very highly, and in applying etching ground to it, the plate is not heated quite so much as is usual with copper. In the application of steel engraving to matters of fine art, the accomplishment of mezzotinting upon steel plates is one of the most important points, as the wear of copper plates engraved in this manner is very rapid.

The cost of engraving upon steel is considerably greater than that of engraving upon copper; yet, as steel plates afford so many more impressions than copper, they enable the publisher, by calculating his returns upon a large instead of a small number, to issue works of art at so low a price as to ensure a very wide circulation.

STEEL MANUFACTURE. Iron possesses many qualities which render it applicable to innumerable purposes in the arts; but there are some uses for which it is not sufficiently hard, and this defect is supplied by converting it into steel. Steel is an intimate compound of iron and charcoal or carbon. There is carbon in soft iron, but in steel it appears to be in more intimate union with the metal.

Hitherto Swedish and Russian bar-iron have been exclusively employed in the manufacture of the best steel. The preference given to this iron is decided, though from what cause it arises has not been satisfactorily made out. We may however remark, that the foreign iron used is made from magnetic iron ore with charcoal; while British iron is obtained mostly from the impure carbonate of iron, or from peroxide of iron, and both of these are reduced by employing coal or coke. *Bar-steel* is made, with few exceptions, from the Swedish and Russian iron, the bars of which are marked *Hoop L*, *G L*, and *Double Bullet*, which are the best kinds. Iron of lower quality is also used, both Russian and Swedish, each kind having its peculiar mark. These steel irons are imported almost exclusively by English merchants residing in Hull. The limited quantity of the fine iron allowed to be produced from the mines of Danemora in Sweden accounts in some degree for the high price at which they are sold. The quantity of iron imported into this country for the manufacture of steel is estimated at 12,000 to 15,000 tons annually, of which at least 9000 come from Sweden.

The usual operation in manufacturing steel is first to cut the bar iron into certain lengths, leaving room in the vessels for the expansion of the iron. The closed vessels in which the bars are heated are usually twelve feet in length, and divided into two pots or troughs, on the bottom of which the workman strews charcoal to the thickness of about an inch, and upon this he places on their flat side a layer of bars; then about three fourths of an inch more of charcoal is added, and upon this he places another layer of bars, and so on till the troughs are filled; these are then covered with a ferruginous earth coming from the Sheffield grinding stones, called *wheelswharf*, to the thickness of about eight inches. All the apertures of the furnace are closed with loose bricks and plastered over with fire-clay. The fire is then lighted, and in four days and nights the furnace is at its full heat, at which it is kept for several days, according to the degree of hardness required. In order to be able to test the progress of the carbonisation, a hole is left in one of the pots near the centre, and three or four bars are placed in the furnace in such a manner, that the ends come through this opening, and after the sixth day one is pulled out. If the iron be then not sufficiently carbonised, the heating is continued from two to four days longer; a bar is drawn every two days, and when the iron is completely converted, the fire is heaped up with small coal, and the furnace is left to burn out and it requires from this period fourteen days' time to cool sufficiently to allow a person to go in and discharge the steel. A *converting furnace*, as it is called, contains generally fifteen tons of iron; and there are some large enough to hold eighteen to twenty tons. The bar-steel, when discharged from the furnace, is partially covered with small raised portions of the metal; and from the resemblance of these to blisters, the steel is called *blistered steel*. The degree of conversion produced depends upon the purpose to which the steel is to be applied.

Bar steel as it comes from the converting furnace is used for various purposes without refining. Those parts which are free from flaws and blisters are broken out and hammered or rolled to the sizes required by the manufacturer for files, edge tools, table knives and forks, coach-springs, and a great variety of common agricultural implements. It is also manufactured into what is called *sheer steel*, which is more homogeneous, tougher, and capable of receiving a finer edge, than bar steel, which is converted into sheer steel by repeated heating, hammering, and welding.

The *cast steel* is comparatively a recent invention; but it is gradually superseding the use of bar and sheer steel, on account of the equality of its temper, and the superior quality as well as beauty of the articles which are made of it. The process adopted is that of taking bar steel converted to a certain degree of hardness, and breaking it into pieces of about a pound each; a crucible charged with these is placed in a melting-furnace, similar to those which are used by brass founders. The furnaces are 20 inches long by 16 inches wide, and 3 feet deep. The most intense heat is kept up for two or three hours, coke being used as fuel. When the furnace requires feeding, the workman takes the opportunity of lifting the lid of each crucible and judging how long the charge of each will be before it is completely melted. All the crucibles are usually ready about the same time. They are taken out of the furnace, and the liquid steel is poured into ingots of the shape and size required. This is considered, we believe, the most fearful process which British manufactures present, in respect to the fierce heat to which the workmen are exposed: the steel is in a perfectly liquid state in the crucibles. The crucibles are immediately returned into the furnace; and when the contents of all have been poured into the moulds, the crucibles are again charged. They are used three times, and then rejected as useless. The ingots are taken to the forge tilt or rolling mill, and hammered into bars or rolled into sheets as may be required. The celebrated *Wootz*, or Indian steel, is cast steel; but it is frequently so imperfect as to resemble cast iron rather than cast steel. It is however made of iron obtained, as the Swedish is, from the magnetic ore. Wootz is made by the natives from malleable iron, packed in small bits with wood in crucibles, which are then covered with some green leaves and clay: about two dozen of these crucibles are packed in one furnace; they are covered with fuel, and a blast given for about two hours and a half, which terminates the operation. When the crucibles are cold, they are broken, and small cakes of steel are obtained in the form in which it is brought to England.

Steel is of a lighter gray colour than iron, so characteristic as to be described as a *steel-gray*. It is susceptible of receiving a very high polish, and this is greater as the grain is finer. Steel is about eight times as heavy as water. When steel is heated to redness and slowly cooled, it is scarcely harder than iron; but by very rapid cooling it becomes hard, and so brittle as to be readily broken. The fracture of steel is usually fine grained; in ductility and malleability it is much inferior to iron, but exceeds it greatly in elasticity and sonorousness. It may be subjected to a full red heat, or 2786° Fahr., without melting, and is therefore less fusible than cast iron, but much more so than wrought iron. Pieces of steel which have not been cast may be readily welded together or with iron: but after casting the operation is more difficult. Steel does not acquire magnetic polarity so readily as iron, but retains it much longer; by exposure however to a moderate degree of heat this power is lost.

In order to give to steel the different degrees of hardness required for the various purposes to which it is applied, it is subjected to the process of what is called *Tempering*. It is found that the higher the temperature to which it is raised, and the more sudden the cooling, the greater is the hardness produced. The steel is usually immersed in a bath of mercury or of oil, having a temperature varying from 430° to 600°. Captain Kater found that 212°, or the heat of boiling water, was the exact point at which the knife edges attached to a pendulum were properly tempered. *Case-hardening* is the operation by which articles made of malleable iron or cast iron are superficially converted into steel by heating them with charcoal in a crucible.

With respect to the composition of steel and the nature of the admixture requisite to constitute it, differences of opinion have long existed, and the question even now is considered by some as hardly decided, whether carbon is indispensably necessary to its formation, and whether certain substances or metals, especially silicon, may not give rise to it. All steel contains a little silicon and phosphorus as well as carbon. Mr. Faraday and Mr. Stodart published in the 'Phil. Trans.' for 1822 a valuable series of experiments on alloys of steel, from which it appears that by combining steel with other metals its quality is improved. A very minute addition was found sufficient to produce a good effect: thus one 500th of silver gave an alloy harder than cast steel; one 100th of nickel gave a very hard alloy, susceptible of a fine polish: alloys of rhodium and platinum were also formed; and these, with the alloys of iridium, osmium, and palladium, formed the most valuable compounds.

STEELYARD. The most common kind of steelyard, which is often called the Roman Balance, is used by suspending the article to be weighed from the end of the shorter arm, or placing it in a scale-dish from thence suspended, and sliding a determinate weight along the longer arm until the instrument remains in equlibrium in an horizontal position; the weight of the substance attached to the short arm of the lever being indicated by observing the position of the moveable balance weight with respect to a graduated scale marked upon the long arm of the steelyard. Many steelyards are supplied with a second fulcrum, the two being placed at different distances from the point to which the hook or scale is attached, and having their respective pointers and suspending hooks on opposite sides of the lever; one is used for light weights and one for heavy.

Various modifications of the steelyard have been contrived for delicate scientific purposes, or for adapting it to the purpose of weighing very heavy bodies. Several ingenious bent-lever balances have been contrived, some of which, from the circumstance of the levers being of unequal arms, resemble the steelyard in principle. These, and the steelyard weighing machines for ascertaining the weight of loaded carriages, are noticed under WEIGHING MACHINE. The balance known as the Danish or Swedish steelyard differs from that above described in having the weight fixed at one extremity of the lever, while the fulcrum itself is moveable. The portable weighing machine, called the spring or pocket steelyard is noticed under SPRING BALANCE.

STENCILLING. [PAPER HANGING.]

STEREOTYPE. Stereotype Printing is printing from cast plates of type-metal instead of moveable letters or types. It was first adopted by William Ged, a goldsmith of Edinburgh, about 1725; but his method fell into disuse. About the year 1780, Mr. Tilloch and Mr. Foulis introduced further improvements. Towards the latter end of the 18th century, many projects were brought forward in France for multiplying engraved blocks or forms of type by processes more or less resembling that of stereotyping, under the names of polytype, stereotype, &c. In some of these the form was imitated by striking upon a mass of soft metal, in the way described under CLICHÉE. Some of the early experiments of Senefelder, the inventor of lithography, were directed to the discovery of a means of stereotyping by which he might be enabled to print his own works with a very small stock of type. He formed a composition of clay, fine sand, flour, and pulverised charcoal, mixed with a little water, and kneaded as stiff as possible; and with this paste he made a mould from a page of type, which became, in a quarter of an hour, so hard that he could take a very perfect cast from it in melted sealing-wax, by means of a hand-press. He states that, by mixing a little pulverised plaster of paris with the sealing wax, the stereotype plates thus produced were much harder than the common type metal of lead and antimony. Professor Wilson, of Glasgow, in 1797, devised a method of multiplying engraved blocks or plates by stereotype or rather polytype impressions in glass or enamel, which, it was anticipated, would prove very durable, and might be applied with advantage to the prevention of forgery. The revival and introduction into common use of the stereotyping process is in a great measure, due to the exertions of the late Earl Stanhope, about the commencement of the present century; the earl assisted with his counsel and purse many of those who were at that time engaged on the subject; and stereotype printing became firmly established about 1809.

In setting up a form intended for stereotyping from, the *spaces*, or short pieces of metal by which the words are separated from each other, and the *quadrats*, or larger spaces by which blank lines are filled up, are cast higher than usual. The types are set up and formed into pages in the usual manner, with the illustrative wood cuts, if there be any; but instead of these pages being arranged into a form of sufficient size to print a whole sheet, each page, if large, or every two or four pages, if small, is separately locked up in a small frame or *chase;* the pages being surrounded by fillets of wood or metal, which serve in the cast to form a border for attaching the plate to its mount. The face of the types is then moistened with oil, to prevent the mould from adhering to them. A brass frame rather larger than the page is laid upon the chase, in order to retain the plaster while in a fluid state, and to regulate the thickness of the mould. The plaster is then poured on the types, and it soon sets into a solid mass, which must be removed from the types with great care, and trimmed on the edges with a knife. The plaster moulds are, in the next place, baked in an oven heated to about 400° Fahr., until they are thoroughly dry and hard. They are placed upright in a rack, and are usually dried in about two hours. Great care is required in this process, especially when the moulds are large, to prevent them from warping.

After being baked, the mould is placed, with its face downwards, upon a smooth plate of iron, called a *floating plate*, which lies at the bottom of a cast iron box rather larger than the mould. The box is then covered in by a lid, the under surface of which is made perfectly flat, and which has the corners cut off to allow the melted metal to enter the box. The cover is firmly held down by a screw, which is attached to an apparatus by which the box is suspended from a crane. It should be observed that the casting box and plate are heated to the same temperature as the mould before it is inserted. The box is then swung by the crane over the metal pit, which is an open iron vessel containing a large quantity of melted metal, resembling in its composition that used for casting types; and it is lowered into the metal in a nearly horizontal position, being a very little inclined, to facilitate the escape of air from tho mould and box. The melted metal runs in at the corners of the box; and by its greater specific gravity, floats up the plate with the mould, forcing the latter tightly against the lid of the box. By this contrivance the metal is forced by hydrostatic pressure into every part of the mould, in the margin of which notches are cut to allow free passage for the metal between it and the floating plate. After remaining immersed in the metal for about ten minutes, the box is gently raised, and removed by the crane to a trough in which its lower part is rapidly cooled by contact with cold water. While the box is cooling, the caster pours in a little metal at the corners, to fill the space left by the contraction of the metal, and so to keep up the necessary pressure upon the cast. When cold, the contents of the box are removed in a mass, from which the superfluous metal is broken off by blows from a mallet. The plaster mould is then broken away from the cast, the face of which is a fac-simile of the types and engravings from which the mould was taken. As the mould is destroyed by this process, it is necessary, when several stereotype plates of the same page are required, to take a distinct plaster mould for each.

The above is the mode of casting usually practised in England; but various modifications of the processes have been brought into use in Edinburgh and elsewhere.

Stereotype plates need careful examination and *picking*, to remove the imperfections in the casting. Small hollows, such as the loops of an a, an e, or an o, are liable to be filled up with metal, owing to blebs of air in the mould, and the fine white lines in wood-engravings are sometimes filled up. Such matters should be corrected by the picker, who should also cut down, with suitable tools, such blank spaces as might be liable to soil in printing. Before printing also, defective letters or words which cannot be corrected by the picker should be cut away, and types inserted in their place. These types are soldered into holes drilled through the plate; their stems being sawn off flush with the back.

Although the plates are cast of as equal a thickness as possible, they require, before printing from, to be accurately flattened at the back by means of a peculiar kind of lathe, in which a steel cutter, or *knife*, mounted in a slide-rest, shaves off the metal from the back of the plate in concentric circles, until it is made perfectly even. They are then mounted upon blocks of wood or metal, to raise them to the same height as common types. The tendency of wood to warp when exposed to changes of temperature, or to occasional wetting, has led to many projects for mounting stereotype plates upon blocks of cement or upon metallic mounts which might be applicable to plates of various sizes. When wooden blocks are used, the plates are usually secured to them by clips at the edges, and sometimes by screws.

The process of stereotyping is one of the most important means by which the production of cheap books has been facilitated of late years. For a work of limited and temporary demand it is unnecessary; but where the demand is very great, and likely to last for several years, it is all-important, since it enables the publisher not only to provide for the regular sales, but also to meet, on short notice, extraordinary demands for the work caused by peculiar circumstances, without the expense of having a very large edition printed at once. In most cases where the demand is uncertain, and in almost all where the demand is sure to be large, it is desirable to resort to stereotyping, because, although it increases the first cost of production, it enables the publisher to avoid, on the one hand, the risk of printing a great number of copies which may prove unsaleable, and, on the other, the outlay necessary for the recomposition of the types, in case the demand should exceed the number of copies first printed.

STILL. [DISTILLATION.]

STIRLINGSHIRE. That part of this county which skirts the Lennox Hills to the south and east, belongs to the coal district of Central Scotland, and yields coal, ironstone, freestone, and limestone, in considerable quantity. The Great Canal, which connects the Forth and the Clyde, has part of its course in this county; by this canal the manufactures of Glasgow are conveyed to the eastern parts of the island, and goods of various kinds conveyed back. The Edinburgh and Glasgow Union Canal, the Edinburgh and Glasgow Railway, and the Scottish Central Railway cross the county, giving access to it from all sides.

In the highland district there are above 4000 acres of natural woods or plantations, the latter being chiefly of oak and larch. The eastern part of the county is the most fertile, and, in an agricultural point of view, the most important. It comprehends the carse or valley of the Forth below Stirling, the soil of which consists principally of a bluish clay mixed with sand. There is here comparatively little waste land; the soil is almost wholly occupied in tillage or in plantations; and the greater facility for obtaining manure which the navigation of the Forth affords has tended to the improvement of agriculture.

Stirlingshire contains several manufacturing towns. *Alva* has manufactures of tartans and blankets. Near *Balfron* is a large cotton-manufactory. *Carronshore* is near the Carron Iron Works, which are among the largest in Europe. There are 4 or 5 blast or smelting furnaces, 4 or 5 cupola furnaces, and about 20 air furnaces; besides mills for grinding fire-clay, boring cylinders, grinding and polishing the metal, &c. The goods manufactured are machinery, agricultural instruments, and warlike implements, as cannon, carronades (which take their name from this place), mortars, shot, and shells. There is abundance of coal in the neighbourhood, but the ironstone and limestone are chiefly brought from a distance. Vessels of 150 tons burthen come up to the village. About 2000 persons are employed at the iron works. *Falkirk* is chiefly indebted for its prosperity to an extensive inland trade, and to the iron works, canals, and collieries, in the neighbourhood. At *Grangemouth* the Grand Canal terminates, in a basin and harbour, and two extensive wood ponds. The basin and harbour admit large vessels, and smaller vessels can proceed by the canal, the traffic on which is considerable. Great efforts have been made of late years to improve the port by the construction of a vast sea-loch, the formation of a wet dock, and the deepening of the river Carron. At *Kilsyth* the manufactures consist almost entirely of handloom weaving to supply orders from Glasgow. *St. Ninians* has manufactures of tartans, shawls, leather, and nails. The county town, *Stirling*, has manufactures of tartan and tartan shawls, yarns, cotton goods, malt, leather, soap, and candles. There are dye-houses for yarns, home-made cloths, and silks, rope yards and breweries. Considerable trade is carried on in corn, wood, coals, bricks, tiles, lime, and wool. About 100 vessels are engaged in the trade up the Forth to Stirling; and there is constant communication by steam with Newhaven, near Edinburgh, and the intermediate places on the Forth.

STOCKHOLM, the capital of Sweden, is the most industrious and commercial town of that country. There are manufactures of cloth, cotton, calico, silk, ribands, sugar, tobacco, leather, cast iron, and soap. Nearly the whole of the superfluous produce of the countries north and west of Stockholm is brought here to be exported to foreign countries; it is mostly shipped in Swedish vessels. The value of the iron exported is as great or greater than the total amount of the other exports, of which the chief are timber, tar, pitch, copper, cobalt, ready built vessels, linseed oil and oil cakes, tobacco, steel, bricks, and a few manufactured articles. The most active commerce is carried on with England, the United States of North America, Denmark, France, Prussia, Portugal, the Netherlands, and Italy. The most important articles of import are sugar, coffee, wine and brandy, rum, woollen and cotton manufactured goods, silk, linens, china and crockery, hemp, cotton, cheese, potash, hides and skins, tallow and candles, train oil, dyeing woods, raisins, almonds, pepper, cinnamon and cassia, tea, butter, and wool.

STOCKINGS. [HOSIERY MANUFACTURE.]

STOCKPORT is one of the principal seats of the cotton manufacture. Orrell's cotton mill, in this town, is one of the finest and largest in the kingdom. The building is nearly 300 feet long, and has about 600 windows. There are six ranges or stories, the lowest of which is 230 feet from front to back. There are four steam engines for working the machines, which consume twenty tons of coal per day. Besides the spinning machinery there are 1,300 power looms.

To the cotton manufacture, which is the staple trade of the town, may be added the manufacture of silk goods, thread, hats, brushes, spindles, and shuttles. There are several iron and brass foundries in the town, and bricks are extensively made in the neighbourhood.

STONE FOR BUILDING. Stone fit for building must in general be freestone firm enough to sustain great pressure, and yet so aggregated as to admit of being worked with facility by ordinary tools, and of receiving correct surfaces in any direction. It must in general yield masses of great dimensions. In the great variety of limestones and sandstones which are adapted for building purposes, we remark, by the aid of the microscope, three principal modes of molecular aggregation: mixtures of grains; segregated concretions of grains; and compacted crystallisations. Mixtures of very unequal or very dissimilar parts, as millstone-grit; concretions which have earthy textures in their interstices, as some oolitic limestones; crystallisations which do not produce compactness, as in some magnesian limestones,—are not in general durable.

The commissioners (Mr. Barry, Sir H. de la Beche, and Dr. W. Smith) who reported on the choice of stone for the construction of the New Houses of Parliament, made valuable experiments as to the hardness, closeness, density, colour, and durability of many varieties of stone. The strength of several sorts of stone, as measured by the weight necessary to be applied for breaking and crushing them, appears below:

	Resistance to fracture.	Resistance to crushing.	Name of Stone.
Sandstones	60	111	Craigleith.
	88	106	Darley Dale.
	56	107	Park Spring.
	48	70	Kenton.
	38	71	Binnie.
Oolites	50	127	Ketton Rag.
	30	55	Portland.
	22	57	Hamhill.
	24	33	Ancaster.
	16	25	Barnack.
	18	21	Box.
Limestones	70	117	Bolsover.
	36	74	Mansfield.
	34	61	Huddlestone.
	24	55	Roche.
	20	23	Cadeby.

Of sixteen specimens selected, the stone most absorbent of water was proved to be the Bath oolite from Box; that most injured by Brard's artificial process of disintegration was the Barnack stone: and that which was most easily crushed was the Bath oolite from Box. Generally speaking, sandstones were least absorbent, magnesian limestones least disintegrating; sandstones appeared to be strongest, though choice magnesian limestones (as that of Bolsover, finally recommended by the Commissioners) were fully equal in this respect, and were almost as little absorbent.

Stones of uniform texture commonly decay by disintegration at the surface, losing grain by grain in proportion to time and exposure. Stones composed of parts unequally mixed suffer unequal waste in different parts. Shells, corals, concretions, and crystallised masses, thus appear prominent from earthy limestones, and indicate the general fact that, in proportion to the force of molecular aggregation in the stone, is the resistance which it offers to decay. It is not the amount but the kind of exposure which governs the decay of stone: the southern and western parts of our cathedrals give way more than the northern and eastern.

STONE WORKING. There are three aspects under which the working in stone presents itself to our notice—quarrying, shaping and preparing the stones, and masonry properly so called.

All statuary marble and all building stone are extracted from the rocks by quarrying. Egypt, Greece, and Italy possessed the quarries from which the great works of the ancients in sculpture and architecture were produced; and nearly every country possesses quarries more or less extensive. The British isles abound with stone of nearly every different kind that can be employed with advantage in architecture and engineering. The *granites* of Aberdeenshire, of Devon and Cornwall, and of Ireland; the *sandstones* of Yorkshire, Lancashire, Derbyshire, and other counties; the *millstone grit* of Yorkshire; the *slate-stones* of Wales, Cumberland, Cornwall, and Ireland; the *limestones* of Portland, Purbeck, Bath, and other counties; the *claystones* of Gloucestershire and Yorkshire; the *ragstone* of Kent—all are plentiful.

In quarrying stone the works are chiefly horizontal or vertical, according as the stone is far below or near the surface. Stone of inferior kind has generally to be removed before the good stone can be reached. The huge masses are often loosened by blasting with gunpowder; but as this shatters the blocks, a slower but less wasteful plan is usually adopted. Most stones present natural layers or places of *cleavage*, which enable it to separato into parallel strata; and the quarrymen employ their picks and jumper-chisels in such a way as to take advantage of this cleavage. After the blocks have been severed from the mass, they are reduced as nearly as possible to a rectangular form; this is done by means of a tool called a *kevel*, pointed at one end and flat at the other, with which the irregular parts are knocked off. The blocks are then usually raised upon low carriages, and drawn on iron railways to the quays or wharfs where the stone is put on shipboard.

The working of stone is similar in principle to that of marble, but does not necessitate so much care. In the common mode of sawing a stone, a man works to and fro a framed saw or cutter, which gradually cuts its way through the stone; the instrument is not really a saw, for it has no teeth; but by the use of sand and water an abrading action is produced which wears a cut in tho stone. In the large marble and stone works, of which a fine example has been established at Pimlico, several stone-saws are framed together in parallel array, and worked by a steam-engine; a block of marble or stone is thus quickly cut up into slabs. Slabs are cut up into smaller pieces by hand-saws, or more expeditiously by circular saws fixed upon a revolving axis—the saws, as in the former case, being in fact blunt knives. By bending these blunt knives into a circular or cylindrical form, and fixing them at the bottom of a vertical revolving shaft, circular pieces of stono are cut. Pillars and hollow cylinders or pipes of stono are shaped by similar means. If, instead of a saw, the horizontal axis be furnished with iron wheels shaped with mouldings on their edges, the forms of architectural mouldings may bo wrought on long slabs of stone.

The smoothing and polishing of stone and marble are effected by the friction either of a smooth iron surface, or of another piece of stone, plentifully wetted during the process.

Masonry is a most important branch of art, as connected both with architecture and with common building, but especially the former. Owing to its expense, masonry is comparatively rarely employed in England, except for public or other buildings of the highest class: the mason's work being in other cases restricted to such parts as door-steps, string courses, facias, plain cornices, pavements, and stairs. Walls which are not of solid masonry throughout, but are built either of brick or inferior stone and rubble, with only an external facing of squared stone laid in courses, are termed *ashler* or *ashlering*.

STONES, METEORIC. If the materials of which these remarkable precipitated bodies consist had become applicable to any useful end, or if their fall illustrated any practical subject, we would touch upon the phenomena here; but they still remain exclusively within the domain of science. The aerolites are chiefly composed of iron, nickel, silica, magnesia, and sulphur, with smaller portions of alumina, lime, manganese, chrome, cobalt, carbon, and soda. It is remarkable that no new substance, nothing with which we were not already acquainted, has evor been discovered in their composition.

STOP. [ORGAN.]

STOP-COCK. [COCK.]

STOVES. Several kinds of fire-places or stoves give out heat by *conduction* chiefly, others do so mainly by *radiation*. Open fire-places are of the latter kind, and a considerable loss of heating-power results from the arrangement. The burning coals radiate heat into the room, and another portion of heat is reflected from the metallic portions of the grate; but the heated air, which ought to contribute to the desired effect, is mainly allowed to escape up the chimney with the smoke and other results of combustion. Dr. Arnott, in his "Treatise on Warming and Ventilation," enumerates about a dozen evils which are more or less inseparable from open fires. Among these are waste of fuel, unequal heating, a stratum of cold air near the floor, tho production of smoke and dust, loss of time in attendance, danger to person and property. Many contrivances have been brought forward to obviate one or other of these inconveniences. Count Rumford suggested the "register-stove," the peculiarity of which consists in narrowing the throat of the chimney by a plate which can be moved to vary the size of the aperture; by this means, particularly if the opening be near the fire, the very hot air directly from the fire enters before it can mix with much colder air from the room, and thus the draught is increased so as to lessen the chance of smoking. But there is a great waste of heat in this as in all other open fire-places.

The common *Dutch stove* is one of the simplest examples of a close stove. It generally consists of a cylindrical case of sheet-iron, within and near the bottom of which is a grating for containing the fuel. There is an ash-pit beneath the grating, and three openings to the interior—one to the ash-pit, one for introducing the fuel above, and one leading to a flue or chimney. In this form of stove the heated iron case warms the air, which thus becomes much more nearly equalised in temperature than it is by a common fire. There is also great economy of fuel, and an absence of smoke and dust; but the air of the room acquires a dry, sulphureous, and unhealthy condition. In *Russian stoves*, earthenware and brickwork are largely used, instead of metal, as a means of making the heat less intense near the stove, and of keeping up a reservoir of heat after the fire is extinguished. The stove is built in a massive style, and consists of a series of chambers, of which the lowest serves as the fire-place, and the upper ones as flues, and being composed almost entirely of brick and porcelain, the outer surface remains at a moderate temperature for a very long period.

Dr. Arnott has the merit of having devised means to prevent the too intense heating of the air near close metallic stoves, by the use of the stove which bears his name. [ARNOTT'S STOVE.] Numerous varieties of the close stove, bearing more or less on the above construction, have been brought forward since the publication of Dr. Arnott's book. Each professes to possess some peculiar merit; but all present these features in common—that the air-hole by which the combustion is fed is very small, and capable of adjustment; that there is a body of air to be warmed, external to the grate or fire-box itself, but confined within an outer case; that the consumption of fuel is much smaller than in any variety of open fire-places; and that the flue for carrying off the smoke and gases is small in diameter, and capable of being carried in any direction. In the different forms of "kitchen-ranges" the open fire-place is combined with what may be deemed a close stove; for the "oven" and "hot-closet" are representatives of the heated space within the outer case of a close stove. The "gas-stoves" and "steam-kitchens" of modern inventors may in like manner be included in the same category, for they are in effect close stoves heated by agents different from common coal.

In the arrangements above described, the stove is in the room which is to be warmed, and its heating effects are calculated with respect to that room alone; but in many factories and other large establishments the fire is in an outer or lower apartment, and the heated air is conveyed thence in a pipe to the apartment to be heated.

In Cundy's patent stove, recently introduced, the air is warmed by passing through channels made of artificial stone; it is intended for use in churches, schools, and other large rooms, and is charged for according to the number of cubic feet of air which it will warm in a given time.

One of the greatest improvements in stoves of recent manufacture is the adoption of such a form in the iron or steel work immediately contiguous to the fire as to reflect out into the room as much as possible of the heat, instead of allowing it to waste by ascending the chimney. In one of these forms, Jobson's patent stove-grate, the reflecting surface entirely surrounds the fire, not only above and at the sides, but also beneath; the ash-pit being so ingeniously arranged as not to interfere with the lower part of the reflector.

Other details relating to heating by stoves, by gas, and by other means, will be found under COOKING APPARATUS, and WARMING and VENTILATION.

STRASBOURG. This large and important city derives so much fame from its exquisite Cathedral, that its industrial features are almost eclipsed thereby. Yet it is a busy place. The trade of the town is very considerable: its manufactures include jewellery, metal buttons, starch, alum, soap, watches and clocks, chemical products, steel, cutlery, pins, combs, cast-iron goods, earthenware, porcelain, enamel, oil from seeds, morocco and other leather, hats, woollen and cotton stuffs, cotton yarn, hosiery, printed flannels, sail-cloth, oil-cloth, thread, carpeting, furs, paper-hangings, playing-cards, &c. There are bleach-grounds, dye-houses, rope-walks, tan-yards, breweries; chicory, mustard, and madder-mills; printing-offices, plaster-kilns, tile-yards, an iron-forge, a type-foundry, sugar-refineries, a snuff-manufactory, &c. There is a considerable trade carried on with Holland, Germany, Switzerland, and Italy; and much business is done in the produce of the surrounding territory, which includes corn, wine, tobacco, madder, hemp, hops, saffron, &c.

STRAW-PLAT MANUFACTURE. It is not known when the manufacture of hats or bonnets of platted straw first became important in Italy, where it has long formed one of the leading pursuits of the agricultural population; but it does not appear to have been followed in England more than seventy or eighty years.

The large size of the wheat-straw used in this country for platting prevented the home manufacture from entering into competition with that of Italy in articles of fine quality; the straw grown for the purpose in Tuscany being much smaller, as well as superior in colour. This difficulty was in some degree overcome by the expedient adopted in England towards the end of the last century, of splitting the straw, and using the narrow *Splints*, or slips of straw, in lieu of whole straws. The operation of splitting is performed by small cutting instruments called *machines*, which have a number of sharp edges so fixed as to divide the straw, by a motion in the direction of its length, into four, five, six, or more equal parts. Before machines were invented, straws were occasionally split with knives by hand. But greatly as the British straw-plat manufacture had been encouraged by the use of split straw, by improvements in bleaching, and by increased care in the selection of straws of uniform size and colour, it was found, when the re-establishment of peace allowed the free importation of Italian straw bonnets, that the home manufacture was unable to compete with the foreign, notwithstanding the heavy protecting duty levied upon hats or bonnets of straw imported from other countries. The Society of Arts therefore, for a long series of years, offered encouragement to attempts for the improvement of the British straw manufacture, which called forth many interesting communications, and led to great improvement.

In plat made of split straw, unless two splints are laid together, with their inside surfaces towards each other, as in the plat called Patent Dunstable, it necessarily happens that the face of the plat exhibits alternately the outer and inner surfaces of the straw, which differ from each other in colour and gloss. Articles made of split straw are also inferior to those of whole straw of equal fineness, in pliability and durability. Another circumstance which greatly increases the beauty of Leghorn plat is the mode of joining it, so as to form, by the combination of several narrow strips, an extended sheet of platted work. British plat is usually joined by making the several rows of plat overlap each other a little, and then stitching through the overlapping with a needle and thread. The surface of a hat or bonnet formed in this manner consists of a series of ridges; and part of each row of plat is concealed by that next above it, so that an unnecessarily large quantity of plat is required to form a given extent of surface. Leghorn plat is formed in such a manner that it may be joined without this loss; the edge of one row of plat being, as it were, knitted into the edge of the other, in such a way that the patterns may appear uninterrupted, and the line of junction may be almost invisible.

The Society of Arts has encouraged the growing of straw similar to that of Leghorn, the platting of the Leghorn straw in England, and every other device which might seem likely to increase the home manufacture. Mr. Parry in 1822 received the Society's large silver medal for his method of manufacturing Leghorn plat from straw imported from Italy. In this method the ears are cut off with a knife, and the straws are then carefully sorted to obtain uniformity in length, thickness, and colour. Thirteen straws are tied together at one end, and then divided into two portions; six straws being towards the left side, and seven to the right, so that the two portions of straw may form a right angle. These are platted over and under each other, so as to form a platted band, about three-eighths of an inch in width. Several of these bands are adjusted in spiral coils, with their adjacent edges knitted together, so as to form the large circular pieces of plat which, under the name of hats, or *flats*, are so extensively exported from the north of Italy.

The straw used in Tuscany is that of *Triticum turgidum*, a variety of bearded wheat, which seems to differ in no respect from the spring wheat grown in the vale of Evesham and in other parts of England. It is grown in Tuscany solely for the straw, and not for the grain; and the upper joint of the straw is that chiefly used for platting. The straw is pulled while the ear is in a soft milky state; the corn having been sown very close, and consequently produced in a thin, short, and dwindling condition. It is then dried by spreading it thinly upon the ground in fine hot weather, and afterwards tied up in bundles and stacked, for the purpose of enabling the heat of the mow to drive off any remaining moisture. After remaining in the mow for about a month, it is spread out in a meadow, and exposed to the action of dew, sun, and air, in order to bleach it. The straw is frequently turned during this operation; and after it is completed, the lower joint of the straw is pulled off, leaving the upper joint, with the ear attached to it, for use. This part is then subjected to the action of steam, and to fumigation with sulphur, in order to complete the bleaching, after which it is ready for use. It is tied up in bundles, and imported to England in this state.

Bleaching the straw with sulphur fumes is commonly practised in this country, and Dr. Ure states that a solution of chloride of lime may be used for the purpose. Straw may be dyed, for ornamental purposes, of many different colours.

The splints, or pieces of split straw, being curved in a way which would impede the operation of platting, require to be flattened between rollers. These, as well as the whole straws used in other kinds of plat, are moistened with water to render them easy to work. It need hardly be observed that cleanliness is indispensable to the beauty of the plat.

In the kind of straw-platting above described, the plat is formed into a narrow strip or riband, which must be formed into a spiral coil, or united edge to edge, to form a hat or bonnet; but in 1834 Mr. T. B. Smith, of St. Alban's, devised a mode of applying Brazilian plat to the manufacture of hats and bonnets of split straw. This kind of plat is not formed in strips, but is at once platted or woven into the required form and size. One advantage claimed for the method is that either the glossy or the dull surface of the split straw may be placed entirely on one side of the plat.

The British straw plat district comprises Bedfordshire, Hertfordshire, and Buckinghamshire; these counties being the most favourable for the production of the wheat-straw commonly used for English plat. The manufacture is also followed in a few places in Essex and Suffolk; but very little in other counties. The principal markets are Luton, Dunstable, and St. Albans.

In 1847, 1,376 lbs. weight of chip hats were imported, and 7,117 lbs. of straw hats; together with 35,530 lbs. of chip-plat, and 13,420 lbs. of straw-plat, for making hats and bonnets; and 892 cwts. of straw-platting.

STRING-COURSE, is a projecting course of masonry forming a string or horizontal line on the face of a wall, and consisting of a series of mouldings, as in Gothic, or a flat surface (either plain or enriched), as in Italian architecture. The string-course itself consists sometimes of only a few narrow and plain mouldings, at others of a variety of them separated by one or more considerable hollows. In Italian architecture, the string-course is either quite plain, or more or less decorated according to the character of the floor to which it belongs.

STRO'NTIUM. This peculiar metal was formerly supposed to be identical with Barytes, but Dr. Hope in 1792 proved them to be distinct bodies. It has not a very high lustre, is fusible with difficulty, and is not volatile. When exposed to the air it attracts oxygen, and becomes converted into *Strontia.* When thrown into water, it decomposes it with great violence, producing hydrogen gas, and forming with the water a solution of strontia.

The salts of strontia are occasionally used in chemical investigations, and in giving a purple flame to fire-works.

STUCCO, is a plaster of any kind used as a coating for walls, and to give them a finished surface. *Stuccatura*, or stucco-work, is the term employed for all interior ornamental plaster work in imitation of carved stone, such as the cornices and mouldings of rooms, and the enrichments of ceilings. Stucco was very much employed by the ancients, and not merely for coating columns, &c., constructed of brick, but in many instances for covering stone, or even marble: for which last purpose it was applied so sparingly as to be no more than a very thin incrustation, for the purpose, it is now supposed, of being painted upon.

The stucco used for internal decorative purposes, such as those above mentioned, is a composition of very fine sand, pulverised marble, and gypsum, mixed with water till it is of a proper consistency. Within a short time after being first applied, it begins to set, or gradually harden, in which state it is moulded, and may at length be finished up with metal tools.

The stucco employed for external work is of a coarser kind, and variously prepared, being now manufactured wholesale as an article of commerce, ready for use; and of which the different sorts are generally distinguished by the name of *cements*. *Adam's* or *Liardet's Cement* is an oil-cement, of which the chief ingredients are fine whiting and calcined oyster-shells, well mixed and ground up in a mill with oil. *Parker's* or *Roman Cement*, that now most in use, consists chiefly of a preparation of argillaceous limestone found on the coast of Essex and Kent, and in the Isle of Sheppey. Of *Bailey's Cement* lime and sharp sand are the principal ingredients. *Mastic Cement*, or *Hamelin's Cement*, is composed of peroxide of lead and oil: *Keene's Cement* is one of recent invention, and of very superior quality, taking a surface and polish almost equal to that of the finest marble; it is in fact a species of scagliola; consequently it is employed, like that, only for interior decoration. Almost every year produces some new kind of stucco.

If perfectly well executed, stucco will be nearly equal in appearance to stone, and even superior to that of stone of inferior quality. There are some who protest against the use of stucco externally, as a spurious and meretricious mode of building with sham material; but it is certain that most of Palladio's edifices, and of what are spoken of as the 'marble palaces' of Venice and Rome, are merely faced with stucco.

STUTTGART, the capital of the kingdom of Würtemberg, has manufactures of linen and woollen cloths, silk, cotton, gloves, carpets, shawls, &c., and is noted for its beautiful works in gold, silver, and bronze; mathematical, philosophical, optical, and musical instruments; cabinet furniture, lackered ware, and carriages. The bark trade is extremely flourishing. The navigation of the Neckar gives Stuttgart water-communication with the Rhine. Lines of railway, partially in operation and rapidly approaching completion, connect it with the Bavarian and Rhine railroads.

STYRIA. The great wealth of this province of Austria consists in its mines, which are confined to the mountainous portion of the country. The most important minerals are—silver, copper, lead, iron (540,000 cwt. a year), alum, cobalt, sulphur, salt, marble, and coal. The most important manufacture is iron. The iron-mines in the Erzberg, in the north of Styria, were well known to the Romans; this mountain does not contain the ore in veins or strata, but presents a solid mass of iron-ore, which has been worked without interruption for eleven centuries. There are a few manufactories of linen, cotton, woollens, and silk, but none of considerable importance. There is a very brisk trade between Upper and Lower Styria: the latter supplies the former with corn, wine, and tobacco, and receives in return iron, timber, and salt. The exports consist of the metals above-named, and of scythes, sickles, steel and iron wares, including razors, and several millions of Jews'-harps. The imports consist of fine cloths, linens, cottons, silks, and jewellery, and colonial produce. The transit trade between Italy and Germany, from Vienna to Trieste, is very important. This trade is greatly facilitated by good common roads, and by the Vienna-Trieste railway now open from Vienna to Laybach.

SUBMARINE DESCENT. A few details on this subject will be found under DIVING BELL.

SU'CCINUM is a bituminous substance of a peculiar kind, procured from amber. It is not now used in the crude state in medicine, but is employed to yield the *Oleum Succini*, or *Oil of Amber*. Volatile oil of amber probably contains a large portion of creasote. One part of rectified oil of amber, and three parts of moderately strong nitric acid, form *Artificial Musk*.

SUET. There are several kinds of suet, according to the species of animal from which it is procured, such as that of the hart, the goat, the ox, and the sheep. When recent, it is white, easily broken, translucent if thin, and almost without smell; it soon becomes yellow and rancid by exposure to the air. The preponderance of stearin renders suet the most solid of animal fats. It liquifies with a gentle heat, and the prepared suet of the Pharmacopœia is obtained by melting it over a slow fire, and straining it to separate the membraneous portion. It is used as an ingredient in cerates, plasters, and ointments. By pouring it when melted over various articles, such as potted char, from which it thoroughly excludes the air, it assists greatly in preserving them.

SUFFOLK produces scarcely any minerals of value. Chalk and Shell-Marl from the crag formation are dug from manures. This county forms one of the best cultivated districts in the southern part of Great Britain. The greater part of the land is under the plough; there being now scarcely such a thing to be seen as a common field. There is no part of England where the implements of husbandry are more perfect than in Suffolk, or where new implements are tried with more readiness and with less prejudice; nowhere is so great a variety of farm-machines used for saving labour.

Suffolk is far from being a manufacturing county; yet it has a few busy and flourishing towns. At *Bungay* a considerable trade is carried on in grain and other articles of provision by means of the Waveney, which is navigable up to Bungay for small barges. At *Ipswich* the manufactures of the town consist chiefly in the spinning of woollen yarn, ship-building, sail-making, &c. Its commerce arises from the exportation of corn, malt, and other produce of the surrounding country. There is, however, one notable establishment, that of Messrs. Ransomes and May, where machinery and agricultural implements are manufactured on a large scale. *Lowestoft* has lately risen into importance on account of the excellent harbour formed there, in connection with the Norfolk railway. Mail steamers have just commenced (April 1851) to run from

Lowestoft to Denmark, under circumstances which promise to be very beneficial to the town. From *Stowmarket* a considerable quantity of corn and malt are sent in river-craft down to Ipswich to be shipped there: timber and deals, coals and slate, are brought up from Ipswich for the supply of the neighbourhood.

SUGAR. Although this valuable commodity is obtainable from various sources, the *sugar cane* is that which yields by far the largest supply. This cane grows in the warm districts both of the old and the new world.

Culture.—The stems vary in height from eight feet up even to twenty feet, and are divided by prominent annular joints into short lengths. The outer part of the cane is hard and brittle; but the inner consists of a soft pith, which contains the sweet juice, and this juice is elaborated separately in each joint. The canes are usually propagated by slips or cuttings, which are planted either in holes dug by hand, or in trenches formed by a plough, about eight to twelve inches deep. The planting usually takes place from August to November, and the cutting in March or April. The maturity of the cane is indicated by the skin becoming dry, smooth and brittle; by the cane becoming heavy; the pith gray, approaching to brown; and the juice sweet and glutinous. The canes which grow immediately from the planted slips are called *plant-canes;* but it is usual, in the West Indies, to raise several crops in successive years from the same roots; the canes which sprout up from the old roots, or *stoles*, being called *rattoons*. The rattoons are not so vigorous as the original plant-canes; but they afford better sugar, and that with less trouble in clarifying and concentrating the juice. The canes are cut as near the ground as possible, because the richest juice is found in the lower joints; and, after cutting them, it is considered well to cut the stumps down a few inches below the surface of the ground, and to cover them up with mould. One or two of the top joints of the cane are cut off, and the remainder is divided into pieces about a yard long, tied up in bundles, and carried immediately to the sugar-mill. The upper branches of the cane are used as food for cattle; and the remainder of the waste forms a valuable manure, for which purpose the *trash*, or waste from the mill, is admirably suited, though much of it is usually consumed as fuel.

Manufacture.—The manufacture of sugar is that train of operations by which the juice is extracted from the canes, and brought to a granulated state. In the West India sugar-mills employed for crushing the canes, a negro applies the canes in a regular layer or sheet to the interval between two rollers, which seize and compress them violently as they pass between them. The ends of the canes are then turned, either by another negro on the opposite side to the feeder, or by a framework of wood called a *dumb returner*, so that they may pass back again between two other rollers placed closer together. Channels are made to receive the liquor expressed from the canes, and to conduct it to the vessels in which it is to undergo the succeeding operations. Improved sugar mills have been lately brought into use.

Cane-juice as expressed by the mill, is an opaque slightly viscid fluid, of a dull gray, olive, or olive-green colour, and of a sweet balmy taste. The juice is so exceedingly fermentable that in the climate of the West Indies it would often run into the acetous fermentation in twenty minutes after leaving the mill, if the process of clarifying were not immediately commenced.

The processes followed in the West Indies for separating the sugar from the juice are as follows. The juice is conducted by channels from the mill to large flat bottomed *clarifiers*, which contain from three hundred to a thousand gallons each. When the clarifier is filled with juice, a little slaked lime is added to it; and when the liquor in the clarifier becomes hot by a fire underneath, the solid portions of the cane-juice coagulate, and are thrown up in the form of scum. The clarified juice, which is bright, clear, and of a yellow wine-colour, is transferred to the largest of a series of evaporating coppers, or pans, three or more in number, in which it is reduced in bulk by boiling; it is transferred from one pan to another, and heated until the sugar is brought to the state of a soft mass of crystals, imbedded in molasses, a thick, viscid, and uncrystallisable fluid. The soft concrete sugar is removed from the coolers into a range of casks, in which the molasses gradually drains from the crystalline portion, percolating through spongy plantain-stalks placed in a hole at the bottom of each cask, which act as so many drains to convey the liquid to a large cistern beneath. With sugar of average quality three or four weeks is sufficient for this purpose. The liquid portion constitutes *molasses*, which is employed to make rum. The crystallised portion is packed in hogsheads for shipment as *Raw*, *Brown*, or *Muscovado Sugar;* and in this state it is commonly exported from our West Indian colonies. The sugar loses usually about 12 per cent. in weight by the drainage of the remaining molasses from it while on ship-board.

Refining.—The refining of sugar is mainly

a bleaching process, conducted on a large scale in England. There are two varieties produced by this bleaching, viz. *clayed* and *loaf* sugar. For clayed sugar, the sugar is removed from the coolers into conical earthen moulds called *formes*, each of which has a small hole at the apex. These holes being stopped up the formes are placed, apex downwards, in other earthen vessels. The syrup, after being stirred round, is left for from fifteen to twenty hours to crystallise. The plugs are then withdrawn, to let out the uncrystallised syrup; and, the base of the crystallised loaf being removed, the forme is filled up with pulverised white sugar. This is well pressed down, and then a quantity of clay, mixed with water is placed upon the sugar, the formes being put into fresh empty pots. The moisture from the clay, filtering through the sugar, carries with it a portion of the colouring matter, which is more soluble than the crystals themselves. By a repetition of this process the sugar attains nearly a white colour, and is then dried and crushed for sale.

But *loaf sugar* is the kind most usually produced by the refining processes. The brown sugar is dissolved with hot water, and then filtered through canvas bags, from which it exudes as a clear, transparent though reddish syrup. The removal of this red tinge is effected by filtering the syrup through a mass of powdered charcoal; and we have then a perfectly transparent and colourless liquid. In the evaporation or concentration of the clarified syrup, which forms the next part of the refining process, the boiling is effected (under the admirable system introduced by Mr. Howard) in a vacuum, at a temperature of about 140° Fahr. The sugar-pan is a large copper vessel, with arrangements for extracting the air, admitting the syrup, admitting steam pipes, and draining off the sugar when concentrated. In using the pan, a quantity of syrup is admitted; and an air-pump is set to work, to extract all the air from the pan, in order that the contents may boil at a low temperature. The evaporation proceeds; and, when completed, the evaporated syrup flows out of the pan through a pipe into an open vessel beneath, called the *granulating vessel*, around which steam circulates, and within which tho syrup is brought to a partially crystallised state. From the granulators the syrup or sugar is transferred into moulds of a conical form, which were formerly made of coarse pottery, but are now usually of iron; in these moulds the sugar crystallises and whitens, the remaining uncrystallised syrup flowing out at an opening at the bottom of the moulds. This syrup is re-boiled with raw sugar, so as to yield an inferior quality of sugar; and when all the crystallisable matter has been extracted from it, the remainder is sold as *treacle*. The loaves of sugar, after a few finishing processes, are ready for sale.

The improvements introduced into the processes of sugar-refining allow loaf sugar to be now sold at a price so little exceeding that of raw sugar, that the manufacture has lately vastly increased.

Sugar-Candy is a kind of crystallised sugar made in China and India. The crystals are formed around small strings or twigs, from which they are afterwards broken off. When heated to 365° Fahr. sugar melts into a viscid colourless liquid which when cooled suddenly, becomes *barley-sugar*.

Beet Root Sugar is briefly described under BEET. The manufacture is not in a flourishing state, as it cannot well compete commercially with that from the sugar-cane. There is a project at present on foot for establishing the beet-sugar manufacture in Ireland. It is proposed to establish a Company with a capital of half a million sterling; and to buy Irish beet root with a view of extracting sugar from it by processes which have recently been patented, and the patents for which are to be held by the Company. The projectors start upon the basis that the climate, soil, and labour-supply of Ireland are highly favourable to the culture; and that the patent processes are calculated to perform the extraction of sugar well and cheaply. It remains to be shewn how far these anticipations are capable of being borne out; if commercially advantageous at all, Ireland must unquestionably be benefited by it. The Company's calculations give 400 tons of sugar and 100 tons of molasses for 6000 tons of beet-root; and shadow forth a flattering rate of prospective dividend. So do the calculations of the Irish Peat Company; and we can only at present express a *wish* that the anticipations may be realised. (April 1851.)

It has just been announced that there are now 303 Beet-Sugar Manufactories in France; and that the produce of French Beet-Sugar in 1850 was 74,628,607 kilogrammes — about 160,917,900 lb.

Sugar Trade. — Before the discovery of America, sugar was a costly luxury used only on rare occasions. About 1459 Margaret Paston, writing to her husband, who was a gentleman and land-owner in Norfolk, begs that he will 'vouchsafe' to buy her a pound of sugar. The consumption has gradually but steadily increased throughout the world.

The sugar trade of 1849 and 1850 exhibited the following results. The importation of sugar amounted to the quantities here stated:

	1849		1850
From West Indies	2,839,912	cwts.	2,584,162
From Mauritius	897,814	,,	1,003,312
From East Indies	1,474,474	,,	1,346,081
Foreign	1,725,149	,,	1,352,476
Refined	304,392	,,	355,387
Molasses	1,311,435	,,	1,249,796
	8,553,176	cwts.	7,891,214

The total quantities of all kinds of sugar and molasses re-exported in the same two years, together with the exports of sugar refined in England, were

	1849		1850
Re-exports	761,286	cwts.	466,219
British refined......	223,273	,,	209,235
	984,559	cwts.	675,454

The gross amount of duty received on the imported sugar was 4,139,999*l.* in 1849, and 4,130,819*l.* in 1850.

The duties on the importation of sugar into this country have varied very considerably. Between the years 1661 and 1815 the duty was gradually raised from 1*s.* 6*d.* to 30*s.* per cwt. on British plantation sugar. From 1815 to 1844 it varied from 24*s.* to 30*s.* East India sugar paid a higher duty than West India until 1836, when the two were assimilated. Foreign sugar paid a duty of 60*s.* to 63*s.* per cwt. until the recent legislative changes. In 1844 a change was made, whereby sugar from certain foreign countries, under certain defined circumstances, might be admitted at 34*s.* instead of 63*s.* duty. In 1845 another act fixed the duty on sugar, from either the East Indies or West Indies, at sums varying from 14*s.* to 21*s.*, according to the quality. By an act passed in 1846, there was to be a gradual reduction of duties from 1846 to 1851, at the expiration of which period the duty on foreign sugar was to be the same as that on East or West India sugar. By another act passed in 1848 this principle of gradual reduction is to extend until July, 1854, after which time sugars from all countries will be placed on the same footing. They will all pay at that time the following import duties per cwt.;

	s.	*d.*
Refined sugar	13	4
White clayed	11	8
Brown clayed	10	0
Brown raw	10	0
Molasses	3	9

SULPHUR, or *Brimstone*, is a solid elementary non-metallic body, which has been known from the remotest antiquity. It is met with pure, and in various states of combination. Sulphur, both crystallised and massive, occurs in beds and veins in Swabia, Hungary, and Switzerland. Volcanic sulphur is found in immense quantities in Italy and Sicily. The volcanic sulphur brought to this country is purified for use. What is called *refined sulphur* is purified by distillation in a large cast-iron still, and it is condensed in an iron receiver kept cool by water; when melted and cast into wooden moulds, it is called *roll* or *stick sulphur;* and when the vaporised sulphur is condensed in a large chamber, it has the form of powder, and is called *sublimed sulphur*, or *flowers of sulphur*.

Sulphur is of a bright yellow colour, resinous lustre, slight odour, and nearly opaque. It is insoluble in water, but dissolves in alcohol and in boiling oil of turpentine. It is very volatile. When sulphur is heated it begins to vaporise before it fuses: at 555° to 600° it is rapidly volatilised, and in close vessels is condensed without change. Some metals when heated in it burn vividly. The fusing-point of sulphur is 232°, and between this and 280° it possesses the highest degree of fluidity: at 320° it begins to thicken, and at 482° is so tenacious that it will not flow from an inverted vessel: from this to 600°, which is its boiling point, it again becomes liquid, but not so perfectly so as at 280°; when boiled in close vessels, an orange-coloured vapour is formed. When poured into water in a fluid state, at about the temperature of 428°, it becomes a brown pasty mass, which readily receives and retains any form given to it, and hence it is employed in taking casts.

The compounds of sulphur with othe bodies are of almost incalculable importance. With oxygen it forms *sulphurous acid gas*, which has powerful bleaching properties. With a further portion of oxygen, it forms *sulphuric acid*, so largely employed in the manufacturing arts. With hydrogen it forms *sulphuretted hydrogen gas*, the powerful constituent of Harrogate and other mineral waters. When sulphur has been brought to the state of sulphuric acid by combining with oxygen, it becomes still more valuable than in any of the above named forms; for it then constitutes the well-known *sulphates*, by combining with various oxides; we thus have the sulphates of soda, potash, ammonia, iron, copper, barytes, lime, magnesia, &c., the practical uses of which are so numerous.

Sulphur Trade.—Although sulphur exists in Iceland, Teneriffe, St. Vincent's, and some other places, the expense of obtaining it is so great, that Sicily alone has furnished the supply required. From 1833 to 1838 England took 49 per cent. of the whole quantity of sulphur exported from Sicily, and France 43 per cent., leaving only 8 per cent. for all other countries; and part of this was shipped for Malta, and eventually reached England. The Sicilian sulphur mines are the property of individuals, and from fifteen to twenty English firms settled in Sicily are engaged in the trade. In 1836 M. Taix, a Frenchman, laid before the Sicilian government a project for establishing a company which was to have the exclusive right during ten years of purchasing Sicilian sulphur at fixed prices, on condition of spending 10,000*l.* a year in constructing roads, and exporting one-third of the quantity produced in Sicilian vessels. The British merchants becoming alarmed, the Sicilian government, in reply to the British ambassador, stated that no such project would be adopted. It would have been in direct contravention to certain commercial treaties between the two governments. The Sicilian government did, however, enter into a contract with M. Taix, and on the 4th of July, 1838, notice was given at Palermo that the monopoly would come into operation on the 1st of August ensuing. The negociations respecting this monopoly were conducted with great secrecy, and it came into operation so suddenly, that twenty-four vessels lost their cargoes. The British lessees of mines, and all others, were compelled to produce only a fixed quantity of sulphur; prices rose more than twofold, contracts could not be completed, the supply became inadequate to the English demand, and other quarters were looked to for a supply. At length the British government took very decided steps to put an end to a monopoly established in the face of commercial treaties; and the trade was then restored to its former footing.

The imports of sulphur during the last three years have been as follows:—

1848	668,392 cwts.
1849	845,388 „
1850	664,630 „

SULPHURATION, or SULPHURING, is the process of bleaching employed to give whiteness to silk and woollens by exposing them to the fumes of burning sulphur. For this process a detached chamber, without a chimney, is made use of, so constructed, that, when required, a current of air may be passed through it. Straw-plat work is also bleached by sulphuring.

SULPHURIC ACID MANUFACTURE. The manufacture of this important acid involves arrangements of great magnitude and interest. At the chemical works of Glasgow, Newcastle, and a few other large towns, the production of sulphuric acid is carried on upon a vast scale. The process consists mainly in bringing sulphur in contact with the air and combining the fumes thus produced with water. As the fumes are very deleterious to the workmen, and as both the fumes and the liquid exert a corrosive action on the vessels which contain them, the apparatus requires to be of a very peculiar kind.

In the first place the Sicilian sulphur is placed in a series of close-fitting iron furnaces, where it is kindled; it combines with oxygen in the act of burning, and produces *sulphurous acid gas*, which gas finds an exit into a hollow wall behind the row of furnaces. The gas passes from thence into vessels which are among the largest known in any department of manufactures. At the Felling chemical works near Newcastle, there are two sulphurous acid chambers, each 200 feet long, 20 wide, and 20 high; and four others about half this length; they are formed of sheet lead, framed strongly together.

In the leaden chambers a conversion takes place of *sulphurous acid* into *sulphuric acid*, and from a gas to a liquid. While the sulphur has been burning in the furnaces, such other ingredients as will yield a little nitrous acid vapour are also heated in the furnace; the nitrous acid vapour accompanies the sulphurous acid gas into the chamber: steam is also admitted into the chamber, and a curious chemical result follows. The acid gas, moistened by the steam, abstracts oxygen from the nitrous acid vapour, and becomes thereby changed from sulphur*ous* into sulphur*ic* acid; and this sulphuric acid, combining with the water of the condensed steam in the bottom of the chamber, becomes a liquid, and then constitutes the sulphuric acid, or *oil of vitriol* of the shops. In order to concentrate the acid for some purposes, it requires to be distilled; but such is its corroding nature, that few materials will resist its action; and hence the costly metal *platinum* is used for the stills for distilling this acid. At the Felling works a platinum still was provided some years ago, which cost one thousand guineas, its weight being about one thousand ounces; it therefore cost about four times its weight in pure silver! Platinum has, however, become less costly in recent years.

SUMACH, or SHUMAC, is a tanning and dye drug procured from the genus of *Rhus* plants. The chief species, *Rhus cotinus*, grows extensively in warm climates. It is made use of, like many other species, for tanning in Italy, where it is called *scotino;* the wood is used by the modern Greeks for dyeing wool of a beautiful rich yellow colour. The *Rhus coriaria* is extensively used for tanning; and it is said that all the leather made in

Turkey is tanned with the bark of this species.

Besides the dye and tan ingredient, many species of sumach tree yield a varnish or japan. The well-known *gum-copal* of commerce, from which *copal varnish* is made, is believed to be procured from the *Rhus copallina.* The celebrated *japan varnish* is produced from the *Rhus vernicifera*, or *varnish-bearing sumach.* The varnish is obtained from those branches of the plant which are about two or three years old, by incision; it is at first white, and of the consistence of cream, but it thickens and blackens after a little exposure; it is exceedingly transparent, and when used a dark surface of finely powdered charcoal is placed underneath it. The Japanese use this varnish, which is very hard, on their doorposts, windows, household furniture, and nearly all their wood-work.

The sumach used by the tanners of Bermondsey, is the powder of the leaves and young branches of the *Rhus coriaria;* it has a fine yellow colour, and is imported from Sicily in cloth bags containing about one cwt. each. For the mode of using it in tanning goat-skins, see LEATHER MANUFACTURE. No less than 12,920 tons of sumach were imported in 1850.

SUMATRA. This is one of the most fertile and important islands in the eastern hemisphere. Rice is cultivated in the lowest plains and in the elevated valleys of the mountain range. The most common esculent vegetables are different kinds of yams, both red and white; the St. Helena yam; sweet potatoes, common potatoes only in the more elevated districts; bredy, a kind of spinach; lobuck, or the Spanish radish; the large purple brinjall, or egg-plant; and many different sorts of beans, with white and green peas, and onions. The peas and onions are articles of export from the north-eastern coast to Penang and Singapore. Chili or capsicum, turmeric, ginger, coriander, and cummin seed, are raised, especially on the western coast. Hemp is extensively cultivated, but only for smoking with tobacco. Tobacco is also grown, and is an article of export from the harbours on the north-eastern coast. Melons are raised on the plains, and sometimes attain an extraordinary size. Sesamum is cultivated for its oil; and the Palma Christi, from which castor-oil is obtained, grows wild. The sugar-cane is only cultivated for chewing; no sugar is manufactured, but it is imported from Java. The plantations of betel-vines are extensive. Indigo and cotton are raised for domestic use only. The fruits are abundant, and include the cocoa-nut, plantains, banana, the bread-fruit tree, jack-tree, mangusteens, durians, mango, different kinds of orange and lemon trees, especially the shaddock: the pine-apple, the jambo, the guava, the papaya, the custard-apple, the pomegranate, and the tamarind The pepper-plant is more abundant in Sumatra than in any other part of the globe. Coffee, sago, cloves, and nutmegs are grown. The forests supply an inexhaustible variety of timber.

Sumatra was once noted for its gold, and a considerable quantity is still exported. Tin occurs in several places on the great plain, but is very little worked, as large quantities are obtained in the Island of Banca, where it is got with less labour. Copper is found between 2° and 3° N. lat., where it occurs in great abundance in an extensive tract. Sumatra contains gold, but it is not much worked. Iron, sulphur, saltpetre, coal, and salt, occur in small quantities.

Nothing perhaps shows more clearly the advanced state of civilization of the inhabitants of Sumatra than their manufacturing industry. The most important manufactures are those of iron and steel, which are carried to a considerable degree of perfection in Menangcabau, where iron has been worked from time immemorial. Silk and cotton fabrics, earthenware, and various works in metal, are among the best of the manufactures.

SUN-DIAL. Up to a comparatively recent period the science of constructing sun-dials, under the name of gnomonics, was an important part of practical science. As long as watches were scarce, and clocks not very common, the dial, which is now only a toy, was in actual use as a timekeeper. Of the mathematical works of the 17th century which are found on book-stalls, none are so common as those on dialling. A sun-dial consists of two parts: the *style*, usually supplied by the edge of a plate of metal, always made parallel to the earth's axis, and therefore pointing towards the north; and the *dial*, which is another plate of metal, horizontal or not, on which are marked the directions of the shadow for the several hours, their halves and quarters, and sometimes smaller subdivisions.

The varieties of sun-dial are numerous; but as the instrument is now little in use, it is unnecessary to describe them.

SUNDERLAND, with its northern suburb of *Monk Wearmouth*, constitutes the busy commercial mouth of the Wear. This river is crossed by an iron bridge of one arch, erected near the close of the last century. The abutments are piers of nearly solid masonry, 24 feet in thickness. The arch is of iron, and forms the segment of a large circle, having a span of 236 feet; the height above low water is 60 feet to the spring, and 94 feet to the centre of the arch, so that ships of 300 tons pass under it very readily by lowering their top-gallant masts. The superstructure is of timber planked over, with flagged footpaths and iron balustrades. This was for many years the most remarkable iron bridge in England.

The preservation and improvement of the port and harbour of Sunderland are entirely owing to the exertions of commissioners who have been appointed under successive acts of parliament for levying certain dues and applying them to the cleansing and improving of the harbour. These works, and particularly the construction of piers on both sides of the mouth of the river, have had so great an effect in improving the port, that ships drawing from 15 to 18 feet of water can now enter and depart from the harbour with great safety. There is a wet-dock comprising nearly 8 acres, with a tidal basin attached to it, on the north side of the river near the entrance of the harbour. In July, 1850, a very large wet-dock was opened on the south side of the river. The works extend from the river to Hendon Bay. First is the tidal harbour of 2½ acres opening from the river; next the half-tide basin (2½ acres), leading from it to the great dock of 20 acres, near the south end of which are the two jetties, one already occupied by four staiths for the shipment of coals, the rest of the accommodation being intended for general traffic. The widths of the entrances between the tidal harbour and the half-tide basin are respectively 45 and 60 feet, and that between the half-tide basin and the great dock 60 feet. In the great dock the depth in the middle at high water of ordinary spring tides is 24 feet, and at neap tides 20 feet 6 inches. Besides the site recovered from the sea, now forming the dock, an area of upwards of 25 acres of land has in like manner been gained from the sea to the eastward of the dock, which will be found exceedingly valuable and available for many useful purposes. The coal traffic is brought by the branch railway to the staiths on the jetties. The access to the dock for other traffic is from the foot of the High Street along the western side of the docks, and to the eastern side by moveable pontoons over the two entrances from the tidal harbour to the half-tide basin. The dock is considered to be the cheapest, as well as one of the best, that has ever been constructed.

The principal manufactures of Sunderland are of bottle and flint glass, anchors, chain-cables, and other iron goods for ships, and cordage. Ship building is carried on to a greater extent than in any other seaport of the British empire. On December 31, 1849, there were 90 ships building, the aggregate burthen of which was 29,210 tons. 5000 tons of shipping more were built in 1849 than in 1848, and 10,000 more in 1850 than in 1849. The number of ships belonging to the port in 1849 was 155 (44,333 tons). About 140 firms are engaged in business in connection with ship-building, as chain-cable manufacturers, sail-cloth manufacturers, anchor and ship-smiths, rope, sail, mast, block, or pump makers; besides ship-owners, brokers, and chandlers. Some of the ropewalks are on a very large scale. Brick-making, coal-mining, and the quarrying of grindstones, are carried on in the neighbourhood; and there are copperas-works, brass-foundries, potteries, hat-manufactories, lime-works, timber-yards, saw-mills, flour-mills, tan-yards, and breweries. The town is, however, more important from its commerce than its manufactures. In shipping coal it is exceeded only by the port of Newcastle, and recently perhaps by Stockton.

The export of lime is another principal branch of trade; also the export of glass and grindstones. The imports are timber and iron from the Baltic; butter, cheese, and flax from Holland; and a variety of goods brought coastwise. A considerable fishery is carried on.

SURREY. The agriculture of this county has immediate reference to the wants of the vast metropolis. The soil varies greatly in different districts; the richest is that which lies along the banks of the rivers, consisting chiefly of a deep alluvial loam. On this soil, in the neighbourhood of London, are some of those extremely productive and highly cultivated market-gardens which supply the metropolis with fruit and vegetables. The immense quantity of manure which is annually laid on the land so occupied, and the deep trenching and digging which are repeated at short intervals, have converted the whole surface, to the depth of three feet or more, into a rich black vegetable mould. On this soil are raised the best and earliest culinary vegetables, which so rapidly succeed each other that five or six different crops are sometimes gathered from the same ground in one year. The well-known hop-grounds in the neighbourhood of Farnham are mostly on a mixed soil of loam and calcareous earth. The greater value of Farnham hops in the market is probably owing partly to the soil being peculiarly suited to this plant, and partly to the greater care with which it is cultivated.

Numerous and attractive as are the towns and villages in Surrey, they owe their importance either to the villa residences which stud them, or to the agricultural markets of which they are the centres; very few of them present a manufacturing character.

SURVEYING is the art of determining the form and dimensions of tracts of ground, the plans of towns and single houses, the courses of roads and rivers, with the boundaries of estates, fields, &c.

Since the measurement of the distance between two objects by means of a rod or chain is very laborious and inaccurate when that distance is considerable, particularly if the ground has many inequalities of level, and is much intersected by walls, hedges, and streams of water, it will seldom be possible to execute even an ordinary survey by such means alone, and instruments for taking angles must be employed, together with the chain, in every operation of importance. A base line of moderate length is measured, and angular observations taken from its two extremities, to determine the relative position of objects.

The surveying instruments are few in number; and the processes are of too mathematical a character to call for description here.

SUSPENSION BRIDGE is a bridge in which the weight of the roadway, instead of resting upon arches of masonry, or on a rigid framework of wood or iron, is supported by the tension of ropes, chains, or rods.

We have no account of the existence of iron suspension-bridges in Europe before the middle of the last century. The earliest appears to have been a small one built across the river Tees, at an elevation of about 60 feet, two miles above Middleton, for foot passengers only. The first iron suspension bridge built in America was that constructed in 1796, by Mr. Finlay, across Jacob's Creek, on the road between Union Town and Greenburgh, the length of which was about 70 feet. Mr. Finlay subsequently, in 1801, obtained a patent for the construction of such bridges, and built several in the United States; one of which, over the Schuylkill, was 306 feet long. In 1807 a scheme was proposed by M. Belu, a French engineer, for crossing the Rhine, between Wesel and Ruderich, by a bridge about 820 feet long, to be supported by a network of wrought-iron chains. In 1814 a bridge of similar construction was proposed for crossing the Mersey at Runcorn Gap, so as to form a direct communication between Runcorn in Cheshire and Liverpool. In 1816 a suspension-bridge was built across Gala Water, made of thin wires, at a cost of only about 40*l.*, although its span was about 111 feet. Another wire bridge of about the same length was built in 1817 across the Tweed, at King's Meadows, at an expense of 160*l.* Sir Samuel Brown soon afterwards introduced an improved method of constructing chains for suspending the roadway. Chains of the ordinary form, with short links, are very defective in strength; and several difficulties, among which is the great extent of surface exposed to oxidation, attend the use of cables consisting of small rods or wires. The plan adopted by Sir S. Brown was to form chains of round or flat bars of iron, several feet long, having either welded eyes or drilled holes at each end, and being connected together by short links and bolt-pins. The first extensive bridge erected upon this plan was the Union Bridge across the Tweed, near Berwick, opened for use in 1820. The length is 449 feet, and the deflection is about 30 feet. There are twelve suspending chains, arranged in pairs side by side, and in three tiers, one above the other; each chain being formed of round rods, 15 feet long, and 2 inches in diameter. The suspension-rods are round, an inch in diameter, and are attached alternately to each of the three tiers of chains. In 1821 Brown commenced the Trinity suspension-pier at Newhaven, near Edinburgh, which consists of three spans of 209 feet each, with 14 feet deflection. In 1818 the Holyhead Road Commissioners applied to Telford for his opinion respecting the erection of an iron suspension-bridge at the Menai. A brief account of this beautiful bridge, and of the yet more extraordinary Britannia Tubular Bridge, recently erected near it by Mr. Robert Stephenson, will be found under MENAI BRIDGES.

While the Menai Bridge was in progress Sir S. Brown constructed the suspension-pier at Brighton, which consists of four openings of 255 feet each, with a deflection of 18 feet; and Mr. W. Tierney Clark commenced in 1824 the Hammersmith suspension-bridge, the first erected in the vicinity of London. The central opening of the Hammersmith Bridge has a chord-line of 422 feet, with a deflection of about 30 feet. The width of the bridge is about 30 feet, there being a carriage-way of 20 feet, and two side foot-paths of 5 feet each. There are eight chains, arranged in four double lines, or in two vertical tiers. The Hungerford suspension-bridge, opened April 18th, 1845, is for foot-passengers only; the chains are borne by two towers in the river, 22 feet square and 80 feet high, the height of the roadway above high-water mark being 32 feet. The span of the centre between the two towers is 676 feet 6 inches, of each of the side arches 333 feet. The roadway is supported by single suspension rods 12 feet apart on each side. It was built under the direction of Mr. I. K. Brunel.

Some suspension-bridges have been erected in which the main chains, instead of passing over a pier or tower at or near each end of the platform, are supported by a single tower in the centre of the bridge, and form what may be called two semi-catenaries. A bridge of this kind was built in 1823 by Sir M. I. Brunel, in the Isle of Bourbon. The bridge consists of two openings of 122 feet each. A few suspension-bridges have been built in which the chains are suspended below the platform, which is supported by framework built upon instead of hanging from them.

Some small bridges of wire have been alluded to already, and Drewry describes several of large dimensions which were erected on the Continent soon after the introduction of suspension-bridges upon an extensive scale in Great Britain. The first large one erected in France was that of Tournon, across the Rhône, between Tain and Tournon, in 1824-5; it consists of two openings of 278 feet each. Another remarkable wire-bridge is that over the Sarine, at Fribourg in Switzerland, which was completed in 1834, by M. Challey. It has a span, from pier to pier, of 870 feet, and is 167 feet above the level of the river, being much longer and higher than the Menai Bridge. The platform is suspended from four cables, arranged in pairs at the sides of the bridge, with a deflection of 55 feet. The wire of which the bridge is composed is about one-twelfth of an inch in diameter, and each cable consists of fifteen bundles of eighty wires each, packed together in a cylindrical form, and bound round at intervals of two or three feet with annealed wire. The wires are not twisted together like the strands of a rope, but each of them extends straight from end to end of the cable. The two pairs of cables are suspended at a distance of 30 feet from each other, but the width between the lower ends of the suspension rods is only 24 feet, so that their position is not quite vertical. These rods are small cables, consisting of thirty wires similar to those of which the cables are composed. The roadway is formed of fir planks, supported by transverse beams, and stiffened by a strong oak railing, or diagonal truss. The bridge was completed at a cost of 24,000*l*., and was publicly opened in 1834.

The use of wire instead of bar-chains in the construction of suspension-bridges is favoured by the simplicity of the apparatus necessary for their erection, and the superior strength, bulk for bulk, of small wires over bars of considerable dimensions. In some instances the chain system and the wire system have been combined. There is a chain bridge at Geneva, in which both the long and short links may be called skeins of wire, bound round into a cylindrical form in the centre, and spread out into broad loops at the ends, where they embrace the hollow bolts. The structure is in fact a chain bridge, of which the chain-bars and linking-plates consist of bundles of wire instead of solid bars.

Several suspension-bridges of small span have been constructed upon an ingenious plan which combines the advantages of the opposite principles of tension and compression. The first of these was the Monk Bridge, across the river Aire at Leeds, which was erected in 1827, by Mr. George Leather, of that place. The platform is supported by vertical suspension-rods, the upper ends of which, instead of being attached to catenarian chains, are supported by rigid arches of cast-iron, which rising between the carriage-way and the footpaths, are elevated above the level of the platform. The suspending rods are of malleable iron, and they sustain transverse cast-iron beams upon which the roadway is laid. Timber bridges have been constructed on a similar principle to the above. Drewry mentions one at Eglisau, near Zürich, in Switzerland, consisting of two arches formed of beams 15 feet long, 10 inches broad, and 1 foot deep, with their abutting ends secured by iron straps. The ends of the arches are tied together by horizontal braces, and the weight of the platform is suspended by vertical bars arranged in pairs, which embrace the wooden arch or rib, and are bolted together above it.

Much attention has been excited by the principle of constructing suspension-bridges introduced by Mr. Dredge of Bath, who obtained a patent for his invention in 1836. The leading features of his plan are the adaptation of every part of the chain to the precise amount of strain to which it is exposed, by diminishing the number of plates, and consequently the weight and strength of the chains, from the points of suspension to the lowest or central point of the catenary; and the position of the suspending rods, which, instead of being vertical, are arranged in oblique lines from their points of attachment to the main chains towards the centre of the catenary. The Victoria Bridge over the Avon, at Bath, which was built on this plan in 1836, contains only twenty-one tons of iron, although it is of 150 feet span. The number of bridges since built on this plan is very considerable. An example of them on a very small scale may be seen in the Regent's Park. In 1827-8 a suspension-bridge of *steel* was erected over the Danube at Vienna, by an engineer named Von Mitis; the bridge alluded to at Vienna has a chord-line of 334 English feet, with a deflection of nearly 21½ feet.

Perhaps the finest suspension bridge ever constructed is that built by Mr. Tierney Clark over the Danube at Pesth. In magnitude and in cost it exceeds all others. It was finished in 1849, and was shortly afterwards traversed by the Austrian and Hungarian armies.

Suspension-bridges are well adapted for many situations in which, from the limited traffic, the expense of ordinary stone bridges would prevent their adoption, and also for places in which, from the great span required, the great elevation, the unfavourable nature of the bottom, or the rapidity of the current to be crossed, the erection of any other kind of bridge would be difficult; but they are not applicable to situations of great and constant traffic, since they are much weaker than arch-bridges, and very liable to injury from the vibration occasioned by what might appear slight forces.

SUSSEX. Few persons are now aware that Sussex was once an iron smelting county. It was in the wealden strata of Sussex, when wood was abundant and when charcoal was employed in smelting iron, that the chief iron-works of Sussex were situated, the iron-ore being extracted from the ironstone of the argillaceous beds. Up to the year 1720 Sussex was the principal seat of the iron manufacture in England; but by degrees the furnaces were disused and the manufacture transferred to districts where coal was abundant. The last furnace, at Ashburnham, was blown out in 1827.

The rich marsh-lands, of which there are about 30,000 acres in the county, make an excellent pasture-ground, on which many oxen and sheep are reared and fatted for market. There are also about 50,000 acres of down-land, which produce excellent pasture for the small sheep known as Southdown sheep. Hops are cultivated to a considerable extent in the eastern part of the county; they have been introduced from Kent, and have gradually extended themselves westward. Upwards of 8000 acres are now under cultivation; the produce however is not so much esteemed in the market as that of Kent.

Sussex, like Surrey, has but few of the characteristics of a manufacturing county; its towns are pleasure towns and agricultural towns, rather than manufacturing towns. Of the former class are Bognor, Brighton, Eastbourne, Hastings, and Worthing. There is, however, a small amount of sea and river traffic at Arundel, Newhaven, Rye, and Shoreham.

SWANSEA. This important Welch town contains groups of furnaces and other works connected with the smelting of copper, for which Swansea is celebrated. The ore is imported from Cornwall, Devonshire, and other parts of Great Britain, and also from various foreign places besides Australia. Besides the works for smelting copper, there are iron-works, zinc-works, tin-plate-works, yards for building and repairing ships, roperies, tanneries, and potteries. The traffic with the country is facilitated by several canals and tram-roads. A canal about 17 miles in length runs along the valley of the Tawe into Brecknockshire; another connects the Neath river and canal with Swansea harbour; and a third communicates with collieries on the N.E. of the town. In 1849 the trade of Swansea was as follows:—Foreign vessels—entered inwards with cargoes, 205, bringing 48,000 tons; outwards, with cargoes, 438, taking 50,000 tons; inwards, with ballast, 112; 9000 tons; outwards, with ballast, 16; 3600 tons. Coasting vessels—entered inwards with cargoes, 4000, bringing 263,000 tons; outwards, with cargoes, 6000, taking 355,000 tons. In addition to the above, about 100 vessels arrived in ballast, and about 200 cleared out in ballast. Eighteen out of the 205 (of a burthen of 600 tons each) entering inwards from foreign parts brought copper ore and wool from South Australia.

The copper ore bought at Swansea by the smelters during the last few years has varied from 600,000*l.* to 900,000*l.* annually in value. It is all purchased by about eight or ten large firms, whose smelting works form the most distinguishing features in the neighbourhood of Swansea. When smelted and reduced to the forms of ingot, bar, sheet, &c., it is distributed throughout every part of the United Kingdom, and indeed throughout the known world. Almost all the copper ore smelted in this country is smelted in and near Swansea. For further details on this subject, see COPPER.

SWEDEN. The climate and soil are less favourable to the growth of grain in Sweden than in most other parts of Europe. The principal objects of cultivation are rye, barley, oats, peas and wheat. The produce of potatoes increased from about 200,000 qrs. in 1805 to about 2,000,000 qrs. in 1840. Other objects of cultivation are hemp, flax, and tobacco; buckwheat, carraway seed, hops and madder. Cherries, apples, and pears, are abundant only in the southern districts; cranberries and other berries abound in the northern districts. The forests are very large, covering altogether more than one-fourth of the whole of the surface of Sweden. The export of timber, though considerable, is not in proportion to the immense extent of the woods. The forests supply fire-wood, of which a great quantity is consumed, as Sweden has no useful coal. Large quantities of charcoal are also used in the mines and factories. Tar and pitch are extracted chiefly from the roots of pine trees, and are minor articles of export. Several kinds of coniferous trees and birch compose the greater part of these forests. Oak and beech grow only in the southern districts. The seas of Sweden contain abundance of fish. Salmon abounds in almost all the rivers and lakes.

Sweden is rich in minerals. Gold is found on the table-land of Småland, at Adelforss, but no mines are worked. Silver-mines are worked at Sala, in Westeras Län, and at some other places, and in Falu Län. The annual produce of the copper-mines amounts to nearly 1000 tons; the richest mines are those at Falun in Falu Län and at Otvidaberg in Linköping Län. Lead mines are worked in Westeras and in Falu. Iron-ore is found in nearly every district of Sweden, and there is no part where it is not worked more or less, with the exception of the plain of Scania, where it seems that no iron ore exists; the best iron is obtained from the mines of Dannemora in Upsala Län. The annual produce of all the iron mines of Sweden amounts to more than 67,000 tons of bar iron. In Orebro Län are rich mines of cobalt, which yield annually more than 600 tons; this metal is found in several other parts of Sweden. At some places alum and vitriol are obtained, but only in small quantities. Some bad brown coal is raised near Cape Kullen in Scania. Porphyry is got at Elfvedal, in the upper valley of the Dal-Elf, and marble in the mountains north of Norrköping.

Manufactures have been fostered in Sweden by a system of prohibitions and severe restrictions. The most important industrial establishments are confined to the large towns. Stockholm has large sugar-refineries, cotton and silk factories, tanyards, woollen-cloth mills, &c. Norrköping is the chief centre of the woollen manufactures. Steam machinery and mill-work are manufactured in Motala, Stockholm, and Nyköping, which last has also large iron-foundries. Tobacco is extensively manufactured in most of the large towns. Other products are paper, cotton-yarn, glass, morocco leather, printed cottons and linens, seed-oils, pottery and chinaware, linen, soap, sail-cloth, silk ribands, &c. Göteborg has important breweries, sugar-refineries, and sail-cloth factories. Very few of the articles named are exported from Sweden, and none to any considerable amount; nor of many of the most important items is the supply sufficient for the demand. The Swedish peasant is of necessity himself a handicraftsman and manufacturer; and very few persons, comparatively speaking, are exclusively devoted to technical trades. The most important articles of peasant industry are—the coarse woollen stuffs of Dalecarlia and West Gothland in which the country people are clad; the linen of West Gothland and Helsingland, and the damasks and fine linens of Angermanland; the stockings, pottery, turnery, and woodwork of West Gothland and Schonen; and the wooden clocks of Dalecarlia; all of which enter largely into the internal trade of the country. Breweries and distilleries are to be found in most of the towns; and most of the towns on the coast have ship-building yards.

The internal commerce, which is considerable, in corn, salt, fish, whisky, bricks and tiles, linens, and other manufactured goods is facilitated by good roads and navigable rivers, and in winter by the whole country being covered with snow — a circumstance which renders the conveyance of goods in sledges easy and expeditious. The Swedes are much given to a seafaring life. Their vessels visit most of the countries contiguous to the Atlantic, and they are also employed in the carrying trade between other countries, especially in the Mediterranean, and on the coasts of South America. The imports consist of fish from Norway; butter, tallow, and provisions from Finland; hemp, flax and hemp seed, linseed oil, hides, tallow, and peltry from Russia; corn, wool, cattle, and provisions from Denmark; colonial produce, dye-stuffs, spices, and manufactured goods, from England and the Hanse towns; fruit, cattle, corn, and manufactured articles from Mecklenburg and Prussia; wine, fruits, oil, and silk from France; tropical fruits and salt (an important article, which Sweden does not produce) from Portugal and Spain; colonial produce and dyestuffs, drugs, hides, tobacco, and rum, from America and the East Indies.

The principal articles of export are—bar and pig iron, nails and other wrought iron; boards, planks, logs and spars, staves, tar; some copper, brass, alum, manganese, paper, and linen and hempen fabrics. The value of the imports in 1844 amounted to 17,487,000 Swedish rix-dollars; the value of the exports in the same year was 21,080,000 rix-dollars. In that year 5445 vessels entered Swedish harbours, 3677 of which were Swedish, and 839 Norwegian; the mercantile marine of Sweden numbered 940 vessels, 738 of which, with 139,990 tons burthen, were engaged in the foreign trade.

In 1850, of Swedish and Norwegian vessels, 1674 entered ports of Great Britain, with an aggregate burthen of 283,061 tons.

The value of the British and Irish produce and manufactures exported to Sweden and Norway in 1849 was 367,363*l*.

SWEEPING MACHINES. Mr. Whitworth's street-sweeping machine deserves to be more extensively adopted than it has yet been; for its operations are more expeditious and more effective than those ordinarily adopted. It was introduced about eight or nine years ago at Manchester. There had before been invented road-scraping machines; but the sweeping machine superseded them. The machine consists of a cart, to the hinder part of which is an endless chain of brushes or brooms, inclining downwards to the ground. The motion of the wheels causes other wheels within the machine to rotate; and these minor wheels act upon the brushes, causing each brush in turn to sweep over the surface of the ground, and to carry up its portion of dirt into the cart. Sloping boards are so adjusted as to facilitate the transfer of the dirt into the cart. The sweepings from 800 to 4000 square yards of street or road suffice to fill the cart, according to the previous state of the ground as to cleanliness. It has been calculated that one of these machines, drawn by two horses, can sweep 24,000 square yards, on an average, per day—a quantity equal to that which twenty men could cleanse in the same time.

Mr. Whitworth patented, in 1849, a new arrangement of the brushes; they are attached to the lower surface of a horizontal disc, which has a revolving motion given to it round a vertical axis, by machinery connected with the ordinary wheels of the cart.

Another street-sweeping machine was patented by Mr. Walker, in 1849. It consists of a cart on four wheels, the front pair of which give motion to two channel brushes, one on each side; while the hinder pair give motion to a large roller brush, as long as the width of the machine. The action of these three brushes is such as to collect the dirt of the street into parallel ridges; and another apparatus then comes into work. This apparatus is something like Whitworth's in respect to sweeping the dirt up a sloping board into a receptacle; but there is also an endless chain of buckets which lifts the dirt from the receptacle into a cart temporarily attached to the machine. The whole contrivance is much more complicated than Whitworth's.

SWITZERLAND. This interesting country does not produce corn enough for its consumption. Flax and hemp are extensively grown; but the chief territorial wealth of the highlands, and indeed of the greater part of Switzerland, consists in its pastures and its cattle. The vine is extensively cultivated in the cantons of Vaud, Geneva, Neufchâtel, Zürich, Schaffhausen, Valais, Ticino, and parts of Aargau, Thurgau, St. Gall, and Basel; but the wine is generally inferior. In the highland cantons cider is made. Kirschwasser is distilled. Mulberry-trees are planted and silk-worms reared in the canton of Ticino and the valleys on the Italian side of the Alps. Chestnut-trees are found in sheltered situations; walnut-trees are more generally diffused; olive-trees grow only in some favoured spots of the canton of Ticino, where also the fig and peach-trees bear abundantly, as well as in some parts of the lower Valais. The highlands abound with timber-trees, especially firs of various kinds, maple, beech, larch, birch, and oak trees. Most of the cottages and farm-houses are built of wood, and the same material is used for fuel, the annual consumption of which is enormous: a great quantity of timber is also exported to France and other countries. Coal-mines are worked in the cantons of Freyberg, Vaud, Basel, and Thurgau, but the coal is mostly of inferior quality. Iron is found in the Jura; and there are furnaces and iron-works of some importance in the cantons of Vaud, Bern, Soleure, Basel, Aargau, and Grisons. In the Grisons there are mines of lead, zinc, and galena. Salt-springs abound, but they are generally neglected, except those of Bex in the canton of Vaud. Switzerland has been a manufacturing country for centuries. In the canton of Zürich the manufacture of silks, taffeta, serges, silk handkerchiefs, and ribands, gives employment to between 12,000 and 13,000 people. The cotton-manufactures of Zürich employ about 12,000 weavers, 5000 spinners, besides 4000 persons engaged in other trades connected with the cotton manufacture. The cantons of St. Gall and Appenzall have important manufactures of cotton cloths, fine muslins, cotton prints, leather, linen, glass, and jewellery. The city of Basel forms another emporium of trade and manufactures, principally of silk ribands, silk thread, taffeta, and satins. Schaffhausen has a manufactory of steel and files, which is in great repute; one of cotton-spinning, and one of cotton prints. It has also a good transit trade with Germany. At the opposite extremity of Switzerland, Geneva is a great mart of trade and industry. The manufactures of Geneva consist chiefly of watches, jewellery, and musical boxes; but include also cabinet work, saddlery, lithography and engraving, cutlery, fire-arms, enamels, &c. The chief industrial occupations in the canton of Neufchâtel are—cotton printing, lace-making, and more especially watch-making, which prevails greatly among the highlands of the Jura, giving employment to about 20,000 persons, who manufacture and export yearly above 120,000 gold and silver watches. The cantons of Thurgau, Glarus, and Aargau manufacture cotton cloth, prints, and muslins of all descriptions, hosiery, silks, and ribands; in Aargau linen and cutlery are also made. The rest of the cantons of Switzerland manufacture merely what is required to supply their own wants. The manufactures find a vent in distant countries by passing through Germany and the Sardinian States to the harbours of Holland and the Mediterranean.

The Great Exhibition affords gratifying proof that the industrial products of Switzerland are varied, ingenious, and valuable.

SWORD MANUFACTURE. Several countries have been celebrated for the excellence of the swords manufactured by the inhabitants. The swords of Toledo were famed even as far back as the time of the Romans. The Milan swords have likewise had a high reputation. But the Damascus swords have had the widest celebrity; though no such manufacture is now carried on in that city, as the Damascus swords now existing are of old date.

About the year 1689 an attempt was made to improve and extend the sword manufacture of England by the incorporation of a company of sword-cutlers for making hollow sword-blades in Cumberland and the adjacent counties. The company was empowered to purchase lands, to erect mills, and to employ a great number of German artificers; yet the project failed. Owing apparently to the parsimony of the manufacturers, which led them to use inferior materials, and to employ unskilful workmen, English sword-blades fell into very ill repute during the 18th century; so much so, indeed, that an English officer would not trust his life to the hazard of the probable failure of a sword of native manufacture. Attention having been drawn to this subject, the late Mr. Gill, of Birmingham, entered into competition with the German sword-cutlers, and produced swords even superior to those of the German makers. The tendency of recent years has been to bring the chief European nations nearly to a level in this manufacture.

The process of manufacturing swords at Birmingham is as follows:—The material of which the blade is wrought should be cast-steel of the very best quality, and wrought with the greatest care. Of this material, besides the quantity prepared at Birmingham, much is obtained from Sheffield in the form of bars, called *sword-moulds*. These bars are heated in the fire, and drawn out upon an anvil by two workmen with hammers, giving alternate strokes. When the blade is required to be concave upon the sides, or to have a reeded back, or some similar ornament, it is hammered between steel bosses or *swages*. The blade is then hardened by heating it in the fire until it becomes worm-red, and is then dipped, point downwards, in a tub of cold water. It is tempered by drawing it through the fire several times until the surface exhibits a bluish oxidation, which takes place at a temperature of about 550° Fahr. The sword is then *set* to the required shape by placing it on a sort of fork upon the anvil, and wrenching it by means of tongs in the direction required to correct any degree of warping which it may have contracted during the hardening. The grinding is performed upon a stone with either a flat or fluted surface, according to the kind of blade; and as the uniformity of the temper is impaired by this process, it is subsequently restored by a slight heating, after which the blade is glazed with emery, and, if the instrument be a fine one, with crocus martis, after the manner of a razor-blade. The sword is then ready for the hilt or handle, the variety of which it is needless to enumerate.

Among the tests to which sword-blades are subjected in order to prove their flexibility and elasticity, is that of bending them into a curve by pressing the side of the blade against six or eight pegs or stout nails driven into a board, in such a manner that, when in contact with all the pegs, the middle of the blade may be bent six or seven inches from a straight line drawn between the point and the hilt. A further test is applied by an apparatus consisting of a vertical pillar rising from a board. The point of the sabre is placed upon the board at the foot of the upright pillar, and the hilt is then pressed down until the middle of the blade bends away from the upright piece to the required degree; the amount of curvature being shown by a peg which projects horizontally from the pillar, about midway between the top and the bottom. The temper is also proved by striking the blade smartly upon a table on both sides, and by severe strokes with the back and edge upon a block. Mr. Inglis, in his 'Spain in 1830,' describes the trials to which sword-blades are subjected at the celebrated manufactory of Toledo. Each sword is there thrust against a plate in the wall, and so bent into an arc forming at least three parts of a circle, and then struck edgeways upon a leaden table with all the force which can be given by a powerful man holding it with both hands. The polishing, according to the same authority, is performed upon a wheel of walnut wood.

The ancient Damascus sword-blades have a peculiar wavy appearance on the surface, which is called *damascene* or *damasking*. [DAMASCENE WORK.] Various modes have been adopted for imitating this appearance; but it is not known whether any of them are identical with the original practice.

SYRIA. In this important region of Western Asia the ordinary farming produce is raised in fair variety and quantity. Cotton, hemp, flax, madder, indigo, and tobacco, are to some extent cultivated. Almost all the fruits both of temperate and of tropical climates are met with in Syria. The forests on the mountains consist of cedars, firs, and pines; those of the table-lands include the oak, walnut, laurel, juniper, scammony, and sumach.

There are no metals found in Syria except iron, which is worked in the Kesrouan in Mar Hanna, west of Beirout, where also coal has been discovered of late years. In the Tyh Beni Israël, and at the southern extremity of the Dead Sea, there are mountains almost entirely composed of rock salt. Bitumen is collected on the western shores of the Dead Sea. In the northern Ghaur pieces of native sulphur are found at a small depth beneath the surface.

Syria is the most manufacturing country in Western Asia. With the exception of hardware and cutlery, there is hardly any manufactured article imported into Syria; but a great variety of goods which are made in Syria are exported to Egypt and Anatolia, and still greater quantities go to the countries farther east, and find their way into Persia, where they meet the articles brought from Hindustan. The most manufacturing town is Damascus. The Phœnicians were probably supplied from Damascus with a great number of manufactured articles for the market of the countries that surround the Mediterranean, and they supplied the manufactures of Damascus with some of the materials used in them. The extent of the manufacturing industry of this town may be conceived from the statement of Schubert, that above 40,000 persons are employed in making silk stuffs, especially satin and silk damasks and brocades; and that caravans frequently go from Damascus to Haleb, which take no other goods but articles of this description. The varieties of manufactures at Damascus are almost countless. Those of Aleppo are considerably smaller, and are mostly limited to cotton and silk stuffs, and gold and silver lace. Some branches of manufacturing industry are carried on in most of the small towns, and even in some villages, such as cotton stuffs for gowns and shirts, the dyeing of cotton, mostly blue and red, tanning leather, and making soap. Such places, however, supply only the neighbourhood, and the Beduins who resort to them for such articles, and they rarely if ever work for a distant market.

The commercial intercourse between Syria and Europe is very small. None of the agricultural products of Europe are in demand in Syria; no kind of grain is imported, with the exception of rice, with which Syria is supplied from Egypt. The manufactured goods of Europe are not in demand, not being adapted to the taste and customs of the East. The only article which is imported to a certain extent is hardware, which is almost exclusively supplied by England: some French cloth is also imported. The chief articles sent from Europe to Syria are supplied by the East and West Indies, and consist of indigo, cochineal, and coffee. The chief exports from Syria to Europe are silk, galls, olive-oil, sponges, fruit, and tobacco. The commerce between Syria and the countries to the east and north of it is very extensive, and is concentrated at Aleppo. Two well-frequented roads lead from Aleppo to Constantinople through Anatolia; and two likewise extend from Aleppo to Persia, which divide at Orfa in Mesopotamia. But the most frequented caravan road between Aleppo and Bagdad lies to the west of the Euphrates, passing by Anuah and Hit.

The objects sent from Syria to the Great Exhibition consist of specimens of the manufacture of silk, gold, silver lace and embroidery, native jewellery, Lebanon horns, petrifactions, oils, different sorts of woods, seeds, the apples of Sodom, &c. The Pacha of Jerusalem sends a few specimens of the Bethlehem work in mother-of-pearl, which is brought by the Hadj from Mecca, such as the crucifixion, and other religious subjects. Mr. Consul Finn sends Palestine flowers arranged in a box of olive wood, and some specimens of Jerusalem marbles contained in a box made of one of the stones of Jerusalem. Colonel Rose, her Majesty's consul-general in Syria, sends with the Syrian specimens a few gold antiquities. One of them is a gold mask found in a Greek sarcophagus near Gebal, which was placed on the face of a femalo corpse, and still retains her features.

SYRINGE, a portable hydraulic instrument of the pump kind, commonly employed for the forcible ejection of fluids. In its simplest form it consists of a cylindrical tube, with a perforated nozzle at one end, and a piston or plunger, to the rod of which a ring or other convenient handle is attached. The tube being held in the left hand, with its nozzle immersed in water, the piston is drawn to the upper end of the tube by tho right hand. The pressure of the atmosphere upon the surface of the water causes it to follow the piston, so that the syringe becomes filled with water. The instrument is then removed from the vessel of water, and, by pushing the piston back towards the nozzle, its contents may be ejected with a force proportionate to the power applied to the piston. Syringes of various sorts are extensively used for surgical, horticultural, and other purposes. The fire-engine, the garden-engine, the air-pump, the stomach-pump, and the school-boy's squirt, are all examples of syringes.

SYRUPS are medicinal solutions of sugar, either in water alone, as in simple syrup, or in liquids charged with some peculiar principle of an active kind, such as senna or buckthorn, or merely grateful from its colour or fragrance, or both, such as syrup of violets. These must be of a proper consistence, either by having a suitable quantity of sugar added to the water first, or by subsequent evaporation of the superfluous water. The former is the preferable mode, as the syrup keeps better. Tho purest and most thoroughly refined sugar should be employed, and generally in the proportion of two parts of sugar to one of fluid.

The variety of syrups is very considerable. Syrups of buckthorn, cochineal, coltsfoot, gum, ginger, horehound, ipecacuanha, lemon, marshmallow, mulberry, orange peel, poppy, rhubarb, rose, rue, saffron, sarsaparilla, senna, squills, tolu, violets—these are some of the many kinds of syrups prepared by druggists.

T

TACHOMETER. This is the name of an apparatus patented by Messrs. Napier, in 1848, for ascertaining the speed with which vessels pass through the water. It consists of a horizontal spindle, moving freely on pivots attached to the side of the vessel beneath the water line, and enclosed in a case open at both ends. The spindle is fitted with vanes, the pitch or angle of which is so regulated, that ten revolutions of the spindle shall equal one fathom. Other wheel-work connects this spindle with a dial and index, so as to measure the number of nautical miles which the apparatus, and consequently the ship itself, has passed through the water.

Messrs. Penn, tho engineers of Greenwich, patented in the same year a tachometer of a very ingenious and peculiar kind. It is to be attached to an auxiliary steam ship; that is, a ship which *sails* only under ordinary circumstances, but which has also facilities for *steaming* in ordinary weather. (Such an auxiliary moving power is described under SCREW PROPELLER.) Messrs. Penn's apparatus is intended, not only to measure the speed of such a vessel through the water, but to strengthen or weaken the steam force according as the sailing force is weak or strong. It is self-acting, like the governor and valve of a steam engine: it feeds itself with steam power, according to its wants. There is a small horizontal paddle-wheel attached to the side of the ship, and the shaft of this wheel is connected, by intervening apparatus, with the steam pipe; as the vessel advances this little wheel rotates, and according as the rotation is fast or slow (depending on the greater or less speed), the steam pipe becomes opened less or more widely.

TALBOTYPE. [CALOTYPE; PHOTOGRAPHY.]

TALC. This remarkable mineral, which consists chiefly of silica and magnesia, presents itself in various forms. It is sometimes crystalline, sometimes laminated in thin plates, and sometimes in greenish gray masses of talc-slate. It is found in beds of clay slate and mica slate, in various parts of Scotland and the Alps. It is used as an ingredient in rouge, as a polisher for soft alabaster, as an ingredient in porcelain paste, and in the manufacture of crayons.

TALLOW is animal fat melted and separated from the membranous matter which is naturally mixed with it. When pure, tallow is white, and nearly tasteless; but the tallow of commerce usually has a yellow tinge.

A very large proportion of the tallow used for making soap and candles in this country is of home production, and is fitted for use by the *renderer*, who chops into pieces the fat and suet received from the butchers, and boils it in water, by which operation the greater part of the fat is melted out from the membranes, and floats to the top, whence it is removed by skimming. The remaining fat is subsequently squeezed from the membranes by a powerful press, leaving the membranous matter in the form of a cake or block, of a dark colour, which is called *graves*, and which, when macerated in warm water, softens and swells, and becomes a wholesome and palatable article of food for poultry, dogs, and other domestic animals. It is extensively used in fattening poultry for the market.

Almost all our imported tallow is brought from Russia, where this article is produced in enormous quantities. 250,000,000 lbs. are annually exported from Russia to various countries, mostly furnished from the steppes of Southern Russia. The cattle are bought by thousands, driven to the Salgans, or tallow factories, and there fattened and slaughtered. After the animals are slaughtered and skinned, a little of the flesh and the intestines are removed, and the rest of the carcass, cut into pieces, is thrown into the boilers, of which there are from four to six in every salgan, each large enough to contain the flesh of ten or fifteen oxen. During the boiling, the fat, as it collects at the top, is skimmed off with large ladles, and before it is quite cold it is poured into the casks in which it is afterwards shipped. The first fat which comes off is the best, and is quite white, while that which follows has a yellowish tinge; and a still coarser tallow is obtained by squeezing the bones and flesh in presses.

An ox in good condition will yield from seven to eight poods (250 to 290 lbs.) of tallow, which is generally worth from eleven to fifteen rubles a pood—about 1½*d.* to 2*d.* per lb. The merchants of St. Petersburg divide the tallow which they receive from the interior into white and yellow candle tallow, and common and Siberian soap-tallow; the latter, which is considered the best tallow for soap-making, being brought by water transit from Siberia. Yellow candle-tallow, when good, should be clean, dry, hard when broken, and of a fine yellow colour throughout. The white candle-tallow, when good, is white, brittle, hard, dry, and clean. The best white tallow is brought from Woronesch.

The chief uses of tallow are noticed under CANDLE and SOAP. Palm-oil has recently come extensively into use as a substitute for tallow in candle-making.

The tallow imported during the last three years amounted to the following quantities:—

1848	1,498,359 cwts.
1849	1,465,629 „
1850	1,241,781 „

Russia, as has been stated, is the great source whence the supply is obtained; but Australia now sends large cargoes of tallow to the mother country.

TAMARINDS. Of the two species of the genus *Tamarindus* the fruit is much larger in the East Indian than the West Indian. The shell being removed, there remains the flat square hard seed, imbedded in a pulp, with membranous fibres running through it. In the East Indies the pulp is either dried in the sun, and used for home consumption, or with salt added it is dried in copper ovens; this kind is sent to Europe. This sort, called natural tamarinds, is much darker and drier than the West Indian, which are called prepared tamarinds.

The West Indian Tamarinds reach maturity in June, July, and August, when they are collected, and the shell being removed, they are put into jars, either with layers of sugar put between them, or boiling syrup poured over them, which penetrates to the bottom. Prepared tamarinds therefore contain much more saccharine matter than the others.

The timber of the East Indian tamarind tree is very firm, hard, and heavy, and is applied to many useful purposes in building.

TAMPING. In mining operations, where the process of blasting with gunpowder is necessary for loosening masses of rock or ore, the powder is pressed in a cavity prepared for its reception by a careful process of ramming; this is called *tamping*. [MINING.]

TANKS. The importance of collecting rain-water for domestic purposes, especially in districts where springs are deficient or lie at a great depth, has been much overlooked in this country. Mr. Waistell urges the importance of placing spouts round all the buildings of a farm to collect the rain-water which falls upon them into a tank or tanks; observing that, besides the value of the supply of water thus obtained, the buildings will be benefited by the walls and foundations being kept drier than when the water from the roof is suffered to fall upon them. He states that the quantity of water that falls annually upon every hundred superficial feet or square of building (in Great Britain) is about 1400 imperial gallons. If, therefore, the external surfaces of roofs were adapted to the collection of the rain water which falls upon them, and means were provided for conveying it to covered tanks, in which it might be preserved from evaporation, and kept free from any admixture of impurities, almost every house might be readily and cheaply supplied with a quantity of wholesome water sufficient for the ordinary wants of its inhabitants. The extensive roofs of churches and other public buildings might be employed in like way to collect water for the supply of ponds or tanks for public use. In some cases even the drainage of lands might also be made available, as the water may be submitted to any required process of filtration before it is allowed to enter the tank.

Tanks or cisterns to hold water for domestic purposes may be conveniently situated beneath the surface of the ground, so that, being paved over, they occupy no valuable space. They are formed of stone slabs grooved into each other and set in cement; of Welsh slate; of large paving-tiles bedded in cement; of brick-work; of plates of cast iron; or of thick wooden planks, protected by charring and pitching, or lined with sheet lead. The brick tanks described by Waistell are circular, the sides being built like a well, with bottoms of an inverted dome-shape, of very slight convexity. The top is also dome-shaped, and has an opening in the centre large enough to receive a man, in order that the tank may be thoroughly cleaned out when necessary. This opening which may be upon the surface of the ground, or a little above it, should be covered with an oak flap pierced with a number of holes, or with an iron grating.

TAPESTRY. This name is commonly applied to the textile fabrics usually composed of wool or silk, and sometimes enriched with gold and silver, woven or embroidered with figures, landscapes, or ornamental devices, and used as a lining or covering for the walls of apartments. It is probable that many of the early tapestries were embroidered by hand or worked with the needle. This kind of work, of which the Bayeux tapestry is a celebrated example, was continued long after the practice of weaving tapestry in the loom had become common

The 16th century, which was an age of general improvement in France, gave a new impulse to the production of tapestry. Francis I. founded the manufactures of Fontainebleau, in which threads of gold and silver were skilfully introduced into the work. It was, we are informed, with this new impulse that the practice was commenced of weaving tapestry in a single piece, instead of composing it, as before, of several small pieces joined together. Francis spared no pains in the encouragement of this department of the fine arts. He engaged Flemish workmen, whom he supplied with silk, wool, and other materials, and paid liberally for their labour; and documents exist to prove that he also patronized the tapestry-makers of Paris. Henry II., the son and successor of Francis, continued to encourage the manufactory at Fontainebleau, and established a manufacture of tapestry on the premises of the Hôpital de la Trinité, which attained its highest celebrity in the reign of Henry IV., and produced many fine tapestries. In 1594 Du Bourg, the most eminent artist connected with this establishment, made there the celebrated tapestries of St. Meri, which were in existence until a recent period; and these pleased Henry IV. so much, that he determined to re-establish the manufacture of tapestry at Paris, where it had been interrupted by the disorders of the preceding reigns. This he did in 1597, bringing Italian workers in gold and silk to assist in the work. In 1605 were laid the foundations of new edifices for the tapestry-weavers, in the horse-market at Paris; and at that time, or a little later, Flemish workmen were engaged to superintend the manufacture. The establishment languished, if it did not become quite extinct, after the death of Henry IV.; but when the royal palaces, especially the Louvre and the Tuileries, were receiving their rich decorations, in the reign of Louis XIV., his minister Colbert revived it, and from that time the celebrated royal tapestry manufactory of the Gobelins dates its origin. Foreign artists and workmen were engaged, laws were drawn up for the protection and government of the manufactory, and everything was done to render it, what it has continued to be, the finest establishment of the kind in the world. Le Brun, when chief director of the establishment, made many designs for working after; and M. de Louvois caused tapestry to be made from some of the finest designs of Raphael, Julio Romano, and other Italian painters. The manufacture declined greatly at the Revolution, but was revived under the government of Napoleon, and has ever since been carried on successfully, though by no means to the same extent as formerly.

The introduction of tapestry-weaving into England is usually attributed to a gentleman named Sheldon, late in the reign of Henry VIII. At Burcheston were worked in tapestry, on a large scale, maps of Oxfordshire, Worcestershire, Warwickshire, and Gloucestershire, some fragments of which were, it is stated, in Walpole's collection at Strawberry Hill. Little more is known of this establishment. James I. endeavoured to revive the manufacture of tapestry by encouraging and assisting in the formation of an establishment at Mortlake, about 1619, under the management of Sir Francis Crane. James I. gave 2000*l*. towards the formation of this establishment. After the Restoration, Charles II. endeavoured to revive the manufacture, and employed Verrio to make designs for it, but the attempt was unsuccessful. During its period of prosperity, this manufacture produced the most superb hangings, after the designs of celebrated painters, with which the palaces of Windsor Castle, Hampton Court, Whitehall, St. James's, Nonsuch, Greenwich, &c., and many of the mansions of the nobility, were adorned.

In the primitive method of working tapestry with the needle, the wool was usually applied to a kind of canvas, and the effect produced was coarse and very defective; but some finer kinds of tapestry were embroidered upon a silken fabric. The process of weaving by the loom, after the manner known as the *haute lisse*, or high warp, was practised in the tapestries of Flanders as early as the 14th and 15th centuries; the only essential difference between these and the productions of modern times being that previously noticed, the comparative size of the pieces woven in the loom. The weaving of tapestry, both by the 'haute lisse' and the 'basse lisse,' appears to be of Oriental invention; and the difference between the two methods may be briefly described. In the 'haute lisse' the loom, or rather the frame with the warp threads, is placed in a perpendicular position, and the weaver works standing; while in the 'basse lisse' the frame with the warp is laid horizontally, and the weaver works in a sitting position. In weaving with the 'basse lisse,' which is now relinquished, the painting to be copied is laid beneath the threads of the warp, which are stretched in a manner resembling that of common weaving, the pattern being supported by a number of transverse threads stretched beneath it. The weaver, sitting before the loom, and leaning over the beam, carefully separates the threads of the warp with his fingers, so that he may see his pattern between them. He then takes in his other hand a kind of shuttle, called a *flûte*, charged with silk or wool of the colour required, and passes it between the threads, after separating them in the usual way by means of treddles worked by the feet. The thread of woof or shoot thus inserted is finally driven close up to the finished portion of the work by means of a reed or comb formed of box-wood or ivory, the teeth of which are inserted between the threads of the warp. In this process the face of the tapestry is downwards, so that the weaver cannot examine his work until the piece is completed and removed from the loom. The frame of the 'haute lisse' loom consists of two upright side-pieces, with large rollers placed horizontally between them. The threads of the warp, which usually consist of twisted wool, are wound round the upper roller, and the finished web is coiled round the lower one. The cartoon, or design to be copied, is placed perpendicularly behind the back or wrong side of the warp, and then the principal outlines of the pattern are drawn upon the front of the warp, the threads of which are sufficiently open to allow the artist to see the design between them. The cartoon is then removed so far back from the warp that the weaver may place himself between them with his back towards the former, so that he must turn round whenever he wishes to look at it. Attached to the upright side-pieces of the frame are contrivances for separating the threads of the warp, so as to allow the *flûte* or broach, which carries the woof, to pass between them. Like the weaver with the 'basse lisse,' the operator works, as it were, blindfolded; but by walking round to the front of the loom he may see the progress of his work, and may adjust any threads which have not been forced into their right position by the reed or comb, with a large needle, called an *aiguille à presser*. The process of working with the 'haute lisse' is much slower than the other, and is indeed almost as slow as that of working with the needle. Lady Wilton, in describing the productions of the Hôtel Royal des Gobelins, observes that 'not the least interesting part of the process was that performed by the *rentrayeurs*, or fine-drawers, who so unite the breadths of the tapestry into one picture, that no seam is discernible, but the whole appears like one design.' Now, however, the pieces are woven so wide that joining is very seldom resorted to, even for the largest pieces.

TAPIOCA. [MANDIOC.]

TAR is obtained from wood or coal by distillation in close vessels, or in piles from which the air is excluded. *Pitch* is obtained by boiling tar until all the volatile matters are driven off. Tar is a viscid brown semi-fluid mass, which long preserves its softness. If it be mixed with water, the water acquires a yellow colour and the taste of tar, with slightly acid properties. This solution is well known by the name of tar-water, and has been used in medicine. Tar is soluble in alcohol, in æther, and in the fixed and volatile oils. Oil of tar, creasote, and many other valuable substances, are obtained from tar.

Tar is extensively manufactured from the roots and branches of pines and firs in Norway, Sweden, Germany, Russia, North America, and other countries in which those trees abound; but that made in the north of Europe is considered far superior to what is produced in the United States. A conical cavity is made in the ground (generally in the side of a bank or sloping hill), and the roots of the fir, together with logs and billets of the same, being neatly trussed in a stack of the same conical shape, are let into this cavity. The whole is then covered with turf, which is well beaten down. The stack of billets is kindled, and a slow combustion of the fir takes place, without flame, as in making charcoal. During this combustion the tar exudes; and a cast-iron pan being at the bottom of the funnel, with a spout which projects through the side of the bank, barrels are placed beneath this spout to collect the fluid as it comes away. As fast as the barrels are filled, they are bunged, and made ready for exportation.

In some parts of France and Switzerland tar is extracted in a kind of oven or kiln, built of stone or brick in the form of an egg, with its smaller end downwards.

As England requires a large quantity of tar for the navy, the supply from foreign countries is an important matter. At different periods the high price of Swedish tar has led to the encouragement by government of the making of tar in the British American colonies. During the American war, attention was paid to the establishment of the manufacture of tar from pitcoal, an object which had been previously attempted; but the manufacture of coal-tar has not proved so important as was at one time anticipated, although for some purposes it is deemed superior to that made from wood. Tar is produced in large quantities in the manufacture of coal-gas; but in some districts its value is considered so trifling that it is mixed with the fuel by which the retorts are heated. It is usually separated from the gas by condensation.

The tar imported in the last three years amounted to the following quantities:

1848................	12,609 lasts.
1849................	15,206 ,,
1850................	12,096 ,,

This last named quantity is equivalent to about 5,000,000 gallons. Tar is free from import duty.

TARTARIC ACID was first obtained in a separate state by Scheele; it exists in several vegetable products, but principally in bitartrate of potash, which is usually called *cream of tartar*, a salt which is deposited from wine.

Tartaric acid is colourless, inodorous, and very sour; it occurs in crystals of a considerable size, the primary form of which is an oblique, rhombic prism; it suffers no change by exposure to the air; water at 60° dissolves about one-fifth of its weight, and at 212° twice its weight. It combines readily with alkalies, earths, and metallic oxides; and these salts are called *tartrates:* many of them are usefully applied in the arts.

Tartaric acid is largely employed as a discharge in calico-printing, and for making what are called sodaic powders, which are imitations of soda-water.

Tartaric acid is entirely confined to the vegetable kingdom, and is found free or uncombined in tamarinds, in the unripe grape, and in pepper; and in combination in tamarinds, ripe grapes, gooseberries, mulberries, squill, dandelion, chenopodium vulvaria, in various species of pines, and as tartrate of lime in the fruit of the *Rhus typhina*.

TEA. Though now so extensively employed, the introduction of tea into Europe is of comparatively recent origin. Pepys in his 'Diary,' writes, Sept., 25, 1661, 'I sent for a cup of tea (a Chinese drink), of which I had never drank before.' The Dutch East India Company probably first introduced it into Europe, and from Amsterdam it was brought to London.

The species of the genus *Thea* are few in number. Some botanists are of opinion that even these are varieties of a single species called *Thea Chinesis;* but there are usually said to be two species yielding green and black tea respectively. The Asam tea-plant, which has lately attracted so much attention, seems to partake of the characters of both of the foregoing, and is regarded by some botanists as a distinct species. Tea is cultivated in China over a great extent of territory. Dr. Wallich mentions it as being cultivated in Cochin-China, in 17° N. lat. We know it is cultivated in the southern provinces of Yunnan and of Canton. If we proceed north we find the principal cultivation of teas for the foreign trade is between 27° and 31° N. Lat.; but tea is said to be produced in several places to the northward of 31°; even in 36°, and also in the Japanese Islands, which extend from 30° to 41° N. lat.

The culture of the tea-plant in China seems simple enough. The plants are raised from seeds, sown in the places where they are to remain. Several are dropped into holes four or five inches deep and three or four feet apart, shortly after they ripen; or in November and December, as they do not preserve well, from their oiliness. The plants rise up in a cluster when the rain comes on, and require little further care, except that of removing weeds, till they are three years old, when they yield their first crop of leaves. They are seldom transplanted, but sometimes four to six plants are put close together, so as to form a fine bush. After growing seven or ten years they are cut down in order that the numerous young shoots which then spring out may afford a more abundant supply of leaves. In some districts the bushes grow unrestrained, in others they are regularly pruned, to keep them low. The gathering of the leaves is performed with great care: they are usually gathered singly, first in March or May (according to the district), when the young leaves are scarcely expanded; the second about two months later, or May and June; and the third in August, or about six weeks after the second; but the times necessarily differ in different districts, as well as the number of crops which are obtained, some avoiding the third for fear of injuring the bushes. When the leaves are gathered they are dried in houses which contain small furnaces, on each of which there is a flat iron pan, and upon this, when heated, the leaves, partially dried by exposure to the sun, are thrown; the leaves require frequent shifting and turning. When all are properly dried, they are quickly removed either by the hand or with a shovel, and either thrown upon a mat or into baskets which are kept ready to receive them. They are then removed to a table where they are rolled and cooled, and the process is repeated; after which they are sifted and sorted into several varieties.

The most difficult part of this question is to determine whether the green and black teas are produced by one or two distinct species of plants, as the statements of apparently equally well qualified judges are not only contradictory, but directly the reverse of each other. The Chinese tea-makers in Asam and those in Java alike state that the black and green trees may be prepared from the same plant.

. Tea having become so extensive an article of commerce, and a source of considerable revenue, various attempts have been made to introduce it into other countries; but the climates are very different in which the several experiments have been made, as in Rio Janeiro and the warm part of Brazil, and latterly in the hilly parts of Java and Brazil, in Penang, Asam, and the Himalayas. Favourable reports are given of the teas grown in the East Indies, but as yet only small quantities are brought into the European markets. [Asam.]

The first importation by the English East India Company took place in 1660 from the Company's factory at Bantam. The directors ordered their servants to 'send home by their ships one hundred pounds weight of the best *Tey* they could get.' In 1678 were imported 4713 lbs., but in the six following years the entire imports amounted to no more than 410 lbs. According to Milburn ('Oriental Commerce'), the consumption in 1711 was 141,995 lbs.; 120,695 lbs. in 1715; and 237,904 lbs. in 1720. In 1745 the amount was 730,729 lbs. In 1844 it was 41,363,770 lbs. The tea consumed in the United Kingdom, and the revenue which it yielded, in 1848, 1849, and 1850, were as follows:—

1848	48,347,789 lbs.	5,329,992*l.*
1849	50,021,576 lbs.	5,471,422*l.*
1850	51,178,215 lbs.	5,597,707*l.*

There have been great changes in the taxes levied on tea. In 1835 the excise duty on tea was repealed from and after July 1, 1836, when a customs' duty of 2*s.* 1*d.* per lb. was levied on all sorts of tea, which, with 5 per cent. added in 1845, makes the duty now paid 2*s.* 2¼*d.* per lb.

For above a century and a half the sole object of the East India Company's trade with China was to provide tea for the consumption of the United Kingdom. The Company had an exclusive trade, and were bound to send orders for tea, and to provide ships to import the same, and always to have a year's consumption in their warehouses. The teas were disposed of in London, where only they could be imported, at quarterly sales. The act of 1834 opened the trade to China. The importation of tea is no longer confined to the port of London, and the trade has increased both in the quantity and variety of the exports to China.

The tea-duty produces about one-twelfth of the total revenue. In 1801 it was 1,423,660*l.*, in 1844, 4,524,193*l.* The amount in later years is stated above. As it was foreseen that on the opening of the tea trade there would be a considerable reduction in price, so that an *ad valorem* duty would not, even with the increased consumption, be so productive as formerly, a fixed duty was imposed. Up to 1836, each of the hundred thousand tea-dealers in the United Kingdom was visited once a month by the officers of excise, who took an account of his stock; and no quantity exceeding 6 lbs. could be sent from his premises without a permit, of which above 800,000 were required in a year. Tea is now sold by the importing merchants by public auction and private sales.

The duty on tea is still too high, and it is certain that an increased consumption would follow a diminution of the duty.

Russia is supplied with about 7,000,000 lbs. of tea annually through Kiakhta; France requires about 2,000,000 lbs.; and Holland about 3,000,000 lbs. With the exception of China no other country consumes so much tea as England. The tea-trade of the United States is, however, rapidly increasing. In 1850 there were 173,317 chests of green tea and 91,017 of black tea exported from Canton to America; these quantities with a further portion purchased from England, made a total of about 23,000,000 lbs. of tea which crossed the Atlantic in 1850.

Tea, like many other commodities is too frequently adulterated with various substances,—tests for detecting which are pointed out by Dr. Normandy. The same authority tells us that the much advertised *veno beno*, for 'improving' the flavour of tea, is nothing more than a mixture of catechu with broken tea leaves.

TEA, PARAGUAY, or **MATÉ,** is the produce of a plant belonging to the family *Aquifoliaceæ*, which is a shrub attaining the size of the orange tree. The leaves of this shrub are in great repute amongst the inhabitants of South America, and are used in infusion in a similar manner to the tea of China. Upwards of 5,000,000 lbs. of the leaves of this tree are annually collected in Paraguay, and are sent to Chili and Buenos Ayres. After the branches have been cut away, the ground is heated by means of a fire, and the leaves, being laid upon the heated ground, are dried, and afterwards they are beaten and pressed into bags, in which state they come into the market. The plant when used is steeped in boiling water, to which a little sugar and sometimes lemon-juice is added. It is drunk out of a vessel called *Maté*, which has a spout perforated with holes for the purpose of preventing the powdered herb from passing out with the fluid. The Creoles are passionately fond of this infusion, and rarely partake of a meal without it. The properties of this plant are sedative and stimulant.

TEAK. The teak-tree is a native of different parts of India, as well as of Birma, chiefly along the banks of the Irawaddy, and of the islands from Ceylon to the Moluccas. The teak-tree grows to an immense size, and is remarkable for its very large leaves, which are from 12 to 24 inches long and from 8 to 16 broad, and are compared by Oriental writers to the ears of the elephant.

From extensive experience teak timber has been found the most valuable timber for ship-building, and has been called the oak of the East. The wood is light, brownish-coloured, easily worked, but at the same time strong and durable. It is soon seasoned, and, from containing a resinous oil, resists the action of water, as well as insects of all kinds.

Some interesting details have lately been published concerning the export of teak-timber from Moulmein in India. Teak is the principal article of export from that province, both in quantity and value. During the year 1849 upwards of 25,000 tons were shipped to various parts of the world, all properly converted, by hand or machinery, of a value estimated in the rough at 100,000*l.* The teak of these provinces and the surrounding foreign states, which finds its way into Moulmein, is of a very superior quality, and unequalled for ship-building purposes by any other wood in the world. The annual supply is more than the demand, in consequence of this port being but little known to the English ship-owners and builders. There is almost an unlimited extent of teak forests in the neighbouring states, of superior quality, and easily worked. The price of first-rate converted squares and planks is 3*l.* per ton of 50 cubic feet, of lengths ranging from 25 feet to 50 feet, and from 10×10 to 24×24 inches square. A vessel arriving here at any time of the year can always procure a cargo, provided she is supplied with funds, or a credit on a good Calcutta house. The time calculated for loading is ten working days for every 100 tons, although a vessel of a large size generally loads much quicker on account of the stowage being easier. In consequence of the abundance of teak to be had at this port, it is likely to become the first building port in India. It has already turned out some of the finest ships now afloat, and as strength and durability are much sought after, this place is most advantageously situated for building good vessels.

TEAZLE (*Dipsacus Fullonum*) is a plant which grows wild in the hedges, but an improved variety is carefully cultivated in those districts of England where cloth is manufactured. It is used for the purpose of forming a species of brush with which the finer hairs of the woollen fabric are drawn to the surface, where they produce what is usually called the *nap* of the cloth. The teazle has a fine hooked awn, which very readily insinuates itself into the woollen web, and draws out with it some of the fine fibres of the wool; these are afterwards shorn smooth, and leave the cloth with the fine velvet-like nap which is its peculiar appearance.

Teazles will grow in any soil; but they grow

strongest and best in a stiff loam. The wild teazle which grows in hedges appears at first sight to be the same as the cultivated variety; but it is of no use to the cloth-worker, from the weakness of the awns, which break off, instead of drawing the wool out of the surface of the web. The growing of teazles is a peculiar trade, and a kind of speculation, for the crop is very precarious. The teazle-grower hires a piece of ground suited to his purpose from the farmer for two years, and pays a considerable rent.

The dressing of a piece of cloth consumes a great number of teazles; as many as 1,500 to 2,000 being required to do the work properly. The teazles are made up in bundles for sale to the clothiers, containing 9,000 or 10,000 each. The price is affected by so many circumstances, that it varies from 4*l.* to 20*l.* per pack or bundle; but when the home price exceeds about 8*l.* the clothier can import more cheaply from abroad.

TELEGRAPH. We may class these useful contrivances in two groups—the *Mechanical* and the *Electro-Mechanical Telegraphs:*—Most of the older telegraphs consisted of boards or wooden arms, which according to the positions assumed, signified the letters of the alphabet. The kind generally used in France at the end of the last century was the T telegraph of M. Chappe. Four arms shaped something like a T were moved on three joints at the upper angles. M. Chappe communicated his intelligence letter by letter, and simplified the movements by using an alphabet of only sixteen letters. Such telegraphs were first erected on a line commencing at the Louvre, in Paris, and proceeding by Montmartre and other elevated points to Lisle, in order to communicate between the Committee of Public Safety and the combined armies in the low countries.

The advantages of such extraordinary celerity of communication were so obvious that, in England and other countries, many plans were immediately brought forward, some of which differed materially from that which had been successfully put in practice in France. These plans are mostly separable into two classes: shutters which open or close certain apertures made to receive them; or arms moveable on pivots. A shutter-apparatus, submitted to the Admiralty in 1795, by Lord George Murray, was adopted in the first government line of telegraphs established in England, in 1796, between London and Dover. It was employed by the Admiralty until 1816.

In 1816 it was determined to change the Admiralty telegraphs into semaphores constructed on the principle of those used in France, with the improvements suggested by Sir Home Popham. These semaphores had been introduced on the French coast in 1803. They consisted of upright posts with two or three moveable arms. Sir Home Popham's telegraph had two arms on one post; but as they were mounted upon separate pivots, each of them could assume six different positions, and the two together were capable of affording 48 signals. This kind of telegraph continued to be used at the government stations till the introduction of the electric telegraph.

Several modes of telegraphic communication without machinery, or with something which may be held in the hands, have been devised, especially for the purpose of directing military operations, or of conveying speedy intelligence in time of war, where no line of ordinary telegraphs can be established. One such method was by circular discs of wood held by men in particular positions; another by a white handkerchief varied in position; another by two small flags; and another by stationing a few men in pre-arranged positions, &c.

Marine telegraphic communication is an object of even greater importance than that on land, since there are many circumstances which render communication between vessels at sea impracticable by any other means than by signals, and that sometimes in cases of the greatest emergency. But, although naval signals have been necessarily long used, and flags of various forms and colours have been extensively employed for the purpose of making them, it was not till within a comparatively recent period that they were reduced to anything like an efficient telegraphic system. Lord Howe proposed a system of numbering the flags used as signals, and also prepared a signal-book which was long used by the Admiralty. An improved code of signals, suggested by Sir Home Popham, was afterwards adopted. A very useful system of flag telegraphing was introduced a few years ago by Mr. Watson, for the use of commercial shipping, and for maintaining communication between a vessel at sea and any of the stations on the coasts of the British islands, whence communication might be made by telegraph inland.

Electric Telegraphs.—It is chiefly to the joint labours of Messrs. W. F. Cooke and Professor Wheatstone that electric telegraphs owe their practical application. Their telegraph, which was patented in 1837, acted upon principles founded on Oersted's celebrated discovery, that a magnetic or compass needle may, through the agency of a voltaic current, be invested with an artificial polarity. The first line was laid down upon the London and

Blackwall Railway; the second from London to West Drayton; and the third (in 1849) from London to Gosport.

In Messrs. Cooke and Wheatstone's first apparatus there were five needles, arranged with their axes in a horizontal line. The needles when at rest hung vertically, by reason of a slight prependerance given to their lower ends. Each electro-magnetic coil was connected with one of the long conducting wires at one end, and was united at the other with a common rod of metal, which joined together the similar ends of all the coils. The current was transmitted from the opposite end of the wires (where an appropriate set of five pairs of finger-keys, for making the connections with the battery, was placed) through two of the wires at once. In accordance with the keys which were pressed down, the needles assumed various positions with respect to each other; and these were made to indicate signals according to the entries in a signal book. The instruments at the two stations were always rendered reciprocating; that is, at each end of the line were placed an instrument, a set of finger-keys, and a voltaic battery, so that either station could transmit or receive a signal. By a beautiful arrangement, a bell or alarum could be rung, when the attention of the clerk at the distant terminus was required. In 1838 Mr. Cooke obtained a patent for some further improvements of this apparatus.

Dr. Steinheil constructed an electric telegraph between Munich and Bogenhausen in 1837. In his telegraph he availed himself of the conducting power of the earth, whereby he was enabled to reduce the cost of erection. The earth in fact occupied the place of the return wire. All that is necessary to enable this to be effected, is that the wire which connects the two ends of the metallic conductor with the earth, shall be carried to a sufficient depth below the surface to be always in contact with moist earth or with water; and that it shall be at this point attached to a plate or piece of metal, of about two or three feet superficial. The electric telegraph invented by Professor Morse, of America, in 1837, was essentially a registering instrument, the various signals being traced on a strip of paper. An electro-magnet was so placed as to be within attracting distance of an armature fixed to the shorter arm of a lever, of which the longer end carried a pencil projecting sideways from it, and pressed lightly against a sheet of paper. This paper was made to travel slowly beneath the pencil. So long as no attractive power was exerted by the electro-magnet, the pencil would continue to trace a straight line as the paper moved onwards; but on momentarily making the circuit with the battery, the armature was drawn to the electro-magnet, and the pencil, carried by the arm of the lever upwards, made an angular mark, like the letter V reversed, on the paper. These angles might either be joined in groups, by rapidly succeeding completions of the circuit, or they might be separated by longer or shorter spaces of straight line. In the telegraph constructed by Morse in 1844, between Baltimore and Washington, a different mode of recording the signals was adopted. The use of the pencil was found objectionable, from its so frequently requiring fresh pointing, and from the risk of breakage. The same arrangements were retained in regard to the paper, but it was made in its course to pass under a roller having a groove around it. The long arm of the lever carried a blunt steel point, standing out from its upper surface, vertically under the groove in the roller. When therefore the arm of the lever was elevated, by the attraction of the magnet upon the armature, the steel point pressed the paper into the groove and produced an indentation. If the attraction were momentary, a depressed point was produced; but if the action were continued for a longer time, a lengthened depression was the result, as the paper was drawn on. The combinations of these two kinds of marks, denoted the various letters and figures.

In the year 1837 Mr. Davy of London obtained a patent for an electric telegraph, the chief peculiarity of which consisted in the method of registering or recording the various communications, by causing the current of a supplementary battery to pass through a riband steeped in a solution of iodide of potassium and starch. The salt being decomposed by the current, a blue spot was produced by the combination of the iodide with the starch, and the position of one or more of these spots across the breadth of the riband determined the nature of the signal transmitted.

In 1840 Professor Wheatstone patented his electro-magnetic telegraph, in which the indicating power was the magnetisation of soft iron by the electric current, instead of the employment of a real or permanent magnet. One part of the apparatus is the Communicator, a wheel or disc, on the edge of which are alternately arranged pieces of iron and of ivory, the one a conductor and the other a non-conductor of electricity. A metal spring presses on this edge while the wheel revolves, and is connected also with the galvanic apparatus, in such a way that when the spring is in contact with the iron, a galvanic circuit is completed, but when in contact with the ivory the circuit becomes broken. Thus alternations of action are produced, which by ingenious mechanism are made the means of transmitting impulses or symbols through the telegraphic wire. This telegraph requires only a single wire for its use, the return of the current being provided by the earth. One application to which Professor Wheatstone found his invention suitable was that of an *Electric Clock*, by adapting his wheel and galvanic apparatus to the action of the escapement wheel of a common clock.

In 1840 Mr. Bain, in conjunction with Mr. Barwise, patented a clock which was to be set in motion by electricity; and in the next following year he brought forward a new electric printing telegraph. The essential principles of this telegraph are two. First, the employment of type, mounted on the periphery of a disc or wheel, capable of revolving with its edge carrying the type very near to a cylinder covered with white paper, between which and the type-wheel a piece of transferring paper or riband is placed; the cylinder has a small movement in a spiral direction communicated to it, after each impression of a signal. The second principle is that of the use of two clocks at the two communicating stations, to rotate the type-wheels with a uniform motion. These clocks, having been adjusted to exactly the same rate, and being started from the same signal, would bring continually, at each station, similar type opposite to the paper cylinders at the samo moment. A hand or index revolving on a dial in front of the machine, at the same rate as the type-wheel, indicates to the operator the signals which are successively in a position ready for printing in his own instrument, and therefore, if the clocks go accurately together, in a similar position in his correspondent's instrument.

In 1842 Mr. Bain patented his proposed plan for working an electric telegraph with a peculiar form of battery. At one end of the line he buried in moist earth a large plate of zinc, and at the other end a plate of copper, iron, or other substance, such as coke or charcoal, which might act the part of a negative plate to the zinc. Then on connecting these distant plates with a wire insulated from the earth, a current of electricity would constantly pass from the one plate to the other. This system has been found insufficient at long distances.

In 1843 Mr. Cooke specified his patent for the mode of insulating the wires by suspending them in the air upon posts or standards of wood or iron; the wires not coming in actual contact with any part of the standard, but passing through rings of porcelain or earthenware. The standards are usually fixed at from forty to sixty yards asunder, and at each quarter of a mile a stouter post is placed, to bear the winding or straining apparatus. The intermediate posts within each quarter of a mile merely supported the wire, without reference to its tension, which depended solely on the winding posts. Instead of the copper wires hitherto employed, iron wires of a larger size were then used. Before this period the wires had been placed in iron tubes buried beneath the ground; but this new form of arrangement was deemed an improvement, and has since been generally acted on in this country.

Since the year last named, the progress of the electro-telegraphic system has been exceedingly rapid. In 1846 an Electric Telegraph Company was formed, by whom the patent rights of Messrs. Cooke and Wheatstone, and some of those of Mr. Bain, were purchased. It is this company which has carried out the greatest part of what has been recently effected in Great Britain. Nearly all the principal railways, except the Great Western, have had lines of telegraphic wire laid by it. A modification of Cooke and Wheatstone's arrangements is generally employed; but the company also possesses a remarkable printing or rather registering telegraph invented by Mr. Bain. A long strip of paper has small holes stamped in it by means of a machine, each hole or group of holes representing a particular letter. This paper is coiled on a wooden roller, from whence it passes to a metal roller, where metallic points act upon it. The arrangement of the mechanism is such, that when the metallic points touch the metal of the roller, through the holes in the paper, a galvanic circuit is completed; but when the points touch the paper itself, the circuit is stopped; and this rapid alternation is made to indicate signals. There is also a recipient apparatus, in which the strip of paper employed has been first soaked in diluted sulphuric acid, and then in a solution of prussiate of potash. Two metallic points press on this paper; and when a galvanic current is passing through these points, they discolour the chemically-prepared paper, and leave a number of dark spots upon it; but when no current is passing, no discolouration is produced. By an ingenious arrangment of mechanism, the recipient apparatus at the end of the telegraphic wire marks with its dark spots the signals which are conveyed by the transmitting apparatus at the other end.

In the form which the English telegraphic system has now assumed, all the stations are placed in connection with the central office in Lothbury. At this office are departments for transmitting messages to and receiving messages from almost all parts of the kingdom. There are several rooms, each of which has its own electric clock, showing Greenwich time, and its own electro-telegraphic machine. Wires pass from the machines to the great hall, and from the hall to the outside of the building, whence they pass under the pavements of the London streets to the great railway termini at Euston Square, Shoreditch, London Bridge, Waterloo Road, &c., as well as to the Admiralty and one or two other Government establishments. Along the lines of railway the telegraphic wires and apparatus are so arranged as to be available both for the railway company's own purposes, and for commercial purposes in general; and a system has been formed whereby information of a commercial character is regularly transmitted to and from the great centres of industry and commerce.

Mr. Whishaw, in a paper communicated to the British Association in 1849, gave an account of the telegraphic systems followed in three countries, Great Britain, Prussia, and the United States. In Great Britain the wires are suspended on poles. The length of railway to which the system had been applied down to July 1849, was about 2000 miles; and the cost was about 150*l.* per mile. In Prussia the telegraphic wires were suspended on the English system until the year 1844, since which date a new plan has been followed. The wires are coated with gutta percha, and laid along under ground, at a distance of about two feet beneath the surface, not only under railways, but under turnpike roads and towing paths. There are at each principal station two telegraphic machines, one colloquial and one printing. The length of Prussian telegraph to July 1849, was about 1500 miles, at a cost of about 40l. per mile. In the United States the telegraphic line is formed by a single iron wire supported from post to post. It is carried not only along railways, but across the open country. There were in July 1849, about 10,500 miles of American telegraph, at a cost of about 20l. per mile.

Various improvements in electro-telegraphic machines have been patented from time to time by Messrs. Brett and Little, and other inventors; but those which seem most likely to be attended with important results relate to Submarine Telegraphs. It has been proved that wires may be so coated with gutta percha and other materials as to act under water. A tube so constructed has been carried under the sea between Dover and Calais; and the first communication by electric telegraph was made from Cape Grisnez to Dover on August 28, 1850. The length from Dover to Cape Grisnez is 21 miles. The copper wire was $\frac{1}{10}$th of an inch in thickness, and was enclosed in a solid cylinder of gutta percha, $\frac{1}{2}$ of an inch in diameter. The entire length of wire was 25 miles, and its weight was 1 ton 2 cwt. 1 quarter $10\frac{1}{2}$ lbs. The weight of the gutta percha was 4 tons 7 cwts. 1 quarter 9 lbs.

Wherever the railway system has extended, there does the electro-telegraphic system find more or less of encouragement; and in the United States the telegraphic wires extend also over vast tracts of country where no railways are yet laid down. In respect to our own country, the contrivances of Messrs. Cooke and Wheatstone have hitherto been those most generally adopted; but there is at the present time (May 1851) an attempt being made to form a new telegraphic company; and if this attempt succeed, we shall probably see many new and efficient mechanical arrangements adopted.

One of the most recent electro-magnetic instruments, partaking of the nature of the electric telegraph in some of its features, is Mr. Shepherd's ingenious clock at the Industrial Palace.

The experiments made in the British Channel have shewn that the submarine Telegraph is practicable; and we shall probably see, ere long, the adoption of the system between England and France, and between England and Ireland. The proposed oceanic telegraph between England and America may well afford to wait till the fruition of the less gigantic schemes.

TELESCOPE. Such telescopes as are constructed with glass lenses only are called *dioptric*, or *refracting* telescopes; whereas those which have a reflecting speculum are the *catoptric*, or *reflecting* telescopes. By these instruments objects even in the remotest depths of space are rendered accessible to human vision; and terrestrial objects faintly visible in the distance are brought as it were close to the eye. There is evidence to show that Roger Bacon, who died in 1292, knew that lenses might be so combined as to make objects seen through them appear to be magnified. No further indications of telescopes are met with till after the middle of the 16th century, when Dr. Dee suggested that the commander of an army, who wants to discover the number and arrangement of an enemy's troops, 'may wonderfully help himself by perspective glasses.' In 1609 Galileo constructed a telescope, with which he discovered the four satellites of the planet

Jupiter. Huygens, Dr. James Gregory, Sir Isaac Newton, Dr. Hooke, Dr. Bradley, Sir Wm. Herschel, Mr. Dollond, and Lord Rosse, have since been the persons most distinguished for the improvements which they have respectively made in the construction of telescopes.

To explain the optical principles which govern the action of telescopes would be beyond the scope of the present volume; but we may briefly explain differences of construction.

The telescope invented by Galileo consisted of one convex lens and one concave lens; the distance between them being equal to the difference between the focal lengths of the two lenses. This is the construction of what is called an *Opera Glass;* and the Galilean telescope is now used chiefly for viewing objects within a theatre, or an apartment; since if considerable magnifying power were given to it the extent of the field of view would be very small.

A simple telescope may also be constructed by means of two convex lenses, which are placed at a distance from one another equal to the sum of their focal lengths.

In order to afford a view of objects in the samo position as they appear to have when seen by the naked eye, Mr. Dollond employed an eye-tube containing four lenses; whereas in the eye-piece invented by Huyghens, which is used in most astronomical telescopes, there are only two lenses, and objects are seen inverted.

In reflecting telescopes, a speculum at one extremity of the tube serves the purpose of the object-glass in refracting telescopes by forming an image at its focus; and the image so formed is viewed by the eye through intermediate reflectors. The *Newtonian* reflecting telescopes have one concave speculum at the bottom of the tube; and the rays reflected from it fall in a convergent state upon a small plane mirror placed so as to make an angle of 45° with the axis of the telescope: after the second reflection the rays unite and form an image which is viewed through a Huygenian eye-piece fixed in the side of the tube, opposite the plane mirror; that is, near the open end of the tube. In the *Gregorian* reflecting *telescope* the second reflection is given by a second concave mirror, the face of which is towards the observer.

The telescope constructed by the late Sir Wm. Herschel differed from the Newtonian telescope only in having no small mirror. The surface of the great speculum, which was 4 feet in diameter, had a small obliquity to the axis, so that the image formed by reflection from it fell near the lower side of tho tube at its open end: at this place there was a sliding apparatus which carried a tube containing the eye-glasses. The observer in viewing was situated at the open end of the tube, with his back to the object, and he looked directly towards the centre of the speculum. The reflecting tolescope executed by Lord Rosse in 1842 is 56 feet long, and its speculum is 6 feet in diameter. It is capable of being directed from the zenith to the horizon towards the south, and from the zenith to a position parallel to the earth's axis towards the north; it has also a movement in azimuth of about 8 degrees on each side of the meridian.

Tho Great Exhibition contains a noble telescope by Mr. Ross, which is, we believe, the largest ever constructed on the *refractive* principle.

TELFORD, THOMAS, was one of those invaluable men whose engineering labours form the best memento of their personal history. He was the son of a shepherd in Eskdale, Dumfriesshire, where he was born in 1757. At the age of fourteen he was apprenticed to a stone-mason in the town of Langholm. In 1780, being then about twenty-three, he went to Edinburgh, where he seems to have devoted much attention both to architecture and drawing. After remaining there about two years, he removed to London, and obtained employment at Somerset House, then erecting by Sir William Chambers. He was employed upon various buildings at Portsmouth dockyard for three years subsequent to 1784; and in 1787 he was employed by Sir William Pulteney to make some alterations at Shrewsbury Castle. He thereupon removed to Shrewsbury, where he was also employed to erect a new gaol, and was subsequently appointed county surveyor, in which office he had to furnish plans for and oversee the construction of bridges and similar works. He erected the iron bridge over the Severn at Buildwas, besides about forty smaller bridges in the same county.

The Ellesmere Canal was the first great work upon which Telford was engaged; and from 1793, in which year the act of parliament for its construction was obtained, his attention was directed almost solely to civil engineering. The aqueduct-bridge over the valley of the Dee, called the Pont-y-Cysylte, is a remarkable work. It consists of a trough of cast-iron plates, securely flanged together, and supported by eighteen piers or pillars of masonry, the elevation of which is 121 feet above the water. These gigantic works were executed between 1795 and 1805. The Caledonian Canal, which was opened throughout in 1823, is another of Telford's principal works. The locks were the largest ever constructed at that time, being 40 feet wide, and from 170 to 180 feet long. Of other canals constructed wholly or partially under Telford's superintendence it is sufficient to mention the Glasgow, Paisley, and Ardrossan; the Macclesfield; the Birmingham and Liverpool Junction; the Gloucester and Berkeley (completed under his direction); the Birmingham, which was completely remodelled, and adapted to the conduct of a very extensive traffic, by him; and the Weaver navigation, in Cheshire. He also constructed a new tunnel, 2,926 yards long, 16 feet high, and 14 feet wide, at Harecastle, on the Trent and Mersey Canal. He also executed many important works connected with the drainage of the fen country, especially of Bedford Level. On the Continent he superintended the construction of the Gotha Canal, in Sweden, a navigation of about 120 miles, of which 55 are artificial canals. For this work a Swedish order of knighthood and other honours were conferred upon him.

The works executed by Telford under the Commissioners of Highland Roads and Bridges were of great importance; and in the improvements of the great road from London to Holyhead, under another parliamentary commission, appointed in 1815, Telford had a further opportunity of carrying into effect his system of road-making. The Menai suspension bridge especially is a noble example of his boldness in designing and practical skill. [Menai Bridges.]

Among other works of Telford are many bridges of considerable size, in which he adopted the important principle of making the spandrils hollow, and supporting the roadway upon slabs laid upon longitudinal walls, instead of filling up the haunches with a mass of loose rubbish, which often proves of serious inconvenience when the masonry of the bridge needs repair.

Telford executed some important harbour works at Aberdeen and Dundee; but his most striking performance of this class is the St. Katherine Docks, London.

In addition to the works which he executed himself, Telford was frequently applied to for his judgment upon important schemes, and in this way he made many reports to parliament. The Russian government frequently applied to him for advice respecting the construction of roads and canals; and the Emperor Alexander acknowledged his sense of his services, in 1808, by sending him a diamond ring with a suitable inscription. He closed his useful life in 1834, and was buried in Westminster Abbey.

TELLU'RIUM, is a metal discovered in 1782 by Müller of Reichenstein. Its colour is silver-white, and it is very brilliant; it is crystalline and brittle, of a lamellar fracture, easily pulverised. Its specific gravity is about 6·13. It is nearly as fusible as antimony, and at a high temperature it boils, and may be distilled. When strongly heated in contact with air, it burns with a lively blue flame, green at the borders, and forms a white vapour, which has an acid odour.

The principal ores of tellurium are *Native Tellurium*, both crystalline and massive, *Graphic* or *Auro-Argentiferous Tellurium*, *Yellow Tellurium*, *Black Tellurium*, *Bismuthic Tellurium* or *Telluret of Bismuth*. But neither the ores nor the various chemical combinations of the metal have yet been applied to many useful purposes.

TEMPERING. [Steel Manufacture.]

TENACITY. This property is a result of the attractions and repulsions which act within the insensible spaces supposed to exist between the particles of bodies: it is consequently different in different materials, and in the same material it varies with the state of the body with respect to temperature and other circumstances. The particles of liquids adhere to one another, and generally to those of solid bodies, by attractive forces which decrease very rapidly; and, at insensible distances from the supposed places of contact, the adhesion entirely disappears. It is on account of the small distance to which the attraction of the fluid molecules extend, and to the freedom with which the particles move on one another, that fluids appear to have so little tenacity; but from the weight which it supports in glass tubes, Dr. Robison has estimated that the mutual attractions of the particles of water on a surface equal to one square inch must far exceed 190 lbs.

Though, when a piece of metal is fractured, the parts will not by simple adjunction adhere together; yet, in some cases, by hammering them upon one another, so many points on their surfaces may be brought within the limits to which the force of cohesion extends, that they will acquire a tenacity equal to that which the metal had in its natural state.

The tenacity of wood is much greater in the direction of the length of its fibres than in the transverse direction, the fibres being united by a substance having little cohesive power. With respect to metals, the processes of forging and wire drawing increase their tenacity in the longitudinal direction; the augmentation of friction and lateral cohesion, arising from the particles being forced together in the transverse direction, more than compensates for the diminution of the attraction which may result from the particles being forced or drawn farther asunder longitudinally. Copper and iron have their tenacity more than doubled; while gold, silver, brass, and lead have it more than tripled, by those metals being drawn into wire.

TENNESSEE. The industry and commerce of this portion of the American Union are briefly adverted to under UNITED STATES.

TERRA COTTA. This is the Italian for *baked earth*, and is the name applied to the material with which many of the coarser varieties of Italian pottery are made. The Etruscan Vases, whatever may be the devices on the surface, are made of Terra Cotta. [ETRUSCAN WARE.] At the Mediæval Exhibition of 1850 there were many fine specimens of terra cotta ware; and in the Etruscan room at the British Museum the collection is especially fine. There is a church near Bolton, in Lancashire, in which the chief material employed, at least in the ornamental parts, is terra cotta; and terra cotta ware finds a fitting place among the articles of pottery at the Great Exhibition.

TESSELLATED FLOORS. Mr. Ward, in the Introductory Essay to Mr. Owen Jones's beautiful work on Mosaic Pavements, says:—"The materials of the best and costliest pavements at Rome (such, for example, as those still remaining in the Baths of Caracalla) are coloured marbles of various kinds, differing considerably from each other in hardness and durability. The inferior pavements, found scattered through Britain, France, and other parts of Europe, and along the western coast of Africa, are usually made of such coloured stones as the neighbourhood happened to supply; with the exception only of the red tesseræ, which are almost invariably of burnt clay. Thus, in the celebrated Roman pavement which was discovered in 1793, at Woodchester in Gloucestershire, the gray tesseræ are of blue lias, found in the vale of Gloucester; the ash-coloured tesseræ of a similar kind of stone, often found in the same masses with the former; the dark brown of a gritty stone, met with near Bristol, and in the Forest of Dean; the light brown of a hard calcareous stone, occurring at Lypiat (two miles from the site of the pavement); and the red tesseræ (as usual) of burnt brick."

The tesseræ, or small cubic pieces of the Roman pavements, are by no means uniform in shape and size; the fissures between them are wide and irregular; and as these fissures are filled up with cement, a muddy hue is given to the general tints.

In the beginning of the present century, Mr. Wyatt introduced the plan of inlaying stone tesseræ with coloured cements. In later methods, *terra cotta* tesseræ have been inlaid in a similar way. Mr. Blashfield adopted the plan of forming the tesseræ of cements coloured with metallic oxides. Bitumen, coloured with metallic oxides, is another material employed. Mr. Singer introduced a plan of forming tesseræ by cutting pieces of the required form out of thin layers of clay; which pieces are afterwards dried and baked, and united by a peculiar cement. In another plan, adopted at the Worcester porcelain works, tiles of two colours are formed by pressing a device on slabs of clay, and pouring liquid clay of another colour into a sunk device on the surface of the former.

In Mr. Prosser's method, small tesseræ are formed by compressing porcelain powder into moulds with great force, in the manner described under BUTTON MANUFACTURE. The tesseræ may be of any colour—white, black, red, blue, yellow, brown; and of any definite form—triangular, quadrilateral, rhomboidal, hexagonal, &c. In the formation of a floor or pavement with such tesseræ, the pieces are first put together in their proper order, placed downward on a smooth surface; and as soon as a sufficient portion of the design is finished, it is backed with fine Roman cement, which is worked in to fill the crevices between the tesseræ. The pavement is thus formed into smooth flat slabs of convenient size, which are laid down on any properly prepared foundation.

Although it belongs more to inlaying or marquetry than to tessellated pavements, we may say a word or two concerning the beautiful floor of the new Coal Exchange. It is a circular floor 60 feet in diameter, and is formed of 4,000 pieces of wood, arranged into a star-like pattern of great beauty, bearing some resemblance to a mariner's compass. All the wood formed portions of living trees within a short period pefore the floor was made; the pieces having been prepared by the Drying or Dessicating process of Messrs. Davison and Symington. In this respect the floor is an exemplar of a highly useful and important manufacturing invention. The kinds of wood employed are ebony, black oak, red oak, common oak, white holly, mahogany, elm, red walnut, white walnut, and mulberry.

TE'SSERA. The Roman tesseræ were small cubes or squares resembling our dice, which were used by the ancients for various purposes, and formed of different materials, as marble, precious stones, ivory, glass, wood, or mother-of-pearl. Such small tesseræ of different colours were used to form the mosaic floors, or pavements in houses, which were hence called *tesselata pavimenta.* (See the preceding article.) The same kinds of cubes were used by the ancients as dice in the games of hazard, just as in our times.

TESTS, CHEMICAL, or Chemical Reagents, are those substances which are employed to detect the presence of other bodies, by admixture with which they are known to produce certain changes in appearance and properties.

TEXAS. This region—once a portion of Spanish America, then a state of republican Mexico, then an independent republic, and now one of the United States—is still in the infancy of its industrial development. Bituminous coal is said to be abundant in the interior, and iron ore is also plentifully distributed. Building stone is abundant in all parts except the sea coast region. Gold, silver, copper, and lead, have been found in the mountainous parts of the State. Oak, pine, and other large timber trees, are abundant along the courses of the rivers and upon the slopes of the mountains. Texas is stated to have climates and soils suitable for maize, wheat, oats, barley, and rice; for apples, pears, figs, melons, and oranges; for the vine, olives, and mulberries; for the sugar-cane and the cotton plant; and in fact for almost every kind of grain, fruit, and vegetable.

The rise of a great commercial community from these elements has yet to take place.

TEXTILE MANUFACTURES. The spinning and weaving of fibres into a web are the general type or representative of textile manufactures. It is difficult to say whether these or metallic manufactures are the most important; but the textile take the lead in respect to our exports. The amount of these exports, and the nature of the processes, are noticed under the names of the respective goods — such as COTTON, FLAX, FUSTIAN, GAUZE, LACE, LINEN, MUSLIN, RIBBON, SHAWL, SILK, VELVET, WOOLLENS, &c.; while the manufacturing statistics are glanced at under FACTORIES, and under the names of the chief textile manufacturing towns and counties.

THAMES. The navigation of this most busy of English rivers commences at Lechlade, where the river is about 258 feet above low-water mark at London Bridge. The Thames and Severn Canal, which follows the valley of the Churn and the Thames from near Cirencester, opens into the Thames at Lechlade, thus connecting it with the Severn and the western coast of the island. At Oxford the Oxford Canal joins the Thames, and opens a communication with the great canal system of the central counties. At Abingdon the Wilts and Berks Canal joins the Thames and, as well as the Kennet and Avon Canal, which joins the Kennet at Newbury (where the navigation of that river commences, 20 miles above its junction with the Thames), opens a communication with the Somersetshire Avon and by it with the Severn. The Thame is navigable from the town of Thame, about 17 miles above its junction with the Thames. The Wey is navigable from Godalming, about 17 miles from its junction; and is connected with the Wey and Arun Canal, and the Basingstoke Canal, the former of which opens a communication with the river Arun and the Sussex coast. The Grand Junction Canal, which unites with the Oxford Canal at Braunston in Northamptonshire opens into the Thames by the mouth of the Brent, the lower part of which is incorporated with the Canal. Below London Bridge the Lea, which is navigable, chiefly by artificial cuts, for 25 miles, opens into the Thames; and just above the Lea, the Regent's Canal, which encircles the north and east side of the metropolis, and communicates with the Paddington Canal, and so with the Grand Junction Canal, also opens into the river.

The Medway is navigable below Rochester Bridge for sea-borne vessels, and from Penshurst, above 43 miles from its mouth, for river craft.

The navigation of the Thames, in its upper part, is kept up by locks and wears, the lowest of which is at Teddington, which is consequently the limit of the tide. Teddington is about 18 or 19 miles above London Bridge. High-water mark at Teddington is about 1¼ feet higher than at London Bridge, and the time of high water is about two hours later. Low-water surface at Teddington is about 16¾ feet higher than at London Bridge. At ebb tide there is a depth of from 12 to 13 feet water nearly or quite up to London Bridge, and the rise of the tide is about 17 feet, or at the extreme springs about 22 feet.

Vessels of 800 tons get up to the St. Catherine's Docks, and those of 1400 tons to Blackwall, about 6 miles below bridge. No other river in the world equals the Thames in its commercial importance. The river for some 2 miles or more below London Bridge is crowded with vessels, chiefly coasters, steam vessels, and colliers, which moor alongside the quays or in tiers in the stream; others are moored lower down, though not in such numbers; and for larger vessels there are several docks excavated on the banks of the river.

There is a dockyard for the navy (now little used) at Deptford, about 4 miles below London Bridge; one at Woolwich, 9 miles below; one at Sheerness, in the Isle of Sheppy, at the junction of the Thames and Medway; and one at Chatham, the most important of the four, on the Medway. The fortifications at Sheerness defend the entrance to both rivers; the passage of the Thames is further protected by Tilbury Fort, and that of the Medway by Gillingham Fort.

Among many engineering schemes for improving the banks of the Thames within the limits of the metropolis, is the following by Mr. W. H. Smith:—It is proposed that a terrace, about 12 feet above high-water mark, designed exclusively for the public, and without any landing places except for passengers, should be carried along the banks of the Thames. The width of the esplanade is to be 60 feet, having a parapet and open railing on the side next the river; thus offering a clear view of the general traffic, but at the same time, by means of the parapet, securing the operations of commerce beneath. This esplanade is connected immediately by carriage approaches with the bridges and main thoroughfares. Where the width of the river is sufficient to admit the space required, it is proposed there should be lines or colonnades of handsome shops, dwellings, or warehouses, according as the situation might require. The goods' traffic of the river is conveyed by transverse arches beneath, descending to within a foot of high water, which are connected with the property of the wharfs and warehouses on the inner side, the river traffic being thus carried on unimpeded and almost invisibly. Immediately beneath is a railway tunnel, in the base of which the required culverts for pure water, gas, rain water, and sewage, would be formed at about low-water mark. It is proposed that the sewage should be entirely cut off from the river, passed longitudinally under the embankment by means of an iron culvert, and carried into the marshes on the southern side of the river beyond the influence of the tide. The probable expense of this great undertaking, extending from Vauxhall to the West India Docks on the north, and from Vauxhall to Deptford on the south, Mr. Smith estimates at about 3,000,000*l*.

THATCH is a covering of straw, rushes, or reeds, as a substitute for tiles or slates for houses, barns, ricks, stacks, and sheds. We will first describe the mode of thatching hay ricks and corn stacks, as the simplest.

The rick or stack having been formed into a proper shape, either with a roof slanting from a ridge, or conical, ending in a central point, the straw is prepared by moistening it, that it may more easily bend without breaking. It is then forked up in a loose heap, the straws lying in every direction, and somewhat matted. Portions are now drawn out from this heap in handfuls, which lays the straws again in a more parallel order: these are placed in a forked stick, which will hold several of these bundles or handfuls, and are thus carried to the thatcher on the top of the rick or stack. He seizes a handful, and bending one end into a kind of a noose, he inserts this into the hay or straw near the bottom of the roof, at one end if it be a square roof, or at any convenient part if it be a round one. He presses down the straw which he has thus inserted to about half its length, in order to form the eaves, which extend a little beyond the lower part of the roof. When he has thus laid several handfuls side by side so as to cover about a yard in width, that is as far as he can conveniently reach without moving his ladder, he begins another row a little above the place where he began, so that the lower end of the straw now inserted may cover the upper part of the first row, as tiles do each other. Thus he proceeds upwards till he comes to the upper ridge of the roof, or to the point of the cone in a round stack. In the latter case the covering diminishes to a point so as to form a triangle. The ladder is now shifted a yard to one side, and the same operation is performed, care being taken that each fresh handful put on shall be interwoven with that which lies beside it, so that no water can possibly pass between them. Thus the work proceeds until the roof is completed, and it only remains to secure the upper ridge in a square stack, or the point of the cone in a round one. In the first case the highest layer of straw is made to extend beyond the ridge on both sides, and the ends are brought together and stand up like the bristles on a hog. A rope of straw has been prepared, and many small rods, about two feet long, and cut sharp at the point: these are inserted just below the ridge, in a line with it, and about a foot apart; one end of the straw rope is inserted into the stack, and twisted firmly round the projecting end of the first rod; it is then wound once round the next rod, and so on the whole length of the ridge: this is done on both sides. The straws which form the ridge are now cut with shears horizontally, to give it a neat finish, and at each end a kind of ornament is usually made by winding a straw rope round a handful of the projecting straw, forming a kind of knot or bow, according to the taste of the thatcher. Rods and straw ropes twisted round them are inserted near the edge of the slanting side and all along the eaves, which prevent the wind from blowing off the thatch.

The only difference in the thatch of a round rick is, that it is brought to one point, where it is tied with straw rope wound round it, and formed into a kind of bow; the rods are inserted a little below in a circle, and a straw rope twisted round them, and likewise around the circular eaves. Barley is generally put into square stacks, and wheat in round ones. When the outside is neatly trimmed and cut smooth, so that no birds can lodge in it, wheat may be kept for years without danger of injury or loss, much better than in a barn, or even in a granary.

In thatching sheds and buildings which are to last many years, the straw is prepared in the same manner, but the ends of the handfuls, as they are put on a lathed roof, are kept down by means of long rods, which are tied to the laths of the roof by means of strong tar twine. A much thicker coat of straw is put on; and rye-straw, which has a solid stem, is preferred, as more lasting, and less liable to be filled with water than hollow straw. Instead of straw ropes, split willow is used, and the rods which are inserted are much nearer each other and more carefully secured. As this kind of thatching is a peculiar trade, it requires a regular apprenticeship to be master of it.

THEIN is the neutral vegetable principle obtained from common tea, and supposed to be identical in its nature with *caffein*, the peculiar principle of coffee. It forms tufts of white delicate silky needles, which have a bitter taste, melt and lose water when heated, and sublime without decomposition.

THEOBROMA. For the best known products of the theobroma plants, see COCOA and CHOCOLATE.

THEODOLITE is the name generally given to the instrument used for measuring horizontal angles. In its simplest form the theodolite consists of a divided circle, which is to be set parallel with the horizon, and a telescope which has so much motion in a vertical plane as to enable the observer to view any object which he may require above or below the horizon.

THEORBO is a musical instrument of the lute kind, which has long fallen into disuse. The upper and middle strings were attached to the lower head or nut; the lower, or base strings, to an upper or additional one. [LUTE.]

THERMO'METER is an instrument by which the temperatures of bodies are ascertained. It consists of a glass tube with a capillary bore containing in general alcohol or mercury. When the liquid expands or contracts by variations in the temperature of the atmosphere, or by the instrument being immersed in the liquid or gas which is to be examined, the state of the atmosphere, liquid, or gas, with respect to caloric, is indicated by a scale which is either applied to the tube or engraven on its exterior surface.

The end proposed by a thermometer is the measurement of the temperature of any body with relation to the temperature of some other substance, as of water at the point of freezing; but the measure so obtained must not be understood to express the absolute quantity or density of caloric in any body, it being well known that different substances, though exhibiting the same apparent temperature, contain very different quantities of caloric according to their *capacities* for that element.

The thermometer was in use in the beginning of the 17th century, but it is not known precisely to whom the honour of the invention is due. A physician of Padua named Santorio, in his 'Commentaries on Avicenna' (1626), claims it for himself. It may however have happened with this, as with other scientific discoveries, that the idea of the instrument occurred to two persons or more about the same time.

The earliest kind of thermometer consisted of a long glass tube containing air, which was hermetically sealed at the upper end, while the lower was made to enter into a vessel of coloured spirit. By the pressure of the atmosphere the spirit was made to occupy part of the tube; and the variations in the temperature of the atmosphere causing the column of spirit to ascend or descend in the tube, allowed the degree of temperature to be measured by a scale applied to the latter. The defects inseparable from such thermometers are, that the dilatations of the air are not proportional to the increments of heat, and that the length of the column of spirit varies with the temperature of the atmosphere. Thus the indications afforded by the thermometer are rendered erroneous, or require corrections which it is difficult to apply.

About the middle of the 17th century the members of the Academia del Cimento caused thermometers to be constructed in which, instead of air, alcohol, or spirit of wine, was employed. Alcohol dilates and contracts considerably with the variations of temperature to which it may be subject, though not in so great a degree as air. It is also capable of measuring very low temperatures but; as it is brought to a boiling state sooner than any other liquid, it cannot be employed to ascertain a high degree of heat.

The idea of employing mercury for the

purpose of measuring degrees of heat by its expansion is supposed to have first occurred to Dr. Halley. The invention is ascribed to Römer, but it was not till 1724 that such a thermometer was known in this country. The advantages of mercury over alcohol and air, as a measure of temperature, are, that its expansions are more nearly proportional to the increments of caloric than those which take place in either of the other fluids; it is easily deprived of air; and its power to conduct heat being considerable, the changes of its volume by changes of temperature in the surrounding medium take place more rapidly than those of any other fluid except the gases.

The scale which has been in general use in this country since the year 1724, is supposed to have been invented by Fahrenheit. It is quite unknown on what ground he made choice of the fixed points on his scale, or the number of graduations between them; but it is thought that one of the fixed points was that of boiling water, and that the other, which is the zero of the scale, was that at which the top of the column stood when the instrument was exposed to an intense cold in Iceland, in 1709. The extent of the scale between this last point and that of boiling water is divided into 212 parts, and the point of freezing water is at the thirty-second division from the zero point. That which is called Réaumur's scale has the interval between the points of freezing and boiling water determined by experiment, and the distance between them is divided into eighty parts, the zero of the scale being at the freezing point. A third scale, called 'Centigrade,' has been much in use among the philosophers of the Continent within the last fifty years. It was invented by Celsius, a Swede, and it differs from that of Réaumur only in the distance between the points of freezing and boiling water being divided into 100 parts. The length of each degree in this thermometer, as well as in that of Réaumur, is greater than in the scale of Fahrenheit.

According to the experiments of Mr. Dalton, mercury does not boil till it has acquired a temperature equal to 660° of Fahrenheit's scale; and it does not freeze till it is subject to a degree of cold expressed by 39 divisions below the zero of that scale, or 71° below the freezing-point of water. Pure alcohol, on the other hand, has never been frozen, though it has been exposed to a degree of cold exceeding that which is expressed by 91° below the zero of Fahrenheit; and therefore a spirit thermometer is to be preferred to one of mercury when it is intended to ascertain the temperature of the air in high northern or southern latitudes: but since the spirit boils in air with a degree of heat expressed by 175° of Fahrenheit, it is unfit for many of the purposes for which a thermometer is required. For instruments capable of measuring very high temperatures, see PYROMETER.

Register Thermometers.—It is of great importance in meteorology that the observer should be able to ascertain the highest or lowest point of a thermometer scale at which the column of mercury may have stood during his absence; and several contrivances have been adopted by artists in order to obtain this end. Of these, one, which is still preferred, was invented by Mr. Six, whose name the instrument bears; it is described in the 'Philosophical Transactions' for 1782. It consists of a long tube bent so as to form three parallel branches, of which the central branch is an elongated bulb, and the rest of the tube has a capillary bore. The lower portion of the bent tube contains mercury, which rises in the two side branches to certain points, and the bulb is filled with spirit of wine, which passing over a bend at the top descends to the upper extremity of the mercury in one of the branches; the upper end of the other branch is also filled with spirit, and this is hermetically sealed. Two small indices of steel, coated with glass, are introduced in the branches, and are capable of being forced upwards by the rising of the column of mercury in either tube, and they have about them a fine wire or a thread of glass; so that they will remain stationary where they happen to be when the heads of the columns recede from them. Their lower extremities consequently indicate the points at which the ends of the columns may have stood before such recess.

Differential Thermometer.—This instrument, which was invented by M. Sturmius, of Altdorf, before the year 1676, and was revived by Professor Leslie in 1804, consists of two thermometer tubes, terminating, at one extremity of each, in a hollow glass ball, and containing coloured sulphuric acid: the opposite extremities are united by the flame af a blow-pipe, and an enlargement of the bore is made, at the place of junction. The tube is then bent so as to form three sides of a rectangle, the two balls, which are of equal diameter forming the upper extremities of two sides; and the instrument is on a stand with the branches of the tube in vertical positions. When the temperature of the air in the two balls is the same, the acid occupies one side and the base, and rises a little way up the other side of the rectangle. To the latter side is attached a graduated scale, with the zero of which the upper extremity of the acid in that branch should coincide. In the event of this adjustment being deranged, it may be restored by causing a small quantity of air to pass from one ball to the other, which is done simply by the warmth of a hand applied to that ball from whence the air is to be driven.

Radiating Thermometer.—[ACTINOMETER.]

THERMOSTAT. This name has been given by Dr. Ure to an apparatus invented by him, for regulating temperature in vaporization, distillation, heating baths or hothouses, ventilating apartments, and other applications of heat. It operates upon this physical principle,—that when two thin metallic bars of different expansibilities are riveted or soldered facewise together, any change of temperatnre in them will cause a sensible movement of flexure in the compound bar, to one side or other; which movement may be made to operate, by the intervention of levers, &c., in any desired degree, upon valves, stop-cocks, stove-registers, air-ventilators, &c. In this way the temperature of the space in which the compound bar is placed may be regulated. Two long rulers, one of steel, and one of hammered brass, answer very well. There are many forms which the apparatus may present, according to the purpose to which it is to be applied.

THIBET. [TIBET.]

THIMBLE. Thimbles are usually formed by means of a stamping machine; but the following method is sometimes practised in France:—Sheet-iron, one twenty-fourth part of an inch thick, after being cut into strips of convenient size, is passed under a punch-press, by which it is cut into circular discs of about two inches diameter. These discs are then made red-hot, and laid in succession upon a series of mandrils, with hollows of successively increasing depth, into which the softened discs are forced by striking them with a round-faced punch, about the size of the finger. After being thus brought to the required shape, the thimble is placed in a lathe, when the inside is polished and the outside is turned and ornamentally finished. Iron rings used in the rigging of ships are in some instances called thimbles.

THRASHING MACHINE. The separation of the grain from the ear in corn is effected in different ways. The finest and ripest grains for seed are extracted by simply beating the corn on a table or flat board. The most usual method is by means of the *flail*, an instrument so formed as to strike a large extent of corn at one time. The flail, by means of its long handle, is swung round the head; and the beating part of it is made to fall horizontally on the straw which is spread on the thrashing floor; and by inserting this part occasionally under the straw, the latter is turned over, and a fresh portion is brought up to be beaten.

In a serene and dry climate, corn may readily be thrashed out in the manner described in the Bible; viz., by levelling a portion of the corn-field, laying the corn in the straw in a large circle, and driving oxen or horses over it till the grain is all trodden out. Such a method as this, however, is not suited for an English climate.

Modern times have seen the introduction of *thrashing machines*, which perform the operation with much rapidity. The general construction may be thus briefly described. A rapid motion is given to a hollow cylinder round a horizontal axis; on the outer surface there are projecting ribs parallel to the axis, at equal distances from each other. Around half the cylinder is a case, the inner surface of which is lined with plates of cast-iron, grooved in the direction of the axis. The ribs or beaters come quite close to these grooves, so that an ear of corn cannot well pass between them without being flattened. The corn is drawn in between two rollers, and the beaters act on the straw so as to beat out most of the corn. The grain falls through the meshes of a sieve, but the straw is retained until removed by rakes.

Many modifications of are adopted by different makers, but the above gives a pretty general idea of the mode of action. Such an apparatus is usually worked by a horse; but there are also hand-machines, which are profitably worked where hand labour is cheap, but where there are no skilful flailmen. There is a peculiar system adopted in some counties, in which a hand-thrashing machine is taken from farm to farm by the owner, who lends and superintends the machine, while the farmer supplies horses and men, a stipulated price being paid to the machine owner, to the mutual advantage of both parties.

The most complete thrashing machines are those which are worked by steam power. In some of the best and largest farms a steam-engine is kept to the thrashing, the chaff-cutter, and other agricultural implements. At the recent agricultural and cattle shows, the thrashing machines made by Garrett, Crosskill, Wedlake, Hensman, &c., have been shewn in great variety; and many such have been sent to the Great Exhibition.

THREAD MANUFACTURE. Sewing-thread, and the various kinds of thread used in the manufacture of bobbin-net, lace, and some other kinds of textile fabric, consist of two or more *yarns*, or simple spun threads, firmly united together by twisting, just as a rope-strand consists of several yarns or distinct cylinders of hemp.

The operation of combining yarns of cotton or linen into thread is performed by a machine called a *doubling* and *twisting frame*, somewhat resembling the throstle of the cotton-spinner. Along the centre of the machine is an elevated creel or frame-work, which supports two parallel rows of cops or bobbins of yarn, one row towards each side of the machine. From the cops the yarns are conducted over horizontal glass rods, which are fixed parallel with the creel, and thence downwards into troughs filled with water or very thin starch-paste, which, by moistening the yarns, facilitates the subsequent process of twisting. After being wetted, the yarns pass over the rounded edge of the trough, which is covered with flannel for the purpose of absorbing the superfluous moisture; and thence under and partly around an iron roller, which is made to revolve with any required velocity by a train of wheel-work. Upon this roller rests another, of box-wood, which revolves solely by contact with the iron roller, its axis playing in vertical slots. In passing under the iron roller, then between it and the wooden roller, and finally over the latter, the yarns required to form the thread are brought together and slightly compressed; and they are finally twisted by apparatus very like that used in throstle spinning. A few details concerning the export of thread are given under the names of the materials employed.

THUNDER-ROD, is a rod of metal attached generally to a side of a building, and extending from below the level of the ground to a point several feet above the highest part of the roof of the building, in order to secure the edifice from the effects of thunder or lightning: the upper extremity of the rod or bar terminating in a point. It is to Dr. Franklin that the world is indebted for the idea of raising pointed rods in order to secure buildings from the effects of atmospherical electricity; and the recommendation was immediately adopted both for edifices on land and ships on the water.

The thunder-rod should be thick enough to carry the electric fluid to the ground without being melted by it; in general a cylindrical rod about half an inch in diameter will be sufficient to prevent this effect from taking place; whether of iron or copper, it should be covered above ground with a coating of paint; and the part under ground is usually formed with two or more branches in order to facilitate the passage of the electric fluid to the earth.

A ship at sea, like an edifice on land, may, when there is an accumulation of electric matter in the upper part of the atmosphere, be struck aloft; or, when the atmosphere is in a contrary state, the lower part of the ship may be struck, the lightning in the latter case ascending along the mast: and ships unfurnished with metallic conductors have frequently suffered serious injury during thunder-storms, while those which have been so provided have generally escaped. The rigid bars of Franklin are considered inapplicable, as conductors, to ships, and instead of them chains of copper have been generally employed; these are attached to the masts at their upper extremities; and, following the standing rigging, they pass down the ship's sides into the water. In 1822 Mr. (now Sir W.) Snow Harris proposed, and subsequently caused to be executed for ships, conductors consisting of slips of copper, of sufficient thickness to prevent them from being fused; these slips are inserted, in two layers, in a groove cut longitudinally along the mast, the joints of one layer being opposite to the middle parts of the other, and they are fastened to the mast by copper screws. The whole line of metal passes down from the copper spindle at the top of the mast-head, and at the junctions of the upper and lower masts the ship is made to join a cylinder of copper which lines each sheave-hole; the lower part of the line is connected with a plate of copper which is fixed on the keelson, at the step, and from thence there is a communication with the water by three copper bolts which pass quite through the keel. This improvement by Sir W. Snow Harris, has proved to be a most valuable one; the safety thereby ensured to the royal shipping, (so far as the effects of lightning are concerned), represents, in money value, a sum which must be immense, however difficult to estimate.

TIA'RA, was a kind of hat, in ancient times worn by the inhabitants of Middle and Western Asia, especially by the Persians, Parthians, Armenians, and Phrygians. There were two kinds of tiaras: the upright tiara was used by kings, priests, and other persons of the highest rank, and the upper part had frequently the shape of a crown; the tiara worn by other people was of a soft and flexible material, so that it hung down on one side, as in the case of the so-called Phrygian bonnet. In modern times the term tiara is applied to the head-dress of the popes, which is worn on solemn occasions, and consists of a triple crown. Hence it is also used in a figurative senso to designate the papal dignity.

TI'BET. Among the minerals of this elevated, but little known region of Asia, are gold, silver, copper, tin; salt, which is taken from the salt-lakes of Jayek and Deng-tsavga; corundum stone, lapis lazuli, turquois, and agate. Besides a great number of grasses which are common in Europe, Tibet produces a kind of barley, grapes, asafœtida, rhubarb, madder, safflower, apples, nuts, apricots, peaches, pomegranates, and figs, in the valleys. The cedar grows in Tibet. Among the animals there are wild oxen with long hair, buffaloes, the buffalo which is called the yak, goats with a very fine fleece, goats with long fine hair, silk-worms, wild cats, tigers, leopards, lynxes, argali with horns of 100 lbs. weight, pigs, white eagles, and swans. Of the industry and commerce of Tibet, we have very little trustworthy information.

TIDE GAUGE. The phenomena of the tides relate too intimately to physicial science to come fittingly under notice in this work; but *tide-gauges*, such as that recently erected at Sunderland, are too important to commerce to be passed over here.

Mr. Meik, the engineer of Sunderland has invented and registered a tide-gauge, for the use of ships entering or leaving a harbour. In a tidal harbour the number of ships which can enter or leave during one tide depends on the time, the depth, and the rapidity of the tidal flow; and Mr. Meik wished to produce some sort of gauge which should indicate these conditions, in a way intelligible to ordinary seamen, at the busy port of Sunderland, by night as well as by day. In conjunction with Mr. Watson, a brass founder at Newcastle, Mr. Meik has carried out his project at Sunderland in the following way.

There is a vertical tube, up which the water rises to a greater or less height according to the state of the tide. A float is borne on the surface of the water; and a copper wire from this float passes upwards to a train of wheels and rollers, which rotate in one or other direction according as the float rises or sinks. A web of wire gauze passes from one roller to another; on this web are painted in large letters the various depths from high to low water; and two fixed pointers also indicate the number of feet and half feet of depth of water, at any hour of the tide, on the bar at the entrance of Sunderland harbour. By day the figures on the web are shown white on a black ground; by night they appear distinctly lighted up, the ground still remaining dark. A white transparent varnish is used for the figures, and an opaque black for the ground.

There are also *tide registering gauges* employed at some ports. There is a vertical tube, into which the water of a river or harbour can enter from beneath, rising to a greater or less height according to the tide. A float is on the surface of the water, and a copper wire passes upwards from the float to a rack which holds a pencil. There is a cylinder, on the surface of which is fastened a sheet of paper, properly ruled for the purpose, and large enough to receive the entries for fourteen days. A time piece gives an equable motion to the cylinder; and as the point of the pencil is in contact with the cylinder, a waving line becomes marked on the paper, passing *round* the cylinder as time progresses, and passing *along* the cylinder according as the tide rises and falls. There thus results a permanent record of the height of the tide at every hour and even minute of the day.

TIFLIS, or TEFLIS, the capital of the Russian province of Georgia, is most favourably situated to be the medium of an extensive transit trade between Europe and Asia; the rich Armenian bankers and merchants of the town have the chief direction of this trade, which however is now carried on mainly through the Turkish port of Trebizond, and thence by caravans to Persia and Bushire. Recent relaxations in the Russian tariff on goods in transit are likely however to turn the course of this trade again through the Georgian port of Redout-Kalé, Tiflis, and the Caspian. The enterprising Armenians of Tiflis trade extensively with Odessa, Trieste, Leipzig, Nishnei-Novgorod, Persia, Bokhara, Thibet, and Cashmere.

TILE MAKING. In the ancient buildings of Greece and Rome, tiles were made of various materials, among which were baked clay, marble, and bronze. They were made flat, or with a raised border along each edge, or semicircular on their lower edges.

The process of making tiles is so similar to that of brick-making [BRICK], that it will be sufficient to observe that only the best qualities of brick-earth are fit for the purpose. The roofing tiles used in this country are chiefly of two sorts, *plane-tiles*, which are flat, of a rectangular form; and *pan-tiles*, which also have a rectangular outline, but are bent in such a manner that, when laid on the roof, the greater part of their surface forms a concave channel for the descent of water, while one side forms a narrow convex ridge, which overlaps the edge of the adjoining tile. Tiles of a semi-cylindrical form, laid in mortar with their convex or concave sides uppermost, respectively, are used for covering ridges and gutters. Drain-tiles are most commonly made in the form of an arch, and laid or bedded upon flat tiles called *soles*.

TILT-HAMMER, is a large hammer worked by machinery, impelled either by a water wheel or a steam engine. Such hammers are extensively used in the manufacture of iron and steel; and the name *Tilt-Mill* is sometimes applied to the mechanism of which they form the principal feature. [STEEL MANUFACTURE.]

TIMBER. The name of timber-trees is most usually applied to such trees as oak, ash, and elm, of the age of twenty years and upwards; but there are many other kinds which may fittingly be designated by the same name. The characteristics of these various sorts of timber are described under the several names [ELM; FIR; OAK; &c.]

The preservation of timber from dry rot and other symptoms of injury is a very important feature in connexion with ship-building and civil engineering. A few details on this subject will be found under the headings ANTISEPTICS and DRY ROT.

The timber subject to Customs Duties on importation is designated by various names according to sizes and forms into which it is cut. *Battens, batten ends, boards, deals, deal ends, planks,* and *staves*, are the principal among these names. The following were the imports in 1850, classified according to the custom-house arrangements:—

Battens, batten ends, boards, deals, deal ends, and planks, entered by tale or No., 34 hundred.

Deals, battens, boards, and other sawn or split timber, entered at per load, 796,108 loads.

Staves, 82,588 loads.

All kinds of timber not included in the above enumeration 870,571 loads.

The gross amount of duty received on these imports was 655,232*l.* Measures are now (May 1851) under consideration of parliament, for a reduction in the timber duties.

TIME-KEEPERS; TIME-PIECES. [CHRONOMETERS; CLOCKS and WATCHES.]

TIN. This metal is one of those which were earliest known, though it occurs in comparatively few countries. It is found in England, Saxony, Bohemia, Hungary, the isle of Banca, the peninsula of Malacca, in Chili, and Mexico. Malacca furnishes the purest tin, and Cornwall the largest quantity. It occurs in two states of combination, the *Peroxide of Tin* and the *Double Sulphuret of Tin and Copper:* this last is rather a rare substance, and it is from the former that the metal is almost entirely obtained.

The peroxide is found in Cornwall in combination with other metals, in *Tin-Stone;* and in loose rounded masses called *Stream-Tin.* The former, when reduced to the metallic state, yields *Block-Tin;* while the latter yields *Grain-Tin*, which is the purer of the two. The tin-stone, which contains 77 per cent. of pure tin, occurs in a crystalline form, as well as in masses; but stream-tin is uncrystallised, and has evidently been derived from the destruction of tin veins or lodes, the lighter portions of stony matter having been carried away by the water, which has rounded the fragments of the ore.

This metal is of a silver-white colour, very soft, and so malleable that it may be reduced into leaves 1-1000th of an inch thick, called tin-foil: it suffers but little change by exposure to the air. Its tenacity is but slight, so that a wire of 1-15th of an inch in diameter is capable of supporting only about 31 lbs.: a bar a quarter of an inch in diameter was broken by 296 lbs. weight. Tin is inelastic, but very flexible, and when bent it produces a peculiar crackling noise. When rubbed it imparts to the fingers a peculiar smell, which remains for a considerable time. Its specific gravity is about 7·29: at 442° Fahr. it fuses, and if exposed at the same time to the air, its surface is tarnished by oxidation, and eventually a gray powder is formed. When heated to whiteness it takes fire, and burns with a white flame, and is converted into peroxide of tin. If slowly cooled after fusion, it exhibits a crystalline appearance on solidifying.

The combinations which tin forms with oxygen, chlorine, sulphur, and iodine, and those which the oxide of tin forms with the various acids, are valuable in calico printing and many other of the practical arts.

Most of the malleable metals are rendered brittle by alloying with tin. It combines readily with potassium and sodium, forming brilliant white alloys, which are less fusible than tin. With arsenic it forms a metallic mass which is whiter, harder, and more sonorous, than pure tin. With antimony tin forms a white, hard, and sonorous alloy. Bismuth forms with tin an alloy which is more fusible than either of the metals separately, a mixture of equal weights melting at 212°; this compound is hard and brittle. Copper and tin form alloys which are well known and highly useful—*Bell Metal* and *Bronze.* With mercury tin readily amalgamates, and the compound is used for silvering mirrors. Tin forms with iron white compounds, which are more or less fusible according to the proportion of iron they contain. Tinplate is of all the alloys of tin the most useful, and the preparation of this and of pewter are the most extensive applications of this very valuable metal.

TIN MANUFACTURE. The ores of tin raised in Cornwall and Devonshire are mostly reduced or smelted within those counties. The smelting-works do not generally belong to the proprietors of the mines, but to other parties who purchase the ore from them, their value being determined by a kind of assay. The smelting is effected by two different methods, according as *tin-stone* or *stream-tin* is to be acted on.

In the former process the prepared ore, which is called *schlich*, is mixed with from one-fifth to one-eighth of its weight of powdered anthracite, or culm, to which a little slaked lime or fluor-spar is sometimes added as a flux. The charge (from 12 to 24 cwts.) is spread upon the concave hearth of the furnace, and then the apertures by which it is inserted are closed and luted, and the furnace is gradually heated, and kept hot for six or eight hours, by which time the reduction of the ore is complete. When the fusion or reduction of the ore is considered to be finished, one of the apertures of the furnace is opened, and the scoriæ removed; after which a channel is opened, by which the melted tin flows from the hearth into a large vessel, where it is allowed to rest for some time, in order that the impurities yet remaining with the metal may separate, by their different specific gravities. When it has settled, the tin is ladled into moulds, so as to form it into large blocks or ingots.

The ingots produced by the above process frequently contain portions of other substances, to remove which the tin is exposed to the process of *refining*. The tin is again melted in another furnace; and into the molten metal billets of green wood are plunged. This occasions the disengagement of considerable volumes of gas from the wood, and thus a kind of ebullition is produced in the tin, which causes the lighter impurities to rise to the surface in a frothy form, and the heavier to fall to the bottom. The scum is removed, and the rest is allowed to settle, whereby all the purest tin rises to the top, and the quality deteriorates thence to the bottom; by which means the tin, poured into moulds, presents many different qualities. The moulds are made of granite, and yield blocks of tin weighing about 3 cwts. each: granite having been found well fitted for this purpose. An inferior kind of tin is produced by remelting the scoriæ. The average quality of the tin ore, as prepared for the smelting-furnaces, is such as to yield 62 to 65 per cent. of pure tin; and the quantity of coal required for producing one ton of tin is about a ton and three-quarters.

The smelting of tin by the blast-furnace, with wood-charcoal, is practised on a limited scale for the production of tin of the greatest possible purity, and from *stream-tin* instead of *tin-stone*. No substance is added to the ore and charcoal, unless it be the residuary matter of a previous smelting; and the proportion of charcoal consumed is about one ton and six-tenths for every ton of tin produced. The melted tin runs from the furnace into an open basin, whence it is run off into a large vessel in which it is allowed to settle. The scoriæ which run with the metal are skimmed off, and separated into two portions, one consisting of such as retain tin oxide, and the other of such as have no oxide, but contain tin in a granulated state. In order to convert the blocks of tin produced by the blast-furnace process into the form known as *grain-tin*, they are heated until they become brittle, and made to fall from a considerable height in a semi-fluid state, thus producing an agglomerated mass of elongated grains.

Tin is rarely employed alone in our metalline manufactures, but when laid in a thin coat upon the surface of sheet-iron by the process of *Tinning*, it produces a material of extensive use in the manufacture of culinary and other articles. Most of the tin used in the manufacture of articles composed exclusively of that metal is that which is expanded by rolling and hammering into leaves of *tin-foil;* this is the substance which is laid upon the back of glass mirrors, and there amalgamated with mercury, so as to form what is called the *Silvering*.

The art of *tinning*, or of coating other metals with a thin layer of tin, so as to protect them from oxidation, was known to the ancients, although it does not appear to have been very extensively practised. The tinning of plate-iron is more modern than that of copper vessels, and is supposed to have been invented either in Bohemia or in Germany, whence it spread to France about 1725, and to England about 1730.

The process of tinning depends upon the strong affinity which exists between tin and the metals to which it is applied. The finest bar-iron, called *tin-iron*, is used for making tin-plates. This material is first made into flat bars, or slabs, about thirty inches long, six inches wide, and weighing eighty pounds; and these bars are rolled until the metal assumes the proper degree of thinness, after which the sheets are cut into pieces measuring usually about thirteen inches by ten.

The removal of every particle of oxide or other impurity from the surface of the plates is then effected by the application of muriatic acid and of heat; and any warping is removed by a process of cold-rolling between very hard rollers. The plates are then immersed singly, in a vertical position, in a fermented steep of bran; whence, after 10 or 12 hours, they are transferred to a leaden vessel containing diluted sulphuric acid. They are then removed into pure water, in which they are scoured with hemp and sand, to remove any remaining oxide. They are next dried by rubbing with bran, greased on both surfaces, and plunged into the metallic bath, which contains a mixture of block and grain-tin, covered with a quantity of grease sufficient to form a layer four inches deep, and heated. When the plates have remained in the tin bath an hour or two, they are lifted out with tongs, and placed upon an iron grating, to allow the superfluous tin to drain off; but as there still remains upon them much more than the proper quantity of tin, they are afterwards subjected to a process called *washing*, which consists in dipping them into a pot containing a quantity of pure grain-tin in a melted state, then rubbing them with a peculiar kind of brush made of hemp, plunging them again for a moment into the melted tin in the wash-pot, and then into a pot filled with clean melted tallow, or lard free from salt. Owing to the vertical position of the plates during the preceding operations, a selvage of tin accumulates along their lower edge, which is partially removed by a re-melting and shaking of the edge. The plates are then cleaned from grease by rubbing them, while yet warm, with dry bran; after which they are packed in boxes of wood or sheet-iron.

The tinning of the inner surfaces of cooking utensils and other vessels of capacity is formed by scouring the surface until it is perfectly bright and clean; then heating the vessel, pouring in some melted tin and rolling it about, and rubbing the tin all over the surface with a piece of cloth or a handful of tow: powdered rosin is used to prevent the formation of oxide. Bridle-bits, stirrups, and many other small articles, are tinned by immersing them in fluid tin.

Tin-Plate Working, or the forming sheets of tinned iron into a variety of useful vessels and utensils, is carried on by means of bench and hand-shears, mallets and hammers, steel heads and wooden blocks, soldering-irons and swages. In the formation of a vessel the first operation is to cut the plate to the proper size and form with shears; and when the dimensions of the article require it, to join them together, which is done either by simply laying the edge of one plate over that of the other, and then soldering them together, or by folding the edges together with laps, and then soldering them. Similar joints are required when gores or other pieces are to be inserted, and also at the junction by which a cylinder is closed in. The usual method of forming laps, bends, or folds for this or other purposes is to lay the plate over the edge of the bench, and to bend it by repeated strokes with a hammer; but a machine is sometimes used for this purpose.

After a tin vessel has been rounded upon a block or mandril, by striking it with a wooden mallet, and the seams finished, all its exterior edges are strengthened by bending a thick iron wire into the proper form, applying it to what would otherwise be the raw edges of the metal, and dexterously folding them over it with a hammer. A superior kind of tin-ware, commonly known as *block-tin ware*, is carefully finished by beating or planishing with a polished steel hammer upon a metal stake. The process of *swaging* is resorted to as a ready means of producing grooved or ridged borders or other embossed ornaments. This process consists in striking the metal between two steel dies, or swages, the faces of which bear the desired pattern, and are made counterparts to each other. Many ornamental articles are produced by embossing or stamping tin-plate, in the same manner as other metallic sheets, with a fly-press or other machinery. Cheap coffin-plates are manufactured at Birmingham in this way; and these and similar articles are sometimes lacquered, painted, or japanned. One particular kind of tin plate is described under MOIRÉ.

Tin forms the principal ingredient in various kinds of pewter and other white metallic alloys, which are manufactured into domestic utensils by casting, stamping, and other processes. *Britannia Metal* is a mixture of tin, antimony, copper, and brass; which is melted, cast into slabs, and rolled into sheets. The principal use of this metal is for candlesticks, tea-pots, coffee-biggins, and other vessels for containing liquids. The feet of candlesticks, the bodies of tea-pots, and other articles containing embossed work, are stamped between dies; while articles of a more globular shape are stamped in two or more pieces, which are afterwards soldered together. The sheet metal has a ductility which enables it to be bent into various curved forms, by pressure on a model or core: this process is called *spinning*.

Many small vessels, spoons, and other articles, are cast in an alloy somewhat harder than that which is rolled into sheets. Articles of this metal are cleaned from the oil, resin, and other impurities acquired during their formation, by boiling in water containing sweet soap; after which they are polished, either by hand, or more commonly by the buff and brush set in motion by a steam-engine; then boiled in a solution of pearlash; and finally hand-brushed and hand-polished by an application of soft soap, a little oil, and powdered rotten-stone.

TINCTURES are solutions of the active principles, mostly of vegetables, sometimes of saline medicines, and more rarely of animal matters, in certain solvents. From possessing more or less of colour, they have obtained this name. They are distinguished according to the kind of solvent employed. When alcohol is used, they are termed *alcoholic tinctures*, or more generally simply *tinctures;* when sulphuric æther is used, they are denominated *ætherial tinctures.* When wine is used, though differing little from pure alcohol, the term *medicated wines* is applied to them; and when the process of distillation is employed to aid the extraction, particularly of volatile oils, the result is termed a *spirit*, such as of rosemary. Ammonia is sometimes conjoined, and the proceeds termed an *ammoniated tincture. Elixirs* differ only from tinctures in being of a greater consistence: they are not unfrequently turbid from the attractive matter suspended in them. The number and variety of tinctures are numerous.

TITA'NIUM. This metal was first recognised by Mr. Gregor, in 1791, as a distinct substance; he detected it in a black sand found in the bed of a rivulet in Cornwall. The form of the crystals of this metal is the cube; their colour resembles that of bright copper; they are sufficiently hard to scratch rock-crystal. Titanium is acted on by very few acids. For fusion an extremely high temperature is required. The metal and its compounds have yet been applied to very few purposes in the arts.

TOBACCO. *Tobacco* was the name used by the Caribbees for the pipe with which they smoked, but was transferred by the Spaniards to the herb itself. The genus *Nicotiana* contains about 40 species, most of them yielding tobacco for smoking, and many of them cultivated in the gardens of Europe.

The cultivation of tobacco is most extensively carried on in the United States of North America. It requires considerable heat to bring it to perfection; but with care and attention, and by treating it as an exotic, it may be very successfully cultivated in much colder climates. In Holland, of which the climate differs little from that of Great Britain, the tobacco-plant is cultivated to a very great extent, even in very poor soils, by great attention to manuring, and by accelerating the growth of the plant.

The seed is sown in a well prepared seed-bed in March, and protected by mats laid over hoops as long as the nights are cold and frost is dreaded. The ground in which the tobacco is to be transplanted is laid in narrow beds with intervals between them; the plants are taken up carefully with a trowel; they are placed slanting in a shallow basket, and are thus carried to the prepared beds. They are inserted into holes made by a proper instrument, so that the fibres of the roots and the adhering earth may be completely buried up to the bottom of the stem. When the leaves acquire a certain size the lower leaves are pinched off. A few plants are left for seed, and of these the heads are allowed to shoot the full length. Tobacco takes about four months from the time of planting to come to perfection. As soon as the colour of the leaves becomes of a paler green inclined to yellow, they are fit to be gathered. The plants are cut down close to the ground, and are then carefully and gradually dried. When the plants are quite dry, they are removed in moist or foggy weather; for if the air is very dry the leaves would crumble. They are laid in heaps on hurdles and covered over, that they may sweat again, and are examined from time to time to see that they do not heat too much; and, according to the season and whether the plants are more or less filled with sap, they remain so a week or a fortnight. If the leaves were not stripped off at first, which is not the most common practice, they are taken off now and sorted; those which grow on the top of the stem, in the middle, and at the bottom, are laid separately, as being of different qualities. They are tied together in bundles of ten or twelve leaves, and again dried carefully, when they are ranged in casks horizontally, and pressed in by means of a lever or screw.

Tobacco is packed in hogsheads for shipment: it is done with the greatest care; and the pressure applied is so great, that a hogshead 48 inches in length, and 30 or 32 inches in diameter, will contain one thousand pounds weight. Upon the arrival of the tobacco in this country, it is conveyed to bonding-warehouses, examined, charged with duty, and sold to the manufacturers.

The manufacture of the tobacco-leaves into the numerous varieties of tobacco for smoking in pipes is commenced by loosening and opening the bundles, and sprinkling the leaves with water. The stalks are then stripped from the leaves; this is effected by women or boys, who fold the leaf along the middle, and, by means of a small instrument, separate the stalks from the leaves, and lay them aside in different heaps. To prepare them for being cut into shreds, the leaves are pressed together in large numbers. When removed from the press to the cutting-engine, the cake of leaves is as hard as a board; yet it retains a slight degree of clamminess or moisture from the leaves having been previously sprinkled. In cutting the tobacco, the cake of leaves is laid upon an iron bed, which is susceptible of a slow progressive motion by means of a screw which passes beneath it, and is connected with a cog-wheel in such a manner that, while the machine is moving, the bed is constantly urged forward. Another part of the mechanism gives motion to the knife, which has a sharp blade, rather longer than the width of the cake, and is pivoted on a hinge or fulcrum at one end, the other rising and falling with the action of the machinery.

The kind called *pig-tail* tobacco is produced by a process similar to spinning, and requires the simultaneous aid of a man and two boys. A bench several yards in length is made use of, with a spinning-wheel at one end, turned by one of the boys. The other boy arranges a number of damp leaves, with the stalks removed, end to end upon the bench, taking care to lay them smooth and open; and the man immediately follows him, and rolls up the leaves into the form of a cord by a peculiar motion of his hand. As fast as this is done, the finished tail is wound upon the spinning-wheel. It is transferred from the spinning-wheel, by the action of the machinery, to a frame connected with it; and subsequently it is wound or twisted up into a hard close ball.

Other forms into which the plant is manufactured are noticed under CIGAR and SNUFF.

Trade.—For the following years the consumption of tobacco, and the duty thereon, were—

	Consumption.	Duty per lb.
1801	16,514,998 lbs	1*s.* 7*d.*
1811	14,923,243	2*s.* 2*d.*
1821	12,983,198	4*s.*
1831	15,350,018	3*s.*
1841	16,000,000	3*s.*

Seven-eighths of all the tobacco brought into this country is grown in the United States. The duties payable are 3*s.* 1$\frac{4}{5}$*d.* per lb. on unmanufactured tobacco; 9*s.* 5$\frac{2}{5}$*d.* per lb. on cigars and manufactured tobacco; and 6*s.* 3$\frac{3}{5}$*d.* per lb. on snuff.

The imports in the last two years have been:

	1849.	1850.
Unmanufactured . . .	42,098,126 lbs.	33,894,506 lbs.
Manufactrd. and Snuff	1,913,474 lbs.	1,532,829 lbs.

The home consumption is about 28,000,000 lbs. annually, the rest being re-exported. The gross duty realised in the two years was 4,425,040*l.* and 4,430,134*l.* respectively.

TOBACCO-PIPES are made of clay, white and coloured earths, porcelain, ivory, and various other substances. The tobacco-pipes commonly used in this country are formed of a fine plastic white clay, which is called from this application, *pipe-clay*. It is procured chiefly from Purbeck, in Dorsetshire; and, after being purified and made into a soft state, is cut into small pieces, each enough for one pipe. Each piece is kneaded thoroughly upon a board, and rolled out to nearly the form and size of a pipe, with a projecting bulb at one end for the formation of the bowl. These pieces are laid aside for some time to dry, and when the clay is sufficiently firm, they are subjected to the curious process of boring. The workman takes the roll of clay in his left hand, and with his right inserts the end of an iron needle, previously oiled, in the small end of the roll, and by dexterous management thrusts the needle through the whole length of the roll, without penetrating the surface. The bulb is then bent into the proper position to form the bowl, and the piece of clay, with the needle remaining in it, is pressed into a mould to complete its form. The moulds are made of metal, in two halves. The bowl is partially hollowed by the finger, and completed by the insertion of an oiled stopper or mould. The wires are now withdrawn, and the pipes are taken out of the moulds, slightly smoothed over, and laid aside to dry. After drying for a day or two, any remaining roughness is removed by means of an instrument of bone or hard wood, and then the pipes are sometimes moulded a second time, and polished with a piece of flint bored with holes, through which the stem is passed repeatedly. The pipe-stems are thus far straight, but before going to the kiln they are slightly bent.

The tobacco-pipe kiln consists of a large but very light cylindrical crucible, with a dome-shaped top, and a circular opening in one side for the insertion of the pipes. This crucible is mounted in a brick furnace, lined with fire-brick, in such a manner as to leave a space of about four inches all round for the circulation of flame. The pipes are placed in the kiln, with their bowls against the circumference, and their ends supported at a considerable elevation upon circular pieces of clay set up in the centre. By this arrangement one furnace may contain fifty gross, or 7,200 pipes, which may all be baked within eight or nine hours.

A different kind of clay or earthen pipe is described under MEERSCHAUM PIPES.

Mr. Skertchley patented a somewhat complicated machine for making tobacco-pipes, in 1848; and Messrs. Steel and Britten patented another machine for the same purpose in the same year.

TOMAHAWK. The tomahawks or hatchets of Indian manufacture are headed with stone, but the ordinary metal blades or heads are of European manufacture, and made expressly for Indian use. The handles are usually made by the Indians themselves, and are often highly ornamented. Some tomahawks are formed with a bowl for burning tobacco in the head, and a hole through the handle to serve for a pipe.

TOMATO. The tomato which is used as a condiment or sauce, is the fruit of one among many species of *Solanum*. It is a native of South America; but it is also well known and much cultivated in the United States, France, Germany, and Italy. The fruit is about the size of a golden pippin; it has an acid flavour, and is used as an addition to soups and sauces, as a preserve, and as a pickle. It is not much used in England; but in Italy whole fields are covered with it; and scarcely a dish is served up into which it does not enter as an ingredient.

TON or TUN. In modern English spelling the *ton* is a weight (twenty hundredweight, or 2240 lbs. avoirdupois), and the *tun* is a measure of wine (two pipes, or 252 gallons).

TOPAZ. The colour of this gem varies from white to a greenish-blue, and is translucent. Fragments exposed to heat emit a blue, green, or yellowish phosphoric light. Topazes occur generally in primitive rocks, and in many parts of the world, as Cornwall, Scotland, Saxony, Siberia, Brazil, &c. &c. They consist of alumina and silica, with a little fluoric acid.

TORMENTIL is a small perennial plant, growing in the whole of Europe and the north of Asia, in forests, bogs, and heaths. The root, or rather the rhizoma, is the most powerful of our indigenous astringents, and more easily assimilated than oak-bark or galls. Valuable as this substance is in medicine, it is of still greater utility in the arts and in agriculture. It may be most beneficially employed to tan leather, both where the oak grows and where it is absent, since one pound and a half of powdered tormentil is equal in strength to seven pounds of tan. It is used in Lapland and the Orkney Isles both to tan and to dye leather.

TORSION is that force with which a thread or wire returns to a state of rest when it has been twisted by being turned round on its axis. In the *torsion-balance* or *torsion-meter* (as it may be termed), the thread or wire, which is suspended vertically, is attached at the upper extremity to some object, and at the lower extremity is a weight with a horizontal index, or a stirrup, which is to carry a needle or bar in a horizontal position. So long as the force of torsion is moderate, its intensity is directly proportional to the angle or arc through which the extremity of the index is moved in twisting the wire, and that the time of a complete oscillation is constant, or that the vibrations are isochronous, like those of a pendulum which is acted upon by gravity. The experiments made with this instrument are chiefly in connection with science; but they have a bearing on civil engineering, insofar as they illustrate the strength and other properties of building materials.

TORTOISE-SHELL is procured from a marine tortoise called the hawk's-bill turtle, or *testudo imbricata*. Each animal furnishes thirteen principal plates, five along the centre of the back, and four on each side; and twenty-five smaller scales or plates, which constitute the margin of the shell. The horny plates which constitute true tortoise-shell are separated from the bony foundation which forms the shell or covering of the animal by the application of heat; the whole shell being commonly placed over a fire until the plates begin to start from the bone, and the separation being completed by the aid of a slender knife. The yellow-coloured shell bears a higher price than that which is mottled.

The processes of manufacturing articles of tortoise-shell are very similar to those described under HORN MANUFACTURE, but on account of the high price of the material (often three guineas per lb.), it is economised as much as possible. In making the frames for eye-glasses, narrow strips of shell are used, in which slits are cut with a saw, the slits being subsequently, while the shell is warm, strained or pulled open, until they form circular or oval apertures, by the insertion of tapering triblets of the required shape. The same yielding or flexible property is made use of in the manufacture of boxes, a round flat disc of shell being gradually forced by means of moulds into the form of a circular box with upright sides. The union of two or more pieces of shell may be effected by carefully scraping the parts that are to overlap, so as to render them perfectly free from grease, even such as might arise from being touched by the finger, softening them in hot water, pressing them together with hot flat tongs, and then plunging the joint into cold water.

In veneering with tortoise-shell, by which very beautiful work may be produced, it is usual to apply fish-glue, mixed with lamp-black, vermilion, green, chrome, white, or other colouring matter, at the back of the shell, both to heighten its effect and to conceal the glue or cement by which it is secured to the wooden foundation.

TOULON. In this maritime French town there are two harbours, one for commerce, the other for the navy, which communicate with each other by a deep channel crossed by a swing bridge. The commercial port, the more eastern of the two, was constructed by Henri IV., and is surrounded by handsome quays. The naval port was formed by Louis XIV., and is surrounded by quays, and on the town side by a naval arsenal, stores, forges, cannon foundries, armories, covered slips for building ships, various naval schools, and all the establishments and machinery necessary for the construction, rigging, and fitting out of ships of war of all sizes. The rope-walk, built with cut stone, and covered with a vaulted roof, is 2000 feet in length. On the south-east and eastern moles of the naval port are the bagnio and hospital for convicts; in front of these are repairing docks. The artillery depôt is on the west side of the harbour, and contains an immense number of guns and projectiles. At the south-eastern angle of the town, new basins, wet docks, and yards for the construction of steam and sailing vessels, have been formed. The industrial products and commerce of Toulon, independent of its connection with the great naval establishment it contains, are not very important. Woollen cloth, hosiery, soap, candles, leather, and chocolate, are the chief manufactured articles; merchant ships are built. The commerce is composed of corn, flour, salt provision, wine, brandy, oil, capers, figs, raisins, and other fruits.

TOULOUSE. The industrial products of this important French city are of great variety, including coarse woollen cloth, blankets, silk goods, gauze, starch, straw-hats, vermicelli, wax candles, musical strings, card and room paper, pottery, scythes, steel, and hardware; it has a large porcelain manufactory, cotton yarn mills, dye-houses, several printing offices, brandy distilleries, copper and iron foundries, tan-yards, cannon foundry, powder-mill, and a tobacco factory. The city is the entrepôt for the iron of Ariège, and has considerable commerce with Spain, Bordeaux, and Marseille. The business done in wheat and flour is very important, causing a circulation of above half a million sterling annually; the commerce in wine and brandy too is very considerable; other articles of trade are colonial produce, oil, soap, salt geese, Spanish wool, broadcloth, hardware, and feathers.

TOY MANUFACTURE. The manufacture of childrens' toys is a remarkable one, which occupies a larger number of persons than would generally be supposed. In one of the excellent papers which have recently appeared in the *Morning Chronicle*, it is well observed:—"The sciences which are laid under contribution in the construction of toys are almost as multifarious as the arts which are employed in the manufacture of them. Optics gives its burning-glass, its microscope, its magic lantern, its stereoscope, its thaumatrope, its phantasmascope, and a variety of others; electricity, its Leyden jars, galvanic batteries, electrotypes, &c.; chemistry, its balloons, fireworks and crackers; mechanics, its clock-work mice—its steam and other carriages; pneumatics contributes its kites and windmills; acoustics, its Jew-harps, musical-glasses, accordions, and all the long train of musical instruments; astronomy lends its orreries; in fine, there is scarcely a branch of knowledge which is not made to pay tribute to the amusement of the young. Nor are the arts and artists that are called into play in the manufacture of toys less numerous. There is the turner, to turn the handles of the skipping-ropes, the ninepins, the peg, the humming, and the whipping tops, the hoop-sticks; the basket-worker, to make dolls' cradles, and babies' rattles, and wicker-work carts and carriages; the tinman, to manufacture tin swords and shields, pea-shooters, carts, money-boxes, and miniature candlesticks; and the pewterer to cast the metal soldiers, and dolls' cups and saucers, and fire-irons, and knives and forks, plates and dishes, chairs and tables, and all the leading furniture of the baby-house; the modeller, to make the skin and composition animals; the glass-blower, to make the dolls' eyes; the wig-maker, to manufacture the dolls' curls; the tallow-chandler, to mould miniature candles for the dolls' houses; the potter, to produce dolls' cups and saucers. Then there are image-men, conjurors, cutlers, card-makers, opticians, cabinet-makers, firework-makers, and, indeed, almost every description of artisan—for there is scarcely a species of manufacture or handicraft that does not contribute something to the amusement of the young."

Considerable imports of foreign toys are made yearly. These are chiefly from France, Germany, and Switzerland. The clock-work and mechanical toys are chiefly from France, where they are better made than in any other country. *Box-toys*, as they are called, that is, numerous little turned or carved toys sold in boxes, are chiefly from Germany—such as Noah's arks, troops of soldiers, tea-sets, farm yards, boxes of skittles, &c. Nürnberg, Frankfort, and the Black Forest, are the principal places in Germany where these toys are made. Women and children make them in the country districts, and take them for sale to the exporting merchants. Low as such labour may be considered to be remunerated in England, the earnings are very much lower in Germany; and it is on this account that such articles can pay the expence of transport from country to country. The Swiss toys are mostly in white wood, and comprise such articles as carved figures and Swiss cottages; they also include the jointed figures used by artists. The conjuring tricks, dissecting puzzles, skeleton maps, &c., are mostly English.

Among the English toy makers the variety is considerable. There are the toy turner, the green wood toy maker, the white wood toy maker, the fancy toy maker, the numerous ramifications of doll makers, the tin toy maker, the lead toy maker, the pewter toy maker, the basket toy maker, the firework maker, the kite maker, the drum and tambourine maker, and others which it would not be easy to range under any particular class. Far more women and children than men are employed in these trades.

A little has been said on one of these toy-departments in a former article. [DOLL MANUFACTURE.]

TRACERY, is a term used to denote that species of pattern-work which is formed or traced in the head of a gothic window by the mullions being made to diverge into arches, curves, and flowing lines, enriched with foliations. The term is also applied to ornamental design of the same character, whether for doors, panelling, or ceilings; the only difference being that in windows the pattern or tracery is perforated, and in other cases closed, that is, is a mere pattern carved on the surface of a solid part. In particular instances, where the tracery on parapets, battlements, turrets, spires, &c., is pierced, it is then named *Open-work*.

TRACTION, in Mechanics, is the act of drawing a body along a plane, usually by the power of men, animals, or steam; as when a vessel is towed on the surface of water or a carriage moved upon a road. The power exerted in order to produce the effect is called the force of traction.

Numerous experiments have been made for the purpose of ascertaining the value of a force so exerted. When men are employed to draw laden boats on canals, it is found that if the work be continued for several days successively, of eight hours each, the force of traction is equivalent to a weight of 31½ lbs., moved at the rate of two feet per second, or 1¼ mile per hour (it being understood that such weight is imagined to be raised vertically by means of a rope passing over a pulley, and drawn in a horizontal direction). The force of traction exerted when, without moving from his place, a man pulls horizontally against a weight so suspended, is estimated at 70lbs. Mr. Tredgold considers that a horse exerts a force of traction expressed by 125 lbs. raised at the rate of 3⅔ feet per second, or 2½ miles per hour. A man or a horse can however double his power of traction for a few minutes without being injured by the exertion; and when the carriage is in motion, so that the friction on the ground is alone to be overcome, a horse can draw, during a short time, on a level road, a weight exceeding 1500 lbs.

Experiments have shown that when the *angle of traction*, as it is called, that is, the angle which the plane of the traces makes with the road on which a carriage is moving, is 15 or 16 degrees, a horse pulls with good effect; and the height of the points at which the traces are attached to a horse's collar being about 4 feet 6 inches from the ground, it follows that, in order to obtain this inclination, the lower extremities of the traces or shafts should be 2 feet 3 inches from the ground. In general however, in two-wheeled carriages, the height of these extremities is about 3 feet.

As an example of the force of traction exerted by steam, it may be stated that on a level line of railway, an engine with an 11-inch cylinder, and having an effective pressure of 50 lbs. per square inch in the boiler, drew 50 tons at the rate of 30 miles per hour, working 10 hours daily; and that the same engine, with an equal pressure in the boiler, drew 160 tons at the rate of 15½ miles per hour.

TRANSIT INSTRUMENT, is an astronomical telescope, made to move in the plane of the meridian, so that the moment of any star passing a vertical wire in the middle of the field of view (and which covers a part of the meridian) may be ascertained. Usually there are several auxiliary wires at equal distances on each side of the middle wire, and the mean of the times at which the several wires are passed, is more accurately the time of meridian passage than that derived from the middle wire itself. The instrument was invented about 1690, by Römer.

The main uses of the transit instrument are either, by means of a star of known right ascension, to determine the time of observation, or else, by means of the observed time at which a star passes the meridian, to determine the star's right ascension. The transit instruments in the principal observatories are specimens of the highest mechanical and optical skill.

TRANSYLVANIA. The products and industry of Transylvania are briefly illustrated under AUSTRIA.

TRAVERTIN, the Italian term for concretionary limestone produced from springs holding carbonate of lime in solution. A large proportion of the most splendid edifices of ancient and modern Rome are built of travertin derived from the quarries of Ponto Leucano.

TREACLE. [MOLASSES; SUGAR.]

TREBIZOND. This town, situated at the south-east corner of the Black Sea, and the north-east corner of Asia Minor, is a place of much commercial importance. The trade has greatly increased since the navigation of the Black Sea was opened to all nations, and especially since the establishment of steamers, by which this town has a direct and regular communication with Constantinople, Odessa, and the Danube. The number of sailing vessels engaged in the commerce of the port in 1849 was 87; and a large trade is carried on by steamers, of which 23 English, 30 Turkish, and 24 Austrian, entered the port in the course of the same year. The entire value of the imports was 53,409,215 francs; the exports amounted to 14,251,406 francs, being an increase on 1848, when the exports amounted to only 6,239,790 francs. The imports shew a decrease on those of 1848, caused by the cheaper and safer means of transit to Persia by the Russian ports of Redut Kalé and Tiflis. The increase in the exports is chiefly owing to the larger quantity of Turkish copper and other produce, and of Persian silks, gall nuts, &c., shipped to Europe from this port. The chief imports are cotton manufactures, sugar, coffee, and other colonial produce. The Austrian Steamboat Company plies regularly between Trieste and Trebizond, and has lately extended its line to Batoom and Redut Kalé, to which latter place Russia aims at diverting the Persian trade, from the old route through Trebizond, Erzeroum, and Bayazid.

TREENAILS. In ship-building the outer planks are fastened to the timbers by thick oak pegs called *treenails*, driven through holes bored in the wood. They are formed of the soundest oak, whose grain is straight and regular. They vary in size from a foot and a half to three feet in length, and from one to two inches in diameter. The pieces of oak which may be selected for this purpose are first sawed to the proper length; the treenail makers then rip each piece into a number of smaller pieces, and finally reduce them to a tolerably cylindrical shape by means of spoke shaves. The treenails are left many months to season before being used.

Treenails are occasionally cut by machinery. Mr. Wilkinson patented an apparatus in 1849 for compressing treenails before use, so as to give them as much solidity and hardness as possible.

TRIBUNALS OF COMMERCE are courts established in all the large towns of France for the quick and inexpensive decision of commercial disputes, and all matters relating to trade and debt. The presidents and judges are chosen from among the most intelligent and respectable merchants of their respective towns, and serve without emolument. A president and two judges form a court, which sits every day except Sunday. The clerks are the only officers who are paid. The expense of these courts for the whole of France does not much exceed 7000*l.* sterling; their decisions are admitted to be highly satisfactory and equitable.

There is a movement now being made towards the establishment of something which, whether called a *Chamber* or a *Tribunal* of Commerce, shall fill a place in London commerce somewhat analogous to those of the French Tribunals.

TRIESTE, at the north-eastern extremity of the Adriatic, has been long a free port, and is the most important and wealthy commercial city in the Austrian dominions. Consuls of almost every nation in Europe reside there. The commerce of Trieste was much increased by the commercial treaty concluded with Greece in 1835, and by the new institution of the Austrian Lloyd's, which is supported by the government. The number of ships engaged in the commerce of Trieste is about 2400, of which, in 1849, 403 were employed on long voyages, and 27 were steamers. The steamers ply to Venice, Greece, Constantinople, Trebizond, and Egypt. A terminus for the Vienna-Trieste Railway, which is now opened nearly throughout, has been lately finished. Among the manufactures, oil-soap, leather, rosoglio, and wax, are the principal. Among the exports are the productions of the mines of Idria, those of Hungary, linens, tobacco, and woollens from different parts of the Austrian dominions, and printed calicoes from

Switzerland. The imports are cotton from Egypt; hides, raisins, silks, rice, and oil from the Levant; wheat from Odessa; and all kinds of tropical and colonial produce from the West and East Indies and Brazil. Ship-building, including the construction of frigates and men-of-war, is carried on to a great extent.

TRIFO'RIUM is a term applied to the upper galleries formed by small open arches above those dividing the nave from the side-aisles of a church, and beneath the clere-story windows: this intermediate tier being within the sloping roof over the aisles. In general the triforium is very shallow or narrow, and the arches in front of it small and low; but there are great differences in these respects even in buildings of the same period and style.

TRIGONOMETRICAL SURVEY. The merit of first applying trigonometry to geodetic operations belongs to Willebrord Snell, who in 1617 undertook a survey of Holland, for the double purpose of establishing the geographical positions of the principal cities in that country, and measuring a degree of the terrestrial meridian. The method which he followed was the same in principle as that which would be adopted at the present time. Having formed a series of triangles extending over the country, he observed their angles with a quadrant, and computed their sides from a base which was carefully measured with wooden perches on the ground. He also determined the direction of the meridian at Leyden, and observed its inclination to a side of one of his triangles, and thereby obtained the bearings of the different angular points. Lastly, by observing the altitude of the pole-star with a five-feet quadrant at Alkmaar, Leyden, and Bergen-op-zoom, he determined the amplitudes of two celestial arcs; and thence deduced the quantities of which he was in quest.

Since that time, trigonometrical or geodetic surveys have been made in various countries. A general survey of the British Islands, under the direction of the master-general of the Ordnance, was begun in 1791, and has been continued to the present time. The first conductors of this national undertaking were Colonel Williams and Captain (afterwards General) Mudge, of the Royal Engineers, and Mr. Dalby, who had previously assisted General Roy. Were it not for the admirable maps which are from time to time issued from the Ordnance map-office, it might be inferred that the survey had been discontinued during the last thirty years. The operation has however never been lost sight of. For some years after the last published account, the triangulation was carried on in Scotland, both along the eastern and western coasts. All the Ordnance maps of Great Britain south of a line from Preston to Hull have been published on a scale of one inch to a mile; but operations have commenced for publishing the northern section on the magnificent scale of 6 inches to a mile.

In respect to Ireland, the survey of that country was begun about 1818. A base was measured on the banks of Lough Foyle, near Londonderry, with an apparatus differing from any which had previously been used, and with precautions to ensure accuracy which probably have never been surpassed. Depending on this base, a net-work of triangles was established over the whole of Ireland. The topography of Ireland has been completed; and the angles of the different chains of primary triangles extending over the whole of Scotland and the adjacent islands have now also been observed. The entire map of Ireland has been published on the six-inch scale.

As one of the results of the various trigonometrical surveys, we give the following table of the lengths of degrees of latitude and longitude in English feet:—

Latitude.	Degree of Meridian.	Degree of Parallel Circle
0°	362748.5	365185.8
10	362858.0	359674.0
20	363173.7	343296.4
30	363658.1	316524.3
40	364254.0	280135.0
45	364575.6	258657.3
50	364889.9	235197.9
60	365489.1	183051.6
70	365978.9	125270.5
80	366299.2	63620.1
90	366410.5	0.0

TRINIDAD. The most remarkable physical feature of Trinidad is the Pitch Lake. It is about a mile and a half in circumference. The pitch at the side of the lake is perfectly hard and cold, but as one walks towards the middle with the shoes off in order to wade through the water, the heat gradually increases, the pitch becomes softer and softer, until at last it is seen boiling up in a liquid state. The air is then strongly impregnated with bitumen and sulphur, and the impression of the feet is left upon the surface of the pitch. During the rainy season it is possible to walk over the whole lake nearly; but in the hot season a great part is not to be approached.

Trinidad possesses some excellent harbours; Chaguaramas, Guaya-guayara, and Puerta d'España. On the last named stands the town called the Port of Spain, the capital of the island. Before 1783 the commerce of

Trinidad was very trifling. In 1787 the first sugar-plantation was established. All the usual productions of tropical countries grow luxuriantly. The nutmeg, cinnamon, and clove, have been introduced, and succeed remarkably well. In 1848 the exports amounted to 282,131*l.*, the imports to 309,257*l.*, and the revenue to 75,874*l.* Sugar, molasses, coffee, and cocoa, are chief articles of export.

The value of the British produce and manufactures exported to Trinidad in 1849 was 247,779*l.*

TRINITY HOUSE. This remarkable corporation has the management of some of the most important interests of the seamen and shipping of England. James II. granted the Trinity House the charter which is now in force, in the first year of his reign. It directs the masters and wardens to examine such boys of Christ's Hospital as shall be willing to become seamen, and to apprentice them to commanders of ships. It also enables them to appoint and license all pilots into and out of the Thames, and prohibits, under penalties, all other persons from exercising that office; it also authorises the corporation to settle rates of pilotage, &c.; to hold courts, &c.; to punish seamen deserting, &c.; and make laws as to other subject-matters not inconsistent with the laws of the kingdom. It also contains many provisions directed to the object of keeping the navigation of the channels secret from foreigners, and renders the officers of the corporation liable to attend when required at the king's bidding. Since that time several acts of parliament have been passed for the purpose of authorising the Trinity House to regulate matters connected with the pilotage, &c., of vessels.

The various provisions in matters of pilotage under the management of the corporation were repealed in 1826, and new arrangements made. At present, besides those under the jurisdiction of the Trinity House and of the lord warden of the Cinque Ports, many independent pilotage establishments exist in various parts of the kingdom; but the expediency of subjecting all these to the uniform management of the Trinity House has been felt for some time past. The inconvenience resulting from the exercise of similar authorities vested in the hands of different parties had been felt with regard to the *lighthouses* on the coast, several of which had been vested in private hands by the crown; while some had been in times past leased out by the corporation itself, the lights in both instances being found to be conducted probably rather with a view to private interest than public utility. By an Act, therefore, of 1827, provision was made for vesting all the lighthouses and lights on the coast of England in the corporation of Trinity House, and placing those of Scotland and Ireland under their supervision. Under this act purchases have been made by the corporation of the whole of the lighthouses not before possessed by that body, the amount expended for which purpose is near 1,000,000*l.*

The annual revenue of the corporation is very considerable, and is derived from tolls paid in respect of shipping, which receives benefit from the lights, beacons, and buoys, and from the ballast supplied. The ballast is raised from such parts of the bed of the river as it is expedient to deepen, by machinery attached to vessels, and worked partly by the power of steam and partly by manual labour. [DREDGING MACHINES.] The revenue is employed upon the necessary expenses of the corporation in constructing and maintaining their lighthouses and lights, beacons and buoys, and the buildings and vessels belonging to the corporation; in paying the necessary officers of their several establishments, and in providing relief for decayed seamen and ballastmen, their widows, &c. The deputy master and elder brethren are employed on voyages of inspection of their lighthouses and lights, beacons and buoys, not unfrequently in most trying weather and seasons; and they are also often engaged in making surveys, &c., on the coast, and reports on such matters of maritime character as are referred to them by the government.

TRIPOD is any article of furniture resting upon three feet, whence the name is given to tables, chairs, moveable altars, and other articles of the same kind. A chair or an altar of this kind must be understood when we read that the Pythia of Delphi gave her oracles from a tripod. We find also mention of tripods containing a certain measure of fluid, and in this case we have to understand a bowl resting upon a pedestal with three feet. The crater, or the vessel in which the wine was mixed with water at the banquets of the ancients, was very frequently a tripod of this description. The tripod was generally of metal and often of exquisite workmanship. Tripods were the most common presents to the temples of Apollo; tripods were given to the victors in the games which were celebrated in honour of Apollo; and tripods appear on innumerable coins which have any relation to the worship of that god. Some ancient tripods are preserved in the British Museum.

TRIPOLI. In this region of Northern Africa, those parts of the country which are moderately fertile produce a variety of grain, fruit, and trees. The wild trees and bushes are only used to make charcoal. Where charcoal is not to be had, camel's dung is used as fuel. Metals do not appear to be found; but salt is collected at a few places.

In *Tripoli*, the chief town and port, the trade is carried on in small vessels, seldom larger than brigs, none of which are now owned in the country. It has no direct trade with England, but an indirect one through Malta. Marseille, Leghorn, and the commercial towns of the Adriatic and the Levant, likewise trade with Tripoli. The trade of Tripoli must greatly depend upon the communication with the interior; and it profits once or twice a year from the passage of the pilgrims from Western Barbary on their way to Mecca. Formerly these caravans, composed partly of penitents and partly of traders, started from Fez, and passing through Tlemsen, Algiers, and Tunis, increasing as they went, on arriving under the walls of Tripoli, amounted sometimes to 3000 persons, and half as many camels and horses, with their goods and merchandise, returning by the same route. But the pilgrims now take a different route; and the caravans which stop at Tripoli in the present day seldom amount to more than a few hundred persons and animals. The cafilas or small caravans from Fezzan and Ghadamis are now the principal medium of inland trade. These people exchange their merchandise for that of Europe, and pay the balance in gold-dust.

TROMBO'NE, the same instrument as the *Sackut*, is a deep-toned trumpet, composed of sliding tubes, by means of which every sound in the diatonic and chromatic scales, being within its compass, is obtained in perfect tune. The trombone is of three kinds—the *alto*, the *tenor*, and the *base*, and these, in orchestral music, are generally used together, forming a complete harmony in themselves.

The scale of the *Alto-Trombone* is from C, the second space in the base, to G, an octave above the treble clef; that of the *Tenor-Trombone* is from B, the second line in the base, to A, the second space in the treble; and that of the *Base-Trombone* is from C, an octave below the second space in the base, to C, the second line in the treble.

TROY WEIGHT. The troy pound is the legal standard, though only actually used in weighing precious metals and stones, and apothecaries' drugs. There is no doubt that it was originally the pound of silver, the pound sterling, and there is evidence that this pound was sometimes described as divided into twenty parts called sterling shillings. The pound troy is now divided, for gold and silver, into twelve ounces, each ounce into twenty pennyweights, and each pennyweight into twenty-four grains. But for medicines, it is divided into twelve ounces, each ounce into eight drams or drachms, each drachm into three scruples, and each scruple into twenty grains. A cubic foot of water weighs 75.7374 pounds troy. [APOTHECARIES WEIGHT; AVOIRDUPOIS WEIGHT.]

TRUCK SYSTEM. This system has much influence on the relation between employers and workmen, in the manufacturing districts. The term truck, which means exchange or barter, is now used to signify the payment of wages of labour in goods, and not in money. By the truck-system is meant this mode of paying wages, together with all its tendencies and results. The Truck Act is an act passed in 1831, which, repealing all the previous acts passed for the same purpose, made stricter provisions for the prevention of payment of wages in truck in the departments of industry therein enumerated. The wages of agricultural labourers and domestic servants are exempted from the operation of the act. The evidence published in the Report of the Select Committee of the House of Commons on this subject, in 1842, shows that, notwithstanding the Truck Act, the truck-system is still in extensive operation in mills, factories, iron-works, collieries, and stone-quarries in the kingdom, and abundantly illustrates the evil tendencies of the system.

The chief part of the evil of what is called the truck-system is incidental, and not essential to the payment of wages in truck, and arises out of the power of the master over the workman, which enables the master to use this mode of paying wages to defraud and oppress the workman. A master may pay the wages of his workmen wholly or in part in truck, in articles of food, clothing, &c., either by agreement or with only the understood consent of his workmen; and if he supply these articles at prices no higher than those at which they are to be procured elsewhere, and study to meet the various wants of the workmen and their families, the utmost harm that can result is the loss to the workmen of the moral and economical lessons which the disbursement by themselves of weekly money-wages is fitted to supply, and the interference with the business and profits of neighbouring retail shopkeepers; and there will always in such cases be some advantage to set against these, so far as they go, evil results. Where the truck-system acts beneficially, it is owing entirely to the justice and benevolence of the individual truck-masters. On the character of the master everything depends. In the hands of masters of opposite character, and under circumstances, whether of scarcity of employment, of isolated situation, or of combination among masters in the same business, or through an extensive district, which place the workman more or less at the mercy of his employer, the payment of wages in truck may be, and continually has been, and is still extensively, used for the defrauding and oppressing of workmen.

TRUMPET. This musical instrument is of the highest antiquity. It is a single tube eight feet long, less in diameter than the horn, doubled up in a parabolic form, sounded by means of a mouthpiece, and subject to the same acoustical laws which govern all instruments of this class. [HORN.] The natural scale of the trumpet extends to about twenty notes; but by the assistance of a small brass tube, called the tuning-pipe, or shank, by which the tube of the trumpet is lengthened, the number of notes may be increased. Music for the trumpet, as in the instance of the horn, is always written in the natural key of C, and the key to which the instrument is to be adapted is pointed out by the composer.

TRUSSING. The rods or bars which are added to a girder for the purpose of trussing or supporting it may be applied in two sets, one on each side of the girder, and connected together by short cross-pieces at the necessary points; or the beam or girder itself may be divided longitudinally into two halves, or flitches, separated just so far as to admit a single truss between them, and held in the right position by the insertion of small blocks. One of the simplest methods of trussing girders is that in which the beam rests upon walls at its extremities, and has two inclined struts, resting on notches in the timber at the lower end, and supported at the centre or junction by a vertical kingpost, screwed by a nut beneath the beam. This form is improved by connecting the lower ends of the inclined bars by an iron rod stretching in a perfectly straight line, and capable of being brought to any required degree of tension by means of screws or keys.

Cast-iron beams are frequently trussed with wrought-iron rods, in a similar manner to those of wood, and are applied to purposes for which great strength is required.

TUBES. Under the heading of PIPES is given a short notice of the different modes of making tubes, pipes, cylinders, and barrels, according to the nature of the material employed and the purposes to which the articles are to be applied. Mr. Hick has recently invented a contrivance for making *taper* tubes; that is, tubes which taper or diminish in diameter from one end to the other. The tubes are first made parallel or cylindrical, and are tapered afterwards. The machine employed effects this by excentric grooved rollers: a greater or less degree of taper being obtained by varying the proportion between the rate at which the tube is drawn through the machine and that at which the rollers revolve.

TUBULAR BRIDGE. [MENAI BRIDGES.]

TUMBREL, or TUMBRIL, was the name of a machine formerly used for the punishment of scolding women, consisting of a stool or chair attached to the end of a long pole, mounted in such a manner that the chair, with the offender placed in it, might be swung over a pond, and immersed as often as might be necessary. The tumbrel was also used as a punishment for brewers and bakers who transgressed the laws relating to them. The name is also applied to the covered carts used to carry tools, &c., in a train of artillery.

TUN. [TON.]

TUNGSTEN. This metal was first obtained in a perfect state by M. d'Elhuyart, in 1781. The name is formed of the Swedish words *tung sten*, 'heavy stone.' It has a grayish-white colour and considerable lustre. It is brittle, and nearly as hard as steel. Its specific gravity is 17.4, and with the exception of platina, gold, and iridium, is the heaviest known metal. It requires a very high temperature for fusion. It is not altered by exposure to the air. When heated to redness in the open air it takes fire, combines with oxygen, and is converted into tungstic acid. Nitric acid produces the same effect.

The chief minerals which contain tungsten are *Tungstic Acid*, or *Schcelic Acid*; *Tungstate of Lime*; *Wolfram*, or *Tungstate of Iron and Magnesia*; and *Tungstate of Lead*.

Tungsten combines with several of the simple substances; but the compounds have not yet been applied to many useful purposes.

TUNING FORK. In tuning the notes of a musical instrument, such as the pianoforte, the first point is to fix upon some one note, by the pitch of which all others may be determined. The only way of retaining a permanent pitch for use is by having an instrument which time will not alter. A standard pitch is usually obtained, or professed to be obtained, by the *tuning fork*, an instrument consisting of two steel prongs extending from a steel handle. When these prongs are sharply struck they vibrate, and if the instrument be then held to the ear, or placed upon the flap of a table, or any other sound board, a low and very pure sound is heard, if the prongs be perfectly equal. These tuning-forks are usually made to sound either C or A, and they would answer their purpose exceedingly well if there really were in existence any rigorous standard from which they were made. But there is not; and the consequence is, that not only do the tuning-forks of different makers frequently vary a little from each other, but the new forks are sensibly higher than the old ones.

In the tuning-forks employed by Mr. Hullah's Singing Classes, the tone is made to correspond to a certain definite number of vibrations in a second, as determined (nearly) by a remarkably delicate little acoustic instrument called the *siren*.

TUNIS. The foreign commerce of Tunis is the most considerable of all the Barbary states. It is not confined to the capital, but is also carried on briskly from the ports of the eastern coast. Among the manufactured articles of export are—soap, marocco leather, shawls, and red skull-caps. Wheat and barley, as well as the inferior grains, olive oil, wool, hides, bees'-wax, dates, and almonds, are the principal articles of produce exported. Those received from the interior of Africa, and afterwards exported, are—ivory, gold dust, ostrich-feathers, senna, and madder-roots. The imports are woollen cloths, cotton-prints, calicoes, muslins, coarse linens, damasks, raw and wrought silks, fine wool, gold and silver tissues, coffee, sugar, spices, iron, tin, lead, hardware, cutlery, arms of all sorts, earthenware, paper, wine, spirits, and tobacco. As ports of loading, those of Sfax and Susa are preferred to Tunis, in consequence of the distance and delay of transporting merchandise in lighters across the lake to the Goletta, where ships generally lie; the commerce of the country is consequently best carried on in vessels under 150 tons burden. The trade with central Africa passes through Gadamis. The caravans arrive at Tozer, Cabes, and Sfax about twice in the year, and barter their merchandise, which is thence introduced in various directions into Tunis.

It is exceedingly interesting to find that this distant, and (comparatively) little known country, has contributed liberally to the display of the world's industry at the Great Exhibition.

TUNNEL, in civil engineering, is an arched passage formed underground to conduct a canal or road on a lower level than the natural surface. Long tunnels are usually made through hills in order to avoid the inconvenience and loss of power occasioned by conducting a canal, road, or railway over elevated ground, and also the enormous expense of such an open excavation as would be necessary in order to preserve the requisite level. Those of less extent are frequently constructed to avoid the opposition of land-owners, or to afford uninterrupted passage under a road, canal, or river.

Rocky strata, if the stone be of a nature to work freely, are usually the cheapest for tunnelling, owing to the absence of lining, and the power of saving labour by the use of gunpowder. Tunnelling in clay is frequently attended with formidable difficulties which render it very expensive. It is, when tough, a difficult material to remove, blasting being of no use, and spades and pick-axes being almost inapplicable. In such cases hatchets may be used to advantage, but cross-cut saws answer best. Tunnels formed through chalk are often impeded by faults or cavities filled with wet gravel or sand, which pour a flood of semifluid matter into the excavation as soon as they are cut into. The irruption of such loose materials, as well as of water alone, has in many cases occasioned difficulties almost insurmountable. Loose sand is perhaps the most difficult stratum that can be met with in tunnelling, but it has been in several instances successfully passed through.

Short tunnels are occasionally excavated from the ends only, but those of considerable length are usually formed by sinking vertical shafts, about nine feet in diameter, down to the level of the tunnel, and excavating in each direction from the bottom of each shaft, until the several parties of workmen meet in the intermediate portions. By this means the work can proceed at any required number of points or faces, so as to bring the execution of the tunnel, whatever may be its length, within a moderate period of time. The number of working shafts in a given length of tunnel is determined by the nature of the ground and the time allowed for excavation. Besides the working-shafts there are usually small air-shafts of three or four feet diameter to prevent the accumulation of foul air in the workings of the tunnel. In very long tunnels one or more large shafts are desirable for the purpose of ventilation, and also to admit some degree of light. When a complete brick lining is required, the bottom is the part first built, and it is completed by a course of stone laid along each side, at the point where the side walls spring from it.

The Thames Tunnel.—Many projects have been started for making a tunnel under the Thames; but the only one put into successful operation is that for which an act was obtained in 1824, with Mr. (afterwards Sir M. I.) Brunel as the engineer. Operations were commenced early in 1825 by the construction of a shaft 50 feet in diameter, at a distance of 150 feet from the south side of the river, at a point about two miles below London Bridge. A similar shaft was sunk on the north side of the river. The excavation for the tunnel was an oblong square, 38 feet wide and 22 feet 6 inches high, presenting a sectional area of 855 square feet. The shield by which the excavation was effected consisted of twelve massive frames of iron, placed side by side, and capable of being slid forward for a short distance independently of each other. The whole apparatus may be compared to a massive cofferdam laid on its side, and capable of being moved forward by the action of screws abutting against the end of the completed brick-work, which followed it up closely. Each frame of the shield consisted of three stories, each of which formed a cell large enough for one man to work in conveniently. The arrangements for supporting the wet clay of the Thames bed while the brickwork was being prepared, were of a very ingenious description.

The excavation of the tunnel was commenced in January, 1826, in a stratum of clay; but several irruptions of the river took place; one, in 1828, was so serious in its consequences that the Company did not resume operations till 1835. The tunnel is 1200 feet in length between the two shafts on the opposite banks of the river. It was not until 1843 that the Thames Tunnel was opened for foot passengers.

This grand undertaking has altogether failed to realise the commercial anticipations of its projectors. It has been, and still is, little more than a penny 'lion' of London; nor is it easy to see any probability that it will acquire trading importance.

TURF. A few details respecting turf will be found under FUEL and PEAT.

TURIN is the name not only of the capital of the Sardinian dominions, but also that of a division of the continental territory of the kingdom of Sardinia. This division has many provinces, which vary in produce and industry. In *Pignerol*, corn, excellent fruits, good wine, chestnuts, and silk, are the chief products. The forests are extensive, and there are many factories of silk, woollen, and leather. In the province of *Torino*, extensive forests and pastures, abundant wheat-crops, wine, and silk, form the elements of the wealth of this country; iron, vitriol, marble, and lime, are the chief minerals. The industrial and commercial activity is considerable. Tho province of *Susa* produces corn, wine, flax, hemp, and mulberries; and there are manufactures of leather, gloves, and thread. In the province of *Ivrea* the soil produces abundantly corn, excellent wine, and hemp. The pastures are good and cattle very numerous; silk is an important product. Iron, copper, marble, slate, and building stone, are the chief minerals. In the capital, *Turin* or *Torino*, the manufactures comprise woollen cloths, silks, hosiery, hats, gloves, optical instruments, chocolate, liqueurs, tobacco, leather, paper, earthen, and china-ware, carriages, arms, and tapestry

TURKEY. The large but ill-organised Turkish Empire is composed of many distinct portions, the produce, industry, and commerce of which have been briefly noticed under various headings relating to those districts and provinces. We may however state that the value of the British produce and manufactures exported in 1849, to European Turkey, exclusive of Wallachia and Moldavia, was 2,371,669.

Of Turkish industry, we have had a few opportunities of judging at the Great Exhibition.

TURKEY-HONE is a slaty, grayish, opaque, soft kind of stone, found in various parts of Europe and Asia. It is composed of silica, lime, alumina, and carbonic acid. When cut and polished, it is used for sharpening small cutting instruments. [GRINDSTONES.]

TURMERIC comprises many species of the *Curcuma* genus of plants. Of the *broad-leaved Turmeric*, the tubers are aromatic, and are used by the Hindoos, not only as a stimulating condiment and a medicine, but as a perfume. Its sensible properties are much like those of ginger, but not so powerful. It is employed in the East in cases of disease, as colic, cramp, torpor, &c., where stimulants are required. It is a native of Bengal, China, and various other parts of Asia, and of the Asiatic Islands. Some of the other species yield a kind of ginger, and some a kind of arrow root. The *common Turmeric* is occasionally wild, and it is also extensively cultivated in China, Java, Malacca, and in Bengal, prospering in a moist but not swampy soil. The Chinese sort is most esteemed, rather on account of its superior richness in colouring matter than from any other cause. Two varieties are found in commerce, the Round Turmeric and Long Turmeric. Turmeric possesses an acrid volatile oil and a colouring matter. It is used on account of the latter principle as a dye. The volatile oil gives it aromatic qualities, which render it useful in languid habits, where digestion is difficult and the circulation slow. It is of some importance as a dye; but it is as a condiment, both in the East and in this country, that it merits notice, as it is an ingredient in all *curry powders* and *curry pastes*.

TURNING is the process of giving a circular form to wood and other materials, by means of a lathe and cutting tools, as in wood and metal turning; or by the thrower's wheel (which is also a species of lathe) and shaping instruments, as in the manufacture of earthenware. The lathe may be described as a machine for moving the material to be wrought in such a manner that, being fixed opposite to the tool, any point in the circumference will act upon the whole circle in precisely the same way

Of all the publications which have appeared relating to the mechanical arts, there are few that we can rank with the late Mr. Holtzapfel's work on turning; for elaborate details, profuse illustrations, and instructive collateral information, it may almost be said to exhaust the subject to which it relates.

TURNTABLE. The *turntables*, or circular iron plates seen at most of the principal railway stations, are platforms on which a locomotive or carriage can be placed in order to be turned round in direction; the platform rotates on a central axis, and the road accompanies it. Where only a locomotive or an ordinary railway carriage are placed on the turntable, the latter need not be of great diameter; but in the instances where both a locomotive and its tender, or such long carriages as are now used on the North Kent and the North Woolwich Railways, are to be reversed, the turntable must be of very large diameter. A description has been lately given at a meeting of the *Institution of Civil Engineers*, of a turntable 42 feet in diameter, used on the Bristol and Exeter Railway. This turntable worked on a ball-pivot, and consisted of two central cast iron arms, or brackets, which carried at their extremities hollow wrought iron transverse girders for supporting the longitudinal timber beams, forming a framing on which were placed the rails—the outer ends being supported by other girders attached to the traversing wheels, which were 3 feet in diameter. It afforded a perfect and equal bearing throughout its entire length, not being depressed more than half an inch when the leading wheels of the engine struck the table; and an engine and tender, together weighing forty tons, were turned by the driver and stoker in three minutes. Tables on this principle have been erected both at Bristol and Exeter, and the cost, with the foundation, has been about 400*l*. each.

TURPENTINE. The common turpentine of commerce is imported from America in barrels and casks. It is a stiff, adhesive, honey-like paste, midway between the solid and the liquid state. It consists of two very different component parts: a clear transparent liquid, which constitutes *oil* or *essence* of *turpentine;* and a yellowish or brownish solid which forms common *resin*. The separation of these two substances is effected at the turpentine works, of which there are several in this country. The thick turpentine is put into a still and exposed to heat; it first melts into a liquid, and then the essential or oily portion rises in vapour, leaving the resinous portion still liquid. The vapour leaves the still, and passes through a refrigerator or cooling vessel, whereby it is brought to a liquid form. When the residue is removed from the still, it forms *black resin* or *yellow resin*, according to the kind of turpentine which had been employed.

The turpentine imported in the last three years amounted to the following quantities:—

1848............	401,787 cwts.
1849............	412,042 ,,
1850............	434,621 ,,

TURQUOISE. This beautiful mineral occurs in masses; it has a greenish blue colour, and is usually opaque. It is found in alluvial clay, near Nishapoor in Persia. It consists chiefly of phosphate of alumina.

TURRET or toweret is used as the diminutive of *tower*, and denotes that what is so described is small in comparison with the main structure, of which it forms a part. Turrets are frequently attached to one or more of the angles of a tower, and contain a winding stair leading to the roof of the tower. Sometimes they are formed on the upper part only of a building.

TUSCANY. About one-sixth part of this Italian State is planted with vines and olive-trees; another sixth is cultivated as arable land; nearly two-sixths are either forests or plantations of chestnut-trees, which afford food to the population of the mountains; and nearly as much again is pasture land. The most common way of letting land is on the 'metayer' system, by which the farmer finds half the seed and implements, and gives the owner half the produce in kind; the landlord stocks the farm, and a valuation is given to the farmer, who is to make all good on leaving.

Tuscany, besides the usual agricultural crops, produces wine, oil, and silk. The other articles of native produce exported are—fruit of various sorts, lamb and kid skins, potash, timber, cork, juniper-berries, marble and alabaster, iron from Elba, borax, sulphur, alum, and anchovies, which are fished off the coast. Nearly the whole trade of Tuscany with other countries is carried on through the port of Leghorn. The mineral products are—iron, from the island of Elba, the ore of which is smelted and cast on the mainland, at Cecina, Valpiana, and Follonica; copper, lead, marble, sulphur, rock-salt, alabaster, and alum. Sea-salt is made chiefly in Elba.

The manufactures of Tuscany consist of woollen, hempen, and linen cloths; woollen caps for the Levant; silk stuffs, paper, glass, leather, wax; coral, which is gathered on the coast of Barbary and worked at Leghorn; iron-ware, alabaster vases, and other ornaments, wrought at Volterra; china and delft ware. The straw-plat manufacture has declined greatly of late years.

The exports of British produce and manufactures to Tuscany in 1849, amounted in value to 777,273*l*.

TUTENAG, is an alloy used in China in the manufacture of the *Gong*. It is white, resembling silver in appearance, and is very sonorous when struck. It consists of copper 40, zinc 25, nickel 32, iron 3. It is susceptible of a fine polish, and does not readily tarnish. At common temperatures, and even at a red heat, it is malleable, but when heated to whiteness it is rendered brittle. The composition is nearly the same as that of German Silver.

TYPE-FOUNDING. In the article PRINTING a general view is given of the various steps in the invention of typography, or the art of printing from moveable types, and a brief notice of the individuals whose ingenuity contributed, more or less, to the perfection of the process of type-founding. Most of the early printers, in England as well as on the Continent, were accustomed to cut and cast their own types. It has since become a separate business

The first and most important operation of a type-foundry is the formation of the *punches*, which are well-tempered pieces of steel, each of which bears on its surface a single letter, formed with the greatest possible accuracy by filing, cutting, and punching the hollows with smaller punches. The face of the punch exactly resembles that of the finished type, the letter being reversed, and in high relief. The punch-cutter has to exercise great care and judgment for making the letter of precisely the right size, form, and thickness, so that it may range well with other letters of the same *Fount*, or set. When the punch is completed and hardened, it is struck into a piece of copper, which, when it has received the impression from the end of the punch, is called a *Matrix*, and forms a mould for the face of the type.

The *Mould* for casting the type consists of two halves, each of which is made of steel, and attached, for convenience of holding, to a piece of wood. The two halves of the mould are so formed that they may be instantaneously fitted together, leaving a square funnel-shaped opening at the top, by which the type-metal is poured into the mould to form the body of the type, with the matrix at the bottom to form the letter or face. The two halves of the mould are capable of adjustment to the varying widths of the letters. The type-metal is usually melted in a small cast-iron pot, set in brickwork with an enclosed fire under it, and is poured into the mould by a very small ladle. The caster then jerks the mould quickly upwards by a peculiar motion of his arm, and thereby expels the air, and forces the fluid metal to enter the cavities of the matrix. Some founders use a small force-pump to aid this operation. When the metal is set, the caster removes the pressure of a long curved spring which is attached to the bottom of the mould, and thereby separates the matrix from the face of the type. The mould is then opened, and the type is removed by the application of a hook attached to the upper part of the mould.

When the types leave the caster, each of them has a small block of metal attached to the shank, or body of the type, being that which filled the throat or funnel of the mould. These are removed by a boy. The next operation is that of rubbing the flat sides of the types upon a piece of gritstone. The types are then set up by boys in long rows or lines, and these are firmly secured in long frames, which hold them together while the dresser scrapes or polishes the flat surface which form the top and bottom of the body, and cuts a groove or channel along their lower ends by means of a small iron plane. While they are in the frame the types are also *bearded*, an operation which consists in planing away to a bevel the upper angle of the body at the feet of the letters. After dressing, the types are tied up in such lines as may be convenient, and the proportionate numbers of every type of which a fount consists are selected. All the types belonging to one fount are distinguished by one or more grooves or *nicks* across the lower edge or bottom face of the body, by which simple contrivance the compositor is enabled to pick up the types and place them all upright without looking at the letter. These nicks are formed by the insertion of one or more wires in the mould. Four casters and two boys can cast, break, and rub 2,000 types in an hour.

The composition of type-metal greatly varies; the chief component however is lead, alloyed by one or more of the following metals—iron, antimony, copper, brass, tin, and bismuth.

As the several letters of the alphabet are, in common printing, required in very different proportions, the number cast of each letter in a fount needs to be carefully regulated. The proportions vary in different languages, and in different kinds of work; but for ordinary English book-work they are about as follows:—

a	8,500	n	8,000	ff	400
b	1,600	o	8,000	fi	500
c	3,000	p	1,700	fl	200
d	4,400	q	500	ffi	150
e	12,000	r	6,200	ffl	100
f	2,500	s	8,000	æ	100
g	1,700	t	9,000	œ	60
h	6,400	u	3,400	,	4,500
i	8,000	v	1,200	;	800
j	400	w	2,000	:	600
k	800	x	400	.	2,000
l	4,000	y	2,000	'	700
m	3,000	z	200		

The names of the various founts, beginning with the smallest and ending with one of the largest used in ordinary book-printing, are—*Diamond, Pearl, Ruby, Nonpareil, Minion, Brevier, Bourgeois, Long Primer, Small Pica, Pica, English, Great Primer.* Larger founts than any of these are occasionally used.

At the Great Exhibition, Messrs. Miller and Richards have displayed type still smaller than *Diamond*, and said by them to be the smallest ever made in this country. The name of *Brilliant* is given to it. Gray's Elegy (32 verses), printed in this type, occupies a space rather less than 4 inches by 3.

The following details have recently been given concerning the types for printing the Great Exhibition Catalogues:—"The first step towards the accomplishment of this vast undertaking was the creation of the type necessary to print four editions—and Messrs. Clowes and Son, being type-founders as well as printers, came to the resolution of having the whole of the type cast specially for the purpose. Their first effort was directed to produce the type for the small English, French, and German catalogues; the quantity cast for the purpose was 16,000 lbs. For the large and illustrated edition they have, in addition to their own foundries, employed those of Messrs. Figgins, Messrs. Bezley and Co., and Mr. Caslon, of London, and Messrs. Miller and Richards, of Edinburgh. The joint exertions of these firms have added 25,000 lbs. more to the general stock set apart for this vast undertaking; making a total of 41,000 lbs. The casting of this large quantity of type gave employment to 250 persons for ten weeks. The number of separate pieces in 20 tons of type amounts to upwards of 26 millions, and each type or piece of metal passes through the hands of five persons in the process of manufacture."

TYROL. In this very interesting country the most fertile lands are in the valleys of the Inn and of the Adige. Wheat, rye, barley, and oats are cultivated; in some parts buckwheat is grown; and millet is also grown, but not extensively. Indian corn is the principal object of agriculture in the southern valleys, and potatoes are nearly as much cultivated as in the northern. Hops grow wild, and tobacco is cultivated to some extent in the southern valleys. Flax and hemp are grown. Fruit-trees abound in the southern valleys, and large quantities of fruit are exported to Bavaria. Near Trent are plantations of fig-trees, and at Roveredo chestnuts are very common. In these parts are also plantations of olive-trees and mulberry-trees. A considerable quantity of silk is annually collected. On the banks of the Lago di Guarda are plantations of oranges. Wine is made in large quantities, and some sorts are very good, but they do not keep. Gold, silver, and copper are found; lead, iron, calamine, and coal mines are worked. There are productive mines of rock-salt near Hall, below Innsbruck. In the southern districts there is a valuable kind of white marble which is much worked.

Though the inhabitants are extremely industrious, Tyrol is not a manufacturing country. The women spin flax, weave linen, knit caps and stockings, make baskets and straw hats; the only manufactures of any importance are carried on in the chief towns. The transit trade of Tyrol is considerable, and much facilitated by the admirable roads. Many of the inhabitants annually migrate as pedlars or hawkers.

U

ULMIC ACID, or ULMINE. Some trees, and more especially the elm, when it is old, secrete a liquid which dries as it exudes; the residue consists principally of mucilaginous matter, with some carbonate or acetate of potash, and eventually the mucilaginous matter undergoes a change, and, combining with the potash, forms a substance which was first examined by Vauquelin and Klaproth, and Dr. Thomson gave it the name of *Ulmin.* It is of a deep brown colour, very brittle, and breaks in angular fragments, and is almost insoluble in water. It may be procured from soils, rotten leaves, bog-earth, wood-soot, or turf. It is an important element in manures and soils; and what is called *moss-water* owes its peculiar properties to its presence. It is a powerful manure, especially when combined with lime or with ammonia.

ULTRAMARINE, is a well-known blue pigment of extraordinary beauty and great permanence.

Ultramarine was originally prepared from the *lapis lazuli* or *lazulite.* This mineral presents itself in small masses of granular structure, in a rock of heterogeneous structure; this rock, which in commerce is called *lapis,* sells for a higher or lower price for pigments according to the proportion of lazulite which it is found to contain. The most perfect specimens of lazulite are used as gems; while the less perfect are used in the preparation of ultramarine. The lazulite is made red hot, quenched, pounded to powder, washed, dried, made into a paste with pure linseed oil and certain resinous substances, kneaded, diffused in hot water, and allowed to settle until the ultramarine (leaving all the other ingredients) falls to the bottom. The whole of these processes require great care.

This colour is now prepared at a very moderate price, and equal in beauty to that obtained from the lazulite. M. Gmelin of Tübingen considers that sulphuret of sodium is the colouring principle both of the natural mineral and the artificial products. The artificial ultramarine is stated to be prepared by adding freshly-precipitated silica and alumina, mixed with sulphur, to a solution of caustic soda, and the mixture is to be evaporated to dryness: the residue is put into a covered crucible and exposed to a white heat, by which, when the air has partial access to it, a dark pure blue mass is obtained. The product is then reduced to impalpable powder. The proportions of materials to be used are, about 36 silica, 36 alumina, 24 soda, and 3 sulphur.

UMBER, is an ore of iron and manganese, employed as a brown pigment. The structure is earthy, and the colour varied from red to brown. It occurs in beds with brown jasper in the Isle of Cyprus.

UNGUENTS. [OINTMENTS.]

UNITED STATES. The following details will illustrate a few among the many aspects under which the produce, industry, and commerce of the United States of America present themselves to our notice.

In the year ending June 1850, the United States imported 247,951 tons of bar iron, 14,706 tons of hammered iron, 10,101 tons of scrap iron, and 74,874 tons of pig iron. New York exported 4,844,574 dollars' worth of produce and commodities in that year, more than two-fifths of which went to Liverpool alone. The cotton exported in the same year was 635,381,604 lbs., being far below the average of recent years.

The exports from the United States in the year ending June 1849 amounted in value to 145,755,820 dollars of which two thirds were in United States' vessels. The imports (paying duty) in the same period were 147,857,439 dollars; of which five-sixths were in United States' vessels. The domestic exports were thus made up:—

	Dollar
Produce of Fisheries (fish, fish-oil, spermaceti, whalebone, &c.	2,547,654
Produce of Forests (timber, bark, dyes, potash, turpentine, tar, &c.) . .	5,917,904
Produce of Agriculture (cattle, meat, butter, cheese, corn, cotton, &c.) . . .	111,059,378
Manufactures and Miscellaneous,	13,141,929
	132,666,955

The remainder of the exports (about 13,000,000 dollars) were re-exported foreign commodities.

More than half of the entire exports of domestic produce were sent to Great Britain.

In the next following year, that is, the year ending June 1850, the exports of domestic produce from the United States was 136,946,912 dollars, of which Great Britain and its dependencies took the enormous value of 81,687,051 dollars; considerably more than half of which was comprised in the single article of cotton.

The following table shows the progress of the population and wealth of New York:—

Year.	Population.	Value of Real and Personal Estate.
1800	60,489	24,486,370 dollars.
1810	93,373	69,530,753 „
1820	123,706	69,530,573 „
1825	166,086	101,160,046 „
1830	202,589	125,283,518 „
1835	270,089	218,723,703 „
1840	312,852	252,843,163 „
1845	371,223	239,938,317 „
1850	517,849	256,217,093 „

To show how the various states of the American Union stand related in respect to shipbuilding, we give the numbers for the year ending June 1850:—

States.	Steamers.	Total—Ships and Steamers.	Total Tonnage.
Maine	6	326	94,211 73
New Hampshire	—	10	6,914 32
Vermont	1	1	77 41
Massachusetts	2	121	35,836 14
Rhode Island	1	14	3,537 15
Connecticut	1	43	4,819 70
New York	32	224	53,342 73
New Jersey	3	57	6,201 68
Pennsylvania	31	185	21,409 93
Delaware	1	16	1,813 82
Maryland	4	150	15,964 80
District of Columbia	—	8	288 17
Virginia	5	34	3,534 04
N. Carolina	5	33	2,691 55
Georgia	3	5	683 82
Florida	—	2	79 75
Alabama	—	3	118 66
Louisiana	4	24	1,582 38
Kentucky	34	34	6,460 69
Missouri	5	5	1,353 82
Illinois	1	13	1,691 21
Ohio	16	31	5,214 62
Michigan	3	14	9,061 63
Texas	1	1	105 54
Oregon	—	2	122 42
Total	150	1,356	270,117 80

In the year ending June 1850, the merchant ships which left ports of the United States amounted to 18,195, of which 8379 were American and 9816 foreign. The tonnage of these vessels was 4,361,002 tons. The tôtal of the crews entered as belonging to those vessels was 195,871. From New York alone the number of ships cleared was no less than 2818, of 1,106,070 tons. In the first nine months of 1850, there were 19 steam ships and 18 sailing vessels launched at New York; and at the end of that period there were 19 other steamers and 12 other sailing vessels building. The numbers of passengers which have arrived at New York during the last ten years are as follow:—

Year.	Passengers.	Vessels.
1841	57,337	2,118
1842	74,949	1,960
1843	46,302	1,832
1844	61,002	2,208
1845	82,960	2,044
1846	115,230	2,289
1847	166,110	3,147
1848	191,909	3,060
1849	221,799	3,237
1850	126,287	3,489
	1,143,885	25,384

In June 1850 the length of the inland mail routes in the United States (not including Oregon and California) was 178,672 miles; and the annual transport on those roads amounted to 46,541,423 miles. The number of post offices in the United States in that month was 18,417.

On January 1, 1851, the length of Railways in the United States amounted to nearly 9000 miles, and the cost to upwards of 60,000,000*l.* sterling. They were distributed among the states in the following ratios:—

	Miles.	Cost.
New York	1402	56,202,060 dollars.
NewHampshire,	452	15,046,080 „
Rhode Island	50	2,614,484 „
Maine	220	5,765,518 „
Vermont	348	10,038,897 „
Massachusetts	1056	48,235,997 „
Connecticut	513	15,245,508 „
New Jersey	259	8,225,000 „
Pennsylvania	917	35,008,033 „
Delaware	17	600,000 „
Maryland	322	13,044,172 „
Virginia	384	7,378,349 „
NorthCarolina,	249	4,000,000 „
SouthCarolina,	271	6,243,678 „
Georgia	716	11,572,280 „
Alabama	114	950,000 „
Florida	54	280,000 „
Mississippi	90	795,600 „
Louisiana	89	603,000 „
Tennessee	33	600,000 „

	Miles.		Cost.	
Kentucky....	77	..	1,480,000	dollars.
Indiana.....	219	..	4,600,000	,,
Ohio........	450	..	7,268,793	,,
Illinois......	117	..	2,100,000	,,
Michigan....	352	..	7,704,633	,,
Wisconsin...	20	..	400,000	,,

URA'NIUM, is the name given to a metal discovered by Klaproth, in 1789, who named it after the planet Uranus, the discovery of which had previously occurred in the same year. The mineral from which it was first obtained is called *Pechblende*, or *Pitchblende*. It is a white lustrous metal. At a moderate degree of heat, in contact with the air, it burns with a white and shining light. The combustion occurs at so low a temperature, that it may take place on paper without causing it to burn. If small particles be shaken from the filter on which the metal in powder has been collected, portions so minute as to be scarcely visible burn with brilliant sparks on coming near the flame of a candle. When heated in a capsule, uranium burns brilliantly and is converted into a deep green-coloured oxide, the bulk of which is considerably greater than that of the metal employed. It does not appear to suffer any alteration by exposure to the air, nor does it decompose water at common temperatures.

The minerals which contain uranium, and from many of which it may be obtained, are numerous. They comprise *Pitchblende* (oxide), *Uranite* (calcareo-phosphate), *Chalcolite* (cupreo-phosphate), *Uran Bloom* (carbonate), *Johannite* (sulphate). The various compounds of the metal with other substances are of but limited use in the arts; the *protoxide*, however, is employed in colouring glass, to which it imparts a fine lemon yellow.

URUGUAY, or *Banda Oriental*, an independent Republic in South America, is of moderate natural richness. A valuable copper mine is worked near San Carlos. The valleys on the west and south are well adapted to a great diversity of production. Wheat, rye, barley, Indian corn, rice, peas, beans, water-melons, and other kinds of melons, with onions, are cultivated; also some cotton, mandioca, and the sugar-cane. Hemp and different qualities of flax grow in great abundance Timber is by no means abundant. More than four-fifths of the country being only fit for pasture, cattle of course constitute the chief wealth. Some cattle are consumed in the country, and others sent to the slaughter-houses of Monte Video, whence hides are exported in large numbers. By far the greatest proportion of the flesh is converted into jerked beef, which is salted without the bones, dried in the sun, and exported to different parts of America, especially Brazil. Every great proprietor breeds also a certain number of horses and mules, and some of them a great number of sheep, which have a fine wool.

UTRECHT, one of the Dutch provinces, is a productive and busy district. The natural productions are—the common domestic animals, poultry, fish, bees, wheat, tobacco, buckwheat, pulse, garden-fruit, culinary vegetables, flax, and hemp. The manufactures are chiefly in the towns, and consist of woollen, cotton, silken, and linen fabrics: there are also breweries and distilleries. The exports are—corn, cattle, swine, butter, cheese, some manufactured goods, bricks, and tiles. The roads in this province, which are remarkably smooth, are paved with clinker bricks. All the heavy traffic is carried on by the canals or railroads to Amsterdam and Arnhem. Another line of railway now unites the town of Utrecht to Rotterdam. In Utrecht, the capital of the province, the inhabitants manufacture woollen cloths, silk, lace, and needles; they have also sugar refineries and bleaching grounds.

V

VACUUM, or VOID. In scientific enquiries the name *vacuum* is given to space wholly free of matter, or perfectly empty. In the common phrase, space is called empty when, so far as air can fill space, it is full of air; and even in a more scientific form of speech, there is said to be a vacuum when there is only such an approach to a vacuum as the operations of philosophy can procure. Thus in the vacuum of the air-pump, however long the attempt at exhaustion may be continued, there is always air left, though in a highly attenuated state; and even in the mercurial vacuum, or in the space which is left over the mercury of the barometer, there is not unfrequently a slight portion of air, and always an atmosphere of the vapour of mercury. Physically speaking, it is perhaps impossible to procure a vacuum: it is most likely that, even if a real vacuum could be procured for an instant, air or other vapour would at once begin to be disseminated from the sides of the vessel in which the vacuum was made, and that the vacuum would thus instantly cease to exist.

In steam machinery, the whole efficacy of the apparatus is dependent on the recurrence, at regular intervals, of a vacuum, or an approximation towards a vacuum, in certain cylinders into which steam passes. [AIR-PUMP; HYDRAULICS; STEAM ENGINE.]

VALENCIA. A large proportion of this beautiful Spanish province is among the most fertile and best cultivated districts in Europe. The plain or vega of Valencia is about 30 miles long and 20 wide; the whole of this district is planted with olive, mulberry, ilex, algaroba, orange, and palm-trees, and has the appearance of an immense garden. Such is the fertility of the soil that two and three crops in the year are generally obtained. The rice crops are the most valuable, and are chiefly produced in the tract which is irrigated by the Albufera, a large lake in the neighbourhood of Valencia. The other chief product is the white mulberry, for the feeding of silkworms: the produce of silk from the vega of Valencia amounts to above one million of pounds yearly, a great part of which is exported in its raw state to France. The export of fruit from Valencia is also considerable; of raisins, the quantity exported has in some years been close upon 150,000 cwts. to England alone. The exports of barilla, almonds, figs, oil, saffron, wool, brandy, and wine, from different ports of Valencia is also very great, particularly the wine called Beni Carlo, which comes from a town of that name.

Mercury, copper, sulphur, arsenic, gold, silver, lead, iron, coal, and antimony, are among the mineral products. Woollen, linen, and silken goods are made in several towns of the province, but chiefly for home consumption. Cordage made from the fibre of the esparto, mats, tiles, soap, glass, paper, pottery, and earthenware, are exported to all parts of Spain. Salt is largely exported to Sweden.

In the city of Valencia, the imports are codfish, bricks, iron, coals, tobacco, colonial produce, hides, manufactured goods, linen, hardware, trinkets, Norway deals, and Dutch cheese. The exports are composed of barilla, wine, raisins, almonds, lead, brandy, oranges, raw silk, saffron, oil, wool, bass mats and ropes, salt, liquorice, and aniseed. The inhabitants are chiefly devoted to agriculture, although many branches of trade flourish in the city. Velvets, taffetas, flowered damask, and other silk stuffs are manufactured for the home market. Woollens, camlets, hats, table-linen, gauzes, artificial flowers, pottery, and earthenware, glass, and paper, are also made in small quantities.

VALERIAN is a herb or undershrub possessing many valuable qualities. It is a native of Europe, and by the sides of rivers and in ditches and moist woods is abundant in Great Britain. The root has a very strong smell, which is dependent on a volatile oil. It is very attractive to cats, and also to rats, and is employed by rat-catchers to decoy rats. It is employed also in medicine at the present day. The root, or more properly the rhizoma, with its root-fibres, is used in medicine. The medicinal action is chiefly due to the volatile oil and extractive.

VALPARAISO, a large town and important seaport of Chile, is yearly rising into rank as one of the leading commercial depôts on the Pacific shore of America. In 1809 only 9 vessels entered the harbour, in 1836 the number averaged 40 per month; in 1849 the total number of foreign vessels that entered was 968. The customs revenue for 1849 was 2,022,577 dollars. There are large ship-building yards, and extensive bonding ware-houses. Many vessels engaged in the Pacific trade come to Valparaiso for provisions, which may be put on board without their dropping an anchor. Valparaiso is the central depôt for the produce of Chile. Large quantities of corn, and other articles of provisions, are shipped here for Callao, Panama, and San Francisco. Besides wheat, the chief exports are—copper (of which 76,515½ quintals were shipped in 1849), gold, and silver; tallow and hides; timber, indigo, wool, sarsaparilla, fruits, &c. The imports are—foreign manufactured goods, chocolate, tea, coffee, sugar, tobacco, hardware, &c., &c. The British exports to Valparaiso exceed a million sterling annually. The French and American commerce with this port is also very important. The trade of Valparaiso has greatly increased since the discovery of gold in California. Steamers ply regularly to Callao and other Pacific ports.

VALVE is the name given to any apparatus by which, in an hydraulic or pneumatic machine, the bore of a pipe or any orifice may be alternately covered and uncovered, in order in the one case to prevent, and in the other to permit, the passage of the fluid.

The ordinary pump-valve, frequently called a *Clack*, consists of a piece of leather rather larger than the bore or orifice. Circular plates of lead or brass are fastened to the upper and lower surfaces of the leather; and the valve thus formed is capable, from the flexibility of the leather, of turning, as on a hinge, at the place of its connection with the rim. After a certain quantity of water has forced its way through the orifice, the valve, by its weight, falls, and closely covers the orifice, so that the water above is in great part prevented from returning.

Frequently a narrow bar of metal is made fast across a circular orifice in the direction of a diameter, and two semicircular valves of leather, each of which is covered above and below with a brass plate of the same form, turn upon the sides of the bar as upon hinges. This is called the *Double-Clack*, or the *Butterfly*-Valve.

The conical or *Spindle* Valve is a metal body in the form of a frustum of a cone, the side of which makes an angle of 45 degrees with a diameter of the base, and its convex surface is ground so as to fit exactly the corresponding side of the orifice. It is usually employed as the safety-valve to the boiler of a steam-engine. The frustum is lifted up vertically by the pressure of the steam, and when the steam has passed, it falls back by its weight.

The valve employed for the usual air-pumps consists merely of a slip of thin bladder thoroughly soaked in oil, its breadth being little more than is necessary to cover the orifice. When the pressure of the atmosphere is in part removed from the barrel, some of the air which is in the receiver forces its way, by its elasticity, through the orifice, and escapes at the sides of the valve. The valves of machines for condensing air are like those of a rarefying pump, but they are placed in contrary positions.

VANA'DIUM, a metal discovered in 1830, has somewhat of a silvery lustre, is extremely brittle, is a conductor of electricity, and at common temperatures is not acted upon by air or water; when heated to low redness in the air, it burns and is converted into black oxide. The compounds which this metal forms with other substances have not yet been applied to much practical use.

VAN DIEMEN'S LAND. The mineral wealth of this British colony is not yet much known. So far as it has been investigated, it includes copper, iron, lead, zinc, manganese, coal, slate, salt, and sandstone. Little has yet been done in mining operations. All grains cultivated in England succeed well. Wheat is of excellent quality, weighing generally from 62 to 64 pounds the bushel: considerable quantities are exported. Barley and oats will only thrive in a good soil. The vegetables and fruits of Europe are cultivated by the colonists in great abundance. The spermaceti whale is very abundant in Bass's Strait, and many of them are annually taken, but more by the inhabitants of Australia than by those of Van Diemen's Land. Black whales abound in all the seas round the island, and a very lucrative fishery is carried on along the southern coast. Whale-bone and train oil are important articles of export. The most useful tree in the colony is the Stringy Bark Tree, which is used for building and fencing; and the Blue Gum Tree, of which most of the boats in the colony are built. The smaller trees are used for masts for small vessels.

The efforts of the local government are rapidly extending improvements over the island. No fewer than 24 bridges were built by the government between 1842 and 1847. In 1847, 5538 emigrants arrived in the colony from Great Britain, and 4787 departed from it (chiefly to Port Philip and South Australia). Among the greatest works now constructing is a bridge over the Derwent, on the high road from Hobart Town to Launceston; it is of wood, and will have twenty bays or arches of 32 feet span each. The manufacturing establishments of Van Diemen's Land in 1847 included 46 breweries, 15 candle factories, 4 dye-works, 17 engineering and foundry works, 80 mills, 3 potteries, 10 printing-offices, 16 ship-yards, and 44 tan-works. The vessels which entered the colony in 1847 were 617 (burthen, 86,940 tons). The vessels built in the colony in that year were 12 (burthen, 1361 tons). The vessels belonging to Hobart Town were 140 (burthen, 11,521 tons); and those to Launceston 44 (burthen, 3373 tons). The value of the fisheries in that year was estimated at 70,000*l.* The live stock comprised 16,212 horses, 82,194 cattle, 1,833,866 sheep, and 2964 pigs. The staple article of produce is wool. A considerable trade is carried on with South Australia and Port Philip, in sheep. Van Diemen's Land produces not only a sufficient supply of grain for domestic consumption, but has contributed for several years to supply the deficiency in New South Wales.

The total exports for 1847 were valued at 600,867*l.*; the four chief items were—wool, 247,240*l.*; wheat, 85,683*l.*; flour, 40,595*l.*; and oil, 63,165*l.* The imports in the same year were valued at 724,593*l.*; the five chief items were—woollens, 108,175*l.*; cottons, 35,679*l.*; apparel and haberdashery, 48,388*l.*; hardware, 41,030*l.*; and sugar, 51,615*l.* The British produce and manufactures imported in 1849, were valued at 315,021*l.*

VANILLA. As the greater portion and the finest kinds of the Vanilla of commerce are imported from Vera Cruz, the most important species must be natives of Mexico. The fruit is the only part of the plant that is used. It has a balsamic odour, and a warm agreeable flavour. For these properties it is indebted to a peculiar volatile oil, and to a considerable quantity of benzoic acid. The fruit is gathered when it gets yellow, and it is first allowed to ferment for two or three days: it is then laid in the sun to dry, and when about half dried it is rubbed over with the oil of cocoa: it is again exposed to the sun to dry, and oiled again a second time. The fruit is then collected in small bundles, and wrapped up in the leaves of the Indian reed. Neither in Guiana nor in Mexico is the vanilla plant cultivated, but the fruit is collected by the natives, who sell it to the Europeans.

VAPOUR consists of ponderable matter combined with sufficient heat to enable it to retain its aëriform state. The difference between *vapour* and *gas* is one of degree only: for when atmospheric air containing, as it always does, the vapour of water, is suddenly cooled by exposure to a colder substance, the water which it contained in the state of invisible vapour it deposited in the state of palpable water on the colder body; and many gaseous bodies which were once considered as permanently elastic have been shown by the important investigations of Dr. Faraday to be reducible to liquids. [EVAPORATION.]

VARNISH is a fluid applied to the surfaces of various articles, as wood, &c., and which, by the evaporation or chemical change of a portion, leaves upon them a shining coating impervious to air and to moisture. Varnishes may be divided into three classes, alcoholic or *spirit* varnishes, *volatile oil* varnishes, and *fixed oil* varnishes.

Spirit varnishes are in general prepared very readily, are easily applied, soon become dry, and emit no disagreeable smell: they are, however, liable to crack or scale off, and are incapable of resisting friction or blows. The following are among the most approved spirit varnishes:—Take of mastich 6 ounces, sandarach 3 ounces, reduced to fine powder, and add 4 ounces of coarsely-powdered glass, which prevents the resins from agglomerating into a mass, or sticking to the bottom of the vessel; digest in a quart of spirit of wine, contained in a loosely-corked vessel for three days in a warm room, shaking the mixture frequently; then add 3 ounces of melted Venice turpentine to the warm solution, stirring thoroughly till mixed; let the mixture remain in a warm room for about a week, and then strain it. This is a strong varnish applied to chairs and other articles of furniture. Another varnish is formed of copal which has been liquified and afterwards very finely powdered, 3 ounces, mastich 2 ounces, and elemi 1 ounce; digest in a warm room in a quart of spirit, and when the solution is complete, add 2 ounces of Venice turpentine. This is a good varnish for violins and other musical instruments. For different purposes the ingredients of spirit varnishes are considerably varied: seed-lac, benzoin, anime, or frankincense, entering into the composition, according to the use to be made of them.

The only essential or volatile oil largely used in varnishes is oil of turpentine, or, as it is commonly called, spirit of turpentine; and one of the best varnishes into the composition of which it enters is copal varnish. This is chiefly used for pictures. Another powerful varnish is prepared by adding to highly rectified oil of turpentine about an eighth of its weight of caoutchouc.

In these varnishes the volatile solvents evaporate, but in the case of fixed oil varnishes, the solvent undergoes a chemical change, and dries with the substance dissolved—these are sometimes termed fat varnishes. One kind of fixed oil varnish consists of a mixture of 4 ounces of copal, which has been liquefied and finely powdered, oil of turpentine, and drying linseed oil, each 10 ounces; digest in a gentle heat till the whole is dissolved; strain it after standing a few days. This forms a solid and nearly colourless glazing, and dries easily at common temperatures.

The *varnish tree* of Birma and Japan abounds in every part with a viscid ferruginous juice, which quickly becomes black by the contact of the atmosphere. The varnish is collected by inserting pointed joints of bamboo, which are closed at the other end, into wounds made in the trunk and principal boughs. The joints of bamboo are removed after from twenty-four to forty-eight hours, and their contents, which rarely exceed a quarter of an ounce, emptied into a basket made of bamboo and rattan, previously varnished over. In Birma almost every article of household furniture intended to contain either solid or liquid food is lacquered by means of this varnish. It is also much employed in the process of gilding: the surface, being first besmeared with this varnish, has then the gold leaf immediately applied to it. The beautiful Pali writing of the Birmese, on ivory, palm-leaves, or metal, is entirely done with this varnish in its native and pure state.

VASES. The most numerous class of ancient vases are those painted vases of dried or baked clay which have of late years been discovered by thousands in Etruria, southern Italy, Sicily, Greece, and some of the Grecian islands. Such vases are frequently found in tombs, catacombs, and other depositories of the dead. The period during which the art of vase painting completed its development from the rudest elements to the highest perfection, is comprised in the three centuries before the Christian æra, from B. C. 600 to about 200.

The most convenient criterion for classifying the ancient vases is their style of painting, which alone affords a very obvious distinction, and also marks the different stages of the art. They may be thus classed as follows:—

1. Vases with paintings in the *Egyptian style*. The vases are of a pale yellow colour, on which the figures, generally of animals or flowers, are painted in a black or brown colour, sometimes with the addition of purple or white tints. Grace is entirely wanting. These vases occur most frequently in the tombs of Volci in Etruria, and in those of Nola; and they are supposed to have been made about B. C. 500.

2. Vases with paintings in the *archaic* or *ancient style*. The vases of this class have black figures on a red ground, and the figures are no longer mere animals and ornaments of the vessels, but contain scenes taken from the stories about the gods and heroes of Greece, and from the occurrences of ordinary life. The form of these vases, which is usually that of the amphora, has a freedom and elegance of proportions which are wanting in those of the first class; and they vary greatly in size. The peculiarities of the designs are strong outlines of the main parts of the human body, and the expression of the highest degree of physical strength. In the representation of animals, especially horses, there is sometimes a considerable degree of boldness and beauty. The majority of vases of this class are generally believed to have been made previous to the year B. C. 430.

3. Vases with painting in *the severe style*. In the vases of this class the figures are red, the natural colour of the clay, on a beautiful black ground. The most striking features in the design are a certain moderation and harmony. The drapery forms varied and rich folds, though they show a conventional regularity. The heads are worked with great care, and sometimes are truly graceful; the hands and feet are better drawn than on the vases of the former classes. The subjects represented are the same as those on the vases of the second class, but repose is more frequent than action. The forms of the vases are elegant, and they present great variations both in shape and size. They occur most frequently in Etruria and at Nola. Vases of this class are commonly assigned to the period from B. C. 460 to 420.

4. Vases with paintings in *the beautiful style*. In all the vases which are regarded as the true representatives of this period, all harshness and severity of style have disappeared: liveliness in the composition, perfect freedom in action and movement, as well as in the drapery, are the essential characteristics of this style. The colour of the figures, as in the third class, is the natural red of the clay, and white is used to represent a variety of things, such as ribbons, garlands, the flames of torches, and the like. The inscriptions too are usually painted in white. Vases of this class are not often found in Etruria: they are most frequent in Nola, Sicily, and Attica. The vases of this class, which show the highest perfection of the art, appear to belong to the period beginning with the year B. C. 400.

5. Vases with paintings in *the rich style*.

These differ but little from the preceding class, and are often difficult to assign with certainty. The designs are frequently executed with considerable carelessness, and show the sinking condition of the art. The best specimens of this class of vases are of extraordinary beauty, but the worst of them are so bad that they can scarcely be regarded as the works of Greeks.

There is a large collection of these vases, including all tho classes, in the British Museum.

VEGETABLE SUBSTANCES. To treat of botanical classification, or of the phenomena of vegetable growth, would be beyond the limits of the present work. In respect to the vegetable substances employed in food, medicine, and the arts, many are described under their proper headings.

When the Commissioners were forming the skeleton for the arrangements of the Great Exhibition, they devoted one of the four sections of the entire collection to *Raw Materials and Produce;* and this section they divided into *animal*, *vegetable*, and *mineral*. It may be useful to give here, in an abridged form, the system on which vegetable substances were divided.

The whole series of vegetable substances, so far as usefully employed, were placed in four groups: 1st. *Substances used chiefly in food;* 2nd. *Materials used chiefly in the chemical or medical arts;* 3rd. *Materials for building, clothing, &c.;* 4th. *Miscellaneous substances.* The first group comprised agricultural produce, such as corn, pulse, oil seeds, &c.; dried fruits and seeds; substances used in the preparation of drinks; spices and condiments; different varieties of starch; different varieties of sugar; fermented liquors and distilled spirits from unusual sources. The second group comprised different varieties of gum; resins, such as balsams, gum resins, and elastic gums; oils, such as volatile oils, fat oils, drying oils, solid oils, and wax; acids and alkalies; dyes and colours; tanning substances; intoxicating drugs; medicinal substances. The third group comprised fibrous substances, such as cordage and clothing materials; cellular substances; timber and fancy woods. The last group, as its name pretty nearly implies, comprised all the substances which could not very well be included under any of the other three, and which were necessarily of a diverse character.

So far as was practicable, this system of classification has been attended to in the arrangement of the Exhibition; but it has unavoidably happened that some of the varieties are less fully represented than others.

VEGETABLE WAX. Various plants yield a substance like wax, which is obtained, like the vegetable butter, by bruising and boiling them in water, when the wax melting floats to the surface, and there concretes on cooling. Of these the most remarkable instance is the *ceroxylon andicola*, the wax palm, palma de cera of the American Spaniards. Myrica gale, candleberry myrtle, or sweet gale, a native of this country, yields a substanco resembling bees'-wax when its catkins or cones are boiled in water: so *myrica cerifera*, a native of North America, yields a similar substance when its berries are thus boiled: candles are made of it also, whence the plant is commonly called tallow-shrub or candleberry tree. *Myrica quercifolia*, a native of the Cape of Good Hope, is another species which yields a vegetable wax. It grows along the coast, on dry sandy plains exposed to the sea-air, where hardly any other plants will vegetate. The wax invests the berries in the form of a rough crust, which is separated by means of boiling water. It is of a greenish colour, but may be bleached. When made into candles it gives a very fine light. A vegetable wax is also obtained in China from *ligustrum lucidum*, which is frequently mentioned as the wax tree in Dr. Abel's and other travels.

VELOCIMETER. Various machines havo been invented and introduced under this name for measuring velocities. Dixon's Velocimeter is intended to measure the speed of railway trains; it is somewhat complicated in arrangement; but when placed in connexion with one of the wheels of the engine or carriage, there is a kind of clock-work mechanism which shows how often the wheels have revolved, and consequently how much space has been passed over in a given time. In one form it simply indicates to the engine driver the speed of the train; but by an additional apparatus it may be made to *register* its results on paper. Mr. Alliot patented a peculiar method, in 1849, of determining the velocity of a railway train by the pressure of water in a chamber or vessel. Mr. Berthon's apparatus for measuring the velocity of a ship's motion through the water is noticed under LOG AND LOGLINE.

VELVET MANUFACTURE. This beautiful substance is mostly a silk fabric, remarkable for the softness of its surface. This softness is owing to a loose *pile* or surface of threads, occasioned by the insertion of short pieces of silk thread doubled under the shoot, weft, or cross threads. These stand upright so thickly as entirely to conceal the interlacing of the warp and shoot. The richness of the velvet depends upon the closeness of the pile-threads. The insertion of these short threads is effected in the following manner:—Instead of having only one row of warp-threads, which will be crossed alternately over and under by the shoot, there are two sets, one of which is to form the regular warp, while the other is to constitute the pile; and these two sets are so arranged in the loom as to be kept separate. The quantity of the pile-thread necessary is very much more than that of the warp-thread; and therefore must be supplied to the loom by a different agency.

If the pile-threads were worked in among the shoot, in the same way as the warp-threads, the fabric would be simply a kind of double silk, but without any kind of pile; the pile-threads are therefore formed into a series of loops, standing up from the surface of the silk; and by subsequently cutting these loops with a sharp instrument, the pile is produced. Thin brass wires are temporarily woven in among the weft-threads, to assist in forming the loops; and by a delicate cut or scission made with a sharp instrument, the loops are cut and the wires liberated. Striped velvets are produced by some of the pile-threads being uncut.

Cotton is now employed, as well as silk, in the manufacture of velvet. The different varieties of *fustian* are a kind of cotton-velvet.

VENEERING is the art of laying thin leaves, called *Veneers*, of a valuable kind of wood upon a ground or foundation of inferior material, so as to produce articles of elegant appearance at smaller cost than if they were composed entirely of the ornamental wood. Small veneers are cut by hand with a thin saw, the block being held firmly in a vice; but large ones are usually cut by machinery. They are carefully brought to the right thickness by fine planes; cut precisely to the required shape; and then glued down to the ground, which should be of dry wood, with strong glue. Precautions are taken to prevent the veneer from springing or loosening before the glue is dry. The work is afterwards finished with very fine planes and scrapers, and polished with fish-skin, wax, and a brush or polisher of shavegrass.

Mr. Meadows patented a veneering machine in 1849, by which, by means of clamps and screws of peculiar kind, he can veneer surfaces much more curved and tortuous than can usually be so treated.

VENEZUELA. This republic of South America is rich in vegetable produce. The articles of cultivation which are grown for exportation are cotton, indigo, cacao, coffee, sugar, tobacco, and cocoa-nuts. Indigo, which was once the most important object of cultivation, is much neglected, and cotton, coffee, and sugar have taken its place; but indigo is still grown in some places within the coast-range. The cocoa-palm is met with to the height of 700 feet, and yields valuable articles of export. The tobacco is of the best quality, and includes the well-known Varinas. Maize is extensively cultivated all over the country, but wheat only in the more elevated tracts. Rice is grown in a few places in the lower tracts, and barley only on the declivity of the Andes. Millet is also an object of cultivation.

Venezuela is not rich in minerals. Gold is found in several places, and a valuable mine has recently been discovered in the mountains south of the Orinoco. Silver, tin, copper, iron, and lead occur; but only the copper ore is worked profitably. Coal, natron, salt, and petroleum are found in different places.

The few manufactures of this country are in the Sierra Nirgua and on the declivities of the Andes, at Tocuyo, Barquicimeto, Trujillo, and Merida, where straw hats, hammocks, coarse cotton cloth, some worsted stuffs, and earthenware, are made. The commerce of Venezuela diminished greatly during the war of independence, but it has since recovered. Custom duties are laid on the importation of hardware, cottons, woollens, silks, linens, and about forty miscellaneous articles. The income and the expenditure of the republic for 1846 were each about 2,000,000 dollars.

The British produce and manufactures exported to Venezuela in 1849 amounted in value to 56,066*l*.

VENICE. This far-famed city has fallen greatly from its once high importance; but it will ever remain a most remarkable place. The islands on which the city stands are about 80 in number, divided from each other by narrow canals, which form the highways of communication, as streets in other towns, and are spanned by 450 bridges. Carriages and horses are useless, and therefore not seen in Venice, and their place is supplied by boats called 'gondole,' which are continually plying in all parts of the town. The city is two miles distant at the nearest point from the main land, and has a circumference of about 8 miles. There is a tide from the Adriatic, which rises a few feet over the lagunes, part of which are left nearly dry at ebb, excepting the 7 large canals, which intersect the lagunes, and keep up the communication between the city and the ports of Malamocco and Chioggia on the Adriatic, and the landing-places of Mestre, Fusina, and others on the main land. The arsenal or dock-yard is surrounded by a high wall, and occupies an area of about three miles in circumference. When the Abbé

Richard saw it (1761-2), there were about forty ships of war, of which twelve were three-deckers, in the docks ready for sea; arms for 150,000 men, 2500 pieces of brass ordnance, besides 1500 iron cannon, and vast stores of provisions; cables, sails, timber for ship-building, brought from the forests of Istria and Dalmatia, and all other appurtenances of such an establishment. The arsenal is now the dockyard for the insignificant Austrian navy. A railroad has been formed between Venice and Verona. The mercantile shipping of the port has assumed a new activity, and trades all over the Mediterranean. The number of vessels which enter the port of Venice yearly is between 1200 and 1300, including small craft; and Venice has seemed within the last ten or twelve years to show symptoms of commercial revival; but the disasters of 1849 gave it a severe check.

VERDIGRIS. [COPPER.]

VERDITER. [COPPER.]

VERMICELLI is a dried paste, manufactured chiefly in Italy, in the form of smooth round strings. The name has been given to it on account of its worm-like appearance, *vermicelli* in Italian signifying 'little worms.' *Maccaroni* is manufactured of the same kind of paste as vermicelli, and in a similar manner; but is rather larger in diameter, and is hollow like the tube of a tobacco-pipe. *Fedelini* is a kind still smaller than vermicelli.

The paste is made of wheat stripped of the husk, and ground roughly into a sort of grit. The kind of wheat preferred by the Italians is a small hard-grained species which they now cultivate on purpose, but which they formerly imported from the coasts of the Black Sea—'Grano di Mar Nero.' The ground wheat is mixed with clear soft water, and made into a paste by kneading it on a large block. The toughness and elasticity of the paste result from a long and powerful process of kneading. The paste is next forced by strong pressure through round holes in the bottom of a cylinder; but, to form maccaroni, a wire extends from a bridge in the upper part of the cylinder through the centre of each of the largest holes, and the paste, being forced through each hole around the wire, is consequently hollow. The strings, several feet in length, whether of maccaroni, vermicelli, or fedelini, having been thoroughly dried, are ready for use.

The Italians manufacture the paste into many other forms; into thin flat strips like ribbons, into thin sheets like paper, into round balls, and into beans and peas. The Neapolitans, who use great quantities of maccaroni as their favourite food, use nothing but the pure paste of wheat and water, but the Genoese mix saffron with it, which gives it a yellow tinge. The French, who also manufacture a good deal of it, frequently season the paste with various condiments.

VERMILLION. [MERCURY.

VERMONT. A few statistical and industrial notices of Vermont will be found under UNITED STATES.

VIENNA. This large and important city, besides being the centre of the Austrian dominions, is likewise the principal seat of commerce and manufactures. Its commerce is with Hungary, Turkey, Italy, and other countries. Since the establishment of the Danube Steam Navigation Company, whose vessels go to Constantinople, Trebizond, and Smyrna, the trade with the Levant has greatly increased. Manufactures of every kind are carried on in Vienna, and employ above 80,000 workmen. The principal are, silk, velvet, shawls, gold and silver lace, cottons, woollens, ribbons, carpets, leather, porcelain, jewellery, mathematical and musical instruments, fire-arms, gold and silver plate, watches; fine cutlery, carriages, gloves, lace, straw hats, paper, &c.

The beautiful specimens of household furniture which adorn the Austrian division of the Great Exhibition are mostly from Vienna.

VINEGAR MANUFACTURE. The relation which vinegar bears to the acetic and pyroligneous acids is noticed under ACETIC ACID. In countries which produce wine vinegar is obtained from the acetous fermentation of wine; but in this country it is usually procured from malt, and the process employed resembles the first stages of the brewer's operations. [BREWING.] The malt is ground and mashed with hot water. The wort, after being cooled, is transferred to the fermenting tun, where by the addition of yeast it undergoes the acetous fermentation; and when this is over the liquor is transferred to small vessels, which are kept warm by means of a stove: in these it remains for a shorter or longer period, according to the temperature of the stove and the strength of the liquor. The process of acetification is assisted by introducing into the casks with the wort what is called *rape*, which is a quantity of the residuary fruit which has served for making domestic wines, or has been preserved by the vinegar-maker from one process to another in his own factory. The use of the rape is to act as an acetous ferment, and thus induce sourness in the wash, it being well impregnated with vinegar and continually kept sour. Acetification is sometimes carried on by transferring the wort, after it has undergone the vinous fermentation, into casks, the bungholes of which are left open and loosely covered with tiles; the casks are then exposed for a long time to the air; but the use of stoves has greatly superseded this mode, has abridged the time of the operation, and rendered it less liable to failure. The vinegar, after it has reached its greatest degree of sourness, is rendered clear and fit for use either by subsidence or by the employment of isinglass.

Vinegar may be prepared in small quantities from the fermentation of a solution of sugar mixed with yeast; or it may be obtained by the fermentation of various fruits; thus the juice of good apples contains a sufficiency of sugar to afford tolerably good vinegar without any addition.

In France vinegar is made from poor wine; and there are two kinds—the white, prepared from white wine; and the red, by the acetification of the red wine: these are finer flavoured and somewhat stronger than the malt vinegar of this country.

Vinegar acts as an effectual preservative from the putrefactive fermentation of dead organic tissues, and is hence employed as the means of forming pickles, or meat in a dried state, by simply immersing the substance in it for a few minutes. Wood vinegar, or pyroligneous acid, is most efficacious for this purpose, owing to the creasote present in it. Crude pyroligneous acid is one of the most effectual applications to timber, both to prevent the dry rot and the ravages of insects. Concentrated acetic acid acts on the living tissues as a caustic poison; applied to the skin it causes heat, redness, and rapid inflammation.

VINES; VINEYARDS. The cultivation of the vine extends from near 55° N. lat. to the equator; but in south latitudes it only extends as far south as 40°. In Middle Germany the vine culture ceases at 1000 to 1500 feet above the level of the sea; on the south slope of the Alps it reaches 2000 feet; in the Apennines and Sicily 5000; and on the Himalaya as much as 10,000 feet.

The spots where the vine flourishes and where vineyards are kept up are said to depend more on the climates of spring and autumn than on those of summer and winter; and this explains many seeming anomalies in the location of vineyards. The vine grows best in a soil where few other shrubs or plants would thrive, such as a deep loose rocky soil. On the steep slopes of hills towards the south, and sheltered from the north-east, the grapes attain the greatest maturity, and the vintage is most certain. The culture of the vine is perhaps one of the most anxious and fatiguing which field labour presents, so numerous are the demands on the time and attention of the grower. The vine will bear any degree of heat, but not heat combined with moisture; hence a wet European season is usually a bad wine season.

Grapes, as is well known, are a favourite fresh fruit. They are also made into *British* or *home-made* wine in this country. In hotter countries they are dried and prepared into *raisins* and *currants*. But the most abundant employment of grapes is in making wine. We may refer for further details to BORDEAUX: CHAMPAGNE; CLARET; CURRANTS; GRAPES; RAISINS; WINE MANUFACTURE; WINE TRADE.

VIOL, was an ancient musical instrument, which may be considered as the parent of all modern instruments of the violin family. It was a fretted instrument, of three sorts—treble, tenor, and base, each furnished with six strings, and played on by a bow. The Treble Viol was rather larger than our violin, and the music for it was written in the treble clef. The Tenor Viol was in length and breadth about the size of the modern viola, but thicker in the body, and its notation was in the soprano or C clef. The Base Viol scarcely differed in dimensions from our violoncello: the music for it was written in the base clef. Other instruments of the viol kind are numerous. The *Viol da Gamba* was the last survivor of the family of viols. It derived its name from being held between the legs. It has been superseded by the violoncello. The *Viola*, or *Tenor Violin*, is a larger kind of violin, to which the part between the second violin and base is assigned. It has four gut strings, the two lowest covered with silver wire, which are tuned A, D, G, and C, an octave above the violoncello. The *Violin* has been known, in some shape, in most countries, and from very early times. The modern violin has four gut strings, the last, or lowest, covered with silver wire. These are tuned in 5ths, E, A, D, G. The wood of which the instrument is made is generally of three sorts: the back, neck, sides, and circles are of sycamore; the belly, bass-bar, sound-post, and six blocks, of deal; the finger-board and tail-piece of ebony. The finest violins are those which were made at Cremona, by the family of the Amati, and by Straduarius and Guarnerius. The *Violoncello* is an instrument of four gut strings, the two lowest covered with silver wire, and tuned in 5ths, A, D, G, and C.

VIRGINAL. This musical instrument is now entirely disused. It was a keyed instrument of one string, jack, and quill, to each note, like a spinet, but in shape resembling the present small pianoforte. The compass was from the 2nd added line below the base to the 2nd added line above the treble, or four octaves.

VIRGINIA. [United States.]

VITRIOL. [Copper; Iron; Zinc.]

VITRIFICATION. Illustrations of the process of vitrification will be met with under Enamel; Glass-Manufacture; Glass-Painting; Pottery and Porcelain.

VOLTAISM; VOLTAIC ELECTRICITY. In so far as this interesting science has a bearing on practical results, the reader will find various details under Electric Light, Electro Metallurgy, Electro Motive Force, Electrotype, and Telegraph.

VOTING MACHINE. A singular contrivance has been lately invented in France for registering the votes of deliberative assemblies. It is primarily intended for taking the votes at the National Assembly; and the Assembly granted 30,000 francs for its construction; but if the principle and the action are found to be correct, many useful applications of the machine will present themselves. The mechanism and arrangement are as follow.

Before the commencement of a sitting of the Assembly, the ushers deposit on the desk of each representative a small case, very closely resembling a domino-box, containing ten small oblong plates of polished steel. Six of these, upon which, with the name of the particular member, the word *pour*, or aye, is engraved, are white in colour: four, which also bear a member's name, are inscribed with *contre*, or no, and are blue. When a division has been demanded and accorded, twelve ushers remove twelve balloting-boxes or urns from the secretaries' desk, and convey them to the different parts of the Chamber. On the upper surface of each urn are two separate apertures, designed to receive the ballots, signifying aye and no respectively.

The edges of the steel balloting plates are milled or grooved, so as to correspond exactly with the apertures; and accordingly, neither an affirmative nor a negative ballot can find its way into the receptacle intended for votes in the contrary sense. As soon as the ushers have made the round of the whole Assembly, the urns are taken to the president. Up to this time they have not exhibited anything which distinguishes them materially from common balloting boxes; but the moment a small door is opened in front of them, the full ingenuity of the invention is disclosed. By a delicate mechanical contrivance, each piece of steel, as it slipped into the compartment proper to it, has been made to fall evenly and horizontally on the top of the ballot inserted immediately before it, so that the whole of the ballots are found to have arranged themselves in two completely regular piles, consisting of white and blue plates respectively. By each pile is a scale of degrees graduated with nearly as many divisions as there are members in the Assembly, and from this scale the president proceeds to read off the height of the piles precisely as we read off the height of the mercurial column from the register of a thermometer. Since the thickness of all the steel ballots is exactly the same, the height of each pile, as determined by the scale, denotes accurately the number of votes which have been given for or against a proposition; and when the results from the several urns have been combined, the general result of a division is known of course immediately.

Another voting machine, having many distinctive features, has been patented in England, and a specimen deposited in the Great Exhibition.

W

WAFER is a small round piece of dried paste, which is used to fasten letters. The piece of consecrated cake which is given by the Roman Catholic priest in extreme unction is also called a wafer; and thin cake formed into a roll, and called wafers, is still sold by pastrycooks. In fact the word was used in England to signify a thin cake long before wafers for sealing letters were invented. *Waffel* is the name given by the Germans to a thin cake made with flour, eggs, sugar, &c.; the Dutch call such a cake *wafel*, and the Danes *vaffel*. The Anglo-Saxons also had the name *waffel*.

In making common wafers for securing letters, wheat flour is mixed with isinglass and white of egg into a paste; the paste is spread evenly over tin plates, several of which are piled one on another and put into an oven. The layer becomes thus both baked and polished. When baked, the layers are taken from the tins, piled into a heap an inch or more in depth, and cut into wafers by means of hollow punches. They are coloured with the usual mineral colouring materials. *Medallion* wafers are made of very pure glue, coloured to any desired tint. A seal or medallion is moistened with a weak solution of either white or coloured gum, which gum is wiped off all except the sunken parts. The glue is then poured over the medallion in a very thin layer; and the result produced is a medallion wafer, either white or coloured, but standing out in relief from a ground of another colour. *Isinglass* or *gelatine* wafers are made of a coloured solution of isinglass, which is poured in a very thin layer on a glass plate, and afterwards cut into any desired form.

WALES. The principal manufacture in Wales is that of iron, and this is chiefly confined to Glamorganshire. Large quantities of ore are raised in that county, where the most extensive smelting furnaces in the empire are to be met with. In 1840 South Wales had 132 furnaces in operation, which consumed during the year about 1,436,000 tons of coal, and produced 505,000 tons of iron. North Wales had 12 furnaces, which consumed about 110,000 tons of coal, and produced 26,500 tons of iron. In 1847 the total quantity produced in Wales was 884,000 tons. The principal iron-works are at and around Merthyr-Tydvil, Tredegar, Aberdare, and Ruabon.

Copper-ore, brought from Cornwall and other parts of England, from Ireland, and foreign countries, is smelted in large quantities at Swansea. The average quantity of ore smelted there in 16 years (1833 to 1848), was 194,142 tons; the average quantity of copper produced was 18,567 tons.

The great coal-field of South Wales affords employment to a number of hands. The quantity of coal exported at the different ports of South Wales and Monmouthshire in 1848 was nearly two million tons. North Wales also yields some coal and iron, from the vicinities of Wrexham and Ruabon in Denbighshire. Lead (with some silver ore) and copper are raised in Anglesey, Cardiganshire, and other parts of Wales, as well as large quantities of slate, limestone, and marble. Various manufactures in lead, iron, copper, and brass are carried on at Holywell in Flintshire. Flannel in considerable quantities, coarse cloth, and stockings are manufactured in Montgomeryshire and other parts of North Wales.

Further illustrations of the industry of Wales will be found under COPPER; GLAMORGAN; IRON; MERTHYR TYDVIL; SWANSEA.

WALES, NEW SOUTH. The produce of this colony is briefly adverted to under AUSTRALIA. The following details relate to its commerce and produce in recent years.

In 1848 the shipping inwards amounted to 199,304 tons; outwards, to 187,322 tons. The wool exported was 22,969,711 lbs., valued at 1,240,144*l*. On Jan. 1, 1849, the total number of sheep in the colony was 11,660,819; of cattle, 1,752,852; of horses, 113,895; of pigs, 70,875. The produce of wheat in 1848 was 1,528,874 bushels; of maize, 262,340 bushels; of barley, 145,219 bushels; of oats, 116,634 bushels; of potatoes, 14,954 tons; of tobacco, 3059 cwts.; of hay, 37,795 tons; of wine, 103,106 gallons; of brandy, 1263 gallons.

The value of the imports and exports in recent years is shown as follows:—

	Imports.	Exports.
1844	931,300*l*.	1,128,100*l*.
1845	1,233,900	1,556,000
1846	1,600,500	1,481,500
1847	1,982,000	1,870,000
1848	1,556,500	1,830,400
1849	1,793,400	1,891,300

In the years 1846 and 1847, the imports exceeded the exports; in the other four the exports exceeded the imports.

The relative value of imports and exports per head of population was as under:—

	Imports per head.	Exports per head.
1844-46 per annum	6*l*. 18*s*.	7*l*. 11*s*.
1847-49 per annum	7*l*. 19*s*.	8*l*. 6*s*.

The following results relate to the countries of which the imports and exports are respectively the produce or manufacture:—

IMPORTS.

Articles the produce or manufacture of the United Kingdom	1,207,800*l*.	
Less re-exported	108,900	
Retained for home consumption		1,098,900*l*.
Articles the produce or manufacture of other British dominions	149,100	
Less re-exported	18,600	
Retained for home consumption		130,500
Articles the produce or manufacture of Foreign States	436,500	
Less re-exported	62,700	
Retained for home consumption		373,800
Total imports retained for home consumption		1,603,200*l*.

EXPORTS.

Articles the produce or manufacture of New South Wales	1,701,100
Net excess of exports over imports.	97,900*l*.

The trade to and from Great Britain was as follows:—

	Imports from.	Exports to.
1844	643,400*l*.	854,000*l*.
1845	777,100	1,254,900
1846	1,119,300	1,130,200
1847	1,347,200	1,503,100
1848	1,084,100	1,483,200
1849	1,371,200	1,572,600

The annual averages of the trade with this country per head of the population were about as follows:—

		Imports per head.	Exports per head.
1844-46	per annum	4*l.* 12*s.* ..	5*l.* 17*s.*
1847-49		5*l.* 13*s.* ..	6*l.* 16*s.*

The value of articles the produce or manufacture of New South Wales exported in the three years 1844-46, was 3,335,200*l.*; the value of those articles exported in the last three years was 4,971,600*l.*, being an increase of 1,636,400*l.*, or more than 39 per cent.

WALNUT-TREE. The uses of the walnut-tree are various. Before the introduction of mohogany and other foreign woods, the wood of the walnut-tree was held in higher estimation than that of any other European tree; and many specimens of furniture and carving still exist, to testify the beauty (somewhat sombre) of the wood. In almost every stage of its growth the fruit of the walnut-tree is used. When young, green, and tender, walnuts are pickled and preserved with the husks on. About the end of June they may be preserved with or without the husks. When the nuts are fully ripe, which is generally at the end of September or the beginning of October, the kernel, deprived of its investing skin, is eaten in great quantities. As long as the skin can be easily removed, they are a nutritious and healthy article of diet; but when they get dry, so that their skins stick to them, they become indigestible. A great number of the walnuts consumed in England are of foreign growth.

The albumen which constitutes the bulk of the seed of the walnut contains an oil, which is used in large quantities, especially on the Continent. It is obtained by reducing the seeds to a pulp by means of a stone wheel and basin, and then expressing the oil, first without heat, and then by the application of heat. The oil obtained by heat is used by artists, and also for lamps.

All parts of the walnut-tree, excepting the albumen of the seed, possess a bitter principle, which acts as a tonic and anthelmintic, and was formerly much esteemed as a medicine.

WARMING AND VENTILATION. Under the headings ARNOTT'S STOVE, COOKING APPARATUS, and STOVE, descriptions are given of various *grates*, *stoves*, and *fire-places*; other modes of warming buildings call for a little notice here.

The employment of steam-boilers in large establishments where steam-engines are worked, is one of the circumstances which have led to the very extensive adoption of the method of warming by steam. A marked difference is observable in the principle of this method, as compared with that of hot-air warming. The steam is not permitted to mingle with the air of the room which is to be warmed, but acts through the medium of the metallic tube which confines it, and which it raises to a temperature sufficient to warm the room. The efficacy of this mode of heating depends on the great capacity for heat which steam possesses, a capacity equal to 1000°; that is, a pound of water at 212° will absorb a thousand degrees of heat in becoming a pound of steam. Mr. Scott Russell calculates that a room containing 500 cubic feet of air, and exposing 400 feet of surface, may be maintained at a temperature of 20° above that of the air without—that is to say, at 60° in the inside of the room when the atmosphere is at 40° without—for a space of twelve hours, by the evaporation of two gallons of water, and at the expense of about three pounds of coal. This mode of heating buildings is adopted to a very large extent in the steam-power factories.

The method of heating by hot water, though not so much adopted in factories as the steam method, is perhaps of more extensive application in other buildings. Where all the apartments to be warmed are on one level, an open boiler may be used; but where it is necessary to carry the pipes to different floors of a building, some of them much above the level of the boiler, the boiler must in that case be closed. When an open boiler is employed, a pipe branches out from the upper part of the side, extends horizontally through the rooms to be warmed (without in any case rising above the level of the water in the boiler), and returns again to the boiler, which it enters at a lower level than the other. Under this arrangement a current of heated water will flow from the boiler at the upper orifice, and, after traversing the tube, return to the lower orifice. The closed boiler is however more extensively useful, since it enables all the stories of a building to be warmed by one apparatus. The whole system, including both tubes and boiler, is filled with water at a valve at the highest point; and when heat is applied to the boiler, a circulation ensues which speedily causes the whole length of tubing to become hot. Various modifications of this hot-water system are adopted in the new Houses of Parliament, in the British Museum, and other public buildings.

Ventilation.—There is an important but often neglected circumstance attending the artificial warming of buildings, viz. that the amount of fresh air, requisite under any condition for animal respiration, must be more and more increased in proportion to the fuel burned in the room; or, more correctly, there must be one portion of air to feed combustion, and another portion to aid respiration. Tredgold, Arnott, Reid, and others, have calculated the quantity of air required for these purposes. Tredgold states that when a room containing several persons is heated to the average and customary degree, it will be necessary to supply four times as many cubic feet of fresh air per minute, as there are persons in the room; that is, four feet for each person. But there must be an outlet for the vitiated air equal to the inlet for pure air; and as it is found that respired air ascends to the upper part of the room, it follows that the ceiling or some neighbouring part is the proper place for an outlet.

In ordinary English houses no steps whatever are taken to regulate either the supply of pure air or the exit of vitiated air; but it is probable that our large fire-places regulate this matter tolerably well. In crowded rooms however, where the amount of vitiated breath bears a much larger ratio to the cubical contents, and where the doors are generally small compared with the height of the room, the impure air cannot escape by these means, and some arrangements must be made near the ceiling for the removal of the air. These methods are chiefly of two different kinds; the one by the use of a revolving wheel or fan-ventilator, and the other by the action of a chimney or tube. At the Reform Club-House, London, a steam-engine works a revolving fan, capable of throwing eleven thousand cubic feet of air per minute into a subterranean tunnel under the basement story; and the steam from the small steam-engine which works the fan supplies three cast-iron chests with the requisite heat for warming the whole building.

The second mode of effecting ventilation, viz. by the use of a tube or chimney opening into the air from the upper part of an apartment, depends for its action on the ascensive power possessed by a lofty aërial column. As the heated air of a furnace-chimney carries up the smoke, &c., more rapidly if the chimney be very lofty, so does a lofty chimney exceed a low one in carrying off vitiated air; and for the same reason, even if no chimney, properly so called, be provided, a lofty room, furnished with appropriate openings in its ceiling, will furnish a draught to carry off impure air more rapidly than a low room; and in many of our public buildings this arrangement is deemed sufficient.

Dr. Arnott has made use of the ascending force of the column of heated air in an ordinary chimney as a means of ventilating ordinary sitting rooms, by placing a balanced valve in an opening from the room into the chimney. He has also introduced very recently a mode of ventilating large buildings by applying the pressure of a column of water to work a forcing air-pump. These admirable contrivances, so worthy of the accomplished physician to whom they are due, are noticed under ARNOTT'S VENTILATOR. Many forms of ship-ventilation depend on the use of an air-pump.

WARWICKSHIRE. The minerals of this county consist chiefly of one small coal field, and some quarries of gritstone. There are no less than 170 miles of canal in this county; and it is also well supplied with railways. Warwickshire stands on the verge of a manufacturing district and contains within itself many busy towns. The two most notable of these, in an industrial point of view, are noticed elsewhere. [BIRMINGHAM; COVENTRY.]

WATCH. [CLOCK AND WATCH MAKING.]

WATER, in its liquid, aëriform, or solid state, is universally diffused through nature. It was once considered as one of the four elements, and is in common language still frequently so termed. Water however is now known to be a compound substance consisting of hydrogen and oxygen. It is colourless, transparent, inodorous, and insipid; it is an imperfect conductor of heat and electricity; it is very slightly compressible, yielding only about 46·65 millionths of its bulk to the pressure of the atmosphere. Its specific gravity is 1, being the unit to which the density of all liquids and solids is referred, as a convenient standard, on account of the facility with which it is obtained in a pure state. Like all other fluids and substances it expands by exposure to an increase of temperature; and with a curious exception, the dilatation within certain limits is proportionate to the degree of heat to which it is subjected. When water is heated to a certain point, which is arbitrarily fixed on the scale of Fahrenheit's thermometer at 212°, it acquires the greatest volume it is capable of assuming; it then boils, and is converted into vapour. Steam at 212° occupies about 1700 times as much space as the water does from which it is generated. It is upon the elastic force of steam communicated by heat, and the instantaneous annihilation of it by cold, that the working of the steam-engine depends.

Water is seldom found in a state of perfect purity, but, from its great solvent and absorbent power, it is impregnated with a variety of saline substances, gases, and animal and vegetable substances, either living or undergoing a process of decomposition. The effect of these is to communicate different properties, and generally give it a peculiar taste, and not unfrequently an odour, which, if not cognisable by the blunted senses of man, is so by animals, especially the camel, which can scent water at a great distance in the desert. The specific gravity is often much increased, especially that of sea-water and of mineral waters, from the saline ingredients, and of some of the great rivers, from the quantity of mud and other matters which they contain.

Rain-Water is commonly reckoned the purest: but it is by no means so free from accidental impregnations as is generally supposed. Whatever foreign ingredients exist in the atmosphere of any place are brought to the ground by the first rain that falls. Rain-water, from its great purity, has high solvent powers, which fit it well for the part it has to perform in the economy of nature, and also for many operations in the laboratory. In this respect it is nearly equal to distilled water. The surface water of sandy districts is the purest that can be obtained naturally.

Dew differs little from rain, save in containing more atmospheric air. *Ice-water* differs when first obtained, from rain, in being destitute of atmospheric air, and hence it cannot sustain respiration in fishes ; it is for the same reason mawkish and insipid; but by exposure to the air it speedily absorbs a due proportion. *Snow-water* is nearly similar.

Spring-water is of various degrees of purity, according to its source and the strata through which it passes. Its most common source is rain, which percolates through some of the superficial strata, and, meeting with some obstacle, is forced up to the surface. *River-water* mostly originates in springs, augmented by rain-water. If it flows over sand or granite, it is found very pure, depositing in its course many earthy salts, especially the calcareous ones, from the escape of carbonic acid. This circumstance renders the water vapid, and less pleasant to drink than spring-water. It possesses however the property of absorbing much oxygen ; hence the surface-water both of rivers and the ocean holds more oxygen than the atmospheric air, to the amount even of 29·1 per cent. This contributes both to the maintenance of the respiration of fishes, and these, in their turn, to the growth of aquatic plants. *Well-water* is generally obtained from a greater depth than spring-water. It is also generally hard, or is apt to become so if kept in a reservoir lined with bricks, unless they be coated with an insoluble cement. The water from old wells is more pure than from recent ones, the soluble particles being all gradually washed away. The pump and well waters in and about London, and chalky districts in general, are mostly hard.

Lake-water varies much in its composition. The main difference depends on the lake possessing an outlet or being destitute of one. The water of the former generally corresponds with that of the rivers which flow into it; but the flow becoming slower, there is more scope for the development of animal and vegetable matters, and for the decomposition of organic remains.

Marsh-water is stagnant, and abounds in animal and vegetable remains, either in a state of decomposition or passing into new combinations, generally of a low grade, as the lowest members of the vegetable kingdom and those of each section of the animal are mostly aquatic. These waters are for the most part unwholesome, both from the gases they emit, and also when used as drink. Impure or putrid water may be rendered pure by adding alum or recently prepared charcoal, or by simply pouring it from one vessel into another in the sun.

Sea-water abounds in saline matters so much, that it is unfit for use internally, except in small quantity as a medicine. Sea-water may be rendered fit for drinking by pressure, filtration, and freezing, or simply by boiling it, and condensing the steam as it arises. For many chemical, pharmaceutical, and even dietetical purposes, water must be of greater purity than it is generally found. For this end it is directed to be distilled, in which process never more than two-thirds of the water put into the still should be allowed to pass over.

Mineral Waters are generally characterised by possessing some principle different from what is found in common water, or some of the ordinary principles in unusual proportion ; yet among these are reckoned certain springs which have no claim to repute beyond what is due to their extreme purity, such as Malvern and Holywell, or to having a higher temperature throughout the year than the mean of the latitude where they are situated. These last are classed among the *thermal* springs, which are properly divided into two sections, the *mineralised hot* springs and the *unmineralised*, among which are some only tepid, such as Matlock, where some springs, are 66° the lowest of the class in Britain, and others cold, presenting this peculiarity, that the tepid springs arise from fifteen to thirty yards above the level of the river Derwent, whilst those which arise either above or below this range are cold.

For practical purposes mineral-waters may be classed under four heads, each susceptible of secondary heads, according as they are hot or cold, or have other peculiarities, viz.: *saline*, *alkaline*, *chalybeate*, and *sulphureous*.

It has never ceased to be an object of interest to determine whether sea-water can be so distilled on board a ship as to yield drinkable fresh-water. Many processes have been devised for this purpose; but all have been wanting in some one or more desired qualities. Some of the government ships have lately been provided with Grant's Distilling and Cooking Galley; during the period it is required to keep the fires alight in these galleys for purposes of cooking, the distillation of salt water is going on so as to yield one gallon of distilled water per man per day. Like all distilled water, it is vapid at first from the loss of oxygen during the process; but the motion of the ship is said to aerate the distilled water in the tanks, by agitation. Experiments have been made in one of the government ships, to see whether the oxygen might be restored to distilled water by an electrical current passed through it; but this seems too complicated an arrangement for the rough usages of a ship.

WATER SUPPLY; WATER WORKS. Before the building of New London Bridge, a considerable part of the metropolis was supplied with water by machinery, placed close to the old bridge; but that machinery being removed, other arrangements for supply have had to be made.

The following are the modes in which London is now supplied with water. The *New River Company* obtains its supply from the rivers Lea and Armwell; the *East London Company* from the river Lea; the *Hampstead Company* from springs near Hampstead; the *Grand Junction Company* from the Thames near Kew; the *West Middlesex Company* from the Thames near Barnes; the *Chelsea Company* from the Thames near Chelsea; the *Southwark and Vauxhall Company* from the Thames near Battersea and the *Lambeth Company* from the Thames near Thames Ditton. When certain new arrangements of the various companies are complete, no supply will be obtained from the Thames at a lower point than Chelsea. Most of the companies have filtering or settling reservoirs, for purifying the water a little before it reaches the service mains.

The agitation for improved and increased water supply is well known to all newspaper readers; some projectors suggest that water should be obtained from a yet higher point in the Thames; some select the Verulam; some the Wandle; some the Colne. Many think that Artesian Wells might supply the whole of London; while a recently proposed plan, which has been received with much favour, is for catching the rain-water over a large sandy surface. The subject is now before the legislature.

See other details under AQUEDUCTS; ARTESIAN WELLS.

WATERFORD. The Waterford mountains contain two varieties of slate: the old transition slate, coloured gray, which is extensively used for roofing, and the newer slate, which rests on the older; the lower portions of its strata consist of alternating beds of brownish-red quartzose conglomerate and coarse red slate. The valleys are occupied by limestone, and there is a clay-slate district, which contains several copper and lead mines, some of which are worked. Iron-ore is also found. Of the entire area of the county (461,553 acres) 325,345 acres are arable, 105,496 uncultivated, 23,408 in plantations, and the rest covered by water or occupied by towns. The common course of tillage is potatoes, wheat, oats, and again potatoes; but some of the better farmers grow only one corn crop in the course. The common Irish cow is the general dairy stock.

In Waterford town the exports are chiefly to England, and almost wholly agricultural—bacon, pork, butter, grain, flour and meal, cattle, sheep, and pigs. The gross produce of the customs' duties in 1848 was 134,897*l*. The sailing vessels registered as belonging to the port in 1848 were 78 under 50 tons, and 123 of 50 tons and upwards; the aggregate burden was 23,244 tons; steamers, 14 (3187 tons).

WATERPROOF COMPOSITIONS. Many patents have been taken out for methods of rendering cloth and leather waterproof. In 1835 Mr. Hellewell, of Salford, took out a patient for a solution, which, by immersion, should render cotton and other fabrics waterproof; it is a composition of rock alum and whiting in water, and its action is aided by a subsequent application of soap and water. Mr. Hall, of Doncaster, patented in 1839 a method of waterproofing cloth by immersion; one solution described consists of alum, white lead, and water; and another of alum, white lead, acetic acid, and water; and the cloth, after steeping in one of these solutions, is passed through a solution of quick lime, and a third time through a solution of boiled Irish moss, which acts as a mucilage. There are other patents of a somewhat similar character to the above, and there have also been numerous methods published but not patented.

The surface-application of a species of varnish has been the subject of many patents. A composition was introduced for this purpose some years ago, formed of linseed oil, pipe-clay, burnt umber, white lead, pounded pumice-stone, and one or two other substances. This was not intended as a waterproof composition for ordinary clothing, but rather for tarpauling, awnings, coach-top covers, boat-cloaks, and other coarse materials. Mr. Newberry's patent, taken out in 1140, is for a mode of applying waterproof composition in such a way as to leave one side of the woven fabric free from its influence, thereby presenting to the eye a texture nearly resembling that of ordinary cloth. The application of a layer of cement, gum, or varnish between two other substances, with a view to render the inner one impervious to water, has been practised under many different modifications, including that which is known by the name of the inventor, *Mackintosh*. In the year 1824 Mr. Weise, of Bermondsey, devised a peculiar kind of fabric, which consists of fibrous materials spun into yarn; the yarn is dipped in caoutchouc solution before weaving; and in order to render the meshes impervious to water, the cloth is drawn over a heated cylinder, whereby the composition is so far melted as to flow into them. The waterproof or Macintosh cloth is made by applying a layer of dissolved caoutchouc to cotton or other cloth. The cloth is stretched upon frames and brushed over with it; and the surfaces of two such pieces, while in a partially damp state, are laid one upon another, and pressed between rollers till they firmly and inseparably unite. The double fabric thus produced is wholly impervious to water, and is at the same time free from any adhesive substance on the surface.

The useful application of air for beds, cushions, seats, and similar articles, is dependent on the formation of air-tight cases; and this air-proof quality is brought about by nearly the same means as waterproofing. When a bag has been made of caoutchouc or similar cloth, and rendered also air-tight by somewhat similar means at the seams, air may be passed into it as a substitute for more solid materials. In practice there are some very neat arrangements adopted in effecting this. Temporary air-seats or cushions are made by forming a bag of air-tight cloth, perfectly enclosed at every part except one corner, where is inserted a small tube and stop-cock, capable of admitting or preventing communication from the interior to the exterior. The cock being opened, and the tube applied to the mouth, air is blown into the cushion, until it expands to the desired degree of fulness; the cock is then closed, and the air remains imprisoned. In this state the cushion is of a more equable kind than any one stuffed with solid materials; and if the envelope be well made, it will retain its efficacy for a long time. When not in use, such a cushion can have the air expressed from it, and may then be folded up into a small space.

It is obvious that seats, cushions, pillows, and beds of various kinds, having a similar object in view in respect to softness, fulness, and elasticity, may be made by similar means. When the quantity of air included in an envelope is greatly increased, it may be made the means of producing actual pressure in a more equable way than by any solid bodies. Thus, an air-tight bandage, so formed, is often used in surgical operations.

The patents for caoutchouc waterproof materials taken out by Mr. Hancock, Mr. Slevier, and other inventors, within the last few years, are so exceedingly numerous that we can only speak of them generally. One patent is for cutting cotton and other fibres into very small fragments, mixing them with dissolved caoutchouc, and forming sheets of material from this mixture. Another patent relates to a method, in which very thin sheets of caoutchouc are cemented by a solution of caoutchouc to gauze, bobbin net, or other open material; and on this, as a ground, and with a similar cement of quick-drying caoutchouc, is laid a stratum of fibres. The fibres are pressed and dressed; and the open and extensible meshes of the gauze or bobbin-net give to the whole an elasticity which closely-woven textures cannot impart.

The attempts to render leather waterproof depend in general on the filling up of the small pores which have previously admitted the tannin, the substance imbibed being such as will repel or resist water. Many such compositions have been proposed at different times, of which the mention of a few will here suffice. Melt over a slow fire a quart of boiled linseed oil, a pound of mutton suet, three-quarters of a pound of yellow bees'-wax, and a half a pound of common resin, or smaller quantities in the like relative proportions; and with this mixture saturate the leather of new boots or shoes, while the latter is slightly warm. Another method is to melt two ounces of yellow bees'-wax, two ounces of

Burgundy pitch, and two ounces of turpentine, in a pint of linseed oil, and with this mixture to saturate the warm leather. Another mixture for this purpose consists of six ounces of caoutchouc boiled for two hours in two quarts of linseed or neat's-foot oil. Lastly, a mode has been much recommended of applying a hot mixture of two parts tallow and one part resin, with which the leather may be completely saturated, the resin imparting an antiseptic quality to the tallow.

WATT, JAMES. Of all the great men whose names are indissolubly connected with the history of the steam-engine, James Watt undoubtedly takes the lead. Watt was born at Greenock in 1736; and in his 16th year he was apprenticed to an instrument maker in Glasgow. At the end of three years he removed to London, in 1755, and placed himself with a mathematical instrument maker; but in little more than twelve months the state of his health compelled him to return to Scotland.

Shortly after his return from London, Watt established himself as an instrument maker within the precincts of Glasgow University. In 1763 Professor John Anderson, who then occupied the chair of natural philosophy in the university, having requested him to examine and repair a small model of Newcomen's steam-engine, which could never be made to work satisfactorily, his sagacity led him to discover and remove the defects of this model; and he also discovered the imperfections of the machine itself, and was led to investigate those properties of steam upon which its action depended. The character of Watt's improvements is briefly noticed in the article STEAM-ENGINE. He next opened a shop in the Salt Market, Glasgow, where he continued to make improvements in the steam-engine; and where, in addition to his employment as a mathematical instrument maker, he devoted much time to the practice of land-surveying. He afterwards adopted the profession of a civil engineer. In 1768 he found in Dr. John Roebuck an individual capable of appreciating the value of his improvements in the steam-engine, and sufficiently enterprising to support him in further experiments. The assistance of this gentleman enabled him to set up an engine, for which he obtained a patent, Jan. 5, 1769. Matthew Boulton, of Soho near Birmingham, purchased Roebuck's share; and in 1774 Boulton and Watt entered into partnership.

At the latter end of 1774 Watt completed at Soho his fourth model engine, which was exhibited to a deputation from the Cornish miners, and to other persons competent to judge of its performances, which were deemed highly satisfactory. Perfect however as was the action of the improved machine, the patentees knew that much remained to be done to bring it into extensive operation; and they succeeded in obtaining an extension of the patent till the year 1800. Of the spirited manner in which Boulton conducted the mercantile department of the great adventure some idea may be formed from the fact, that upwards of 47,000*l*. was spent before the patentees began to receive any return; but at length their remuneration began to pour in, and in no scanty stream. They were, however, put to great expense by legal proceedings against infringements of their patent, and in defence of the patent itself.

At a social meeting of scientific men, a suggestion was thrown out which led Watt to the invention of the useful little machine known as the *Copying Press*, for which he obtained a patent. Towards the latter end of 1786, on a visit to Paris, undertaken at the instance of the French government for the purpose of suggesting improvements on the Machine de Marly, Watt became acquainted with Berthollet, whose method of bleaching with chlorine he brought to this country, and introduced, with certain improvements of his own, in the bleach-works of Mr. Macgrigor, near Glasgow, whose daughter he had married in 1775.

Concerning Watt's share in the discovery of the composition of water, an investigation in which he, Cavendish, and Lavoisier, were engaged about the same time, we must refer those who are curious to Arago's Life or 'Eloge' of Watt, and to the 'Historical Account of the Discovery of the Composition of Water,' by Lord Brougham.

One of the last of the projects to which Watt devoted his attention after his retirement from business was a machine for copying sculpture, with which he proceeded so far as to execute several specimens.

In acknowledgment of his invaluable services it was intimated to Watt a few years before his death, that 'the highest honour usually conferred in England on men of literature and science (knighthood) was open to him, if he expressed a wish to that effect;' but while he felt flattered by the intimation, he determined to decline it. He became a member of the Royal Society of Edinburgh in 1784, of that of London in the following year, of the Batavian Society in 1787, and in 1808 a correspondent of the French Institute; and in 1814 the 'Académie des Sciences' of the Institute elected him one of its eight foreign associates. In 1806, by a spontaneous vote, the university of Glasgow conferred upon him the honorary degree of LL.D. In 1824 a subscription was entered into for a statue, which was sculptured by Chantrey, and is now in Westminster Abbey. Another statue by Chantrey adorns an elegant chapel erected by Watt's only surviving son, at the parish church of Handsworth, near Birmingham, in the chancel of which he was interred. Other statues have been erected in St. George's Square, Glasgow, and in the university of Glasgow.

Every Exhibition of manufactures owes a debt to James Watt, of which it would be in vain to attempt to determine the value.

WAX. There are several varieties of this substance. *Bees' Wax* is a secretion from the ventral scales of the bee. With this substance the comb is constructed. From the comb the wax is extracted chiefly by pressure and by melting it in hot water, in which the impurities subside, after which the wax is poured into moulds. The wax has a yellowish or orange colour, and a peculiar odour. Even in winter it is soft enough to be indented by the nail, and in summer it is much softer. It melts at about 143° to 150° Fahr.

White Wax is obtained by melting yellow wax by means of steam, running it off into a perforated trough called a Cradle, from which it falls into water. By this means the wax is solidified and converted into a kind of ribbon; it is afterwards bleached, re-melted, re-bleached, and refined. Pure wax thus obtained is nearly devoid of smell, and is white with a yellowish tint; it is brittle and insipid; its melting point is 158° Fahr., and it solidifies at 149°.

Sealing Wax is not properly a wax. It is composed of shel-lac (4 parts), Venice Turpentine (1 part), and cinnabar (3 parts). The round sticks of sealing-wax are made by hand on a smooth slab of marble, which is kept at a moderate temperature by a brazier or chafing-dish placed beneath it. A quantity sufficient to make about six sticks is rolled out on the slab into one long stick, which, when of proper diameter, is cut into lengths. The sticks are then rolled on a cold slab beneath a smooth piece of wood or metal, and are afterwards polished by gently fusing the surface, and devices are stamped upon them. Sticks of a more complicated shape are cast in moulds. For the best black sealing-wax, the finest ivory-black is substituted for the cinnabar. Inferior materials are used for cheap wax. Soft sealing-wax contains bees'-wax in the place of the shell-lac.

A peculiar kind of wax is yielded by the *Ceroxylon Andicola*, or *Wax-Palm* of South America. Near the Andes this tree grows in all its grandeur, elevating its majestic trunk, coated with a thick incrustation of wax, to the height of 180 feet among the most rugged precipices of the wild region which it inhabits. It does not extend over more than 15 or 20 leagues of country altogether. The trunk is distinctly marked by rings caused by the fall of the leaves, which are from 18 to 20 feet long. The spaces between the rings are pale yellow, and smooth like the stems of a reed, and covered with a thick coating of wax and resin. This substance, melted with a third of fat, makes excellent candles. Vauquelin ascertained that this vegetable matter consists of two-thirds resin, and one-third-wax, which is only a little more brittle than bees'-wax.

WEATHER GLASS. [Barometer.]

WEAVING. We shall glance rapidly over this subject in the following order:—*Plain Weaving; Pattern Weaving; Double Weaving; Cross Weaving; Chain Weaving; Pile Weaving; Power Weaving.*

Plain Weaving.—Calico, Irish linen, and plain silk, are good representatives of this kind of weaving. In the language of weavers, the long threads are called, according to circumstances, *warp, twist, caine*, or *organzine*; while the cross threads are called *weft, woof, shoot*, or *tram*. We shall here use the simple terms *warp* and *weft*. The warp is always affixed to the loom or weaving machine; while the weft is contained in the shuttle, a small boat-like instrument.

The first operation consists in laying the requisite number of threads together to form the width of the cloth: this is called *warping*. Supposing there to be 1000 threads in the width of a piece of cloth; then the yarn, wound on the bobbins as it leaves the hand of the spinner, must be so unwound and laid out as to form 1000 lengths, constituting, when laid parallel, the warp of the intended cloth. The ancient method was to draw out the warp from the bobbins at full length in an open field; and this is still practised in India and China; but the *warping-frame* is now employed, in which the threads are arranged by means of a frame revolving on a vertical axis. When the warp is arranged around this machine, the warper takes it off and winds it on a stick into a ball, preparatory to the process of *beaming*, or winding it on the beam of the loom. The threads, in this latter process, are wound as evenly as possible on the beam; a separator, ravel, or comb being used to lay them parallel, and to spread them out to about the intended width of the cloth. Arrangements are then made for *drawing*, or attaching the warp-threads individually to certain mechanism of the loom. In this process all the threads are attached to stays fixed to two frames called *heddles*, in such a manner that all the alternate threads (1st, 3rd, 5th, &c.) can be drawn up or down by one heddle, and all the rest (2nd, 4th, 6th, &c.) by the other.

There are three movements attending every thread of weft which the weaver throws across the warp. In the first place he presses down one of the two *treadles*, by which one of the two heddles is depressed, thereby forming a kind of opening called the *shed*. Into this shed, at the second movement, he throws the shuttle containing the weft-thread, with sufficient force to drive it across the whole web. Then, at the third movement, he grasps the *batten*, which is a kind of frame carrying at its lower edge a comb-like piece having as many teeth as there are threads in the warp, and with this he drives up the thread of weft close to those previously thrown. One thread of weft is thus completed, and the weaver proceeds to throw another in a similar way, but in a reverse order, that is, by depressing the left treadle instead of the right, and by throwing the shuttle from left to right, instead of from right to left. In the commonest mode of weaving the shuttle is thrown by both hands alternately; but about a century ago John Kay invented the *fly-shuttle*, in which a string and handle are so placed that the weaver can work the shuttle both ways with one hand.

In weaving plain silks, calicoes, and other webs of moderate width, there are two leaves of heddles and two treadles, for dividing the warp into two parcels. In weaving broader webs, such as floor-cloth canvas, the heddles and treadles are more powerful. In weaving ribbons, galloons, &c., the *engine-loom* is employed, noticed under RIBAND.

Pattern Weaving. — Pattern-weaving has many varieties, in which different colours are combined by weaving. If all the threads of the warp are of one colour, and all those of the weft another colour, it produces the peculiar effect called *shot* patterns. A *stripe* is a pattern in which parallel lines run either along or across the warp; while a *check* is an alternation of rectangles like a chess-board, or more properly like the varieties of Scotch plaid. The production of a stripe depends either upon the warper or the weaver; the production of a check depends upon both. [CHECK.] In the *twill*, which includes satin, bombazeen, kerzeymere, &c., the weft-threads pass over one warp-thread and under two, over one and under three, or over one and under eight or ten, according to the kind of twill; the effect of this is, to produce a kind of diagonal ribbed appearance, either on the 'right' or the 'wrong' side of the cloth, and a smooth and glossy appearance on the other, according as the one thread is crossed above or below by the weft. [BOMBAZEEN; CHECK.] To produce such results, more than two leaves of heddles are required, and more than two treadles to work them; and the weaver's loom is a much more complicated machine than that for plain weaving.

When, instead of, or in addition to a twill, the weaver has to produce sprigs, flowers, spots, or any kind of figure, a great increase of complexity occurs. The weft may pass over four and under one at one part of the width of the cloth; over two and under two at another; over one and under four at another; according to the part of the figure which may happen to occur at any particular part of the width of the cloth. The complex movements thus rendered necessary gave rise to the invention of the *draw-loom*, in which strings are so arranged that a boy can draw down the requisite warp-threads preparatory to the movement of the shuttle. Early in the present century two inventions were made with the view of rendering the draw-loom more automatic. One of these, called the *draw-boy*, not only superseded the necessity of employing a boy to pull the handles, but removed, by the unerring certainty of its operation, all possible chance of mistake in pulling the wrong handle. The other was the *automatic carpet-loom* of Mr. Duncan, in which the threads were moved by pins inserted in a rotating barrel, somewhat on the principle of the musical box.

But the draw-loom, the draw-boy, and the barrel-loom, have been alike eclipsed by the exquisite apparatus of M. Jacquard. [JACQUARD.]

Double Weaving.—In all the fabrics hitherto noticed, there is but one layer of threads, formed by the intersection of the weft among the warp, both weft and warp being individually single. But there has long been practised the weaving of a kind of double cloth, composed of two webs, each consisting of separate warp and weft, but both sets interwoven at intervals. The junction of the two webs is formed by passing each of them occasionally through the other, so that each particular part of both is sometimes above and sometimes below. [CARPET MANUFACTURE.]

Cross Weaving.—*Gauze* and *Bobbin-Net* may be taken as the chief representatives of this kind of fabric. *Net* is the generic name for these goods; and according as slight deviations were made in the mode of crossing the threads, so were distinctive names given to the material produced; such as *whip-net*, *mail-net*, *patent-net*, *drop-net*, *spider-net*, *Paris-net*, *balloon-net*,

&c. All these varieties are produced at the loom, with warp-threads stretched horizontally, and weft-threads thrown across by means of a shuttle; and the difference between them depends on the manner in which the warp-threads were made to cross one another, and in which the weft-thread was thrown. [GAUZE; LACE MANUFACTURE.]

Chain-Weaving.—We may apply this term to a mode of using threads in which a series of loops is formed by a continuous thread, each loop or link being so connected with others as to form a kind of chain; and this chain-work may either be worked upon a ground woven at the loom, or may constitute the woven material itself. *Sampler work, lace running, tambouring, pillow lace, rug work, Berlin work, tapestry,*—all may be regarded as varieties of chain-work. The manufacture of *stockings,* whether by the humble process of knitting, or by the use of the stocking-frame, is in strictness to be called *chain-weaving;* for the fabric itself is produced by a series of links or loops in a thread of worsted, cotton, or silk. In the process of knitting, still carried on to a small extent in secluded country districts, polished steel needles or wires are used to link threads together into a series of loops, closely resembling in their character the loops produced in tambouring. But this method has been almost entirely superseded by the ingenious *stocking-frame.* Various kinds of chain-weaving are noticed under BERLIN WORK; EMBROIDERY; HOSIERY MANUFACTURE; LACE MANUFACTURE; TAPESTRY.

Pile-Weaving.—If we examine *velvet, fustian, velveteen, moleskin, doeskin,* or a *Turkey* or *Wilton carpet,* we shall find that in all of these fabrics the warp and weft threads are almost concealed by a kind of down, nap, or pile, which imparts a peculiarly soft and smooth texture to them. Fustians are in fact a kind of cotton velvet, as Turkey carpeting is a woollen velvet. A few details respecting this kind of weaving will be found under CARPET; FUSTIAN; VELVET.

Power-weaving.—In 1678 M. de Gennes invented a rude kind of weaving machine, intended to increase the power of the common loom; and other looms were invented which were to be worked by a winch, by water-power, or by some contrivance more expeditious than the common hand-weaving; but a greater step in advance was made by the invention of Dr. Cartwright's power-loom in 1785. [CARTWRIGHT.] One cause which delayed the adoption of power-looms was the necessity for stopping the machine frequently, in order to dress the warp with paste or size, as it unrolled from the beam, which operation required a man to be employed for each loom, so that there was no saving of expense. But the successive inventions of Radcliffe, Horrocks, Marsland, Roberts, and others, have since brought the dressing-machine and the power-loom to a high state of efficiency.

Taking a piece of calico as the representative of plain fabrics generally, the mode of proceeding in power-loom factories may be shortly sketched as follows;—The *warping-frame* is so arranged as to be worked by steam-power, and to bring the yarns into a parallel layer, which is transferred to the *dressing-machine.* This latter is a large piece of mechanism, in which the threads dip into paste on their way to the warp-beam; undergoing a process of brushing after the dipping. After this dressing the *drawing* and mounting for the loom are attended to. When the warp is properly arranged in the loom, steam-power does all the rest: it forms the shed or division of the warp into two parts; it throws the shuttle; it drives up the weft with the batten; it unwinds the warp from the warp-roller; and winds the woven material on the cloth-roller.

WEDGE-PRESS. [OIL-MILL.]

WEDGWOOD, JOSIAH will ever be associated with the history of the porcelain and pottery manufacture in this country. He was born in 1730 at Burslem, in Staffordshire, where his father, Thomas Wedgwood, and some other members of his family, were engaged in the manufacture of pottery, a branch of industry then in a very imperfect state. His education was very limited; and at the age of eleven years Josiah worked in his elder brother's pottery. The small-pox, which left an incurable lameness in his right leg, so as afterwards to require amputation, compelled him to relinquish the potter's wheel. After a time he left Burslem, and entered into partnership with a person named Harrison, at Stoke; and during this partnership his talent for the production of ornamental pottery is said to have first developed itself. He returned to Burslem in 1759, and set up for himself. His business being prosperous, he took a second manufactory, where he made white stone-ware, and a third, at which was produced the improved cream-coloured ware by which he gained so much celebrity. Wedgwood presented some articles to Queen Charlotte, who ordered a complete table service, and appointed him her potter. He soon afterwards opened a warehouse in the metropolis for the sale of his productions. One of his principal works was his imitation of the Portland Vase, of which he made fifty copies. But though these were sold for fifty guineas each, that sum did not, it is said, repay him for his expenditure. He succeeded in producing the most delicate cameos, medallions, and miniature pieces of sculpture, in a substance so extremely hard, that they appear likely to exceed even the bronzes of antiquity in durability. Another important discovery made by him was that of painting on vases and similar articles, without the glossy appearance of ordinary painting on porcelain or earthenware; an art which appears to have been lost since the time of Pliny. The fame of his operations was such that his works at Burslem, and subsequently at Etruria, a village erected by him near Newcastle-under-Lyne, and to which he entirely removed in 1771, became a point of attraction to numerous visitors from all parts of Europe. The result of Wedgwood's talent and energy not only obtained for him extensive patronage and an ample fortune, but were of the highest importance to the commercial interests of his country.

In addition to the attention bestowed by Wedgwood upon this manufacture, he deserves remembrance for the public spirit displayed by him in the encouragement of various useful schemes. Among these the Trent and Mersey Canal is conspicuous. Wedgwood's pyrometer is noticed elsewhere. [PYROMETER.] He died at Etruria in 1795.

WEIGHING-MACHINE, is any contrivance by which the weight of an object may be ascertained. Under the words BALANCE, GOLD WEIGHING-MACHINE, SPRING-BALANCE, and STEELYARD, the machines by which materials of comparatively small magnitude are weighed are explained. The Weighing-Machine, which is usually employed at the toll-gates on roads for the purpose of determining the weights of laden carriages, may be described as a platform sunk on a level with the road, and made to rest at four points on a double lever of the second kind. [LEVER.] The extremities of the arms of these levers rest upon a third lever, which may be of the first or second kind; and this last lever may either serve as a steelyard, or may be connected with one arm of an ordinary balance, or with the extremity of a steelyard.

Mr. Elliott has sent to the Great Exhibition a new form of weighing-machine, somewhat on the principle of a steelyard, but with certain new features of construction. With one ball or weight of 4 lbs., the instrument will determine all weights from a quarter of a pound to 56 lbs. It is also graduated with *kilogrammes*, to measure French weights.

WEIGHTS AND MEASURES. Under APOTHECARIES' WEIGHT, AVERDUPOIS WEIGHT, STANDARD, and TROY WEIGHT, many details are given on this subject. We will here give a few brief notices concerning *Foreign* weights and measures, as they are often useful while reading industrial statistics of foreign countries.

France.—The new French system is called *metrical*, as derived from the measurement of the earth. Its first measure, the *metre*, is presumed to be the ten-millionth part of a line drawn from the pole to the equator, and is 39.37079 English inches. All the multiples and subdivisions of every measure are decimal, and are formed by the same prefixes. For 10, 100, 1000, and 10,000, the syllables *Deca*, *Hecto*, *Kilo*, and *Myria* are prefixed; and for tenths, hundredths, thousandths, the syllables *Deci*, *Centi*, *Milli*. Latin prefixes indicate division, Greek prefixes multiplication. Thus the hectometre is 100 metres, and the centimetre the hundredth part of a metre. The metre being thus settled, the other fundamental measures are formed as follows:—For surface or area, the *Are*, which is a decametre square, or 100 square metres, or .02471143 of an English acre, or 3.9538 English perches. For solidity, the *stere*, or cubic metre, 35.32 cubic feet English, or 220.09687 imperial gallons English. For liquid measures the *litre*, or cubic decimetre, .22009687 of an imperial gallon, or a very little more than a pint and three quarters English. For weight, the *gramme*, a cubic centimetre of distilled water at the freezing point, .00220606 of an English pound averdupois, or 15.442 grains English. The *kilogramme* is therefore 2.2 pounds averdupois, or, roughly, 50 kilogrammes make a hundredweight. The *franc*, the unit of money, is divided into 10 decimes, and each decime into 10 centimes. The *sous* is 5 centimes.

Austria. The metrical system is introduced in the Italian dominions. In Austria proper gold and silver are weighed by the *Vienna marc* of 4333 grains. The *pfund* is 1.235 lb. averdupois. The *metzen* is 1.691 of the English bushel. The *eimer* is 12.444 gallons. The *foot* is 12.45 inches; the *ell*, 30.66 inches. The *joch* is 1 acre, 1 rood, 28 perches.

Bavaria. The *Augsburg marc* is 3643 grains; 24 lb. *commercial* weight is 25 lb. averdupois, and 24 lb. *carriers'* weight is 26 lb. averdupois, nearly. The *metzen* is 1.515 of the English bushel; the *fuder* is 31.24 bushels. The *foot* (half the short ell) is 11.667 inches. The *long ell* is 24 inches. The German *geographical mile* is 4.6 miles English.

Belgium. The French metrical system.

Constantinople. The *chequee* is 4957 grains. The *oke* is 2.832 pounds averdupois. The *killow* (dry) is 7.296 gallons. The *almud* is 1.150 of the English gallon. The *pike* is 27 inches.

Denmark. The *pound* for gold and silver is 7266 grains. The *commercial pound* is 1.1028 lb. averdupois. The *barrel* is 3.8264 bushels. The *viertel* is 1.701 of the English gallon. The *foot, or half-ell,* is the Rhineland foot of 12.356 English inches. The *toende* of corn is 5½ acres.

Florence and Leghorn. The *cantaro* is 150 pounds of .74864 lb. averdupois each. The *stajo* is .6702 of the English bushel. The *barile* is 10.033 gallons. The *braccio* is 22.98 English inches. The *saccata* is 1 acre 36 perches.

Frankfort. For gold and silver the *Cologne marc.* The common *pound* is 1.03 lb. averdupois. The *centner* is 112.25 lb. averdupois. The *malter* is 2.9705 bushels. The *ohm* is 32.454 gallons. The *foot* is 11.27 inches, the *ell* 21.24 inches.

Genoa. The *pound sottile* for gold and silver is 4891.5 grains. The *pound grosso* is .76875 lb. averdupois. The *mina* is 3.321 bushels. The *mezzarola* is 32.57gallons. The *palma* is 9.725 inches.

Hamburg. The *Cologne marc* is 3608 grains; the *pound troy* is two marcs. The *commercial pound* is 1.068 lb. averdupois. The *last* of wheat (30 scheffels) is 10.9 quarters; the *ahm* is 31.85 gallons. The *foot* is 11.289 inches. The *scheffel* of land is 1 acre 6 perches.

Holland. The *marc* is 3798 grains; the *pound* is 2 marcs; but the *commercial pound* is 1.0893 lb. averdupois. The *last* is 10.231 quarters. The *aam* is 34.16 gallons. The *Rhineland foot* is 12.36 inches. The *Rhineland perch* is 12 Rhineland feet; and the *Rhineland morgen* or *acre* is 2 acres 16 perches.

Lübeck. For gold and silver, as at Hamburg. The *commercial pound* is 1.0685 lb. averdupois. The *scheffel* is .92 of the English bushel. The *ahm* is 31.85 gallons. The *foot* or *half-ell* is 11.346 inches.

Malta. The *pound* for gold and silver is 4886 grains. The *commercial pound* is 1.745 lb. averdupois. The *salma* is 7.968 bushels. The *foot* is 11.167 inches. The *canna* (8 palmi) is 81.9 inches.

Milan. The *mark* is 3627 grains. The *pound sottile* is .7206 lb. averdupois; the *pound grosso* is 1.682 lb. averdupois. The *moggio* (32 quartari) is 4.0234 bushels. The *brenta* (12 quartari) is 15.71 gallons. The *braccio* is 23.42 inches. The metrical system is also introduced.

Naples. The *pound* for gold and silver is 4950 grains. The *cantaro grosso* is 196.5 pounds averdupois, the *cantaro piccolo* 106 pounds averdupois. The *tomolo* is 1.407 of the English bushel. The *barile* is 9.172 gallons. The *palmo* is 10.38 inches. The *moggia* is 3 roods 12 perches.

Netherlands. The French metrical system.

Portugal. The *marc* is 3541.5 grains. The *commercial pound* is 1.0119 lb. averdupois. The *moyo* is 22.39 bushels. The *almude* is 3.6407 gallons. The *foot* is 12.944 inches.

Prussia. The *Cologne marc* is 3609 grains 2 marcs are a *commercial pound*, or 1.0311 lb. averdupois. The *scheffel* is 1.5116 of the English bushel. The *eimer* is 15.11 gallons. The *foot* is 12.356 inches; the *ell* two-thirds of a metre. The *morgen* or *acre* is 2 roods 21 perches.

Rome. The *pound* is 5234 grains, or .7477 lb. averdupois. The *rubbio* (4 quarte) is 8.1012 bushels. The *barile* (32 boccali) is 12.841 gallons. The *foot* is 11.72 inches; The *builders' canna,* of 10 palms, is 87.96 inches.

Russia. There is but one *pound,* .9026 lb. averdupois. The *pood* is 36 lb. averdupois. The *chertwert* is 5.7698 bushels. The *vedro* is 2.7048 gallons. The *inch* is the English one; the *arshine* is 28 inches; the *foot* is 13¾ inches; but the English foot is in common use. The Russian *verst,* or *werst,* is 0.664 (or about two-thirds) of an English mile. The *desselina* is 2 acres, 2 roods, 32 perches.

Sardinia has lately adopted the French metrical system.

Saxony. For gold and silver the *Cologne marc.* The *commercial pound* is 1.0294 lb. averdupois. The *Dresden wispel* (24 scheffels) is 69.85 bushels; the *Leipzic wispel,* 91.747 bushels. The *Dresden eimer* is 14.89 gallons; the *Leipzic eimer* 16.75 gallons. The *Dresden foot* is 11.14 inches; the *Leipzig foot* is 11.13 inches. The *acre* is 1 acre, 1 rood, 18 perches.

Sicily. The *pound* is 7 pounds averdupois. The *cantaro grosso* is 192.5 pounds averdupois; the *cantaro sottile* is 175 lb. averdupois. The *salma grossa* is 9.46 bushels; the *salma generale* 7.59 bushels. The salma of wine is 19.23 litres. The *palmo* is 9.5 inches.

Smyrna. The *chequee* is 4958 grains. The *rottolo* is 1.2748 lb. averdupois. The *killow* is 11.3 gallons. The *pike* is 27 inches.

Spain. The *Castilian marc* for gold and silver is 4800 grains. The *commercial pound* is 1.0144 lb. averdupois. The *fanega* is 1.55 of the English bushel. The *arroba* of wine is 3.538 gallons. The *foot* is 11.128 inches; the *vara* is 33.384 inches. The *fanegada* (for corn-land) is 1 acre, 21 perches.

Sweden. The *Mint marc* is 3252 grains. The *commercial pound* is .9376 lb. averdupois. The dry *tunna* is 4.028 bushels; the *liquid tunna* is 48 *kanns* of .5756 of the English gallon each. The *foot, or half-ell,* is 11.684

inches. The *tunneland* is 1 acre 35 perches.

Switzerland adopted the French metrical system by a law passed in 1849.

United States. The weights and measures are those of England before the introduction of the imperial standard.

WEIR, or WEAR, is a dam erected across a river, either for the purpose of taking fish, of conveying a stream to a mill, or of maintaining the water at the level required for the navigation of it. By the laws of England, no weirs can be maintained on any rivers to the prejudice of the public, or even of individuals, except such as have existed time out of mind, or such as have been erected under local acts of parliament for the navigation of particular rivers.

WELLS. [ARTESIAN WELLS; BORING.]

WEST INDIES. With the exception of Hispaniola or Hayti, which is an independent republic, the islands composing the West Indies are subject to six different European nations — the Spaniards, English, French, Danes, Dutch, and Swedes.

The Spanish possessions are the largest, and comprehend more than half the area of the archipelago; they consist of Cuba, Puerto Rico, Culebra, and Bique. The English possessions are next in extent. They consist of Jamaica, the Bahamas, the Virgin Islands, (Tortola, &c.), Anguilla, Barbuda, Antigua, St. Christopher, Nevis, Montserrat, Dominica, Santa Lucia, Barbadoes, St. Vincent, Grenadines, Grenada, Tobago, and Trinidad. The French possess only a few of the Lesser Antilles, namely Guadaloupe, with several smaller islands in its vicinity, and Martinique. The Danes possess three of the Virgin Islands, viz. St. John, St. Thomas, and Santa Cruz. The Dutch possessions consist of three Lesser Antilles, viz. St. Eustatius, Saba, and St. Martin.

Since the abolition of negro slavery in the British West Indies in 1834, immigrants and liberated Africans have arrived there to assist in cultivating the sugar estates. Their number from 1834 to 1849, was, in—

Jamaica	14,519
Trinidad	13,356
Grenada	1,476
St. Vincent	1,197
Antigua	1,075
Dominica	732
Nevis	427
St. Kitt's	95
	32,877

The British produce and manufactures exported to the British West Indies in 1849 were valued at 1,521,954*l.*

The imports from the British West Indies and Honduras in 1849 included—

Cocoa	3,159,086 lbs.
Coffee	3,596,839 lbs.
Molasses	605,628 cwts.
Rum	4,329,640 galls.
Sugar	2,897,837 cwts.

The imports from the foreign West Indies and Hayti in 1848 included—

Coffee	3,639,108 lbs.
Molasses	95,893 cwts.
Rum	156,185 galls.
Sugar	957,015 cwts.
Tobacco	573,316 lbs.

A few further industrial and commercial statistics will be found under the names of the principal islands.

WESTERN AUSTRALIA dates its history as a British colony from the year 1829. Its progress has hitherto been comparatively slow. The imports in 1848 were valued at 45,411*l.*; the exports at 29,598*l.* The shipping inwards was estimated at 15,494 tons; outwards at 13,957 tons. The wool exported amounted to 301,965 lbs., valued at 9666*l.* The gross revenue was 18,188*l.*, but this included a sum of 7695*l.* voted by the British parliament for the service of the colony. Western Australia is, as yet, one of the poorest of the British Colonies; and little can be said concerning its produce, industry, or commerce.

WESTMORELAND. Geologically, this county may be regarded as consisting of three parts. The slate rocks of the Cumbrian mountain group form the first part or division; the formations of the great carboniferous and mountain limestone series of the north of England, of which formations the Pennine Chain forms the western outcrop, constitute the second division; and the new red sandstone of the valley of the Eden forms the third division. Westmoreland contains some very fertile valleys, in which there are many well-cultivated farms. The soil in the valley is mostly a dry gravelly mould, composed different earths washed down from the hil and forming a soil well fitted for the culti tion of turnips, of which great crops are rais on some well-managed farms. Near Kend a great breadth of potatoes is planted for the supply not only of the immediate neighbourhood, but also of the adjacent counties, many thousand loads being annually sent into Lancashire and Yorkshire. Grass land being abundant and the climate favourable to pasthres, a great portion of the soil is devoted to the maintenance of cattle; good meadows let at a high rent, and are carefully manured with composts; and great crops of hay are made in favourable years.

Westmoreland is not a manufacturing county; but considerable manufactures are carried on at Kendal of cotton checks, kerseys and other woollens, linsey, blanketing, fancy waistcoating, carpets, girths, hosiery, sacking, and worsted.

WESTPHALIA, is one of the richest and busiest of the Prussian provinces. The vegetable products are—corn of all kinds, peas, beans, garden vegetables, fruit, hemp and flax (which are staple articles), hops, and timber. The minerals are—iron, copper, lead, calamine, marble, slate, freestone, salt, and coal: there are extensive turf-moors. The manufactures include linen, cotton, woollen cloth, silk, leather, hosiery, and paper. There are numerous iron, copper, and steel works, and manufactories of all kinds of cutlery and copper, brass and iron goods. There are also many sugar refineries, brandy distilleries, and tanneries in the province. The commerce in the products indicated and in hams is important. The Cologne-Minden railway, with branches to Münster and Paderborn, traverses the province, and connects it with Berlin, Hanover, Hamburg, and Bremen.

WEXFORD. The agriculture of Wexford is generally in a creditable state, considering the natural disadvantages of the soil. The crops consist of the various kinds of grain, of which barley is the principal, beans, tares, rape, turnips, and potatoes, the last being the staple crop, and that upon which most manuring is bestowed. Dairies are numerous, and much butter is exported. The great extent of sea-coast and the numerous banks in the vicinity render the fisheries of Wexford very important to its population, many of whom are engaged in them; the coast presents very numerous creeks capable of accommodating open boats, and at most of these some fishermen are resident, but there are no harbours suitable for large vessels. The manufactures of the county are of little importance; woollen cloths, checks, and coarse linens are made, but on a small scale.

WHALE FISHERY. Whales are sought after for many useful purposes which they render to man. The flesh of the *Manatee* whale is excellent eating. The *Narwhal*, a kind of whale, is valued for its blubber and its ivory tusk. The *Sperm Whale* yields eight or ten barrels of spermaceti, besides oil and whalebone. To the Esquimaux and the Greenlander the *Greenland Whale* is all in all. They eat the flesh and fat with indescribable relish. The membranes of the abdomen serve them for clothing, and the thin transparent peritoneum admits light through the windows of their huts, whilst it keeps out the weather. The bones are made into props for their tents, or aid in the formation of their boats, and supply them with harpoons and spears for the capture of the narwhal, the seal, and greater sea birds. The sinews divided into filaments are used as thread for sewing their dress, &c. To civilised nations, the oil made from its fat or blubber, and the whalebone, have long made it a great commercial object.

The Arctic regions, between the northern parts of America and Europe, have for some centuries been the chief seat of the Whale Fishery. The whales were so abundant that the fishing was easy and the profits great; but in later years the whales have evidently lessened in number, and the fishery has become gradually more precarious. At first there were settlements on the shores of Greenland and other lands in the north, where the whale blubber was boiled down into oil, and in that state sent to England; but in later years it has been the practice to bring the blubber itself to England, and there boil it down. Between 1815 and 1834 the number of English ships engaged in the northern whale fishery varied from 76 to 159; the annual capture of whales varied from 161 to 2018 (so very uncertain is the success of this employment); the annual yield of oil, 2199 to 18,745 tuns; and of whalebone, 119 to 946 tons. So hazardous are these enterprises, that there were not less than 99 whale ships lost in the above-named twenty years, of which 19 were lost in the disastrous year 1830. Hull and Peterhead are the chief British ports to which the whalers belong; but the northern whale fishery has materially declined in the seventeen years since 1834.

The Whale Fishery of the Southern Ocean has sprung into importance as that of the Northern has declined. The relation which the newly-settled Auckland Isles bear to the Southern Whale Fishery is noticed in an earlier article [AUCKLAND ISLANDS]. The southern fishery is prosecuted energetically by the United States, as well as by Britain and other countries.

The following are the numbers of vessels engaged in the American whale fisheries, and the quantities of sperm oil and whale oil procured, in the last 10 years:—

	Ships.	Barrels—Sperm.	Barrels—Whale.
1850	177	86,157	191,752
1849	188	99,433	256,183
1848	196	108,531	243,876

1847	253	121,410	320,545
1846	199	92,877	219,763
1845	242	158,484	274,843
1844	(?)	138,585	267,082
1843	145	167,134	205,861
1842	207	163,697	163,816
1841	222	157,643	205,164
1840	213	156,445	203,441

Whalebone also forms an important item in the products of the fisheries. The quantities imported into the United States during the last ten years have been as follow :—

1850	2,242,012 lbs.
1849	1,990,640 „
1848	1,755,892 „
1847	3,450,124 „
1846	2,723,939 „
1845	3,116,100 „
1844	3,015,145 „
1843	1,933,321 „
1842	1,329,234 „
1841	1,942,885 „

The year 1850 was a very profitable one in the southern fishery, and more than usually unprofitable in the northern.

WHARF, is a place constructed or set apart for the loading and unloading of goods. In this sense the word includes the quays of all sea-ports at which goods are required to be shipped or landed. The sea-beach or natural ground on the banks of a river or canal, is not a wharf. Wharfs in docks and similar situations are made legal by special acts of parliament, as the London Docks, &c., and there are some places which are deemed wharfs from immemorial usage. For the use of a wharf certain rates are usually charged, which are called *wharfage*. The wharfs of the port of London were established in 1558, in the first year of the reign of Queen Elizabeth. Several *sufferance wharfs* have been since added to these, under the authority of the commissioners of customs, and other sufferance wharfs are occasionally authorised for the landing and keeping of goods by the custom-house till the duties are paid or the goods bonded.

No goods except diamonds and bullion, fresh fish of British taking, and turbots and lobsters fresh, however taken or imported, are allowed to be unshipped from any ship arriving from foreign parts beyond seas, or landed or put on shore, except at legal quays appointed by her majesty for landing of goods, or at some wharf appointed by the commissioners of customs. Goods entitled to drawback or bounty are only to be shipped in Great Britain by wharfingers appointed by the commissioners of customs.

WHEAT. The species and varieties of wheat are numereus ; but there are three principal kinds, so different in appearance that they claim peculiar attention. These are the *hard* wheats, the *soft* wheats, and the *Polish* wheats. The hard wheats are the produce of warm climates, such as Italy, Sicily, and Barbary. The soft wheats grow in the northern parts of Europe as in Belgium, England, Denmark, and Sweden. The Polish wheats grow in the country from which they derive their name, and are also hard wheats. It is from their external form that they are distinguished from other wheats. The hard wheats have a compact seed nearly transparent, which, when bitten through, breaks short, and shows a very white flour within. The soft wheats are those usually cultivated in Britain ; they have an opaque coat or skin ; which, when first reaped, gives way readily to the pressure of the thumb and finger. These wheats require to be well dried and hardened before they can be conveniently ground into flour. The Polish wheat has a long chaff which is much longer than the seed, a large oblong seed, and an ear cylindrical in appearance. It is a delicate spring wheat, and not very productive in the climate of England.

The hard wheats contain much more gluten than the soft wheats. It is this quantity of gluten which causes the Italian wheats to be used exclusively for the pastes which form so large a portion of the food of that nation. [VERMICELLI.] The soft wheats contain the greatest quantity of starch, which fits them for the vinous fermentation, by its conversion into sugar and alcohol : for brewing or distilling, therefore, the soft wheats are the best.

The distinction between the *winter* and *summer* wheats is one which arises entirely from the season in which they have been usually sown ; for they can readily be converted into each other, by sowing earlier or later, and gradually accelerating or retarding their growths. The difference in colour between *red* and *white* wheats is owing chiefly to the soil ; white wheats gradually become darker and ultimately red in some stiff wet soils, and the red wheats lose their colour and become first yellow and then white on rich, light, and mellow soils.

The quantity of wheat imported in 1849 was 3,872,134 quarters ; the quantity entered for home consumption was 4,509,626 quarters. The gross amount of duty received was 226,785*l*.

WHEEL AND AXLE is a machine consisting usually of a cylinder to which a wheel is firmly united, so that the axes of both are coincident. The *capstan*, the *windlass*, and the *helm-wheel* of a ship are only so many different forms of the same class of machines. Frequently also the axle is made to carry a wheel with teeth on its circumference, in order that, by revolving, motion may be communicated to machinery: such are the *wind-mills* and *water-mills* which are employed for grinding corn.

Considered as a mechanical aid in locomotion, lifting, transference of power, &c., the wheel and axle act like a lever of the first kind.

WHEELS. In machinery, wheels are generally used for transmitting motion, regulating velocity, converting one species of motion into another, reducing friction, or equalizing the effect of forces applied in an intermittent or irregular manner.

The simplest mode of transmitting motion from one wheel to another is by causing their peripheries to revolve in contact and pressing them together, in order to prevent slipping. Another mode of transmitting rotatory motion more effectually than by simple contact is by the use of endless bands or straps passing over the peripheries of the wheels which are intended to revolve together. Straps or belts are much used in cotton-factories, and other works in which moving-power has to be communicated to a great number of machines in different parts of a building, and they are preferred to cog-wheels in cases where sudden strains are liable to occur, because of the yielding character of the connection effected by them. Such straps were formerly made of leather; but caoutchouc and gutta percha are now largely used. Sometimes a chain of links is used instead of a band.

To convert rotatory motion into rectilinear, or rectilinear into rotatory, various forms of the rack and pinion are used. In its simplest form this contrivance is applied in raising sluice-gates, in lifting-jacks, and various other machines in which a fixed pinion or small toothed wheel is made to give motion to a straight toothed bar capable of moving in the direction of its length. A crank is also applied in various ways for converting rotatory motion into rectilinear, or rectilinear motion into rotatory. Of the *Excentric* and other wheels for producing rectilinear or irregular motion from a revolving axis, or for producing uniform rotation from an intermittent force, the varieties are numerous.

The escapement-wheels of clocks and wheels furnish types of another important class of wheels for modifying motion; and snail-wheels, pin-wheels, ratchet-wheels, and fusee wheels, are among the ingenious contrivances by which the rotatory motion of a wheel and axle may be made to set in motion a train of complicated machinery, or to regulate and vary motion at pleasure. Another class of wheels, called *Friction-Wheels* are intended to lessen the evils of friction in machinery.

Wheels introduced into machinery for the purpose of overcoming inertia, or of rendering uniform and steady a motion derived from an intermittent or variable source, are called *Fly-Wheels.* Since they owe their effect to their weight, fly-wheels are usually heavy, and as much as possible of their weight is disposed in the rim, where, owing to the effect of centrifugal force, it is of far more value than when near the centre. The steam-engine, the stamping-press, the common lathe, the coffee-mill, and a variety of other machines exhibit the useful application of a fly-wheel. In roasting-jacks, musical-boxes, the striking-apparatus of clocks, and various other contrivances in which a retarding force is required to prevent the moving power of a spring or weight from running down too rapidly, wheels with projecting vanes, which encounter sufficient resistance from the air to moderate their velocity, are used under the name of *Flys* or *Flyers.*

A small wheel having cylindrical staves or spindles fixed between two circular boards or plates of metal, in positions parallel to the axis of rotation, is called a *lantern wheel:* and when a wheel acts with one which is smaller in diameter, whatever be the form of the teeth, the latter is usually called a *pinion.* Wheels having the teeth formed on their circumferences so as to project from thence in the direction of the radii are called *spur-wheels:* but when the teeth are perpendicular to the plane of the wheel, the latter is called a *crown* or *contrate wheel.* If the teeth are cut on the circumference of a wheel in a direction oblique to its plane, the wheel is said to be *bevilled;* and two wheels may have their teeth so bevilled as to revolve in planes making any angles with one another.

WHETSTONE, is a smooth flat stone used for whetting or sharpening edged instruments by friction. Whetstones, of which a peculiar kind for sharpening razors are called *Hones,* are made of various kinds of hard close-grained stone, and are moistened, when in use, with either oil or water. [GRINDSTONES; TURKEY HONE.]

WHISKEY. [DISTILLATION; RECTIFYING; SPIRIT TRADE.]

WHITE-LEAD MAFUFACTURE. This branch of industry exhibits many interesting features, both on account of the chemical relations which govern it, and the mechanical arrangements adopted.

White lead is made from common metallic

sheet lead; it is a *carbonate*, and is produced in the following way. The lead is first cast into the form of flat pieces, about 20 inches long, by 5 broad, ⅛th of an inch thick, and weighing 5 lbs. In a large lofty room a pile is built up, formed in the following singular way; a layer of fine ashes is strewed over the floor: then comes a layer of tanner's spent bark, two or three feet thick; then a layer of earthen pots, about five inches in diameter, each containing a pint of strong vinegar; then a layer of the leaden plates, five or six in depth, over the open mouths of the pots; then a layer of boards; then a second layer of tan, vinegar pots, lead plates, and boards—then a third layer of tan, vinegar pots, lead plates, and boards, and so on, until the room is filled to the ceiling, a height of perhaps 20 feet. The whole is called a *stack*, which consists of as many *beds* as there are recurrences of the above series, perhaps seven or eight. A stack usually comprises about 30 tons of lead plates besides the weight of the pots, vinegar, &c. The room is then closed up, and left untouched for many weeks.

During this period a somewhat complicated chemical process goes on. The spent bark, by fermenting, gives off heat, which raises the general temperature to 180° Fahr. The vinegar, at this temperature, evaporates slowly, and gives off an acid vapour which acts upon the lead; the lead first becomes an oxide, then it becomes an acetate by combining with the acetic acid vapour, and this is transformed to a carbonate by carbonic acid arising from the tan. This action takes place in about one half of the thickness of the lead, at the two surfaces; the central part remaining unacted upon. The door is then opened, the stack taken down, and all the lead plates removed. Each piece is passed between two brass rollers, which crush and remove the earthy carbonate from the surface; the remaining metallic lead is remelted, to be used again; and the carbonate goes through further processes. The carbonate is mixed with water, brought to the state of a fine cream, evaporated, and dried: it then constitutes *white lead*, which is brought to market either in the earthy state, or ground up with oil as a paint.

There are other and more expeditious methods which have been patented within the last few years, but the above is the general method, as practised at Newcastle.

See further on this point under ZINC PAINT.

WICKLOW. This Irish county is rich in minerals. Galena green and white lead ore, and copper pyrites are found in the granitic districts. The ore is smelted in small blast-furnaces, with the aid of turf, lime, and a small portion of the purest blind-coal. In the clay-slate tract are found gold, silver, copper, iron, lead, zinc, tin, tungsten, manganese, arsenic, and antimony. The discovery of native gold near Croaghan Kinshela Mountain took place about 1796, and many hundred people assembled daily to search for it in the bed and on the banks of the Ballinvalley, or Goldmine River, a stream which rises in the mountain, and joins the Daragh just above its junction with the Ovoca. Government took up the matter, and regular stream-works were established, but they were destroyed in the insurrection of 1798. They were resumed in 1801, with the addition of works for the discovery of auriferous veins; but the search was unsuccessful, and the whole of the works were abandoned.

The soil of Wicklow is very fertile in the lower tracts and along the river-courses. The crops are oats, potatoes, and some wheat. Pasturage is also much attended to. The occupations of the people are generally agricultural: manufactures being at a very low ebb.

WILLOW. The *timber* willow, the *weeping* willow, the *osier* willow, and many other kinds, render a singular variety of uses to man. The leaves, flowers, and young shoots are eaten as food by various domestic animals. The dried inner bark is mixed with oatmeal in Norway. The twigs are extensively used in Russia and Sweden as thongs and cords. The bark is used in the same countries for shoes, buckets, boxes, roof coverings, and other articles; it is also used as a tanning ingredient and when separated into fibres it is woven into cloth.

The willow timber is soft, smooth and light; it is employed in making cutting boards for tailors and shoemakers; for cork-cutters sharpening boards; for turnery; for flooring and rafters; for lining waggons and carts; for paddle-boards, water-wheels, and small vessels and boats. The smaller timber and shoots are used for ladder-poles, hop-poles, vine-props, clothes-props, rake-handles, hurdles, crates, hampers, hay-racks, hoop-barrels. In France, hats are made from strips or shavings of the white willow. Sheets of woven material called *Willow*, consist of a fabric woven with fine strips of willow wood, subsequently stiffened; they are in common use for the framework of bonnets, and of light or 'gossamer' hats. A downy substance which envelopes the willow seed is used in Germany as a wadding for ladies' dresses. The willow makes very excellent charcoal.

The best known use of the willow, however,

is in making baskets. For this purpose the kind called *osiers* is chiefly selected. The principal plantations of basket-osiers in this country, and indeed in every other, are made along the banks of rivers and streams. In England the Thame and the Cam are the most celebrated in this respect; in both these rivers small islands are frequently planted entirely with osiers, and are called *osier-holts*. There are many such islands in the Thames, between Reading and London. The largest plantation of these willows is near Reading. The most extensive willow plantations in fields (instead of river banks and islands) are in the fenny districts of Cambridge and Huntingdon counties.

The application of these willows or osiers is described under BASKET MAKING.

WILNA, a government of West Russia, is somewhat rich in agricultural produce. Rye is the principal grain crop; barley, wheat, oats, buck-wheat, peas, beans, hops, flax, and hemp are likewise grown, and a considerable quantity exported. Bees are kept in great numbers, and the quality of the honey is very superior. The forests not only furnish large quantities of timber and fuel, but supply material for building every year about 3000 craft for the navigation of the Düna, Wilia, and Niemen, which never come back. Charcoal pitch, tar, potashes, and lamp-black are made. The minerals are bog-iron, saltpetre, marble, granite, sandstone, jasper, agates, and chalcedony. The manufactures are unimportant, being entirely of a domestic kind. The exports, consisting of the produce already named, are sent partly to Riga on the Düna, still more by land-carriage to Libau, and a considerable quantity by the Niemen to Prussia. The inland trade is almost exclusively in the hands of the Jews.

WILTSHIRE. There are very few mineral deposits worked in this county. In respect to commerce, the navigation of the Thames, the Kennet, and the Bristol Avon, does not commence until after those rivers have quitted the county; but the want of river-navigation is partially supplied by canals, of which three lines are connected with this county. These are the Thames and Severn canal, the Kennet and Avon Canal, and the Wilts and Berks Canal. Many of the principal towns are now accommodated with railway facilities.

In an agricultural point of view Wiltshire may be divided into two districts; a southern district comprehending all the Wiltshire Downs, with their intersecting valleys; and a northern district. The soil on the downs produces excellent short herbage, very well suited for sheep pasture. The proportion which has been converted into arable land is comparatively small, and chiefly on the borders of the valleys. In the northern district, where the top soil is thin, it is chiefly cultivated as arable land; but where it is deep and rich, there are some of the finest pastures in England, such as those about Chippenham, and thence southward to Melksham and Trowbridge, where the largest oxen may be fatted. This district is essentially a dairy country. The grass land forms the greater portion of the north-west part of Wiltshire, and the cheese made there is justly celebrated; it is mostly bought up by factors for the supply of London and other large towns.

Wiltshire is one of the most manufacturing counties in the West of England; the carpets of Wilton, and the woollen-cloths of Bradford, Trowbridge, &c. have been long celebrated, though they have been eclipsed in late years (in quantity but not in quality) by the productions of the West Riding.

WINCH AND AXLE is a machine constituting a small windlass, and consisting of a cylinder of wood which is capable of turning on its axis between two upright posts of the same material, or between the ends of a cast-iron frame. A lever at one or at each extremity of the cylinder is attached to an iron axle which passes through the cylinder, and is turned at right angles to its direction, and again turned, so as to furnish a handle parallel to the cylinder. When of a simple form it is employed to raise water from a well, earth from the shaft of a small mine, &c.; but when the cylinder or barrel is turned by the intervention of toothed wheels and pinions, in which case the machine is called a *Crab*, it is frequently employed to raise casks or heavy packages from the ground to the upper part of a building. [WHEEL AND AXLE; WINDLASS.]

WIND MEASURER. [ANEMOMETER.]

WINDLASS. The *Winch and Axle*, the *Windlass* by which on board of small ships the anchors are weighed, and even the *Capstan*, are so many different forms of the same machine. In the last two of these machines the power of men is applied at the extremities of handspokes or levers inserted at their opposite extremities in holes made in the axle or barrel to receive them. In the capstan, the axis of the barrel being vertical, the handspokes are in horizontal positions, and the men exert a continuous pressure against them while walking round.

In the machine to which the name of windlass is more particularly applied, the barrel is a horizontal cylinder. In order to turn the cylinder on its axis the men mounting on it plant their handspokes vertically in a series of holes formed at intervals for the purpose; then grasping them as high as they can reach, they pull towards themselves: when the cylinder is turned nearly a quarter round, the handspokes being almost in horizontal positions, the men throw upon them the whole weight of their bodies, and by the weight the cylinder is still further turned. After this the handspokes are drawn out and planted in other holes, which now are in vertical positios, and the like exertions of muscular force and pressure are repeated till the anchor is weighed or the weight raised. The machine permits the power of men to be applied, in one position of the handspokes, in the most advantageous manner; and in this respect it may be considered superior to the capstan.

The vertical windlass, or *capstan*, was originally a short cylindrical column turning on its axis by means of levers or bars of considerable length which passed quite through the perforations made to receive them at the top of the column; the pivot or axle upon which it turned, entered, as at present, into the floor or deck upon which the machine was placed. It appears to have been introduced into the British navy in the time of Queen Elizabeth. It is now generally made in the form of a frustum of a cone, or rather the body is cylindrical, and about it, at equal intervals, are ribs or buttresses which, projecting from the cylinder less at top than at bottom, give to the part about which the rope turns a pyramidal figure. Both the windlass and the capstan are furnished with catches, or *Paulls*, each consisting of an arm of metal turning on a pivot, and as the barrel revolves falling into notches formed in a ring of wood or metal placed round one end of the barrel.

WINDMILL. Windmills are of two kinds: in one the wind is made to act upon vanes or sails, generally four, which are disposed so as to revolve by that action in a plane which is nearly vertical; and in the other, the axis of revolution being precisely vertical, any point on the surface of a vane revolves in a horizontal plane. The former is called a *Vertical* Windmill and the latter a *Horizontal* Windmill.

The building for a Vertical Windmill is generally a wall of timber or brickwork in the form of a frustum of a cone, and terminated above by a wooden dome which is capable of revolving horizontally upon it. A ring of wood, forming the lower part of the dome, rests upon a ring of the same material at the top of the wall, and the surfaces in contact being made very smooth, the dome may easily be turned round upon the wall; and is prevented from sliding off by a rim which projects from it, and descends over the interior circumference of the lower ring. The dome in turning carries with it the windsails and their axle; and thus the windsails may be made to coincide with the direction of the wind, or the plane in which the radii of the sails turn may be made perpendicular to that direction. The revolution is sometimes accomplished by the force of a man applied to a winch near the ground; but in general the wind itself is made to turn the dome or the mill by means of a set of small vanes which are situated at the extremity of a long horizontal arm projecting from the dome in a plane passing through the vertical shaft of the mill, and on the side opposite to the great sails.

A Horizontal Windmill is a great cylindrical frame of timber, which is made to revolve about a vertical axis, and its convex surface is formed of boards attached in vertical positions to the upper and lower parts of the frame. The whole is inclosed in a fixed cylinder having the same vertical axis as the other: this consists of a screen formed by a number of boards which are disposed so that, in whatever direction the wind may blow, it may enter between them on one side only of a vertical plane passing through the axis, and thus give motion to the interior cylinder. The effective power of the Vertical Windmill is however so much greater than that of the Horizontal Windmill that the latter is now seldom constructed.

WINE MANUFACTURE. Wine is the result of the fermentation of saccharine fluids, either existing naturally in the juices of plants or artificially blended together. The roots of plants, such as the parsnip and beet; the stems of plants, such as the birch and the cocoa palm; the leaves of plants, such as the vine; the fruit of plants, such as the grape and other well-known kinds—all yield juices which may be fermented into wine. Though alcohol or spirit is present in all wines, yet many other principles exist in them also; the number of which, and the manner in which they are combined, as well as their relative proportion, give to different wines their distinctive properties.

The grape is in most countries the source whence wine is chiefly prepared, and the vintage or wine manufacture is always regarded as an important part of the national industry in the countries of central and southern Europe. It has been found that, in respect to Claret, Port, and Rhenish wines, a season which is good for one is not necessarily so for others; thus the year 1825 was very good for Claret, bad for Port, and about an average for Rhenish wines; while 1840 was middling for Claret, very fine for Port, and bad for Rhenish wines. Locality, aspect, soil, and climate all have to do with this question of quality and quantity. In respect to the modes of manufacture, a few details will be found under the names of the chief wines, and of the provinces and French departments where the most celebrated vintages are situated.

When wine contains much alcohol, it is called strong; when otherwise, *light* or *weak.* When it contains much sugar undecomposed, it is *sweet* or *luscious;* when little, *dry.* When it contains much free acid, it is *acescent;* when much carbonic acid, *sparkling* or *mousseux.* In strong wines of cheap price, spirit is added; but never in good wines, as it destroys the finer qualities.

British or *home-made* wines consist of the fermented juices of fruits, sweetened and otherwise flavoured. They are in principle analogous to real wine from grapes, but requiring much less care and attention, as no attempt is made to obtain those delicate varieties of flavour which distinguish choice wines.

WINE TRADE. The duty at present on all foreign wines is 5*s.* 6*d.* per gallon; on Cape wines, 2*s* 9*d.* The following statement shows the number of gallons imported into the United Kingdom during the year ending Jan. 5, 1850, together with the number retained for home consumption, after deducting the quantity exported subsequently to the payment of duty:—

Wines.	Imported. *Gallons.*	Retained. *Gallons.*
Cape	264,106	241,845
French	466,169	331,690
Portugal	3,004,043	2,648,242
Spanish	3,310,206	2,448,107
Madeira	165,463	71,097
Rhenish	63,380	46,405
Canary	151,239	19,868
Fayal	12,163	67
Sicilian & other sorts	533,298	444,541
Total	7,970,067	6,251,862

The stock of foreign wine in bond in London, on March 1, 1851, was as follows:—

	Pipes.
London Docks	18,346
St. Katherine's ditto	3,853
	22,199

WIRE DRAWING. Wire is a metal elongated into the form of a slender rod, generally cylindrical, but not necessarily so. In early times, metals were probably beaten out with a hammer into thin plates or leaves, which were then divided into small slips by means of scissors or some other cutting instrument, these slips being subsequently rounded by a hammer and file, so as to form threads or wires. So long as wire was formed by the hammer, the artists of Nürnberg, by whom it was fabricated, were styled 'wire smiths,' but subsequent to the introduction of the drawing process their designation was changed to 'wire drawers.' Beckmann conceives that the invention of wire drawing must be assigned to the 14th century. Previous to 1565 all English iron wire appears to have been drawn by manual strength. The first wire-mill in England was set up at Sheen, near Richmond, by a Dutchman, in 1662.

For the manufacture of iron wire the very best and toughest iron is selected. Before the process of rolling with grooved rollers had become common, the iron was prepared for use by a slow and tedious process. At the present day the preparing of iron for the wire-drawers is performed by means of rollers, which are generally 7 or 8 inches in diameter, and are sometimes made to perform 350 revolutions in a minute. A bar of steel 30 inches long and an inch square, heated to redness, is passed between the rollers, through grooves successively diminishing in size, eight times in less than a minute, and is thereby elongated to from 20 to 30 feet. For ordinary wire the rods are commonly reduced to a thickness of about one-eighth of an inch by this process; and these rods themselves are used as wire for some purposes. The kind of cast-steel wire of which the best needles and some other articles are made, is not usually submitted to the rolling process, but, after being tilted to about a quarter of an inch square, it is rounded on an anvil previous to elongation by the draw-plate.

The drawing of wire is thus managed. The draw-plate is usually formed of a stout piece of shear-steel, about six inches long and an inch and a half in diameter, but being somewhat reduced in thickness towards each end, like a cucumber, and flattened on one side. It is pierced transversely with several conical holes, the larger orifices of which open upon the flattened surface of the plate, while their smaller orifices are carefully finished to the size to which it is intended to reduce the wire drawn through them. In drawing wire by hand the draw-plate is laid against two upright pillars fixed on a bench or table, and, the extreme end of the wire to be drawn being so reduced as to enable it readily to pass through the hole, a small portion is drawn through by a lever apparatus, and attached to a cylindrical drum, mounted on a vertical axis. The workman then takes in one hand the coil of thick wire to be reduced, and in the other a lever handle attached to the drum; and while he turns the drum so as to wind the wire upon its circumference, and consequently to draw it through the plate, he imparts a kind of twist to the wire which enters the plate, by a peculiar motion of the hand in which the coil is supported.

The size of wire is commonly measured by means of a gauge, which consists of a plate of steel with a series of deep notches or slits at each edge, varying slightly from each other in width, and numbered according to the number given to wire of corresponding size.

The use of wire in manufactures has largely extended within the last few years, principally owing to the success with which a weaving process has been applied to it. The following are only some among the many applications of wire now generally adopted:—Wire netting for enclosing young plantations; strong wire netting for sheep folds, or for enclosures generally in farms; ornamental wire fences for pleasure grounds; pheasantries and hencoops; garden bordering; plant guards; hurdles for horse and cattle pastures; fences and gates; plant trainers; arbours and arches; plant umbrellas and canopies; flower stands and stages; garden chairs; bedsteads; wire gauze blinds; sieves and riddles; Venetian blinds; bird cages; fire guards; safety lamps and lanterns; meat covers and safes. Lastly, we may mention *wire ropes*, of the use of which a few illustrations have been given under ROPE MAKING and SUSPENSION BRIDGES.

WOAD. This is a plant cultivated for the sake of the leaves, which, after being properly prepared, are used as an ingredient in dyeing blue, and as a basis for black. Three or four crops are obtained in a year. When the leaves have been gathered, they are ground in a mill to a sort of paste, which is then pressed into heaps. A blackish crust forms on the outside. After thus lying for about a fortnight the heaps are opened, the crust rubbed and mixed with the interior portions, and the whole formed into oval balls, which are pressed close and solid in wooden moulds. The balls are dried for the market. When about to be used in dyeing, the balls are broken in fragments, and allowed to ferment, by which a thick fœtid fume is given off. By steeping the leaves in water, an infusion is obtained which will impart a green dye, and this green changes to blue by exposure to the air.

WOOD. The uses of wood in the arts are illustrated in the articles CARVING; DRY ROT; SHIP BUILDING; TIMBER; &c., and under the names of the principal timber trees.

WOOD ENGRAVING is the art of producing raised surfaces, by excision, on blocks of wood, from which impressions can be transferred by means of a coloured pigment to paper, or other suitable medium, and generally applied to pictorial representations of objects.

The art of cutting both upon metal and wood for other purposes than those which are now understood as printing, ascends to a very remote antiquity. The Egyptians indeed seem to have made a very close approximation to printing, in their wooden stamps used for impressing characters on clay or other ductile material; and printing from engraved wood blocks has been practised by the Chinese probably from the 10th century.

In Europe the first application of the art of wood-engraving took place in Germany about the beginning of the 15th century. It was probably first used for the production of playing-cards, the outlines of which were formed by impressions from wood-cuts, and the colouring filled up by hand. The first wood-cut with a date known to be in existence is of 1423; it represents St. Christopher carrying our Saviour on his shoulders across a river. The next great step was the production of block books and the adoption of moveable letters; and without entering into the disputed question of the dates of the 'Biblia Pauperum,' the 'Speculum Salvationis,' and others, they sufficiently prove the extension of its use, and many of the early books with moveable types were illustrated with pictorial wood-cuts. Maps also were engraved on wood. In an edition of Ptolemæus, printed in 1482 at Ulm, there are twenty-seven; and in a later edition, printed at Venice in 1511, the outline, with the mountains and rivers, is in wood, while the names are printed with type, and in two colours, no doubt by separate workings. In 1486 the improvement known as 'cross-hatching,' by which the bold and free effect of a pen-drawing was endeavoured to be attained, was shown in Breidenberg's 'Travels,' printed at Mentz. This invention has been usually attributed to Michael Wohlgemuth, the master of Albert Dürer. The art had now attained an excellence which induced artists of celebrity and talent to select it as the means of conveying their designs to the world. Among the most distinguished in this line was Albert Dürer, whose productions as a painter, and an engraver on copper and wood, are so numerous as to excite a doubt whether he was actually an engraver on wood himself, or whether he only put the designs on the blocks, leaving them for other hands to execute.

In the early part of the 16th century several artists of celebrity were either designers on wood or engravers. Books were also at this period profusely illustrated. The art was chiefly practised in Germany, where it was patronised by the Emperor Maximilian, for whom Burgmair produced the great work called 'The Triumphs of Maximilian.' The next great name in the annals of wood-engraving is Hans Holbein, whose 'Dance of Death' was printed at Lyon, in 1538, though Bartsch and Jackson deny that he engraved on wood, and Mr. Douse even questions his being the designer. From about 1545 to 1580 wood-engraving continued to be much used for the illustrating of books. From this period there is little to be recorded of essential importance, till the appearance of Bewick, to whom the revival of wood-engraving is chiefly to be attributed.

WOOL; WOOL TRADE. The term 'wool' is now applied almost exclusively to the fleece of the sheep. The distinction between wool and hair is more easily understood than described. Wool compared with hair is generally softer, more flexible, and more disposed to undergo the felting process, which imparts to it so much value in manufactures. Many of the wilder animals, such as the beaver, the racoon, the wild-cat, and the otter, produce both hair and wool, the hair forming the long and conspicuous outer fibres, and the shorter fibres of wool lying hidden beneath. The goats of Angora, or Ancyra, of Tibet, and of Cashmere, yield woolly fibres of great beauty, which are peculiarly suited for the weaving of shawls. For the manufacture of all kinds of woollen fabrics, except these shawls, the wool of the sheep is used. [SHEEP.]

In the time of Edward I. a duty was imposed on the exportation of British wool, and in 1337 an act was passed for prohibiting the exportation. From that time down to the reign of Charles I. the exportation of British wool was sometimes prohibited and sometimes allowed under certain restrictions and duties. From 1660 down to 1824 the exportation was strictly prohibited. In the meantime duties, sometimes more, sometimes less, were laid on the importation of foreign wool. At length, in 1824, an act was passed making the duty on importation and exportation the same, viz., 1*d.* per lb. The duty on exportation was soon afterwards removed, and in 1844 the duty on the importation of foreign wool ceased altogether.

All the finer wools used to be brought from Spain; but in 1765 the Elector of Saxony imported into his dominions a few Merino sheep, which have had a most surprising influence on the trade of wool. The Saxony Merinos, instead of degenerating, improved upon their Spanish progenitors, and the wool afforded by them has almost driven the Spanish wool out of the English market. But the most remarkable circumstance in the recent history of the wool-trade is the rapid increase in the quantity of wool imported from Australia. This is shown by comparing the quantities imported in the three following years:—

1829	1,838,642 lbs.
1839	10,128,774 ,,
1849	35,870,171 ,,

The quantity imported from various countries in 1849 was as follows:—

Australia	35,870,171 lbs.
Spain	127,559 ,,
Germany	12,750,011 ,,
Other European Countries	11,432,354 ,,
South America	6,014,525 ,,
Cape of Good Hope	5,377,495 ,,
East Indies	4,182,853 ,,
All other parts	1,004,679 ,,
Total......	76,768,647

In 1848 the quantity of wool exported was 4,000,000 lbs.

WOOLLEN AND WORSTED MANUFACTURES. Wools are divided into two great classes—*Clothing-Wools* and *Combing-Wools*, or *Short-Wools* and *Long-Wools;* and the fabrics woven from them are termed *Woollens* or *Worsteds*, according as the one or the other is employed. Clothing wools possess in high perfection that peculiar property which enables the fibres to 'felt' or interlace one among another, and to form thereby the dense compact material of which men's garments are so largely made in this country; whereas combing-wools, though long in fibre, are deficient in the felting property, and are therefore employed for stuffs, merinos, hosiery, and a large number of fabrics which do not undergo the felting process.

Woollen Manufacture.—The sorting of the wool is the first operation. Each pack of wool contains many different qualities, according to the part of the fleece whence it was taken, and other circumstances; and much tact and discrimination are called for in the separation. The sorter has to make his selection in relation to the *fineness*, the *softness*, the *strength*, the *colour*, the *cleanness* and the *weight* of the wool; and in reference to these qualities he separates the wool into many parcels. When the proper kinds are selected, they are next *washed* or *scoured* with soap and alkali, to free them from the grease which invariably attaches to them.

If the cloth is dyed in the wool, that operation succeeds the scouring; but if dyed in the piece, many other processes intervene; and it depends a good deal on the kind of colour as to which plan is followed. Supposing the dyeing to be completed, however, the wool undergoes the process of *willying* or *willowing*, which is somewhat analogous to the *batting* or *scutching* in the cotton-manufacture; the object being to open and disentangle the locks of wool, and cleanse them from sandy and other loose impurities. The willowing machine contains a number of revolving spikes which tear asunder the fibres of the wool, and a fan which blows away the dust from them. There are frequently impurities which cannot be removed by the willy, and such are afterwards picked out by boys or women, called *Wool-Moaters*, or *Wool-Pickers*. A further opening of fibres results from the process of *scribbling;* but before this is effected, the wool undergoes that of *oiling;* it being spread out on a floor, sprinkled with olive-oil, and well beaten with staves. The *scribbling-machine* is very similar in its principle of action to the *carding-engine*. [COTTON SPINNING.]

The cardings into which the wool is brought by this operation, and which are short pieces in the form of rolls or sticks, are then spun into yarn for the use of the woollen-weaver; the process of spinning being generally effected by means of the *slubbing-billy* or *slubbing-machine*, and afterwards by the common jenny or mule-spinning machine; the slubbing-billy bringing the wool to the state of a soft weak thread, and the spinning-machine giving it the proper firmness and hardness for yarn.

The process next following that of spinning is weaving, by which the yarn is worked up into a textile fabric. [WEAVING.] Formerly woollen cloths were principally woven by hand-weavers; but the power-loom is every year superseding moro and more the common loom.

As the wool has been dressed with oil before spinning, and with size before weaving, it becomes necessary to cleanse it from these impurities immediately after the weaving. This is the object of a second scouring process, in which the cloth is beaten with wooden mallets in a kind of trough or mill; soap and water being let in upon it first, and then clear water. Being then carried to the drying-room, or the tenter-ground, it is stretched out by means of hooks on rails, and allowed to dry in a smooth and extended state. It is then taken into a room and examined by *Burlers*, who pick out all irregular threads, hairs, or dirt. After this it is ready for the important process of *fulling* or *felting*, which imparts to woollen goods that peculiarity of surface whereby they are distinguished from all others. A large mass of cloth folded into many plies is put into the fulling-mill, where it is exposed to the long-continued action of two heavy wooden mallets or stocks. Superfine cloth has four fullings of three hours each, a thick solution of soap being spread between each layer of cloth every time. This process, besides felting or interlacing the fibres together, thickens the cloth remarkably, but diminishes it both in length and breadth nearly one-half.

In the fulled state the cloth presents a woolly and rough appearance, to improve which it goes through the process of *teazling* or *raising*, and *shearing* or *cutting*, the object of the first being to raise the ends of the fibres above the surface, and of the second to cut them off to a uniform level. The raising of the fibres is effected by thistle-heads, teazling-cards, or wire-brushes. Teazles are the seed-pods of the *Dipsacus Fullonum*, and are used by hand [TEAZLE]; but sometimes wire-cards are used, fixed to a machine called a *gig-mill*.

When the ends of the fibres have been thus raised to the surface, they are next sheared or cropped, a process of great beauty and singularity. Originally this process was performed by means of large hand-shears, the cloth being stretched over a stuffed table, and the workman proceeding to clip the ends of the fibres in a regular and equable manner; but the process is now more frequently conducted by a machine, which causes a revolving circular furnished with cutters to travel horizontally over the cloth, and shear it.

When the cloth has been raised and sheared (which operations are repeated two or threo times for superfine cloth), it is brushed by a machine consisting of a system of brushes affixed to cylinders; the cloth being exposed at the same time to the action of the brushes and of steam. A few subsequent operations are carried on, having for their object the imparting of smoothness, gloss, &c., to the cloth, preparatory to its being placed in the hands of the dealers.

Worsted Manufacture.—All combing-wools are longer in fibre than the clothing-wools, but they are subject to the division into 'long' and 'short' combing wools; the long, varying from 6 to 12 inches in length, being used principally for coarse worsted goods, and the short, from 4 to 7 inches, being used for hosiery and some other purposes.

After the wool has been sorted, washed,

and scoured from the adherent grease, and dried in a heated room, it is carried to a machine called a *plucker*, containing a pair of spiked rollers, by the action of which the wool is cleansed, separated, and the fibres straightened, preparatory to the process of *combing*. This combing is sometimes performed by hand, by means of two instruments filled with spikes, between which the wool is drawn till the fibres assume a regular arrangement; but a very efficient machine, somewhat on the principle of the carding machine, is now frequently used for this purpose.

When the wool has been combed either by hand or machine, it is transferred to the *breaking-frame*, the object of which is to open out any fibres which may have escaped the action of the combs, and to bring the wool into the form of a roll or narrow belt. This roll is then lapped round a large bobbin or cylinder; then passed a second time through a breaking-frame; and then subjected to the action of a machine analogous in principle to the drawing-frame of the cotton manufacture; the object being to extend the length, diminish the thickness, and equalise the number of fibres of the roll or sliver. Hitherto the woolly fibres are merely slightly coherent, without having any twist; but they are now passed through a *roving-machine*, preparatory to the process of spinning. The roving and spinning are conducted much in the manner described in the article COTTON SPINNING. When spun, the worsted yarn is wound on a reel, and is then made up into hanks.

Here terminate the operations of a worsted mill. The dyeing of the yarn, and the weaving into the various kinds of textile fabrics, lead us to other departments of industry. [DYEING; WEAVING.]

Woollen Trade. Plain *broad cloth* is a specimen of plain weaving, followed by the fulling process; whereas *kerseymere* is a twilled fabric, similarly fulled. *Serges* are twills having worsted warp and coarse woollen weft. *Blankets* are made of very soft yarn, afterwards worked up into a kind of pile by milling; and many varieties of coarse cloth are of analogous structure. *Bombazeen* is a twilled mixture of worsted and silk; *Poplin* is an untwilled mixture, showing more silk than worsted at the surface. Goods called *Saxonies* and *Orleans* are made of woollen, sometimes mixed with cotton, and afterwards printed. *Stuff* is made wholly of worsted; while *Merino* is a fine woollen twill, sometimes printed. The material called *Cashmere*, if properly so named, is made of the shawl-goat wool, much in the same way as merino; but most of the fabrics so called are made of sheep's wool. *Challis* is a mixture of woollen weft with silk warp, and is generally printed. *Mousseline-de-Laine* was originally all wool, but is now frequently mixed with cotton, and generally printed. *Norwich Crape*, unlike common crape, is composed of wool and silk, something like challis, but without being printed. *Crêpe de Lyon* is formed of worsted and silk; and *Italian Net* of worsted only. These examples are only intended to indicate the sources of the varieties in woollen and worsted goods, for to enumerate all the varieties themselves would be nearly impossible. This is particularly the case in respect to Waistcoatings, where fancy weaving adds to the sources of diversity.

Mr. McCulloch made a rough estimate, a few years ago, that the value of woollen and worsted goods made in the United Kingdom averages about 23,000,000*l.* yearly; that about two-fifths of this sum are paid in wages; and that about 350,000 persons are directly employed in it. But it is admitted that the data for forming such estimates are very insufficient.

The value of all kinds of woollens, worsteds, worsted hosiery, and woollen and worsted yarn, exported from Great Britain in 1830 was estimated at 4,728,666*l.*; in 1840, at 5,327,853*l.*; and in 1849, at 8,420,342*l.*

WOOLWICH DOCKYARD. The Royal Dockyard at Woolwich much resembles those already described as existing elsewhere. [CHATHAM; PLYMOUTH; PORTSMOUTH.] The same groupings of manufacturing arrangements are to be met with in all of them, subject to certain minor differences. Woolwich is also rich in other government establishments; but they belong rather to military than to manufacturing operations, and scarcely come within the scope of this volume.

WORCESTERSHIRE. There are coal deposits of various degrees of richness in this county. The town of Dudley stands on the thicker coal-measures. In the neighbourhood of Droitwich and Stoke Prior are saliferous beds, from which a large quantity of salt is manufactured. The northern part of the county is well supplied with railways and canals. In respect to agriculture, the average produce of wheat in Worcestershire is higher than in many other counties. Potatoes are raised in great abundance for the supply of Birmingham and other large towns. Wolverley Sands have long been famous for the growth of carrots, and for raising carrot seed. Orchards are numerous, but many of the trees are old.

The northern part of the county contains many manufacturing towns. The industry of Bromsgrove, Droitwich, Dudley, and Kidderminster, is briefly noticed in separate articles. Redditch is the great seat of the needle manufacture; and Stourbridge has extensive manufactures in iron, glass, and fire-bricks.

WORMWOOD (*Artemisia absinthium*), is an indigenous perennial plant met with on waste places, but that which is required for medical uso is mostly cultivated. The upper part of the stem, with the leaves and unexpanded flowers, should be collected, for these parts possess the peculiar aroma, with a strong bitter taste; while the lower part of the stem is merely aromatic, and devoid of bitterness. Wormwood possesses the properties common to aromatic bitters, but it seems to possess also some peculiar ones rendering it worthy of more attention than it receives. The bitter principle is readily absorbed, so that the flesh of animals fed upon it becomes manifestly bitter. Ale in which wormwood has been steeped (purl) is more heady than other ale.

WORSTED. [Woollen and Worsted Manufactures.]

WÜRTEMBERG is one of the most fruitful countries of Germany, and agriculture is on the whole carried on upon a good system. A manifest improvement in tho breed of cattle and horses is remarked at every new cattle-show at Cannstadt, where a fête is held Sept. 26, in each year. The chief agricultural products aro spelt, maize, oats, barley, rye, wheat, peas, beans, vetches, potatoes, flax, hemp, rape-seed, poppies, hops, and tobacco. Of the vineyards more than three-fifths are in the circle of the Neckar, the rest are chiefly on the Tauber and the lake of Constanz; the wines of these last districts are very different from the Neckar wines, rather resembling Rhenish. The metals and minerals are copper, lead, zinc, iron, marble, mill-stone-grit, freestone, quartz, precious stones, porcelain earth, potters'-clay, fullers' earth, chalk, salt, and a little coal. The salt works are the property of government, which has the monopoly of the salt trade; the annual produce is about 24,000 tons.

The manufactures include linen and woollen cloths, calicoes, silks, lace, hosiery, muslin, carpets, leather, paper, porcelain, earthenware, iron and steel ware, gold and silver plate, tobacco, tobacco pipes, and gunpowder; there are likewise numerous distilleries and breweries, and chemical factories. Würtemberg has a very considerable trade in its natural productions and manufactures, its horned cattle, horses, sheep, timber, wool, and printed books. The imports consist of raw cotton and cotton manufactures, silks, glass wares, wine, fruit, cheese, china, earthenware, and all kinds of colonial produce. There is likewise a very great transit trade. The inland navigation is important, especially on the Neckar, which becomes navigable at Cannstadt; above 2000 vessels are employed in it.

X

XANTHIAN MARBLES. These interesting marbles form one of the most attractive portions of the collection of antiquities in the British Museum. They consists of a large collection of sepulchral marbles of various ages, which were first made known to the European public by Mr. Fellows (now Sir Charles), who discovered them in 1838. They were all found in or near Xanthus, the ancient capital of Lycia.

Y

YARN is the general name given to the threads which are woven into the various kinds of textile fabrics, whether, cotton, silk, flax, hemp, wool, or worsted; the terms *twist*, *mule-weft*, *organzine*, *tram*, *abb*, *line*, &c., being particular names applied to particular sorts. [COTTON SPINNING; FLAX MANUFACTURE; SILK MANUFACTURE; SPINNING; WOOLLEN AND WORSTED MANUFACTURES.]

The exportation of yarn has now become very large, the perfection of English spinning-machines enabling foreign weavers to buy ready-spun yarn cheaper, in many cases, than they can spin it themselves. The quantities exported and the estimated values, in 1848, were as follows:—

Cotton Yarn ..	135,831,162 lbs.	5,927,831*l.*
Linen Yarn ..	11,722,182	493,449
Woollen Yarn .	8,429,152	776,975
	155,982,496 lbs.	7,198,255*l.*

YEAST, BARM, or FERMENT, is a substance which is deposited in an insoluble state during the fermentation of wine, beer, and vegetable juices. This substance, as is well known, is employed to produce fermentation in saccharine solutions. [BREAD; BREWING; FERMENTATION.]

YEW. The timber of the yew tree is applied to many useful purposes. In the days of archery, yew was almost exclusively employed for making bows; but various ornamental woods from South America are now substituted for it in this respect. Yew-tree wood is extensively used in cabinet making, as being hard, compact, and of a very fine close grain. It is also much used by turners for making snuff-boxes, musical instruments, &c.

YORKSHIRE. This county is rich in minerals. The lower red sandstone, or Pontefract Rock, near Pontefract, is usually a mass of yellowish sands, of the greatest excellence for the use of the metal-founder in the construction of his moulds. From beneath the magnesian deposits rise the sandstones, shales, ironstones, and coal of the West Riding of Yorkshire, and fill an enormous area in the valleys of the Aire, Calder, Went, Dearn, Dove, and Don. The whole of this large area (not less than 600 square miles) yields coal. The whole series of strata is about 4000 feet thick; and of the coal which lies in this series there are about 20 workable beds, yielding about 40 feet of coal, generally of good quality. Ironstones of excellent quality accompany the lower parts of this coal deposit. The seam of coal are worked in the west of Yorkshire as thin as 18 inches (near Halifax and Penistone), and one as thick as 8, 9, or 10 feet (Barnsley), but the average is from 3 to 6 feet. The most characteristic rock in the millstone grit of the West Riding is the quartzose conglomerate, used in making millstones.

Yorkshire is excellently supplied with canals and railways, in aid of its manufactures and commerce. The manufactures of the county are of great importance. The manufacture of woollen cloths, at Leeds, Bradford, Halifax, Wakefield, and Huddersfield, has been brought to such a degree of perfection as to compete with the woollens of the West of England, while it far exceeds them in quantity. The iron-works are very extensive. Sheffield is the great seat of the manufacture of cutlery of all kinds, as well as of tools and plated goods. Linens are extensively manufactured at Barnsley, blanketing at Dewsbury, and glass and iron at Rotherham. Hull, Whitby, and Goole, are the chief ports. Under the names of the principal towns of the West Riding, a few details will be found illustrative of the manufacturing industry of the county.

YTTRIUM, a peculiar metal discovered by Gadolin in 1794, in the state of oxide, which is named *Yttria*. It presents the aspect of small brilliant scales, having a perfect metallic lustre. After being washed and dried, it is a brilliant blackish gray powder, composed of small metallic scales. It does not oxidise either by the action of air or water, at common temperatures; but when heated to redness in the air, it takes fire, burns with much splendour, and is converted into yttria. Yttrium has not yet been applied to many useful purposes.

Z

ZEALAND, NEW. In these islands copper, manganese, and coal, have been found. The soil on the table-lands, in the valleys, and near the coasts, is generally fertile, and the surface is well wooded. The sides of the mountains are generally bare of wood, but overgrown with ferns and grasses. The New Zealand flax-plant *(Phormium tenax)*, an edible fern (*Pteris esculenta*), the sweet potato, and a variety of timber-trees, are the chief vegetable productions. Wheat, maize, and other grains and vegetables have been introduced by the colonists, and the grazing grounds afford pasture all the year round.

ZINC. This metal, in commerce frequently called *Spelter*, does not occur in the native state, but is obtained from its ores, which are chiefly the sulphuret and carbonate of zinc. Zinc has a brilliant metallic lustre and a bluish white colour. It is so hard as to be filed with some difficulty, and its toughness is such as to require very considerable force to break it when the mass is considerable. The specific gravity of zinc varies from 6·86 to 7·21. It undergoes little alteration, even by the combined operation of air and moisture, at common temperatures. When heated to between the temperature of boiling water and 300° Fahr., it becomes both malleable and ductile, so that it may be rolled into sheets and drawn into wire. It fuses at 773° Fahr., and when cautiously cooled crystallises, assuming the prismatic form. Exposed to a white heat, out of the contact of air, it sublimes and is condensed unchanged.

The ores of zinc comprise the *Sulphuret*, or *Blende;* the *Oxisulphuret*, or *Voltzite;* the *Carbonate*, or *Calamine;* the *Hydrous Carbonate;* the *Sulphate;* the *Phosphate;* the *Silicate;* the *Hydrous Silicate;* the *Aluminate;* the *Oxide of Zinc and Manganese;* the *Sulphuret of Zinc and Iron.* Some of these ores are crystalline, some massive. The largest specimen ever procured, perhaps, is that which has been sent from America to the Great Exhibition, and which weighs 16,000 lbs.

The combinations of zinc with other substances are numerous, and many of them valuable. The Sulphate of Zinc constitutes *White Vitriol.* Zinc combined with copper forms *Brass;* and with iron it forms a very hard alloy. If plates of hot iron be dipped into melted zinc, they acquire the appearance of tin-plate, and the iron is prevented from rusting; the coating of zinc is sometimes applied by galvanic agency.

ZINC PAINT. An attempt is now being made to find a substitute for white lead in house-painting. White lead forms the basis of nearly all the pigments used by the house-painter; and though it is known to produce very injurious effects upon the health of those who use it, yet white lead possesses so many valuable properties, that it has outlived all the objections urged against it, and all the attempts made to supersede it. It remains to be seen whether the 'Patent White Zinc Paint' will be more successful. According to the patentees, it is free from all poisonous qualities; is unchangeable in tint by noxious gases; is so lustrous as to need no varnish; is more economical than white lead; and is easier to use. Time must test the validity of these claims. The French government is said to have adopted the White Zinc Paint in all the public works.

ZIRCO'NIUM, is a peculiar metal obtained from the earth or metallic oxide *Zirconia.* Under the burnisher it assumes the lustre of iron, and is compressed into scales resembling graphite. When heated in the air, even below redness, it takes fire; and by combining with oxygen is converted into oxide of zirconium, or Zirconia. *Zircon*, the mineral from which the earth and the metal have been named, occurs in prysmatic crystals, and consists of zirconia and silica. Zircon, like most of these new metals, has yet scarcely been brought into useful application.

LIST OF ILLUSTRATIONS.

The Wood Engravings which appear in this Work have reference chiefly to large departments, and occasionally localities, of British Industry; but they also illustrate distinct branches of those departments. For this latter reason it has been thought less desirable to attempt to place them in connection with any particular articles, than to group them together at the end of the volume. It is optional on the part of each purchaser, however, to have the engravings re-arranged by the binder in any other order.

The following table will elucidate the several pages of engravings. In the first column is given the number of the cut, as printed on the left-hand bottom corner; in the next is a brief description of the subjects; while in the third is a reference to such articles in the body of the work as receive illustration from the engravings in question.